TRANSFER CASES
Section 16

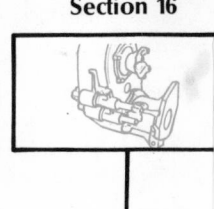

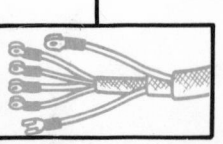

WIRING DIAGRAMS
Section 5

BONUS
Special MEDIUM and HEAVY DUTY
ENGINE SECTION at the rear
of this manual

GENERAL
INDEX

QUICK-CHECK TUNE-UP SPECS.
SECTION T

TUNE-UP
SECTION 1

FUEL SYSTEMS
SECTION 2

EMISSION CONTROL
SECTION 3

ELECTRICAL
SECTION 4

WIRING DIAGRAMS
SECTION 5

ACCESSORIES & EQUIPMENT
SECTION 6

ENGINES
SECTION 7

CLUTCHES
SECTION 8

DRIVE AXLES
SECTION 9

BRAKES
SECTION 10

WHEEL ALIGNMENT
SECTION 11

SUSPENSION
SECTION 12

STEERING
SECTION 13

AUTOMATIC TRANSMISSIONS
SECTION 14

LATEST CHANGES
& CORRECTIONS

PREFACE

This is the 1981 edition of Mitchell Manuals'
Light Truck Service & Repair Manual.
This book, like the many Mitchell publications which have preceded it,
represents our commitment to professionalism
in the automotive service market.

The automotive industry advances every year,
and Mithcell Manuals pledges to advance and improve its products
as we maintain the quality and usefulness of all Mitchell Manuals' publications.

We cordially acknowledge the good will
and mutual goals that exist in the automotive business,
and it is in this spirit that we thank the automotive manufacturers,
distributors, dealers and the entire automotive industry
for their fine cooperation and assistance
which have made this publication possible.

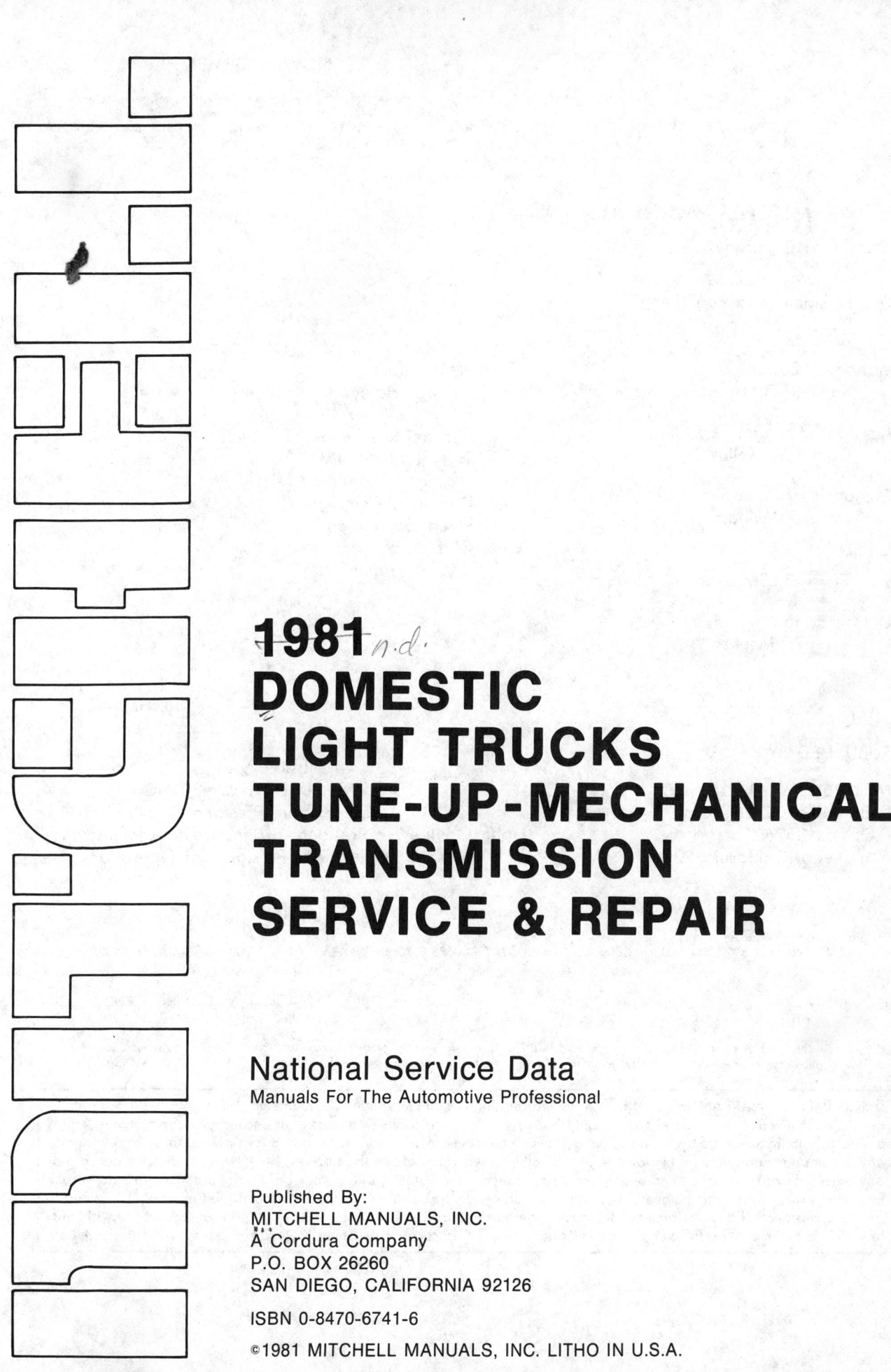

1981 ~~1981~~ n.d.
DOMESTIC
LIGHT TRUCKS
TUNE-UP-MECHANICAL
TRANSMISSION
SERVICE & REPAIR

National Service Data
Manuals For The Automotive Professional

Published By:
MITCHELL MANUALS, INC.
A Cordura Company
P.O. BOX 26260
SAN DIEGO, CALIFORNIA 92126

ISBN 0-8470-6741-6

ACKNOWLEDGEMENT

Mitchell Manuals thanks the automotive and equipment manufacturers,
distributors, dealers and the entire automotive industry for their fine
cooperation and assistance which makes the publication of this manual possible.

MITCHELL MANUALS, INC.

A Cordura Company

Vice President and Publisher
Richard M. Harris

Managing Editor
Kenneth A. Young

Assistant Managing Editor
Daniel M. Kelley

Composition Manager
Doris J. Williams

Art Director
Eloise S. Stiverson

Detroit Editor
Lynn D. Meeker

Technical Editors
Gary L. Haley
Daryl F. Visser
Michael Roeder
Terry L. Blomquist
Thomas L. Landis
Daniel D. Fleming
Philip G. Wallan
Cliff Herrin
Eric M. Hamm

PUBLISHED BY

MITCHELL MANUALS, INC.
9889 Willow Creek Road
P.O. Box 26260
San Diego, California 92126

a subsidiary of
CORDURA PUBLICATIONS, INC.
C.L. Kobrin, President
John Opelt, Vice President of Finance & Administration
Malcolm Ferrier, Vice President of Operations

For Subscription Information:
CALL TOLL FREE 800 - 854-7030. In California CALL COLLECT 714-578-8770. Or WRITE: P.O. Box 26260, San Diego, CA 92126

ISBN 0-8470-6741-6

©1981 MITCHELL MANUALS, INC. LITHO IN U.S.A.

Introduction

You now have the most complete and up to date Service and Repair Manual currently available to the professional mechanic. Our staff of experts has spent many hundreds of hours gathering and processing service and repair information from sources throughout the automotive industry. More than 200 separate articles provide specific step-by-step Testing, Adjusting and Repair procedures for 1981 Domestic Light Trucks.

To use this manual in the most efficient and profitable way possible, please take the time to read the following section, "How To Find The Information." This will enable you to quickly locate the car model and the mechanical procedure you need, without wasting time thumbing through unnecessary pages.

HOW TO FIND THE INFORMATION
3 Quick Steps

① On the inside cover, you'll find the contents of this manual. Locate the section you want, and notice that it has a black square next to it.

THUMB INDEX SPOT

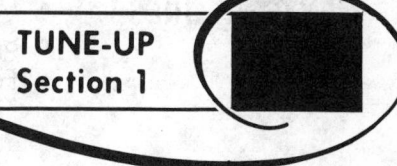

TUNE-UP
Section 1

② Looking along the right edge of the book, you'll notice additional black squares.

Match the black square of the section listed on the cover with the black square in line with it on the book's edge, then turn directly to that section.

③ Review the section contents page.

After locating the specific article and starting page needed, turn to the beginning of the article.

OR...

Go directly to the GENERAL INDEX located at the front of the book.
Use this alphabetical guide as you would any type of reference index.

Section Highlights

GENERAL INDEX

The first section of the Domestic Light Duty Truck manual is the GENERAL INDEX. This section is a quick, easy reference to help you locate the information you need. It is arranged alphabetically and is broken down into all of the vehicle's major components and then divided into models under component headings.

TUNE-UP SPECIFICATIONS

Section T

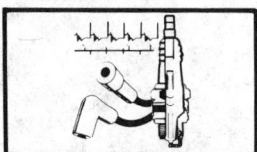

In this section, you will find all 1981 model Tune-Up Specifications listed in chart form. This is for fast reference when you need Ignition or Fuel System Specifications.

KEY FEATURES

- Models with electronic ignition are called out.
- Special notes to specific engines are called out.
- Federal and California models are listed separately.

TUNE-UP

Section 1

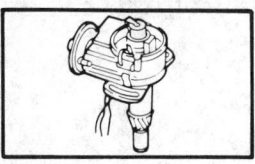

The TUNE-UP section in this manual is divided alphabetically by manufacturer and then by engine size. Included in this section are Engine Identification, to determine precisely what engine you are working on; Complete Servicing Tables which cover such items as Belt Adjustment; Filter and Cleaner Service Intervals and Refill Capacities.

KEY FEATURES

- Complete Tune-Up adjustment procedures are included.
- Illustrations and Diagrams showing Timing Marks, Firing Order and Distributor Rotation.
- Trouble Shooting tables to quickly locate problems.

FUEL SYSTEMS

Section 2

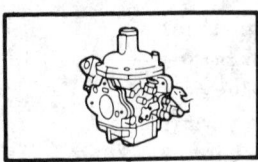

The FUEL SYSTEMS section covers such vital points as: Trouble Shooting, Carburetors and Diesel Fuel Injection. Complete Specification Tables and exploded views of carburetors are included in this section. Step-by-step procedures, supported by precise and detailed illustrations, make any Fuel System repair easier and faster.

KEY FEATURES

- Coverage of Diesel Fuel Injection Systems.
- Motorcraft 7200 VV carburetor used with EEC system.
- Specific tool requirements are called out.

EMISSION CONTROL

Section 3

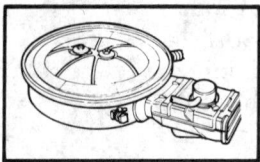

Within the EMISSION CONTROL section you will find comprehensive information on all Emission Systems for Light Duty Trucks in 1981. This includes, Catalytic Converters, Thermostatic Air Cleaners, EGR Valves and Fuel Evaporation Systems.

KEY FEATURES

- Complete coverage of Computerized Engine Control Systems (C-4, CEC, MCU, and EEC)
- Chrysler Aspirator Air System is detailed.
- Individual articles on Thermostatic Air Cleaners.

ELECTRICAL

Section 4

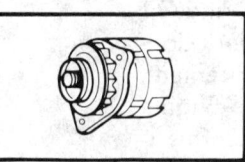

Within the ELECTRICAL section you'll find comprehensive Distributor Applications and Specifications. Testing, Adjustment and Overhaul procedures for Ignition Systems as well as Alternators, Regulators and Starters are included here.

KEY FEATURES

- Starting and Charging Systems Trouble Shooting.
- Electronic Ignition Systems are covered.
- Distributor Advance Specifications.

WIRING DIAGRAMS

Section 5

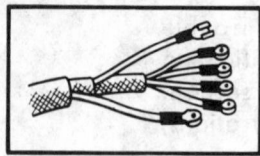

The WIRING DIAGRAM section covers Chassis Wiring for all Light Duty Trucks for 1981. Full Schematics are spread across several pages for easy reading and comprehension. This year, all electrical sub-systems are included in the full schematic diagrams so locating sub-system wiring is made easier and faster. In addition, complete Fuse and Circuit Breaker information is presented at the end of the section.

KEY FEATURES

- A Fuse and Flasher location quick reference chart is included.
- Diesel Fuel Injection Wiring Diagrams are included.
- Power accessories are clearly labeled.

ACCESSORIES & EQUIPMENT

Section 6

The ACCESSORIES & EQUIPMENT section covers the Description, Operation, Adjustment, Testing and Removal and Installation of major Accessories and Equipment found on 1981 model trucks. Many articles include system and system testing Wiring Diagrams to help you diagnose and correct electrical problems. The articles are arranged alphabetically by accessory.

KEY FEATURES

- Air Conditioning Servicing is included.
- Fuel Selector Valves for auxiliary fuel tanks are covered.
- Complete Instrument Panel Servicing.

ENGINES

Section 7

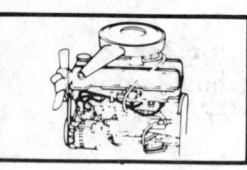

Within the ENGINE section you will find detailed articles covering Oil Pan Removal, Engine Removal, Valve Servicing, Crankshaft and Connecting Rod Bearing Fitting and Camshaft Inspection and Replacement. At the end of each article you will find tables listing complete Engine Component Specifications as well as Tightening Specifications. This makes it easier to find Specifications when procedural information is not required.

KEY FEATURES

- General Motors Diesel Engine coverage.
- Oil Pan Removal procedures are included.
- Engine Cooling systems are at the end of the section.

CLUTCHES

Section 8

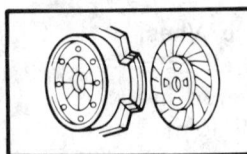

KEY FEATURES

In the CLUTCH section you will find thorough Removal, Adjustment and Inspection procedures for Clutches on all models. This coverage includes Release Bearings and hydraulic clutch component overhaul.

- Jeep 4 Cyl. Hydraulic Clutch System.
- Tightening Specifications are included.
- Descriptions of Clutch Systems used in all models.
- Trouble Shooting Tables to diagnose Clutch problems.

DRIVE AXLES

Section 9

KEY FEATURES

The DRIVE AXLE section includes information on Positive Traction Differentials, Propeller Shaft Alignment and Universal Joints. In addition, at the front of the section you will find a trouble shooting guide to help diagnose problems.

- Drive Axle Ratio Identification is included.
- Clear disassembled views make repair easier.
- Gear Tooth Contact Patterns plus illustrations.

BRAKES

Section 10

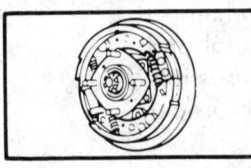

At the beginning of the BRAKE section, you will find a Trouble Shooting guide to help you locate and solve most problems associated with Brake Systems. Individual articles include Master Cylinder and Power Brake Unit coverage, with detailed explanations for Removal, Adjustment, Overhaul and Installation of both Drum and Disc Brake Systems. At the end of each article you'll find Specifications listed for Disc Brake Rotors and Brake Drums, as well as Tightening Specifications.

KEY FEATURES

- Complete Brake Bleeding procedures.
- Complete Service and Overhaul procedures for Bendix Hydro-Boost Power Brake Units.
- Hydraulic System Control Valves are included.

WHEEL ALIGNMENT

Section 11

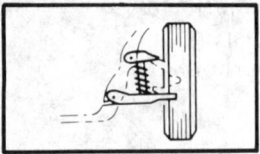

In the WHEEL ALIGNMENT section you will find comprehensive Wheel Alignment Specifications at the beginning of the section, as well as a Trouble Shooting guide for correct diagnosis. Procedures covered include: Wheel Alignment, Wheel Bearing Adjustment, and Ball Joint Checking.

KEY FEATURES

- Camber and Caster adjustment procedures.
- Wheel Alignment specifications listed in tables.
- Wheel Lug Nut Tightening Specifications.

SUSPENSION

Section 12

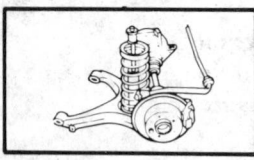

This section covers all Front Suspension components with complete Removal, Adjustment and Overhaul procedures. Such items as Coil Springs, Strut Assemblies, Stabilizer Bars and Control Arms are given detailed procedural coverage. Large and easy to understand illustrations which show proper positioning of suspension components eliminate guesswork.

KEY FEATURES

- Ford Motor Co. Four-Wheel Drive Suspension.
- Trouble Shooting table at the front of the section.
- Complete Tightening Specifications.

STEERING

Section 13

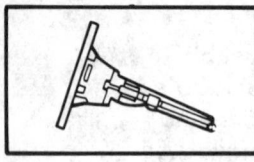

The STEERING section covers all aspects of steering components. Steering Columns, Steering Gears and Linkage as well as a comprehensive guide to Power Steering. At the front of the section is a Manual and Power Steering Gear Trouble Shooting guide to locate possible problems. Detailed diagrams and illustrations clearly show the proper positioning of steering assemblies and steering columns.

- Tilt Steering Columns for all models are covered.
- Steering Column Switches are included.
- Alignment and Adjustment procedures.

KEY FEATURES

AUTOMATIC TRANSMISSIONS

Section 14

In the AUTOMATIC TRANSMISSION section, complete Lubrication, Adjustment, Removal, Installation and Overhaul procedures allow you to perform all service necessary for Automatic Transmissions. In addition, an Oil Pan Gasket Identification article is included, as well as Cut-Away and Exploded View Illustrations and Tool Use Tips.

KEY FEATURES

- Automatic Transmission Servicing is included.
- A Trouble Shooting section is at the beginning.
- Shift Speeds and Hydraulic Pressure Charts.
- Ford Automatic Overdrive Transmission (AOT) complete Servicing and Overhaul procedures.

MANUAL TRANSMISSIONS

Section 15

In the MANUAL TRANSMISSION section, you will find complete coverage of all Manual Transmissions used in 1981 Light Duty Trucks. This coverage includes procedures for Removal, Installation, Overhaul, Adjustment and Lubrication. Shift Linkages are also covered in this section, as well as Refill Capacities. At the front of the section is a Trouble Shooting section to help you diagnose problems before beginning servicing.

KEY FEATURES

- Jeep's T-176 and SR-4 4-Speeds are covered.
- Manual Transmission Removal for all models.
- New Process A-833 is included.

TRANSFER CASES

Section 16

In the TRANSFER CASE section, detailed procedures for servicing and repairing all Transfer Cases are included. Also included are detailed Exploded Illustrations to make Overhaul of a transfer case easier and faster. Complete Tightening Specifications are included with each article.

KEY FEATURES

- Full Time differential type transfer cases are included.
- Service Intervals and Capacities.
- Complete Trouble Shooting Tables are included.

LATEST CHANGES & CORRECTIONS

This section is printed on blue paper and contains manufacturers changes and corrections which were received too late to be included among the regular articles. This information may also pertain to previous model trucks which were covered in earlier editions of Mitchell's Light Duty Truck Manual.

MEDIUM & HEAVY DUTY TRUCK SPECIFICATIONS

This section is a special feature of Mitchell's Light Duty truck Manual. Since many of the servicemen who work on light duty trucks also do some Heavy and Medium Duty truck work, this section is a fast, easy reference for tune-up and engine specifications.

KEY FEATURES

- Tune-Up Specifications
- Engine Overhaul Specifications

1981 Light Truck
Model Identification

The various Light Truck models included in this manual will be referred to by the manufacturer's model and/or series designation. When a specific model does not have a designated model and/or series designation, it will be referred to by the model name.

CHEVROLET

C10	½ Ton Conventional Cab 2-WD①
C20	¾ Ton Conventional Cab 2-WD①
C30	1 Ton Conventional Cab 2-WD
K10	½ Ton Conventional Cab 4-WD & Blazer①
K20	¾ Ton Conventional Cab 4-WD①
K30	1 Ton Conventional Cab 4-WD
G10	½ Ton Van
G20	¾ Ton Van
G30	1 Ton Van②
P10	½ Ton Parcel Delivery Van
P20	¾ Ton Parcel Delivery Van
P30 (42)	1 Ton Parcel Delivery Van

① — Includes Suburban Models.
② — Includes Front Section Models and Hi-Cube Models

GMC

C1500	½ Ton Conventional Cab 2-WD①
C2500	¾ Ton Conventional Cab 2-WD①
C3500	1 Ton Conventional Cab 2-WD
K1500	½ Ton Conventional Cab 4-WD & Jimmy①
K2500	¾ Ton Conventional Cab 4-WD①
K3500	1 Ton Conventional Cab 4-WD
G1500	½ Ton Van
G2500	¾ Ton Van
G3500	1 Ton Van②
P1500	½ Ton Parcel Delivery Van
P2500	¾ Ton Parcel Delivery Van
P3500 (42)	1 Ton Parcel Delivery Van

① — Includes Suburban Models.
② — Includes Front Section Models and Hi-Cube Models.

NOTE — When General Motors is referred to within this manual (rather than Chevrolet or GMC), the numerical vehicle series designations will be abbreviated for common reference to both Chevrolet and GMC. Chevrolet will use numerical series designations as listed. GMC models will be identified as follows: 10 = 1500; 20 = 2500; 30 = 3500

DODGE

D150	Heavy Duty ½ Ton Conventional Cab 2-WD
D250	¾ Ton Conventional Cab 2-WD
D350	1 Ton Conventional Cab 2-WD
D450	Heavy Duty 1 Ton Conventional Cab 2-WD
W150	Heavy Duty ½ Ton Conventional Cab 4-WD
W250	½ Ton Conventional Cab 4-WD
W350	1 Ton Conventional Cab 4-WD
W450	Heavy Duty 1 Ton Conventional Cab 4-WD
AD150	Ramcharger 2-WD
AW150	Ramcharger 4-WD
B150	½ Ton Van
B250	¾ Ton Van
B350	1 Ton Van
CB350	1 Ton Van (Kary Van)
CB450	1½ Ton Van (Kary Van)
MB250	¾ Ton Van (Front Section)
MB350	1 Ton Van (Front Section)
MB450	1½ Ton Van (Front Section)

FORD

F100	½ Ton Conventional Cab 2-WD
F150	H.D. ½ Ton Conventional Cab 2 & 4-WD
F250	¾ Ton Conventional Cab 2 & 4-WD
F350	1 Ton Conventional Cab 2 & 4-WD
Bronco	Family 4-WD Wagon
E100	½ Ton Van
E150	Heavy Duty ½ Ton Van
E250	¾ Ton Van
E350	1 Ton Van①

① — Includes Front Section Models and Parcel Delivery Models.

JEEP

J10	½ Ton Conventional Cab 4-WD
J20	¾ Ton Conventional Cab 4-WD
CJ5	84" Wheelbase Utility Vehicle 4-WD
CJ7	94" Wheelbase Utility Vehicle 4-WD
Cherokee	Cherokee 4-WD
Scrambler	104" Wheelbase Utility Vehicle 4-WD
Wagoneer	Wagoneer 4-WD

PLYMOUTH

PB150	½ Ton Van
PB250	¾ Ton Van
PB350	1 Ton Van
PD150	Trailduster 2-WD
PW150	Trailduster 4-WD

GENERAL INDEX

The first step in using these pages is to locate the listed components that you require information on. Go down the list under the specific component heading to the model or engine size of the vehicle you are working on. On the righthand side of the column will appear the corresponding page number of the article, specification, or wiring diagram you require.

NOTE – ALSO SEE INDIVIDUAL SECTION CONTENTS PAGE.

NOTE — ALSO SEE INDIVIDUAL SECTION CONTENTS PAGE.

NOTE – ALSO SEE INDIVIDUAL SECTION CONTENTS PAGE.

NOTE — ALSO SEE INDIVIDUAL SECTION CONTENTS PAGE.

NOTE – ALSO SEE INDIVIDUAL SECTION CONTENTS PAGE.

NOTE – ALSO SEE INDIVIDUAL SECTION CONTENTS PAGE.

NOTE — ALSO SEE INDIVIDUAL SECTION CONTENTS PAGE.

NOTE – ALSO SEE INDIVIDUAL SECTION CONTENTS PAGE.

NOTE – ALSO SEE INDIVIDUAL SECTION CONTENTS PAGE.

NOTE – ALSO SEE INDIVIDUAL SECTION CONTENTS PAGE.

Section T

QUICK-CHECK
TUNE-UP SPECS.
1981

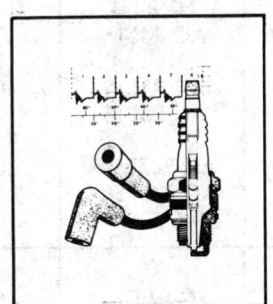

IMPORTANT

Because of the great number of model names used by vehicle manufacturers, accurate identification of models is important.
See Model Identification at the front of this publication.

1981 Light Truck Tune-Up

ENGINE	IGNITION TIMING@RPM*		SPARK PLUGS		CARBURETOR	No.
	Man. Trans.	Auto. Trans	Type	Gap	Make & Type	
CHRYSLER CORP.						
3.7L (225") 6 Cyl.						
Fed.	12@600	16@600	CH RBL16Y	.035"	Holley 1945	1
Calif.	12@800	16@800	CH RBL16Y	.035"	Holley 1945	2
5.2L (318") V8 2-Bbl.	10@650	10@650	CH RN11Y	.035"	Holley 2280	3
5.2L (318") V8 4-Bbl.						
Fed.	8@750	16@650①	CH RN11Y	.035"	Carter Thermo-Quad	4
Calif.	12@750	16@750	CH RN11Y	.035"	Carter Thermo-Quad	5
5.9L (360") V8						
Light Duty	12@600④	16@750	CH RN12Y	.035"	Carter Thermo-Quad	6
Heavy Duty	4@700⑧	4@700⑧	CH RF-10	.035"	Carter Thermo-Quad	7
FORD						
4.9L (300") 6 Cyl.						
Light Duty	6@800	10@800	AL BSF-42	.044"	Carter YFA①	8
Heavy Duty	10@800	12@800	AL BSF-42	.044"	Carter YFA	9
4.2L (255") V8	4@800	10@800	AL ASF-42	.044"	MCFT 2150	10
5.0L (302") Fed. V8⑫	8@800	8@800	AL ASF-42	.044"	MCFT 2150	11
5.8L (351") M V8	10@800	6@800③	AL ASF-42	.044"	MCFT 2150	12
5.8L (351") W V8						
Fed.	10@600⑥	10@600⑥⑦	AL ASF-52	.044"	MCFT 2150	13
Calif. Hvy. Duty⑫	.....	6@800	AL ASF-52	.044"	MCFT 2150	14
6.6L (400") V8	6@800⑩	3@800⑪	AL ASF-52	.044"	MCFT 2150	15
7.5L (460") V8	.....	8@800	AL ASF-42	.044"	Holley 4180-C	16
GENERAL MOTORS						
4.1L (250") 6-Cyl.	10@750	10@650①	AC R45TS	.035"	Roch 2SE	17
4.8L (292") 6-Cyl.	8@700	8@700	AC R44T	.035"	Roch 1ME	18
5.0L (305") V8 2-Bbl.	8@700	8@600	AC R45TS	.045"	Roch M2ME	19
5.0L (305") V8 4-Bbl.						
Fed.	4@700②	8@650③	AC R45TS	.045"	Roch M4ME	20
Calif.	.....	8@650	AC R45TS	.045"	Roch M4ME	21
5.7L (350") V8						
Fed.	8@700④	8@600④	AC R45TS⑤	.045"	Roch M4MC	22
Calif.	.....	6@650⑥	AC R45TS⑤	.045"	Roch M4MC	23
7.4L (454") V8	4@700	4@700	AC R44T	.045"	Roch M4MC	24
JEEP						
2.5L (151") 4-Cyl.	10@900	12@700①	AC R44TSX	.060"	Roch 2SE②	25
4.2L (258") 6-Cyl.	8@650③	8@550④	CH RFN14LY	.035"	Carter BBD	26
5.0L (304") V8	8@600⑤	10@600	CH RN12Y	.035"	MCFT 2150	27
6.0L (360") V8	10@600	10@600	CH RN12Y	.035"	MCFT 2150	28

SPARK PLUGS: AC — AC Delco: **AL** — Autolite; **CH** — Champion.

CARBURETORS: MCFT — Motorcraft; **Roch** — Rochester.

No.	HOT IDLE ★		FAST IDLE †			Remarks
	Man. Trans.	Auto. Trans.	Man. Trans. RPM	Cam Step	Auto. Trans. RPM	
1	600/800	600/800	1600	2nd High	1800	① — 8° on Nationwide models.
2	800/800	800/800	1600	2nd High	1800	② — 750/800 RPM on Nationwide models.
3	650/800	650/800	1500	2nd High	1500	③ — 1800 RPM on Nationwide models.
4	650/800②	650/800②	1800	2nd High	1500③	④ — Set at 725 RPM on Calif. models.
5	750/800	750/800	1500	2nd High	1600	⑤ — 725/800 RPM on Calif. models.
						⑥ — 750/800 RPM on Calif. models.
6	600/800⑤	600/800⑥	1500⑦	2nd High	1700	⑦ — 1700 RPM on Calif. models.
7	700/800⑥	700/800⑥	1800	2nd High	1500	⑧ — 10°@750 on Calif. models.
8	600/700	550	1400	2nd	1400	① — YFA Feedback on Calif. models.
9	500/700	500/600	1500	2nd	1600	② — 1350 RPM on Calif. models.
10	750	575/650	2200	High	2000	③ — 10° on Hvy. Duty Emissions.
11	700	575/650	2200	High	2000②	④ — 1750 RPM on Calif. models.
12	650	550/625	2000④	High	2000⑤	⑤ — 2200 RPM on High Alt. models.
						⑥ — 8°@800 RPM on High Alt. models.
13	575/650	575/650	1700	2nd⑧	2000⑨	⑦ — 6°@800 RPM on Hvy. Duty Emission.
14	.....	525/600	.....	High	1700	⑧ — Highest step on Hvy. Duty Emission.
15	600	500/600	1750	High	2000	⑨ — 1700 RPM on Hvy. Duty Emission.
16	.....	650	.....	High	1600	⑩ — 3° on E250/350 models.
						⑪ — 6° on Calif. models.
						⑫ — Calif. Lt. Duty 5.0L & 5.8L W use 7200VV Carb. & EEC III.
17	450/750	450/650	2000	High	2200	① — 8° for Decals AAC & ADC.
18	450/700	450/700	2400	High	2400	② — 6° on Vans.
19	600/700	500/600	1300	High	1600	③ — 6° for Decal AAN; 2° for Decal AAS.
20	700	500/600	1300	High	1600	④ — 4° on Hvy. Duty Emission.
21	.....	550/650	.....	High	1800	⑤ — R44T for Hvy. Duty Emission.
22	700	500	1300	High	1600	⑥ — 8° on Vans.
23	.....	550/650	.....	High	1800	
24	700	700	1900	High	1900	
25	500/900	500/700	2400	High	2000	① — 10° on Calif. models.
26	650/750	550/650	1700	2nd	1850	② — E2SE Feedback carb. for Calif. models.
27	500/600	500/600	1500	2nd	1600	③ — 4° on Calif. models.
28	500/600	500/600	1500	2nd	1600	④ — 6° on Calif. models.
						⑤ — 10° on High Alt. models.

* — All Specifications given are Before Top Dead Center (BTDC); Auto. Trans. in "D" unless otherwise specified.

★ — When idle solenoid is used, lower RPM is with solenoid disconnected, higher RPM is with solenoid connected.

† — All specifications are with transmission in Neutral unless otherwise noted.

Contents

Section 1
TUNE-UP

NOTE — ALSO SEE GENERAL INDEX.

IMPORTANT

*Because of the great number of model names used by vehicle manufacturers, accurate identification of models is important.
See Model Identification at the front of this publication.*

1981 Tune-Up

TUNE-UP TROUBLE SHOOTING

CONDITION & POSSIBLE CAUSE	CONDITION & POSSIBLE CAUSE

SPARK PLUG DIAGNOSIS

Normal Spark Plug Condition

- Light tan or gray deposits on insulator.
- Electrode not burned or fouled.
- Gap tolerance not significantly changed.

Cold Fouling or Carbon Deposits

- Over rich air-fuel mixture, possibly from a faulty choke, clogged air cleaner, improper idle adjustment or dirty carburetor.
- Faulty ignition wires.
- Prolonged operation at idle.
- Sticking valves or worn valve guide seals.

Wet Fouling or Oil Deposits

- Worn rings and pistons.
- Excessive cylinder wear.
- Excessive valve guide clearance.
- Worn or loose bearings.

Gap Bridged

- Deposits in combustion chamber becoming fused to electrode under high heat.

Blistered Electrode or Overheating

- Engine overheating.
- Wrong type of fuel.
- Loose spark plugs.
- Over-advanced ignition timing.

Pre-ignition or Melted Electrodes

- Incorrect type of gasoline.
- Incorrect ignition timing.
- Burned valves.
- Engine overheating.
- Wrong type of spark plug, too hot.

Chipped Insulators

- Severe detonation.
- Improper gapping procedure.

Rust Colored Deposits

- Additives in unleaded fuel may create this condition. It may be misdiagnosed as water in the combustion chamber. These deposits do not affect plug performance.

ELECTRONIC IGNITION DIAGNOSIS

Before diagnosing an electronic ignition system, ensure that all wiring is connected properly between distributor, wiring connector and spark plugs. Ignition problems will show up either as: engine will not start or engine runs rough.

Engine Will Not Start

- Open circuit between distributor and bulkhead connector.
- Open circuit between bulkhead connector and ignition switch.
- Open circuit between ignition switch and starter solenoid.

Engine Runs Rough

- Fuel lines leaking or clogged.
- Initial timing incorrect.
- Centrifugal advance malfunction.
- Worn or defective spark plugs.
- Worn or defective secondary wiring.

If the above checks do not locate the problem, check the components listed below.

Component Failure

- Spark arc-over on distributor cap, rotor or coil.
- Defective pick-up coil.
- Defective ignition coil.
- Defective vacuum unit.
- Defective control module.

ELECTRONIC IGNITION DIAGNOSIS BY OSCILLOSCOPE PATTERN

Firing Voltage Lines are the Same, but Abnormally High

- Retarded ignition timing.
- Too lean of a fuel mixture.
- High resistance in coil wire.
- Corrosion in coil tower terminal.
- Corrosion in distributor coil terminal.

Firing Voltage Lines are the Same, but Abnormally Low

- Too rich of a fuel mixture.
- Breaks in coil wire causing arcing.
- Cracked coil tower causing arcing.
- Low coil output.
- Low engine compression.

TUNE-UP TROUBLE SHOOTING (Cont.)

CONDITION & POSSIBLE CAUSE

One or More, but Not All Firing Voltage Lines are Higher Than the Others

- Carburetor idle mixture not balanced.
- EGR valve stuck open.
- High resistance in spark plug wire.
- Cracked or broken spark plug insulator.
- Intake vacuum leak.
- Defective spark plugs.
- Corroded spark plug terminals.

One or More, but Not All Firing Voltage Lines are Lower Than the Others

- Curb idle mixture not balanced.
- Breaks in spark plug wires causing arcing.
- Cracked coil tower causing arcing.
- Low compression.
- Defective spark plugs, or spark plugs fouled.

One or More Cylinders Not Firing

- Cracked distributor cap terminals.
- Shorted spark plug wire.
- Mechanical problem in engine.
- Defective spark plugs.
- Spark plugs fouled.

GENERAL DIAGNOSIS

Hard Starting

- Binding carburetor linkage, choke linkage or choke piston.
- Restricted choke vacuum.
- Worn or dirty needle valve and seat.
- Float sticking.
- Incorrect choke adjustment.
- Defective coil.
- Improper spark plug gap.
- Incorrect ignition timing.

Detonation

- Over-advanced ignition timing.
- Defective spark plugs.
- Fuel lines clogged.
- EGR system malfunction.
- PCV system malfunction.
- Vacuum leaks.
- Loose fan belts.
- Restricted air flow.
- Vacuum advance malfunction.

CONDITION & POSSIBLE CAUSE

Dieseling

- Binding carburetor linkage, throttle linkage, choke linkage or fast idle cam.
- Defective idle solenoid.
- Improper base idle speed.
- Incorrect ignition timing.
- Incorrect idle mixture setting.

Faulty Acceleration

- Incorrect ignition timing.
- Engine cold and choke too lean.
- Defective spark plugs.
- Defective coil.

Faulty Low Speed Operation

- Clogged idle transfer slots.
- Restricted idle air bleeds and passages.
- Clogged air cleaner.
- Defective spark plugs.
- Defective ignition cables.
- Defective distributor cap.

Faulty High Speed Operation

- Incorrect ignition timing.
- Defective distributor centrifugal advance.
- Defective distributor vacuum advance.
- Incorrect spark plugs or plug gap.
- Faulty choke operation.
- Clogged vacuum passages.
- Improper size or clogged main jet.
- Restricted air cleaner.
- Defective distributor cap, rotor or coil.
- Worn distributor shaft.

Misfire at All Speeds

- Defective spark plugs.
- Defective spark plug wires.
- Defective distributor cap, rotor or coil.
- Cracked or broken vacuum hoses.
- Vacuum leaks.
- Fuel lines clogged.

Hesitation

- Cracked or broken vacuum hoses.
- Vacuum leaks.
- Binding carburetor linkage, throttle linkage, choke linkage or fast idle cam.
- Improper float setting.
- Cracked or broken ignition wires.

TUNE-UP TROUBLE SHOOTING (Cont.)

CONDITION & POSSIBLE CAUSE	CONDITION & POSSIBLE CAUSE

Rough Idle, Missing or Stalling

- Incorrect curb idle or fast idle speed.
- Incorrect basic timing.
- Improper idle mixture adjustment.
- Improper feedback system operation.
- Incorrect spark plug gap.
- Moisture in ignition components.
- Loose or broken ignition wires.
- Damaged distributor cap or rotor.
- Faulty ignition coil.
- Fuel filter clogged or worn.
- Damaged idle mixture screw.
- Improper fast idle cam adjustment.
- Improper EGR valve operation.
- Faulty PCV valve air flow.
- Choke binding, or improper choke setting.
- Vacuum leak.
- Improper float bowl fuel level.
- Clogged air bleed or idle passages.
- Clogged or worn air cleaner.
- Faulty choke vacuum diaphragm.
- Exhaust manifold heat valve inoperative.
- Improper distributor spark advance.
- Leaking valves or valve components.
- Improper carburetor mounting.
- Excessive play in distributor shaft.
- Loose or corroded wiring connections.

Engine Surges

- Improper PCV valve air flow.
- Vacuum leaks.
- Clogged main jets.
- Clogged air bleeds.
- EGR valve malfunction.
- Restricted air cleaner.
- Cracked or broken vacuum hoses.
- Cracked or broken ignition wires.
- Vacuum advance malfunction.
- Defective or fouled spark plugs.

Ping or Spark Knock

- Incorrect ignition timing.
- Distributor centrifugal or vacuum advance malfunction.
- Carburetor setting too lean.
- Vacuum leak.
- EGR valve malfunction.

Poor Gasoline Mileage

- Cracked or broken vacuum hoses.
- Vacuum leaks.
- Defective ignition wires.
- Incorrect choke setting.
- Defective vacuum advance.
- Defective spark plugs.
- Binding carburetor power piston.
- Dirt in carburetor jets.
- Incorrect float adjustment.
- Defective power valves.

Power Not Up to Normal

- Incorrect ignition timing.
- Defective distributor cap, rotor, coil or ignition wires.
- Incorrect spark plug gap.
- Incorrect idle speeds.
- Improper float level.
- Leaking needle valve and seat.
- Choke sticking.

Engine Stalls

- Incorrect idle speed.
- Improper float level.
- Leaking needle valve and seat.
- Sticking choke.
- Carburetor mounting gasket air leaks.
- Vacuum leaks.
- Defective ignition wires, distributor cap or rotor.
- Loose condensor.
- Shorted distributor wires.
- Defective spark plugs.
- Clogged fuel filter.

TUNE-UP

ENGINE IDENTIFICATION

The engine can be identified by a number stamped on right side of block below No. 1 spark plug. The first digit indicates model year; the next 3 digits indicate cubic inch displacement. The engine can also be identified by the 8th digit of the Vehicle Identification Number (VIN). The VIN number is located on a label on the driver's door post.

VIN Engine Codes

Application	VIN Code
3.7L (225") 1-Bbl.	E

TUNE-UP NOTES

NOTE — *In order to comply with emission standards, specifications shown on engine compartment emission control tune-up decal must be used in all instances.*

CAUTION — *When performing tune-up on vehicles equipped with catalytic converters, do not allow or create a condition of engine misfire in more than one cylinder for an extended period of time. Damage to converter may occur due to loading converter with unburned air/fuel mixture.*

CAUTION — *On vehicles equipped with catalytic converters do not add fuel system cleaning agents to fuel tank or carburetor as their use may be detrimental to the catalytic converter.*

NOTE — *For other items affecting Tune-Up, see FUEL SYSTEMS Section or EMISSION CONTROL Section.*

CAUTION — *Before making a compression test or cranking engine using a remote starting switch, disconnect coil wire from distributor and secure to a good ground.*

ENGINE COMPRESSION

Compression Ratio	8.4:1
Compression Pressure	Min. 100 psi
Maximum Pressure Variation	25 psi

With engine warm, spark plugs removed and throttle wide open, compression pressure should be as specified.

VALVE CLEARANCE

All engines are equipped with hydraulic valve lifters.

Hydraulic Lifters	Zero Lash

VALVE ARRANGEMENT

E-I-E-I-E-I-I-E-I-E-I-E (Front to rear).

SPARK PLUGS

Application	Gap (In.)	Torque (Ft. Lbs.)
All Models	.035	10

Spark Plug Type

Application	Champion No.
All Models	RBL16Y

HIGH TENSION WIRE RESISTANCE

Carefully remove spark plug wire from spark plug and install the proper adapter between wire and spark plug. Carefully remove wire from distributor cap. Connect an ohmmeter between spark plug adapter and opposite end of wire. If resistance is not within specifications, replace wire. To check coil wire resistance, remove distributor cap from distributor without removing wire from cap or coil. Connect an ohmmeter between center contact in cap and either primary terminal at coil. If resistance is not within specifications, remove coil wire at coil tower and check cable resistance. If resistance is now within specifications, check for a loose connection at coil tower or a faulty coil. If resistance is not within specifications, replace wire.

Resistance (Ohms)

Application	Maximum
Coil Wire	
Installed	25,000
Removed	15,000
Spark Plug Wire	
To 25" Length	30,000
Over 25" Length	50,000

DISTRIBUTOR

All models are equipped with Chrysler Electronic Spark Advance system with dual pick-up distributor. No adjustments are required.

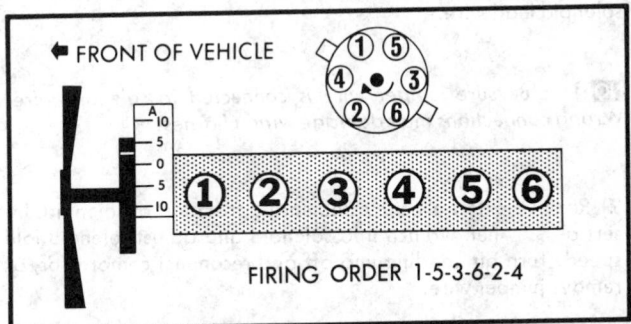

Fig. 1 Firing Order and Timing Marks

IGNITION TIMING

NOTE — *All models are equipped with socket for magnetic timing equipment, located at 10° ATDC. Do not use this location for timing with a conventional timing light.*

TUNE-UP (Cont.)

1) Connect timing light to number 1 cylinder. Connect tachometer to engine. Start engine, set parking brake and place transmission in Neutral. Bring engine to normal operating temperature.

2) Disconnect and plug vacuum hoses to EGR valve and at distributor. Disconnect PCV valve and vapor canister purge hose at carburetor, leaving connections open. Idle set RPM should be within ±100 RPM of specifications. To adjust, use idle speed screw.

3) Reconnect PCV valve and purge hose and check timing. If not within ±2°, loosen distributor hold-down screw and adjust timing until within specifications. Tighten hold-down screw when timing is correct. Recheck idle set RPM and timing.

CAUTION — *DO NOT use distributor vacuum advance unit as a handle when turning distributor housing.*

4) If timing was adjusted or idle speed screw was turned, perform propane enrichment procedure. Unplug and reconnect all vacuum hoses and remove all test equipment.

Ignition Timing Specifications
(Degrees BTDC@RPM)

Application	Man. Trans.	Auto. Trans.
3.7L		
Federal	12@600	16@600
Calif.	12@800	16@800

HOT (SLOW) IDLE RPM

1) Set parking brake, place transmission in neutral and warm engine to normal operating temperature. Turn on air conditioning and disconnect compressor clutch wire. If not equipped with air conditioning, connect a jumper wire between 12V and solenoid lead wire.

NOTE — *Be sure jumper wire is connected to solenoid wire. Wrong connections may damage wiring harness.*

2) Remove external screw and spring from top of solenoid. Insert a 1/8" Allen wrench into solenoid and adjust solenoid idle speed. Turn air conditioning off and reconnect compressor, or remove jumper wire.

3) Disconnect and plug EGR valve hose, distributor vacuum hose, and 3/16" control hose at canister. Pull PCV valve from valve cover and allow to draw fresh air.

4) Allow engine to run at least 2 minutes, then check idle speed. Replace idle speed screw on solenoid and adjust curb idle. Stop engine, remove test equipment and reconnect all hoses.

Idle Speed (RPM)

Application	Curb Idle	Solenoid Energized
3.7L		
Federal	600	800
Calif.	800	800

IDLE MIXTURE

MIXTURE SCREW PLUG REMOVAL

1) Remove carburetor. Remove throttle body from carburetor and clamp in padded vise with mixture screw facing up.

2) Drill a 1/16" pilot hole in casting directly above roll pin. Redrill hole to 1/8" and drive out roll pin with punch.

3) On bottom side of throttle body, drill a 1/16" pilot hole in casting at a 45° angle toward mixture screw plug. Redrill hole to 1/8" and drive out plug with punch.

4) Position a new roll pin partially into place from bottom of throttle body, but so mixture screw is still accessible. Reassemble and install carburetor.

PROPANE ENRICHMENT PROCEDURE

1) Warm engine to operating temperature and place transmission in neutral. Disconnect and plug vacuum hoses at EGR valve, distributor and control line at canister (3/16" hose). Remove PCV valve from valve cover and allow to draw fresh air. Disconnect heated air cleaner hose from carburetor and connect propane supply hose.

2) With air cleaner in place, open propane valve slowly until maximum engine speed is reached. Adjust idle speed screw on solenoid to obtain mixture RPM, then adjust propane carefully to highest possible speed. Readjust idle speed screw to mixture RPM.

3) Turn off propane and allow engine to stabilize. Slowly adjust mixture screw to obtain smooth idle at curb idle speed. Turn on propane again and adjust to obtain highest possible RPM. If more than 25 RPM from mixture RPM specification, repeat procedure.

4) Turn off propane. Adjust fast idle speed. Stop engine and remove test equipment, then reconnect all hoses. Install roll pin.

Mixture Adjustment RPM

Application	Mixture RPM
3.7L	
Federal	675
Calif.	900

COLD (FAST) IDLE RPM

1) Warm engine to operating temperature and place transmission in neutral. Disconnect and plug hoses at EGR valve, dis-

TUNE-UP (Cont.)

tributor and canister (³⁄₁₆" hose). Remove PCV valve from valve cover and allow to draw fresh air.

2) Place fast idle adjustment screw on 2nd highest step of fast idle cam. Adjust fast idle speed by turning screw. Remove test equipment and reconnect all hoses.

Fast Idle Speed (RPM)①

Application	Man. Trans.	Auto. Trans.
3.7L	1600	1800

① — Set fast idle speed screw on 2nd highest step of cam.

AUTOMATIC CHOKE

Vehicles over 6000 lbs. GVW are equipped with a nonadjustable thermostatically controlled automatic choke using engine heat only in positioning valve. All other vehicles have an electric assist choke requiring no adjustment.

FUEL PUMP

Pressure (At Idle) .... 3.5-5 psi
Volume (At Idle) .... 1 quart in 1 minute

MANIFOLD HEAT CONTROL VALVE

Every 30,000 miles (light duty) or 18,000 miles (heavy duty), apply a suitable solvent to both ends of valve shaft where it rotates in bushing. Work valve back and forth several times.

CAUTION — *Apply solvent only when manifold is cold.*

EMISSION CONTROL SYSTEMS

See appropriate article in Emission Control Section.

GENERAL SERVICING

IGNITION

DISTRIBUTOR

All models are equipped with Chrysler Electronic Spark Advance system with dual pick-up. No adjustments are necessary.

Other Data & Specifications — *See Tune-Up and Chrysler Corp. Distributors in ELECTRICAL Section.*

IGNITION COIL

Coil Resistance (Ohms@75°F)

Application	Primary	Secondary
Essex	1.34-1.55	9000-12,200
Prestolite	1.60-1.79	9400-11,700
Ballast Resistor		1.1-1.3 ohms

FUEL SYSTEMS

CARBURETORS

Application	Carburetor
All Models	Holley 1945 1-Bbl.

Other Data & Specifications — *See Tune-Up and Holley Carburetors in FUEL SYSTEMS Section.*

ELECTRICAL

BATTERY

Application	Cold Cranking Amps@0° F	Reserve Capacity Minutes
Standard	305	68
Optional	375	86
Optional	430	100
Optional	500	125

STARTER

All models use a Chrysler Corp. Reduction Gear type starter.

Starter Specifications

Application	Volts	Amps	Test RPM
All Models	11	90	3700

Other Data & Specifications — *See Chrysler Corp. Starters in ELECTRICAL Section.*

ALTERNATORS

All models use Chrysler Corp. alternator.

Tag Color	Rated Amp. Output
Violet	41
Yellow	
"D","W","AD","AW" & "PW"	117
All Other Models	60

Other Data & Specifications — *See Chrysler Corp. Alternators in ELECTRICAL Section.*

ALTERNATOR REGULATOR

All models use Chrysler Corp. Electronic Voltage Regulator. Unit is nonadjustable.

GENERAL SERVICING (Cont.)

Operating Voltage (@80°F)........................ 13.9-14.6 Volts

Other Data & Specifications — *See Chrysler Corp. Electronic Regulator in ELECTRICAL Section.*

REPLACEMENT INTERVALS

Component	Interval (Miles)
Oil Filter	15,000
Air Filter	30,000
Fuel Filter	30,000
PCV Valve	30,000
Spark Plugs	
With Converter	30,000
Without Converter	15,000

BELT ADJUSTMENTS

Tension (Lbs.) Using Strand Tension Gauge

Application	New Belt	①Used Belt
All	120	70

① — Any belt operated for 15 minutes.

CAPACITIES

Application	Quantity
Crankcase	①5.0 qts.
Cooling System	
Standard	②12.0 qts.
Optional	②13.0 qts.
Automatic Transmission (Dexron II)	③7.7 pts.
Manual Transmission	
4-Speed Overdrive (A-833) (Dexron II)	7.5 pts.
4-Speed N.P. 435 (SAE 80W-90)	7.0 pts.
Transfer Case	
N.P. 205 (SAE 80W-90)	4.5 pts.
N.P. 208 (Dexron II)	6.0 pts.
Rear Axle (SAE 80W-90)	
8⅜" Ring Gear	4.5 pts.
9¼" Ring Gear	4.5 pts.
9¾" Ring Gear	6.0 pts.
10½" Ring Gear	6.5 pts.
Front Axle (SAE 80W-90)	
Model 44	3.5 pts.
Model 60	6.5 pts.
Fuel Tank	
Van Models	
B150, 250, 350	22.0 or 36.0 gals.
CB350, 450 & MB250	22.0 or 45.0 gals.
MB350, 450	45.0 gals.
Pickup Models	20.0 or 30.0 gals.

① — Add 1 quart with filter change.
② — Add 1 quart with rear heater.
③ — Without torque converter drain.

TUNE-UP

ENGINE IDENTIFICATION

Engine identification number is stamped on left front of block below cylinder head. First digit indicates model year, then the next 3 digits indicate engine size in cubic inches. Engine can also be identified by the 8th digit in the Vehicle Identification Number (VIN). VIN is located on a plate attached to driver's door post.

VIN Engine Codes

Application	VIN Code
5.2L (318") 2-Bbl.	P
5.2L (318") 4-Bbl.	M
5.9L (360") 4-Bbl.	T
5.9L (360") 4-Bbl. Heavy Duty Single Exhaust	U
5.9L (360") 4-Bbl. Heavy Duty Dual Exhaust	V

TUNE-UP NOTES

CAUTION — *When performing tune-up on vehicles equipped with a catalytic converter, do not allow or create a condition of engine misfire in one or more cylinders for an extended period of time. Damage to converter from overheating may occur due to loading with unburned fuel.*

NOTE — *Due to production changes, always refer to Engine Tune-Up Decal in engine compartment before attempting tune-up. In the event of a conflict between specifications given in this manual and decal specifications, use the decal specifications.*

CAUTION — *On vehicles equipped with catalytic converters do not add fuel system cleaning agents to fuel tank or carburetor as their use may be detrimental to the catalytic converter.*

CAUTION — *Before making a compression test or cranking engine using a remote starting switch, disconnect coil wire from distributor and secure to a good ground.*

NOTE — *For other items affecting Tune-Up, see FUEL SYSTEMS Section or EMISSION CONTROL Section.*

NOTE — *For tune-up purposes, "Light Duty" refers to vehicles 8500 lbs. GVW or less and "Heavy Duty" refers to vehicles over 8500 lbs. GVW.*

ENGINE COMPRESSION

Compression Ratio	
5.2L	8.6:1
5.9L	8.5:1
Minimum Compression Pressure	100 psi
Maximum Pressure Variation	40 psi

Test compression with engine warm, all plugs removed and throttle wide open.

VALVE CLEARANCE

All (Hydraulic)	Zero Lash

VALVE ARRANGEMENT

E-I-I-E-E-I-I-E (Front to rear, both banks).

SPARK PLUGS

Application	Gap (In.)	Torque (Ft. Lbs.)
5.2L	.035	30
5.9L Light Duty	.035	30
5.9L Heavy Duty	.035	10

Spark Plug Type

Application	Champion No.
5.2L	RN-11Y
5.9L Light Duty	RN-12Y
5.9L Heavy Duty	RF-10

HIGH TENSION WIRE RESISTANCE

1) Carefully remove spark plug wire from spark plug and install proper adapter between wire and spark plug. Remove distributor cap with wires attached. Connect an ohmmeter between spark plug adapter and opposite end of wire. If resistance is not within specifications, remove wire from cap and retest. If not within specifications, replace wire.

2) To check coil wire resistance, remove distributor cap from distributor (with wires still attached). Do not remove wire from coil. Connect an ohmmeter between center contact in cap and either primary terminal at coil. If combined resistance of coil and cable is not within specifications, remove coil wire at coil tower and check cable resistance.

3) If resistance is now within specifications, check for a loose connection at coil tower or for a faulty coil. If resistance is not within specifications, replace wire.

Resistance (Ohms)

Application	Maximum
Coil Wire	
Installed	25,000
Removed	15,000
Spark Plug Wire	
To 25" Length	30,000
Over 25" Length	50,000

DISTRIBUTOR

All models are equipped with Chrysler Electronic Ignition system and no adjustments are required. Automatic transmission models use a dual pick-up distributor, while manual transmission vehicles have a single pick-up.

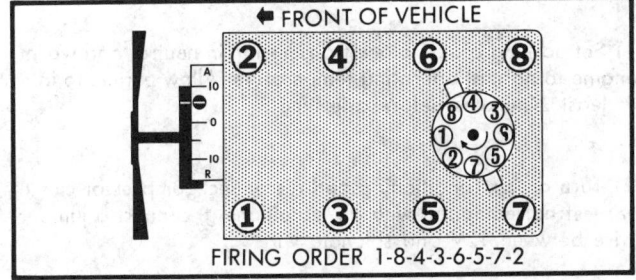

Fig. 1 Firing Order and Timing Marks (5.2L & 5.9L)

TUNE-UP (Cont.)

IGNITION TIMING

NOTE — *All models are equipped with a receptacle for magnetic timing light equipment, located 10° ATDC. Do not use this location for timing with a conventional timing light.*

1) Connect timing light to number 1 cylinder and tachometer to engine. Start engine, set parking brake and place transmission in Neutral. Bring engine to normal operating temperature.

2) Disconnect and plug vacuum hoses to EGR valve and at distributor. Disconnect PCV valve from grommet and vapor canister purge hose at carburetor, leaving connections open. Idle set RPM should be within ±100 RPM of specifications. To adjust, use idle speed screw.

3) Reconnect PCV valve and purge hose and check timing. If not within ±2°, loosen distributor hold-down screw and adjust timing until within specifications. Tighten hold-down screw when timing is correct. Recheck idle set RPM and timing.

CAUTION — *DO NOT use distributor vacuum advance unit as a handle when turning distributor housing.*

4) If timing was adjusted or idle speed screw was turned, perform propane enrichment procedure. Unplug and reconnect all vacuum hoses and remove all test equipment.

Ignition Timing Specifications
(Degrees BTDC@RPM)

Application	Man. Trans.	Auto. Trans.
5.2L 2-Bbl.	10@650	16@650
5.2L 4-Bbl.		
Federal	.....	16@650
Calif.	12@750	16@750
Nationwide	8@750	8@750
5.9L 4-Bbl.		
Light Duty		
Federal	12@600	.....
Calif.	12@725	16@750
Heavy Duty		
Federal	4@700	4@700
Calif.	10@750	10@750

HOT (SLOW) IDLE RPM

1) Set parking brake, place transmission in neutral and warm engine to normal operating temperature. Allow engine to idle at least 2 minutes before adjusting.

2) Turn on air conditioning and disconnect compressor clutch wire. If not equipped with air conditioning, connect a jumper wire between 12V and solenoid wire.

CAUTION — *Be sure jumper wire is connected to solenoid wire. Wrong connections may damage wiring harness.*

3) On 2-Bbl. models, remove external screw and spring from top of solenoid. Insert 1/8" Allen wrench into solenoid and adjust to solenoid RPM. On 4-Bbl. models, use screw on throttle lever to adjust solenoid RPM.

4) Turn air conditioning off and reconnect compressor clutch (or remove jumper wire). Disconnect and plug hoses at EGR valve, distributor and 3/16" hose at canister. Remove PCV valve from valve cover and allow to draw air. Disconnect 5/16" hose (red stripe) at canister and allow to draw air.

5) Allow engine to idle for 2 minutes. Adjust curb idle speed using screw on solenoid. Reconnect all hoses and remove test equipment.

Idle Speed (RPM)

Application	Curb Idle	Solenoid Energized
5.2L 2-Bbl.	650	800
5.2L 4-Bbl.		
Federal	650	800
Calif.	750	800
Nationwide	750	800
5.9L 4-Bbl.		
Light Duty		
Federal	600	800
Calif.		
Man. Trans.	725	800
Auto. Trans.	750	800
Heavy Duty		
Federal	700	800
Calif.	750	800

IDLE MIXTURE

MIXTURE SCREW PLUG REMOVAL

2-Bbl. Carburetors — **1)** Remove carburetor. Remove throttle body from carburetor and clamp in a padded vise. Drill a 1/16" pilot hole above both roll pins, then redrill to 1/8" and drive out roll pins with punch.

2) Drill a 1/16" pilot hole into casting at a 45° angle toward plug. Redrill hole to 1/8" and drive out plug with a blunt punch. Position roll pins partially in holes, then reassemble and install carburetor.

4-Bbl. Carburetors — **1)** Remove carburetor and clamp in a padded vise with mixture screws facing up. Drill a 1/16" pilot hole at a 45° angle towards concealment plugs in the side of screw housings.

2) Redrill hole with 1/8" drill, then use punch to drive out plugs. Use a punch inserted through screw openings to remove roll pins. Position new pins from bottom of throttle body but leave screws accessible. Reinstall carburetor.

PROPANE ENRICHMENT PROCEDURE

1) Warm engine to normal operation temperature. Place transmission in neutral and turn all accessories off. Disconnect and plug hoses at EGR valve, distributor and 3/16" hose at canister.

1981 Chrysler Corp. V8 Tune-Up 1-11

TUNE
UP

TUNE-UP (Cont.)

2) Disconnect vacuum hose from heated air cleaner to carburetor and connect propane bottle to carburetor port. Pull PCV valve from valve cover and allow to draw fresh air. Disconnect 5/16" hose (red stripe) from canister and allow to draw fresh air.

3) Open propane valve. Adjust propane until maximum engine speed is reached (with air cleaner in place). When maximum RPM is attained, adjust idle speed screw on solenoid to obtain mixture RPM specification.

4) Readjust propane level to increase RPM as high as possible, then readjust idle speed screw to maximum RPM again. Turn off propane. Then turn mixture screws evenly (with air cleaner in place) until curb idle is reached.

5) Turn on propane again and adjust for highest RPM. If it differs more than 25 RPM from mixture speed, repeat adjustment procedure. Turn off engine and remove all test equipment. Reconnect all hoses. Use a screwdriver to press roll pin into place, then reinstall mixture screw plugs.

Mixture Adjustment RPM

Application	Man. Trans.	Auto. Trans.
5.2L 2-Bbl.	740	740
5.2L 4-Bbl.		
Federal	.....	740
Calif.	830	830
Nationwide	810	810
5.9L 4-Bbl.		
Light Duty		
Federal	680	.....
Calif.	825	850
Heavy Duty		
Federal	800	800
Calif.	810	810

COLD (FAST) IDLE RPM

1) Warm engine to operating temperature and place transmission in neutral. Disconnect and plug hoses at EGR valve, distributor and 3/16" hose at canister. Disconnect PCV valve and 5/16" hose at canister (red stripe) and allow both to draw fresh air.

2) Remove air cleaner, place fast idle screw on 2nd highest step of cam and adjust fast idle speed with screw. Reconnect all hoses, remove test equipment and install air cleaner.

Fast Idle Speed (RPM)

Application	Man. Trans.	Auto. Trans.
5.2L 2-Bbl.	1500	1500
5.2L 4-Bbl.		
Federal		1500
Calif.	1500	1600
Nationwide	1800	1800
5.9L 4-Bbl.		
Light Duty		
Federal	1500	.....
Calif.	1700	1700
Heavy Duty		
Federal	1500	1500
Calif.	1500	1500

AUTOMATIC CHOKE SETTING

All models use an electric assist choke which requires no adjustment.

FUEL PUMP

Pressure (At Idle)	5-7 psi
Volume (At Idle)	1 quart in 1 minute

MANIFOLD HEAT CONTROL VALVE

Every 30,000 (Light Duty) or 18,000 (Heavy Duty) miles, apply a suitable solvent to both ends of valve shaft where it rotates in bushing. Work valve back and forth a few times.

NOTE — Apply solvent only when manifold is cool.

EMISSION CONTROL SYSTEMS

See appropriate article in Emission Control Section.

GENERAL SERVICING

IGNITION

DISTRIBUTOR

All models are equipped with Chrysler Corp. Electronic Ignition System. Units are entirely self-contained and require no outside adjustments.

Other Data & Specifications — See Tune-Up and Chrysler Corp. Distributors in ELECTRICAL Section.

IGNITION COIL

Coil Resistance (Ohms@75°F)

Application	Primary	Secondary
Essex	1.34-1.55	9000-12,200
Prestolite	1.60-1.79	9400-11,700
Ballast Resistor		1.1-1.3 ohms

1981 Chrysler Corp. V8 Tune-Up

GENERAL SERVICING (Cont.)

FUEL SYSTEMS

CARBURETORS

Application	Carb. Model
5.2L 2-Bbl.	Holley 2280
5.2L 4-Bbl.	Carter Thermo-Quad
5.9L 4-Bbl.	Carter Thermo-Quad

Other Data & Specifications — *See Tune-Up and Holley or Carter Carburetors in FUEL SYSTEMS Section.*

ELECTRICAL

BATTERY

Application	Cold Cranking Amps@0°F	Reserve Capacity Minutes
Standard	305	68
Optional	375	86
Optional	430	100
Optional	500	125

STARTER

All models use a Chrysler Corp. reduction gear type starter.

Starter Specifications

Application	Volts	Amps	Test RPM
All Models	11	90	3700

Other Data & Specifications — *See Chrysler Corp. Starters in ELECTRICAL Section.*

ALTERNATORS

All models use Chrysler Corp. alternator.

Tag Color	Rated Amp. Output
Violet	41
Yellow	60
Yellow ("D", "W", "AD", "PD", "AW" & "PW")	117

Other Data & Specifications — *See Chrysler Corp. Alternator in ELECTRICAL Section.*

ALTERNATOR REGULATOR

All models use Chrysler Corp. Electronic Voltage Regulator. Unit is nonadjustable.

Operating Voltage (@80°F) — 13.9-14.6 Volts

Other Data & Specifications — *See Chrysler Corp. Electronic Regulators in ELECTRICAL Section.*

BELT ADJUSTMENT

NOTE — *Do not use either the gauge or torque method when checking belt adjustment. Instead, use belt deflection method.*

Application	Deflection New Belt①	Deflection Used Belt①
All	¼ - ½"	¼ - 5⁄16"

① — With 10 pounds deflection pressure midway between pulleys. Used belts are any operated more than 15 minutes.

COOLING CAPACITIES

Application	Quantity (Qts.)
5.2L	①16.0
5.9L	①14.5

① — Add 1 quart for A/C or increased cooling.

REPLACEMENT INTERVALS

Component	Light Duty Interval (Miles)	Heavy Duty Interval (Miles)
Oil Filter	15,000	12,000
Fuel Filter	30,000	18,000
Air Filter	30,000	①24,000
PCV Valve	30,000	24,000
Spark Plugs	30,000	18,000

① — Clean at 12,000 mile intervals.

CAPACITIES (EXCEPT COOLING)

Application	Quantity
Crankcase	①5.0 qts.
Automatic Transmission (Dexron II)	②7.7 pts.
Manual Transmission	
4-Speed Overdrive (A-833) (Dexron II)	7.5 pts.
4-Speed N.P. 435 (SAE 80W-90)	7.0 pts.
Transfer Case	
N.P. 205 (SAE 80W-90)	4.5 pts.
N.P. 208 (Dexron II)	6.0 pts.
Rear Axle (SAE 80W-90)	
8⅜" Ring Gear	4.5 pts.
9¼" Ring Gear	4.5 pts.
9¾" Ring Gear	6.0 pts.
10½" Ring Gear	6.5 pts.
Front Axle (SAE 80W-90)	
Model 44	3.5 pts.
Model 60	6.5 pts.
Fuel Tank	
Van Models	
B150/350	22.0 or 36.0 gals.
CB350/450 & MB250	22.0 or 45.0 gals.
MB350/450	45.0 gals.
Pickup Models	22.0 or 30.0 gals.
All Other Models	35.0 gals.

① — Add 1 quart with filter change.
② — Without torque converter drain.

TUNE-UP

ENGINE IDENTIFICATION

The engine can be identified by the eighth digit of the Vehicle Identification Number. The number is located on the Safety Compliance label (on left front door pillar) and on a metal plate riveted to the driver's side of the dash and visible through windshield.

VIN Engine Code

Application	Code
4.9L (300") 1 Bbl.	E

MODEL IDENTIFICATION

Model identification can be found on bottom line of Safety Compliance label located on left front door pillar.

TUNE-UP NOTES

NOTE — *For other items affecting Tune-Up, see FUEL SYSTEMS Section or EMISSION CONTROL Section.*

CAUTION — *When performing tune-up on vehicles equipped with a catalytic converter, do not allow or create a condition of engine misfire in one or more cylinders for an extended period of time. Damage to converter from overheating may occur due to loading with unburned fuel.*

NOTE — *Due to production changes, always refer to Engine Tune-Up Decal in engine compartment before attempting tune-up. In the event of a conflict between specifications given in this manual and decal specifications, use the decal specifications.*

NOTE — *For tune-up purposes, "Light Duty" refers to vehicles up to 8500 lbs. "Heavy Duty" refers to vehicles exceeding 8500 lbs.*

NOTE — *In some applications within this article it will be necessary to refer to engine calibration number. To determine location of calibration number decal on engine, refer to Ford Motor Co. Vacuum Diagrams in EMISSION CONTROL Section.*

ENGINE COMPRESSION

Compression Ratio
4.9L 8.9:1

Test compression with all spark plugs removed and engine at normal operating temperature. Crank engine through at least five compression strokes before recording reading. Maximum compression variation should not exceed 25% between highest and lowest cylinder.

VALVE CLEARANCE

Application	Clearance
4.9L	①.100-.200"

① — Clearance allowable with tappet collapsed. Desired clearance is .125-175".

VALVE ARRANGEMENT

E-I-E-I-E-I-E-I-E-I-E-I (front to rear).

SPARK PLUGS

Application	Gap (In.)	Torque (Ft. Lbs.)
4.9L	.042-.046	15-25

Spark Plug Type

Application	Autolite No.
4.9L	BSF-42

HIGH TENSION WIRE RESISTANCE

1) Loosen wires from spark plugs by twisting spark plug boot carefully to loosen seal on spark plug. Remove wires by pulling on plug boot. Remove distributor cap from distributor, leaving wires connected to cap.

2) Using an ohmmeter, check resistance of each wire by connecting one ohmmeter lead to spark plug terminal and other lead to distributor cap insert. Replace any wire with over 5000 ohms resistance per inch. New wires should have a resistance of 7000 ohms per foot.

NOTE — *Whenever a high tension wire is disconnected, the interior of spark plug terminal boot must be coated with dielectric silicone grease before connection.*

DISTRIBUTORS

All models are equipped with Dura Spark II ignition system and no adjustments are required.

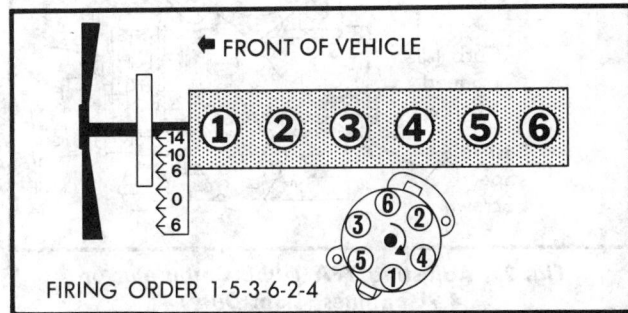

Fig. 1   Firing Order and Timing Marks

IGNITION TIMING

NOTE — *Engines are equipped with a receptacle for use with magnetic pick-up timing lights, located at 135°ATDC. Do not use this location for timing with a conventional timing light.*

TUNE-UP (Cont.)

1) Place mark on proper degree line of damper (or of pointer and damper notch). Disconnect vacuum lines at distributor and plug lines.

2) Connect timing light using adaptor or inductive pick-up. Do not puncture spark plug leads. Connect an accurate tachometer.

3) Start engine and warm to operating temperature. With engine idling in neutral, check timing. If within ±2°, do not reset. If outside specifications, loosen distributor hold-down bolt and rotate to set timing. Recheck after tightening bolt.

Ignition Timing Specifications
(Degrees BTDC@RPM)

Application	Man. Trans.	Auto. Trans.
4.9L		
Light Duty	6@800	10@800
Heavy Duty	10@800	12@800

HOT (SLOW) IDLE RPM

LIGHT DUTY

1) Place transmission in "Neutral" or "Park", with engine at normal operating temperature. Turn A/C Heat Selector off.

2) Allow engine speed to stabilize and measure curb idle speed. To set curb idle speed, adjust curb idle speed screw to obtain specified reading. See *Fig. 2.*

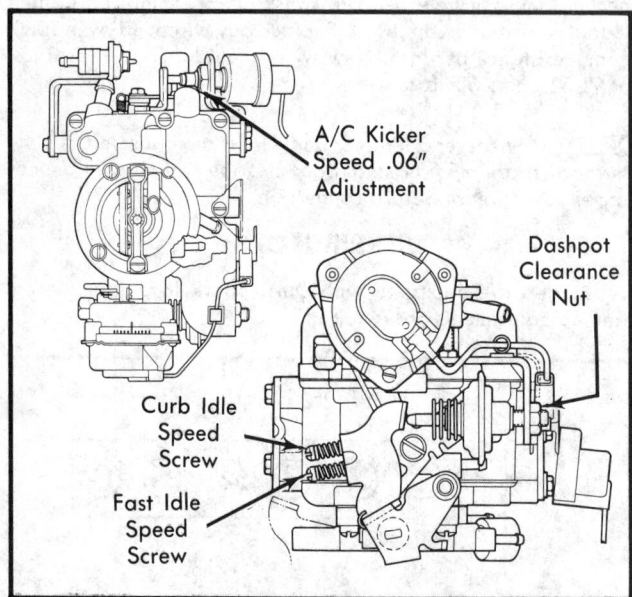

Fig. 2   *Adjusting YFA 1-Bbl. Carburetor on 4.9L Engines (Light Duty)*

3) Place transmission in "Neutral" or "Park". Speed up engine momentarily, and recheck curb idle RPM. Readjust if necessary.

4) Check dashpot clearance, adjusting if necessary. Move AC Heat Selector to maximum cooling (blower switch in high position). Disconnect A/C clutch wire. Check and adjust for A/C-On RPM.

Light Duty Idle Speed (RPM)①

Application	Curb Idle	②Solenoid/Kicker Energized
4.9L		
Man. Trans.	600③	700
Auto. Trans.	550④	.....

① — Subtract 50 RPM if engine has less than 100 hours use.
② — A/C-On reading.
③ — A/C-Off or Non-A/C reading.
④ — Non-A/C reading.

HEAVY DUTY

1) Place transmission in "Neutral" or "Park", with engine at normal operating temperature. Turn A/C Heat Selector off.

2) Activate Throttle Solenoid Positioner (TSP). Set curb idle to specification by screwing solenoid in or out. See *Fig. 3.*

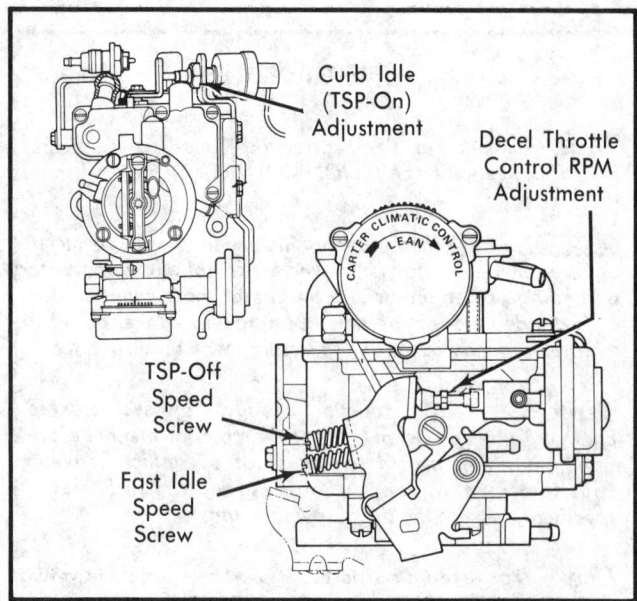

Fig. 3   *Adjusting YFA 1-Bbl. Carburetor on 4.9L Engines (Heavy Duty)*

3) With transmission selector lever in either "Neutral" or "Park" position, increase engine speed momentarily, letting it return to normal curb idle. Check RPM and readjust if required.

4) To set TSP-Off RPM, bring engine to normal operating temperature. Place A/C Heat Selector in "Off" position. Disconnect TSP wire. Place transmission in "Neutral". Using TSP-Off adjusting screw, set TSP-Off RPM to specifications. Reconnect TSP wire to terminal.

Heavy Duty Idle Speed (RPM)

Application	Curb Idle (TSP-On)	TSP-Off RPM
4.9L		
Man. Trans.	700	500
Auto. Trans.	550①	500

① — 600 RPM for Calibration No. 5-77-R1; 700 RPM for Calibration No. 9-77J-R12.

TUNE-UP (Cont.)

COLD (FAST) IDLE RPM

LIGHT DUTY

1) Place transmission in "Neutral". Bring engine to normal operating temperature. Disconnect vacuum hoses at EGR, purge valve or purge solenoid valve and plug hoses.

2) Disconnect vacuum hose from cold start vacuum switch (orange vacuum switch on valve corner). Plug hose. Using a slave vacuum hose, connect manifold vacuum to cold start vacuum switch.

3) Place fast idle screw on second step (kickdown) of fast idle cam. Adjust fast idle speed to specifications. See Fig. 2. Remove plugs from vacuum hoses and restore all hoses to their original locations.

Light Duty Fast Idle Speed (RPM)

Application	①RPM	Cam Step
4.9L		
Man. Trans.	1400	2nd (Kickdown)
Auto. Trans.	1400	2nd (Kickdown)

① — Subtract 150 RPM if engine has less than 100 miles use.

HEAVY DUTY

NOTE — Procedure includes setting Decel Throttle Control.

1) Place transmission in "Neutral". Bring engine to normal operating temperature. Disconnect vacuum hoses at EGR, purge valve, or purge solenoid valve. Plug hoses.

2) Disconnect and plug vacuum hose to decal throttle control diaphragm. Place fast idle adjusting screw on second step (kickdown) of fast idle cam. See Fig. 3. Adjust fast idle speed to specifications.

3) Using a slave vacuum hose, connect manifold vacuum to decal throttle control diaphragm. Adjust diaphragm shaft length until specified RPM is obtained. Remove plugs and restore vacuum hoses to their original locations.

Heavy Duty Fast Idle Speed (RPM)

Calibration Number	Fast Idle Speed	Decel Throttle Control Speed
5-77-R1, 5-78-R1, 9-78J-R0	1500	
9-77J-R11	1600	1950 + 50
9-77J-R12, 9-77S-R10	1600	1450 + 50

IDLE MIXTURE

NOTE — If adjustments to the air/fuel mixture are made that require removing the idle limiter caps, it is imperative that the BLUE SERVICE LIMITER CAPS be installed. Idle mixture should be adjusted only during carburetor repair or when necessary as a result of government inspection laws.

PROPANE ENRICHMENT PROCEDURE

NOTE — For specifications for Propane Enrichment Procedure, see Emission Control Tune-Up Decal. If no decal can be located, use specifications at end of instructions.

1) Leave all vacuum signal hoses attached to air cleaner assembly when relocating air cleaner for carburetor adjustments. Air cleaner MUST be installed for engine speed checks.

CAUTION — Do not let engine idle for extended periods, as catalyst overheating may cause excessive underbody temperatures.

2) Apply parking brake and block wheels. Disconnect automatic brake release and plug vacuum connection. Connect tachometer (20362 or equivalent).

3) Disconnect and plug fuel evaporative purge valve signal hose at engine. Disconnect purge hose at air cleaner and plug nipple.

4) Disconnect flexible fresh air tube from air cleaner duct or adapter. Insert hose from propane enrichment tool (Rotunda T75L-9600-A) about ¾ the way into duct or fresh air tube. Disconnect PCV valve from grommet and allow valve to draw underhood air during adjustment.

5) For vehicles equipped with thermactor, disconnect and plug hoses of dump valves equipped with two fittings. If valves have one fitting, remove and plug hose at valve. Connect slave hose to dump valve and intake manifold vacuum source.

6) Be sure idle mixture limiter(s) is set to maximum rich position (counterclockwise against stop). With engine at normal operating temperature, check curb idle speed or A/C-Off RPM. Adjust as necessary. Run engine at 2500 RPM for 15 seconds before each mixture check. Check ignition timing, and adjust as necessary.

7) With engine idling in neutral, gradually open propane tool valve and watch for engine speed gain on tachometer. When speed reaches maximum and begins to drop off, note amount of speed gain.

NOTE — Propane cartridge must be in vertical position. If engine speed will not drop off, check bottle gas supply. If necessary, repeat test with new bottle.

8) Compare measured speed gain with specifications. If mixture adjustment is necessary, adjust so gain is within "Reset RPM" specifications. If propane enrichment speed gain is within "RPM Gain" specifications, proceed to step 11).

9) If measured speed gain is greater than specification, turn mixture screws counterclockwise in equal amounts and recheck until measured speed rise is within "Reset RPM" specifications. Then proceed to step 11).

TUNE-UP (Cont.)

10) If measured speed gain is less than specification, turn mixture screws clockwise in equal amounts and recheck until measured speed rise is within "Reset RPM" specifications. Then proceed to step 11).

11) Check curb idle and remove all test equipment. Reconnect hoses in original positions and connect PCV valve.

Idle Mixture Specifications
(Propane Enrichment)

Calibration Number①	RPM Gain (Check)	Reset RPM (Adjust)
Light Duty		
1-52K-R0, R10 &		
1-52L-R0, R10	20-110	60
All Others	10-50	20
Heavy Duty	②	②

① — Calibration No. is located on an identification label on front of valve cover. On some engines, label may be on same component as Emission Certification Decal.

② — See Emission Control Decal.

DASHPOT ADJUSTMENT

Each time curb idle speed is adjusted, check dashpot clearance. Collapse dashpot stem and check clearance between dashpot stem and throttle lever pad. To adjust, remove air cleaner and loosen lock nut on dashpot. Turn dashpot in or out to achieve specified clearance. Tighten lock nut. See *Fig. 2.*

Dashpot Clearance Specifications①

Calibration Number	Clearance (Inches)
1-51D-R0, 1-51D-R10,	
1-51D-R12	.105-.135
All Others	.055-.085

① — Light Duty models only.

GENERAL SERVICING

IGNITION

DISTRIBUTOR

All units are equipped with Motorcraft Dura-Spark II Ignition system. Units are self-contained and require no outside adjustments.

Other Data & Specifications — *See Tune-Up and Motorcraft Distributors in ELECTRICAL Section.*

IGNITION COIL

Resistance
Primary	1-2 ohms
Secondary	7700-9600 ohms
Primary Ballast Resistance Wire	1.05-1.15 ohms

Coil Reserve Voltage .... 28 Kv minimum.

AUTOMATIC CHOKE ADJUSTMENT

NOTE — *Some 1981 carburetors may have tamperproof choke assemblies.*

Drill heads from 2 rivets and remove rivets. Loosen remaining screw, and turn choke cover in direction indicated on cover to specified setting. Install new rivets and tighten screw.

Automatic Choke Specifications

Calibration Number	Choke Setting
Light Duty	Non-Adjustable
Heavy Duty	
5-77-R1 & 5-78-R1	1 Rich
All Others	Index

FUEL PUMP

Check fuel pump at idle RPM with engine in normal operating temperature and transmission in neutral.

Pressure	5.0-7.0 psi
Volume	One Pint in 20 seconds

EMISSION CONTROL

See appropriate article in EMISSION CONTROL Section.

FUEL SYSTEMS

CARBURETOR

Application	Carb. Model
4.9L Engine	
Light Duty	
Federal	Carter YFA 1-Bbl.
Calif.	Carter YFA 1-Bbl. Feedback
Heavy Duty	Carter YFA 1-Bbl.

Other Data & Specifications — *See Tune-Up and Carter Carburetors in FUEL SYSTEMS Section.*

TUNE-UP (Cont.)

ELECTRICAL

BATTERY

Application	Amp. Hr. Rating
Standard	
Federal	36
Calif.	45
Optional	45, 48, 54, 63, 71, 77, 81

STARTER

Motorcraft positive engagement type with either a 4" or 4½" armature.

Engine Cranking Speed	
4" Armature	180-250 RPM
4½" Armature	150-290 RPM
Starter Current Draw	
4" Armature	150-200 amps.
4½" Armature	150-180 amps.

Other Data & Specifications — *See Motorcraft Starters in ELECTRICAL Section.*

ALTERNATORS

All Models use Motorcraft Alternators.

I.D. Color	Rated Amp. Output
Rear Terminal	
Orange	40
Green	60 or 65
Side Terminal	
Black	70
Red	100

Other Data & Specifications — *See Motorcraft Alternators in ELECTRICAL Section.*

ALTERNATOR REGULATORS

Two Motorcraft Electronic Voltage Regulators are used on 4.9L engines. Although both look alike, they are not interchangeable.

Application	Color Coding
Used with Ammeter	Blue label
Used with Indicator Lamp	Black label

Other Data & Specifications — *See Motorcraft Alternators in ELECTRICAL Section.*

CAPACITIES (EXCEPT FUEL & COOLING)

Application	Quantity
Crankcase	①6.0 qts.
Drive Axles (Hypoid Gear Lube)②	
Front	3.9 pts.
Rear	6.5 pts.
Transfer Case (Dexron II)	
Warner 1435	6.5 pts.
New Process 208	7.0 pts.
Auto. Trans. (Dexron II)③	
C-4	9.6 qts.
C-6	
2-WD	11.9 qts.
4-WD	13.4 qts.
AOT	12.0 qts.
Man. Trans. (SAE 80W-90)	
Ford 3.03	3.5 pts.
T-18	7.0 pts.
New Process 435	7.0 pts.
New Process 435 w/Ext	6.5 pts.
4-Speed Overdrive	4.5 pts.

① — Includes 1 quart for filter change.
② — Fill to bottom of filler plug hole.
③ — Use Auto. Trans. dipstick for exact refill.

FUEL TANK CAPACITIES

Application	Gallons
F100, F150, F250 (Short W.B.)	
Standard	16.5
Auxiliary	19.0
F100, F150, F250, F350 (Long W.B.)	
Standard	19.0
Auxiliary	19.0
E100, E150, Club Wagon (Short W.B.)	
Standard	18.0
Auxiliary	18.0
All Other "E" Models (Long W.B.)	
Standard	22.1
Auxiliary	18.0
Bronco	
Standard	25
Optional	32

GENERAL SERVICING (Cont.)

COOLING CAPACITIES

Application	Quarts
"E" Models①	
With Heater	15.0
With Heater & A/C	20.0
"F" Models & Bronco	
With Heater	13.0
With Heater & A/C	14.0

① — Add .8 quart for auxiliary heater.

BELT ADJUSTMENT

Tension (Lbs.) Using Strand Tension Gauge

Application	New Belt	①Used Belt
¼" Belts	50-80	40-60
All Others	120-160	75-120

① — Any belt operated for 10 minutes or more.

FILTERS & CLEANERS

Filter or Cleaner	Service Interval (Miles)
Oil Filter	
E100, E150, F100, F150	Replace 10,000
All Others	Replace 15,000
Air Filter	Replace 30,000
PCV Filter	Replace 30,000

TUNE-UP

ENGINE IDENTIFICATION

Engine can be identified by the eighth digit of Vehicle Identification Number. Number is stamped on metal plate, which is riveted to upper left corner of instrument panel and visible through left side of windshield.

VIN Engine Codes

Application	Code
4.2L (255″) 2-Bbl.	D
5.0L (302″) 2-Bbl.	F
5.8L (351″) M 2-Bbl.	G
5.8L (351″) W 2-Bbl.	W
6.6L (400″) 2-Bbl.	Z
7.5L (460″) 4-Bbl.	L

MODEL IDENTIFICATION

On all models, the model identification can be found on bottom line of Safety Compliance Certification label located on lock face of left front door.

TUNE-UP NOTES

NOTE — *In some applications within this article it will be necessary to refer to the engine calibration number. To determine location of calibration number decal on engine, refer to Ford Motor Co. Vacuum Diagrams in EMISSION CONTROL Section. Most numbers for V8 engines are located on an identification label on front of right valve cover.*

NOTE — *For Tune-Up purposes, "Light Duty" refers to vehicles up to 8500 lbs. "Heavy Duty" refers to vehicles exceeding 8500 lbs.*

NOTE — *When connecting a tachometer to SSI coil, install the alligator clip on tachometer into the "DEC" (TACH TEST) cavity.*

NOTE — *For other items affecting Tune-Up, see FUEL SYSTEMS Section or EMISSION CONTROL Section.*

NOTE — *Due to production changes, always refer to Engine Tune-Up Decal in engine compartment before attempting tune-up. In the event of a conflict between specifications given in this manual and decal specifications, use the decal specifications.*

CAUTION — *When performing tune-up on vehicles equipped with a catalytic converter, do not allow or create a condition of engine misfire in one or more cylinders for an extended period of time. Damage to converter from overheating may occur due to loading with unburned fuel.*

CAUTION — *IDLE SPEED ADJUSTMENT: Procedures and specifications for idle speed adjustment must be followed exactly as outlined. See "Hot (Slow) Idle RPM" under Tune-Up.*

ENGINE COMPRESSION

Compression Ratio .... ①

① — Information not available from manufacturer.

Test compression with all spark plugs removed and engine at normal operating temperature. Crank engine through at least five compression strokes before recording reading. Maximum compression variation should not exceed 25% between highest and lowest cylinder.

VALVE CLEARANCE

Hydraulic Lifters .... Zero Lash

VALVE ARRANGEMENT

All Models

E-I-E-I-E-I-E-I (Left bank, front to rear.)
I-E-I-E-I-E-I-E (Right bank, front to rear.)

SPARK PLUGS

Application	Gap (In.)	Torque (Ft. Lbs.)
7.5L	.042-.046	5-10
All Other Engines	.042-.046	10-15

Spark Plug Type

Application	Autolite No.
5.8L M & 6.6L	ASF-52
All Other Engines	ASF-42

HIGH TENSION WIRE RESISTANCE

1) Loosen wires from spark plugs by twisting spark plug boot carefully to loosen seal on spark plug. Remove wires by pulling on plug boot. Remove distributor cap from distributor, leaving wires connected to cap.

NOTE — *DO NOT disconnect wires from distributor cap unless replacement is necessary.*

2) Using an ohmmeter, check resistance of each wire by connecting one ohmmeter lead to spark plug terminal and other lead to distributor cap insert. Replace any wire with over 5,000 ohms resistance per inch.

NOTE — *Whenever a high tension wire is disconnected, the interior of spark plug terminal boot must be coated with dielectric silicone grease before connection.*

1981 Ford V8 Tune-Up

TUNE-UP (Cont.)

DISTRIBUTOR

All models are equipped with Motorcraft Dura Spark II ignition system and no adjustments are required.

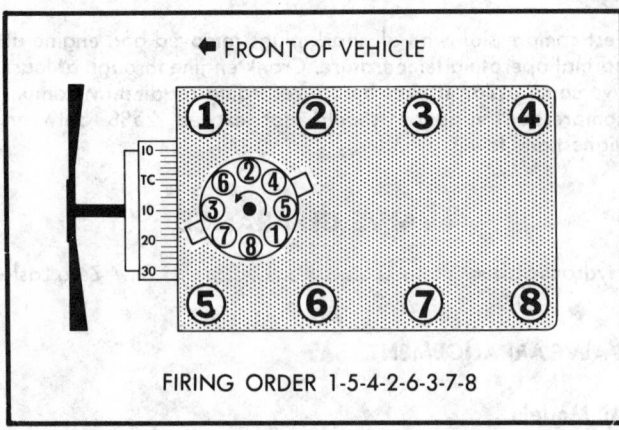

Fig. 1 4.2L, 5.0L & 7.5L Firing Order & Timing Mark Identification

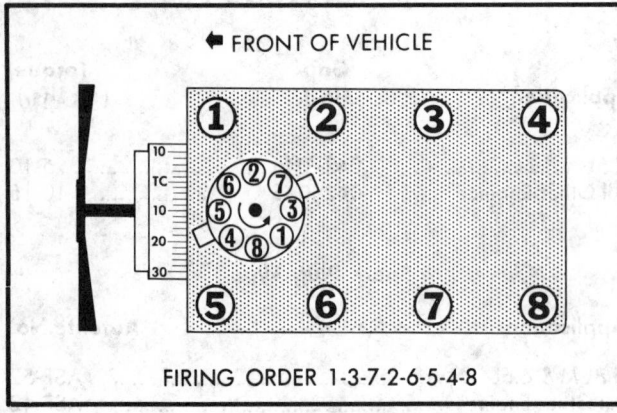

Fig. 2 5.8L & 6.6L Firing Order & Timing Mark Identification

IGNITION TIMING

NOTE — *Magnetic probe timing device may be used if instrument is available and engine is so equipped. Timing probe offset is 135°ATDC on all V8 engines.*

1) Determine specified timing and mark degree line on damper (some vehicles mark both pointer and damper notch). Disconnect vacuum line(s) at distributor and plug lines.

2) Connect tachometer (Rotunda 20362 or equivalent). Connect timing light (Rotunda 270001 or equivalent) to No. 1 spark plug wire. Set timing to specifications if more than ±2° variation is found.

3) To adjust, loosen distributor hold-down bolt and rotate distributor to align marks in step **1)**. Tighten hold-down bolt and recheck timing.

Ignition Timing Specifications
(Degrees BTDC@RPM)

Application	Man. Trans.	Auto. Trans.
4.2L	4@800	10@800
5.0L (Federal)③	8@800	8@800
5.8L (351") M		
Light Duty	10@800	6@800
Heavy Duty	10@800	10@800
5.8L (351") W		
F150/350 & Bronco	①	①
E100	10@600	10@600
E150/250		
Federal	10@600	②10@600
Calif.	③	③
High Alt.	8@800	8@800
E350		
Heavy Duty		6@800
6.6L		
F250/350		
Federal	6@800	3@800
Calif.	6@800	6@800
E250/350		
Federal	3@800	3@800
Calif.		6@800
7.5L	8@800	8@800

① — Information not available from manufacturer.

② — 6@800 on Heavy Duty Emission models.

③ — Calif. 5.0L & 5.8L W engines are equipped with Electronic Engine Control (EEC III) system and no adjustment is required.

HOT (SLOW) IDLE RPM

NOTE — *Calif. 5.0L & 5.8L W engines are equipped with Motorcraft 7200VV 2-Bbl. carburetor and the Electronic Engine Control (EEC III) system. Adjustments are computer-controlled.*

NOTE — *On engines that idle smoothly but become rough at 1000-2000 RPM, check for crossed orange and purple primary ignition wires between distributor and module. To check, turn ignition key off and set engine at initial timing mark firing point. One spoke of distributor armature should be opposite stator pole. If pole is between spokes, primary wires are probably crossed.*

4.2L & FEDERAL 5.0L ENGINES

Curb Idle — 1) With transmission in "NEUTRAL" (Man. Trans.) or in "PARK" (Auto. Trans.), start engine and let it run until it reaches normal operating temperature.

2) Place air conditioning and heater in "OFF" position. Disconnect and plug vacuum hose at thermactor air by-pass valve.

3) Place transmission in specified gear position and check curb idle RPM. If adjustment is necessary, adjust to specifications by turning curb idle speed screw.

4) Place transmission in "NEUTRAL" (Man. Trans.) or in "PARK" (Auto. Trans.) and increase engine speed momentarily. Again place transmission in specified gear position, and recheck curb idle RPM. Readjust if necessary. Check and or adjust dashpot clearance to .090-.140".

TUNE-UP (Cont.)

5) Unplug and reconnect vacuum hose at thermactor air by-pass valve.

Kicker RPM — 1) With engine at normal operating temperature, place air conditioner in maximum cooling position and blower in high position.

2) Disconnect air conditioner compressor clutch wire, and place transmission in specified gear position.

3) Check and or adjust air conditioner "ON" (AC-On) RPM to specifications by turning saddle bracket adjusting screw. Reconnect air conditioner compressor clutch wire.

FEDERAL 5.8L (351") W ENGINES
LIGHT DUTY VEHICLES

Curb Idle — 1) With transmission in "NEUTRAL" (Man. Trans.) or in "PARK" (Auto. Trans.), start engine and let it run until it reaches normal operating temperature.

2) Check purge hose for vacuum on canister side of evaporator purge solenoid and reconnect hose.

3) With transmission in specified gear position, check curb idle RPM. If RPM is not to specification, adjust as necessary by turning curb idle screw.

4) Place transmission in "NEUTRAL" (Man. Trans.) or in "PARK" (Auto. Trans.) and increase engine speed momentarily. Place transmission in specified gear position, and recheck curb idle. Readjust if necessary.

5) Check and adjust TSP (Throttle Solenoid Positioner) to specifications.

5.8L (351") & 6.6L (400") ENGINES
HEAVY DUTY VEHICLES

Curb Idle — 1) With transmission in "NEUTRAL" (Man. Trans.) or in "PARK" (Auto. Trans.), start engine and let it run until it reaches normal operating temperature.

2) Place air conditioner and heater switch in "OFF" position. Disconnect and plug vacuum hose from throttle kicker or from throttle kicker portion of TSP (Throttle Solenoid Positioner)

3) Install a slave vacuum hose from throttle kicker portion of TSP to intake manifold vacuum. Speed up engine momentarily. Check and adjust the decel throttle kicker RPM to specification by turning saddle bracket adjusting screw.

4) Disconnect slave vacuum hose from throttle kicker and intake manifold vacuum. Increase engine speed momentarily and check and adjust curb idle speed (TSP-On) by adjusting bolt sticking out from back of TSP.

5) Disconnect Blue electrical wiring clip connecting TSP to engine wiring harness. Check and adjust TSP-Off RPM to specifications by turning throttle stop adjusting screw on 5.8L (351") W or by turning curb idle screw on 5.8L (351") M and 6.6L.

6) Remove plug and reconnect vacuum hose to throttle kicker or throttle kicker portion of TSP. Reconnect Blue electrical clip to TSP wire.

5.8L (351") M & 6.6L ENGINES
LIGHT DUTY VEHICLES

Curb Idle — 1) With transmission in "NEUTRAL" (Man. Trans.) or in "PARK" (Auto. Trans.), start engine and let it run until it reaches normal operating temperature. Place air conditioner and heater switch in "OFF" position.

2) Disconnect and plug vacuum hose at thermactor air by-pass valve. If thermactor air by-pass valve has 2 hoses, disconnect hose closest to front of vehicle. Install a slave hose between manifold vacuum and thermactor air by-pass valve.

3) Check and adjust curb idle RPM to specification by turning curb idle screw on Man. Trans. models. On Auto. Trans. models, depress dashpot then check and adjust curb idle RPM to specification by turning curb idle screw. Also check and adjust dashpot clearance to specification on Auto. Trans. models.

4) Remove slave vacuum hose between manifold vacuum and thermactor air by-pass valve. Unplug and reconnect thermactor air by-pass valve vacuum hose to thermactor by-pass valve.

7.5L ENGINES

Curb Idle and Decel Throttle Control Speed — 1) With transmission in "PARK" or "NEUTRAL" and air conditioner in "OFF" position, start engine and let it run until it reaches normal operating temperature.

2) Remove air cleaner. Disconnect and plug decel throttle control kicker diaphragm vacuum hose. Connect a slave vacuum hose from intake manifold vacuum to decel throttle control kicker.

3) Run engine at 2500 RPM for 15 seconds, and then release throttle. If decel throttle control RPM is not within 50 RPM of specified RPM, adjust decel throttle control kicker until specified RPM is reached.

4) Allow engine to return to curb idle by removing slave vacuum hose. Adjust curb idle, if necessary, by turning curb idle adjusting screw.

5) Unplug and reconnect vacuum hose to decel throttle control kicker diaphragm and reinstall air cleaner.

ALL MODELS

NOTE — *If specified idle speed cannot be obtained by normal adjustments on vehicles with speed control, disconnect accelerator cable at carburetor throttle lever. If specified idle speed can now be obtained with linkage disconnected, check speed control installation.*

Engine Service After Speed Checks — 1) Reconnect all vacuum lines or hoses to their original positions. Reinstall air cleaner assembly. Run engine at 2500 RPM for 15 seconds and recheck curb idle speed.

2) Final curb idle speed check must be made with air cleaner installed. Adjust as necessary and recheck dashpot clearance.

TUNE-UP (Cont.)

Curb Idle Speed (RPM)

NOTE — *Calif. 5.0L & 5.8L W engines are equipped with Motorcraft 7200VV 2-Bbl. carburetor and the Electronic Engine Control (EEC III) system. Adjustments are computer-controlled.*

Application	Curb Idle & TSP-Off①	TSP-On
4.2L		
Man. Trans.	750	
Auto. Trans.	575	650
5.0L (Federal)		
Man. Trans.	700	
Auto. Trans.	575	②650

Application	Curb Idle A/C-On	Curb Idle A/C-Off or Non-A/C
5.8L (351") M		
Man. Trans.	650	650
Auto. Trans.	625	550
5.8L (351") W (Federal)		
Auto. Trans.	625	550

Application	Curb Idle	TSP-Off
6.6L		
Man. Trans.	600	
Auto. Trans.	600	500
7.5L	650	

① — Subtract 50 RPM on engines with less than 100 miles.
② — E100/250 Federal Auto. Trans. — no TSP. Calif. Auto. Trans. models are equipped with EEC III system and have VOTM, not TSP, (VOTM-On = 650 RPM, VOTM-Off = 575 RPM).

COLD (FAST) IDLE RPM

NOTE — *Before adjusting Cold (Fast) Idle RPM, perform Hot (Slow) Idle RPM preliminary adjustments.*

4.2L & 5.0L ENGINES

1) With transmission in "NEUTRAL" (Man. Trans.) or in "PARK" (Auto. Trans.), start engine and let it run until it reaches normal operating temperature.

2) Disconnect and plug hoses at both EGR valve and thermactor air by-pass valve. Disconnect vacuum hose and electrical connector on EVAP purge solenoid.

3) Place fast idle adjusting screw on first step of fast idle cam. Check and or adjust fast idle to specified RPM.

4) Reconnect vacuum hoses and electrical connector removed in step **2)**.

FEDERAL 5.8L (351") W ENGINES LIGHT DUTY VEHICLES

1) With transmission in "NEUTRAL" (Man. Trans.) or in "PARK" (Auto. Trans.), start engine and let it run until it reaches normal operating temperature.

2) On California models, disconnect purge hose on canister and ensure that purge vacuum is present, reconnect hose.

3) Disconnect and plug vacuum hose at EGR valve and purge valve. Place fast idle adjusting screw on first step of fast idle cam.

4) Check and or adjust fast idle to specified RPM. Unplug and reconnect vacuum hoses removed in step **3)**.

5.8L (351") W ENGINES HEAVY DUTY VEHICLES

1) With transmission in "NEUTRAL" (Man. Trans.) or in "PARK" (Auto. Trans.), start engine and let it run until it reaches normal operating temperature.

2) Disconnect and plug vacuum hose at EGR valve. Place fast idle adjusting screw on first step of fast idle cam.

3) Check and or adjust fast idle to specified RPM by turning fast idle adjusting screw.

4) Unplug and reconnect EGR valve vacuum hose to EGR valve.

5.8L (351") M & 6.6L ENGINES

1) With transmission in "NEUTRAL" (Man. Trans.) or in "PARK" (Auto. Trans.), start engine and let it run until it reaches normal operating temperature.

2) Disconnect and plug vacuum hose at thermactor by-pass valve. If valve has vacuum hoses, disconnect and plug hose closest to front of vehicle. Install a slave vacuum hose between thermactor by-pass valve and intake manifold vacuum.

3) Disconnect and plug vacuum hose that connects carburetor spacer plate to purge valve. Plug nipple on carburetor spacer plate. Disconnect and plug vacuum hose at EGR valve.

4) Disconnect and plug vacuum hose at throttle kicker or at throttle kicker portion of TSP.

5) Place fast idle adjusting screw on first step of fast idle cam and adjust fast idle to specified RPM by turning fast idle adjusting screw.

6) Unplug and reconnect all vacuum hoses removed in steps **2), 3)** and **4)**.

7.5L ENGINES

1) With transmission in "PARK" or "NEUTRAL" and air conditioner in "OFF" position, start engine and let it run until it reaches normal operating temperature. Remove air cleaner.

2) Disconnect and plug throttle decel control diaphragm vacuum hose and EGR valve vacuum hose.

3) Depress throttle lever and turn fast idle cam, by hand, until fast idle adjusting screw sets on first step of fast idle cam. Adjust fast idle to specified RPM by turning fast idle adjusting screw.

4) Unplug and reconnect all vacuum hoses removed in step **2)**, and reinstall air cleaner.

TUNE-UP (Cont.)

Fast Idle Speed (RPM)①

Application	Man. Trans.	Auto. Trans.
4.2L	2200	2000
5.0L		
Federal	2200	2000
Calif.	.....	1350
5.8L (351″) M		
Light Duty	2000	2000
Heavy Duty	1750	2000
F150/250 & Bronco Hi. Alt.	.....	2200
5.8L (351″) W		
Federal	1700②	2000
Calif.	1700②	1650②
Heavy Duty	.....	1700
6.6L	1750	2000
7.5L	.....	1600

① — Set fast idle speed screw on highest step of cam.
② — Set fast idle speed screw on kickdown step of cam.

DASHPOT ADJUSTMENT

With idle speed and mixture properly adjusted, remove air cleaner and loosen dashpot lock nut. With choke open, hold throttle plate closed (idle position), and check clearance between throttle lever pad and dashpot plunger tip. Plunger MUST be completely collapsed to check clearance. Turn dashpot in or out to obtain .090-.140″ clearance. Tighten lock nut.

IDLE MIXTURE

NOTE — *No idle mixture adjustment is possible on vehicles with 7200VV 2-Bbl. carburetors. If engine performance is unsatisfactory, see Ford Electronic Engine Control in EMISSION CONTROL Section.*

NOTE — *If adjustments to the air/fuel mixture are made that require removing the idle limiter caps, BLUE Service Limiter Caps must be installed. Idle mixture should be adjusted only during carburetor repair or when necessary as a result of government inspection laws.*

PROPANE ENRICHMENT PROCEDURE

1) Leave all vacuum signal hoses attached to air cleaner assembly when relocating air cleaner for carburetor adjustments. Air cleaner MUST be installed for engine speed checks.

CAUTION — *Do not let engine idle for extended periods, as catalyst overheating may cause excessive underbody temperatures.*

2) Apply parking brake and block wheels. Disconnect automatic brake release and plug vacuum connections. Connect tachometer (Rotunda 20362 or equivalent).

3) Disconnect and plug fuel evaporative purge valve return hose at engine. Disconnect evaporative emission purge hose at air cleaner. Plug nipple.

NOTE — *Check and make sure correct PCV valve is installed and that air cleaner element is clean, as an excessively dirty air cleaner element could cause an erroneous propane reading.*

4) Disconnect flexible fresh air tube from air cleaner duct or adapter. Insert hose from propane enrichment tool (Rotunda T75L-9600-A) into duct or fresh air tube.

5) For vehicles equipped with thermactor, disconnect and plug hoses of dump valves equipped with two fittings. If valves have one fitting, remove and plug hose at valve. Connect slave hose to dump valve and intake manifold vacuum source.

6) Be sure idle mixture limiter(s) is set to maximum rich position (counterclockwise against stop). Check curb idle speed or A/C "OFF" RPM and set as specified. Remove PCV valve from grommet, leaving connection open.

NOTE — *If idle mixture limiter caps have been previously removed from 2-Bbl. or 4-Bbl. carburetors, shut off engine, turn mixture screws clockwise until seated and then back (counterclockwise) 2 turns. Start engine and proceed to step 7).*

7) With shift lever in "NEUTRAL" (Man. Trans.) or "PARK" (Auto. Trans.), run engine at 2500 RPM for 15 seconds before each mixture check.

8) With engine idling at normal operating temperature, place transmission shift lever in "NEUTRAL" (Man. Trans.) or "DRIVE" (Auto. Trans.). Gradually open propane tool valve and watch for engine speed gain on tachometer. When speed reaches maximum and begins to drop off, note amount of speed gain.

NOTE — *If engine speed will not drop off, check bottle gas supply. If necessary, repeat test with new bottle.*

9) Compare measured speed gain to specifications. If idle mixture adjustment is necessary, adjust to "Reset RPM." If speed increase is within "RPM Gain" specification, proceed to step **16)**.

10) If measured speed gain is zero RPM and minimum speed gain specification is zero RPM, proceed to step **13)**.

11) If measured speed gain is GREATER than specification, turn mixture screw(s)/limiter(s) counterclockwise in equal amounts and repeat steps **6)** through **9)** until measured speed rise meets "Reset RPM" specifications. After final adjustment, proceed to step **16)**.

12) If measured speed gain is LESS than specification, turn mixture screw(s)/limiter(s) clockwise in equal amounts and repeat steps **6)** through **9)** until speed rise meets "Reset RPM" specifications. After final adjustment, proceed to step **16)**.

13) If there is ZERO increase in RPM and the minimum speed gain specification is zero RPM, perform the following speed drop test. While watching tachometer, adjust mixture screw(s)/limiter(s) clockwise by number of turns specified. Note drop in engine speed.

14) If measured speed is EQUAL TO or drops off MORE THAN speed drop specifications, return mixture limiter(s) to maximum rich position or mixture screw(s) to position prior to adjustment. Then proceed to step **16)**.

15) If measured speed drop is LESS THAN the specified minimum, leave mixture limiter(s) in adjusted position and

16) Check curb idle speed and remove all test equipment. Install PCV valve in grommet. Reconnect and/or install all components and reinstall air cleaner.

NOTE — *Idle mixture adjustment by propane enrichment not required for heavy duty vehicles.*

TUNE-UP (Cont.)

Idle Mixture Specifications

Application	RPM Gain/Reset RPM
4.2L	
Man. Trans.	10-80/40
Auto. Trans.	20-100/60
5.0L	
Man. Trans.	10-50/30
Auto. Trans.	
Federal	20-100/60
Calif.	N/R
5.8L (351") M	
Man. Trans.	20-80/50
Auto. Trans.	30-100/60
F150/250 High Alt. Auto. Trans.	40-110/60
5.8L (351") W	
Man. Trans.	N/R
Auto. Trans.	
Federal	30-80/50
Calif.	N/R
6.6L	N/R
7.5L	N/R

FUEL PUMP

Check mechanical fuel pump at curb idle RPM with engine at normal operating temperature and transmission in "NEUTRAL."

Pressure	6-8 psi
Volume	One pint in 20 seconds

AUTOMATIC CHOKE ADJUSTMENT

Loosen choke cover screws and turn choke cover in desired direction as indicated on cover to specified setting.

Automatic Choke Specifications

Application	Setting
4.2L	①
5.0L	
All Except Calif. Auto. Trans.	①
Calif. Auto. Trans.	Rich
5.8L (351") M	
All Except Heavy Duty Models	①
Heavy Duty Models	3 Rich or "V"
5.8L (351") W	
E150/250 High Alt.	Index
Heavy Duty Auto. Trans.	3 Rich or "V"
All Other Models	①
6.6L	
Calif. F250 Heavy Duty	
Man. Trans.	2 Rich or "V"
All Other Models	3 Rich or "V"
7.5L	5 Rich

① — Non-Adjustable

EMISSION CONTROL

See appropriate article in EMISSION CONTROL Section.

GENERAL SERVICING

IGNITION

DISTRIBUTORS

All units are equipped with Motorcraft Dura-Spark II Ignition system. Units are self-contained and require no outside adjustments.

Other Data & Specifications — *See Tune-Up and Motorcraft Distributors in ELECTRICAL Section.*

IGNITION COIL

Resistance

Primary	1.13-1.23 ohms
Secondary	7,700-9,300 ohms
Resistor Wire	1.05-1.15 ohms

Reserve Voltage	28 Kv minimum

FUEL SYSTEMS

CARBURETORS

Application	Model
All 4.2L, 6.6L &	
Federal 5.0L & 5.8L (351") W	Motorcraft 2150 2-Bbl.
Calif. 5.0L & 5.8L (351") W	Motorcraft 7200VV 2-Bbl.
7.5L	Holley 4180-C 4-Bbl.

Other Data & Specifications — *See Tune-Up and Holley or Motorcraft Carburetors in FUEL SYSTEMS Section.*

ACCELERATOR LINKAGE ADJUSTMENT

All Models — Linkage is cable type and no adjustment is necessary.

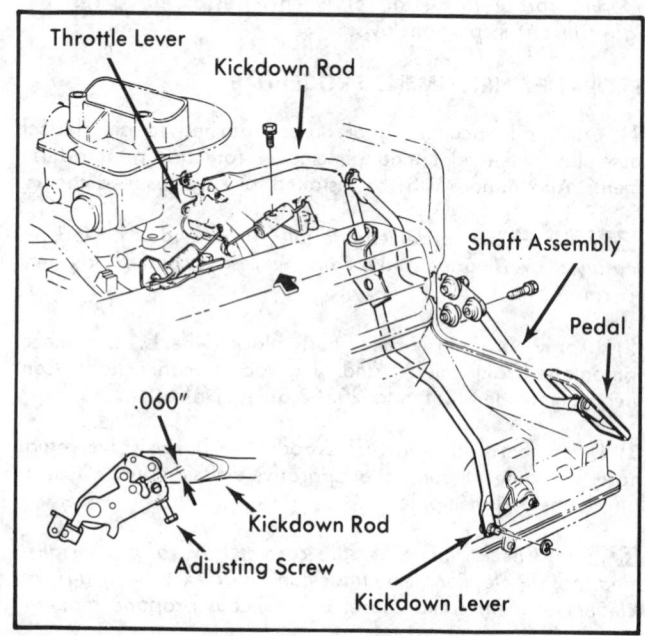

Fig. 3 View of Typical Accelerator Linkage

GENERAL SERVICING (Cont.)

DOWNSHIFT LINKAGE ADJUSTMENT

With accelerator linkage correctly adjusted, hold throttle lever in wide open position. Place a .060" feeler gauge between throttle lever and adjusting screw. Loosen adjusting screw lock nut and turn adjusting screw until downshift lever on transmission is against internal stop. Tighten adjusting screw lock nut.

ELECTRICAL

BATTERY

Application	Amp. Hr.
Maintenance Free	36, 45, 48, 54, 63, 71
Conventional	77 & 81

STARTER

Motorcraft positive engagement type with either a 4" or 4½" armature.

Application	Cranking RPM	Cranking Amps.
4" Armature	180-250	150-200
4½" Armature	150-290	150-180

Other Data & Specifications — *See Motorcraft Starters in ELECTRICAL Section.*

ALTERNATORS

All Models use Motorcraft Alternator

I.D. Color	Rated Amp. Output
Rear Terminal	
Orange	40
Green	60
Side Terminal	
Black	70
Red	100

Other Data & Specifications — *See Motorcraft Alternators in ELECTRICAL Section.*

ALTERNATOR REGULATOR

Motorcraft Electronic Regulators are externally mounted. Two different models are color coded as they are not interchangeable, but similar in appearance.

Application	Color of Plate
Vehicles with Ammeters	Blue
Vehicles with Indicator Lights	Black

Other Data & Specifications — *See Motorcraft Alternators in ELECTRICAL Section.*

BELT ADJUSTMENTS

Tension (Lbs.) Using Strand Tension Gauge

Application	New Belt	①Used Belt
¼" Belt	50-80	40-60
All Other Belts	120-160	90-120

① — Any belt operated for 10 minutes or more.

REPLACEMENT INTERVALS

Component	Interval (Miles)
Oil Filter	
"F" & "E" Models	10,000
Bronco	①15,000
Air Filter	30,000
Fuel Filter	15,000
PCV Valve	30,000
Spark Plugs	30,000

① — Change filter after first 7,500 miles.

OIL & FUEL CAPACITIES

Application	Quantity
Crankcase (including filter)	
All Engines	①6.0 qts.
Fuel Tank	
F100/150 & F150/250 Super Cab	
Short Wheel Base	
Standard	16.4 gal.
Auxiliary	19.0 gal.
All Other "F" Models	
Standard & Auxiliary	19.0 gal.
Bronco	
Standard	25.0 gal.
Auxiliary	32.0 gal.
E100 Van & Club Wagon, E150 Van (W/124" W.B.)	
Standard	18.0 gal.
Auxiliary	18.0 gal.
All Other "E" Models	
Standard	22.1 gal.
Auxiliary	18.0 gal.

① — Use engine oil dipstick for exact refill capacity.

1981 Ford V8 Tune-Up

GENERAL SERVICING (Cont.)

TRANSMISSION & DIFFERENTIAL CAPACITIES

Application	Quantity
Man. Trans. (SAE 80W-90)	
3-Speed Ford	3.5 pts.
4-Speed New Process 435	
With Extension	7.0 pts.
Without Extension	6.5 pts.
4-Speed Warner T-18	7.0 pts.
4-Speed Overdrive	4.5 pts.
Auto. Trans. (Motorcraft Dexron II Series D)	
C-4	
2-WD Only	19.2 pts.
C-6	
2-WD	23.8 pts.
4-WD	26.8 pts.
Rear Axle (Hypoid Gear Lube)	
Ford Standard & Traction-Lok	6.5 pts.
Dana 60	5.0 pts.
Dana 61-1	6.0 pts.
Dana 61-2	6.0 pts.
Dana 70	
Standard & Heavy Duty	6.5 pts.
Front Axle (Hypoid Gear Lube)	
Dana 44-IFS	
F150 & Bronco	3.9 pts.
F250	3.8 pts.
Dana IFS	4.1 pts.
4-WD Transfer Case (Motorcraft Dexron II Series D)	
Warner 1345	6.5 pts.
New Process 208	7.0 pts.

COOLING CAPACITIES

Application	Quantity
4.2L V8	
F100	
Standard or Extra Cooling	13.0 qts.
Super Cooling	14.0 qts.
5.0L V8	
F150/350 & Bronco	
Standard or Extra Cooling	13.0 qts.
Super Cooling 14.0 qts. E100/250	
Standard Cooling	15.0 qts.
Extra Cooling	17.5 qts.
Super Cooling	18.5 qts.
5.8L (351") W V8	
E100/250 Calif. Only	
Standard or Extra Cooling	20.0 qts.
Super Cooling	21.0 qts.
5.8L (351") M V8	
F150/350 & Bronco	
Standard or Extra Cooling	15.0 qts.
Super Cooling	16.0 qts.
6.6L V8	
F250/350 & Bronco	
Standard Cooling	15.0 qts.
Super Cooling	16.0 qts.
7.5L V8	
E350	
All Models	28.0 qts.

TUNE-UP

ENGINE IDENTIFICATION

Engines can be identified by the 8th digit of the Vehicle Identification Number (VIN). The VIN number is stamped on a plate located at the base of the steering column on "P" models, and on the upper left corner of the dash on all other models.

VIN Engine Codes

Application	VIN Code
4.1L (250") 2-Bbl	D
4.8L (292") 1-Bbl	T

TUNE-UP NOTES

CAUTION — *IDLE SPEED ADJUSTMENT: Procedures and specifications for idle speed adjustment must be followed exactly as outlined. See "Hot (Slow) Idle RPM" under Tune-Up.*

NOTE — *For other items affecting Tune-Up, see FUEL SYSTEMS Section or EMISSION CONTROL Section.*

NOTE — *Due to changes and corrections, always refer to Engine Tune-Up Decal in engine compartment before attempting Tune-Up. In the event of a conflict between specifications given in this manual and decal specifications, decal specifications prevail.*

CAUTION — *When performing tune-up on vehicles equipped with a catalytic converter, do not allow or create a condition of engine misfire in one or more cylinders for an extended period of time. Damage to converter from overheating may occur due to loading with unburned fuel.*

NOTE — *SERIES IDENTIFICATION: The vehicle series numbers used in this article have been abbreviated for common reference to both Chevrolet and GMC models. Chevrolet models use numerical designation as listed; GMC models are identified as follows: 10 = 1500; 20 = 2500; 30 = 3500.*

NOTE — *For tune-up purposes, "Light Duty" refers to vehicles up to 8500 lbs. "Heavy Duty" refers to vehicles exceeding 8500 lbs.*

ENGINE COMPRESSION

Compression Ratio	
4.1L	8.3:1
4.8L	8.0:1
Compression Pressure	130 psi
Maximum Pressure Variation Between Cylinders	30 psi

When making compression checks, disconnect ignition switch pink wire from High Energy Ignition system. With air cleaner removed and throttle and choke wide open, crank engine through at least four compression strokes.

VALVE CLEARANCE

Hydraulic Lifters .... One turn down from zero lash.

VALVE ARRANGEMENT

E-I-I-E-E-I-I-E-E-I-I-E

SPARK PLUGS

Application	Gap (In.)	Torque (Ft. Lbs.)
All Models	.035	17-27

Spark Plug Type

Application	AC No.
4.1L	R45TS
4.8L	R44T

HIGH TENSION WIRE RESISTANCE

Carefully remove ends of wire from spark plug and distributor. Using an ohmmeter, check resistance while gently twisting wire. If resistance is not to specifications, or fluctuates from infinity to any value, replace cable.

Resistance (Ohms)

Wire Length	Maximum
Under 24"	30,000 Max.
Over 24"	50,000

DISTRIBUTOR

All models are equipped with High Energy Ignition systems and no adjustments are required.

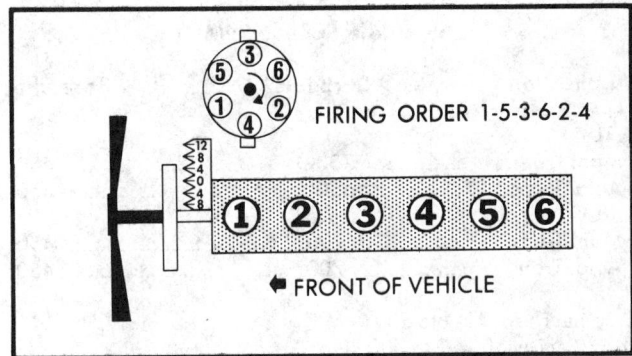

FIRING ORDER 1-5-3-6-2-4

FRONT OF VEHICLE

Fig. 1   Firing Order and Timing Marks

IGNITION TIMING

NOTE — *Engines are equipped with a receptacle for magnetic probe timing equipment, located 10° ATDC. Do not use this location for timing with a conventional light.*

1) Install timing light with an adapter between No. 1 spark plug and No. 1 spark plug wire, or use an inductive type pickup. Do not puncture wire.

2) Check or adjust ignition engine timing with engine at normal operating temperature, distributor advance line disconnected and plugged, and automatic transmission in "D". On heavy duty vehicles, leave transmission on all models in neutral.

TUNE-UP (Cont.)

Ignition Timing Specifications
(Degrees BTDC@RPM)

Application	Man. Trans.	Auto. Trans.
4.1L	10@750	①10@650
4.8L	8@700	8@700

① — Set Decal AAC and ADC to 8°.

HOT (SLOW) IDLE RPM

4.1L — 1) Warm engine to normal operating temperature and place transmission selector in "D". Disconnect and plug EGR and canister purge hoses at carburetor.

2) Open throttle slightly to allow solenoid to extend, then adjust curb idle by turning screw in back of solenoid. Disconnect solenoid wire and set base idle speed with idle speed screw. Reconnect solenoid wire and all hoses.

4.8L — 1) Warm engine to normal operating temperature. Leave transmission in neutral on all models. Adjust solenoid idle speed by turning solenoid assembly in or out.

2) Disconnect solenoid wire and set base idle speed by turning hex head screw in rear of solenoid. Reconnect solenoid wire.

3) Connect hose from hand vacuum pump to throttle return control (if equipped). Apply 20 in. Hg and adjust plunger to obtain 1500 RPM. Reconnect hoses and remove test equipment.

Slow Idle Speed (RPM)

Application	Curb Idle	Base Idle
4.1L		
Man. Trans.	750①	450
Auto. Trans.	650②	450
4.8L		
Man. Trans.	700	450
Auto. Trans.	700	450

① — Set Decal ADA to 800 RPM.
② — Set Decal AAC to 700 RPM.

IDLE MIXTURE

NOTE — *Idle mixture should be adjusted only after major carburetor overhaul, throttle body replacement, or failure of emissions test.*

PROPANE ENRICHMENT PROCEDURE
4.1L MODELS ONLY

1) Set parking brake and block drive wheels. On vehicles equipped with vacuum parking brake release, disconnect and plug hose at brake. With engine at normal operating temperature, air conditioning "OFF", and vacuum advance hoses disconnected and plugged at distributor, connect tachometer to engine.

2) Set timing to specifications and reconnect vacuum advance hose. Set idle speed to specifications. Disconnect crankcase ventilation tube from air cleaner. Using tool J-26911 (or equivalent), insert hose with rubber stopper (from propane valve) into ventilation tube opening in air cleaner. Be sure propane cartridge is vertical.

3) With engine idling in "D" or neutral, open propane supply control valve slowly. Add propane until engine speed begins to drop from over-richness. Note maximum engine speed.

NOTE — *If rich speed drop cannot be obtained, check for empty propane cartridge.*

4) Engine speed should rise above normal idle by amount specified. If so, mixture is correct. Proceed to step **7)**.

5) If speed is not within specifications, remove idle mixture screw plugs. (On 2SE, carburetor must be removed and punch driven through bottom of throttle body to remove plug.) Seat screws, then back out until engine just runs. Place transmission in "D", then back out screw slowly until maximum idle speed is reached. Then set idle to enriched idle specification.

6) Turn each mixture screw in (clockwise) 1/8 turn at a time until idle speed reaches specification. Recheck enriched speed with propane. If not within specification, repeat steps **5)** and **6)**, beginning with shift lever placement. Then, check and adjust fast idle speed.

7) Turn off engine. Remove propane tool, connect crankcase ventilation tube and reconnect all vacuum hoses.

Propane Enriched RPM

Application	Man. Trans.	Auto. Trans.
4.1L Engines		
Federal	100①	20-30
Calif.	100	30

① — Set carburetor No. 17081621 to 75 RPM, 17081627 to 130 RPM, and 17081629 to 150 RPM.

LEAN DROP PROCEDURE
4.8L MODELS ONLY

1) Set parking brake and block drive wheels. Remove air cleaner for access to carburetor, but keep vacuum hoses connected. Disconnect and plug other hoses as directed on Emission Control Tune-Up decal in engine compartment.

2) With engine at normal operating temperature, choke open, air conditioning "OFF", connect a tachometer to engine. Disconnect and plug distributor vacuum advance hose. Check ignition timing and adjust if necessary. Reconnect vacuum advance hose.

3) Using care not to bend idle mixture screw, remove limiter cap from screw. Lightly seat mixture screw, then back out just enough so engine will run. Place transmission in neutral.

4) Back out mixture screw slowly until maximum idle speed is obtained. Adjust idle speed screw so enriched RPM is 0-75 RPM faster than idle speed. Turn mixture screw in until specified idle RPM is reached. Reconnect all hoses and install air cleaner, then recheck idle speed.

TUNE-UP (Cont.)

COLD (FAST) IDLE RPM

4.1L — Place fast idle screw on high step of fast idle cam. Turn screw to adjust fast idle RPM.

4.8L — Place cam follower on high step of fast idle cam. Support lever with pliers and bend tang in or out to adjust fast idle RPM.

NOTE — *On models with manual choke, rotate fast idle cam clockwise to farthest "UP" position.*

Fast Idle Speed (RPM)

Application	Man. Trans.	Auto. Trans.
4.1L	2000	2200
4.8L	2400	2400

AUTOMATIC CHOKE

All choke caps are retained with rivets and are non-adjustable.

FUEL PUMP PRESSURE & VOLUME

For pressure test, pinch off fuel return line (if equipped), connect pressure gauge to fuel line at carburetor, and hold pressure gauge at level of pump outlet. For vacuum test, disconnect fuel line at carburetor, install hose on line and route gas back to tank.

Pressure (At Idle) .... 4.5-6.0 psi
Volume (At Cranking Speed) .... 1 pt. in 30 seconds or less

EMISSION CONTROL

See appropriate article in EMISSION CONTROL Section.

GENERAL SERVICING

IGNITION

DISTRIBUTOR

Delco .... High Energy Ignition

Other Data & Specifications — *See Tune-Up and Delco distributors in ELECTRICAL Section.*

IGNITION COIL

Coil Resistance (Ohms@75° F)

Application	Primary	Secondary
All Models	0.4-1.0	6000-30,000

Coil Output

At all engine speeds .... 25-35KV Minimum

IGNITION PICKUP COIL

Resistance .... 500-1500 ohms

FUEL SYSTEMS

CARBURETOR

Application	Model
4.1L	Rochester 2SE 2-Bbl.
4.8L	Rochester 1ME 1-Bbl.

Other Data & Specifications — *See Tune-Up and Rochester Carburetors in FUEL SYSTEMS Section.*

ELECTRICAL

BATTERY

Application	Cold Cranking Amps@0° F	Reserve Capacity Minutes
Standard		
4.1L	275	60
4.8L	350	80
Optional	430	100

STARTER

Delco .... Overrunning Clutch

Starter Specifications

Application	Volts	Amps	Test RPM
4.1L	9	50-80	5500-10,500
4.8L	9	50-80	3000-6000

Other Data & Specifications — *See Delco Starters in ELECTRICAL Section.*

ALTERNATOR

Delco .... Integral Regulator

Application	Rated Amp. Output
Standard	
4.1L	37
4.8L	
G20, G30 & "P" Models	42
All Others	37
Optional (All)	61, 80

Other Data & Specifications — *See Delco Alternators in ELECTRICAL Section.*

GENERAL SERVICING (Cont.)

ALTERNATOR REGULATOR

Delco — Nonadjustable, integral with alternator.

Operating Voltage @85° .... 12.5-15.5 volts

Other Data & Specifications — See Delco Alternators and Regulators in ELECTRICAL Section.

BELT ADJUSTMENT

Tension (Lbs.) Using Strand Tension Gauge

Application	New Belt	①Used Belt
Air Conditioning	135-145	90-100
All Others	120-130	70-80

① — One that has been rotated at least one complete revolution of the engine pulley.

REPLACEMENT INTERVALS

Components	Intervals (Miles)
Oil Filter	15,000
Fuel Filter	15,000
Spark Plugs	22,500
PCV Valve and Filter	30,000
Air Filter	30,000

CAPACITIES (COOLING)

Application	Quantity (Qts.)
4.1L	
Van Models	17.0 qts.
All Other Models	15.0 qts.
4.8L	
"P" Models	13.5 qts.
All Other Models	15.0 qts.

CAPACITIES (EXCEPT COOLING)

Application	Quantity
Crankcase	
4.1L	①4.0 qts.
4.8L	①5.0 qts.
Automatic Transmission (Dexron)	
THM 350	
Overhaul	10.0 qts.
Refill	6.0 pts.
THM 400	
Overhaul	11.0 qts.
Refill	7.0 pts.
Manual Transmission (SAE 80W-90)	
3-Speed	3.0 pts.
4-Speed	4.0 qts.
Transfer Case (SAE 10W-30)	5.0 pts.
Front Axle (SAE 80W-90)	5.0 pts.
Rear Axle (SAE 80W-90)	②
Power Take-Off (SAE 80W-90)	5.0 qts.
Fuel Tank	
Pickup Models	
Short Wheelbase (Each Tank)	16.0 gals.
Long Wheelbase (Each Tank)	20.0 gals.
Van Models	
Standard	22.0 gals.
Optional	33.0 gals.
Suburban Models	
Standard	25.0 gals.
Optional	31.0 or 40.0 gals.
Blazer Models	
Standard	25.0 gals.
Optional	31.0 gals.
"P" Models	
Standard	31.0 gals.
Optional	40.0 gals.

① — Add one quart with filter change.
② — Fill to bottom of filler hole.

TUNE-UP

ENGINE IDENTIFICATION

Engines can be identified by 8th digit of Vehicle Identification Number (VIN). Number is located on plate at top left corner of dashboard and at base of steering column on van models. Engine code numbers are located at front of block, at right cylinder head on 5.0 and 5.7L engines and in front of intake manifold on 7.4L engines.

VIN Engine Codes

Application	VIN Code
5.0L (305") 2-Bbl.	G
5.0L (305") 4-Bbl.	
Federal	H
Calif.	F
5.7L (350") 4-Bbl.	
Light Duty	L
Heavy Duty	M
7.4L (454") 4-Bbl.	
Heavy Duty	W

TUNE-UP NOTES

NOTE — *For other items affecting Tune-Up, see FUEL SYSTEMS Section or EMISSION CONTROL Section.*

NOTE — *Due to changes and corrections, always refer to Engine Tune-Up Decal in engine compartment before attempting Tune-Up. In the event of a conflict between specifications given in this manual and decal specifications, decal specifications prevail.*

NOTE — *SERIES IDENTIFICATION: The vehicle series numbers used in this article have been abbreviated for common reference to both Chevrolet and GMC models. Chevrolet models use numerical designation as listed; GMC models are identified as follows: 10 = 1500; 20 = 2500; 30 = 3500.*

NOTE — *For Tune-Up purposes, "Light Duty" refers to vehicles up to 8500 lbs. "Heavy Duty" refers to vehicles exceeding 8500 lbs.*

CAUTION — *When performing tune-up on vehicles equipped with a catalytic converter, do not allow or create a condition of engine misfire in one or more cylinders for an extended period of time. Damage to converter from overheating may occur due to loading with unburned fuel.*

ENGINE COMPRESSION

Compression Ratio
5.0L 2-Bbl. 8.5:1
5.0L 4-Bbl.
  Federal 9.2:1
  Calif. 8.6:1
5.7L 4-Bbl. 8.2:1
7.4L 4-Bbl. 8.5:1
Compression Pressure .... 150 psi
Maximum Pressure Variation .... 20 psi

When making compression checks, disconnect the ignition switch connector pink wire from high energy ignition system. With air cleaner removed and throttle and choke wide open, crank engine through at least four compression strokes.

VALVE CLEARANCE

Hydraulic Lifters .... One turn down from zero lash.

VALVE ARRANGEMENT

5.0L & 5.7L
  E-I-I-E-E-I-I-E (Both banks, front to rear.)
7.4L
  E-I-E-I-E-I-E-I (Left bank, front to rear.)
  I-E-I-E-I-E-I-E (Right bank, front to rear.)

SPARK PLUGS

Application	Gap (In.)	Torque (Ft. Lbs.)
All Models .... .045 17-27		

Spark Plug Type

Application	AC No.
Light Duty Emissions	R45TS
Heavy Duty Emissions	R44T

HIGH TENSION WIRE RESISTANCE

Carefully remove ends of wire from spark plug and distributor. Using an ohmmeter, check resistance while gently twisting wire. If resistance is not to specifications, or fluctuates from infinity to any value, replace cable.

Resistance (Ohms)

Wire Length	Resistance
0-24"	30,000 Max.
Over 24"	50,000 Max.

DISTRIBUTOR

5.0L Federal engines are high compression (9.2:1) models and use an Electronic Spark Control (ESC) ignition system with detonation sensor. All other models are equipped with High Energy Ignition systems and no adjustments are required.

IGNITION TIMING

NOTE — *Engines are equipped with a receptacle for magnetic probe timing lights, located 10°ATDC. Do not use this location for timing with a conventional light.*

TUNE-UP (Cont.)

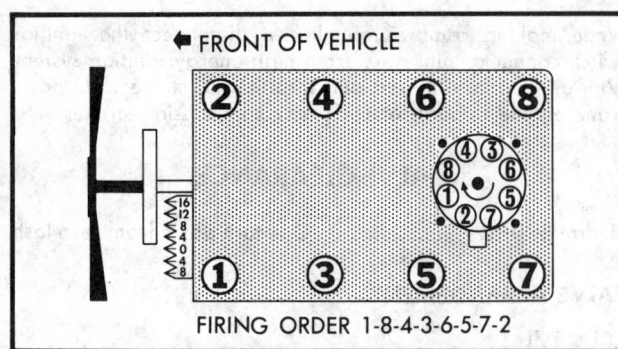

← FRONT OF VEHICLE

FIRING ORDER 1-8-4-3-6-5-7-2

Fig. 1 Firing Order and Timing Marks
(All Engines)

1) Connect an adapter between No. 1 spark plug and No. 1 spark plug wire or use an inductive type pickup. Do not puncture wires.

2) Connect timing light according to manufacturer's instructions. Check or adjust ignition timing with engine at normal operating temperature, distributor vacuum line disconnected and plugged. Place transmission in neutral, except for Light Duty models with automatic which should be in "D". Set timing to specifications.

3) To adjust timing, loosen distributor hold down bolt and rotate distributor until timing is to specifications. Tighten hold down bolt.

Ignition Timing Specifications
(Degrees BTDC@RPM)

Application	Man. Trans.	Auto. Trans.
Light Duty		
5.0L 2-Bbl.	8@700	8@600
5.0L 4-Bbl.		
Federal	① 4@700	② 8@650
Calif.	.....	8@650
5.7L 4-Bbl.		
Federal	8@700	8@600
Calif.	.....	③ 6@650
Heavy Duty		
5.7L 4-Bbl.		
Federal	4@700	4@700
Calif.	6@700	6@700
7.4L 4-Bbl.	4@700	4@700

① — Set Van to 6° BTDC.
② — Set Decal AAN to 6° BTDC; Decal AAS to 2° BTDC.
③ — Set Van to 8° BTDC.

HOT (SLOW) IDLE RPM

NOTE — See engine compartment Emission Control Tune-Up Decal to prepare engine for idle speed adjustment.

1) Set ignition timing to specifications. Disconnect lead from idle solenoid (if equipped). Adjust idle speed to specifications using idle speed screw. Transmission should be in "D" for Light Duty automatic, and in neutral on all others.

2) Disconnect lead from air conditioning compressor. Reconnect lead at idle solenoid, then turn air conditioning "ON".

Open throttle slightly to allow solenoid to fully extend. Adjust solenoid idle speed by turning solenoid screw.

3) If equipped with throttle return control, connect a hand vacuum pump to control diaphragm. With engine idling, apply at least 20 in. Hg vacuum. Open throttle slightly to allow plunger to fully extend. Screw plunger in or out as necessary to obtain 1600 RPM on Federal models and 1500 RPM on Calif. models.

Idle Speed (RPM)

Application	Curb Idle	Solenoid Energized
Light Duty		
5.0L 2-Bbl.		
Man. Trans.	600	700
Auto. Trans.	500	600
5.0L 4-Bbl.		
Federal		
Man. Trans.	700	.....
Auto. Trans.	500	600
Calif.	550	650
5.7L 4-Bbl.		
Federal		
Man. Trans.	700	.....
Auto. Trans.	500	.....
Calif.	550	650
Heavy Duty		
5.7L 4-Bbl.	700	.....
7.4L 4-Bbl.	700	.....

IDLE MIXTURE

PROPANE ENRICHMENT PROCEDURE
(LIGHT DUTY MODELS ONLY)

1) With engine at normal operating temperature, choke fully open and A/C "OFF" (if equipped), set parking brake and block drive wheels. Disconnect and plug hoses as directed on Emission Control/Tune-Up decal.

2) Connect tachometer to engine. Disconnect vacuum advance and set timing to specification. Reconnect vacuum advance. Disconnect crankcase ventilation tube from air cleaner. Insert hose with rubber stopper (tool J-26911 or equivalent) from propane valve into PCV tube opening in air cleaner.

3) Propane bottle must be in vertical position. slowly open control valve until maximum engine speed is reached with transmission in "D" (automatic) or neutral (manual).

NOTE — Too much propane will cause engine speed to drop.

4) Observe propane flow meter to ensure propane cartridge is full. With propane flowing, adjust idle speed screw or solenoid so speed rises above normal idle by specified amount. Readjust propane flow to be certain of maximum engine speed and adjust idle speed if necessary.

5) Turn off propane. Run engine at 2000 RPM in neutral for 30 seconds, return to idle, and place in "D". Check idle speed. If correct, no adjustment of mixture is necessary. If not correct, proceed with adjustment procedure.

TUNE-UP (Cont.)

6) If idle speed is too low, carefully remove cap(s) from mixture screw(s) and back out screws (richen) $\frac{1}{8}$ turn at a time until correct speed is reached. If speed is too high, turn screw(s) in (leaner) $\frac{1}{8}$ turn at a time until correct speed is reached.

7) Turn propane on again to check maximum engine idle speed. If speed does not meet specifications, readjust idle speed screw or solenoid screw to obtain specified enriched RPM with propane flowing. Turn off propane, place transmission in neutral and run engine at 3000 RPM for 30 seconds. Recheck idle speed and repeat procedure if necessary.

Propane Enriched RPM
(Light Duty Only)

Application	Man. Trans.	Auto. Trans.
5.0L 2-Bbl.	150	50
5.0L 4-Bbl.		
Federal	①100	40
Calif.		20
5.7L 4-Bbl.	100	20-50

①-150 RPM on 4-sp overdrive.

BEST IDLE PROCEDURE
(HEAVY DUTY MODELS ONLY)

1) Set parking brake and block drive wheels. Remove air cleaner after engine reaches normal operating temperature. Place transmission in neutral and connect tachometer.

2) As a starting point, turn idle mixture screws in lightly to seat and then back out 2 turns. Do not turn screw tightly against seat or damage may result.

3) With engine running, choke open, and transmission in neutral, adjust idle speed to specifications. Then adjust mixture screw to obtain maximum RPM.

4) Readjust idle speed screw to specifications and readjust mixture screw to obtain highest RPM. Shut down engine, remove gauges and install air cleaner.

COLD (FAST) IDLE RPM

1) Place transmission in neutral. Move cam follower onto highest step of fast idle cam. Disconnect and plug vacuum hose to EGR valve.

2) Start engine without touching throttle. Turn fast idle speed screw to adjust speed to specifications.

Fast Idle Speed (RPM)

Application	Man. Trans.	Auto. Trans.
Light Duty		
5.0L 2-Bbl.	1300	1600
5.0L 4-Bbl. & 5.7L 4-Bbl.		
Federal	1300	1600
Calif.		1800
Heavy Duty		
All Engines	1900	1900

AUTOMATIC CHOKE

The choke cover on all engines is riveted in place and no adjustments are possible or necessary.

FUEL PUMP PRESSURE

Pressure (At Idle)	
With Vapor Return Line	
7.4L	7.5-9.0 psi
All Others	5.5-7.0 psi
Without Vapor Return Line	7.5-9.0 psi
Volume	1.0 pt. in 30 seconds or less

EMISSION CONTROL

See appropriate article in EMISSION CONTROL Section.

GENERAL SERVICING

IGNITION

DISTRIBUTOR

5.0L 4-Bbl. Federal engines use Electronic Spark Timing (EST) system with detonation sensor and 5-pin module. All other models use a standard HEI system with 4-pin module.

NOTE — *High energy ignition system module must be replaced as a unit. A liberal coat of silicone grease MUST be applied to both the module and the surface on which it will be mounted.*

Other Data & Specifications — *See Tune-Up and Delco Distributors in ELECTRICAL Section.*

IGNITION COIL

Coil Resistance (Ohms@68°F)

Application	Primary	Secondary
All Models	0.4-1.0	6000-30,000
Coil Output		
At all engine speeds		30 KV Min.

FUEL SYSTEMS

CARBURETORS

Application	Model
Light Duty	
5.0L 2-Bbl.	Rochester M2ME
5.0L & 5.7L 4-Bbl.	Rochester M4ME
Heavy Duty	
All	Rochester M4MC

GENERAL SERVICING (Cont.)

Other Data & Specifications — *See Tune-Up and Rochester Carburetors in FUEL SYSTEMS Section.*

ELECTRICAL

BATTERY

Application	Cold Crank Amps@0° F	Reserve Capacity Minutes
5.0L & 5.7L		
Standard	350	80
Optional	430	100
7.4L	465	125

STARTER

Delco .... Overrunning Clutch

Starter Specifications

Application	Volts	Amps	Test RPM
5.0L	9	50-80	5500-10,500
5.7L & 7.4L	9	65-96	7500-10,500

Other Data & Specifications — *See Delco Starters in ELECTRICAL Section.*

ALTERNATOR

Delco .... Integral Regulator

General Motors offers either a 37 amp, 42 amp, 61 amp or an 80 amp alternator as standard or optional equipment.

Other Data & Specifications — *See Delco Alternators in ELECTRICAL Section.*

ALTERNATOR REGULATOR

Delco — Non Adjustable, Integral with Alternator.
Operating Voltage (@85°F)................................. 13.8-14.8

Other Data & Specifications — *See Delco Alternators & Regulators in ELECTRICAL Section.*

REPLACEMENT INTERVALS

Component	Interval (Miles)
Oil Filter	15,000
Fuel Filter	15,000
PCV Filter & Valve	15,000
Air Filter	30,000
Spark Plugs	30,000

BELT ADJUSTMENT

Tension (Lbs.) Using Strand Tension Gauge

Application	New Belt	Used Belt
Air Conditioning	135-145	90-100
All Others	120-130	70-80

CAPACITIES (EXCEPT COOLING)

Application	Quantity
Crankcase	
5.0L & 5.7L	① 4.0 qts.
7.4L	① 6.0 qts.
Automatic Transmission (Dexron)	
THM 350	
Overhaul	10.0 qts.
Refill	6.0 pts.
THM 400	
Overhaul	11.0 qts.
Refill	7.0 pts.
Manual Transmission (SAE 80W-90)	
3-Speed	3.0 pts.
4-Speed	4.0 qts.
Transfer Case (SAE 10W-30)	5.0 pts.
Front Axle (SAE 80W-90)	5.0 pts.
Rear Axle (SAE 80W-90)	②
Power Take-Off (SAE 80W-90)	5.0 qts.
Fuel Tank	
Pickup Models	
Short Wheelbase (Each Tank)	16.0 gals.
Long Wheelbase (Each Tank)	20.0 gals.
Van Models	
Standard	22.0 gals.
Optional	33.0 gals.
Suburban Models	
Standard	25.0 gals.
Optional	31.0 or 40.0 gals.
Blazer Models	
Standard	25.0 gals.
Optional	31.0 gals.
"P" Models	
Standard	31.0 gals.
Optional	40.0 gals.

① — Add 1 quart for filter change.
② — Fill to bottom of filler hole.

CAPACITIES (COOLING)

Application	Quantity
5.0L	
Pickup	17.5 qts.
Van	19.0 qts.
5.7L	
Pickup	17.5 qts.
Van	17.0 qts.
"P" Models	20.0 qts.
7.4L	24.0 qts.

TUNE-UP

ENGINE IDENTIFICATION

Engine can be identified by the 8th digit of Vehicle Identification Number (VIN) which is stamped on a tag at top left corner of dashboard. The engine is also identified by code letters which are located on a label at rear of left valve cover, and stamped into block on left front corner.

VIN Engine Codes

Application	VIN Code
5.7L (350") Diesel	Z

TUNE-UP NOTES

NOTE — *Due to late changes and corrections, always refer to Engine Tune-Up Decal in engine compartment before attempting tune-up. If the decal specifications are different than the specifications presented here, use the decal specifications.*

CAUTION — *Adjustment of injectors or internal adjustments of injection pump must be done in a properly equipped injector shop with clean environment.*

ENGINE COMPRESSION

NOTE — *Prior to checking compression, be sure battery is fully charged to avoid battery run-down. When turning engine over during test, 6 "puffs" per cylinder should be used to obtain reading.*

Compression Ratio	22.5:1
Compression Pressure	275 psi (min.)
Max. Pressure Variation	①

① — Lowest cylinder must read within 70% of highest.

1) Remove air cleaner and install screen cover over air crossover. Disconnect electrical wire from fuel injection pump solenoid terminal.

2) Disconnect glow plug wiring and remove all glow plugs. Use compression gauge (J-26999) to test individual cylinders.

CAUTION — *Do not add oil to cylinders during compression check as extensive engine damage will result.*

VALVE CLEARANCE

Lifters are hydraulic and are not adjustable. They should have zero lash.

NOTE — *Some engines were produced with both standard and .010" oversize lifters installed. Oversize lifters can be identified by an "O" etched on side of lifter boss. Diesel engine lifters are NOT interchangeable with gasoline engine lifters.*

GLOW PLUGS

Glow plugs are small 6-volt heaters operated by an electronic relay. They cycle on and off, powered by 12 volts to give rapid heating. Glow plug light on dash should cycle on and off as plugs do. If test lamp is connected to glow plugs and ground, it should flash on and off. Relay can be heard clicking on and off after ignition has been on for approximately 6 seconds.

All Models	GM Part No. 5613680
Torque	12 Ft. Lbs.

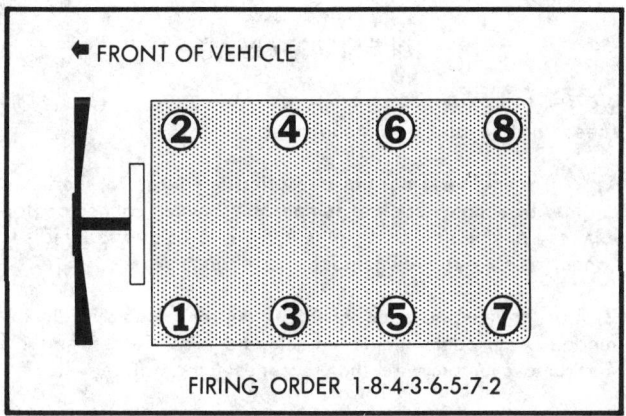

◄ FRONT OF VEHICLE

FIRING ORDER 1-8-4-3-6-5-7-2

Fig. 1   Firing Order Illustration

INJECTOR TIMING

1) Check alignment of injection pump marks. If marks are not within tolerance shown in *Fig. 2*, timing is necessary. Loosen 3 retaining nuts (use J-26987) and turn pump with ¾" wrench on boss at front of pump. Tighten nuts and adjust throttle linkage.

2) Disconnect cruise control and transmission linkage. Disconnect pump rod, loosen lock nut, and shorten rod several turns. Rotate throttle lever to full-throttle position and lengthen rod until it fits with lever just contacting full-throttle stop. Reconnect linkage from cruise control or transmission.

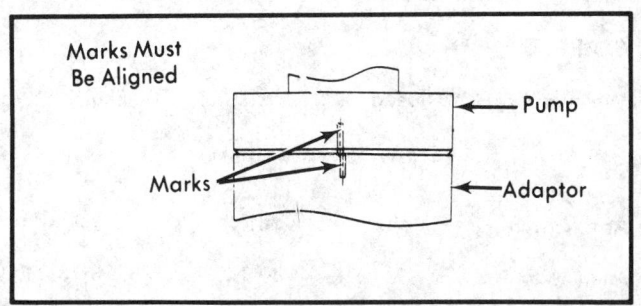

Marks Must
Be Aligned

Pump

Marks

Adaptor

Fig. 2   Timing Marks on Injection Pump & Adaptor

TUNE-UP (Cont.)

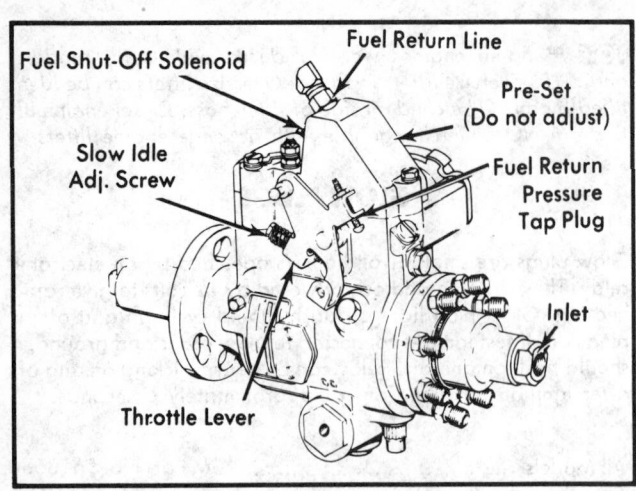

Fig. 3   Diesel Injection Pump Adjustment Locations

IDLE SPEED (RPM)

NOTE — *Use magnetic tachometer (J-26925) to check idle speed. Insert probe in timing indicator hole.*

1) Warm engine to normal operating temperature, then stop engine. Disconnect coolant temperature switch connector (top left rear of engine). Use a jumper wire to bridge terminals in connector. Do not allow jumper wire to touch ground.

2) Start engine and open throttle to ensure solenoid is fully extended. Adjust solenoid to set solenoid RPM. Turn engine off and remove jumper wire, then reconnect temperature switch.

3) Start engine and check curb idle speed. Adjust with slow idle screw if necessary. Remove test equipment.

	Idle Speed (RPM)	
Application	**Curb Idle**	**Solenoid Energized**
Federal	575	650
Calif.	600	750

INJECTION NOZZLES

If engine starts, but idles roughly, check injection nozzles as described:

1) Start engine. Loosen injection line fitting at each nozzle, one at a time. Be sure to direct fuel away from sources which could cause fire.

2) If, when an injection line fitting is loosened, idle speed or quality does NOT change, replace that nozzle and repeat test.

3) Disconnect fuel return system from nozzles on one bank of engine at a time. Start engine and observe fuel seepage from each nozzle. Replace any nozzle that leaks excessively. Torque nozzle clamp bolt to 25 ft. lbs.

GENERAL SERVICING

FUEL INJECTION

All models are equipped with General Motors Diesel Fuel Injection.

Other Data & Specifications — *See GM Diesel Fuel Injection article in FUEL SYSTEMS Section.*

ELECTRICAL

BATTERIES

Two 89-5 12 volt negative (−) ground sealed top units. One battery is located on each side of engine compartment and they are wired in parallel.

STARTER

Minimum Cranking Speed .... 100 Engine RPM

Starter Specifications

Application	Volts	Amps	Test RPM
All Models	9	40-140	8000-13,000

Other Data & Specifications — *See Delco Starters in ELECTRICAL Section.*

ALTERNATOR

Alternator supplies current to both batteries. There are no switches or relays in charging circuit.

Application	Amp. Output
Standard	63

Other Data & Specifications — *See Delco Alternators in ELECTRICAL Section.*

ALTERNATOR REGULATOR

Delco non-adjustable integral with alternator.
Operating Voltage (at 85° F) .... 13.8-14.8 V

Other Data & Specifications — *See Delco Alternators and Regulators in ELECTRICAL Section.*

BELT ADJUSTMENT

Tension (Lbs.) Using Strand Tension Gauge

Application	New Belt	Used Belt
Air Conditioning	135-165	85-95
All Others	110-140	70-80

GENERAL SERVICING (Cont.)

CAPACITIES

Application	Quantity
Crankcase	①7.0 qts.
Auto. Trans. (Dexron)	②6.0 pts.
Rear Axle (SAE 80W-90)	③
Cooling System	18.0 qts.
Fuel Tank	
Short W.B. (Main or Auxiliary)	16.0 gals.
Long W.B. (Main or Auxiliary)	20.0 gals.

① — Includes filter. Oil MUST be designated BOTH SE & CC. If CD appears anywhere on can, do not use.

② — Total fill is 10.0 quarts.

③ — Fill to bottom of filler hole.

REPLACEMENT INTERVALS

Component	Interval (Miles)
Oil Filter	3000
Air Cleaner Element	30,000
Fuel Filter	15,000
Automatic Transmission Filter	100,000
Breather Cap and Filter	Check 6000
	Replace 30,000
Ventilation Regulator Valve	Replace 30,000

TUNE-UP

ENGINE IDENTIFICATION

VEHICLE IDENTIFICATION NUMBER CODE

Engine can be identified by the 4th digit of the Vehicle Identification Number (VIN), which is stamped on a plate attached to top left corner of instrument panel.

VIN Engine Code

Application	Code
2.5L (151") 2-Bbl.	B

ENGINE IDENTIFICATION NUMBER CODE

Engine code is stamped into a pad on the left rear upper corner of the engine block. On engines built for sale in Georgia and Tennessee, a second code number is stamped into the left rear flange.

TUNE-UP NOTES

NOTE — *In order to comply with emission standards, specifications shown on engine compartment emission control tune-up decal must be used in all instances.*

CAUTION — *When performing tune-up on vehicles equipped with catalytic converters, do not allow or create a condition of engine misfire in more than 1 cylinder for an extended period of time. Damage to converter may occur due to loading converter with unburned air/fuel mixture.*

ENGINE COMPRESSION

Compression Ratio	8.2:1
Compression Pressure	140 psi
Maximum Variation Between Cylinders	30 psi

Check compression pressure with engine at normal operating temperature, all spark plugs removed, and throttle and choke valves wide open.

VALVE CLEARANCE

Hydraulic Lifters	Zero Lash

VALVE ARRANGEMENT

I-E-I-E-E-I-E-I

SPARK PLUGS

Application	Gap (In.)	Torque (Ft. Lbs.)
All Models	.060	 7-15

Spark Plug Type

Application	AC No.
All Models	R44TSX

HIGH TENSION WIRE RESISTANCE

Do not puncture spark plug wires with any type of probe. Remove spark plug wire and check resistance using an ohmmeter.

Resistance (Ohms)

Wire Length	Minimum	Maximum
0-15"	3000	 10,000
15-25"	4000	 15,000
25-35"	6000	 20,000
Over 35"	8000	 25,000

DISTRIBUTOR

All models are equipped with a Delco High Energy Ignition system distributor and no adjustments are necessary.

IGNITION TIMING

NOTE — *Engines are equipped with a receptacle for a magnetic probe timing light, located 9.5°ATDC. Do not use this location for timing with a conventional light.*

Check or adjust ignition timing with engine at normal operating temperature, distributor vacuum hose disconnected and plugged, and engine at curb idle speed.

Ignition Timing Specifications
(Degrees BTDC@RPM)

Application	Man. Trans.	①Auto. Trans.
Federal	10@900	.... 12@700
Calif.	10@900	.... 10@700

① — Auto. Trans. in "D".

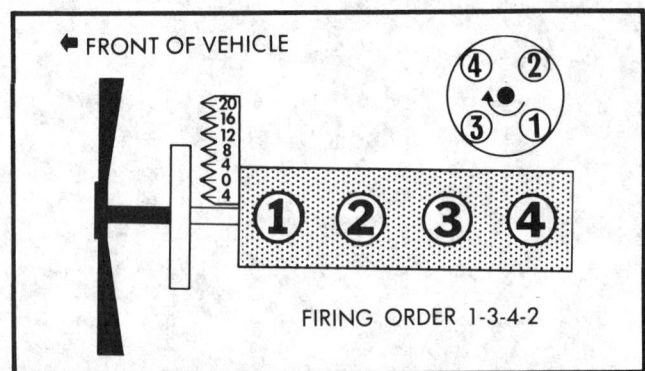

Fig. 1   Firing Order and Timing Marks

HOT (SLOW) IDLE RPM

NOTE — *Do not idle engine for over 3 minutes at a time. If idle adjustment is not completed within 3 minutes, run engine at 2000 RPM for 1 minute before continuing, repeat as necessary.*

TUNE-UP (Cont.)

1) Warm engine to normal operating temperature and connect tachometer. Place automatic transmission in "D". Turn nut on solenoid plunger to obtain solenoid RPM.

2) Disconnect solenoid wire and use curb idle screw to set curb idle. Reconnect solenoid wire and remove test equipment.

Idle Speed (RPM)

Application	Curb Idle	Solenoid Energized
Man. Trans.	500	 900
Auto. Trans.①	500	 700

① — Auto. Trans. in "D".

IDLE MIXTURE

NOTE — *Do not idle engine for over 3 minutes at a time. If idle mixture adjustment is not completed within 3 minutes, run engine at 2000 RPM for 1 minute before continuing, repeat as necessary.*

MIXTURE SCREW PLUG REMOVAL

NOTE — *Mixture adjustment is not a normal tune-up procedure. DO NOT remove idle mixture plugs unless vehicles fails emissions testing or throttle body has been disassembled.*

1) Remove carburetor and drain fuel. Place upside down on holding fixture. Place a punch in locator point in throttle body (beneath mixture plug).

2) Drive punch through locator until plug breaks, then drive out loose pieces by holding punch at a 45° angle. Reinstall carburetor and make adjustments using a thin wall 3/16" deep socket.

LEAN DROP PROCEDURE (FEDERAL VEHICLES ONLY)

1) Connect an accurate tachometer, start engine, and warm to normal operating temperature.

2) Place manual transmission in neutral and automatic transmission in "D". Starting from full rich position, turn mixture screw leaner (clockwise) until a noticeable RPM loss is indicated.

3) Turn mixture screw richer (counterclockwise) until highest RPM reading is obtained. Do not turn screw any further than point at which highest RPM is first obtained.

4) As final adjustment, turn mixture screw clockwise to obtain specified drop in engine RPM. If final RPM differs more than ±30 RPM from specified curb idle speed, reset curb idle to specification and repeat mixture adjustment.

Specified RPM Drop

Application	RPM Drop
All Federal Models	100

DWELL METER PROCEDURE (CALIFORNIA VEHICLES ONLY)

1) Remove mixture screw plug. While carburetor is removed from vehicle, turn mixture screw in until lightly seated, then back out 2½ turns (Man. Trans.) or 3 turns (Auto. Trans.). If plug in air horn which covers idle air bleed is already removed, turn screw in until seated and back out 1½ turns. If plug is in place, DO NOT remove.

2) Remove vent stack screen to reach lean mixture screw. Turn lean mixture screw in until seated and back out 3 turns. Install carburetor on engine.

3) Disconnect bowl vent line at carburetor. Disconnect EGR and canister purge line at carburetor and plug carburetor port. Connect dwell meter (set on 6 cyl. scale) to mixture solenoid test lead near carburetor. Connect tachometer to connector on distributor side of noise filter.

4) Place transmission in neutral and start engine. Operate at fast idle for at least 3 minutes to allow oxygen sensor to warm up, and system to shift to Closed Loop operation.

5) Operate engine at 3000 RPM and adjust lean mixture screw (below vent stack screen) carefully to obtain 35° dwell reading. Back screw out to raise dwell; turn screw in to lower dwell reading. Allow engine to operate between adjustments to stabilize readings. Return engine to idle and adjust to 700 RPM.

6) Adjust idle mixture screw to obtain average dwell of 25°. Back screw out slowly to raise dwell reading; turn screw in to lower reading. Allow engine to stabilize between adjustments.

7) Disconnect mixture control solenoid wire and check that idle speed drops at least 50 RPM. If not, check idle air bleed circuit. Connect solenoid and recheck 3000 RPM dwell reading. If not correct, repeat adjustment procedure.

8) Replace all hoses and set idle speed to specification. Remove test equipment. Be sure vent stack screen is replaced.

COLD (FAST) IDLE RPM

Set fast idle with engine at normal operating temperature and EGR disconnected. Position fast idle screw on high step of fast idle cam and turn to obtain fast idle RPM.

Fast Idle (RPM)

Application	RPM
Man. Trans.	2400
Auto. Trans.	2600

AUTOMATIC CHOKE

Choke coil cover is riveted in place and no adjustment is necessary.

FUEL PUMP

Perform fuel pump test with air cleaner removed and fuel inlet line or filter disconnected at carburetor. Disconnect fuel return line at fuel filter and plug nipple or filter. Make all tests at idle speed.

TUNE-UP (Cont.)

Fuel Pump Specifications

Pressure .... 6.5-8.0 psi
Volume .... 1 pint in 30 seconds
Vacuum .... 10" minimum

EMISSION CONTROL

See appropriate article in EMISSION CONTROL Section.

GENERAL SERVICING

IGNITION

DISTRIBUTOR

Delco High Energy Ignition System.

Other Data & Specifications — See Tune-Up and Delco Distributors in ELECTRICAL Section.

IGNITION COIL

Resistance
  Primary (at 75°F) .... 0.4-1.0 ohms
  Secondary (at 75°F) .... 6000-30,000 ohms
Coil Output
  All Models .... 25-35 KV Minimum
Current Draw
  Engine Stopped .... .25 amps
  Engine Idling .... 1.0 amps

CARBURETION

CARBURETOR

Application	Model
All Models	
Federal	Rochester 2SE
California	Rochester E2SE

Other Data & Specifications — See Tune-Up and Rochester Carburetors in FUEL SYSTEMS Section.

ELECTRICAL

BATTERY

Application	Cold Cranking Amps@0°F	Reserve Capacity Minutes
Standard	380	75
Optional	450	90

STARTER

Delco-Remy solenoid actuated with overrunning clutch.

Starter Specifications

Application	Volts	Amps	Test RPM
All Models	9	45-70	7000-11,900

Other Data & Specifications — See Delco-Remy Starters in ELECTRICAL Section.

ALTERNATOR

Application	Rated Amp. Output
Standard	42
Optional	63

Other Data & Specifications — See Delco Alternators and Regulators in ELECTRICAL Section.

ALTERNATOR REGULATOR

Delco-Remy non-adjustable, integral with alternator.

  Operating Voltage (at 50-100°F) 13.9-14.9

Other Data & Specifications — See Delco Alternators and Regulators in ELECTRICAL Section.

BELT ADJUSTMENT

Tension (lbs.) Using Strand Tension Gauge

Application	New Belt	Used Belt
All Belts	125-155	90-115

REPLACEMENT INTERVALS

Component	Interval (Miles)
Oil Filter	15,000
Fuel Filter	15,000
Air Filter	30,000
PCV Filter & Valve	30,000
Oxygen Sensor (Calif.)	30,000
Charcoal Canister Filter (Fed.)	30,000
Spark Plugs	30,000

CAPACITIES

Application	Quantity
Crankcase (Includes Filter)	3.0 qts.
Cooling System	7.8 qts.
Man. Trans. (SAE 80W-90)	3.0 pts.
Transfer Case (SAE 10W-30)	4.0 pts.
Front Axle (SAE 85W-90)	2.5 pts.
Rear Axle (SAE 85W-90)	4.75 pts.
Fuel Tank	14.8 gals.

TUNE-UP

ENGINE IDENTIFICATION

Engine can be identified by the 4th digit of engine Build Date Code number, located on a tag attached to right side of block between No. 2 and 3 cylinders. The same code letter is also the 4th digit in the Vehicle Identification Number (VIN), located at top left corner or dashboard.

VIN Engine Code

Application	Code
4.2L (258") 2-Bbl	C

TUNE-UP NOTES

CAUTION — *When performing tune-up on vehicles equipped with a catalytic converter, do not allow or create a condition of engine misfire in one or more cylinders for an extended period of time. Damage to converter from overheating may occur due to loading with unburned fuel.*

NOTE — *Due to production changes, always refer to Engine Tune-Up Decal in engine compartment before attempting tune-up. In the event of a conflict between specifications given in this manual and decal specifications, use the decal specifications.*

ENGINE COMPRESSION

Compression Ratio	8.0:1
Compression Ratio	120-140 psi
Maximum Variation Between Cylinders	30 psi

Measure compression pressure with engine at normal operating temperature, spark plugs removed, throttle and choke valves wide open and engine at cranking speed.

VALVE CLEARANCE

Hydraulic Lifters ....Zero Lash

VALVE ARRANGEMENT

E-I-I-E-I-E-E-I-E-I-I-E (front to rear).

SPARK PLUGS

Application	Gap (In.)	Torque (Ft. Lbs)
All Models	.035	7-15

Spark Plug Type

Application	Champion No.
All Models	RFN14LY

HIGH TENSION WIRE RESISTANCE

Do not puncture spark plug wires with any type of probe. Remove spark plug wire and check resistance using an ohmmeter.

	Resistance (Ohms)	
Wire Length	Minimum	Maximum
0-15"	3000	10,000
15-25"	4000	15,000
25-35"	6000	20,000
Over 35"	8000	25,000

DISTRIBUTOR

All models are equipped with Solid State Ignition (S.S.I.) systems and no adjustments are required.

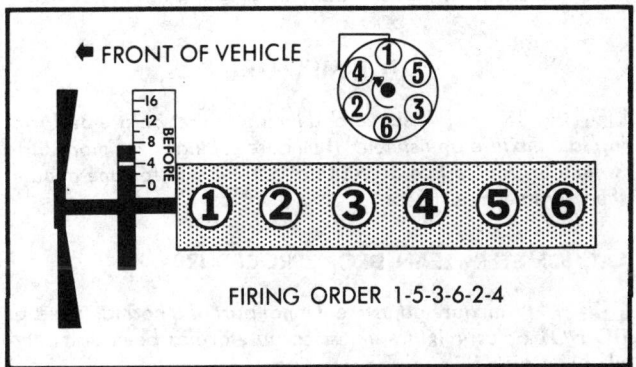

Fig. 1   Firing Order and Timing Marks

IGNITION TIMING

NOTE — *Engines are equipped with a receptacle for a magnetic probe timing light, located 10°ATDC. Do not use this location to check timing with a conventional light.*

1) Connect timing light using inductive pickup or adaptor. Do not puncture spark plug wire. Connect tachometer, then disconnect and plug vacuum hose at distributor.

2) Start engine and adjust idle speed to specifications. Set timing at idle by loosening distributor clamp bolt and turning distributor. Recheck timing after clamp bolt is tightened.

Ignition Timing Specifications
(Degrees BTDC@RPM)

Application	Man. Trans.	Auto. Trans.
All Models		
Federal	8@650	8@550
Calif.	4@650	6@550

HOT (SLOW) IDLE RPM

1) Warm engine to normal operating temperature. Set parking brake and place automatic transmission selector in "D". Disconnect solenoid wire and electrical connection. Adjust curb idle screw to obtain correct curb idle.

2) Apply direct manifold vacuum to vacuum actuator. Adjust screw on throttle lever to set vacuum actuator RPM. Disconnect vacuum.

TUNE-UP (Cont.)

3) Apply battery voltage to solenoid with a jumper wire. Turn on air conditioning and open throttle to allow solenoid to extend fully. Adjust hex-head screw to obtain solenoid RPM. Reconnect solenoid connector and vacuum hose.

Idle Speed Adjustment (RPM)

Application	Curb Idle	Vacuum Actuator	Solenoid Energized
Man. Trans.	650	900	750
Auto. Trans.	550	800	650

IDLE MIXTURE

NOTE — Be sure idle speed and timing are set before performing idle mixture adjustment. If mixture setting takes more than 3 minutes, run engine at 2000 RPM in neutral for one minute, then resume adjustment.

TACHOMETER (LEAN DROP) PROCEDURE

NOTE — Idle mixture adjustment is not part of a normal tune-up. DO NOT adjust mixture unless carburetor has been disassembled or vehicle fails emissions testing.

1) Remove carburetor and locate roll pins blocking idle mixture screws. Drill through throttle body on closed end of roll pin hole, then drive pins out with punch. Reinstall carburetor.

2) Warm vehicle to operating temperature and adjust idle speeds. Place automatic transmission selector in "D". Turn mixture screws in (lean) until RPM drops, then turn screw out until highest RPM is reached.

3) Turn mixture screws in until specified "Lean Drop" is obtained. Adjust both screws equally. When mixture is correctly adjusted, replace roll pin to block adjustment screws.

NOTE — If final RPM differs more than 30 RPM from specified curb idle speed, reset curb idle and repeat mixture adjustment.

Lean Drop RPM

Application	Man. Trans.	Auto. Trans.
All Models	50	50

COLD (FAST) IDLE RPM

Disconnect EGR solenoid vacuum line and plug carburetor ports. With engine running at normal operating temperature, place fast idle screw on second step of fast idle cam and against shoulder of high step. Turn screw to adjust fast idle speed.

Fast Idle Speed RPM

Application	Man. Trans.	Auto. Trans.
All Models	1700	1850

AUTOMATIC CHOKE SETTING

To adjust automatic choke, loosen coil housing retaining screws and rotate housing in direction indicated by arrows. Adjust to 1NR and tighten screws.

FUEL PUMP PRESSURE & VOLUME

Pressure (at Idle)	4.0-5.0 psi
Volume (at Idle)	1 pint in 30 seconds
Vacuum (at Idle)	10 In. Hg (Minimum)

EMISSION CONTROL

See appropriate article in EMISSION CONTROL Section.

GENERAL SERVICING

IGNITION

DISTRIBUTOR

Motorcraft .... Breakerless Solid State

Other Data & Specifications — See Tune-Up & Motorcraft Distributors in ELECTRICAL Section.

IGNITION COIL

Resistance

Primary	1.13-1.23 ohms
Secondary	7700-9300 ohms
Coil Output	24 KV minumum

FUEL SYSTEMS

CARBURETORS

Application	Model
All Models	Carter BBD 2-Bbl.

Other Data & Specifications — See Tune-Up and Carter Carburetors in FUEL SYSTEMS Section.

ELECTRICAL

BATTERY

Application	Cold Cranking Amps @ 0° F	Reserve Capacity Minutes
Standard	380	75
Optional	450	90
Police	440	135

STARTER

Motorcraft.................................... Positive Engagement Type

Starter Specifications

Application	Volts	Amps	Test RPM
All Models	12	77	8900-9600

GENERAL SERVICING (Cont.)

Other Data & Specifications — *See Motorcraft Starters in ELECTRICAL Section.*

ALTERNATOR

Delco .... Solid State, Integral Regulator

Application	Rated Amp. Output
Standard	42
Optional	63, 70
Police	85

Other Data & Specifications — *See Delco Alternators in ELECTRICAL Section.*

ALTERNATOR REGULATORS

Delco .... Solid State, Integral With Alternator (Non-Adjustable)

Other Data & Specifications — *See Delco Alternators in ELECTRICAL Section.*

REPLACEMENT INTERVALS

Component	Interval (Miles)
Oil Filter.................	7500
Air Filter	30,000
PCV Valve	30,000
Spark Plugs	30,000

CAPACITIES

Application	Capacity
Cooling System (Includes Heater).......................	10.5 qts.
Crankcase (Includes Filter)	5 qts.
Man. Trans. (SAE 85W-90)	
SR4	3.0 pts.
T176	3.5 pts.
Auto. Trans. (Dexron)	
Refill	8.5 pts.
Overhaul	17.0 pts.
Transfer Case	
CJ Series (SAE 85W-90)	4.0 pts.
Quadra-Trac (SAE 10W-30)	4.0 pts.
All Others (SAE 10W-30)	6.0 pts.
Drive Axles .... Fill to bottom of filler plug hole	
Fuel Tank	
CJ Series	14.8 gals.
Cherokee & Wagoneer	20.3 gals.
Truck	19.0 gals.

BELT ADJUSTMENT

Tension (Lbs.) Using Strand Tension Gauge

Application	New Belt	Used Belt
Air Pump & Pwr. Strg.① ..	65-75	60-70
Serpentine (Calif.)	180-200	140-160
All Other Belts	125-155	90-115

① — ⅜" belt only.

1981 Jeep V8 Tune-Up

TUNE-UP

ENGINE IDENTIFICATION

Engine can be identified by the 4th digit of engine Build Date Code, located on a tag attached to the right cylinder head cover. The same code letter is also used as the 4th digit of Vehicle Identification Number (VIN), located on a plate attached to top left corner of instrument panel.

VIN Engine Codes

Application	Code Letter
5.0L (304") 2-Bbl.	H
6.0L (360") 2-Bbl.	N

TUNE-UP NOTES

NOTE — *Due to production changes, always refer to Engine Tune-Up Decal in engine compartment before attempting tune-up. In the event of a conflict between specifications given in this manual and decal specifications, use the decal specifications.*

CAUTION — *When performing tune-up on vehicles equipped with a catalytic converter, do not allow or create a condition of engine misfire in one or more cylinders for an extended period of time. Damage to converter from overheating may occur due to loading with unburned fuel.*

ENGINE COMPRESSION

Compression Ratio	
5.0L	8.4:1
6.0L	8.3:1
Compression Pressure	120-140 psi
Maximum Pressure Variation	30 psi

Measure compression pressure with engine at normal operating temperature, spark plugs removed, throttle and choke valves wide open and engine at cranking speed.

VALVE CLEARANCE

Hydraulic Lifters ....Zero Lash

VALVE ARRANGEMENT

E-I-I-E-E-I-I-E (both banks, front to rear).

SPARK PLUGS

Application	Gap (In.)	Torque (Ft. Lbs.)
All Models	.035	 16-26

Spark Plug Type

Application	Champion No.
All	N-12Y or RN-12Y

HIGH TENSION WIRE RESISTANCE

Do not puncture spark plug wires with any type of probe. Remove spark plug wire and check resistance using an ohmmeter.

Resistance Ohms

Wire Length	Minimum	Maximum
0-15	3000	10,000
15-25	4000	15,000
25-35"	6000	20,000
Over 35"	8000	25,000

DISTRIBUTOR

All models are equipped with Solid State Ignition (S.S.I.) systems and no adjustments are required.

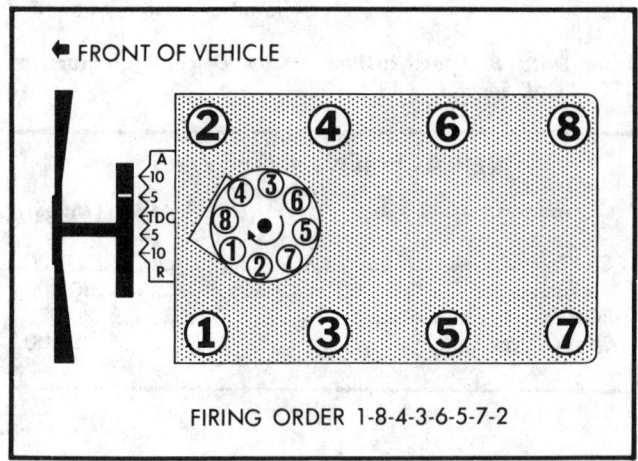

Fig. 1   Firing Order and Timing Marks

IGNITION TIMING

NOTE — *Engines are equipped with a receptacle for a magnetic probe timing light, located 9.5°ATDC. Do not use this location for timing with a conventional light.*

Warm engine and allow to idle. Disconnect and plug distributor vacuum line, then check ignition timing. Adjust by turning distributor.

Ignition Timing Specifications
(Degrees BTDC@RPM)

Application	Man. Trans.	Auto. Trans.
5.0L	8@600①	10@600
6.0L	10@600	10@600

① — 10° on High Alt. models.

HOT (SLOW) IDLE RPM

1) Set parking brake and block drive wheels. Warm engine to operating temperature and place in neutral (manual) or "D" (automatic).

TUNE-UP (Cont.)

2) Turn hex head screw on solenoid carriage to adjust solenoid RPM. Disconnect solenoid wire and adjust idle speed screw to obtain curb idle.

3) If equipped with dashpot, depress stem fully and measure clearance between stem and throttle lever. Turn dashpot to adjust to .032". Tighten locknut and remove test equipment.

Idle Speed RPM

Application	Curb Idle	Solenoid Energized
All Models	500	600

IDLE MIXTURE

NOTE — *Be sure idle speed and timing are set before performing idle mixture adjustment. If mixture setting takes more than 3 minutes, run engine at 2000 RPM in neutral for one minute, then resume adjustment.*

TACHOMETER (LEAN DROP) PROCEDURE

NOTE — *Idle mixture adjustment is not part of a regular tune-up. DO NOT adjust mixture unless carburetor has been disassembled or vehicle fails emissions testing.*

1) Warm engine to normal operating temperature. Turn idle mixture screws to full counterclockwise position, note position of screw slot, and remove limiter caps. If screw moved during cap removal, adjust to prior position.

2) Start engine and run in neutral (manual) or "D" (automatic). Turn mixture screw clockwise (leaner) until engine speed begins to drop. Then turn screw counterclockwise (richer) until highest RPM reading is obtained. This is lean best idle. Finally, turn screw clockwise until specified "Lean Drop" is obtained.

NOTE — *If final RPM differs more than 30 RPM from specified curb idle speed, reset curb idle and repeat mixture adjustment.*

3) Carefully install new limiter caps with tabs positioned against full rich stop. Press caps fully into place.

Lean Drop RPM

Application	Man. Trans.	Auto. Trans.
All Models	50	20

COLD (FAST) IDLE RPM

Disconnect EGR vacuum line and plug carburetor port. With engine idling at normal operating temperature, place fast idle screw on second step of fast idle cam and against shoulder of high step. Adjust screw to set fast idle RPM.

Fast Idle Speed RPM

Application	Man. Trans.	Auto. Trans.
All Models	1500	1600

AUTOMATIC CHOKE SETTING

To adjust automatic choke, loosen cover retaining screws and rotate cover in direction indicated by arrow on face of cover. Adjust to specified setting.

Automatic Choke Setting

Application	Man. Trans.	Auto. Trans.
5.0L	2NR①	1NR
6.0L	2NR	2NR

① — 1NR on High Alt. models.

FUEL PUMP PRESSURE & VOLUME

Pressure (at Idle)	5.0-6.5 psi
Volume (at Idle)	1 pint in 30 seconds
Vacuum (at Idle)	10 In. Hg (Minimum)

EMISSION CONTROL

See appropriate article in EMISSION CONTROL Section.

GENERAL SERVICING

IGNITION

DISTRIBUTOR

Motorcraft	Breakerless Solid State

Other Data & Specifications — *See Tune-Up & Motorcraft Distributors in ELECTRICAL Section.*

IGNITION COIL

Resistance

Primary	1.13-1.23 ohms
Secondary	7700-9300 ohms

Coil Output	24 KV min.

FUEL SYSTEMS

CARBURETORS

Application	Model
5.0L	Motorcraft 2150 2-Bbl.
6.0L	Motorcraft 2150 2-Bbl.

Other Data & Specifications — *See Tune-Up and Motorcraft Carburetors in FUEL SYSTEMS Section.*

1981 Jeep V8 Tune-Up

GENERAL SERVICING (Cont.)

ELECTRICAL

BATTERY

Application	Cold Cranking Amps@0° F	Reserve Capacity Minutes
Standard	380	75
Optional	450	90
Police	440	135

STARTER

Motorcraft.. Positive Engagement

Starter Specifications

Application	Volts	Amps	Test RPM
All Models	12	77	8900-9600

Other Data & Specifications — *See Motorcraft Starters in ELECTRICAL Section.*

ALTERNATORS

Delco .... Solid State, Integral Regulator

Application	Rated Amp. Output
Standard	42
Optional	63,70
Police	85

Other Data & Specifications — *See Delco Alternators in ELECTRICAL Section.*

ALTERNATOR REGULATORS

Delco .... Solid State, Integral With Alternator (Non-Adjustable)

Other Data & Specifications — *See Delco Alternators in ELECTRICAL Section.*

BELT ADJUSTMENT

Tension (Lbs.) Using Strand Tension Gauge

Application	New Belt	Used Belt
All Belts	125-155	90-115

REPLACEMENT INTERVALS

Component	Interval (Miles)
Oil Filter	7500
Fuel Filter	15,000
Air Filter	30,000
PCV Valve	30,000
Charcoal Canister Filter	30,000
Spark Plugs	30,000

CAPACITIES

Application	Quantity
Cooling System	
5.0L	13.0 qts.
6.0L	14.0 qts.
Crankcase (Includes Filter)	5.0 qts.
Man. Trans. (SAE 85W-90)	
SR4	3.0 pts.
T176	3.5 pts.
T18	6.5 pts.
Auto. Trans. (Dexron)	
Refill	8.5 pts.
Overhaul Fill	17.0 pts.
Transfer Case	
CJ Series (SAE 85W-90)	4.0 pts.
Quadra-Trac (SAE 10W-30)	4.0 pts.
All Others (SAE 10W-30)	6.0 pts.
Drive Axles	Fill to bottom of filler plug hole
Fuel Tank	
CJ Series	14.8 gals.
Cherokee & Wagoneer	20.3 gals.
Truck	19.0 gals.

Contents

Section 2

FUEL SYSTEMS

NOTE — ALSO SEE GENERAL INDEX.

IMPORTANT

Because of the great number of model names used by vehicle manufacturers, accurate identification of models is important. See Model Identification at the front of this publication.

1981 Fuel Systems

CARBURETOR TROUBLE SHOOTING

CONDITION & POSSIBLE CAUSE	CONDITION & POSSIBLE CAUSE
No Start — Cold • No fuel in carburetor bowl. • Choke binding, stuck closed, or improperly adjusted. • Clogged air bleeds or idle passages. • Choke vacuum diaphragm leaking. • Engine flooding (see flooding). **Hard Start — Cold** • Cold enrichment or choke system not functioning. • Incorrect choke adjustment. • Restricted choke vacuum and hot air passages. • Accelerator pump not functioning properly. • Leaking intake or carburetor gaskets. **Rough Idle — Cold** • Cold enrichment or choke system not functioning. • Vacuum leak. • Improper throttle stop adjustment. • Improper fast idle cam adjustment. • Choke linkage binding, throttle plates sticking. • Choke pulldown diaphragm leaking. **Stall, Hesitation, Stumble — Cold** • Accelerator pump not functioning. • Cold enrichment or choke system not functioning. • Low fuel pump volume. • Clogged fuel filter. • Power valve stuck closed. • Leaking or misaligned float. • Improper or obstructed main jets. • Choke plate improperly adjusted. **No Start — Hot** • No fuel in carburetor bowl. • Fuel lines vapor locked. • Cold enrichment or choke system not functioning. • Flooding or loading (see flooding). **Hard Start — Hot** • Cold enrichment or choke system not functioning. • Choke improperly adjusted. • Bowl vents plugged. • Flooding or loading (see flooding). • Restricted choke vacuum or hot air passages. • Leaking intake manifold or carburetor gaskets.	**Rough Idle — Hot** • Cold enrichment or choke system not functioning. • Improper throttle stop adjustment. • Throttle plates stuck open. • Choke pulldown diaphragm not functioning. • Hot idle compensator stuck closed. • External vent blocked. • Improper idle adjustment. • Damaged tip on idle mixture screws. • Clogged air bleeds or idle passages. • Clogged or malfunctioning PCV system. • Improper fuel level in carburetor. • Vacuum leak. • Leaking carburetor gaskets. **Stall, Hesitation, Stumble — Hot** • Cold enrichment or choke system not functioning. • Vacuum leak at intake manifold, carburetor, or vacuum lines. • Weak or damaged accelerator pump. • Restricted air cleaner or exhaust system. • Low fuel pump volume. • Carburetor bowl vents plugged. • Clogged fuel filter. • Secondary throttle plate sticking open (4-Bbl.) • Power valve stuck closed. • Improper or obstructed main jets. **Stalls on Deceleration or Quick Stops** • Idle speed low. • Throttle positioner not functioning. • Venturi valve not functioning. • Clogged air bleeds or idle passages. • Leaking intake manifold or carburetor gaskets. **Hesitation or Stall on Acceleration** • EGR valve stuck open. • Weak or improperly adjusted accelerator pump. • Air valve sticking or binding (4-Bbl.). • Control vacuum regulator set high. • Secondary throttle plates sticking or binding (4-Bbl.). • Plugged accelerator pump discharge nozzle. • Restricted fuel filter. • Discharge nozzle gasket leaking. • Vacuum leaks. • Improper float setting. • Restricted exhaust system. • Main metering system plugged, contaminated fuel.

CARBURETOR TROUBLE SHOOTING (Cont.)

CONDITION & POSSIBLE CAUSE	CONDITION & POSSIBLE CAUSE
Reduced Top Speed/Power • Clogged or defective PCV system. • Low fuel pump volume. • Heat valve stuck. • Plugged manifold heat passages. • Binding throttle linkage. • Restricted air cleaner or exhaust system. • Incorrect float drop. • Secondary throttle plates stuck open or not opening (4-Bbl.). • Clogged fuel filter. • Metering jets bent, dirty, or incorrect size. • Power valve stuck closed. • Throttle plate not opening fully. **Surge at Cruising Speed** • Plugged or malfunctioning PCV system. • Plugged fuel filter. • Restricted air cleaner or exhaust system. • Improper float level. • Low fuel pump pressure or volume. • Main metering jets dirty, loose, or wrong size. • Contaminated fuel. • Primary metering rods bent. • Blocked air bleeds. **Engine Diesels (After Run)** • Vacuum hoses off or leaking. • Incorrect idle adjustment. • Not coming off fast idle cam. • Excessively lean idle mixture.	**Flooding** • Leaking float. • Improper float level setting. • Damaged fuel inlet. • Float needle valve loose, sticking, or loose seat. • Fuel pump pressure too high. • Internal or cross circuit leakage. **Low Fuel Mileage** • Accelerator pump discharge ball not seating. • Power piston stuck or bent. • Main metering jets plugged, loose, or improper size. • Leaking carburetor gaskets. • Poor driving habits. • Choke linkage binding or maladjusted. • Carburetor flooding or loading (see flooding). • Fuel leaks other than at carburetor. **Evidence of Fuel Loss, or Fuel Vapor Ordor** • Leaking fuel level sending unit or gasket. • Leaking fuel filler or cap. • Leaking fuel tank. • Leaking fuel system to carburetor. • Inoperative bowl vent valve. • Damaged fuel vapor hoses or canisters.

DIESEL FUEL INJECTION TROUBLE SHOOTING

CONDITION & POSSIBLE CAUSE	CONDITION & POSSIBLE CAUSE

Engine Cranks But Will Not Start

- Incorrect starting procedure.
- No voltage to fuel solenoid.
- Faulty glow plugs or glow plug control system.
- Plugged fuel return system.
- No fuel to nozzles.
- No fuel to injection pump.
- Clogged fuel tank filter.
- Incorrect or contaminated fuel.
- Incorrect pump timing.

Engine Starts But Stalls at Idle

- Incorrect slow idle adjustment.
- Faulty fast idle solenoid.
- Plugged fuel return system.
- Glow plugs turn off too soon.
- Incorrect pump timing.
- Limited fuel to injection pump.
- Air in injection lines to nozzles.
- Incorrect or contaminated fuel.
- Faulty injection pump.
- Fuel solenoid closes in "RUN" position.

Engine Starts, Idles Rough Without Unusual Noise Or Smoke

- Incorrect slow idle adjustment.
- Leaking injection line.
- Plugged fuel return line.
- Air in lines to nozzles.
- Internal fuel leak at nozzles.
- Faulty nozzle.
- Improper or contaminated fuel.
- Uneven fuel distribution.

Engine Starts and Idles Rough With Excessive Noise and/or Smoke

- Incorrect pump timing.
- Air in injection lines to nozzles.
- Faulty nozzles.
- Improperly installed high pressure lines.

Engine Idles Correctly, But Misfires Above Idle

- Plugged fuel filter.
- Incorrect pump timing.
- Incorrect or contaminated fuel.

Engine Will Not Return To Idle

- Linkage binding or maladjusted.
- Defective injection pump.

Fuel Leaks on Ground, No Other Engine Malfunction

- Loose or broken fuel line or connection.
- Internal seal leak at injection pump.

Low Engine Power

- Restricted air intake.
- Plugged fuel filter.
- Restricted fuel return system.
- Restricted fuel supply from tank to pump.
- Incorrect or contaminated fuel.
- Restricted fuel tank filter.
- Compression leaks at nozzles or glow plugs.
- Plugged nozzle(s).

"Rapping" Noise From One or More Cylinders

- Air in fuel system.
- Air in high pressure lines.
- Nozzle sticking in open position; low nozzle opening pressure.

Excessive Combustion Noise With Black Smoke

- Incorrect pump timing.
- Incorrect pump housing pressure.
- Defective injection pump.

Engine Will Not Shut Off With Key

- Injection pump fuel solenoid does not return to "OFF" position.

CARTER YFA & YFA FEEDBACK SINGLE BARREL

CARBURETOR APPLICATION

FORD MOTOR CO.

Application	Ford Carburetor Number	
	Man. Trans.	Auto. Trans.
4.9L (300") 6 Cyl.		
Bronco		
With A/C	E1TE-AD	
Without A/C	E1TE-ANA	
E100/150		
Federal	E1TE-ARA	E1TE-AUA
	E1TE-UA	
Calif.	E1TE-GA	E1TE-AZA
E250		
Federal	E1TE-ANA	E1TE-AUA
Calif.		E1TE-AZA
E350		
Federal	EOTE-AMA	EOTE-FA
Calif.	D9TE-CA	
F100		
Federal	E1TE-ANA, E1TE-DA,	E1TE-VA
	E1TE-EA, E1TE-TA	
Calif.	E1TE-GA	E1TE-AZA
F150/250		
Federal	E1TE-ANA	E1TE-VA
	E1TE-AD	
Calif.	E1TE-GA	E1TE-AZA
F350		
Federal	EOTE-AMA	EOTE-FA
Calif.	D9TE-CA	

CARBURETOR IDENTIFICATION

A carburetor identification tag is attached to carburetor. The tag contains part number prefix and suffix. A design change code (if any) is also stamped into tag. An assembly date code (year, month, and day) is also stamped into tag. To obtain replacement parts, it is necessary to know identification number prefix and suffix, and in some instances, the design change code.

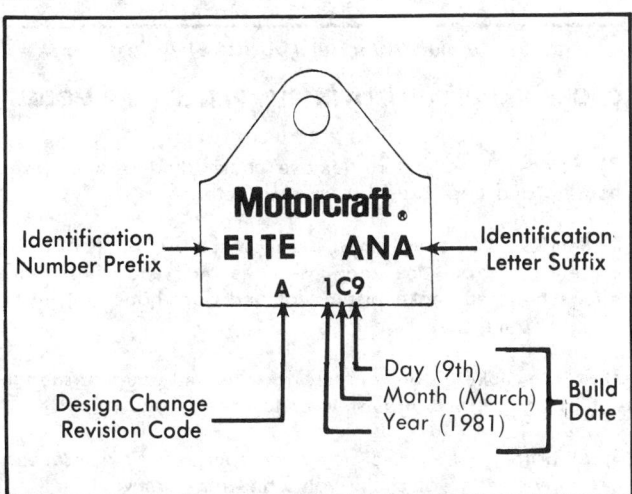

Fig. 1   Ford Motor Co. Carburetor Identification Tag

DESCRIPTION

Carter YFA and YFA Feedback carburetors are made up of three main assemblies: air horn, main body, and throttle body. YFA model carburetors have an adjustment limiting vacuum diaphragm type automatic choke with an electric assist choke cap. The main body contains a temperature compensated accelerator pump which has a thermostatic disc designed to open and close within a specified range.

The YFA Feedback carburetor differs from the YFA in its addition of a feedback solenoid. This solenoid is used to meter air into both the idle and main circuits for improved engine performance. A Microprocessor Control Unit (MCU) senses various engine needs and supplies feedback fuel as required by forcing air into fuel bowl, and in turn more fuel into carburetor air stream.

ADJUSTMENT

HOT (SLOW) IDLE RPM

See appropriate article in TUNE-UP SERVICE PROCEDURES.

VACUUM THROTTLE KICKER (DECEL THROTTLE DIAPHRAGM)

See appropriate article in TUNE-UP SERVICE PROCEDURES.

IDLE MIXTURE

See appropriate article in TUNE-UP SERVICE PROCEDURES.

COLD (FAST) IDLE RPM

See appropriate article in TUNE-UP SERVICE PROCEDURES.

FLOAT LEVEL

All Models — 1) Remove air cleaner assembly. Remove air horn and gasket from top of carburetor.

2) Turn air horn assembly upside-down. Measure distance between top of float (at free end) and gasket surface of air horn.

NOTE — *Float arm should be resting gently on needle. Do not apply pressure against needle to prevent damage to tip.*

3) Bend float arm as necessary to obtain correct clearance. DO NOT bend tab at end of float arm as this would stop the float travel to bottom of fuel bowl when empty.

4) When adjustment is completed, reinstall air horn and gasket. Start engine and check for fuel leaks. Install air cleaner.

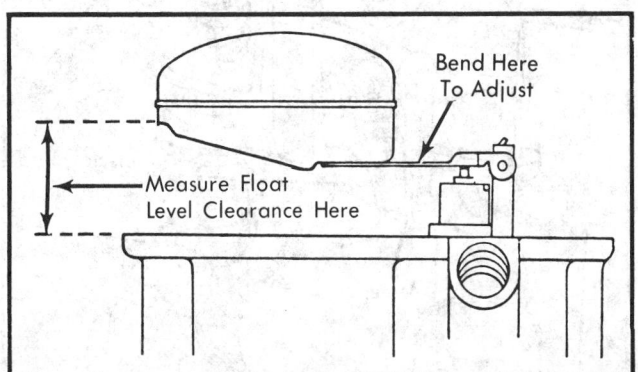

Fig. 2   Float Level Clearance Adjustment

1981 Carter Carburetors

CARTER YFA & YFA FEEDBACK SINGLE BARREL (Cont.)

FLOAT DROP

All Models – 1) Remove air cleaner, carburetor air horn and gasket from top of carburetor.

2) Hold air horn in upright position. Allow float to hang free. Measure minimum clearance from tip of float to bottom of air horn casting with a suitable gauge. See *Fig. 3.*

3) Bend tab at end of float arm to adjust. After completing adjustment, install gasket and air horn on carburetor. Start engine and check for fuel leaks. Install air cleaner.

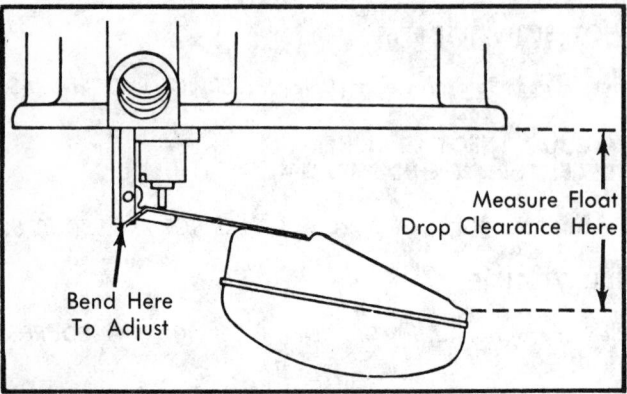

Fig. 3   Float Drop Clearance Measurement

METERING ROD

All Models – 1) Remove air cleaner, air horn and gasket from carburetor.

2) Back out idle speed adjusting screw until throttle plate is tightly closed in throttle bore.

3) Press down on end of pump diaphragm shaft until assembly bottoms. While holding diaphragm assembly in this position, turn rod adjustment screw counterclockwise until metering rod gently bottoms in body casting. See *Fig. 4.*

4) Now turn metering rod adjustment screw clockwise (IN) ONE turn for final adjustment.

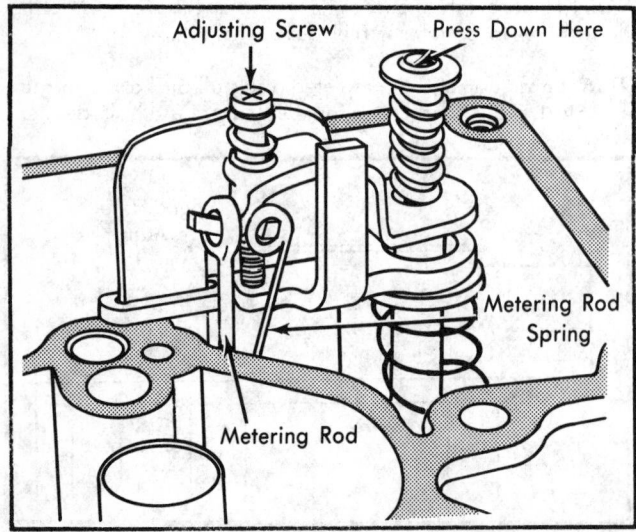

Fig. 4   Metering Rod Adjustment

5) Install air horn and gasket on carburetor. Start engine and check for fuel leaks. Install air cleaner.

CHOKE UNLOADER (DECHOKE)

All Models – 1) Remove air cleaner. Hold throttle valve in fully open position without forcing it. Press choke valve toward closed position.

2) Measure clearance between lower edge of choke valve and air horn wall .

3) Adjust by bending unloader tang which contacts the fast idle cam. See *Fig. 5.*

4) Bend tang (arm) upward to increase clearance; bend downward (away from fast idle cam) to decrease clearance.

5) Operate throttle to check for binding or clearance interference. Install air cleaner.

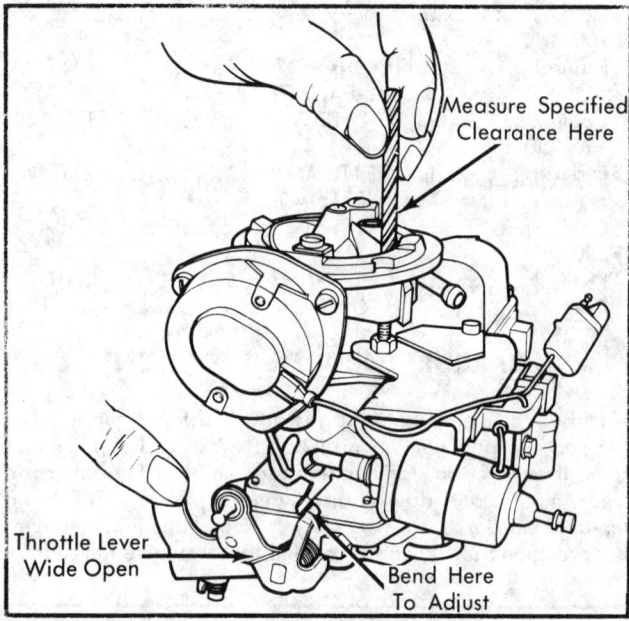

Fig. 5   Choke Unloader (Dechoke) Adjustment

CHOKE VALVE PULL-DOWN CLEARANCE (YFA MODEL)

1) Remove air cleaner. Remove choke thermostatic spring housing and heat baffle from carburetor.

2) Bend a .026″ diameter wire gauge at a 90° angle approximately ⅛″ from one end. Insert the bent end of the wire gauge between choke piston slot and right hand slot in the choke housing. See *Fig. 6.*

3) Rotate choke piston counterclockwise until gauge is snug in slot. Hold pressure against lever to keep gauge in place.

4) Measure choke valve pull-down specified clearance between lower edge of choke valve and air horn wall.

5) To adjust, bend choke lever. Bend lever toward piston to decrease clearance; bend lever away from piston to increase clearance.

NOTE – *Do not distort piston link while adjusting or erratic choke operation will result.*

CARTER YFA & YFA FEEDBACK SINGLE BARREL (Cont.)

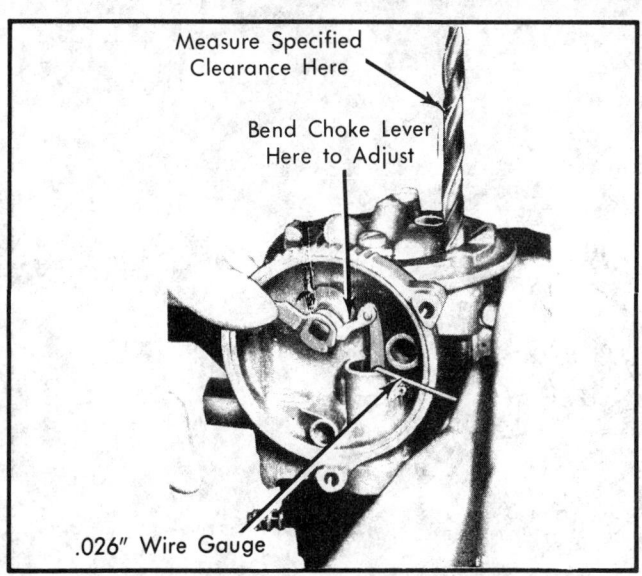

Fig. 6   Choke Valve Pull-Down Clearance Adjustment

CHOKE VALVE PULL-DOWN CLEARANCE (YFA FEEDBACK MODEL)

1) Remove air cleaner. Remove choke thermostatic spring housing and heat baffle from carburetor.

2) Temporarily rotate choke housing to rich setting to lightly close choke plate, then increase an additional 90°.

3) Activate pulldown motor by applying an external vacuum source. Check clearance between lower edge of choke valve and air horn wall.

4) To adjust, bend choke diaphragm link as required. Reinstall choke thermostat housing using 2 No. 6-32 screws in place of rivets. Replace air cleaner.

FAST IDLE CAM INDEX

1) Place fast idle speed screw on kickdown step of fast idle cam, against shoulder of highest step. *See Fig. 7.*

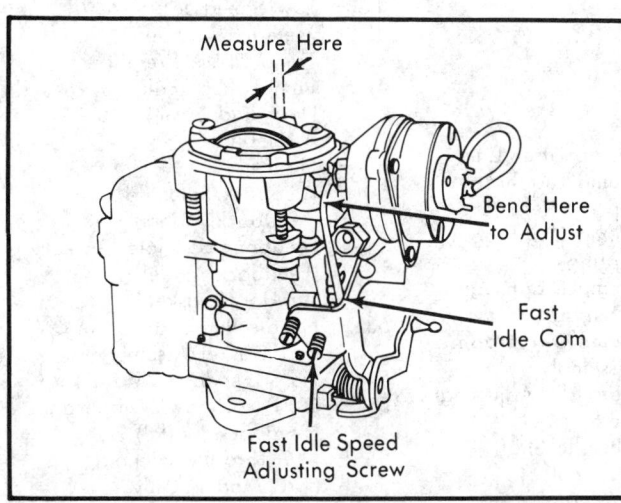

Fig. 7   Fast Idle Cam Index Adjustment

2) Measure specified clearance between lower edge of choke valve and air horn wall.

3) If clearance is not to specification, adjust by bending fast idle cam link.

AUTOMATIC CHOKE

NOTE — *Although automatic choke is of tamper-proof design, these steps are used if automatic choke is damaged or when carburetor is rebuilt.*

1) Loosen choke thermostat cover retaining screws.

2) Rotate cover assembly in "Rich" or "Lean" direction to align reference mark on cover with specified scale graduation on housing. Tighten cover screws.

OVERHAUL

DISASSEMBLY

NOTE — *Use new gaskets and seals. Make sure that new gaskets fit correctly and that all holes and slots are punched through and correctly located.*

All Models — **1)** Remove carburetor from engine. Remove thermostatic spring housing assembly, spring housing gasket, baffle plate, and fast idle link. Remove EGR WOT dump valve and bracket. If equipped, remove air conditioning throttle solenoid.

2) Remove air horn assembly screws and dashpot. If YFA Feedback model, remove feedback solenoid and bracket assembly. Lift air horn away from main body and remove gasket. Turn air horn upside down and remove float pin, float, and lever assembly.

3) Turn air horn right side up and catch needle pin, spring and needle as they fall out. Remove needle seat and gasket.

4) Remove air cleaner bracket. If necessary, file staked (burred) ends of choke plate attaching screws and remove. Be sure to use new screws when assembling. Remove choke plate from air horn. Remove choke link lever and attaching screw.

5) Turn choke shaft and piston assembly counterclockwise until choke piston comes out of choke piston cylinder. Remove assembly from air horn. Remove piston pin and piston from choke piston lever and shaft assembly.

6) Remove spring retainer from mechanical fuel bowl vent flapper valve. Remove vent shaft rod and spring, and flapper valve. Note position of spring on rod for reassembly.

7) Turn main body upside-down and catch accelerator pump check ball and weight. Remove bowl vent lever screw in end of throttle shaft. Remove spring washer, actuating lever, operating lever and clip. Loosen throttle shaft arm screw. Remove arm and accelerator pump connector link. Remove fast idle cam and screw. Remove throttle kicker (if equipped).

8) Remove accelerator pump diaphragm housing screws, lift out pump diaphragm assembly, pump lifter link and metering rod as a unit.

9) Disengage metering rod arm spring from metering rod. Remove metering rod from rod arm assembly. Be sure to note

1981 Carter Carburetors

CARTER YFA & YFA FEEDBACK SINGLE BARREL (Cont.)

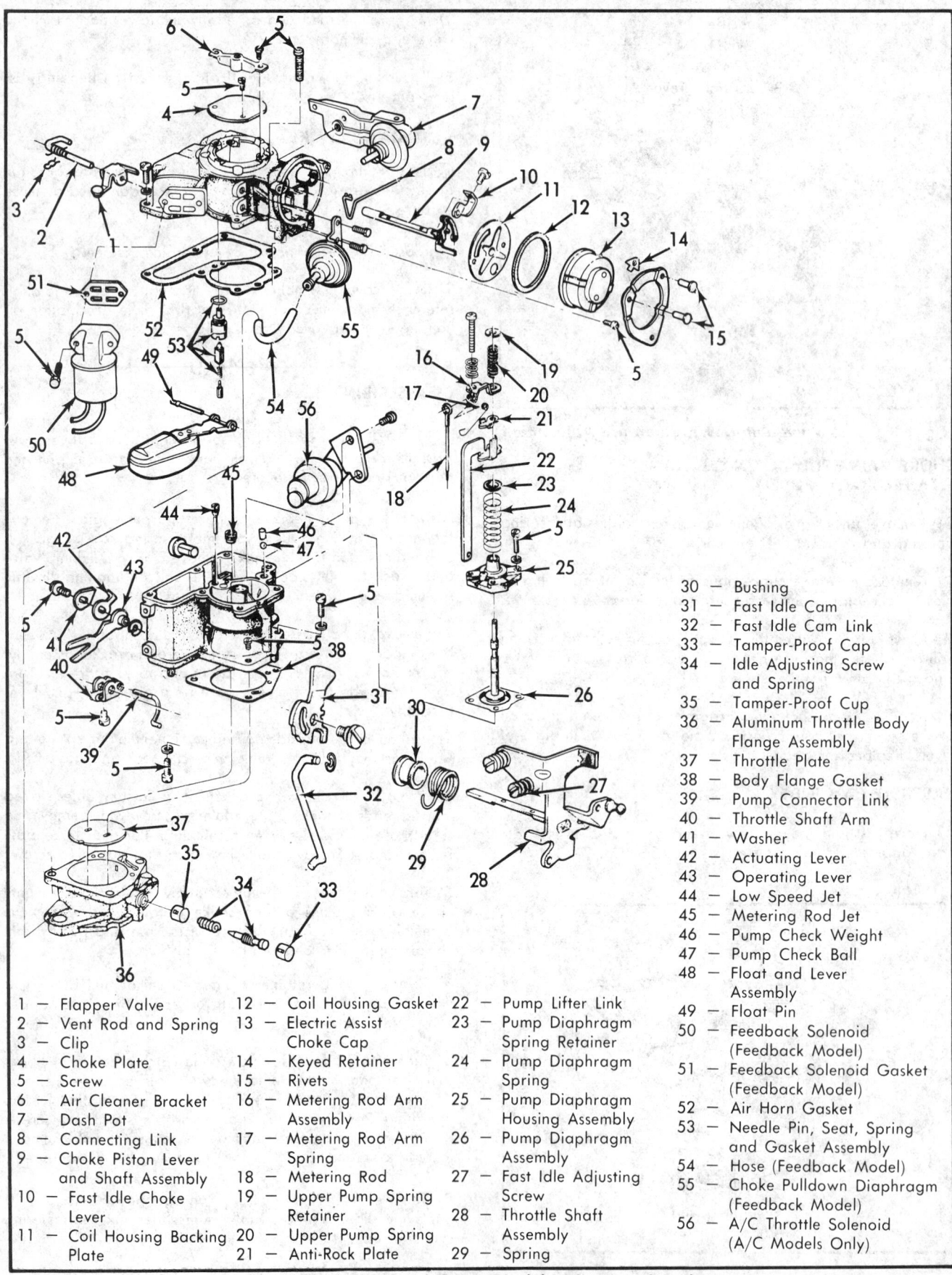

1 — Flapper Valve	12 — Coil Housing Gasket	22 — Pump Lifter Link
2 — Vent Rod and Spring	13 — Electric Assist Choke Cap	23 — Pump Diaphragm Spring Retainer
3 — Clip	14 — Keyed Retainer	24 — Pump Diaphragm Spring
4 — Choke Plate	15 — Rivets	25 — Pump Diaphragm Housing Assembly
5 — Screw	16 — Metering Rod Arm Assembly	26 — Pump Diaphragm Assembly
6 — Air Cleaner Bracket	17 — Metering Rod Arm Spring	27 — Fast Idle Adjusting Screw
7 — Dash Pot	18 — Metering Rod	28 — Throttle Shaft Assembly
8 — Connecting Link	19 — Upper Pump Spring Retainer	29 — Spring
9 — Choke Piston Lever and Shaft Assembly	20 — Upper Pump Spring	
10 — Fast Idle Choke Lever	21 — Anti-Rock Plate	
11 — Coil Housing Backing Plate		

30 — Bushing
31 — Fast Idle Cam
32 — Fast Idle Cam Link
33 — Tamper-Proof Cap
34 — Idle Adjusting Screw and Spring
35 — Tamper-Proof Cup
36 — Aluminum Throttle Body Flange Assembly
37 — Throttle Plate
38 — Body Flange Gasket
39 — Pump Connector Link
40 — Throttle Shaft Arm
41 — Washer
42 — Actuating Lever
43 — Operating Lever
44 — Low Speed Jet
45 — Metering Rod Jet
46 — Pump Check Weight
47 — Pump Check Ball
48 — Float and Lever Assembly
49 — Float Pin
50 — Feedback Solenoid (Feedback Model)
51 — Feedback Solenoid Gasket (Feedback Model)
52 — Air Horn Gasket
53 — Needle Pin, Seat, Spring and Gasket Assembly
54 — Hose (Feedback Model)
55 — Choke Pulldown Diaphragm (Feedback Model)
56 — A/C Throttle Solenoid (A/C Models Only)

Fig. 8 *Exploded View of Carter Model YFA 1-Barrel Carburetor (YFA Feedback Model Illustrated, YFA Similar)*

CARTER YFA & YFA FEEDBACK SINGLE BARREL (Cont.)

location of any washers that were used for shimming either spring (for reassembly). Compress upper pump spring and remove spring retainer.

10) Remove upper spring, metering rod arm assembly, anti-rock plate (if equipped), and pump lifter link from pump diaphragm shaft.

11) Compress pump diaphragm spring, remove pump diaphragm spring retainer, spring and pump diaphragm assembly from pump diaphragm housing.

12) Using proper size jet tool or screwdriver, remove metering rod jet and low speed jet. Remove screws and separate throttle body flange assembly from main body casting. Remove gasket.

13) Remove throttle plate retaining screws. File staked (burred) ends if necessary, and use new screws at reassembly. Slide throttle shaft and lever assembly out of throttle body.

NOTE — *Location of torsion spring ends on throttle shaft is important to know for reassembly.*

14) When removing idle mixture limiter cap, be sure to note the position of the tab. After removing limiter cap, count number of turns to lightly seat needle. When assembling, install screw in same location.

CLEANING & INSPECTION

- Use a regular carburetor cleaning solution. Soak components long enough to thoroughly clean all surfaces and passages of foreign matter.

- Do not soak any components containing rubber or leather.

- Remove any residue after cleaning by rinsing components in a suitable solvent.

- Blow out all passages with dry compressed air.

REASSEMBLY

NOTE — *Use new gaskets. Make sure that new gaskets fit correctly and that all holes and slots are punched through and correctly located.*

To reassemble carburetor, reverse disassembly procedures and note the following:

1) If throttle valve was removed, make sure notch in throttle valve is aligned with idle port in body flange. Make sure throttle plate does not bind or stick. Restake or peen throttle plate screws.

2) Make sure vacuum passage in accelerator pump housing is aligned with vacuum passage in main body.

3) Make sure bowl vent rod engages forked actuating lever when air horn is installed.

CARBURETOR ADJUSTMENT SPECIFICATIONS

Application	Float Level Setting	Choke Unloader Setting	Choke Pull-Down Setting	Fast Idle Cam Setting	Auto. Choke Setting
D9TE - CA	.69″	.280″	.290″	.140″	Index
E0TE - AMA	.69″	.280″	.290″	.140″	Index
E0TE - FA	.69″	.280″	.290″	.140″	Index
E1TE - EA	.78″	.280″	.300″	.140″	Index
E1TE - DA	.78″	.280″	.300″	.140″	Index
E1TE - ANA	.78″	.280″	.300″	.140″	Index
E1TE - UA	.78″	.280″	.230″	.140″	Index
E1TE - ARA	.78″	.280″	.230″	.140″	Index
E1TE - TA	.78″	.280″	.300″	.140″	Index
E1TE - GA	.78″	.330″	.320″	.140″	2 Rich
E1TE - AZA	.78″	.330″	.320″	.140″	2 Rich
E1TE - VA	.78″	.280″	.300″	.140″	2 Rich
E1TE - AUA	.78″	.280″	.300″	.140″	2 Rich

CARTER BBD 2-BARREL

CARBURETOR APPLICATION

JEEP

	Jeep Code No.	
Application	Man. Trans.	Auto. Trans.
4.2L (258")		
Federal	BBD-8309	BBD-8308
	BBD-8312	BBD-8312
California	BBD-8303	BBD-8302
	BBD-8307	BBD-8306
High Altitude	BBD-8311	BBD-8302

CARBURETOR IDENTIFICATION

Carter Carburetors are identified by a code number and build date. Both numbers are stamped on a tag attached to carburetor by an air horn screw. Each carburetor build month is coded alphabetically beginning with letter "A" (for January), and ending with "M" (for December). Letter "I" is not used. Second number on tag is year in which carburetor was built, and third and fourth are for build day. There may be a revision letter following build day numbers if needed.

DESCRIPTION

The Carter carburetor model BBD is a 2-barrel downdraft type. The carburetor incorporates three basic metering systems: The Float (Fuel Inlet) system; Idle (Low Speed) system; and the Main (High Speed) system. Accelerator pump system provides additional fuel for acceleration. It is important that the fuel inlet system maintains the correct fuel level in the float bowl as the fuel metering system is calibrated to deliver the proper mixture only at this level.

In addition to the fuel systems, the carburetor uses an automatic choke and choke diaphragm which temporarily richens the mixture while starting, but also prevents overchoking. On all models, choke is assisted by an electric heating element. This provides for shorter choke duration during warm weather. Choke diaphragm prevents overchoking by opening choke valve when engine is being cranked.

Vehicles built for California are equipped with an electronically controlled stepper motor which controls air flow through metered air bleeds located in each main fuel metering circuit. Stepper motor is activated through an on-board computer. Computer receives information from various sensors located on engine and in exhaust system. Computer then signals stepper motor to retract metering rods from air bleeds (lean) or extend metering rods farther into air bleeds (rich).

All Jeep vehicles use a vacuum and electrically operated solenoid called a solevac. It is used to keep engine idle constant when load is placed on engine, such as air conditioning or rear window defroster.

ADJUSTMENTS

HOT (SLOW) IDLE RPM

See appropriate article in TUNE-UP SERVICE PROCEDURES.

IDLE MIXTURE

See appropriate article in TUNE-UP SERVICE PROCEDURES.

COLD (FAST) IDLE RPM

See appropriate article in TUNE-UP SERVICE PROCEDURES.

DASHPOT (MAN. TRANS.)

See appropriate article in TUNE-UP SERVICE PROCEDURES.

VACUUM THROTTLE POSITIONER

See appropriate article in TUNE-UP SERVICE PROCEDURES.

FLOAT LEVEL (BENCH ADJUSTMENT)

1) Remove air horn. Hold float lip gently against needle. See *Fig. 1.*

2) Using straightedge, place across float bowl to measure float level. If adjustment is needed, release float and then bend float tip to obtain correct clearance.

CAUTION — *Do not bend lip while float is resting against needle to avoid damaging synthetic rubber tip.*

3) Reinstall air horn.

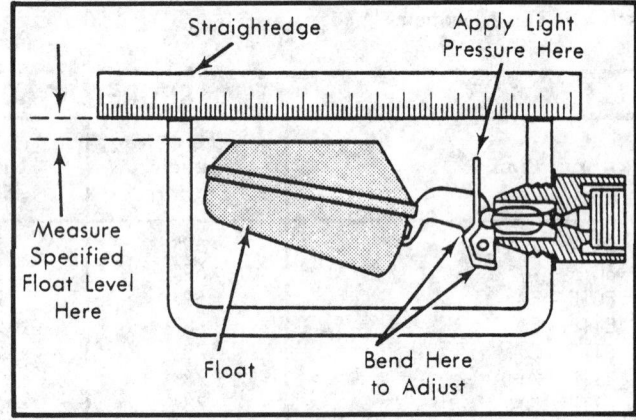

Fig. 1   Adjusting Float Level

VACUUM STEP-UP PISTON GAP QUALIFICATION

NOTE — *This adjustment is required if step-up piston is removed or if piston lifter position is changed on actuating rod. This adjustment (qualification) places piston in a centered "mean" position.*

1) Remove step-up piston cover plate and gasket. Remove lifter lock screw and remove piston step-up assembly.

2) Measure piston gap. See *Fig. 2.* If not to specification, adjust by turning Allen head screw on top of piston.

3) Record number of turns and direction to obtain proper dimension, or this must be reset to its original position after vacuum step-up piston adjustment has been made.

CARTER BBD 2-BARREL (Cont.)

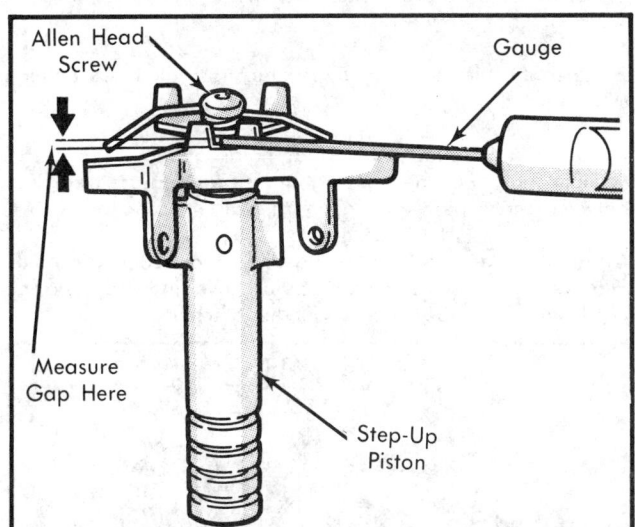

Fig. 2 *Vacuum Step-Up Piston Gap Qualification*

VACUUM STEP-UP PISTON ADJUSTMENT

NOTE — *Perform Vacuum Step-Up Piston Gap Qualification adjustment before adjusting vacuum step-up piston.*

1) With vacuum piston installed, back off idle speed screw until throttle valves are completely closed. Count number of turns so that screw can be returned to its original position. *See Fig. 3.*

2) Fully depress step-up piston while holding moderate pressure on rod lifter tab. While in this position, tighten rod lifter lock screw.

3) Release piston and rod lifter, then return idle speed set screw to its original position.

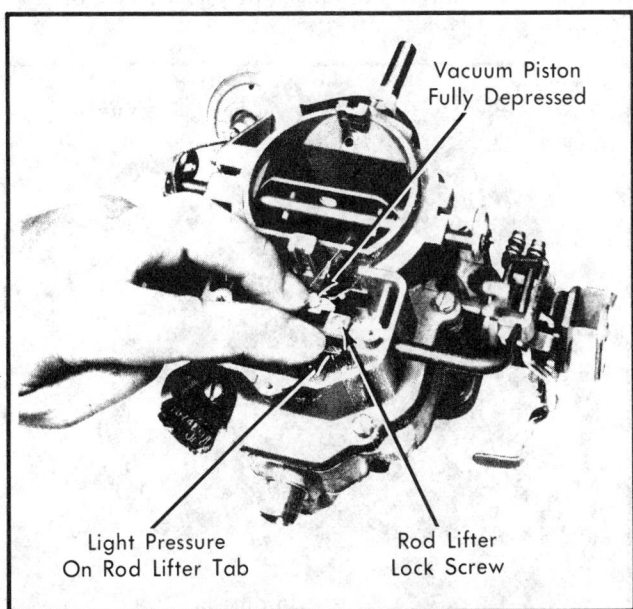

Fig. 3 *Adjusting Step-Up Piston*

4) Reset Allen head calibration screw on top of step-up piston to its original position as recorded under Vacuum Step-Up

Piston Gap Qualification. If this adjustment is changed, the step-up piston must be requalified.

SOLEVAC ADJUSTMENT

NOTE — *Three adjustments are required on BBD carburetor solevacs, and must be made in proper order.*

1) Disconnect vacuum hose from solenoid vacuum unit and plug hose. Disconnect electric wire to solenoid and adjust normal curb idle with RPM screw.

2) Using a hand vacuum pump, apply vacuum to solenoid vacuum unit and adjust to proper RPM with screw located on the throttle lever. Remove vacuum pump.

3) Energize solenoid and adjust RPM to specifications using screw located on rear of solenoid.

Solevac Adjusting Specifications	
Adjustment Step	**Idle RPM**
Normal Curb Idle	550
Vacuum Actuated	800
Solenoid Energized	650

ACCELERATOR PUMP STROKE ADJUSTMENT

1) Remove step-up piston cover plate and gasket. Back off curb idle screw to fully close throttle valves. Fast idle cam must be in open position. *See Fig. 4.*

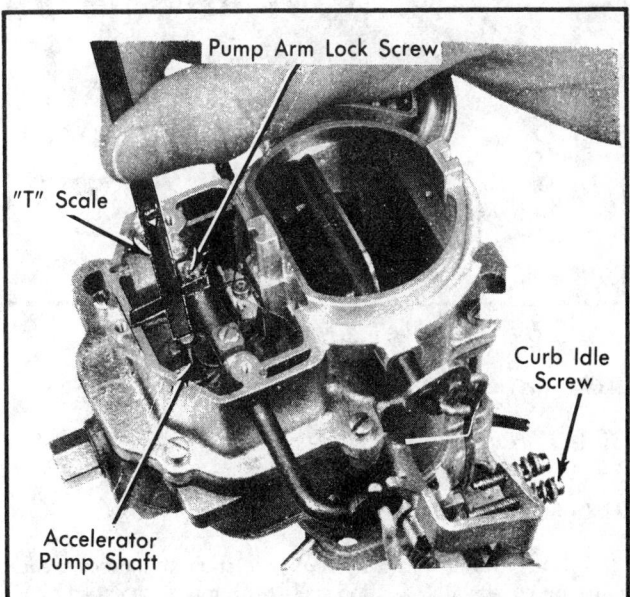

Fig. 4 *Adjusting Accelerator Pump Stroke*

2) Now turn curb idle screw until it just touches stop. Continue 2 more complete turns. Measure distance between surface of air horn and top of accelerator pump shaft.

3) If adjustment is needed, loosen pump arm adjusting lock screw and turn sleeve to adjust pump travel. When correct measurement is obtained, tighten lock screw. Install step-up piston cover plate and gasket.

CARTER BBD 2-BARREL (Cont.)

FAST IDLE CAM POSITION

NOTE — *To meet Federal regulations, all carburetors incorporate tamper-proof choke, choke pull-off, and idle adjusting screws. Adjustments given are for after a major carburetor overhaul, or if carburetor components are damaged.*

1) Remove torque-head screws and position choke cover ¼ turn rich. Retain with 1 straight-slot screw to hold choke cover in position. *See Fig. 5.*

2) Place fast idle adjusting screw on second step of fast idle cam. With specified drill or pin gauge, measure clearance between upper edge of choke valve and air horn wall.

3) Adjust by bending fast idle connecting rod down to increase measurement or up to decrease measurement. Loosen housing cover screw, reset choke to specified index and tighten all retaining screws.

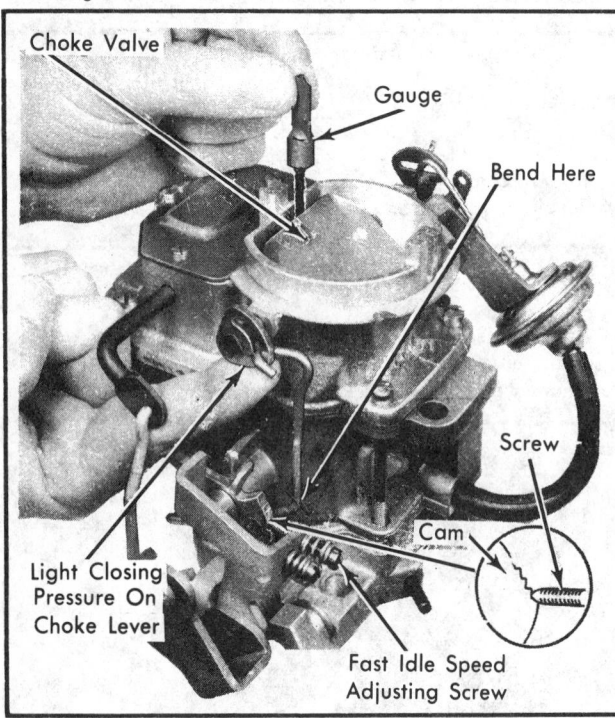

Fig. 5   Adjusting Fast Idle Cam Position

AUTOMATIC CHOKE

NOTE — *Normally, no readjustment is necessary from factory setting. Perform adjustment only after a major overhaul.*

1) Loosen choke thermostat cover retaining screws.

2) Rotate cover in "Rich" or "Lean" direction to align reference mark on cover with specified scale graduation on choke housing. Tighten retaining screws.

INITIAL CHOKE VALVE CLEARANCE

NOTE — *To meet Federal regulations, all carburetors incorporate tamper-proof choke, choke pull-off, and idle adjusting screws. Adjustments given are for after a major overhaul, or if carburetor components have been damaged.*

1) Grind off torque-head screw heads and remove remaining portions of screws by turning counterclockwise with locking pliers. Turn choke cover ¼ turn rich. Retain in this position with 1 straight slot screw.

2) Open throttle valve slightly to place fast idle screw on high step of cam. *See Fig. 6.*

3) Using a vacuum source that holds at least 19 in. Hg. vacuum, pull in diaphragm against stop. Measure clearance between choke plate and air horn wall.

4) Adjust clearance by bending diaphragm connecting link. Remove straight slot screw and adjust cover index to specified notch. Install replacement torque-head screws.

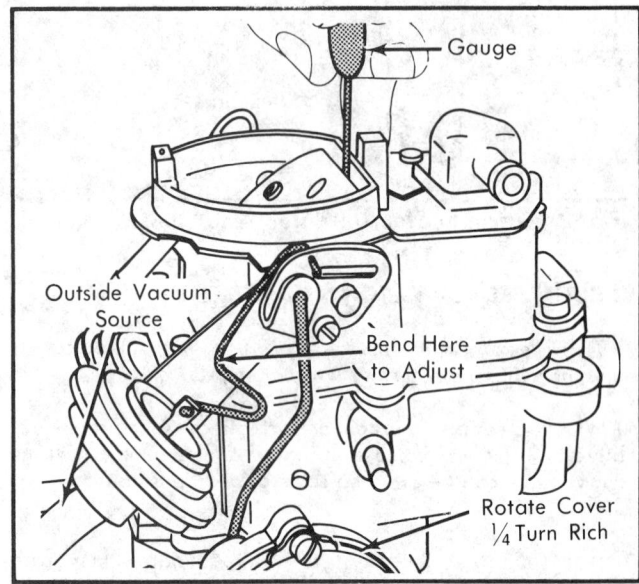

**Fig. 6   Adjusting Choke Diaphragm
(Initial Choke Valve Clearance)**

CHOKE UNLOADER

1) Hold throttle valves wide open. Apply light closing pressure to choke valve lever. *See Fig. 7.*

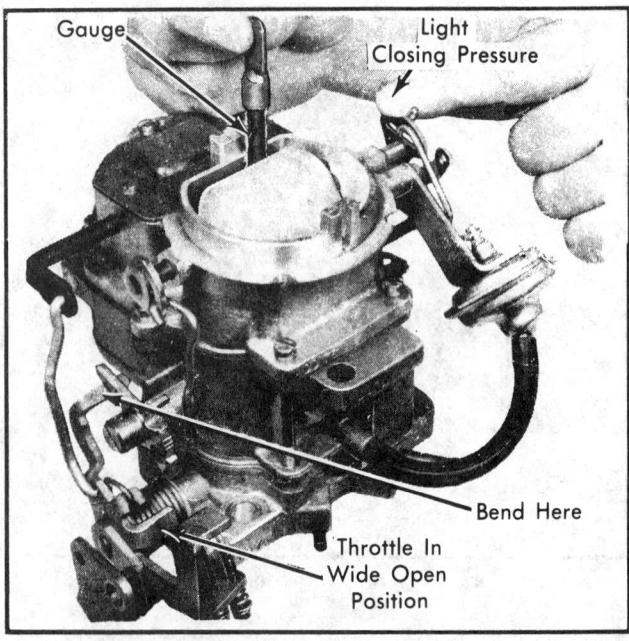

Fig. 7   Adjusting Choke Unloader

CARTER BBD 2-BARREL (Cont.)

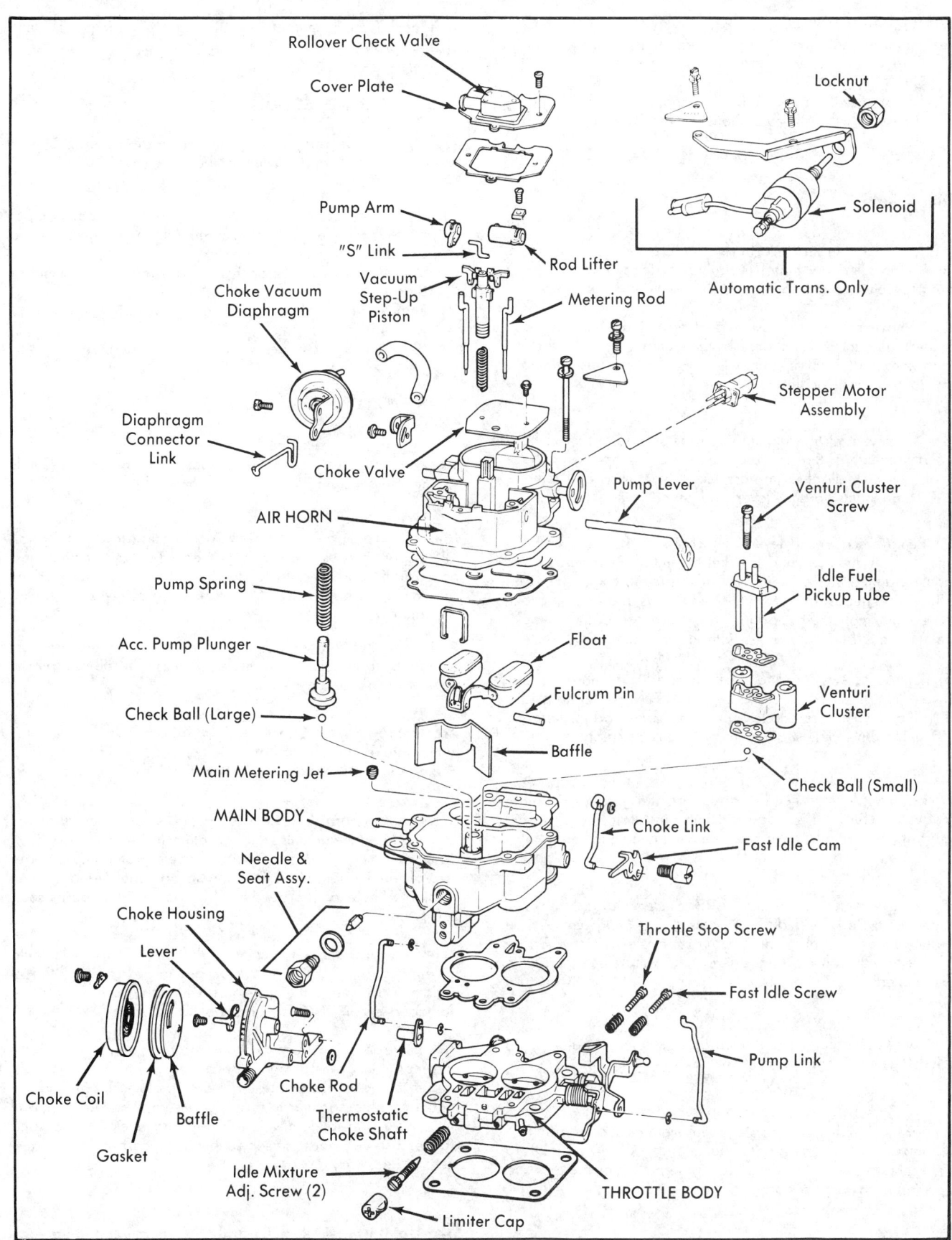

Rollover Check Valve

Cover Plate

Locknut

Solenoid

Pump Arm

"S" Link

Rod Lifter

Vacuum Step-Up Piston

Metering Rod

Automatic Trans. Only

Choke Vacuum Diaphragm

Diaphragm Connector Link

Choke Valve

Stepper Motor Assembly

AIR HORN

Pump Lever

Venturi Cluster Screw

Pump Spring

Idle Fuel Pickup Tube

Acc. Pump Plunger

Float

Check Ball (Large)

Fulcrum Pin

Venturi Cluster

Main Metering Jet

Baffle

Check Ball (Small)

MAIN BODY

Choke Link

Needle & Seat Assy.

Fast Idle Cam

Choke Housing

Lever

Throttle Stop Screw

Fast Idle Screw

Choke Coil

Choke Rod

Pump Link

Gasket

Baffle

Thermostatic Choke Shaft

Idle Mixture Adj. Screw (2)

THROTTLE BODY

Limiter Cap

Fig. 8 Exploded View of Carter Model BBD 2-Barrel Carburetor

CARTER BBD 2-BARREL (Cont.)

2) Measure choke unloader specified clearance between upper edge of choke valve and air horn wall. Clearance can be checked using a specified drill or pin gauge.

3) To adjust, bend choke unloader tang. Make sure tang does not interfere with other components after it is adjusted.

OVERHAUL

DISASSEMBLY

All Models — 1) Place carburetor on a suitable repair stand, and remove stepper motor if equipped. Remove retaining clip from accelerator pump arm link and remove link.

2) Remove cover and gasket from top of air horn. Remove screws and locks from accelerator pump arm and vacuum piston rod lifter. Slide pump lever out of air horn. Remove pump arm and rod lifter.

3) Lift vacuum piston and step-up rods up and out of air horn as an assembly. Remove the vacuum piston spring. Remove choke vacuum diaphragm hose. Disconnect clips and remove link from choke housing lever and choke lever.

4) Remove screw and lever from choke shaft. Remove choke diaphragm, linkage, and bracket assembly. Remove fast idle cam retaining screw. Remove fast idle cam, choke link, and clip. Grind heads off of torque-head screws and remove choke cover assembly and housing from throttle body. Remove remaining portion of screws with locking pliers.

5) Remove screws securing air horn and lift air horn up and away from main body. Discard gasket. Turn air horn upside-down and compress accelerator pump drive spring. Remove "S" link from pump shaft. Remove pump assembly.

6) Remove fuel inlet needle valve, seat and gasket from main body. Carefully lift out float fulcrum pin retainer and baffle. Lift out floats and fulcrum pin. Remove the main metering jets.

7) Remove venturi cluster screws. Lift cluster and gaskets away from main body and discard gaskets. DO NOT remove idle orifice tubes or main vent tubes from cluster as they can be cleaned with solvent and dried with compressed air while assembled.

8) Turn carburetor upside-down and catch accelerator pump discharge and intake check balls as they fall out.

9) Turn idle limiter caps to stop. Remove plastic caps from idle air mixture screws. Be sure to count number of turns it takes to seat screws to ease reassembly adjustment. Remove screws and springs from throttle body.

10) Remove screws and separate throttle body from main body. Discard gasket. Check choke plate in air horn for freedom of movement. If any sticking or binding is evident, clean thoroughly.

CLEANING & INSPECTION

NOTE — *Do not apply compressed air to diaphragm. Do not use wire or drill to clean jets or passageways.*

- Use a regular carburetor cleaning solution. Soak components long enough to thoroughly clean all surfaces and passages of foreign matter.
- Do not soak any components containing rubber, leather or plastic.
- Remove any residue after cleaning by rinsing components in a suitable solvent.
- Blow out all passages with dry compressed air.

REASSEMBLY

Use all new gaskets and reverse disassembly procedures while noting the following;

Idle Mixture Screw & Limiter Cap Installation — 1) Install idle mixture screws and springs in body. Tapered portion must be straight and smooth. If tapered portion is grooved or ridged, use a new screw. DO NOT use a screwdriver for installation.

2) Turn screws lightly against their seats with fingers. Back off number of turns counted at disassembly and install new plastic caps with tab against stop.

Accelerator Pump Check Ball Installation — Accelerator pump intake and discharge check balls are different sizes. Make sure large check ball is installed in float bowl. See *Fig. 9.*

Accelerator Pump Assembly — 1) Check operation as follows: Pour clean unleaded gasoline into carburetor bowl approximately ½" deep. Operate accelerator pump plunger several times to expel air from pump passage. Using a small brass rod, hold discharge check ball down firmly on its seat. See *Fig. 10.*

2) Again raise plunger and press downward. No fuel should be emitted from either intake or discharge passage. If fuel does escape from either passage, check that ball seat is not damaged or dirty. Clean passages and retest.

3) If leakage is still present, attempt to form a new seat. This is accomplished by installing a new discharge check ball in leaking seat. Place a piece of drill rod on top of check ball and tap it lightly with a hammer to form a new seat. Remove check ball and discard. Install a new check ball and retest as described above. If service does not correct problem, carburetor replacement is necessary.

Step-Up Piston & Rod Assembly — Be sure step-up rods move freely each side of vertical position. Carefully guide step-up rods into main metering jets.

CARTER BBD 2-BARREL (Cont.)

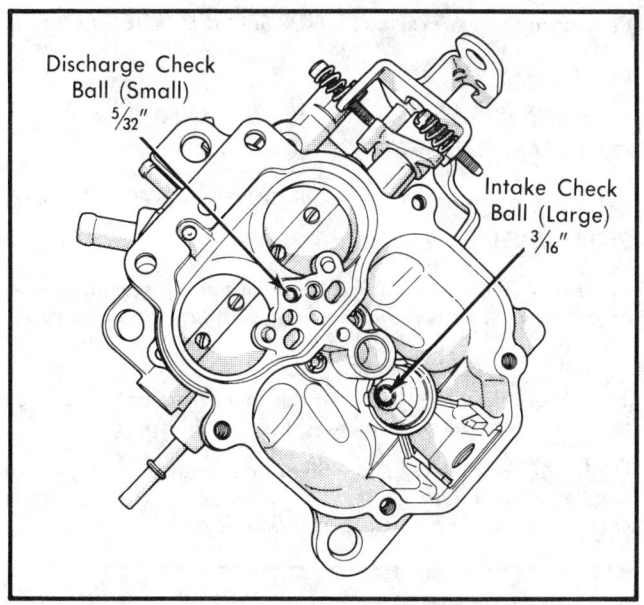

Fig. 9 *Installing Accelerator Pump Intake and Discharge Check Balls*

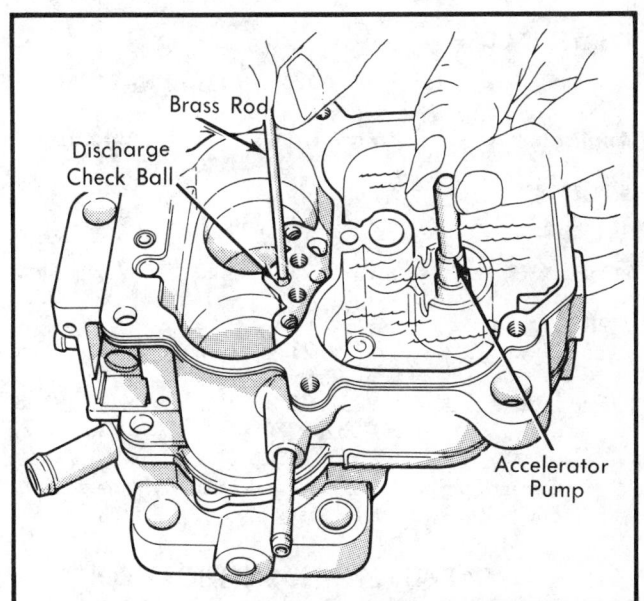

Fig. 10 *Testing Accelerator Pump Intake and Discharge*

CARBURETOR ADJUSTMENT SPECIFICATIONS							
Application	Float Level Setting	Vacuum Piston Gap Setting	Accel. Pump Stroke Setting	Fast Idle Cam Setting	Choke Vacuum Kick Setting	Choke Unloader Setting	Auto. Choke Setting
BBD-8302	.25″	.035″	.520″	.095″	.140″	.280″	1 Rich
BBD-8303	.25″	.035″	.520″	.095″	.140″	.280″	1 Rich
BBD-8306	.25″	.035″	.520″	.095″	.140″	.280″	1 Rich
BBD-8307	.25″	.035″	.520″	.095″	.140″	.280″	1 Rich
BBD-8308	.25″	.025″	.500″	.095″	.128″	.280″	2 Rich
BBD-8309	.25″	.035″	.520″	.093″	.128″	.280″	2 Rich
BBD-8311	.25″	.035″	.520″	.085″	.120″	.280″	1 Rich
BBD-8312	.25″	.035″	.500″	.095″	.140″	.280″	1 Rich

1981 Carter Carburetors

CARTER THERMO-QUAD 4-BARREL

CARBURETOR APPLICATION

CHRYSLER CORP.

Application	Carter Carb. No.①	
	Man. Trans.	Auto. Trans.
5.2L (318")		
Federal	9357, 9371	9311, 9357, 9371
Calif.	9330, 9367	9329, 9365, 9368
5.9L (360")		
Federal	9314, 9359, 9366	9359, 9366
Calif.	9332, 9358, 9369, 9370	9331, 9358, 9369, 9370

① — Carburetor numbers are preceeded by letters "TQ", and followed by the letter "S".

CARBURETOR IDENTIFICATION

Carburetor identification number is stamped on left rear foot of throttle body on vertical surface near bolt hole.

DESCRIPTION

Thermo-Quad carburetors have 3 main parts; the air horn, main body, and throttle body. Air horn houses choke valve, air valve for secondaries, fuel inlet system (2 floats, inlet needles and seats), and accelerator pump system. Also housed in air horn are primary boost venturis, vacuum controlled step-up piston and metering rods, and high and low speed fuel metering system (secondary jets, fuel discharge nozzles, and air bleeds).

Main body houses primary jets and is constructed of phenolic resin for cooler fuel temperatures. Throttle body houses throttle valves and linkage.

All Thermo-Quad carburetors installed on vehicles equipped with an EGR system have a venturi vacuum port on the side of the carburetor. This is the only vacuum port located in the main body. All other vacuum pick-up points are located in the throttle body.

ADJUSTMENT

Thermo-Quad carburetors have unique features which require extra caution during adjustment. The vacuum kick diaphragm provides 2 separate functions. It still provides for vacuum kick, but also controls the secondary air valve. Because of the separate nature of these functions, separate but interrelated adjustments are necessary, and must be performed in proper sequence.

NOTE — *All carburetors incorporate tamper-proof choke, choke pull-off, and air/fuel mixture adjusting screws. Adjustments are only to be performed after a major overhaul, or if carburetor has received component damage.*

HOT (SLOW) IDLE RPM

See appropriate article in TUNE-UP SERVICE PROCEDURES

IDLE MIXTURE

See appropriate article in TUNE-UP SERVICE PROCEDURES.

COLD (FAST) IDLE RPM

See appropriate article in TUNE-UP SERVICE PROCEDURES.

FLOAT LEVEL

1) Turn air horn upside down. Place air horn gasket in position on air horn. Make sure floats are against seated needle valve. *See Fig. 1.*

2) Measure float level specified clearance from bottom side of float to gasket surface. To adjust, bend float lever.

CAUTION — *DO NOT allow lip of float lever to press against needle when adjusting. This will damage needle and cause carburetor flooding and incorrect float level.*

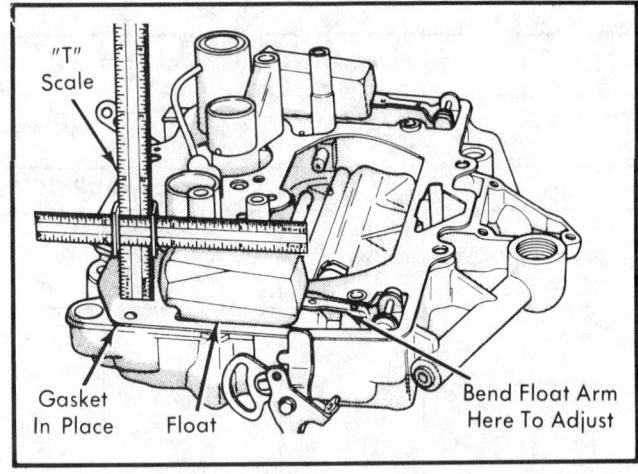

Fig. 1 Adjusting Float Level

SECONDARY THROTTLE LINKAGE

1) Hold fast idle lever in curb idle position. Turn carburetor upside down. Open throttle valves wide open. See *Fig. 2.*

Fig. 2 Adjusting Secondary Throttle Linkage

CARTER THERMO-QUAD 4-BARREL (Cont.)

2) Primary and secondary levers should both contact stops at the same time. To adjust, bend secondary throttle operating rod at point shown in illustration.

NOTE — *Check linkage for interference and smooth movement after bending linkage rod.*

SECONDARY AIR VALVE ALIGNMENT

1) Observe carburetor from directly above. See *Fig. 3*.

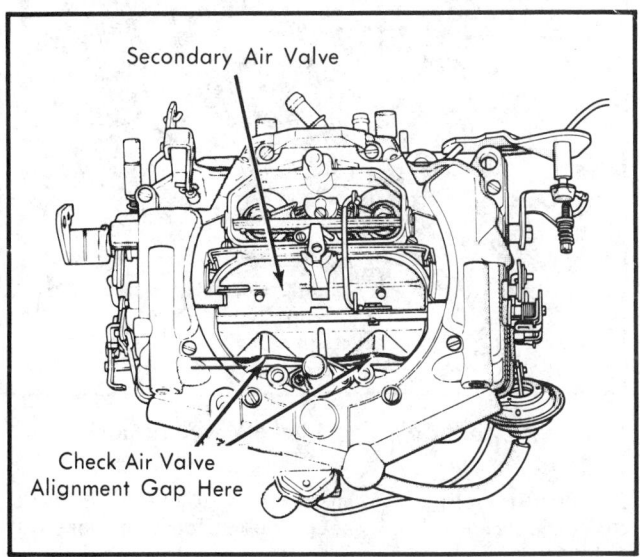

Fig. 3   Checking Secondary Air Valve Alignment

2) With air valve in closed position, gap between air valve and air horn wall must be at its maximum and parallel with air horn gasket.

SECONDARY AIR VALVE OPENING

1) Hold secondary air valve wide open. Measure specified gap between raised edge (short side) of air valve and air horn wall. See *Fig. 4*.

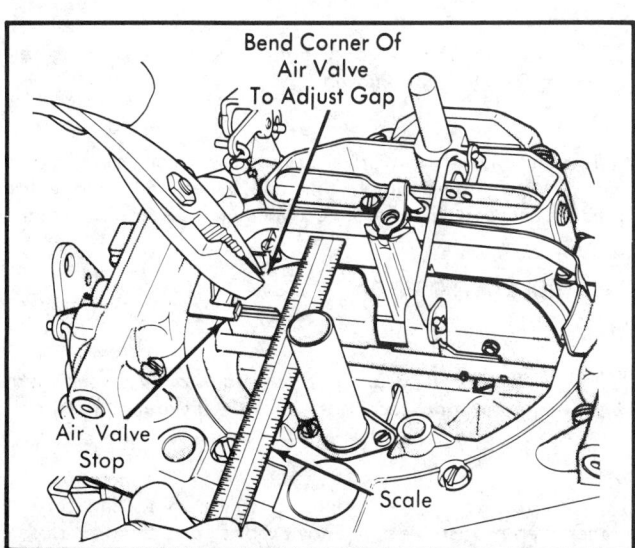

Fig. 4   Adjusting Air Valve Gap

2) To adjust, bend short side of air valve with pliers until specified gap is obtained. Corner of air valve is notched to aid in adjustment.

SECONDARY AIR VALVE SPRING TENSION

CAUTION — *When performing this adjustment, hold air valve adjustment plug with screwdriver when loosening lock plug. If not, spring may snap out of position. This would require taking the carburetor apart to get the spring out.*

1) Loosen air valve lock plug. Turn air valve adjustment plug clockwise. This allows air valve to move to wide open position. See *Fig. 5*.

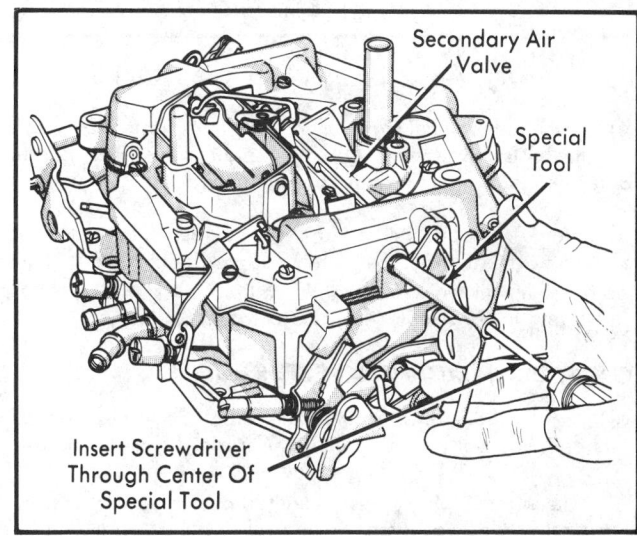

Fig. 5   Adjusting Secondary Air Valve Spring Tension

2) Insert a long slender screwdriver through center of special valve spring adjustment tool (C-4152-B or equivalent).

3) With special tool positioned on air valve lock plug, turn adjustment plug counterclockwise until air valve lightly touches stop.

4) Lightly press air valve against stop with finger. Now turn adjustment plug additional amount of specified turn(s) counterclockwise. Hold adjustment plug with screwdriver and tighten lock plug with special tool.

CHOKE CONTROL LEVER

NOTE — *If choke control lever adjustment is changed, vacuum kick, fast idle cam position and choke unloader adjustments must also be reset.*

1) Place carburetor on a flat surface. Make sure bottom of throttle body is flush with flat surface and that flat surface extends out under choke control lever. See *Fig. 6*.

2) Close choke by pushing on choke lever with throttle partly open. Measure vertical distance from top of rod hole in control lever to flat surface.

3) Adjust choke control lever by loosening the screw (left-hand threads) holding outer countershaft lever in place. Remove countershaft lever screw.

CARTER THERMO-QUAD 4-BARREL (Cont.)

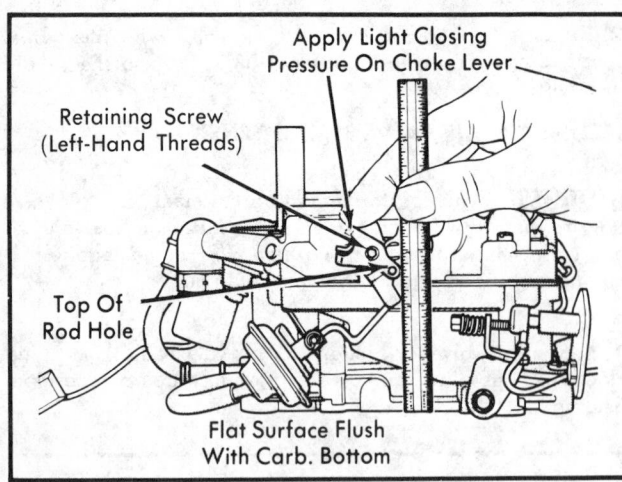

Apply Light Closing Pressure On Choke Lever

Retaining Screw (Left-Hand Threads)

Top Of Rod Hole

Flat Surface Flush With Carb. Bottom

Fig. 6   Adjusting Choke Control Lever

4) Loosen outer choke shaft lever enough to rotate it on shaft. Do this by lightly prying out with a small screwdriver. Rotate outer choke lever to proper specification.

5) Holding the opposite end of choke countershaft, seat outer lever onto shaft taper by lightly tapping with a very small hammer. Install screw and tighten to 8-15 INCH lbs. DO NOT use screw to force outer lever onto taper of shaft.

CHOKE DIAPHRAGM CONNECTOR ROD

NOTE — If choke diaphragm connector rod adjustment is changed, vacuum kick adjustment must also be reset.

1) Make sure diaphragm is securely mounted to carburetor. Using an outside vacuum source, apply at least 15 in. Hg of vacuum to diaphragm. Make sure diaphragm stem is fully seated. See Fig. 7.

2) Apply light opening (downward pressure) on secondary air valve. Measure specified clearance between air valve and stop. To adjust, bend connector rod at point shown.

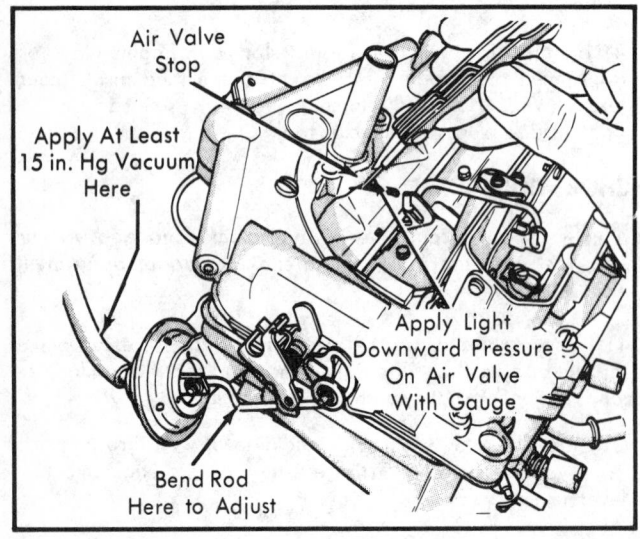

Air Valve Stop

Apply At Least 15 in. Hg Vacuum Here

Apply Light Downward Pressure On Air Valve With Gauge

Bend Rod Here to Adjust

Fig. 7   Adjusting Choke Diaphragm Connector Rod

CHOKE VACUUM KICK

1) Open throttle and close choke. Now close throttle to trap fast idle cam at closed position. See Fig. 8.

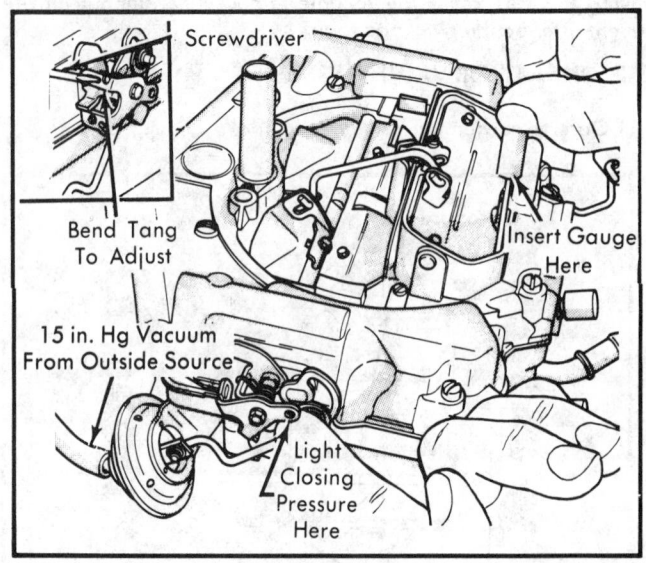

Screwdriver

Bend Tang To Adjust

Insert Gauge Here

15 in. Hg Vacuum From Outside Source

Light Closing Pressure Here

Fig. 8   Adjusting Choke Vacuum Kick

2) Apply an outside vacuum source of at least 15 in. Hg to choke diaphragm. Apply enough closing force on choke control lever to move vacuum kick adjustment tang against stop without distorting linkage.

NOTE — A weak torsion spring will easily be deflected. Vacuum kick adjustment tang must be at stop for proper adjustment.

3) Measure choke vacuum kick specified clearance between lower edge of choke valve and air horn wall at throttle lever side. Measurement can be checked using a specified drill or pin gauge.

NOTE — Make sure clearance does not change as drill or pin gauge is inserted or removed.

4) To adjust, insert screwdriver in slot in vacuum kick tang and twist. Do not adjust diaphragm rod. Check all linkage for freedom of movement. Reconnect vacuum hose to diaphragm.

FAST IDLE CAM POSITION

NOTE — If fast idle cam position adjustment is changed, choke unloader and secondary throttle lockout adjustments must also be reset.

1) With fast idle speed adjusting screw contacting second highest step of fast idle cam, move choke valve towards closed position using light pressure on fast idle control lever. See Fig. 9.

CARTER THERMO-QUAD 4-BARREL (Cont.)

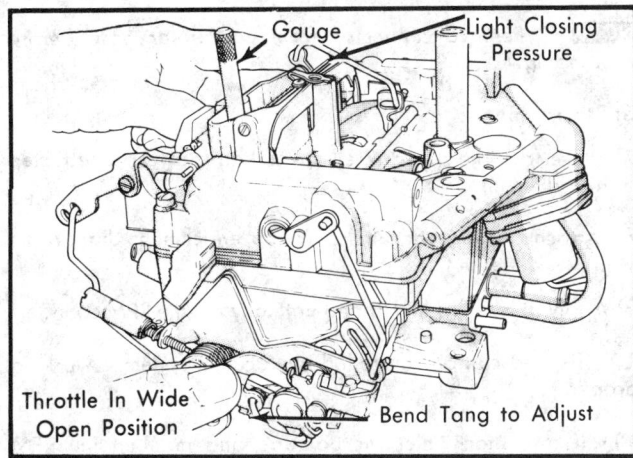

Fig. 9   Adjusting Fast Idle Cam Position

2) Measure clearance by inserting specified gauge between bottom of choke valve and air horn wall at throttle lever side.

NOTE — *Make sure clearance does not change as drill or pin gauge is inserted or removed.*

3) To adjust, bend fast idle cam connector rod at point shown until correct valve opening is obtained.

CHOKE UNLOADER

1) Open throttle valves wide open. Apply light closing pressure on fast idle cam lever to close choke valve. See *Fig. 10*.

2) Measure specified clearance between lower edge of choke valve and air horn wall at throttle lever side. Measurement can be checked using a specified drill or pin gauge.

NOTE — *Make sure clearance does not change as drill or pin gauge is inserted or removed.*

3) To adjust, bend tang on fast idle lever until specified clearance is obtained.

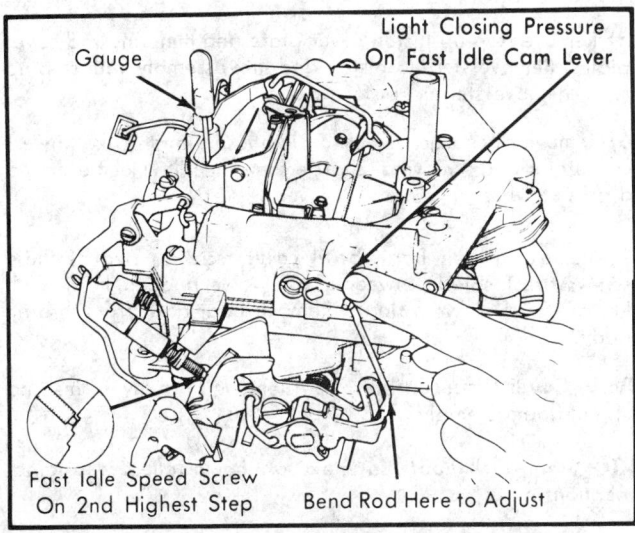

Fig. 10   Adjusting Choke Unloader

SECONDARY THROTTLE LOCKOUT

1) Move fast idle control lever to wide open choke position. Measure specified clearance between lockout lever and stop. Clearance can be checked using a specified drill or pin gauge. See *Fig. 11*.

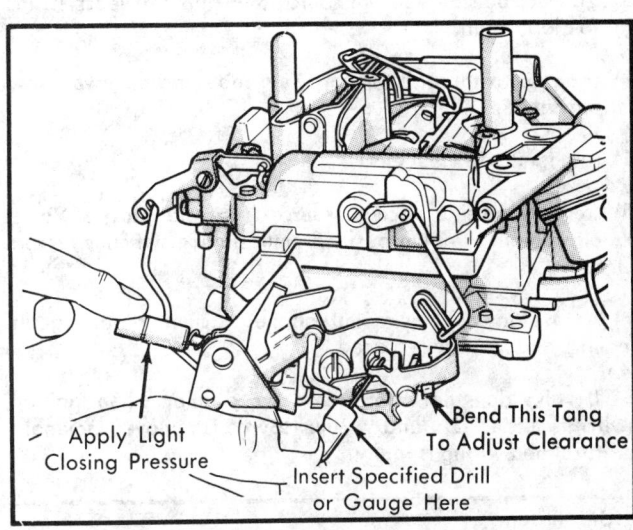

Fig. 11   Adjusting Secondary Throttle Lockout

2) To adjust, bend tang on lower end of fast idle control lever until specified clearance is obtained.

ACCELERATOR PUMP STROKE

NOTE — *Accelerator pump stroke is determined by measurement of accelerator pump plunger height above air horn surface AT CURB IDLE.*

1) Be sure throttle connector rod is in specified hole of pump arm.

2) Use a scale to measure height of accelerator pump plunger stem (from stem top to air horn surface) at curb idle.

3) Adjust plunger height by bending throttle connector rod as shown in *Fig. 12*.

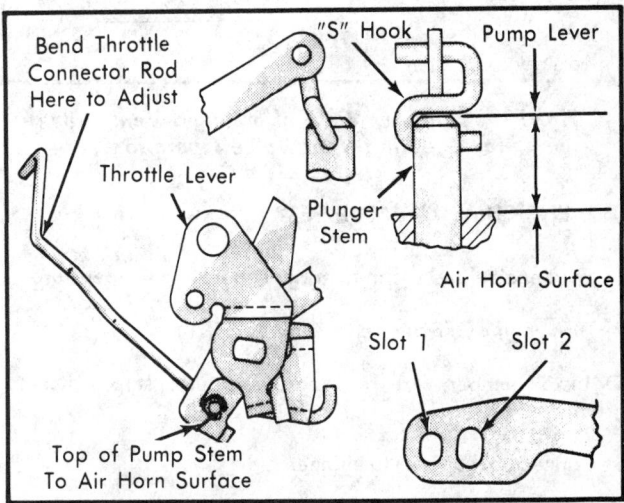

Fig. 12   Adjusting Accelerator Pump Stroke

CARTER THERMO-QUAD 4-BARREL (Cont.)

SOLENOID BOWL VENT VALVE TEST

1) Remove air cleaner assembly.

2) Disconnect hose to solenoid bowl vent diaphragm.

3) Connect outside vacuum source and apply at least 15 in. Hg to diaphragm.

4) Look down through air horn vent tube and observe valve movement. *See Fig. 13.*

5) Turn ignition switch ON.

6) Remove outside vacuum source from diaphragm. Valve should remain in down position until ignition switch is turned OFF.

7) If valve does not move with applied vacuum, diaphragm is leaking and must be replaced.

8) If valve does not remain in down position when ignition switch is turned ON and vacuum source is removed, solenoid or its related wiring is faulty.

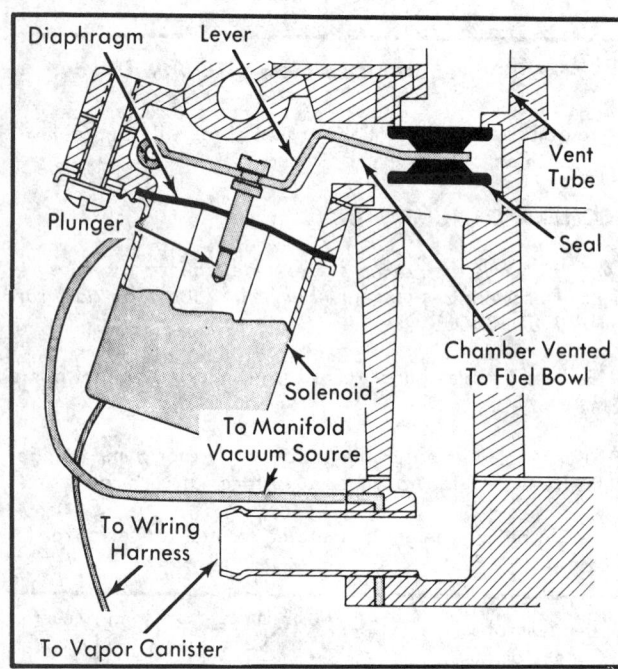

Fig. 13 Cutaway View of Solenoid Vent Valve for Checking Vent Valve Operation

IDLE ENRICHMENT VALVE TEST

1) Start engine and warm to normal operating temperature.

2) Turn engine OFF and remove air cleaner.

3) Install jumper wire from carburetor idle stop switch to ground.

4) Connect tachometer to engine.

5) Disconnect hose to idle enrichment system diaphragm at plastic connector.

NOTE — *Remove connector from carburetor hose before proceeding.*

6) Start engine.

7) Place fast idle speed screw on setting (slowest speed) step of fast idle cam.

8) Attach outside vacuum source to enrichment diaphragm with 3 or 4 feet of hose.

9) Apply at least 15 in. Hg and note any engine RPM change.

10) If speed can be controlled by vacuum, system is working properly.

11) If not, block inlet air passage and note engine RPM change. If speed can be controlled in this manner, diaphragm is leaking and/or air valve is stuck open.

12) If speed cannot be controlled, air valve is stuck closed.

13) Clean air valve and repeat steps **9)** and **10)**.

14) If speed cannot be controlled, replace the enrichment diaphragm.

OVERHAUL

DISASSEMBLY

1) Place carburetor on a suitable repair stand. Remove idle enrichment valve assembly.

2) Remove rod retainers that hold throttle connector rod to accelerator pump arm and throttle lever. Remove connector rod from carburetor.

3) Remove accelerator pump arm screw, disengage pump arm from "S" link and remove pump arm. Leave "S" link connected to pump rod.

4) Remove retainers and washers holding choke diaphragm connecter rod to vacuum diaphragm and air valve lever. Remove retainer holding rod to choke countershaft.

5) Remove step-up piston cover plate and metering rod cover plates. Remove step-up piston and link assembly with step-up rods. Remove step-up piston spring.

6) Remove discharge pump nozzle housing and gasket. Invert carburetor and remove discharge check needle. Needle should drop out when carburetor is inverted.

7) Remove 10 air horn (bowl cover) screws. Two of these screws are located between choke valve and air horn wall. Remove air horn with floats. Remove float bowl from throttle body.

Bowl Cover Disassembly — 1) Remove float lever pins and lift out float assembly.

NOTE — *Mark floats so they can be installed in original locations.*

2) Remove 2 needle valves from seats, marking them for reassembly location.

CARTER THERMO-QUAD 4-BARREL (Cont.)

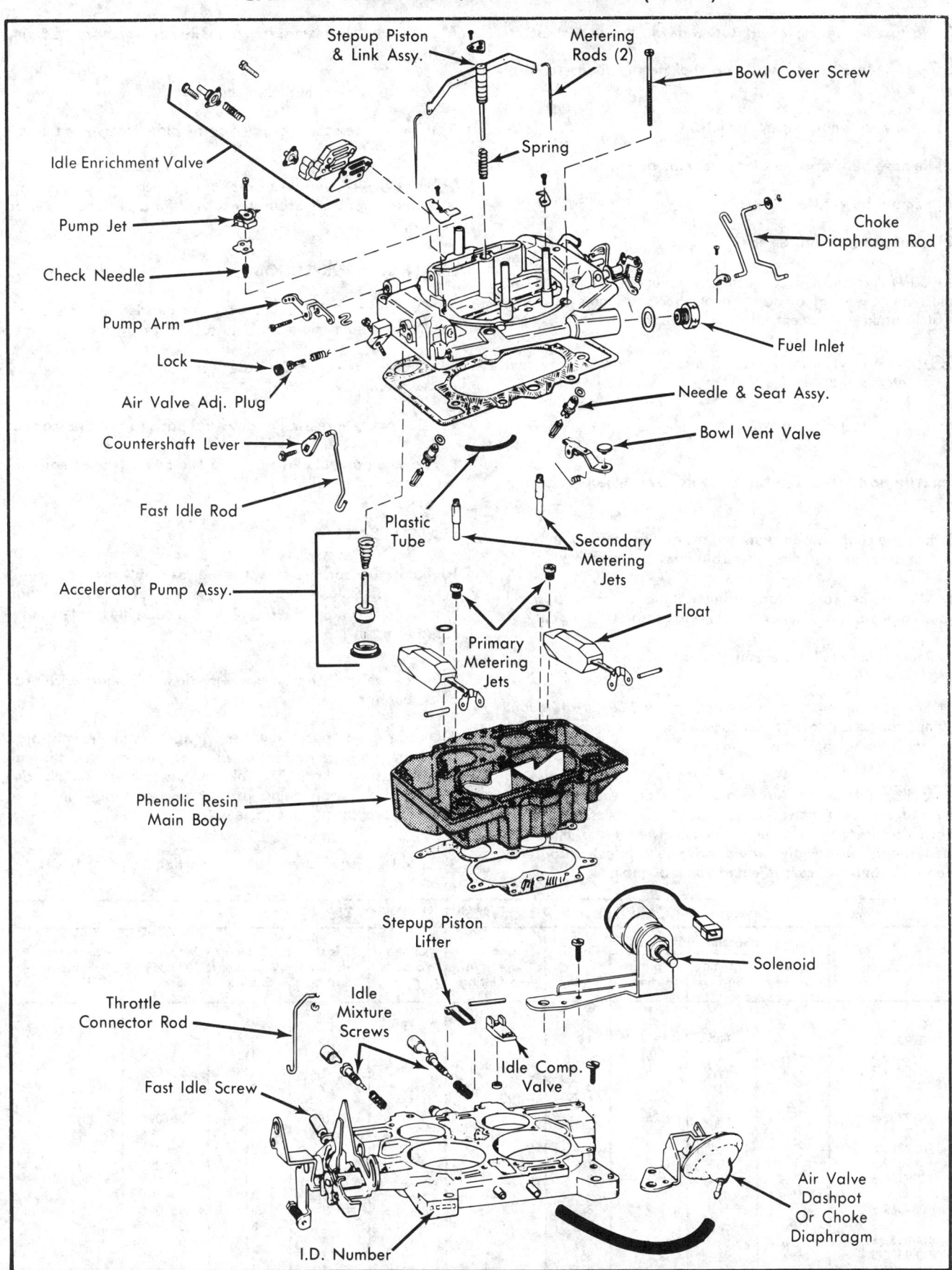

Stepup Piston & Link Assy.

Metering Rods (2)

Bowl Cover Screw

Spring

Idle Enrichment Valve

Choke Diaphragm Rod

Pump Jet

Check Needle

Pump Arm

Fuel Inlet

Lock

Air Valve Adj. Plug

Needle & Seat Assy.

Countershaft Lever

Bowl Vent Valve

Fast Idle Rod

Plastic Tube

Secondary Metering Jets

Accelerator Pump Assy.

Float

Primary Metering Jets

Phenolic Resin Main Body

Stepup Piston Lifter

Solenoid

Throttle Connector Rod

Idle Mixture Screws

Fast Idle Screw

Idle Comp. Valve

Air Valve Dashpot Or Choke Diaphragm

I.D. Number

Fig. 14   Exploded View of Carter Thermo-Quad 4-Barrel

CARTER THERMO-QUAD 4-BARREL (Cont.)

3) Remove needle valve seats (use wide blade screwdriver).

NOTE — *Be sure to match original needle to its seat for reassembly.*

4) Remove secondary metering jets.

5) Remove plastic accelerator pump passage tube.

6) Remove bowl cover gasket.

7) Remove pump rod "S" link.

8) Carefully remove accelerator pump plunger assembly. Care must be taken not to damage plunger shaft hole in cover. Catch intake check seat, plunger and spring.

NOTE — *Always install a new check seat and plunger when carburetor is reassembled.*

9) Remove fuel inlet fitting and gasket.

Throttle Body Disassembly — 1) Remove step-up actuating lever.

2) Remove choke diaphragm and bracket assembly with hose. Do not place this assembly in carburetor cleaning solvent.

NOTE — *The carburetor vacuum fitting contains a small vacuum passage restriction. Clean with compressed air only.*

3) Remove (carefully) idle limiter caps.

4) Remove idle mixture screws and springs. Be sure to count number of turns it takes to seat screws so they may be installed in their original positions.

CAUTION — *Manufacturer does not recommend removal of throttle shafts or valves unless absolutely necessary. These parts are precisely adjusted at factory. The slightest misalignment upon reassembly would adversely affect carburetor operation between curb idle and about 30 mph.*

Main Body Disassembly — 1) Remove primary "O" ring seals and discard.

2) Remove primary metering jets.

3) It is not necessary to remove baffle plate from main body.

CAUTION — *No further disassembly is recommended. Do not leave main body in carburetor solvent for a prolonged period of time.*

CLEANING & INSPECTION

- Do not soak choke diaphragm or plastic parts in solvent. Do not leave main body in solvent for too long a time.

- Rinse parts with HOT water after using solvent. Blow dry with compressed air.

- Do not use wire, drill or any hard parts to clean passages.

- Be sure gasket holes match up and all parts are clean and ready for installation.

REASSEMBLY

To reassemble carburetor, reverse disassembly procedures, using new gaskets and seals. Make sure gaskets fit correctly and that all holes are punched through and correctly located. Also, note the following:

1) Install pump discharge check needle with point toward base of carburetor.

2) Install upper pump plunger spring in cylinder with large end first. Lubricate and install plunger, pushing stem through hole in casting. Install "S" link with lower open end toward choke valve. Install pump arm and screw before installing pump intake check valve assembly.

3) Install 10 bowl cover screws and tighten to 35 INCH lbs.

		Secondary Air Valve								
Application	Float Level Setting	Opening Setting	Spring Tension①	Choke Lever Setting	Choke Diaphragm Rod Setting	Choke Vacuum Kick	Fast Idle Cam Setting	Choke Unloader Setting	Secondary Throttle Lockout	Accelerator Pump Hole
TQ-9311-S	29/32"	27/64"	2½	3⅜"	.04"	.15"	.10"	.31"	.06-.09"	#2
TQ-9314-S	29/32"	7/16"	2½	3⅜"	.04"	.15"	.10"	.31"	.06-.09"	#2
TQ-9325-S	29/32"	27/64"	2½	3⅜"	.04"	.15"	.10"	.31"	.06-.09"	#2
TQ-9329-S	29/32"	27/64"	2½	3⅜"	.04"	.15"	.10"	.31"	.06-.09"	#2
TQ-9330-S	29/32"	27/64"	2½	3⅜"	.04"	.15"	.10"	.31"	.06-.09"	#2
TQ-9331-S	29/32"	7/16"	2½	3⅜"	.04"	.15"	.10"	.31"	.06-.09"	#2
TQ-9332-S	29/32"	7/16"	2½	3⅜"	.04"	.15"	.10"	.31"	.06-.09"	#2
TQ-9357-S	29/32"	3/8"	2	3⅜"	.04"	.13"	.13"	.31"	.06-.09"	#2
TQ-9358-S	29/32"	3/8"	2	3⅜"	.04"	.18"	.13"	.31"	.06-.09"	#2
TQ-9359-S	29/32"	7/16"	2	3⅜"	.04"	.13"	.13"	.31"	.06-.09"	#2
TQ-9365-S	29/32"	3/8"	2	3⅜"	.04"	.13"	.13"	.31"	.06-.09"	#2
TQ-9366-S	29/32"	3/8"	2	3⅜"	.04"	.13"	.13"	.31"	.06-.09"	#2
TQ-9367-S	29/32"	3/8"	2	3⅜"	.04"	.13"	.13"	.31"	.06-.09"	#2
TQ-9368-S	29/32"	3/8"	2	3⅜"	.04"	.13"	.13"	.31"	.06-.09"	#2
TQ-9369-S	29/32"	3/8"	2	3⅜"	.04"	.13"	.13"	.31"	.06-.09"	#2
TQ-9370-S	29/32"	3/8"	2	3⅜"	.04"	.13"	.13"	.31"	.06-.09"	#2
TQ-9371-S	29/32"	3/8"	2	3⅜"	.04"	.13"	.13"	.31"	.06-.09"	#2

CARBURETOR ADJUSTMENT SPECIFICATIONS

① — Specification is amount of turns counterclockwise after air valve contacts stop.

HOLLEY MODEL 1945 SINGLE BARREL

CARBURETOR APPLICATION

CHRYSLER CORP.

Application	Holley Carb. No. Man. Trans.	Auto. Trans.
3.7L (225")		
Federal	R-9152-A	R-9131-A
Calif.	R-9153-A	R-9132-A

DESCRIPTION

Holley 1945 is single venturi of concentric downdraft design. Internally, fuel bowl completely surrounds venturi. Carburetor consists of three main parts: bowl cover, main body, and throttle body. Carburetor includes four basic metering systems: idle and transfer, main metering system, accelerating system and power enrichment system. Other systems include fuel inlet and electric assist choke systems.

CARBURETOR IDENTIFICATION

Carburetor is identified by a part number stamped into main body, or by tag attached to carburetor top.

ADJUSTMENTS

HOT (SLOW) IDLE RPM

See appropriate article in TUNE-UP SERVICE PROCEDURES.

COLD (FAST) IDLE RPM

See appropriate article in TUNE-UP SERVICE PROCEDURES.

IDLE MIXTURE

See appropriate article in TUNE-UP SERVICE PROCEDURES.

FLOAT LEVEL

1) With air horn removed, turn main body upside down with gasket installed. Using a straightedge, check that ends of floats, away from the fuel inlet, just contact the straightedge. See Fig. 1.

2) To adjust, bend float tang on float arm that contacts fuel inlet needle.

ACCELERATOR PUMP STROKE

1) Place throttle lever in curb idle position. Make sure accelerator pump rod link is installed in correct hole in throttle lever. See Fig. 2.

2) Measure accelerator pump stroke specified distance between center of rod in throttle lever and center of rod in accelerator pump arm.

3) To adjust, bend the accelerator pump rod at the point shown in Fig. 2.

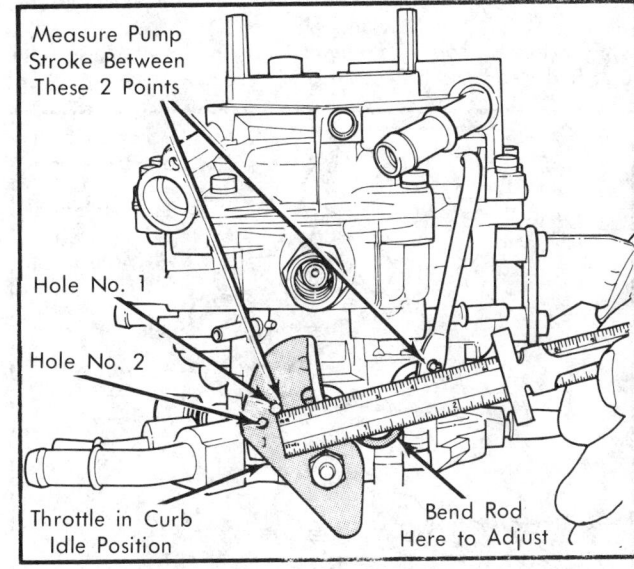

Fig. 2   Adjusting Accelerator Pump Stroke

FAST IDLE CAM POSITION

1) Position fast idle speed screw on second step of fast idle cam. Apply light finger pressure on choke shaft lever to close choke valve. See Fig. 3.

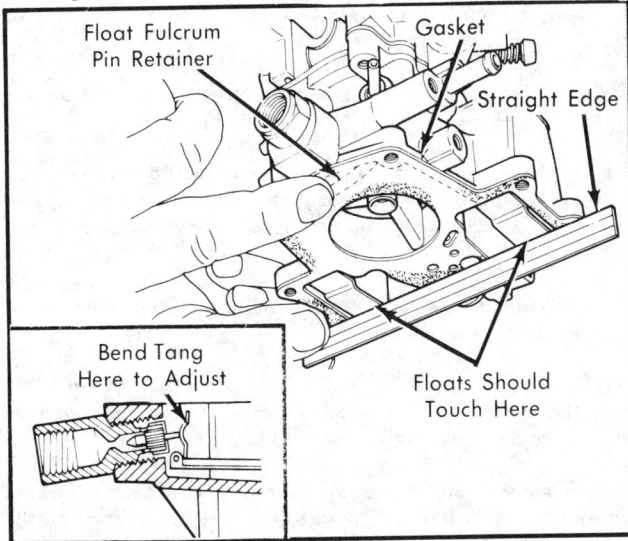

Fig. 1   Adjusting Float Level

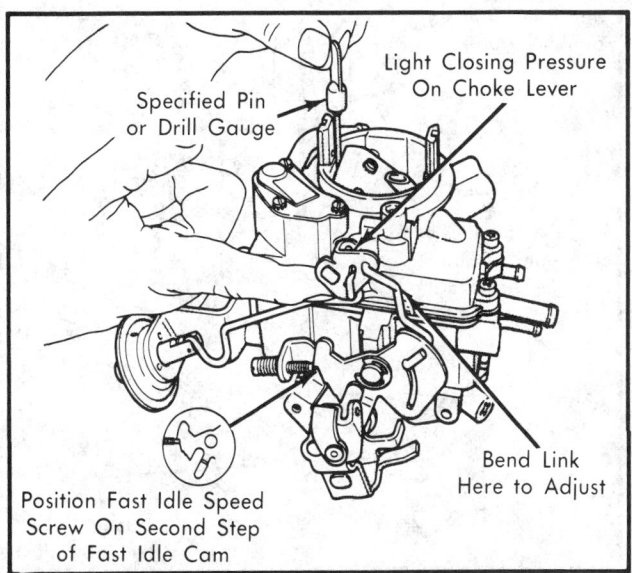

Fig. 3   Adjusting Fast Idle Cam Position

HOLLEY MODEL 1945 SINGLE BARREL (Cont.)

2) Measure fast idle cam specified clearance between top of choke valve and air horn wall at throttle lever side. Measure clearance using a suitable drill or pin gauge of specified clearance.

3) To adjust, bend fast idle cam connector rod at point shown.

CHOKE UNLOADER

1) Hold throttle valves in wide open position. Apply light finger pressure on the choke shaft lever to close choke valve. See Fig. 4.

2) Measure choke unloader specified clearance between top edge of choke valve and air horn wall at throttle lever side. Clearance can be checked using a specified drill or pin gauge.

3) To adjust, bend choke unloader tang on throttle lever until specified clearance is obtained.

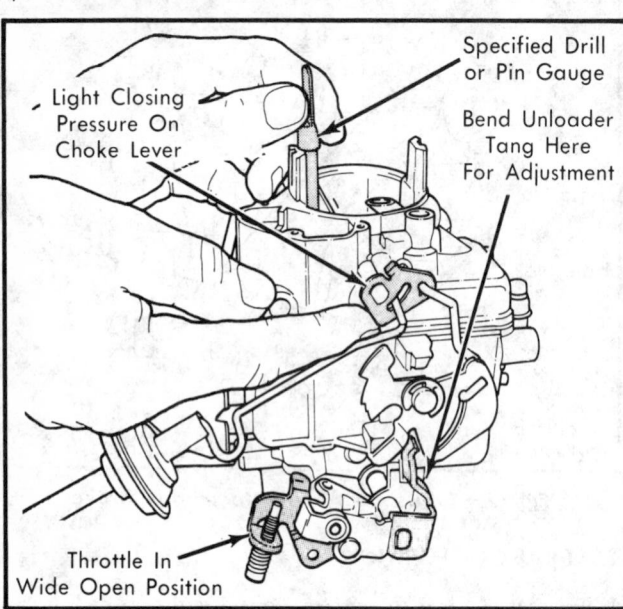

Fig. 4   Adjusting Choke Unloader

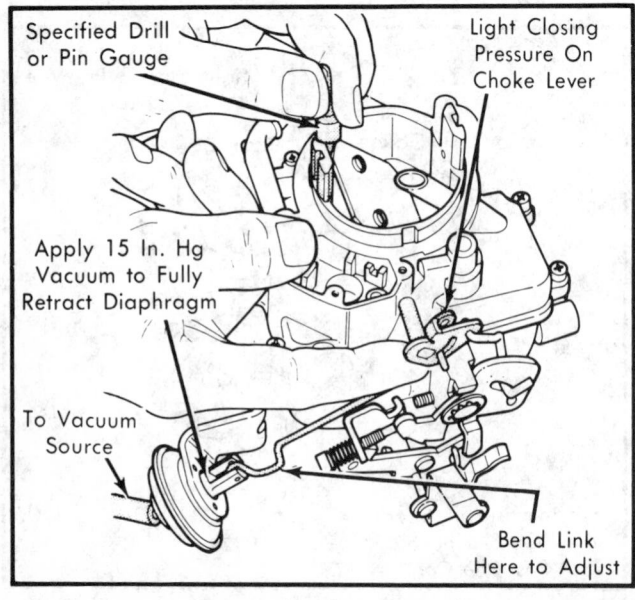

Fig. 5   Adjusting Choke Vacuum Kick

CHOKE VACUUM KICK

1) Open throttle and close choke. Now close throttle to trap fast idle cam in closed choke position. See Fig. 5.

2) Connect an outside vacuum source to choke vacuum diaphragm. Apply a minimum of 15 in. Hg. Apply light finger pressure on choke shaft lever to compress spring in diaphragm without distorting linkage.

NOTE — Diaphragm stem reaches a stop as spring is compressed.

3) Measure choke vacuum kick specified clearance between upper edge of choke valve and air horn wall. Clearance can be measured using a specified drill or pin gauge.

4) To adjust, bend vacuum diaphragm rod at existing "U" bend to obtain specified clearance. Check all linkage for freedom of movement. Install vacuum hose on diaphragm.

OVERHAUL

DISASSEMBLY

1) Place carburetor in a suitable holding device for disassembly. Remove cover over bowl vent solenoid and solenoid idle stop (SIS).

2) Remove fast idle cam retaining clip, fast idle cam and connector rod. Remove rod from fast idle cam.

3) Remove choke vacuum diaphragm bracket screws. Disconnect diaphragm rod from slot in choke lever. Remove diaphragm and rod.

4) Remove throttle lever and link, noting hole position of lever. Remove air horn screws. Remove air horn from main body by lifting straight up until vacuum piston, accelerator pump and main well tube clears main body.

5) Remove air horn gasket. Remove accelerator pump rod retainer screw and retainer. Remove accelerator pump retainer screw and remove accelerator pump.

6) Remove accelerator pump operating rod and grommet from air horn. Remove 3 screws and remove power valve diaphragm assembly.

NOTE — Do not attempt to remove main well tube from air horn.

7) Remove fuel inlet fitting from main body. Remove float pin retainer, float pin and float assembly. Turn main body upside down and catch accelerator pump discharge check ball and weight.

8) Remove main jet using a screwdriver with a blade at least 3/8" wide.

9) Depress power valve with a 3/8" wide screwdriver until screwdriver blade fits into slot in top of valve and remove valve, needle seat, and spring.

10) Remove 3 throttle body springs and separate throttle body from main body. Remove idle speed screw from throttle body. Remove idle limiter cap from mixture screw. Remove mixture screw and spring.

HOLLEY MODEL 1945 SINGLE BARREL (Cont.)

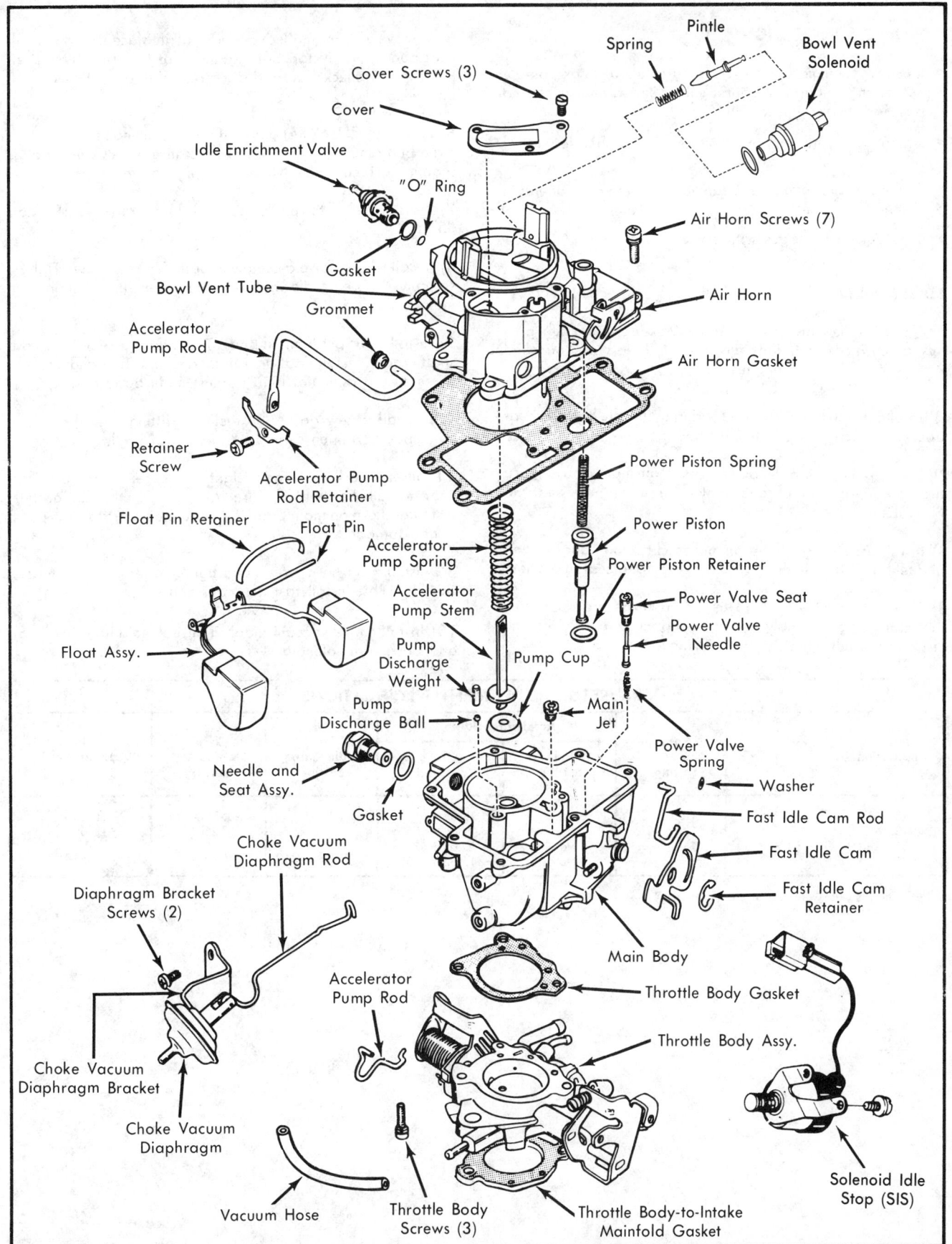

Fig. 6 *Exploded View of Holley Model 1945 Single Barrel Carburetor*

HOLLEY MODEL 1945 SINGLE BARREL (Cont.)

CLEANING & INSPECTION

- Use a regular carburetor cleaning solution. Soak components long enough to thoroughly clean all surfaces and passages of foreign matter.

- Do not soak any components containing rubber, leather or plastic.

- Remove any residue after cleaning by rinsing components in a suitable solvent.

- Blow out all passages with dry compressed air.

REASSEMBLY

NOTE — *Use new gaskets and seals. Make sure that new gaskets fit correctly and that all holes and slots are punched through and correctly aligned.*

1) Install idle mixture screw and spring in throttle body. Ensure tapered portion is straight and smooth.

2) Install a new throttle body gasket on main body. Place throttle body in position and tighten 3 retaining screws to 30 INCH lbs.

3) Install accelerator pump discharge check ball and weight. Fill fuel bowl with clean fuel to check ball and seat operation.

4) Hold ball and weight down with a brass rod. Place accelerator pump assembly in well and operate by hand. If no resistance is felt, check ball is leaking.

5) Remove weight and leave check ball in place. Using a small drift punch, lightly tap ball against seat to form a new seal. Remove old check ball and discard. Install a new check ball and weight.

6) Perform fuel leak test again. If there is still no resistance felt, main body must be replaced. If resistance is felt, check ball is seating correctly. Remove check ball and weight.

7) Install accelerator pump, pump rod, and rod retainer in air horn.

8) Install power valve assembly in bottom of fuel bowl. Tighten securely. Ensure needle valve operates freely. Install main jet in main body.

9) Install float pin in main body. Place float assembly in float shaft cradle. Install float pin retainer. Check float alignment to make sure it does not bind against main body casting.

10) Install a new gasket on fuel inlet fitting. Install fitting in main body. Tighten securely. Check float level.

11) Insert check ball and weight into accelerator pump discharge well. Position air horn gasket on air horn. Carefully install air horn on main body. Make sure accelerator pump cup is not damaged.

12 Install 7 air horn screws and tighten alternately in steps to 30 INCH lbs. Install fast idle cam and link.

13) Install choke vacuum diaphragm, solenoid idle stop (SIS), and bowl vent solenoid.

CARBURETOR ADJUSTMENT SPECIFICATIONS						
Application	Float Level Setting	Accelerator Pump		Fast Idle Cam Setting	Choke Unloader Setting	Choke Vacuum Kick Setting
		Hole Setting	Stroke Setting			
R-9131-A	Flush①	No. 2	1.605-1.625"	.090"	.250"	.130"
R-9132-A	Flush①	No. 2	1.605-1.625"	.090"	.250"	.130"
R-9152-A	Flush①	No. 2	1.605-1.625"	.080"	.250"	.130"
R-9153-A	Flush①	No. 2	1.605-1.625"	.080"	.250"	.130"

① — Setting is flush with top of casting to .050" above.

HOLLEY MODEL 2280 2-BARREL

CARBURETOR APPLICATION

CHRYSLER CORP.

Application	Chrysler Corp. Carb. No. Man. Trans.	Auto. Trans.
5.2L (318") Federal	R-9151-A	R-9135-A, R-9136-A

CARBURETOR IDENTIFICATION

Carburetor part number is stamped on main body flange in front of lever controlled by throttle position transducer under choke vacuum diaphragm.

DESCRIPTION

The Holley model 2280 2-bbl. carburetor uses 4 basic fuel metering systems; basic idle system, accelerator pump system, main meteringg and power enrichment systems. The idle system provides mixture at idle and low speed engine operation. The accelerator pump system provides an additional predetermined amount of fuel for acceleration. The main metering provides an economical mixture for normal cruising. And the power enrichment system provides a richer mixture when high power output is required (full throttle operation).

ADJUSTMENTS

HOT (SLOW) IDLE RPM

See appropriate article in TUNE-UP SERVICE PROCEDURES.

IDLE MIXTURE

See appropriate article in TUNE-UP SERVICE PROCEDURES.

COLD (FAST) IDLE RPM

See appropriate article in TUNE-UP SERVICE PROCEDURES.

FLOAT LEVEL

1) Install float and hinge pin in main body. Install hinge pin retainer. Install float needle valve, seat and gasket in main body. Tighten securely. See Fig. 1.

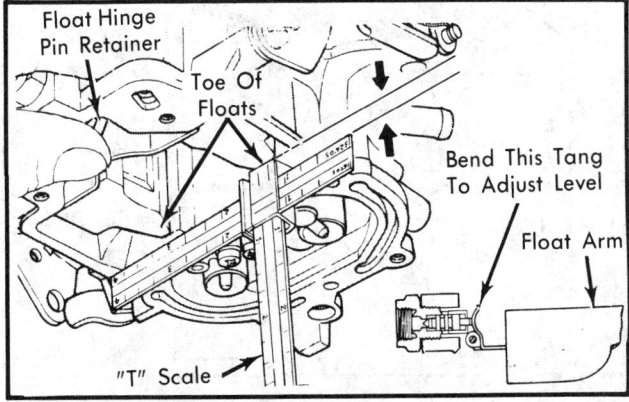

Fig. 1 Adjusting Float Level

2) Invert main body. Catch accelerator pump intake check ball if previously installed. Hold retainer in place with finger to fully seat float pin in cradle.

3) Using a "T" scale, measure float level specified clearance from air horn gasket surface on main body to toe of each float. To adjust, bend float tang. If necessary, bend either float arm to equalize float positions.

ACCELERATOR PUMP STROKE

1) Remove bowl vent cover plate and gasket.

2) With all pump links and levers installed, adjust the accelerator pump cap nut for zero clearance.

3) Check that wide open throttle can be reached without binding. Install gasket and bowl vent cover plate.

NOTE — *If accelerator pump adjustment is changed, then mechanical power valve must be readjusted also.*

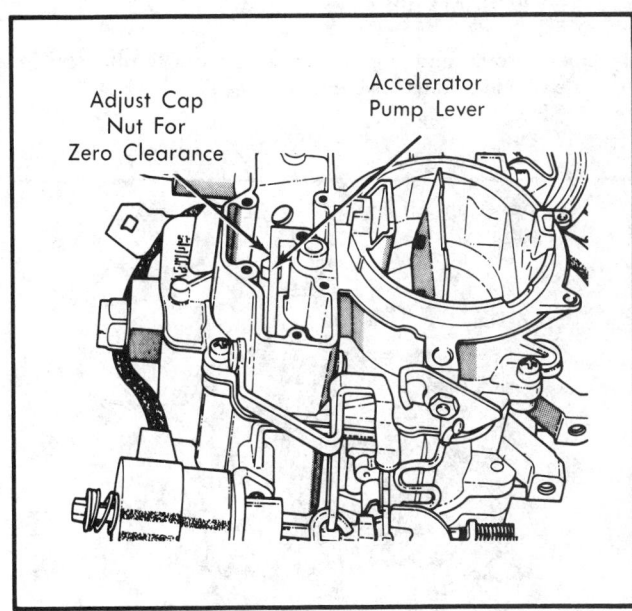

Fig. 2 Adjusting Accelerator Pump Stroke

CHOKE UNLOADER

1) Hold throttle valves in wide open position. Close choke valve by applying light closing pressure on choke control lever. See Fig. 3.

2) Measure choke unloader specified clearance between upper edge of choke valve and air horn wall. To adjust, bend choke unloader tang on accelerator pump lever.

HOLLEY MODEL 2280 2-BARREL (Cont.)

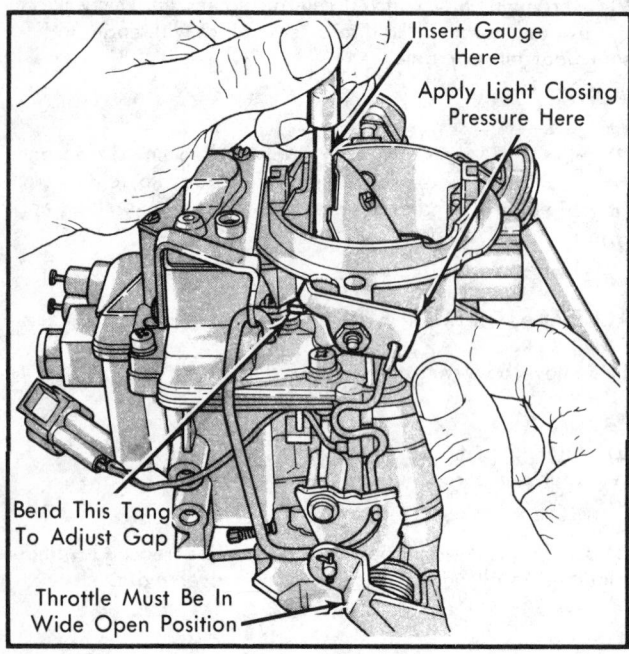

Fig. 3   Adjusting Choke Unloader

CHOKE VACUUM KICK

1) Open throttle and close choke. Now close throttle to trap fast idle cam in closed choke position. *See Fig. 4.*

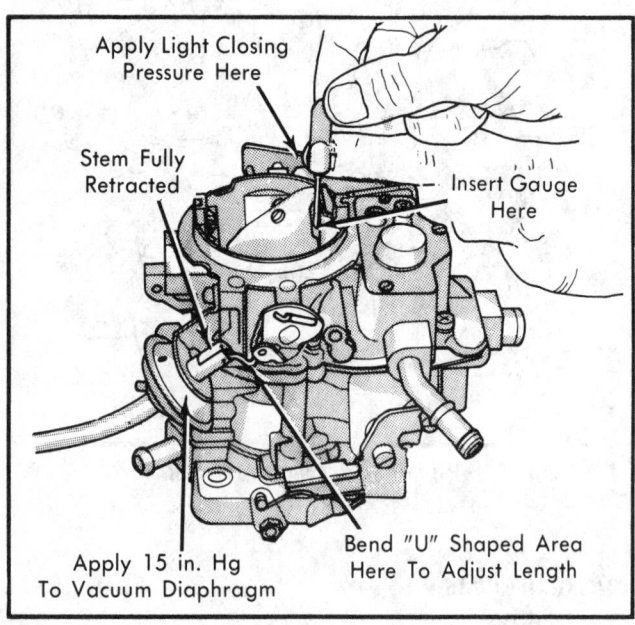

Fig. 4   Adjusting Choke Vacuum Kick

2) Connect an outside vacuum source to choke vacuum diaphragm. Apply a minimum of 15 in. Hg of vacuum. Apply enough closing force on choke valve with finger to compress spring in diaphragm without distorting linkage.

NOTE – *Diaphragm stem reaches a stop as spring is compressed.*

3) Measure choke vacuum kick specified clearance between upper edge of choke valve and air horn wall. Clearance can be measured using a specified drill or pin gauge.

4) To adjust, bend vacuum diaphragm rod at existing "U" bend to obtain specified clearance. Check all linkage for freedom of movement. Install vacuum hose on diaphragm.

FAST IDLE CAM POSITION

1) Position fast idle speed screw on second highest step of fast idle cam. Close choke valve by applying light pressure with finger on choke shaft lever. *See Fig. 5.*

2) Measure fast idle cam specified clearance between upper edge of choke valve and air horn wall. Clearance can be measured using a specified drill or pin gauge.

3) To adjust, bend fast idle cam connector rod at existing bend as shown in illustration.

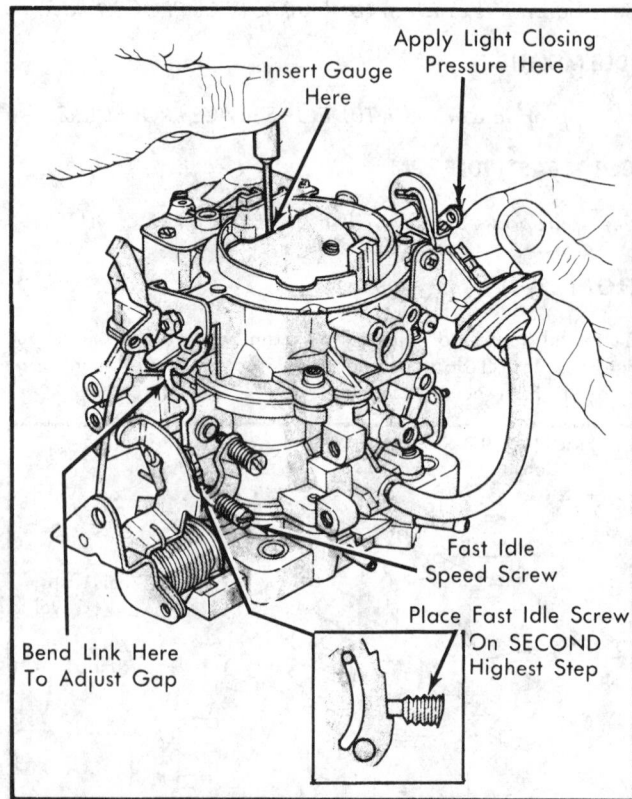

Fig. 5   Adjusting Fast Idle Cam Position

HOLLEY MODEL 2280 2-BARREL (Cont.)

MECHANICAL POWER VALVE

1) Remove bowl vent valve cover and hold throttle lever in wide open position. *See Fig. 6.*

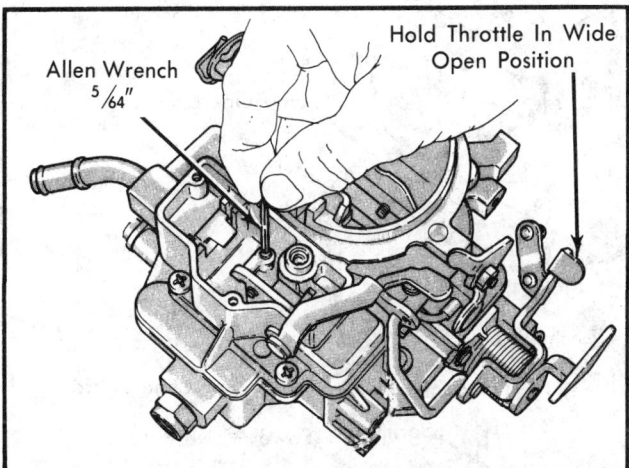

Fig. 6 Adjusting Mechanical Power Valve

2) Insert a 5/64" Allen wrench in mechanical power valve adjustment screw. Push down on screw, then release to determine if there is any clearance. If so, turn screw clockwise until there is no clearance.

3) To make final adjustment, turn screw counterclockwise 1 full turn from zero clearance. Install bowl vent valve cover plate and gasket.

NOTE — *If accelerator pump adjustment is changed, mechanical power valve adjustment must be reset also.*

OVERHAUL

DISASSEMBLY

1) Position carburetor on a suitable holding fixture. Remove air cleaner bolt and retainer. Remove accelerator pump link arm.

2) Remove bowl vent cover plate and bowl vent solenoid assembly. Remove choke vacuum diaphragm, linkage, and bracket. Remove electronic throttle control.

3) Remove nut and washer securing fast idle cam lever to choke valve shaft. Disconnect fast idle cam rod from lever and fast idle cam.

4) Remove 6 air horn screws. Lift air horn straight up from main body. Remove air horn gasket. Remove bowl vent valve

seal. Disconnect spring and lift valve lever, spring and pin out of air horn.

5) Remove link connecting accelerator pump plunger to operating lever. Remove accelerator pump plunger.

6) Gently pry up vacuum piston retaining ring tangs. Remove vacuum power valve piston. Remove clip securing accelerator pump operating shaft and remove shaft. Remove pump arm and internal pump lever.

7) Gently pry off mechanical power valve push rod plastic cap and remove clip. Remove mechanical power valve push rod and spring assembly.

8) Remove fuel inlet fitting and gasket. Remove float hinge pin retainer, hinge pin, float baffle and float assembly. Remove main metering jets.

9) Using special tool (C-4231) remove vacuum power valve and mechanical power valve. Make sure blade of tool is squarely seated in slots of valves to avoid damage.

NOTE — *Do not get 2 power valve assemblies mixed up. Mechanical power valve needle is about .050" longer than vacuum power valve needle. Mechanical power valve is located on choke side of carburetor. Do not mix up valve seats. Assemblies must be reinstalled in original locations.*

10) Remove venturi cluster screws. Lift cluster and gasket away from main body. Do not remove idle well tubes. Turn main body upside down and catch accelerator pump weight and check ball.

11) Remove 4 throttle body screws. Separate throttle body from main body and discard gasket.

12) Remove clip securing fast idle cam and slide cam off stub shaft. Carefully remove idle limiter caps from idle mixture screws. Remove mixture screws and springs from throttle body.

CLEANING & INSPECTION

- Do not soak choke diaphragm or plastic parts in solvent.

- Rinse all metal parts with HOT water after using solvent. Blow dry with compressed air.

- Do not use wire, drill or any hard parts to clean passages and orifices in carburetor.

- Be sure gasket holes match up and all parts are clean and ready for installation.

1981 Holley Carburetors

HOLLEY MODEL 2280 2-BARREL (Cont.)

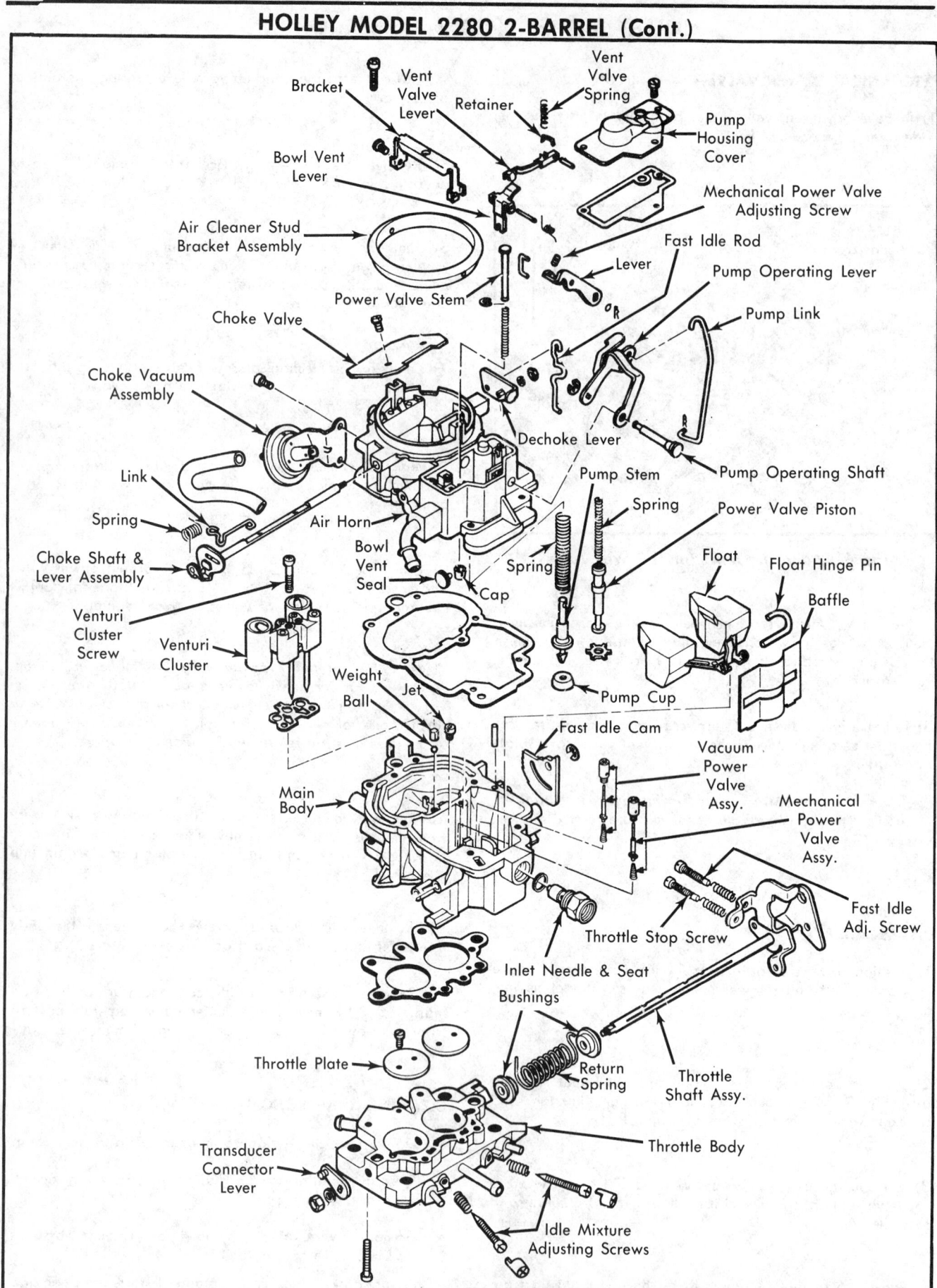

Fig. 7 Exploded View of Holley Model 2280 2-Barrel Carburetor

HOLLEY MODEL 2280 2-BARREL (Cont.)

REASSEMBLY

Throttle Body — Install idle mixture screws and springs. Gently seat both mixture screws by hand. Now back out 1 full turn as a preliminary idle mixture adjustment.

Main Body — 1) Install fast idle cam on shaft with steps facing fast idle speed screw. Install retaining clip.

2) Turn main body upside down. Place throttle body gasket in position. Position throttle body on main body. Install 4 attaching screws and tighten to 30 INCH lbs.

3) Install accelerator pump discharge check ball and weight. Fill fuel bowl with clean fuel and check ball and seat operation.

4) Hold ball and weight down with a brass rod. Place accelerator pump plunger in well and operate by hand. If no resistance is felt, check ball is leaking.

5) Remove weight and leave check ball in place. Use a small drift punch and lightly tap ball against seat to form a new seal. Remove old check ball and discard. Install a new ball and weight.

6) Perform fuel leak test again. If there is still no resistance felt main body must be replaced. If resistance is felt, check ball is seating correctly.

7) Install new venturi cluster gaskets. Install venturi cluster in position in main body. Install screws and tighten securely.

8) Install main metering jets. Use tool outlined during disassembly and install mechanical and vacuum power valves. Take care not to damage power valve needles. Make sure valves are installed in original positions as noted during disassembly.

9) Install hinge pin in float. Insert hinge pin through slot in float baffle. Tabs in baffle should point down. Place assembly in cradle in main body. Install hinge pin retainer.

10) Install fuel inlet fitting with new gasket. Adjust float level at this time.

Air Horn — 1) Install vacuum power piston spring and piston. Install retaining ring over piston and carefully seat in place. Check piston operaton for binding or sticking. If piston binds or sticks, install new piston.

2) Install mechanical power valve push rod spring, rod and retaining clip. Install plastic cap on push rod.

3) Install accelerator pump assembly through air horn and install cap nut.

4) Install new air horn gasket. Carefully lower air horn into position on main body. Care must be taken not to damage accelerator pump plunger.

5) Install air horn screws. Starting from center and working out, tighten screws to 25 INCH lbs.

6) With pump override spring retainer contacting air horn boss, adjust cap nut for a clearance of .310" between housing surface and cap nut. Install accelerator pump lever and operating shaft.

7) Connect plain end of fast idle cam connector rod to slot in fast idle cam from inside of cam. Engage other end of link in choke lever.

8) Open choke valve wide open. Align flats and slide choke lever onto choke shaft. Install lockwasher and tighten nut.

9) Connect choke vacuum break diaphragm rod to slot in choke lever. Install diaphragm assembly and tighten screws. Install electronic throttle control.

10) Install bowl vent assembly, and using a new gasket, fit bowl vent cover plate to air horn.

11) Install accelerator pump lever using a new cotter pin. Install air cleaner bolt and retainer, and install carburetor on vehicle.

CARBURETOR ADJUSTMENT SPECIFICATIONS					
Application	Float Level Setting	Accel. Pump Setting	Choke Unloader Setting	Choke Vac. Kick Setting	Fast Idle Cam Setting
R-9135-A	9/32"	Flush①	.310"	.130"	.070"
R-9136-A	9/32"	Flush①	.310"	.110"	.070"
R-9151-A	9/32"	Flush①	.310"	.110"	.070"

① — Flush with top of bowl vent casting.

HOLLEY 4180-C 4-BARREL

CARBURETOR APPLICATION

FORD

Application	Ford Carb. No.	
	Man. Trans.	Auto. Trans.
460" V8 Federal	....	D9TE-BKA

CARBURETOR IDENTIFICATION

A carburetor identification tag is attached to carburetor. The tag contains part number prefix and suffix. Basic part number for all carburetors is 9510. A design change code (if any) is also stamped on the tag. An assembly date code (year, month and day) is also stamped on the tag.

DESCRIPTION

The Holley 4180-C 4-Barrel is a downdraft 2 stage carburetor. It can be considered as 2 separate carburetors: one supplying air/fuel mixture throughout entire range of engine operation (primary stage), and the other functioning only when a greater supply of air/fuel is needed (secondary stage).

The primary stage (front section) of carburetor contains a fuel bowl, metering block, and accelerator pump assembly. The secondary (rear) section of carburetor contains a fuel bowl, metering body, and secondary throttle operating diaphragm assembly.

This model carburetor has a Modulated Power Valve System. This system ensures power valve opening when manifold vacuum increases (during full acceleration) beyond the point where power valve would start to close. Vacuum will bleed off whenever throttle valve opening is 50° or more.

Vehicles over 8500 lbs. GVW use a decel throttle modulator which keeps throttle plates from closing on deceleration for improved emission control. All models use a hot air operated automatic choke system.

ADJUSTMENT

HOT (SLOW) IDLE RPM

See appropriate article in TUNE-UP SERVICE PROCEDURES.

DECEL THROTTLE MODULATOR

See appropriate article in TUNE-UP SERVICE PROCEDURES.

IDLE MIXTURE

See appropriate article in TUNE-UP SERVICE PROCEDURES.

COLD (FAST) IDLE RPM

See appropriate article in TUNE-UP SERVICE PROCEDURES.

ACCELERATOR PUMP LEVER

1) Open throttle valves wide open. Using a feeler gauge, measure specified clearance between the lever adjustment screw head and pump arm with the pump arm manually open. *See Fig. 1.*

2) To adjust, loosen adjustment screw lock nut. Turn adjusting screw in to increase clearance and out to decrease clearance. Tighten lock nut.

NOTE — *One-half turn of adjustment screw is equal to .015".*

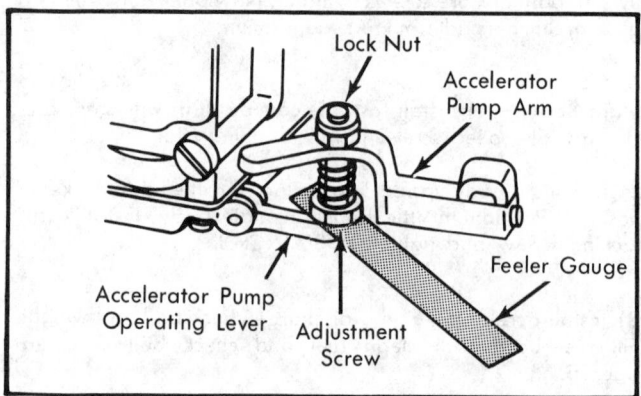

Fig. 1 Accelerator Pump Lever Adjustment

ACCELERATOR PUMP STROKE

NOTE — *Accelerator pump stroke has been preset at factory. Setting should not be changed. If original setting has been changed, adjust as follows:*

1) Check that plastic accelerator pump cam is aligned with correct hole (top or bottom) in throttle lever.

2) If not aligned with correct hole, remove screw. Reposition in correct hole. Install and tighten screw.

FLOAT LEVEL (DRY SETTING)

NOTE — *Dry float setting is a preliminary adjustment only. Final adjustment (wet setting) must be made after carburetor is installed on vehicle.*

1) Remove float bowl. Hold upside down. Float is adjusted correctly if top of float is parallel with float bowl. *See Fig. 2.*

2) To adjust, loosen lock nut and turn adjusting nut until float is parallel.

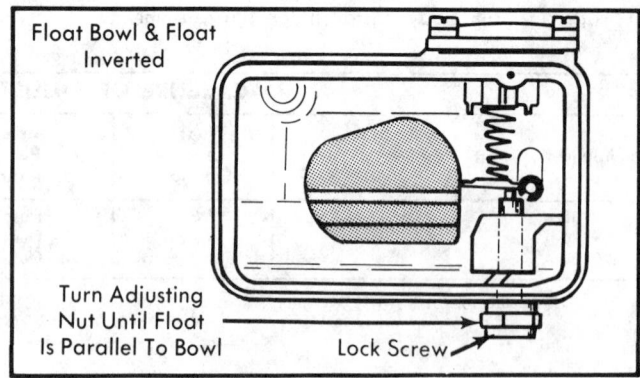

Fig. 2 Float Level Adjustment (Dry Setting)

FLOAT LEVEL (WET SETTING)

1) With engine at normal operating temperature, place vehicle on a flat, level surface. Remove air cleaner. Check fuel level at each float bowl separately. *See Fig. 3.*

HOLLEY 4180-C 4-BARREL (Cont.)

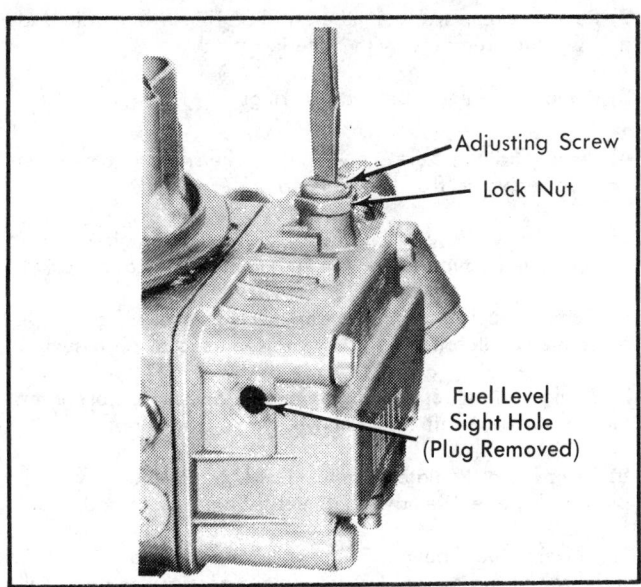

Fig. 3 Float Level Adjustment (Wet Setting)

Adjusting Screw
Lock Nut
Fuel Level Sight Hole (Plug Removed)

2) Place a container under primary float bowl sight plug. With engine running remove plug and gasket. Fuel level should be at lower edge of plug opening.

3) If float level is too high, stop engine and drain fuel bowl by removing one of the lower float bowl screws. Drain fuel into a container. Tighten fuel bowl screw.

NOTE — *Engine should be restarted to fill fuel bowl. This will make sure that foreign material did not cause a temporary flooding condition.*

4) If float level is still too high, it should be lowered then raised to correct level. Remove both secondary and primary sight plugs and gaskets.

5) Loosen float adjustment lock screw on top of primary float bowl. Turn adjustment nut clockwise to lower fuel level below sight plug opening.

6) Now turn adjustment nut counterclockwise until fuel level just reaches lower edge of sight plug hole. Tighten lock screw. Allow fuel level to stabilize to check for correct level. Install sight plug and gasket.

7) If the float level was too low during original checking procedure, follow step **6)**.

SECONDARY THROTTLE VALVES

1) Hold secondary throttle valves closed. Turn secondary throttle valve stop screw out until secondary throttle valves seat in throttle bores.

2) Now turn screw in until screw just contacts secondary throttle valve lever.

CHOKE PULLDOWN

1) Remove choke thermostat housing, gasket and retainer. Insert a .026" wire gauge into choke piston bore. This moves piston down against stop screw. See *Fig. 4*.

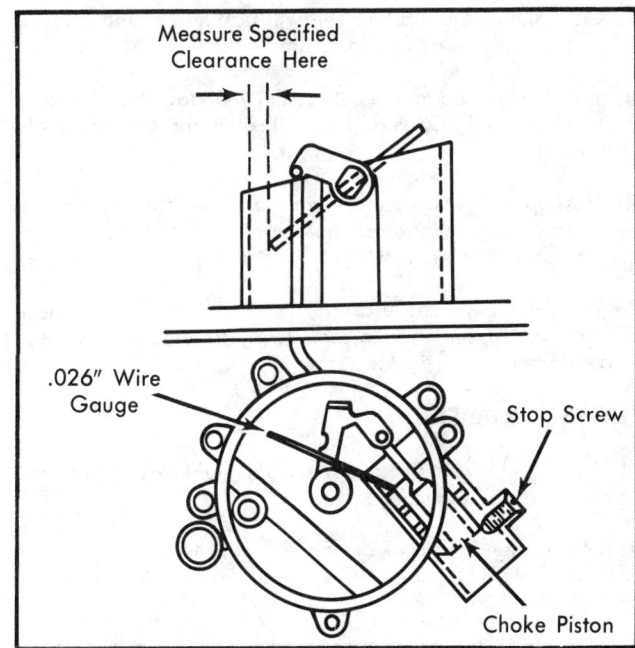

Fig. 4 Choke Pulldown Adjustment

Measure Specified Clearance Here
.026" Wire Gauge
Stop Screw
Choke Piston

2) Hold choke valve toward closed position. Measure specified choke pulldown clearance between lower edge of choke valve and air horn wall.

3) If adjustment is necessary, remove putty covering stop screw. Turn screw clockwise to increase clearance and counterclockwise to decrease clearance.

FAST IDLE CAM

1) Loosen choke thermostat housing screws. Rotate housing 45° counterclockwise (rich) to close choke valve. Tighten choke housing screws. See *Fig. 5*.

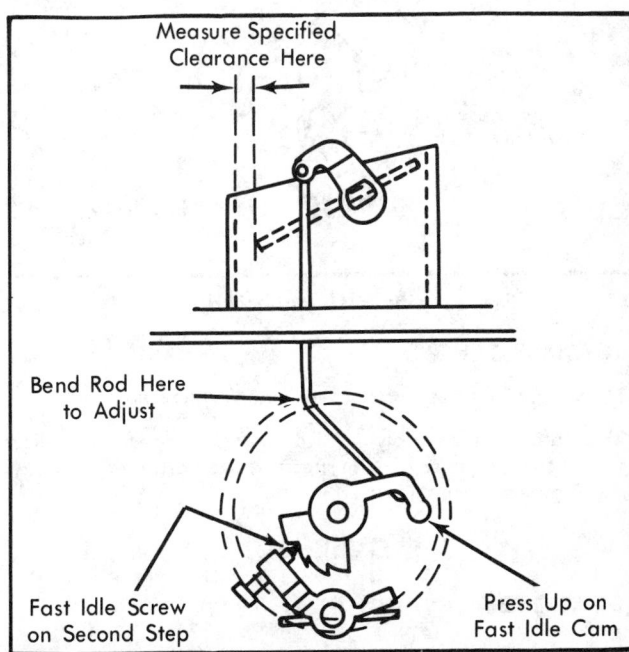

Fig. 5 Fast Idle Cam Adjustment

Measure Specified Clearance Here
Bend Rod Here to Adjust
Fast Idle Screw on Second Step
Press Up on Fast Idle Cam

HOLLEY 4180-C 4-BARREL (Cont.)

2) Open then close throttle. This will postition fast idle speed screw on top step of fast idle cam.

3) Insert a specified gauge between lower edge of choke valve and air horn wall. Open and close throttle and allow fast idle cam to drop.

4) Press up on fast idle cam. There should be little or no movement. This indicates that fast idle screw is on second (kickdown) step of cam, against first step.

5) To adjust, bend choke control rod until fast idle screw is in correct position on fast idle cam. Readjust automatic choke to correct setting and tighten screws.

CHOKE UNLOADER

1) Hold throttle valves wide open. Apply light closing pressure on choke valve. *See Fig. 6.*

2) Measure specified choke unloader clearance between lower edge of choke valve and air horn wall. To adjust, bend pawl on fast idle cam lever.

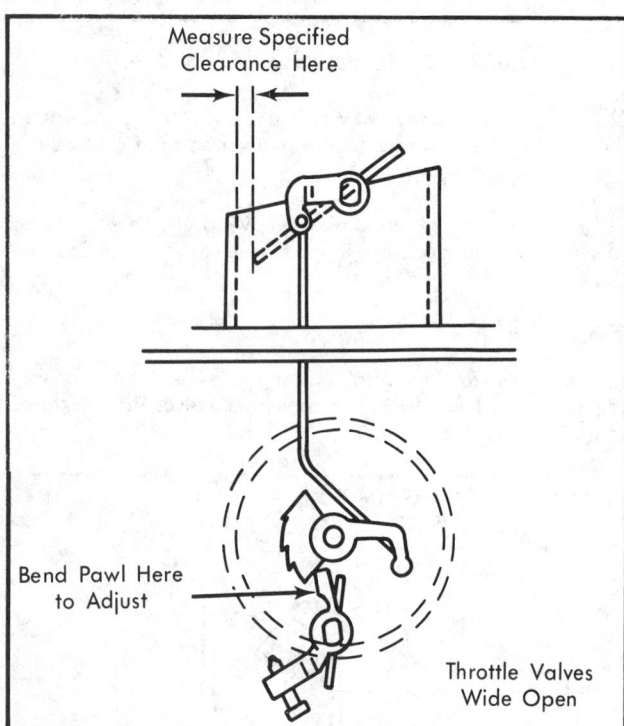

Measure Specified Clearance Here

Bend Pawl Here to Adjust

Throttle Valves Wide Open

Fig. 6   Choke Unloader Adjustment

AUTOMATIC CHOKE

1) Loosen choke thermostat cover retaining screws.

2) Rotate cover assembly in "Rich" or "Lean" direction to align reference mark on cover with specified scale grauation in housing. Tighten cover screws.

OVERHAUL

DISASSEMBLY

Primary Fuel Bowl & Metering Block — 1) Remove primary fuel bowl and gasket. Remove metering block and gasket.

2) Remove pump transfer tube and "O" rings from main body if it was not removed with metering block.

3) Remove fuel line tube and "O" rings.

4) Remove idle mixture screws and gaskets. Remove main jets and power valve from metering block.

5) Remove fuel level adjustment lock screw and gasket. Turn adjusting nut counterclockwise and remove nut and gasket.

6) Remove fuel inlet needle and seat assembly. Do not disassemble needle and seat, they are replaced as an assembly.

7) Remove float retainer using a pair of needle nose pliers. Slide float off shaft and remove spring from float.

8) Remove baffle plate from fuel bowl. Remove fuel level sight plug and gasket. Remove fuel inlet fitting, gasket and screen.

9) Invert fuel bowl. Remove accelerator pump cover, diaphragm and spring. Do not remove accelerator pump inlet check ball.

Secondary Fuel Bowl & Metering Block — 1) Remove fuel bowl. Using a clutch type screwdriver, remove metering block screws. Remove metering block, plate and gasket.

2) Remove balance tube, washer and "O" ring seal. Disassemble fuel bowl by following steps **5** through **8)** in Primary Fuel bowl assembly.

Main Body — 1) Remove air cleaner stud. Remove secondary diaphragm link retainer.

2) Disassemble fuel bowl by following steps **5)** through **8)** in *Primary Fuel Bowl disassembly procedures.*

3) Remove choke rod retainer from choke housing shaft and lever assembly. Remove choke cover, thermostatic spring and gasket. Remove choke main housing and gaskets.

4) Remove choke housing shaft nut, lock washer and spacer. Remove shaft and fast idle cam. Remove choke piston and lever assembly.

NOTE — *If it is necessary to remove choke valve and shaft, tips of choke valve screws may have to be filed as they are staked into shaft.*

5) If it is necessary, remove choke valve screws. Remove choke valve and slide out choke shaft.

6) Remove secondary diaphragm housing and gasket. Remove diaphragm housing cover, spring diaphragm and vacuum check ball.

NOTE — *The secondary diaphragm housing must be removed before attempting to remove cover.*

7) Remove accelerator pump discharge nozzle screw. Lift off discharge nozzle and gasket. Invert main body and catch accelerator pump discharge needle as it falls out of bore in main body.

HOLLEY 4180-C 4-BARREL (Cont.)

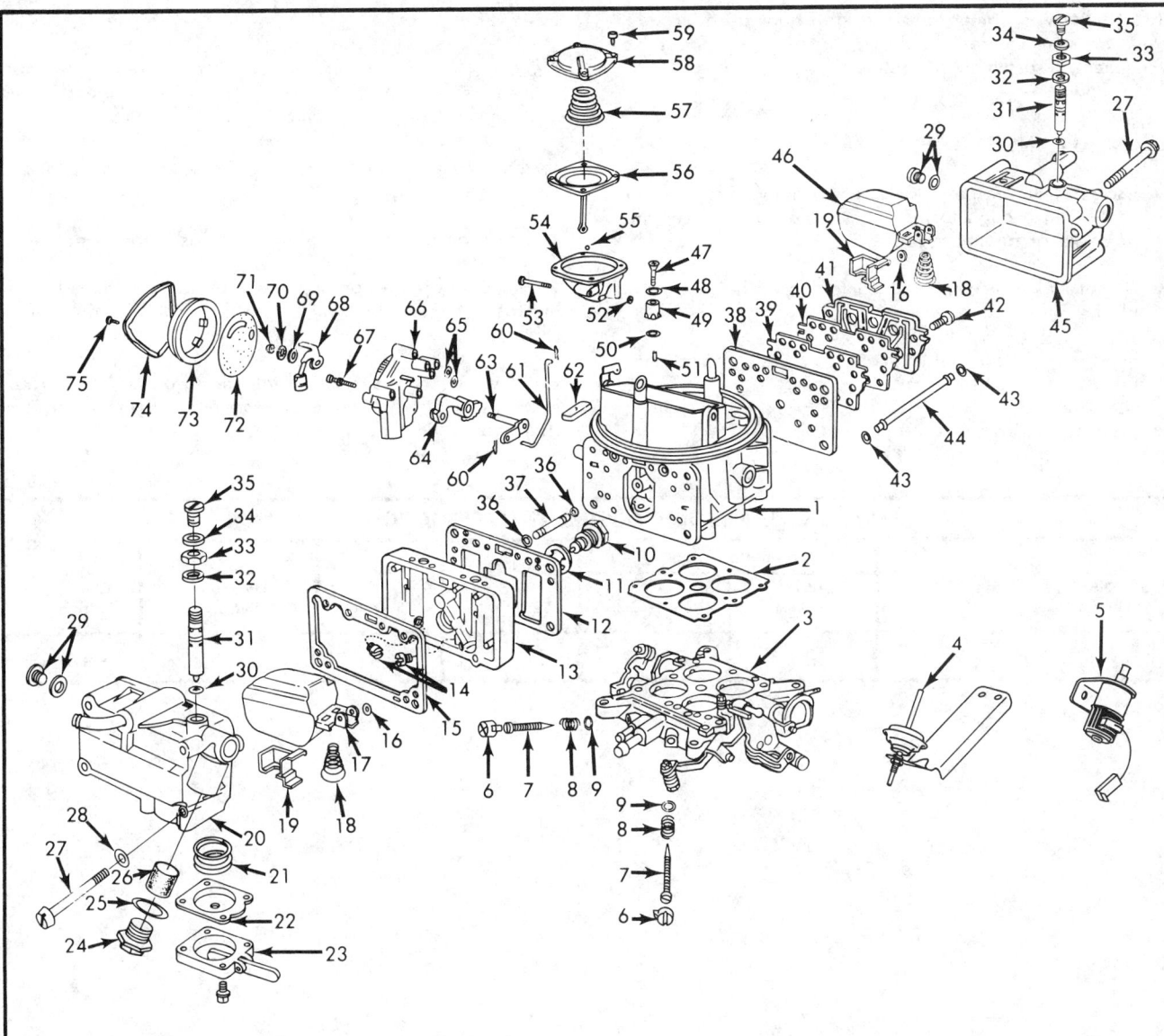

1. Main Body
2. Throttle Body Gasket
3. Throttle Body
4. Decel Throttle Modulator (Vehicles Over 8500 Lbs. GVW)
5. Solenoid Throttle Positioner (Vehicles Under 8500 Lbs. GVW)
6. Idle Limiter Cap
7. Idle Mixture Screw
8. Idle Mixture Screw Spring
9. Idle Mixture Screw Gasket
10. Power Valve
11. Power Valve Gasket
12. Primary Metering Block Gasket
13. Primary Metering Block
14. Main Jets
15. Primary Fuel Bowl Gasket
16. Float Retainer
17. Primary Float
18. Float Spring
19. Baffle Plate
20. Primary Float Bowl
21. Accel. Pump Spring
22. Accel. Pump Diaphragm
23. Accel. Pump Cover
24. Fuel Inlet Fitting
25. Fuel Inlet Fitting Gasket

26. Fuel Filter
27. Fuel Bowl Screw
28. Fuel Bowl Screw Gasket
29. Fuel Bowl Sight Plug & Gasket
30. Needle & Seat "O" Ring
31. Needle & Seat Assy.
32. Fuel Level Adjustment Nut Gasket
33. Fuel Level Adjustment Nut
34. Fuel Level Adjustment Lock Screw Gasket
35. Fuel Level Adjustment Lock Screw
36. Accel. Pump Transfer Tube "O" Ring
37. Accel. Pump Transfer Tube
38. Secondary Plate Gasket
39. Secondary Plate
40. Secondary Metering Block Gasket
41. Secondary Metering Block
42. Secondary Metering Block Screw
43. Fuel Transfer Tube "O" Ring
44. Fuel Transfer Tube
45. Secondary Float Bowl
46. Secondary Float
47. Accel. Pump Discharge Nozzle Screw
48. Accel. Pump Discharge Nozzle Screw Gasket
49. Accel. Pump Discharge Nozzle
50. Accel. Pump Discharge Nozzle Gasket
51. Accel. Pump Discharge Needle
52. Secondary Vacuum Diaphragm Housing Gasket

53. Secondary Vacuum Diaphragm Housing Screw
54. Secondary Vacuum Diaphragm Housing
55. Secondary Vacuum Diaphragm Check Ball
56. Secondary Vacuum Diaphragm
57. Secondary Vacuum Diaphragm Spring
58. Secondary Vacuum Diaphragm Cover
59. Secondary Vacuum Diaphragm Cover Screw
60. Choke Rod Clip
61. Choke Rod
62. Choke Rod Seal
63. Choke Rod Shaft & Lever
64. Fast Idle Cam
65. Choke Housing Gasket
66. Choke Housing
67. Choke Housing Screw
68. Choke Thermostat Lever & Piston
69. Washer
70. Spacer
71. Nut
72. Choke Thermostat Cover Gasket
73. Choke Thermostat Cover
74. Choke Thermostat Cover Retainer
75. Choke Thermostat Cover Retainer Screw

Fig. 7   Exploded View of Holley Model 4180-C 4-Barrel Carburetor

HOLLEY 4180-C 4-BARREL (Cont.)

Throttle Body — Components of throttle body are matched to meet emission control standards. Manufacturer does not recommend disassembly of throttle body.

CLEANING & INSPECTION

- Use a regular carburetor cleaning solution. Soak components long enough to thoroughly clean all surfaces and passages of foreign matter.

- Do not soak any components containing rubber, leather or plastic.

- Remove any residue after cleaning by rinsing components in a suitable solvent.

- Blow out all passages with dry compressed air.

REASSEMBLY

NOTE — *Use new gaskets and seals. Make sure that new gaskets fit correctly and that all holes and slots are punched through and correctly located.*

To reassemble carburetor, reverse disassembly procedure and note the following:

1) Apply petroleum jelly to all "O" rings before installation.

2) Make sure projection on the choke rod is positioned under the fast idle cam. This will ensure that fast idle cam will be raised up when the choke valve closes.

3) It will be necessary to install the secondary diaphragm housing cover and all 4 screws before diaphragm housing is installed onto main body.

	CARBURETOR ADJUSTMENT SPECIFICATIONS					
	Accelerator Pump		Choke Pulldown Setting	Fast Idle Cam Setting	Choke Unloader Setting	Auto. Choke Setting
Carb. No.	Lever (Clearance)	Stroke (Hole No.)				
D9TE-BKA	.015"	No. 1	.195-.225"	.210"	.295-.335"	5 Rich

MOTORCRAFT MODEL 2150 2-BARREL

CARBURETOR APPLICATION

FORD

Application	Ford Part No. Man. Trans.	Auto. Trans.
4.2L (255")		
Federal	E1TE-BVA	E1TE-CSA
5.0L (302")		
Federal		
Without A/C	E1UE-GA, E1TE-BVA	E1TE-CRA, E1TE-CNA, E1TE-CKA, E1TE-CLA
With A/C	E1UE-GA	E1TE-CPA, E1TE-CMA
5.8L (351") M		
Federal	E1TE-BFA, E1TE-CFA	E1TE-CHA, E1TE-CDA, E1TE-BGA
Calif.	E1TE-CEA	E1TE-CCA
High Alt.	E1TE-BHA	E1TE-BJA, E1TE-BFA
5.8L (351") W		
Federal	E1UE-KA,	
6.6L (400")		
Federal	E1TE-CBA, E1TE-BYA	E1TE-BYA
Calif.	E1TE-BZA	E1TE-CAA

JEEP

Application	Jeep Code No. Man. Trans.	Auto. Trans.
5.0L (304")		
Federal	DMJ2	DA2J
Hilly Terrain	DM2A	
6.0L (360")		
Federal	RHM2	RHA2

CARBURETOR IDENTIFICATION

Ford Motor Co. — A carburetor identification tag is attached to carburetor. The tag contains part number prefix and suffix. Basic part number for all carburetors is 9510. A design change code (if any) is also stamped on the tag. An assembly date code (year, month and day) is also stamped on the tag.

Jeep — A carburetor identification tag is attached to carburetor. The tag contains the Jeep carburetor code number. An assembly date code (year, month and day) is also stamped on the tag.

DESCRIPTION

Motorcraft 2150 carburetors have 2 main assemblies: the air horn and main body. Air horn contains choke plate, fuel bowl vent, and hot idle compensator. Main body houses throttle plate, accelerator pump assembly, float assembly, power valve and fuel bowl. Each bore contains main and boost venturis, main fuel discharge, and accelerator pump discharge orifices.

On some applications, booster venturis contain variable high speed bleed control system, which allows control of air/fuel mixture for improved high speed operation and low speed responses.

Vehicles sold for high altitude use (above 4000 ft.) contain an altitude compensator. This circuit compensates for thinner air by metering an additional amount of air into the air/fuel mixture, preventing an over-rich situation. An automatic device (aneroid) reacts to atmospheric pressure and overrides the compensation feature at lower altitudes.

ADJUSTMENT

HOT (SLOW) IDLE RPM

See appropriate article in TUNE-UP SERVICE PROCEDURES.

VACUUM THROTTLE KICKER (DECEL THROTTLE MODULATOR)

See appropriate article in TUNE-UP SERVICE PROCEDURES.

IDLE MIXTURE

See appropriate article in TUNE-UP SERVICE PROCEDURES.

COLD (FAST) IDLE RPM

See appropriate article in TUNE-UP SERVICE PROCEDURES.

ACCELERATOR PUMP STROKE

Accelerator pump stroke has been preset at the factory. Additional holes are provided for different engine applications. For normal operations, accelerator pump rod should be in the inner hole of pump lever. Install connecting rod to specified hole of overtravel lever. See Fig. 1.

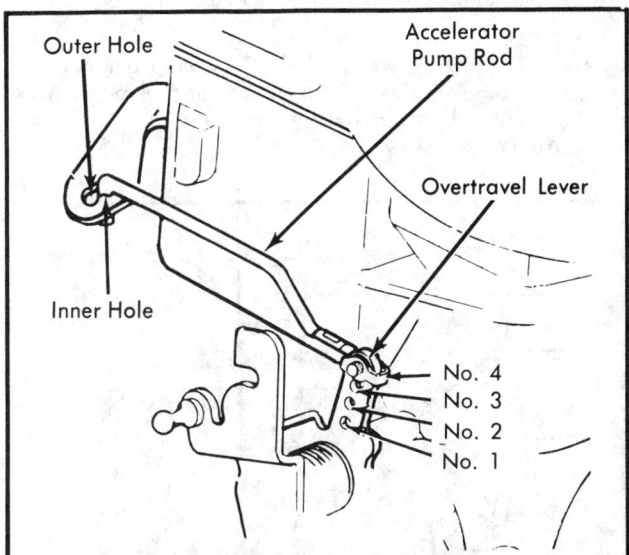

Fig. 1   Accelerator Pump Stroke

FLOAT LEVEL (DRY SETTING)

NOTE — Dry float setting is preliminary adjustment only. Final adjustment must be made after carburetor is installed on vehicle.

MOTORCRAFT MODEL 2150 2-BARREL (Cont.)

With air horn removed, raise float by depressing float tab until fuel inlet needle is lightly seated. Measure distance from top of main body (gasket removed) to flat portion of free end of float. If adjustment is necessary, carefully bend float tab.

NOTE — *Do not allow float tab to contact needle while making adjustment as Viton needle tip may be damaged.*

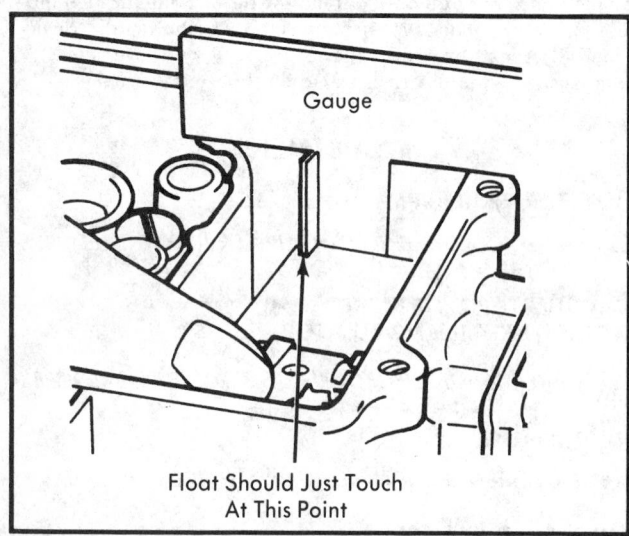

Fig. 2   Adjusting Float Level (Dry Setting)

FLOAT LEVEL (WET SETTING)

1) Warm up engine to operating temperature. Ensure vehicle is on flat, level surface. Stop engine and remove air cleaner and air horn attaching screws. Leave air horn in position on carburetor. Start engine. *See Fig. 3.*

2) Allow engine to idle for a few minutes to stabilize fuel level. With engine idling, remove air horn and gasket.

3) Measure distance, with suitable "T" scale, from machined surface of main body to level of fuel in fuel bowl. Make measurement at least ¼" away from sides of bowl to be sure of accurate reading.

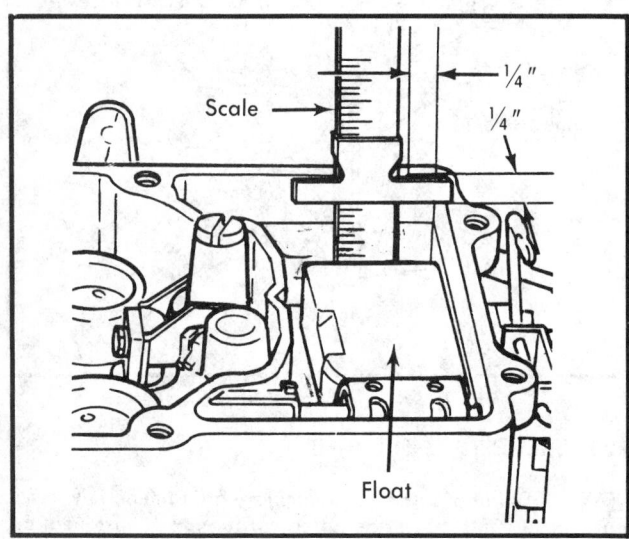

Fig. 3   Adjusting Float Level (Wet Setting)

4) If level is not within specifications, adjustment is needed. Stop engine before adjusting to avoid fire danger from fuel spray. Bend float tab (contacting inlet valve) up to raise fuel level and down to lower level.

5) After each adjustment, install air horn with 2 screws. Start engine and idle long enough for fuel level to stabilize to new setting. Stop engine and recheck fuel level.

6) When correct level is obtained, install new air horn gasket; replace air horn (install I.D. tag). Be sure plastic dust seal on choke rod is positioned properly and does not bind rod.

CHOKE VALVE PULL-DOWN

NOTE — *Most applications have a tamper-proof choke, incorporating a sealed pull-down motor and break-away choke cap screws. Adjustments given are used when a major overhaul is performed or if components are damaged.*

1) Loosen choke cover retainers. Open throttle and rotate choke cover until choke valve is held closed. Tighten choke cover.

2) Close throttle with fast idle speed adjustment screw on top step of fast idle cam.

3) Apply vacuum to hold choke diaphragm against set screw. Do not press on links.

NOTE — *If vacuum is applied to choke diaphragm with a hand pump, an air leak may be detected. This is normal.*

4) Measure clearance between lower edge of choke valve and air horn. If adjustment is required, turn screw at rear of diaphragm housing to achieve proper clearance. *See Fig. 4.*

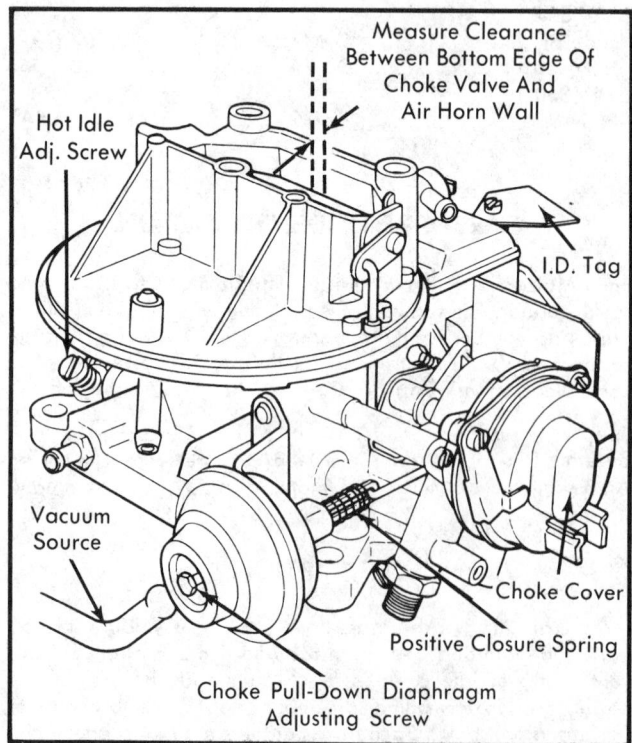

Fig. 4   Adjusting Choke Pull-Down Clearance

MOTORCRAFT MODEL 2150 2-BARREL (Cont.)

FAST IDLE CAM LINKAGE

NOTE — *Adjust choke vacuum pull-down adjustment before adjusting fast idle cam linkage.*

1) Perform steps 1) through 4) of *Choke Pull-Down* adjustment section.

2) Push down on fast idle cam lever until fast idle speed adjustment screw is in contact with second step and against shoulder of high step.

3) Measure clearance between upper edge of air horn wall and upper edge of choke valve. *See Fig. 5.*

4) If adjustment is required, turn fast idle cam lever screw to achieve correct adjustment. Reset automatic choke to proper adjustment notch.

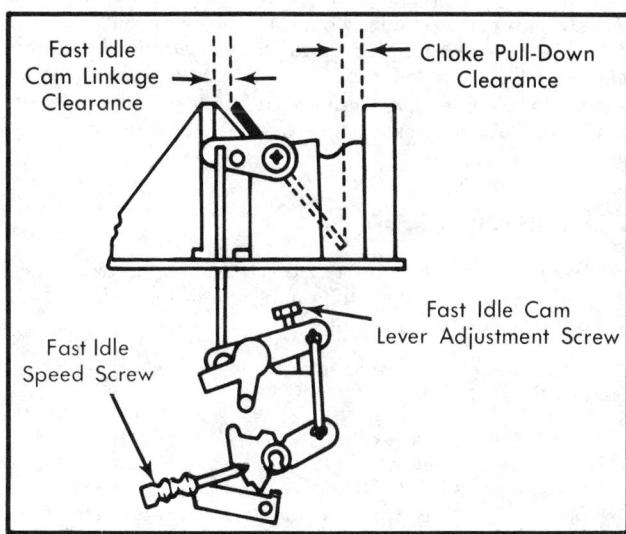

Fig. 5   Clearance Locations for Fast Idle Cam and Choke Valve Pull-Down Adjustment

CHOKE UNLOADER

1) Hold throttle fully open, and apply pressure on choke valve toward closed position. Measure specified choke unloader clearance between lower edge of choke valve and air horn wall.

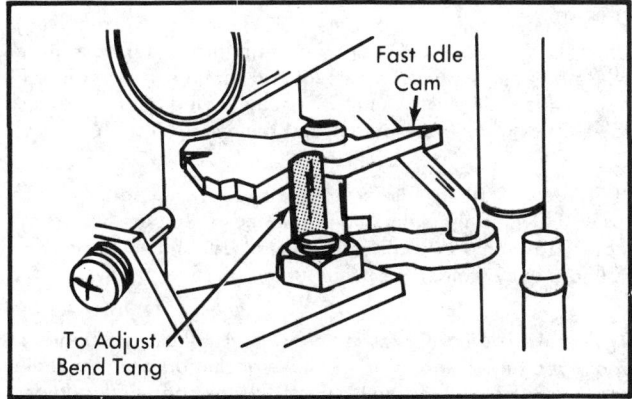

Fig. 6   Unloader Tang-to-Fast Idle Cam Clearance

2) To adjust, bend choke unloader tang that contacts fast idle cam. Bend tang toward cam to increase clearance and away from cam to decrease clearance. *See Fig. 6.*

3) After correct adjustment is obtained, open throttle until unloader tang is directly under fast idle cam pivot. Make sure there is .070" clearance between unloader tang and fast idle cam. *See Fig. 7.*

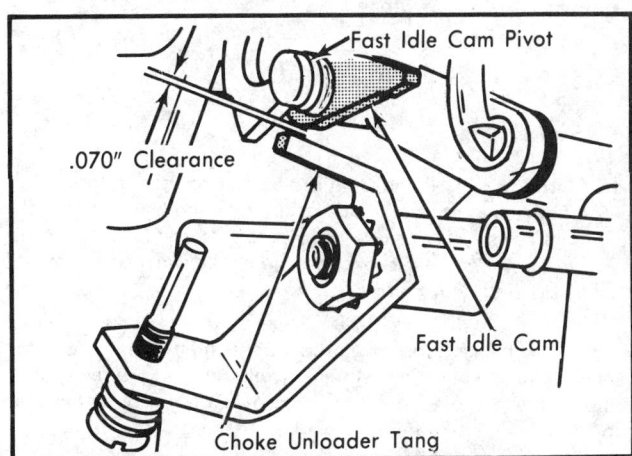

Fig. 7   Unloader Tang-to-Fast Idle Cam Clearance

4) Operate throttle and make sure that tang does not stick or bind against any portion of the linkage or carburetor casting.

AUTOMATIC CHOKE

1) Loosen choke thermostat cover retaining screws.

2) Rotate cover assembly in "Rich" or "Lean" direction to align reference mark on cover with specified scale graduation on housing. Tighten cover screws.

FUEL BOWL VENT

NOTE — *This is not a precise adjustment. It is made only to ensure that vent is open at idle and that it closes as throttle opens. Adjustment can be made with carburetor on or off vehicle.*

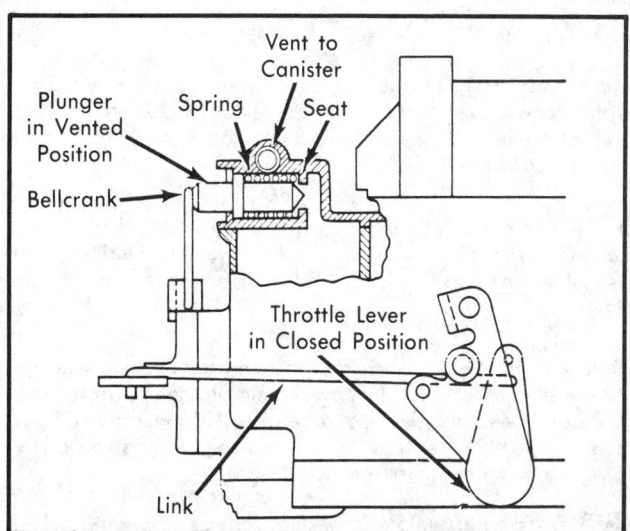

Fig. 8   Fuel Bowl Vent

MOTORCRAFT MODEL 2150 2-BARREL (Cont.)

1) If carburetor is installed on vehicle, make sure ignition is off. Make sure throttle is completely off fast idle cam.

2) Manually depress stem of bowl vent valve. Measure clearance between end of stem and flat on end of bell crank. See Fig. 8.

3) If clearance is not to specification, bend bell crank. Do not bend lever on accelerator pump.

OVERHAUL

DISASSEMBLY

Air Horn — 1) Remove air cleaner anchor screw and automatic choke control rod retainer. Remove air horn attaching screws, lockwashers, carburetor I.D. tag and air horn. Remove screw securing choke lever to choke shaft and remove choke rod and seal from air horn.

2) Remove choke diaphragm assembly, then if necessary to remove choke valve, file staking from retaining screws and remove screws. Remove choke valve by sliding it out from the top of the air horn. Remove choke shaft from air horn.

3) On models equipped with altitude compensator, the bypass choke plate is removed in same way as main choke plate. To remove shaft, remove link retainer and slide shaft out of air horn.

Automatic Choke — 1) Remove fast idle cam retainer, thermostatic choke coil housing screws and then remove clamp and gasket.

NOTE — *Some models are equipped with rivets retaining choke coil cover to prevent tampering with factory adjustment. To remove rivets, align a .128" (No. 30) drill on rivet head and drill only enough to remove rivet head. Using an ⅛" punch, drive remaining portion of rivet from housing. Repeat for remaining rivets.*

2) Remove choke housing screws, choke housing, gasket and fast idle cam rod from cam lever. Remove choke lever retaining screw and washer, then remove choke lever and fast idle cam lever.

Main Body — 1) Pry float shaft retainer from fuel inlet seat with a screwdriver, then remove float, float shaft retainer and fuel inlet needle assembly. Remove retainer and float shaft from float lever.

2) Remove fuel inlet needle seat, filter screen, and main jets. Remove booster venturi screw, booster venturi, metering rod assembly, and gasket. Remove filter screen from booster venturi screw.

3) Invert main body and catch accelerator pump discharge weight and check ball. Remove accelerator pump operating rod from overtravel lever and retainer by pressing ends of retainer together, while at the same time, pressing rod away from retainer until it is free.

NOTE — *To disassemble metering rod assembly on 2150 models, remove lift spring retaining clip and spring. Do not remove metering rod hanger from lift rod.*

4) Remove accelerator pump cover screws. Remove bowl vent bell crank and bracket, accelerator pump cover diaphragm and spring. If necessary to remove Elastomer valve, grasp firmly, from outside main body, and pull out.

NOTE — *If tip of Elastomer valve broke off, make sure it is removed from fuel bowl. Elastomer valve must be replaced whenever it is removed.*

5) Remove enrichment valve cover and gasket, then remove enrichment valve using a box wrench. Remove mixture needle limiter caps, mixture needles and springs. If necessary, remove nut and washer securing fast idle adjusting lever and remove lever. Remove throttle positioner solenoid (if equipped).

NOTE — *To remove tamper-resistant plugs from idle adjustment screws, support the area under limiter plug and tap plug forward.*

6) If necessary to remove throttle plates, mark each throttle plate with its corresponding bore for reassembly. Slide throttle shaft from main body. Mechanical high speed bleed actuator will drop out. It is located between throttle plates in main body. On altitude compensated carburetors, remove 4 attaching screws and remove aneroid and valve assembly.

CLEANING & INSPECTION

- Use a regular carburetor cleaning solution. Soak components long enough to thoroughly clean all surfaces and passages of foreign matter.

- Do not soak any components containing rubber, leather or plastic.

- Remove any residue after cleaning by rinsing components in a suitable solvent.

- Blow out all passages with dry compressed air.

REASSEMBLY

NOTE — *Use new gaskets and seals. Make sure that new gaskets fit correctly and that all holes and slots are punched through and correctly located. Replace Elastomer valve if removed from main body.*

To reassemble carburetor, reverse disassembly procedure and note the following:

1) When installing Elastomer check valve (if removed), lubricate tip of new valve and insert tip into center hole of accelerator pump cavity. Use needle nose pliers inserted in fuel bowl and pull valve in until it is fully seated. Cut off excess valve tip at retaining shoulder and remove tip from fuel bowl.

2) When installing idle mixture needles and springs, turn screws in with fingers until lightly seated. Then back screws off seated position 1½ turns for an initial adjustment. Do not install idle screw limiter caps until final adjustments have made.

3) If choke coil cover was removed, reinstall using 3 beads of epoxy sealant to each side of choke gasket adjacent to choke cap screw bosses. Position gasket, choke cap, and retainer, and mount using break-away screws.

MOTORCRAFT MODEL 2150 2-BARREL (Cont.)

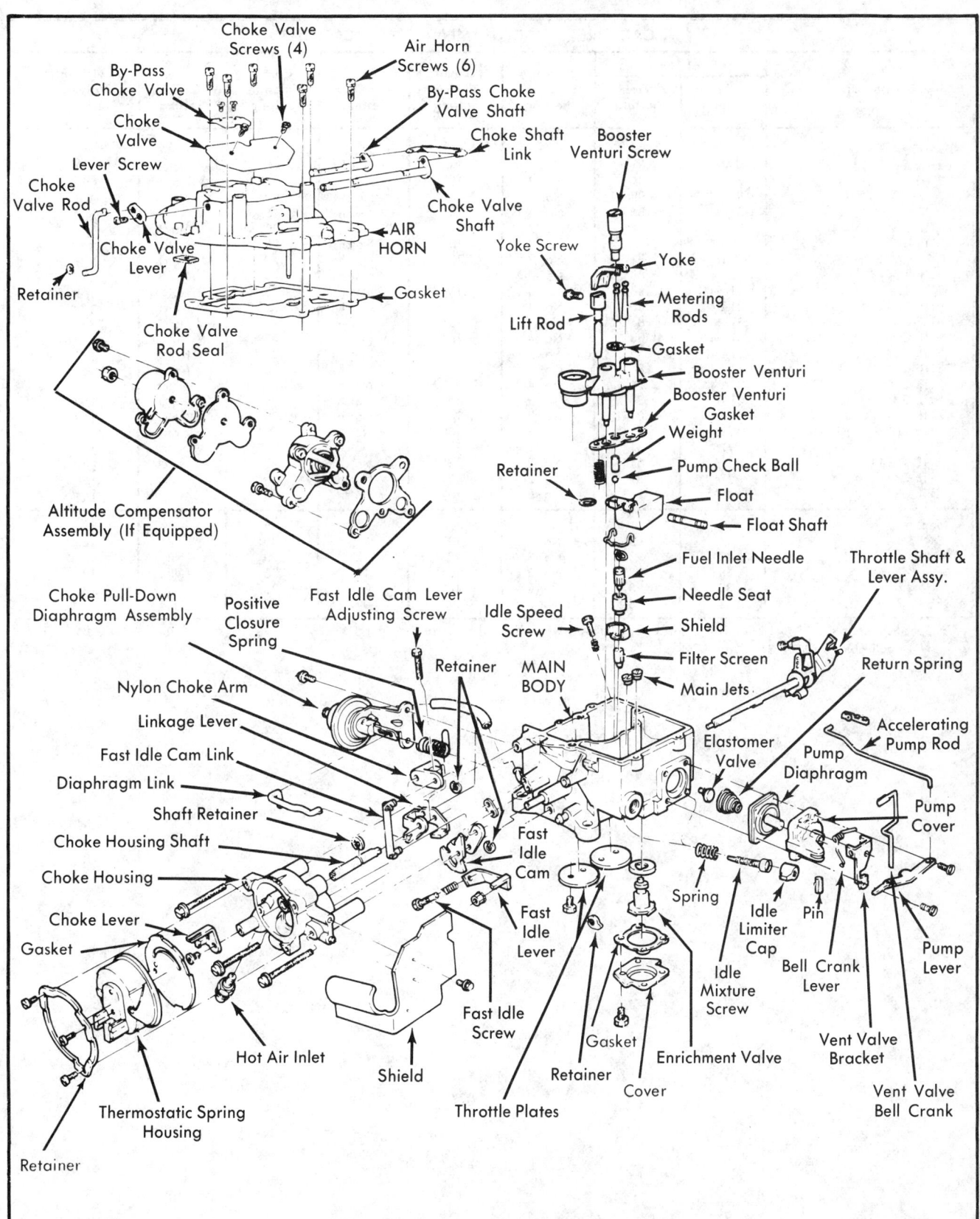

Fig. 9 Exploded View of Motorcraft Model 2150 Carburetor

1981 Motorcraft Carburetors

MOTORCRAFT MODEL 2150 2-BARREL (Cont.)

| | Float Level | | | | | | | |
Application	Dry Setting	Wet Setting	Accel. Pump Setting	Choke Pull-Down Setting	Fast Idle Cam Setting	Choke Unloader Setting	Auto. Choke Setting	Bowl Vent Valve Setting ①
CARBURETOR ADJUSTMENT SPECIFICATIONS								
Ford								
E1UE-GA	7/16″	.81″	No. 2	.13″	V Notch	.20″	V Notch	3/8″
E1UE-KA	31/64″	.86″	No. 3	.18″	V Notch	.25″	V Notch	3/64″
E1TE-BFA	31/64″	.88″	No. 2	.14″	V Notch	.20″	V Notch	3/8″
E1TE-BGA	31/64″	.86″	No. 3	.15″	V Notch	.25″	V Notch	.....
E1TE-BHA	31/64″	.86″	No. 2	.14″	V Notch	.20″	V Notch	3/8″
E1TE-BJA	31/64″	.88″	No. 3	.15″	V Notch	.25″	V Notch	3/8″
E1TE-BVA & E1TE-CSA	7/16″	.81″	No. 2	.13″	V Notch	.20″	V Notch	3/8″ ②
E1TE-BYA	31/64″	.88″	No. 4	.18″	V Notch	.25″	V Notch	.....
E1TE-BZA	31/64″	.88″	No. 4	.18″	V Notch	.25″	V Notch	3/8″
E1TE-CAA	31/64″	.86″	No. 4	.18″	V Notch	.25″	V Notch	3/8″
E1TE-CBA	31/64″	.88″	No. 4	.18″	V Notch	.25″	V Notch	.....
E1TE-CCA	31/64″	.88″	No. 4	.16″	V Notch	.25″	V Notch	.....
E1TE-CDA	31/64″	.88″	No. 4	.16″	V Notch	.25″	V Notch	.....
E1TE-CEA	31/64″	.86″	No. 4	.16″	V Notch	.20″	V Notch	.....
E1TE-CFA	31/64″	.86″	No. 4	.16″	V Notch	.20″	V Notch	.....
E1TE-CHA	31/64″	.88″	No. 3	.15″	V Notch	.25″	V Notch	3/8″
E1TE-CKA	7/16″	.81″	No. 2	.13″	V Notch	.20″	V Notch	3/8″
E1TE-CLA	7/16″	.81″	No. 2	.13″	V Notch	.20″	V Notch	.....
E1TE-CMA	7/16″	.81″	No. 2	.13″	V Notch	.20″	V Notch	3/8″
E1TE-CNA	7/16″	.81″	No. 2	.13″	V Notch	.20″	V Notch	3/8″
E1TE-CPA	7/16″	.81″	No. 2	.13″	V Notch	.20″	V Notch	3/8″
E1TE-CRA	7/16″	.81″	No. 2	.13″	V Notch	.20″	V Notch	3/8″
Jeep								
DMJ2	.38″	.93″	No. 3	.13″	.12″	.30″	2NR	.12″
DA2J	.38″	.93″	No. 3	.13″	.12″	.30″	1NR	.12″
DM2A	.38″	.93″	No. 3	.13″	.12″	.36″	1NR	.12″
RHM2	.38″	.93″	No. 3	.10″	.08″	.35″	2NR	.12″
RHA2	.38″	.93″	No. 3	.11″	.09″	.35″	2NR	.12″

① — Specification is size of fuel bowl vent tube except E1UE-KA, which is bowl vent valve setting.

② — Not applicable to E1TE-CSA.

MOTORCRAFT MODEL 7200 VV 2-BARREL

CARBURETOR APPLICATION

FORD

Application	Ford Carburetor No.	
	Man. Trans.	**Auto. Trans.**
5.0L (302") Calif.		E1TE-YA, E1TE-ABA
5.8L (351") W Federal	E1TE-ZA	E1TE-ZA
Calif.		E1TE-AHA

CARBURETOR IDENTIFICATION

Carburetor Part number identification is stamped on top of carburetor on flat surface of venturi valve cover plate.

DESCRIPTION

Motorcraft model 7200 variable venturi carburetor differs from other standard type carburetors in that it has the ability to change the area of the venturi for varying engine speed and load conditions. This is accomplished by dual venturi valves controlled by engine vacuum and throttle position. Depending upon engine speed and load conditions, the position of the venturi valves moving in and out of the air stream determine the air flow to the 2 carburetor throats. The venturi valves are connected to 2 tapered main metering rods which ride in the main metering jets, varying the amount of fuel flow through the carburetor.

Systems on the 7200 carburetor include a fuel inlet, main metering, control vacuum, cold enrichment, accelerator pump system and an all electric dual-stage choke. The 7200 carburetor is equipped with a "Feedback" control system. This system works in conjunction with an on-board electronic engine control computer. The air bleed feedback system uses a stepper motor to regulate bleed air admitted into main metering system. This provides a more precise metering of the air/fuel ratio as dictated by the computer through a series of sensors.

ADJUSTMENTS

NOTE — *When performing any adjustment requiring that the engine be running, make sure wheels are blocked and parking brake is engaged. If vehicle is equipped with a vacuum parking brake release, disconnect line to parking brake control and plug line. Engine must be at normal operating temperature for all engine running adjustments.*

HOT (SLOW) IDLE RPM

See appropriate article in TUNE-UP SERVICE PROCEDURES.

IDLE MIXTURE

See appropriate article in TUNE-UP SERVICE PROCEDURES.

COLD (FAST) IDLE RPM

See appropriate article in TUNE-UP SERVICE PROCEDURES.

ACCELERATOR PUMP LEVER LASH

1) Make sure curb idle speed is correctly adjusted. Measure clearance between accelerator pump stem and pump operating link with a feeler gauge. *See Fig. 1.*

2) If clearance is not to specification, tighten or loosen nut on end of link to obtain specified clearance.

NOTE — *This adjustment must be checked whenever curb idle speed is adjusted.*

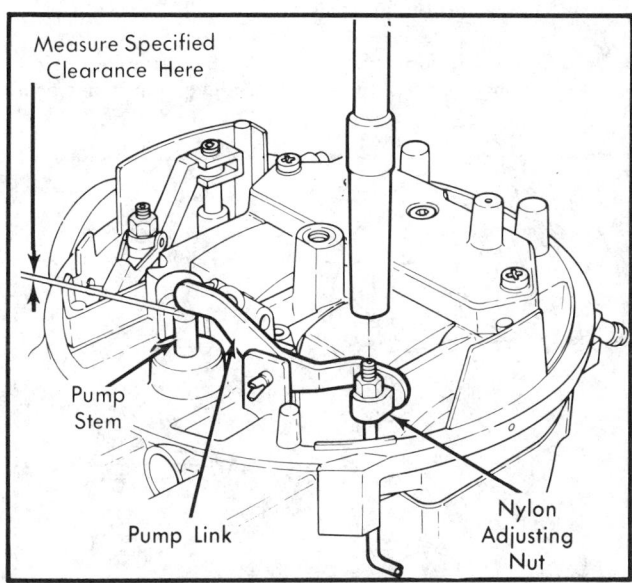

Fig. 1   Adjusting Accelerator Pump Lever Lash

FLOAT LEVEL

1) With upper body and gasket removed, turn upper body assembly upside down. *See Fig. 2.*

2) Construct a gauge (as shown in *Fig. 2.*) to specified float level setting. Using gauge, measure distance from cast surface of upper body to bottom of float.

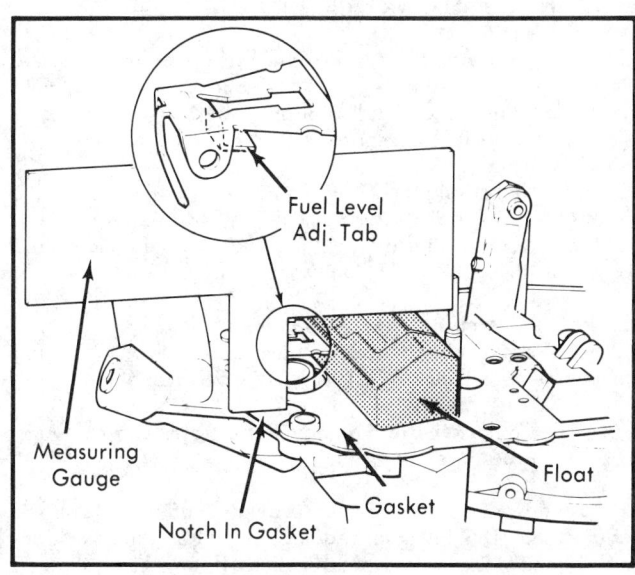

Fig. 2   Adjusting Float Level

MOTORCRAFT MODEL 7200 VV 2-BARREL (Cont.)

3) To adjust, bend adjustment tab on float arm away from inlet needle to decrease setting and toward inlet needle to increase setting.

FLOAT DROP

1) With upper body and gasket removed, hold upper body in upright position and allow float to hang. See Fig. 3.

2) Construct a gauge (as shown in Fig. 3.) to specified float drop setting. Using gauge, measure distance from cast surface of upper body to bottom of float.

3) To adjust, bend float lever stop tab on float arm away from hinge pin to increase setting and toward hinge pin to decrease setting.

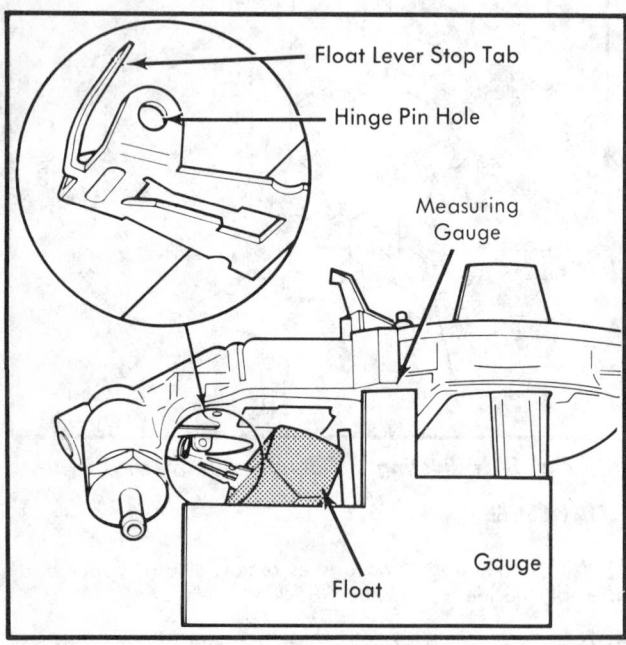

Fig. 3   Adjusting Float Drop

COLD ENRICHMENT METERING ROD

Checking Procedure — 1) Remove carburetor from vehicle. Perform steps 1) and 2) of Automatic Choke adjustment procedure. Position dial indicator on carburetor with indicator stem on top surface of enrichment rod.

2) Install choke weight (T77L-9848-A7 or equivalent) on choke bimetal lever. Install stator cap (T77L-9848-A or equivalent) and rotate stator cap to index. Dial indicator reading should be within the "CER 75°F Run" specification.

3) Rotate thermostat lever clockwise until CER travel stop screw is bottomed on upper body. Dial indicator reading should be within the "CER 0°F Start" specification.

NOTE — Do not remove dial indicator or reset to zero during checking procedure.

4) Push down on control vacuum regulator rod until it bottoms against seat. Dial indicator reading should be within the "Control Vacuum Regulator" specification. If any 1 of these 3 settings is out of specification, reset to specifications following Setting Procedure.

NOTE — If Control Vacuum Regulator is being adjusted, remove stator cap but do not remove dial indicator. Do not reset dial indicator to zero after removing stator cap. Also, if Control Vacuum Regulator, Choke Control Diaphragm or Fast Idle Cam are being adjusted, do not install choke cover.

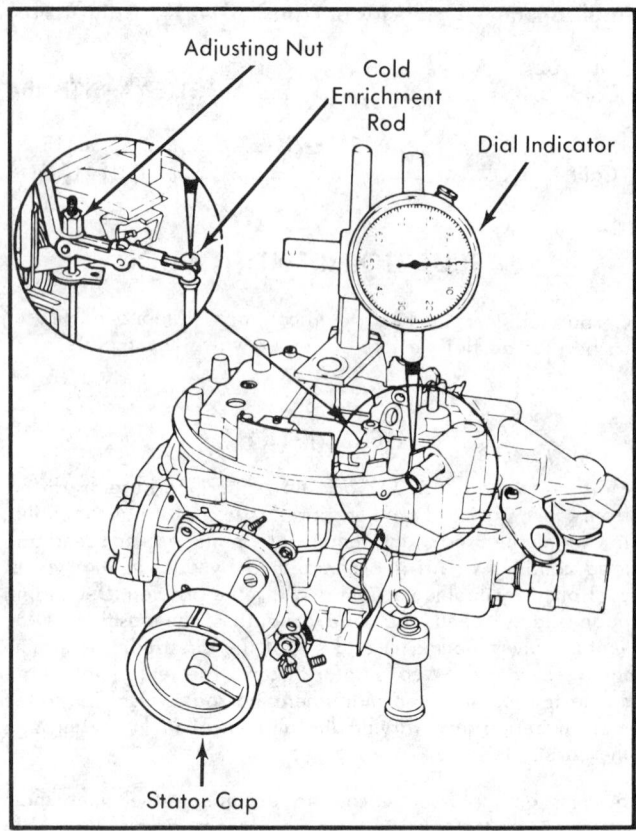

Fig. 4   Adjusting Cold Enrichment Metering Rod

Setting Procedure — 1) Turn CER adjusting nut counterclockwise until nut disengages from choke control rod. Remove CER lever "E" clip and hinge pin. Remove CER lever, control vacuum regulator adjusting swivel and adjusting nut as an assembly.

NOTE — Adjusting nuts are filled with epoxy sealer after final adjustment is made by manufacturer. To adjust, new parts must be installed. Also, choke control rod has undercut groove designed to break at 10 INCH. lbs. torque. If rod breaks during setting procedure, new rod must be installed.

2) Install new CER lever, control vacuum regulator adjusting swivel and adjusting nut. Tighten CER adjusting nut to lower and locate into position. Connect lever to control vacuum regulator adjusting swivel and install hinge pin and "E" clip.

3) Install choke weight (T77L-9848-A7 or equivalent) on choke bimetal lever. Install stator cap (T77L-9848-A or equivalent) and rotate stator cap to index. Turn CER adjustment nut until dial indicator reading is within the "CER 75°F Run" specification. See Fig. 4.

4) Rotate thermostat lever clockwise until CER travel stop screw is bottomed on upper body. Turn CER travel stop screw until dial indicator reading is within the "CER 0° F Start" specification. See Fig. 5.

MOTORCRAFT MODEL 7200 VV 2-BARREL (Cont.)

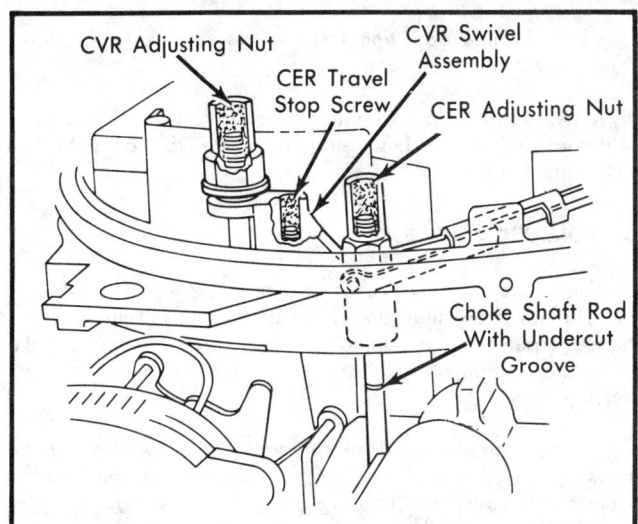

Fig. 5 **Adjusting Control Vacuum Regulator Swivel Assembly**

5) Push down on control vacuum regulator rod until it bottoms against seat. Position a ³⁄₈" wrench over the control vacuum rod adjusting nut to prevent from turning.

6) Using a ³⁄₃₂" Allen wrench, turn the control vacuum rod counterclockwise to increase travel and clockwise to decrease travel. When adjustments are complete, apply epoxy sealer to adjusting nuts and stop screw. See Fig. 6.

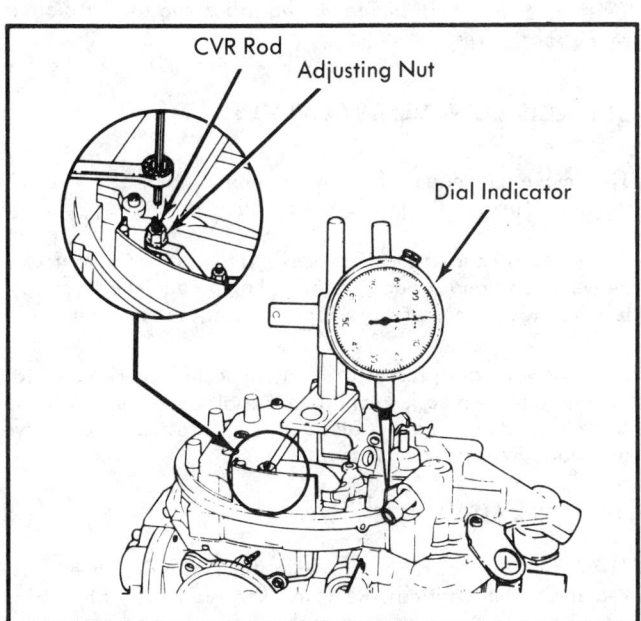

Fig. 6 **Adjusting Control Vacuum Regulator**

NOTE — If these were the only adjustments necessary, install choke cover, performing steps 3) and 4) of Automatic Choke adjustment procedure. Remove tools and reinstall carburetor on vehicle. If not, proceed as follows:

7) Depress choke control diaphragm by pushing in on choke diaphragm rod (do not push on fast idle intermediate lever) until diaphragm bottoms on diaphragm cover adjusting screw. See Fig. 7.

8) Rotate thermostat lever clockwise until choke shaft lever pin touches fast idle intermediate lever. Dial indicator reading should be within the "CER 0°F Run" specification.

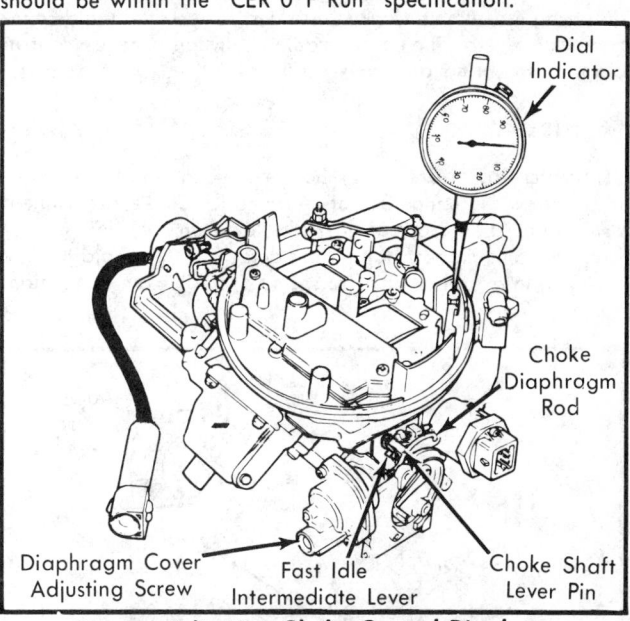

Fig. 7 **Adjusting Choke Control Diaphragm (At CER 0°F Run Position)**

9) To adjust, remove lead ball covering choke control diaphragm cover adjusting screw. Turn adjusting screw clockwise to increase height and counterclockwise to decrease height. Install a new lead ball over adjusting screw.

10) Center punch choke control diaphragm cover retaining screw heads. Align a ¼" drill on screw head and drill only enough to remove screw head. Repeat for remaining screw head. Remove choke control diaphragm cover and spring.

11) Remove remaining portion of retaining screws from choke control diaphragm housing using small pliers. Manually seat choke control diaphragm assembly in direction of fast idle cam. See Fig. 8.

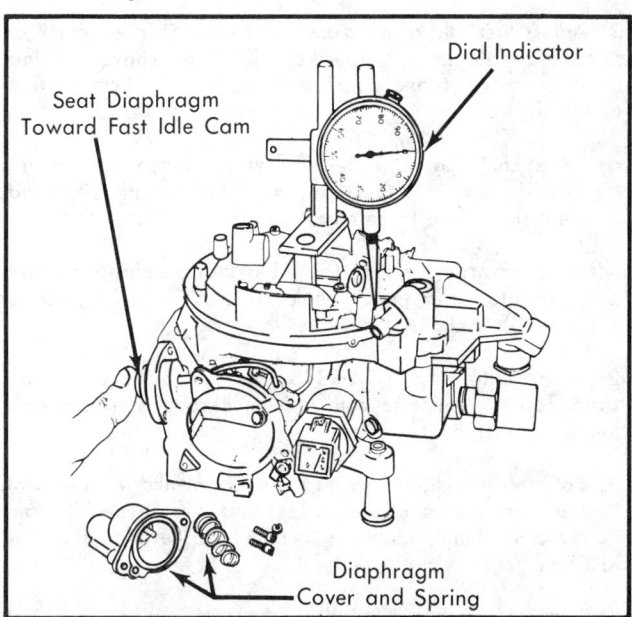

Fig. 8 **Adjusting Choke Control Diaphragm (At CER 75°F Start Position)**

MOTORCRAFT MODEL 7200 VV 2-BARREL (Cont.)

12) With dial indicator installed, reading should be within the "CER 75°F Start" specification. To adjust, rotate choke diaphragm assembly clockwise to decrease reading and counterclockwise to increase reading. Install choke control diaphragm spring and cover using new breakaway screws.

FAST IDLE CAM

Standard Procedure — 1) Before making adjustment, perform steps **1)** and **2)** of Automatic Choke adjustment procedure. Then, position fast idle lever on specified step of fast idle cam. Highest step is considered 1st step. Hold throttle closed with a rubber band to secure fast idle cam in position. See *Fig. 9*.

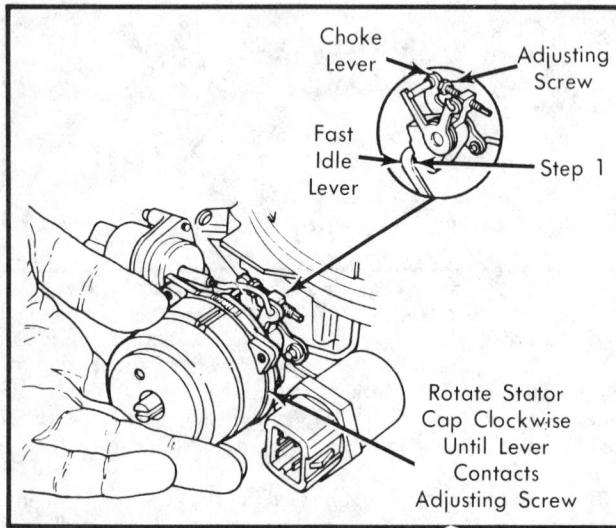

Fig. 9 Adjusting Fast Idle Cam

2) Install stator cap T77L-9848-A (or equivalent) in place of choke cover. Rotate stator cap clockwise until fast idle speed screw contacts lever.

3) Adjust fast idle cam adjusting screw until index mark on stator cap aligns with specified notch on choke housing. Remove stator cap and install choke cover. Adjust choke cover to specified setting.

4) Adjust choke cover to specified setting. When adjustment is completed, perform steps **3)** and **4)** of Automatic Choke adjustment procedure to complete this adjustment.

Alternate Procedure — 1) Leave dial indicator installed. Zero dial indicator and install choke weight (T77L-9848-A7 or equivalent) on choke bimetal lever.

2) Install stator cap (T77L-9848-A or equivalent) and rotate stator cap to index to set cold enrichment rod to the "CER 75°F Run" specification.

3) Hold throttle slightly open to allow free linkage movement. Position fast idle cam lever on specified step of fast idle cam. Rotate choke bimetal lever until choke shaft lever contacts fast idle cam screw.

4) Dial indicator reading should be as specified. To adjust, turn adjusting screw clockwise to increase reading and counterclockwise to decrease reading.

NOTE — *Turning adjusting screw in clockwise direction turns cam in counterclockwise direction.*

5) When adjustment is completed, perform steps **3)** and **4)** of Automatic Choke adjustment procedure to complete this adjustment.

AUTOMATIC CHOKE

1) Center punch choke cover retaining screw heads. Align a ¼" drill on screw head and drill only enough to remove screw head. Repeat for remaining 2 screw heads. Remove choke cover by inserting sharp, flat chisel between choke cover gasket layers.

2) Remove remaining portion of retaining screws from choke housing using small pliers. Carefully clean epoxy and gasket from choke cover and housing using gasket scraper.

NOTE — *Remove choke cover carefully. Choke cover and gasket are sealed to housing with epoxy sealer.*

3) Apply ½" bead of epoxy sealer to each side of choke cover gasket adjacent to the 3 screw bosses. Install gasket and choke cover using new breakaway screws.

4) Rotate cover assembly in "Rich" or "Lean" direction to align reference mark on choke cover with specified scale graduation on housing. Tighten each breakaway screw until head of screw breaks off.

NOTE — *Ensure that bimetal spring tab is engaged in slotted choke shaft lever.*

SOLENOID BOWL VENT VALVE TEST

1) Remove air cleaner, then turn ignition on and off. A "click" should be heard if solenoid is operating properly.

2) If not, disconnect electrical lead, and connect a voltmeter between lead and ground. Turn ignition on and check for battery voltage. If not present, repair wiring as required.

3) If 12 volts are present at lead connector, check valve for binding and/or plugged condition. Repair as required. If valve is not binding and/or plugged, replace solenoid valve assembly. Reinstall air cleaner.

VENTURI VALVE LIMITER

1) With carburetor removed, remove venturi valve cover, gasket and roller bearings. Remove expansion plug at rear of main body on throttle side of carburetor with a center punch.

2) Remove venturi valve limiter stop screw with a 5/32" Allen wrench. Hold throttle valves wide open. Apply light closing pressure on venturi valve.

3) Measure venturi valve limiter specified clearance between venturi valve and air horn wall. To adjust, move venturi valve to wide open position.

4) Insert a 5/64" Allen wrench in hole that stop screw was removed from. Turn screw clockwise to increase gap and counterclockwise to decrease gap.

MOTORCRAFT MODEL 7200 VV 2-BARREL (Cont.)

5) Remove Allen wrench. Apply light closing pressure on venturi valve and recheck specified clearance between valve and air horn wall.

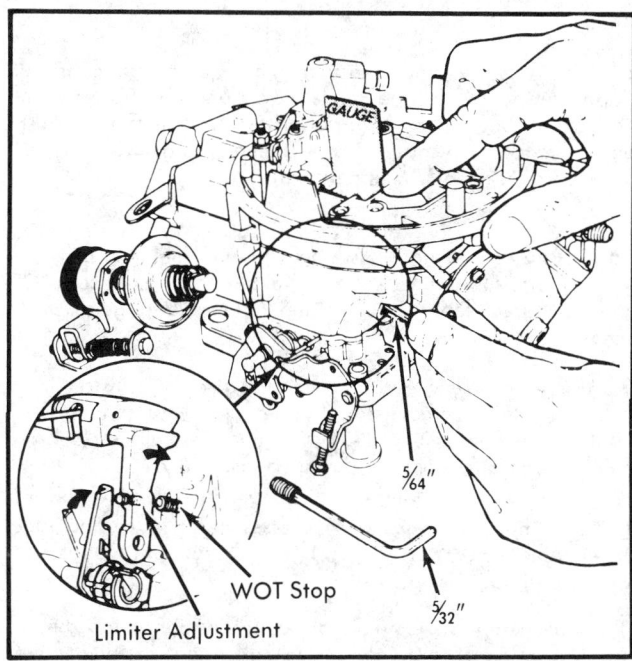

WOT Stop

Limiter Adjustment

5/64"

5/32"

Fig. 10 Adjusting Venturi Valve Limiter

6) Install stop screw and turn in until it contacts venturi valve. Hold venturi valve wide open and measure specified venturi valve limiter stop clearance between venturi valve and air horn wall. To adjust, turn stop screw.

7) Install a new expansion plug in access hole. Install venturi roller bearings, gasket and valve cover. Install carburetor.

OVERHAUL

DISASSEMBLY

Upper Body — 1) Mount carburetor in a suitable holding fixture. Remove fuel inlet fitting, filter, gasket and spring. Remove clip from accelerator pump and choke control rods. Disconnect rods.

2) Remove air cleaner stud. Remove 7 screws and remove upper body. Note position of 2 long screws. Remove float hinge pin and float assembly. Remove upper body gasket.

3) Remove fuel inlet valve, seat and gasket. Remove accelerator pump rod, dust seal, pump link retaining pin and link. Remove pump swivel and adjusting nut.

4) Disconnect choke rod. Remove retainer and carefully lift out dust seal. Remove choke hinge pin. Remove cold enrichment rod nut, lever, swivel, control vacuum regulator and adjusting nut as an assembly.

NOTE — *Disassembly of cold enrichment rod assembly is only required if parts replacement is necessary.*

5) Slide cold enrichment rod from casting and seal. Remove venturi valve cover plate and roller bearings. Drive air bypass plug out of venturi valve cover. Remove venturi air bypass screw.

6) Using a suitable plug removal tool (T77P-9928A or equivalent), press tapered plugs out of venturi valve pivot pins. Push out pivot pins.

7) Slide venturi valve to rear to remove. Remove pivot pin bushings. Remove metering rod pivot pins (on outer side of venturi valve), metering rods and springs.

NOTE — *Mark or identify the rods as to choke or throttle side of carburetor.*

8) Using jet plug removal tool (T77L-9533-B or equivalent), remove main jet plugs recessed in upper body casting.

NOTE — *The main metering jet setting is important to the overall performance of the carburetor. Use the following step to remove the main metering jets.*

9) Using a suitable jet wrench (T77L-9533A or equivalent), turn each metering jet clockwise counting number of turns required to seat them in bottom of casting. Record number of turns to nearest 1/4 turn. Now turn jet assemblies counterclockwise to remove. Remove "O" rings. Mark or identify main metering jets as to choke or throttle side.

10) Remove accelerator pump plunger assembly. Remove internal vent valve from plunger stem. Remove accelerator pump cup and spring.

11) Remove venturi valve limiter adjusting screw from throttle side of venturi valve. If necessary for cleaning, remove 1/8" pipe plug in fuel inlet casting boss.

Main Body — 1) Remove venturi valve diaphragm cover, spring guide and spring. Carefully loosen diaphragm and slide out of main body. Remove diaphragm adjusting screw by center punching until loose.

2) Remove venturi valve diaphragm adjusting screw. Remove venturi valve limiter stop screw plug by center punching until loose. Remove venturi valve limiter stop screw.

3) Remove "Feedback" stepper motor using a 1 5/8 socket. Remove gasket pintle valve and pintle spring. Turn main body upside down and catch check ball and weight as they fall out. Remove 5 throttle body screws. Remove throttle body and gasket.

Throttle Body — 1) Remove any throttle return control device and bracket. Disconnect kickdown spring.

2) Center punch choke cover retaining screw heads. Align a 1/4" drill on screw head and drill only enough to remove screw head. Repeat for remaining 2 screw heads. Remove choke cover by inserting sharp, flat chisel between choke cover gasket layers.

3) Remove retaining ring, choke cover and gasket. Remove remaining portion of retaining screws from choke housing using small pliers.

4) Remove choke thermostatic lever screw and remove lever. Slide choke shaft and lever assembly out of casting and remove fast idle cam.

5) Remove the fast idle intermediate lever. Center punch choke control diaphragm cover retaining screw heads. Align a 1/4" drill on screw head and drill only enough to remove screw head.

MOTORCRAFT MODEL 7200 VV 2-BARREL (Cont.)

6) Repeat for remaining screw head. Remove choke control diaphragm cover and spring. Remove choke control diaphragm and rod. Disconnect rod from diaphragm.

7) If necessary to remove choke housing bushing, file off staking from around bushing. Carefully press bushing out while supporting casting.

8) Remove choke heat tube fitting. Remove off idle (TSP) adjusting screw. Remove throttle shaft retaining nut. Remove fast idle adjusting lever, fast idle lever and adjusting screw.

9) If it is necessary to remove throttle valves, scribe alignment mark along shaft and identify the throttle valves as to choke side or throttle side.

10) Throttle valve screws are staked in place. Staking must be removed before removing screws. Remove screws and throttle valves. To remove throttle shaft, it will be necessary to drive limiter lever stop pin down until it is flush with shaft.

11) Slide throttle shaft out of casting. Remove transmission kickdown adjustment screw. Remove venturi valve limiter lever and bushing.

REASSEMBLY

Throttle Body — 1) Support throttle shaft assembly and drive out venturi valve limiter stop pin. Discard pin. Position venturi valve limiter assembly in throttle body and slide throttle shaft into place.

2) Place throttle valves in correct position (noted during disassembly). Install new screws and tighten until just snug. Close throttle and tap plates to center. Tighten throttle plate screws and stake into position.

3) Drive venturi valve limiter stop pin into shaft. Leave $1/8$" of pin exposed. Install fast idle lever, adjusting lever and fast idle screw. Install throttle shaft nut and tighten.

4) Install off idle (TSP) adjusting screw. Install choke heat tube fitting. Install choke shaft bushing in housing. Support housing when installing bushing. Stake into position.

5) Install fast idle intermediate lever. Install fast idle cam. Install choke control diaphragm and rod and connect rod to lever.

6) Install choke shaft and lever assembly. Install choke thermostatic lever in position. Install and tighten lever retaining screws.

7) Install choke control diaphragm spring, cover and new breakaway cover screws. Apply $1/2$" bead of epoxy sealer to each side of choke cover gasket adjacent to the 3 screw bosses. Install gasket, choke cover and retaining ring using new breakaway screws.

8) Install throttle control device and bracket in position.

Main Body — 1) Position throttle body gasket in position on main body. Assemble main body to throttle body. Install screws and tighten securely. Drop accelerator pump check ball and weight into position in main body.

NOTE — *Do not install venturi valve limiter stop screw and plug at this time. They are installed after carburetor is assembled and venturi valve limiter is adjusted.*

2) Slide venturi valve diaphragm into position. Install diaphragm spring, spring guide, cover and cover screws. Install venturi valve diaphragm adjustment screw (final adjustment is made on vehicle). Install pintle spring, gasket pintle valve and "Feedback" stepper motor.

Upper Body — 1) Install $1/8$" pipe plug in fuel inlet boss. Install venturi valve limiter screw in venturi valve. Lubricate "O" rings with mild soapy solution and install "O" rings on main metering jets.

2) Using jet wrench used during disassembly, install main metering jets in correct holes. Turn jets clockwise until they are lightly seated in casting. Now turn each jet counterclockwise number of turns recorded during disassembly.

3) Drive main jet plugs into recesses in casting using plug driver tool (T77L-9533-C). Tap lightly on tool until plugs bottom in casting.

4) Install metering rods and springs in position noted during disassembly on venturi valve. Install metering rod pivot pins. Install venturi valve, carefully guiding metering rods into jets. If springs are correctly installed, metering rods will spring back up when depressed.

5) Install venturi valve bushings and pivot pins. Install tapered plugs in pivot pins using tool used to remove plugs during disassembly.

6) Install venturi air valve bypass screw. Turn clockwise 4 turns to allow clearance for cover plate. Install plug in venturi valve cover plate.

7) Install venturi valve cover plate roller bearings, gasket and cover plate. Install and tighten screws. Install accelerator pump swivel and adjusting nut into pump link.

8) Install accelerator pump link and retaining pin. Install accelerator pump operating rod and dust seal. Install fuel inlet valve seat gasket, seat and valve.

9) Install upper body gasket. Place float in position and install hinge pin. Install accelerator pump return spring, cup, plunger, internal vent valve and retainer. Place pump piston assembly in position in hole in upper body.

10) Install upper body on main body. Guide accelerator pump piston assembly into cavity in main body. Make sure venturi valve diaphragm stem engages venturi valve.

11) Install fuel filter spring, filter, inlet fitting gasket and inlet fitting. Install air cleaner stud. Install choke control rod dust seal. Tap seal gently to straighten retainer.

12) Slide cold enrichment rod into upper body. Assemble cold enrichment rod adjusting nut, lever, swivel, control vacuum regulator and adjusting nut. Install assembly on carburetor.

MOTORCRAFT MODEL 7200 VV 2-BARREL (Cont.)

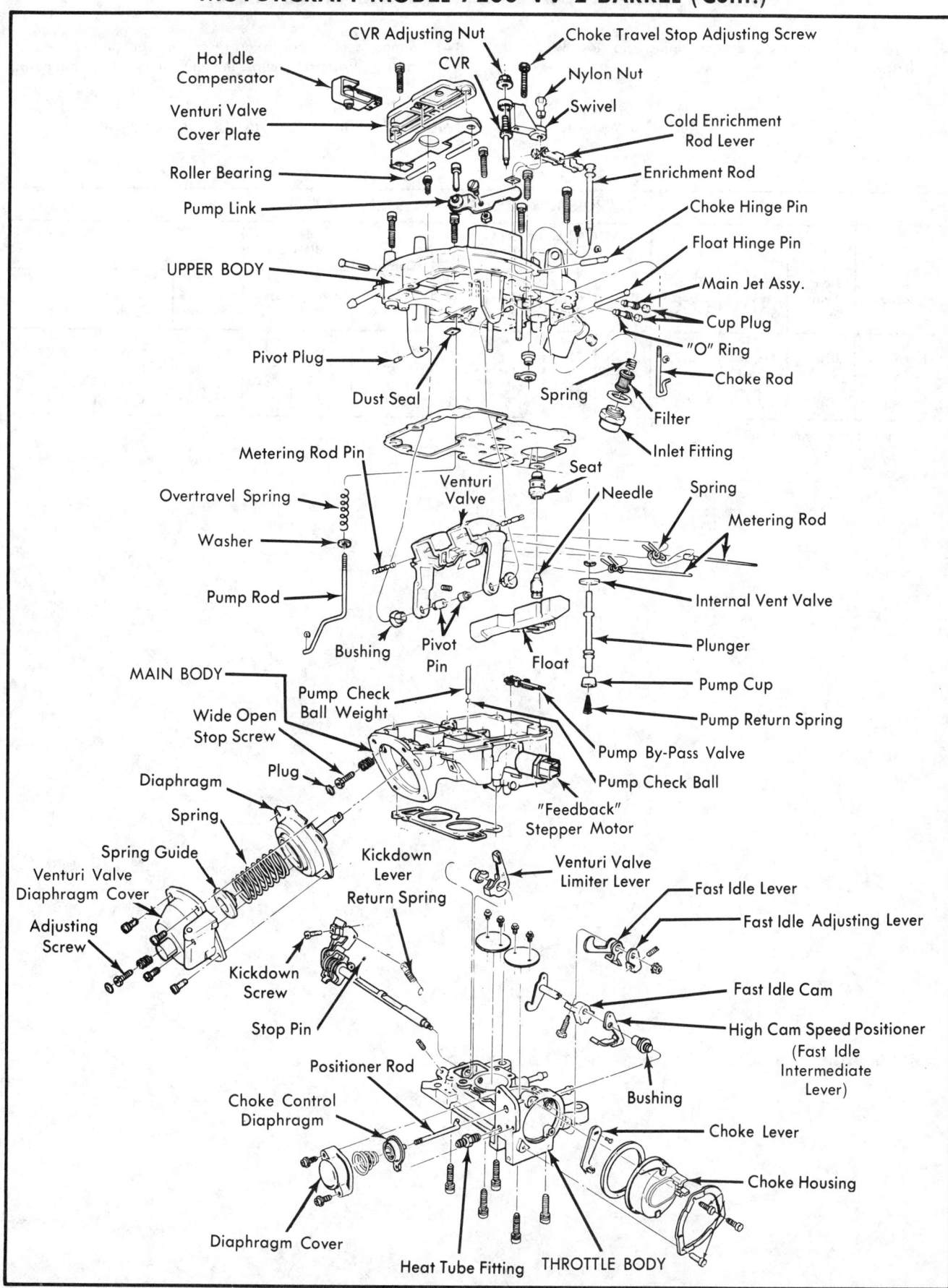

Fig. 11   Exploded View of Model 7200 VV Carburetor

1981 Motorcraft Carburetors

MOTORCRAFT MODEL 7200 VV 2-BARREL (Cont.)

13) Install choke hinge pin and retaining clip. Install choke control rod.

NOTE — *Perform Cold Enrichment Rod adjustment now.*

14) Connect accelerator pump operating rod and choke control rod. Install retaining clips. Install venturi valve limiter stop screw.

NOTE — *Perform Venturi Valve Limiter adjustment now.*

Application	Accel. Pump Setting	Fuel Level Setting	Float Drop Setting	Cold Enrichment Rod Specifications				Control Vacuum Regulator Setting	Fast Idle Cam		Choke Cover Setting	Venturi Limiter	
				0°F Start	0°F Run	75°F Start	75°F Run		Setting	Stop		Maximum Open	Wide Open on Throttle
E1TE-YA	.010"①	1-3/64"	1-15/32"	.525"	.350"	.445"	.125"	.250"	.360"	2	Index	1.00"	.400"
E1TE-ZA	.010"①	1-3/64"	1-15/32"	.525"	.350"	.445"	.125"	.250"	.360"	2	Index	1.00"	.500"
E1TE-ABA	.010"①	1-3/64"	1-15/32"	.525"	.350"	.445"	.125"	.250"	.360"	2	Index	1.00"	.400"
E1TE-AHA	.010"①	1-3/64"	1-15/32"	.525"	.350"	.475"	.125"	.250"	.360"	2	Index	1.00"	.500"

CARBURETOR ADJUSTMENT SPECIFICATIONS

① — Plus 1 turn counterclockwise.

ROCHESTER 1ME SINGLE BARREL

CARBURETOR APPLICATION

CHEVROLET & GMC

Application	Rochester Carb. No.

4.8L (292")
Federal
C, K, & P20/30 17081009
C & K20/30 17081309
Calif.
P30 17081329

CARBURETOR IDENTIFICATION

The carburetor model identification is stamped on a vertical portion of the float bowl, adjacent to the fuel inlet nut. If replacing float bowl, follow manufacturer's instructions contained in service package so that the identification number can be transferred to the new float bowl.

DESCRIPTION

The Rochester model 1ME carburetor is a single bore downdraft type carburetor using a triple venturi in conjunction with a plain tube nozzle. This model carburetor incorporates an electrically activated integral automatic choke system. The choke vacuum diaphragm is mounted externally to carburetor air horn and is connected to thermostatic coil lever through a connector link. An electrically actuated idle stop solenoid and dual throttle return springs are used on all models.

ADJUSTMENT

HOT (SLOW) IDLE RPM

See appropriate article in TUNE-UP SERVICE PROCEDURES.

IDLE MIXTURE

See appropriate article in TUNE-UP SERVICE PROCEDURES.

COLD (FAST) IDLE RPM

See appropriate article in TUNE-UP SERVICE PROCEDURES.

FLOAT LEVEL

1) Remove air horn. Hold float pin firmly in place. Push down on end of float arm against top of float needle. See Fig. 1.

2) With gasket removed, use a depth or "T" scale to measure distance from top of casting to index point at toe of float.

3) If adjustment is needed, gently bend float arm up or down. Do not force needle against needle seat to avoid damage.

4) Install new gasket, replace air horn. Start engine and check for leaks.

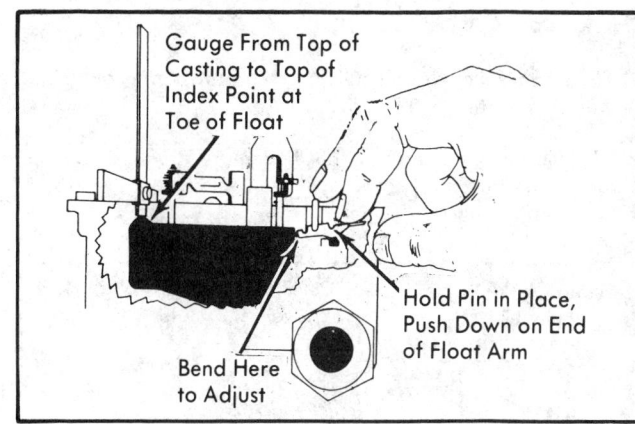

Fig. 1   Adjusting Float Level

METERING ROD ADJUSTMENT

1) Remove air horn and gasket. Hold throttle valve wide open. Push down on metering rod against spring tension. See Fig. 2.

2) Slide metering rod out of slot in holder and remove from main metering jet.

3) Back out idle stop solenoid. Hold throttle valve in fully closed position.

4) Press down on power piston. Swing metering rod holder over flat surface of bowl casting next to bore.

5) Measure specified clearance between rod holder and carburetor surface. Measurement can be made using a drill or pin gauge.

6) If adjustment is needed, gently bend holder arm up or down. Recheck clearance.

7) Reassemble carburetor. Install new air horn-to-body gasket. Check for leaks.

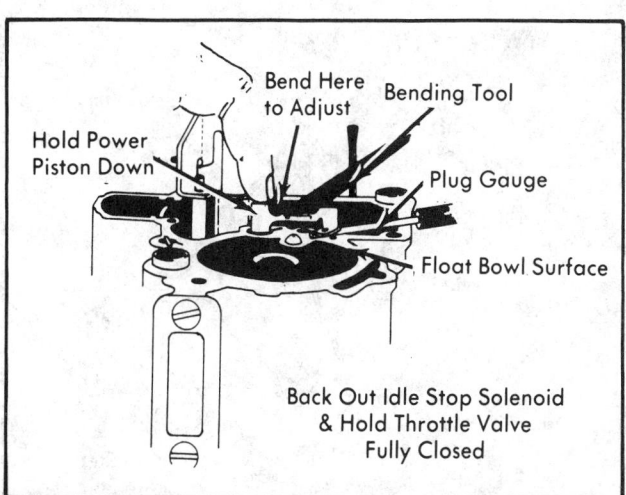

Fig. 2   Adjusting Metering Rod

ROCHESTER 1ME SINGLE BARREL (Cont.)

CHOKE COIL LEVER

1) Place cam follower on HIGHEST step of fast idle cam. Hold choke valve closed. *See Fig. 3.*

2) If adjustment is correct, specified plug gauge should be able to pass through hole in lever and enter hole in casting. Bend connector link to adjust.

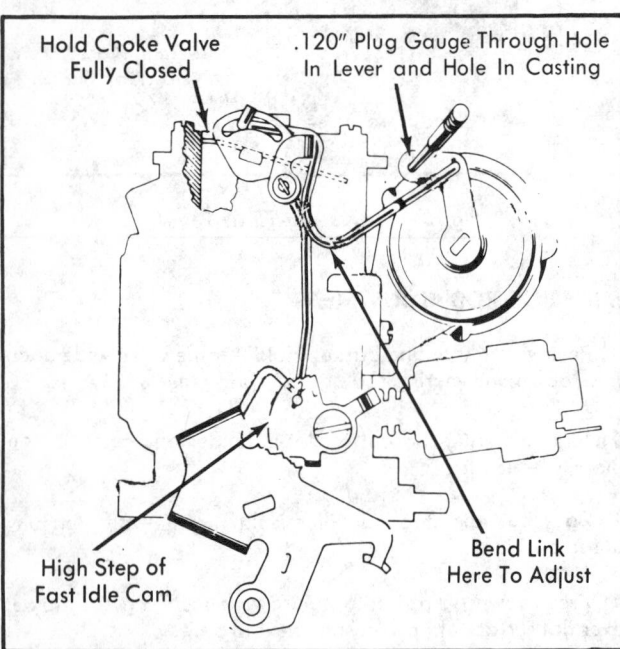

Hold Choke Valve Fully Closed

.120" Plug Gauge Through Hole In Lever and Hole In Casting

High Step of Fast Idle Cam

Bend Link Here To Adjust

Fig. 3   Adjusting Choke Coil Lever

CHOKE COIL ROD (FAST IDLE CAM)

1) Make sure fast idle speed is correctly set. Place fast idle cam follower on SECOND step of fast idle cam, against HIGHEST step. *See Fig. 4.*

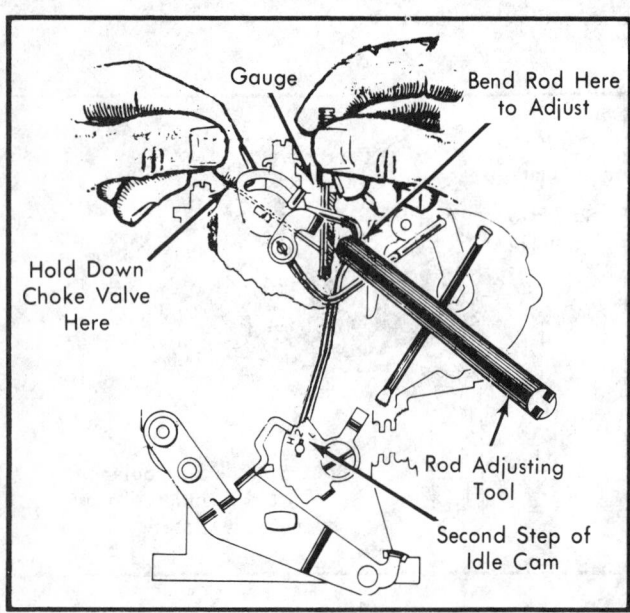

Gauge

Bend Rod Here to Adjust

Hold Down Choke Valve Here

Rod Adjusting Tool

Second Step of Idle Cam

Fig. 4   Adjusting Choke Coil Rod

2) Apply light closing pressure to choke valve. Measure specified clearance between lower edge of choke valve and air horn wall. Measurement can be made with a specified drill or pin gauge. To adjust, bend fast idle cam rod.

AUTOMATIC CHOKE

NOTE — *Choke coil cover uses rivets in place of retaining screws. If necessary to remove choke coil cover, refer to Disassembly and Reassembly procedures in this Section.*

VACUUM BREAK

1) Place cam follower on HIGHEST step of fast idle cam. Use outside vacuum source and apply enough vacuum to seat diaphragm. *See Fig. 3.*

2) Diaphragm plunger should be IN and seated. If used, bucking spring should be fully compressed.

3) Push up on choke coil lever. Rod should be snug in end of diaphragm plunger slot. On models equipped with delay feature, cover purge bleed hole in vacuum break end cover with masking tape.

4) Measure specified clearance between lower edge of choke valve and air horn wall. Measurement can be made with a specified drill or pin gauge. *See Fig. 5.*

5) To adjust, bend "U" shaped portion of vacuum diaphragm connector link. Remove masking tape. Check linkage for binding.

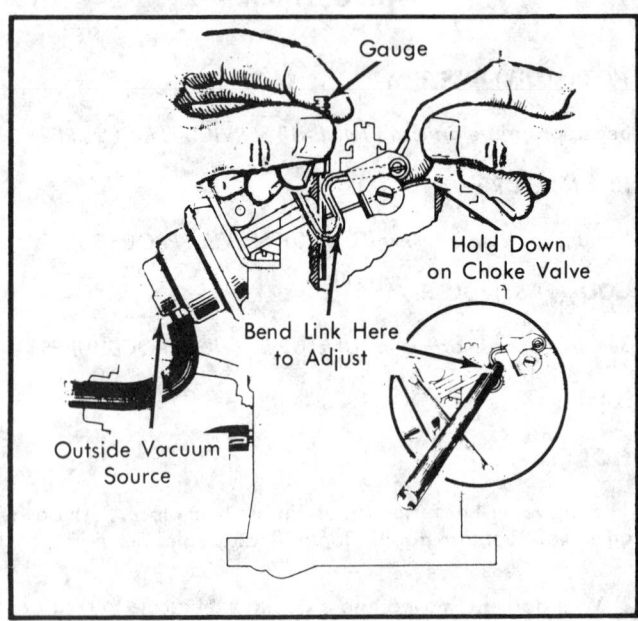

Gauge

Hold Down on Choke Valve

Bend Link Here to Adjust

Outside Vacuum Source

Fig. 5   Adjusting Vacuum Break

CHOKE UNLOADER

1) Install choke coil in housing and index properly.

NOTE — *If choke is warm, cool down to point where choke valve will close fully.*

ROCHESTER 1ME SINGLE BARREL (Cont.)

2) Hold throttle valve wide open. Measure specified clearance between lower edge of choke valve and air horn wall.

3) Measurement can be made using a specified drill or pin gauge. If adjustment is required, bend choke unloader tang to achieve proper clearance.

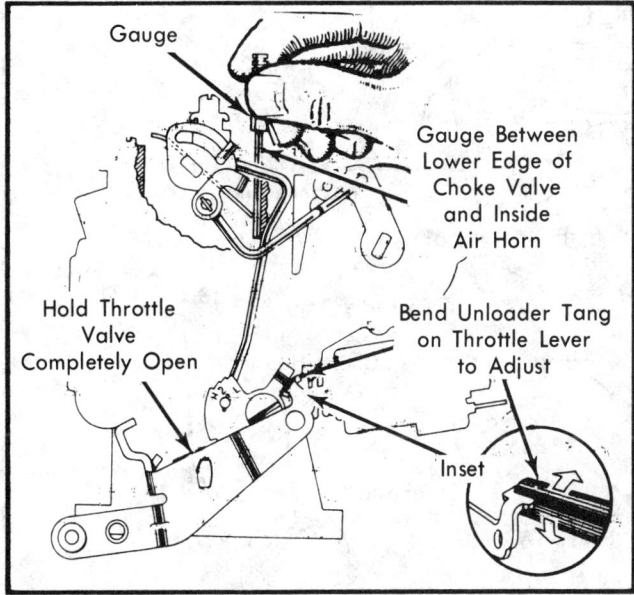

Fig. 6   Adjusting Choke Unloader

OVERHAUL

DISASSEMBLY

Air Horn — 1) Place carburetor on suitable stand to prevent damage to throttle valve. Pull off vacuum break diaphragm hose. Remove diaphragm assembly from air horn (2 attaching screws).

2) Slide diaphragm plunger stem from choke lever link. Do not attempt to remove screw that retains vacuum break lever to choke shaft. This screw is installed with thread-locking compound and should not be removed unless choke shaft replacement is required.

NOTE — *Do not remove choke housing unless replacement of housing is necessary.*

3) Remove fast idle cam. Remove choke rod from choke coil lever. Remove 3 choke coil housing attaching screws from float bowl.

NOTE — *Two screws have lock washers. Screw facing choke housing has tapered head for locating housing.*

4) If necessary to remove choke coil cover, drill rivet heads from cover retainer using a .159" (No. 21) drill. Remove cover retainer and cover. Carefully remove remaining pieces of rivets from housing.

5) Remove (4) remaining air horn-to-float bowl screws and lockwashers (3 long and 1 short). Carefully remove air horn by lifting and twisting back towards choke housing. Disengage choke coil lever link from choke coil lever at choke housing.

6) Turn air horn upside-down. If required, remove choke valve and choke shaft by removing screw retaining vacuum break lever to choke shaft. Be sure to apply Loctite or suitable torque retaining compound to this screw upon assembly. Now remove (2) choke valve attaching screws. Remove choke valve and shaft from air horn.

NOTE — *Choke valve screws are staked in place. File off staking for removal and restake during assembly. Use care not to bend choke shaft when staking screws.*

Float Bowl — 1) Remove air horn gasket. Lift upward on float hinge pin to extract float assembly from bowl. Remove hinge pin from float arm. Withdraw float needle from seat. Disconnect accelerator pump and power piston actuator lever from end of throttle shaft by removing lever attaching screw. Hold down power piston while removing lever. Power piston and metering rod assembly may now be removed.

2) Remove lower end of power piston link from actuator lever by rotating until tang on rod slides out of notch in lever. Remove actuator lever from lower end of accelerator pump link in same manner. Push down on accelerator pump and remove actuator link by rotating until tang on rod is aligned with slot on pump plunger lever. Remove the link.

3) Remove pump assembly from float bowl. Remove pump return spring and power piston spring from float bowl. Extract "T" guide and pump discharge spring. Invert bowl and collect pump discharge ball and idle tube. Remove main metering jet from bottom of fuel bowl. Remove float needle seat and gasket. Idle stop solenoid can now be removed. Remove fuel inlet nut and gasket, filter and relief spring.

Throttle Body — Invert float bowl on bench and remove two throttle body-to-bowl attaching screws. Remove gasket. No further disassembly of throttle body is necessary unless idle mixture needle is damaged or idle channels need cleaning. If necessary to remove idle mixture needle, cut tang from plastic limiter cap. Do not install replacement.

NOTE — *Due to close tolerance fit of throttle valve in bore of throttle body, do not remove throttle valve or shaft.*

NOTE — *California models have seals built into float bowl to seal the power piston drive rod and pump lever to prevent escape of fuel vapors to the atmosphere. Remove these seals and retainer prior to immersing float bowl in carburetor cleaner.*

CLEANING & INSPECTION

- Use a regular carburetor cleaning solution. Soak components long enough to thoroughly clean all surfaces and passages of foreign matter.

- Do not soak any components containing rubber, leather or plastic.

- Remove any residue after cleaning by rinsing components in a suitable solvent.

- Blow out all passages with dry compressed air.

1981 Rochester Carburetors

ROCHESTER 1ME SINGLE BARREL (Cont.)

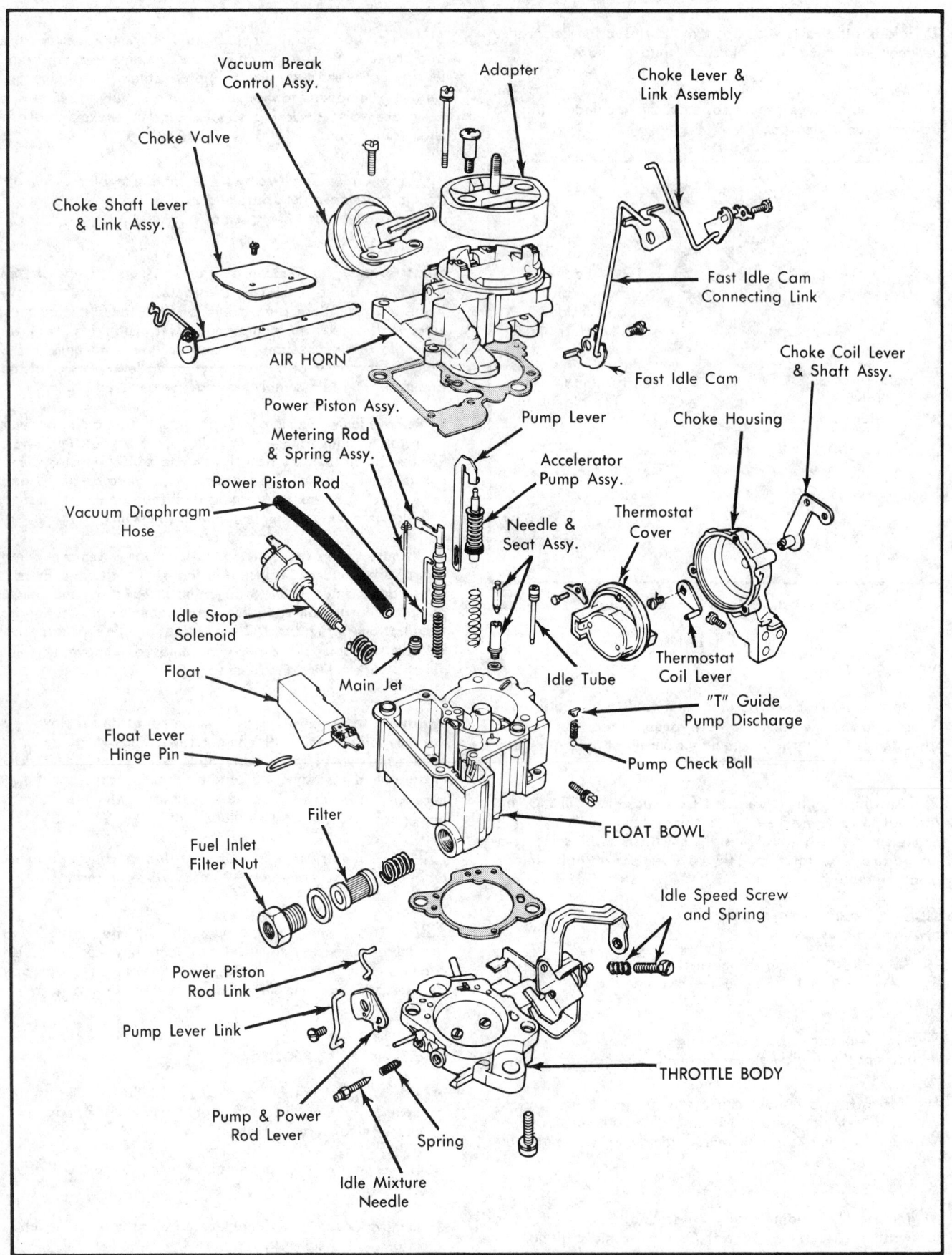

Fig. 7 Exploded View of Rochester Model 1ME Single Barrel Carburetor

ROCHESTER 1ME SINGLE BARREL (Cont.)

REASSEMBLY

NOTE — *Use new gaskets and seals. Make sure that new gaskets fit correctly and that all holes and slots are punched through and correctly located.*

To reassemble carburetor, reverse disassembly procedure noting the following:

1) Adjust float level and metering rod before installing air horn. All other adjustments are made with carburetor assembled.

2) Install metering rod with spring above power piston.

3) Thermostatic spring in idle compensator must hold valve closed after installation. Replace unit if spring is bent or distorted. Do not attempt to straighten or adjust spring.

4) Use two tapered head screws for mounting and locating diaphragm bracket. Install and tighten air horn screws evenly and in sequence shown in *Fig. 8.*

NOTE — *If choke coil cover was removed, it will be necessary to install replacement rivets supplied in service kit. Do not use a gasket between choke housing and cover, as direct contact is needed to ground electric coil housing.*

5) Place fast idle screw on high step of fast idle cam. Install choke coil cover, aligning notch in cover with raised boss on housing cover flange. Install self-tapping screws and tighten.

NOTE — *When torquing carburetor after removal, tighten bolts in a clockwise direction to 198 INCH lbs. When retorquing at recommended intervals, retorque to 144 INCH lbs. maximum.*

CAUTION — *Do not use a gasket between choke housing and electric coil. Coil is grounded through housing.*

6) Install vacuum diaphragm hose to diaphragm tube and connect to vacuum extension on bowl.

NOTE — *When installing carburetor on intake manifold, install insulator, then carburetor. Tighten 2 nuts to 36 INCH lbs., then tighten nuts to 18 ft. lbs.*

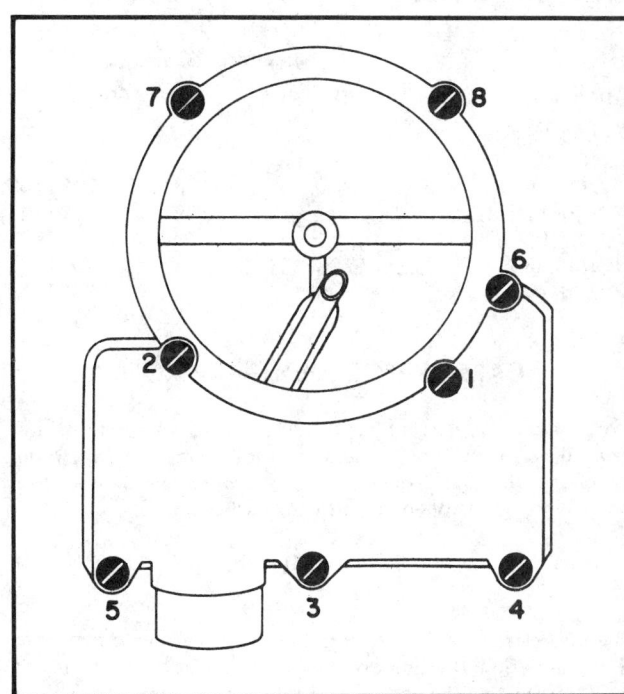

Fig. 8   Air Horn Tightening Sequence

CARBURETOR ADJUSTMENT SPECIFICATIONS							
Application	Float Level Setting	Metering Rod Setting	Choke Coil Lever Setting	Auto. Choke Setting	Choke Coil Rod Setting	Vacuum Break Setting	Choke Unloader Setting
17081009	11/32″	.090″	.120″	.....	.275″	.400″	.520″
17081309	11/32″	.090″	.120″	.....	.275″	.400″	.520″
17081329	11/32″	.090″	.120″	.....	.275″	.400″	.520″

1981 Rochester Carburetors

ROCHESTER M2ME 2-BARREL

NOTE — *SERIES IDENTIFICATION: The vehicle numbers used in this article have been abbreviated for common reference to both Chevrolet and GMC models. Chevrolet models use numerical designations as listed; GMC models are identified as follows: 10 = 1500; 20 = 2500; 30 = 3500.*

CARBURETOR APPLICATION

CHEVROLET & GMC

	Rochester Carb. No.	
Application	**Man. Trans.**	**Auto. Trans.**
5.0L (305") Federal		
C10/20		
Without A/C		17081142, 17081143
With A/C		17081144, 17081145
G10/20		
Without A/C	17081101	17081142
With A/C	17081103	17081144

CARBURETOR IDENTIFICATION

Carburetor model identification is stamped vertically on left rear corner of float bowl. Be sure to follow manufacturer's instructions on transferring identification number if new float bowl is to be installed on original carburetor.

DESCRIPTION

The Rochester M2ME carburetor is of single stage, downdraft, 2-barrel design. It is equipped with an Adjustable Part Throttle (APT) screw which accurately meters fuel flow through the main jets for improved emission control. This screw is preset at the factory, and is non-adjustable.

The choke system has an electric thermostat and coil assembly, and has factory tamper-proofing. A single float, brass needle seat, and rubber-tipped float valve are used to control fuel level in the float chamber.

ADJUSTMENT

HOT (SLOW) IDLE RPM

See appropriate article in TUNE-UP SERVICE PROCEDURES.

IDLE MIXTURE

See appropriate article in TUNE-UP SERVICE PROCEDURES.

COLD (FAST) IDLE RPM

See appropriate article in TUNE-UP SERVICE PROCEDURES.

ANGLE GAUGE ADJUSTMENT TOOL

Manufacturer recommends that some carburetor adjustments be performed using a choke valve angle gauge (Kent-Moore tool No. J-26701). While preparations and actual adjustments may vary with each individual adjustment, the procedure for using the angle gauge to check the choke valve angle remains the same. Use the following procedure to perform adjustments requiring the use of the choke valve angle gauge.

1) Rotate degree scale on angle gauge so that 0° mark is opposite pointer.

2) With choke valve closed, place angle gauge magnet squarely on choke valve.

3) Rotate leveling bubble on angle gauge until it is centered.

4) Rotate degree scale until specified degree mark is opposite pointer.

5) Now perform individual adjustment preparations as outlined in the following carburetor adjustments requiring angle gauge. If bubble is centered, adjustment is correct. If not, adjust carburetor as outlined.

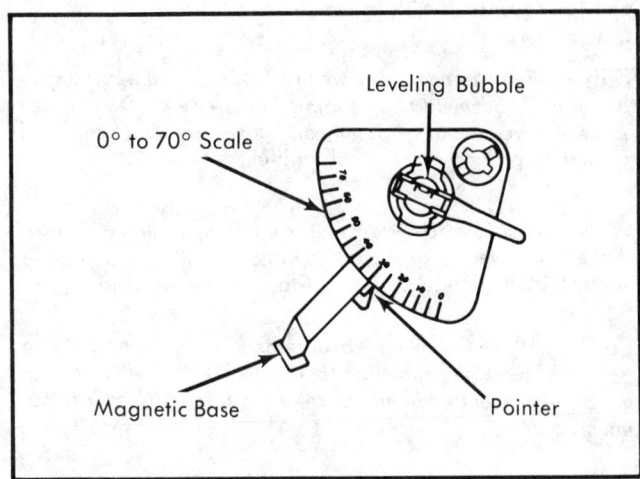

Fig. 1 Choke Valve Angle Gauge

FLOAT LEVEL

1) Remove air horn and gasket from float bowl. Hold float retainer firmly down. *See Fig. 2.*

2) Position a "T" measuring scale over toe of float at point 3/16" from end of float at toe. Measure distance from float bowl casting to float.

3) To adjust, remove float and bend arm. Check to make sure float is correctly aligned after adjustment.

ACCELERATOR PUMP

1) Close throttle valves completely. Make sure fast idle speed screw is off fast idle cam. *See Fig. 3.*

2) Make sure accelerator pump rod is in specified hole (inner or outer) of accelerator pump lever.

3) Using a "T" scale, measure accelerator pump specified distance from top of choke valve wall (next to vent stack) to top of accelerator pump stem.

ROCHESTER M2ME 2-BARREL (Cont.)

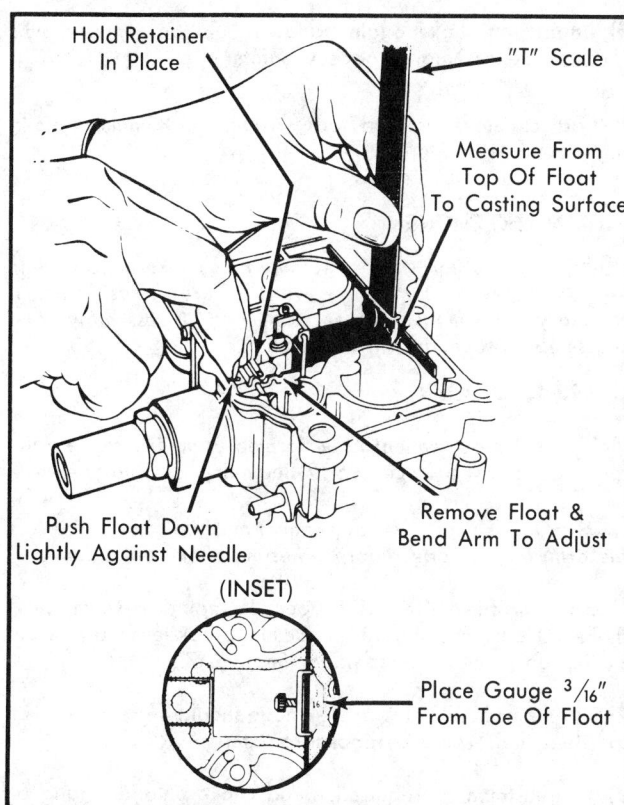

Fig. 2 Adjusting Float Level

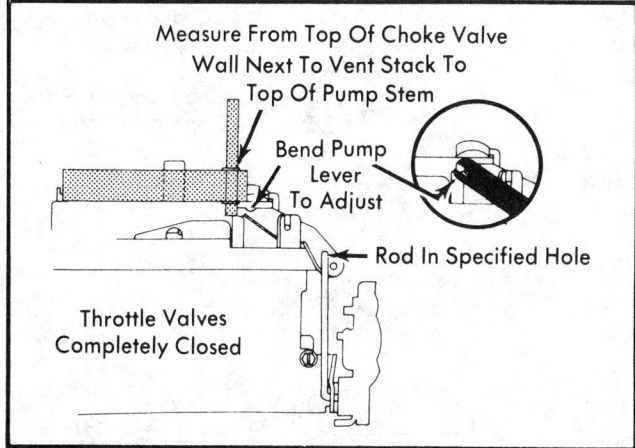

Fig. 3 Adjusting Accelerator Pump

4) To adjust, support accelerator pump lever with a screwdriver and bend pump arm at point shown.

CHOKE COIL LEVER

NOTE — *Choke coil cover is retained on choke housing with rivets to prevent tampering with factory adjustments. If necessary to remove cover, refer to Disassembly and Reassembly procedures in this Section.*

1) Drill out and remove retaining rivets. Remove choke cover and thermostatic coil from choke housing. See *Fig. 4*.

2) Position fast idle speed cam follower on high step of fast idle cam.

3) Push up (counterclockwise) on choke coil tang until choke valve is closed.

4) Insert a specified drill or pin gauge in hole provided in choke housing. Choke lever inside housing should just touch drill or pin gauge.

5) To adjust, bend choke rod at point shown.

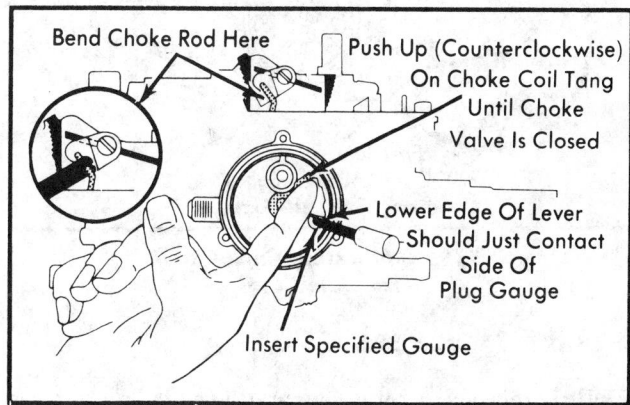

Fig. 4 Adjusting Choke Coil Lever

FAST IDLE ADJUSTMENT (BENCH SETTING)

NOTE — *This is a preliminary adjustment only. It is required to ensure that other adjustments are made with fast idle speed approximately correct. Final Cold (Fast) Idle Speed adjustment must be made with carburetor installed and engine running. See appropriate article in TUNE-UP SERVICE PROCEDURES.*

1) Position fast idle speed cam follower on highest step of fast idle cam. Back off fast idle speed screw until throttle valves are completely closed.

2) Turn fast idle screw in until it just contacts lever, then turn in an additional 4½ turns.

CHOKE ROD (FAST IDLE CAM)

NOTE — *Fast idle adjustment (bench setting) and choke coil lever must be adjusted first. This adjustment is performed using choke angle gauge, see procedure at beginning of Adjustments.*

1) Place fast idle speed cam follower on second step of fast idle cam against shoulder of highest step. See *Fig. 5.*

2) Close choke by pushing up on choke coil lever or vacuum break lever tang. Hold choke closed with a rubber band.

3) Bubble in choke angle gauge should be centered with specified angle mark opposite pointer.

4) If adjustment is required, bend tang on fast idle cam until bubble is centered.

ROCHESTER M2ME 2-BARREL (Cont.)

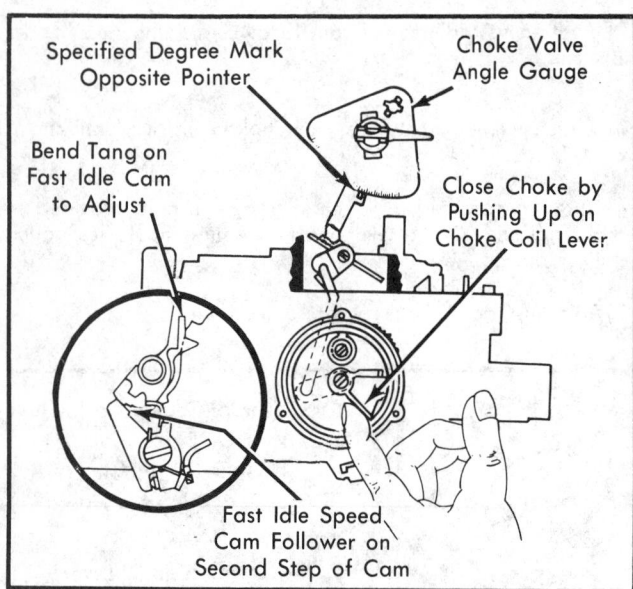

Specified Degree Mark Opposite Pointer

Choke Valve Angle Gauge

Bend Tang on Fast Idle Cam to Adjust

Close Choke by Pushing Up on Choke Coil Lever

Fast Idle Speed Cam Follower on Second Step of Cam

Fig. 5   Adjusting Choke Rod (Fast Idle Cam)

PRIMARY VACUUM BREAK

NOTE — *This adjustment is performed using the choke angle gauge, see procedure at beginning of Adjustments.*

1) Using an outside vacuum source of at least 15 in. Hg, seat primary vacuum break diaphragm. *See Fig. 6.*

NOTE — *On models equipped with air bleed, remove rubber cover from filter and plug vacuum tube with a piece of tape. If bleed hole is in end of diaphragm, plug hole in end of diaphragm with a piece of tape. Remove tape after completing adjustment.*

2) Close choke by pushing upon choke coil lever or vacuum break lever tang. Hold choke closed with a rubber band.

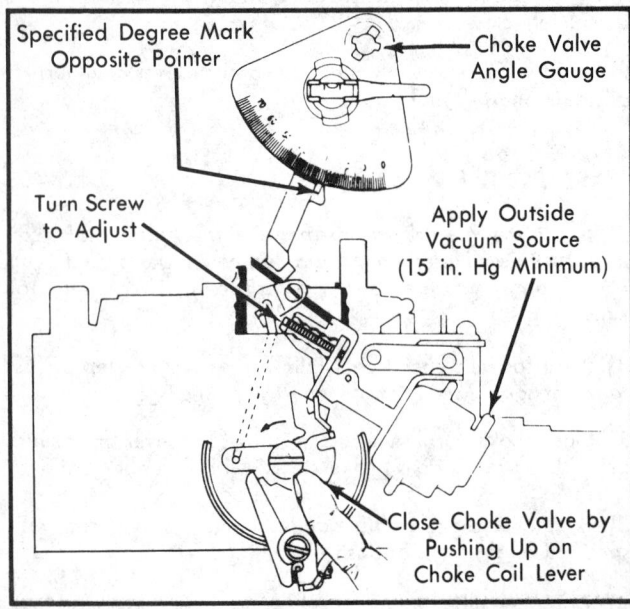

Specified Degree Mark Opposite Pointer

Choke Valve Angle Gauge

Turn Screw to Adjust

Apply Outside Vacuum Source (15 in. Hg Minimum)

Close Choke Valve by Pushing Up on Choke Coil Lever

Fig. 6   Adjusting Primary Vacuum Break

3) Bubble on choke angle gauge should be centered with specified degree mark opposite pointer.

4) If adjustment is required, turn vacuum break until bubble in angle gauge is centered.

AUTOMATIC CHOKE

NOTE — *Choke coil cover is retained on choke housing with rivets to prevent tampering with factory adjustments. If necessary to remove cover, refer to Disassembly and Reassembly procedures in this Section.*

CHOKE UNLOADER

NOTE — *This adjustment is performed using the choke valve angle gauge, see procedure at beginning of adjustments.*

NOTE — *Choke coil lever adjustment must be correct and fast idle adjustment made before adjusting choke unloader.*

1) Hold throttle valves wide open. If engine is warm, close choke valve by pushing up on vacuum break lever tang. Hold in position with a rubber band. *See Fig. 7.*

2) Bubble in choke valve angle gauge should be centered with specified degree mark opposite pointer.

3) If adjustment is required, bend choke unloader tang on throttle lever until bubble in angle gauge is centered.

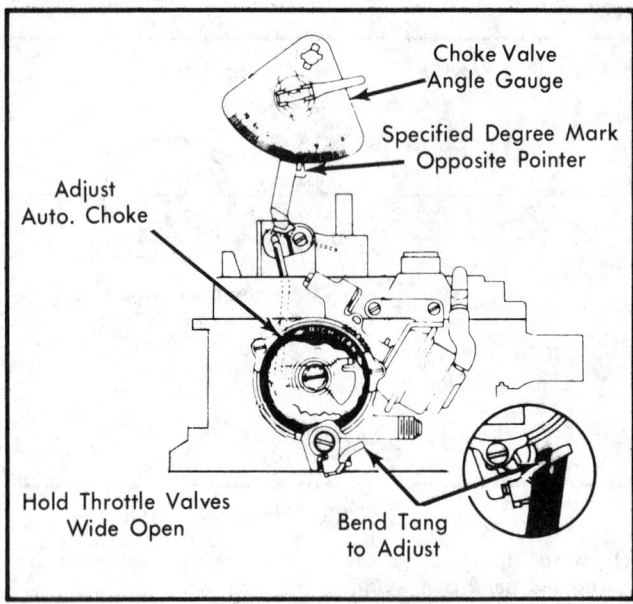

Choke Valve Angle Gauge

Specified Degree Mark Opposite Pointer

Adjust Auto. Choke

Hold Throttle Valves Wide Open

Bend Tang to Adjust

Fig. 7   Adjusting Choke Unloader

OVERHAUL

DISASSEMBLY

NOTE — *Place carburetor on a suitable working stand to avoid damaging throttle valves during overhaul.*

Air Horn — 1) Remove solenoid and bracket assembly.

2) Remove screw and upper choke from end of choke shaft.

ROCHESTER M2ME 2-BARREL (Cont.)

3) Rotate upper choke lever to remove choke rod from slot in lever.

4) Remove choke rod from lower lever inside bowl casting.

NOTE — *Hold lever outward and twist rod counterclockwise to remove.*

5) Using suitable driver, drive pump lever pivot pin inward until pump lever can be removed from air horn.

6) Remove pump lever from pump rod, noting location of pump rod for reassembly.

CAUTION — *Be careful when removing roll pin to avoid damage to pump lever bosses.*

7) Remove 9 air horn screws. Remove air horn by lifting straight up and away from float bowl.

NOTE — *Two of the 9 air horn screws are countersunk and are located next to the venturi.*

8) Remove front vacuum break assembly. Remove accelerator pump plunger stem seal by inverting air horn and removing staking that holds seal retainer in place.

9) No further disassembly of air horn is required unless choke valve or shaft is to be replaced. If so, remove 2 staked choke valve screws, choke valve and shaft.

Float Bowl — 1) Remove air horn gasket.

NOTE — *When lifting gasket tab from under power piston hanger, use care not to bend springs holding main metering rods.*

2) Remove pump plunger and return spring from pump well.

3) Remove power piston and metering rods by depressing piston stem and allowing it to snap free. Repeat if necessary.

CAUTION — *Do not use pliers to remove power piston.*

4) Remove power piston spring from well.

CAUTION — *The A.P.T. metering rod adjustment screw is preset at factory. Do not change this adjustment. If float bowl is to be replaced, new bowl will already have a preset A.P.T. screw installed.*

5) Disconnect tension spring from top of each metering rod. Rotate rods to remove from hanger. Note position of rods for reassembly.

6) Remove plastic filler block over float valve.

7) Remove float and float needle by pulling up on retaining pin. Remove needle seat and gasket with suitable tool (J-22769).

8) Remove main metering jets only if necessary.

9) Remove pump discharge check ball retainer and check ball. Remove pump well fill slot only if necessary.

10) Align a .159″ (No. 21) drill on choke cover retaining rivet and drill only enough to remove rivet head. Repeat for remaining rivets. Remove cover and coil assembly. Remove pieces of rivets from choke housing.

11) Remove screw and washer inside choke housing and remove housing assembly from float bowl.

12) Invert float bowl and remove lower choke lever.

13) Remove coil lever screw at end of shaft inside choke housing. Remove coil lever from flats on choke shaft.

14) Remove intermediate choke shaft from housing by sliding outward.

15) Remove fast idle cam from choke shaft.

CAUTION — *If housing is to be soaked in solvent, remove cup seal from inside choke housing shaft hole. Remove cup seal from insert to clean float bowl. Do not remove insert.*

16) Remove fuel inlet nut, gasket, check valve filter assembly, and spring.

17) Remove throttle body from float bowl.

18) Remove throttle body-to-bowl insulator gasket.

Throttle Body — 1) Remove accelerator pump rod from throttle lever.

NOTE — *It is not necessary to disassemble throttle body any further. Do not remove idle mixture screw plugs unless it is necessary to replace mixture screws or cleaning and air pressure fails to clean idle mixture passages. If necessary to remove, proceed as follows:*

2) Using a hacksaw, make 2 parallel cuts in throttle body on either side of locator points beneath the idle mixture needle plug (manifold side). Cuts should reach down to steel plug, but should not extend more than $\frac{1}{8}$″ beyond locator points.

3) Place a flat punch at a point near the ends of saw marks in throttle body. Holding punch at a 45° angle, drive casting away until steel plug is exposed.

4) Holding a center punch vertically, drive it into steel plug. Angle center punch and drive plug out of casting. Hardened plug will break rather than remain intact.

5) Remove enough of plug to allow mixture screw adjusting tool (J-28706) or a thin walled $\frac{3}{16}$″ deep socket to be used to remove mixture screws and springs. Remove mixture screws and springs.

CLEANING & INSPECTION

- Use a regular carburetor cleaning solution. Soak components long enough to thoroughly clean all surfaces and passages of foreign matter.

- Do not soak any components containing rubber, leather or plastic.

- Remove any residue after cleaning by rinsing components in a suitable solvent.

- Blow out all passages with dry compressed air.

1981 Rochester Carburetors

ROCHESTER M2ME 2-BARREL (Cont.)

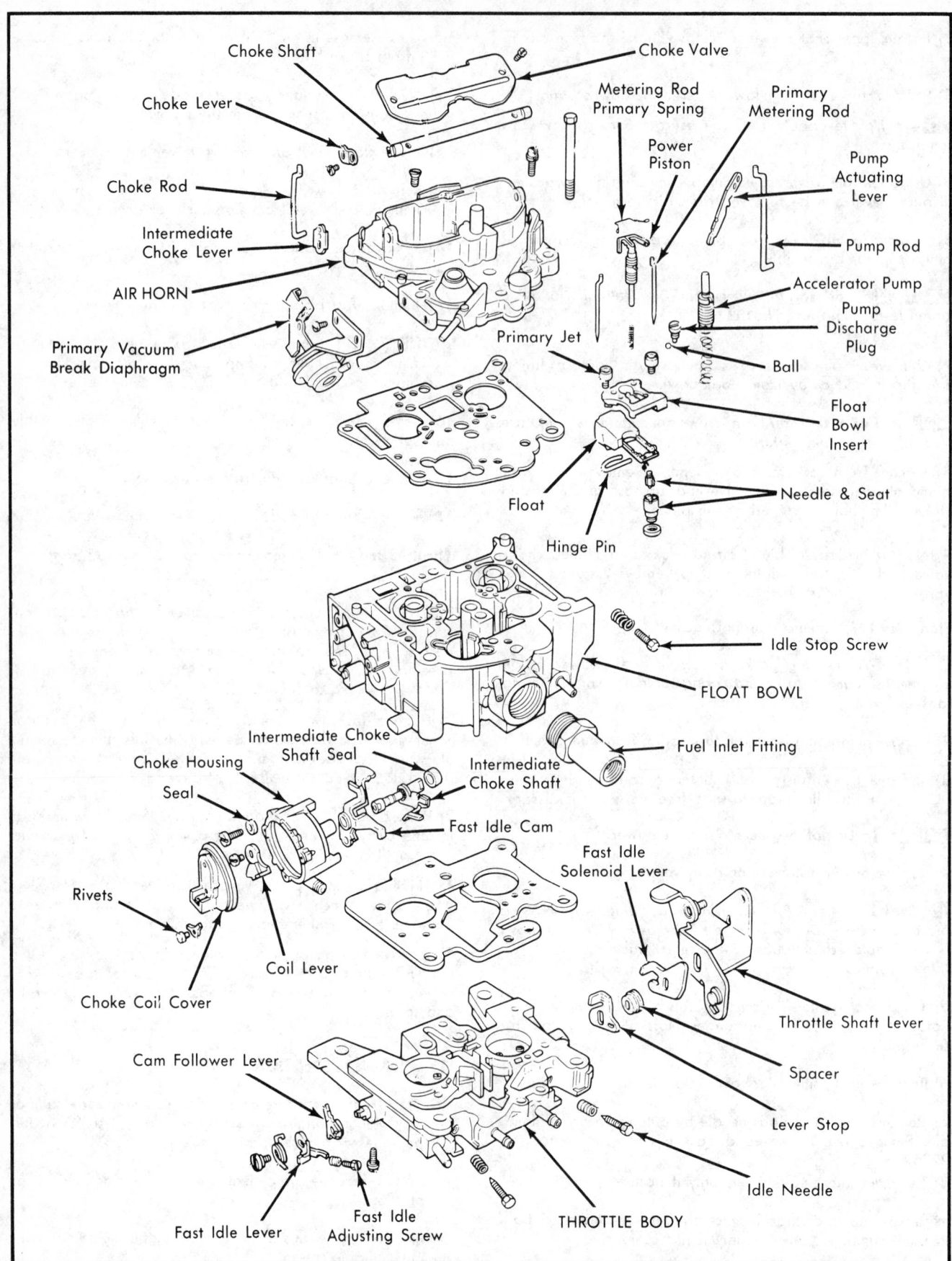

Choke Shaft

Choke Valve

Choke Lever

Metering Rod
Primary Spring

Primary
Metering Rod

Choke Rod

Power
Piston

Pump
Actuating
Lever

Intermediate
Choke Lever

Pump Rod

AIR HORN

Accelerator Pump

Pump
Discharge
Plug

Primary Vacuum
Break Diaphragm

Primary Jet

Ball

Float
Bowl
Insert

Float

Needle & Seat

Hinge Pin

Idle Stop Screw

FLOAT BOWL

Intermediate Choke
Shaft Seal

Fuel Inlet Fitting

Choke Housing

Intermediate
Choke Shaft

Seal

Fast Idle Cam

Fast Idle
Solenoid Lever

Rivets

Throttle Shaft Lever

Coil Lever

Spacer

Choke Coil Cover

Lever Stop

Cam Follower Lever

Idle Needle

Fast Idle Lever

Fast Idle
Adjusting Screw

THROTTLE BODY

Fig. 8 Exploded View of Rochester Model M2ME Carburetor

ROCHESTER M2ME 2-BARREL (Cont.)

REASSEMBLY

NOTE — *Use new gaskets and seals. Make sure that new gaskets fit correctly and that all holes and slots are punched through and correctly located.*

To reassemble carburetor, reverse disassembly procedures and note the following:

1) Inside thermostatic choke coil lever is properly aligned when both inside and outside levers face toward fuel inlet.

2) The intermediate choke shaft lever and fast idle cam are correctly aligned when the tang on lever is beneath fast idle cam.

3) When installing fuel inlet needle valve pull clip over edge of flat on float arm, do not hook clip in holes in float arm.

NOTE — *If choke coil cover was removed, it will be necessary to install service rivet retaining kit. Before installing cover, place fast idle screw on high step of fast idle cam. Align notch in cover with raised boss on housing cover flange and install rivets. Do not use a gasket between choke housing and electric choke assembly, as a ground contact is needed for choke assembly.*

4) Place fast idle screw on high step of fast idle cam. Install choke coil cover, aligning notch in cover with raised boss on housing cover flange.

5) Install 9 air horn screws and tighten evenly and in correct sequence. *See Fig. 9.*

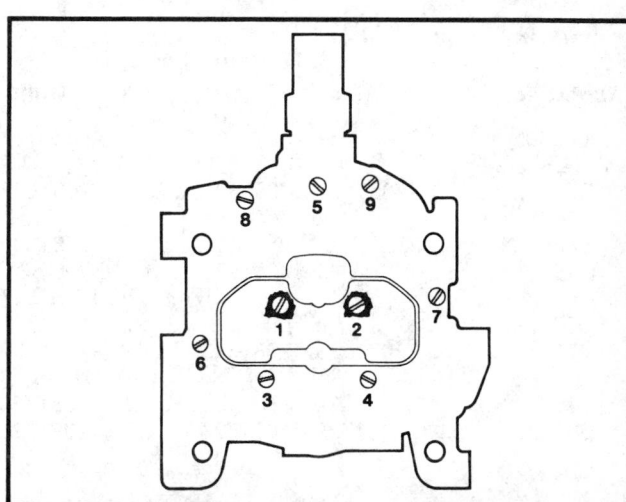

Fig. 9   Air Horn Tightening Sequence

CARBURETOR ADJUSTMENT SPECIFICATIONS								
Application	Float Level Setting	Accelerator Lever Setting	Pump Hole Setting	Choke Coil Lever Setting	Choke Rod Setting	Primary Vac. Break Setting	Auto. Choke Setting	Choke Unloader Setting
17081101	13/32"	5/16"	Inner	.120"	38°	25°	TR	38°
17081103	13/32"	5/16"	Inner	.120"	38°	25°	TR	38°
17081142	13/32"	5/16"	Inner	.120"	38°	25°	TR	38°
17081143	13/32"	5/16"	Inner	.120"	38°	25°	TR	38°
17081144	13/32"	5/16"	Inner	.120"	38°	25°	TR	38°
17081145	13/32"	5/16"	Inner	.120"	38°	25°	TR	38°

TR — Tamper Resistant.

ROCHESTER MODELS 2SE & E2SE 2-BARREL

NOTE — *SERIES IDENTIFICATION: The vehicle numbers used in this article have been abbreviated for common reference to both Chevrolet and GMC models. Chevrolet models use numerical designations as listed; GMC models are identified as follows: 10 = 1500; 20 = 2500; 30 = 3500.*

CARBURETOR APPLICATION

CHEVROLET & GMC

	Rochester Carb. No.	
Application	Man. Trans.	Auto. Trans.
4.1L (250")		
Federal (2SE)		
C10	17081621, 17081625	17081622
	17081629	
C20	17081625	17081630
G10/20	17081623, 17081627	17081624,
	17081626, 17081627	
G30	17081725	17081725
K10	17081625, 17081633	17081630
California (2SE)		
C10	17081721	17081720
G10/20	17081725, 17081727	17081726

JEEP

	Jeep Carb. No.	
Application	Man. Trans.	Auto. Trans.
2.5L (151")		
Federal (2SE)	17081790	17081791
California (E2SE)	17081796	17081797

CARBURETOR IDENTIFICATION

The Rochester 2SE and E2SE carburetor numbers are stamped vertically on the float bowl next to the vacuum tube. If float bowl is replaced, follow manufacturer's instructions contained in service package, so that part number is transferred to new float bowl.

DESCRIPTION

The Rochester models 2SE & E2SE are 2-stage, 2-barrel downdraft carburetors. The primary stage consists of a triple venturi with a 35 mm bore. The secondary stage has a 46 mm bore and is equipped with an air valve with a single tapered metering rod. Both are equipped with integral electronically activated chokes, a choke vacuum break diaphragm and an idle speed solenoid.

The E2SE model is used in conjunction with the Computer Controlled Catalytic Converter System (C-4). The carburetor is equipped with an electrically actuated mixture control solenoid mounted in the air horn. Fuel metering is controlled by the mixture control solenoid plunger opening and closing and fuel passage to the main metering jet.

This opening and closing action causes a variable restriction of fuel to the main metering circuit, changing air/fuel ratio. Also, air metered to the idle system is controlled by the movement of the mixture control solenoid plunger.

The solenoid is activated by an electronic signal from the Electronic Control Module (ECM). The ECM responds to a signal from the oxygen sensor in the exhaust, then energizes the

solenoid to move the plunger down to a lean position or de-energizes solenoid to move plunger up to a rich position. Air metered (by solenoid plunger) to idle system is controlled by an idle air bleed valve located in the air horn. This valve follows movement of the mixture control solenoid.

On E2SE models, a Throttle Position Sensor (TPS) is used to signal the ECM of throttle position changes as they occur. When throttle position is changed, a tang on the pump lever moves TPS plunger. This signals the ECM to hold the last known air/fuel ratio to aid in throttle response.

ADJUSTMENT

HOT (SLOW) IDLE RPM

See appropriate article in TUNE-UP SERVICE PROCEDURES.

COLD (FAST) IDLE RPM

See appropriate article in TUNE-UP SERVICE PROCEDURES.

IDLE MIXTURE

See appropriate article in TUNE-UP SERVICE PROCEDURES.

IDLE AIR BLEED VALVE (E2SE ONLY)

See appropriate article in TUNE-UP SERVICE PROCEDURES.

ANGLE GAUGE ADJUSTMENT TOOL

Manufacturer recommends that some carburetor adjustments be performed using a choke valve angle gauge (Kent-Moore tool no. J-26701). While preparations and actual adjustments may vary with each individual adjustment, the procedure for using the angle gauge to check the choke valve angle remains the same. Use the following procedure to perform adjustments requiring the use of the choke angle gauge.

1) Rotate degree scale on angle gauge so that 0° mark is opposite pointer.

2) With choke valve closed, place angle gauge magnet squarely on choke valve.

3) Rotate leveling bubble on angle gauge until it is centered.

4) Rotate degree scale until specified degree mark is opposite pointer.

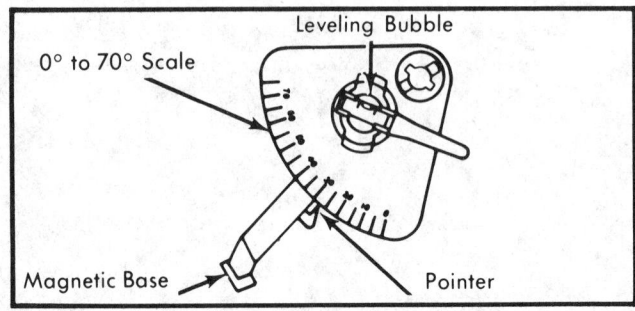

Fig. 1   Choke Valve Angle Gauge

5) Now perform individual adjustment preparations as outlined in the following carburetor adjustments requiring angle

ROCHESTER MODELS 2SE & E2SE 2-BARREL (Cont.)

gauge. If bubble is centered, adjustment is correct. If not, adjust carburetor as outlined.

FLOAT LEVEL

1) Remove air horn and gasket from float bowl. Hold float retainer firmly down while pushing float down against needle. See Fig. 2.

2) Position a "T" scale over toe of float at point furtherest away from float hinge. Measure distance from float bowl casting to float.

3) To adjust, remove float and bend float arm. Check to make sure float is correctly aligned after adjustment.

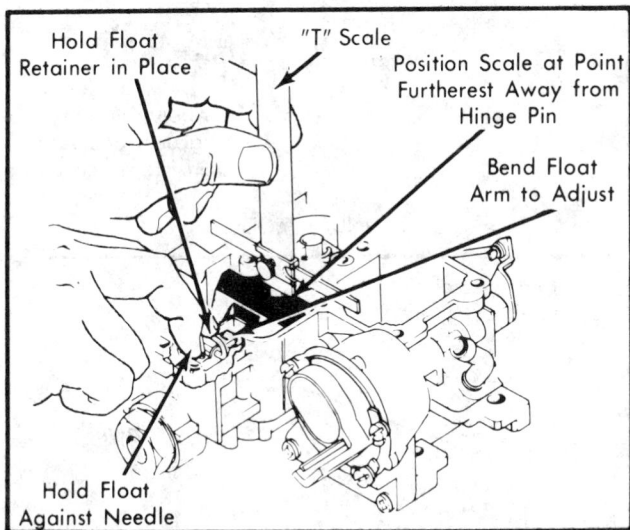

Fig. 2 Adjusting Float Level

ACCELERATOR PUMP

NOTE — *Accelerator pump setting should not be changed from original factory setting unless measurement shows a variation from specification. Do not attempt to bend pump lever unless absolutely necessary as it is made of hardened steel and extremely difficult to bend.*

1) Close throttle valves completely. Make sure fast idle speed screw is off fast idle cam. See Fig. 3.

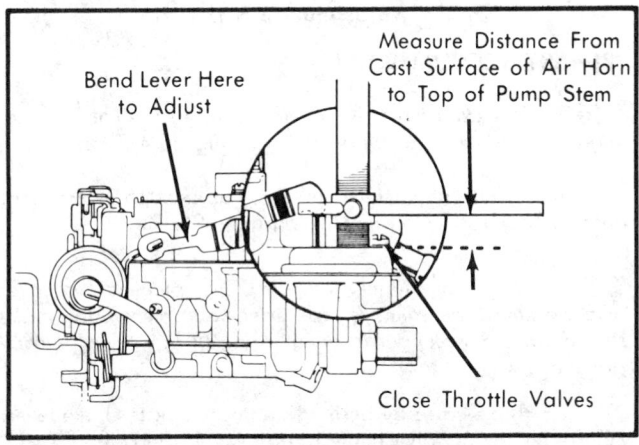

Fig. 3 Adjusting Accelerator Pump

2) Using a "T" scale, measure accelerator pump specified distance from cast surface of air horn to top of pump stem.

3) To adjust, remove pump lever screw and washer. Remove pump lever by rotating lever and removing from pump rod. Secure lever in a vise and bend end of lever at small segment.

4) Install pump lever and tighten screw. Recheck specified distance. Open and close throttle and check for freedom of movement.

CHOKE COIL LEVER

NOTE — *Choke coil cover is retained on housing with rivets to prevent tampering with factory adjustment. If necessary to remove cover, refer to Disassembly and Reassembly procedures in this Section.*

1) Remove choke thermostatic cover from choke housing. Place fast idle speed screw on high step of fast idle cam. See Fig. 4.

2) Push in on intermediate choke lever until choke valve is fully closed.

3) Insert a specified drill or pin gauge in hole provided in choke housing. Choke lever inside housing should just touch drill or pin gauge.

4) To adjust, bend intermediate choke rod at point shown in illustration. Reinstall choke cover and adjust.

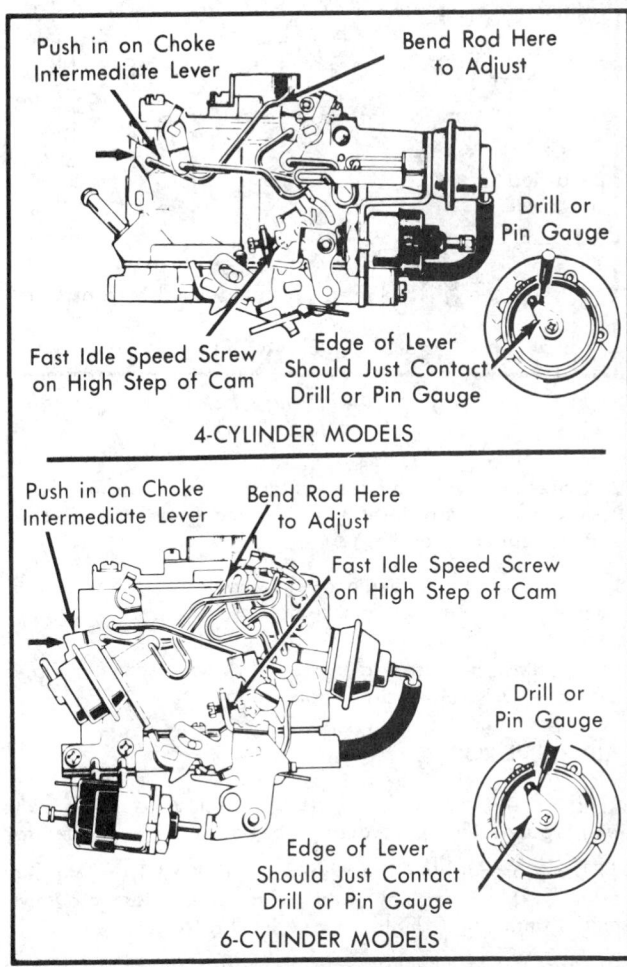

Fig. 4 Adjusting Choke Coil Lever

ROCHESTER MODELS 2SE & E2SE 2-BARREL (Cont.)

CHOKE ROD
(FAST IDLE CAM)

NOTE — *Before adjusting choke rod, choke coil lever adjustment must be correct, and fast idle adjustment made. Use an angle gauge adjustment tool to perform adjustments. See Angle Gauge Adjustment Tool at beginning of Adjustments.*

1) Place fast idle speed screw on second step of fast idle cam against shoulder of highest step. See *Fig. 5*.

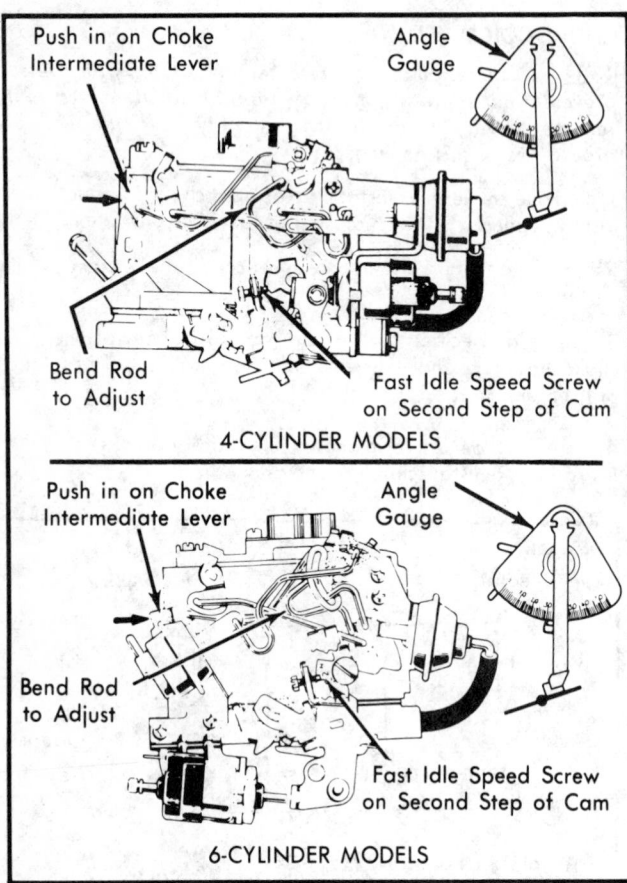

Fig. 5 **Adjusting Choke Rod**
(Fast Idle Cam)

2) Close choke valve by pushing on intermediate choke lever. Push vacuum break lever toward open choke until lever is against rear tang on choke lever.

3) Bubble on choke angle gauge should be centered with specified degree mark opposite pointer.

4) To adjust, bend fast idle cam rod at point shown in *Fig. 5* until bubble is centered in angle gauge.

AIR VALVE ROD

NOTE — *This adjustment is made by using the choke valve angle gauge. See procedure at beginning of Adjustments.*

1) Using an outside vacuum source of at least 15 in. Hg, seat primary choke vacuum break diaphragm. Close air valve, mount and adjust angle gauge. See *Fig. 6*.

2) Apply light opening pressure to air valve shaft. Set to specified angle by bending air valve rod at a point near its

connection to primary vacuum break (models equipped with primary vacuum break only) or at a point near its connection to air valve lever (models equipped with primary and secondary vacuum breaks).

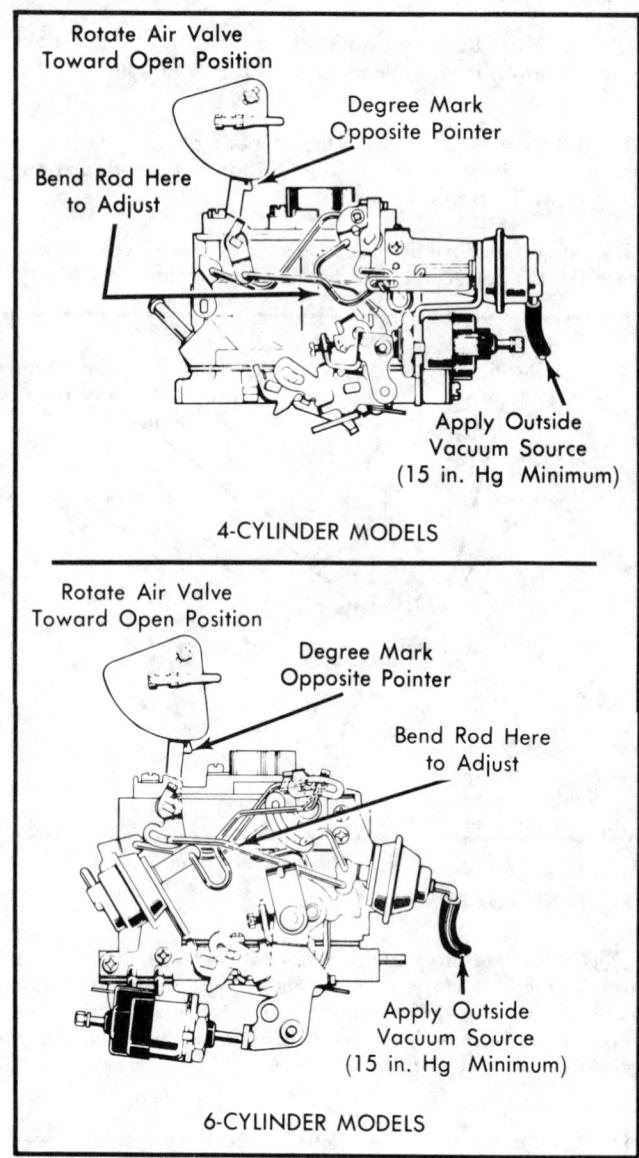

Fig. 6 **Adjusting Air Valve Rod**

PRIMARY VACUUM BREAK

NOTE — *This adjustment is performed using the choke valve angle gauge, see procedure at beginning of Adjustments.*

1) Using an outside vacuum source of at least 15 in. Hg, seat primary choke vacuum break diaphragm. See *Fig. 7*.

NOTE — *On delay models with air bleed, plug hole in cover with masking tape. Remove tape after adjustment. Also, make sure diaphragm plunger bucking spring (if equipped) is compressed.*

2) Close choke valve by pushing on intermediate choke lever. Bubble on choke valve angle gauge should be centered with specified degree mark opposite pointer.

ROCHESTER MODELS 2SE & E2SE 2-BARREL (Cont.)

3) For adjustment on 4-cylinder models, bend primary vacuum break rod at point illustrated until angle gauge bubble is centered.

NOTE — *Prior to adjustment on 6-cylinder models, vacuum break must be removed from carburetor and adjustment screw access cover ground off. Place bracket in a vise, carefully grind off adjusting screw access cap, and reinstall vacuum break on carburetor.*

4) For 6-cylinder model adjustment, use a 1/8" hex wrench. Turn screw in or out until bubble of angle gauge is centered. Apply a bead of sealer to over screw to seal adjustment.

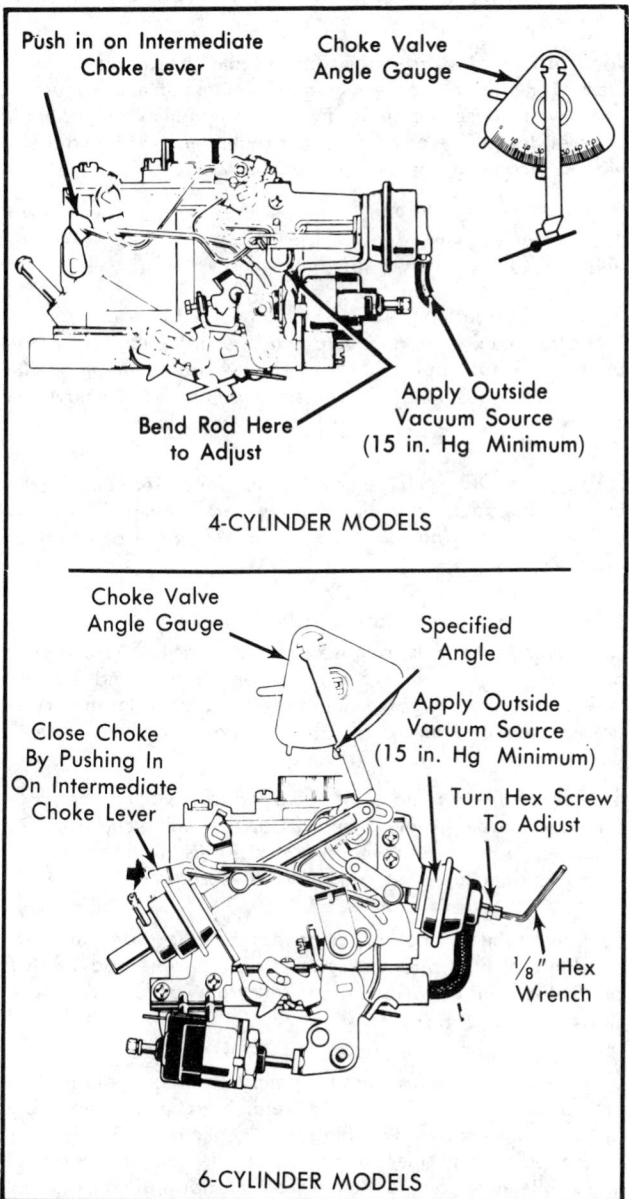

4-CYLINDER MODELS

6-CYLINDER MODELS

Fig. 7   Primary Vacuum Break Adjustment

SECONDARY VACUUM BREAK

NOTE — *This adjustment is made using the choke valve angle gauge, see procedure at beginning of Adjustments.*

1) Using an outside vacuum source of at least 15 in. Hg , seat secondary choke vacuum break diaphragm. *See Fig. 8.*

2) Close choke valve by pushing on intermediate choke lever. Make sure bucking spring on diaphragm plunger (if equipped) is fully compressed and seated.

3) Bubble on choke valve angle gauge should be centered with specified degree mark opposite pointer.

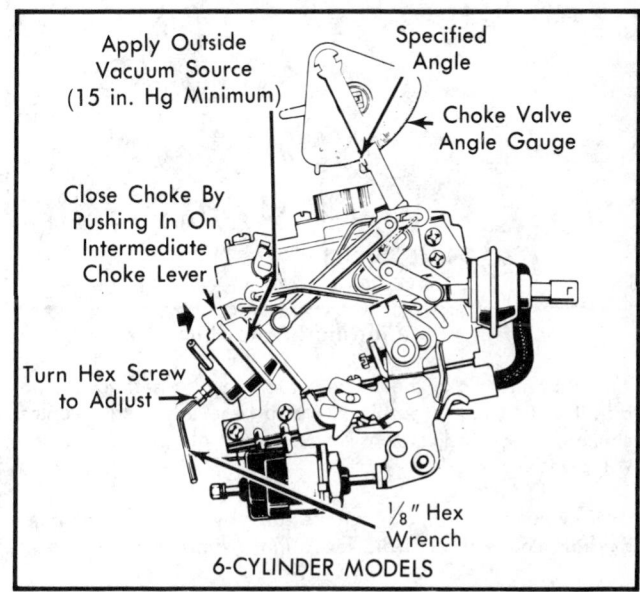

6-CYLINDER MODELS

Fig. 8   Adjusting Secondary (Rear) Vacuum Break

NOTE — *Prior to adjustment, vacuum break bracket must be removed from carburetor and adjustment screw access cover ground off. Place bracket in a vise, carefully grind off adjusting screw access cap, and install vacuum break bracket back on carburetor.*

4) After access screw cover has been ground off, place an accelerator pump plunger cup (Varajet or equivalent) over screw to plug end cover.

5) Adjust vacuum break using a 1/8" hex wrench. Turn adjusting screw in or out until bubble in angle gauge is centered. Remove accelerator pump plunger cup from adjusting screw and apply a bead of epoxy sealer to cover screw and seal adjustment.

AUTOMATIC CHOKE

NOTE — *Choke coil cover is retained on housing with rivets to prevent tampering with factory adjustment. If necessary to remove cover, refer to Disassembly and Reassembly procedures in this Section.*

CHOKE UNLOADER

NOTE — *This adjustment is performed using the choke valve angle gauge, see procedure at beginning of adjustments.*

ROCHESTER MODELS 2SE & E2SE 2-BARREL (Cont.)

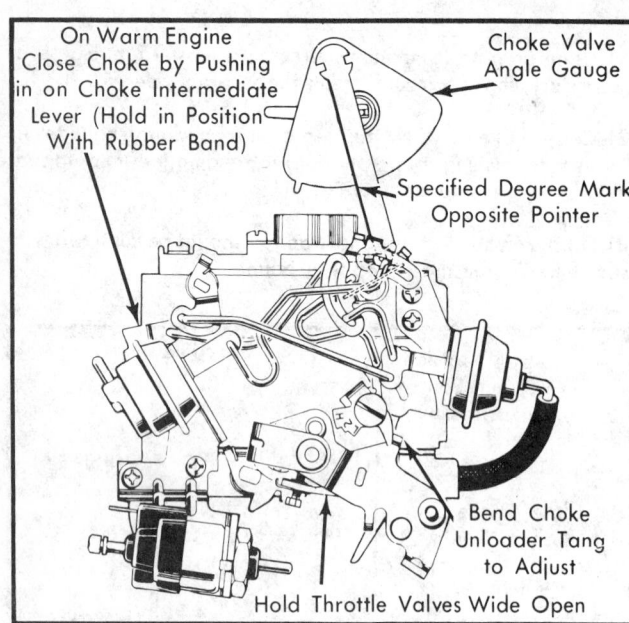

On Warm Engine Close Choke by Pushing in on Choke Intermediate Lever (Hold in Position With Rubber Band)

Choke Valve Angle Gauge

Specified Degree Mark Opposite Pointer

Bend Choke Unloader Tang to Adjust

Hold Throttle Valves Wide Open

Fig. 9   Adjusting Choke Unloader

1) Automatic choke should be set to specified setting. Do not adjust setting unless carburetor is to be overhauled or unless choke coil lever adjustment is necessary. Hold primary throttle valve wide open. See Fig. 9.

2) If engine is warm, close choke valve by pushing in on intermediate choke lever. Hold in position with a rubber band.

3) Place vacuum break lever against rear tang on choke lever. To adjust, bend tang on throttle lever until bubble in angle gauge is centered.

SECONDARY LOCK OUT

1) Hold choke valve wide open by pushing out on choke intermediate lever. See Fig. 10.

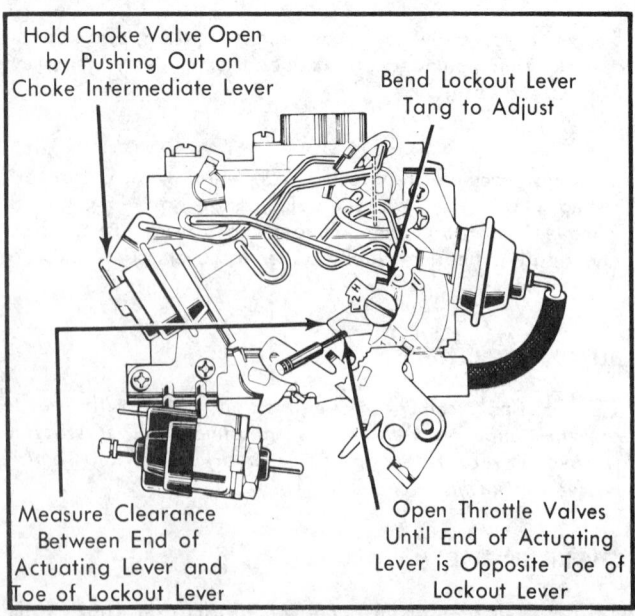

Hold Choke Valve Open by Pushing Out on Choke Intermediate Lever

Bend Lockout Lever Tang to Adjust

Measure Clearance Between End of Actuating Lever and Toe of Lockout Lever

Open Throttle Valves Until End of Actuating Lever is Opposite Toe of Lockout Lever

Fig. 10   Adjusting Secondary Throttle Lockout

2) Open throttle valves until end of secondary actuating lever is opposite toe of lockout lever.

3) Measure specified clearance between end of actuating lever and toe of lockout lever. Measurement can be checked using a drill or pin gauge of specified size.

4) To adjust, bend lockout lever tang contacting fast idle cam.

OVERHAUL

DISASSEMBLY

NOTE — *Before disassembling carburetor, mount unit in a suitable holding fixture to prevent damage to throttle valves or linkage.*

Air Horn — 1) Bend back tabs on idle speed solenoid lock washer. Remove large solenoid retaining nut. Care must be taken when loosening nut to avoid damaging linkage, solenoid bracket, throttle lever or vacuum break. Remove solenoid and washer from bracket.

NOTE — *On models with Idle Speed Control, remove control bracket (to vacuum break) attaching screws. Remove control and bracket as an assembly.*

2) On 2SE models (NOT USING a clip to secure the accelerator pump rod), remove pump lever retaining screw from air horn. Rotate pump lever to remove from pump rod. On E2SE models (using a clip to secure pump rod), remove clip and remove pump rod from hole in pump lever.

CAUTION — *DO NOT remove pump lever retaining screw from E2SE models using clip as pump rod retainer. Pump lever and washer must not be removed from air horn assembly on these models.*

3) Remove hose from vacuum break assembly or assemblies. On 6-cylinder models, remove bracket attaching screws from air horn only. Then, rotate vacuum break and bracket assembly to disengage vacuum break link from slot in vacuum break lever, and air valve rod from slot in air valve lever.

4) If necessary to remove air valve rod from vacuum break on 6-cylinder models, remove and discard retaining clip from end of air valve. New retaining clip must be used on reassembly. Plastic bushing used on rod may be reused.

5) On 6-cylinder models, remove secondary vacuum break bracket assembly attaching screws from throttle body. Rotate bracket to remove vacuum break link from vacuum break lever slot.

6) Remove and discard retaining clip from intermediate choke rod at choke lever. Use a new retaining clip at reassembly. Remove choke rod and bushing from choke lever. Bushing may be reused. If equipped, remove hot idle compensator valve screws. Remove valve and seal from air horn, discarding seal. Valve removal is necessary to gain access to short air horn-to-bowl attaching screw.

7) On E2SE models, remove 3 mixture control solenoid screws and remove mixture control solenoid using a light twisting motion. Remove and discard solenoid gasket, plunger seal and plunger seal retainer.

ROCHESTER MODELS 2SE & E2SE 2-BARREL (Cont.)

8) Remove all air horn-to-float bowl screws and lock washers. Remove vent and screen assembly. Rotate fast idle cam up as far as possible. Rotate air horn and tilt to disengage fast idle cam rod from slot in fast idle cam and pump rod from hole in pump lever.

9) Disconnect fast idle cam rod from choke lever by aligning tang on rod with slot in lever. Lift off air horn assembly.

10) On 6-cylinder models, remove TPS plunger by pushing through seal in air horn. Remove seal retainer and seal. Remove accelerator pump plunger seal from air horn.

NOTE — *Use fingers only (no tools) when removing plunger to prevent damage to sealing surface. Use care in removing plunger seal retainer and plunger stem seal retainer to prevent damage to air horn. Discard seals and retainers.*

11) It is not necessary to remove choke valve and shaft unless bent or damaged. Choke valve screws are staked in place. Staking must be removed before screws are removed.

Float Bowl — 1) Remove air horn gasket. Remove pump plunger and pump spring from pump well. Remove plastic filler block from float valve.

2) Remove float assembly and float valve, pulling up on retaining pin. Remove float needle seat, gasket and extended metering jet from float bowl. Use suitable tool (J-22769) or screwdriver that fully fits slot in top of jet.

3) On E2SE models, push up from bottom on electrical connector and remove TPS and connector from float bowl. Remove spring from bottom of TPS well in bowl. On 2SE models, press down on power piston stem and allow it to snap up. Repeat this until plastic retainer is dislodged and remove power piston and metering rod assembly.

4) Remove spring from power piston bore. If necessary to remove metering rod from hanger, compress spring on metering rod and align groove on rod with slot in holder. Care must be taken not to damage tip of metering rod.

5) Remove main metering jet using a screwdriver that fits tight in groove. Using a small slide hammer, remove plastic retainer holding pump discharge spring and check ball in place in float bowl. Discard retainer.

6) If it is necessary to remove the tamper-resistant choke cover and coil assembly, align a .125" (1/8") drill on choke cover retaining rivets and drill only enough to remove rivet heads. Remove rivets, choke cover and coil assembly. Remove screw from end of intermediate choke shaft in choke housing. Remove choke coil lever from shaft.

7) Slide intermediate choke shaft out of float bowl. Remove choke housing screws and remove choke housing. Remove fuel inlet nut, gasket, check valve/filter and spring.

8) Remove 4 screws securing throttle body to float bowl. Remove throttle body. Remove throttle body insulator gasket.

Throttle Body — 1) Hold throttle valves wide open. Disengage pump rod from throttle lever by rotating rod until tang on rod aligns with slot in lever.

2) Do not remove plug covering idle mixture screw unless it is necessary to replace mixture screw or normal soaking and air pressure fails to clean idle mixture passages. Remove curb idle and fast idle speed screws and springs if necessary.

NOTE — *It is not necessary to disassemble throttle body any further. Throttle valve screws are permanently staked in. Do not remove idle mixture screw plug unless it is necessary to replace mixture screw or cleaning and air pressure fails to clean idle mixture passage. If necessary to remove, proceed as follows:*

3) Invert throttle body and position on a holding fixture with manifold side up. Using a small hacksaw, make 2 small cuts, one on either side of mixture screw plug location. Position a small flat punch on throttle body between cuts.

4) Drive punch down and break out portion of throttle body between the 2 cuts. Hold punch at a 45° angle and drive out hardened steel plug.

NOTE — *Plug will shatter when struck. Remove loose pieces to allow the use of adjusting tool (J-28706) or thin walled deep 3/16" socket to remove adjusting screw and spring.*

5) Turn mixture screw in carefully, counting turns needed to seat screw. Record number to be used in reassembly, then remove mixture screw.

CLEANING & INSPECTION

- Use a regular carburetor cleaning solution. Soak components long enough to thoroughly clean all surfaces and passages of foreign matter.

- Do not soak any components containing rubber, leather or plastic. Definitely do not soak idle speed solenoid or control, mixture control solenoid, throttle position sensor, electric choke, diaphragms, pump plunger and plastic filler block. Plastic bushings in end of vacuum break link and air valve rod on 4-cylinder models will withstand normal cleaning.

- Remove any residue after cleaning by rinsing components in a suitable solvent.

- Blow out all passages with dry compressed air.

REASSEMBLY

NOTE — *Use new gaskets and seals. Make sure new gaskets fit correctly and all holes are punched through and properly located.*

To reassemble carburetor, reverse disassembly procedure and note the following:

1) Install fuel inlet needle pull clip over edge of flat on float arm facing float. Do not hook clip in holes in float arm.

1981 Rochester Carburetors

ROCHESTER MODELS 2SE & E2SE 2-BARREL (Cont.)

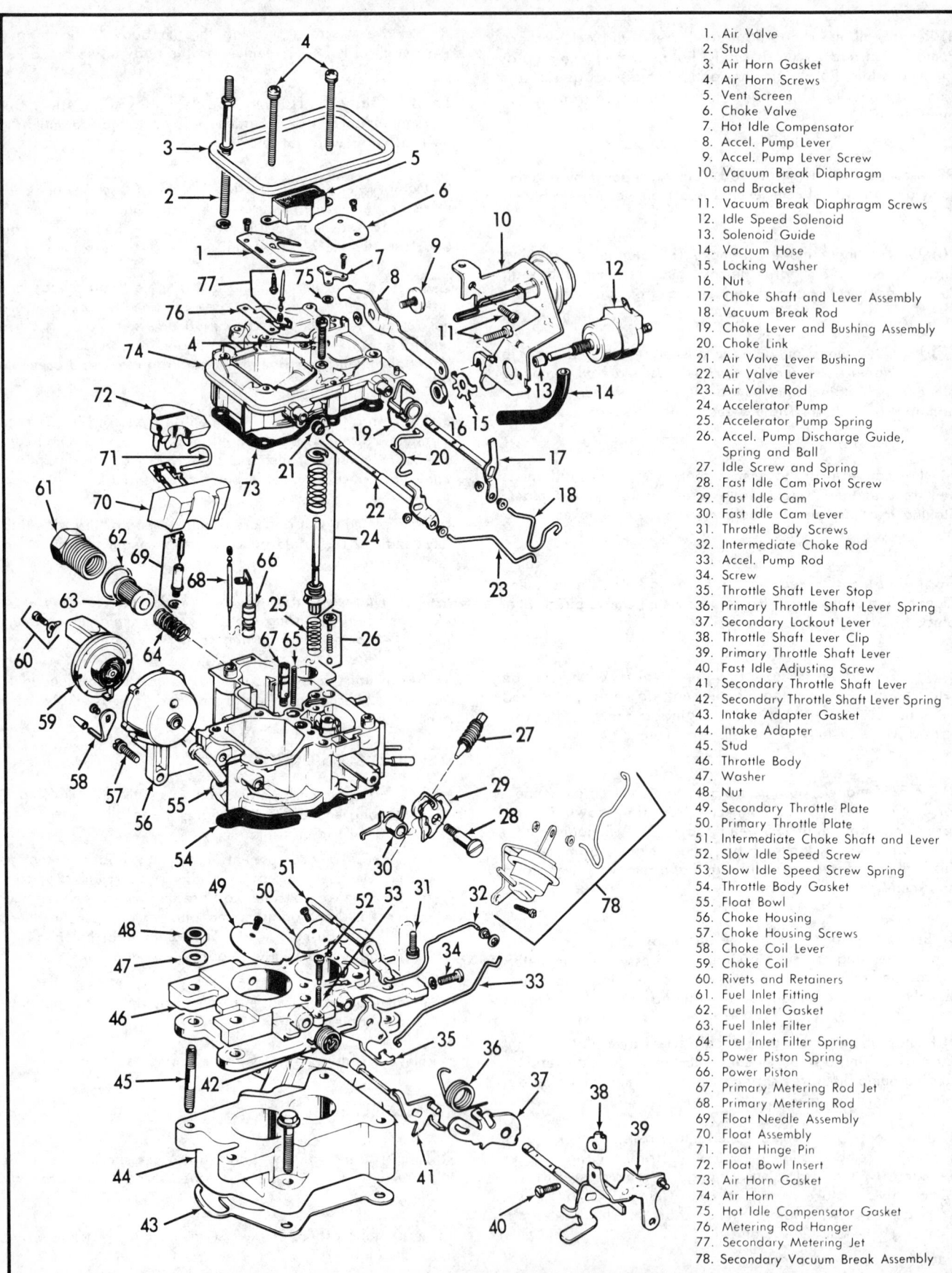

1. Air Valve
2. Stud
3. Air Horn Gasket
4. Air Horn Screws
5. Vent Screen
6. Choke Valve
7. Hot Idle Compensator
8. Accel. Pump Lever
9. Accel. Pump Lever Screw
10. Vacuum Break Diaphragm and Bracket
11. Vacuum Break Diaphragm Screws
12. Idle Speed Solenoid
13. Solenoid Guide
14. Vacuum Hose
15. Locking Washer
16. Nut
17. Choke Shaft and Lever Assembly
18. Vacuum Break Rod
19. Choke Lever and Bushing Assembly
20. Choke Link
21. Air Valve Lever Bushing
22. Air Valve Lever
23. Air Valve Rod
24. Accelerator Pump
25. Accelerator Pump Spring
26. Accel. Pump Discharge Guide, Spring and Ball
27. Idle Screw and Spring
28. Fast Idle Cam Pivot Screw
29. Fast Idle Cam
30. Fast Idle Cam Lever
31. Throttle Body Screws
32. Intermediate Choke Rod
33. Accel. Pump Rod
34. Screw
35. Throttle Shaft Lever Stop
36. Primary Throttle Shaft Lever Spring
37. Secondary Lockout Lever
38. Throttle Shaft Lever Clip
39. Primary Throttle Shaft Lever
40. Fast Idle Adjusting Screw
41. Secondary Throttle Shaft Lever
42. Secondary Throttle Shaft Lever Spring
43. Intake Adapter Gasket
44. Intake Adapter
45. Stud
46. Throttle Body
47. Washer
48. Nut
49. Secondary Throttle Plate
50. Primary Throttle Plate
51. Intermediate Choke Shaft and Lever
52. Slow Idle Speed Screw
53. Slow Idle Speed Screw Spring
54. Throttle Body Gasket
55. Float Bowl
56. Choke Housing
57. Choke Housing Screws
58. Choke Coil Lever
59. Choke Coil
60. Rivets and Retainers
61. Fuel Inlet Fitting
62. Fuel Inlet Gasket
63. Fuel Inlet Filter
64. Fuel Inlet Filter Spring
65. Power Piston Spring
66. Power Piston
67. Primary Metering Rod Jet
68. Primary Metering Rod
69. Float Needle Assembly
70. Float Assembly
71. Float Hinge Pin
72. Float Bowl Insert
73. Air Horn Gasket
74. Air Horn
75. Hot Idle Compensator Gasket
76. Metering Rod Hanger
77. Secondary Metering Jet
78. Secondary Vacuum Break Assembly

Fig. 11   Exploded View of Rochester Model 2SE Carburetor (6-Cylinder Model Shown, 4-Cylinder Model Similar)

ROCHESTER MODELS 2SE & E2SE 2-BARREL (Cont.)

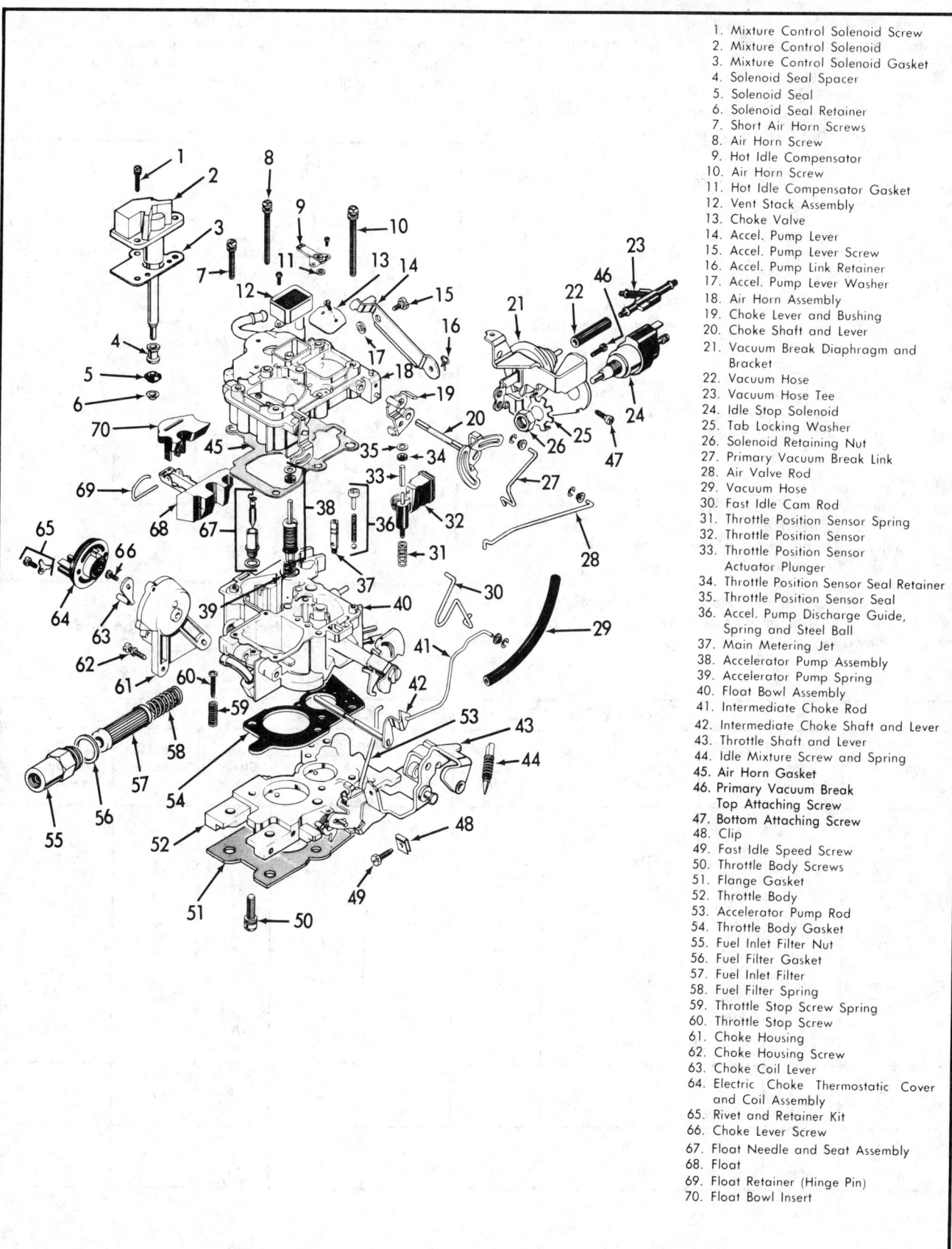

1. Mixture Control Solenoid Screw
2. Mixture Control Solenoid
3. Mixture Control Solenoid Gasket
4. Solenoid Seal Spacer
5. Solenoid Seal
6. Solenoid Seal Retainer
7. Short Air Horn Screws
8. Air Horn Screw
9. Hot Idle Compensator
10. Air Horn Screw
11. Hot Idle Compensator Gasket
12. Vent Stack Assembly
13. Choke Valve
14. Accel. Pump Lever
15. Accel. Pump Lever Screw
16. Accel. Pump Link Retainer
17. Accel. Pump Lever Washer
18. Air Horn Assembly
19. Choke Lever and Bushing
20. Choke Shaft and Lever
21. Vacuum Break Diaphragm and Bracket
22. Vacuum Hose
23. Vacuum Hose Tee
24. Idle Stop Solenoid
25. Tab Locking Washer
26. Solenoid Retaining Nut
27. Primary Vacuum Break Link
28. Air Valve Rod
29. Vacuum Hose
30. Fast Idle Cam Rod
31. Throttle Position Sensor Spring
32. Throttle Position Sensor
33. Throttle Position Sensor Actuator Plunger
34. Throttle Position Sensor Seal Retainer
35. Throttle Position Sensor Seal
36. Accel. Pump Discharge Guide, Spring and Steel Ball
37. Main Metering Jet
38. Accelerator Pump Assembly
39. Accelerator Pump Spring
40. Float Bowl Assembly
41. Intermediate Choke Rod
42. Intermediate Choke Shaft and Lever
43. Throttle Shaft and Lever
44. Idle Mixture Screw and Spring
45. Air Horn Gasket
46. Primary Vacuum Break Top Attaching Screw
47. Bottom Attaching Screw
48. Clip
49. Fast Idle Speed Screw
50. Throttle Body Screws
51. Flange Gasket
52. Throttle Body
53. Accelerator Pump Rod
54. Throttle Body Gasket
55. Fuel Inlet Filter Nut
56. Fuel Filter Gasket
57. Fuel Inlet Filter
58. Fuel Filter Spring
59. Throttle Stop Screw Spring
60. Throttle Stop Screw
61. Choke Housing
62. Choke Housing Screw
63. Choke Coil Lever
64. Electric Choke Thermostatic Cover and Coil Assembly
65. Rivet and Retainer Kit
66. Choke Lever Screw
67. Float Needle and Seat Assembly
68. Float
69. Float Retainer (Hinge Pin)
70. Float Bowl Insert

Fig. 12   Exploded View of Rochester Model E2SE Carburetor

ROCHESTER MODELS 2SE & E2SE 2-BARREL (Cont.)

2) After throttle body is installed on float bowl, make sure secondary lockout tang is in correct position to engage secondary lockout lever.

3) Install new accelerator pump discharge check ball and spring plastic retainer. Insert end of retainer in spring and place in position in float bowl. Lightly tap retainer into position until it is flush in float bowl.

4) Make sure holes in fuel filter face toward fuel inlet fitting when filter is installed.

5) Some linkage retaining clips are dished. Make sure portion of clip that bends outward is toward end of rod. Make sure clip makes full contact with rod.

6) Place fast idle screw on high step of fast idle cam. Install choke coil cover, aligning notch in cover with raised boss on housing cover flange.

NOTE — *If choke cover and coil assembly was removed from housing, a service rivet kit must be installed to restore tamper-resistant feature.*

CAUTION — *On E2SE models, be sure coil pick-up lever is located inside choke coil tang. Also, on electric chokes, the ground contact is provided by a metal plate at rear of choke cover assembly. Do not install a choke cover gasket between electric choke assembly and choke housing.*

7) Install air horn screws, noting location and type of screw for correct installation. Tighten all screws evenly, securely and in sequence shown in Fig. 13.

8) On E2SE models, install mixture control solenoid seal on solenoid stem. Using a 3/16" socket and hammer, lightly tap retainer in place, on stem, leaving a slight clearance between retainer and seal. Apply silicone grease to seal before installation of solenoid.

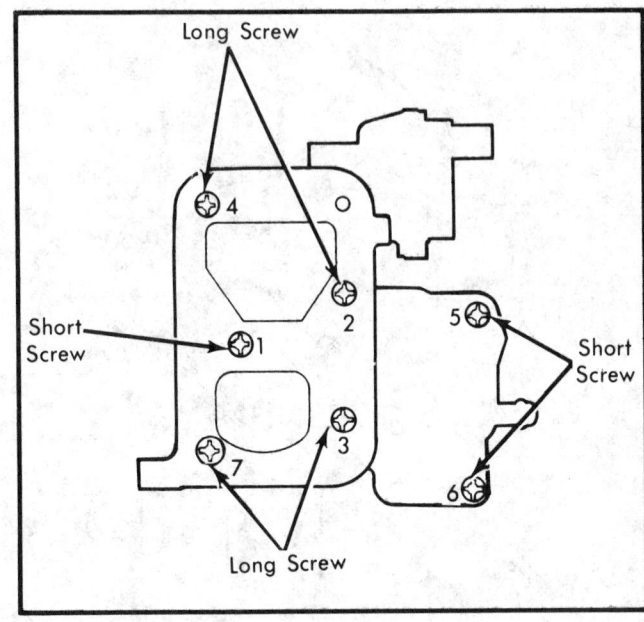

Fig. 13 Air Horn Screw Location and Tightening Sequence

						Vacuum Break				
Application	Float Level Setting	Accel. Pump Setting	Choke Coil Lever Setting	Choke Rod Setting	Air Valve Rod Setting	Primary Setting	Secondary Setting	Auto. Choke Setting	Choke Unloader Setting	Secondary Lockout Setting
GM (2SE)										
17081621	3/16"	5/8"	.085"	15°	1°	26°	38°	TR	38°	.025"
17081622	3/16"	5/8"	.085"	15°	1°	26°	38°	TR	38°	.025"
17081623	3/16"	5/8"	.085"	15°	1°	26°	38°	TR	38°	.025"
17081624	3/16"	5/8"	.085"	15°	1°	26°	38°	TR	38°	.025"
17081625,626	3/16"	5/8"	.085"	15°	1°	26°	38°	TR	38°	.025"
17081627	3/16"	5/8"	.085"	15°	1°	26°	38°	TR	38°	.025"
17081629	3/16"	5/8"	.085"	15°	1°	24°	34°	TR	41°	.025"
17081630	3/16"	5/8"	.085"	15°	1°	26°	38°	TR	38°	.025"
17081633	3/16"	5/8"	.085"	15°	1°	26°	38°	TR	38°	.025"
17081720	3/16"	5/8"	.085"	15°	1°	30°	37°	TR	41°	.025"
17081721	3/16"	5/8"	.085"	15°	1°	30°	37°	TR	41°	.025"
17081725	3/16"	5/8"	.085"	15°	1°	30°	37°	TR	41°	.025"
17081726	3/16"	5/8"	.085"	15°	1°	30°	37°	TR	41°	.025"
17081727	3/16"	5/8"	.085"	15°	1°	30°	37°	TR	41°	.025"
Jeep (2SE)										
17081790	.208"	.128"	.065"	25°	2°	19°	.....	TR	32°	.065"
17081791	.256"	.128"	.085"	25°	2°	19°	.....	TR	32°	.085"
Jeep (E2SE)										
17081796	.208"	.128"	.065"	25°	2°	19°	.....	TR	32°	.065"
17081797	.208"	.128"	.085"	25°	2°	19°	.....	TR	32°	.085"

(Table title: CARBURETOR ADJUSTMENT SPECIFICATIONS)

ROCHESTER MODELS M4MC & M4ME 4-BARREL

CARBURETOR APPLICATION

CHEVROLET & GMC

Application	Rochester Carb. No.	
	Man. Trans.	Auto. Trans.
5.0L (305")		
Without A/C		
C10	17081205	17081200, 17081201
C & G10/20, K10	17081227	17081220, 17081524
With A/C		
C10	17081206	.....
C & G10/20, K10	17081226, 17081526	.....
5.7L (350")		
Federal		
Without A/C		
C20, K10	17081506	.....
C & K10, G10/20, K20	17081290	17081291
C & K20/30	17080213	.....
P20/30		17080213
G30	17080298	17080298
P30		17080215
With A/C		
C20, K10	17081508	.....
C & K10, G10/20, K20	17081292	.....
California		
Without A/C		
C & K10, G10/20, K20	17081506	.....
C & K20/30		17080513
G30		17080507
P30	17080513	.....
With A/C		
C & K10, G10/20, K20	17081508	.....
7.4L (454")		
Federal		
C, K, & P20/30	.....	17080212
California		
C & K20/30	17080512	.....
P30	17080513	.....

CARBURETOR IDENTIFICATION

The Rochester M4MC and M4ME carburetor identification number is stamped on a vertical section of float bowl, near secondary throttle. If bowl needs replacing, follow manufacturer's instructions contained in service package to ensure carburetor number is transferred to new float bowl.

DESCRIPTION

The M4MC carburetor is a two stage type of downdraft design. The primary side has a triple venturi system. The secondary side is composed of two large bores using the air valve principle, in which fuel is metered in direct proportion to amount of air passing through the secondary bores. A baffle is attached to the secondary side of the air horn above the main well bleed tubes to deflect incoming air to improve secondary nozzle operation on heavy acceleration. This model uses the bowl-mounted choke housing with thermostatic control assembly. For light-duty emission vehicles model M4ME is used, which is basically the same carburetor, except for the deletion of the aneroid cavity and the use of an electric rather than hot air choke.

ADJUSTMENTS

HOT (SLOW) IDLE RPM

See appropriate article in TUNE-UP SERVICE PROCEDURES.

IDLE MIXTURE

See appropriate article in TUNE-UP SERVICE PROCEDURES.

COLD (FAST) IDLE RPM

See appropriate article in TUNE-UP SERVICE PROCEDURES.

ANGLE GAUGE ADJUSTMENT TOOL

Manufacturer recommends that some carburetor adjustments be performed using a choke valve angle gauge (Kent-Moore tool no. J-26701). While preparations and actual adjustments may vary with individual adjustment, the procedure for using the angle gauge to check the choke valve angle remains the same. Use the following procedure to perform adjustments requiring the use of the choke valve angle gauge.

1) Rotate degree scale on angle gauge so that 0° mark is opposite pointer.

2) With choke valve closed, place angle gauge magnet squarely on choke valve.

3) Rotate leveling bubble on angle gauge until it is centered.

4) Rotate degree scale until specified degree mark is opposite pointer.

5) Now perform individual adjustment preparations as outlined in the following carburetor adjustments requiring angle gauge. If bubble is centered, adjustment is correct. If not, adjust carburetor as outlined.

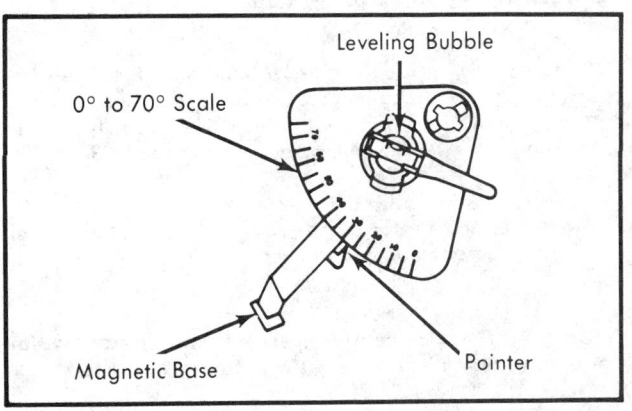

Fig. 1 Choke Valve Angle Gauge

ROCHESTER MODELS M4MC & M4ME 4-BARREL (Cont.)

FLOAT LEVEL

1) Remove air horn. Remove gasket from main body casting. Hold float retainer firmly in place. *See Fig. 2.*

2) Apply light finger pressure to push float gently against needle. Measure distance with "T" scale from top of casting to top of float. Gauging point should be 3/16" back from end of float at toe.

3) If adjustment is needed, REMOVE float from main body of carburetor. Bend float arm up or down. Install float and recheck float level.

4) Be sure to check float alignment after adjusting operation. Install new gasket and reinstall air horn.

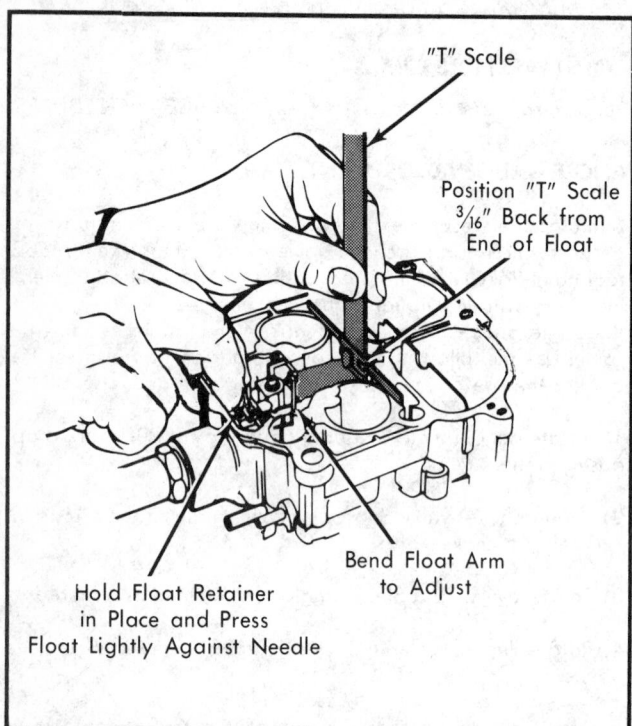

"T" Scale

Position "T" Scale 3/16" Back from End of Float

Bend Float Arm to Adjust

Hold Float Retainer in Place and Press Float Lightly Against Needle

Fig. 2   Adjusting Float Level

ACCELERATOR PUMP ROD

1) Close throttle valves completely. Make sure fast idle cam follower is off fast idle cam steps. Bend secondary throttle closing tang to make sure primary throttle valves are fully closed. Readjust after accelerator pump adjustment. *See Fig. 3.*

2) Make sure accelerator pump rod is in specified hole (inner or outer) in accelerator pump lever.

3) Using a "T" scale, measure specified distance from top of choke valve wall (next to vent stack) to top of pump stem.

4) To adjust, bend accelerator pump lever at point shown.

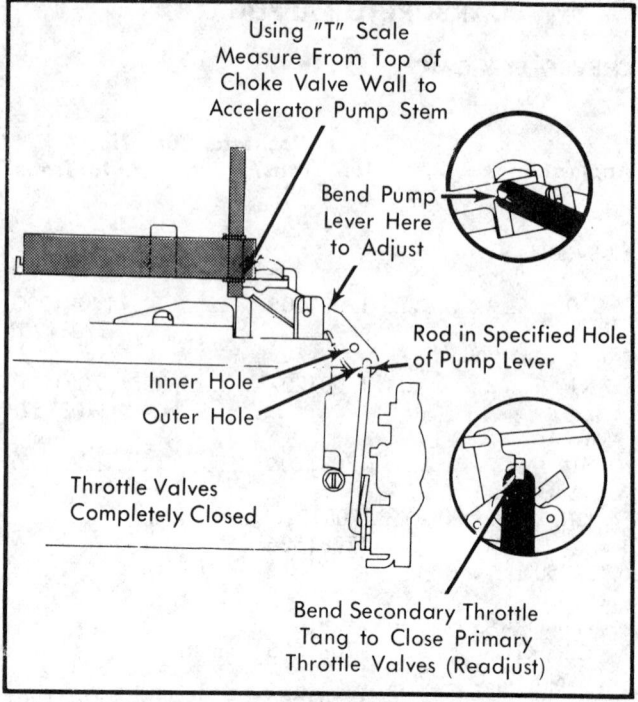

Using "T" Scale Measure From Top of Choke Valve Wall to Accelerator Pump Stem

Bend Pump Lever Here to Adjust

Rod in Specified Hole of Pump Lever

Inner Hole
Outer Hole

Throttle Valves Completely Closed

Bend Secondary Throttle Tang to Close Primary Throttle Valves (Readjust)

Fig. 3   Adjusting Accelerator Pump

CHOKE COIL LEVER

1) Drill out rivets retaining choke cover assembly, and remove choke cover. Remove coil assembly from choke housing. Press upward (counterclockwise) on thermostatic coil tang until choke valve is closed. *See Fig. 4.*

2) Make sure choke rod is in bottom of slot in choke lever. Insert a drill or pin gauge of specified size into hole in choke housing casting.

3) Lower edge of lever should just contact drill or pin gauge. Bend choke rod at point shown to adjust. *See Fig. 4.* Install choke cover and coil, using self-tapping screws supplied in service kit.

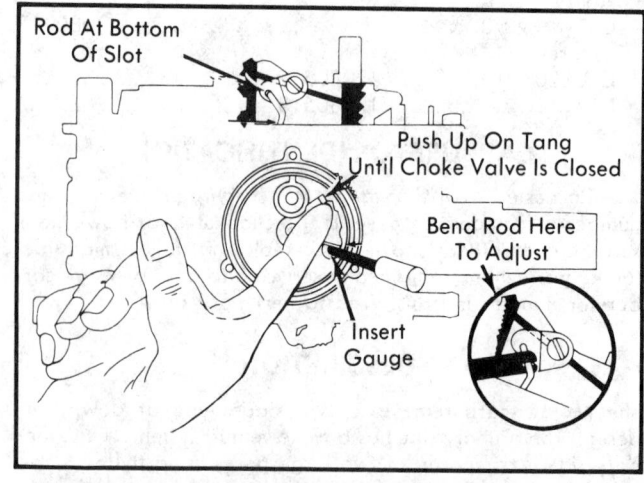

Rod At Bottom Of Slot

Push Up On Tang Until Choke Valve Is Closed

Bend Rod Here To Adjust

Insert Gauge

Fig. 4   Adjusting Choke Coil Lever

ROCHESTER MODELS M4MC & M4ME 4-BARREL (Cont.)

FAST IDLE ADJUSTMENT (BENCH SETTING)

NOTE — *This is a preliminary adjustment only. It is required to ensure that other adjustments are made with fast idle speed approximately correct. Final Cold (Fast) Idle Speed adjustment must be made with carburetor installed and engine running. See appropriate article in TUNE-UP SERVICE PROCEDURES.*

1) Place fast idle speed cam follower on high step of fast idle cam. Back off fast idle speed screw until throttle valves are completely closed.

2) Turn screw in until it contacts lever, then turn in an additional 4½ turns.

CHOKE ROD (FAST IDLE CAM)

NOTE — *Fast idle adjustment (bench setting) and choke coil lever must be adjusted first. This adjustment is performed using choke angle gauge, see procedure at beginning of adjustment.*

1) Place fast idle speed cam follower on second step of fast idle cam against shoulder of highest step. See *Fig. 5*.

2) Close choke by pushing up on choke coil lever or vacuum break lever tang. Hold choke closed with a rubber band.

3) Bubble on choke angle gauge should be centered with specified angle mark opposite pointer.

4) To adjust, bend tang on fast idle cam until bubble of choke valve angle gauge is centered.

AIR VALVE ROD — FRONT

1) Using an outside vacuum source, seat primary (front) choke vacuum break diaphragm. Plug purge bleed hole (if equipped) with masking tape. Hole is found in end of diaphragm. See Fig. 6.

2) Make sure air valve is completely closed. Insert a .015″ drill or pin gauge between rod and end of slot in lever.

3) Bend rod at point shown to adjust clearance in slot. Remove tape and reconnect vacuum hose to diaphragm.

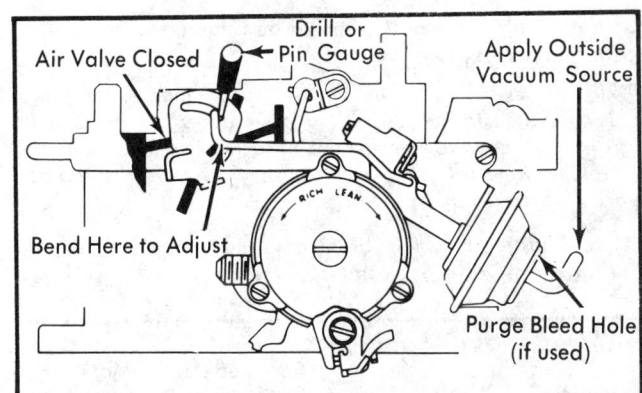

Fig. 6   Adjusting Air Valve Rod — Front

AIR VALVE ROD — REAR

NOTE — *This adjustment procedure is for Federal vehicles equipped with M4ME carburetors.*

1) Using an outside vacuum source, seat secondary (rear) choke vacuum break diaphragm. See Fig. 7.

2) Make sure air valve is completely closed. Insert a .015″ drill or pin gauge between rod and end of slot in lever.

3) Bend rod at point shown to adjust clearance in slot. Reconnect vacuum hose to diaphragm.

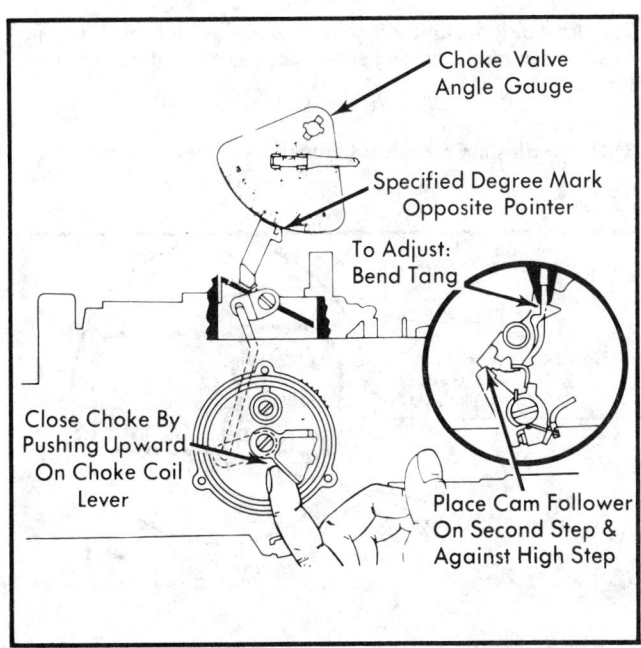

Fig. 5   Adjusting Choke Rod (Fast Idle Cam)

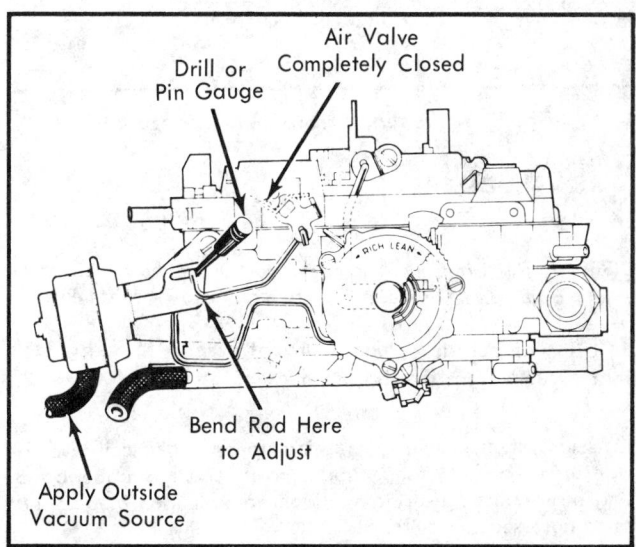

Fig. 7   Adjusting Air Valve Rod — Rear

1981 Rochester Carburetors

ROCHESTER MODELS M4MC & M4ME 4-BARREL (Cont.)

FRONT VACUUM BREAK

NOTE — *This adjustment is performed using the choke angle gauge, see procedure at beginning of Adjustments.*

1) Using an outside vacuum source of at least 15 in. Hg, seat front vacuum break diaphragm. See *Fig. 8*.

NOTE — *Plug purge bleed hole (if equipped) with masking tape. Hole is found in end of diaphragm.*

2) Close choke by pushing up on choke coil lever or vacuum break lever tang. Hold choke closed with a rubber band.

3) Bubble on angle gauge should be centered with specified degree mark opposite pointer.

NOTE — *Certain earlier models will have tamper-proof plugs over the adjustment screws. To gain access to adjustment screws, remove vacuum break bracket from carburetor. Carefully grind off plugs over adjustment screws and replace vacuum break diaphragm.*

4) To adjust, turn vacuum break adjustment screw in until bubble of choke valve angle gauge is centered.

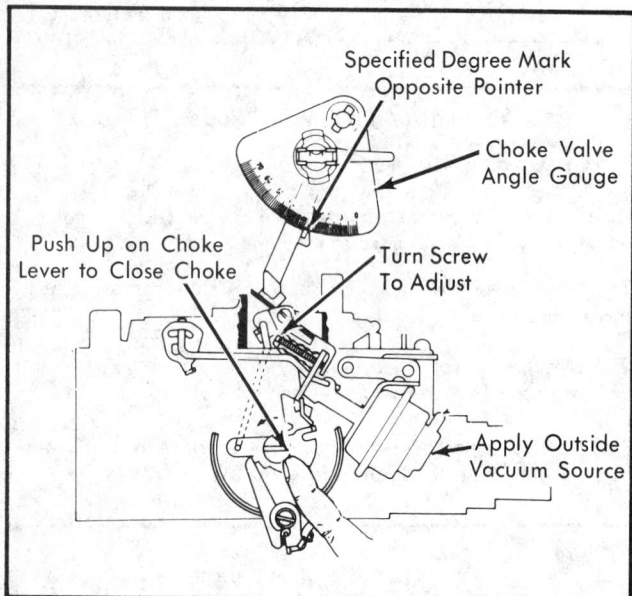

Fig. 8   Adjusting Front Vacuum Break

REAR VACUUM BREAK

NOTE — *This adjustment is performed using the choke valve angle gauge, see procedure at beginning of Adjustments.*

1) Using an outside vacuum source of at least 15 in. Hg, seat rear vacuum break diaphragm. See *Fig. 9*.

2) Close choke valve by pushing up on choke coil lever or vacuum break lever tang. Hold in position with a rubber band. Make sure bucking spring on diaphragm plunger (if equipped) is compressed and seated.

3) Bubble on choke valve angle gauge should be centered with specified degree mark opposite pointer.

4) If adjustment is required, turn screw at end of vacuum diaphragm until bubble in angle gauge is centered. Seal adjustment by applying a drop of silicone sealant or equivalent to head of screw.

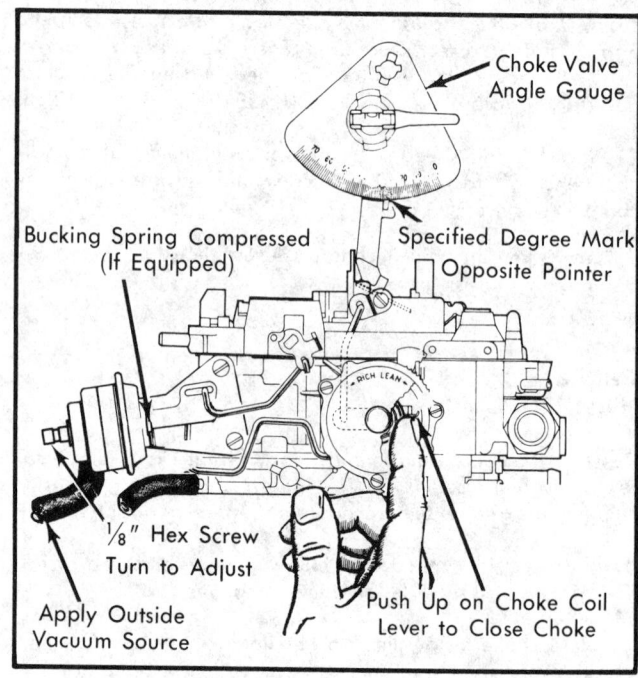

Fig. 9   Adjusting Rear Vacuum Break

AIR VALVE SPRING

1) Use hex wrench to loosen lock screw. Turn tension adjusting screw counterclockwise until air valve opens part way.

2) Turn tension adjusting screw clockwise until air valve just closes. Then turn adjusting screw clockwise specified number of turns.

3) Hold adjusting screw and tighten lock screw.

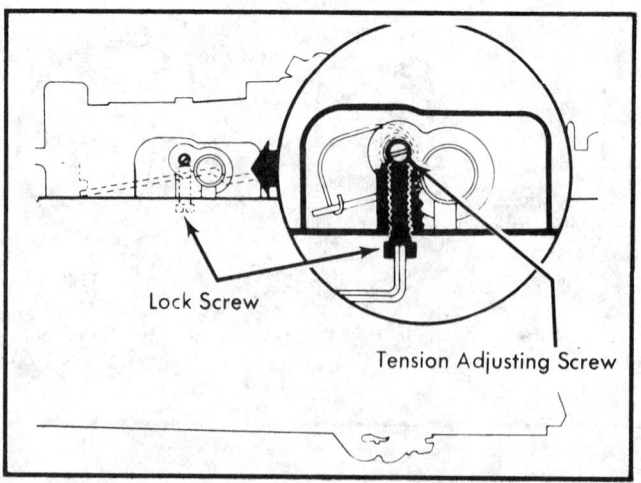

Fig. 10   Adjusting Air Valve Spring

ROCHESTER MODELS M4MC & M4ME 4-BARREL (Cont.)

AUTOMATIC CHOKE

NOTE — *Choke coil cover is retained on housing by rivets to prevent tampering with factory adjustment. If necessary to remove cover, refer to Disassembly and Reassembly procedures in this section.*

CHOKE UNLOADER

NOTE — *This adjustment is performed using the choke valve angle gauge. See procedure at beginning of Adjustments.*

1) Choke coil lever must be adjusted correctly, and fast idle adjustment must be set before proceeding.

2) Hold throttle valves wide open. See *Fig. 11*. If engine is warm, close choke valve by pushing up on vacuum break lever tang. Hold in position with a rubber band.

3) Bubble on choke valve angle gauge should be centered with specified degree mark opposite pointer.

4) To adjust, bend choke unloader tang on throttle lever until bubble of choke valve angle gauge is centered.

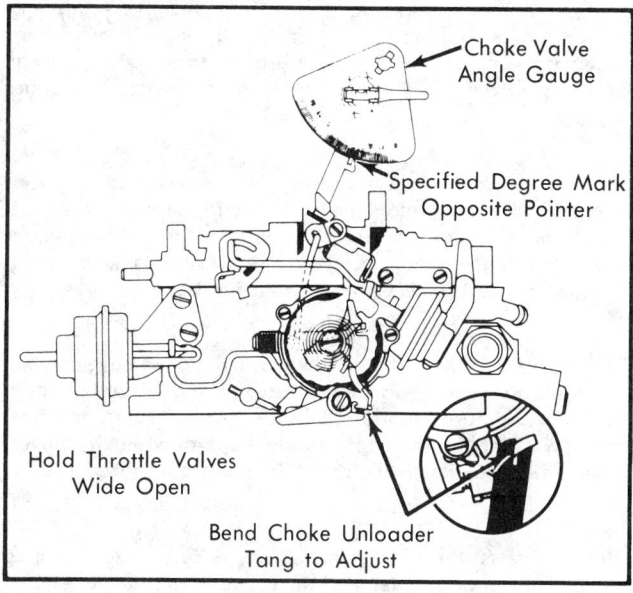

Fig. 11   Adjusting Choke Unloader

SECONDARY THROTTLE VALVE LOCKOUT

Lockout Lever Side Clearance — **1)** Hold choke valve and throttle valves closed completely. See *Fig. 12*.

2) Measure secondary throttle valve lockout specified side clearance between pin and lockout lever.

3) Specified clearance is .015". To adjust, bend pin.

Lockout Lever Opening Clearance — **1)** Push down on tail of fast idle cam and open choke valve completely. See *Fig. 12*.

2) Measure secondary throttle valve lockout specified opening clearance between end of pin and toe of lockout lever.

3) Specified clearance is .015". To adjust, file end of lockout pin. Make sure all burrs are removed.

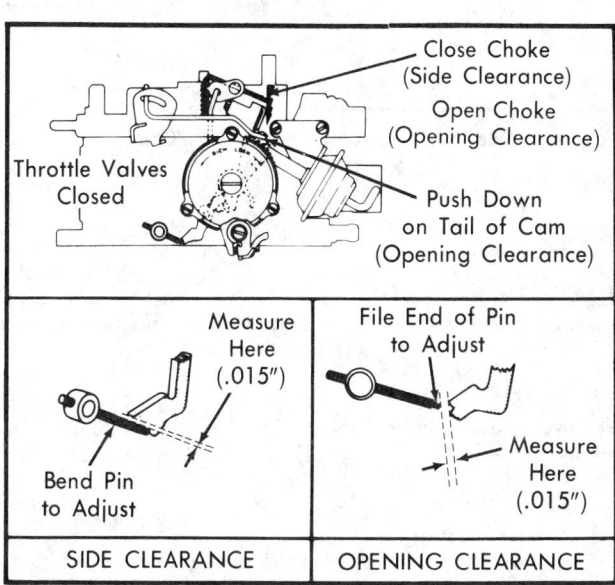

Fig. 12   Adjusting Secondary Throttle Valve Lockout

SECONDARY CLOSING LINKAGE

1) Engine idle speed must be correctly adjusted. Hold choke valve wide open and make sure fast idle cam follower is off fast idle cam steps. See *Fig. 13*.

2) Make sure secondary closing lever is against tang. Measure specified clearance between secondary throttle link and slot in secondary throttle lever.

3) Specified clearance is .020". To adjust bend tang.

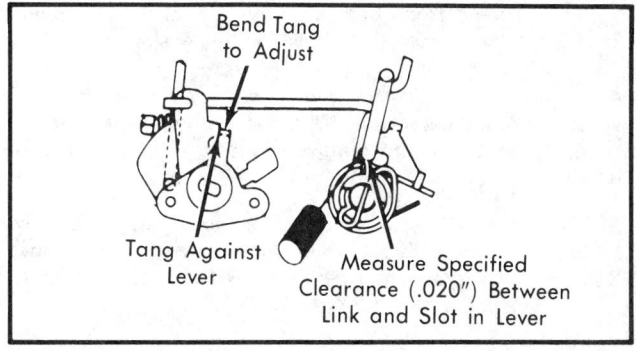

Fig. 13   Adjusting Secondary Throttle Closing Linkage

SECONDARY OPENING LINKAGE

1) Open primary throttle valves until secondary throttle link just contacts tang on secondary throttle lever. See *Fig. 14*.

2) Link should be centered in slot of secondary throttle lever. To adjust, bend tang on secondary throttle lever.

1981 Rochester Carburetors

ROCHESTER MODELS M4MC & M4ME 4-BARREL (Cont.)

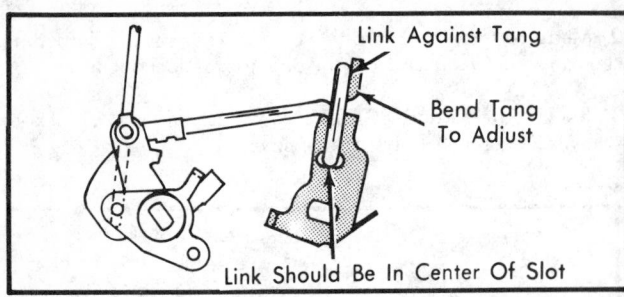

Fig. 14 Measuring Secondary Throttle Opening Linkage

OVERHAUL

DISASSEMBLY

NOTE — *Before performing any service on carburetor, it is essential that carburetor be placed on a holding fixture (J-8328) to prevent damage to throttle valves.*

Idle Stop Solenoid — If equipped with idle stop solenoid, remove screws securing solenoid and bracket to float bowl and remove assembly.

Air Horn Removal — 1) Remove upper choke lever from end of choke shaft by removing retaining screw. Then rotate upper choke lever to remove choke rod from slot in lever. Remove choke rod from lower lever inside float bowl casting.

NOTE — *Remove rod by holding lower lever outward with small screwdriver and twisting rod counterclockwise.*

2) Remove vacuum hose from front vacuum break unit. Remove secondary metering rods by removing the small screw in top of metering rod hanger. Lift upward on metering rod hanger until secondary metering rods are completely out of air horn. Metering rods may be disassembled from hanger by rotating ends out of holes in end of hanger.

3) Drive pump lever pivot pin inward until pump lever can be removed, then disconnect pump rod from pump lever. Remove air horn-to-float bowl attaching screws. Remove secondary air baffle deflector from beneath center 2 attaching screws. Remove air horn from float bowl by lifting straight up.

4) Remove front vacuum break attaching screws and front vacuum break diaphragm. Disconnect diaphragm from air valve dashpot rod and remove dashpot rod from air valve lever.

5) It is not necessary to remove choke valve and shaft unless bent or damaged. Choke valve screws are staked in place. Staking must be removed before screws are removed.

NOTE — *Air horn should not be disassembled any further. Air valve screws are permanently staked in place. However, a repair kit is available for air valve closing spring and center plastic eccentric cam.*

Float Bowl Disassembly — 1) Remove air horn gasket by lifting out of dowel locating pins and lifting tab of gasket from beneath power piston hanger, being careful not to distort springs holding main metering rods.

2) Remove pump plunger and return spring from pump well. Remove power piston and metering rods by depressing piston stem and allowing it to snap free. Repeat until piston force dislodges retainer. Remove power Piston spring from well.

CAUTION — *Do not use pliers on metering rod hanger to remove power piston.*

3) Remove metering rods from power piston by disconnecting tension spring from top of each rod and rotating out of hanger.

4) Remove plastic filler block located over float valve. Remove float assembly and fuel inlet needle by pulling up on retaining pin. Remove inlet seat and gasket. Remove aneroid cavity from float bowl if equipped.

NOTE — *The APT metering rod adjustment screw is preset at the factory, and no attempt should be made to alter its setting. If a new float bowl is required, it will contain a preset APT metering screw.*

5) Remove primary main metering jets. Remove pump discharge check ball retainer and check ball. Remove rear vacuum break attaching screws and rotate vacuum break assembly to remove vacuum break rod from slot in plunger head.

6) Align a .159" (No.21) drill on choke cover retaining rivet and drill only enough to remove rivet head. Repeat for remaining 2 rivets. Remove choke cover and coil assembly. Remove choke housing retaining screw located inside choke housing. Slide complete choke assembly from float bowl.

7) Remove fuel inlet nut, gasket and filter. Remove throttle body-to-float bowl attaching screws and throttle body. Remove secondary throttle valve lockout lever from float bowl and lower choke lever from inside float bowl cavity (invert bowl to remove). Remove plastic tube seal from choke housing.

Choke Disassembly — Remove choke coil lever retaining screw from end of intermediate choke shaft. Remove thermostatic coil lever from flats on intermediate choke shaft and remove shaft. Fast idle cam can now be removed from intermediate choke shaft.

Throttle Body — 1) Remove accelerator pump rod from throttle lever.

NOTE — *It is not necessary to disassemble throttle body any further. Do not remove idle mixture screw plugs unless it is necessary to replace mixture screws or cleaning and air pressure fails to clean idle mixture passages. If necessary to remove, proceed as follows:*

2) Invert throttle body and position on a holding fixture with manifold side up. Position a punch in between 2 locator points on manifold side of throttle body. There are 2 locator points adjacent to each mixture screw.

ROCHESTER MODELS M4MC & M4ME 4-BARREL (Cont.)

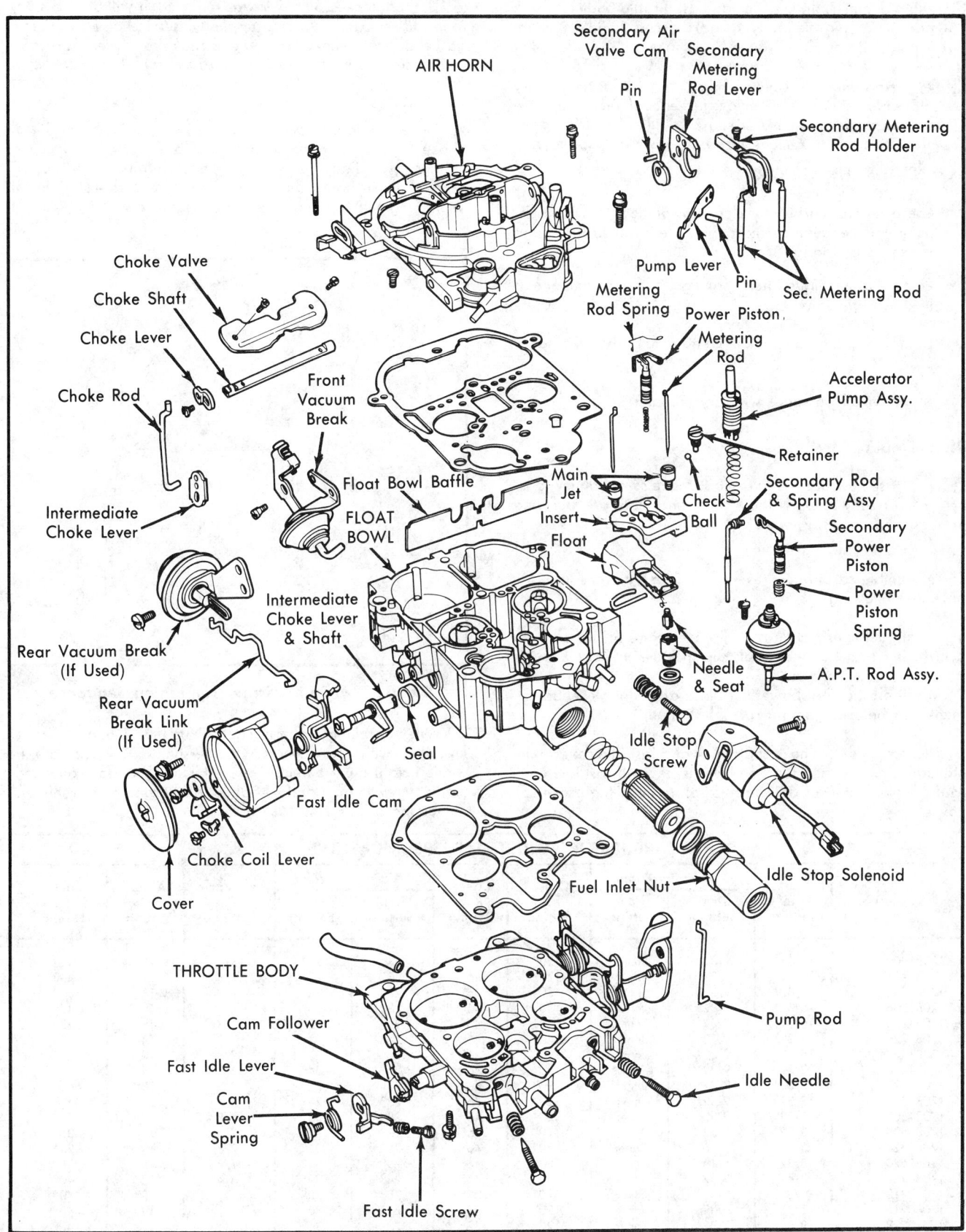

Fig. 15 *Exploded View of Rochester Model M4MC 4-Barrel Carburetor*

ROCHESTER MODELS M4MC & M4ME 4-BARREL (Cont.)

3) Using a hammer, drive punch against throttle body to break out portion of throttle body to gain access to idle mixture screw plugs. Drive out hardened steel plugs.

NOTE — *Hardened steel plugs will shatter. It is not necessary to remove plug completely. Remove just enough pieces to allow idle mixture adjusting tool (J-28706) or a thin walled 3/16" deep socket to be used to remove mixture screws and spring.*

CLEANING & INSPECTION

- Use a regular carburetor cleaning solution. Soak components long enough to thoroughly clean all surfaces and passages of foreign matter.

- Remove any residue after cleaning by rinsing components in a suitable solvent.

- Do not soak any components containing rubber, leather or plastic.

- Blow out all passages with dry compressed air.

REASSEMBLY

NOTE — *Use new gaskets and seals. Make sure that new gaskets fit correctly and that all holes and slots are punched through and correctly located.*

To reassemble carburetor, reverse disassembly procedure and note the following:

1) Install fuel inlet needle pull clip over edge of flat on float arm facing float. Do not hook clip in holes in float arm.

2) Install plastic float bowl filler block after float level adjustment and before metering rod installation.

3) The intermediate choke shaft lever and fast idle cam are installed correctly when tang on lever is beneath fast idle cam. Make choke coil lever adjustments before installing choke coil cover.

NOTE — *If choke coil cover was removed, it will be necessary to install replacement rivets supplied in service kit. Do not use a gasket between choke housing and choke coil cover, as surface contact is needed to provide a ground for electric choke.*

4) Place fast idle screw on high step of fast idle cam. Install choke coil cover, aligning notch in cover with tab on cover retainer (supplied in service kit). Install retainer with tab into screw hole in housing nearest to front of carburetor. Install remaining self tapping screws and tighten.

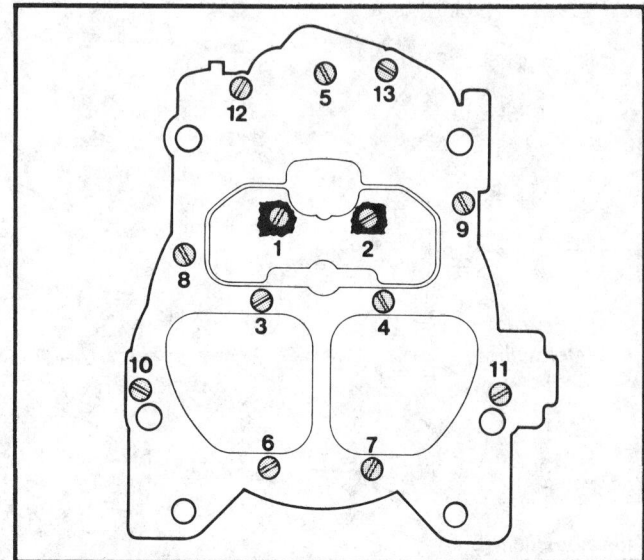

Fig. 16   Air Horn Screw Tightening Sequence

5) When installing air horn screws, note that 2 long screws are installed with lockwashers. Countersunk screws (2) are installed right next to venturi area. Install secondary air baffle under screws No. 2 and 4. Tighten air horn screws evenly and in sequence. *See Fig. 16.*

		Accelerator Pump		Choke	Choke	Vacuum Break		Air Valve	Auto.	Choke
Application	Float Level Setting	Stem Setting	Hole Setting	Coil Lever Setting	Rod Setting	Front Setting	Rear Setting	Spring Setting①	Choke Setting	Unloader Setting
17081200	15/32"	9/32"	Inner	.120"	46°	24°	23°	7/8	TR	42°
17081201	15/32"	9/32"	Inner	.120"	46°	23°	23°	7/8	TR	42°
17081205	15/32"	9/32"	Inner	.120"	46°	23°	23°	7/8	TR	42°
17081206	15/32"	9/32"	Inner	.120"	46°	23°	23°	7/8	TR	42°
17081220	15/32"	9/32"	Inner	.120"	46°	23°	23°	7/8	TR	42°
17081226	15/32"	9/32"	Inner	.120"	46°	24°	23°	7/8	TR	42°
17081227	15/32"	9/32"	Inner	.120"	46°	24°	23°	7/8	TR	42°
17081290	13/32"	9/32"	Inner	.120"	46°	23°	24°	7/8	TR	42°
17081291	13/32"	9/32"	Inner	.120"	46°	23°	24°	7/8	TR	42°
17081292	13/32"	9/32"	Inner	.120"	46°	23°	24°	7/8	TR	42°
17081506	13/32"	9/32"	Inner	.120"	46°	23°	36°	7/8	TR	36°
17081508	13/32"	9/32"	Inner	.120"	46°	23°	36°	7/8	TR	36°
17081524	13/32"	5/16"	Outer	.120"	46°	25°	36°	7/8	TR	38°
17081526	13/32"	5/16"	Outer	.120"	46°	25°	36°	7/8	TR	38°
17080212	3/8"	9/32"	Inner	.120"	46°	24°	30°	3/4	TR	40°
17080213	3/8"	9/32"	Inner	.120"	37°	23°	30°	1	TR	40°
17080215	3/8"	9/32"	Inner	.120"	37°	23°	30°	1	TR	40°
17080298	3/8"	9/32"	Inner	.120"	37°	23°	30°	1	TR	40°
17080507, 513	3/8"	9/32"	Inner	.120"	37°	23°	30°	1	TR	40°
17080512	3/8"	9/32"	Inner	.120"	46°	24°	30°	3/4	TR	40°

CARBURETOR ADJUSTMENT SPECIFICATIONS

① — Specification is amount of turns.
TR — Tamper Resistant.

GENERAL MOTORS DIESEL FUEL INJECTION

DESCRIPTION

Diesel mechanical fuel injection systems differ greatly from electronic fuel injection systems. In this diesel system, a mechanical high pressure rotary pump, gear driven by the camshaft at camshaft speed, injects a precisely metered amount of fuel to each cylinder at the proper time. The pump is mounted on top of the engine and provides necessary timing advance under all operating conditions.

Eight high pressure fuel pipes carry fuel from pump to an injection nozzle in each cylinder. All eight pipes are exactly the same length to ensure that there is no variance in timing. Engine RPM is controlled by a rotary fuel metering valve. As the accelerator pedal is pushed down, a throttle cable opens the metering valve and allows increased fuel delivery. A built-in low pressure transfer pump delivers fuel to the main injection pump.

A fuel filter is located between the mechanical fuel pump (mounted on the side of the engine block) and the injection pump. Any excess fuel is returned to the tank by a fuel return system.

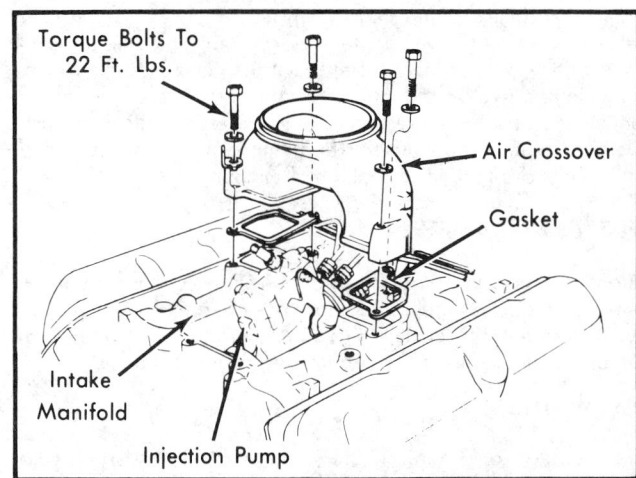

Fig. 2   Air Crossover Assembly (Federal Models)

FUEL TANK-TO-PUMP SYSTEM

Diesel fuel, NOT gasoline, is drawn from the fuel tank by an engine mounted mechanical fuel pump. This pump is driven by an eccentric cam mounted on the crankshaft and puts out about $5\frac{1}{2}$-$6\frac{1}{2}$ psi to the main injection pump. A small screen type filter is located in the fuel tank at the pickup. A larger sealed 11-12 micron fuel filter is located on the rear of the engine between fuel pump and main injection pump. Diesel fuel arrives at the center inlet fitting on the injection pump after leaving the filter. A fuel return line is provided to return any excess fuel to the tank.

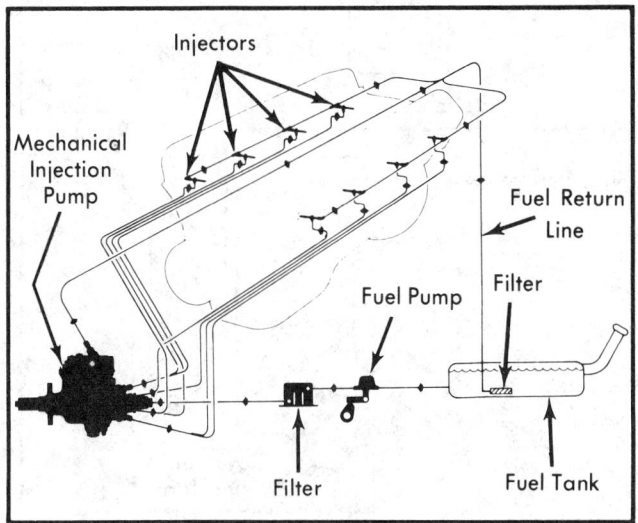

Fig. 1   Diesel Injection System Fuel Circuit

OPERATION

AIR INDUCTION SYSTEM

An air crossover housing is located on top of the engine over the injection pump. It is bolted to the intake manifold with 4 bolts and serves as the only air inlet in the system. No fuel passes through the crossover. It is an open-chambered housing with a single inlet drawing air through an air filter assembly mounted above. The crossover unit has two branches, one leading to each side of the intake manifold. Gaskets are installed between crossover and manifold to prevent vacuum leaks. Federal and California models use different crossovers to accomodate specific EGR systems. Starter fluid should never be used or sprayed into crossover. If crossover is removed, air screens must be installed.

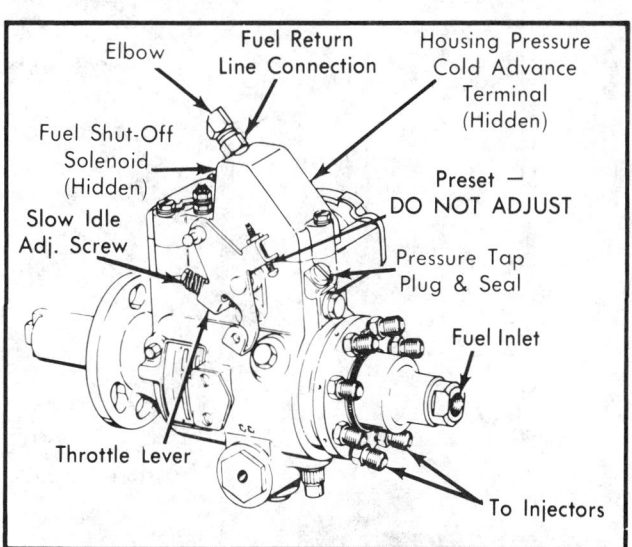

Fig. 3   Diesel Injection Pump

DIESEL INJECTION PUMP

The high pressure diesel injection pump is mounted to the top of the engine below the air crossover. The pump is cam driven at speed equal to the camshaft. Because of this, the pump can precisely govern time and amount of fuel injection.

A built-in fuel pressure regulator and transfer pump picks up fuel at the pump inlet, and pushes it through a passage to the

GENERAL MOTORS DIESEL FUEL INJECTION (Cont.)

pump head. The pump head distributes fuel, still at transfer pump pressure (8-12 psi), to metering valve, governor and automatic advance mechanisms. Fuel then passes to the rotary fuel metering valve and into a charging passage. As the pump shaft rotates, fuel is fired, under high pressure, through each delivery pipe to an injector. The pump is not serviceable and must be exchanged in case of a malfunction.

FUEL DELIVERY PIPES

Eight high pressure pipes are routed from injection pump to an injector in each cylinder. The pipes are of equal length but are bent differently to achieve this equal length. Pipes are not interchangeable and are pre-bent by the manufacturer.

GLOW PLUGS

Glow plugs are small heaters provided to assist in cold starting. The glow plug controller and relay cycle 12 volts to these 6 volt heaters, which causes them to heat rapidly. After the engine starts, the glow plugs remain on for about a minute, then shut off. If the ignition is turned on and the engine is not started, the glow plugs will continue to cycle until the batteries are discharged.

CAUTION — *Do not manually by-pass glow plug relay, or glow plugs will be ruined instantly.*

NOTE — *A burned out FAST GLOW glow plug tip may break off and drop into the pre-chamber when removed. Cylinder head must be removed and pre-chamber removed from head to remove broken tip.*

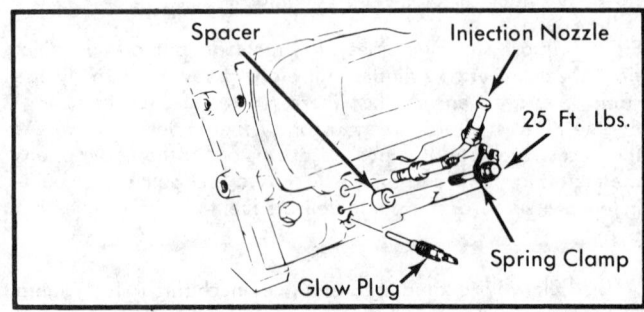

Fig. 5   Glow Plug and Injection Nozzle Location (Federal Model)

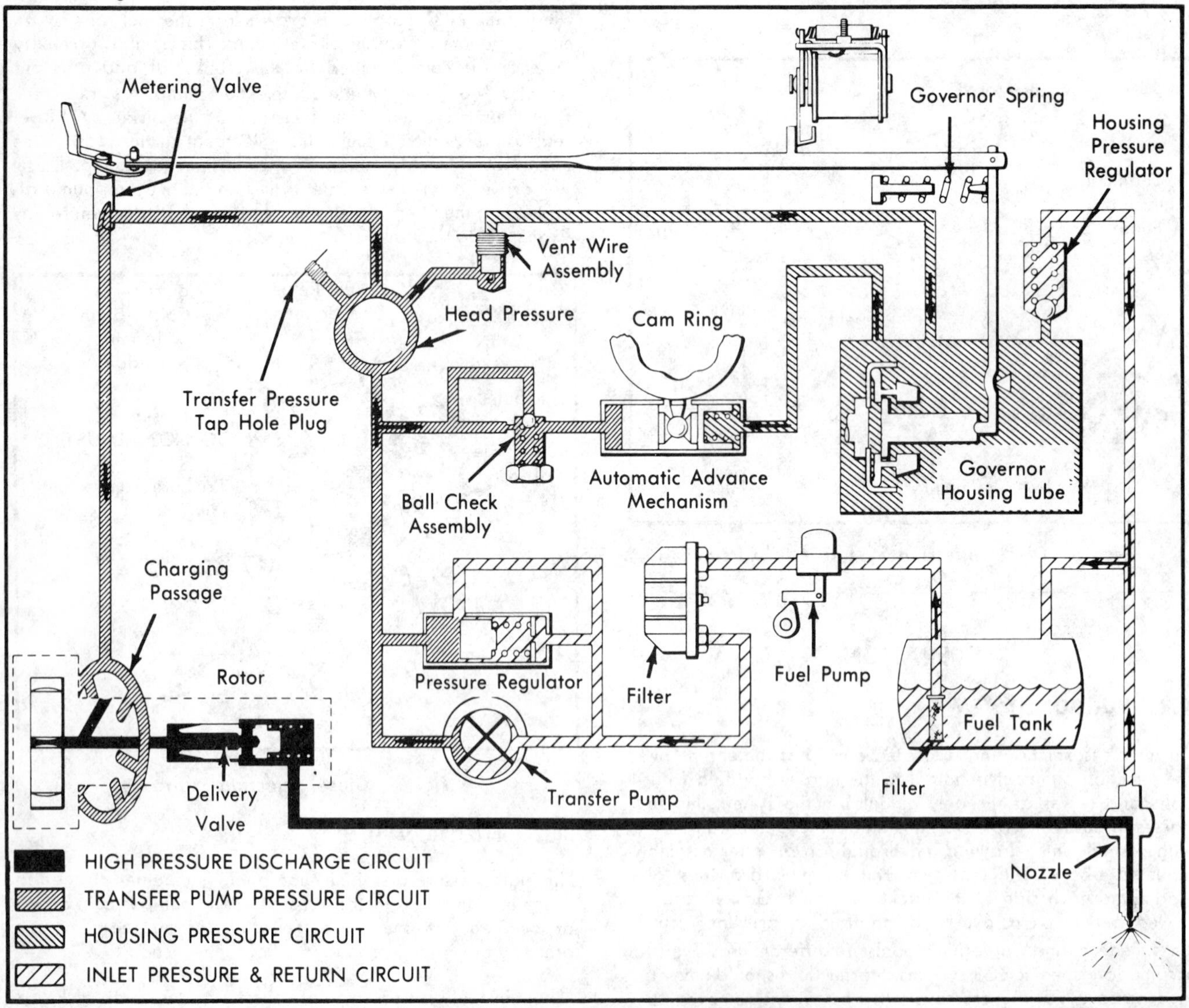

HIGH PRESSURE DISCHARGE CIRCUIT

TRANSFER PUMP PRESSURE CIRCUIT

HOUSING PRESSURE CIRCUIT

INLET PRESSURE & RETURN CIRCUIT

Fig. 4   Diesel Injection Pump Fuel Circuit Diagram

GENERAL MOTORS DIESEL FUEL INJECTION (Cont.)

INJECTION NOZZLES

Diesel Equipment/C.A.V. Lucas — One injection nozzle is located in each combustion chamber. It has a single fuel inlet fitting and is threaded into the cylinder head as are the glow plugs. Injection nozzles are spring loaded and calibrated to open at specified fuel line pressure. The combustion chamber end of the nozzle has a replaceable copper compression seal.

Two types of injection nozzles are used. The inlet fitting in the body of the injector must be tightened to the correct torque when installed or checked.

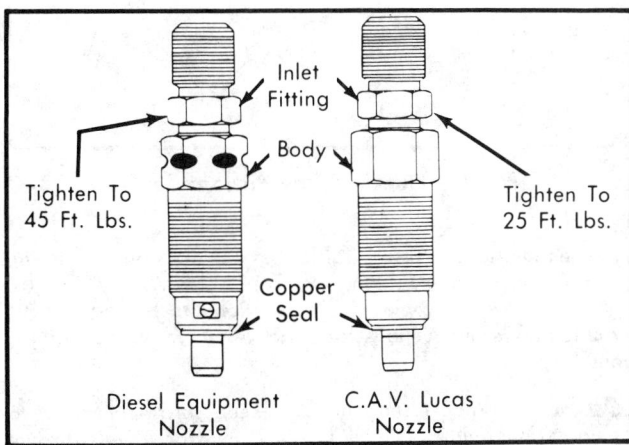

Fig. 6   Diesel Injection Nozzle Identification (California Models)

Roosa-Master — One injection nozzle is located in each combustion chamber. It has a single fuel inlet fitting and a return line for removal of excess fuel. Nozzle is retained in head by a bolt and clamp and is not threaded as glow plugs are. Injection nozzles are spring loaded and calibrated to open at a specified fuel pressure. The engine end of nozzle has a replaceable compression seal and carbon stop seal.

NOTE — *Never try to interchange pickup and passenger car injectors.*

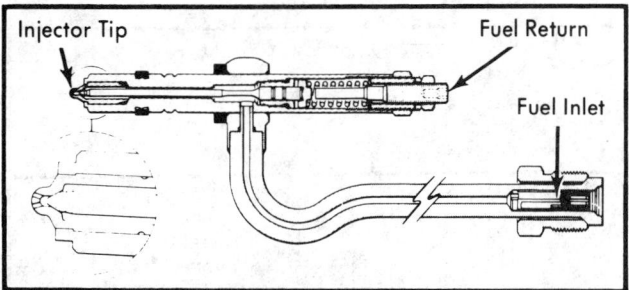

Fig. 7   Cutaway View of Roosa-Master Injection Nozzle (Federal Models)

VACUUM PUMP

Vacuum to operate accessory systems on diesel vehicles is provided by a vacuum pump which is located at the rear of the block and driven by the cam. The engine should never be operated without the vacuum pump in place as it is also the oil pump drive.

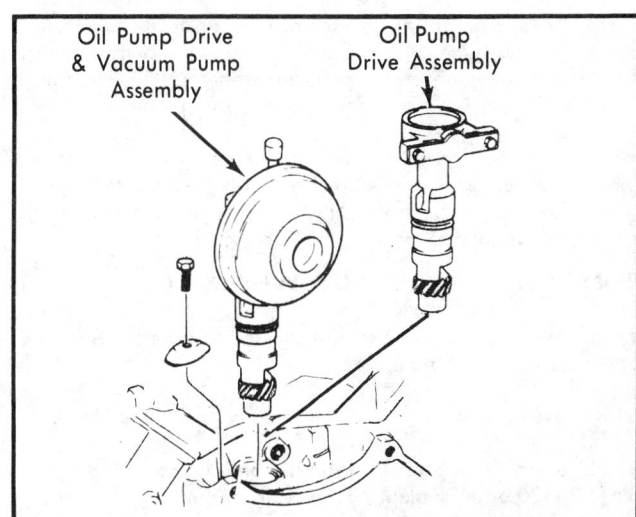

Fig. 8   Vacuum and Oil Pump Drive Units

HOUSING PRESSURE COLD ADVANCE (HPCA)

The HPCA is used to improve cold starting and emission control. The solenoid is controlled by the engine temperature switch and advances injection timing by 3° when the engine is cold. It does this by decreasing the housing pressure from 10 psi to zero. At the same time, the fast idle solenoid is activated. When the temperature switch opens (125° F), the HPCA solenoid is de-energized and housing pressure rises, retarding pump timing.

DIESEL FUEL HEATER (OPTIONAL)

This option is used to heat the fuel during low temperature (below 20° F) operation. This prevents wax crystals from building up and blocking the fuel filters. The filter is located along the right side of the intake manifold and uses a resistance wire spiraled around the fuel line. The filter has a bypass valve which allows fuel to flow to the fuel heater when the filter is covered with wax.

TESTING

GLOW PLUG RESISTANCE TEST

1) Start engine and allow to warm up; then remove all glow plug wires. Using idle speed screw on side of injection pump, adjust idle to roughest speed (but do not exceed 900 RPM). Allow engine to run for 1 minute.

2) Attach jumper wire between voltmeter ground lead and engine lift point on left side of intake manifold. DO NOT use any other point for ground connection. Check resistance by touching positive lead of voltmeter to glow plug terminals (with engine running). Write down values obtained in firing order sequence (1-8-4-3-6-5-7-2).

3) If ohm reading on any cylinder is about 1.2-1.3 ohms, make a compression check on that cylinder before continuing fuel injection diagnosis. Most cylinders should measure between 1.8-3.4 ohms. If more than .3 ohms difference is observed between

GENERAL MOTORS DIESEL FUEL INJECTION (Cont.)

2 consecutive cylinders in firing order, remove injectors and check opening pressure.

4) To improve rough idle, switch nozzles as necessary. Install nozzles with a higher opening pressure to lower ohm reading, and a lower opening pressure to raise ohm reading. A change of about 30 psi will vary ohm reading by .1 ohm.

5) Repeat procedure to confirm idle improvement. Be sure to check glow plug resistance at the same idle speed both times. If no improvement is observed, injection line replacement or injection pump calibration may be necessary.

INJECTION PUMP HOUSING FUEL PRESSURE

1) Remove air crossover assembly. Install screened covers over openings in intake manifold.

2) Remove pressure tap plug from injector pump. See *Fig. 3.*

3) Place seal from pressure tap plug onto pressure tap adapter (J-28526 or equivalent). Screw adapter into pump housing in place of plug.

4) Connect a low pressure gauge to adapter. Install magnetic pickup tachometer.

5) Start engine. Run engine at 1000 RPM with transmission in PARK. Observe gauge.

6) Pressure should be 8-12 psi with no more than 2 psi fluctuation.

7) If equipped with HPCA and pressure is zero, remove electrical connector from HPCA. If pressure remains zero, remove injection pump cover and check advance solenoid for binding and replace parts as needed.

8) If pressure returned to normal with HPCA electrical connector removed, check operation of temperature switch.

9) If pressure is still high, fuel return system may be restricted. Remove fuel return line at injection pump. Install fitting and short piece of hose to allow fuel return to empty into small container.

10) If pressure is lower, correct restriction in fuel line. If pressure still high, replace fuel return line connector assembly.

11) Recheck pressure. If pressure is still not correct, remove injection pump for repair. Pump is not serviceable and must be exchanged for another unit.

12) Remove tachometer, pressure gauge and adapter. Install a NEW pressure tap plug seal on plug. Install tap plug into pump.

13) Remove screened covers from manifold. Install air crossover assembly.

INJECTION NOZZLE

CAUTION — *Do not use a steel brush or a motorized brush to clean nozzles. Damage to nozzle tip may result.*

Spray Pattern Test — 1) Remove injection nozzles. Clean carbon from tip of nozzle with a soft brass brush. Check torque of inlet fitting to nozzle body and correct as necessary.

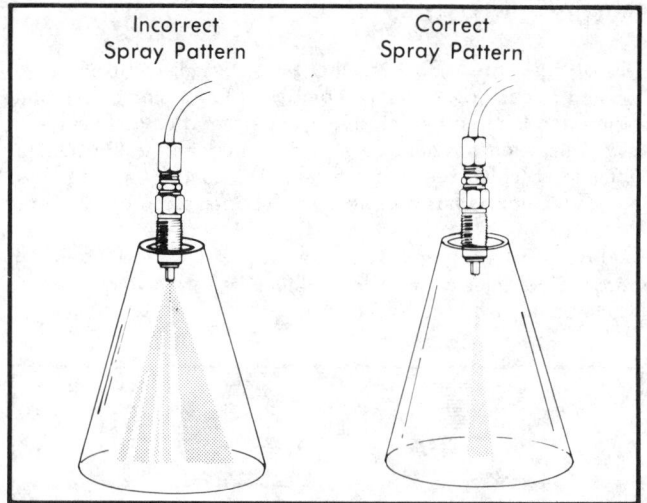

Fig. 9   Nozzle Spray Pattern Test

2) Assemble nozzle to a suitable diesel injection nozzle tester using a connecting line (high pressure) 12" long by ¼" O.D by ¹⁄₁₆" I.D. between nozzle and tester. Refer to test equipment manufacturers' instructions for exact tester operating instructions.

CAUTION — *When testing nozzles, keep spray contained to avoid serious injury. DO NOT allow injector to release line pressure on hands, arms or any part of body. Pressure of atomized test spray has sufficient penetrating power to puncture flesh.*

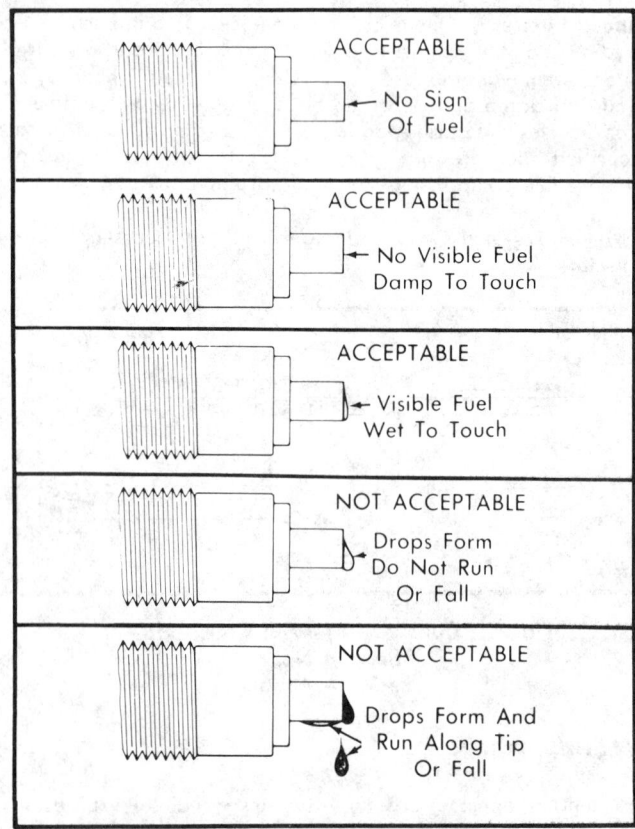

Fig. 10   Injection Nozzle Seat Tightness Test

GENERAL MOTORS DIESEL FUEL INJECTION (Cont.)

3) Build nozzle pressure slow enough to determine exact minimum opening pressure of nozzle. Minimum opening pressure is 1750-1900 psi (Roosa-Master) or 870 psi (Diesel Equipment/C.A.V. Lucas). When nozzle releases pressure, note spray pattern and compare with examples shown. If incorrect, or if a liquid stream, replace nozzle. See *Fig. 9.*

Seat Tightness Test — Decrease pressure to at least 290 psi BELOW actual opening pressure. Dry nozzle tip with compressed air, then increase pressure slowly to 1300-1400 psi (Roosa-Master) or 652 psi (Diesel Equipment/C.A.V. Lucas). Maintain pressure for 5 seconds and compare fuel leakage to examples. See *Fig. 10.*

Chatter Test — Operate tester rapidly to put nozzle under extreme load conditions. Chatter should be audible and should also be felt through handle of tester. Chatter does not occur in engine. It is an indication of valve freedom, proper seat width and interference angle.

Fuel Return Test — **1)** Loosen connector nuts and reposition nozzle tip slightly above horizontal plane. Tighten connector nuts and raise pressure to 1500 psi. Nozzle should not open. Maintain 1500 psi and observe fluid from nozzle return. After first drop forms on fuel return end of nozzle, there should be 3-10 more drops in 30 seconds.

2) Replace defective nozzles or have them serviced by manufacturer. Reinstall all nozzles carefully and tighten to recommended torque.

REMOVAL & INSTALLATION

NOTE — *Manufacturer does not recommend disassembly of pump. However, pump cover, guide stud, and throttle shaft seals may be replaced to eliminate leaks. For all other problems, pump must be removed and taken to an authorized repair station.*

INJECTION PUMP SEAL REPLACEMENT

1) Disconnect ground cables from both batteries, then remove air cleaner and crossover. Install screens over air intakes. Disconnect fuel return line and wiring from injection pump.

2) Clean injection pump cover and area around throttle rod and guide stud. Place rags in engine valley to catch fuel. Remove vacuum regulator valve, throttle rod, and return springs. Remove throttle cable bracket.

3) Install tool (J-29601) over throttle shaft with slots of tool engaging pin. Put spring clip of tool over throttle shaft advance cam and tighten wing nut. Without loosening wing nut, pull tool off shaft. This provides a reference for proper alignment during reassembly.

4) Drive pin from throttle shaft and remove advance cam and fiber washer. Remove any burrs that may have been caused by pin removal. Remove injection pump cover and remove screws from cover.

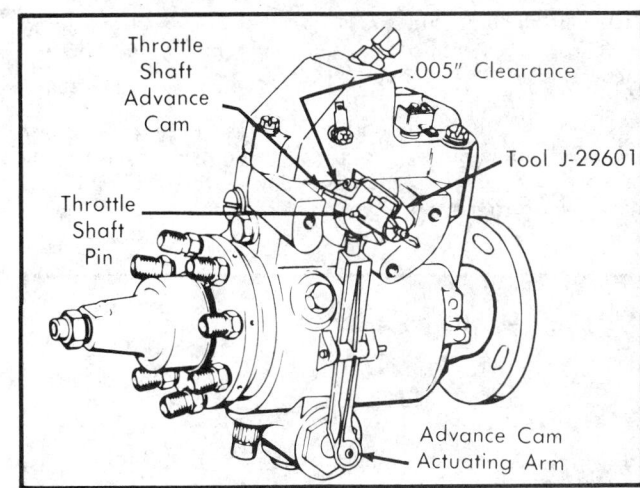

Fig. 11 Injection Pump With Advance Cam Tool Installed

CAUTION — *Do not allow any dirt or foreign objects to drop into injection pump. Engine damage will result.*

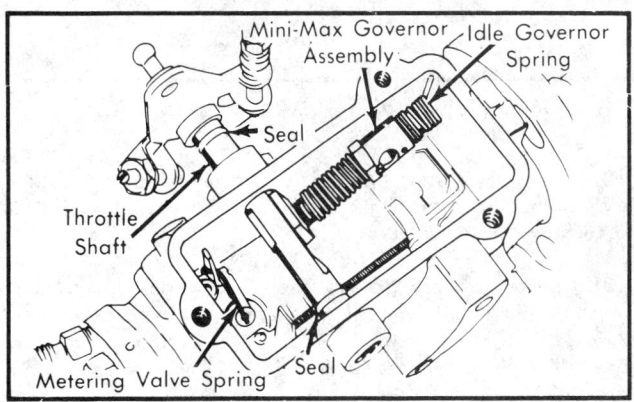

Fig. 12 Injection Pump With Cover Removed

5) Note position of metering valve spring over top of guide stud. This position must be exactly duplicated during reassembly. Remove guide stud and washer, then rotate mini-max governor assembly up and remove from throttle shaft.

6) Remove throttle shaft and inspect. If damaged or worn, replace. It may be necessary to loosen and rotate pump slightly to remove throttle shaft. Inspect shaft bushings. If replacement is necessary, pump must be sent to authorized repair dealer.

7) Remove throttle shaft seals. Do not cut off, as a nick on shaft will cause leakage. Coat new seals lightly with grease and install on shaft.

8) Slide shaft into pump until mini-max governor will slip onto throttle shaft. Rotate governor downward, hold in position, and side shaft and governor cam into place.

9) Install new fiber washer, throttle shaft advance cam (do not tighten screw) and throttle shaft drive pin. Realign advance cam in original position with tool (J-29601), place a .005" feeler gauge between fiber washer and cam, and tighten cam screw.

GENERAL MOTORS DIESEL FUEL INJECTION (Cont.)

10) Reinstall guide stud with new washer. Ensure that metering valve spring extension rides on top of guide stud. Tighten guide stud to 85 INCH Lbs.

11) Hold throttle in idle position and install new pump cover seal. Do not insert screws in cover; position cover slightly forward and above pump. Carefully move cover rearward and downward into position, taking care not to damage seal.

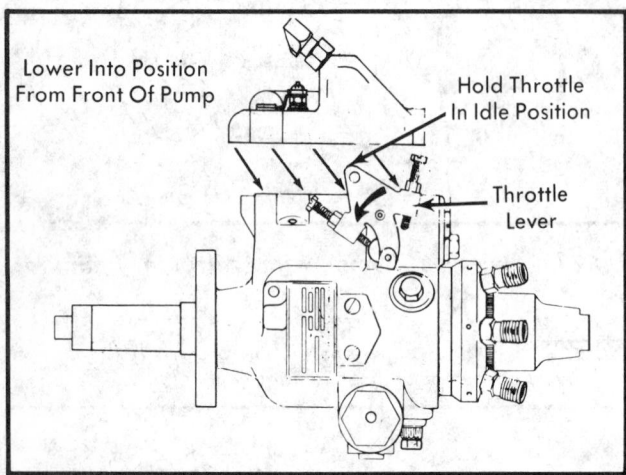

Fig. 13   Installing Injection Pump Cover

12) Insert screws, using flat and lock washers with flat washers against pump cover. Tighten to 33 INCH Lbs., then install vacuum regulator valve.

13) Connect battery ground cables, turn ignition on, and touch pink solenoid wire to solenoid terminal. A clicking sound should be heard as solenoid operates. If not, remove cover and check for solenoid operation.

CAUTION — *If clicking sound is not heard as solenoid wire is connected, DO NOT start engine. Throttle may be stuck in wide-open position.*

14) To check solenoid, ground solenoid lead opposite hot lead and connect pink wire. Turn ignition to "run" position. Solenoid should move linkage. If not, check that voltage across solenoid terminals is at least 12 volts. Replace solenoid if linkage does not move and voltage is 12 volts.

15) Repeat step **14)** and install cover. See Fig. 13.

16) If solenoid clicks, connect all wires to pump housing. Reinstall throttle cable bracket and throttle rod. Reinstall throttle cable and return springs.

17) Adjust pump timing and throttle linkage. Install fuel return line and check that all fuel lines are tight. Start engine and check for leaks. Allow engine to idle for several minutes to purge air bubbles and smooth out idle. It may be necessary to stop engine for several minutes to allow air to rise and be purged.

18) Adjust vacuum regulator valve. See *VACUUM REGULATOR VALVE LINKAGE ADJUSTMENT.* Replace air crossover.

AIR CROSSOVER

Removal — Remove air cleaner, then remove filters and pipes from air crossover. Remove bolts and washers and lift crossover from manifold. Place screened covers over intake manifold openings.

Installation — Reverse removal procedure. Torque air crossover bolts to 22 ft. lbs. Be sure to install new gaskets between crossover and intake manifold.

INJECTION PUMP FUEL LINES

Removal — 1) Remove air cleaner and crossover, then install screened covers (J-26996-2 California or J-26996-10 Federal) over openings in intake manifold.

2) Remove injection pump line clamps. It is not necessary to use a back-up wrench when removing lines from pump.

3) Remove injection pump lines and cap open lines.

4) Using a back-up wrench on upper injector nozzle hex, disconnect injection pump lines at nozzle inlet fittings.

5) It is not necessary to remove pump to replace a line(s).

Installation — 1) Install new injection pump line(s) loosely. Position line properly.

2) Torque all high pressure fuel lines to 25 ft. lbs.

NOTE — *Use a back-up wrench when tightening fuel lines to fuel inlet fittings on injector nozzles.*

3) Install line clamps. Start engine and check for fuel leaks.

NOTE — *If several lines are to be replaced, start by connecting lower lines first.*

4) Remove screened covers from intake manifold and install air crossover and air filter assembly.

INJECTION PUMP

Removal — 1) Remove air cleaner and crossover, then install screened covers over openings in intake manifold.

2) Disconnect throttle rod and return spring.

3) Remove bellcrank. Remove throttle and T.V. cables from intake manifold brackets. Position cables away from engine.

4) Remove lines to fuel filter and remove filter.

5) Disconnect fuel line at fuel pump. On models equipped with A/C, remove rear compressor brace.

6) Remove fuel line to injection pump.

7) Disconnect fuel return line at injection pump.

8) Remove injector fuel lines at pump, using 2 wrenches.

9) Use special wrench (J-26987 or equivalent) to remove 3 nuts securing injection pump. Remove pump and cap all open lines and nozzles.

Installation — 1) Position cylinder No. 1 at TDC by lining up crankshaft pulley mark with indicator. Remove caps placed over fittings.

GENERAL MOTORS DIESEL FUEL INJECTION (Cont.)

2) Line up offset tang on pump driveshaft with pump driven gear and install pump.

3) Install 3 nuts and lockwashers securing pump but DO NOT tighten yet.

4) Connect pump lines at nozzles and tighten to 25 ft. lbs. with TWO wrenches.

5) Connect fuel return line to injection pump.

6) Align mark on injection pump with line on adapter. Tighten retaining nuts to 18 ft. lbs.

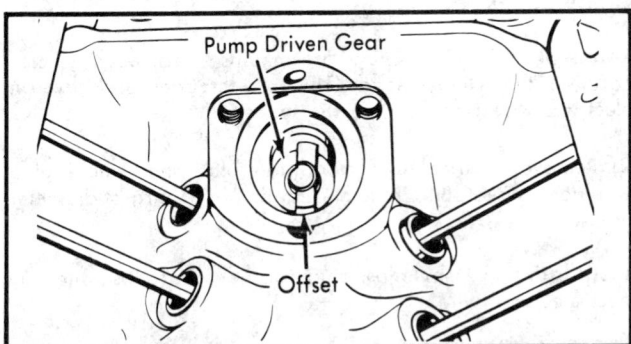

Fig. 14   Pump Driven Gear Offset at TDC (Shown with Intake Manifold Removed)

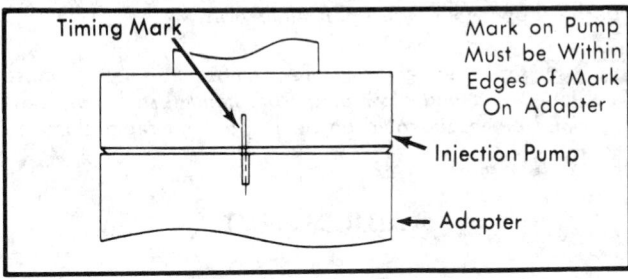

Fig. 15   Aligning Timing Marks on Pump & Adapter

NOTE — *Use a ¾" wrench on boss at front of injection pump to help in rotating pump while aligning marks.*

7) Adjust throttle rod. *See Linkage Adjustment in this article.*

8) Install fuel line from fuel pump to fuel filter. On A/C models, install rear compressor brace.

9) Install bellcrank and clip. Install throttle and T.V. cables to intake manifold. Attach cables to bellcrank.

10) Adjust T.V. cable (See Linkage Adjustment.) Connect throttle rod and return spring, then start engine and check for leaks.

11) Let engine run 2 minutes, then shut-off for 2 minutes to bleed air from pump.

12 Start engine and check for fuel leaks.

13) Remove screened covers and install air crossover and filter assembly.

INJECTION PUMP ADAPTER, SEAL & NEW ADAPTER TIMING MARK

Removal — 1) Remove air cleaner, air crossover, injection pump and lines.

2) Remove injection pump adapter. Remove seal from pump adapter.

Installation — 1) File timing mark off of injection pump ADAPTER.

CAUTION — *DO NOT file timing mark off of injection pump.*

2) Rotate engine to place No. 1 piston at TDC. Align mark on balancer with ZERO mark on indicator See *Fig. 14* for position of driven gear.

NOTE — *Index is offset to the right with No. 1 at TDC.*

3) Apply chassis lube to seal area on adapter, taper edge and seal area in intake manifold. Install adapter and leave loose.

4) Thoroughly lube seal, inside and out, with chassis lube. Install seal on seal installation tool (J-28425).

5) Push seal onto pump adapter using the installation tool.

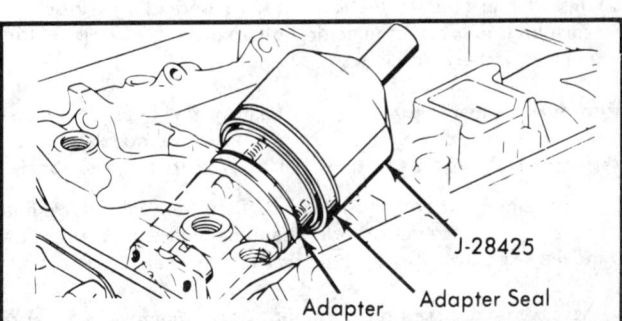

Fig. 16   Installation of New Adapter Seal

6) Remove tool. Observe seal for proper positioning. Torque adapter bolts to 25 ft. lbs.

7) Install timing tool (J-26896) into injection pump adapter. Torque tool in direction of No. 1 cylinder to 50 ft. lbs.

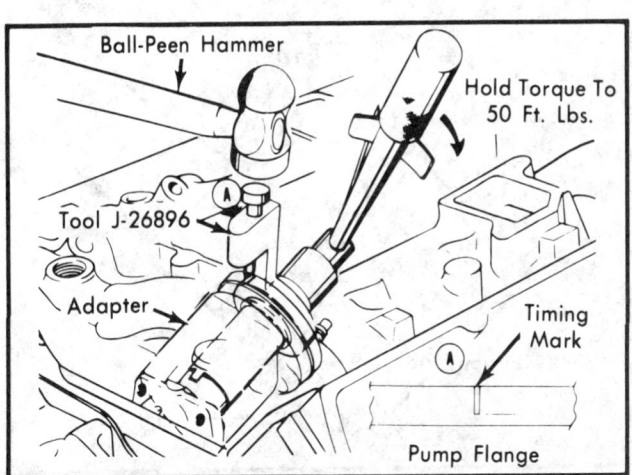

Fig. 17   Stamping Timing Mark on Adapter

1981 Diesel Fuel Injection

GENERAL MOTORS DIESEL FUEL INJECTION (Cont.)

8) While holding torque, stamp timing mark on injection pump adapter. See *Fig. 17*.

9) Remove tool. Install injection pump, lines, and air crossover assembly.

INJECTION NOZZLES

Removal (Diesel Equipment/C.A.V Lucas) — 1) Remove fuel lines from injection pump-to-nozzle on bank of engine where nozzle is to be serviced. Use back-up wrench on nozzle inlet fitting hex. DO NOT bend lines out of way to remove nozzle.

2) Cap open fittings and nozzles. Remove nozzle, using wrench on largest hex of injector nozzle. Make sure copper compression seal is removed with nozzle.

NOTE — *Tip of nozzle must be protected from any damage or dirt.*

Installation — 1) Use new copper compression seal and install nozzle. Tighten to 25 ft. lbs. (C.A.V. Lucas nozzle) or 45 ft. lbs. (Diesel Equipment nozzle). See *Fig. 6*.

2) Install fuel lines to fuel inlet fittings and using a back-up wrench on upper hex of injector, tighten lines to 25 ft. lbs. Start engine and check for leaks.

Removal (Roosa-Master) — 1) Remove fuel lines from injection pump-to-nozzle on bank of engine where nozzle is to be serviced. DO NOT bend lines out of way to remove nozzle.

2) Cap open fittings and nozzles. Remove fuel return line clamps from all nozzles on side of engine where nozzle is to be removed. Remove appropriate fuel return line(s).

3) Remove nozzle spring clamp and spacer. Remove nozzle using removal tool (J-26952). Cap nozzle inlet line and nozzle tip.

NOTE — *Tip of nozzle must be protected from any damage or dirt.*

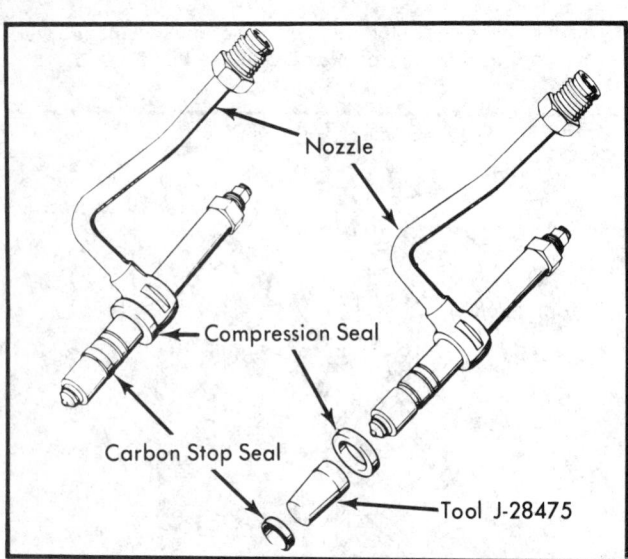

Fig. 18 Roosa-Master Injection Nozzle Seals (Federal Models)

Installation — 1) If old nozzle is to be reinstalled after removal, remove old carbon stop seal and compression seal. Install NEW carbon stop and compression seals.

2) Remove caps from open fittings and lines. Install nozzle, spring clamp and spacer. Torque bolt to 25 ft. lbs.

3) Reinstall fuel return lines and clamps.

4) Install fuel delivery lines from pump-to-nozzles.

5) Start engine and check for leaks.

GLOW PLUGS

Removal — 1) Glow plugs are mounted near each injector nozzle in the cylinder heads. They are threaded and have an electrical wire plugged into the top end.

2) Remove electrical wire from glow plug and remove plug with deep socket. Be sure to engage socket on largest diameter hex surfaces.

Installation — Install glow plug, torque to 12 ft. lbs., and connect electrical wire.

PRE-CHAMBER

NOTE — *Cylinder head must be removed to remove pre-chamber. There is one pre-chamber for each combustion chamber in cylinder head. Pre-chamber is opposite glow plug and can be tapped out with small blunt drift.*

CAUTION — *When removing pre-chamber, be sure to remove injection nozzle and glow plug from head first. If not, glow plug and/or nozzle could be bent and need replacement.*

ADJUSTMENT

HOT (SLOW) IDLE RPM

See *appropriate article in TUNE-UP Section.*

COLD (FAST) IDLE RPM

See *appropriate article in TUNE-UP Section.*

INJECTION TIMING

Engine is properly timed when mark on injection pump is aligned with mark on adapter. See *Fig. 15*. If marks are not aligned, adjustment is necessary. Engine must be off for adjustment.

1) Loosen 3 pump retaining nuts with wrench (J-26987). Align mark on pump with mark on adapter and tighten nuts to 19 ft. lbs.

NOTE — *Use ¾" wrench on boss at front of pump to turn pump while aligning marks.*

2) Adjust throttle rod and linkage.

GENERAL MOTORS DIESEL FUEL INJECTION (Cont.)

LINKAGE ADJUSTMENT

Throttle Rod Adjustment — 1) With engine off, check pump timing. If equipped with cruise control, remove clip from cruise control throttle rod and disconnect rod from throttle lever.

2) Disconnect transmission T.V. or detent cable from throttle assembly. Loosen lock nut on pump rod and shorten by several turns. Rotate lever to full throttle position and hold.

3) Lengthen rod until injection pump lever just contacts full throttle stop. Release lever and tighten lock nut. Remove pump rod from lever assembly.

4) Reconnect transmission T.V. or detent cable. Depress and hold metal lock tab on upper end of cable, then move slider away from lever assembly until it stops against metal fitting.

5) Release metal tab, rotate lever assembly to full throttle stop and release lever assembly. Reconnect pump rod and cruise control rod. Adjust idle speed.

Vacuum Regulator Valve — 1) Remove air crossover and install screen covers over openings. Remove throttle rod from throttle lever. Loosen vacuum regulator valve-to-pump bolts.

2) Install carburetor angle gauge to injection pump throttle lever. Rotate throttle lever to wide-open throttle position and set angle gauge to zero degrees, then center bubble.

3) Set angle gauge to 58°, then rotate throttle lever until bubble is centered. Attach vacuum pump to port "A" of vacuum regulator valve and vacuum pump to port "B". See *Fig. 21.*

4) Apply 18-22 in. Hg vacuum to port "A", then rotate vacuum valve clockwise to obtain 8.5-9.0 in. Hg. Tighten bolts and connect throttle rod. Remove vacuum pump and angle gauge.

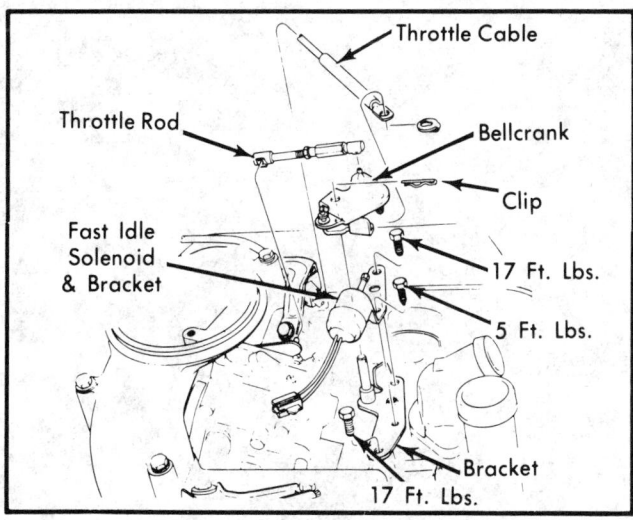

Fig. 19   Disassembled View of Throttle Linkage

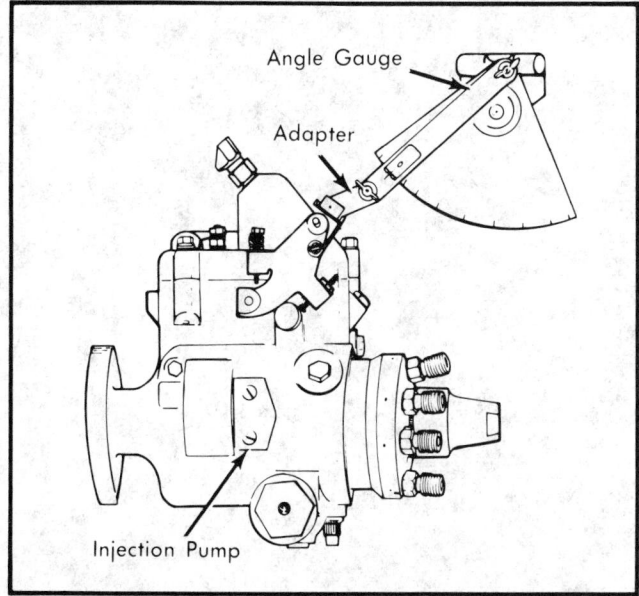

Fig. 20   Vacuum Regulator Valve Adjustment

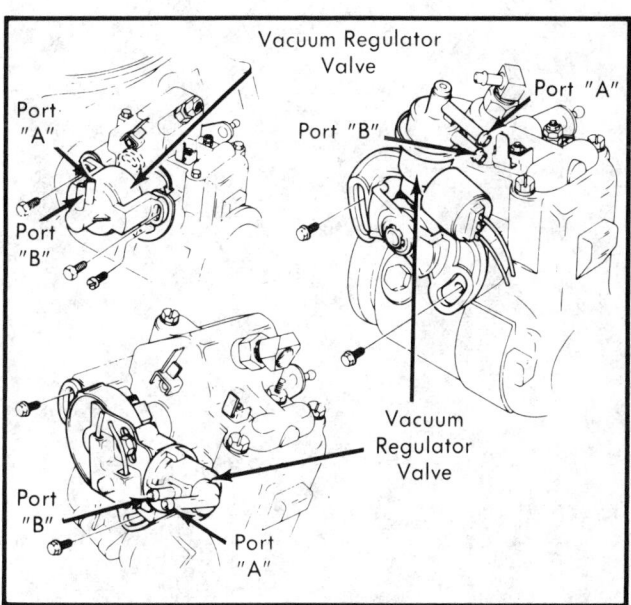

Fig. 21   Vacuum Regulator Valve Port Locations

TIGHTENING SPECIFICATIONS

Application	Ft. Lbs.
Fuel Pump-to-Block Bolt/Nut	25
Injection Pump Attaching Nuts	19
Injection Line Nut-to-Pump	25
Injection Pump Adapter Bolts	25
Injection Line Nut-to-Nozzle	25
Inj. Pump Fuel Filter Inlet	20
Inj. Pump Fuel Filter Outlet	18
Injection Pump Fuel Inlet Line	20
Nozzle Clamp	25
Glow Plug	12
Injection Nozzle (Calif.)	
Diesel Equipment	45
C.A.V. Lucas	25
Glow Plug	12
Air Crossover Bolts	22

Section 3

EMISSION CONTROL

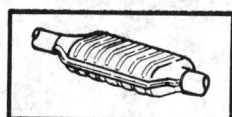

Contents

NOTE — ALSO SEE GENERAL INDEX

IMPORTANT

*Because of the great number of model names used by vehicle manufacturers, accurate identification of models is important.
See Model Identification at the front of this publication.*

1981 Emission Control Application

1981 CHRYSLER CORP.

Engines	Emission Control Systems & Devices	Remarks
1981 Chrysler Corp. Light Duty Emissions 3.7L (225") 6-Cyl.	AAS, AIR, APDV, CAT, CCV, CCEGR, EAC, ECS, EGR, HADV, TAC	① — California models only. ② — Federal models only.
5.2L (318") V8	AAS, AIR, APDV, CAT, CCV, CCEGR, EAC, ECS, EGR, HADV①, OSAC, PHDV①, PHV①, TAC, TIDC	
5.9L (360") V8	AAS, AIR, APDV, CAT, CCV, CCEVS②, EAC, ECS, EGR, OSAC, TAC, TIDC	
Heavy Duty Emissions 5.2L (318") V8	AAS, AIR, APDV, CAT, CCV, CCEGR, ECS, EGR, EGR-DV, OSAC, TAC, TIDC, TP	
5.9L (360") V8	AAS, AIR, APDV, CAT, CCV, CCEGR, ECS, EGR, EGR-DV, OSAC, TAC, TIDC, TP	

Light Duty Emissions: Are vehicles up to 8500 GVW. **Heavy Duty Emissions:** Are vehicles over 8500 GVW.

AAS — Aspirator Air System
AIR — Air Injection Reactor
APDV — Air Pump Diverter Valve
CAT — Catalytic Converter
CCC — Crankcase Control Valve

CCEGR — Coolant Controlled Exhaust Gas Recirculation
CCEVS — Coolant Controlled Engine Vacuum Switch
EAC — Electric Assist Choke

ECS — Evaporation Control System
EGR — Exhaust Gas Recirculation
EGR-DV — EGR Delay Valve
HADV — Heated Air Delay Valve
OSAC — Orifice Spark Advance Control

PHDV — Power Heat Delay Valve
TAC — Thermostatic Air Cleaner
TIDC — Thermostatic Ignition Distributor Control
TP — Throttle Positioner

1981 FORD

Engines	Emission Control Systems & Devices	Remarks
1981 Ford Light Duty Emissions 4.9L (300") 6-Cyl.	AIR, AIR-BPV, A/CL-BM, A/CL-CWM①, A/CL-DV, TAC, DV-TW, EAC, EGR, FVEC, PCV, PG-CV, TAC, TVS, TVV, VCV, VRDV, V-RSR③, V-RST①③	① — California models only. ② — Federal models only. ③ — Manual transmission only. ④ — Automatic transmission only. ⑤ — Some models only. ⑥ — A/C models only.
4.2L (255") V8	AIR, AIR-BPV, EGR, VCV, TAC, VRDV, V-RST, VDV④	
5.0L (302") V8	AIR, AIR-BPV, A/CL-BM, A/CL-DV, BV, CAT, DV-TW⑤, EAC, EGR, FVEC, IVV③, PCV, PG-CV, SV-CBV①, TAC, TVS, TVV②, VCV, VDV⑤, VRDV, V-RSR⑤, VRV④⑤	
5.8L (351") "M" V8	AIR, AIR-BPV, A/CL-BM, A/CL-DV, BV, CAT, EAC, EGR, FVEC, IVV③, LCV⑤, PCV, PG-CV, SV-CBV①, TAC, TVS, TVV②④, VCkV⑤, VCV, VRDV, V-RSR, V-RST⑤	
5.8L (351") "W" V8	AIR, AIR-BPV, A/CL-CWM, A/CL-DV, BV, CAT, DV-TW⑤, EAC, EGR, FVEC, HIC⑥, PCV, PG-CV, SV-CBV①, TAC, TVS, TV-RST①, TVV②, VCV, VRDV, V-RSR	

Light Duty Emissions: Are vehicles up to 8500 GVW. **Heavy Duty Emissions:** Are vehicles over 8500 GVW.

AIR — Air Injection System
AIR-BPV — AIR-Bypass Valve
A/CL-BM — Air Cleaner Bi-Metal Sensor
A/CL-CWM — Air Cleaner Cold Weather Modulator
A/CL-DV — Air Cleaner Duct Valve Vacuum Motor
BV — Bowl Vent Port
CAT — Catalytic Converter
DV-TW — Delay Valve-Two Way
EAC — Electric Assist Choke
EGR — Exhaust Gas Recirculation
FVEC — Fuel Vapor Emission Control

HIC — Hot Idle Compensator
IVV — Idle Vacuum Valve
LCV — Load Control Valve
PCV — Positive Crankcase Ventilation
PG-CV — Purge Control Valve
SA-FV — Separator Assembly - Fuel/Vacuum
Sol-V — Solenoid Valve
SV-CBV — Solenoid Valve - Carb. Bowl Vent
TAC — Thermstatic Air Cleaner
TK — Throtte Kicker
TV-RST — Hose Tee Vacuum Restrictor

TVS — Thermal Vacuum Switch
TVV — Thermal Vent Valve
V-CkV — Vacuum Check Valve
VCV — Vacuum Control Valve
VDV — Vacuum Delay Valve
VOTM — Vacuum Operated Throttle Modulator
VRDV — Vacuum Retard Delay Valve
V-RSR — Vacuum Reservoir
V-RST — Vacuum Restrictor
VVA — Venturi Vacuum Amplifier (EGR-VVA)

1981 FORD (Cont.)

Engines	Emission Control Systems & Devices	Remarks
1981 Ford (Cont.) Light Duty Emissions (Cont.) 6.6L (400") V8	AIR, AIR-BPV, A/CL-BM, A/CL-DV, BV, CAT, EAC, EGR, FVEC, PCV, PG-CV, SV-CBV①, TAC, TVS, VCV, V-RST	① — California models only. ② — Federal models only. ③ — Manual transmission only. ④ — Automatic transmission only. ⑤ — Some models only. ⑥ — A/C models only.
Heavy Duty Emissions 4.9L (300") 6-Cyl.	AIR, AIR-BPV, A/CL-BM, A/CL-DV, PCV, SA-FV, Sol-V, TAC, VCV, VOTM, V-RSR, VVA	
5.8L (351") "M" V8	AIR, AIR-BPV, A/CL-BM, A/CL-DV, EGR, FVEC①, LCV, PCV, SA-FV, Sol-V, TAC, TK, VCV, VDV, VRDV, V-RSR, VVA	
5.8L (351") "W" V8	AIR, AIR-BPV, A/CL-BM, A/CL-CWM, A/CL-DV, EGR, LCV, PCV, SA-FV, Sol-V, TAC, VCV, VDV, VOTM, VRDV, V-RSR, VVA	
6.6L (400") V8	AIR, AIR-BPV, A/CL-BM, A/CL-DV, EGR, LCV, PCV, SA-FV, Sol-V, TAC, TK, VCV, VDV, VRDV, V-RSR, VVA	
7.5L (460") V8	AIR, AIR-BPV, A/CL-BM, A/CL-DV, EGR, PCV, Sol-V, TAC, TK, VCV, VDV, V-RSR, VVA	

Light Duty Emissions: Are vehicles up to 8500 GVW. **Heavy Duty Emissions:** Are vehicles over 8500 GVW.

AIR – Air Injection System
AIR-BPV – AIR-Bypass Valve
A/CL-BM – Air Cleaner Bi-Metal Sensor
A/CL-CWM – Air Cleaner Cold Weather Modulator
A/CL-DV – Air Cleaner Duct Valve Vacuum Motor
BV – Bowl Vent Port
CAT – Catalytic Converter
DV-TW – Delay Valve-Two Way
EAC – Electric Assist Choke
EGR – Exhaust Gas Recirculation
FVEC – Fuel Vapor Emission Control

HIC – Hot Idle Compensator
IVV – Idle Vacuum Valve
LCV – Load Control Valve
PCV – Positive Crankcase Ventilation
PG-CV – Purge Control Valve
SA-FV – Separator Assembly - Fuel/Vacuum
Sol-V – Solenoid Valve
SV-CBV – Solenoid Valve - Carb. Bowl Vent
TAC – Thermstatic Air Cleaner
TK – Throttle Kicker
TV-RST – Hose Tee Vacuum Restrictor

TVS – Thermal Vacuum Switch
TVV – Thermal Vent Valve
V-CkV – Vacuum Check Valve
VCV – Vacuum Control Valve
VDV – Vacuum Delay Valve
VOTM – Vacuum Operated Throttle Modulator
VRDV – Vacuum Retard Delay Valve
V-RSR – Vacuum Reservoir
V-RST – Vacuum Restrictor
VVA – Venturi Vacuum Amplifier (EGR-VVA)

1981 GENERAL MOTORS

Engines	Emission Control Systems & Devices	Remarks
1981 GM Light Duty Emissions 4.1L (250") 6-Cyl.	A/CL, A.I.R.②, CAT, DC-VLV①, DCP-TVS, DLCk-VLV, DVTR-VLV③, EFE, EFE-TVS, EGR, EGR-TVS, PCV, SVBrk, SRDD-VLV, TrC-TVS, TrC-VS, VBrk, VR-VLV	① — Except Federal models with auto. trans. ② — Used on some models. ③ — Used with A.I.R. only.
5.0L (305") V8	A/CL, A.I.R.②, CAT, CkDL-VLV, DC-VLV, DDL-VLV, DVTR-VLV③, EFE, EFE-TVS, EGR, EGR-TVS, PCV, SVBrk, TrC-VS, VBrk	

Light Duty Emissions: Are vehicles up to 8500 GVW. **Heavy Duty Emissions:** Are vehicles over 8500 GVW.

A/CL – Air Cleaner
A.I.R. – Air Injection Reactor
APD-VLV – Air Pump Diverter Valve
CAT – Catalytic Converter
CkDL-VLV – Check Delay Valve
Ck-VLV – Check Valve
DCP-TVS – Distributor and Canister Purge Thermal Vacuum Switch
DC-VLV – Deceleration Valve
DDL-VLV – Distributor Delay Valve
DLCk-VLV – Delay Check Valve
DVTR-VLV – Diverter Valve

EFE – Early Fuel Evaporation
EFE-TVS – Early Fuel Evaporation Thermal Vacuum Switch
EGR – Exhaust Gas Recirculation
EGR-TVS – Exhaust Gas Recirculation Thermal Vacuum Switch
PCV – Positive Crankcase Ventilation
SVBrk – Secondary Vacuum Break Actuator
SRD-VLV – Spark Retard Delay Valve
SP-TVS – Spark Thermal Vacuum Switch
TLA – Throttle Lever Actuator

TrC-TVS – Transmission Lock-up Converter Thermal Vacuum Switch
TrC-VS – Transmission Lock-up Converter Vacuum Switch
TRC-SOL-CVLV – Throttle Return Control Solenoid – Control Valve
TRC-TLA – Throttle Return Control – Throttle Lever Actuator
TRC-VLV – Throttle Return Control – Valve
TVS – Thermal Vacuum Switch
VBrk – Vacuum Break Actuator
VR-VLV – Vacuum Regulator Valve

1981 GENERAL MOTORS (Cont.)

Engines	Emission Control Systems & Devices	Remarks
1981 GM (Cont.) Light Duty Emissions (Cont.) 5.7L (350") V8	A/CL, A.I.R.②, CAT, CkDL-VLV, CkVLV, DDL-VLV, DC-VLV, DVTR-VLV③, EFE, EFE-TVS, EGR, EGR-TVS, PCV, SVBrk, SP-TVS, TLA, TrC-VS, TRC-VLV, TVS, VBrk	① — Except Federal models with auto. trans. ② — Used on some models. ③ — Used with A.I.R. only.
Heavy Duty Emissions 4.8L (292") 6-Cyl.	A/CL, A.I.R., APD-VLV, CAT, DL-VLV, PCV, TLA, TRC-VLV	
5.0L (305") V8	A/CL, A.I.R.②, Ck-VLV, DDL-VLV, DLTR-VLV, DLCk-VLV, EFE, EFE-TVS, EGR, EGR-TVS, TrC-VS	
5.7L (350") V8	A/CL, A.I.R.②, Ck-VLV, DVTR-VLV, EFE, EFE-TVS, PCV, SP-TVS, SVBrk, TLA, TRC-VLV, TRC-SOL-CVLV, TVS, VDL-VLV	
7.4L (454") V8	A/CL, A.I.R., Ck-VLV, DVTR-VLV, EFE, EFE-TVS, PCV, SVBrk, SP-TVS, TRC-SOL-CVLV, TRC-TLA, TVS	

Light Duty Emissions: Are vehicles up to 8500 GVW. **Heavy Duty Emissions:** Are vehicles over 8500 GVW.

A/CL – Air Cleaner
A.I.R. – Air Injection Reactor
APD-VLV – Air Pump Diverter Valve
CAT – Catalytic Converter
CkDL-VLV – Check Delay Valve
Ck-VLV – Check Valve
DCP-TVS – Distributor and Canister Purge Thermal Vacuum Switch
DC-VLV – Deceleration Valve
DDL-VLV – Distributor Delay Valve
DLCk-VLV – Delay Check Valve
DVTR-VLV – Diverter Valve
EFE – Early Fuel Evaporation

EFE-TVS – Early Fuel Evaporation Thermal Vacuum Switch
EGR – Exhaust Gas Recirculation
EGR-TVS – Exhaust Gas Recirculation Thermal Vacuum Switch
PCV – Positive Crankcase Ventilation
SVBrk – Secondary Vacuum Break Actuator
SRD-VLV – Spark Retard Delay Valve
SP-TVS – Spark Thermal Vacuum Switch
TLA – Throttle Lever Actuator
TrC-TVS – Transmissionm Lock-up Converter Thermal Vacuum Switch

TrC-VS – Transmission Lock-up Converter Vacuum Switch
TRC-SOL-CVLV – Throttle Return Control Solenoid – Control Valve
TRC-TLA – Throttle Return Control – Throttle Lever Actuator
TRC-VLV – Throttle Return Control – Valve
TVS – Thermal Vacuum Switch
VBrk – Vacuum Break Actuator
VR-VLV – Vacuum Regulator Valve

1981 JEEP

Engines	Emission Control Systems & Devices	Remarks
1981 Jeep 2.5L (151") 4-Cyl.	CAT, C-4①, Decel-V①, EGR, EGR-CTO, EGR-TVS, HDSP-CTO②, MCU①, PCV, RDV, SP-CTO, TSD, VSA①	① — California only. ② — Federal only. ③ — Heavy Duty. ④ — Some Models. ⑤ — J-10 Manual transmission. ⑥ — Automatic transmission.
4.2L (258") 6-Cyl.	A.I.R., ASV①, BPV, CAT, CEC①, CTO, Decel-V, DLV①, DVTRV, EGR, EGR-CTO, EGR-TVS, FDV, HDC-CTO③, MCU①, NLRV④, PCV, RDV, SL, SLV, SP-CTO, VR, VR-CkV, VSA①	
5.0L (304") Fed. V8	A.I.R., CAT, CTO, DVTRV, EGR, EGR-CTO, EGR-TVS, EGR-FDLV⑤⑥, FDV, HDC-CTO, NLRV, RDV, TSD, PCV	
6.0L (360") Fed. V8	A.I.R., CAT, CTO, DVTRV, EGR, EGR-CTO, EGR-TVS, EGR-FDLV, HDSP-CTO③, NLRV, RDV, TSD, PCV, VSD	

A.I.R. – Air Injection Reactor
ASV – Air Switch Valve
BPV – By-Pass Valve
CAT – Catalytic Converter
CEC – Computerized Emission Control
CTO – Coolant Temperature Override
C-4 – Computer Controlled Catalytic Converter
Decel-V – Deceleration Valve
DLV – Delay Valve
DVTRV – Diverter Valve
EGR – Exhaust Gas Recirculation

EGR-CTO – Exhaust Gas Recirculation Coolant Temperature Override
EGR-FDLV – Exhaust Gas Recirculation Forward Delay Valve
EGR-TVS – Exhaust Gas Recirculation Thermal Vacuum Switch
FDV – Forward Delay Valve
HDC-CTO – Heavy Duty Cooling Coolant Temperature Override
HDSP-CT – Heavy Duty Spark Coolant Temperature Override
MCU – Micro Computer Unit

NLRV – Non-Linear Valve
PCV – Psitive Crankcase Ventilation
RDV – Reverse Delay Valve
SP-CTO – Spark Coolant Temperature Override
SLV – Solevac
SL – Solenoid
TSD – Throttle Solenoid
VR – Vacuum Reservoir
VR-CkV – Vacuum Reverse Check Valve
VSA – Vacuum Switch Assembly
VSD – Vacuum Switch Dump

POSITIVE CRANKCASE VENTILATION SYSTEMS – PCV

All Models

DESCRIPTION

The crankcase ventilation system is designed to prevent contaminating hydrocarbons from escaping to the atmosphere. This is accomplished by routing the vapors from the crankcase through a vacuum controlled ventilating valve (PCV Valve) into the intake manifold, where they mix with the air-/fuel mixture and are burned in the combustion process.

OPERATION

Air is supplied to the crankcase ventilation system through a crankcase ventilating filter assembly located in the carburetor or on rocker arm cover.

When the engine is operating, fresh air enters the positive crankcase ventilation system through the air cleaner and filter.

The air then flows into the rocker arm cover and valve compartment. It combines with blow-by gas and unburned air/fuel mixture and burns in combustion chamber. See Fig. 1.

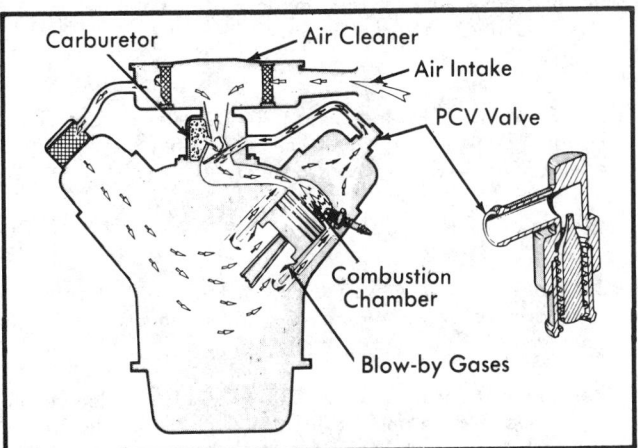

Fig. 1 Typical Crankcase Ventilation System

The ventilator valve is constructed so it is held closed by spring pressure when engine is not running. See Fig. 2. This prevents an accumulation of hydrocarbon fumes from collecting in the intake manifold, which results in hard starting.

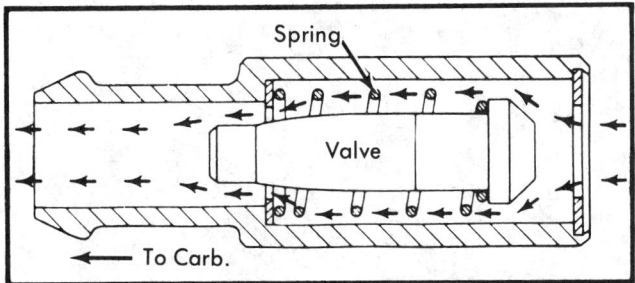

Fig. 2 Typical PCV Valve & Airflow

As the engine is started, manifold vacuum pulls the valve open against spring pressure. As long as there is engine vacuum, the valve floats, permitting crankcase fumes to enter the intake manifold.

A baffle in the rocker arm prevents oil from being drawn into the intake manifold through the ventilator valve.

In the event of an engine backfire through the intake manifold, the ventilator valve shuts, preventing any flow through it. This action prevents the ignition of fumes in the crankcase.

During certain engine operations more blow-by is created than the ventilator valve can handle. The excess amount is returned to air cleaner and carburetor through the rocker arm cover and breather assembly, then burned in the engine.

The breather assembly acts as a separator to keep oil from being drawn into the air cleaner during this operation.

TESTING

ALL MODELS (EXCEPT JEEP)

To test crankcase ventilation system, start engine and allow it to reach normal operating temperature. Make sure engine is idling at normal curb idle and perform following checks:

1) Remove PCV valve from its mounting. If valve is functioning properly, a hissing noise will be heard as air passes through. A strong vacuum should be felt when finger is placed over valve inlet. While finger is over inlet, check for vacuum leaks in hose line and at all connections. Re-install PCV valve, then remove crankcase air inlet hose at air cleaner.

2) Loosely hold a piece of stiff paper over opening at end of inlet hose. Paper should be sucked against hose opening with a noticeable force after sufficient time has elapsed for crankcase pressure to lower (usually about a minute).

3) As a final check; stop engine, remove PCV valve and shake it, a metallic clicking noise should be heard, indicating valve is free.

NOTE — *If system passes both the engine running and stopped tests, it is functioning properly and no further tests are required. If it has failed either test, replace appropriate components and retest. If it does not pass on second try, clean system.*

JEEP

1) Remove PCV valve from grommet in rocker arm cover on 4 and 6 cylinder models, or from hose behind carburetor on V8 models.

2) Connect valve to PCV valve tester (J-23111 or equivalent). Four cylinder valves require an adapter for the tester.

3) Connect a vacuum gauge to read intake manifold vacuum.

NOTE — *PCV valve must be in a horizontal position and lightly tapped during tests (holding tester in a vertical position).*

4) Start engine, allow to idle, compare vacuum and tester reading to flow chart. A valve that flows above or below chart specification must be cleaned or replaced.

1981 Crankcase Ventilation

POSITIVE CRANKCASE VENTILATION SYSTEMS – PCV (Cont.)

Jeep PCV Flow Rates①

Vacuum (In. Hg)	Flow Rate for 4-Cyl.	Flow Rate for 6-Cyl.	Flow Rate for V8
16		.0-.20	1.34-1.63
15	.50-1.00		
13		1.30-1.90	
11		.90-2.00	
7			2.70-3.79
6	1.05-1.85		
5		1.50-2.50	
3	1.50-2.50		3.30-4.39
2		1.28-2.56	

① — Flow rate given in cubic feet per minute (cfm).

MAINTENANCE

NOTE — An engine may idle slow or rough due to clogged ventilator valve or system; therefore never adjust carburetor idle without first checking valve and system.

If the ventilator valve or system becomes clogged, all crankcase ventilation will stop and serious engine damage could result.

Although the following manufacturers' service procedures give specific intervals, it is recommended the crankcase ventilation system be checked more frequently if vehicles are operated under severe conditions (extreme dust, prolonged idling, trailer hauling or short trips in cold weather).

CHRYSLER CORP.

PCV Valve — On Light Duty Emission models (up to 8,500 GVW), check every 15,000 miles and replace every 30,000 miles. On Heavy Duty Emission models (over 8,500 GVW), check every 12,000 miles and replace every 24,000 miles.

Filter Element — On Light Duty Emission models, clean crankcase inlet air cleaner every 30,000 miles. On Heavy Duty Emission models, clean every 12,000 miles.

FORD

PCV Valve — Valve is located on rocker covers. On all models replace every 30,000 miles. Under extreme conditions service will be more frequent.

Filter Element — Filter is located in air cleaner housing. Replace crankcase filter on 6 cylinder engines every 30,000 miles. On V8 engines, "E" & "F" 350 models replace every 30,00 miles. All other models not required.

GENERAL MOTORS

PCV Valve — Check every 15,000 miles and replace every 30,000 miles on Light Duty emission models (up to 8,500 lbs. GVW); check every 12,000 miles and replace every 24,000 miles on Heavy Duty emission models (over 8,500 lbs. GVW). Valve is located on rocker cover.

Filter Element — Replace every 30,000 miles on Light Duty emission models, every 24,000 miles on Heavy Duty emission models. Filter is located in carburetor.

JEEP

PCV Valve — Replace every 30,000 miles. Valve is located on rocker arm cover on 4 and 6 cylinder models, on intake manifold on V8 models.

Filter Element — Clean every 30,000 miles. Filter is located inside air cleaner on 4 and 6 cylinder models, in oil filler cap on V8 models.

CHRYSLER CORP.

DESCRIPTION

The evaporation control system prevents gasoline vapors from the fuel tank and carburetor from escaping into the atmosphere. The systems are all dual canister types.

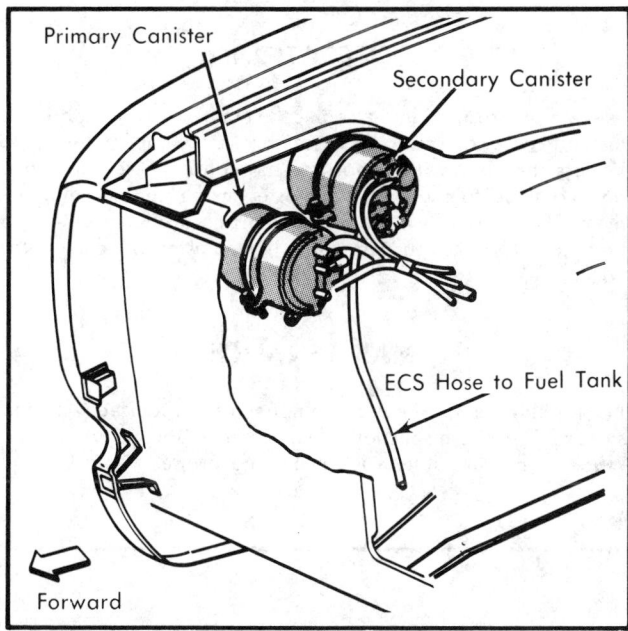

Fig. 1   Typical Dual Canister Mounting on "D" & "W" Models

OPERATION

When fuel evaporates in the carburetor float chamber or fuel tank, vapors pass through vent hoses or tubes to the charcoal canister. Fuel vapors are held on the activated charcoal surface until they are drawn into the intake manifold when the engine is running. A vacuum port in the carburetor base controls vapor flow to the engine.

On the two-canister system, fuel vapors from the primary canister are purged through the carburetor port. Vapors from the secondary canister are purged through the PCV hose to the carburetor using a distributor vacuum signal applied to the purge switch.

MAINTENANCE

There is no required service on the fuel evaporation control system except replacement of the filter element in the charcoal canister. Replace filters every 18,000 miles on Heavy Duty emission models (over 8,500 lbs. GVW). On all other models replace filter every 30,000 miles.

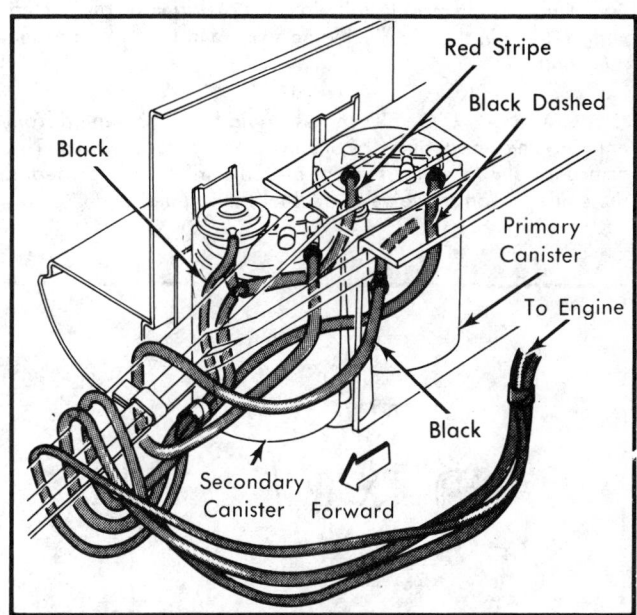

Fig. 2   Typical Vapor Hose Routing for Dual Canister "B" & "PB" Models

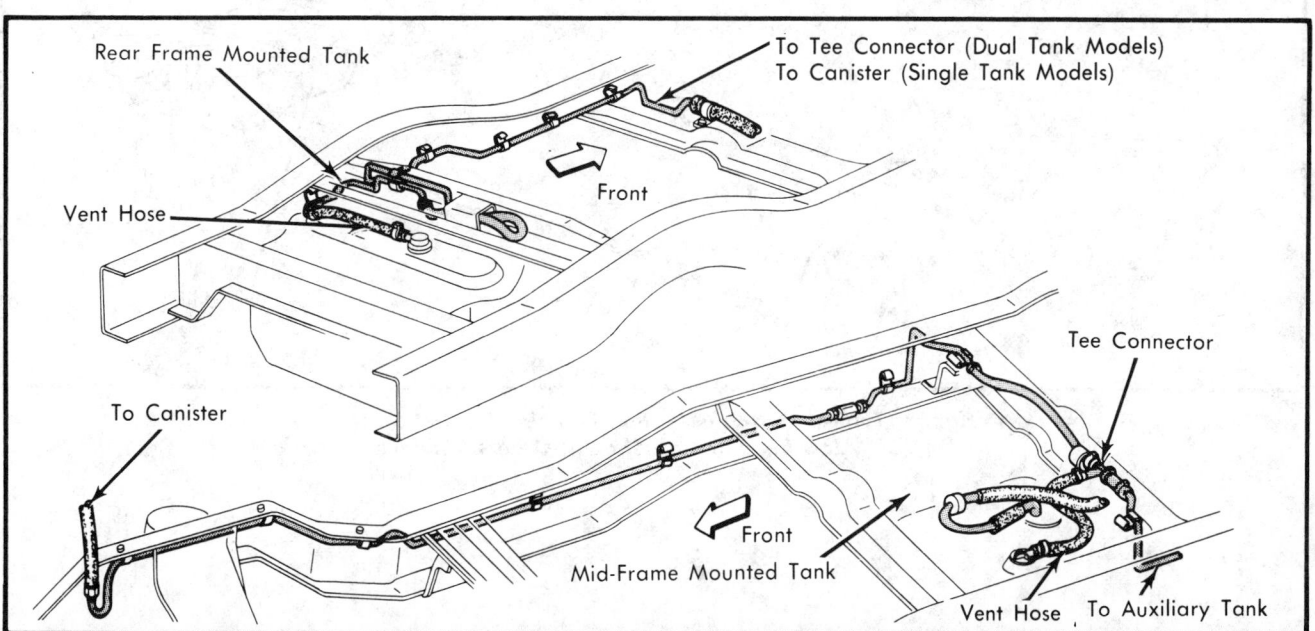

Fig. 3   Typical Evaporation Control System Hose Routing for "D" & "W" Models

FORD

DESCRIPTION

All models are equipped with fuel evaporation emission control systems. This closed system is designed to limit the amount of fuel vapor released to the atmosphere. The system consists of a special fuel filler cap, a specially designed fuel tank, a carbon-filled canister, an orifice valve and necessary fuel vent vapor lines. All 6 cylinder models with dual fuel tanks, and all V8 models use 2 carbon canisters.

Fuel Filler Cap — The fuel filler cap has a one-way vent, this prevents tank collapse by allowing air to enter the tank as fuel is consumed.

Fuel Tank — In most installations the fuel tank is constructed with a dome in the top. Fuel vapors rise and tend to gather in this dome.

Orifice Valve — On all vehicles, liquid fuel is prevented from entering the vapor lines by means of restricted orifices. This orifice usually takes the form of a .050 orifice valve located in the emission control valve in the fuel tank dome.

Carbon Canister — The carbon filled canister acts as a storage system for fuel vapors vented from the fuel tank and carburetor. The outlet of the canister is connected to the carburetor bowl vent.

OPERATION

Fuel vapors trapped in the sealed fuel tank are vented through the orifice vapor separator assembly in the top of the tank. Vapors then leave the separator through a single vapor line and continue to the carbon canister in the engine compartment. There they are absorbed by carbon granules, until such time as they are purged from the canister by carburetor vacuum.

MAINTENANCE

No regular replacement of components is required with this system. Periodic inspection of system components should be made to be sure system is functioning properly.

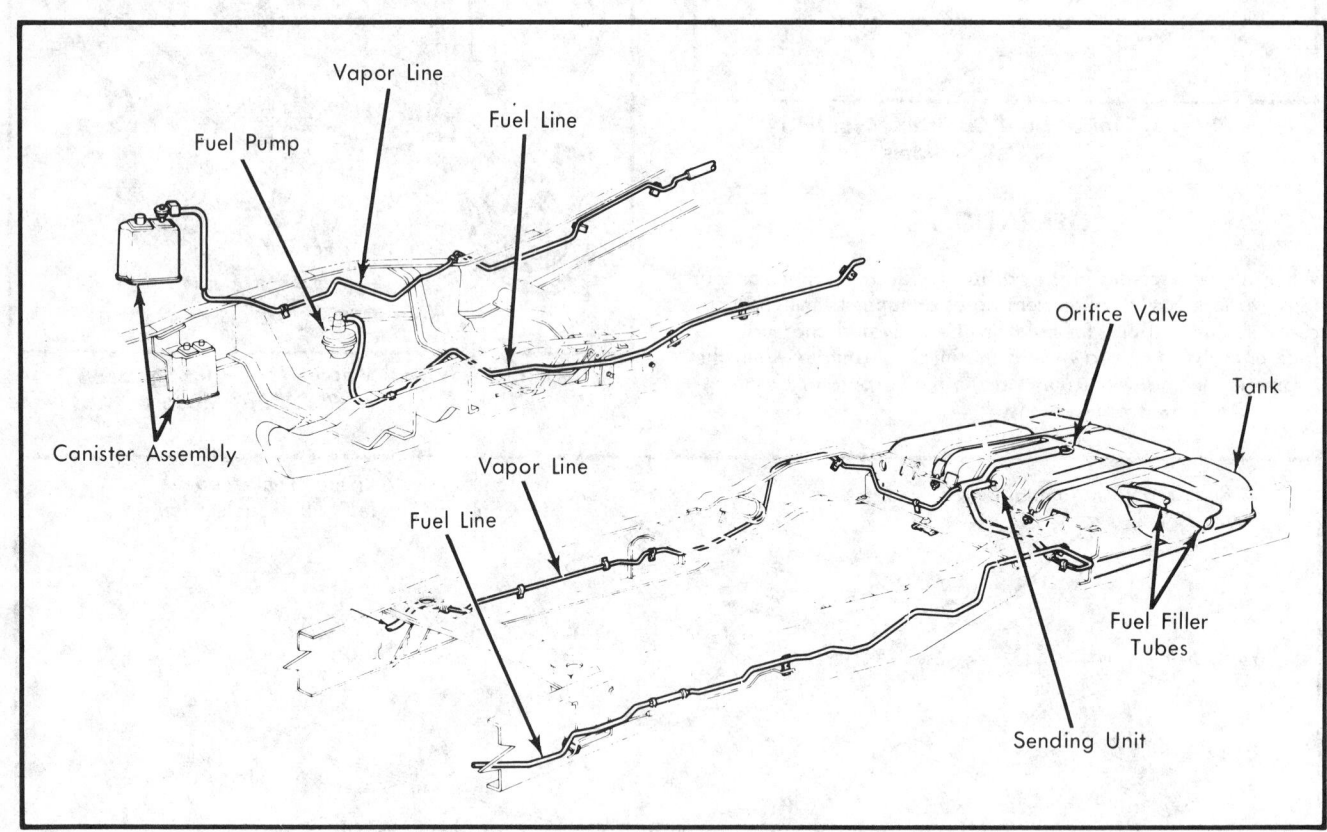

**Fig. 1   Typical Ford Evaporation Emission Control System
(F100/250 Regular Cab Shown, Others Similar)**

GENERAL MOTORS

DESCRIPTION

All Light and some Heavy Duty emissions models are equipped with an Evaporative Control System (ECS) designed to prevent raw fuel vapors from escaping to the atmosphere. System consists of a special fuel tank with a expansion section, a venting system which allows only vaporous fuel to be drawn into the system, a pressure-vacuum relief valve in the gas cap to control tank pressure and a vapor-storing charcoal canister.

OPERATION

During periods of engine operation, vapors are drawn through the system vent lines and into the intake manifold of the engine for burning. When engine is off, fuel vapors are stored in the charcoal of the vapor storage canister, and then drawn into the engine when it is running.

TESTING

PURGE VALVE (ON CANISTER)

1) Remove purge valve control vacuum line. Check for vacuum at line with engine running at approximately 1500 RPM. If there is no vacuum present, check EGR system.

2) Apply external vacuum to the valve. Vacuum should hold. If not, replace the canister assembly. If vacuum holds, remove purge line and check for vacuum. If no vacuum, check PCV system.

BOWL VENT VALVE

1) Remove bowl vent vapor hose from carburetor. Check open condition of valve by connecting to a manual vacuum pump. It should not be possible to draw more than 0.5" Hg if valve is open (as when engine is off).

2) If high resistance or plugged system is found, check for plugged or restricted hose. Hose may be cleared with com-pressed air. If hose is clear, remove canister filter. If restriction persists, replace canister.

3) To check valve closed position, run engine at idle. Manifold vacuum will be applied to valve through control line. Bowl vent line should exhibit a plugged condition.

4) If valve is not closed, remove control vacuum line and check for vacuum. If no vacuum, check for hose restriction or leak. Replace hose if required. If vacuum is present, replace canister assembly.

MAINTENANCE

The charcoal canister is the only serviceable item. It should be replaced every 24 months or 30,000 miles on Light Duty Emission models and every 24 months or 24,000 miles on Heavy Duty Emission models. If operated in severe conditions, more frequent replacement may be required.

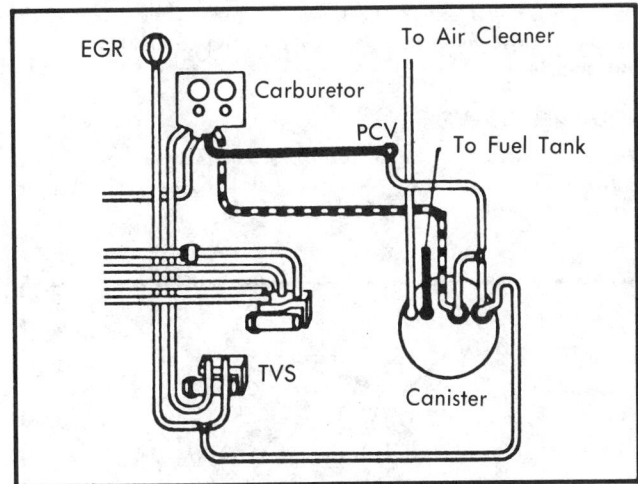

Fig. 1   Vacuum Hose Routing for Single-Canister Evaporative Control System

JEEP

DESCRIPTION

The fuel evaporation control system is used on all models. It is designed to retain raw fuel vapors, which would normally escape to the atmosphere, and transfers them to the intake manifold for burning. System consists of a special fuel tank, sealed gas cap, liquid check valve ("CJ" & Scrambler models only), rollover check valve, charcoal canister, and connecting lines and hoses.

OPERATION

During periods of non-operation, raw vapors from the fuel tank and carburetor are channeled to the charcoal canister where they are stored. When the engine is running, this canister is purged of these vapors which are taken into the intake manifold and burned. On "CJ" & Scrambler models, a liquid check valve prevents liquid fuel from entering canister. The rollover valve prevents fuel flow from tank in the event of vehicle rollover.

LIQUID CHECK VALVE

The liquid check valve incorporates a float and needle assembly. If fuel enters check valve, float will rise and force needle to close vent passage, preventing liquid fuel from entering canister.

ROLLOVER VALVE

Valve consists of a plunger and a stainless steel ball. When valve is inverted, the stainless steel ball pushes the plunger against its seat, blocking fuel flow through valve.

CHARCOAL CANISTER

All models are equipped with a dual-purge type canister. Two inlets are provided: 1 for the carburetor fuel bowl vapors and 1 for the fuel tank vapors. The outlet is connected to intake manifold vacuum and a fourth nipple (secondary purge) connects to the carburetor spark port.

When the engine is running, manifold vacuum draws fresh air through the inlet filter in the bottom of the canister and purges stored vapors. When ported vacuum reaches 12 in. Hg, the secondary purge circuit is opened and canister is purged at a much higher rate.

CARBURETOR BOWL VENT

The carburetor bowl vent used on all models provides an outlet for fuel vapors when the engine is not running. When the engine is running, the fuel bowl is vented to the inside of the air cleaner. The bowl vent is automatically closed by a mechanical link to the throttle when the engine is started.

MAINTENANCE

No adjustments are required with this system. The air inlet filter in the bottom of the charcoal canister should be replaced every 30,000 miles. A regular inspection of system components should be made and defective components replaced as necessary.

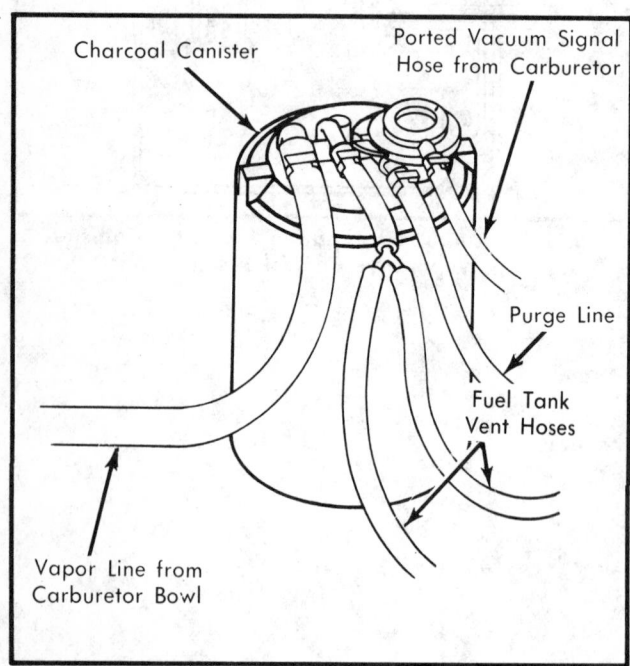

Fig. 1   Typical Charcoal Canister Connections

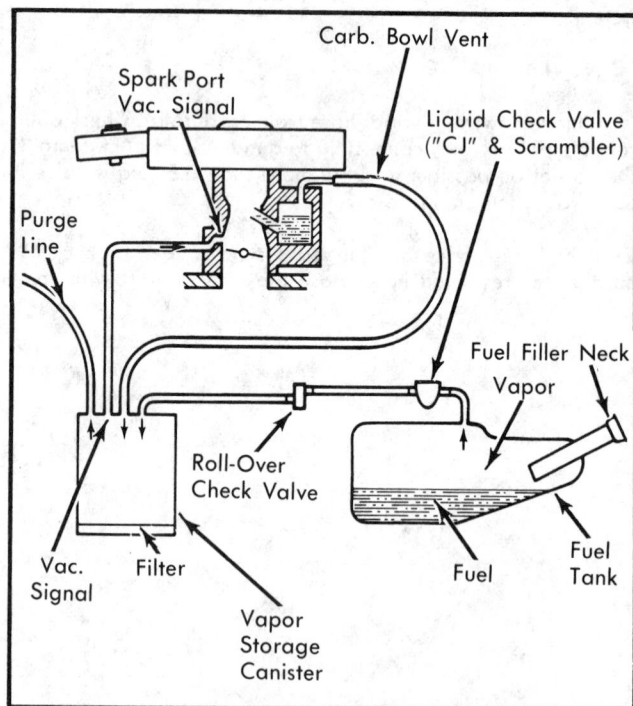

Fig. 2   Typical Jeep Evaporation Control System

AIR INJECTION SYSTEMS — AIR PUMP TYPE

All Models

DESCRIPTION

The air injection systems, used on many applications (may vary according to engine and equipment), are designed to reduce carbon monoxide and hydrocarbon emissions. This is done by injecting fresh air at critical points in the exhaust manifold to burn those gases which passed through the combustion cycle. System consists of an air pump with integral filter, diverter/bypass valve, check valve(s), external or internal injection tubing and connecting hoses. Some Ford and all Chrysler models use additional valves, depending on applications. They are explained below.

OPERATION

AIR PUMP

The air pump uses an eccentric (off-center) vane to draw in fresh air, compress it and pass it on through the system. The pump is belt driven. *Fig. 1.*

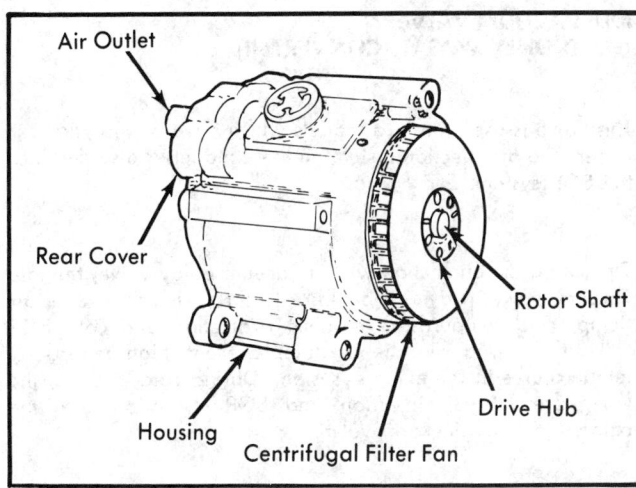

Fig. 1   Typical Air Injection Pump

DIVERTER VALVE

After the air leaves the air pump, it goes immediately into the diverter valve. This valve serves to prevent backfire by stopping air injection flow during periods of high increase in manifold vacuum (such as during deceleration). The diverter valve will dump the air supply to the atmosphere for the first few seconds of deceleration. Most diverter valves also have a pressure relief valve built in which bleeds off excessive air pump pressure to prevent damage to the system.

Diverter valves used on many applications are similar to the one shown in *Fig. 2.*

Ford & Jeep Timed Bypass Valve — This is a normally-open valve. During normal operation, vacuum is equalized on both sides of the diaphragm. Spring pressure holds the valve open, allowing fresh air to the exhaust. On deceleration, manifold vacuum pulls the diaphragm so that air is directed to the atmosphere. A small orifice in the diaphragm will allow the pressure to quickly equalize again. See *Fig. 3.*

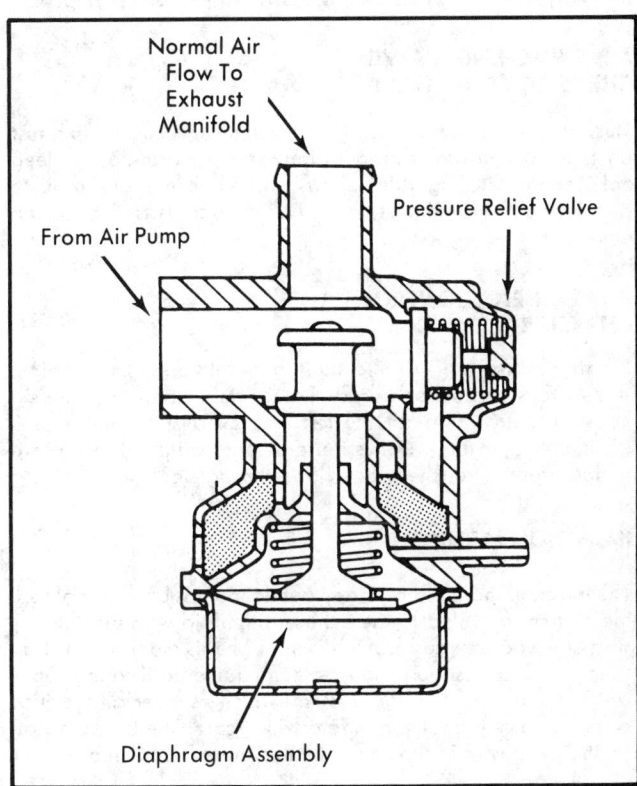

Fig. 2   Typical Diverter Valve Chevrolet, GMC & Chrysler Corp.

Ford Normally-Closed Bypass Valve — When no vacuum is applied, all air pump air is diverted to the atmosphere to protect the converter. When vacuum is received, air then passes to the exhaust ports.

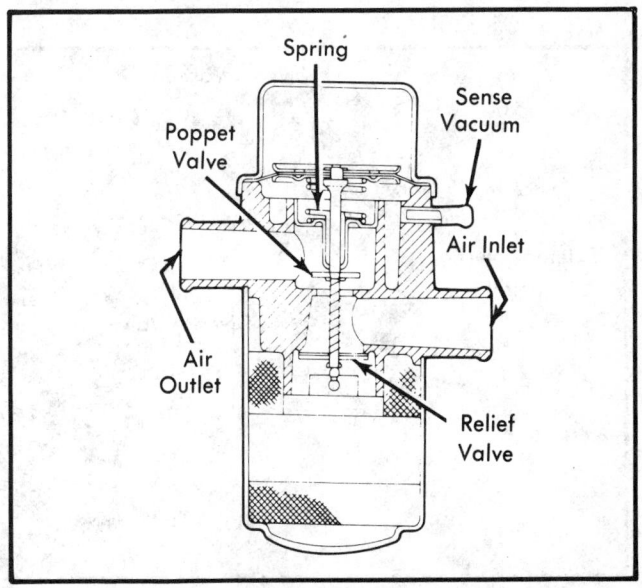

Fig. 3   Typical Diverter Valve Ford & Jeep (Bypass Valve)

AIR INJECTION SYSTEMS — AIR PUMP TYPE (Cont.)

Ford & Jeep Timed & Vented Bypass Valve — Valve operation is similar to that of the timed valve described earlier. When vacuum signal is 8" Hg or more, the valve will continuously vent air pump air to the atmosphere. See *Fig. 4*.

AIR SWITCHING VALVE
CHRYSLER CORP. ONLY

This valve is used to switch the injection air from the exhaust ports to a point downstream after engine warm-up. A bleed hole in the switching valve allows a small portion of the air to be injected at the exhaust ports at all times to assist in reducing emissions.

POWER HEAT CONTROL VALVE
CHRYSLER CORP. ONLY

Located between the right exhaust manifold and exhaust pipe, this valve is vacuum operated and directs a majority of the exhaust gas flow through the left side exhaust manifold until engine temperature reaches a pre-determined point. After that temperature is reached, gas flows through both manifolds.

INJECTION MANIFOLD

The injection manifold on many applications is an external tubing system, mounted to the exhaust manifold with air delivery ports for each exhaust port. It is through this manifold that air pump air reaches the exhaust system. Some applications have an internal air injection system which is specially drilled passages in the intake manifold which carry the air pump air to the exhaust ports. This eliminates the external tubing.

CHECK VALVE

The check valve is a one-way flow valve. It prevents air from the exhaust manifold from backing up through the system and reaching the air pump. The check valve will be found either in the tubing leading to the injection manifold or as an integral part of the manifold.

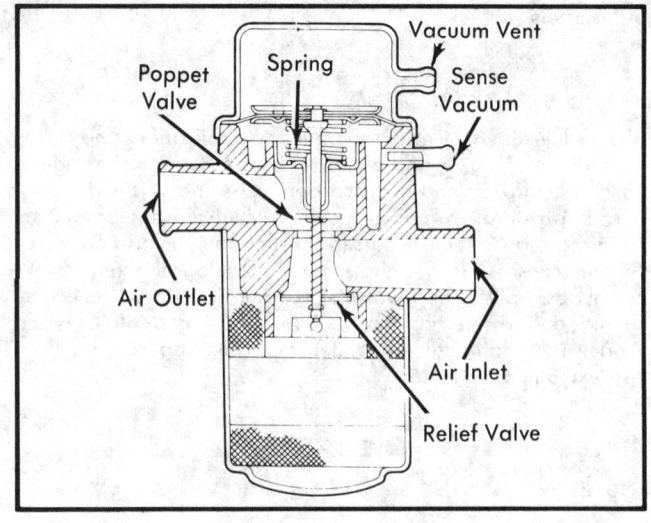

Fig. 4   Ford & Jeep Timed & Vented Bypass Valve

IDLE VACUUM VALVE
(FORD ONLY W/CAT. CONVERTER)

This valve is used on Ford models which have a catalytic converter. The air injection system on these models is also tied into the EGR system. See *Fig. 6*.

Operating in conjunction with a vacuum delay valve, the idle vacuum valve provides backfire control, full-time idle air dump, cold temperature catalyst protection and cold EGR lockout. On long idle, the air dump prevents high underbody temperatures in the exhaust system. During cold engines, the valve prevents air injection and EGR operation until the catalyst and engine are warm.

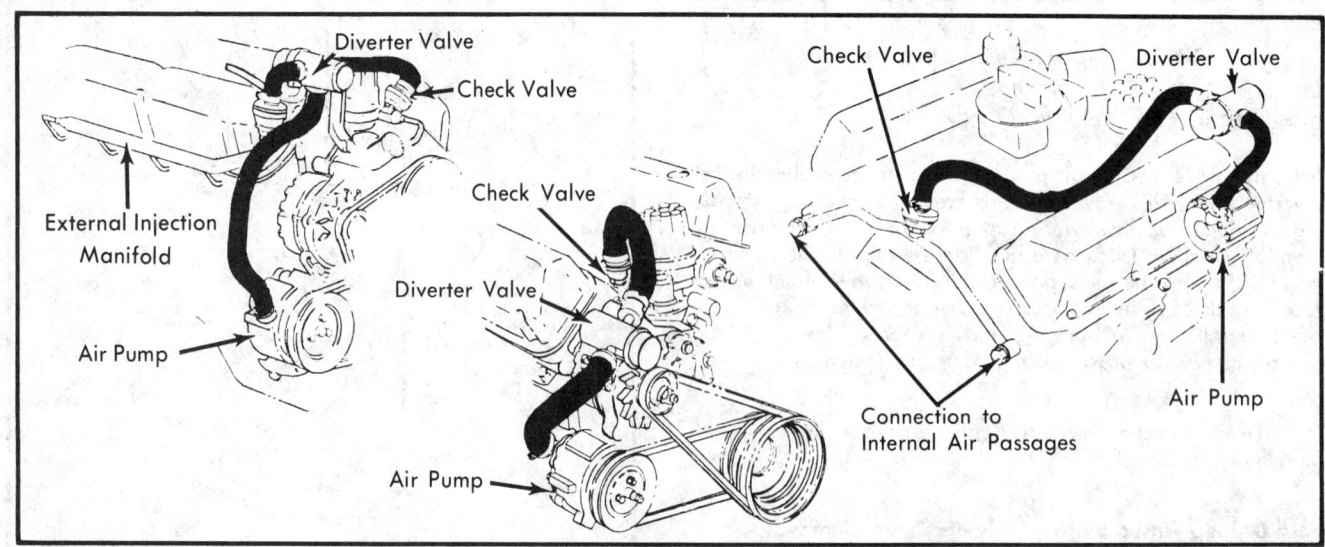

Fig. 5   Typical Air Injection System Installation Configurations

AIR INJECTION SYSTEMS — AIR PUMP TYPE (Cont.)

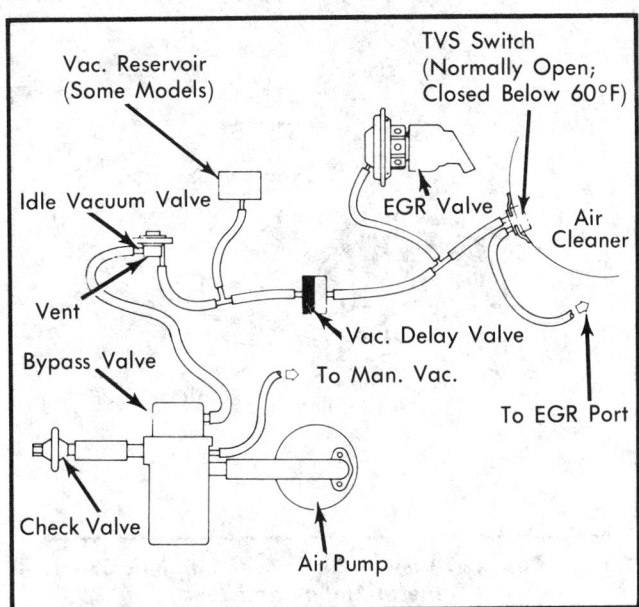

Fig. 6 Schematics of Ford Air Injection System with Idle Vacuum Valve

TROUBLE SHOOTING

Excessive Belt Noise — Loose pump drive belt or seized pump.

Excessive Pump Noise — Leak in hose, loose hose, hose touching other engine parts, diverter valve or by-pass valve failure, check valve failure, pump mounting loose, pump or impeller damaged.

No Air Supply — Loose drive belt, leak in hose or hose fitting, diverter valve or by-pass valve failure, check valve failure, pump failure.

Exhaust Backfire — Incorrect engine tune-up, engine vacuum leaks, faulty diverter valve or check valve.

NOTE — *Proper operation of the Air Injection System is dependent upon proper engine tune-up. See individual car models for specifications and procedures.*

TESTING

Diverter Valve Test — Check valve by accelerating engine and allowing throttle to close rapidly; a momentary rush of air should be noted at diverter air outlet.

Check Valve Test — To check operation of this valve, remove air supply hose from pump at distribution manifold. With engine operating listen for exhaust leakage at check valve which is connected to distribution manifold.

MAINTENANCE

Approximately every 15,000 miles, air injection system components should be checked for proper operation and condition. No regular parts replacement schedule is required. Service is limited to replacement of air pump filter if it becomes clogged.

Centrifugal Fan Filter — To replace, remove drive belt, pulley mounting bolts, and pulley. Break off remaining portions of centrifugal fan filter from pump hub, being careful that fragments do not enter air intake hole. Install new filter by drawing it on with the pulley and pulley bolts. Do not attempt to hammer or press filter on.

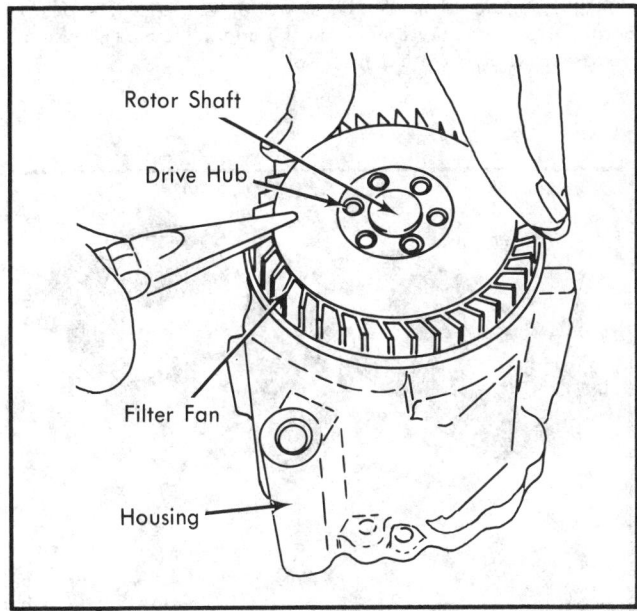

Fig. 7 Removing Centrifugal Fan Filter from Air Injection Pump with Pulley Removed

NOTE — *After new filter is installed, it may squeal during operation until its outside diameter has worn in. This may require 20 to 30 miles of operation.*

CAUTION — *If engine or engine compartment is to be cleaned with steam or high pressure detergent, centrifugal filter fan should be masked off to prevent liquids from entering air pump.*

Exhaust Emission System Cleaning — DO NOT attempt to clean diverter valve. Do not blow compressed air through check valve.

Air Pump Overhaul — Overhaul of air pump is not recommended since internal components of pump are not serviceable. However, certain service items can be replaced as follows:

Pump Exhaust Tube Replacement — Remove by placing tube in a vise or use a suitable pair of pliers to pull tube with a twisting motion. Insert new tube into hole and tap in with a block of wood to protect tube. Approximately 7/8" of tube should extend above cover.

CATALYTIC CONVERTERS

All Light Duty Emissions Models

NOTE — *Light Duty Emission vehicles are those vehicles whose Gross Vehicle Weight (GVW) does not exceed 8,500 lbs.*

DESCRIPTION & OPERATION

The catalytic converter(s) is installed in the exhaust system in front of the muffler so that all exhaust gas must pass through the converter(s). The converter is a stainless steel muffler shapped device that reduces exhaust emissions. The catalyst reduces hydrocarbons (HC) and carbon monoxide (CO) emissions. The material inside the converter is one of 2 types: a coated 1-piece honeycombed block (monolithic type), or small beads of catalyst-coated material.

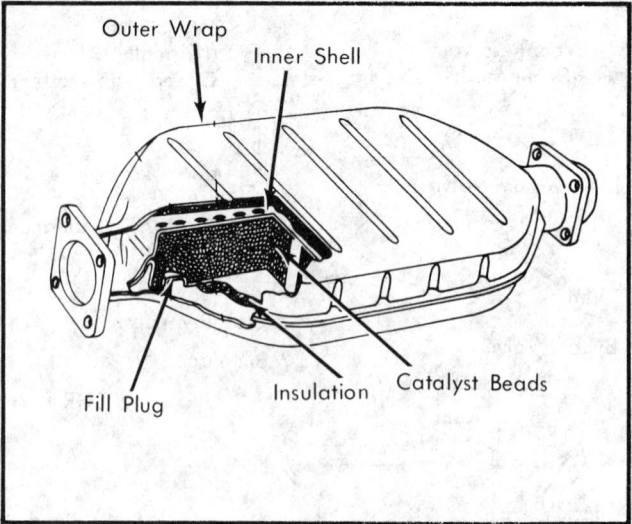

Fig. 2   Cutaway View of Bead-Type Catalytic Converter General Motors and Jeep

SERVICE

MAINTENANCE

There is no scheduled maintenance required for catalytic converters. However, on General Motors and Jeep with bead-type converters, bead removal and replacement is possible.

BOTTOM COVER REPLACEMENT (GENERAL MOTORS ONLY)

1) Remove bottom cover by making a shallow, close cut to bottom outside edge.

NOTE — *A shallow cut is required to avoid damage to inner shell.*

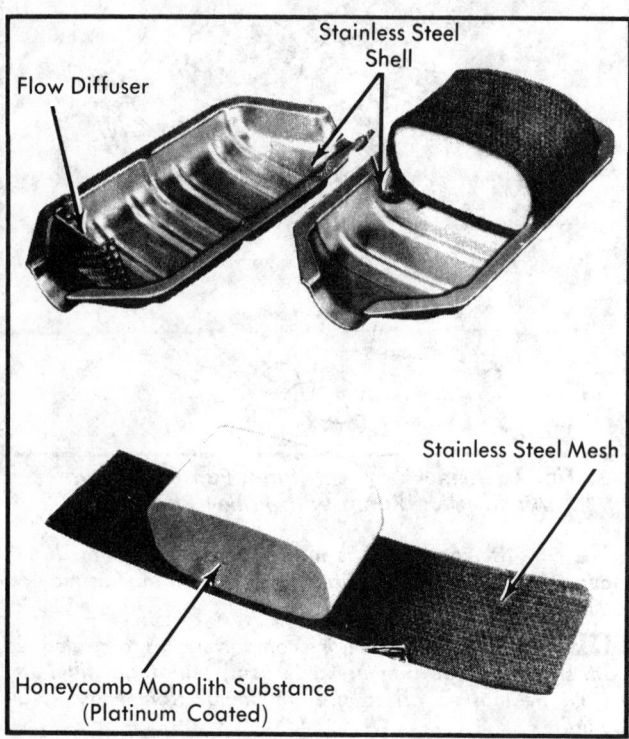

Fig. 1   Cutaway View of Monolithic Catalytic Converter Chrysler Corp. Shown, Ford is Similar

NOTE — *Use unleaded fuel only on vehicles using catalytic converters. If leaded fuel is used, the Tetra Eythel Lead will coat the palladium, platinim and rhodium, rendering these catalysts inoperative. If this happens, the converter must be replaced.*

HEAT SHIELDS

The combustion reaction, which is furthered by the converter, releases additional heat. Temperature in the catalytic converter can reach 1600° F under normal conditions. Special heat shields are used to protect underbody and components from this extreme heat.

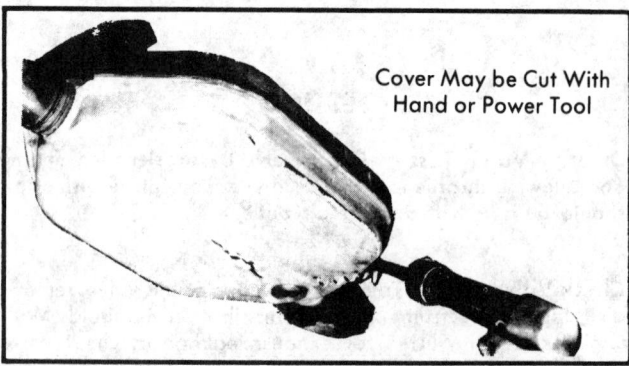

Fig. 3   Removal of Converter Bottom Cover on General Motors Vehicles Only

2) Remove insulation and check inner shell for damage. If damage is found, entire converter must be replaced.

CATALYTIC CONVERTERS (Cont.)

3) If no damage is found, position new insulation into replacement cover. Apply suitable sealer (8998245 or equivalent) around edge of cover, using extra sealer at front and rear pipe openings.

4) Install replacement cover on converter and position retaining channel along edges. Complete the installation by attaching clamps (provided with replacement cover) to both ends of converter.

CATALYST REPLACEMENT (JEEP ONLY)

1) Raise vehicle and attach vacuum aspirator device (J-25077-01 or equivalent) to exhaust pipe as shown in *Fig. 4.*

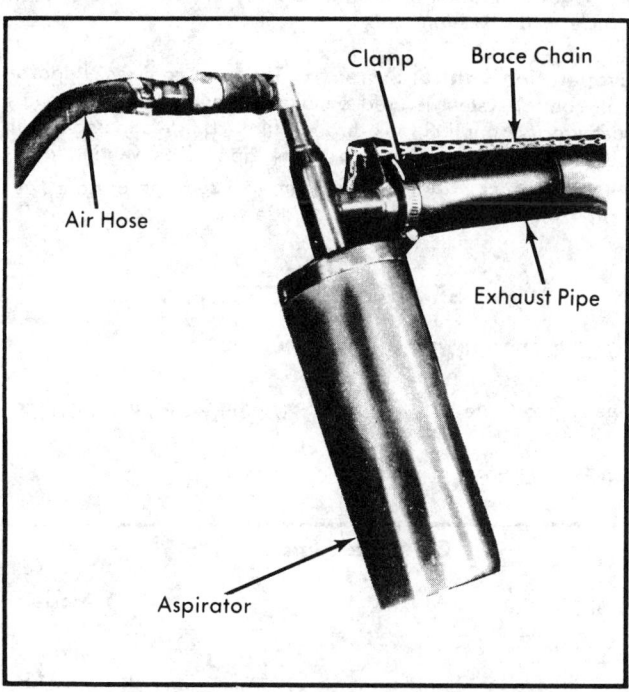

Fig. 4   Vacuum Aspirator Installation Jeep Vehicles Only

2) Apply enough air pressure (minimum 80 lbs.) to hold catalyst beads in place while converter fill plug is removed.

3) Clamp on vibrator and catalyst receptacle as shown in *Fig. 5.* Disconnect air supply from vacuum aspirator and attach it to vibrator unit.

4) Using similar air pressure, vibrator should operate to empty the converter of the catalytic beads in about 10 minutes.

5) When all catalyst material is removed, disconnect air supply and remove container from converter and discard beads.

6) Fill container with approved replacement catalyst and install a fill tube fixture to the vibrator device.

7) Attach air supply to both vibrator and aspirator. With container attached to fill tube, catalyst will begin to move into converter.

8) When catalyst stops flowing, disconnect air supply to vibrator and note level of catalyst. It should be even with fill plug. Add more catalyst if required.

9) Apply nickle-base, anti-seize compound to fill plug. Install plug and tighten to 60 ft. lbs. If equipped with press-type fill plug, install "bridge-and-bolt" type service plug and torque to 28 ft. lbs.

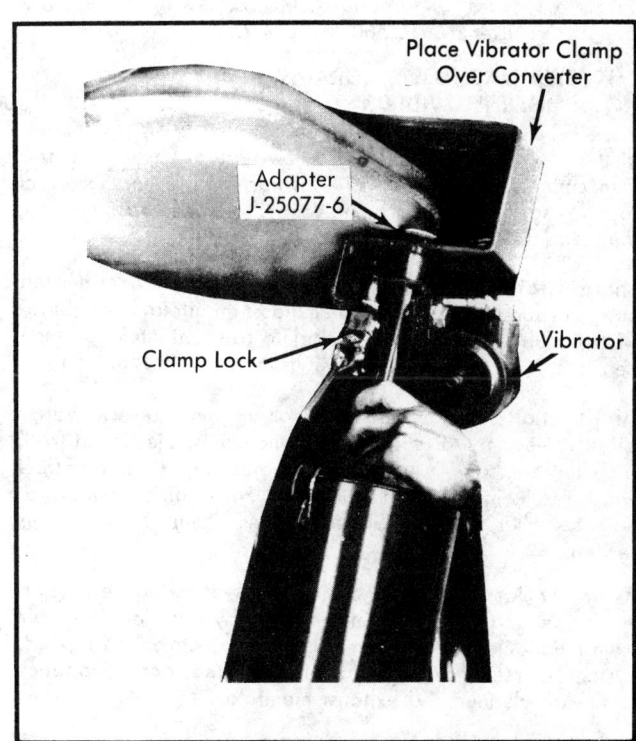

Fig. 5   Placement of Vibrator & Catalyst Container Jeep Vehicles Only.

CATALYST REPLACEMENT (GENERAL MOTORS ONLY)

1) With converter removed from vehicle, remove fill plug by driving a small chisel between converter shell and fill plug. Continue to deform plug until it can be removed with pliers.

CAUTION — *Do no pry plug from opening as damage to plug sealing surface may result.*

2) Hold converter over a container, and by shaking it, remove catalyst beads.

3) Raise front of converter to 45° and fill through opening with new catalyst beads. Light tapping on the converter side belt will facilitate bead installation.

4) Install bridge into fill plug opening and thread bolt into bridge. Move bridge back and forth to loosen catalyst and position bridge.

5) Remove bolt, and place washer and fill plug (with dished side out) in place. Install bolt and tighten to 28 ft. lbs.

CHRYSLER CORP. SYSTEMS & SERVICE PROCEDURES

DESCRIPTION

Control of exhaust emissions is accomplished by a combination of engine modifications and special system components. Component usage varies according to model, engine, states, and emissions cycle application.

NOTE — *There are 2 light duty truck emission control standards classifications: Light Duty and Heavy Duty. Light Duty refers to vehicles up through 8,500 lbs. GVW; Heavy Duty refers to vehicles over 8,500 lbs. GVW.*

CHRYSLER VACUUM DIAGRAMS NO LONGER PROVIDED

NOTE — *Chrysler vehicles use a new type of vacuum harness with connectors at each end. This harness prevents incorrect routing, so Chrysler Corp. no longer provides vacuum hose diagrams.*

Thermostatic Air Cleaner (TAC) — System provides heated air to carburetor (from stove on exhaust manifold) in combination with underhood air to maintain a constant intake air temperature for more efficient combustion and emission control.

Air Injection — System consists of an air pump, diverter valve, check valves and various air distribution lines. Injection of fresh air adjacent to exhaust valves creates an afterburn effect which results in lower emission levels. *For additional information, see "Air Injection Systems — Air Pump Type" in this section.*

Aspirator Air System — System is used to reduce carbon monoxide and hydrocarbon emissions by drawing fresh air from the air cleaner and allowing it to mix with exhaust gases. System consists of an aspirator air valve and connecting tubes to the air cleaner and exhaust manifold.

Exhaust Gas Recirculation (EGR) — System allows a predetermined amount of hot exhaust gas to recirculate and dilute air/fuel mixture in order to aid combustion and reduce NOx emissions.

Electric Assist Choke — System is designed to give faster choke openings at temperatures above 60°F and slower choke openings below 60°F.

Orifice Spark Advance Control (OSAC) — System is used on some Light Duty emissions engines to aid in control of oxides of nitrogen (NOx). It controls vacuum to distributor vacuum advance unit in response to changes in throttle position.

Idle Enrichment System — System is used on some Light Duty emissions models with automatic transmission to reduce cold engine stalling. System enriches carburetor mixture at curb idle and fast idle during cold or semi-cold operation.

Vacuum Throttle Positioner — System is used on Heavy Duty emissions vehicles. Throttle positioner prevents unburned hydrocarbons from entering atmosphere by preventing full throttle closure during deceleration from high engine speeds.

Catalytic Converter — Converter brings about combustion type reaction to further consume unburned elements in the engine exhaust. Converter is located in exhaust system ahead of muffler. Vehicles equipped with catalytic converters must use unlead fuel only. *For additional information, see Catalytic Converter article in this section.*

Positive Crankcase Ventilation (PCV) — System is used on all cars to eliminate fumes and vapors from crankcase by directing them back through the combustion chamber to be burned. *For additional information, see Crankcase Ventilation article in this section.*

Evaporation Control System — The dual canister evaporation control system is used on all vehicles. The system routes fuel vapors from fuel tank through filter canisters to engine for burning. This closed system prevents vapors from venting to the atmosphere. *For additional information see appropriate Fuel Evaporation System article in this section.*

SERVICE PROCEDURES

IGNITION TIMING

See appropriate article in TUNE-UP SERVICE PROCEDURES.

CARBURETION

Carburetor Applications	
Application	**Model**
3.7L (225") 6-Cyl.	
1-Bbl.	Holley 1945
5.2L (318") V8	
2-Bbl.	Holley 2280
4-Bbl.	Carter Thermo-Quad
5.9L (360") V8	
2-Bbl.	Holley 2280
4-Bbl.	Carter Thermo-Quad

IDLE SPEED & MIXTURE

See appropriate article in TUNE-UP SERVICE PROCEDURES.

CHRYSLER CORP. THERMOSTATIC AIR CLEANER

All Models

DESCRIPTION

All Chrysler Light Duty Truck models use a heated air inlet system. This system is part of the air cleaner and controls the temperature so that the carburetor can be calibrated leaner to control hydrocarbon emissions and improve warm-up characteristics. The system consists of an air cleaner assembly, a temperature sensor, an air control valve, a vacuum diaphragm, a duct system and a shroud on the exhaust manifold.

OPERATION

When the ambient air temperature is less than 50°F, carburetor intake air flows through the shroud, into a flexible connector, through the vacuum diaphragm and into the carburetor. When the temperature rises to operating temperature, the vacuum diaphragm shuts off the air coming from the shroud and allow fresh air to enter the carburetor. When the temperature is between the minimum and maximum, the air will flow through both circuits.

TESTING

1) Ensure that all vacuum hoses, flexible duct hose and air cleaner duct are in good condition. With engine cold, the heat control door in the air cleaner snorkel should be up, in the heat on position.

2) With engine running at normal operating temperature, the door should be in the down, or heat off position.

3) Turn off engine and allow to cool to 50°F. Remove air cleaner and apply 20 in. Hg vacuum with an external vacuum source to the temperature sensor. The door should be in the up position. If not, check vacuum diaphragm for proper operation.

4) Apply 20 in. Hg vacuum to diaphragm. The diaphragm should not bleed down more than 10 in. in 5 minutes. The door should not lift off the bottom at less than 5 in. Hg, and should be in the full up position at no more than 8.5 in. Hg.

5) If vacuum diaphragm does not meet specifications, replace it and repeat steps 1) and 2). If diaphragm performs as specified, but proper temperature is not maintained, replace temperature sensor and repeat temperature checks.

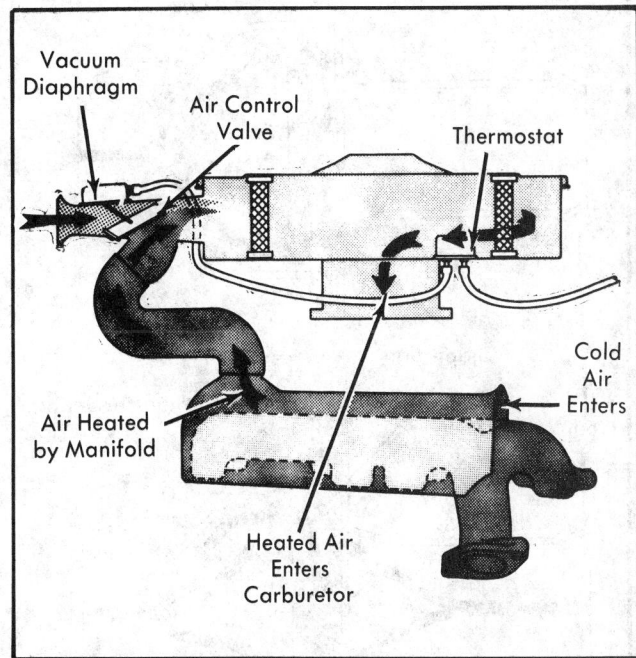

Fig. 1   Typical Chrysler Corp. Thermostatic Air Cleaner

1981 Exhaust Emission Systems

CHRYSLER CORP. ASPIRATOR AIR SYSTEM

DESCRIPTION

The aspirator air system consists of an aspirator valve and an aspirator tube assembly. The valve uses exhaust pressure pulsation to draw air into the exhaust system to reduce carbon monoxide (CO), and hydrocarbon (HC) emissions. The tube assembly connects the aspirator valve to the air cleaner at one end, and the exhaust manifold at the other end.

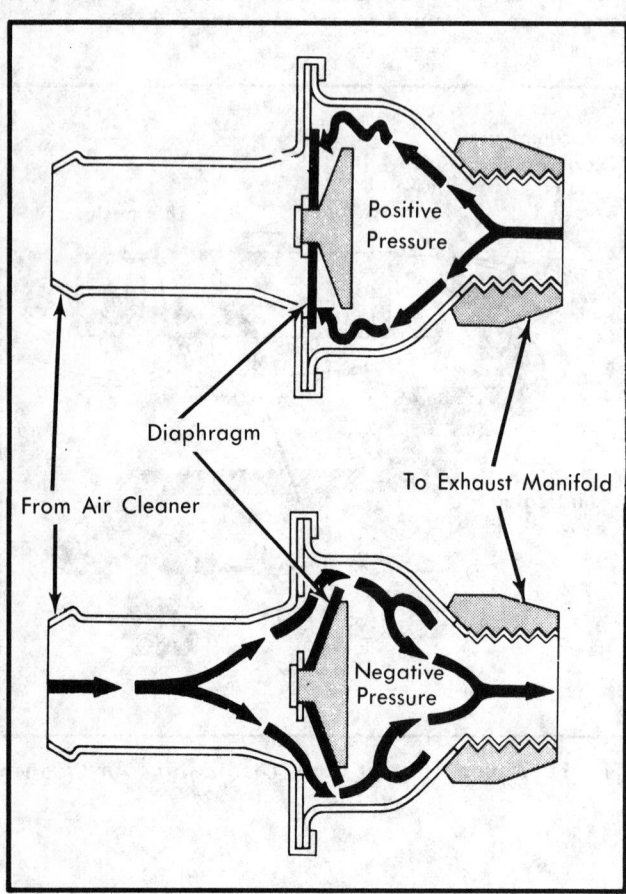

Fig. 1 *Aspirator Valve Air Flow*

OPERATION

The aspirator valve draws fresh air from the "clean" side of the air cleaner past a one-way, spring loaded diaphragm made of rubber. The diaphragm opens to allow fresh air to mix with the exhaust gases during negative pressure (vacuum) pulses which occur at the exhaust ports and manifold passages. If the pressure is positive, the diaphragm closes, and no exhaust gas is allowed to flow past the valve and into the "clean" side of the air cleaner. The valve works best at idle and slightly off-idle, when the negative pulses are at maximum. At higher engine speeds the valve remains closed.

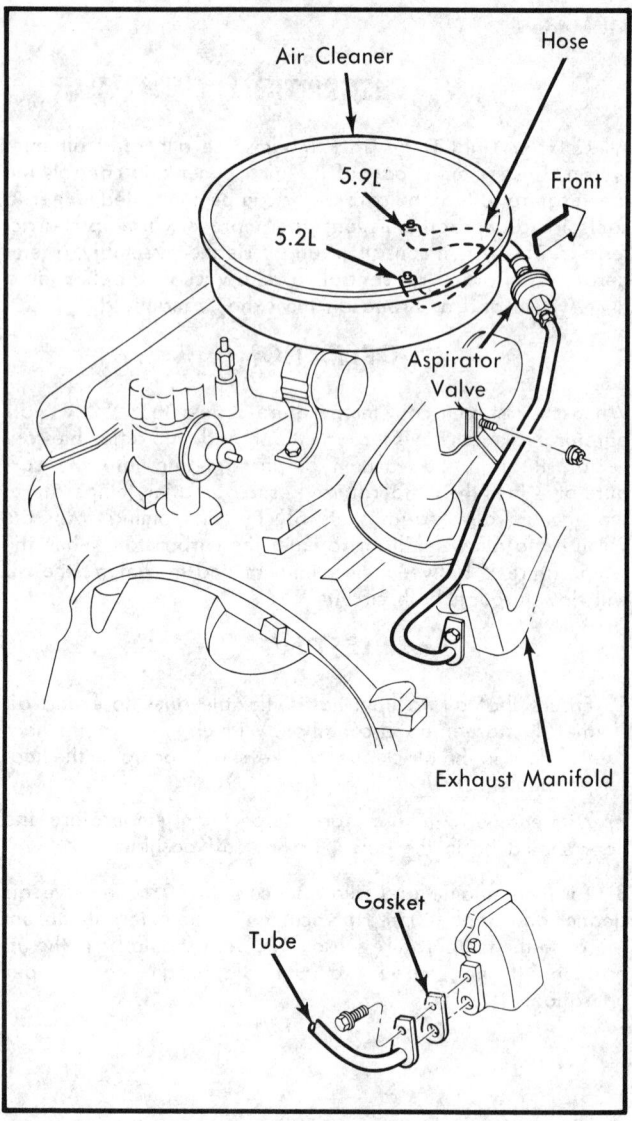

Fig. 2 *Aspirator Air System Assembly
(V8 Shown — 6-Cylinder Similar)*

TESTING

The aspirator valve is not repairable. If the valve fails, it must be replaced. Check all connections for proper assembly. If leakage is noted at any joints, repair before testing valve.

To test aspirator valve, disconnect hose from aspirator inlet. With engine idling in neutral, vacuum exhaust pulses should be felt at the aspirator inlet. If hot exhaust gas is escaping from the inlet, the valve is defective and must be replaced.

CHRYSLER CORP. EXHAUST GAS RECIRCULATION

DESCRIPTION

Exhaust gas recirculation allows a predetermined amount of hot exhaust gas to recirculate and dilute incoming air/fuel mixture. This reduces peak flame temperature during combustion, thereby reducing NOx emission. System consists of an EGR valve, timer, vacuum solenoid, vacuum amplifier, charge temperature switch (light duty), CCEGR valve (heavy duty) and an EGR maintenance reminder.

OPERATION

EGR system controls vacuum under varying conditions to EGR valve. The EGR valve is a vacuum actuated poppet type used to modulate exhaust gas flow from manifold crossover into incoming air/fuel mixture.

A vacuum tap at throat of carburetor venturi is used to provide control vacuum. Because of the low amount of vacuum, it is necessary to use a vacuum amplifier to increase vacuum to the level required for EGR valve operation.

Elimination of recycle at wide open throttle is accomplished by a dump diaphragm which compares venturi and manifold vacuum to determine when wide open throttle is reached. At wide open throttle, the internal reservoir is "dumped", limiting output to EGR valve opening point. Opening point is set above manifold vacuum available at wide open throttle, allowing closure of EGR valve at wide open throttle.

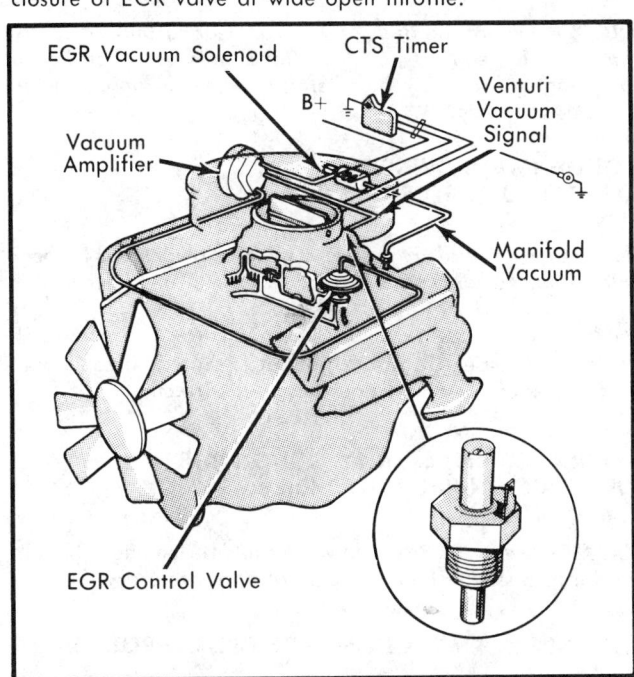

Fig. 1   Chrysler Corp. Exhaust Gas Recirculation System Schematic

EGR TIMER

The EGR timer is a delay system consisting of an electrical timer mounted on dash panel in engine compartment which controls an engine-mounted solenoid. Solenoid is connected by vacuum hoses between carburetor venturi signal nipple and vacuum amplifier. Purpose of timer system is to prevent EGR operation for a short period after ignition is turned on. Time interval is between 35 and 90 seconds, depending upon application. Timer operation is overridden by CCEGR valve. On CTS systems, timing function begins after switch opens to permit EGR operation.

NOTE — *Although similar in appearance, timers used on CTS systems are not interchangeable with those used on CCEGR systems.*

COOLANT CONTROL EGR (CCEGR) VALVE (HEAVY DUTY EMISSIONS ONLY)

CCEGR valve is used with EGR system to delay EGR operation until engine warm-up is achieved. Valve location and opening temperature varies according to vehicle model and engine type. On models with CCEGR valve in the radiator tank, opening temperature is 59°F. On models with valve in thermostat housing, opening temperature is 108-125°F.

CHARGE TEMPERATURE SWITCH (CTS) (LIGHT DUTY EMISSIONS ONLY)

A Charge Temperature Switch (CTS) is installed on a branch of engine intake manifold. When air/fuel mixture temperature is below 60°F, as sensed by CTS, switch closes, allowing no EGR timer function and no EGR valve operation. Above 60°F, air-/fuel mixture temperature, timer and EGR switch operation are allowed.

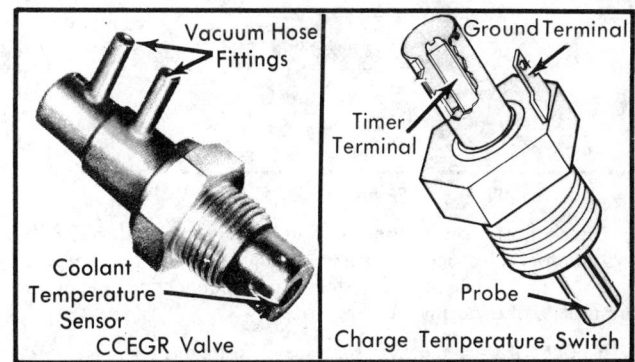

Fig. 2   CCEGR Valve & Charge Temperature Switch

TESTING

EGR SYSTEM OPERATION

1) With transmission in neutral, parking brake on and engine at normal operating temperature, allow engine to idle with throttle closed. Then, quickly accelerate engine to approximately 2,000 RPM while watching EGR valve stem. Stem should move when engine is accelerated. If not, refer to "Trouble Shooting" in this article.

2) Once EGR valve movement has been obtained, it is necessary to determine if EGR is actually taking place. On CCEGR systems, disconnect EGR valve-to-CCEGR valve hose at CCEGR valve. On CTS systems, disconnect hose from EGR valve-to-CTS valve. On all systems, disconnect air cleaner-to-carburetor hose at carburetor.

3) With engine idling at normal operating temperature, hold free end of EGR valve hose tightly against opening of carburetor connector (from which air cleaner hose was removed). With hose on connector, engine idle speed should drop about 150 RPM and may stall. This shows that EGR is taking place.

4) If speed does not change or change is less than minimum, exhaust deposits are in EGR valve or intake manifold passages. Remove valve for inspection and cleaning. Inspect manifold passages and clean as required.

CHRYSLER CORP. EXHAUST GAS RECIRCULATION (Cont.)

NOTE — *When cleaning valve, do not allow cleaning solvents on diaphragm. Do not push on diaphragm to operate valve, use vacuum only.*

EGR DELAY SYSTEM TEST

1) If equipped with Delay System, stop engine, then restart. Immediately open throttle to approximately 1,000 RPM and watch EGR valve stem for movement.

2) If it moves during first 30 seconds after starting, EGR time delay system is defective.

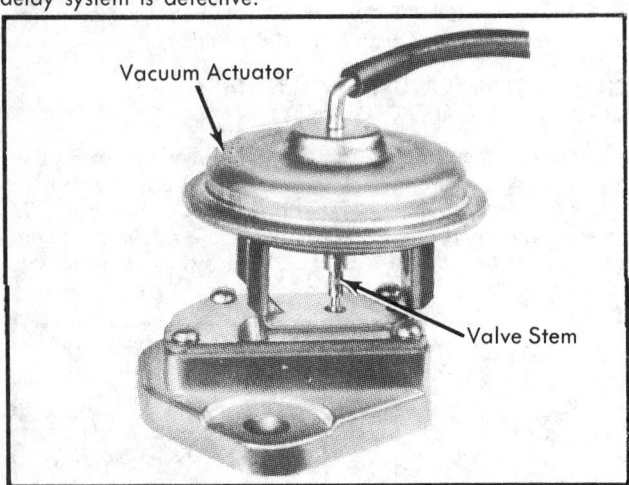

Fig. 3 Chrysler Corp. EGR Valve

3) Check hose connections to time delay solenoid valve. If okay, detach electrical plug from solenoid valve and energize valve by grounding either terminal and connecting the other terminal to the positive battery post.

4) If EGR valve stem moves on this test, solenoid valve is defective and must be replaced.

5) If EGR valve stem did not move, EGR timer control should be replaced. If this does not correct the problem, check wiring for proper connections.

TROUBLE SHOOTING

EGR VALVE STEM DOES NOT MOVE ON SYSTEM TEST

1) Check for correct hose connections and leak check to confirm all hoses are in good condition.

2) Check EGR valve for ruptured diaphragm or frozen valve stem by connecting external vacuum source of 10 in. Hg or greater to valve diaphragm. If no valve movement occurs, replace valve. If valve opens 1/8", pinch off supply hose to check for diaphragm leakage. Valve should remain open 30 seconds or longer. If leakage occurs, replace valve.

EGR VALVE STEM DOES NOT MOVE ON TEST; OPERATES OKAY WITH EXTERNAL VACUUM APPLIED

1) Check for defective CCEGR valve or CTS as follows:

- On CCEGR systems, by-pass CCEGR valve and connect vacuum amplifier directly to EGR valve. If EGR valve now operates normally, replace CCEGR valve.
- On CTS systems, by-pass EGR solenoid and connect vacuum amplifier directly to EGR valve. If EGR valve operates normally, reconnect EGR solenoid hoses and remove wire from timer terminal of CTS. If EGR valve operates within 90 seconds, replace CTS.

2) In Venturi Vacuum Control System, remove venturi vacuum hose from carburetor nipple. With engine at idle, apply two in. Hg vacuum to hose. Engine speed should drop 150 RPM or more and EGR valve stem should move $\frac{1}{8}$" or more. If this does not occur, replace vacuum control valve.

3) If vacuum control amplifier operates normally in previous test, plugged vacuum tap to carburetor is indicated. Use suitable carburetor solvent to remove deposits from passage and clear with light air pressure.

NOTE — *Do not use drills or wires to clear carburetor control passages for either type of control system as calibration of precision orifices may be altered resulting in unsatisfactory vehicle operation.*

ROUGH IDLE, SLOW IDLE, OR STALL ON RETURN TO IDLE

1) Disconnect hose from EGR valve and plug hose. Recheck idle. If satisfactory, replace vacuum control amplifier.

2) If vacuum hose removal does not correct, remove EGR valve and inspect to insure poppet is seated. Clean poppet seat, replace if poppet does not seat correctly.

POOR COLD DRIVEABILITY, ROUGH IDLE OR STALLS ON RETURN TO IDLE

CCEGR valve or EGR control valve could be leaking. Check by performing leak test and replace valves as necessary.

WEAK PERFORMANCE ON WIDE OPEN THROTTLE

Disconnect hose from EGR valve and plug hose. Road test vehicle, if performance is restored, replace vacuum control amplifier.

CHRYSLER CORP. ELECTRIC ASSIST CHOKE

DESCRIPTION

All Light Duty emissions models are equipped with an electric assist choke system to help control hydrocarbon (HC) and carbon monoxide (CO) emissions and to shorten warm-up time. The electric assist choke system consists of an electric heating element, a bimetal spring, a thermostatic choke coil and connecting linkage.

OPERATION

The choke thermostatic coil spring reacts to engine temperature; however, an electric heating element (located next to a bimetal spring inside the choke well) will assist engine heat during both summer and winter operations to shorten choke on time.

This single-stage electric assist choke is designed to give a more rapid choke opening at temperatures above about 60°F, and slower choke opening below this temperature.

A wire from the choke heater is connected to an electrical control switch. Above 60°F, the control switch will energize the choke heater.

Since the heater control switch is mounted to the engine, some cold weather operation may energize the choke heater. This could occur after the choke has opened without benefit of electric heat. No adverse reaction will occur.

TESTING

CONTROL SWITCH TEST

1) Check test light, before starting test, by connecting between battery terminals. Note light intensity.

2) Before starting engine, detach ignition harness electrical connector from heater control switch.

3) Connect test light to load (choke) terminal of control switch and to ground.

4) Start engine and allow to reach normal operating temperature.

5) Apply 12 volts to ignition harness terminal of control switch. If test light does not light or have same intensity as when first tested, control switch is defective and must be replaced.

CHOKE HEATING ELEMENT TEST

1) Disconnect only the B+ wire at the control switch. Connect an ohmmeter lead to the choke housing or choke retainer screw.

2) Touch other meter lead to a bare portion of choke wire connector at switch (not B+ terminal). A meter reading of 4 to 12 ohms indicates heater is electrically functional. An open or short circuit are cause for installing a new choke assembly.

NOTE — *Heater element must not be immersed in any fluid, as an electrical short to choke heater is also a short circuit to ignition system.*

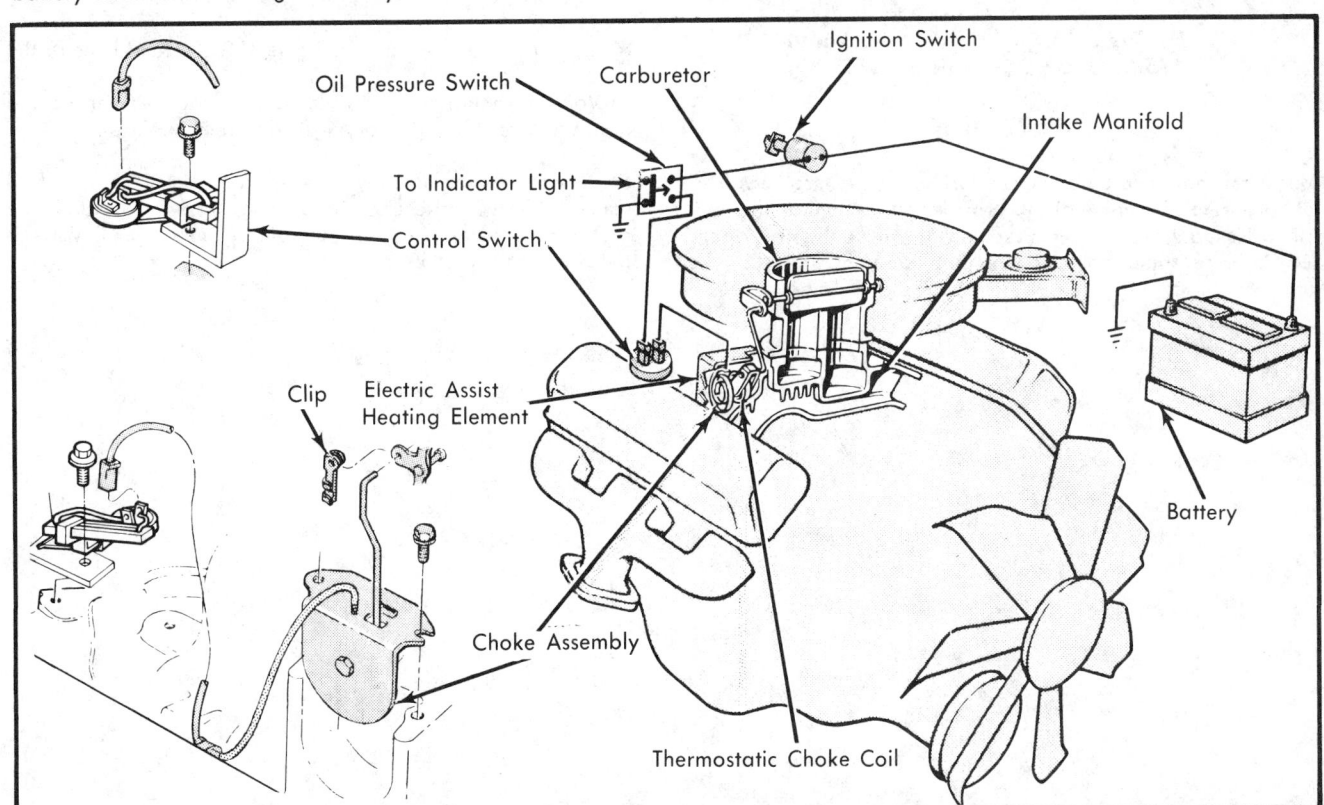

Fig. 1 Chrysler Corp. Electric Assist Choke System

CHRYSLER CORP. OSAC VALVE

DESCRIPTION

Orifice Spark Advance System (OSAC) is used on most Light Duty emission models to aid in control of oxides of nitrogen (NOx). It controls vacuum to vacuum advance actuator of distributor. A tiny orifice incorporated in OSAC valve delays change in ported vacuum to distributor by about 10 seconds when going from idle to part throttle. When going from part throttle to idle, change in ported vacuum to distributor will be instantaneous.

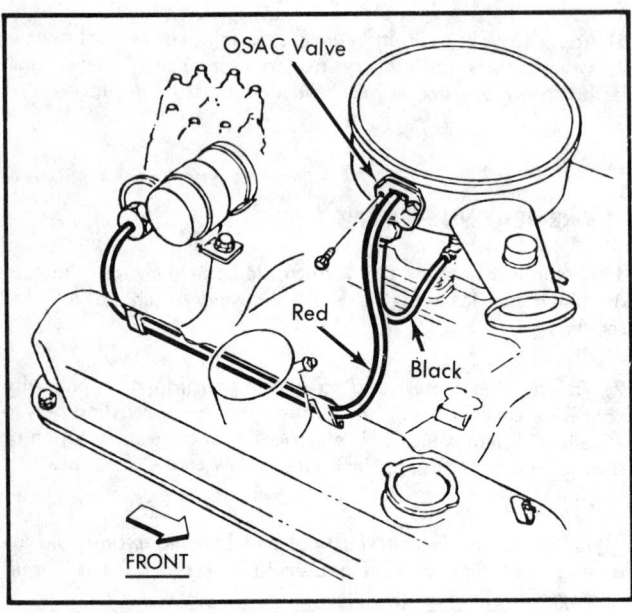

Fig. 1   Typical OSAC Valve Hose Routing (5.2L & 5.9L Engines Shown)

OPERATION

Vacuum is obtained by a vacuum tap just above throttle valves of carburetor. This type of tap provides no vacuum at idle, but provides manifold vacuum as soon as throttle valves are opened slightly. Proper operation requires air tight fittings.

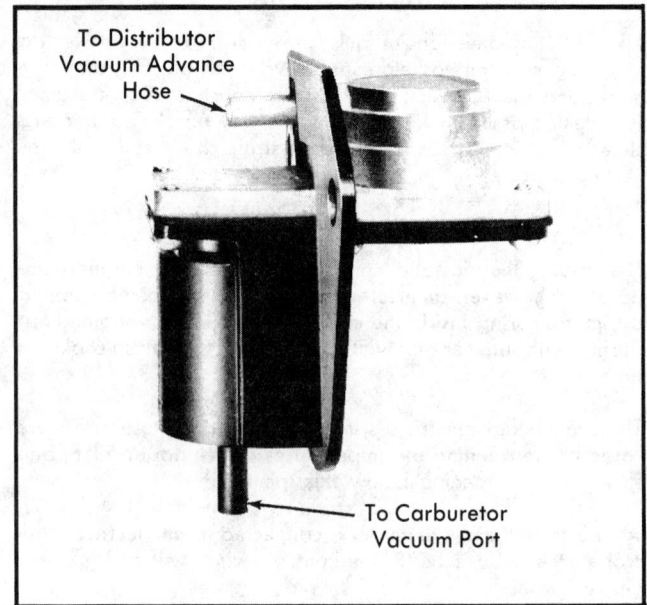

Fig. 2   Close-Up View of OSAC Valve

TESTING

1) Inspect all hoses for leakage or damage. Replace as necessary.

2) Warm engine to normal operating temperature. Tee a vacuum gauge into red hose at OSAC valve leading to distributor.

3) Set parking brake and run engine at 2,000 RPM in neutral.

4) Vacuum should gradually increase, in about 20 seconds, to a stable level (this will vary with different engines).

5) If vacuum immediately rises to same level as manifold vacuum, OSAC valve is not operating properly and must be replaced. If there is NO increase in vacuum, OSAC valve is defective and must be replaced.

CHRYSLER CORP. IDLE ENRICHMENT SYSTEM

DESCRIPTION

Idle Enrichment System is designed to reduce cold engine stalling by use of a metering system related to the basic carburetor instead of choke. It is used on some vehicles with automatic transmissions and Light Duty cycle emissions. System enriches carburetor mixtures in curb idle and fast idle area during cold or semi-cold operation. System consists of a vacuum idle enrichment valve, coolant vacuum switch or solenoid vacuum switch and electric timer combination.

OPERATION

When vacuum is applied to enrichment valve diaphragm, idle air is reduced. As a result of less idle air, air/fuel mixture is enriched. On coolant vacuum switch; when engine is cold, switch is open and vacuum is applied to enrichment valve. When engine warms to 98°F, switch closes and engine returns to normal lean mixture condition. On solenoid vacuum valve; switch receives its vacuum signal from a solenoid valve which is operated by an electric timer. Enrichment duration is approximately 35 seconds after engine start or until switch closes at 150° F (98° F on some models). All switches open approximately 12° F below closing temperature.

TESTING

System Test — 1) With engine at normal operating temperature, remove air cleaner but DO NOT cap any vacuum fittings opened by hose removal (leakage needed for test).

2) Disconnect hose to idle enrichment valve at plastic connector (connector has a filtered bleed which will interfere with test, so it must be removed). Start engine place fast idle screw on slowest step of fast idle cam. Connect 3-4' length of hose to enrichment valve .

3) Apply vacuum with a hand pump to end of hose and listen for engine speed change. If engine speed can be controlled by vacuum, diaphragm and air valve are operating correctly. If speed cannot be controlled by vacuum, replace valve assembly (Holley carburetors) or proceed to next step (Carter carburetors).

4) Place finger on the other plug over air inlet passage and listen for engine speed change. If speed can be controlled, diaphragm is leaking or air valve is stuck open. If speed cannot be controlled, air valve is stuck closed. Clean air valve or replace diaphragm as necessary.

NOTE — *In the following procedure on some vehicles, timing module and solenoid valve serve a dual function of controlling both EGR delay and idle enrichment duration.*

Time Delay Test — 1) With ignition switch off, remove wiring connector from time delay solenoid valve. Place a test light across connector terminals.

2) Start engine, test light should come on and stay on for approximately 60 seconds after engine starts. If light does not come on or stays on indefinitely, replace timer.

NOTE — *Test light current should not exceed .5 amps. or damage to timer may occur.*

Coolant Vacuum Switch — 1) Disconnect molded connector from valve and attach a ⅛" I.D. hose to bottom port of valve. With radiator top tank warm to touch (no warmer than 75°F), blow through hose. If air cannot be blown through valve, replace valve.

2) Bring engine to normal operating temperature. Attach a vacuum pump and gauge to bottom port of valve. Apply ten inches of vacuum. If vacuum level drops more than one inch in 15 seconds, replace valve.

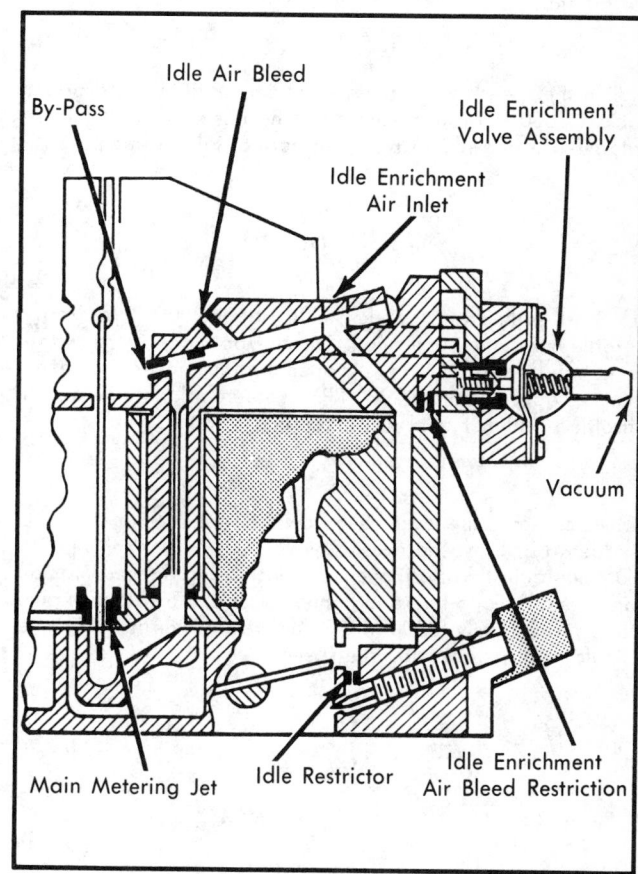

**Fig. 1   Sectional View of Chrysler Corp.
Idle Enrichment System**

CHRYSLER CORP. VACUUM THROTTLE POSITIONER

DESCRIPTION

Some Heavy Duty emissions models have a carburetor equipped with a vacuum throttle positioner. This system prevents unburned hydrocarbon (HC) emissions during periods of rapid deceleration from high engine speeds. System consists of an electronic speed switch, a vacuum solenoid valve and a vacuum throttle positioner.

OPERATION

The electronic speed switch receives an ignition pulse through the ballast resistor, which is connected to the electronic ignition control unit. It then senses when engine speed is above 2,000 RPM and energizes the throttle positioner. By energizing, the throttle positioner plunger extends slightly and will hold the throttle blades open at 1750 RPM upon sudden deceleration. This will prevent an overly rich mixture from flowing into the carburetor.

When the speed switch senses that engine RPM has dropped below 2000 RPM, it de-energizes the positioner and throttle blades are allowed to return to normal idle position.

ADJUSTMENT

1) Start engine and accelerate to about 2000 RPM. Verify throttle positioner operation. Throttle positioner must withstand hand pressure. Manually open throttle until engine speed reaches approximately 2000 RPM. Loosen lock nut and adjust throttle positioner until it just contacts throttle lever.

2) Release throttle lever, then slowly adjust positioner until a sudden drop in speed occurs (over 1000 RPM). At this point, continue adjusting positioner in a decreasing direction for an additional $\frac{1}{4}$ of a turn and tighten lock nut. Accelerate engine to approximately 2300 RPM and release throttle. Engine should return to normal idle speed.

TESTING

1) Check all wiring and hose connections in system. Repair or replace as necessary.

2) Apply vacuum from an external source to vacuum throttle positioner. If positioner does not extend, replace it. If it does, pinch off vacuum hose and observe plunger. If it remains extended for one minute or more, unit is okay.

3) Apply external vacuum to the manifold supply hose connection on the solenoid valve. Disconnect wiring harness from solenoid and ground one terminal of the solenoid. Connect 12 volt source to the other terminal. Watch throttle positioner.

4) If plunger does not cycle as voltage is applied, replace solenoid. If it does, replace speed switch.

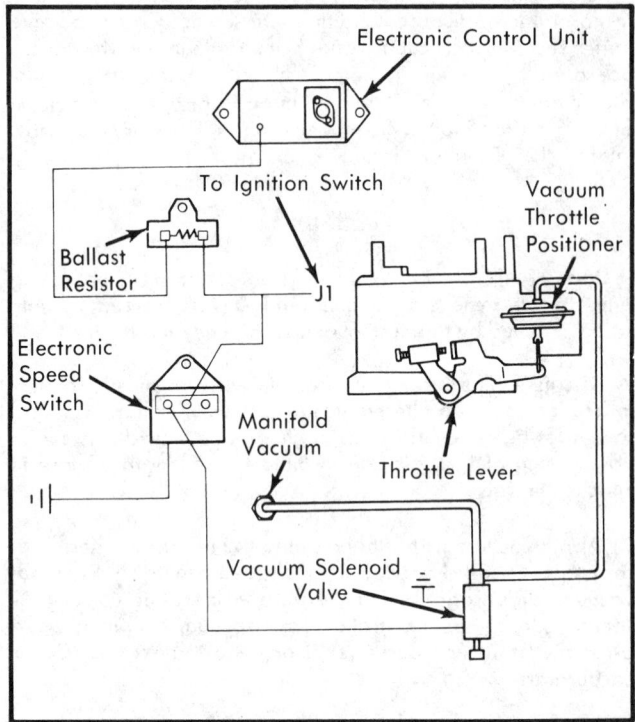

Fig. 1   Schematic of Vacuum Throttle Positioner System for Chrysler Corp. Vehicles

FORD SYSTEMS & SERVICE PROCEDURES

DESCRIPTION

Several systems are used to control emission of pollutants. System usage depends on model, engine, and transmission combinations. Each system is designed to control a particular vehicle emission. In addition, specially calibrated carburetors, distributors, and modified combustion chambers are used with these systems.

NOTE — *There are 2 light duty truck emission control standards classifications: Light Duty and Heavy Duty. Light Duty refers to vehicles up through 8,500 lbs. GVW; Heavy Duty refers to vehicles over 8,500 lbs. GVW.*

Thermostatic Air Cleaner — Regardless of type of thermostatic air cleaner used; air valve or thermostat, function is the same, and that is to provide hot air from exhaust manifold shroud to carburetor during warm-up conditions.

Air Injection — Air injection system consists of an air pump, diverter valve, check valve, and various air distribution lines necessary to inject fresh air adjacent to exhaust valves. Injection of fresh air adjacent to exhaust valves creates an afterburn which further consumes unburned material in engine's exhaust. *For additional information, see "Air Injection Systems — Air Pump Type" in this section.*

EGR — Exhaust gas recirculation system uses a vacuum operated EGR valve to introduce metered amounts of exhaust gas into engine's combustion chambers. This introduction of inert exhaust gas lowers peak combustion temperatures and lowers NOx formations.

Electronic Engine Control System (EEC III) — This system is used on California light duty emission models with 5.0L (302″) and 5.8L (351″) W engines. Sensors monitor crankshaft position, EGR valve position, throttle position, manifold and barometric pressure, engine coolant temperature and exhaust gas oxygen. Information is sent to the Electronic Control Assembly (ECA) where it is analyzed. ECA then computes correct operating modes and signals other modules to adjust timing, air/fuel ratio, EGR flow rate, thermactor air flow, canister vapor flow and idle speed.

Microprocessor Control Unit (MCU) System — Used on California models with 4.9L (300″) engine, this system is named for and commanded by a micro-computer. This micro-computer is located in the engine compartment and is capable of controlling engine air/fuel ratios, air injection, and on some models, canister purge, spark retard and idle speed.

Electric Assist Choke — This unit is supplied power from a stator terminal on alternator. Contained in choke cap is an electric heating element. At underhood temperatures above 54°F, choke mechanism heats up, causing a more rapid choke opening time. This helps to lean mixtures much sooner. Below 54°F, normal choking action occurs.

Decel Throttle Modulator —This unit holds the throttle partly open during deceleration to reduce emissions of hydrocarbons (HC).

Spark Delay Valves — These valves delay air flow in the vacuum lines to control spark advance or retard functions. Delay valves are also used to control air flow to other vacuum-operated equipment. Amount of time delay depends upon application.

Vacuum Exhaust Heat Control Valve — This vacuum operated valve directs exhaust gases through a passage in intake manifold to rapidly heat incoming air/fuel mixture to promote better cold engine emissions.

Catalytic Converter — This unit, used on all Light Duty emissions models, is connected into exhaust system so exhaust gas passes through converter. Inside converter, a chemical reaction takes place which reduces exhaust emissions. *For additional information, see Catalytic Converter article in this section.*

Positive Crankcase Ventilation — Positive crankcase ventilation system is used to control crankcase blow-by gases. This system takes blow-by gases from crankcase and recirculates them back into combustion chamber for reburning. Key device in PCV system is vacuum-controlled PCV valve. *For additional information, see Crankcase Ventilation article in this section.*

Evaporative Emission Control — Fuel evaporative control system consists of a special fuel tank, a liquid vapor separator, a non-vented filler cap, a charcoal filled storage canister located in engine compartment, and plumbing necessary to direct fuel vapors to charcoal canister for storage. With this system fuel vapors are not allowed to evaporate from carburetor or fuel tank, instead they are routed to charcoal canister for storage. Carburetor vacuum later purges canister of stored fuel vapors. *For additional information, see appropriate Fuel Evaporation System article in this section.*

SERVICE PROCEDURES

IGNITION TIMING

See appropriate article in TUNE-UP SERVICE PROCEDURES.

CARBURETION

Carburetor Models	
Application	**Model**
4.9L (300″) 6-Cyl.	
Light Duty	
Federal	Carter YFA 1-Bbl.
Calif.	Carter YFA 1-Bbl. Feedback
Heavy Duty	Carter YFA 1-Bbl.
4.2L (255″) V8	Motorcraft 2150 2-Bbl.
5.0L (302″) & 5.8L (351″) V8	
Federal	Motorcraft 2150 2-Bbl.
Calif.	Motorcraft 7200VV 2-Bbl.
6.6L (400″) V8	Motorcraft 2150 2-Bbl.
7.5L (460″) V8	Holley 4180-C 4-Bbl.

IDLE SPEED & MIXTURE

See appropriate article in TUNE-UP SERVICE PROCEDURES.

1981 Exhaust Emission Systems

FORD THERMOSTATIC AIR CLEANER

All Models

DESCRIPTION

Fresh air or heated air is made available to the engine by a system of ducting which directs air into the air cleaner assembly. Air temperature is controlled by a temperature sensitive vacuum system that operates the duct valve. The vacuum-operated duct can select cool air from the outside through a pickup tube, or warm air from a shroud around the exhaust manifold. The system consists of a shroud around the exhaust manifold, an air cleaner assembly with a vacuum motor, a duct and valve assembly, a temperature sensor and on some models a cold-weather modulator.

OPERATION

When the engine is cold, air is selected from the exhaust manifold shroud because the heat sensor in the air cleaner is cold. Vacuum is applied to the vacuum motor that operates the duct valve, and the duct valve is opened to allow heated air to enter the air cleaner. As the engine warms up, the sensor operates, preventing vacuum from being applied to the vacuum motor. The duct valve then opens and allows air from the outside to flow through the pickup tube into the air cleaner. A cold-weather modulator, on some models, controls operation of the duct valve under certain air temperature conditions for improved emission control.

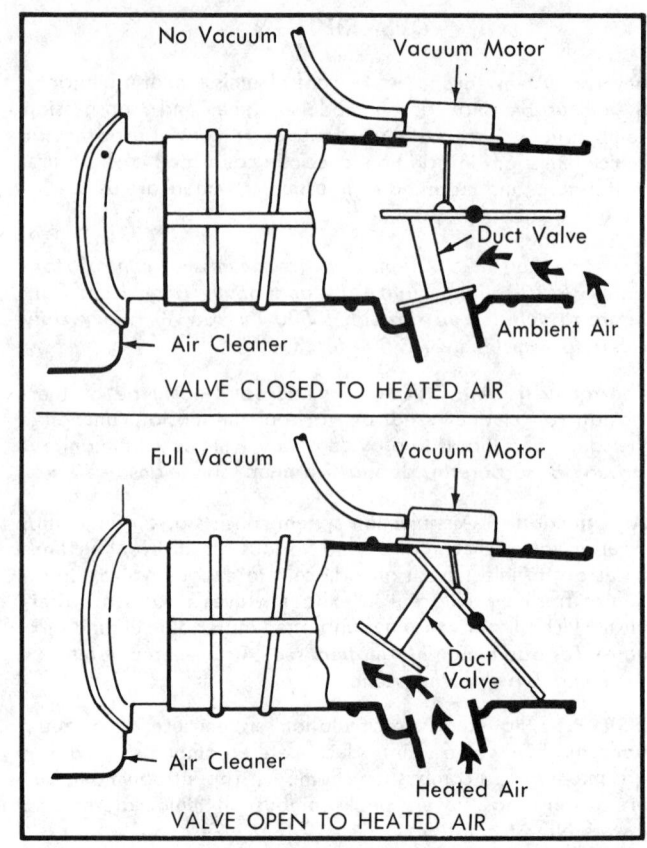

Fig. 2   Operation of Vacuum Controlled Duct Valve

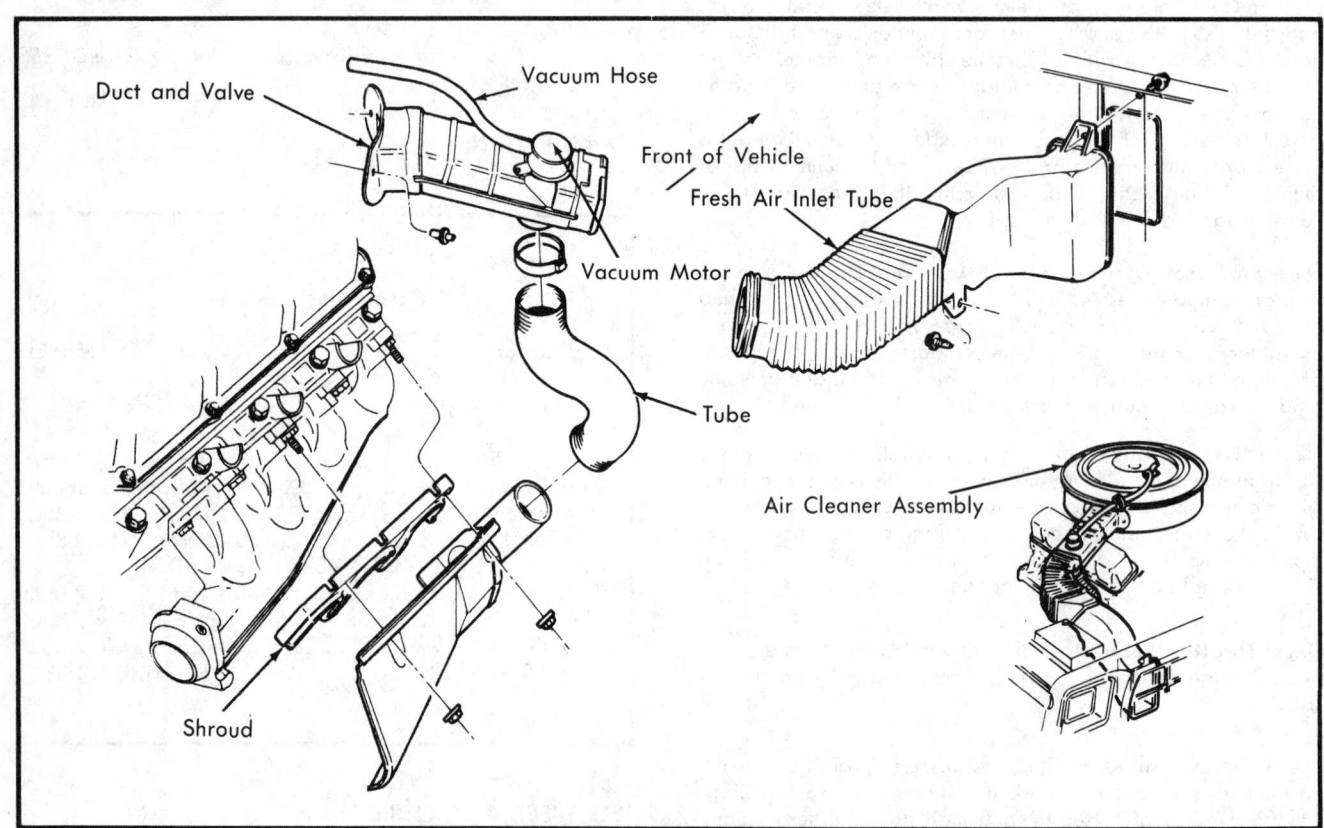

**Fig. 1   Ford Vacuum Operated Air Cleaner Assembly
(Typical V8 Assembly Shown - Others Similar)**

FORD THERMOSTATIC AIR CLEANER (Cont.)

TESTING

DUCT & VALVE ASSEMBLY WITHOUT VACUUM OVERRIDE

NOTE — *This check must be performed with outside temperature at least 60°F. If vehicle is equipped with a cold-weather modulator or vacuum delay valve, by-pass these systems by connecting the 2 vacuum lines together.*

1) Check to see that the duct door is open with the engine not running. If door is closed, check for binding. Place a magnetic thermometer as close as possible to the temperature sensor on the air inlet side.

2) Start engine. If duct door is closed, proceed to *step 3*. If duct door is open, turn off engine and cool the temperature sensor by spraying it with R-12 refrigerant.

CAUTION — *Do not spray R-12 on sensor with engine running. Heated R-12 vapors produce poisonous phosgene gas. Always perform this step in a well ventilated area.*

3) Start engine. Observe how long it takes the duct door to open. It should open within 5 minutes. If not, check thermometer temperature. If greater than 110°F, replace sensor. If less than 110°F, warm engine again to correct temperature. If door still fails to open, replace sensor.

DUCT & VALVE ASSEMBLY WITH VACUUM OVERRIDE

1) Disconnect duct and valve assembly from air cleaner. Check door for free operation. With outside temperature less than 73°F, connect an external vacuum source to vacuum motor.

2) At zero vacuum on vacuum motor, the door must be within .060" or less of heat-off position. If door does not close to this position within 10 minutes, replace duct and valve assembly.

3) Apply 1-5 in. Hg of vacuum to the vacuum motor. The duct door should start to move to the heat-on position. If not, replace or repair as required.

4) Apply 7-12 in. Hg of vacuum to vacuum motor. The duct door should be in the heat-on position. If door does not move to this position within 1 minute, repair or replace as necessary.

VACUUM MOTOR

Disconnect vacuum hose from vacuum motor connector tube. Apply 16 in. Hg of vacuum and trap. Vacuum motor should remain closed for 60 seconds. If not, replace duct and valve assembly.

1981 Exhaust Emission Systems

FORD EXHAUST GAS RECIRCULATION

DESCRIPTION

The exhaust gas recirculation (EGR) system is used to reduce NOx emissions. This is accomplished by recycling exhaust gases back into the intake manifold, which results in cooler combustion temperatures and controlled NOx emissions.

The EGR system used in Ford vehicles consists of an EGR valve, a vacuum amplifier, a vacuum reservoir, ported vacuum switch (PVS) and connecting lines and hoses.

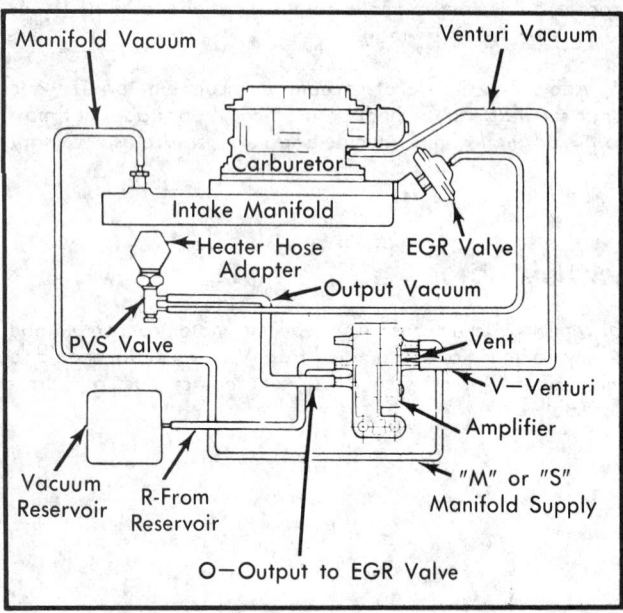

Fig. 1   Typical Ford EGR System Schematic

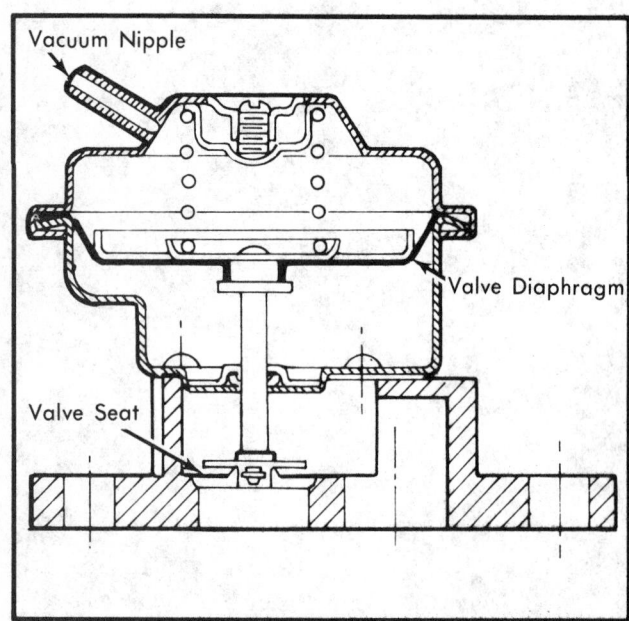

Fig. 2   Sectional View of Typical EGR Valve without Backpressure Transducer

OPERATION

The EGR system is controlled by the EGR valve. When the valve is open, exhaust gas enters the manifold passages. When closed, no gas is allowed to enter the intake manifold. Vacuum signals control the opening and closing of the EGR valve.

Some EGR systems use a Backpressure Transducer to aid in controlling exhaust gas recirculation. This unit senses exhaust gas backpressure and modulates the vacuum signal to the EGR valve in response to the amount of backpressure (this tells the transducer engine operation modes).

Light Duty emissions EGR systems use a backpressure transducer to aid in controlling exhaust gas recirculation. This unit senses exhaust gas backpressure and modulates the vacuum signal to the EGR valve in response to the amount of backpressure. Backpressure is used to provide information on engine operation modes. The backpressure transducer is integral with the EGR valve.

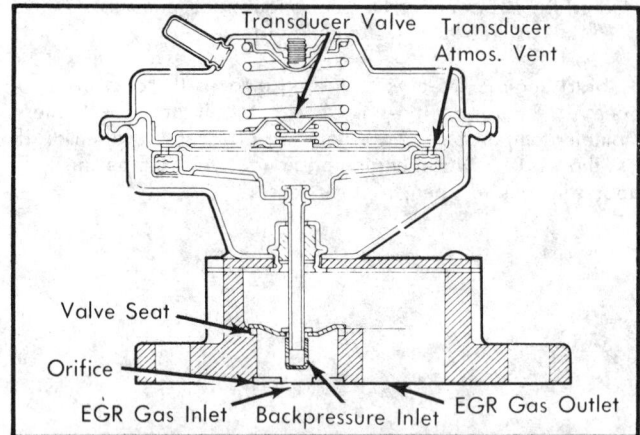

Fig. 3   Integral Type Backpressure Transducer and EGR Valve

TESTING

EGR VALVE WITHOUT BACKPRESSURE TRANSDUCER

NOTE – *This test applies only to EGR systems which DO NOT have backpressure transducer.*

1) Start and run engine to normal operating temperature (to be sure PVS is open).

2) Check all vacuum hoses for proper condition and that they are tightly seated on connectors.

3) Remove vacuum supply hose from EGR valve and plug hose. Attach another vacuum hose to EGR valve and attach a vacuum gauge to hose (preferably one calibrated in 1 in. Hg increments).

4) Gradually apply 8 in. Hg to EGR valve and watch EGR valve stem. At idle, it should take no more than 1 in. Hg to cause stem to move (begin to open). If stem does not start to move, replace EGR valve.

5) Turn engine off and apply 8" Hg to EGR valve and hold it. Vacuum should remain (within 1") for at least 30 seconds. If not, replace EGR valve.

FORD EXHAUST GAS RECIRCULATION (Cont.)

6) Restart engine and idle. Apply 8" Hg to EGR valve. Valve stem should move full length of travel and idle condition will get rough, RPM decrease and possibly stall. If not, EGR is not functioning and system is plugged. Clean as required.

7) Reconnect all hoses to original (normal) positions, restart engine and idle at normal operating temperature. If idle is not acceptable, EGR valve may not be sealing.

8) Install new gasket and adjust curb idle. Recheck idle condition. If no improvement, problem is elsewhere, reinstall original EGR valve and perform other engine diagnosis to seek out problem area.

CARBURETOR EGR PORT

1) Attach vacuum gauge directly to EGR carburetor port, using suitable hose. Start engine and quickly open throttle to about halfway position and close.

2) Observe vacuum gauge for quick rise and fall as throttle is open and closed. If definite vacuum is evident, port is okay. If not, port is clogged and must be cleaned.

EGR VALVE WITH INTEGRAL BACKPRESSURE TRANSDUCER

1) Loosen air cleaner and move aside without disconnecting vacuum hose from thermal vacuum switch on air cleaner housing.

2) Inspect EGR system for proper hose routing, hoses in good condition and all connections tight. See "Ford Vacuum Diagrams" in this Section.

3) Check EGR valve assembly for obvious damage, looseness, or exhaust "blowouts" at gaskets. Repair or replace as required.

4) Warm up engine to normal operating temperature. Place transmission in neutral. Slowly open and close throttle and watch valve stem. It should move up, oscillate and move down with throttle movement. If so, system is okay.

5) If unable to see stem movements, open and hold steady throttle at 2000-2500 RPM. Remove and pinch off vacuum hose to EGR valve. Engine speed should increase.

6) If valve operates as described above, the transducer is functioning properly. If not, replace the EGR valve.

7) To test for leakage, remove and cap the EGR valve vacuum hose. Start the engine. If engine idle improves noticeably, check vacuum hose routing, as valve may have vacuum supply at idle.

8) If engine idle does not improve, remove EGR valve. Block EGR passages with a plate. Start engine. If idle quality is still bad, the problem is elsewhere. Reinstall EGR valve. If idle quality improves, replace EGR valve.

PORTED VACUUM SWITCH

PVS with 2 Connections — 1) Detach both vacuum hoses from PVS and connect a vacuum gauge to top port on PVS. Connect other PVS nipple to manifold vacuum or external vacuum supply of at least 10 in. Hg.

2) Start engine and warm up until PVS opening temperature is reached. See chart. If no vacuum reading is noted, PVS should be replaced. If vacuum is present, PVS is okay.

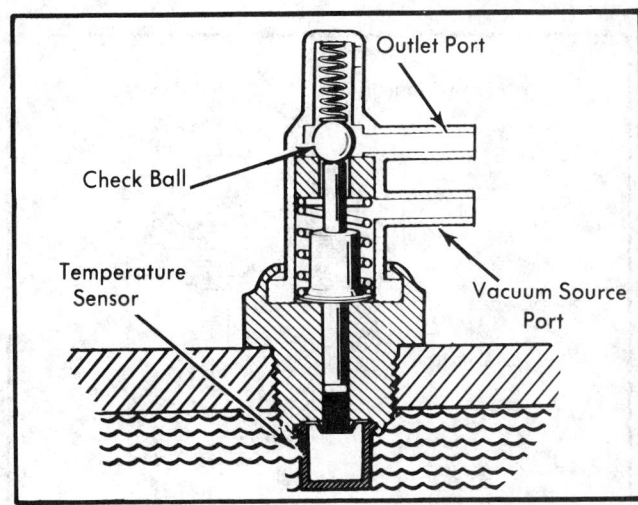

Fig. 4   Sectional View of 2-Port PVS

PVS with 3 Connections — 1) Disconnect EGR vacuum hose from PVS and connect manifold vacuum or external vacuum source to lowest port on PVS.

2) Detach distributor supply hose from center port and attach vacuum gauge to center port.

3) Start engine and warm up until PVS opening temperature is reached. See chart. If no vacuum is present, replace PVS. If present, PVS is okay.

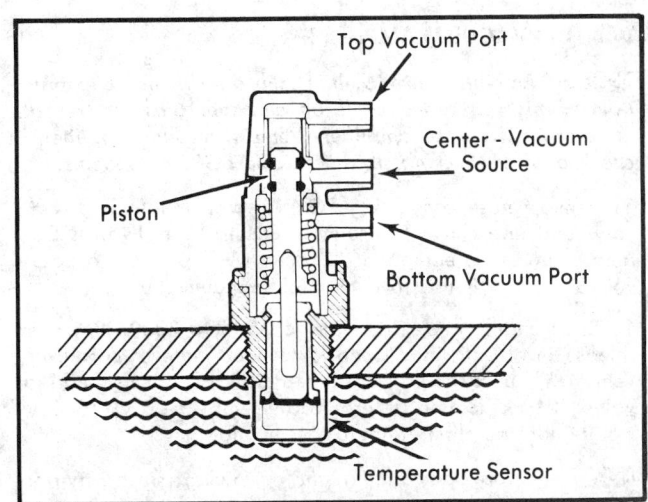

Fig. 5   Sectional View of 3-Port PVS

FORD EXHAUST GAS RECIRCULATION (Cont.)

PVS with 4 Connections — 1) Disconnect vacuum hoses at PVS valve. Connect a vacuum gauge to top port of the PVS. Connect external vacuum source to the second port.

2) Start engine and warm up until PVS opening temperature is reached. *See chart*. If no vacuum, this portion of the PVS is damaged and valve should be replaced. If vacuum, proceed to next step.

3) Connect gauge to the third port and vacuum supply to the bottom port. If vacuum is noted, PVS is okay. If no vacuum, replace PVS.

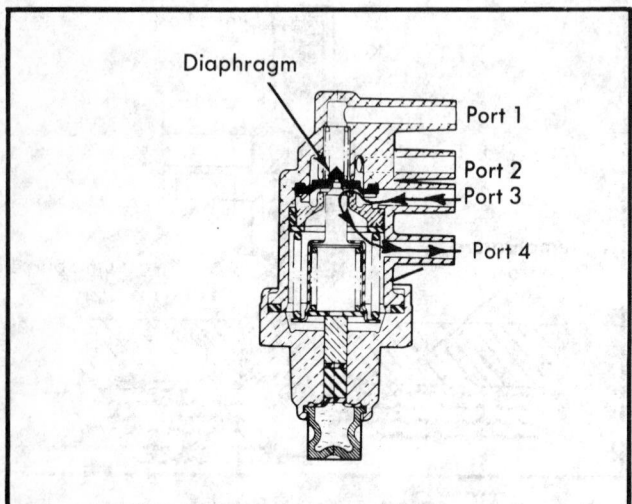

Fig. 6   Sectional View of 4-Port PVS

PVS Opening Temperatures	
Color Code	**Temp. (°F)**
Pink or Natural	Above 90
Black	Above 100
Blue or Plain	Above 133
Yellow or Gray	Above 155

VENTURI VACUUM AMPLIFIER

NOTE — *Amplifiers have built-in calibrations, and no external adjustments are required. If an amplifier bias test reveals malfunction, replace amplifier. Venturi vacuum amplifier is checked after checking all other basic EGR components.*

1) Remove hose connecting EGR valve to amplifier at EGR valve end and connect vacuum gauge to hose. By-pass EGR delay valve, if so equipped. Disconnect vacuum hose at reservoir and "T" this line to a manifold vacuum source.

2) Start engine and accelerate to 1500 to 2000 RPM, then release throttle to idle speed. Disconnect hose at carburetor venturi. Vacuum should be within ±.3 in. Hg of specified bias value. If specification is zero, vacuum may read up to .5 in. Hg. Replace amplifier if not to specification.

NOTE — *Before performing the following steps, by-pass vacuum solenoid valve or vacuum operated switch, if so equipped.*

3) Accelerate engine to 1500 to 2000 RPM then release throttle to idle speed. If vacuum gauge increased more than 1 in. Hg during acceleration, replace amplifier. Reconnect venturi hose to carburetor. If output vacuum increases more than .5 in. Hg, check idle speed. If idle speed is too high, output vacuum could increase due to increase in venturi vacuum.

4) Accelerate engine to 1500 to 2000 RPM and check vacuum gauge. Vacuum should measure above 4 in. Hg during acceleration and return to specified bias when throttle is released. If vacuum does not return to specified bias, replace amplifier.

5) Connect "R" nipple to manifold vacuum source, "S" nipple to spark port vacuum, "V" nipple to venturi vacuum, and "O" nipple to vacuum gauge. Accelerate engine to 1500 to 2000 RPM and release throttle to idle speed. Remove vacuum hose at carburetor venturi, and check spark port vacuum. If vacuum is greater than 2 in. Hg, amplifier output vacuum could increase. Vacuum gauge reading should be less than .5 in. Hg for all amplifiers. If not to specification, replace amplifier.

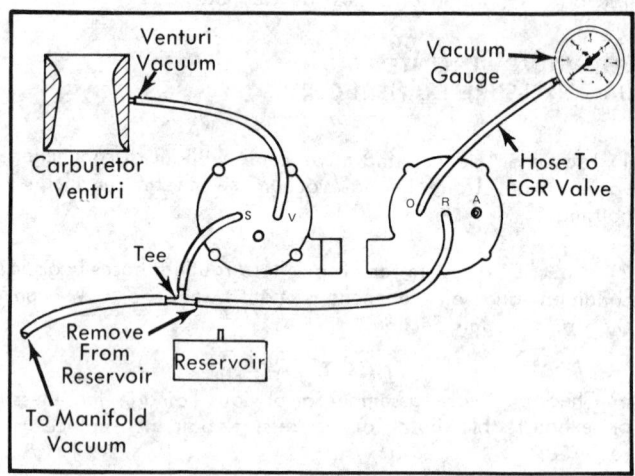

Fig. 7   Testing Venturi Vacuum Amplifier

VACUUM AMPLIFIER RESERVOIR

1) If reservoir does not have an external check valve, disconnect hose to amplifier and connect an external vacuum source to reservoir. Apply 14" Hg to reservoir. Charge reservoir with 14" vacuum. Vacuum should hold, with no more than 1" Hg drop, for at least one minute. If vacuum drops, replace reservoir.

2) If reservoir does have an external check valve, apply an external vacuum source 15 in. Hg to "T" between check valve and reservoir at amplifier side of "T". Vacuum should not vary more than 1 in. Hg for one minute. If vacuum drops, replace reservoir.

3) Remove hose to reservoir "T" and charge reservoir with an external vacuum source of 15 in. Hg. Vacuum should not vary more than 1 in. Hg for one minute. If vacuum varies, replace reservoir. To test check valve, disconnect hose to check valve at "T", and apply an external vacuum source of 15 in. Hg. Vacuum should not vary more than 1 in. Hg for one minute. If vacuum varies more, replace check valve.

FORD ELECTRONIC ENGINE CONTROL III (EEC III)

Ford
Calif. Models with
5.0L (302") & 5.8L (351") W Engines

DESCRIPTION

Ford Electronic Engine Control III (EEC III) with 7200VV Feedback Carburetor is used on California light duty Ford models with 5.0L and 5.8L W engines.

The EEC system consists of an Electronic Control Assembly (ECA), several sensors located on the engine or in the various engine systems, special actuators governed by the ECA, and various connecting electrical and vacuum lines. This system adjusts the engine to the best settings for various conditions of load, speed, temperature and altitude by controlling the following functions:

- Ignition Timing
- Carburetor Air/Fuel Ratio
- Engine Speed At Idle
- Exhaust Gas Recirculation (EGR) Flow Rate
- Secondary (Thermactor) Air Flow Rate
- Fuel Evaporation Canister Purging

OPERATION

ELECTRONIC CONTROL ASSEMBLY (ECA)

The ECA is a solid-state, micro-computer consisting of a processor assembly and a calibration assembly. This unit is located in the passenger compartment under the instrument panel, to the left of the steering column. The ECA is the "brain" of the EEC system.

Processor Assembly — The processor assembly is housed in an aluminum case and contains circuits designed to:

- Continuously sample input signals from the sensors.
- Calculate the proper spark advance, air/fuel ratio, EGR flow and thermactor air flow.
- Send out control signals to adjust spark timing, air/fuel ratio, EGR flow, thermactor air mode, evaporation canister purge and idle speed.

The processor assembly also provides a continuous reference voltage of 9.0 volts to the sensors.

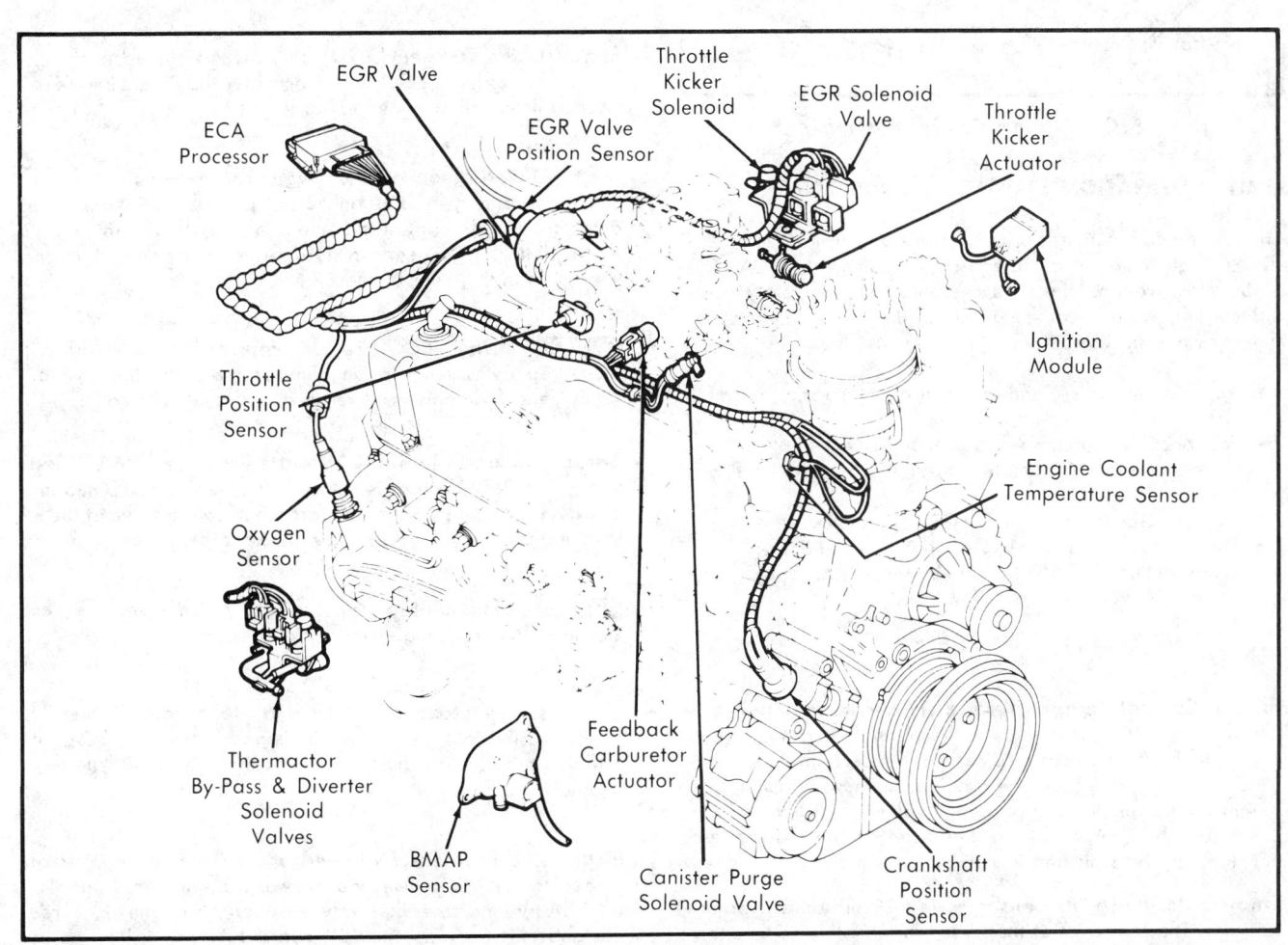

Fig. 1 Electronic Engine Control Component Locations

FORD ELECTRONIC ENGINE CONTROL III (EEC III) (Cont.)

Calibration Assembly — The calibration assembly is contained in a black plastic housing which is attached to the top of the processor assembly. It contains the "memory" and programming used by the processor assembly and is capable of:

- Providing operating information for that particular vehicle, for use by the processor assembly.
- Recalling information from its memory when required.

Power Relay — Activated by the ignition switch to supply battery voltage to the EEC. Attached to the lower right side of the ECA mounting bracket. Also protects ECA from possible damage due to reversed voltage polarity.

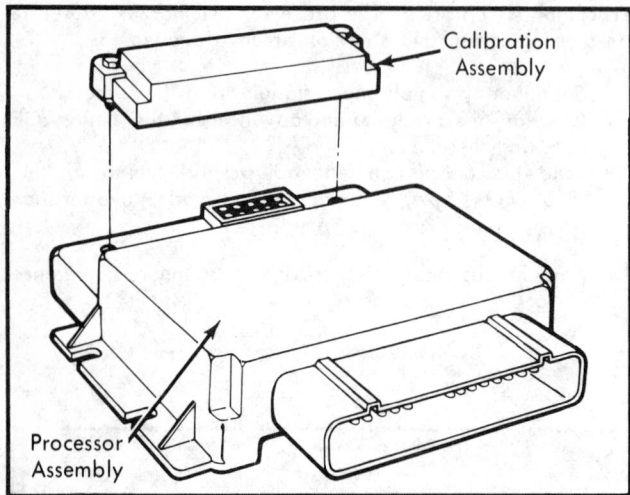

Fig. 2   EEC Electronic Control Assembly (ECA)

LIMITED OPERATION STRATEGY (LOS) MODE

The LOS mode functions during engine start, or upon failure of the ECA detected by a "safeguard" circuit in the ECA. This mode allows continued vehicle operation (with reduced performance) until repairs can be made. In this mode the actuator functions are set as follows:

- Ignition Module Timing: Minimum spark advance (10° BTDC).
- Feedback Carburetor Actuator (FBCA): Locked at last controlled position. On startup, the FBCA is driven full rich and then slightly lean.
- Exhaust Gas Recirculation (EGR): No EGR.
- Thermactor Air (TAB): Bypass (dump) position.
- Canister Purge (CANP): Canister sealed, no purge.
- Throttle Kicker (TK): Low RPM idle.

SENSORS

Engine Coolant Temperature (ECT) Sensor — Installed in heater outlet fitting at front of intake manifold near right valve cover, the ECT sensor converts coolant temperature to an electrical signal for the ECA. The brass sensor housing contains a thermistor (a resistor that changes value according to temperature). The ECA is able to determine engine coolant temperature by the resistance value of the sensor.

Throttle Position (TP) Sensor — The TP sensor is a potentiometer. The resistance of the sensor varies with throttle opening. The ECA applies a reference voltage to the sensor and the resultant sensor output voltage allows the ECA to determine throttle position (closed throttle, part throttle or wide open throttle). This information is used by the ECA in determining the proper amount of spark advance, EGR flow, air/fuel ratio and the proper thermactor air mode.

NOTE — The throttle position (TP) sensor mounting holes are slotted to permit rotational adjustment. If sensor is replaced, it must be correctly positioned or erroneous throttle information will be sent to the ECA.

Crankshaft Position (CP) Sensor — To provide the EEC system with an accurate timing reference (when pistons reach 10° BTDC), the crankshaft vibration damper is fitted with a 4-lobe "pulse ring".

As the crankshaft rotates, the pulse ring interrupts a magnetic field at the tip of the CP sensor (mounted on right front of engine). When the field is interrupted, an output signal is generated and sent to the ECA. The ECA uses these signals to determine the exact position of the crankshaft. From the frequency of the pulses, the ECA can determine engine RPM. By knowing these two factors, the ECA can determine the appropriate ignition timing advance required for best engine operation.

NOTE — Once the CP sensor is installed, no field adjustment is necessary.

Exhaust Gas Oxygen (EGO) Sensor — Installed in the exhaust manifold, the EGO sensor provides the ECA with the oxygen concentration of the exhaust gas.

The EGO sensor monitors the oxygen concentration of the exhaust gas and generates an output of .6 to 1.1 volts when detecting a rich exhaust gas mixture, and less than .2 volts when detecting a lean mixture. The constantly changing voltage signal is sent to the ECA for analysis.

CAUTION — The EGO sensor resistance CANNOT be measured by connecting an ohmmeter directly to its output lead. Sensor damage will result if this is attempted.

Barometric and Manifold Absolute Pressure (BMAP) Sensor — The BMAP sensor is actually two sensors combined into one assembly. This sensor monitors the absolute value of the intake manifold pressure and atmospheric pressure.

NOTE — Manifold absolute pressure is the difference between barometric pressure and manifold pressure.

Changes in atmospheric pressure and intake manifold pressure are converted into electrical signals and sent to the ECA. The signals are used to adjust spark advance and EGR rate to fit engine conditions.

EGR Valve Position (EVP) Sensor — The EVP sensor is attached to the EGR valve and provides an electrical signal to the ECA that indicates EGR valve position. Using the input from this and other sensors, the ECA can regulate EGR flow by activating or deactivating a pair of solenoid valves.

FORD ELECTRONIC ENGINE CONTROL III (EEC III) (Cont.)

THROTTLE KICKER SYSTEM

The throttle kicker system consists of a Throttle Kicker Solenoid (TKS) and a Throttle Kicker Actuator (TKA). The system is designed to increase engine RPM when the A/C is on, at high altitude, and when coolant temperature is above or below a specific range.

With A/C "ON", the ECA energizes the TKS allowing intake manifold vacuum to reach the TKA. The TKA is positioned on the carburetor against the throttle lever. With vacuum applied, the TKA will increase engine RPM for increased cooling and smoother idle. The TKA is also energized during engine warm-up or if an engine overheat condition exists.

EXHAUST GAS RECIRCULATION (EGR) SYSTEM

The EGR system used with EEC-III has 3 major components: an EGR valve and sensor assembly, an EGR cooler, and a 2-solenoid EGR control assembly.

Utilizing engine manifold vacuum to operate the EGR valve, the ECA controls EGR gas flow. When EGR valve is open, exhaust gas from exhaust manifold is directed into the intake manifold and becomes part of the combustion cycle, helping to reduce NOx emissions levels.

EGR Valve and Sensor Assembly — The EGR valve is mounted to the intake manifold under the carburetor. The valve controls EGR flow through a pintle valve and seat. An EGR valve position sensor (EVP) is attached to the valve and provides an electrical signal to the ECA indicating EGR valve position. The EGR valve, unlike standard EGR valves, has no opening to observe pintle valve movement. The EGR valve and position sensor are serviced as individual units.

Dual EGR Control Solenoids — EGR valve flow rate is controlled by two solenoid valves mounted on the left valve cover. Proper control of vacuum needed to operate the EGR valve requires two types of solenoid valves:

- A vent valve, which is normally open; that is, the outlet port is normally connected to the inlet port when the solenoid is not energized.
- A vacuum valve, which is normally open; that is, the outlet port is normally blocked when solenoid is not energized.

Utilizing input from the various sensors, the ECA directs the vacuum and vent solenoids to: (1) Increase EGR flow by applying vacuum to the EGR valve, (2) Maintain the EGR flow by

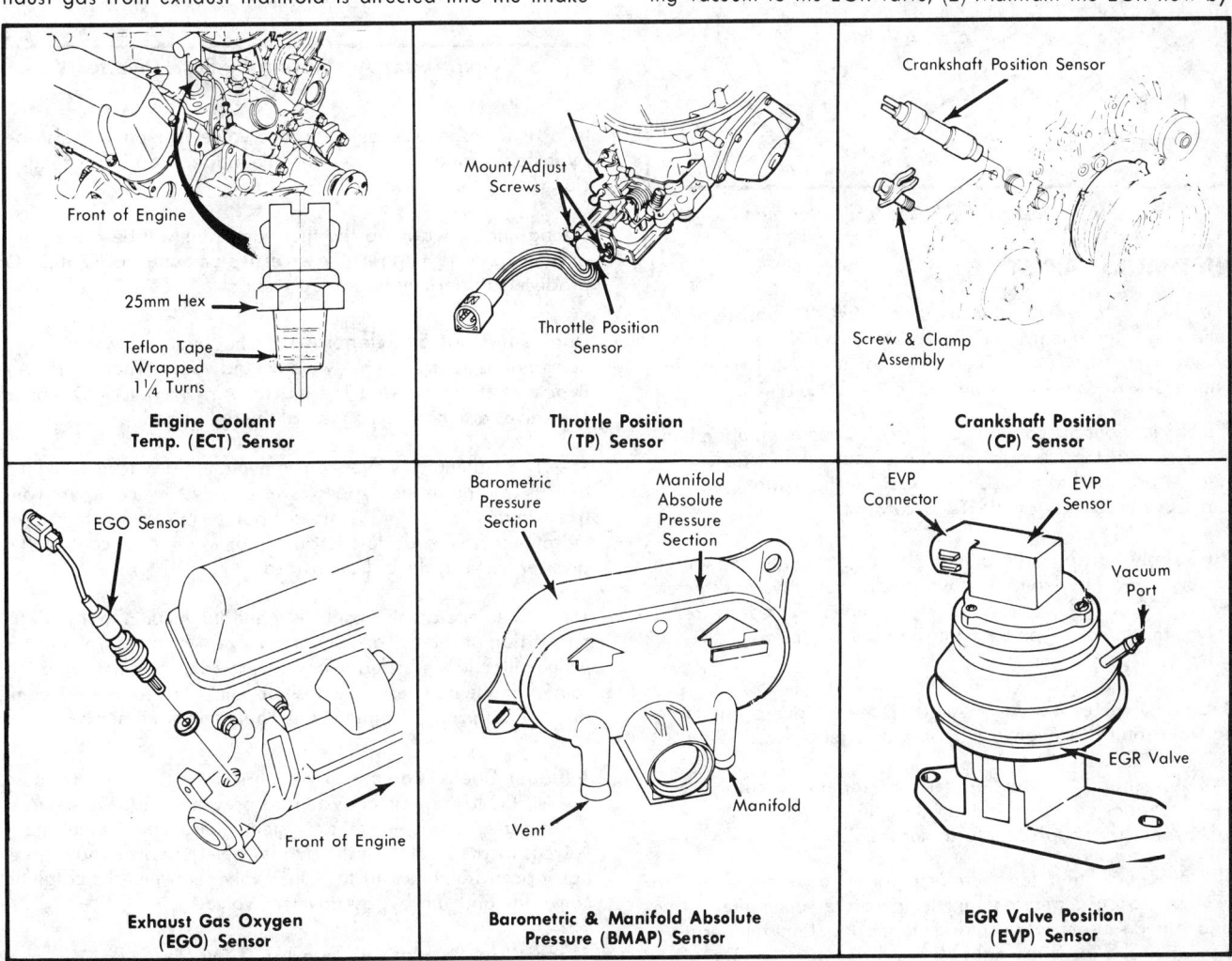

Fig. 3   Electronic Engine Control Sensors

FORD ELECTRONIC ENGINE CONTROL III (EEC III) (Cont.)

trapping vacuum in the system, and (3) Decrease EGR flow by venting the system to the atmosphere.

EGR Cooler Assembly — An EGR gas cooler is used to reduce EGR gas temperature, thus providing improved flow characteristics, better engine operation and EGR valve durability.

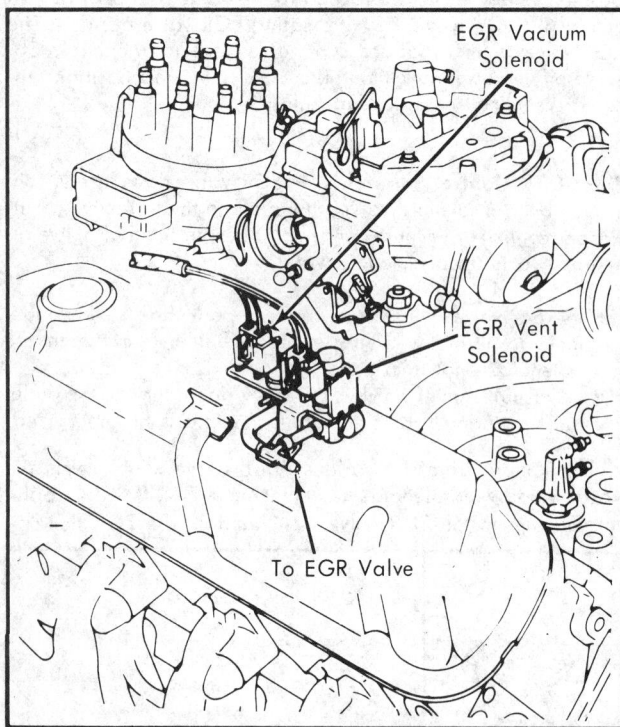

Fig. 4 Dual EGR Control Solenoids

THERMACTOR AIR SYSTEM

The Thermactor Air System used with EEC-III consists of the following components: an air supply pump, Thermactor By-pass/Diverter valve, dual Thermactor solenoids, 2 check valves, and a 3-way converter (referred to as COC/TWC).

The efficiency of the catalytic converter is dependent upon temperature and the chemical makeup of the exhaust gases. Air must be provided to the COC catalyst for the oxidation of HC and CO byproducts of the TWC catalyst.

Air Supply Pump — This belt driven pump provides the source of air to be controlled by the bypass/diverter valve as directed by the ECA. The air pump does not have a pressure relief valve, this function being controlled by the bypass/diverter valve.

Bypass/Diverter Valve — Air from the air pump has three possible routes through the bypass/diverter valve:

- Downstream air (air injected into three-way catalyst).
- Upstream air (air injected into exhaust manifold).
- Bypass (air bypassed to atmosphere).

The proper routing for thermactor air is determined by the ECA based on engine coolant temperature versus time curve and other sensor data. During normal coolant temperature operation the air is normally directed downstream. The air is bypassed when the closed throttle time exceeds a set time value, or if the time between the Exhaust Gas Oxygen

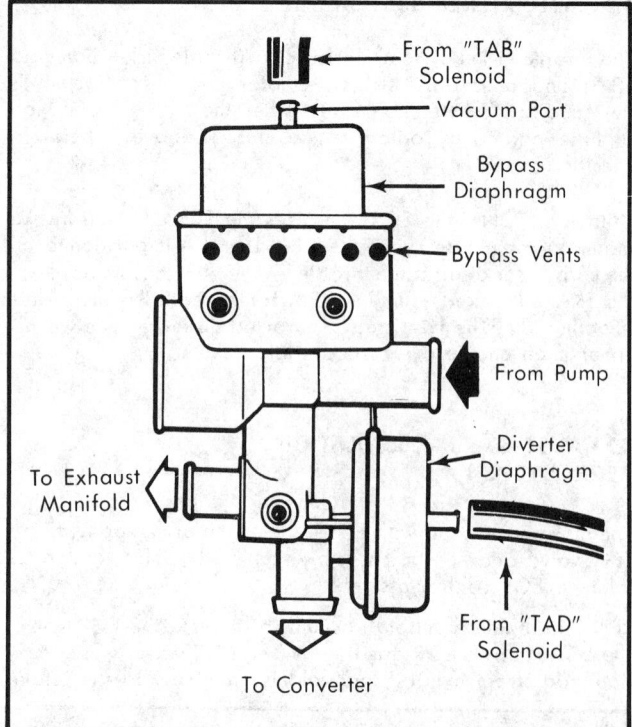

Fig. 5 Thermactor Air System By-Pass/Diverter Valve

lean/rich sensor exceeds a set time value. The air will also be bypassed during wide open throttle mode or during extended closed throttle operation.

During engine warm-up the thermactor air will be routed upstream. This is to help remove excessive amounts of HC and CO produced during the warm-up period.

Dual Air Control Solenoids — The bypass/diverter valve operation is controlled by two solenoid valves: Thermactor Air Bypass (TAB) valve, and Thermactor Air Diverter (TAD) valve. The valves are mounted on top of the right hand fender apron.

The TAB solenoid valve controls manifold vacuum to the bypass portion of the bypass/diverter valve, which in turn controls whether air from thermactor pump is bypassed to the atmosphere (solenoid de-energized) or routed to control the diverter valve (solenoid energized).

The TAD solenoid valve controls manifold vacuum to the diverter portion of the bypass/diverter valve, which in turn controls which direction (upstream or downstream) thermactor air is routed. In the de-energized position, air is routed downstream. In the energized position, air is routed upstream.

Exhaust Check Valve — Two exhaust check valves are used in the EEC II Thermactor system to prevent reverse flow of exhaust gases in the event of system malfunction. One check valve is located between the bypass/diverter valve and the exhaust port drillings, and the other valve between the catalytic converter and the bypass/diverter valve.

Three-Way Catalytic Converter (COC/TWC) — This is a dual catalytic converter consisting of two converters in one shell, with a mixing chamber between the two. Each converter

FORD ELECTRONIC ENGINE CONTROL III (EEC III) (Cont.)

is composed of a ceramic "honeycomb" coated with catalyst material.

The front, or "three-way catalyst" (TWC) converter acts on exhaust gases as they arrive from the engine. As gases flow from the TWC converter to the rear, or "conventional oxidation catalyst" (COC) converter, they mix with air from the thermactor pump injected into the mixing chamber. This air is required for proper oxidation of HC and CO in the COC converter.

FEEDBACK CARBURETOR ACTUATOR (FBCA)

The FBCA controls air/fuel ratio on signal from the ECA by adjusting the position of a vacuum bleed metering rod in the carburetor. This actuator is not a solenoid but a combination motor and leadscrew. The leadscrew changes the rotary motion of the motor to a linear (in and out) motion of the actuator shaft.

The FBCA actuator shaft can be set by ECA signal to any position between fully retracted and fully extended. When the actuator shaft is fully extended, the vacuum bleed metering rod is seated, permitting the slightly rich mixture to enter the engine unchanged.

When the actuator shaft is retracted, the metering rod bleeds vacuum from the control vacuum chamber into the fuel bowl. This lowers the air pressure in the fuel bowl, which leans out the air/fuel mixture.

Distributor — The EEC distributor eliminates conventional mechanical and vacuum advance mechanisms. All timing is controlled by the ECA, which is capable of firing the spark plug at any point within a 50° range depending on calibration. This increased spark capability requires greater separation of adjacent distributor cap electrodes to prevent cross-fire.

Bi-Level Rotor and Distributor Cap — Both the rotor and cap have upper and lower electrode levels. As the rotor turns, one of the high voltage electrode pickup arms aligns with one spoke of the distributor cap center electrode plate, allowing high voltage to pass from the plate, through the rotor to the terminal on the cap and on to the spark plug.

The numbers molded into the top of the distributor cap are wire identification numbers. Due to the unique design of the cap and rotor, the wires ARE NOT arranged in the cap in firing order. The outer ring of numbers is for 5.8L engine and the inner ring is for the 5.0L engine Actual firing order for 5.0L is 1-5-4-2-6-3-7-8 and for 5.8L is 1-3-7-2-6-5-4-8.

NOTE — *Do not attempt to remove any silicone coating from the rotor lower electrode blades or from the distributor cap electrodes (including the center plate electrodes). With age, this silicone compound has the appearance of being a contaminant of the cap and electrodes. This condition is normal and will not affect the performance.*

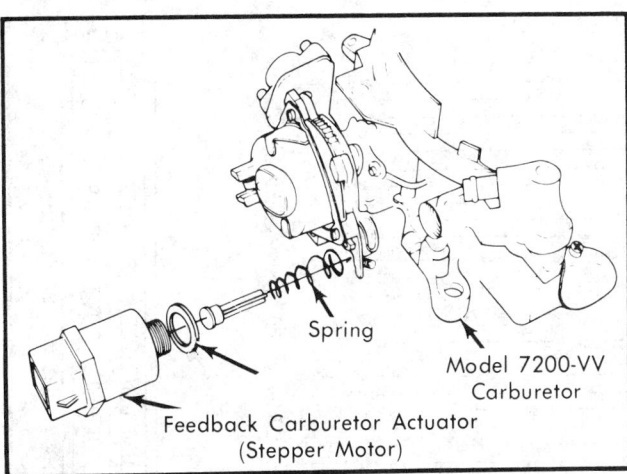

Fig. 6 EEC III Feedback Carburetor Actuator

CANISTER PURGE SYSTEM

Canister Purge (CANP) Solenoid — This solenoid is a combination solenoid and valve. Located in the line between the intake manifold purge fitting and the carbon canister, the CANP solenoid controls the flow of vapors from the canister to the intake manifold during various engine operating modes. The valve is opened and closed by a signal from the ECA.

DURA-SPARK III IGNITION SYSTEM

The EEC-III system uses a Dura-Spark III module (Brown grommet where wires emerge) and a Dura-Spark II ignition coil. A resistance wire is also used in the primary circuit.

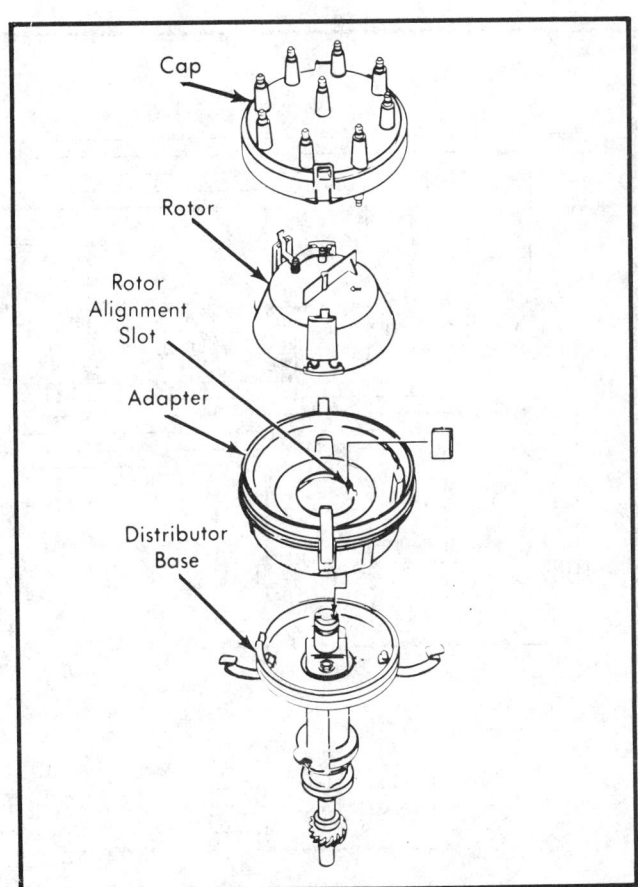

Fig. 7 EEC III Ignition Distributor Assembly

1981 Exhaust Emission Systems

FORD ELECTRONIC ENGINE CONTROL III (EEC III) (Cont.)

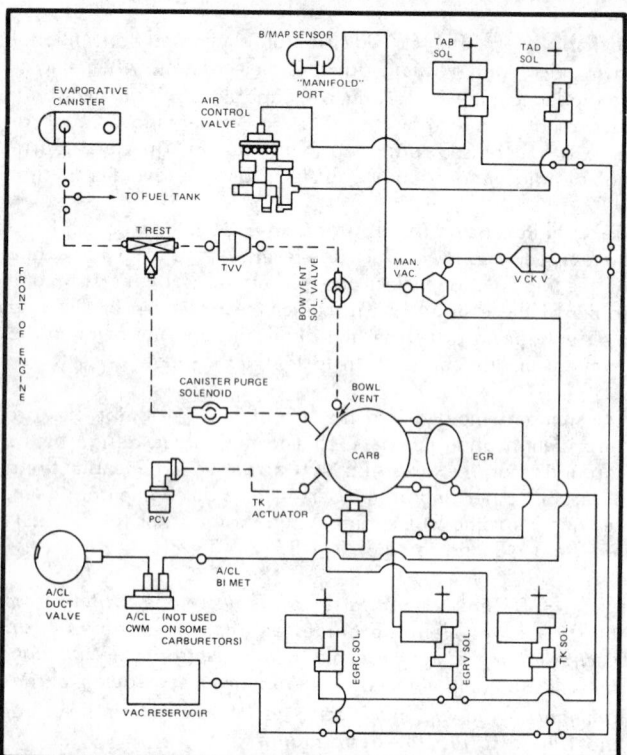

Fig. 8   Typical EEC III Vacuum Schematic

DIAGNOSIS & TESTING

NOTE – *Due to the complexity of the EEC III system, full testing cannot be done unless a special tester is used. Instructions for testing come with the tester, which is available from Owatonna Tool Co. However, some checks can be made using regular shop equipment. These checks are outlined in the following procedures.*

TESTING NOTES & CAUTIONS

NOTE – *No repairs or adjustments can be made to the ECA components. If diagnosis shows Processor or Calibration units are not functioning properly, they must be replaced.*

CAUTION – *Shorting the wiring harness across a solenoid valve can burn out circuitry in the ECA that controls the solenoid valve actuator.*

CAUTION – *The EEC system contains transistors which CANNOT tolerate excessive voltage surges or transient voltage. Never try to jump-start the vehicle with 24 volts.*

CAUTION – *The Exhaust Gas Oxygen (EGO) sensor resistance CANNOT be measured by connecting an ohmmeter directly to its output lead. Sensor damage will result if this is attempted.*

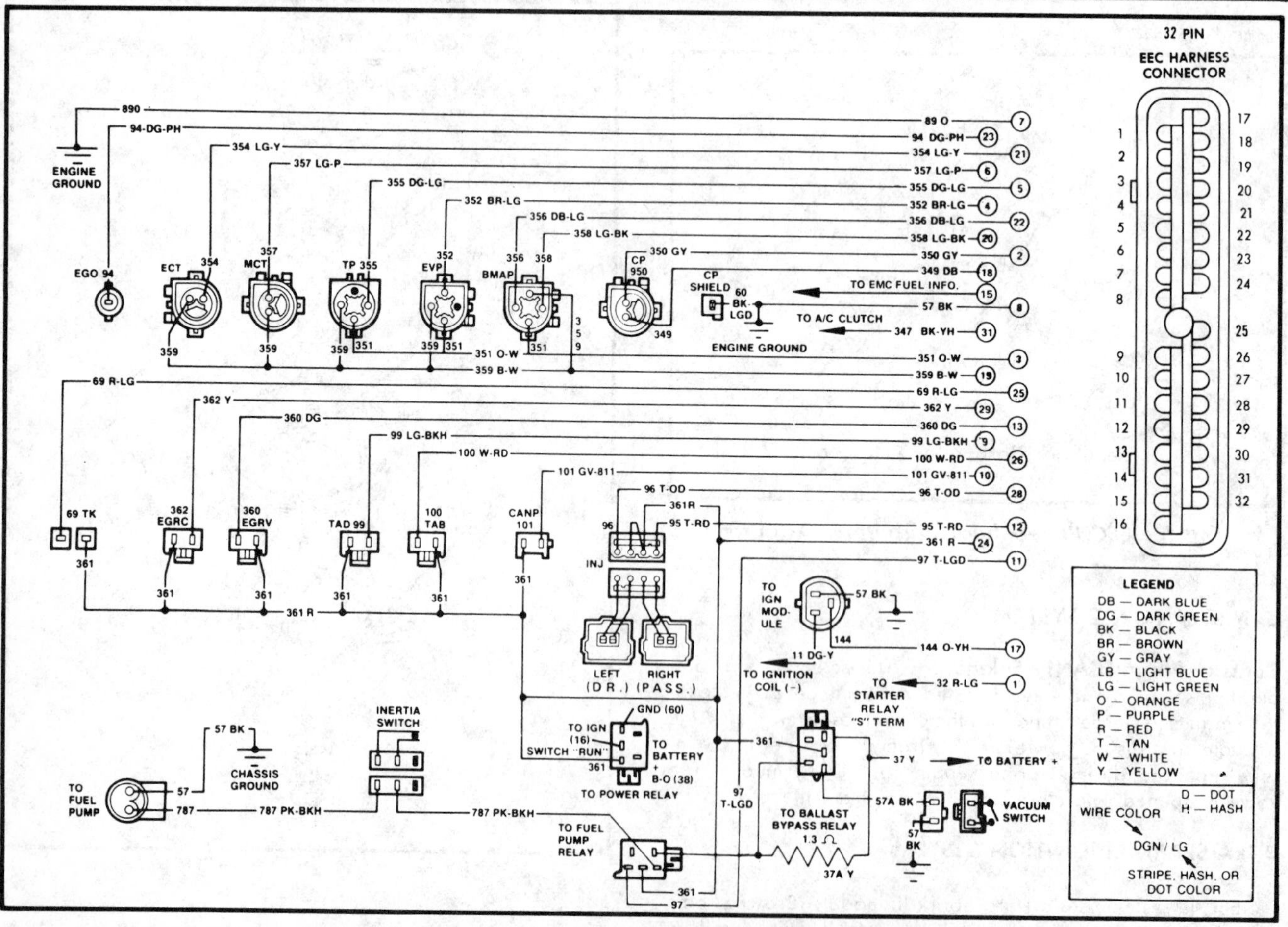

Fig. 9   Electronic Engine Control System Wiring Diagram

FORD ELECTRONIC ENGINE CONTROL III (EEC III) (Cont.)

BASIC EEC TROUBLE SHOOTING

1) Perform basic fuel system and ignition system checks, to ensure there is gas and spark.

2) Remove air cleaner assembly and inspect all vacuum and pressure hoses for proper connection to fittings, or any broken, cracked or pinched conditions.

3) Inspect EEC sub-system harness for proper connections to EGR solenoid valves. Red wire to both, yellow wire to vacuum solenoid and green wire to vent solenoid.

4) Check for any loose or detached connectors or broken or detached wires. Ensure all terminals are completely seated.

5) Check for partially broken or frayed wires at connectors or any shorting between wires. Also clean up any corrosion detected.

6) Inspect sensors for evidence of physical damage.

7) Repair items as required. Replace air cleaner.

8) Check vehicle electrical system. Check for full battery charge and check battery cable connections for tightness.

9) Inside passenger compartment, check to make sure the power relay is securely attached and making a good ground connection.

10) Use an ohmmeter to check resistance of the system sensors and solenoids. If any component fails to meet specifications, replace it. Be sure to disconnect component from system before measuring resistance.

OXYGEN SENSOR TEST

1) With engine at operating temperature but stopped, disconnect oxygen sensor connector. Start engine and run on high step of fast idle cam for 1 minute.

2) Connect voltmeter between ground and sensor, then depress carburetor control vacuum regulator (CVR) rod for 10 seconds. Voltage should be more than 0.5 volts.

3) Run engine at fast idle for 1 minute with PCV valve disconnected. Measure oxygen sensor voltage. Voltage should be less than 0.5 volts.

4) If oxygen sensor does not function as described, retest. If voltage readings are still incorrect, replace sensor. Tighten sensor to 27-33 ft. lbs.

REMOVAL & INSTALLATION

BMAP SENSOR

Removal — Disconnect wiring harness from BMAP sensor. Disconnect vacuum hose, remove retaining nuts, and remove sensor.

Installation — Position sensor and tighten retaining nuts. Connect vacuum hose to "Manifold" port. Do not connect any hose to "Vent" port. Connect wiring harness.

CANISTER PURGE SOLENOID VALVE

Removal — Remove air cleaner. Disconnect 2-wire connector and 2 vacuum hoses from solenoid. Remove valve.

Installation — Connect hose from manifold to nipple at end of valve. Connect hose from "T" to nipple toward middle of valve. Position valve so end with wires faces upward, then connect wiring and install air cleaner.

CRANKSHAFT POSITION (CP) SENSOR

Removal — Disconnect both sensor connectors. Remove sensor retaining clamp and pull sensor carefully out of holder.

Installation — Clean holder, then insert sensor fully (clamping surface about .025" from holder surface). Install retaining

---

EEC III COMPONENT RESISTANCE VALUES

Component	Wire Colors	Resistance (Ohms)
Crankshaft Position (CP) Sensor	Gray—Dk Blue	100-640
Engine Coolant (ECT) Sensor	Lt Grn/Yel—Blk/Wht	1100-8000
Air Charge Temperature (ACT) Sensor	Lt Grn/Ppl—Blk/Wht	1700-60,000
Throttle Position (TP) Sensor		
Closed Throttle	Org/Wht—Blk/Wht	3000-5000
Closed Throttle	Dk Grn/Lt Grn—Blk/Wht	550-1100
Wide Open Throttle	Dk Grn/Lt Grn—Blk/Wht	More than 2100
EGR Control Solenoid	Red—Yel	More than 30
EGR Vent Solenoid	Red—Dk Grn	More than 30
TK Solenoid	Red—Red/Lt Grn	More than 45
TAB Solenoid	Red— Wht/Red	45-90
TAD Solenoid	Red—Lt Grn/Blk	45-90
Fuel Pump Relay	Red—Tan/Lt Grn	More than 40
By-Pass Ballast Resistor	.....	Less than 3
Feedback Motor (FBCA)	①	32-150

① — Measured from center terminal (above blank) to each other terminal.

1981 Exhaust Emission Systems

FORD ELECTRONIC ENGINE CONTROL III (EEC III) (Cont.)

clamp and tighten to 70-100 INCH Lbs. Route wires up water pump and under spark plug wires along manifold to right of carburetor.

ELECTRONIC CONTROL ASSEMBLY

Removal — 1) Remove 10 mm retaining bolt and remove harness connector. Remove 2 bracket nuts, then remove gasket around connector.

2) From inside passenger compartment, remove 2 screws holding ECA to bracket. Slide out ECA and remove 2 screws to lift off calibration assembly.

Installation — 1) Attach calibration assembly with 2 screws. Slide ECA into bracket, engaging clip in ECA flange. Position connector surface through firewall, then install 2 mounting screws.

2) Install gasket carefully and replace bracket mounting nuts. Install connector and tighten retaining bolt to 40 INCH Lbs.

ENGINE COOLANT TEMPERATURE (ECT) SENSOR

Removal — Disconnect wiring and remove sensor with 25 mm socket.

Installation — Install sealing tape on threads of sensor. Install sensor, tightening to 8-18 ft. lbs. Reconnect wiring.

OXYGEN SENSOR

Removal — Allow exhaust manifold to cool. Disconnect wiring and remove sensor with crow's foot socket or special tool (T79P-9472-A).

Installation — Clean mounting surface and install sensor with fingers. Use tool to tighten sensor until compression washer crushes (27-33 ft. lbs.), then connect wiring.

EGR VALVE POSITION SENSOR

Removal — Disconnect wiring connector. Remove 3 fasteners at perimeter of sensor. Lift sensor and "O" ring seal. Cover valve to prevent foreign material from entering.

Installation — Clean top of valve and "O" ring groove. Lubricate "O" ring with silicone grease, then install in groove. Install sensor and secure with 3 self-tapping screws. Connect wiring.

TAB/TAD SOLENOID ASSEMBLY

Removal — Remove wiring connector from solenoids. Remove vacuum source hose at "T" and disconnect both solenoid hoses. Remove bolts from underneath fender and remove valve assembly.

Installation — Install assembly and tighten screws. Connect vacuum source hose to "T". Connect air by-pass hose to TAB solenoid (toward front of engine), then connect air diverter hose to TAD solenoid (toward firewall). Install wiring connectors.

FORD MCU ENGINE CONTROL SYSTEM

Calif. Models With 6-Cylinder Engines

DESCRIPTION

The MCU control system is named for and commanded by a Microprocessor Control Unit. This micro-computer is located in the engine compartment and is capable of controlling engine air/fuel ratios, air injection, and on some models, canister purge, spark retard and idle speed.

The MCU system is used on 6-cylinder trucks in California. The system consists of the MCU module, air/fuel control and air injection solenoids, engine sensors, and related circuitry.

OPERATION

MICROPROCESSOR CONTROL UNIT (MCU)

The MCU is a solid-state micro-computer located on the left fender panel. It is the "brain" of the system and receives inputs and sends signals through a 24-pin connector. The MCU is capable of operating in 3 modes: Intialization, Open-Loop and Closed-Loop.

Initialization mode occurs when the engine is started. In this mode the MCU richens the fuel mixture for easy starting.

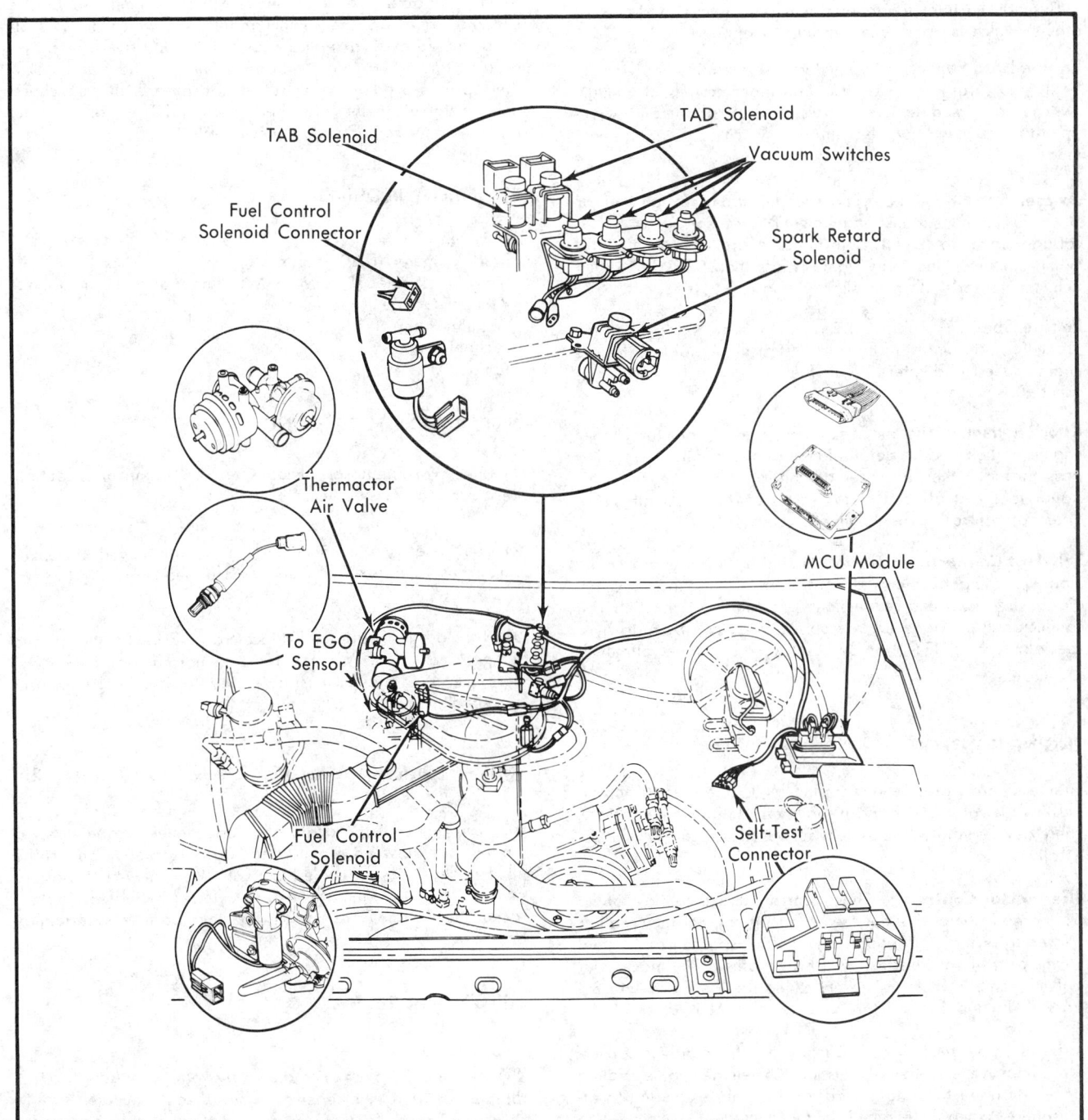

Fig. 1   MCU System Schematic for Calif. 6-Cylinder Engines

FORD MCU ENGINE CONTROL SYSTEM (Cont.)

Open-Loop operation is controlled by MCU programming. Air/fuel ratio is fixed at a pre-determined level and allows good driveability at idle, moderate-to-heavy acceleration, and deceleration. Closed-Loop operation occurs when the engine is warm and vehicle is operated at light load conditions. In closed loop, the MCU controls the air/fuel mixture in response to signals from an oxygen sensor in the exhaust manifold.

ENGINE SENSORS

Coolant Temperature — Various switches are used to signal temperature changes to the MCU. On 6-cylinder engines, a PVS sends vacuum to an electrical switch (mounted with 3 others) which is open when vacuum is applied.

Engine Load Sensor — Engine load is determined by vacuum level, and throttle position. On 6-cylinder models, 3 vacuum switches are used to signal cruise, deceleration, and wide-open-throttle condition. No throttle switch is used on these models.

Oxygen Sensor — All 6-cylinder models use an oxygen sensor mounted in the exhaust manifold. This sensor sends a low voltage signal to the MCU to indicate rich or lean mixture. When mixture is lean, the signal is less than 0.2 volts. When rich, the sensor voltage is slightly above 0.6 volts.

Engine Speed — The MCU receives a direct signal from the "Tach Test" terminal on the coil. It uses this signal to calculate engine speed and alters its air/fuel correction based on this speed.

Knock Sensor — The knock sensor is used on some 6-cylinder engines to help reduce detonation. It allows a voltage signal to pass through when it senses detonation. The MCU uses this signal to bleed off distributor vacuum. The MCU otherwise does not control ignition timing.

Self-Test Connector — The MCU can self-diagnosis most common operating problems. In order to initiate and read the diagnostic program, connections are made to the Self-Test connector. It provides voltage pulses which can be read by a specialized tester (Rotunda 07-0004) or a dial-type voltmeter.

ENGINE CONTROLS

Engine controls are the devices the MCU operates to accomplish its task of improving driveability and reducing emissions. These devices vary with engine type, but are all controlled electrically.

Thermactor Controls — These controls direct the flow of air from an air pump to either the exhaust manifold, the catalytic converter, or the atmosphere. On all models, a pair of solenoid valves control vacuum flow which operates a Thermactor Air Valve assembly. These valves are called the Thermactor Air Bypass (TAB) and Thermactor Air Diverter (TAD) valves.

In normal operation, the air is injected in the catalytic converter to improve reduction of emissions. When the engine is idling or decelerating for long periods of time, air is diverted to atmosphere. When the engine is first warming, air is injected into the exhaust manifold to help heat exhaust gases before they reach the converter.

Air/Fuel Controls — In 6-cylinder applications, the MCU provides a pulsed voltage signal which operates a fuel control solenoid. The engine is controlled directly by the solenoid which is a part of the carburetor.

Canister Purge Solenoid — A canister purge solenoid is controlled by the MCU. When engine conditions are optimum, the solenoid is opened and the fuel vapor canister is purged.

DIAGNOSIS & TESTING

The MCU system is capable of diagnosing some problems which may occur. To determine which components should be checked, perform the "Functional Test" which follows. If problems do exist, a service code will be displayed (as pulses on a voltmeter). Locate the appropriate test chart and follow the repair procedure as instructed. Do not use the test charts unless referred to them by the "Functional Test", or you may replace some components unnecessarily.

EQUIPMENT REQUIRED

All Systems
  Dial Voltmeter (0-20v scale)
  Digital Voltmeter (DVOM — Min. impedance 10 megohms)
  Vacuum Gauge (0-30 in. Hg)
  Vacuum Pump
  Tachometer
  Jumper Wire

PREPARATION FOR TESTING

1) Check vacuum hoses for leaks, cracks, or improper routing. Repair or replace as necessary.

2) Check electrical connections. Repair any frayed or broken wires. Ensure that all connections are clean and tight.

3) Turn all accessories off. Place transmission in neutral and set parking brake. Warm engine to normal operating temperature. If air cleaner must be moved, leave all vacuum hoses attached.

NOTE — *If vehicle will not start, see No Start Test (No. 2).*

4) Turn ignition off. Locate Self-Test connector and insert a jumper wire between ground and Trigger sockets. Connect the positive lead of a needle-type voltmeter to vehicle battery positive terminal, and the negative lead to Self-Test output socket. Set voltmeter on 15-20 volt scale. Battery voltage may be shown.

FUNCTIONAL TEST

NOTE — *Service codes are shown by voltage pulses. The first digit is indicated by a series of pulses, then the needle drops to zero for 2 seconds, then the second digit of the code is displayed. After all service codes are displayed, a 4 second pause will occur and then the codes will be repeated.*

FORD MCU ENGINE CONTROL SYSTEM (Cont.)

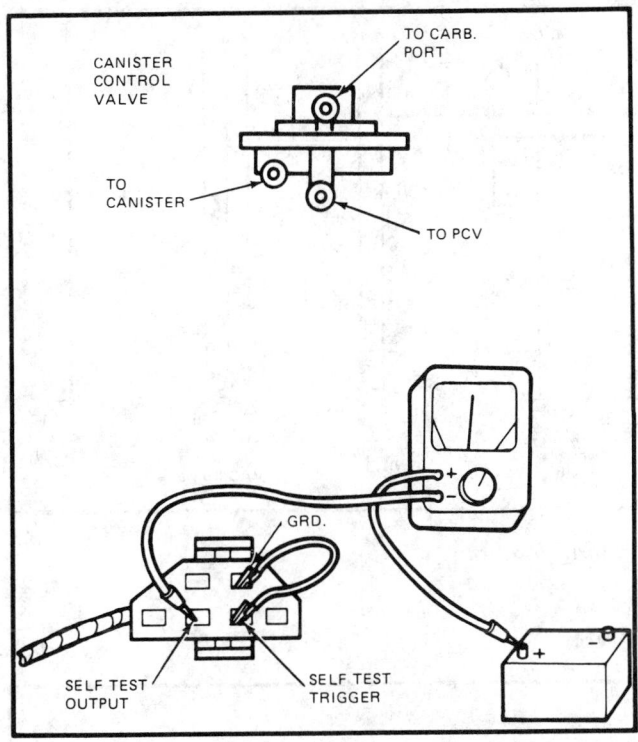

CANISTER CONTROL VALVE

TO CARB. PORT

TO CANISTER

TO PCV

GRD.

SELF TEST OUTPUT

SELF TEST TRIGGER

Fig. 2 Connections for Functional Test

Key On, Engine Off Test — Turn key on, but do not start engine. Watch voltmeter for code pulses which should appear within 30 seconds. Ignore any initial surge of voltage. Record code(s).

NOTE — *If voltmeter does not pulse, but shows steady high or low readings, see test 1, Functional Test Not Operating.*

Engine Running Test — 1) Start engine and raise speed to 2500-3000 RPM within 20 seconds after start. Hold RPM until 3 initial pulses appear. Continue holding speed until code pulses begin (10-40 seconds).

NOTE — *If more than 3 initial pulses occur, go to test 14 to check for an open circuit in the tachometer signal.*

2) Return engine to idle when codes begin. Codes will be repeated once. Record codes, then stop engine and reconnect canister purge hose. Refer to code chart to locate appropriate test.

NON-CODE TESTS

Perform the following tests after vehicle has passed all other diagnosed tests.

Canister Purge Check — Tee in vacuum gauge between canister and canister purge solenoid. Stop engine, then restart and raise RPM to initiate Self-Test. Observe vacuum gauge during initial pulses. If vacuum pulses 3 times between 0-1 in. Hg, go to Spark Retard Solenoid Check. If vacuum is always high or low, go to test 12, Canister Purge Solenoid test.

Spark Retard Solenoid Check — Remove vacuum gauge from canister purge hose and reconnect hose. Remove filter from spark retard solenoid and connect vacuum gauge to port. Turn engine off, then restart it and increase RPM to initiate Self-Test. If gauge pulses 3 times, system and MCU are O.K. If vacuum remains high or low, go to test 13, Spark Retard Solenoid test.

Cold Drive Complaint — If complaint occurred when engine was cold, recheck coolant temperature switch for proper operation. Go to Low Temperature Vacuum Switch test, step 4).

Closed or Light Throttle Drive Complaint — Check resistance between Self-Test output socket and ground. If continuity is found, repair short to ground.

SERVICE CODES & SUB-ROUTINE TESTS

6-Cylinder Test	Code
1 Functional Test Not Operating	None
2 No Start Test System OK	No Start 11
3 Running Test Not Initiated	33
4 Fuel Always Lean	41
5 Fuel Always Rich	42
6 Thermactor System	44
7 Thermactor Air Diverter	45
8 Thermactor Air By-Pass	46
9 Low Temperature Vacuum Switch	51
10 Vacuum Switch	52, 53, 56, 62, 63 & 66
11 Low Temperature Switch	51
12 Canister Purge	None
13 Spark Solenoid	None
14 Tachometer Lead	None

INSTRUCTIONS FOR USING SUB-ROUTINE TESTS

Sub-routines are the following checks which are performed to correct a service code. Be sure to perform check as instructed. After replacing components or repairing circuits, repeat "Functional Test" and check engine operation.

Observe the following instructions when performing sub-routines:

- Do not measure voltage or resistance at MCU module, or connect test lamps to it (unless specific instructions say to do so).

- Disconnect both ends of a circuit when looking for continuity or shorts. Be sure ignition is turned off.

- Disconnect solenoids and switches from harness before measuring resistance or continuity.

- When more than one service code is indicated, start service with the first code received.

- Use wiring diagrams to locate pin locations and connectors.

FORD MCU ENGINE CONTROL SYSTEM (Cont.)

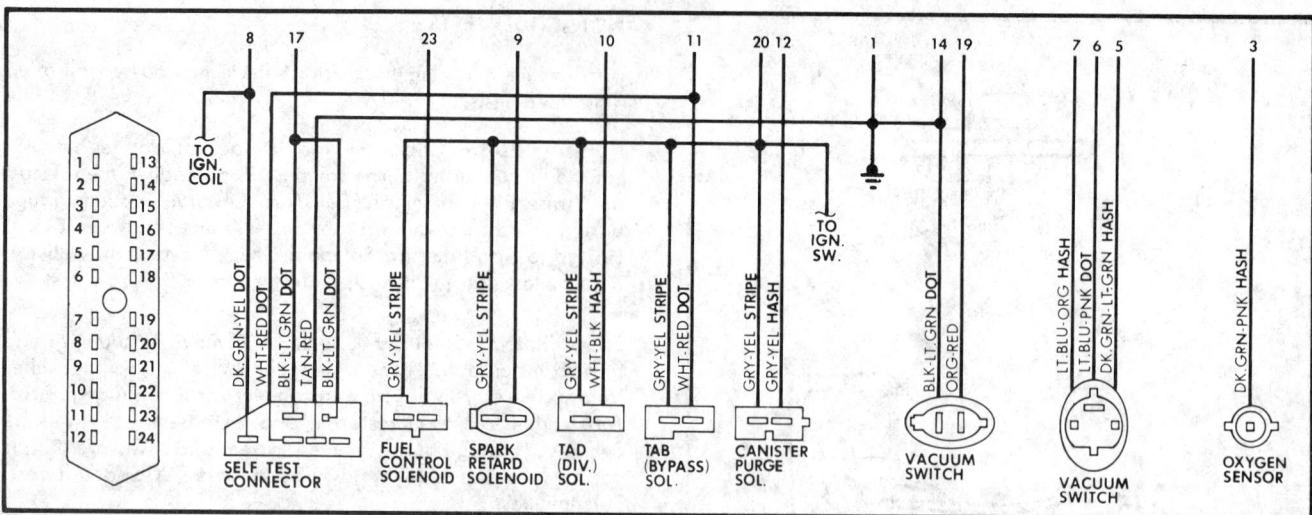

Fig. 3   MCU System Wiring Diagram

SUB-ROUTINES

1   FUNCTIONAL TEST NOT OPERATING

1) Ensure that test connections, jumper wires, and VOM were all correctly hooked up.

2) Disconnect MCU connector. With ignition on, battery voltage should be present at pin 20. If not, check fuse. With ignition off, pin 14 should have continuity to ground. If not, repair. If wiring is okay, go to next step.

3) Check for continuity between Self-Test connector and MCU. See wiring diagram at end of this test for wire connections. Check to ensure circuit from MCU to TAB solenoid is not shorted to ground.

4) Measure TAB solenoid resistance. If within 50-110 ohms, replace MCU module. If not within 50-110 ohms, replace solenoid. Repeat "Functional Test".

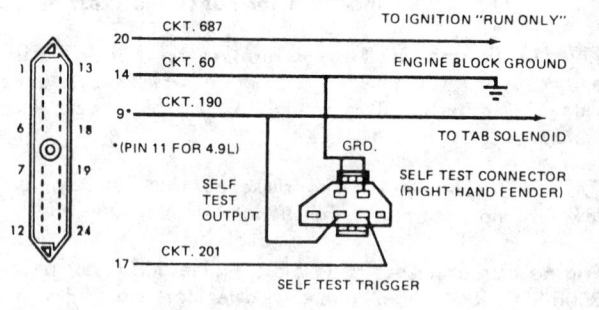

2   NO START TEST

This test detects faults in the MCU only.

1) Check Tach lead for a ground short. Leave harness connected to MCU; disconnect coil and ignition module connectors. Measure resistance between ground and self-test connector, then Tach connector. If resistance is less than 1000 ohms, go to step 2). If higher than 1000 ohms, MCU is not shorted.

2) Disconnect harness from MCU and measure resistance again. If resistance is less than 1000, repair circuit. If greater than 1000, replace MCU module.

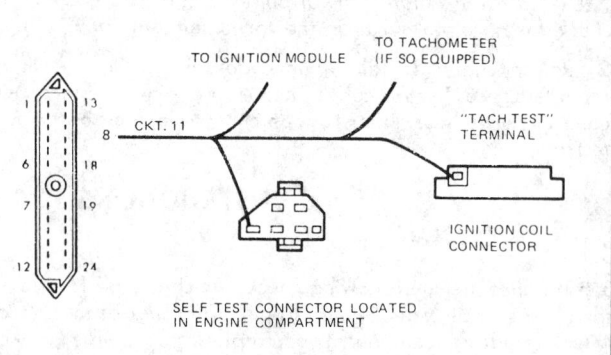

3   RUNNING TEST NOT INITIATED
(CODE 33)

It is necessary to increase speed to more than 2500 RPM within 20 seconds after start in order to initiate "Functional Test". Turn key off and repeat procedure.

FORD MCU ENGINE CONTROL SYSTEM (Cont.)
SUB-ROUTINES

4

FUEL ALWAYS LEAN
(CODE 41)

After starting engine, allow at least 40 seconds before testing. Disconnect "Functional Test" trigger jumper.

1) Disconnect oxygen sensor and MCU connector. Turn all accessories off. Check resistance between MCU connector pin 3 and ground, then pin 23 and ground. If resistance in either circuit is less than 1000 ohms, repair short to ground. If resistance is greater than 1000 ohms, go to next step.

2) Check continuity between pin 1 of MCU connector and ground, then continuity between pin 3 and oxygen sensor connector. If either circuit measures more than 5 ohms, repair wiring. If both are less than 5 ohms resistance, go to next step.

3) Connect voltmeter to back of Fuel Control Solenoid (FCS) connector. Start engine and run at 2500 RPM. Observe voltage after 15 seconds. If less than 10 volts, go to next step. If greater than 10 volts, replace MCU module.

4) Reconnect oxygen sensor and MCU connector. Disconnect Thermactor hose from air pump and plug hose. Set engine at 2500 RPM and hold choke valve 3/4 closed to force engine rich. With voltmeter still connected at FCS, observe voltage after 15 seconds. If less than 10 volts, go to next step. If greater than 10 volts, MCU is okay. Check Thermactor and carburetor.

5) Turn ignition off and disconnect harness from oxygen sensor. Measure resistance between oxygen sensor wire (harness side) and ground. If resistance is less than 1000 ohms, replace MCU module. If greater than 1000 ohms, go to next step.

6) With oxygen sensor still disconnected, start engine. With engine idling, connect a jumper wire to harness side of oxygen sensor connector. Be sure this connection cannot touch ground. Connect other end of jumper to battery positive terminal, then raise engine speed to 2500-2800 RPM. If voltage at FCS is less than 10 volts, replace MCU module. If greater than 10 volts, replace oxygen sensor.

EGO SENSOR

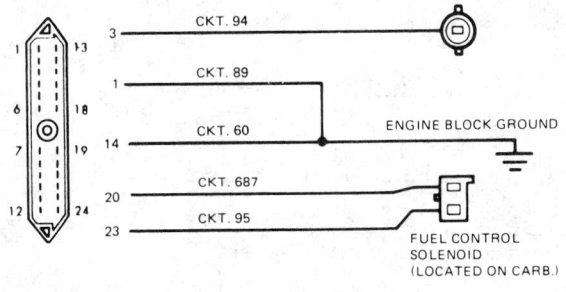

5

FUEL ALWAYS RICH
(CODE 42)

After starting engine, allow at least 40 seconds before testing. Disconnect "Functional Test" trigger jumper.

1) Check choke valve for sticking or binding, and repair as necessary.

2) Disconnect connector at MCU and connector at Fuel Control Solenoid (FCS). Measure resistance between pin 20 in MCU connector and 1 pin at FCS connector, then between pin 23 at MCU connector and other pin at FCS connector. Resistance should be less than 5 ohms in both cases. If not, repair wiring. If okay, go to next step.

3) Check resistance across terminals of FCS. If within 15-33 ohms, go to next step. If not, replace FCS.

4) Connect a voltmeter to the back of FCS connector. Start engine and run at 2500 RPM. Check voltage after 15 seconds. If less than 10 volts, replace MCU module. If greater than 10 volts, go to next step.

CAUTION − *For the following step, a digital VOM must be used which has an input impedance of at least 10 megohms.*

5) Disconnect oxygen sensor and connect DVOM between sensor and ground, with switch in lowest voltage position. Start engine and run at 2000 RPM for 1 minute to warm up sensor. Turn engine off and immediately check DVOM reading. If greater than 0.4 volts, go to next step. If less than 0.4 volts, check carburetor (too rich).

6) Purge exhaust system immediately by disconnecting coil "horseshoe" connector and cranking engine for 10 seconds with throttle wide open. Observe voltage reading. If greater than 0.4 volts, replace oxygen sensor. If less than 0.4 volts, check carburetor (too rich).

EGO SENSOR

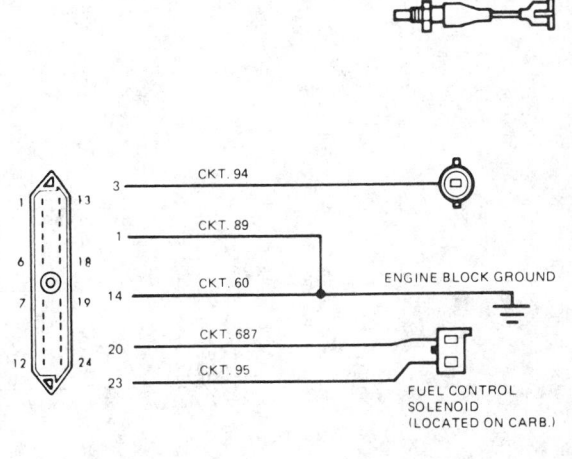

FORD MCU ENGINE CONTROL SYSTEM (Cont.)
SUB-ROUTINES

6

THERMACTOR SYSTEM
(CODE 44)

1) Remove vacuum hose from TAB valve and connect gauge to hose. Start, increase RPM above 2500 to activate "Functional Test" and observe vacuum gauge. If vacuum pulses are above and below 5 in. Hg, go to next step. If pulses are always above 5 in. Hg, go to next step. If pulses are below 5 in. Hg, go to step 10.

2) Reconnect hose to TAB. Disconnect hose at TAD valve and connect vacuum gauge. Start engine and raise RPM above 2500 to start "Functional Test". Observe vacuum readings. If above and below 5 in. Hg, go to next step.

3) Reconnect hose to TAD valve. Remove upstream air hose at TAD valve. Start engine and raise RPM above 2500 to start "Functional Test". Hold engine speed and feel for air at TAD valve nipple 20 seconds after test starts. Air will flow for 6 seconds. If okay, go to next step. If not, check air pump.

4) Turn engine off and reconnect air hose. Disconnect harness from oxygen sensor and insert jumper wire between connector and ground. Start engine, raise RPM to begin "Functional Test" and maintain RPM until output code is received. If code 41 is read on voltmeter, check choke system, then go to next step. If code 44 is received, replace MCU module.

CAUTION — *For the next step, a digital VOM must be used which has an input impedance of at least 10 megohms.*

5) Place DVOM selector in lowest voltage position and connect it between oxygen sensor and ground. Start engine and run at 2000 RPM for 1 minute to warm up sensor. Turn engine off and immediately check DVOM. If voltage is less than 0.4 volts, check carburetor (too rich). If voltage is greater than 0.4 volts, go to next step.

6) Immediately purge exhaust system. Disconnect coil "horseshoe" connector and crank engine for 10 seconds with throttle wide open. If voltage is greater than 0.4 volts, replace oxygen sensor. If voltage is less than 0.4 volts, check carburetor (too rich).

7) Disconnect MCU connector, then connectors at TAD and TAB solenoids. Check continuity between MCU connector pin 20 and TAD solenoid, then between pin 11 and TAB solenoid. If less than 5 ohms resistance, go to next step. If greater than 5 ohms resistance is measured, repair wiring.

8) Measure resistance of TAB solenoid. If between 50-110 ohms, go to next step. If not within 50-110 ohms, replace TAB solenoid.

9) Check at TAB solenoid output to be sure vacuum is not present when solenoid is energized (12 volts). If vacuum is present, replace TAB solenoid. If no vacuum, replace MCU module.

10) Check vacuum hose between TAD and TAB solenoid, then between source and TAB solenoid. Repair as ncessary. If hoses are okay, go to next step.

11) Check vacuum switch (TVS) and retard delay valve (RDV) for proper installation and operation. Check vacuum schematic for usage and location. Service valves if necessary, otherwise go to next step.

12) Check at TAB solenoid output to be sure vacuum is present when the solenoid is energized (12 volts). If vacuum is not present, replace TAB solenoid. If vacuum is present, go to next step.

13) Disconnect TAB solenoid connectors and MCU connector. Measure resistance between pin 20 and TAB connector, then pin 11 and TAB solenoid. If resistance is less than 5 ohms, replace MCU module. If higher than 5 ohms, repair circuits.

14) Disconnect MCU connector. Measure resistance from pin 20 to ground. If greater than 1000 ohms, go to next step. If less than 1000 ohms, repair short to ground.

15) Check at TAD solenoid to be sure vacuum is not present when solenoid is deactivated. If vacuum is present, replace TAD solenoid. If vacuum is not present, replace MCU module.

16) Check vacuum hoses between TAD valve and TAD solenoid, then between TAD solenoid and vacuum source. Repair if necessary. If vacuum source and hoses are okay, go to next step.

17) Check retard delay valve (RDV) for proper installation and operation. Check thermal vacuum switch (TVS) for proper installation and operation (if used on vehicle). Replace if necessary. If okay, go to next step.

18) Measure resistance of TAD solenoid. If not between 50-110 ohms, replace solenoid. If resistance is okay, go to next step.

19) Check at TAD solenoid to be sure vacuum is present when solenoid is energized (12 volts). If vacuum is not present, replace solenoid. If vacuum is present, go to next step.

20) Disconnect wiring at TAD solenoid and MCU. Measure between MCU pin 20 and TAD solenoid, then between pin 10 and solenoid. If resistance is greater than 5 ohms, repair wiring. If less than 5 ohms, replace MCU module.

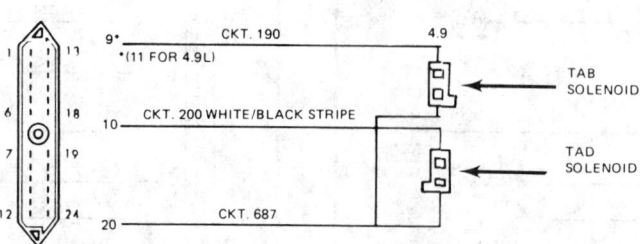

FORD MCU ENGINE CONTROL SYSTEM (Cont.)
SUB-ROUTINES

7

THERMACTOR AIR DIVERTER (CODE 45)

1) Remove vacuum hose from TAD valve and connect vacuum gauge to hose. Start engine and raise RPM to above 2500 to begin "Functional Test". Observe gauge during initial pulses. If pulses are above and below 5 in. Hg, MCU is okay — check Thermactor pump. If pulses are always above 5 in Hg, go to step 6. If pulses are always below 5 in Hg, check Thermactor pump.

2) Check vacuum hoses between vacuum source, TAD solenoid, and TAD valve. If vacuum source or hoses are faulty, repair. If okay, go to next step.

3) Measure resistance of TAD solenoid. If within 50-110 ohms, go to next step. If not, replace TAD solenoid.

4) Check at TAD solenoid output for vacuum when solenoid is energized (12 volts). If no vacuum, replace solenoid. If vacuum is present, go to next step.

5) Disconnect MCU connector and TAD connector. Measure resistance between MCU pin 10 and TAD connector, then between pin 20 and TAD connector. If resistance is less than 5 ohms, replace MCU module. If resistance is greater than 5 ohms, repair circuit.

6) Check at TAD solenoid output to ensure vacuum is not present when solenoid is deactivated. If vacuum is present, replace solenoid. If no vacuum, go to next step.

7) Measure resistance between MCU pin 10 and ground. If resistance is greater than 1000 ohms, replace MCU module. If resistance is less than 1000 ohms, repair short circuit to ground.

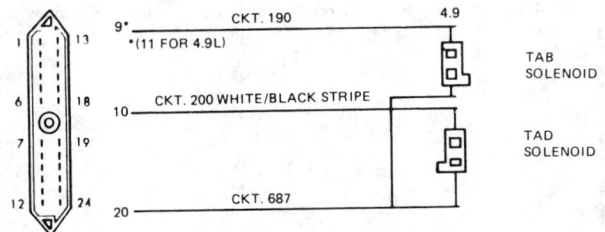

8

THERMACTOR AIR BY-PASS (CODE 46)

1) Remove vacuum hose at TAB valve and connect gauge to hose. Start engine and raise RPM to above 2500 to start "Functional Test". Observe gauge during initial pulses. If pulses are above and below 5 in. Hg, MCU is okay — check Thermactor pump. If pulses are always above 5 in. Hg, go to step 5. If pulses are always below 5 in. Hg, check Thermactor pump.

2) Check vacuum hoses between vacuum source, TAB solenoid, and TAB valve for leaks or blockage. Repair if necessary. If hoses are okay, go to next step.

3) Check at TAB solenoid output to be sure vacuum is present when solenoid is deactivated. If no vacuum is present, replace solenoid. If vacuum is present, go to next step.

4) Disconnect MCU and TAB solenoid connectors. Measure resistance between ground and MCU pin 9. If resistance is less than 1000 ohms, repair short to ground. If resistance is greater than 1000 ohms, replace MCU module.

5) Check TAB solenoid output to make sure vacuum is not present when solenoid is deactivated. If vacuum is present, replace solenoid. If vacuum is not present, go to next step.

6) Disconnect MCU and TAB solenoid connectors. Measure resistance between ground and MCU pin 11. If resistance is less than 1000 ohms, repair short to ground. If greater than 1000 ohms, replace MCU module.

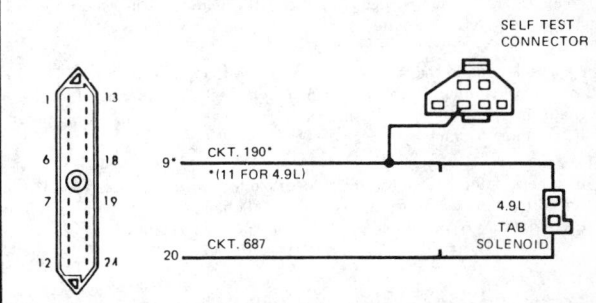

9

LOW TEMPERATURE VACUUM SWITCH (CODE 51)

1) Check vacuum switch contacts without vacuum applied. Measure resistance across switch. If less than 5 ohms, go to next step. If greater than 5 ohms, replace switch.

2) Vacuum at switch should be less than 1 in. Hg with engine hot. If vacuum is too high, replace PVS. If vacuum level is correct, go to next step.

3) Check continuity between switch connector pins and MCU connector pins 5 and 14. If resistance is greater than 5 ohms, repair circuit. If less than 5 ohms and code is still present after "Functional Test", replace MCU module.

NOTE — The following steps are to be used when referred here by "Functional Test" Cold Drive Complaint procedure.

4) Disconnect harness from vacuum switch and repeat "Functional Test" section that produced code 51. If another code appears, go to step **8)**. If code 51 reappears, go to next step.

5) Apply more than 4 in. Hg to switch. Measure resistance to be sure contacts are open. If resistance is less than 5 ohms, replace switch. If greater than 5 ohms, go to next step.

6) Ensure that vacuum is present at vacuum switch when coolant is below 95° F. If vacuum is present, MCU is okay. Check for other problems. If no vacuum, go to next step.

7) Check vacuum hoses for blockage or leaks, and check PVS for proper operation. Repair problems as necessary. If vacuum leak or block is not found, MCU is okay, check for other problems.

8) Check resistance between MCU connector pin 5 and ground. If less than 1000 ohms, repair short to ground. If higher than 1000 ohms, replace MCU module.

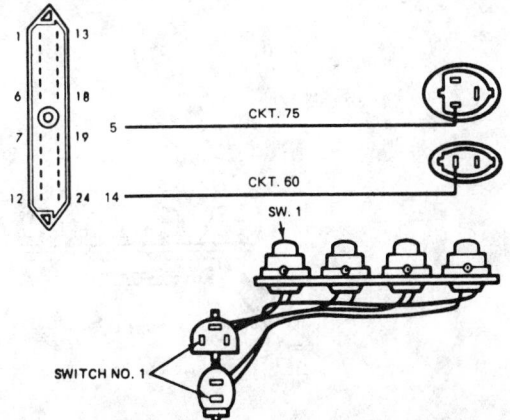

FORD MCU ENGINE CONTROL SYSTEM (Cont.)
SUB-ROUTINES

10

VACUUM SWITCH

Use chart to identify code, switch, and pin connections. Use proper pin connection when directed by test procedures.

Code	Switch Name/Number	MCU Pin
52 or 62	Wide Open Throttle #2	6
53 or 63	Crowd #3	7
56 or 66	Closed Throttle #6	19

1) Verify correct amount of vacuum is present at switch (use vacuum gauge). At least 8 in. Hg at switches 2 & 3; at least 4 in. Hg at switch 6. Check switch 6 at 2500 RPM; all others at idle. If vacuum level is too low, check vacuum lines and thermal switches. If vacuum is okay, go to next step.

2) Check switch contacts. Continuity should be present without vacuum. If resistance is greater than 5 ohms, replace vacuum switch. If less than 5 ohms, go to next step.

3) Check switch contacts with vacuum applied to switch (at least 8 in. Hg). If resistance is less than 5 ohms, replace switch. If greater than 5 ohms, go to next step.

4) Check continuity from pin 14 in MCU connector to bottom pin in 2-wire connector at vacuum switch (circuit 60). If resistance is less than 5 ohms, go to next step. If greater than 5 ohms, repair wiring.

5) Check continuity of switch circuit from MCU connector to switch. Use MCU pin identified in chart, and switch connector pin identified in wiring diagram at end of test. If resistence is greater than 5 ohms, repair circuit. If less than 5 ohms, go to next step.

6) Check same circuit for short to ground. Measure between MCU pin and ground. If resistance is less than 1000 ohms, repair short in circuit. If greater than 1000 ohms, MCU module must be replaced.

11

LOW TEMPERATURE SWITCH
(CODE 51)

1) Ensure water temperature was above 95° F during Self-Test when code was observed.

2) Check contacts of low temperature switch (should be closed above 95° F). If resistance measures less than 5 ohms, go to step **3)**. If above 5 ohms, replace low temperature switch.

3) Measure resistance in wiring between MCU (pins 5 & 14) and low temperature switch. If resistance is less than 5 ohms, replace MCU module. If greater than 5 ohms, repair wiring.

4) Disconnect harness from low temperature switch and rerun "Functional Test". If service code other than 51 is recorded, go to appropriate test. If not, go to next step.

NOTE — The following steps are to be used when referred here by "Functional Test" Cold Drive Complaint procedure.

5) Check contacts of low temperature switch (should be open below 95° F). If resistance is greater than 5 ohms, go to next step. If less than 5 ohms, replace low temperature switch.

6) Check wire from pin 5 to switch for continuity with ground. Measure between pin 5 in MCU connector and ground. If resistance is less than 1000 ohms, repair circuit. If resistance is greater than 1000 ohms and code 51 still appears, replace MCU module.

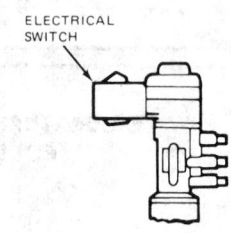

ELECTRICAL SWITCH

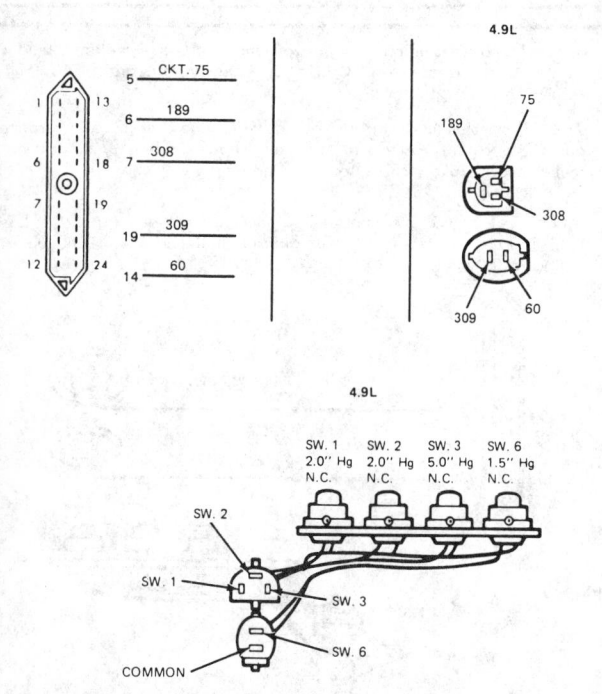

4.9L

4.9L

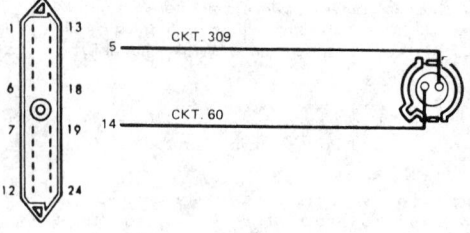

FORD MCU ENGINE CONTROL SYSTEM (Cont.)
SUB-ROUTINES

12 CANISTER PURGE SOLENOID

1) Check vacuum hoses for leaks and blockage. Check vacuum source. Repair as necessary.

2) Check to ensure Canister Purge solenoid passes vacuum when energized (12 volts) and blocks vacuum when deactivated. If solenoid does not operate as indicated, replace. If solenoid operates correctly, go to next step.

3) Disconnect connectors at MCU and Canister Purge solenoid. Check continuity between MCU pin 12 and solenoid connector, then pin 20 and solenoid connector. If resistance is less than 5 ohms, go to next step. If more than 5 ohms, repair open circuit.

4) Measure resistance between MCU pin 12 and ground. If resistance is less than 1000 ohms, repair short to ground. If greater than 1000 ohms, replace MCU module.

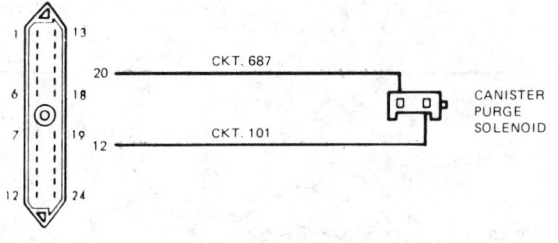

13 SPARK RETARD SOLENOID

1) Check vacuum hoses for leaks or blockage, then check vacuum source at 2500 RPM. Repair or clean as necessary.

2) Hold engine at 2000 RPM. Make sure vacuum is present at Spark Retard Solenoid output when solenoid is activated (12 volts) and no vacuum present when deactivated. If solenoid does not operate properly, replace it. If operation is okay, go to next step.

3) Disconnect MCU connector and Spark Retard Solenoid connector. Measure resistance between MCU pin 20 and solenoid connector, then pin 9 and solenoid connector. If resistance is more than 5 ohms, repair wiring. If less than 5 ohms, go to next step.

4) Measure resistance between MCU connector pin 9 and ground. If resistance is less than 1000 ohms, repair short to ground. If greater than 1000 ohms, replace MCU module.

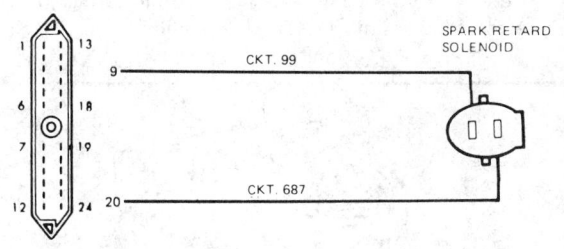

14 TACHOMETER LEAD

Disconnect MCU connector and "horseshoe" connector at ignition coil. Check continuity between pin 8 in MCU connector and "Tach Test" terminal in coil connector. If circuit is open, repair. If continuity is found, replace MCU module.

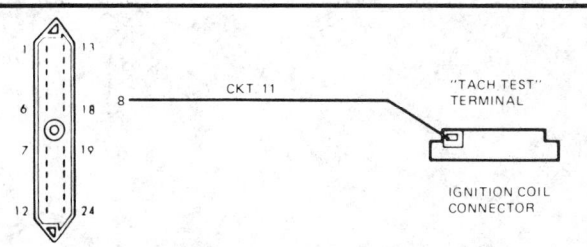

FORD ELECTRIC ASSIST CHOKE

DESCRIPTION

All Light Duty emissions models use an electrically heated choke thermostat spring housing as an aid to fast choke release. The heater operates from a terminal on the alternator, but only when the engine is actually running. The choke system consists of a choke cap, thermostatic spring, a bimetal temperature sensing disc and a positive temperature coefficient (PTC) ceramic heater.

OPERATION

Current is constantly supplied to the temperature sensing switch. The system is grounded through a ground strap connected to the carburetor body. At temperatures below about 54°F, the switch is open and no current is supplied to the ceramic heater located within the thermostatic spring, allowing normal choking action to occur. At temperatures from 54-74°F, depending on engine requirements, switch will remain open or will close to supply current to the ceramic heater. The switch will always be closed at temperatures above 74°F. As the heater warms, it causes the thermostatic spring to pull the choke plate open with in 1 to 1.5 minutes.

TESTING

1) Remove air cleaner, check choke plate and choke linkage for free operation. Remove hot air supply tube at choke housing, and install a suitable choke tester (LRE34618 or equivalent). Perform hot and cold choke function per instructions contained in tester kit.

2) With engine running, disconnect the stator lead at connector and connect a 0-3 amp. ammeter or test lamp between the choke lead connector and stator lead. If light does not glow, replace choke cap assembly.

3) Operate engine for about 5 minutes. A current reading of .3 to 1 amp. should be noted. If reading not correct, check alternator for proper operation and if good, replace choke cap.

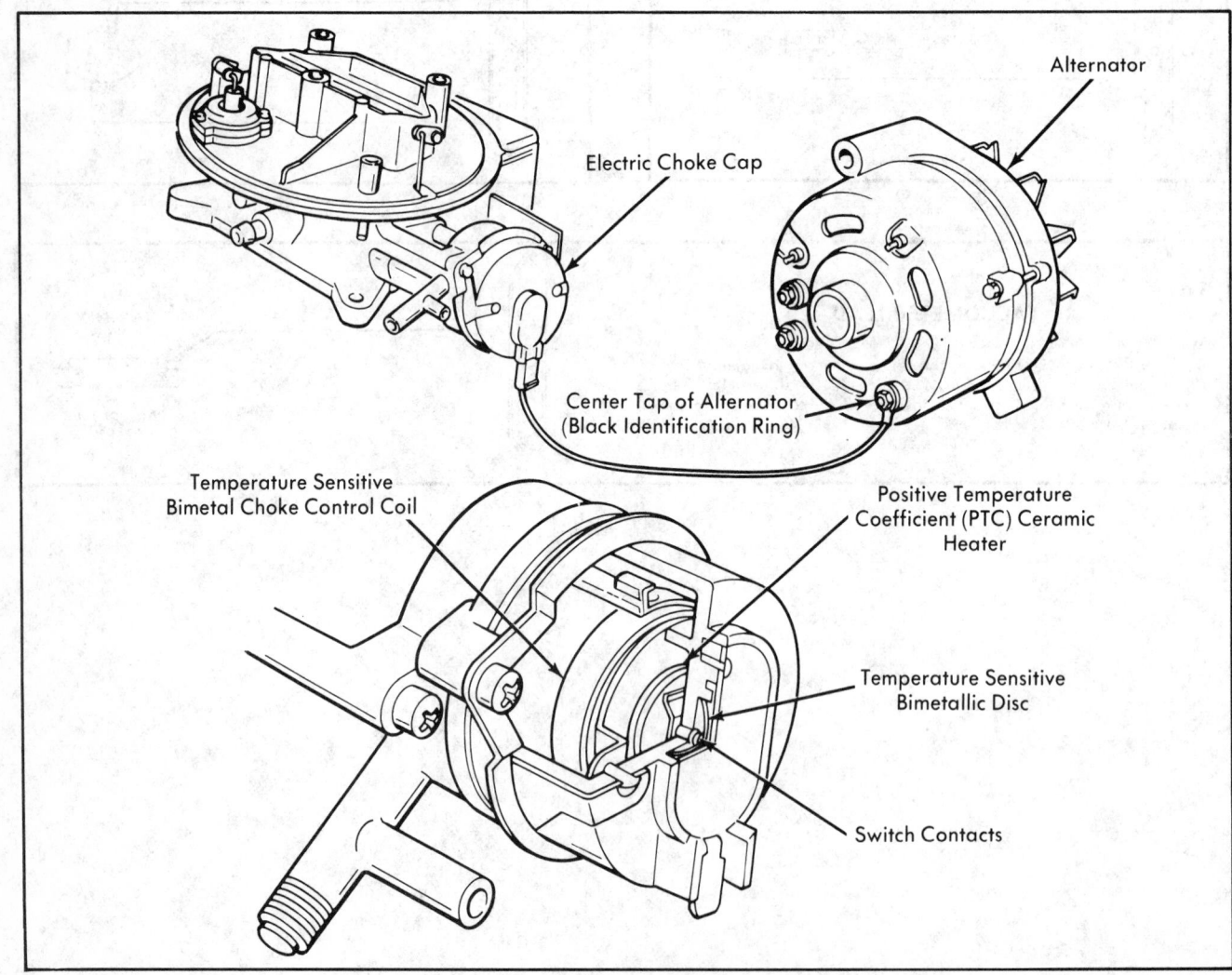

Fig. 1   Ford Electric Assist Choke Assembly

FORD DECEL THROTTLE MODULATOR

DESCRIPTION

The decel throttle modulator system keeps the throttle valves open slightly during sudden deceleration to help reduce emissions. System consists of a speed sensor, solenoid vacuum valve, throttle modulator on throttle linkage, a ported vacuum switch, and electrical wiring and vacuum hoses. The system is electrically connected to the "B+" terminal of the ignition switch and to the "+" terminal of ignition coil.

OPERATION

Manifold vacuum is routed through a PVS valve and a solenoid vacuum valve, which is normally closed, to the vacuum throttle modulator. Power is available to solenoid vacuum valve through an electronic sensor, but the sensor ground circuit is open. As engine reaches 1850 RPM, ground circuit in sensor is completed, allowing solenoid vacuum valve to open. Vacuum pulls throttle modulator diaphragm which pushes throttle to high idle position during deceleration. Engine coolant must be above 125°F to allow vacuum to reach solenoid vacuum valve.

ADJUSTMENT

NOTE — *This adjustment is to be performed when replacing components found defective during "Testing" sequence.*

1) With engine at normal operating temperature, set transmission in neutral (all transmissions).

2) Adjust carburetor to specified curb idle speed. On Auto. Trans. vehicles, this will be set to 150 RPM higher than specified curb idle speed (as with transmission in "DRIVE"), although transmission will remain in neutral. This is to keep minimum load on engine

3) Disconnect system vacuum hose from throttle modulator diaphragm and plug hose. Using a "slave" hose, connect manifold vacuum source to diaphragm.

4) Allow one minute for engine speed to stabilize. If engine speed is within specifications, the modulator is properly set. Go to step **7**).

5) If RPM was not within specification, adjust throttle modulator by loosening lock nut and turning until speed is within limits. Retighten lock nut.

NOTE — *On Carter 1-barrel carburetors, avoid damage to diaphragm by holding diaphragm shaft with ¼" wrench while turning adjusting screw with ⅜" wrench.*

6) Detach manifold vacuum hose from modulator diaphragm and allow engine to return to idle condition. Repeat procedure from step **2**) as required until proper function occurs.

7) Disconnect manifold vacuum hose from modulator diaphragm and allow engine to return to normal idle. Remove plug from original hose and reconnect it to throttle modulator fitting.

8) On Auto. Trans. vehicles, reset idle to specifications with transmission in "DRIVE".

9) On all vehicles, stop engine. Install air cleaner assembly.

TESTING

PRE-TEST SET UP

1) If vehicle is equipped with spark delay valves, test for proper operation per instruction given in "Ford Spark Delay Valve" article in this Section.

2) Remove air cleaner and plug vacuum line. Check primary and secondary throttle linkage and choke linkage for freedom of movement. Connect tachometer to engine.

NOTE — *Perform testing in sequence given.*

THROTTLE MODULATOR DIAPHRAGM CHECK

1) Disconnect vacuum line from diaphragm. Connect external vacuum source to diaphragm. Apply and trap 19 in. Hg.

2) If diaphragm does not respond, or will not hold vacuum, replace the diaphragm.

3) Remove external vacuum source. If the diaphragm does not return within 5 seconds, replace the diaphragm. Reconnect vacuum line.

PORTED VACUUM SWITCH TEST

1) Disconnect hose from PVS to solenoid vacuum valve and connect external vacuum source.

2) Start engine and let it idle long enough to reach normal operating temperature. At normal temperature, there should be vacuum indicated on gauge.

3) If no vacuum is present, check vacuum hose for leaks. If hose is not leaking, replace the PVS. Reconnect vacuum line.

SOLENOID VACUUM VALVE TEST

1) With engine at normal operating temperature, engine idling and transmission in neutral, make sure choke plate is fully open.

2) Turn off air conditioner or power take-off if equipped. Disconnect vacuum supply hose at solenoid valve and check for vacuum. If no vacuum is present, clean or replace hose as required.

3) If a vacuum delay valve is used, remove valve and install a straight connector. Disconnect wires to solenoid valve. With a jumper wire, apply battery voltage to one of the solenoid terminals. The engine speed should not increase. If it does, replace the valve.

4) Using a second jumper wire, ground the other terminal of the valve. The engine speed should increase, if not, replace valve.

5) Remove the ground jumper wire. The engine should return to idle within 15 seconds. If not, replace the valve.

FORD DECEL THROTTLE MODULATOR (Cont.)

ELECTRONIC SPEED SENSOR TEST

1) Check the harness connection at the module. Start engine and run long enough to reach normal operating temperature.

2) While watching the vacuum diaphragm assembly, accelerate slowly. The diaphragm should extend at speeds above 1850 RPM (±100), and retract at speeds below 1600 RPM. If not, perform the harness connector checks as follows. Number the harness terminals from 1 to 6 (or 8) from the key side of the connector.

3) On models without electronic governor, turn key "ON" and connect one lead of voltmeter to terminal "1" and other lead to ground. Battery voltage should be indicated. Repeat test on terminals 4 and 6.

4) Turn ignition off. Connect one lead on an ohmmeter to terminal "3" of connector and the other lead to terminal "1".

Meter should read continuity. Repeat test, connecting terminal "5" to "1".

5) On models with electronic governor, connect one lead of tachometer to terminal "1" and the other lead to terminal "2". Tachometer should read engine RPM.

6) Connect one lead of voltmeter to terminal "1" and the other lead to terminal "8". With key "ON", voltmeter should read battery voltage.

7) Connect one lead of ohmmeter to terminal "4" and the other lead to terminal "6". With key "OFF", ohmmeter should read continuity. Repeat test betweem terminals "5" and "7".

8) If any of the terminals fail any of the tests, repair the wiring as required. If harness meets all specifications, replace the speed sensor module.

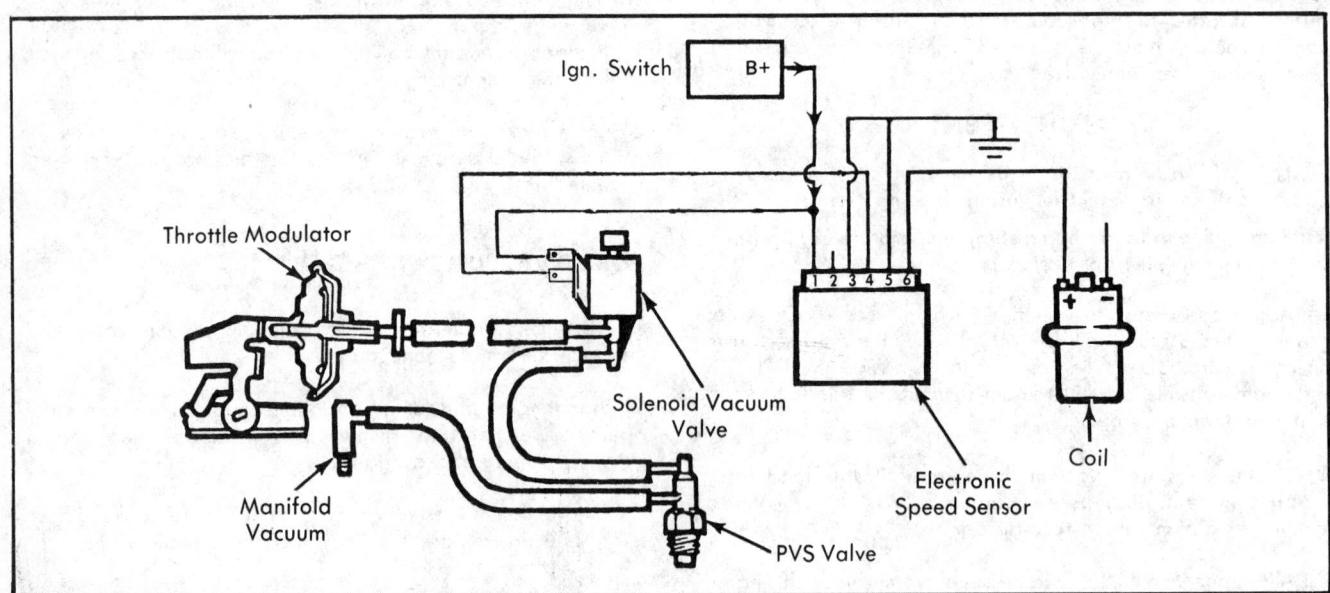

Fig. 1   Schematic of Ford Decel Throttle Modulator System

FORD SPARK DELAY VALVES

DESCRIPTION

Spark Delay Valves (SDV) are used on many engine applications to permit closer control of vacuum-operated emission control equipment. All SDVs have internal sintered orifices to permit a restricted air flow in one direction, a check valve to allow free air flow in the other direction, and a filtering device to keep dirt and moisture from the emission control equipment.

NOTE — *For location and names of various SDVs, refer to appropriate "Ford Vacuum Diagram" in this section.*

OPERATION

By slowing, or restricting, vacuum signals to their respective emission control devices, the SDVs help modulate and regulate the vacuum signal being applied. Since engine vacuum levels vary with engine operating modes, it is important to control the vacuum signal by some means. The SDVs aid in this control.

TROUBLE SHOOTING

If valve is defective or installed backwards, engine will idle roughly, ping, and increase fuel consumption. When blowing air through valve by mouth, air will appear to flow in one direction. This should not be misinterpreted as direction of vacuum flow.

NOTE — *It is very important that Black or inlet side of Spark Delay Valve and By-Pass Check Valve be connected to vacuum line leading to carburetor.*

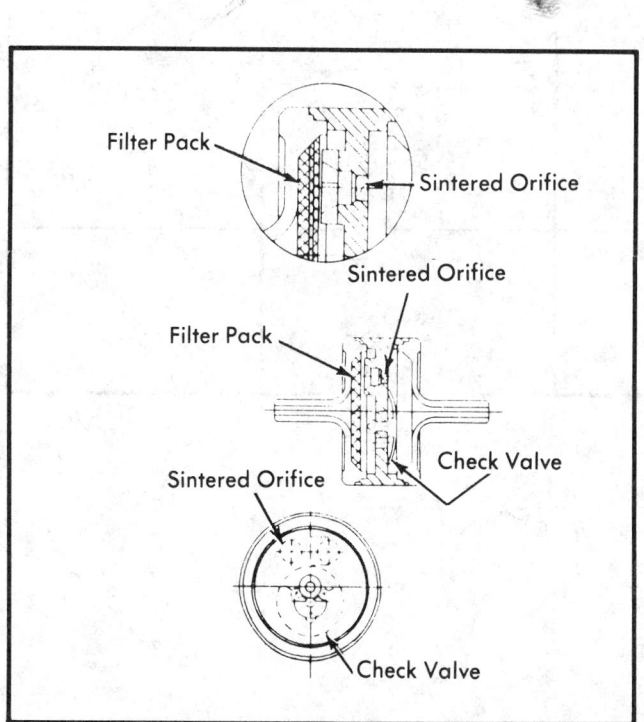

Fig. 1 Sectional Views of Typical Spark Delay Valve

TESTING

DELAY VALVE TIME TEST

1) Connect appropriate side of delay valve to an external vacuum source set at 10″ Hg. See *chart below.*

2) Connect a 24″ length of vacuum hose and vacuum gauge to the other side of the delay valve.

3) Apply vacuum, observe gauge and note time, in seconds, required to go from 0-8″ Hg.

NOTE — *A steady 10″ Hg must be applied by external vacuum source during this test.*

4) Compare time to appropriate time chart below. If delay valve tested does not come within time limits, replace valve and repeat test.

Delay Valve Testing Attachments

Valve Type	Vac. Source Side	Vac. Gauge Side
Vacuum	Black	Color
Retard	Color	White
Two-Way		
Vacuum Vent	I.D. No.	
Air Cleaner	Color	White

Delay Valve Time Specifications (in Seconds)

Application	Min. Delay	Max. Delay
Vacuum Delay Valve		
Black & Gray	0.6	1.6
Black & Brown	1.0	3.0
Black & White	2.7	9.3
Black & Yellow	4.5	13.2
Black & Blue	6.8	18.8
Black & Green	8.0	26.0
Black & Orange	11.6	38.0
Black & Red	14.0	47.2
Retard Delay Valve		
White & Red	14.0	47.2
White & Blue	8.0	26.0
Two-Way Delay Valve		
Brown	1.0	3.0
White	2.7	9.3
Yellow	4.5	13.2
Green	8.0	26.0
Red	14.0	47.2
Vacuum Vent Delay Valve		
I.D. No. 5	7	13.7
I.D. No. 20	16	36.8
I.D. No. 40	28	67.6
Air Cleaner Delay Valve		
White & Red	14.0	47.2
White & Green	8.0	26.0
White & Blue	8.0	26.0

1981 Exhaust Emission Systems

FORD VACUUM DIAGRAMS

FORD MOTOR CO. VACUUM DIAGRAM INDEX			
Engine & Model	Transmission	Calibration No.	Fig. No.
4.9L (300″) 6-Cylinder			
Federal			
F100	Man.	1-51D-R0	1
F100	Man.	1-51D-R10	4
F100/150	Man.	1-51G-R0	2
F100/150	Man.	1-51G-R10	4
F100/150	Man.	1-51H-R0	2
F100/150	Auto.	1-52G-R0	5
F100/150	Auto.	1-52G-R10	6
F100/150	Auto.	1-52H-R0	5
F100/150	Auto.	1-52H-R10	6
F250	Man.	1-51E-R0	1
F250	Man.	1-51E-R10	4
F250	Man.	1-51F-R0	1
F250	Man.	1-51F-R10	4
F250	Auto.	1-52L-R0	6
F250	Auto.	1-52L-R10	6
Bronco	Man.	1-51F-R0	1
Bronco	Man.	1-51F-R10	4
Bronco	Man.	1-51G-R0	2
Bronco	Man.	1-51G-R10	4
E100/150	Man.	1-51K-R0	3
E100/150	Man.	1-51K-R10	4
E100/250	Man.	1-51L-R0	3
E100/250	Man.	1-51L-R10	4
E100/150	Auto.	1-52K-R0	5
E100/150	Auto.	1-52K-R10	6
E100/250	Auto.	1-52L-R0	6
E100/250	Auto.	1-52L-R10	6
Calif.			
F100/150	Man.	1-51S-R0	7
F100/150	Man.	1-51S-R10	8
F100	Auto.	1-52S-R0	8
E100/150	Man.	1-51T-R0	8
E100/250	Auto.	1-52T-R0	8
4.2L (255″) V8			
Federal			
F100	Man.	1-57G-R0	9
F100	Man.	1-57G-R10	10
F100	Auto.	1-58G-R0	11

FORD VACUUM DIAGRAMS (Cont.)

FORD MOTOR CO. VACUUM DIAGRAM INDEX

Engine & Model	Transmission	Calibration No.	Fig. No.
5.0L (302") V8			
Federal			
F100/150	Man.	1-53G-R0	12
F100/150	Man.	1-53G-R10	13
F100/150	Man.	1-53G-R12	17,18
F100/150	Auto.	1-54G-R0	24
F150/250	Man.	1-53D-R0	14
F150/250	Man.	1-53D-R10	13
F150/250	Man.	1-53D-R12	15,16
F150/250	Man.	1-53K-R0	14
F150/250	Man.	1-53K-R10	13
F150/250	Man.	1-53K-R13	19,20
F150/250	Auto.	1-54K-R0	27
F250	Auto.	1-54L-R2	28
F250	Auto.	1-54L-R10	29
Bronco	Man.	1-53D-R0	14
Bronco	Man.	1-53D-R10	13
Bronco	Man.	1-53D-R12	15,16
Bronco	Man.	1-53K-R0	14
Bronco	Man.	1-53K-R10	13
Bronco	Man.	1-53K-R13	19,20
Bronco	Auto.	1-54D-R0	24
E100/150	Man.	1-53H-R0	23
E100/150	Man.	1-53H-R11	23
E150	Man.	1-53F-R0	21
E150	Man.	1-53F-R11	22
E100	Auto.	1-54H-R0	26
E100/150	Auto.	1-54F-R0	25
Calif.			
F100/250	Auto.	1-54P-R0	30
F100/250	Auto.	1-54P-R10	30
F150/250	Auto.	1-54R-R0	30
F150/250	Auto.	1-54R-R10	30
Bronco	Auto.	1-54R-R0	30
Bronco	Auto.	1-54R-R10	30
E100/250	Auto.	1-54R-R0	30
E100/250	Auto.	1-54R-R10	30
5.8L (351") W V8			
Federal			
E100/150	Auto.	1-64G-R1	33
E150/250	Auto.	1-64H-R2	34
E250/350	Auto.	7-76J-R11	31
Calif.			
F150/250	Man.	1-63T-R0	50
F150/250	Auto.	1-64S-R0	36
F150/250	Auto.	1-64T-R0	37
Bronco	Auto.	1-64T-R0	37
E150/250	Auto.	1-64R-R1	35
High Alt.			
E150/250	Auto.	1-64A-R0	32

1981 Exhaust Emission Systems

FORD VACUUM DIAGRAMS (Cont.)

FORD MOTOR CO. VACUUM DIAGRAM INDEX			
Engine & Model	Transmission	Calibration No.	Fig. No.
5.8L (351") M V8			
Federal			
F150	Man.	1-59G-R0	38
F150	Man.	1-59G-R10	39
F150	Man.	1-59K-R0	40
F150	Man.	1-59K-R10	39
F150/250	Man.	1-59H-R0	40
F150/250	Man.	1-59H-R10	39
F150	Auto.	1-60J-R0	41
F150	Auto.	1-60J-R10	42
F150	Auto.	1-60K-R0	41
F150	Auto.	1-60K-R10	42
F150/250	Auto.	1-60H-R1	41
F150/250	Auto.	1-60H-R10	42
F250	Auto.	9-72J-R11	43
Bronco	Man.	1-59G-R0	38
Bronco	Man.	1-59G-R10	39
Bronco	Man.	1-59H-R0	40
Bronco	Man.	1-59H-R10	39
Bronco	Man.	1-59K-R0	40
Bronco	Man.	1-59K-R10	39
High Alt.			
F150/250	Man.	1-59A-R0	38
F150/250	Man.	1-59B-R0	38
F150/250	Man.	1-59B-R10	39
F150/250	Auto.	1-60A-R0	41
F150/250	Auto.	1-60A-R10	42
F150/250	Auto.	1-60B-R0	41
F150/250	Auto.	1-60B-R10	42
Bronco	Man.	1-59A-R0	38
Bronco	Man.	1-59B-R0	38
Bronco	Man.	1-59B-R10	39
Bronco	Auto.	1-60B-R0	41
Bronco	Auto.	1-60B-R10	42
6.6L (400") V8			
Federal			
E250/350	Man.	9-73J-R11	44
E250/350	Auto.	9-74J-R11	46
Calif			
F250	Man.	9-73J-R12	45
F250/350	Auto.	9-74J-R12	47
7.5L (460") V8			
F250/350	.....	9-97J-R0	48
F250/350	.....	9-97J-R12	49

FORD VACUUM DIAGRAMS (Cont.)

CALIBRATION NUMBER IDENTIFICATION

Locate engine emission control label and determine engine size and model year. Label is Gold or Silver in color and located in engine compartment. Next, find engine code label and determine calibration base number and revision number. Code labels are Yellow or White and located on engine valve cover. Use engine size, vehicle body style and calibration number to locate vacuum diagrams in index, then refer to proper illustration for vacuum diagram.

NOTE — Some calibration numbers are carried over from previous years and may not start with a number 1, which indicates 1981 calibration.

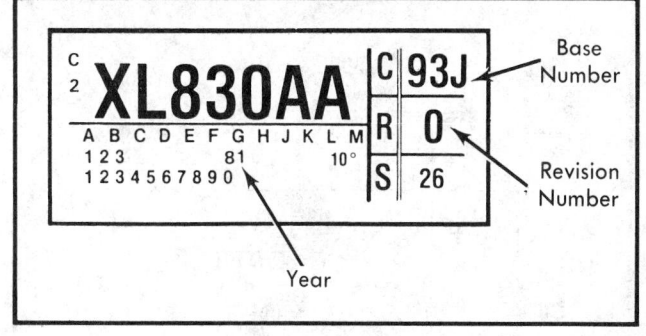

Engine Code Label

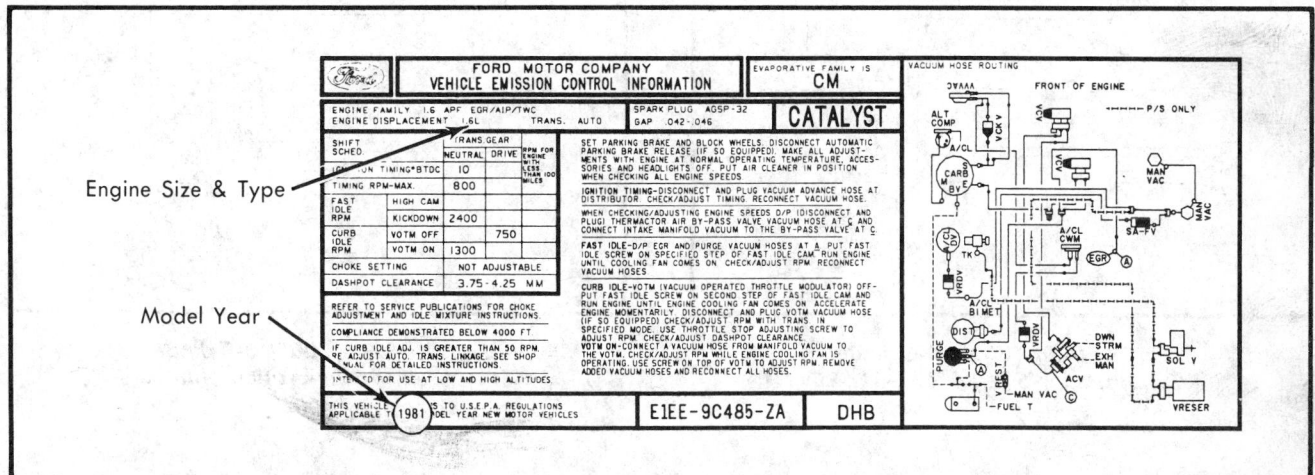

Emission Control Label

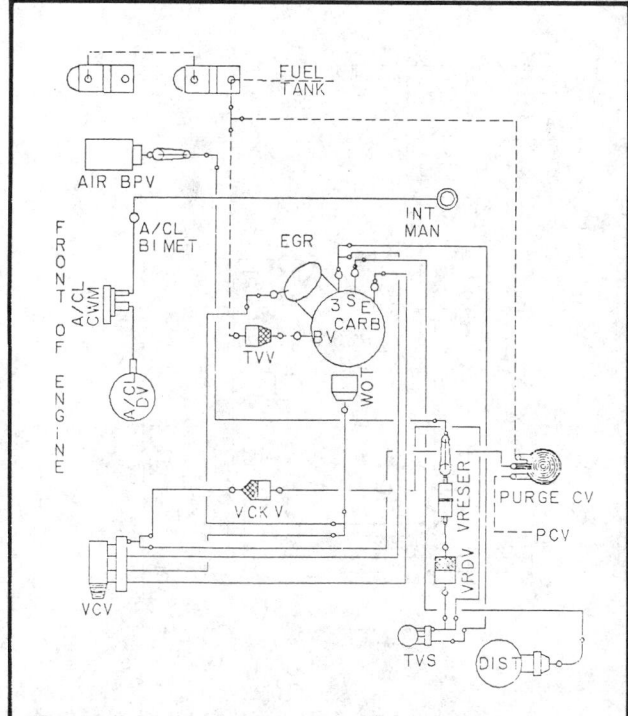

**Fig. 1 4.9L (300") 6-Cylinder
(See Index for Calibration Numbers)**

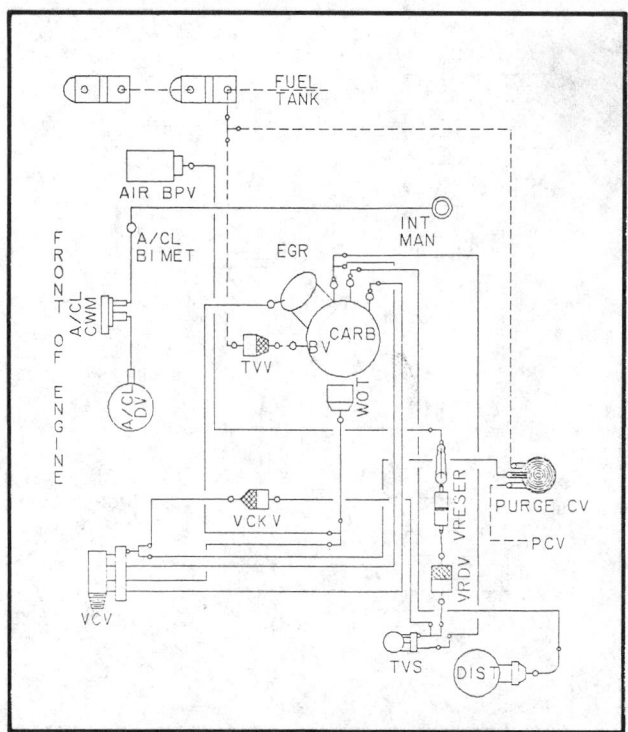

**Fig. 2 4.9L (300") 6-Cylinder
Calibration 1-51G-R0 & 1-51H-R0**

1981 Exhaust Emission Systems

FORD VACUUM DIAGRAMS (Cont.)

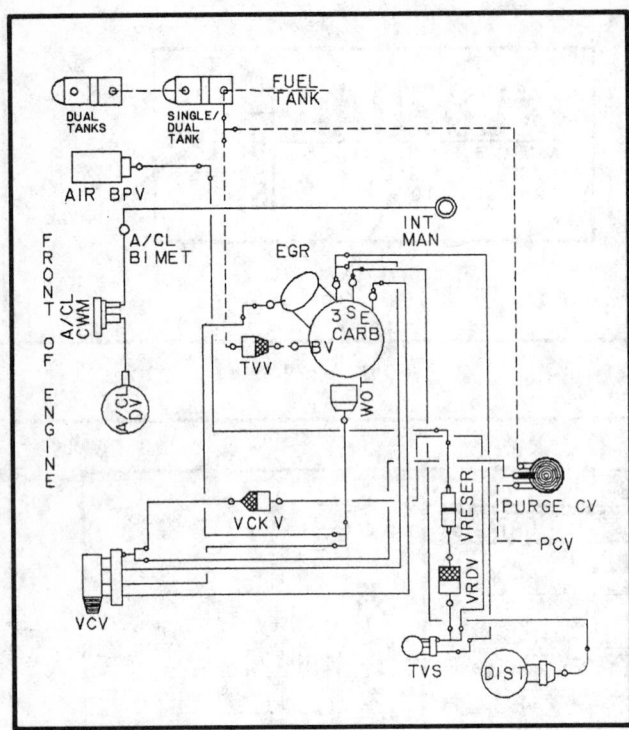

**Fig. 3 4.9L (300") 6-Cylinder
Calibration 1-51K-R0 & 1-51L-R0**

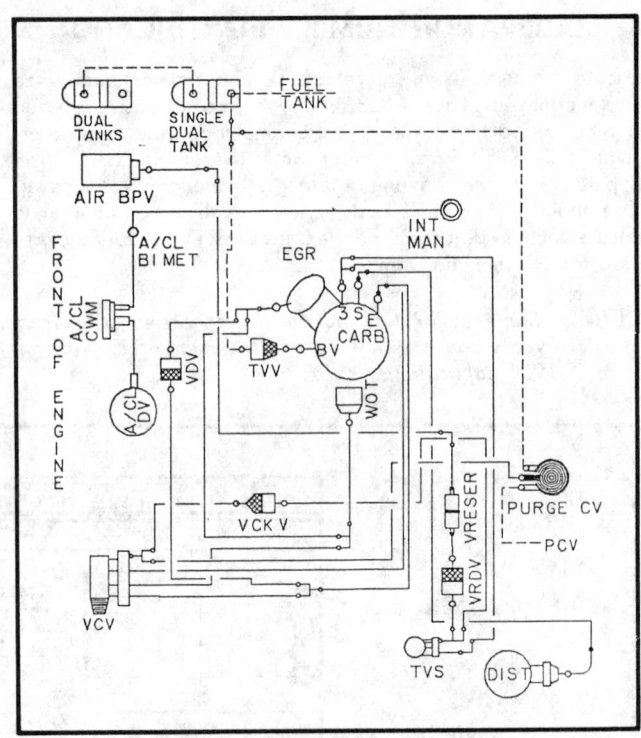

**Fig. 4 4.9L (300") 6-Cylinder
(See Index for Calibration Numbers)**

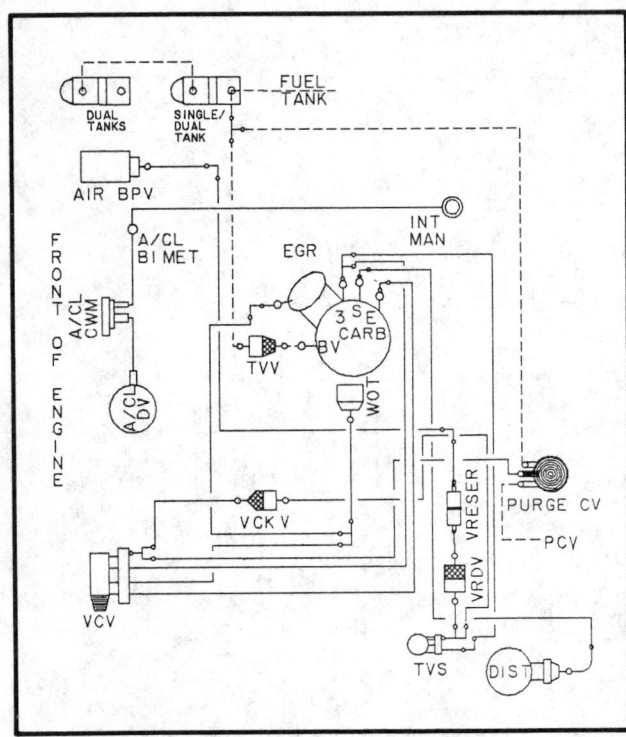

**Fig. 5 4.9L (300") 6-Cylinder
(See Index for Calibration Numbers)**

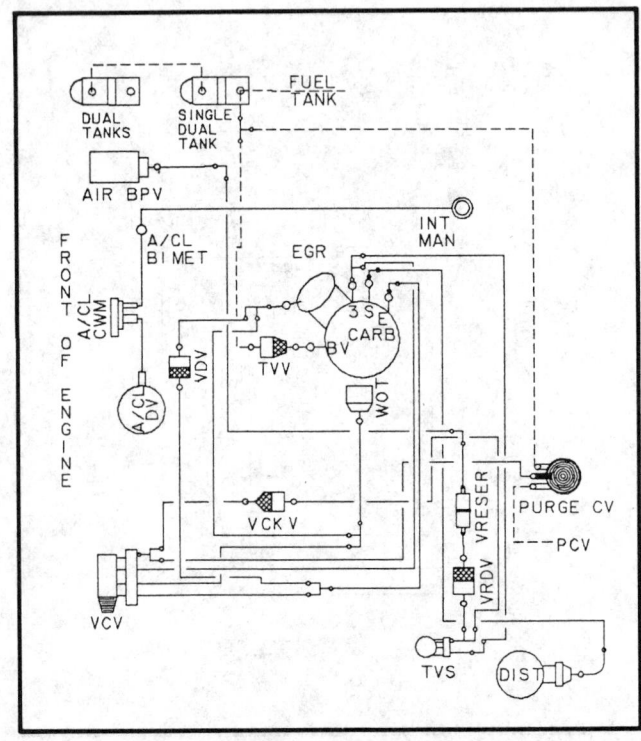

**Fig. 6 4.9L (300") 6-Cylinder
(See Index for Calibration Numbers)**

FORD VACUUM DIAGRAMS (Cont.)

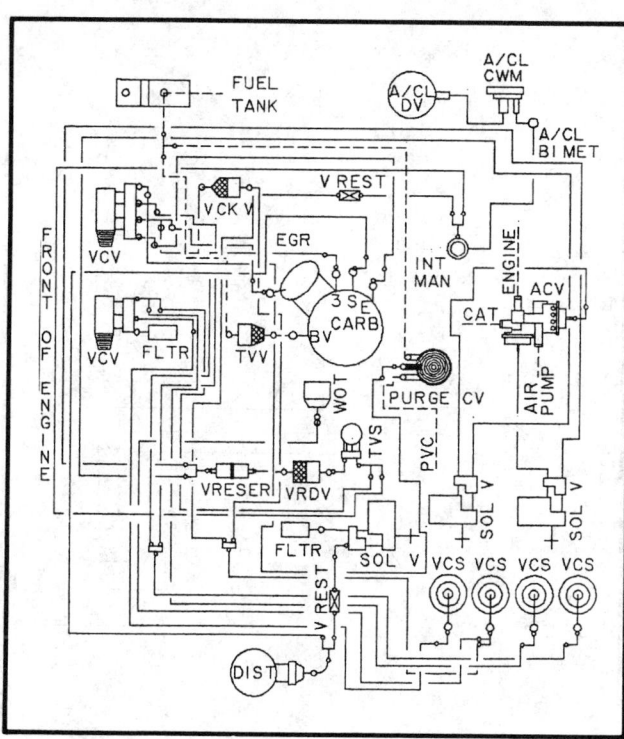

Fig. 7 4.9L (300") 6-Cylinder
Calibration 1-51S-R0

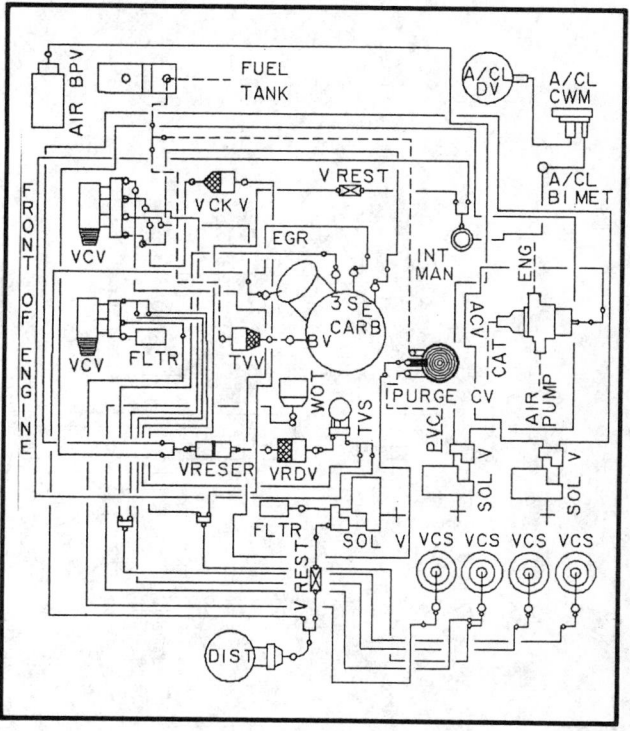

Fig. 8 4.9L (300") 6-Cylinder
(See Index for Calibration Numbers)

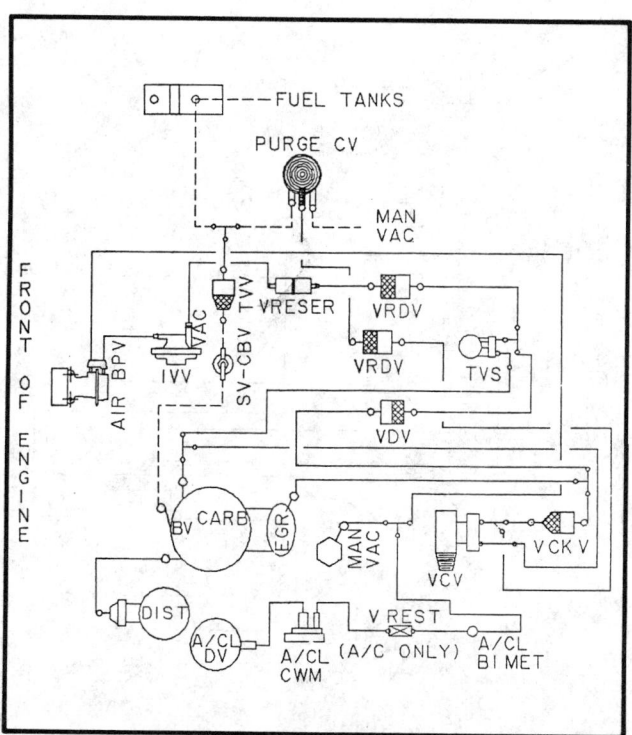

Fig. 9 4.2L (255") V8
Calibration 1-57G-R0

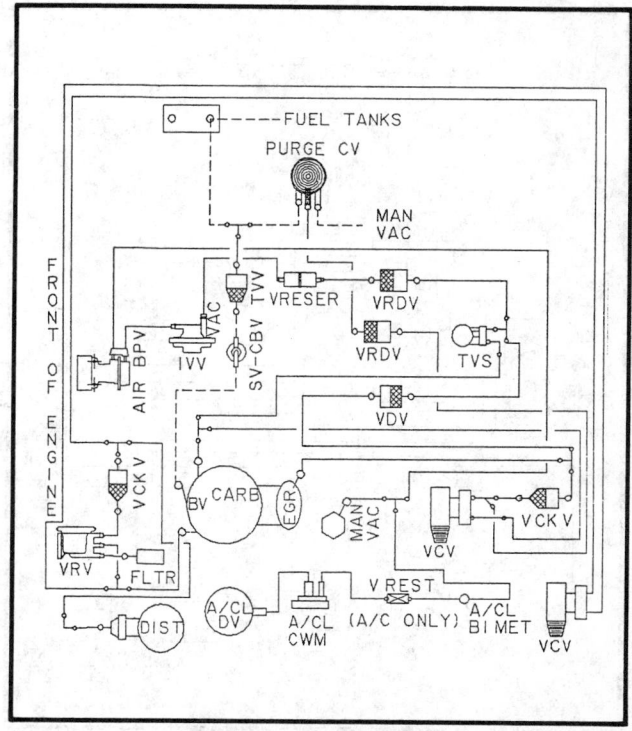

Fig. 10 4.2L (255") V8
Calibration 1-57G-R10

1981 **Exhaust Emission Systems**

FORD VACUUM DIAGRAMS (Cont.)

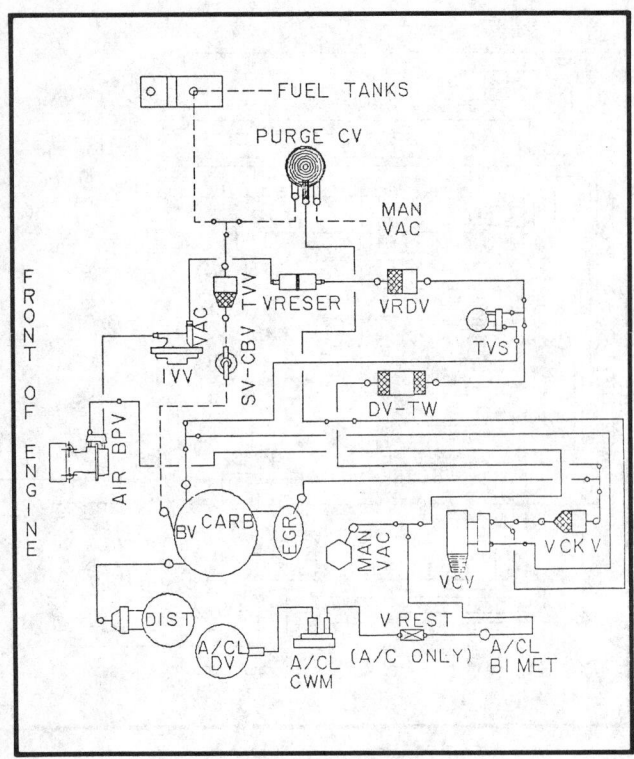

Fig. 11   4.2L (255") V8
Calibration 1-58G-R0

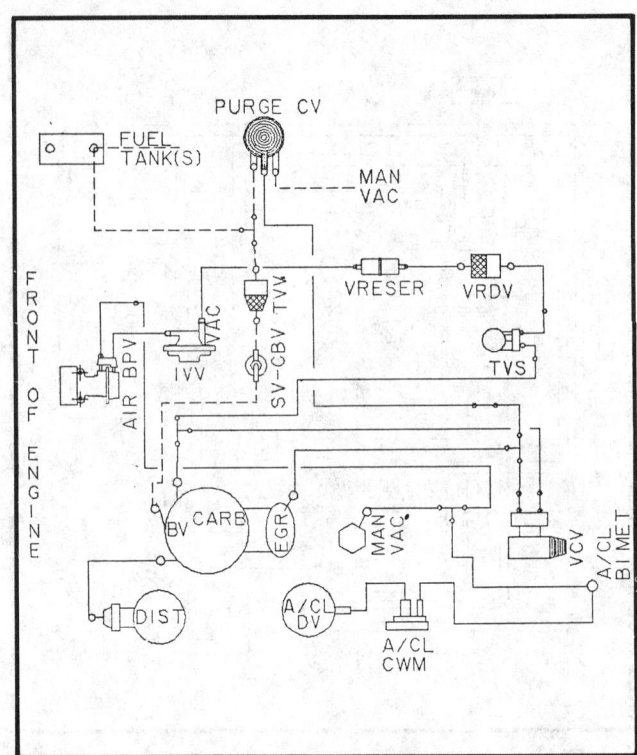

Fig. 12   5.0L (302") V8
Calibration 1-53G-R0

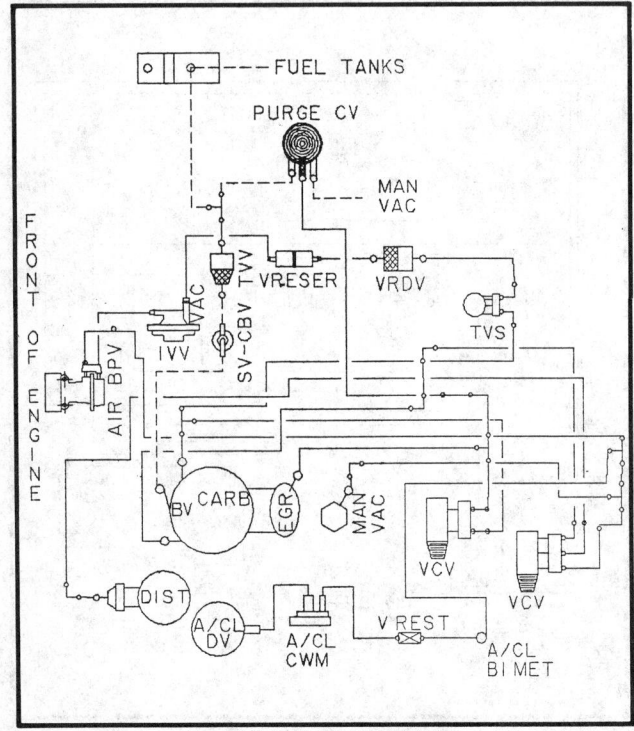

Fig. 13   5.0L (302") V8
(See Index for Calibration Numbers)

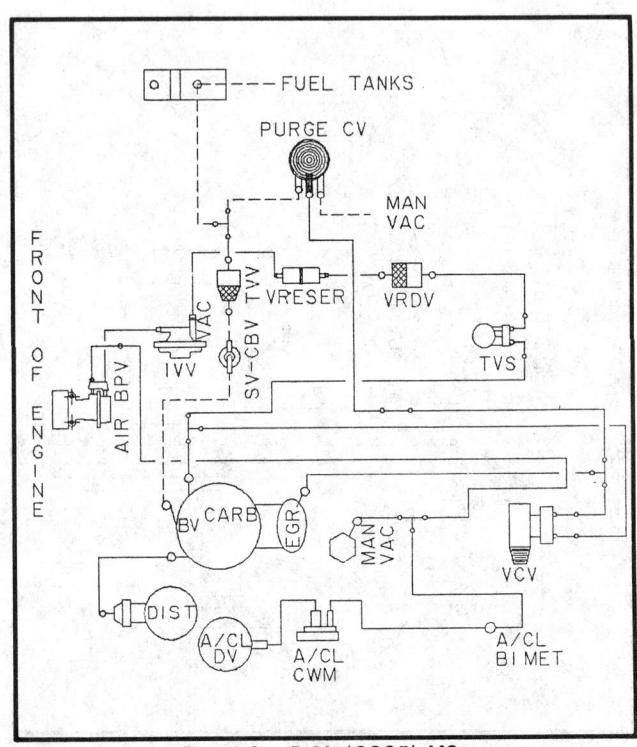

Fig. 14   5.0L (300") V8
Calibration 1-53D-R0 & 1-53K-R0

FORD VACUUM DIAGRAMS (Cont.)

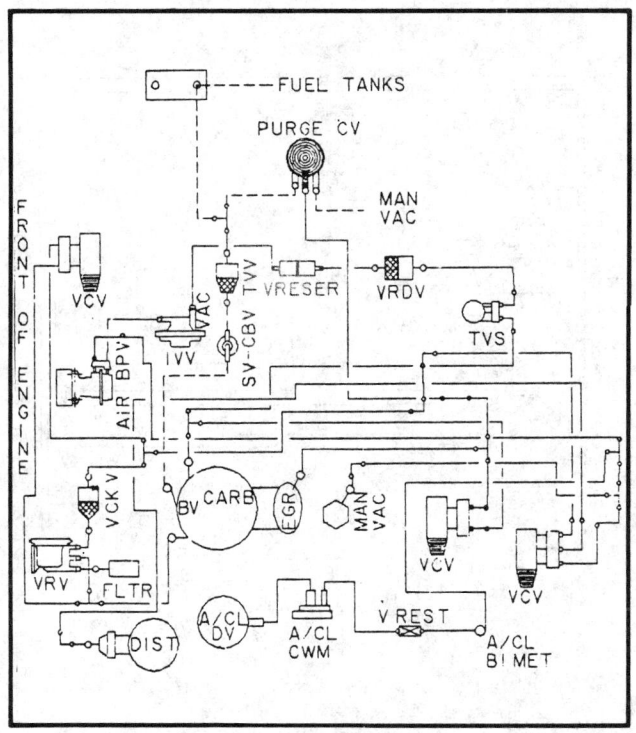

Fig. 15   5.0L (300") V8
Calibration 1-53D-R12 with A/C

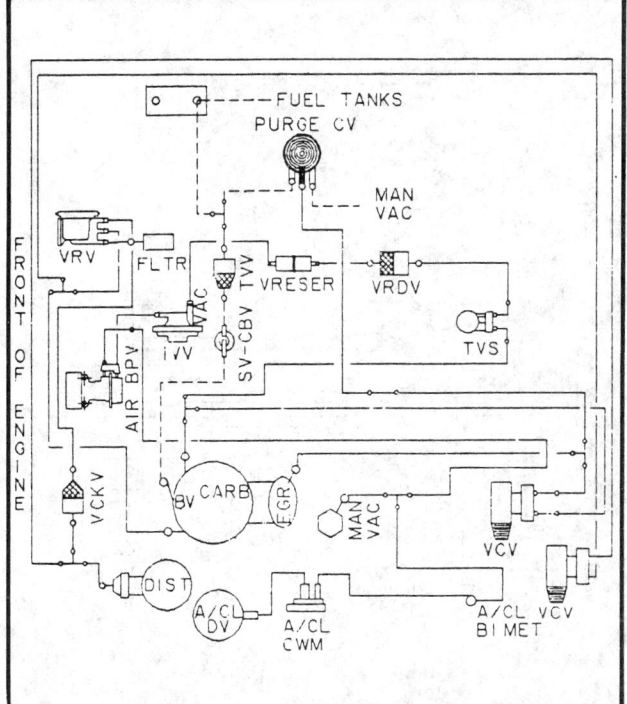

Fig. 16   5.0L (302") V8
Calibration 1-53D-R12 without A/C

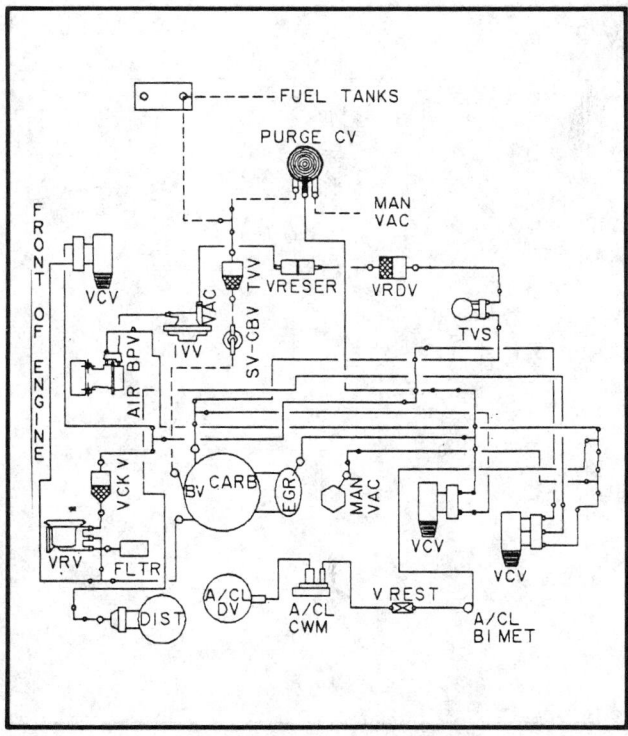

Fig. 17   5.0L (302") V8
Calibration 1-53G-R12 with A/C

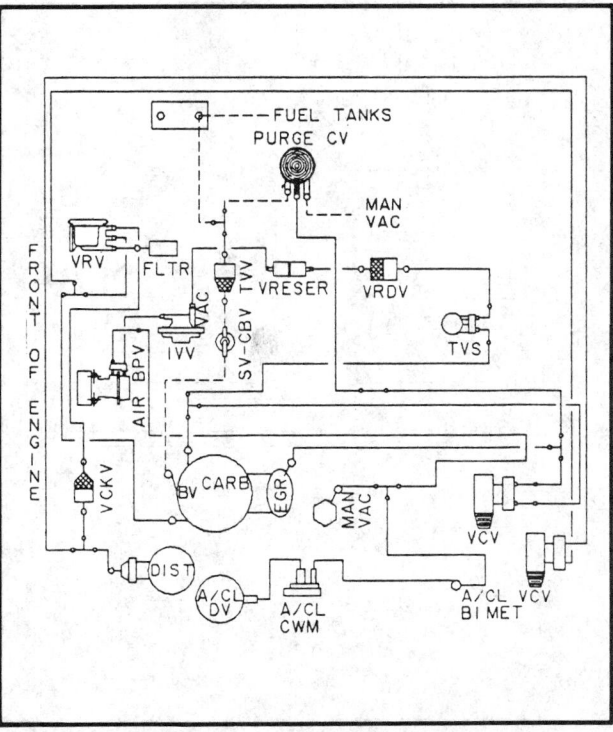

Fig. 18   5.0L (302") V8
Calibration 1-53G-R12 without A/C

1981 Exhaust Emission Systems

FORD VACUUM DIAGRAMS (Cont.)

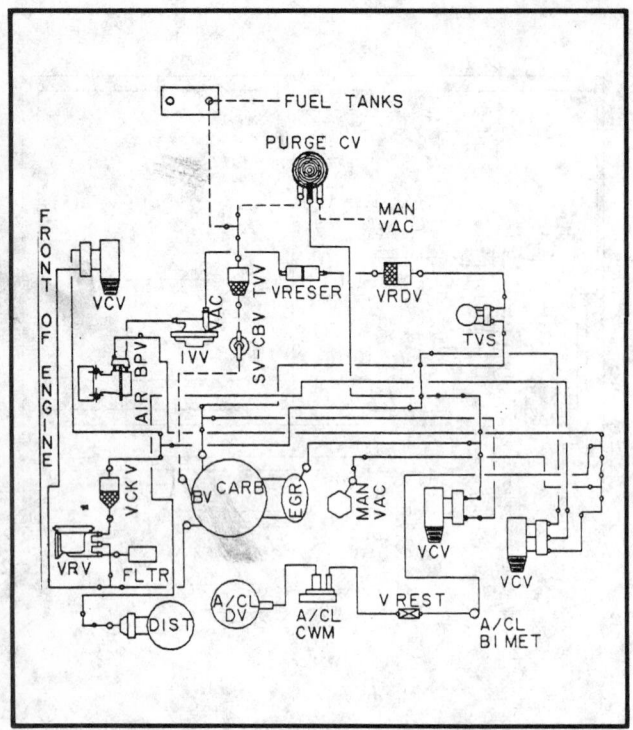

Fig. 19 5.0L (302") V8
Calibration 1-53K-R13 with A/C

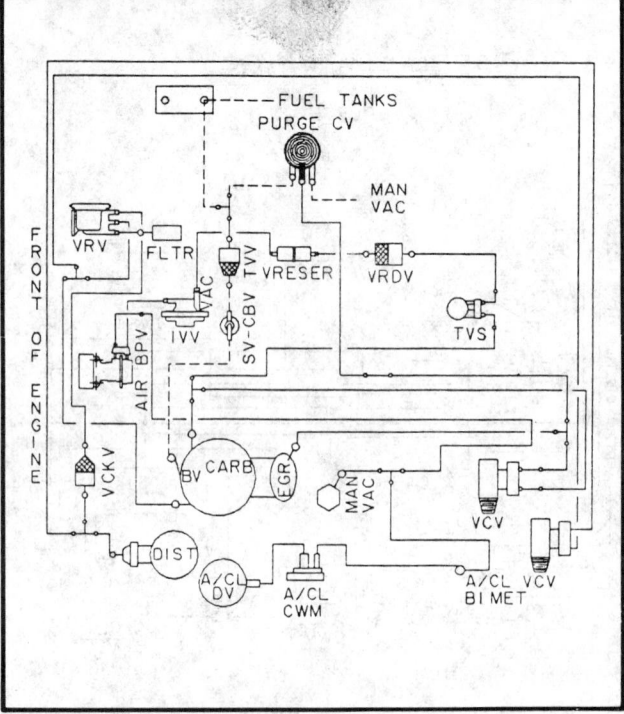

Fig. 20 5.0L (302") V8
Calibration 1-53K-R13 without A/C

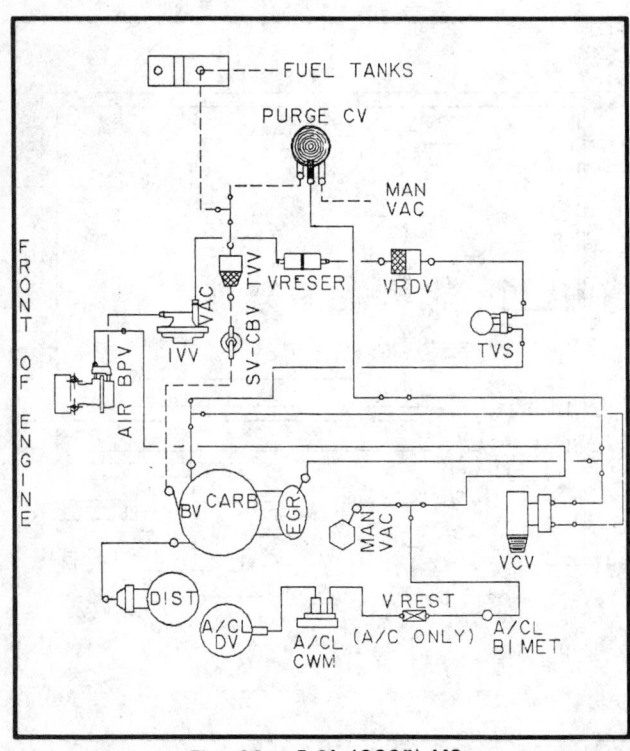

Fig. 21 5.0L (302") V8
Calibration 1-53F-R0

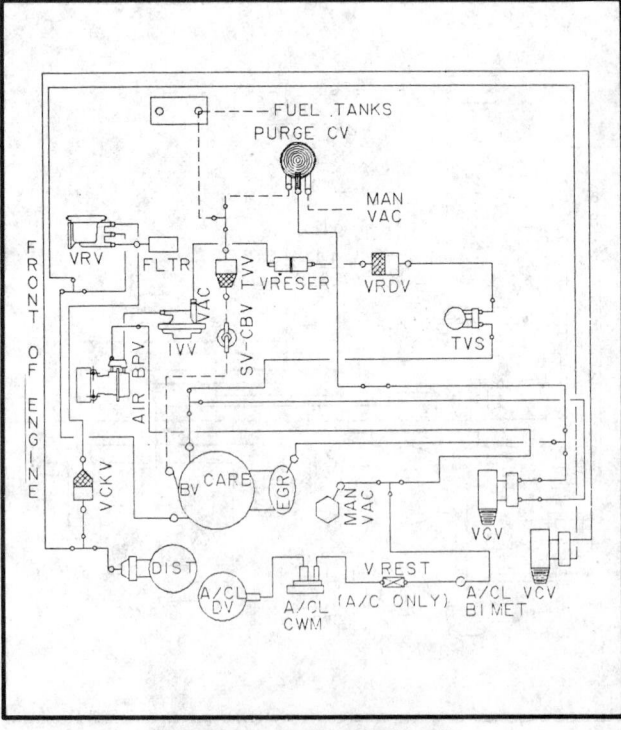

Fig. 22 5.0L (302") V8
Calibration 1-53F-R11

FORD VACUUM DIAGRAMS (Cont.)

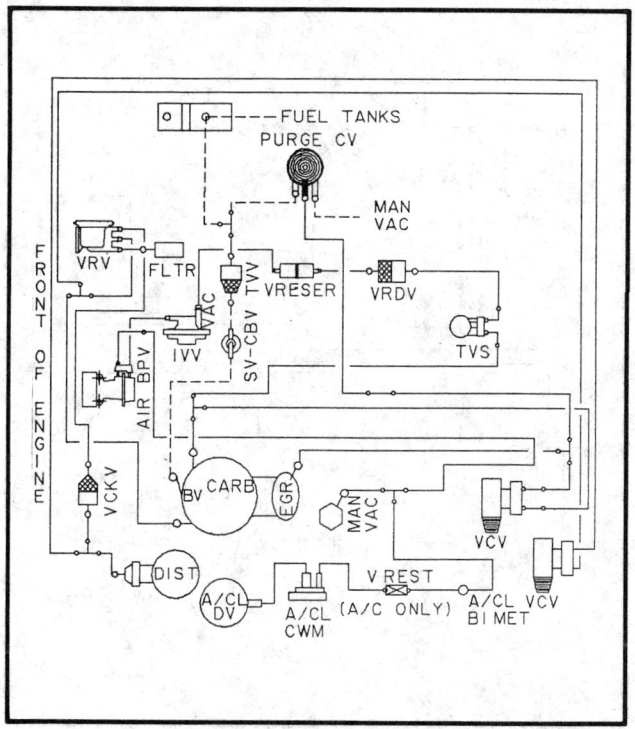

Fig. 23 5.0L (302") V8
Calibration 1-53H-R0 & 1-53H-R11

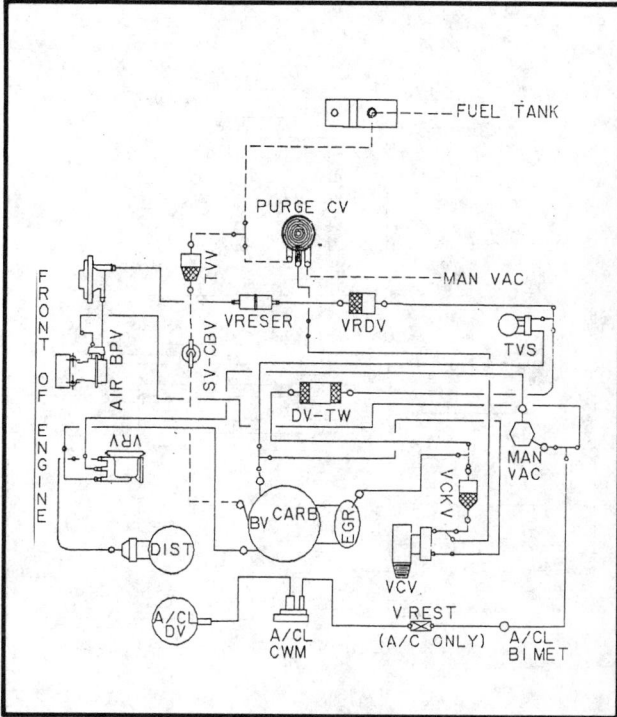

Fig. 24 5.0L (302") V8
Calibration 1-54D-R1 & 1-54G-R0

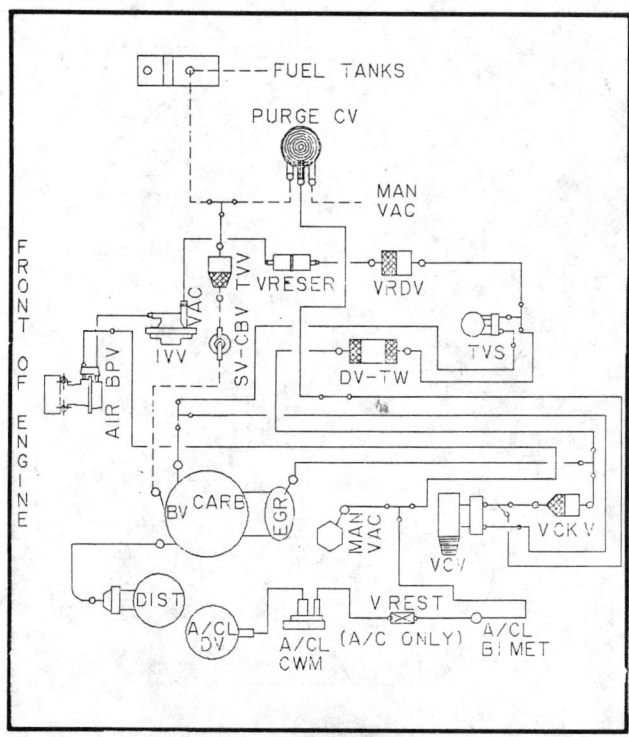

Fig. 25 5.0L (302") V8
Calibration 1-54F-R0

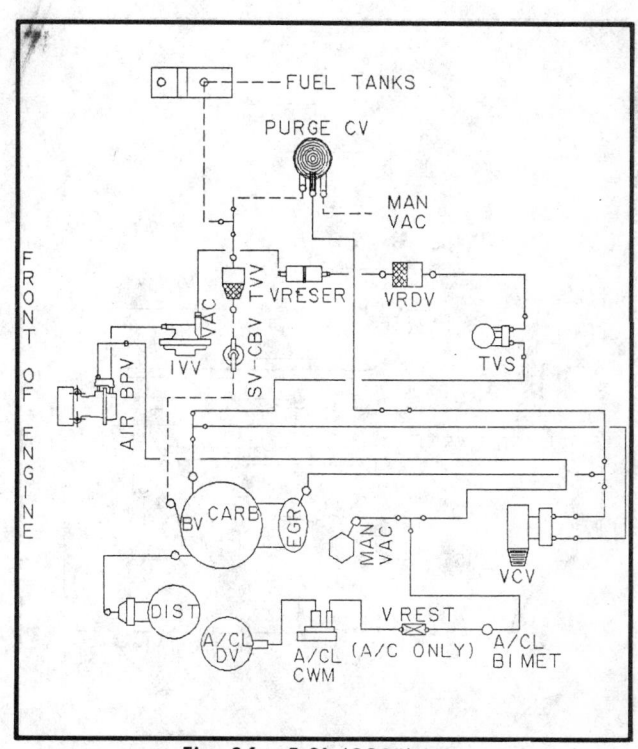

Fig. 26 5.0L (302") V8
Calibration 1-54H-R0

1981 Exhaust Emission Systems

FORD MOTOR CO. VACUUM DIAGRAMS (Cont.)

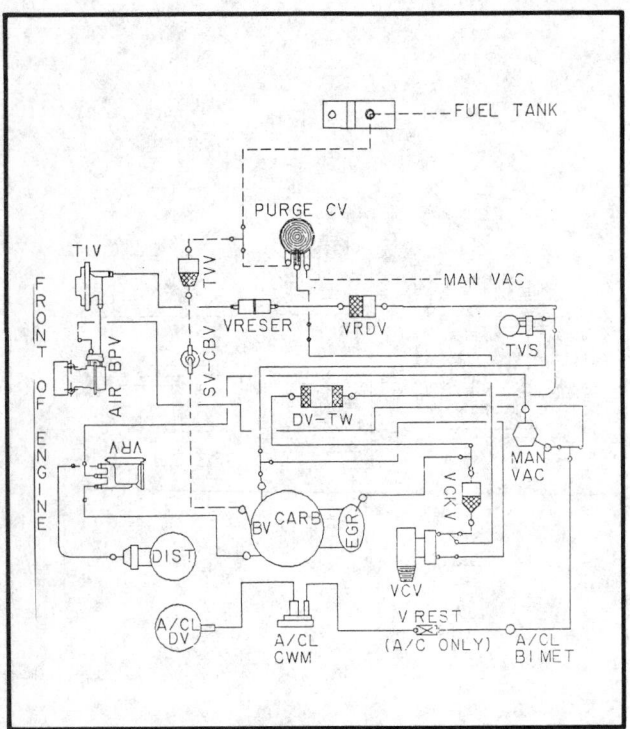

Fig. 27   5.0L (302") V8
Calibration 1-54K-R0

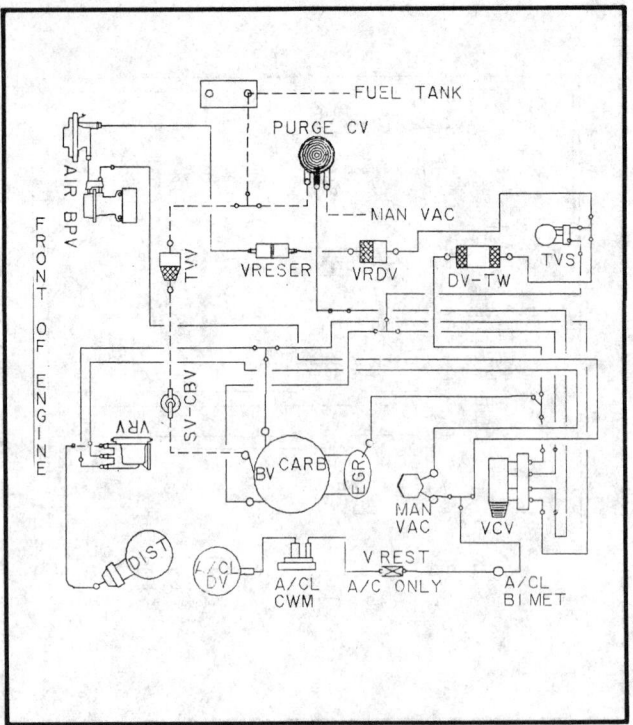

Fig. 28   5.0L (302") V8
Calibration 1-54L-R2

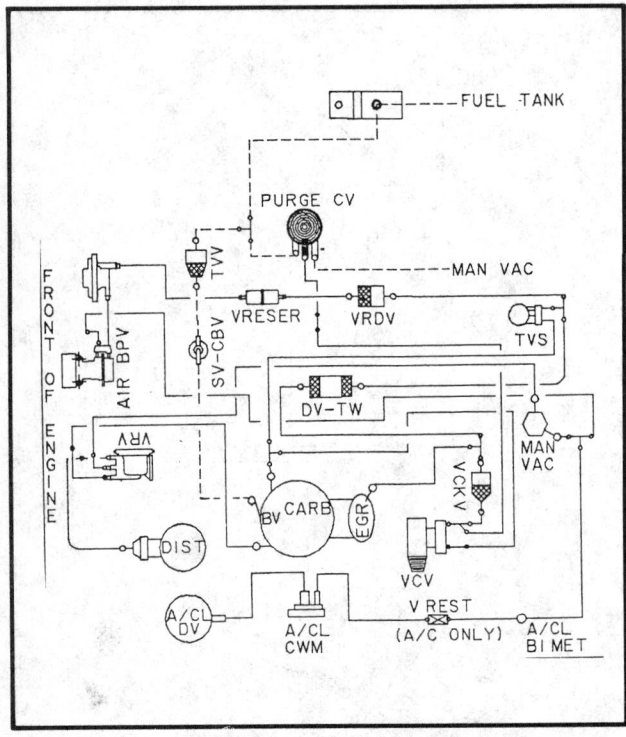

Fig. 29   5.0L (302") V8
Calibration 1-54L-R10

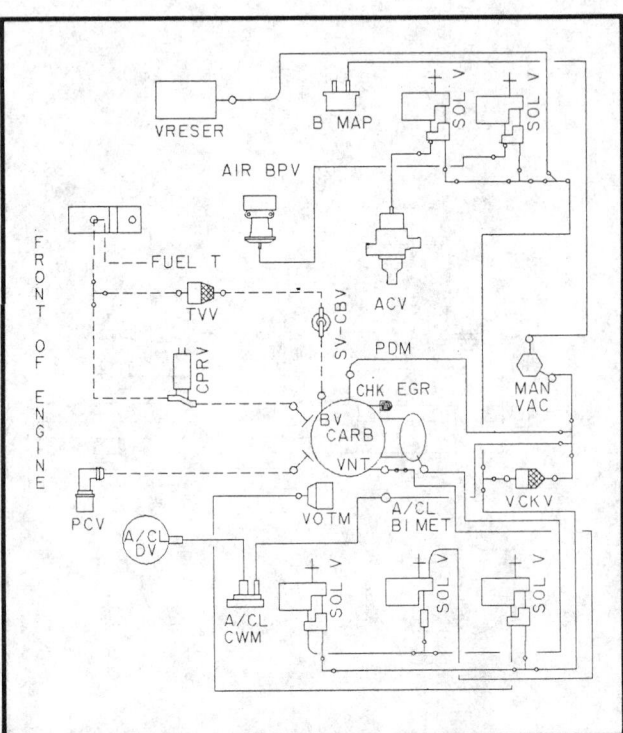

Fig. 30   5.0L (302") V8
(See Index for Calibration Numbers)

FORD VACUUM DIAGRAMS (Cont.)

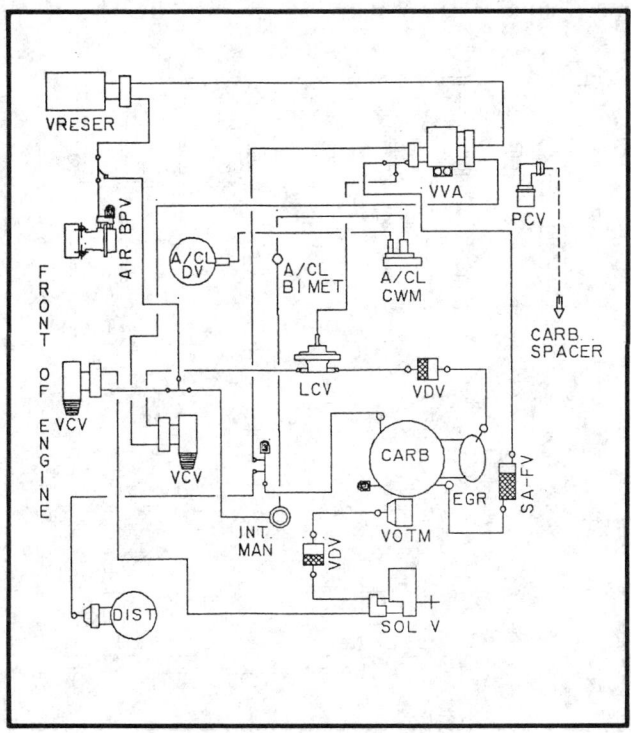

**Fig. 31   5.8L (351") W V8
Calibration 7-76J-R11**

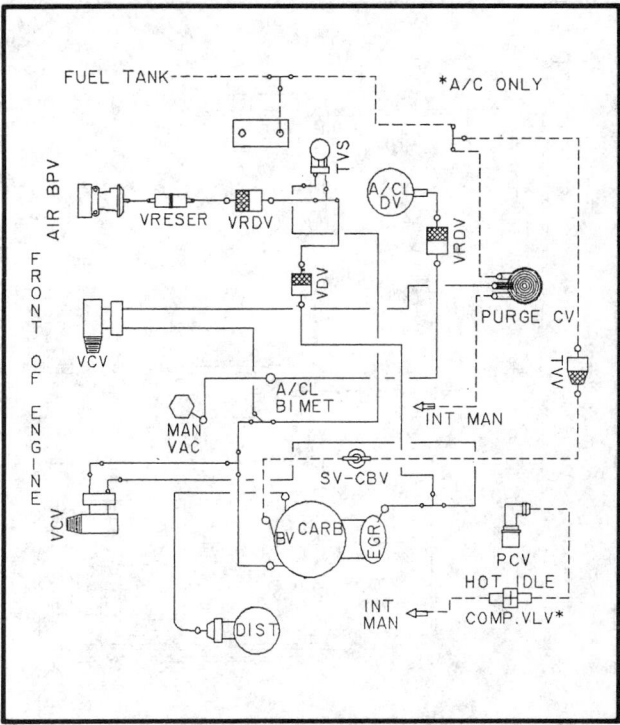

**Fig. 32   5.8L (351") W V8
Calibration 1-64A-R0**

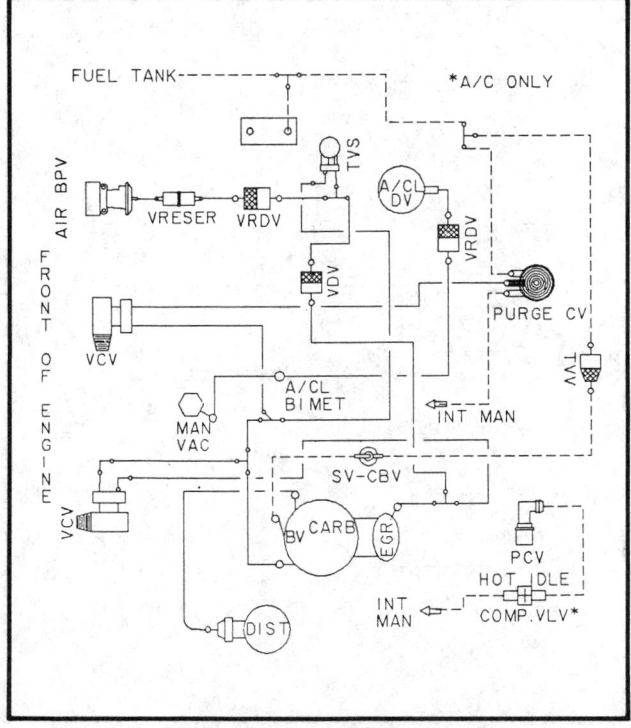

**Fig. 33   5.8L (351") W V8
Calibration 1-64G-R1**

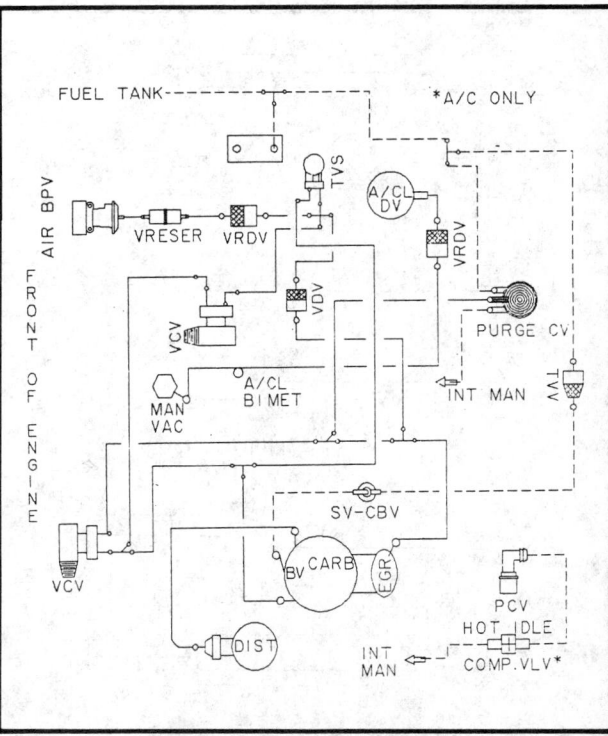

**Fig. 34   5.8L (351") W V8
Calibration 1-64H-R2**

1981 Exhaust Emission Systems

FORD MOTOR CO. VACUUM DIAGRAMS (Cont.)

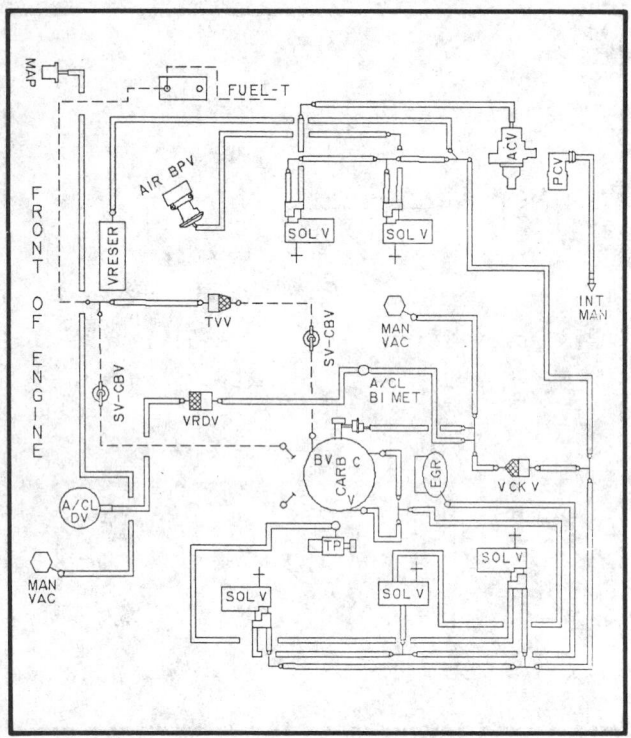

Fig. 35 5.8L (351") W C8
Calibration 1-64R-R1

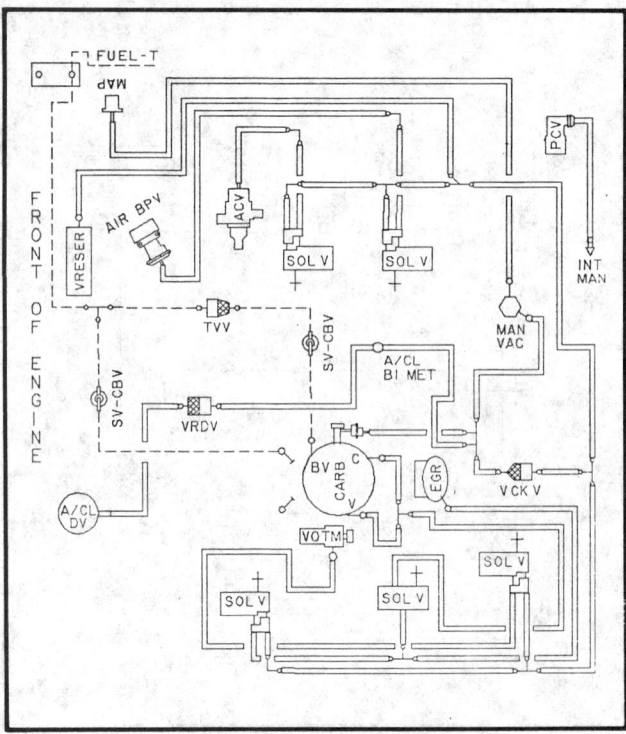

Fig. 36 5.8L (351") W V8
Calibration 1-64S-R0

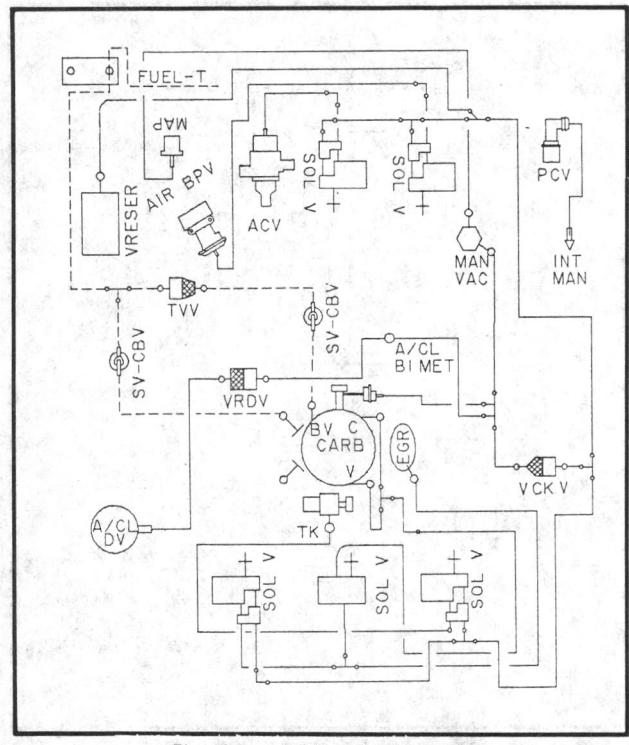

Fig. 37 5.8L (351") W V8
Calibration 1-64T-R0

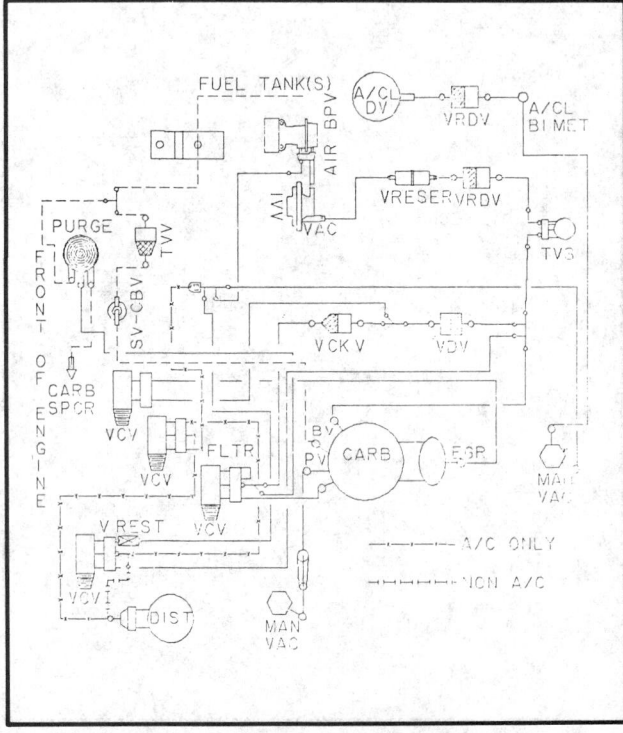

Fig. 38 5.8L (351") M V8
(See Index for Calibration Numbers)

FORD VACUUM DIAGRAMS (Cont.)

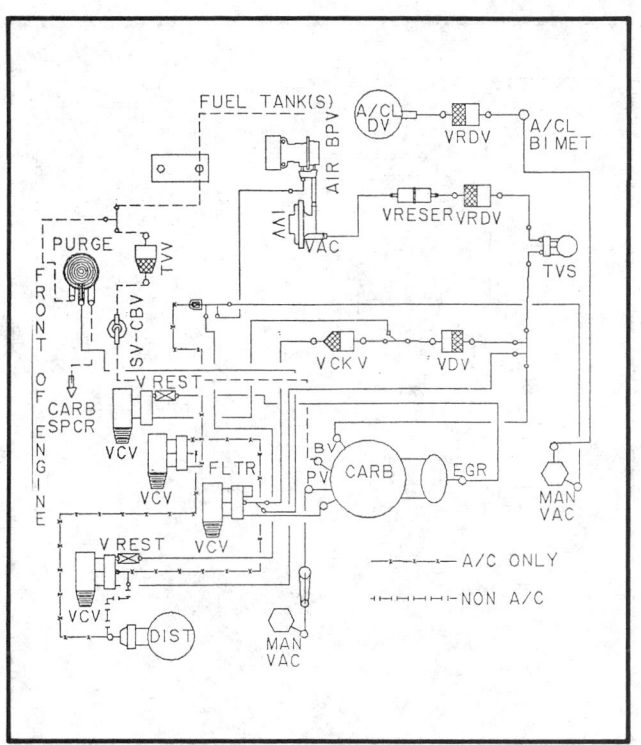

Fig. 39   5.8L (351") M V8
(See Index for Calibration Numbers)

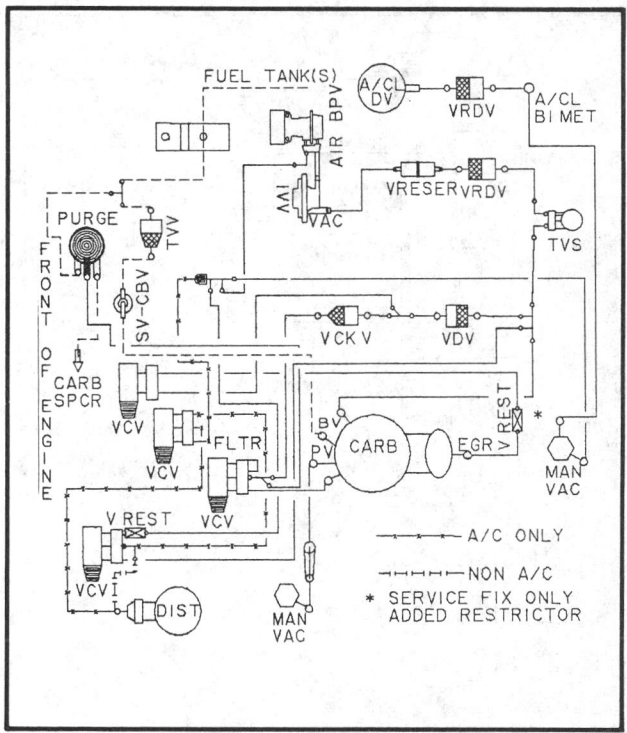

Fig. 40   5.8L (351") M V8
Calibration 1-59H-R0 & 1-R9K-R0

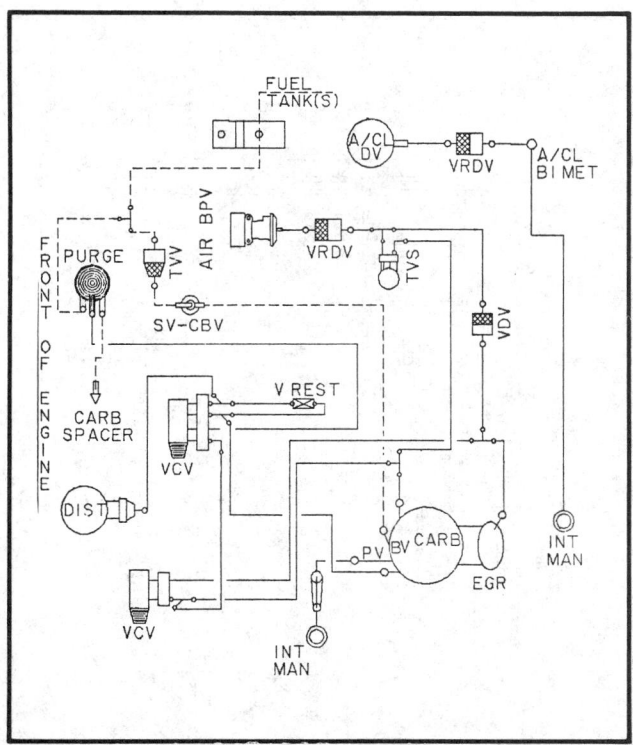

Fig. 41   5.8L (351") M V8
(See Index for Calibration Numbers)

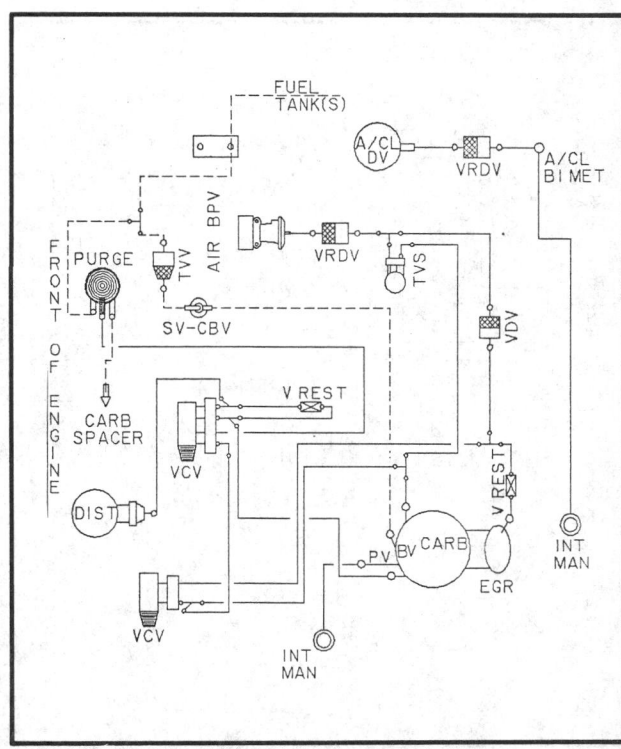

Fig. 42   5.8L (351") M V8
(See Index for Calibration Numbers)

1981 Exhaust Emission Systems

FORD VACUUM DIAGRAMS (Cont.)

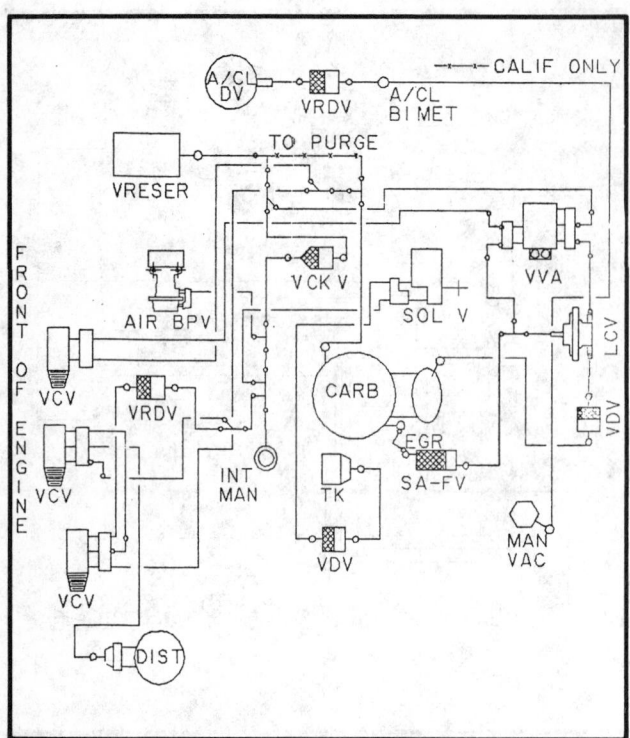

Fig. 43   5.8L (351") M V8
Calibration 9-72J-R11

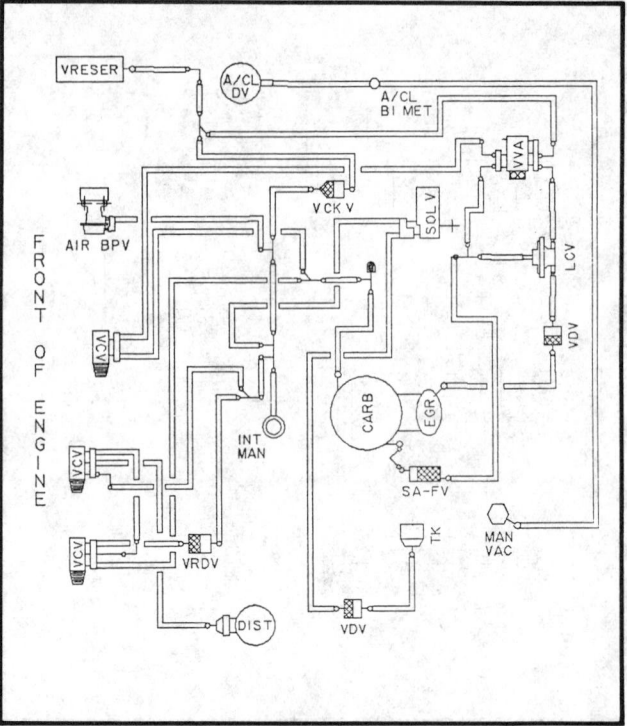

Fig. 44   6.6L (400") V8
Calibration 9-73J-R11

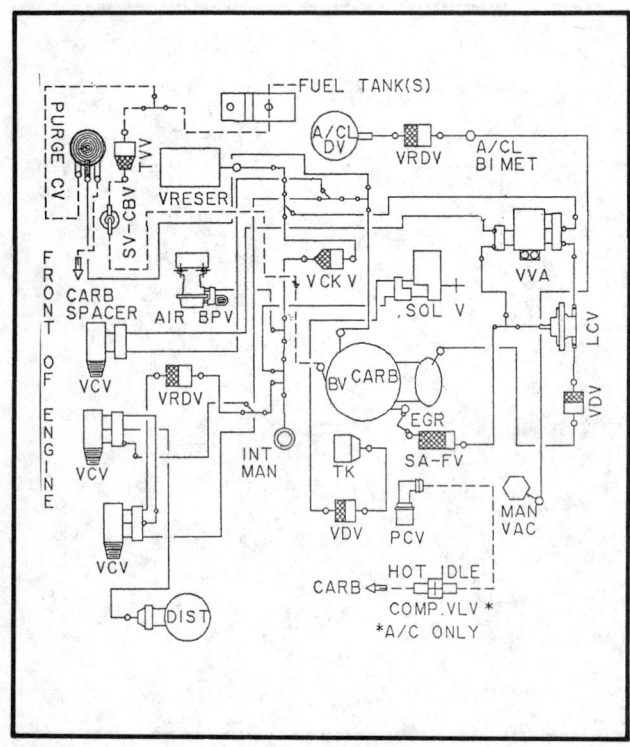

Fig. 45   6.6L (400") V8
Calibration 9-73J-R12

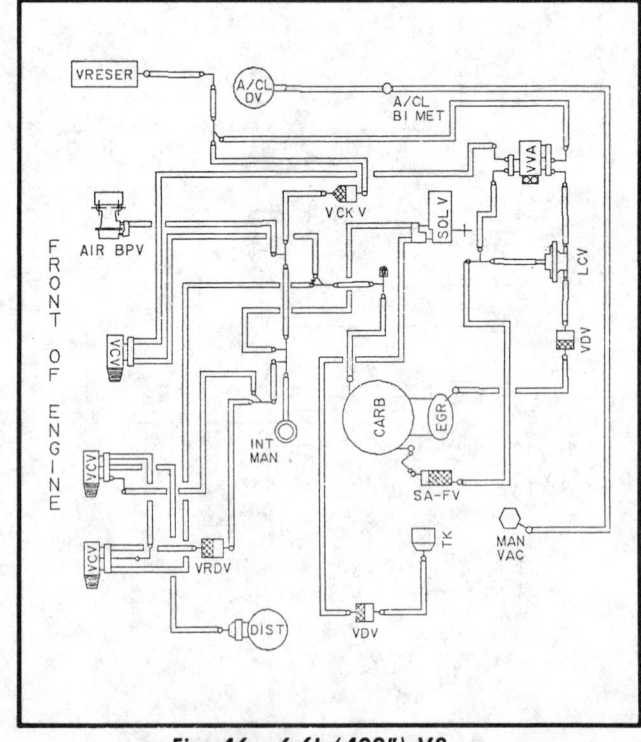

Fig. 46   6.6L (400") V8
Calibration 9-74J-R11

FORD VACUUM DIAGRAMS (Cont.)

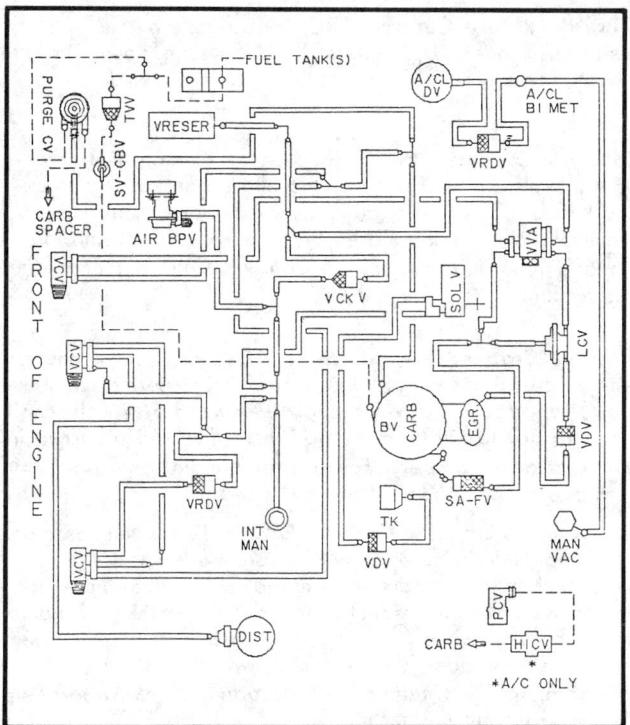

**Fig. 47   6.6L (400") V8
Calibration 9-74J-R12**

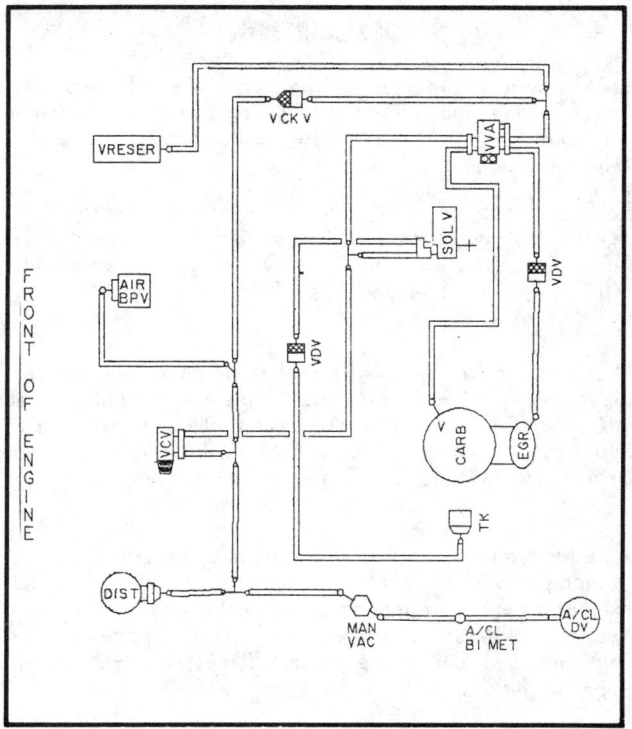

**Fig. 48   7.5L (460") V8
Calibration 9-97J-R0**

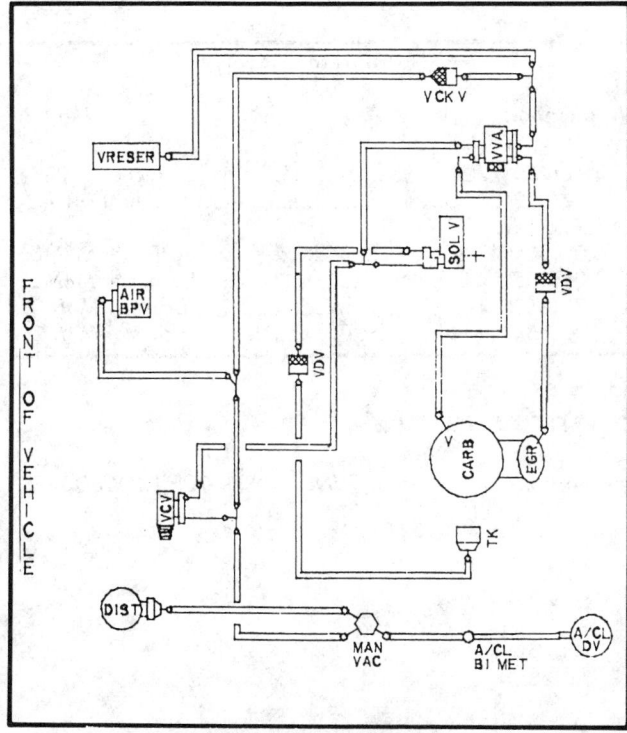

**Fig. 49   7.5L (460") V8
Calibration 9-97J-R12**

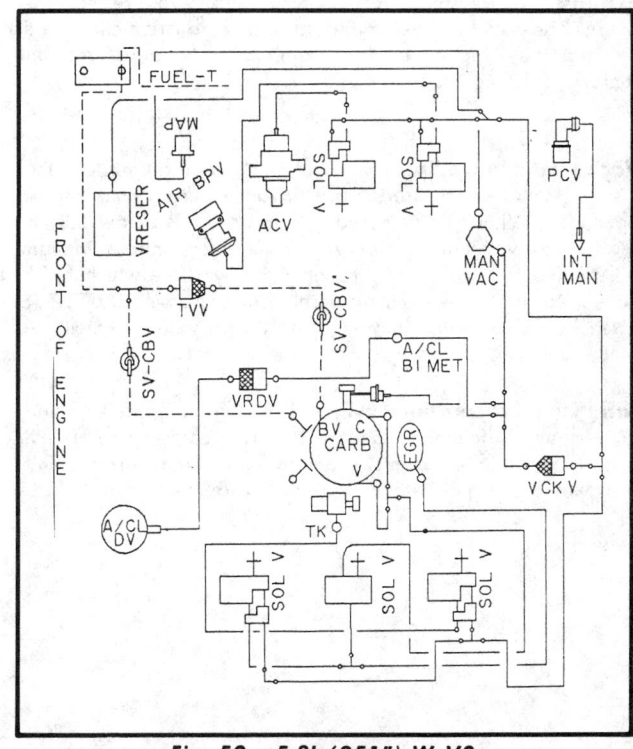

**Fig. 50   5.8L (351") W V8
Calibration 1-63T-R0**

1981 Exhaust Emission Systems

GENERAL MOTORS SYSTEMS & SERVICE PROCEDURES

DESCRIPTION

Several systems are used to control emission of pollutants. System usage depends on model, engine and transmission combination. Each system is designed to control a particular vehicle emission.

NOTE — *There are 2 light duty truck emission control standard classifications: Light Duty and Heavy Duty. Light Duty refers to vehicles up through 8,500 lbs. GVW; Heavy Duty refers to vehicles over 8,500 lbs. GVW.*

Thermac Air Cleaner (TAC) — Used on all models, this unit is designed to aid engine in more complete burning of air/fuel mixture and smoother operation by controlling temperature of intake air. Heated or cooled portions of air are fed into air cleaner assembly as temperature sensor regulates.

Air Injection Reactor (A.I.R.) — This system uses an air pump to supply additional fresh air to exhaust ports, further burning exhaust gases before they reach exhaust system. This reduces hydrocarbon (HC) and carbon monoxide (CO) emissions. *For additional information, see "Air Injection Systems — Air Pump Type" in this section.*

Pulse Air Injection Reactor (PAIR) — This system, used on 250" 6-cylinder models, allows additional fresh air into exhaust system without using an air pump. A special set of check valves is used to respond to exhaust system pulses and draw in fresh air. As with the A.I.R. system, HC and CO emissions are reduced.

Exhaust Gas Recirculation (EGR) — This system recirculates exhaust gases into intake manifold and combustion chambers. This has the effect of lowering combustion temperatures and thereby lowering NOx emissions.

Vacuum Advance Spark Control — Used on all models, this system provides increased spark advance during cold engine operation. When engine coolant temperature is below 100°F, the thermal vacuum switch (TVS) closes and manifold vacuum is supplied to distributor through a delay valve which holds vacuum at high levels during acceleration. Above 100°F, TVS opens, causing manifold vacuum to by-pass delay valve.

Early Fuel Evaporation (EFE) — Used on all Light Duty and some Heavy Duty emissions models. During cold engine operation, system allows exhaust gases to base of carburetor. This improves driveability while reducing exhaust emissions.

Throttle Return Control (TRC) — Used on all Heavy Duty emissions models. Upon deceleration, system opens throttle slightly, thus reducing hydrocarbons during coastdown.

Catalytic Converter (CAT) — Used on all Light Duty emissions models, this unit is connected into exhaust system so exhaust gas passes through converter. Inside converter, a chemical reaction takes place which reduces exhaust emissions. *For additional information, see Catalytic Converter article in this section.*

Positive Crankcase Ventilation (PCV) — System removes engine crankcase vapors which result from normal combustion. Vapors are drawn through a metered PCV valve and routed back to intake manifold where they are reburned in con.bustion chamber. *For additional information, see Crankcase Ventilation article in this section.*

Evaporative Emission Control (EEC) — This system, used on all except Federal Heavy Duty Emissions models, is designed to keep fuel system vapors from escaping to atmosphere. This sealed system separates fuel vapors and routes them to engine to be burned, while retaining liquid fuel in tank. A carbon canister stores vapors until engine draws them off for burning. *For additional information, see appropriate Fuel Evaporation System article in this section.*

SERVICE PROCEDURES

IGNITION TIMING

See appropriate article in TUNE-UP SERVICE PROCEDURES.

CARBURETION

Carburetor Models	
Application	**Model**
6-Cyl. Engines	
4.1L (250") 2-Bbl.	Rochester 2SE
4.8L (292") 1-Bbl.	Rochester 1ME
V8 Engines	
5.0L (305") 2-Bbl.	Rochester M2ME
5.0L (305") 4-Bbl.	Rochester M4ME
5.7L (350") 4-Bbl.	Rochester M4MC
7.4L (454") 4-Bbl.	Rochester M4MC

IDLE SPEED & MIXTURE

See appropriate article in TUNE-UP SERVICE PROCEDURES.

GENERAL MOTORS THERMOSTATIC AIR CLEANER

All Models

DESCRIPTION

All light trucks use a system for preheating the air entering the carburetor. This device is part of the air cleaner and maintains the air temperature at a point where the carburetor can be calibrated much leaner to reduce hydrocarbon (HC) emissions and also improve warm-up operations and reduce carburetor icing.

System consists of an air cleaner assembly, intregal air control door, vacuum control temperature sensor, vacuum motor, heat shroud (on exhaust manifold) with connecting pipe and vacuum hoses. Some models use additional controls, such as vacuum traps and cold weather modulators.

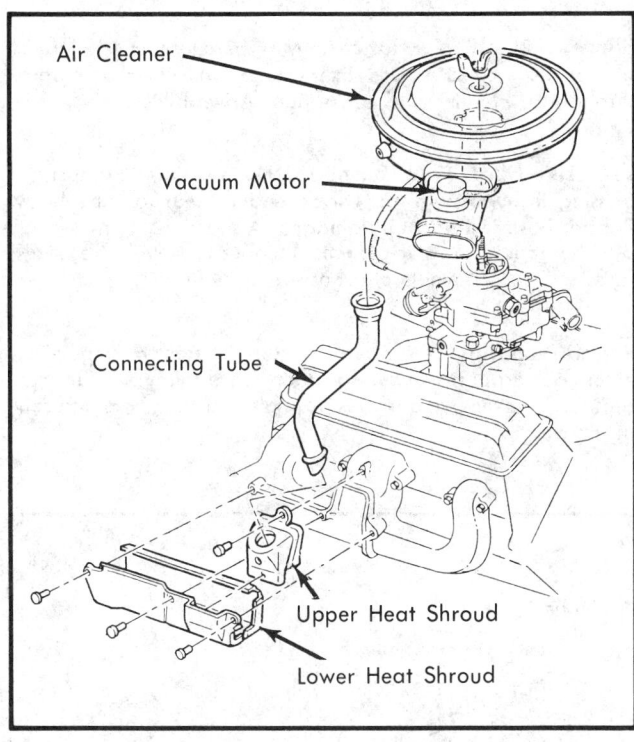

Fig. 1 Typical V8 Engine Air Cleaner Assembly

OPERATION

When temperature of air entering air cleaner is less than the setting of temperature sensor, sensor closes to allow engine vacuum to operate vacuum motor which closes damper assembly to outside air. Air is then drawn from around exhaust manifold, through heat shroud and into air cleaner as heated air. As air inside air cleaner warms, sensor valve begins to open. This bleeds off vacuum to vacuum motor. As vacuum to vacuum motor drops, air control door begins to open, allowing outside air to enter air cleaner. When air entering air cleaner reaches a specified temperature, air control door opens completely, thus closing off heated air from around exhaust manifold.

TESTING

VACUUM CONTROL TEMPERATURE SENSOR TEST

1) With engine cold, check damper door. It should be in the open snorkel position. Place thermometer inside air cleaner, close to sensor.

2) With engine temperature below 80°F, start engine and idle. Damper door should be in the closed snorkel position. When door starts to open, read thermometer in air cleaner. Temperature should be 80-120°F. If door does not begin to open at this temperature, replace sensor.

VACUUM MOTOR TEST

1) Check all hoses and connections for proper hook-up. With engine off, observe damper door through snorkel opening. The door should be open to outside air.

2) With an external vacuum unit, apply 7 in. Hg of vacuum to diaphragm assembly through hose disconnected at sensor. Damper door should close when vacuum is applied. If not, check for vacuum leak, or binding linkage.

3) With vacuum applied, bend hose to trap vacuum in diaphragm assembly. Damper door should remain closed. If not, replace diaphragm assembly.

1981 Exhaust Emission Systems

GENERAL MOTORS PULSE AIR INJECTION

General Motors
4.1L (250") Engine

DESCRIPTION

The Pulse Air Injection Reaction (Pair) system is used on General Motors models with 4.1L 6-cylinder engines. It is a non-pump type air injection system which uses engine exhaust pulses to draw fresh air into the exhaust system. This helps to oxidize HC and CO emissions. System consists of a grouping of check valves in 2 plenum chambers (located on valve covers) and related tubing.

OPERATION

Each one of the check valves in plenum chambers is connected to an exhaust port. The firing of the engine creates a pulsating flow of exhaust gases. When positive exhaust pressure is felt, the check valve will be forced closed and no exhaust gas will flow past the valve into the fresh air supply line. With negative exhaust pressure (vacuum), the check valve will open and fresh air will be drawn and mixed with exhaust gases. During high engine RPM, the check valve will remain closed (such as under heavy acceleration).

TESTING

FUNCTIONAL TEST

1) Remove air cleaner-to-plenum pipe hose from plenum pipe. Slide a length of tight-fitting ¾" hose onto plenum pipe and, using an adapter, connect a hand vacuum pump to hose.

2) Apply 17 in. Hg. Note time required for vacuum level to drop from 17 in. Hg to 6 in. Hg. If less than 2 seconds, remove check valves and test individually. Replace check valve(s) which fail leak-down test.

NOTE — *If system fails leak-down test, ensure that failure is not due to a leaking test hose or connection.*

TROUBLE SHOOTING

FAILURE DIAGNOSIS

Short Hissing Noise — May indicate a defective check valve or improper torque at manifold. Inspect check valves.

Surge or Poor Performance — May be caused by failure of one or more check valves. Exhaust gas will enter carburetor through air cleaner and cause poor driveability.

Excessive Heat; Paint Burned Off of Valve — Exhaust gas passing through pulse air valve, sending heat to valve body. Rubber hose will also be damaged. A short hissing noise may also be noticed. Repair plenum chamber-to-valve cover seals, and replace grommets and hose as required.

Poor Driveability — Rubber hose deteriorated. Hose particles entering carburetor causing poor driveability. Clean carburetor, and remove particles from plenum chambers and connecting pipe.

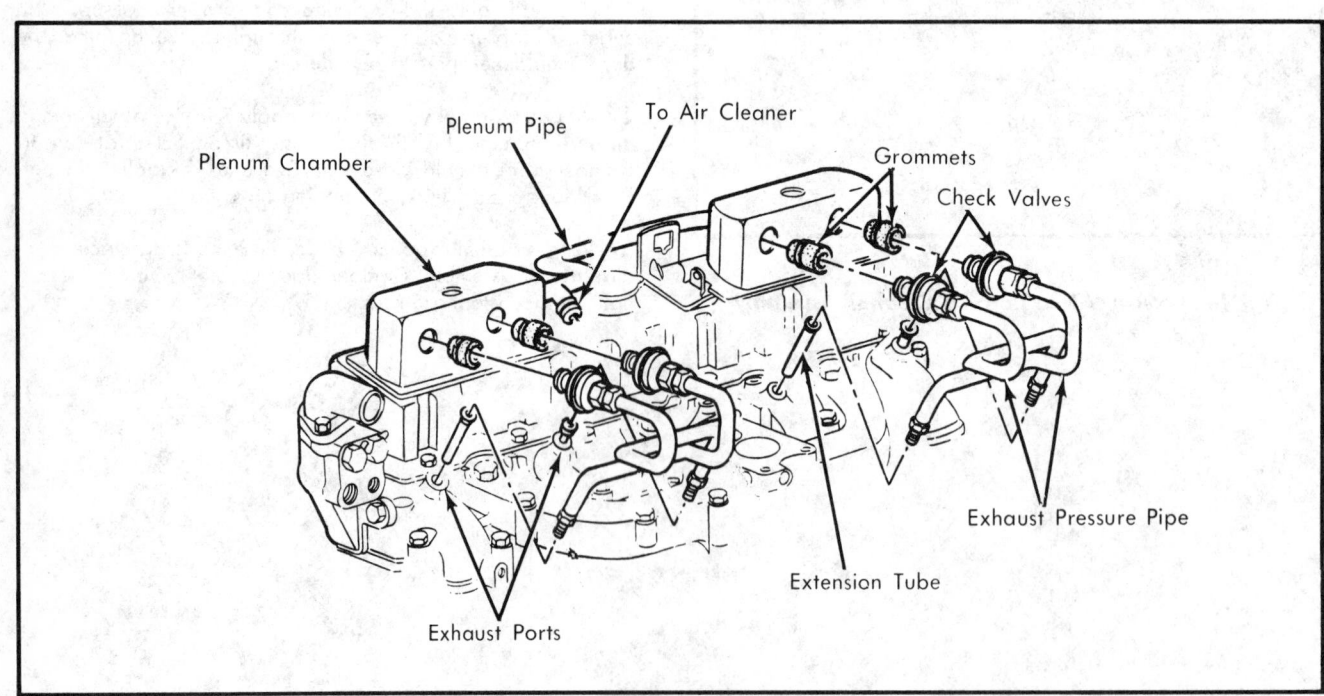

Fig. 1   Pulse Air Injection Reactor (PAIR) System Components

GENERAL MOTORS EXHAUST GAS RECIRCULATION

DESCRIPTION

Exhaust gas recirculation (EGR) is used on all Light Duty emissions models to reduce oxides of nitrogen (NOx) emissions. This process is accomplished by lowering the combustion temperatures of burning gases. Recirculated and metered amounts of exhaust gases are reintroduced into the engine through the intake manifold, where they are mixed with the air/fuel mixture.

The back pressure modulated system regulates the timed vacuum according to the exhaust back pressure level. A special control valve within the EGR valve housing responds as a pressure regulator.

OPERATION

BACK PRESSURE EGR SYSTEM

Two types of back pressure type EGR valves are used by General Motors: a Positive Back Pressure EGR valve (used on Federal V8 models) and a Negative Back Pressure EGR valve (used on some 6-cylinder and most California V8 models). Operation of these 2 systems is explained as follows:

Positive Back Pressure EGR Valve — A small diaphragm control valve inside the EGR valve assembly acts as a pressure regulator. The control valve receives an exhaust back pressure signal through the hollow shaft which exerts a force on the bottom of the control valve diaphragm, opposed by a light spring. A metal deflector plate prevents hot exhaust gases from flowing directly on the diaphragm.

Vacuum is applied to the EGR valve assembly from the carburetor spark port, to assure no exhaust gas recirculation at idle. During off-idle operation, manifold vacuum is applied to the vacuum chamber through a restriction in the signal tube.

When engine load is light, and back pressure is low, the control valve is open, allowing air to flow from the 6 bleeds in diaphragm plate, through control valve orifice, into the vacuum chamber. The air bleeds off vacuum, decreasing signal trying to open EGR valve. Therefore, if back pressure does not close the control valve, sealing off air flow, there will not be any vacuum built up to open the EGR valve for exhaust gas recirculation.

When power demands are made on the engine, and exhaust gas recirculation is needed, exhaust gas back pressure increases, closing the control valve, thereby shutting off air flow through valve. Vacuum builds up in the vacuum chamber until the spring force holding the EGR valve closed is overcome.

Once the EGR valve opens, the exhaust pressure decreases because some of the exhaust gas is flowing into the intake manifold through the EGR passage. In actual operation, the system will reach a balanced condition providing optimum EGR operation.

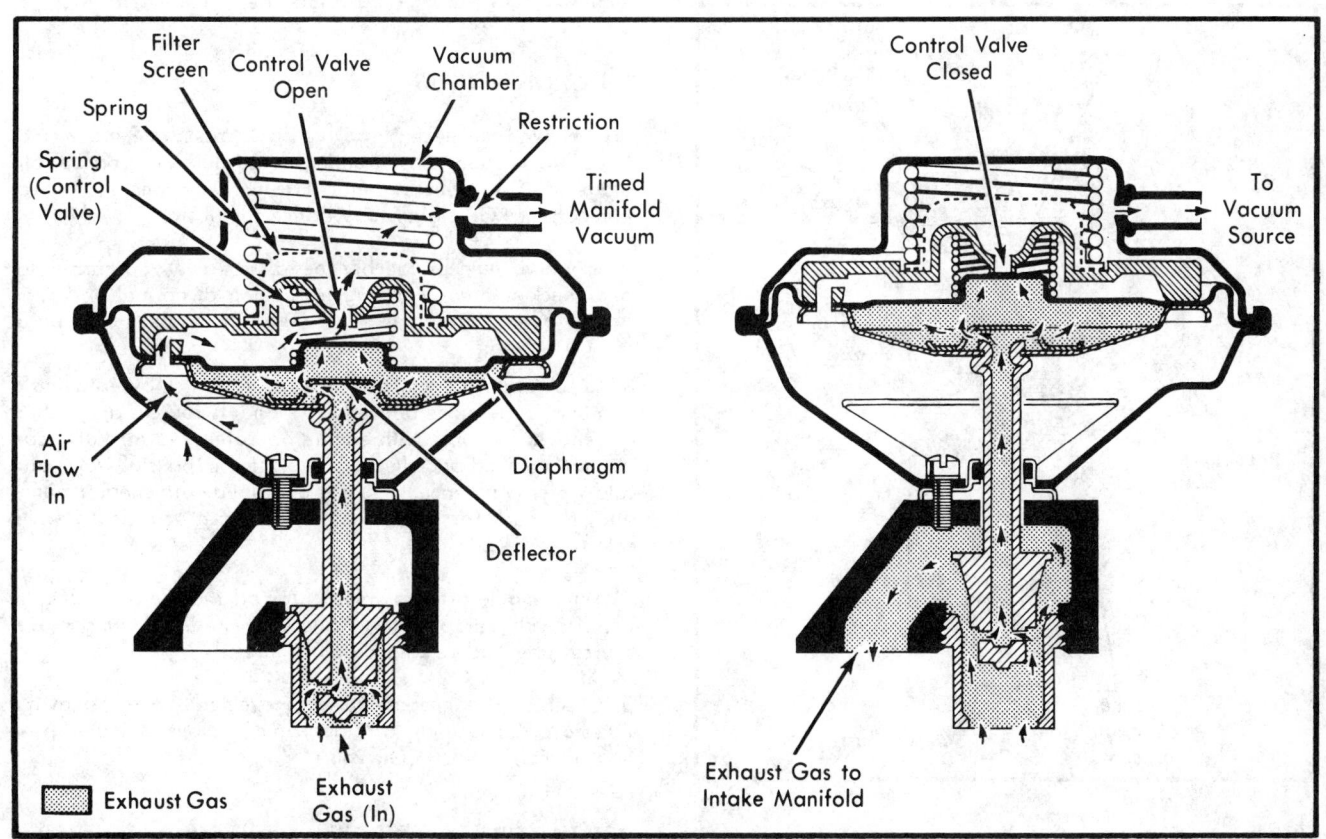

Fig. 1 Cutaway View of Positive Back Pressure EGR Valve

GENERAL MOTORS EXHAUST GAS RECIRCULATION (Cont.)

Any increase in engine load will momentarily increase the exhaust signal, causing the control valve to close, allowing a stronger vacuum signal. The system will then stabilize at a greater EGR flow.

At maximum engine load, when manifold vacuum is nearly zero, momentarily, there will be no EGR operation. This is because of insufficient vacuum to pull the valve open, even though high exhaust back pressure has closed the control valve.

Negative Transducer Back Pressure EGR Valve — The negative transducer back pressure EGR valve assembly has the same function as the positive back pressure EGR valve except the transducer is designed to allow the valve to open with negative exhaust back pressure.

The flow of the valve is controlled by manifold vacuum, negative exhaust back pressure and the carburetor ported vacuum signal. The control valve spring in the transducer is placed on the bottom side of the diaphragm.

When the carburetor ported vacuum signal is applied to the main vacuum chamber partially opening the valve, the vacuum signal from the manifold side (reduced by exhaust back pressure) is transmitted up the hollow stem of the valve. This enables the signal to act on the diaphragm, opening the bleed and causing the transducer to modulate providing a specific valve flow. Thus the flow of the valve is a constant percentage of engine air flow.

EGR THERMAL VACUUM (TVS)

The EGR TVS, used on all models, closes to prevent EGR operations when engine coolant temperature is below 85°. This improves cold engine driveability. When coolant temperature rises above 85°F, TVS opens to allow vacuum to be directed to EGR valve.

TESTING

SYSTEM OPERATION

1) With engine at normal operating temperature, set engine speed to fast idle (or high enough to obtain at least 5 in. Hg at EGR valve). Place gloved finger beneath EGR valve so diaphragm movement can be felt.

2) Disconnect vacuum hose from EGR valve and watch for diaphragm movement. Diaphragm should move downward (valve closed) and an increase in engine RPM should be noticed.

3) Reconnect vacuum hose. Diaphragm should move upward (valve open) and engine RPM should decrease.

4) If no diaphragm movement is noticed during test, check for vacuum at hose. If vacuum is present, replace EGR valve. If no vacuum is present, check for plugged or leaking hose or carburetor port.

5) If diaphragm moves with no change in engine RPM, check manifold EGR passages for blockage.

FUNCTIONAL TESTS

EGR Valve Installed (Negative Back Pressure Types) — 1) Check for proper hose routing, according to appropriate diagrams. *See "General Motors Vacuum Diagrams" in this Section.* Check EGR signal tube orifice for obstructions.

2) Hook vacuum gauge between EGR valve and carburetor and check vacuum with engine running at normal operating temperature. With engine at 3,000 RPM, there should be at least 5 in. Hg.

3) Check operation of Thermal Vacuum Switch by installing a vacuum gauge inline between TVS and its sources and noting presence of vacuum with engine operating warm. Valve can also be removed and checked by placing in pails of warm and cold water (with vacuum source and gauge attached on either side) to check for valve open while warm and closed while cold.

4) With engine off and valve on or off the vehicle, manually depress valve diaphragm. While depressed, hold finger over source tube and release diaphragm.

5) Check for diaphragm and seat movement. Valve is okay if it takes over 20 seconds for diaphragm to move to seated position. If less, replace EGR valve.

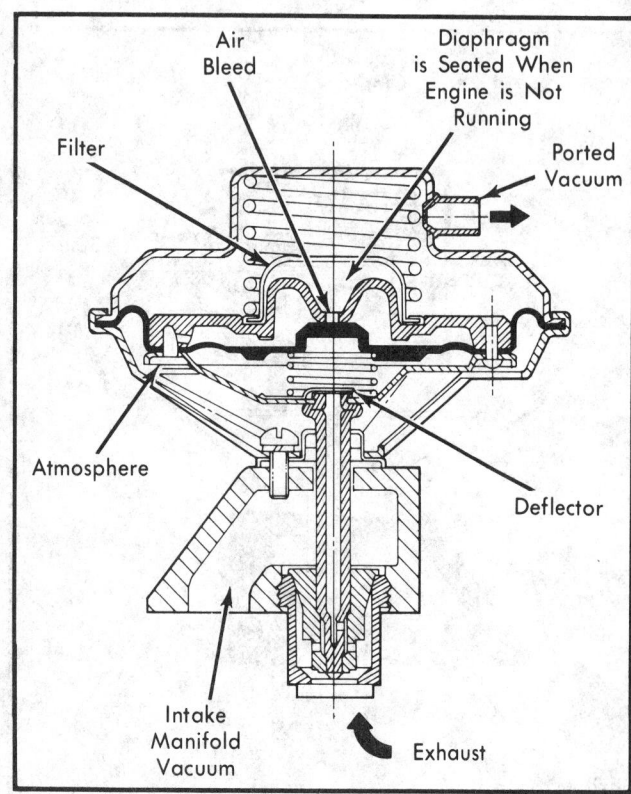

Fig. 2 Cutaway View of Negative Transducer Back Pressure EGR Valve

EGR Valve Removed (Positive Back Pressure Type Valve Only) — 1) Apply external vacuum (10 in. Hg or more) to EGR valve signal tube.

GENERAL MOTORS EXHAUST GAS RECIRCULATION (Cont.)

NOTE — *A constant vacuum supply must be used.*

2) Valve should not open. If it does, control valve is stuck closed and EGR valve must be replaced.

3) With vacuum still applied, apply a stream of air from a low pressure source into the EGR valve exhaust gas intake passage. Valve should open completely. If it does not open at all, control valve is stuck open or exhaust passages are plugged. Replace EGR valve.

4) If EGR valve and control valve are both functioning properly, clean the mounting surfaces, then using a new gasket, install valve on engine. Reconnect vacuum hose.

EGR-TVS Test (Hot) — 1) Remove EGR valve vacuum hose at EGR valve and connect hose to a vacuum gauge. Start engine. With transmission in Park or Neutral, open throttle partially. As throttle is opened, the vacuum gauge should respond with an increase in vacuum reading. If operation is satisfactory, remove gauge and reconnect hose to EGR valve. If gauge does not respond to throttle opening, proceed to step **2)**.

2) Remove carb-to-switch hose from switch and connect hose to vacuum gauge. Start engine. With transmission in Park or Neutral open throttle partially. If vacuum gauge responds to throttle opening, then switch is defective. Remove switch and replace with new part. If gauge does not respond to throttle opening, then check for plugged hose or defective carburetor.

EGR-TVS Test (Cold) — 1) Engine coolant must be below 85°F. Drain coolant to below level of switch. Disconnect vacuum lines and remove switch. Inspect switch to make sure it is in good condition.

2) Connect a vacuum hose to lower nipple of switch, marked "C" or "CARB". Connect a vacuum gauge to upper nipple, marked "E" or "EGR". Place switch in water at 75°F and submerge completely for 2 minutes while agitating water thoroughly. Apply 12 in. Hg vacuum to hose on lower nipple of switch. Under this condition, the switch should be closed.

NOTE — *Leakage of up to 2 in. Hg of vacuum in 2 minutes is allowable and does not mean a defective switch.*

3) If operation is satisfactory, reinstall switch. If switch is defective, replace with a new part. Replace coolant and check level.

MAINTENANCE

EGR PASSAGE CLEANING

If inspection of EGR passages in intake manifold indicates excessive build up of exhaust deposits, the passages should be cleaned. Care should be taken to ensure that all loose particles are completely removed to prevent them from clogging the EGR valve or from being ingested into the engine.

GENERAL MOTORS VACUUM ADVANCE SPARK CONTROL

DESCRIPTION

TRAPPED VACUUM SPARK

Trapped vacuum spark is used on all models. A thermal vacuum switch (TVS) is mounted in cylinder head and used to sense engine coolant temperature. A vacuum check valve is mounted between manifold vacuum, distributor and thermal vacuum switch. The system maintains high vacuum levels to the distributor during cold engine operation and cold engine acceleration.

SPARK VACUUM DELAY

The spark vacuum delay is used on 350" and 400" V8 engines with Heavy Duty Emissions. It is installed between the TVS check valve and the distributor.

OPERATION

TRAPPED VACUUM SPARK

When engine temperature is below a pre-set specified value, the manifold vacuum signal is routed through the check valve

to the distributor. Ports on TVS are blocked. The check valve will keep distributor vacuums at levels higher than manifold depression during vehicle acceleration. A small sintered iron bleed orifice is provided in the check valve to allow for a leakdown to enable engine to be restarted if it stalls. (This applies to all models except: Light Duty California and Altitude Emissions; 350" and 400" V8 with Heavy Duty Emissions; all 454" V8 engines.)

When engine temperature is above pre-set value, TVS ports will be open to allow manifold vacuum to the distributor. During this mode of operation, the check valve will act as a connector.

SPARK VACUUM DELAY

As manifold vacuum increases, the check valve opens and allows distributor vacuum to increase to same level. When vacuum decreases during vehicle acceleration, the check valve closes and distributor vacuum will decrease at a rate controlled by the internal bleed.

1981 Exhaust Emission Systems

GENERAL MOTORS EARLY FUEL EVAPORATION SYSTEM

DESCRIPTION

An early fuel evaporation (EFE) system is used on all Light Duty and some Heavy Duty emissions models. System provides improved cold driveability while reducing exhaust emissions.

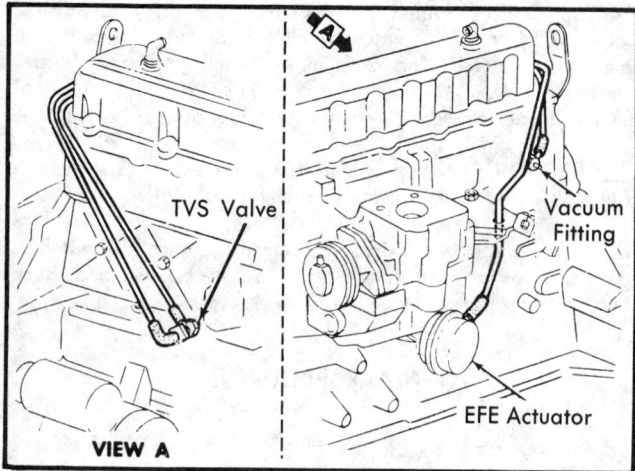

Fig. 1   Early Fuel Evaporation System 6-Cylinder Engines

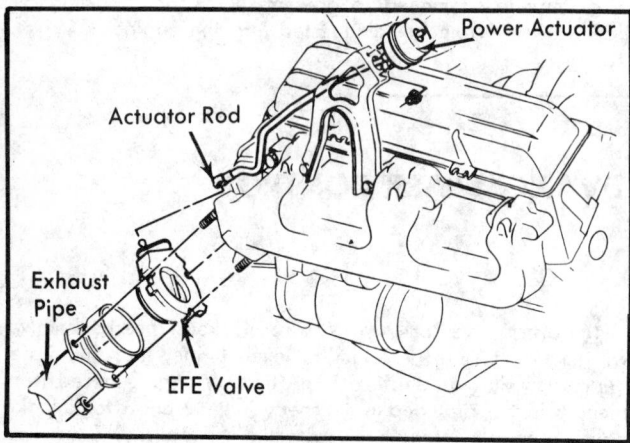

Fig. 2   Early Fuel Evaporation System 5.0L & 5.7L V8 Engines

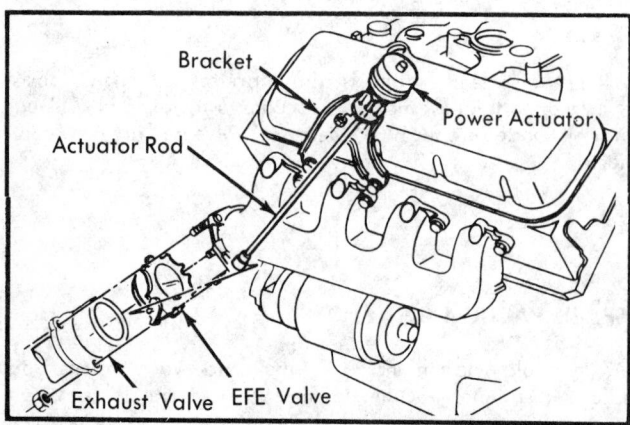

Fig. 3   Early Fuel Evaporation System 7.4L V8 Engines

System consists of an EFE valve, an actuator and a thermal vacuum switch (TVS). The TVS is coolant temperature controlled on V8 engines and oil temperature controlled on 6-cylinder engines.

OPERATION

6-Cylinder Engines — The thermal vacuum switch is a normally closed switch which is sensitive to oil temperature. With a cold engine, below 150°F, TVS is closed which allows manifold vacuum to the actuator valve. Vacuum pulls the diaphragm in the actuator, closing the EFE Valve. This causes the hot exhaust gases to be routed to the base of carburetor. When oil temperature is above 150°F, the thermal vacuum switch opens. This stops vacuum to actuator. Without vacuum, a spring pushes actuator diaphragm to its at rest position and opens the EFE valve.

V8 Engines — On V8 engines the TVS is located in the coolant outlet housing and directly controls vacuum. With coolant temperatures below 180°F, manifold vacuum is applied to actuator which closes the EFE valve. This routes hot exhaust gases to base of carburetor. When temperctures reach 180°F, vacuum to the actuator is stopped. This allows a spring to return the actuator to its at rest position, opening the EFE valve.

TESTING

1) With engine cold, position transmission in "NEUTRAL" or "PARK" and apply parking brake. Start engine and observe movement of actuator rod and exhaust heat valve. Valve should move to its closed position.

2) If valve does not close, disconnect hose at actuator and check for vacuum. If there is vacuum, replace actuator. If no vacuum is found, disconnect hose at TVS-to-vacuum source. If there is vacuum at hose, replace TVS. If no vacuum, check hose for leaks.

3) When coolant temperature reaches 180° F (V8) or oil temperature reaches 150° F (6 cylinder), exhaust heat valve should move to the open position.

4) If valve does not open, disconnect hose at actuator and check for vacuum. If there is vacuum, replace TVS. If no vacuum is present, replace actuator.

MAINTENANCE

Periodically inspect vacuum hoses for damage, actuator for proper operation, linkage for binding and EFE valve for smooth operation.

GENERAL MOTORS THROTTLE RETURN CONTROL SYSTEM

DESCRIPTION

A throttle return control (TRC) system is used on all Heavy Duty emissions models. Upon deceleration, system opens throttle slightly to reduce hydrocarbon emissions. System consists of a throttle lever actuator, a solenoid vacuum control valve and an electronic speed sensor.

OPERATION

Manifold vacuum is routed through the solenoid vacuum valve, which is normally closed, to the throttle lever actuator. Upon vehicle deceleration, electronic speed sensor signals solenoid vacuum valve to open when engine speed is above a preset RPM. When valve opens, manifold vacuum is directed to throttle lever acutator, which extends to open throttle slightly. When engine speed drops below the preset RPM, solenoid valve closes, retracting throttle lever actuator and returning throttle to curb idle position.

TESTING & ADJUSTMENT

SYSTEM OPERATION

1) Connect a tachometer accurate to within ±10 RPM. Start engine and open throttle until tachometer reads 1890 RPM. Throttle lever actuator should be extended at this speed. Decrease engine speed to 1700 RPM. Throttle actuator should be retracted at this speed.

2) If throttle actuator operates at specified engine speeds, system is functioning. If actuator operates outside of RPM limits, replace speed sensor. If actuator does not operate at any speed, proceed with the following steps.

3) Using a voltmeter, check for battery voltage at voltage wire terminal on solenoid valve and speed sensor. If voltage is present at 1 component only, repair wiring harness as required. If no voltage at both components, check engine harness connections at distributor and bulkhead connector and repair as required.

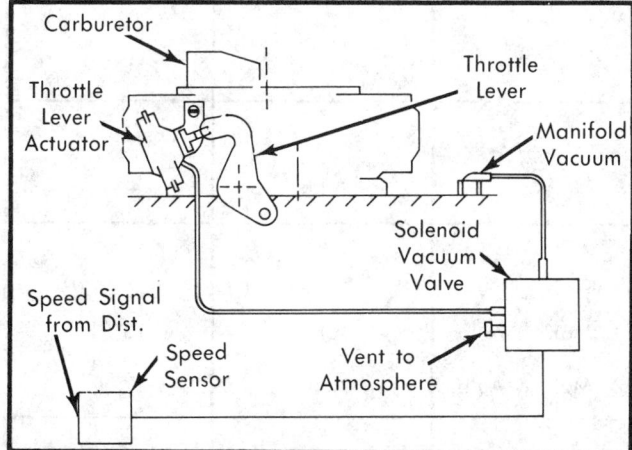

Fig. 1   Schematic of G.M. Throttle Return Control System

4) If battery voltage is present at solenoid valve and speed sensor, start engine and use a jumper wire to ground solenoid-to-speed sensor connecting wire terminal at speed sensor. Throttle actuator should extend.

- If actuator did not extend, remove throttle actuator hose from solenoid and check solenoid orifice for blockage. If orifice is plugged, clean as required. If orifice is clear, replace solenoid.
- If actuator did extend, ground solenoid-to-switch wire terminal at speed switch. If actuator does not extend, repair speed switch-to-solenoid wire. If it extends, ensure speed switch ground wire reads ground with engine running and check speed switch-to-distributor wire connections. If actuator still does not extend with all wires properly connected and engine speed above 1890 RPM, replace speed sensor.

5) If throttle actuator remains extended at all speeds, remove electrical connector from solenoid.

- If actuator remains extended, check actuator vacuum orifice on solenoid valve for blockage. Clean orifice, and reconnect system. If actuator again remains extended, remove solenoid connector. If actuator does not retract, replace solenoid valve.
- If actuator retracts with connector removed, reconnect and then remove speed switch connector. If actuator retracts, replace speed switch. If actuator does not retract, solenoid-to-switch wire is shorted to ground in harness. Repair wire.

THROTTLE LEVER ACTUATOR

1) Disconnect valve-to-actuator hose at valve and connect to an external vacuum supply, with a vacuum gauge installed near the actuator.

2) Apply 20 in. Hg to the actuator and seal off vacuum source. If vacuum gauge reading drops, actuator is leaking and must be replaced.

3) To check actuator for proper operation, first ensure throttle lever, shaft and linkage work without binding. Start engine and run to normal operating temperature. Turn off air conditioner and note idle RPM.

4) Apply 20 in. Hg to the actuator. Manually open throttle slightly and allow it to close against extended actuator plunger. Note engine RPM.

5) Release throttle and reapply 20 in. Hg to actuator and note RPM to which engine speed increases (do not assist the actuator).

6) If RPM as just noted is not within 150 RPM of speed noted in Step 4), then actuator plunger is binding. Clean around plunger to see if condition can be corrected. If not, replace actuator.

7) Release vacuum from actuator and engine speed should return to within 50 RPM of idle speed noted in Step 3). If not, plunger may be binding and should be cleaned. If problem cannot be corrected, replace actuator.

8) If engine RPM noted in Step 4) is not to specified TRC speed, actuator must be adjusted.

9) To adjust actuator, apply 20 in. Hg to actuator. Manually, open throttle slightly and allow it to close against extended actuator plunger. Turn hex-end of plunger to obtain specified speed.

NOTE — *See Emission Control Tune-Up decal for throttle lever actuator adjustment speeds.*

1981 Exhaust Emission Systems

GENERAL MOTORS VACUUM DIAGRAMS

MODEL IDENTIFICATION

Truck models, listed in tables, are identified using manufacturers letter and number designations. The letters identify the vehicle model series (i.e., "C" is conventional chassis, including Pickup, Blazer and Suburban). The number reference identifies the vehicles load capacity. Refer to following charts for actual letter and number designations.

VEHICLE SERIES IDENTIFICATION	
Vehicle Series	I.D. Letter
Conventional Chassis (2-WD)	C
Conventional Chassis (4-WD)	K
Conventional Van Chassis	G
Forward Control/Stepvan Chassis	P

VEHICLE LOAD CAPACITY		
Chevrolet Number	GMC Number	Ton Capacity
10	1500	1/2
20	2500	3/4
30	3500	1

GENERAL MOTORS VACUUM DIAGRAM REFERENCE CHART

Vehicle Model, Series & Engine	Application	Transmission	Equipment Note	Figure Number
LIGHT DUTY 4.1L (250") 6-Cyl. C10/20	Fed.	Man.		1
	Fed.	Man.	Aux. Tk.	2
	Fed.	Auto.		①
	Fed.	Auto.	Aux. Tk.	3
	Fed. & Calif.	Man.	A.I.R.	4
	Fed. & Calif.	Man.	Aux. Tk. & A.I.R.	5
	Fed. & Calif.	Auto.	A.I.R.	6
	Fed. & Calif.	Auto.	Aux. Tk. & A.I.R.	7
	Fed.	Man.		8
	Fed.	Man.		9
	Calif.	Auto.		①
	Fed.	Man.	Aux. Tk.	10
K10/20	Fed.	Auto.		①
	Fed.	Auto.	Aux. Tk.	3
	Fed.	Man.		1
G10/20	Fed.	Man.		1
	Fed.	Auto.		11
MEDIUM DUTY 4.1L (250") 6-Cyl. C10 & K10	Calif.	Man.	A.I.R.	4
HEAVY DUTY 4.8L (292") 6-Cyl. C20/30 & K20/30	Fed. & Calif.	Man. & Auto.	A.I.R.	12
	Fed & Calif.	Man. & Auto.	A.I.R.	13
P20/30	Fed. & Calif.	Man. & Auto.	A.I.R.	12
LIGHT DUTY 5.0L (305") V8 C10/20 & K10/20	Fed.	Man.		14
	Fed.	Auto.		①
	Fed.	Man.		15
	Fed.	Auto.		16
	Fed.	Man.	A.I.R.	17
	Fed. & Calif.	Auto.	A.I.R.	18
	Calif.	Auto.	A.I.R.	19

1981 Exhaust Emission Systems 3-77

GENERAL MOTORS VACUUM DIAGRAMS (Cont.)

GENERAL MOTORS VACUUM DIAGRAM REFERENCE CHART				
Vehicle Model, Series & Engine	Application	Transmission	Equipment Note	Figure Number
LIGHT DUTY (Cont.) G10/20	Fed.	Man.		14
	Fed. & Calif.	Auto.	A.I.R.	18
	Fed. & Calif.	Auto.	A.I.R.	19
MEDIUM DUTY 5.0L (305″) V8 C20	Calif.	Auto.	A.I.R.	19
LIGHT DUTY 5.7L (350″) V8 C10/20 & K10/20	Calif.	Auto.		①
	Fed.	Man.		①
	Fed.	Auto.	A.I.R.	20
	Fed.	Auto.	A.I.R.	18
G10/20	Fed.	Man.	A.I.R.	21
	Fed.	Auto.	A.I.R.	22
	Fed. & Calif.	Auto.	A.I.R.	19
5.7L (350″) Diesel V8	Fed. & Calif.	Auto.		①
MEDIUM DUTY 5.7L (350″) V8 C10/20	Calif.	Auto.	A.I.R.	18
G10/20	Calif.	Auto.	A.I.R.	19
HEAVY DUTY 5.7L (350″) V8 C20/30 & K20/30	Fed.	Man. & Auto.	A.I.R.	23
	Fed.	Man. & Auto.	A.I.R.	24
	Fed. & Calif.	Man. & Auto.	A.I.R.	25
G30 & P20/30	Fed.	Man. & Auto.	A.I.R.	24
	Fed. & Calif.	Man. & Auto.	A.I.R.	25
	Fed.	Man.	A.I.R.	26
HEAVY DUTY 7.4L (454″) V8 C20/30 & K20/30	Fed. & Calif.	Man. & Auto.	A.I.R.	27
	Fed. & Calif.	Man. & Auto.	A.I.R.	28

① – Diagrams not available from General Motors.

EMISSION CONTROL DEVICE ABBREVIATIONS

AIR – Air Injection Reactor
DVTR – Diverter Valve
EFE – Early Fuel Evaporation
EGR – Exhaust Gas Recirculation
PCV – Positive Crankcase Ventilation
TRC – Throttle Return Control
TVS – Thermal Vacuum Switch

1981 Exhaust Emission Systems

GENERAL MOTORS VACUUM DIAGRAMS (Cont.)

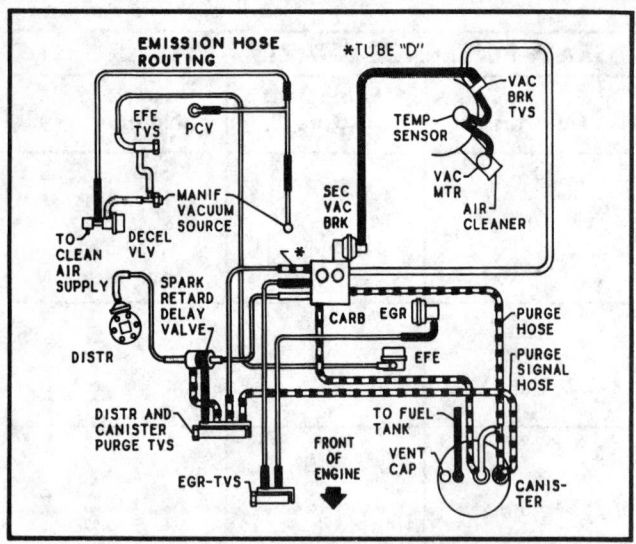

Fig. 1 4.1L 6-Cyl. Federal Manual Transmission

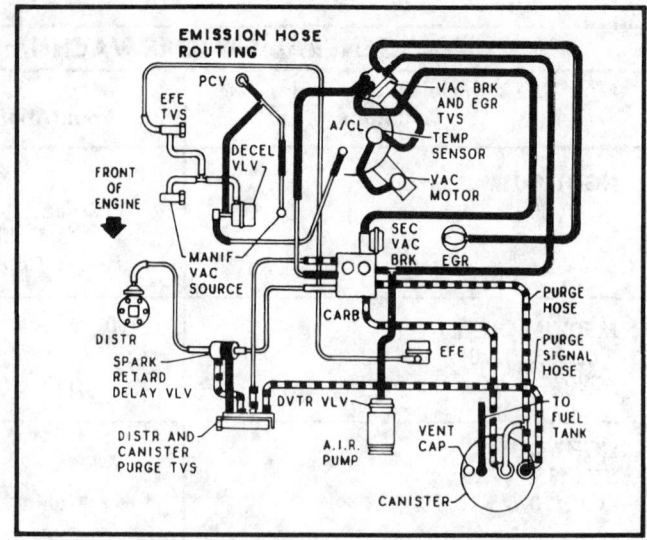

Fig. 4 4.1L 6-Cyl. Federal & California Manual Transmission

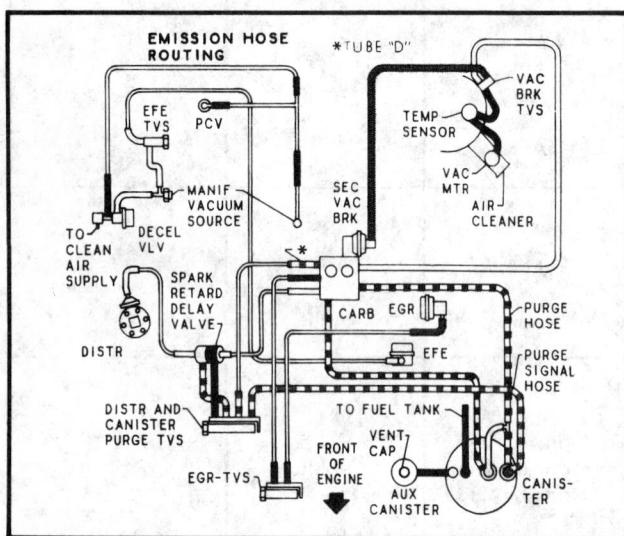

Fig. 2 4.1L 6-Cyl. Federal Manual Transmission & Auxiliary Tank

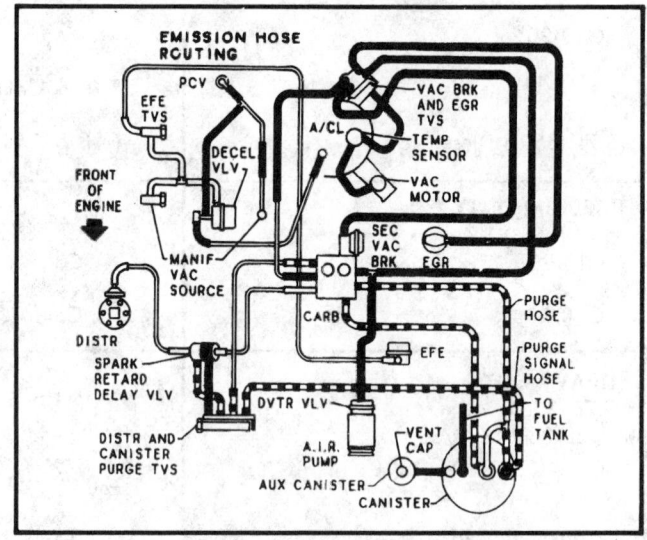

Fig. 5 4.1L 6-Cyl. Federal & California Manual Transmission & Auxiliary Tank

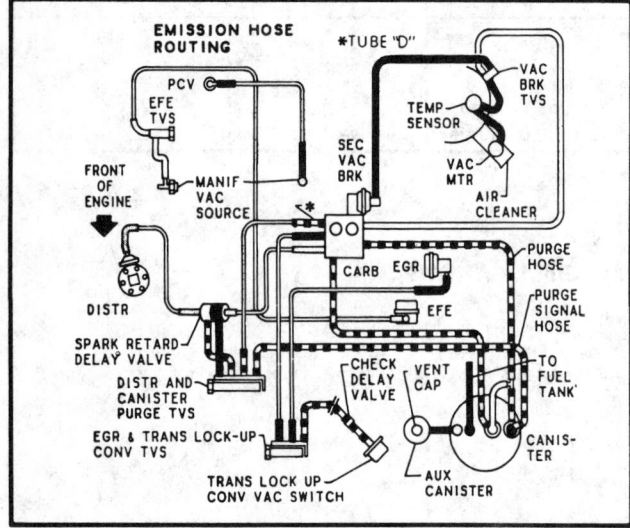

Fig. 3 4.1L 6-Cyl. Federal Automatic Transmission & Auxiliary Tank

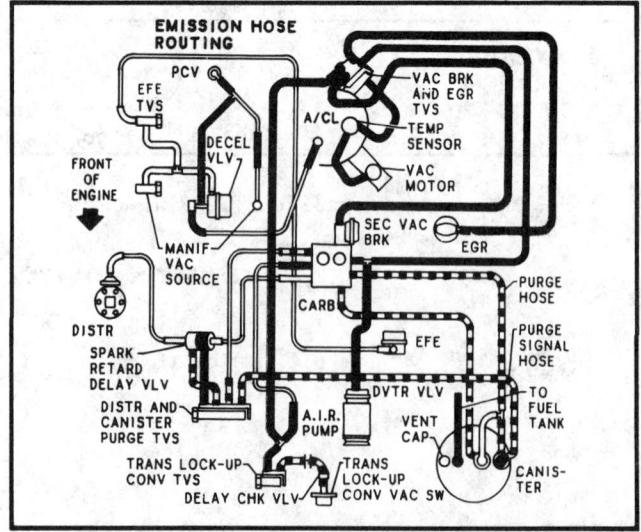

Fig. 6 4.1L 6-Cyl. Federal & California Automatic Transmission

GENERAL MOTORS VACUUM DIAGRAMS (Cont.)

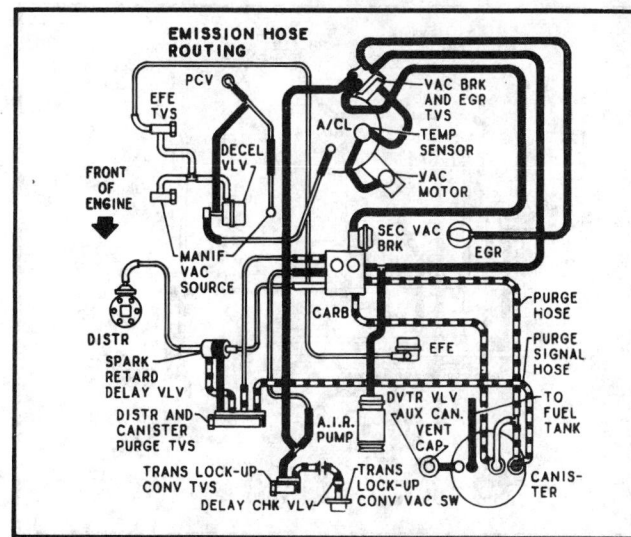

Fig. 7   4.1L 6-Cyl. Federal & California Automatic Transmission & Auxiliary Tank

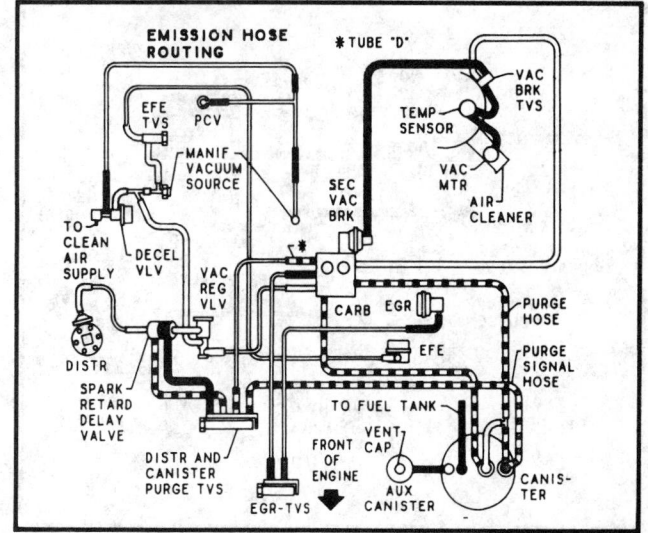

Fig. 10   4.1L 6-Cyl. Federal Manual Transmission & Auxiliary Tank

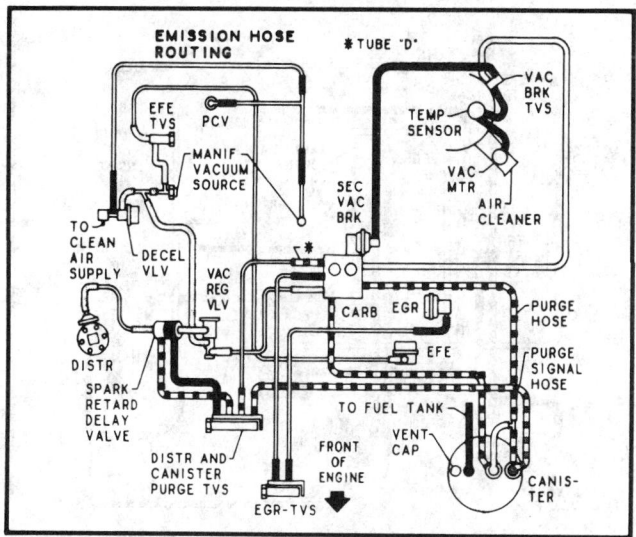

Fig. 8   4.1L 6-Cyl. Federal Manual Transmission

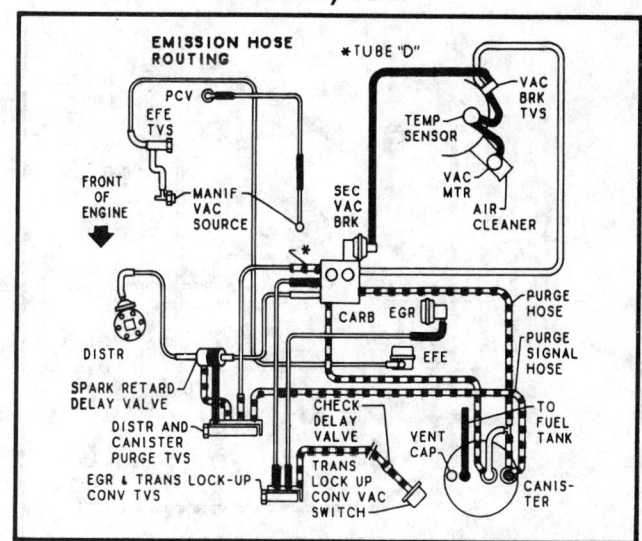

Fig. 11   4.1L 6-Cyl. Federal Automatic Transmission

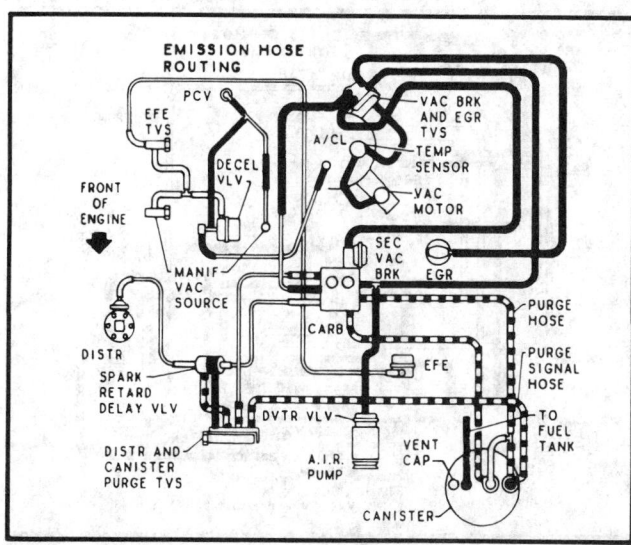

Fig. 9   4.1L 6-Cyl. Federal Manual Transmission

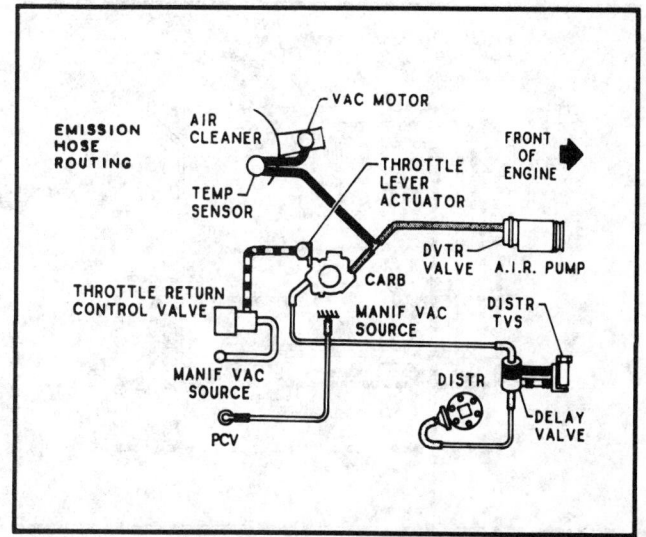

Fig. 12   4.8L 6-Cyl. Federal & California Manual & Automatic Transmission

1981 Exhaust Emission Systems

GENERAL MOTORS VACUUM DIAGRAMS (Cont.)

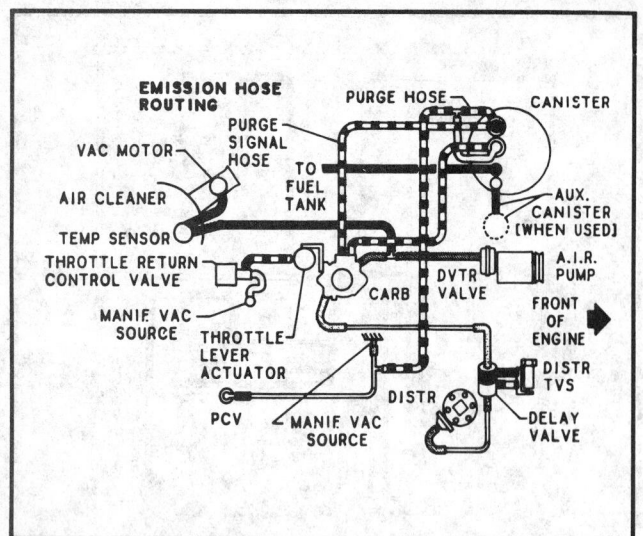

Fig. 13   4.8L 6-Cyl. Federal & California Manual & Automatic Transmission

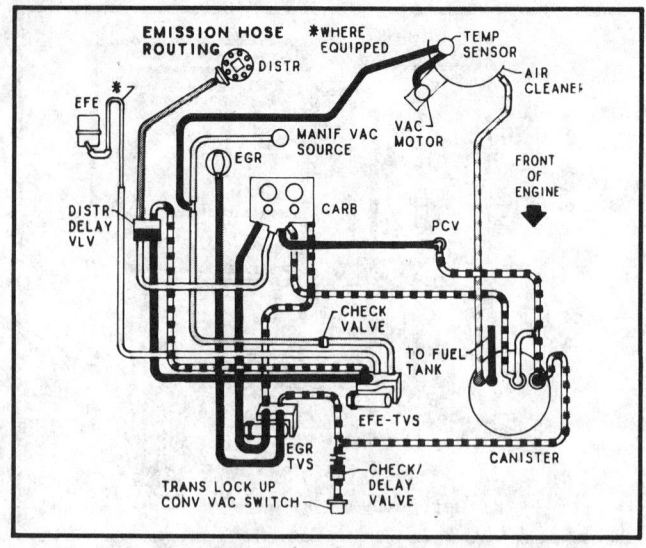

Fig. 16   5.0L V8 Federal Automatic Transmission

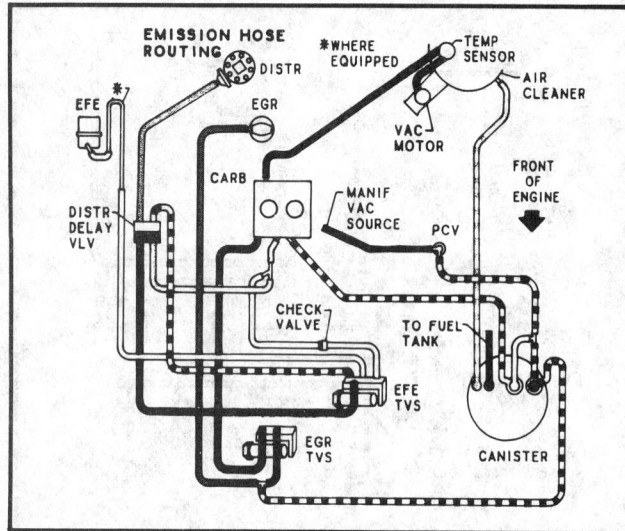

Fig. 14   5.0L V8 Federal Manual Transmission

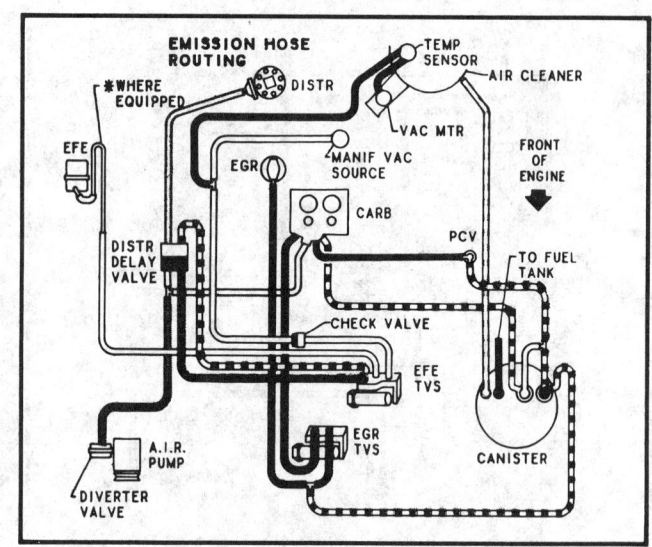

Fig. 17   5.0L V8 Federal Manual Transmission

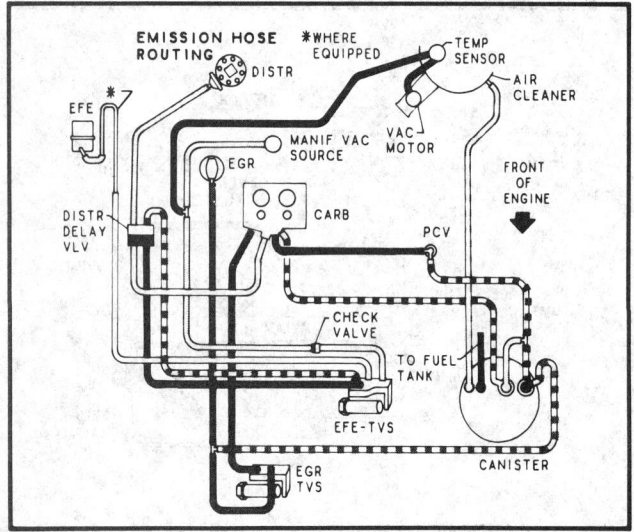

Fig. 15   5.0L V8 Federal Manual Transmission

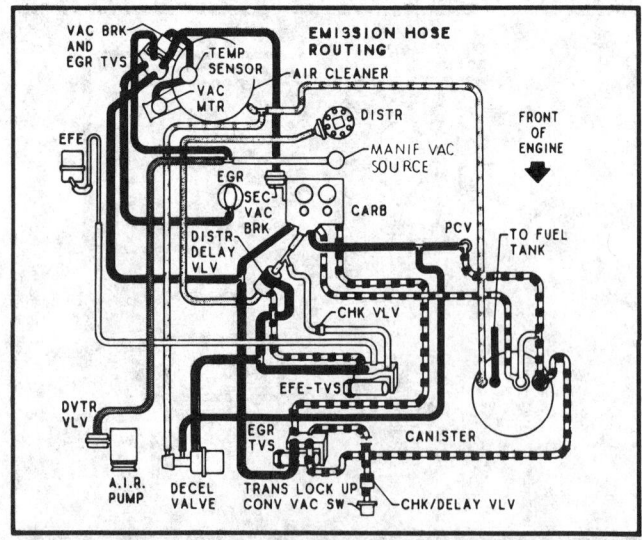

Fig. 18   5.0L V8 Federal & California Automatic Transmission

GENERAL MOTORS VACUUM DIAGRAMS (Cont.)

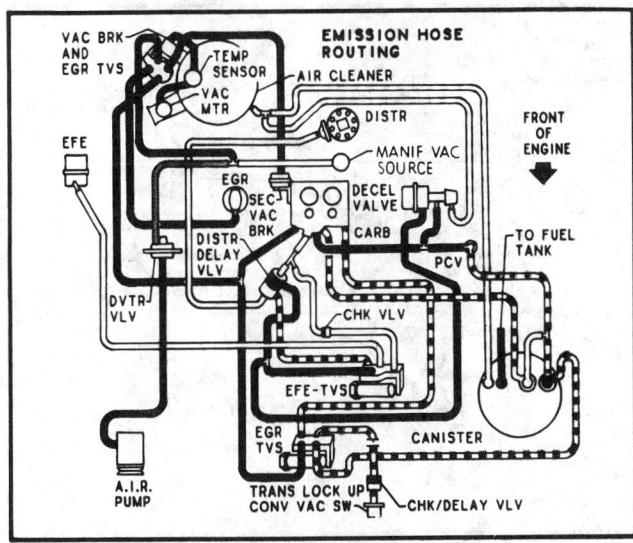

Fig. 19   5.0L V8 Federal & California Automatic Transmission

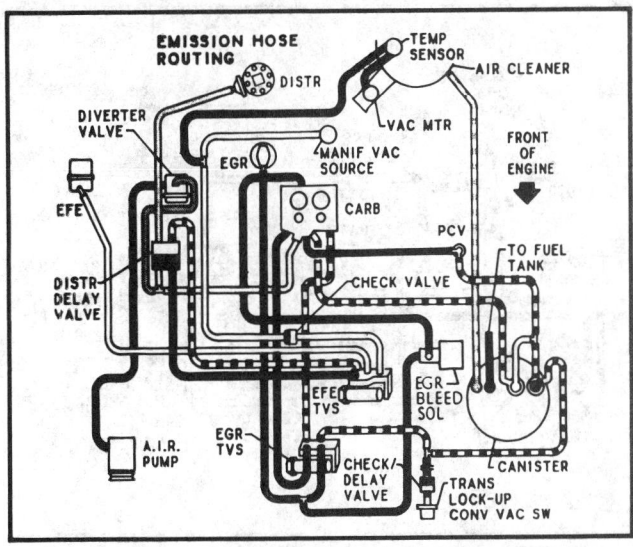

Fig. 22   5.7L V8 Federal Automatic Transmission

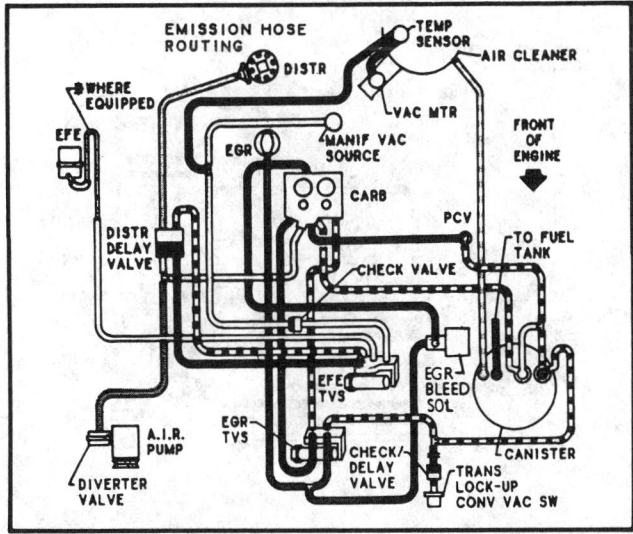

Fig. 20   5.7L V8 Federal Automatic Transmission

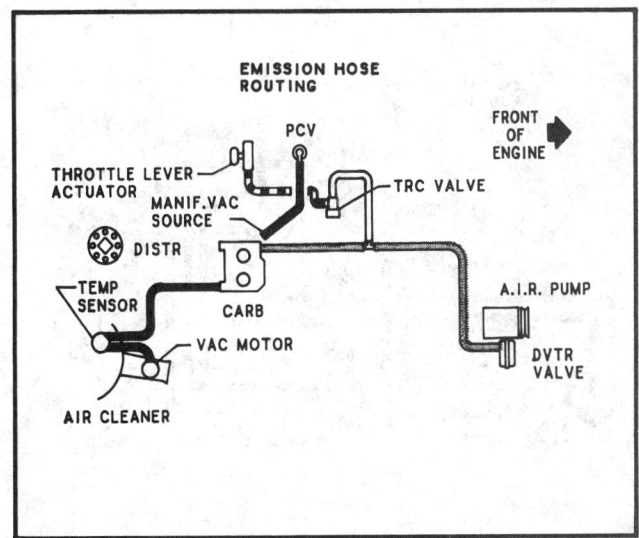

Fig. 23   5.7L V8 Federal Manual & Automatic Transmission

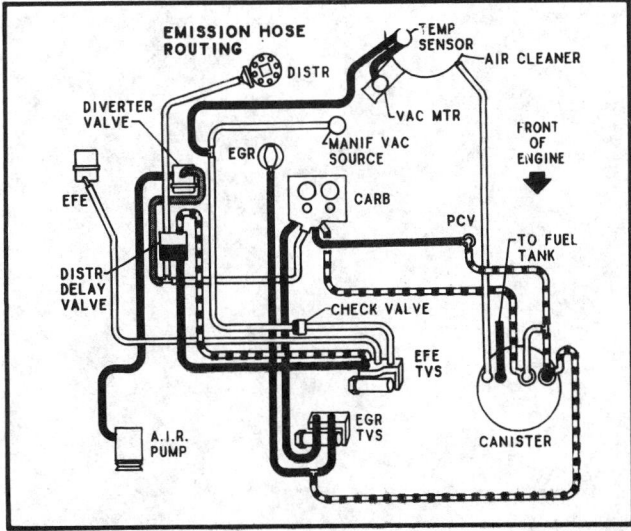

Fig. 21   5.7L V8 Federal Manual Transmission

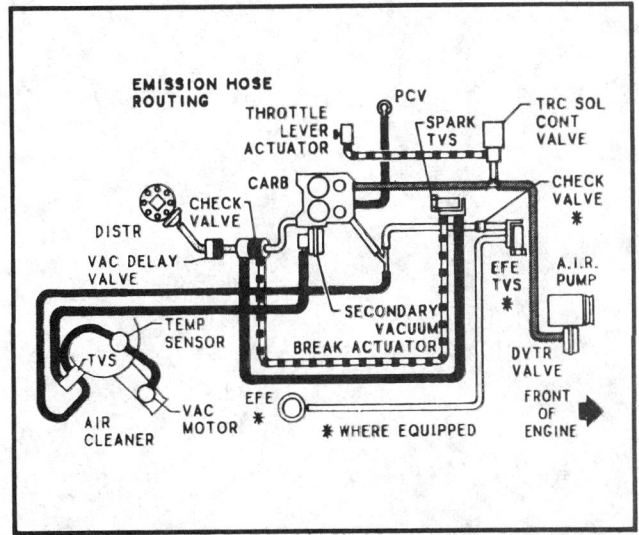

Fig. 24   5.7L V8 Federal Manual & Automatic Transmission

1981 Exhaust Emission Systems

GENERAL MOTORS VACUUM DIAGRAMS (Cont.)

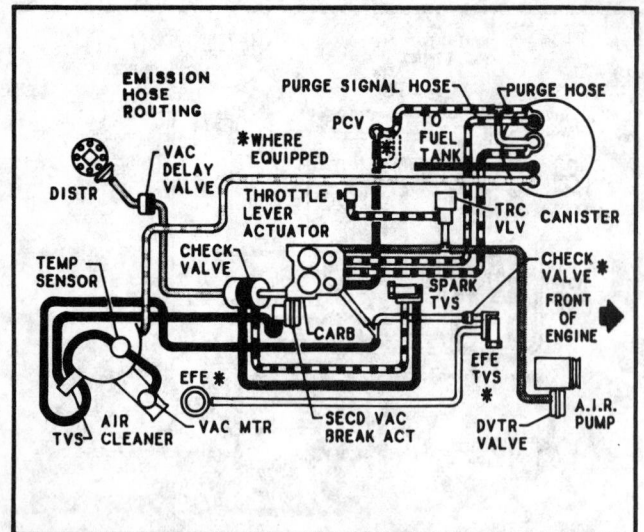

Fig. 25 *5.7L V8 Federal & California Manual & Automatic Transmission*

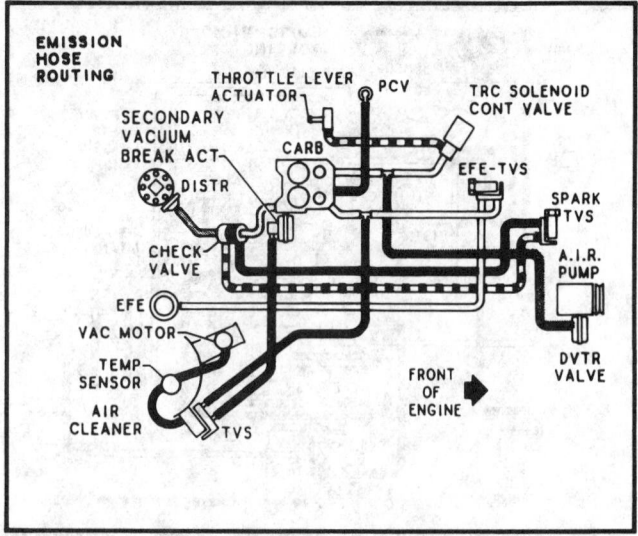

Fig. 27 *7.4L V8 Federal & California Manual & Automatic Transmission*

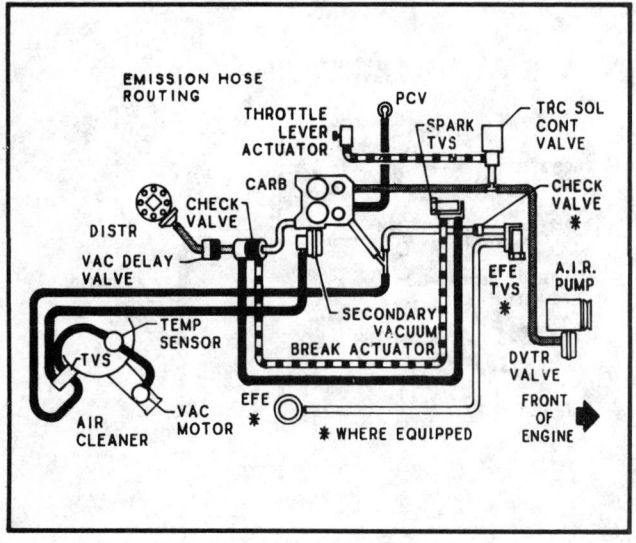

Fig. 26 *5.7L V8 Federal Manual Transmission*

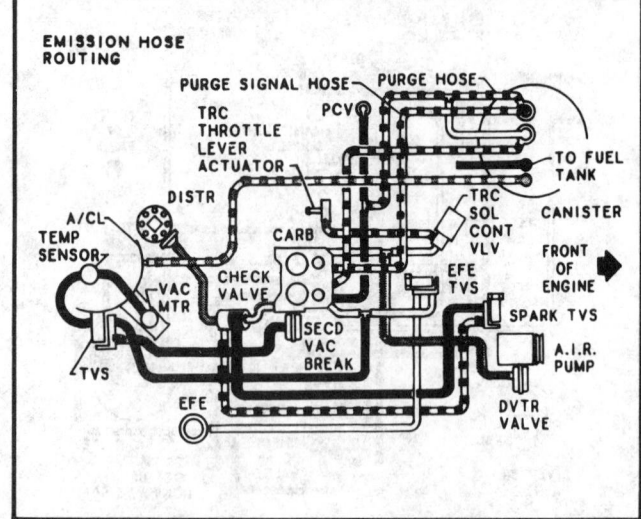

Fig. 28 *7.4L V8 Federal & California Manual & Automatic Transmission*

JEEP SYSTEMS & SERVICE PROCEDURES

DESCRIPTION

Several systems are used to control emission of pollutants. System usage depends on model, engine, and transmission combinations. Each system is designed to control a particular vehicle emission. In addition, specially calibrated carburetors, distributors and modified combustion chambers are used with these systems.

Thermostatic Air Cleaner — The TAC assembly is used to keep the incoming air in the carburetor at a stable temperature which is able to promote complete combustion (resulting in fewer emissions). The system consists of a heat shroud at the exhaust manifold, a hot air hose, an air cleaner assembly with a thermal sensor, an air door, a vacuum motor and a delay valve on all models. *For additional information, see "Jeep Thermostatic Air Cleaners" in this section.*

Air Injection — Air injection system consists of an air pump, diverter valve, check valve, and various air distribution lines necessary to inject fresh air adjacent to exhaust valves. Injection of fresh air adjacent to exhaust valves creates an afterburn which further consumes unburned material in engine's exhaust. *For additional information, see "Air Injection Systems— Air Pump Type" in this section.*

EGR — Exhaust gas recirculation system uses a vacuum operated EGR valve to introduce metered amounts of exhaust gas into engine's combustion chambers. This introduction of inert exhaust gas lowers peak combustion temperatures and thus lowers NOx formations.

C-4 Computer Emission System — Use on 4 cylinder California "CJ" & Scrambler models, this system reduces exhaust emissions by maintaining an optimum air/fuel mixture. System consists of an Electronic Control Module, an oxygen sensor in the exhaust manifold, a mixture control solenoid, 4 sensors to monitor engine conditions and a 3-way catalytic converter.

Computerized Emission Control (CEC) System — Used on 6-cylinder models, the CEC system closely controls air/fuel ratio through a feedback system from an oxygen sensor in the exhaust system. The major components of this system include an exhaust gas oxygen sensor, vacuum switches, temperature switches, a Micro Computer Unit (MCU) and a special carburetor with a stepper motor that controls air/fuel mixture.

Spark Control Systems — Jeep spark control systems are designed to control vacuum spark advance operation. Two systems are used: Coolant Temperature Override (CTO)and Non-Linear Vacuum Regulator (NLVR). The CTO system improves driveability by alternating vacuum advance source between manifold vacuum and carburetor ported vacuum, depending upon temperature. The NLVR system supplies vacuum advance unit with a regulated combination of manifold and carburetor ported vacuum when engine load is low and switches to supply only carburetor ported vacuum as load increases. In addition, a forward delay valve, a reverse delay valve, a thermal vacuum spark control valve and a vacuum spark control delay valve are used with various applications.

Catalytic Converter — The converter is installed in the vehicle's exhaust system to aid in the reduction of exhaust emissions. This unit changes unburned hydrocarbons (HC) and carbon monoxide (CO) into water vapor and carbon dioxide. *For additional information, see Catalytic Converter article in this section.*

Positive Crankcase Ventilation — Positive crankcase ventilation system is used to control crankcase blow-by gases. This system takes blow-by gases from crankcase and recirculates them back into combustion chamber for reburning. Key device in PCV system is vacuum-controlled PCV valve. *For additional information, see Crankcase Ventilation article in this section.*

Evaporative Emission Control — All models use this closed tank (sealed) system, which retains raw fuel vapors and routes them to intake manifold for burning. A carbon canister stores vapors until they are burned. *For additional information, see appropriate Fuel Evaporation System article in this section.*

SERVICE PROCEDURES

IGNITION TIMING

See appropriate article in TUNE-UP SERVICE PROCEDURES.

CARBURETION

Carburetor Models	
Application	**Models**
2.5L (151") 4-Cyl. 2-Bbl.	
Federal	Rochester 2SE
Calif.	Rochester E2SE
2.5L (258") 6-Cyl. 2-Bbl.	Carter BBD
5.0L (304") V8 2-Bbl.	Motorcraft 2150
6.0L (360") V8 2-Bbl.	Motorcraft 2150

IDLE SPEED & MIXTURE

See appropriate article in TUNE-UP SERVICE PROCEDURES.

JEEP THERMOSTATIC AIR CLEANER

All Models

DESCRIPTION

All Jeep vehicles use a system for pre-heating the air entering the carburetor. This system is part of the air cleaner and maintains air temperature at a point where the carburetor can be calibrated at a leaner setting to reduce hydrocarbon emissions and improve engine performance during warm-up.

Jeep systems are vacuum operated and consist of a heat shroud on the exhaust manifold, a hot air duct, a thermal sensor switch, a vacuum motor, an air valve assembly and a reverse delay valve.

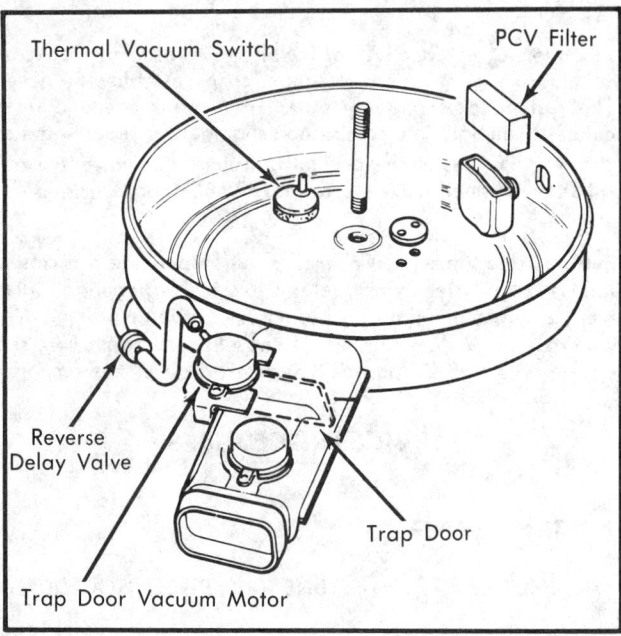

Fig. 1   Jeep Thermostatic Air Cleaner Assembly

OPERATION

During engine warm-up, the temperature sensor switch applies vacuum to the vacuum motor. The air diverter valve is held in the ON position. Exhaust manifold heated air flows to the air cleaner. As the temperature of incoming air increases to 90°F, the temperature sensor opens the vacuum line to the atmosphere allowing spring pressure to push the valve to the OFF position. Air now flows from the outside, through the air cleaner duct to the carburetor.

AIR CLEANER TRAP DOOR

On California vehicles, a spring-loaded trap door is built-in to the air cleaner to close off the air cleaner when the engine is shut-off. The door is vacuum operated.

REVERSE DELAY VALVE

A reverse delay valve is installed in the vacuum line in some vehicles to prevent the trap door from closing during low engine vacuum periods. The valve provides about 9 seconds delay before allowing the trap door to close completely.

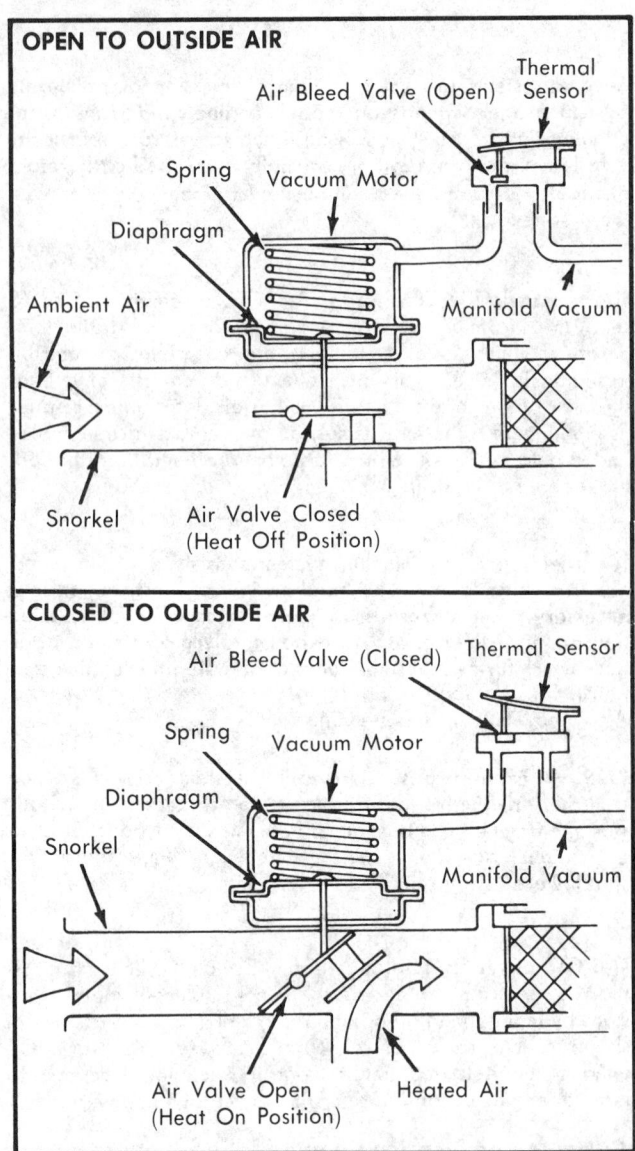

Fig. 2   Cross Section of Jeep Thermostatic Air Cleaner Assembly

TESTING

VACUUM MOTOR & TEMPERATURE SENSOR

1) Remove air cleaner assembly from vehicle and allow to cool to room temperature. Sight through air cleaner duct and observe position of air diverter valve. It should be fully open to outside air.

2) Reinstall assembly on carburetor and connect hot air duct and manifold vacuum hose. Start engine and observe position of air diverter valve. It should be fully closed to outside air.

3) Move throttle lever rapidly to ½ to ¾ opening and release. Air diverter valve should open and then close again. Allow engine to warm to operating temperature and observe position of air diverter valve. It should be fully open to outside air.

JEEP THERMOSTATIC AIR CLEANER (Cont.)

4) If valve does not move to fully close off outside air at 83°F or less with vacuum applied, check for binding of the duct, vacuum leaks in hose connections or disconnected vacuum motor. If valve mechanism operates freely and no vacuum leaks are detected, connect a hose from intake manifold vacuum source directly to vacuum motor.

5) If diverter valve now moves to close off outside air, replace thermal sensor switch. If valve still does not move to close off outside air, replace air cleaner assembly and vacuum motor assembly.

TRAP DOOR

1) With engine off, remove air cleaner and check position of trap door. It should be closed.

2) Remove vacuum hose from intake manifold vacuum source and apply an external vacuum source of approximately 2-4 in. Hg. Trap door should open.

3) If door does not open, apply vacuum directly to vacuum motor. If door does not open, check for binding and adjust as necessary. If door swings freely, replace vacuum motor.

4) If door opens during step **3)**, check vacuum hose for blockage, cracks or leaks. Correct as necessary and retest as specified in step **2)**.

5) If hoses are not defective, remove reverse delay valve, join vacuum hose and retest from step **2)**. If door opens, replace reverse delay valve.

REVERSE DELAY VALVE

Remove vacuum hose from red end of valve and apply an external vacuum source of approximately 2-4 in. Hg. With clock, or watch in view, measure time required for vacuum to be eliminated through valve. If time is less than 4.5 seconds, or more than 13.2 seconds, replace reverse delay valve.

1981 Exhaust Emission Systems

JEEP EXHAUST GAS RECIRCULATION

DESCRIPTION

The purpose of the exhaust gas recirculation (EGR) system is to limit the formation of oxides of nitrogen (NOx) emissions. This is done by reducing the high peak combustion temperatures at which NOx is formed. By reintroducing some exhaust gas back into the combustion chamber, the high temperatures are avoided and thus NOx emission formation is reduced.

System consists of a vacuum-operated EGR valve and a coolant temperature override (CTO) switch. In addition, some models are equipped with an air cleaner-mounted thermal vacuum switch (TVS), and some models are equipped with an EGR vacuum dump valve.

OPERATION

When EGR valve receives a vacuum signal from the carburetor, through the CTO switch, EGR valve opens and meters gases from exhaust manifold into intake manifold. Individual component operation follows:

EGR VALVE

The EGR valve is mounted on a spacer plate located beneath the carburetor on 4 cylinder models, on a machined surface at the rear of the intake manifold on V8 models, and on the side of the intake manifold on 6 cylinder models. Exhaust gas is drawn from the exhaust crossover passage in V8 and 4 cylinder engines and from an area near the heat riser in 6 cylinder engines. Two types of EGR valves are used: a valve without back-pressure sensor and a valve with integral back-pressure sensor.

EGR Valve w/o Integral Back-Pressure Sensor — EGR valves are calibrated by the use of different shapes of the valve pintles. The valve is normally held closed by a spring (above the diaphragm). The valve opens by overcoming spring tension when vacuum is sensed through the coolant temperature override switch (CTO) and the back-pressure sensor (if used).

EGR Valve w/Integral Back-Pressure Sensor — Calibration is accomplished by the use of different diaphragm spring loads and flow control orifices. This integral type unit combines the EGR valve and back-pressure sensor functions into one component. A restrictor plate is required with some engines.

Exhaust gas exerts back-pressure inside the exhaust manifold whenever the engine is running. This pressure is conducted through the hollow pintle stem into the EGR diaphragm control chamber. If this pressure is great enough to overcome spring tension against the diaphragm, the diaphragm is moved against the bleed valve and exhaust gas flow begins.

CTO SWITCH

The coolant temperature override (CTO) switch is located in the coolant passage at right rear of cylinder head on 4 cylinder engines, at the coolant passage of the intake manifold, or at right rear corner of intake manifold near EGR valve on V8 engines, or at left front side of cylinder block on 6 cylinder engines. The inner port of the switch is connected to the EGR spark port on the carburetor and the outer port is connected to the EGR valve, or TVS.

Switch opens at 100°F for 4 cylinder engines, or 115°F for 6 and 8 cylinder engines. Below these temperatures, no EGR is possible.

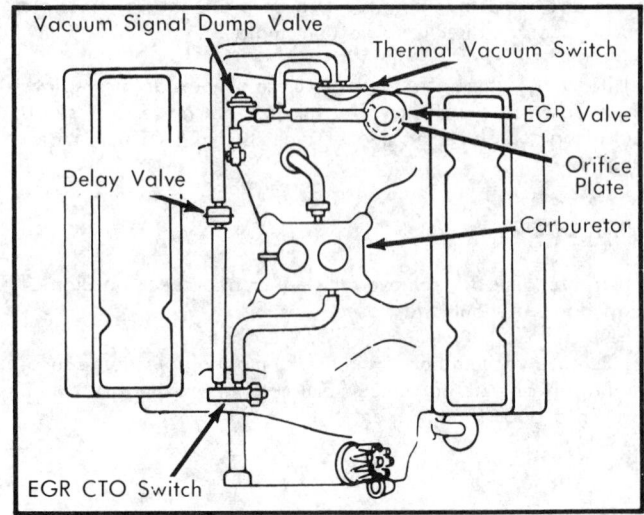

Fig. 1   Typical V8 Engine EGR System

THERMAL VACUUM SWITCH (TVS)

Used only on 6 and 8 cylinder engines, this switch is located in the air cleaner and acts as an on-off switch for the EGR system. It is controlled by ambient temperature in the air cleaner. The switch controls vacuum passage between CTO switch and the EGR valve. Below a pre-set temperature, TVS blocks passage of vacuum, delaying EGR operation and improving cold driveability.

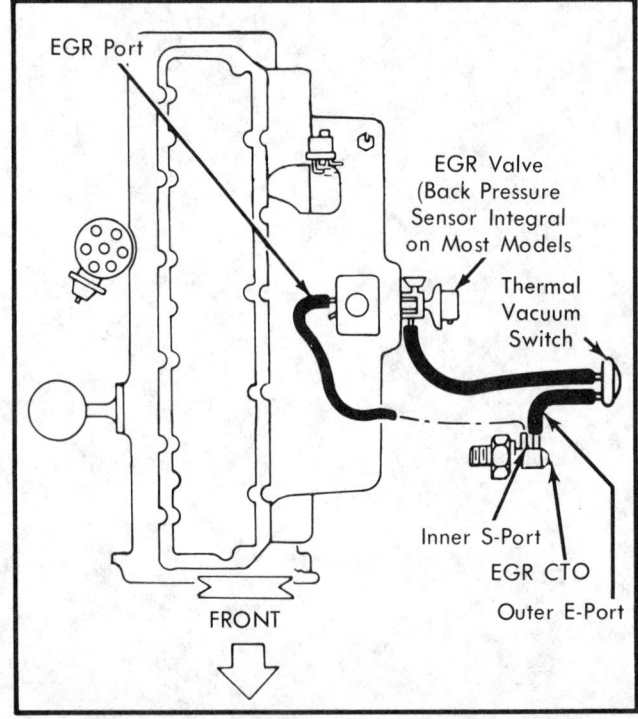

Fig. 2   Typical 6 Cylinder Engine EGR System

JEEP EXHAUST GAS RECIRCULATION (Cont.)

EGR DUMP VALVE

Used on some models, the EGR dump valve is connected in series with the vacuum source and the EGR valve. Valve is used to eliminate EGR function at low vacuum levels. When vacuum drops below a predetermined level, the valve "dumps" vacuum rather than allowing it to flow to EGR valve.

FORWARD DELAY VALVE

The forward delay valve is located between the EGR CTO switch and the EGR valve. It modifies the initial vacuum signal applied to the EGR valve by delaying the full vacuum force.

TESTING

EGR VALVE

Valve Opening Test — 1) With engine at normal operating temperature and at curb idle, rapidly open and close throttle (open throttle sufficiently to obtain at least 1500 RPM). A definite movement should be noticed in the EGR diaphragm.

2) If diaphragm does not move, probable causes are: faulty vacuum signal to EGR; defective EGR diaphragm or defective back-pressure sensor diaphragm (if equipped); or leaks in vacuum lines or connections.

Valve Closing Test — 1) With engine at normal operating temperature and at curb idle, manually depress EGR valve diaphragm. This should cause an immediate engine speed drop, indicating that EGR valve had been properly cutting off exhaust gas flow at idle.

2) If there is no change in RPM and engine is idling properly, exhaust gases are not reaching combustion chamber. There is probably a plugged passage between the EGR valve and the intake manifold.

3) If engine idles poorly and RPM is not greatly affected by moving the diaphragm, EGR valve is not closing off exhaust gas flow. Defective hoses, hose routing, or EGR valve is the problem.

CTO SWITCH

NOTE — *Engine coolant temperature must be below 100°F to perform this test.*

1) Check vacuum lines for leaks and correct routing. Disconnect vacuum line at back-pressure sensor (if equipped) or at EGR valve, and attach this line to a vacuum gauge.

2) Operate engine at 1500 RPM. No vacuum should be indicated on gauge. If vacuum is shown, replace CTO switch.

3) Idle engine until coolant temperature exceeds 100°F on 4 cylinder engines, or 115°F on 6 and 8 cylinder engines.

4) Accelerate engine to 1500 RPM. Carburetor ported vacuum should be shown on gauge. If not, replace CTO switch.

DUMP VALVE

1) With engine at normal operating temperature, remove dump valve vacuum hose from manifold and plug manifold connection.

2) Accelerate engine to 2000 RPM. Vacuum should be present at exhaust ports on bottom of valve. If not, replace valve.

3) Reconnect vacuum hose to manifold and accelerate engine to 2000 RPM. No vacuum should be felt at exhaust ports on bottom of valve. If vacuum is present, replace valve.

THERMAL VACUUM SWITCH

1) With air cleaner temperature below 40°F, disconnect vacuum hoses from TVS and connect vacuum source to large outlet.

2) Apply vacuum to TVS. Vacuum should be held. If not, replace TVS.

3) Start engine and warm air cleaner to 55°F, or above. Vacuum should not be held. If it is held, replace TVS.

1981 Exhaust Emission Systems

JEEP COMPUTER CONTROLLED CATALYTIC CONVERTER (C-4) SYSTEM

DESCRIPTION

The Computer Controlled Catalytic Converter (C-4) system is used on all California Jeep models equipped with 151" 4-cylinder engines. The C-4 system closely controls air/fuel ratio through a feedback system from an oxygen sensor mounted in the exhaust manifold. The major components of this system include an exhaust gas oxygen sensor, an electronic control module (ECM), a special electronically controlled carburetor (Rochester Model E2SE) and a three-way catalytic converter.

OPERATION

OXYGEN SENSOR

This unit is positioned in the exhaust manifold so it can sense exhaust gas composition as it comes from the engine. The sensor detects oxygen content in order to relay a signal to the ECM. This sensor is actually a (Zirconia) battery which reacts to oxygen levels by generating a voltage signal (100 to 900 millivolts) that is inversely proportionate to the amount of oxygen. If the oxygen content of exhaust gas is high (indicating a lean mixture), the voltage signal created by the sensor will be low. If oxygen content is low (indicating a rich mixture), the voltage signal to the ECM is high. The oxygen sensor should be replaced every 30,000 miles to ensure proper function.

ELECTRONIC CONTROL MODULE (ECM)

The ECM reads and computes the signal from the oxygen sensor. In response, it sends a proportionate signal to the mixture control solenoid (in carburetor), which creates either a lean or rich mixture, as required. The signal which is sent from the ECM to the mixture control solenoid is also modified by inputs from throttle position vacuum switches and coolant temperature sensor (CTS).

The ECM contains a replaceable integrated circuit "chip" which has stored data unique to each vehicle (i.e., axle ratio, body style, etc.). This is called a Programmable Read Only Memory (PROM). This PROM's memory system stores an average set of operating conditions with the ideal air/fuel ratio for these conditions. If any settings change from these stored conditions (as determined by engine sensors), the ECM will make necessary adjustments to bring engine back to the "ideal" set of conditions.

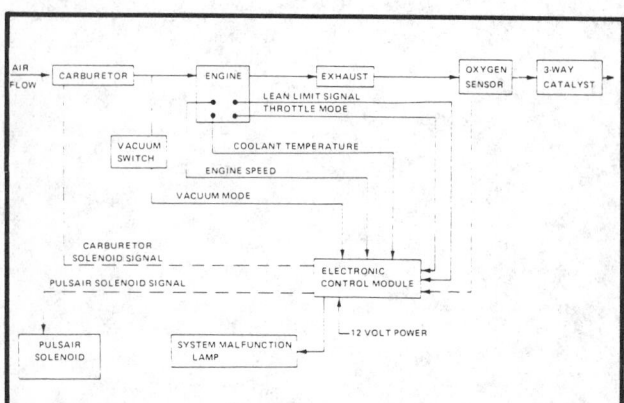

Fig. 1 Typical C-4 Flow Diagram Showing Operating Relationships

Before the ECM can begin in governing the air/fuel ratio, it is important to note that a minimum of 10 seconds must have elapsed after startup before any C-4 operation begins, engine coolant temperature must be above 150° F, and the oxygen sensor must be sufficiently hot (600° F) and putting out sufficient voltage before the ECM can react. During cold engine startup, the ECM is off-line and a fixed carburetor condition is maintained until proper warmup occurs.

CARBURETOR

Carburetors used in conjunction with the C-4 system are designed with an electrically operated solenoid in the fuel bowl. In the Rochester E2SE carburetor, this solenoid provides a controlled restriction to the main metering system. This solenoid responds to impulses (cycles) generated from the ECM to make the mixture leaner or richer, as determined by the system of engine sensors and switches.

NOTE – *For additional information, including adjustments and specifications, see Rochester E2SE carburetor article in FUEL SYSTEMS section of this manual.*

CATALYTIC CONVERTER

Proper emission control is accomplished with the special three-way catalytic converter which converts all 3 major pollutants (HC, CO and NOx). In order for this catalytic converter to be effective, precise control of the oxygen content of gases entering the converter is necessary, thus the need for the oxygen sensor, ECM and special carburetor.

ENGINE SENSORS & SWITCHES

Coolant Temperature Sensor (CTS) – The CTS senses engine coolant temperature and sends a proportionate signal to the ECM. It does not allow C-4 system operation (closed loop) while coolant temperature is below 150° F.

Wide Open Throttle (WOT) – This switch is used to detect full throttle condition. When activated, a signal from the WOT to ECM sets a temporary full rich mixture until throttle moves off wide open position. At which time, the C-4 system returns to pre-WOT operating conditions. This switch is closed at wide open throttle and opens with 5 in. Hg or more of ported vacuum.

Closed Throttle Switch – This switch detects closed or part throttle conditions and sends appropriate signal to ECM. This switch is used in conjunction with WOT to determine intermediate throttle positions. This switch is normally closed until 12 in. Hg or more manifold vacuum is present.

COMPONENT REPLACEMENT

OXYGEN SENSOR

Every 30,000 miles, it is necessary to replace oxygen sensor to prevent system failure. Replace sensor as follows:

Removal – Disconnect sensor electrical connector and spray sensor threads with suitable heat riser valve lube. Allow to soak for at least 5 minutes, then carefully unscrew oxygen sensor and remove.

JEEP COMPUTER CONTROLLED CATALYTIC CONVERTER (C-4) SYSTEM (Cont.)

Installation — Coat threads of new sensor with anti-seize compound and carefully install. Tighten to 25 ft. lbs.

VACUUM SWITCHES

Removal & Installation — Note vacuum hose position and disconnect hoses from switch assembly. Disconnect electrical connectors. Remove switch and bracket assembly from fender panel. Replace vacuum switch assembly as a unit (both switches and bracket). Install by reversing removal procedure.

ELECTRONIC CONTROL MODULE

Removal & Installation — Remove ECM and mounting bracket as an assembly from left kick panel near parking brake. Disconnect electrical connectors. Remove ECM from mounting bracket. Install new ECM to mounting bracket, connect electrical connectors and install assembly to kick panel. DO NOT ground bracket. Bracket is insulated from vehicle ground.

PROGRAMMABLE READ ONLY MEMORY (PROM)

Removal — 1) Remove ECM from vehicle. Remove access cover screw and cover from ECM. PROM "chip" removal and insertion tool will be included with replacement unit. Remove tool from replacement kit.

2) Starting at opposite end from reference mark ("U2" stamped in ECM next to PROM and rectangular impression and paint stripe on PROM unit), gently work tang of removal tool beneath PROM unit with slight side to side rocking motion. DO NOT attempt to lift out PROM at this time. Remove extraction tool.

3) At reference end, push tang of tool beneath unit (above mating socket), making sure tang is completely under unit. Grasp PROM unit with thumb and forefinger and pull straight up and out.

Installation — 1) Place replacement PROM with leads pointing downward on a flat hard surface. Check part number of new unit to be sure it is the same as one being replaced.

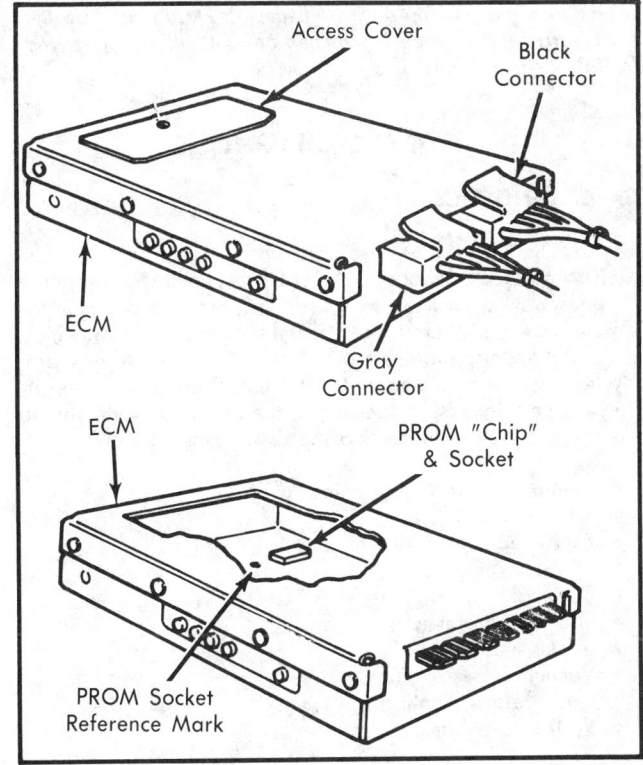

Fig. 2 PROM "Chip" Location

2) Press insertion tool firmly onto unit with reference paint stripe visible. Locate reference end of PROM to reference end of socket ("U2" stamped next to socket). Lightly mate unit with socket.

3) Inspect unit to be sure it is aligned properly and that no pins are bent. Now, fully install unit by pressing down firmly on insertion tool. Remove tool, install access cover and install ECM to vehicle. Start engine and observe "CHECK CARB" display for trouble codes.

NOTE — *If trouble code 51 is present after replacement, new unit is either installed backwards, is defective, is not fully*

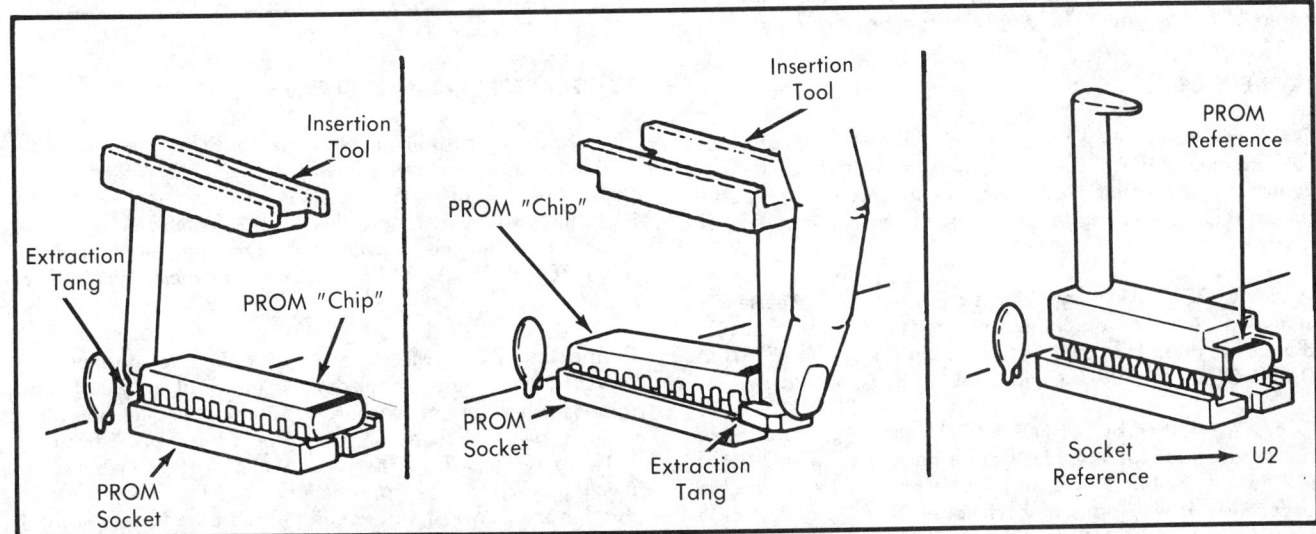

Fig. 3 PROM Removal and Installation Procedure Showing Insertion/Extraction Tool

JEEP COMPUTER CONTROLLED CATALYTIC CONVERTER (C-4) SYSTEM (Cont.)

seated or has bent pins. Whenever PROM is installed backwards and ignition is switched on, unit will be destroyed. In this event, replace unit.

TESTING & DIAGNOSIS

C-4 DIAGNOSTICS

The C-4 system may be suspected when engine performance, fuel economy or exhaust emissions are improper. A built-in diagnostic system is likely to activate if a problem occurs in the system (however, there is the possibilty of this not happening). If the C-4 system contains a problem, a "CHECK CARB" warning light will be activated on the instrument panel. If, however, the warning light is not activated, the following items should be checked before inspecting the C-4 system further:

- Ignition system (dist., timing, plugs, etc.)
- Air cleaner system
- Fuel evaporation system
- PCV system
- EGR valve
- Engine compression
- Intake manifold
- Vacuum hoses
- Carburetor mounting bolts
- Restricted exhaust

WARNING LIGHT CHECK

1) To test warning light and be sure the diagnostic system is operating, turn off the ignition switch, leave engine stopped and ground trouble code test lead located beneath dash (white wire with tracer, attached to ECM harness).

2) If the system is operating properly, when the ignition switch is turned to the "ON" position the "CHECK CARB" light will flash a code 12. Code 12 indicates proper operation of diagnostic system. The 12 will be flashed as follows: One flash, followed by a pause, and then two more flashes. After a longer pause, the code will repeat two more times.

NOTE — If fault is intermittent, "CHECK CARB" light may come on and then go out; however, fault problem will be stored in ECM memory so diagnosis can be performed.

TROUBLE CODES

C-4 diagnostic system is programmed to flash a series of codes through the "CHECK CARB" light. After light becomes activated by the system, it is necessary to ground the trouble code test lead, with engine running, so system can flash proper trouble code.

When "CHECK CARB" light comes on, trouble in C-4 system is indicated. A series of codes are programmed to assist in diagnosis and correction of problem. See C-4 SYSTEM DIAGNOSTIC TROUBLE CODES table for explanation.

Codes are flashed by "CHECK CARB" light after trouble code test lead is grounded. Codes will be flashed as follows: Light will flash 1, 2, 4 or 5 times to indicate first number of trouble code; then, it will (after a short pause) flash 1, 2, 3, 4 or 5 more times to indicate second number of code. After a longer pause, signal will repeat itself two more times.

FOR EXAMPLE — With trouble code test lead grounded and engine running, if problem is a shorted coolant sensor circuit, Code 14, light will flash one time, pause, then flash four times. A long pause, then repeat one-and-four flashes, a long pause and repeat again.

If more than one trouble spot is detected, one code series will flash, then the other code series will flash.

C-4 SYSTEM DIAGNOSTIC TROUBLE CODES	
Trouble Code	Area of Malfunction
12	No tach or reference signal to ECM.
13	Oxygen sensor circuit.
14	Shorted coolant sensor circuit.
15	Open coolant sensor circuit.
21 & 22	(At same time) Grounded WOT switch circuit.
22	Grounded closed throttle or WOT switch circuit.
23	Defective mixture control solenoid circuit.
44	Lean oxygen sensor.
44 & 45	(At same time) Faulty oxygen sensor.
45	Rich oxygen sensor.
51	Faulty PROM unit.
52 & 53	"CHECK CARB" light off — Intermittent ECM problem. "CHECK CARB" light on — Faulty ECM.
54	Faulty mixture control solenoid and/or ECM.
55	Faulty oxygen sensor circuit or ECM.

SYSTEM PERFORMANCE CHECK

Since it is not possible to store a code for every possible problem, one may develop in which the "CHECK CARB" light does NOT come on. If C-4 system is suspected, make a System Performance Check, using a dwell meter, ohmmeter, test light, voltmeter, tachometer, vacuum gauge and jumper wires. *Refer to SYSTEM PERFORMANCE CHECK chart later in this article.*

Connecting Dwell Meter — Set to 6-Cylinder position and connect dwell meter to mixture control solenoid test lead (green connector at carburetor). On normally operating engines, dwell at both idle and at part throttle will fluctuate between 10-50°. This is the "closed loop" system, meaning the dwell is varying due to reaction from the oxygen sensor through the ECM. At wide open throttle or cold engine dwell will be fixed (needle steady). This is "open loop" since oxygen sensor has no effect upon dwell.

JEEP COMPUTER CONTROLLED CATALYTIC CONVERTER (C-4) SYSTEM (Cont.)

CAUTION — *When attaching dwell meter, do not allow lead to touch ground. This includes hoses, since they are conductive.*

DIAGNOSTIC PROCEDURES

Follow the sequence given in the following "Diagnostic Charts" until proper problem identification and correction can be made. Refer to wiring diagram in this article to aid in diagnosis.

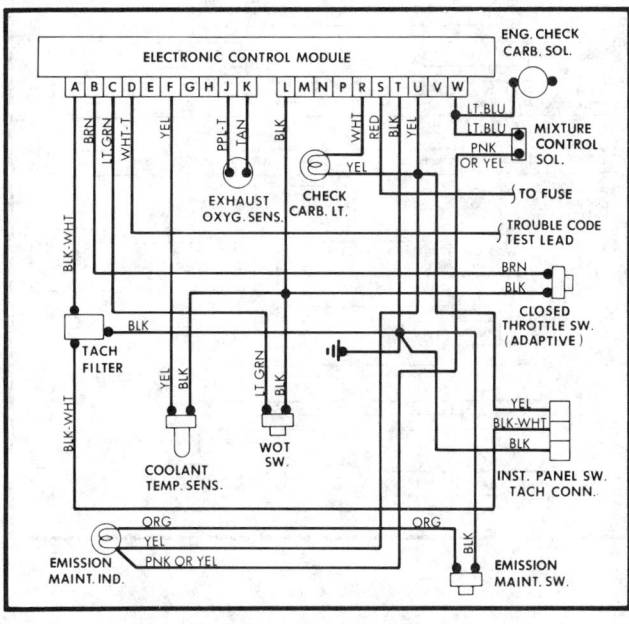

Fig. 4   C-4 System Wiring Diagram for 1981 California Jeep 4-Cylinder Models

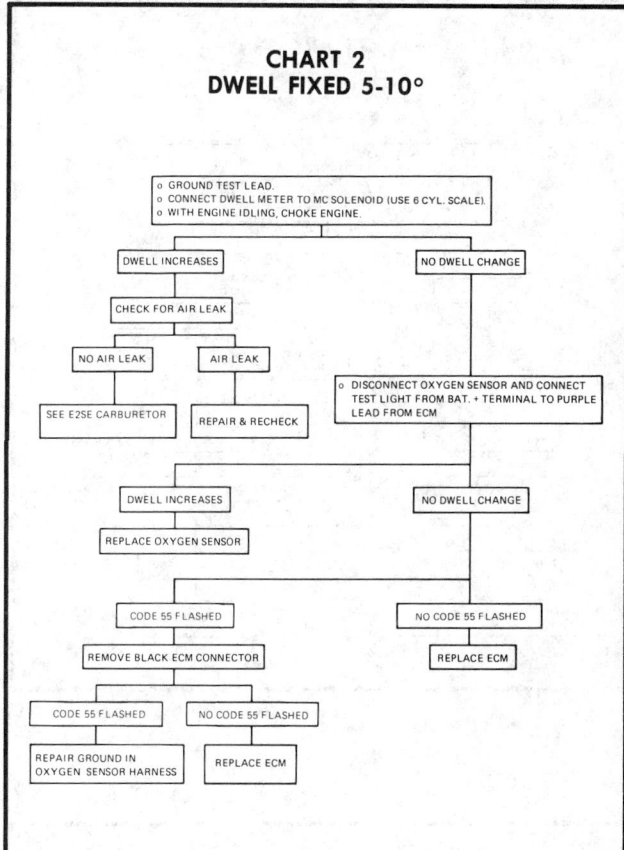

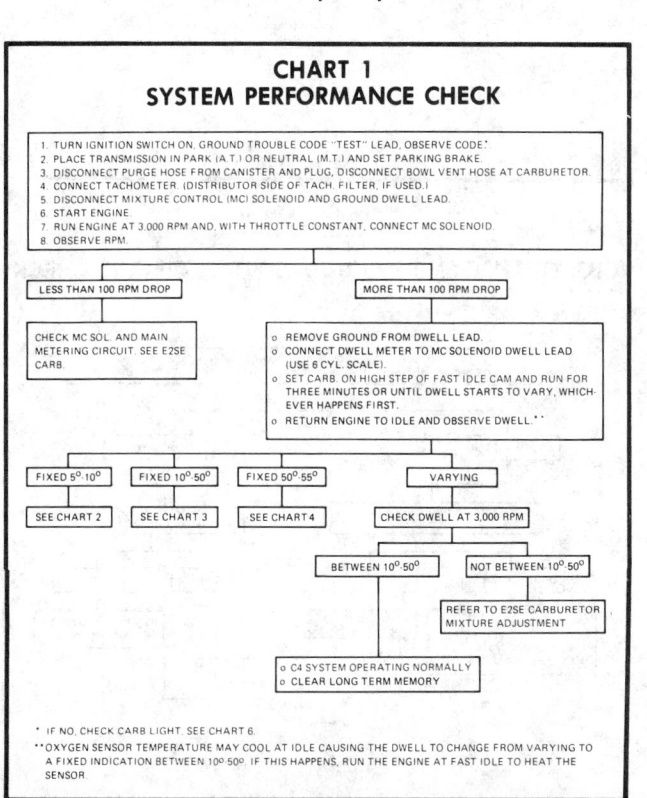

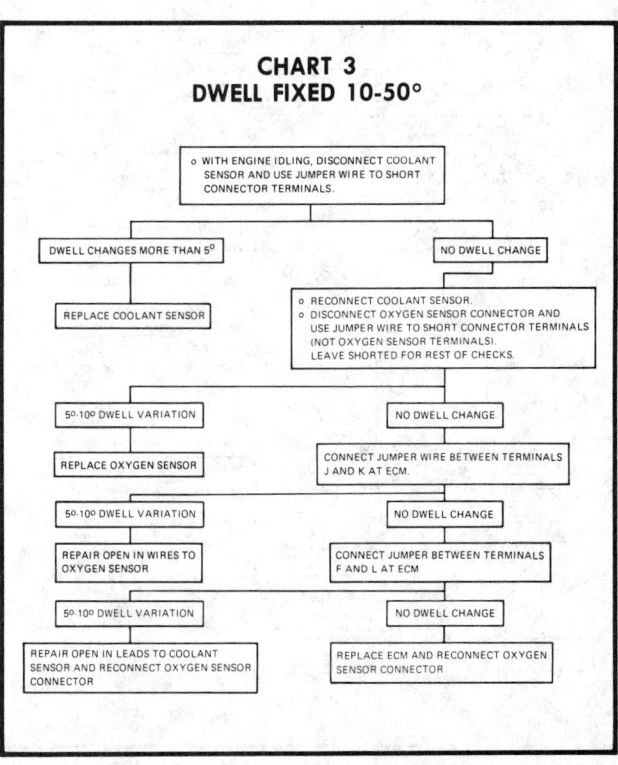

JEEP COMPUTER CONTROLLED CATALYTIC CONVERTER (C-4) SYSTEM (Cont.)

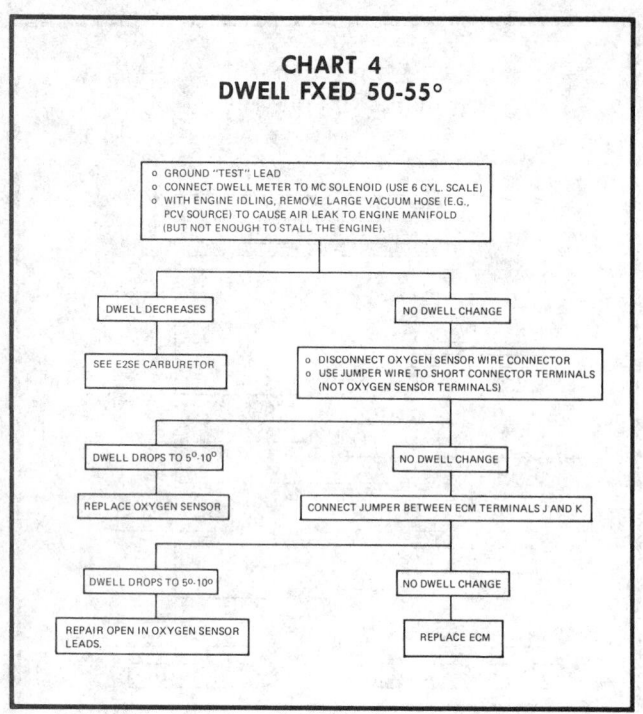

CHART 4
DWELL FXED 50-55°

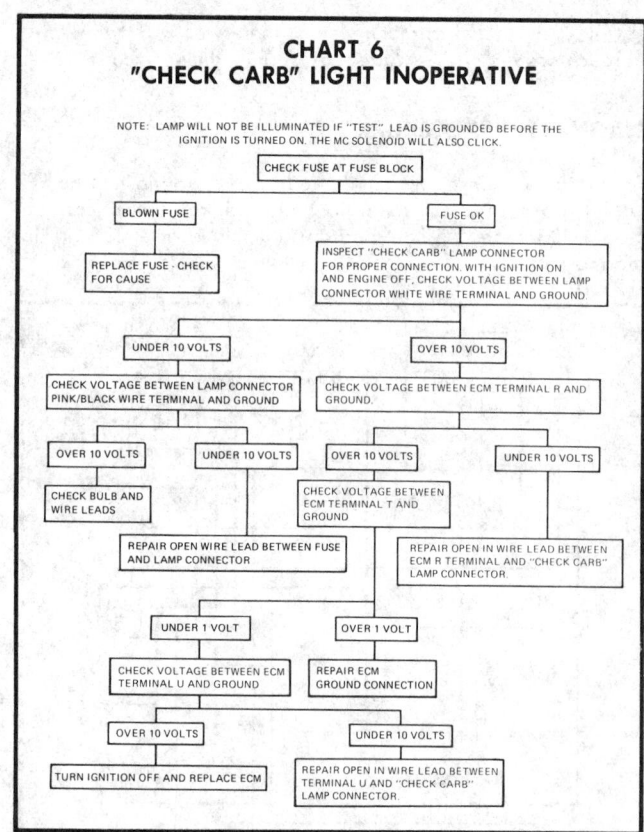

CHART 6
"CHECK CARB" LIGHT INOPERATIVE

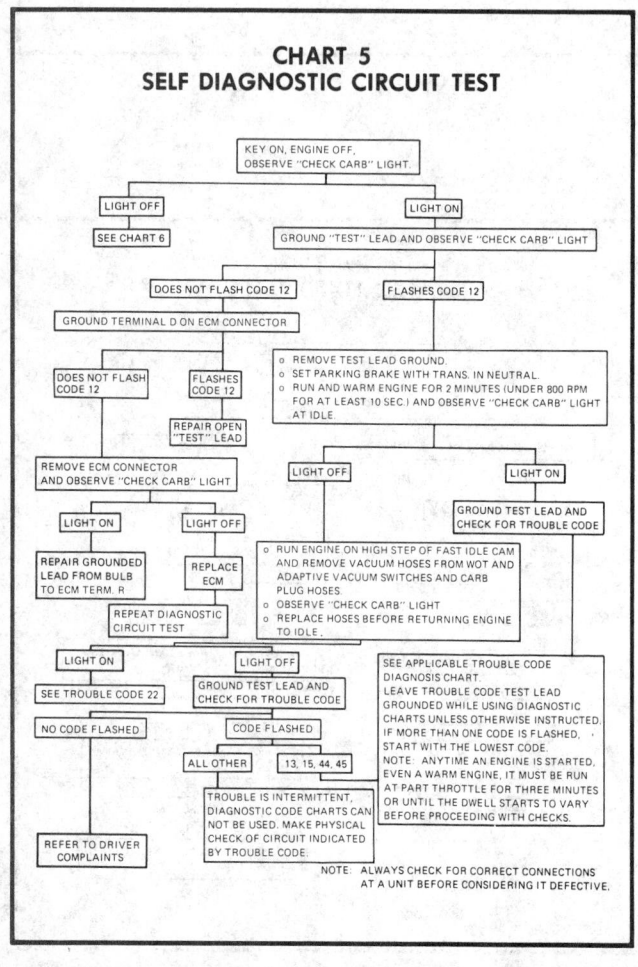

CHART 5
SELF DIAGNOSTIC CIRCUIT TEST

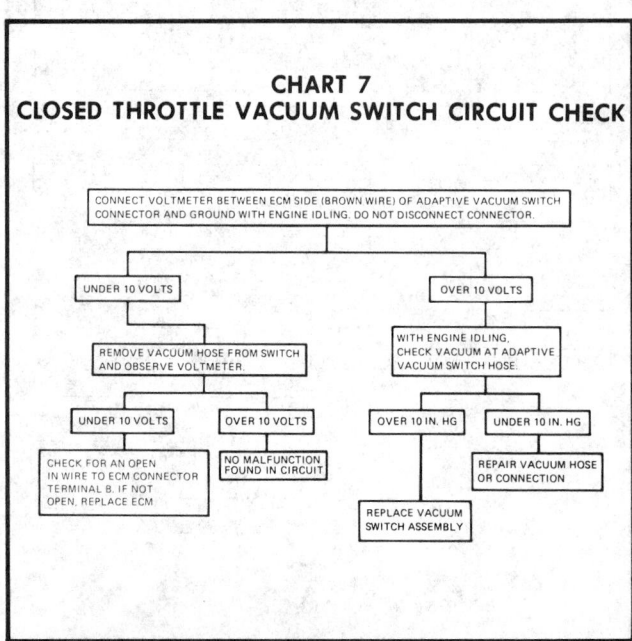

CHART 7
CLOSED THROTTLE VACUUM SWITCH CIRCUIT CHECK

JEEP COMPUTER CONTROLLED CATALYTIC CONVERTER (C-4) SYSTEM (Cont.)

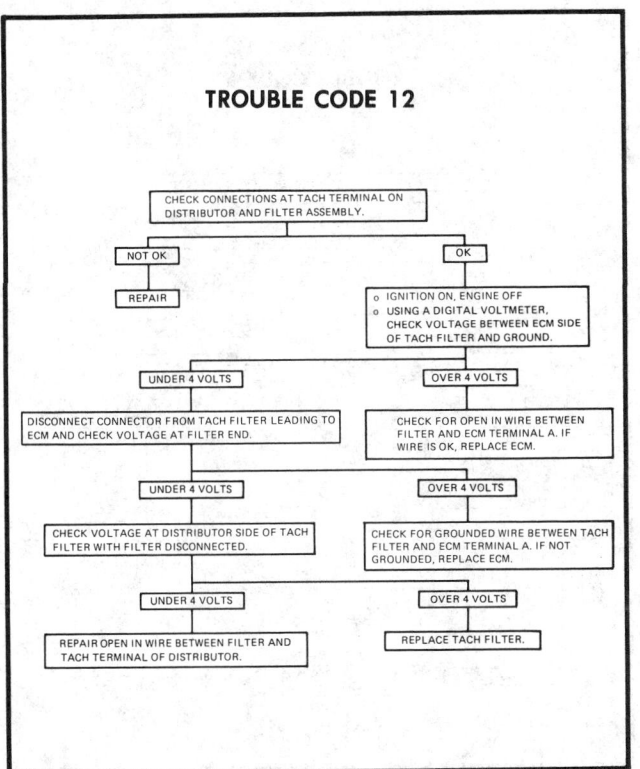

TROUBLE CODE 12

CHECK CONNECTIONS AT TACH TERMINAL ON DISTRIBUTOR AND FILTER ASSEMBLY.

NOT OK → REPAIR

OK
- IGNITION ON, ENGINE OFF
- USING A DIGITAL VOLTMETER, CHECK VOLTAGE BETWEEN ECM SIDE OF TACH FILTER AND GROUND.

UNDER 4 VOLTS → DISCONNECT CONNECTOR FROM TACH FILTER LEADING TO ECM AND CHECK VOLTAGE AT FILTER END.

OVER 4 VOLTS → CHECK FOR OPEN IN WIRE BETWEEN FILTER AND ECM TERMINAL A. IF WIRE IS OK, REPLACE ECM.

UNDER 4 VOLTS → CHECK VOLTAGE AT DISTRIBUTOR SIDE OF TACH FILTER WITH FILTER DISCONNECTED.

OVER 4 VOLTS → CHECK FOR GROUNDED WIRE BETWEEN TACH FILTER AND ECM TERMINAL A. IF NOT GROUNDED, REPLACE ECM.

UNDER 4 VOLTS → REPAIR OPEN IN WIRE BETWEEN FILTER AND TACH TERMINAL OF DISTRIBUTOR.

OVER 4 VOLTS → REPLACE TACH FILTER.

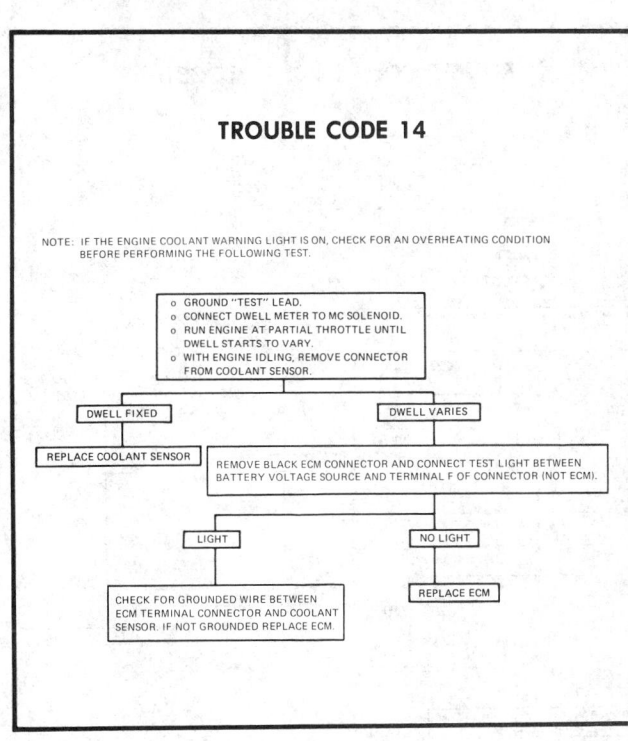

TROUBLE CODE 14

NOTE: IF THE ENGINE COOLANT WARNING LIGHT IS ON, CHECK FOR AN OVERHEATING CONDITION BEFORE PERFORMING THE FOLLOWING TEST.

- GROUND "TEST" LEAD.
- CONNECT DWELL METER TO MC SOLENOID.
- RUN ENGINE AT PARTIAL THROTTLE UNTIL DWELL STARTS TO VARY.
- WITH ENGINE IDLING, REMOVE CONNECTOR FROM COOLANT SENSOR.

DWELL FIXED → REPLACE COOLANT SENSOR

DWELL VARIES → REMOVE BLACK ECM CONNECTOR AND CONNECT TEST LIGHT BETWEEN BATTERY VOLTAGE SOURCE AND TERMINAL F OF CONNECTOR (NOT ECM).

LIGHT → CHECK FOR GROUNDED WIRE BETWEEN ECM TERMINAL CONNECTOR AND COOLANT SENSOR. IF NOT GROUNDED REPLACE ECM.

NO LIGHT → REPLACE ECM

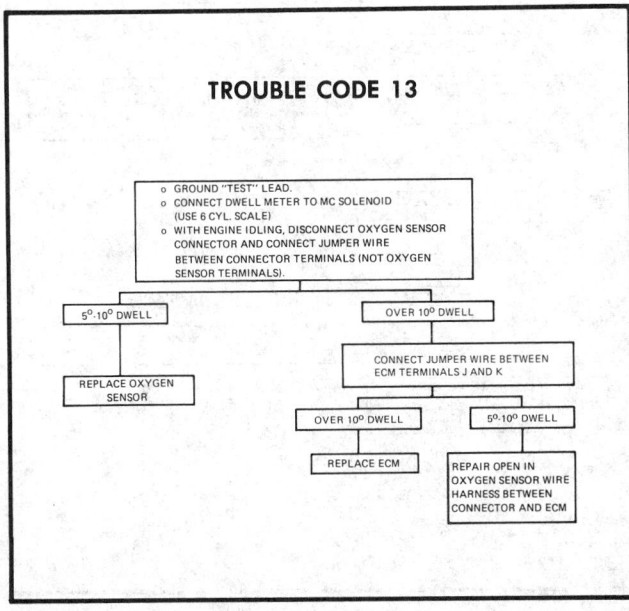

TROUBLE CODE 13

- GROUND "TEST" LEAD.
- CONNECT DWELL METER TO MC SOLENOID (USE 6 CYL. SCALE)
- WITH ENGINE IDLING, DISCONNECT OXYGEN SENSOR CONNECTOR AND CONNECT JUMPER WIRE BETWEEN CONNECTOR TERMINALS (NOT OXYGEN SENSOR TERMINALS).

5°-10° DWELL → REPLACE OXYGEN SENSOR

OVER 10° DWELL → CONNECT JUMPER WIRE BETWEEN ECM TERMINALS J AND K

OVER 10° DWELL → REPLACE ECM

5°-10° DWELL → REPAIR OPEN IN OXYGEN SENSOR WIRE HARNESS BETWEEN CONNECTOR AND ECM

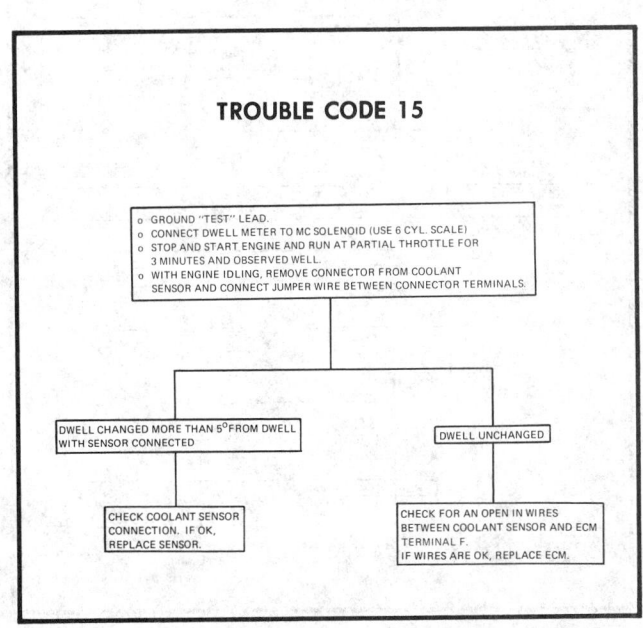

TROUBLE CODE 15

- GROUND "TEST" LEAD.
- CONNECT DWELL METER TO MC SOLENOID (USE 6 CYL. SCALE)
- STOP AND START ENGINE AND RUN AT PARTIAL THROTTLE FOR 3 MINUTES AND OBSERVED WELL.
- WITH ENGINE IDLING, REMOVE CONNECTOR FROM COOLANT SENSOR AND CONNECT JUMPER WIRE BETWEEN CONNECTOR TERMINALS.

DWELL CHANGED MORE THAN 5° FROM DWELL WITH SENSOR CONNECTED → CHECK COOLANT SENSOR CONNECTION. IF OK, REPLACE SENSOR.

DWELL UNCHANGED → CHECK FOR AN OPEN IN WIRES BETWEEN COOLANT SENSOR AND ECM TERMINAL F. IF WIRES ARE OK, REPLACE ECM.

1981 Exhaust Emission Systems

JEEP COMPUTER CONTROLLED CATALYTIC CONVERTER (C-4) SYSTEM (Cont.)

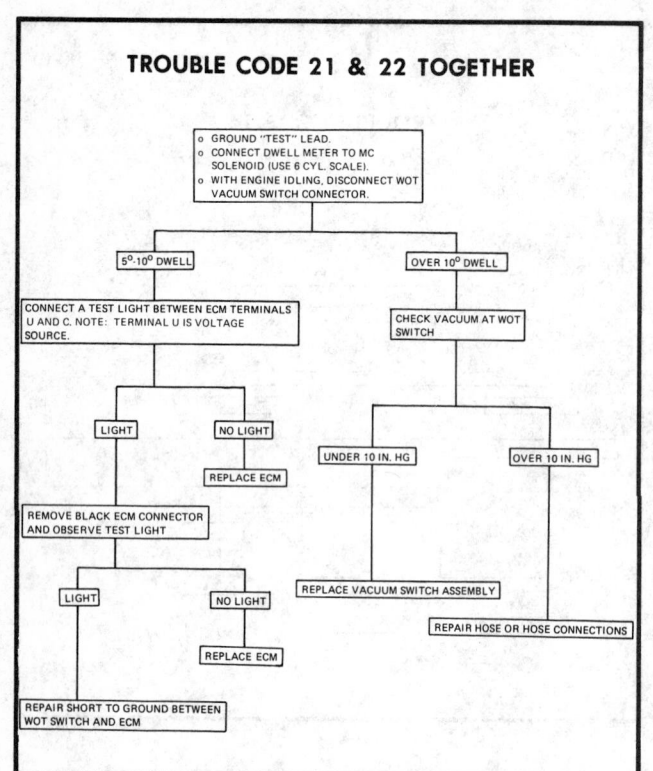

TROUBLE CODE 21 & 22 TOGETHER

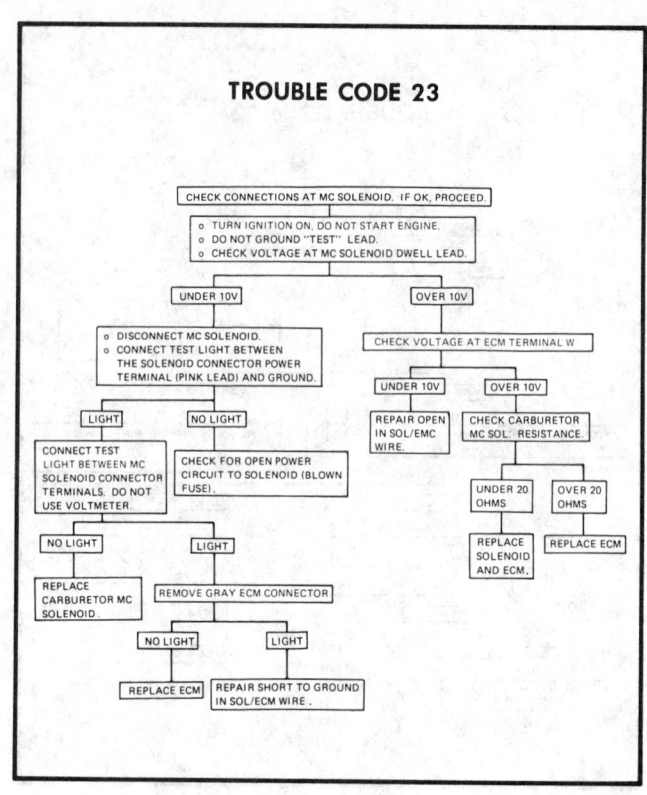

TROUBLE CODE 23

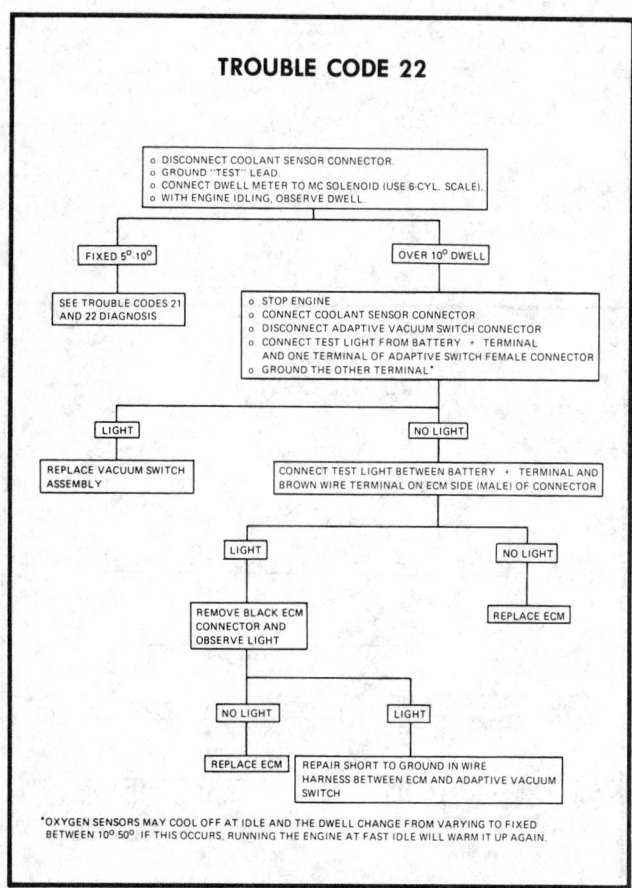

TROUBLE CODE 22

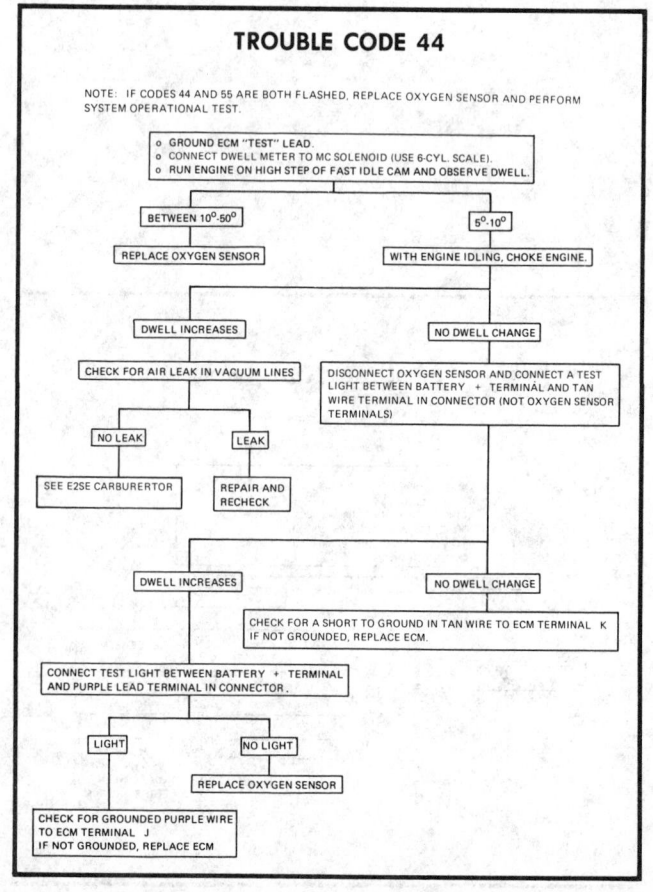

TROUBLE CODE 44

JEEP COMPUTER CONTROLLED CATALYTIC CONVERTER (C-4) SYSTEM (Cont.)

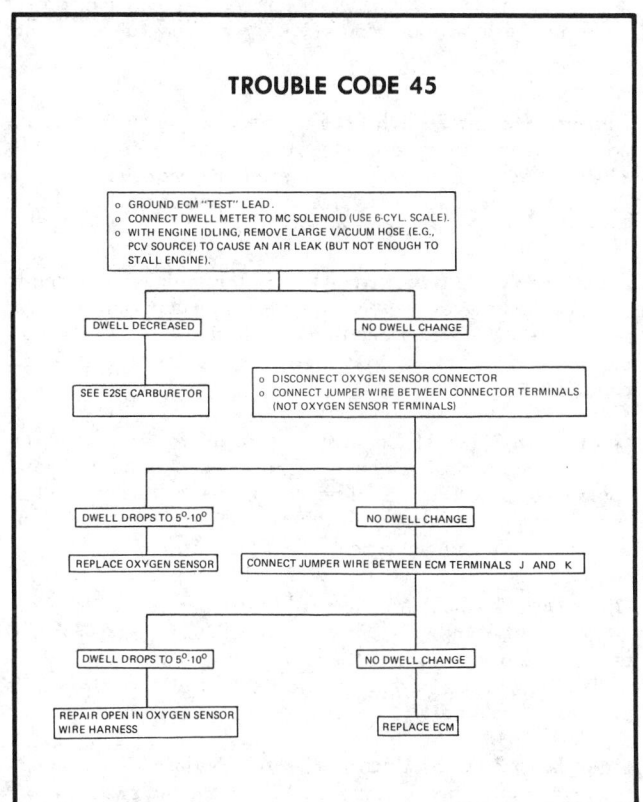

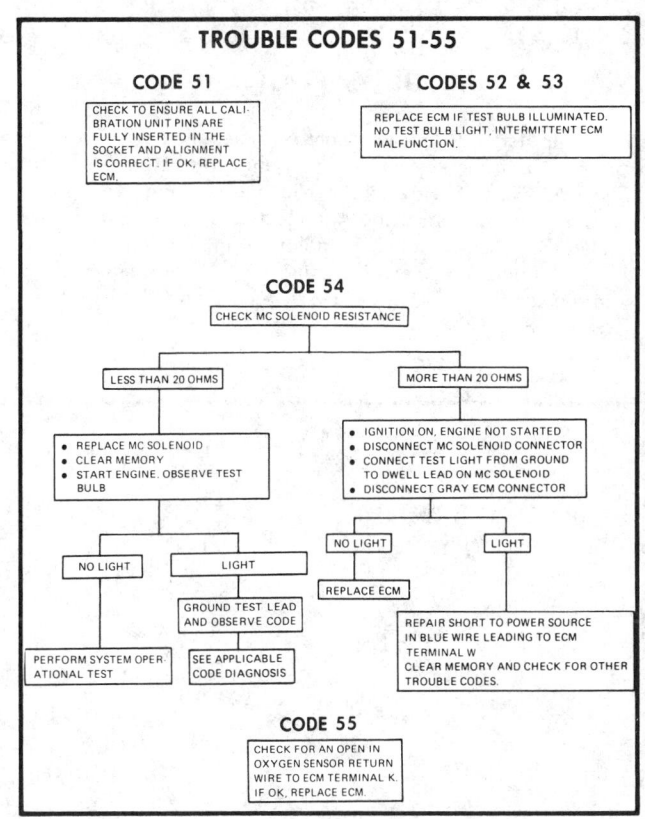

1981 Exhaust Emission Systems

JEEP COMPUTERIZED EMISSION CONTROL

**All Models
(6-Cyl.)**

DESCRIPTION

The Computerized Emission Control system (CEC) is an electronically controlled system that closely controls air/fuel ratio to lower exhaust emissions while maintaining good fuel economy and to control the AIR injection system. Primary objective of the CEC system is to maintain an ideal air/fuel ratio of 14.7:1 under all operating conditions. When ideal ratio is maintained, the catalytic converter can effectively control NOx, HC and CO.

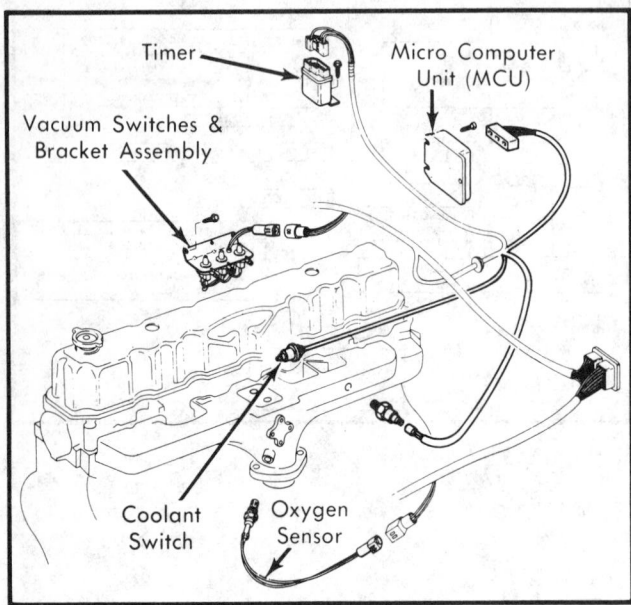

Fig. 1   Jeep 6-Cylinder CEC System

OPERATION

The CEC system consists of 5 sub-systems: Fuel control, data sensors, Micro Computer Unit (MCU), catalytic converter and diagnostic system.

FUEL CONTROL

All models are equipped with feedback carburetors which contain an electronically operated stepper motor. The stepper motor controls the metering pins that vary the size of idle and main air bleed orifices in carburetor body. The stepper motor moves the pins in and out of the orifices in steps, in response to signals received from MCU. The motor has a range of 100 steps, but normal operating area is mid-range.

When the metering pins are "stepped" in direction of orifices, the air/fuel mixture becomes richer. When the pins are "stepped" away from orifices, mixture becomes leaner.

DATA SENSORS

Oxygen Sensor — The oxygen sensor is located in the exhaust manifold to measure oxygen content of exhaust gases. As more oxygen is sensed (lean mixture indication), electrical signal

generated by sensor drops in voltage. A lower oxygen content (rich mixture indication) causes an increase in voltage signal output.

Thermal Electric Switch (TES) — This switch is attached inside air cleaner to provide either a ground circuit for MCU to indicate necessity for cold weather engine start-up (air temperature below calibrated value) or an open circuit to indicate normal start-up (air temperature above calibrated value).

Adaptive Vacuum Switch (AVS) — This switch is mounted in a bracket with 2 other vacuum switches on right inner fender panel. The AVS is controlled by manifold vacuum and is normally closed. When closed, this switch indicates an engine idle condition.

Open Loop 1 (OL1) Coolant Temperature Switch — This switch is an integral component of the intake manifold heater coolant temperature control switch. This switch is controlled by coolant temperature and is normally closed. When open, the switch indicates engine is cold (less than 160°F).

Open Loop 2 (OL2) Mechanical Switch — This switch is an integral part of the Wide Open Throttle (WOT) switch, located at the base of carburetor. The OL2 switch is mechanically controlled and has a normally closed electrical switch which is opened by 3.5-4.5" Hg vacuum.

Open Loop 3 (OL3) Vacuum Switch — This switch is mounted on the same bracket as the AVS switch. This switch is controlled mechanically and has a normally closed electrical switch (indicating a closed throttle position). The electrical switch is opened with 2.5-3.5" Hg of carburetor ported vacuum.

Open Loop 4 (OL4) Vacuum Switch — This switch is mounted on same bracket as the AVS switch and is controlled by manifold vacuum. This switch is normally open. When open, the switch indicates a near full throttle condition.

Wide Open Throttle Switch (WOT) — This mechanically operated electrical switch is located on carburetor and is controlled by the throttle position to indicate a wide open throttle condition. This switch is normally open.

Engine RPM Voltage — This voltage is supplied from the tach terminal on the distributor. Until a voltage equal to a predetermined RPM is received by the MCU, the system remains in open loop mode of operation. The result is a fixed rich air/fuel mixture for engine starting.

Timer — This timer is activated whenever system is operating in open loop 2 mode (wide open throttle). This timer remains active for a preset period of time. If a "lean limit" condition (altitude jumper wire installed) occurs, the timer becomes inoperative. The timer has multi-function abilities, in addition to OL2 mode, it is used as a WOT timer and start-up timer.

MICRO COMPUTER UNIT (MCU)

The MCU is located in the engine compartment, on the left-hand inner fender panel. The MCU monitors the CEC system data sensors and, based upon mode of operation, generates

JEEP COMPUTERIZED EMISSION CONTROL (Cont.)

an output control signal to the stepper motor, mounted in carburetor. The MCU allows the following 3 modes of operation:

Initialization — This function occurs when ignition switch is turned on. This sets initial air bleed metering rod position by signaling the stepper motor to drive them first to a full rich position (fully toward front of vehicle) and then, by a pre-programmed number of steps, in lean direction (toward rear of vehicle). This serves as a starting point of mixture control operation.

Open Loop — In this mode, the MCU determines the air/fuel mixture based upon engine operation rather than oxygen sensor input signals. There are 5 open loop modes of operation and each has a specific metering pin position. However, because each condition may be present at the same time, the MCU is programmed with a priority ranking for each operation. The MCU complies with the highest priority. The open loop priorities (listed from highest to lowest) are as follows:

- **Cold Weather Start-Up & Operation** — If air cleaner air temperature is below calibrated value of TES, the stepper motor positions the metering pins a pre-determined number of steps richer than that at initialization. Air injection is diverted "upstream". Lean air/fuel mixtures are not permitted for a preset period, following a cold weather start.

- **Open Loop 2 (Wide Open Throttle)** — Open Loop 2 (OL2) is selected whenever air cleaner air temperature is above calibrated value of the TES and the WOT switch has been engaged. In OL2 mode, the stepper motor drives the metering pins to a calibrated number of steps rich of initialization and the air control valve diverts air "downstream". The timer is activated in this mode.

NOTE — *If a "lean limit" condition (altitude jumper wire installed) is selected, the air is diverted "upstream". The timer is inoperative if "lean limit" is selected.*

- **Open Loop 4** — This mode is selected whenever manifold vacuum falls below a preset value. During OL4 operation, the stepper motor is positioned at the initialization position. Air injection is switched "upstream"; however, air is diverted "downstream" if the extended OL4 timer is activated or "lean limit" (altitude jumper wire) is not installed. Air is also diverted "downstream" if the WOT timer is activated.

- **Open Loop 3** — This mode is selected when spark advance vacuum level falls below a preset level. In OL3 mode, engine RPM is also determined. If the RPM voltage is greater than the calibrated value, an engine deceleration condition is assumed to exist. If the RPM voltage is less than calibrated value, an engine idle condition is assumed to exist.

NOTE — *Both deceleration and idle conditions are independently selectable to be either an open loop or closed loop condition. If selected as an open loop operation, air is diverted "upstream".*

- **Open Loop 1** — This mode will be selected if air cleaner temperature is above calibrated value, OL2, OL3 or OL4 is not selected and if engine coolant temperature is below calibrated value. The OL1 mode operates instead of normal closed loop operation during cold engine operating

condition. In this mode, 1 of 2 pre-determined metering pin positions are chosen, dependent if the "lean limit" (altitude circuit) jumper wire is installed.

NOTE — *With each engine start-up, a start-up timer is activated. During this interval, if engine operating condition would otherwise trigger normal closed loop operation, OL1 mode is selected.*

Closed Loop — When all input data and engine operation meet programmed criteria (after OL1, OL2, OL3 and OL4 modes have been selected and start-up timer has deactivated), the CEC system goes into closed loop operation. In this mode, oxygen sensor input signals are accepted by MCU to determine proper air/fuel mixture based upon oxygen content of exhaust gases. Air injection is routed "downstream" during this mode to aid in oxidation of HC and CO. The predetermined "lean mixture ceiling" is selected for a preset length of time at the start of closed loop operation.

NOTE — *Closed loop operation is characterized by constant movement of the metering pins. The MCU is constantly making small corrections in air/fuel ratio in an attempt to create the ideal air/fuel ratio.*

Open Loop Position Variation — An additional function of the MCU is to correct for a change in ambient conditions (altitude). During closed loop operation, the MCU stores the number of steps and direction that the metering pins are driven to correct oxygen content of exhaust gases. If the movements are consistently to the same position, the MCU will vary all open loop operation preset metering pin positions a corresponding amount. This function allows the open loop air-/fuel mixture ratios to be adjusted to the existing ambient condition during each uninterrupted use of the system to optimize emission control and engine performance.

CATALYTIC CONVERTER

Proper emission control is accomplished with special catalytic converters used with the Computerized Engine Control (CEC) system. A COC pellet-type converter is used with all 6-cylinder engine exhaust systems except California "CJ", Scrambler, Cherokee, and Wagoneer models. These vehicles use a dual-bed COC and TWC monolithic-type converter with "downstream" air injection. The injection of air between the 2 beds provides more complete oxidation of air and CO in the closed loop mode. In order for these converters to be effective, precise control of the oxygen content of gases entering converter is necessary. This is accomplished by the oxygen sensor, MCU and feedback carburetor.

DIAGNOSTIC SYSTEM

The MCU of the CEC system is equipped with a self-diagnostic system which detects system failures or abnormalities. When a fault is detected in the CEC system, the MCU will cause the "CHECK ENGINE" lamp on instrument panel to flash a trouble code. Trouble codes will only be displayed when a malfunction exists. The MCU does not have a long term memory; therefore, all faults detected MUST be corrected. Trouble codes will be flashed 5 times. The series of code flashes will not be repeated.

NOTE — *Trouble codes are lost when ignition is turned off.*

As a routine bulb and system check, the "CHECK ENGINE" lamp will be illuminated when the ignition is turned on (engine off). This indicates that diagnostic system is functioning

JEEP COMPUTERIZED EMISSION CONTROL (Cont.)

properly. When the engine is started, the "CHECK ENGINE" lamp should go out after a few seconds.

DIAGNOSIS & TESTING

NOTE — *The self-diagnostic system does not detect all possible faults. The absence of a trouble code does not indicate that there is no problem with the CEC system. To determine this, a system operational test is made when the "CHECK ENGINE" lamp does not indicate a problem but the system is suspected because no other reason can be found for a specific complaint.*

CEC DIAGNOSIS

When the "CHECK ENGINE" lamp flashes a trouble code, the following procedures should be followed to correct the identified fault. When the malfunction is corrected, the "CHECK ENGINE" lamp will go out. In all instances the ignition must be on or the engine running.

Trouble Code "11" ("FLASH", pause, "FLASH") — Indicates no RPM voltage to MCU, loss of full battery voltage or a bad ground, a short in "CHECK ENGINE" circuit or defective MCU. Perform Test No. 3 and 4 to isolate problem.

NOTE — *If the "CHECK ENGINE" lamp remains on constantly, use the procedure given for trouble code "11" to diagnose the problem.*

Trouble Code "12" ("FLASH", pause, "FLASH", "FLASH") — 1) This indicates that the engine coolant temperature has been greater than 160°F for at least 8 minutes and the air cleaner thermal electric switch (TES) indicates that air cleaner air is still cold. This could be caused by a faulty coolant switch, faulty TES or defective MCU.

2) To isolate the problem, perform Test No. 1; warm engine for 4 minutes or until coolant temperature has stabilized; perform Test No. 12; perform Test No. 9. If the problem is not isolated after completion of this test procedure, fault is intermittent and system cannot be diagnosed until fault becomes continuous.

Trouble Code "14" ("FLASH", pause, "FLASH", "FLASH", "FLASH", "FLASH") — 1) This code reflects that the WOT switch (mounted on carburetor) indicates a wide open throttle condition while the adaptive vacuum switch indicates engine vacuum to be greater than 10 in. Hg.

2) This condition indicates a failure in 1 of the following areas: WOT switch stuck in actuated position; adaptive vacuum switch fails to close when vacuum is removed; short in WOT switch wiring harness; open in adaptive vacuum switch wiring harness or defective MCU.

3) To isolate the problem, perform Test No. 1; warm engine for 4 minutes or until engine temperature has stabilized, then turn engine off. Perform Tests No. 9 and 10. If problem is not isolated after completion of this test procedure, malfunction is intermittent and cannot be diagnosed until fault becomes continuous.

Trouble Code "21" ("FLASH", "FLASH", pause, "FLASH") — 1) This code indicates that MCU input shows that an engine idle condition exists with less than 10 in. Hg of manifold vacuum present.

2) This condition may be caused by a failure in 1 of the following areas: Faulty OL3 vacuum switch or an open in wiring to switch; faulty adaptive vacuum switch or a short in wiring to switch; air leak into manifold or ported vacuum or defective MCU.

3) To isolate the problem, perform Test No. 1; warm engine for 4 minutes or until engine temperature has stabilized, then turn engine off; perform Tests No. 9, 10 and 14. If problem is not isolated after completion of this test procedure, malfunction is intermittent and cannot be diagnosed until fault becomes continuous.

Trouble Code "23" ("FLASH", "FLASH", pause, "FLASH", "FLASH", "FLASH") — 1) This code indicates that MCU input shows that manifold vacuum has been less than 4 in. Hg for more than 10 minutes or that WOT condition has existed for more than 10 minutes.

2) This condition may be caused by a failure in 1 of the following areas: Defective OL4 and adaptive vacuum switches; defective WOT switch; manifold vacuum not present at vacuum switches or defective MCU.

3) To isolate the problem, perform Test No. 1; warm engine for 4 minutes or until engine temperature has stabilized, then turn engine off; perform Tests No. 9 and 10. If problem is not isolated after completion of this test procedure, malfunction is intermittent and cannot be diagnosed until fault becomes continuous.

Trouble Code "24" ("FLASH", "FLASH", pause, "FLASH", "FLASH", "FLASH", "FLASH") — 1) This code indicates that the coolant temperature switch shows that coolant temperature has reached 160°F after 20 minutes of operation.

2) This condition may be caused by a failure in 1 of the following areas: Coolant temperature switch for intake manifold heater and OL1 or open circuit in wiring harness for OL1, OL2 and OL4 switches input wire.

3) To isolate the problem, perform Test No. 1; warm engine for 4 minutes or until temperature stabilizes, then turn engine off; perform Test No. 9. If problem is not isolated after completion of this test procedure, malfunction is intermittent and cannot be diagnosed until fault becomes continuous.

TESTING

The steps listed in the following charts will provide a systematic evaluation of each component that could cause the indicated trouble code or malfunction. After completing a repair, repeat the test to ensure the malfunction has been eliminated.

If after completing any test procedure and the problem persists, other engine associated systems that can affect air/fuel mixture, combustion efficiency or exhaust gas composition may be causing the fault. These systems include:

- Basic carburetor adjustments.
- Mechanical engine operation (plugs, valves, rings).
- Ignition system.
- Intake manifold, carburetor or base plate gaskets.
- Loose vacuum hoses or fittings.

JEEP COMPUTERIZED EMISSION CONTROL (Cont.)

Test Equipment — 1) The test equipment required to perform the tests include: Tachometer, hand vacuum pump, digital volt-ohmmeter with minimum 10 megohm impedance and a No. 158 bulb with socket and jumper wire.

2) Before beginning any of the tests, a clear air cleaner cover must be fabricated from clear acrylic plastic at least .25" thick. This is secured with air cleaner wing nut after top of air cleaner has been removed to observe operation and position of metering pins. *See Fig. 2.*

NOTE — *The metering pins operate in tandem. Only the upper pin is visible.*

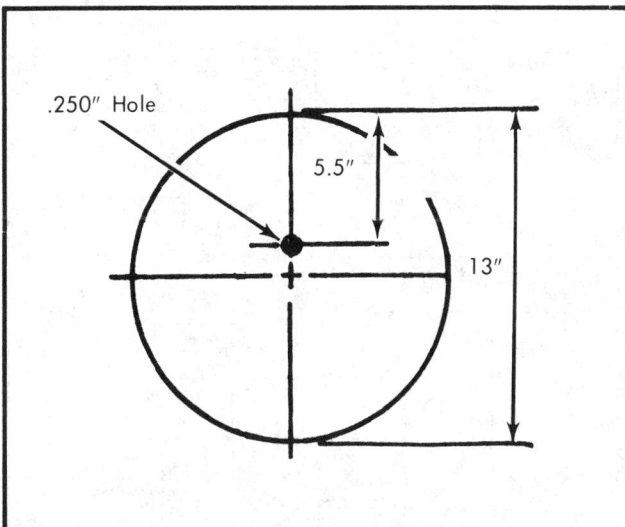

Fig. 2   Dimensions for Fabricating Clear Air Cleaner Cover for Observing Metering Pins

TEST CHARTS

Chart	Condition
No. 1	Initialization test.
No. 2	System operation test.
No. 3	"CHECK ENGINE" lamp test.
No. 4	"CHECK ENGINE" lamp remains on or trouble code "11".
No. 5	Oxygen sensor and closed loop test.
No. 6	AIR injection test.
No. 7	Divert solenoid test.
No. 8	"Upstream" solenoid test.
No. 9	Open loop switches test.
No. 10	Adaptive switch test.
No. 11	Altitude circuit test.
No. 12	Thermal electric switch (TES) test.
No. 13	Closed loop operational test.
No. 14	Vacuum switch functional test.

TEST NO. 1

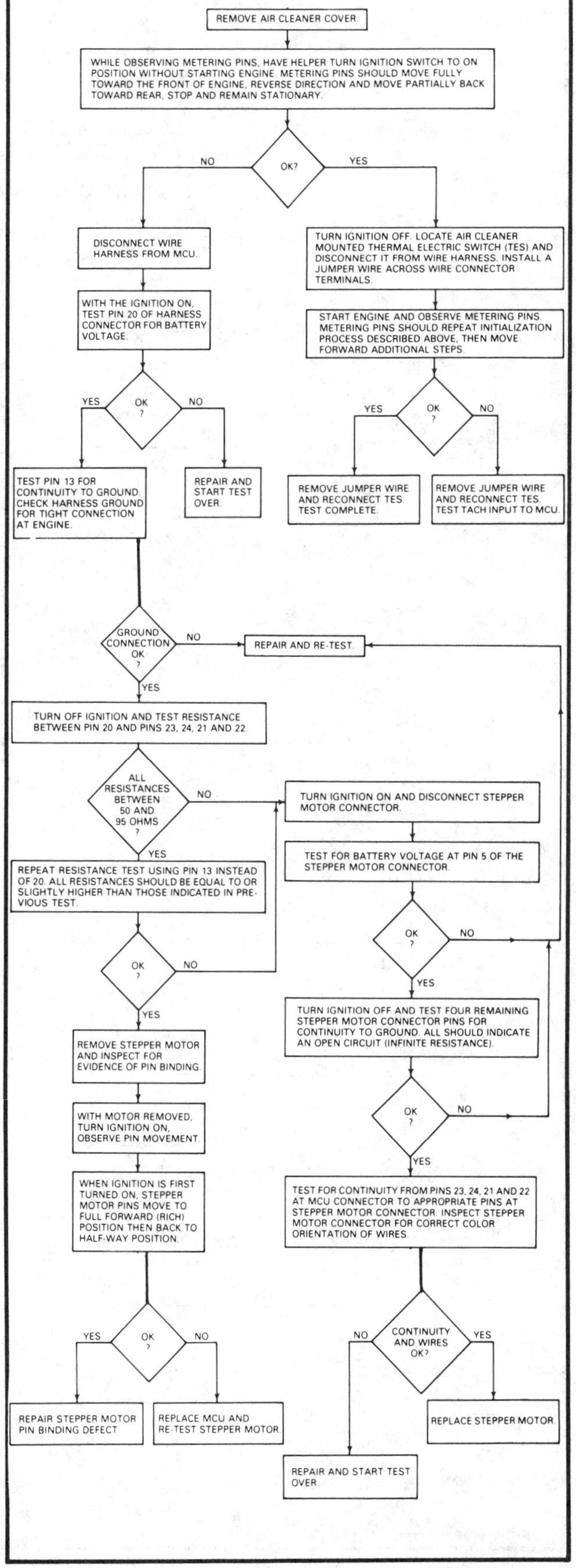

REMOVE AIR CLEANER COVER.

WHILE OBSERVING METERING PINS, HAVE HELPER TURN IGNITION SWITCH TO ON POSITION WITHOUT STARTING ENGINE. METERING PINS SHOULD MOVE FULLY TOWARD THE FRONT OF ENGINE, REVERSE DIRECTION AND MOVE PARTIALLY BACK TOWARD REAR, STOP AND REMAIN STATIONARY.

OK? — NO / YES

NO → DISCONNECT WIRE HARNESS FROM MCU.

WITH THE IGNITION ON, TEST PIN 20 OF HARNESS CONNECTOR FOR BATTERY VOLTAGE.

OK? — YES / NO

NO → REPAIR AND START TEST OVER.

YES → TEST PIN 13 FOR CONTINUITY TO GROUND. CHECK HARNESS GROUND FOR TIGHT CONNECTION AT ENGINE.

GROUND CONNECTION OK? — NO / YES

NO → REPAIR AND RE-TEST.

YES → TURN IGNITION OFF. LOCATE AIR CLEANER MOUNTED THERMAL ELECTRIC SWITCH (TES) AND DISCONNECT IT FROM WIRE HARNESS. INSTALL A JUMPER WIRE ACROSS WIRE CONNECTOR TERMINALS.

START ENGINE AND OBSERVE METERING PINS. METERING PINS SHOULD REPEAT INITIALIZATION PROCESS DESCRIBED ABOVE, THEN MOVE FORWARD ADDITIONAL STEPS.

OK? — YES / NO

YES → REMOVE JUMPER WIRE AND RECONNECT TES. TEST COMPLETE.

NO → REMOVE JUMPER WIRE AND RECONNECT TES. TEST TACH INPUT TO MCU.

TURN OFF IGNITION AND TEST RESISTANCE BETWEEN PIN 20 AND PINS 23, 24, 21 AND 22.

ALL RESISTANCES BETWEEN 50 AND 95 OHMS? — NO / YES

NO → TURN IGNITION ON AND DISCONNECT STEPPER MOTOR CONNECTOR.

TEST FOR BATTERY VOLTAGE AT PIN 5 OF THE STEPPER MOTOR CONNECTOR.

OK? — YES / NO

YES → TURN IGNITION OFF AND TEST FOUR REMAINING STEPPER MOTOR CONNECTOR PINS FOR CONTINUITY TO GROUND. ALL SHOULD INDICATE AN OPEN CIRCUIT (INFINITE RESISTANCE).

OK? — YES / NO

YES → TEST FOR CONTINUITY FROM PINS 23, 24, 21 AND 22 AT MCU CONNECTOR TO APPROPRIATE PINS AT STEPPER MOTOR CONNECTOR. INSPECT STEPPER MOTOR CONNECTOR FOR CORRECT COLOR ORIENTATION OF WIRES.

CONTINUITY AND WIRES OK? — NO / YES

YES → REPLACE STEPPER MOTOR.

NO → REPAIR AND START TEST OVER.

YES (ALL RESISTANCES) → REPEAT RESISTANCE TEST USING PIN 13 INSTEAD OF 20. ALL RESISTANCES SHOULD BE EQUAL TO OR SLIGHTLY HIGHER THAN THOSE INDICATED IN PREVIOUS TEST.

OK? — YES / NO

YES → REMOVE STEPPER MOTOR AND INSPECT FOR EVIDENCE OF PIN BINDING.

WITH MOTOR REMOVED, TURN IGNITION ON, OBSERVE PIN MOVEMENT.

WHEN IGNITION IS FIRST TURNED ON, STEPPER MOTOR PINS MOVE TO FULL FORWARD (RICH) POSITION THEN BACK TO HALF-WAY POSITION.

OK? — YES / NO

YES → REPAIR STEPPER MOTOR PIN BINDING DEFECT

NO → REPLACE MCU AND RE-TEST STEPPER MOTOR.

1981 Exhaust Emission Systems

JEEP COMPUTERIZED EMISSION CONTROL (Cont.)

TEST NO. 2

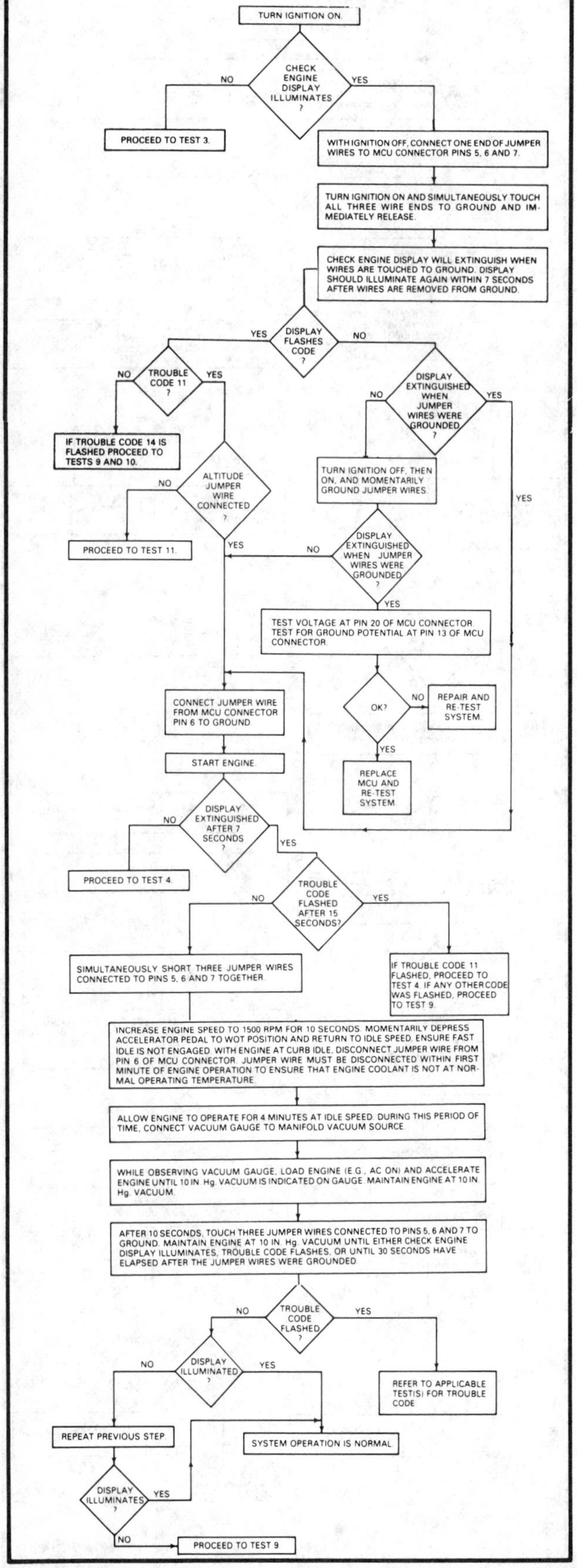

TURN IGNITION ON.

CHECK ENGINE DISPLAY ILLUMINATES ?

NO → PROCEED TO TEST 3.

YES → WITH IGNITION OFF, CONNECT ONE END OF JUMPER WIRES TO MCU CONNECTOR PINS 5, 6 AND 7.

TURN IGNITION ON AND SIMULTANEOUSLY TOUCH ALL THREE WIRE ENDS TO GROUND AND IMMEDIATELY RELEASE.

CHECK ENGINE DISPLAY WILL EXTINGUISH WHEN WIRES ARE TOUCHED TO GROUND. DISPLAY SHOULD ILLUMINATE AGAIN WITHIN 7 SECONDS AFTER WIRES ARE REMOVED FROM GROUND.

DISPLAY FLASHES CODE ?

YES → TROUBLE CODE 11 ?

NO → IF TROUBLE CODE 14 IS FLASHED PROCEED TO TESTS 9 AND 10.

YES → ALTITUDE JUMPER WIRE CONNECTED ?

NO → PROCEED TO TEST 11.

YES →

NO (DISPLAY FLASHES CODE) → DISPLAY EXTINGUISHED WHEN JUMPER WIRES WERE GROUNDED ?

NO → TURN IGNITION OFF, THEN ON, AND MOMENTARILY GROUND JUMPER WIRES.

DISPLAY EXTINGUISHED WHEN JUMPER WIRES WERE GROUNDED ?

NO

YES → TEST VOLTAGE AT PIN 20 OF MCU CONNECTOR. TEST FOR GROUND POTENTIAL AT PIN 13 OF MCU CONNECTOR.

OK? → NO → REPAIR AND RE-TEST SYSTEM.

YES → REPLACE MCU AND RE-TEST SYSTEM.

CONNECT JUMPER WIRE FROM MCU CONNECTOR PIN 6 TO GROUND.

START ENGINE.

DISPLAY EXTINGUISHED AFTER 7 SECONDS ?

NO → PROCEED TO TEST 4.

YES → TROUBLE CODE FLASHED AFTER 15 SECONDS?

NO → SIMULTANEOUSLY SHORT, THREE JUMPER WIRES CONNECTED TO PINS 5, 6 AND 7 TOGETHER

YES → IF TROUBLE CODE 11 FLASHED, PROCEED TO TEST 4. IF ANY OTHER CODE WAS FLASHED, PROCEED TO TEST 9.

INCREASE ENGINE SPEED TO 1500 RPM FOR 10 SECONDS. MOMENTARILY DEPRESS ACCELERATOR PEDAL TO WOT POSITION AND RETURN TO IDLE SPEED. ENSURE FAST IDLE IS NOT ENGAGED. WITH ENGINE AT CURB IDLE, DISCONNECT JUMPER WIRE FROM PIN 6 OF MCU CONNECTOR. JUMPER WIRE MUST BE DISCONNECTED WITHIN FIRST MINUTE OF ENGINE OPERATION TO ENSURE THAT ENGINE COOLANT IS NOT AT NORMAL OPERATING TEMPERATURE.

ALLOW ENGINE TO OPERATE FOR 4 MINUTES AT IDLE SPEED. DURING THIS PERIOD OF TIME, CONNECT VACUUM GAUGE TO MANIFOLD VACUUM SOURCE.

WHILE OBSERVING VACUUM GAUGE, LOAD ENGINE (E.G., AC ON) AND ACCELERATE ENGINE UNTIL 10 IN. Hg. VACUUM IS INDICATED ON GAUGE. MAINTAIN ENGINE AT 10 IN. Hg. VACUUM.

AFTER 10 SECONDS, TOUCH THREE JUMPER WIRES CONNECTED TO PINS 5, 6 AND 7 TO GROUND. MAINTAIN ENGINE AT 10 IN. Hg. VACUUM UNTIL EITHER CHECK ENGINE DISPLAY ILLUMINATES, TROUBLE CODE FLASHES, OR UNTIL 30 SECONDS HAVE ELAPSED AFTER THE JUMPER WIRES WERE GROUNDED.

TROUBLE CODE FLASHED ?

NO → DISPLAY ILLUMINATED ?

YES (TROUBLE CODE FLASHED) → REFER TO APPLICABLE TEST(S) FOR TROUBLE CODE

DISPLAY ILLUMINATED ?

NO → REPEAT PREVIOUS STEP.

YES → SYSTEM OPERATION IS NORMAL.

DISPLAY ILLUMINATES ?

YES → (back up)

NO → PROCEED TO TEST 9.

TEST NO. 3

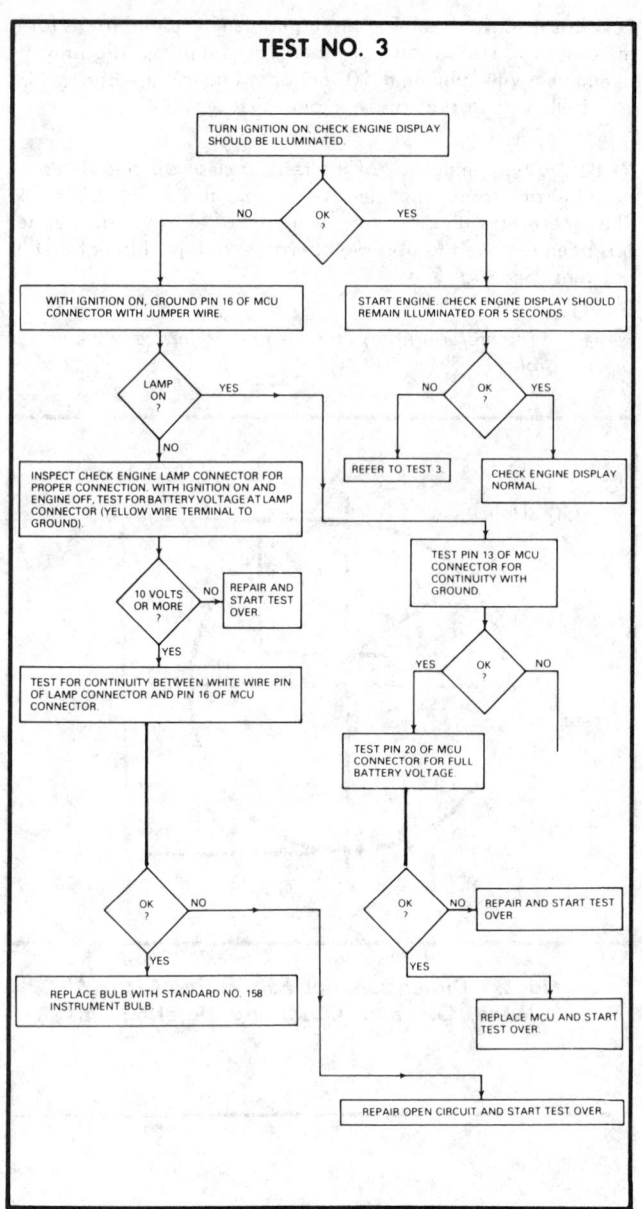

TURN IGNITION ON. CHECK ENGINE DISPLAY SHOULD BE ILLUMINATED.

OK ?

NO → WITH IGNITION ON, GROUND PIN 16 OF MCU CONNECTOR WITH JUMPER WIRE.

LAMP ON ?

YES → INSPECT CHECK ENGINE LAMP CONNECTOR FOR PROPER CONNECTION. WITH IGNITION ON AND ENGINE OFF, TEST FOR BATTERY VOLTAGE AT LAMP CONNECTOR (YELLOW WIRE TERMINAL TO GROUND).

10 VOLTS OR MORE ?

NO → REPAIR AND START TEST OVER.

YES → TEST FOR CONTINUITY BETWEEN WHITE WIRE PIN OF LAMP CONNECTOR AND PIN 16 OF MCU CONNECTOR.

OK ?

NO →

YES → REPLACE BULB WITH STANDARD NO. 158 INSTRUMENT BULB.

YES (OK) → START ENGINE. CHECK ENGINE DISPLAY SHOULD REMAIN ILLUMINATED FOR 5 SECONDS.

OK ?

NO → REFER TO TEST 3.

YES → CHECK ENGINE DISPLAY NORMAL.

TEST PIN 13 OF MCU CONNECTOR FOR CONTINUITY WITH GROUND.

OK ?

YES → TEST PIN 20 OF MCU CONNECTOR FOR FULL BATTERY VOLTAGE.

NO →

OK ?

NO → REPAIR AND START TEST OVER

YES → REPLACE MCU AND START TEST OVER.

REPAIR OPEN CIRCUIT AND START TEST OVER.

JEEP COMPUTERIZED EMISSION CONTROL (Cont.)

TEST NO. 4

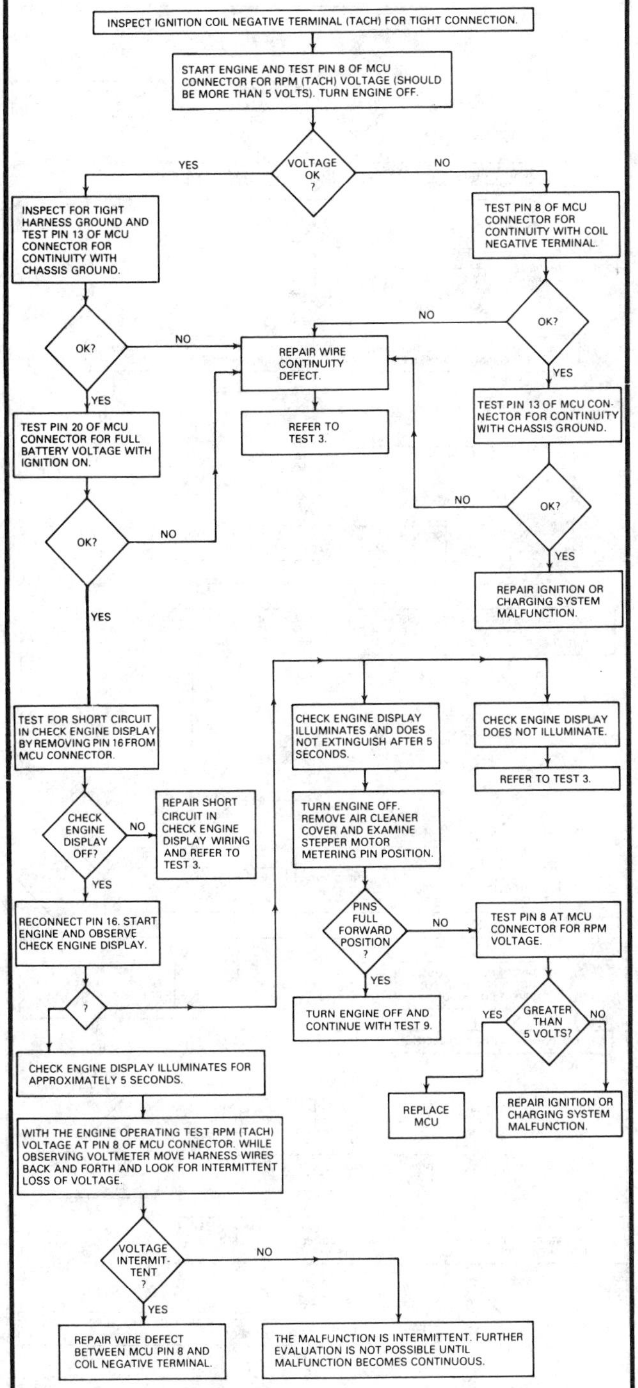

INSPECT IGNITION COIL NEGATIVE TERMINAL (TACH) FOR TIGHT CONNECTION.

START ENGINE AND TEST PIN 8 OF MCU CONNECTOR FOR RPM (TACH) VOLTAGE (SHOULD BE MORE THAN 5 VOLTS). TURN ENGINE OFF.

VOLTAGE OK ?

YES — INSPECT FOR TIGHT HARNESS GROUND AND TEST PIN 13 OF MCU CONNECTOR FOR CONTINUITY WITH CHASSIS GROUND.

NO — TEST PIN 8 OF MCU CONNECTOR FOR CONTINUITY WITH COIL NEGATIVE TERMINAL.

OK?

NO → REPAIR WIRE CONTINUITY DEFECT. → REFER TO TEST 3.

YES → TEST PIN 13 OF MCU CONNECTOR FOR CONTINUITY WITH CHASSIS GROUND.

OK?

NO → REPAIR WIRE CONTINUITY DEFECT.

YES → REPAIR IGNITION OR CHARGING SYSTEM MALFUNCTION.

OK?

NO → REPAIR WIRE CONTINUITY DEFECT.

YES → TEST PIN 20 OF MCU CONNECTOR FOR FULL BATTERY VOLTAGE WITH IGNITION ON.

OK?

NO → REPAIR WIRE CONTINUITY DEFECT.

YES → TEST FOR SHORT CIRCUIT IN CHECK ENGINE DISPLAY BY REMOVING PIN 16 FROM MCU CONNECTOR.

CHECK ENGINE DISPLAY OFF?

NO → REPAIR SHORT CIRCUIT IN CHECK ENGINE DISPLAY WIRING AND REFER TO TEST 3.

YES → RECONNECT PIN 16. START ENGINE AND OBSERVE CHECK ENGINE DISPLAY.

?

CHECK ENGINE DISPLAY ILLUMINATES AND DOES NOT EXTINGUISH AFTER 5 SECONDS.

CHECK ENGINE DISPLAY DOES NOT ILLUMINATE. → REFER TO TEST 3.

TURN ENGINE OFF. REMOVE AIR CLEANER COVER AND EXAMINE STEPPER MOTOR METERING PIN POSITION.

PINS FULL FORWARD POSITION?

NO → TEST PIN 8 AT MCU CONNECTOR FOR RPM VOLTAGE.

GREATER THAN 5 VOLTS?

YES → REPAIR IGNITION OR CHARGING SYSTEM MALFUNCTION.

NO → REPLACE MCU.

YES → TURN ENGINE OFF AND CONTINUE WITH TEST 9.

CHECK ENGINE DISPLAY ILLUMINATES FOR APPROXIMATELY 5 SECONDS.

WITH THE ENGINE OPERATING TEST RPM (TACH) VOLTAGE AT PIN 8 OF MCU CONNECTOR. WHILE OBSERVING VOLTMETER MOVE HARNESS WIRES BACK AND FORTH AND LOOK FOR INTERMITTENT LOSS OF VOLTAGE.

VOLTAGE INTERMITTENT ?

NO → THE MALFUNCTION IS INTERMITTENT. FURTHER EVALUATION IS NOT POSSIBLE UNTIL MALFUNCTION BECOMES CONTINUOUS.

YES → REPAIR WIRE DEFECT BETWEEN MCU PIN 8 AND COIL NEGATIVE TERMINAL.

TEST NO. 5

WITH ENGINE OFF, REMOVE AIR CLEANER AND PLUG ALL VACUUM HOSES.

TURN IGNITION ON FOR 4 SECONDS THEN TURN OFF.

DISCONNECT MCU CONNECTOR. START ENGINE AND OPERATE UNTIL TEMPERATURE GAUGE POINTER IS AT MIDRANGE (OR 4 MINUTES).

CONNECT POSITIVE PROBE OF DIGITAL VOLTMETER (OR VOLTMETER WITH GREATER THAN 1 MEGOHM INPUT IMPEDANCE) TO PIN 3 AT HARNESS SIDE OF MCU CONNECTOR AND NEGATIVE PROBE TO PIN 13 (GROUND).

INCREASE ENGINE SPEED TO APPROXIMATELY 1200 RPM AND MAINTAIN. CLOSE CHOKE VALVE AND OBSERVE VOLTMETER. (CLOSE VALVE FOR AT LEAST 15 SECONDS BUT DO NOT EXCEED 30 SECONDS.)

GREATER THAN 0.6 VOLTS

YES — TURN ENGINE OFF AND CONNECT MCU CONNECTOR. START ENGINE AND OPERATE FOR A MINIMUM OF 1 MINUTE.

INCREASE ENGINE SPEED TO MORE THAN 1200 RPM. HOLD THE CHOKE VALVE CLOSED FOR AT LEAST 20 SECONDS AND TURN IGNITION OFF WITH VALVE CLOSED.

OBSERVE STEPPER MOTOR METERING PINS. PINS SHOULD BE IN LEAN POSITION (TOWARD REAR OF ENGINE).

POSITION OK ?

YES → (continues)

NO → STEPPER MOTOR PINS ARE AT MIDWAY TO FULL RICH POSITION. REPLACE MCU AND RE-TEST STEPPER MOTOR PIN POSITION.

NO — TURN ENGINE OFF. DISCONNECT AND PLUG AIR HOSE CONNECTED TO EXHAUST MANIFOLD.

START ENGINE AND OPERATE FOR 1 MINUTE. TEST OXYGEN SENSOR VOLTAGE (PIN 3 OF MCU CONNECTOR).

GREATER THAN 0.6 VOLTS ?

YES → PROCEED WITH TEST 6.

NO → DISCONNECT OXYGEN SENSOR CONNECTOR AND TEST VOLTAGE AT OXYGEN SENSOR.

GREATER THAN 0.6 VOLTS ?

YES → REPAIR WIRE HARNESS BETWEEN O₂ CONNECTOR AND MCU CONNECTOR.

NO → INSPECT FOR LARGE AIR LEAK INTO MANIFOLD VACUUM. IF OK, REPLACE OXYGEN SENSOR.

START ENGINE AND OPERATE FOR 40 SECONDS. INCREASE ENGINE SPEED TO MORE THAN 1000 RPM AND LOAD ENGINE (E.G., AC ON). OBSERVE STEPPER MOTOR PIN MOVEMENT. PINS SHOULD MOVE FORE AND AFT OF A FIXED POINT.

RESTRICT AIR HOSE CONNECTED TO EXHAUST MANIFOLD AND OBSERVE AVERAGE POSITION OF STEPPER MOTOR PINS.

AVERAGE POSITION CHANGED ?

YES → PROCEED TO TEST 6.

NO → PROCEED TO TEST 7.

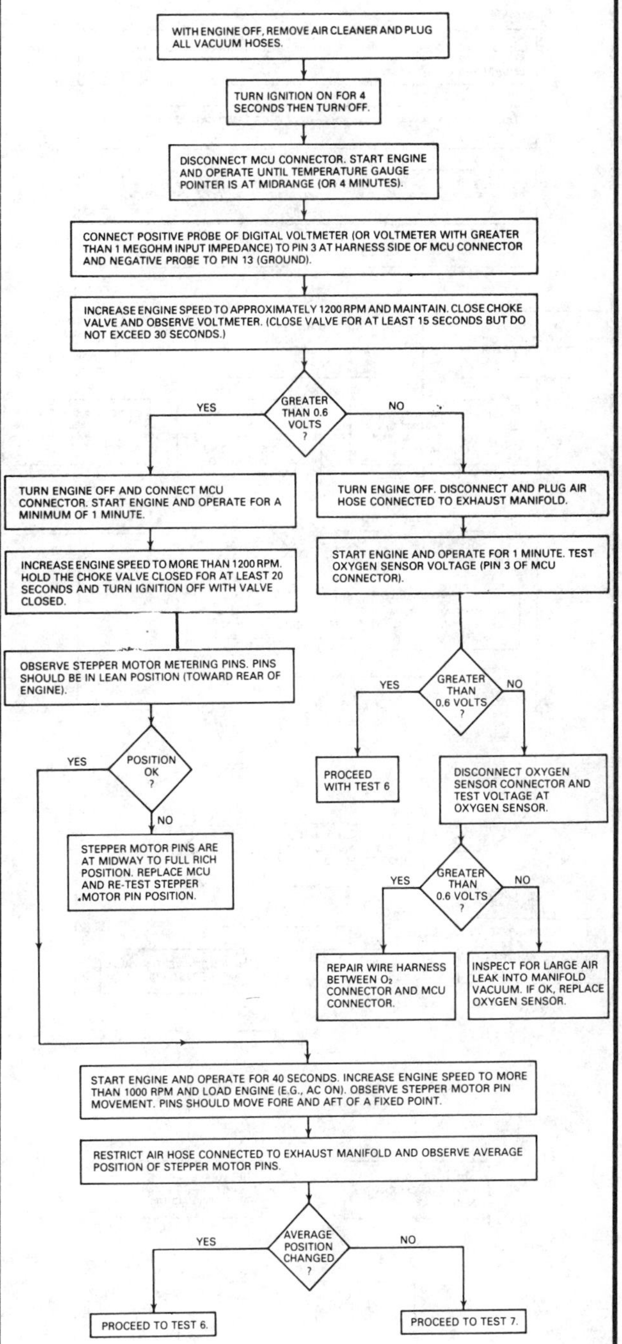

JEEP COMPUTERIZED EMISSION CONTROL (Cont.)

TEST NO. 6

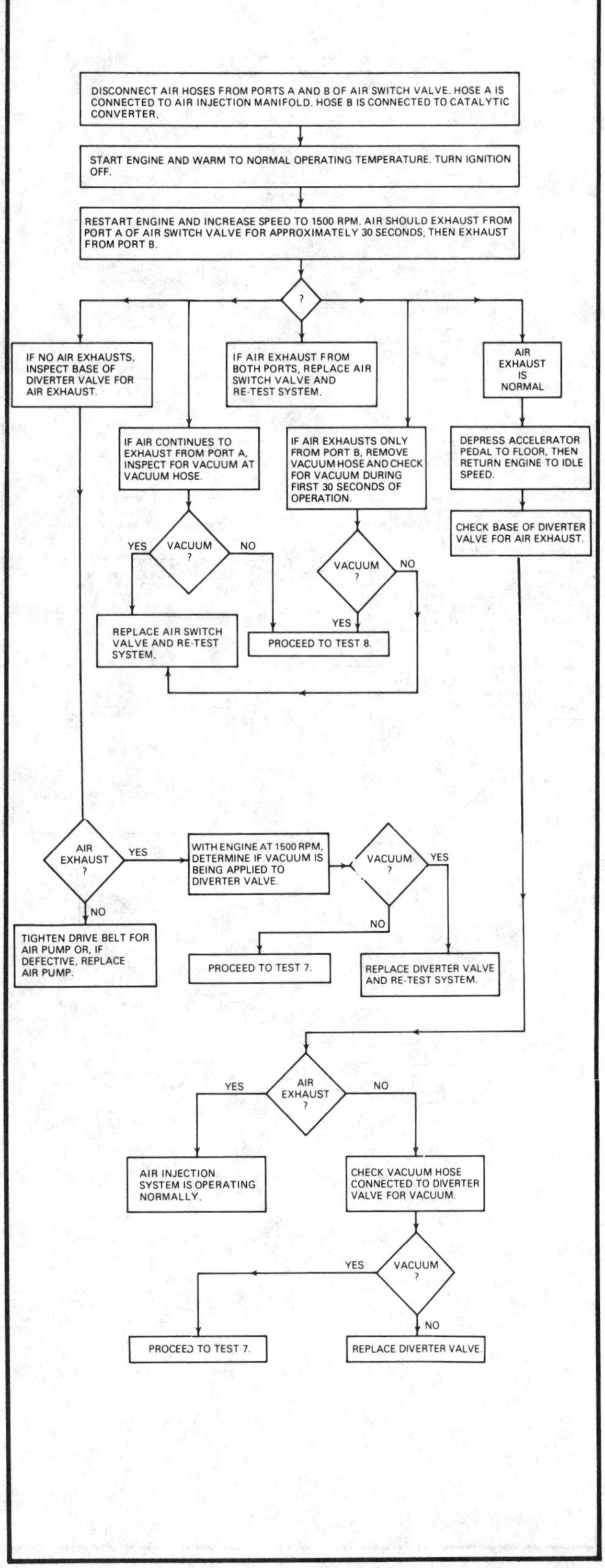

DISCONNECT AIR HOSES FROM PORTS A AND B OF AIR SWITCH VALVE. HOSE A IS CONNECTED TO AIR INJECTION MANIFOLD. HOSE B IS CONNECTED TO CATALYTIC CONVERTER.

START ENGINE AND WARM TO NORMAL OPERATING TEMPERATURE. TURN IGNITION OFF.

RESTART ENGINE AND INCREASE SPEED TO 1500 RPM. AIR SHOULD EXHAUST FROM PORT A OF AIR SWITCH VALVE FOR APPROXIMATELY 30 SECONDS, THEN EXHAUST FROM PORT B.

?

IF NO AIR EXHAUSTS, INSPECT BASE OF DIVERTER VALVE FOR AIR EXHAUST.

IF AIR EXHAUST FROM BOTH PORTS, REPLACE AIR SWITCH VALVE AND RE-TEST SYSTEM.

AIR EXHAUST IS NORMAL

IF AIR CONTINUES TO EXHAUST FROM PORT A, INSPECT FOR VACUUM AT VACUUM HOSE.

IF AIR EXHAUSTS ONLY FROM PORT B, REMOVE VACUUM HOSE AND CHECK FOR VACUUM DURING FIRST 30 SECONDS OF OPERATION.

DEPRESS ACCELERATOR PEDAL TO FLOOR, THEN RETURN ENGINE TO IDLE SPEED.

CHECK BASE OF DIVERTER VALVE FOR AIR EXHAUST.

VACUUM ? — YES / NO

VACUUM ? — NO / YES

REPLACE AIR SWITCH VALVE AND RE-TEST SYSTEM.

PROCEED TO TEST 8.

AIR EXHAUST ? — YES / NO

WITH ENGINE AT 1500 RPM, DETERMINE IF VACUUM IS BEING APPLIED TO DIVERTER VALVE.

VACUUM ? — YES / NO

TIGHTEN DRIVE BELT FOR AIR PUMP OR, IF DEFECTIVE, REPLACE AIR PUMP.

PROCEED TO TEST 7.

REPLACE DIVERTER VALVE AND RE-TEST SYSTEM.

AIR EXHAUST ? — YES / NO

AIR INJECTION SYSTEM IS OPERATING NORMALLY.

CHECK VACUUM HOSE CONNECTED TO DIVERTER VALVE FOR VACUUM.

VACUUM ? — YES / NO

PROCEED TO TEST 7.

REPLACE DIVERTER VALVE.

TEST NO. 7

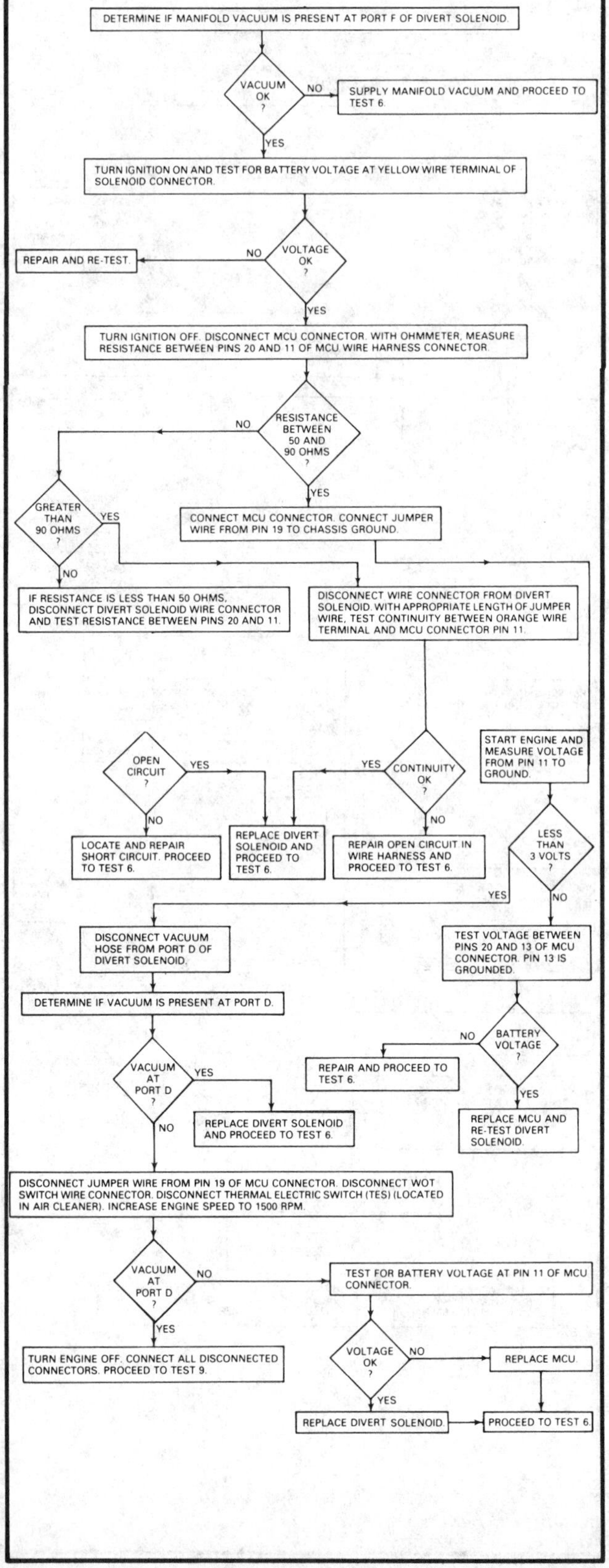

DETERMINE IF MANIFOLD VACUUM IS PRESENT AT PORT F OF DIVERT SOLENOID.

VACUUM OK ? — NO / YES

SUPPLY MANIFOLD VACUUM AND PROCEED TO TEST 6.

TURN IGNITION ON AND TEST FOR BATTERY VOLTAGE AT YELLOW WIRE TERMINAL OF SOLENOID CONNECTOR.

VOLTAGE OK ? — NO / YES

REPAIR AND RE-TEST.

TURN IGNITION OFF. DISCONNECT MCU CONNECTOR. WITH OHMMETER, MEASURE RESISTANCE BETWEEN PINS 20 AND 11 OF MCU WIRE HARNESS CONNECTOR.

RESISTANCE BETWEEN 50 AND 90 OHMS ? — NO / YES

GREATER THAN 90 OHMS ? — YES / NO

CONNECT MCU CONNECTOR. CONNECT JUMPER WIRE FROM PIN 19 TO CHASSIS GROUND.

IF RESISTANCE IS LESS THAN 50 OHMS, DISCONNECT DIVERT SOLENOID WIRE CONNECTOR AND TEST RESISTANCE BETWEEN PINS 20 AND 11.

DISCONNECT WIRE CONNECTOR FROM DIVERT SOLENOID. WITH APPROPRIATE LENGTH OF JUMPER WIRE, TEST CONTINUITY BETWEEN ORANGE WIRE TERMINAL AND MCU CONNECTOR PIN 11.

OPEN CIRCUIT ? — YES / NO

CONTINUITY OK ? — YES / NO

START ENGINE AND MEASURE VOLTAGE FROM PIN 11 TO GROUND.

LOCATE AND REPAIR SHORT CIRCUIT. PROCEED TO TEST 6.

REPLACE DIVERT SOLENOID AND PROCEED TO TEST 6.

REPAIR OPEN CIRCUIT IN WIRE HARNESS AND PROCEED TO TEST 6.

LESS THAN 3 VOLTS ? — YES / NO

DISCONNECT VACUUM HOSE FROM PORT D OF DIVERT SOLENOID.

TEST VOLTAGE BETWEEN PINS 20 AND 13 OF MCU CONNECTOR. PIN 13 IS GROUNDED.

DETERMINE IF VACUUM IS PRESENT AT PORT D.

VACUUM AT PORT D ? — YES / NO

REPLACE DIVERT SOLENOID AND PROCEED TO TEST 6.

BATTERY VOLTAGE ? — NO / YES

REPAIR AND PROCEED TO TEST 6.

REPLACE MCU AND RE-TEST DIVERT SOLENOID.

DISCONNECT JUMPER WIRE FROM PIN 19 OF MCU CONNECTOR. DISCONNECT WOT SWITCH WIRE CONNECTOR. DISCONNECT THERMAL ELECTRIC SWITCH (TES) (LOCATED IN AIR CLEANER). INCREASE ENGINE SPEED TO 1500 RPM.

VACUUM AT PORT D ? — NO / YES

TEST FOR BATTERY VOLTAGE AT PIN 11 OF MCU CONNECTOR.

TURN ENGINE OFF. CONNECT ALL DISCONNECTED CONNECTORS. PROCEED TO TEST 9.

VOLTAGE OK ? — NO / YES

REPLACE MCU.

REPLACE DIVERT SOLENOID → PROCEED TO TEST 6.

JEEP COMPUTERIZED EMISSION CONTROL (Cont.)

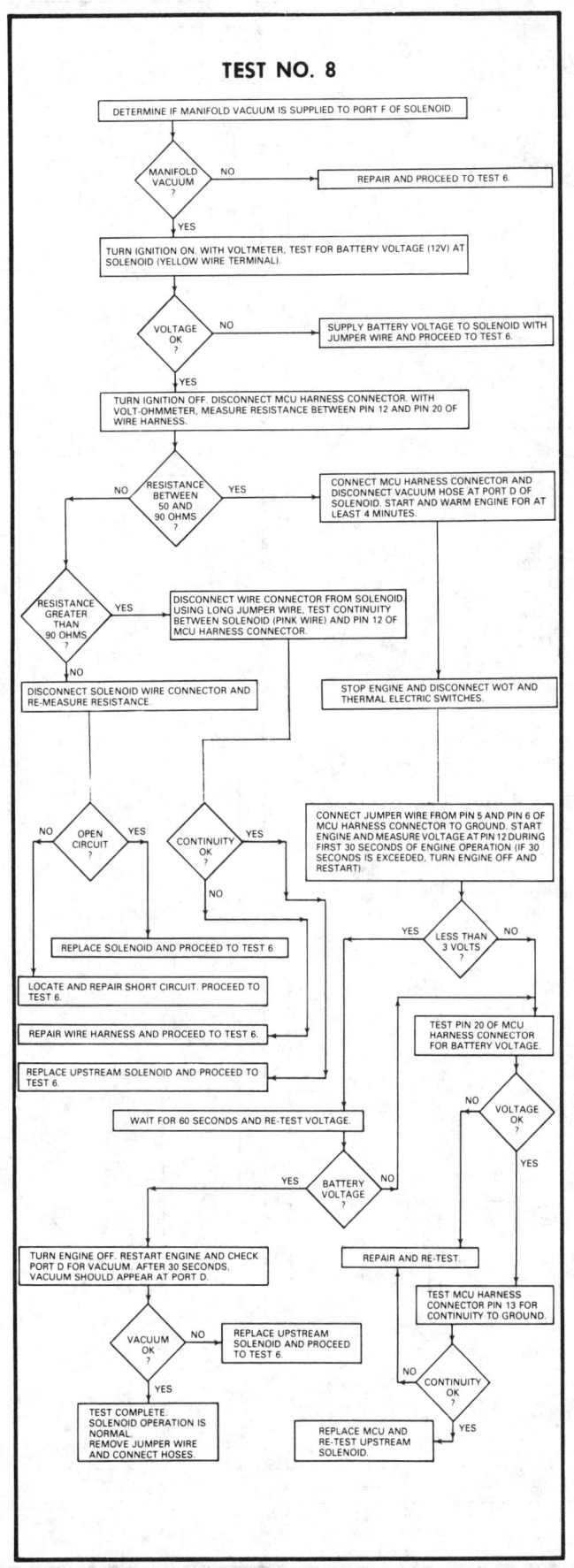

TEST NO. 8

JEEP COMPUTERIZED EMISSION CONTROL (Cont.)

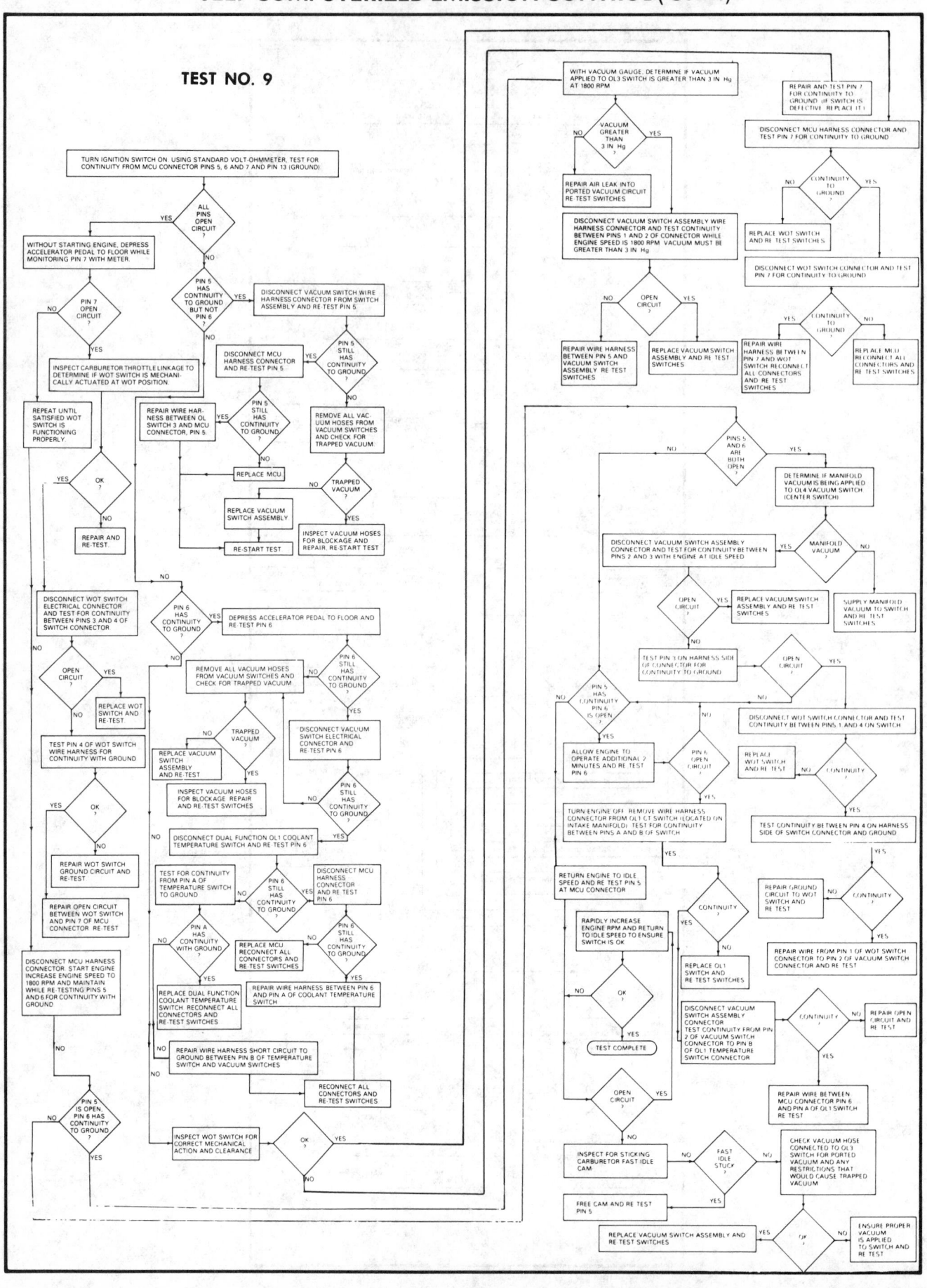

JEEP COMPUTERIZED EMISSION CONTROL (Cont.)

TEST NO. 10

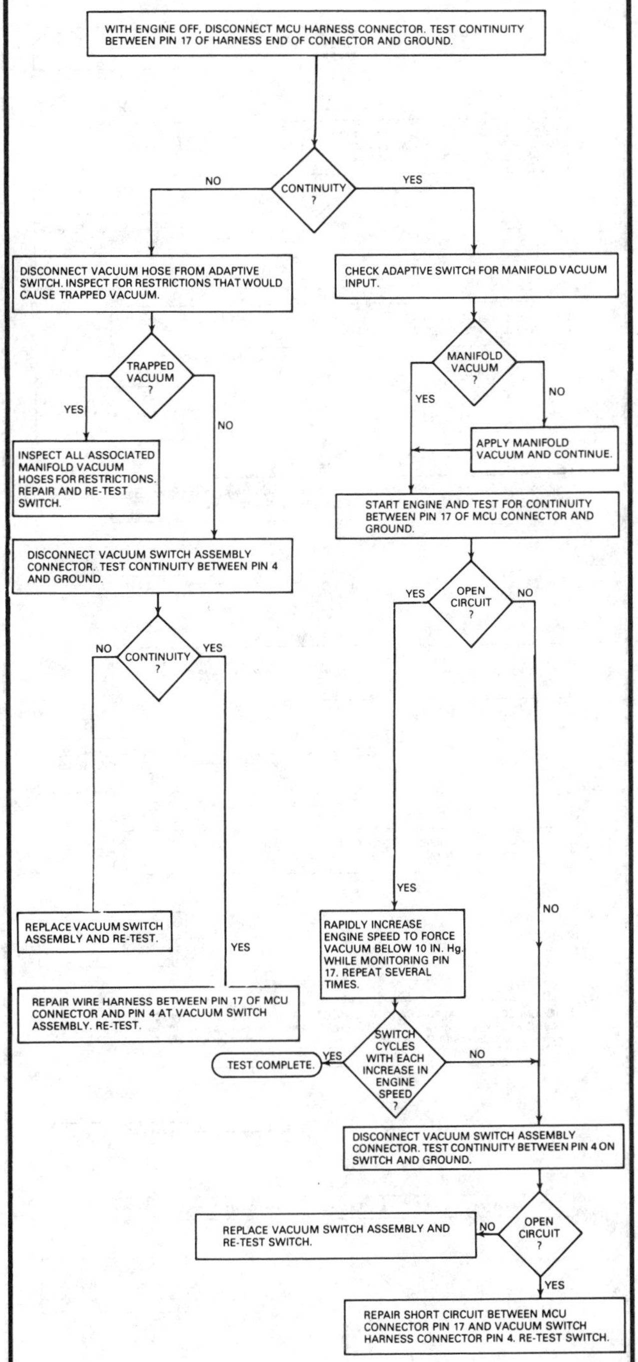

WITH ENGINE OFF, DISCONNECT MCU HARNESS CONNECTOR. TEST CONTINUITY BETWEEN PIN 17 OF HARNESS END OF CONNECTOR AND GROUND.
CONTINUITY ?
NO
YES
DISCONNECT VACUUM HOSE FROM ADAPTIVE SWITCH. INSPECT FOR RESTRICTIONS THAT WOULD CAUSE TRAPPED VACUUM.
TRAPPED VACUUM ?
YES
NO
INSPECT ALL ASSOCIATED MANIFOLD VACUUM HOSES FOR RESTRICTIONS. REPAIR AND RE-TEST SWITCH.
DISCONNECT VACUUM SWITCH ASSEMBLY CONNECTOR. TEST CONTINUITY BETWEEN PIN 4 AND GROUND.
CONTINUITY ?
NO
YES
REPLACE VACUUM SWITCH ASSEMBLY AND RE-TEST.
YES
REPAIR WIRE HARNESS BETWEEN PIN 17 OF MCU CONNECTOR AND PIN 4 AT VACUUM SWITCH ASSEMBLY. RE-TEST.
CHECK ADAPTIVE SWITCH FOR MANIFOLD VACUUM INPUT.
MANIFOLD VACUUM ?
YES
NO
APPLY MANIFOLD VACUUM AND CONTINUE.
START ENGINE AND TEST FOR CONTINUITY BETWEEN PIN 17 OF MCU CONNECTOR AND GROUND.
OPEN CIRCUIT ?
YES
NO
RAPIDLY INCREASE ENGINE SPEED TO FORCE VACUUM BELOW 10 IN. Hg. WHILE MONITORING PIN 17. REPEAT SEVERAL TIMES.
SWITCH CYCLES WITH EACH INCREASE IN ENGINE SPEED ?
YES
TEST COMPLETE.
NO
DISCONNECT VACUUM SWITCH ASSEMBLY CONNECTOR. TEST CONTINUITY BETWEEN PIN 4 ON SWITCH AND GROUND.
OPEN CIRCUIT ?
NO
REPLACE VACUUM SWITCH ASSEMBLY AND RE-TEST SWITCH.
YES
REPAIR SHORT CIRCUIT BETWEEN MCU CONNECTOR PIN 17 AND VACUUM SWITCH HARNESS CONNECTOR PIN 4. RE-TEST SWITCH.

TEST NO. 11

WITH ENGINE PREVIOUSLY WARMED, START ENGINE. WITH ENGINE AT CURB IDLE SPEED, DISCONNECT ADAPTIVE SWITCH VACUUM HOSE AND PLUG. OBSERVE CHECK ENGINE DISPLAY.
TROUBLE CODE 21 FLASHES ?
YES
NO
ALTITUDE JUMPER WIRE INSTALLED ?
NO
SYSTEM OK.
YES
WITH OHMMETER, TEST CONTINUITY BETWEEN PINS 18 AND 13 OF MCU CONNECTOR.
CONTINUITY ?
YES
NO
REPLACE MCU AND RE-TEST.
INSTALL JUMPER WIRE BETWEEN PIN 18 AND GROUND. RE-TEST.
ALTITUDE JUMPER WIRE INSTALLED ?
YES
SYSTEM OK.
NO
WITH OHMMETER, TEST CONTINUITY BETWEEN PINS 18 AND 13 AT MCU CONNECTOR.
CONTINUITY ?
NO
YES
REPAIR SHORT CIRCUIT TO GROUND FROM PIN 18 OF MCU CONNECTOR. RE-TEST.
PROCEED TO TESTS 9 AND 10 IF NOT PREVIOUSLY PERFORMED. IF RESULTS OF TESTS 9 AND 10 ARE OK, REPLACE MCU AND RE-TEST CIRCUIT.

TEST NO. 12

WARM ENGINE UNTIL AT NORMAL OPERATING TEMPERATURE. IF VEHICLE HAS BEEN RECENTLY EXPOSED TO ENVIRONMENT WITH TEMPERATURE BELOW 40°F (4.5°C), ALLOW 2 EXTRA MINUTES FOR ENGINE WARM-UP. WITH OHMMETER, TEST CONTINUITY BETWEEN PIN 19 AND CHASSIS GROUND.
OPEN CIRCUIT ?
YES
NO
SWITCH OK.
DISCONNECT AIR CLEANER MOUNTED TES CONNECTOR AND RE-TEST.
CONTINUITY TO GROUND ?
NO
REPLACE TES AND RE-TEST.
YES
DISCONNECT MCU CONNECTOR AND TEST PIN 19 TO GROUND.
CONTINUITY TO GROUND ?
YES
REPAIR SHORT CIRCUIT IN WIRE HARNESS BETWEEN PIN 19 AND GROUND. RE-TEST SWITCH.
NO
REPLACE MCU AND RE-TEST SWITCH.

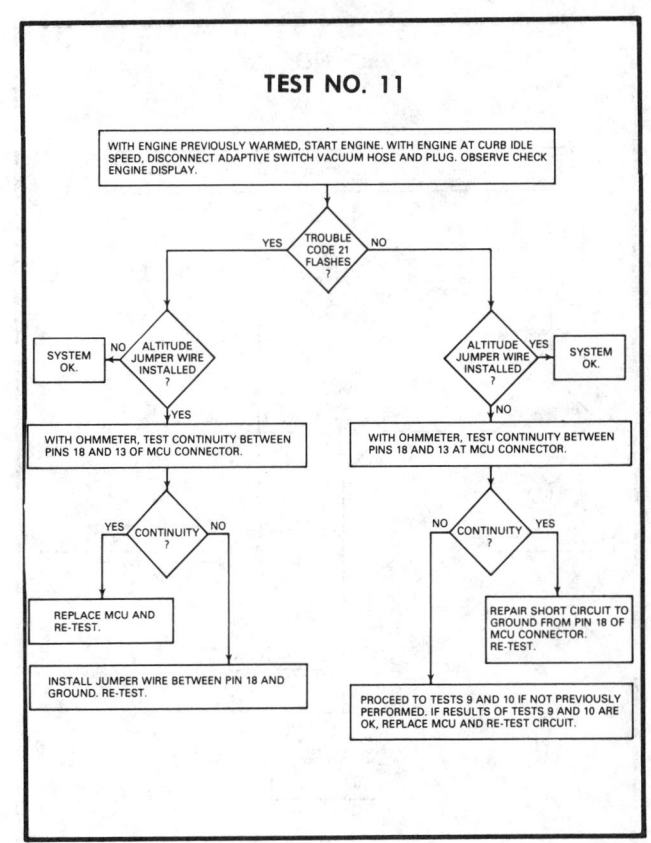

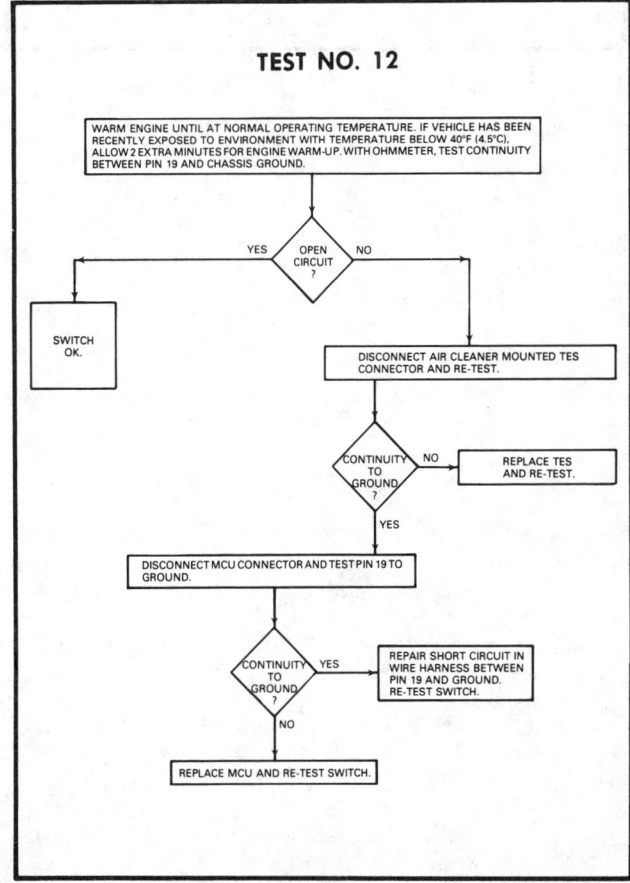

1981 Exhaust Emission Systems

JEEP COMPUTERIZED EMISSION CONTROL (Cont.)

TEST NO. 13

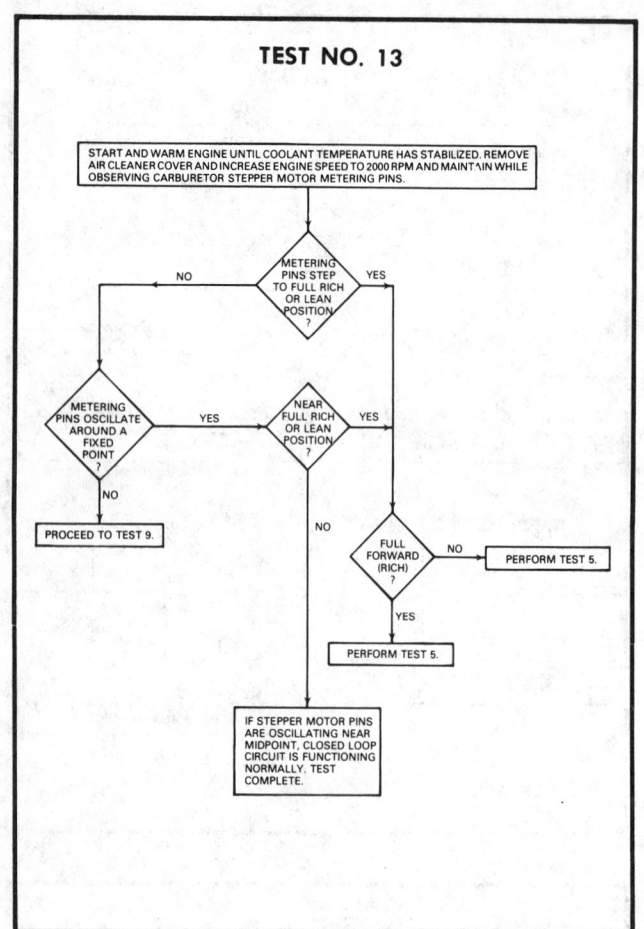

START AND WARM ENGINE UNTIL COOLANT TEMPERATURE HAS STABILIZED. REMOVE AIR CLEANER COVER AND INCREASE ENGINE SPEED TO 2000 RPM AND MAINTAIN WHILE OBSERVING CARBURETOR STEPPER MOTOR METERING PINS.

METERING PINS STEP TO FULL RICH OR LEAN POSITION ?

METERING PINS OSCILLATE AROUND A FIXED POINT ?

NEAR FULL RICH OR LEAN POSITION ?

FULL FORWARD (RICH) ?

PROCEED TO TEST 9.

PERFORM TEST 5.

PERFORM TEST 5.

IF STEPPER MOTOR PINS ARE OSCILLATING NEAR MIDPOINT, CLOSED LOOP CIRCUIT IS FUNCTIONING NORMALLY. TEST COMPLETE.

TEST NO. 14

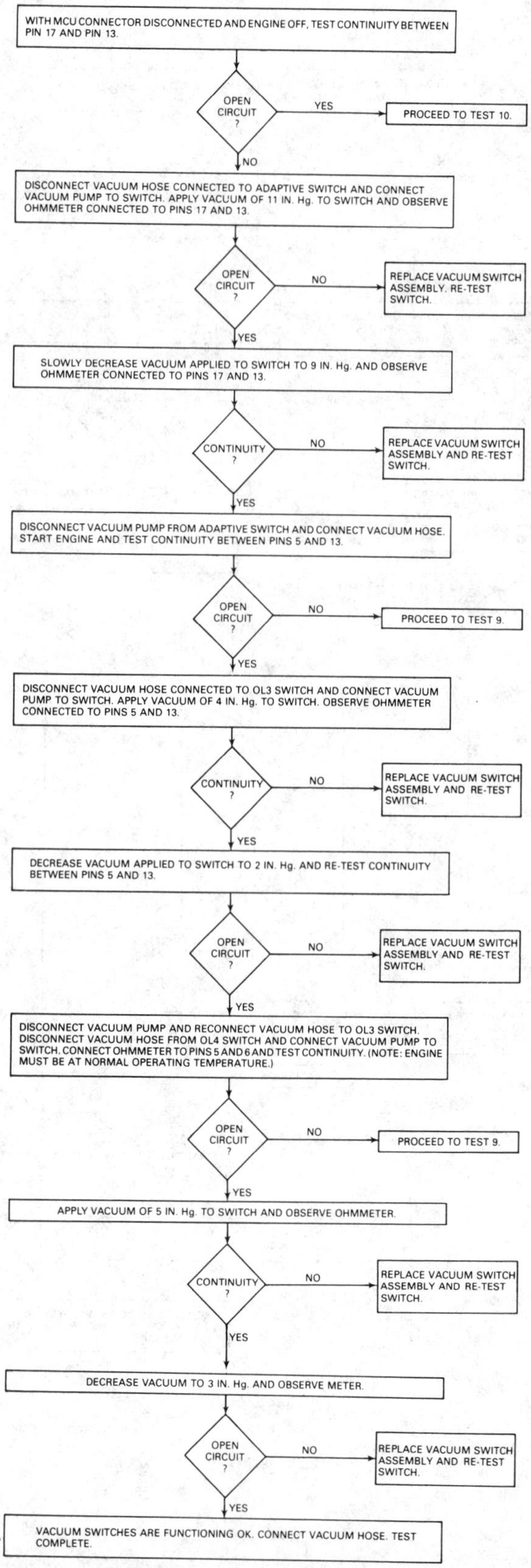

WITH MCU CONNECTOR DISCONNECTED AND ENGINE OFF, TEST CONTINUITY BETWEEN PIN 17 AND PIN 13.

OPEN CIRCUIT ? — YES → PROCEED TO TEST 10.

DISCONNECT VACUUM HOSE CONNECTED TO ADAPTIVE SWITCH AND CONNECT VACUUM PUMP TO SWITCH. APPLY VACUUM OF 11 IN. Hg. TO SWITCH AND OBSERVE OHMMETER CONNECTED TO PINS 17 AND 13.

OPEN CIRCUIT ? — NO → REPLACE VACUUM SWITCH ASSEMBLY. RE-TEST SWITCH.

SLOWLY DECREASE VACUUM APPLIED TO SWITCH TO 9 IN. Hg. AND OBSERVE OHMMETER CONNECTED TO PINS 17 AND 13.

CONTINUITY ? — NO → REPLACE VACUUM SWITCH ASSEMBLY AND RE-TEST SWITCH.

DISCONNECT VACUUM PUMP FROM ADAPTIVE SWITCH AND CONNECT VACUUM HOSE. START ENGINE AND TEST CONTINUITY BETWEEN PINS 5 AND 13.

OPEN CIRCUIT ? — NO → PROCEED TO TEST 9.

DISCONNECT VACUUM HOSE CONNECTED TO OL3 SWITCH AND CONNECT VACUUM PUMP TO SWITCH. APPLY VACUUM OF 4 IN. Hg. TO SWITCH. OBSERVE OHMMETER CONNECTED TO PINS 5 AND 13.

CONTINUITY ? — NO → REPLACE VACUUM SWITCH ASSEMBLY AND RE-TEST SWITCH.

DECREASE VACUUM APPLIED TO SWITCH TO 2 IN. Hg. AND RE-TEST CONTINUITY BETWEEN PINS 5 AND 13.

OPEN CIRCUIT ? — NO → REPLACE VACUUM SWITCH ASSEMBLY AND RE-TEST SWITCH.

DISCONNECT VACUUM PUMP AND RECONNECT VACUUM HOSE TO OL3 SWITCH. DISCONNECT VACUUM HOSE FROM OL4 SWITCH AND CONNECT VACUUM PUMP TO SWITCH. CONNECT OHMMETER TO PINS 5 AND 6 AND TEST CONTINUITY. (NOTE: ENGINE MUST BE AT NORMAL OPERATING TEMPERATURE.)

OPEN CIRCUIT ? — NO → PROCEED TO TEST 9.

APPLY VACUUM OF 5 IN. Hg. TO SWITCH AND OBSERVE OHMMETER.

CONTINUITY ? — NO → REPLACE VACUUM SWITCH ASSEMBLY AND RE-TEST SWITCH.

DECREASE VACUUM TO 3 IN. Hg. AND OBSERVE METER.

OPEN CIRCUIT ? — NO → REPLACE VACUUM SWITCH ASSEMBLY AND RE-TEST SWITCH.

VACUUM SWITCHES ARE FUNCTIONING OK. CONNECT VACUUM HOSE. TEST COMPLETE.

JEEP COMPUTERIZED EMISSION CONTROL (Cont.)

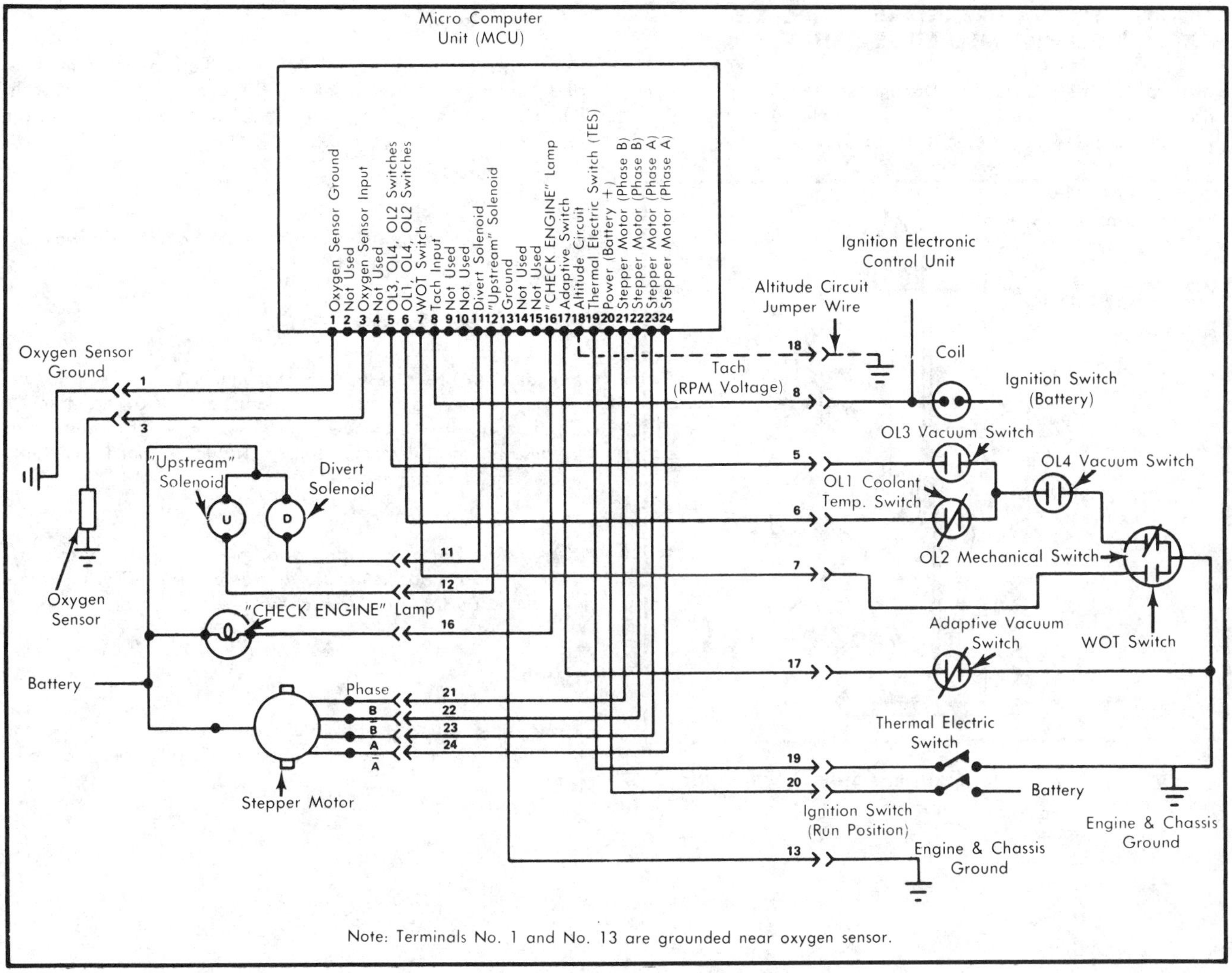

Micro Computer Unit (MCU)

Oxygen Sensor Ground
Not Used
Oxygen Sensor Input
Not Used
OL3, OL4, OL2 Switches
OL1, OL4, OL2 Switches
WOT Switch
Tach Input
Not Used
Not Used
Divert Solenoid
"Upstream" Solenoid
Ground
Not Used
Not Used
"CHECK ENGINE" Lamp
Adaptive Switch
Altitude Circuit
Thermal Electric Switch (TES)
Power (Battery +)
Stepper Motor (Phase B)
Stepper Motor (Phase B)
Stepper Motor (Phase A)
Stepper Motor (Phase A)

1 2 3 4 5 6 7 8 9 10 11 12 13 14 15 16 17 18 19 20 21 22 23 24

Oxygen Sensor Ground
Oxygen Sensor
Battery
"Upstream" Solenoid
Divert Solenoid
"CHECK ENGINE" Lamp
Stepper Motor
Phase
B
B
A
A

21 22 23 24

11 12 16

1 3

Tach (RPM Voltage)

Ignition Electronic Control Unit
Altitude Circuit Jumper Wire
Coil
Ignition Switch (Battery)

OL3 Vacuum Switch
OL1 Coolant Temp. Switch
OL4 Vacuum Switch
OL2 Mechanical Switch
WOT Switch
Adaptive Vacuum Switch
Thermal Electric Switch

Ignition Switch (Run Position)
Battery
Engine & Chassis Ground
Engine & Chassis Ground

18 8 5 6 7 17 19 20 13

Note: Terminals No. 1 and No. 13 are grounded near oxygen sensor.

Fig. 3   Jeep CEC System Wiring Diagram

MAINTENANCE

The CEC system does not require periodic maintenance. However, when vehicle is raised for other services, check condition of catalytic converter, oxygen sensor and exhaust system.

REMOVAL & INSTALLATION

MICRO COMPUTER UNIT (MCU)

Removal & Installation — Remove MCU attaching bolts. Disconnect electrical plug connector. To install MCU, reverse removal procedure and ensure terminal ends are not forced out of position when connecting plug.

STEPPER MOTOR

CAUTION — Do not drop metering pins and spring when removing stepper motor.

Removal & Installation — Remove air cleaner and disconnect motor connector. Remove retaining screw and unit from carburetor. To install, reverse removal procedure and tighten screw to 25 INCH Lbs.

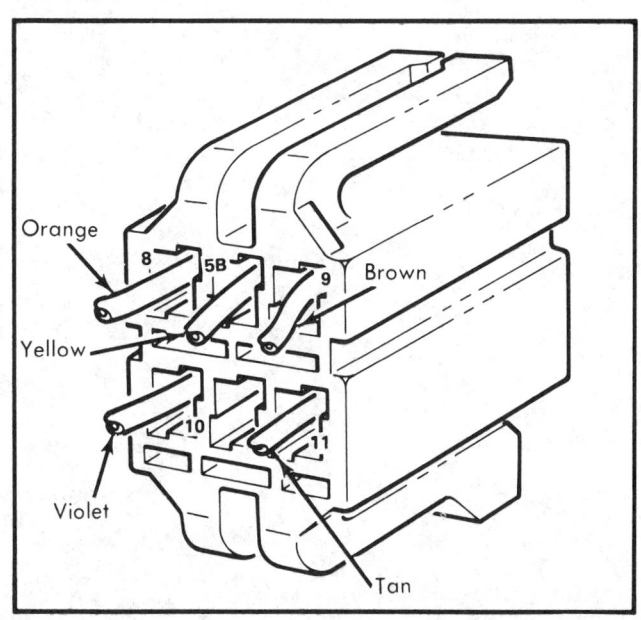

Orange
Brown
8   5B   9
Yellow
10   11
Violet
Tan

Fig. 4   Stepper Motor Connector Terminal Identification

JEEP COMPUTERIZED EMISSION CONTROL (Cont.)

COOLANT TEMPERATURE/INTAKE MANIFOLD HEATER COOLANT TEMPERATURE SWITCH

Removal & Installation — Disconnect electrical connector and remove switch. Install replacement switch and tighten to 72 INCH Lbs. Reconnect electrical lead.

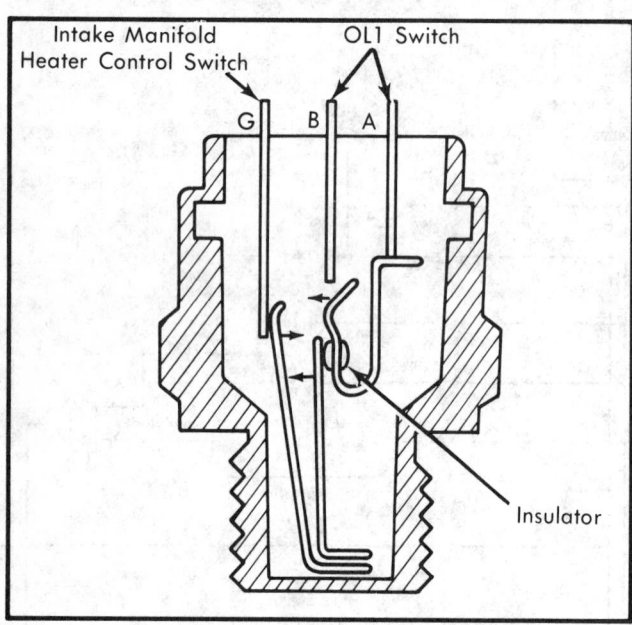

Fig. 5 Coolant Temperature Switch Schematic

VACUUM SWITCHES

Removal & Installation — Note positions of vacuum hoses and disconnect from switches. Disconnect electrical leads. Remove vacuum switches and bracket assembly. To install, reverse removal procedure.

NOTE — *Vacuum switches are not serviced individually. Replace as component set.*

OXYGEN SENSOR

Removal & Installation — Disconnect electrical lead and remove sensor from manifold. Clean threads of manifold. To install, coat threads of new oxygen sensor with anti-seize compound and carefully install sensor. Tighten sensor to 31 ft. lbs. Reconnect electrical lead.

NOTE — *Do not push rubber boot down on sensor body more than ½" above base. Also, oxygen sensor pigtail wires cannot be spliced or soldered. If broken, replace sensor.*

TIMER

Removal & Installation — Disconnect electrical connector. Remove mounting screw and timer. To install, reverse removal procedure.

JEEP SPARK CONTROL SYSTEMS

DESCRIPTION

Jeep vehicles use spark control devices to assist the ignition system in controlling exhaust emissions. They are the Spark Control Temperature Override (CTO) valve, the Non-Linear Vacuum Regulator (NLVR) valve, a Forward Delay Valve, A Reverse Delay Valve, and on 4 cylinder engines, a Vacuum Spark Control Delay Valve and a Thermal Vacuum Spark Control valve. System application depends upon engine size, emissions category and vehicle model.

SPARK COOLANT TEMPERATURE OVERRIDE SYSTEM

This system alternates distributor vacuum advance vacuum source between carburetor ported vacuum and manifold vacuum, depending upon coolant temperature. Two types of CTO switch are used: a single-function switch for models with standard cooling systems, and a single-function switch for heavy duty cooling systems. The CTO switch is threaded into the left rear of block on 6 cylinder engines, and into the thermostat housing on 4 and 8 cylinder engines. On some models, this system is used in conjunction with the NLVR valve.

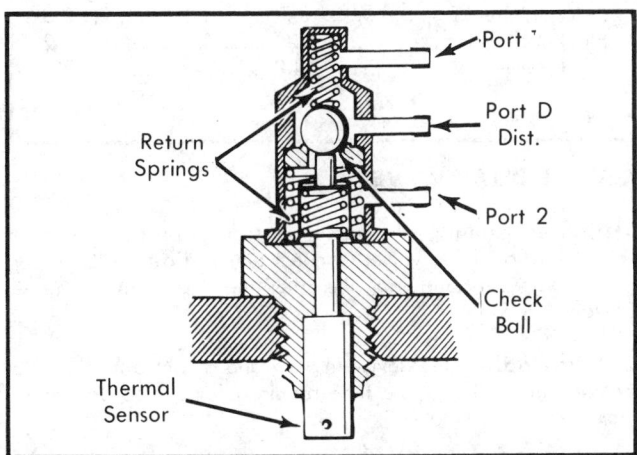

Fig 1   Sectional View of Single-Function CTO Switch

NON-LINEAR VACUUM REGULATOR VALVE

Used on some models, this valve supplies vacuum advance unit with a regulated combination of manifold and carburetor ported vacuum when engine load is low and switches to supply only carburetor ported vacuum as load increases.

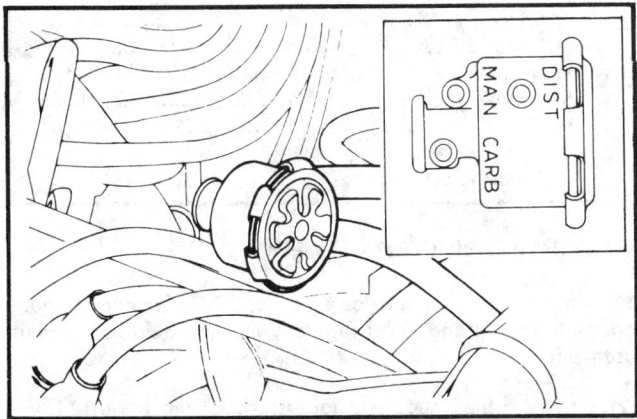

Fig. 2   Non-Linear Vacuum Regulator Valve

OPERATION

SPARK COOLANT TEMPERATURE OVERRIDE SWITCH

Single-Function for Standard Cooling — When coolant temperature is below 149°F on 6 and 8 cylinder engines, or 120°F on 4 cylinder engines, the check ball is held against inner seat by spring tension. Manifold vacuum enters through port "1" and is applied through port "D". When temperature goes above specified limits, the check ball is moved up in the valve and manifold vacuum is applied from port "2" to port "D" on 4 cylinder engines, or carburetor ported vacuum is applied from port "2" to port "D" on 6 and 8 cylinder engines.

Single-Function for Heavy-Duty Cooling — Valve is used to prevent engine overheating at high ambient temperatures. When coolant temperature is below 220°F, carburetor ported vacuum enters port "1" and is applied through port "D". This allows full ported vacuum to distributor. Above 220°F, port "1" is blocked and manifold vacuum enters through port "2" and connects to port "D". Manifold vacuum then controls spark advance. *Fig. 1.*

NON-LINEAR VACUUM REGULATOR VALVE

There are 2 input ports on the NLVR: intake manifold vacuum and carburetor ported vacuum. One outlet port connects to the distributor vacuum unit. At curb idle, regulated vacuum is supplied to the advance unit, when manifold vacuum is high and ported vacuum is very low. The NLVR regulates the vacuum signal so it is between these two vacuum source levels at idle. As engine load increases and vacuum signal is above 7.5 in. Hg, regulator valve switch to ported vacuum output.

FORWARD DELAY VALVE

Some engines use this valve to improve driveability and reduce hydrocarbon emissions. The valve functions to delay the effects of sudden increases in vacuum. This prevents sudden spark advance during deceleration.

REVERSE DELAY VALVE

Some engines use this valve to improve cold driveability and reduce hydrocarbon emissions. The valve is installed in the vacuum line to delay the effects of manifold vacuum decrease which causes ignition timing to be retarded.

THERMAL VACUUM SPARK CONTROL VALVE

This valve is used on California 4 cylinder engines and is located in the air cleaner. It passes manifold vacuum to port "1" of the CTO valve and distributor vacuum advance mechanism only when the air cleaner intake is below 63°F. At temperatures above 63°F, manifold vacuum is prevented from reaching the CTO valve until the coolant temperature reaches the spark CTO valve switching point.

VACUUM SPARK CONTROL DELAY VALVE

This valve is used on 4 cylinder engines to improve driveability when the engine is cold. It is located in the vacuum advance circuit. When vacuum is greater at port "4" than at port "1", air must flow through the orifice to equalize the pressure. This creates a momentary delay that prevents a sudden decrease in spark advance. When vacuum is greater at port "1" than at

JEEP SPARK CONTROL SYSTEMS (Cont.)

port "4", air flows freely through the check valve and pressure is instantly equalized.

MAINTENANCE

Periodic maintenance is not normally required; should any switch or valve fail to function properly it should be replaced.

TESTING

SPARK COOLANT TEMPERATURE OVERRIDE SWITCH

Single-Function For Standard Cooling (6 and 8 Cylinder) — Connect a vacuum gauge to center port "D" of CTO switch. When coolant is below 165°F, manifold vacuum should register. Above 165°F, carburetor ported vacuum should register. If valve does not meet these requirements, it must be replaced.

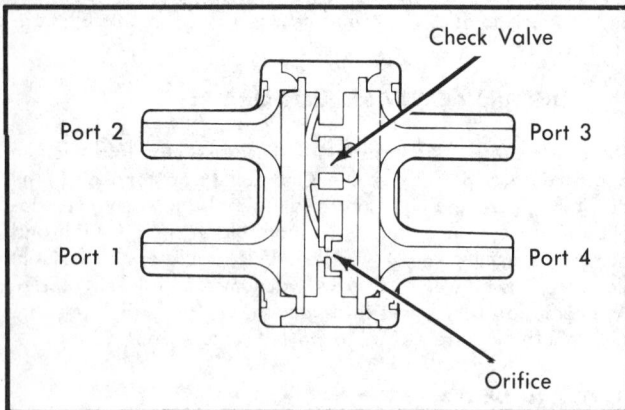

Fig. 3   Vacuum Spark Control Delay Valve (4 Cylinder Engines)

Single-Function for Standard Cooling (4 Cylinder) — Disconnect vacuum hose from distributor vacuum advance mechanism and connect a vacuum gauge to hose. Start engine. With coolant temperature below 120°F, manifold vacuum should register. Disconnect vacuum hose from port "4" of delay valve and cap. Manifold vacuum should not register until coolant temperature reaches 120°F. If valve fails these tests it must be replaced.

NOTE — *Ported vacuum is not available with throttle closed. Ported vacuum is available at part throttle (equivalent of 1000 RPM).*

Single-Function for Heavy-Duty Cooling — Connect a vacuum gauge to center port ("D") of CTO switch. When coolant is below 220°F, carburetor ported vacuum should register. Above 220°F, manifold vacuum should be indicated.

NON-LINEAR VACUUM REGULATOR VALVE

Connect vacuum gauge to distributor port ("DIST") on NLVR. With engine at idle speed, a vacuum reading of 7 in. Hg should be shown. As throttle is opened and engine speed increases, ported vacuum level should be indicated. If not, replace NLVR.

FORWARD DELAY VALVE

1) Connect an external vacuum source to port on black (or red) side of delay valve. Connect one end of a 24" section of rubber hose to vacuum gauge and the other end to the port on colored side of valve.

2) With elapsed time device in view and a constant 10 in. Hg of vacuum applied, note time required for gauge pointer to move from 0 in. Hg to 8 in. Hg.

3) If valve fails to meet time limits, replace valve. If valve meets specifications, install so that black (or red) side is toward vacuum source.

Forward Delay Valve Time Limits[1]		
Valve Color	**Min. Time**	**Max. Time**
Black/Purple	0.3	0.7
Black/Gray	0.6	1.6
Black/Brown	1.0	3.0
Red/Blue	1.9	5.7
Black/White	2.7	9.3
Black/Yellow	4.5	13.2
Black/Green	14.0	47.2

[1] — Time in seconds.

REVERSE DELAY VALVE

1) Connect external vacuum source to port on colored (non-white) side of delay valve. Connect one end of a 24" rubber hose to vacuum gauge and the other end to port on white side of valve.

2) With elapsed time device in view and a constant 10 in. Hg of vacuum applied, note time required for gauge pointer to move from 0 in. Hg to 8 in. Hg.

3) If valve fails to meet time limits, replace valve. If valve meets specifications, install with non-white side toward vacuum source.

Reverse Delay Valve Time Limits[1]		
Valve Color	**Min. Time**	**Max. Time**
White/Purple	0.3	0.7
White/Gray	0.6	1.6
White/Gold	0.8	2.3
White/Brown	1.0	3.0
White/Yellow	4.5	13.2
White/Red	14.0	47.2

[1] — Time in seconds.

VACUUM SPARK CONTROL DELAY VALVE

1) Connect a tee fitting at ports "1" and "4". Connect vacuum gauge to each fitting. Start engine. Vacuum should be equal at both ports.

2) When throttle is suddenly depressed, vacuum at port "1" will instantly decrease and vacuum at port "4" should be maintained momentarily. If valve fails these tests, replace valve.

JEEP SPARK CONTROL SYSTEMS (Cont.)

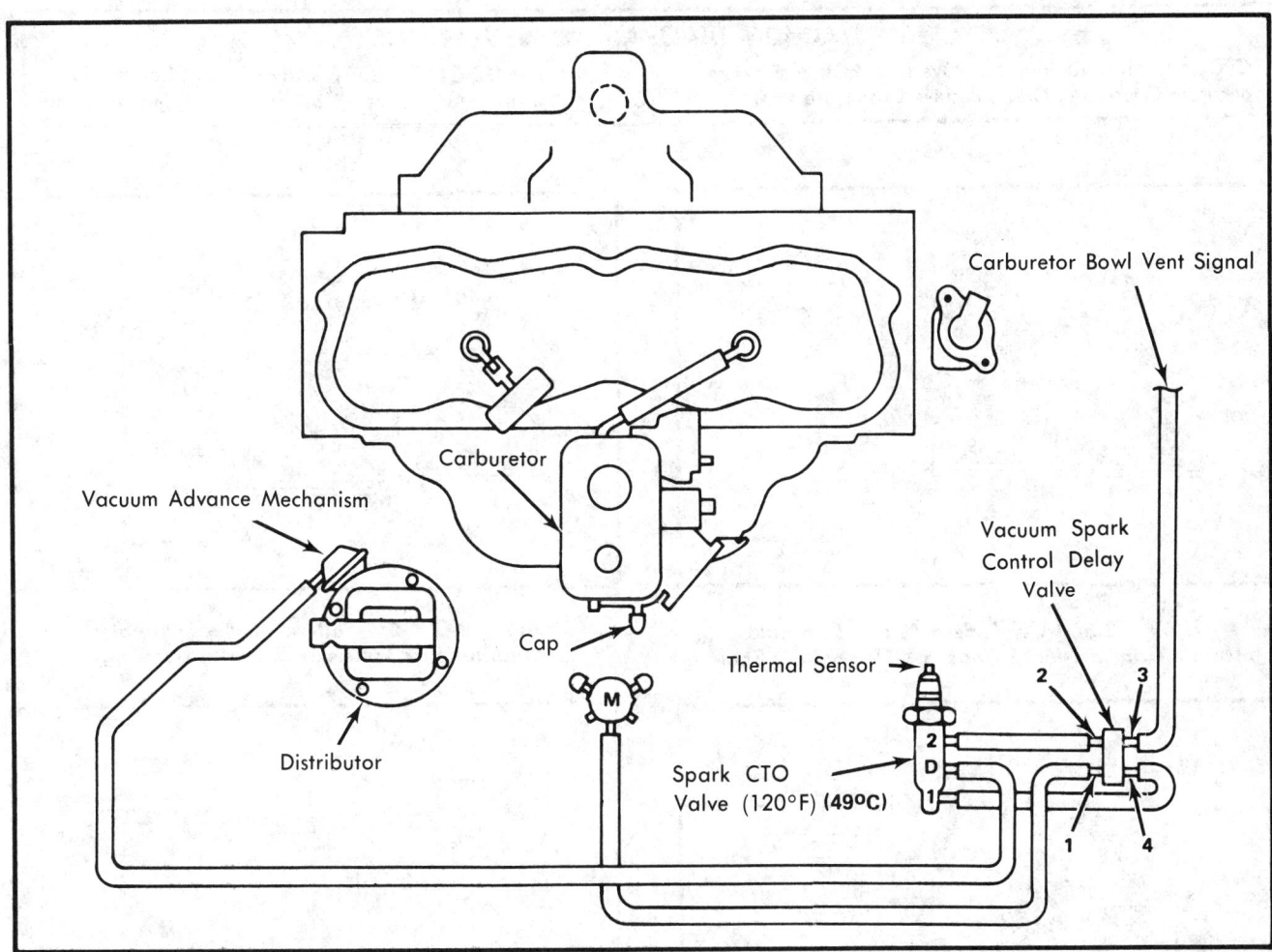

Carburetor Bowl Vent Signal

Vacuum Spark Control Delay Valve

Vacuum Advance Mechanism

Carburetor

Cap

Distributor

Thermal Sensor

Spark CTO Valve (120°F) **(49°C)**

Fig. 4   California 4-Cylinder Spark Control System

JEEP VACUUM DIAGRAMS

JEEP VACUUM DIAGRAM ABBREVIATIONS

CTO – Coolant Temperature Override; **EGR** – Exhaust Gas Recirculation; **HDC CTO** – Heavy Duty Cooling, Coolant Temperature Override; **PCV** – Positive Crankcase Ventilation; **TAC** – Thermostatic Air Cleaner; **VSD** – Vacuum Signal Dump

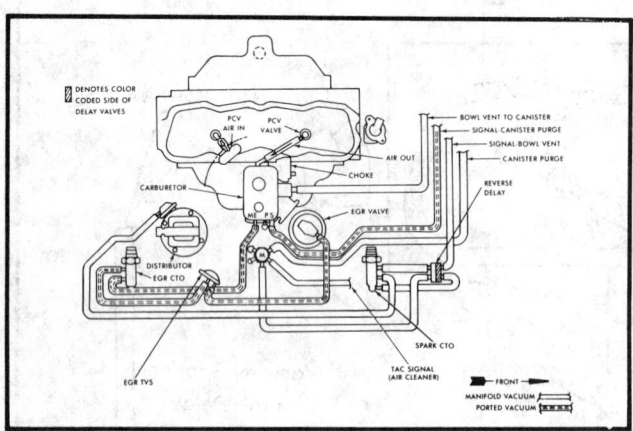

Fig. 1   2.5L 4-Cyl. Federal "CJ" & Scrambler
Manual Transmission, Standard & Heavy Duty Cooling

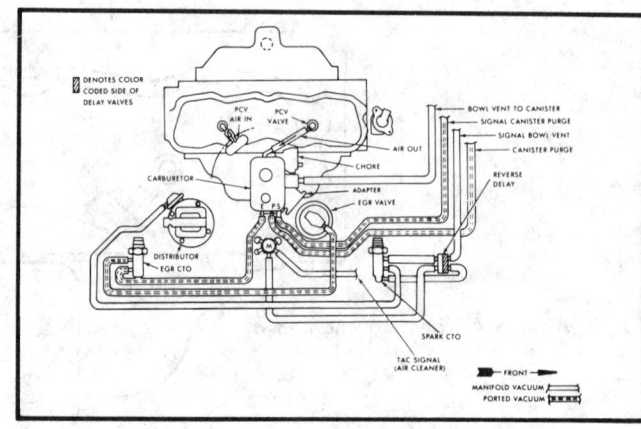

Fig. 2   2.5L 4-Cyl. Federal "CJ" & Scrambler
Automatic Transmission, Standard Cooling

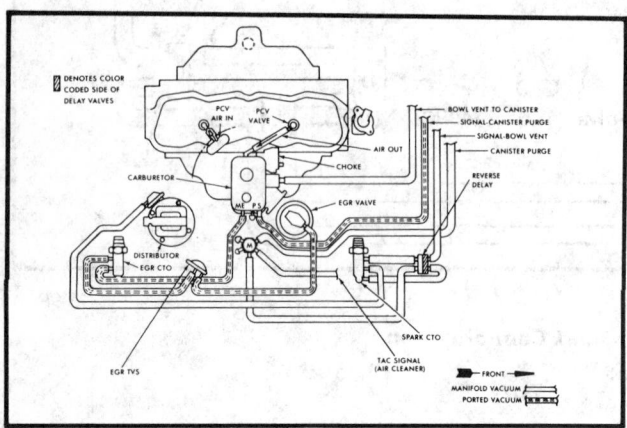

Fig. 3   2.5L 4-Cyl. Federal "CJ" & Scrambler
Automatic Transmission, Heavy Duty Cooling

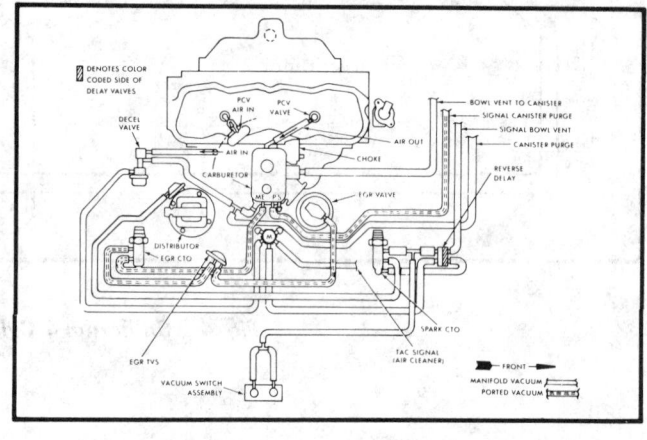

Fig. 4   2.5L 4-Cyl. Calif. "CJ" & Scrambler
Manual Transmission, Standard & Heavy Duty Cooling

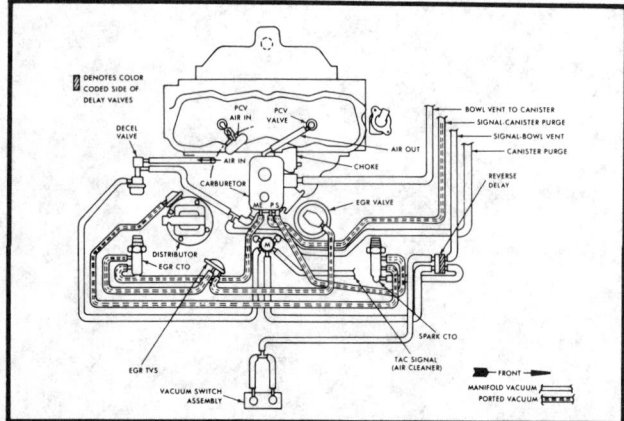

Fig. 5   2.5L 4-Cyl. Calif. CJ-7
Automatic Transmission, Standard & Heavy Duty Cooling

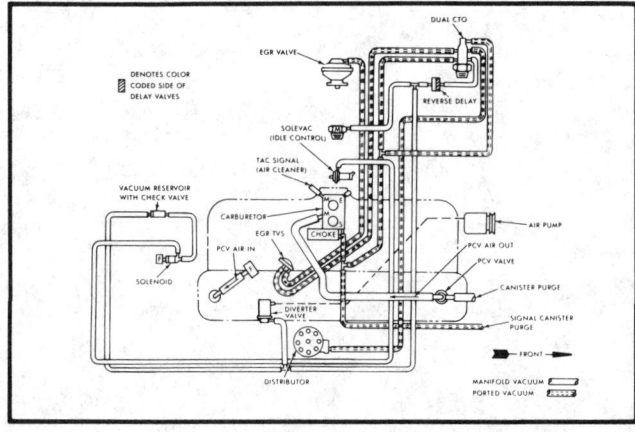

Fig. 6   4.2L 6-Cyl. Federal All Models
Manual Transmission, Standard Cooling

JEEP VACUUM DIAGRAMS (Cont.)

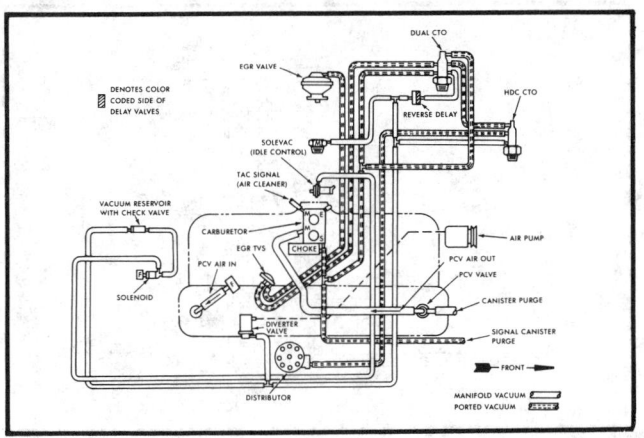

Fig. 7   4.2L 6-Cyl. Federal All Models
Manual Transmission, Heavy Duty Cooling

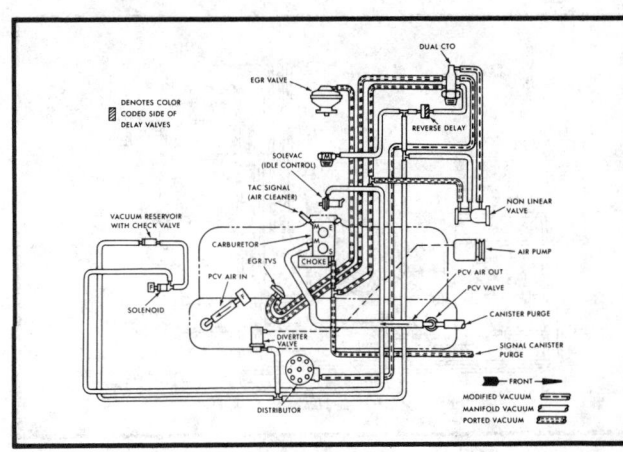

Fig. 8   4.2L 6-Cyl. Federal All Models
Automatic Transmission, Standard Cooling

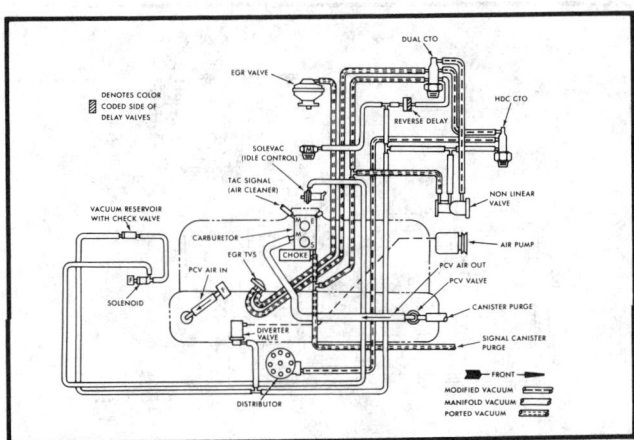

Fig. 9   4.2L 6-Cyl. Federal All Models
Automatic Transmission, Heavy Duty Cooling

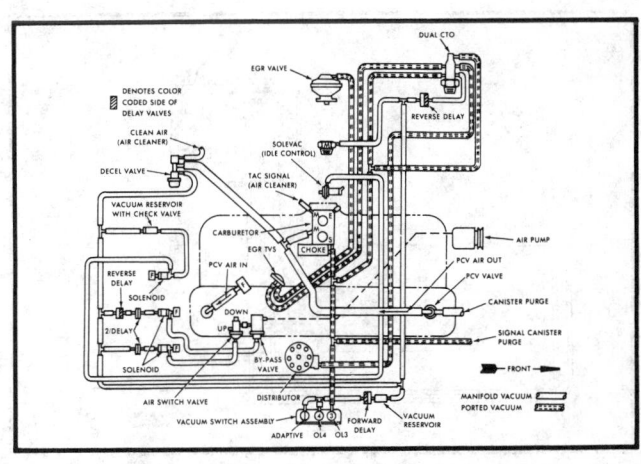

Fig. 10   4.2L 6-Cyl. Calif. All Models
Manual Transmission, Standard Cooling

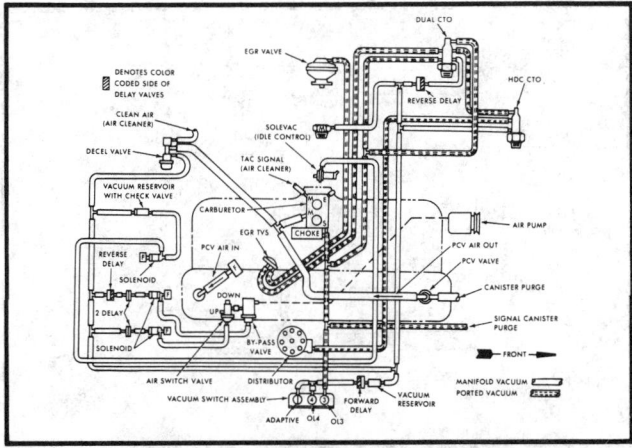

Fig. 11   4.2L 6-Cyl. Calif. All Models
Manual Transmission, Heavy Duty Cooling

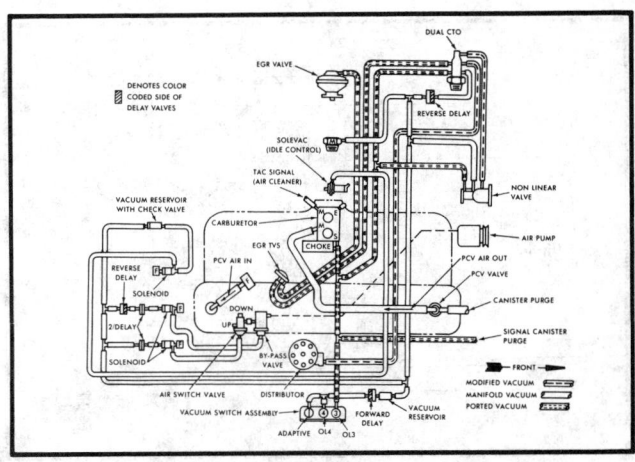

Fig. 12   4.2L 6-Cyl. Calif. All Models
Automatic Transmission, Standard Cooling

1981 Exhaust Emission Systems

JEEP VACUUM DIAGRAMS (Cont.)

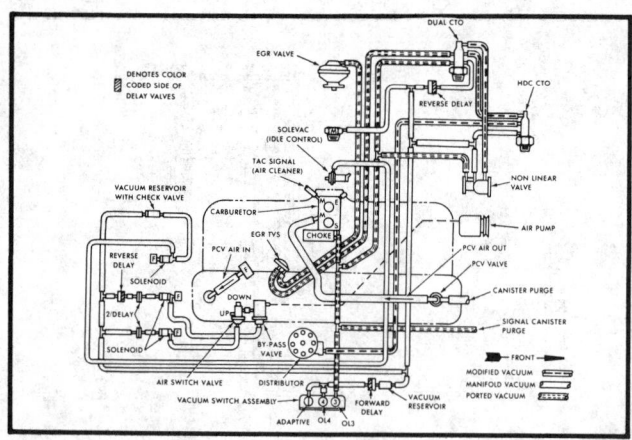

Fig. 13   4.2L 6-Cyl. Calif. All Models
Automatic Transmission, Heavy Duty Cooling

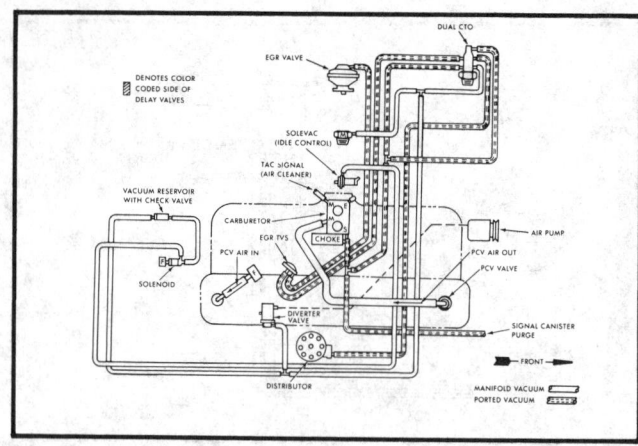

Fig. 14   4.2L 6-Cyl. High Altitude All Models
Manual Transmission, Standard Cooling

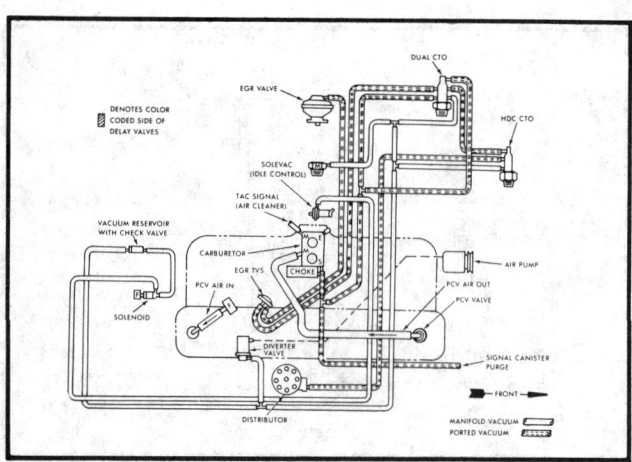

Fig. 15   4.2L 6-Cyl. High Altitude All Models
Manual Transmission, Heavy Duty Cooling

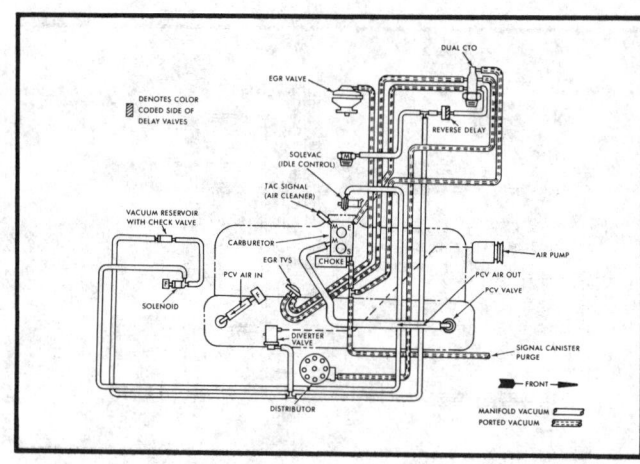

Fig. 16   4.2L 6-Cyl. High Altitude All Models
Automatic Transmission

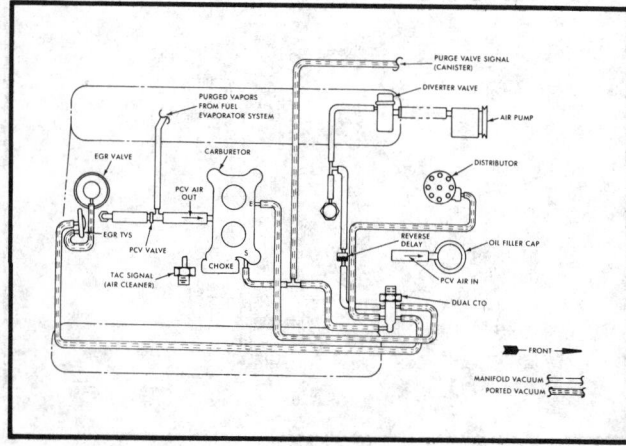

Fig. 17   5.0L V8 Federal "CJ" & Scrambler
Manual Transmission, Standard Cooling

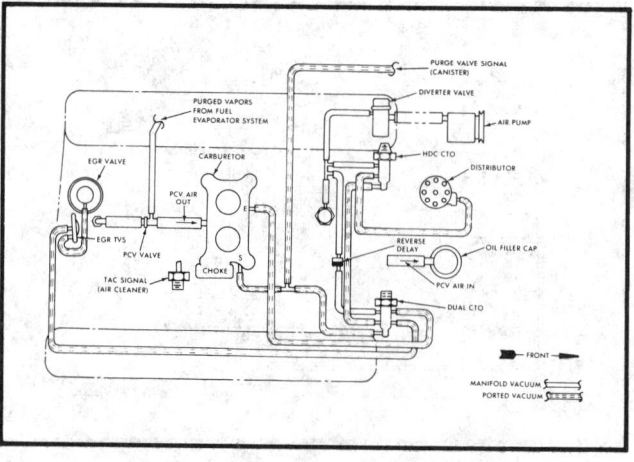

Fig. 18   5.0L V8 Federal "CJ" & Scrambler
Manual Transmission, Heavy Duty Cooling

JEEP VACUUM DIAGRAMS (Cont.)

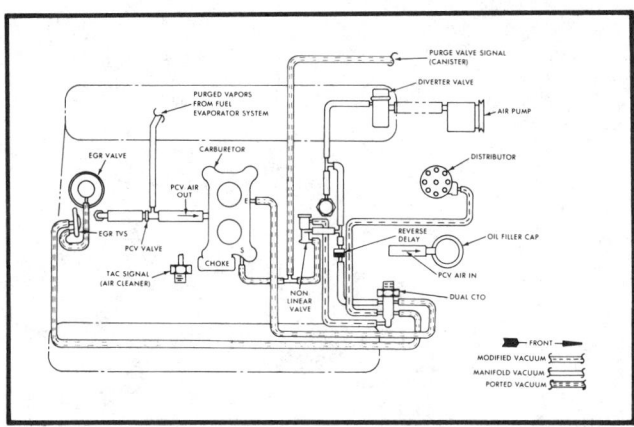

Fig. 19   5.0L V8 Federal "CJ" & Scrambler
Automatic Transmission, Standard Cooling

Fig. 20   5.0L V8 Federal "CJ" & Scrambler
Automatic Transmission, Heavy Duty Cooling

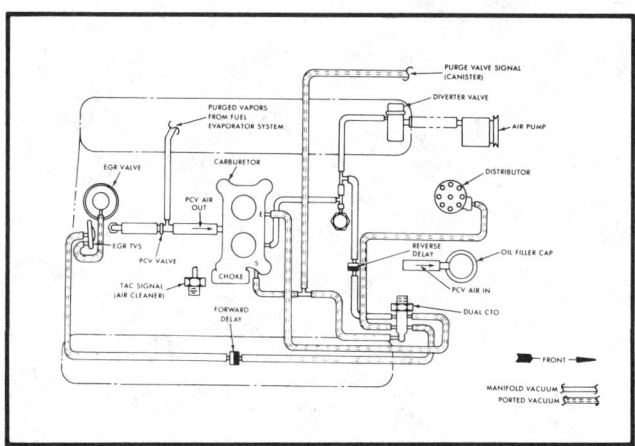

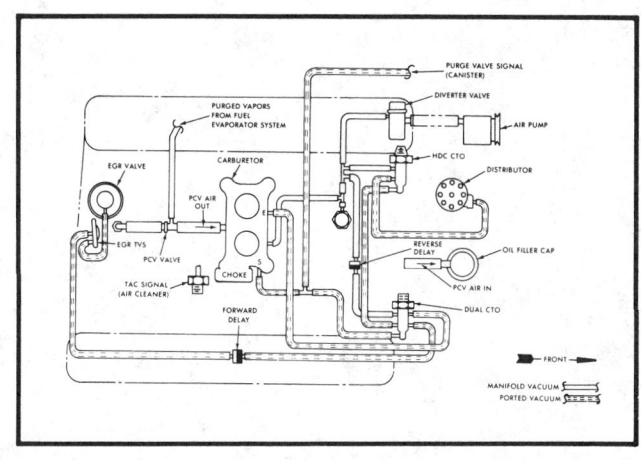

Fig. 21   5.0L V8 High Altitude "CJ" & Scrambler
Manual Transmission, Standard Cooling

Fig. 22   5.0L V8 High Altitude "CJ" & Scrambler
Manual Transmission, Heavy Duty Cooling

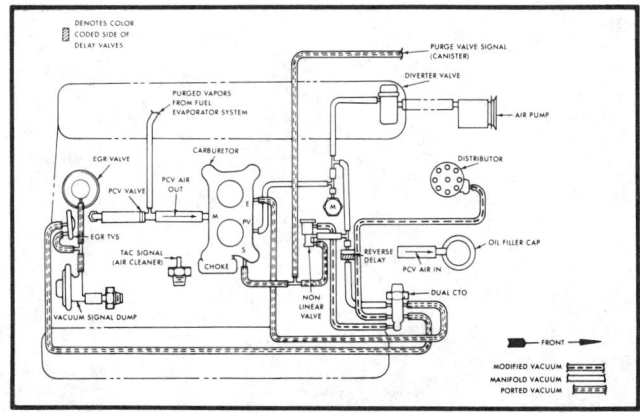

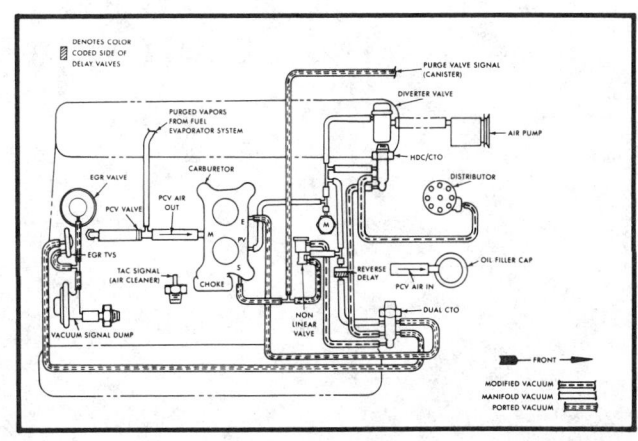

Fig. 23   6.0L V8 Federal Cherokee, Wagoneer & Truck
Manual & Automatic Transmission, Standard Cooling

Fig. 24   6.0L Federal Cherokee, Wagoneer & Truck
Manual & Automatic Transmission, Heavy Duty Cooling

Section 4
ELECTRICAL

Contents

NOTE — ALSO SEE GENERAL INDEX.

IMPORTANT

*Because of the great number of model names used by vehicle manufacturers, accurate identification of models is important.
See Model Identification at the front of this publication.*

Ignition Systems

IGNITION SYSTEM TROUBLE SHOOTING

IGNITION SECONDARY QUICK CHECK CHART

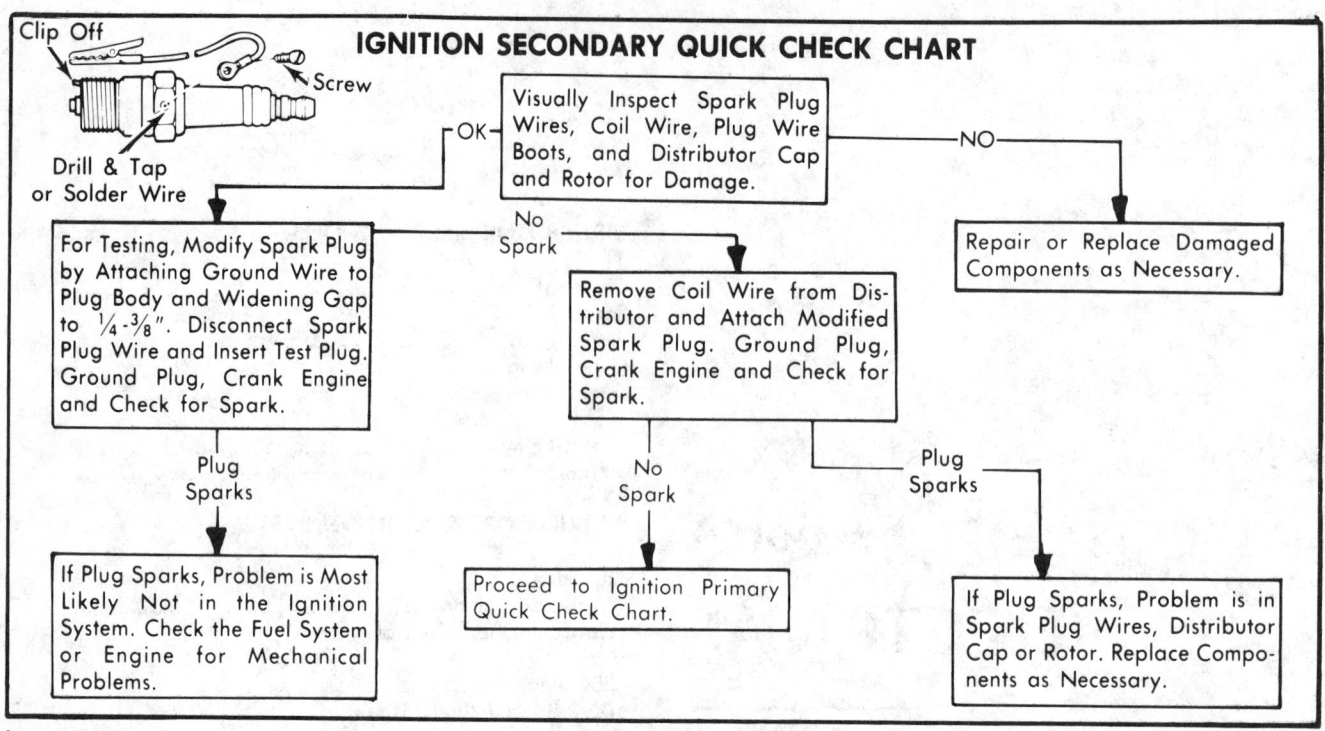

Clip Off

Screw

Drill & Tap
or Solder Wire

Visually Inspect Spark Plug Wires, Coil Wire, Plug Wire Boots, and Distributor Cap and Rotor for Damage.

OK

NO

Repair or Replace Damaged Components as Necessary.

For Testing, Modify Spark Plug by Attaching Ground Wire to Plug Body and Widening Gap to ¼-⅜". Disconnect Spark Plug Wire and Insert Test Plug. Ground Plug, Crank Engine and Check for Spark.

No Spark

Remove Coil Wire from Distributor and Attach Modified Spark Plug. Ground Plug, Crank Engine and Check for Spark.

Plug Sparks

No Spark

Plug Sparks

If Plug Sparks, Problem is Most Likely Not in the Ignition System. Check the Fuel System or Engine for Mechanical Problems.

Proceed to Ignition Primary Quick Check Chart.

If Plug Sparks, Problem is in Spark Plug Wires, Distributor Cap or Rotor. Replace Components as Necessary.

IGNITION PRIMARY QUICK CHECK CHART

Inspect All Ignition Secondary Wiring for Broken, Frayed, Split or Cut Wires. Also Check for Loose, Corroded or Disconnected Connectors.

OK

NO

Repair or Replace Components as Necessary.

Check Battery Voltage. Should Be 11.5 Volts or Above.

OK

Check for Battery Voltage at Positive Terminal of Coil.

NO

Replace or Recharge Battery.

OK

NO

Check Air Gap of Pick-Up Coil in Distributor.

Check Wires from Battery/Ignition Switch to Coil. Also Check Coil Primary and Secondary Resistance.

OK

Check Resistance of Ballast Resistor (If Used) for Correct Value.

OK

NO

Check Pick-Up Coil Resistance for Correct Value.

Adjust or Repair as Necessary.

NO

Replace Ballast Resistor if Value is Not to Specification.

NO

OK

Check Control Module for Good Ground Connections.

Replace Pick-Up Coil if Not to Specifications.

OK

If Vehicle Still Fails to Run, Turn to Appropriate Article in this Manual for Complete Primary Ignition Checks with Specifications.

Charging Systems

CHARGING SYSTEMS TROUBLE SHOOTING

CONDITION & POSSIBLE CAUSE	CONDITION & POSSIBLE CAUSE
Car Will Not Start • Dead battery. • Loose or corroded battery connections. • Ignition switch malfunction. **Generator Light Stays ON With Engine Running** • Loose or worn drive belt. • Loose generator wiring connections. • Short in generator light wiring. • Defective generator stator or diodes. • Defective regulator. **Generator Light Stays OFF With Ignition ON** • Blown fuse. • Defective generator. • Defective indicator light bulb. • Defective indicator light bulb socket. **Generator Light Stays ON With Ignition OFF** • Short in generator wiring. • Defective rectifier bridge. **Lights or Fuses Burn Out Frequently** • Defective generator wiring. • Defective regulator. • Defective battery. **Generator Light Flickers While Vehicle is Being Driven** • Loose or worn generator belt. • Loose or improper wiring connections. • Defective generator. • Defective regulator. **Ammeter Gauge Shows Discharge** • Loose or worn drive belt. • Defective wiring. • Defective generator or regulator. • Defective ammeter, or improper ammeter wiring connections. • Add-on electrical accessories exceeding generator capacity.	**Noisy Generator** • Loose or worn generator drive belt. • Loose drive pulley. • Loose mounting bolts. • Worn or dirty bearings. • Defective diodes or stator. • Bent pulley flanges. • Interference between rotor fan and stator leads. • Rotor fan or rotor damaged. • Rectifiers shorted open. • Open, grounded, or shorted rectifier wiring. • Defective regulator. **Battery Does Not Stay Charged** • Loose or worn drive belt. • Loose or corroded battery connections. • Loose generator connections. • Defective generator or battery. • Electrical accessories left ON. • Defective generator stator or diodes. • Add-on electrical accessories exceeding generator capacity. • Low speed driving of short duration, insufficient to charge battery. **Battery Overcharged - Uses Too Much Water** • Defective battery. • Defective generator. • Defective regulator caused by shorted field windings. • Battery overheated. • Excessive generator voltage. • Low speed driving of short duration. **Generator Current Output Low (with Excessive Charging)** • Grounded generator field wire, field terminal, or connections. • Generator field internally grounded. • Regulator sensing circuit open. **Generator Current Output Low (with Unsteady or Low Charging)** • Corroded or shorted cables. • High resistance across fusible link.

Starting Systems

STARTING SYSTEMS TROUBLE SHOOTING

CONDITION & POSSIBLE CAUSE	CONDITION & POSSIBLE CAUSE

Starter Fails to Operate

- Dead battery or bad connections between starter and battery.
- Ignition switch faulty or misadjusted.
- Open circuit between starter switch and ignition terminal on starter relay.
- Starter relay or starter defective.
- Open solenoid pull-in wire.

**Starter Does Not Operate
and Headlights Dim**

- Weak battery or dead battery cell.
- Loose or corroded battery connections.
- Internal ground in windings.
- Grounded starter fields.
- Armature rubbing on pole shoes.

**Starter Turns but Engine
Does Not Rotate**

- Starter clutch slipping.
- Broken clutch housing.
- Pinion shaft rusted or dry.
- Engine basic timing incorrect.
- Broken teeth on engine ring gear.

Starter Will Not Crank Engine

- Faulty overrunning clutch.
- Broken clutch housing.
- Broken ring gear teeth.
- Armature shaft sheared or reduction gear teeth stripped.
- Weak battery.
- Faulty solenoid.
- Starter spins slowly and draws high current.
- Poor grounds.
- Engine siezed.
- Ignition switch faulty or misadjusted.
- Burned fusible link in main wire feed to ignition switch.
- Defective starter relay.

Starter Cranks Engine Slowly

- Battery weak or defective.
- Engine overheated.
- Engine oil too heavy.
- Poor battery-to-starter connections.
- Current draw too low or too high.
- Tight engine bearings or pistons.
- Bent armature, loose pole shoe screws or worn bearings.
- Burned solenoid contacts.
- Faulty starter.

Starter Engages Engine Only Momentarily

- Engine timing too far advanced.
- Overrunning clutch not operating.
- Broken starter clutch housing.
- Broken teeth on engine ring gear.
- Weak drive assembly thrust spring.
- Weak hold-in coil.

Starter Drive Will Not Engage

- Defective point assembly.
- Poor point assembly ground.
- Defective pull-in coil.

Starter Drive Will Not Disengage

- Starter motor loose on mountings.
- Worn drive end bushing.
- Damaged ring gear teeth.
- Drive yoke return spring broken or missing.
- Defective starter motor drive.
- Foreign metal object in dash connector.
- Faulty ignition starter switch.
- Solenoid contact switch plunger stuck.
- Faulty relay.
- Insufficient clearance between winding leads to solenoid terminal and main contact in solenoid.
- Starter clutch not disengaging.
- Ignition starter switch contacts sticking.

Starter Relay Does Not Close

- Dead battery.
- Faulty wiring.
- Neutral safety switch faulty.
- Starter relay faulty.

**Starter Relay Operates
but Solenoid Does Not**

- Faulty solenoid switch, switch connections or switch wiring.
- Broken lead or loose soldered connections.

**Solenoid Plunger Vibrates
When Switch is Engaged**

- Weak battery.
- Solenoid contacts corroded.
- Faulty wiring.
- Broken connections inside switch cover.
- Open hold-in wire.

Low Current Draw

- Worn brushes or weak brush springs.

**High Pitched Whine During Cranking
Before Engine Fires but Engine Fires
and Cranks Normally**

- Distance too great between starter pinion and flywheel.

**High Pitched Whine After Engine
Fires With Key Released. Engine
Fires and Cranks Normally**

- Distance too small between starter pinion and flywheel. Flywheel runout contributes to the intermittent nature.

CHRYSLER CORP. DISTRIBUTORS

DODGE & PLYMOUTH

Application ①	Part No.
3.7L (225") 6-Cylinder	
All Models	4145751
5.2L (318") 2-Bbl. V8	
Federal	
Man. Trans.	4111950
Auto. Trans.	4145602
5.2L (318") 4-Bbl. V8	
Federal	
Man. Trans.	4111501
Auto. Trans.	4111501, 4145602
Calif.	
Man. Trans.	4111501
Auto. Trans.	4111501, 4145602

DODGE & PLYMOUTH (Cont.)

Application ①	Part No.
5.9L (360"-1) 4-Bbl. V8	
Man. Trans.	4145364
Auto. Trans.	
Light Duty	4145604
Heavy Duty	
Federal	4091661
Calif.	4111950
5.9L (360"-3) 4-Bbl. HD V8	
Federal	4091661
Calif.	
Without Catalyst	4091661
With Catalyst	4111950

① – "Light Duty" and "Heavy Duty" refer to emission control standards classifications. "Light Duty" refers to vehicles of 8,500 lbs. GVW or less. Vehicles over this weight are referred to as "Heavy Duty".

DELCO-REMY DISTRIBUTORS

CHEVROLET & GMC

Application	Part No.
4.1L (250") 6-Cylinder	
Federal	
Man. Trans.	
C10	1110589, 1111388
K10	1110590, 1110753
G10/20	1110589
G10/30	1110749
Auto. Trans.	1110589
Calif.	
All Models	1110749
4.8L (292") 6-Cylinder	
All Models	1110753
5.0L (305") V8 (LG9)	
Federal	
Man. Trans.	
C10	1103381
G10/20	1103369
Auto. Trans.	
C10 & G10/20	1103381
5.0L (305") V8 (LE9)	
Federal	
Man. Trans.	
C10/20 & K10	1103464
C10	1103465
G10/20	1103464
Auto. Trans.	
All Models	1103464
5.0L (305") V8 (LF3)	
Calif. Auto. Trans.	
C10	1103432

CHEVROLET & GMC (Cont.)

Application	Part No.
5.7L (350") V8 (LS9)	
Federal	
Man. Trans.	
C10, K10/20, & G10/20	1103353
Auto. Trans.	1103353
Calif.	
Auto. Trans.	
C10, K10 & G10	1103433
C20, K20 & G20	1103433
C20 & K20	1103339
5.7L (350") V8 (LT9)	
Federal	
All Models	1103375
Calif.	
All Models	1103420
7.4L (454") V8	
All Models	1103376

JEEP①

Application	Part No.
2.5L (151") 4-Cylinder	
"CJ" & Scrambler	
Federal	
Man. Trans.	1110560
Auto. Trans.	1110561
Calif.	
All Models	1110560

① – For Jeep distributors for 6 cylinder and V8 engines, see MOTORCRAFT DISTRIBUTORS.

Distributor Applications

MOTORCRAFT DISTRIBUTORS

FORD

Application	① Part No.
4.9L (300") 6-Cylinder	
E100/150	
Federal	
Man. Trans.	E1TE-HA, E1TE-JA
Auto. Trans.	E1TE-FA
Calif.	
Man. Trans.	E1TE-RA
Auto. Trans.	E1TE-VA
E250	
Federal	
Man. Trans.	E1TE-HA
Auto. Trans.	E1TE-FA
F100	
Federal	
Man. Trans.	E1TE-HA, E1TE-JA, E1TE-ZA, E2TE-EA
Auto. Trans.	E1TE-FA
Calif.	
Man. Trans.	E1TE-RA
Auto. Trans.	E1TE-GA, E1TE-VA
F150 2-WD	
Federal	
Man. Trans.	E1TE-HA, E1TE-JA
Auto. Trans.	E1TE-FA, E1TE-GA
Calif. Man. Trans.	E1TE-RA
F150 4-WD	
Man. Trans.	E1TE-JA
F250 2-WD	
Federal	
Man. Trans.	D9TE-AEA, E1TE-JA
Auto. Trans.	D9TE-ADA, E1TE-FA
Calif.	
Man. Trans.	D9TE-AEA
Auto. Trans.	E1TE-VA
F250 & Bronco 4-WD	
All Models	E1TE-JA
4.2L (255") V8	
F100	
Man. Trans.	E1TE-UA
Auto. Trans.	E1TE-ABA
5.0L (302") V8	
E100/150	
Federal	
Man. Trans.	E0TE-RA
Auto. Trans.	E1UE-DA
Calif.	
Man. Trans.	E0TE-RA
Auto. Trans.	E1AE-MA
E250	
Federal Auto. Trans.	E1UE-DA
Calif. Auto. Trans.	E1AE-MA
F100/F150 2-WD	
Federal	
Man. Trans.	E0TE-RA
Auto. Trans.	E1TE-SA
AOT	E1TE-TA
Calif.	
Man. Trans.	E0TE-RA
Auto. Trans.	E1TE-SA
AOT	E1AE-MA

FORD (Cont.)

Application	① Part No.
F150 4-WD	
Federal	
Man. Trans.	
Without Overdrive	E0TE-RA
With Overdrive	E0TE-KA, E1TE-KA
Auto. Trans.	E1TE-SA
Calif	
Auto. Trans.	E1AE-MA
F250 2-WD	
Federal	
Man. Trans.	
Without Overdrive	E0TE-RA
With Overdrive	E0TE-KA, E1TE-KA
Auto. Trans.	E1TE-SA
AOT	E1TE-ACA
Calif.	
Man. Trans.	
Without Overdrive	E0TE-RA
With Overdrive	E0TE-KA, E1TE-KA
Auto. Trans.	E1AE-MA
AOT	E1AE-MA
F250 4-WD	
Auto. Trans.	E1AE-MA
Bronco	
Federal	
Man. Trans.	
Without Overdrive	E0TE-RA
With Overdrive	E0TE-KA, E1TE-KA
Auto. Trans.	E1TE-SA
Calif.	
Man. Trans.	
Without Overdrive	E0TE-RA
With Overdrive	E0TE-KA, E1TE-KA
Auto. Trans.	E1AE-MA
5.8L (351") M V8	
F150 2-WD & 4-WD	
Man. Trans.	E1TE-EA
Auto. Trans.	E0UE-CA
F250 2-WD	
Heavy Duty	D7TE-AHA
Light Duty	
Man. Trans.	E1TE-EA
Auto. Trans.	E0UE-CA
F250 4-WD & Bronco	
Man. Trans.	E1TE-EA
Auto. Trans.	E0UE-CA
5.8L (351") W V8	
E100	
All Models	E1UE-EA
E150	
Federal	E1UE-EA, E1UE-GA
Calif.	E1AE-LA
E250	
Federal	
Man. Trans.	E1UE-GA
Auto. Trans.	D7UE-JA, E1UE-GA
Calif.	E1AE-LA
High Alt.	E1UE-FA
E350	
Auto. Trans.	D7UE-JA

MOTORCRAFT DISTRIBUTORS (Cont.)

FORD (Cont.)

Application	①Part No.
F150 2-WD & 4-WD	
All Models	E1AE-LA
F250 4-WD	
All Models	E1AE-LA
Bronco	
All Models	E1AE-LA
6.6L (400") V8	
E250/350	
Federal	D7TE-ALA
Calif.	D9TE-ATA
F250	
Federal	
Man. Trans.	D7TE-AMA
Auto. Trans.	D7TE-ALA
Calif	
Man. Trans.	D9TE-ATA
F350	
Calif.	
Auto. Trans.	D9TE-ATA

① — Basic part number is 12127. Table gives prefix and suffix only.

JEEP①

Application	Part No.
4.2L (258") 6-Cylinder	
All Models	3235141
5.0L (304") V8	
"CJ" & Scrambler	
Federal	
Man. Trans.	3237198
Hilly Terrain	3237198
Auto. Trans.	3237199
5.9L (360") V8	
Cherokee, Wagoneer & Truck Models	
All Models	3233174

① — For Jeep distributors for 4 cylinder engines, see DELCO-REMY DISTRIBUTORS.

ELECTRICAL

CHRYSLER CORP. DISTRIBUTOR ADVANCE SPECIFICATIONS

NOTE — FOR DISTRIBUTOR RPM AND DEGREES, DIVIDE SPECIFICATIONS BY 2.

Distributor Part No.	Rot. ①	Automatic Advance (Engine Degrees & RPM)						Vacuum Advance (Engine Deg. & In. of Hg)			
		Deg.	RPM	Deg.	RPM	Deg.	RPM	Deg.	In. Hg	Deg.	In. Hg
4091661	C	3-6	1100	11-15	1700	22-26	4000	1-4	7	12-16	15
4111501	C	1-3	1400	3-7	1800	15-20	4400	2-5	7	20-24	15
4111783	C	2-5	1100	8-10	1800	23-27	4200	1-5	10	15-19	15
4111950	C	1-5	1100	5-9	1800	16-20	4400	2-5	7	20-24	15
4145364	C	2-6	1000	7-11	1800	12-16	4200	0-2	6	20-24	13
4145602	C	1-5	1800	5-7	2400	11-15	4400	0-2	6	20-24	13
4145604	C	2-5	1200	3-7	2000	8-12	4400	0-2	6	20-24	13
4145751	C	Electronic Spark Advance									

① — C (Clockwise), CC (Counterclockwise) viewed from rotor end.

DELCO-REMY DISTRIBUTOR ADVANCE SPECIFICATIONS

NOTE — FOR DISTRIBUTOR RPM AND DEGREES, DIVIDE SPECIFICATIONS BY 2.

Distributor Part No. ①	Rot. ②	Automatic Advance (Engine Degrees & RPM)						Vacuum Advance (Engine Deg. & In. of Hg)			
		Deg.	RPM	Deg.	RPM	Deg.	RPM	Deg.	In. Hg	Deg.	In. Hg
1103339	C	0	1100	16	2400	22	4600	0	4	10	8
1103353	C	0	1100	16	2400	22	4600	0	4	20	10
1103369	C	0	1200	8	2000	20	4200	0	3	16	6.5
1103375	C	0	1150	17	2900	22	4200	0	4	10	8
1103381	C	0	1100	14	2800	20	4200	0	8	10	13
1103381	C	0	1200	8	2000	20	4200	0	3	10	7.5
1103420③	C	0	1000	17	1000	22	4200	0	4	15	10
1103420④	C	0	1800	—	1600	24	4000	0	10	10	13
1103432	C	0	1000	10	2000	14	4000	0	4	15	12
1103433	C	0	1100	16	2400	22	4600	0	4	15	12
1110560	C	0	800	8	2400	14	4400	6	6	20	12
1110589	C	0	1100	14	2300	24	4100	0	3	16	6.5
1110590	C	0	1100	14	2300	24	4100	0	4	15	10
1110749	C	0	1100	7	2300	16	4200	0	4	10	8
1110753	C	0	1100	14	2300	24	4100	0	4	10⑤	8⑤
1111388	C	0	1100	14	2300	24	4100	0	3	20	7.5
1103464	C	Electronic Spark Control									
1103465	C										

① — Part numbers apply to GMC and Chevrolet except for 1110560, used on Jeep 4 cylinder 2.5L (151") engine.
② — C (Clockwise), CC (Counterclockwise) viewed from rotor end.
③ — Calif. Auto. Trans.
④ — Calif. Man. Trans.
⑤ — Specification is for 4.8L (292") engine. On 4.1L (250") engine, vacuum is 15° @ 10 in. Hg.

MOTORCRAFT DISTRIBUTOR ADVANCE SPECIFICATIONS①

NOTE – FOR DISTRIBUTOR RPM AND DEGREES, DIVIDE SPECIFICATIONS BY 2.

Distributor Part No.②	Rot. ③	Automatic Advance (Engine Degrees & RPM)						Vacuum Advance (Engine Deg. & In. of Hg)			
		Deg.	RPM	Deg.	RPM	Deg.	RPM	Deg.	In. Hg	Deg.	In. Hg
JEEP											
3233174	C	0	800	10	2400	14	4000	3	4	24	14
3237198	C	0	800	10	2400	18	4000	3	4	22	14
3237199	C	0	800	10	2400	18	4000	3	4	32	14
3235141	C	0	800	8	2400	10	4000	6	6	23	16

① – Ford specifications not available from manufacturer.

② – For Jeep specifications on 4 cylinder 2.5L (151") engine, see Delco-Remy Distributor Advance Specifications.

③ – C (Clockwise), CC (Counterclockwise) viewed from rotor end.

CHRYSLER CORP. ELECTRONIC IGNITION

**Dodge & Plymouth
All V8 Models**

DESCRIPTION

All Dodge and Plymouth vehicles with V8 engines use Chrysler Corp. Electronic Ignition. This system consists of an electronic control unit, an ignition coil, a 1.25 ohm ballast resistor and a distributor with both vacuum and centrifugal advance mechanisms. *See Fig. 1 and 2.*

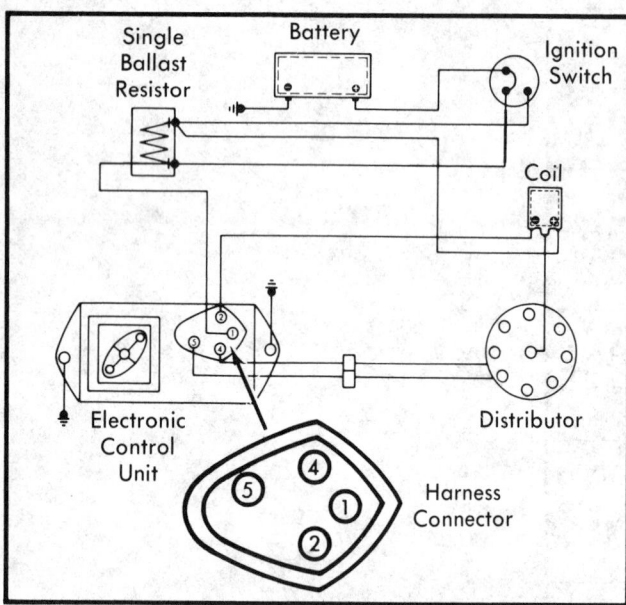

**Fig. 1   *Electronic Ignition Wiring Diagram for V8 Engines with Single Pick-Up Coil
(NOTE: No Terminal No. 3)***

Distributors may vary between models, as some have a reluctor and single pick-up coil assembly, while other models have a reluctor and 2 pick-up coil assemblies. Models with dual pick-up coil assemblies also have a dual pick-up start-run relay, located between the electronic control unit and the distributor.

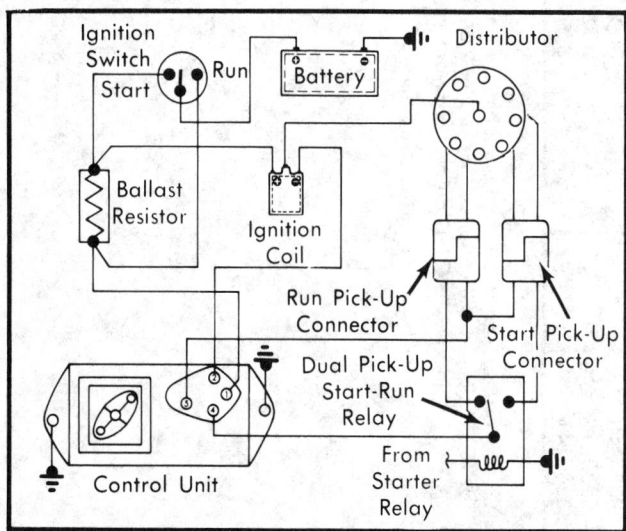

**Fig. 2   *Electronic Ignition Wiring Diagram for V8 Engines with Dual Pick-Up Coil
(NOTE: No Terminal No. 3)***

The dual pick-up start-run relay permits use of a dual pick-up distributor without electronic spark advance. This results in improved timing and increased fuel economy.

The control unit is connected to the rest of the system through a 4-wire connector. The distributor is connected to the control unit by a 2-wire or by two 2-wire connectors (dual pick-up models).

NOTE — *There is no terminal 3 on the control unit.*

OPERATION

DISTRIBUTOR

Single Pick-Up Models — The distributor has a toothed wheel, called a reluctor, having one tooth for each of the engine's 8 cylinders. *See Fig. 3.* As the reluctor rotates with the distributor shaft, its teeth approach, become aligned with, and pass the center pole piece of the pick-up coil. This interruption of the magnetic field around the pick-up coil creates an electronic signal.

This signal is transmitted to the control unit, which shuts off current flow to the primary circuit of the ignition coil as each signal is received.

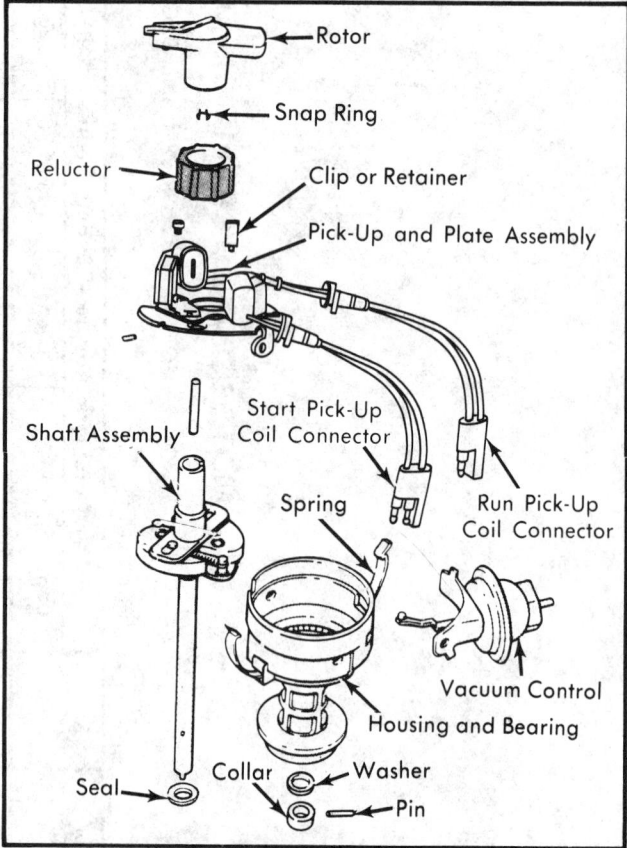

Fig. 3   *Exploded View of Distributor Used on Dual Pick-Up System for V8 Engines*

Dual Pick-Up Models — This system operates identically to single pick-up models with one exception. Signals are sent by different pick-up coils during cranking and normal running conditions.

CHRYSLER CORP. ELECTRONIC IGNITION (Cont.)

When cranking, the system operates through the start pick-up circuit of the dual pick-up start-run relay. Once the engine begins to run, the relay switches back to the run pick-up circuit. Only one pick-up coil operates at a time. Distributor pick-up coil connectors can be identified by their terminals. Run pick-up connectors have one male and one female terminal; start pick-up connectors have 2 male terminals.

ELECTRONIC CONTROL UNIT

The electronic control unit is located in a metal housing on the firewall. A switching transistor is exposed on top for more efficient cooling. The control unit is connected to the rest of the system by a wiring harness and a 4-wire connector. The control unit functions whenever the ignition switch is turned to the "START" or "RUN" positions.

The control unit furnishes current to the distributor pick-up coil directly on single pick-up models. On dual pick-up models, current flows through the dual pick-up start-run relay to either the start or run pick-up assembly, depending on whether ignition switch is in the "START" or "RUN" position.

The signal created, as the reluctor teeth pass the "live" pick-up coil, is transmitted by the control unit to the primary circuit of the ignition coil. As current to the primary is cut off, the magnetic field there collapses, causing a voltage surge in the secondary windings. This fires the spark plugs.

The length of time current is permitted to flow through the coil's primary circuit (dwell time) is determined by the control unit and is not adjustable.

BALLAST RESISTOR

A single 2-pin ballast resistor is used. During cranking, the resistor is by-passed, allowing full battery voltage to flow to the coil. In low speed operation, the ballast resistor limits voltage to the coil, protecting it from overheating. As engine speed increases, the ballast resistor allows the coil to charge faster to prevent voltage loss.

ADJUSTMENT

PICK-UP COIL AIR GAP

NOTE — *On models with a single pick-up coil assembly, adjust air gap in same manner outlined for start pick-up coils. See Fig. 5.*

1) To set **start** pick-up coil air gap, loosen hold-down screw and align one reluctor tooth with pick-up coil pole. Install .006" non-magnetic feeler gauge between reluctor tooth and pick-up coil pole. See Fig. 4. Move pick-up coil assembly until contact is made between pick-up coil pole, feeler gauge and reluctor tooth. Tighten hold-down screw and remove feeler gauge. Gauge should not require force during removal.

2) Check air gap of **start** pick-up coil using an .008" non-magnetic feeler gauge. It should not fit in gap. Do not force it to fit. Apply vacuum to vacuum unit and rotate distributor shaft. Pick-up coil pole should not strike reluctor teeth. If so, gap is incorrectly set. If pick-up coil pole strikes teeth only on one side, distributor shaft is probably bent, requiring replacement.

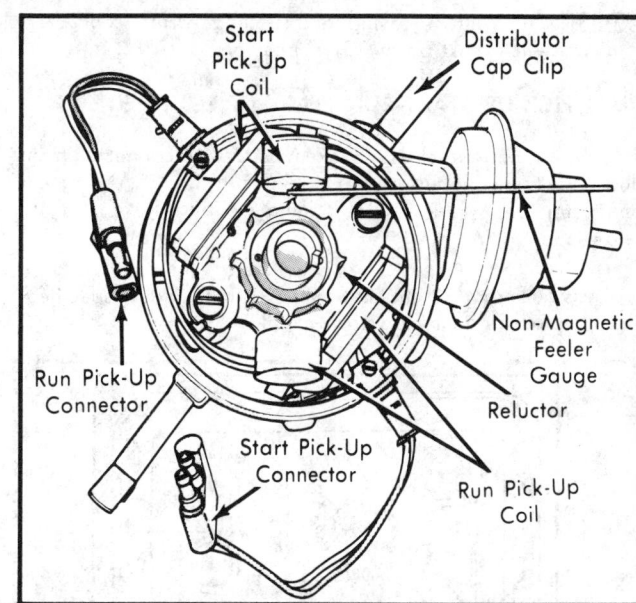

Fig. 4   Checking Air Gap of Dual Pick-Up Distributor Start Pick-Up Coil

NOTE — *To adjust run pick-up coil air gap, use same procedure as for start pick-up coil, except set gap with a .012" feeler gauge and check it with a .014" gauge.*

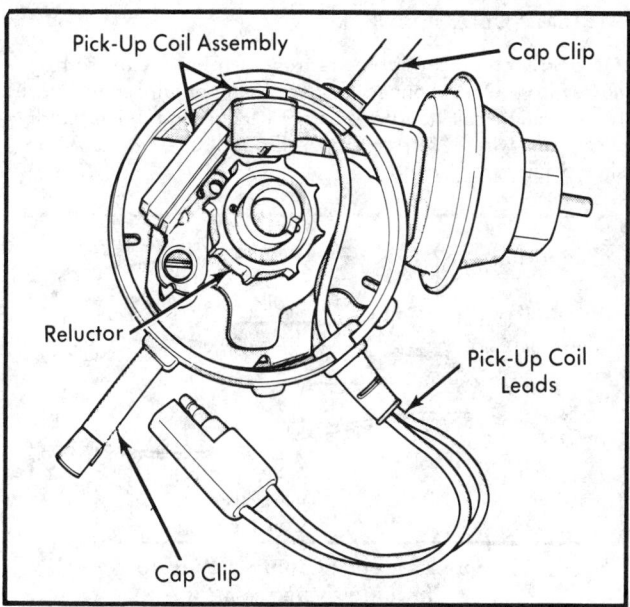

Fig. 5   Checking Air Gap of Single Pick-Up Distributor Pick-Up Coil

TESTING

NOTE — *If a suitable tester (C-4166 with adapter C-4166-1 or C-4166-A, or tester C-4503 with adapter C-4503-3) is available, use tester and follow manufacturer's instructions. If tester is not available, proceed as follows:*

Check that all secondary cables, primary wire at coil and ballast resistor are not loose and not cracked excessively. Use a voltmeter with a 20,000 ohm/volt rating and an ohmmeter which uses a 1½ volt battery for its operation. Check calibration of both meters. Check and record battery voltage reading using voltmeter. Proceed with following tests.

CHRYSLER CORP. ELECTRONIC IGNITION (Cont.)

CAUTION — *When removing or installing wiring connector, ignition switch must be in "OFF" position.*

DUAL PICK-UP START-RUN RELAY (IF EQUIPPED)

1) Turn ignition switch "OFF". Remove 2-wire connector from dual pick-up start-run relay terminals 4 and 5. Using an ohmmeter, connect leads to terminals 4 and 5 of start-run relay. See Fig. 6.

2) Resistance reading should be 20-30 ohms. If not to specifications, replace dual pick-up start-run relay.

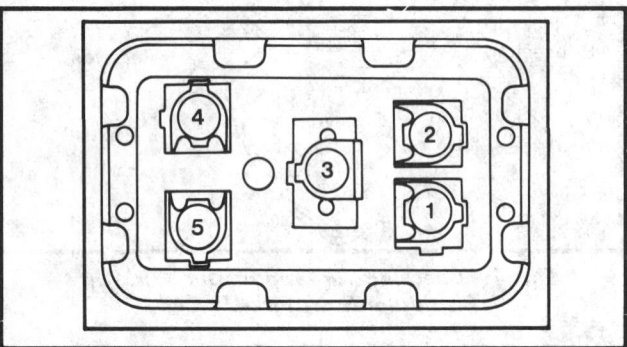

Fig. 6   Dual Pick-Up Start-Run Relay Terminal Locations

SYSTEM VOLTAGE CHECK

1) Remove coil secondary wire from distributor cap. Turn ignition switch "ON". Connect a special jumper wire momentarily from ignition coil negative terminal to ground, while holding secondary wire 1/4" from engine ground. See Fig. 7. A spark should jump to ground.

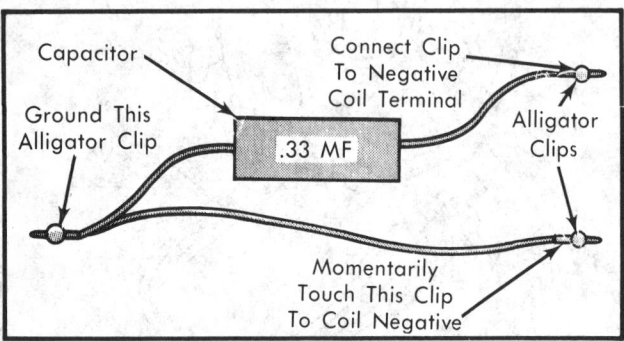

Fig. 7   Special Jumper Wire for Checking System Voltage

2) If spark was present, proceed to "Wiring Harness and Connector." If no spark was obtained, turn ignition switch "OFF". Disconnect 4-wire harness connector from electronic control unit.

3) Turn ignition switch "ON". Repeat step 1). If spark now results with connector removed, replace electronic control unit.

4) If no spark was obtained in step 3), measure voltage at coil positive terminal. It should be within 1 volt of battery voltage. If so, check for battery voltage at coil negative terminal. If you get battery voltage but no spark in step 3), replace ignition coil.

5) If no battery voltage was present at ignition coil positive terminal in step 4), replace starter relay and check wiring bet-

ween battery positive terminal and coil positive terminal. If continuity does not exist, replace ballast resistor and repeat Step 4).

WIRING HARNESS & CONNECTOR

Measure voltage across battery terminals, record this measurement. Turn ignition switch "OFF", then disconnect harness connector from control unit. Connect voltmeter negative lead to a good ground and then turn ignition "ON". Make checks as follows.

1) Connect voltmeter positive lead to control unit harness connector cavity 1. Reading should be battery voltage. If not, check and repair wires and components from harness connector cavity 1 back to battery. See Figs. 8 and 9.

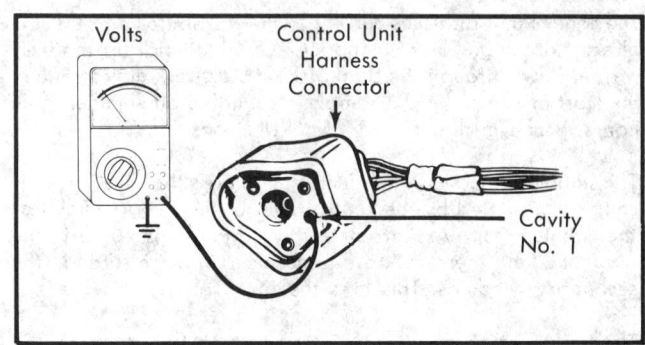

Fig. 8   Checking Voltage at Cavity No. 1

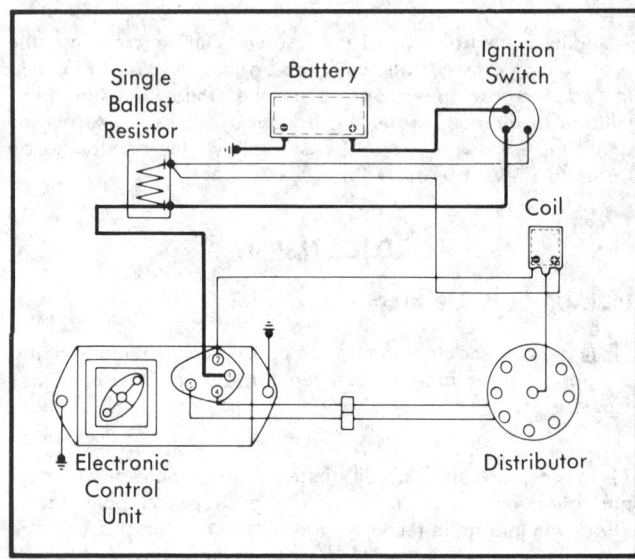

Fig. 9   Circuitry Checked if Cavity No. 1 Reading is Not to Specifications

2) With voltmeter negative lead still connected to ground, connect positive lead to harness connector cavity 2. Voltmeter should again read battery voltage. If reading is not to specification, check voltage at each connection (coil negative terminal, coil positive terminal, ballast resistor, ignition switch, etc.) back to battery. Repair wiring or replace components as necessary. See Figs. 10 and 11.

CHRYSLER CORP. ELECTRONIC IGNITION (Cont.)

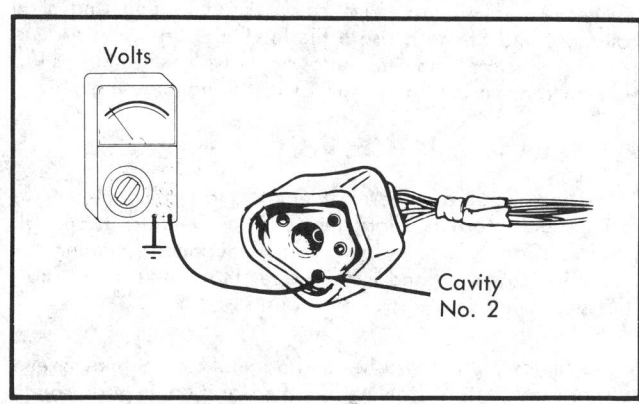

Fig. 10   Checking Voltage at Cavity No. 2

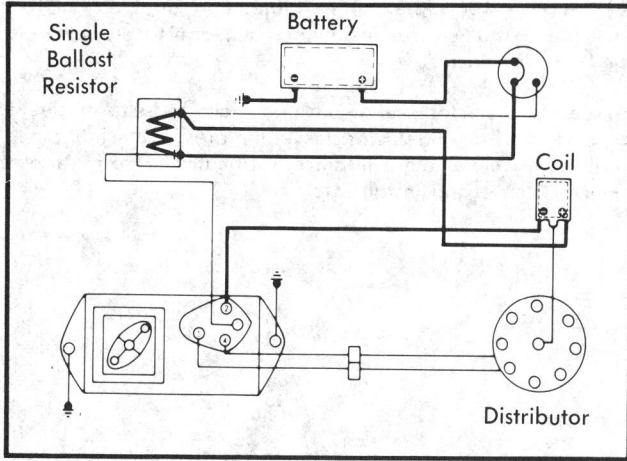

Fig. 11   Circuitry Checked if Cavity No. 2 Reading Is Not to Specifications

3) If reading jumped to battery voltage on positive side of ignition coil, check coil primary and secondary resistance. If coil is bad, replace it. Also check ballast resistor by disconnecting wires from resistor and then taking an ohmmeter reading across its 2 terminals. Resistance should be 1.12-1.38 ohms. If reading is not to specifications, replace ballast resistor. See Fig. 12.

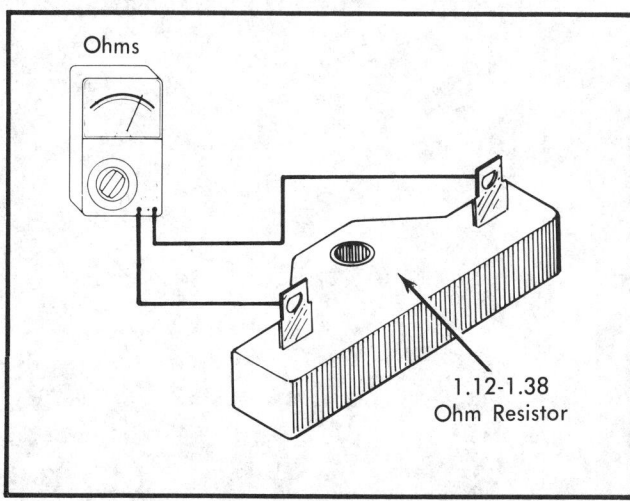

Fig. 12   Checking Ballast Resistor Resistance

DISTRIBUTOR PICK-UP COILS

1) Turn ignition switch "OFF". Disconnect control unit harness connector. Connect ohmmeter leads to cavities 4 and 5 of harness connector. See Fig. 13. Ohmmeter reading should be 150-900 ohms. If reading is not to specifications, make same check at 2-wire connector(s) leading to distributor. If readings at pick-up coils are now correct, start-run relay or harness from control unit to distributor is defective. If readings are still not correct, replace faulty pick-up coil assembly.

NOTE – *On distributors with single pick-up coil assemblies, there will be only one 2-wire connector to check.*

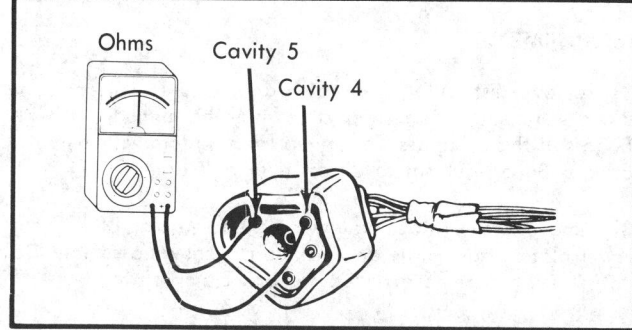

Fig. 13   Checking Resistance at Cavities No. 4 and 5 (Pick-Up Coil Resistance)

2) Connect one ohmmeter lead to a good ground (distributor housing). Connect other lead to either terminal of start pick-up coil distributor connector, then to either terminal of run pick-up coil connector. If ohmmeter shows a reading for either test, replace faulty pick-up coil and adjust air gap.

ELECTRONIC CONTROL UNIT GROUND CIRCUIT

1) Connect one ohmmeter lead to a good ground and other lead to control unit connector pin 5 (not cavity 5 of harness connector). Ohmmeter should show full continuity.

2) If not, make sure control unit is making good contact with ground at hold-down bolts. If it is, replace control unit.

CENTRIFUGAL ADVANCE CURVE

Install distributor in test stand. It is important that appropriate adapter for checking electronic type distributors be used. Adjust tester speed control to operate distributor at speeds called for in distributor tables. If advance is not according to specifications, replace distributor shaft assembly (shaft, reluctor sleeve, governor weights).

IGNITION COIL RESISTANCE

1) Coil is designed to operate with an external ballast resistor. When testing ignition coil for output and resistance, also make ballast resistor tests. See Fig. 12. Inspect coil for external cracks and arcing at same time.

2) To check coil primary resistance, isolate coil from rest of system. Connect ohmmeter leads to positive and negative primary terminals. To check secondary resistance, connect ohmmeter leads to coil negative terminal and coil tower.

3) If resistance readings are not to specifications, replace ignition coil.

CHRYSLER CORP. ELECTRONIC IGNITION (Cont.)

Resistance Specifications	
Application	**Ohms@70-80°F**
Primary Resistance	
Prestolite	1.60-1.79
Essex	1.34-1.55
Secondary Resistance	
Prestolite	9400-11,700
Essex	9000-12,200
Single Ballast Resistor	
Resistor Resistance	1.12-1.38

OVERHAUL

DISASSEMBLY

1) Remove distributor cap, rotor and vacuum control unit. Remove reluctor. Some reluctors may be pulled off with fingers. If this is impossible, pry up from bottom with 2 screwdrivers. Be careful not to distort reluctor teeth.

2) Remove screws attaching lower plate to housing and lift out lower plate, upper plate and pick-up coils as an assembly. Do not attempt to remove distributor cap clamp springs.

3) Remove distributor drive collar retaining pin and slide collar off end of shaft. Use a file to clean burrs from around pin hole in shaft, and remove lower thrust washer. Push shaft up and remove it through top of distributor housing.

REASSEMBLY

1) Test operation of governor weights and inspect the weight springs for distortion. Lubricate governor weights. Inspect all bearing surfaces and pivot pins for roughness, binding, or looseness. Lubricate and install upper thrust washer on shaft and slide shaft into distributor housing.

2) Install lower thrust washer and original collar on lower end of shaft, and install retaining pin. If collar is not in good condition, replace it.

3) Install lower plate, upper plate, and dual pick-up coil assembly. Attach vacuum advance unit arm to pick-up plate and install attaching screws.

4) Position reluctor keeper pin into place on reluctor sleeve. Slide reluctor down reluctor sleeve and press firmly into place. Make sure keeper pin is in place. Lubricate felt pad in top of reluctor sleeve and install rotor.

CHRYSLER CORP. ELECTRONIC SPARK CONTROL SYSTEM

**Dodge & Plymouth
3.7L (225") 6-Cylinder Engines**

DESCRIPTION

The Electronic Spark Control (ESC) system is governed by a Spark Control Computer (SCC), 6 engine sensors, a specially calibrated carburetor and a dual pick-up distributor. The ESC system is designed to burn a lean air/fuel mixture, with a minimum of emissions. See *Fig. 1*.

SPARK CONTROL COMPUTER

The Spark Control Computer (SCC) is the heart of the entire system. It gives the system the capability of igniting a lean fuel mixture according to different modes of engine operation by delivering an infinite amount of variable advance curves. The computer determines the exact instant when ignition is required, then signals the ignition coil to produce the spark required to fire the spark plugs.

The computer consists of one electronic printed circuit board which receives signals from all the sensors and within milliseconds computes them so that proper advance or retard is immediately achieved.

SENSORS

The electronic Spark Control Computer, mounted on the air cleaner, uses 6 engine sensors to determine when to fire the spark plugs. See *Fig. 2*. These include 2 distributor pick-up coils, coolant temperature sensor, carburetor switch, vacuum transducer, and a charge temperature switch. Sensor signals are processed by a microprocessor in the computer. Sensor functions are as follows:

Fig. 2   Electronic Spark Control Computer

Magnetic Pick-Up Assembly — The pick-up coil assembly is located in the distributor. The start pick-up coil supplies a signal to the computer, which will cause the spark plugs to fire at a fixed amount of advance during cranking only. Once the engine begins to run, the run pick-up coil takes over, supplying advance information to the computer. The computer then modifies advance information to reflect other engine operating conditions supplied by the remaining sensors.

Coolant Temperature Sensor — The coolant sensor is located in the cylinder head. It informs the computer when the engine has reached a predetermined temperature. This information is necessary to determine correct spark advance until engine reaches operating temperature.

Vacuum Transducer — This sensor, located on the spark control computer, signals the computer to inform it of engine operating vacuum. Vacuum is one of the factors used to determine whether the computer will advance or retard ignition timing or change the air/fuel ratio.

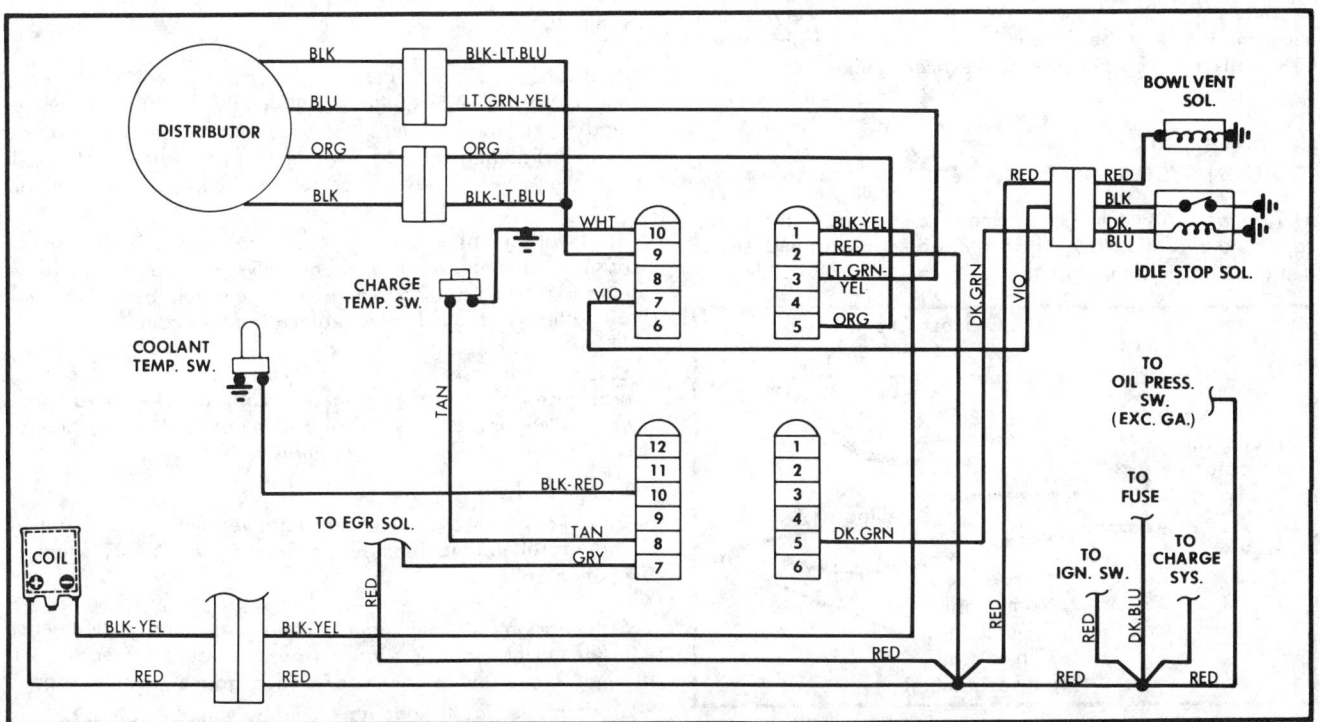

*Fig. 1   Wiring Diagram for Chrysler Corp. Electronic Spark Control System
(Vehicles with 3.7L (225") 6-Cylinder Engines)*

CHRYSLER CORP. ELECTRONIC SPARK CONTROL SYSTEM (Cont.)

Carburetor Switch — Located on the end of idle stop, the carburetor switch informs the computer when the engine is at idle. When carburetor switch contacts throttle lever ground, the computer will cancel spark advance and prevent air/fuel ratio from being adjusted.

Charge Temperature Switch — This sensor is located in the No. 6 branch runner of the intake manifold. The switch will be closed when intake charge (air/fuel mixture) is below 60° F. This permits no EGR timer function and no EGR valve operation. When temperature is above 60° F, the switch is open, allowing EGR timer to time out and EGR valve to operate.

OPERATION

The Spark Control Computer has two functional modes, "Start" and "Run". The "Start" mode operates while cranking and starting only. The "Run" mode operates after engine has started and during normal engine operation. The two modes never operate at the same time. When cranking and starting the pick-up coil sends a signal to the computer which is in the "Start" mode, the "Run" mode is by-passed. During this time a fixed advance is used. Advance is determined by distributor position (basic timing). After engine starts, the pick-up coil continues to send a signal to the computer, but the computer is now in the "Run" mode and "Start" mode is by-passed. The amount of timing advance is now controlled by the computer, based upon information received from the engine sensors.

The amount of spark advance is determined by two factors, engine speed and engine vacuum. At what point it occurs depends upon computer programming. Advance from vacuum will be provided when carburetor switch is open. The amount is programmed into the computer and is proportional to the amount of vacuum and engine RPM. Advance from speed will be given by the computer when the carburetor switch is open and is programmed to engine RPM.

If for some reason, there is a failure of the "Run" mode of the computer, the "Start" mode will come back into service and allow the vehicle to be driven. Performance and economy will be greatly reduced because of the fixed timing.

TESTING

IGNITION SYSTEM STARTING TEST

1) Turn ignition switch "ON". Remove coil wire from distributor cap. Hold end of wire ¼ " from a good engine ground. Using a special jumper, intermittently jump coil negative terminal to

ground. Watch for spark at coil wire. If there is a spark, it must be constant and bright blue. *See Fig. 3.*

2) If spark is good, continue to intermittently jumper coil negative terminal to ground, while slowly moving coil wire away from ground. Check for arcing at coil tower. If arcing occurs, replace ignition coil.

3) If spark is weak or not constant, or if there is no spark, proceed to "Failure to Start Test."

4) If spark is good and there is no arcing at coil tower, ignition system is producing necessary high secondary voltage. Make sure this spark is getting to plugs by checking distributor rotor, cap, spark plugs, and plug wires.

5) If all this checks out, but engine will still not start, the ignition system is not the problem. It will be necessary to check fuel system and engine mechanical components.

FAILURE TO START TEST

NOTE — *Perform "Ignition System Starting Test" first. Failure to do so may result in lost diagnostic time or incorrect test results. If a good spark is obtained in this test, proceed to step* **6**).

1) Measure and record battery voltage. Measure specific gravity, which must be at least 1.220 (temperature corrected) to deliver proper voltage.

2) Turn ignition switch "OFF", and disconnect 10-wire connector from spark control computer. Repeat Ignition System Starting Test, step **1**). If spark results, replace spark control computer.

3) If no spark is obtained, check voltage at coil positive terminal. With ignition switch "ON", connect positive voltmeter lead to coil positive terminal and negative lead to a good ground. Reading should be within 1 volt of battery voltage. If not, check wiring between battery and coil positive terminal.

4) If voltage at positive coil terminal was correct, connect positive voltmeter lead to coil negative terminal and negative lead to a good ground. Again, voltage should be within 1 volt of battery voltage. If not, replace ignition coil.

NOTE — *You may wish to check coil primary and secondary resistance before replacing ignition coil. However, if you have battery voltage on positive side, but not on negative side of coil, ignition coil normally requires replacement.*

5) If voltage was correct at negative coil terminal, but no spark resulted in Ignition System Starting Test, step **1**), replace ignition coil.

6) If spark results, but engine will not start, turn ignition switch to the "RUN" position. Connect positive voltmeter lead to terminal 1 of 10-wire connector and negative lead to a good ground. *See Fig. 4.* Reading should be within 1 volt of battery voltage. If not, check wire for open and repair it, repeating step **6**) once more. Reconnect 10-wire connector to computer.

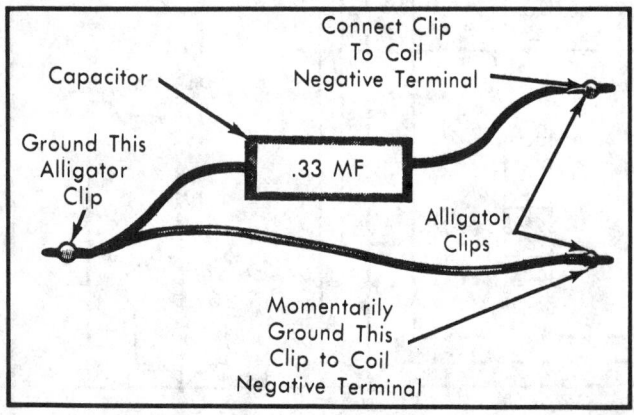

Fig. 3   Components of Special Jumper Wire for Ignition System Starting Test

Distributors & Ignition Systems

CHRYSLER CORP. ELECTRONIC SPARK CONTROL SYSTEM (Cont.)

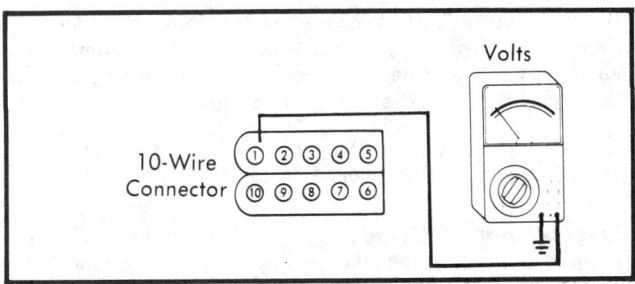

**Fig. 4   Voltmeter Hookup for Checking
Terminal 1 Voltage**

7) If battery voltage was recorded in step **6)**, place a thin insulator (piece of paper) between curb idle adusting screw and carburetor switch or make sure screw does not touch switch. See *Fig. 5*. Connect negative lead of voltmeter to a good ground. Turn ignition switch to "RUN" position, and touch positive voltmeter lead to carburetor switch terminal. Reading should be approximately 5 volts. If so, proceed to step **10)**.

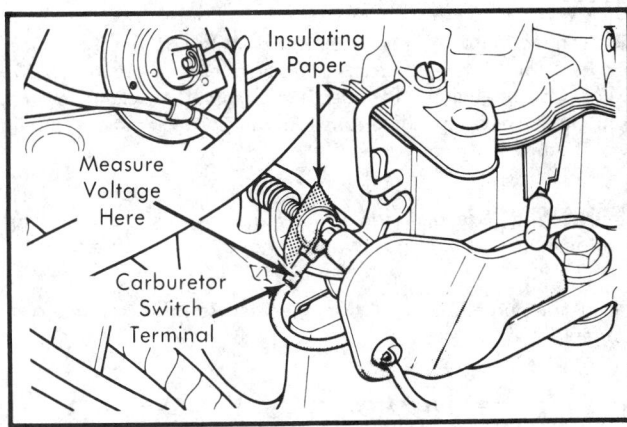

Fig. 5   Checking Voltage at Carburetor Switch

8) If voltage was not at least 5 volts, turn ignition switch "OFF". Disconnect 10-wire connector from computer. Turn ignition switch back to "RUN" position. Connect positive voltmeter lead to terminal 2 of 10-wire connector and negative lead to ground. See *Fig. 6*. Voltage reading should again be within 1 volt of battery voltage. If not correct, check wiring between terminal 2 and ignition switch for opens, shorts or poor connections.

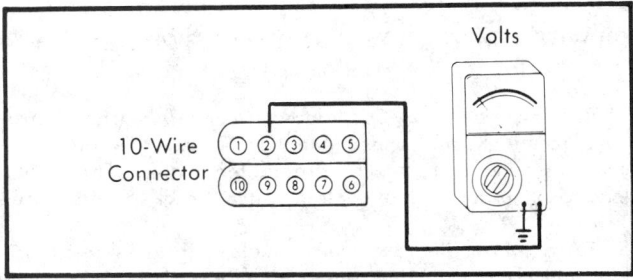

**Fig. 6   Voltmeter Hookup for Checking
Terminal 2 Voltage**

9) If voltage at terminal 2 was correct, turn ignition switch "OFF". Using an ohmmeter, check continuity between terminal 7 of 10-wire connector and carburetor switch terminal. See

Fig. 7. Continuity should exist. If not, check wire between connections for opens, shorts or poor connections. If continuity is present, use an ohmmeter with leads attached to terminal 10 and engine ground to check continuity of ground circuit. See *Fig. 8*. If there is continuity, replace computer. If there is no continuity, check wire from terminal 10 to ground. If engine fails to start, proceed to next step.

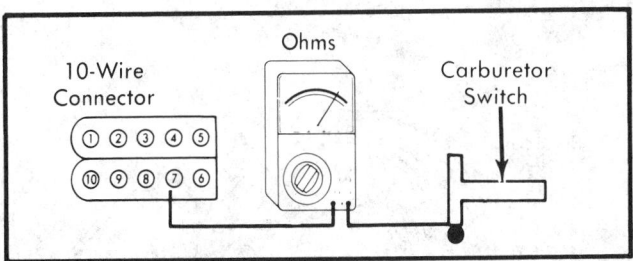

**Fig. 7   Ohmmeter Hookup for Checking
Carburetor Switch Wiring Harness**

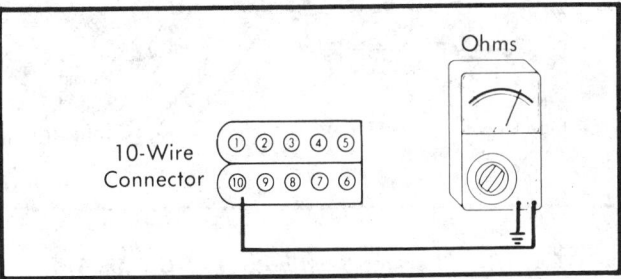

**Fig. 8   Ohmmeter Hookup for Checking
Computer Ground Circuit**

10) Turn ignition switch "OFF". Attach ohmmeter leads to terminals 5 and 9 of 10-wire harness connector to check run pick-up coil resistance and to terminals 3 and 9 to check start pick-up coil resistance. See *Fig. 9*. Resistance should be 150-900 ohms. If so, proceed to step **12)**.

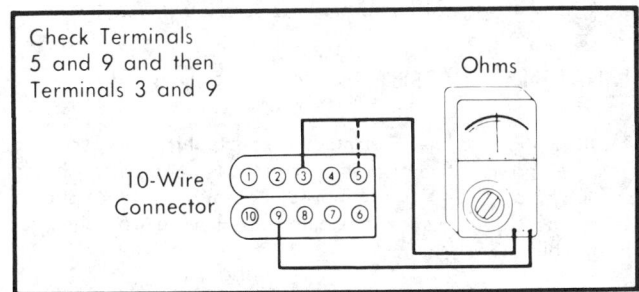

**Fig. 9   Ohmmeter Hookup for Checking
Pick-Up Coil Resistance**

11) If not, disconnect distributor connectors, and attach ohmmeter leads to run pick-up coil leads and then to start pick-up coil leads coming from distributor. If resistance is now okay, wiring harness is defective. If resistance is still not 150-900 ohms, replace pick-up coils, as necessary.

12) Next, connect one lead of an ohmmeter to engine ground and touch other lead to each terminal of leads coming from 2 distributor pick-up coils. There should be no continuity. If continuity is indicated, replace pick-up coil assembly.

Distributors & Ignition Systems

CHRYSLER CORP. ELECTRONIC SPARK CONTROL SYSTEM (Cont.)

13) Remove distributor cap and check each reluctor-to-pick-up coil air gap. When setting start pick-up coil gap, use a .006" non-magnetic feeler gauge. Check gap using an .008" gauge. When setting run pick-up gap, set with .012" gauge and check with .014" gauge. Larger gauges should not fit in gap. See Fig. 10.

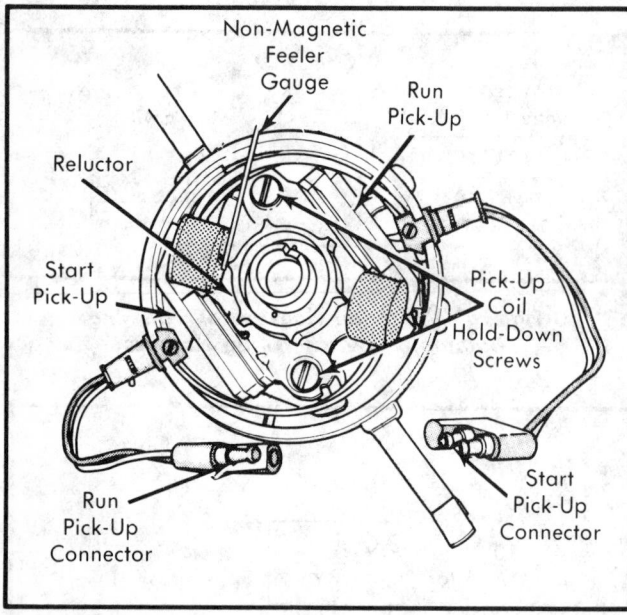

Fig. 10   Checking Distributor Pick-Up Air Gap

NOTE — To adjust gap, loosen pick-up coil hold-down screws, move pick-up coil against feeler gauge resting against reluctor tooth. Tighten hold-down screw, remove feeler gauge, and recheck gap.

14) Install distributor cap and reinstall all wiring. If engine fails to start, replace spark control computer. If it still fails to start, install original computer and retest.

IGNITION COIL RESISTANCE CHECKS

1) If ignition coil is suspected, connect ohmmeter leads to positive and negative primary terminals. Ignition switch should be "OFF" and coil wires removed. Primary resistance should read 1.60-1.79 ohms for Prestolite coils; 1.34 to 1.55 ohms for Essex coils.

2) Then move ohmmeter leads to coil negative terminal and coil tower. Ohmmeter resistance reading should be 9,400-11,700 for Prestolite coils, 9,000-12,200 ohms for Essex coils.

3) Replace ignition coil if either specification is not obtained.

POOR PERFORMANCE TESTS

Basic Advance Timing Test — 1) Connect an adjustable timing light to engine so that total timing advance at crankshaft can be checked. Connect a jumper wire between carburetor switch and a good ground.

2) Be sure vacuum line is connected to vacuum transducer on computer. Observe timing mark on crankshaft damper immediately after engine starts to run. Adjust timing light so basic timing signal is seen at timing plate.

3) The meter on timing light should then show amount of advance, as indicated on vehicle emission control label.

Spark Advance of Computer — 1) Start engine and allow it to warm to normal operating temperature. Put transmission in neutral and set parking brake.

NOTE — The Spark Control Computer has various spark advance schedules incorporated into its microprocessor for operation at differing engine temperatures. Therefore, be sure engine is at normal operating temperature before testing.

2) Place a thin insulator (piece of paper) between curb idle adjusting screw and carburetor switch, or make sure screw is not touching switch. See Fig. 4. Remove and plug vacuum line at vacuum transducer.

3) Connect an auxiliary vacuum supply to vacuum transducer and set for 16 in. Hg vacuum. Increase engine speed to 2000 RPM, wait one minute for specified accumulator clock up time, and then check specifications. Advance specifications are in addition to basic advance.

CAUTION — Use a metal exhaust tube for this test, as high temperatures could cause rubber hose to catch fire.

4) If computer fails to obtain specified settings, replace computer.

CARBURETOR SWITCH TEST

1) Grounding the carburetor switch eliminates all spark advance. Turn key off and disconnect 10-wire harness connector from computer. With throttle completely closed, check continuity between terminal 7 and a good ground. If no continuity is indicated, check wire and carburetor switch. Recheck basic timing.

2) With throttle opened, check continuity between terminal 7 and a good ground. There should be no continuity.

CHARGE TEMPERATURE & COOLANT SWITCH

1) Turn ignition switch "OFF" and disconnect wire from charge temperature switch. Connect one lead of ohmmeter to a good engine ground (or to switch's ground terminal). Connect other lead to center terminal of coolant switch. Check for continuity.

2) For a cold engine, continuity should be present (resistance less than 100 ohms). If not, replace the switch. The charge temperature switch must be cooler than 60°F to obtain this reading.

3) For an engine at normal operating temperature, the terminal should show no continuity. If it does, replace coolant switch.

CHRYSLER CORP. ELECTRONIC SPARK CONTROL SYSTEM (Cont.)

ELECTRONIC EGR SYSTEM TEST

The Spark Control Computer also incorporates an electronic EGR control system. Check that engine temperature sensors are working properly, and proceed as follows:

1) With engine cold and ignition switch turned off, connect voltmeter positive lead to EGR solenoid Gray wire and negative lead to ground. Start engine.

2) Voltage should be less than 1 volt, remaining 1 volt until engine reaches normal operating temperature and electronic EGR schedule has timed out. Solenoid will then de-energize, and voltmeter should read charging system voltage.

3) If not to specification, replace solenoid and repeat test. If voltmeter indicates charging voltage before EGR schedule is complete, replace computer or externally mounted timer.

4) If an engine is started with engine hot, EGR solenoid will be energized for the length of time delay schedule only. It will then de-energize.

ELECTRONIC THROTTLE CONTROL SYSTEM TEST (FEDERAL ONLY)

The Spark Control Computer also incorporates an electronic throttle system on Federal 6-cylinder models. A solenoid, mounted on the carburetor, is energized when the A/C, heater, electronic backlite, or electronic timers are activated. The two timers, incorporated in the ignition system, operate when throttle is closed, plus a time delay of 2 seconds, or after an engine start condition (EGR time delay).

1) To test system, connect a tachometer to engine. Start engine. Depress accelerator and let it up. A higher than curb idle speed should be seen for the length of EGR schedule.

2) If vehicle is equipped with A/C or electronic backlite, turn system on and depress accelerator for a brief period. A higher than curb idle speed should result. Turn system off and normal idle speed should return.

NOTE — *A/C clutch will cycle as it is running. This should not be mistaken as part of electronic control.*

3) If speed increases do not occur, disconnect 3-way connector at carburetor. Check solenoid with ohmmeter, measuring resistance from terminal that contained Black wire to ground. Resistance should read 15-35 ohms. If not, replace solenoid.

4) Start vehicle and before delay has timed out, measure voltage of Black wire at 3-way connector. Charging voltage should be observed. If not, replace computer or Gray start timer.

5) After time delay, turn A/C or backlite on. Charging voltage should be read. If not, check wiring back to instrument panel for an open circuit.

OVERHAUL

Disassembly — 1) Remove distributor cap. Using 2 screwdrivers, pry off rotor from shaft. Remove reluctor by prying up from bottom of reluctor using 2 pry bars or screwdrivers with a maximum width of $7/16$". Be careful not to distort or damage reluctor teeth.

2) Remove 2 screws and lock washers attaching lower plate to housing, and lift out lower plate and pick-up coils as an assembly. Do not attempt to remove distributor cap clamps, as they are peened in place.

3) If distributor has excessive shaft side play (more than .006"), replace housing shaft and reluctor sleeve by removing shaft, retaining pin and sliding drive gear off end of shaft.

NOTE — *Prior to removing shaft, scribe a line on end of shaft from center of shaft to edge. Line should align with space between 2 gear teeth.*

4) Use a file to clean burrs from around pin hole in shaft and remove lower thrust washer. Push shaft up and remove shaft through top of distributor housing.

Reassembly — To assemble, reverse disassembly procedure.

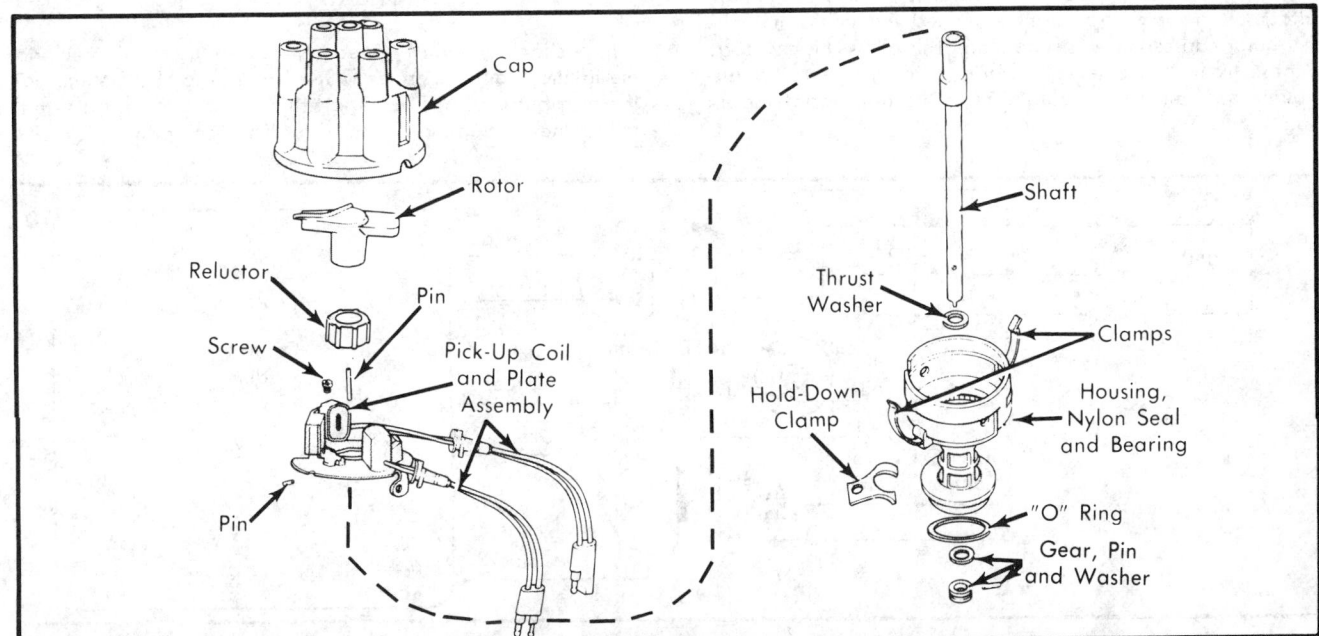

Distributor for 6-Cylinder Vehicles

Distributors & Ignition Systems

MOTORCRAFT EEC III IGNITION SYSTEM

Ford
Calif. Models with
5.0L (302") & 5.8L (351") W Engines

DESCRIPTION

The Electronic Engine Control System (EEC III) is used on California model trucks with 5.0L and 5.8L W engines. All other Ford models use the Dura-Spark II Ignition System.

The ignition portion of the EEC III system is referred to as Dura-Spark III, a solid state system which provides power switching of the ignition coil. Dura-Spark III input signals are controlled by the EEC system.

The EEC distributor, unlike Dura-Spark II, has no centrifugal or vacuum advance. Also, it has no armature (reluctor) or stator (pick-up coil). See Fig. 1. Secondary wires and spark plugs are the same, however, as used in Dura-Spark II systems.

Although control modules appear similar, they must not be interchanged. Dura-Spark III control modules have no purple wire and can also be identified by a brown grommet (Dura-Spark II modules have a blue grommet).

Ignition timing is determined by the crankshaft position (CP) sensor and 6 other engine sensors, which feed information to the EEC III system Electronic Control Assembly (ECA) through a special 32-pin connector.

These other sensors may include exhaust gas oxygen (EGO), engine coolant temperature (ECT), EGR valve position (EVP), throttle position (TP), and barometric manifold absolute pressure (BMAP) sensors and a power relay.

Unlike conventional distributors that are restricted to approximately 20° advance, the EEC system permits up to 50° distributor advance. Both distributor cap and rotor have upper and lower electrode levels. As the rotor turns, one of the high voltage electrode pick-up arms is aligned with one arm of the distributor cap center electrode plate. This allows high voltage to pass from the center plate arms through the rotor, distributor cap, and spark plug wire to the appropriate spark plug.

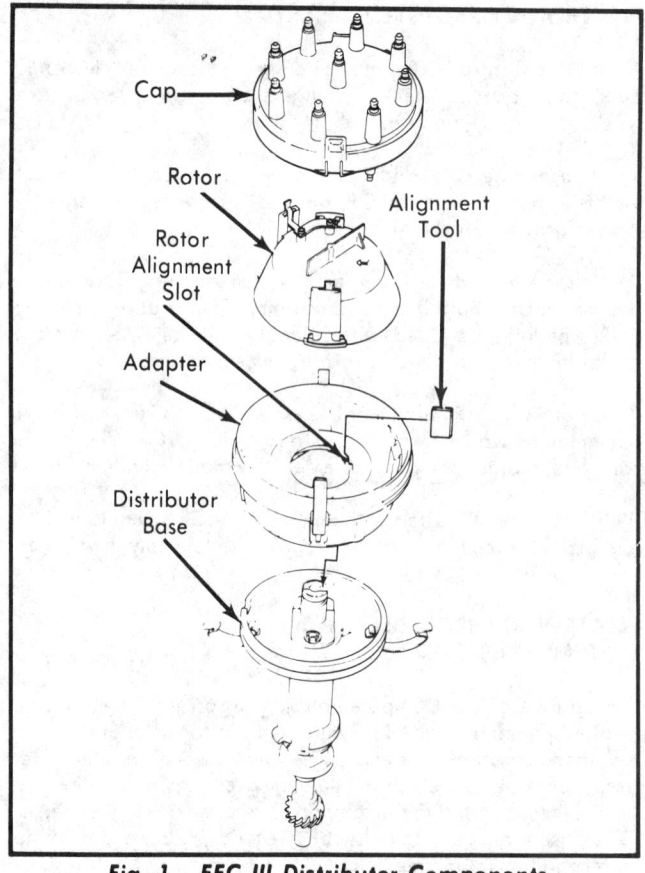

Fig. 1 EEC III Distributor Components

NOTE — *The numbers on top of the distributor cap are for spark plug wire or cylinder identification only. The engine firing order cannot be read from the top of the distributor cap, due to the rotor's 2-level electrode design. In EEC III system, the upper and lower level electrodes fire alternately in a pattern jumping from one side of the cap to the other.*

OPERATION

With the ignition switch turned on, the primary circuit is on and the ignition coil is energized. See Fig. 2. The EEC system (not the distributor as in Dura-Spark II systems) provides a signal telling the ignition module to turn off the coil primary circuit.

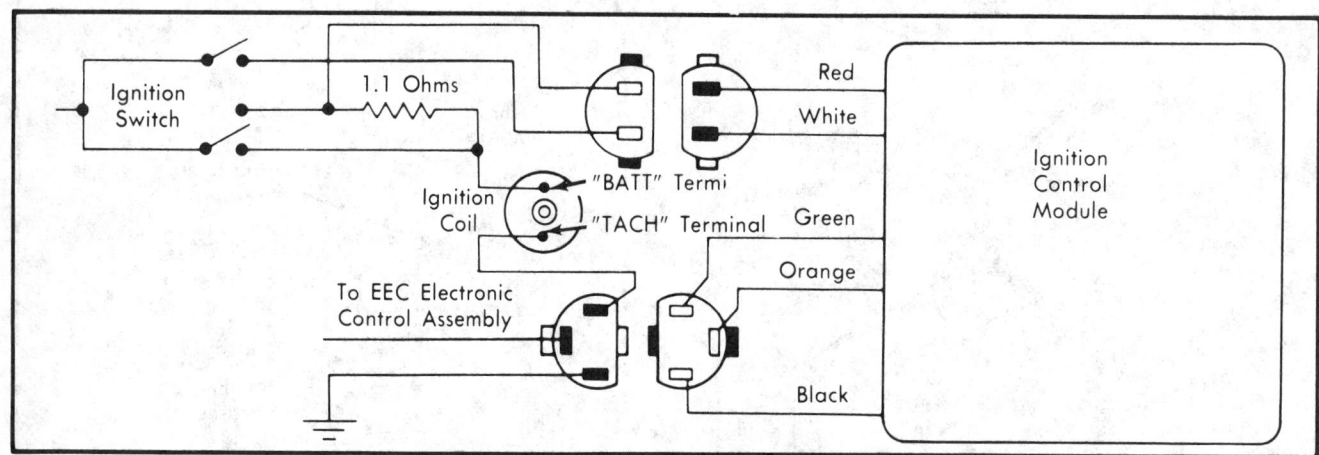

Fig. 2 EEC III Ignition System Schematic

ELECTRICAL

MOTORCRAFT EEC III IGNITION SYSTEM (Cont.)

The length of time the primary circuit is turned on or off is controlled by the EEC Electronic Control Assembly (ECA). *See Fig. 3.* When the current is on, it flows from the battery through the ignition switch, primary windings of ignition coil, and ignition module circuits to ground.

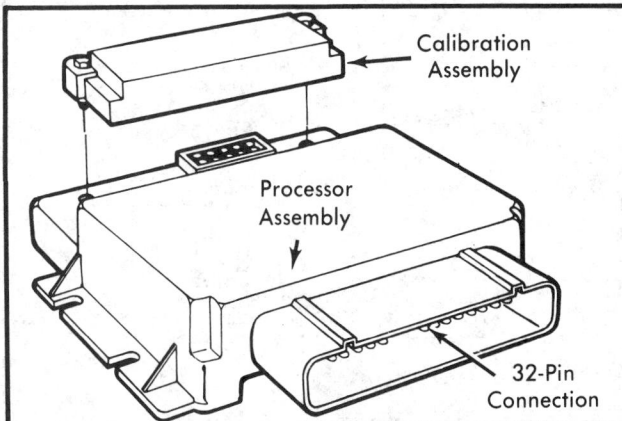

Fig. 3   EEC III Electronic Control Assembly

When the current is turned off, the magnetic field which built up in the ignition coil collapses, inducing high voltage to the secondary windings of the coil. This high voltage, produced each time the magnetic field builds and collapses, is transmitted by the coil to the distributor, rotor and cap to individual spark plugs.

The function of the electronic control assembly and engine sensors follows:

Electronic Control Assembly — The ECA is the "brain" of the EEC system. It is a solid-state, pre-programmed microcomputer, consisting of a processor assembly and a calibration assembly. The ECA is located under the instrument panel to the left of the steering column.

Processor Assembly — The processor assembly contains circuits designed to:

- Continuously sample the 7 engine sensor input signals for analysis. See *Fig. 4.*
- Convert the input signals to a form usable by the computer section in calculations.
- Choose the proper operating strategy (base engine, modulator, or limited operational) for the operating conditions.
- Perform spark, EGR, air/fuel ratio, canister purge, throttle kicker, thermactor air control and other functions.
- Send electrical output signals to the fuel injectors, ignition module, and control solenoids to adjust timing and dwell, air/fuel ratio, canister purge mode, EGR flow rate, thermactor air mode, throttle kicker mode and fuel control.

The processor assembly also provides a continuous reference voltage (about 9 volts) to the sensors.

Calibration Assembly — The calibration assembly is attached to the top of the processor assembly and contains electronic circuits in its black plastic case. It is capable of:

- Providing calibration information necessary for that particular vehicle, for use by the processor assembly.
- Recalling appropriate data previously stored in the memory bank, as vehicle requires.

Power Relay — A power relay is attached to the lower right side of ECA mounting bracket. It supplies battery voltage to the EEC system.

Crankshaft Position Sensor — A crankshaft pulse ring with 4 lobes is pressed onto the vibration damper at the front of the crankshaft. The 4 lobes are spaced 90° apart. The EEC ring is positioned 10° BTDC on the crankshaft. As the crankshaft rotates, the pulse ring lobes pass the tip of the crankshaft position sensor. The sensor contains a permanent magnet and coil. As the lobes cut through the magnetic field of the sensor, an output voltage is generated in the coil and sent to the ECA. The ECA converts these signals to crankshaft (piston) position for spark timing and into RPM for spark advance calculation. The sensor is attached to the engine block and locked in place by a clip and screw. The sensor has no adjustment.

NOTE — *A broken sensor or open wiring will prevent the ECA from receiving a position signal and prevent the engine from starting.*

Barometric & Manifold Absolute Pressure Sensor — The barometric and manifold absolute pressure (BMAP) sensor is actually an assembly containing 2 sensors. The BMAP sensor monitors the value of intake manifold absolute pressure and atmospheric pressure. Manifold absolute pressure is defined as barometric pressure minus manifold vacuum. Barometric and manifold pressure are converted into electrical signals for use by the ECA, in calculating spark advance, EGR flow and air/fuel ratio. The sensor is located on the right-hand fender apron.

Air Charge Temperature Sensor — Sensor is located on left rear side of fuel injection unit and is not used on carbureted models. Threaded into a cylinder runner of the intake manifold, the sensor provides EFI system with air/fuel mixture temperature information. It is used both as a density corrector to air flow calculation and to proportion the cold enrichment fuel flow.

Coolant Temperature Sensor — The sensor converts engine coolant temperature to an electrical signal to the ECA. The ECA then controls EGR operation. Also, if the engine overheats, the ECA will advance ignition timing. The sensor is located in the heater outlet fitting at the front of the intake manifold, near the right-hand valve cover.

Throttle Position Sensor — The sensor is a variable resistor control, mounted on a bracket on the right side of the carburetor. With a reference voltage applied by the ECA, a signal is sent to the ECA, which classifies the signal into one of 3 modes:

- Closed throttle (idle or deceleration).
- Part throttle (cruise).
- Wide open throttle (maximum acceleration).

The sensor has slotted mounting holes to permit rotational adjustment. If sensor is replaced or if curb idle speed is adjusted, sensor must be positioned correctly or erroneous throttle position information will be sent to the ECA.

EGR Valve Position Sensor — Sensor monitors EGR valve position. This signals ECA on the amount of EGR flow. It is located at base of carburetor.

Exhaust Gas Oxygen Sensor — Sensor is threaded into the right-hand exhaust manifold directly in the path of exhaust gas stream. EGO sensor provides information to the ECA

Distributors & Ignition Systems

MOTORCRAFT EEC III IGNITION SYSTEM (Cont.)

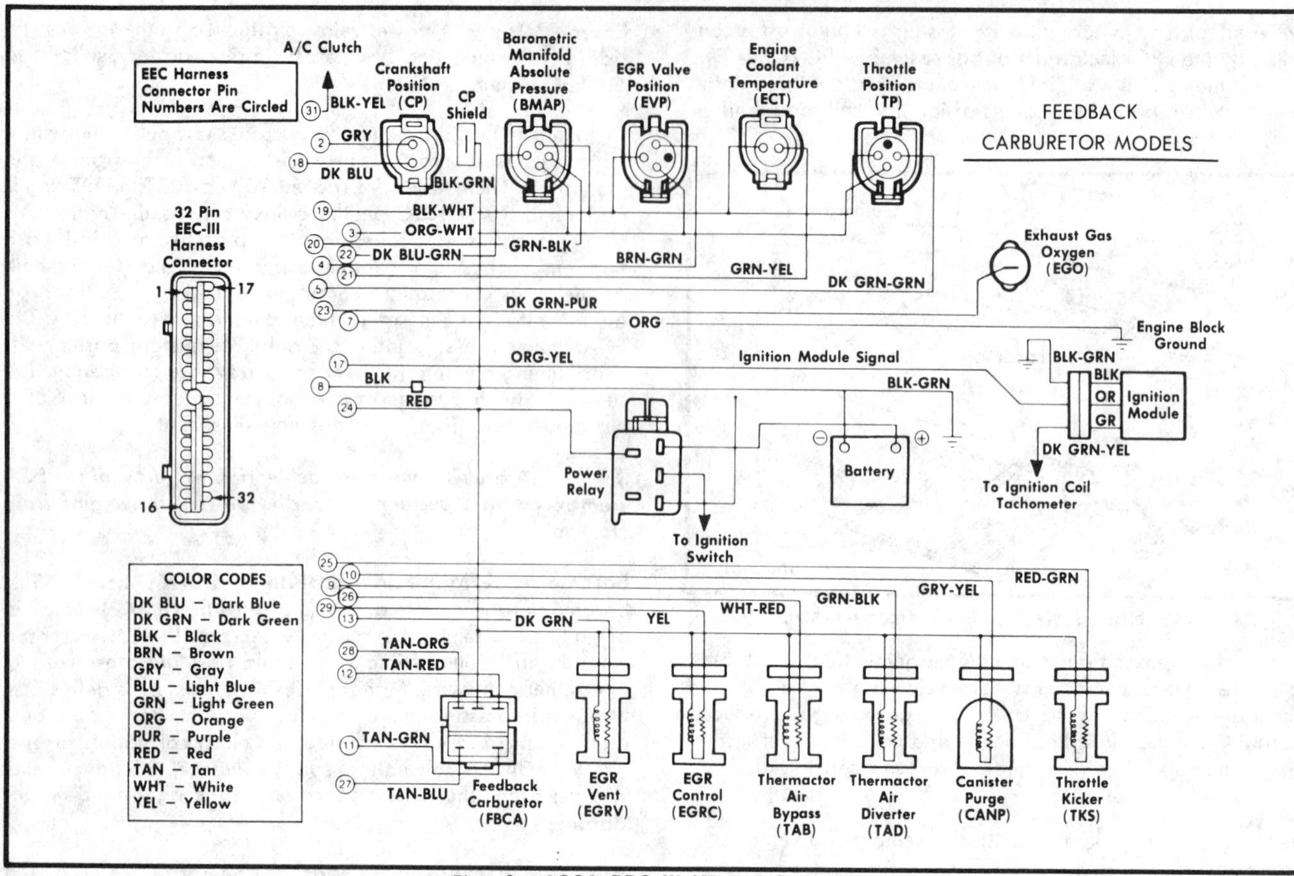

Fig. 4 1981 EEC III Wiring Diagram

about air/fuel ratio (rich or lean) as indicated by oxygen concentration of the exhaust gases.

TESTING

NOTE — *The following tests (Spark Plug Required Voltage, Coil Reserve Voltage and Distributor Rotor to Cap Voltage Drop) are designed to diagnose poor operating characteristics. If vehicle cranks, but will not start, proceed to Secondary Voltage Check to begin testing.*

SPARK PLUG REQUIRED VOLTAGE CHECK

1) Connect diagnostic console to display "parade" pattern. Connect timing light to No. 1 spark plug wire. Attach clamp-on voltage pick-up to coil high tension wire. Start engine and run at approximately 2000 RPM for 2 minutes.

NOTE — *If vehicle will not start, test while cranking.*

2) Apply 25 in. Hg vacuum to "BP" port of BMAP sensor. Read highest spark plug required voltage for each cylinder. If reading is 6,000-20,000 volts, required voltage is OK.

3) If timing is 27-30° BTDC, timing is OK. If not, timing cannot be adjusted. Check lobes on pulse ring for damage, check gap (.075") between crankshaft position sensor and pulse ring. If no problem is found, correct problem in non-ignition portion of EEC system.

4) If voltage was less than 6,000 volts, proceed to Fouled Spark Plug Check. If voltage was greater than 20,000 volts or 50 per cent higher than other cylinders, proceed to Ignition

Coil Primary Voltage Check. If both voltage and timing are correct, proceed to next test.

NOTE — *If an abnormal scope pattern is evident, remove distributor cap and rotor. Check for damaged components or internal arcing. Also check rotor alignment.*

COIL RESERVE VOLTAGE

1) Disconnect wire from either No. 2 or No. 4 spark plug. Connect a spark tester to spark plug wire. See Fig. 5.

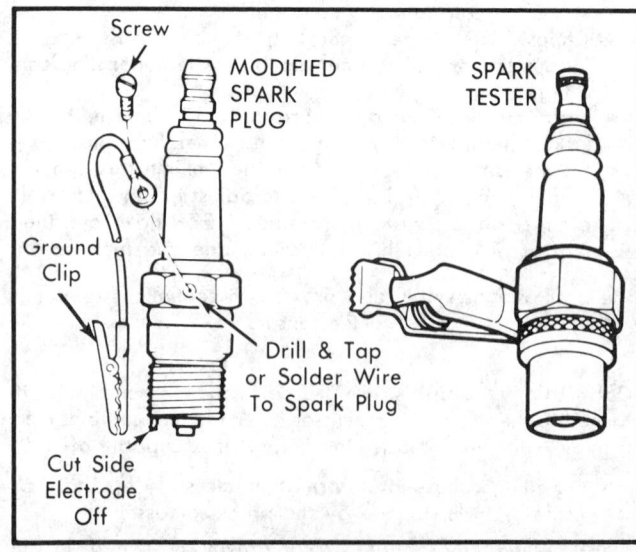

Fig. 5 Modified Spark Plug and Spark Tester

MOTORCRAFT EEC III IGNITION SYSTEM (Cont.)

NOTE — *If no tester is available, modify spark plug by attaching ground to metal case and clip off outer electrode.*

2) Start engine and run at approximately 1000 RPM. Limit engine operation to 30 seconds to prevent damage to emission system components. If spark occurs at plug, coil reserve voltage is OK. Proceed to next test.

3) If no spark occurs, remove distributor cap, rotor and adapter (in order) and check components. Then proceed to Secondary Voltage Check.

DISTRIBUTOR ROTOR-TO-CAP VOLTAGE DROP CHECK

1) Connect diagnostic console. Remove spark tester from spark plug wire and ground wire. Connect clamp-on voltage pick-up to coil high tension wire. Start engine and run at idle.

NOTE — *If high voltage secondary spike is negative going on the scope, the "BATT" lead and "TACH" lead could be reversed at the coil connection or coil could be worn or damaged.*

2) If reading is 8,000 volts maximum, distributor rotor-to-cap voltage drop is OK. If more than 8,000 volts, remove distributor cap and inspect for worn or damaged rotor or for silicone grease leak on rotor. Measure resistance of coil wire. Replace wire if resistance is more than 5,000 ohms per inch.

3) If an abnormal scope pattern appears, inspect for worn or damaged distributor components or for a misaligned rotor.

SECONDARY VOLTAGE CHECK

1) Connect timing light to No. 1 spark plug wire. Crank engine with timing light pointing at mark on timing pointer. Refer to engine decal for proper timing.

2) If light flashes and timing marks line up on damper, proceed to Start Check. If light flashes, but marks do not line up, remove distributor cap and check for rotor damage or misalignment. If light does not flash, proceed to Ignition Coil Output Check.

3) Connect a spark tester to No. 2 or No. 4 spark plug wire. If spark occurs, proceed to Fouled Spark Plug Check and then Start Check. If no spark occurs, proceed to Ignition Coil Output Check.

START CHECK

Attempt to start engine. If it starts, problem is resolved. If engine does not start, proceed to next test and check fuel system.

IGNITION COIL OUTPUT CHECK

1) Connect spark tester to ignition coil high tension wire's distributor end. Crank engine. If spark occurs, check distributor cap, rotor and secondary wires for damage. Service as necessary and rerun test. If problem still exists, proceed to Ignition Coil Primary Voltage Check.

2) If no spark resulted, remove distributor cap, crank engine, and check for rotor movement. If none, check distributor and engine for damage. Then, proceed to next test.

TRIGGER CHECK

1) Disconnect ignition control module's 3-pin connector (Black, Orange and Green wires). Install diagnostic test adapter (T79P-12127-A) between 3-pin module and harness connectors. See Fig. 6.

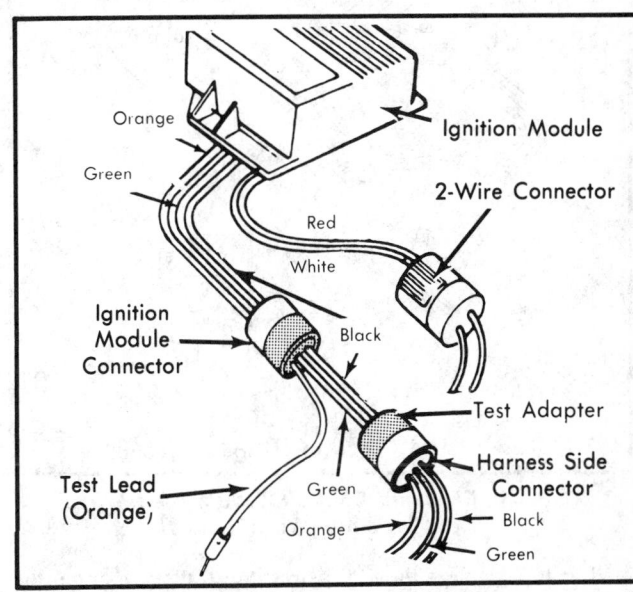

Fig. 6 Installation of Test Adapter or Jumper Wires for Performing EEC III Diagnosis

NOTE — *If adapter is not available, use jumper wires. Connect Black and Green wires to their mating harness wires. Attach jumper wire to Orange module wire, but do not attach this wire to its mating harness wire. Leave it free for testing.*

2) Remove coil high tension wire from distributor. Install spark tester on end of wire. Turn ignition switch to "RUN" position. Tap the adapter diagnostic lead wire (jumper wire to Orange module wire) against battery positive terminal. A spark should occur at spark tester each time diagnostic lead touches battery.

3) If spark results, ignition system is OK. Check other parts of EEC system. Then check fuel system. If no spark results, proceed to next test after reconnecting all vehicle wiring.

IGNITION COIL PRIMARY VOLTAGE CHECK

1) Turn ignition switch to "RUN" position. Measure battery voltage at coil positive ("BATT") terminal.

2) If more than 8 volts is read, proceed to Ground Circuit Check. If 5-8 volts, ignition primary is OK. Proceed to next test. If less than 5 volts, proceed to Wiring Harness Shorts Check and then Ignition Coil Circuit Check. Then check for open power feed wires (battery positive wire to ignition coil and module). If problem still is not solved, check non-ignition portion of EEC system.

MODULE RUN CIRCUIT VOLTAGE CHECK

1) Turn ignition switch to "RUN" position. Using a small straight pin, puncture Red wire between control module and connector. See Fig. 7. Attach positive voltmeter lead to straight pin and negative lead to ground. Do not let pin touch ground.

MOTORCRAFT EEC III IGNITION SYSTEM (Cont.)

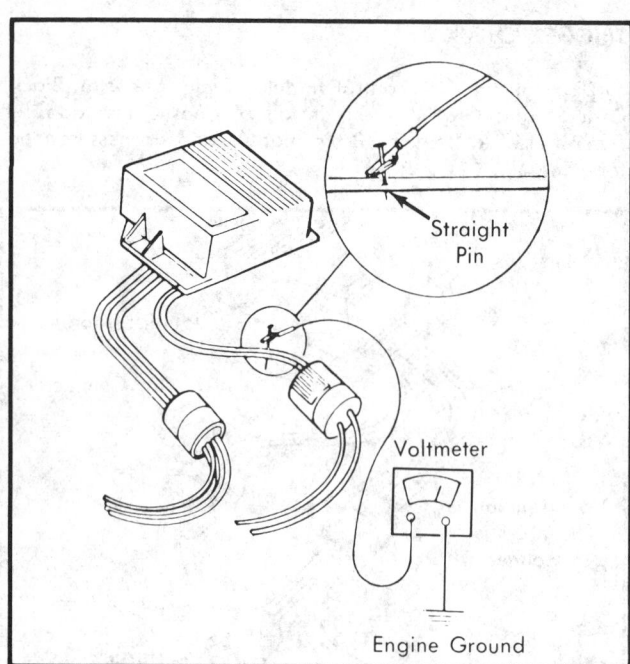

**Fig. 7   Checking Control Module Feed Wires
(Red or White Wire Circuits)**

2) If voltage is more than 90 per cent of battery voltage, the module run circuit is OK. Proceed to next test. If less than 90 percent, check for an open wire in run circuit.

MODULE START CIRCUIT VOLTAGE CHECK

1) If starter relay has an "I" terminal, disconnect cable from relay to starter motor. If there is no "I" terminal, disconnect wire at "S" terminal.

2) Hold ignition switch in "START" position. Connect voltmeter positive lead to coil positive ("BATT") terminal and negative lead to ground. *See Fig. 8.* Record reading. Then puncture White wire with a straight pin between control module and connector. *See Fig. 7.* Attach positive voltmeter lead to pin and negative lead to ground. Do not let pin touch ground.

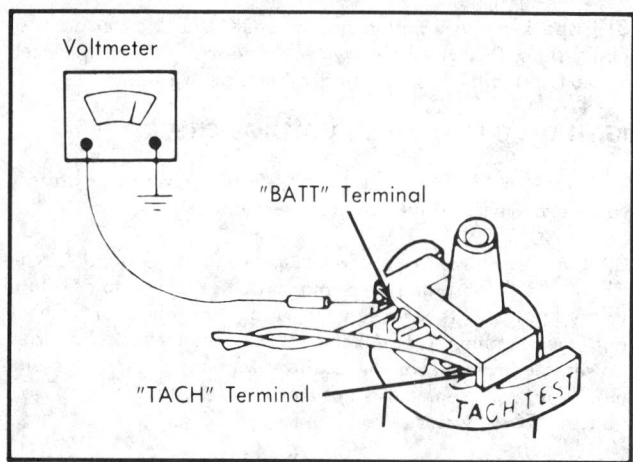

Fig. 8   Checking Battery Voltage at Coil

3) If voltage is more than 90 percent of battery voltage (measured at coil), module start circuit is OK. Proceed to Module Output Check.

4) If voltage is less than 90 percent of battery voltage, proceed to next test. Then check for an open ballast resistor by-pass wire or for an open condition in the module White wire circuit. Also check ignition switch connections and switch condition.

WIRING HARNESS SHORTS CHECK

1) Disconnect and check ignition module, ignition coil and EEC electronic control assembly connectors for dirt or damage. Check also for overheated, burned or bare wires connecting to Red, White or Green control module wires or to "BATT" or "TACH" terminals of coil connector.

2) Set parking brake and place transmission lever in "NEUTRAL" or "PARK" position. Connect ohmmeter leads to module wiring harness Orange wire and to ground.

3) Connect an ohmmeter, in turn, between harness connector wires that would mate with control module harness Red and White wires, Red and Green wires, Red and Orange wires, White and Green wires, and White and Orange wires.

4) If resistance is greater than 70,000 ohms, proceed to Ignition Coil Circuit Check. If less than 70,000 ohms, repair or replace wires as necessary.

GROUND CIRCUIT CHECK

1) Disconnect 3-pin module connector and inspect it for dirt or damage. Connect ohmmeter leads to ground and to harness connector terminal that mates with control module Black wire.

2) If resistance is less than 1 ohm, proceed to next test. If more than 1 ohm resistance, inspect ground strap connecting to battery for poor connection or open condition.

IGNITION COIL CIRCUIT CHECK

1) Disconnect control module and coil connectors and inspect for dirt or damage. Connect one ohmmeter lead to harness connector terminal mating with control module Green wire. Connect other lead to end of same wire disconnected from coil "TACH" terminal.

2) If less than 2 ohms, resistance is OK. Proceed with test. If more than 2 ohms, service open in wiring harness "TACH" wire and inspect for corrosion.

3) Connect ohmmeter leads in same manner to harness terminal connecting with control module Red wire and to other end of wire disconnected from coil "BATT" terminal.

4) If less than 2 ohms, resistance is OK. Proceed to next test. If greater than 2 ohms, service ballast resistor wire for open or corrosion.

MODULE OUTPUT CHECK

1) Be sure all wires and harnesses are connected. Connect positive lead of voltmeter to coil "TACH" terminal and negative lead to ground. Set voltmeter on highest scale. Ground distributor cap end of coil high tension wire. Crank engine, and while cranking, switch voltmeter to lowest scale.

2) Meter needle should oscillate. If so, module output is OK. Proceed to Ignition Coil Primary Resistance Check. If needle does not oscillate, proceed to next test.

MOTORCRAFT EEC III IGNITION SYSTEM (Cont.)

NOTE – *If voltmeter is not available, connect test light across coil terminals. Check for light flashing instead of needle oscillation.*

MODULE OPERATION CHECK

1) Disconnect 3-pin control module connector. Connect positive voltmeter lead to wiring harness terminal that mates with control module Green wire. Attach negative lead to ground. Turn ignition switch to "RUN" position and check voltage.

2) If reading is greater than 90 percent of battery voltage, turn switch to "OFF" position and replace ignition control module. If reading is less than 90 percent of battery voltage, turn switch to "OFF" position and proceed to next test.

"TACH" WIRE CONTINUITY CHECK

1) Connect one ohmmeter lead to harness terminal that mates with control module Green wire. Connect other end to coil "TACH" wire in coil connector (do not remove connector).

2) If less than 1 ohm, wire is OK. Proceed to next test. If more than 1 ohm, service open wire between control module harness connector and "TACH" terminal of coil.

IGNITION COIL PRIMARY RESISTANCE CHECK

1) Disconnect ignition coil connector. Attach ohmmeter leads to "BATT" and "TACH" terminals of coil (not connector).

2) If reading is greater than 1 ohm, but less than 2 ohms, primary resistance is OK. Proceed to next test. If reading is not 1-2 ohms, replace ignition coil.

IGNITION COIL SECONDARY RESISTANCE CHECK

1) With coil connector still removed from coil, connect ohmmeter leads to "TACH" terminal and to coil tower (with high tension wire removed).

2) If resistance is 7,700-9,600 ohms, secondary resistance is OK. If not within specified range, replace ignition coil.

FOULED SPARK PLUG CHECK

1) Remove distributor cap. Connect 500V DC megohmmeter between each spark plug wire at distributor and engine ground.

NOTE – *If megohmmeter is not available, proceed to Power Balance Check.*

2) If reading is more than 50 megohms, spark plug is OK. If less than 50 megohms, check spark plug wire. If good, replace spark plug.

POWER BALANCE CHECK

1) Connect tachometer to ignition coil. Start engine and let it run at idle until engine reaches normal operating temperature. Remove spark plug wire at distributor.

2) If RPM drops approximately 100-200 RPM, spark plug tested is OK. Proceed until all plugs have been tested. If all plugs test OK, check fuel system for problems. If engine RPM

does not drop when spark plug wire is removed, check spark plug and wire as instructed in next test.

SPARK PLUG WIRE CHECK

1) Disconnect spark plug end of suspected wire or wires. Remove distributor cap. Measure resistance of spark plug wires by touching ohmmeter probes to each end of wire. Measure from inside distributor cap. If resistance is less than 5,000 ohms per inch, wire is OK.

2) If resistance is more than 5,000 ohms per inch, remove wire from cap and measure resistance of wire only. If it is less than 5,000 ohms, wire is OK. Check distributor cap and spark plug terminal for corrosion. Also check spark plug. If more than 5,000 ohms, replace spark plug wire.

ELECTRONIC CONTROL ASSEMBLY AND SENSOR CHECK

Due to the complexity of the EEC system, 2 special diagnostic aids are required. One is a Digital Volt/Ohmmeter. This is a highly accurate, high input impedance meter that is more accurate than conventional needle-type Volt/Ohmmeters.

The second diagnostic aid is the special EEC System Diagnostic Tester (Rotunda T79L-50-EEC II or T80L-50-EEC II). The tester plugs into the vehicle harness between the electronic control assembly and its harness. Testing instructions are provided in the operator's manual furnished with the tester. Specifications required are on vehicle emission control information decal on engine valve cover.

Other equipment necessary for testing includes a timing light compatible with Dura-Spark systems, a pressure/vacuum gauge, tachometer, spark tester, jumper wire, EFI pressure gauge (T80L-9974-A) and EFI adapter harness (T80L-50-EFI).

OVERHAUL

ROTOR

Removal – Remove distributor cap. Remove rotor by pulling up on rotor pull tab. Rotor is held in place by a spring clip.

NOTE – *Rotor removal is only necessary when replacing rotor or adapter or when checking rotor condition. No adjustment to distributor is needed when rotor is replaced.*

Installation – 1) Coat rotor lower electrode blade only (not upper blades) using silicone grease. Coat all 4 distributor cap center blade arms to a $\frac{1}{32}$" thickness.

2) To check rotor alignment, set No. 1 piston on compression stroke, rotate crankshaft until rotor alignment tool (T79P-12200A) can be inserted into alignment slots in rotor and center of shaft. See *Fig. 9.* Read timing mark on damper that is aligned with pointer. If timing mark is within 4° of specification, do not reset rotor alignment. EEC models with feedback carburetors should be adjusted to TDC; those with EFI to 5° ATDC. Either adjustment may be ±4°.

3) If alignment is not within 4° of specified timing or when installing rotor, remove alignment tool, position crank at proper timing mark and loosen 2 sleeve assembly adjustment screws. Rotate sleeve until alignment tool fits into alignment slots. Tighten adjustment screws and remove tool.

MOTORCRAFT EEC III IGNITION SYSTEM (Cont.)

4) Align arrow molded into top of rotor with large key way slot in distributor sleeve. Press down on rotor until retaining spring snaps into place.

NOTE — *Since EEC distributors have no vacuum or centrifugal advance mechanisms, overhaul is limited to removal, inspection and alignment of rotor or removal and inspection of cap.*

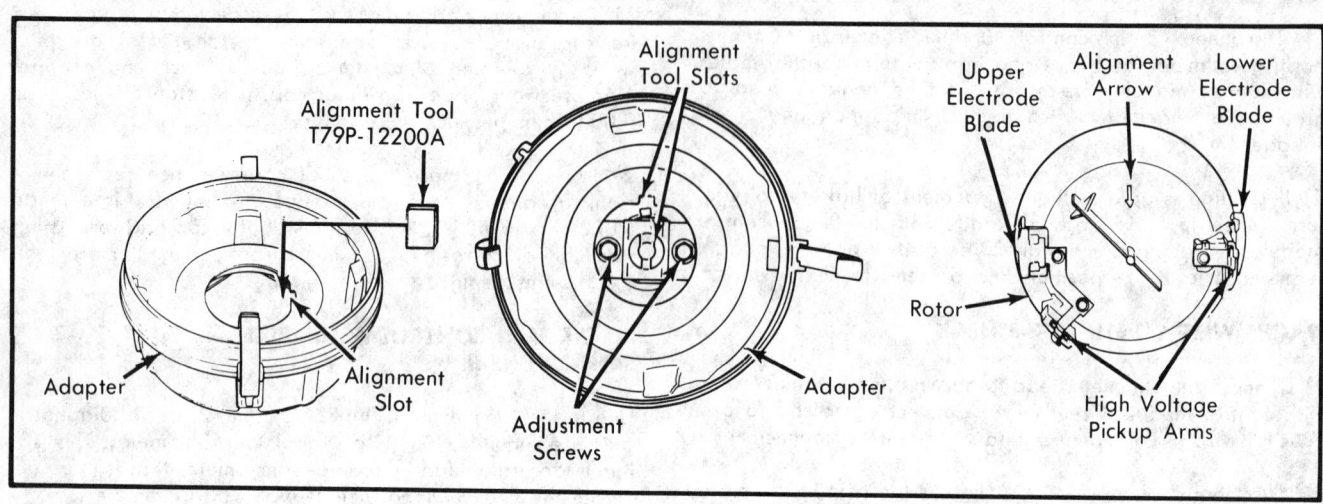

Fig. 9   EEC III Rotor, Adapter and Alignment Procedure

MOTORCRAFT DURA-SPARK II IGNITION SYSTEMS

Ford
All Except Calif. Models with
5.0L (302″) and 5.8L (351″) W Engines

DESCRIPTION

Dura-Spark II — Dura-Spark II is basically a solid-state ignition system, consisting of a breakerless distributor, electronic control module, ignition coil, battery, ignition switch, secondary wires and various wiring harnesses. See Figs. 2 and 4.

All models use a larger rotor, a distributor cap and adapter, secondary wires, and wide gap spark plugs to take advantage of higher energy produced.

Dura-Spark II system can be identified by blue grommet on electronic control module and by module's 2-wire and 4-wire connectors. See Fig. 3.

Dura-Spark II with Dual Mode Timing — Some models have a special electronic control module with a third connector having 3 wires. See Fig. 1. This connector attaches to a special ignition barometric pressure switch, used on altitude calibration vehicles.

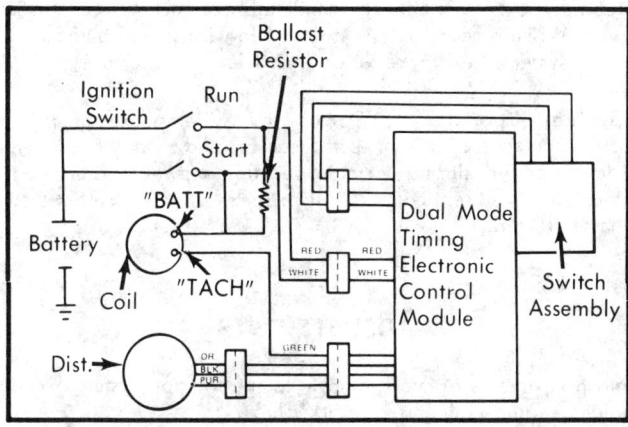

Fig. 1   Dura-Spark II System with Dual Mode Timing Electronic Control Module (Altitude Models)

This switch allows base engine timing to be modified to suit altitude conditions. All other operating charactics of the module are the same as for Dura-Spark II systems without the special switch.

OPERATION

The Dura-Spark II systems contain a distributor, electronic control module and ignition coil and function much the same as other solid state systems. See Figs. 1 and 2. An armature on the distributor shaft rotates past a stator (pick-up coil). See Fig. 8.

The armature has the same number of teeth as the engine has cylinders. As the teeth rotate past the pick-up coil, a signal is sent to the electronic control module.

The module then determines when to turn current off and on in the primary windings of the ignition coil. This current collapse in the primary, causes a high voltage surge in the secondary, which is routed to the spark plugs through the rotor, distributor cap and spark plug wires. System components include the following:

Electronic Control Module — Each Dura-Spark II module has 6 wires. (A 2-wire and 4-wire connector). See Fig. 3. Modules with dual mode timing have 9 wires; See Fig. 1. The Red and White wires are the ignition feed wires — the White circuit is for cranking; the Red circuit, for operation after the engine begins to run. The Red wire circuit contains a 1.1 ohm wire resistor. The current to the primary circuit of the ignition coil is turned off and on through the Green wire. The Orange and Purple wires transmit signals to the module from the armature and stator in the distributor. The Black wire is used to ground the distributor. The module is "ON" whenever the ignition switch is in the "ON" or "START" position.

Distributor — An armature, containing the same number of teeth as the engine has cylinders, turns with the distributor shaft. A stator (pick-up coil) contains a permanent magnet, causing a magnetic field around the stator's pick-up coil. As the teeth of the armature pass the stator, the magnetic field builds and collapses, causing a signal to be sent to the electronic control module. In turn, the control module turns the ignition coil off and on.

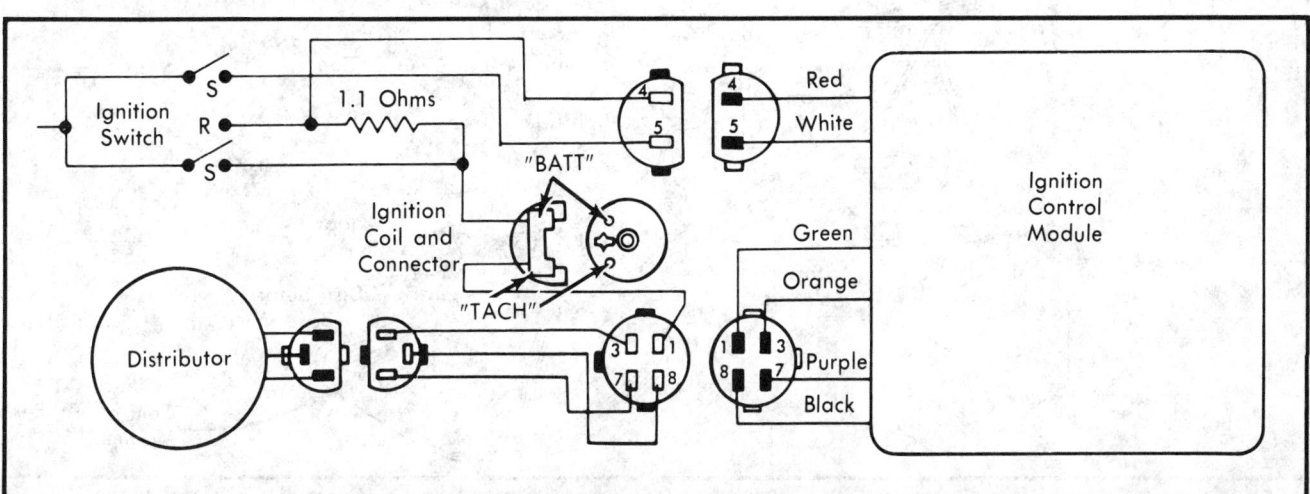

Fig. 2   Dura-Spark II Ignition System Wiring Diagram

Distributors & Ignition Systems

MOTORCRAFT DURA-SPARK II IGNITION SYSTEMS (Cont.)

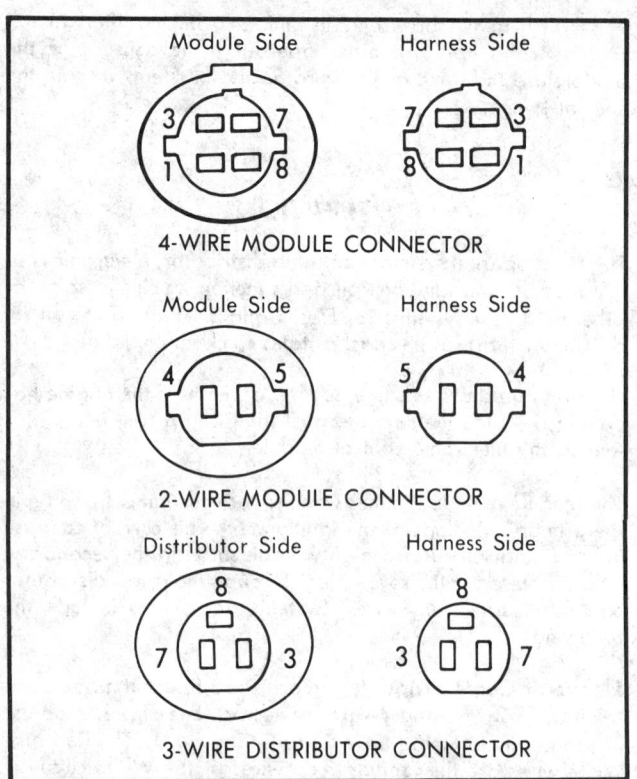

Fig. 3   Control Module and Distributor Connectors for Dura-Spark II

Dura-Spark II systems have an adapter between the distributor housing and cap. See Fig. 4. Caps are larger than for conventional distributors and have male terminals. Distributors have both centrifugal and vacuum advance units.

On single diaphragm vacuum units, increased vacuum causes the movable stator to pivot on lower plate assembly, advancing spark timing. On dual diaphragm vacuum units, the outer (primary) diaphragm operates from carburetor vacuum to provide timing advance during normal off idle driving conditions. It is connected to the stator assembly.

The inner (secondary) diaphragm operates from intake manifold vacuum and acts to retard ignition timing. The inner diaphragm is connected to the outer diaphragm by means of sliding linkage. Stronger intake manifold vacuum can override carburetor vacuum during closed throttle operation, retarding spark timing.

Distributors on 6-cylinder models rotate clockwise, those on V8 models, counterclockwise.

Ignition Coil — Coils are oil filled and are energized whenever the ignition switch is in the "ON" or "START" position. They contain a positive "BATT" terminal and a negative "TACH" (sometimes called "DEC") terminal and a single secondary terminal. A special connector attaches the Green wire from the control module to the negative terminal ("TACH") and the wire from the ignition switch to the positive terminal ("BATT"). The wire from the ignition switch contains a 1.1 ohm resistance wire.

NOTE — "DEC" refers to Distributor Electronic Control. This terminal is also referred to as the "Tach Test" terminal.

Resistance Wire — The special ignition resistance wire in the Red wire circuit must be of specified length and diameter to reduce operating voltage. Under no circumstances should it be replaced by any other wire other than correct service resistor wire. When a new wire is installed, old wire should be isolated from system. Resistance value is 1.0-1.1 ohms.

System Protection — Dura-Spark systems are protected against electrical currents produced or used by any other vehicle component during normal operation. However, damage to the ignition system can occur if proper testing procedures are not followed.

ADJUSTMENTS

No adjustments are to be made to the ignition system except initial engine timing and spark plug gap.

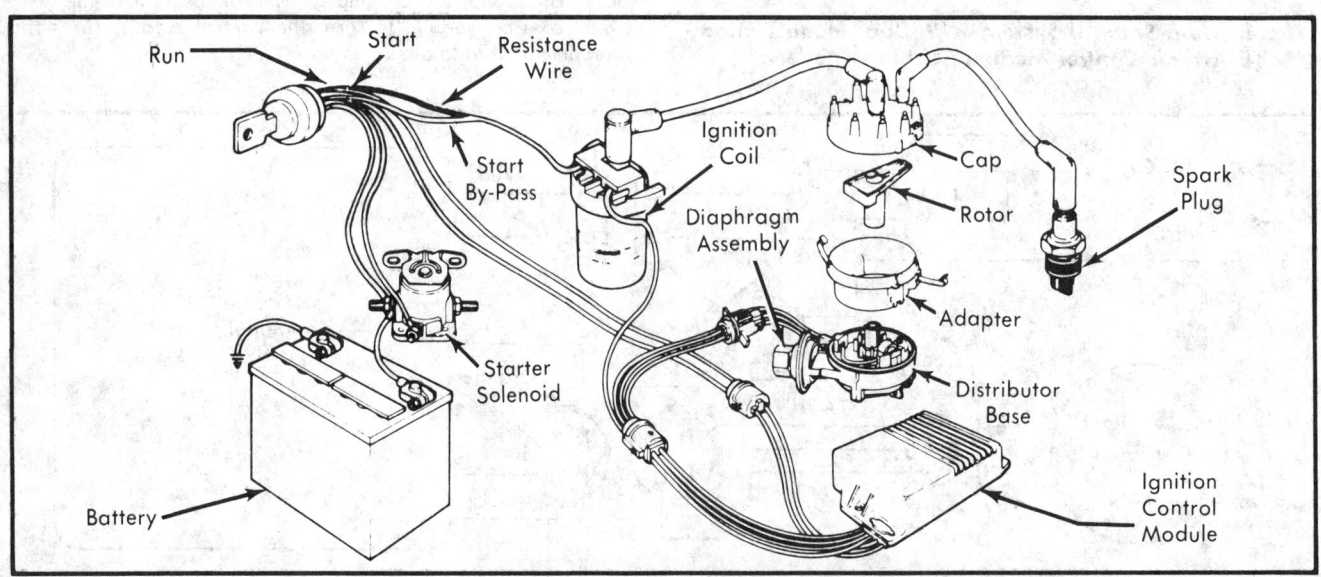

Fig. 4   Schematic of Dura-Spark II Ignition System

MOTORCRAFT DURA-SPARK II IGNITION SYSTEMS (Cont.)

DURA-SPARK II SYSTEM PRECAUTIONS

Since the electronic control module and ignition coil are "ON" whenever the ignition switch is in the "ON" or "START" position, the system will generate a spark whenever the ignition switch is turned "OFF". This feature may be used as a diagnostic tool to check for continuity of circuit, coil and ignition switch. As spark may occur if distributor cap is removed with switch "ON", keep switch "OFF" during underhood operations, unless you plan to start the engine or perform a test requiring the switch to be "ON". This will prevent accidental engine rotation during service or test procedures.

Silicone dielectric grease must be applied to all insulating areas at distributor, coil and spark plug boots.

A ¾" clearance must be maintained at distributor cap mounting edge, spark plug wire terminals, and coil tower to prevent high voltage arc to ground.

To help prevent radio frequency interference, coat the entire brass rotor tip with silicone dielectric grease to a thickness of 1/32". Do not remove this grease, even if discolored, as the grease will maintain its insulating properties.

When replacing spark plug wires, insure wire made of the same material is used for a replacement. Silicone/Silicone wire can be identified by the letters "SS" appearing on the wire in WHITE lettering. Silicone/EPDM wire can be identified by the letters "SE" appearing on the wire in BLACK lettering. The "SS" wire is used on cylinders subject to very high engine temperatures.

When removing distributor cap and adapter, always remove the distributor cap first, then the adapter.

TESTING

NOTE — *All wire colors shown refer to colors of ignition control module wires. When making tests, wires must be traced back to control module for proper color identification. Also, when a test is completed and a problem is disclosed, make the repair necessary and repeat failed test to be sure problem has been corrected. All tests are based on the fact that engine cranks but will not start.*

CAUTION — *When checking the secondary voltage, do not remove the following spark plug wires while the engine is running or cranking:*

Plug No. 1 or 8 on V8 Engines.
Plug No. 3 or 5 on 6-Cylinder engines.

NOTE — *On vehicles with a catalytic converter, do not run engine for more than 30 seconds with a spark plug wire removed.*

TEST SPARK PLUG

Either use a spark tester tool or modify a spark plug (cut off side terminal and install spring clip for grounding plug housing) for use in testing ignition system. See Fig. 5.

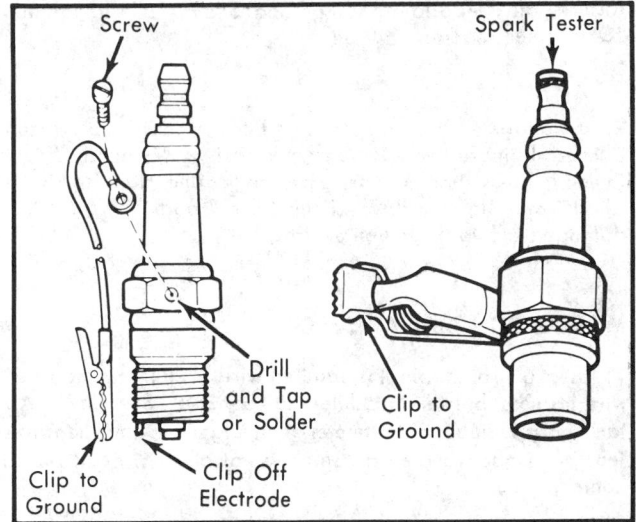

Fig. 5   Modified Spark Plug and Spark Tester

IGNITION COIL OUTPUT VOLTAGE CHECK

1) Connect spark tester between ignition coil high tension wire and engine ground. Crank engine. Disconnect tester and reconnect coil wire to distributor cap.

2) If spark occurs, ignition coil output voltage is OK. Check distributor cap and rotor for damage or lack of silicone grease. Then proceed to "Fouled Spark Plugs."

NOTE — *Do not apply silicone grease to center spring portion of rotor. Apply 1/32 of silicone grease on complete surface (top, bottom, and edges) of rotor blade tip.*

3) If there was no spark in step 1), measure resistance of ignition coil wire. Attach ohmmeter leads to each end of wire. Replace if greater than 5,000 ohms per inch resistance is encountered. Remove distributor cap, crank engine, and check for distributor rotation. If none, check distributor. Proceed to "Ignition Coil Primary Voltage Check".

IGNITION COIL PRIMARY VOLTAGE CHECK

1) Turn ignition switch to "RUN" position. Connect positive lead of voltmeter to ignition coil positive ("BATT") terminal. At-

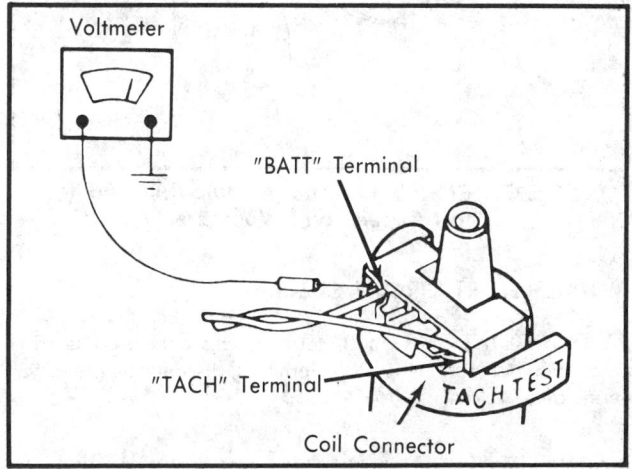

Fig. 6   Checking for Battery Voltage at Ignition Coil Positive ("BATT") Terminal

MOTORCRAFT DURA-SPARK II IGNITION SYSTEMS (Cont.)

tach negative lead to a good ground. *See Fig. 6.* Turn ignition "OFF" after reading voltage.

2) If voltage is 6-8 volts, proceed to "Module Run Circuit Check." If more than 8 volts, proceed to "Ground Circuit Check." If less than 6 volts, perform "Wiring Harness Shorts Check" and "Ignition Coil Circuit Check" and then check for damaged or worn ignition switch.

MODULE RUN CIRCUIT CHECK

1) Insert a straight pin through Red wire of ignition module 2-wire harness, between module and connector. *See Fig. 7.* Attach positive lead of voltmeter to straight pin and negative lead to a good engine ground. Do not allow straight pin to contact ground.

2) Turn ignition switch to "RUN" position, take reading and turn switch "OFF".

3) If reading is at least 90 percent of battery voltage, proceed to "Module Start Circuit Check." If reading is below 90 percent, proceed to "Wiring Harness Shorts Check." Service and replace wires, as necessary.

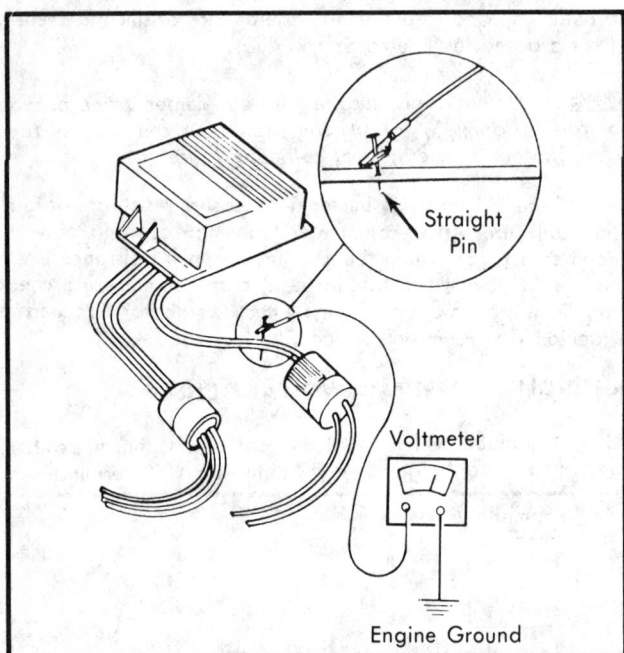

Fig. 7 Checking Control Module Run and Start Circuits with Voltmeter

MODULE START CIRCUIT CHECK

1) If starter relay has an "I" terminal, disconnect cable from relay to motor. If there is no "I" terminal, disconnect wire at "S" terminal of relay.

2) Hold ignition switch in "START" position. Connect voltmeter positive lead to ignition coil positive ("BATT") terminal and negative lead to ground. *See Fig. 6.* Take reading. Then insert

a straight pin in White wire of ignition module 2-wire harness, between module and connector. *See Fig. 7.* Attach positive lead of voltmeter to pin, with negative lead still grounded. Again, do not let pin touch ground. Turn ignition switch "OFF" and reattach starter relay wires.

3) Readings in both instances should be 90 percent of battery voltage while cranking. If so, proceed to "Distributor Stator Assembly Check." If less than 90 percent, proceed to "Wiring Harness Shorts Check." Also check ballast resistor by-pass circuit, replace damaged wiring harnesses, and check for worn or damaged ignition switch.

WIRING HARNESS SHORTS CHECK

1) Inspect wiring harness for overheated, burned or bare wires, connecting to control module Red, White, and Green wires or to primary ("BATT" and "TACH") terminals of ignition coil connector.

2) Check control module and ignition coil connectors for dirt, corrosion or damage. Connect one lead of ohmmeter to engine ground and other lead to terminals in 4-wire connector that mate with Orange and Purple module wires.

3) Check resistance, in turn, between the sets of wires in the harness connectors that mate with Red and White wires, Red and Green wires, Red and Orange wires, Red and Purple wires, White and Green wires, and White and Purple wires. Remove ohmmeter and reconnect all connectors.

4) If more than 70,000 ohms, proceed to "Distributor Stator Assembly Check." If less than 70,000 ohms, service or replace defective wires.

GROUND CIRCUIT CHECK

1) Disconnect 3-wire distributor connector and 4-wire module connector. Check for dirt, corrosion or damage. Connect one ohmmeter lead to Black wire in distributor connector and other lead to ground. Wiggle distributor grommet during measurement.

2) Then connect ohmmeter leads to each end of Black wire, between 4-wire and 3-wire connectors. Remove ohmmeter and reconnect connectors.

3) If there is less than 1 ohm resistance, proceed to "Ignition Coil Circuit Check." If more than 1 ohm resistance, check for loose, broken or missing distributor ground screw. Replace defective wires.

IGNITION COIL CIRCUIT CHECK

1) Disconnect ignition coil connector and module connectors. Inspect for dirt, corrosion or damage. Connect ohmmeter leads to "TACH" terminal of ignition coil connector and to terminal in wiring harness connector that mates with module Green wire.

2) If less than 1 ohm resistance, proceed to step **3)**. If greater than 1 ohm, repair or replace wire.

3) Connect ohmmeter leads to "BATT" terminal of ignition coil connector and to terminal in 2-wire connector that mates with

MOTORCRAFT DURA-SPARK II IGNITION SYSTEMS (Cont.)

module Red wire. If resistance is 0.6-1.6 ohms, proceed to "Distributor Stator Assembly Check." If either is more or less than specified range, replace ballast resistor wire.

DISTRIBUTOR STATOR ASSEMBLY CHECK

1) Disconnect 4-wire module connector and check for dirt, corrosion or damage. Clean as required. Connect ohmmeter leads to terminals in 4-wire harness connector that mate with module's Orange and Purple wires.

2) Resistance should be 400-1,000 ohms. If so, proceed to "Distributor Stator Assembly Output Voltage Check." If not within specified range, disconnect distributor connector and check for dirt, corrosion or damage.

3) Connect ohmmeter leads to Orange and Purple wires in distributor connector, take reading and reconnect connector. If reading is now 400-1000 ohms, stator assembly is OK and wiring harness between 3-wire and 4-wire connectors is defective.

4) If resistance reading at distributor connector is still not within specified range, replace stator assembly.

DISTRIBUTOR STATOR ASSEMBLY OUTPUT VOLTAGE CHECK

1) Connect a voltmeter, set in a 2V DC range, so that leads connect to terminals of 4-wire harness connector that mate with Orange and Purple module wires. Crank engine and read voltage. Reconnect harness connector.

2) If voltmeter needle oscillates, proceed to "Module Output Check." If needle does not oscillate, replace stator assembly.

MODULE OUTPUT CHECK

1) Connect positive lead of voltmeter to "TACH" terminal of ignition coil and negative lead to engine ground. Ground distributor cap end of coil high tension wire. Set voltmeter to 50V DC range.

2) Crank engine and while cranking, switch voltmeter to 2V DC range. Observe reading and reconnect coil wire to distributor.

3) If voltmeter needle oscillates, proceed to "Ignition Coil Primary Resistance Check." If needle does not oscillate, proceed to "Module Input Check."

NOTE — If voltmeter testing does not obtain a usable conclusion, substitute a 12V DC test light. If light flashes, module output is OK.

MODULE INPUT CHECK

1) Disconnect 4-wire module connector. Connect positive lead of voltmeter to terminal in harness connector that mates with

module Green wire. Connect negative lead to engine ground. Turn ignition switch to "ON" position, take reading and turn switch "OFF".

2) If voltage is less than 90 percent of battery voltage, proceed to "Coil Harness Continuity Check." If more than 90 percent of battery voltage but engine will not start, suspect control module.

COIL HARNESS CONTINUITY CHECK

1) Connect ohmmeter leads to coil "TACH" terminal and to 4-wire harness connector terminal that mates with control module Green wire.

2) If resistance is less than 1 ohm, proceed to "Ignition Coil Primary Resistance Check." If more than 1 ohm, repair or replace Green wire from coil to 4-wire harness connector.

IGNITION COIL PRIMARY RESISTANCE CHECK

Disconnect ignition coil connector. Connect ohmmeter leads to coil "BATT" and "TACH" primary terminals. If resistance is 1-2 ohms, proceed to "Ignition Coil Secondary Resistance Check." If not 1-2 ohms, replace ignition coil.

IGNITION COIL SECONDARY RESISTANCE CHECK

1) With coil connector removed from coil, connect ohmmeter leads to coil "BATT" terminal and to coil tower (high tension wire removed).

2) If reading is 7,700-9,600 ohms, resistance is OK. If resistance is outside specified range, replace ignition coil.

FOULED SPARK PLUG CHECK

1) Remove distributor cap, leaving spark plug wires attached. Connect megohmmeter leads to engine ground and, in turn, to each spark plug wire terminal inside distributor cap.

NOTE — If no megohmmeter is available, proceed to "Power Balance Check."

2) If resistance reading is greater than 50 megohms, proceed to "Spark Plug Wire Resistance Check." If below 50 megohms, spark plugs are fouled and must be cleaned or replaced.

POWER BALANCE CHECK

Perform power balance according to equipment manufacturer's instructions. If RPM drops, check fuel system instead of ignition. If RPM does not drop, proceed to "Spark Plug Wire Resistance Check."

SPARK PLUG WIRE RESISTANCE CHECK

1) Remove distributor cap and disconnect spark plug end of suspected wire or wires. Connect ohmmeter leads to spark plug terminal and terminal inside distributor cap (each end of wire).

CAUTION — Never puncture a spark plug wire when measuring resistance.

MOTORCRAFT DURA-SPARK II IGNITION SYSTEMS (Cont.)

2) If resistance is less than 5,000 ohms, visually inspect wires for damage and remove spark plug for inspection or replacement. If resistance is greater than 5,000 ohms, disconnect suspected wire from distributor cap and again connect ohmmeter leads to each end of wire.

3) If resistance is now less than 5,000 ohms per inch, inspect distributor cap and spark plug wire terminals for damage. Repair as necessary. If resistance is still greater than 5,000 ohms per inch, replace wire(s).

OSCILLOSCOPE PATTERNS

For typical Dura-Spark II ignition oscilloscope patterns, see article on MOTORCRAFT SOLID STATE IGNITION SYSTEM (JEEP) in this section.

OVERHAUL

Disassembly — **1)** Remove distributor cap, adapter and rotor. Disconnect distributor wiring harness plug. Using a small gear puller or two screwdrivers, carefully pry armature from sleeve and plate assembly. Remove spring pin.

CAUTION — *Do not pinch stator wires when removing armature.*

2) On V8 engines, remove large wire retaining clip from base plate annular groove. Remove ground screw base and pull up to remove rubber grommet from base. Remove "E" clip securing diaphragm rod advance link to stator assembly. Lift diaphragm rod off post on stator assembly, and move it out against housing. Remove stator assembly.

3) On 6-cylinder models, remove "E" clip washer and wave washer securing stator assembly to lower plate. Remove stator assembly ground screw and lift assembly from distributor.

Reassembly — Reverse disassembly procedure, but use new roll pin and install roll pin in different groove, 180° from original groove.

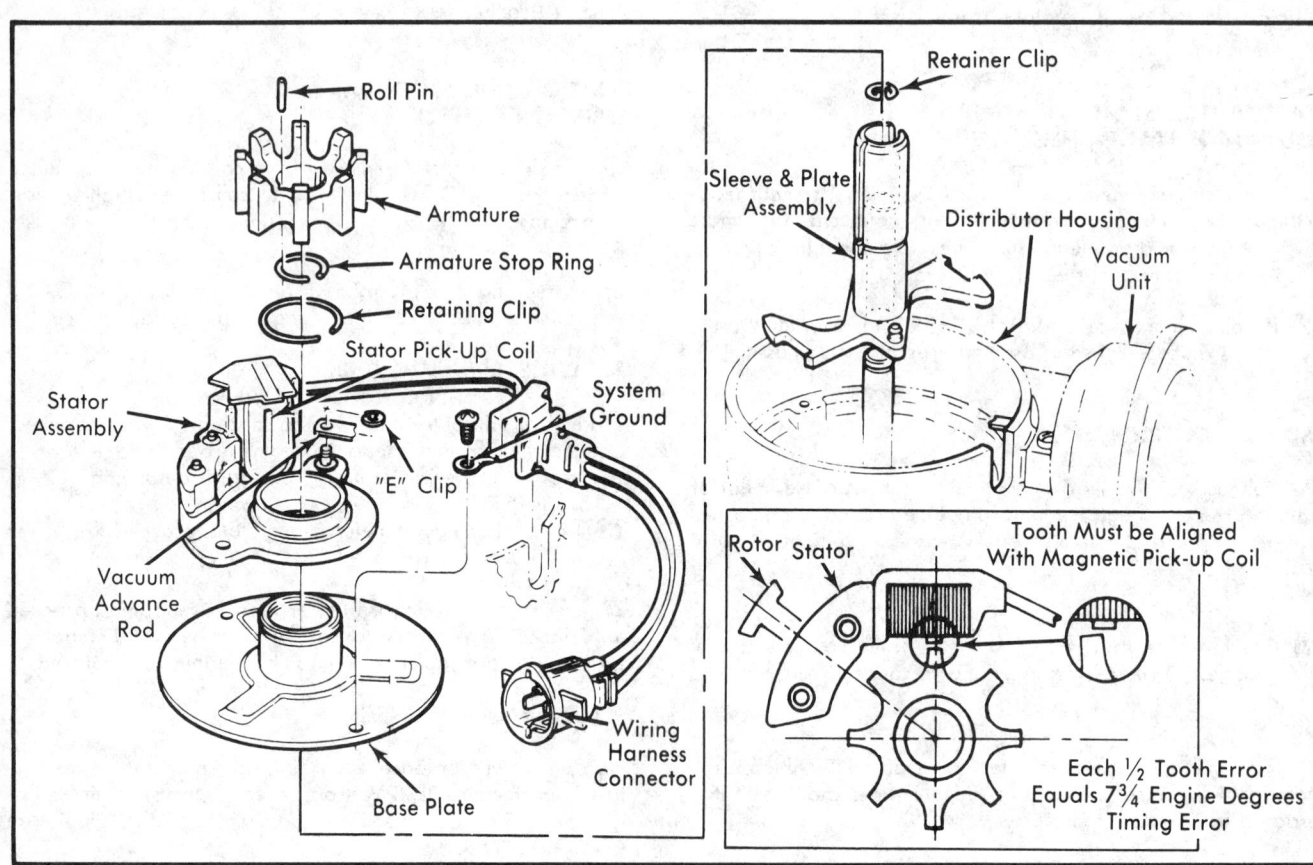

Fig. 8 Components of Dura-Spark II Distributor (V8 Shown)

DELCO-REMY HIGH ENERGY IGNITION

Chevrolet
GMC
Jeep
  4 Cylinder

DESCRIPTION

NOTE — *Some Chevrolet and GMC light truck models with 5.0L VIN H engines are equipped with Electronic Spark Control to combat detonation.*

The Delco-Remy High Energy Ignition system consists of a battery, ignition switch, spark plugs, primary and secondary wiring and a special distributor assembly.

The distributor housing and cap contain vacuum and centrifugal advance mechanisms, an electronic control module, pick-up coil, pole piece (with internal teeth), timer core (with external teeth), rotor, distributor shaft and a capacitor for radio noise suppression.

Full battery voltage is present at the battery terminal of the distributor in either the "START" or "RUN" position, as no ballast resistance wire is used.

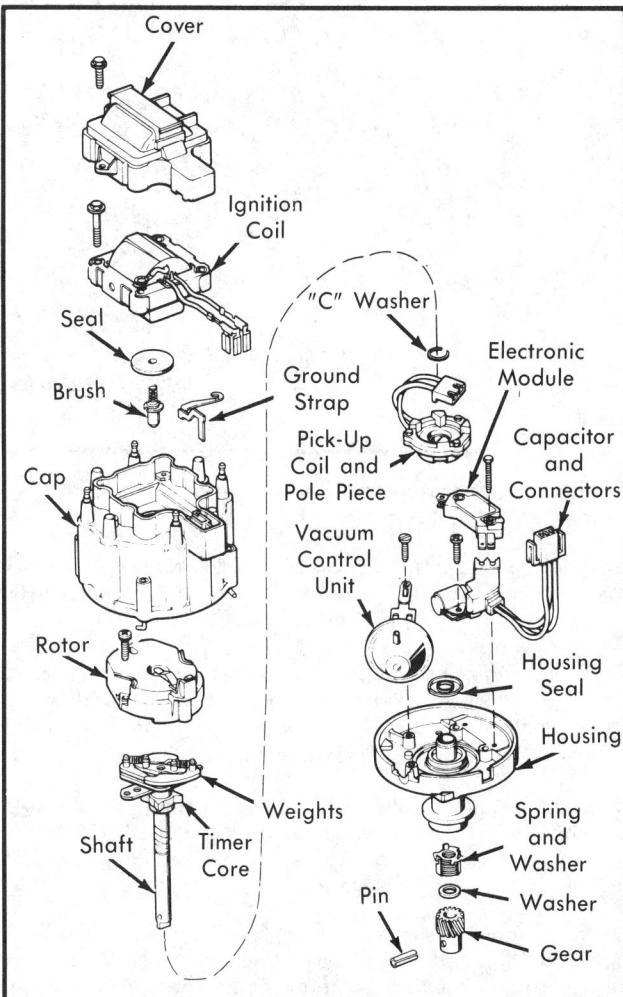

Fig. 1   Exploded View of Integral Coil Type HEI Distributor (Jeep 4-Cylinder Shown)

OPERATION

The pick-up coil assembly consists of a permanent magnet, a pole piece and a pick-up coil. The pick-up coil assembly is stationary, unless it is shifted by the vacuum control unit. The timer core position can also be shifted by the centrifugal weights.

The timer core, mounted on the distributor shaft, rotates with the shaft inside the pole piece portion of the pick-up coil assembly. When the external teeth of the timer core line up with the internal teeth of the pole piece, a voltage is induced in the pick-up coil. This signals the electronic module inside the distributor, which opens the ignition coil primary circuit. See Fig. 2.

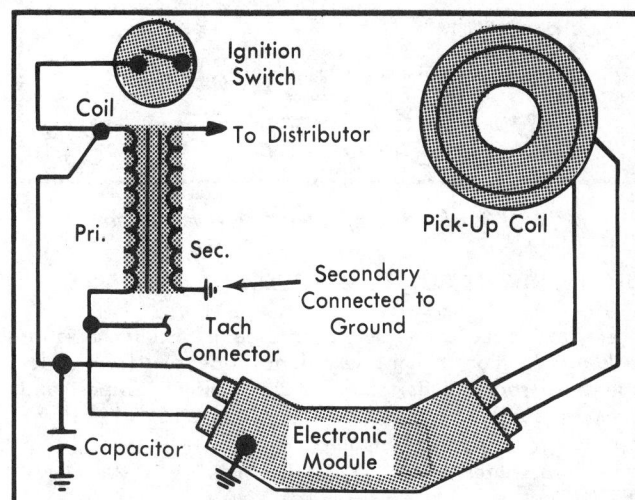

Fig. 2   Delco-Remy High Energy Ignition System Basic Wiring Diagram

The magnetic field in the ignition coil primary circuit collapses, inducing high voltage in the coil's secondary circuit. This travels through the distributor cap contact, rotor and secondary wires to fire the spark plugs.

The electronic module automatically controls dwell period, stretching it with increasing engine speed. Dwell is not adjustable and periodic checks of dwell are unnecessary. The HEI system features a longer spark duration, which is desirable for firing lean and EGR diluted mixtures.

TESTING

NOTE — *During testing procedures, the following precautions must be observed. Do not ground tachometer terminal of distributor connector. Disconnect ignition switch connector at distributor before making compression checks. To remove spark plug wires, twist boot ½ turn and pull on boot (not on wire). When using a timing light connect at plug end of number 1 spark plug wire (do not pierce plug boot).*

Check that wiring connector is properly attached to connector at side of distributor cap and that spark plug leads are properly connected at both ends before continuing with test procedures.

ENGINE WILL NOT START

NOTE — *If engine is difficult to start or misses, check position of battery terminal connector at distributor cap. Terminal must be inserted on side of connector opposite hold-down clip.*

Connect voltmeter between "BAT" terminal lead on distributor connector and ground. Turn ignition switch on. If voltage is zero, check system for open circuit. If reading is battery

Distributors & Ignition Systems

DELCO-REMY HIGH ENERGY IGNITION (Cont.)

voltage, connect a modified spark plug (plug that has ground electrode cut off) to center brush contact in distributor cap. Crank engine, if spark occurs trouble is not in ignition system. Check fuel system, spark plugs and wires for trouble. If sparking does not occur, *follow procedures under SYSTEM TESTING or COMPONENT TESTING. See Fig. 3.*

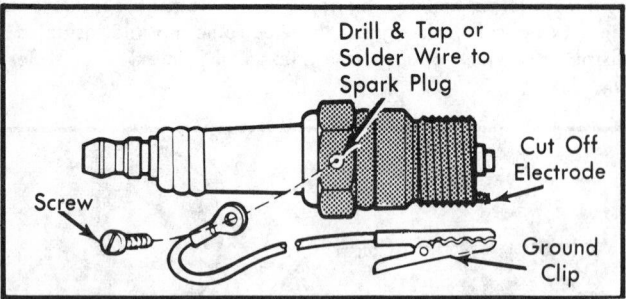

Fig. 3   Modifying Spark Plug for Testing

ENGINE STARTS BUT RUNS ROUGH

Check for proper fuel delivery to carburetor, vacuum hoses for leakage, ignition timing, centrifugal advance for proper operation, spark plugs for defects, and visually inspect and listen for sparks jumping to ground or to other wires. If no defects are found or condition continues after correction, *follow procedures under SYSTEM TESTING or COMPONENT TESTING.*

SYSTEM TESTING

1) Connect voltmeter positive lead to distributor battery terminal and negative lead to ground. Crank engine. If voltage is under 7 volts, repair or replace wiring or components back to battery, including ignition switch and all connections.

2) If voltmeter reading in step 1) was 7 volts or more, connect positive lead of voltmeter to "TACH" terminal of distributor, while leaving negative lead attached to ground. If reading is 10 volts or more, proceed to step 4).

3) If reading in step 2) was under 1 volt, replace ignition coil. If reading was 1-10 volts, replace electronic HEI module in distributor and check for spark as instructed in step 7). If spark results, system is OK. If no spark results, replace ignition coil in addition to the module.

4) If reading in step 2) was 10 volts or more, remove distributor cap, but leave wiring harness attached to cap connector. Connect spark tester (ST-125) or modified spark plug so terminal touches center contact of cap. Ground tester ground wire, and crank engine. *See Fig. 4.*

5) If spark occurs, inspect cap for water, cracks, or other defects. If cap is OK, replace rotor. If no spark occurred in step 4), remove pick-up coil leads (Green and White wires) from module. Again, check voltage at "TACH" terminal of distributor cap. Attach voltmeter positive lead to terminal and negative lead to ground. *See Fig. 5.* Turn ignition switch on. Observe voltmeter reading as you attach test light to battery positive terminal and momentarily (no more than 5 seconds) touch other test light lead to module terminal "G" (small terminal).

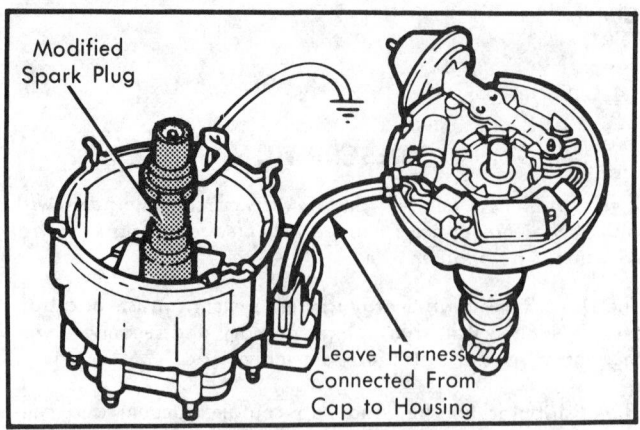

Fig. 4   Checking for Spark at Ignition Coil Output Terminal

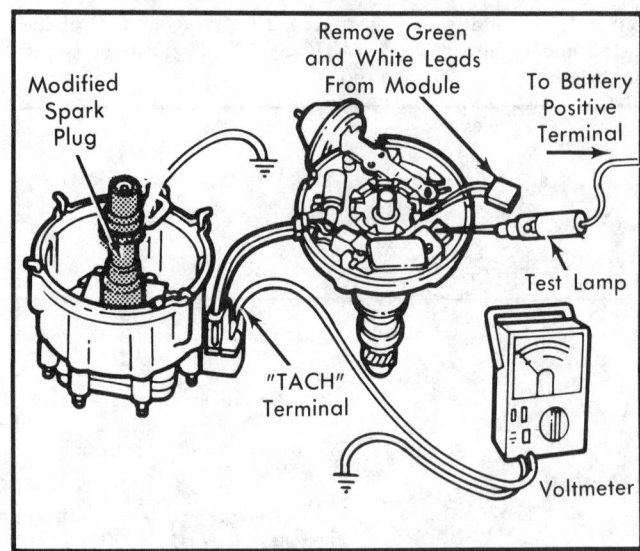

Fig. 5   Checking Distributor Components with Voltmeter and Test Light

6) If voltage did not drop, check module ground. Also check for open in wires from distributor to cap. If OK, replace HEI module.

7) If voltage dropped in step 5) when test light was connected, or if 1-10 volts was recorded in step 2), check for spark at coil center contact (using spark tester as before) as test light is removed from module's "G" terminal.

8) If spark results, replace pick-up coil assembly. If no spark, appears use module tester to test HEI module. If OK, check ignition coil ground. If ground is OK, replace ignition coil. If module is defective, replace it.

9) If no module tester is available, check ignition coil ground circuit. If OK, replace ignition coil and repeat step 7). If spark results, system is OK. If no spark results, original coil is OK. Replace module.

INTERMITTENT SYSTEM PROBLEMS

1) Using a spark tester or modified spark plug, check for spark at 2 spark plug wires. If no spark results, *see SYSTEM TES-*

DELCO-REMY HIGH ENERGY IGNITION (Cont.)

TING. If spark is noted on one or both wires, check for dwell increase from low to high RPM.

2) Check pick-up coil with ohmmeter leads attached to Green and White wires, removed from HEI module. If reading does not fall between 500-1500 ohms, replace pick-up coil. If pick-up coil reading was satisfactory, and dwell did not increase, replace electronic module.

3) If pick-up coil was satisfactory, but dwell increased, check fuel, spark plug wires, distributor cap, rotor or spark plugs.

COMPONENT TESTING

Distributor Cap & Coil Testing — 1) Remove distributor cap and coil assembly by removing wiring harness connector, battery lead, and cap-to-housing latches. Inspect rotor, cap and coil assembly for arc-over. Replace parts as necessary.

2) To test coil primary resistance, connect one ohmmeter lead to battery terminal on distributor cap. See Fig. 6. Connect other lead to tach terminal of distributor cap. Ohmmeter reading should be 0.4-1.0 ohm. Connect ohmmeter leads to tach terminal and ground. Reading should be infinity. If either reading is not to specifications, replace ignition coil.

3) To test coil secondary resistance, connect one ohmmeter lead to coil secondary contact (cap button). See Fig. 6. Connect other lead to tach terminal. Ohmmeter reading should be infinity.

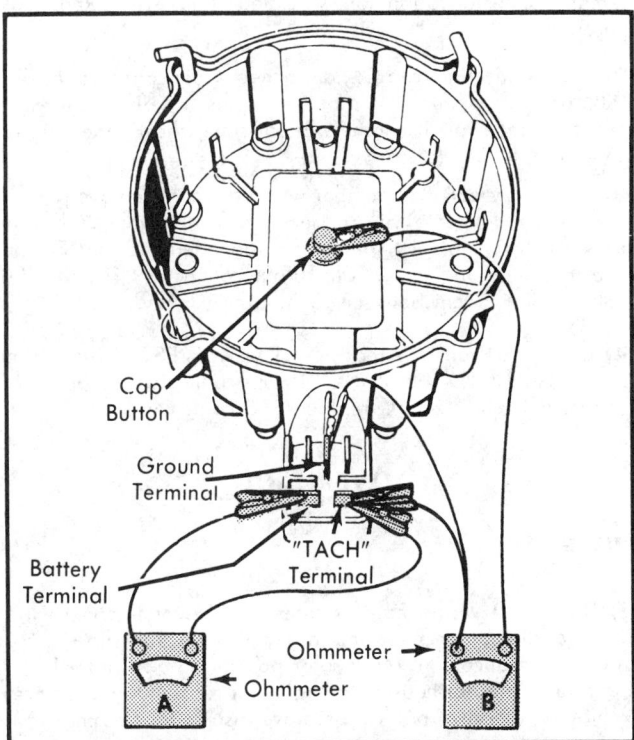

Fig. 6   Distributor Cap and Coil Testing Connections for Delco-Remy HEI Distributor

4) Move ohmmeter lead from tach terminal and attach it to ground terminal. Secondary-to-ground ohmmeter reading should be 6,000-30,000 ohms. If these tests are not to specifications, replace ignition coil.

NOTE — Replace ignition coil only if readings in both steps **3)** and **4)** are infinity.

Pick-Up Coil — 1) Connect test stand vacuum source to vacuum advance unit. If vacuum advance unit is inoperative, replace unit. To check pick-up coil for shorts, connect ohmmeter leads as shown by meter "A" in Fig. 7. Set on middle scale of meter. Operate vacuum advance through range. Reading should be infinite at all times. If not, replace pick-up coil.

2) To check pick-up coil resistance, connect ohmmeter leads as shown by meter "B" in Fig. 7. Again use the middle scale. Operate vacuum advance through its range. Ohmmeter reading should be 500-1500 ohms in all advance positions. If readings are not as specified, replace pick-up coil.

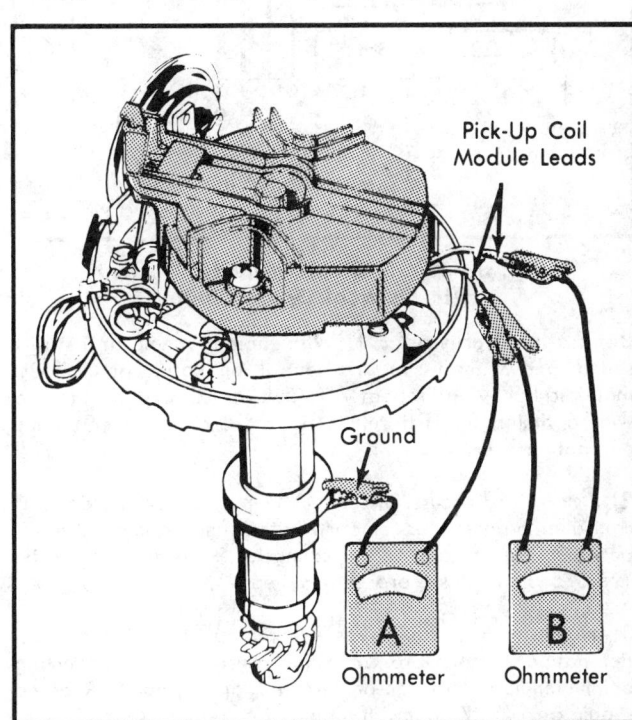

Fig. 7   Distributor Pick-Up Coil Testing Connections

Capacitor — Set ohmmeter in x1000 scale. Disconnect capacitor. Touch ohmmeter leads to capacitor terminal and to ground. The needle should move slightly, but very quickly, and return to infinity. Any continuous reading other than infinity indicates defective capacitor.

Electronic Module — If engine operation remains rough after preceding test procedures are completed, replace the electronic module.

NOTE — When installing a new HEI module, use silicone lubricant on back of module and on housing under module.

ELECTRONIC SPARK CONTROL TESTING

NOTE — Electronic Spark Control is used on some Chevrolet and GMC models using the 5.0L VIN H engine.

DELCO-REMY HIGH ENERGY IGNITION (Cont.)

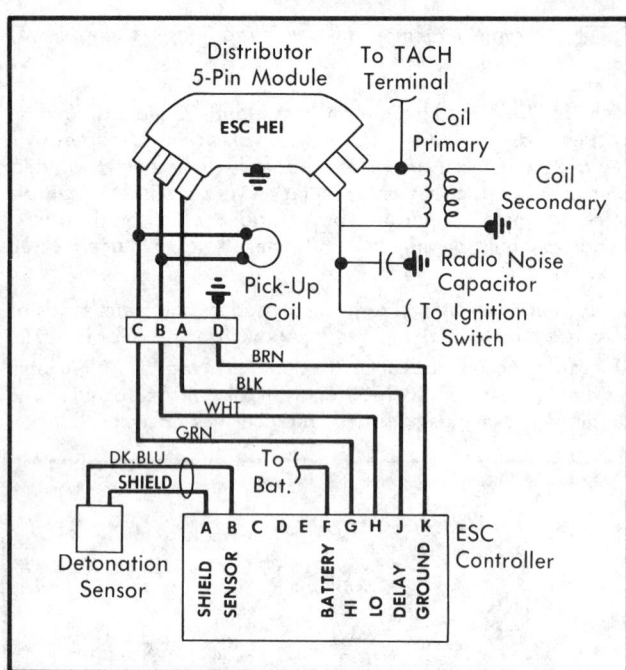

Fig. 8   Wiring Diagram for HEI System with Electronic Spark Control

Detonation Problems — 1) With engine running at fast idle speed and transmission in Neutral or Park, tap exhaust manifold lightly and repeatedly. Check for spark timing retard with a timing light. If retard is noted, check other engine detonation causes.

2) If no retard occurs, disconnect 10-pin connector from ESC controller in passenger compartment. Connect ohmmeter leads between pins "B" and "K" of connector. Resistance should be 175-375 ohms. If so, proceed to step **4)**.

3) If resistance reading was either high or low, disconnect detonation sensor wire. Measure resistance by connecting ohmmeter leads to sensor terminal and ground. Reading should be 175-375 ohms. If high or low, replace sensor. If OK, check wires from pins "A", "B", and "K" of 10-pin connector for opens or shorts. If OK, repair sensor connector. If not OK, replace or repair wiring harness.

4) If resistance reading in step **2)** was OK, try to start engine with 10-pin connector disconnected. If it starts, replace distributor's HEI module.

5) If engine will not start, reconnect 10-pin connector to controller. Disconnect sensor wire from sensor, and insert a jumper wire into sensor wire connector. With engine running at fast idle speed, lay wire on top of distributor over ignition coil. If spark timing retard occurs. replace sensor.

6) If no spark retard occurs, connect voltmeter positive lead to pin "H" of 10-pin connector and negative lead to pin "K". With ignition switch on, voltage should read more than 0.2 volt. If voltage is more than 0.2 volt, replace ESC controller. If less than 0.2 volt, repair open wire from pin "H" in ESC harness.

Poor Engine Performance Problems — 1) Disconnect 4-pin connector at distributor and install a jumper wire between pins "A" and "C" of distributor connector. If problem remains, check other causes of poor engine performance.

2) If problem disappeared, remove jumper wire and reconnect 4-pin connector. Without disconnecting 10-pin ESC connector, attach jumper wire from pin "A" to pin "B". If problem remains, proceed to step **5)**.

3) If problem disappeared in step **2)**, remove jumper wire and disconnect 10-pin connector at controller. Connect ohmmeter leads to pins "B" and "K". Resistance should read 175-375 ohms. If OK, check for engine noises other than detonation that might cause input to sensor.

4) If resistance reading was either high or low in step **3)**, disconnect wire from sensor. Measure resistance from terminal to ground, checking again for 175-375 ohms. If high or low, replace sensor. If OK, check sensor wire and shield for open circuit. If OK, repair sensor connector. If not OK, repair harness.

5) If in step **2)**, the problem still existed, remove jumper wire from pins "A" and "B". With engine running, connect positive voltmeter lead to pin "F" and negative lead to pin "K" of 10-pin connector. If reading is under 11.6 volts, repair alternator charging circuit.

6) If over 11.6 volts, check wires in ESC harness from pins "H" and "K" for open circuits or poor connections. If OK, replace ESC controller; if not, replace or repair harness.

Engine Starting Problems — 1) Check all ESC harness connections, including 10-pin connector, 4-pin connector at distributor, 2-blade male connector to distributor, and 2-blade female connector to ignition switch lead (Pink wire). Repair as necessary.

2) If all connections are OK, disconnect 4-pin connector at distributor. Install jumper wire between pins "A" and "C" of distributor connector. If engine will not start, check other causes of engine failing to start.

3) If engine starts with jumper wire attached, remove jumper wire and reconnect 4-pin connector to distributor. With ignition switch on, connect voltmeter positive lead to pin "F" and negative lead to Pin "K" on 10-pin connector. If under 7.0 volts, repair circuit between ignition switch and pin "F".

4) If over 7.0 volts are read, check wires in ESC harness from pins "G", "H", "J" and "K" of 10-pin connector for opens or shorts. If harness is OK, replace ESC controller.

OVERHAUL

DISASSEMBLY

1) Disconnect wiring harness from cap. Disconnect coil wire. Remove distributor cap and disconnect vacuum hose from vacuum advance unit. Mark rotor position to distributor housing and distributor housing to engine for reassembly reference. Remove hold-down bolt and remove distributor housing from engine.

2) Remove rotor, two advance springs, weight retainer and advance weights. Mark distributor shaft and gear so they may be assembled in same position. Drive out roll pin from drive gear while supporting gear so no damage will occur to distributor shaft. Remove gear, shim and tanged washer from distributor shaft and clean any burrs from shaft. Remove distributor shaft from housing.

DELCO-REMY HIGH ENERGY IGNITION (Cont.)

NOTE – *Do not attempt to service shaft bushings in housing.*

3) Remove 2 attaching screws holding module-to-housing and position module to disconnect pick-up coil and wiring harness connectors. Remove "C" washer from housing and lift pick-up coil assembly from advance unit and distributor shaft.

4) Remove 2 attaching screws and remove vacuum advance mechanism. Disconnect capacitor lead, remove attaching screw and capacitor. Remove wiring harness from position in distributor housing.

5) Remove 3 coil cover attaching screws and lift off cover. Remove 4 ignition coil attaching screws, disconnect coil leads and remove coil from cap. Remove ignition coil arc seal.

REASSEMBLY

Reverse disassembly procedures while noting following: Ensure there is special silicone lubricant between module and distributor base to provide heat transfer for module cooling. Lubricate felt washer with a few drops of engine oil. After installation of distributor shaft, rotate to check for even clearance between external timer core teeth and internal pole piece teeth. Notch on side of rotor must engage tab on cam weight base.

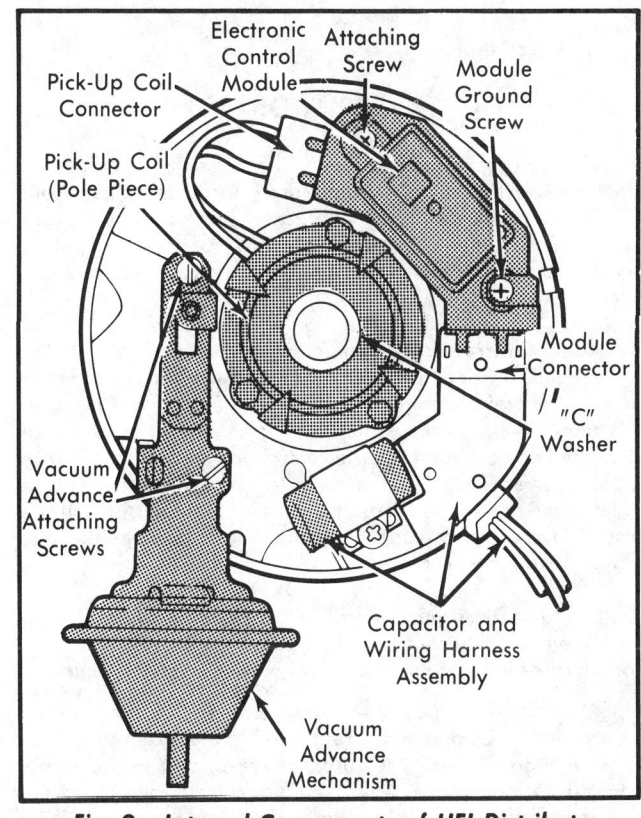

Fig. 9 Internal Components of HEI Distributor

TYPICAL DELCO-REMY HIGH ENERGY IGNITION OSCILLOSCOPE PATTERNS

PRIMARY PATTERNS (TYPICAL)

Scope Instructions for Primary Parade Only:
NOTE – *Also refer to scope manufacturers' instructions.*

1) Scope secondary pick-up cannot be connected because coil center terminal is inside distributor.
2) Connect pick-up to No. 1 spark plug wire as usual.
3) Connect primary pick-up to "Tach" terminal at distributor connector plug.

Reading Scope Primary Pattern

A) Spark Zone — spark plug arcing.
B) Coil and Condenser Zone
B1) Firing Zone — no plug arc.
C) Dwell Zone — displays current through coil primary with module turned on.

SECONDARY PATTERNS (TYPICAL)

NOTE – *A special adapter placed on top of the coil-cap assembly may be used with some scopes to view the secondary pattern. The output voltage will read low with the adapter; this is normal. Refer to the scope manufacturers' instructions.*

Secondary Voltage Patterns:

It is normal if dwell time varies from cylinder to cylinder. A 40 to 60 percent variation is shown below. It could be more, or it could be less. The voltage ripple shown may or may not appear; either is normal. Variation in dwell time or voltage ripple, as shown, does not necessarily indicate a bad module.

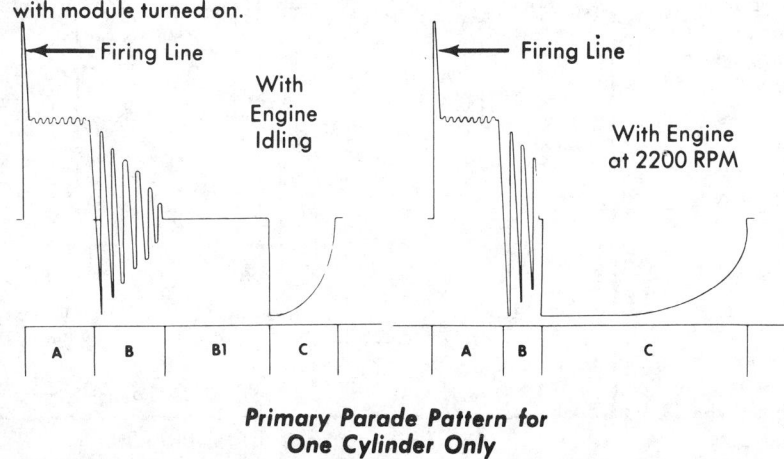

Primary Parade Pattern for One Cylinder Only

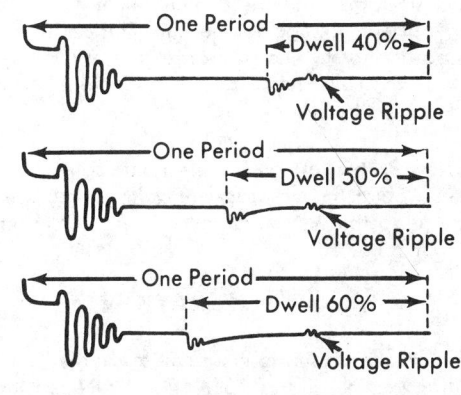

Typical Secondary Scope Patterns. See Scope Instructions for Actual Patterns

MOTORCRAFT SOLID STATE IGNITION

Jeep
Except 4-Cylinder Models

DESCRIPTION

The Solid State Ignition system, often called SSI, features a solid state distributor, electronic control unit, an ignition coil, and conventional distributor cap, rotor, spark plug wires and spark plugs. Other components include the battery, ignition switch, starter solenoid and primary resistance wires and by-pass wire.

Electronic Control Unit — There are 6 wires leading from the control unit, 2 to one connector and 4 to the other. The white wire and red wire leading to the 2-wire connector are the ignition feed circuits — the white wire for cranking, the red wire after the engine is running. The control unit uses the green wire to turn power to the ignition coil off and on. The orange and violet wires are used to transmit signals from the distributor's sensor to the control unit. The black wire supplies the distributor ground circuit.

NOTE — *The electronic control unit is permanently sealed to resist moisture, vibration, dirt and atmospheric conditions. It is not repairable and must be serviced as a complete unit.*

Distributor — Components are divided into 3 groups, the sensor and trigger wheel, the spark advance, and the cap and rotor. The trigger wheel which has 6 or 8 teeth (one per cylinder), rotates with the distributor shaft. The sensor is a coil of fine wire mounted around a permanent magnet. There are no contacting surfaces between the trigger wheel and sensor. Dwell is not adjustable and is controlled electronically. Centrifugal advance is controlled by engine speed, vacuum spark advance by carburetor ported vacuum, supplied to the distributor's vacuum unit. Distributor cap and rotor are of conventional design.

Ignition Coil — Coils are oil-filled and, sealed and contain a primary and secondary circuit. As in any system, the coil's basic function is to convert battery voltage applied to the primary circuit into high secondary voltage for firing the spark plugs. The coil has positive and negative primary terminals and a single secondary terminal. A special coil connector slides over the primary terminals.

Resistance Wire — A wire with 1.3-1.4 ohms resistance is provided in the red wire (engine running) circuit to supply less than battery voltage to the coil. This resistance wire is by-passed during starting so that full battery voltage may be applied to the coil. The by-pass is accomplished through the "I" terminal of the starter solenoid.

System Protection — The electronic control unit has built-in reverse polarity and transient voltage protection. However, damage to the system can occur if proper testing procedures are not followed.

OPERATION

The control unit and ignition coil are turned on whenever the ignition switch is in the "START" or "ON" position. When the engine begins turning the distributor shaft, the trigger wheel rotates with it. As each tooth passes the sensor, it interrupts the magnetic field around the sensor. This continual build-up and collapse of the magnetic field provides a signal to the control unit. The control unit receives this signal and turns the power to the ignition coil's primary circuit off and on as each tooth passes the sensor. The collapse of the magnetic field in the ignition coil primary circuit induces a high voltage surge in the secondary, causing current to flow from the coil to the distributor, rotor, cap and spark plug wires.

SOLID STATE IGNITION SYSTEM NOTES

When disconnecting wire from spark plug or distributor cap, twist rubber boot slightly to loosen. Grasp boot (not wire) and pull off with steady, even force.

When disconnecting control unit connectors, pull apart with firm, straight pull. Do not attempt to pry apart with screwdriver. When connecting, press together firmly to overcome hydraulic pressure of grease. If connector locking tabs weaken or break off, it is unnecessary to replace connector. Just press together firmly and bind with electrical tape or a harness tie strap to assure good connection.

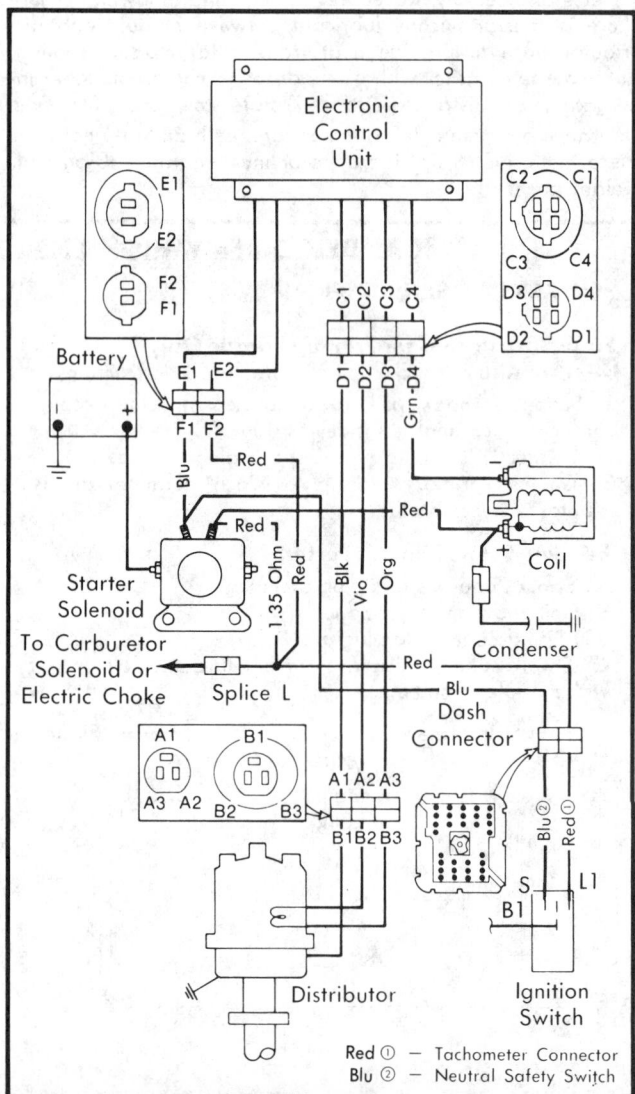

Fig. 1   Jeep Solid State Ignition System Wiring Diagram

MOTORCRAFT SOLID STATE IGNITION (Cont.)

TESTING

SECONDARY CIRCUIT CHECK

CAUTION — *When checking the secondary voltage, do not remove spark plug wires from spark plugs No. 1 or 5 on 6-cylinder engines nor from spark plugs No. 3 or 4 on V8 engines.*

1) Disconnect coil wire from distributor cap. Use insulated pliers to hold wire approximately ½ inch from engine block or intake manifold.

2) Crank engine and check for spark at gap. If no spark occurs, turn off ignition switch, and check resistance of secondary coil windings. *See IGNITION COIL RESISTANCE CHECK, Secondary Resistance.* Replace ignition coil if outside specifications.

3) If spark occurred in step **2)**, connect coil wire to distributor cap. Remove wire from one spark plug. Using insulated pliers, hold wire ½ inch from engine head while cranking engine. Check for spark. If spark occurs, check for fuel problems or incorrect timing. If no sparks occur, check for defective rotor or distributor cap or for defective spark plug wires.

CURRENT FLOW CHECK

1) Remove connector from ignition coil. Remove positive wire from connector, then negative wire. Connect ammeter between positive terminal of coil and disconnected positive wire. Connect jumper wire from negative terminal to good ground.

2) Turn ignition switch "ON". Current flow should be approximately 7 amps., but should not exceed 7.6 amps. If more than 7.6 amps., replace ignition coil.

3) With ammeter still connected to coil positive terminal, remove jumper wire from negative terminal. Connect coil green wire to negative terminal. Current flow should be approximately 4 amps. If less than 3.5 amps., check for poor connections in 4-wire and 3-wire connectors or for poor ground at distributor ground screw.

4) If current flow is greater than 5 amps., the control unit is defective and must be replaced. Start engine. Normal current flow with engine running is 2.0-2.4 amps. If outside of specifications, replace control unit.

COIL OUTPUT CHECK

1) Connect oscilloscope to engine. Start engine and observe secondary winding spark voltage. Remove one spark plug wire (not wire No. 1 or 5 on 6-cylinder engine nor wire No. 3 or 4 on V8 engines) from distributor cap. Run engine at 1000 RPM.

2) Observe voltage on oscilloscope. This voltage, referred to as open circuit voltage, should be 24,000 volts minimum.

NOTE — *Do not operate engine with spark plug disconnected for more than 30 seconds or damage may result to catalytic converter.*

SPARK PLUG REQUIRED VOLTAGE

1) Attach secondary voltage pick-up over coil high tension wire. Run engine at approximately 1000 RPM. Firing voltage should be relatively even and between 5,000-16,000 volts.

2) If firing voltage is bad, check each cylinder. Maximum variation between cylinders is 3,000 to 5,000 volts.

IGNITION COIL RESISTANCE CHECK

Primary Resistance — Remove connector from positive and negative coil terminals. Be sure ignition switch is "OFF." Set an ohmmeter on low scale and connect ohmmeter leads to positive and negative terminals. Ohmmeter reading should be 1.13-1.23 ohms at 75°F. With coil temperature at 200°F, a 1.5 ohm reading is acceptable.

Secondary Resistance — Turn ignition switch "OFF". Set ohmmeter to high scale (x 1000 scale) and connect one lead to coil negative terminal and other lead to coil tower (remove coil secondary wire). Ohmmeter reading should be 7,700-9,300 ohms with coil temperature at 75° F. With coil temperature at 200° F or above, a maximum reading of 12,000 ohms is acceptable.

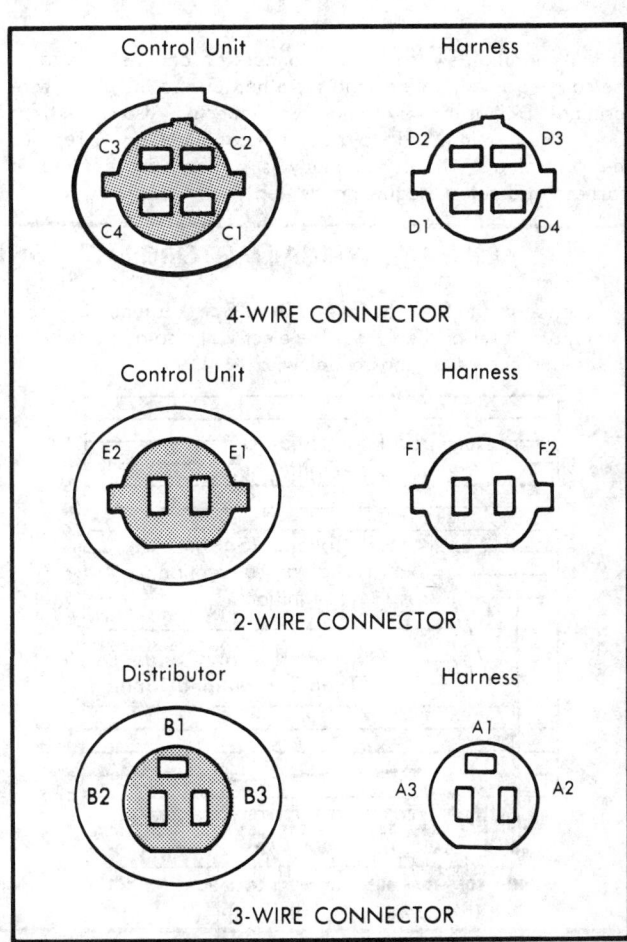

Fig. 2 Solid State Ignition Connectors

Distributors & Ignition Systems

MOTORCRAFT SOLID STATE IGNITION (Cont.)

COIL PRIMARY CIRCUIT CHECK

1) Connect a voltmeter to coil positive terminal and ground. Turn ignition switch to "ON" position. Reading should be 5.5-6.5 volts. If voltage is too high (battery voltage), proceed to step **4)**. If voltage is too low (below 5.5 volts), disconnect condenser lead. If voltage is now correct, replace condenser. If voltage is still low, proceed to step **7)**.

2) If voltage was 5.5-6.5 volts in step **1)**, turn ignition switch to "START" position. Voltage should be the same as battery cranking voltage. If correct, check other systems (fuel, mechanical, etc.) for problems. If voltage is not correct, proceed to next step.

3) Check wire connected to starter solenoid "I" terminal for shorts or opens. If wire is OK, check for defective starter solenoid. Replace solenoid if necessary.

4) With ignition switch in "ON" position, voltmeter still connected to coil positive terminal, disconnect wire connected to starter solenoid "I" terminal. If voltage drops to 5.5-6.5 volts, replace starter solenoid.

5) If voltage remains high, connect a jumper wire from coil negative terminal to ground. If voltage drops to 5.5-6.5 volt range, proceed to step **6)**. If voltage does not drop, resistance wire is defective. Replace resistance wire and retest, beginning with step **2)**.

6) With ignition switch "OFF", connect an ohmmeter lead to the coil negative terminal and the other lead to the green wire terminal "D4" of the 4-wire harness connector. Also check from black wire terminal "D1" to ground. If continuity is OK, replace the control unit. If no continuity is present, repair wire in harness and retest beginning at step **2)**.

7) With ignition switch "OFF", connect ohmmeter leads between coil positive terminal and dash connector "AV" (red wire). If resistance is not 1.3-1.4 ohms, replace resistance wire. If ohmmeter reading is to specifications, proceed to next step.

8) With ignition switch still "OFF", connect ohmmeter leads between dash connector "AV" (red wire) and ignition switch terminal "L1". Resistance should be less than 0.1 ohm. If reading is to specifications, repair feed wire or replace ignition switch.

9) If resistance is more than 0.1 ohm, check for opens in wire or for poor connections at connectors. Repair or replace as necessary.

CONTROL UNIT & SENSOR CHECK

1) Disconnect high tension coil wire from distributor cap. Attach a modified spark plug to coil wire (side electrode of plug cut off and ground wire attached to side of plug casing). If plug is not available, hold coil wire ½" from engine block, using insulated pliers.

2) Turn ignition switch "ON" and disconnect 4-wire connector from control unit. Watch for spark at modified spark plug, as connector is disconnected. If sparking occurs, proceed with next step. If no sparking occurs, proceed to step **6)**.

3) Turn ignition switch "OFF" and disconnect 4-wire connector at control unit. Connect an ohmmeter between the orange and violet wire terminals "D2" and "D3" of harness connector. Ohmmeter reading should be 400-800 ohms. If reading is correct, proceed to step **8)**. If reading is not correct, proceed to next step.

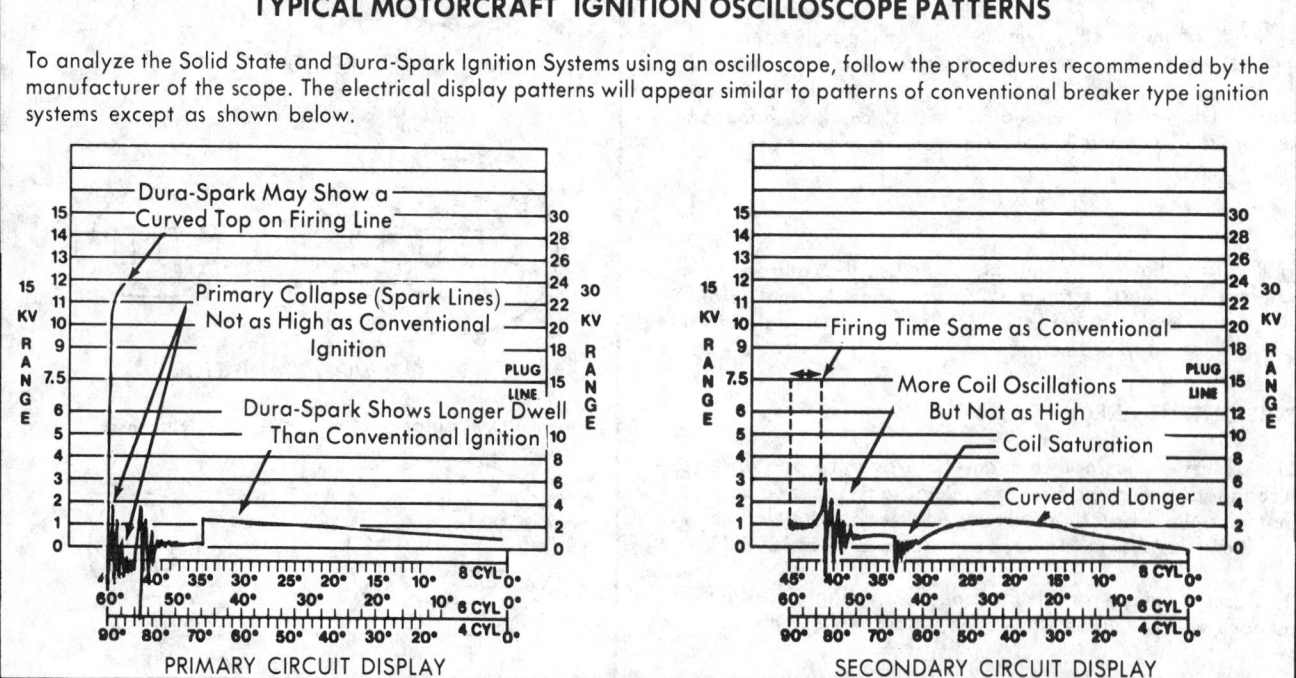

TYPICAL MOTORCRAFT IGNITION OSCILLOSCOPE PATTERNS

To analyze the Solid State and Dura-Spark Ignition Systems using an oscilloscope, follow the procedures recommended by the manufacturer of the scope. The electrical display patterns will appear similar to patterns of conventional breaker type ignition systems except as shown below.

PRIMARY CIRCUIT DISPLAY

SECONDARY CIRCUIT DISPLAY

Fig. 3   Normal Oscilloscope Patterns Shown for Solid State Ignition Systems
(Also Applies to Motorcraft Dura-Spark II Systems)

MOTORCRAFT SOLID STATE IGNITION (Cont.)

4) Disconnect and reconnect the 3-wire connector at the distributor. If ohmmeter reading is now correct, proceed to step **8)**. If reading is still not correct, proceed to next step.

5) Disconnect 3-wire connector at the distributor and connect ohmmeter leads between the orange and violet wire terminals "B2" and "B3" of distributor connector. If reading is now 400-800 ohms, repair harness between 3-wire and 4-wire connectors. If reading is still out of specifications, replace sensor in distributor.

6) With ignition switch "OFF" and 4-wire connector disconnected, connect ohmmeter leads to battery negative terminal (ground) and black wire terminal "D1" in harness connector. Ohmmeter reading should be nearly zero (less than .002 ohms).

7) If ohmmeter reading is OK, recheck system starting at step **3)**. If reading is above specifications, check for the source of the bad ground (ground cable resistance, distributor-to-engine block resistance, or ground screw in distributor to black wire terminal "D1").

8) With ignition switch "ON" and voltmeter connected to harness side of 4-wire connector orange and violet wire terminals "D2" and "D3", crank engine. Voltmeter reading should fluctuate. If no voltage fluctuation occurs, check for defective trigger wheel, distributor shaft not turning, or missing trigger wheel retaining pin (shaft turning but not trigger wheel).

CONTROL UNIT POWER FEED CHECK

NOTE — *Before making this check, always check ignition coil primary circuit first.*

1) Disconnect 2-wire connector at control unit. Connect voltmeter negative lead to ground and positive lead to red wire harness connector terminal "F2". Turn ignition switch "ON". Voltage reading should be battery voltage (within 0.2 volts). If reading is correct, replace control unit. If not, proceed to next step.

2) Locate and repair cause of voltage reduction (corroded connectors, defective ignition switch, etc.). If connectors are repaired and there is spark at coil wire, start engine. If connectors are repaired and there is no spark at coil wire, replace control unit.

3) Connect voltmeter negative lead to ground and positive lead to light blue wire at harness connector terminal "F1" in 2-wire connector. Crank engine. Voltmeter reading should be within 1 volt of battery cranking voltage. If not, check for bad connections, ignition switch or starter solenoid.

4) Turn ignition switch "OFF", connect 2-wire connector and disconnect 4-wire connector. Connect an ammeter to black wire terminal "C1" of control unit (not harness) connector and to ground. Turn ignition switch "ON". Reading should be 0.9-1.1 amps. If reading is higher or lower than specified, replace control unit.

OVERHAUL

DISTRIBUTOR

Disassembly — **1)** Remove distributor cap and rotor. Using suitable gear puller (J-28509), remove trigger wheel (two screwdrivers can be used to pry trigger wheel upward). Remove pin.

2) On 6 cylinder engines, remove sensor retainer and washers from pivot pin on base plate. On V8 engines, remove sensor snap ring from shaft. Remove retainer from vacuum unit-to-sensor drive pin and move vacuum lever aside.

3) Remove ground screw from harness tab. Lift sensor assembly from distributor housing. Only remove vacuum unit when it is to be replaced.

Reassembly — Reverse disassembly procedure, being sure to coat brass surface of rotor with silicone grease. If sensor or vacuum unit was replaced, check ignition timing.

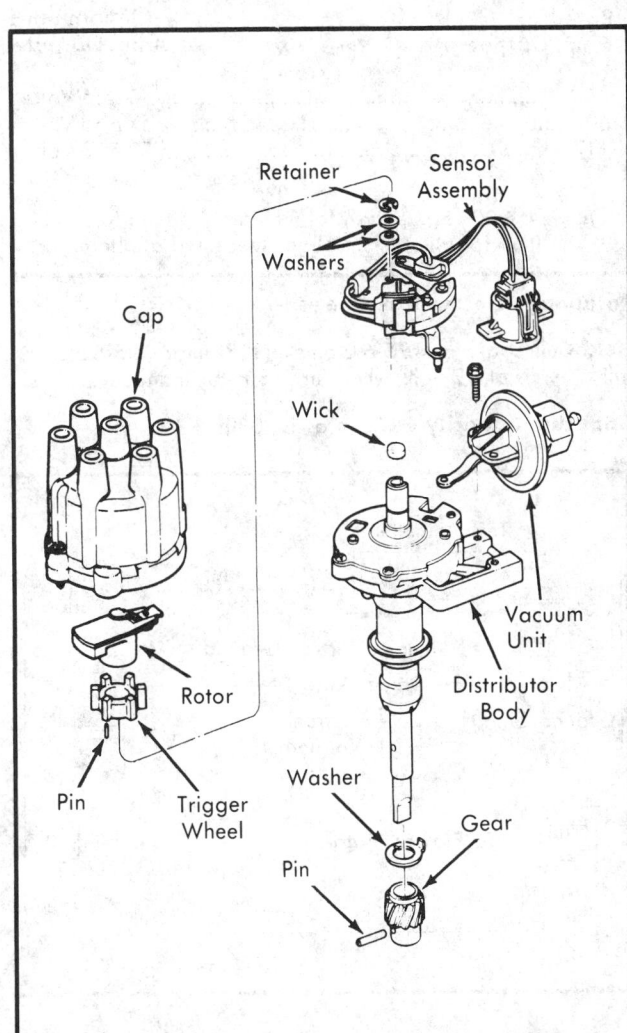

Fig. 4 Exploded View of Jeep SSI Distributor

CHRYSLER CORP. ALTERNATORS

Dodge
Plymouth

DESCRIPTION

Alternator main components are the stator, rotor, rectifiers, end shield and drive pulley. The built-in silicon rectifiers convert A.C. current into D.C. output current. The 117 amp. model has 12 silicon rectifiers, all others have 6 rectifiers.

IDENTIFICATION

Chrysler Corp. Part No.	Tag Color	Rated Amp. Output
4111928	Violet	41
4091563	Violet	41
4091568	Yellow	60
4091727	Yellow	60
4091460	Yellow	117
4091461	Yellow	117

SPECIFICATIONS

Rated Amp. Output	①Minimum Amp. Output
41	40@15 Volts
60	57@15 Volts
117	72@13 Volts

① — At 900 engine RPM for 117 amp. alternator; 1250 RPM for all others. Voltage measured at alternator.

Rotation — Clockwise at drive end.

Field Coil Draw — 4.75-6.0 amps. (117 amp.); 4.5-6.5 amp. (all others); at 12 volts while turning rotor manually.

Capacitor Capacity — .50 mfd. ± 20%.

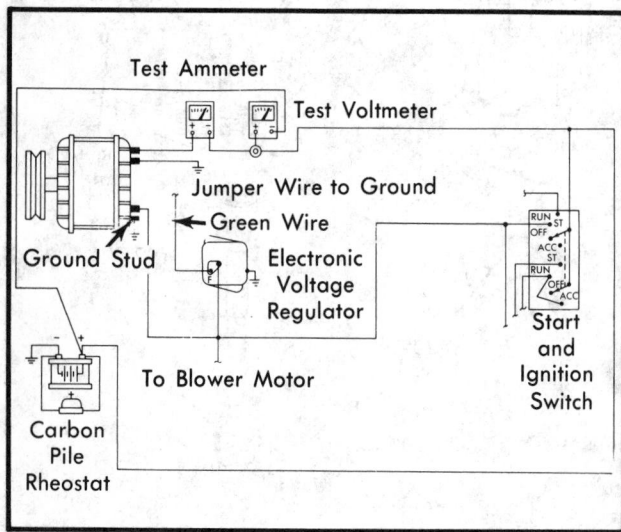

Fig. 1   Diagram Showing Meter Connections for Charging Circuit Resistance Test

ON VEHICLE TESTS

CHARGING CIRCUIT RESISTANCE

NOTE — *Before making test connections, disconnect battery ground cable at battery negative post to avoid accidental shorting of charging or field circuits.*

1) Disconnect "BAT" lead at alternator and connect a 0-100 ampere scale D.C. ammeter in series between alternator "BAT" terminal and disconnected "BAT" lead. Connect positive lead of D.C. voltmeter to disconnected "BAT" lead and connect negative voltmeter lead to battery positive terminal. Disconnect Green regulator field lead from alternator. Connect a jumper lead from alternator field terminal to ground. Connect a tachometer and reattach battery ground cable. Connect a variable carbon pile (set in open or off position) to battery terminals. *See Fig. 1.*

2) Start engine and immediately reduce engine speed to idle. Adjust engine speed and carbon pile to obtain 20 amps. flowing in circuit. Voltmeter reading should not exceed 0.7 volts. If a higher voltage drop is indicated, inspect, clean and tighten all connections in charging circuit.

NOTE — *If necessary, test voltage drop at each connection to locate connection with excessive resistance.*

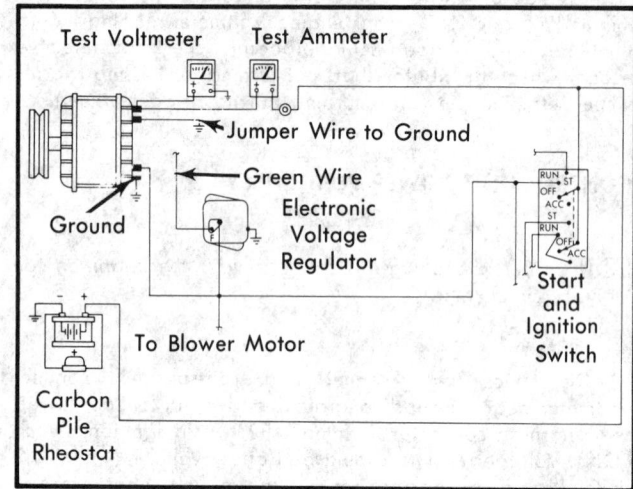

Fig. 2   Diagram Showing Meter Connections for Alternator Current Output Test

CURRENT OUTPUT

1) With test connections made as for "Charging Circuit Resistance", move negative lead of voltmeter to a good ground, then move the positive lead of voltmeter to "BAT" terminal of alternator. *See Fig. 2.* Connect positive ammeter lead to alternator "BAT" terminal and negative lead to disconnect "BAT" lead. Start engine and operate at idle speed.

CAUTION — *To avoid damage, reduce engine speed to idle immediately after starting.*

2) Adjust engine speed and carbon pile until a speed of 900 RPM (117 amp.) or 1250 RPM (all others) and a voltmeter reading of 13 volts (117 amp.) or 15 volts (all others) is obtained. Do not increase engine speed enough to allow voltage to exceed 16 volts. Observe ammeter, current output should be

CHRYSLER CORP. ALTERNATORS (Cont.)

within specifications. If output is less than specified, remove the alternator from the vehicle and bench test it.

BENCH TESTING

FIELD COIL DRAW

1) Connect a jumper wire between one field terminal of alternator and negative terminal of a fully charged battery. Connect ammeter positive lead to the other field terminal of alternator, with ammeter negative lead contacting battery positive terminal.

2) Connect a jumper wire from negative terminal of battery to end shield. See Fig. 3. Slowly rotate alternator by hand. Observe ammeter reading. Field coil draw should be 4.75-6.0 amps. for 117 amp. alternator or 4.5-6.5 amps. for other models at 12 volts.

3) A low coil draw is an indication of high resistance in field coil (brushes, slip rings or rotor). A higher coil draw indicates possible shorted rotor coil or grounded rotor. No reading indicates an open rotor or defective brushes.

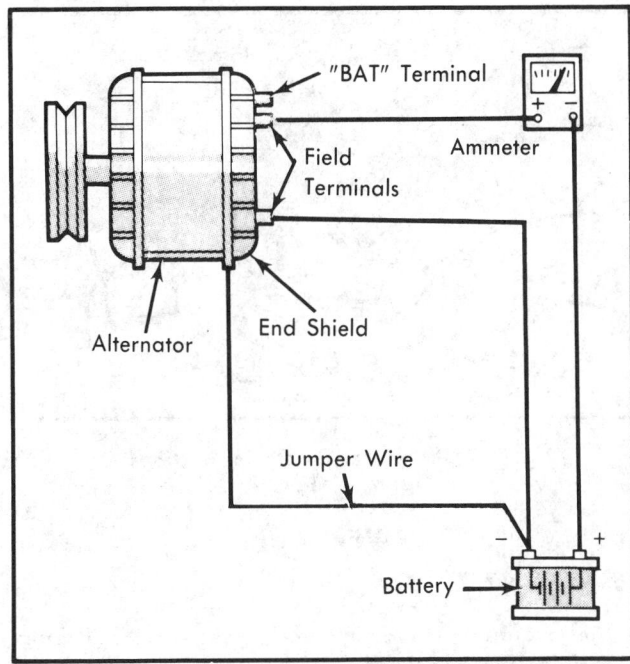

Fig. 3   Ammeter Connections for Field Coil Current Draw Test

RECTIFIER (DIODE) TESTS

NOTE — Do not break plastic cases of diodes, cases are for protection against corrosion. Always touch test probe to metal strap nearest diode. Rectifier diodes may be tested with a test lamp or tester C-3829A as follows:

Test Lamp Method — With rectifier end shield and stator assembly separated, test rectifiers with a 12V battery and suitable test lamp (No. 67 bulb, 4 candle power). Connect test lamp to battery positive terminal and to one test probe. Touch other test probe to battery negative terminal. Measure rectifier continuity with probes touching heat sink and rectifier top strap. Then reverse probes. If lamp lights with current flow in

one direction only, rectifier is satisfactory. If lamp lights with probes either way, rectifier is shorted. If lamp does not light at all, rectifier is open. Test each rectifier and both assemblies in same manner.

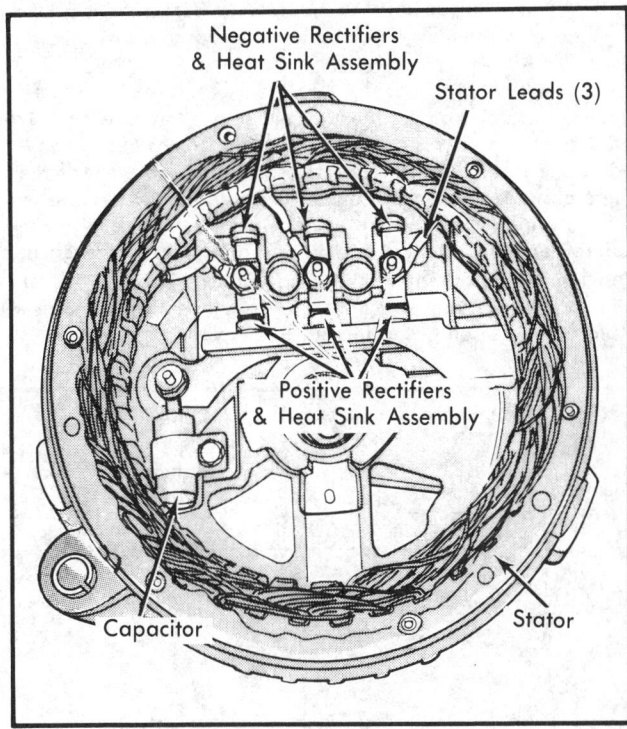

Fig. 4   View of Rectifier End Shield

Tool C-3829A Method — Remove alternator brushes and through bolts. Separate rectifier end housing and stator from drive end housing and rotor. Test rectifiers as follows:

Positive Rectifiers — With alternator on an insulated surface, connect test lead clip to alternator "BAT" output terminal and plug tool into 110 volt A.C. power supply. Touch exposed bare metal connections of each positive case rectifier with test probe. Reading for satisfactory rectifiers will be 1¾ amperes or more and should be approximately the same for each rectifier. When two rectifiers are good and one is shorted, reading taken at good rectifiers will be low and reading at shorted rectifier will be zero. Disconnect lead to rectifier reading zero and retest. Reading of good rectifiers will now be within satisfactory range. When one rectifier is open, it will read approximately 1 ampere. Two good rectifiers will read within satisfactory range.

Negative Rectifiers — Connect test lead clip to rectifier end housing. Touch exposed connection of each negative rectifier with test probe. Test specifications and results will be approximately the same as for positive case rectifiers, except meter will read on opposite side of scale.

NOTE — If a negative rectifier shows shorted condition, remove stator from rectifier end shield and retest. Stator winding could be grounded to stator laminations or rectifier end shield, indicating a shorted negative rectifier.

CHRYSLER CORP. ALTERNATORS (Cont.)

STATOR TEST

NOTE — *On 117 amp. alternators, stator windings are "Delta" wound and cannot be checked for opens and shorts with common shop equipment. If stator is not grounded, and all other components check correctly, suspect an open or a short in stator.*

Separate stator from both end shields. Press test probe firmly onto any pin on stator frame. Be sure varnish has been removed so the pin is bare. Press test probe firmly to each of the three phase lead terminals one at a time. If lamp lights stator lead is grounded. Now press test probe firmly on one phase control lead and contact each of the other two stator leads. Test lamp should light when probe contacts each of the terminals. If lamp does not light, stator is open. Install a new stator if it is open or grounded. See Fig. 5.

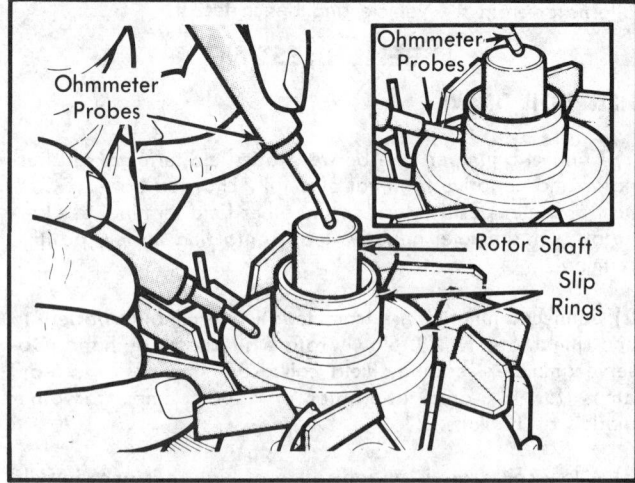

Fig. 6   Ohmmeter Probe Connections for Rotor Ground Test

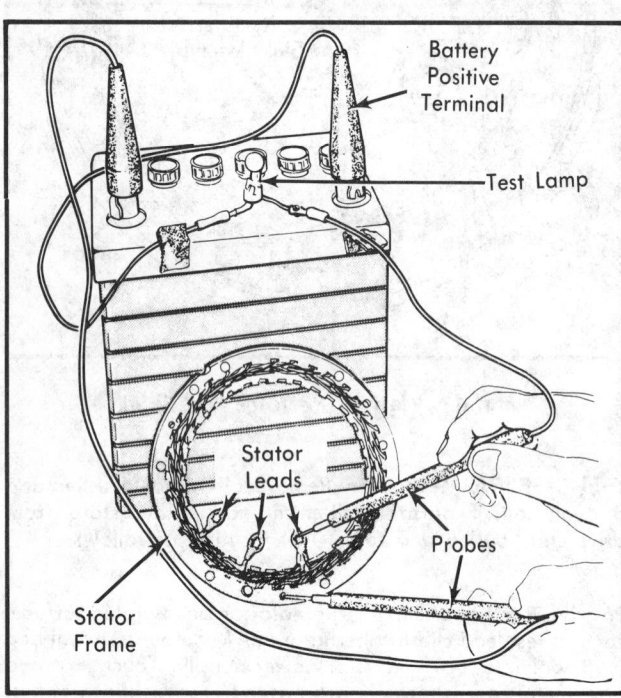

Fig. 5   Test Lamp Connections for Stator Ground Test

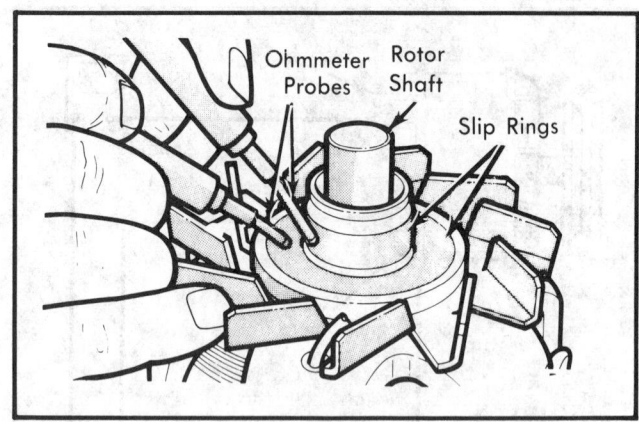

Fig. 7   Ohmmeter Probe Connections for Open or Short Tests

ROTOR TEST

1) Test rotor for grounded, open or shorted field coils, using an ohmmeter. See Figs. 6 and 7. Test for grounds between each slip ring and rotor shaft. No continuity should exist.

2) Check for open field by connecting ohmmeter leads across slip rings. Normal resistance reading with rotor at room temperature is 1.7-2.1 ohms for 117 amp. alternator; 1.5-2.0 ohms for all other models.

3) Readings between 2.5 and 3.0 ohms would result from rotors operating at higher engine compartment temperatures. Readings above 3.5 ohms indicate high resistance, possibly requiring rotor replacement. If reading is below 1.7 ohms (117 amp. alternator) or 1.5 ohms (all other models), the field coil is shorted.

OVERHAUL

DISASSEMBLY

1) Remove brush screws, insulating washers, and lift brush assemblies from end shield.

CAUTION — *Stator is laminated. Do not burr stator or end shield.*

2) Remove thru bolts and pry between stator and drive end shield with blade of screwdriver, using slot provided. Carefully separate drive end shield, pulley and rotor assembly away from stator and rectifier end shield assembly.

NOTE — *If negative heat sink diode straps are on top of positive heat sink straps, remove 4 hex head screws on negative rectifier and heat sink assembly. Remove heat sink assembly and proceed to step 3).*

3) On all except 117 amp. alternators, remove nut, washer and insulator from output (BAT) terminal on outside of end shield. Turn end shield over and remove capacitor, insulated

CHRYSLER CORP. ALTERNATORS (Cont.)

washer and positive heat sink assembly. Remove insulator from "BAT" terminal hole.

4) On 117 amp. alternators, from inside rectifier end shield remove nut and insulator attaching positive heat sink to end shield. Remove capacitor screw, capacitor and insulator. From outside end shield, remove nut and insulator attaching positive heat sink to end shield. Remove screws attaching negative heat sink to end shield. Remove positive and negative heat sink assemblies, noting location of insulators. Remove terminal block attaching screws and terminal block.

5) On all except 117 amp. alternators, remove mica insulator from end shield and loosen four hex head screws on negative rectifier and heat sink assembly. Remove two outer screws and remove heat sink assembly.

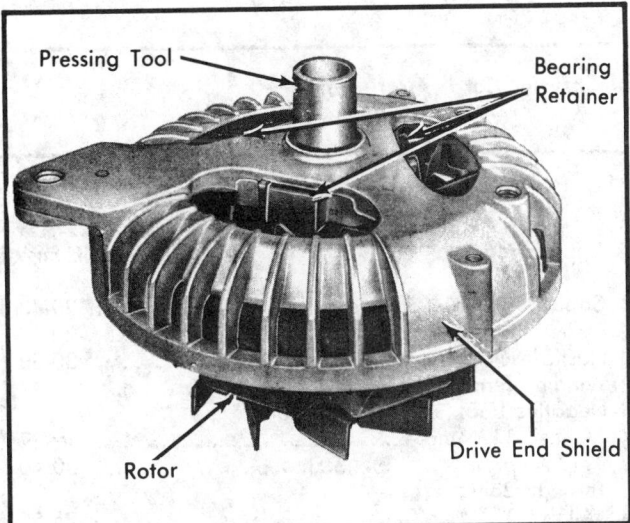

Fig. 8 Installing Drive End Shield Bearing

6) Using a puller (C-4068 or C-4333; C-4467 on 117 amp. models), remove drive pulley from shaft. Remove screws attaching bearing retainer to drive end shield on 117 amp. alternators. Separate bearing retainer from end shield. Support end shield and tap rotor shaft with plastic hammer to separate rotor from end shield.

7) Using suitable puller, remove drive end ball bearing. If needle roller bearing in rectifier and shield must be replaced, it can be pressed out of a properly supported end shield.

SLIP RING REPLACEMENT

Slip rings are not serviced as a separate item, only as part of the rotor assembly.

REASSEMBLY

All Exc. 117 Amp. – 1) Place grease retainer on rotor shaft and press retainer onto shaft until suitable tool (C-3921) bottoms on shaft. Position rectifier end shield bearing on base of tool C-4201-1. Place end shield on top of bearing so it is

properly aligned. With top part of tool C-4201-2 placed on end shield, press into place until it bottoms.

NOTE – *New bearings are prelubricated and should require no additional lubrication.*

2) Insert drive end bearing in drive end shield and install bearing retainer plate to hold bearing in place. A metal spacer is supplied with replacement rotors and replacement ball bearings (but is not a part of original alternator assembly). Place spacer on pulley end of rotor shaft first. Position bearing and drive end shield on rotor shaft. While supporting base of rotor shaft, press bearing end shield into position with an arbor press and adapter (C-3858).

CAUTION – *Make sure bearing is installed squarely.*

3) Install pulley on rotor shaft. Shaft of rotor must be supported so all pressing force is on pulley hub and rotor shaft, and not on bearings. Do not apply more than 6800 pounds force or hammer pulley on.

4) If removed, install output terminal stud and insulator thru end shield. Be sure mica insulators are in place and undamaged. Install positive heat sink assembly over studs; guide rectifier straps over studs on terminal block. Install capacitor. Slide negative rectifier and heat sink assembly into place, position straps and install screws.

5) Position stator over rectifier end shield and install winding terminals on terminal block and press stator pins into each end shield. Route leads so they cannot contact rotor or sharp edge of negative heat sink. Position rotor and drive end shield over stator and rectifier end shield and install through bolts. Compress both ends manually and tighten through bolts evenly to 25-55 INCH lbs.

6) Install field brushes in insulated holders. Position vertical and horizontal field brushes in proper location in rectifier end shield. Place an insulating washer on each field brush terminal and install lockwashers. Be sure that brushes are not grounded. Rotate pulley slowly by hand to be sure rotor fan blades do not hit stator winding leads.

117 Amp. Only – 1) Position rectifier end shield bearing on base of tool C-4330-1. Place end shield on top of bearing, so that it is properly aligned. With tool C-4330-2 placed on end shield, press into place until end shield touches base of press.

NOTE – *New bearings are prelubricated and should require no additional lubrication.*

2) Insert drive end bearing in end shield, position retainer in place and tighten mounting screws, ensuring that rotor spacer is in position. Position bearing and drive end shield on rotor shaft and press end shield into position with arbor press and tool C-3858.

3) Install pulley on rotor shaft. Support shaft so that pressing force is on pulley hub. Press pulley on shaft until it contacts inner race of drive end bearing. Position insulator and capacitor on positive heat sink mounting stud and tighten attaching screw. Do not exceed 6800 pounds of force or hammer pulley on.

CHRYSLER CORP. ALTERNATORS (Cont.)

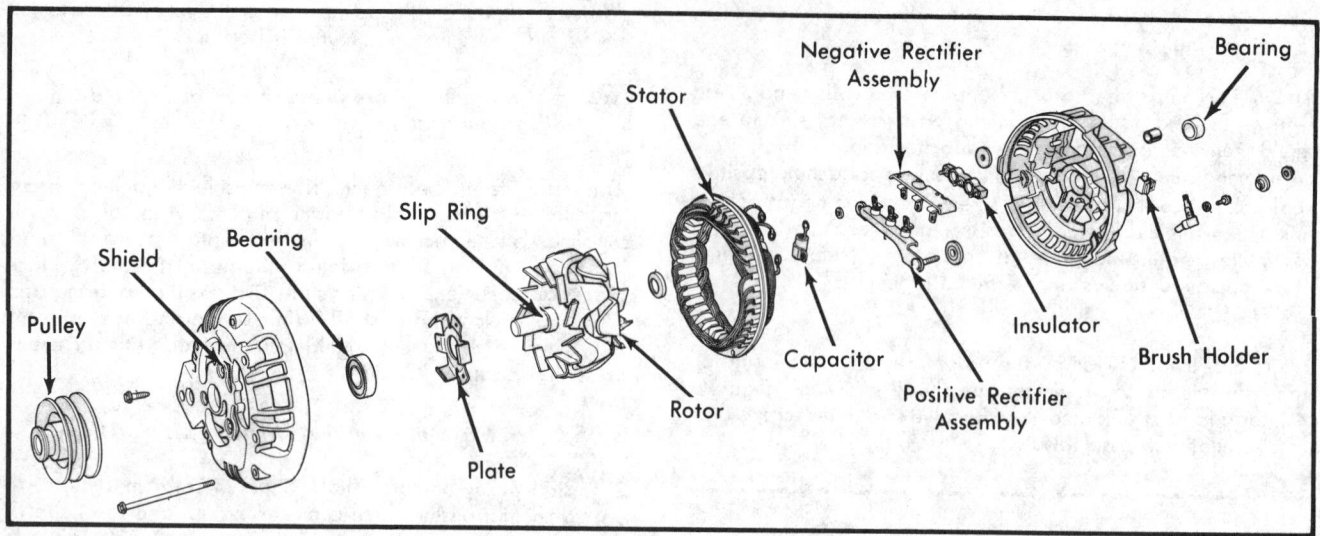

Fig. 9 *Exploded View of Typical Chrysler Corp. Alternator*

4) Position terminal block in rectifier end shield and tighten screws. Position negative heat sink in end shield ensuring that metal straps are properly positioned over studs on terminal block. Install mounting screws and tighten.

5) Install insulator on positive heat sink stud and place assembly into end shield ensuring that metal straps are properly positioned over studs on terminal block. From inside end shield install insulator on positive heat sink stud and tighten nut.

6) From outside of end shield, install insulator on stud and tighten mounting bolt. Position stator over end shield and install terminals on terminal block, routing leads so they cannot contact rotor or sharp edges of negative heat sink.

7) Position rotor and drive end shield over end shield assembly and align through bolts. Compress stator and both end shields manually, install and tighten through bolts. Install field brushes in brush holder with long terminal on bottom and short terminal on top. Install insulators and mounting screw.

8) Position brush holder assembly to end shield making sure it is properly seated and tighten mounting screw. Rotate pulley by hand to ensure rotor poles do not hit stator winding leads.

TIGHTENING SPECIFICATIONS

Application	INCH Lbs.
Capacitor Bracket Screws	30-40
Positive Heat Sink Stud Nut	20-30
Plastic Insulator Nut	30-50
Winding Terminal Nut	11-17
Negative Heat Sink Mount Screw	
All Exc. 117 Amp.	19-29
117 Amp.	30-40
Through Bolts	
All Exc. 117 Amp.	25-55
117 Amp.	40-60
Field Brush Screws	
All Exc. 117 Amp.	15-35
117 Amp.	30-40
End Bearing Mount Screws	
117 Amp.	19-29
Terminal Block Mount Screws	
117 Amp.	30-40

CHRYSLER CORP. ELECTRONIC REGULATOR

Dodge
Plymouth

DESCRIPTION

Regulates electrical system voltage by limiting output voltage generated by alternator. This is accomplished by controlling amount of current that is allowed to pass through alternator field winding. Regulator has no moving parts and requires no adjustment after it is set at factory. Unit contains several semiconductor components, transistors and diodes plus some resistors and a capacitor. A large transistor is placed in series with alternator field winding and a control circuit which senses system voltage and turns transistor on and off as required.

As alternator speed and electrical system load conditions change, control circuit is turning transistor on and off many times per second most of the time engine is in operation. The only time transistor is not turning on and off rapidly is during low engine speed operation when high electrical loads are present. This requires the alternator field to be in the "ON" state continuously. Electronic regulator control circuit can also vary the regulated system voltage up or down as temperatures change.

TESTING

NOTE — *Battery specific gravity should be above 1.200 for a properly regulated voltage check. Charge battery or use a good test battery before testing regulator.*

NOTE — *Where tester (C-4133) is available, use an adapter (C-4341) to switch circuit of regulator to be tested. The adapter has a three position switch to select regulator part number or regulator installed. Follow manufacturers test procedure.*

1) Connect positive lead of a voltmeter to terminal of single ignition ballast resistor having the Red wire. *See Fig. 1.* DO NOT remove connector from ballast resistor. Connect negative lead of voltmeter to a good ground. Start and run vehicle at 1250 RPM with all lights and accesories turned off. Check voltmeter, noting that regulator is working properly if voltage readings are within specifications.

2) If voltage is not within limits or is fluctuating, check that regulator has a good ground. With engine off, disconnect regulator terminals. Turn ignition on, but do not start engine.

3) Battery voltage should be present at both regulator harness terminals. If so, replace regulator and repeat test.

Specifications	
Ambient Temperature①	**Voltage Range**
−20°F	14.9-15.9
80°F	13.9-14.6
140°F	13.3-13.9
Above 140°F	Less than 13.6

① — Ambient temperature is measured ¼" from regulator.

ADJUSTMENT

The Electronic Voltage Regulator cannot be adjusted. If specifications are not obtained and investigation has shown the rest of electrical system to be satisfactory, then regulator must be replaced.

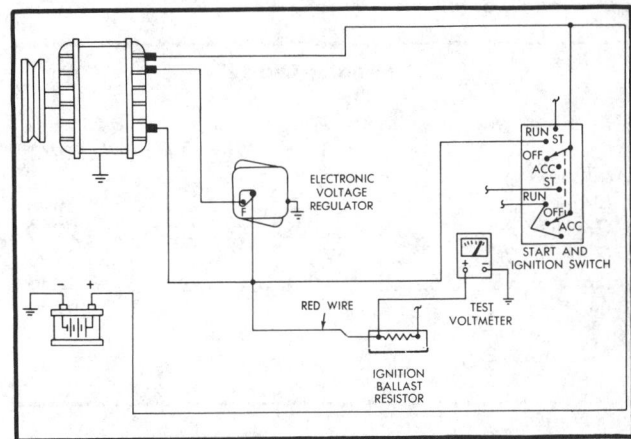

Fig. 1   Test Connections for Voltage Regulator Test

MOTORCRAFT ALTERNATORS

Ford

DESCRIPTION

Ford light trucks use 2 similar alternators, a rear terminal model and a side terminal model. *See Figs. 1 and 2.* Rated outputs range from 40 to 100 amps. depending upon model used. Some models are equipped with indicator lights, others with ammeters.

Alternator is belt driven from engine. Current is supplied from Alternator-Regulator system to rotating field of alternator through two brushes to two slip rings. Power is produced in the form of alternating current which is rectified to direct current by six diodes. Alternator regulator automatically adjusts alternator field current to maintain alternator output voltage within prescribed limits to correctly charge battery. Charging systems are equipped with a fuse link between the starter relay and alternator "BAT" terminal.

IDENTIFICATION & SPECIFICATIONS

Alternator is color-ink stamped with "Motorcraft" trademark. Color stamp is code for rated amperage output. Rated amperage is also stamped on end frame (40A, 60A, etc.). Color code is as follows:

Alternator Output		
Application	Amperage @15V	Rated Output Speed (Engine RPM)
Orange	40	2900
Green	60	2900
Green	65	2900
Black	70	①1640
Red	100	①2900

① — Rated cold output.

Alternator Specifications	
Alternator	Specifications
Field Current at 12 Volts (All)	4.0 Amps
Slip Rings (All)	
Minimum Diameter	1.22"
Maximum Runout	.0005"
Brush Length Wear Limit	
40 Amp.	5/16"
60 Amp.	5/16"
65 Amp.	3/16"
70 Amp.	1/4"
100 Amp.	1/4"
Pulley Nut Torque (All)	60-100 ft. lbs.

ADJUSTMENTS

ALTERNATOR REGULATOR

An electronic regulator is used on all charging systems. It is factory calibrated and cannot be adjusted.

TESTING

CAUTION — *When testing or servicing alternator or regulator, take following precautions to avoid damage to components.*

Battery — Do not reverse battery connections. Negative terminal must be connected to ground. When charging battery, cables must be disconnected from battery before connecting charger. Do not use charger as a booster for starting engine. If booster battery is used to start engine, negative cable of booster must be connected to negative cable of vehicle battery.

Alternator — Do not ground field circuit between alternator and regulator, or operate alternator on an open circuit with field winding energized. Do not ground output terminal or attempt to polarize alternator as polarization is not required.

Regulator — Turn ignition switch off when working on regulator. Use care to prevent a short circuit between regulator relay and regulator base while working on components. Use insulated tools when making adjustments.

VOLTMETER TEST PROCEDURES

NOTE — *When performing charging system test with a voltmeter, turn off all lights and electrical components. Be sure battery specific gravity is at least 1.200.*

1) Connect negative lead of voltmeter to negative battery post and positive lead to positive battery post. Record battery voltage.

2) Attach suitable tachometer and start engine. Operate at 1500 RPM with no electrical load. Voltmeter reading should increase 1-2 volts above battery voltage. Reading should be taken when voltmeter needle stops moving.

3) With engine operating, turn on heater or A/C blower motor to "HIGH" position. Turn on headlights to high beam. Increase engine speed to 2000 RPM. Voltmeter should indicate a minimum of .5 volt increase over battery voltage. If system conforms to these readings, operation is normal.

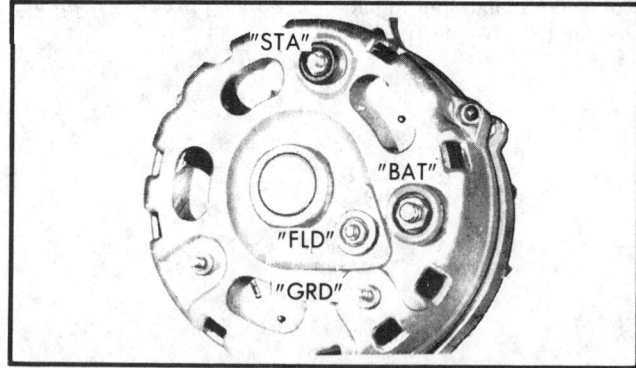

Fig. 1   View Showing Alternator Terminal Location on Rear Terminal Models

TEST RESULTS

1) If voltmeter reading indicates over-voltage (more than two volts above battery voltage), shut off engine and check ground connections between regulator and alternator and/or regulator and engine. Clean and tighten connections, then repeat tests.

MOTORCRAFT ALTERNATORS (Cont.)

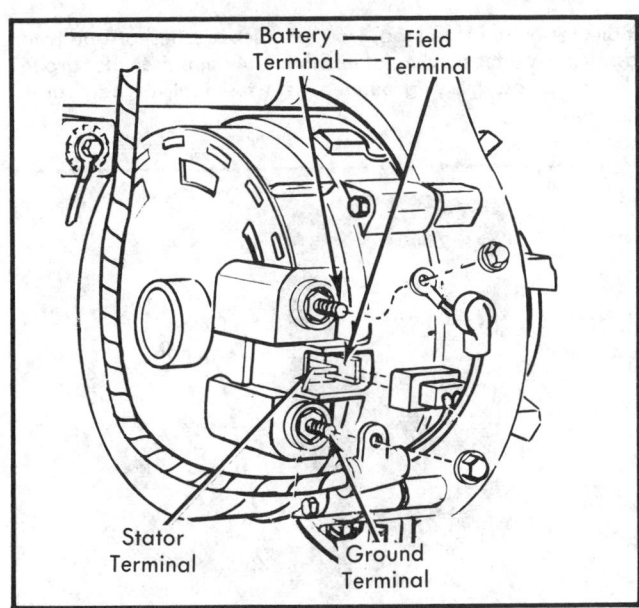

Fig. 2   View Showing Alternator Terminal Location on Side Terminal Models

2) If over-voltage condition still exists, disconnect regulator wiring plug and repeat steps **2)** and **3)** of *"Voltmeter Test Procedures"*. If condition is corrected, replace regulator and repeat test.

3) If over-voltage still exists with regulator disconnected, a short is indicated in wiring harness between alternator and regulator (Circuits "A" and "F"). Repair short circuit, and then replace regulator, repeating tests with regulator plug connected.

UNDER VOLTAGE & FIELD CIRCUIT TESTS

1) To determine if the jumping procedure is safe, the field circuit should be checked with the regulator wiring plug disconnected and an ohmmeter connected from the "F" terminal of the wiring plug to the battery ground. The ohmmeter should indicate 3-250 ohms. See *Fig. 3*.

2) If the load voltage did not increase one-half volt above base voltage, connect a jumper wire across the "A" and "F" terminals of the wiring plug and repeat test procedures.

3) If the voltage is still under base voltage, remove jumper wire from wiring plug and leave the plug disconnected from the regulator. Connect jumper wire to "FLD" and "BAT" terminals on alternator and repeat test. If voltage increases more than one-half volt above battery voltage, repair wiring harness or replace regulator.

4) If voltmeter still indicates under voltage, stop engine and move positive voltmeter lead to "BAT" terminal. If voltmeter now indicates base voltage reading, repair alternator. If voltmeter indicates zero volts, repair "BAT" wire or replace fuse link.

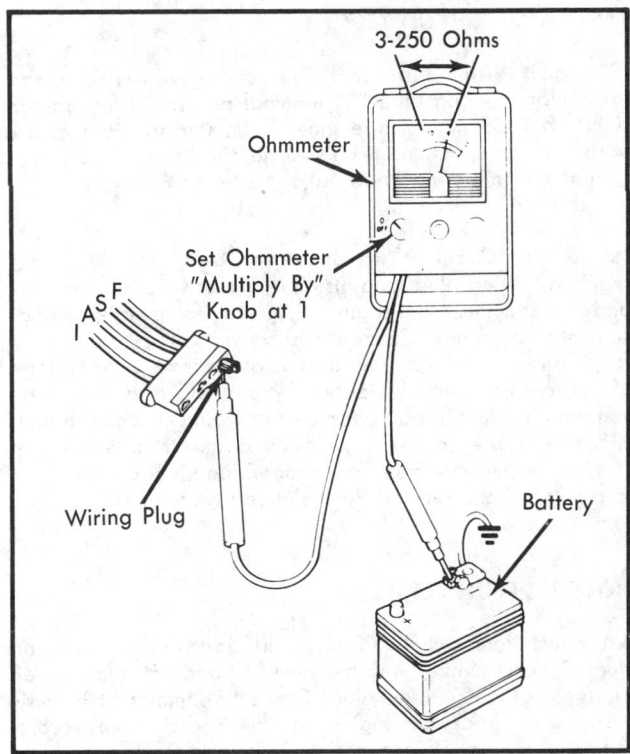

Fig. 3   Test Connections for Field Circuit Test

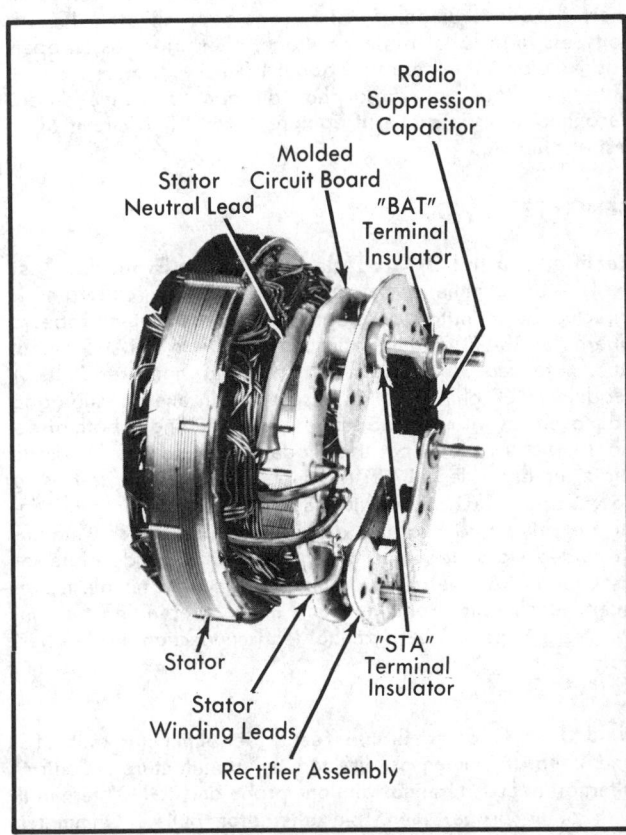

Fig. 4   View Showing Stator Lead Connections on Rear Terminal Models

MOTORCRAFT ALTERNATORS (Cont.)

REGULATOR CIRCUIT TESTS

"S" Circuit With Ammeter — Connect positive voltmeter lead to regulator wiring plug "S" terminal position. Turn ignition "ON", but do not start engine. Voltmeter should indicate battery voltage. If there is no voltage, the "S" wire lead from ignition switch is open. Repair and retest system.

"S" & "I" Circuit With Indicator Light — Disconnect regulator wiring plug, and install a jumper wire between "A" and "F" terminals. With engine idling, connect negative lead of voltmeter to ground. Connect positive voltmeter lead, in turn, to "S" and then "I" terminals of regulator wiring plug. Voltage of "S" circuit should be about ½ that of "I" circuit. If no voltage is present, repair alternator or wiring circuit at fault. If circuit tests are satisfactory, install a new regulator. Then remove jumper wire from regulator wiring plug, connect plug to regulator, and repeat *"Voltmeter Test Procedures"* No Load test.

DIODE TEST (ON VEHICLE)

Disconnect electric choke (if equipped) and voltage regulator plug. Connect jumper wire between "A" and "F" terminals of voltage regulator wiring plug. Connect voltmeter to battery posts, start and run engine at idle speed, then record voltmeter reading. Move positive voltmeter lead to "S" terminal of alternator and note voltmeter reading. If meter reads ½ of battery voltage, diodes are in working order. If meter reads approximately 1.5 volts, alternator has shorted negative diode or grounded stator winding. If meter reads approximately 1.5 volts less than battery voltage, alternator has shorted positive diode. If meter reads approximately 1.0-1.5 volts less than ½ of battery voltage, alternator has an open positive diode. If meter reads about 1.0-1.5 volts more than ½ battery voltage, alternator has an open negative diode. Reconnect electric choke (if equipped) back into circuit after test is completed.

BENCH TESTS

Rectifier Shorted Or Grounded and Stator Grounded Test — Use an ohmmeter, set knob at "10", and calibrate as directed by manufacturer. Connect one ohmmeter probe to alternator "BAT" terminal and other probe to "STA" terminal and note reading. Reverse probes and note reading. A reading of 60 ohms should be observed in one direction and no movement with terminals reversed. A reading in both directions indicates a bad positive diode, grounded positive diode plate, or grounded "BAT" terminal. Perform same test using "STA" and "GRD" terminals. Readings in both directions indicate either bad negative diode, grounded stator winding, grounded stator terminal, grounded positive diode plate, or grounded "BAT" terminal. Infinite reading (no needle movement) in all four probe positions in the preceeding tests indicates an open "STA" terminal lead connection inside alternator. See Fig. 4.

Field Open Or Short Circuit Test — Set ohmmeter knob at 1 and calibrate meter as directed by manufacturer. Contact alternator "FLD"terminal with one probe and "GND" terminal with other probe, then spin alternator pulley. Ohmmeter should read between 2.4 and 100 ohms, and should fluctuate while pulley is spinning. Infinite reading (no needle movement) indicates open brush lead, worn or stuck brushes, or bad rotor assembly. Meter reading of less than 2.4 ohms indicates grounded brush assembly, grounded field terminal, or bad rotor. See Fig. 5.

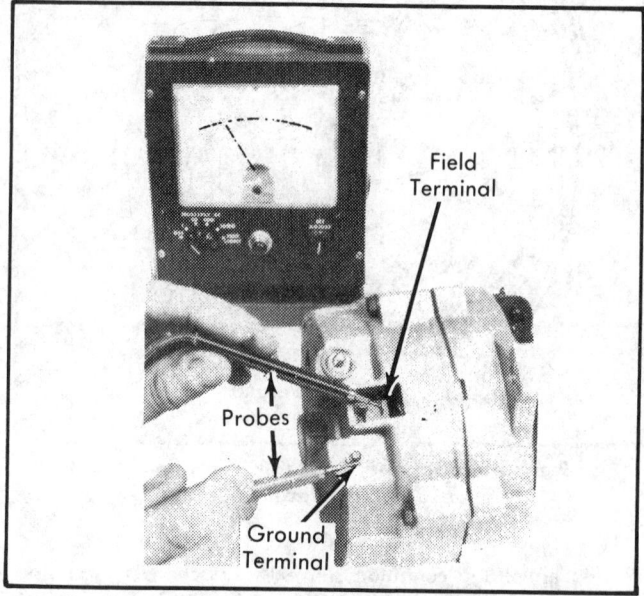

Fig. 5   Test Connections for Field Open or Short Circuit Test (Side Terminal Model Shown)

Diode Test — Remove rectifier assembly from alternator. Set ohmmeter knob at 10. Calibrate meter. To test one set of diodes, contact one probe to terminal bolt and contact each of three stator lead terminals with other probe. Reverse probes and repeat test. All diodes should show readings of about 60 ohms in one direction, and infinite readings with probes reversed. Repeat test for other set of diodes, moving first probe to other terminal screw. If meter readings are not as specified, replace rectifier assembly.

Stator Coil Grounded Test — Set ohmmeter knob at 1000. Contact meter probes to one of stator leads and to stator laminated core. Meter should show infinite reading (no needle movement). If meter needle moves, stator winding is shorted to core and must be replaced. Repeat test for each one of stator leads.

Rotor Open or Short Circuit Test — Disassemble front housing and rotor from rear housing. Set ohmmeter knob at 1 and calibrate meter. Contact each probe to a rotor slip ring. Meter reading should be 2.0-3.5 ohms. Higher reading indicates damaged slip ring solder connection or broken wire. Lower reading indicates shorted wire or slip ring. Replace rotor if damaged. Contact one meter probe to slip ring and other probe to rotor shaft. Meter reading should be infinite (no needle deflection). Reading other than infinite indicates rotor is shorted to shaft. Replace rotor if shorted and beyond repair.

NOTE — *Slip ring terminals or solder touching rotor shaft will cause shorted condition.*

MOTORCRAFT ALTERNATORS (Cont.)

OVERHAUL

REAR TERMINAL MODELS

Disassembly — **1)** Mark both housings and stator with scribe for reassembly. Remove through bolts and separate front housing and rotor from stator and rear housing. Remove all nuts and insulators from rear housing. Remove rear housing from stator and rectifier assembly. *See Fig. 6.*

2) Remove brush holder mounting screws, holder, brushes, springs, insulator, and terminal. If replacement is necessary, press bearing from rear housing, supporting housing on inner boss. If rectifier assembly is being replaced, unsolder stator leads from rectifier terminals and separate stator from rectifier assembly.

NOTE — *Use suitable 100 watt soldering iron.*

3) Original production alternators will have one of two types of rectifier assembly boards; one has circuit board spaced away from diode plates with diodes exposed. The other type is single circuit board with built-in diodes. If alternator rectifier has exposed diode board, remove screws from rectifier by rotating bolt heads ¼ turn clockwise to unlock, and then remove screws. Push stator terminal straight out on a rectifier with diodes built into circuit board. Avoid turning screw while removing to make certain straight knurl will engage insulators when installing. Do not remove grounded screw.

4) Remove drive pulley nut, using suitable tool. Then, pull lock washer, pulley, fan, and spacer from rotor shaft. Remove rotor from front housing, and remove front bearing spacer. Do not remove rotor stop ring from shaft unless it is damaged.

5) Remove 3 screws holding front end bearing retainer and remove retainer. If bearing has lost lubricant or is damaged, support housing close to bearing boss and press out old bearing.

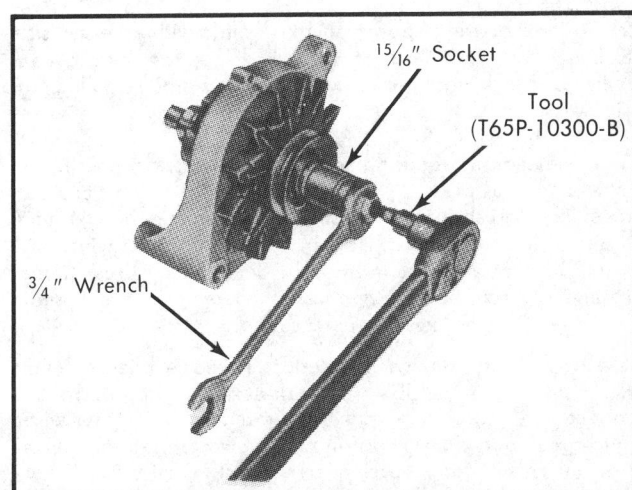

Fig. 7 Pulley Removal Procedure

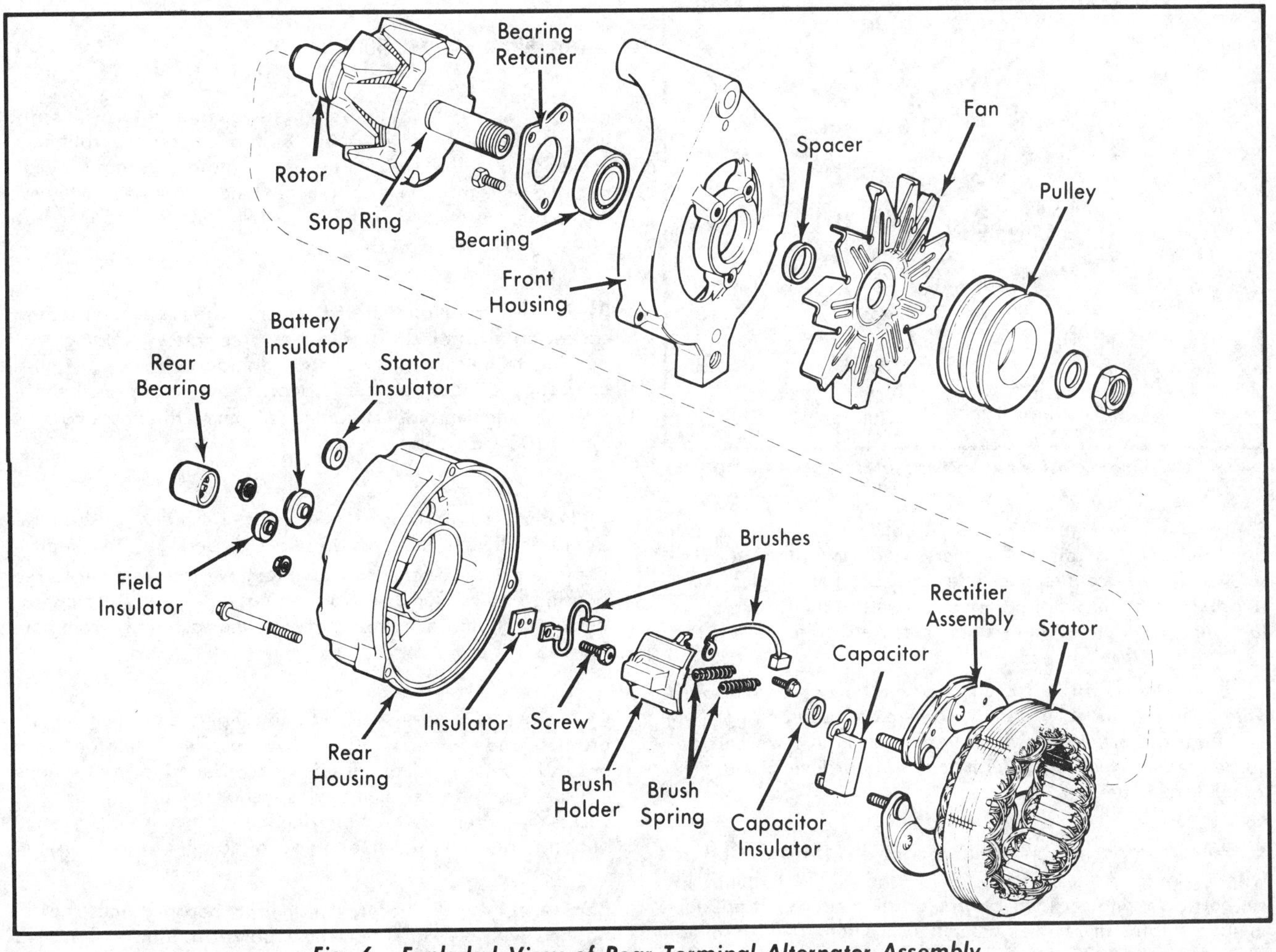

Fig. 6 Exploded View of Rear Terminal Alternator Assembly

MOTORCRAFT ALTERNATORS (Cont.)

Reassembly — 1) Rotor, stator and bearing must not be cleaned with solvent. Wipe these parts off with a clean, lint-free cloth. Press front bearing in front housing bearing boss, putting pressure on bearing outer race only. Install bearing retainer. If stop-ring on rotor drive shaft is damaged, install new stop-ring. Push new ring on shaft and into groove.

NOTE — *Do not open ring with snap ring pliers, as permanent damage will result.*

2) Position bearing spacer on rotor shaft with recessed side against stop ring. Position front housing, fan spacer, fan, pulley and lock washer on rotor shaft and install retaining nut. Tighten nut.

3) If rear housing bearing was removed, support housing on inner boss and press a new bearing flush with outer end surface. Place brush springs, brushes, brush terminal and terminal insulator in brush holder. Hold brushes in position by inserting small piece of stiff wire in brush holder. Position brush holder assembly in rear housing and install mounting screws. Position brush leads in holder. See Figs. 8 and 9.

4) Wrap three stator winding leads around rectifier terminals and solder using suitable 100 watt soldering iron and resin-core solder. On 65 amp models, push terminals of stator wires onto circuit board terminals and solder. Position stator neutral lead eyelet on stator terminal screw and install screw in rectifier assembly. See Fig. 4.

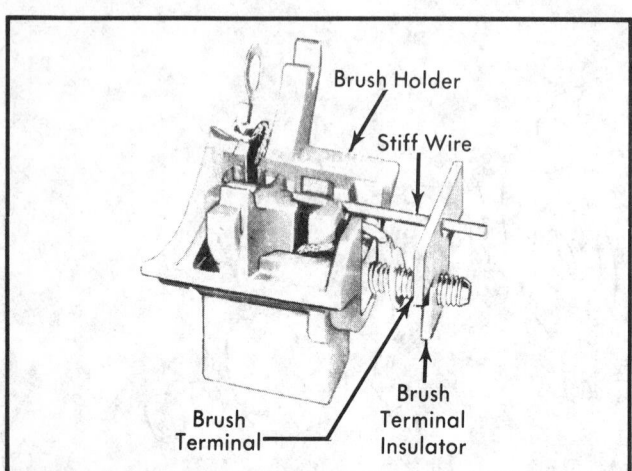

Fig. 8   Assembled View of Brush Holder Assembly

5) For rectifier with diodes exposed, insert special screws through wire lug, dished washers, and circuit board. Turn screw ¼ turn counterclockwise to lock. For single circuit boards with built-in diodes, insert screws straight through wire lug, insulating washer and rectifier, into insulator.

NOTE — *Dished washers are to be used only on circuit board with exposed diodes. If dished washers are used on single circuit board, short circuit will occur. Flat insulating washers are to be used between stator terminal and board when single circuit board is used.*

6) Position capacitor on rectifier terminals. On circuit board with exposed diodes, install "STA" and "BAT" terminal insulators. On single circuit board, position square stator terminal insulator in rectifier assembly. Position "BAT" terminal insulator on "BAT" terminal. Position stator and rectifier

assembly in rear housing. Make certain all terminal insulators are seated properly in appropriate recesses. Position "STA" (black), "BAT" (red), and "FLD" (orange) insulators on terminal bolts and install retaining nuts.

7) Wipe rear end bearing of rotor shaft with clean, lint free cloth. Position rear housing and stator assembly over rotor and align scribe marks made during initial disassembly. Seat machined portion of stator core into step in both end housings. Install housing through bolts. Remove brush retracting wire, and put small amount of water-proof cement over hole to seal from moisture.

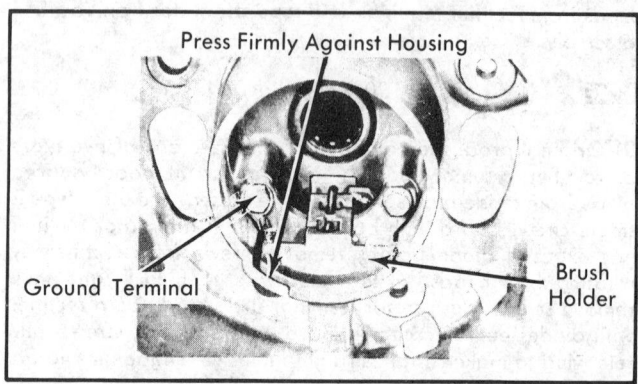

Fig. 9   View Showing Brush Lead Wire Routing

SIDE TERMINAL MODELS

Disassembly — 1) Mark both housings and stator with scribe for reassembly. Remove through bolts and separate front housing and rotor from rear housing and stator. Do not separate rear housing from stator at this time. Remove drive pulley nut; then, remove lock washer, pulley, fan and fan spacer from rotor shaft. See Fig. 10.

2) Remove rotor and shaft from front housing, then remove spacer from rotor shaft. Remove three screws holding front bearing to housing. If bearing is damaged or has lost lubricant, support housing close to bearing boss and press bearing from housing. Unsolder stator leads from rectifier assembly, using a 100 watt soldering iron.

3) Remove stator from rear housing. Unsolder brush holder from rectifier, using a 100 watt soldering iron. Remove capacitor lead-to-rectifier screw. Remove four rectifier-to-rear housing screws. Remove two terminal nuts and insulator from outside of housing, then remove rectifier assembly from housing.

4) Remove two brush holder-to-housing screws, then remove brushes and holder. Remove two rectifier insulators from bosses in housing. Clean all sealing compound from rear housing and brush holder. Remove capacitor from rear housing. If necessary to replace rear bearing, support rear housing near bearing boss and press bearing out of housing from the inside.

Reassembly — 1) Rotor, stator, and bearings must not be cleaned with solvent. Wipe these parts off with a clean, lint-free cloth. Press front bearing into front housing, putting

MOTORCRAFT ALTERNATORS (Cont.)

pressure on bearing outer race only. Install bearing retaining screws. Install inner spacer on rotor shaft and install shaft into front housing and bearing.

2) Install fan spacer, fan, pulley, lock washer, and nut onto rotor shaft. Tighten pulley nut. If rear bearing was removed, press new bearing in until it is flush with boss outer surface. Position brush terminal, springs, and brushes in brush holder and hold in position by inserting a small piece of stiff wire in brush holder.

3) Install brush holder to rear housing and install attaching screws. Push brush holder toward rotor shaft opening and tighten screws. Install capacitor to rear housing and install attaching screw. Install two rectifier insulators on bosses inside rear housing. Install insulator on "BAT" terminal of rectifier, then position rectifier in rear housing.

4) Install outside insulator on "BAT" terminal, then install nuts on "BAT" and "GRD" terminals finger tight. Install four rectifier attaching screws but do not tighten. Tighten terminal nuts on "BAT" and "GRD" terminals, then tighten four rectifier screws. Secure capacitor lead to rectifier. Press brush holder lead on rectifier pin and solder, using a 100 watt soldering iron.

5) Install stator in rear housing and align scribe marks. Press three stator leads onto rectifier pins and solder, using a 100 watt soldering iron. Position rotor and front housing into stator and rear housing while aligning scribe marks. Install four through bolts and tighten. Spin fan and pulley to ensure nothing is binding inside alternator. Remove brush retracting wire, and put small amount of water-proof cement over hole to seal from moisture.

BRUSH REPLACEMENT

70 Amp. Alternator — 1) Remove brush holder and cover assembly from rear housing. Remove terminal bolts from brush holder and cover assembly and remove brush assemblies. Position new brush terminals on terminal bolts. Assemble terminals, bolts, and brush holder washers and nuts. Insulating washer mounts under "FLD" terminal nut. Entire brush and cover assembly is also available for service.

2) Depress brush springs in brush holder cavities and insert brushes on top of springs. Hold brushes in position by inserting a stiff wire in brush holder. Position brush leads as required. Install brush holder and cover assembly to rear housing. Remove brush retracting wire and seal with small amount of water-proof cement.

Except 70 Amp. Alternator — 1) Mark both end housings and stator with a scribe. Remove four through bolts and separate front housing and rotor from rear housing and stator. Use a 100 watt soldering iron to unsolder and detach brush holder lead from rectifier. Remove brush holder attaching screws and remove holder from rear housing. Remove any sealing compound.

2) To install, position holder to rear housing and insert wire, to retract brushes, through hole in rear housing. Install holder attaching screws, push holder toward rotor shaft and tighten screws. Press holder lead on rectifier pin and solder using a 200 watt soldering iron. Install front housing and rotor to rear housing and stator while aligning scribe marks. Install four through bolts, then spin fan and pulley to ensure nothing is binding inside alternator. Remove wire, retracting brushes, and seal with a small amount of water-proof cement.

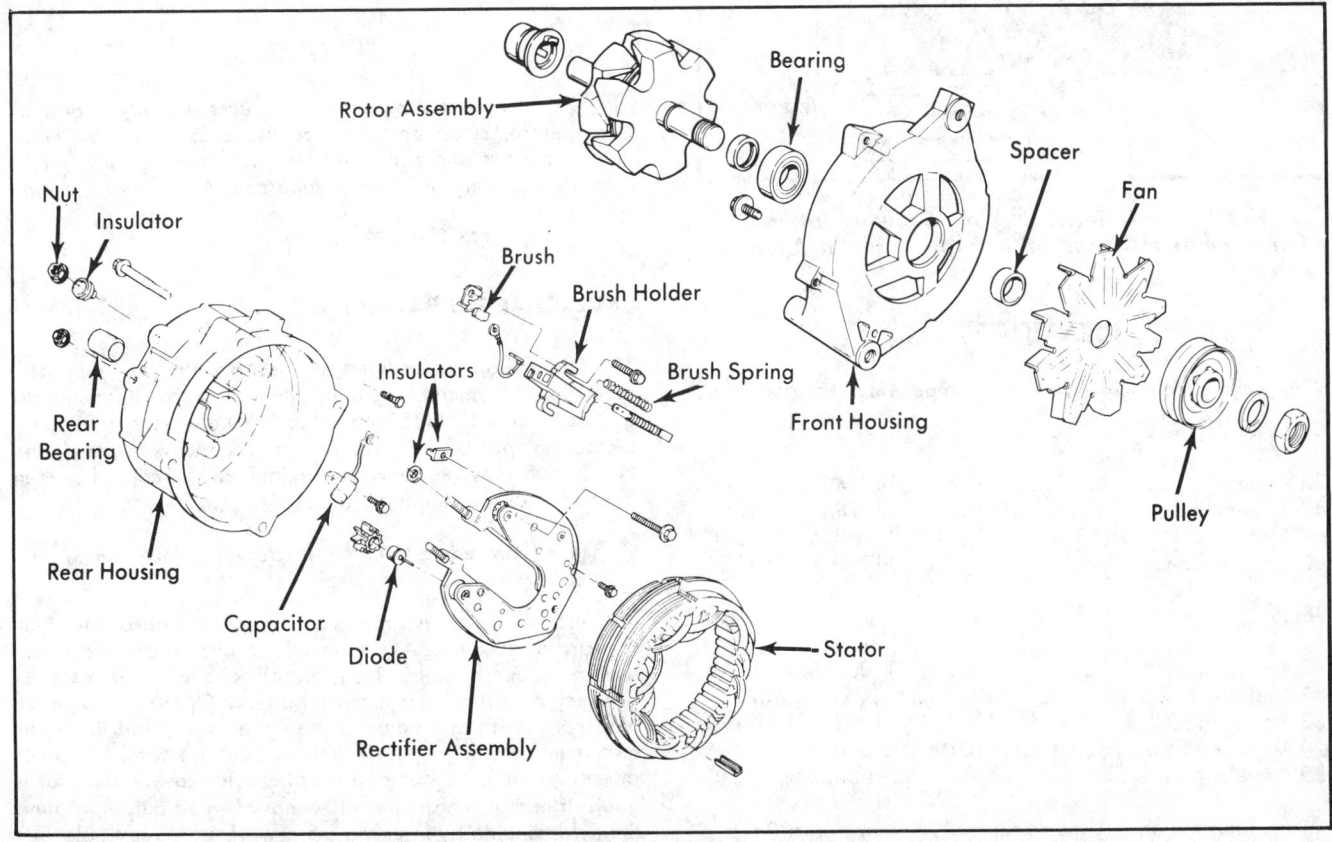

Fig. 10   Exploded View of Side Terminal Alternator Assembly (100 Amp. Shown)

Alternators & Regulators

DELCO-REMY WITH INTEGRAL REGULATOR

Chevrolet
GMC
Jeep

DESCRIPTION

Delco 10SI, 15SI and 27SI Integral regulator alternators feature a solid state regulator mounted inside the alternator. These alternators are available with different outputs at idle and different maximum outputs.

Delcotrons consist of 2 separate housings (end frame assemblies), a rotor, stator, brushes, slip rings and diodes. Rotor is supported in drive end frame by ball bearings and in slip ring end frame by roller bearings. Bearings contain enough lubrication to eliminate need for periodic lubrication.

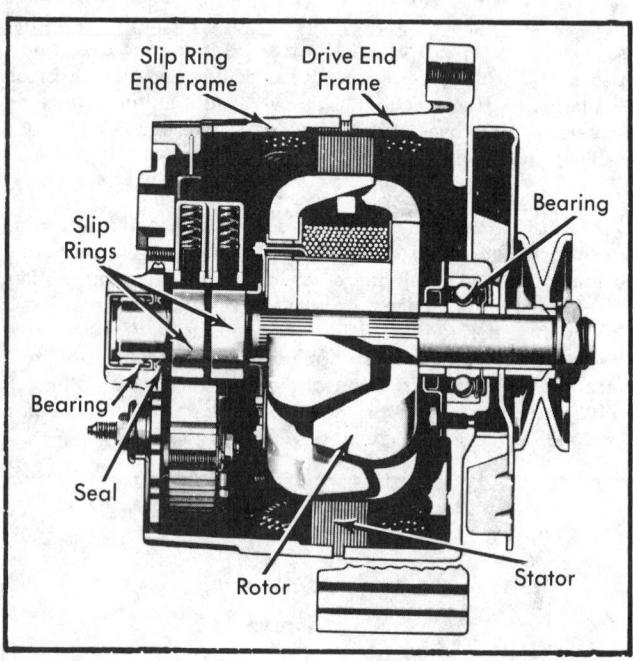

Fig. 1   Cross Sectional View Showing Internal
Components of Delcotron Integral Regulator Alternator

IDENTIFICATION

Alternator rated ampere output is stamped on alternator case.

CHEVROLET & GMC

37 Ampere	1102394, 1102491, 1102889
42 Ampere	1102485, 1102841, 1102887
61 Ampere	1102480, 1102486, 1102886, 1102888
80 Ampere	1101016, 1101028

JEEP

42 Ampere	1100158, 1100159
55 Ampere	1103155
63 Ampere	1100129, 1100132, 1103196
70 Ampere	1101087, 1101093, 1101094, 1101436
85 Ampere	①

① — Information not available from manufacturer. Police option.

OPERATION

Two brushes carry current through the slip rings to and from the field coil mounted on the rotor. The stator windings are assembled on the inside of a laminated core that forms part of the alternator frame.

A rectifier bridge, connected to the stator windings, contains 6 diodes (3 positive and 3 negative) molded into an assembly. This rectifier bridge changes stator A.C. voltage into D.C. voltage, which appears at the output terminal.

The blocking action of the diodes prevents battery discharge back through the alternator. Because of this blocking action, the need for a cutout relay is eliminated. Generator field current is supplied through a diode trio which is also connected to the stator windings. A capacitor is mounted in the end frame, protecting rectifier bridge and diodes from high voltages and suppressing radio interference noise. Some vehicles are equipped with ammeters, others with voltmeters.

ADJUSTMENTS

No periodic adjustments or maintenance of any kind is required on alternator assembly. Regulator voltage is preset, and no adjustment is possible.

CAUTION — *Do not attempt to polarize alternator. Do not short or ground any terminals except as instructed. Never operate alternator with battery out of circuit or output terminal open. Alternator and battery must share same ground polarity.*

TESTING

NOTE — *Before making electrical checks, visually inspect all terminals for clean and tight connections. Check alternator mounting bolts and drive belt tension. Do not ground No. 2 lead wire. Battery must be in good condition to test charging system.*

UNDERCHARGED BATTERY

1) With ignition switch "ON", connect a voltmeter from alternator "BAT" terminal to ground, then from No. 1 terminal to ground, and last, No. 2 terminal to ground. A zero reading indicates an open between connection and battery. Opens in the No. 2 lead may be between terminals at the crimp between harness wire and terminal, or in wire. See Fig. 2.

NOTE — *If preceding test is satisfactory, continue to next step.*

2) Disconnect battery ground cable. Connect an ammeter in the circuit at the "BAT" terminal of alternator. Reconnect battery ground cable. Turn on all available accessories. Connect a carbon pile across battery. Operate engine at moderate speed and adjust carbon pile as required to obtain maximum current output. If ampere output is within 10 amps of rated output as stamped on alternator case, alternator is good. If output is not within 10 amps of rated output, ground the field winding by inserting a screwdriver into test hole. See Fig. 3.

DELCO-REMY WITH INTEGRAL REGULATOR (Cont.)

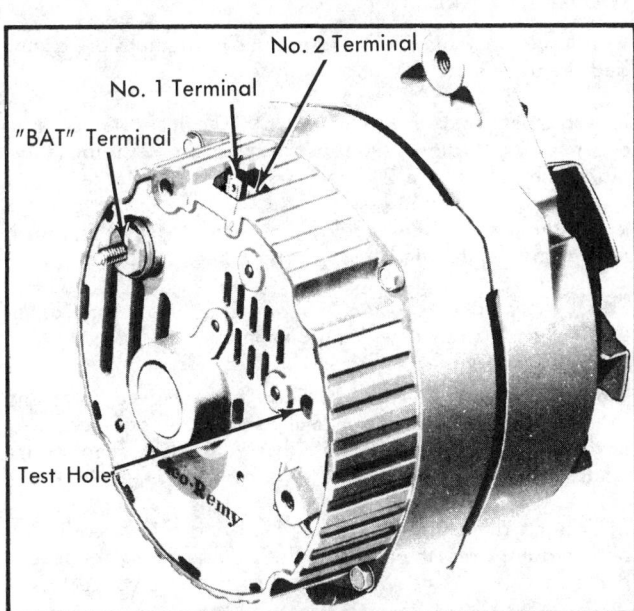

Fig. 2   Identification of Delcotron Terminal Locations

CAUTION — *Tab is within ¾" of casting surface. Do not force screwdriver deeper than 1" into end frame. If test hole is not accessible, proceed to "Testing (On Bench)" as described under Overhaul.*

3) Operate engine at moderate speed as required and adjust carbon pile for maximum output. If output is now within 10 amps of rated output with fields grounded, regulator is defective and requires replacement. If output is still not within 10 amps of rated output, check field winding, diode trio, rectifier bridge, and stator.

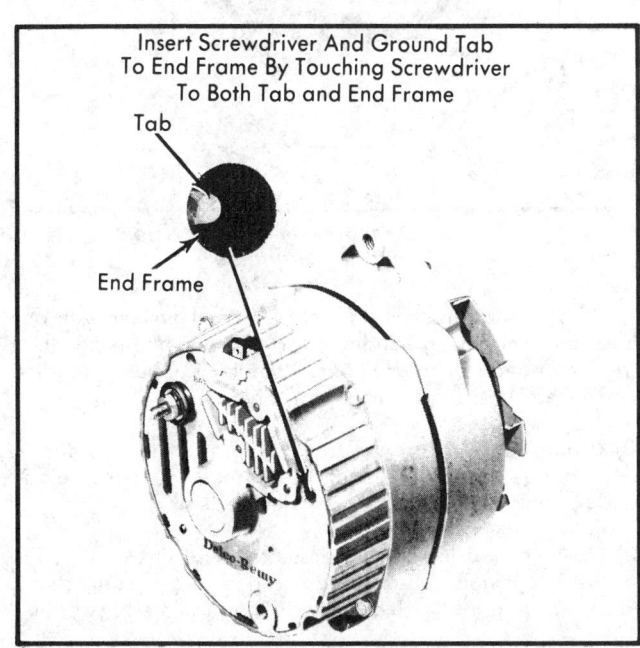

Insert Screwdriver And Ground Tab
To End Frame By Touching Screwdriver
To Both Tab and End Frame

Tab

End Frame

**Fig. 3   View Showing Field Ground Tab Accessible
Through Hole in End Frame**

OVERCHARGED BATTERY

Connect a voltmeter from alternator terminal No. 2 to ground. If reading is zero, No. 2 lead circuit is open. If battery and No. 2 lead circuit check out good, alternator will have to be disassembled for further checks. *See Overhaul.*

OVERHAUL

DISASSEMBLY

NOTE — *As rotor and drive end housing are separated from slip ring housing, brushes will spring out onto rotor shaft and contact lubricant. Clean brushes immediately to avoid contamination by lubricant, otherwise they will have to be replaced.*

1) Scribe marks on housings for reassembly reference. Remove through bolts connecting housings. Separate front and rear housings by prying apart with screwdriver.

2) Place a piece of tape over slip ring end frame bearing to prevent entry of dirt. At this point brushes may drop onto rotor shaft and become contaminated with bearing lubricant, clean brushes as soon as possible with a suitable cleaner (acetone) to keep them from becoming grease soaked.

3) Place rotor in vise and tighten vise only enough to permit removal of shaft nut. Remove shaft nut, washer, pulley, fan and collar. Separate front housing from rotor shaft. Remove 3 stator lead attaching nuts and remove stator leads from bridge terminal.

4) Separate stator from rear housing. Remove diode trio lead clip attaching screw and remove diode trio. Remove capacitor attaching screw and remove capacitor lead from bridge rectifier.

5) Remove bridge rectifier and battery terminal attaching screws and remove bridge rectifier. Remove 2 brush holder screws and 1 diode trio lead strap screw. Remove brush holder and brushes. Note location of brushes for reassembly.

6) Remove voltage regulator. Remove front bearing retaining plate screws. Press front bearing out of housing with suitable collar. Press out rear bearing from housing by inserting collar inside housing and pressing bearing toward the outside.

INSPECTION

Wash all metal parts except bearings, stator, and rotor. Inspect rotor slip rings. They may be cleaned with 400 grain polishing cloth, while rotor is being rotated. Slip rings may be lathe turned to .002" maximum indicator reading.

Slip rings are not replaceable. Excessive damage will require rotor replacement. Inspect brushes for wear, replacing them if more than 50% worn.

TESTING (ON BENCH)

Rotor Field Winding Test — 1) Check rotor for grounds or an open circuit, using a 110-volt test lamp or an ohmmeter. *See Fig. 4.* To check for grounds, connect ohmmeter leads to shaft and slip ring (each ring in turn). No continuity should exist.

Alternators & Regulators

DELCO-REMY WITH INTEGRAL REGULATOR (Cont.)

2) To test for open field, connect ohmmeter leads to each slip ring. Continuity should be indicated.

3) To test for shorts, connect a 12-volt battery and ammeter in series with both slip rings. Current draw is used for this test, resistance should be 2.5-3.0 ohms. Excessive amperage draw or low resistance indicates shorted windings. If rotor tests okay, but alternator output is low, continue with tests.

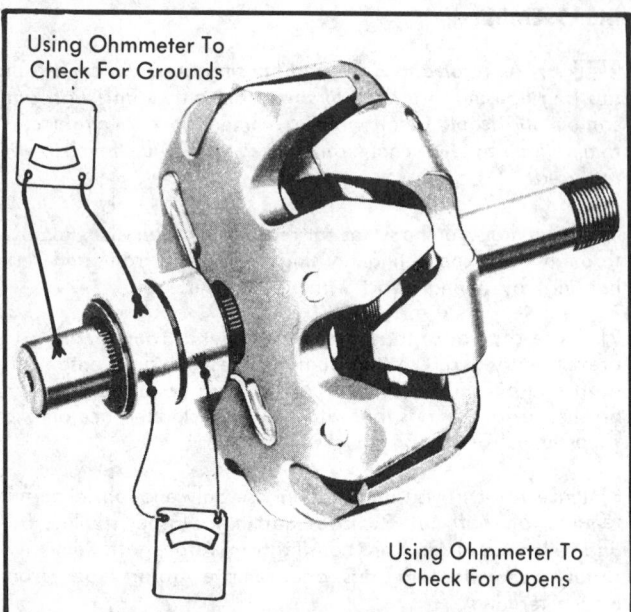

Using Ohmmeter To Check For Grounds

Using Ohmmeter To Check For Opens

Fig. 4   Bench Testing Rotor For Opens or Grounds Using an Ohmmeter

Stator Ground Test — 1) Connect leads of a 110-volt test lamp or an ohmmeter (x1000 scale) to any stator lead and to stator frame. Ohmmeter reading should be infinite. See Fig. 5.

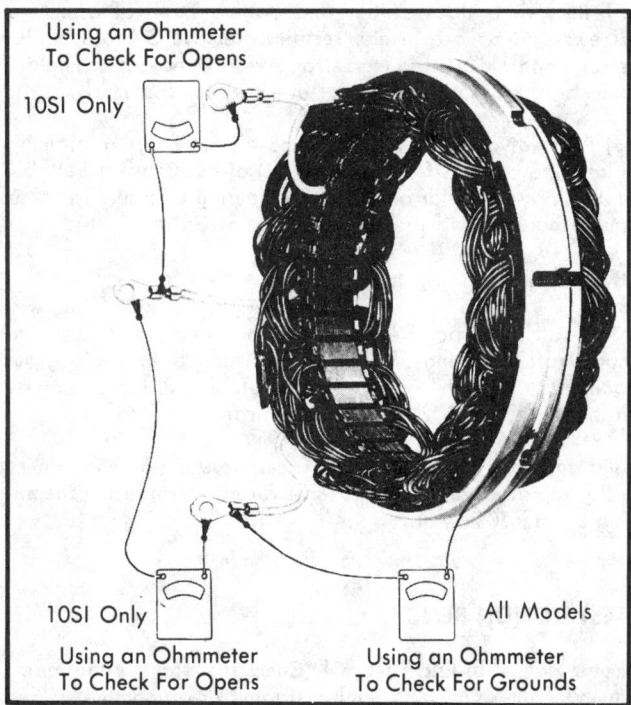

Using an Ohmmeter To Check For Opens

10SI Only

10SI Only

All Models

Using an Ohmmeter To Check For Opens

Using an Ohmmeter To Check For Grounds

Fig. 5   Bench Testing Stator for Open or Grounded Circuits Using an Ohmmeter

2) If test lamp lights or if resistance is low, windings are grounded. Replace stator assembly.

Stator Open Test — 1) Connect a 110-volt test lamp or an ohmmeter (x1 scale) with leads touching any 2 stator leads. Make checks between 2 different sets of stator leads.

2) Readings should be equal. If test lamp does not light or if resistance is high, windings are open. See Fig. 5.

NOTE — *Delta windings on 15SI and 27SI alternators cannot be checked for opens with an ohmmeter.*

Diode Trio Test — 1) With diode trio removed from end frame, connect an ohmmeter to the single connector and to 1 of the 3 connectors. See Fig. 6. Observe reading, then reverse leads.

2) A good diode trio will give 1 high and 1 low reading. If both readings are the same, replace diode trio. Repeat tests between single connector and each of other 2 connectors.

NOTE — *Before replacing diode trio, also check rectifier bridge. Do not use high voltage, such as 110-volt test lamp, when testing diode trio.*

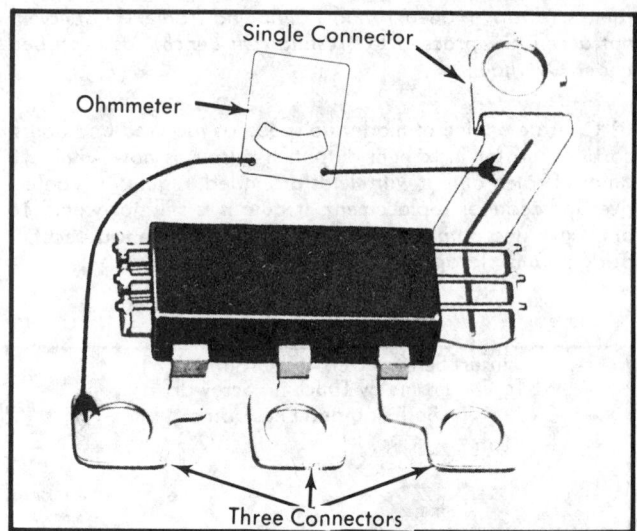

Single Connector

Ohmmeter

Three Connectors

Fig. 6   Bench Testing Diode Trio Using an Ohmmeter

Rectifier Bridge Test — 1) Connect an ohmmeter with one lead touching the grounded heat sink and the other lead touching flat metal on one of the 3 terminals. Observe reading and reverse test lead connections. See Fig. 7.

2) If both readings are the same, replace rectifier bridge. A good bridge will give 1 high and 1 low reading. Repeat test on all terminals (6 tests using grounded heat sink).

3) Now, connect test leads to insulated heat sink and 1 edge of the 3 terminals. Observe reading and reverse connections. Repeat test on all terminals (6 tests with insulated heat sink).

4) When all 12 tests have been made, testing is complete. Do not use high voltage, such as 100-volt test lamp to check bridge. Do not replace diode trio or rectifier bridge unless at least 1 pair of readings is the same (with leads reversed).

Alternators & Regulators

DELCO-REMY WITH INTEGRAL REGULATOR (Cont.)

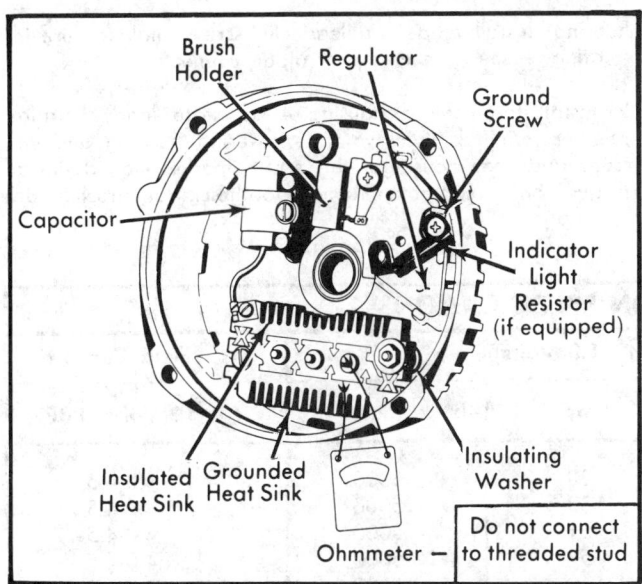

Fig. 7 Bench Testing Rectifier Bridge and Identification of End Frame Components

Alternator/Regulator Circuit Test — Voltage regulator tester CTW-1170 must be used for this check. With alternator in vehicle, turn tester off. Plug the on-vehicle testing cable in place on the tester. Disconnect regulator connector from alternator. Plug the on-vehicle testing cable in its place. Connect ground lead to alternator case. Test circuit using steps 2, 3, 4 and 15 under instructions listed on tester cover. If proper voltage indication is not obtained or lamps flicker off and on when performing test, the regulator must be removed from vehicle for further testing.

REASSEMBLY

1) Fill cavity between retainer plate and bearing ¼ full with suitable lubricant (Delco-Remy 1948791 or equivalent). Assemble bearing and slinger (flat washer on some models) in front housing. Press bearing in with suitable collar that fits over outer race. If bearing retainer plate felt seal is hardened, replace retainer plate.

2) Install retainer plate and screws. Press rotor into end frame. Assemble collar, fan, pulley, washer and nut.

3) If rear bearing was removed, support inside of rear housing with hollow cylinder. On 10SI and 27SI models, place flat plate over bearing. Press bearing into housing from outside, until bearing is flush with end frame. On 15SI models, use thin wall tube in space between grease cup and housing to push bearing in until flush with housing. Oil lip of replacement bearing seal, and press seal in with lip away from bearing.

4) Install springs and brushes in brush holder. Install wooden toothpick in hole at bottom of holder to retain brushes. Install voltage regulator. Attach brush holder into rear housing, noting stack-up of parts. Allow toothpick to protrude through hole in rear housing.

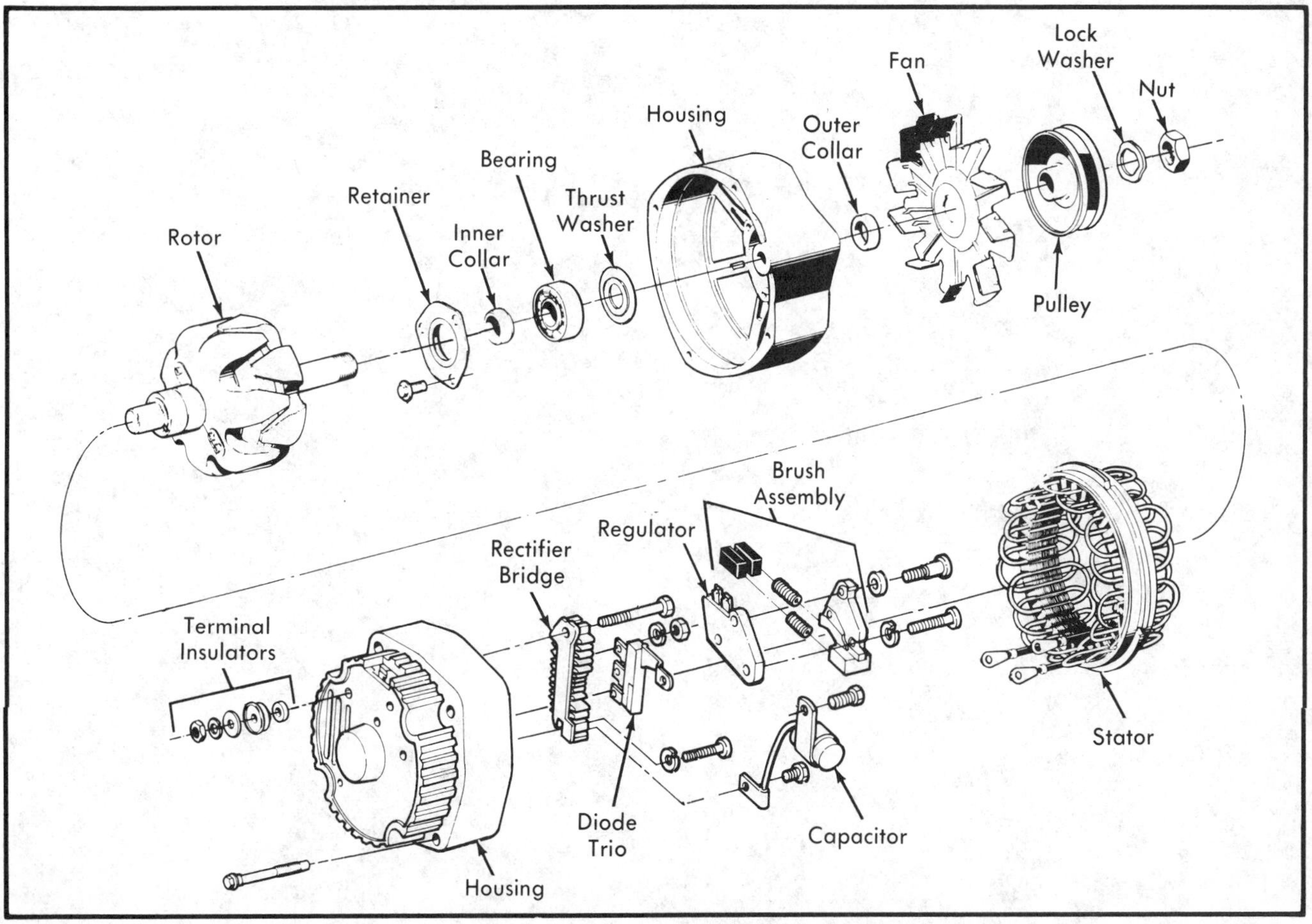

Fig. 8 Exploded View of 10 SI Delcotron Alternator

Alternators & Regulators

DELCO-REMY WITH INTEGRAL REGULATOR (Cont.)

5) Install diode trio lead strap attaching screw and washer. Tighten brush holder screws. Position bridge rectifier on rear housing with insulator between heat sink and rear housing.

6) Install bridge rectifier and battery terminal screws. Connect capacitor lead to bridge rectifier. Position diode trio on end

housing. Install diode trio lead clip screw, making sure insulating washer is over top of diode connector.

7) Install stator on rear housing. Attach stator leads to bridge rectifier terminals. Remove tape covering bearing and join front and rear housings with scribe marks aligned. Install through bolts and tighten. Remove toothpick from brush holder assembly.

DELCO-REMY DELCOTRON SPECIFICATIONS					
Stamped Rated Amp. Output	Test Specification (At 14.0 Volts)				Field Current (Amps.) 12 Volts, 80F
	Amps.	RPM	Amps.	RPM	
37	22	2000	33	5000	4.0-4.5
42	25	2000	38	5000	4.0-4.5
55	30	2000	51	5000	4.0-4.5
61	30	2000	57	5000	4.0-4.5
63	32	2000	60	5000	4.0-4.5
70	55	2000	70	5000	4.0-4.5
80	55	2000	76	5000	4.0-4.5
85	①	①	①	①	①

① — Information not available from manufacturer. Police option.

CHRYSLER CORP. GEAR REDUCTION

Dodge
Plymouth

DESCRIPTION

The starter motor consists of 4 series parallel fields, 4 brushes and a solenoid-shifted, overrunning clutch. The starter has a 3.5 to 1 reduction gear set, built into the starter assembly, and located in a die cast aluminum housing. The starter consists of 2 separate circuits: the supply circuit which provides the heavy current to the motor and the control circuit which activates the solenoid.

TESTING

STARTER CONTROLS

NOTE – *Test solenoid and relay in order as described. Before performing any test, disconnect coil wire from distributor cap and secure to a good ground to prevent engine from starting.*

Starter Solenoid – Connect a heavy jumper wire on starter relay between battery and solenoid terminals. If engine cranks, solenoid is good. Proceed to starter relay test. If engine does not crank or solenoid chatters, check wiring and connections from relay to starter for loose or corroded connections. Repeat test and if starter still fails to crank, starter must be removed for repairs.

Starter Relay – Position automatic transmission gear selector in "N" or "P" position and manual transmission in neutral. Connect a jumper wire on starter relay between battery and ignition terminals. If engine cranks, the starter relay is good. If engine does not crank, connect a second jumper wire to starter relay ground terminal and a good ground. If engine still does not crank, replace starter relay. If engine does crank, relay is functioning, but transmission linkage is out of adjustment (automatic transmission) or neutral safety switch is defective (automatic transmission) or there is a poor ground between relay housing and its mounting surface.

CRANKING CIRCUIT RESISTANCE TESTS

Make the following tests with the engine cranking and all terminals connected. Connect a voltmeter at the following locations: Positive lead to battery positive post and negative lead to battery terminal on starter; positive lead to starter housing and negative lead to negative post on battery; positive lead to engine block and negative lead to battery ground cable. Each of these three connections should show a voltmeter reading of .2 volts or less. If reading exceeds .2 volts, clean or repair cables and connections in circuit. Connect a voltmeter at the following locations: Positive lead to battery positive post and negative lead to cable clamp; positive lead to battery negative post and negative lead to cable clamp. If reading is other than zero on voltmeter, clean or repair cables and connections in circuit.

AMPERAGE DRAW TEST

NOTE – *Engine should be up to operating temperature before performing this test. Heavy oil or a tight engine will increase starter draw amperage.*

1) Connect a suitable battery-starter tester and a remote starter jumper, both according to manufacturer's instructions. Turn variable resistor control knob to off or zero position. Crank engine long enough to read cranking voltage on voltmeter.

CAUTION – *Do not crank engine excessively, or starter may overheat.*

2) Without cranking engine, turn variable resistor control knob on tester until voltmeter reads cranking voltage of previous test. With same voltage reading indicated, amperage reading will be equivalent to starter amperage draw test. See *Starter Specifications.*

SOLENOID WINDINGS

Connect solenoid to a 6 volt DC power supply with an ammeter in series. Connect positive lead of power supply to solenoid terminal and positive lead of ammeter to solenoid sleeve. Connect negative lead of power supply to other ammeter terminal. Turn current on and check draw against hold-in specifications. Check pull-in coil the same way, except connect positive ammeter lead to solenoid lead terminal. Check draw against specifications. If either winding does not meet specifications, or if winding looks burnt or damaged, replace solenoid assembly.

NO LOAD TEST (ON BENCH)

Connect a test ammeter and carbon pile rheostat in series with battery positive post and starter terminal. Connect a voltmeter across starter. Rotate carbon pile to full resistance position. Connect battery cable from battery negative post to starter frame. Adjust rheostat until battery voltage shown on voltmeter reads 11 volts. Amperage draw should be as shown in specifications.

LOCKED RESISTANCE TEST

Mount starter in test bench. Follow test equipment manufacturer's instructions. With battery voltage adjusted to 4 volts, amperage draw should be as shown in specifications.

Starter Specifications	
Application	**Amps.**
Amperage Draw Test	
3.7L and 5.2L	165-180
5.9L	180-200
Solenoid Winding Test (6 Volts@77° F)	
Pull-In Circuit	13-15
Hold-In Circuit	8-9
No Load Test (110 Volts@3700 RPM Minimum)	90
Locked Resistance Test (4 Volts)	475-550

OVERHAUL

DISASSEMBLY

1) Remove through bolts and end head assembly. By pulling outwards, remove armature from gear housing and field frame assembly. Carefully pull field frame assembly from gear housing just far enough to expose terminal screw. Remove terminal screw, then completely remove field frame assembly.

2) Remove nuts and separate solenoid and brush plate assembly from gear housing. Remove nut, steel washer and sealing washer from solenoid terminal. Unwind solenoid lead wire from brush terminal. Remove screws attaching solenoid to brush plate. Remove solenoid from brush plate.

3) On brush plate, remove nut from battery terminal, then remove terminal. From solenoid, remove solenoid contact and plunger assembly. Remove return spring from inside of solenoid moving core. Remove dust cover from gear housing.

CHRYSLER CORP. GEAR REDUCTION (Cont.)

4) Release retainer clip that positions driven gear on pinion shaft.

CAUTION — *Retainer is under tension. Place cloth over assembly to catch it as it flies off.*

5) Remove pinion shaft "C" clip. Push shaft toward rear of housing, and remove retainer ring and thrust washers, clutch and pinion assembly, and 2 shift fork nylon actuators as an assembly. Remove driven gear and friction washer. Pull shifting fork forward, and remove solenoid moving core. Remove shifting fork retainer pin and shifting fork assembly.

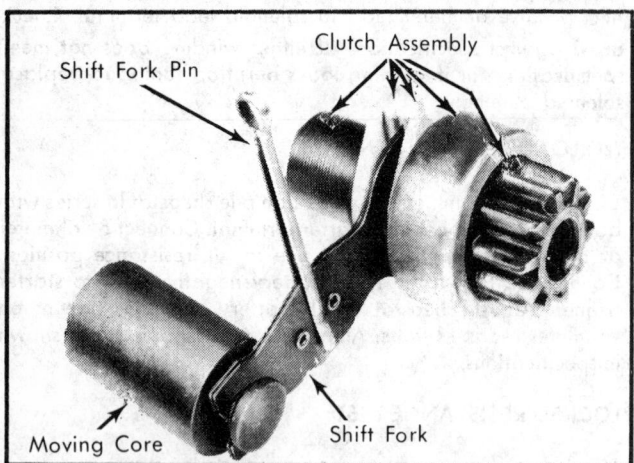

Fig. 1 Assembled View of Shift Fork and Clutch Assembly

PARTS REPLACEMENT & TESTING

Brushes and Springs — Replace brushes if oil soaked or worn more than 1/2 length of new brushes. When soldering solenoid lead, use high temperature solder and resin flux. Measure spring tension with spring scale attached under spring near end. Pull on line parallel to edge of brush and note reading just as spring end leaves brush. Replace if tension is not within specifications.

Spring Tension	
Application	**Tension**
All Models	32-36 ozs.

Starter Shaft Bushings — Inspect bearing surfaces for wear. Insert starter shaft into bushing and check for side play. Replace end head if its bushing is worn. Replace other bushings, using a suitable puller (C-3944). Service bushings are presized and do not require burnishing or reaming.

Starter Clutch Unit — Pinion should rotate smoothly in one direction (not necessarily easy) and should not rotate in the opposite direction. If not functioning properly, or if pinion worn, chipped or burred, replace assembly.

CAUTION — *Do not immerse in cleaning solvent, as the unit is pre-lubricated and lubricant will wash out.*

Armature — Check for shorted armature coils in a growler. Check for grounded coils by touching one test light probe to armature shaft and other probe to each commutator bar. Lamp should not light. If lamp lights, armature coils are grounded and armature must be replaced. Commutator should be smooth and clean, and runout must not exceed .004". If runout is excessive, reface in a lathe.

Field Coil Assembly — With field frame removed from starter, drill out rivet attaching field coil lead and shunt coil lead to frame, then insulate leads from frame. Test for ground with 110V test lamp by touching one probe to field coil lead and other probe to field frame. Lamp should not light, if lamp lights, field coils are grounded. Replace field coils and field frame as an assembly.

CLEANING

Do not immerse parts in cleaning solvent. Clutch outer housing and pinion gear may be cleaned with a cloth moistened with cleaning solvent and then wiped dry. Clean all corrosion from solenoid assembly and inside of solenoid housing. Clean terminal contacts and contactor with crocus cloth.

REASSEMBLY

1) Ensure that shift fork plates have approximately 1/16" side movement, then lubricate sparingly between plates with SAE 10 engine oil. Position shift fork in housing then bend one tip of pin at a 15° angle away from housing. Fork and retainer pin must operate freely after tip of pin is bent. Install solenoid moving core and engage shifting fork.

2) Start pinion shaft into drive housing, then install friction washer and drive gear, clutch and pinion assembly, thrust washer, retaining ring and thrust washer. Shift fork must engage clutch actuators properly and friction washer must be positioned on shoulder of pinion shaft splines before driven gear is positioned. Install driven gear, retainer clip, pinion shaft "C" clip and starter solenoid return spring into bore of movable core.

3) Install solenoid contact plunger assembly into solenoid. Contact spring must be positioned on shaft of solenoid contact and plunger assembly. Assemble battery terminal stud in brush holder. Position seal on brush holder plate. Start solenoid lead wire through hole in brush holder, then install solenoid stud, insulating washer, flat washer, and nut.

4) Wrap lead wire tightly around brush terminal post, then solder with high temperature resin core solder and resin flux. Install brush holder to solenoid attaching screws. Install solenoid coil and brush plate assembly into starter gear housing, then install and tighten nuts.

5) Install armature thrust washer in brushes with brushes resting on washer tabs (washer will hold brushes out and facilitate armature installation). Install brush terminal screw. Position field frame in correct position on gear housing and install armature in field frame and gear housing. Carefully engage splines of shaft with reduction gear by rotating armature slightly. Install thrust washer on armature shaft. Position starter end head assembly and tighten through bolts securely.

Starters

CHRYSLER CORP. GEAR REDUCTION (Cont.)

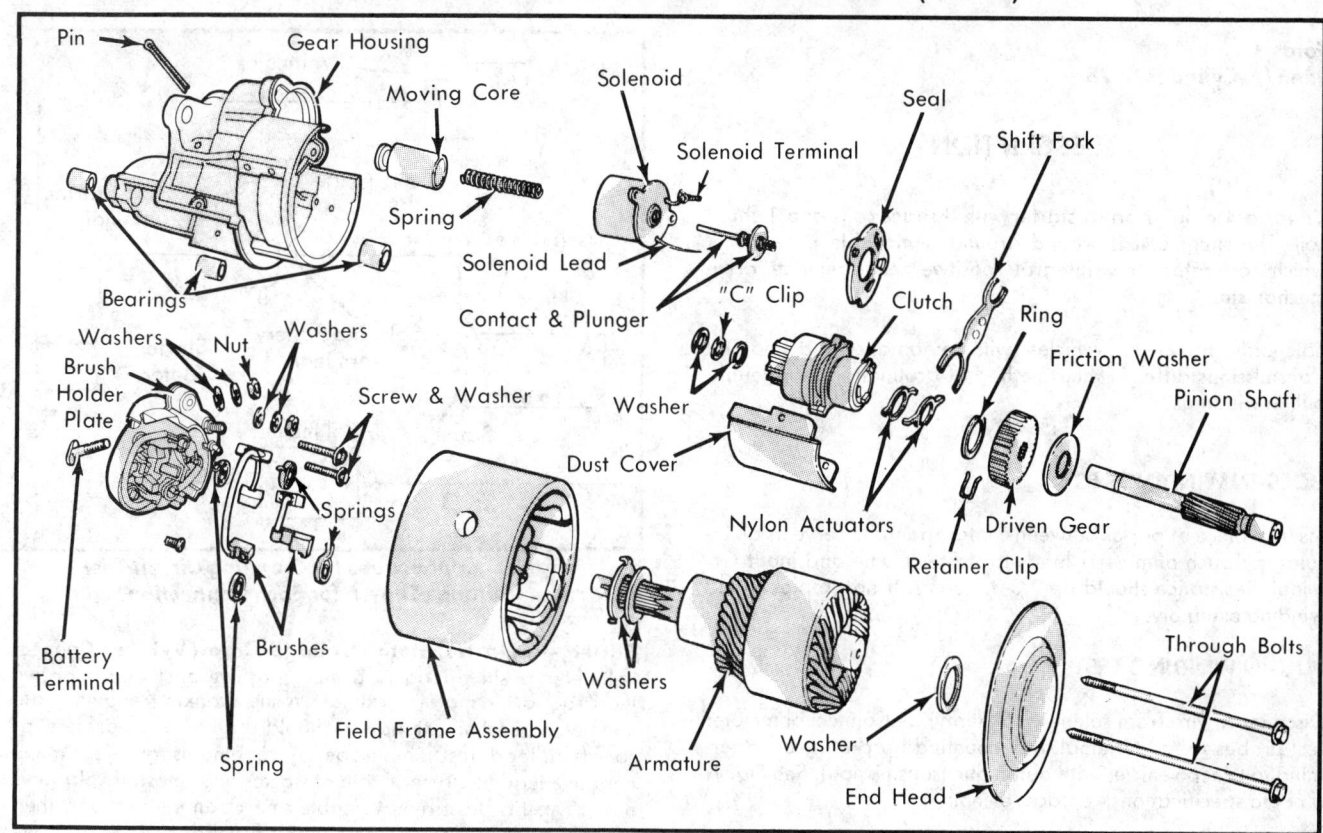

Fig. 2 Exploded View of Chrysler Corp. Reduction Gear Starter

MOTORCRAFT POSITIVE ENGAGEMENT

Ford
Jeep (6-Cylinder & V8)

DESCRIPTION

Unit is a 4-pole, 4-brush starter with 3 series coils and 1 shunt coil. The shunt coil is wound around a movable pole piece, which operates the integral positive engagement drive mechanism.

Solenoids for Jeep vehicles with automatic and manual transmissions differ in their method of grounding the solenoid pull-in windings.

TESTING

HOLD-IN WINDING TEST

Insert a piece of paper between contact points to serve as an insulator. Touch ohmmeter leads to starter frame and input terminal. Resistance should be 2.0-3.5 ohms. If not, replace field winding assembly.

PULL-IN WINDING TEST

Disconnect wire from solenoid "S" terminal. Connect ohmmeter test probes to "S" terminal and mounting bracket (ground terminal on Jeep vehicles with automatic transmission). See Fig. 1. If not to specifications, replace solenoid.

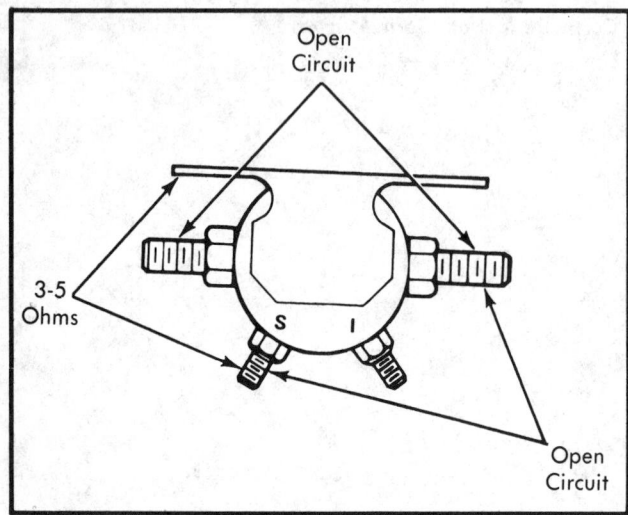

Fig. 1   Ohmmeter Test Connections for Solenoid

NOTE — Check for a poor ground by connecting ohmmeter leads to battery negative terminal and "S" terminal. If reading is greater than results received between "S" terminal and mounting bracket, solenoid has poor ground.

STARTER CRANKING CIRCUIT TESTS

Before performing tests, remove and ground coil secondary wire (disconnect at distributor). Place transmission in neutral or park and apply parking brake. Be sure battery is fully charged. When making voltmeter connections, be sure to connect leads to battery posts or threaded terminals and not just to cable ends.

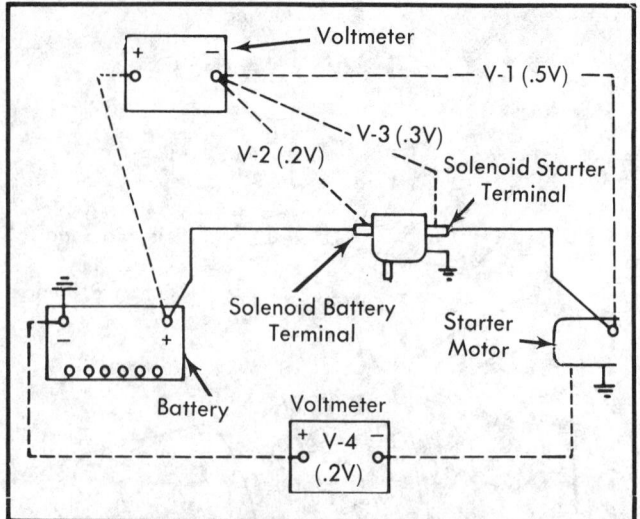

**Fig. 2   Connections for Cranking Circuit Test
(Voltages Shown for Each Connection)**

Battery-to-Starter Motor Voltage Drop (V-1) — Connect voltmeter positive lead to battery positive post and negative lead to starter motor terminal. While cranking engine, note voltmeter reading. Reading should be .5 volts or less at specified load test amperage. If reading is greater, move negative lead to starter cable at starter and retest. If voltage is now .5 volt or less, remove cable and clean connections, then retest at starter motor terminal. If voltage is still above specifications, test individual cables between battery and starter as follows:

Battery-to-Solenoid Voltage Drop (V-2) — Connect voltmeter positive lead to battery positive post and negative lead to battery terminal of solenoid. While cranking engine, note voltmeter reading. Reading should be .2 volt or less at specified load test amperage. If just below or at specification, repair solenoid. If reading is greater, remove cable, clean connections, and retest. If reading is still above maximum (.2V), replace cable.

Solenoid Voltage Drop (V-3) — Connect voltmeter positive lead to battery positive post and negative lead to starter CABLE at solenoid. While cranking engine, note voltmeter reading. Reading should be .3 volt or less at specified load test amperage. If at or just below maximum reading, repair solenoid-to-starter cable. If reading is above maximum, move negative lead to starter TERMINAL at solenoid and retest. If reading is now .3 volt or less, remove and clean cable connector, then retest. If still in excess of .3 volt, replace solenoid. If battery-to-starter circuit (V-1) reading is now greater than .5 volt, replace solenoid-to-starter cable.

Starter Motor Ground Voltage Drop (V-4) — Connect voltmeter negative lead to starter motor housing and positive lead to battery negative post. While cranking engine, note voltmeter reading. Reading should be .2 volt or less at specified load test amperage. If more, move the positive lead to ground cable attaching bolt at engine and retest. If reading is now less than .2 volt, check starter motor for loose mounting bolts, corrosion or dirt on mounting surface. If reading is now more than .2 volt, examine ground cable for bad connections or bad cable.

MOTORCRAFT POSITIVE ENGAGEMENT (Cont.)

STARTER LOAD TEST

Connect a tester and battery into starter circuit. *See Fig. 3.* Crank engine with ignition coil secondary wire grounded and note voltage on tester. Stop cranking engine and turn load control knob until voltage reading is exactly the same as it was when engine was cranking. Read current draw on ammeter scale. If not within specifications, starter is defective and must be overhauled.

NOTE — *Do not take amperage draw reading until starter has obtained maximum RPM.*

Load Test Specifications	
Application	**Amperes**
Ford	
4" Starter	150-200
4½" Starter	150-180
Jeep	
6 Cyl.	150-180
8 Cyl.	160-210

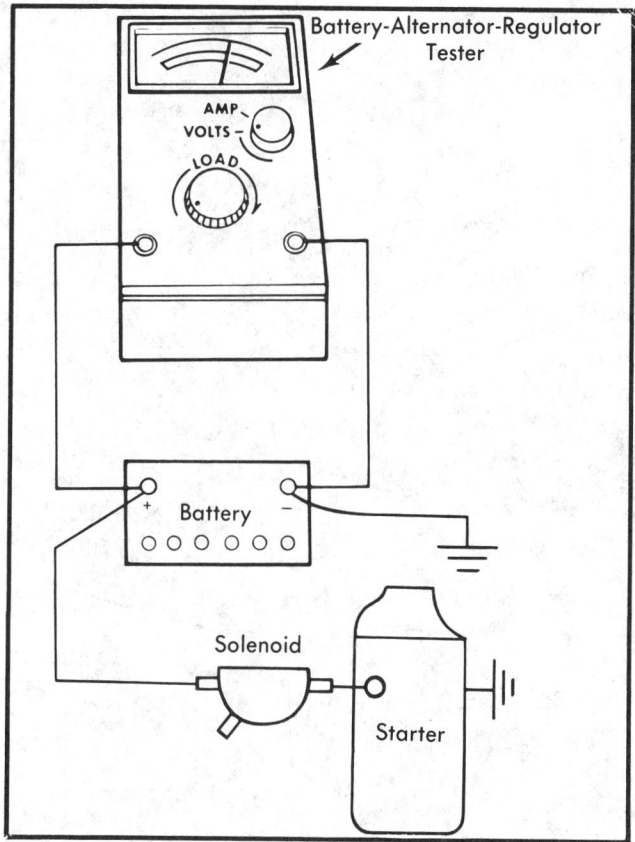

Fig. 3   Connections for Load Test

STARTER NO-LOAD TEST

With a tester and battery connected to starter, operate starter motor and note voltage reading and tachometer reading. *See Fig. 4.* Disconnect the starter from battery. Turn load control knob until voltage reading is same as when starter is connected. Read the amperage draw, and if

amperage reading is less than specifications, starter has high electrical resistance. If starter RPM is less than specifications, worn bushings or bent armature shaft is indicated.

No-Load Specifications	
Application	**Specifications**
Voltage	12 Volts
Amperage	
Ford	
4" Starter	70 Amps.
4½" Starter	80 Amps.
Jeep	77 Amps.
RPM Range	8900-9600

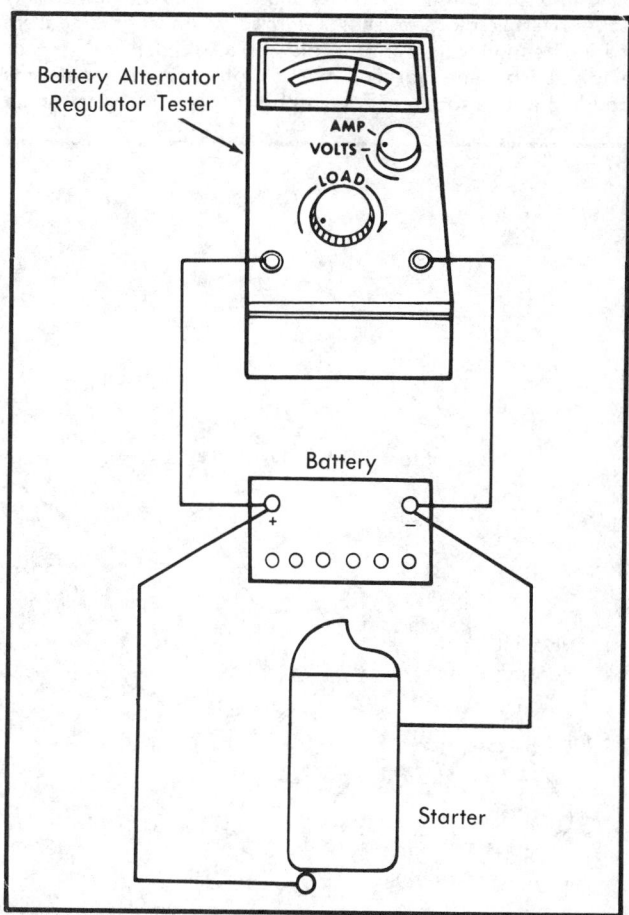

Fig. 4   Connections for No-Load Test

OVERHAUL

DISASSEMBLY

1) Remove cover screw, cover, through bolts, starter drive end housing and starter drive plunger lever return spring. Remove pivot pin retaining plunger lever and remove plunger lever and armature.

2) Remove stop ring retainer, stop ring from starter drive gear and starter drive gear assembly. Remove brush end plate and

Starters

MOTORCRAFT POSITIVE ENGAGEMENT (Cont.)

insulator assembly, then remove brushes from brush holder and lift out brush holder. Note location of brush holder with respect to end terminal.

3) Remove ground brushes-to-frame retaining screws. On the field coil which operates drive gear actuating lever, bend the edges on the retaining sleeve and remove sleeve and retainers.

4) Remove 3 coil retaining screws with tool 10044-A and an arbor press. Cut the field coil connection at the switch post lead and remove small diameter ground wire from upper tab riveted to frame. Remove pole shoes and coils from frame. Cut the positive brush leads from fields coils as close to the field connection point as possible.

PARTS REPLACEMENT & TESTING

Brushes & Springs — Check brush holders for broken springs and insulated brush holders for shorts to ground. Tighten any loose rivets. Replace brushes if worn to ¼" in length. Measure spring tension with spring scale hooked under spring near end, pull on line parallel to edge of brush and note the reading just as spring end leaves brush. Spring tension should be 40 ozs. on 4" starters, 80 ozs. on 4½" starters. If replacing brushes, use a 300 watt soldering iron and rosin core solder.

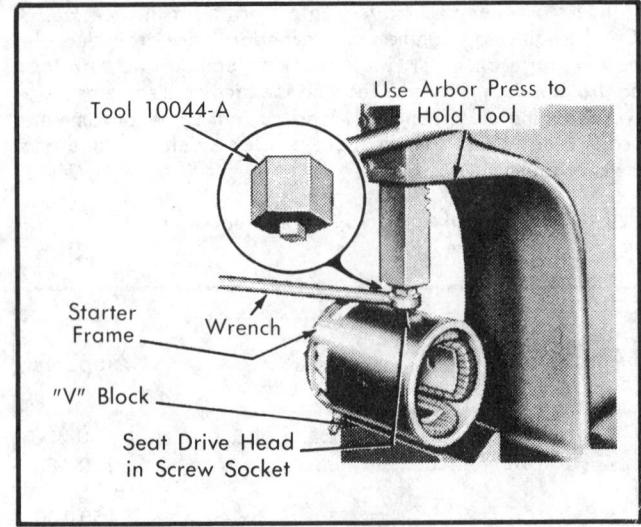

Fig. 5   Removing Pole Shoe Screw

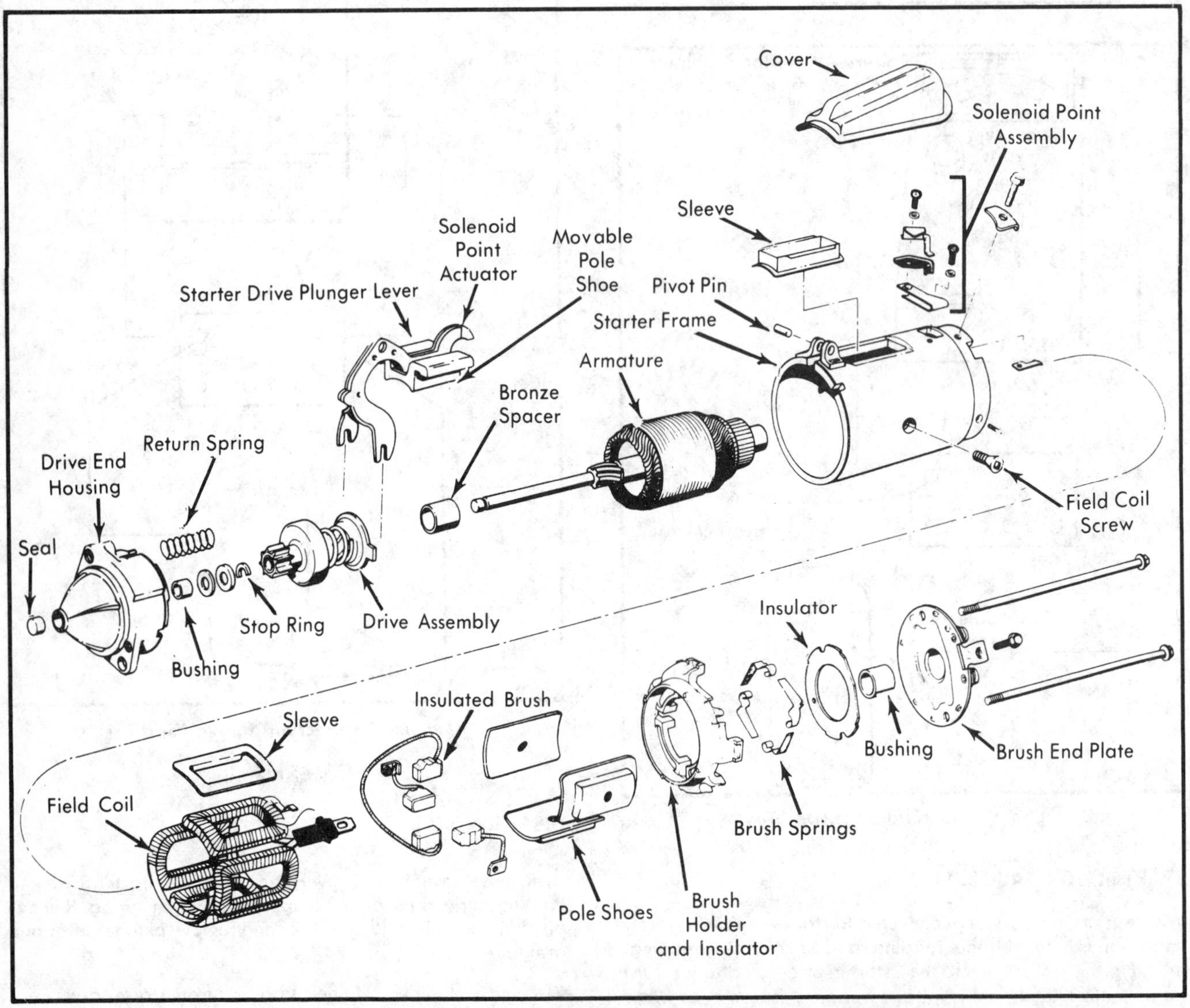

Fig. 6   Exploded View of Motorcraft Starter Motor Assembly

MOTORCRAFT POSITIVE ENGAGEMENT (Cont.)

Field Coil Assembly — Inspect the field coils for burned or broken insulation and continuity. Check field brush connections and lead insulation. Check for grounds in the field coil windings.

Armature — Check armature for shorted coils with a growler and a test light. Touch one test lead to armature core and the other to each commutator bar one at a time. If light lights, armature is shorted to ground and must be replaced. Place switch on growler in GROWLER position and hold steel blade parallel to and touching armature core. Rotate armature and if blade vibrates at any point, that area is shorted and armature must be replaced. Inspect armature shaft for excessive wear. Inspect windings for broken or burned insulation. If commutator is rough or more than .005" out of round, turn down in a lathe, removing only enough material to provide a smooth, even surface.

REASSEMBLY

1) Position 3 coils and pole pieces and install attaching screws. As pole shoe screws are tightened, strike the frame with a soft hammer to seat and align pole shoes, then stake the screws.

2) Install the remaining coil and retainer and bend the tabs to secure coil to frame. Position the new field brush lead on field coil terminal. Install clip to hold brush lead to terminal. Solder lead, clip and terminal together with a 300 watt iron and rosin core solder.

3) Ground the coil around the retaining sleeve by placing the small diameter wire from the coil under the copper tab which attaches the contact to frame. Install ground brushes to frame with screws. Lubricate armature shaft splines with Lubriplate (or equivalent). Install the drive gear assembly on the armature shaft. Install new retaining stop ring and stop retainer.

4) Install armature in frame. Partially fill drive end housing bearing bore with grease and position drive gear plunger lever to frame and starter drive assembly and install pivot pin. Install plunger lever return spring and drive end housing to frame. Install brush holder, brushes and springs. Install brush holder insulator.

5) Position end plate to frame and align plate locator with frame slot. Install and tighten through bolts. DO NOT pinch brush leads when installing end plate. Position drive gear plunger lever cover on starter and tighten cover screw.

Starters

DELCO-REMY ENCLOSED HOUSING

Chevrolet
GMC
Jeep (4-Cylinder Only)

DESCRIPTION

Starter is a 12-volt, 4-pole unit of conventional design and has a solenoid pinion shaft (overrunning clutch) with entire mechanism enclosed within the housing. Field assembly consists of four series coils or combination of series coils with one or more shunt coils. Brush assemblies are completely enclosed within field frame at commutator end so entire starter and drive assembly is protected.

Starter solenoid is flange mounted on drive end housing and has a compression-type return spring located inside the solenoid case. Jeep models use the 5MT starter. All others except diesel Chevrolet and GMC models use the 10MT starter. Diesel models use the 20MT starter, which differs only in that it uses a center bearing.

Jeep "CJ" and Scrambler models with 4-cylinder engine and automatic transmission have a starter motor relay, which is energized when ignition key is in "START" position and transmission selector lever is in either "NEUTRAL" or "PARK" position. Battery voltage is then applied to pull-in and hold-in windings.

APPLICATION

Vehicle	Delco-Remy Part No.
Chevrolet & GMC	
4.1L (250")	
"C" & "K" Models	1108778
All Other Models	1108779
4.8L (292")	
All Models	1108780
5.0L (305")	
"C" & "K" Models	1109056
All Other Models	1109798
5.7L (350")	
Gasoline Models	1109052
Diesel Models	1109216
7.4L (454")	
All Models	1108776
Jeep	
2.5L (151")	1109526

TESTING

SOLENOID WINDINGS TEST

NOTE — Tests are performed with all leads disconnected. Complete tests in minimum amount of time to prevent solenoid from overheating.

Hold-In Winding — Connect an ammeter, voltmeter and battery into starter circuit. See Fig. 1. Use a carbon pile to decrease battery voltage to 10 volts. Ammeter should read 14.5-16.5 amperes. If amperage is above 16.5, then winding is shorted or grounded. If amperage draw is below 14.5 amperes, excessive resistance is indicated.

NOTE — On Jeep 4-cylinder engines, specifications are 15-20 amps. at 10 volts for hold-in windings; 20-30 amps. at 5 volts for pull-in windings.

Both Windings in Parallel — Ground the "M" terminal and connect a 10 volt source (in series with ammeter) to solenoid switch terminal and ground. Current draw should be 40.5-47.5 amps.

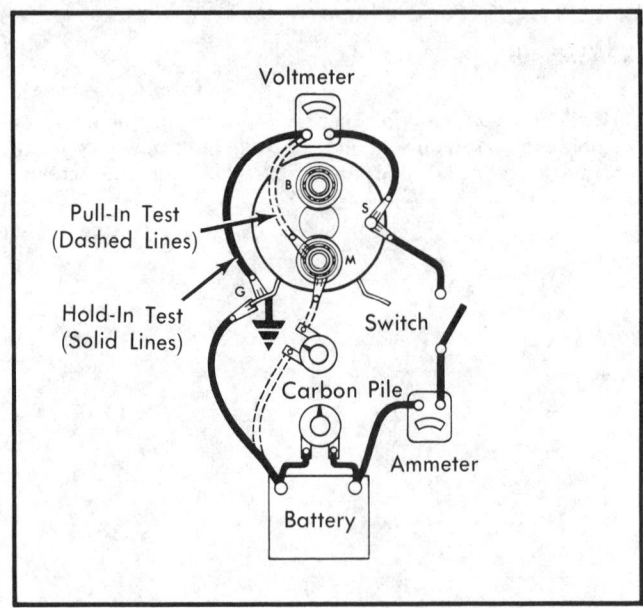

Fig. 1   Connections for Testing Solenoid Windings

STARTER NO LOAD TEST

To perform test, connect a tachometer, ammeter and voltmeter into starter circuit. See Fig. 2. Adjust carbon pile to voltage indicated in Delco-Remy Starter Specifications, then read current draw and armature speed to ensure they are within specifications.

CAUTION — Do not apply voltage greater than specified, as excessive voltage may cause armature to throw windings due to excessive speed.

NOTE — Low free speed and high current draw indicates too much friction, shorted armature, or grounded armature or fields. Failure to operate with high current draw indicates a direct ground in terminal or fields or frozen bearings. Failure to operate with no current draw indicates an open field, open armature coils, or broken brush springs, worn brushes, or high commutator insulation. If no-load speed is low and there is low current draw, suspect high internal resistance due to poor connection, defective leads, or dirty commutator. A high free speed and high current draw usually indicates shorted fields.

DELCO-REMY ENCLOSED HOUSING (Cont.)

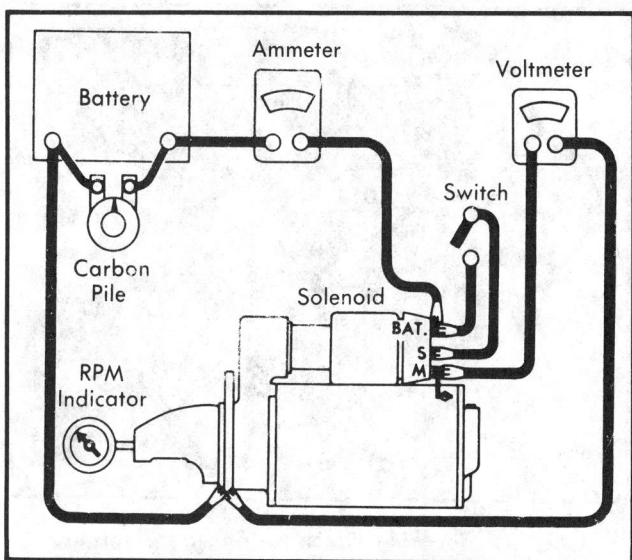

Fig. 2   Connections for No Load Test

DELCO-REMY STARTER SPECIFICATIONS

Delco-Remy Number	No Load Test		
	Amps. ①	RPM	Volts
1108776	65-95	7,500-10,500	9
1108778	50-80	5,500-10,500	9
1108779	50-80	5,500-10,500	9
1108780	50-80	3,500-6,000	9
1109052	65-95	7,500-10,000	9
1109056	50-80	5,500-10,000	9
1109216	.....	.....	.....
1109526	45-70	7,000-11,900	9
1109798	50-80	5,500-10,500	9

① — Includes the solenoid.

OVERHAUL

DISASSEMBLY

1) Disconnect field coil connector from solenoid motor terminal. On diesel models, remove solenoid mounting screws and rotate solenoid 90° and remove along with solenoid plunger spring.

2) Remove 2 through bolts, commutator end frame, field frame assembly, and washer. On diesel models, remove insulator. On gasoline models, remove armature assembly from drive housing and thrust collar from armature shaft.

3) On diesel models, remove shift lever pivot bolt, center bearing screws and drive gear housing from armature shaft. Shift lever and plunger assembly will now fall away from starter clutch.

4) Slide a ⅝" deep socket over pinion shaft and with a hammer, strike the socket against the retainer to drive the retainer off the snap ring. Remove snap ring from groove in armature shaft.

5) On diesel models, remove retainer, clutch assembly, fiber washer and center bearing. Remove roll pin and remove shift

lever and plunger. On gasoline models, roller clutches are serviced as an assembly only.

CLEANING

Clean all parts by wiping with clean cloth. Do not clean armature, field coils, or drive assembly in any type of grease dissolving solvent as this will damage insulation and wash lubricant out of drive assembly.

PARTS REPLACEMENT & TESTING

Armature — Test armature for shorted coils with a growler. Check for grounded coils with a 110 volt test lamp. Place one test lead on armature core or shaft, and other test lead on commutator. Lamp should not light. If lamp lights, armature is grounded and should be replaced.

CAUTION — *Some starters have molded-type commutator, and insulation must not be undercut on these models as this may cause serious damage to commutator.*

Field Coils — Check with 110 volt test light. Place one test lead on field coil terminal strap, touch other test lead to field coil brush lead (check series coils and shunt coils separately at appropriate terminals). Lamp should light. If lamp does not light, coils are open. Check for grounds by placing one test lead on field armature strap, touch other lead to armature core or shaft. If lamp lights, 1 or more coils are grounded.

CAUTION — *Shunt coil ground lead must be disconnected and all field terminals insulated from frame when making this test.*

Brushes, Springs, & Holders — Replace brushes if worn to one-half of original length, or if oil-soaked or pitted. Check brush spring tension and replace springs if weak or distorted. Deformed or bent brush holders can be replaced by service units which are installed with screws and nuts.

Drive & Pinion Assembly — Pinion should turn freely in overrun direction and should not slip in drive direction. Check spring for correct tension and drive collar for wear (these parts can be removed for replacement by forcing collar toward clutch and removing lock ring from end of tube). Replace drive assembly if pinion teeth are worn, chipped, or cracked.

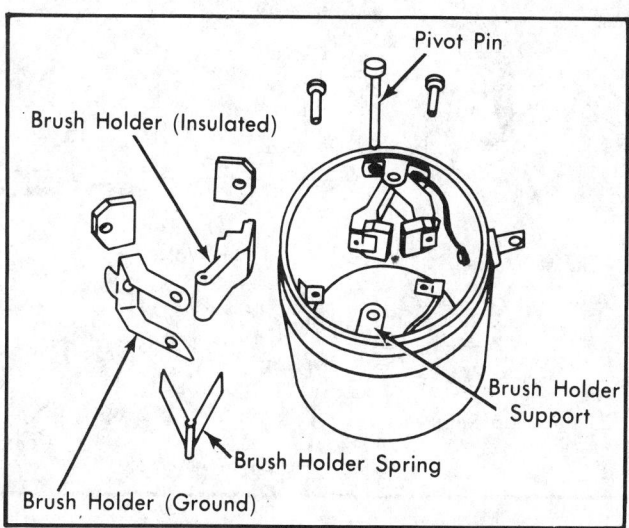

Fig. 3   Brush Holder and Assembly

DELCO-REMY ENCLOSED HOUSING (Cont.)

Overrunning Clutch Slippage — With clutch attached to armature, wrap the armature in a shop towel and place in a vise. Using a $^{15}/_{16}$" 12 point deep socket and torque wrench, place socket on clutch and turn counterclockwise. The clutch should not slip with up to 50 ft. lbs. of torque applied. If it slips, replace clutch.

Pinion Clearance — Disconnect motor field coil connector and insulate it carefully. Connect a battery from the solenoid switch terminal to solenoid frame. Momentarily flash a jumper lead from motor terminal to solenoid frame. This shifts pinion into cranking position. Push pinion back toward commutator end to eliminate slack. Measure distance between pinion and pinion stop. When installing starter, check clearance between pinion and flywheel ring gear teeth. Insert gauge (.200" diameter wire, about 3" long, with a ¼ to ½" 90° bend in end) between pinion tooth and ring gear. Center pinion tooth between flywheel teeth when making measurement.

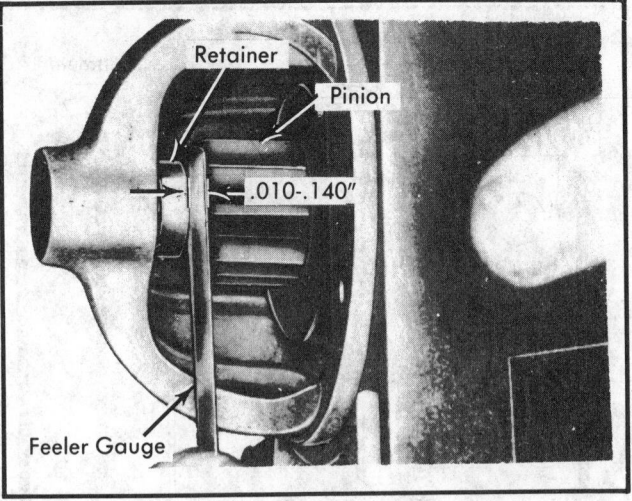

Fig. 4 Checking Pinion-to-Housing Clearance

Pinion Clearance	
Application	**Clearance**
Pinion-to-Housing	①.010-.140"
Pinion-to-Flywheel Clearance	.200"

① — Measured between pinion stop (retainer) with pinion in engaged position.

REASSEMBLY

1) On diesel model starters, assemble armature and clutch as follows: Lubricate drive end of armature shaft with silicone

lubricant and install center bearing, fiber washer and clutch assembly onto armature, with pinion away from armature. Slide retainer onto shaft and install snap ring and thrust washer.

2) Position retainer and thrust washer with snap ring in between. Using pliers, grip retainer and washer and squeeze until snap ring is forced into retainer and is held in groove in armature shaft.

3) On all models, lubricate drive gear housing bushing with silicone lubricant. Engage shift lever yoke with clutch and slide complete assembly into drive gear housing.

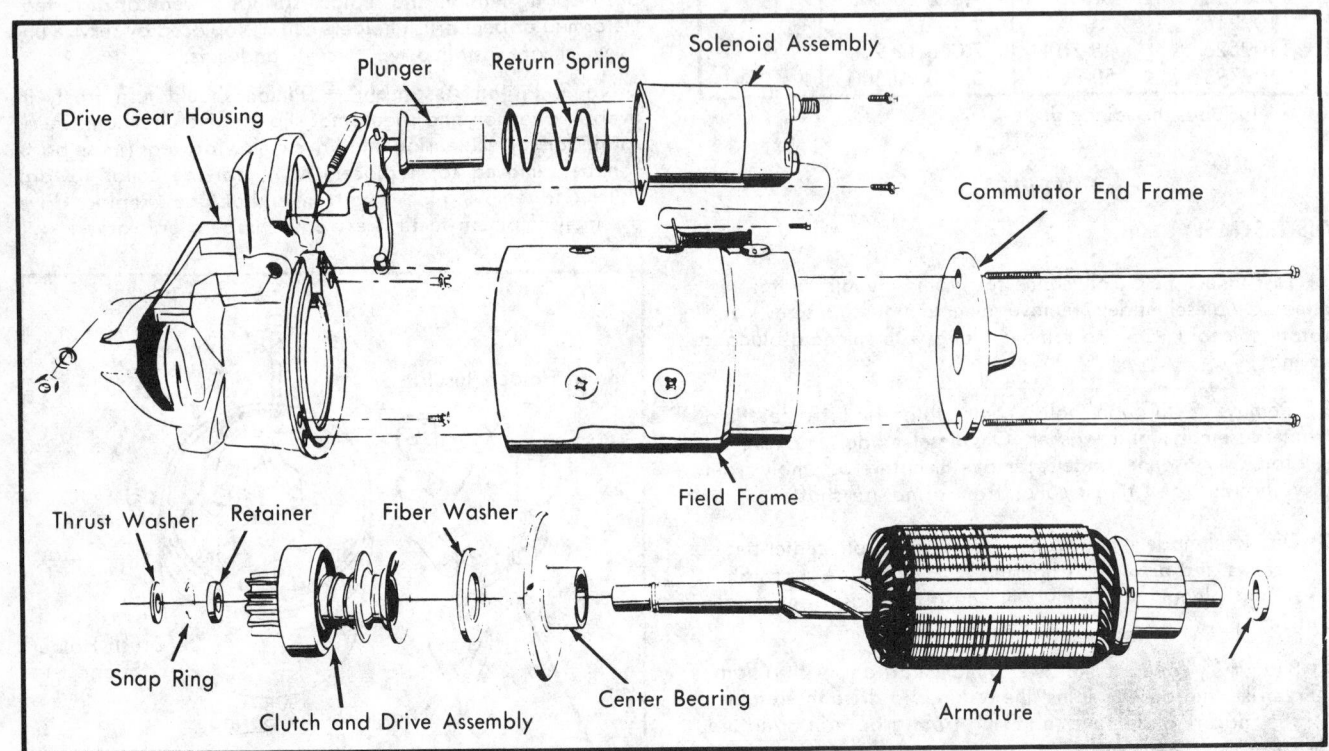

Fig. 5 Exploded View of Delco-Remy 20MT Starter Assembly
(5 and 10MT Starters Similar Except without Center Bearing)

DELCO-REMY ENCLOSED HOUSING (Cont.)

4) Install center bearing screws (diesel only) and shift lever pivot bolt. Tighten securely. Install solenoid assembly on drive gear housing. Apply sealer (No. 1050026) to solenoid flange where it meets the drive housing and field frame, using care not to damage brushes.

5) Position field frame against drive gear housing on alignment pin using care not to damage brushes. Lubricate commutator end frame bushing with silicone lubricant. Install washer on armature shaft and slide end frame onto shaft and install through bolts. On diesel models, install insulator and then end frame onto shaft. Then install through bolts, making sure they pass through bolt holes in insulator.

6) Connect the field coil connector to the solenoid terminal. Check pinion clearance as outlined under Parts Replacement and Testing in this article.

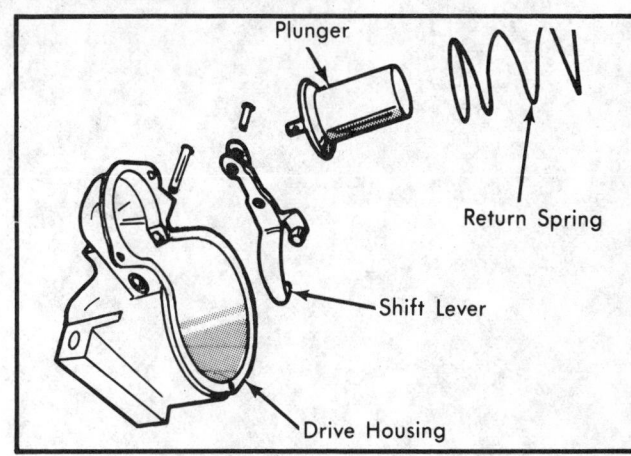

Fig. 6 Exploded View of Shift Lever Assembly

Section 5

WIRING DIAGRAMS

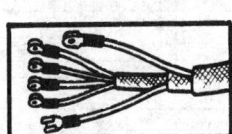

Contents

ARRANGEMENT OF DATA

The Wiring Diagram Section contains chassis wiring diagrams spread across four pages for efficient reading. The diagrams are arranged alphabetically by vehicle make and model.

NOTE — ALSO SEE GENERAL INDEX

IMPORTANT

Because of the great number of model names used by vehicle manufacturers, accurate identification of models is important.
See Model Identification at the front of this publication.

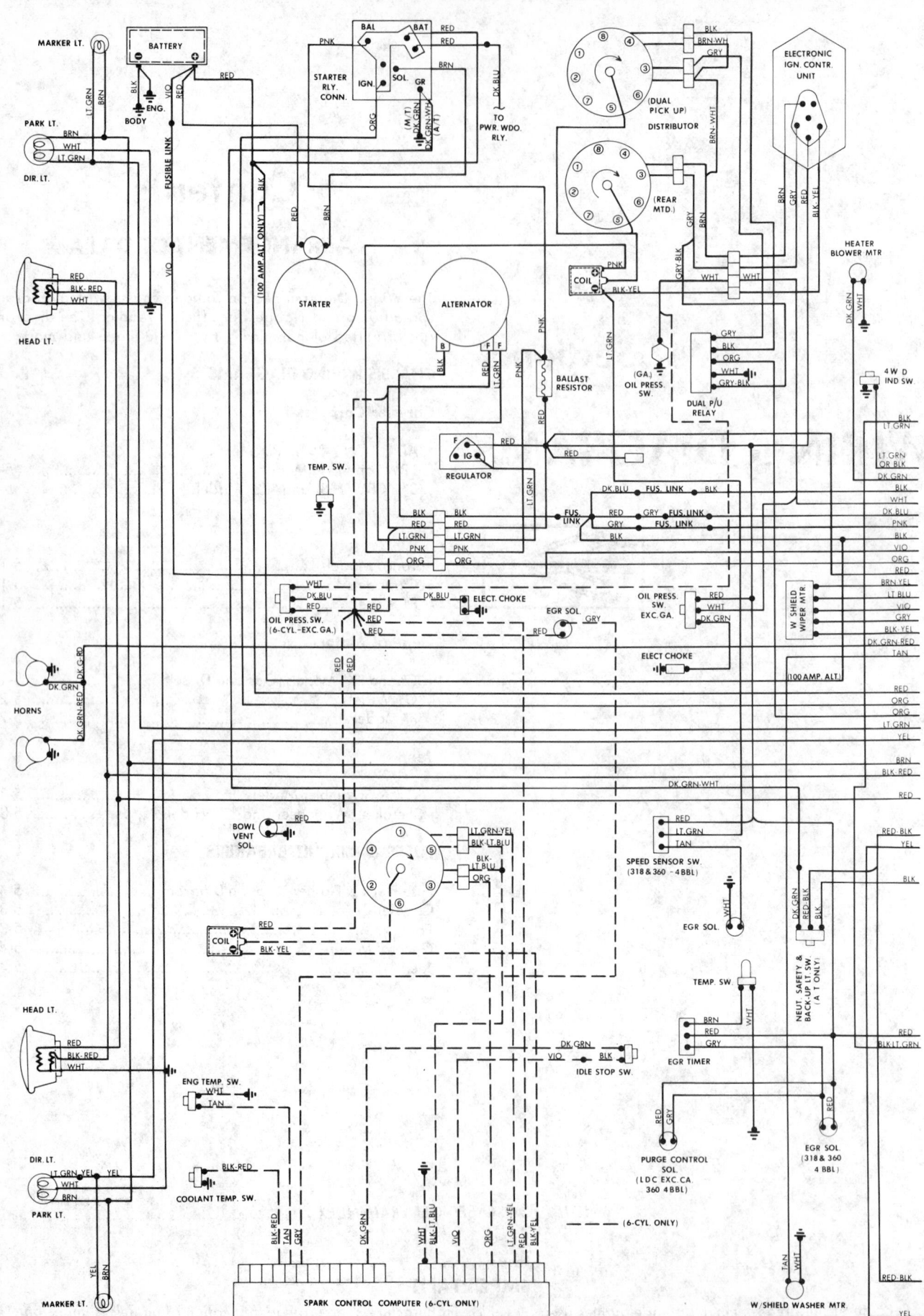

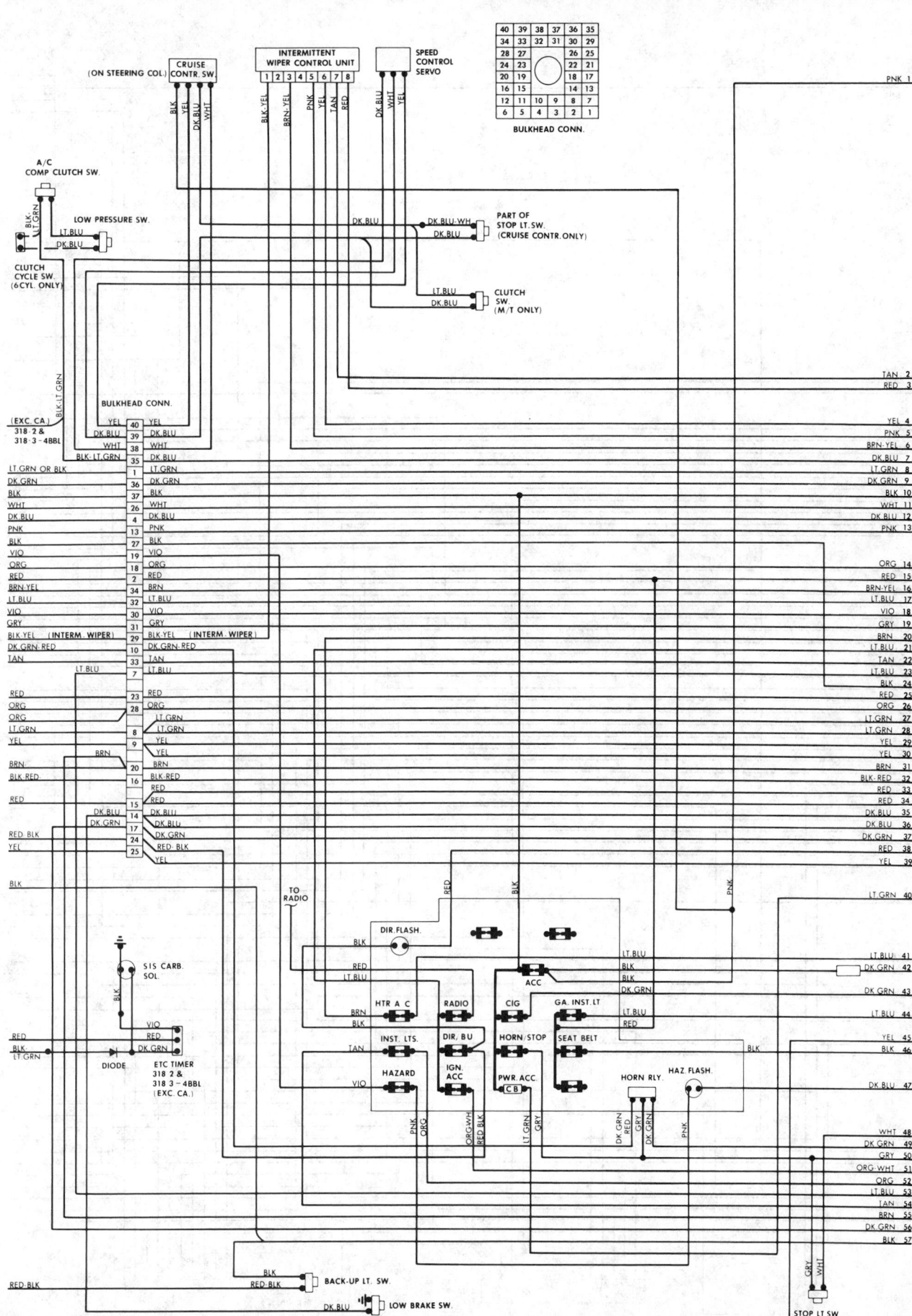

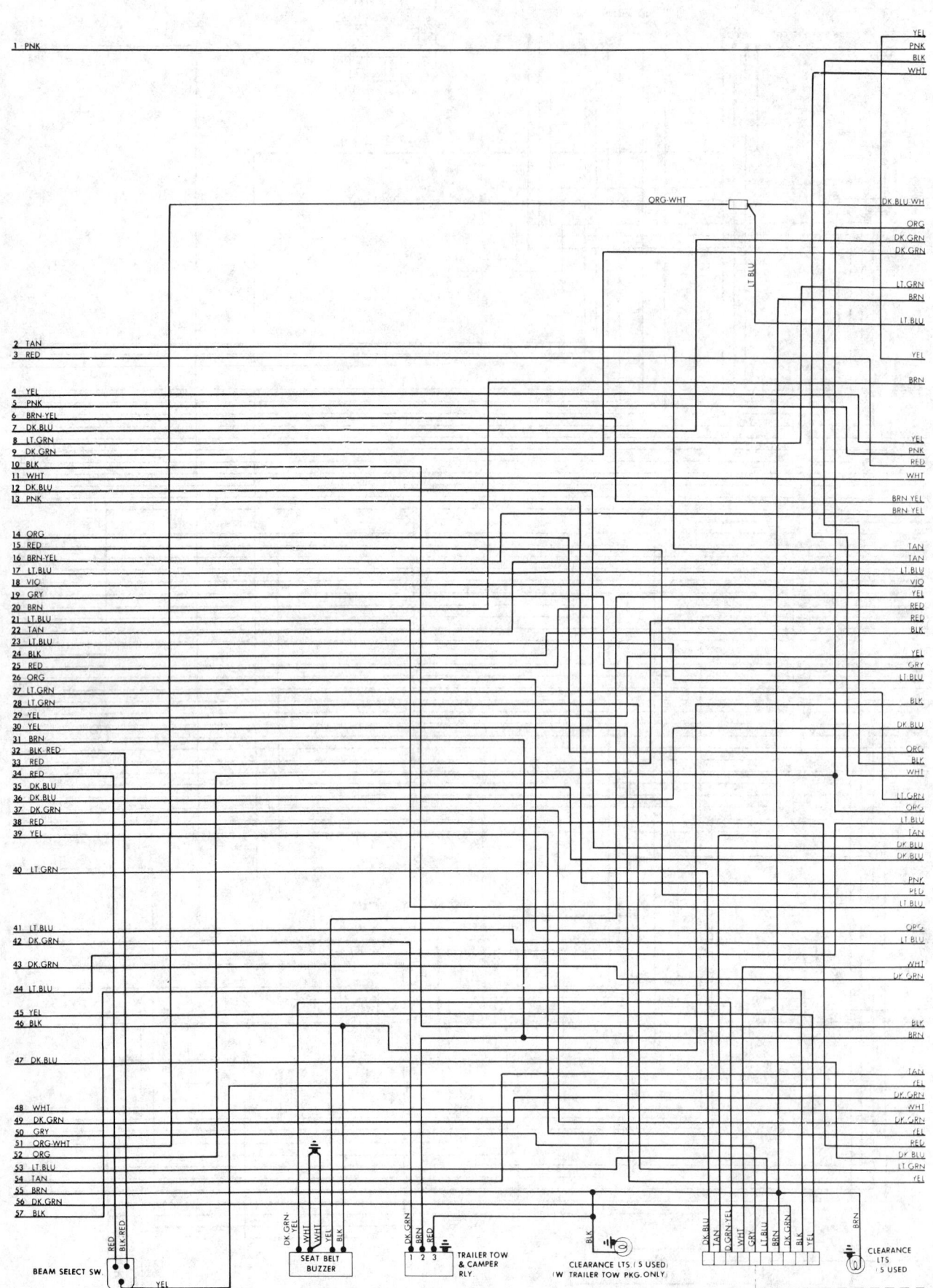

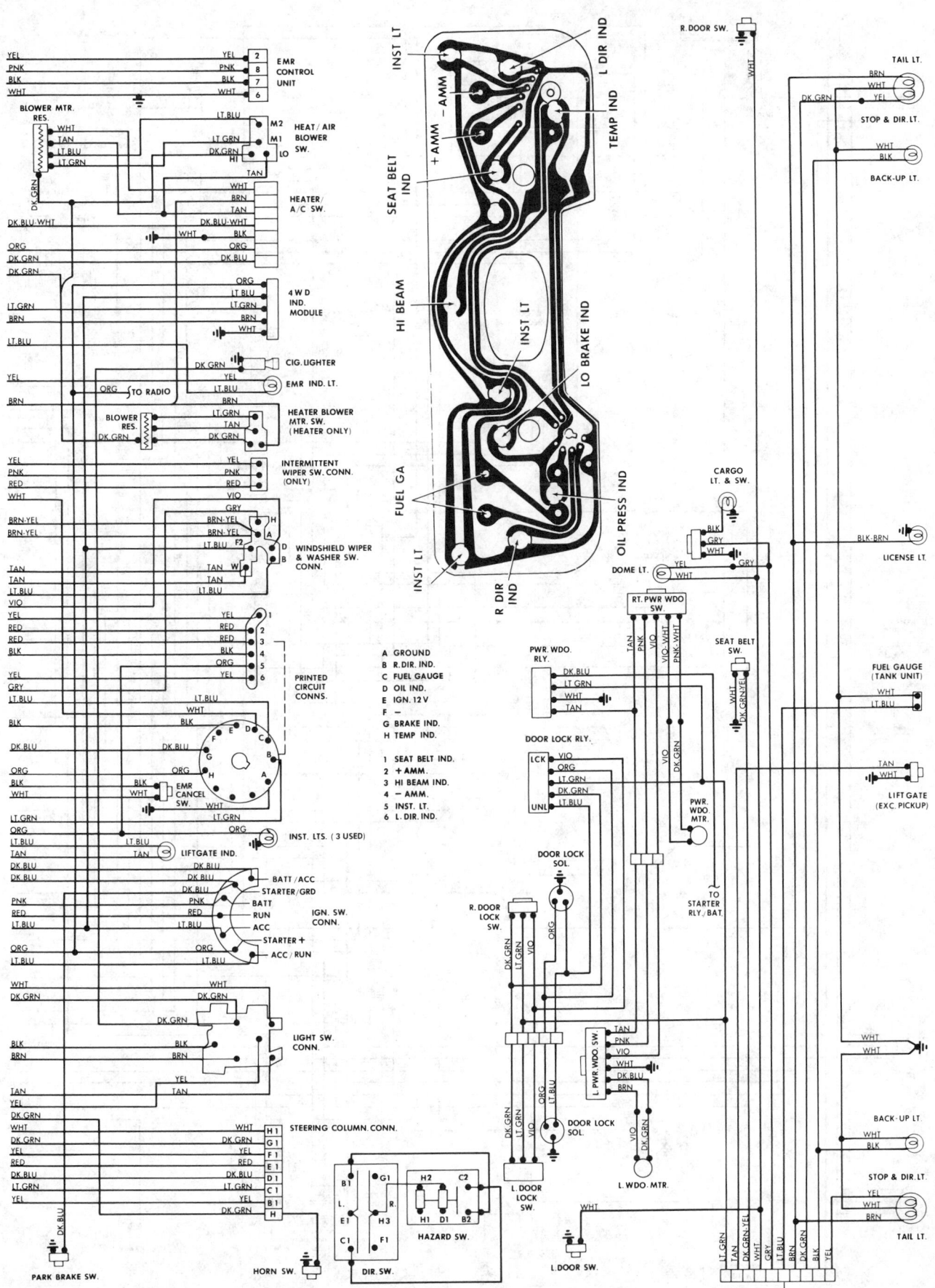

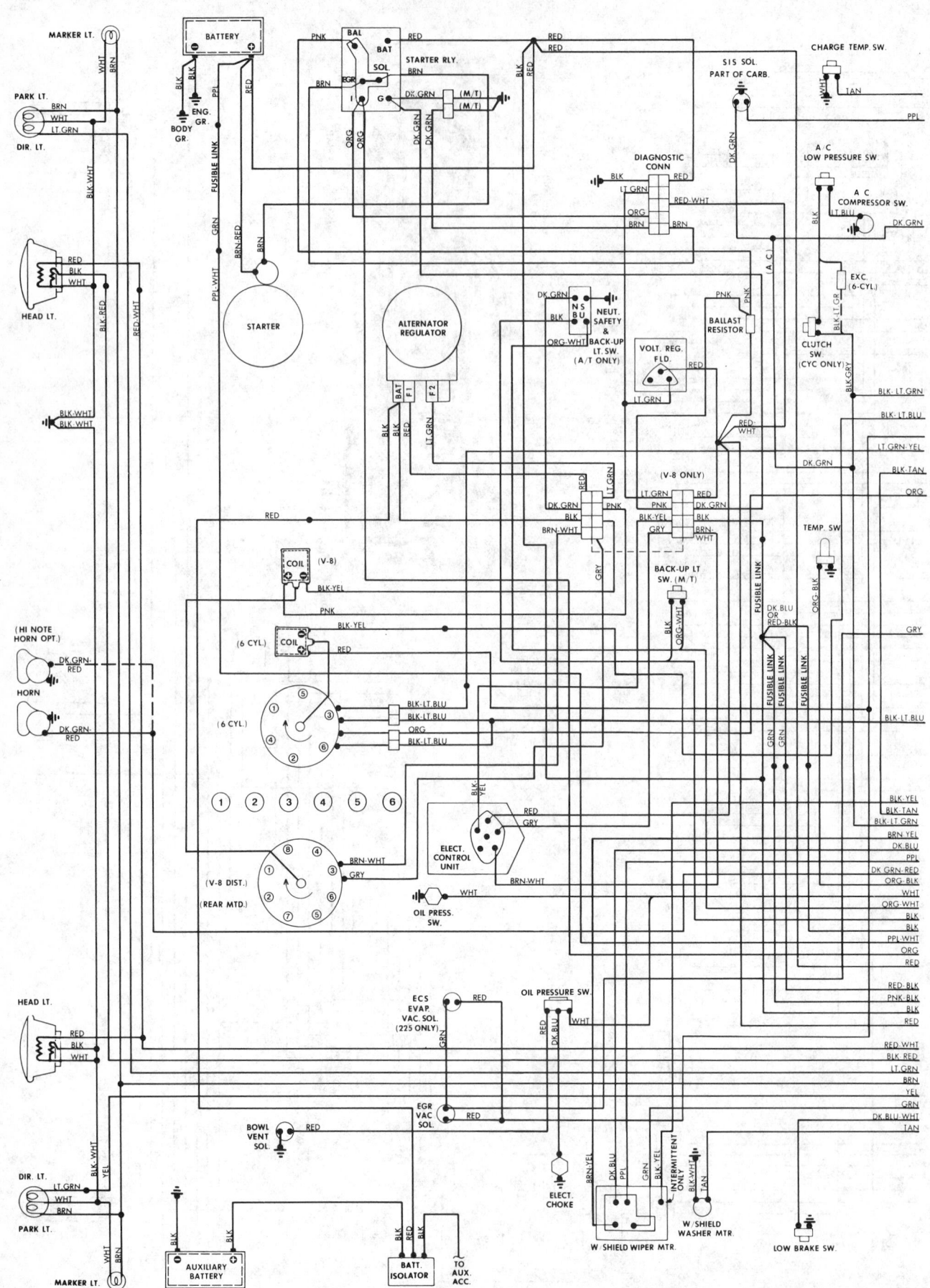

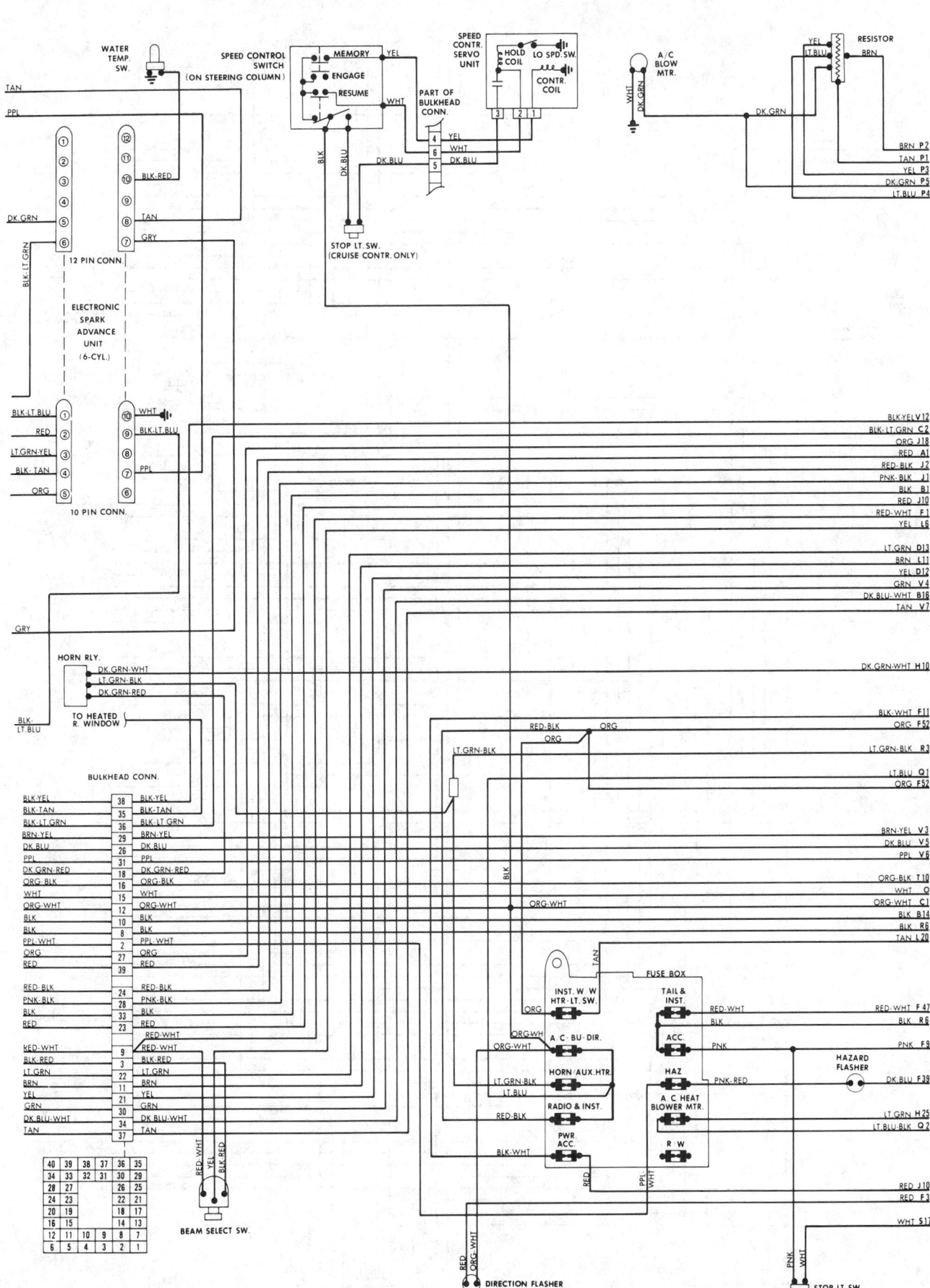

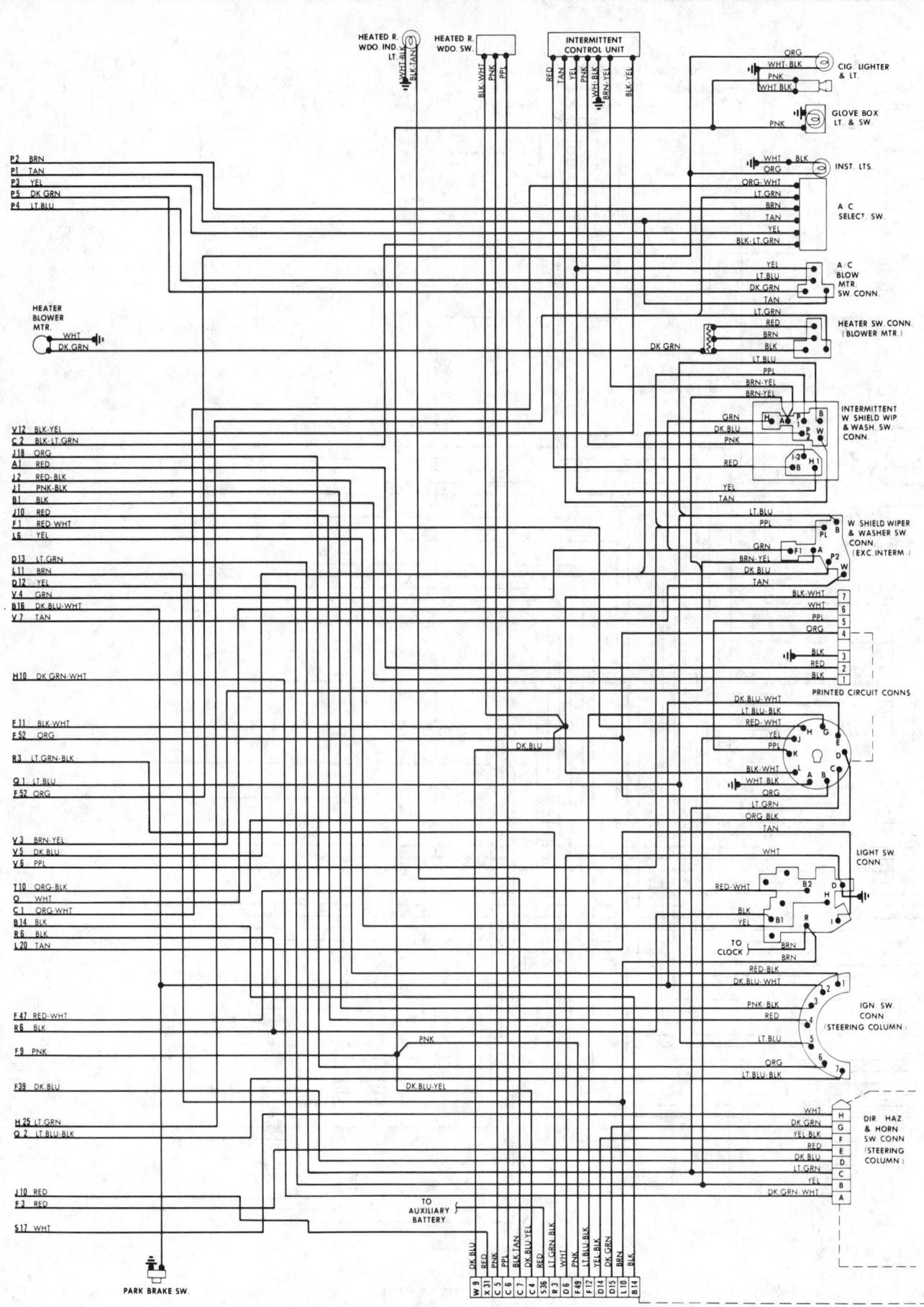

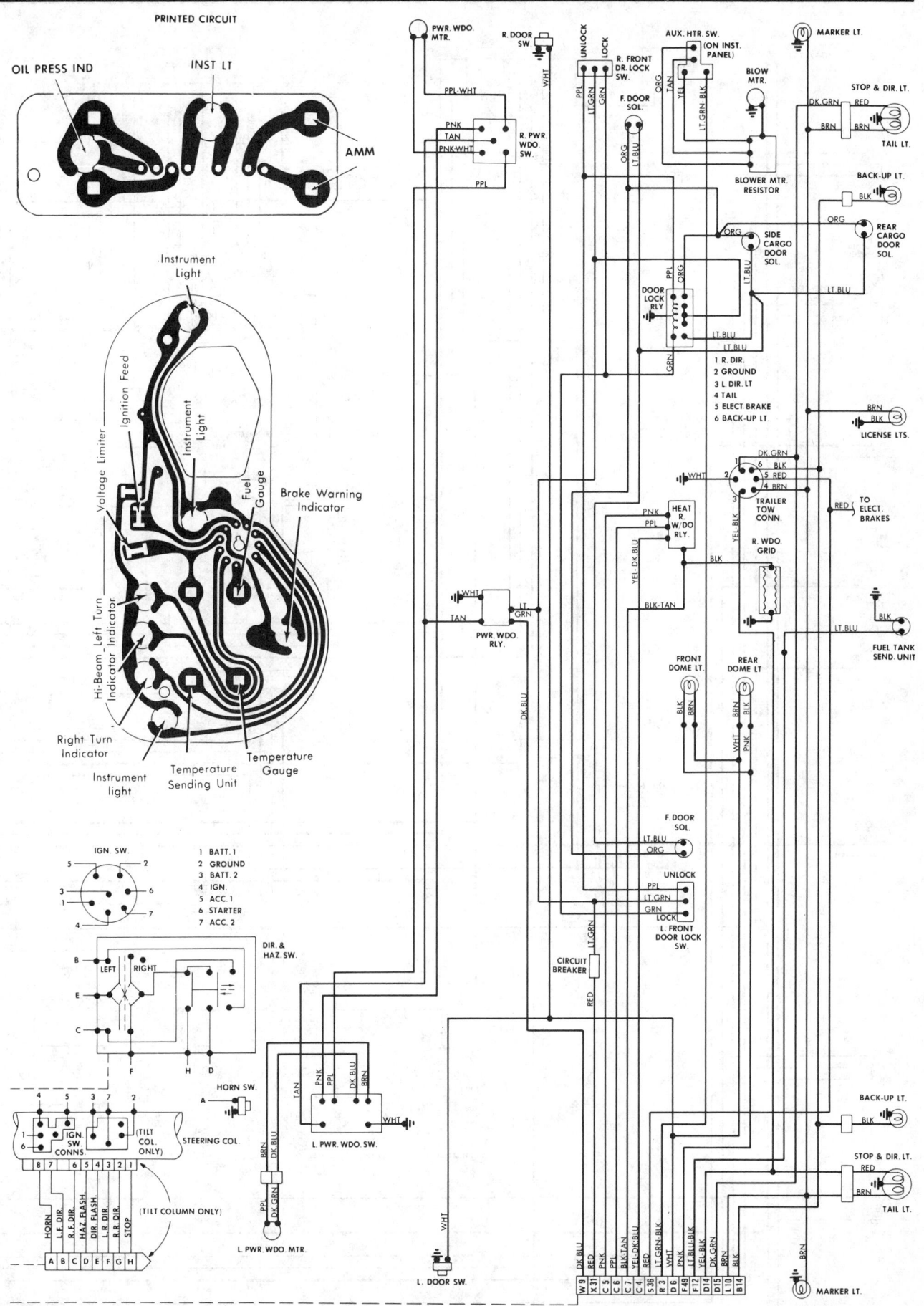

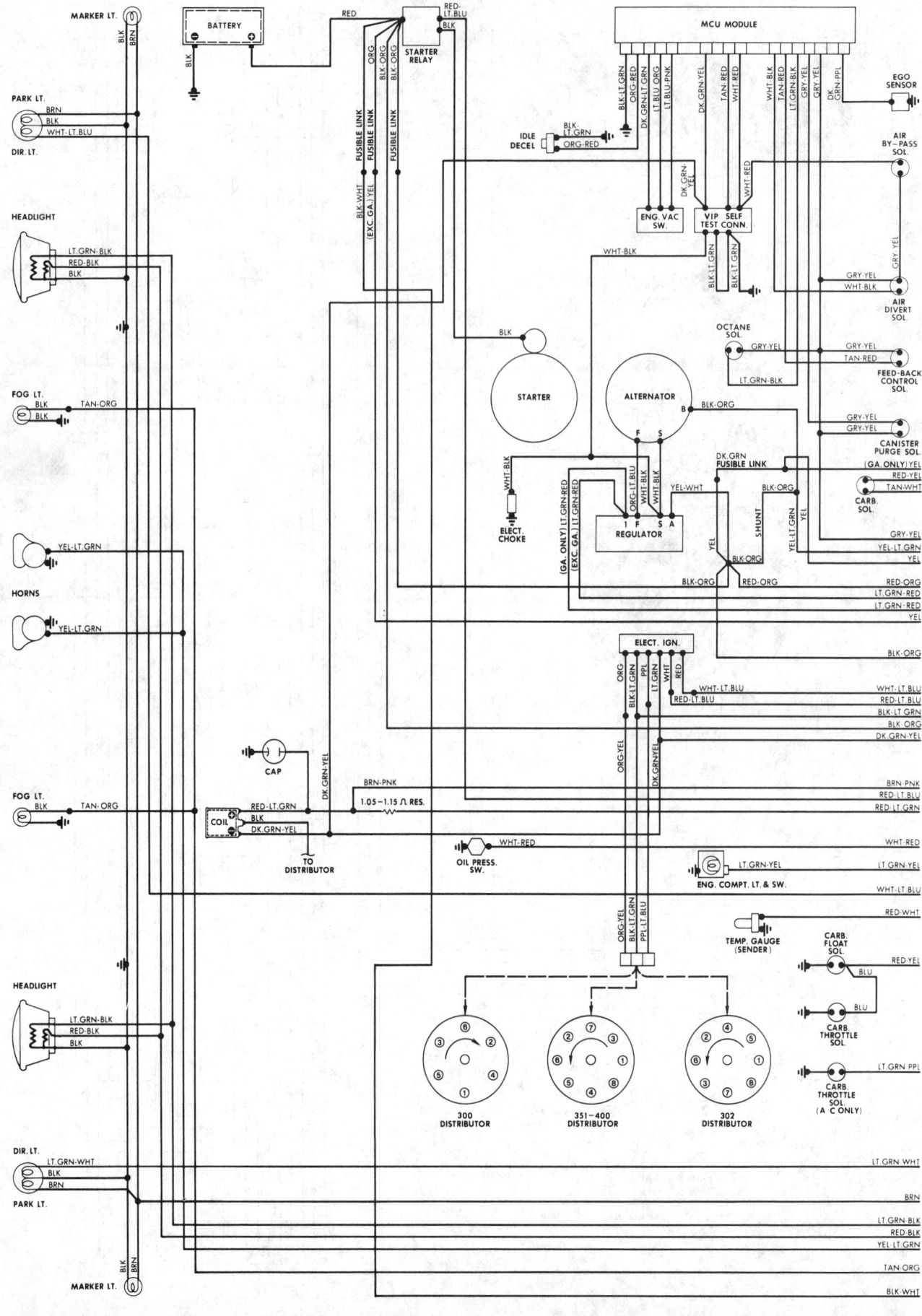

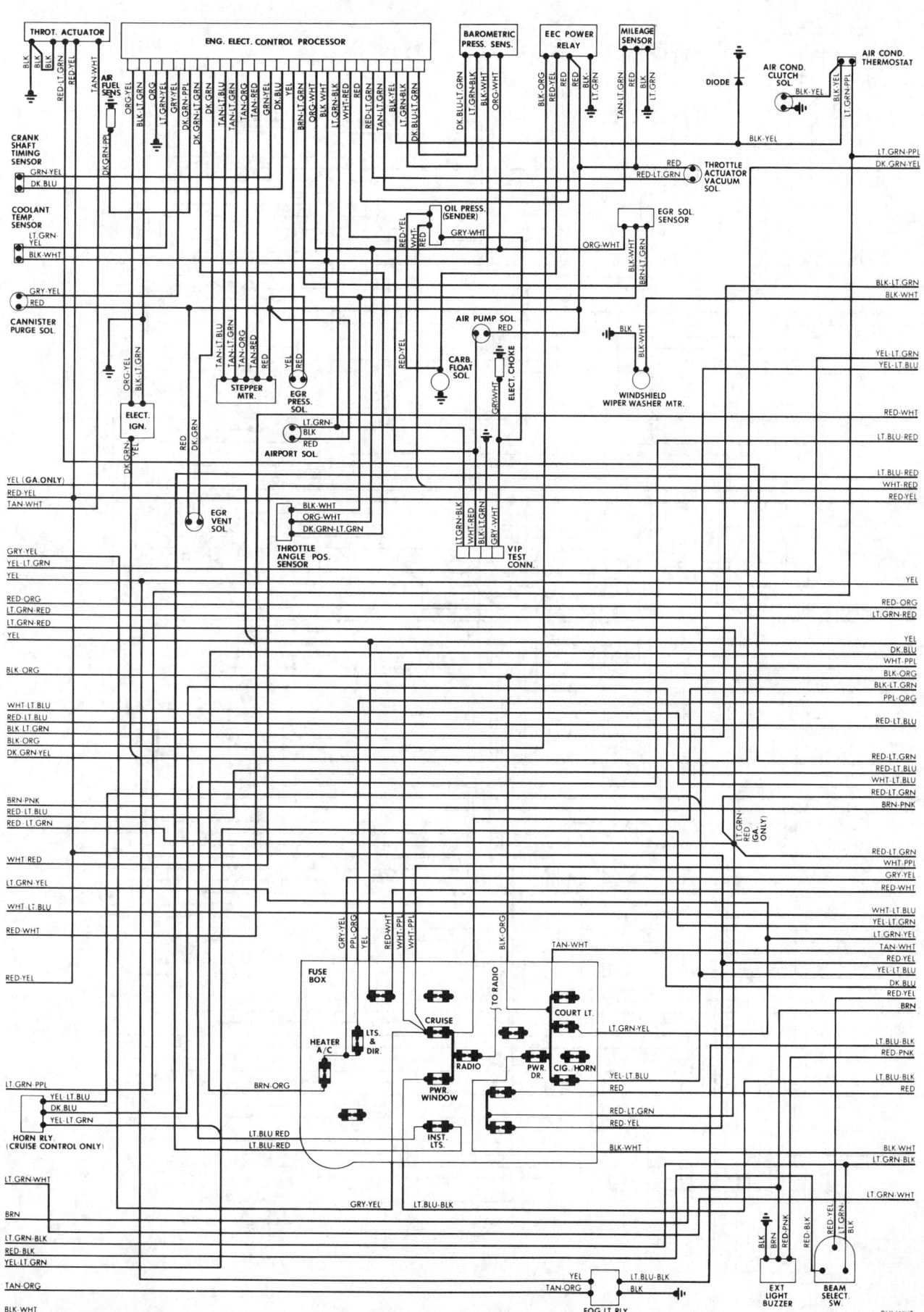

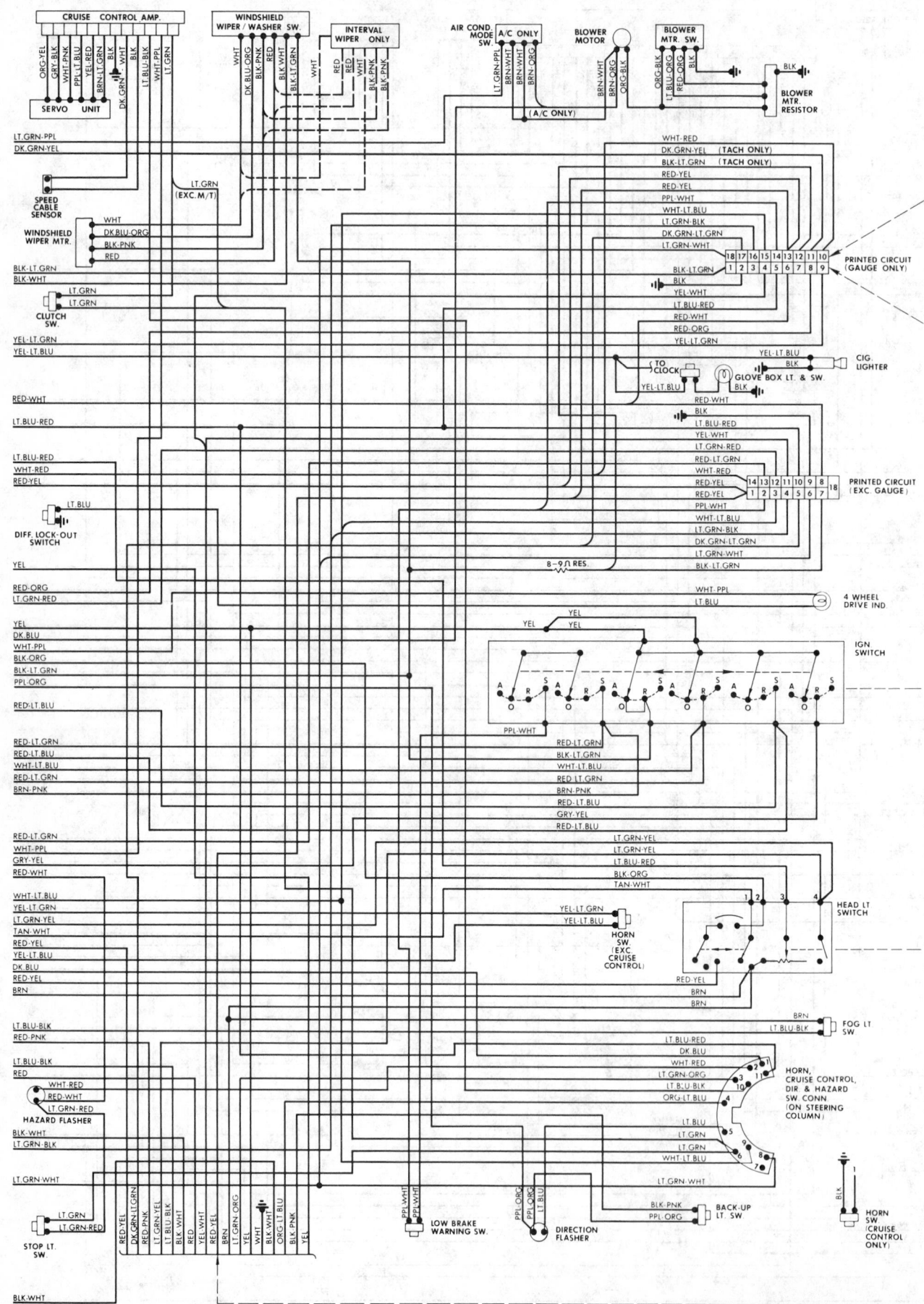

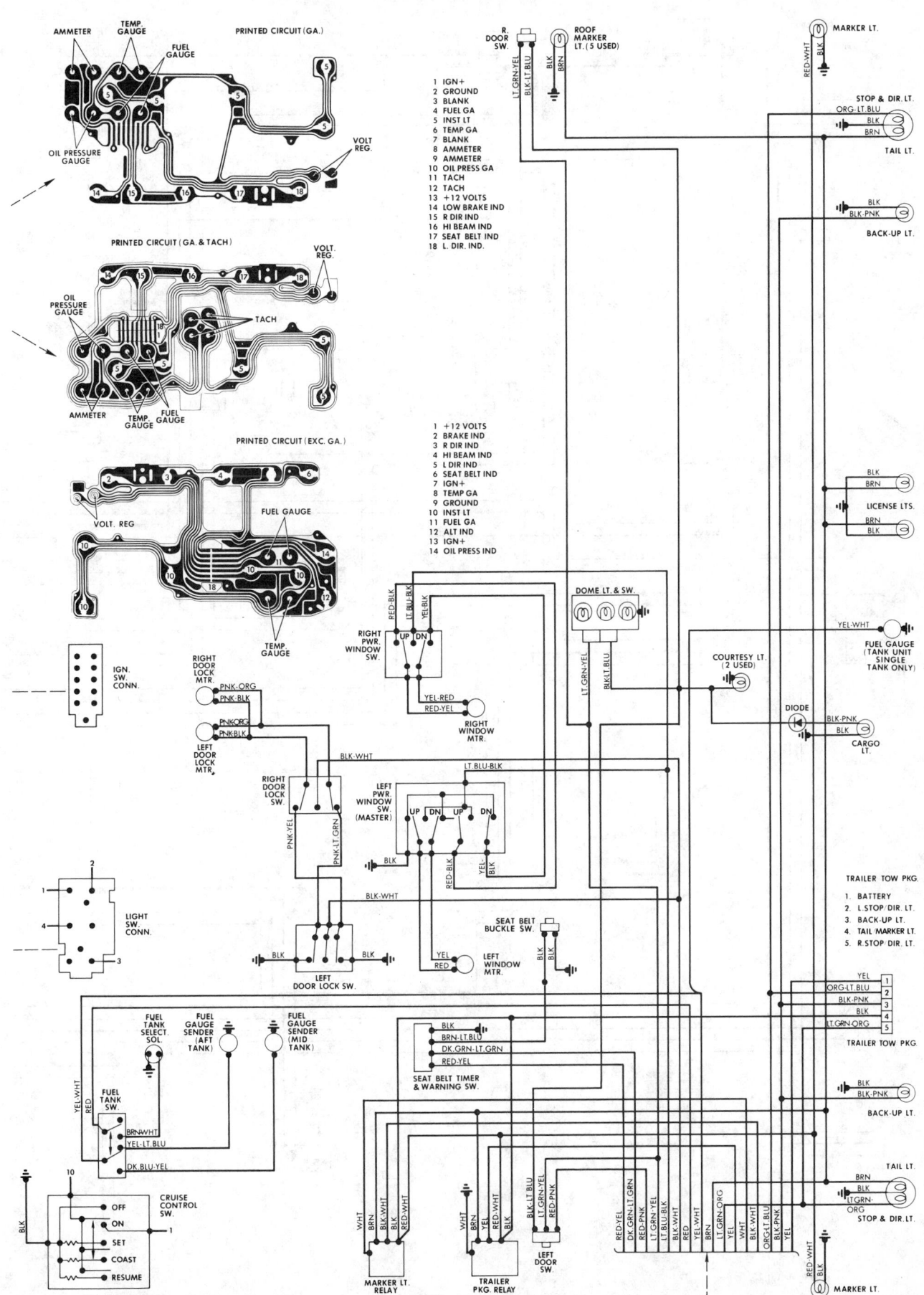

PRINTED CIRCUIT (GA.)

AMMETER — TEMP. GAUGE — FUEL GAUGE

OIL PRESSURE GAUGE

VOLT. REG.

PRINTED CIRCUIT (GA. & TACH)

VOLT. REG.

OIL PRESSURE GAUGE — TACH

AMMETER — TEMP. GAUGE — FUEL GAUGE

PRINTED CIRCUIT (EXC. GA.)

VOLT. REG. — FUEL GAUGE — TEMP GAUGE

1 IGN+
2 GROUND
3 BLANK
4 FUEL GA
5 INST LT
6 TEMP GA
7 BLANK
8 AMMETER
9 AMMETER
10 OIL PRESS GA
11 TACH
12 TACH
13 +12 VOLTS
14 LOW BRAKE IND
15 R DIR IND
16 HI BEAM IND
17 SEAT BELT IND
18 L. DIR. IND.

1 +12 VOLTS
2 BRAKE IND
3 R DIR IND
4 HI BEAM IND
5 L DIR IND
6 SEAT BELT IND
7 IGN+
8 TEMP GA
9 GROUND
10 INST LT
11 FUEL GA
12 ALT IND
13 IGN+
14 OIL PRESS IND

IGN. SW. CONN.

RIGHT DOOR LOCK MTR.

PNK-ORG
PNK-BLK
PNK-ORG
PNK-BLK

LEFT DOOR LOCK MTR.

RIGHT DOOR LOCK SW.

PNK-YEL
PNK-LT.GRN

LIGHT SW. CONN.

RIGHT PWR. WINDOW SW.

RED-BLK
LT.BLU-BLK
YEL-BLK

UP DN

YEL-RED
RED-YEL

RIGHT WINDOW MTR.

BLK-WHT

LEFT PWR. WINDOW SW. (MASTER)

LT.BLU-BLK

UP DN UP DN

BLK
RED-BLK YEL-BLK

BLK-WHT

BLK BLK

LEFT DOOR LOCK SW.

YEL RED

SEAT BELT BUCKLE SW.

BLK BLK

LEFT WINDOW MTR.

R. DOOR SW.
LT.GRN-YEL BLK-LT.BLU BLK BRN

ROOF MARKER LT. (5 USED)

DOME LT. & SW.

LT.GRN-YEL BLK-LT.BLU

COURTESY LT. (2 USED)

DIODE

MARKER LT.
RED-WHT BLK

STOP & DIR. LT.
ORG-LT.BLU
BLK
BRN

TAIL LT.

BLK
BLK-PNK

BACK-UP LT.

BLK
BRN

BRN
BLK

LICENSE LTS.

YEL-WHT

FUEL GAUGE (TANK UNIT SINGLE TANK ONLY)

BLK-PNK
BLK

CARGO LT.

TRAILER TOW PKG.
1. BATTERY
2. L.STOP/DIR. LT.
3. BACK-UP LT.
4. TAIL MARKER LT.
5. R.STOP/DIR. LT.

YEL   1
ORG-LT.BLU   2
BLK-PNK   3
BLK   4
LT.GRN-ORG   5

TRAILER TOW PKG.

BLK
BLK-PNK

BACK-UP LT.

BRN
BLK
ORG

TAIL LT.

STOP & DIR. LT.

FUEL TANK SELECT. SOL.

FUEL GAUGE SENDER (AFT TANK)

FUEL GAUGE SENDER (MID TANK)

YEL-WHT RED

FUEL TANK SW.

BRN-WHT
YEL-LT.BLU
DK.BLU-YEL

BLK

10

CRUISE CONTROL SW.

OFF
ON
SET
COAST
RESUME

1

WHT
BRN
BLK-WHT
BLK
RED-WHT

MARKER LT. RELAY

WHT
BRN
YEL
RED-WHT
BLK

TRAILER PKG. RELAY

BLK
BRN-LT.BLU
DK.GRN-LT.GRN
RED-YEL

SEAT BELT TIMER & WARNING SW.

BLK-LT.BLU
LT.GRN-YEL
RED-PNK

LEFT DOOR SW.

RED-YEL
DK.GRN-LT.GRN
RED-PNK
LT.GRN-YEL
LT.BLU-BLK
BLK-WHT
RED
BRN
LT.GRN-ORG
WHT
ORG-LT.BLU
BLK-PNK
YEL

RED-WHT BLK

MARKER LT.

1981 Ford

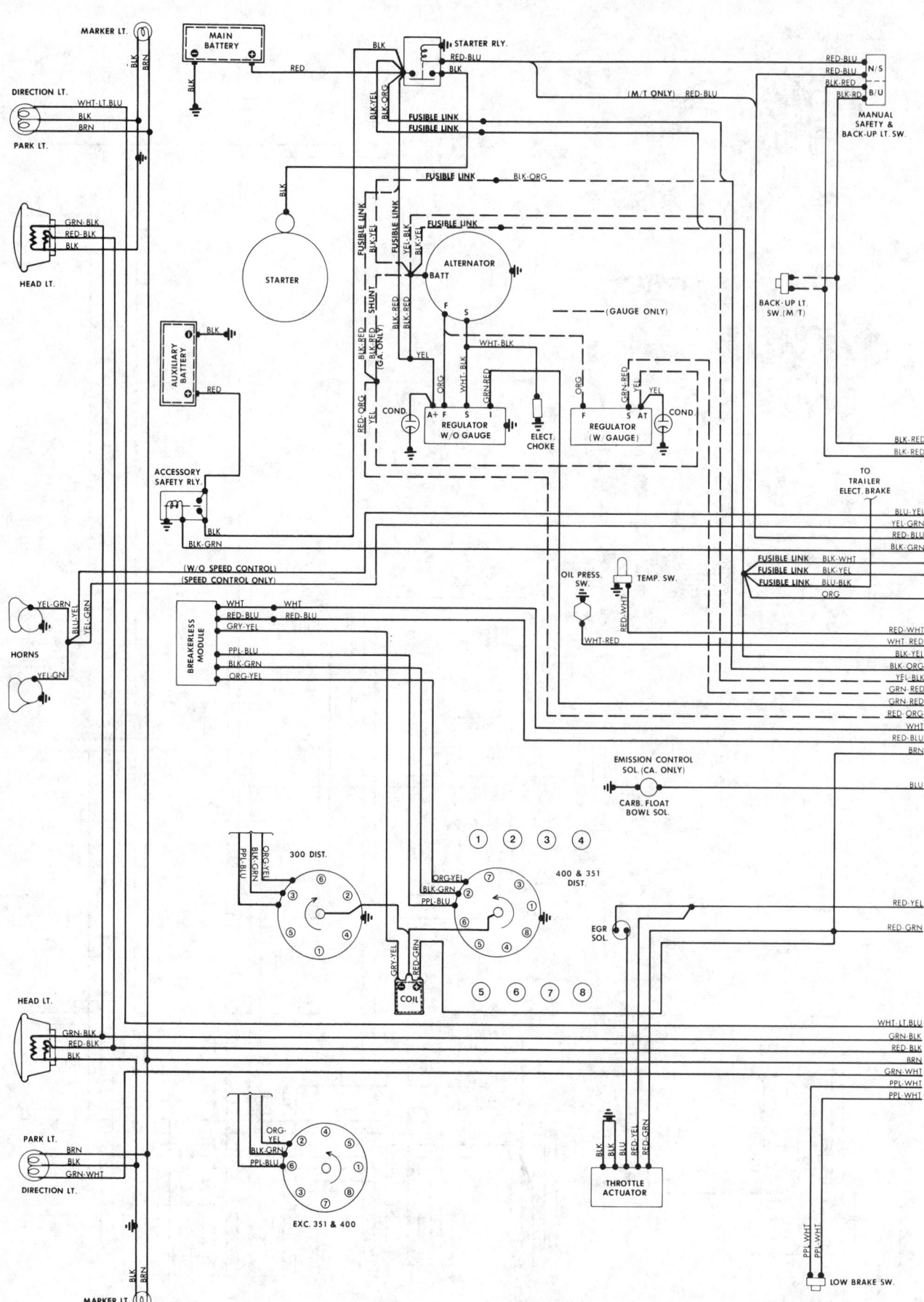

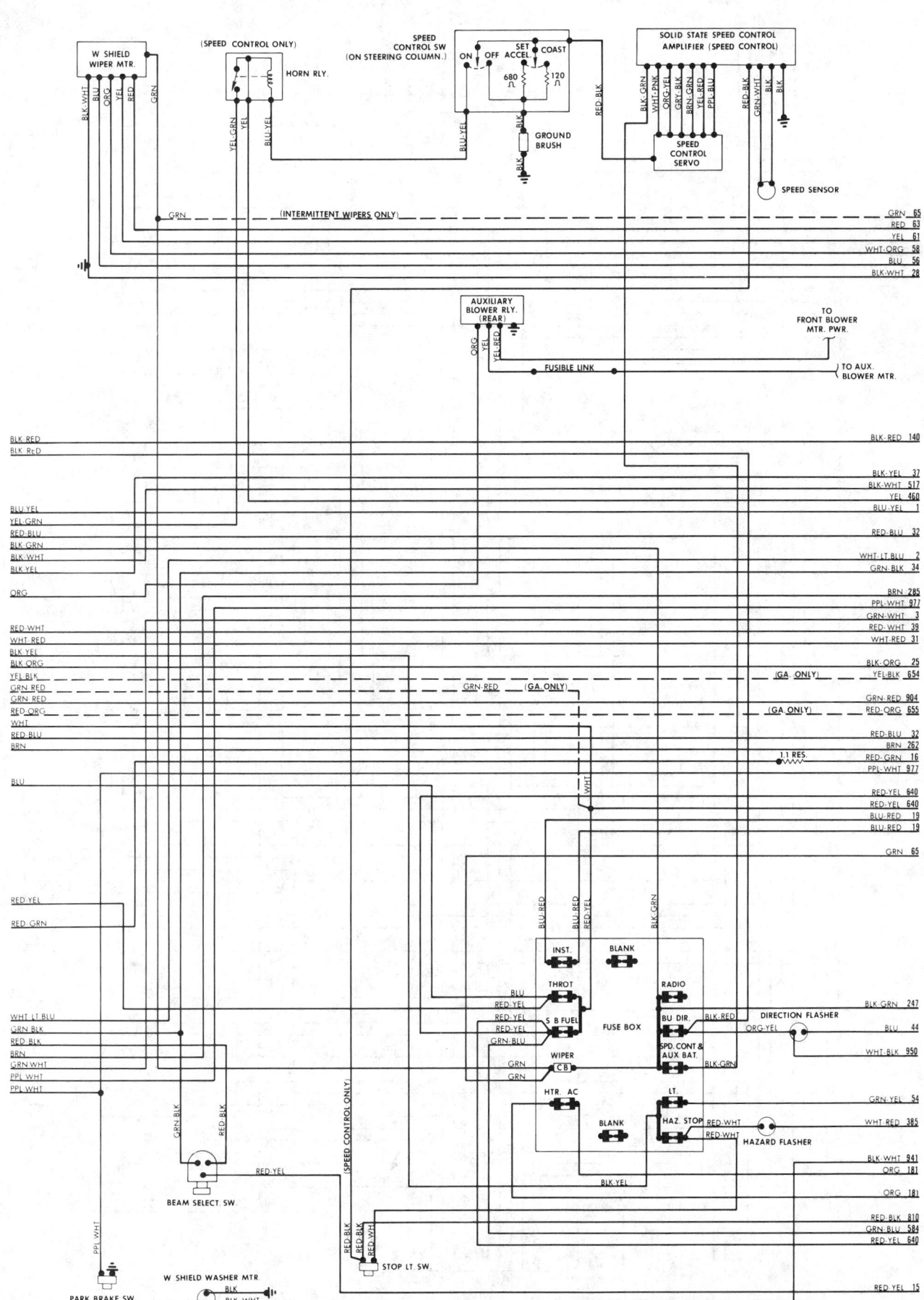

1981 Ford

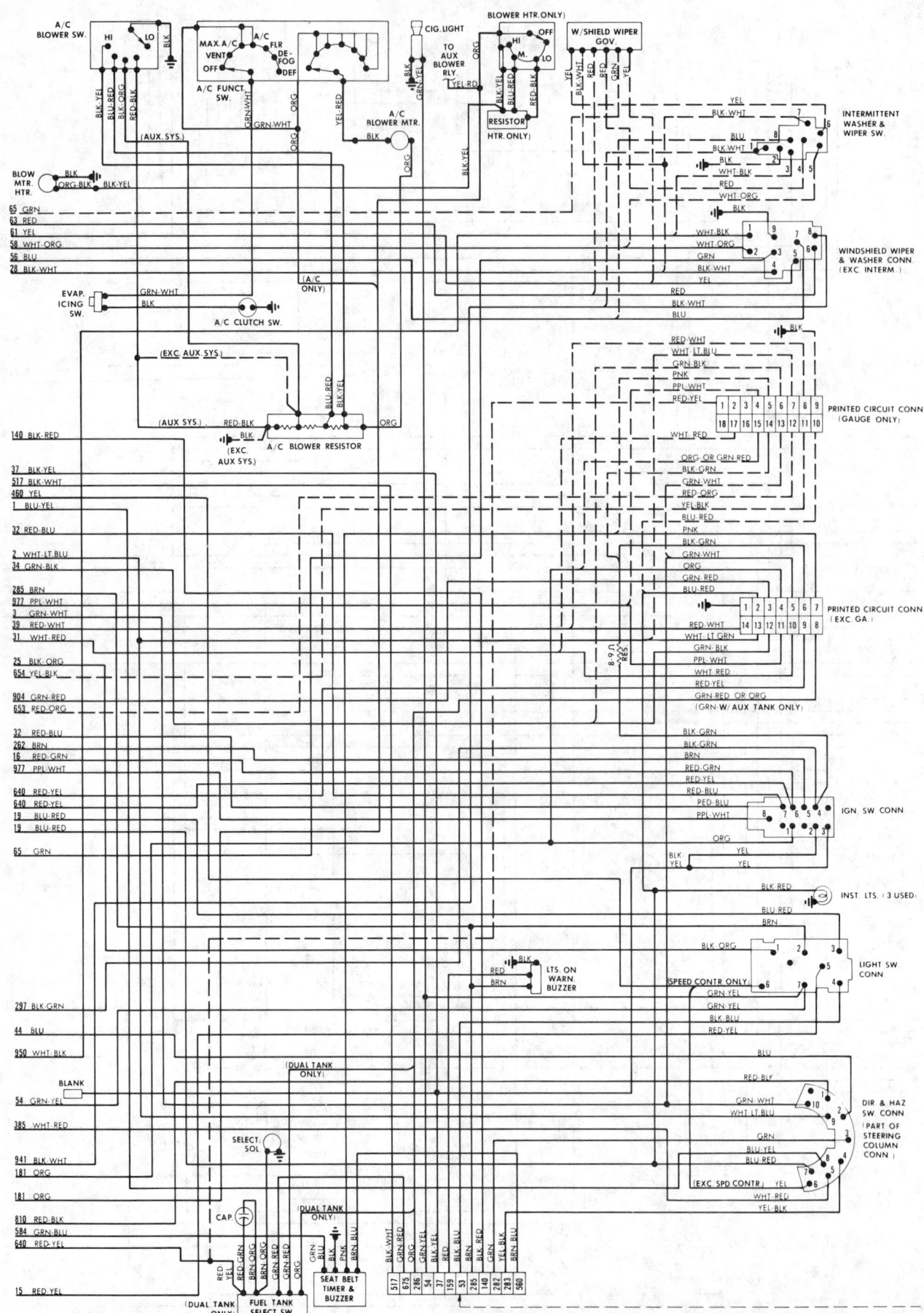

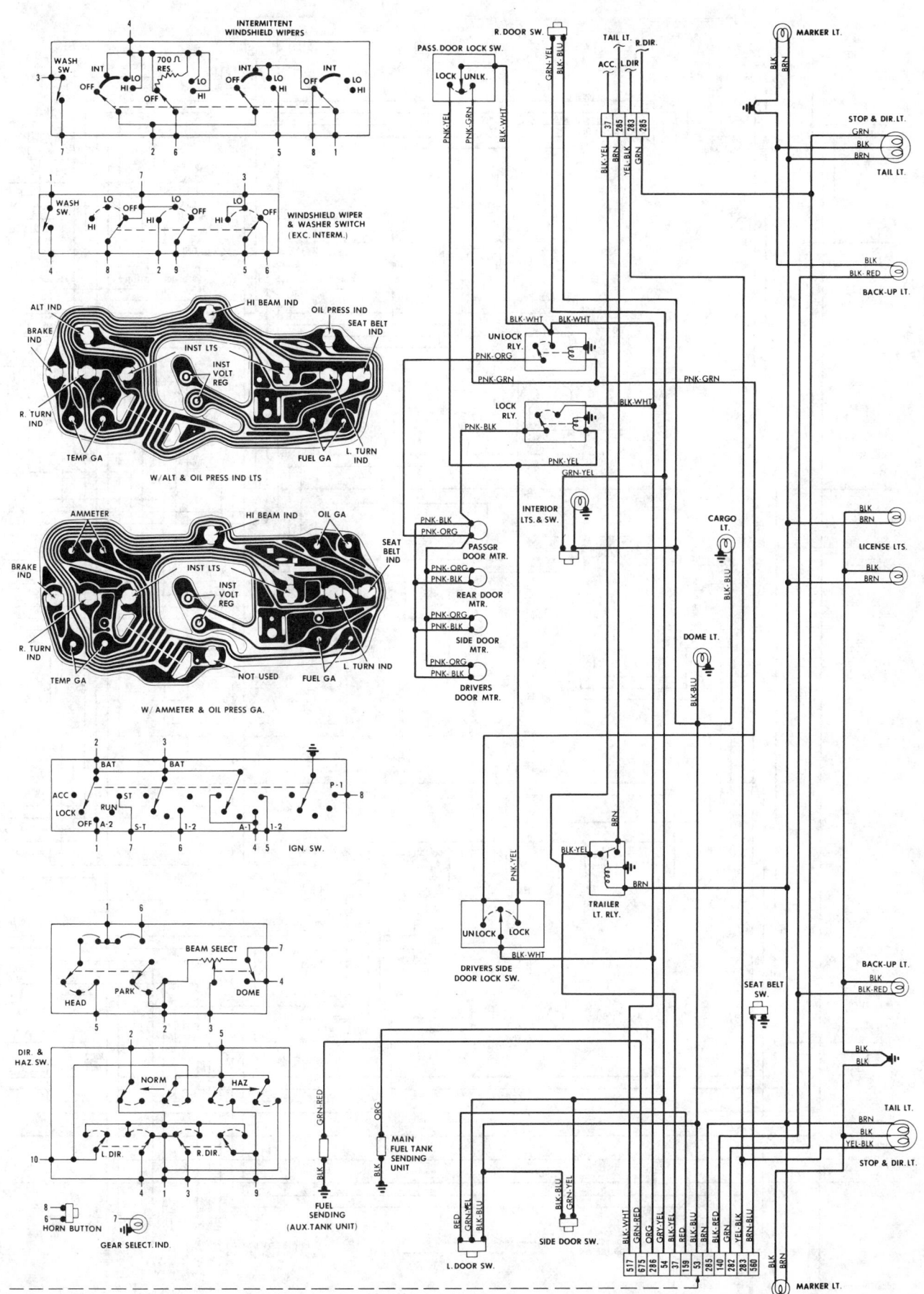

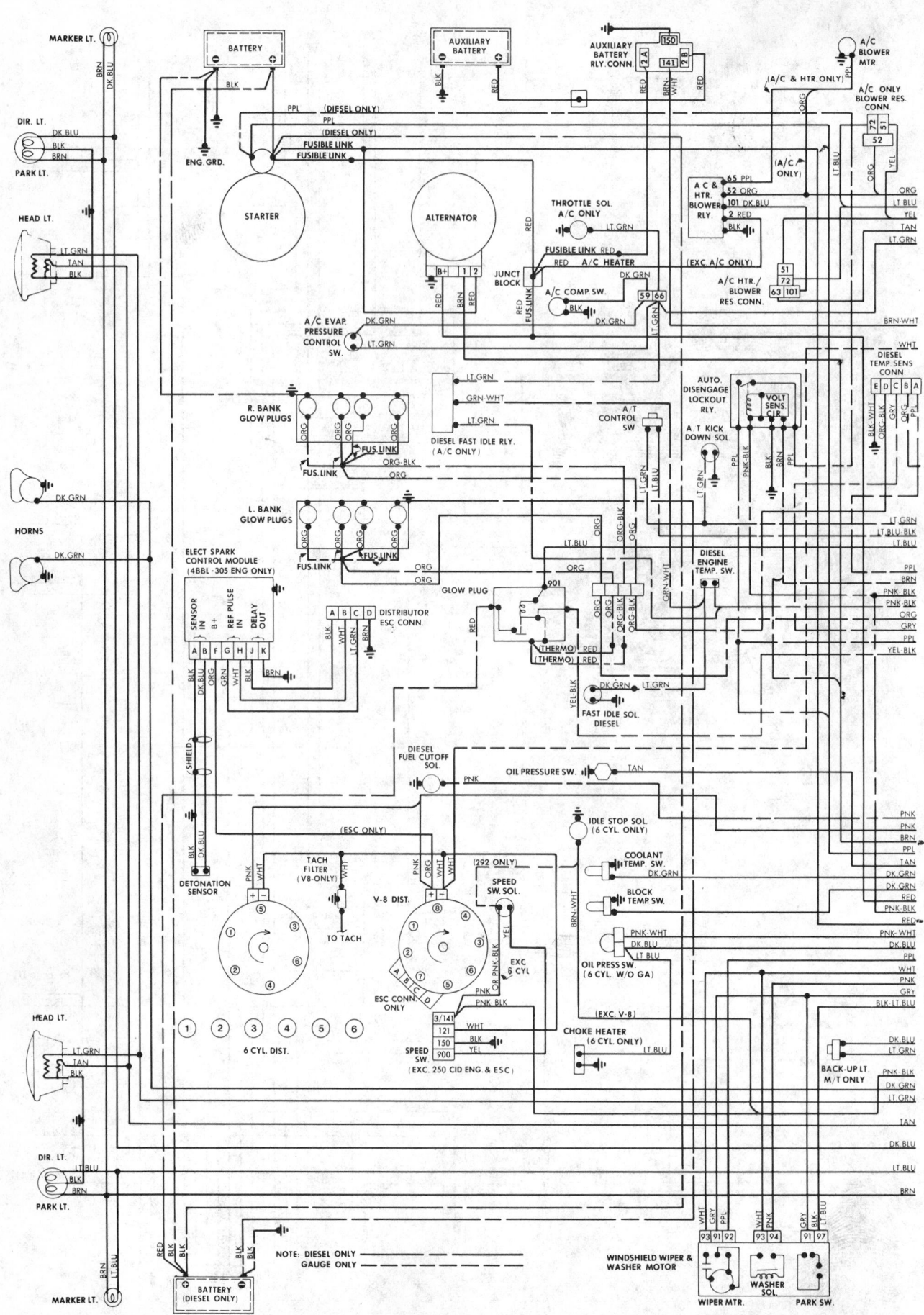

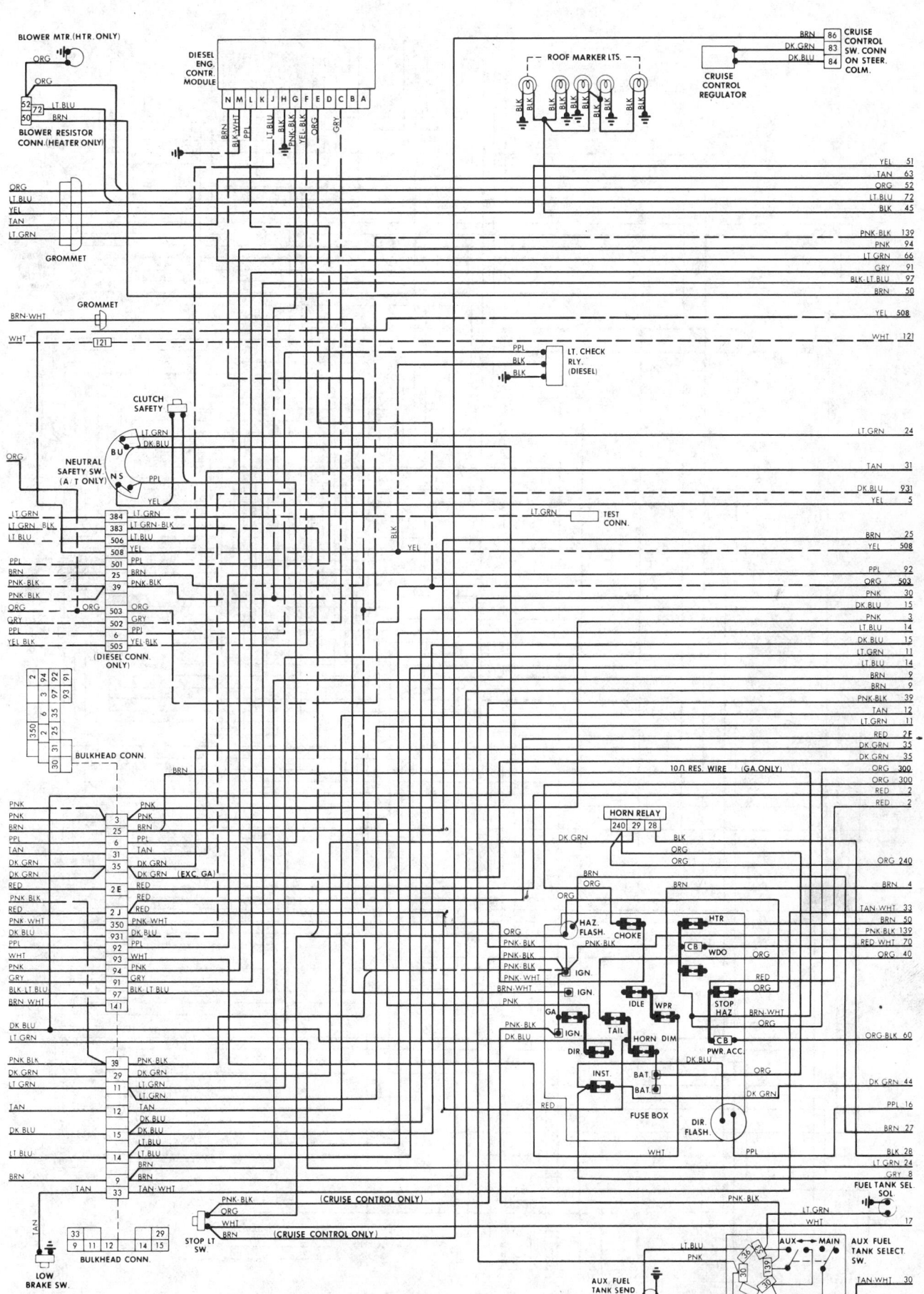

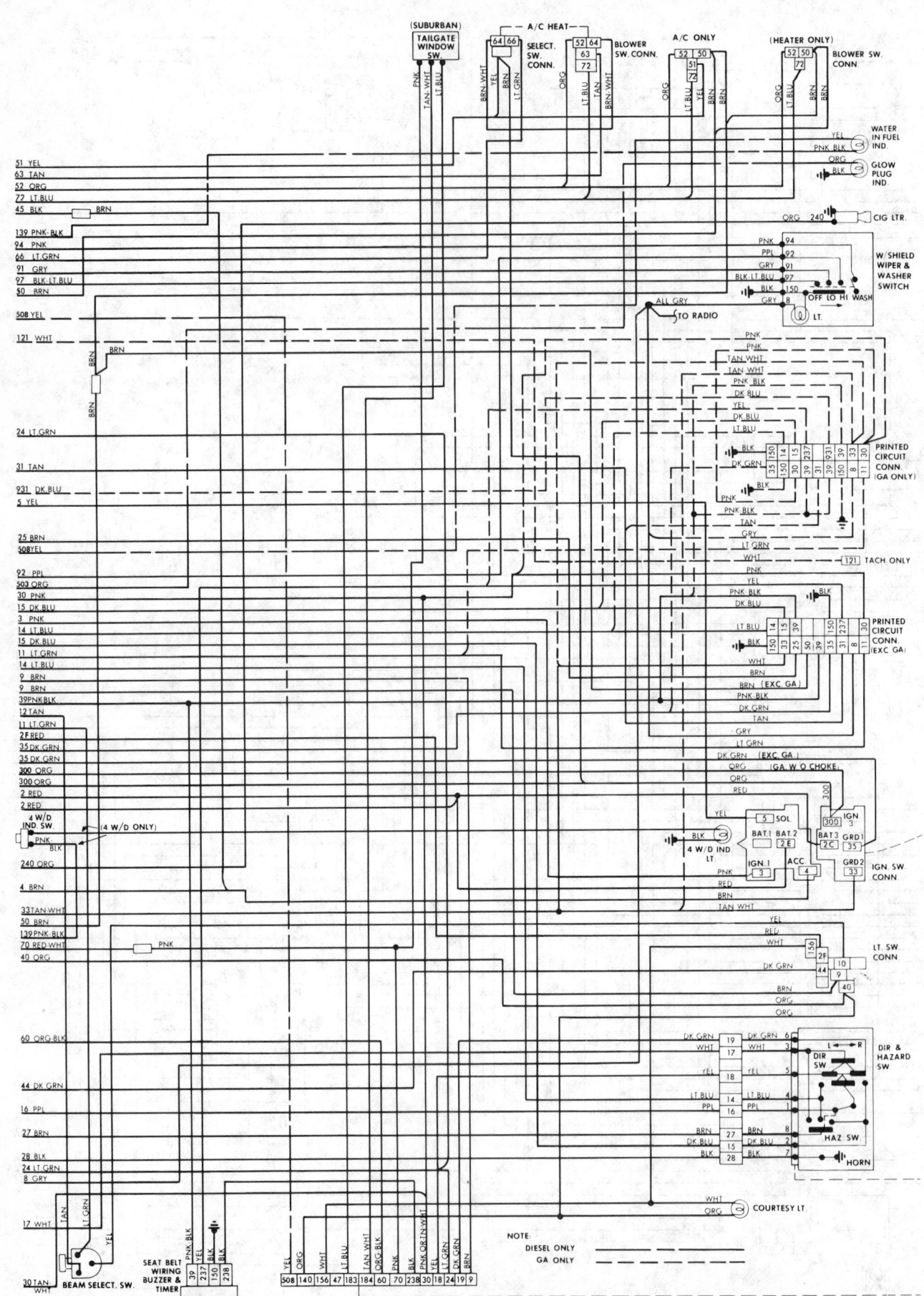

WIRING DIAGRAMS

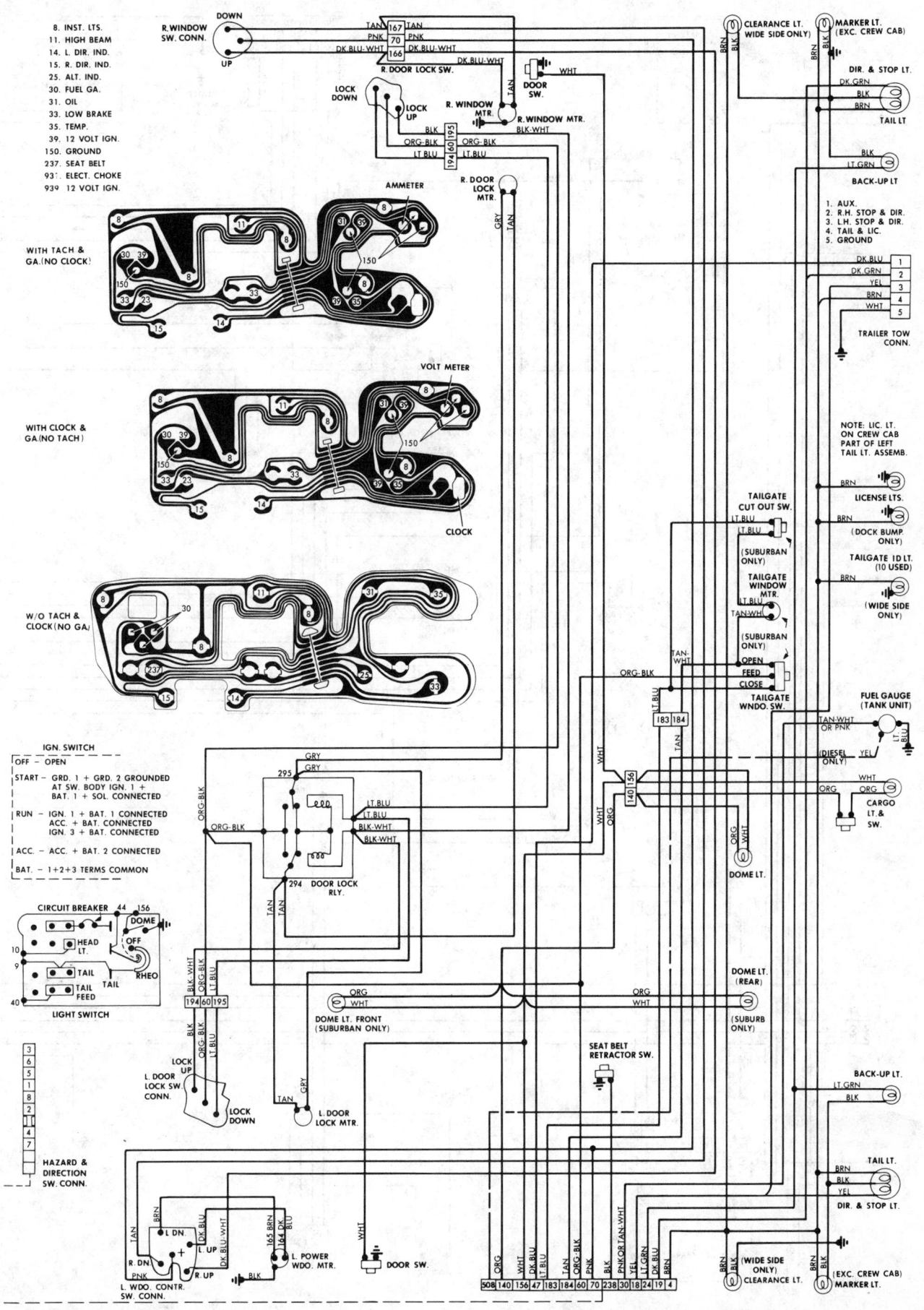

1981 General Motors

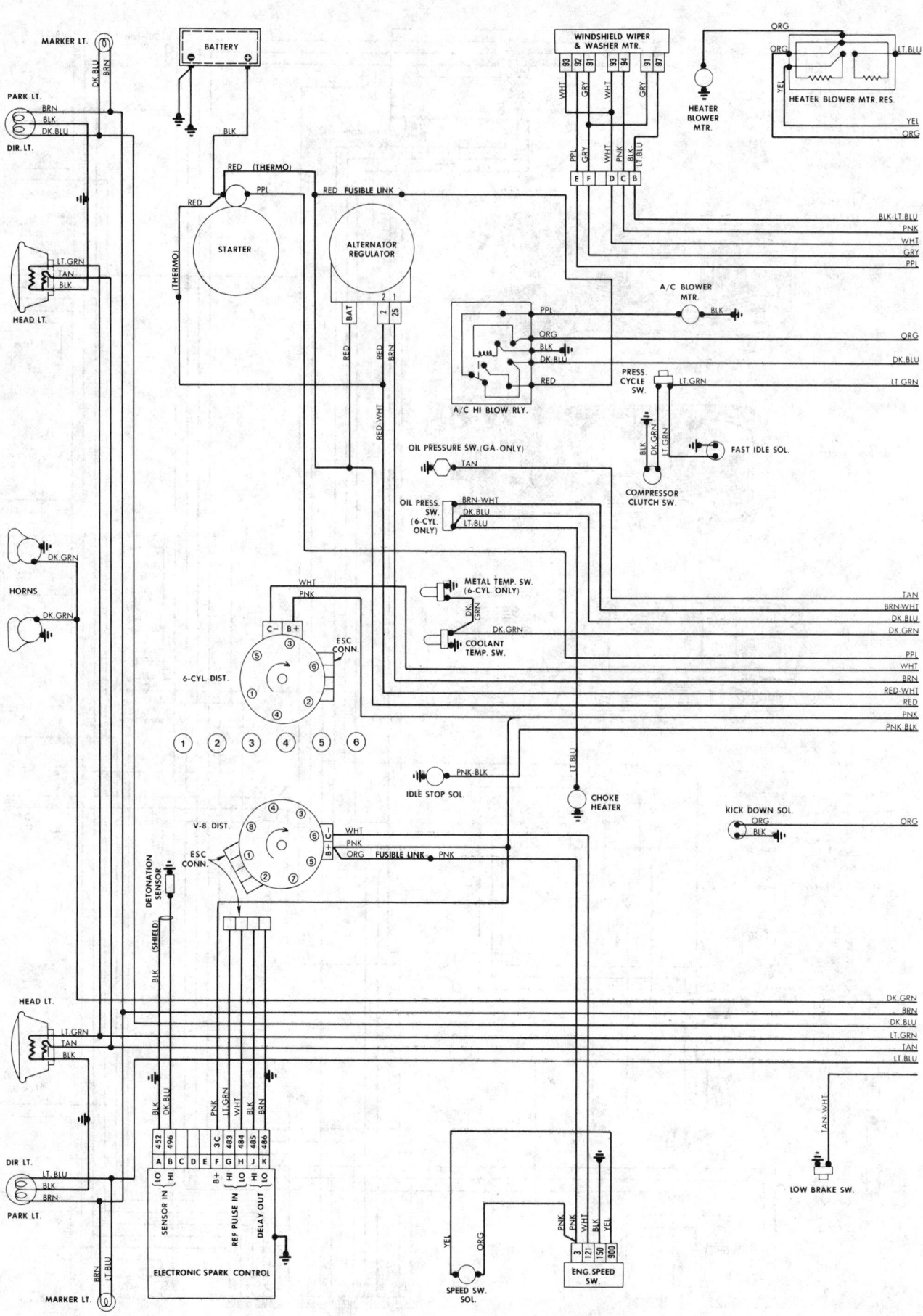

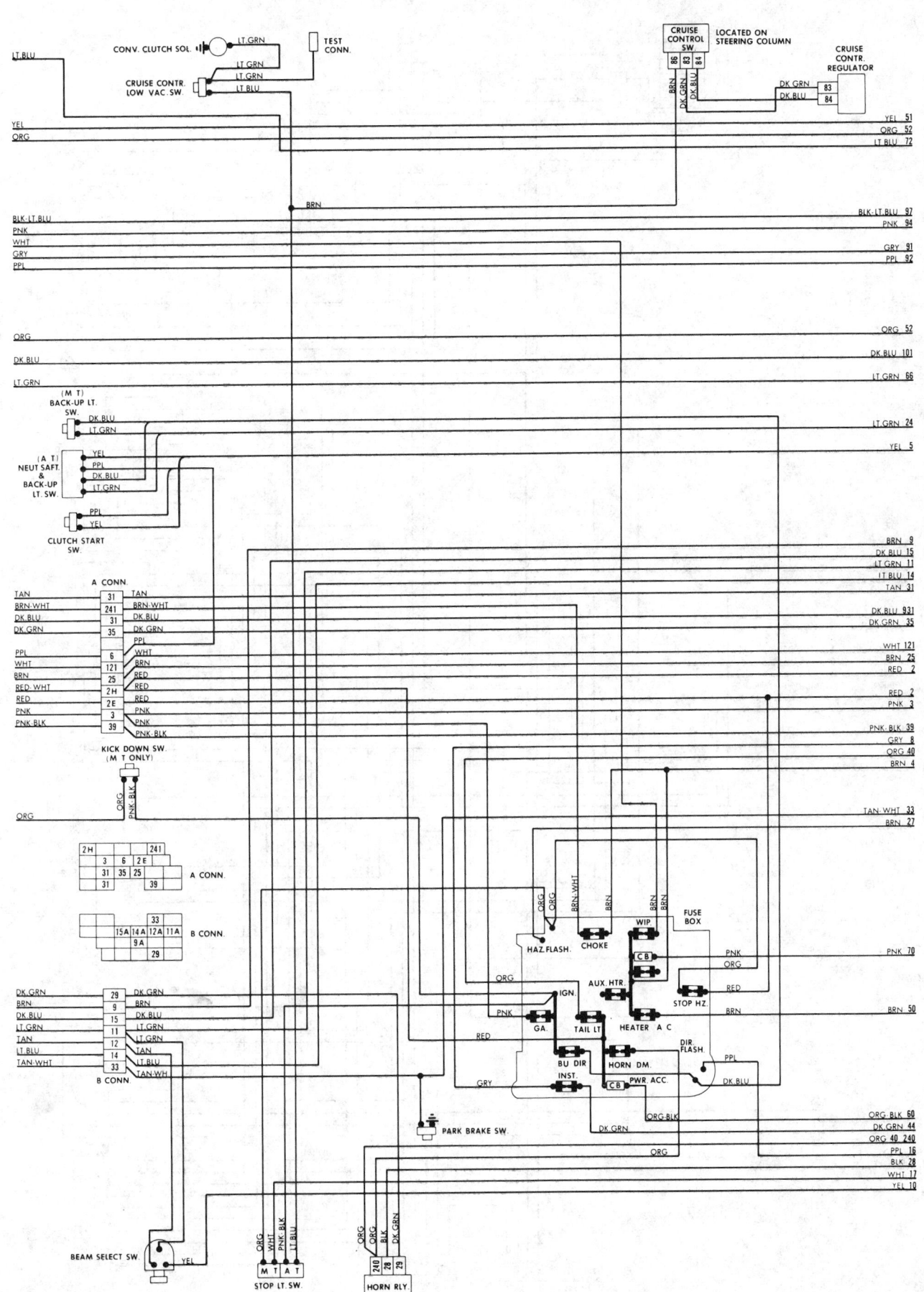

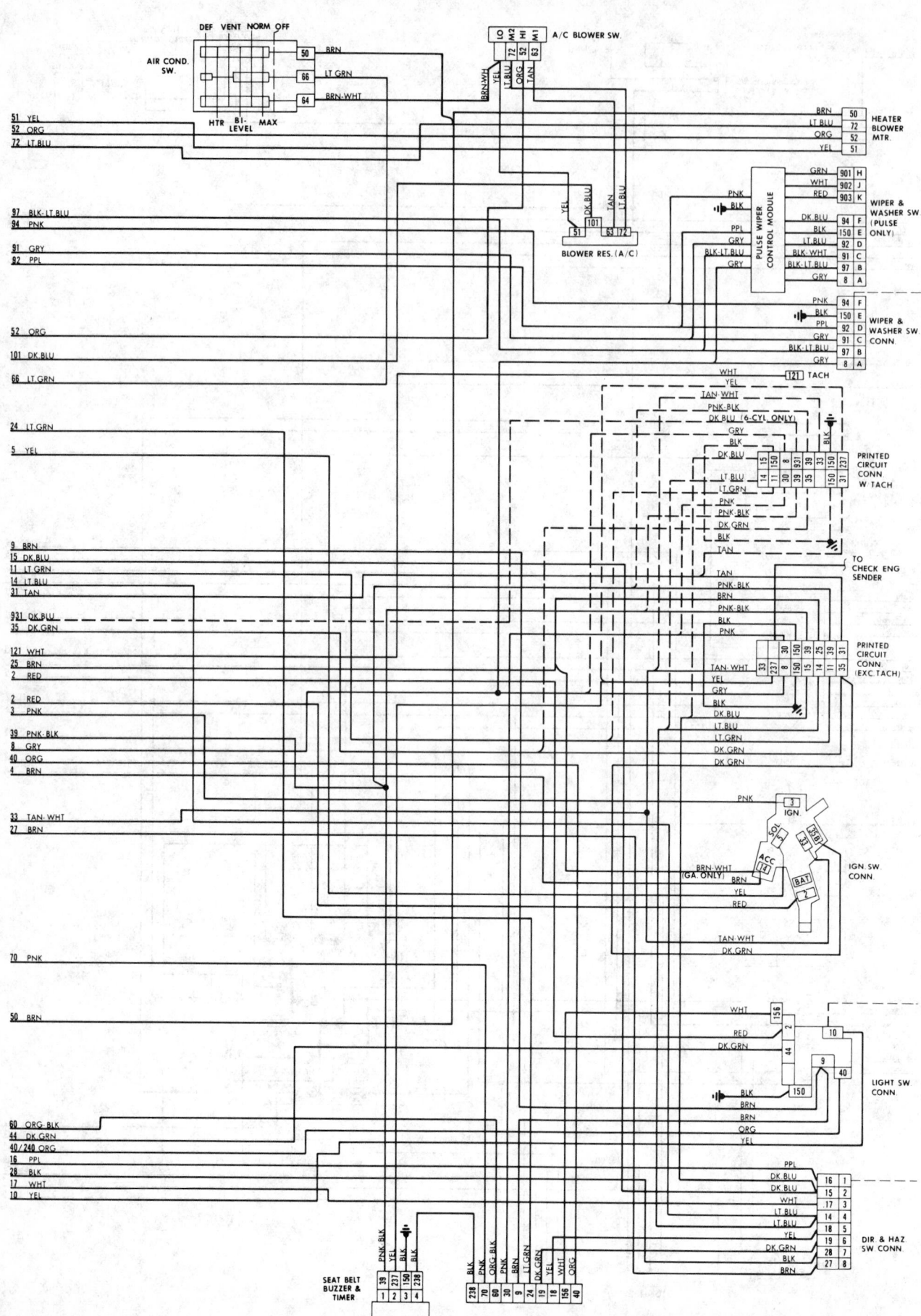

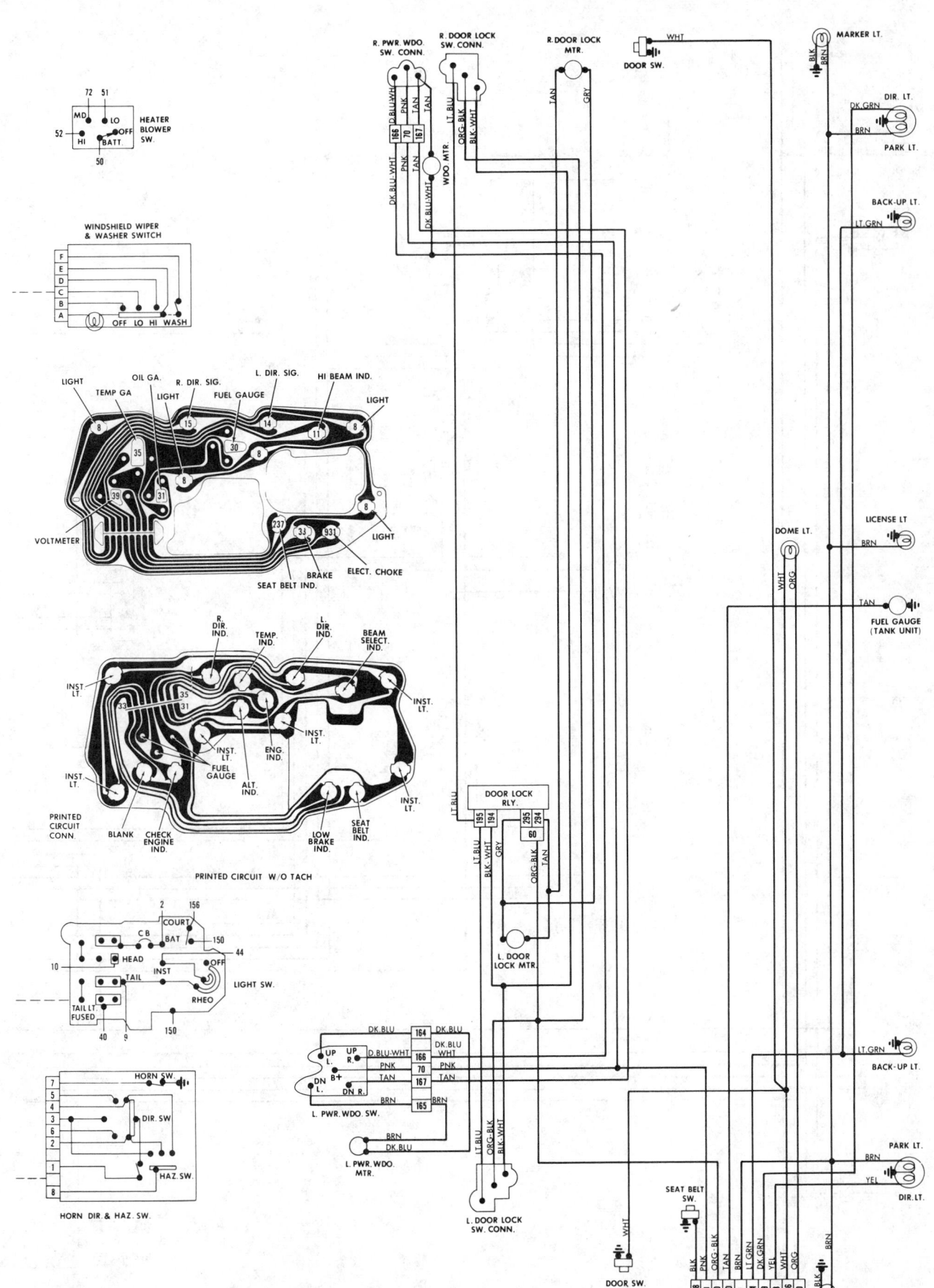

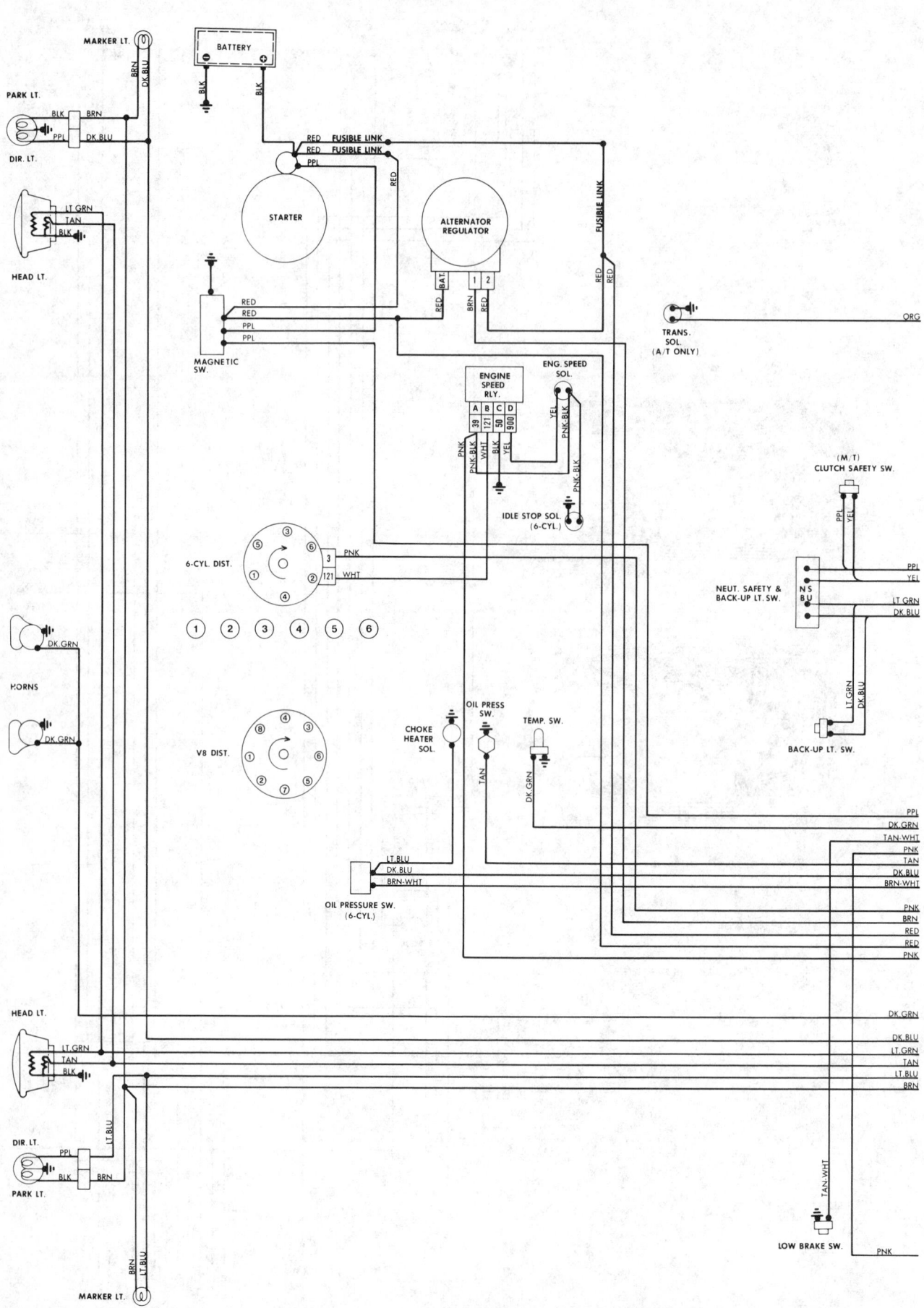

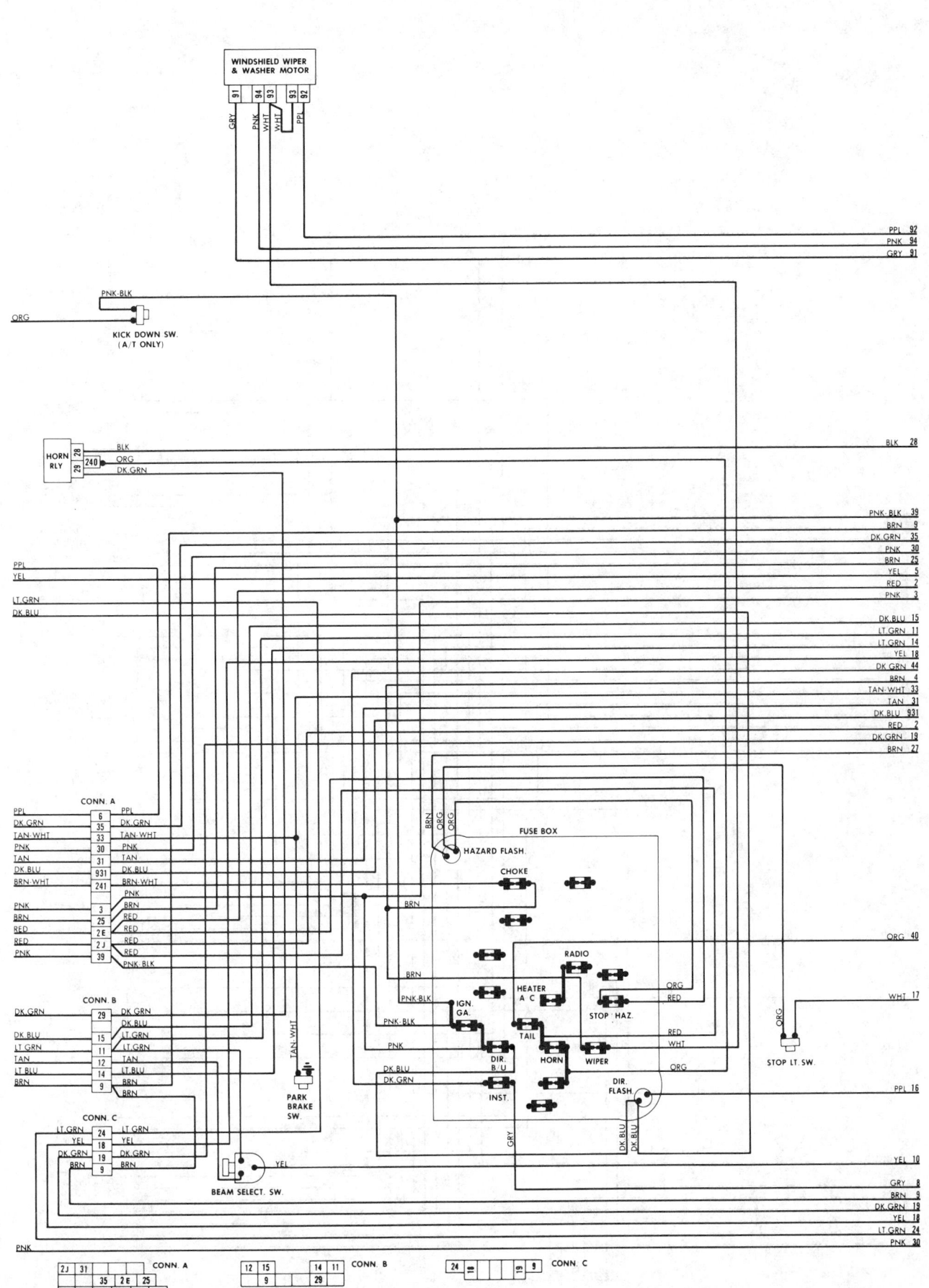

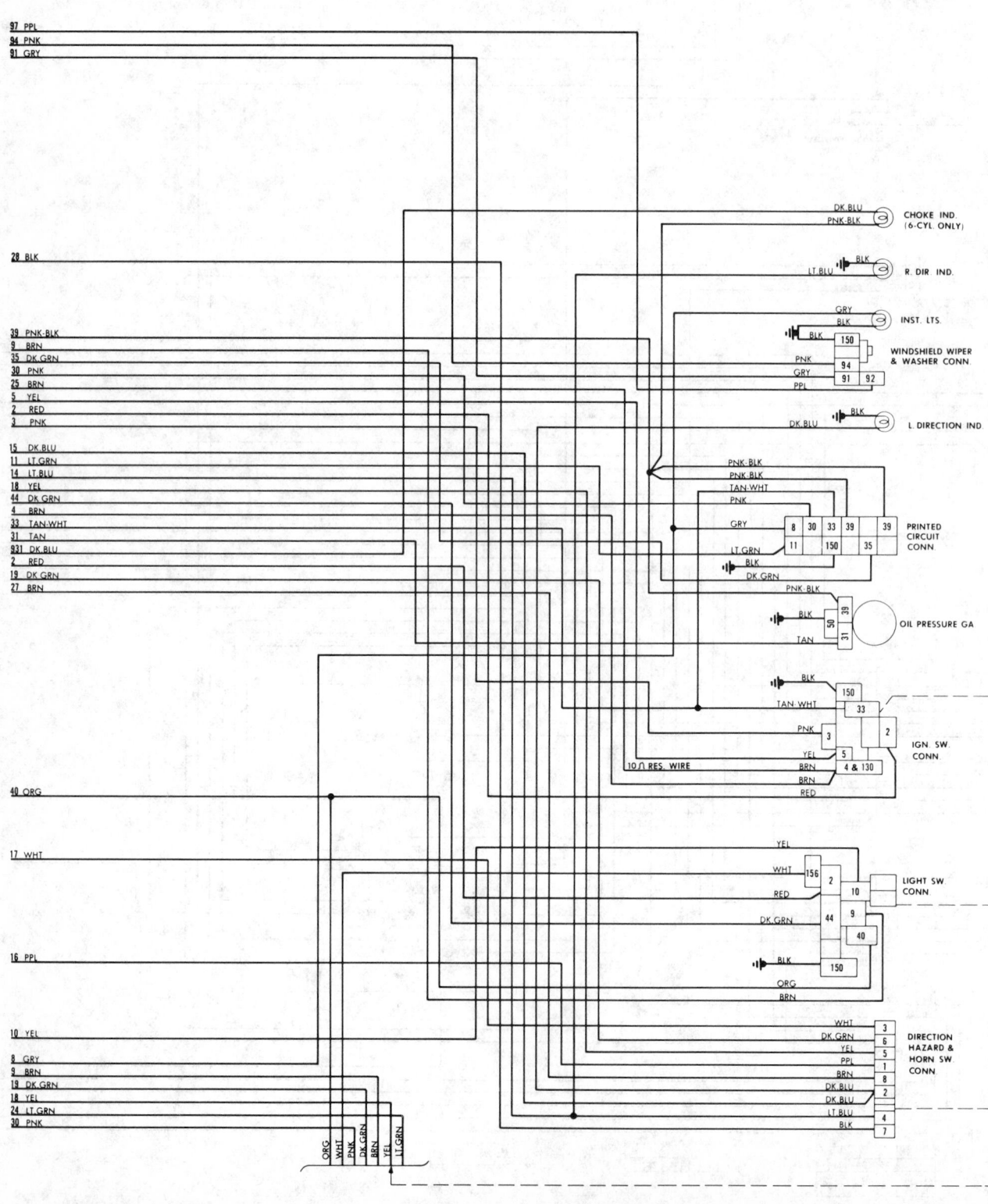

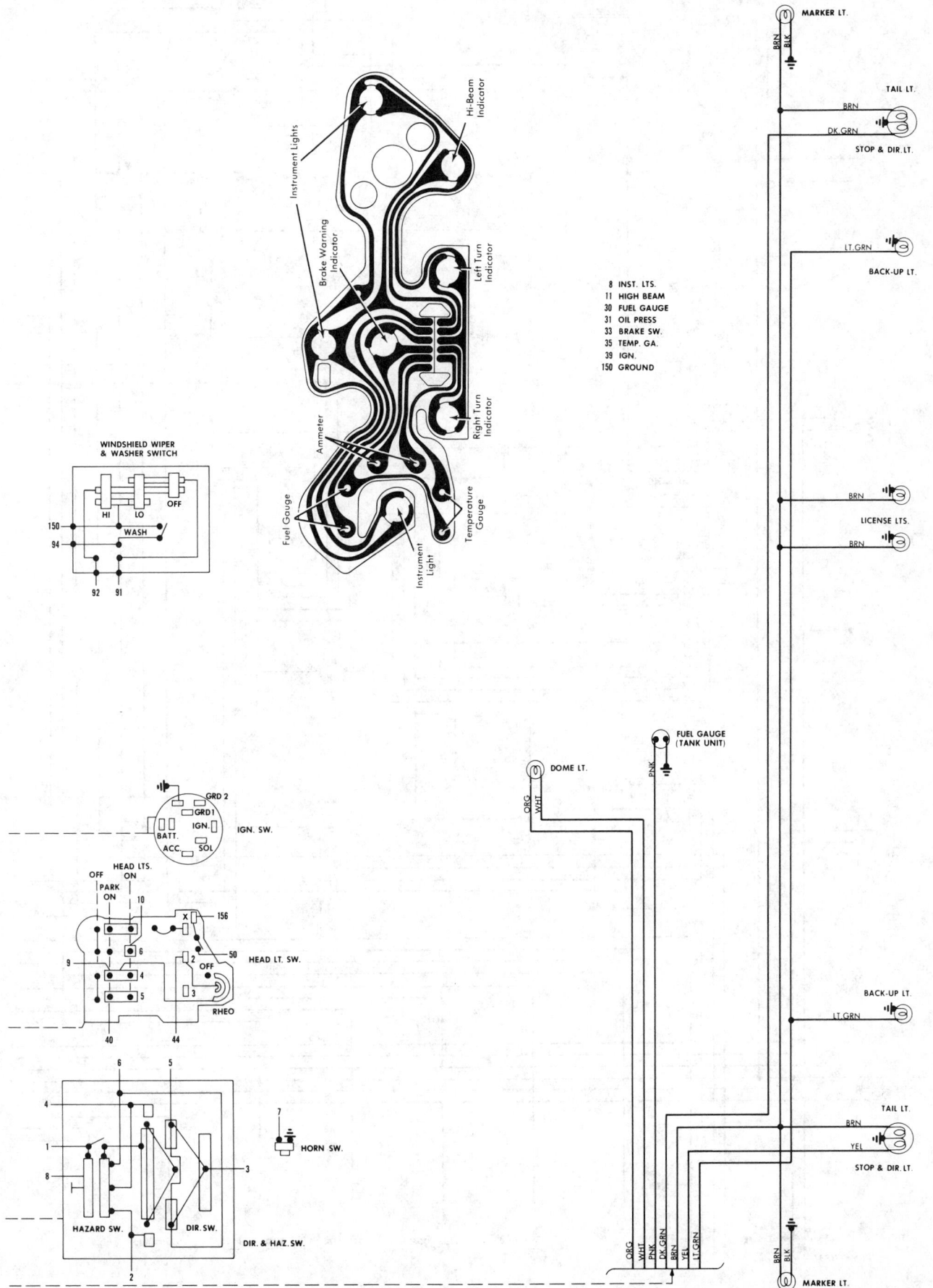

MARKER LT.

BRN BLK

TAIL LT.

BRN

DK.GRN

STOP & DIR. LT.

LT.GRN

BACK-UP LT.

8   INST. LTS.
11   HIGH BEAM
30   FUEL GAUGE
31   OIL PRESS
33   BRAKE SW.
35   TEMP. GA.
39   IGN.
150   GROUND

Hi-Beam Indicator

Instrument Lights

Brake Warning Indicator

Left Turn Indicator

Right Turn Indicator

Ammeter

Fuel Gauge

Temperature Gauge

Instrument Light

BRN

LICENSE LTS.

BRN

WINDSHIELD WIPER & WASHER SWITCH

HI   LO   OFF

150

94

WASH

92   91

FUEL GAUGE (TANK UNIT)

DOME LT.

PNK

ORG WHT

GRD 2
GRD 1
IGN.
BATT.
ACC.   SOL

IGN. SW.

HEAD LTS.
OFF   ON
PARK ON
10
X   156
6
9
2   50
OFF
4
3
5
RHEO

HEAD LT. SW.

40   44

BACK-UP LT.

LT.GRN

6   5

4

7

1

HORN SW.

8

3

TAIL LT.

BRN

YEL

STOP & DIR. LT.

HAZARD SW.   DIR. SW.

DIR. & HAZ. SW.

2

ORG
WHT
PNK
DK.GRN
BRN
YEL
LT.GRN

BRN
BLK

MARKER LT.

1981 Jeep

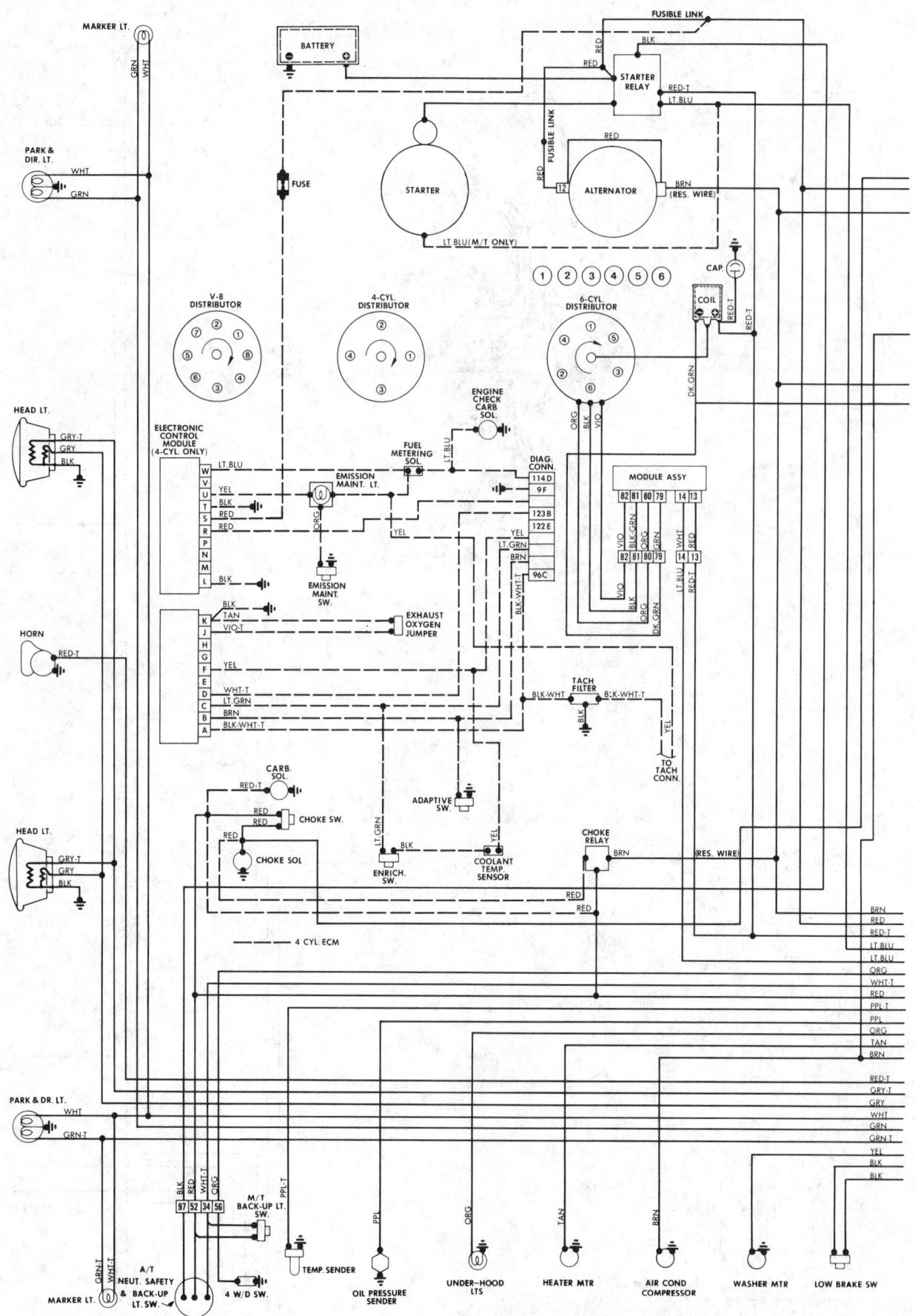

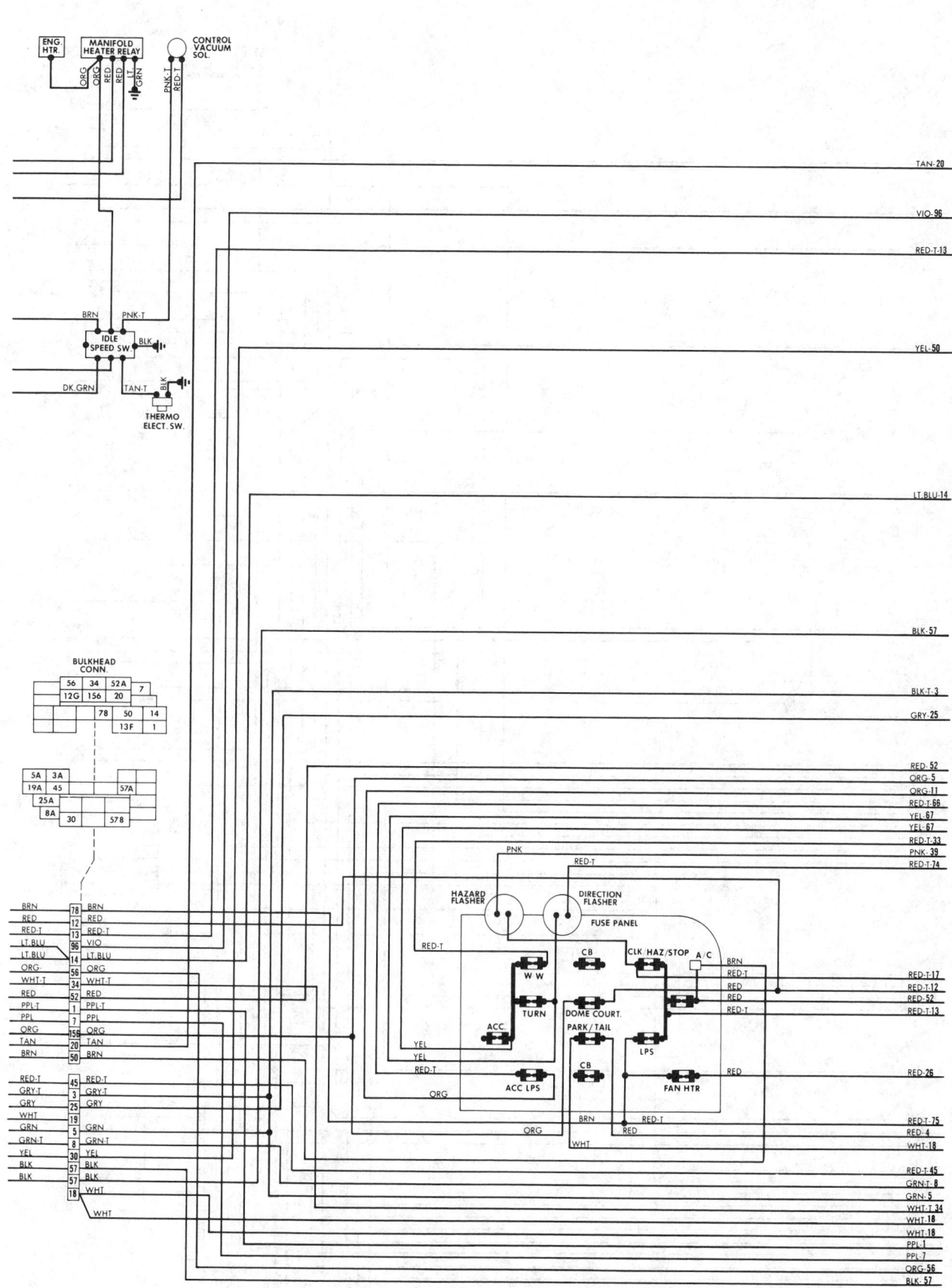

1981 Jeep

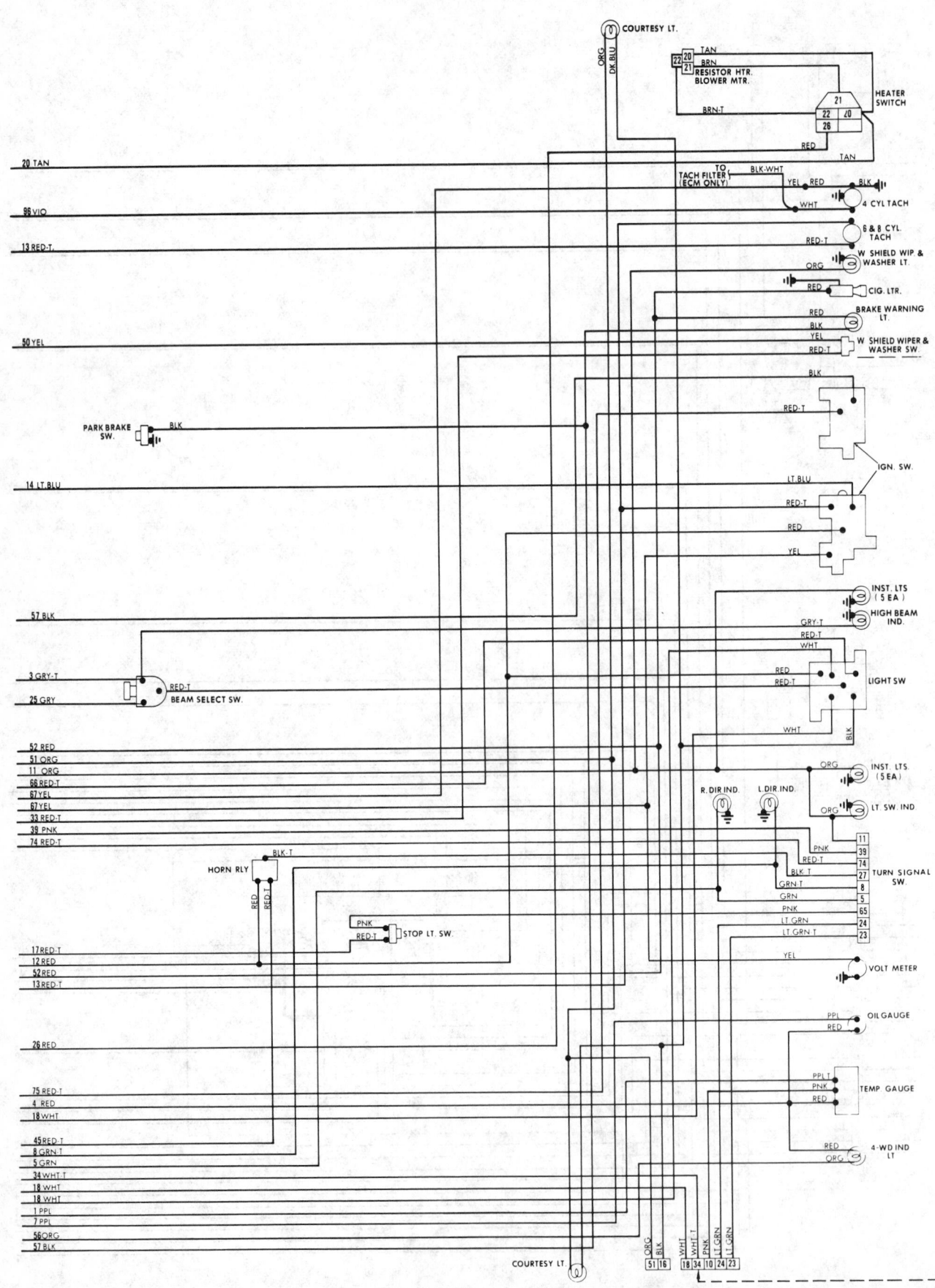

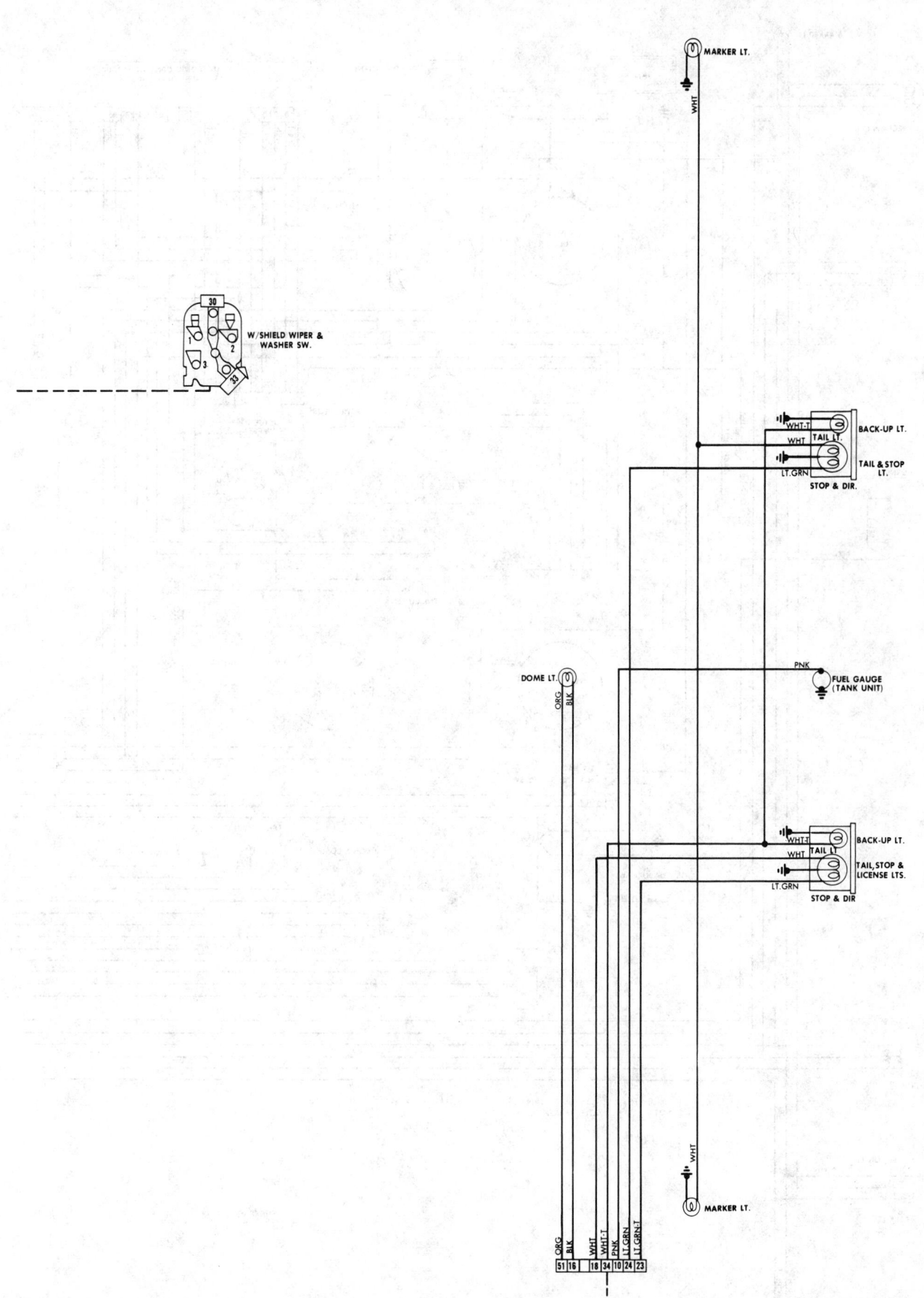

MARKER LT.

WHT

W/SHIELD WIPER & WASHER SW.

30
1
2
3
33

WHT-T   BACK-UP LT.
WHT   TAIL LT.
LT.GRN   TAIL & STOP LT.
STOP & DIR.

PNK   FUEL GAUGE (TANK UNIT)

DOME LT.

ORG   BLK

WHT-T   BACK-UP LT.
WHT   TAIL LT.
LT.GRN   TAIL, STOP & LICENSE LTS.
STOP & DIR

WHT

MARKER LT.

ORG   BLK   WHT   WHT-T   PNK   LT.GRN   LT.GRN-T
51   16   18   34   10   24   23

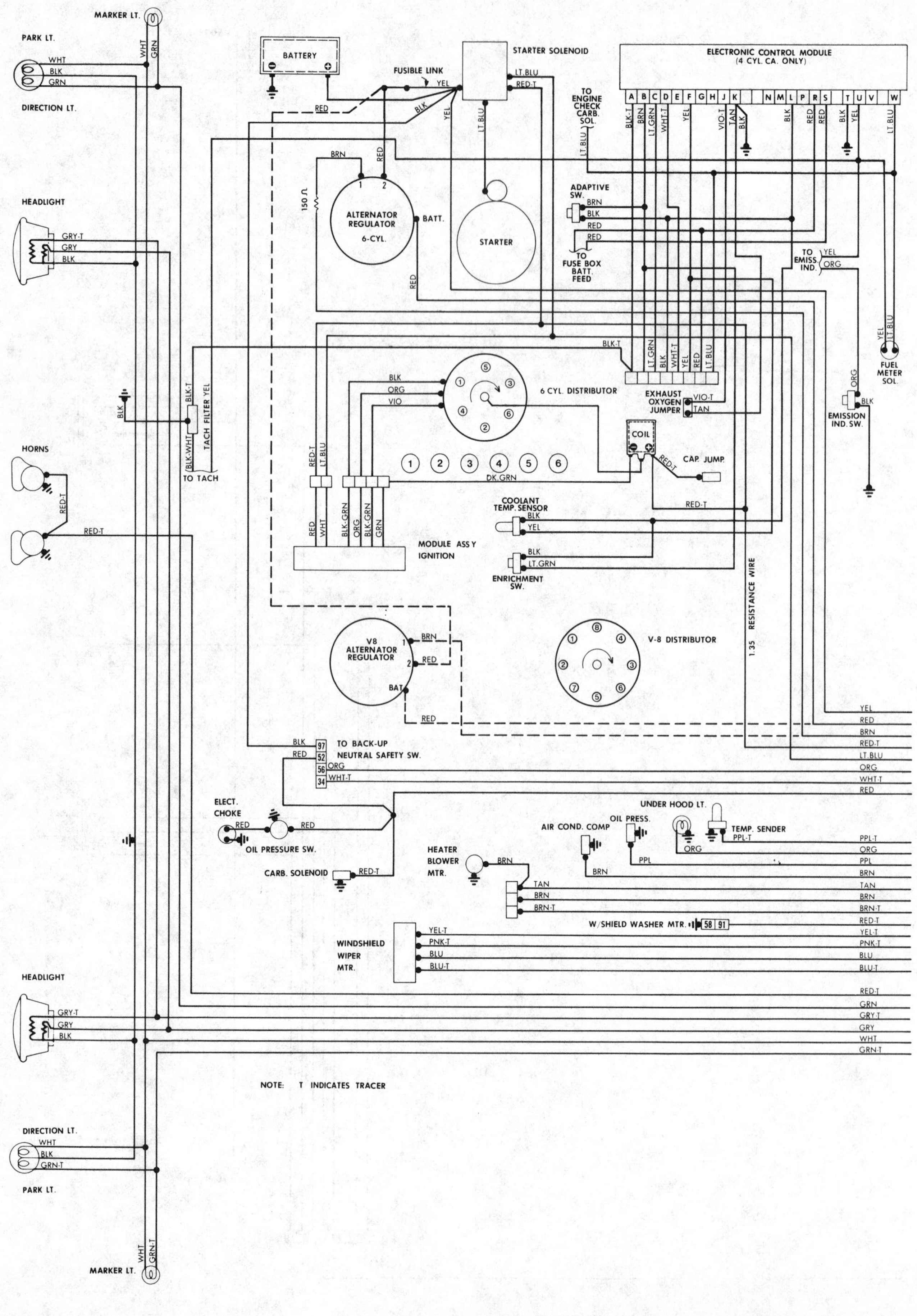

NOTE: T INDICATES TRACER

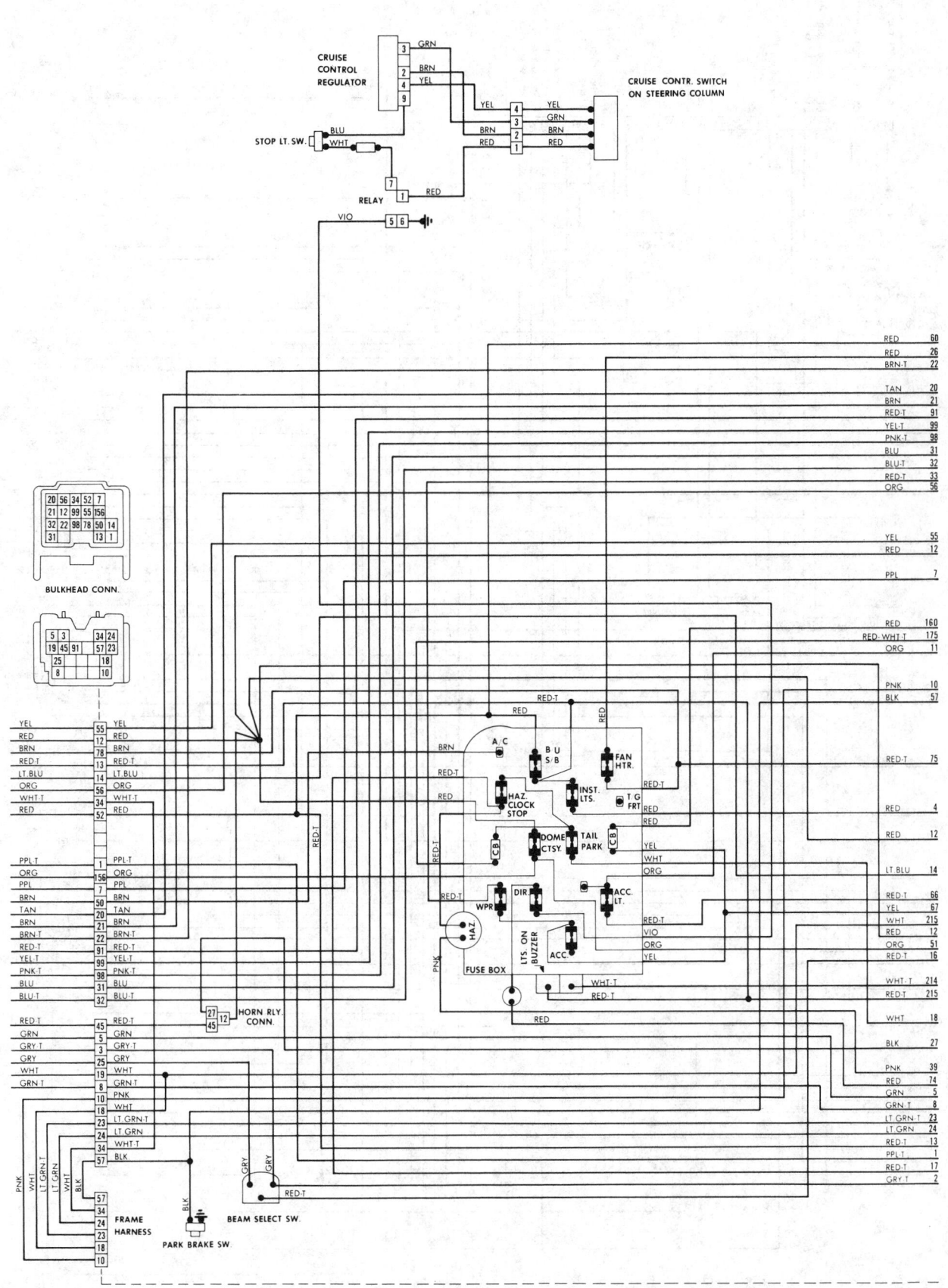

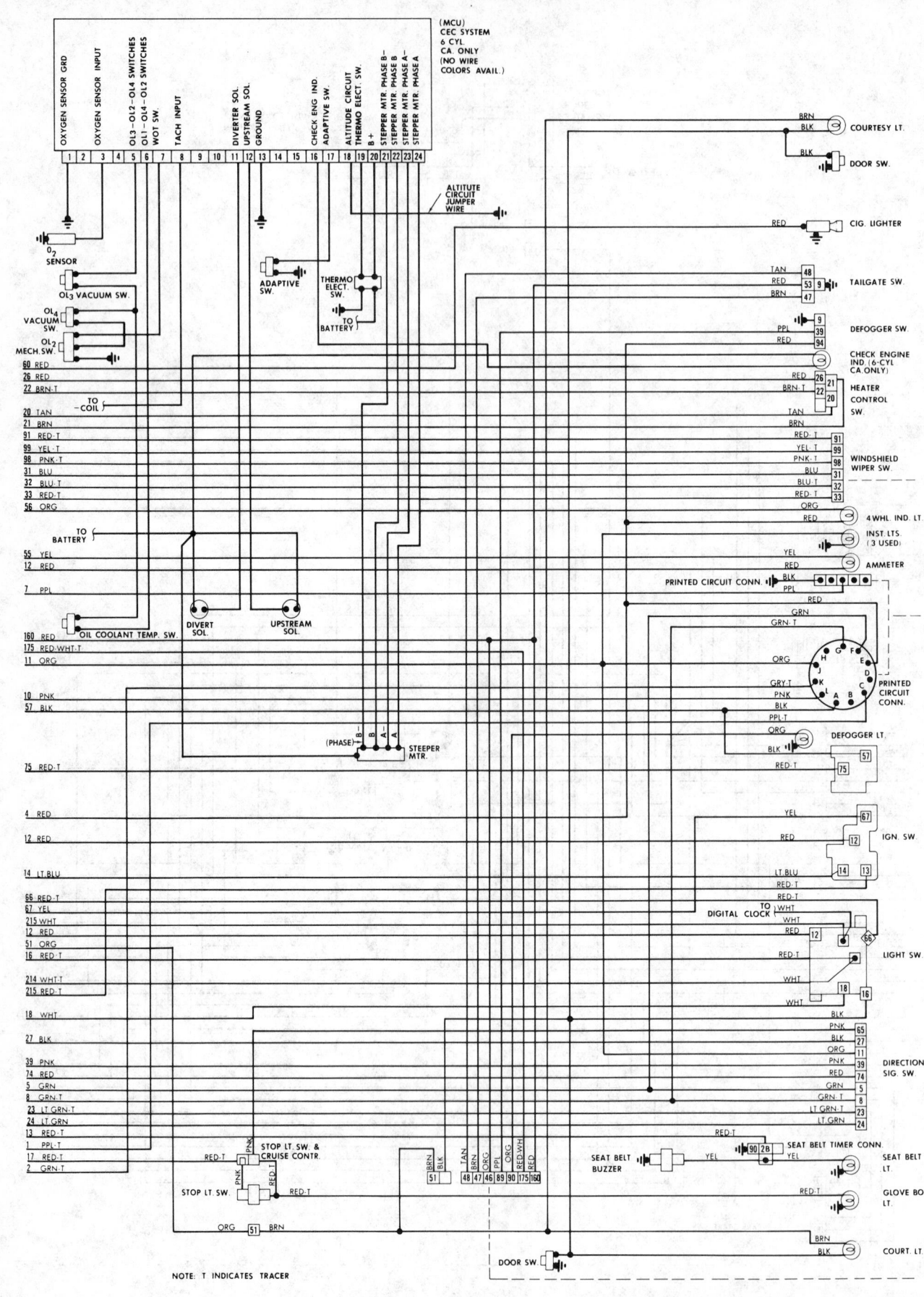

NOTE: T INDICATES TRACER

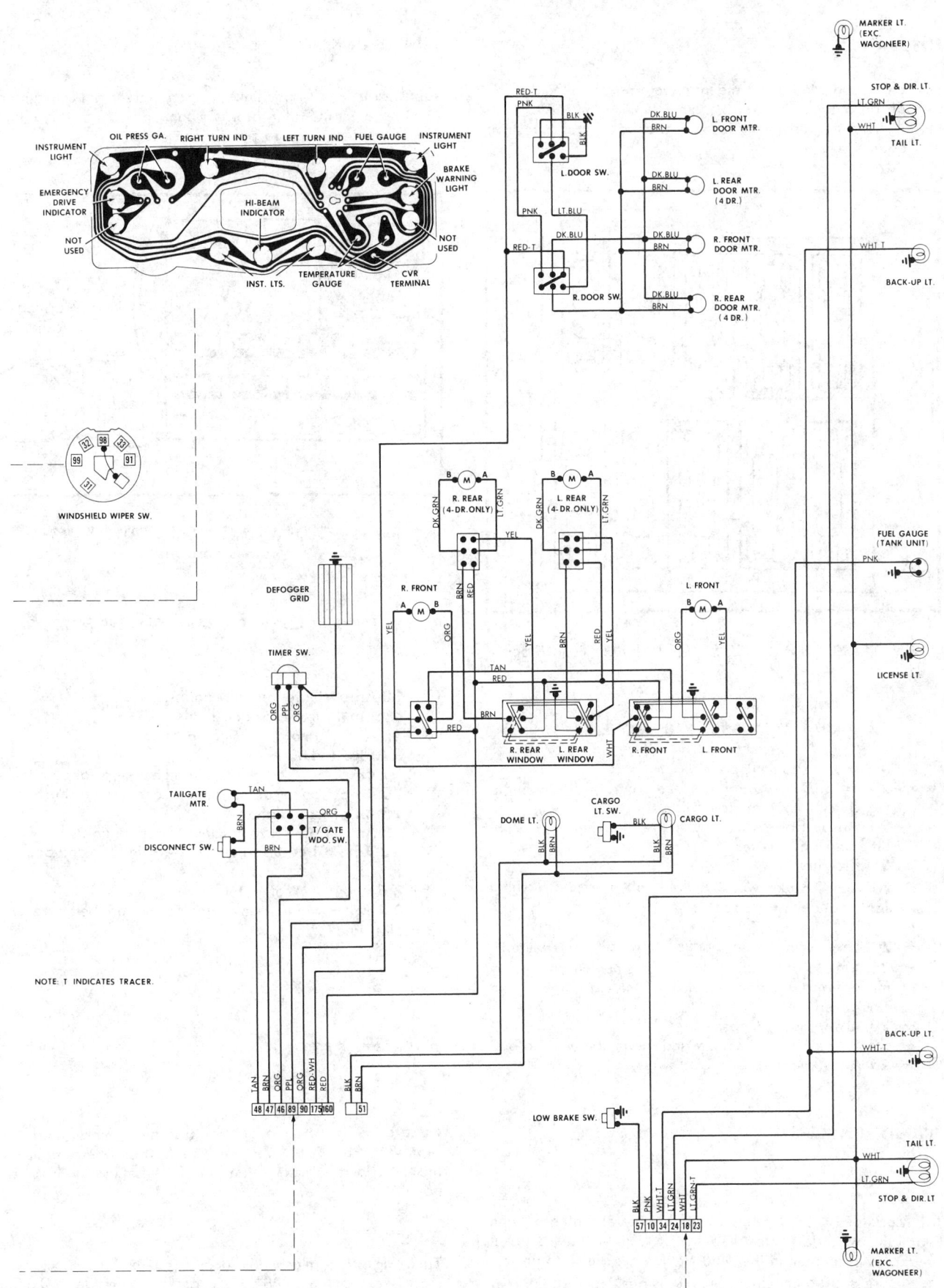

Fuses & Circuit Breakers

CHRYSLER CORP.

FUSE PANEL

Fuse block is located under the instrument panel on the driver's side on all models except "B", "PB", "CB" and "MB". These models have the fuse block located in a box under the glove box door.

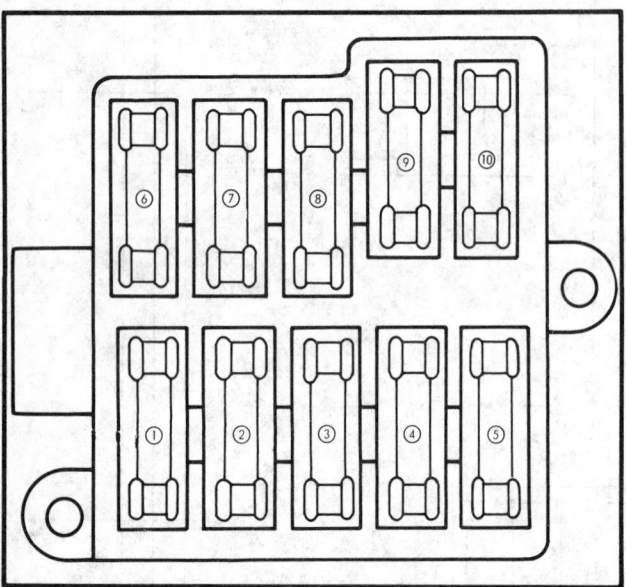

Fig. 1 "B", "PB", "CB" & "MB" Models Fuse Block

"PB", "B", "CB" & "MB" MODELS

① — **5 Amp.** Instrument panel lights.
② — **20 Amp.** Back-up lights, speed control, air conditioning clutch and turn signal lights.
③ — **20 Amp.** Horn, auxiliary heater, auxiliary air conditioning and heater.
④ — **5 Amp.** Radio.
⑤ — **20 Amp.** Brake warning light, oil pressure warning light, gauges and clock.
⑥ — **20 Amp.** Tail, license, parking and side marker lights.
⑦ — **25 Amp.** Dome, stop, glove box, stepwell and vanity mirror lights. Ignition time delay light, cigar lighter and clock feed.
⑧ — **20 Amp.** Hazard flashers.
⑨ — **30 Amp.** Air conditioning and heater blower motors.
⑩ — **25 Amp.** Heated rear window.

CIRCUIT BREAKERS

All Models — A 20 amp. circuit breaker is integral with headlight switch to protect headlight circuit. A 6 amp. circuit breaker is positioned in the windshield wiper switch to protect the wipers. A 20 amp. circuit breaker is positioned at the rear of the ammeter on pickup models, or in the fuse block on van models to protect trailer towing or camper options.

FUSIBLE LINKS

All Models — A fusible link is placed in the main charging circuit to protect the alternator. On some models, a fusible link is placed in the wiring to protect the radio.

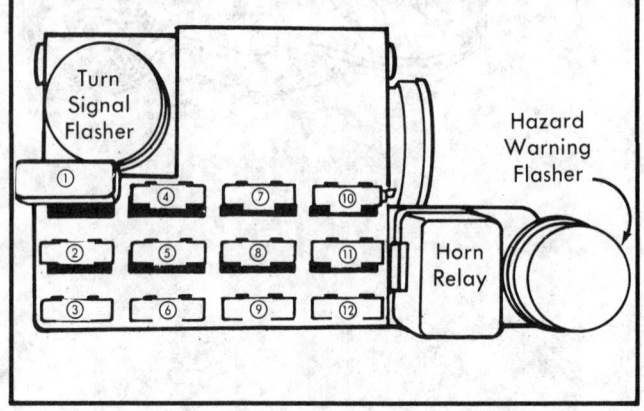

Fig. 2 "A", "W", "AD", "PD", "AW" & "PW" Models Fuse Block

"A", "W", "AD", "PD", "AW" & "PW" MODELS

① — **30 Amp.** Heater and air conditioning.
② — **5 Amp.** Instrument panel lights.
③ — **15 Amp.** Hazard warning flashers.
④ — **5 Amp.** Radio.
⑤ — **15 Amp.** Turn signal flasher and back-up lights.
⑥ — **20 Amp.** Speed control and air conditioning clutch.
⑦ — **25 Amp.** Cigar lighter.
⑧ — **25 Amp.** Horn relay, cargo and interior lights.
⑨ — **30 Amp. Circuit Breaker.** Power windows and door locks.
⑩ — **3 Amp.** Travel computer.
⑪ — **3 Amp.** Instrument cluster lamps and seat belt buzzer.
⑫ — Not Used.

FLASHER LOCATION

Hazard — Flasher is located on fuse block on all models except "B", "PB", "CB" and "MB" models. On these models the flasher is located next to the fuse block behind the instrument panel.

Turn Signal — Flasher is located on the fuse block on all models except "B", "PB", "CB" and "MB" models. On these models the flasher is located next to the fuse block behind the instrument panel.

FORD

FUSE PANEL

All Models — Fuse block is located under instrument panel to the left of the steering column.

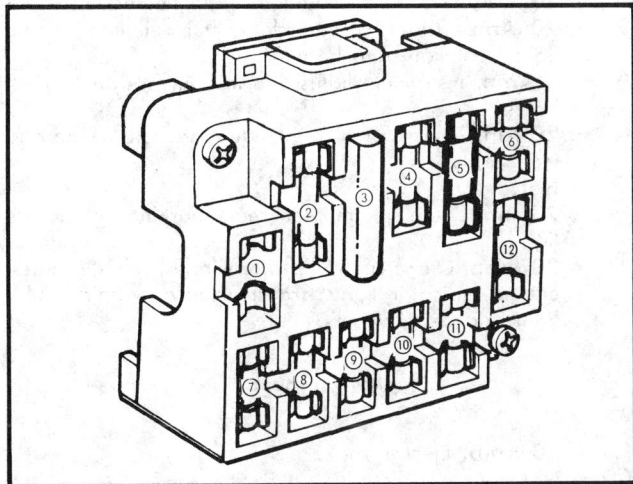

Fig. 1 "E" Models Fuse Panel

"E" MODEL FUSE BLOCK CIRCUITS

① — Not Used.
② — **35 Amp.** Heater and/or air conditioning.
③ — **7.5 Amp.** Circuit breaker. Windshield wipers.
④ — **7.5 Amp.** Seat belt warning.
⑤ — **7.5 Amp.** Throttle solenoid.
⑥ — **3 Amp.** Instrument panel, cluster, ash tray, gear selector, radio, heater/A/C, headlight and windshield wiper illumination lights.
⑦ — **20 Amp.** Hazard flasher and stop lights.
⑧ — **15 Amp.** Dome, cargo and courtesy lights, and cigar lighter.
⑨ — **20 Amp.** Accessory feed and speed control.
⑩ — **15 Amp.** Turn signal and back-up lights, and windshield washer.
⑪ — **7.5 Amp.** Radio and CB radio.
⑫ — Not used.

CIRCUIT BREAKERS

"E" Models — A circuit breaker for protection of windshield wiper system is located in the fuse panel and rated at 7.5 amps. A 15 amp. circuit breaker is located in the headlight switch to protect the tail, license, parking and marker lights and the horn. An 18 amp. circuit breaker is integral with the headlight switch to protect the headlight circuit.

"F" & Bronco Models — An 18 amp. circuit breaker is integral with the headlight switch to protect the headlight circuit. A circuit breaker is integral with the windshield wiper switch to protect the wiper circuit.

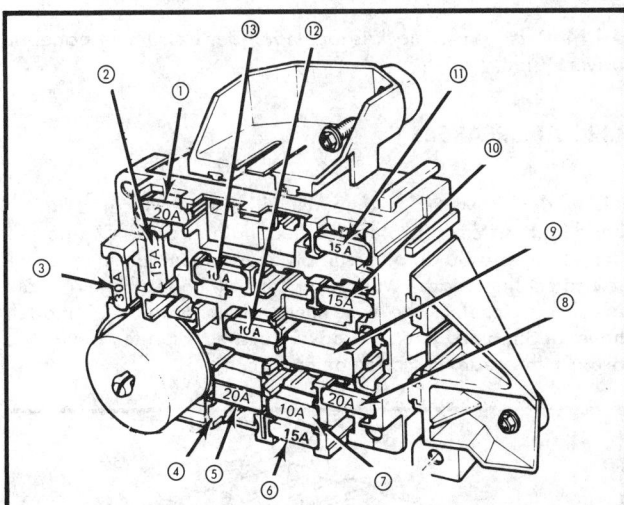

Fig. 2   Bronco & "F" Models Fuse Block

BRONCO & "F" MODELS FUSE BLOCK CIRCUITS

① — **20 Amp.** Hazard warning and stop lights.
② — **15 Amp.** Turn signal and back-up lights.
③ — **30 Amp. Circuit Breaker.** Heater blower motor.
④ — **5 Amp.** Instrument panel lights.
⑤ — **20 Amp. Circuit Breaker.** Power windows, tailgate and door locks.
⑥ — **15 Amp.** Emission control.
⑦ — **10 Amp.** Auxiliary fuel tank (pickup).
⑧ — **20 Amp.** Horn and cigar lighter.
⑨ — **30 Amp. Circuit Breaker.** Power door locks and tailgate.
⑩ — **15 Amp.** Courtesy lights.
⑪ — **15 Amp.** Tail and parking lights.
⑫ — **10 Amp.** Radio.
⑬ — **15 Amp.** Accessories and windshield wipers.

IN-LINE FUSES

"E" Models — A 5 amp. in-line fuse is used to protect the electric mirror.

FUSIBLE LINKS

"E" Models — Fusible links are used to protect the following circuits. Separate links in the starter motor relay to protect air conditioner, alternator, dual batteries and fog lights. Alternator is also protected by a link located at the electric choke.

"F" & Bronco Models — Fusible links are used to protect the following circuits. Separate links at the starter relay protect the alternator and trailer towing package. A link at the junction block protects the marker lights on F250/350 camper special and F350 with dual wheels. Alternator is protected by a link located at the electric choke.

FLASHER LOCATION

Hazard — Flasher is located at rear of fuse block on "F" and Bronco models, and under left side of dashboard on "E" models.

Turn Signal — Flasher located at front of fuse block on Bronco and "F" models. Flasher located on left side cowl on "E" models.

Fuses & Circuit Breakers

GENERAL MOTORS

FUSE PANEL

All Models — Fuse block is located under instrument panel on driver's side.

CIRCUIT BREAKERS

All models have a 15 amp. circuit breaker located in the headlight switch to protect the headlight circuit. "C" and "K" models have a 30 amp. circuit breaker located on the firewall to protect the tailgate window motor. All models have a circuit breaker to protect the windshield wiper motor. "G" models have a 35 amp. circuit breaker located on the firewall to protect the rear air conditioning circuit.

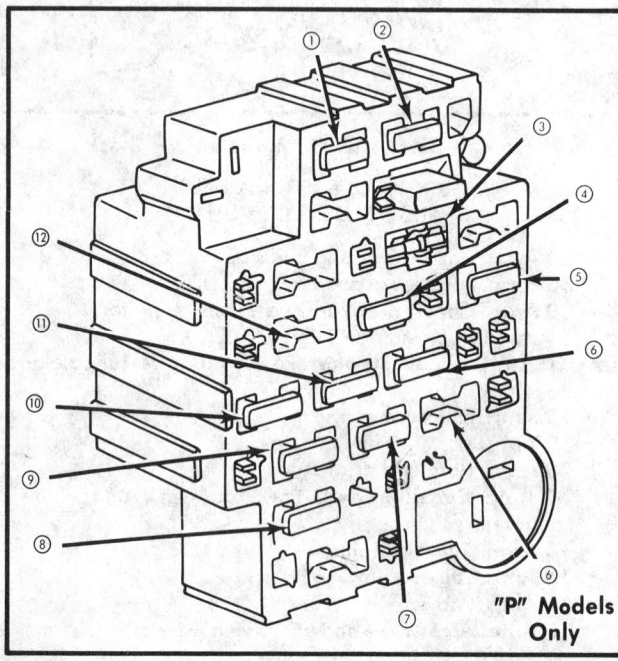

"P" Models Only

Fig. 1 Fuse Panel All Models

"C" & "K" MODELS

① — **20 Amp.** Electric choke.
② — **20 Amp.** Heater, air conditioner, alternator warning light and heavy duty heater (if equipped).
③ — **25 Amp.** Auxiliary heater or air conditioner.
④ — **15 Amp.** Radio, idle stop solenoid and auxiliary battery.
⑤ — **15 Amp.** Turn signal, hazard and stop lights.
⑥ — **25 Amp.** Windshield wiper and washer.
⑦ — **20 Amp.** Cigar lighter, clock and horn. Dome, cargo and spot lights.
⑧ — **5 Amp.** Instrument panel lights and headlight warning buzzer.
⑨ — **15 Amp.** Turn signal (front), side marker and backup lights.
⑩ — **20 Amp.** Cruise control, gauges and engine warning indicators. Four-wheel drive indicator light, auxiliary fuel tank, transmission downshift (M40) and seat belt warning buzzer.
⑪ — **20 Amp.** Courtesy, roof, license, parking, side marker, tail, clearance and side clearance lights.
⑫ — Not used.

"G" MODELS

① — **20 Amp.** Electric choke heater.
② — **25 Amp.** Windshield wipers.
③ — **10 Amp.** Radio, auxiliary battery and idle stop solenoid.
④ — **25 Amp.** Rear air conditioner or auxiliary heater.
⑤ — **20 Amp.** Turn signal, stop and hazard lights.
⑥ — **20 Amp.** Front air conditioner and heater.
⑦ — **20 Amp.** Cigar lighter, clock, stepwell light, dome light, spot light and horn.
⑧ — **5 Amp.** Instrument lights and instrument panel switch lights.
⑨ — **20 Amp.** Turn signal, front side marker, back-up and stop lights.
⑩ — Not used.
⑪ — **20 Amp.** Tail, side marker (rear), parking and license lights.
⑫ — **20 Amp.** Cruise control, power window relay, gauges, engine indicator lights, transmission downshift (M40) light and delay wipers.

"P" MODELS

① — **20 Amp.** Electric choke.
② — Not used.
③ — **10 Amp.** Radio.
④ — **25 Amp.** Air conditioning and heater blower motor.
⑤ — **15 Amp.** Turn signal, stop and hazard lights.
⑥ — **25 Amp.** Windshield wipers and washer.
⑦ — **15 Amp.** Horn, cigar lighter, clock, courtesy and dome lights.
⑧ — **5 Amp.** Instrument panel lights.
⑨ — **15 Amp.** Turn signal, back-up and stop lights, and auxiliary battery.
⑩ — **10 Amp.** Idle stop solenoid, gauges, indicator lights, speed switch solenoid and relay and transmission downshift.
⑪ — **20 Amp.** Tail, license, parking, side marker, clearance and identification lights.
⑫ — Not used.

IN-LINE FUSES

An in-line fuse is used on all models to protect the auxiliary heater circuit. On "C" and "K" models, an in-line fuse protects the engine compartment light and front and rear air conditioning circuits. On "G" models, an in-line fuse protects the ammeter.

FUSIBLE LINKS

Fusible links are incorporated into the wiring harness on all models to protect the following circuits: Headlight high-beam indicator, horn, ignition and air conditioning high blower motor. On all models except "G", a link is placed in the starter solenoid circuit.

FLASHER LOCATION

Hazard — Located on fuse block on all models.

Turn Signal — Located behind instrument panel near steering column on all models.

Anti-Theft — On "G" models only, a flasher is located to left of steering column near parking brake.

Fuses & Circuit Breakers

JEEP CORP.

FUSE PANEL

All Models — Located under the instrument panel on the driver's side of the vehicle.

CIRCUIT BREAKERS

All Models — A 24 amp. circuit breaker is located in the headlight switch to protect headlight circuit. A 7 amp. circuit breaker is located in the wiper switch to protect the wipers. Cherokee and Wagoneer models have two 30 amp. circuit breakers located in the fuse block to protect the electric tailgate window. One protects the instrument panel switch circuit and the other protects the tailgate switch circuit.

IN-LINE FUSES

All Models — Six-cylinder models have a 4 amp. in-line fuse protecting the cruise control. Eight-cylinder models have a 1.5 amp. in-line fuse protecting the cruise control.

FUSIBLE LINKS

All Models — A fusible link is located in alternator wiring harness for protection of the system.

FLASHER LOCATION

Hazard — Flasher is located on fuse block on all models.

Turn Signal — Flasher is located on fuse block on all models.

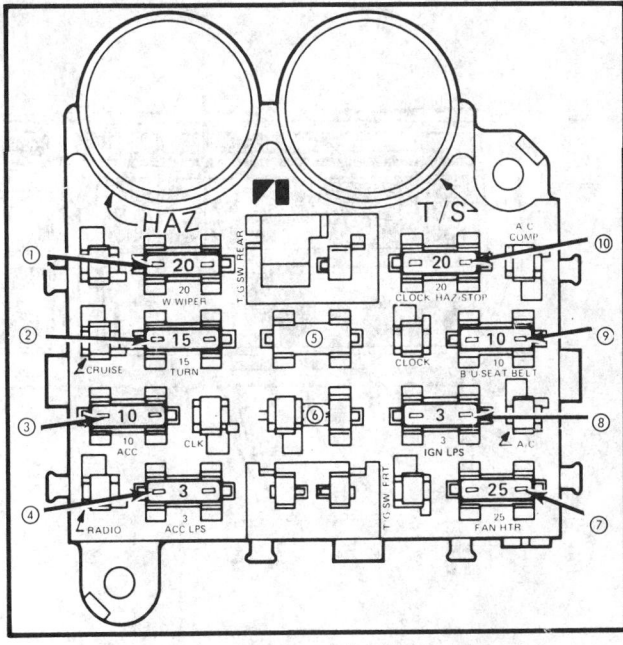

Fig. 1   Fuse Panel All Models

"CJ", CHEROKEE, WAGONEER & TRUCK

① — **20 Amp. All Except "CJ" & Scrambler.** Windshield wipers. **4.5 Amp. "CJ" & Scrambler Only.** Windshield wipers.

② — **15 Amp.** Turn signals.

③ — **10 Amp.** Accessories.

④ — **3 Amp.** Instrument and accessory lights.

⑤ — **20 Amp.** Interior lights.

⑥ — **20 Amp.** Brake, tail and parking lights.

⑦ — **25 Amp.** Air conditioning, heater and electric fan.

⑧ — **3 Amp.** Instruments.

⑨ — **25 Amp. All Except "CJ" & Scrambler.** Seat belt warning and back-up lights. **10 Amp. 6-Cyl. "CJ" & Scrambler.** Seat belt warning and back-up lights. **20 Amp. 4-Cyl. "CJ" & Scrambler.** Seat belt warning and back-up lights.

⑩ — **20 Amp.** Hazard flasher, clock and stop lights.

Fuse Block & Flasher Locations

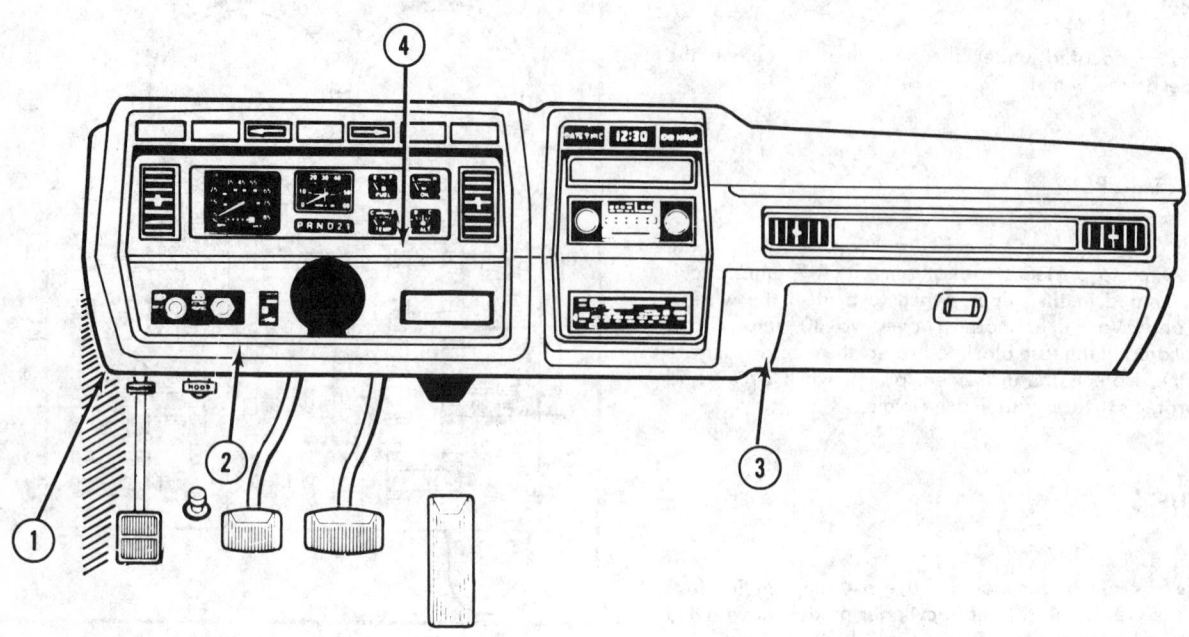

Manufacturer and Model	Fuse Block	Hazard Flasher	Turn Signal Flasher
Chrysler Corp.			
All Pick-Up Models All Van Models	②Left of Steering Column ③Behind Instrument Panel	On Fuse Block ③Next to Fuse Block	On Fuse Block ③Next to Fuse Block
Ford Motor Co.			
"F" 100 — 350 Models "E" 100 — 350 Models Bronco Models	②Left of Steering Column ②Left of Steering Column ②Left of Steering Column	Back of Fuse Block ①Left Wiring Harness Back of Fuse Block	On Fuse Block ①Left Wiring Harness On Fuse Block
General Motors			
"C" and "K" Models "P" Models "G" Models	②Left of Steering Column ②Left of Steering Column ②Left of Steering Column	On Fuse Block On Fuse Block On Fuse Block	②Near Fuse Block ②Near Fuse Block ②Near Fuse Block
Jeep			
"CJ5", "CJ7" & Scrambler Models Cherokee, Wagoneer & Truck Models	②Left of Steering Column ②Left of Steering Column	On Fuse Block On Fuse Block	On Fuse Block On Fuse Block

Section 6
ACCESSORIES & EQUIPMENT

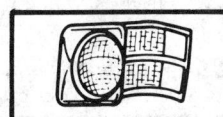

Contents

NOTE – *ALSO SEE GENERAL INDEX.*

IMPORTANT

Because of the great number of model names used by vehicle manufacturers, accurate identification of models is important. See Model Identification at the front of this publication.

Air Conditioning Servicing

COMPRESSOR OIL CHECK

GENERAL NOTES

AIR TEMP, TECUMSEH & YORK COMPRESSORS

Oil level on these compressors may be checked with compressor mounted in vehicle. If these compressors are equipped with stem-type service valves, compressor may be "isolated", thereby avoiding necessity of discharging entire system.

NOTE — *See Compressor Isolating or related paragraphs in this Section.*

FRIGIDAIRE COMPRESSORS

When checking oil level on these compressors, it may be necessary to remove compressor from vehicle, as filler plug is located near bottom of compressor. After oil level is checked, system must be evacuated and recharged.

NOTE — *See Frigidaire Compressor in this Section.*

COMPRESSOR ISOLATING

On York and Tecumseh compressors with stem-type service valves (at compressor suction and discharge ports), it will not be necessary to discharge entire system in order to service compressor.

NOTE — *See York & Tecumseh Compressors and Compressor Replacement in this Section.*

REFRIGERATION OIL

Only new, pure, moisture-free refrigeration oil should be used in the air conditioning system. This oil is highly refined and dehydrated (moisture content less than 10 parts per million) to a point well below contamination factor. Refrigeration oil container must be kept tightly closed at all times when not in use, or moisture will be absorbed from the air and introduced into the refrigeration system.

AIR-TEMP COMPRESSOR

CHRYSLER CORP.

Oil capacity is 10-12 oz. in 2-cylinder compressors. 6-cylinder compressors, 9-10 oz. Oil level need not be checked each time system is discharged, unless refrigerant charge has been lost or significant oil loss is indicated. Quantity of oil in compressor sump is measured using dipstick. See *Fig. 1*.

2-Cylinder (RV-2) Oil Level Check — 1) Slowly discharge system. This will prevent oil from escaping with refrigerant. Near completion of discharge, oil dipstick should be flushed with freon on insure a clean dipstick.

2) Slowly remove compressor filler plug (some residual pressure will remain after discharge). Insert oil lever dipstick until it bottoms in sump. Oil lever on stick must be 3-3.4". If necessary, add recommended oil to bring level to specifications. Do not exceed specified amount. Install filler plug and recharge system.

6-Cylinder (C-171) Oil Level Check — 1) Slowly discharge system. With system discharged, disconnect suction and discharge lines from compressor and remove compressor.

2) Drain oil from suction port and discard. Add 9 oz. of new refrigerant oil through suction port. Clean drain plug and put a light coat of sealant on threads. Install drain plug and tighten to 90-130 INCH lbs.

3) Install compressor, connect suction and discharge lines and tighten, using new gaskets to prevent leakage.

4) Evacuate system and recharge to specification.

Oil Level Check After Discharge — If using fast discharge method (with oil collector can attached to center discharge hose), measure amount of oil in can. Replace this amount with new oil. If following components are replaced, add specified additional amounts of oil:

Evaporator	2 oz.
Condenser	1 oz.
Receiver-Drier	1 oz.

NOTE — *After this is completed, use standard dipstick method to determine exact oil level before recharging system.*

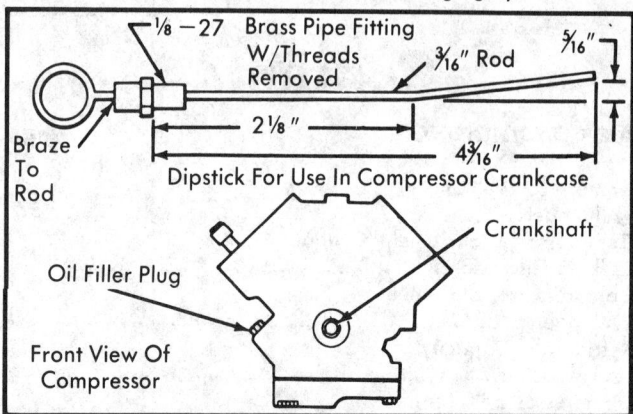

Fig. 1   Air-Temp Compressor Oil Check Point and Dipstick for Chrysler

FRIGIDAIRE COMPRESSOR

GENERAL MOTORS
4 & 6-CYLINDER COMPRESSOR

A/C system with 6-cylinder compressor is fully charged with 10 oz. refrigerant oil. 4-cylinder compressor is fully charged with 6 oz. Optional overhead A/C system is fully charged with 13 oz. Adding additional oil is not required unless a definite oil loss has occurred due to a ruptured line, leaking compressor seal, replacement of system component, compressor overhaul, or collision.

NOTE — *Do not reuse old oil; add only new refrigerant oil to system.*

On-Car Checking After Minor Repairs — 1) With compressor in normal position (not removed) and system fully discharged, loosen oil plug far enough to determine if it will run out. If oil starts to run out, do not add additional oil other than amount shown for component replacement (as performed).

2) If oil does not run out and there is visible evidence of considerable oil loss somewhere in the system, add 4 ounces of new oil to the compressor after repairing leak and adding oil to replaced component (as required).

3) If oil does not run out and there is no visible evidence of a large oil leak, add 2 ounces of new oil to the compressor after repairing leak and adding proper amount to replaced components (as required).

4) Oil can be added without removing the compressor, by using a special oil injector (J-7605-03) or by using the A/C service station unit as recommended by the manufacturer. If these are not available, remove compressor and pour proper amount of oil into compressor.

COMPRESSOR OIL CHECK (Cont.)

Off-Car Checking After Major Repair — 1) Before performing repairs, if system is operable, run A/C for several minutes to stabilize system. Turn off air conditioner and engine, discharge system completely, and remove compressor. Slowly remove oil drain plug, then drain and measure oil from compressor, and replace amounts as outlined below. If new compressor is being installed, drain and measure oil from old compressor and add new oil to replacement compressor using described method below; if compressor is being overhauled, add one additional ounce of oil to amount being replaced.

2) If quantity drained is less than 4 ounces, add 6 ounces of replacement oil. If quantity drained is between 4 and 6 ounces, oil is properly distributed throughout the system; add same amount as drained. If quantity drained is more than 6 ounces, add ONLY 6 ounces

NOTE — *A-6 system will have 6 oz. of oil in accumulator and/or compressor. This is why BOTH have to be measured.*

3) If compressor is inoperable, use the following method: Remove compressor, drain, measure, and discard the oil. If amount drained is more than 1½ ounces, and the system shows no sign of a major leak, add amount drained. If less than 1½ ounces is drained and system appears to have lost excessive oil, add 6 ounces to replacement compressor, or 7 ounces if compressor is being overhauled.

4) When repairing system leaks by replacing components, add additional amounts of oil as specified:

Evaporator	3 oz.
Condenser	1 oz.
Receiver-Drier	1 oz.
Accumulator	1 oz.①

① — R-4 accumulator holds 2 oz. plus 1 oz. for desiccant.

NOTE — *If oil drained contains metal chips or other foreign material, replace receiver-drier and flush or replace other components as necessary.*

TECUMSEH & YORK COMPRESSORS

FORD W/SCHRADER SERVICE VALVES

Check compressor oil level only if any portion of refrigerant system is being replaced, or if system was discharged due to a leak.

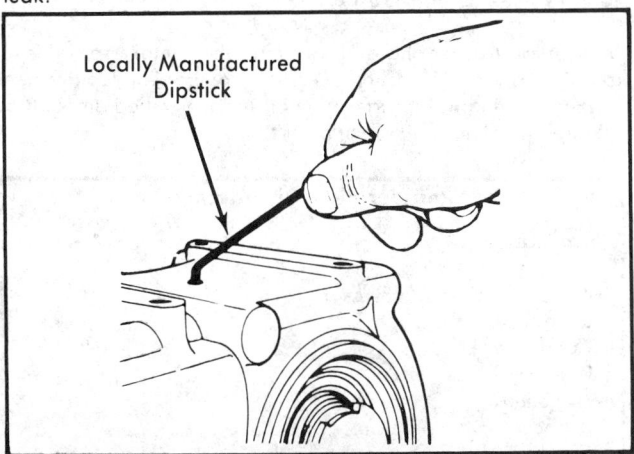

Locally Manufactured Dipstick

Fig. 2   Checking Compressor Oil Level Horizontally Mounted Unit

On horizontally mounted compressors, oil check hole is located on side of crankshaft which faces up. On opposite or downward side there is a corresponding boss provided on inner wall as an alternate oil check hole, for different mounting. When checking oil level on such a compressor, angle the dipstick such that it bottoms against lower side of compressor and not against boss.

1) After system has been charged, operate for approximately 10 minutes, or until pressures have stabilized (with ambient temperature of 60°F or higher).

2) Stop engine and discharge entire system using a suitable Schrader-Type service valve. Fabricate a suitable dipstick according to specifications *(see Fig. 3)*. Remove oil filler plug and insert dipstick until it bottoms. If necessary, slightly rotate compressor crankshaft by hand so that dipstick will clear. Level on dipstick must be within specifications.

Tecumseh Compressor Oil Level	
Application	**Measurement**
All Models	
Horizontal Mount	⅞-1 ⅝ "
Vertical Mount	⅞-1 ⅜ "

FORD & JEEP W/STEM TYPE SERVICE VALVES

Oil level should be checked whenever the system is discharged for service part replacement, or if system has self-discharged due to component malfunction. Oil level is checked with compressor in its operating position.

It is important when checking oil level that system has been operated and car interior temperature has cooled to desired setting. This is necessary to stabilize amount of oil in the system.

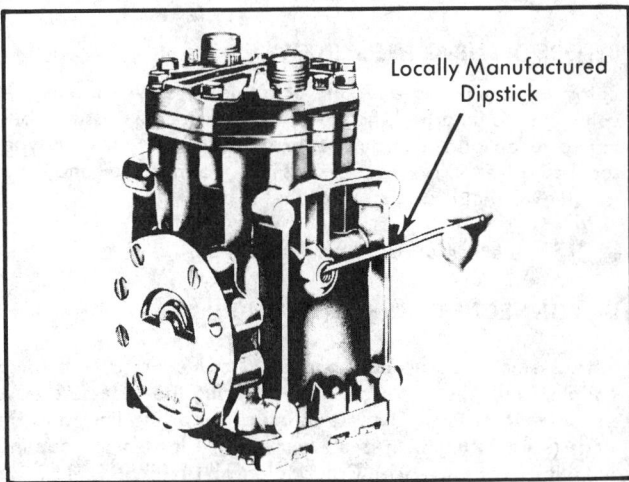

Locally Manufactured Dipstick

Fig. 3   Checking Oil on Vertically Mounted York Compressor

NOTE — *The following oil checking procedure details isolating the compressor prior to checking; however, it is possible to discharge the entire system and then check the oil level.*

Air Conditioning Servicing

COMPRESSOR OIL CHECK (Cont.)

York Compressor Oil Level	
Application	**Measurement**
Ford	
Horizontal Mount	$^{13}/_{16}$-$1^{13}/_{16}$"
Vertical Mount	$^{7}/_{8}$-$1^{1}/_{8}$"
Jeep	
Horizontal Mount	$^{13}/_{16}$-$1^{13}/_{16}$"
Vertical Mount	$^{7}/_{8}$-$1^{1}/_{8}$"

1) Turn both the high and low pressure service valve clockwise as far as possible (front-seat position). Loosen cap on the high pressure service valve and bleed residual pressure from compressor.

CAUTION — *Only loosen cap a small amount and DO NOT remove cap until pressure is totally relieved.*

NOTE — *Oil level check plugs are located on either side of compressor crankcase; use check plug which is most convenient when checking oil level with compressor on car.*

2) Fabricate a suitable dipstick according to specifications. Using proper end of dipstick, check oil level. Add clean refrigerant oil if necessary. Install new "O" ring seal on filler plug.

3) When oil check is complete, compressor must be purged of air before operating the system.

NOTE — *See procedure as outlined in Compressor Replacement in COMPONENT REPLACEMENT Section.*

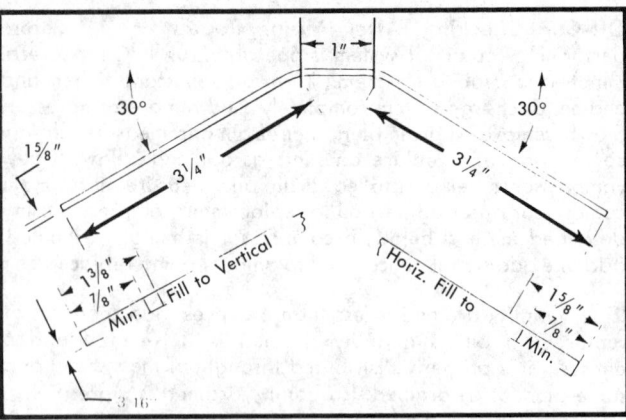

Fig. 4   Dimensions for Locally Made Tecumseh Compressor Oil Level Dipstick

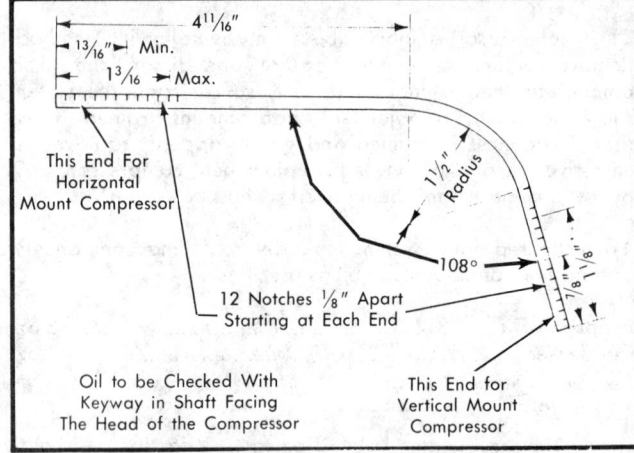

Fig. 5   Dimensions for Locally Made York Compressor Oil Level Dipstick

COMPONENT REPLACEMENT CAUTIONS

BEFORE OPENING THE SYSTEM

Before disconnecting any lines or fittings, the system must be completely discharged; however, if only the compressor is being removed and the compressor is equipped with stem-type service valves (York or Tecumseh) , compressor may be isolated without discharging the system.

NOTE — *See Compressor Isolation Method.*

DISCONNECTING LINES & FITTINGS

After system is discharged, carefully clean entire area around coupling nut to prevent dirt from entering the system. Always use two wrenches to avoid twisting or distorting lines and fittings (hold fitting with one wrench while loosening coupling nut with second wrench). Cap or plug all LINES and FITTINGS immediately to prevent entry of air and moisture into system and do not remove these caps until connections are being made.

See following pages for removal and installation of each component. After replacement or repaired component is installed, connect lines as directed below.

COMPONENT REPLACEMENT

See following pages for removal and installation of each component. After replacement or repaired component installed, connect lines as directed below.

In addition to checking and adjusting the compressor oil level (see Compressor Oil Check), certain component replacement requires additional refrigeration oil. Add specified amounts of oil directly to the component prior to installation.

Refrigeration Oil Addition	
Application	**Amount**
With Frigidaire Compressor	
Evaporator	3 oz.
Condenser	1 oz.
Receiver-Drier	1 oz.
With Air-Temp Compressor	
Evaporator	2 oz.
Condenser	1 oz.
Receiver-Drier	1 oz.

COMPRESSOR REPLACEMENT

CONNECTING LINES & FITTINGS

A new "O" ring should be used in all instances when connecting lines and fittings (dip "O" ring in clean refrigeration oil and make certain it is not twisted during installation). Always use two wrenches to avoid twisting or distorting lines and fittings, tighten coupling nuts securely.

PLACING SYSTEM IN OPERATION

After component replacement and/or system servicing has been completed and all connections have been made, proceed as follows:

1) Evacuate the system using a vacuum pump.

2) Charge the system with new R-12 (refrigerant) according to each individual vehicle manufacturers procedure as outlined in this Manual.

NOTE – *Also see Refrigerant Capacity in this Section.*

3) Leak test the system, with particular attention to all new connections and components.

4) Make a performance test of the system.

COMPRESSOR ISOLATION METHOD

On systems which have compressors equipped with stem-type service valves (York and some Tecumseh), it is possible to isolate the compressor for removal as detailed below.

Isolating (Ford) – Turn both high and low pressure manual valves to extreme clockwise (front seat) position. Loosen cap on high pressure manual valve connection to compressor and allow gas to escape until compressor is relieved of pressure.

Isolating (Jeep) – 1) Connect pressure gauge and manifold assembly (J-23575). Close both gauge hand valves and mid-position both service valves. Start engine and operate A/C.

2) Turn suction service valve slowly clockwise toward front-seat position. When suction pressure is reduced to zero or less, stop engine and compressor and quickly finish frontseating suction service valve.

3) Front-seat discharge service valve. Loosen oil check plug slowly to release any internal pressure in compressor. Compressor is now isolated from system.

Removal – 1) Carefully remove service valves from compressor by unscrewing the mounting bolts. Do not disturb line connections and do not turn valve stems with valve assemblies disconnected from compressor (to prevent system discharge). Cap service valves and plug compressor openings to prevent entry of dirt and moisture.

2) If compressor clutch is to be removed (for installation on replacement compressor), energize compressor clutch with engine NOT running and remove clutch mounting bolt from end of compressor shaft, then install ⅜-11 bolt in driveshaft hole and tighten bolt to loosen clutch from shaft with clutch energized, disconnect clutch lead. Remove drive belt and clutch.

3) Remove service valve caps and shipping plugs from compressor valve ports and immediately install service valves on compressor using new "O" rings.

4) Remove compressor mounting bolts and lift compressor off engine. Remove clutch field assembly from compressor (on early compressors with rotating field, remove brush assembly).

Installation – 1) Position compressor on engine, install compressor clutch using new retaining bolt and washer (energize clutch to hold shaft while tightening nut).

2) Make necessary compressor oil level check and add oil if necessary.

NOTE – *See Compressor Oil Check in this Section.*

3) Drain and measure compressor oil level. Retain measurement to make proper oil adjustment during installation.

4) Leak test compressor, and then evacuate it and connect it back into system. Recheck compressor oil level, adding or removing oil as necessary for correct oil level.

COMPRESSOR DISCHARGE METHOD

This procedure is to be used on vehicles which have compressor equipped with Schrader service valves. In these cases, the compressor cannot be isolated and the system must be discharged prior to compressor removal.

Removal (Chrysler Corp.) – 1) Discharge system. Measure and record refrigerant level so that it can be refilled to exact level in replacement or repaired compressor. Disconnect suction and discharge lines and cap openings.

2) Disconnect magnetic clutch-to-control unit wire and on Air-Temp compressors, remove clutch assembly. Remove compressor-to-bracket attaching bolts and remove compressor. On C-171 compressors, drain oil from suction and discharge ports.

Installation (Chrysler Corp.) – 1) Reverse removal procedures noting the following; On C-171 compressors, add oil to bring level to 5 ounces. On Air-Temp compressors, rotate crankshaft assembly by hand at least 2 revolutions to clear oil accumulation from compressor head before energizing clutch, or damage to reed valves will result.

2) On all models, evacuate and charge air conditioning system.

Removal (General Motors "C" & "K") – Discharge system. Remove connector attaching bolt. Remove connector and cap openings. Disconnect wiring to clutch actuating coil. Remove drive belt. Remove compressor mounting brackets and compressor. Drain and measure oil in compressor.

Installation (General Motors "C" & "K") – Replace oil in compressor with exact amount drained. Reverse removal procedures, installing new "O" rings on connector. Evacuate and charge system. Check operation.

Removal (General Motors "G" Models) – 1) Disconnect battery ground cable and compressor clutch connector. Purge system of refrigerant. Release belt tension and remove drive belt.

COMPRESSOR REPLACEMENT (Cont.)

2) Remove 2 bolts and 2 clamps holding engine cover and remove engine cover. Remove air cleaner, fitting and muffler assembly and cap openings.

3) Remove compressor-to-bracket bolts. Remove engine oil tube support bracket bolt and nut from compressor. Remove clutch ground wire and remove compressor. Drain and measure oil in compressor.

Installation (General Motors "G" Models) — Replace oil in compressor with same amount as that removed. Reverse removal procedures, installing new "O" rings on connectors. Evacuate and charge system.

REFRIGERANT CAPACITY

O.E.M. REFRIGERANT TABLE

Application	Capacity (Lbs)	Application	Capacity (Lbs)
Chrysler Corp.		General Motors	
"B", "PB", "CB" & "MB" Models		Standard System	
W/Standard System	3⅜	"C" & "K" Models	3¾
W/Auxiliary Rear System	4	"G" Models	3
All Remaining Models	2⅝	Overhead System	
Ford		"C" & "K" Models	5¼
All Models Exc. "E" Models	3½	"G" Models	5
"E" Series Models		Jeep Corp.	
W/Standard System	3½	"CJ" Models	2½
W/Auxiliary Rear System	4¼	Cherokee, Wagoneer & Trucks	2¼

COMPRESSOR BELT TENSION

BELT TENSION TABLE

Application	New Belt	①Tension (Lbs.) Used Belt
Chrysler Corp.	¼-½"②	½-5⁄16"②
Ford	120-160	75-120
General Motors	135-145	90-100
Jeep	125-155	90-115

① — Using standard strand tension gauge unless otherwise indicated.

② — Chrysler Corp. recommends adjusting belt tension using the deflection method. Deflection is measured under a 10 pound load.

GENERAL MOTORS

"G" Models

DESCRIPTION

Anti-theft system consists of a warning horn mounted to the fender, relays and flasher located under instrument panel at left side, protective switches located at each door and the hood and an "ON-OFF" arming switch with an anti-tamper switch located on the outside fender.

OPERATION

With the switch in the "OFF" position and all protective switches open, no ground path exists for the energizing of the relay coils. When the driver leaves the vehicle and closes the doors, the protective switches open. When the arming switch is turned clockwise to a closed position, the system is activated.

If an attempt is made to break into the vehicle, the opening of any door will close the protective switches and complete a path to ground for relay coil A. See Fig. 1. The plus terminal of this coil is "HOT" (12V) at all times. When relay A is energized, the relay coil closes the relay contacts, providing a path to ground for relay B. At the same time, the closed contacts of relay A provide a ground path through the key switch to terminal 3 of relay A which activates the alarm.

Terminal 3 was initially grounded by the closing of a protective switch. If the door were closed however, the ground path would be broken and the alarm would cease. To prevent this, a Diode is installed in the wiring to hold the alarm on. As long as the ground path is unbroken the relay remains energized, and closing the door will not break this path.

As terminal 3 of the relay is grounded, the relay pulls in, closing the contacts and completing the flasher/horn circuit to positive 12 volts. The flasher then opens and closes the pulsating anti-theft horn, which will continue to sound until the battery is exhausted, or the alarm is disarmed with the key switch.

An anti-tamper switch is installed in terminal 3 of relay B. This switch closes if an attempt is made to remove or force the key switch, whether the alarm is set or not. When the switch closes a ground path is provided for terminal 3 and the alarm sounds. No other components are involved in this circuit and the only way to stop the alarm is to depress the plunger of the anti-tamper switch, or remove power from the relay.

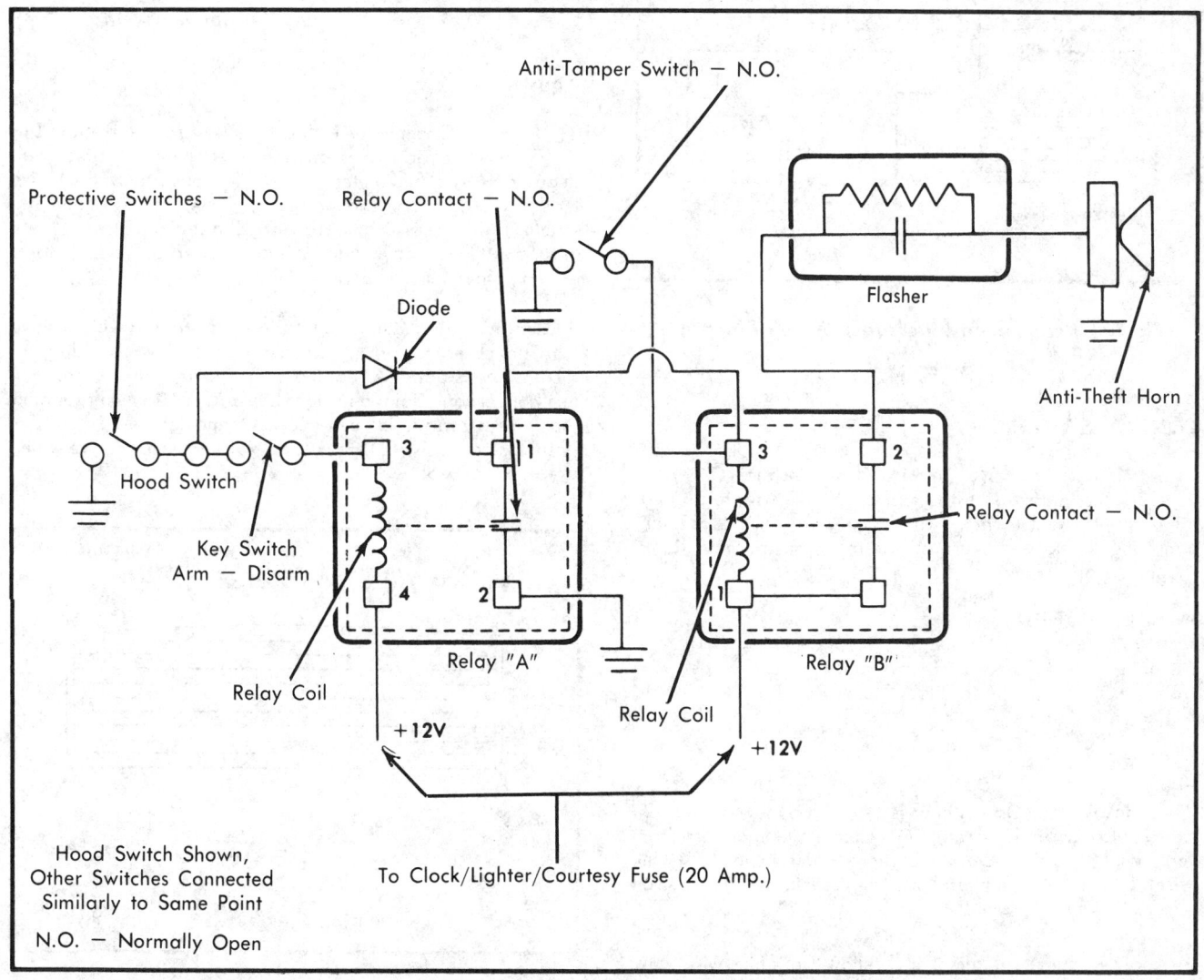

Fig. 1 *Wiring Diagram Circuit of Anti-Theft Alarm*

CHRYSLER CORP. REAR WINDOW DEFOGGER

Van Models

DESCRIPTION

Heated rear window is available on van models. The system consists of 2 bus bars, heating elements baked on inside of glass, a control switch, 25 ampere fuse and continuous or timed relay.

OPERATION

With ignition and control switch turned "ON", continuous relay will remain on until ignition or switch is turned "OFF". Timed relay will operate 8½ to 11½ minutes. Relay is mounted to right of switch on lower dash panel. An indicator lamp on dash indicates when system is in operation.

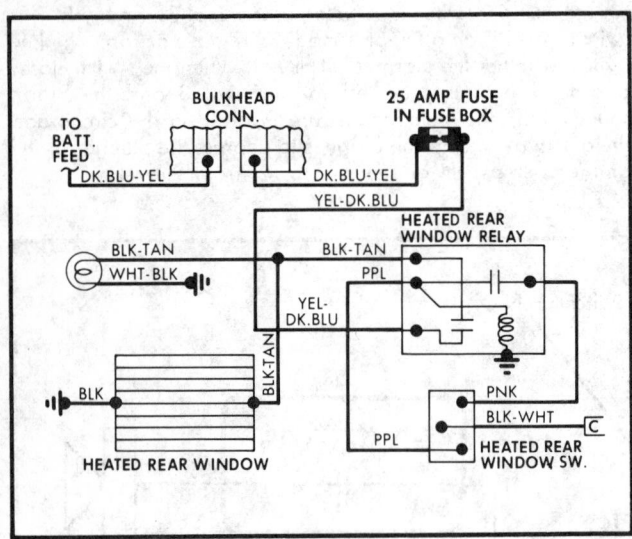

Fig. 1 Rear Window Defogger Wiring Diagram

TESTING

CONTROL SWITCH

Turn ignition switch "ON", move control switch to "ON" position. Connect a 12-volt test lamp from Purple wire to ground, lamp should light. When switch moves to normal position, lamp should stay on. Turn switch to "OFF" position, lamp should go off.

INDICATOR LIGHT

Disconnect Black/Tan wire from lamp. Connect jumper wire from "ACC" terminal to Black/Tan wire. Turn ignition to "ACC", lamp should light.

RELAY

1) Remove relay. On continuous relay, ground housing. On timed relay ground terminal "G". Connect jumper wire from terminal "B" (Yellow/Dark Blue wire) to terminal "Y" (Pink wire). Connect a 12-volt test lamp from terminal "L" (Black/Tan wire) of relay to ground.

2) Apply 12 volts to terminal "B" (Yellow/Dark Blue wire), test lamp should not light. If lamp comes on, replace relay.

3) Short terminal "B" (Yellow/Dark Blue wire) and terminal "P" (Ground wire) for a few seconds, lamp should light and stay on for 8½ to 11½ minutes on timed relays and until turned off on continuous relays. If lamp does not light, replace relay.

Fig. 2 Relay Terminals

GRID

1) Using a DC voltmeter with a 0-15 volt range, contact bus bar connecting grid lines on right (Feed) side of glass with negative lead of voltmeter. Contact left bus bar with positive lead. Turn ignition and control switches "ON". Voltmeter should read 10-14 volts. Lower voltage indicates a poor ground. With negative lead, contact a good ground. Voltage reading should not change.

2) Contact negative lead to left side bus bar and with positive lead, touch each grid line at midpoint. A 6 volt reading indicates line is good. A reading of 0 volts indicates a break in line between midpoint and right bus bar. A 10-14 volt reading indicates a break between midpoint and left bus bar. Move positive lead toward break and voltage will change when break is crossed.

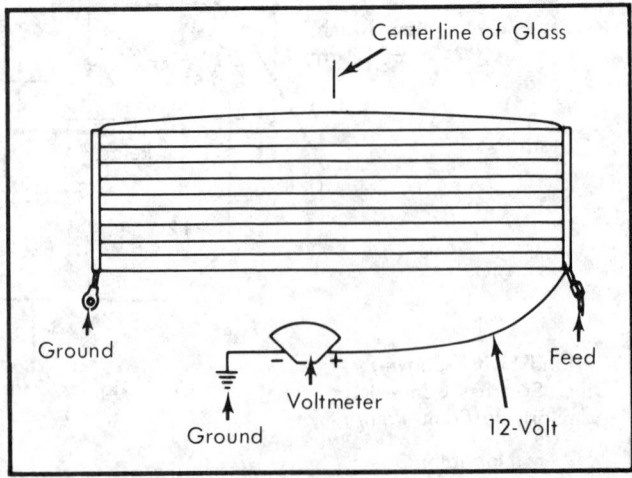

Fig. 3 Voltmeter Connections For Grid Continuity

JEEP TAILGATE WINDOW DEFOGGER

Jeep
Cherokee
Wagoneer

DESCRIPTION

A heated tailgate window defogger system is available on Cherokee and Wagoneer models. The system consists of 2 vertical bus bars and horizontal rows of heating elements fused to inside of glass, a control switch, pilot light, and timer relay. Braided wire serves as the electrical feed and ground for the grid. The grid feed wire is attached to the timer relay located inside tailgate. The timer relay receives its power from the fuse panel power tailgate terminal. A 30-ampere circuit breaker protects the circuit.

OPERATION

A separate control circuit, connected to the heater control switch, operates the relay and timer. With the control switch on instrument panel and ignition switch "ON", the defogger relay contacts close. A timer, enclosed in relay case will allow the defogger to operate for about 8 to 12 minutes, depending upon ambient temperature, or until the control switch or ignition switch is turned "OFF". A pilot lamp on the instrument panel indicates when the system is in operation.

NOTE — *Defogger switch and electric tailgate switch are serviced as an assembly.*

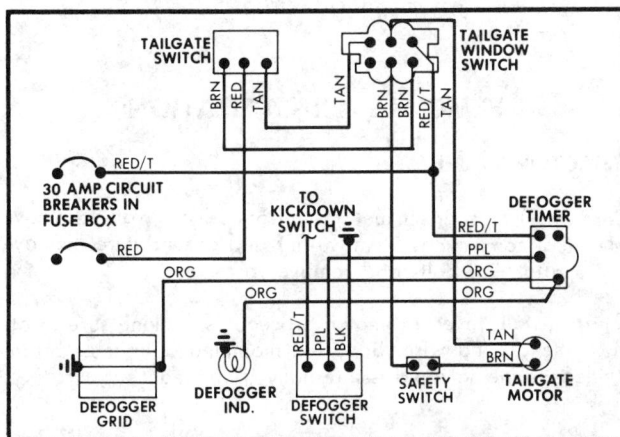

Fig. 1   Jeep Wiring Diagram for Rear Window Defogger

TESTING

CONTROL SWITCH

Turn ignition switch "ON" and press defogger switch. Separate wiring harness at connector under dash. Connect a 12-volt test lamp from Purple wire to ground, test lamp should light. Turn defogger switch "OFF", test lamp should not light.

INDICATOR LIGHT

Disconnect Orange wire from lamp. Connect jumper wire from accessory terminal to Orange wire. With ignition turned to "Accessory", lamp should light.

RELAY

1) Attach negative lead of voltmeter to ground. Touch red wire with voltmeter positive lead. Battery voltage should be indicated. If no voltage is indicated, operate tailgate window. If window operates, the wire between the relay and window switch is open.

2) Touch orange wire with voltmeter positive lead. No voltage should be indicated. Turn ignition switch "ON". Voltmeter should indicate voltage. If not, relay is defective or not receiving voltage from purple wire. If relay operates properly, it should remain energized for 8 to 12 minutes before opening. If time period is too short or long, relay is defective.

3) If relay did not energize, connect a jumper wire to a known good 12 volt source in tailgate and touch relay purple terminal. If relay clicks, trace purple wire for open or short. If relay does not click, check relay ground. If ground is satisfactory, replace relay.

GRID

1) Use a 12-volt meter and connect positive lead to right (Feed) side of vertical element on inside of glass. Connect negative lead to left side of vertical element. Voltage on meter should read 11 to 13 volts with ignition "ON".

2) Connect negative lead to ground, disconnect positive lead and touch each grid at center of window.

3) Voltage drop of 6 volts indicates good grid. Voltage drop of 12 volts at center indicates break in grid between positive lead and ground. No voltage drop at center indicates break in grid between center and feed wire.

4) Exact location of break can be located by moving positive lead to left or right until an abrupt change in voltage is noticed. Repair to grid can then be made.

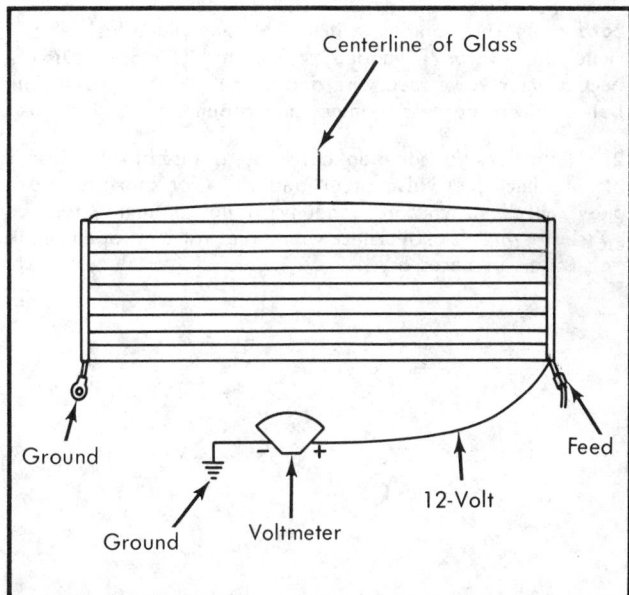

Fig. 2   Voltmeter Connections and Voltage Drop for Grid Continuity

FORD & GENERAL MOTORS

Ford
("F" & "E" Models Only)
General Motors
("C" & "K" Models Only)

DESCRIPTION

Fuel tank selector valves are used in conjunction with auxiliary fuel tanks on subject models. Systems consist of a main and auxiliary fuel tank, a selector valve to route fuel from desired tank through fuel pump, a selector switch to choose tanks, necessary fuel lines and electrical wiring.

OPERATION

Ford — The electrically actuated fuel selector valve is spring loaded and in the de-energized state feeds the fuel pump from the front tank on "F" models, and the rear tank on "E" models. When activated by a minimum of 9.5 volts by the selector switch, the fuel feed transfers to the rear tank on "F" models and the front tank on "E" models.

General Motors — Two types of valves are used on GM trucks. Those models with a fuel return system use a 6 port valve, while those without a fuel return system use a 3 port valve. Valve operation is the same for both valves. When instrument panel switch is in the Aux. (left hand) position, selector valve solenoid is energized. When switch is in Main (right hand) position, selector valve solenoid is de-energized.

The dash switch is energized only when the ignition is on. When vehicle is operated in Aux. position, fuel in feed lines as well as return lines (if equipped) will always return to main tank when ignition is turned off. Operation of Aux. switch position with main tank full will result in overfilling of main tank.

TESTING

Ford — 1) Turn ignition switch "ON" and place fuel selector switch on rear for "F" models, or front for "E" models. Disconnect selector valve feed wire and connect a 12 volt test light between wire harness terminal and ground.

2) If light does not come on, check fuse at fuse block. If fuse is blown, check fuel valve circuit and valve for short. If fuse is okay, check switch for continuity. If no continuity, replace switch. If switch is okay, check wiring and valve for open circuit and repair as necessary.

3) If test light comes on, reconnect feed wire and place a paper clip on end of valve opposite port end. Paper clip should adhere to valve. If not, ground valve case to frame rail with short piece of wire and repeat paper clip test.

4) If paper clip does not adhere, replace valve and solenoid assembly. If paper clip adheres, remove valve mounting bolts and clean mounting surface. Install new mounting bolts that are zinc or cadmium plated.

5) If the paper clip adhered in step **3)** position selector switch on front for "F" models, or rear for "E" models. Pinch off fuel hose from valve to main tank and remove fuel line from carburetor and place end in a container. Remove battery feed from coil and crank engine.

6) If fuel flows continuously, remove and replace valve solenoid assembly. If no fuel flows into container, unpinch fuel hose and crank engine to reestablish fuel flow.

7) Place selector switch on rear for "F" models, or front for "E" models. Pinch off hose from valve to rear tank on "F" models, or front tank on "E" models. Crank engine and observe fuel flow.

8) If fuel flows continuously, replace solenoid and valve assembly. If no fuel flows, system is operating correctly and problem has been misdiagnosed.

NOTE — *Testing procedures for General Motors vehicles were not available from manufacturer.*

REMOVAL & INSTALLATION

SELECTOR VALVE

Ford — 1) Disconnect fuel hoses from selector valve. Remove electrical connections. Remove nut and ground wire. Remove valve attaching bolts and remove valve.

2) To install, reverse removal procedures, making sure to attach the ground wire. Specified mounting bolts must be installed as the solenoid is internally grounded.

NOTE — *Removal and installation procedures for General Motors vehicles were not available from maufacturer.*

Ignition Switch & Lock Cylinders

ALL MANUFACTURERS

All Models

DESCRIPTION

Ignition switches are typically mounted on steering columns and are actuated by ignition key locking cylinders. Neutral safety switches are typically mounted on lower end of steering columns.

SERVICING

Chrysler Corp. vehicles with column mounted ignition switches and lock cylinders require that steering wheel and turn signal switch be removed before ignition components are accessible.

On General Motors and Jeep Corp. vehicles, steering column must be removed or lowered. Steering wheel and turn signal switch must be removed before ignition components are accessible.

CAUTION — *Lock plate is under strong spring pressure. Do not remove snap ring without using compressor tool. If steering shaft has American threads, use compressor tool J-23653; if shaft has metric threads use Metric Forcing Screw J-23653-4.*

Ford vehicles require that steering column be lowered before servicing the ignition switch or lock cylinder.

CAUTION — *Some steering columns are collapsible and special care must be taken to avoid bumping, jolting or hammering on steering shaft and gearshift tube.*

REMOVAL & INSTALLATION

LOCK CYLINDER REMOVAL

Chrysler Corp. — Place lock in "LOCK" position and remove key. Insert thin tool (machinist's scale or knife blade) into lock cylinder slot. Push in to release spring loaded lock retainer. Remove lock cylinder from housing.

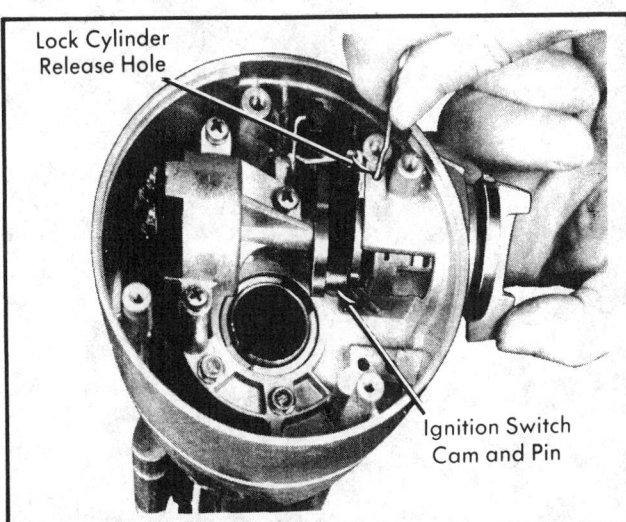

Ford — On non-tilt models, remove steering wheel and trim pad. Place gear selector in "P" on automatic transmission models, or any position on manual transmission models. Insert key and turn cylinder to "ON" position. Insert an 1/8" diameter pin in hole on outside of steering column casting near hazard warning button on tilt models, or in hole near base of lock cylinder on non-tilt models. Depress pin while pulling out on lock cylinder to remove.

General Motors — Place lock in "RUN" position. Remove lock plate, turn signal switch and buzzer switch. Remove lock retaining screws and lock cylinder.

Jeep — Place lock in "ON" position (manual transmission) or in "OFF-LOCK" position (automatic transmission). Insert thin tool (machinist's scale or knife blade) into lock cylinder slot. Push in to release spring loaded lock retainer. Remove lock cylinder from housing.

LOCK CYLINDER INSTALLATION

Chrysler Corp. — Place lock in "LOCK" position and remove key. Insert cylinder into housing. Press cylinder in until contact is made with pin on ignition switch cam. Insert key into lock and rotate until slot in cylinder plate aligns with pin. Push cylinder in and lock retainer will snap into slot in lock housing.

Ford — Turn lock cylinder to "ON" position. Depress retaining pin and insert cylinder into housing. Ensure that cylinder is fully seated and aligned with interlocking washer. Turn key and check operation of lock cylinder.

General Motors — Place lock in housing. Turn key to "RUN" position while holding cylinder. Align cylinder with keyway in housing. Push lock in and install retaining screw.

Jeep — 1) Insert key in lock. Hold cylinder sleeve and turn key clockwise until key stops.

2) Align lock cylinder retaining tab with keyway in housing and insert cylinder into column.

3) Push cylinder in until it contacts lock sector. Rotate cylinder to engage lock sector and push in until cylinder retaining tab engages in housing groove.

IGNITION SWITCH REMOVAL

Chrysler Corp. — Ignition switch is in upper end of steering column. With lock cylinder removed, remove 3 retaining screws and switch.

Ford — Disconnect negative battery cable. Remove steering column shroud and lower column. Disconnect switch wiring at multiple plug. Remove nut securing switch to steering column. Lift switch vertically to disengage actuator and remove switch.

General Motors — Lower steering column and support column to avoid causing damage. Remove lock cylinder, pull switch actuating rod up until there is a definite stop, then move rod down one detent to place lock in "LOCK" position. Remove two switch screws and switch assembly from vehicle.

Fig. 1 Typical Column Type Ignition Switch Lock Cylinder Removal

ALL MANUFACTURERS (Cont.)

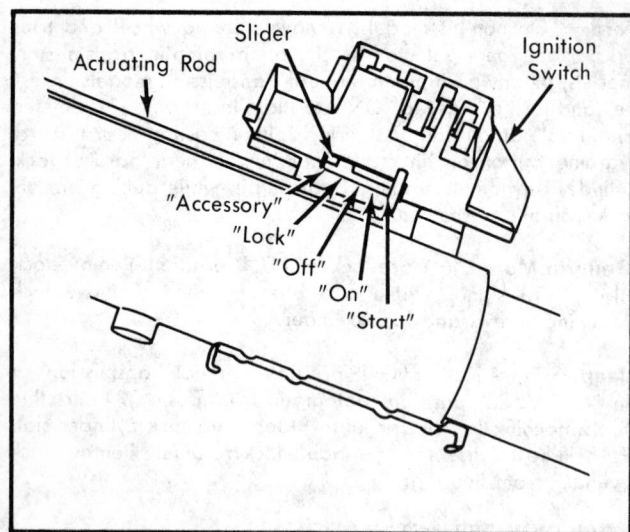

**Fig. 2   Rod Actuated Ignition Switch
(Common to All Models)**

Jeep — Place lock in "OFF-LOCK" position and remove 2 mounting screws. Disconnect switch from remote rod, harness connector and remove switch.

IGNITION SWITCH INSTALLATION

Chrysler Corp. — Install ignition switch to column ensuring that key in housing is indexed with slot in steering jacket. Install retaining screws and tighten, making sure not to change switch position.

Ford — With lock cylinder and switch in "LOCK" position, engage actuator rod in switch. Position switch on column and install retaining nuts, but do not tighten. Move switch up and down along column to locate mid-position of rod lash and then tighten retaining nuts.

General Motors — Place lock and switch in "LOCK" position. Install actuating rod into switch and install switch using mounting screws. Tighten, making sure not to change switch position.

Jeep — Move switch slider to "ACC" position. Move switch slider back two clicks to "OFF-UNLOCK" position. Engage remote rod in switch slider and position switch on column. Do not move slider. Install and tighten screws.

NEUTRAL SAFETY SWITCH REMOVAL

NOTE — *Chrysler Corp., Ford and General Motors "G" & "P" models have the neutral safety switch located on the transmission. See Section 14, AUTOMATIC TRANSMISSIONS for servicing these vehicles.*

General Motors "C" & "K" Models — Disconnect negative battery cable and electrical harness at neutral switch. Remove mounting screws and remove switch.

Jeep — With parking brake on, disconnect wire connector from safety switch. Remove attaching screws and remove switch.

NEUTRAL SAFETY SWITCH INSTALLATION

General Motors "C" & "K" Models — Place switch shift lever in neutral gate notch. Insert a .096" gauge pin to a depth of $\frac{3}{8}$" into switch gauge hole. Place switch in position on column and install mounting screws. Remove gauge pin and move switch lever out of neutral gate notch and into park gate position to shear off switch internal plastic pin. Return shift lever to neutral gate notch. Rotate switch on column and insert a .096" gauge pin to a depth of $\frac{3}{8}$". Tighten attaching screws and remove pin.

Jeep — Move selector lever to "PARK" and "NEUTRAL" positions. Inspect switch operating lever fingers to ensure they are properly centered in switch opening. Install switch and seal on transmission case and tighten to 24 ft. lbs.

Power Door Locks

CHRYSLER CORP. — SOLENOID ACTUATED

All Models

DESCRIPTION

The electric door lock system is solenoid actuated at each door and can be locked or unlocked electrically by operating either left or right front locking knobs. Side and rear doors, when electrically equipped can be actuated by operation of front locking knobs. All doors must be closed before locking. They can be locked or unlocked manually with key or electrically as described. The system combines a relay, circuit breaker, and "button" head terminals in door and post panels to combine all door wiring into 1 wiring harness. The relay and circuit breaker are mounted to steering column support bracket on underside of dash. All components are serviced as complete assemblies.

ELECTRICAL TESTS

1) With battery in normal operating condition and solenoid adjusted properly, connect positive lead of voltmeter to buss bar on relay assembly and negative lead to ground.

2) With no load, voltage should be approximately 12.5 volts. When locks are operated, voltage should be 11 volts. If no voltage is read at relay, test circuit breaker as follows:

3) Connect positive voltmeter lead to light green terminal of circuit breaker, and negative lead to ground. If reading of 12.5 volts is not obtained, connect positive lead to battery side of circuit breaker.

4) If 12.5 volts are obtained, the circuit breaker is defective and should be replaced. If 12.5 volts are not obtained, check for broken feed wire or loose connection.

5) To check for faulty solenoids, disconnect the solenoid connectors one at a time while operating the door lock switch. If none of the solenoids work, the problem may be a shorted solenoid of faulty relay. If defective solenoid is found, disconnecting it will allow the remaining solenoids to operate, provided the relay is not damaged.

ADJUSTMENT

DOOR LOCK SOLENOID

Remove door trim panel. Loosen solenoid attaching screws. While pressing down on the lock knob, push up on the solenoid until the solenoid plunger bottoms out in the solenoid. Tighten screws and test operation before installing trim panel.

REMOVAL & INSTALLATION

DOOR LOCK SOLENOID

1) Remove inside door release handle, window regulator handle and door trim panel.

2) Roll door water shield away from lower rear corner of door to reveal inside panel access opening.

3) Remove solenoid link at solenoid. Disconnect solenoid lead wires. Remove mounting bracket attaching screws and remove solenoid from mounting.

4) To install, reverse removal procedure and adjust if necessary.

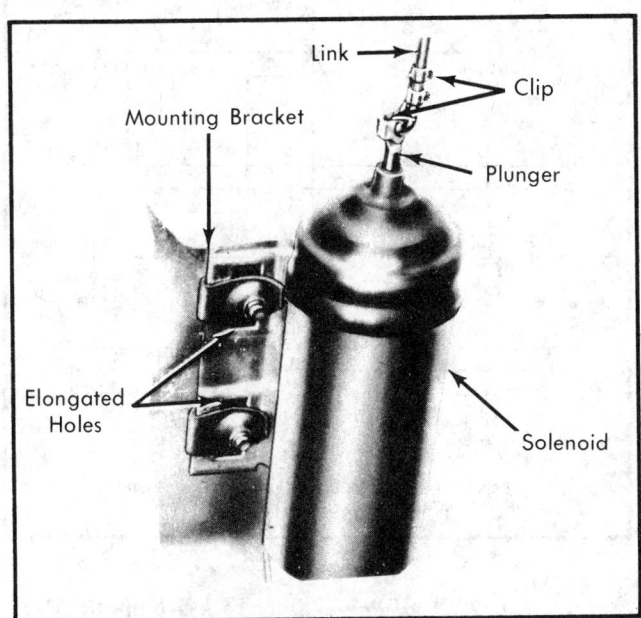

Fig. 1 Electric Door Lock Solenoid

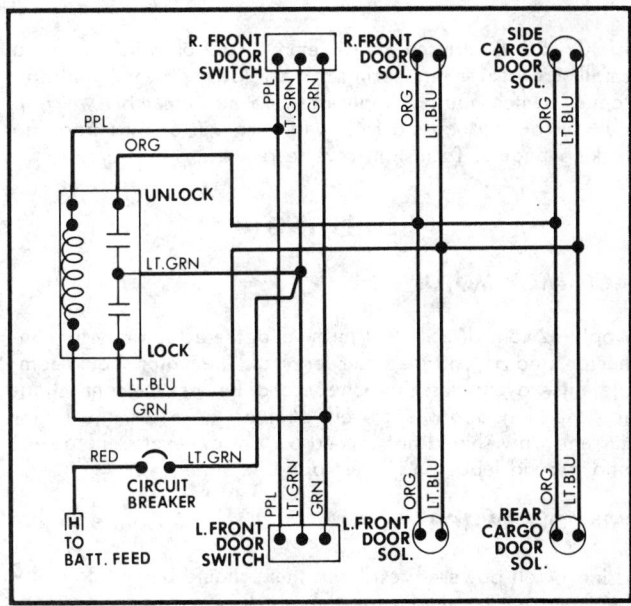

*Fig. 2 Chrysler Corp. Light Truck
Power Door Lock Wiring Diagram*

FORD — MOTOR ACTUATED

All Models

DESCRIPTION

The power door lock system uses electric switches controlled by the front door lock push buttons. Relays direct the current to the door lock actuator motors to lock or unlock the doors. The system includes contact buttons at the side cargo door and key-locked rear door. The buttons provide an electrical link for actuator motor operation in the remote doors.

REMOVAL & INSTALLATION

ACTUATOR MOTOR

Remove door trim panel. Disconnect actuator link from door latch. Remove actuator motor and swivel bracket from door by drilling out retaining rivet. Disconnect wiring at connector and remove motor. To install, reverse removal procedure noting that new pop rivet must retain actuator bracket securely.

DOOR LOCK CONTROL SWITCH

E100/350 — 1) Remove door trim panel. Detach switch from door latch and/or bellcrank. Disengage push button rod from latch.

2) Disengage wiring connector from switch by depressing tab on connector with screwdriver. Pry locking tab up from the flange of the connector and pull apart.

3) To install, reverse removal procedures, making sure that switch is not binding with sheet metal, or wires.

F100/350 & Bronco — To remove control switch, insert a small screwdriver into spring tab slot located at top and bottom of switch housig. Apply pressure and assembly will pop out. Disconnect housing from wiring connector by separating locking fingers. To install, reverse removal procedure.

TESTING

ACTUATOR MOTOR

Apply 12 volts directly to 1 terminal of the actuator motor connector, and ground the other terminal. The motor should complete its travel in less than one second. Reverse the connections for checking opposite travel. With an ammeter, the motor current draw should not exceed 6.2 amps. Reverse the power and ground leads and retest opposite side.

WINDOW SWITCH

Using a self-powered test light, there should be no continuity between any terminals with the switch in its normal position. With the switch in the down (lock) position, continuity should exist between terminals A and B. See *Fig.* 2. With the switch in the up (unlock) position, there should be continuity between terminals A and C.

RELAY

To perform relay tests, remove both relay connectors. The relays are located on the lower left side of the instrument panel reinforcer. Ensure that terminal 1 of the relay is grounded. If not, check relay case-to-ground screws for tightness. If screws are tight, replace the relay. With a test light connected between terminals 1 and 2, apply power to terminals 2 and 4 of each relay. Do not leave light connected for more than 2 minutes. The test light should light, if not, replace the relay.

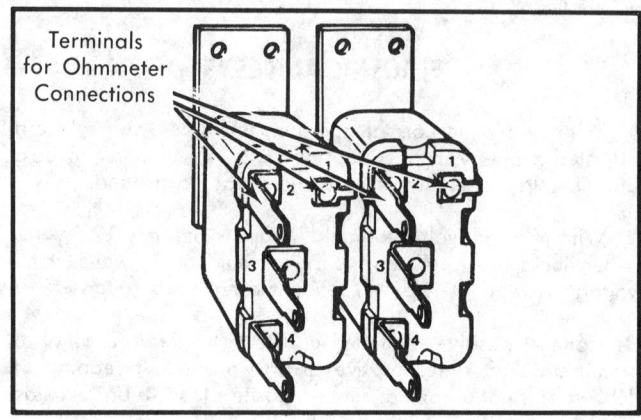

Fig. 1   Power Door Lock Relay Terminals

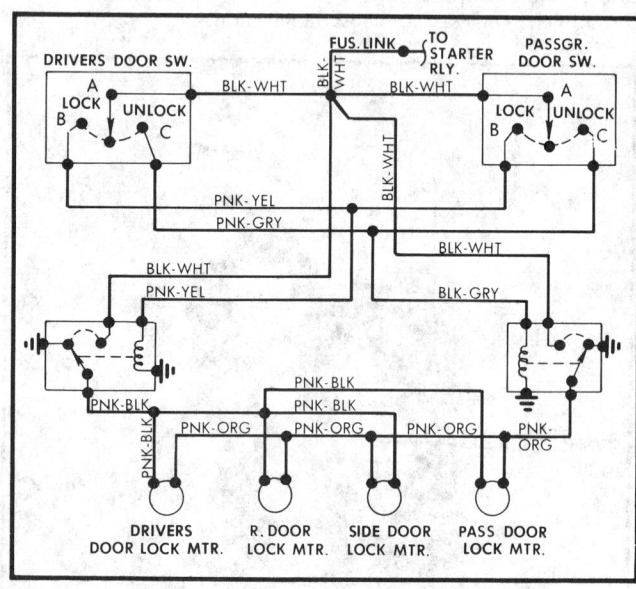

Fig. 2   Ford Power Door Lock Schematic

Power Door Locks

GENERAL MOTORS – MOTOR ACTUATED

Chevrolet
GMC

DESCRIPTION

The electric door lock system consists of a lock actuator assembly at each door, conventional switches and a relay. All doors lock and unlock manually or from the door control switches. All components are serviced as complete assemblies. The motor is a permanent magnet, 12 volt reversible type that is protected by an internal circuit breaker which may require 1 to 3 minutes to reset. A 30 ampere circuit breaker also protects the door lock feed circuit to relay wiring. The relay assembly is a double-pole, double-throw relay externally grounded to body beneath the right side of the instrument panel behind glove compartment. The control switch is a three-pin rocker type mounted on door armrests. The feed circuit to the lock switches is protected by a 20 ampere fuse.

TROUBLE SHOOTING

DOOR LOCKS INOPERATIVE FROM BOTH CONTROL SWITCHES, COURTESY LAMP FUSE BLOWN

Install new courtesy lamp fuse and press door lock switch to "Lock" position. If fuse blows, check for short in Light Blue wire between relay and switches. If system remains operative, check for short in Orange wire and in both Light Blue and Black wires between source and cross bar harness.

DOOR LOCKS INOPERATIVE, COURTESY LAMP OPERATES

With a test lamp grounded, check Orange/Black wire at relay connector. If light remains off, check circuit breaker and circuit to relay. With light on, press switch to lock position. If light remains off, check ground to the body. If grounded, replace relay.

DOORS WILL UNLOCK BUT WILL NOT LOCK

With a test lamp grounded, check Light Blue wire terminal at relay. Press switch to "Lock" position. If light comes on but system does not operate, replace relay. If light does not come on, check for short between relay and cross-body wiring harness

DOORS WILL LOCK BUT WILL NOT UNLOCK

With a test lamp grounded, check Black wire at relay. Press switch to "Unlock" position. If light comes on but system does not operate, replace relay. If light does not come on, check or open in Black wire between relay and cross-body harness.

DOOR LOCKS OPERATE EXCEPT FOR ONE DOOR

Check for loose connection of Gray and Tan wires, or short in circuit. If both leads check to the actuator motor, replace the motor.

DOOR LOCKS OPERATE NORMALLY EXCEPT ONE DOOR WILL NOT UNLOCK/LOCK

Check ground and if correct, check for open in Light Blue wire between switch and cross-body harness.

DOOR LOCKS INOPERATIVE AND RELAY CLICKS WHEN ACTIVATED

Check Light Blue and Black wires between switch and relay.

DOOR LOCKS INOPERATIVE OR LOCKS PULSATE AND RELAY CHATTERS WHEN SWITCH IS ACTIVATED

Gray and Tan wires are making contact between relay and lock actuator motor.

REMOVAL & INSTALLATION

DOOR LOCK MOTOR

1) Disconnect battery cable, remove door trim panel and disconnect electrical connector from motor.

2) Remove screws attaching motor to door. Remove door lock lever from rubber mount at top of motor actuator and remove motor through access hole. To install, reverse removal procedure.

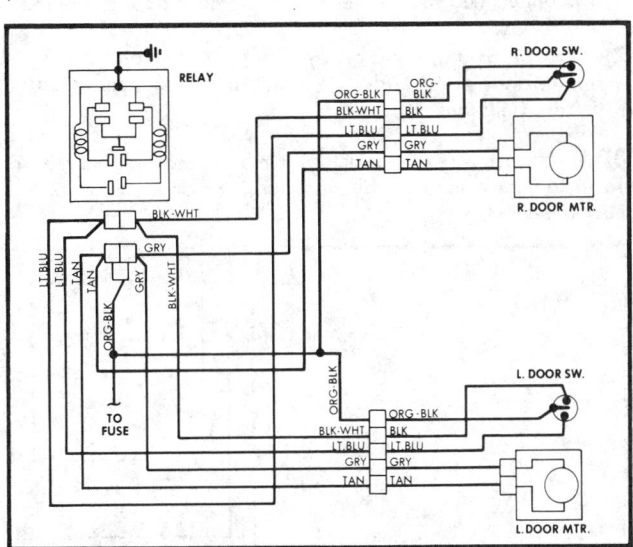

Fig. 1   General Motors Light Truck Power Door Lock Wiring Diagram

JEEP — MOTOR ACTUATED

All Models

DESCRIPTION

Jeep vehicles with power door locks use a battery powered, motor actuated lock system controlled by two rocker switches. Pressing up on the switch unlocks doors, or pressing down on the switch locks the doors. Power door locks are protected by a 30 amp. circuit breaker located in the fuse block. Two-door models have the wiring harness running from door-to-door and is secured at the instrument panel with retainers. Four-door models have the wiring harness for the back doors connected to the front door harness at the side cowl panels.

REMOVAL & INSTALLATION

DOOR LOCK SWITCH

1) Disconnect negative battery cable. Remove door trim panel. Remove switch housing from inner door panel.

2) Disconnect wiring and remove switch assembly. Pry clips holding connector up, to disconnect. Depress retainer clips through holes in switch housing and remove switch.

3) To install, reverse removal procedures.

ACTUATOR MOTOR

1) Disconnect negative battery cable. Remove door trim panel.

2) Remove actuator motor by drilling out rivets attaching motor to door panel with a ¼" drill bit. Disconnect actuator rod from bellcrank.

3) Disconnect wires from actuator motor and remove motor. To install, reverse removal procedures making sure to install new rivets.

TESTING

SWITCH

Test switches for continuity using an ohmmeter. Connect ohmmeter across terminals as shown in *Fig. 1*. Continuity should exist between terminals in all positions.

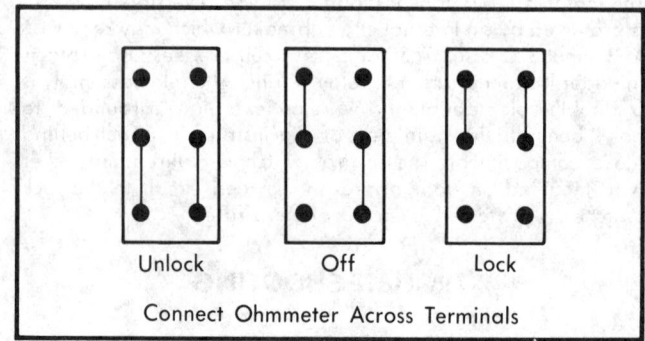

Connect Ohmmeter Across Terminals

Fig. 1   Checking Switch for Continuity

ACTUATOR MOTOR

Connect ammeter to motor terminals and operate door switch. If current draw exceeds 8 amps. at room temperature or if actuator does not complete its travel within 1 second, replace actuator motor.

CIRCUIT BREAKER

Disconnect harness connector from fuse block. Test fuse block connection with test light. If light operates, battery voltage is present. If light stays off, remove circuit breaker and test with ohmmeter. If circuit breaker tests okay, check for battery voltage at circuit breaker connection at fuse block. If no battery voltage at connection, check for breakage of fusible link in engine compartment.

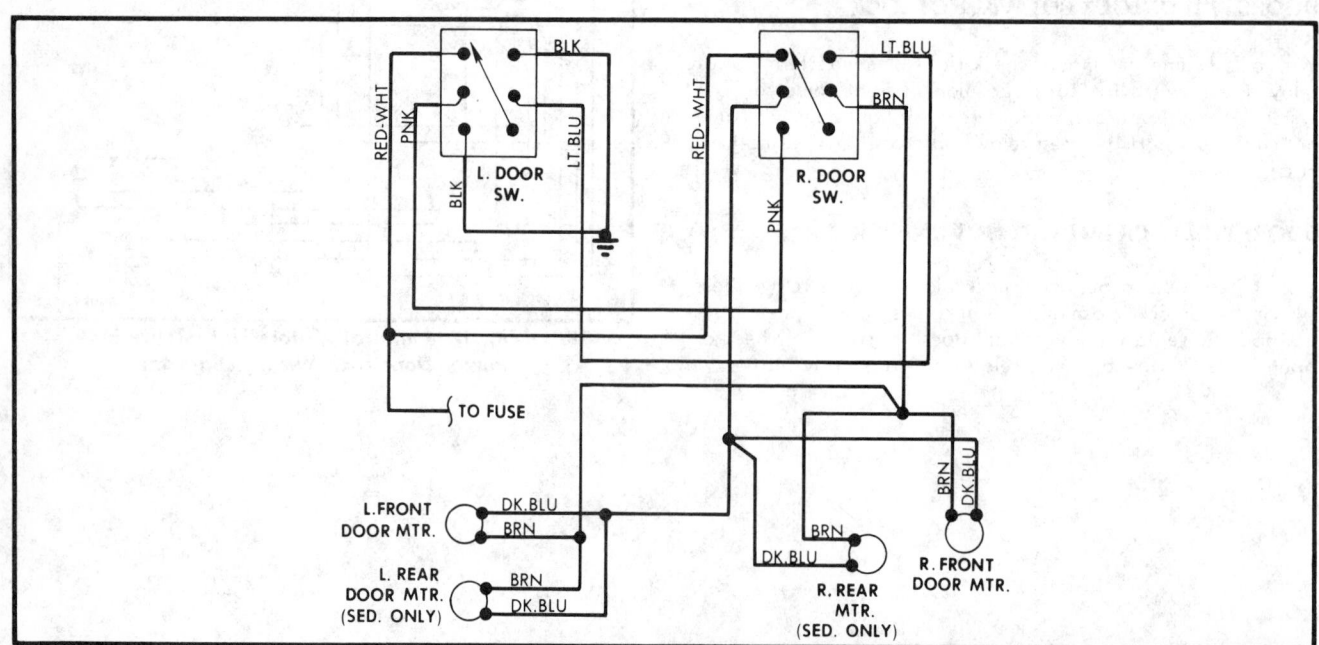

Fig. 2   Wiring Diagram For Jeep Power Door Locks
(2-Door and 4-Door Models)

Power Mirrors

FORD

All Models

DESCRIPTION

Power rearview mirror assemblies consist of door-mounted mirrors with internal motor drive and backing plate. System includes a door panel switch and necessary wiring components.

TROUBLE SHOOTING & TESTING

ONE MIRROR DOES NOT FUNCTION

1) Working underneath mirror, remove head of plastic rivet using a ¼" drill. Remove rivet stem remnants. Remove screw from cover, remove cover and disconnect plug. Check function of mirror by connecting 12 volts to terminals of wire plug. Yellow and Green wires provide up-down movement; Black and White wires, right-left movement.

2) If mirror does not function, replace motor drive. See *Motor Drive Removal* in this Article. If mirror functions when tested, but does not operate when connected to feed wire, remove left door panel and test feed wire for continuity at switch plug. Then, apply 12 volts to feed wire. If mirror functions through feed wire, but fails to respond to switch operation, replace switch.

BOTH MIRRORS DO NOT FUNCTION

1) Remove left door inner trim panel. Unplug accessory feed wire (Black and Yellow with Red stripe) and check for voltage. Turn ignition switch to "ON" position on "E" models. If no voltage is observed, remove instrument panel on "E" models or instrument panel pad on "F" models. Check hot wire, in-line fuse, and ground connections. Repair as necessary.

2) If voltage is present at accessory feed wire plug, reconnect wire and check mirror functions. If satisfactory, install trim panel. If no voltage is observed, disconnect and check continuity of wiring, step-by-step, from hot wire lead to cowl/door harness connection, to switch wire feed connection, and to mirror feed wire connection. Replace or repair damaged wiring.

REMOVAL & INSTALLATION

MIRROR GLASS & MOTOR DRIVE

Removal — Break out and remove center of mirror glass and expose mounting screw attaching backing plate to motor drive. See *Fig. 1*. Remove and discard mirror remnants and backing plate, saving 3 stabilizer bars. Remove 4 screws attaching motor drive to mirror assembly. See *Fig. 1*. Unplug wires from motor drive by pushing connector retainer tab, separating connectors. Remove motor drive assembly.

Installation — Connect wiring connector to motor drive assembly. Insert stabilizer bars into motor drive. See *Fig. 2*. Install new backing plate to motor drive with center screw, and snap stabilizer ball joints in sockets of backing plate. Install motor drive/backing plate assembly to bracket and tighten screws. Remove paper backing from new mirror replacement glass, and press firmly into backing plate.

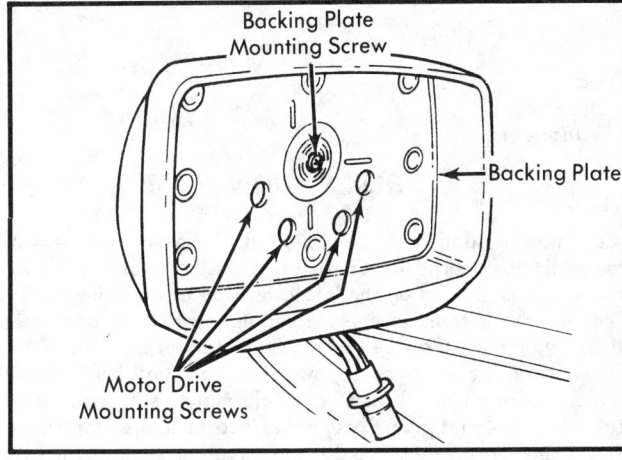

Fig. 1   Electric Mirror Mounting Screws

MIRROR ASSEMBLY

Removal — Using a ¼" drill bit, remove head of plastic rivet securing cover on mirror assembly. Remove rivet stem remnants. Remove screw from cover, and remove cover. Disconnect electrical connector. Remove screws attaching mirror assembly to door, and remove mirror assembly.

Installation — To install, reverse removal procedure.

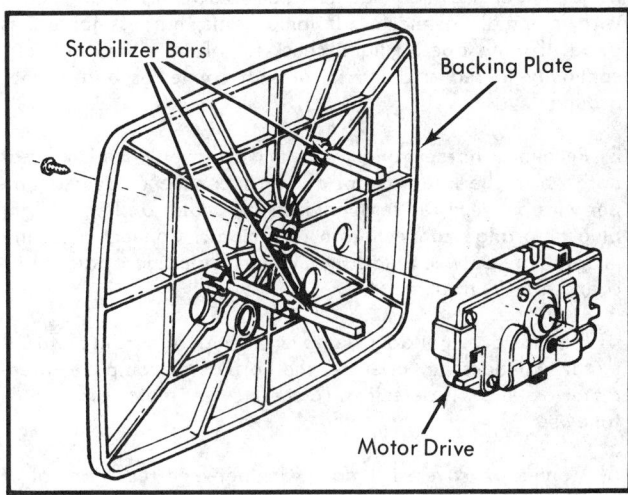

Fig. 2   Motor Drive Stabilizer Bars

MIRROR SWITCH ASSEMBLY

Removal & Installation — Remove left door inner trim panel. Disconnect wiring harness from both switch wiring assemblies. Remove 2 bezel nuts securing bezel and switch assembly to door. Remove bezel and switch from door. To install, reverse removal procedure.

NOTE — *Some "F" models may use a snap-in bezel-switch assembly. Insert screwdriver in slots at bezel edge to release retention springs. Then, disconnect wiring harness from switch, loosen set screw, and remove switch.*

JEEP

Jeep
Cherokee
Wagoneer

DESCRIPTION

Jeep power seats can be adjusted six ways; up, down, forward, backward, tilt forward and tilt backward. The control switch is located on the left lower side of the drivers seat. The switch has three levers; the middle lever raises or lowers the complete seat, as well as moving it forward or rearward. The two side levers raise or lower the front and back of the seat. A permanent magnet reversible motor is connected by cables to rack and pinion assemblies located in the seat tracks. The circuit is protected by a 30 amp. circuit breaker on the fuse block.

TESTING

ELECTRICAL CIRCUITS

1) With battery fully charged and all electrical connections cleaned and tightened, turn dome light on and operate seat switch. If dome light dims, seat may be jamming. Check for binding. If dome light does not dim, proceed with tests.

2) Using a 12 volt test light, disconnect wiring harness at connector under seat. Connect test light between red and black wire in female connector. If lamp lights, harness to seat is good. If lamp doesn't light, check for blown circuit breaker, continuity in red and black wires at connector and proper ground.

3) Reconnect harness under seat and remove switch from seat harness. To check rear motor of switch, connect a covered jumper wire between red terminal in center motor and either light blue or orange connection in rear motor. Connect a second jumper wire between black terminal in center motor and open connection in front motor.

4) If motor does not operate, reverse jumpers in front motor. If motor still does not operate, the harness or complete three-motor assembly is defective. To check center motor proceed as follows;

5) Connect a covered jumper wire between red terminal of center motor and white or tan terminal of center motor. Connect a second jumper wire between black terminal of center motor and open connection in center motor. If motor does not operate, reverse white and tan wires. If motor still does not operate, harness or three-motor assembly is defective.

6) To check front motor, connect covered jumper wire between red terminal in center motor and green or yellow connection of rear motor. Connect second jumper wire between black terminal of center motor and open connection in rear motor. If motor does not operate, reverse wires on rear motor. If motor

still does not operate, harness or three-motor assembly is defective. If all motors and seat operate properly, the switch is bad and should be replaced.

REMOVAL & INSTALLATION

SEAT ASSEMBLY

1) Disconnect negative battery cable. Remove nuts attaching seat assembly to floorpan.

2) Tilt seat and disconnect wiring harness. Remove seat assembly from vehicle. To install, reverse removal procedure.

MOTOR

NOTE — *Whenever the motor, cable and housing assemblies are removed or serviced, they must be synchronized to ensure proper operation.*

1) Remove seat assembly as previously outlined. Lay seat assembly on its back on a clean surface.

2) Remove motor mounting screws. Disconnect housings and cables from motor assembly and remove motor. To install, reverse removal procedures.

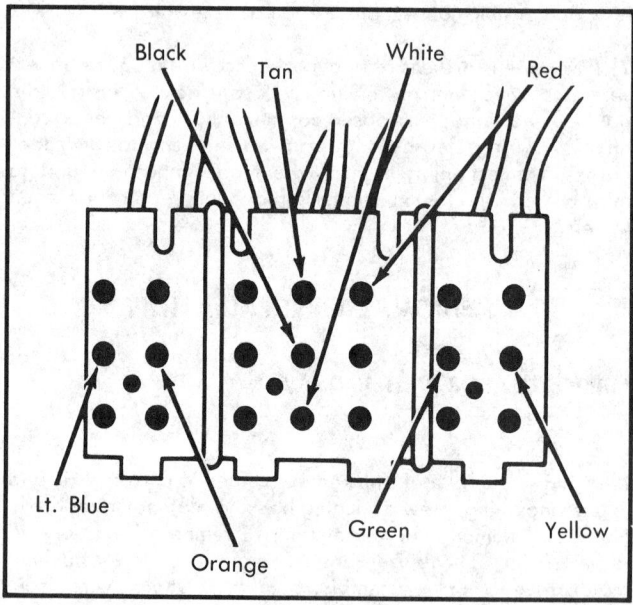

Fig. 1   Electrical Test Connections

CHRYSLER CORP. SIDE WINDOWS

All Models

DESCRIPTION

Chrysler Corp. electric window system consists of motors in each front door, switches to operate the motors, wiring harnesses and necessary connections. Window motors are permanent magnet type with a positive and negative connection. Each motor is grounded through the master switch by a white wire.

REMOVAL & INSTALLATION

WINDOW REGULATOR

1) Disconnect wiring connector from motor. Remove 3 attaching rivets which hold regulator to inner panel.

2) Remove screws holding motor tie-down bracket to inner panel (if equipped). Disengage the drive arm slider from glass lift channel by manuvering the regulator assembly by hand. Remove from door.

3) To install, reverse removal procedures.

MOTORS

Remove regulator as previously described. Secure in a vise to prevent sector gear from rotating. Remove counterbalance spring. Remove 3 motor attaching screws and remove motor. To install, reverse removal procedures, noting that counterbalance spring must be installed after motor is attached to regulator.

OVERHAUL

REGULATOR

Disassembly — 1) Secure regulator in vise to prevent sector gear from rotating. Remove counterbalance spring.

2) Remove 3 screws holding motor to regulator, and remove motor.

Inspection — Check regulator sector gear for chipped or broken teeth, or severe wear. Check that all sliders and rivets are securely attached. Parts must not be bent or cracked. Check that sector gear rotates freely.

Reassembly — Reverse disassembly procedure for reassembly, noting that counterbalance spring must be installed after motor is attached to regulator.

TESTING

MOTOR LIFT

1) Connect positive lead of test battery to either of the 2 terminals of motor. Connect other lead to remaining terminal. Motor should now rotate in one direction to move window up or down.

2) If window is in up position, and leads are connected so motor rotates in up direction, no movement should occur. The reverse holds if leads are connected so motor rotates in down direction, and window is already down.

3) Reverse battery leads. Window should now move in desired direction. If not, remove motor and replace. If motor moved window, reverse leads again and ensure that motor moves window in both directions.

SWITCH VOLTAGE

1) Remove switch from trim panel. Separate multiple terminal block on wiring harness from switch body. Connect one lead of test light to battery wire terminal and other lead to ground wire terminal.

2) If test light comes on, wiring circuit is okay. If light does not light, check 30 amp. circuit breaker in fuse block for failure, check for broken wire or poor ground.

MOTOR SWITCH

1) Connect one lead of jumper wire to battery lead and other lead to "UP" terminal of left multiple connector. See *Fig. 1.* Connect a second jumper wire with one lead to "DOWN" terminal of switch and other lead to ground terminal. Connect 2 jumper wires to right motor switch connector to operate switch.

2) If motor operates, voltage to motor is okay. Install switch to multiple connector and operate switch. If motor fails to operate, replace switch body. Test each switch.

3) Connect one lead of jumper wire to battery terminal, and other lead to "DOWN" terminal of switch. Connect second jumper wire with one lead to "UP" terminal, and other lead to ground terminal. Connect 2 jumpers wires to right motor switch connector to operate switch.

4) Test results are the same as in step 2). If motor fails to run, perform Motor Lift test.

ACCESSORIES & EQUIPMENT

Power Windows

CHRYSLER CORP. SIDE WINDOWS (Cont.)

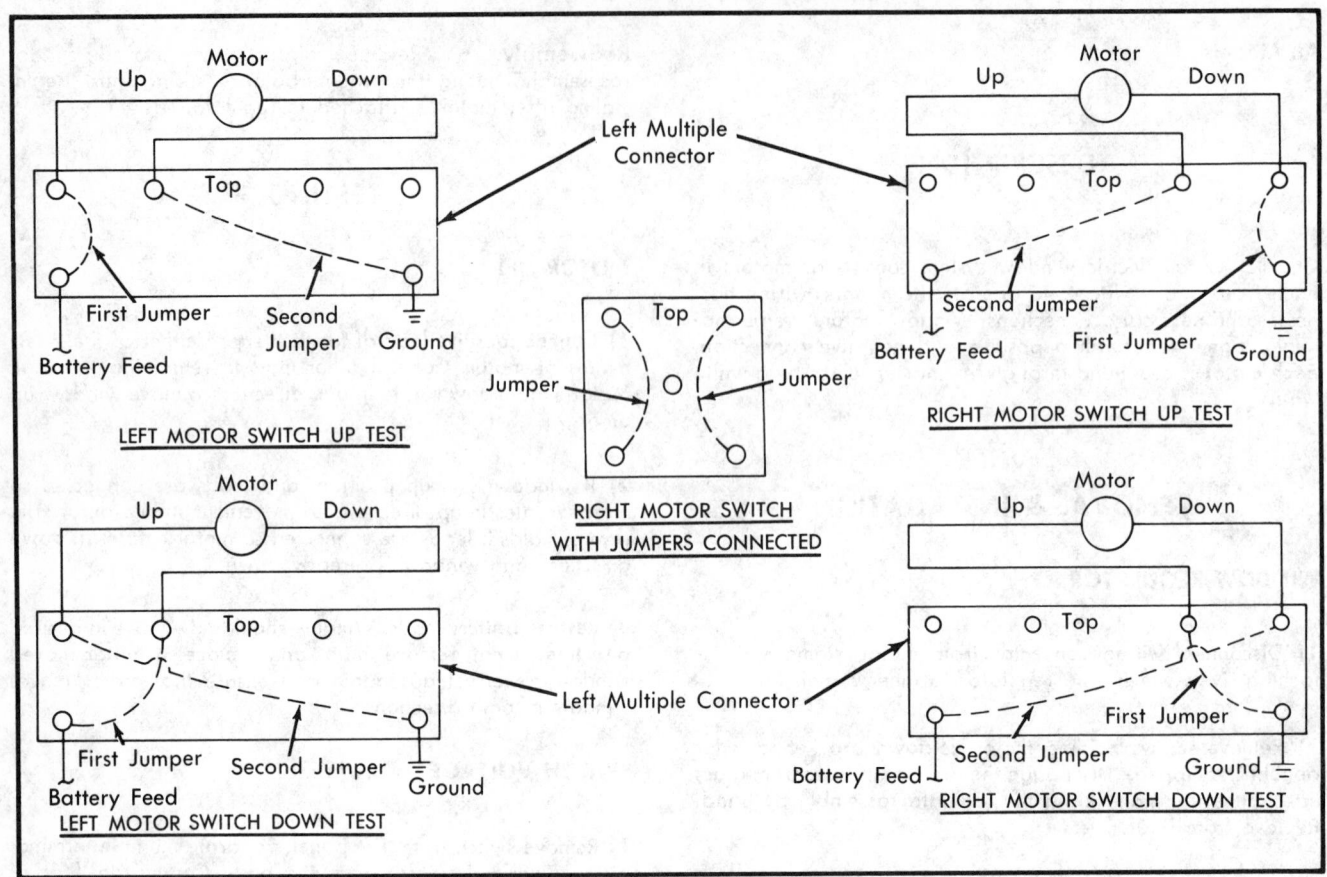

Fig. 1 Connections for Motor Switch Test

FORD SIDE WINDOWS

**Bronco
"F" Models**

DESCRIPTION

Ford power window system consists of reversible 12 volt motors in each front door, switches to operate motors, wiring harness and necessary connections. Driver's door has a multiple switch to control both windows.

REMOVAL & INSTALLATION

MOTORS

1) Disconnect battery cable. Remove door trim panel. Disconnect power window motor wire from harness connector. Using a ½" diameter drill bit, drill 2 holes in door inner panel at drill dimples located opposite 2 unexposed motor drive retaining screws.

NOTE — *Check before drilling to make sure no wires are in line with holes to be drilled.*

2) Remove 3 motor mount retainer screws using 2 drilled holes and existing access holes. Push motor outward to disengage motor and drive from rectangular gear. After motor and drive are disengaged, prop window up. Remove motor and drive.

3) To install, reverse removal procedure, noting the following: Tighten screws to 50-85 INCH lbs. Cover drilled holes with suitable body tape. Ensure that door drain holes are open.

POWER WINDOW SWITCH

1) Insert a thin screwdriver between bezel and trim panel at either side of bezel. Carefully pry bezel from trim panel and housing assembly will snap out. On left side switch, remove 2 retaining screws from bottom side of connector. Unsnap right side connector from housing.

2) Pry switch from connector with a small screwdriver. To install, positon switch in connector and press firmly. Reverse removal procedure to complete installation.

SWITCH CONNECTOR WIRE

If replacement of a switch wire or switch connector is necessary, insert a needle-like tool into edge of pin hole and bend terminal in. Pull wire and terminal from connector. To install terminal in connector, open terminal and insert it in connector.

TESTING

MOTOR

1) Remove motor and drive assembly from vehicle. Connect a power source (battery or power-pac) to motor with an ammeter in series. Operate motor and observe current draw.

2) Current draw should not exceed 4 amps and should not fluctuate. Reverse motor wire connections to observe reversed motor rotation. Replace motor if current draw exceeds 4 amps.

MULTIPLE SWITCH

1) Remove switch from vehicle. Using an ohmmeter or test light, clip a test probe on pin No. 6 which is grounded. See *Fig. 1*.

Place both switches in neutral position and test for continuity between pin No. 6 and pins No. 1 through No. 4.

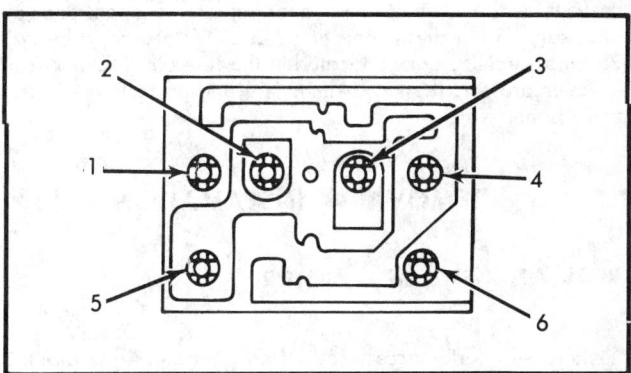

Fig. 1   Multiple Switch Pin Location

2) Push both switches upward. Both No. 1 and No. 3 should lose continuity to pin No. 6. Push switches downward. No. 2 and No. 4 should lose continuity to pin No. 6.

3) Remove test probe from No. 6 and connect to feed pin (No. 5). With both switches in neutral position, no continuity should exist at remaining terminals. Push switches upward. No. 2 and No. 4 should show continuity with No. 5. If any switch does not test as indicated, replace complete switch assembly.

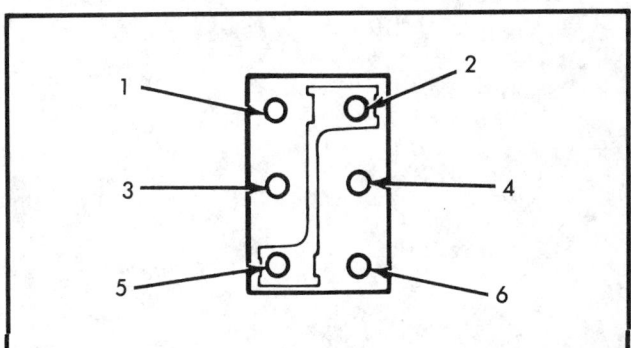

Fig. 2   Single Switch Pin Locations

SINGLE SWITCH

1) With the switch in the neutral position, use an ohmmeter to test switch. Continuity should exist between terminals 1, 2, 3, and 5. Continuity should also exist between 4 and 6. See *Fig. 2*.

2) With switch pushed downward, continuity should exist between 2, 4 and 5. Continuity should also exist between 1 and 3. Terminal 6 should be disconnected from all other terminals.

3) With switch pushed upward, there should be continuity between terminals 2, 3, and 5; also 4 and 6. Terminal 1 should be disconnected from all other terminals. If switch does not operate as indicated in any test, replace switch.

Power Windows

FORD TAILGATE WINDOW

Bronco

DESCRIPTION

Power tailgate window system consists of a motor and regulator assembly inside the tailgate, a key operated switch at the tailgate, an instrument panel switch, a limit switch to prevent window operation when tailgate is open and all necessary wiring and connections. Circuit is protected by two 25 amp. circuit breakers located in the fuse block. One circuit breaker protects the key switch, and one protects the instrument panel switch.

REMOVAL & INSTALLATION

REGULATOR SWITCH & MOTOR

1) Remove interior access cover from tailgate. Raise glass to full "UP" position.

2) Disconnect wiring harness from switch and/or motor. Remove clip attaching switch to lock cylinder and remove switch. Remove motor mounting screws and remove motor.

3) To install, reverse removal procedures making sure to check operation of switch and motor before replacing access cover.

WINDOW REGULATOR

Raise glass to full "UP" position. If glass cannot be raised, lower tailgate and remove interior access cover. Using fingers, locate and remove 4 glass attaching nuts and screws at bottom edge of access opening. Slowly slide glass from tailgate. Remove regulator attaching screw and washer assemblies. Remove regulator. To install, reverse removal procedure, tightening screws to 6-11 ft. lbs.

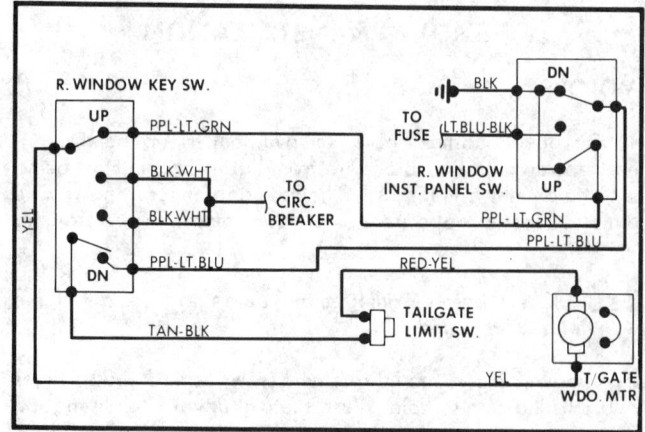

Fig. 1   Ford Bronco Power Tailgate Window Wiring Diagram

Power Windows

GENERAL MOTORS SIDE WINDOWS

Chevrolet
GMC

DESCRIPTION

DOOR WINDOWS

Window regulators are individually powered by a 12 volt reversible motor located in each door. The motor contains an internal circuit breaker requiring 1 to 3 minutes to reset. The motor, bolted to the regulator assembly, utilizes a selflocking gear drive. A 2-way control switch is located on each door, with a master control switch located on left door. The window cannot be operated from the door control switches until the ignition is turned on.

CIRCUIT BREAKER

A 30 ampere circuit breaker of the plug-in type is mounted on the fuse panel for all Chevrolet and GMC light trucks.

CONTROL SWITCHES

In addition to individual control switches adjacent to individual windows, a master control switch is mounted on the left door trim pad.

ACCESSORY JUNCTION BLOCK

Located on the reinforcement at the left shroud and used to supply current to power operated circuits. Current is supplied to junction block from the circuit breaker. The power window harness plugs into the junction block.

TROUBLE SHOOTING

WINDOWS WILL NOT OPERATE WITH IGNITION ON

Open circuit or short in power feed circuit. Switch defective.

RIGHT WINDOW OPERATES WITH MASTER SWITCH BUT WILL NOT OPERATE WITH RIGHT CONTROL SWITCH, LEFT WINDOW OPERATES

Open circuit or short in front harness feed circuit.

TESTING

CIRCUIT BREAKER

Check power feed to circuit breaker, with no power available, feed wire is open or shorted. Test breaker output terminal, if power fails, breaker is inoperative

MASTER CONTROL SWITCH

Check power feed Pink wire at switch, if power fails, test wire between relay and master switch.

WINDOW CONTROL SWITCH

1) Connect one lead of test lamp to switch connector feed wire and ground other lamp lead. If lamp does not light, an open short circuit exists between switch and power source.

2) Insert one end of a jumper wire in switch connector and other end of jumper to motor lead in connector. Repeat procedure for motor lead terminal. If motor operates with jumper wire but does not operate with switch, replace switch.

WINDOW SWITCH TO WINDOW HARNESS

Disconnect harness connector from motor. Insert one end of a jumper wire in switch connector and other end of jumper to motor lead in connector. Using a test lamp, check for current at motor connector. If lamp does not light, switch to motor harness is shorted or has open circuit. Check other terminal using same procedure.

WINDOW MOTOR

Check Power feed to motor terminals, if power is available, check motor ground. Inspect window regulator and channels for possible binding. Connect a jumper wire to the other motor terminal. Motor should operate window up and down, if not, replace motor.

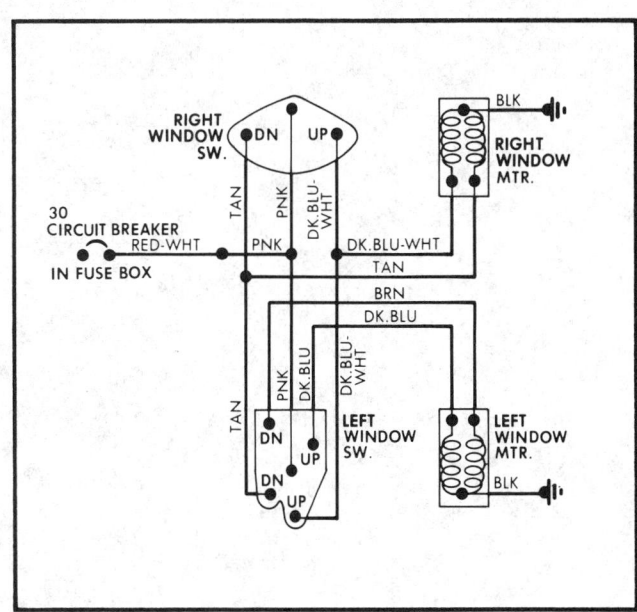

*Fig. 1 General Motors Light Truck
Power Window Wiring Diagram*

GENERAL MOTORS SIDE WINDOWS (Cont.)

REMOVAL & INSTALLATION

WINDOW REGULATOR & MOTOR

CAUTION — *Disconnect electrical connections before removing regulator assembly from window or injury may result.*

1) Raise window to full "UP" position and tape glass to door frame to prevent it from falling. Disconnect negative battery cable and remove door trim panel.

2) Remove remote control bolts and place control assembly aside. Remove regulator-to-door panel attaching screws. Disconnect harness from regulator.

3) Slide regulator assembly rearward, disengaging rollers from sash panel. Remove regulator assembly.

4) Drill a hole through sector gear and back plate. Do not drill closer than ½" to edge of sector gear or back plate. Install sheet metal screw into hole to lock sector gear.

5) Remove motor-to-regulator attaching screws and remove regulator from motor.

6) To install, reverse removal procedures, noting that the motor drive gear and regulator sector gear should be lubricated with an approved lubricant that is effective down to —20°F.

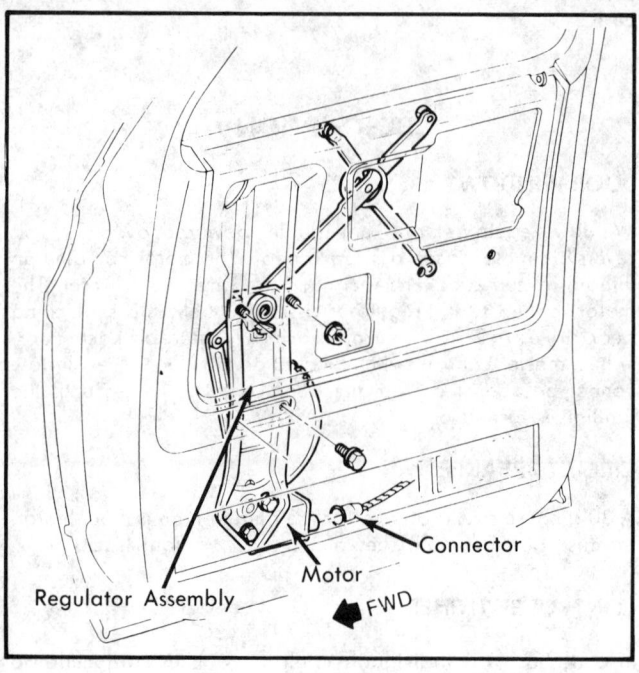

Fig. 2 General Motors Power Window Regulator, Motor and Connector

GENERAL MOTORS TAILGATE

Chevrolet
GMC

DESCRIPTION

Tailgate window system consists of a 12 volt reversible direction motor, that is protected by an internal circuit breaker which may require 1 to 3 minutes to reset. Window is controlled by a jackscrew type regulator. Window is operated by an instrument panel switch with the ignition switch at "ON" position, or an external key switch located in the tailgate door. A cut-out switch prevents operation of the window by either switch when tailgate is open. Window will retract into tailgate door. Circuit is protected by a 30-ampere circuit breaker located at fuse block.

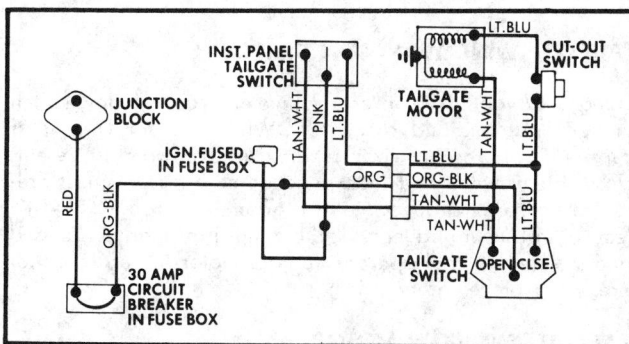

Fig. 1 General Motors Tailgate Power Window Wiring Diagram

TESTING & TROUBLE SHOOTING

TAILGATE POWER WINDOW INOPERATIVE FROM PANEL OR TAILGATE KEY SWITCH

Check circuit breaker and replace if bad. If good, check motor ground. If good, check the Tan/White and Lt. Blue wires for short. If not shorted, replace window motor.

TAILGATE POWER WINDOW INOPERATIVE FROM PANEL SWITCH, OPERATES FROM TAILGATE KEY SWITCH

If current from fuse block is good, press switch to window "UP" position. Check Lt. Blue wire at back of switch. If no continuity exists, replace switch. If continuity is good, press switch to "DOWN" position and check Tan/White wire for continuity. If open, replace switch. If good, check window motor ground to body and Lt. Blue and Tan/White wires between switch and motor.

NOTE — If switch operation is reversed, use same test procedure and replace tailgate key switch if necessary.

TAILGATE WINDOW WILL NOT CLOSE FROM PANEL SWITCH, OTHERWISE OPERATES

With ignition switch "ON", tailgate door open, put panel switch in "UP" position. Check Lt. Blue wire at back of switch. If no continuity exists, replace panel switch. If good, check Lt. Blue wire at cutout switch, also between cutout switch and motor. If wire is good, replace cutout switch.

TAILGATE WINDOW WILL NOT OPEN FROM TAILGATE KEY SWITCH, OTHERWISE OPERATES

Open tailgate door, turn key switch to "DOWN" position and check continuity of Tan/White wire between key switch and window motor. If open, replace key switch.

NOTE — If window will not close, place switch in "UP" position and check Lt. Blue wire. If open, replace key switch.

REMOVAL & INSTALLATION

WINDOW MOTOR

1) Secure window regulator lift arms and remove window glass from lift arms. Drill a 1/8" hole through the sector gear and backplate. Install a sheet metal screw into the hole locking the sector gears in position.

2) Disconnect drive cable at regulator. Remove motor attaching screws, motor and detach harness.

3) To install, reverse removal procedure.

CUT-OUT SWITCH

1) Disconnect left side remote control rod from center control by removing retaining clip. Remove side latch retaining screws and disconnect cut-out switch wiring.

2) Remove side latch assembly and screws holding latch to switch. To install, reverse removal procedures.

JACKSCREW REGULATOR

CAUTION — If window glass is removed, or disengaged from regulator lift arms, the regulator lift arms must be secured before removing jackscrew. Regulator lift arms are under spring pressure and may cause injury if not secured.

1) Drill an 1/8" hole through sector gear and back plate, and install a sheet metal screw in hole to secure sector gears in position.

2) Disconnect drive cable at jackscrew. Remove regulator jackscrew attaching screws and remove jackscrew assembly. To install, reverse removal procedures.

Power Windows

JEEP ELECTRIC WINDOWS

**Cherokee
Wagoneer**

DESCRIPTION

System consists of an electrically operated tailgate window and individual motors at all side windows. Tailgate window operates on two circuits: an instrument panel switch or an external key switch at tailgate. Side windows are operated by individual switches at each door, or by a complete set of control switches at the instrument panel.

Electric tailgate window system consists of a safety switch, gearbox-type regulator, 12 volt DC motor, wiring and connections and a 30 amp. circuit breaker at fuse block. Electric side window system consists of regulator motors, switches, actuators and actuator rods, wiring and connections and a 30 amp. circuit breaker located at the fuse block.

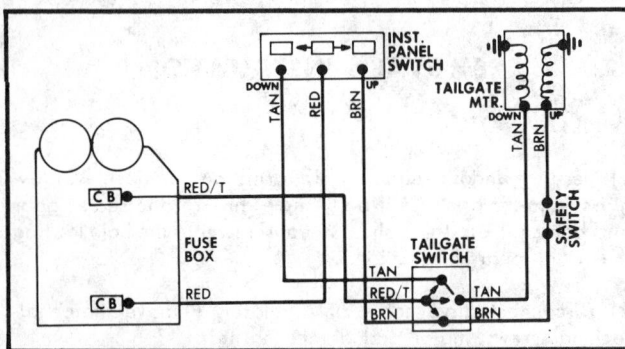

Fig. 1   Jeep Instrument Panel Tailgate Wiring Diagram Cherokee & Wagoneer

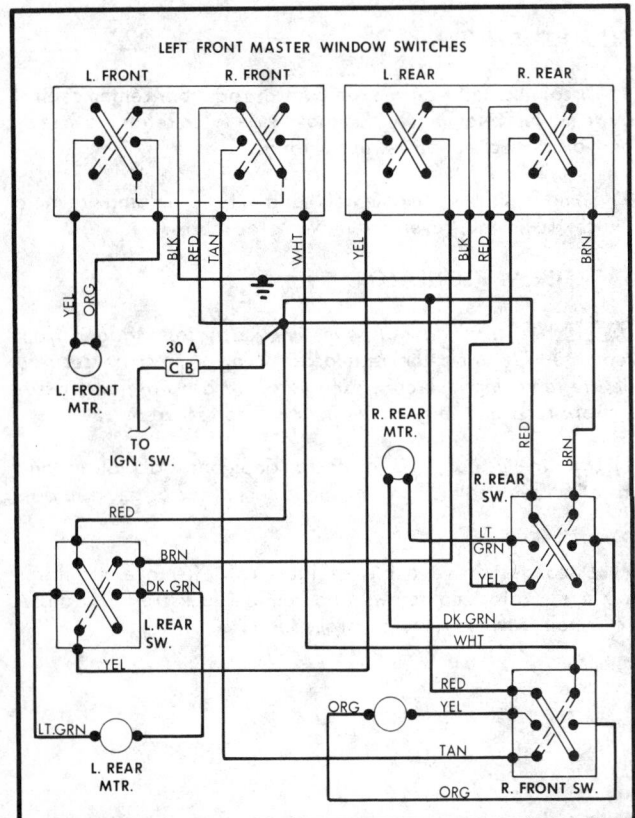

Fig. 2   Jeep Power Window Wiring Diagram

TESTING

INSTRUMENT PANEL & TAILGATE SWITCH

Turn ignition switch to "ON" position. Using a 12 volt test lamp or a voltmeter, connect one end of test equipment to ground and probe the "RED" lead. If current is not available, repair feed circuit. If current is present, probe "BROWN" lead with switch in "UP" position. If current is present move switch to "DOWN" position and check the "TAN" lead for current. If current is not present, replace switch. If current is present check window switch in the tailgate using the same procedure.

NOTE – *If vehicle is equipped with a tailgate window defogger, the defogger and tailgate switches are serviced as one assembly. Both switches must be replaced when either is defective.*

TAILGATE WINDOW SAFETY SWITCH

Using a 12 volt test lamp or a voltmeter, place window switch in "UP" position and check "BROWN" lead for current. If current is not present, repair feed circuits. If current is present, close safety switch and check lead at motor. If current is present check motor ground. Motor is grounded through "BLACK" lead at instrument panel switch. If motor is properly grounded and system does not operate, replace motor. If current is not present, replace safety switch.

TAILGATE WINDOW MOTOR

Using a 12 volt test lamp or a voltmeter, connect one lead of test equipment to ground and probe "TAN" lead. Close safety switch and turn tailgate window switch to "DOWN" position. If current is not present, repair feed circuit. Probe "BROWN" wire at motor, close safety switch and place switch in "UP" position. If current is not present, repair feed wire. If current is present in both tests but motor does not operate, replace motor.

MASTER SWITCH CIRCUITS

1) Remove escutcheon and housing from master switch. Separate terminal plate by releasing retainer hooks to expose terminal ends.

2) Turn ignition switch to "ON" position. Using a 12 volt test lamp, connect one lead to black wire and other lead to red terminal. Repeat test at second black wire.

3) If lamp does not light in either test, remove black lead and connect to chassis ground. If lamp lights, an opening exists between master switch and ground. If lamp does not light, it indicates a defective circuit breaker or an opening in the red wire from circuit breaker to master switch.

CONTROL SWITCH & MOTOR CIRCUITS

1) Connect test lamp between terminals of "ORANGE" and "YELLOW" wire. Operate control switch "UP" and "DOWN".

2) If lamp lights in both positions, wires and door switch are not defective. Disconnect "WHITE" and "GREEN" motor leads at terminal plate and connect to "GREEN" and "WHITE" leads.

3) Operate master switch. If window goes up and down, motor is okay, but switch is defective. If motor does not

JEEP ELECTRIC WINDOWS (Cont.)

operate, check connections and leads to motor. If motor operates, switch is defective.

SIDE WINDOW MOTOR

Connect test battery positive lead to one of the motor terminals. Connect negative lead to other terminal. Motor should now rotate in one direction to go "UP" or "DOWN".

SWITCH VOLTAGE TEST

1) Connect one lead of a jumper wire to "RED" lead, and the other lead to "UP" terminal of switch. Connect one lead of a second jumper wire to ground terminal of switch and other lead to "DOWN": terminal. This will test "UP" operation of switch.

2) If motor runs, voltage is present to motor. Connect switch to multiple connector and operate switch. If motor fails to run, replace switch. Test all switches in this manner.

3) To test "DOWN" operation of switch, make connections as stated in step 1) except connect second lead of first jumper wire to "DOWN" terminal, and second lead of second jumper wire to "UP" terminal. Repeat tests on all switches. Results are the same as "UP" test.

REMOVAL & INSTALLATION

TAILGATE WINDOW REGULATOR & MOTOR

1) Remove carpet and tailgate access cover plate. Remove retainers attaching regulator arms to channel. Disengage regulator arm pins from channel and raise glass.

2) Carefully support glass in raised position. If regulator attaching screws are covered by sector gears, disconnect motor drive from gear regulator. Grasp regulator arm as far outboard as access hole will allow.

3) Push down on arm until holes in sector gears align with attaching screws and motor. Hold regulator in this position and wedge a ¼" screw between meshing teeth. Remove regulator attaching screws, regulator and motor. Release spring tension by using a large screwdriver to snap spring from under tension bracket.

4) To install, reverse removal procedure.

SIDE WINDOW MASTER SWITCH

1) Disconnect negative battery cable. Remove retaining screws and escutcheon. Remove switch housing screws.

2) Pull switch out to expose wires. Disconnect terminal plate from switch. Depress retainer clips through holes in switch housing and remove switch.

FRONT & REAR DOOR REGULATORS & MOTORS

1) Raise window half way up. Disconnect negative battery cable. Remove door trim panel and water shield.

2) Insert a drift punch into hole in door inner panel, or use masking tape to hold window half way up. Remove regulator arm retainer clip and remove arm from bottom window channel.

3) Disconnect wires from motor. Remove nuts and bolts from inner door panel-to-regulator and remove regulator and motor assembly.

4) To install, reverse removal procedures.

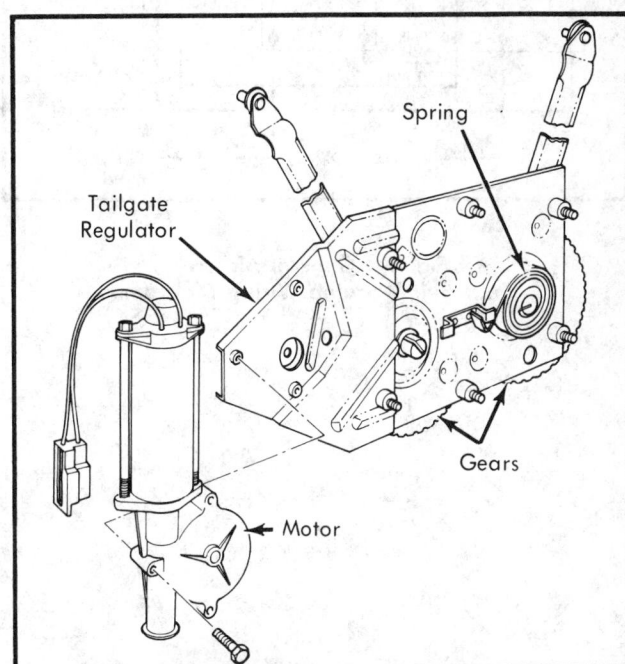

Fig. 3 Power Tailgate Regulator and Motor

Seat Belt Warning Systems

FORD MOTOR CO. & GENERAL MOTORS

Ford
 All Models
General Motors
 "C" & "K" Models

DESCRIPTION & OPERATION

If drivers seat belt is not buckled and ignition is turned to "ON" or "START" position, seat belt warning system will turn on "FASTEN SEAT BELTS" indicator light and sound buzzer for 4 to 8 seconds. If the drivers belt is buckled after buzzer sounds, buzzer will remain on until timer turns it off. When ignition is turned to "ON" position, current is supplied through timer to buzzer circuit and indicator light circuit. Light will always remain on until timer turns off current. Buzzer will only sound if single space drivers seat belt is not buckled before turning on ignition.

NOTE — Ford 2 point seat belt system does not have a warning system (lap belts only).

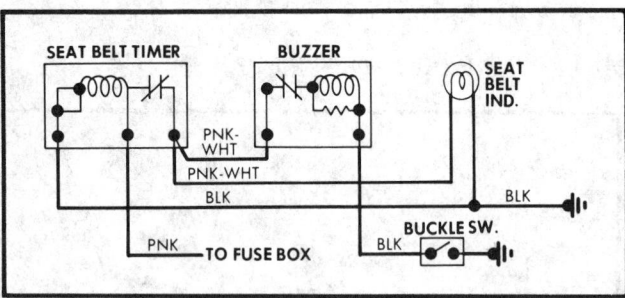

**Fig. 1   General Motors
Seat Belt Warning Wiring Diagram**

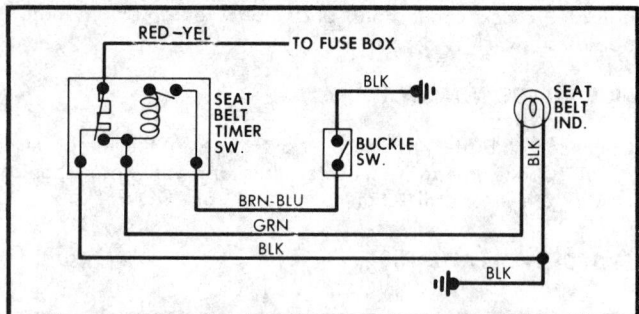

Fig. 2   Ford Seat Belt Warning Wiring Diagram

TROUBLE SHOOTING

BUZZER & INDICATOR LIGHT INOPERATIVE

Check fuse. Check for open circuit in timer feed wire. Check seat belt switch for good ground. Check for defective timer or ignition switch.

BUZZER INOPERATIVE

Check for defective buzzer, open circuit in seat belt switch or defective wire. Check connections at seat belt switch and buzzer. Check seat belt switch ground.

INDICATOR LIGHT INOPERATIVE

Check light and wiring for shorts, open circuits, or poor connections.

BUZZER & INDICATOR LIGHT REMAIN ON

Check for open circuit in timer ground lead. Check for a defective timer.

CHRYSLER CORP.

Dodge
Plymouth

DESCRIPTION

System is electrically actuated and vacuum operated. Turn signal lever on steering column incorporates a slide switch which has three positions: "OFF", "ON" and "RESUME SPEED". A speed set button is located in the end of lever. System will not function under 30 MPH.

OPERATION

Engaging System — Move slide switch to "ON" position, attain desired speed, then momentarily depress and release speed set button. Remove foot from accelerator and speed will be maintained at selected level. Moving slide switch from "OFF" to "ON" while car is in motion establishes memory without system engagement at that speed.

Disengaging System — Normal brake application or a soft tap on brake pedal will disengage control unit without erasing speed memory. Moving slide switch to "OFF" or turning ignition off also disengages system and in addition, erases speed memory.

Resuming Speed — Move slide switch to "RESUME" position.

Changing Speed Setting — To increase speed, accelerate to desired speed and momentarily depress and release speed set button. When unit is engaged, tapping button will increase speed in small amounts. To decrease speed, tap brake pedal lightly to disengage system. When desired speed has been obtained, depress and release speed set button. Decrease in speed can also be obtained by holding set button depressed until desired speed is attained. Releasing button engages system at that speed.

Accelerating for Passing — Depress accelerator as necessary. When passing is completed, release accelerator and vehicle will return to previous speed.

TROUBLE SHOOTING

NO SPEED CONTROL WHEN BUTTON PRESSED

Slide switch in "OFF" position. Fuse blown. Faulty electrical circuit. Vacuum leak. Insufficient brake switch clearance. Speed control throttle cable disconnected.

NO RESUME WHEN SLIDE SWITCH MOVED

Insufficient movement of slide switch. Faulty electrical circuit.

NO AUTO. RELEASE WITH PEDAL DEPRESSED

Speed control cable kinked or damaged. Improper adjustment of brake switch. Faulty electrical circuit.

SPEED CONTROL ENGAGES WITHOUT ACTUATING SPEED SET BUTTON

Faulty electrical circuit.

CARBURETOR DOES NOT RETURN TO NORMAL IDLE

Speed control cable kinked or damaged. Speed control cable improperly adjusted. Standard throttle linkage faulty.

SPEEDOMETER NOISE, EXCESSIVE NEEDLE FLUTTER OR ERRATIC SERVO LOCK-IN PERFORMANCE

Speedometer cable kinked or damaged. Cable core bent or too long. Cable ferrule nut loose at speedometer head, transmission or speed control servo. No lubrication on speedometer cable or core. Noisy speedometer head assembly.

SPEED SETTING AFTER LOCK-IN, TOO HIGH OR TOO LOW

Improper speed control throttle cable adjustment. Vacuum leak. Improper speed control lock-in adjustment.

UNIT DISENGAGES ON ROUGH ROAD

Insufficient brake switch clearance.

RESUME SPEED POSSIBLE BELOW 20 MPH

Faulty low speed inhibit switch in servo unit. Faulty electrical circuit.

SPEED CONTROL ENGAGES WHEN ENGINE STARTED OR DOES NOT DISENGAGE WITH PEDAL DEPRESSED

Faulty electrical circuit.

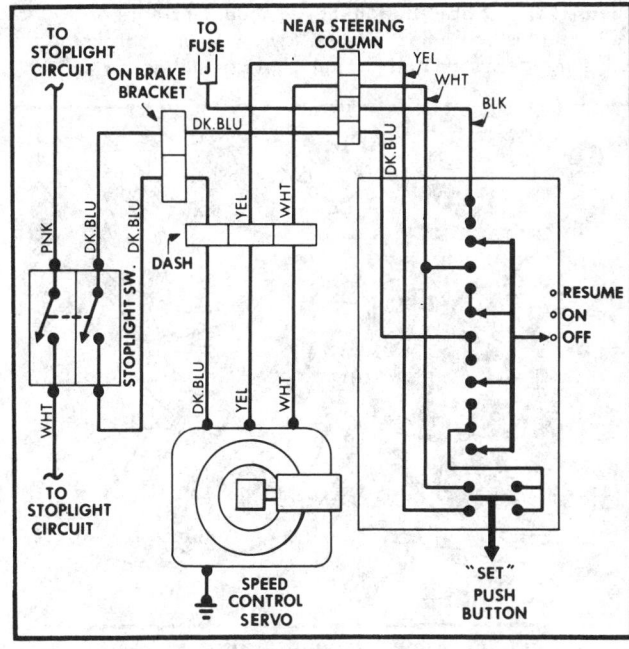

Fig. 1   Wiring Diagram of Chrysler Corp. Speed Control System

TESTING

SPEED CONTROL SWITCH

1) Disconnect 4-wire connector at steering column. Connect a 12 volt positive source to black wire terminal in speed control

CHRYSLER CORP. (Cont.)

harness connector (male). With switch in "ON" position, connect a test lamp between connector yellow wire and ground. Lamp should light and then go out when "SPEED SET" button is depressed.

2) Move test lamp lead to connector blue wire. Lamp should light with switch in "ON" position and go out when switch is turned to "OFF" position. With switch in "ON" position, move test lamp lead to connector white wire. Lamp should light by either depressing "SPEED SET" button or by moving switch to "RESUME" position.

BRAKE SWITCH

Disconnect double connector at switch pigtail and connect a 12 volt source to either terminal, then connect a test lamp from other terminal to ground. Test lamp should light with brake pedal in normal position. Test lamp light should go out when brake pedal is depressed a maximum of ½" if switch is correctly adjusted.

SERVO UNIT

Locking Coil Test — Turn ignition switch to "ACC" or "ON" position and move slide switch to "ON" position. Momentarily disconnect and connect the double connector at terminals at servo. A clicking sound should be detected in servo. If no clicking sound is heard, replace servo.

Holding Coil & Low Speed Switch Test — Without removing connectors at servo, place one test lamp lead to terminal with black wire (with tracer) and other lead to ground. Block front wheels, raise rear of vehicle, start vehicle and accelerate to 35 MPH. With slide switch in "ON" position, depress and release "SPEED SET" button. Speed should increase above 35 MPH and test lamp light should stay on. Depress brake pedal to disengage system and test lamp light should go out.

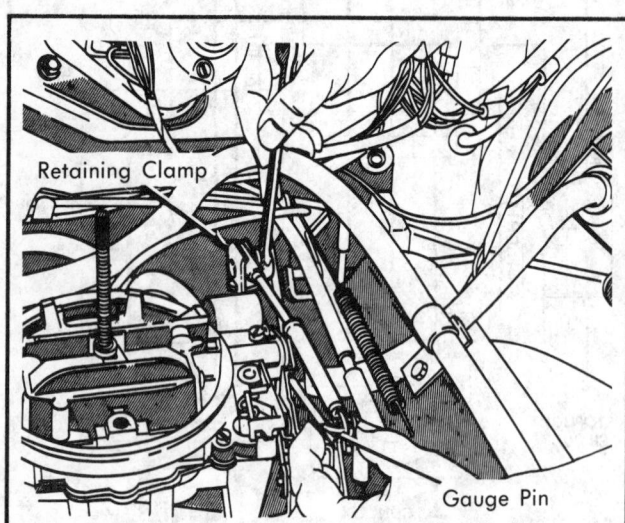

Fig. 2 View Showing Adjustment of Servo Throttle Cable

ADJUSTMENTS

SPEED CONTROL THROTTLE CABLE

Remove spring clip and insert a 1/16" diameter pin between forward end of slot in cable and carburetor linkage pin. With choke in full open position and carburetor at curb idle, pull back on cable (toward dash panel), without moving carburetor linkage, until all free play is removed. Tighten cable clamp bolt to 45 INCH lbs., remove pin and install clip.

BRAKE LIGHT/SPEED CONTROL SWITCH

Loosen switch mounting bracket. Insert .140" feeler gauge between brake push rod and switch, with brake pedal in fully released position. Push switch bracket assembly toward brake push rod until plunger is fully depressed and switch body contacts spacer. Tighten switch bracket bolt to 100 INCH lbs. Remove feeler gauge.

SERVO UNIT (LOCK-IN SCREW ADJUSTMENT)

NOTE — *Lock-in accuracy will be affected by engine being out of tune, adverse power-to-weight ratio, and improper slack in throttle control cable.*

If speed drops more than 2 to 3 MPH when speed control is activated, lock-in adjusting screws should be turned counterclockwise approximately ¼ turn for each 1 MPH correction required. If speed increases more than 2 to 3 MPH, turn screw clockwise approximately ¼ turn for each 1 MPH correction required. If screw is loose, stake side of servo housing adjacent to screw to ensure a snug fit.

CAUTION — *Screw should never be turned more than 2 turns in either direction or damage to servo unit may occur.*

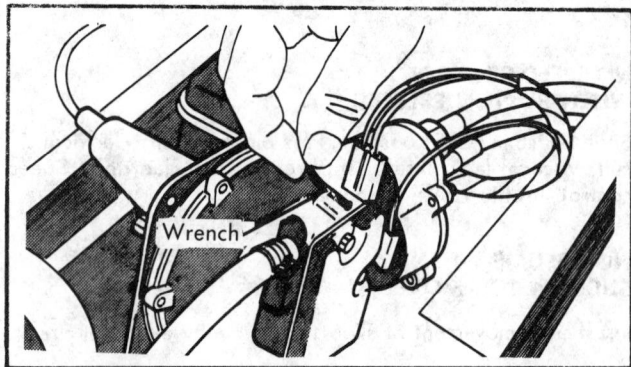

Fig. 3 View Showing Adjustment of Lock-In Screw

FORD

"E" Models
"F" Models
Bronco

DESCRIPTION

Speed control system consists of "ON-OFF", "SET-ACCEL", "COAST", and "RESUME" switches, servo assembly, speed control sensor, clutch position sensor switch (man. trans.), amplifier, wire harness, vacuum dump valve, and vacuum hoses to connect components. The switches are located in steering wheel spokes. The amplifier is located under the instrument panel and the servo assembly is attached to the engine intake manifold. The speed sensor is located on the left side of dash panel.

OPERATION

This system is operational at speeds over 30 MPH. When "ON-OFF" switch is actuated to "ON" position and "SET-ACCEL" switch is activated, the vehicle speed will be maintained until a new speed is set, brake pedal is depressed, clutch pedal is depressed (man. trans.), or system is turned off. The purpose of having the clutch position sensor switch (man. trans.) disengage the speed control is to prevent engine overspeed when the clutch pedal is depressed.

To decrease set speed, apply brake and reset speed using the preceding method or depress the "COAST" switch. When the vehicle has slowed to the desired speed, release switch and the new speed is set into system.

To increase set speed, accelerate until desired speed is reached, then depress and release the "SET-ACCEL" switch. Speed may also be increased by depressing "SET-ACCEL" switch and holding in that position while vehicle automatically increases in speed. When desired speed is reached, release switch and new speed will be set into system.

When the speed control system is deactivated by depressing brake pedal, vehicle speed before system deactivation may be resumed by depressing "RESUME" switch. Speed control memory of vehicle speed and "RESUME" switch will not function if "OFF" switch is depressed, or ignition is turned off, or vehicle speed drops below 30 MPH.

TESTING

NOTE — *Horn and/or speed control may operate intermittently if ground brush is missing.*

CONTROL SWITCH

1) Disconnect six-way connector at amplifier. Check battery voltage at light blue/black hash wire when "ON" switch is depressed. Battery voltage should be available from light blue/black hash wire leading from control switches.

2) Connect an ohmmeter between light blue/black hash wire and ground. Check wire for continuity to ground with "OFF" switch depressed. If resistance higher than 1 ohm is found, the wiring, slip rings or switch is at fault, or steering column may not be properly grounded. To check steering column ground, connect an ohmmeter between a good body ground and steering column upper flange. Resistance should be less than 1/2 ohm. Rotate steering wheel and check flexible coupling resistance. If resistance higher than 3 ohms is noted, clean horn brush contacts and ground brush. A resistance less than 1 ohm must be obtained before performing the remaining tests.

3) With ohmmeter connected between light blue/black hash wire and ground, depress "SET-ACCEL" switch. A reading of approximately 680 ohms should be indicated on ohmmeter. Depress "COAST" switch and a reading of approximately 120 ohms should be indicated on ohmmeter. Depress and hold "RESUME" switch. A reading of approximately 2200 ohms should be indicated.

SPEED SENSOR

Disconnect sensor wires from amplifier and connect an ohmmeter between wire connector terminals (dark green stripe and black on "E" models, dark green/white stripe and black on "F" and Bronco models) at sensor end. A reading of about 40 ohms should be obtained. A reading of "zero" ohms indicates a shorted coil, and a maximum reading indicates an open coil. Replace sensor in either case. If reading is 40 ohms and speedometer operates properly, speed sensor is probably good. A new sensor can be substituted to check for proper operation.

SERVO ASSEMBLY

1) Disconnect ball chain from throttle linkage. Separate eight-way connector at amplifier, then connect an ohmmeter between the orange/yellow hash wire and gray/black hash wire at the connector. A resistance of approximately 85 ohms should be obtained. Connect ohmmeter between the orange/yellow hash wire and white/pink hash wire at connector. A resistance of approximately 85 ohms should be obtained. Reconnect the ball chain to carburetor.

2) Start the engine with the servo-to-amplifier connector disconnected. Connect orange/yellow hash wire of servo to battery positive terminal, connect white/pink hash wire to ground, and then momentarily touch gray/black hash wire of servo to ground. Servo throttle actuator should tighten bead chain and open throttle. Throttle should hold in that position or slowly release tension on chain.

3) When white/pink hash wire is removed from ground, servo should release bead chain tension immediately. If servo fails any of the preceding tests, replacement of the servo is necessary. If orange/yellow hash wire is shorted to either white/pink hash wire or gray/black hash wire, it may be necessary to replace amplifier.

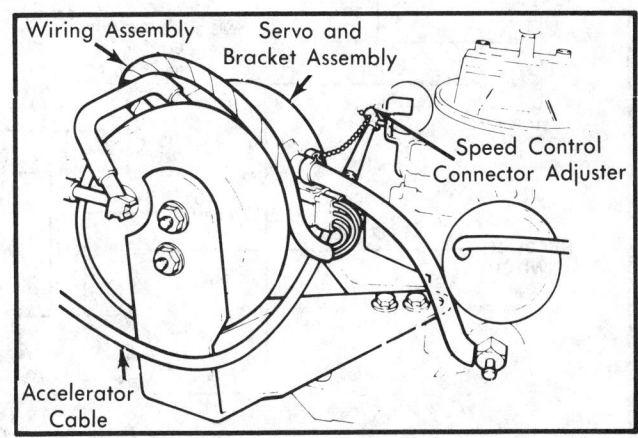

Fig. 1 Engine Compartment Servo and Bracket Installation for "E" Models ("F" Models are Similar)

FORD (Cont.)

AMPLIFIER

CAUTION — *DO NOT use a test light to perform amplifier tests as excessive current draw will damage electronic components. Use only a voltmeter of 5000 ohm/volt rating or higher.*

"ON" Circuit Test — Turn ignition "ON" and connect a voltmeter between ground and light blue/black hash wire at amplifier six-way connector. Voltmeter should read 12 volts when "ON" switch in steering wheel is depressed and held. If no voltage is available, conduct Horn Relay Circuit Test and Control Switch Test. Release "ON" button. A 7.8 volt reading should remain on voltmeter indicating the "ON" circuit is engaged. If voltage does not remain, check for ground at amplifier, fuse and/or circuit breaker. Insert a known good amplifier and recheck "ON" circuit if necessary.

"OFF" Circuit Test — With ignition "ON" and voltmeter connected to light blue-black hash wire at amplifier six-way connector, depress the "OFF" switch on steering wheel. Voltage should drop to zero indicating "ON" circuit is de-energized. If voltage does not drop to zero, perform Control Switch Test. If switches test good, install a known good amplifier and retest.

"SET-ACC" Circuit Test — With ignition "ON" and voltmeter connected to light blue/black hash wire at amplifier six-way connector, depress the "ON" switch, then hold "SET-ACC" button on steering wheel. Voltmeter should indicate approximately 4.5 volts. Rotate steering wheel and watch voltmeter for variation. If voltage varies more than .5 volts, perform Control Switch Test.

"COAST" Circuit Test — With ignition "ON" and voltmeter connected to light blue/black hash wire at amplifier six-way connector, depress the "ON" switch and hold "COAST" button down on steering wheel. Voltmeter should indicate about 1.5 volts. If all functions check good, perform Servo Assembly Test. Insert a known good amplifier and recheck system if necessary.

CAUTION — *DO NOT substitute a new amplifier until actuator coils have been tested. See Servo Assembly Test.*

"RESUME" Circuit Test — With ignition "ON" and voltmeter connected to light blue/black hash wire at amplifier six-way connector and ground, depress and hold "RESUME" switch. Voltmeter should indicate approximately 6.5 volts. If all functions check good, perform Servo Assembly Test. Insert a known good amplifier and recheck system if necessary.

HORN RELAY CIRCUIT TEST

NOTE — *Electrical connectors must remain connected during horn relay testing.*

1) Locate yellow wire ("E" models) or yellow/light blue dot wire ("F" and Bronco models) at connector "X" and check for battery voltage on pin side of connector. *See Fig. 2.*

2) Locate blue/yellow stripe wire ("E" models) or dark blue wire ("F" and Bronco models) at connector "Y" and check for battery voltage on socket side of connector. With voltmeter still connected to socket, depress horn switch. Horn should sound but voltmeter should indicate "zero" volts. If voltmeter still indicates battery voltage when horn switch is depressed, check horn switch or steering column wiring for an open circuit.

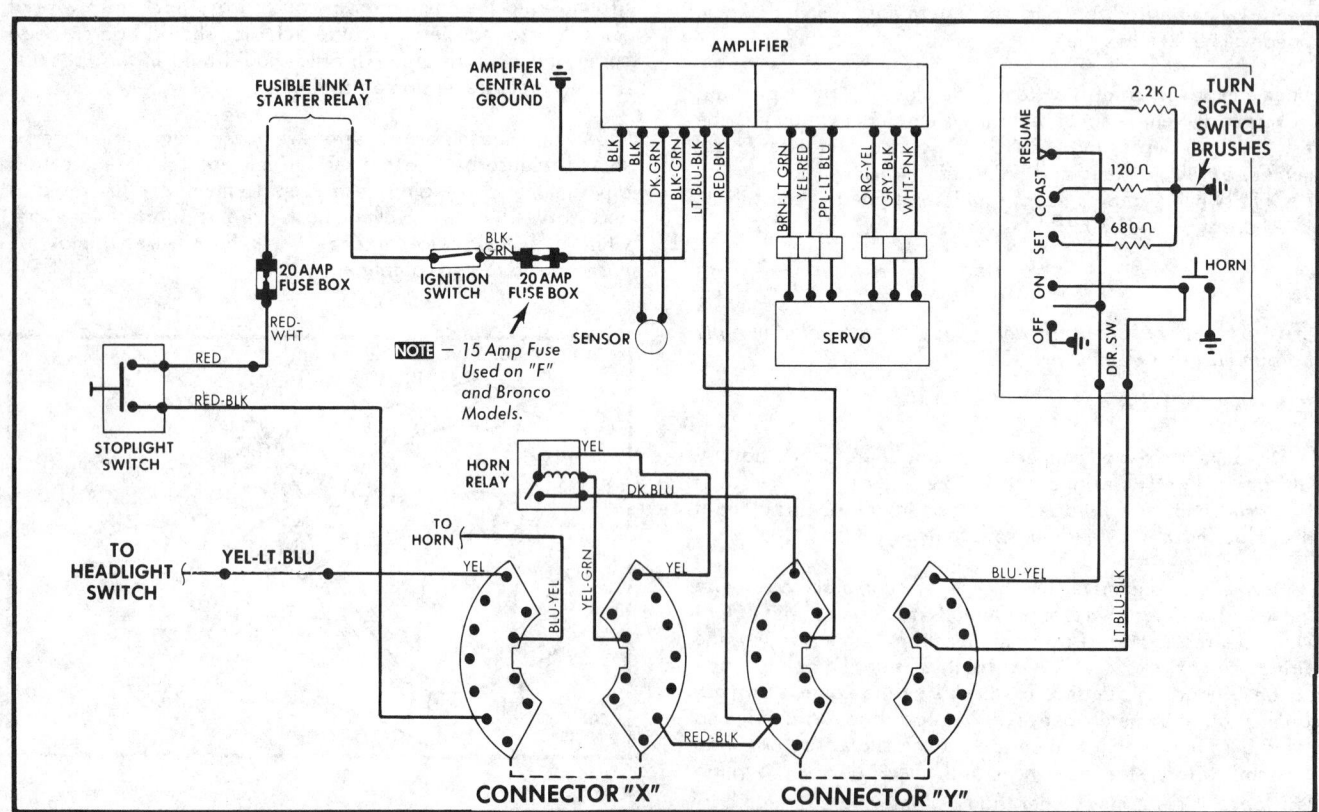

Fig. 2   Wiring Diagram of Ford Automatic Speed Control System ("E" Model Shown)

FORD (Cont.)

3) To bypass horn switch and check horn relay, momentarily ground blue/yellow stripe wire ("E" models) or dark blue wire ("F" and Bronco models) on socket side of connector "Y".

4) If horn still does not sound, check yellow/green stripe wire ("E" models) or yellow/light green wire ("F" and Bronco models) at connector "X" for battery voltage while relay is activated. If battery voltage is present when relay is activated, an open circuit is present between connector "X" and horn.

5) If battery voltage is present in step 1) and horn relay fails to operate in step 3), replace relay.

CLUTCH SWITCH TEST (MANUAL TRANSMISSION "F" AND BRONCO MODELS)

NOTE — *Automatic transmission models use a shorting plug instead of a clutch switch.*

CAUTION — *Switch operates magnetically. Do not use magnetized tools near switch. Use only a voltmeter of 5,000 ohm/volt rating or higher to test switch. Test lamp will not indicate switch condition.*

1) Check if clutch switch plunger is depressed (switch closed) when clutch pedal is released. Speed control will not operate unless this condition exists.

2) Disconnect clutch switch connector from speed control harness connector and connect an ohmmeter to switch connector terminals. With clutch pedal released in "full-up" position and switch plunger depressed (switch closed), resistance should be less than 5 ohms. With clutch pedal depressed and switch plunger fully extended (switch open), resistance should be "infinity".

BRAKE STOP LIGHT SWITCH & CIRCUIT TEST

NOTE — *This test should be performed whenever brake application will not disengage speed control. If both stop lights are not working it will cause speed control malfunctions.*

Check for stop light operation with a maximum brake pedal effort of 6 lbs. Check brake pedal actuation and stop light switch if pedal effort required is in excess of specification. If stop lights operate correctly, check battery voltage at black/green stripe wire at six-way connector. Depress pedal until stop lights are lit and check voltage at red/black stripe wire at six-way connector. If voltage readings differ by more than 1.5 volts, high resistance exists in stop light circuit and must be corrected. If stop lights do not work, the stop light switch, supply circuit and bulbs must be checked for correct operation.

VACUUM DUMP VALVE TEST

Vacuum dump valve should be checked whenever brake application does not release speed control. Disconnect vacuum hose from the dump valve to the servo at the servo. Connect hand vacuum pump to hose and pump up a vacuum. If vacuum cannot be obtained, the hose or dump valve leaks and should be replaced. Depress brake pedal. Vacuum should be released. If not, adjust or replace dump valve.

ADJUSTMENT

LINKAGE ADJUSTMENT

Adjust bead chain to obtain .06-.25" actuator arm free travel when engine is at hot idle. Adjustment should be made to eliminate as much slack as possible without restricting carburetor lever from returning to idle. Cut off chain in excess of four beads. On vehicles equipped with solenoid anti-diesel valve, perform this adjustment with ignition switch in "OFF" position.

VACUUM DUMP VALVE ADJUSTMENT

Check that brake pedal is against stop in "released" position. Move dump valve forward in retaining clip until ⅛" or less of valve plunger is exposed. Tip of valve plunger should contact brake pedal adapter. Check again if brake pedal is against stop in "released" position. Step on brake pedal. If vacuum still does not release, replace vacuum dump valve.

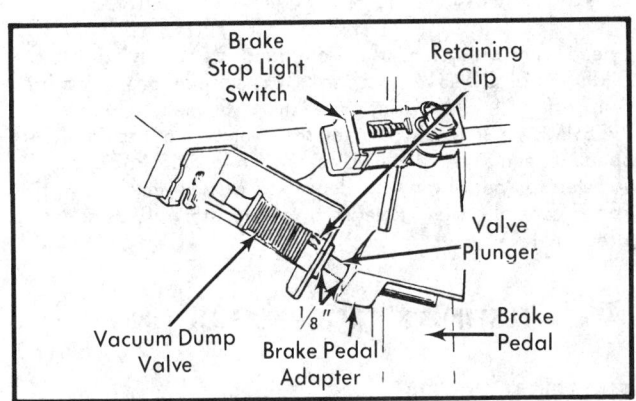

Fig. 3 Vacuum Dump Valve Adjustment

GENERAL MOTORS CRUISE MASTER

Chevrolet
GMC

DESCRIPTION

System uses manifold vacuum to power a throttle servo unit. When speed adjustment is necessary, servo moves the throttle by receiving a varying amount of controlled vacuum from transducer. Speedometer cable from transmission drives transducer and a cable from transducer drives instrument panel speedometer. There are 2 control switches operating speed control. The first is a "CRUISE" slide switch with "OFF", "ON", and "RESUME" positions. The second is a "SET-COAST" button switch located on end of turn signal lever. It controls engagement of transducer. Two brake release switches are provided. An electric switch disengages transducer and a vacuum valve (switch) decreases vacuum in servo unit to quickly return throttle to idle position when brake pedal or clutch is depressed.

OPERATION

This system is designed to operate at speeds above 30 MPH. "CRUISE" switch must be in "ON" position to activate speed control system. Driver accelerates to desired speed, then partially depresses and slowly releases speed control "SET-COAST" switch button. To change speed setting to higher speed, depress accelerator until desired speed is reached, then fully depress and slowly release "SET-COAST" switch. To change speed setting to lower speed, depress "SET-COAST" switch fully and hold in this position until vehicle has decelerated to new desired speed setting. Then, release "SET-COAST" switch slowly to re-engage speed control.

Speed control system is disengaged by applying brakes. Sliding "SET-COAST" switch to "OFF" position or turning ignition off will also disengage the system and erase the "RESUME" memory. To accelerate vehicle to previously set speed in memory, slide "CRUISE" switch to "RESUME" position. Accelerator pedal may be depressed at any time to override speed control system. Release of accelerator returns speed to previous level.

TESTING & TROUBLE SHOOTING

ELECTRICAL SYSTEM

1) Check fuse and connector. Unplug electric brake switch connector at switch and connect ohmmeter at two terminals on switch. Ohmmeter must indicate no continuity when pedal is depressed and continuity when pedal is released. Replace switch if necessary. Check clutch release brake switch in same manner.

NOTE — *Check if transducer is well grounded.*

2) Disconnect "SET-COAST" switch wire harness connector from main harness connector (red, brown/white, and white wires). Connect ohmmeter between brown/white striped wire in main wiring harness and ground. Ohmmeter should read 42-49 ohms. If resistance is not within specifications, disconnect the connector from transducer and measure resistance of brown/white striped wire. Resistance should be 38-42 ohms. If not within specifications, replace main wiring harness.

3) Measure solenoid coil circuit resistance between "Hold" terminal and ground. Resistance should be 5-6 ohms. A reading of less than 4 ohms indicates shorting of coil circuit and a reading of more than 7 ohms indicates excessive coil circuit resistance. Either high or low condition indicates replacement of transducer assembly. Check White wire of main harness from engagement switch to transducer for continuity.

CONTROL SWITCHES

To test "SET-COAST" and "CRUISE" switches, refer to Fig. 1.

SERVO & VACUUM CHECK

To determine condition of diaphragm, remove hose from servo unit and apply 15" of vacuum to tube opening and hold in for one minute. Vacuum should not leak down more than 5" in one minute. If leakage is excessive, replace servo. To utilize engine as vacuum source, proceed as follows: Disconnect servo cable or bead chain and hose from servo unit, then connect engine vacuum directly to servo fitting. Note position of servo diaphragm and start engine. Diaphragm should pull in. Clamp off engine vacuum supply line and check unit for leakage.

ERRATIC CRUISE PERFORMANCE

Check servo, brake release switch, and vacuum release switch adjustments. Check for operation of engagement switch. Check for pinched, kinked, plugged or damaged vacuum hoses. Check speedometer cable routing and ensure that the turning radius of cable is not less than a 6" radius. Check for binding throttle linkage. Check for plugged transducer filter. Check if transducer has correct part number.

INOPERATIVE CRUISE CONTROL

NOTE — *Make all tests with transmission shift lever in "PARK" position and parking brake "ON".*

1) Check "Gauges" fuse. If fuse is blown, check speed control wiring for short circuit. If fuse is not the problem and *Erratic Cruise Performance Trouble Shooting* checks out O.K., turn ignition to "RUN" position. Slide "CRUISE" switch to "ON" position.

2) Disconnect the 2 wire connector from transducer. Connect 12 volt test light to "Engage" terminal in connector and ground.

3) Repeat step 2) using "Hold" connector terminal.

4) If test light is off in step 2) or 3), check for open circuit in wire. *See Fig. 1 and perform "SET-COAST" Switch Test.*

5) If test light is "on" in step 2) and 3), check if transducer is well grounded. If transducer is grounded, remove it for repair.

6) If test light is "off" in step 2) and 3), check for open circuit in wire (brown) between engagement switch connector and brake switch. Check brake switch for voltage at both terminals with ignition in "RUN" position and "CRUISE" switch in "ON" position. Check for open circuit in wire from brake release switch to "CRUISE" switch to fuse panel plug-in. Check engagement switch operation and replace if necessary.

GENERAL MOTORS CRUISE MASTER (Cont.)

ADJUSTMENTS

BRAKE RELEASE SWITCHES

The design of the electric switch and vacuum valve mounting provides for automatic adjustment when brake pedal is manually returned to its stop. Depress brake pedal fully and push switch and valve forward until they stop against bracket or arm. Pull brake pedal back up toward its stop with 15-20 lbs. of force.

SERVO UNIT

1) Disconnect idle stop solenoid. With air conditioning off, adjust engine curb idle speed to 500 RPM. Shut engine off.

2) To check bead chain slack, unsnap swivel from ball stud and pull chain tight. Center of swivel on chain should extend $\frac{1}{8}$" beyond center of ball stud. To adjust bead chain slack, remove retainer from chain and swivel. Adjust chain in swivel to remove slack and re-install retainer.

TRANSDUCER

1) Before adjusting transducer, be sure servo adjustment is correct. Check all hoses for proper routing and good condition. Ensure electric and vacuum release switches are properly adjusted.

2) To adjust transducer, note cruising speed. If it is lower than engagement speed, loosen orifice tube lock nut and turn tube outward. If cruising speed is high, turn tube inward. Each $\frac{1}{4}$ turn will change engagement speed by 1 MPH. Tighten lock nut and check operation.

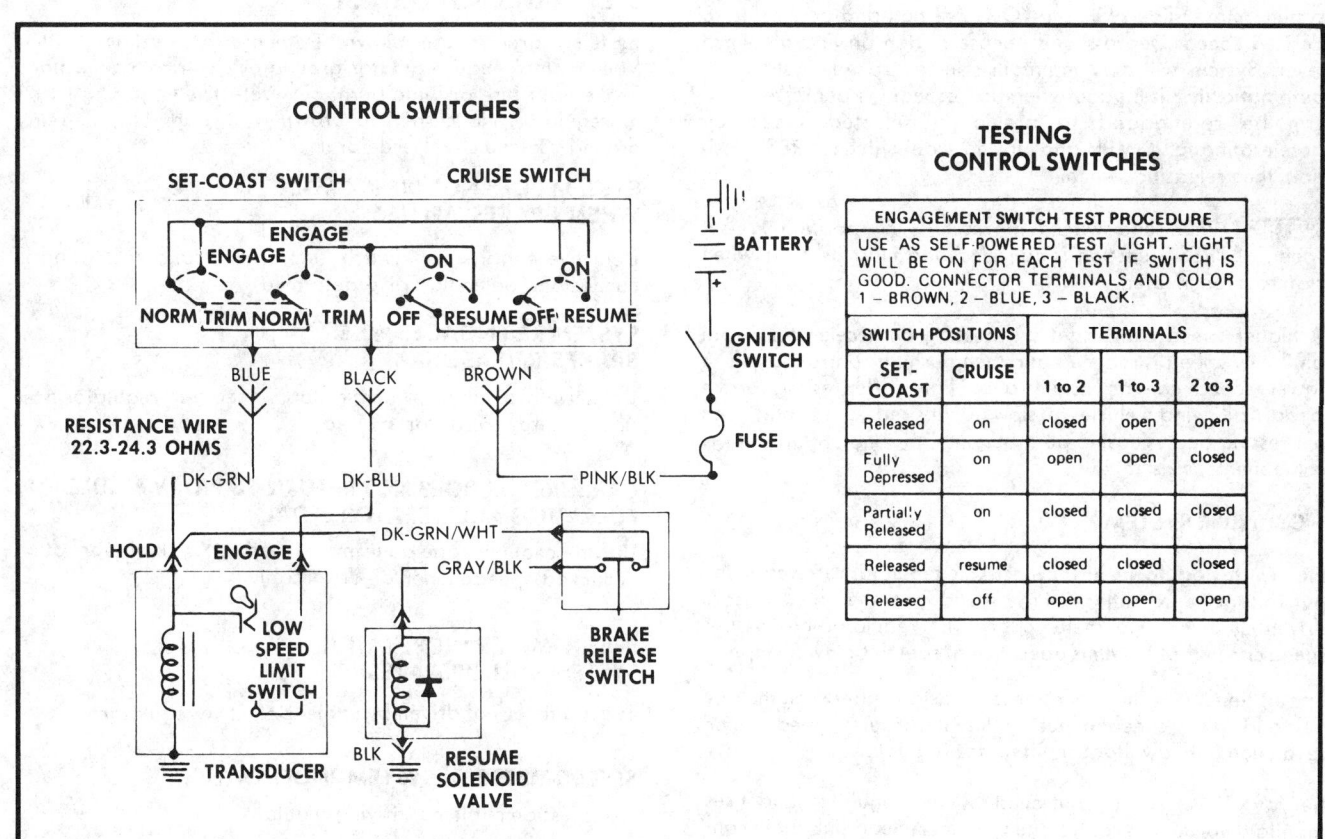

ENGAGEMENT SWITCH TEST PROCEDURE				
USE AS SELF-POWERED TEST LIGHT. LIGHT WILL BE ON FOR EACH TEST IF SWITCH IS GOOD. CONNECTOR TERMINALS AND COLOR 1 – BROWN, 2 – BLUE, 3 – BLACK.				
SWITCH POSITIONS		TERMINALS		
SET-COAST	CRUISE	1 to 2	1 to 3	2 to 3
Released	on	closed	open	open
Fully Depressed	on	open	open	closed
Partially Released	on	closed	closed	closed
Released	resume	closed	closed	closed
Released	off	open	open	open

Fig. 1   General Motors Cruise Master Wiring Diagram

JEEP CRUISE COMMAND

All Models

DESCRIPTION

Jeep vehicles use 2 automatic speed control systems; an automatic system for V8 engines and an electro-mechanical system for 6-cylinder engines. The V8 system consists of a regulator, relay, bellows, control switch assembly and a release circuit. The 6-cylinder system consists of an electronic regulator, speed sensor, servo, control switch assembly and a release system.

OPERATION

Cruise Command control is an integral part of the directional switch lever and consists of two separate switches. The first is "OFF-ON" and "RES" (resume) slide switch located on the flat of directional switch lever. Second is a push button switch located at the end of directional switch lever. To engage system, move slide switch to "ON" position and accelerate to desired speed. Depress and release button on end of switch lever. System will now maintain selected speed. System will automatically disengage when brake pedal is depressed and can be re-engaged to previously selected speed by accelerating to 30 MPH and moving slide switch to "RES" position, then releasing switch.

NOTE — *When slide switch is moved to "OFF" position, Pre-set speed of "RES" function is canceled and must be reset when system is reactivated.*

A higher speed can be set by pressing on accelerator pedal until new speed is reached and then pushing control button. A lower speed can be achieved by lightly depressing brake pedal, allowing vehicle to slow to desired speed and then depressing and releasing push button. Operation of individual components is as follows:

6-CYLINDER SYSTEM

Electronic Regulator — The electronic regulator receives an input voltage representing vehicle speed from the speed sensor, driven by the speedometer cable. The regulator has a low speed circuit that prevents operation at speeds below 30 mph.

Speed Sensor — The speed sensor is installed between the upper and lower speedometer cables. It converts speedometer revolutions into a voltage input for the regulator.

Servo — The servo is controlled by the regulator and uses manifold vacuum to control the throttle. A bead-link chain connects the servo cable to the throttle linkage.

Control Switch — The control switch assembly is an integral part of the turn signal switch lever.

Release System — The release deactivates the cruise command system when the brake pedal is depressed. Either a servo vent valve or a mechanical vacuum vent switch admits atmospheric pressure into the servo when the brake pedal is depressed.

V8 SYSTEM

Regulator — Senses speed through speedometer cable located between transmission and regulator. Fly-weight type governor reacts to cable speed and engages low speed switch at approximately 30 MPH. When low speed switch is closed, driver may engage system. Regulator is serviced as an assembly.

Vacuum Servo — A neoprene bellows that receives modulator vacuum and actuates throttle to control vehicle speed.

Control Switch — An integral part of turn signal lever, when actuated, it will energize either solenoid valve or coupling coil (or both), thereby controlling speed.

Relay — Relay is energized when ignition switch is turned to "ON" position. It prevents battery drain when ignition switch is turned to "OFF."

Release Switch — Disengages system when brake pedal is depressed.

TROUBLE SHOOTING & DIAGNOSIS

SYSTEM WILL NOT ENGAGE

System harness fuse blown. Defective brake light switch. Vacuum leak. Bad regulator ground or electrical connections. Brake light fuse or lamp burnt out. Defective engaging switch or regulator. No current to brown wire. Bad relay or relay ground. Solenoid valve deformed.

SYSTEM DOES NOT DISENGAGE WHEN BRAKES APPLIED

Defective engagement switch. Improper location of wiring in connectors. Solenoid valve deformed.

SYSTEM RE-ENGAGES WHEN BRAKES RELEASED

Defective brake light switch, collapsed servo-to-regulator hose or 250 mfd. capacitor shorted.

CARBURETOR DOES NOT RETURN TO NORMAL IDLE, PULSATING ACCELERATOR PEDAL

Throttle chain linkage adjustment incorrect. Lack of lubrication or kinked speedometer or drive cable.

SPEEDOMETER INOPERATIVE, SYSTEM STILL OPERATES

Speedometer not driven by cable. Defective regulator.

SPEEDOMETER & SYSTEM INOPERATIVE

Transmission cable not driving regulator.

SPEED 3 OR MORE MPH ABOVE OR BELOW SELECTED SPEED

Adjustment of regulator incorrect.

SYSTEM DISENGAGES ON LEVEL ROAD WITHOUT APPLYING BRAKE

Loose electrical connections or ground. Loose hoses. Broken servo linkage chain or slipped throttle clevis. Oversensitive stop lamp switch.

ERRATIC OPERATION OF SYSTEM

Inspect vacuum servo or vacuum hoses. Inspect regulator.

JEEP CRUISE COMMAND (Cont.)

SYSTEM CONTINUES TO ACCELERATE AFTER ENGAGEMENT

Open circuit in green wire attached to No. 4 terminal at regulator

VEHICLE LOSES SPEED ON HILLS

Excessive slack in servo chain. Lack of engine manifold vacuum.

STOP LIGHT FUSES BLOWING

Shorted 250 mfd. capacitor.

BLOWING FUSES

Short or ground in system wiring circuit.

SYSTEM DISENGAGES WHEN TURN SIGNAL SWITCH IS OPERATED

Open 250 mfd. capacitor. Stop or turn lamp bulb burned out on side opposite direction of turn.

TESTING

All tests of system should be performed as part of diagnosis of malfunction and to determine procedure(s) required for system repair. Five separate circuits are used in system. These circuits are: slide switch in "ON" position, push button depressed, push button released, brake release, and slide switch in "RESUME" position.

NOTE — *Whenever a unit is disconnected for testing, it should be reconnected before next unit is tested.*

CONTROL SWITCH CONTINUITY

Control switch continuity test is performed at steering column using an ohmmeter. Refer to following chart to determine switch continuity condition. When using the ohmmeter, the ignition switch must be OFF, otherwise the ohmmeter will be internally damaged.

NOTE — *Pushbutton cannot be depressed with slide switch in "RES" position.*

Control Switch Continuity Conditions

Application	Switch Position	Condition
Red/Brown	"OFF"	Open
Red/Green	"OFF"	Open
Red/Yellow	"OFF"	Open
Red/Brown	"ON"	Closed
Red/Green	"ON"	Closed
Red/Yellow	"ON"	Open
Red/Brown	"RES"	Closed
Red/Green	"RES"	Closed
Red/Yellow	"RES"	Closed
Red/Brown	"ON"①	Closed
Red/Green	"ON"①	Open
Red/Yellow	"ON"①	Closed

① — Pushbutton depressed.

ELECTRICAL TESTS

NOTE — *If system is inoperative, it is not always necessary to remove regulator.*

1) Disconnect both single and triple push-on connectors at regulator. Turn ignition switch to "ACC" and move slide switch to "ON" position. Perform the following tests using a suitable test lamp.

2) Ground one test lamp lead and touch other to brown wire and then green wire at connectors. Test lamp should light at both wires. If lamp does not light, check fuse, speed control relay, engagement switch, and connection at power source.

3) Hold "SET SPEED" button all the way in. Ground one test lamp lead and touch other to each wire in connector. Lamp should light at brown and yellow wires and should not light at green or blue wires. Release "SET SPEED" button.

4) Hold slide switch in "RES" position. Ground one test lamp lead and touch other to each wire in connector. Lamp should light at all wires except blue wire. Blue wire connects to brake lamp side of brake lamp switch.

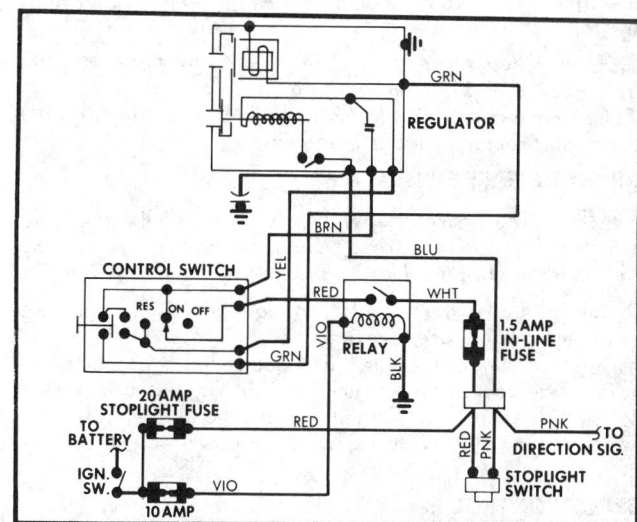

Fig. 1 V8 Cruise Command Wiring Diagram

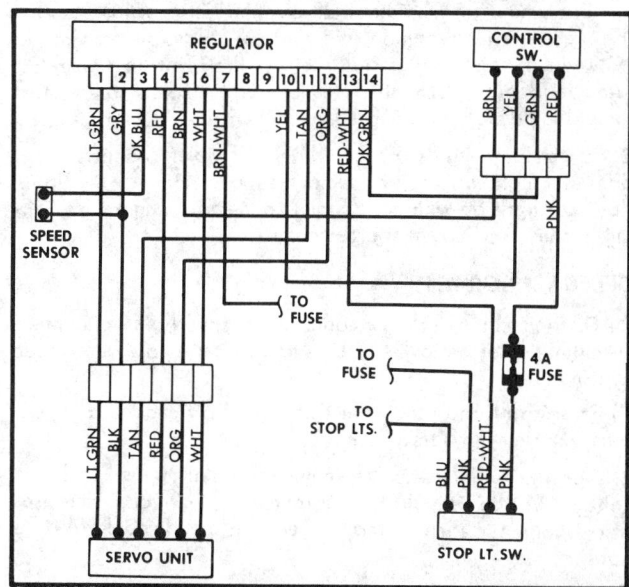

Fig. 2 6-Cylinder Cruise Command Wiring Diagram

JEEP CRUISE COMMAND (Cont.)

NOTE — *The following tests need not be done if preceding tests checked out. If the preceding tests did not check out, perform the following tests.*

5) Disconnect engagement switch from wiring harness at multiple connector in passenger compartment. Attach a jumper wire from a 12 volt power source to engagement switch red lead.

6) Move slide switch to "OFF" position. Ground one test lamp lead and touch other (in turn) to brown wire, green wire and then yellow wire. Lamp should not light at any wire.

7) Move slide switch to "ON" position. Ground one test lamp lead and touch other to brown wire and then green wire. Lamp should light on both wires. Touch test lamp lead to yellow wire. Lamp should not light.

8) Hold "SET SPEED" button all the way in. Ground one test lamp lead and touch other to brown wire and yellow wire. Lamp should light on both wires. Touch test lamp lead to green wire. Lamp should not light. Release "SET SPEED" button.

9) Hold slide switch in "RES" position. Ground one test lamp lead and touch other (in turn) to brown wire, yellow wire and then green wire. Lamp should light at all wires. Release slide switch.

NOTE — *If test procedures 1) through 4) do not check out, but procedures 5) through 9) do check out, replace Cruise Command system wiring harness. If all test procedures do not check out, replace engagement switch.*

BRAKE RELEASE SWITCH TEST

NOTE — *The brake release switch is part of the stoplamp switch. The stoplamp circuit must be operating correctly before testing brake release switch.*

Disconnect triple wire connector at regulator. Using a suitable test lamp, ground one test lamp lead and touch other to blue wire. Lamp should not light. If it does, wire is connected to wrong side of stoplamp switch. With brake pedal depressed ¼ ", test lamp should light. If not, check fuse, stoplamp switch, wiring harness to regulator or power source connection.

SPEED CONTROL RELAY TEST

1) The speed control relay is mounted close to fuse panel under instrument panel. Check all electrical connections before testing relay. Turn ignition switch on and move slide switch to "ON" position. Using a suitable test lamp, ground one test lamp lead and touch other to each connector at relay. Test lamp should light at each connector wire except ground.

2) If test lamp lights on the white and violet connectors but does not light on red connector, replace relay. If test lamp does not light on white and violet connectors, check fuse, wiring harness and power source connection.

SPEED SENSOR TEST

1) Disconnect wire harness connector at speed sensor. Connect a voltmeter set on low AC scale to wire terminals from speed sensor.

2) Raise front and rear wheels of vehicle off ground and support vehicle with safety stands.

3) Operate engine (wheels spinning freely) at 30 mph and note voltage. Voltage should be approximately 0.9 volts. Increases of 0.1 volts per each 10 mph increase in speed should also be noticed.

4) Turn off engine and stop wheels. Lower vehicle. Connect speed sensor wire harness.

ADJUSTMENT

VACUUM SERVO CHAIN

NOTE — *Before adjusting servo chain, carburetor throttle must be at idle position, ignition must be off and choke valve fully open.*

Inspect and ensure that bellows bracket screws are tight. Adjust chain at bellows hook end, one bead at a time, until a free pin fit is obtained at the throttle lever. When properly adjusted, there should be a slight deflection in the chain without moving either the throttle lever or bellows. After chain is adjusted, bend bellows hook tabs together.

NOTE — *Chain must be free in hook after bending tabs.*

CENTERING SPRING

NOTE — *Adjustment of centering spring is extremely sensitive. Adjustment screw must never be turned more than ⅛ turn in either direction.*

Cruise command system is designed to maintain speed selected by driver, within 3 mph. System operation is checked at 50 mph. Speed adjustment is made by turning centering adjusting screw on regulator. If speed control holds speed more than 3 mph above selected speed, turn centering screw counterclockwise on 6-cylinder systems or clockwise on V8 systems. If speed is more than 3 mph below selected speed, turn centering screw clockwise on 6-cylinder systems, or counterclockwise on V8 systems.

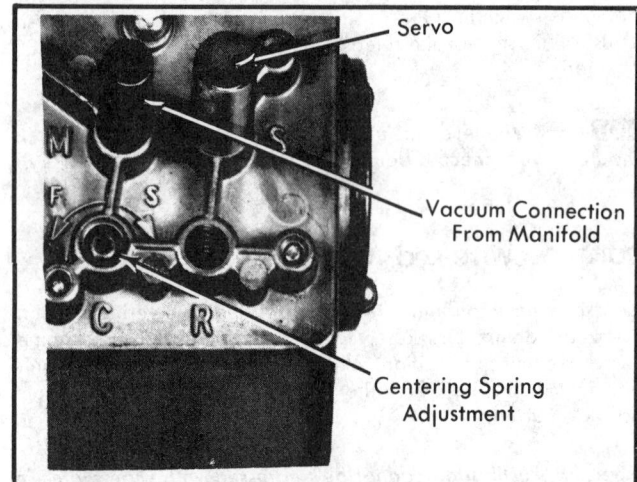

Fig. 3   V8 System Centering Adjustment Screw

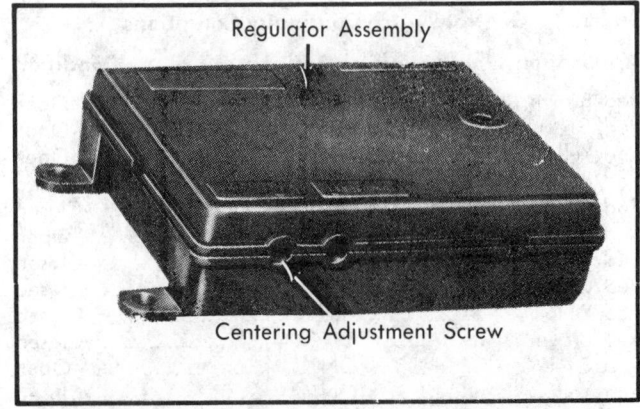

Fig. 4   6-Cylinder System Centering Adjustment Screw

JEEP POWER SUNROOF

Wagoneer

DESCRIPTION

Jeep electric sunroof features a sliding glass panel operated by an electric motor and a manually operated sun screen. System consists of sun roof assembly, electric motor mounted in the forward portion of the sun roof housing, a 2-position switch mounted in the windshield header and all necessary wiring. Electrical feed is through air conditioning terminal of fuse block. Circuit is protected by air conditioning fuse and a 20 amp. in-line fuse located in the wiring harness just below the "A" pillar.

ADJUSTMENT

MOTOR CLUTCH

1) Remove motor cap to gain access to adjusting screw. Cap is located in headlining just above and at center of windshield.

2) Loosen clutch plate adjusting screw jam nut using a deep socket. Tighten adjusting screw to 50 INCH lbs. Tighten jam nut and install motor cap.

GLASS PARALLEL ALIGNMENT

NOTE — *Do not operate electric motor while the glass panel or cables are removed as cable damage could occur.*

1) Open glass about ½". Determine how much out of line front edge of glass is in relation to forward edge of roof panel opening. Note variation.

2) Open panel about 8" to gain access to cable and drive gear mechanism. Remove cable front cover and drive gear plate. Remove one cable from track.

3) Move one side of glass panel slightly forward or backward as required to obtain parallel alignment with roof edge. Install cable in front track and insert cable in drive gear teeth.

4) Install drive gear plate and cable front cover. Close glass to within ¼" of roof panel edge and check alignment. Repeat steps as necessary to obtain proper parallel alignment.

REMOVAL & INSTALLATION

HALO ASSEMBLY

Removal & Installation — 1) Open glass panel partially and remove halo assembly attaching screws. *See Fig. 1.* Grasp center of halo assembly and pull assembly downward to disengage front tabs from track.

2) Close glass panel fully, slide halo assembly forward and remove assembly from vehicle. To install, reverse removal procedures.

GLASS PANEL

Removal & Installation — 1) With halo assembly removed, close glass panel and remove outboard screws from front guide shoe assemblies. Loosen inboard screws and rotate guide shoes to disengage slide portion froom track.

2) Release rear slide tension springs by rotating them to inboard position. Remove screws attaching rear guide shoes and retainers to tabs in glass panel and remove retainers.

3) From outside of vehicle, raise front of glass panel and slide panel forward and out of vehicle. To install, reverse removal procedures noting that rear slide tension springs must be positioned under the spring lock roller.

SUNSCREEN

Removal — Remove halo assembly and glass panel. Open sunscreen fully. Working from outside of vehicle, push sunscreen upward at center of screen and slide screen forward and upward to removed.

Installation — Working from outside of vehicle, curve sunscreen upward at center of screen and slide screen rearward and downward into roof opening. Install glass panel and halo assembly.

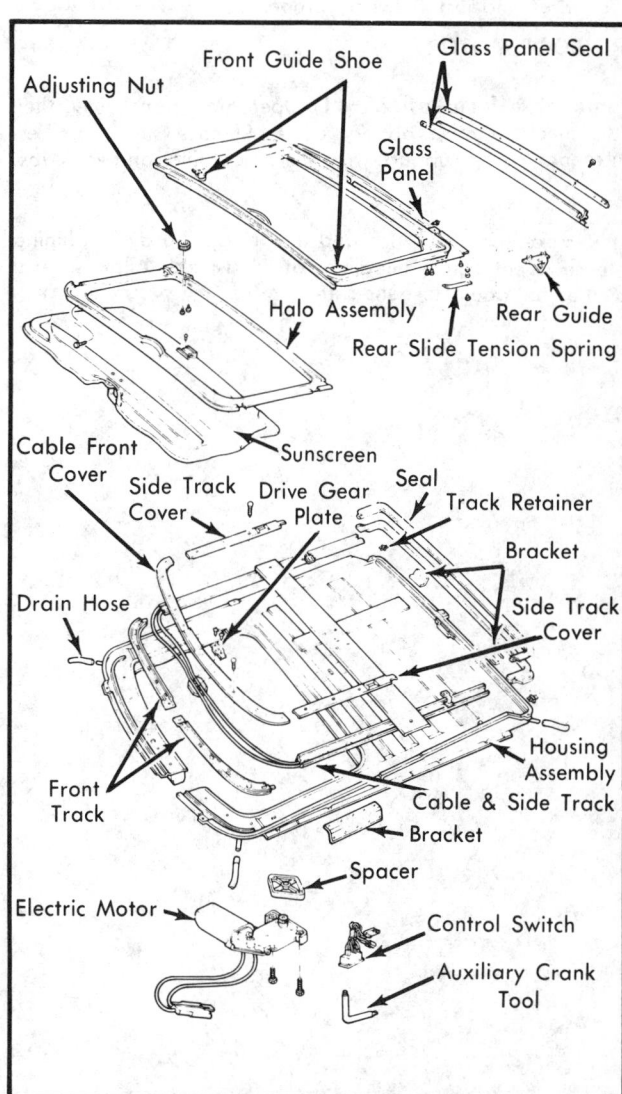

Fig. 1   Exploded View of Jeep Power Sunroof Assembly

JEEP POWER SUNROOF (Cont.)

CABLE & SIDE TRACK

Removal & Installation — 1) Remove halo assembly, glass panel and sunscreen. Remove screws attaching cable front cover and remove cover.

2) Remove drive gear plate. Remove side track cover screws and remove side track cover.

3) Disengage cable from front track and motor gear and remove cable by pulling it up and out. Lift side track up and remove.

4) To install, reverse removal procedures noting the following: Make sure track retainer is seated in hole at rear of housing. If both cables have been removed, make sure rear guide shoes are in contact with side track covers before installing cables.

SUNROOF SWITCH

Removal & Installation — Pull switch straight down from windshield header and disconnect switch wires. To install, connect wires and install switch in opening.

SUNROOF MOTOR

Removal & Installation — 1) Open glass panel fully, then disconnect negative battery cable. Remove sun visors, escutcheons, center support, windshield mouldings and end caps.

2) Remove sunroof switch and motor cap. Spray headlining release agent across headliner at windshield. Allow several minutes for agent to penetrate.

NOTE — When removing headliner, use care to avoid separating foam backing from headliner. If backing begins to separate, apply more release agent.

3) Pull front edge of headliner downward. Remove motor mounting screws and remove motor.

4) To install, reverse removal procedures noting the following: Mask off top of windshield and spray trim adhesive on roof panel along top of windshield and install headliner. Check sunroof operation and and adjust motor clutch if necessary.

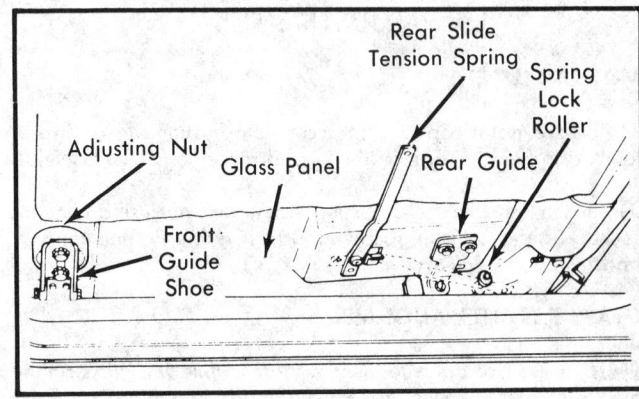

Fig. 2 Front Guide Shoe and Rear Tension Spring

CHRYSLER CORP.

Dodge
Plymouth

DESCRIPTION & OPERATION

Fuel, temperature and oil pressure gauges operate on the constant voltage principle through a common voltage limiter which provides intermittent current to the gauge system.

Fuel Level Gauge — A hinged float arm in fuel tank raises or lowers depending on fuel level, and contacts a variable resister in the fuel gauge sending unit. This provides a change of resistance in the fuel gauge circuit. This resistance registers on instrument panel gauge in the form of a level reading.

Temperature & Oil Pressure — The operation of temperature and oil pressure indicating systems is identical in operation to the fuel system, with the exception of the method of varying resistance of the sending units.

In temperature, the resistance of the disc in sending unit varies with a direct relation to coolant temperature. When coolant temperatures are high, resistance is low, when coolant temperatures are low, resistance is high.

In oil pressure, the sending unit resistance is controlled by a diaphragm. The diaphragm is actuated as oil pressure increases or decreases.

Oil Pressure Warning Light — The oil pressure switch is mounted on the engine (location depends on engine). When oil pressure is high (normal) switch is held in "OFF" or "OPEN" position, allowing no current to flow to the indicator light. When oil pressure is low, switch is in "ON" or "CLOSED" position allowing current to flow to the indicator light.

Alternator Indicator System — Alternator gauge is an ammeter which senses the direction and rate of flow of electrical current to or from battery, thereby indicating whether battery is being charged or discharged.

Tachometer — Tachometer is a self-contained electronic unit connected to the ignition coil. The tachometer senses ignition firings and counts their number. This is shown on the face of the gauge which is marked off in RPM increments.

TESTING

VOLTAGE LIMITER

To quickly test voltage limiter in vehicle, connect one lead of a voltmeter or test light to temperature sending unit and other lead to a good ground. Leave sending unit wire attached to sending unit. Turn ignition switch "ON". A fluctuating voltmeter or a flashing light indicates voltage limiter is operating.

FUEL GAUGE (WITH TESTER)

NOTE — *Allow 2 minutes at each test point for gauge to settle. Tapping instrument cluster will help position needle.*

1) Disconnect wire at fuel tank unit. Connect one lead of a suitable gauge tester (C-3826A) to wire terminal, and other lead to a good ground. Turn ignition "ON", turn tester knob to "F" position and observe instrument panel gauge. Gauge should read "FULL", plus two pointer widths minus one pointer width. Turn tester knob to ½, gauge should read ½ plus or minus two pointer widths. Turn knob to "E", gauge should read "EMPTY", plus one pointer width minus two pointer widths.

2) If panel gauge does not perform as prescribed, continuity of circuit from tank sending unit to panel unit should be tested with special attention to printed circuit board before replacing gauge. If panel performs properly when tested but fails to operate properly when connected to vehicle system, fuel tank sending unit ground strap should be inspected for proper installation on fuel line. If ground continuity is good, remove tank unit for testing.

FUEL GAUGE (WITHOUT TESTER)

1) Disconnect wire from terminal on fuel tank sending unit. Attach wire to known good sending unit. Connect jumper wire

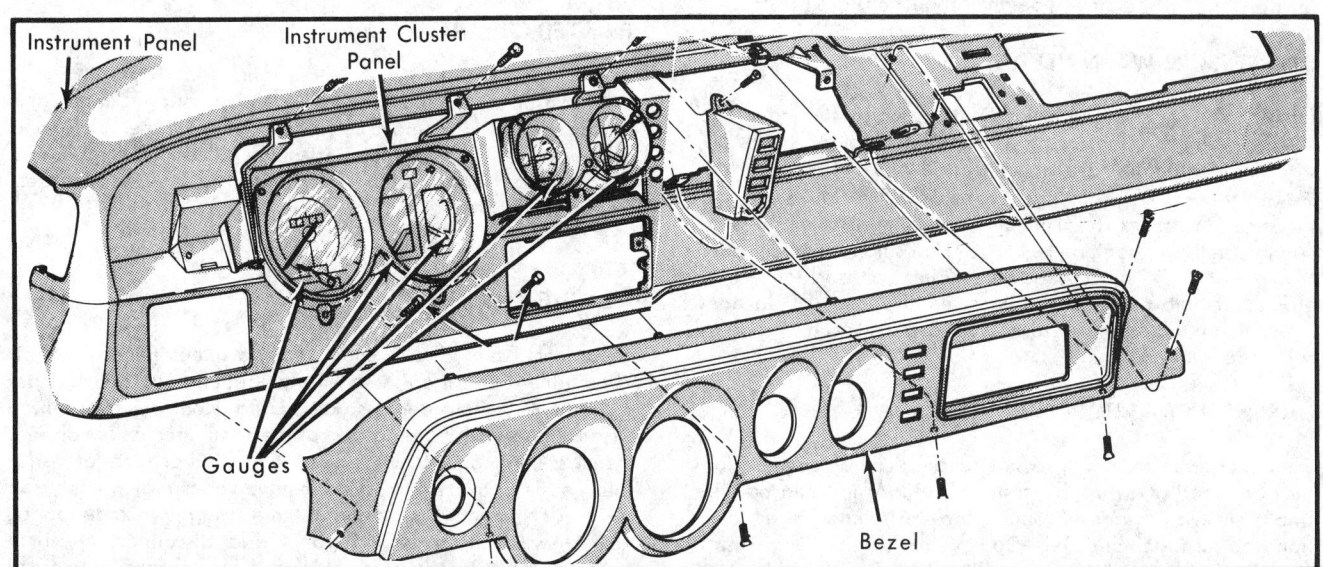

Fig. 1 **Chrysler Corp. Instrument Cluster & Bezel (Van Models Shown — Pick-Up Models Similar)**

CHRYSLER CORP. (Cont.)

between sending unit fuel pick up tube and a good ground. To check fuel gauge, allow at least 2 minutes at each test point for gauge to settle. Clip float arm of sending unit to its empty stop and turn ignition key to "ON" position. Gauge should read "EMPTY" plus one pointer width, minus two pointer widths. Move and clip sending unit float arm to full stop. Gauge should read "FULL" plus two pointer widths, minus one pointer width.

2) If fuel gauge does not perform as indicated, continuity of circuit from tank sending unit to panel should be tested with special attention to printed circuit board. Also check voltage limiter before replacing gauge. If panel gauge performs satisfactorily with Tester C-3826A or known good sending unit, check fuel tank and original fuel gauge sending unit by removing sending unit from tank. Connect sending unit wire and jumper wire as in step 1). If fuel gauge now checks within specifications, original unit is electrically okay.

3) Check ground strap from sending unit to fuel line for continuity, check for deformed sending unit, improper installation, deformed mounting flange on fuel tank, or deformed bottom of fuel tank. Then recheck sending unit.

TEMPERATURE GAUGE

Disconnect terminal from temperature sending unit on engine. Connect one test lead of suitable tester (C-3826) to terminal and other lead to good ground. Turn ignition "ON", turn tester knob to "E" and temperature gauge should show "C", plus or minus $\frac{1}{8}$". Turn tester knob to $\frac{1}{2}$, pointer should advance to driving range left of $\frac{1}{2}$ position of dial. Turn tester knob to "F", gauge pointer should move to "H" position on dial. If gauge responds as stated, but does not operate with terminal attached to sending unit, replace sending unit. If gauge does not respond, check for loose connections, broken wire, open printed circuit or faulty gauge.

AMMETER GAUGE

Turn headlights "ON" (do not start engine). Ammeter needle should move toward the "D" or discharge scale. If no movement of the needle is observed, check terminals for loose wires. If terminals are secure, ammeter is defective. If needle moves toward the "C" or charge side, the connections are reversed.

OIL PRESSURE WARNING LIGHT

Check low oil pressure warning light system by turning key to "ON" position and observing pressure light. If light comes on, start engine. If light stays on, immediately turn off engine and use direct pressure gauge to check oil pressure. If pressure is to specifications, check for grounded wire or replace oil pressure sending unit. With ignition key in "ON" position, and light does not come on, disconnect lead of sending unit and touch it to ground. If bulb comes on, replace sending unit. If bulb does not come on, light bulb is burned out or bulb socket, wiring or connections are faulty.

OIL PRESSURE GAUGE

Disconnect wire from oil pressure sending unit on engine. Connect one lead of a suitable tester (C-3826A) to removed wire and other lead to good ground. Place tester knob in "E" position and turn ignition "ON". Do not start engine. Oil pressure gauge should read "L" plus or minus $\frac{1}{8}$". Turn tester knob to $\frac{1}{2}$ position, oil pressure gauge should advance to $\frac{1}{2}$ position

on dial. With tester knob in "F" position, gauge should also advance to "H" position. Should gauge respond to above tests, but fail to operate when connected to vehicle system, indications are of a defective sending unit. Should gauge fail to respond to above tests, check for loose connection, broken wire or faulty gauge.

BRAKE WARNING LIGHT

Brake warning system light comes on when ignition switch is "ON" with parking brake applied, when one of the two service brake systems fails or when ignition switch is positioned to "START". Test system by hoisting vehicle with helper inside to depress brake pedal and observe warning light. Light should come on when bleeder port on wheel cylinder is opened. If light fails to operate, inspect for burned out bulb, disconnected socket, broken or disconnected wiring.

REMOVAL & INSTALLATION

SPEEDOMETER & GAUGES

Remove instrument panel cluster, lens plastic mounting clips, and lens. Remove mask, and mounting nuts to gauge being serviced. Remove gauge through front of cluster. To install, reverse removal procedure.

INSTRUMENT CLUSTER

Disconnect fusible link under hood and remove screws fastening instrument panel hood and bezel assembly. Pull bezel off upper retaining clips and remove cluster screws. On truck models, remove steering column cover and transmission select indicator (if equipped). Loosen heater and air conditioner control and pull rearward to clear cluster housing. On all cluster models, carefully pull cluster out far enough to disconnect speedometer cable, circuit board connectors and gauge wiring. Remove cluster assembly. To install, reverse removal procedure.

PRINTED CIRCUITS

With instrument cluster removed, remove voltage limiter and radio capacitor. Remove all lamp socket assemblies and gauges except speedometer. Remove attaching screws and printed circuit board from vehicle. To install, reverse removal procedures.

HEADLIGHT SWITCH

Disconnect fusible link in engine compartment. Remove left air conditioner and air outlet assembly (if equipped). Reach under instrument panel, depress knob and stem release button located on switch housing and at the same time pull knob and stem assembly out of switch housing located on front of instrument panel. On truck models, remove wiper switch knob. On all models, remove spanner nut mounting switch to panel. Lower switch from behind panel and disconnect electrical leads. Remove switch from vehicle. To install, reverse removal procedure.

FORD

All Models

DESCRIPTION & OPERATION

Ammeter Gauge — Gauge senses the direction and rate of flow of electrical current to or from the battery indicating whether the battery is being charged or discharged.

A shunt-type ammeter is used for Bronco and "E" and "F" Series vehicles. Ammeters are non-adjustable and must be replaced as a unit.

Fuel Gauge — Gauge pointer is operated by current flow heating a wire-wound bi-metal strip in gauge. Current flow is controlled by a variable resistor float type sending unit in the fuel tank. As the amount of fuel decreases, more resistance is placed in the circuit, allowing less current flow and heat at the bi-metal strip, causing the pointer to move a shorter distance.

Instrument Voltage Regulator — IVR is used in conjunction with all gauges (exc. ammeter). It controls and maintains an average pulsating value of five volts at gauge. A supression choke is connected in series between printed circuit and IVR to prevent radio interference.

Oil Pressure Gauge — Oil pressure gauge circuit consists of an IVR, oil pressure gauge and a pressure-operated sending unit. As oil pressure increases, resistance in sending unit decreases causing an increase in current flow and gauge pointer movement.

Oil Pressure Indicator Light — The light is connected between the oil pressure switch unit on the engine and the coil terminal of the ignition switch. The light should come on when the ignition switch is first turned to the "R" or "RUN" position. It should go out after engine is started, indicating oil pressure has reached a safe value. The light should also come on any time pressure drops below a safe level.

Temperature Gauge — System consists of a variable resistance type sending unit and a gauge. As coolant temperature increases, resistance in sending unit decreases allowing an increase of current flow and gauge pointer movement. It is possible, under certain driving conditions, for pointer to read at the top of the normal band and still have coolant temperature within limits.

TESTING

GAUGES

Oil Pressure Indicator Light — Turn on ignition switch, but do not start engine. The light should come on. Start engine and light should go out within seconds. To test oil pressure switch, turn ignition switch to "ON", but do not start engine. Indicator light should come on. If not, disconnect wire from oil pressure switch terminal and touch to ground. If light now comes on, oil pressure switch is defective. If light does not come on, check for bad bulb or open circuits to bulb.

Oil Pressure Gauge — 1) Disconnect connector from oil pressure sender unit and connect to matching terminals on tester (Rotunda 21-0015 or equivalent). Attach tester ground

wire to vehicle frame. Turn vehicle ignition switch to "ACCESSORY" position.

2) Turn tester switch to IVR Check position. A flashing light indicates IVR and wiring are functional. Turn tester switch to either High or Low position. The center line of gauge pointer should be within the oil pressure white band of tester. If center of pointer registers in white band after 2 minutes, system is operating properly and oil pressure sending unit must be replaced.

3) If pointer center line falls outside low band, replace gauge. If outside high band, replace IVR and repeat test. If still outside high band, replace gauge and reinstall original IVR.

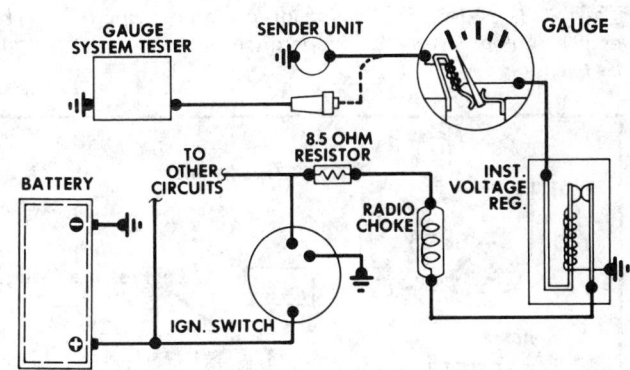

Fig. 1 Testing IVR, Fuel, Oil or Temperature Gauge

Ammeter — 1) Turn headlights on; engine off. Meter pointer should move toward the "D" or discharge side of the gauge. If no pointer movement is noted, check rear of meter housing for loose connections, printed circuit connections and multiple connector at printed circuit.

2) If connections are good, replace ammeter. Should ammeter pointer move toward "C" with lights on and engine off, ammeter connections are reversed.

Fuel Level Gauge — 1) Using proper tester (Rotunda Instrument Gauge System Tester Model 21-0015 or equivalent), test fuel level gauge with instrument voltage regulator (IVR). Disconnect connector from fuel sender and attach to tester. Turn ignition switch to "ACCESSORY" position.

2) Set tester switch to IVR Check position. If light flashes on and off, the IVR and wiring are functional. If IVR Check light is on steady, check IVR ground screw. If ground screw is secure, replace IVR. If IVR Check light does not come on, check for open circuit in gauge and/or circuit wiring.

3) With tester switch in either High or Low position, center line of gauge pointer should be within "F" or "E" white band of tester. If so, fuel indicating system is working properly and replacement of fuel sender is necessary. If pointer is outside the

FORD (Cont.)

"E" white band, replace fuel gauge. If outside "F" white band, replace IVR and retest. If still outside, replace fuel gauge and reinstall original IVR.

Temperature Gauge — 1) Disconnect connector from temperature sender and connect to tester (Rotunda 21-0015 or equivalent). Attach other tester lead to ground on vehicle. Turn vehicle ignition switch to "ACCESSORY" position.

2) Turn tester switch to IVR Check position. A flashing light indicates IVR and wiring are functional. Place tester switch in either high or low position. Center line of pointer should be within white temperature level test band, indicating system is operating properly and that sender unit requires replacement. If center line is outside high white band, replace IVR and retest. If outside low white band, replace gauge and retest.

NOTE — If system still does not perform properly, check engine coolant level, proper operation of thermostat and fan belt tension.

REMOVAL & INSTALLATION

SPEEDOMETERS & GAUGES

All Models — Instrument cluster must be removed to allow any repair or replacement of speedometer or gauges.

INSTRUMENT CLUSTER

"E" Models — 1) Disconnect battery ground, remove seven screws retaining cluster to instrument panel. Position cluster part way out of panel for access to rear of cluster. At back of cluster, disconnect speedometer cable.

NOTE — It may be necessary to remove 2 steering column shroud to panel retaining screws. Loosen bolts attaching column to Band C support to provide additional clearance for cluster removal. In some cases, it may prove necessary to remove speedometer cable at the transmission, pulling cable through cowl.

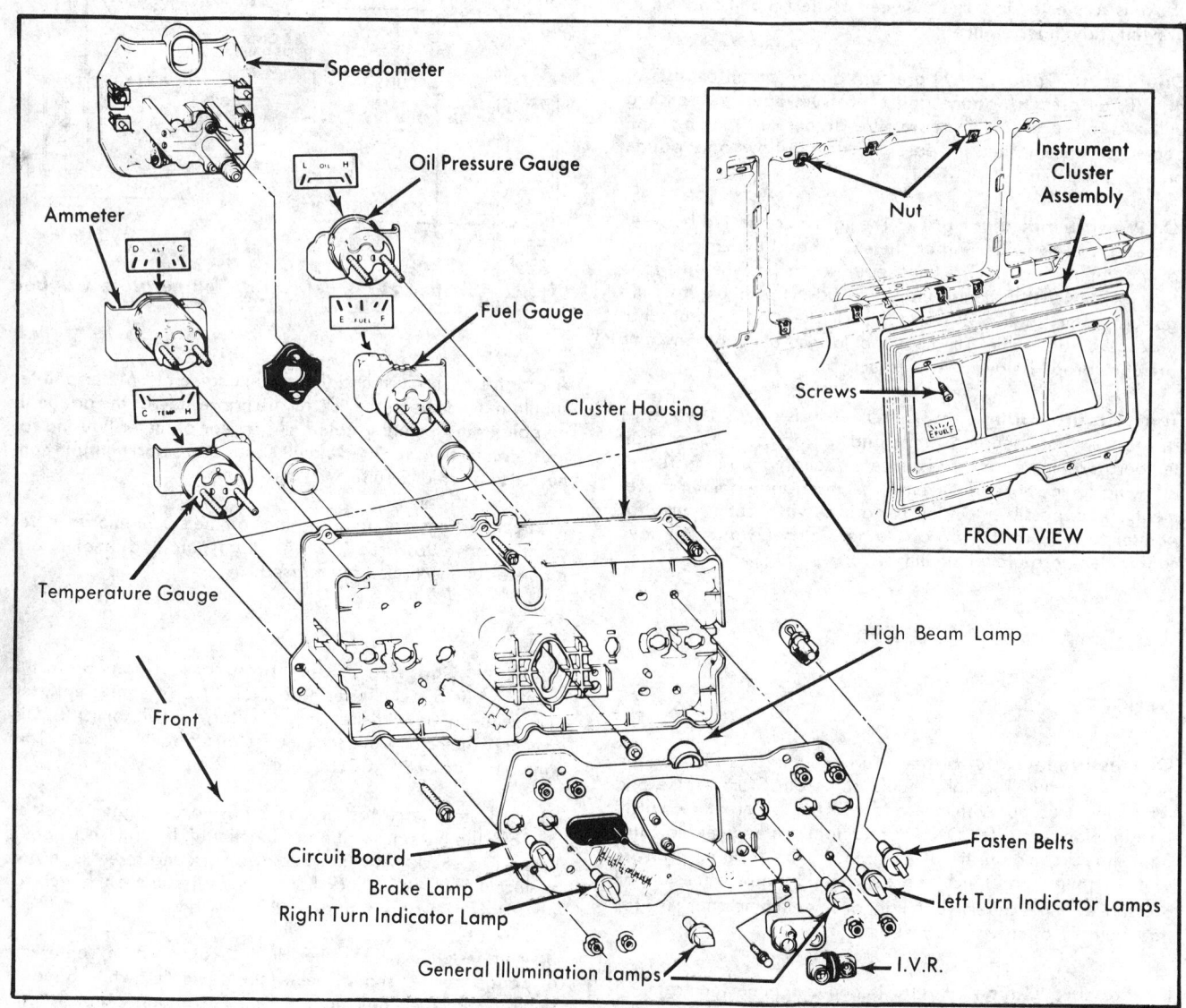

Fig. 2 Exploded View of "E" Models Instrument Cluster

FORD (Cont.)

2) Disconnect multiple feed plug from printed circuit board and remove the cluster assembly from instrument panel.

3) To install, reverse removal procedure while noting the following: Apply approximately $\frac{3}{16}$" diameter ball of suitable silicone lubricant in drive hole of speedometer head.

"F" Models & Bronco — 1) Disconnect battery ground cable. Pull knobs from radio shafts (if equipped), fuel gauge switch knob, heater control knobs and wiper/washer knob. Use a hook tool to release each knob lock tab. Remove knob and shaft from light switch.

2) Remove steering column shroud. On automatic transmission vehicles remove loop on selector indicator cable assembly from retainer pin. Remove bracket screw from cable bracket and slide bracket out of slot in tube.

3) Remove cluster trim cover and 4 cluster attaching screws. Disconnect speedometer cable, wire connector from printed circuit and 4x4 indicator light (if equipped). Remove instrument cluster. To install, reverse removal procedure.

INSTRUMENT VOLTAGE REGULATOR & PRINTED CIRCUIT

All Models — 1) Remove instrument panel cluster. Disconnect (snap off) printed circuit connector buttons from instrument voltage regulator.

2) Disconnect multiple feed plug and remove the one attaching screw, then remove the IVR from cluster assembly. Remove gauge retaining nuts, light bulbs, and printed circuit board from cluster.

3) To install, reverse removal procedure while noting the following: Printed circuit board must be carefully positioned to back of cluster and engaged with the plastic locating pins.

HEADLIGHT SWITCH

All Models — Disconnect battery ground cable. On "F" and Bronco models, remove knob from switch shaft, remove center finish panel and remove switch from back side of instrument panel. On "E" models, remove knob and shaft by pressing the knob release button on switch housing, with knob in full "ON" position. Pull knob and shaft out of switch, unscrew mounting nut, remove bezel and switch and then remove wiring connector. To install, reverse removal procedure.

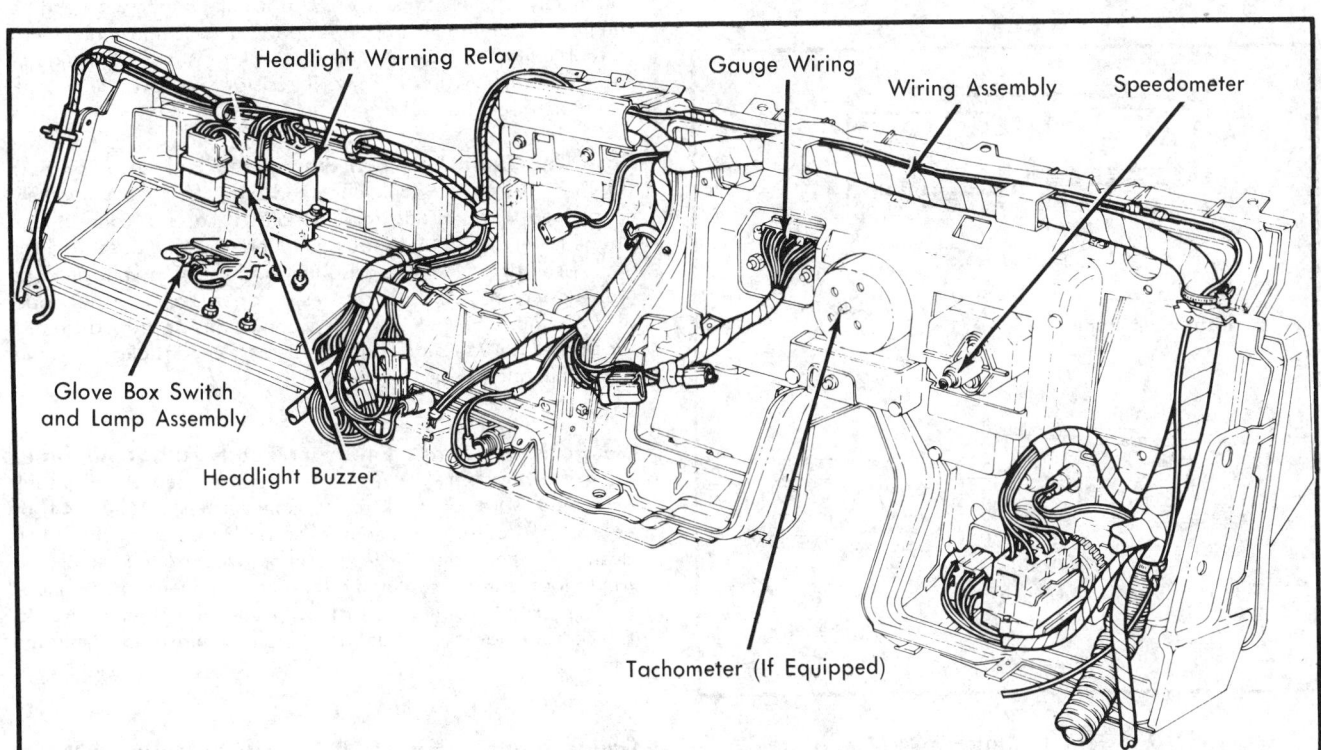

Fig. 3   Exploded View of "F" Models & Bronco Instrument Cluster (Back View)

GENERAL MOTORS

Chevrolet
GMC

DESCRIPTION

All instruments and gauges are installed in the instrument cluster and "C" & "K" models can be serviced in the vehicle. "G" models require removal of the entire instrument cluster from the vehicle prior to servicing. Indicator lamps and illuminating bulbs may be replaced on all models without removing instrument cluster from vehicle.

TESTING & TROUBLE SHOOTING

INDICATOR WARNING LIGHTS

Oil Pressure Indicator — 1) Indicator light is inoperative with ignition switch on and engine not running. Check for burned out bulb, open light circuit or defective oil pressure switch.

2) Indicator light is on and engine is running above idle speed. Indicates low oil pressure, defective oil pressure switch or ground condition between light and switch.

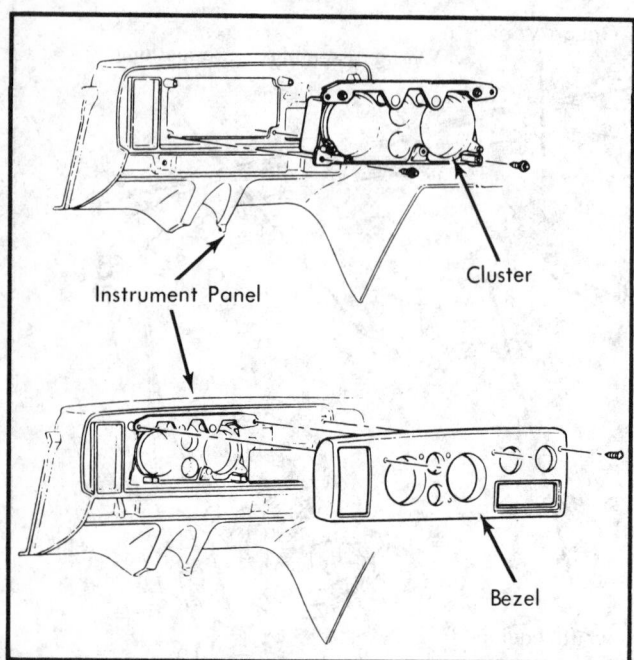

Fig. 1   General Motors "G" Models Instrument Cluster

Temperature Indicator — 1) If "HOT" indicator light is inoperative when cranking engine, check for burned out light bulb, open light circuit or a defective ignition switch.

2) When light is on with engine running, check for coolant temperature above 258°F, grounded condition between light and switch, defective temperature or ignition switch.

Charging System Indicator — 1) If light is on with ignition "OFF", check for shorted positive diode. If light is not on with ignition "ON" but engine not running, check for burned out bulb, open in light circuit or open in field.

2) If light is on with engine running above idle speed, check for no generator output, shorted negative diode or loose or broken generator belt.

FUEL GAUGE

Use a suitable Gas Gauge Tester (J-22344 or equivalent). Disconnect feed wire from the gas gauge tank terminal and connect one test lead to the wire and ground the other lead. Switch tester to "EMPTY" and "FULL" positions and fuel gauge should read the same as the tester. If not, proceed with the following tests with ignition in "ON" position.

Dash Unit Never Reads Full — Connect tester (J-22344) to tank unit feed wire and observe dash unit. If gauge does not read full, check cluster fuse, dash unit and printed circuit connections, opens in printed circuits or shorts due to pinched wires in body harness. Remove dash unit and check. If dash unit reads okay, reconnect tank unit feed wire to tank unit and completely fill fuel tank. Note dash unit pointer with engine running. If pointer still does not go to full, disconnect feed wire to tank unit. Using an ohmmeter, check resistance of tank unit for 88-92 ohms with full tank. If resistance is low, check tank mounting area for damage.

Dash Unit Dead Between Empty and Full with Ignition "ON" — Disconnect tank unit feed wire. Using a voltmeter, check feed wire voltage for 3-4 volts. If correct, connect gas gauge tester (J-22344) to tank unit feed wire and observe dash unit. If still dead, remove dash unit and check. If voltage does not register on meter, it indicates an open circuit on HOT side of dash unit. Check cluster fuse, connections at printed circuits for both dash unit and panel harness. If circuits okay, remove dash unit and check.

Gauge Never Reads Empty or Reads Full at All Times with Ignition "ON" — Check for disconnected or loose tank unit feed wire at tank unit. Connect tester (J-22344 or equivalent) to tank unit feed wire and observe dash unit. If dash unit reads okay, check ground wire from tank unit to trunk floor pan for continuity. If no improvement, check cluster fuse or proper connections at dash unit and printed circuits. Check trunk harness to flat wire. Finally, remove dash unit and check.

Gauge Reads Empty At All Times with Ignition "ON" — Disconnect tank unit feed wire. Dash unit should now read full. If not, check cluster fuse, printed circuit connections, and wiring for pinched condition in body harness. Finally, remove dash unit and check. If gauge reads full, check for grounded tank unit lead. Remove tank unit and check.

Erratic Gauge Readings — If operation is erratic (fluctuation during acceleration and deceleration is normal), check dash unit mounting screws, harness to printed circuit, panel harness to flat wire, flat wire to trunk harness, feed wire to tank unit and tank unit ground to body.

GENERAL MOTORS (Cont.)

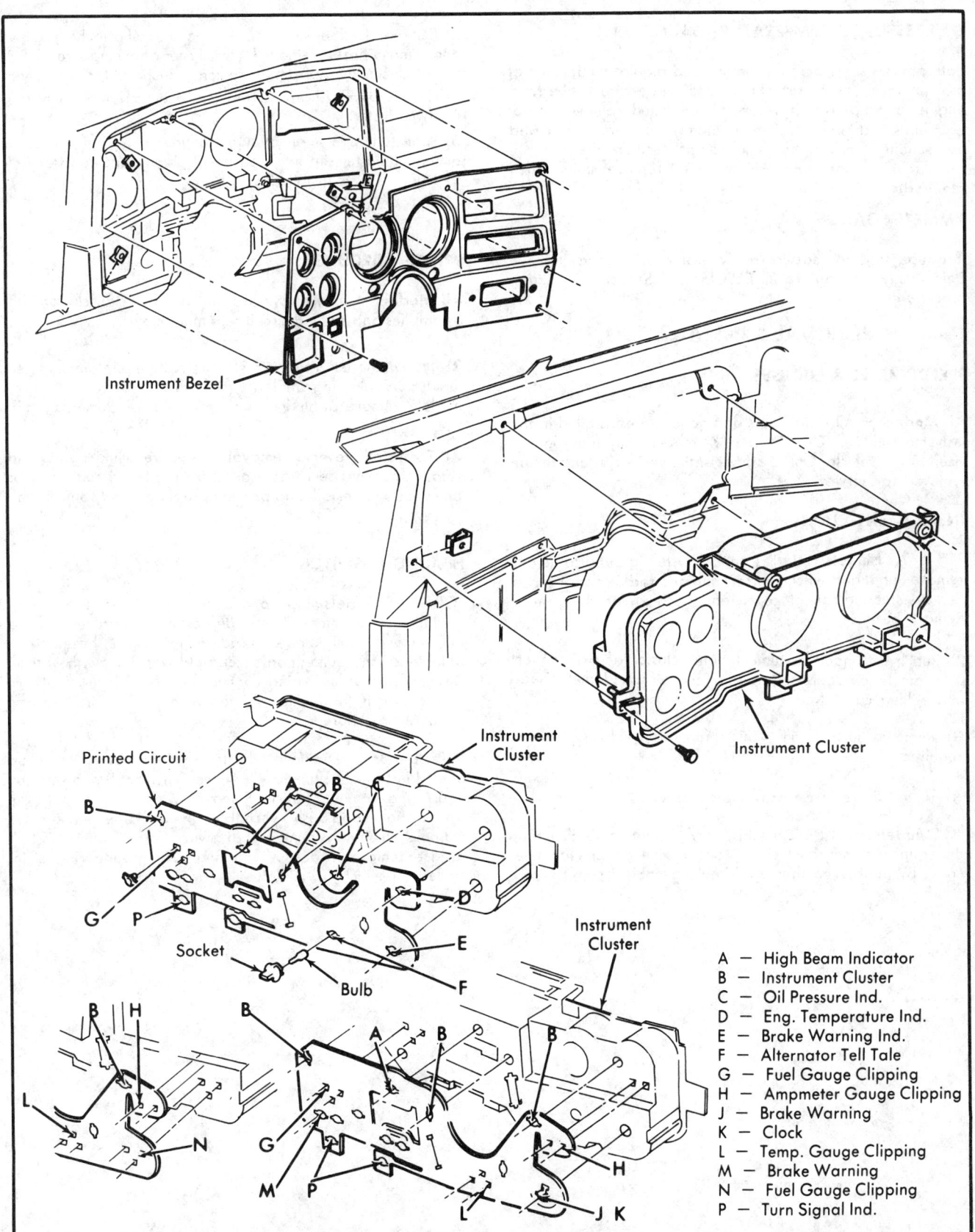

Instrument Bezel

Instrument Cluster

Instrument Cluster

Printed Circuit

Instrument Cluster

Socket

Bulb

A — High Beam Indicator
B — Instrument Cluster
C — Oil Pressure Ind.
D — Eng. Temperature Ind.
E — Brake Warning Ind.
F — Alternator Tell Tale
G — Fuel Gauge Clipping
H — Ampmeter Gauge Clipping
J — Brake Warning
K — Clock
L — Temp. Gauge Clipping
M — Brake Warning
N — Fuel Gauge Clipping
P — Turn Signal Ind.

Fig. 2   General Motors "C" & "K" Models
Instrument Cluster

GENERAL MOTORS (Cont.)

OIL PRESSURE & TEMPERATURE GAUGE

Both gauges show actual readings and require a minimum of maintenance. The oil pressure gauge uses a direct tube from engine to gauge and if it becomes restricted, remove tube at both ends and blow out the line. Both gauges are electric and use sending units to transmit engine temperature and oil pressure. Do not repair either unit, replace units when required.

AMMETER GAUGE

If gauge fails to read correctly, test charging system. *See Delco-Remy Alternators in ELECTRICAL Section for testing procedures.*

REMOVAL & INSTALLATION

SPEEDOMETER & GAUGES

All Models — All instruments and gauges are installed in the instrument cluster. On "C" and "K" models they may be serviced in the vehicle. On "G" models, the entire cluster must be removed for service.

INSTRUMENT CLUSTER

"C" & "K" Models — 1) Disconnect battery ground cable and remove headlight switch control knob and radio control knobs. Remove steering column cover, and 8 screws attaching bezel. Remove bezel.

2) Reach up under instrument panel cluster and disconnect speedometer by depressing tang on rear of speedometer head and pulling cable free.

3) Remove cluster from vehicle for further disassembly as required.

4) To install, reverse removal procedure.

"G" Models — 1) Disconnect battery ground cable. Reach up under instrument panel cluster and disconnect speedometer cable by depressing tang while pulling cable free.

2) Remove clock set stem knob. Remove bezel attaching screws and remove bezel. Remove lower cluster attaching screws. Pull top of cluster away from instrument panel and lift out bottom of cluster. Unplug harness connector from printed circuit and remove cluster.

3) To install, reverse removal procedure making sure that clips at top of cluster slip into instrument panel opening after bottom of cluster is installed.

PRINTED CIRCUITS

All Models — 1) Remove instrument cluster, all cluster light assemblies and printed circuit retaining screws.

2) On "G" Models, remove fuel, temperature and ammeter terminal nuts retaining printed circuits to rear of cluster. On all models, remove printed circuits from rear of cluster.

3) To install, reverse removal procedure while noting that retaining screws serve as ground for printed circuit and must be properly reinstalled to provide proper ground connection.

HEADLIGHT SWITCH

"C" & "K" Models — Disconnect battery ground cable. Reach up behind instrument cluster, depress shaft retaining button and remove switch knob and rod. Remove cluster bezel screws at left end, and pull out on bezel. Hold switch nut with wrench. Disconnect multiple wiring connectors at switch terminals. To remove switch, turn while holding switch nut. To install, reverse removal procedure.

"G" Models — Disconnect battery ground cable. Reach up behind instrument panel and remove switch knob and shaft by depressing retaining button. Remove switch retaining nut from front of panel and push switch through panel opening. Remove multiple electrical connector at switch terminals. To install, reverse removal procedure making sure ground ring is installed on switch.

JEEP

All Models

DESCRIPTION

"CJ" & Scrambler Models — Instrument panel is composed of speedometer housing, panel lights, high beam indicator, turn signal indicators, brake failure/parking brake warning indicator, Emergency Drive indicator, temperature gauge, and combination fuel gauge and constant voltage regulator (CVR). Other gauges include tachometer, voltmeter and oil pressure gauge.

Cherokee, Wagoneer & "J" Models — Instrument cluster is composed of speedometer housing, panel lights, high beam indicator, turn signal indicators, ammeter, oil pressure gauge, temperature and fuel gauges, constant voltage regulator (CVR), brake failure warning bulb, lockout warning bulbs (Quadra-Trac), heater control lights, wiper/washer control lights and blower motor fan switch.

OPERATION

Ammeter — Used to indicate current flow into and out of battery, depending on vehicle electric load. Regular equipment on all but "CJ" and Scrambler models.

Temperature Gauge — System consists of gauge and sending unit, appropriate wiring and constant voltage regulator (CVR). Gauge is grounded through variable resistance of sending unit. Changes in coolant temperature vary resistance in sending unit, increasing or decreasing indication on gauge.

Fuel Level Gauge — System consists of a fuel gauge, sending unit in fuel tank, appropriate wiring and constant voltage regulator (CVR). Gauge is grounded through variable resistance of sending unit. A float attached to a slide rheostat follows fuel level and varying resistance increases or decreases indicator reading.

Voltmeter — Used on "CJ" and Scrambler models only, system consists of a voltmeter and related wiring. Voltmeter indicates regulated voltage to provide an indication of the charging systems ability to maintain battery charge.

Oil Pressure Gauge — Consists of magnetic type gauge, a variable resistance sending unit and wiring on all "CJ" and Scrambler models. There are 2 coils in gauge, one directly grounded, the other connected to sending unit. Resistance is controlled in sending unit by oil pressure. Magnetic fields are created around both coils in gauge. Needle is attracted to coil having greater current flow. On all other models, oil pressure gauge system consists of CVR-powered gauge, variable resistance sending unit, and CVR. Gauge needle, attached to bi-metal strip, responds to temperature changes. It moves as current flows from CVR through heating coil around bi-metal strip, and to ground at sending unit on engine.

Constant Voltage Regulator — 1) On "CJ" and Scrambler models, CVR is built into fuel gauge. On all other models it is built into temperature gauge. CVR provides equal regulated voltage to each gauge.

2) The CVR's function is to regulate the variable input voltage available from car battery, or charging system to provide a constant 5 volt output to gauges. The CVR does not produce a steady DC voltage output, but rather a pulsating voltage averaging 5 volts. Output voltage averaging lower or higher than 5 volts will result in proportionately higher or lower gauge readings.

TESTING

OIL PRESSURE GAUGE

1) To test accuracy of oil pressure gauge, use a variable resistance tester (J-24538 or equivalent).

2) Disconnect wire from sending unit on engine. Turn ignition switch "ON". Connect one lead of tester to ground and other leading to sending unit wire. Compare results with specifications shown in table.

Oil Pressure Gauge Test Readings		
Application	**Psi**	**Ohms**
"CJ" & Scrambler Models	0	73
	40	20
	80	10
Cherokee, Wagoneer & "J" Models	0	69-77
	10	35-38
	60	13-15
	80	9.5-10.5

FUEL & TEMPERATURE GAUGE

1) Using a variable resistance tester (J-24538 or equivalent), attach one lead to fuel tank sending unit and other lead to sending unit ground wire. Move float arm and mark arm location at each of the appropriate resistance values.

2) Disconnect sending wire from sending unit. Connect one lead of tester to sending wire and other lead to ground. Turn ignition to "ON" position. Adjust tester to known ohm values and observe gauge indication at each ohm setting.

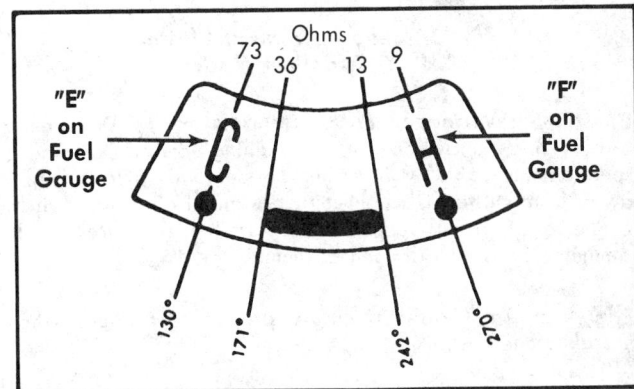

Fig. 1 Fuel and Temperature Gauge Test Band by Ohms and Needle Position

JEEP (Cont.)

VOLTMETER

Connect voltmeter of known accuracy across battery terminals. Turn ignition switch "ON" and compare indication of test voltmeter with indication of vehicle voltmeter. Replace if readings vary.

NOTE – *Fuel and temperature gauge indications may vary width of needles at any specific resistance value. Preceding test applies to both gauges.*

REMOVAL & INSTALLATION

SPEEDOMETER & GAUGES

All Models – Instrument panel must be removed to gain access to speedometer and gauges for repair or replacement.

INSTRUMENT CLUSTER

"CJ" & Scrambler Models – Disconnect battery ground cable. Separate speedometer cable from speedometer head. Remove 4 attaching nuts and pull cluster from mounting studs. Note position of all lamps and wires. Remove gauge wires and lamps. To install, reverse removal procedures.

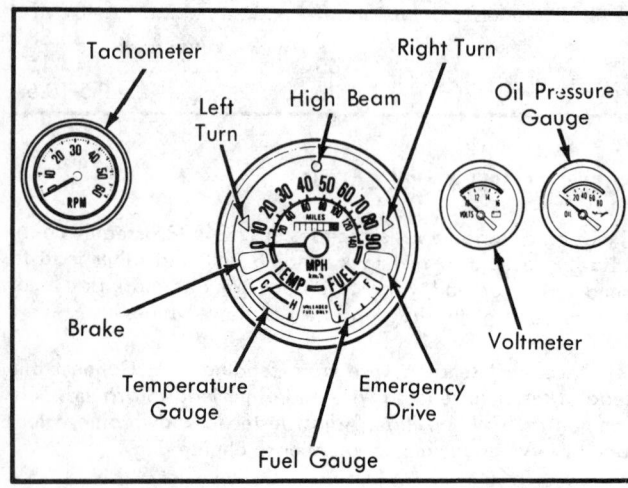

Fig. 2 Jeep Instrument Cluster ("CJ" & Scrambler Models)

Cherokee, Wagoneer & "J" Models – 1) Disconnect battery and remove six cluster retaining screws. Disconnect speedometer cable. Pull cluster pin terminal plug straight away from cluster. Disconnect four-terminal plug, fan switch connector plug, and vacuum hoses from heater control. Mark ammeter wires and disconnect them.

NOTE – *Tag hoses to ensure proper connections when installing the cluster.*

2) Remove two heater control panel lights, and disconnect temperature control wire from lever. Remove instrument cluster assembly. To install, reverse removal procedure.

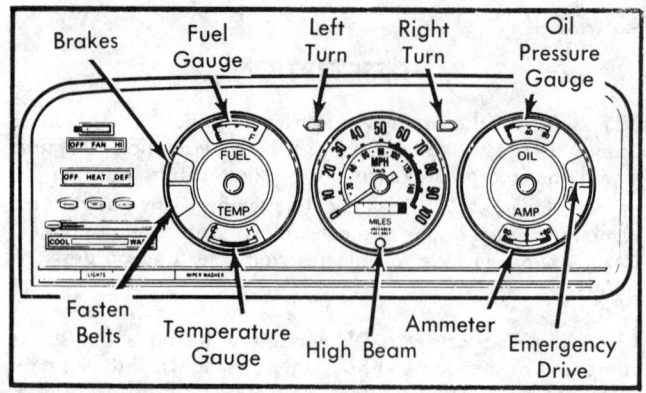

Fig. 3 Jeep Instrument Cluster (Cherokee, Wagoneer & "J" Models)

PRINTED CIRCUITS

NOTE – *Only Cherokee, Wagoneer & "J" Models use printed circuit board. "CJ" and Scrambler models use direct wiring for all gauges and cluster lamps.*

Cherokee, Wagoneer & "J" Models – Remove instrument cluster, radio noise suppressor, and all lamps from cluster (twist counterclockwise to remove). Remove circuit board and gauge assembly. Remove retaining nuts from ammeter and oil pressure gauges. Lift ammeter, oil pressure gauge and plate out of cluster as an assembly. Remove retaining nuts from fuel and temperature gauges. Remove large ground screw from circuit board above speedometer. Remove speedometer, fuel gauge, and temperature gauge as an assembly. To install, reverse removal procedure, checking gauge lenses for fingerprints.

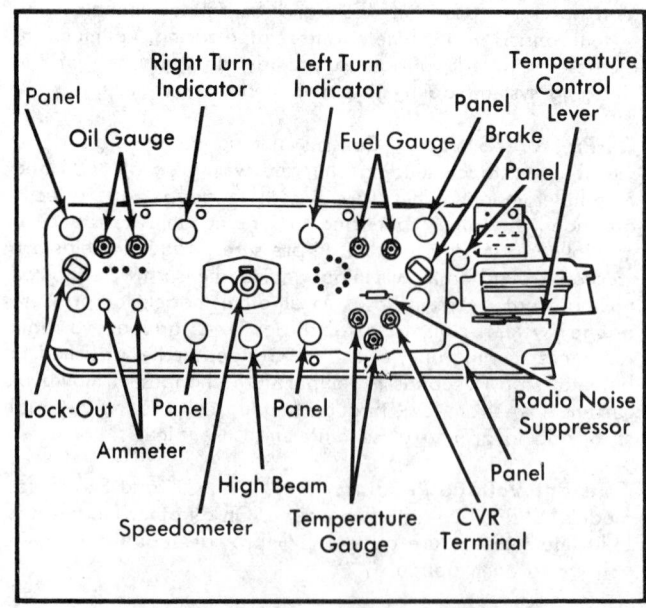

Fig. 4 Rear View of Jeep Instrument Cluster (Cherokee, Wagoneer & "J" Models)

JEEP (Cont.)

CONSTANT VOLTAGE REGULATOR

CVR is integral part of fuel gauge on "CJ" and Scrambler models and of temperature gauge on other models. If regulator requires replacement, entire gauge must be replaced.

HEADLIGHT SWITCH

All Models — Disconnect connector plug from switch, pull control knob out to second position. From behind instrument panel, depress knob release button and pull knob out of switch. Remove retaining nut and bezel. Remove switch through rear of instrument panel. To install, reverse removal procedures.

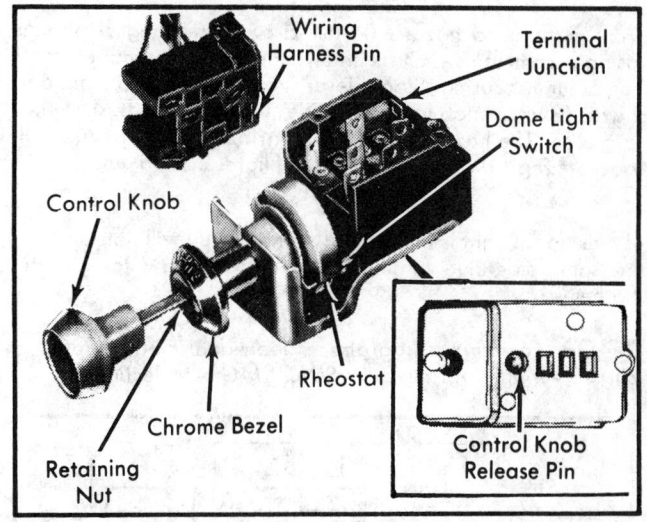

Fig. 5 Jeep Headlight Switch & Harness Connector

ALL MANUFACTURERS

DESCRIPTION

Turn signal and hazard flasher circuits are integral systems using a common switch assembly mounted within upper steering column housing. Signal lever is on left side of column and hazard switch knob is on right side. Two different flasher units are used. The hazard flasher is a variable load type and will operate regardless of the number of lights burned out.

If one signal light is burned out, signal circuit will not function on same side due to insufficient current draw to operate flasher.

NOTE — *For wiring diagrams of individual models, refer to chassis wiring diagrams in WIRING DIAGRAM Section.*

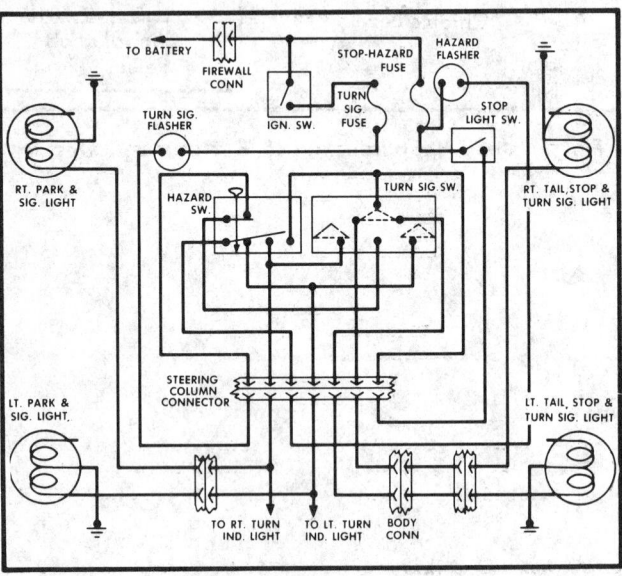

Fig. 1 *Wiring Diagram of Typical Turn Signal and Hazard Flasher System*

OPERATION

Turn Signals — Signal systems operate only when ignition switch is turned on. Normal frequency of signal lights are about 60-120 flashes per minute. Switch has two detent positions for each signal direction. With signal lever in first detent, lights will blink, but will go off if switch lever is released. Second switch detent will hold signal on, until steering wheel canceling fingers automatically turn signal off.

Hazard Flasher — With knob activated, all park and stop lights flash simultaneously regardless of ignition switch position. Depressing brake pedal will override flasher operation until pedal is released. During hazard switch operation with some vehicles, the turn signal should be off to avoid electric feed back through accessory circuits causing intermittent operation of circuits left turned on.

FLASHER LOCATION

CHRYSLER CORP.

Hazard — Located to the right of the fuse block on all models.

Turn Signal — Located to the right of the fuse block on all models.

FORD MOTOR CO.

Hazard — Located on back side of fuse block on "F" and Bronco models, or in wiring harness near left side cowl on "E" models.

Turn Signal — Located on fuse block on "F" and Bronco models, or on wiring harness near left side cowl on "E" models.

GENERAL MOTORS

Hazard — Mounted on the fuse panel.

Turn Signal — Located near fuse block at left of steering column on all models.

JEEP CORP.

Hazard — Mounted on the fuse panel.

Turn Signal — Mounted on the fuse panel.

TESTING & TROUBLE SHOOTING

CAUTION — *If equipped with Air Cushion Restraint System, do not attempt any service on turn signal switch until ignition switch is in "LOCK" position and battery ground cable is disconnected and taped.*

TURN SIGNAL & HAZARD SYSTEM

Turn Signals Inoperative — Turn on hazard system, if all lights operate, inspect for blown turn signal fuse or defective flasher. If fuse is open, check for shorts between fuse and lamps. If turn signal fuse and flasher are satisfactory, check wire terminals in harness connector for continuity and power feed to and from switch. To determine if switch is bad, connect a known good switch in column to chassis connector and operate switch by hand. If signals now operate, replace switch.

Turn Signals Inoperative (One Side) — Turn on hazard system, if one or more lights are inoperative, replace lights as necessary. Test light sockets for power or poor ground connection. If all lights operate with hazard system on, inspect for improper lamp or inoperative turn signal switch. If turn signal flasher can be heard, but lights fail, check for a short circuit.

Hazard Flasher Inoperative — Turn on signal switch, check all lights, and service as required. Check power to hazard circuit fuse and test fuse. If fuse is blown, check for shorts and/or replace fuse. If fuse is satisfactory, check power to hazard flasher. Replace with a good flasher, if system still fails. check power to hazard switch in steering column. Repair circuit between hazard flasher element and switch if necessary. To determine if switch is at fault, connect a known good switch in column to chassis connector and operate switch by hand. If hazard system now operates, repair or replace switch.

REMOVAL & INSTALLATION

TURN SIGNAL & HAZARD SWITCH ASSEMBLY

See Steering Wheel, Horn Button & Turn Signal Switch Removal in STEERING Section.

Wiper/Washer Systems

CHRYSLER CORP.

All Models

DESCRIPTION

Standard two-speed and intermittent wiper motors have permanent magnetic fields and are controlled by feeding power to different brushes for low and high speed. Motor speed is selected by rotating switch knob. A 6-ampere circuit breaker is integral with wiper switch in protecting wiper system. Washer system is electrically operated and consists of an electric pump, sealed motor, reservoir, rubber hoses and nozzles.

NOTE — *Wiper motors are basically the same. The intermittent wiper system does employ the following additions: Delay mode of 2-15 seconds, high speed is higher than standard, with a extra wipe after wash.*

TROUBLE SHOOTING

WIPER SYSTEM

Wiper Inoperative — Binding linkage. Faulty wiper switch. Open or grounded wiring. Faulty motor.

Motor Runs But Output Crank Does Not Turn — Stripped intermediate gear or output gear. Output gear slips on output shaft. Crank arm not fastened properly to output gear shaft.

Motor Does Not Shut Off — Defective park switch.

Blades Will Not Park — Motor park switch open. Faulty instrument panel switch. Arm set at incorrect position. Open park wiring circuit.

Motor Will Not Run, Circuit Breaker Does Not Cycle — Open circuit in wiring. Loose Bulkhead connector. Motor not grounded. Faulty circuit breaker, instrument panel switch or motor.

Motor Will Not Run, Circuit Breaker Cycles — Grounded wiring. Binding linkage. Faulty motor or instrument panel switch circuit breaker.

Motor Stops In Any Position When Switch Turned Off — Motor park switch open. Open park wiring circuit. Faulty instrument panel switch.

Motor Will Not Stop When Switch Turned Off — Defective park switch.

WASHER SYSTEM

Pump Runs But No Fluid Comes Out — No fluid in reservoir. Nozzle jet plugged or under intake grille. Broken hose or faulty pump.

System Operates Intermittently — Loose wiring connections. Faulty switch or motor.

System Output Low — Low aimed nozzles. Leaking hoses. Poor electrical connections. Defective motor.

Pump Motor Does Not Run — Broken wires. Faulty motor or switch. Poor ground. Loose wiring terminals.

TESTING

MOTOR WILL NOT RUN

1) Position panel switch in low-speed position. If motor can be heard running, check motor output shaft. If shaft is not turning, gearbox assembly requires replacement. If the shaft is turning, check drive link to output shaft for worn parts or disconnected components. If motor cannot be heard running, connect a voltmeter or test lamp between motor terminal "L" and ground.

2) If voltage is present and panel switch circuit breaker is not cycling, check for open ground circuit. Ground strap must make good contact. If motor runs, panel switch is not grounded, switch is faulty or there is an open in wiring. Common brush may not be making good contact with commutator and may require freeing-up or repositioning of spring. Armature may have an open circuit.

3) If voltage is present only part of the time, the circuit breaker is cycling. Problem may be a faulty circuit breaker or a short in the wiring, motor, or switch panel. Remove wiper arms and blades, disconnect harness at the motor and connect an ammeter between battery and terminal "L". If motor runs with average ammeter reading below six amperes, motor is good and trouble is in switch panel or wiring. If motor does not run and draw is more than six amperes, check wiper linkage for binding. Disconnect drive link from motor. If motor runs and draws less than three amperes, repair linkage. If motor fails to run or draws more than three amperes, check motor and gearbox for internal jamming. If no internal jamming exists, check motor for brush leads shorting to housing or armature for burned or blackened windings which could indicate an internal short.

MOTOR RUNS AT LOW SPEED ONLY

Position switch in high position and connect test lamp between terminal "H" and ground. If lamp does not light, an open exists in wiring or switch. If lamp lights, brush is not making contact with armature.

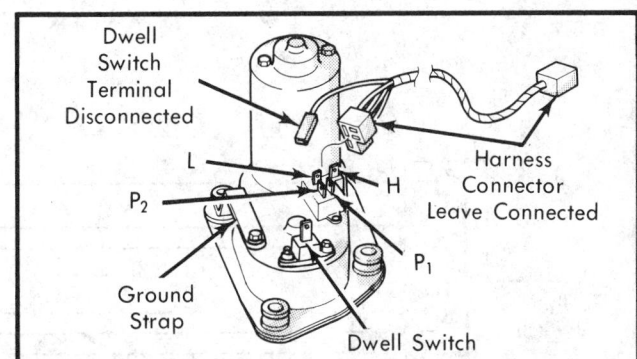

Fig. 1 Two Speed Intermittent Wiper Motor Terminal Identification (Standard Terminal Similar)

MOTOR RUNS AT HIGH SPEED ONLY

Position switch in low position and connect test lamp between terminal "L" and ground. If lamp does not light, an open exists in wiring or switch. If lamp lights at terminal "L", brush is not making contact with armature.

CHRYSLER CORP. (Cont.)

MOTOR CONTINUES TO RUN WITH SWITCH IN OFF OR PARK POSITION

Remove wiring harness and connect a jumper wire from terminal "P2" to terminal "L", then connect a jumper from "P1" to battery. If motor now runs to park position and stops, panel switch is defective. If motor continues to run and does not park, gearbox assembly requires replacement.

MOTOR WILL NOT STOP IN PARK POSITION WHEN SWITCH IS IN OFF POSITION

Remove wiring connector and clean terminals. If problem continues, place switch in park position and connect a voltmeter or test lamp between terminal "P1" and "L". If 12 volts are present or test lamp lights, check for voltage at "P2". If voltage is zero or test lamp does not light, motor park switch is defective and must be replaced. If 12 volts are present or lamp lights, an open exists in panel switch or wiring.

WIPER SWITCH (2-SPEED)

Disconnect wiring from switch and remove switch from instrument panel. Use a continuity tester or ohmmeter to check for continuity between contact terminals of switch as shown in table. For test purposes, first position is "OFF", "LOW" is first detent from "OFF" position and "HIGH" is second detent from "OFF" position. Ground is the case of wiper switch.

Switch Continuity

Off	Low	High
B to B/U	B to B/U	B to B/U
B to P1	B to P1	B to P1
A to P2	B to A	B to H
H-Open	P2-Open	P2-Open
	H-Open	A-Open

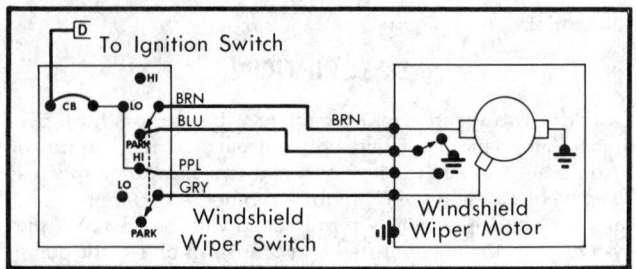

Fig. 2 Chrysler 2-Speed Wiper Wiring Diagram

WIPER SWITCH (INTERMITTENT WIPE)

Disconnect wiring from switch and remove switch from instrument panel. Use a continuity tester or ohmmeter to check for continuity between contact terminals of switch as shown in table. For test purposes, first position is "OFF", next is slide for "DELAY WIPE", "LOW" is first detent and "HIGH" is second detent. Ground is the case of wiper switch.

Intermittent Switch Continuity

Off	Delay	Low/High
$B-P_1$	$B-I_1$	B-A
A-G	$R-I_1$	P_2-G
	P_2-G	①H-G

① — Measured on high scale.

Resistance at maximum delay position should be between 270,000 ohms and 330,000 ohms.

Resistance at minimum delay position should be zero with ohmmeter set on the high ohm scale and positive of ohmmeter

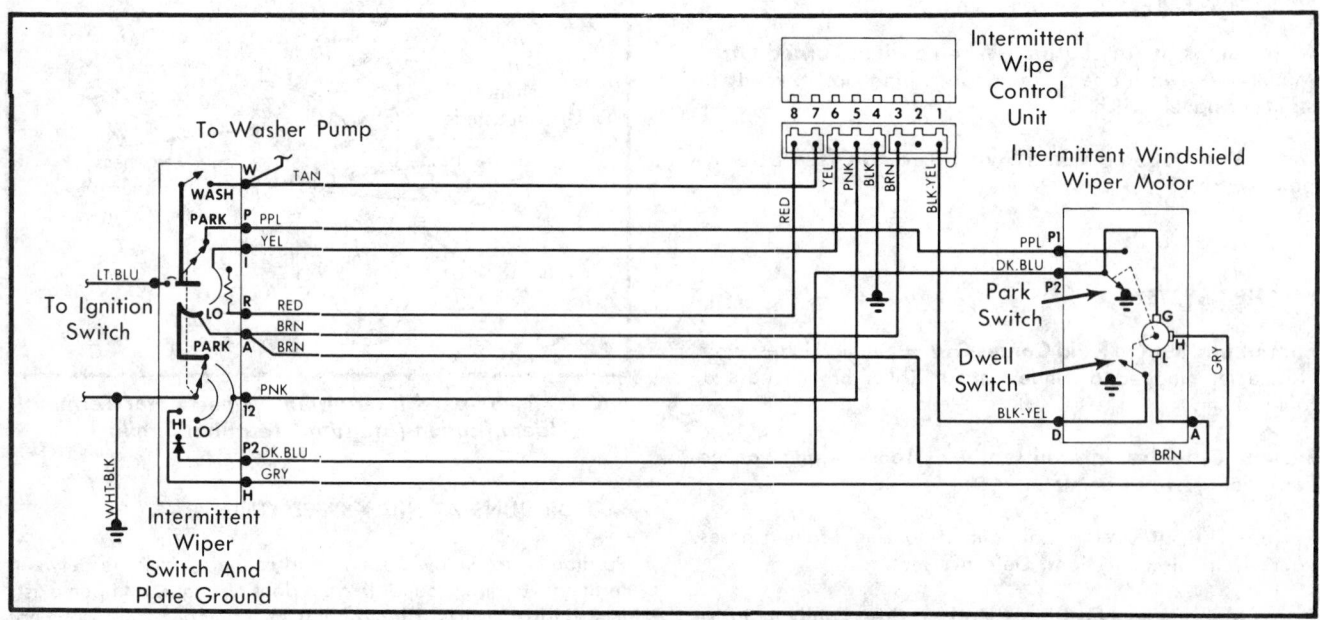

Fig. 3 Chrysler Intermittent Wiper Wiring Diagram

CHRYSLER CORP. (Cont.)

connected to "P₂" and negative connected to "G" should show low resistance.

Negative of ohmmeter connected to "P₂" and positive connected to "G" should show an open circuit or very high resistance. If same reading in both tests, switch is defective.

REMOVAL & INSTALLATION

WIPER MOTOR

Disconnect battery cable, and wiring connector from motor and remove motor mounting screws. Lower motor far enough to gain access to crank arm-to-drive link retainer bushing. Remove crank arm by prying retainer bushing from crank arm pin. Remove motor and nut attaching crank arm to motor drive shaft. Remove crank arm from motor. To install, reverse removal procedure.

WASHER PUMP

Drain fluid from reservoir. Remove reservoir mounting screws, reservoir and pump assembly. Disconnect electrical lead and rubber hose from bottom of pump. Using an extension and deep socket, remove pump mounting nut and plastic washer by reaching through reservoir neck. Remove pump and rubber grommet from reservoir. To install, reverse removal procedures.

OVERHAUL

WIPER MOTOR

Disassembly — Hold wiper motor in a vise and remove housing through bolts. Remove housing and armature assembly. Remove flat washers and spring washer.

Reassembly — 1) Hold gear box in vise with brush holder up. Pull brushes back in brush slots and push brush lead into holding notch. Clean commutator with ink eraser. Install flat washer, spring washer and flat washer on armature shaft.

2) Place armature shaft in brush holder assembly. Release brush leads from brush holder notches, (ensuring that brushes are spring loaded against commutator). Align the window in the motor housing with the brush holder. Install housing quickly over armature so magnets do not pull armature out of brush holder.

3) Make sure motor housing is flush with gear housing and over the four detents. Install through bolts. Install part number tag and retaining screw. Bench test motor by connecting 12 volt power source. Connect positive lead in series with ammeter to terminal "L". On 2-speed motor, ground the ground strap with a jumper wire. On intermittent wipe motors, connect a jumper wire from terminal "P2" to ground. On all models, tap the assembly gently with mallet to align bearings. Stop tapping when meter reads less than 2.5 amps. Install bulkhead seal.

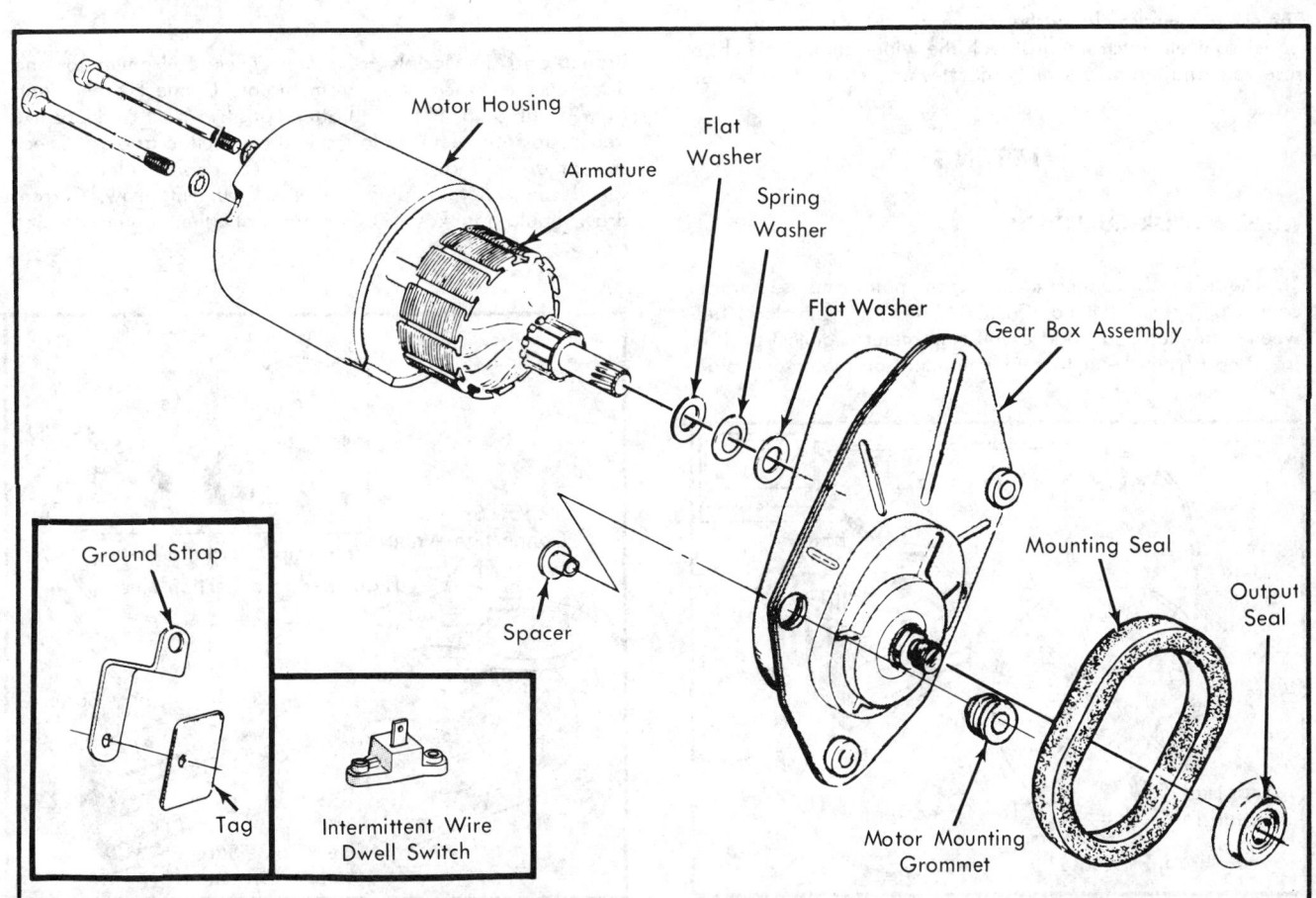

Fig. 4   Wiper Motor Exploded View

Wiper/Washer Systems

FORD

All Models

DESCRIPTION

Two speed permanent magnet windshield wiper motor is used. The two speed motor uses a three brush plate and switch assembly. When control selector is in low position, grounded brush and white wire brush are used to operate motor at low speed. When control selector is in high position, grounded brush and blue wire brush are used to operate motor at high speed. When control selector is moved to park position, motor will continue at low speed until park switch lower contacts open, stopping motor in park position. Optional interval wipers are available on "E" models, "F" models and Bronco. Intermittent operation is controlled by a variable resistor in the windshield wiper control switch, combined with the electronic governor allows a variable pause between wiping cycles.

For normal operation on "F" models, turn wiper control knob to right for low or high speed. For intermittent operation, rotate wiper control knob to left. The more knob is rotated to left, the greater the time interval between wiper blade sweeps. On "E" models the wiper switch knob slides toward the right with the first position being intermittent, the second is low and the third is high. As the control is moved to the left of intermittent position the interval between blade sweeps is at a maximum and as it moves to the right of intermittent detent, the blade sweep interval is reduced.

The electric windshield washer system consists of an instrument panel control switch integral with the wiper control switch, a reservoir and motor assembly, nozzles and connecting hoses.

TESTING

WIPER MOTOR CURRENT DRAW

"E" Models — Disconnect linkage from motor and use suitable connector sleeves (kit no. C4AZ-14294-B or equivalent) between motor terminals and a volt-amp meter. Connect positive (red) lead from meter to center terminal on motor end plate

and green lead from meter to battery positive post. Connect a jumper wire from negative post of battery to low speed terminal on motor end plate and check current draw. Move jumper wire from low speed to high speed terminal and check current draw. Current draw should not exceed 3.5 amperes. If current draw is excessive, check output arm and windlatch mechanism for binding or damage before replacing motor. See Fig. 1.

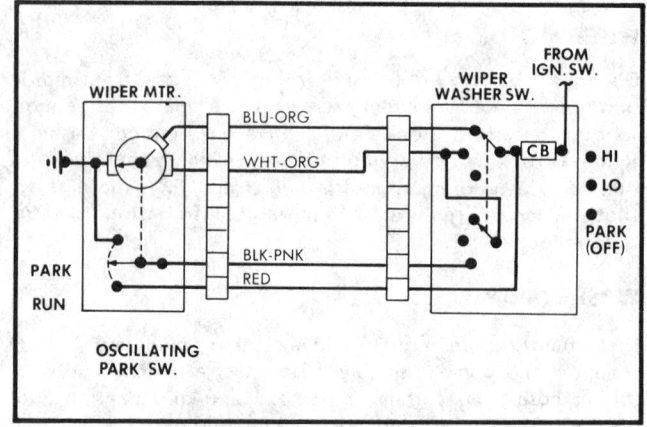

Fig. 2   Wiring Diagram 2-Speed Non-Interval "F" Series and Bronco

Bronco and "F" Models — Disconnect linkage from motor and disconnect electrical plug from motor. Connect green lead from a volt-amp meter to battery positive post and positive (red) lead from meter to low speed connection at plug. Check current draw. Move positive (red) lead from meter to high speed connection at plug and check current draw. Current draw should not exceed 3.0 amperes at either connection. See Fig. 3.

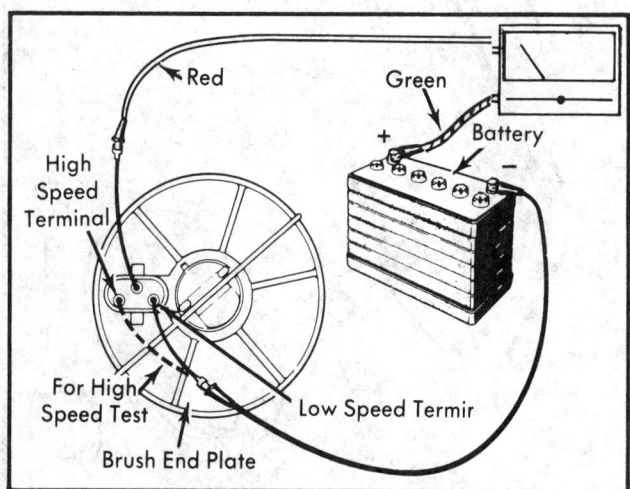

Fig. 1   Motor Current Draw Test "E" Models

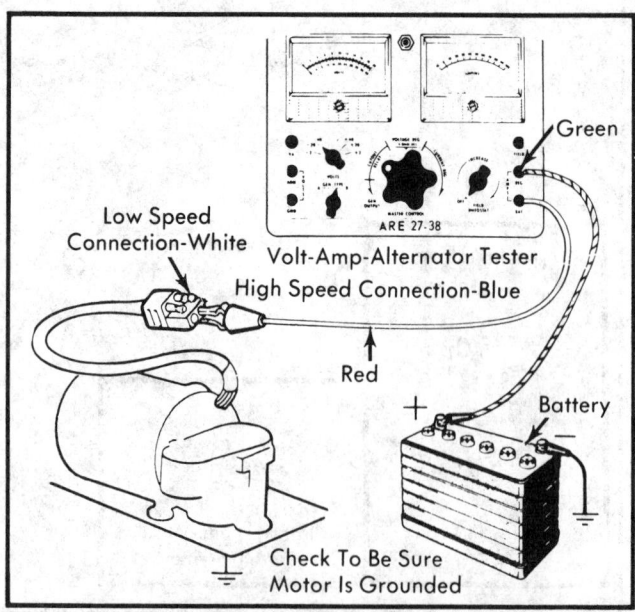

Fig. 3   Motor Current Draw Test Bronco and "F" Models

FORD (Cont.)

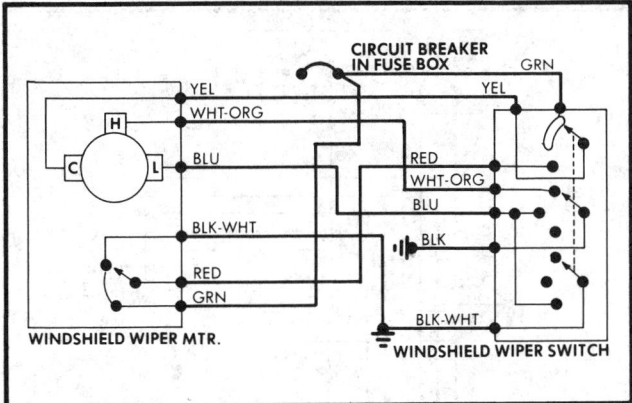

Fig. 4   Wiring Diagram 2-Speed Non-Interval "E" Models

CIRCUIT BREAKER

Circuit breaker is located in wiper control switch on all rotary switches and in fuse panel for slide wiper control switches. On models with the circuit breaker located in the fuse panel, the rating is 7.5 amps. The circuit breaker integral with the switch is rated at 7 amps. The following test does not apply to vehicles with the circuit breaker located in the fuse panel. *See Fig. 5.*

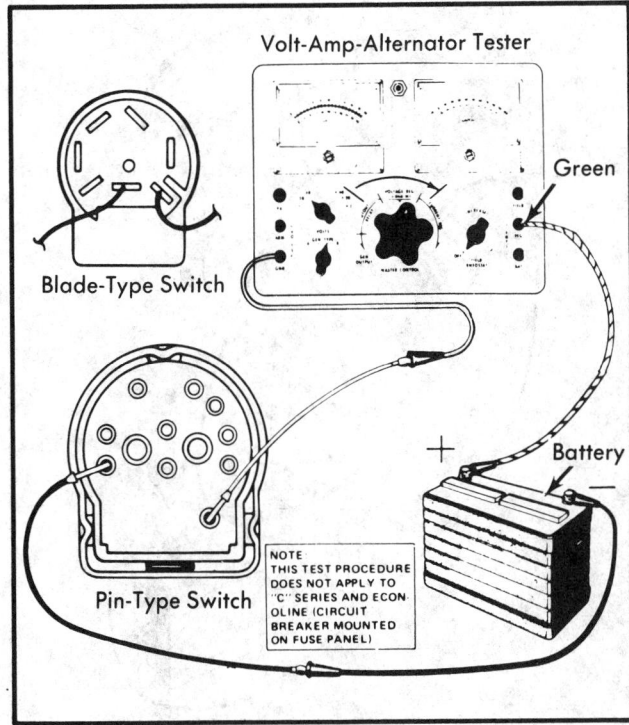

Fig. 5   Circuit Breaker Test

1) Before connecting tester leads as shown in illustration, short tester leads together and adjust current draw until it equals circuit breaker rating. Connect switch to tester and leave switch connected for ten minutes. Current reading should remain at rated current. If circuit breaker opens during the ten minutes, replace wiper switch assembly.

2) Short tester leads together and adjust current draw until it is twice rated current. Connect switch to tester and current reading on ammeter should drop to zero within 20 seconds. If it takes longer than 20 seconds for breaker to open, replace wiper switch assembly.

WIPER SWITCH CONTINUITY TEST

Check continuity between switch terminals as shown in illustrations. Either a self powered test light or an ohmmeter can be used to test a standard two speed switch. An ohmmeter must be used to test a switch with the intermittent system. To detect marginal operation of switch, rotate knob or slide switch while each reading is being taken. If switch does not exhibit continuity as shown or poor continuity exists, replace switch.

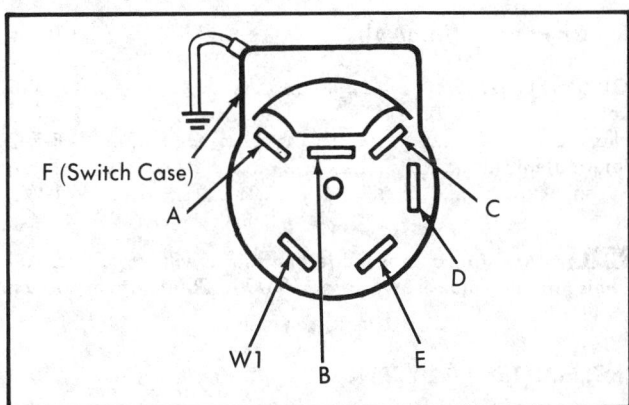

Fig. 6   Blade Type Switch Connector Non-Interval

Switch Position	Terminals
Off (Park)	C-D, A-B
Low	A-B-C
High	A-B-E
Wash	A-B-W1

Intermittent Switch Position	Intermittent Terminals
Off (Park)	A-B, D-E
Low	A-B, D-E-F
High	D-E-F, A-B-C
Intermittent	①E-F, A-B
Wash	A.B-W1

① — Variable resistance between terminals D-E should be minimum 200-1000 ohms and maximum 5600-8400 ohms.

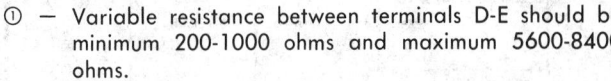
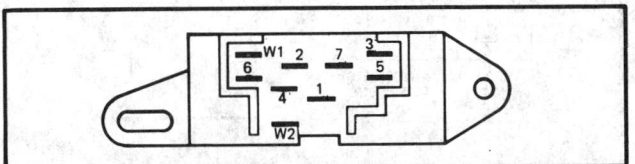

Fig. 7   Blade Type (Slide Switch) Connector Non-Interval

FORD (Cont.)

Switch Position (Non-Interval)	Terminals
Off (Park)	1-5,3-7
Low	1-4,2-7
High	1-4,2-6
Wash	W1-W2

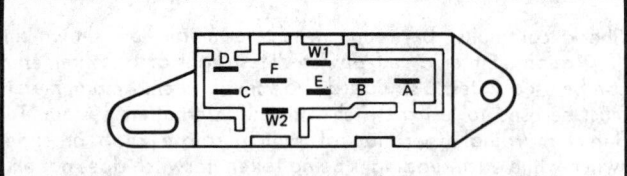

**Fig. 8   Blade Type (Slide Switch) Connector
Interval**

Switch Position (Interval)	Terminals
Off (Park)	A-E
Low	B-E-F-C
High	D-B-F-C
Intermittent	B-E-F
Wash	W1-W2

NOTE — *Resistance between terminals F-C will vary 500±400
ohms at minimum dwell to 10,000±2000 at maximum
dwell.*

INTERMITTENT GOVERNOR

If intermittent operation is unsatisfactory, check motor current
draw, then check control switch and all connecting wires for
continuity. If motor, switch and connecting wires are satisfactory, replace electronic governor assembly.

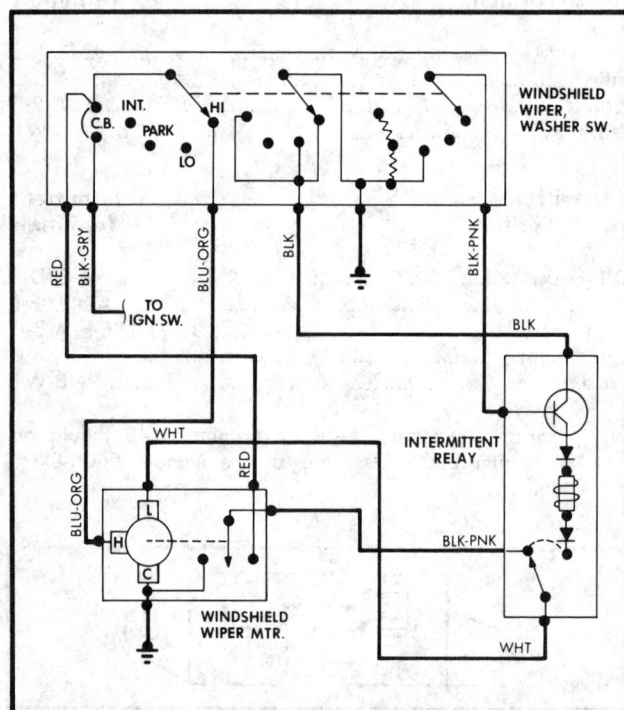

**Fig. 9   Wiring Diagram 2-Speed Interval
Bronco and "F" Models**

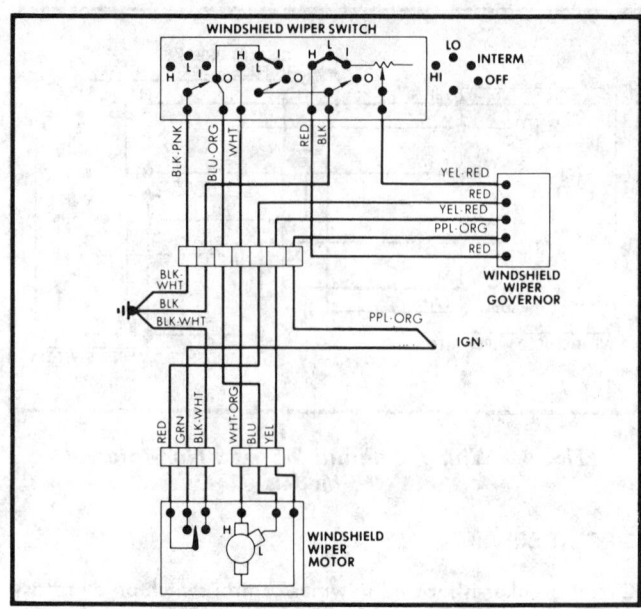

**Fig. 10   Wiring Diagram 2-Speed Interval
(Depressed Park) "E" Models**

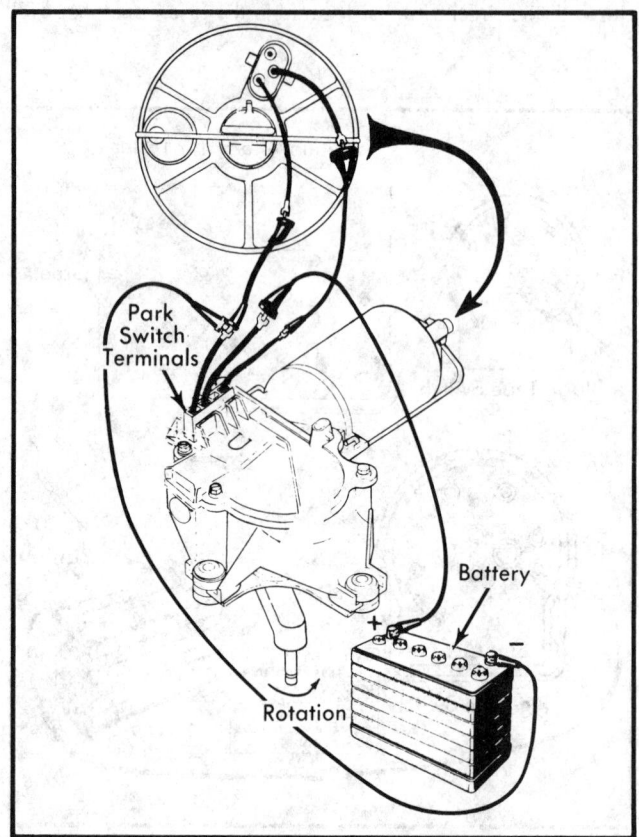

**Fig. 11   Motor Park Test
"E" Models**

WASHER PUMP CURRENT DRAW

Connect test leads of ammeter as shown in *Fig. 12.* The current
draw should not exceed 4 amps., or be less than 1.7 amps.,
while the washer pump is pumping fluid.

FORD (Cont.)

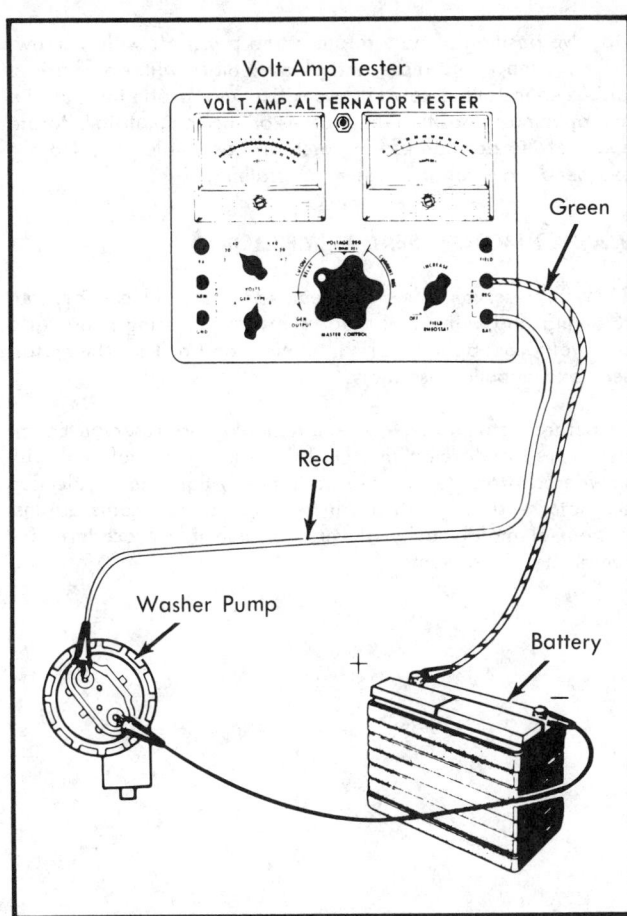

Fig. 12 Washer Pump Current Draw Test

REMOVAL & INSTALLATION

WIPER MOTOR

"E" Models — Disconnect battery ground cable, remove fuse panel and bracket assembly. Then disconnect wires at motor brush cap and gear box cover. Remove wiper arm blade assemblies from pivot shaft, outer air inlet cowl and clip retaining motor drive arm to linkage mounting arm and pivot shaft assembly. Remove motor attaching bolts and remove motor from vehicle. To install, reverse removal procedures while noting the following: If a new motor is installed, motor must be in park position.

Bronco & "F" Models — 1) Disconnect negative battery cable. Remove wiper arms and blade assemblies. Remove cowl grille attaching screws and raise cowl. Disconnect washer nozzle hose and remove cowl grille.

2) Remove wiper linkage clips from motor output arm. Disconnect motor wiring connector. Remove motor attaching screws and remove motor. To install, reverse removal procedure.

WIPER CONTROL SWITCH

"E" Models — Disconnect battery ground cable and remove windshield wiper switch knob. Remove ignition switch bezel.

Depress button on top of headlight switch and pull knob and shaft from switch. Remove screws at bottom of finish panel and pry two upper retainers away from instrument panel assembly. Disconnect connector from wiper switch, remove switch attaching bolts and remove switch from vehicle. To install, reverse removal procedures.

Bronco and "F" Models — Disconnect battery ground cable and remove wiper switch knob, bezel nut and bezel. Pull switch out from under instrument panel and disconnect plug connector from switch. Remove switch from vehicle. To install, reverse removal procedure.

INTERMITTENT GOVERNOR

"E" and "F" Models — Governor is mounted on lower flange of instrument panel. Disconnect wire connectors from governor, remove attaching screws and remove governor. To install, reverse removal procedure.

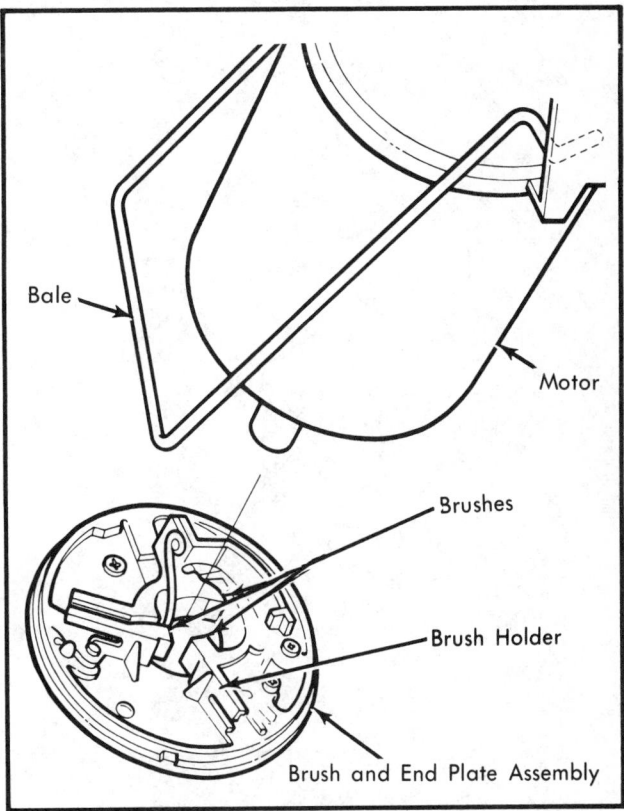

Fig. 13   Motor Brush End Plate Assembly, "E" Models

WASHER PUMP & RESERVOIR

1) Disconnect lock tab wire connector using a small screwdriver. Remove hose and drain reservoir. Remove retaining screws and lift motor from vehicle.

2) With reservoir drained, remove reservoir attaching screw and remove reservoir. To install, reverse removal procedure, noting that reservoir must be filled before connecting electrical connections or operating pump.

FORD (Cont.)

OVERHAUL

WIPER MOTOR

NOTE — *The wiper motor for "F" and Bronco models is not serviceable. It must be replaced as a complete assembly. Wiper motor for "E" models is serviceable only in kits of major sub-assemblies. The kits available are for the cover and switch assembly and the brush end plate.*

COVER & SWITCH ASSEMBLY

Remove four cover retaining screws and remove assembly. Replace with appropriate kit. Be sure that ground strap is under the cover screw. Tighten screws to 15-25 INCH lbs.

BRUSH END PLATE

NOTE — *"E" model switch assembly is identified by the letter "U" stamped on the outside surface.*

Observe position of bale retainer and pry it off with a screwdriver. Remove end plate and plug. Replace with appropriate kit. When installing new kit, use a fine wire probe through the hub opening to position the brushes on the commutator. Rotate end plate to position key in notch and assemble plug. Do not overbend bale retainer when reinstalling.

WASHER MOTOR, SEAL & IMPELLOR

1) With reservoir assembly removed from vehicle, pry out retaining ring with small blade screwdriver. Using pliers, grip one wall around the electrical terminal and pull out the motor, seal and impellor assembly.

2) Before installing new assembly, make sure reservoir chamber is free of foreign matter. Lubricate outside of seal with powdered graphite before installation. Align small projection on motor end cap with slot in reservoir so seal seats against bottom of motor cavity. Reverse disassembly procedures for remaining components.

GENERAL MOTORS — INTEGRAL WIPER/WASHER MOTOR

All Exc. "P" Models

NOTE — *For "P" Model applications, see "General Motors — Square Motor" article in this section.*

DESCRIPTION

Two speed motor, permanent magnet type, consists of partsfield magnets, armature and drive gear within upper and lower housings. The washer pump is assembled on the outside surface of the upper half of the housing and is an integral part of the wiper motor assembly. Wiper motor is protected by an automatic reset circuit breaker. Vehicle wiring is protected by fuse in fuse block.

OPERATION

The basic washer pump is a spring loaded piston enclosed in a plastic cylinder housing with an actuator plate extending from the cylinder housing. A valve assembly, consisting of two exhaust and one intake check valve, is attached to the end of the cylinder housing. A tang on the piston actuator plate holds the plate in a lock-out position, (no pumping action). To start the pump, push washer button which will energize the relay. This pulls the relay armature toward the coil allowing the ratchet gear pawl to engage the ratchet gear and begin rotation. This sequence starts pumping action.

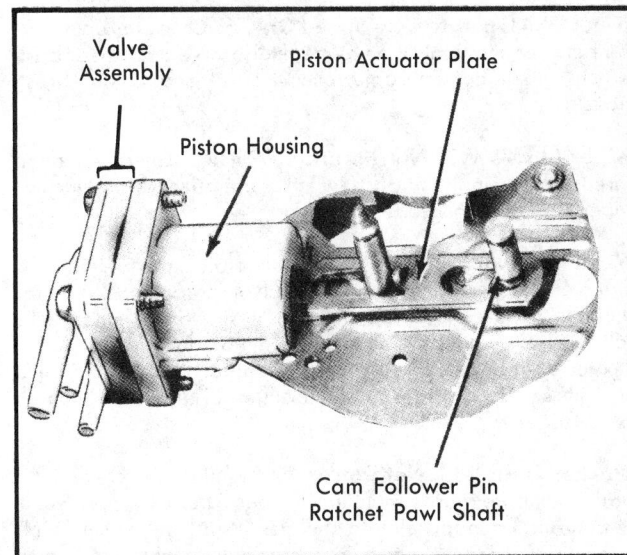

Fig. 2 Washer Actuator Plate and Valve Assembly

TROUBLE SHOOTING

Wiper Inoperative — Check fuse, wiring harness, wiper ground and dash connections.

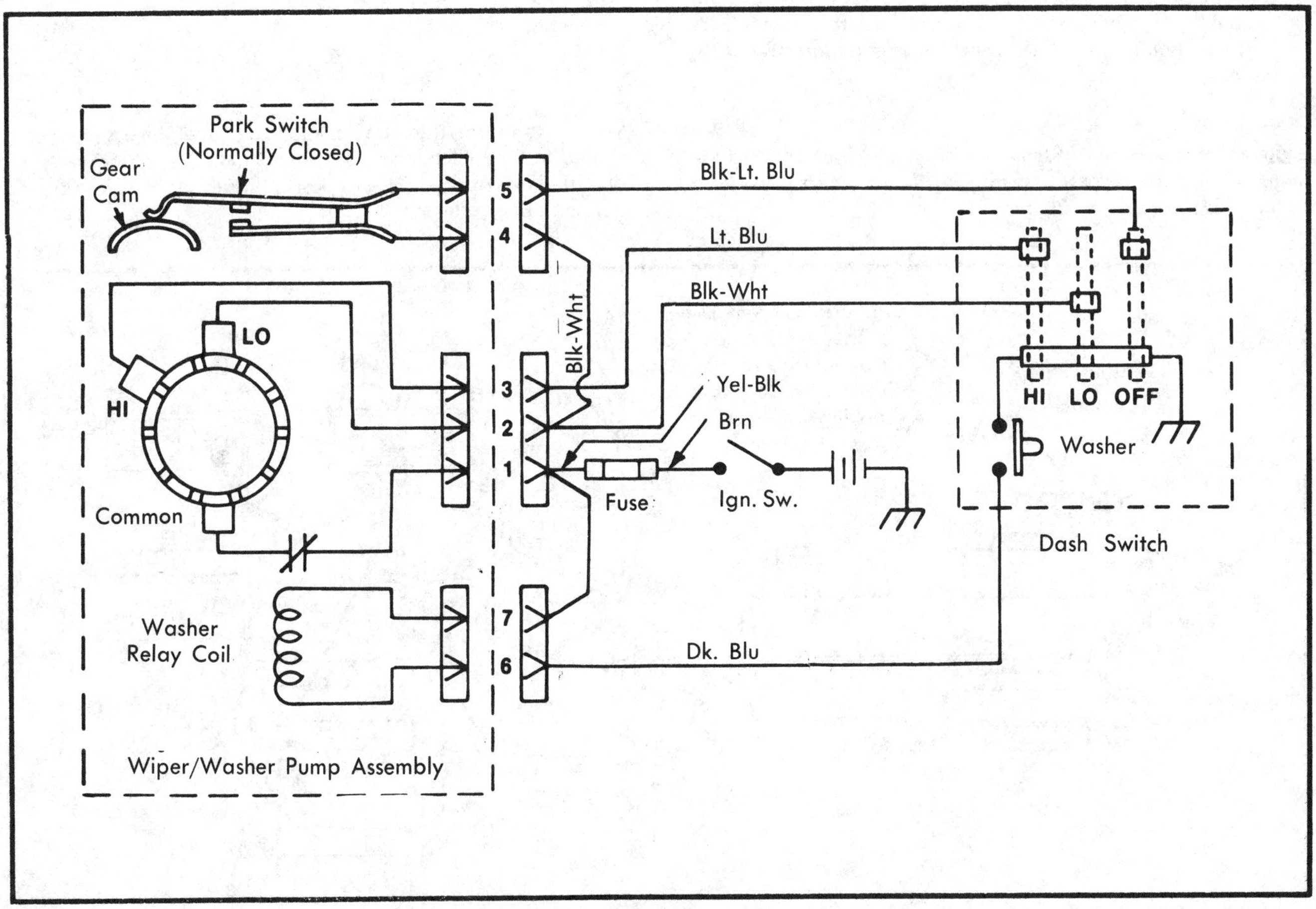

**Fig. 1   General Motors Truck Wiper Motor and
Integral Washer System Wiring Diagram**

Wiper/Washer Systems

GENERAL MOTORS – INTEGRAL WIPER/WASHER MOTOR (Cont.)

Wiper Will Operate One Speed Only – Check for open wiring between terminals 2 or 3 and the dash switch. Check dash switch and if not operable, check "Low" and "High" brush leads.

Wiper Blades Will Not Return To Park – Check for open wire from terminal 5 to dash switch. If not open, dash switch or wiper park switch needs replacing.

Wiper Will Not Shut Off – Disconnect wiring from terminals 4 and 5. Replace park switch assembly if motor stops. If motor still runs, remove wires from terminals 1, 2 and 3. Connect a 12 volt lead to terminal 1 only and if motor does not run it indicates a ground in wires from wiper motor to terminal 2 or 3 at dash switch. If it runs, check for internal ground in high or low brushes.

Washer Pump Will Not Run – Turn ignition switch to "ON" position. Insure washer solution is adequate, then push wash button and listen for relay to energize. With ignition still "ON" and wiring connected to wiper terminals, connect test lamp lead to ground and probe terminals 6 and 7.

- Light "OFF" at both terminals; check for open in circuit to the pump.
- Light "ON" at one terminal, replace coil-park switch assembly.
- Light "ON" at both terminals, but one light is dim; ground the dim light terminals. If pump runs, check for open in wire between pump and dash switch or for a defective dash switch.

NOTE – *Delay wiper system is available as optional equipment. A separate control assembly is utilized which provides a variable delay of 1 to 20 seconds.*

REMOVAL & INSTALLATION

WIPER MOTOR (EXC. "G" MODELS)

Removal & Installation – Ensure wiper motor is in park position, then disconnect ground cable from battery, electrical harness at motor and hoses at washer pump. Reach through access hole in cowl grille and loosen wiper drive rod attaching screws. Remove drive rod from wiper motor crank arm. Remove wiper motor-to-dash panel attaching screws and remove motor assembly. To install, reverse removal procedure while noting the following: Lubricate crank arm pivot prior to reinstallation.

WIPER MOTOR ("G" MODELS ONLY)

Removal – Ensure wiper motor is in park position, then disconnect battery ground cable and remove wiper arms. Remove cowl panel cover. Loosen nuts holding linkage to crank arm and lift linkage off arm. Disconnect wiring to motor. Remove left dash defroster outlet from flex hose and position hose to one side. Remove screw securing left hand heater duct to engine cover shroud and slip heater duct down and out. Remove washer hoses, then remove screws securing wiper motor to cowl and lift wiper motor from under dash.

Installation – To install, reverse removal procedures while noting the following: Ensure wiper motor is in park position before installing. Lube wiper motor crank arm pivot prior to installation.

OVERHAUL

Repairs to motor/gear box section of the wiper assembly are limited to the switch, armature, cap and brush holder assembly plus the external parts, crankarm, spacer/seal (plastic) and output shaft seal.

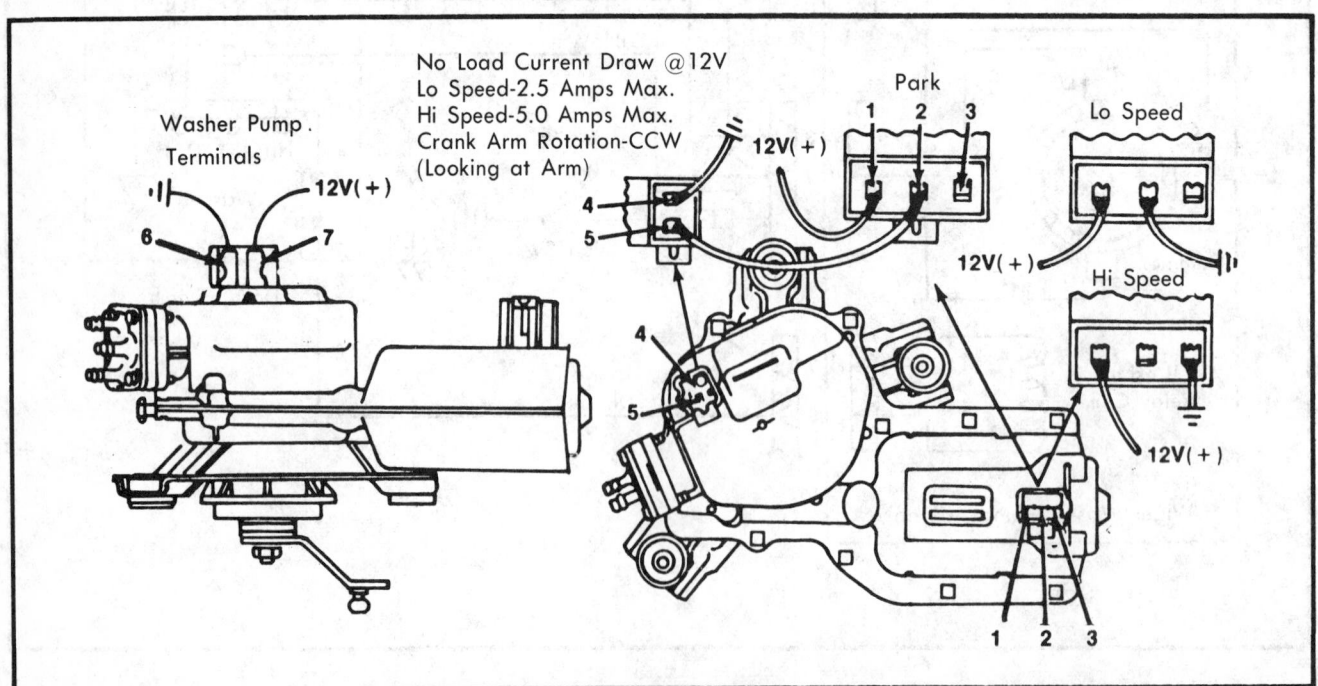

Fig. 3 Wiper/Washer Motor Terminal Check Diagram

Wiper/Washer Systems

GENERAL MOTORS — SQUARE MOTOR

Chevrolet
"P" Models
GMC
"P" Models

DESCRIPTION

Two speed motor is a compound wound (series and shunt) type. Gear train consists of a helical gear at end of armature shaft which drives an intermediate gear and pinion assembly. Pinion drives output gear and shaft; and crank arm, attached to output gear shaft, drives wiper transmissions through connecting link arms. Circuit protection for wipers is through a fuse on fuse block. Windshield washer pump is a positive displacement type using a piston arrangement. Pump is mounted on shaft of wiper output gear.

TESTING & TROUBLE SHOOTING

WIPER ON CAR

Wiper Inoperative — Check wiring harness, wiper ground strap and dash switch for proper connections and mounting. Check fuse. With ignition switch on, check for 12 volts at harness terminal which connects to No. 2 terminal. To bypass switch, disconnect wiring at motor and connect jumper wire from No. 1 and 3 terminals to ground and a 12 volt source to No. 2 terminal. If wiper does not operate, disconnect transmissions from crank arm. If wiper still does not operate, remove from vehicle and test unit. *See Wiper Off Car.*

Wiper Will Not Shut Off — Determine whether wiper has both speeds, low speed only or high speed only, then operate wiper by bypassing switch as previously outlined. *See Wiper Inoperative.* If wiper operates correctly and has both speeds, lead to switch from No. 1 terminal is grounded or switch is faulty. If wiper has low or high speed only, lead to switch from No. 3 terminal is open or switch is faulty. If wiper still does not operate, remove from vehicle and test unit. *See Wiper Off Car.*

Operates Low Speed Only & Shuts Off With Dash Switch In High Position — Reverse harness leads connected to No. 1 and 3 terminals.

Does Not Return To Park With Wiper Off — Check ground strap connection and park switch contacts may be dirty, bent or broken.

Speed Normal In Low, But Too Fast In High — Terminal board resistor may be open. Remove from vehicle to test terminal board.

Wiper Operates Intermittently — Loose ground strap or dash switch mounting.

WIPER OFF CAR

NOTE — *Use ammeter with reading of 30 amperes (minimum) in feed wire circuit.*

Wiper Inoperative — Connect an ammeter and battery to No. 2 terminal and a jumper wire from No. 1 and 3 terminals to ground. Wiper should operate at low speed. If ammeter reading is 0, check for loose splice joints or loose solder connection at No. 2 terminal. If reading is 1-1.5 amperes, check

for sticking brushes, open armature or loose splice joint. If reading is 11 amperes, check for broken gear or other stalling condition.

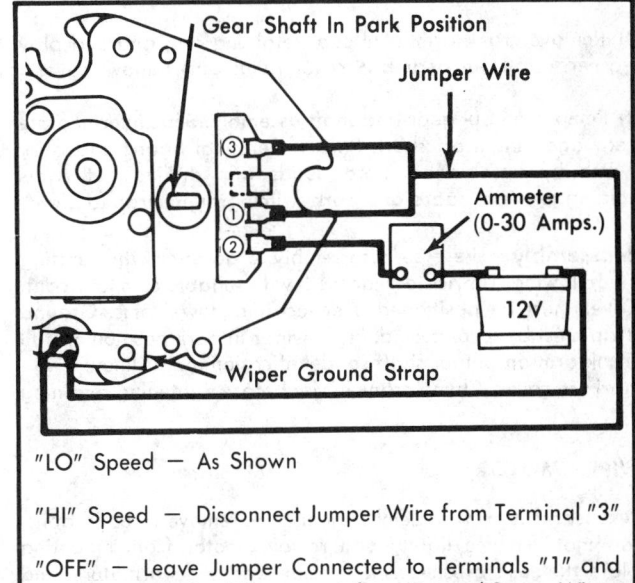

"LO" Speed — As Shown

"HI" Speed — Disconnect Jumper Wire from Terminal "3"

"OFF" — Leave Jumper Connected to Terminals "1" and "3", But Disconnect It from Ground Strap. Wiper Should Stop with Gear Shaft Flats as Shown.

Fig. 1   Test Jumper Wire Connections

Wiper Will Not Shut Off — If wiper has both speeds, park switch contacts may not be opening or internal motor lead to No. 1 terminal is grounded. If wiper has low speed only, shunt field coil may be grounded or internal wiper lead to No. 3 terminal is grounded. If wiper has high speed only, shunt field is open or internal lead to No. 3 terminal is open.

Wipers Operate Intermittently — Check for sticking brushes, loose splice joints or other loose connections.

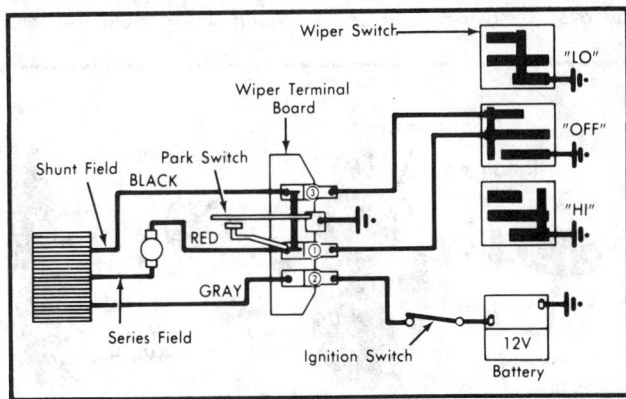

Fig. 2   General Motors Square Motor Wiper System Wiring Diagram

OVERHAUL

GEAR BOX

Disassembly — 1) Remove washer pump, if equipped. Remove pump drive cam by wedging off shaft with two screwdrivers. Clamp crank arm in vise and remove retaining nut.

GENERAL MOTORS – SQUARE MOTOR (Cont.)

NOTE – *Arm must be secure in vise to avoid stripping wiper gears.*

2) Remove crank arm, seal cap, retaining ring and end play washers. Drill out gear box cover rivets and remove cover.

3) Remove output gear and shaft assembly. Slide intermediate gear and pinion off shaft. Remove terminal board and park switch by unsoldering motor leads and drilling out rivets holding terminal board and park switch ground strap to plate.

Reassembly – Reverse disassembly procedure while noting the following: Lubricate gear teeth with suitable cam lubricant. Cover must be positioned over locating dowel pins. Ground strap must be reconnected. Place wiper in park position, install crank arm on output shaft so identification marks line up with marks in cover. Clamp crank in vise before tightening retaining nut.

WIPER MOTOR

Disassembly – Disassemble gear box, remove through bolts, tap motor frame lightly and remove motor from mounting plate. Release brush spring tension and slide armature and end plate from motor frame. Pull end plate from armature. Remove end play adjusting washers and note arrangement for proper reassembly.

NOTE – *A thrust plug is located between armature shaft and end plate.*

Reassembly – Reverse disassembly procedure while noting the following: Lubricate armature shaft bushings with light machine oil. Install washers with concave side of washers toward each other. End play is automatically controlled by proper installation of washers.

WASHER PUMP (PISTON TYPE)

Solenoid Assembly (Ratchet Dog) – Squeeze cover to remove. Remove ratchet dog retaining screw. Hold solenoid plunger in position and lift solenoid assembly and ratchet dog from pump frame. Separate ratchet dog from solenoid mounting plate as required. To install, reverse disassembly procedure.

Ratchet Pawl – Disconnect ratchet pawl spring, remove pawl retaining ring and slide ratchet pawl off cam follower shaft. To install, reverse removal procedure.

Ratchet Wheel – Remove ratchet dog from pump frame, move ratchet wheel spring out of shaft groove and slide ratchet wheel off its shaft. To install, reverse removal procedure.

Pump And Actuator Plate Assembly – Remove solenoid assembly, ratchet dog, ratchet pawl and ratchet wheel. To separate pump and pump actuator plate from frame, pull pump housing in direction of arrow until grooves in housing clear the frame. Remove actuator plate from ratchet wheel and cam follower shafts. To install, reverse removal procedure.

Valve Assembly – Remove screws attaching valve assembly to pump housing. During reassembly, gasket must be properly positioned between housing and valve plate in the housing and valve plate grooves. Triple "O" ring must be properly installed between valve body and pipe assembly.

MOTOR SPECIFICATIONS

Application	Specification
Operating Voltage	12 Volts
Current Draw (No Load Max.)	
"Low" Speed	4 Amps.
"High" Speed	3.5 Amps.
Current Draw (Stall, Cold)	12 Amps.
Crank Arm Speed (Minimum)	
"Low" Speed	31 RPM
"High" Speed	55 RPM

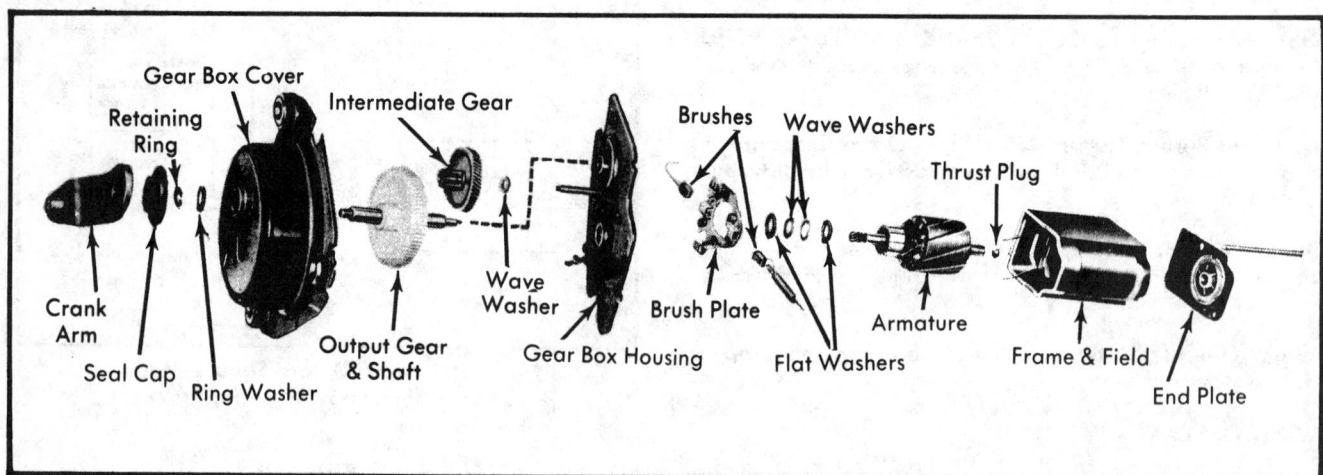

Fig. 3   Exploded View of Wiper Motor and Drive Assembly

JEEP

All Models

DESCRIPTION

Jeep vehicles use a two-speed electric motor which is a compound wound (series and shunt) type. A crank arm is attached externally to gear shaft and operates linkage which activates the wiper blades. All models except "CJ" and Scrambler have an optional intermittent feature. All models use an electric washer system which consists of a motor, reservoir and necessary hoses and nozzles. The pump assembly is mounted in the bottom of the reservoir. The motor case is grounded to the vehicle body and is energized by a feed wire from the control switch.

TESTING & TROUBLE SHOOTING

**2-SPEED WIPER (ON VEHICLE)
"CJ" & SCRAMBLER MODELS**

NOTE — *The wiper motor must be grounded for proper operation and during all of the following test procedures.*

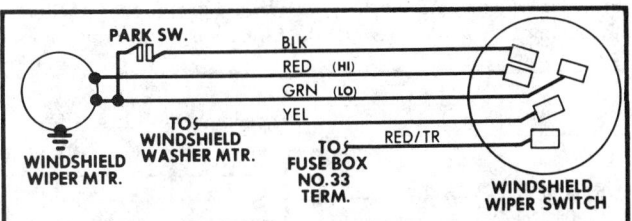

**Fig. 1   Jeep 2-Speed Wiper System
Wiper Diagram ("CJ" & Scrambler Models)**

1) Place ignition switch in "ON" position and use a suitable test lamp to check for 12 volts at switch terminal B. *See Fig. 2.* If test lamp lights but motor does not operate, ensure ground is

good by connecting a jumper wire from motor ground strap to a good body ground. If motor still will not operate, disconnect jumper wire. Disconnect wiring from switch.

2) Connect a jumper wire between terminals number 2 and B which should give low speed operation of motor. If motor does not operate on low speed, possible causes are an open condition in green wire leading from switch, a loose internal connection in motor or a stuck low speed brush.

3) Connect a jumper wire between terminals number 3 and B which should give high speed operation of motor. If motor does not operate on high speed possible causes are an open condition in red wire leading from switch, a loose internal connection in motor or a stuck high speed brush.

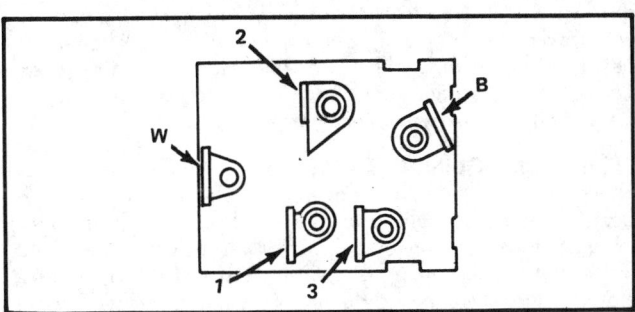

**Fig. 2   Jeep Identification of Test Connections
("CJ" & Scrambler Models)**

4) Position wiper blades in a position other than park and connect a jumper wire between terminals number 1 and B Motor should run on low speed and stop with blades in park position. If motor does not run with jumper connected, possible causes are an open in black wire from switch, a loose internal connection in motor, a bad connection between park point set to low speed brush, or a misaligned or damaged set of con-

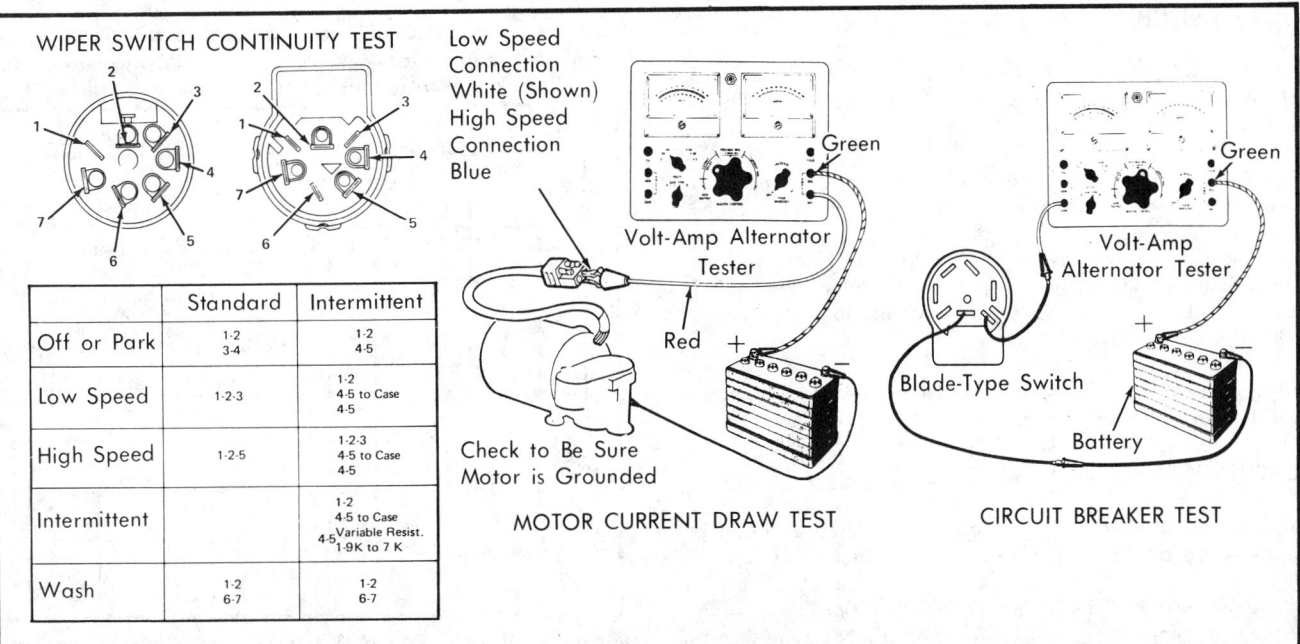

**Fig. 3   Testing Wiper/Washer System
(Cherokee, Wagoneer & "J" Models)**

JEEP (Cont.)

tact points. If motor runs but does not position wipers in park position, cam on drive gear is not breaking contact points sufficiently.

2-SPEED WIPER (ON CAR)
CHEROKEE, WAGONEER & "J" MODELS

Wiper Inoperative or Operates at One Speed Only — Foreign objects interfering with linkage. Open circuit in ignition switch, wiper switch, harness or terminals. Loose or misaligned connection between wiring harness plug and motor plug. Faulty ground strap connection.

Wipers Do Not Park — Disconnect wiper motor and connect black lead to white lead and feed 12 volts to red lead. Replace motor if it fails to park. If it parks, turn ignition switch "ON" and wiper switch to "PARK". Connect test light to pink wire with tracer (at motor plug) and ground. Also check continuity between yellow wire with tracer and blue wire with tracer. Check harness connections between motor and instrument panel switch. If okay, replace panel switch.

Wiper Motor Quits While Wiping — With engine idling, blower motor on high, operate wipers at high setting for 5 cycles (3 seconds of water and 57 seconds of drying). If motor struggles to a complete stop, clean glass, replace blades, and test circuit breaker in panel switch. As a last resort, replace motor. If motor stopped suddenly in original test, check circuit breaker first.

No Intermittent Wiper (Other Functions Okay) — If blades stop and start erratically, test circuit breaker, wiper switch continuity and continuity of wiring between switch, governor, wiper motor and ground. If operation is intermittent on low speed only, check for loose connections at governor.

Windshield Washer Does Not Operate — Check fluid level, condition of hoses, and for restrictions (particularly ice or dirt in jet opening). Check fuse in panel and for good connection at plug terminal.

WIPER SWITCH TEST

1) Check wiper switch continuity, using a continuity light (J-21008 or equivalent) or an ohmmeter. Continuity should exist at switch positions indicated in *Fig. 3*.

2) Using an ohmmeter, check variable resistance between No. 4 and 5 terminals of intermittent system if intermittent wipe cycle is not working, but system operates properly on low and high speeds. Turn switch knob counterclockwise as far as possible. Ohmmeter should indicate 5600-8400 ohms. As knob is turned clockwise, resistance should decrease to a minimum of 100-900 ohms.

3) Replace switch if continuity or resistance tests fail. If operation is proper, check wiring.

CIRCUIT BREAKER TEST

Two tests are available for the 7 amp. circuit breaker. Connect wiper switch as shown in *Fig. 3*, and test as follows:

1) Adjust current draw until it equals circuit breaker rating. Leave switch connected for 10 minutes. Current reading on ammeter should remain at rated current. If circuit breaker opens during 10 minute period, replace switch assembly.

2) Adjust current draw until it is twice the circuit breaker rating (14 amps.). Current reading on ammeter should drop to zero within 15 seconds. If it takes longer, replace switch assembly.

INTERMITTENT GOVERNOR TEST

To check governor requires special electronic testing equipment. However, check all other components in event of unsatisfactory intermittent wiper cycle. If all components function properly, install new governor. The 6-inch governor lead plugs into wiper control switch and shorter 4-inch lead plugs into instrument panel switch.

CURRENT DRAW TEST

1) Remove wiper arms and blades and disconnect motor lead. Connect negative lead of ammeter to positive battery post. See *Fig. 3*. Connect other ammeter test lead to blue wire with tracer (low speed) of motor harness. Current draw should be approximately 1 amp., but not more than 3 amps.

2) Connect blue wire terminal (high speed). Current draw should remain about the same, but never over 3 amps.

PARK TEST

1) Disconnect motor from harness connection. Temporarily contact a battery feed to either blue or blue with tracer wire to move wiper arms and blades away from normal park position. Insert jumper wire from white to black wire terminals.

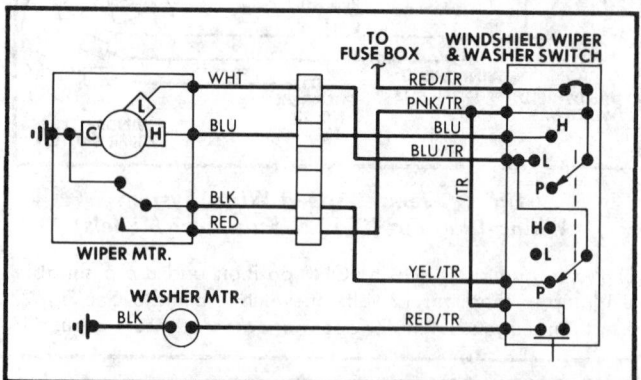

*Fig. 4 Jeep 2-Speed Wiper System Wiring Diagram
(Cherokee, Wagoneer & "J" Models — Standard)*

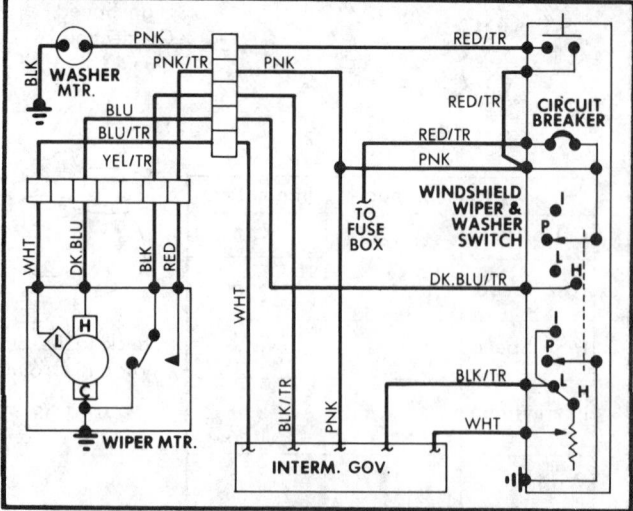

*Fig. 5 Jeep 2-Speed Wiper System Wiring Diagram
(Cherokee, Wagoneer & "J" Models
With Intermittent Governor)*

JEEP (Cont.)

2) Contact a battery feed to red wire terminal of motor harness. Motor should operate until wipers have reached normal park position. If not, replace wiper motor.

REMOVAL & INSTALLATION

WIPER MOTOR

"CJ" & Scrambler Models — Remove necessary components from windshield frame. Remove windshield hold-down knobs and fold windshield down. Remove left access hole cover and disconnect drive link from left wiper pivot. Disconnect wiper motor wire harness from switch. Remove attaching screws and wiper motor. To install, reverse removal procedures.

Cherokee, Wagoneer & "J" Models — Remove motor adapter plate-to-dash panel screws. Disconnect wiper wiring harness at motor. Pull motor and linkage out of opening so that drive link-to-crank stud retaining clip can be removed with screwdriver. Remove motor assembly. To install, reverse removal procedure.

OVERHAUL

WIPER MOTOR
CHEROKEE, WAGONEER & "J" MODELS ONLY

Disassembly — 1) Using care not to damage ceramic magnets, mark position of drive crank with respect to output shaft. Remove drive crank, mounting bracket, and ground strap. Remove gear housing cover and gasket, idler gear and pinion, motor through bolts and motor housing. Remove end play spring, output gear and shaft, switch lever, washer and seal from gear housing.

2) Disassemble brushes, harness and springs from end head (terminal board). Remove end head assembly, parking lever pin, and all old lubricant. Inspect gear housing and all components, replacing parts as necessary. Lubricate all bearing surfaces and gears.

Reassembly — 1) Install switch washer and lever in gear housing with cam rider pointing toward output shaft hole. Install seal and output gear and shaft in gear housing. Be sure switch lever is clear of cam and gear assembly. Place idler gear and

pinion on shaft and insert shaft through switch lever and washer into gear housing. Maintain .001-.007" clearance between push nut and gear.

2) Install end spring, parking lever pin, and attach brush terminals and switch terminals to end head. Attach end head to gear housing. Install springs and brushes in end head. Lightly lubricate armature end shaft and ball. Install armature in gear housing. Plastic thrust button in end play spring should bear against end of armature shaft.

3) Install motor housing over armature. Align motor housing and gear housing marks and install through bolts. Lubricate gear housing cavity generously, and install gasket and cover on gear housing. Attach ground strap and mounting bracket. Install grommets in mounting bracket and secure motor assembly to bracket. Install plain washer and spring washer on output shaft, and position drive crank on output shaft in previously marked position. Tighten nut to 10 ft. lbs.

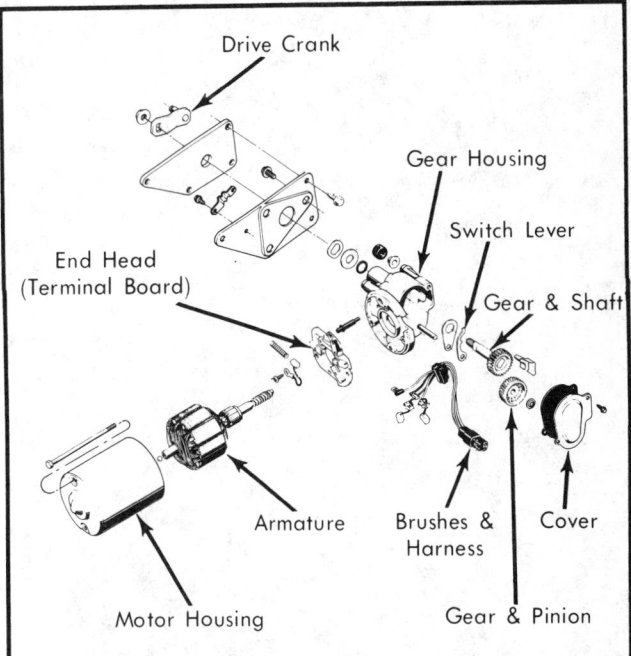

Fig. 6 Exploded View of Wiper Motor Assembly (Cherokee, Wagoneer & "J" Models)

Section 7

ENGINES

Contents

NOTE — ALSO SEE GENERAL INDEX.

IMPORTANT

Because of the great number of model names used by vehicle manufacturers, accurate identification of models is important.
See Model Identification at the front of this publication.

Engine Trouble Shooting

GASOLINE ENGINE TROUBLE SHOOTING

The following Trouble Shooting guide covers all mechanical problems which relate to all engines in general. For specific Trouble Shooting problems relating to Diesel engines, see Diesel Engine Trouble Shooting in this section.

CONDITION & POSSIBLE CAUSE	CONDITION & POSSIBLE CAUSE

Engine Lopes While Idling

- Intake manifold-to-head leaks.
- Blown head gasket.
- Worn timing gears, chain or sprocket.
- Worn camshaft lobes.
- Overheated engine.
- Blocked crankcase vent valve.
- Leaking EGR valve.
- Faulty fuel pump.

Engine Has Low Power

- Leaking fuel pump.
- Sticking valves, weak valve springs, incorrect valve timing or worn camshaft lobes.
- Excessive piston-to-bore clearance.
- Blown head gasket.
- Improper power steering glow control valve operation.
- Clutch slipping on manual transmission.
- Engine overheating.
- Improper pressure regulator valve operation on automatic transmission.
- Improper automatic transmission fluid level.
- Improper operation of diverter valve.
- Vacuum leaks.
- Leaking piston rings.

Faulty High Speed Operation

- Low fuel pump volume.
- Leaking engine valves, or faulty valve springs.
- Incorrect valve timing.
- Intake manifold restricted.
- Worn distributor shaft.

Faulty Acceleration

- Improper fuel pump stroke.
- Incorrect basic ignition timing.
- Inoperative pump discharge check ball or needle.
- Faulty elastomer valve.
- Worn or damaged pump diaphragm or piston.
- Leaking engine valves.

Intake Backfire

- Improper ignition timing.
- Faulty accelerator pump discharge.
- Improper choke operation.
- Defective EGR valve.
- Too lean fuel mixture.
- Initial choke valve clearance too large.

Exhaust Backfire

- Vacuum leak.
- Faulty diverter valve.
- Faulty choke operation.
- Exhaust system leak.

Engine Detonation

- Overadvanced timing or faulty ignition system.
- Spark plugs loose or cracked.
- Fuel lines, fuel filter or fuel pump clogged or faulty.
- EGR valve inoperative.
- PCV system inoperative.
- Vacuum leaks.
- Excessive combustion chamber deposits.
- Leaking, sticking or broken valves.

External Oil Leakage

- Improperly seated fuel pump, or worn gasket.
- Improperly seated or broken push rod cover gasket.
- Improperly seated or broken oil filter gasket.
- Improperly seated or broken oil pan gasket, or bent oil pan gasket surface.
- Improperly seated or broken timing chain cover gasket.
- Improperly seated or worn rear main bearing oil seal.
- Loose oil line plugs.
- Improperly seated oil pan drain plug.
- Obstructed camshaft rear bearing drain hole.
- Oil pressure sending switch leaking.

GASOLINE ENGINE TROUBLE SHOOTING (Cont.)

CONDITION & POSSIBLE CAUSE	CONDITION & POSSIBLE CAUSE

Excessive Oil Consumption

- Intake or exhaust valve "O" ring seal damaged or has excessive looseness.
- Worn valve stems or guides.
- Plugged oil drain back holes.
- Improper PCV valve operation.
- Engine oil level too high.
- Engine oil too thin.
- Valve stem oil deflectors missing or damaged.
- Piston rings improperly installed or incorrect size.
- Piston rings out-of-round, broken or scored.
- Piston ring gaps not staggered.
- Piston ring tension insufficient due to engine overheating.
- Piston ring grooves or oil return slots clogged.
- Piston rings sticking in ring grooves.
- Ring grooves worn excessively.
- Compression rings installed upside down.
- Excessively worn or scored cylinder walls.
- Mismatch of oil ring expander and rail.
- Intake gasket dowels too long.
- Excessive main or connecting rod bearing clearance.

No Oil Pressure

- Low oil level.
- Oil pressure gauge or sending unit broken.
- Oil pump malfunction.
- Oil pressure relief valve sticking.
- Oil passages on pressure side of pump blocked.
- Oil pickup screen or tube blocked.
- Loose oil inlet tube.
- Excessive clearance at main or connecting rod bearing.
- Loose camshaft bearings.
- Internal leakage at oil passages.

Low Oil Pressure

- Low engine oil level, or engine oil too thin.
- Oil pressure relief spring weak or stuck.
- Oil pickup tube and screen blocked, or has air leak.
- Excessive oil pump clearance.
- Excessive main, rod or camshaft bearing clearance.

High Oil Pressure

- Improper grade of oil.
- Oil pressure gauge or sending unit inaccurate.
- Oil pressure relief valve sticking closed.

Noisy Main Bearings

- Inadequate oil supply.
- Excessive main bearing clearance.
- Excessive crankshaft end play.
- Loose flywheel or torque converter.
- Loose or damaged vibration damper.
- Eccentric or out-of-round crankshaft journals.
- Excessive belt tension.

Noisy Connecting Rods

- Inadequate oil supply.
- Excessive bearing clearance or missing bearing.
- Crankshaft connecting rod journal out-of-round.
- Misaligned connecting rod or cap.
- Improperly tightened connecting rod bolts.

Noisy Pistons and Rings

- Excessive piston-to-cylinder wall clearance.
- Cylinder walls excessively tapered or out-of-round.
- Piston ring broken.
- Piston pin loose or seized.
- Connecting rods misaligned.
- Piston ring side clearance excessively loose or tight.
- Excessive carbon build-up on piston.

Noisy Valve Train Components

- Insufficient oil supply.
- Worn or bent push rods.
- Worn rocker arms, or bridged pivots.
- Dirt or chips in hydraulic valve lifters.
- Excessive valve lifter leak down.
- Valve lifter face worn.
- Broken or cocked valve springs.
- Excessive valve stem-to-guide clearance.
- Valve bent.
- Loose rocker arms.
- Excessive valve seat runout.
- Missing valve lock.
- Push rod rubbing or contacting cylinder head.

Engine Trouble Shooting

GASOLINE ENGINE TROUBLE SHOOTING (Cont.)

CONDITION & POSSIBLE CAUSE	CONDITION & POSSIBLE CAUSE
Noisy Valve Train Components (Cont.) • Excessively worn camshaft lobes. • Plugged valve lifter oil feed holes. • Faulty valve lifter check ball. • Rocker arm retaining nut installed up-side down. • Valve lifters incorrectly fitted to bore size. • Faulty valve lifter plunger, or push rod seat. • Improper valve lash. **Burned, Sticking or Broken Valves** • Weak valve springs. • Improper valve lifter clearance. • Improper valve guide clearance, or worn guides. • Out-of-round valve seats, or improper valve seat width. • Deposits or gum formation on valve stems, seats or guides. • Warped valves or faulty valve forgings.	**Burned, Sticking or Broken Valves (Cont.)** • Exhaust back pressure. • Improper spark timing. **Broken Pistons and/or Rings** • Undersize pistons. • Wrong type or size of rings. • Tapered or eccentric cylinder bore. • Improper connecting rod alignment. • Excessively worn ring grooves. • Improperly assembled piston pins. • Insufficient ring gap clearance. • Engine overheating. • Incorrect ignition timing. **Excessive Exhaust Noise** • Leaks at exhaust pipe joints. • Burned or blown out muffler or exhaust pipe. • Exhaust pipe leaking at manifold flange. • Exhaust manifold cracked or broken. • Leak between manifold and cylinder head. • Obstruction in muffler or tail pipe.

DIESEL ENGINE TROUBLE SHOOTING

Diesel engine mechanical diagnosis is the same as that for gasoline engines for such items as noisy lifters, rod bearings, main bearings, valves, rings and pistons. The following trouble shooting guide cover those items which apply only to diesel engines.

CONDITION & POSSIBLE CAUSE	CONDITION & POSSIBLE CAUSE
Engine Does Not Crank • Loose or corroded battery cables, or dead batteries. • Loose starter connections or faulty starter. **Engine Cranks Slowly but Does Not Start** • Loose or corroded battery cables, or batteries do not have a sufficient charge. • Wrong weight engine oil in engine.	**Engine Cranks Normally but Does Not Start** • Glow plugs not functioning. • Glow plug control system not functioning. • Fuel not being injected into cylinders. • No fuel going to injection pump. • Fuel filter blocked. • Fuel tank filter blocked. • Fuel pump not operating. • Fuel return system blocked. • No voltage to fuel solenoid. • Incorrect or contaminated fuel.

DIESEL ENGINE TROUBLE SHOOTING (Cont.)

CONDITION & POSSIBLE CAUSE	CONDITION & POSSIBLE CAUSE
Engine Cranks Normally but Does Not Start (Cont.) • Incorrect injection pump timing. • Low compression. • Injection pump malfunction. **Engine Starts but Will Not Run at Idle** • Incorrect slow idle adjustment. • Fast idle solenoid not functioning. • Fuel return system blocked. • Glow plugs turning off too soon. • Injection pump timing incorrect. • Insufficient fuel going to injection pump. • Incorrect or contaminated fuel. • Low compression. • Injection pump malfunction. • Fuel solenoid closes in "RUN" position. **Engine Starts and Idles Rough Without Abnormal Smoke or Noise** • Incorrect slow idle adjustment. • Injection line fuel leaks. • Fuel return system blocked. • Air in fuel system. • Incorrect or contaminated fuel. • Injector nozzle malfunction. **Engine Starts and Idles Rough Without Abnormal Smoke or Noise, but Clears After Warm-Up** • Injection pump timing incorrect. • Engine has not fully broken in. • Air in fuel system. • Injector nozzle malfunction. **Engine Misfires Above Idle but Idles Correctly** • Blocked fuel filter. • Injection pump timing incorrect. • Incorrect or contaminated fuel. **Engine Will Not Return to Idle** • External linkage binding or adjusted wrong. • Fast idle adjustment incorrect. • Internal injection pump malfunction. **Fuel Leaking on Ground** • Loose or broken fuel line or connection. • Internal injection pump seal leak.	**Knocking Noise from Cylinders** • Injector nozzles sticking open. • Very low nozzle opening pressure. **Noticeable Loss of Engine Power** • Restricted air intake. • EGR valve malfunction. • Restricted or damaged exhaust system. • Blocked fuel tank filter • Blocked fuel filter, or fuel tank vacuum vent in gas cap. • Restricted fuel supply from tank to injection pump. • Restricted fuel return system. • Incorrect or contaminated fuel. • External compression leaks. • Blocked injector nozzles. • Low compression. **Excessive Black Smoke and Loud Engine Noise** • Basic timing incorrect. • EGR valve malfunction. • Injector pump housing pressure not to specifications. • Internal injection pump malfunction. **Engine Overheating** • Cooling system leaks. • Belt slipping or damaged. • Thermostat stuck closed. • Head gasket leaking **Oil Light On at Idle** • Oil cooler, or oil cooler line restricted. • Low oil pump pressure. **Engine Will Not Shut Off** • Injector pump fuel solenoid doesn't return fuel valve to "OFF" position. **VACUUM PUMP DIAGNOSIS** **Excessive Noise** • Loose screws between pump and drive assembly. • Loose tube on pump assembly. • Valves not functioning properly. **Oil Leakage** • Loose end plug. • Bad crimp.

3.7L 6-CYLINDER ENGINE

IDENTIFICATION CODING

ENGINE IDENTIFICATION

Engine Identification number is stamped on block below No. 6 spark plug. First letter indicates model year (A). Next 3 numbers designate engine cubic inch displacement.

Engine Identification	
Application	Code
3.7L (225″) 1-Bbl.	225

SPECIAL ENGINE MARKS

Information identifying undersize and oversize components will be found on various locations on engine. Coding and location is as follows:

- "M" or "R" followed by number indicates main or rod journals .001" undersize. Found on center counterweight.

- "M-10" or "R-10" indicates all main or rod journals are .010" undersize. Found on center counterweight.

"A" — Indicates all cylinder bores .020" oversize. Found on top of front pad on right side of block.

"♦" — Indicates .008" oversize valve lifters. Found on top of front pad on right side of block.

"O/S" — Indicates .005" oversize valve stems and is stamped on the thermostat boss at front of cylinder head.

ENGINE REMOVAL

See Engine Removal at end of ENGINE Section.

CYLINDER HEAD & MANIFOLDS

MANIFOLD ASSEMBLY

Removal — Disconnect all lines, hoses and linkage to air cleaner and carburetor. Remove air cleaner and disconnect exhaust pipe at manifold. Remove carburetor and manifolds as an assembly. Remove three screws securing intake manifold to exhaust manifold and separate.

Installation — 1) Install new gasket between intake and exhaust manifold and install three screws securing manifolds together. DO NOT tighten screws at this time. Position manifold assembly on cylinder head using new gasket.

2) Install steel conical washers with cup side against manifolds. Snug all nuts to approximately 20 INCH Lbs. Tighten bolts holding manifold together to specifications. Tighten inner nut first.

3) Start at center of manifold assembly and work outward, tightening manifold nuts. Reinstall carburetor, linkage, hoses and air cleaner.

CYLINDER HEAD

Removal — 1) Drain cooling system and remove air cleaner. Remove all wiring, hoses, lines and linkage from carburetor, distributor, manifolds and cylinder head.

2) Disconnect exhaust pipe at manifold. Remove rocker cover, rocker arm and shaft assembly. Remove push rods and identify to insure installation in original location. Remove cylinder head bolts, cylinder head and manifolds as an assembly.

Installation — Clean all gasket surfaces and coat new gasket with suitable sealer. Install gasket and cylinder head on block. Install cylinder head bolts and tighten in 2 steps to specifications. See Fig. 1. To complete installation, reverse removal procedure.

NOTE — Do not retighten bolts after engine has been operated when steel head gaskets are used.

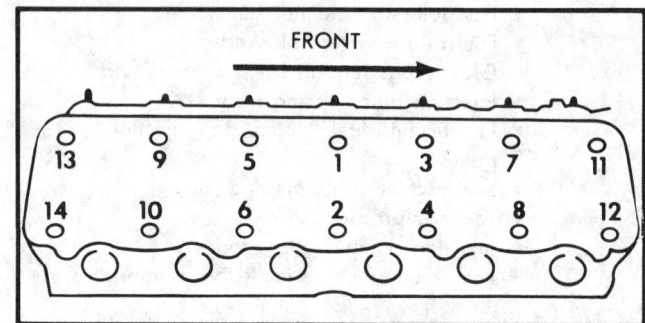

Fig. 1 Cylinder Head Tightening Sequence.

VALVES

VALVE ARRANGEMENT

E-I-E-I-E-I-I-E-I-E-I-E (front to rear).

VALVE GUIDE SERVICING

Wear Check — 1) Remove valve spring and install suitable sleeve tool (C-3973) over valve stem and install valve in cylinder head. Attach dial indicator to cylinder head and position at right angle to valve stem being measured.

2) Total sideplay should not exceed .017". If dial reading is excessive or stems are scuffed or scored, ream guides for installation of valves with oversize stems.

Servicing — Ream guides to next oversize valve stem if necessary. Oversize valves are available in .005", .015" and .030" oversize.

NOTE — Do not attempt to ream guides from standard to .030" oversize in one step. Use step procedure to obtain the .030" oversize.

Fig. 2 Measuring Valve Stem-to-Guide Clearance.

3.7L 6-CYLINDER ENGINE (Cont.)

VALVE STEM OIL SEALS

Cup type seal is used on all valves. Long seal is used on intake valve and short seal is used on exhaust valve. If seals are removed for any reason, new seals should be used upon installation. *See Valve Springs in this Story.*

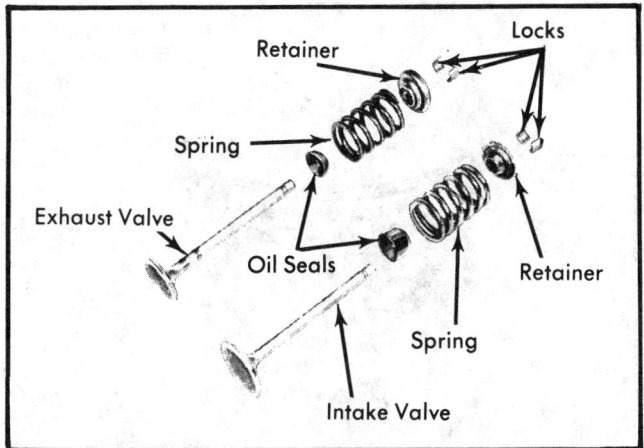

Fig. 3   Intake & Exhaust Valve Assemblies

VALVE SPRINGS

Removal — With cylinder head removed, compress valve springs using valve spring compressor C-3422A (or equivalent). Remove valve retaining locks, spring retainers, springs and cup seals.

NOTE — *Remove burrs from valve stem lock grooves to prevent damage to valve guides if valves are removed.*

Inspection — 1) Valve springs should be tested whenever they are removed from cylinder head. Using valve spring tester C-647 (or equivalent), check springs against specifications. *See Valve Spring Table. See Fig. 4.*

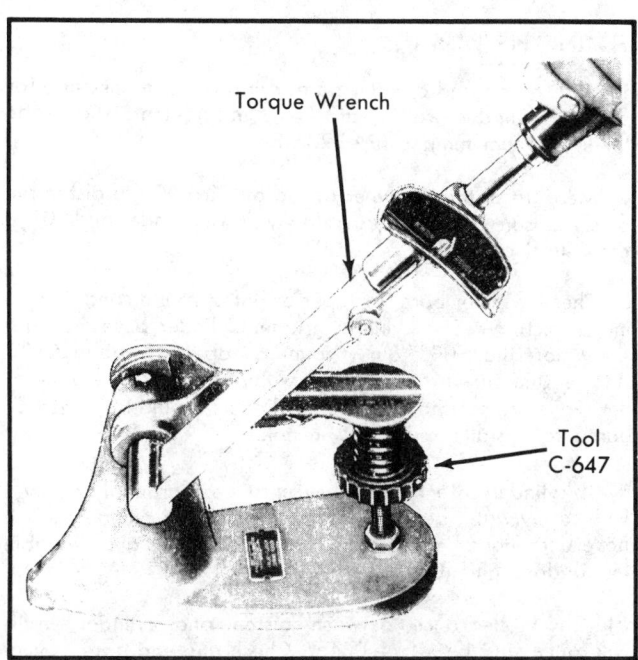

Fig. 4   Testing Valve Spring Tension

2) Replace springs if they do not meet specifications. Inspect each spring for squareness using a steel square and flat surface. Replace spring if more than $\frac{1}{16}$" out-of-square.

Installation — 1) Coat valve stems with engine oil and insert in cylinder head. Install new cup seals, valve springs and retainers.

2) Install springs so closed coils are against cylinder head. Compress valve springs using compression tool and install retaining locks.

VALVE SPRING INSTALLED HEIGHT

1) If valves or seats are reground, measure installed height of springs. Measurement is taken from bottom surface of spring seat in cylinder head to bottom surface of spring retainer.

NOTE — *If spacers are installed, measure from top of spacer.*

2) Installed height should be $1\frac{11}{16}$"-$1\frac{5}{8}$". If valve height is greater than $1\frac{43}{64}$", install $\frac{1}{16}$" spacer at head counterbore to correct spring height.

ROCKER ARM ASSEMBLY

Stamped steel rocker arms are arranged on single rocker arm shaft. Hardened steel spacers are used between pairs of rocker arms. Shaft is supported and attached to seven mounts on cylinder head. *See Fig. 5* for assembly of parts, noting the following:

* The flat end of shaft and oil hole must be installed upward and toward front of engine.
* Install long retainer at center position and long shaft bolt at rear of engine.
* Shaft retainers must seat on rocker shaft and not on extended bushing of rocker arm.

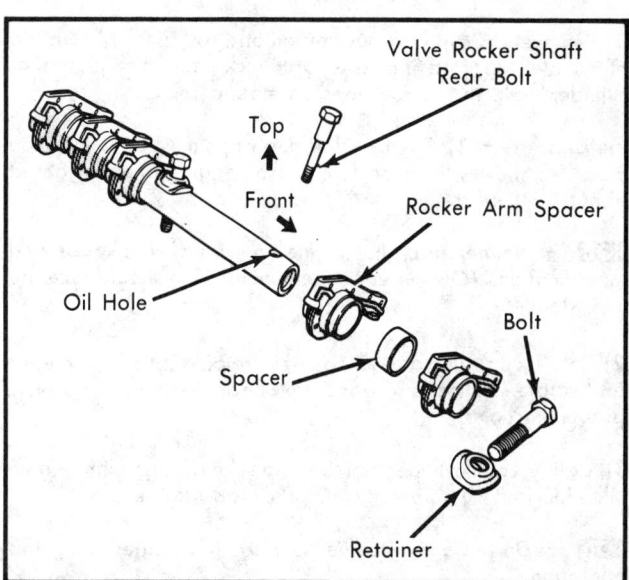

Fig. 5   Rocker Arm and Shaft Assembly

Chrysler Corp. 6 Engines

3.7L 6-CYLINDER ENGINE (Cont.)

HYDRAULIC VALVE LIFTERS

To test, remove cap from plunger and plunger from lifter body. See Fig. 6. Fill lifter body with clean kerosene and install plunger. Unseat check valve with a brass rod to permit complete installation of plunger and replace cap. Place lifter upright in Lifter Testing Tool (C-4343). Test leakdown by compressing tool. If plunger collapses immediately, disassemble, clean and retest. If rapid leakdown still occurs, replace lifter. Use a straightedge to check all lifters for negative crown. If negative crown (dish) is observed, replace lifter.

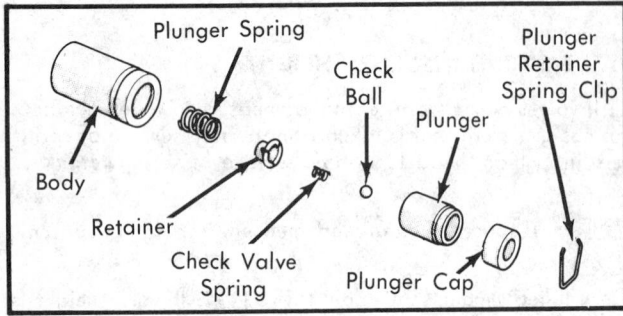

Fig. 6   Exploded View of Hydraulic Lifter Assembly

PISTONS, PINS & RINGS

OIL PAN

See Oil Pan Removal at end of Engine Section.

PISTON & ROD ASSEMBLY

Removal — 1) With cylinder head and oil pan removed, use ridge cutter C-3012 (or equivalent), to remove any ridge or deposits on upper end of cylinder bore.

NOTE — *Piston must be at bottom of stroke and covered with cloth to collect cuttings.*

2) Inspect connecting rods and caps for cylinder identification and mark as necessary. Rotate crankshaft so each connecting rod is centered in cylinder bore for removal.

3) Remove rod cap and push piston and rod assembly out top of cylinder block, taking care not to nick crankshaft journal or cylinder wall. Install rod caps on mating rods.

Installation — 1) Compression ring gaps must be located on piston so they will be on left side of engine and staggered about 60° apart.

NOTE — *Neither gap should line up with oil ring gaps and identification "TOP" on each compression ring should face top of piston.*

2) Rotate oil ring expander so gaps are on right side of engine and rotate steel rails so gaps are opposite (positioned above piston pin holes).

3) Lightly coat cylinder bores, pistons and rings with engine oil, slide ring compressor over piston and tighten.

NOTE — *Do not allow position of rings to change during this operation.*

4) Install each piston and rod assembly, with notch on head of piston head facing front of engine and oil hole in connecting rod toward right side of engine, in its respective bore and guide connecting rod onto crankshaft journal. See Fig. 7.

5) Tap piston head lightly with hammer handle to seat connecting rod and bearing against crankshaft. Install rod cap with bearing, nut and tighten.

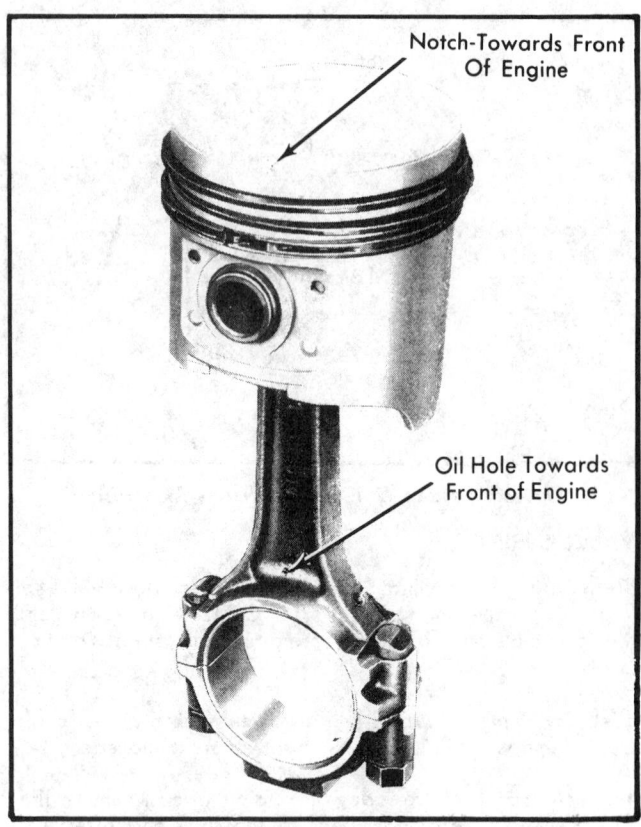

Fig. 7   View Showing Correct Assembly of Rod-to-Piston

FITTING PISTONS

1) With piston and cylinder bores dry and clean, measure for piston-to-cylinder wall clearance. Measurements should be taken at room temperature (70° F).

2) Measure piston diameter at top of skirt, 90° to piston pin axis. Measure cylinder bore halfway down cylinder and 90° to crankshaft center line.

3) Check cylinder bore for taper or out-of-round condition using a micrometer or cylinder gauge. Cylinder bore must not show more than .005" out-of-round or taper more than .010". If taper and out-of-round are not within specifications, or cylinder walls are scuffed or scored, cylinders should be honed or bored for installation of new pistons.

4) If cylinders are honed, they must be thoroughly washed with soapy water before installing pistons. For cylinders which have been honed or rebored, piston assemblies are available in standard and .020" oversize.

5) Check clearance between piston and cylinder walls, clearance must be .0005-.0015". Check ring end gap in cylinder bore with a feeler gauge. Ring must be square in bore and about 2" from bottom of cylinder bore.

3.7L 6-CYLINDER ENGINE (Cont.)

6) Check ring side clearance in ring groove of piston with a feeler gauge. Steel rail service oil ring should be free in groove and all ring grooves in piston must be clean. *See Fig. 8.*

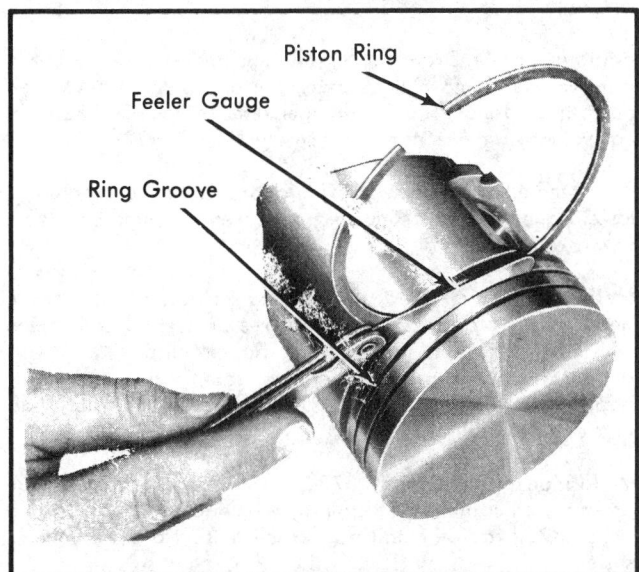

Fig. 8   Measuring Ring Side Clearance

PISTON PINS

Removal — Arrange piston pin removal tool C-3724 (or equivalent), as shown in *Fig. 9.* Spring must be removed from anvil. Install nut loosely on main screw. When pin falls from connecting rod, stop press to prevent damage to bottom of anvil.

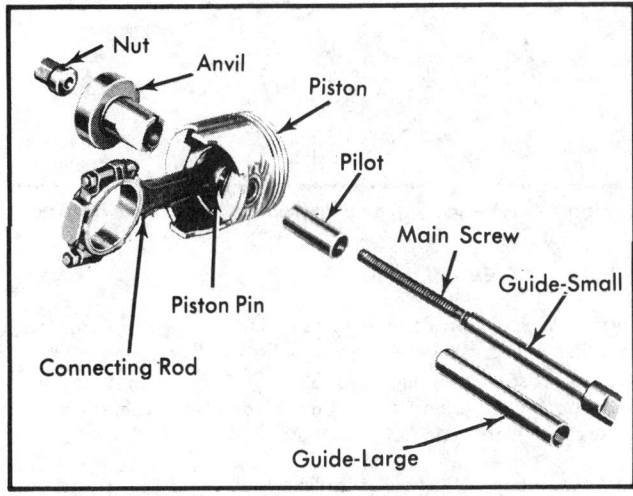

Fig. 9   Removing Piston Pin

Installation — **1)** Measure piston pin fit in the piston. If pin is not a sliding fit in piston at 70° F, piston and piston pin must be replaced as an assembly. Lubricate piston pin holes and connecting rods. Arrange pin removal tool C-3724 parts for installation of piston pin as shown in *Fig. 10*

2) Install spring inside pilot and install spring and pilot in the anvil. Position piston with notch up and oil hole in connecting rod so hole faces front of engine. Press pin into position until pin bottoms against pilot on tool.

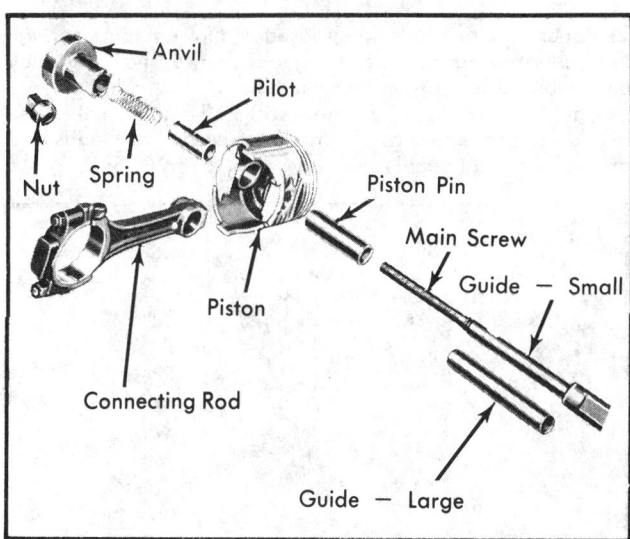

Fig. 10   Installing Piston Pin

Checking Pin Fit — Arrange piston pin tool parts as for removal of pin. Place assembly in vise, attach torque wrench to nut and test torque up to 15 ft. lbs. If connecting rod moves downward on piston pin, replacement is necessary.

CRANKSHAFT & ROD BEARINGS

MAIN & CONNECTING ROD BEARINGS

NOTE — *Use Plastigage method for checking bearing clearances. The following procedures are with oil pan and pump removed.*

Connecting Rod Bearings — **1)** After ensuring rod caps are marked for cylinder identification, remove rod caps. Rotate crankshaft until connecting rod to be checked starts moving toward top of engine. Place strip of Plastigage across full width of lower insert at center of cap. Install bearing cap and tighten to 45 ft. lbs. Remove cap and measure width of Plastigage with INCH scale furnished.

2) New bearings are available in standard, .001", .002", .003", .010" and .012" undersize. Taper or out-of-round on any crankshaft journal should not exceed .001". Always install new bearings in pairs.

NOTE — *Never use a new bearing with an old bearing on same journal.*

3) Install bearings so small formed tang fits into machined groove in connecting rod. Install rod caps and tighten nuts.

Main Bearings — **1)** Use Plastigage method to check main bearing clearances one at a time. This can be accomplished by placing a shim (minimum .010" thick) between bearing shell and bearing cap of bearings adjacent to one being checked. Tighten adjacent bearing caps to 10-15 ft. lbs. Place strip of Plastigage across full width of lower insert, 1/4" off center and away from oil holes. Install bearing cap and tighten to 85 ft. lbs. Remove cap and measure width of Plastigage with INCH scale furnished. New bearings are available in standard, .001", .002", .003", .010" and .012" undersize.

NOTE — *Never use a new bearing with an old bearing on the same journal.*

3.7L 6-CYLINDER ENGINE (Cont.)

2) Upper main bearings are grooved and lower main bearings are plain and are not interchangeable. Lower main bearings one, two and four are interchangeable. Upper main bearings one, two and four are interchangeable. The number 3 upper and lower main bearings are flanged to carry thrust loads and are not interchangeable with any other bearing. See Fig. 11.

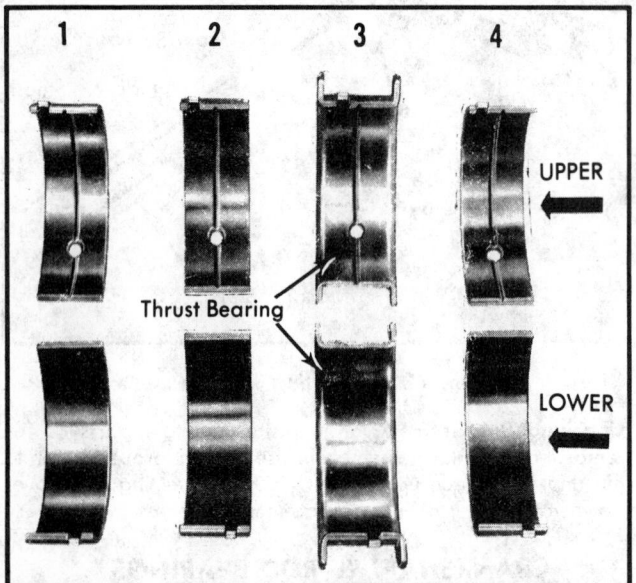

Fig. 11   Main Bearing Identification Showing Location of Thrust Bearing

3) If bearing clearances are not within limits, remove bearing cap and insert pin tool C-3059 in the oil hole of crankshaft. Rotate crankshaft clockwise to remove upper bearing. To install new bearing, slightly chamfer sharp edges from plain side and start bearing in place. Insert tool and slowly rotate crankshaft counterclockwise, sliding bearing in place. Install main bearing cap with new bearing installed and tighten.

4) Check crankshaft end play and if not within specifications, change number three main bearing. This bearing carries thrust load.

REAR MAIN BEARING OIL SEAL

New split type rubber service seals may be installed without removing the crankshaft. New type seals must be installed as a pair and cannot be used or combined with original rope type seals.

Removal — With oil pan removed, remove rear seal retainer and rear main bearing cap. Remove lower seal by pushing end with a small screwdriver. Remove upper seal by pressing carefully on end with a small screwdriver, or turning seal removal tool (C-4148) into end of seal and turning out, being careful not to damage crankshaft.

Installation — 1) Oil upper seal lightly with engine oil. Hold seal (with paint stripe to rear) tightly against crankshaft with thumb and rotate crankshaft while sliding seal into groove.

CAUTION — Sharp edge of groove in block may shave or nick the back of seal. Care must be exercised not to damage seal lip.

2) Install lower half of seal into lower seal retainer with paint stripe to rear. Install main bearing cap and tighten. Install 2 side seals into grooves in seal retainer.

NOTE — Do not use sealer or cement on seal ends or lip.

CAMSHAFT

ENGINE FRONT COVER

Removal — 1) Drain cooling system and remove radiator from vehicle. Remove drive belts, fan and pulley from water pump hub. Using vibration damper removal tool C-3732A (or equivalent), remove damper. See Fig. 12.

2) Loosen oil pan bolts to provide clearance between pan and lower flange of cover. Remove front cover attaching bolts and cover.

Installation — 1) Check that mating surfaces of front cover and cylinder block are clean and free of burrs. Install cover with new gasket and tighten bolts. Tighten oil pan bolts with gaskets in place. Lubricate front cover seal lip with Lubriplate, position vibration damper hub slot key in crankshaft and slide hub onto crankshaft.

2) Position installing tool C-3732A and press vibration damper assembly on crankshaft. Install drive belt pulley, fan and drive belts. Install radiator and adjust belt tension and fill cooling system.

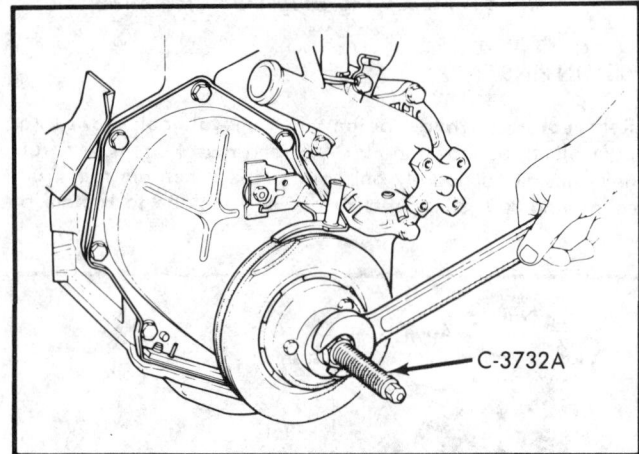

Fig. 12   Removing and Installing Vibration Damper

FRONT COVER OIL SEAL

Removal — Drain cooling system and remove radiator and fan. Remove power steering crankshaft pulley. Remove vibration damper using puller C-3732A. See Fig. 12. Pry seal out from behind lip, being careful not to damage crankshaft seal surface of front cover.

Installation — Use seal installing tool C-4351 to press seal into front cover. Seal is properly installed when seal case is tight against face of front cover. To complete installation, reverse removal procedure.

TIMING CHAIN

Checking For Stretch — 1) Position scale next to timing chain, to measure any movement of the chain. Place torque wrench with socket over camshaft sprocket bolt and apply torque in direction of crankshaft rotation to remove slack. See Fig. 13.

NOTE — Do not permit the crankshaft to move.

3.7L 6-CYLINDER ENGINE (Cont.)

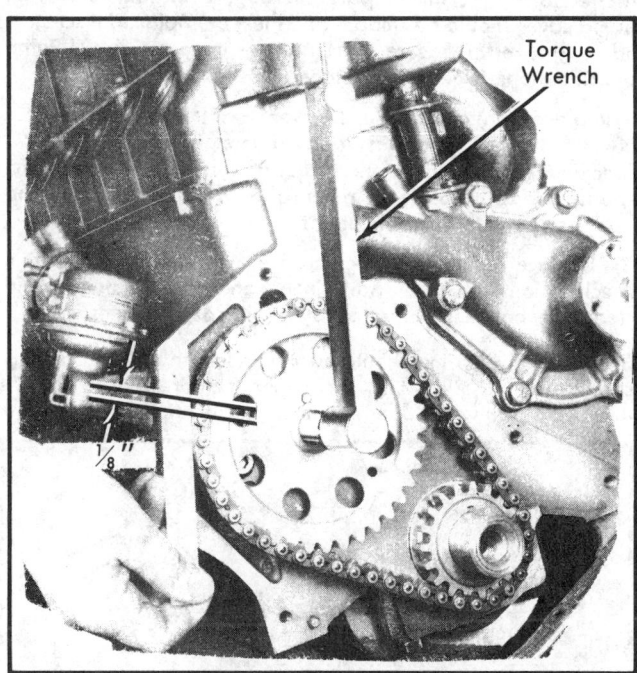

Fig. 13   Measuring Timing Chain Stretch

2) Torque should be 30 ft. lbs. with cylinder head installed and 15 ft. lbs. with head removed. Apply same torque in reverse direction and measure amount of chain movement. If movement exceeds $\frac{1}{8}$", replace timing chain. See Fig. 13.

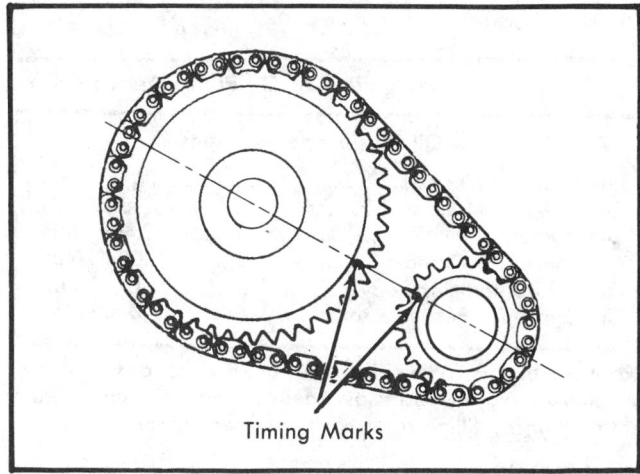

Fig. 14   Timing Chain Sprocket Alignment

Removal & Installation — Remove camshaft sprocket attaching bolt and remove timing chain with camshaft sprocket. Turn crankshaft to line up centerline of camshaft and crankshaft with timing mark on crankshaft sprocket. See Fig. 14. Install camshaft sprocket and timing marks aligned. Tighten camshaft sprocket bolt.

CAMSHAFT

Removal — With engine removed from vehicle, remove cylinder head and tappets. Remove fuel pump, distributor and oil pump. Remove front cover and timing chain. Install long bolt into front of camshaft and carefully remove camshaft.

CAUTION — Take care not to damage bearings with cam lobes.

Installation — 1) Lubricate camshaft lobes and bearing journals and insert camshaft into cylinder block. Check all tappets with a straight edge for crown. If any negative crown (dishing) is observed, tappet must be replaced. Install timing chain and sprockets, front cover, fuel pump and oil pump. Install tappets and cylinder head.

2) Install distributor, timing the engine as follows: Rotate crankshaft until mark on inner edge of crankshaft pulley is in line with the TDC mark on front cover. No. 1 piston should be at top dead center of compression stroke (both valves closed). With distributor "O" rings in position, hold distributor over mounting pad and turn rotor to point forward. Install distributor so that when fully seated on engine, the gear has spiraled to bring rotor to 5 o'clock position. Turn distributor so rotor is positioned directly under No.1 tower of distributor cap. Install and tighten distributor hold-down bolt.

CAMSHAFT BEARINGS

Removal — With camshaft removed, drive out rear cam bearing welch plug. Install proper size adapters and horseshoe washers of tool C-3132A, at back of each bearing and drive out bearing shells.

Installation — 1) Using camshaft bearing installer tool C-3132A, slide bearing over adapter, install horseshoe lock and drive bearing into place.

NOTE — Camshaft bearing oil hole must be in exact alignment with drilled oil passage of main oil bearing.

2) Insert remaining bearings in similar manner. No. 1 bearing must be installed $\frac{3}{32}$" inward from front face of block. Apply sealing compound such as Loctite Stud and Bearing Mount to new welch plug at rear of camshaft. Be sure plug does not leak.

ENGINE OILING

Crankcase Capacity — On all models, capacity is 5 quarts. Add one quart when changing filter.

Oil Filter — Replace at first oil change and every other change thereafter.

Normal Oil Pressure — 30-70 psi at 2000 RPM.

Pressure Regulator Valve — In oil pump body. Not adjustable.

ENGINE OILING SYSTEM

1) Rotor type oil pump mounted externally on right side of crankcase. Oil pump assembly consists of oil pump, oil filter and oil pressure regulator. Pump draws oil from pan through fixed strainer and intake pipe screwed into crankcase wall at pump mounting pad. See Fig. 15.

2) Pump delivers oil directly into main oil gallery extending along right side of crankcase.

Chrysler Corp. 6 Engines

3.7L 6-CYLINDER ENGINE (Cont.)

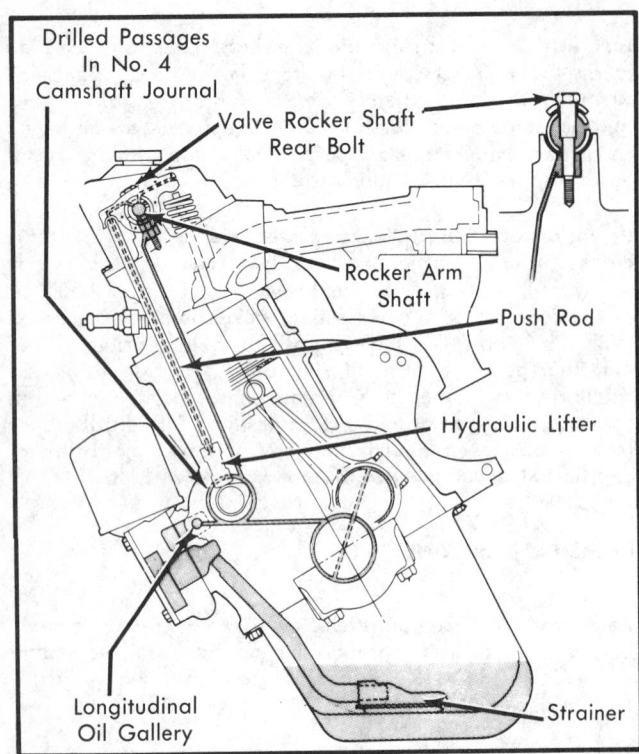

Fig. 15 Engine Oiling System

Valve Mechanism — Oil is continuously applied from circular groove in number 4 camshaft journal through passages to valve rocker shaft and into valve rockers. Full flow through push rods reaches valve lifters, and reduced metered flow reaches valve tips.

Crankshaft Bearings — All main bearings are lubricated as shown in illustration. Connecting rod bearings are lubricated by holes drilled in the crankshaft between main and connecting rod journals.

OIL PUMP

Disassembly — Remove pump cover and seal ring. Press off drive gear while supporting gear to eliminate load on aluminum body of pump. Remove outer rotor and inner rotor with shaft. Remove oil pressure relief valve plug, spring and valve. *See Fig. 16.*

Inspection — Clean all parts thoroughly. Mating face of oil pump cover should be smooth and must be replaced if scratched or grooved. Measure all clearances indicated in Oil Pump Specifications table and replace parts as follows:

1) Replace front cover if pump cover wear is excessive. Replace outer rotor if thickness and diameter are not within specifications. Replace inner rotor if thickness is not within specifications. Replace oil pump body if outer rotor-to-pump body is not within specifications.

2) Replace pump body if clearance over rotors is not within specifications. Replace both inner and outer rotors if tip clearance between rotors is not within specifications.

3) Relief valve spring should have free length of $2\frac{1}{4}$". Spring should test to 22.3-23.3 lbs. when compressed to $1\frac{11}{32}$". Replace spring which does not meet specifications.

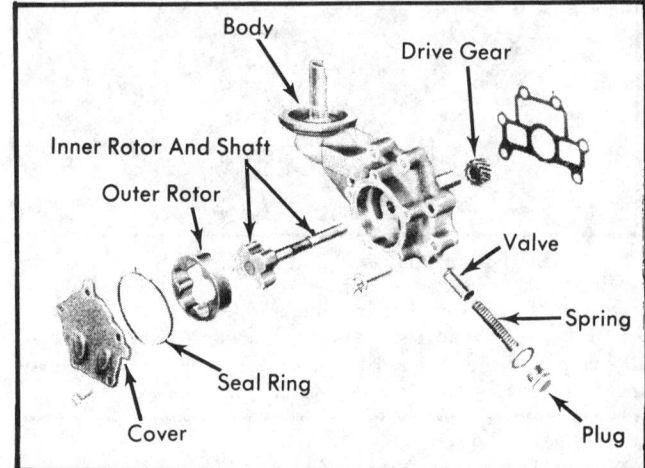

Fig. 16 Exploded View of Oil Pump Assembly

Oil Pump Specifications

Pump Cover Wear	.0015" Max.
Inner and Outer Rotor Thickness	.825" Min.
Outer Rotor Diameter	2.469" Min.
Clearance Over Rotors	.004" Max.
Outer Rotor-to-Pump Body	.014" Max.
Tip Clearance Between Rotors	.010" Max.

Reassembly — Assemble pump in reverse order of disassembly using new parts as required. Prime oil pump before installation by filling rotor cavity with engine oil.

ENGINE SPECIFICATIONS

GENERAL SPECIFICATIONS

Year	Displ. Cu. Ins.	Carburetor	HP at RPM	Torque (Ft. Lbs. at RPM)	Compr. Ratio	Bore	Stroke
1981	225"	1-Bbl.	.....	.....	8.4:1	3.40"	4.125"

VALVES

Engine & Valve	Head Diam.	Face Angle	Seat Angle	Seat Width	Stem Diameter	Stem Clearance	Valve Lift
3.7L Int.	1.615-1.625"	45°	45°	.0625-.0938"	.372-.373"	.001-.003"	.378"
Exh.	1.355-1.365"	43°	45°	.0156-.0625"	.371-.372"	.002-.004"	.378"

3.7L 6-CYLINDER ENGINE (Cont.)

ENGINE SPECIFICATIONS (Cont.)

PISTONS, PINS, RINGS						
	PISTONS	PINS		RINGS		
Engine	Clearance	Piston Fit	Rod Fit	Rings	End Gap	Side Clearance
3.7L	.0005-.0015″	.00035-.00085″	.0007-.0017″	1 & 2 3	.010-.020″ .015-.055″	.0015-.003″ .0002-.005″

CRANKSHAFT MAIN & CONNECTING ROD BEARINGS							
	MAIN BEARINGS				CONNECTING ROD BEARINGS		
Engine	Journal Diam.	Clearance	Thrust Bearing	Crankshaft End Play	Journal Diam.	Clearance	Side Play
3.7L	2.7495-2.7505″	.0010-.0025″	No. 3	.0035-.0095″	2.1870″	.0010-.0022″	.007-.013″

VALVE SPRINGS			
	Free Length	PRESSURE (LBS.)	
Engine		Valve Closed	Valve Open
3.7L	1.92″	49-57@1¹¹⁄₁₆″	137-150@1⁵⁄₁₆″

CAMSHAFT			
Engine	Journal Diam.	Clearance	Lobe Lift
3.7L		.001-.003″	.....
No.1	1.998-1.999″		
No.2	1.982-1.983″		
No.3	1.967-1.968″		
No.4	1.951-1.952″		

TIGHTENING SPECIFICATIONS

Application	Ft. Lbs.
Camshaft Lock Bolt	50
Connecting Rod Cap Nuts	45
Cylinder Head Bolts	①70
Exhaust Manifold Nuts	10
Front Cover Bolts	17
Fuel Pump Bolts	30
Intake-to-Exh. Manifold Bolts	②20
Main Beaing Cap Bolts	85
Manifold-to-Cylinder Head Bolts	10
Oil Pump Attaching Bolts	17
Oil Pump Cover Bolts	8
Rear Main Bearing Seal Retainer	30
Rocker Arm Shaft Bolts	25
Water Pump Bolts	30
Rocker Arm Cover Bolts	③7
Oil Pan Bolts	17

① – Tighten in 2 steps; First to 35 ft. lbs., then to 70 ft. lbs. *See Fig. 1.*

② – Tighten Intake-to-Exh. Manifold Stud to 30 Ft. Lbs.

③ – Tighten within 10 minutes of application of RTV sealer.

Chrysler Corp. V8 Engines

5.2L & 5.9L V8 ENGINES

IDENTIFICATION CODING

ENGINE IDENTIFICATION

Engine identification number is stamped on left front of block below cylinder head. First two digits are year and manufacturing plant code. Next three digits are cubic inch displacement. Four following numbers are build date and the last four digits are engine sequence numbers.

Engine Code	
Engine	**Code**
5.2L (318")	318
5.9L (360")	360

SPECIAL ENGINE MARKS

Information identifying special engine marks is stamped on the cylinder block after the serial number and is decoded as follows:

"M" or "R" — Followed by number, indicates which main or rod bearing journal is .001" undersize. This mark will be stamped on No. 8 crankshaft counterweight on 5.2L engines and on No. 3 counterweight on 5.9L engines.

"MX" or "RX" — Indicates **ALL** main or rod bearing journals .010" undersized. Marked on counterweight.

"A" — Indicates .020" oversize cylinder bores.

"◆" — Indicates .008" oversize lifters.

"X" — Indicates .005" oversize valve stems.

ENGINE REMOVAL

See Engine Removal at end of Engine Section.

CYLINDER HEAD & MANIFOLDS

INTAKE MANIFOLD

Removal — Remove air cleaner and disconnect fuel line. Disconnect accelerator linkage, heater hose, by-pass hose and radiator hose. Disconnect coil wires and vacuum hose between carburetor and distributor. Remove intake manifold, coil and carburetor as an assembly.

Installation — 1) Place a drop of suitable sealer into each corner between the cylinder head gasket tabs. Coat intake manifold side gaskets with sealer (5.2L only).

NOTE — On 5.9L engines, DO NOT use sealer on side composition gaskets.

2) Position intake manifold on engine. Inspect seals for correct positioning and install attaching bolts finger tight. Tighten caps one through 12 to 25 ft. lbs. in sequence shown in *Fig. 1.* Then retighten cap screws 1 through 4 to 40 ft. lbs. and follow by retightening the remaining cap screws to 45 ft. lbs. in sequence.

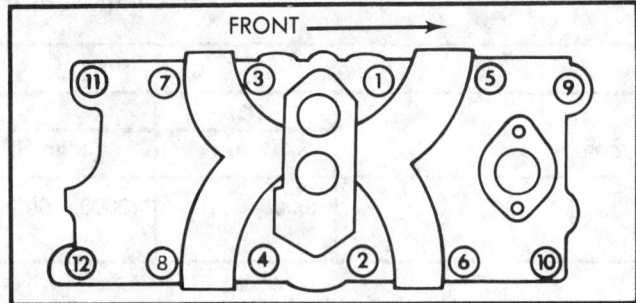

Fig. 1   Intake Manifold Tightening Sequence

CYLINDER HEAD

Removal — 1) Drain cooling system and disconnect battery ground cable. Remove alternator, air cleaner, distributor wires and cap. Disconnect fuel line, accelerator linkage, vacuum control hose between carburetor and distributor, coil wires, and temperature sending unit wire. Disconnect heater hoses, by-pass hose and radiator hose.

2) Remove closed ventilation system, evaporation control system and rocker arm covers. Remove water by-pass tube between intake manifold and water pump (if equipped). Remove intake manifold, coil and carburetor as an assembly. Remove exhaust manifolds from cylinder heads.

3) Remove rocker arm shaft assemblies, then pull push rods from cylinder heads after identifying location for reinstallation in original positions. Remove attaching bolts and cylinder heads from engine.

Installation — Clean all gasket surfaces of cylinder block and head. Coat new gasket with suitable sealer. Install gasket and cylinder head on block. Apply sealer to cylinder head bolts, install bolts and tighten to specifications in 2 steps. Use tightening sequence shown in *Fig. 2.*

Tightening Specifications		
Application	**Step 1 (Ft. Lbs.)**	**Step 2 (Ft. Lbs.)**
All Models	50	 95

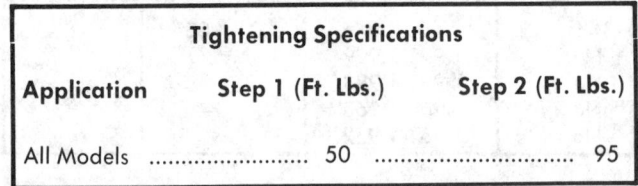

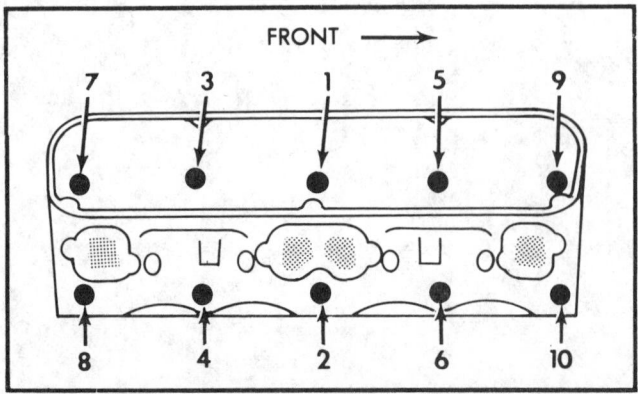

Fig. 2   Cylinder Head Tightening Sequence

5.2L & 5.9L V8 ENGINES (Cont.)

VALVES

VALVE ARRANGEMENT

E-I-I-E-E-I-I-E (Both banks, front to rear).

VALVE GUIDE SERVICING

Wear Check — Remove valve springs and install a locking sleeve over valve stem and install valve in cylinder head. Attach a dial indicator to cylinder head and position indicator at right angle to valve stem being measured. Total sideplay should not exceed .017". If dial indicator reading is excessive or stems are scuffed or scored, ream guides to correct size for installation of valves with oversize stems.

Servicing — Ream guides to next oversize valve stem if necessary. Oversize valve stems are available in .005", .015" and .030" oversize.

NOTE — Do not attempt to ream guides from standard diameter to .030" oversize in one step. Use step procedure to obtain .030".

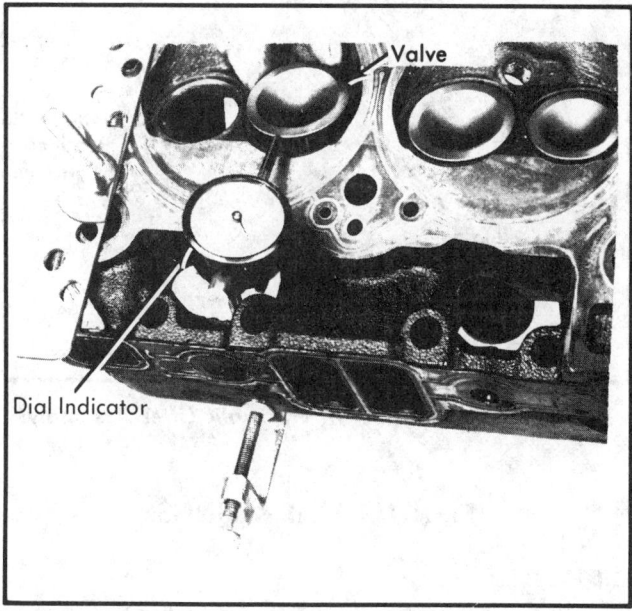

Fig. 3 Measuring Valve Stem to Guide Clearance

VALVE STEM OIL SEALS

Cup type seal is used on all valves. If seals are removed for any reason, new seals must be used upon assembly.

VALVE SPRINGS

Removal — With the cylinder head removed, compress valve springs using valve spring compressor. Remove valve retaining locks, valve spring retainers, valve rotators (if equipped), valve springs and valve stem cup seals. Before removing valves, remove any burrs from valve stem lock grooves to prevent damage to the valve guides. Identify valves to insure installation in original location. See Fig. 4.

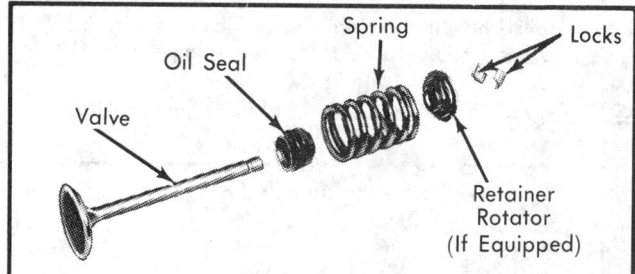

Fig. 4 Exploded View of Valve Assembly

Inspection — Whenever valve springs have been removed, they must be tested. Using a suitable tester, valve springs must be within specifications. Replace springs which do not meet specifications. Inspect each valve spring for squareness using a steel square and surface plate. If spring is more than 5/64" out-of-square, a new spring must be installed.

Installation — 1) Coat valve stems with lubricant and position in cylinder head. If valve or seats have been reground, check valve stem height using gauge C-3968. If valve is too long, grind material off valve stem tip until length is within limits. See Fig. 5.

NOTE — If engine is equipped with rotators, do not grind valve stems.

2) Install new oil seals on all valves, reinstall valve springs and retainers. Use spring compressor to compress springs, then install valve locks.

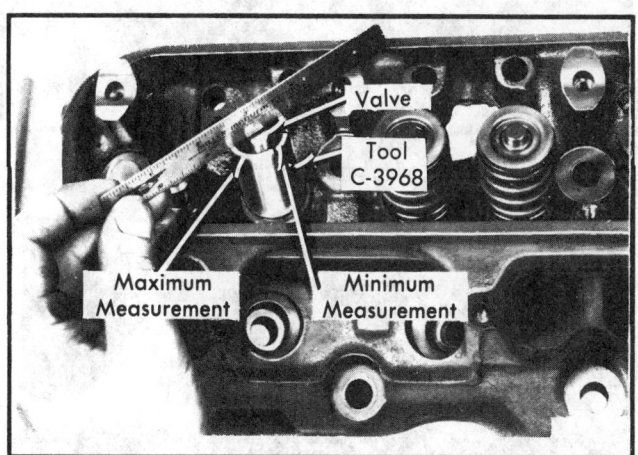

Fig. 5 Measuring Valve Stem Length

VALVE SPRING INSTALLED HEIGHT

1) If valves and/or seats are reground, measure installed height of springs. Measurement is taken from bottom of spring seat in cylinder head to bottom surface of spring retainer.

NOTE — If spacers are installed, measure from top of spacer.

5.2L & 5.9L V8 ENGINES (Cont.)

2) If installed height is not within specifications, install a 1/16" spacer at head counterbore to correct spring height.

`CAUTION` — *Do not shim to a height less than specification.*

Valve Spring Installed Height	
Application	**Height**
Without Rotators	1⅝-1¹¹⁄₁₆"
With Rotators	1²⁹⁄₆₄-1³³⁄₆₄"

ROCKER ARM ASSEMBLY

1) Rocker arms are stamped steel type. Arms are mounted on shaft attached to cylinder head at five support brackets which are cast into cylinder head. Rocker arms have right and left positions. *See Fig. 6.* If rocker arm assemblies were disassembled, reassemble with rocker arms in correct position on shaft. *See Fig. 7.*

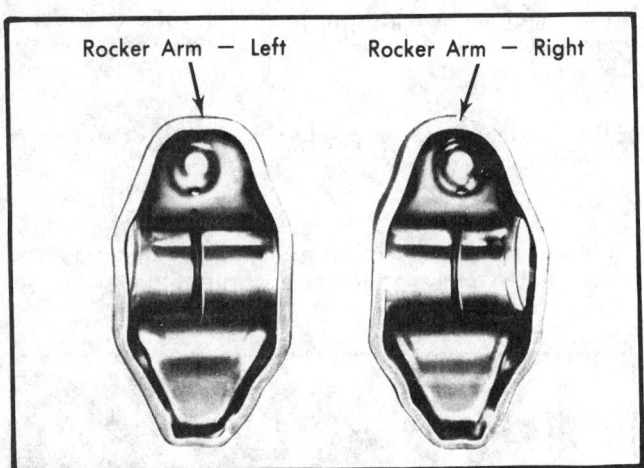

Fig. 6   *Rocker Arm Identification*

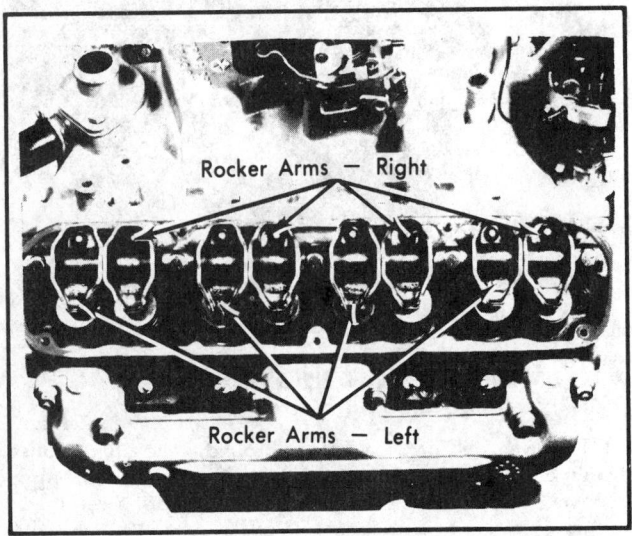

Fig. 7   *Rocker Arm Location on Rocker Arm Shaft*

2) Install rocker arms and shaft to engine while noting the following: Notch on end of rocker arm shaft must point to centerline of engine and toward engine front on left hand bank, or to rear of engine on right hand bank. Long, stamped retainers must be in number two and four positions.

HYDRAULIC VALVE LIFTER ASSEMBLY

`NOTE` — *Lifters are serviced as complete assemblies only. Parts are not interchangeable between lifters. If any component of lifter is worn or damaged, complete lifter must be replaced.*

To test, remove cap from plunger and plunger from lifter body, *See Fig. 8.* Fill lifter body with clean kerosene and install plunger and cap. Place lifter upright in Lifter Testing Tool (C-4343), and check leak down. If lifter collapses immediately, disassemble, clean and retest. If rapid leak down still occurs, replace lifters. Use straightedge to check all lifters for a negative crown. If a negative crown is observed, lifter must be replaced.

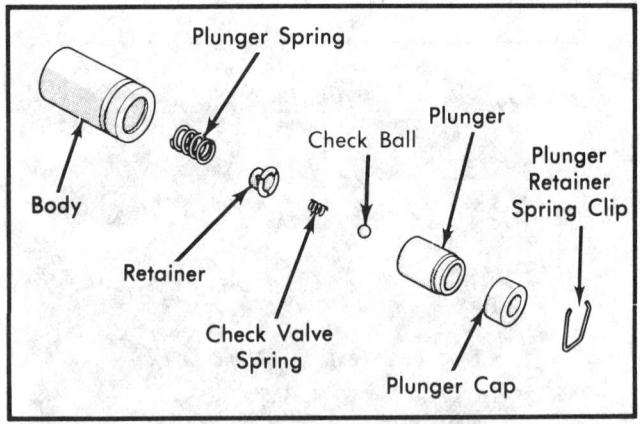

Fig. 8   *Exploded View of Hydraulic Lifter Assembly*

PISTONS, PINS & RINGS

OIL PAN

See Oil Pan Removal at end of Engine Section.

PISTON & ROD ASSEMBLY

`NOTE` — *Following procedures are with cylinder head and oil pan removed.*

Removal — 1) Remove ridge at top of cylinder bores using suitable tool before removing pistons from block.

`NOTE` — *Keep tops of pistons covered during this procedure.*

2) Rotate crankshaft and inspect connecting rods and rod caps for cylinder identification. Identify them if necessary. Remove rod cap and push each piston and rod assembly out top of cylinder bore being careful not to nick crankshaft journals. Install rod caps on mating rods.

5.2L & 5.9L V8 ENGINES (Cont.)

Installation — 1) Before installing piston and connecting rod assemblies into cylinder block, compression ring gaps must be staggered so neither is in line with oil ring rail gaps and "TOP" must be facing top of piston. Oil ring expander ends should be positioned under the notch on piston. Oil ring rail gaps should be facing middle of engine upon installation and spread 3" apart. See *Fig. 9*.

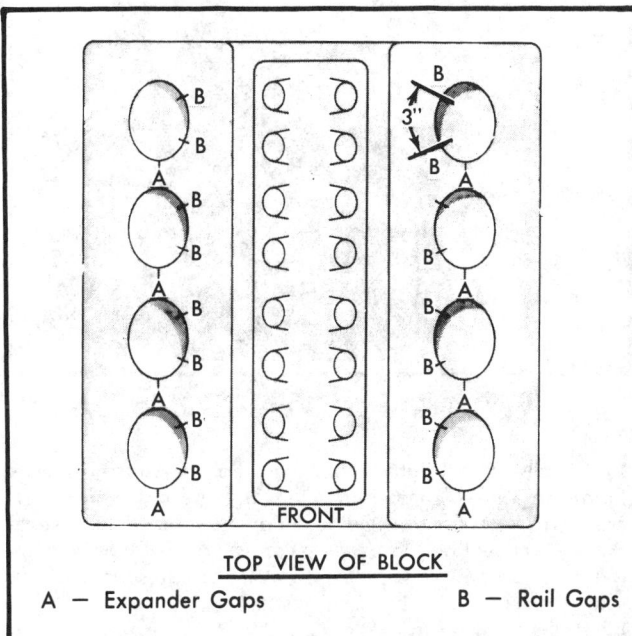

Fig. 9   Positioning Oil Rings for Installation

2) Immerse piston head and rings in clean engine oil and slide suitable ring compressor over piston and tighten.

NOTE — *Do not allow position of rings to change during ring compressor installation and tightening.*

3) Install connecting rod bolt protectors on rod bolts. The long protector should be installed on the numbered side of the connecting rod.

4) Rotate crankshaft so connecting rod journal is in center of cylinder bore. Insert rod and piston assembly into cylinder bore and guide rod over the crankshaft journal, taking care not to nick the journal.

NOTE — *Notch on top of piston must face front of engine and larger chamfer of connecting rod bore must be installed toward crankshaft journal fillet.*

5) Tap piston into cylinder bore using wooden handle of a hammer and guide connecting rod into place on crankshaft journal. Install rod cap and tighten. Repeat procedure for each remaining piston assembly.

FITTING PISTONS

Pistons should be measured 90° to piston pin axis at top of skirt. Measure cylinder bore halfway down the bore 90° to crankshaft center line. Pistons and cylinder bores should be measured at normal room temperature, 70°F.

PISTON PINS

Removal — Use suitable tool for piston pin removal as follows: Install pilot on main screw and install screw through piston pin. See *Fig. 10*. Install anvil (with spring removed) over threaded end of main screw with small end of anvil against piston boss. Install nut loosely on main screw and place assembly on a press. Press piston pin out off connecting rod. Remove tool from piston.

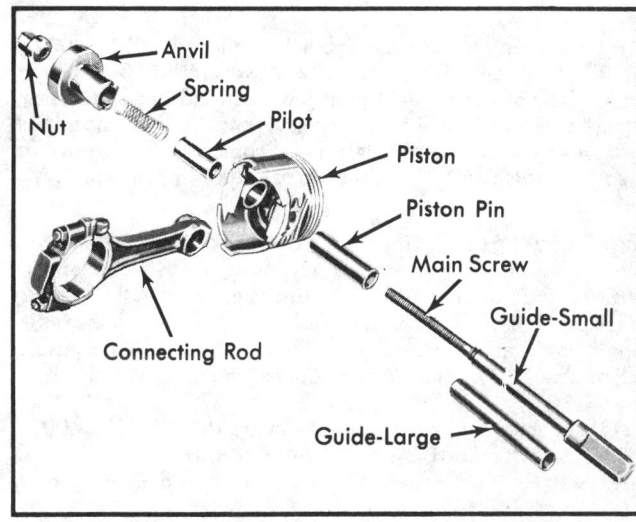

Fig. 10   Exploded View of Piston Pin Removal & Installation Tool

Installation — 1) Lubricate piston pin holes in piston and connecting rod and use suitable tool to install pin. Install tool spring inside pilot and install spring and pilot in the anvil. Install piston pin over main screw.

2) Place piston (with notch up) and connecting rod over pilot so pilot extends through piston pin holes. Assemble rods to pistons of the right cylinder bank (2,4,6 and 8) with indent on piston head opposite to larger chamfer on large bore end of connecting rod. Assemble rods to pistons of the left cylinder bank (1,3,5 and 7) with indent on piston head on the same side as the large chamfer on large bore end of connecting rod.

3) Install main screw and piston pin in piston and install nut on main screw to hold assembly together. Place assembly in a vise. Press piston pin in until piston pin bottoms on the pilot.

Checking Pin Fit — Assemble suitable tool in same manner as for piston pin removal and place assembly in a vise. Attach a torque wrench to nut and test torque to 15 ft. lbs. If connecting rod moves downward on piston pin, reject connecting rod and piston pin combination. Install a new connecting rod and recheck. If connecting rod does not move under 15 ft. lbs. torque, piston pin fit is satisfactory.

CRANKSHAFT & ROD BEARINGS

MAIN & CONNECTING ROD BEARINGS

NOTE — *Plastigage method is used for checking bearing clearances. The following procedures are with oil pan and oil pump removed.*

5.2L & 5.9L V8 ENGINES (Cont.)

Connecting Rod Bearings — 1) After ensuring rod caps are marked for cylinder identification, remove rod caps. Turn crankshaft until connecting rod to be checked starts moving toward the top of the engine. Place Plastigage across width of bearing shell in cap approximately ¼″ off center and away from oil holes. Tighten bearing cap. Remove bearing cap and compare width of flattened Plastigage with inch scale on package. Difference in readings between the ends indicates amount of taper present. Compare readings with specifications.

2) New bearings are available in standard, .001″, .002″, .003″, .010″ and .012″ undersize. Always install bearings in pairs. Do not use a new bearing with an old bearing. Install connecting rod bearings so formed tang fits into machined groove in connecting rod. Install rod caps, with "V" groove of bearing matching "V" groove of cap, and tighten nuts.

Main Bearings — 1) The total clearance of the main bearings can only be determined by removing the weight of the crankshaft. Place a .010″ cardboard shim between the bearing shell and the bearing cap of the bearings adjacent to the bearing being checked. Tighten caps to 10-15 ft. lbs., then measure clearance as explained under Connecting Rod Bearings.

2) New bearings are available in standard, .001″, .002″, .003″, .010″ and .012″ undersize. A new .001″ bearing may be used in combination with a new standard bearing or a .002″ with a .001″.

NOTE — *Always use smaller diameter bearing as upper bearing on journal.*

3) If bearing clearances are not within limits, remove bearing cap, insert suitable tool (C-3509) in oil hole journal and rotate crankshaft clockwise to remove upper bearing. To install new upper bearing, slightly chamfer sharp edges from plain side and start bearing in place. Insert tool and slowly rotate crankshaft counterclockwise, sliding bearing in place. Install main bearing cap with new bearing installed and tighten.

NOTE — *Upper main bearings are grooved and lower main bearings are plain. Upper and lower are not interchangeable.*

4) Check crankshaft end play and if not within specifications, change number 3 main bearing. This bearing carries thrust load.

REAR MAIN BEARING OIL SEAL

New split rubber type seals may be used for replacement without removing crankshaft. New type must be installed as paired upper and lower seals and cannot be used or combined with old type rope seals.

Removal W/Crankshaft Installed — With oil pan removed, remove rear seal retainer and rear main bearing cap. Remove upper seal by turning suitable tool (C-4148) into end of seal and pulling seal out with tool (do not mar crankshaft). Remove lower seal by prying carefully from the side with small screwdriver. See Fig. 11.

Installation — 1) On 5.2L engines, insert cap seals into slots in bearing cap. Seal with yellow paint goes in right side of cap, with cap in engine position. Make sure seals are installed with narrow sealing edges up. Also make sure that edge of cap

seals line up exactly with shoulder in bearing cap or seals will leak. Install seal edge toward inside of shoulder and pull outward on small end of seal until edges line up with shoulder.

Fig. 11   Removing Upper Rear Main Oil Seal

2) On all models, lightly oil sealing lips of crankshaft seals. Rotate upper seals into block, making sure paint stripe is to rear. Care must be taken not to cut or shave seal outer surface. Place lower seal half in bearing cap, making sure paint stripe is in rear. On 5.9L engines, apply sealer on cap surface next to rear main seal. On all models, install cap and tighten bolts to 85 ft. lbs.

CAMSHAFT

ENGINE FRONT COVER

Removal — 1) Drain cooling system and remove radiator and water pump assembly. Remove power steering pump (if equipped). Remove pulley from vibration damper. Remove bolt and washer securing vibration damper on crankshaft. Using suitable tool (C-3688), remove damper from end of crankshaft.

2) Remove fuel lines and fuel pump. Loosen oil pan bolts and remove front bolt at each side. Remove cover attaching bolts, cover and gasket using care not to damage oil pan gasket.

NOTE — *It is normal to find neoprene particles collected between crankshaft seal retainer and oil slinger.*

Installation — Check that mating surfaces of cover and cylinder block are clean and free from burrs. Lubricate seal lip with Lubriplate and install cover with new gasket. Install attaching bolts and tighten. Tighten oil pan bolts and install fuel pump, lines and power steering pump. Install vibration damper, water pump assembly and radiator. Fill cooling system and adjust drive belt tension.

FRONT COVER OIL SEAL

Removal — Remove belts from pulleys and remove fan and shroud from engine. Remove crankshaft pulley and vibration damper. Use suitable tool behind seal lips, pry outward being careful not to damage crankshaft seal surface of cover.

5.2L & 5.9L V8 ENGINES (Cont.)

Installation − Install new seal by using seal installing tool C-4251 (or equivalent). Install threaded shaft part of tool into threads of crankshaft. Place seal into opening with springs towards inside of engine. Place adapter with thrust bearing and nut on shaft. Tighten nut until tool is flush with cover. Reinstall vibration damper, crankshaft pulley, fan, shroud and belts. *See Fig. 12.*

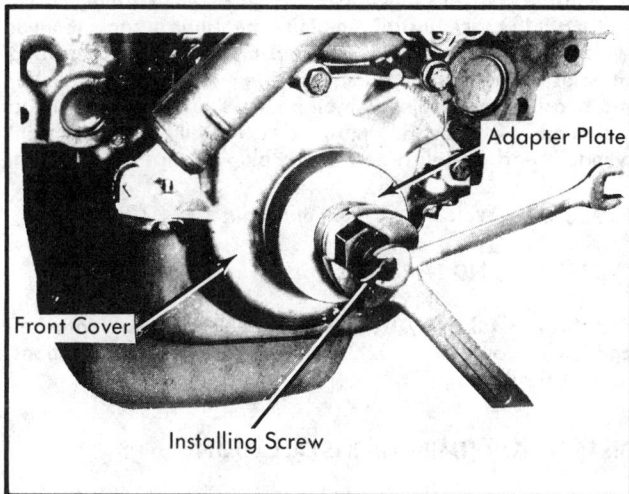

Fig. 12   Installing Front Cover Seal

TIMING CHAIN

Checking For Stretch − 1) Position scale next to timing chain to measure any movement of chain, *See Fig. 13.* Place torque wrench with socket over camshaft sprocket lock bolt and apply torque in direction of crankshaft rotation to remove slack. Torque should be 30 ft. lbs. with cylinder heads installed or 15 ft. lbs. with cylinder heads removed.

NOTE − *Do not permit crankshaft to move.*

2) Apply same torque in reverse direction and measure amount of chain movement. If movement exceeds 1/8", install new timing chain.

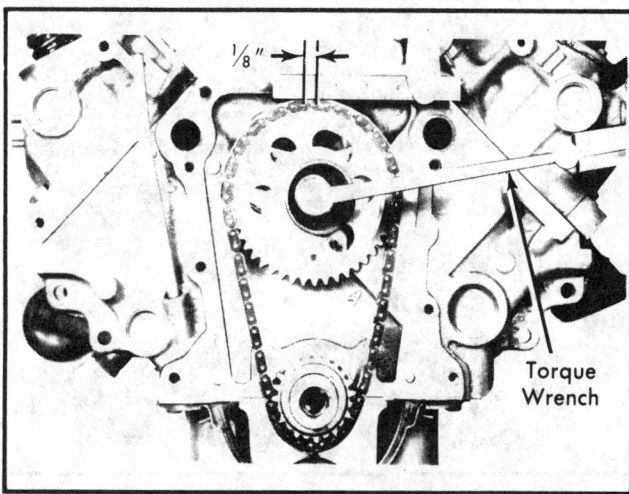

Fig. 13   Measuring Timing Chain Stretch

Removal − With front cover removed, remove camshaft sprocket attaching bolt, washer and fuel pump eccentric. Remove timing chain with crankshaft and camshaft sprockets.

Installation − 1) When installing timing chain, use a suitable tool (C-3509) to prevent camshaft from contacting welch plug in rear of engine block. Remove distributor and oil pump distributor drive gear. Locate tool against rear side of cam gear and attach tool with distributor retainer plate bolt. Proceed as follows:

2) Place camshaft and crankshaft sprockets on bench with timing marks on an imaginary centerline through bore of both sprockets. Place timing chain around both sprockets. Turn crankshaft and camshaft to line up with keyway location in sprockets.

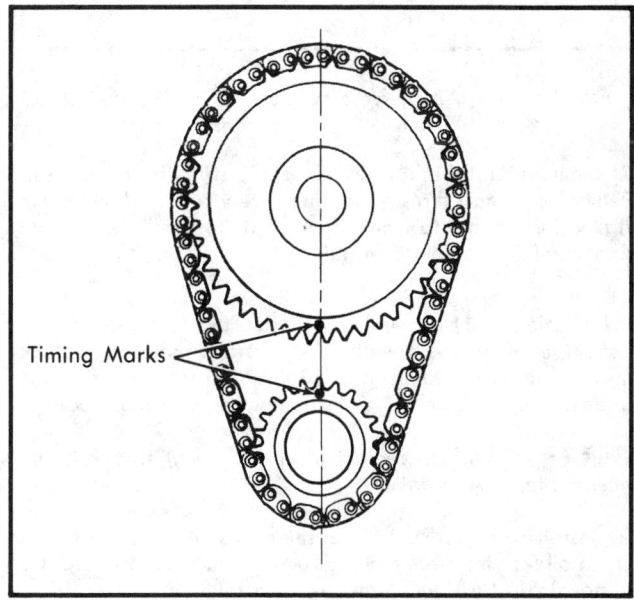

Fig. 14   Timing Chain Sprocket Alignment Marks

3) Slide both sprockets evenly over their respective shafts (with new chain installed on sprockets). Use a straightedge to measure alignment of timing marks. Install fuel pump eccentric, cup washer and camshaft bolt. Tighten bolt and check camshaft end thrust. Slide crankshaft oil slinger over shaft and up against sprocket (flange away from sprocket). Install front cover. *See Fig. 14.*

CAMSHAFT

NOTE − *Whenever a new camshaft is installed; inspect and check, with a straightedge, all tappet faces for "dishing". Replace any tappet with a negative crown.*

Removal − 1) With engine removed from vehicle, remove intake manifold, front cover and timing chain. Remove rocker arm and shaft assemblies. Remove push rods and tappets.

NOTE − *Identify push rods and tappets for reinstallation in original location.*

5.2L & 5.9L V8 ENGINES (Cont.)

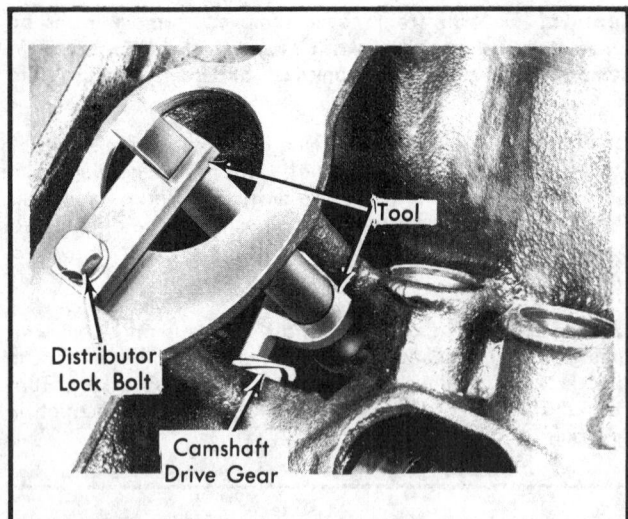

Fig. 15   Camshaft Holding Tool (C-3509) Installed

2) Remove distributor and lift out distributor drive shaft. Remove camshaft thrust plate and note location of oil tab. Install a long bolt into front of camshaft to facilitate removal, and carefully remove camshaft.

Installation — 1) Lubricate camshaft lobes and bearing journals. Insert camshaft to within 2" of its final position in block. Install camshaft holding tool C-3509 in distributor drive hole and hold in position using distributor retainer plate bolt.

NOTE — *Tool should remain in position until sprockets and timing chain are installed.*

2) Install camshaft to final position. Install thrust plate and chain oil tab. Install remaining components in reverse order of removal. See *Distributor Timing and Installation.*

CAUTION — *Top edge of tab should be flat against thrust plate to provide oil for chain lubrication.*

CAMSHAFT BEARINGS

Removal — With engine completely disassembled, drive out rear cam bearing welch plug. Install proper size adapters and horseshoe washers (C-3132A) at rear of each bearing to be removed and drive out bearings.

Installation — Slide new rear bearing over proper adapter of suitable tool, install horseshoe lock and carefully drive bearing into place. Install remaining bearings in same manner while noting the following: Bearings must be aligned to bring oil holes in line with oil passages from main bearing. Number two bearing must index with oil passage to left cylinder head and number four bearing must index with oil passage to right cylinder head. Install a new welch plug at rear of camshaft.

CAUTION — *Welch plug must not leak.*

CAMSHAFT END THRUST

End thrust is taken by thrust plate behind camshaft sprocket. End play should be .002-.010". If not within specifications, replace thrust plate.

DISTRIBUTOR TIMING & INSTALLATION

Distributor Timing — Before installing distributor-oil pump drive shaft, time engine as follows: Rotate crankshaft so number one cylinder is at top dead center on firing stroke. Straight line on vibration damper should be under "O" on timing indicator. Coat shaft and drive gear with engine oil. Install shaft so that when gear spirals into place, it will index with oil pump shaft, so slot in top of drive gear will point in a direction parallel to the centerline of the crankshaft. See *Fig. 17.*

Distributor Installation — Hold distributor over mounting pad of cylinder block with vacuum chamber pointing toward right of engine. Turn rotor to point forward and approximately toward location of number one terminal in distributor cap. Place distributor gasket in position, lower distributor and engage shaft in slot of distributor drive shaft gear. Turn distributor clockwise until breaker points are just separating and install hold down clamp.

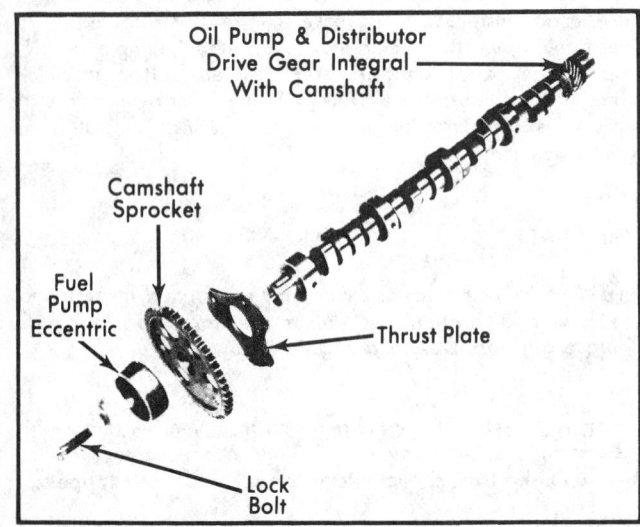

Fig. 16   Exploded View of Camshaft Assembly

Fig. 17   Alignment of Distributor Gear with Engine for Distributor Timing

5.2L & 5.9L V8 ENGINES (Cont.)

ENGINE OILING

Crankcase Capacity — Capacity of all engines is 5 quarts. On all engines, add 1 quart with filter change.

Oil Filter — Change at first oil change and every second oil change after that.

Pressure Regulator Valve — In oil pump. Not adjustable.

Normal Oil Pressure (Hot)	
Application	PSI @ RPM
All Engines......................................	30-80@2000

ENGINE OILING SYSTEM

System has a rotor type oil pump and full flow type oil filter. Oil is forced by the pump through a series of oil passages in engine to provide lubrication to engine components. Oil is supplied to hollow rocker arm shaft (left side) from No. 2 camshaft bearing and to hollow rocker arm shaft (right side) from No. 4 camshaft bearing through indexed holes in camshaft. Oil enters rocker arm shaft through second rocker arm bracket from front (left side) and second bracket from rear (right side) to lubricate rocker arm assembly. Valve assembly is lubricated by oil spray from drilled holes in rocker arms. See *Fig. 18.*

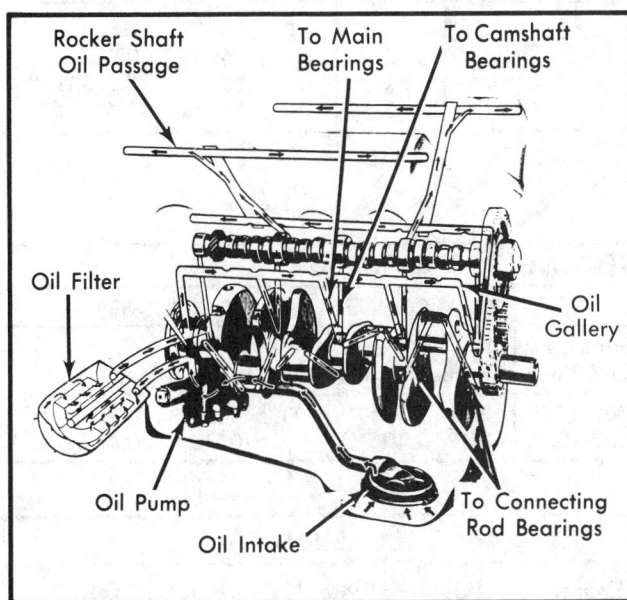

**Fig. 18   Chrysler Corp. 5.2L & 5.9L
Engine Oiling System**

OIL PUMP

Disassemble, clean and inspect all parts for proper clearances See *Oil Pump Specifications.*

NOTE — *Inner rotor and shaft assembly can only be replaced if outer rotor is replaced, as units are a matched assembly. See Fig. 19.*

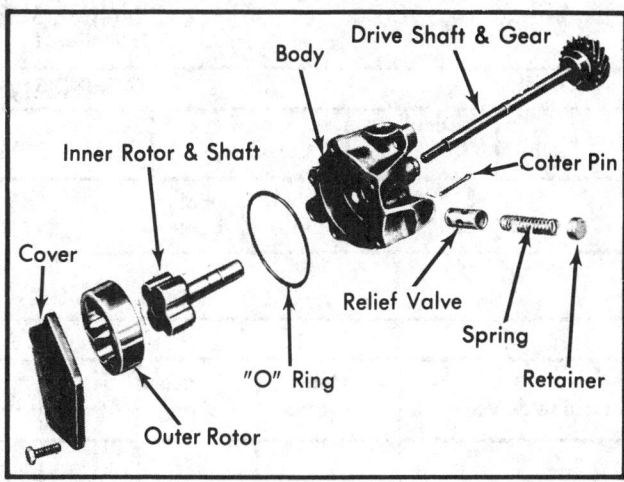

Fig. 19   Exploded View of Oil Pump Assembly

Oil Pump Specifications	
Application	Specifications
Clearance Over Rotors	.0015" Max.
Inner & Outer Rotor Thickness	
5.2L Engine	.825" Min.
5.9L Engine	.943" Min.
Outer Rotor Diameter	2.469" Min.
Outer Rotor-to-Pump Body	.014" Max.
Rotor Tip Clearance	.010"

Pressure Relief Valve Spring — Spring has a free length of $2\frac{1}{32}$-$2\frac{3}{64}$". Spring should test 16.2-17.2 lbs. when compressed to $1\frac{11}{32}$". Replace springs which do not meet specifications.

TIGHTENING SPECIFICATIONS

Application	Ft. Lbs.
Camshaft Sprocket Bolt	50
Camshaft Thrust Plate	18
Front Cover Bolt	35
Connecting Rod Nut	45
Crankshaft Damper Bolt	100
Cylinder Head Bolt	105
Exhaust Manifold	
Screw	20
Nut	15
Flywheel-to-Crankshaft	55
Intake Manifold Bolt	40
Main Bearing Cap Bolt	85
Oil Pan	
Screw	17
Bolt	20
Oil Pump Attaching Bolt	30
Rocker Arm Shaft Retaining Bolt	17

Chrysler Corp. V8 Engines

5.2L & 5.9L V8 ENGINES (Cont.)

ENGINE SPECIFICATIONS

GENERAL SPECIFICATIONS

Year	Displ. Cu. Ins.	Carburetor	HP at RPM	Torque (Ft. Lbs. at RPM)	Compr. Ratio	Bore	Stroke
1981	318" (5.2L)	2-Bbl. & 4-Bbl.	.....	.....	8.6:1	3.91"	3.31"
	360" (5.9L)	2-Bbl. & 4-Bbl.	.....	.....	8.5:1	4.00"	3.58"

VALVES

Engine & Valve	Head Diam.	Face Angle	Seat Angle	Seat Width	Stem Diameter	Stem Clearance	Valve Lift
5.2L							
Int.	1.780"	45°	45°	.065-.085"	.372-.373"	.001-.003"	.373"
Exh.	1.500"	45°	45°	.080-.100"	.371-.372"	.002-.004"	.400"
5.9L							
Int.	1.880"	45°	45°	.065-.085"	.372-.373"	.001-.003"	.410"
Exh.	1.600"	45°	45°	.080-.100"	.371-.372"	.002-.004"	.410"

PISTONS, PINS, RINGS

Engine	PISTONS	PINS		RINGS		
	Clearance	Piston Fit	① Rod Fit	Rings	End Gap	Side Clearance
5.2L	.0005-.0015"	.000-.0005"	.0007-.0014"	1 & 2	.010-.020"	.0015-.0030"
				3	.015-.055"	.0002-.005"
5.9L	.0005-.0015"	.00025-.00075"	.0007-.0014"	1 & 2	.010-.020"	.0015-.0030"
				3	.015-.055"	.0002-.005"

① — Press fit

CRANKSHAFT MAIN & CONNECTING ROD BEARINGS

Engine	MAIN BEARINGS				CONNECTING ROD BEARINGS		
	Journal Diam.	Clearance	Thrust Bearing	Crankshaft End Play	Journal Diam.	Clearance	Side Play
5.2L	2.4995-2.5005"	.0005-.0020"	3	.002-.007"	2.124-2.125"	.0005-.0025"	.006-.014"
5.9L	2.8095-2.8105"	.0005-.0020"	3	.002-.009"	2.124-2.125"	.0005-.0025"	.006-.014"

CAMSHAFT

Engine		Journal Diam.	Clearance	Lobe Lift
5.2L	No. 1	1.998-1.999"	.001-.003"	.....
	No. 2	1.982-1.983"		
	No. 3	1.967-1.968"		
	No. 4	1.951-1.952"		
	No. 5	1.5605-1.5615		
5.9L	No. 1	1.998-1.999"	.001-.003"	.....
	No. 2	1.982-1.983"		
	No. 3	1.967-1.968"		
	No. 4	1.951-1.952"		
	No. 5	1.5605-1.5615"		

VALVE SPRINGS

Engine	Free Length	PRESSURE (LBS.)	
		Valve Closed	Valve Open
5.2L, 5.9L			
Int.	2.00"	78-88@1¹¹⁄₁₆"	170-184@1⁵⁄₁₆"
Exh.	1.81"	80-90@1³¹⁄₆₄"	181-197@1¹⁄₁₆"

4.9L 6-CYLINDER ENGINE

IDENTIFICATION CODING

ENGINE IDENTIFICATION

Engine is identified by a letter code, eigth digit of Vehicle Identification Number, located inside windshield on left upper side of instrument panel. The VIN number is also located on the Safety Compliance Certification Label located on left door lock pillar.

Engine Identification Codes	
Application	**VIN Code**
4.9L (300″)	E

ENGINE REMOVAL

See Engine Removal at end of ENGINE Section.

CYLINDER HEAD & MANIFOLD

INTAKE MANIFOLD

Removal — 1) Remove air cleaner, disconnect choke cable and accelerator cable or rod at carburetor. Remove accelerator retracting spring.

2) Remove kick-down rod retracting spring (vehicles with automatic transmission), remove accelerator rod bellcrank assembly.

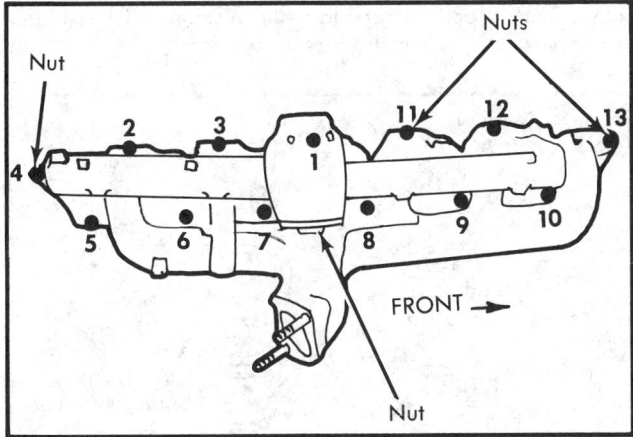

Fig. 1   Intake & Exhaust Manifold Tightening Sequence

3) Disconnect and label all vacuum lines at carburetor. Disconnect fuel inlet line at carburetor. Disconnect muffler inlet pipe from exhaust manifold. Disconnect crankcase vent hose clamp at manifold inlet tube and remove hose. Disconnect power brake vacuum line, if equipped.

4) Remove bolts and nuts retaining both manifolds to cylinder head. Lift manifold assemblies from engine. Remove and discard gaskets. Separate manifolds by removing nuts joining both pieces. Discard gaskets between manifolds.

Installation — 1) Clean joining surfaces of cylinder head and manifolds. If one of the manifolds is to be replaced remove tube fittings from discarded part and install on new part as required, also install new studs in replacement part.

2) If intake manifold and exhaust manifold have been separated, coat mating surfaces lightly with graphite grease, and position exhaust manifold over studs on intake manifold. Install lock washers and nuts, then tighten finger tight. Install new intake manifold gasket.

3) Coat mating surfaces lightly with graphite grease, place manifold assemblies in position against cylinder head. Make sure gaskets have not become dislodged. Install attaching washers, bolts and nuts. Torque bolts and nuts to specification in sequence shown in *Fig. 1.* If intake and exhaust manifolds were separated, tighten nuts joining both parts.

4) Position new gasket on muffler inlet pipe and connect inlet pipe to exhaust manifold. Torque nuts to specifications. Connect crankcase vent hose to intake manifold inlet tube, and position hose clamp.

5) Connect accelerator cable to carburetor and install retracting spring. Connect choke cable to carburetor. Install bellcrank assembly and kickdown rod retracting spring on models with automatic transmission. Adjust transmission control linkage as necessary. Install air cleaner, adjust engine idle speed and idle fuel mixture.

CYLINDER HEAD

Removal — If cylinder head is to be replaced, disassemble and transfer all valves, springs, rocker arms, etc. to new cylinder head. Clean and inspect all components, reface valves and check valve guide clearances before assembling used parts to new cylinder head. To remove cylinder head from engine block, proceed as follows:

1) Drain cooling system and remove air cleaner. Remove PCV valve from rocker cover, and disconnect vent tube at intake manifold inlet tube. Disconnect and remove carburetor fuel inlet line. Disconnect and label all vacuum lines at carburetor. Disconnect choke cable at carburetor and position choke cable and housing to one side.

2) Remove accelerator cable retracting spring, and disconnect accelerator cable from carburetor. On vehicles with automatic transmission, disconnect kickdown rod at carburetor. Disconnect upper radiator hose and heater hose at coolant outlet elbow. Remove coil bracket retaining bolt and position coil to one side.

3) Disconnect muffler inlet pipe from exhaust manifold, and discard inlet pipe gasket. Remove rocker arm cover, loosen rocker arm stud nuts, and rotate rocker arms to one side. Remove and identify push rods in sequence, permitting reinstallation in original locations. Disconnect spark plug wires at spark plugs.

4) Remove cylinder head bolts and attach lifting eyes to cylinder head. Position a floor crane or other suitable lifting device and attach lifting sling to eyes. Raise cylinder head and manifold assembly from engine.

CAUTION — *Do not pry between cylinder head and block when freeing head assembly as gasket surface may be damaged.*

Installation — 1) Clean cylinder head and cylinder block gasket surfaces. Clean gasket surfaces on exhaust manifold and muffler inlet pipe.

Ford 6 Engines

4.9L 6-CYLINDER ENGINE (Cont.)

2) If cylinder head was removed for head gasket replacement, check flatness of block and head gasket surfaces, then position new gasket over dowel pins on cylinder block.

3) Install lifting eyes on cylinder head in previous locations used to detach head assembly. Use suitable hoist to lift cylinder head over block, lowering carefully until head assembly is properly positioned on block and dowel pins. Remove hoist and lifting eyes.

4) Coat threads of head bolts with engine oil and install bolts. Tighten cylinder head bolts, in steps, in sequence shown in *Fig. 2*. Reverse removal procedure to install remaining components.

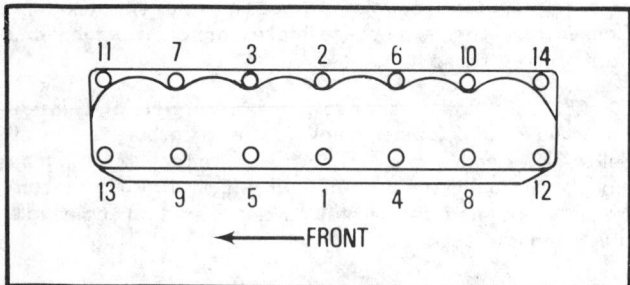

Fig. 2   Cylinder Head Tightening Sequence

VALVES

VALVE ARRANGEMENT

E-I-E-I-E-I-E-I-E-I-E-I (Front to rear).

VALVE GUIDE SERVICING

To ream valve guides (for installation of valves with oversize stems), always use reamers in proper sequence and reface valve seat after valve guide has been reamed. Reamers are available .003" oversize with standard diameter pilots; .015" oversize with .003" oversize pilot; .030" oversize with .015" oversize pilot.

NOTE — *Always break sharp corner (ID) at top of valve guide after reaming.*

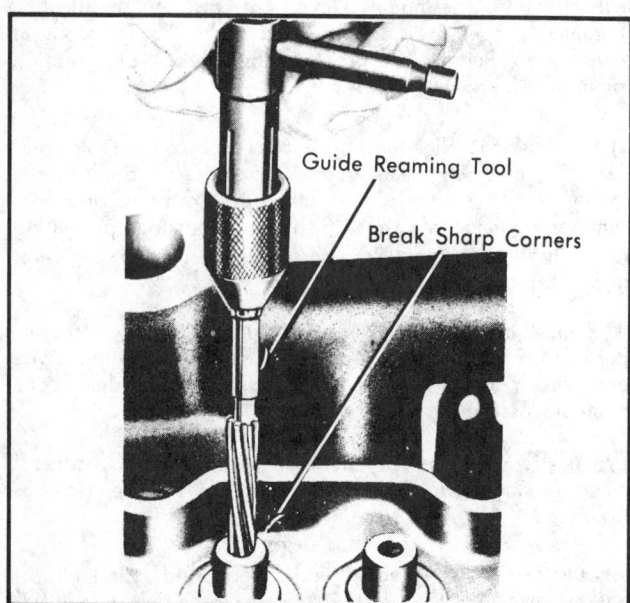

Fig. 3   Reaming Valve Guides

VALVE STEM OIL SEALS

Cup type teflon oil seals are used on valves. Install cupped side down, below upper spring retainer.

VALVE SPRINGS

Removal — 1) Remove air cleaner, accelerator cable retracting spring, and disconnect accelerator and choke cables at carburetor. Remove PCV valve from rocker arm cover, and remove rocker arm cover.

2) Remove spark plug from cylinder to be serviced. Crank engine to position cylinder on TDC after compression stroke. Install an air line and adapter to spark plug hole and apply air pressure.

3) Remove rocker arm stud nut, fulcrum seat, rocker arm, and push rod. Install a spring compressor to compress spring; then remove valve locks. Remove tool, spring retainer, valve spring and valve stem seal.

CAUTION — *Do not remove air pressure until all components are reinstalled.*

Installation — 1) Install new valve stem seal, position spring over valve and install spring retainer. Apply lubriplate to fulcrum seat and socket. Install retainer locks.

NOTE — *Closed end of spring faces cylinder head.*

2) Install push rod, rocker arm, fulcrum seat and stud nut. Adjust valve clearance. Remove air line and adapter, then install spark plug. Install rocker arm cover with new gasket and PCV valve. Connect accelerator cable, choke cable and accelerator cable retracting spring. Install air cleaner.

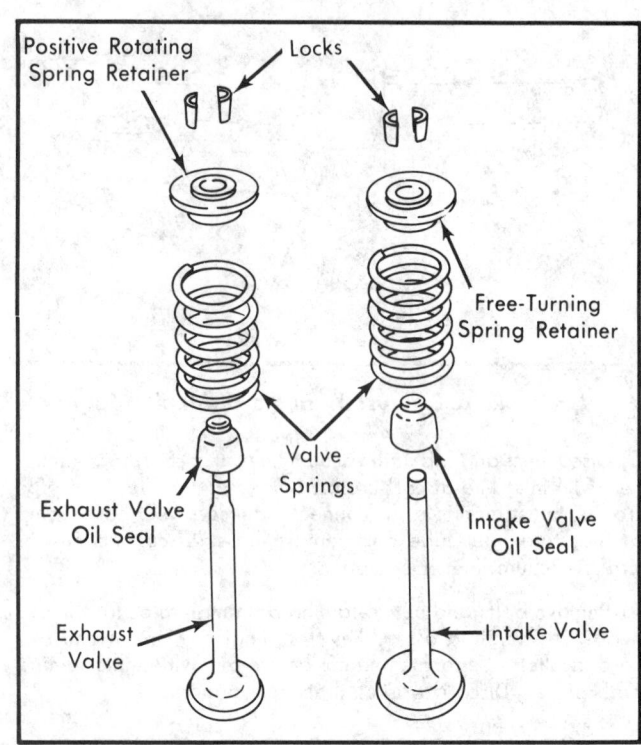

Fig. 4   Exploded View of Valve Assemblies

4.9L 6-CYLINDER ENGINE (Cont.)

VALVE SPRING INSTALLED HEIGHT

1) Check valve springs for squareness using steel square and surface plate. Stand spring against edge of square and rotate spring slowly observing space between top coil of spring and square. If spring is out of square more than 5/64", spring must be replaced.

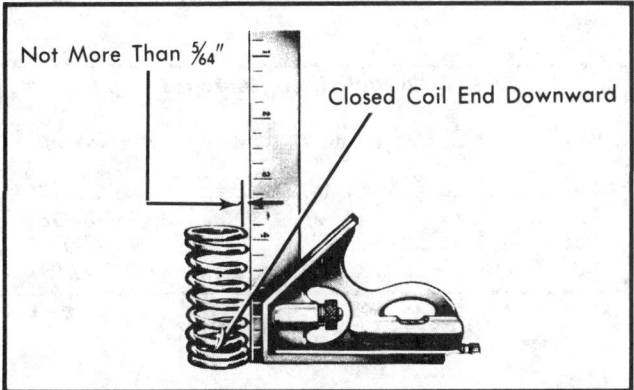

Not More Than 5/64"

Closed Coil End Downward

Fig. 5 Checking Valve Spring Squareness

2) Measure assembled height of valve spring from surface of cylinder head spring pad to underside of spring retainer using dividers. Check divider against scale, if assembled height of spring is greater than specified height, install necessary .030" spacers between cylinder head spring pad and valve spring to bring assembled height to recommended dimensions.

CAUTION — *Do not install spacers unless necessary to meet specifications. Excess use of spacers will result in overstressing of valve spring assembly, and will overload camshaft lobes, causing possible spring breakage and/or camshaft wear.*

Underside Of Spring Retainer

Surface of Spring Pad

Fig. 6 Checking Valve Spring Height

Valve Spring Installed Height Specfications		
Application	**Intake Valve**	**Exhaust Valve**
4.9L	1 11/16-1 23/32"	1 9/16-1 19/32"

ROCKER ARM STUDS

Removal — 1) Use suitable stud pulling tool kit (T79T-6527-A) to facilitate removal of faulty studs. Follow instructions of manufacturer for proper use.

2) If rocker arm stud was broken off flush with stud boss, use suitable screw extractor to remove broken stud.

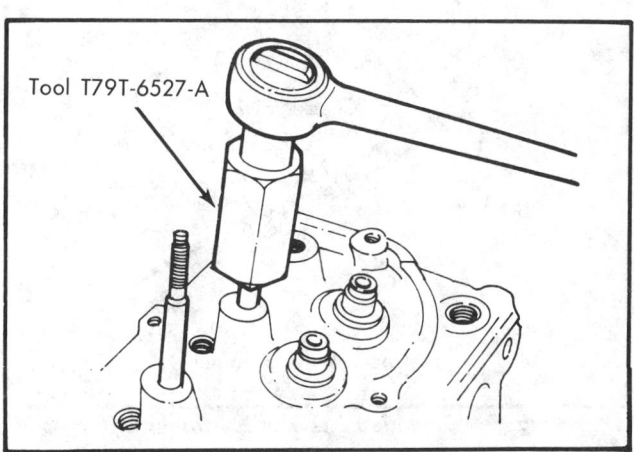

Tool T79T-6527-A

Fig. 7 Removing Rocker Arm Stud

Installation — 1) Replacement studs may be pressed into head using suitable stud replacement tool (T79T-6527-B). Align stud and replacement tool with stud bore and tap sliding driver on tool until tool contacts stud boss, indicating stud is installed to proper height.

2) If rocker arm stud being replaced was loose, check rocker stud bore diameter. If not within specification (.3685-.3695 Std.), ream stud bore using proper reamer (or reamers in sequence) for selected oversize stud. Studs are available in oversizes of .006", .010" and .015". Install rocker arm stud using same replacement tool as for standard size stud.

CAUTION — *Make sure metal particles from reaming process of stud bore do not enter valve area.*

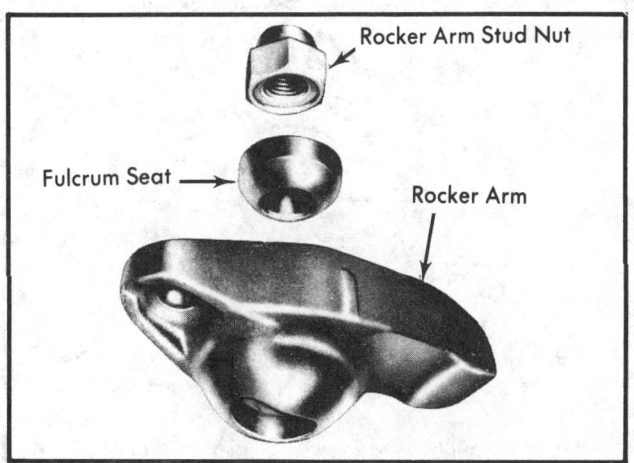

Rocker Arm Stud Nut

Fulcrum Seat

Rocker Arm

Fig. 8 Rocker Arm Assembly

4.9L 6-CYLINDER ENGINE (Cont.)

HYDRAULIC VALVE LIFTER ASSEMBLY

Lifters should be serviced as an assembly only. Parts are not interchangeable. Leak down rate on all lifters is 10-15 seconds at $\frac{1}{16}$" plunger travel using suitable lifter leak down testing device. Replace lifter assembly if any sign of malfunction is noticed.

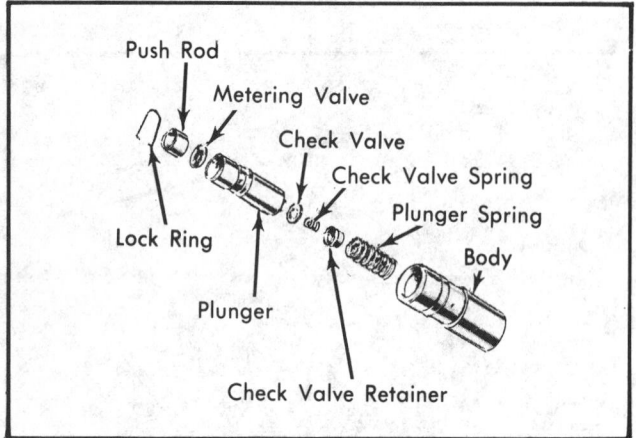

Fig. 9   Exploded View of Hydraulic Lifter

HYDRAULIC VALVE LIFTER ADJUSTMENT

1) Make two chalk marks on crankshaft pulley spaced approximately 120° apart, which together with timing marks, will divide damper pulley into three equal parts. Rotate crankshaft until number one piston is on TDC at end of compression stroke.

2) Adjust intake and exhaust valve clearance for number one cylinder by loosening rocker arm stud nut until there is end clearance in push rod, then tighten nut to just remove all push rod to rocker arm clearance (determined by rotating or moving push rod with fingers as nut is tightened).

3) When push rod to rocker arm clearance has been eliminated, tighten stud nut an additional one turn to place hydraulic lifter piston in desired range.

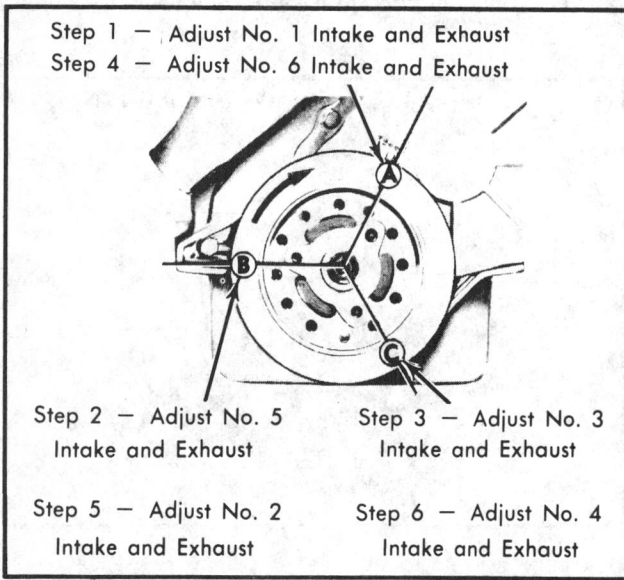

Step 1 — Adjust No. 1 Intake and Exhaust
Step 4 — Adjust No. 6 Intake and Exhaust

Step 2 — Adjust No. 5 Intake and Exhaust

Step 3 — Adjust No. 3 Intake and Exhaust

Step 5 — Adjust No. 2 Intake and Exhaust

Step 6 — Adjust No. 4 Intake and Exhaust

Fig. 10   Crankshaft Pulley Marking for Valve Clearance Adjustment

4) Repeat procedure for remaining set of valves, turning engine with auxiliary starter switch 1/3 turn at a time, in direction of rotation, while adjusting valves in firing order sequence of 1-5-3-6-2-4.

5) Start engine and check for rough engine idle or noisy lifters. Valve clearance set too tight will cause rough idle and valve clearance set too loose will cause noisy lifters. Readjust if necessary.

Collapsed Lifter Clearance		
Application	**Allowable**	**Desired**
4.9L	.100-.200"	.125-.175"
Red	....	3.9982-3.9988"
Blue	....	3.9994-4.0000"
.003" Oversize	....	4.0008-4.0014"

PISTONS, PINS & RINGS

OIL PAN

See Oil Pan Removal at end of ENGINE Section.

PISTON & ROD ASSEMBLY

NOTE — *Following procedures are performed with oil pan and oil pump removed.*

Removal — 1) Turn crankshaft until piston to be removed is at bottom of stroke. Place cloth or shop towel lightly soaked with oil on head of piston to collect metal cutting from cylinder ridge.

2) Remove any ridge and deposits from upper end of cylinder bore using suitable ridge cutter. Follow instructions furnished by tool manufacturer.

CAUTION — *Never cut into ring travel area in excess of $\frac{1}{32}$" when removing ridges.*

3) Make sure all connecting rod caps are marked to the appropriate pistons to ensure installation in original locations. Remove connecting rod cap.

4) Push connecting rod and piston out of top of cylinder using handle end of a hammer. Avoid damage to crankshaft journal or cylinder wall when removing piston and rod.

Installation — 1) Oil piston rings, piston, and cylinder wall with light engine oil. Install piston into original cylinder making sure ring gaps are spaced properly on piston as shown in *Fig. 12*. Install a ring compressor on piston.

2) Insert rod and piston assembly into cylinder bore and guide rod over crankshaft journal. Tap piston into cylinder bore us-

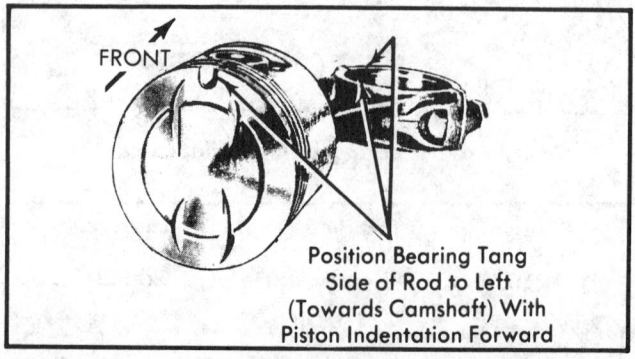

FRONT

Position Bearing Tang Side of Rod to Left (Towards Camshaft) With Piston Indentation Forward

Fig. 11   Piston and Connecting Rod Assembly

4.9L 6-CYLINDER ENGINE (Cont.)

ing wooden handle tool until rod seats on crankshaft journal, install and tighten rod cap. Repeat procedure for each piston removed.

NOTE — *Indentation on piston top must be installed towards front of engine.*

FITTING PISTONS

Measure piston at centerline of piston pin bore 90° to pin bore axis. Measure cylinder bore at right angle to centerline of crankshaft, below ring travel. Piston-to-bore clearance should be as shown in Pistons, Pins & Rings table. Check Piston Size Code Chart to determine correct size. Make sure both piston and cylinder block are at normal room temperature (70°F) when fitting.

Piston Size Code Chart	
Code	**Size**
Red	3.9982-3.9988"
Blue	3.9994-4.0000"
.003" Oversize	4.0008-4.0014"

PISTON PINS

Removal — Using arbor press and pin removal tool T68P-6135-A, press piston pin from piston and connecting rod.

Installation — Start piston pin in piston and connecting rod. Using arbor press and suitable tool (T65L-6135-C), press piston pin through piston and connecting rod until pin is centered in connecting rod.

FITTING RINGS

1) Position ring in the cylinder bore that it will be used in. Push ring down to point in bore where ring wear is not encountered. Use head of piston to position ring squarely in bore.

2) Measure gap between ends of ring using feeler gauge, if not to specification, substitute another ring set until rings are within specification.

NOTE — *Use care to avoid damage to ring or cylinder bore.*

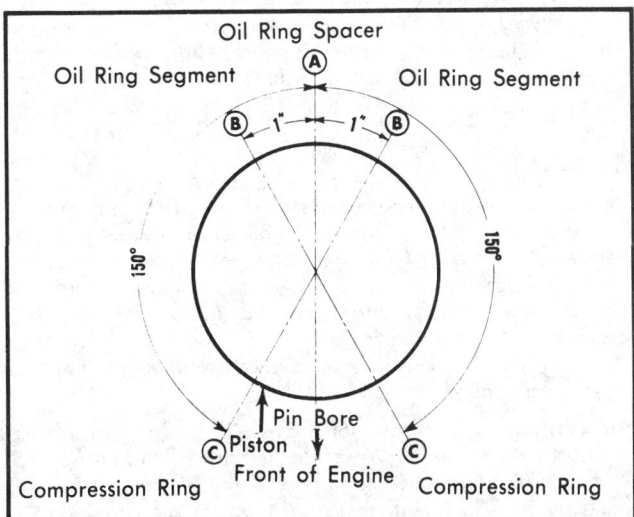

Fig. 12 Correct Spacing for Piston Rings

CRANKSHAFT & ROD BEARINGS

MAIN & CONNECTING ROD BEARINGS

NOTE — *Following procedures are performed with oil pan and oil pump removed.*

Connecting Rod Bearings — After ensuring rod caps are marked for cylinder identification, remove rod caps (with crankshaft journal of cylinder to be checked at bottom of throw). Use Plastigage method to check for proper clearances. New bearings are available in standard, .001" and .002" undersize. Selective fitting is required on each rod. A standard bearing half may be used in combination with a .001" undersize or a .002" undersize with a .001" undersize. Coat bearing surfaces with oil, install rod cap and tighten. Rotate crankshaft after bearing replacement to ensure that bearings are not too tight.

Main Bearings — 1) Mark main bearing caps for identification before removal. Remove bearing caps and upper half of main bearing. Rotate crankshaft slowly in direction of engine rotation to force upper half of bearing out.

NOTE — *Replace one bearing at a time, leaving other bearings secured until ready to be changed.*

2) Determine crankshaft bearing journal clearance using Plastigage method. When checking main bearings, place jack under counterweight adjoining bearing being checked. Place Plastigage on bearing surface over full width of cap and about ¼" off center. Install cap and tighten to specified tightness. Remove cap and check with gauge provided. New bearings are available in standard, .001" and .002" undersize.

3) To install upper main bearing, lubricate bearing with engine oil and place plain end of bearing over shaft on locking tang side of block. Insert bearing and rotate crankshaft in opposite direction of engine rotation until bearing tang is seated. Install bearing cap and tighten.

THRUST BEARING ALIGNMENT

Install thrust bearing cap after all other main caps have been tightened. Install thrust bearing cap with bolts finger tight. Pry crankshaft forward against thrust surface of upper half of bearing. Hold crankshaft forward and pry thrust bearing cap to rear. This will align thrust surfaces of both halves of bearing. Retain forward pressure on crankshaft and torque cap bolts to specifications.

REAR MAIN BEARING OIL SEAL

NOTE — *The seal may be replaced without removing crankshaft on this engine. If oil seal is being replaced at same time as rear main bearing replacement, engine must be removed from vehicle.*

Removal — Loosen all main bearing cap bolts and lower crankshaft slightly but do not exceed 1/32". Remove rear main bearing cap and seal by punching two holes in rear oil seal with an awl and install sheet metal screws in each hole. Use two large screwdrivers and pry against both screws at the same time. Use caution to avoid damaging the crankshaft or oil seal surface.

Installation — Install seal using installing tool T65L-701-A (or equivalent) making sure undercut (lip) side of seal is toward front of engine. Press seal into place until it contacts cylinder block surface. Inspect seal for possible damage.

4.9L 6-CYLINDER ENGINE (Cont.)

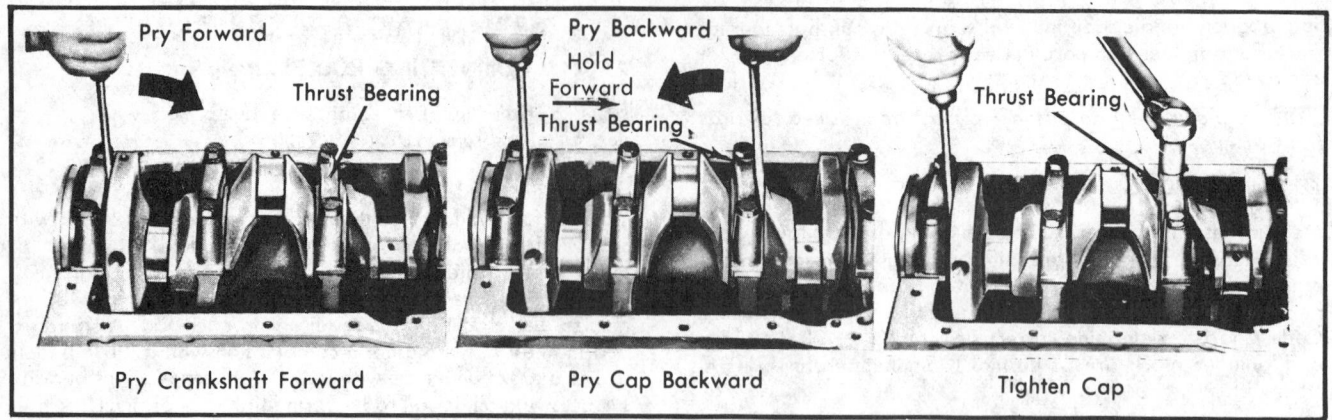

Pry Forward — Thrust Bearing

Pry Backward — Hold Forward Thrust Bearing

Thrust Bearing

Pry Crankshaft Forward

Pry Cap Backward

Tighten Cap

Fig. 13   Aligning Thrust Bearing

CAMSHAFT

ENGINE FRONT COVER

Removal — Drain cooling system and crankcase, then remove radiator. Remove alternator adjusting arm bolt, drive belt, and then swing adjusting arm to one side. Remove crankshaft damper. Remove oil pan, oil pump screen and inlet tube assembly. Remove front cover and gasket.

Installation — Replace front cover oil seal. Install an alignment tool into bore of front cover, then install cover, gasket, and alignment tool to engine. Install and tighten front cover attaching bolts. Install remaining components in reverse of removal procedure.

FRONT COVER OIL SEAL

Removal & Installation — With front cover removed from engine, drive oil seal out of cover using suitable pin punch. Clean out recess in cover. Coat new seal with grease and drive in seal until seal is fully seated in front cover recess. Check seal after installation to see that spring is properly positioned in seal.

Timing Marks

Fig. 15   Aligning Timing Marks

Crank engine over until timing marks are aligned as shown in *Fig. 15*. Use a gear puller to remove camshaft and crankshaft gears.

2) Ensure that key and spacer are properly installed. Align gear keyway with key and install camshaft gear and crankshaft gear. Check that timing marks line up on camshaft and crankshaft gears. Install front cover and related components.

CAMSHAFT

Removal — Drain cooling system and crankcase. Remove radiator, valve lifters, front cover, oil pump and oil pan. Disconnect fuel lines at fuel pump, remove fuel pump attaching bolts, and position fuel pump to one side. Disconnect wires and vacuum line to distributor, then remove distributor. Turn crankshaft to align timing marks. Remove camshaft thrust plate screws, then carefully remove camshaft taking care not to damage camshaft lobes.

Installation — Coat camshaft lobes with Lubriplate and coat journals with engine oil. Assemble key, spacer and thrust plate to camshaft. Align gear keyway with key and install gear as an assembly. Be sure timing marks are aligned and tighten thrust plate attaching screws. Replace oil seal in front cover. Reverse removal procedures for remaining components.

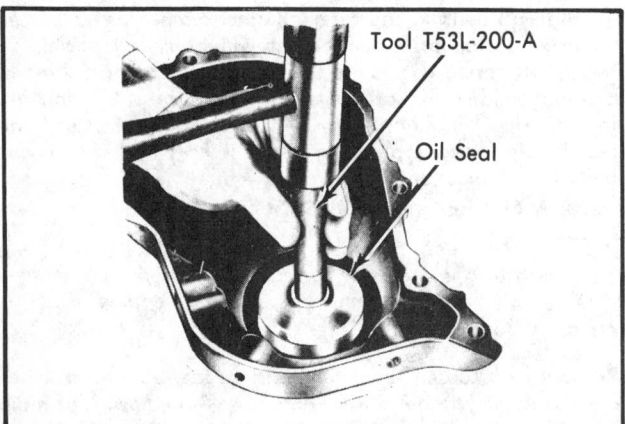

Tool T53L-200-A

Oil Seal

Fig. 14   Installing Front Cover Oil Seal

TIMING GEARS

Removal & Installation — **1)** Drain cooling system and crankcase. Remove front engine cover as previously outlined. Check camshaft end play with dial indicator. End play should not exceed .009". Clearance should be between .001-.007".

4.9L 6-CYLINDER ENGINE (Cont.)

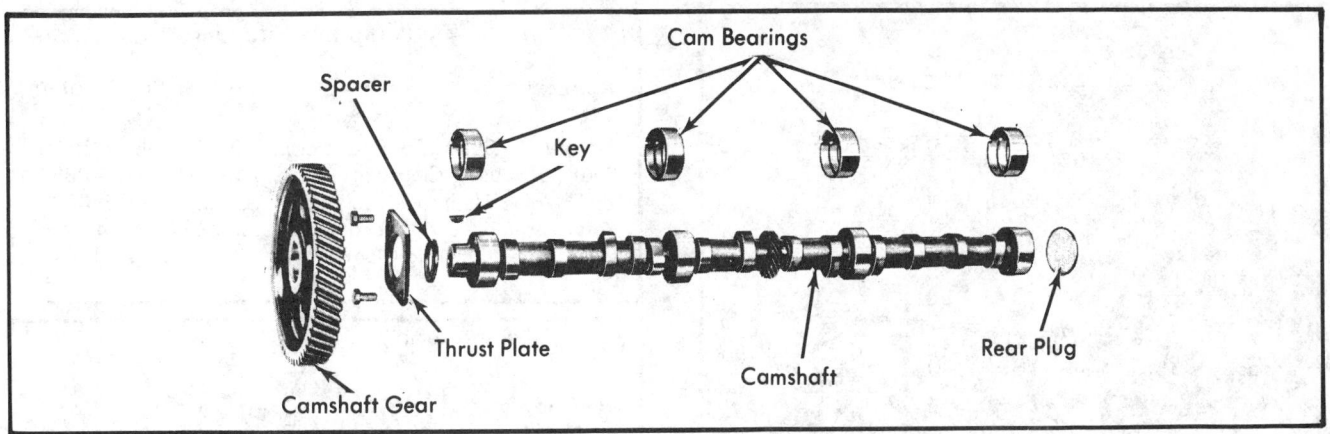

Fig. 16   Exploded View of Camshaft Assembly

CAMSHAFT BEARINGS

Removal & Installation — Remove engine from vehicle and remove flywheel. Remove camshaft and rear bearing bore plug. Remove crankshaft and push pistons to top of cylinders. Using a driver-puller tool (T65L-6250-A), remove camshaft bearings. Position new bearings at bearing bores and press into place while noting the following: Oil holes in bearings must be aligned with oil holes in cylinder block. Front bearing must be installed below front face of cylinder block at a distance of .020-.035".

CAMSHAFT END THRUST

With engine front cover removed, push camshaft toward rear of engine and install dial indicator so indicator point is on camshaft sprocket cap screw. Zero the dial indicator. Position large screwdriver between camshaft sprocket and block. Pull camshaft forward and then release. If dial indicator reading is not within specifications, replace thrust plate.

CAM LOBE LIFT

Remove rocker arm cover, stud nut, fulcrum seat and rocker arm. Check lift of each lobe in consecutive order. Using a dial indicator, position point on end of push rod and in same plane as push rod movement. Rotate crankshaft until lifter and push rod are at lowest position and zero dial indicator. Rotate crankshaft slowly until push rod is in fully raised position. Check that total lift recorded with indicator is within specifications. Maximum allowable lift loss is .005". If lift on any lobe is below specifications, camshaft and valve lifter operating on worn lobes must be replaced.

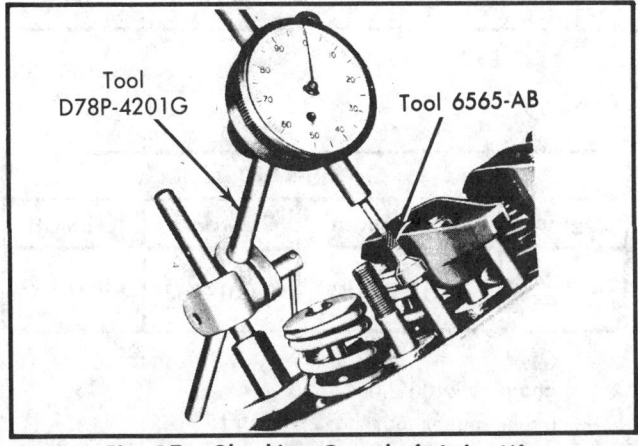

Fig. 17   Checking Camshaft Lobe Lift

ENGINE OILING

Crankcase Capacity — Capacity is 5 quarts. Add one quart with filter change.

Oil Filter — Replace filter at first oil change, then every second oil change thereafter.

Normal Oil Pressure — Oil pressure at 2000 RPM should be 40-60 psi.

Pressure Regulator Valve — Located in pump body. Nonadjustable.

ENGINE OILING SYSTEM

Oil supply is picked up from pan by oil pump which routes oil through filter element to passages in block supplying crankshaft bearings, camshaft bearings, and lifters. Oil is moved up to top of engine by means of push rods from the lifters. Rocker arms are lubricated in this fashion. Oil is returned to pan through drain holes in head assembly which lead back down to oil pan.

Timing Gears — Lubricated by splash method from oil pan.

Oil Filter — Full flow externally mounted type located on left side of engine. Filter has integral by-pass valve and anti-drain back diaphragm. Filter is disposable, throw-away type.

OIL PUMP

Removal & Disassembly — Remove oil pan, oil pump attaching bolts and oil pump from engine. Remove oil inlet tube cover attaching screws and cover. Remove inner rotor and shaft assembly, remove outer race. Drill small hole into oil pressure relief spring valve chamber cap, insert self-threading sheet metal screw into cap and pull from chamber. Remove spring and plunger.

Reassembly — 1) Clean, inspect and oil all parts thoroughly. Install relief plunger, spring and new cap. Stake cap into position. Install outer race, inner rotor and shaft with identification marks facing bottom of pump.

NOTE — Inner rotor, shaft and outer race are serviced as an assembly.

2) Install cover and tighten attaching bolts to specifications. Position oil inlet tube on oil pump, install new gasket and tighten attaching bolts to specifications. Submerge inlet port in oil and rotate shaft until oil flows from outer port.

Ford 6 Engines

4.9L 6-CYLINDER ENGINE (Cont.)

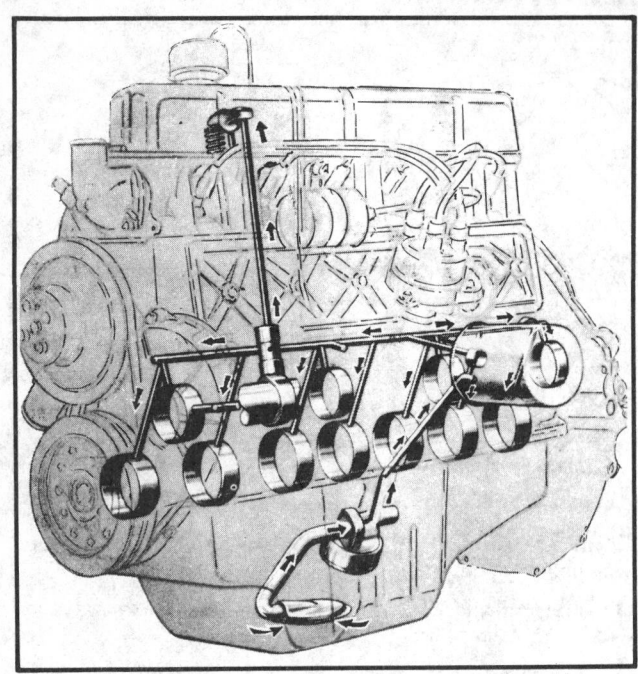

Fig. 18 Engine Oiling System

Oil Pump Specifications

Application	Specification
Relief Valve Spring Tension	20.6-22.6 lbs.@2.490"
Shaft-to-Housing Clearance	.0015-.0030"
Relief Valve Clearance	.0015-.0030"
Rotor Assembly End Clearance	.004" Max.
Outer Race-to-Housig Clearance	.001-.013"

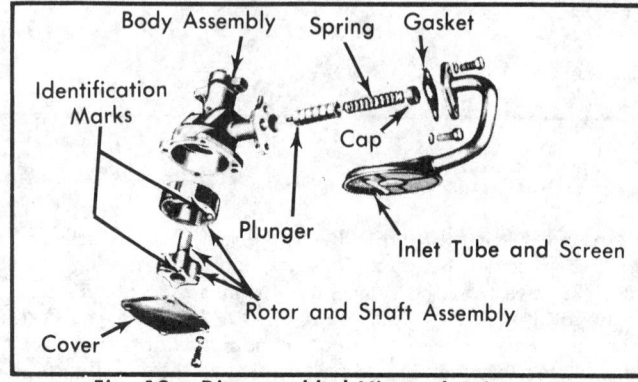

Fig. 19 Disassembled View of Oil Pump

ENGINE SPECIFICATIONS

GENERAL SPECIFICATIONS

Year	Displ. Cu. Ins.	Carburetor	HP at RPM	Torque (Ft. Lbs. at RPM)	Compr. Ratio	Bore	Stroke
1981	300"	1-Bbl.	.....	.....	8.9:1	4.00"	3.98"

VALVES

Engine & Valve	Head Diam.	Face Angle	Seat Angle	Seat Width	Stem Diameter	Stem Clearance	Valve Lift
4.9L							
Int.①	1.772-1.790"	44°	45°	.060-.080"	.3416-.3423"	.0010-.0027"	.403"
Exh.①	1.551-1.569"	44°	45°	.070-.090"	.3416-.3423"	.0010-.0027"	.403"

① — Do Not remove more than .010" from end of stem.

VALVE SPRINGS

Engine	Free Length	PRESSURE (LBS.)	
		Valve Closed	Valve Open
4.9L			
Int.	1.99"	76-85@1.700"	187-207@1.300"
Exh.	1.87"	77-85@1.580"	182-202@1.180"

CAMSHAFT

Engine	Journal Diam.	Clearance	Lobe Lift
4.9L	2.017-2.018"	①.001-.003"	②.2490"

① — End play is .001-.007".

② — Intake and exhaust have same lift.

4.9L 6-CYLINDER ENGINE (Cont.)
ENGINE SPECIFICATIONS (Cont.)

PISTONS, PINS, RINGS						
	PISTONS	PINS		RINGS		
Engine	Clearance	Piston Fit	Rod Fit	Rings	End Gap	Side Clearance
4.9L	.0014-.0022"	.0002-.0004"	Interference Fit	1 2 3	.010-.020" .010-.020" .010-.035"	.0019-.0036" .002-.004" Snug

CRANKSHAFT MAIN & CONNECTING ROD BEARINGS						
	MAIN BEARINGS				CONNECTING ROD BEARINGS	
Engine	Journal Diam.	Clearance	Thrust Bearing	Crankshaft End Play	Journal Diam.	Clearance	Side Play
4.9L	2.3982-2.3990"	.0008-.0015"	No. 5	.004-.008"	2.1228-2.1236"	.0008-.0015"	.006-.013"

TIGHTENING SPECIFICATIONS	
Application	Ft. Lbs.
Cylinder Head①	85
Manifold-to-Cylinder Head	
Intake	22-32
Exhaust	28-33
Oil Pickup Tube	10-15
Main Bearing Caps	60-70
Connecting Rod Caps	40-55
Vibration Damper	130-150
Flywheel	75-85
Rocker Arm Nut	17-23
Engine Front Cover	12-18
Rocker Arm Cover	4-7
Oil Pan-to-Block	10-15
Water Pump	12-18
Oil Pump	10-15
Camshaft Thrust Plate	9-12

① — Tighten cylinder head bolts in three steps as follows: Step One — 55 ft. lbs.; Step Two — 65 ft. lbs.; Step Three — 85 ft. lbs.

4.2L, 5.0L & 5.8L (W) V8 ENGINES

IDENTIFICATION CODING

ENGINE IDENTIFICATION

Engine is identified by a letter code, eighth digit of Vehicle Identification Number, located inside windshield on left upper side of instrument panel. The VIN number is also located on the Safety Compliance Certification Label located on left door lock pillar.

Engine Identification Codes	
Application	**VIN Code**
4.2L (255") 2-Bbl.	D
5.0L (302") 2-Bbl.	F
5.8L (351" W) 2-Bbl.	W

ENGINE REMOVAL

See Engine Removal at end of ENGINE Section.

CYLINDER HEAD & MANIFOLD

INTAKE MANIFOLD

Removal — 1) Drain cooling system. Remove air cleaner and duct assembly. Disconnect accelerator rod, choke cable, speed control and kickdown rod at carburetor. Remove accelerator retracting spring. Disconnect high-tension lead and wires from coil. Disconnect spark plug wires from plugs, then remove distributor cap and wires as an assembly.

2) Remove fuel line at carburetor. Disconnect fuel evaporation hoses. Disconnect distributor vacuum lines and remove distributor. Disconnect radiator and heater hoses at intake manifold and water pump. Disconnect temperature sending unit wire. Disconnect crankcase vent hose at rocker arm cover. Remove intake manifold attaching bolts, then remove manifold and carburetor as an assembly. Remove and discard gaskets and seals. Discard attaching bolt sealing washers.

Installation — 1) Clean all gasket surfaces thoroughly and apply suitable oil resistant sealer at 4 points of gasket-to-gasket contact. Position manifold gaskets (valley baffle on 5.8L) on surface of cylinder heads. Lock front and rear sealing gaskets into tabs on manifold gaskets. Check that all gaskets are aligned properly.

2) Lower manifold into position taking care not to misalign manifold gaskets. Install manifold bolts, tighten in two steps in sequence shown in *Fig. 1*. Reverse removal procedure to install remaining components. Warm engine to normal operating temperature, shut off engine, and retighten manifold bolts to specifications.

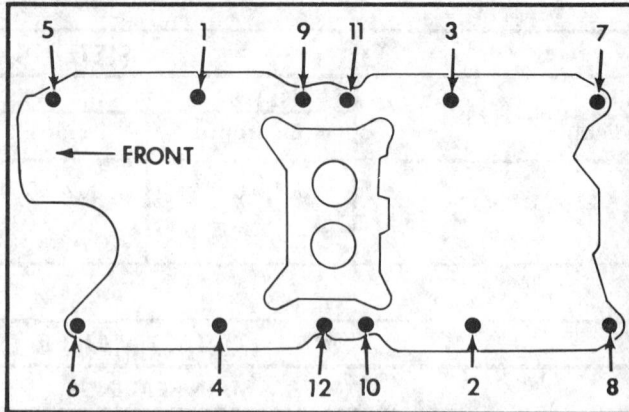

Fig. 1   Tightening Sequence for Intake Manifold

CYLINDER HEAD

Removal — 1) Remove intake manifold and rocker arm covers. If right cylinder head is to be removed, remove alternator and air pump mounting bracket bolts and swing alternator out of way. Remove ignition coil and air cleaner inlet duct. If left cylinder head is to be removed, remove bolts from A/C bracket at front of cylinder head.

2) Remove oil dipstick and tube. Disconnect speed control brackets from cylinder head and disconnect exhaust manifold from muffler pipe. Remove rocker arm fulcrum bolts and remove rocker arm and push rods in sequence for reinstallation in original positions. Remove exhaust valve caps and cylinder head attaching bolts and lift head off engine.

Installation — 1) Clean all gasket surfaces thoroughly. Check cylinder head and block for flatness if cylinder head was removed for gasket replacement. Position new cylinder head gasket over dowel pins on block surface.

NOTE — *A specially treated composition gasket is used and does not require sealer.*

2) Install cylinder heads and bolts. Tighten 5.8L (W) head bolts in 3 steps and all others in 2 steps. Tighten bolts in sequence shown in *Fig. 2*. Reverse removal procedure for installation of remaining components.

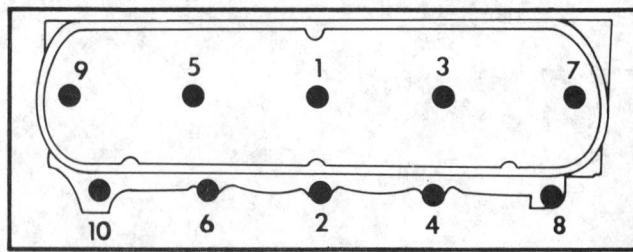

Fig. 2   Tightening Sequence for Cylinder Head

VALVES

VALVE ARRANGEMENT

E-I-E-I-E-I-E-I (Left bank, front to rear).
I-E-I-E-I-E-I-E (Right Bank, front to rear).

VALVE GUIDE SERVICING

To ream guides for installation of valves with oversize stems, always use reamers in size sequence and reface valve seat after valve guide is reamed. Reamers are furnished .003" oversize with standard diameter pilot; .015" oversize with .003" oversize pilot; and .030" oversize with .015" oversize pilot.

NOTE — *Use suitable scraper tool to break sharp corner (ID) at top of valve guide after reaming.*

VALVE STEM OIL SEALS

Cup or umbrella type oil seals are used on all valves. Lubricate valve stem with engine oil and install new valve stem seal with cup side down over valve guide using $\frac{5}{8}$" deep well socket and light mallet to seat seal on valve stem.

VALVE SPRINGS

Removal — **1)** Remove air cleaner, crankcase ventilation regulator valve, and any Thermactor air hoses (if equipped) as necessary from rocker arm cover(s), remove cover(s). Remove spark plug from any cylinder to be serviced.

2) Install air line with adapter into spark plug hole. Remove appropriate rocker arm(s) and push rod(s). Remove exhaust valve stem caps and use spring compressing tool to remove retainer locks. Remove and discard valve stem seal after removing spring retainer and valve spring.

NOTE — *If air pressure fails to hold valve closed, remove cylinder head for inspection of valve seat area.*

CAUTION — *Do not remove air pressure from cylinder as this will allow valve to fall into cylinder if piston has been forced to bottom of cylinder.*

Fig. 3   Compressing Valve Springs for Removal

Installation — **1)** With valve stem seals installed, place spring in position over valve and position spring retainer and sleeve. Compress valve spring and install retainer locks.

2) Apply Lubriplate (or equivalent) to end of push rods and tip of valve stem. Install valve stem caps, rocker arms and tighten. Replace all parts removed in reverse of removal procedure.

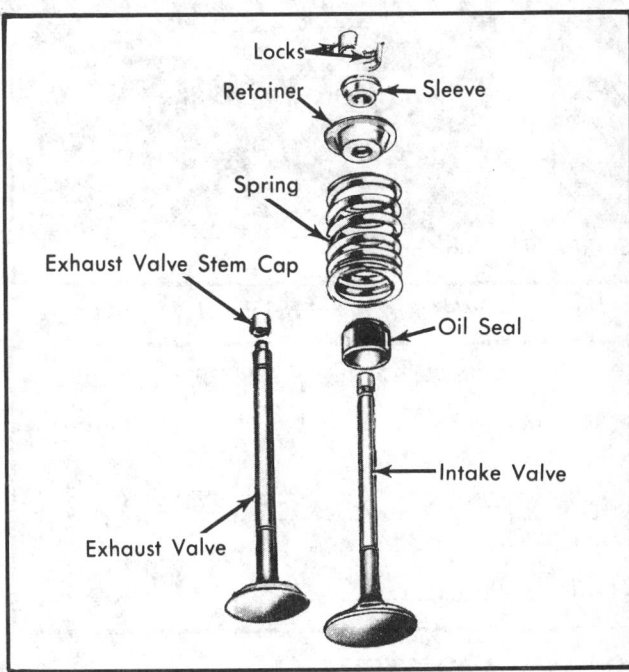

Fig. 4   Exploded View of Valve Assemblies

VALVE SPRING INSTALLED HEIGHT

Valve spring ends must be square within $\frac{5}{64}$" tolerance. Installed height of valve spring must not exceed specifications. Measure spring height from surface of cylinder head pad to underside of spring retainer. If height is greater than specified, install .030" spacer on head under spring to bring height within limits.

CAUTION — *Install spacers only if necessary and do not use more than two spacers as any more will overstress springs and overload camshaft lobes.*

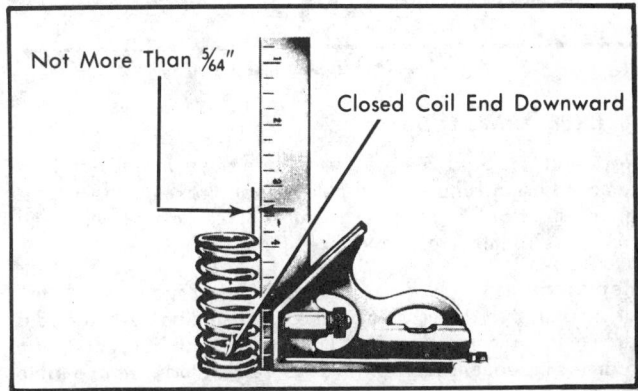

Fig. 5   Checking Valve Spring Squareness

Ford V8 Engines

4.2L, 5.0L & 5.8L (W) V8 ENGINES (Cont.)

Fig. 6   Checking Installed Height of Valve Spring

Valve Spring Installed Height Specifications	
Application	Specifications
4.2L & 5.0L	
Int.	$1\frac{43}{64}$"-$1\frac{45}{64}$"
Exh.	$1\frac{37}{64}$"-$1\frac{39}{64}$"
5.8L (W)	
Int.	$1\frac{49}{64}$"-$1\frac{51}{64}$"
Exh.	$1\frac{37}{64}$"-$1\frac{39}{64}$"

ROCKER ARM ASSEMBLY

Inspect rocker arms, fulcrum seats, rocker arm studs, rocker arm stud nuts and fulcrum guides for undue or excessive wear. Replace all parts which show wear.

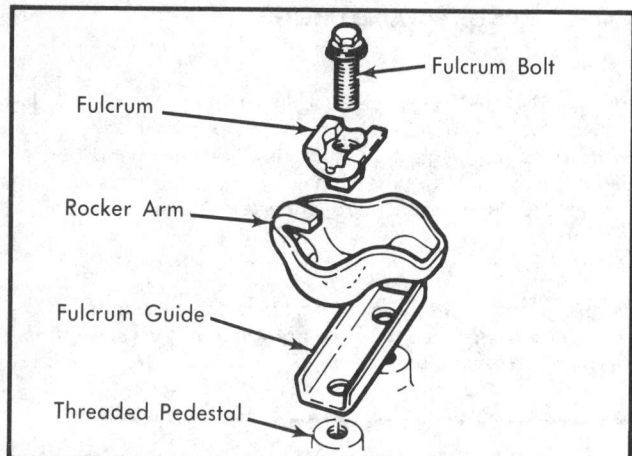

Fig. 7   Rocker Arm Assembly

ROCKER ARM STUDS

Removal — Studs with worn or damaged threads can be removed using suitable stud pulling tool. Broken studs will require use of drill or screw extractor tool. Loose studs will need stud boss reamed to fit oversize studs.

Replacement — Normal stud replacement requires only use of suitable stud driver which will contact stud boss when stud is driven in to correct height. If oversize stud is needed, use reamers in sequence to obtain correct size. Studs are available in .006", .010", and .015" oversizes. Use suitable stud driver to install oversize stud to correct height.

HYDRAULIC VALVE LIFTER ASSEMBLY

Lifters should be serviced as assemblies only, internal parts are matched sets and cannot be interchanged. Leak down rate on hydraulic lifters is 10-50 seconds at $\frac{1}{16}$" plunger travel using suitable leak down tester. Replace lifter assembly if any sign of malfunction occurs.

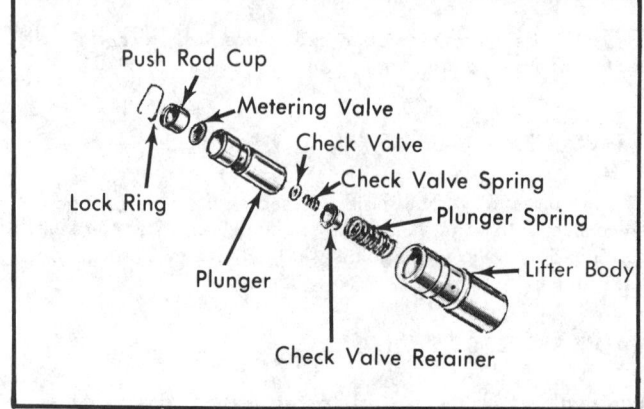

Fig. 8   Disassembled View of Hydraulic Valve Lifter

HYDRAULIC VALVE LIFTER ADJUSTMENT

1) Positive stop rocker arm stud eliminates necessity of adjusting valve clearance, but to obtain specified valve clearance, it is important that all valve components be in serviceable condition and installed properly. With crankshaft in positions designated in following procedure, slowly apply pressure to bleed down tappet until plunger is completely bottomed, using suitable tappet compressor.

2) Check clearance between rocker arm and valve stem tip with feeler gauge. If clearance is less than specified, install a shorter push rod. If clearance is greater than specifications, install longer push rod.

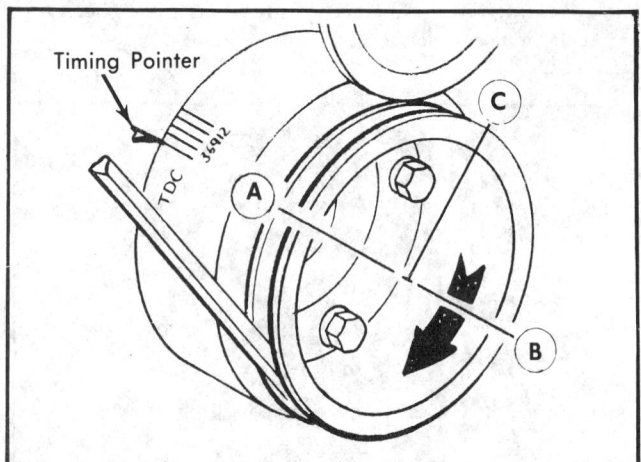

Fig. 9   Crankshaft Positions for Adjusting Hydraulic Valve Lifters

4.2L & 5.0L Engines — **1)** With No. 1 piston on TDC at end of compression stroke (position A in *Fig. 9*), check valve clearance on the following valves: No. 1 intake, No. 1 exhaust, No. 7 intake, No. 5 exhaust, No. 8 intake, No. 4 exhaust.

4.2L, 5.0L & 5.8L (W) V8 ENGINES (Cont.)

2) Rotate crankshaft to position B (see *Fig. 9*) by rotating crankshaft 180° clockwise from TDC position. Check clearance on the following valves: No. 5 intake, No. 2 exhaust, No. 4 intake, No. 6 exhaust.

3) Rotate crankshaft to position C (see *Fig. 9*) by rotating crankshaft 270° clockwise from position B. Check clearance on the following valves: No. 2 intake, No. 7 exhaust, No. 3 intake, No. 3 exhaust, No. 6 intake, No. 8 exhaust.

5.8L (W) Engine — 1) With No. 1 piston on TDC at end of compressionstroke (position A in *Fig. 9*), check valve clearance on the following valves: No. 1 intake, No. 1 exhaust, No. 4 intake, No. 4 exhaust, No. 8 intake, No. 7 exhaust.

2) Rotate crankshaft to position B (see *Fig. 9*) by rotating crankshaft 180° clockwise from the TDC position. Check clearance on the following valves: No. 3 intake, No. 2 exhaust, No. 7 intake, No. 6 exhaust.

3) Rotate crankshaft to position C (see *Fig. 9*) by rotating crankshaft 270° clockwise from position B. Check clearance on the following valves: No. 2 intake, No. 4 exhaust, No. 5 intake, No. 5 exhaust, No. 6 intake, No. 8 exhaust.

Collapsed Lifter Clearance		
Application	**Allowable**	**Desired**
4.2L & 5.8L (W)	.071-.193"	.096-.165"
5.0L	.098-.198"	.123-.173"

PISTON, PINS & RINGS

OIL PAN

See Oil Pan Removal at end of ENGINE Section.

PISTON & ROD ASSEMBLY

Removal — 1) With cylinder head and oil pan removed, use ridge reamer to remove any ridge or deposit on upper end of cylinder bore. Place piston at bottom of stroke and place shop towel or cloth lightly soaked in oil over piston dome to collect cuttings.

NOTE — *Never cut more than 1/32" from bore in ring travel area.*

2) Inspect connecting rods and caps for cylinder identification and mark as necessary. Remove rod cap and push piston and rod assembly out of top of cylinder taking care not to nick crankshaft journal or to score cylinder wall.

Installation — 1) Lightly coat cylinder bore, piston and rings with engine oil. Ensure that ring gaps are properly spaced as shown in *Fig. 11*. Install a ring compressor on piston.

NOTE — *Be sure largest chamfer at bearing end of rod is positioned towards crank pin thrust face of crankshaft.*

2) Install each piston and rod assembly (with notch on piston head facing front of engine) in respective bore, guide connecting rod onto crankshaft journal while tapping piston dome with suitable wooden handle to seat connecting rod against crankshaft. Install rod caps and tighten.

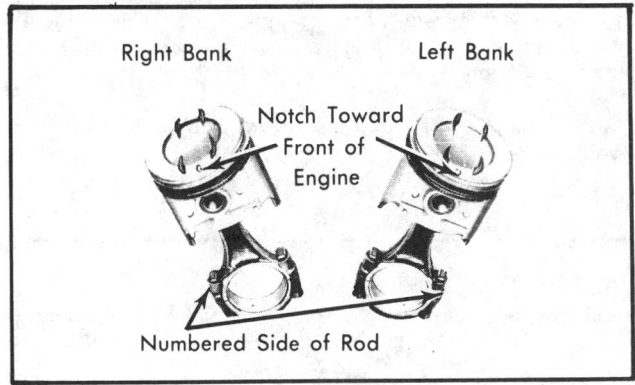

Fig. 10   Piston and Connecting Rod Assembly

FITTING PISTONS

Measure piston at centerline of piston pin bore 90° to pin bore axis. Measure cylinder bore at right angle to centerline of crankshaft, below ring travel. Piston-to-bore clearance should be as shown in Pistons, Pins & Rings table. Check Piston Size Code Chart to determine correct size. Make sure both piston and cylinder block are at normal room temperature (70°F) when fitting.

Piston Size Code Chart	
Code	**Piston Size**
4.2L	
Red	3.6784-3.6790"
Blue	3.6798-3.6804"
.003" Oversize	3.6812-3.6818"
5.0L	
Red	3.9984-3.9990"
Blue	3.9960-4.0000"
.003" Oversize	4.0008-4.0014"
5.8L	
Red	3.9978-3.9984"
Blue	3.9990-3.9996"
.003" Oversize	4.0002-4.0008"

PISTON PINS

Removal — Using arbor press and piston pin removal tool T68P-6135A (or equivalent), press piston pin from piston and connecting rod.

Installation — Start piston pin in piston and connecting rod. Using arbor press and installing tool T68P-6135A (or equivalent), press piston pin through piston into connecting rod until pin is centered in connecting rod.

FITTING RINGS

1) Position ring in the cylinder bore that it will be used in. Push ring down to point in bore where ring wear is not encountered. Use head of piston to position ring squarely in bore.

Ford V8 Engines

4.2L, 5.0L & 5.8L (W) V8 ENGINES (Cont.)

2) Measure gap between ends of ring using a feeler gauge, if not to specification, substitute another ring set until rings are within specification.

CAUTION — *Use care to avoid damage to ring or cylinder bore.*

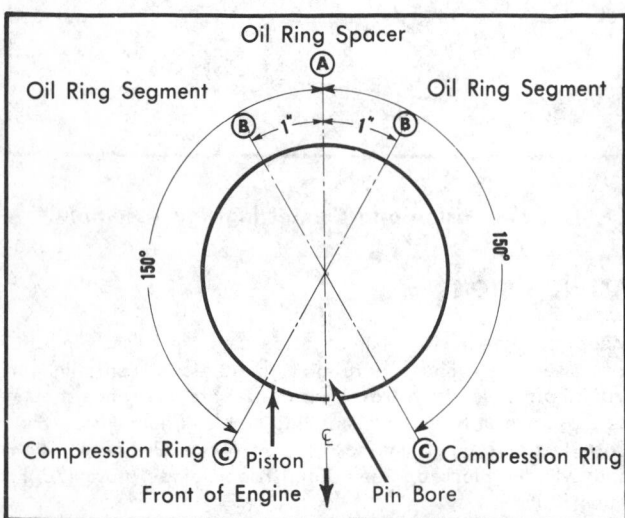

Fig. 11   Correct Spacing for Piston Rings

CRANKSHAFT & ROD BEARINGS

MAIN & CONNECTING ROD BEARINGS

Connecting Rod Bearings — 1) To change connecting rod bearings, remove and inspect caps for cylinder identification to ensure correct position for replacement. With crankshaft lined up in center of cylinder bore, push piston upward into block enough to allow removal of upper half of bearing.

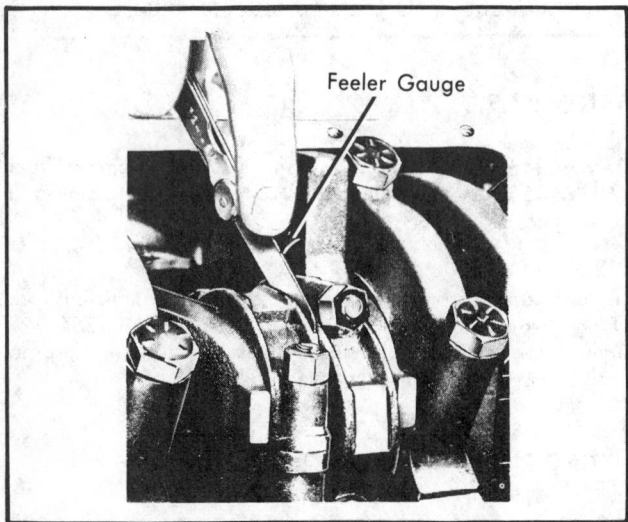

Fig. 12   Measuring Connecting Rod Side Clearance

2) After rod bearings have been fitted using Plastigage method, apply light coat of engine oil to journals and bearings. With crankshaft throw at bottom of stroke and upper half of bearing installed, move piston down until connecting rod bearing seats on crank journal. Install connecting rod cap and tighten. Check connecting rod side clearance.

Main Bearings — 1) Mark main bearing caps for identification before removal from block. Remove upper half of main bearing by inserting removal tool 6331 (or equivalent) in oil hole of crankshaft and slowly rotate crankshaft in direction of engine rotation.

NOTE — *Replace one bearing at a time leaving other bearings secured until ready to change.*

2) Determine journal clearance by using Plastigage method. When checking main bearings, place a jack under counterweight adjoining bearing being gauged to avoid erroneous reading.

3) If bearing clearance is excessive, a .001″ or .002″ undersize bearing half may be used in combination with a standard size half. If .002″ undersize bearings are used on more than one journal, they may be positioned in engine block rather than bearing cap. If standard and .002″ undersize combination did not bring bearing clearance within specified limits, crankshaft will have to be refinished and suitable undersize bearings installed.

4) To install upper main bearing, lubricate bearing with engine oil and place plain end of bearing over crankshaft on locking tang side of block. Partially insert bearing to allow tool 6331 to be inserted into oil hole in crankshaft journal. Rotate engine in opposite direction of engine rotation until bearing tang is seated. Remove tool and install bearing cap and tighten.

THRUST BEARING ALIGNMENT

Install thrust bearing cap after all other main caps have been tightened. Install thrust bearing cap with bolts finger tight. Pry crankshaft forward against thrust surface of upper half of bearing. Hold crankshaft forward and pry thrust bearing cap to rear, this will align thrust surfaces of both halves of bearing. Retain forward pressure on crankshaft and torque cap bolts to specifications. *See Fig. 13.*

REAR MAIN BEARING OIL SEAL

Removal — 1) Complete seal can be replaced without removing crankshaft. Remove oil pan and oil pump (if required), loosen all main bearing cap bolts to lower crankshaft slightly, but not to exceed $\frac{1}{32}$″.

2) Remove rear main bearing cap and remove oil seal from bearing cap and block. On block half of seal, use seal removing tool or place small metal screw in one end of seal and pull on screw to remove seal. Prevent scratching or damage to

3) Remove oil seal retaining pin from bearing cap if so equipped, as replacement seal does not use pin. Discard pin.

4.2L, 5.0L & 5.8L (W) V8 ENGINES (Cont.)

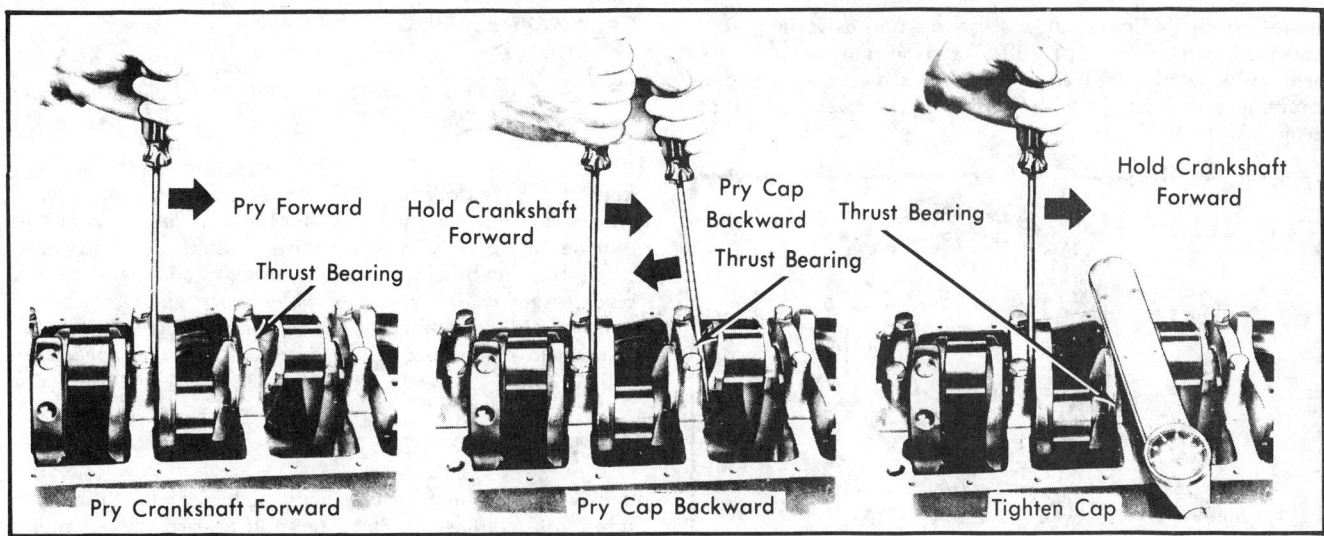

Pry Forward

Thrust Bearing

Pry Crankshaft Forward

Hold Crankshaft Forward

Pry Cap Backward

Thrust Bearing

Pry Cap Backward

Thrust Bearing

Hold Crankshaft Forward

Tighten Cap

Fig. 13 Aligning Thrust Bearing

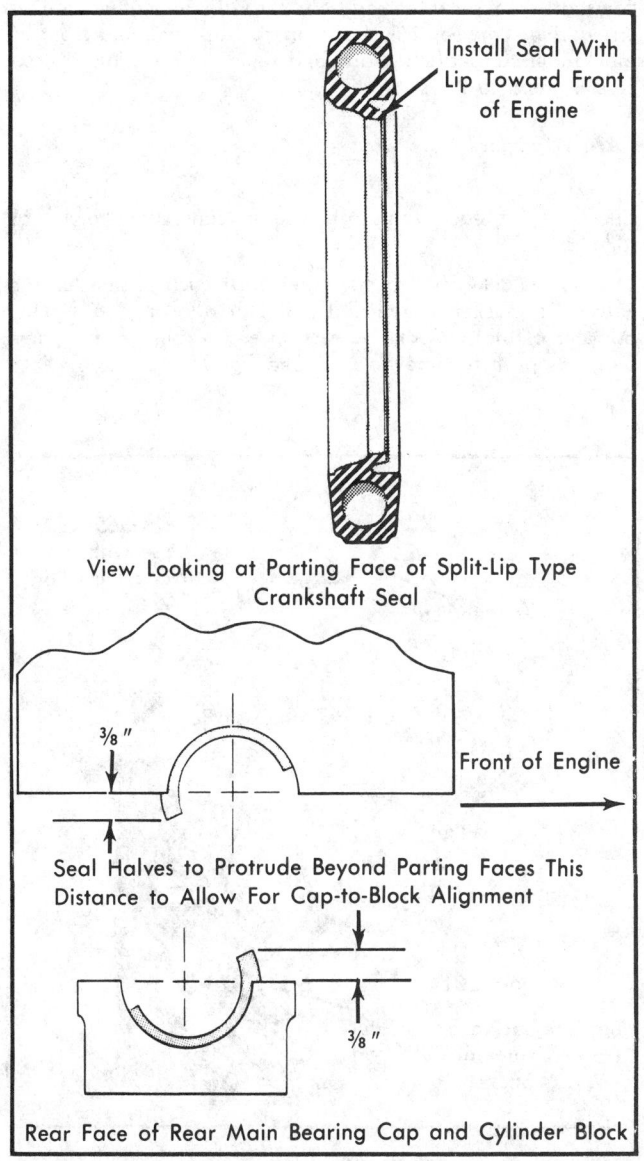

Install Seal With Lip Toward Front of Engine

View Looking at Parting Face of Split-Lip Type Crankshaft Seal

3/8"

Front of Engine

Seal Halves to Protrude Beyond Parting Faces This Distance to Allow For Cap-to-Block Alignment

3/8"

Rear Face of Rear Main Bearing Cap and Cylinder Block

Fig. 14 Installing Crankshaft Rear Oil Seal

Installation — 1) Clean oil seal groove, dip split-lip seal halves in engine oil. Carefully install block upper seal into groove. Ensure undercut (lip) side of seal is toward front of engine. Install by rotating seal on crankshaft journal until approximately 3/8" of seal protrudes from parting surface. See Fig. 14.

CAUTION — *Avoid shaving any rubber from outside diameter of seal by bottom edge of groove. Do not allow any oil to get into sealing area.*

2) Tighten remaining bearing cap bolts to torque specifications. Install lower seal in rear main bearing cap with undercut side of seal toward front of engine, allowing seal to protrude approximately 3/8" above parting surface to mate with upper seal when cap is installed.

3) Apply suitable oil-resistant sealer to bearing edges and install rear main bearing cap. Torque cap bolts to specifications and reinstall oil pump, oil pan, and all other related parts.

CAMSHAFT

ENGINE FRONT COVER

Removal — Drain cooling system and crankcase. Remove fan, spacer and all hoses or brackets attaching to water pump. Remove crankshaft pulley and use suitable puller to remove vibration damper. Disconnect fuel pump outlet line from fuel pump, remove fuel pump bolts and move pump to one side. Remove front cover bolts and cut oil pan gasket flush with cylinder block. Remove front cover and water pump as an assembly.

Installation — Clean all gasket surfaces. Use suitable sealer and install gaskets and seals. Use suitable tool to center front cover on crankshaft, install bolts and tighten. Install all related parts.

FRONT COVER OIL SEAL

Removal — Remove front cover following procedure given in Front Cover Removal. Using suitable pin punch, drive out old seal taking care not to damage seal surface.

4.2L, 5.0L & 5.8L (W) V8 ENGINES (Cont.)

Installation — Coat seal with grease and drive into front cover using suitable tool (T58P-6700-B or equivalent). Check seal to make sure that edges are fully seated and spring is properly positioned in seal. Reassemble in reverse order of removal.

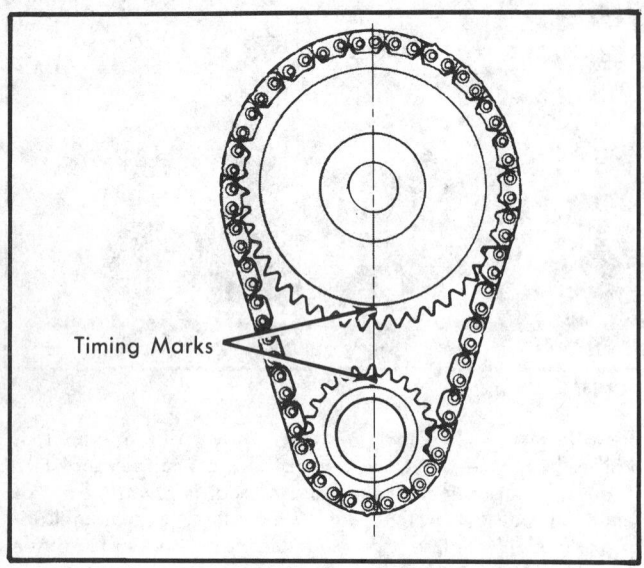

Fig. 15   Aligning Timing Marks

TIMING CHAIN

Removal & Installation — Crank engine until timing marks are positioned properly. See Fig. 15. Remove camshaft sprocket cap screw, washers and fuel pump eccentric. Slide both sprockets and timing chain forward off key ways and remove as an assembly. To install, position timing chain on sprockets with timing marks aligned. Slide timing chain and sprockets onto crankshaft and camshaft as an assembly. Install fuel pump eccentric, washers and sprocket cap screw. Tighten bolt and then oil timing chain.

CAMSHAFT

Removal & Installation — **1)** Drain cooling system, remove radiator, front cover, timing chain and related parts. Remove intake manifold and related parts. Remove valve covers and loosen rocker arms. Remove push rods and valve lifters in sequential order so as to return to original location. Remove grille on "E" models.

CAUTION — Do not scar or mark camshaft lobes or bearing journals while removing camshaft. See Fig. 17.

2) Remove thrust plate and carefully pull camshaft out through front of engine. Oil camshaft journals with engine oil and apply Lubriplate to lobes. Carefully slide camshaft through cam bearings and install camshaft thrust plate. Reassemble engine in reverse of removal procedures.

CAUTION — Do not attempt to pry camshaft back and forth in block with valve train load on camshaft.

CAMSHAFT BEARINGS

NOTE — Camshaft bearings are not interchangeable from one bore to another.

Removal & Installation — Remove camshaft, flywheel and crankshaft. Push pistons to top of cylinders. Remove camshaft rear bearing bore plug and remove camshaft bearings. Using a suitable cam bearing installation tool, fit cam bearings into block assembly. Make sure oil holes are properly aligned in each journal. Be sure front bearing is installed to specified distance below front face of cylinder block. Distance specified is .005-.020".

CAMSHAFT END THRUST

Rocker arm stud nuts or bolts must be loosened sufficiently to free load on camshaft. Push camshaft toward rear of engine and install dial indicator. Position indicator so that point is on camshaft sprocket attaching bolt. Zero dial indicator. Position screwdriver between camshaft sprocket or gear and front of block. Pull camshaft forward and release, if end play is excessive, replace thrust plate.

CAM LOBE LIFT

Check lift of each camshaft lobe in consecutive order as follows:

1) Remove all rocker arms. Make sure each push rod is in valve lifter socket. Install dial indicator allowing ball socket adapter of dial indicator to rest on end of push rod in same plane as push rod movement. See Fig. 16.

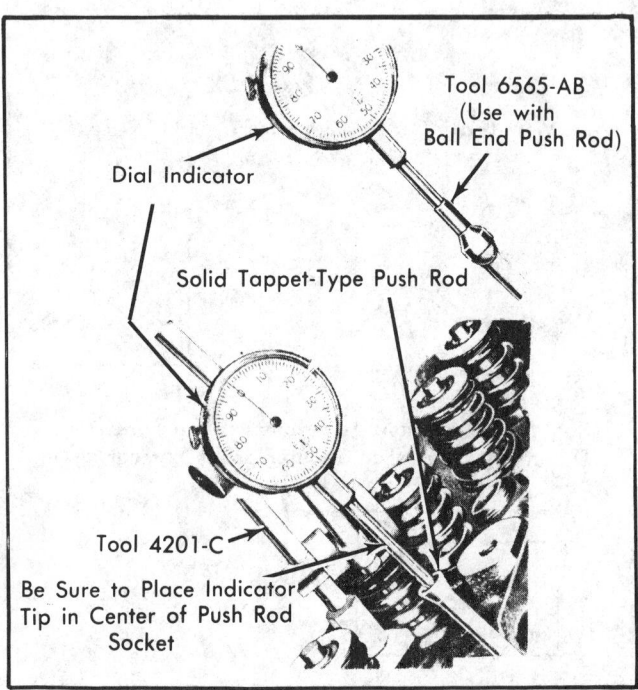

Fig. 16   Checking Camshaft Lobe Lift

4.2L, 5.0L & 5.8L (W) V8 ENGINES (Cont.)

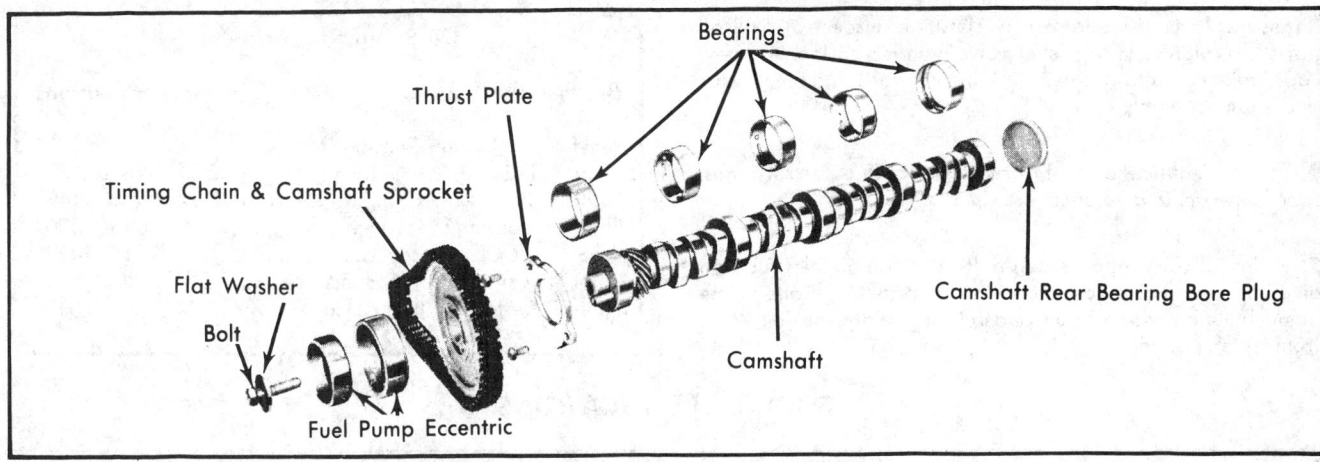

Fig. 17 Exploded View of Camshaft Assembly

2) Using remote starter switch (with ignition OFF), turn engine until valve lifter being checked is on base circle of camshaft lobe indicating lowest point of push rod travel.

3) Zero dial indicator and continue to rotate engine until push rod is in fully raised position giving highest indicator reading. Continue same procedure for each camshaft lobe. Compare camshaft lift from dial indicator readings with specifications.

4) To check accuracy of dial indicator readings, continue to rotate engine until dial indicator reads zero. If lift on any camshaft lobe is .005" less than specifications, valve lifters are operating on worn camshaft lobes, indicating need for camshaft replacement.

ENGINE OILING

Crankcase Capacity — 5 quarts. Add 1 quart with filter change.

Oil Filter — Replace at first oil change and every second oil change following.

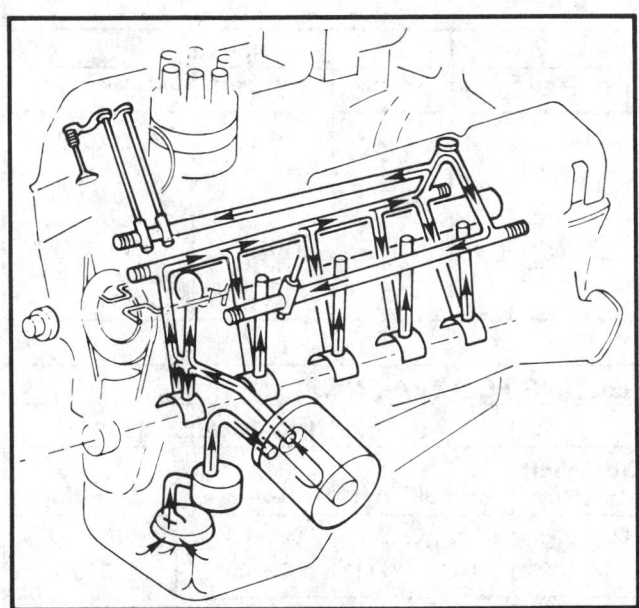

Fig. 18 Engine Oiling System

Normal Oil Pressure — 4.2L & 5.0L engines have 40-60 psi at 2000 RPM, 5.8L (W) engines have 40-65 psi at 2000 RPM.

Pressure Regulator Valve — Housed in oil pump body on all engines. Not adjustable.

ENGINE OILING SYSTEM

System is pressure feed from rotor type oil pump in left forward section of engine. Oil flows through full flow oil filter before entering main oil gallery on right side of camshaft. Oil from main gallery enters main bearings through drilled passages in block, passes through main bearings up to camshaft bearings. Oil moves through secondary drilled passages from main bearings to lifter galleries, push rods pick oil up from lifters and through rotation of push rod moves oil up to top of head assembly to rocker arms. Oil is returned through drain holes in head assemblies back down into crankcase. *See Fig. 18.*

OIL PUMP

Removal & Disassembly — Remove oil pan, attaching bolts and oil pump from engine. Remove oil inlet tube, cover attaching screws, and cover. Remove inner rotor and shaft assembly, remove outer race. Drill small hole into oil pressure relief spring valve chamber cap. Insert self-threading sheet metal screw into the cap and pull from chamber. Remove the spring and plunger. *See Fig. 19.*

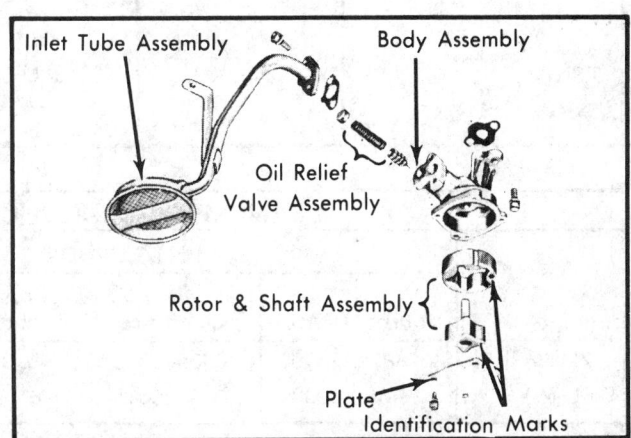

Fig. 19 Disassembled View of Oil Pump

Ford V8 Engines

4.2L, 5.0L & 5.8L (W) V8 ENGINES (Cont.)

Reassembly & Installation — **1)** Clean, inspect and oil all parts thoroughly. Install relief valve plunger, spring and new cap. Stake cap into position. Install outer race and inner rotor and shaft assembly.

NOTE — *Identification mark on rotor and on outer race must face outward and to same side.*

2) — Install cover and tighten bolts. Position oil inlet tube on oil pump, install new gasket and tighten attaching bolts. Prime pump by submerging in oil and rotating shaft until oil flows from outer port.

Oil Pump Specifications

Application	Specifications
Relief Valve Spring Tension	
4.2L & 5.0L	10.6-12.2 lbs.@1.74"
5.8L (W)	18.2-20.2 lbs.@2.49"
Shaft-to-Housing Clearance	.0015-.0030"
Relief Valve Clearance	.0015-.0030"
Rotor Assembly End Clearance	.004" Max.
Outer Race-to-Hsg. Clearance	.001-.013"

ENGINE SPECIFICATIONS

GENERAL SPECIFICATIONS

Year	Displ. Cu. Ins.	Carburetor	HP at RPM	Torque (Ft. Lbs. at RPM)	Compr. Ratio	Bore	Stroke
1981	255"	2-Bbl.	.....	.....	.....	3.68"	3.00"
	302"	2-Bbl.	.....	.....	.....	4.00"	3.00"
	351" (W)	2-Bbl.	.....	.....	.....	4.00"	3.50"

VALVES

Engine & Valve	Head Diam.	Face Angle	Seat Angle	Seat Width	Stem Diameter	Stem Clearance①	Valve Lift
4.2L & 5.0L							
Int.	1.690-1.694"	44°	45°	.060-.080"	.3416-.3423"	.0010-.0027"	.382"
Exh.	1.439-1.463"	44°	45°	.060-.080"	.3411-.3418"	.0015-.0032"	.398"
5.8L (W)							
Int.	1.770-1.794"	44°	45°	.060-.080"	.3416-.3423"	.0010-.0027"	.4186"
Exh.	1.453-1.458"	44°	45°	.060-.080"	.3411-.3418"	.0015-.0032"	.4186"

① — Service clearance — .0055"

PISTONS, PINS, RINGS

Engine	PISTONS Clearance	PINS Piston Fit	PINS Rod Fit	Rings	RINGS End Gap	RINGS Side Clearance
4.2L & 5.0L	.0018-.0026"	.0002-.0004"	Interference Fit	1	.010-.020"	.0019-.0036"
				2	.010-.020"	.0020-.0040"
				3	.010-.035"	Snug
5.8L (W)	.0018-.0026"	.0003-.0005"	Interference Fit	1	.010-.020"	.0019-.0036"
				2	.010-.020"	.0020-.0040"
				3	.010-.035"	Snug

CRANKSHAFT MAIN & CONNECTING ROD BEARINGS

Engine	MAIN BEARINGS Journal Diam.	MAIN BEARINGS Clearance	Thrust Bearing	Crankshaft End Play	CONNECTING ROD BEARINGS Journal Diam.	CONNECTING ROD BEARINGS Clearance	Side Play
4.2L & 5.0L	2.2482-2.2490"	①.0005-.0015"	No. 3	②.004-.008"	2.1228-2.1236"	.0008-.0015"	.010-.020"
5.8L (W)	2.9994-3.0002"	.0008-.0015"	No. 3	②.004-.008"	2.3103-2.3111"	.0008-.0015"	.010-.020"

① — No. 1 is .0001-.0015".

② — Service limit — .012"

Ford V8 Engines

4.2L, 5.0L & 5.8L (W) V8 ENGINES (Cont.)

ENGINE SPECIFICATIONS (Cont.)

VALVE SPRINGS

Engine	Free Length	PRESSURE (LBS.)	
		Valve Closed	Valve Open
4.2L			
Int.	2.04"	74-82@1.78"	190-212@1.36"
Exh.	1.85"	76-84@1.60"	190-210@1.36"
5.0L			
Int.	2.04"	74-82@1.78"	196-212@1.36"
Exh.	1.85"	76-84@1.60"	190-210@1.20"
5.8L (W)			
Int.	2.04"	74-82@1.78"	190-210@1.36"
Exh.	1.85"	76-84@1.60"	190-210@1.20"

CAMSHAFT

Engine	Journal Diam.	Clearance	Lobe Lift
4.2L, 5.0L & 5.8L (W)		①	
No.1	2.0805-2.0815"	.001-.003"	Int. .2375"②
No.2	2.0655-2.0665"		Exh. .2470"②
No.3	2.0505-2.0515"		Int. .2600"③
No.4	2.0355-2.0365"		Exh. .2600"③
No.5	2.0205-2.0215"		

① — End Play is .001-.007".
② — 4.2L & 5.0L engines.
③ — 5.8L (W) engine.

TIGHTENING SPECIFICATIONS

Application	Ft. Lbs.
Cylinder Head	
4.2L & 5.0L	
Step One	55-65
Step Two	65-72
5.8L (W)	
Step One	85
Step Two	95
Step Three	105-112
Intake Manifold	23-25
Exhaust Manifold	18-24
Flywheel-to-Crankshaft	75-85
Main Bearing Caps	
4.2L & 5.0L	60-70
5.8L (W)	95-105
Connecting Rod Caps	
4.2L & 5.0L	19-24
5.8L (W)	40-45
Pulley-to-Damper	35-50
Rocker Arm Cover Bolts	3-5
Damper-to-Crankshaft	70-90
Camshaft Thrust Plate	9-12
Rocker Arm Stud Nut	18-25
Camshaft Sprocket	40-45
Oil Filter Insert-to-Block	20-30
Oil Pump-to-Cylinder Block	22-32
Oil Pan Bolts	9-11

Ford V8 Engines

5.8L (M) & 6.6L V8 ENGINES

IDENTIFICATION CODING

ENGINE IDENTIFICATION

Engine is identified by a letter code, eighth digit of Vehicle Identification Number, located inside windshield on left upper side of instrument panel. The VIN number is also located on the Safety Compliance Certification Label located on left door lock pillar.

Engine Identification Codes	
Application	**VIN Code**
5.8L (351" M) 2-Bbl.	G
6.6L (400") 2-Bbl.	Z

ENGINE REMOVAL

See Engine Removal at end of ENGINE Section.

CYLINDER HEAD & MANIFOLD

INTAKE MANIFOLD

Removal — 1) Remove air cleaner and air inlet duct. If equipped with air conditioning, isolate and remove compressor. Disconnect all electrical connections on manifold and position harness out of way.

2) Disconnect spark plug wires from spark plugs. Disconnect wires from valve cover brackets. Remove distributor cap and wires as a unit. Disconnect fuel inlet line at carburetor. Disconnect vacuum lines from intake manifold.

3) Remove heater hoses from retainers and position out of way. Remove coil, vacuum solenoid valve and bracket. Disconnect PCV hose from valve cover. Disconnect vacuum hose at distributor. Remove hold down clamp and remove distributor. Place a clean shop towel over hole.

4) Disconnect accelerator linkage, speed control cable and transmission downshift linkage (if equipped) at carburetor. Remove carburetor, manifold bolts and manifold. Remove and discard intake manifold gasket.

Installation — 1) Clean all gasket surfaces thoroughly. Apply a ⅛" bead of RTV silicone sealer to the four points at corner of heads that contact seal mounting surface of block.

2) Install a new seal on block and press locating extensions into holes in mating surface. Apply a 1/16" bead of silicone sealer to end of each seal. Place manifold gasket in position, making sure all alignment notches are under dowels on cylinder head. Make sure holes in gasket are aligned with holes in head.

CAUTION — *Do not apply sealer to waffle section of end seals as sealer will rupture end seals.*

3) Place manifold in position on engine. Tighten bolts to specification in 2 steps in sequence shown in *Fig. 1.* After completion of intake manifold installation, retighten manifold bolts in sequence with engine at normal operating temperature.

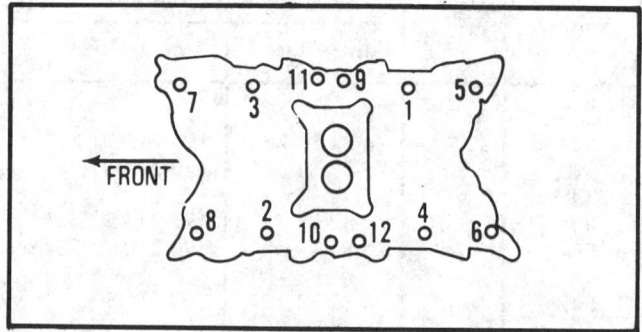

Fig. 1   Intake Manifold Tightening Sequence

CYLINDER HEAD

Removal — 1) Remove intake manifold as previously outlined. Remove valve covers. If left cylinder head is being removed on a vehicle equipped with air conditioning, isolate and remove compressor.

2) If left cylinder head is being removed on a vehicle with power steering, disconnect pump bracket from cylinder head. Remove pump drive belt. Place pump out of way, sitting up straight to prevent fluid loss.

3) If right cylinder head is being removed, remove alternator mounting bracket through bolt and air inlet duct. Disconnect ground wire from rear of head. Disconnect exhaust pipes at manifolds.

4) Remove rocker arm bolts, oil deflectors, fulcrum seats, rocker arms and push rods in sequence. Same components must be installed in original position. Remove cylinder head bolts and remove cylinder head.

NOTE — *On E150/350 models, it may be necessary to remove left-hand cylinder head with forward bolt installed due to closeness of body flange.*

Installation — 1) Clean all gasket surfaces. Check cylinder head and block for flatness if cylinder head was removed for gasket replacement. Place a new gasket over dowel pins on block.

NOTE — *A specially treated composition gasket is used and does not require sealer.*

2) Install cylinder heads and bolts. Tighten head bolts to specifications in 2 steps in sequence shown in *Fig. 2.* Reverse removal procedure to complete installation.

NOTE — *On E150/350 models, it may be necessary to install left-hand cylinder head with forward bolt already installed due to closeness of body flange.*

5.8L (M) & 6.6L V8 ENGINES (Cont.)

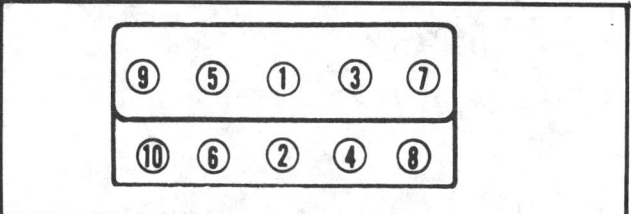

Fig. 2   Cylinder Head Tightening Sequence

VALVES

VALVE ARRANGEMENT

E-I-E-I-E-I-E-I (left bank, front to rear.)
I-E-I-E-I-E-I-E (right bank, front to rear.)

VALVE GUIDE SERVICING

To ream guides for installation of valves with oversize stems, always use reamers in size sequence and reface valves and valve seats after guide is reamed. Reamers are furnished .003" oversize with standard diameter pilot; .015" oversize reamer with .003" oversize pilot; and .030" oversize reamer with .015" oversize pilot.

NOTE — *Use suitable scraper tool to break sharp corner (ID) at top of valve guide after reaming.*

VALVE STEM OIL SEALS

Cup or umbrella type oil seals are used on valves. Lubricate valve stem with engine oil and install seal with cup side down over valve guide using $\frac{5}{8}$" deep well socket and light mallet to seat seal on valve stem.

VALVE SPRINGS

Removal — 1) Remove air cleaner. Remove valve cover and spark plug for cylinder being serviced. Install an air line with adapter in spark plug hole.

NOTE — *If air pressure fails to hold valve closed, remove cylinder head for inspection of valve seat.*

2) Remove required rocker arm and push rod. Using a suitable spring compression tool, compress valve spring and remove spring retainer locks. Release spring compressor. Remove retainer and valve spring. Remove valve stem seal.

CAUTION — *Do not release air pressure as this will allow valve to fall into cylinder if piston is at bottom of stroke.*

Installation — 1) With valve stem seal installed, place spring in position over valve. Install spring retainer. Compress spring with spring compressor and install retainer locks.

2) Apply Lubriplate (or equivalent) to end of push rods and tip of valve stem. Install rocker arm and tighten fulcrum bolt to specification. Install valve cover.

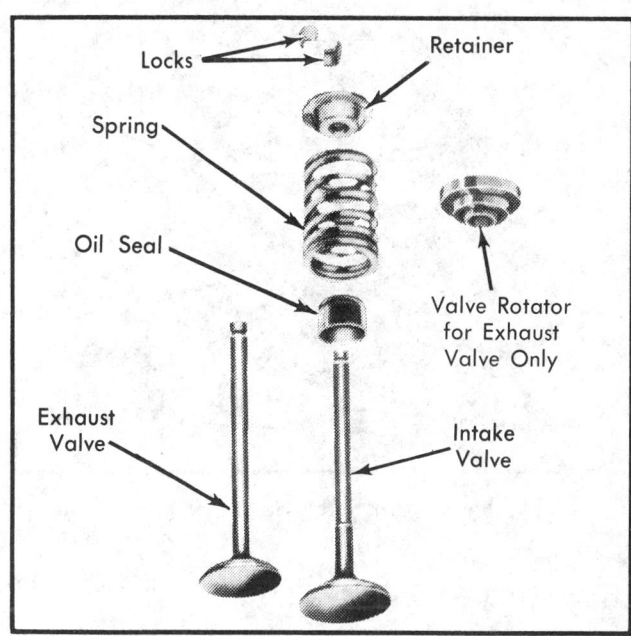

Fig. 3   Exploded View of Valve Assemblies

VALVE SPRING INSTALLED HEIGHT

Valve spring ends must be square within $\frac{5}{64}$" tolerance. Installed height of valve spring must not exceed specifications. Measure spring height from surface of cylinder head pad to underside of spring retainer. If height is greater than specified, install a .030" spacer on head under spring to bring height within limits.

CAUTION — *Install spacer only if necessary and do not use more than two spacers as any more will overstress springs and overload camshaft lobes.*

Valve Spring Installed Height Specifications	
Application	**Installed Height**
5.8L (M) & 6.6L	
Int.	$1\frac{13}{16}$-$1\frac{27}{32}$"
Exh.	$1\frac{11}{16}$-$1\frac{24}{32}$"

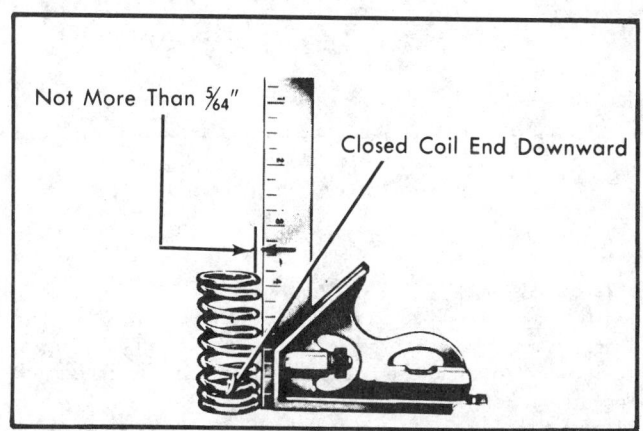

Fig. 4   Checking Valve Spring Squareness

Ford V8 Engines

5.8L (M) & 6.6L V8 ENGINES (Cont.)

Fig. 5   Checking Installed Height of Valve Spring

ROCKER ARM ASSEMBLY

Inspect rocker arms, fulcrum seats and fulcrum bolts for excessive wear. Replace components as necessary.

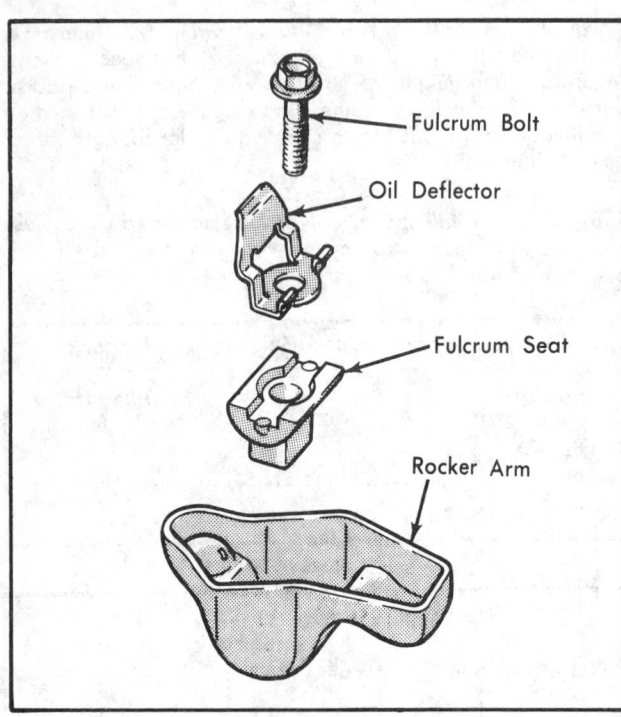

Fig. 6   Rocker Arm Assembly

HYDRAULIC VALVE LIFTER ASSEMBLY

Lifters should be serviced as assemblies only, integral components are matched sets and cannot be interchanged. Leak down rate on hydraulic lifters is 10-50 seconds at 1/16" plunger travel using a suitable leak down rate tester. Replace lifter assembly if any sign of malfunction occurs. See Fig. 7.

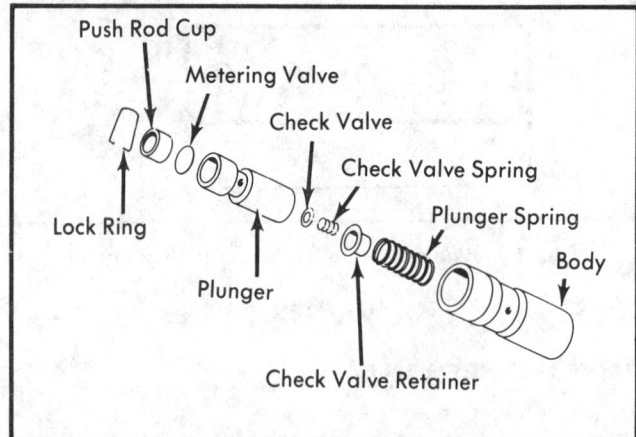

Fig. 7   Disassembled View of Hydraulic Valve Lifter

HYDRAULIC VALVE LIFTER ADJUSTMENT

Repeated valve (seat and face) reconditioning operations will decrease valve stem to rocker arm clearance to a point that if compensation is not made, valve lifters will cease to function. To compensate for any dimensional changes in valve mechanism, a shorter or longer replacement push rod is available.

1) To determine whether or not a longer or shorter push rod is necessary, clearance between rocker arm and valve stem must be checked.

NOTE — Valve lifter must be completely collapsed when checking valve clearance.

2) Using a suitable tool, slowly collapse lifter until plunger is bottomed. Hold lifter down while checking clearance.

3) Rotate crankshaft until No. 1 piston is at TDC (point 1 in Fig. 8) after compression stroke, as indicated by timing mark on crankshaft damper and pointer. Make chalk mark on damper 180° (point 2) from TDC mark and another chalk mark 90° (point 3) clockwise from TDC mark.

4) With damper at point 1, check clearance on intake valves 1, 4 and 8 and exhaust valves 1, 3 and 7.

5) Rotate crankshaft 180° clockwise from point 1 so point 2 is opposite pointer. Check clearance on intake valves 3 and 7 and exhaust valves 2 and 6.

6) Rotate crankshaft 270° clockwise from point 2 so point 3 is opposite pointer. Check clearance on intake valves 2, 5 and 6 and exhaust valves 4, 5 and 8.

Collapsed Lifter Clearance		
Application	Desired	Allowable
5.8L (M) & 6.6L	.125-.175"	.100-.200"

5.8L (M) & 6.6L V8 ENGINES (Cont.)

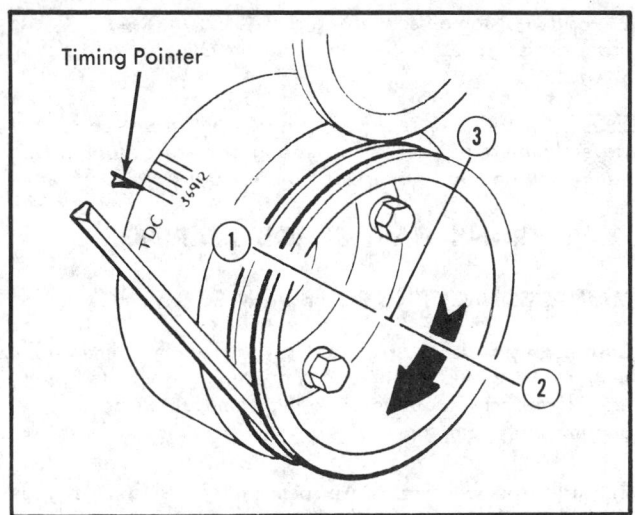

Fig. 8 Crankshaft Positions for Adjusting Hydraulic Valve Lifters

PISTON, PINS & RINGS

OIL PAN

See Oil Pan Removal at end of ENGINE Section.

PISTON & ROD ASSEMBLY

NOTE — *New pistons must be installed in same cylinders for which they were fitted and used pistons in same cylinder from which they were removed.*

Removal — 1) With cylinder head and oil pan removed, use a ridge reamer to remove any ridge or deposits on upper end of cylinder bore. Piston must be at bottom of stroke and covered with cloth to collect cuttings.

NOTE — *Never cut more than 1/32" from ring travel area of bore when removing ridge.*

2) Inspect connecting rods and caps for cylinder identification and mark as necessary. Remove rod cap and push piston and rod assembly out top of block, taking care not to nick crankshaft journal or cylinder wall.

Installation — 1) Lightly coat cylinder bores, pistons and rings with engine oil. Make sure ring gaps are properly spaced. *See Fig. 10.*

2) Compress piston rings with a ring compressor. Install each piston and rod assembly in cylinder bore with notch or arrow on piston toward front of engine and numbered side of rod facing away from camshaft.

3) Guide connecting rod onto crankshaft journal while tapping piston head with hammer handle to seat connecting rod bearing against crankshaft. Install connecting rod cap, aligning numbers. Tighten nuts to specification.

FITTING PISTONS

Measure piston at centerline of piston pin bore 90° to pin bore axis. Measure cylinder bore at right angle to centerline of

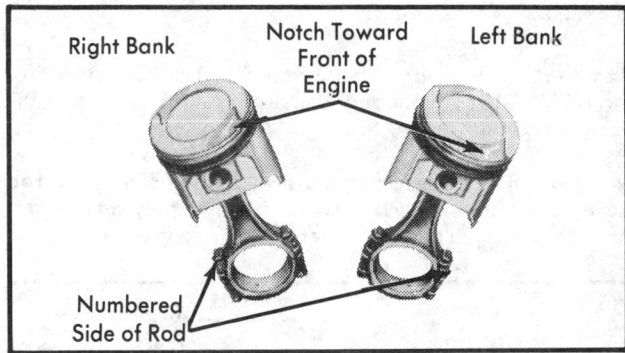

Fig. 9 Fitting Piston and Connecting Rod Assembly

crankshaft, below ring travel. Piston-to-bore clearance should be as shown in Pistons, Pins & Rings table. Check Piston Size Code Chart to determine correct size. Make sure both piston and cylinder block are at normal room temperature (70°F) when fitting.

Piston Size Code Chart	
Code	**Piston Size**
Red	3.9982-3.9988"
Blue	3.9994-4.0000"
.003" Oversize	4.0006-4.0012"

FITTING RINGS

1) Position ring in the cylinder bore that it will be used in. Push ring down to point in bore where ring wear is not encountered. Use head of piston to position ring squarely in bore.

2) Measure gap between ends of ring using a feeler gauge, if not to specification, substitute another ring set until rings are within specification.

CAUTION — *Use care to avoid damage to ring or cylinder bore.*

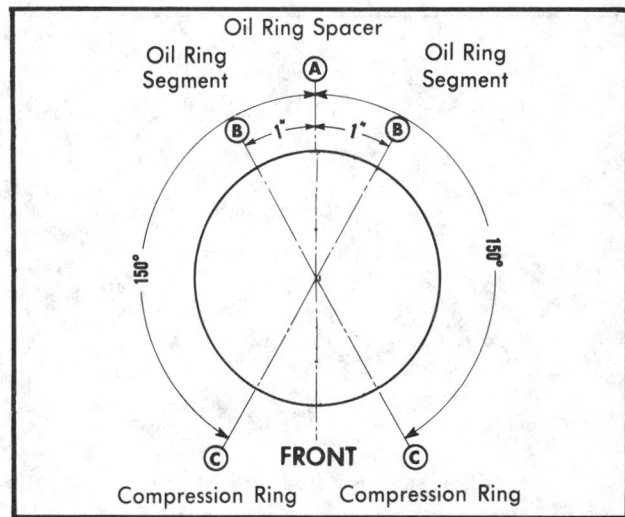

Fig. 10 Correct Spacing for Piston Ring Gaps

Ford V8 Engines

5.8L (M) & 6.6L V8 ENGINES (Cont.)

PISTON PINS

Removal — Using an arbor press and removal/installation tool (T68P-6135-A) and adapters, press piston out of connecting rod and piston. *See Fig. 11.*

Installation — **1)** Make sure piston pin and connecting rod have correct interference fit specifications. Apply a light coat of oil to piston pin and to pin bore in rod and in piston.

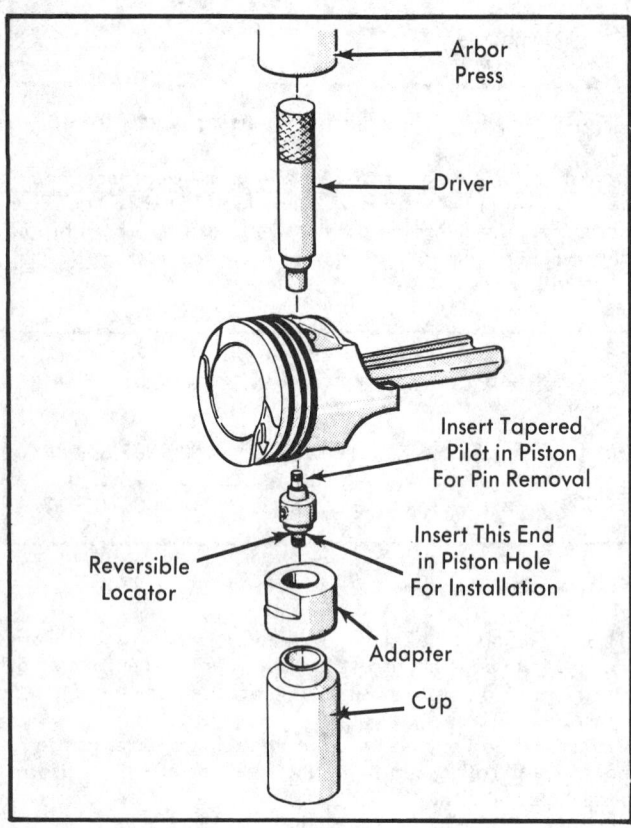

Fig. 11   Removing and Installing Piston Pins

2) Position piston on connecting rod as shown. *See Fig. 9.* Use arbor press to press piston pin into connecting rod and piston. *See Fig. 11.*

NOTE — *If rods are replaced, position piston on rod so that large chamfered side of rod bearing bore faces forward on right bank and faces rearward on left bank.*

CRANKSHAFT & ROD BEARINGS

MAIN & CONNECTING ROD BEARINGS

Connecting Rod Bearings — **1)** With crankshaft lined up in center of bore, push piston and connecting rod up into bore to gain clearance for upper bearing removal. Remove lower bearing half from cap.

2) After rod bearings have been fitted using Plastigage method, apply light coat of engine oil to journals and bearings. With crankshaft throw at bottom of stroke, move piston down until connecting rod bearing seats on crankshaft journal. Install connecting rod cap and nuts and tighten to specification checking connecting rod side clearance.

Main Bearings — **1)** Mark main bearing caps for identification before removal from block. Remove upper half of main bearing by inserting removal tool 6331 (or equivalent), into oil hole of crankshaft and slowly rotate crankshaft in direction of engine rotation.

NOTE — *Replace one bearing at a time leaving other bearings secured until ready to change.*

2) If bearing clearance is excessive, a .001" or .002" undersize bearing half may be used in combination with a standard size half. If .002" undersize bearings are used on more than one journal, they may be positioned in engine block rather than bearing cap. If standard and .002" undersize combination did not bring bearing clearance within specified limits, crankshaft will have to be refinished and suitable undersize bearings installed.

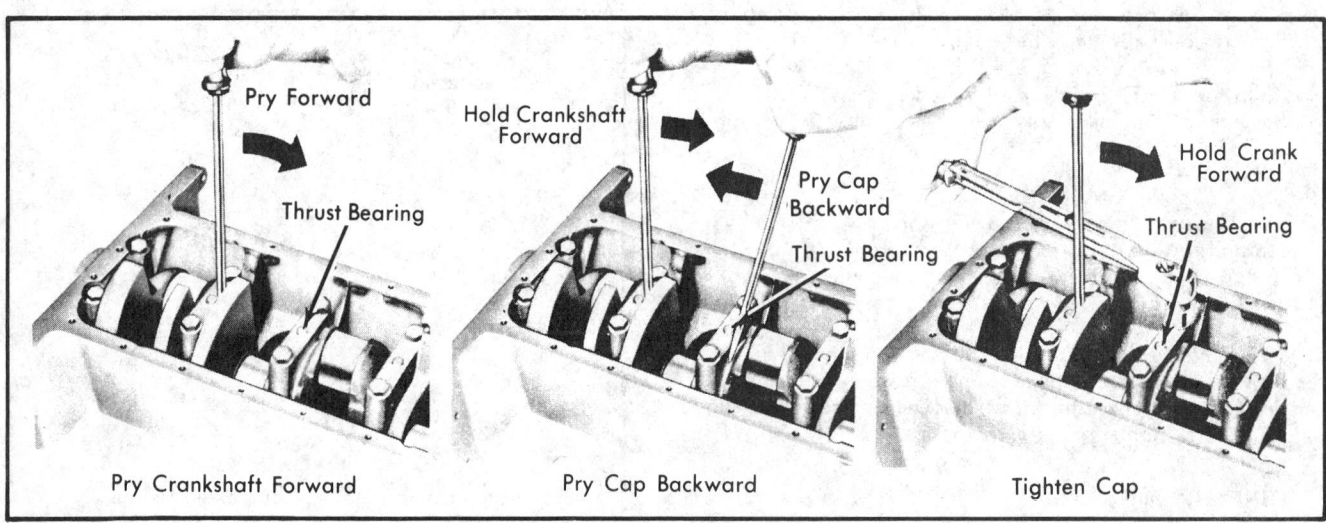

Fig. 12   Aligning Thrust Bearing

5.8L (M) & 6.6L V8 ENGINES (Cont.)

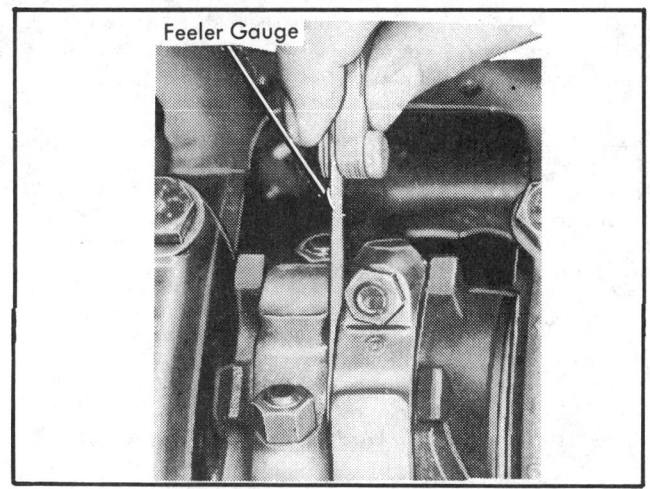

Fig. 13   Measuring Connecting Rod Side Clearance

3) To install upper main bearings, lubricate bearing with engine oil and place plain end of bearing over crankshaft on locking tang side of block. Partially insert bearing to allow suitable tool (6331) to be inserted into oil hole in crankshaft journal. Rotate crankshaft in opposite direction of engine rotation until bearing is seated. Remove installer tool. Install bearing cap and tighten bolts.

THRUST BEARING ALIGNMENT

Install thrust bearing cap after all other main caps have been tightened. Install thrust bearing cap with bolts finger tight. Pry crankshaft forward against thrust surface of upper half of bearing. Hold crankshaft forward and pry thrust bearing cap to rear. This will align thrust surfaces of both halves of bearing. Retain forward pressure on crankshaft and tighten cap bolts to specification.

REAR MAIN BEARING OIL SEAL

Removal — 1) Complete seal can be replaced without removing crankshaft. Remove oil pan and oil pump. Loosen all main bearing cap bolts and allow crankshaft to drop slightly, but not to exceed $\frac{1}{32}$".

2) Remove rear main bearing cap and remove oil seal from bearing cap and block. On block half of seal, use seal removing tool or place small metal screw in one end of seal and pull on screw to remove seal. Care must be taken to prevent scratching or damage to crankshaft seal surface.

3) Remove oil seal retaining pin from bearing cap (if equipped). Replacement seal does not use pin. Discard pin after removal.

Installation — 1) Clean oil seal groove. Dip new seal halves in engine oil. Carefully install block upper seal half into groove. Make sure undercut (lip) side of seal is toward front of engine. Install by rotating seal on journal of crankshaft until approximately $\frac{3}{8}$" of seal protrudes from parting surface.

CAUTION — *Avoid shaving any rubber from outside diameter of seal by bottom edge of groove. Do not allow oil to get into sealing area.*

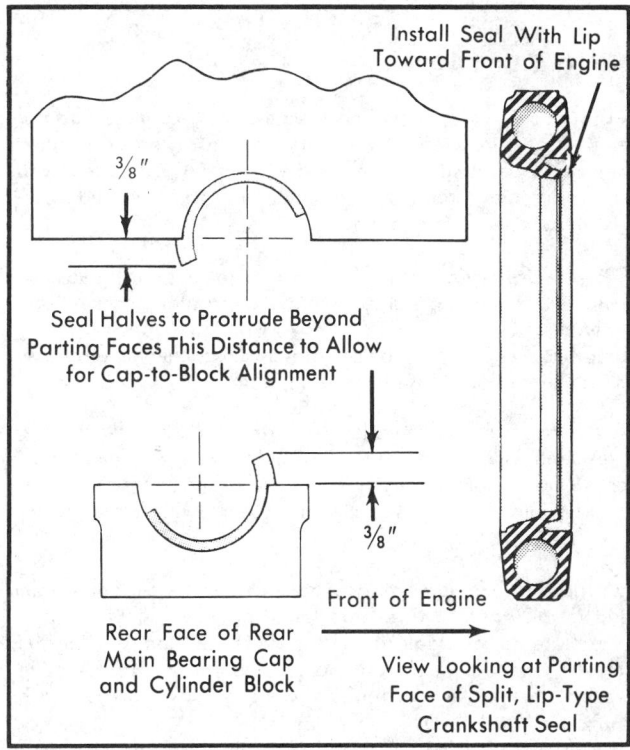

Fig. 14   Installing Crankshaft Rear Oil Seal

2) Tighten remaining bearing cap bolts to specification. Install lower seal in cap with undercut side of seal toward front of engine. Allow seal to protrude $\frac{3}{8}$" above parting surface to mate with upper seal when cap is installed.

3) Apply suitable RTV silicone sealer to areas shown in *Fig. 15*. Install bearing cap and tighten bolts.

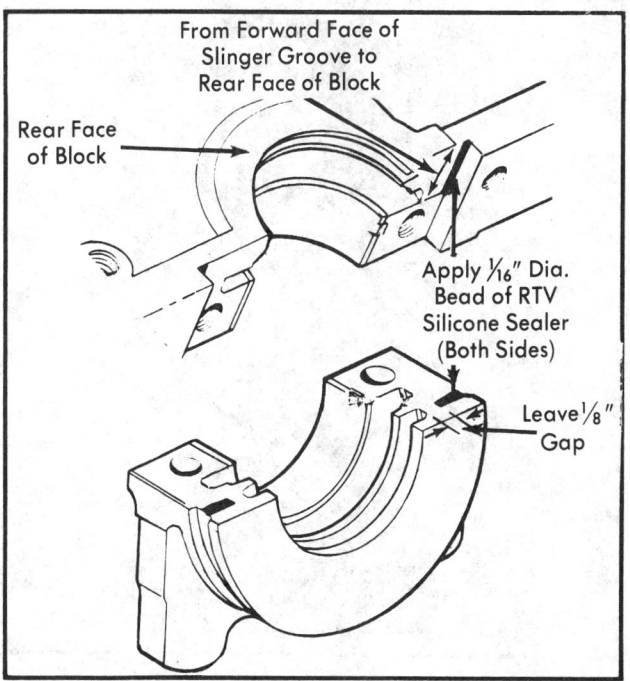

Fig. 15   Applying Sealer to Main Bearing Cap and Block

5.8L (M) & 6.6L V8 ENGINES (Cont.)

CAMSHAFT

ENGINE FRONT COVER

Removal — 1) Drain cooling system and disconnect battery. Remove fan shroud attaching bolts and move shroud to rear. Remove fan and spacer from water pump. If equipped with air conditioning, remove belt, lower idler pulley and compressor to water pump mount.

2) Remove alternator drive belt and power steering drive belt. Remove water pump pulley. Remove alternator bracket from water pump and position out of way. Remove power steering pump bracket and position out of way. Disconnect heater hose and lower radiator hose from water pump.

3) Remove crankshaft pulley from damper. Remove damper screw and pull off damper with a puller. Remove timing pointer. Remove bolts securing front cover and water pump to cylinder block and remove front cover (with water pump attached).

Installation — Clean all gasket surfaces. Use suitable sealer and install gaskets. Coat threads of bolts with sealer. Apply Lubriplate to oil seal running surface on damper. Tighten screws. Oil pan must be removed and a new front seal installed when cover is removed. Reverse removal procedure to complete installation.

FRONT COVER OIL SEAL

Removal — 1) Remove fan shroud bolts and slide back over engine. Remove water pump belt. Remove fan, spacer and shroud. Remove remaining drive belts. Remove crankshaft pulley from vibration damper.

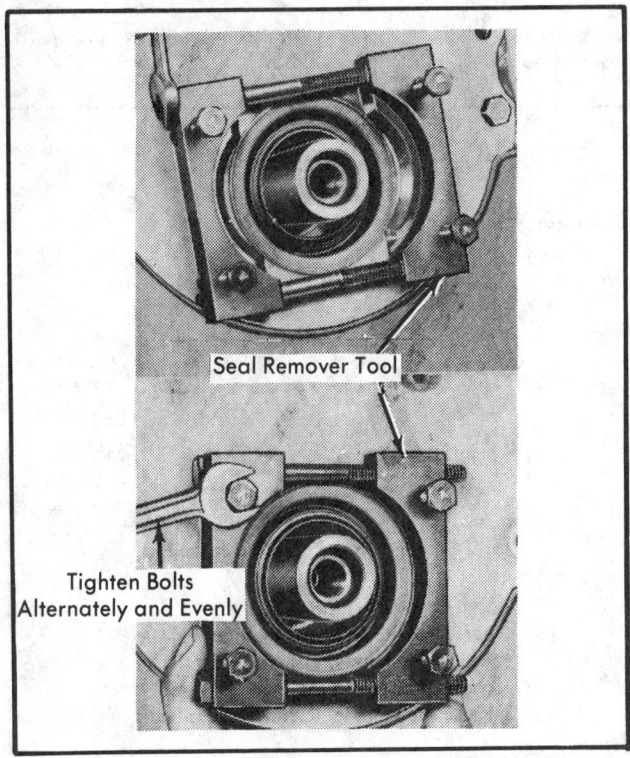

Fig. 16 Removing Front Cover Oil Seal

2) Remove vibration damper bolt. Pull off damper with a puller. Attach seal remover tool (T70P-6B070-B) to lip of front seal. Tighten puller bolts and remove seal. See *Fig. 16.*

Installation — Coat a new front cover oil seal with Lubriplate. Position seal on cranksaft against seal bore in front cover. Position a suitable seal installation sleeve (T70P-6B070-A) on crankshaft. Tighten tool bolt into crankshaft and turn tool nut against screw to push seal into place. Reverse removal procedure to complete installation.

TIMING CHAIN

Removal — Remove front engine cover as previously outlined. Remove fuel pump outlet line and mounting bolts. Lay fuel pump to side. Crank engine over until timing marks are aligned as shown in *Fig. 17.* Remove camshaft sprocket bolt. Remove washer and 2-piece fuel pump eccentric. Slide both sprockets and timing chain forward to remove.

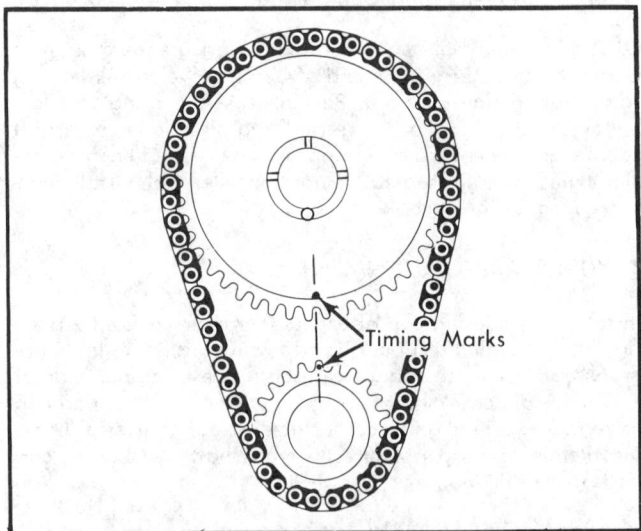

Fig. 17 Aligning Timing Sprocket Marks

Installation — 1) Position timing chain on sprockets, aligning timing marks as shown in *Fig. 17.* Slide timing chain and sprockets onto camshaft and crankshaft as an assembly.

2) Install 2-piece fuel pump eccentric, washers and camshaft sprocket bolt. Tighten bolt to specifications. Reverse removal procedure to complete installation.

CAMSHAFT

Removal — 1) Drain cooling system. Disconnect upper and lower radiator hoses at radiator. Disconnect oil cooler lines at radiator (if equipped). Remove radiator. Remove air conditioning condenser (if equipped) after discharging system. Remove front engine cover and timing chain as previously outlined.

2) Remove intake manifold as previously outlined. Remove valve covers. Loosen but do not remove rocker arm fulcrum bolts. Rotate rocker arms to side and remove push rods. Mark or identify push rods to ensure that they are installed in original position. Remove valve lifters. Mark or identify lifters to ensure that they are installed in original position.

5.8L (M) & 6.6L V8 ENGINES (Cont.)

3) Turn engine over until number one piston is at TDC. Remove camshaft thrust plate bolts and remove thrust plate. Carefully pull camshaft toward front to remove. Care must be taken when withdrawing camshaft to avoid damaging camshaft bearings or camshaft lobes.

Installation — Coat camshaft lobes with Lubriplate and bearing journals with heavy engine oil. Carefully install camshaft in engine. Install thrust plate and tighten bolts. Install timing chain as previously outlined. To complete installation, reverse removal procedure.

CAMSHAFT BEARINGS

NOTE — *Engine must be removed from vehicle and flywheel, crankshaft, and camshaft must be removed. Bearings are not interchangeable from one bore to another.*

Removal — Drive out camshaft rear plug and all camshaft bearings using a suitable driver and mandrels of correct size.

Installation — Drive new bearing into position, making sure oil holes are aligned. Make sure front bearing is installed .040-.060" below front edge of cylinder block. Install camshaft rear plug.

CAMSHAFT END THRUST

Rocker arm fulcrum bolts must be loosened to free load on camshaft. Push camshaft toward rear of engine. Install a dial indicator so that plunger is on camshaft sprocket bolt. Zero dial indicator. Position a screwdriver between camshaft sprocket and cylinder block. Pry camshaft forward and release. If end play exceeds .009", replace thrust plate.

CAMSHAFT LOBE LIFT

Check lift of each camshaft lobe in consecutive order as follows:

1) Remove all fulcrum bolts, oil deflector, fulcrum seats and rocker arms. Mark or identify rocker arms to ensure installation in original position. Make sure each push rod is in valve lifter socket. Install a dial indicator allowing ball socket adapter of dial indicator to rest on end of push rod in same plane as push rod movement.

2) Using a remote starter (with ignition switch in "OFF" position), turn engine until valve lifter being checked is on base circle of camshaft lobe, indicating lowest point of push rod travel.

3) Zero dial indicator and continue to rotate engine until push rod is in fully raised position giving highest indicator reading. Continue same procedure for each camshaft lobe. Compare camshaft lift from dial indicator readings with specifications.

4) To check accuracy of dial indicator readings, continue to rotate engine until dial indicator reads zero. If lift on any camshaft lobe is .005" less than specifications, camshaft lobes are worn. Camshaft and lifter must be replaced.

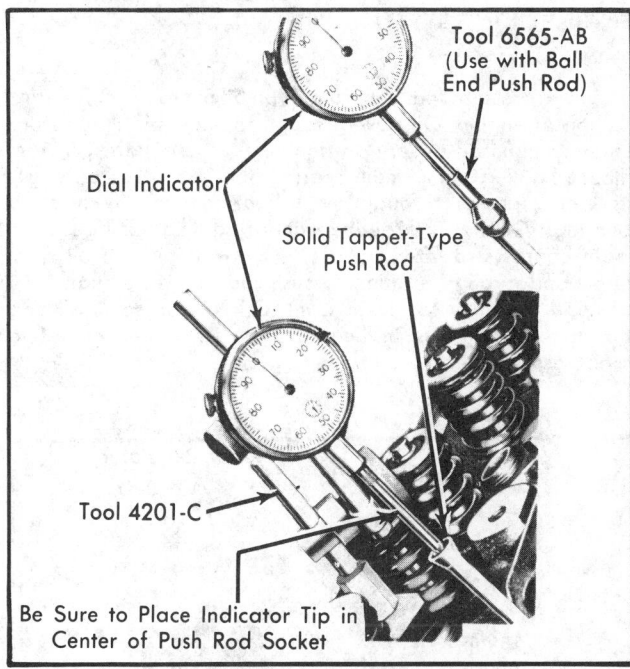

Fig. 18 Checking Camshaft Lobe Lift

ENGINE OILING

Crankcase Capacity — 5 quarts. Add 1 quart with filter change.

Oil Filter — Replace at first oil change and every second oil change after that.

Normal Oil Pressure — Oil pressure should be 50-75 psi at 2000 RPM.

Pressure Regulator Valve — In oil pump body on all engines. Not adjustable.

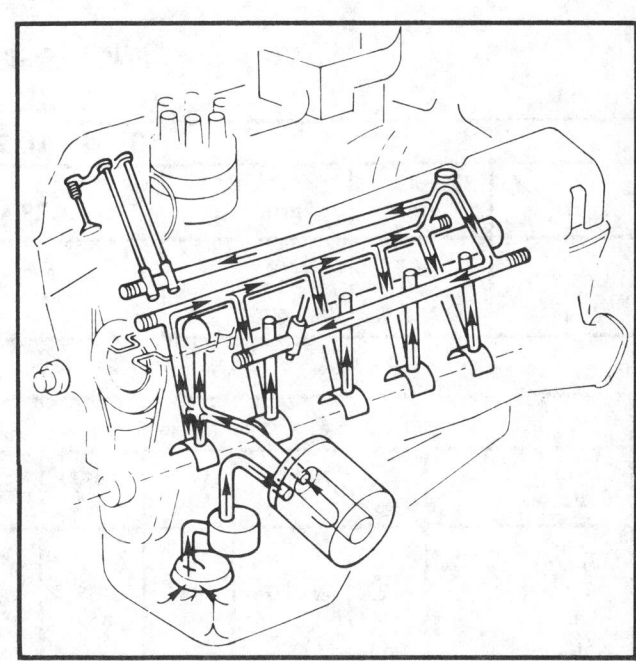

Fig. 19 Engine Oiling System

Ford V8 Engines

5.8L (M) & 6.6L V8 ENGINES (Cont.)

ENGINE OILING SYSTEM

System is pressure fed from rotor type oil pump in left forward section of engine. Oil flows through full-flow oil filter before entering main oil gallery on right side of camshaft. Oil from main oil gallery enters main bearings through drilled passages in block, passes through main bearings up to camshaft bearings. Oil moves through secondary drilled passages from main bearings to lifter galleries. Push rods pick up oil from lifters and through rotation of push rods, moves oil up to top of head assembly to rocker arms. Oil is returned to oil pan through drain holes in head assemblies back down into crankcase.

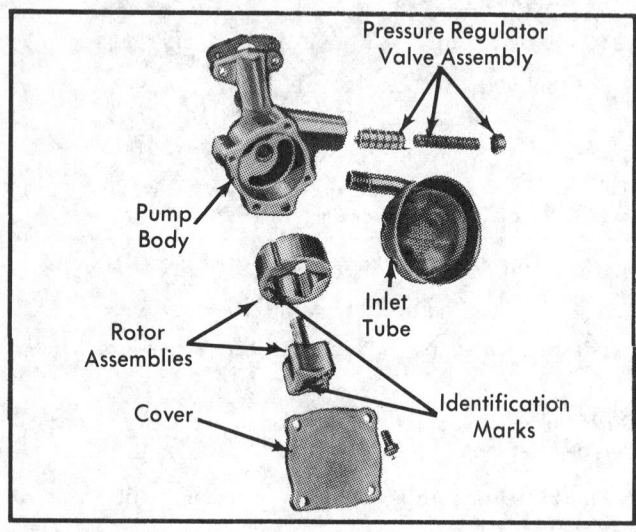

Fig. 20   Exploded View of Oil Pump

OIL PUMP

Removal & Disassembly — With oil pan removed, remove pump bolts and remove pump. Remove oil inlet tube from pump. Remove cover screws and cover. Remove inner rotor and shaft assembly, then remove outer rotor. Remove cotter pin from pump housing. Drill a small hole in pressure regulator valve plug. Screw in a self threading sheet metal screw then pull plug out of bore. Remove spring and plunger.

Inspection & Reassembly — Clean, inspect and oil all components thoroughly. Install pressure regulator valve plunger, spring and a new cap. Stake cap into position. Install inner and outer rotor. Make sure identification marks on inner and outer rotor are facing outward and to same side. Check various oil pump clearances as outlined in specifications. Install cover and tighten bolts. Install oil inlet tube using new gasket. Submerge inlet tube in oil and prime pump by rotating shaft until oil emerges from outer port.

Oil Pump Specifications	
Application	**Specifications**
Pressure Regulator Valve	
Spring Tension	20.6-22.6 lbs.@2.49"
Shaft-to-Housing Clearance	.0015-.0030"
Pressure Regulator Valve Clearance	.0015-.0030"
Rotor Assembly End Clearance	.004" Max.
Outer Rotor-to-Housing Clearance	.001-.013"

ENGINE SPECIFICATIONS

GENERAL SPECIFICATIONS							
Year	Displ. Cu. Ins.	Carburetor	HP at RPM	Torque (Ft. Lbs. at RPM)	Compr. Ratio	Bore	Stroke
1981							
5.8L (M)	351"	2-Bbl.	.....	.....	.....	4.00"	3.50"
6.6L	400"	2-Bbl.	.....	.....	.....	4.00"	4.00"

VALVES							
Engine & Valve	Head Diam.	Face Angle	Seat Angle	Seat Width	Stem Diameter	Stem Clearance	Valve Lift
5.8L (M)							
Int.	2.032-2.050"	44°	45°	.060-.080"	.3416-.3423"	.0010-.0027"	.4325"
Exh.	1.6495-1.6595"	44°	45°	.070-.090"	.3411-.3418"	.0015-.0032"	.4325"
6.6L							
Int.	2.032-2.050"	44°	45°	.060-.080"	.3416-.3423"	.0010-.0027"	.4325"
Exh.	1.6495-1.6595"	44°	45°	.070-.090"	.3411-.3418"	.0015-.0032"	.4325"

5.8L (M) & 6.6L V8 ENGINES (Cont.)
ENGINE SPECIFICATIONS (Cont.)

CRANKSHAFT MAIN & CONNECTING ROD BEARINGS

Engine	MAIN BEARINGS				CONNECTING ROD BEARINGS		
	Journal Diam.	Clearance	Thrust Bearing	Crankshaft End Play	Journal Diam.	Clearance	Side Play
5.8L (M) &6.6L	2.994-3.0002"	.0008-.0015"	No. 3	.004-.008"	2.3103-2.3111"	.0008-.0015"	.010-.020"

PISTONS, PINS, RINGS

Engine	PISTONS	PINS		RINGS		
	Clearance	Piston Fit	Rod Fit	Rings	End Gap	Side Clearance
5.8L (M) & 6.6L	.0014-.0022"	.0003-.0005"	Interference Fit	1	.010-.020"	.0019-.0036"
				2	.010-.020"	.002-.004"
				3	.010-.035"	Snug

VALVE SPRINGS

Engine	Free Length	PRESSURE (LBS.)	
		Valve Closed	Valve Open
5.8L (M) & 6.6L			
Int.	2.06"	76-84@1.82"	215-237@1.39"
Exh.	1.93"	79-87@1.68"	215-237@1.39"

CAMSHAFT

Engine	Journal Diam.	Clearance	Lobe Lift
5.8L (M) & 6.6L		①	
No. 1	2.1238-2.1248"	.001-.003"	.250"
No. 2	2.0655-2.0665"		
No. 3	2.0505-2.0515"		
No. 4	2.0355-2.0365"		
No. 5	2.0205-2.0215"		

① — Camshaft end play is .001-.006"

TIGHTENING SPECIFICATIONS

Application	Ft. Lbs.
Cylinder Head	
Step One	75
Step Two	95-105
Oil Pan	
¼" Bolts	7-9
⁵⁄₁₆" Bolts	11-13
Intake Manifold	
⁵⁄₁₆" Bolts	19-25
¾" Bolts	22-32
Exhaust Manifold	18-24
Flywheel-to-Crankshaft	75-85
Main Bearing Caps	95-105
Connecting Rod Caps	40-45
Pulley-to-Damper	35-50
Damper-to-Crankshaft	70-90
Camshaft Thrust Plate	9-12
Camshaft Sprocket Bolt	40-45
Rocker Arm Fulcrum Bolt	18-25
Rocker Arm Cover Bolts	3-5
Oil Filter Insert-to-Block	20-30
Oil Pump-to-Cylinder Block	22-32

Ford V8 Engines

7.5L V8 ENGINE

IDENTIFICATION CODING

ENGINE IDENTIFICATION

Engine is identified by a letter code, eighth digit of Vehicle Identification Number, located inside windshield on left upper side of instrument panel. The VIN number is also located on the Safety Compliance Certification Label located on left door lock pillar.

Engine Identification Codes	
Application	**VIN Code**
7.5L (460")	L

ENGINE REMOVAL

See Engine Removal at end of ENGINE Section.

CYLINDER HEAD & MANIFOLD

INTAKE MANIFOLD

Removal – 1) Drain cooling system. Remove air cleaner and duct assembly, disconnect radiator and heater hoses at intake manifold and water pump and position out of way.

2) Disconnect and tag all vacuum lines for proper installation. Disconnect PCV valve and hose at right rocker arm valve cover. Disconnect spark plug wires at spark plugs and disconnect coil high-tension lead at coil. Remove distributor cap and spark plug wires as an assembly. Remove distributor.

3) Disconnect accelerator linkage at carburetor and speed control linkage bracket, if equipped, and position linkage out of way. Disconnect fuel line at carburetor.

4) Disconnect any electrical wiring to intake manifold and position out of way. Remove coil and bracket assembly. Remove attaching bolts and nuts and remove intake manifold and carburetor as an assembly.

Installation – 1) Clean and inspect manifold for cracks, damaged gasket surfaces, or other defects. Thoroughly clean all gasket surfaces and apply an oil resistant sealer to intake manifold and block seal surfaces (4 corners).

2) Position front and rear seals on cylinder block and new gaskets on cylinder heads. Ensure that holes in gaskets are aligned with holes in cylinder heads. Position gaskets in slots with end tabs over ribs on seals.

3) Lower intake manifold on engine and check for correct positioning of gaskets and seals before installing attaching bolts and nuts. Install bolts and nuts, then tighten in sequence shown in *Fig. 1*.

4) To install remaining components, reverse removal procedure. After engine has been started and allowed to reach normal operating temperature, retighten manifold attaching bolts and nuts.

CYLINDER HEAD

Removal – 1) Drain cooling system. Remove intake manifold as previously outlined. Disconnect exhaust pipe from exhaust manifold and remove bolt attaching alternator bracket to cylinder head.

2) If equipped with air conditioning, shut off compressor at service valves and remove valves and hoses from compressor. Remove nuts attaching compressor support bracket to water pump and bolts attaching compressor to upper mounting bracket and position compressor out of way. Remove upper mounting bracket from cylinder head.

3) If not equipped with air conditioning, remove bolts attaching power steering reservoir bracket to cylinder head. Position reservoir and bracket out of way.

4) Remove rocker arm covers. Remove rocker arms and push rods in sequence so they can be installed in their original positions. Remove cylinder head attaching bolts and remove cylinder heads and exhaust manifold as assemblies.

Installation – Clean old gasket material from cylinder heads and block. Position head gaskets on block and install cylinder heads. Tighten all head bolts in sequence in three steps. See *Fig. 2*. To install remaining components, reverse removal procedure. Adjust valve clearance.

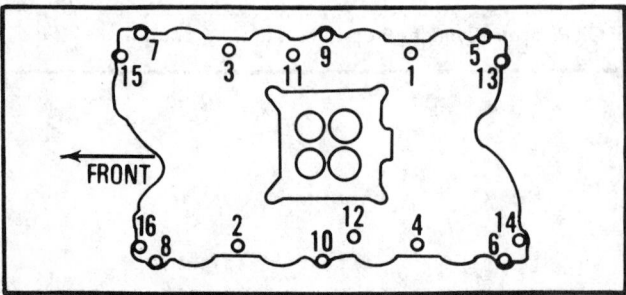

Fig. 1 Intake Manifold Tightening Sequence

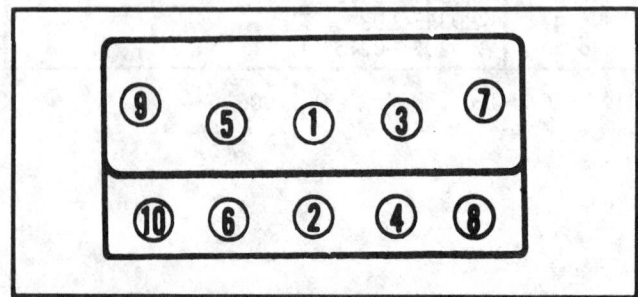

Fig. 2 Cylinder Head Tightening Sequence

7.5L V8 ENGINE (Cont.)

VALVES

VALVE ARRANGEMENT

E-I-E-I-E-I-E-I (Left side, front to rear).
I-E-I-E-I-E-I-E (Right side, front to rear).

VALVE GUIDE SERVICING

To ream guides for installation of valves with oversize stems, always use reamers in sequence and always reface valve seats after valve guides are reamed. Reamers are available .003" oversize with standard size pilot; .015" oversize reamer with .003" oversize pilot; .030" oversize reamer with .015" oversize pilot.

VALVE STEM OIL SEALS

Umbrella type oil seals are used on all valves. Lubricate valve stem with engine oil and install new valve stem seal with cup side down over valve guide using 5/8" deep well socket and light mallet to seat seal on valve stem.

VALVE SPRINGS

Removal — 1) Remove air cleaner and duct assembly. Remove rocker arm cover, spark plug, rocker arms and push rod from cylinder to be serviced.

2) Install air line with adapter into spark plug hole. Use spring compressing tool to compress valve spring and remove retainer lock. See *Fig. 3*.

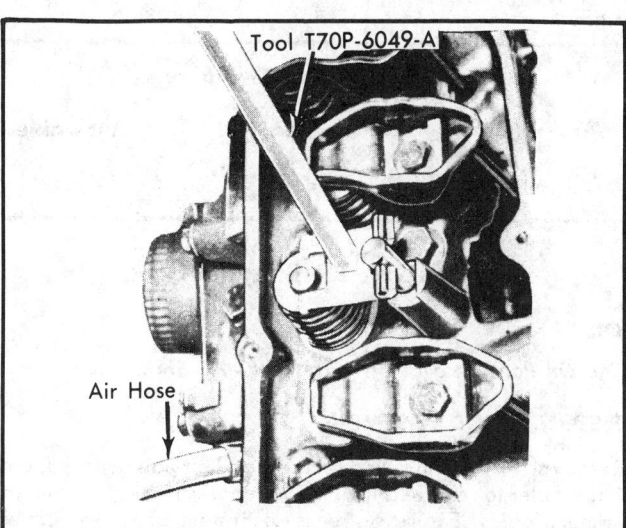

Fig. 3 Compressing Valve Spring for Removal

NOTE — *If air pressure fails to hold valve closed, remove cylinder head and inspect valve seat area for damage. Remove and discard valve stem oil seal after removing spring retainer and valve spring.*

CAUTION — *Do not remove air pressure from cylinder as this will allow valve to drop into cylinder if piston has been forced to bottom of cylinder.*

Installation — 1) With valve stem seals installed, place spring in position over valve and position spring retainer. Compress valve spring and install retainer locks.

2) Apply Lubriplate or equivalent to end of push rods and tip of valve stem. Install rocker arms and tighten bolts. To install remaining components, reverse removal procedure.

VALVE SPRING INSTALLED HEIGHT

Valve spring ends must be square within 5/64" tolerance. Installed height of valve spring must not exceed specifications. Measure spring height from surface of cylinder head pad to underside of spring retainer. If installed height exceeds specifications, install spacer(s) below spring to reduce height to specified dimension. See *Fig. 5*.

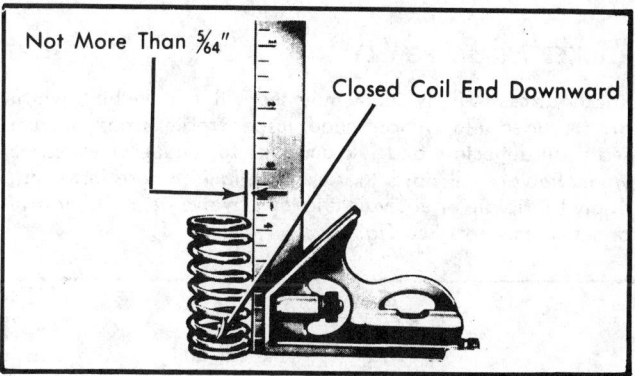

Not More Than 5/64"

Closed Coil End Downward

Fig. 4 Checking Valve Spring Squareness

CAUTION — *Reducing installed height below specifications can cause spring breakage and rapid wear of cam lobe.*

Valve Spring Installed Height Specifications	
Application	**Installed Height**
7.5L (All Valves)	1 51/64-1 53/64"

Underside Of Spring Retainer

Surface of Spring Pad

Fig. 5 Checking Valve Spring Installed Height

HYDRAULIC VALVE LIFTER ASSEMBLY

Lifters should be serviced as assemblies only as internal parts are matched sets and cannot be interchanged. If any part of lifter needs replacing, replace entire assembly. Leak down rate on lifters is 10-50 seconds at 1/16" plunger travel using suitable leak down tester. See *Fig. 6*.

7.5L V8 ENGINE (Cont.)

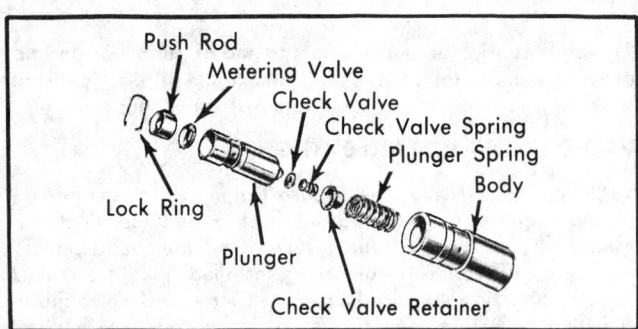

Fig. 6 Disassembled View of Hydraulic Valve Lifter

ROCKER ARM ASSEMBLY

Rocker arms are individually mounted with fulcrum bolts which are threaded into cylinder head. Inspect rocker arms, fulcrum seats, oil deflectors and fulcrum bolts for undue or excessive wear. Replace all parts that show fatigue. Before installing, apply Lubriplate or equivalent to top of valve stem, rocker arm and fulcrum seat. See Fig. 7.

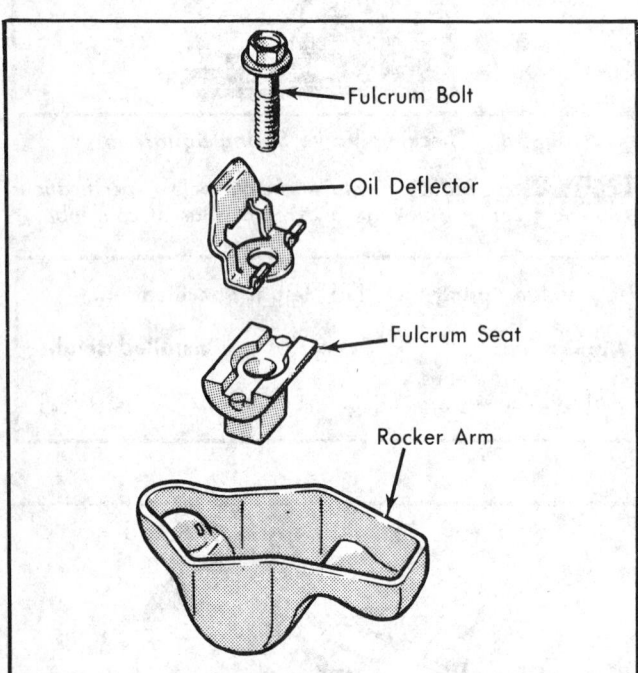

Fig. 7 Rocker Arm Assembly

HYDRAULIC VALVE LIFTER ADJUSTMENT

Repeated valve seat and face reconditioning will decrease valve stem to rocker arm clearance to point that if not compensated for, hydraulic valve lifters will cease to function. To compensate for dimensional changes in valve mechanism, a .060" shorter or .060" longer replacement push rod is available.

NOTE — *Valve lifters must be completely collapsed when checking valve clearance.*

1) Use suitable tool (T71P-6513-A or equivalent) to slowly collapse valve lifter until plunger is bottomed. Hold lifter down while checking valve clearance.

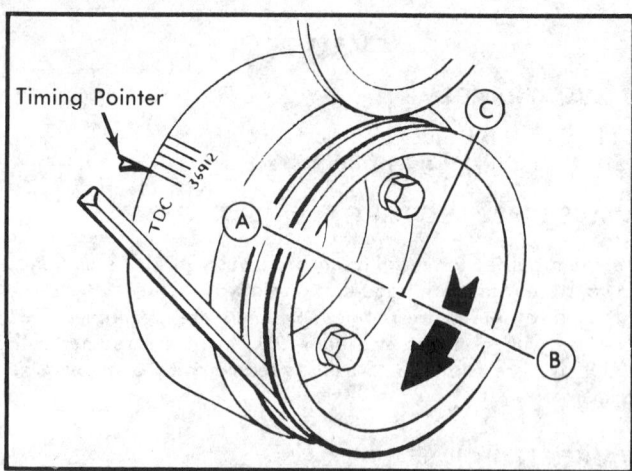

Fig. 8 Crankshaft Positions for Adjusting Hydraulic Valve Lifters

2) With No. 1 piston on TDC at end of compression stroke (position A in *Fig. 8*), check valve clearance on the following valves: No. 1 intake, No. 1 exhaust, No. 7 intake, No. 5 exhaust, No. 8 intake, No. 4 exhaust.

3) Rotate crankshaft to position B as shown in *Fig. 8* and check valve clearance on the following valves: No. 4 intake, No. 2 exhaust, No. 5 intake, No. 6 exhaust.

4) Rotate crankshaft to position C as shown in *Fig. 8* and check valve clearance on the following valves: No. 2 intake, No. 3 exhaust, No. 3 intake, No. 7 exhaust, No. 6 intake, No. 8 exhaust.

Callapsed Lifter Clearance		
Application	**Desired**	**Allowable**
7.5L (All Valves)	.100-.150"	.075-.175"

PISTON, PINS & RINGS

OIL PAN

See Oil Pan Removal at end of ENGINE Section.

PISTON & ROD ASSEMBLY

Removal — 1) With cylinder heads and oil pan removed, use ridge cutter to remove any ridge or deposits from upper end of cylinder bores. Ensure piston is at bottom of stroke. Cover piston with cloth to collect cuttings.

NOTE — *Never cut more than 1/32" from ring travel area of bore when removing ridge.*

2) Ensure that all connecting rods and caps are marked so they can be installed in their original positions. Remove rod cap and push piston and rod assembly out top of cylinder taking care not to damage crankshaft journal or cylinder wall.

Installation — 1) Lightly coat cylinder bore, piston and rings with engine oil. Ensure that ring gaps are properly spaced as shown in *Fig. 11*. Install a ring compressor on piston.

7.5L V8 ENGINE (Cont.)

2) Install piston into respective cylinder bore with notch in piston head towards front of engine. Carefully push piston into cylinder until it is slightly below top of cylinder. Install connecting rod bearings. Coat bearings and crankshaft journal with oil. Pull piston and rod assembly down onto journal and install rod cap. Install rod cap nuts and tighten. See Fig. 9.

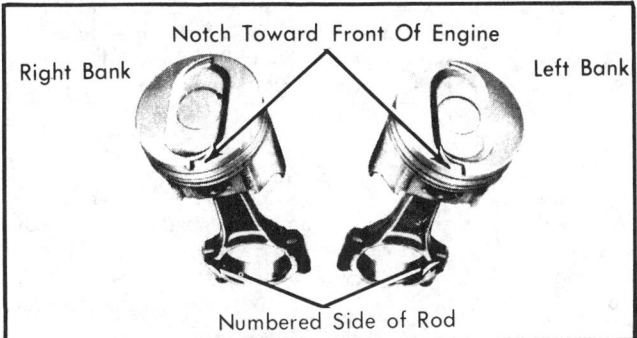

Fig. 9 Piston and Connecting Rod Assembly

FITTING PISTONS

Measure piston at centerline of piston pin bore 90° to pin bore axis. Measure cylinder bore at right angle to centerline of crankshaft, below ring travel. Piston-to-bore clearance should be as shown in Pistons, Pins & Rings table. Check Piston Size Code Chart to determine correct size. Make sure both piston and cylinder block are at normal room temperature (70°F) when fitting.

Piston Size Code Chart	
Code	**Piston Size**
Red	4.3585-4.3591″
Blue	4.3597-4.3603″
.003″ Oversize	4.3609-4.3615″

PISTON PINS

Pins are a press fit in connecting rods. Use a suitable tool (T65L-6135-A) and arbor press as shown in Fig. 10 for removal and installation of piston pins. Pins are pressed through piston body and connecting rod until end of pin is $\frac{1}{16}$-$\frac{1}{8}$″ below chamfer of pin bore in piston.

FITTING RINGS

1) Position ring in the cylinder bore that it will be used in. Push ring down to point in bore where ring wear is not encountered. Use head of piston to position ring squarely in bore.

2) Measure gap between ends of ring using a feeler gauge, if not to specification, substitute another ring set until rings are within specification.

CAUTION — Use care to avoid damage to ring or cylinder bore.

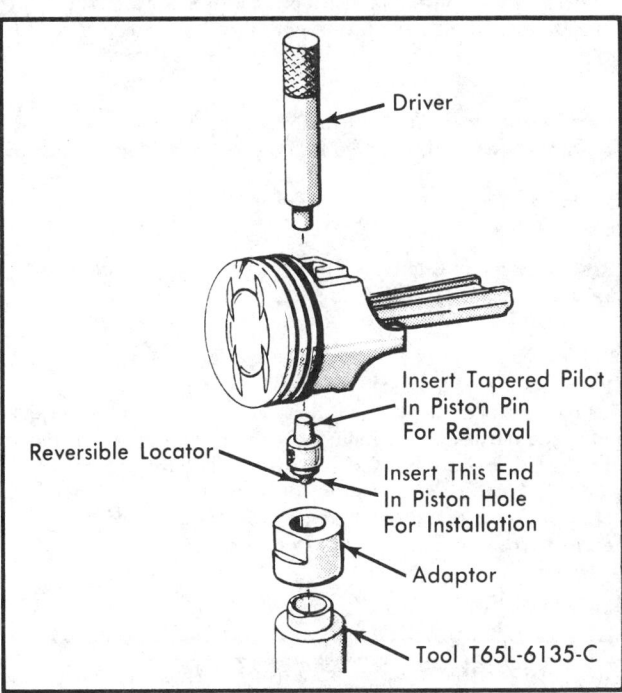

Fig. 10 Removing and Installing Piston Pin

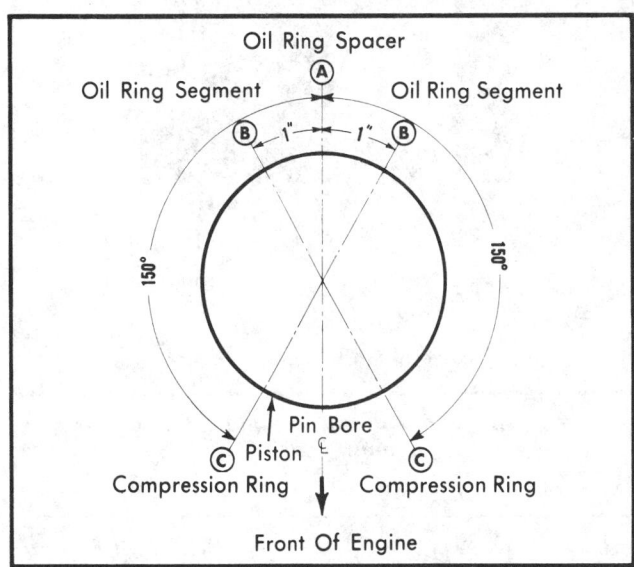

Fig. 11 Correct Spacing For Piston Rings

CRANKSHAFT & ROD BEARINGS

MAIN & CONNECTING ROD BEARINGS

Connecting Rod Bearing — After ensuring rod caps are marked for cylinder identification, remove rod caps (with crankshaft journal of cylinder to be checked at bottom of throw). Use Plastigage method to check for proper clearances. New bearings are available in standard, .001″ and .002″ undersize. Selective fitting is required on each rod. A standard bearing half may be used in combination with a .001″ undersize or a .002″ undersize with a .001″ undersize. Coat bearing

7.5L V8 ENGINE (Cont.)

surfaces with oil, install rod cap and tighten. Rotate crankshaft after bearing replacement to ensure that bearings are not too tight.

Main Bearings — 1) Mark main bearing caps for identification before removal. Remove bearing caps and upper half of main bearing. Rotate crankshaft slowly in direction of engine rotation to force upper half of bearing out. See Fig. 12.

NOTE — Replace one bearing at a time, leaving other bearings secured until ready to be changed.

2) Determine crankshaft bearing journal clearance using Plastigage method. When checking main bearings, place jack under counterweight adjoining bearing being checked. Place Plastigage on bearing surface over full width of cap and about 1/4" off center. Install cap and tighten to specified tightness. Remove cap and check with gauge provided. New bearings are available in standard, .001" and .002" undersize.

3) To install upper main bearing, lubricate bearing with engine oil and place plain end of bearing over shaft on locking tang side of block. Insert bearing and rotate crankshaft in opposite direction of engine rotation until bearing tang is seated. Install bearing cap and tighten.

THRUST BEARING ALIGNMENT

Install all bearing caps except thrust bearing cap and tighten bolts. Install thrust bearing cap with bolts finger tight. Pry crankshaft to front of engine and hold it forward while prying thrust cap to rear. Hold crankshaft forward and tighten cap bolts. Check crankshaft end play. See Fig. 13.

REAR MAIN BEARING OIL SEAL

Removal — 1) Complete seal can be replaced without removing crankshaft. Remove oil pan and oil pump. Loosen all main bearing cap bolts and allow crankshaft to drop slightly, but not to exceed 1/32".

2) Remove rear main bearing cap and remove oil seal from bearing cap and block. On block half of seal, use seal removing tool or place small sheet metal screw in one end of seal and pull on screw to remove seal. Extreme care must be taken to prevent scratching or damaging crankshaft seal surface.

3) Remove oil seal retaining pin from bearing cap and discard (if equipped). Replacement seal does not use pin.

Installation — 1) Clean oil seal groove. Dip new seal halves in engine oil. Carefully install block upper seal half into groove. Ensure undercut (lip) side of seal is toward front of engine. Install by rotating seal on crankshaft journal until approximately 3/8" of seal protrudes from parting surface. See Fig. 14.

2) Tighten remaining bearing caps. Install lower half of seal in rear main bearing cap so that 3/8" protrudes above parting surface. Apply light coat of oil resistant sealer to rear of top mating surface of bearing cap. Install cap and tighten bolts.

CAUTION — Avoid shaving any rubber from outside diameter of seal by bottom edge of groove. Do not allow oil to get into seal area.

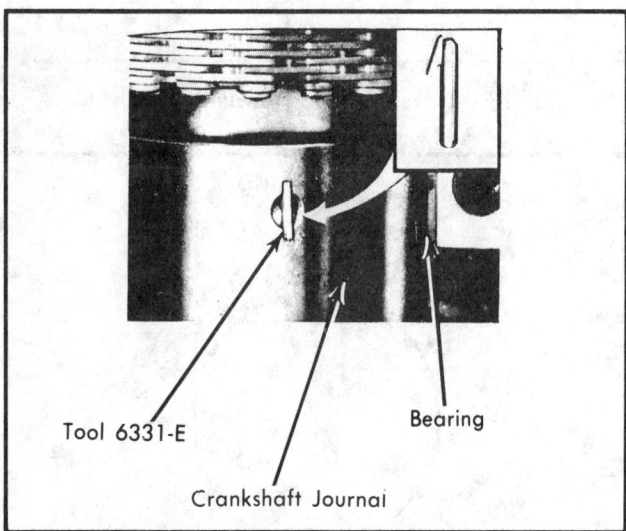

Tool 6331-E

Bearing

Crankshaft Journal

Fig. 12 Removal and Installation of Upper Main Bearing

1 — Pry Crankshaft Forward And Hold
2 — Pry Cap Rearward
3 — Tighten Cap Bolts While Holding Crankshaft Forward

Fig. 13 Aligning Thrust Bearing

7.5L V8 ENGINE (Cont.)

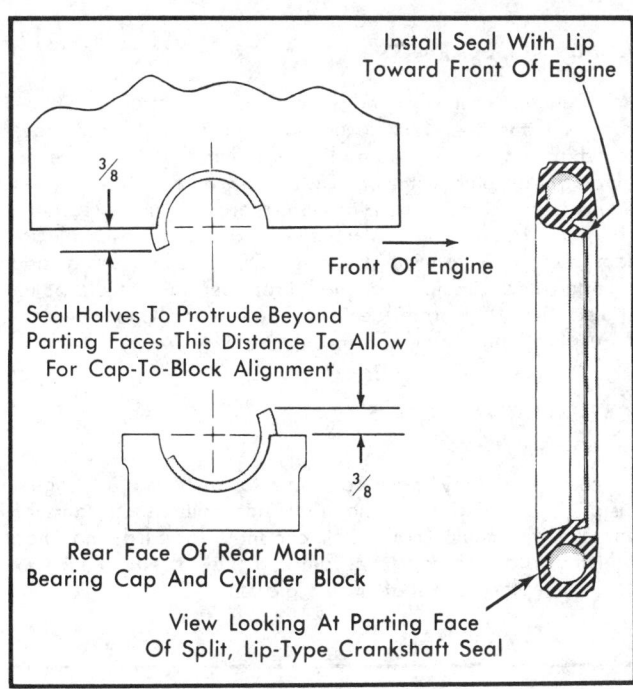

Install Seal With Lip Toward Front Of Engine

Front Of Engine

Seal Halves To Protrude Beyond Parting Faces This Distance To Allow For Cap-To-Block Alignment

Rear Face Of Rear Main Bearing Cap And Cylinder Block

View Looking At Parting Face Of Split, Lip-Type Crankshaft Seal

Fig. 14   Installing Crankshaft Rear Oil Seal

CAMSHAFT

ENGINE FRONT COVER

NOTE — *Always replace front cover oil seal after removing front cover.*

Removal — 1) Drain cooling system and crankcase. Remove fan and radiator shroud. Disconnect radiator hoses at engine and oil cooler lines at radiator and remove radiator.

2) Remove all drive belts and water pump pulley. Remove air conditioning compressor support (if equipped). Remove crankshaft pulley from vibration damper. Remove bolt attaching crankshaft damper and remove damper using suitable puller. Remove Woodruff key.

3) Loosen by-pass hose at water pump and disconnect heater return tube at water pump. Disconnect and plug fuel lines at fuel pump and remove fuel pump.

4) Remove bolts attaching front cover to cylinder block. Using a thin blade knife, cut oil pan seal flush with cylinder block face prior to separating cover from block. Remove front cover and water pump as an assembly.

Installation — 1) Coat gasket surface of oil pan with sealer. Cut and position required section of a new seal on oil pan. Apply sealer to front cover and cylinder block gasket surfaces.

2) Position front cover on cylinder block. Install front cover to seal alignment tool in proper position as shown in *Fig. 15*.

NOTE — *Use care when installing cover to avoid seal damage or possible misalignment.*

3) Install cover attaching bolts, and while pushing in on alignment tool, tighten oil pan-to-cover bolts, and cover-to-cylinder block bolts. To install remaining components, reverse removal procedure.

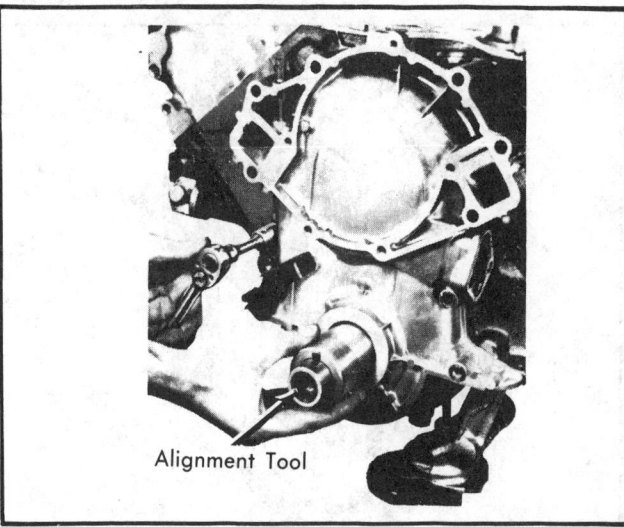

Alignment Tool

Fig. 15   Aligning Front Cover

FRONT COVER OIL SEAL

With engine front cover removed, drive out old oil seal with pin punch and clean seal recess in front cover. To install, coat new seal with grease and install seal using installing tool T68P-6700-A (or equivalent). *See Fig. 16.*

NOTE — *After installation, ensure seal spring remains in proper position.*

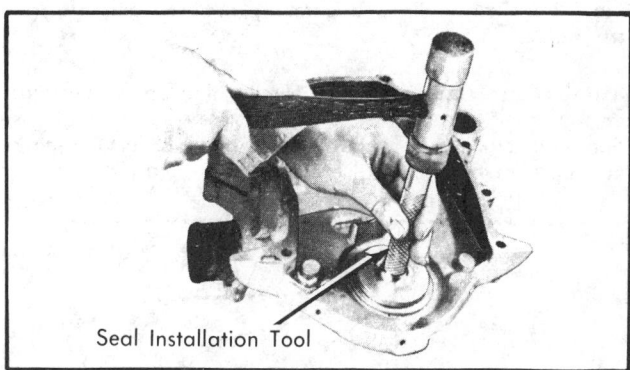

Seal Installation Tool

Fig. 16   Installing Front Cover Oil Seal

TIMING CHAIN & SPROCKETS

Removal — With engine front cover removed, crank engine until timing marks on sprockets are aligned as shown in *Fig. 17*. Remove camshaft sprocket cap screw, washer, 2-piece fuel pump eccentric and front oil slinger. Slide timing chain and sprockets forward and remove as an assembly.

Installation — Assemble timing chain and sprockets so sprocket timing marks are aligned as shown in *Fig. 17*. Install chain and sprockets as an assembly to crankshaft and camshaft. To install remaining components, reverse removal procedure and lubricate timing chain with engine oil.

7.5L V8 ENGINE (Cont.)

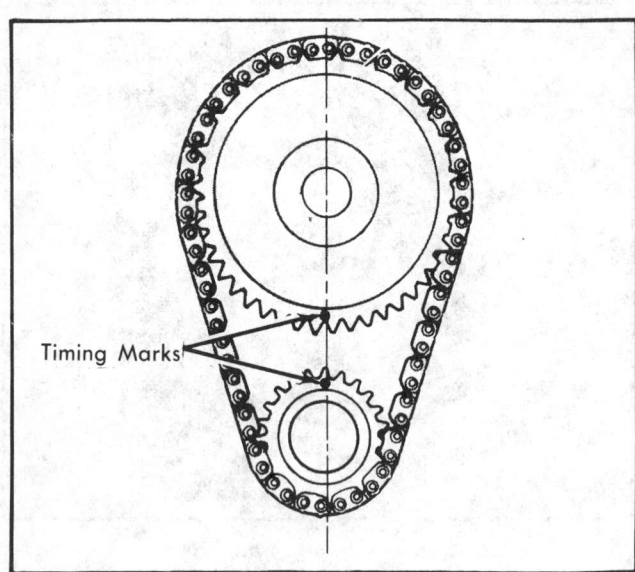

Fig. 17 Aligning Timing Marks

CAMSHAFT

Removal — 1) Remove timing chain and sprockets and intake manifold. Remove rocker arm covers and back off all rocker arm bolts. Turn rocker arms sideways and remove push rods and valve lifters, keeping them in order for installation in their original positions.

2) Remove radiator and bolts attaching air conditioning condenser (if equipped) to chassis. Carefully move condenser to rest on left fender. Remove grille. Remove camshaft thrust plate attaching bolts and carefully remove camshaft from front of engine.

Installation — Oil camshaft journals and apply Lubriplate or equivalent to cam lobes. Carefully slide camshaft into position and install thrust plate attaching bolts. To install remaining parts, reverse removal procedure. See Fig. 18.

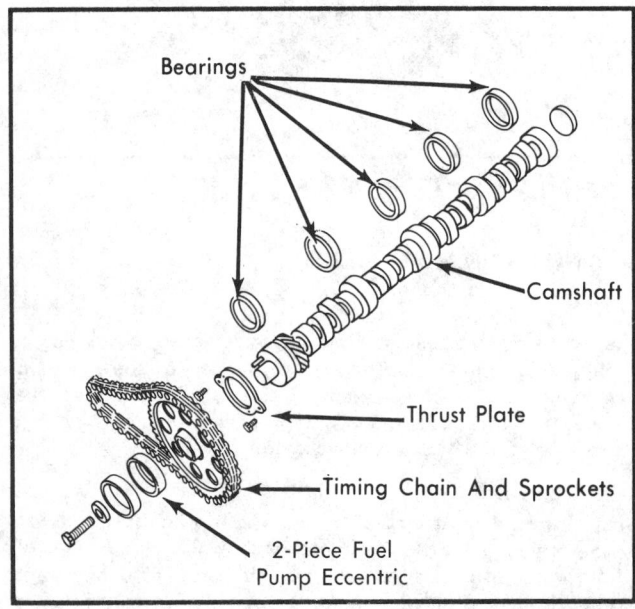

Fig. 18 Exploded View of Camshaft Assembly

CAMSHAFT BEARINGS

With engine removed and placed in work stand, remove camshaft, flywheel, rear cover plate and crankshaft. Remove camshaft rear bearing bore plug by drilling ½" hole in center of plug. Pull plug with tool T59L-100-B and T50T-100-A (or equivalent). Remove bearing using proper size expanding collet and back-up nut assembled on expanding mandrel. Use same procedure to install bearings. Oil holes in bearings and cylinder block should be aligned. Front bearings should be installed .040-.060" from face of cylinder block. Coat new rear bore plug with sealer and install. See Fig. 19.

CAMSHAFT END THRUST

To check end play, push camshaft towards rear of engine. Install dial indicator so that indicator point is on camshaft sprocket attaching screw. Pull camshaft forward and check dial indicator reading to obtain end play. If end play is excessive, replace camshaft thrust plate.

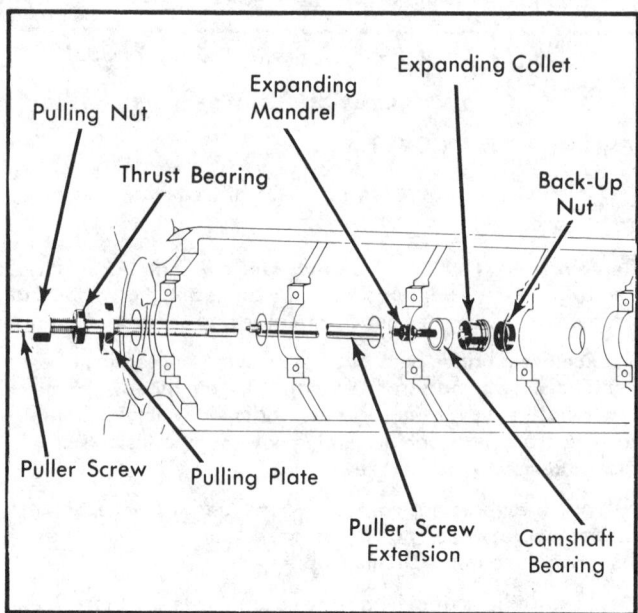

Fig. 19 Replacing Camshaft Bearings

ENGINE OILING

Crankcase Capacity — 5 qts., add 1 qt. with filter change.

Oil Filter — Change filter after first 6,000 miles and at alternate oil changes thereafter. To install, coat gasket with oil, screw filter onto adapter by hand until snug, then tighten an additional ½ turn.

Normal Oil Pressure — With engine at normal operating temperature, oil pressure should be 40-65 psi at 2,000 RPM.

Pressure Regulator Valve — In pump body. Not adjustable.

7.5L V8 ENGINE (Cont.)

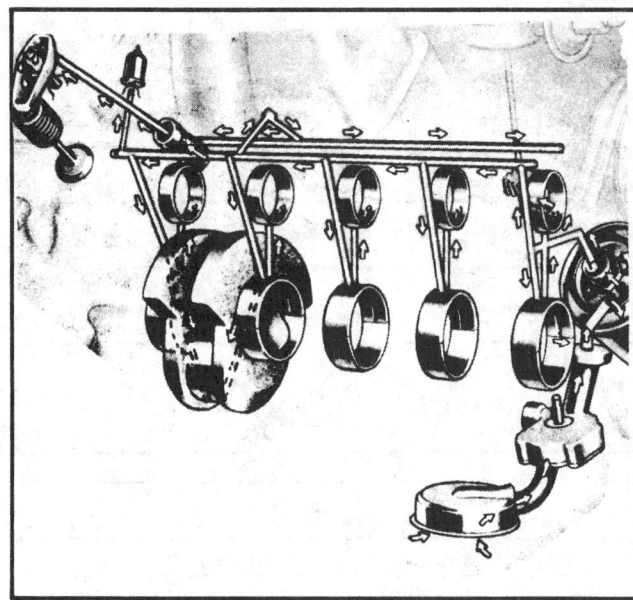

Fig. 20 Engine Oiling System

NOTE — *Identification marks should face same direction. Rotor and shaft assembly, and outer rotor are serviced as an assembly.*

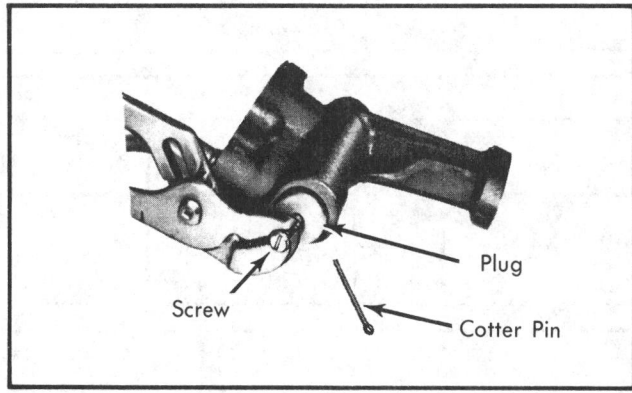

Fig. 21 Removing Oil Pump Relief Valve Plug

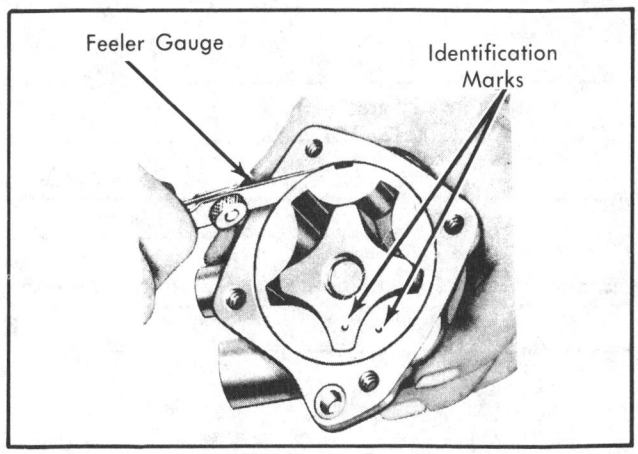

Fig. 22 Checking Clearance for Outer Race-to-Housing

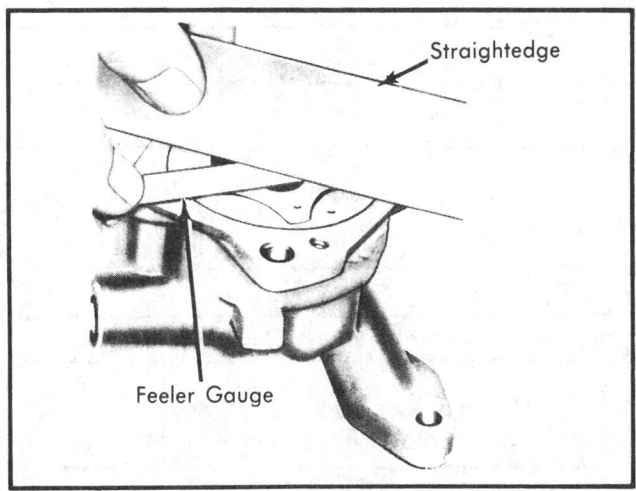

Fig. 23 Checking Rotor End Play

ENGINE OILING SYSTEM

Distributor driven oil pump provides full pressure lubrication to all camshaft and crankshaft bearings. Engine feeds oil through hydraulic valve lifters and hollow push rods to rocker arms and upper valve train area. Timing chain and sprockets are lubricated by drainage from No. 1 camshaft bearing. See *Fig. 20.*

OIL PUMP

Oil pump is rotor type, mounted inside oil pan on lower left corner of block. Oil pump is driven by distributor through an intermediate shaft.

Disassembly — 1) With oil pump removed, remove cover screws and separate cover from pump body. Remove oil pump outer rotor and rotor shaft assembly from pump housing.

2) Remove cotter pin securing relief valve plug. To remove plug, drill a small hole in plug and insert a self-tapping screw. Use pliers to remove plug from housing as shown in *Fig. 21.* Remove spring and valve from housing.

Reassembly — 1) Clean, inspect and oil all parts thoroughly. Check all clearances (see specification chart). Install relief valve, spring and plug in housing.

2) Press plug in until it seats, then install cotter pin. Install outer rotor and rotor shaft into housing. Install cover and tighten cover bolts.

Oil Pump Specifications	
Application	**Specification**
Relief Valve Spring Tension	20.6-22.6 lbs.@2.49"
Relief Valve Clearance	.0015-.0030"
Drive Shaft-to-Housing Clearance	.0015-.0030"
Rotor End Play Clearance	.004" Max.
Outer Race-to-Housing Clearance	.001-.013"

Ford V8 Engines

7.5L V8 ENGINE (Cont.)
ENGINE SPECIFICATIONS

GENERAL SPECIFICATIONS

Year	Displ. Cu. Ins.	Carburetor	HP at RPM	Torque (Ft. Lbs. at RPM)	Compr. Ratio	Bore	Stroke
1981	460″	4-Bbl.	.....	.....	.....	4.36″	3.85″

VALVES

Engine & Valve	Head Diam.	Face Angle	Seat Angle	Seat Width	Stem Diameter	Stem Clearance	Valve Lift
7.5L Int.	2.075-2.090″	44°	45°	.060-.080″	.3416-.3423″	.0010-.0027″	.436″
Exh.	1.646-1.661″	44°	45°	.060-.080″	.3416-.3423″	.0010-.0027″	.481″

PISTONS, PINS, RINGS

Engine	PISTONS Clearance	PINS Piston Fit	PINS Rod Fit	RINGS Rings	RINGS End Gap	RINGS Side Clearance
7.5L	.0022-.0030″	.0002-.0004″	Interference Fit	1	.010-.020″	.0019-.0036″
				2	.010-.020″	.002-.004″
				3	.010-.035″	Snug

CRANKSHAFT MAIN & CONNECTING ROD BEARINGS

Engine	MAIN BEARINGS Journal Diam.	MAIN BEARINGS Clearance	MAIN BEARINGS Thrust Bearing	MAIN BEARINGS Crankshaft End Play	CONNECTING ROD BEARINGS Journal Diam.	CONNECTING ROD BEARINGS Clearance	CONNECTING ROD BEARINGS Side Play
7.5L	2.9994-3.0002″	① .0008-.0015″	No. 3	② .004-.008″	2.4992-2.5000″	③ .0008-.0015″	.010-.020″

① — Allowable clearance is .0008-.0026″.
② — Service limit is .012″.
③ — Allowable clearance is .0008-.0025″

VALVE SPRINGS

Engine	Free Length	PRESSURE (LBS.) Valve Closed	PRESSURE (LBS.) Valve Open
7.5L	2.06″	76-84 @ 1.81″	218-240 @ 1.33″

CAMSHAFT

Engine	Journal Diam.	① Clearance	Lobe Lift
7.5L Int.	2.1238-2.1248″	.001-.003″	.252″
Exh.	2.1238-2.1248″	.001-.003″	.278″

① — End play is .001-.006″

TIGHTENING SPECIFICATIONS

Application	Ft. Lbs.
Cylinder Head Bolts	
Step One	80
Step Two	110
Step Three	130-140
Main Bearing Cap Bolts	95-105
Connecting Rod Cap Bolts	40-45
Intake Manifold Bolts	22-32
Exhaust Manifold Bolts	28-33
Flywheel-to-Crankshaft Bolts	75-85
Engine Front Cover Bolts	
5/16″	12-18
7/16″	45-55
Camshaft Sprocket Bolts	40-45
Crankshaft Pulley Bolts	35-50
Oil Pan-to-Cylinder Block Bolts	
1/4″	7-9
5/16″	9-11
Rocker Arm Cover Bolts	5-6
Camshaft Thrust Plate	9-12
Damper-to-Crankshaft	70-90
Oil Filter Insert-to-Block	45-55
Oil Pump-to-Cylinder Block	22-32
Rocker Arm Bolt-to-Cylinder Head	18-25

4.1L & 4.8L 6-CYLINDER ENGINES

IDENTIFICATION CODING

ENGINE IDENTIFICATION

Engines have a portion of the vehicle identification number and build date code stamped on cylinder block. Number for 6 cylinder engine is stamped on pad located on right side of block next to distributor. Third character is engine code.

Engine Identification Codes		
Application	Man. Trans.	Auto. Trans.
4.1L (250") 2-Bbl.		
Federal	TUA, TUC	TUB, TUD
Calif.	TUF, TUL, TUR	TUH, TUM, TUS
4.8L (292") 1-Bbl.		
All Models	TSA	TSB

ENGINE REMOVAL

See *Engine Removal* at end of ENGINE Section.

CYLINDER HEAD & MANIFOLDS

INTAKE & EXHAUST MANIFOLD (4.8L Engine)

Removal — 1) Remove air cleaner, disconnect both throttle rods at bellcrank and remove throttle return spring. Disconnect fuel line, vacuum lines and choke cable (if equipped) at carburetor. Disconnect crankcase vent hose at rocker arm cover and remove vapor hose at canister.

2) Disconnect exhaust pipe at flange and remove manifold attaching bolts and clamps. Remove intake and exhaust manifold as an assembly.

Installation — Ensure gasket surfaces are clean. Place manifold in position with new gasket, tighten center clamp bolts and then tighten end bolts. Reverse removal procedure to complete installation.

EXHAUST MANIFOLD (4.1L Engine)

NOTE — *Intake manifold is integral with cylinder head on 4.1L engine.*

Removal — 1) Remove air cleaner. Remove power steering pump, A.I.R. pump and brackets. Remove A.I.R. tubing manifold.

2) Raise vehicle and disconnect exhaust pipe. Unhook converter bracket at transmission and lower vehicle. Remove manifold.

Installation — Ensure gasket surfaces are clean and straight. Place manifold in position with new gasket. Install manifold

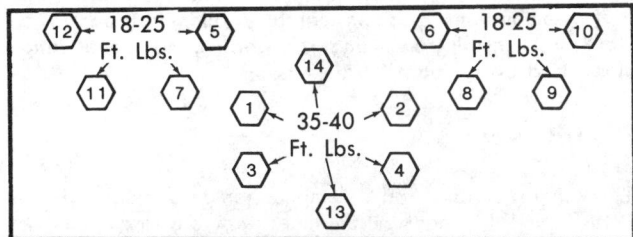

Fig. 1   Exhaust Manifold Tightening Sequence (4.1L Engine)

bolts and tighten to specification. Reverse removal procedure to complete installation. See *Fig. 1.*

CYLINDER HEAD

Removal — 1) Remove intake manifold as previously outlined. Disconnect all wires, fuel and vacuum lines from rocker arm cover clips. On 4.1L engines, remove pulse air pipes and disconnect accelerator linkage from bracket. On all models, remove rocker arm cover.

NOTE — *On 4.1L engine, disconnect exhaust pipe at manifold.*

2) Drain cooling system and remove fuel and vacuum line from clip at water outlet. Disconnect radiator hose at water outlet and battery ground strap. Disconnect air injection hose at check valve (if so equipped) of A.I.R. pipe. Remove cylinder head bolts and cylinder head.

Installation — Ensure that gasket surface on cylinder head and block are clean and all head bolt threads and threads in block are clean. To install cylinder head, reverse removal procedure. Do not apply sealer to composition steel asbestos gaskets. Coat threads of head bolts with sealer. Tighten bolts in sequence as shown in *Fig. 2.* Install push rods and adjust hydraulic valve lifters. See *Hydraulic Valve Lifter Adjustment.*

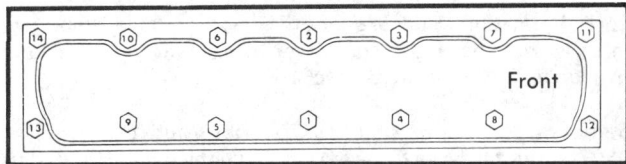

Fig. 2   Cylinder Head Tightening Sequence

VALVES

VALVE ARRANGEMENT

E-I-I-E-E-I-I-E-E-I-I-E (Front to rear.)

VALVE GUIDES

Valve guides are integral with cylinder head. If guide is worn, it must be reamed for valve with oversize stem. Valves are available with stems .003, .015 and .030" oversize. Use suitable reamers to ream valve guide bore to specified clearance for oversize stems.

VALVE STEM OIL SEALS

A small "O" ring type seal is installed in second groove in valve stem before valve keepers are installed. See *Valve Springs.*

VALVE SPRINGS

Removal — With cylinder head removed, compress valve spring with a suitable spring compressor. Remove valve keepers and release spring compressor. Remove spring retainer (valve rotating retainer is used on exhaust valves), shield, spring and damper, and any shims under spring.

Installation — To install valve spring, place shims, spring and damper, shield and retainer on the valve stem. Compress the spring with a spring compressor tool. Install new "O" ring type

4.1L & 4.8L 6-CYLINDER ENGINES (Cont.)

seal in second groove on valve stem. Install valve keepers in upper groove on valve stem and release spring compressor.

NOTE — Damper is not used on 4.1L engines.

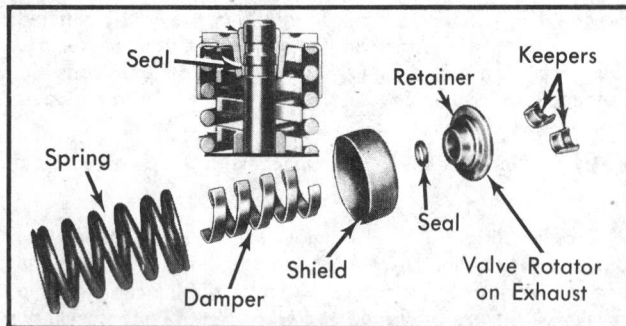

Fig. 3   Exploded View of Valve Spring Assembly

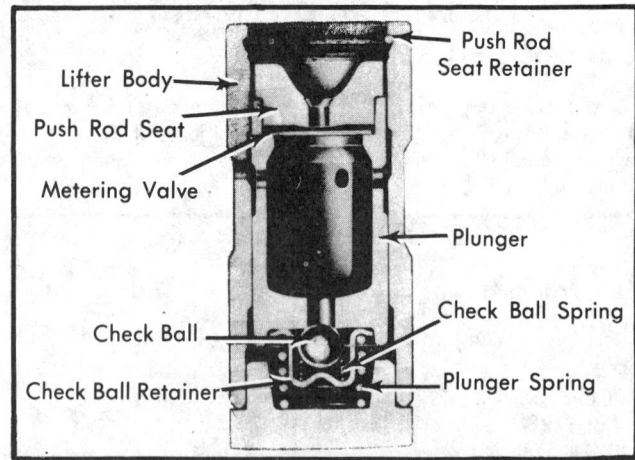

Fig. 4   Cutaway of Hydraulic Valve Lifter Assembly

VALVE SPRING INSTALLED HEIGHT

Using a narrow thin scale, check valve spring installed height by measuring from top of shim or spring seat in head to top of valve spring or shield. If height exceeds specified height, install a 1/16" thick shim under spring. Installed height should never be less than specified height.

ROCKER ARM STUDS

Rocker arm studs that are loose in head or have damaged threads can be replaced with oversize studs. Studs are available .003" and .013" oversize.

Removal — Remove stud using suitable stud extractor (J-5802-A). Install extractor over stud and tighten nut until stud is pulled from cylinder head.

Installation — Ream hole for oversize studs with a suitable reamer (J-5715 for .003" oversize and J-6036 for .013" oversize). Coat press fit area of stud with hypoid axle grease. Drive rocker stud into place with a suitable driver (J-6880) and a hammer. When driver bottoms on head, stud is at correct height.

HYDRAULIC VALVE LIFTER ASSEMBLY

Disassembly — Depress plunger in lifter with a push rod and pry out retainer with a small blade screwdriver. Remove push rod seat and metering valve. Remove plunger, ball check valve and assembly, and plunger spring. Remove ball check valve and spring by prying ball retainer loose with a small blade screwdriver. See Fig. 4.

Reassembly — 1) Thoroughly clean and inspect all components. If any components are worn and/or damaged, complete lifter assembly must be replaced.

2) Position check ball on small hole in bottom of plunger. Insert check ball spring on seat in ball retainer and position retainer on ball so that spring seats on ball. Using a screwdriver, press plunger into position.

3) Slide lifter body over spring and plunger, lining up oil feed holes. Fill assembly with SAE 10 oil and depress plunger to stop. With plunger depressed, insert a 1/16" drift punch into feed holes. Release plunger and refill with SAE 10 oil. Install metering valve, push rod seat and retainer. Depress push rod seat and remove drift punch.

HYDRAULIC VALVE LIFTER ADJUSTMENT

Rotate engine until rotor is at number 1 cylinder position. With engine at this position, adjust intake valves 1, 2, and 4 and exhaust valves 1, 3 and 5. Back off rocker arm nuts until lash is felt, then tighten nut until all lash is removed and tighten 1 full additional turn. Now rotate engine until rotor is at number 6 position. Following same procedure, adjust intake valves 3, 5 and 6 and exhaust valves 2, 4 and 6.

PISTON, PINS & RINGS

OIL PAN

See Oil Pan Removal at end of ENGINE Section.

PISTON & ROD ASSEMBLY

Removal — With oil pan, oil pump and cylinder head removed, remove any ridge in top of cylinder bore with a suitable ridge reamer. Check connecting rod and cap for identification marks or numbers and identify if necessary. Remove connecting rod cap nuts and rod cap. Push piston and rod assembly up and out of cylinder block. It will be necessary to rotate crankshaft to various positions to aid in removing piston and rod assemblies.

Installation — Before installing piston and rod assembly, place ring end gaps in positions shown in illustration. Ensure that cylinder bores are clean and oiled before installing piston and rod assemblies. Lubricate crankshaft journal and rod bearings. Compress piston rings with a suitable ring compressor. Position piston and rod assembly in bore with notch in top of piston facing toward front of engine. Push piston and rod assembly into position carefully aligning bearing on crankshaft. Install connecting rod cap noting identification marks and evenly tighten rod nuts.

FITTING PISTONS

1) With piston and rod assemblies removed, wipe cylinder bore clean and measure diameter with dial indicator. Set gauge so that thrust pin must be forced in 1/4" to enter cylinder bore. Center gauge in cylinder and set indicator to zero.

4.1L & 4.8L 6-CYLINDER ENGINES (Cont.)

2) Work gauge carefully up and down cylinder and turn in different directions to determine out-of-round and taper. Out-of-round must not exceed .002" and taper .005". Cylinder may be honed and .001" oversized pistons installed if measurements do not exceed specifications. Oversized pistons are available if cylinders are bored.

3) To check fit of rings in cylinder bore, insert ring in cylinder bore and push ring into bore 2" with head of piston and measure ring end gap with a feeler gauge. Before installing rings on pistons, ensure ring grooves are clean of carbon and inspect grooves for nicks or burrs. Install rings with gaps positioned as shown. *See Fig. 5.*

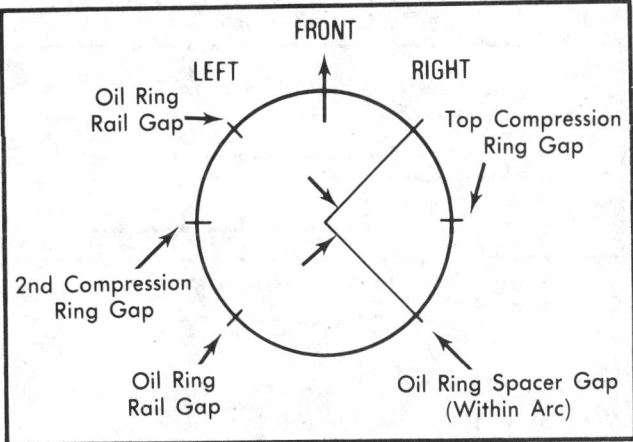

Fig. 5   Desired Ring Gap Locations

PISTON PINS

Removal – With piston and rod assembly removed, press out piston pin using removal and installation tool set J-24086 (or equivalent) and an arbor press. Separate piston from connecting rod. *See Fig. 6.*

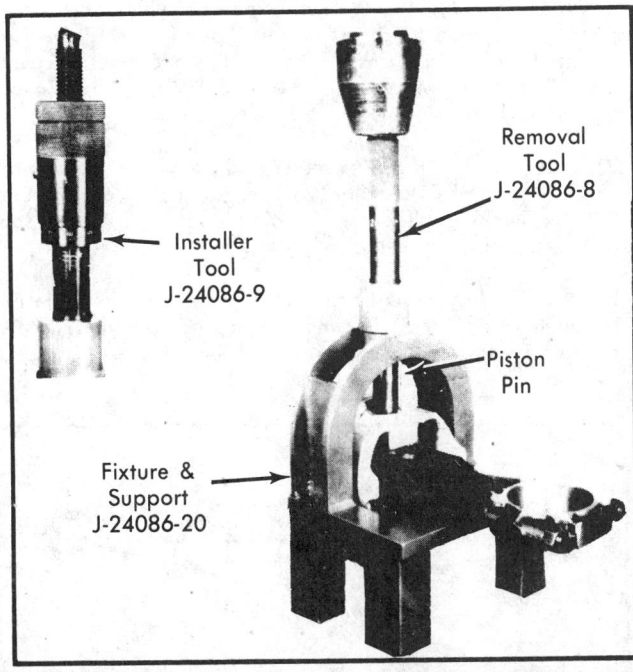

Fig. 6   Removing and Installing Piston Pin

Installation – Check clearance of piston pin in piston. If clearance exceeds .001" over specified clearance, piston and pin must be replaced. Position piston on rod so that bearing tangs face away from camshaft and notch on top of piston is toward front of engine. Lubricate piston pin and press in using same tools as outlined in removal procedure. Check piston for freedom of movement on piston pin.

CRANKSHAFT & ROD BEARINGS

MAIN & CONNECTING ROD BEARINGS

NOTE – *Following procedures are performed with oil pan and oil pump removed.*

Connecting Rod Bearings – **1)** Mark or identify rod cap to rod before removing rod cap nuts. With rod nuts removed, remove rod cap and bearing. Push up on piston and rod assembly and remove bearing from rod. Inspect bearings for wear or damage and replace as necessary.

2) Check crankshaft rod bearing journal for out-of-round or taper conditions. If crankshaft is out-of-round or tapers more than .001", crankshaft must be removed and ground for undersize bearings.

3) Check rod bearing clearance using the Plastigage method. If clearance exceeds specifications, a .001" or .002" undersize bearing may be installed to obtain correct clearance. If clearance is still excessive, crankshaft must be removed and ground for undersize bearings. Connecting rod bearings are available .010" and .020" undersize.

4) To install bearings, clean crankshaft journal and bearing surface in rod. Insert bearing halves in rod and cap. Lubricate journal and pull piston and rod assembly down, aligning bearing on journal. Install rod cap noting identification marks and evenly tighten rod nuts.

Main Bearings – **1)** Main bearings are selective fit by manufacturer during production. A standard size bearing half may be used in combination with a .001" undersize bearing half to obtain correct clearance. This combination will decrease clearance .0005".

2) If correct clearance could not be obtained during production, a crankshaft with .009" undersize main bearing journals is fitted. A .009" and .010" bearing half combination may be used to obtain correct clearance.

3) Engines fitted with reground crankshafts may be identified by a "9" stamped on counterweight and a large spot of light green paint next to affected bearing. Also main bearing cap will be painted light green for that bearing.

4) Main bearings may be removed and replaced with crankshaft still installed. Mark or identify main bearing caps to cylinder block before removing caps. With the exception of rear main bearing, main bearings are removed from cylinder block by inserting a bearing removal and installing tool in oil hole in crankshaft and rotating crankshaft clockwise. To remove rear main bearing, drive bearing partly out with a drift punch and hammer. Using a pair of pliers with taped jaws, grab bearing thrust surface and slinger on crankshaft and rotate crankshaft to remove bearing.

4.1L & 4.8L 6-CYLINDER ENGINES (Cont.)

5) Crankshaft clearance, taper or out-of-round conditions can be checked using the Plastigage method. If clearance exceeds specifications, a .001" or .002" undersize bearing may be installed to obtain correct clearance. Both bearing halves must be replaced.

6) If correct clearance can not be obtained or if journal is tapered or is out-of-round more than .001", crankshaft must be removed and ground for undersized bearings. Bearings are available in standard, .001", .002", .009", .010" and .020" undersize.

Fig. 7   Using Feeler Gauge to Check Crankshaft End Play

7) To install bearings, ensure crankshaft journal and bearing surface in cap and block are clean. Lubricate journal and install bearing in cap. If bearings were removed with crankshaft still installed, use bearing removal and installation tool inserted in crankshaft oil hole to install upper bearing half. To install rear upper main bearing, place in position and use plier procedure, as previously described, to install bearing. Install main caps noting identification marks and evenly tighten main bearing bolts.

THRUST BEARING ALIGNMENT

Pry crankshaft forward as far as possible and check crankshaft end play with a feeler gauge inserted between front of rear main bearing and crankshaft. Replace rear main bearing if end play not to specifications. See Fig. 7.

REAR MAIN BEARING OIL SEAL

Removal — Remove rear main bearing cap and pry out old seal. Remove upper half of seal by tapping end with brass punch until end of seal protrudes enough to be removed with pliers.

Installation — 1) Fabricate installation tool as shown in illustration. Coat seal lips and seal bead of upper seal with

motor oil. Keep ends of seal dry of oil and position tool between crankshaft and seal seat in cylinder block. Position seal between tip of tool and crankshaft.

2) Roll seal around crankshaft, using tool as a "shoehorn" to protect seal from sharp corner of seal seat surface. Tool must remain in position until seal is positioned with both ends flush with block. Make sure seal lip is positioned toward front of engine and remove tool. See Fig. 8.

3) Install lower half of seal in bearing cap, using tool as a "shoehorn". Feed seal into cap using light pressure with thumb and finger. Install bearing cap with sealant applied to face, taking care to keep sealant off of split line.

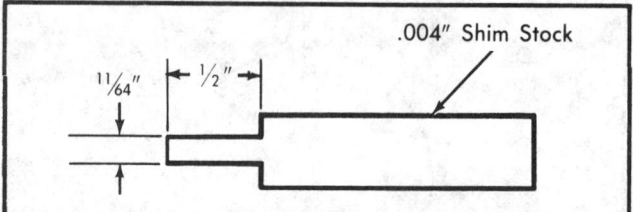

Fig. 8   Rear Main Oil Seal Installation Tool

CAMSHAFT

ENGINE FRONT COVER

Removal — 1) Remove fan belt, fan, pulley and radiator shroud. Remove radiator and accessory drive pulley. Remove harmonic balancer pulley bolt (if equipped).

2) Pull off harmonic balancer with suitable puller (J-23523). Remove front cover and oil pan-to-cover retaining screws and remove cover with gasket. Use sharp cutting tool to cut oil pan front seal flush with block. See Fig. 9.

NOTE — 4.8L engines do not use front rubber seal. RTV or equivalent is used.

Installation — 1) Clean gasket surfaces on cylinder block and crankcase cover. Cut tabs from new oil pan front seal. See Fig. 9. Install seal to front cover, pressing tips into holes in cover. On 4.1L engines, place a 3/16" bead of RTV sealant on cover sealing surface.

2) Coat gasket with gasket sealer and position on cover. Apply 1/8" bead of RTV sealant to joint formed by oil pan and cylinder block. Install centering tool (23042) in front cover seal and install cover to cylinder block.

3) Install and partially tighten oil pan-to-cover screws. Install remaining cover screws, remove centering tool and tighten screws. To install remaining components, reverse removal procedure.

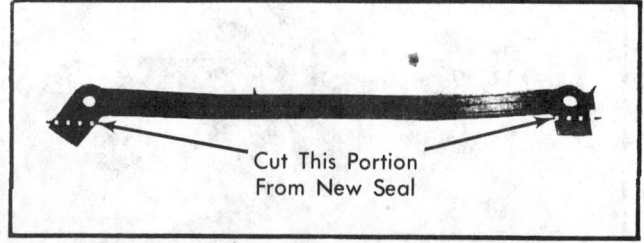

Fig. 9   Oil Pan Front Seal Modification

4.1L & 4.8L 6-CYLINDER ENGINES (Cont.)

FRONT COVER OIL SEAL

With Cover Removed — Pry seal out of cover with a screwdriver. Install new seal with open end of seal toward inside of cover and drive into position with a suitable driver (J-23042) and a hammer. Support cover at seal area before driving in seal.

With Cover Installed — With harmonic balancer removed, pry seal out front of cover. Install seal with open end of seal toward engine and drive into place with a suitable driver (J-23042) and a hammer.

CAMSHAFT

Removal — 1) Drain cooling system and remove radiator. Remove front grille assembly. Remove valve cover and loosen all rocker arm nuts. Rotate rocker arms to side and withdraw all push rods.

2) Remove coil, side cover and all valve lifters. Remove front engine cover as previously outlined. Rotate engine until timing marks on camshaft gear and crankshaft gear are aligned. Remove distributor, noting position of rotor. Remove two camshaft thrust plate screws and carefully pull camshaft out front of engine to remove. See Fig. 10.

Installation — To install camshaft, reverse removal procedure. Carefully install camshaft in cylinder block to prevent damage to camshaft lobes or bearings. Make sure marks on timing gears are aligned. See Fig. 11.

TIMING GEARS

With camshaft installed, check gear backlash with a narrow feeler gauge. Backlash should be not less than .004" nor more than .006" for new gears or no more than .008" for old gears. Check both gears for runout with a dial indicator. If camshaft gear runout exceeds .004", or crankshaft gear runout exceeds .003", gears must be replaced.

Removal — With camshaft removed, position camshaft and a suitable mandrel (J-971) in a press and press camshaft out of gear. Make sure thrust plate is positioned so that Woodruff key will not damage it when camshaft is pressed out of gear. To remove crankshaft gear from crankshaft pull off with a suitable puller. See Fig. 12.

Fig. 10 View Showing Location of Camshaft Thrust Plate Screws

Fig. 12 Pressing Camshaft From Gear

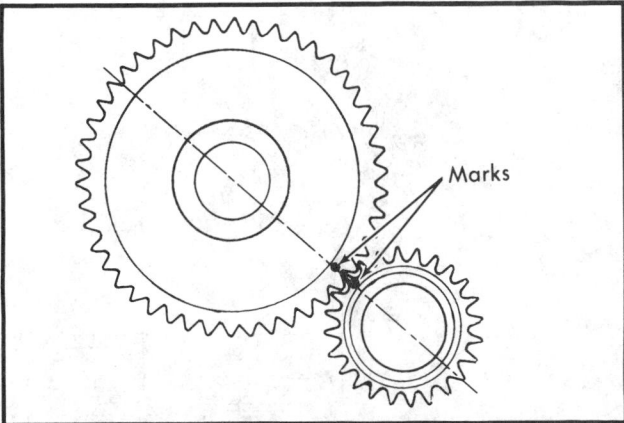

Fig. 11 Alignment of Timing Gear Marks

4.1L & 4.8L 6-CYLINDER ENGINES (Cont.)

Installation — To install crankshaft gear, align gear on key and drive gear onto crankshaft with a suitable driver. To install camshaft gear, position camshaft in a press with camshaft supported at back of front journal. Place gear spacer ring and thrust plate over camshaft and install Woodruff key in keyway. Press gear onto shaft until clearance between thrust plate and gear is .001-.005".

CAMSHAFT BEARINGS

Removal — 1) With oil pump and pan removed, drive out camshaft rear plug from block. Following manufacturers instructions for tool set (J-6098) remove center bearings first.

2) Front and rear bearings are removed by assembling drive handle to tool set (J-6098) and driving bearings towards center of block.

Installation — 1) Install front and rear bearings first to act as guide for pilot of tool (J-6098) and to center remaining bearings being pulled into place.

NOTE — *Oil holes in cam bearings must be aligned with oil holes in cam bore.*

2) Install new camshaft rear plug flush to 1/32"(.80mm) deep and parallel with rear surface of engine block.

CAMSHAFT END THRUST

Check camshaft end play with feeler gauge, if end play exceeds .005", gear, thrust plate or both must be replaced. See Fig. 13.

Fig. 13   Checking Camshaft End Play

CAM LOBE LIFT

With valve cover removed, remove rocker arm. Mount dial indicator on rocker arm stud and position dial indicator stem on push rod using a suitable ball adapter (J-8520). Rotate engine slowly in direction of rotation until lifter is on heel of camshaft and set dial indicator to zero. Rotate engine until push rod is fully raised. This is camshaft lobe lift. Continue to rotate engine until indicator reads zero. This will check accuracy of original reading. See Fig. 14.

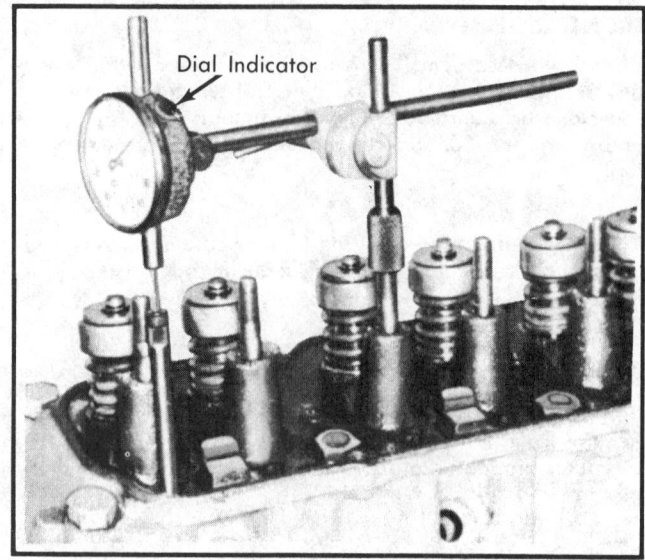

Fig. 14   Checking Camshaft Lobe Lift

ENGINE OILING

Crankcase Capacity — 4.1L engine, 4 quarts. 4.8L engines, 5 quarts. Add 1 quart with filter change.

Oil Filter — Replaced every other oil change or more often under dusty or severe conditions.

Oil Pressure — With engine at normal operating temperature, oil pressure should be 40 psi at 2000 RPM.

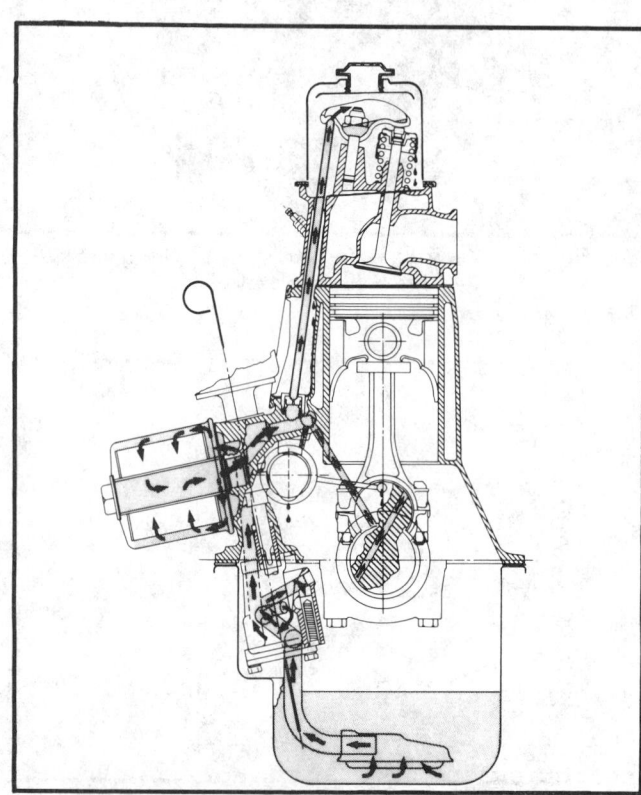

Fig. 15   Engine Oiling System

4.1L & 4.8L 6-CYLINDER ENGINES (Cont.)

ENGINE OILING SYSTEM

The gear type pump provides full pressure lubrication through full flow oil filter. Oil is drawn by pick up screen, pressurized through pump and routed to oil filter. A bypass valve allows oil flow to main gallery in case backpressure is encountered at filter. This rifle drilled passage supplies oil to camshaft bearings, lifters and main bearings. Connecting rod bearings are supplied oil from crankshaft main bearings by cross drilled passages. *See Fig. 15.*

OIL PUMP

The valve train receives lubrication from valve lifters through hollow push rods. Oil drains back to crankcase through drain holes. Timing gears are lubricated through nozzle from front camshaft bearing. The distributor drive gear is oiled by drainage from valve lifter compartment. *See Fig. 16.*

Removal — Mark gears so they may be reassembled with the same teeth indexing. Do not disturb pickup screen on pipe. Screen is serviced as an assembly.

NOTE — *If pump gears or body are damaged or worn, replacement of entire pump assembly is required.*

Installation — Apply sealer to end of pipe and tap into place. Install idler gear in pump body with smooth side of gear toward cover opening.

NOTE — *Bottom of screen must be parallel with bottom of pan.*

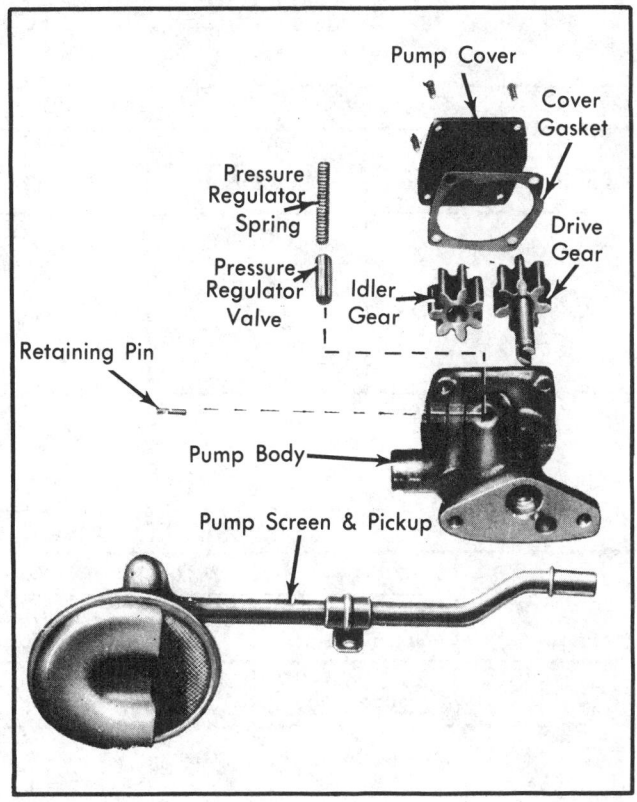

Fig. 16 Exploded View of Engine Oil Pump

ENGINE SPECIFICATIONS

GENERAL SPECIFICATIONS							
Year	Displ. Cu. Ins.	Carburetor	HP at RPM	Torque (Ft. Lbs. at RPM)	Compr. Ratio	Bore	Stroke
1981	250″	2-Bbl.	.....	.....	8.25:1	3.876″	3.53″
	292″	1-Bbl.	.....	.....	8.0:1	3.876″	4.12″

VALVES							
Engine & Valve	Head Diam.	Face Angle	Seat Angle	Seat Width	Stem Diameter	Stem Clearance	Valve Lift
4.1L & 4.8L							
Int.	1.720″	45°	46°	.031-.063″	.3410-.3417″	.0010-.0027″	①.388″
Exh.	1.500″	46°	46°	.063-.094″	.3410-.3417″	.0015-.0032″	.405″

① — 4.8L engine intake valve lift is .405″.

General Motors 6 Engines

4.1L & 4.8L 6-CYLINDER ENGINES (Cont.)

ENGINE SPECIFICATIONS (Cont.)

PISTONS, PINS, RINGS						
	PISTONS	PINS		RINGS		
Engine	Clearance	Piston Fit	①Rod Fit	Rings	End Gap	Side Clearance
4.1L	.0010-.0020″	.00015-.00025″	.0008-.0016″	1	.010-.020″	.0012-.0027″
				2	.010-.020″	.0012-.0032″
				3	.015-.055″	.000-.005″
4.8L	.0026-.0036″	.00015-.00025″	.0008-.0016″	1	.010-.020″	.0020-.0040″
				2	.010-.020″	.0020-.0040″
				3	.015-.055″	.005-.0055″

① — Interference fit.

CRANKSHAFT MAIN & CONNECTING ROD BEARINGS							
	MAIN BEARINGS				CONNECTING ROD BEARINGS		
Engine	Journal Diam.	Clearance	Thrust Bearing	Crankshaft End Play	Journal Diam.	Clearance	Side Play
4.1L	2.2979-2.2994″	①.0010-.0024″	No.7	.002-.006″	1.999-2.000″	.0010-.0026″	.006-.017″
4.8L	2.2979-2.2994″	①.0010-.0024″	No.7	.002-.006″	2.099-2.100″	.0010-.0026″	.006-.017″

① — Journals 1-6. No. 7 Journal is .0016-.0035″.

VALVE SPRINGS			
Engine	Free Length	PRESSURE (LBS.)	
		Valve Closed	Valve Open
4.1L & 4.8L	2.08″	78-86@1.66″	170-180@1.26″

CAMSHAFT			
Engine	Journal Diam.	Clearance①	Lobe Lift
4.1L	1.8677-1.8697″	.0015-.0035″	②.2217″
4.8L	1.8677-1.8697″	.0015-.0035″	.2315″

① — Camshaft end play is .003-.008″.
② — Exhaust lobe lift is .2315″.

TIGHTENING SPECIFICATIONS

Application	Ft. Lbs.
Cylinder Head Bolts	95
Intake Manifold-to-Head (4.8L)	40
Exhaust Manifold Bolts	①30
Main Bearing Cap Bolts	65
Connecting Rod Cap Nuts	
4.1L	35
4.8L	40
Camshaft Thrust Plate Screws	6.6
Flywheel Bolts	
4.1L	60
4.8L	110
Oil Pump	9.6
Harmonic Balancer Bolt (4.8L)	60
Rocker Arm Cover	3.7
Push Rod Cover	4.1

① — Non integral head.

5.0L & 5.7L V8 ENGINES

IDENTIFICATION CODING

ENGINE IDENTIFICATION

Engine code letters are suffix of Engine Identification Number. Number is stamped in pad on front right side of cylinder block.

Engine Identification Codes	
Application	**Code**
5.0L (305") 2-Bbl.	UAA, UAB, UAC, UAD, UAF, UAH
5.0L (305") 4-Bbl.	UAJ, UAK, UAT, UAU, UAW, UAX, UAY, UAZ, UBA, UBB, UBC, UBD
5.7L (350") 2-Bbl.	UKA, UKB
5.7L (350") 4-Bbl.	UJA, UJB, UJC, UJD, UJF, UJH, UJJ, UJK, UJL, UJM, UJR, UJS, UJT, UJU, UJW, UHA, UHB, UHC, UHD, UHF, UHH, UHJ, UHL, UHM, UHR, UHS, UHT, UHU, UHW, UHX, UHY, UHZ

ENGINE REMOVAL

See Engine Removal at end of ENGINE Section.

CYLINDER HEAD & MANIFOLD

INTAKE MANIFOLD

Removal — 1) Drain cooling system and remove air cleaner. Disconnect battery cables at battery, upper radiator hose and heater hose at engine. Disconnect gas line, all vacuum lines and accelerator linkage at carburetor.

2) Remove distributor cap, note position of rotor with chalk and remove distributor. Remove (if equipped or necessary) oil filler bracket, coil, air compressor and bracket, accelerator bellcrank, and accelerator return spring and bracket.

3) Remove alternator upper mounting bracket. Remove all manifold retaining bolts and pry intake manifold loose from cylinder heads. Remove intake manifold and carburetor as an assembly.

Installation — To install intake manifold, clean all gasket surfaces and apply sealer at all water passages and at positions where seals butt together. Install manifold and tighten bolts in sequence shown in *Fig. 1*. Install distributor noting marked position of rotor. To complete installation, reverse removal procedure.

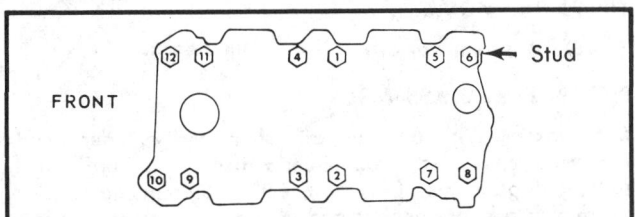

Fig. 1   Intake Manifold Tightening Sequence

CYLINDER HEAD

Removal — 1) Remove intake manifold as previously outlined. Remove alternator lower mounting bolt and lay unit aside.

Remove carburetor air heater from exhaust manifold (if equipped). Remove spark plug shields. Disconnect exhaust pipes at exhaust manifolds. Remove exhaust manifolds.

2) If equipped with air conditioning, remove compressor (without disconnect lines) and lay out of way. Remove forward mounting bracket. If equipped with A.I.R., disconnect rubber hose at check valve. It will not be necessary to remove A.I.R. tubing manifolds from cylinder heads.

3) Disconnect ventilation hose from valve cover. Remove valve covers. Loosen rocker arm nuts and pivot rocker arms to side. Remove push rods. Mark or identify push rods to ensure that they are installed in original positions.

4) Drain cylinder block of coolant. Remove all cylinder head bolts. Pry cylinder head loose from cylinder block and remove head.

Installation — Gasket surfaces of both head and cylinder block must be clean. Use sealer if equipped with steel gasket. If asbestos gasket is being used, sealer is not required. Position heads and gaskets on cylinder block. Coat threads of bolts with a sealing compound. Tighten cylinder head bolts in sequence shown in *Fig. 2*. To complete installation, reverse removal procedure.

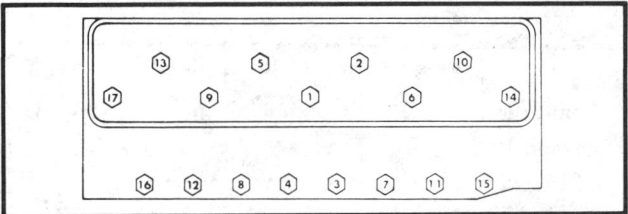

Fig. 2   Cylinder Head Tightening Sequence

VALVES

VALVE ARRANGEMENT

E-I-I-E-E-I-I-E (Both sides, front to rear.)

VALVE GUIDE SERVICING

If valve stem to guide clearance is excessive, valves with oversize stems are available. Oversize valve stems are available .003", .015" and .030" oversize. Using a suitable reamer (Reamer Kit No. J-5830) ream guides to correct size for oversize valve stems.

VALVE STEM OIL SEALS

A small "O" ring type seal is installed in second groove of valve stem before keepers are installed. *See Valve Springs.*

VALVE SPRINGS

Removal — With cylinder head removed, compress valve spring with a suitable spring compressor and remove keepers. Release spring compressor and remove retainer (valve rotating retainer is used on exhaust valves), shield, spring and damper, and any shims under spring. *See Fig. 3.*

General Motors V8 Engines

5.0L & 5.7L V8 ENGINES (Cont.)

Installation — To install valve springs, reverse removal procedure. Install seal in second groove of valve stem before installing keepers and releasing spring compressor.

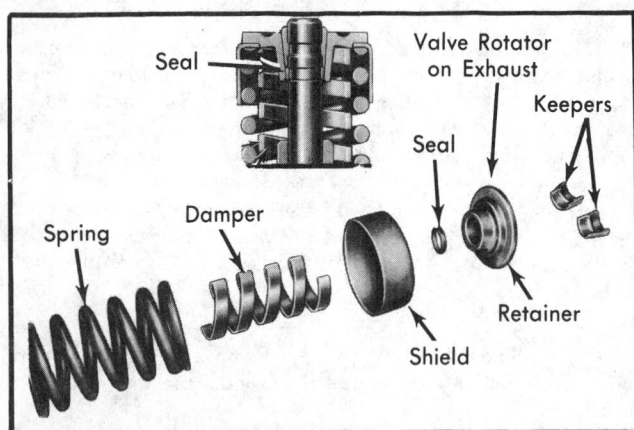

Fig. 3   Exploded View of Valve Spring Assembly

VALVE SPRING INSTALLED HEIGHT

Valve spring installed height is measured from top of shim, at bottom of spring, or spring seat to top of valve spring or spring shield. If distance exceeds specified height, install a 1/16" thick shim. Installed height should never be more than 1/16" less than specified height.

Valve Spring Installed Height	
Application	**Height**
All Models	
Int.	1 23/32"
Exh.	1 19/32"

ROCKER ARM STUDS

Rocker arm studs that are loose in head or have damaged threads can be replaced with oversize studs. Studs are available .003" and .013" oversize.

Removal — Remove stud using a suitable stud extractor (J-5802-1). Install extractor over stud and tighten nut until stud is pulled from cylinder head.

Installation — Ream hole for oversize studs with a suitable reamer (J-5715 for .003" oversize and J-6036 for .013" oversize). Coat press fit area of stud with hypoid axle grease. Drive rocker stud into place with a suitable driver (J-6880) and a hammer. When driver bottoms out on head, stud is at correct height.

HYDRAULIC VALVE LIFTER ASSEMBLY

Disassembly — Depress plunger in lifter with a push rod and pry out retainer with a small blade screwdriver. Remove push rod seat and metering valve. Remove plunger, ball check valve assembly and plunger spring. Remove ball check valve and spring by prying ball retainer loose with a small blade screwdriver. See Fig. 4.

Reassembly — 1) Thoroughly clean and inspect all components. If any components are worn or damaged, complete lifter must be replaced. Position check ball on small hole in bottom of plunger. Insert check ball spring on seat in ball

retainer and position retainer on ball so that spring seats on ball. Using a screwdriver, press plunger into position.

2) Slide lifter body over spring and plunger, lining up oil feed holes. Fill assembly with SAE 10 oil and depress plunger to stop. With plunger depressed, insert a 1/16" drift punch into feed holes. Release plunger and refill with SAE 10 oil. Install metering valve, push rod seat and retainer. Depress push rod seat and remove drift punch.

NOTE — *Before installing lifters in engine, coat bottoms with "Molykote" or equivalent.*

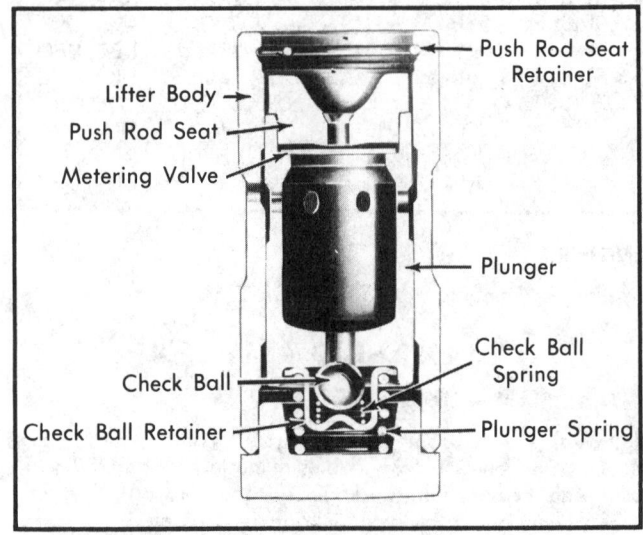

Fig. 4   Cutaway View of Hydraulic Valve Lifter Assembly

HYDRAULIC VALVE LIFTER ADJUSTMENT

1) Rotate engine until engine is at number 1 firing position. Back off rocker arm adjusting nuts on number 1 intake and exhaust rocker arms until play in push rod is detected. Now tighten rocker arm nuts until play in push rod is just eliminated then tighten adjusting nuts one full turn more. With engine at number 1 firing position, adjust intake valves 1, 2, 5 and 7 and exhaust valves 1, 3, 4 and 8.

2) Rotate engine to number 6 firing position and follow same procedures for adjusting valves. With engine at number 6 firing position, adjust intake valves 3, 4, 6 and 8 and exhaust valves 2, 5, 6 and 7.

PISTONS, PINS & RINGS

OIL PAN REMOVAL

See Oil Pan Removal at end of ENGINE Section.

PISTON & ROD ASSEMBLY

Removal — With oil pan, oil pump and cylinder heads removed, remove any ridge in top of cylinder bore with a suitable ridge reamer. Check connecting rod and cap for identification marks or numbers and identify if necessary. Remove connecting rod cap nuts and rod cap. Push piston and rod assembly up and out of cylinder block. It will be necessary to rotate crankshaft to various positions to aid in removing piston and rod assemblies.

NOTE — *DO NOT wire brush any part of piston assembly during cleaning.*

5.0L & 5.7L V8 ENGINES (Cont.)

Installation – Before installing piston and rod assembly, place ring gaps in positions shown in illustration. Place connecting rod in bore with bearing tang slots facing away from camshaft. Compress piston rings with a suitable ring compressor. With rod bearings and crankshaft rod journal lubricated, push piston and rod assembly into position and install rod cap to respective rod. Install and tighten rod nuts.

FITTING PISTONS

1) With piston and rod assemblies removed, wipe cylinder bores clean and measure diameter of cylinder with a dial indicator. If cylinder is worn or tapered more than .005", cylinder must be bored for oversize pistons.

2) If bore is worn or tapered less than .005", cylinder can be cleaned and honed, and .001" oversize pistons installed. See oversize piston table for oversize pistons available from manufacturer.

Oversize Pistons	
Application	**Size**
All	.030"

3) To check fit of rings in cylinder bore, insert ring in cylinder bore and push ring into bore 2" with head of piston. Measure ring end gap with a feeler gauge. Before installing rings on pistons, ensure ring grooves are clean of carbon and inspect grooves for nicks or burrs. Install rings with gaps positioned as shown in *Fig. 5*.

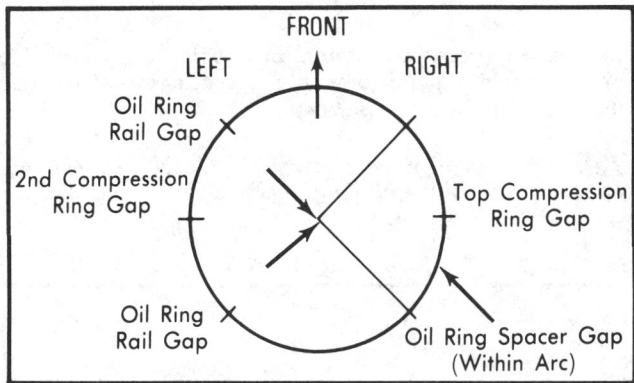

Fig. 5   Desired Ring Gap Location

PISTON PINS

Removal – With pistons and rod assembly removed, press out piston pin using removal and installation tool J-24086 with adapters and arbor press. Separate piston from connecting rod. See *Fig. 6*.

Installation – Check clearance of piston pin in piston. If clearance exceeds .001" over specified clearance, piston and pin must be replaced. Position piston on rod correctly. See *Piston and Rod Positioning*. Lubricate piston pin and press in using same tools as outlined in removal procedure. Check piston for freedom of movement on piston pin.

PISTON & ROD POSITIONING

Position piston on rod so that bearing tang notch in rod is aligned with side "A" of piston (see illustration) for cylinders 2, 4, 6, and 8 and aligned with side "B" for cylinders 1, 3, 5 and 7. See *Fig. 7*.

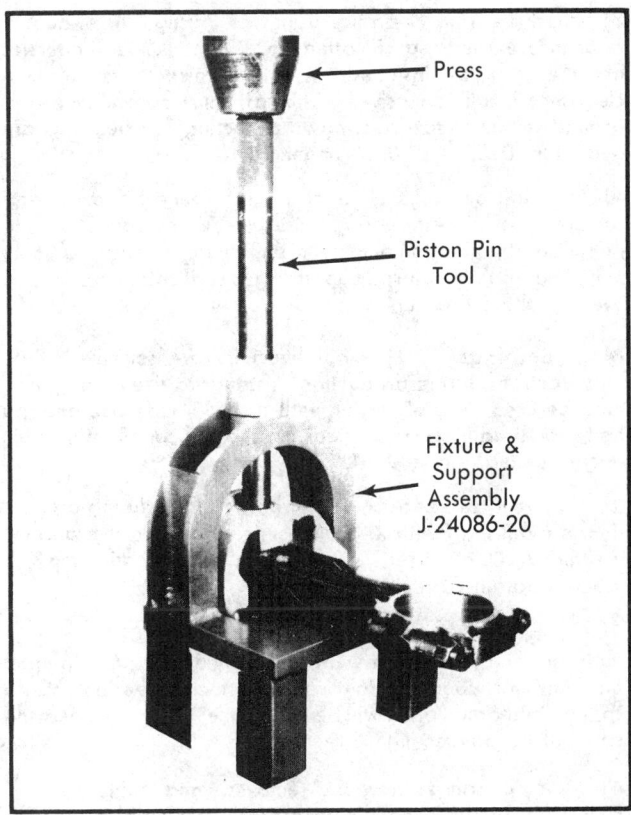

Fig. 6   Removing and Installing Piston Pin

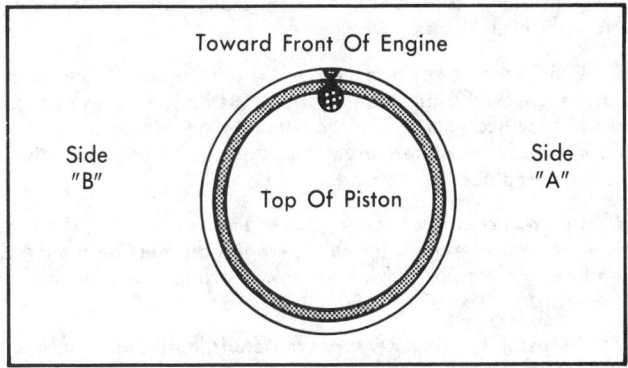

Fig. 7   Piston and Rod Positioning

CRANKSHAFT & ROD BEARINGS

MAIN & CONNECTING ROD BEARINGS

NOTE – *Following procedures are performed with oil pan and oil pump removed.*

Connecting Rod Bearings – **1)** Mark or identify rod cap to rod before removing rod cap nuts. With rod nuts removed, remove rod cap and bearing. Push up on piston and rod assembly and remove bearing from rod. Inspect bearings for wear or damage and replace as necessary.

2) Check crankshaft rod bearing journal for out-of-round or taper conditions. If crankshaft is out-of-round or tapers more than .001", crankshaft must be removed and ground for undersize bearings.

5.0L & 5.7L V8 ENGINES (Cont.)

3) Check bearing clearance using the Plastigage method. If clearance exceeds specifications, a .001" or .002" undersize bearing may be installed to obtain correct clearance. If clearance is still excessive, crankshaft must be removed and ground for undersize bearings. Connecting rod bearings are available .010" and .020" undersize.

4) To install bearings, clean crankshaft journal and bearing surface in rod. Insert bearing halves in rod and cap. Lubricate journal and pull piston and rod assembly down, aligning bearing on journal. Install rod cap noting identification marks and evenly tighten rod nuts.

Main Bearings — **1)** Main bearings are selective fit by manufacturer during production. A standard size bearing half may be used in combination with a .001" undersize bearing half to obtain correct clearance. This combination will decrease clearance .0005".

2) If correct clearance could not be obtained during production, a crankshaft with .009" undersize main bearing journals is fitted. A .009" and .010" bearing half combination may be used to obtain correct clearance.

3) If engine is fitted with a crankshaft with .009" undersize main bearing journals, it will be identified by a "9" stamped on crankshaft counterweight next to affected bearing. Also a spot of light green paint will be next to the "9" and the bearing cap will be painted light green.

4) Main bearings may be removed and replaced with crankshaft still installed in engine. Mark or identify main bearing caps to cylinder block before removing caps. Bearings are removed from cylinder block by inserting a bearing removal and installing tool in oil hole in crankshaft and rotating crankshaft clockwise.

5) Crankshaft clearance, taper or out-of-round conditions can be checked using the Plastigage method. If clearance exceeds specifications, a .001" or .002" undersize bearing may be installed to obtain correct clearance. Both bearing halves must be replaced.

6) If correct clearance cannot be obtained or journal tapers or is out-of-round more than .001", crankshaft must be removed and ground for undersize bearings. Bearings are available in Standard, .001", .002", .009", .010" and .020" undersize.

7) To install bearings, ensure crankshaft journal and bearing surface in cap and block are clean. Lubricate journal and install bearing in cap. If bearings were removed with crankshaft still installed, use bearing removal and installation tool inserted in crankshaft oil hole to install upper bearing half. Install main cap noting identification marks and evenly tighten main bearing bolts.

THRUST BEARING ALIGNMENT

Pry crankshaft forward as far as possible and check crankshaft end play with a feeler gauge inserted between front of rear main bearing and crankshaft. Replace rear main bearing if end play not to specifications. See Fig. 8.

REAR MAIN BEARING OIL SEAL

Removal — Remove rear main bearing cap and pry out old seal. Remove upper half of seal by tapping end with brass punch until end of seal protrudes enough to be removed with pliers.

Fig. 8 Checking Crankshaft End Play

Installation — **1)** Fabricate installation tool as shown in *Fig. 9*. Coat seal lips and seal bead of upper seal with engine oil. Keep ends of seal dry of oil and position tool between crankshaft and seal seat in cylinder block. Position seal between tip of tool and crankshaft.

2) Roll seal around crankshaft, using tool as a "shoehorn" to protect seal from sharp corner of seal seat surface. Make sure that oil seal lip is positioned towards front of engine.

NOTE — *Installation tool must remain in position until seal is positioned with both ends flush with block. Remove tool taking care not to remove seal.*

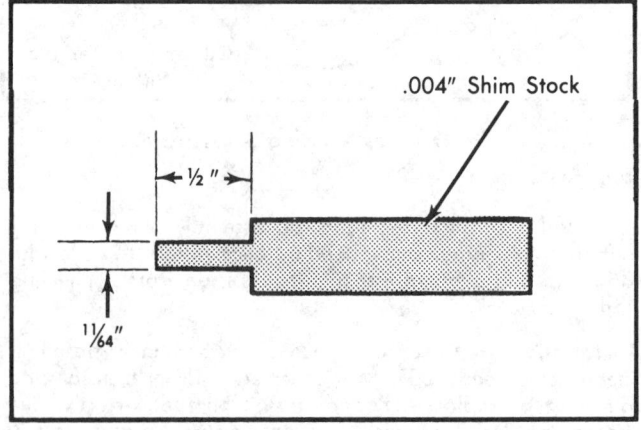

Fig. 9 Rear Main Oil Seal Installation Tool

3) Install lower half of seal in bearing cap, using tool as a "shoehorn". Feed seal into cap using light pressure with thumb and finger. Install bearing cap with sealant applied to face, taking care to keep sealant off split line.

5.0L & 5.7L V8 ENGINES (Cont.)

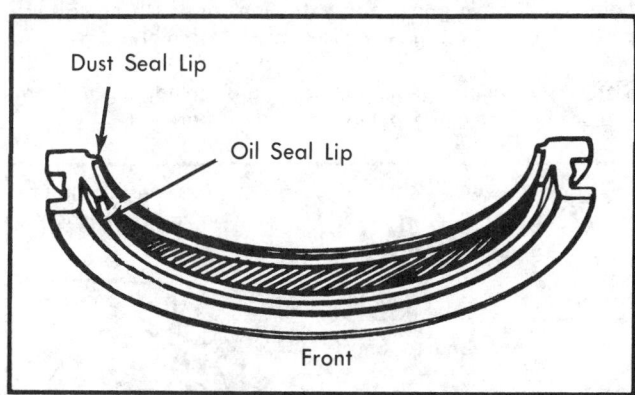

Fig. 10 Identifying Rear Main Oil Seal

CAMSHAFT

ENGINE FRONT COVER

Removal — Remove fan belt, fan and pulley. Remove radiator shroud and accessory drive pulley. Remove harmonic balancer pulley bolt (if equipped). Pull off harmonic balancer with a suitable puller (J-23523). Remove water pump and front cover retaining screws. Remove cover and gasket.

Installation — 1) Make sure gasket surface on cover and cylinder block are clean. Using a sharp knife, remove any excess gasket protruding from between oil pan and cylinder block. Apply a ⅛" bead of silicone rubber sealer to oil pan and cylinder block junction and oil pan front lip.

2) Coat front cover gasket with sealer and position on cover. Position cover on cylinder block. Loosely install cover-to-block upper attaching screws. Tighten screws alternately and evenly while pressing downward on cover so that dowels in block are aligned with holes in cover.

3) Install remaining cover screws and torque to specifications. Install harmonic balancer using suitable tool (J23523). Reverse removal procedures to install remaining components.

FRONT COVER OIL SEAL

With Cover Removed — Pry seal out of cover with a screwdriver. Install new seal with open end of seal toward inside of cover and drive into position with a suitable driver (J-23042) and a hammer. Support cover at seal area before driving in seal.

With Cover Installed — With harmonic balancer removed, pry seal out front of cover. Install seal with open end of seal toward engine and drive into place with a suitable driver (J-23042) and a hammer.

TIMING CHAIN & SPROCKETS

Removal — Remove engine front cover as previously outlined. Crank engine over until timing marks on camshaft and crankshaft sprockets are aligned. Remove bolts securing camshaft sprocket to camshaft and pull off sprocket with timing chain. Camshaft sprocket is a light fit on camshaft. A light blow with a plastic hammer will dislodge sprocket.

Installation — To install new crankshaft sprocket, pull into place with a bolt or drive into place with suitable driver and hammer. Install camshaft sprocket and timing chain making

sure timing marks on sprockets are aligned. Install and tighten sprocket bolts. See *Fig. 11.*

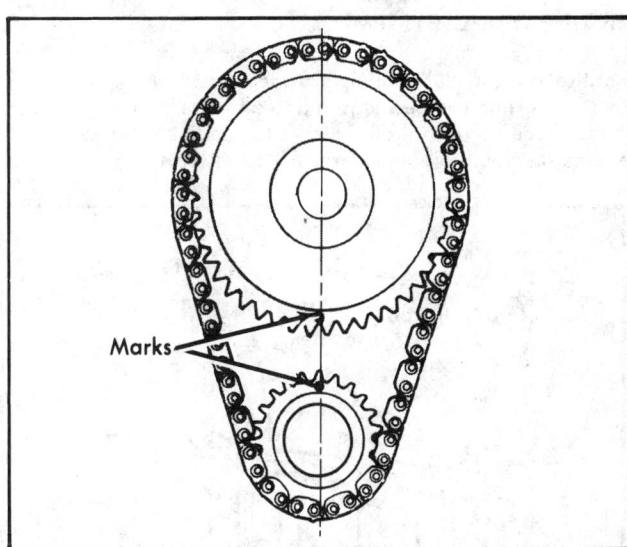

Marks

Fig. 11 Timing Chain Sprocket Alignment

CAMSHAFT

Removal — Remove intake manifold, engine front cover and timing chain as previously outlined. Remove valve covers and loosen all rocker arms until push rods can be removed. Remove grille and radiator if necessary. Remove fuel pump and push rod. Screw two bolts into camshaft and withdraw camshaft.

Installation — Lubricate camshaft journals and lobes with motor oil. If a new camshaft is being installed, coat camshaft lobes with Molykote. Position camshaft to align timing marks on sprockets. Install remaining components as previously outlined. Adjust hydraulic valve lifters.

CAMSHAFT BEARINGS

Position number 1 cam bearing oil holes equal distance from 6 o'clock position. Position number 2, 3 and 4 bearings at 5 o'clock from left side of engine and even with bottom of cylinder bore. Position number 5 bearing oil hole at 12 o'clock.

CAM LOBE LIFT

With valve cover removed, remove rocker arm. Mount dial indicator on cylinder head and position indicator stem on a suitable ball socket adapter (J-8520) on push rod. Rotate engine slowly until lifter is on heel of camshaft and set dial indicator to zero. Rotate engine slowly until push rod is at fully raised position. Dial indicator will give total camshaft lobe lift. Lift should be within specifications.

NOTE — *Valve lift can be figured by multiplying lobe lift by rocker arm ratio.*

ENGINE OILING

Crankcase Capacity — Capacity is 4 quarts, add 1 quart with filter change.

Oil Filter — Replaced every other oil change or more often under dusty or severe conditions.

5.0L & 5.7L V8 ENGINES (Cont.)

Oil Pressure – With engine at normal operating temperature, oil pressure should be 40 psi at 2000 RPM.

ENGINE OILING SYSTEM

Positive pressure lubrication provided to all main, camshaft, and connecting rod bearings and to all valve lifters and rocker arms. Three horizontal oil galleries located in "V" at center of engine distribute oil under pressure to all parts. See Fig. 12.

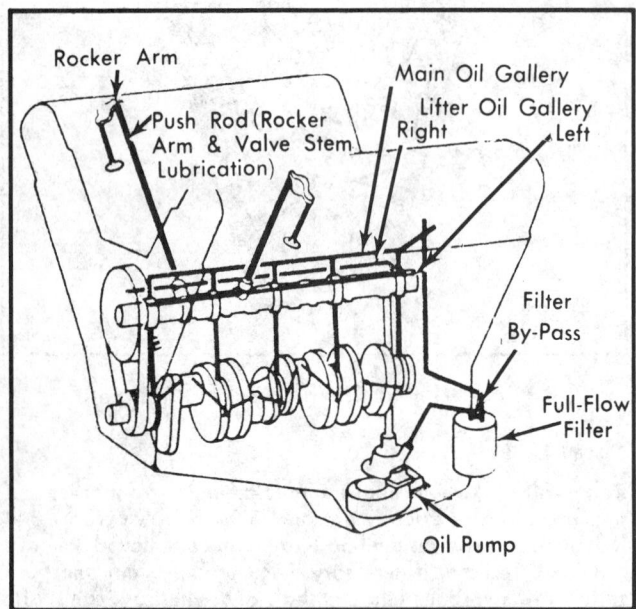

Fig. 12 Engine Oiling System

Valve Lifters – Oil passage from rear camshaft bearing supplies oil to lifter galleries. Both mechanical and hydraulic lifters intersect the gallery. Recess in mechanical lifter permits oil to pass into lower end of push rod. A larger passage in rear camshaft bearing permits more oil pressure for lubrication of hydraulic lifters. Hydraulic lifters contain an inertia valve which opens permitting oil to pass to hollow pushrods.

Rocker Arms and Valve Stems – Oil passes up through hollow pushrods to a hole in upper end that matches hole in rocker arm. Oil sprayed out this hole and across rocker arm lubricates valve stem tip.

OIL PUMP

Removal – Mark gears so they may be reassembled with same teeth indexing. Remove pump-to-rear main bearing cap

bolt and remove pump and extension shaft. Do not disturb pickup screen. Screen is serviced as an assembly.

NOTE – *If pump gears or body are damaged or worn, replacement of entire pump assembly is necessary.*

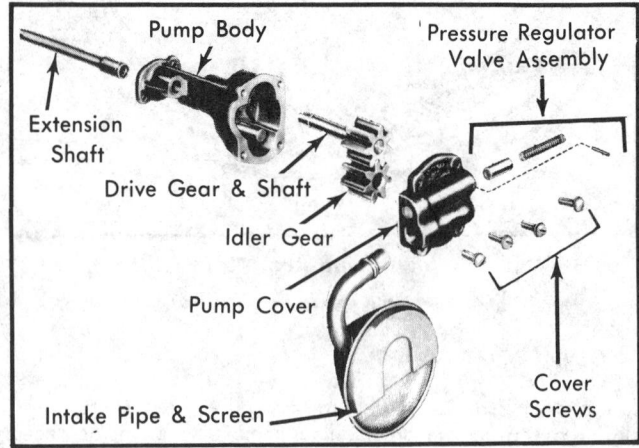

Fig. 13 Exploded View of Engine Oil Pump

Installation – Apply sealer to end of pipe and tap in place. Install idler gear in pump body with smooth side of gear towards cover opening.

NOTE – *Bottom of screen must be parallel with bottom of pan.*

TIGHTENING SPECIFICATIONS

Application	Ft. Lbs.
Cylinder Head Bolts	65
Main Bearing Cap Bolts①	80
Connecting Rod Nuts	45
Camshaft Sprocket Bolts	20
Intake Manifold Bolts	30
Exhaust Manifold Bolts②	20
Water Pump Bolts	30
Flywheel Bolts	60
Harmonic Balancer Bolt	60
Oil Pump Bolt	65
Rocker Arm Cover Screws	4
Oil Pan Bolts	
¼"	7
5/16"	14

① – Outer bolts on 4 bolt caps 70 ft. lbs.
② – Two center bolts on 350" engine 30 ft. lbs.

ENGINE SPECIFICATIONS

GENERAL SPECIFICATIONS

Year	Displ. Cu. Ins.	Carburetor	HP at RPM	Torque (Ft. Lbs. at RPM)	Compr. Ratio	Bore	Stroke
1981							
5.0L	305"	2-Bbl.	.....	.....	8.5:1	3.736"	3.480"
	305"	4-Bbl.	.....	.....	8.6:1①	3.736"	3.480"
5.7L	350"	2-Bbl.	.....	.....	.....	4.000"	3.480"
	350"	4-Bbl.	.....	.....	8.2:1②	4.000"	3.480"

① – VIN code F shown, VIN code H; 9.2:1.
② – VIN code L shown, VIN code M; 8.3:1.

General Motors V8 Engines

5.0L & 5.7L V8 ENGINES (Cont.)
ENGINE SPECIFICATIONS (Cont.)

VALVES							
Engine & Valve	Head Diam.	Face Angle	Seat Angle	Seat Width	Stem Diameter	Stem Clearance	Valve Lift
5.0L & 5.7L Int. Exh.	1.940" 1.500"	45° 45°	46° 46°	.031-.063" .063-.094"	.3410-.3417" .3410-.3417"	.0010-.0027" .0010-.0027"	....

PISTONS, PINS, RINGS						
	PISTONS	PINS		RINGS		
Engine	Clearance	Piston Fit	Rod Fit ①	Rings	End Gap	Side Clearance
5.0L & 5.7L	.0007-.0017"	.00025-.00035"	.0008-.0016"	1 2 3	.010-.020" .010-.025" .015-.055"	.0012-.0032" .0012-.0032" .002-.007"

① — Interference fit.

CRANKSHAFT MAIN & CONNECTING ROD BEARINGS							
	MAIN BEARINGS				CONNECTING ROD BEARINGS		
Engine	Journal Diam.	Clearance	Thrust Bearing	Crankshaft End Play	Journal Diam.	Clearance	Side Play
5.0L & 5.7L	①2.4484-2.4493" ②2.4481-2.4490" ③2.4479-2.4488"	①.0008-.0020" ②.0011-.0023" ③.0017-.0032"	No.5	.002-.006"	2.0988-2.0998"	.0013-.0035"	.008-.014"

① — Journal No. 1.
② — Journal Nos. 2, 3 and 4.
③ — Journal No. 5.

VALVE SPRINGS			
	Free Length	PRESSURE (LBS.)	
Engine		Valve Closed	Valve Open
5.0L, 5.7L Int. Exh.	2.03" 2.03"	76-84@1.70" 76-84@1.61"	194-206@1.25" 194-206@1.16"

CAMSHAFT			
Engine	Journal Diam.	Clearance	Lobe Lift
5.0L Int. Exh.	1.8682-1.8692"	.....	.2484" .2667"
5.7L Int. Exh.	1.8682-1.8692"	.....	.2600" .2733"

5.7L V8 DIESEL ENGINE

IDENTIFICATION CODING

ENGINE IDENTIFICATION

Engines may be identified by codes found stamped on pad at lower left front side of cylinder block. An alternate location for engine codes is lower left rear side of cylinder block (just above starter). Code letters are suffix of engine Identification Number.

Engine Identification Codes	
Application	**Code**
5.7L (350") Diesel	
Federal	VLC
Calif.	VLD

ENGINE REMOVAL

See Engine Removal at end of ENGINE Section.

CYLINDER HEAD & MANIFOLDS

INTAKE MANIFOLD

Removal — 1) Drain cooling system, remove air cleaner and disconnect all hoses and wiring as necessary. Remove breather pipes and air crossover. Cap intake manifold with cover screens (J-26996-2 for Calif. or J-26996-10 for Federal).

2) Disconnect throttle rod, spring and remove retaining clip from bellcrank. Remove throttle cable from bracket and position away from engine. Remove alternator and A/C bracket as necessary.

3) Disconnect fuel lines to fuel pump, filter, nozzles and injection pump. Remove injection pump, fuel filter and brackets. Cap all open fuel lines and fittings.

4) Remove vacuum pump, drain tube, intake manifold and injection pump adapter.

CAUTION — *DO NOT bend injection pump lines.*

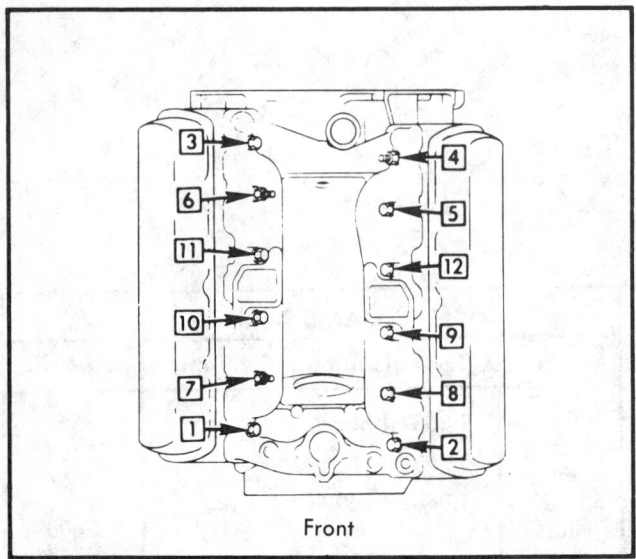

Front

Fig. 1 Intake Manifold Tightening Sequence

Installation — 1) Clean machined surfaces of manifold and head. Use suitable sealer to coat both sides of intake manifold gasket and position on head. Install end seals and intake manifold making sure that ends are positioned under cylinder head. Before installing bolts, connect thermostat bypass hose to water hose.

2) Dip manifold bolts in oil and tighten in 2 steps. *See Fig. 1.* Install drain tube and apply chassis lube to seal area on injection pump adapter, taper edge and seal area of manifold. Use seal installing tool (J-28425) to properly position seal on adapter, then tighten bolts to specifications.

NOTE — *When replacing original injection pump with new pump, only use injection pumps with part number 22510362 for Federal vehicles or injection pumps with part number 22510363 for Calif. vehicles.*

3) Align offset tang on pump drive shaft with offset in pump driven gear and install injection pump. Align mark on injection pump with mark on adapter. Install fuel filter bracket and fuel filter. Connect fuel lines and fuel return line to injection pump.

4) Install vacuum pump and vacuum lines, then reverse removal procedure to complete installation.

EXHAUST MANIFOLD

Removal — Remove air cleaner and lower alternator bracket. Raise vehicle, remove crossover pipe and disconnect exhaust pipe from manifold. Remove right side manifold. Lower vehicle and remove left side manifold.

Installation — To install manifolds, reverse removal procedure.

CYLINDER HEAD

Removal — 1) Drain cooling system and remove or disconnect all necessary lines, hoses, brackets and linkage. Remove intake and exhaust manifolds. Remove rocker arm assemblies and push rods.

NOTE — *Keep rocker arms, pivots and push rods in order of removal. They must be installed in their original positions.*

2) Remove engine block drain plug on same side as cylinder head being removed. Remove cylinder head bolts and cylinder head. If necessary to remove pre-chamber, remove the glow plug and injection nozzle, then tap out with a small blunt drift punch.

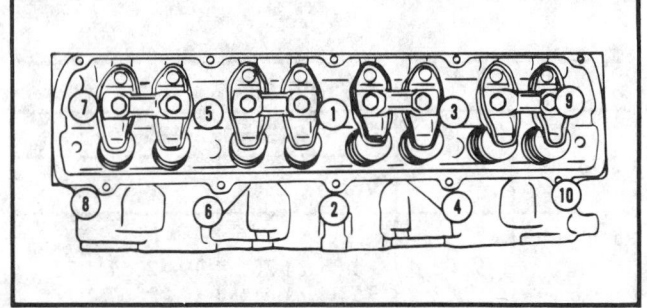

Fig. 2 Cylinder Head Tightening Sequence

5.7L V8 DIESEL ENGINE (Cont.)

Installation — 1) Install head gasket WITHOUT sealer. Install pre-chamber (if removed) to the head. Pre-chamber must not be recessed or protrude more than .003". Install glow plug, injection nozzle, and head to engine block.

NOTE — *On early 1981 diesel engines the head gasket can be installed upside down. To prevent this, later models have a 3rd dowel pin in engine block. On early models, install head gasket with the prechamber shield (on gasket) facing toward cylinder head.*

2) Clean and dip cylinder head bolts in engine oil and tighten in 2 steps. *See Fig. 2.*

VALVES

VALVE ARRANGEMENT

I-E-I-E-E-I-E-I (Both banks, front to rear)

VALVE GUIDE SERVICING

Intake and exhaust valve guides are integral with cylinder head. Valves are available in Standard, .003", .005", .010" and .013" oversize.

NOTE — *Use .003" oversize reamer for Standard and .003" oversize valves. Use .005" oversize reamer for .005" oversize and .013" oversize reamer for .010" and .013" oversize valves.*

VALVE STEM OIL SEALS

Install oil seal down as far as possible on valve stem. Seals will correctly position when engine is started. The valve stem oil seals are color coded as follows:

Intake — Gray: Standard to .005" oversize.
          Orange: .010" to .013" oversize.
Exhaust — Ivory: Standard to .005" oversize.
          Blue: .010" to .013" oversize.

VALVE SPRINGS

Removal — With cylinder head removed, remove valve keys using valve spring compressing tool (J-5892-1) to compress spring. Remove retainers, spring and seal. Keep components separate for reinstallation in original location.

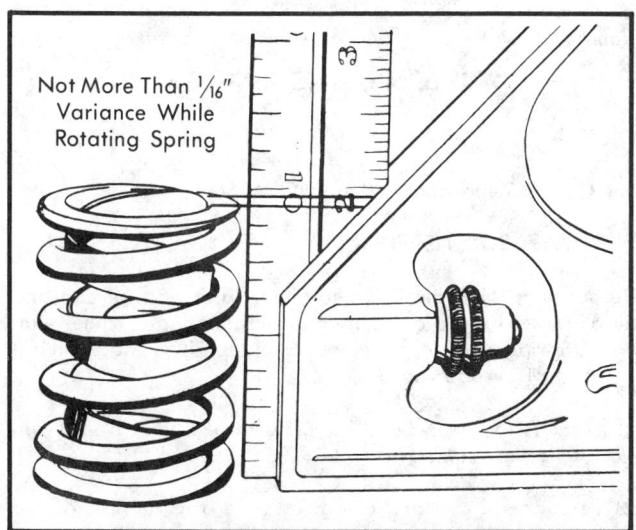

Fig. 3   Checking Valve Spring Squareness

Inspection — Check for squareness of valve spring as shown in *Fig. 3.* Spring must be within 1/16" square in free position.

Installation — 1) Reverse removal procedure and note the following: Check spring and keys to be sure they are properly installed.

2) Measure valve stem height whenever new valve is installed or after grinding valve. Use valve stem height gauge (J-25289) shown in *Fig. 4.* There should be at least .015" clearance between gauge and valve stem. If clearance is less than .015", grind tip as required.

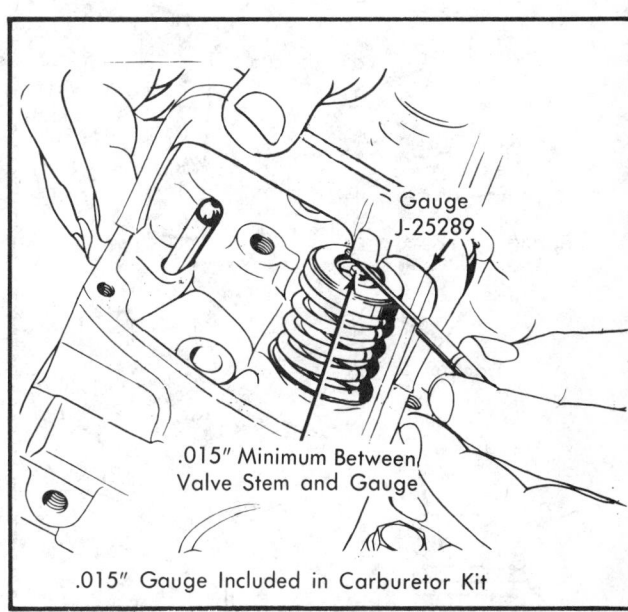

Fig. 4   Measuring Valve Stem Height

3) Measure clearance between gauge and valve rotator. Clearance must be .030" minimum. If any valve is less than .005" above rotator, valve is too short and must be replaced. *See Fig. 5.*

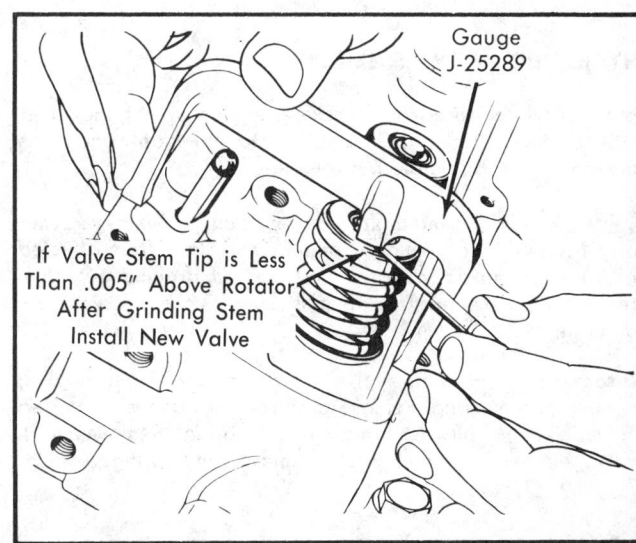

Fig. 5   Measuring Rotator Height

ROCKER ARM ASSEMBLY

Removal & Installation — Remove valve cover, rocker arm flanged bolts, pivot and rocker arms. Remove each set (one set

5.7L V8 DIESEL ENGINE (Cont.)

per cylinder) as a unit. To install, position one set of rocker arms in proper location. Lubricate wear points with suitable lubricant and install pivots. Install flanged bolts and tighten alternately to proper torque.

NOTE — *Refer to "Valve Lifter Bleed Down" as lifters must be bled down to prevent piston from hitting valves.*

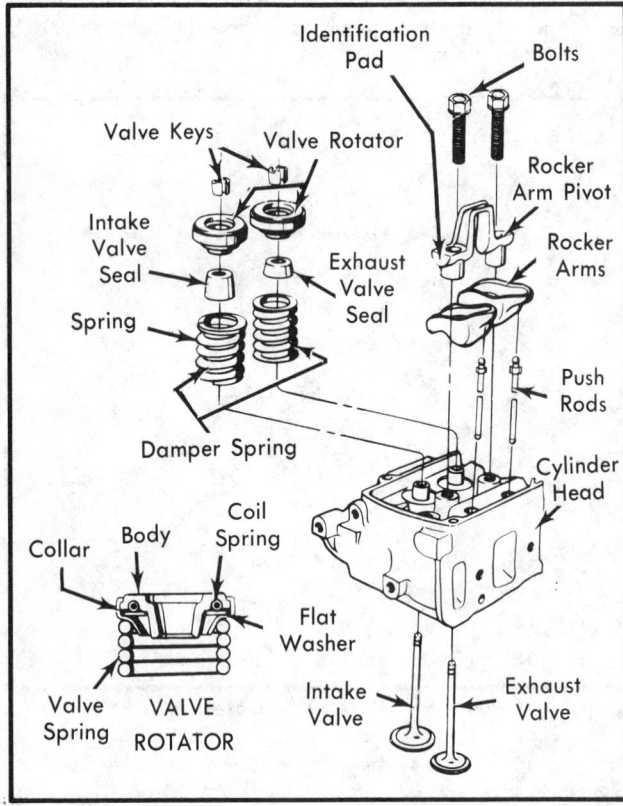

Fig. 6   Exploded View of Valve Assembly

HYDRAULIC LIFTER ASSEMBLY

Hydraulic lifters used on the diesel engine are of the roller type. Lifters are serviced as complete assemblies only and parts are not interchangeable between lifters.

NOTE — *If intake manifold was removed and if any rocker arm assembly was removed or loosened, the lifters affected MUST be removed, disassembled and oil drained out, then reassembled. Failure to do this could cause valve train damage.*

Disassembly — With valve lifter removed from engine, remove retainer ring. Remove push rod seat and oil metering valve. Remove plunger and plunger spring. Remove check valve retainer from plunger and remove valve spring. *See Fig. 7.*

Inspection — Clean all parts in clean solvent or diesel fuel. Check for nicks, burrs or scoring on parts. Make sure lifter roller operates smoothly and without excessive play.

Reassembly — Coat all parts with clean engine oil, then reverse disassembly procedure.

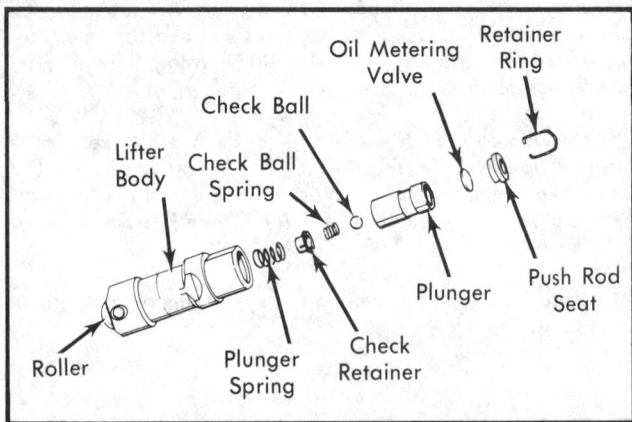

Fig. 7   Exploded View of Valve Lifter Assembly

NOTE — *Oversize lifters are used and are identifiable by raised "O" on lifter bore casting on block. Oversize is .010".*

VALVE LIFTER BLEED DOWN

If intake manifold was not removed but some or all of the rocker arm assemblies were loosened or removed, proceed as follows:

1) Before installing any rocker arm assembly, rotate crankshaft until number 1 cylinder is 32° BTDC. This is ½" beyond end of timing indicator. Remove glow plug for number 1 cylinder to check correct positioning of crankshaft.

2) If removed or loosened, install number 5 cylinder rocker arm assembly first. Tighten rocker arm bolts evenly and alternately until exhaust valve just starts to open.

CAUTION — *Do not tighten rocker arm assemblies, for cylinders 3, 5 and 8, beyond the point where valves are fully open or damage to valve train will occur.*

3) Install remaining removed or loosened rocker arms. Tighten bolts until valves are in the fully open position. Then finish tightening rocker arm for cylinder number 5 until valve is in fully open position.

CAUTION — *It will take approximately 45 minutes for lifters to bleed down. During this time, DO NOT rotate engine or damage to valve train and/or engine will occur.*

PISTONS, PINS & RINGS

OIL PAN

See Oil Pan Removal at end of ENGINE Section.

PISTON & ROD ASSEMBLY

Removal — 1) Remove intake manifold, heads, oil pan and oil pump. Mark rod and caps for reinstallation in same cylinder. Use ridge reamer to remove any deposits or ridge on upper end of cylinder bore.

NOTE — *Pistons must be at bottom of stroke and covered with cloth to collect cuttings.*

2) Remove rod cap and use guide hose over threads of rod bolts to prevent damage to journals and threads. Remove rod and pistons out top of block.

5.7L V8 DIESEL ENGINE (Cont.)

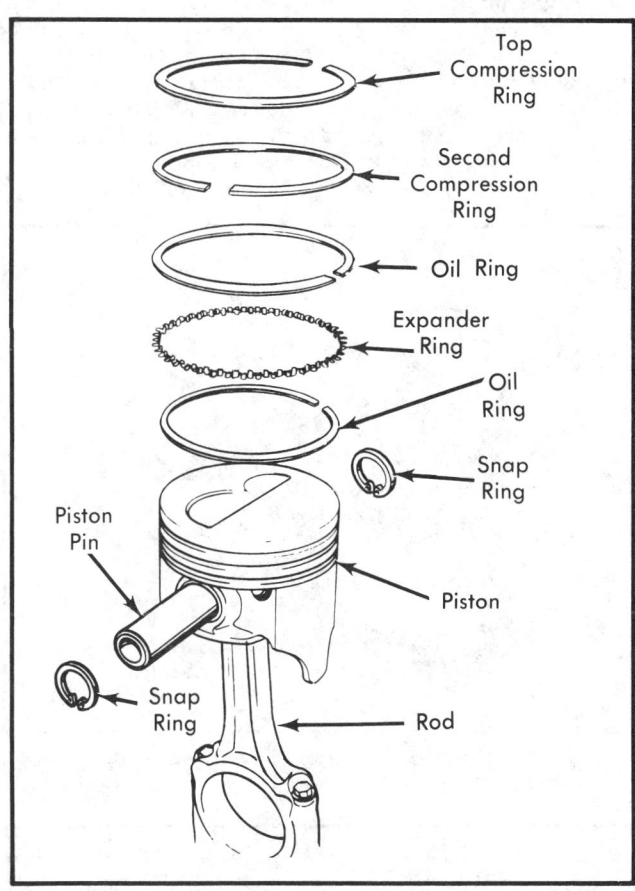

Fig. 8 Exploded View of Piston and Rod Assembly Showing Piston Ring Positions

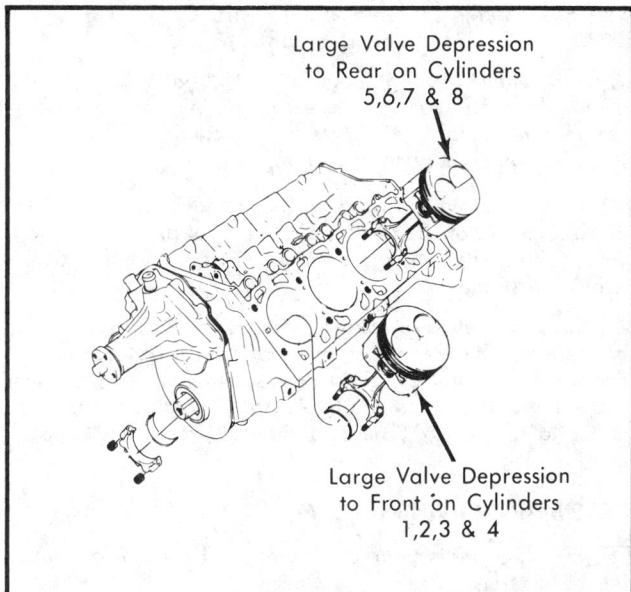

Fig. 9 Installation of Piston Assemblies in Engine Showing Positioning of Piston Valve Depressions

Installation — 1) Lightly coat pistons, rings and cylinder walls with engine oil. Position rings as shown in *Fig. 8*. Make sure the marks on piston rings are toward top of piston. Using piston ring compressor, install piston with valve depression in top of piston turned toward inner side of engine. See *Fig. 9*.

2) On cylinders 1, 2, 3 & 4, the larger valve depression goes toward the front of engine. On cylinders 5, 6, 7 & 8, the larger depression goes toward rear of engine. See *Fig. 9*.

FITTING PISTONS

NOTE — *Each piston is fitted to its individual cylinder and should be marked for that cylinder.*

1) Measure cylinder bores. Maximum taper and/or out-of-round is .001". Measure piston (with pin removed) for taper at pin centerline and at bottom of skirt. Measure for size ¾" below pin centerline. Maximum taper is .002". Piston-to-bore clearane should be .005-.006".

2) If clearance is not to specifications, bore may have to be honed or bored. Pistons are available in standard, high standard and .010" oversize. Mark piston and cylinder for oversize pistons.

NOTE — *Vehicles may have oversize pistons fitted at factory, these pistons will be .010" oversize and marked.*

PISTON PINS

Piston pin is free floating and can be inserted into piston or rod with hand pressure. Piston pin-to-rod clearance should be .0003-.0013". Piston pin-to-piston clearance should be .0003-.0005". Piston rod may be installed in the piston with either side facing up.

CRANKSHAFT & ROD BEARINGS

CONNECTING ROD & MAIN BEARINGS

NOTE — *.010" undersized crankshafts are used and are identified by a .010" stamped on number 6 counterweight.*

Connecting Rod Bearings — 1) These bearings are designed to have slight projection above the rod and cap faces to ensure positive contact. They may be replaced without removing rod and piston assembly from engine.

2) Measure connecting rod journals with a micrometer to check out-of-round. Maximum out-of-round must not exceed .0015". Use Plastigage method to check bearing clearance. Maximum bearing clearance should be .0035". Coat bearings with engine oil before installation.

NOTE — *All rods must be connected to journals before rotating crankshaft to prevent damage to engine.*

3) Measure connecting rod side clearance by spreading rods with screwdriver and inserting feeler gauge. Clearance should be .006-.020".

Main Bearings — 1) Check bearing clearance. On engines not removed from vehicle, use floor jack or other support to hold crankshaft against upper bearing half.

2) Use Plastigage across full width of bearing. Install cap with bearing and tighten to 120 ft. lbs. Determine bearing

General Motors V8 Engines

5.7L V8 DIESEL ENGINE (Cont.)

clearance by removing cap and check flattened Plastigage with graduations on container. If clearance is greater than .0035", replace BOTH bearing halves as a set.

NOTE — *Main bearing clearance of .0035" is maximum allowable, but if bearing noise exists with this clearance, bearings must be replaced to reduce bearing clearance. NEVER use shims to reduce bearing clearance.*

3) To replace main bearing halves, remove caps and lower shell. Insert a flattened cotter pin or rollout pin in oil passage hole of crankshaft. Rotate crankshaft in opposite direction of cranking rotation.

4) Check journals for roughness and wear. Out-of-round may be measured by inside micrometer or crankshaft caliper. Upper half must be removed when measuring journals. Maximum allowable out-of-round is .0015". Apply suitable lubricant to thrust flanges of No. 3 bearing. Reverse procedures to install new bearing halves.

REAR MAIN BEARING OIL SEAL

NOTE — *Rear main bearing oil seal can be installed without removing crankshaft.*

1) Drain oil, remove oil pan and rear main bearing cap. Use packing tool (BT-6433) against end of seal and drive oil seal into groove until it is packed tight. This may vary from ¼" to ¾", depending on amount of pack required. Repeat on other end of seal.

2) Measure amount seal was driven up on one side; add ¹⁄₁₆", then cut this length from old seal removed from bearing cap. Repeat on other side, again adding ¹⁄₁₆", then cut this length off old seal.

3) Place a drop of suitable sealer on each end of seal. Using 2 small screwdrivers, work these 2 pieces (one on each side) into block seal groove. Use packing tool to force short pieces into block.

4) Form a new rope seal in main bearing cap, packing by hand. Use rear main seal installing tool (J-28693) and hammer seal into groove.

NOTE — *Seal is fully seated if undercut area of tool slides over seal. If tool butts against seal, drive seal further into groove.*

5) Rotate tool before cutting off excessive packing. Reinstall main bearing cap and tighten.

CAMSHAFT

FRONT COVER

Removal — Drain cooling system and remove radiator and by-pass hoses. Remove belts, fan and fan pulley, crankshaft pulley, harmonic balancer and accessory brackets. Remove cover attaching bolts, cover, timing indicator and water pump. Remove both dowel pins.

Installation — 1) Grind a chamfer on one end of dowel pin. Cut excessive material from end of oil pan gasket on each side of block. Clean all mating surfaces with solvent. Trim ⅛" from each end of new pan seal. Install new front cover gasket on block and new seal on front cover. Apply suitable sealer to gasket around coolant holes and place on block.

2) Apply suitable sealer at junction of block, pan and front cover. See *Fig. 10.* Install front cover, pressing downward to compress seal. Rotate cover left and right to guide pan seal into cavity using a small screwdriver. See *Fig. 11.* Install 2 bolts and tighten finger tight. Install dowel pins (chamfered end first), into timing indicator and water pump and tighten bolts. Lubricate timing cover seal and install harmonic balancer. Reverse removal procedure to complete installation.

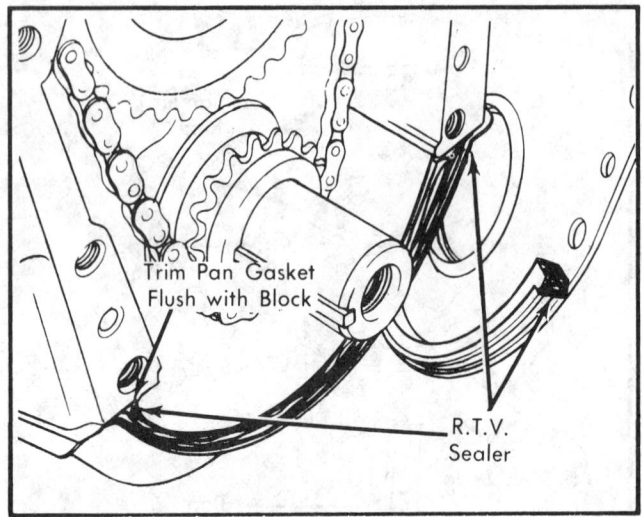

Fig. 10 **Oil Pan and Front Cover Seal Installation**

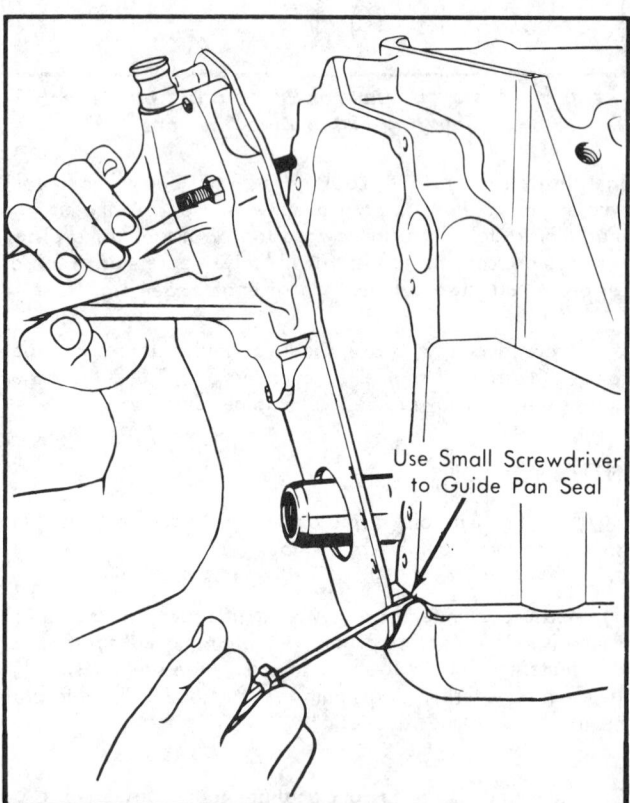

Fig. 11 **Installation of Front Cover**

FRONT COVER OIL SEAL

Removal — Remove belts, harmonic balancer, crankshaft pulley and hub. Remove front cover oil seal.

5.7L V8 DIESEL ENGINE (Cont.)

Installation — Apply sealer to outside of seal. Use seal installer (J-25264 and J-23952) to position and install seal. Reinstall components removed in removal procedure.

TIMING CHAIN

Removal — Remove front cover, oil slinger, cam gear, crankshaft gear and key. Remove timing gear. Remove fuel pump eccentric only if replacement is necessary.

Installation — **1)** Install key in crankshaft and fuel pump eccentric if removed. Install camshaft gear, crankshaft gear and timing chain together. When installing these components, make sure timing marks on both gears are aligned. See *Fig. 12.* Install oil slinger.

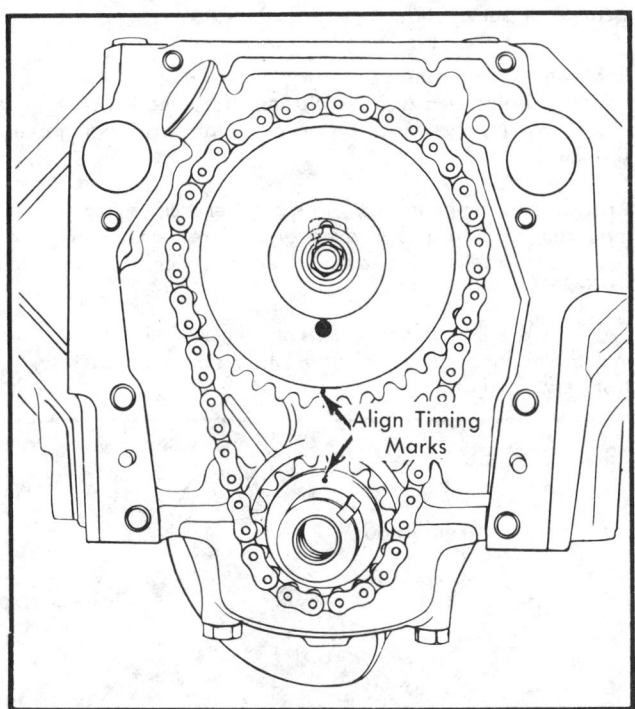

Fig. 12   Aligning Crankshaft and Camshaft Gear Timing Marks

NOTE — *When the 2 marks are aligned, No. 6 cylinder is at TDC. To obtain TDC for No. 1 cylinder, slowly rotate crankshaft 1 revolution. This will bring cam mark to top. No. 1 cylinder will then be in firing (TDC) position.*

2) If timing chain or gears were replaced, engine will have to be retimed and marking on injection pump adaptor will have to be filed off and remarked. To retime engine proceed as follows:

3) File off the original mark on injection pump adapter. DO NOT file off mark on injector pump. Place engine at TDC on No. 1 cylinder and align mark on balancer with zero mark on indicator.

NOTE — *The index is offset to the right when number 1 cylinder is at TDC.*

4) Install special timing tool (J-26896) into pump adapter. Tighten tool, toward No. 1 cylinder, to 50 ft. lbs. Then, while

holding this torque, mark injection pump adapter. Remove tool. *See Fig. 13.*

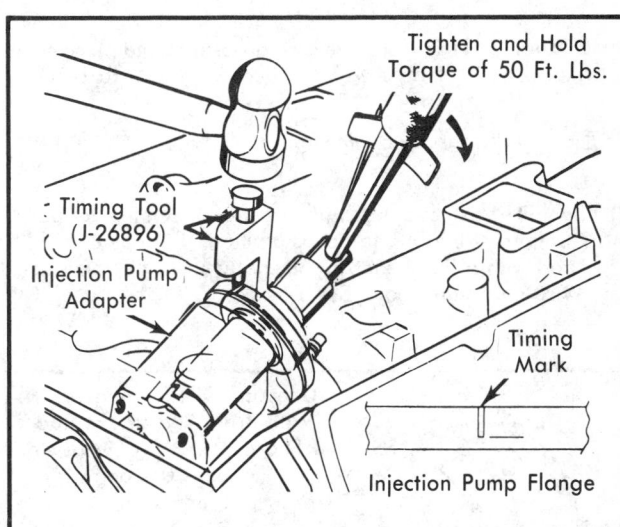

Fig. 13   Marking Injection Pump Adapter When Retiming Engine

CAMSHAFT

Removal — **1)** Disconnect battery, drain cooling system, disconnect radiator hoses, cooler lines and remove radiator. Remove air crossover, all hoses, lines, wiring and linkage to intake manifold and remove manifold.

2) Remove fan, belts, balancer pulley, harmonic balancer, front cover, rocker arm covers, rocker arms, push rods and hydraulic lifters, keeping them in sequence for reassembly. If equipped with air conditioning, discharge system and remove condenser. Remove timing chain and gears.

3) Position camshaft dowel at 3 o'clock position. Hold camshaft to rear and remove pump drive gear by sliding off camshaft while rocking pump driven gear. Remove injection pump adapter, then remove snap ring and selective washer. Remove driven gear and spring. Remove camshaft carefully sliding out front of engine.

NOTE — *Do not force shaft as damage can occur to bearings.*

Installation — To install camshaft, reverse removal procedure. Apply suitable lubricant to camshaft and bearings prior to installation.

CAMSHAFT BEARINGS

Removal — **1)** Oil pan must be removed to replace camshaft bearing.

NOTE — *Camshaft bearings are replaced as a complete set only. All bearings must be removed first before installing new bearings.*

2) Remove camshaft. Use bearing remover set (J-6098-01) and handle (J-8092) to drive out camshaft bearings. Remove bearings in sequence, starting with No. 1.

5.7L V8 DIESEL ENGINE (Cont.)

3) To remove injection pump driven gear bushings, drive both bushings out at the same time from rear to front of block, using pump drive shaft tool (J-28439-2 & J-8092).

Installation − **1)** To install, reverse procedure and place each bearing in front of bore with tapered edge toward block.

NOTE − *Install bearings beginning with No. 5.*

2) Align oil hole in bearings with center of oil slot in each bore. Mark bottom of bearing to act as a guide. Use a piece of 3/32" brass rod with a 90° bend at one end to check oil hole opening. Wire must enter hole. See *Fig. 14*.

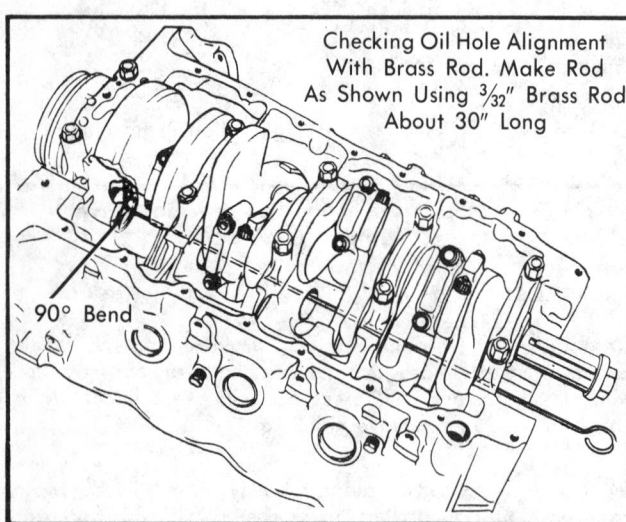

Checking Oil Hole Alignment With Brass Rod. Make Rod As Shown Using 3/32" Brass Rod About 30" Long

90° Bend

Fig. 14   *Checking Cam Bearing Oil Hole Alignment Using Brass Rod*

ENGINE OILING SYSTEM

Oil pump is gear type driven by camshaft gear through hexagonal drive shaft. Oil is delivered to right gallery where it is distributed to the five main bearings. The right bank valve lifters receive oil from this gallery through eight feed holes that intersect gallery. Camshaft bearings are lubricated from vertical passages intersecting main bearing oil passages and the left bank lifters receive oil through connecting passages from right gallery. The injection pump driven gear gets oil from passages in front camshaft bearing.

Rear driven gear bearing receives oil from passage in shaft of driven gear and vacuum pump is oiled by orifice in rear oil gallery plug. An orifice in front of right gallery lubricates the timing chain and fuel pump eccentric. Rocker arms and valve tips are lubricated through lifters and hollow push rods. Vacuum pump driven gear is oiled through left rear gallery and connecting rod bearings receive oil from drilled passages in crankshaft. Grooves around each main bearing furnish oil to drilled crankshaft passages.

OIL PUMP

Disassembly − Remove oil pump drive shaft extension. Place shop towel or wooden block over pressure regulator bore, then remove cotter pin. Remove spring and pressure regulator valve. Remove oil pump cover, gasket, drive gear and idler gear from pump body. See *Fig. 15*.

Reassembly − **1)** Install idler and drive gear in pump body. Check gear end clearance by placing straightedge over gears and measuring clearance between straightedge and gasket surface.

2) Clearance must be .0005-.0075". If end clearance is near maximum reading, check cover for scoring. Reinstall pressure regulator valve, spring and cotter pin. Replace parts as necessary.

NOTE − *When installing extension, the end nearest washer must be inserted into drive shaft. Make sure washer is 1 11/32" from end of shaft.*

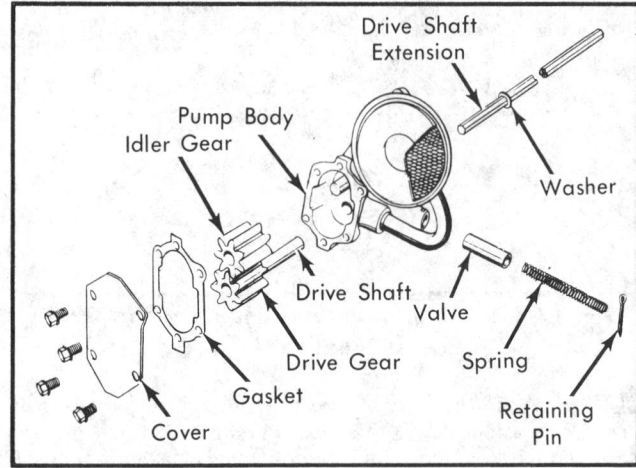

Drive Shaft Extension

Pump Body

Idler Gear

Washer

Drive Shaft

Valve

Drive Gear

Spring

Gasket

Retaining Pin

Cover

Fig. 15   *Exploded View off Oil Pump*

ENGINE SPECIFICATIONS

GENERAL SPECIFICATIONS							
Engine	Cycle	Displ. Cu. Ins.	Compr. Ratio	Bore	Stroke	Firing Order	Inj. Timing
5.7L	4	350"	22.5:1	4.057"	3.385"	1-8-4-3-6-5-7-2	.....

5.7L V8 DIESEL ENGINE (Cont.)

ENGINE SPECIFICATIONS (Cont.)

VALVES

Engine & Valve	Head Diam.	Face Angle	Seat Angle	Seat Width	Stem Diameter	Stem Clearance	Valve Lift
5.7L							
Int.①	1.875″	44°	45°	.075-.098″	.3425-.3432″	.0010-.0027″	.....
Exh.	1.625″	30°	31°	.037-.075″	.3420-.3427″	.0015-.0032″	.....

① — Induction hardened valve seat used.

PISTONS, PINS, RINGS

Engine	PISTONS	PINS		RINGS		
	Clearance	Piston Fit	Rod Fit	Rings	End Gap	Side Clearance
5.7L	.005-.006″	.0003-.0005″	.0003-.0013″	1	.015-.025″	.005-.007″
				2	.015-.025″	.0018-.0038″
				3	.015-.055″	.001-.005″

CRANKSHAFT MAIN & CONNECTING ROD BEARINGS

Engine	MAIN BEARINGS				CONNECTING ROD BEARINGS		
	Journal Diam.	Clearance①	Thrust Bearing	Crankshaft End Play	Journal Diam.	Clearance	Side Play
5.7L	2.9993-3.0003″	.0005-.0021″	No. 3	.0035-.0135″	2.1238-2.1248″	.0005-.0026″	.006-.020″

① — Journals 1,2,3 & 4. No. 5 journal .0015-.0031″

VALVE SPRINGS

Engine	Free Length	PRESSURE (LBS.)	
		Valve Closed	Valve Open
5.7L	2.09″	85-95@1.67″	203-207@1.30″

CAMSHAFT

Engine	Journal Diam.	Clearance①	Lobe Lift
5.7L			
No.1	2.0357-2.0365″	.0020-.0058″	.....
No.2	2.0157-2.0165″	.0020-.0058″	.....
No.3	1.9957-1.9965″	.0020-.0058″	.....
No.4	1.9757-1.9765″	.0020-.0058″	.....
No.5	1.9557-1.9565″	.0020-.0058″	.....

① — End play is .011-.077″.

TIGHTENING SPECIFICATIONS

Application	Ft. Lbs.
Camshaft Sprocket Bolt	65
Connecting Rod Nut	42
Cylinder Head①	130
Exhaust Manifold-to-Head Bolts②	25
Flywheel-to-Crankshaft	60
Flywheel-to-Converter	40
Injection Pump Adapter	25
Injection Pump Nuts	19
Intake Manifold ①③	40
Main Bearing Cap Bolt①	120
Oil Pump Bolts	35
Oil Pump Cover Bolts	8
Rocker Arm Pivot Bolts	28
Vibration Damper	200-300

① — Dip entire bolt in engine oil before installing.
② — Left side exhaust manifold forward bolt is tightened to 30 ft. lbs.
③ — Intake is tightened in 2 steps; Step 1 — 15 ft. lbs. Step 2 — 40 ft. lbs.

7.4L V8 ENGINE

IDENTIFICATION CODING

ENGINE IDENTIFICATION

Engine code letter is suffix of Engine Identification Number. Number is stamped on pad at front top center of cylinder block, forward of intake manifold.

Engine Identification Codes	
Application	**Code**
7.4L (454") 4-Bbl.	TRL,TRK,TRM,UCA,UCB,UCD

ENGINE REMOVAL

See Engine Removal at end of ENGINE Section.

CYLINDER HEAD & MANIFOLD

INTAKE MANIFOLD

Removal — 1) Drain cooling system. Remove air cleaner. Disconnect battery ground cable. Disconnect upper radiator hose and heater hose at manifold. Disconnect water pump by-pass at water pump. Disconnect PCV line at valve cover.

2) Disconnect accelerator linkage and fuel inlet line at carburetor. Disconnect vacuum line at distributor. Remove distributor cap and mark rotor position. Remove distributor. Remove air cleaner bracket, accelerator return spring bracket and accelerator bellcrank.

3) If equipped with air conditioning, remove compressor and bracket without disconnecting lines and lay aside. Remove upper alternator mounting bracket. Remove intake manifold bolts and pry manifold loose. Remove manifold with carburetor attached and discard all gaskets.

Installation — To install intake manifold, clean all gasket surfaces and install gaskets on cylinder heads. Install new end seals on cylinder block. Install manifold and tighten bolts in sequence shown in *Fig. 1*. Install distributor noting marked position of rotor. To complete installation, reverse removal procedure.

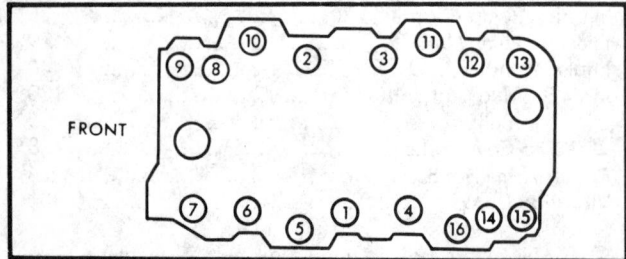

Fig. 1 Intake Manifold Tightening Sequence

CYLINDER HEAD

Removal — 1) Remove intake manifold as previously outlined. Remove alternator lower mounting bolt and lay alternator aside. Remove carburetor air heater from exhaust manifold (if equipped). Remove spark plugs, disconnect exhaust pipes at manifolds and remove manifolds.

2) Disconnect PCV hose from valve cover. Remove valve covers. Loosen rocker arm nuts and pivot rocker arms to side. Remove push rods. Mark or identify push rods to ensure that they are installed in original positions.

3) Drain cylinder block of coolant. Remove all cylinder head bolts. Pry cylinder head loose from cylinder block and remove cylinder head.

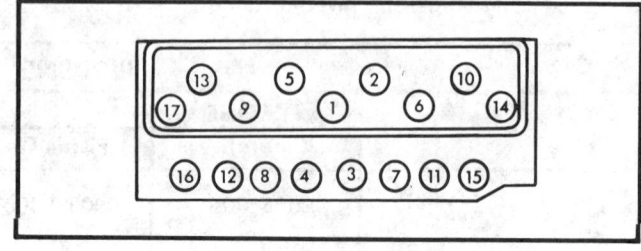

Fig. 2   Cylinder Head Tightening Sequence

Installation — Reverse removal procedure to install cylinder heads. Ensure that gasket surfaces on head and cylinder block are clean and that cylinder head bolts threads and threads in block are clean. If cylinder head gasket is steel type, coat both sides with a suitable sealer. Asbestos gasket requires no sealer. Coat cylinder head bolt threads with sealer. Tighten cylinder head bolts in sequence shown in illustration.

VALVES

VALVE ARRANGEMENT

E-I-E-I-E-I-E-I (Left bank, front to rear).
I-E-I-E-I-E-I-E (Right bank, front to rear).

VALVE GUIDE SERVICING

If valve stem-to-guide clearance is excessive, guides are removable and can be replaced, or valves with oversize stems are available. Use a suitable reamer (J-7049) to ream guides to correct size for oversize valve stems.

VALVE STEM OIL SEALS

An umbrella type oil seal is installed on valve stem before valve spring is installed. *See Valve Springs.*

VALVE SPRINGS

Removal — With cylinder head removed, compress valve spring with a suitable spring compressor and remove valve keepers. Release spring compressor and remove retainer, spring, damper, seal and valve rotators (if equipped on exhaust).

Installation — To install valve springs, reverse removal procedure. Lubricate and install valve stem oil seal on valve stem before installing remaining components.

7.4L V8 ENGINE (Cont.)

VALVE SPRING INSTALLED HEIGHT

Valve spring installed height is measured from top of shim at bottom of spring, or spring seat to top of valve spring. If distance exceeds specified height, install a 1/16" thick shim. Installed height should never be more than 1/16" less than specified height.

Valve Spring Installed Height	
Application	**Height**
All	1 51/64"

ROCKER ARM STUDS

Push rod guides are attached to cylinder head by rocker arm studs. Replace as necessary and torque studs. Coat threads on cylinder head end of new stud with sealer.

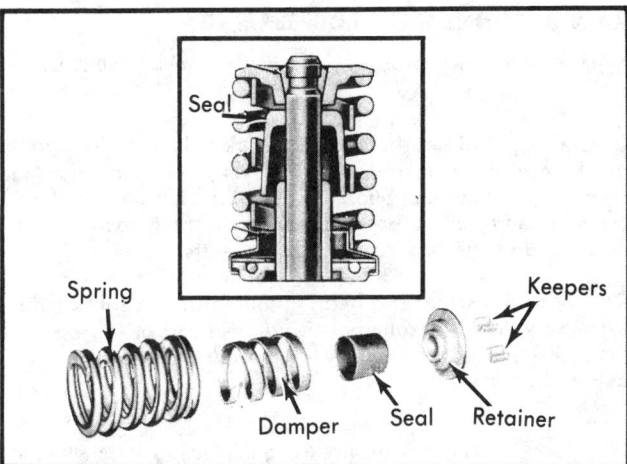

Fig. 3   Exploded View of Valve Spring Assembly

HYDRAULIC VALVE LIFTER ASSEMBLY

Disassembly — Depress plunger in lifter with a push rod and pry out retainer with a small blade screwdriver. Remove push rod seat and metering valve. Remove plunger, ball check valve assembly and plunger spring. Remove ball check valve and spring by prying ball retainer loose with a small blade screwdriver.

Reassembly — **1)** Thoroughly clean and inspect all components. If any components are worn or damaged, complete lifter must be replaced. Position check ball on small hole in bottom of plunger. Insert check ball spring on seat in ball retainer and position retainer on ball so that spring seats on ball. Using a screwdriver, press plunger into position.

2) Slide lifter body over spring and plunger, lining up oil feed holes. Fill assembly with SAE 10 oil and depress plunger to stop. With plunger depressed, insert a 1/16" drift punch into feed holes. Release plunger and refill with SAE 10 oil. Install metering valve, push rod seat and retainer. Depress push rod seat and remove drift punch.

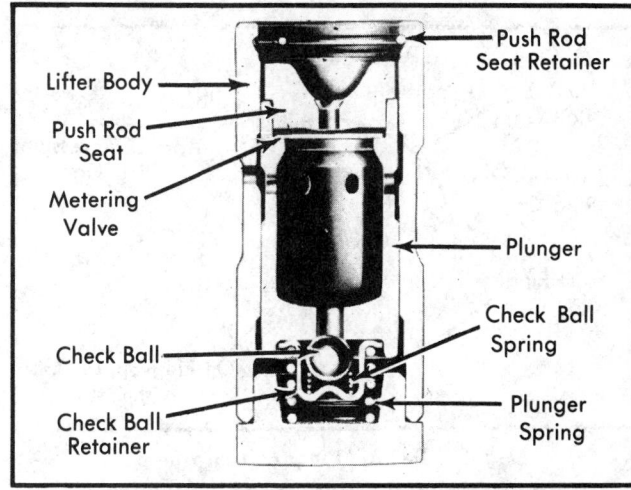

Fig. 4   Cutaway of Hydraulic Valve Lifter Assembly

VALVE CLEARANCE ADJUSTMENT

1) Rotate engine until timing marks are aligned and No. 1 cylinder is in firing position. Back off rocker arm adjusting nuts on number one intake and exhaust rocker arms until play in push rod is detected. Now tighten rocker arm nut until play in push rod is just eliminated, then tighten adjusting nut one full turn more. With engine at number one firing position, adjust intake valves 1, 2, 5 and 7 and exhaust valves 1, 3, 4 and 8.

2) Rotate engine to number 6 firing position and follow same procedures for adjusting valves. With engine at number 6 firing position, adjust intake valves 3, 4, 6 and 8 and exhaust valves 2, 5, 6 and 7.

PISTONS, PINS & RINGS

OIL PAN REMOVAL

See Oil Pan Removal at end of ENGINE Section.

PISTON & ROD ASSEMBLY

Removal — With oil pan, oil pump and cylinder heads removed, remove any ridge in top of cylinder bore with a suitable ridge reamer. Check connecting rod and cap for identification marks or numbers and identify if necessary. Remove connecting rod cap nuts and rod cap. Push piston and rod assembly up and out of cylinder block. It will be necessary to rotate crankshaft to various positions to facilitate removing piston and rod assemblies.

NOTE — *When cleaning pistons, DO NOT wire brush any part of piston assembly.*

Installation — **1)** Before installing piston and rod assembly, position ring gaps in positions shown in illustration. Place connecting rod in bore with bearing tang slots facing away from camshaft.

2) Compress piston rings with suitable ring compressor. With rod bearings and crankshaft journal lubricated, push piston and rod assembly into position and install rod cap to respective rod. Install and tighten rod cap nuts to specifications.

7.4L V8 ENGINE (Cont.)

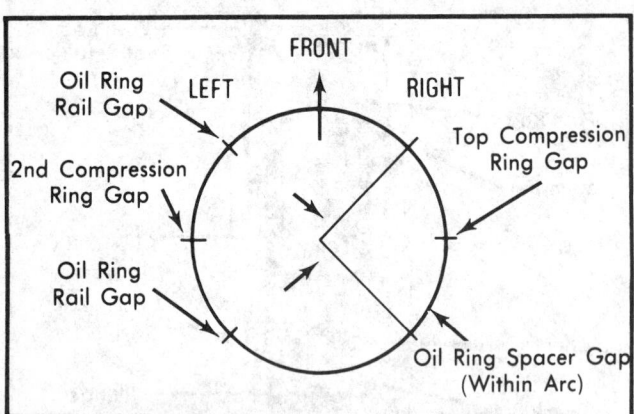

Fig. 5   Desired Ring Gap Locations

FITTING PISTONS

1) With piston and rod assemblies removed, wipe cylinder bores clean and measure diameter of cylinder with a dial indicator. If cylinder is worn or is tapered more than .005", cylinder must be bored for oversize pistons.

2) If bore is worn or tapered less than .005", cylinder can be cleaned and honed, and .001" oversize pistons may be installed. If cylinders are bored, various oversize pistons are available.

3) To check fit of rings in cylinder bore, insert ring in cylinder bore and push ring into bore 2" with head of piston and measure ring end gap with a feeler gauge. Before installing rings on pistons, ensure ring grooves are clean of carbon and inspect grooves for nicks or burrs. Install rings with gaps positioned as shown in *Fig. 5*.

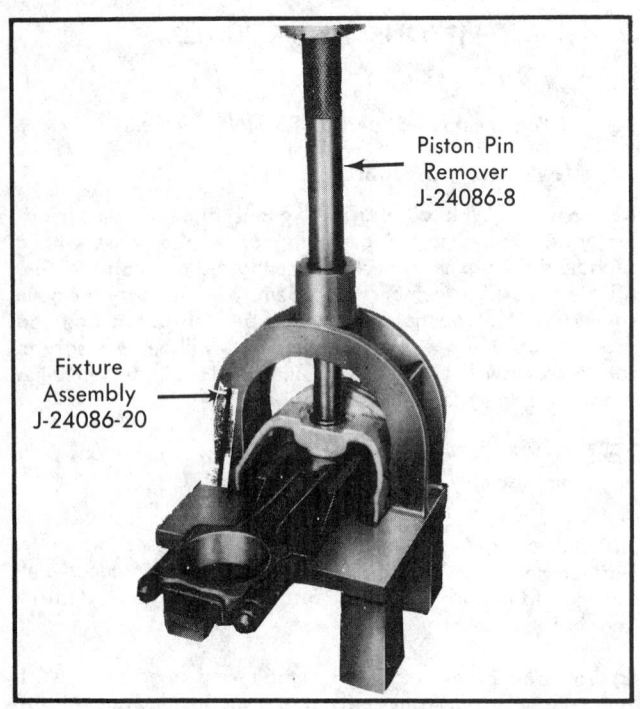

Fig. 6   Removal/Installation of Piston Pin

PISTON PINS

Removal — With piston and rod assembly removed, press out piston pin using removal and installation tool J-24086 (or equivalent), and an arbor press. Separate piston from connecting rod.

Installation — Check clearance of pin in piston. If clearance exceeds .001" over specified clearance, piston and pin must be replaced. Position piston on rod so that valve notch in top of piston faces to opposite side of bearing tang slots in connecting rod. Lubricate piston pin and press in using same tools as outlined in removal procedure. Check piston for freedom of movement on piston pin.

CRANKSHAFT & ROD BEARINGS

MAIN & CONNECTING ROD BEARINGS

NOTE — *Following procedures are performed with oil pan and oil pump removed.*

Connecting Rod Bearing — 1) Mark or identify rod cap to rod before removing rod cap nuts. With rod nuts removed, remove rod cap and bearing. Push up on piston and rod assembly and remove bearing from rod. Inspect bearings for wear or damage and replace as necessary.

2) Check crankshaft rod bearing journal for out-of-round or taper conditions. If crankshaft is out-of-round or tapers more than .001", crankshaft must be removed and ground for undersize bearings.

3) Check crankshaft clearance using the Plastigage method. If clearance exceeds specifications, a .001" or .002" undersize bearing may be installed to obtain correct clearance. If clearance is still excessive, crankshaft must be removed and ground for undersize bearings. Connecting rod bearings are available .010" and .020" undersize.

4) To install bearings, clean crankshaft journal and bearing surface in rod. Insert bearing in rod and cap. Lubricate journal and pull piston and rod assembly down, aligning bearing on journal. Install rod cap noting identification marks and tighten rod nuts evenly and to specifications.

Main Bearings — 1) Main bearings are selective fit by manufacturer during production. A standard size bearing may be used in combination with a .001" undersize bearing to obtain correct clearance. This combination will decrease clearance .0005".

2) If correct clearance could not be obtained during production, a crankshaft with .009" undersize main bearing journals is fitted. A .009" or .010" bearing may be used to obtain correct clearance.

3) If engine is fitted with a crankshaft with .009" undersize main bearing journals, it will be identified by a "9" stamped in crankshaft counterweight along with large spot of light green paint. The bearing cap will also be painted.

7.4L V8 ENGINE (Cont.)

4) Main bearings may be removed and replaced with crankshaft still installed in engine. Mark or identify main bearing caps to cylinder block before removing caps. Bearings are removed from cylinder block using a bearing removal tool. Install tool in oil hole in crankshaft and rotate crankshaft clockwise.

5) Crankshaft clearance, taper or out-of-round conditions can be checked using the Plastigage method. If clearance exceeds specifications, a .001" or .002" undersize bearing may be installed to obtain correct clearance. Both bearings must be replaced on any journal not within specifications.

6) If correct clearance cannot be obtained or journal tapers or is out-of-round more than .001", crankshaft must be removed and ground for undersize bearings. Bearings are available in standard, .001", .002", .009", .010" and .020" undersize.

7) To install bearings, ensure crankshaft journal and bearing surface in cap and block are clean. Lubricate journal and install bearing cap. If bearings were removed with crankshaft still installed, use bearing removal and installation tool inserted in crankshaft oil hole to install upper bearing. Install main cap noting identification marks and tighten main bearing bolts evenly and to specifications.

THRUST BEARING ALIGNMENT

Pry crankshaft forward as far as possible and check crankshaft end play with a feeler gauge inserted between front of rear main bearing and crankshaft. Replace rear main bearing if end play is not to specification.

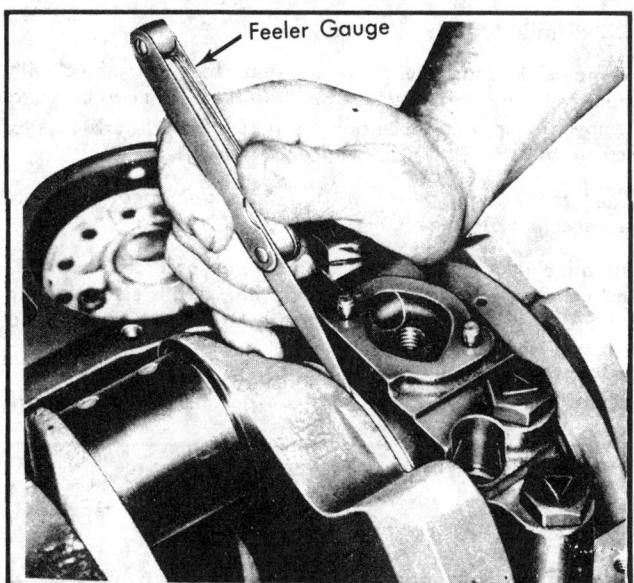

Fig. 7   Using Feeler Gauge to Check Crankshaft End Play

REAR MAIN BEARING OIL SEAL

Removal — Remove rear main bearing cap and pry out old seal. Remove upper half of seal by tapping end with brass punch until end of seal protrudes enough to be removed with pliers.

Installation — 1) Fabricate an installation tool as shown in illustration. Coat seal lips and seal bead of upper seal with motor oil. Keep ends of seal dry of oil and position tool between crankshaft and seal seat in cylinder block. Position seal between tip of tool and crankshaft.

NOTE — *Installation tool must remain in position until seal is positioned with both ends flush with block.*

2) Roll seal around crankshaft, using tool as a "shoehorn" to protect seal from sharp corner of seal seat surface. Make sure oil seal lip is positioned towards front of engine.

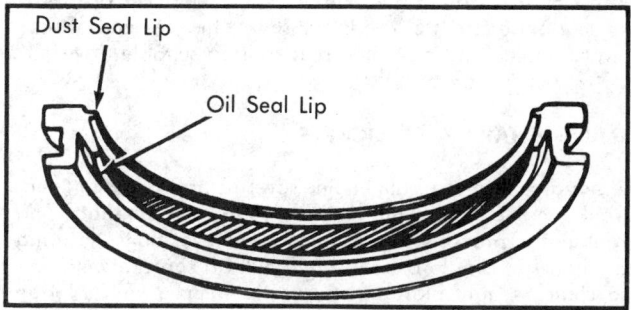

Fig. 8   Identifying Rear Main Oil Seal

3) Remove tool, taking care not to remove seal. Install lower half of seal in bearing cap, using tool as a "shoehorn" again, feed seal into cap using light pressure with thumb and finger.

4) Install bearing cap with sealant applied to face, taking care to keep sealant off split line.

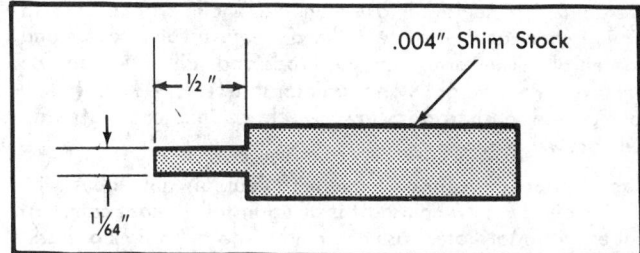

Fig. 9   Rear Main Oil Seal Installation Tool

CAMSHAFT

ENGINE FRONT COVER

Removal — Remove fan belt, fan and pulley. Remove radiator shroud and water pump. Remove accessory drive pulley and harmonic balancer retaining bolt. Remove harmonic balancer with a suitable puller (J-23523). Remove cover retaining screws and pull cover forward slightly. Using a sharp knife, cut oil pan front seal flush with cylinder block. Remove cover and gasket.

Installation — 1) Clean cover, oil pan and cylinder block gasket surfaces. Cut tabs off new oil pan front seal. Install seal in front cover, pressing seal tips in holes provided in cover. Apply a ⅛" bead of RTV sealer to joint formed at oil pan and cylinder block. Install new cover gasket and coat with sealer.

2) Position front cover over crankshaft, press downward against oil pan and push over dowel pins. Slightly tighten two bolts in oil pan, install and tighten remaining bolts. Tighten

General Motors V8 Engines

7.4L V8 ENGINE (Cont.)

two oil pan bolts. Oil seal contact surface on harmonic balancer and pull into position using a suitable puller. Install and tighten harmonic balancer bolt. Reverse removal procedure to install remaining components.

FRONT COVER OIL SEAL

With Cover Removed — Pry seal out of cover with a screwdriver. Install new seal with open end of seal toward inside of cover and drive into position with suitable tool (J-22102). Support cover at seal area before driving in seal.

With Cover Installed — With harmonic balancer removed, pry seal out of front cover. Install seal with open end of seal toward engine and drive into place with a suitable driver (J-22102) and a hammer.

TIMING CHAIN & SPROCKETS

Removal — Remove front engine cover as previously outlined. Crank engine over until timing marks on camshaft and crankshaft sprockets are aligned. Remove bolts securing camshaft sprocket to camshaft and pull off sprocket with timing chain. A light blow with a plastic hammer will dislodge sprocket.

Installation — To install new crankshaft sprocket, pull into place with mounting bolts. Install camshaft sprocket and timing chain, making sure timing marks on sprockets are aligned. See *Fig. 10*. Install and tighten sprocket bolts.

CAMSHAFT

Removal — Remove intake manifold, engine front cover and timing chain as previously outlined. Remove valve covers and loosen all rocker arms until push rods and valve lifters can be removed. Remove grille and radiator if necessary. Remove fuel pump and push rod. Screw two bolts into camshaft and withdraw camshaft.

Installation — Lubricate camshaft journals and lobes with motor oil. If a new camshaft is being installed, coat camshaft lobes with Molykote. Position camshaft to align timing marks on sprockets. Install remaining components as previously outlined. Adjust hydraulic valve lifters.

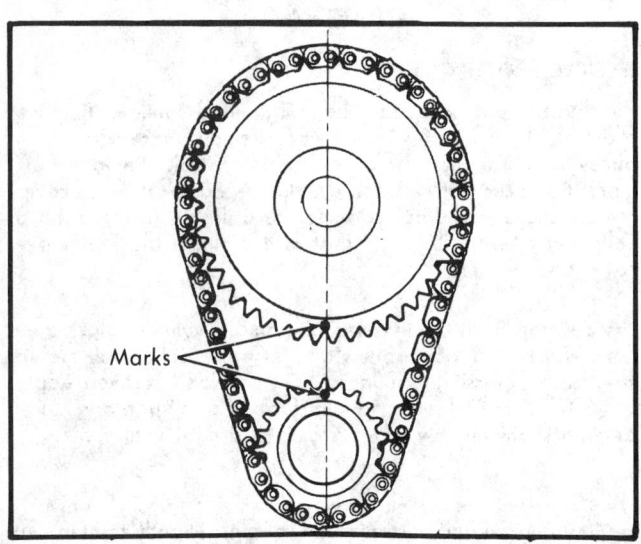

Fig. 10 Timing Chain Sprocket Alignment

CAMSHAFT BEARINGS

Use camshaft bearing installation and removal tool (J-6098) to remove bearings. Install front and rear bearings first by driving toward center of cylinder block. Align oil holes in first 4 bearings with oil holes in bearing bore in block. Position rear camshaft bearing oil hole at or near the 6 o'clock position.

CAM LOBE LIFT

With valve cover removed, remove rocker arm. Mount dial indicator on cylinder head. Position indicator stem on push rod with a suitable adapter (J-8520). Rotate engine slowly until lifter is on heel of camshaft and set dial indicator to "0". Rotate engine slowly until push rod is at fully raised position. Dial indicator will give total camshaft lobe lift. Lift should be within specifications.

ENGINE OILING

Crankcase Capacity — P-30 Step Van, 4 quarts. Add 1 quart with filter change. All other engines 6 quarts. Add 1 quart with filter change.

Oil Pressure — 40 psi at 2000 RPM.

Oil Filter — Replaced every other oil change or more often under dusty conditions.

Pressure Regulator Valve — In oil pump body, nonadjustable.

ENGINE OILING SYSTEM

Full pressure lubrication through a full flow oil filter is supplied by a gear-type oil pump. Main oil gallery feeds oil through drilled passages to camshaft and crankshaft to lubricate bearings. Valve lifter gallery feeds the valve lifters, which feed the rocker arms through hollow push rods.

OIL PUMP

Removal — Mark gears so they may be reassembled with same teeth indexing. Remove pump to rear main cap bolt and remove pump and extension shaft. Do not disturb pickup screen on pipe. Screen is serviced as an assembly.

NOTE — *If pump gears or body are damaged or worn, replacement of entire pump assembly is necessary.*

Installation — Apply sealer to end of pipe and tap into place. Install idler gear in pump body with smooth side of gear towards cover opening. To complete installation, reverse removal procedure.

NOTE — *Bottom of screen must be parallel with bottom of pan.*

TIGHTENING SPECIFICATIONS

Application	Ft. Lbs.
Cylinder Head Bolts	80
Intake Manifold	30
Exhaust Manifold	20
Main Bearing Caps	110
Flywheel	65
Connecting Rod Caps	50
Camshaft Sprocket	20
Rocker Arm Stud	50
Water Pump	30
Oil Pump	65
Harmonic Balancer Bolt	85

7.4L V8 ENGINE (Cont.)

ENGINE SPECIFICATIONS

GENERAL SPECIFICATIONS							
Year	Displ. Cu. Ins.	Carburetor	HP at RPM	Torque (Ft. Lbs. at RPM)	Compr. Ratio	Bore	Stroke
1981	454"	4-Bbl.	.....	.....	8.5:1	4.250"	4.000"

VALVES							
Engine & Valve	Head Diam.	Face Angle	Seat Angle	Seat Width	Stem Diameter	Stem Clearance	Valve Lift
7.4L Int.	2.065"	45°	46°	.031-.063"	.3715-.3722"	.0010-.0027"	.398"
Exh.	1.720"	45°	46°	.063-.094"	.3713-.3720"	.0012-.0029"	.430"

PISTONS, PINS, RINGS						
	PISTONS	PINS		RINGS		
Engine	Clearance	Piston Fit	① Rod Fit	Rings	End Gap	Side Clearance
7.4L	.003-.004"	.00025-.00035"	.0013-.0021"	1 2 3	.010-.020" .010-.020" .015-.055"	.0017-.0032" .0017-.0032" .005-.0065"

① — Interference fit.

CRANKSHAFT MAIN & CONNECTING ROD BEARINGS							
	MAIN BEARINGS				CONNECTING ROD BEARINGS		
Engine	Journal Diam.	Clearance	Thrust Bearing	Crankshaft Endplay	Journal Diam.	Clearance	Sideplay
7.4L	①2.7481-2.7490" ②2.7476-2.7486"	①.0013-.0025" ②.0024-.0040"	No.5	.006-.010"	2.1990-2.200"	.0009-.0025"	.013-.023"

① — Journal No. 1, 2, 3 & 4.   ② — Journal No. 5.

VALVE SPRINGS			
Engine	Free Length	PRESSURE (LBS.)	
		Valve Closed	Valve Open
7.4L	2.12"	84-96@1.80"	210-230@1.40"

CAMSHAFT			
Engine	Journal Diam.	Clearance	Lobe Lift
7.4L Int.	1.9482-1.9492"	.....	.2343"
Exh.	1.9482-1.9492"	.....	.2530"

2.5L 4-CYLINDER ENGINE

IDENTIFICATION CODING

ENGINE IDENTIFICATION

The 3 character engine identification code is stamped into the rear top left-hand corner of engine block. In addition, engines built for sale in Georgia and Tennessee have a non-repeating number stamped into the left rear block flange.

Engine Identification Codes	
Application	**Code**
2.5L (151")	
Federal Man. Trans. without A/C	WCP, WFM
Calif. Man. Trans. without A/C	WCU
Federal Auto. Trans. without A/C	WCT, WFP
Calif. Auto. Trans. without A/C	WCW, WFS

ENGINE REMOVAL

See *Engine Removal* at end of ENGINE Section.

CYLINDER HEAD & MANIFOLDS

INTAKE MANIFOLD

Removal — **1)** Disconnect battery cable. Remove air cleaner and PCV valve. Drain cooling system. Disconnect throttle linkages, vacuum lines, fuel lines, and electrical connections to carburetor. Remove carburetor and carburetor spacer.

2) Remove heater hose at intake manifold. Remove alternator noting position of spacers for installation. Remove manifold-to-cylinder head bolts, and remove manifold.

Installation — **1)** Install manifold and gasket on cylinder head. Start all bolts and finger tighten only.

2) Torque manifold-to-cylinder head bolts using torque sequence shown in *Fig. 1*. Reverse removal procedure to complete installation.

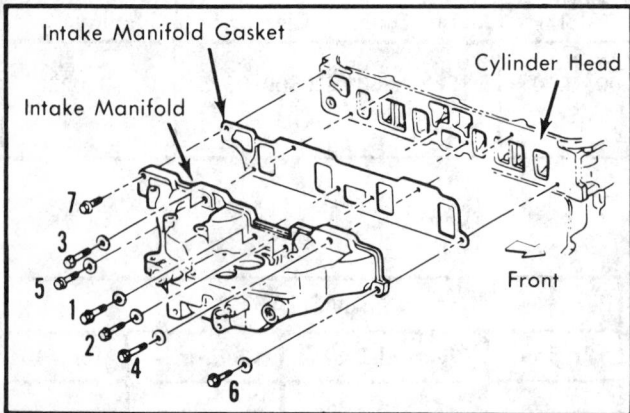

Fig. 1   Intake Manifold Bolt Torque Sequence

EXHAUST MANIFOLD

Removal — **1)** Remove air cleaner and carburetor preheat tube. If equipped, remove oxygen sensor. Remove oil dipstick tube attaching bolt.

2) Disconnect exhaust pipe from manifold. Remove exhaust manifold bolts, and remove manifold.

Installation — **1)** Install manifold and gasket on cylinder head. Start all bolts and finger tighten only.

2) Torque manifold-to-cylinder head bolts using torque sequence shown in *Fig. 2*. Reverse removal procedure to complete installation.

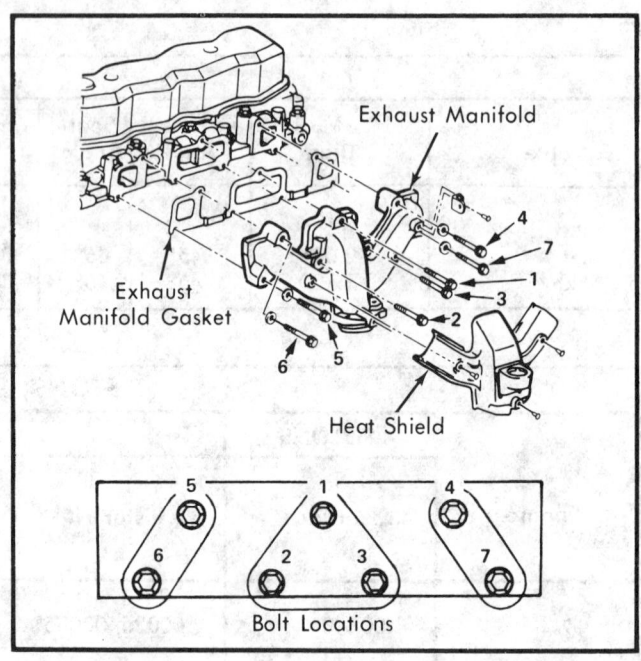

Fig. 2   Exhaust Manifold Bolt Torque Sequence

CYLINDER HEAD

Removal — **1)** Disconnect battery cable. Remove air cleaner, PCV valve, spark plugs and wires, and cylinder head cover.

2) Drain cooling system and remove upper radiator hose. Remove intake and exhaust manifolds as previously described.

3) Remove alternator. Remove air conditioning and power steering units if equipped. Disconnect and identify all electrical leads and connections to cylinder head. Remove oil dipstick.

4) Remove rocker arm assemblies and push rods. Note and mark their positions for installation in their original positions.

5) Remove cylinder head bolts and dislodge cylinder head by inserting a bar into alternator bracket and prying upward. Place cylinder head on 2 blocks of wood to prevent damage to valves.

Installation — **1)** Make sure gasket surfaces are clean of foreign matter and free of nicks. Install new gasket in position over dowel pins on cylinder block. Carefully install cylinder head over dowel pins and gasket.

NOTE — *Make sure all cylinder head bolt threads are clean and oiled. (If the threads are dirty correct torque cannot be achieved).*

2) Coat threads and underside of cylinder head bolts with sealer and install in cylinder head finger tight. Gradually tighten bolts following the sequence in *Fig. 3*. Reverse removal procedures to complete installation.

2.5L 4-CYLINDER ENGINE (Cont.)

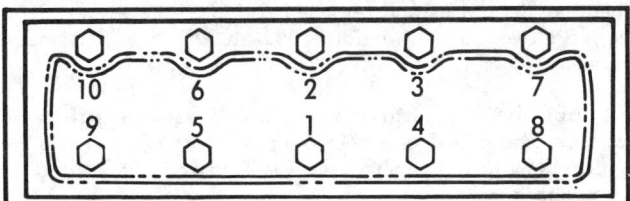

Fig. 3 Cylinder Head Tightening Sequence

VALVES

VALVE ARRANGEMENT

I-E-I-E-E-I-E-I

VALVE GUIDE SERVICING

1) With cylinder head and rocker assemblies removed, use spring depressing tool (J-5892-1 or equivalent) to depress valve springs and remove locks. Release tool and remove spring cap, spring shield, spring, and oil seal. Remove valves from cylinder head and place in rack in proper sequence.

2) After cleaning, measure valve stem diameters at top, middle, and at bottom. Exhaust valves are tapered, and are approximately .001" larger at the top than at head end. Using a telescoping gauge, measure valve guide bore diameter and subtract reading from bore diameter reading.

3) If clearance is not within specifications, use next oversize valve stem size, and ream valve guide to fit using a suitable reamer. Valves are available in standard, .003", and .005" oversize.

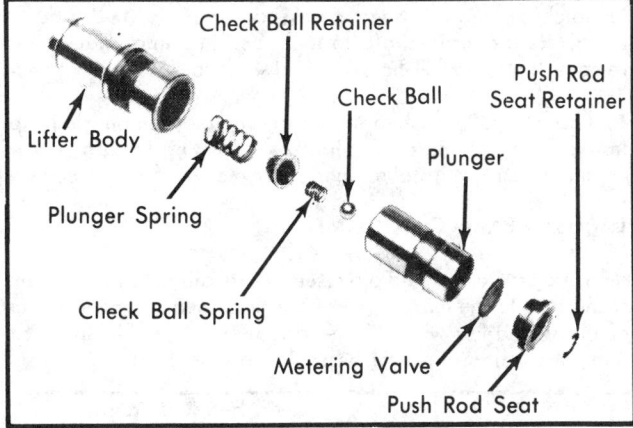

Fig. 4 Hydraulic Valve Lifter Assembly

VALVE STEM OIL SEALS

Oil seals are used on all valve stems, and should be replaced when valve service is performed. To install, set valve shield, spring, and cap in place. Compress valve spring with compressing tool (J-5892-1). Install oil seal in lower groove of stem ensuring it is flat and not twisted. Install locks and release compressing tool.

VALVE SPRINGS

NOTE — *Although normal maintainance is perfomed with head removed, it is possible to replace stem seals, keepers, retainers, or broken springs with cylinder head installed.*

Removal — **1)** Remove cylinder head cover and rocker arm of valve to be serviced. Remove spark plug and install adaptor (J-

22974 or equivalent) in spark plug hole. Apply a minimum constant air pressure of 90 psi.

2) Using a spring compressor (J-5892-1 or equivalent) compress valve spring and remove locks. Remove tool, cap, shield, spring, and oil seal.

Installation — To complete installation, reverse removal procedures.

VALVE SPRING INSTALLED HEIGHT

Installed height of valve spring must not exceed specifications. Measure spring height from surface of cylinder head pad to underside of spring retainer. If installed height exceeds specifications, install spacer(s) below spring to reduce height to specifications.

HYDRAULIC VALVE LIFTERS

Valve lifters are serviced as complete units, and parts are not interchangable between lifters. Inspect for signs of scuffing on barrel and face of lifter body. Inspect lifter face and cam lobe for concave wear or pitting, and if present, replace camshaft or lifters as necessary. If lifters are disassembled for cleaning or inspection, (see Fig. 4 for arrangement of parts) they should be tested using a suitable leak-down tester according to manufacturers instructions. Leak-down should take between 12 and 90 seconds. Replace any lifter not within specification.

PISTONS, PINS & RINGS

OIL PAN

See Oil Pan Removal at end of ENGINE Section.

PISTON & ROD ASSEMBLY

NOTE — *New pistons must be installed in same cylinders for which they were fitted. Install used pistons in same cylinders from which they were removed.*

NOTE — *Piston should be at bottom of stroke and covered with a cloth to collect cuttings.*

Removal — **1)** With cylinder head and oil pan removed, use a ridge reamer to remove any ridge or deposits from upper end of cylinder bore.

2) Check connecting rod and piston for proper identification and mark if neccessary. Remove bearing cap. Remove piston and rod assembly through top of cylinder block, taking care not to damage cylinder wall or crankshaft journal.

Installation — **1)** Lightly coat cylinder bores and pistons with oil. Insure ring gaps are evenly spaced and marked side of compression ring is facing upward.

2) Install ring compressor on piston, insuring ring gap spacing does not change. Using suitable tool, gently tap piston assembly into correct cylinder bore, taking care not to damage cylinder bore.

NOTE — *Notches in top of piston must face front of engine, and raised notch on bearing end of connecting rod points to rear of engine.*

3) Install bearing caps and tighten nuts. Reverse removal procedure to complete installation.

2.5L 4-CYLINDER ENGINE (Cont.)

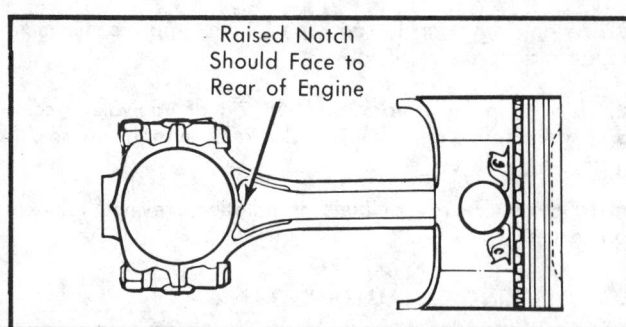

Fig. 5 Making Sure Connecting Rod and Piston Assembly are Properly Indexed

FITTING PISTONS

1) Using an inside micrometer, measure bore of each cylinder crosswise to block to determine smallest diameter. Measure piston skirt diameter perpendicular to piston boss approximately 2" from crown. If clearance is excessive, reboring and oversize pistons are necessary.

NOTE — *Measure block and pistons at room temperature, or improper fitting will result.*

2) Pistons and rings are available in standard, .005", .010", .020", and .030" oversize. When selecting rings, make sure they correspond to the piston size. Check end gap by placing a ring in lower end of ring travel area in cylinder bore. Level ring and check end gap with a feeler gauge.

NOTE — *An incorrect ring gap indicates the wrong rings are being used. It should not be necessary to alter ring gap by filing.*

3) Install rings with end gaps 120° apart using appropriate ring installation tool. Check side clearance of rings in ring groove. If side clearance is excessive, it is necessary to replace piston.

PISTON PINS

Piston pins are a press fit in rods. The piston pin specification for fit in piston is .0002-.0004". When determining fit, piston and pin must be at room temperature, and pin must gravity fall from piston.

CRANKSHAFT AND ROD BEARINGS

NOTE — *Bearings may be replaced with either the crankshaft installed or removed from engine. Always replace bearings in pairs. Do not shim or mix bearing size, or use a new bearing with an old one.*

MAIN & CONNECTING ROD BEARINGS

Connecting Rod Bearings — 1) Before removal of rod caps, stamp side of connecting rod and cap with corresponding cylinder number to assure matched reassembly. With oil pan and oil pump removed, turn crankshaft and rod to be serviced to bottom of stroke.

2) Remove connecting rod cap and bearing and push piston assembly up far enough to remove upper bearing shell.

3) Measure crankshaft journal for out-of-round and taper, and check for any damage. Using Plastigage method, measure

bearing clearances and replace bearings as necessary. Bearings are available in standard, .001", .002", and .003" undersize.

4) Coat bearing surfaces with oil, and install inserts in rod and bearing cap. Tap each rod lightly (parallel to journal) to ensure they have proper clearance. Reverse removal steps to complete installation.

Main Bearings (Crankshaft Removed) — 1) Remove main bearing inserts from engine block and bearing caps. Measure main bearing journals with a micrometer and check for excessive wear or damage. Using Plastigage method, measure bearing clearances and replace bearings as necessary.

2) Coat bearings with oil and position in engine block and main bearing caps. Install crankshaft and caps with arrows pointing towards rear of engine.

Main Bearings (Crankshaft Installed) — 1) With oil pan, oil pump and spark plugs removed, remove cap from main bearing requiring replacement and remove lower bearing insert from cap.

2) Insert upper main bearing insert removal and installation tool in oil hole in crankshaft journal. If tool is not available, tool may be fabricated from a 7/64" cotter pin. See Fig. 6.

3) Rotate crankshaft clockwise as viewed from front of engine. This will roll upper bearing insert out of block.

4) Apply oil to replacement bearing insert and position plain (unnotched) end between crankshaft and notched side of block. Rotate crankshaft to pull bearing into place, and remove tool from oil hole in crankshaft journal.

5) Apply oil to lower bearing insert, and place in bearing cap. Install main bearing cap with arrows pointing toward rear of engine. Complete installation in reverse of removal procedure.

THRUST BEARING ALIGNMENT

Measure crankshaft end play (see specifications) by forcing the crankshaft to the extreme front position. Measure at front end of thrust bearing with a feeler gauge, if not within specifications thrust bearing must be replaced.

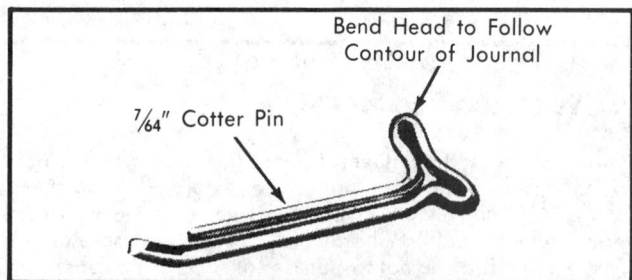

Fig. 6 Fabricated Upper Main Bearing Removal and Installation Tool

REAR MAIN BEARING OIL SEAL

Removal — 1) Remove transmission, clutch housing and flywheel.

2) Remove rear main bearing oil seal by prying it out with a screwdriver taking care not to scratch crankshaft.

2.5L 4-CYLINDER ENGINE (Cont.)

Installation — Coat new seal with engine oil and install with lip toward front of engine. Seat seal firmly in place. Install flywheel, clutch housing and transmission.

CAMSHAFT

FRONT COVER

Removal — **1)** Remove alternator and fan belts, or power steering belt if equipped. Remove crankshaft vibration pulley center bolt and slide damper and damper hub from shaft.

2) Remove alternator bracket, fan, and shroud. Remove oil pan-to-timing case cover bolts. Pull cover slightly foreward, only enough to permit cutting of oil pan seal.

3) Using a sharp knife or other suitable cutting device, cut oil pan front seal flush with engine block at both sides of cover. Remove front cover.

Installation — **1)** Clean mating surfaces of block and front cover. Cut tabs from replacement oil pan front seal, (see *Fig. 7*) and install seal on front cover. Coat gasket with sealer and place in position on cover. Apply a $\frac{1}{8}''$ bead of sealant to joint formed at cylinder block and oil pan.

2) Install alignment tool (J-23042 or equivalent) in front cover seal, and position front cover to block. Install and partially tighten 2 oil pan-to-front cover bolts.

NOTE — *Use of an alignment tool is necessary so seal damage does not result from vibration damper installation, and to ensure correct seal position around hub.*

3) Install and tighten all cover-to-block attaching bolts, and remove alignment tool. Reverse steps to complete installation.

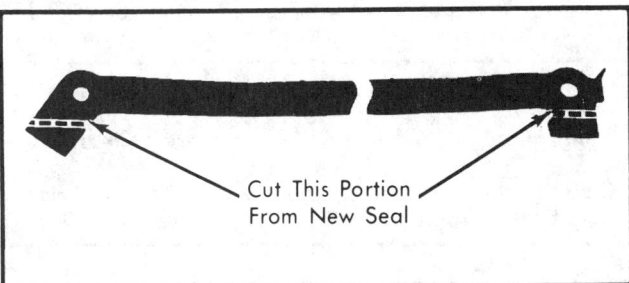

Fig. 7   Oil Pan Seal Modification

Cut This Portion From New Seal

FRONT COVER OIL SEAL

Removal & Installation — **1)** With vibration damper removed, pry oil seal from front cover using care not to damage cover.

2) Position new seal with lip toward rear of engine. Drive into cover using installer (J-23042 or equivalent).

3) Lightly coat oil seal contact area of balancer with engine oil. Position balancer on crankshaft and push it onto the crankshaft until it bottoms, install center bolt and torque. Reverse removal procedure to complete installation.

NOTE — *Apply a locking agent to damper-to-hub bolts before installation.*

CAMSHAFT & TIMING GEAR

Removal — **1)** Remove air cleaner and drain cooling system. Remove front cover. Disconnect radiator hoses, and remove radiator. Remove valve cover, rocker arms, push rods, and hydraulic lifters, making sure to place them in proper order for installation. Remove distributor, fuel pump, and oil pump drive (see *Fig. 8*).

2) Remove 2 camshaft thrust plate bolts through holes in camshaft gear (see *Fig. 9*). Remove camshaft assembly by pulling out through front of block. Support camshaft carefully when removing to prevent damage to camshaft bearings.

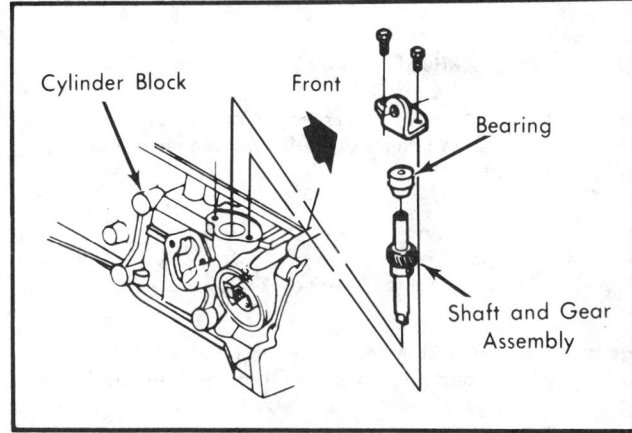

Cylinder Block   Front   Bearing   Shaft and Gear Assembly

Fig. 8   Removing Oil Pump Drive Shaft

3) If gear must be removed from camshaft, use press plate and appropriate adaptor with hydraulic press. Press shaft out of gear.

NOTE — *Thrust plate must be properly aligned to ensure Woodruff key in camshaft does not damage thrust plate when the shaft is pressed out of gear.*

Installation — **1)** Install gear spacer ring and thrust plate over end of camshaft, and install Woodruff key in shaft keyway.

Camshaft Gear

Fig. 9   Removing Thrust Plate Attaching Bolts

2.5L 4-CYLINDER ENGINE (Cont.)

2) Install camshaft gear and press onto camshaft until it bottoms against spacer ring. Measure end clearance of thrust plate, It should be .0015-.005". If less than .0015", spacer ring should be replaced. If more than .005", thrust plate should be replaced.

3) Coat camshaft journals with engine oil and install camshaft in engine block being careful not to damage camshaft bearings. Align timing marks by rotating camshaft and crankshaft until valve timing marks on gear teeth will line up. Engine is now timed in the number 4 cylinder firing position.

4) Install 2 camshaft thrust screws and torque to 7 ft. lbs. Reverse removal procedure to complete assembly.

CAMSHAFT BEARINGS

Removal — 1) Remove engine and place on suitable stand. Remove flywheel and camshaft, drive out rear expansion plug from inside out.

2) Using bearing remover J-21473-1, drive out front bearing toward rear and rear bearing toward front. Install extension J-21054-1 and drive center bearing out toward rear.

Installation — 1) Install bearings using reverse procedure, ensuring that oil holes line up in camshaft and engine block.

2) Install front camshaft bearing approximately ⅛" behind front of engine block to expose oil hole for timing gear oil nozzle. Reverse removal procedures to complete installation.

ENGINE OILING

Crankcase Capacity — 3 quarts, with or without oil filter.

Oil Filter — Disposable, full-flow. Change every 15,000 miles or 15 months.

Normal Oil Pressure — 36-40 psi at 2000 RPM with engine at normal operating temperature.

Pressure Regulator Valve — Non-adjustable; located in oil pump body.

ENGINE OILING SYSTEM

Engine lubrication is accomplished through a gear type pump which picks up oil from the oil pan sump, pumps it through the full flow oil filter and into oil passage which runs along the right side of the block and intersects the lifter bosses. Oil is then routed to the camshaft and crankshaft bearings through smaller drilled passages. Oil is supplied to the rocker arms through the hydraulic lifters which feed oil up the push rod tubes to the rocker arms. Bypass valves are located in the pickup screen, oil filter mounting and oil pump to allow for any clogged or restricted conditions. Many internal parts have no direct oil feed and rely on gravity or splash oiling from other direct feed components. Oil returns to the sump through oil return holes in cylinder head and block. *See Fig. 10.*

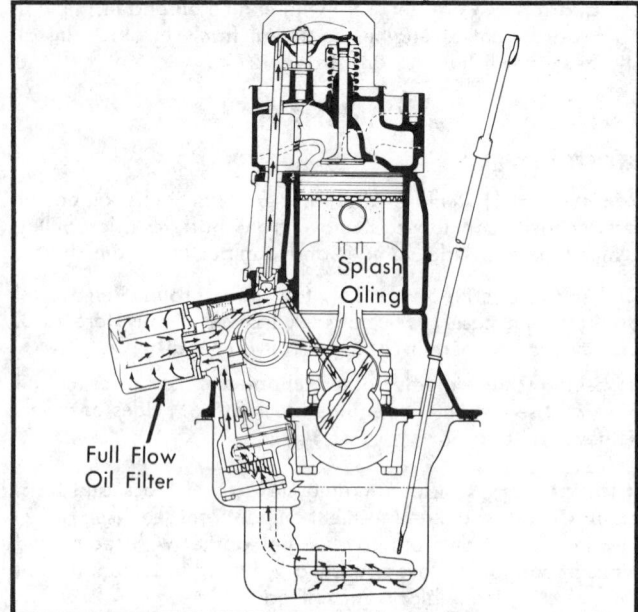

Fig. 10   Engine Oiling System

OIL PUMP

1) Oil pump is located in oil sump, oil pan must be removed for access. See *Oil Pan Removal at end of ENGINE Section.*

2) Remove 2 flange bolts and nut from main bearing cap bolt. Remove oil pump and screen as an assembly. Do not disturb oil pickup tube on screen or pump body. Disassemble pump and inspect for excessive wear or cracks. Replace oil pump as a unit if parts are defective or not within specifications. *See Fig. 11.*

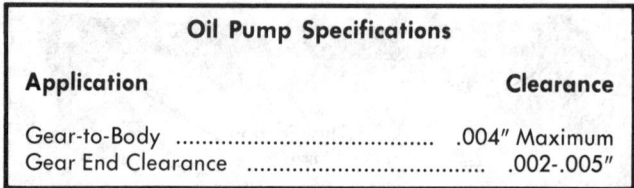

Oil Pump Specifications	
Application	**Clearance**
Gear-to-Body	.004" Maximum
Gear End Clearance	.002-.005"

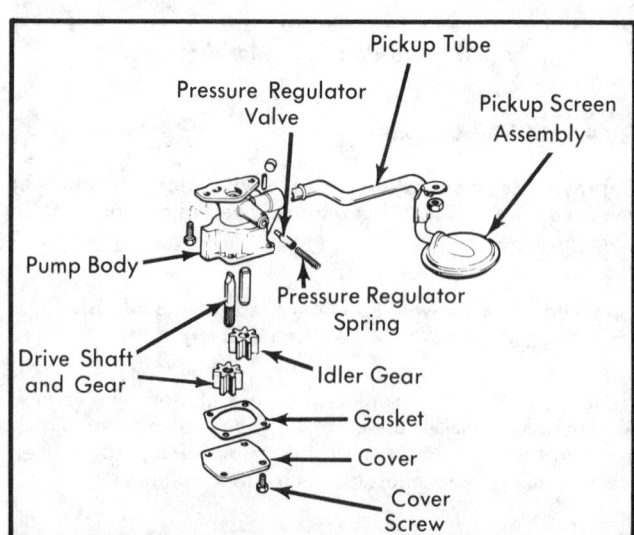

Fig. 11   Exploded View of Engine Oil Pump Assembly

2.5L 4-CYLINDER ENGINE (Cont.)
ENGINE SPECIFICATIONS

GENERAL SPECIFICATIONS						
Engine	Net HP at RPM	Torque (Ft. Lbs. at RPM)	Compr. Ratio	Bore	Stroke	Displ. Cu. Ins.
2.5L	86@4000	128@2800	8.24:1	4.00"	3.00"	151"

VALVES								
Engine & Valve	Head Diam.	Face Angle	Seat Angle	Seat Width	Stem Diameter	Stem Clearance	Valve Lift
2.5L Int.	1.72"	45°	46°	.0353-.0747"	.3418-.3425"	.0010-.0027"	.406"
Exh.	1.50"	45°	46°	.0580-.0971"	.3418-.3425"	① .0010-.0027"	.406"

① — Measured at top of guide. Bottom is .0020-.0037".

PISTONS, PINS, RINGS						
Engine	PISTONS	PINS		RINGS		
	Clearance	Piston Fit	Rod Fit	Rings	End Gap	Side Clearance
2.5L	① .0025-.0033"	.0003-.0005"	Press Fit	1	.010-.022"	.003"
				2	.010-.028"	.003"
				3	.015-.055"	.003"

① — Top clearance. Bottom clearance is .0017-.0041".

CRANKSHAFT MAIN & CONNECTING ROD BEARINGS							
Engine	MAIN BEARINGS				CONNECTING ROD BEARINGS		
	Journal Diam.	Clearance	Thrust Bearing	Crankshaft End Play	Journal Diam.	Clearance	Side Play
2.5L	2.2988"	.0005-.0022"	No. 5	.0035-.0085"	2.000"	.0005-.0026"	.017"

VALVE TIMING				
Engine	INTAKE		EXHAUST	
	Open (BTDC)	Close (ABDC)	Open (BBDC)	Close (ATDC)
2.5L	33°	79°	74°	38°

VALVE SPRINGS			
Engine	Free Length	PRESSURE (LBS.)	
		Valve Closed	Valve Open
2.5L	.....	78-86@1.66"	172-180@1.254"

CAMSHAFT			
Engine	Journal Diam.	Clearance ①	Lobe Lift
2.5L	1.869"	.0007-.0027"	.230"

① — End play .0015-.1150".

TIGHTENING SPECIFICATIONS	
Application	Ft. Lbs.
Cylinder Head	① 92
Flywheel-to-Crankshaft	68
Cam Thrust Plate-to-Block	7
Connecting Rod	30
Harmonic Balancer	160
Engine Front Cover	6
Intake Manifold-to-Cyl. Head	37
Exhaust Manifold-to-Cyl. Head	39
Main Bearings	65
Oil Pan-to-Block	6
Oil Pump-to-Block	18
Water Pump	17
Thermostat Housing	22
Carburetor-to-Manifold	13
Rocker Arm-to-Stud	20

① — Requires thread sealer.

Jeep 6 Engines

4.2L 6-CYLINDER ENGINE

IDENTIFICATION CODING

ENGINE IDENTIFICATION

Engine code is stamped on a machined surface on right side of engine block between No. 2 and No. 3 cylinders. The code numbers identify the month, day, and year of engine manufacture. The code letter identifies engine displacement (cu. in.), carburetor type, and compression ratio.

Engine Identification Codes	
Application	Code
4.2L (258") 2 Bbl.	C

SPECIAL ENGINE MARKS

Some engines are produced at factory with oversize or undersize components. These engines are identified by a letter code stamped on a boss between ignition coil and distributor. Letters are decoded as follows:

B — All cylinder bores .010" oversize.
C — All camshaft bearing bores .010" oversize.
M — All main bearing journals .010" undersize.
P — All connecting rod journals .010" undersize.

ENGINE REMOVAL

See Engine Removal at end of ENGINE Section.

CYLINDER HEAD & MANIFOLDS

INTAKE & EXHAUST MANIFOLDS

Removal — 1) Remove air cleaner. Disconnect fuel pipe, carburetor air horn vent hose, choke heater wire, and solenoid wire (if equipped). Disconnect throttle cable from throttle bellcrank. If equipped, disconnect throttle valve rod. Disconnect PCV vacuum hose and heater wire from manifold.

2) Drain coolant and remove hoses from intake manifold. Disconnect vacuum hoses from spark CTO valve and EGR valve. Disconnect EGR tube fittings from intake and exhaust manifolds.

3) Disconnect air injection hoses at air pump and air injection manifold check valve. Disconnect diverter valve vacuum hose and remove diverter valve with hoses attached. Remove air pump and if equipped, remove power steering pump with hoses attached. Remove air pump/power steering mounting bracket.

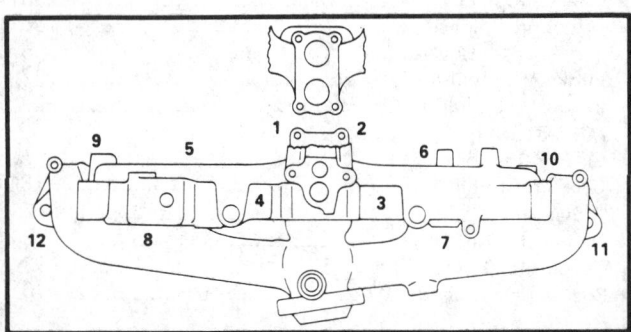

Fig. 1   Manifold Tightening Sequence

4) If equipped with air conditioning, remove drive belt idler pulley. Disconnect exhaust header pipe. Remove oxygen sensor if equipped. Remove manifold attaching nuts and remove manifold.

Installation — 1) Clean mating surfaces of manifolds and cylinder head. Position exhaust manifold and positioning sleeves over end studs. Secure exhaust manifold to cylinder head at positions 1 and 2, tighten bolts to 23 ft. lbs, and remove positioning sleeves. See *Fig. 1.*

2) Loosely connect EGR tube to intake manifold. Position intake manifold gasket over dowels and flush against cylinder head. Fit intake manifold over dowels and flush against gasket. Loosely connect EGR tube to exhaust manifold. Secure intake manifold at positions 3 and 4 and tighten bolts to 23 ft. lbs.

3) Install remaining nuts and bolts and tighten in sequence as shown in *Fig. 1.* To complete installation, reverse removal procedures.

CYLINDER HEAD

NOTE — *Rocker arm cover is made of molded plastic. Extreme care must be used when removing and installing to prevent it from cracking.*

Removal — 1) Drain cooling system and disconnect radiator hose at thermostat housing. Remove rocker arm cover. Remove rocker arms and bridged pivot assembly by backing each screw off one turn at a time to avoid damage to bridge, then remove push rods. Remove intake and exhaust manifold assembly from cylinder head.

NOTE — *Retain push rods, bridged pivots and rocker arms in order for reinstallation in original location.*

2) If equipped with air conditioning, remove drive belt idler bracket from cylinder head. Remove compressor mounting bracket bolts and position compressor and mount off to side without disconnecting lines. Remove spark plugs and disconnect temperature sending unit wire. Disconnect battery ground cable. Remove ignition coil and bracket. Remove cylinder head bolts, cylinder head and gasket.

Installation — Clean gasket mounting surfaces of cylinder head and engine block. Apply an even coat of sealing compound to both sides of cylinder head gasket, and position on block with word "TOP" facing upward. Carefully set head in place and install bolts. Tighten bolts in sequence. See *Fig. 2.* Reverse removal procedures to complete installation.

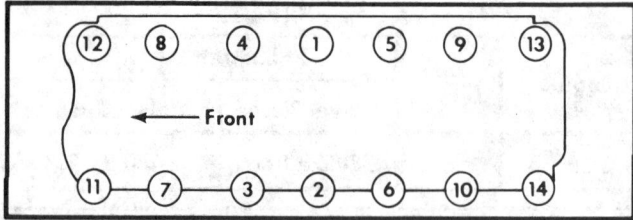

Fig. 2   Cylinder Head Tightening Sequence

VALVES

VALVE ARRANGEMENT

E-I-I-E-I-E-E-I-E-I-I-E (front to rear).

4.2L 6-CYLINDER ENGINE (Cont.)

VALVE GUIDE SERVICING

1) Valve guides are an integral part of cylinder head and are not replaceable. If stem-to-guide clearnace is excessive, use next oversize valve and ream valve guide bore to accomodate. Valves are available in .003", .015", and .030" oversize.

2) To check stem-to-guide clearance, install a valve in its guide so head is barely off seat. Place a dial indicator against top of stem and rock valve back and forth. If indicated movement is greater than .003", an oversize valve and valve guide bore reaming is necessary.

NOTE — *Ream valve guides in steps, starting with .003" over-size reamer, and progressing to size required.*

VALVE STEM OIL SEALS

A nylon valve stem oil seal is used on all valves to keep engine oil from entering combustion chambers through valve guides. Replace oil seals if deteriorated, or when valve service is performed.

NOTE — *If valves with oversize stems are used, then oversize oil seals are also required.*

VALVE SPRINGS

NOTE — *Although normal service is performed with cylinder head removed, it is possible to replace seals, keepers, retainers, or broken springs with cylinder head installed.*

Removal — 1) Remove rocker arm cover. Remove bridge and pivot assemblies, rocker arm, and push rod of valve to be serviced. Remove spark plug and install 14 mm (thread size) air adaptor in spark plug hole. Connect an air hose and maintain a constant pressure of at least 90 psi.

2) Using a valve spring compressing tool (J-22534-01 or equivalent), compress valve spring and remove locks. Remove valve spring retainer, valve spring, and oil seal.

Installation — Use a suitable valve spring tester to check each spring for tension value. Replace if necessary. To complete installation, reverse removal procedures noting the following: Use a 7⁄16" deep socket to lightly tap valve stem oil seals into place on valve stem. Tap each valve spring from side to side to ensure spring is seated properly.

HYDRAULIC VALVE LIFTER ASSEMBLY

Lifters are serviced as complete assemblies only and parts are not interchangeable between lifters. Inspect for signs of scuffing on barrel and face of tappet body. Inspect tappet face for concave wear and if present, replacement of camshaft and tappets is necessary. If lifters are disassembled for cleaning and inspection, after reassembly (see illustration for arrangement of parts), they should be tested using suitable leak-down tester according to manufacturers instructions. Leak-down should take 20-110 seconds with a load travel of .125". Discard tappets not within specifications.

NOTE — *Do not fill tappet assemblies with engine oil prior to installation as they will charge themselves within 3-8 minutes of engine operation.*

ROCKER ARM ASSEMBLY

Both intake and exhaust rocker arms for individual cylinders are on a bridged pivot connected to cylinder head by two screws. Rocker arms are removed by removing screws and lifting rocker arms and pivot from cylinder head. Mark or position rocker arms and pivots to ensure that they are installed in original position. Check pivot surface on rocker arm and pivot for wear or scoring. Check valve contact surface on rocker arm for wear or scoring. To install, reverse removal procedure.

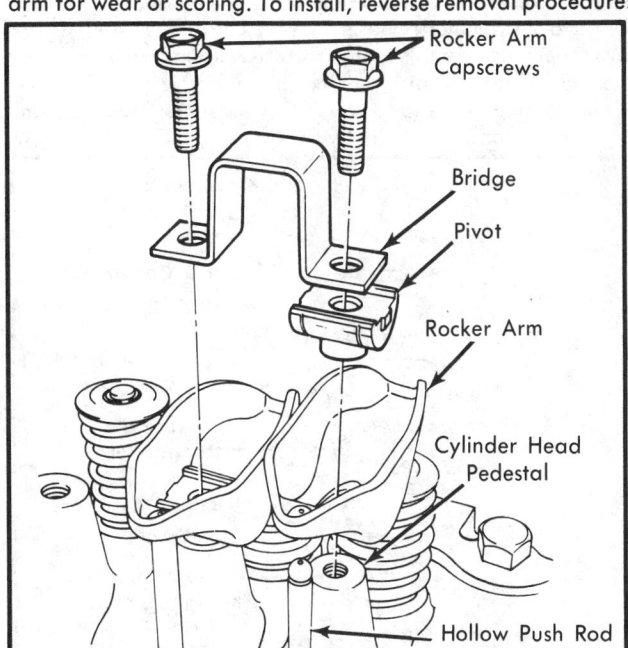

Fig. 4   Detailed View of Rocker Arm Assemblies

PISTONS, PINS & RINGS

OIL PAN

See Oil Pan Removal at end of ENGINE Section.

PISTON & ROD ASSEMBLY

NOTE — *New pistons must be installed in same cylinders for which they were fitted, and used pistons in same cylinder from which they were removed.*

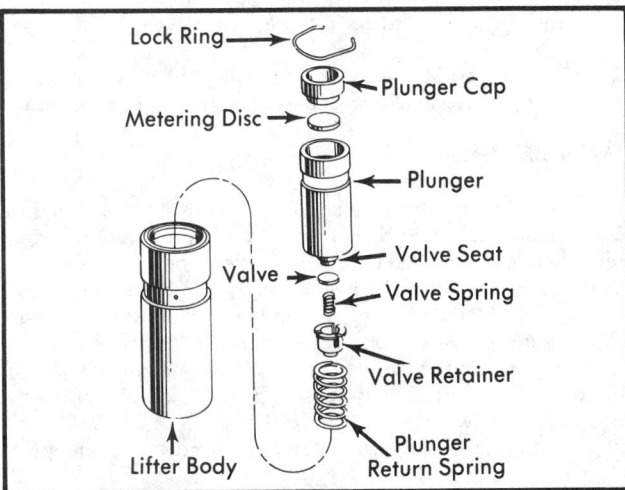

Fig. 3   Exploded View of Hydraulic Valve Lifter Assembly

4.2L 6-CYLINDER ENGINE (Cont.)

Removal — 1) With cylinder head and oil pan removed, use ridge reamer to remove any ridge or deposits on upper end of cylinder bore.

NOTE — *Piston must be at bottom of stroke and covered with cloth to collect cuttings.*

2) Remove connecting rod bearing caps and retain in same order as removed. Install rubber hose over connecting rod studs to protect cylinder walls and push piston and rod assembly out top of cylinder block.

NOTE — *Caps and rods are stamped with corresponding cylinder number.*

Installation — 1) Lightly coat pistons, rings, and cylinder walls with engine oil. Install suitable ring compressor on pistons, making sure not to change position of piston rings. With connecting rod studs covered to protect cylinder walls, install each piston and rod assembly in its respective bore with arrow pointing toward front of engine.

2) Guide connecting rod onto crankshaft journal while tapping piston head with a hammer handle to seat connecting rod against crankshaft journal. Install mating cap and tighten connecting rod cap nuts.

FITTING PISTONS

1) With piston removed, check each cylinder bore with an inside micrometer approximately 2 $\frac{5}{16}$" below top of cylinder. Using a micrometer, measure piston at right angle (90°) to piston pin at centerline of pin. Difference between cylinder bore diameter and piston diameter is piston-to-pin clearance. If clearance exceeds specifications, cylinder must be bored and oversize pistons and rings used.

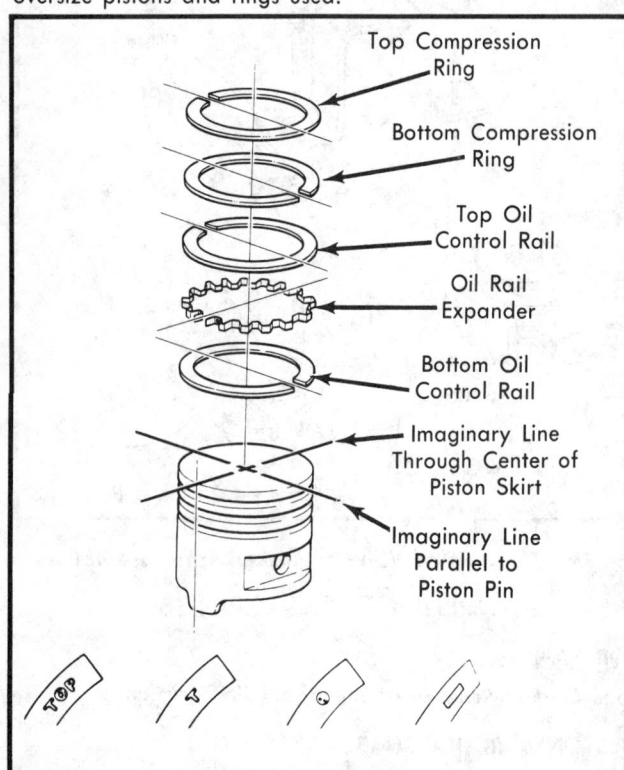

Fig. 5 Piston Ring Gap Positions and Ring Markings

2) Position a piston ring squarely at bottom end of piston ring travel in cylinder bore and check ring end gap with a feeler gauge. End gap should be .010-.020" for compression rings, and .010-.025" for oil control rings.

3) Position piston rings as shown in *Fig. 5*. Ring gaps may vary 20° from position illustrated. Make sure markings on compression rings point up. *See Fig. 5.* When installing oil control rings, insert expander ring first, then side rails. Check ring side clearance with a feeler gauge. If found to be excessive, replace piston.

PISTON PINS

Removal — 1) Using a suitable driver, arbor press and support, press piston pin completely out of piston assembly.

NOTE — *Never reuse a piston pin after it has been installed in and removed from a connecting rod.*

2) To check replacement piston pin for fit, position piston so pin bore is in a vertical position. At room temperature replacement pin should slide completely through pin bore without using force. If pin jams in bore, replace piston.

Installation — Use arbor press to press piston pin through connecting rod and piston until pin is centered in connecting rod within .031". The piston pin requires a 2000 lb. press fit. If little effort is required to install piston pin in connecting rod, or if rod moves along pin, replace connecting rod.

MAIN & CONNECTING ROD BEARINGS

CONNECTING ROD BEARINGS

Removal — With oil pan removed, rotate crankshaft as required to position 2 connecting rods at a time at bottom of stroke. Note each rod cap marking for proper replacement. Using Plastigage method, check bearings for proper clearance. Install new bearings if clearance is excessive.

Installation — 1) Rod journal size is identified in production by a color coded paint mark located on rear side of adjacent counterweight. When required, upper and lower bearing inserts of different sizes may be used as a pair to achieve desired clearance. Do not use pair of bearings with more than .001" difference in size on same journal.

2) Lubricate bearing surface of each insert with clean oil. Install bearing inserts, caps, and retaining nuts and tighten.

MAIN BEARINGS

Main bearing caps are numbered 1 to 7 front to rear, and an arrow indicates forward position. Main bearing journal size is identified in production by a color coded paint mark on adjacent cheek toward rear of crankshaft except for rear main journal, which has a paint mark on the crankshaft rear flange. When required, upper and lower bearing inserts of different sizes may be used to obtain correct bearing clearance. Do not use a pair of inserts with greater than .001" difference in size. Bearings are available in standard, .001", .002", .010", and .012" undersize. Insert size is stamped on back of each insert.

NOTE — *When replacing bearing inserts, all odd sized inserts must be either on top (in block) or on bottom (in main bearing caps).*

4.2L 6-CYLINDER ENGINE (Cont.)

Main Bearings (Crankshaft Removed) — Note each main bearing cap marking and remove main bearing cap. Using Plastigage method, check each bearing for proper clearance. Replace those bearings found to be excessively worn. To install, coat each bearing lightly with oil and fit to engine block and caps. Install crankshaft and bearing caps with arrows pointing toward front of engine.

Main Bearings (Crankshaft Installed) — **1)** With oil pan and spark plugs removed, remove cap from bearing requiring replacement and remove lower bearing insert. Loosen remaining main bearing caps slightly. Insert upper main bearing removal tool in oil hole in crankshaft journal. If tool is not available, one may be fabricated from a 7/64" cotter pin. See Fig. 6.

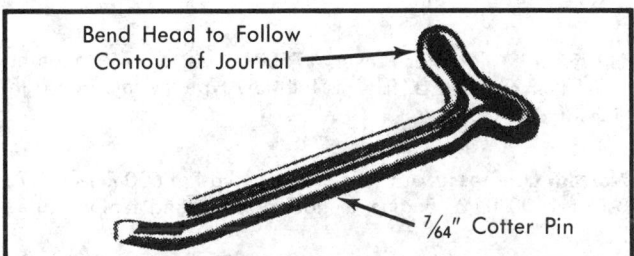

Fig. 6   Fabricated Upper Main Bearing Removal and Installation Tool

2) With cotter pin in place, rotate crankshaft so that upper main bearing insert rotates out in direction of its locking tab and out of block.

3) Because there is no oil hole in No. 4 main journal, use a tongue depressor or similar soft faced tool to push bearing insert out of block.

4) Apply a light film of oil to replacement bearing insert and position in block. Use cotter pin tool to pull upper main bearing into place by rotating crankshaft in opposite direction as for removal. Fit lower bearing to cap and install with arrow pointing forward. Tighten remaining bearing caps.

THRUST BEARING ALIGNMENT

When replacing thrust bearings (located at No. 3 main bearing journal), crankshaft should be moved fore and aft to align thrust faces of bearings.

REAR MAIN BEARING OIL SEAL

Removal — Remove oil pan and rear main bearing cap. Loosen all remaining main bearing bolts. Using a brass drift, tap upper seal until seal is protruding enough to permit pulling it out completely. Remove lower seal from bearing cap.

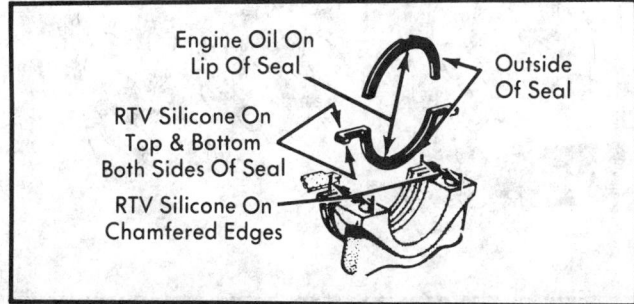

Fig. 7   Exploded View of Rear Main Bearing Oil Seal

Installation — Reverse removal procedure while noting following: Lip of seal must face front of engine. Make sure seal is firmly seated in bearing cap recess. Use suitable sealer and apply as indicated in illustration.

CAMSHAFT

ENGINE FRONT COVER

Removal — **1)** Remove drive belts, fan and hub assembly, and vibration damper. Remove oil pan-to-front cover bolts and cover-to-block bolts. Remove front cover and gasket.

2) Cut off oil pan gasket end tabs flush with front face of engine block and remove tabs. Clean all gasket surfaces.

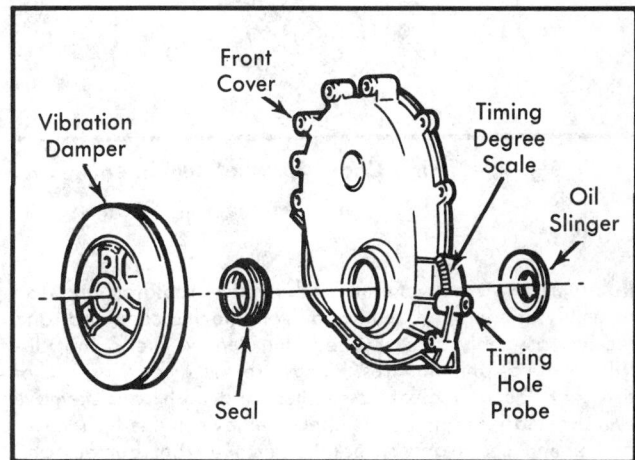

Fig. 8   Exploded View of Engine Front Cover Assembly

Installation — **1)** Apply a suitable sealing compound to both sides of replacement gasket and fit front cover gasket to block. Cut end tabs off replacement oil pan gasket to correspond to pieces cut off of original gasket and cement to oil pan.

2) Position front cover to engine. Place front cover alignment tool in crankshaft opening of front cover and install mounting bolts. Tighten all bolts and remove alignment tool. Reverse removal procedures to complete installation.

FRONT COVER OIL SEAL

Removal & Installation — Remove drive belt(s), accessory drive pulley and vibration damper. Remove oil seal using tool (J-9256). To install new seal, apply light film of suitable sealer on outside diameter of seal and position on cover with seal lip facing outward. Use alignment and seal installation tool (J-22248) with screw from tool (J-9163) to press seal into cover until it bottoms. Apply light film of engine oil on seal lip and install vibration damper, accessory drive and drive belt(s).

TIMING CHAIN

Removal — Remove engine front cover. Remove camshaft sprocket retaining bolt and washer. Rotate crankshaft until timing mark on sprocket is aligned with camshaft sprocket timing mark (see illustration). Remove sprockets and timing chain as an assembly.

Installation — Assemble timing chain, crankshaft sprocket, and camshaft sprocket with timing marks aligned (see illustration). Install assembly to crankshaft and camshaft. Install camshaft sprocket retaining bolt and washer, then tighten.

4.2L 6-CYLINDER ENGINE (Cont.)

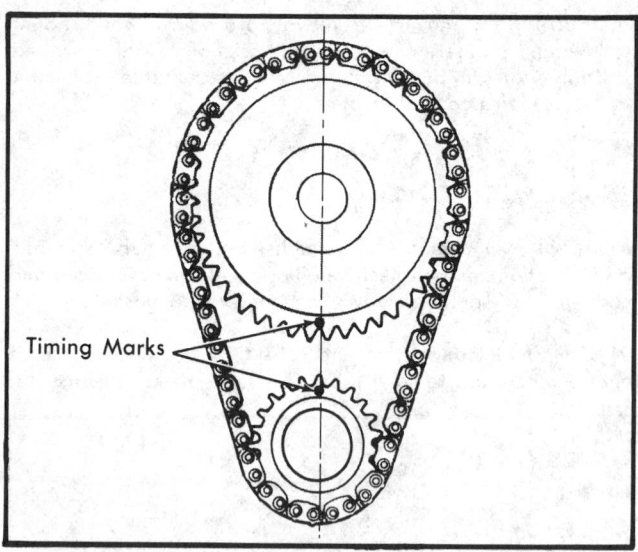

Fig. 9   Timing Chain Sprocket Alignment

(Timing Marks)

CAMSHAFT

Removal — Drain coolant and remove radiator and fan assembly. If equipped, remove air conditioning condensor and receiver assembly as a charged unit. Remove fuel pump, distributor, and ignition wires. Remove rocker arm cover, rocker arms, bridge and pivot assemblies, and push rods. Remove cylinder head and hydraulic lifters. Remove engine front cover and timing chain and sprockets. Remove front bumper and grille as required and carefully remove camshaft.

Installation — Reverse removal procedure while noting following: Lubricate camshaft with suitable oil supplement and install camshaft carefully to avoid damage to camshaft lobes.

CAMSHAFT BEARINGS

NOTE — *When installing cam bearings, use a screw-type cam bearing installation tool, one that provides steady pressure. Do Not use a driver-type cam bearing installation tool.*

CAM LOBE LIFT

Remove rocker arm cover, rocker arms and pivots. Remove spark plugs and proceed as follows:

1) Using suitable clamping or mounting fixture, attach dial indicator to cylinder head so indicator probe rests on top of push rod with indicator and probe in a vertical position over push rod.

CAUTION — *If using an auxiliary starter switch, distributor primary lead must be disconnected from negative post of coil.*

2) Rotate crankshaft slowly until valve lifter is on heel of cam lobe. At this point, push rod will be at its lowest point.

3) With push rod at lowest position, zero dial indicator and rotate engine until push rod is in fully raised position. Compare total lift recorded with specifications. If less than specifications, camshaft is defective. Check all remaining lobes of camshaft in same manner.

VALVE TIMING

Remove spark plugs, rocker arm cover, and rocker arms and bridged pivot from No. 1 cylinder. Rotate crankshaft until No. 6 piston is at TDC on compression stroke. Rotate crankshaft counterclockwise 90°. Install dial indicator with indicator point touching No. 1 cylinder intake push rod, then set dial indicator to zero. Rotate crankshaft clockwise until dial indicator shows .016" lift. Timing mark on vibration damper should index with TDC mark on engine front cover. If timing mark is more than ½" off TDC in either direction, valve timing is incorrect.

ENGINE OILING

Crankcase Capacity — 4 quarts without filter change, 5 quarts with filter change.

Oil Filter — Replace every 7500 miles or 7½ months, whichever comes first. Filter is full-flow type mounted on right side of crankcase.

Normal Oil Pressure — Minimum of 13 psi at 600 RPM; 37-75 psi at 1600 RPM. Engine at normal operating temperature.

Pressure Regulator Valve — Located in pump body. Not adjustable.

ENGINE OILING SYSTEM

Oil under pressure is directed from gear type oil pump to a full-flow oil filter. In case filter becomes clogged and restricts full flow of oil, a by-pass valve is located in filter mounting base. From oil filter, oil flow is directed as follows:

Crankshaft & Camshaft Bearings — Main and camshaft bearings receive oil from main oil gallery. From main bearings oil passes through passage in crankshaft to connecting rod bearings. Oil throw-off from each connecting rod bearing lubricates cylinder walls, piston pins, camshaft lobes and distributor drive gear.

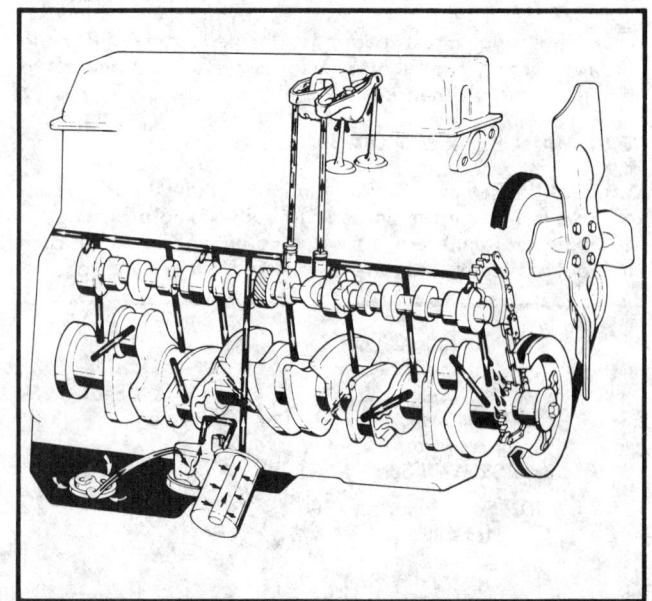

Fig. 10   Engine Oiling System

4.2L 6-CYLINDER ENGINE (Cont.)

Hydraulic Valve Tappets — Lubricated directly from main oil gallery.

Timing Chain & Sprockets — Oil is received from front camshaft bearing and returns to crankcase through cavity under front main bearing cap.

Rocker Arms & Push Rods — Oil from main oil gallery is fed to hydraulic valve lifters. Lifters meter oil to hollow push rods which lubricate rocker arms and pivots. Holes cast in cylinder head return oil to crankcase through lifter area.

OIL PUMP

Oil pump is driven by distributor drive shaft. Removal of pump will not affect ignition timing, as distributor gear remains meshed with camshaft gear. Pump must be filled with petroleum jelly prior to installation of oil pump cover.

CAUTION — *Oil inlet tube position must be changed to allow removal of relief valve; therefore, pickup tube assembly must be replaced upon installation and suitable sealer used.*

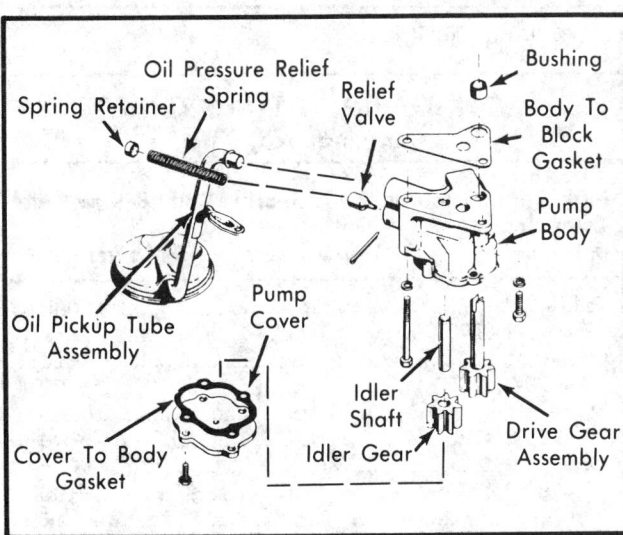

Fig. 11 Exploded View of Oil Pump Assembly

Oil Pump Specifications

Application	Specifications
Gear-to-Body Clearance	.0005-.0025"
Gear End Clearance	① .004-.008"

① — With feeler gauge method. Plastigage method; .002-.006".

TIGHTENING SPECIFICATIONS

Application	Ft. Lbs.
Camshaft Sprocket	45-55
Clutch Housing-to-Block	
Top	22-30
Bottom	37-47
Connecting Rod Nut	30-35
Cylinder Head Bolts	80-90
Drive Plate-to-Converter	20-25
Engine Front Cover	
Screw	4-8
Stud	13-19
Exhaust Manifold Bolt	18-28
Flywheel-to-Crankshaft	95-120
Fuel Pump	13-19
Intake Manifold Bolts	18-28
Main Bearing Cap Bolts	75-85
Oil Pan	
¼" Bolts	5-9
5/16" Bolts	9-13
Oil Pump Cover	5-7
Oil Pump Screw	
Short	12-20
Long	12-20
Rocker Arm Capscrews	16-26
Thermostat Housing	10-18
Vibration Damper	70-90
Water Pump Screws	9-18

ENGINE SPECIFICATIONS

GENERAL SPECIFICATIONS

Year	Displ. Cu. Ins.	Carburetor	HP at RPM	Torque (Ft. Lbs. at RPM)	Compr. Ratio	Bore	Stroke
1981	258"	2-Bbl.	.....	.....	8.0:1	3.75"	3.895"

VALVES

Engine & Valve	Head Diam.	Face Angle	Seat Angle	Seat Width	Stem Diameter	Stem Clearance	Valve Lift
4.2L							
Int.①	1.782-1.792"	29°	30°	.040-.060"	.3715-.3725"	.001-.003"	.397"
Exh.①	1.401-1.411"	44°	44.5°	.040-.060"	.3715-.3725"	.001-.003"	.397"

① — Do not remove more than .010" from end of valve stem.

Jeep 6 Engines

4.2L 6-CYLINDER ENGINE (Cont.)
ENGINE SPECIFICATIONS (Cont.)

PISTONS, PINS, RINGS

| Engine | PISTONS | PINS | | RINGS | | |
	Clearance	Piston Fit	Rod Fit	Rings	End Gap	Side Clearance
4.2L	.0009-.0017"	.0003-.0005"	Press Fit	1	.010-.020"	.0017-.0032"
				2	.010-.020"	.0017-.0032"
				3	.010-.025"	.001-.008"

CRANKSHAFT MAIN & CONNECTING ROD BEARINGS

| Engine | MAIN BEARINGS | | | | CONNECTING ROD BEARINGS | | |
	Journal Diam.	Clearance①	Thrust Bearing	Crankshaft End Play	Journal Diam.	Clearance	Side Play
4.2L	2.4986-2.5001"	.0005-.0030"	No. 3	.0015-.0065"	2.0934-2.0955"	.0010-.0025"	.010-.019"

① — For journals No. 2-6; Journal No. 1 — .0005-.0026"; Journal No. 7 — .0011-.0035".

MAIN BEARING FITTING CHART
(Journals 1-6)

| Main Bearing Journal Color Code & Diameter | Bearing Color & Size Code | |
	Upper Insert	Lower Insert
Yellow 2.5001-2.4996"	Yellow Std.	Yellow Std.
Orange 2.4996-2.4991"	Yellow Std.	Black —.001"
Black 2.4991-2.4986"	Black —.001"	Black —.001"
Green 2.4986-2.4981"	Black —.001"	Green —.002"
Red 2.4901-2.4896"	Red —.010"	Red —.010"

MAIN BEARING FITTING CHART
(Journal No. 7)

| Main Bearing Journal Color Code & Diameter | Bearing Color & Size Code | |
	Upper Insert	Lower Insert
Yellow 2.4995-2.4990"	Yellow Std.	Yellow Std.
Orange 2.4990-2.4985"	Yellow Std.	Black —.001"
Black 2.4985-2.4980"	Black —.001"	Black —.001"
Green 2.4980-2.4975"	Black —.001"	Green —.002"
Red 2.4895-2.4890"	Red —.010"	Red —.010"

CONNECTING ROD BEARING FITTING CHART

| Connecting Rod Journal Color Code & Diameter | Bearing Color & Size Code | |
	Upper Insert	Lower Insert
Yellow 2.0948-2.0955"	Yellow Std.	Yellow Std.
Orange 2.0941-2.0948"	Yellow Std.	Black —.001"
Black 2.0934-2.0941"	Black —.001"	Black —.001"
Red 2.0848-2.0855"	Red —.010"	Red —.010"

VALVE SPRINGS

| Engine | Free Length | PRESSURE (LBS.) | |
		Valve Closed	Valve Open
4.2L Int.	1.99"	64-72@1.786"	188-202@1.411"
Exh.	1.99"	80-88@1.625"	210-226@1.188"

CAMSHAFT

Engine	Journal Diam.	Clearance	Lobe Lift
4.2L No. 1	2.029-2.030"	.001-.003"	.253"
No. 2	2.019-2.020"		
No. 3	2.009-2.010"		
No. 4	1.999-2.000"		

VALVE TIMING

| Engine | INTAKE | | EXHAUST | |
	Open (BTDC)	Close (ABDC)	Open (BBDC)	Close (ATDC)
4.2L	9°	73°	57°	25°

5.0L & 6.0L V8 ENGINES

IDENTIFICATION CODING

ENGINE IDENTIFICATION

Engine code number located on tag attached to valve cover, right bank. Letter contained in code number designates CID, carburetor, and compression ratio. Coding is as follows:

Engine Identification Codes	
Application	**Code**
5.0L (304")	H
6.0L (360")	N

SPECIAL ENGINE MARKINGS

Some engines are produced at factory with oversize or undersize components. Letters found stamped adjacent to engine code number, indicate following deviation from standard specifications:

B — All cylinder bores .010" oversize.
M — All main bearings .010" undersize.
F — All connecting rod bearings .010" undersize.
PM — All connecting rod and main bearings .010" undersize.
C — All camshaft bearing bores .010" oversize.

ENGINE REMOVAL

See Engine Removal at end of ENGINE Section.

CYLINDER HEAD & MANIFOLD

INTAKE MANIFOLD

Removal — 1) Drain cooling system and remove air cleaner. Disconnect spark plug wires, upper radiator hose and by-pass hose from manifold. Remove ignition wire plastic separators from rocker arm cover brackets. Disconnect and move out of way temperature sending unit wire and ignition coil assembly.

2) Disconnect heater hose from rear of manifold. Mark all hoses, pipes and wires on carburetor, then disconnect them and place out of way. Disconnect throttle valve and linkage from carburetor and manifold. Disconnect air hoses from air injection manifolds.

3) Disconnect diverter valve from air pump. Remove carburetor. Remove intake manifold bolts, manifold, metal gaskets and end seals. Make sure gasket mating surfaces are clean and that gasket material does not fall into intake or exhaust ports of cylinder heads.

Installation — 1) Coat both sides of new metal gaskets with non-hardening sealant and attach gaskets to cylinder head locating studs. Apply Permatex No. 2 to seal ends and install them to engine block.

2) Install intake manifold and bolts to engine. Make sure all bolts are seated before tightening. Install diverter valve and attach air pump output hose. Connect air hoses to air injection manifolds. Connect all hoses, pipes, wires and linkages to carburetor and manifold.

3) Install ignition coil and bracket assembly. Connect upper radiator hose and bypass hose. Install ignition wire plastic separators, then connect spark plug wires. Install air cleaner assembly and add coolant.

CYLINDER HEAD

Removal — 1) Disconnect battery ground. Drain cooling system and remove rocker arm cover, rocker arm assemblies and push rods. Disconnect spark plug wires and remove spark plugs. Remove intake manifold and exhaust manifold.

NOTE — *Keep rocker arm assemblies and push rods in same order as removed.*

2) Loosen all drive belts and remove compressor mount bracket and battery negative cable from cylinder head. Disconnect alternator support brace, air pump, and power steering pump mount bracket from cylinder head. Remove retaining bolts and remove cylinder head and gasket.

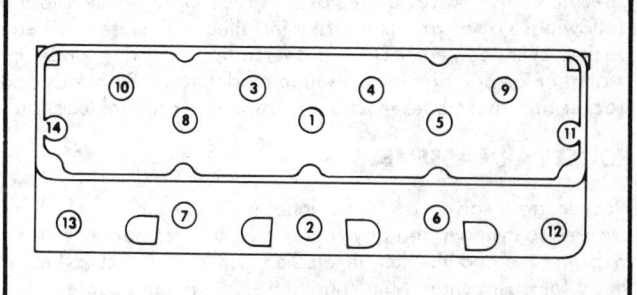

Fig. 1 Cylinder Head Tightening Sequence

Installation — 1) Clean all gasket surfaces. Apply a thin coat of sealing compound to both sides of head gaskets.

2) Position gasket on block with stamped word "TOP" facing up. Install cylinder head and retaining bolts. Tighten bolts in sequence. To complete cylinder head installation, reverse removal procedure. *See Fig. 1.*

NOTE — *DO NOT apply sealing compound on head and block surfaces or allow sealer to enter cylinder bores.*

VALVES

VALVE ARRANGEMENT

All — E-I-I-E-E-I-I-E (front to rear, both banks).

VALVE GUIDE SERVICING

Guides are an integral part of cylinder head and cannot be replaced. If valve guide is out of round more than .0025" or if valve guide bore is worn more than .003", valve guides must be reamed to next oversize and oversize valves installed. Oversize valves are available in .003", .015" and .030" oversize. Valve guide reamers are available for these oversizes.

NOTE — *Guides must be reamed in steps, starting with .003" oversize reamer and progressing to size desired.*

VALVE STEM OIL SEALS

Nylon valve stem seals are used on each valve stem and should be replaced whenever seals become deteriorated or valve service is performed. Use a 7/16" deep socket and light mallet to seat valve seals on stems.

Jeep V8 Engines

5.0L & 6.0L V8 ENGINES (Cont.)

VALVE SPRINGS

Removal — 1) Remove rocker arm cover, rocker arm assemblies and push rods. Remove spark plug on cylinder to be serviced and install suitable air line adaptor to spark plug port. Apply air pressure to hold valves in place.

NOTE — *Retain rocker arm assemblies, push rods, bridge and pivot assemblies in order of removal for reinstallation in original location.*

2) Using suitable spring compressor (J-22534-1,4 & 5), compress valve spring and remove valve keeper locks. Remove valve spring and retainer. Remove and discard oil seal.

Installation — Use suitable valve spring tester (J-8056) to test valve springs. Replace those that are not within specifications. Reverse removal procedures while noting following: Valve springs must be installed with closed coil end facing cylinder head. Do not overcompress spring upon installation as damage may result to oil deflector. Push rods and rocker arm assemblies must be reinstalled in original locations.

ROCKER ARM ASSEMBLY

Rocker arms pivot on a bridged pivot assembly which is secured to cylinder head by cap screws. It is not normal to find a pattern along the length of the push rod. Check cylinder head for obstruction if this condition exists. If valve contact surface on rocker arm is worn severely, rocker arm must be replaced.

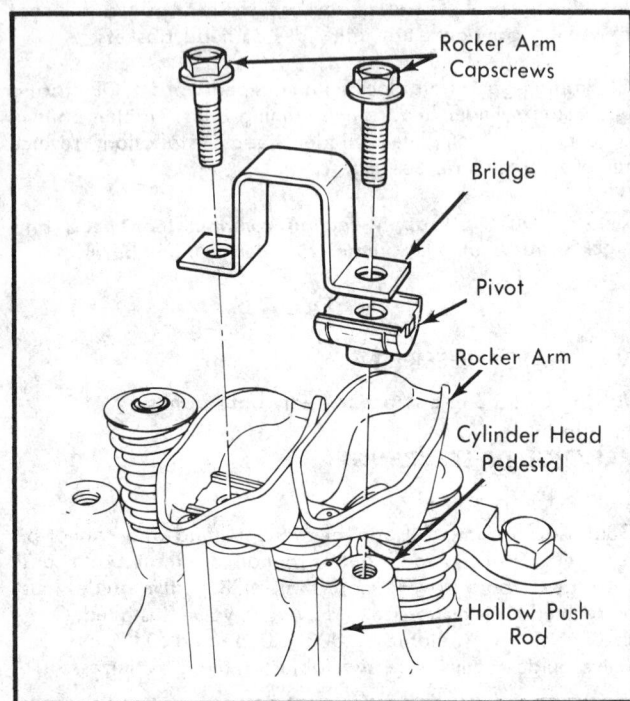

Fig. 2   Rocker Arm Assembly

HYDRAULIC VALVE LIFTER ASSEMBLY

Lifters are serviced as complete assemblies only and parts are not interchangeable between lifters. Inspect for signs of scuffing on barrel and face of tappet body. Inspect face for concave wear and if present, replacement of camshaft and tappet is necessary. If lifters are disassembled for cleaning and inspection, after reassembly they should be tested using suitable leak-down tester according to manufacturers' instructions. Leak-down should take 20-110 seconds with a load travel of .125". Discard tappets not within specifications.

NOTE — *DO NOT fill tappet assemblies with engine oil prior to installation as they will charge themselves within 3-8 minutes of engine operation.*

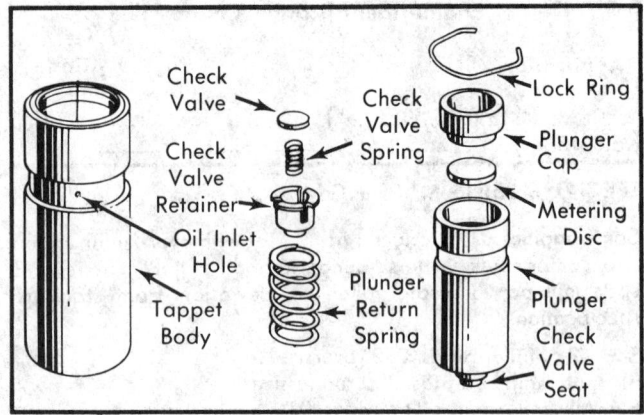

Fig. 3   Exploded View of Hydraulic Valve Lifter Assembly

PISTONS, PINS & RINGS

OIL PAN

See Oil Pan Removal at end of ENGINE Section.

PISTON & ROD ASSEMBLY

NOTE — *New pistons must be installed in same cylinders for which they were fitted and used pistons in same cylinder from which they were removed.*

Removal — 1) With cylinder head and oil pan removed, use a suitable ridge reamer to remove any ridge or deposits on upper end of cylinder bore.

NOTE — *Piston must be at bottom of stroke and covered with cloth to collect cuttings.*

2) Remove connecting rod bearing caps and retain in same order as removed. Cover connecting rod studs to protect cylinder walls and push piston and rod assembly out top of block.

NOTE — *Caps and rods are stamped with corresponding cylinder number.*

Installation — 1) Piston rings must be positioned as follows: No. 1 compression ring gap must be 180° from No. 2 compression ring gap. Oil control ring spacer expander gap must be at least 90° from No. 2 compression ring gap. Oil control ring gaps must be 90° from expander gap with at least 30° between each ring gap. Upper and lower compression ring markings indicate top side of ring.

2) Lightly coat pistons, rings and cylinder walls with engine oil. Install suitable ring compressor on pistons making certain ring gap positions do not change. With connecting rod studs covered for cylinder wall protection, install each piston and rod assembly (with notch on piston head towards front of engine) in its respective bore. Guide connecting rod onto crankshaft journal while tapping piston head with hammer handle to seat connecting rod against crankshaft. Install mating rod cap, nuts and tighten to specifications.

5.0L & 6.0L V8 ENGINES (Cont.)

NOTE — *With pistons installed, cylinder number should be outboard and squirt hole inboard.*

FITTING PISTONS

Measure cylinder bore diameter 2⁵⁄₁₆" below top of cylinder bore. Measure piston at right angles to piston pin at centerline of pin. If clearance is not within specifications, replace piston.

PISTON PINS

Removal — Place piston on support tool (J-21872-1) and use removal tool (J-21872), press piston pin out with arbor press. Note position of pin through gauge window of remover support.

Installation — Using pilot tool (J-21872-2), and support (J-21872-1), press piston pin through connecting rod and piston until pin pilot indexes with mark on support. Pin should be centered in rod ±¹⁄₃₂".

NOTE — *If little effort is required to install piston pin in connecting rod, or if rod moves along pin, a new connecting rod is required. Check piston for freedom of movement on pin.*

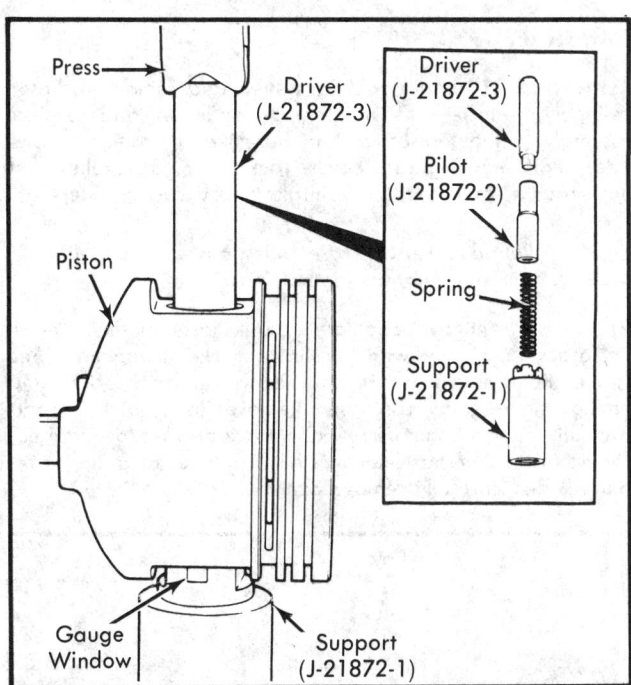

Fig. 4 Piston Pin Removal & Installation

MAIN & CONNECTING ROD BEARINGS

NOTE — *Following procedure is with oil pan removed.*

Connecting Rod Bearings — 1) After ensuring rod caps are marked for cylinder identification, remove rod caps. Use Plastigage method to check for proper bearing clearances. If not within specifications, new bearings must be installed. New bearings are available in standard and .001", .002", .010" and .012" undersize.

2) Selective fitting is required on each connecting rod. A standard bearing may be used in combination with a .001" under-

size, or a .002" undersize in combination with a .001" undersize. Coat bearing surfaces with oil, install rod cap, nuts and tighten to specifications.

NOTE — *Never use a new bearing with a used bearing. Never use a pair of bearings with more than .001" difference in size on same journal.*

Main Bearings — 1) Support crankshaft at counterweight adjacent to main bearing being checked and ensure that all bearing caps other than one being checked are tight. Starting with rear main bearing cap and working forward, remove one cap at a time and check bearing clearances, using Plastigage method.

2) If clearances are not within specifications, bearings are available in standard and .001", .002", .010" and .012" undersize. A standard bearing may be used in combination with a .001" undersize, or a .002" undersize in combination with a .001" undersize.

NOTE — *Never use a new bearing with a used bearing. Never use a pair of bearings with more than .001" difference in size on same journal.*

3) Remove all upper bearings by inserting suitable tool in oil hole of crankshaft journal and rotating crankshaft clockwise to roll bearing from engine. Oil new bearing and rotate crankshaft so bearing will rotate in direction of its locating tang. Install bearing cap with lower bearing and tighten bolts.

THRUST BEARING ALIGNMENT

When replacing thrust bearings (located at No. 3 main bearing journal), crankshaft should be moved fore and aft to align thrust faces of bearings.

REAR MAIN BEARING OIL SEAL

Removal — Remove oil pan and rear main bearing cap. Loosen all remaining main bearing bolts. Using a brass drift, tap upper seal until it is protruding enough to permit pulling it out completely. Remove lower seal from bearing cap.

Installation — Reverse removal procedure while noting the following: Lips of seal must face toward front of engine. Ensure seal is firmly seated in bearing cap recess. Use suitable sealer.

CAMSHAFT

FRONT COVER

Removal — 1) Drain cooling system and disconnect radiator hoses and by-pass hose. Remove drive belts, fan and hub assembly, distributor, fuel pump, drive pulley and vibration damper. Remove A/C compressor and power steering pump without disconnecting hoses and position on one side.

2) Remove alternator and mounting bracket from engine. Remove 2 front oil pan bolts. Remove bolts securing front cover to block. Pull cover forward until free of locating dowel pins.

NOTE — *Bolts vary in length and must be installed in same location as removed.*

Jeep V8 Engines

5.0L & 6.0L V8 ENGINES (Cont.)

Installation — **1)** Remove lower locating dowel pin from engine block and clean all gasket surfaces. Cut both sides of oil pan gasket flush with engine block. Using old gasket as a guide, trim new gasket to correspond to amount cut off at oil pan. Apply suitable sealer to both sides of gasket and install on front cover.

2) Install front oil pan seal and align tongues of new oil pan gasket pieces with seal and cement into place on cover. Apply suitable sealer to cut-off edges of original oil pan gaskets and place cover into position, then install 2 front oil pan bolts.

3) Tighten bolts slowly and evenly until cover aligns with upper locating dowel. Install lower dowel through cover and drive into corresponding hole in engine block. Install cover retaining bolts in same location as they were removed from and tighten.

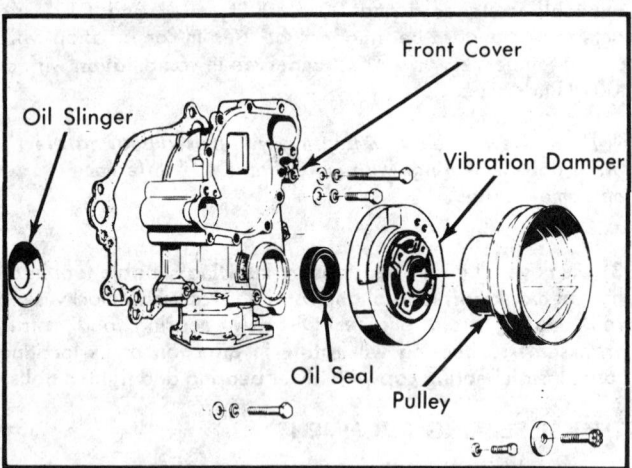

Fig. 5   Exploded View of Engine Front Cover

FRONT COVER OIL SEAL

Removal — The oil seal may be installed from either side of the front cover. It is not necessary to remove cover for seal replacement. Use removal tool (J-9256) to remove seal.

Installation — Clean seal bore and apply light coat of suitable sealer to outer surface of new seal. Drive new seal into place using tool (J-26562), until seal contacts outer flange of cover. Apply light coat of engine oil to lip of neoprene seal.

TIMING CHAIN

Removal — Remove front cover and crankshaft oil slinger. Remove camshaft sprocket retaining bolt and washer, distributor drive gear and fuel pump eccentric. Rotate crankshaft until timing mark on sprocket is aligned with camshaft sprocket timing mark. See Fig. 6. Remove crankshaft sprocket, camshaft sprocket and timing chain as an assembly.

Installation — **1)** Assemble timing chain, crankshaft sprocket and camshaft sprocket with timing marks aligned. Install fuel pump eccentric and distributor drive gear. See Fig. 7.

NOTE — *Fuel pump eccentric must be installed with stamped word "REAR" facing camshaft sprocket.*

2) Install camshaft sprocket washer and retaining bolt. Check for correct installation of timing chain by rotating crankshaft until timing mark on camshaft sprocket is at 3 o'clock position.

Beginning with pin next to camshaft sprocket timing mark, ensure that the crankshaft timing mark lies between pins 20 and 21. Install oil slinger, new cover gasket and front cover.

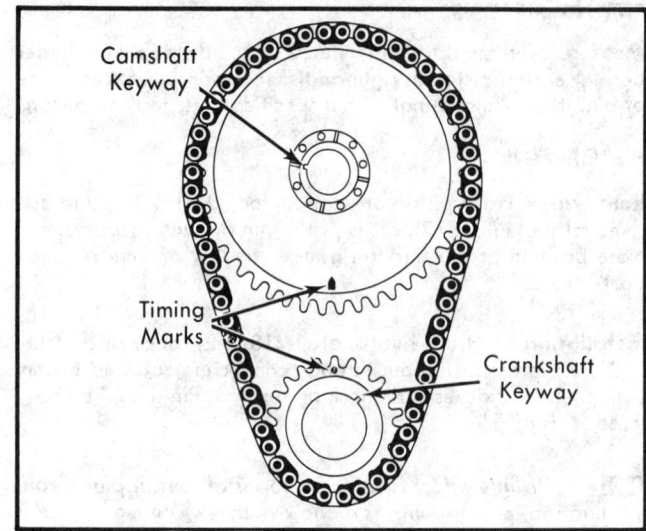

Fig. 6   Aligning Timing Marks

CAMSHAFT

Removal — **1)** Drain cooling system and remove radiator assembly. remove air conditioning condenser and receiver assembly (without disconnecting hoses) and position to one side. Remove rocker arm cover, rocker arm assemblies and push rods. Remove intake manifold and hydraulic lifters.

NOTE — *Retain rocker arm assemblies, push rods and lifters in order for reinstallation in original location.*

2) Remove front cover and rotate crankshaft until timing mark on sprocket is aligned with camshaft sprocket timing mark. See Fig. 6. Remove crankshaft sprocket, camshaft sprocket, and timing chain as an assembly. Remove hood latch support bracket upper retaining screw and move bracket (as required) for access to camshaft. Remove front bumper or grille (as required) and carefully remove camshaft.

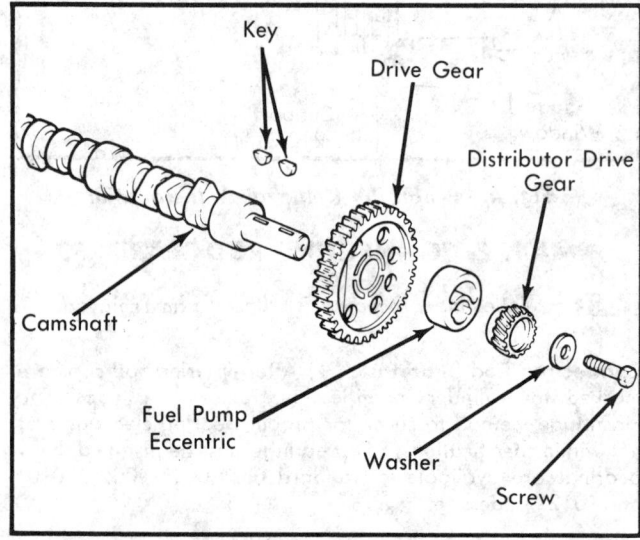

Fig. 7   Exploded View of Camshaft Assembly

5.0L & 6.0L V8 ENGINES (Cont.)

Installation — Reverse removal procedure while noting following: Lubricate camshaft with suitable oil supplement and install camshaft carefully to avoid damage to camshaft lobes.

CAMSHAFT BEARINGS

NOTE — *When installing bearings, use a screw-type cam bearing installation tool, one that provides steady pressure. DO NOT use a driver-type cam bearing installation tool.*

CAM LOBE LIFT

Remove rocker arm cover, bridged pivot, rocker arms and spark plugs, then proceed as follows:

1) Use suitable clamping or mounting fixture, attach dial indicator to cylinder head so indicator probe rests on top of push rod with indicator and probe in a vertical position over push rod. Rotate crankshaft slowly until valve lifter is on heel of cam lobe. At this point, push rod will be at its lowest point.

CAUTION — *If using an auxiliary starter switch, distributor primary lead must be disconnected from negative post of coil.*

2) With push rod at lowest position, zero dial indicator and rotate engine until push rod is in fully raised position. Compare total lift recorded, with specifications. Check all remaining lobes of camshaft in same manner.

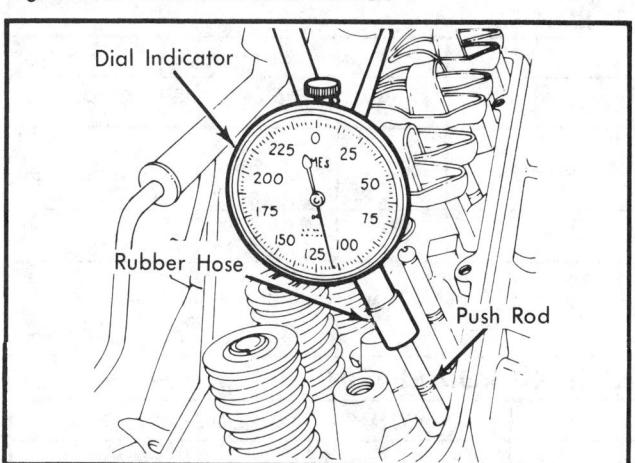

Fig. 8 Measuring Camshaft Lobe Lift

VALVE TIMING

1) Remove spark plugs, rocker arm covers, and rocker arm assemblies from No. 1 cylinder. Rotate crankshaft until No. 6 piston is at TDC on compression stroke and rotate crankshaft counterclockwise 90° from this position. Install a dial indicator on No. 1 intake valve rocker arm push rod end. Set dial indicator to zero.

2) Crank engine slowly in clockwise direction until dial indicator shows a lift of .020". Timing marks on vibration damper should be in line with TDC or zero marking on timing chain cover. If variation of more than ½" in either direction exists, remove timing chain cover and inspect timing chain installation.

ENGINE OILING

Crankcase Capacity — 4 quarts. Add 1 quart with filter change.

Oil Filter — Replace oil filter every 5000 miles or 5 months, whichever comes first.

Normal Oil Pressure — 13 psi minimum at 600 RPM and 37-75 psi maximum at 1600+ RPM.

Pressure Regulator Valve — Located in pump body. Not adjustable.

ENGINE OILING SYSTEM

Oil is drawn from oil pan into gallery at lower right side of engine. A passage in timing chain cover channels oil into oil pump. Oil then flows through oil filter equipped with by-pass valve and to gallery extending to left front of engine. Oil passes directly to right main gallery and intersects with short passage leading to left main gallery. Engine components are then lubricated as follows:

Crankshaft & Camshaft Bearings — Passages extend down from main oil galleries to each camshaft bearing and to each upper main bearing. Passages in crankshaft allow oil flow from main bearing journal to adjacent connecting rod journal. A squirt hole in connecting rod bearing cap distributes oil on cylinder walls, pistons and piston pins.

Hydraulic Valve Lifters — Lubricated directly from main oil galleries.

Rocker Arms & Push Rods — Oil is delivered from hydraulic lifters and passes through hollow push rods to rocker arms. Rocker arms direct oil onto valve train and oil returns to pan through channels in cylinder head.

Timing Chain & Sprockets — Oil is received from front camshaft bearing. Oil is thrown off to lubricate distributor gear and fuel pump eccentric. Oil returns to pan through cavity under front main bearing.

OIL PUMP

Oil pump is driven by distributor drive shaft. Removal of pump will not affect ignition timing, as distributor gear remains in time with camshaft. Pump must be filled with petroleum jelly (do not use grease of any type) prior to installation of oil pump cover. To measure oil pump gear clearances, proceed as follows:

1) To measure pump gear end clearance, two methods can be used; Plastigage method (preferred) and feeler gauge method (alternate). To use the Plastigage method, remove pump cover and gasket. Place a strip of Plastigage across each gear end and install pump cover with gasket. Tighten screws to 55 INCH lbs. Remove screws, cover and gasket. Measure Plastigage width for correct specifications.

2) To use feeler gauge method, remove pump cover and gasket. Place a straight edge across pump body and gear ends. Insert a feeler gauge that fits snug and check feeler gauge thickness against specifications.

3) To check pump housing to gear tooth clearance, insert feeler gauge that fits snug between gear tooth and pump body. Check feeler gauge thickness against specifications.

Oil Pump Specifications	
Application	**Specifications**
Gear-to-Body Clearance	.0005-.0025"
Gear End Clearance	
Plastigage Method	.002-.008"
Feeler Gauge Method	.004-.008"

Jeep V8 Engines

5.0L & 6.0L V8 ENGINES (Cont.)

ENGINE SPECIFICATIONS

GENERAL SPECIFICATIONS

Year	Displ. Cu. Ins.	Carburetor	HP at RPM	Torque (Ft. Lbs. at RPM)	Compr. Ratio	Bore	Stroke
1981			.....	.....			
5.0L	304″	2-Bbl.	.....	.....	8.4:1	3.75″	3.44″
6.0L	360″	2-Bbl.			8.25:1	4.08″	3.44″

VALVES

Engine & Valve	Head Diam.	Face Angle	Seat Angle	Seat Width	Stem Diameter	Stem Clearance	Valve Lift
5.0L							
Int.	1.782-1.792″	29°	30°	.040-.060″	.3715-.3725″	.001-.003″	.426″
Exh.	1.401-1.411″	44°	44.5°	.040-.060″	.3715-.3725″	.001-.003″	.426″
6.0L							
Int.	2.020-2.030″	29°	30°	.040-.060″	.3715-.3725″	.001-.003″	.426″
Exh.	1.675-1.687″	44°	44.5°	.040-.060″	.3715-.3725″	.001-.003″	.426″

PISTONS, PINS, RINGS

Engine	PISTONS	PINS		RINGS		
	Clearance	Piston Fit	Rod Fit	Rings	End Gap	Side Clearance
5.0L	.001-.0018″	.0003-.0005″	Press Fit	1 & 2	.010-.020″	.0015-.003″ ①
				3	.010-.025″	.001-.008″
6.0L	.0012-.002″	.0003-.0005″	Press Fit	1 & 2	.010-.020″	.0015-.003″ ②
				3	.015-.045″	0-.007″

① — Ring No. 1 side clearance is .0015-.0035″.   ② — Ring No. 2 side clearance is .0015-.0035″.

CRANKSHAFT MAIN & CONNECTING ROD BEARINGS

Engine	MAIN BEARINGS				CONNECTING ROD BEARINGS		
	Journal Diam.	Clearance	Thrust Bearing	Crankshaft End Play	Journal Diam.	Clearance	Side Play
5.0L, 6.0L	①2.7474-2.7489″	②.001-.003″	No. 3	.003-.008″	2.0934-2.0955″	.001-.003″	.006-.018″

① — For bearings 1-4. No. 5 bearing 2.7464-2.7479″.   ② — For bearings 1-4. No. 5 bearing .002-.004″.

MAIN BEARING FITTING CHART

Main Bearing Journal Color Code & Diameter	Bearing Color & Size Code	
	Upper Insert	Lower Insert
Yellow	Yellow	Yellow
2.7484-2.7489″	Std.	Std.
Orange	Yellow	Black
2.7479-2.7484″	Std.	−.001″
Black	Black	Black
2.7474-2.7479″	−.001″	−.001″
Green	Black	Green
2.7469-2.7474″	−.001″	−.002″
Red	Red	Red
2.7384-2.7389″	−.010″	−.010″

CONNECTING ROD FITTING CHART

Connecting Rod Journal Color Code & Diameter	Bearing Color & Size Code	
	Upper Insert	Lower Insert
Yellow	Yellow	Yellow
2.0948-2.0955″	Std.	Std.
Orange	Yellow	Black
2.0941-2.0948″	Std.	−.001″
Black	Black	Black
2.0934-2.0941″	−.001″	−.001″
Red	Red	Red
2.0848-2.0855″	−.010″	−.010″

5.0L & 6.0L V8 ENGINES (Cont.)

ENGINE SPECIFICATIONS (Cont.)

CAMSHAFT

Engine	Journal Diam.	Clearance	Lobe Lift
5.0L, 6.0L		.001-.003"	.266"
No. 1	2.1195-2.1205"		
No. 2	2.0895-2.0905"		
No. 3	2.0595-2.0605"		
No. 4	2.0295-2.0305"		
No. 5	1.9995-2.0005"		

VALVE SPRINGS

Engine	Free Length	PRESSURE (LBS.)	
		Valve Closed	Valve Open
5.0L, 6.0L	1.99"	64-72 @ 1.786"	202-220 @ 1.356"

VALVE TIMING

Engine	INTAKE		EXHAUST	
	Open (BTDC)	Close (ABDC)	Open (BBDC)	Close (ATDC)
5.0L, 6.0L	14.75°	68.75°	56.75°	26.75°

TIGHTENING SPECIFICATIONS

Application	Ft. Lbs.
Cylinder Head Bolts	110
Intake Manifold Bolts	43
Exhaust Manifold Bolts	
Center (2)	25
Outer (4)	15
Oil Pan Bolts	
1/4"	7
5/16"	11
Main Bearing Cap Bolts	100
Connecting Rod Nuts	33
Flywheel-to-Crankshaft Bolts	105
Vibration Damper Bolt①	90
Camshaft Sprocket Bolt	30
Rocker Arm Cap Screws	19
Engine Front Cover Bolts	25
Thermostat Housing Bolts	13
A.I.R. Tube-to-Manifold Nuts	38
Oil Pump Cover Bolts	5
Oil Relief Valve Cap	28
Water Pump Bolts	4

① — Bolt is lubricated.

Oil Pan Removal

CHRYSLER CORP.

6-CYLINDER ENGINES

3.7L (225") ENGINE

1) Disconnect battery ground cable. Remove engine oil dipstick. Raise vehicle and drain engine oil.

2) Remove engine-to-transmission support strut. Remove torque converter inspection cover plate (if equipped with automatic transmission). Remove oil pan attaching bolts and oil pan.

NOTE — When installing, use 1/8" bead of sealer on 4 corners of rubber seal and cork gasket. California engines require a high temperature left side oil pan gasket.

V8 ENGINES

5.2L (318") & 5.9L (360") ENGINES

1) Disconnect battery ground cable. Remove engine oil dipstick. Raise vehicle and drain crankcase.

2) Remove exhaust crossover pipe and remove left engine-to-transmission support strut. Remove torque converter cover (if equipped with automatic transmission).

3) Remove oil pan bolts and remove oil pan.

NOTE — When installing, apply a drop of sealer to corners where cork and rubber gaskets meet. On 5.9L (360") engines, ensure notches in side gaskets align with corresponding notches in engine block.

TIGHTENING SPECIFICATIONS

Oil Pan Attaching Bolts	INCH Lbs.
All Models	200

NOTE — Torque specifications for components other than oil pan attaching bolts may be found in Engine Removal Section.

FORD

6-CYLINDER ENGINES

"E" MODELS WITH 4.9L (300") ENGINE

1) Remove engine cover, air cleaner and carburetor. If equipped with air conditioning, discharge refrigerant and remove compressor. Remove EGR valve and upper radiator hose. On E350 models, remove thermactor check valve.

2) Remove fan shroud. If equipped with automatic transmission, remove filler tube. Remove nuts holding exhaust pipe to exhaust manifold, and raise vehicle. Disconnect and plug fuel pump inlet line.

3) Remove alternator, splash shield and front engine mount nuts. Disconnect lower radiator hose and transmission cooler lines. Remove power steering return line clip located in front of crossmember.

4) Remove starter and dip stick tube. Raise engine and place 3" blocks under engine mounts. Lower engine and remove jack. Remove oil pan bolts and pick-up tube with screen from oil pump. Remove oil pan.

NOTE — When installing, use a suitable sealer on pan gaskets. Tighten 3 oil pan-to-front cover bolts last.

"F" MODELS & BRONCO WITH 4.9L (300") ENGINE

1) Drain crankcase and cooling system. Remove radiator and raise vehicle on hoist. On F 100-250 vehicles, remove starter. Remove front engine mount nuts then raise front of engine with transmission jack.

2) Place 1" block of wood under engine mounts. Lower engine on blocks and remove jack. Remove oil pan bolts and lower pan to crossmember. Remove oil pump inlet tube bolts and lay tube in bottom of pan. Remove oil pan.

V8 ENGINES

"F" MODELS & BRONCO WITH 4.2L (255"), 5.0L (302") & 5.8L (351") W ENGINES

1) Remove oil dipstick (on pan entry models only). Remove fan shroud and position over fan. Disconnect engine mounts. On automatic transmission models, disconnect oil cooler line at left side of radiator. Raise engine and place wooden blocks under engine supports.

2) Drain engine oil, remove oil pan attaching bolts, and lower oil pan onto engine crossmember. Remove 2 bolts holding oil pump pickup tube to oil pump. Remove nut attaching oil pickup tube to No. 3 main bearing cap stud. Lower pickup tube and screen assembly into oil pan and remove pan from vehicle.

"E" MODELS WITH 4.2L (255") 5.0L (302") & 5.8L (351") W ENGINES

1) Disconnect battery and remove engine cover. Remove air cleaner and drain cooling system. If equipped with air conditioning or power steering, remove compressor or power steering pump and position out of way. Disconnect upper radiator hose. Remove fan shroud bolts and oil filler tube. Remove oil dipstick-to-exhaust manifold bolt. Raise vehicle on hoist.

2) Remove splash shield under alternator. Disconnect lower radiator hose and if equipped, disconnect automatic transmission lines at radiator. Disconnect engine mounts and fuel line at fuel pump. Drain engine oil and remove dipstick tube from oil pan. Detach exhaust pipe from exhaust manifolds. If equipped, remove automatic transmission dipstick and tube. Disconnect manual linkage at transmission. Remove center driveshaft support and remove driveshaft from transmission.

FORD (Cont.)

3) Place a transmission jack under oil pan and raise engine 4 inches measured from front engine mounts. Insert wooden blocks between engine and mounts to support engine.

NOTE — *Engine and transmission assembly will pivot around rear engine mount. Engine must remain centered in engine compartment to obtain the required 4 inch lift.*

4) Remove oil pan attaching bolts and lower oil pan. Unbolt oil pump and pickup tube and lay in pan (except on E100-E350 models with 5.8L engine). Remove nut attaching pickup tube to No. 3 bearing cap stud, and remove pan from vehicle.

"E" MODELS WITH 5.8L (351") M & 6.6L (400") ENGINES

1) Disconnect battery and remove engine cover. Remove air cleaner and drain cooling system. Disconnect upper radiator hose and remove fan shroud bolts. Remove oil filler tube and dipstick-to-manifold mounting bolt. Raise vehicle on hoist.

2) Remove splash shield under alternator. If equipped with automatic transmission, remove cooler lines at radiator. Disconnect lower radiator hoses and fuel line at pump. Remove engine mount nuts and oil dipstick tube from oil pan. Disconnect exhaust crossover pipe from exhaust manifolds.

3) If equipped, remove automatic transmission dipstick and filler tube. Disconnect manual linkage at transmission. Remove center driveshaft support and remove driveshaft from transmission.

4) Place a transmission jack under oil pan and raise engine 2 inches measured from front engine mounts. Insert wooden blocks between engine and mounts to support engine.

NOTE — *Engine and transmission assembly will pivot around rear engine mount. Engine must remain centered in engine compartment to achieve required lift. DO NOT raise engine more than 2 inches, or damage to air conditioning main and auxiliary suction lines will result.*

5) Remove oil pan attaching bolts and lower oil pan onto crossmember. Unbolt oil pump and pickup tube and lay in oil pan. Remove oil pan from vehicle.

"F" MODELS & BRONCO WITH 5.8L (351") M & 6.6L (400") ENGINES

1) Remove oil dipstick. Remove fan shroud attaching bolts and position shroud over fan. Raise vehicle and drain engine oil. Disconnect starter cable and remove starter. Place a jack under engine and remove engine front support. Place wooden blocks between engine and chassis brackets. Remove jack.

2) If vehicle is equipped with automatic transmission, remove oil cooler lines and position out of way. Remove oil pan attaching bolts and remove oil pan from vehicle.

"E" MODELS WITH 7.5L (460") ENGINE

1) Remove engine cover, disconnect battery and drain cooling system. Remove air cleaner assembly, then disconnect throttle and transmission linkage at carburetor. Disconnect power brake vacuum line. Disconnect fuel line, choke lines, and air cleaner adapter from carburetor.

2) Disconnect radiator hoses, transmission oil cooler lines, then remove fan assembly, shroud, and radiator. Remove power steering pump and position to one side with hoses connected. Remove oil dipstick tube and engine mount attaching bolts. Remove oil filler tube and bracket.

3) If equipped, remove air conditioning lines or rotate them downward at rear of compressor to clear dashboard. Raise vehicle, drain crankcase, and remove oil filter. Remove exhaust crossover pipe from exhaust manifolds. Disconnect manual and kickdown linkage from transmission. Remove drive shaft and coupling shaft assembly. Remove transmission tube assembly.

4) Remove dipstick and tube from oil pan. Position a jack under oil pan and raise engine until transmission touches floor board (approximately 4 inches). Insert wooden blocks between engine and mounts to support engine.

NOTE — *Engine and transmission will pivot around rear engine mount. Engine must remain centered in engine compartment to achieve desired lift.*

5) Remove oil pan attaching bolts and lower oil pan onto crossmember. Remove oil pump and pickup tube assembly and lay in oil pan. Remove oil pan rearward from vehicle.

TIGHTENING SPECIFICATIONS

Oil Pan Attaching Bolts	Ft. Lbs.
4.9L (300")	10-12
4.2L (255"), 5.0L (302"), & 5.8L (351") W	9-11
5.8L (351") M & 6.6L (400")	7-9
7.5L (460")	7-11

NOTE — *Torque specifications for components other than oil pan attaching bolts may be found in Engine Removal Section.*

GENERAL MOTORS

6-CYLINDER ENGINES
"G" VAN MODELS WITH 4.1L (250") & 4.8L (292") ENGINES

1) Disconnect battery cable and remove engine cover. Remove air cleaner and studs. Remove fan guard. Remove radiator upper supports. Raise vehicle.

2) If vehicle is equipped with a standard transmission, perform the following steps before continuing: Disconnect clutch cross shaft from left front mount bracket. Remove transmission-to-bell housing upper bolt. Remove transmission rear mount bolts and install two 7/16" X 3" bolts. Raise transmission using jack and install 2" block between mount and crossmember.

3) Remove starter and drain engine oil. Remove engine mount bolts. Raise engine sufficiently to insert wooden blocks between engine mounts and crossmember brackets.

4) Remove flywheel splash shield or torque converter cover as applicable. Remove oil pan attaching bolts and remove oil pan.

Oil Pan Removal

GENERAL MOTORS (Cont.)

ALL MODELS WITH 4.1L (250") & 4.8L (292") ENGINES (EXCEPT "G" VAN)

1) Disconnect battery cable, raise vehicle, and drain engine oil. Remove starter and flywheel splash shield or torque converter housing underpan as applicable.

2) Remove bolts from front engine mount. Raise front of engine, reinstall mount bolts, and lower engine. Remove oil pan bolts, and remove oil pan from vehicle.

V8 ENGINES

ALL MODELS WITH 5.0L (305") & 5.7L (350") GAS ENGINES

1) Raise vehicle on hoist and drain engine oil. Remove exhaust crossover pipe. On vehicles with automatic transmissions, remove converter housing underpan.

2) On "K" models with automatic transmission, remove strut rods at engine mounts. Remove oil pan mounting bolts and remove oil pan from vehicle.

ALL MODELS WITH 7.4L (454") ENGINE

1) Disconnect battery negative cable, loosen fan shroud and remove air cleaner and distributor cap. Raise vehicle and drain oil. On models equipped with manual transmission, remove starter.

2) Remove flywheel splash shield/converter cover. Remove oil filter. On gauge equipped models, remove oil pressure line from block. Remove front engine mount through bolts, raise engine and remove oil pan bolts and remove oil pan.

ALL MODELS WITH 5.7L (350") DIESEL ENGINE

1) Disconnect battery cable and remove oil dipstick. Remove oil pump drive and vacuum pump. Remove upper radiator support and fan shroud attaching bolts.

2) Raise vehicle and drain engine oil. Remove flywheel cover. Disconnect exhaust and crossover pipes. Remove oil cooler lines at filter base and remove starter assembly.

3) Remove engine mounts from engine block and install a jack under engine. Remove oil pan mounting bolts and remove oil pan from vehicle.

TIGHTENING SPECIFICATIONS

Oil Pan Attaching Bolts	Ft. Lbs.
4.1L (250") & 4.8L (292") Engines	
Oil Pan-to-Block	
1/4-20 Bolts	6-7
5/16-18 Bolts	6-7
Oil Pan-to-Front Cover	4-5
5.0L (305") & 5.7L (350") Gas Engines	
Oil Pan-to-Block	
1/8-20 Bolts	6-7
5/16-18 Bolts	13-14
7.4L (454")	
Oil Pan-to-Block	11-12
Oil Pan-to-Front Cover	4-5
5.7L (350") Diesel	
Oil Pan-to-Block	9-11

NOTE — *Torque specifications for components other than oil pan attaching bolts may be found in Engine Removal Section.*

JEEP

4-CYLINDER ENGINES

Disconnect battery negative cable. Raise vehicle and drain oil. Remove starter. Remove oil pan bolts and remove oil pan.

6-CYLINDER ENGINES

Disconnect battery negative cable. Raise vehicle and drain oil. Remove starter. On "CJ" and Scrambler models, position a floor jack under transmission housing, disconnect right support cushion bracket from block and raise engine enough to gain clearance for oil pan removal. On all models, remove oil pan attaching bolts and remove oil pan, seals, and side gaskets.

V8 ENGINES

Disconnect battery cable and drain engine oil. On "CJ" and Scrambler models, remove frame crossmember and automatic transmission cooler lines (if equipped). If necessary, cut corner of right side engine mount to provide clearance for removal of oil pan. On all models, bend tabs down on dust shield if equipped with manual transmission. Remove oil pan attaching bolts and remove oil pan from engine.

TIGHTENING SPECIFICATIONS

Oil Pan Attaching Bolts	Ft. Lbs.
All Engines	
1/4-20 Bolts	7
5/16-18 Bolts	11

NOTE — *Torque specifications for components other than oil pan attaching bolts may be found in Engine Removal Section.*

CHRYSLER CORP.

6-CYLINDER ENGINES

"B","CB","MB", & "PB" MODELS

1) Disconnect battery and remove oil dipstick. Raise vehicle and remove air pump tube from exhaust pipe, then remove pipe. Remove inspection cover from transmission and drain crankcase, remove engine-to-transmission strut. Remove oil pan, it may be necessary to turn the crankshaft to clear the front of the oil pan. Turn the oil pick-up tube upwards to protect it from damage. Remove flex plate-to-torque converter bolts and transmission housing bolts. Remove right motor mount nut.

2) Lower vehicle and drain cooling system. Remove engine cover, carburetor air cleaner and carburetor. If equipped with air conditioning, discharge system and disconnect condenser lines. Remove fan shroud, windshield washer and overflow reservoirs. Remove front bumper, grille and support brace. Disconnect radiator hoses and remove radiator and support as an assembly. Remove steering pump bracket bolts and set pump to one side. Remove air pump and disconnect throttle linkage, all hoses, electrical connections and lines to coil, alternator and other engine accessories.

3) Remove alternator with brackets, fan blade, pulley and drive belts. Disconnect flexible fuel pump line and cap openings. Remove starter attaching bolts and set starter aside. Remove distributor cap and left engine mount nut. Attach suitable lifting fixture to engine and place jack under transmission. Remove remaining transmission housing bolts and remove engine from front of vehicle.

ALL OTHER MODELS

1) Scribe hood hinge for reinstallation and remove hood. Drain cooling system and remove battery. Remove radiator hoses and radiator. Set fan shroud to one side and discharge air conditioning system (if equipped). Remove air cleaner, vacuum lines, distributor cap and wiring.

2) Remove carburetor, linkage, starter wiring and oil pressure wire. Remove starter, alternator, charcoal canister and horns. Remove air conditioning and power steering hoses (if equipped). Remove exhaust pipe at manifold. Remove transmission housing and inspection plate bolts.

3) Attach "C" clamp to front of housing to prevent torque converter from coming out. Remove torque converter drive plate bolts and mark converter and drive plate to aid in reassembly. Support transmission with stand (C-3201-A) and disconnect engine from torque converter drive plate. Install engine lifting fixture and attach chain. Remove engine front mount bolts and remove engine from engine compartment.

V8 ENGINES

"B", "CB", "MB" & "PB" MODELS

1) Disconnect battery and remove oil dipstick. Raise vehicle and remove exhaust crossover and pipes from manifolds. Remove inspection cover from transmission. Drain engine oil and remove strut from transmission (if equipped). Remove oil pan (it may be necessary to rotate engine to clear front of pan). Remove flex plate to torque converter bolts and (if necessary), oil pump. Remove starter retaining bolts and set starter aside. Remove lower transmission housing bolts and engine mount nuts. Lower vehicle and drain cooling system.

2) Remove engine cover and discharge air conditioning system. Remove air cleaner and carburetor (318" & 360" engines). Disconnect condenser lines and remove front bumper, grille and support brace. Disconnect radiator hoses and remove condenser, radiator and support as an assembly. Remove air conditioning compressor bracket bolts and set compressor aside (remove if necessary). Remove air pump and power steering pump brackets and position pumps to one side (remove if necessary).

3) Disconnect throttle linkage, heater and vacuum hoses and all electrical connections to coil, alternator and other engine accessories. Remove alternator, fan blade (or fluid fan unit), pulley and drive belts. Disconnect flexible line to fuel pump and cap line. Remove left exhaust manifold heat shield and remove spark plug wires and distributor cap. On 318" and 360" engines, attach a suitable lifting fixture to intake manifold. Place floor jack under transmission and remove upper transmission housing bolts. Use lifting device to remove engine from front of vehicle.

ALL OTHER MODELS

1) Scribe hood hinges for reassembly and remove hood. Drain cooling system and remove battery and air cleaner. Remove radiator hoses and remove radiator. Discharge air conditioning system (if equipped) and remove vacuum lines, distributor cap and wiring. Remove carburetor, linkage, starter wires and oil pressure wire. Remove air conditioning hoses and power steering hoses (if equipped). Remove starter, alternator, charcoal canister and horns.

2) Remove exhaust pipe at manifold, and transmission housing bolts. Remove inspection plate and attach "C" clamp to front of transmission torque converter housing to prevent converter from falling out. Remove drive plate and mark converter and drive plate to aid in reassembly. Support transmission with stand and disconnect engine from torque converter drive plate. Install engine lifting fixture and device and remove engine from engine compartment.

TIGHTENING SPECIFICATIONS

Application	Ft. Lbs.
Exhaust Manifold Nuts	
6 Cyl.	20
V8	15
Exhaust Pipe Flange	
6 Cyl.	35
V8	24
Flex Plate-to-Converter	23
Flex Plate-to-Crankshaft	55
Flywheel-to-Crankshaft	55
Front Mount-to-Engine	
6 Cyl.	75
V8	65
Rear Mount-to-Engine	50
Starter Mount Bolt	50

Engine Removal

FORD

6-CYLINDER ENGINES

NOTE — *Procedures are for engine removal without transmission attached.*

ALL "E" MODELS

1) Open hood and door, remove engine cover. Drain coolant, remove air cleaner and disconnect battery. Remove front bumper, then remove grille and lower gravel deflector as an assembly. Disconnect radiator hoses at engine and remove A/C compressor.

2) Remove alternator splash shield, disconnect transmission oil cooler lines at radiator (if equipped), remove radiator and shroud. Disconnect heater hoses and alternator wiring at alternator. Remove power steering pump drive belt, then remove power steering pump (with support) from engine. Disconnect and plug fuel line at fuel pump.

3) Disconnect distributor wiring, brake booster hose, and accelerator cable and bracket from engine. Disconnect automatic transmission kickdown (if equipped) at bell crank. Remove exhaust manifold heat deflector and inlet pipe-to-manifold nuts. Disconnect both ends of transmission vacuum line at intake manifold and junction.

4) Remove upper transmission-to-engine bolts. If so equipped, remove automatic transmission dipstick tube support at intake manifold. Raise vehicle on hoist, drain crankcase and remove oil filter. Disconnect and remove starter and flywheel inspection cover. Remove four converter nuts (if automatic transmission), then remove front engine support nuts. Remove remainder of transmission-to-engine bolts. Lower vehicle, install suitable lift chain and remove engine from vehicle.

ALL "F" MODELS

1) Drain cooling system and crankcase. Remove hood and mark hinge positions for reassembly. Disconnect battery cables, radiator and heater hoses and fuel line from fuel pump. Remove radiator, fan and water pump pulley. Disconnect accelerator cable at carburetor and remove retracting spring. Disconnect engine wiring, transmission kickdown rod at bellcrank assembly (automatic transmissions only). Disconnect engine ground strap and exhaust pipes at manifolds. On vehicles with power brakes, disconnect vacuum line at intake manifold.

2) Remove alternator mounting bolts and position alternator to one side leaving wires attached. If equipped with power steering, remove pump from mounting brackets and place to one side leaving lines attached.

3) Raise vehicle on hoist. Remove starter, automatic transmission fluid filler tube bracket and engine rear plate upper right bolt. On vehicles with manual transmission, remove flywheel housing lower retaining bolts and disconnect clutch retracting spring.

4) On vehicles with automatic transmission, remove converter housing access cover, flywheel to converter nuts and then secure converter assembly in housing. Remove transmission oil cooler lines from clip at engine and converter housing to engine lower retaining bolts.

5) Remove insulator-to-intermediate support bracket nut from each front engine mount. On F100/F350 and Bronco models, remove the insulator-to-intermediate support bracket nut from each engine front support. Lower vehicle and support transmission with a floor jack. Remove remaining flywheel or converter-to-engine bolts. Attach a suitable lifting device to engine, raise engine slightly and pull from transmission, then remove engine from vehicle.

V8 ENGINES

ALL "F" MODELS

1) Drain cooling system and crankcase. Disconnect radiator hoses, transmission oil cooler lines (if equipped), then remove fan shroud, radiator, fan, spacer and pulley. Disconnect battery and alternator ground wires at cylinder block. Remove air cleaner and intake duct assembly. Remove alternator attaching bolts and position to one side. Disconnect fuel line at fuel tank line, vacuum lines, heater hoses, electrical wiring and ground straps to cylinder block. Remove A/C compressor and vent hose from crankcase and carbon cannister hose.

2) Disconnect accelerator rod and transmission shift rod from carburetor, then remove retracting spring (if equipped). Remove flywheel housing-to-engine upper bolts. Remove starter, then disconnect exhaust pipes from manifolds. Disconnect motor mounts from brackets at frame and remove remaining flywheel housing-to-engine bolts. If equipped with automatic transmission, remove converter inspection plate and converter-to-flywheel attaching bolts.

3) Lower vehicle and support transmission with suitable floor jack. Install suitable lifting brackets on front of left cylinder head and rear of right cylinder head. Attach lifting sling and carefully raise engine and pull it from transmission. Lift engine from vehicle taking care that rear cover plate is not bent or other components damaged.

ALL "E" MODELS

1) Remove engine cover, open hood and disconnect battery. Drain cooling system, remove grille assembly and upper grille support bracket. Remove hood lock support and condenser upper mounting brackets. Remove condenser and disconnect lines at air conditioning compressor. Disconnect heater hoses, radiator hoses, and oil cooler lines (if equipped).

2) Remove radiator, fan shroud and fan assembly. Disconnect alternator lead wires at alternator, loosen adjusting bolt and pivot alternator toward engine. Remove air cleaner assembly, duct and valve assembly, and exhaust manifold shroud. Disconnect throttle and transmission linkage at carburetor, then remove accelerator cable bracket from engine.

3) Disconnect fuel, choke, and vacuum lines to carburetor, then remove carburetor. Raise vehicle on hoist. Drain crankcase and remove oil filter. Disconnect exhaust pipes at exhaust manifolds. Disconnect automatic transmission fill tube

Engine Removal

FORD (Cont.)

at cylinder head. Remove engine mount attaching bolts and starter. Remove clutch housing-to-engine bolts on manual transmission models.

4) On models with automatic transmission, remove converter inspection cover and remove converter-to-flex plate attaching nuts. Remove adapter plate-to-converter housing bolts and converter housing-to-engine lower bolts.

5) Remove ground cable-to-cylinder block. Lower vehicle and support transmission using a floor jack. Loosen power steering pump bracket and remove front bracket bolts. Disconnect vacuum line at rear of intake manifold, and engine wire loom. Remove speed control servo and accelerator cable bracket from intake manifold and position to one side.

6) Disconnect air conditioning compressor wire. Install lifting brackets to intake manifold and connect a lifting hoist.

TIGHTENING SPECIFICATIONS

Application	Ft. Lbs.
Front Mount-to-Engine	
6-Cyl. "F" Models & Bronco	60-80
6-Cyl. "E" Models	50-70
V8	50-70
Rear Mount-to-Engine	
6-Cyl. "F" Models & Bronco	40-60
6-Cyl. "E" Models	50-70
V8	55-65
Converter Housing-to-Engine	
C-4 Transmission	28-38
C-6 Transmission	40-50
Converter-to-Flywheel	20-30
Flywheel Housing-to-Engine	
New Process 435 4-Speed Transmission	33-45
Ford 3.03 3-Speed & Warner T-8 4-Speed Transmission	40-50

GENERAL MOTORS

**Chevrolet
GMC**

6-CYLINDER ENGINES

"C", "K", & "P" MODELS

1) Disconnect battery cables and drain cooling system, then remove air cleaner. Remove hood and engine compartment cover ("P" models only). Disconnect radiator hoses, transmission cooler lines (if equipped) and remove radiator and shroud from vehicle. Remove battery from vehicle on "P" models.

2) Disconnect wiring, lines, linkage and hoses from engine. Raise vehicle and remove starter, flywheel or converter splash shield and exhaust pipe from manifold. If equipped with automatic transmission, remove converter-to-flex plate bolts.

NOTE — On "K" models, remove strut rods at motor mounts.

3) Remove clutch housing to engine retaining bolts and support transmission with chain. Lower vehicle and attach lifting device. Remove engine.

"G" MODELS

1) Disconnect battery and drain cooling system. Remove engine cover and air cleaner. Disconnect accelerator linkage from carburetor and remove carburetor. Remove grille and crossbrace. Remove windshield washer jar and disconnect radiator hoses. If equipped with automatic transmission, remove oil cooler lines and remove radiator.

NOTE — If equipped with air conditioning, remove A/C compressor, vacuum reservoir and swing condenser out of way.

2) Remove all hoses, wiring, linkage and lines from engine. Raise vehicle, drain crankcase and remove propeller shaft. Remove exhaust pipe at manifold and linkage from transmission. Remove speedometer cable and engine mount bolts.

NOTE — If equipped with manual transmission, disconnect clutch linkage and remove clutch cross shaft.

3) Lower vehicle and attach lifting device. Raise engine slightly to remove right hand motor mount. Remove engine with transmission.

V8 ENGINES

"C", "K", & "P" MODELS

1) Disconnect battery ground cable and drain cooling system. Remove hood, air cleaner and accessory drive belts and pulleys. Disconnect all hoses, lines, linkage and wiring from engine. If equipped with A/C, remove compressor and lay aside.

2) Disconnect transmission oil cooler lines (if equipped) and remove radiator with shroud. If equipped with power steering, remove pump and lay aside. Raise vehicle and drain crankcase.

NOTE — On "K" models with automatic transmission, remove strut rod at motor mounts.

3) Disconnect tail pipe from exhaust manifold. Remove flywheel or converter cover. Remove starter and wiring along right pan rail. Remove gas gauge wiring. If equipped with automatic transmission, remove converter-to-flex plate attaching bolts.

4) Support transmission and remove clutch housing-to-engine bolts. Remove lower engine mount bracket-to-frame bolts. Lower vehicle and attach lifting device. Remove engine.

"G" MODELS

1) Remove battery cable and drain cooling system. Remove grille, upper radiator support and lower grille valance. Disconnect transmission oil cooler lines (if equipped), and radiator hoses. Remove washer jar with bracket and remove radiator. Remove air cleaner, air stove pipe and accelerator cable from carburetor.

2) If equipped with power steering, remove pump and lay aside. Disconnect wiring from firewall connection and remove carburetor. Remove thermostat housing, oil fill pipe and disconnect heater hoses. If equipped with cruise control, remove servo, transducer and bracket.

3) Raise vehicle and drain crankcase. Disconnect tail pipe at manifold. Remove propeller shaft and shift linkage. Disconnect fuel line from pump and speedometer cable. Remove transmission mount bolts and engine mount bracket-to-frame bolts.

4) Remove engine mount through bolts. Raise engine slightly and remove engine mounts. Block up engine with wooden block between oil pan and crossmember. Lower vehicle and install lifting device. Remove engine.

TIGHTENING SPECIFICATIONS

Application	Ft. Lbs.
Flywheel Housing-to-Engine	30
Transmission Case-to-Engine	35
Oil Cooler Pipe Connections	11
Center Support Bolt	23
Converter-to-Flywheel Bolts	35
Rear Mount-to-Transmission	40
Rear Mount-to-Crossmember Bolt	40
Crossmember Mounting Bolt	25

JEEP

All Models
4 & 6-CYLINDER ENGINES

ALL MODELS

NOTE — *Engine is removed without transmission.*

1) Drain cooling system. On all models (except CJ & Scrambler), remove hood. Mark hinge location for installation alignment. Remove air cleaner. Disconnect and plug fuel line at pump. Disconnect fuel return line at frame. On CJ & Scrambler models, disconnect heater hoses at front of engine. On all others, disconnect at heater.

2) Disconnect accelerator cable at carburetor. Disconnect all electrical connections at engine and alternator. Disconnect all vacuum lines at engine. Identify for reassembly if necessary. On all models except CJ & Scrambler, battery must be removed.

3) Remove radiator, fan and shroud. Remove starter. Remove motor mount to frame nuts. Disconnect exhaust pipe at manifold. If equipped with manual transmission, remove clutch housing bolts, clutch linkage and shield.

4) If equipped with automatic transmission, remove transmission cover and mark position of converter on flex plate. Remove converter bolts. Remove bolts securing transmission converter housing to engine. Disconnect oil cooler lines from transmission oil pan.

5) On all models, support transmission with a floor jack. If equipped with power steering, disconnect hoses at steering gear and tie up out of way to prevent leakage. If equipped with air conditioning, disconnect lines at compressor after seating service valves and bleeding lines. Attach a sling to engine and remove from vehicle.

V8 ENGINES

NOTE — *Engine is removed without transmission.*

ALL MODELS

1) Mark hinge positions on hood and remove hood on all models except CJ. Remove air cleaner and drain cooling system. Disconnect radiator hoses and transmission oil cooler lines. **NOTE** — *If equipped with radiator shroud, separate shroud from radiator.* Remove radiator and fan.

2) Drain fluid from power steering pump reservoir and disconnect hoses. If equipped with air conditioning, turn both service valves clockwise to front seated position and bleed refrigerant charge by slowly loosening service valve fittings. Disconnect condenser and evaporator lines from compressor and receiver outlet at disconnect coupling. Remove condenser and receiver assembly.

3) Remove Cruise Command vacuum servo bellows and mounting bracket as an assembly. Remove battery on all models except CJ. Disconnect all wires, lines, linkage and hoses connected to engine. On automatic transmissions, disconnect filler tube bracket from right cylinder head, fuel return line at fuel filter, and fuel bowl pressure vent line at carburetor. Use suitable lifting device to support engine and remove front support to frame bolts.

4) Remove left front support and bracket from engine on CJ models. On CJ models with manual transmission, remove transfer case shift lever boot, floor mat, and transmission access cover. On all models remove upper bolts securing transmission to engine adapter plate or clutch housing to engine. Disconnect exhaust pipe at manifold and support bracket, then remove starter.

5) Support transmission using a floor jack. On models equipped with automatic transmission, remove adapter plate inspection covers and mark assembled position of converter and flex plate. Remove converter to flex plate bolts and remaining bolts securing transmission.

6) On models equipped with manual transmission remove clutch housing lower cover and remaining bolts securing clutch housing to engine. Raise engine and pull forward to remove from vehicle.

TIGHTENING SPECIFICATIONS

Application	Ft. Lbs.
4-Cylinder	
Automatic Transmission-to-Block	35
Clutch Housing-to-Block	54
Drive Plate-to-Converter	40
Drive Plate or Flywheel-to-Crankshaft	58
Exhaust Pipe-to-Manifold	35
Front Support Bracket-to-Block	35
Front Support Cushion-to-Crossmember	37
Rear Support Bracket-to-Transmission	33
6-Cylinder	
Automatic Transmission-to-Block	35
Clutch Housing-to-Block	
Top	35
Bottom	45
Drive Plate-to-Converter	26
Drive Plate or Flywheel-to-Crankshaft	105
Exhaust Pipe-to-Manifold	23
Front Support Bracket-to-Block	35
Front Support Cushion-to-Crossmember	37
Rear Support Bracket-to-Transmission	33
V8	
Automatic Transmission-to-Block	35
Clutch Housing-to-Block	30
Drive Plate-to-Converter Screw	22
Drive Plate or Flywheel-to-Crankshaft	105
Exhaust Pipe-to-Manifold	20
Front Support Bracket-to-Block	35
Front Support Bracket-to-Crossmember	37
Rear Support Bracket-to-Transmission	33

Engine Cooling Systems

GENERAL COOLING SYSTEM SERVICING

DESCRIPTION

The basic liquid cooling system consists of a radiator, water pump, thermostat, cooling fan, pressure cap, heater (if equipped), various connecting hoses, and cooling passages in the block and cylinder head. In addition, many cars use a fan clutch, which may incorporate a thermostatic control, or a flexible blade fan, or both, to reduce noise and power requirements at higher engine speeds. Some models, with exhaust emission control, use a thermostatic vacuum switch to advance ignition timing in the event of overheating. As most new models require the use of a permanent (ethylene glycol) type anti-freeze, year round, coolant recovery systems are being used more commonly to prevent coolant loss.

MAINTENANCE

DRAINING

Remove radiator cap, open heater control valve to maximum heat position (if equipped), open drain cocks or remove plugs in bottom of radiator and in engine block. In-line engines usually have one plug or cock, while V-engines will have two, one in each bank of cylinders.

CLEANING

A good cleaning compound will remove most rust and scale. Follow manufacturer's instructions in the use of the cleaner. If considerable rust and scale will have to be removed, flushing will be necessary. Also, clean radiator air passages by blowing out with compressed air from back to front of radiator.

FLUSHING

Back flushing is a very effective means of removing rust and scale from a cooling system. For best results the radiator, engine and heater core should be flushed separately. To flush radiator, connect flushing gun to water outlet of radiator and disconnect water inlet hose. Use a leadaway hose, connected to radiator inlet, to prevent flooding the engine. Use air in short bursts only, as a clogged radiator could be easily damaged. Continue flushing until water runs clear. To flush engine, first remove thermostat and replace housing. Connect flushing gun to water outlet of engine. Disconnect heater hoses from engine. Flush using short air bursts until water runs clean. Flush heater core as described for radiator. Make sure heater valve is set to maximum heat position before flushing heater.

REFILLING

Engine should be running while refilling cooling system to prevent air from being trapped in engine block. After system is full, continue running engine until thermostat is open, then recheck fill level. Do not overfill system. Refer to appropriate story for correct fill level.

TESTING

THERMOSTAT

Visually inspect thermostat for corrosion and proper sealing. If this is satisfactory, suspend thermostat and a thermometer in a container of water. Do not allow either thermostat or thermometer to touch bottom of container as this concentration of heat could cause an incorrect reading. Heat water until thermostat just begins to open.

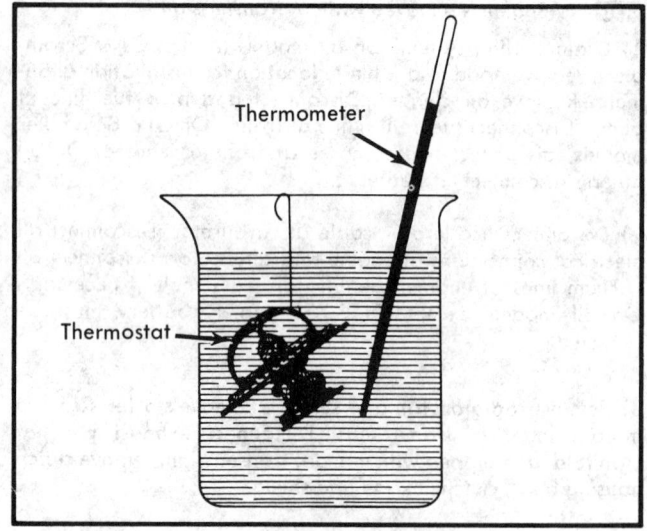

Fig. 1   Testing Thermostat

PRESSURE TESTING

A pressure testing tool is used to test both radiator cap and complete cooling system. Test as follows, following tool manufacturer's instructions.

Radiator Cap — Visually inspect radiator cap, dip cap in water and connect to tester. Pump tester to bring pressure to upper limit of cap specifications. If cap fails to hold pressure within specifications, replace cap.

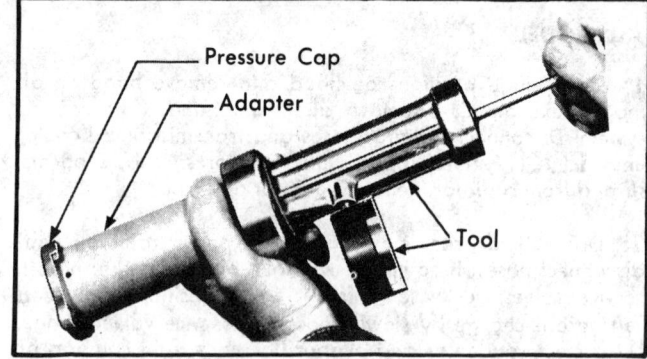

Fig. 2   Testing Radiator Pressure Cap

Cooling System — With engine stopped, wipe radiator filler neck seat clean. Fill radiator to correct level. Attach cooling system tester to radiator and pump until pressure is at upper level of radiator rating. If pressure drops, inspect for internal leaks. If no leaks are apparent, detach tester and run engine until normal operating temperature is obtained. Reattach tester and pump until pressure reaches approximately 7 psi. Race engine. If needle on tester fluctuates it indicates a combustion leak.

Engine Cooling Systems

GENERAL COOLING SYSTEM SERVICING (Cont.)

CAUTION — *Pressure may build up fast. Release any excess pressure above the upper limit of pressure cap specifications or cooling system damage may result.*

If needle does not fluctuate, race engine a few more times and check for water at tailpipe. Excessive water would indicate a faulty head gasket, cracked block or cylinder head near exhaust ports. Next, remove oil dipstick and if water globules appear in the oil, a serious internal leak is indicated.

ANTI-FREEZE CONCENTRATION

Test anti-freeze concentration using a suitable anti-freeze tester. The tester should have a temperature compensating feature, as failing to take temperature into consideration could cause an error as large as 30° F in freeze or overheating protection. Follow manufacturer's instructions for correct use of tester.

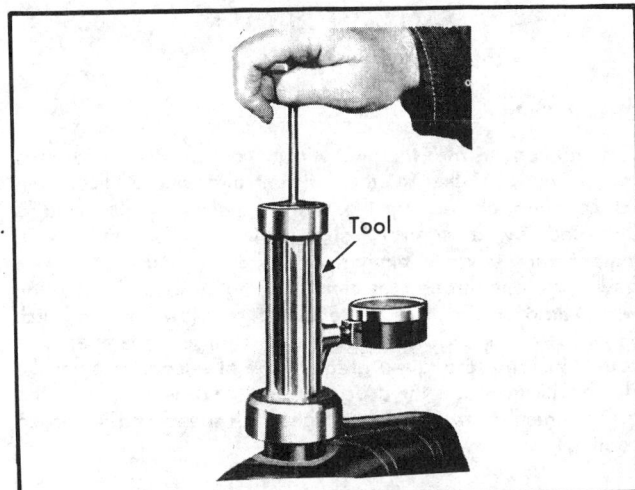

Fig. 3   Pressure Testing Cooling System

COOLANT RECOVERY SYSTEMS

DESCRIPTION

A coolant recovery system differs from a normal cooling system in that an overflow bottle is connected to the radiator overflow hose. The overflow bottle is transparent or translucent to permit checking of coolant level without removing radiator cap. No adjustment or test is required beyond keeping vent hole or hose clean and checking pressure relief of radiator cap.

OPERATION

As coolant temperature rises and pressure in system exceeds pressure relief valve of radiator cap, due to expansion of coolant, excess coolant flows into overflow bottle. As engine cools and coolant contracts, vacuum is formed in system, drawing coolant, stored in overflow bottle, back into radiator. As a result, in a properly maintained cooling system, the only coolant losses will be through evaporation.

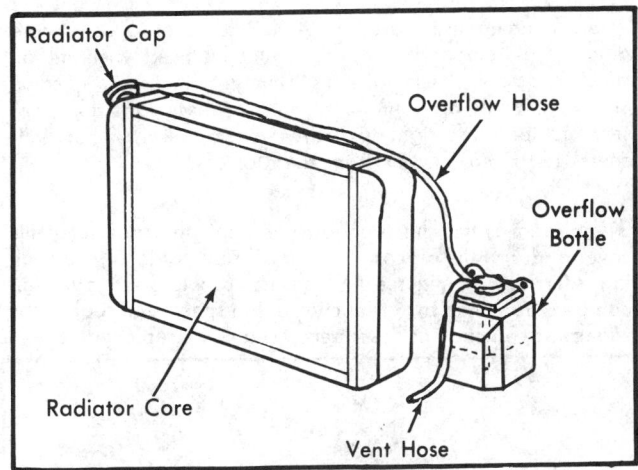

Fig. 1   Coolant Recovery System

RADIATOR CAPS

DESCRIPTION

The radiator cap consists of a pressure valve and a vacuum valve. The cap has several different functions: It prevents coolant loss when vehicle is in motion; prevents impurities from entering cooling system minimizing corrosion; allows atmospheric pressure to eliminate the vacuum that occurs in system during cooldown; and raises coolant boiling point approximately 2°F per psi of pressure by maintaining a constant cooling system pressure. For radiator cap testing procedures, see article on *GENERAL COOLING SYSTEM SERVICING*.

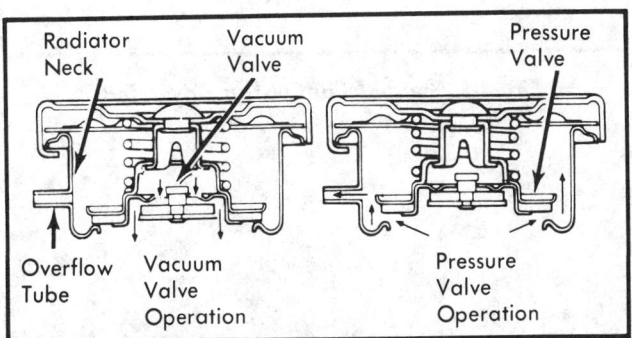

Fig. 1   Radiator Cap Operation

VARIABLE SPEED COOLING FANS

FAN CLUTCH WITH THERMOSTATIC CONTROL

DESCRIPTION

This unit consists of a thermostatically controlled fluid fan and torque control clutch. The thermal control drive is a silicone filled coupling connecting the fan to the fan pulley and is operated by a control valve (which is operated by a temperature sensitive bimetal coil or strip) and controls the flow of silicone through the clutch. During periods of operation when radiator discharge air temperature is low, the fan clutch limits the fan speed. High radiator discharge air temperature causes bimetal to allow a greater flow of silicone to enter the clutch. This increases the drag between the driven member and driving member resulting in a higher fan speed and increased cooling.

TESTING

In cases of engine overheating or insufficient air conditioning, proceed with the following:

1) Start with a cool engine to ensure complete fan clutch disengagement. Cover radiator grille sufficiently to induce high engine temperature.

2) Start engine and operate at 2000 RPM and turn on air conditioning (if equipped). A fan roar will be noticed when the fan clutch engages. It will take 5-10 minutes for fan to become engaged. While operating engine under these conditions, observe temperature light to prevent overheating. If hot light comes on, remove cover from radiator grille.

3) As soon as the clutch engages, remove the radiator grille cover and turn the air conditioning off to assist in engine cooling. After several minutes the fan clutch should disengage. This can be determined by a reduction in fan speed and roar. If the fan fails to function as described, it should be replaced.

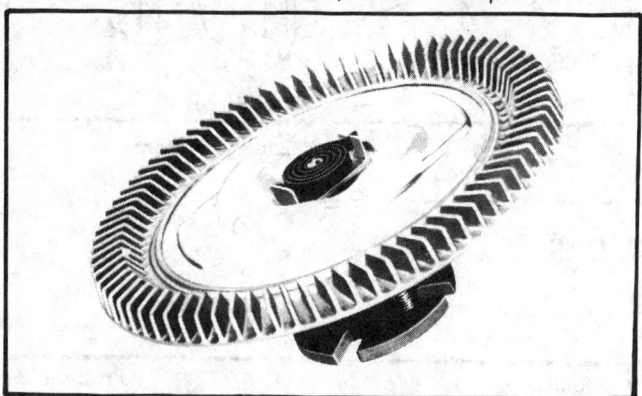

Fig. 1   Thermal Control Fan Drive Unit

FAN CLUTCH WITHOUT THERMOSTATIC CONTROL

DESCRIPTION

This unit is basically the same as the thermostatically controlled fan clutch except it is not controlled by a temperature sensitive coil. It allows the fan to be driven in normal manner at low speeds while limiting the top speed of the fan to a predetermined level at higher speeds. The silicone in the clutch housing provides a more positive drive at lower speeds and allows greater slippage between the driven member and driving member at higher engine speeds.

TESTING

In case of engine overheating during low car speed or idle operation, increase engine speed to approximately 1000 RPM in neutral gear. If condition is not corrected by increasing engine speed, replace fan drive unit with a unit that is known to be operating properly and test by operating vehicle under same conditions. Replace unit assembly if trouble is corrected with test unit. All units are non-adjustable and if damaged or not operating properly they must be replaced.

FLEX-BLADE FAN

DESCRIPTION

This unit is a fixed blade assembly designed to flex the blades as the engine RPM increases. As RPM increases, blade pitch decreases thereby saving power and decreasing noise level. No adjustment or test is required beyond keeping the fan belt adjusted to the proper tension and ensuring that unit is not damaged.

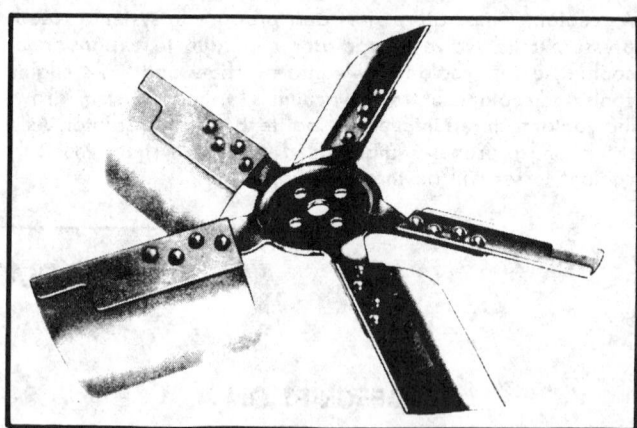

Fig. 2   Flex-Blade Fan

CHRYSLER CORP.

COOLING SYSTEM CAPACITIES			
	Approximate Capacity (Qts.)①		
Application	Standard System	With Air Conditioning	With Maximum Cooling Option②
3.7L (225")			
B & PB150/250			
Automatic Transmission	14	14	14
Manual Transmission	12	14	14
5.2L (318")			
B & PB150/250			
Automatic Transmission	16	17	18
Manual Transmission	16	17	18
B, PB & CB350,			
CB450 & MB250/450			
Automatic Transmission	16	18	19
Manual Transmission	.....	.....	19
5.9L (360")			
B & PB150/250			
Automatic Transmission	14.5	15.5	15.5
Manual Transmission	.....	.....	.....
B, PB & CB350,			
CB450 & MB250/450			
Automatic Transmission	17	18	19
Manual Transmission	.....	.....	.....

① — Add 1 quart if vehicle is equipped with auxiliary heater.
② — Includes trailer towing option.

PRESSURE CAP

Application	psi
All Models	16

THERMOSTAT

Application	①Initial Open	①Full Open
3.7L All Models	195	219
5.2L All Models	195	219
5.9L All Models	195	219

① — Specifications are in °F.

WATER PUMP

"AD", "AW", "PD", "PW", "D" & "W" Models

Removal (3.7L Engines) — Drain cooling system. Loosen alternator, power steering pump or idler pulley, and remove all drive belts. Remove fan, spacer, pulley and bolts as an assembly. Position by-pass hose lower clamp in center of hose and disconnect hose. Remove water pump retaining bolts and remove pump assembly.

Installation — Clean all gasket surfaces, install new hoses (as required) and gaskets. Reverse removal procedure, tighten bolts, adjust drive belt tension and refill cooling system.

Removal (5.2L & 5.9L Engines) — 1) Drain cooling system. If equipped with air conditioning, remove radiator. Loosen power steering and air pumps if equipped. Loosen alternator adjusting bolt and pivot bolt. Remove all drive belts.

2) On vehicles without air conditioning, remove alternator bracket bolts from water pump. Swing alternator out of the way and tighten pivot bolt. On vehicles with air conditioning, remove alternator adjusting bracket and power steering pump bolts and set aside.

3) Remove fan blade, spacer or fluid unit, pulley and bolts as an assembly. Disconnect heater and by-pass hoses. Remove air conditioning compressor pulley and field coil assembly.

CAUTION — *To prevent silicone fluid from draining into fan drive bearing and ruining the lubricant, do not place drive unit with shaft pointing downward.*

4) Remove water pump-to-compressor front mount bracket bolts, and remove bracket. Remove pump retaining bolts and water pump assembly.

Installation — Clean all gasket surfaces, install new hoses (as required) and gaskets. Reverse removal procedure, tighten bolts, adjust drive belt tension and refill cooling system.

"B", "PB", "CB", & "MB" MODELS

Removal (3.7L Engines) — Drain cooling system, loosen alternator, power steering pump or idler pulley, then remove all drive belts. Remove fan spacer, pulley and bolts as an assembly. Position by-pass hose lower clamp in middle of hose and disconnect hose. Remove water pump retaining bolts and remove water pump assembly.

Installation — Clean all gasket surfaces, install new hoses (as required) and gaskets. Reverse removal procedure, tighten bolts, adjust drive belt tension and refill cooling system.

CHRYSLER CORP. (Cont.)

Removal (5.2L & 5.9L Engines) − **1)** Drain cooling system and if equipped with air conditioning, remove radiator and shroud. Loosen alternator adjusting bolts and pivot bolt. Loosen power steering bolts. Remove all drive belts. On engines without air conditoning remove alternator bracket-to-water pump bolts. Swing alternator out of way and tighten pivot bolt.

2) On engines with air conditioning, remove idler pulley assembly, alternator and adjusting bracket. On all models, remove fan, spacer or fluid drive, pulley and bolts as an assembly.

CAUTION − *To prevent silicone fluid from draining into fan drive bearing and ruining lubricant, do not place drive unit with shaft pointing downward.*

3) Disconnect heater, by-pass and radiator hoses. Remove compressor clutch assembly, compressor-to-front mounting bracket bolts and water pump-to-compressor front mount

bracket bolts and bracket. Remove water pump attaching bolts and water pump assembly.

Installation − Clean all gasket surfaces, install new hoses (as required) and gaskets. Reverse removal procedure, tighten bolts, adjust drive belt tension and refill cooling system.

TIGHTENING SPECIFICATIONS

Application	Ft. Lbs.
Water Pump Attaching Bolts	30
Fan Attaching Bolts	15-18
Fluid Fan Drive Bolts	15-18

FORD MOTOR CO.

COOLING SYSTEM CAPACITIES

Application	Approximate Capacity (Qts.)			
	Standard System	Extra Cooling	Super Cooling Option	With Air Conditioning
4.2L (255″) & 5.0L (302″)				
F100/250 & Bronco				
Automatic Transmission	13	14	14	14
Manual Transmission	13	13	14	14
E100/350				
Automatic Transmission	.....	17.5	18.5	18.5
Manual Transmission	15	15	18.5	12.5
4.9L (300″)				
F100/350 & Bronco				
Automatic Transmission	13	13	14	14
Manual Transmission	13	13	14	14
E100/350				
Automatic Transmission	15③	.....	.....	20①②
Manual Transmission	15③	.....	.....	20①②
5.8L (351″)				
F100/350 & Bronco				
Automatic Transmission	15	15	16	16
Manual Transmission	15	15	16	16
E100/150				
Automatic Transmission	20③	20③	21	21
Manual Transmission	.....	.....	.....	15①②
E250/350				
Man. & Auto. Transmission	20	21	28	21
6.6L (400″)				
F350				
Automatic Transmission	16	16	16	16
Manual Transmission	15	15	16	16
E250/350				
Man. & Auto. Transmission	20	21	28	21
7.5L (460″)				
E350				
Man. & Auto. Transmission	28①②	28①②	28①②	28①②

① − Add 1 quart for heater. ② − Add 1.8 quarts for auxiliary heater. ③ − Without air conditioning.

FORD MOTOR CO. (Cont.)

PRESSURE CAP

Application	psi
All Models	13

THERMOSTAT

NOTE – *Due to the different variations of emission control devices and the geographical areas for which the vehicles are manufactured, the thermostats will vary from one model to another. Either a 160°, 180° or a 190° thermostat may be used.*

WATER PUMP

4.9L "E" & "F" MODELS

Removal – Drain cooling system. Loosen alternator adjusting arm bolt and remove drive belt. Remove air conditioning drive belt (if equipped). Remove fan, pulley and bolts from water pump hub. Disconnect heater hose and lower radiator hose at water pump. Remove water pump attaching bolts and water pump assembly.

Installation – Clean all gasket surfaces, install new hoses (as required) and gaskets. Reverse removal procedure, tighten bolts, adjust drive belt tension and refill cooling system.

5.0L & 5.8L (W) F100/250 & BRONCO MODELS

Removal – Drain cooling system. Remove bolts securing fan shroud (if equipped) to radiator and position shroud over fan. Disconnect lower radiator hose, heater hose, and by-pass hose at water pump. Remove drive belts, fan, spacer, pulley and bolts from water pump hub. Remove fan shroud. Loosen alternator pivot bolt and adjusting arm-to-water pump bolt. Remove water pump attaching bolts and water pump assembly.

Installation – Clean all gasket surfaces, install new hoses (as required) and gaskets. Reverse removal procedure, tighten bolts, adjust drive belt tension and refill cooling system.

4.2L, 5.0L, & 5.8L (W) E100/350 MODELS

Removal – **1)** Remove air cleaner and intake duct assembly including closed crankcase ventilation hose and oil breather cap. Drain cooling system. Disconnect radiator hoses at radiator and oil cooler lines (if equipped). Remove radiator attaching bolts and remove radiator.

2) Remove drive belts, fan, spacer, pulley and bolts from water pump hub. Disconnect heater hose and by-pass hose at water pump. Remove water pump attaching bolts and water pump assembly.

Installation – Clean all gasket surfaces, install new hoses (as required) and gaskets. Reverse removal procedure, tighten bolts, adjust drive belt tension and refill cooling system.

5.8L (M) & 6.6L "E", "F", & BRONCO MODELS

Removal – **1)** Drain cooling system and disconnect battery ground cable. Remove fan shroud bolts and position back over engine. Remove fan and spacer from pump. Remove air conditioning drive belt, lower idler pulley and compressor mounting bracket (if equipped).

2) Loosen alternator and remove drive belt. Loosen power steering pump and remove drive belt. Remove water pump pulley. Remove alternator and bracket without disconnecting wires and position out of way.

3) Remove radiator and heater hoses from water pump. Remove water pump attaching bolts and water pump.

Installation – Clean all gasket surfaces, install new hoses (if required) and gasket. Reverse removal procedure, tighten bolts, adjust drive belt tension and refill cooling system.

7.5L "E" MODELS

Removal – **1)** Drain cooling system and remove fan shroud bolts. Remove fan assembly from water pump and remove shroud. Loosen power steering pump bolts. If equipped with air conditioning, loosen compressor top bracket bolts and remove bracket. Remove air conditioning idler arm and bracket assembly. Remove compressor and power steering drive belts.

2) If equipped with air pump, remove pump pulley and belt. Disconnect by-pass hose and remove pump pivot bolt. Loosen adjustment arm and remove air pump. Loosen alternator pivot bolt and remove attaching bolts and spacer. Remove adjustment arm bolt and remove alternator and bracket as an assembly.

3) Remove power steering pump and lay aside. Disconnect radiator lower hose and heater hose from water pump. Loosen by-pass hose clamp at pump and remove attaching bolts and remove water pump.

Installation – Clean all gasket surfaces, install new hoses (as required) and gaskets. Reverse removal procedure, tighten bolts, adjust drive belt tension and refill cooling system.

TIGHTENING SPECIFICATIONS

Application	Ft. Lbs.
All Models	
Water Pump Attaching Bolts	
4.2L, 4.9L, 5.0L, 5.8L, & 6.6L	12-18
7.5L	15-21
Fan-to-Hub Bolts	12-18

GENERAL MOTORS

COOLING SYSTEM CAPACITIES

Application	Approximate Capacity①		
	Standard System Manual Transmission	Heavy Duty Radiator	With Air Conditioning
4.1L (250")			
C & K10	15	15	15.5
C20	15	15	15.5
G10/30	17	17	17
4.8L (292")			
C20	15	15	15.5
C & K30	14	14	15
P10/30	13.5	13.5	.....
5.0L (305")			
C & K10	17.5	17.5	17.5
G10	19	19	20
5.7L (350")			
C & K10/30	17.5	18	18
P20	16.5	17	.....
G10/30	.....	20	20
6.5L (400")			
K20	18	19	20
G20	20	20	20
G30	21	21	21
7.4L (454")			
C20/30	23	23	24
P30	24.5	24.5	24.5

① — Add .5 qt. for automatic transmission.

PRESSURE CAP

Application	psi
All Models	15

THERMOSTAT

Application	① Rating °F
All	195

① — Thermostat should be full open at 25°F above stamped rating and fully closed at 10°F below stamped rating.

WATER PUMP

Removal — 1) Disconnect battery cable and drain cooling system. Remove accessory drive belts and disconnect water hoses from water pump. Remove fan (or fan clutch) to water pump hub attaching bolts and remove fan and pulley.

NOTE — *On some vehicles, it may be necessary to loosen or remove alternator and (if equipped) air conditioning, power steering brackets to prevent removal interference.*

2) Remove pump-to-block attaching bolts and remove water pump.

Installation — Clean mating surfaces of water pump and engine block. Using a new gasket, install water pump making sure attaching bolts are tightened uniformly.

NOTE — *On V8 gasoline engines, apply a ⅛" bead of RTV sealer to sealing edges of water pump legs before installing.*

TIGHTENING SPECIFICATIONS

Application	Ft. Lbs.
Water Pump Attaching Bolts	
6 Cyl. Engines	15
V8 Engines	30
V8 Diesel Engines	13

JEEP

COOLING SYSTEM CAPACITIES

Application	Quarts
All Models	
2.5L Engines	8
4.2L Engines	11
5.0L Engines	13
6.0L Engines	14

PRESSURE CAP

Application	psi
4 Cylinder Engines	14
6 & 8 Cylinder Engines	15

THERMOSTAT

Application	① Initial Open	① Full Open
All Models	192-198	218

① — Specifications are in °F.

WATER PUMP

ALL 4-CYLINDER MODELS

Removal — Drain coolant. Remove drive belts and fan. Disconnect radiator hoses from water pump. Remove water pump attaching bolts, and remove pump.

Installation — Clean gasket surfaces, install new hoses (as required) and gaskets. Reverse removal procedure, tighten bolts, adjust drive belt tension, refill system and check for leaks.

ALL 6-CYLINDER MODELS

Removal — 1) Drain cooling system and disconnect all hoses at water pump. Remove drive belts and separate fan shroud (if equipped) from radiator.

2) Remove fan and hub assembly and remove fan shroud. Remove water pump and gasket.

NOTE — *On some models, fan removal may be easier if shroud is rotated ½ turn.*

Installation — Clean gasket surfaces, install new hoses (as required) and gaskets. Reverse removal procedure, tighten bolts, adjust drive belt tension and refill cooling system.

CAUTION — *California engines with a single drive belt have a reverse rotating water pump and viscous (Tempatrol) fan drive assembly. Components are identified by the words "REVERSE" stamped on the cover of viscous drive and inner side of fan, and "REV" cast into water pump body. Do not install components that are intended for non-single drive belts.*

ALL V8 MODELS

Removal — 1) Drain cooling system and disconnect negative battery cable. Disconnect upper radiator hose at radiator. Loosen all drive belts. Separate fan shroud (if equipped) from radiator and position rearward on engine.

2) Remove fan and hub from water pump. Remove fan and shroud assembly (if equipped) from engine compartment.

3) If equipped with air conditioning, install a double nut on compressor bracket-to-water pump stud and remove stud. This eliminates having to remove the mounting bracket. Remove alternator and mounting bracket assembly (position to one side with wires attached). If equipped with power steering, remove nuts attaching pump to rear half of mounting bracket. Remove bolts attaching front half of bracket to rear half.

4) Remove remaining upper bolt from inner air pump support brace, loosen lower bolt and drop brace away from power steering front bracket. Remove front half of power steering bracket from water pump mounting stud. Disconnect heater hose, by-pass hose and lower hose at water pump. Remove water pump attaching bolts and water pump assembly.

Installation — Clean all gasket surfaces, install new hoses (as required) and gaskets. Reverse removal procedure, tighten nuts and bolts, adjust drive belt tension and refill cooling system.

CAUTION — *Check to be sure wire coil is installed in lower radiator hose. Failure to install this coil will result in the hose collapsing at high engine RPM.*

TIGHTENING SPECIFICATIONS

Application	Ft. Lbs.
Water Pump-to-Block	
2.5L (151″ Engines)	18-33
4.2L (258″ Engines)	9-18
5.0L (304″ Engines)	18-33
6.0L (360″ Engines)	18-33
Front Cover to Engine	
Block Through Water Pump (V8 only)	18-33
Fan Blade-to-Hub	12-25
Thermostat Housing	
2.5L Engines	17-23
All Others	10-18

Section 8

CLUTCHES

CONTENTS

NOTE — ALSO SEE GENERAL INDEX.

IMPORTANT

*Because of the great number of model names used by vehicle manufacturers, accurate identification of models is important.
See Model Identification at the front of this publication.*

Clutches

CLUTCH TROUBLE SHOOTING

CONDITION & POSSIBLE CAUSE	CONDITION & POSSIBLE CAUSE
Chattering or Grabbing • Incorrect Lever Adjustment. • Oil or Grease on Facings. • Loose "U" Joint Flange. • Worn Input Shaft Spline. • Binding Pressure Plate. • Binding Release Lever. • Binding Disc Hub. • Glazed Facings. • Unequal Pressure Plate Contact. • Bent Clutch Disc. • Uneven Spring Pressure. • Incorrect Transmission Alignment. • Incorrect Facings. • Scored Pressure Plate. • Worn Pressure Plate, Disc or Flywheel. • Clutch Disc Hub Sticking on Shaft. • Worn or Binding Release Levers. • Broken or Weak Pressure Springs. • Sticking Clutch Pedal. • Incorrect Disc Facing. • Engine loose in Chassis. **Spinning** • Dry or Worn Bushing. • Misaligned Clutch Housing. • Bent or Distorted Clutch Disc. • Warped Pressure Plate. • Excessive Pedal Free Play. **Dragging** • Oil or Grease on Facings. • Incorrect Lever Adjustment. • Incorrect Pedal Adjustment. • Dust or Dirt on Clutch. • Worn or Broken Facings. • Bent Clutch Disc. • Clutch Disc Hub Binding on Shaft. • Binding Pilot Bushing. • Sticking Release Bearing Sleeve. • Warped Pressure Plate. **Whirring** • Incorrect Pedal Free Play. • Incorrect Transmission Alignment.	**Rattling** • Weak or Broken Release Spring. • Damaged Pressure Plate. • Broken Clutch Return Spring. • Worn Splines in Clutch Disc Hub or Transmission Input Shaft. • Worn Clutch Release Spring. • Dry or Worn Pilot Bushing. • Incorrect Pedal Free Play. • Warp Clutch Disc. **Slipping** • Pressure Springs Worn or Broken. • Worn Facing. • Incorrect Clutch Adjustment. • Oil or Grease on Facings. • Warped Clutch Disc. • Warped on Scored Pressure Plate. • Binding Release Levers. • Binding Clutch Pedal. **Squeaking** • No Lubrication in Release Bearing. • Worn Release Bearing. • Dry or Worn Pilot Bearing. • Pilot Bearing Turning in Crankshaft. • Worn Input Shaft Bearing. • Incorrect Transmission Alignment. • No Lubrication Between Clutch Fork and Pivot. • No Lubrication in Torque Shaft. **Heavy Stiff Pedal** • Dry or Binding Linkage Components. • Sticking Release Bearing Sleeve. • Dry or Binding Pedal Hub. • Pedal Interference With Floorboard or Mats. • Rough, Dry or Binding Pivot Ball, or Fork Pivots. **Grinding** • Dry Release Bearing. • Worn or Dry Pilot Bearing. • Worn Input Shaft Bearing.

CHRYSLER CORP.

Dodge
Plymouth

DESCRIPTION

Clutches used on all Chrysler Corp. vehicles are the single, dry disc type of Borg and Beck design. Adjustment for wear is not provided in clutch itself, however clutch pedal linkage is adjustable to maintain specified pedal free play. Clutch linkage on all models is mechanical type.

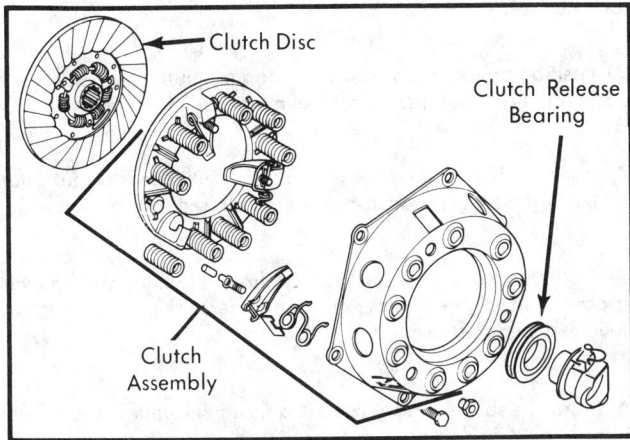

Fig. 1 Exploded View of Chrysler Corp. Borg and Beck Type Clutch Assembly

REMOVAL & INSTALLATION

CLUTCH

NOTE — *For Transfer Case and Manual Transmission removal, see appropriate articles in TRANSFER CASE AND MANUAL TRANSMISSION SERVICING Sections.*

Removal — 1) Remove transfer case (if equipped), transmission and clutch housing pan. Disconnect clutch fork return spring. Remove fork rod spring washer from pin and remove fork rod, adjusting nut, washer and insulator. Remove clutch fork and release bearing (if not removed with transmission).

2) Mark position of clutch cover on flywheel for reassembly. Remove clutch cover bolts by loosening 1 or 2 turns at a time until all bolts are removed. Remove clutch cover and disc from flywheel.

Installation — Make sure clutch surface on flywheel is clean. Align clutch cover and disc using a suitable aligning tool. Make sure clutch cover is installed in original position on flywheel. Tighten clutch cover bolts a few turns at a time, alternately and evenly. Fill bearing sleeve cavity with grease, and apply a thin film to release fork pads. Lubricate clutch fork fingers and pivot contact area. To complete installation, reverse removal procedure.

PILOT BEARING (BUSHING)

Removal — Thread a suitable tapered pilot into bushing, and install puller screw into pilot. Turn puller screw until bushing is removed from crankshaft.

Installation — Soak new bushing in oil before installing. Using suitable tool (SP-3549 or C-4171 on head SP-3551), drive new bushing into crankshaft flush to end. Place one-half teaspoon of grease in the crankshaft cavity forward of the bushing, and coat inner surface of bushing with a light film of grease.

CLUTCH HOUSING ALIGNMENT

NOTE — *If clutch housing is removed while making adjustments or repairs, it will be necessary to check and/or align housing.*

1) Remove 1 flywheel-to-crankshaft bolt and replace with bolt approximately 3" long. Mount dial indicator (C-3339 or equivalent) on bolt using "C" clamp. Position stem of dial indicator on face of clutch housing.

2) Pry crankshaft forward until bottomed against crankshaft thrust bearing. Zero dial indicator. Rotate flywheel using tool (C-771 or equivalent) and note indicator reading, runout should not exceed .006".

3) If runout is greater than .006", loosen housing bolts and insert correct thickness shim between clutch housing and block at point of maximum runout. Reposition stem of dial indicator to inside of pilot bore of clutch housing.

4) Zero dial indicator. Rotate flywheel using tool (C-771 or equivalent) and note indicator reading. Runout should not exceed .008". If runout is greater than .008", offset dowels must be installed in pairs of same size.

5) Determine amount of runout. If runout is between .009-.020", use a .007" offset dowel. If runout is between .022-.034", use a .014" offset dowel and if runout is between .036-.050", use a .021" offset dowel.

6) Remove clutch housing and original dowels from rear face of engine block. Install offset dowels with slots parallel to point of maximum runout and seated in block up to shoulder of offset.

7) Install clutch housing and shim (if used), remount dial indicator and check runout again. Minimum adjustment can be made by turning dowel with a screwdriver until runout is within specification.

ADJUSTMENTS

CLUTCH LINKAGE

Adjust clutch fork push rod to obtain specified free play at clutch fork push rod pivot pin. This free play will provide correct pedal free play of approximately 1".

Clutch Fork Free Play	
Application	**Free Play**
All Models	3/32"

TIGHTENING SPECIFICATIONS	
Application	**Ft. Lbs.**
Clutch Cover-to-Flywheel Bolts	
5/16"	17
3/8"	30
Clutch Fork Pivot Bolts	17
Flywheel Bolts	55
Housing-to-Engine Block Bolts	
7/16"	50
3/8"	30
Transmission-to-Clutch Housing	50

Clutches

FORD

DESCRIPTION

Two different types of clutches are used in Ford vehicles. Both types are single plate, dry types, with one being non-centrifugal and the other being semi-centrifugal. Clutch release is accomplished through mechanical linkage. The pedal pressure is transmitted through a series of rods and an equalizer shaft.

REMOVAL & INSTALLATION

CLUTCH

Removal & Installation — Raise and support vehicle under frame. Disconnect clutch fork return spring and clutch fork push rod at clutch fork. Remove transmission. *See appropriate article in MANUAL TRANSMISSION SERVICING Section.* Remove starter and clutch housing. Mark flywheel and clutch cover for reassembly, then loosen clutch cover attaching bolts evenly until clutch cover spring tension is released. Remove bolts and remove clutch assembly from vehicle. To install, clean flywheel surface, and reverse removal procedure. Tighten bolts evenly and alternately to specification.

ADJUSTMENT

CLUTCH PEDAL FREE TRAVEL

All Models — 1) The amount of pedal movement from full stop to point where clutch release bearing contacts clutch fingers is pedal free travel.

2) Specified pedal free travel is ¾-1½". If not to specification, adjust as follows: Remove retracting spring. Loosen both lock nuts on rod.

3) Position bullet end of rod tight against clutch release lever. Push rod tight against arm to eliminate all free play.

4) Insert a .135" thick spacer or gauge between lock nut and bullet. Tighten nut against spacer with all free play eliminated.

5) Tighten second lock nut against first, finger tight. Remove spacer and tighten lock nuts together. This should give specified pedal free play.

6) If not to specification, repeat adjustment until correct free play is obtained.

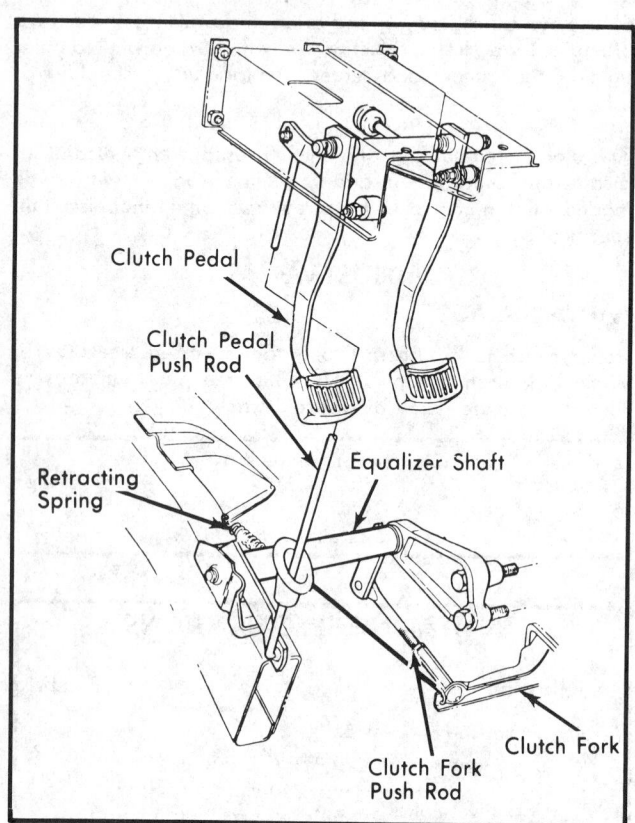

Fig. 1 Assembled View of Typical Clutch Linkage

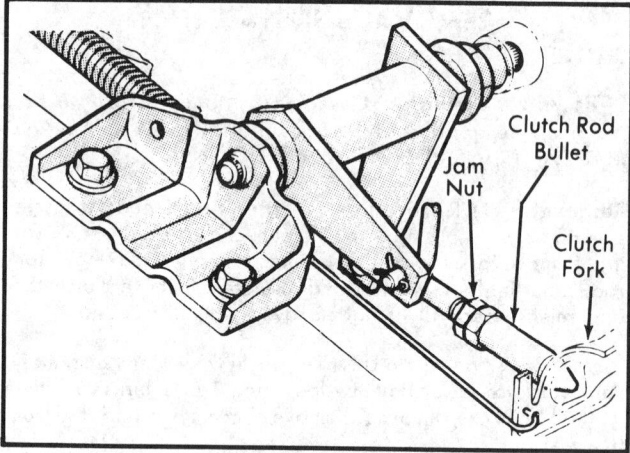

Fig. 2 Clutch Pedal Free Travel Adjustment

TIGHTENING SPECIFICATIONS

Application	Ft. Lbs.
Clutch Cover-to-Flywheel	20-29
Clutch Housing-to-Engine Block	40-50
Transmission-to-Clutch Housing	42-50
Adjusting Nut Lock Nuts	15-20

GENERAL MOTORS

Chevrolet
GMC

DESCRIPTION

Chevrolet and GMC vehicles incorporate two types of clutches. Both a coil spring and a diaphragm spring type clutch is used. Coil spring type clutch utilizes three release levers to provide pressure plate actuation, and coil springs to provide pressure plate tension. Diaphragm spring type clutch utilizes a single, slotted diaphragm type spring to provide both pressure plate action and tension. All vehicle models use a mechanical type linkage to actuate clutch. Removal and installation procedures and adjustments are the same for both Chevrolet and GMC.

REMOVAL & INSTALLATION

CLUTCH

Removal & Installation — Raise and support vehicle under frame and remove transmission. See *appropriate article in MANUAL TRANSMISSION SERVICING Section.* Disconnect rod and return spring at clutch fork. Remove throw-out bearing from clutch fork and remove clutch fork. Mark position of clutch cover on flywheel for reassembly. Install a suitable tool (J-5824) in clutch disc for support. Loosen clutch plate bolts one or two turns at a time until clutch plate spring tension is released. Remove clutch pilot tool and remove clutch plate and disc. To install, reverse removal procedure, making sure clutch hub and pilot bearing are aligned.

ADJUSTMENT

CLUTCH PEDAL FREE PLAY

"G" Models — Disconnect return spring at clutch fork. Loosen clutch fork swivel lock nut, and force push rod toward rear until clutch throw-out bearing just contacts clutch release levers. Rotate push rod adjusting nut until ¼" clearance between nut and swivel is obtained. Tighten clutch fork swivel lock nut, and check pedal free travel.

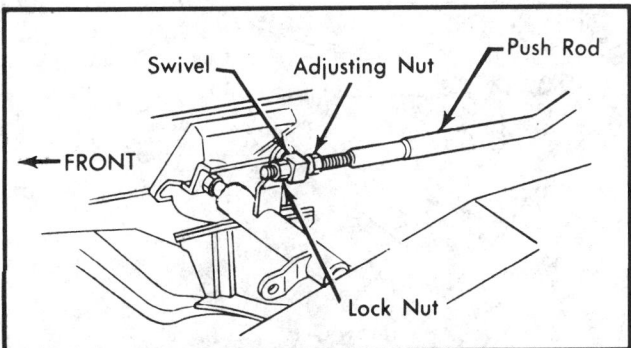

Fig. 1   "G" Models Free Play Adjustment

P30 W/Propeller Shaft Parking Brake — Disconnect clutch fork return spring, and loosen clutch swivel lock nut. Move clutch fork toward rear until throw-out bearing just contacts clutch release levers. Rotate clutch equalizer shaft until clutch pedal is seated against pedal stop. Turn clutch fork push rod in swivel to obtain ¼ -5⁄16" clearance between adjustment nut and shoulder on clutch fork push rod. Tighten swivel lock nut, and check pedal free play.

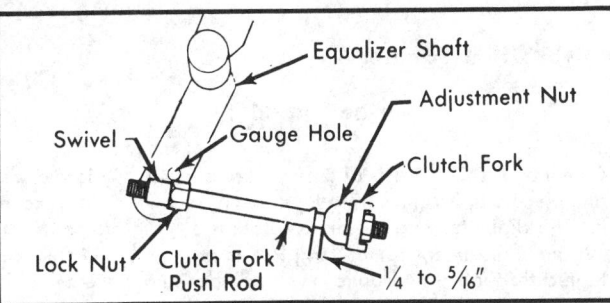

Fig. 2   P30 With Propeller Shaft Parking Brake Free Play Adjustment

All Other Models — Disconnect clutch pedal return spring at clutch fork. Rotate clutch equalizer shaft until clutch pedal is seated against pedal stop. Force clutch fork push rod toward rear until throw-out bearing just contacts clutch release levers. Loosen clutch swivel lock nut, and adjust swivel until swivel can be easily inserted in gauge hole of equalizer shaft. Remove swivel from gauge hole and install in equalizer shaft lower hole. Tighten swivel lock nut and check pedal free play.

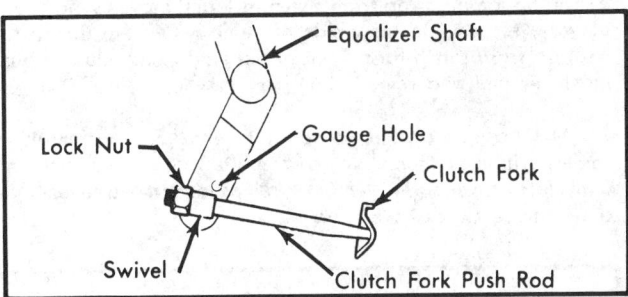

Fig. 3   "C" and "K" Models Free Play Adjustment

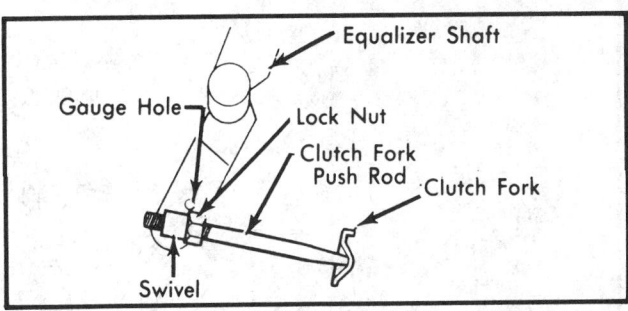

**Fig. 4   P10 & P30 Models Free Play Adjustment
(Exc. Motor Home)**

Clutch Pedal Free Play	
Application	**Free Play**
"C" & "K" Models	1⅜"-1⅝"
P30 W/Propeller Shaft Parking Brake	1⅜"-1⅝"
All Other Models	1¼"-1½"

TIGHTENING SPECIFICATIONS	
Application	**Ft. Lbs.**
Clutch Cover-to-Flywheel Bolts	30
Clutch Housing-to-Engine Bolts	30
Transmission-to-Clutch Housing Bolts	
3 Speed Transmission	75
4 Speed Transmission	75

JEEP — HYDRAULIC

4-Cyl. "CJ" & Scrambler

DESCRIPTION

Clutch assembly consists of a single dry-disc driven plate and a one-piece diaphragm spring type clutch cover. The clutch cover is 9" in diameter and the driven plate is 8½" in diameter. No internal adjustment for driven plate is provided. Clutch is actuated through a hydraulic clutch cylinder and slave cylinder.

REMOVAL & INSTALLATION

CLUTCH ASSEMBLY

Removal — 1) Raise and support vehicle under frame and remove transmission. *See appropriate article in MANUAL TRANSMISSION SERVICING Section.* Remove bolts attaching slave cylinder to clutch housing.

2) Disengage push rod from clutch fork and move cylinder out of way, securing to underside of vehicle. Remove throw-out bearing from clutch fork. Remove bolts attaching clutch housing to engine and remove housing.

3) Mark position of clutch cover on flywheel for reassembly in same position. Loosen clutch cover bolts 1 or 2 turns at a time until clutch cover spring tension is released. Remove cover bolts and remove clutch cover and disc.

Installation — Check all components for wear or damage and replace as necessary. Using a suitable clutch alignment tool, align clutch disc and loosely install clutch cover, noting alignment marks made during removal. To avoid warping the clutch cover, tighten the cover attaching bolts a few turns at a time only. Tighten clutch cover bolts alternately and evenly to 23 ft. lbs. Reverse removal procedures to complete installation.

Removal — 1) Disconnect hydraulic line at clutch master cylinder and cap line and cylinder opening to prevent dirt from entering. From inside vehicle, remove cotter pin and washer retaining cylinder push rod on clutch pedal.

2) Slide push rod off pedal pivot. Remove nuts attaching clutch master cylinder to mounting studs on dash panel and remove cylinder.

Installation — Reverse removal procedure and bleed hydraulic system.

CLUTCH SLAVE CYLINDER

Removal — 1) Disconnect hydraulic line at clutch slave cylinder and cap line to prevent fluid loss. Remove clutch fork lever-to-cylinder push rod retaining spring.

2) Remove bolts attaching slave cylinder to clutch housing and remove slave cylinder, heat shield, clutch fork pivot, washer and seal.

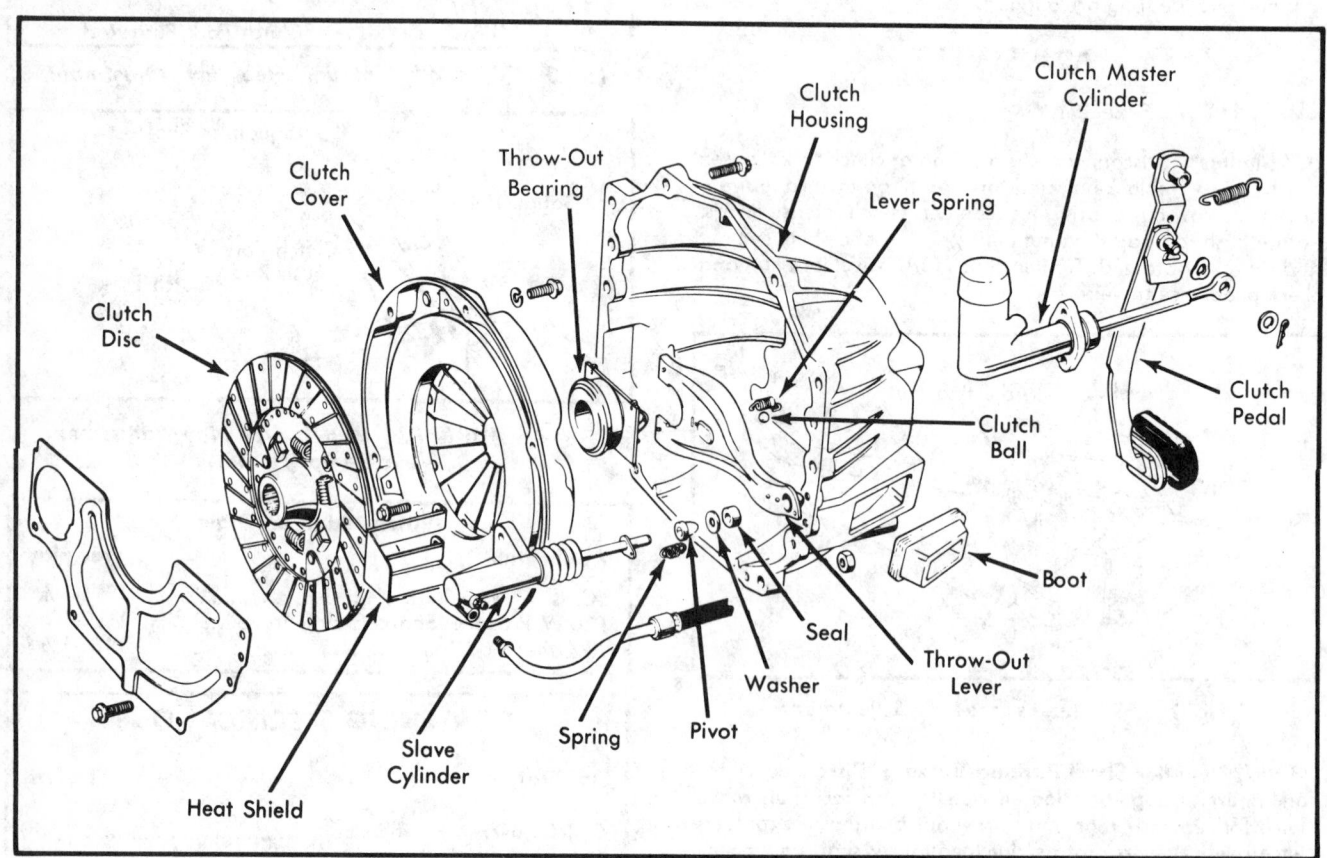

Fig. 1 Exploded View of Hydraulic Clutch Assembly ("CJ" & Scrambler With 4-Cylinder Engine)

JEEP — HYDRAULIC (Cont.)

Installation — Reverse removal procedure and bleed hydraulic system.

OVERHAUL

CLUTCH MASTER CYLINDER

Disassembly — 1) Remove reservoir cap and rubber cover. Remove push rod dust cover using screwdriver to pry cover off cylinder and discard dust cover. Remove snap ring retaining push rod in cylinder bore and discard snap ring.

2) Remove push rod, retaining washer and seal as an assembly. Discard push rod seal. Remove plunger, valve spring and valve stem assembly from cylinder bore by lightly tapping cylinder body on wood block.

3) Compress valve spring slightly and pry tab of valve stem retainer upward to release retainer, spring and stem assembly from plunger. Remove seal from plunger and discard. Remove spring retainer and valve stem from valve spring.

NOTE — *Retainer tab is located in rectangular slot in side of stem retainer. Use thin blade screwdriver to pry upward.*

4) Remove valve stem from retainer and remove spring washer and stem tip seal from end of valve stem amd discard stem tip seal and spring washer. Clean all parts thoroughly with brake fluid or brake cleaning solvent only. Inspect cylinder bore for wear and/or nicks, scores or damage. Replace if necessary.

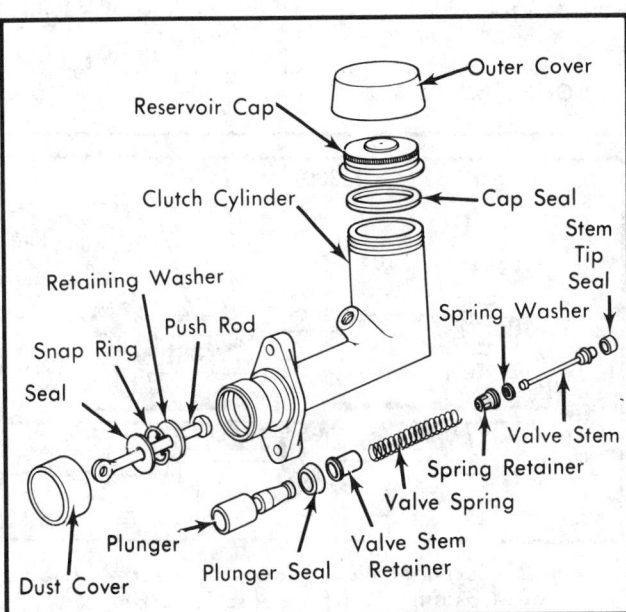

Fig. 2 Exploded View of Clutch Master Cylinder Assembly

Reassembly — Reverse disassembly procedure and note the following:

1) Lubricate cylinder bore with brake fluid. Make sure lip of plunger seal faces stem end of plunger and stem tip seal is installed so seal shoulder fits in undercut at end of valve stem.

2) When end of valve stem passes through stem retainer and seats in small bore in end of plunger, bend retainer tab downward to lock stem and retainer on plunger.

CLUTCH SLAVE CYLINDER

Disassembly — 1) Clean cylinder exterior thoroughly. Remove dust boot from cylinder. Remove cylinder push rod, plunger and spring as an assembly. Remove spring and seal from plunger.

2) Remove snap ring retaining push rod in plunger and remove push rod and boot. Remove boot from push rod. Clean all parts thoroughly with brake fluid or brake cleaning solvent. Inspect cylinder bore for wear and/or nicks, scores or damage. Replace if necessary.

Reassembly — Reverse disassembly procedure and note the following: Lubricate cylinder bore and seal with brake fluid and assemble.

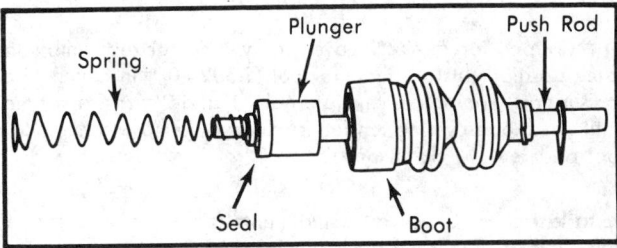

Fig. 3 Exploded View of Clutch Slave Cylinder

ADJUSTMENT

NOTE — *Due to automatic wear adjustment, no adjustment is necessary except bleeding of hydraulic system.*

HYDRAULIC SYSTEM BLEEDING

1) Make sure clutch master cylinder is full of brake fluid (SAE J-1703 or DOT 3 or equivalent). Compress slave cylinder plunger by pushing forward on clutch fork as far as possible. Attach rubber hose to bleeder screw, then immerse other end of hose in glass container ½ full of brake fluid.

2) Loosen bleeder screw. Depress and hold clutch pedal to end of its travel. Tighten bleeder screw and release pedal. Repeat bleeding operation until fluid entering container is free of bubbles. Refill clutch master cylinder to level mark on reservoir.

NOTE — *DO NOT allow reservoir to run out of fluid during bleeding operation.*

TIGHTENING SPECIFICATIONS

Application	Ft. Lbs.
Clutch Cover-to-Flywheel Bolts	23
Clutch Housing-to-Engine Bolts	54
Clutch Housing-to-Transmission Bolts	54
Flywheel-to-Engine Bolts	65
Clutch Cylinder-to-Dash Panel	11
Clutch Cylinder-to-Clutch Housing	15

JEEP — MECHANICAL LINKAGE

All Models
Except 4-Cyl. "CJ" & Scrambler

DESCRIPTION

Clutch assembly consists of a single dry-disc driven plate, 2 types of clutch covers; a 10½" diameter direct spring pressure type; and an 11" semi-centrifugal type. No internal adjustment for clutch disc wear is provided, but release lever height should be checked and adjusted. Clutch is actuated through mechanical type linkage.

REMOVAL & INSTALLATION

CLUTCH

Removal — 1) Raise and support vehicle under frame and remove transmission. See appropriate article in MANUAL TRANSMISSION SERVICING Section. Disconnect rod and return spring at clutch fork. Remove throw-out bearing from clutch fork, then remove clutch fork.

2) Mark position of clutch cover on flywheel for reassembly in same position. Install aligning tool (J-5824-01) in clutch disc for support. Loosen clutch plate bolts 1 and 2 turns at a time until clutch plate spring tension is released. Remove clutch pilot tool and remove clutch and disc.

Installation — Check all components for wear or damage and replace as necessary. Using a suitable clutch alignment tool and noting alignment marks made during removal, align clutch disc and loosely install pressure plate. Reverse removal procedure to complete installation.

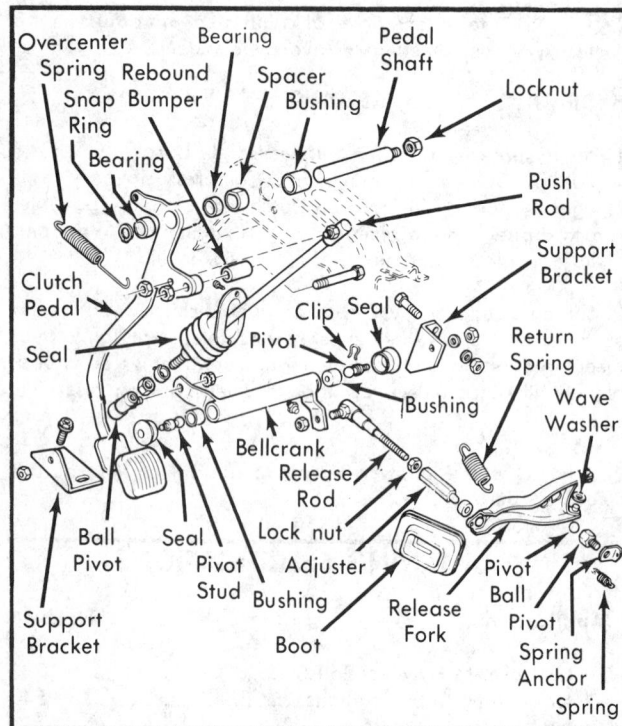

Fig. 1   Exploded View of Clutch Linkage Assembly Cherokee, Wagoneer and Truck Shown ("CJ" & Scrambler Models Similar)

ADJUSTMENT

CLUTCH LINKAGE

Raise clutch pedal up to stop and adjust lower ball pivot assembly on pedal-to-bellcrank rod until inner bellcrank lever is parallel with front face of clutch housing. Adjust clutch fork release rod to obtain specified pedal free play.

Clutch Pedal Free Play Specifications	
Application	**Specification**
"CJ" & Scrambler	1-1¼"
All Others	⅜-⅝"

CLUTCH RELEASE LEVER

Position a suitable gauge plate (J-1048) on flywheel. Position clutch cover over gauge plate with release fingers aligned with machined lands on plate. Gauge plate hub should be centered between release levers. Attach cover to flywheel, tightening cover screws in rotation, one or two turns at a time. Set each release lever by depressing two or three times. Measure height of each lever in relation to plate hub using a suitable height gauge tool (J-23330). Tool has four different dimensional settings. Turn adjusting lever nuts until all three levers are at specified height. Work levers up and down two or three times and recheck measurements.

Clutch Release Lever Height Specifications	
Application	**Height**
"CJ" & Scrambler	3/32-7/64"
All Others	3/16"

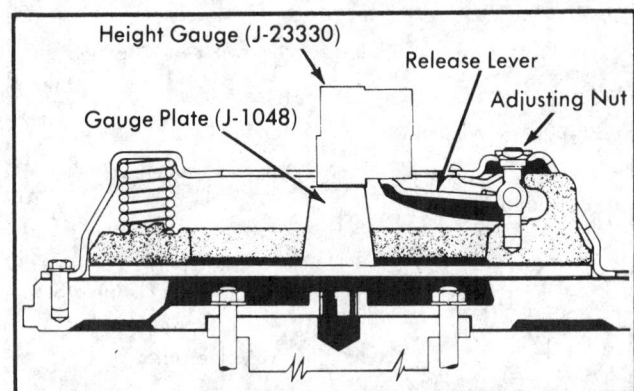

Fig. 2   Sectional View Showing Correct Method of Measuring Clutch Release Lever Height

TIGHTENING SPECIFICATIONS	
Application	**Ft. Lbs.**
Clutch Cover-to-Flywheel Bolts......................................	40
Clutch Housing-to-Engine Bolt	
6 Cylinder Models Top..	35
6 Cylinder Models Bottom....................................	45
8 Cylinder Models...	30
Transmission-to-Clutch Housing Bolts	55

Section 9
DRIVE AXLES

Contents

NOTE — ALSO SEE GENERAL INDEX

IMPORTANT

Because of the great number of model names used by vehicle manufacturers, accurate identification of models is important. See Model Identification at the front of this publication.

Drive Axles

DRIVE AXLE TROUBLE SHOOTING

CONDITION & POSSIBLE CAUSE	CONDITION & POSSIBLE CAUSE
Rear Wheel Noise • Wheel Loose • Faulty, Worn Wheel Bearings **Axle Shaft Noise** • Misaligned Axle Housing • Bent or Sprung Axle • Pinion Bearing End Play • Excessive Ring Gear Backlash • Incorrect Pinion Bearing Adjustment • Loose Companion Flange Nut • Incorrect Wheel Bearing Adjustment • Scuffed Tooth Contact Surfaces **Rear Axle Breakage** • Incorrect Wheel Bearing Adjustment • Misaligned Axle Housing • Vehicle Overloaded • Clutch Grabs **Differential Case Breakage** • Incorrect Differential Bearing Adjustment • Excessive Ring Gear Clearance • Vehicle Overloaded • Erratic Clutch Operation **Broken Differential Side Gear** • Excessive Housing Deflection • Worn Thrust Washers • Misaligned Axle Housing	**Differential Gears Scored** • Insufficient Lubricant • Incorrect Lubricant • One Wheel Spins Excessively **Ring Gear and Pinion Tooth Breakage** • Vehicle Overloaded • Erratic Clutch Operation • Ice Spotted Pavement • Normal Fatigue • Incorrect Adjustment **Rear Axle Noise** • Insufficient Lubricant • Incorrect Ring Gear and Pinion Adjustment • Worn Ring Gear or Pinion Teeth • Loose Pinion Bearings • Loose Differential Gear Bearings • Misaligned Ring Gear • Loose Carrier Bolts **Loss of Lubricant** • Lubricant Level Too High • Worn Axle Shaft Seals • Cracked Housing • Worn Drive Pinion Seal • Scored or Worn Companion Flange **Unit Overheats** • Lubricant Level Low • Incorrect Lubricant • Bearings Adjusted Too Tight • Insufficient Ring Gear to Pinion Clearance

Drive Axles

GEAR TOOTH CONTACT PATTERNS

PRELIMINARY INSPECTION

Wipe lubricant from internal parts, then rotate gears and inspect for wear or damage. Mount a dial indicator to housing and check backlash at several points around ring gear. Backlash must be within specifications at all points. If no defects are found, check gear tooth pattern.

GEAR TOOTH CONTACT PATTERN

NOTE — *Drive pattern should be well centered on ring gear teeth. Coast pattern should be centered but may be slightly toward toe of ring gear teeth.*

Paint ring gear teeth with a suitable marking compound, then wrap a cloth or rope around drive pinion flange to act as a brake. Rotate ring gear until a clear tooth pattern is obtained. Gear tooth contact pattern will disclose whether correct pinion bearing mounting shim has been installed and drive gear backlash set properly. Backlash between drive gear and pinion must be maintained within specified limits until correct tooth pattern is obtained.

GEAR BACKLASH & PINION SHIM CHANGES

NOTE — *Backlash is adjusted by shifting shims from one side of differential case to the other or by turning adjusting nuts on which differential side bearings ride. Changing pinion shims changes distance from top of pinion to centerline of ring gear.*

1) With no change in backlash, moving pinion further from ring gear moves drive pattern toward heel and top of tooth, and moves coast pattern toward toe and top of tooth.

2) With no change in backlash, moving pinion closer to ring gear moves drive pattern toward toe and bottom of tooth, and moves coast pattern toward heel and bottom of tooth.

3) With no change in pinion shim thickness, an increase in backlash moves ring gear further from pinion. Drive pattern moves toward heel and top of tooth, and coast pattern moves toward heel and top of tooth.

4) With no change in pinion shim thickness, a decrease in backlash moves ring gear closer to pinion gear. Drive pattern moves toward toe and bottom of tooth, and coast pattern moves toward toe and bottom of tooth.

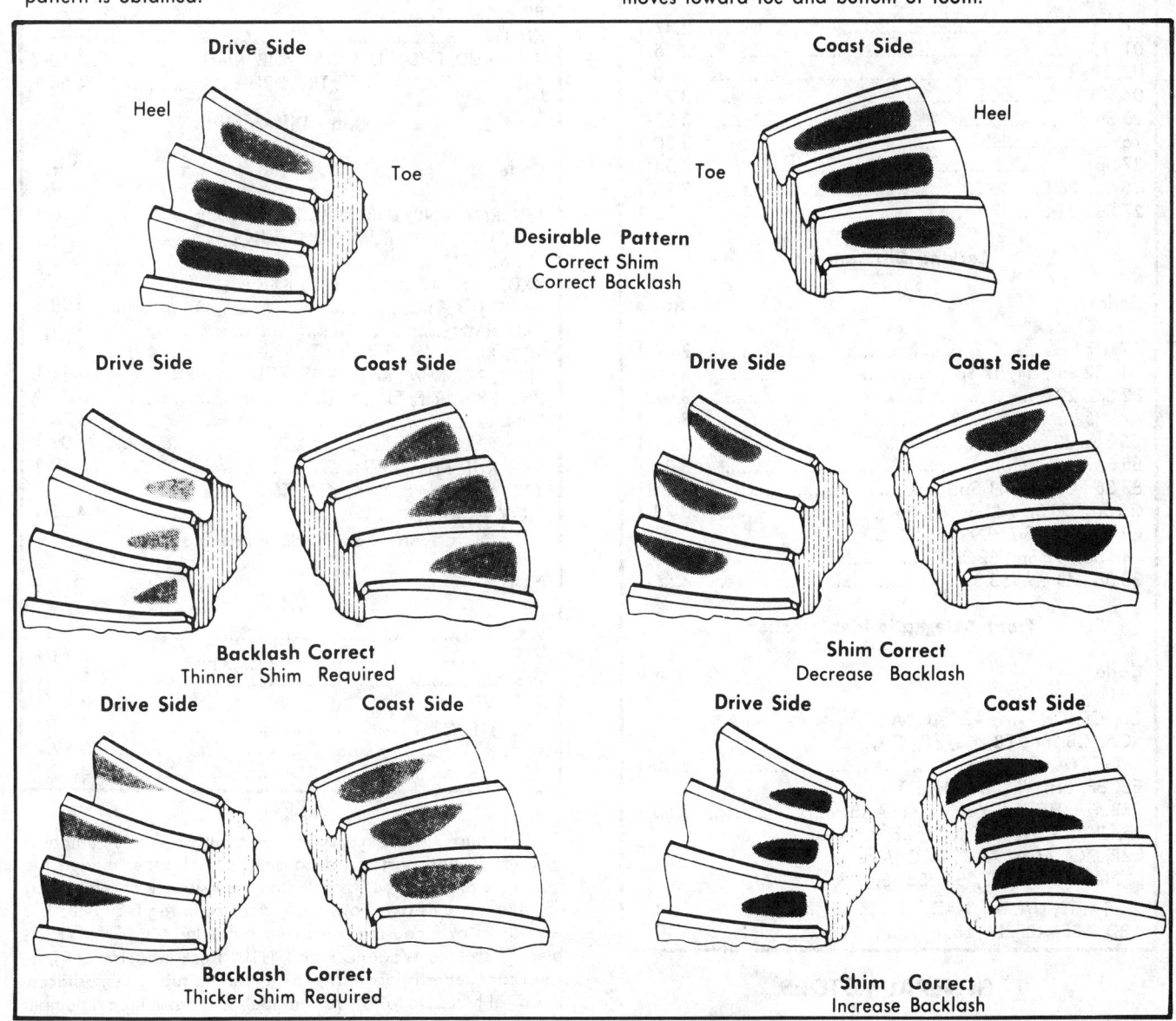

Fig. 1 Drive Axle Gear Tooth Pattern

Drive Axles

AXLE RATIO IDENTIFICATION

CHRYSLER CORP.

A metal tag is attached to one of the rear axle housing cover bolts. Tag gives number of teeth for ring gear and pinion gear. To obtain gear ratio, divide larger number by smaller number.

FORD

The axle ratio code is stamped on the Vehicle Rating Plate located on the rear face of left door on all model except Bronco. On Bronco models plate is located on the inside panel of glove box door. Models with Spicer (Dana) rear axles have an additional tag bolted to drive axle that contains drive axle ratio code. Code designations are as follows:

Rear Axle Ratio Identification (Ford) Conventional Differentials

Code	Ratio
07, 17	2.47:1
01, 13	2.75:1
02, 14, 32 Sp.	3.00:1
04, 15	3.25:1
25 Sp.	3.33:1
16	3.50:1
37 Sp.	3.54:1
36 Sp., 38 Sp., 46 Sp.	3.73:1
27 Sp., 31 Sp., 47 Sp.	4.10:1

Locking Differentials

Code	Ratio
A7, H7	2.47:1
A1, C2 Sp., H4, 32 Sp.	3.00:1
B2 Sp., 22 Sp.	3.07:1
A4, H5	3.25:1
C3 Sp., 23 Sp.	3.31:1
B5 Sp.	3.33:1
B7 Sp., C7 Sp., 41 Sp.	3.54:1
C6 Sp., D6 Sp., 42 Sp. 51 Sp.	3.73:1
C1 Sp., D3 Sp., D7 Sp., E2 Sp., 43 Sp., 52 Sp., 62 Sp.	4.10:1
28 Sp., 44 Sp., 53 Sp.	4.56:1

Front Axle Ratio Identification

Code	Ratio
CE, CF, CH, AA, AB, AC, AG, CA, CB, FA, FB, FC, FF, GA, GC, YA, YD	3.00:1
EE, EF, EH, VE, VF, VH, EA, EB, HA, HC, KA, KB, KC, KF, AAB	3.50:1
JE, JF, JG, NE, NF, NG, ZE, ZF, ZG, ACA, ACB, ACC, MA, NA, RA, RB, RF, SA, SB, SF, TA, TE, UA, UD, AAD	3.54:1
ABD, ABE, ABF, LA, LB, LF	4.10:1

GENERAL MOTORS

Identification code for rear axles is stamped on rear surface of right rear axle tube. Identification code for front axles is stamped on top rear of left axle tube. On Dana built front axles, axle ratio code is on tape stripe around right front axle tube.

Rear Axle Ratio Identification (General Motors) Conventional Differentials

Code	Ratio
TFR, TFM, TFD, TFT, TFC, TNA, RNA, TFW, TEX	2.56:1
TAJ, TDA, TAY, TAA, TDF, RUR, TAF, TDJ	2.73:1
TBA, TBK, KXC, KXA, KXJ, KXM, RYJ, TBW, TBF	3.08:1
RMR, KKA, RMM	3.21:1
TKK, TKM, TKN, TKR	3.23:1
TCH, RCA, RCX, RKB, KHN, KHU, KDB, RCH, RZK, KHJ, KMK, TCD, RCS	3.42:1
RBZ, RJB, RBC, KBM, RKJ, TJK, KBK, TJN, TJS	3.73:1
RRM	3.75:1
KND	4.09:1
RHN, KUD, RHD, KUN, RHC, KUB, KMH	4.10:1
TRB, KSF, KSZ, KRJ, KFT, TRB, KRU	4.56:1

Locking Differentials

Code	Ratio
TFU, RNA, RNB, TNB, RNC, TFY, TFZ	2.56:1
TDB, TDD, RUK, RUM, TDH, RUN, TDM, TDN	2.73:1
KXD, KXH, KXK, RYA, RYF, KXR, RYH, TBY, TBB	3.08:1
KKD, RMN	3.21:1
RCB, RCZ, KZH, RZH, KHT, KDA, RCR, RZJ, KHM, KHW, KHS, RCU	3.42:1
RBD, KBW, RJF, TJM, KKU, TJR, TJT	3.73:1
RRN	3.75:1
KNF	4.09:1
RHR, KUF, RHM, KUR	4.10:1
TRC, KSH, KWB, KRK, KFZ, TRC, KRW, KSU	4.56:1

Front Axle Ratio Identification

Code	Ratio
WK	2.56:1
WA	2.73:1
WB	3.08:1
WC, WD	3.23:1
WF, WH, WJ	3.42:1
WM, WW	3.73:1
WY	4.10:1

JEEP

On "CJ" and Scrambler models, the front axle code number is cast into bottom surface of housing. On all other models the front axle code number is cast into upper surface of reinforcing rib at left side of axle housing. A gear ratio tag is attached to left side of axle housing cover on front axles. On "CJ", Scrambler, Cherokee, Wagoneer and "J10" truck models, rear axle ratio code letter is located on axle housing tube boss, adjacent to dowel hole. On "J20" truck models, rear axle model number is cast into boss on lower right side of axle housing, adjacent to housing cover.

Drive Axles

AXLE RATIO IDENTIFICATION (Cont.)

<table>
<tr><td colspan="2">Axle Ratio Identification
(Jeep)
Conventional Differential</td></tr>
<tr><td>Code</td><td>Ratio</td></tr>
<tr><td>AA</td><td>2.73:1</td></tr>
<tr><td>BB</td><td>3.31:1</td></tr>
<tr><td>A</td><td>3.54:1</td></tr>
<tr><td>GG</td><td>3.73:1</td></tr>
</table>

<table>
<tr><td colspan="2">Axle Ratio Identification
(Jeep)
Trac-Lok Differential</td></tr>
<tr><td>Code</td><td>Ratio</td></tr>
<tr><td>DD</td><td>2.73:1</td></tr>
<tr><td>CC</td><td>3.31:1</td></tr>
<tr><td>N</td><td>3.54:1</td></tr>
<tr><td>Q</td><td>3.73:1</td></tr>
</table>

CHRYSLER CORP. 8⅜″ & 9¼″ RING GEAR

**Dodge & Plymouth
All 150 Models**

DESCRIPTION

The axle assembly is the hypoid gear type with an integral carrier housing. It is used on light duty vehicles with semi-floating axles. The pinion bearing preload adjustment is made with a collapsible spacer. The differential bearing preload adjustment is made with the adjusting nuts on which the bearing cups seat. A removable housing cover permits inspection and minor servicing of differential without removal from vehicle. Service procedures are the same for both size assemblies, except for some tightening specifications and special tool numbers.

AXLE RATIO & IDENTIFICATION

A small metal tag attached to rear axle housing cover bolt identifies axle ratio. Chrysler Corp. also uses Spicer (Dana) axles for some applications. To distinguish these models from Chrysler Corp. models, refer to *Spicer (Dana) axle articles in this Section.*

REMOVAL & INSTALLATION

AXLE SHAFTS & BEARINGS

Removal — 1) Raise vehicle, then remove wheel, tire and brake drum. Loosen housing cover attaching bolts to drain lubricant, then remove housing cover. Remove pinion shaft lock screw and differential pinion shaft. Force axle shaft toward center of vehicle, then remove "C" washer lock from groove in axle shaft.

2) Pull axle shaft out of housing, using care not to damage roller bearing. Remove oil seal from housing bore. To remove the axle shaft bearing from the axle housing, use suitable tool (C-4167). Attach tool (C-637) to end of selected remover, using a slide hammer motion, remove axle shaft bearing and inspect. Discard if axle or bearing shows any signs of brinnelling, spalling or pitting. Dents caused by axle shaft splines should be polished smooth, or rubber on outside diameter of seal will be torn and seal leakage will result. Inspect both axle and bearing. If either show signs of excessive wear, discard bearing.

NOTE — *Always install new axle shaft oil seal.*

Installation — 1) Clean all parts thoroughly. Install axle shaft bearing squarely into housing bore, making sure bearing is bottomed against shoulder in bore. Oil and install oil seal in housing bore. Slide axle shaft into place being careful not to damage oil seal.

2) Install "C" washer lock into groove in axle shaft, then pull outward on axle shaft so that "C" washer lock seats in counterbore of differential side gear.

3) Install differential pinion shaft through case and pinions, aligning hole in shaft with lock screw hole in case. Install pinion shaft lock screw and tighten securely. Install housing cover and identification tag.

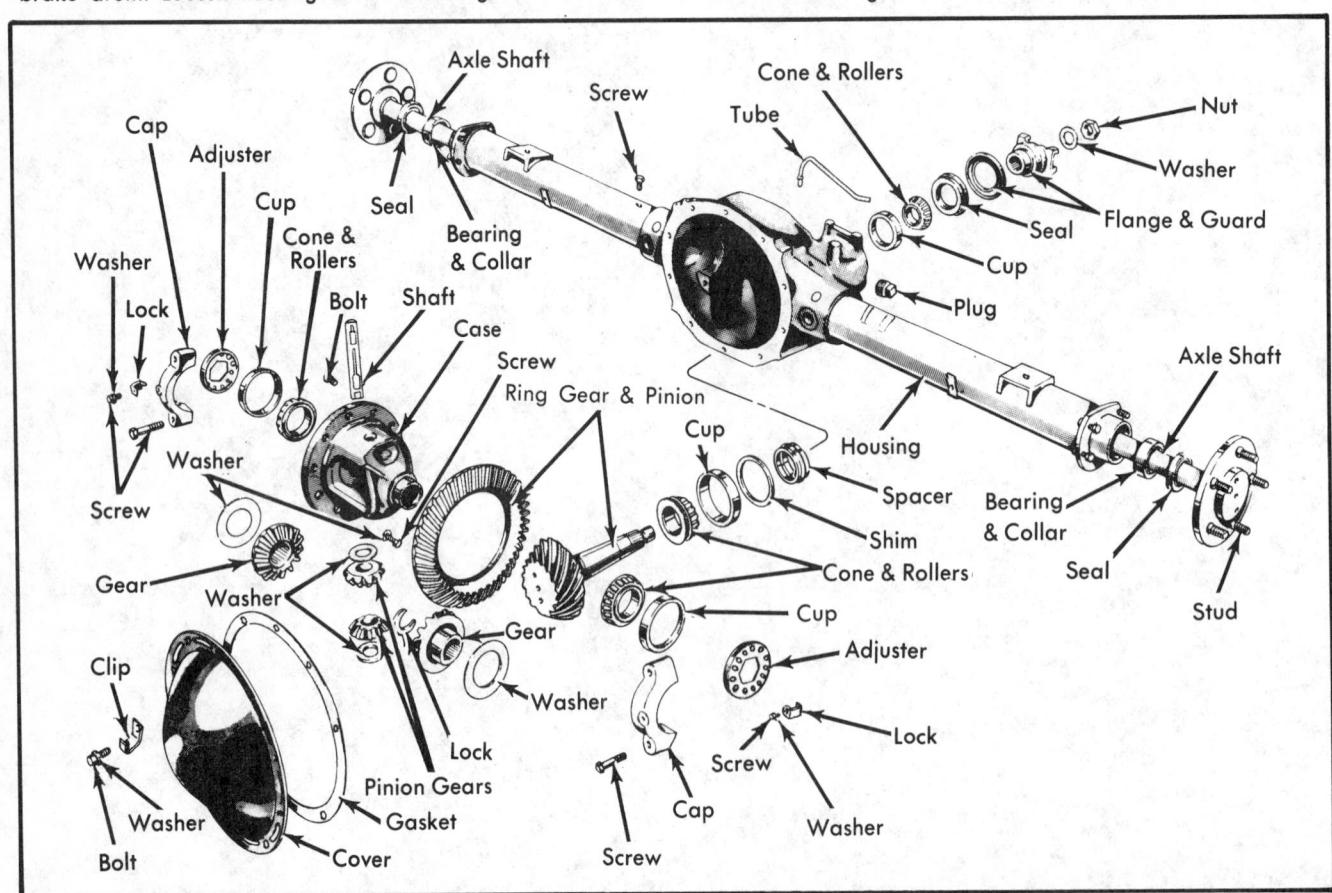

**Fig. 1 Exploded View of Chrysler Corp. Drive Axle Assembly
(8⅜″ Shown — 9¼″ Similar)**

CHRYSLER CORP. 8⅜" & 9¼" RING GEAR (Cont.)

PINION FLANGE & SEAL

Removal — 1) Raise vehicle, mark propeller shaft universal joint, drive pinion flange and pinion stem for reassembly. Disconnect propeller shaft and tie out of way.

2) Remove rear wheels and brake drums to prevent false preload reading. Using an INCH Lb. torque wrench, measure and record pinion bearing preload. Remove drive pinion nut and pull off flange using a suitable puller. Pry out oil seal, taking care not to damage machined surface.

Installation — 1) Install new pinion oil seal squarely into bore in housing until seal flange seats against housing flange face. Position pinion flange on pinion stem, making sure marks are aligned, then install pinion washer (convex side out) and nut. Tighten nut to specifications and rotate pinion through several revolutions to be sure bearing rollers are properly seated.

NOTE — *Outside diameter of seal is precoated with a special sealer, so no sealing compound is required.*

2) Measure pinion bearing preload. Continue tightening pinion nut until preload is same as that noted before disassembly. Under no circumstances should preload be more than 10 INCH lbs. over original setting.

CAUTION — *Under no circumstances should pinion nut be backed off to lessen preload. If desired preload is exceeded, a new collapsible spacer MUST be installed, and nut retightened until proper preload is obtained.*

AXLE ASSEMBLY

Removal & Installation — 1) Raise vehicle and block brake pedal in "Up" position. Remove wheels, tires and brake drums. Disconnect brake lines at wheel cylinders and cap to prevent fluid loss. Disconnect parking brake cables.

2) Mark propeller shaft universal joint, drive pinion flange and pinion stem for reassembly. Disconnect propeller shaft and tie out of way. Remove shock absorbers, rear spring "U" bolts and remove rear axle assembly. To install, reverse removal procedure.

OVERHAUL

DISASSEMBLY

NOTE — *It is not necessary to remove complete rear axle assembly to overhaul differential.*

1) Remove wheels and brake drums. Mark propeller shaft and universal joint for reassembly, remove propeller shaft and tie out of way. Drain lubricant and remove housing cover. Measure and record axle shaft end play.

2) Insert feeler gauge between each end of axle shaft and pinion shaft. Record maximum thickness that can be inserted in each side. If end play is less than .005", measure side gear clearance.

3) Using 2 feeler gauges of equal thickness, insert one above and one below side gear hub next to thrust surface. If clearance is more than .012", replace side gear. Remove axle shafts as previously described.

4) Measure and record differential side play, ring gear runout and pinion bearing preload. Mark differential gear and case

at point of maximum runout. There should be no side play and ring gear runout should not exceed .005".

5) If ring gear runout exceeded .005", differential case flange runout must be checked. Using tool (C-4164 or equivalent) tighten adjusters until all case side play is eliminated.

6) Mount dial indicator to housing and place indicator stem on ring gear flange of differential case. Rotate case several times, checking reading on dial indicator. If reading varies more than .005" replace differential case.

7) Remove drive pinion flange and seal as previously described. Mark side bearing caps and axle housing for reassembly. Remove adjuster locks, loosen but do not remove bearing caps. Insert tool (C-4164 or equivalent) through axle tube and loosen hex adjuster on each side.

8) Remove bearing caps, adjusters and differential case assembly, keeping bearing cups and adjusters with respective bearing cones. Using soft drift punch and hammer, drive pinion shaft out of housing.

NOTE — *Bearing cones, cups, collapsible spacer and shim(s) MUST be replaced after driving out pinion.*

9) Drive bearing cups out of housing using a hammer and soft drift punch, remove shim(s) from behind rear cup and record thickness. Remove bearing cones from pinion shaft using suitable puller (C-293-P and C-293-42 or equivalent).

10) Mount differential case assembly in a soft jawed vise. Remove and discard ring gear bolts (left-hand thread). Using a soft faced hammer, drive ring gear off differential case.

NOTE — *DO NOT remove ring gear from differential case unless either case or gear set is replaced.*

CLEANING & INSPECTION

- Clean all components in suitable cleaning solvent. Inspect all machined surfaces for smoothness or raised edges, polish or flatten as required.
- Inspect all bearings and cups for wear and/or pitting and replace as a set. Inspect all gear teeth for wear and/or chipping and replace as a matched set only. Inspect all splined components for wear or damage and replace as required.

REASSEMBLY & ADJUSTMENT

Case Assembly — 1) Install thrust washers on differential side gears and position gears in differential case. Place thrust washers on differential pinion gears and position gears in case such that they are 180° apart when they are in mesh with side gears.

2) Rotate side gears until holes in pinion gears are in alignment with pinion shaft holes in case. Install differential pinion shaft, making sure hole in shaft is aligned with lock screw hole in case.

NOTE — *Use care not to damage pinion thrust washers.*

Drive Axles

CHRYSLER CORP. 8⅜" & 9¼" RING GEAR (Cont.)

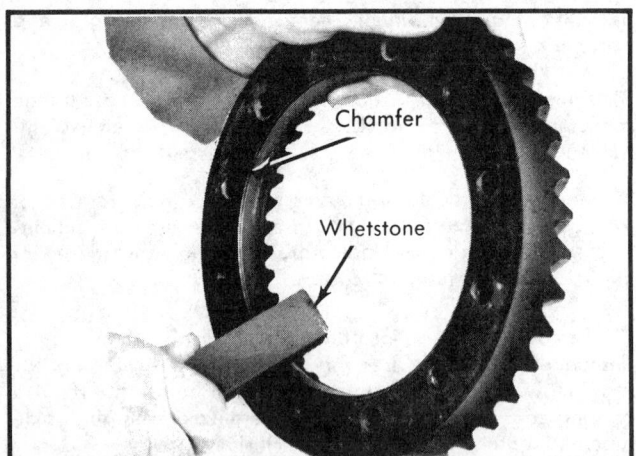

Fig. 2   Relieving Ring Gear Chamfer

3) Make sure contact surface of ring gear and case flange is clean and free of all nicks and burrs. Using a fine whetstone, relieve the sharp edge of the chamfer on inside diameter of ring gear. See Fig. 2.

NOTE — *Relieving chamfer insures that no burrs will become imbedded between case flange and ring gear causing ring gear distortion.*

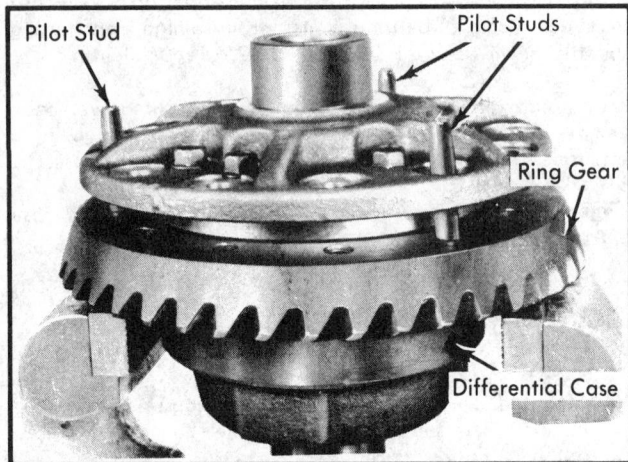

Fig. 3   Installing Ring Gear on Differential

4) Heat ring gear using heat lamp, hot oil or water; not to exceed 300°F. Do not use torch to heat ring gear. Install 3 equally spaced pilot studs on ring gear, place heated ring gear on jaws of vise and install case using new left-hand threaded bolts. See Fig. 3.

5) Tighten ring gear-to-case bolts alternately and evenly to specifications. Install side bearings on case using suitable tool (C-4340 & C-4171; 8⅜" ring gear. C-4213 & C-4171; 9¼" ring gear). Lubricate assembly with hypoid gear lubricant.

Drive Pinion Depth — **1)** Install both drive pinion bearing cups into axle housing bores. Assemble pinion locating spacer (SP-60-30) over body of main stem (SP-5385) followed by rear pinion bearing cone. Insert assembly into axle carrier from rear.

NOTE — *Tool numbers used apply to 8⅜" ring gear axles. For equivalent tool numbers for 9¼" ring gear axles, see Equivalent Tool Numbers Chart.*

2) On 8 3/8" assembly, hold spacer and main stem assembly in position and install front pinion bearing over spacer (SP-5382) and position over main stem of tool. On 9 1/4" assembly, position spacer and main stem assembly in housing, then install front pinion bearing cone and washer (SP-6022). Procedure from this point is same for both assemblies except for tool numbers (see note in preceding step). Position suitable compression sleeve (SP-3194B), centralizing washer (SP-534), and main screw nut (SP-3193) on main stem. Hold compression sleeve with tool (C-3281) and tighten nut. Allow tool to rotate while nut is being tightened to prevent damaging bearings and cups. See Fig. 4.

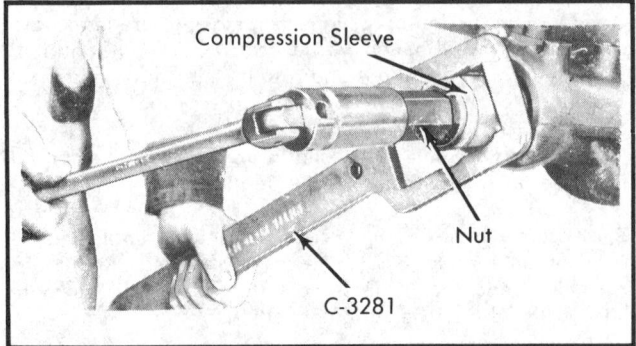

Fig. 4   Seating Pinion Bearing Cups

3) Loosen tool nut, then retighten to obtain pinion bearing preload of 10-30 INCH lbs. (15-25 INCH lbs. with 9 1/4" assembly). Rotate tool after tightening to properly seat pinion bearings. Install suitable gauge block (SP-5383) on main tool and tighten screw.

4) Position cross bore arbor (SP-6029) in housing side bearing seats and center arbor in bore. Position bearing caps on carrier pedestals and insert .002" spacer between arbor and each cap. Install cap bolts and tighten to 10 ft. lbs.

5) Use feeler gauge to determine proper thickness of shims that will fit snugly between arbor and gauge block. This fit must be snug but not excessively tight.

6) To select correct shim pack, read markings on end of pinion head. When marking is minus, add that amount of thickness to feeler gauge thickness to obtain thickness of correct shim pack. When marking is plus, subtract that amount of thickness. Remove all tools and REAR pinion bearing cup from housing. See Fig. 5.

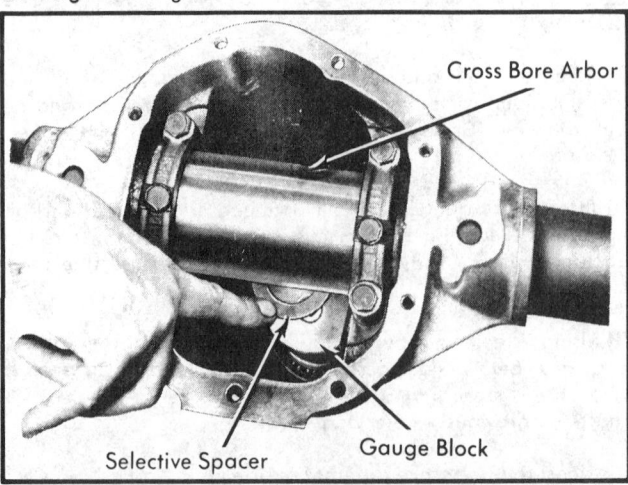

Fig. 5   Determining Correct Shim Pack Thickness

CHRYSLER CORP. 8⅜″ & 9¼″ RING GEAR (Cont.)

Equivalent Tool Number Chart

Application	8⅜″	9¼″
Spacer	SP-6030	SP-6017
Main Stem	SP-5385	SP-526
Spacer	SP-5382	SP-1730
Washer	SP-6022	SP-6022
Comp. Sleeve	SP-3194B	SP-535A
Cent. Washer	SP-534	SP-534
Nut	SP-3193	SP-533
Holding Tool	C-3281	C-3281
Gauge Block	SP-5383	SP-6020
Cross Bore Arbor	SP-6029	SP-6018
Bearing Installer	DD-955	DD-955

Pinion Bearing Preload — 1) Place selected shim in pinion shaft bore and reinstall rear pinion bearing cup. Lubricate rear pinion bearing and press into position on drive pinion stem.

2) Insert drive pinion assembly through axle housing, then install collapsible spacer and front pinion bearing onto stem of gear. Install pinion flange and nut and tighten nut until front bearing is seated.

NOTE — *Use care NOT to callapse spacer. If spacer is collapsed, new spacer MUST be installed.*

3) With front bearing fully seated, remove pinion flange and install new pinion oil seal into housing so flange of seal is fully seated against housing flange face.

4) Install pinion flange, Belleville washer (convex side out) and nut on pinion stem. While rotating pinion assembly (to insure proper bearing seating), tighten pinion flange nut until all end play is removed.

5) Tighten pinion nut to specified torque and measure pinion bearing preload by rotating pinion through several revolutions with an INCH lb. torque wrench. Continue tightening pinion flange nut in small increments until correct bearing preload is obtained.

CAUTION — *Do not back off nut to lessen bearing preload. If desired preload is exceeded, a new collapsible spacer MUST be installed and nut retightened until proper preload is obtained.*

Backlash & Side Bearing Preload — 1) Two precautions must be observed when checking and adjusting ring gear backlash and differential bearing preload. **a)** Permissible backlash variation is .003″. For example if backlash at minimum point is .006″ and backlash at maximum point is .009″, variation is correct. It is important to index gears so that same teeth are meshed during all backlash measurments. **b)** It is also important to maintain specified adjuster torque to obtain accurate differential bearing preload.

2) Using suitable tool (C-4164) turn each adjuster until bearing freeplay is eliminated with approximately .010″ backlash. Seat differential roller bearings.

NOTE — *Differential bearings do not always move with adjusters. To ensure accurate adjustment, bearings MUST be seated by oscillating drive pinion ½ turn in each direction 5-10 times each time adjusters are moved.*

3) Install dial indicator on cover flange. Position indicator stem against drive side of ring gear. Check backlash every 90° to find point of minimum backlash. Mark each position so backlash readings will be taken with same teeth meshed. Rotate ring gear to point of minimum backlash.

4) Loosen right adjuster and tighten left adjuster until backlash is .003-.004″ with each adjuster tightened to 10 ft. lbs. Seat bearings as previously described. Tighten bearing cap bolts to 100 ft. lbs. Using adjuster tool (C-4164), tighten right adjuster to 70 ft. lbs. Seat bearings and continue to tighten right adjuster until torque remains constant at 70 ft. lbs.

5) Check backlash again with indicator. If backlash is not between .006-.008″, increase torque on right adjuster and seat bearings. Continue this operation until backlash is .006-.008″. Tighten left adjuster to 70 ft. lbs. and seat bearings. With adjustments completed, install adjuster locks. Make sure lock teeth are engaged in adjuster threads. Tighten lock screws to 90 INCH lbs.

Final Inspection & Assembly — With pinion bearing preload and ring gear backlash properly adjusted, make a tooth pattern contact check. When pattern is satisfactory, install axle shafts, brake drums, wheels and tires, axle housing cover and refill with hypoid gear lubricant.

AXLE ASSEMBLY SPECIFICATIONS

Application	Specifications
Ring Gear Backlash	.006-.008″
Pinion Bearing Preload	
New Bearings	20-35 INCH Lbs.
Used Rear, New Front Bearing	10 INCH Lbs.
Maximum Ring Gear Runout	.005″

TIGHTENING SPECIFICATIONS

Application	Ft. Lbs.
Ring Gear-to-Diff. Case Bolts①	70
Drive Pinion Nut (Minimum)	210
Axle Housing Cover Bolts	15-25
Side Bearing Cap Bolts	100
Bearing Adjuster Lock Bolts	8

① — Left-hand threaded bolts.

FORD SEPARATE HOUSING

Bronco
E100/150
F100/150

DESCRIPTION

The axle has a banjo-shaped housing with a removable carrier. Drive pinion is straddle mounted and pinion depth is adjusted by shims. Ring gear and differential case are mounted on the removable carrier. The pre-load on side bearings is set by adjusting nuts on which bearing cups rest. This unit is distinguishable from Dana/Spicer units by its removable carrier and lack of rear cover plate. It is used with semi-floating axles in all applications. Ring gear diameter is 9.0".

AXLE RATIO & IDENTIFICATION

Axle ratio and model identification numbers may be found on the metal tag attached to axle by 1 carrier bolt. Other information included on tag includes date code, ring gear diameter and assembly plant code. The information on this tag must be used to order replacement parts.

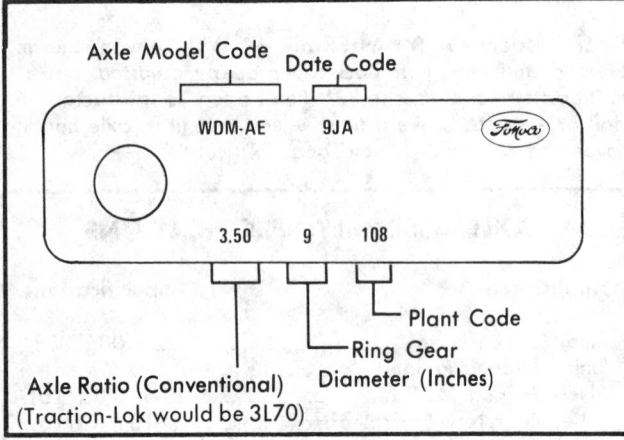

Fig. 1   Drive Axle Identification Tag

REMOVAL & INSTALLATION

AXLE SHAFTS

Models W/Ball Type Bearing — Remove wheel, tire and brake drum. Working through hole in axle flange, remove 4 wheel bearing retainer nuts. Using a slide hammer connected to axle, pull out axle and bearing. Remove backing plate and suspend from frame with wire. Replace oil seal using seal remover (1175-AC) and slide hammer. To install, reverse procedure. Use new bearing retainer gasket. Make sure bearing is firmly seated in axle housing.

Models W/Tapered Roller Bearing — Follow same procedure as outlined for ball bearing removal. Use a slide hammer to remove bearing cup from axle housing. To install, reverse removal procedure. Place bearing cup over tapered bearing before sliding axle into housing.

NOTE — If axle is removed for service or overhaul, a new oil seal must be installed.

AXLE BEARINGS & SEALS

Models W/Ball Type Bearing — 1) With axle removed, drill a ¼-½" hole in bearing retainer ring. Drill hole to a depth of ¾ the thickness of retainer ring.

CAUTION — DO NOT drill through ring into axle shaft.

2) Place a chisel across drilled hole. Strike with a hammer until ring separates. Remove ring and press bearing from axle shaft using a press and axle bearing plate (T75L-1165-B). Press a new bearing and retainer onto axle shaft. Drive new seal into axle housing.

NOTE — DO NOT attempt to press new bearing and retaining ring onto axle at the same time.

Models W/Tapered Roller Bearing — 1) With axle removed, drill a ¼-½" hole in bearing retainer ring. Drill hole to a depth of ¾ the thickness of retainer ring.

CAUTION — DO NOT drill through ring into axle shaft.

2) Place a chisel across drilled hole. Strike with a hammmer until ring separates and can be removed. Remove bearing cup from housing and place over bearing.

3) Place removal collet (T75L-1165A, B or C, or equivalent) over bearing. Place axle shaft in press, position over a support plate and press off bearing.

NOTE — If removal collet is not used, bearing MUST be discarded.

4) Install retainer plate on axle shaft (if removed). Lubricate new seal and bearing. Place seal and bearing on axle making sure cup rib ring is facing axle flange.

5) Press bearing onto axle, making sure it is fully seated. Do not attempt to press bearing retainer on at the same time. Press on a new bearing retainer.

PINION FLANGE & SEAL

Removal — Mark propeller shaft end yoke and pinion flange for reassembly reference, then disconnect propeller shaft and tie out of way. Scribe marks on pinion shaft and pinion flange for reassembly reference, then measure and record pinion bearing preload. Remove pinion nut, washer and flange, then remove oil seal with slide hammer and seal remover.

Installation — 1) Press new oil seal into bore in bearing retainer and seal outer edge with oil resistant sealer. Install pinion flange, washer and new nut. Tighten pinion shaft nut slowly while rotating pinion flange to insure proper seating of pinion bearings.

2) Continue tightening nut, taking frequent preload readings. If recorded preload reading was less than specifications, tighten to specifications. If recorded reading was more than specification, tighten to original reading. Install drive shaft.

CAUTION — DO NOT back off pinion nut to lessen preload. If backed off, a new spacer must be installed.

FORD SEPARATE HOUSING (Cont.)

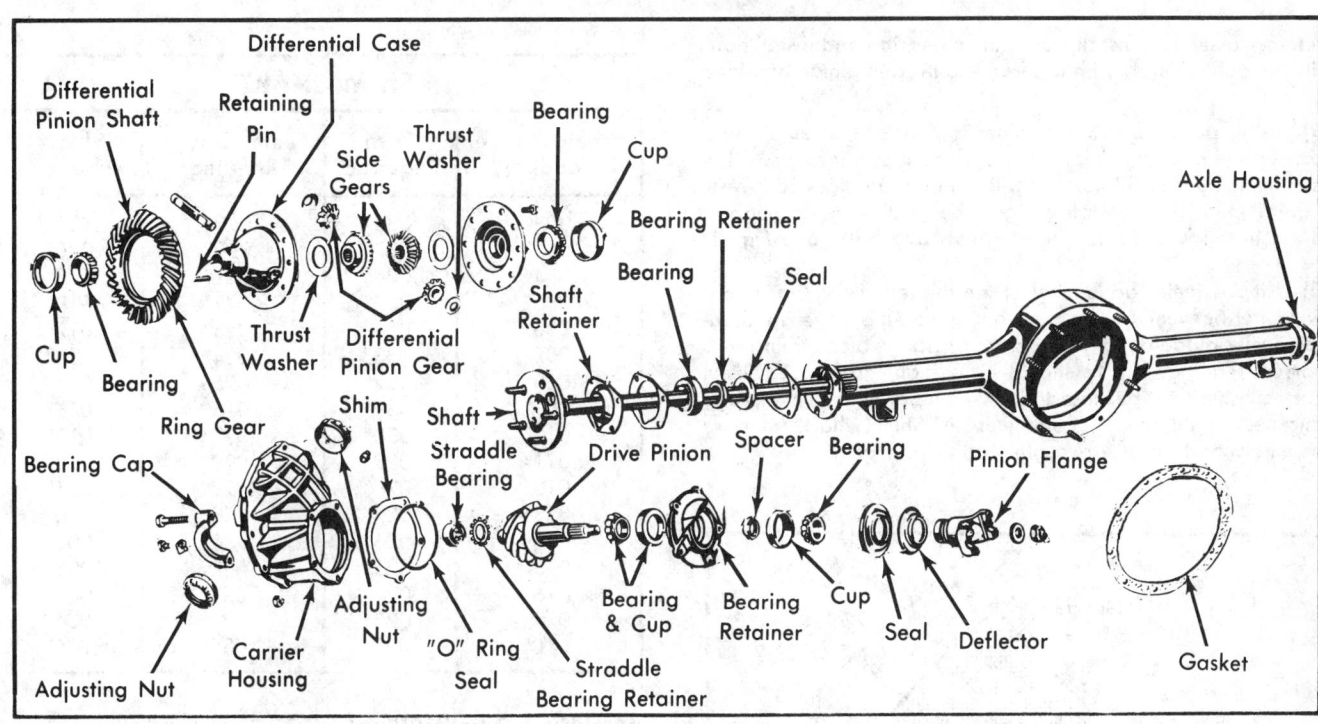

Fig. 2 Exploded View of Ford Separate Housing Drive Axle Assembly

DIFFERENTIAL CARRIER

Remove both axle shafts, then mark propeller shaft end yoke and pinion flange for reassembly reference and remove propeller shaft. Drain rear axle lubricant, then remove carrier attaching bolts and differential carrier. To install, reverse removal procedure.

OVERHAUL

DISASSEMBLY

1) Mark differential bearing caps for reassembly reference, then remove adjusting nut locks, bearing caps and adjusting nuts. Remove differential case from carrier. Remove differential side bearings from case. Remove ring gear attaching bolts and discard. Tap ring gear from case using a soft faced hammer.

2) Drive out differential pinion shaft retaining pin. Mark case halves for reassembly reference and separate case. Using brass drift, drive out pinion shaft. Remove differential side gears, pinion gears and thrust washers from case.

3) Remove pinion shaft nut, washer, pinion flange and seal from carrier. Remove pinion shaft and bearing retainer, noting number and thickness of shims between retainer and carrier. Remove straddle bearing and retainer from carrier using suitable driver and press pinion bearings from pinion shaft. Press bearing cups from bearing retainer.

REASSEMBLY & ADJUSTMENT

NOTE – *Lubricate all parts with hypoid gear lubricant during assembly.*

Differential Case Assembly — Place differential side gear and thrust washer into differential case bore. From outside of case, drive differential pinion shaft into case just far enough to retain pinion thrust washer and pinion gear, then place second pinion thrust washer and gear into position in case. Drive pinion shaft into place, making sure shaft retainer holes are in alignment with holes in case. Install second side gear and thrust washer, assemble case halves and install retainer pin. Install differential side bearings and ring gear and tighten ring gear bolts to specifications.

NOTE – *Ring and pinion gears should not be used if numbers do not match.*

Drive Pinion Depth — 1) Press new pinion bearing cups into pinion retainer housing until fully seated, making sure a .0015" feeler gauge cannot be inserted between bearing cup and bottom of bore.

2) Install new straddle bearing and retainer (with concave side up) in carrier and fully seat bearing and retainer. Press rear pinion bearing onto pinion shaft.

3) Determine pinion shim thickness as follows: If same ring and pinion gears are being reused, install original shim pack. If new ring and pinion gears are being installed, use "nominal" thickness shim and make tooth contact pattern to see if additional shims are required.

4) Adjust pinion depth using rear axle pinion depth gauge (T79P-4020-A or equivalent) as follows: Assemble aligning adapter and gauge disc over threaded shaft. Install gauge block on threaded shaft and tighten securely. Insert gauge assembly and NEW rear pinion bearing into pinion bearing

FORD SEPARATE HOUSING (Cont.)

retainer assembly. Install front pinion bearing and install handle on tool assembly with tapered end in front pinion bearing.

5) Install pinion bearing retainer and gauge assembly into carrier (without a pinion shim). Tighten retainer assembly mounting bolts to 30-45 ft. lbs. Rotate gauge block so it rests against pilot boss. Install gauge tube in differential bearing bore. Install and tighten bearing cap and bolts. See Fig. 3.

6) Using a feeler gauge, select the thickest feeler blade that will enter between gauge block and gauge tube. See Fig. 3. Insert feeler blade directly along top of gauge block to insure a correct reading. The fit should be a slight drag-type. Select correct shim to be inserted by comparing feeler gauge thickness with shim requirement in Shim Chart. Remove assembly and install drive pinion and ring gear.

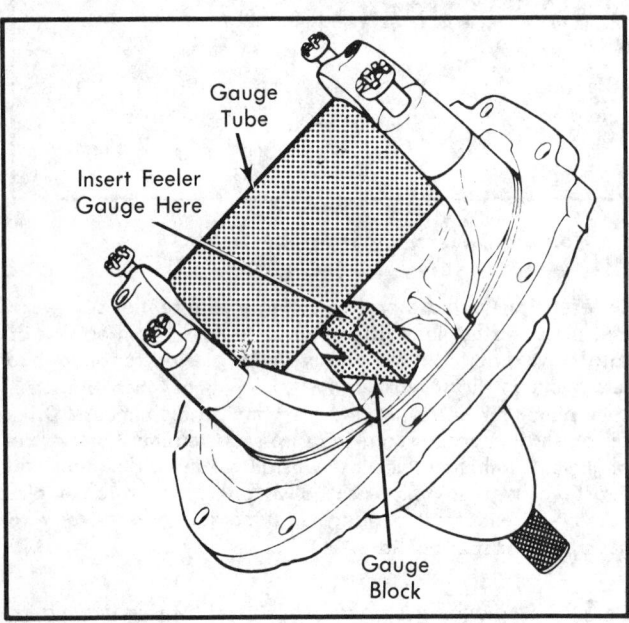

Fig. 3   Measuring Pinion Depth With Gauge (T79P-4020-A)

Pinion Bearing Preload (W/Collapsible Preload Spacer) —
1) Place NEW preload spacer on drive pinion shaft. Install front pinion bearing and bearing retainer. Press bearing into position being careful not to crush spacer. Install "O" ring in groove in bearing retainer, place selected pinion depth shim on carrier housing, then install pinion assembly and tighten bolts.

2) Install pinion flange, washer and nut. Tighten pinion flange nut to 175 ft. lbs. Check pinion bearing preload. Continue to tighten pinion flange nut until proper preload is obtained.

CAUTION — *DO NOT exceed 175 ft. lbs. at this time. DO NOT back off nut to obtain preload. If torque on pinion shaft is less than 175 ft. lbs. after preload is set, a new collapsible spacer MUST be installed.*

SHIM CHART			
Feeler Gauge Reading	Shim Required	Feeler Gauge Reading	Shim Required
.002"	.038"	.019"	.021"
.003"	.037"	.020"	.020"
.004"	.036"	.021"	.019"
.005"	.035"	.022"	.018"
.006"	.034"	.023"	.017"
.007"	.033"	.024"	.016"
.008"	.032"	.025"	.015"
.009"	.031"	.026"	.014"
.010"	.030"	.027"	.013"
.011"	.029"	.028"	.012"
.012"	.028"	.029"	.011"
.013"	.027"	.030"	.010"
.014"	.026"	.031"	.009"
.015"	.025"	.032"	.008"
.016"	.024"	.033"	.007"
.017"	.023"	.034"	.006"
.018"	.022"	.035"	.005"

Backlash & Side Bearing Preload — 1) Place cups on differential side bearings and set differential case in carrier. Slide assembly along bores until a slight amount of backlash is felt between gear teeth. Set adjusting nuts in bores so nuts just contact bearing cups (each nut should be engaging approximately same number of threads).

2) Carefully position bearing caps on carrier, install bearing cap bolts and tighten to 70-85 ft. lbs. Make sure adjusting nuts turn freely as bolts are tightened. If not, remove caps and inspect for damaged threads. Loosen cap bolts and retorque to 25 ft. lbs.

3) Loosen right adjusting nut until it is away from cup. Tighten left nut until ring gear is just forced into pinion with no backlash. Make sure right nut is still loose. Install dial indicator as shown in Fig. 4. Tighten right nut until it first contacts bearing cup. Then, continue tightening until side bearing preload (case spread) is to specifications. Turn pinion gear several times in each direction to seat bearings and make sure no bind is evident.

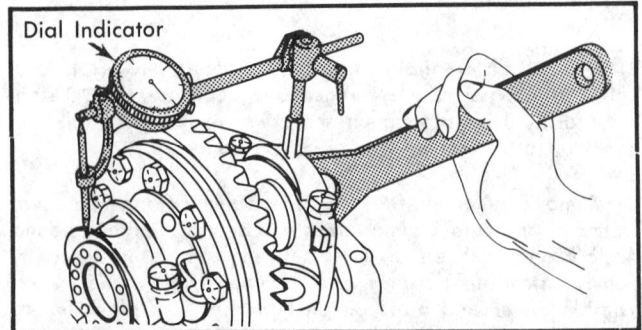

Fig. 4   Adjusting Side Bearing Preload

4) Tighten bearing cap bolts to 70-85 ft. lbs. Install a dial indicator on carrier so contact tip of indicator bears against face of gear tooth on outer diameter of ring gear. Measure

FORD SEPARATE HOUSING (Cont.)

backlash at several locations on ring gear. If backlash measurements vary more than .004", there is excessive runout in gear or mounting.

5) If backlash is not correct, loosen 1 adjusting nut and tighten opposite nut an equal amount. This will move ring gear into adjustment. After this procedure, always check case spread specifications.

6) When side bearing preload and ring gear backlash are correctly set, perform gear tooth pattern check and install carrier into axle housing.

NOTE — *When moving adjusting nuts, final movement should always be made in a tightening direction. If nut must be loosened 1 notch, loosen 2 notches and then tighten 1 notch.*

AXLE ASSEMBLY SPECIFICATIONS

Application	Specification
Ring Gear Backlash	.008-.012"
Ring Gear Runout (Maximum)	.003"
Backlash Variation (Maximum)	.004"
Side Bearing Preload (Case Spread)	
New Bearings	.008-.012"
Used Bearings	.005-.008"
Pinion Bearing Preload (Rotating Torque)	
Collapsible Spacer	
New Bearings	8-14 INCH Lbs.
Used Bearings	16-29 INCH Lbs.
Side Gear Thrust Washer Thickness	.030-.032"
Pinion Gear Thrust Washer Thickness	.030-.033"
Nominal Pinion Shim Thickness	.015"

TIGHTENING SPECIFICATIONS

Application	Torque (Ft. Lbs.)
Side Bearing Cap Bolts	70-85
Ring Gear Bolts	70-85
Pinion Flange Nut	
Collapsible Spacer (Minimum)	175
Pinion Bearing Retainer-to-Carrier	30-45
Carrier-to-Housing	25-40
Adjusting Nut Lock Bolts	12-25
Bearing Retainer Plate Bolt	20-40

Drive Axles

GENERAL MOTORS 8½", 8⅞", 9½" RING GEAR

**Chevrolet & GMC
C, K, G and P10 Models
G20 Models
K10/20 Models (Front Axle Only)**

NOTE — *FRONT AXLE USAGE — The General Motors 8½" ring gear drive axle is used as the front drive axle on K10 and K20 models. For removal and installation instructions, see articles on Locking Hubs and 4-Wheel Drive Steering Knuckles. These models may also be equipped with a Spicer front drive axle. See appropriate article in this section.*

DESCRIPTION

The axle assembly is the hypoid gear type with integral carrier housing. It is used on light-duty vehicles with semi-floating axles. The pinion bearing preload is made with a collapsible spacer. The differential side bearing preload adjustment and the drive pinion depth adjustment are made by shims. A removable 10-bolt housing cover permits inspection and minor servicing of differential without removal from vehicle. Service procedures are the same for all 3 assemblies, except for tightening specifications and special tool numbers.

AXLE RATIO & IDENTIFICATION

General Motors uses several types of axles. The 8½", 8⅞" and 9½" axle can be distinguished from others by the configuration of their housing covers and by the number of attaching bolts. To determine drive axle ratio, see *article on Drive Axle Ratio Identification in this section.*

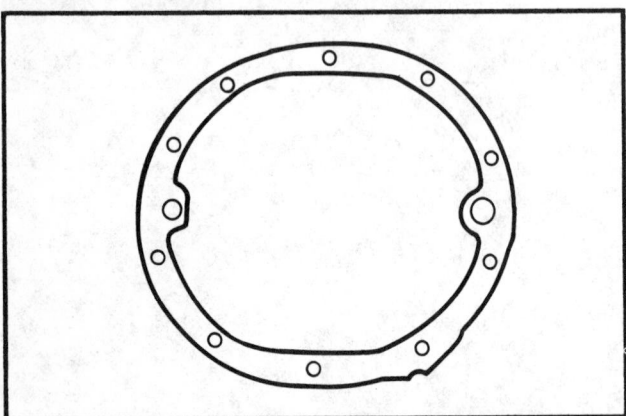

Fig. 1   8½", 8⅞" and 9½" Ring Gear Housing Cover Gasket for Axle Identification Purposes

REMOVAL & INSTALLATION

AXLE SHAFTS & BEARINGS

NOTE — *For front axle shaft and bearing removal, see articles on Spicer (Dana) Full-Floating Axles or 4-Wheel Drive Steering Knuckles in this section.*

Removal — **1)** Raise vehicle. Remove wheel and tire, and brake drum. Drain lubricant from drive axle. Remove housing cover. Remove differential pinion shaft lock screw.

NOTE — *On vehicles equipped with 8⅞" ring gear and Eaton positive traction differential, proceed to step 3). On all remaining models, proceed as follows:*

2) Remove differential pinion shaft. Push flanged end of axle shaft toward center of vehicle. Remove "C" lock from splined end of axle shaft and remove axle shaft.

3) On vehicles with 8⅞" ring gear and Eaton positive traction differential, remove pinion shaft lock screw. Partly withdraw pinion shaft.

4) Rotate differential case until pinion shaft touches edge of housing. See *Fig. 2.*

Fig. 2   Positioning Case for Axle Removal

5) Reach into case with screwdriver and rotate "C" lock until open end points directly inward. When "C" lock is correctly positioned, axle shaft can be pushed inward, allowing "C" lock to be removed. Remove axle shaft. See *Fig. 3.*

CAUTION — *Do not hammer on axle shaft. It should slide easily when "C" lock is correctly positioned. When removing the axle shaft on the 9½" ring gear axle, be sure the thrust washer in the differential case does not slip out.*

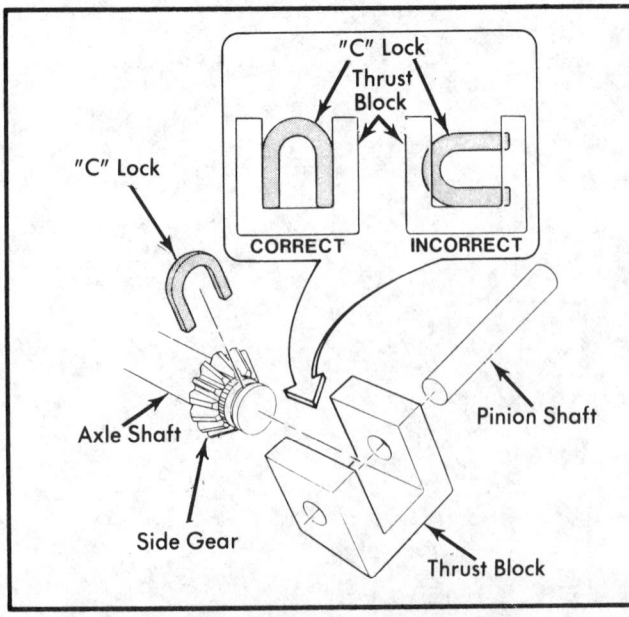

Fig. 3   View Showing Correct Positioning of "C" Lock for Removal

GENERAL MOTORS 8½", 8⅞", 9½" RING GEAR (Cont.)

6) With axle shaft removed, insert bearing removal tool (J-23689 or equivalent) into axle housing behind bearing. Attach slide hammer to tool and remove bearing and seal.

Installation — Reverse removal procedure and note the following:

1) Install axle shaft housing bearing until it bottoms against housing. Install axle shaft housing seal until flush with outer edge of axle tube.

2) After installing axle shaft and "C" lock, pull axle shaft outward so "C" lock seats in side gear counterbore. On models equipped with Eaton positive traction differential, make sure "C" lock is correctly positioned in thrust block. *See Fig. 3.*

PINION FLANGE & SEAL

1) Raise vehicle and allow axle to hang free. Disconnect universal joint and tie propeller shaft out of the way. Note and record pinion bearing preload by rotating pinion shaft through several revolutions using an INCH lb. torque wrench. Then mark relationship of pinion flange and shaft for reassembly. Count the number of threads on pinion shaft. Hold yoke with a suitable tool (J-8614-11), and remove self-locking nut. Remove yoke using a suitable puller. Pry old seal out of housing.

2) Pack seal lip cavity with lithium-base extreme pressure lubricant. Place seal in bore. Using suitable gauge plate (J-22804-1) and seal driver (J-21057) drive seal into place. Make sure seal is square in carrier. Pack cavity between end of pinion splines and pinion flange with a non-hardening sealer.

3) Using a suitable installation tool (J-8614-11) install flange on pinion shaft. Install washer and nut. Install nut in original position taking note of scribe marks and number of exposed threads. Measure pinion preload. Tighten nut in small increments until preload exceeds original figure by 1-5 INCH lbs. Install propeller shaft and lower vehicle.

CAUTION — *Do not attempt to hammer flange onto pinion shaft, as it will damage ring gear and pinion.*

AXLE ASSEMBLY

Removal — 1) Raise vehicle. Raise axle until tension is released from springs and shock absorbers. Disconnect propeller shaft from flange. Tie propeller shaft out of way.

2) Disconnect shock absorbers at lower mounts. Disconnect vent hose from vent connector. Disconnect and plug brake hose at connector on axle housing.

3) Remove rear brake drums. Disconnect parking brake cable at actuating levers and at flange plate. Remove "U" bolt nuts, washers, spacers and clamp plates. Lower axle assembly and remove from vehicle.

Installation — To install axle assembly, reverse removal procedure. Bleed brake system.

OVERHAUL

DISASSEMBLY

NOTE — *Check and record ring gear backlash and pinion bearing preload before disassembly.*

1) Remove lock screws retaining pinion shaft, and remove pinion shaft. Remove axle shafts, and roll out differential pinions and thrust washers, marking pinions and thrust washers for reassembly. Remove side gears and thrust washers, marking side gears and thrust washers for reassembly also.

2) Mark differential bearing caps and housing for reassembly. Loosen bearing cap bolts and tap surface of bearing caps to loosen. Using suitable pry bar inserted in differential carrier, pry against housing to remove carrier.

NOTE — *Be careful as carrier bearings are preloaded and carrier will fall free after being pried past certain point. Bearing caps are loosely installed to support carrier at this point.*

3) After removing carrier, place bearing cups with appropriate shims. Install bearing caps onto housing in their original position, prior to removal. Using puller tool (J-22888 & J-8107-4 or J-8107-3 for the 9½" ring gear), remove differential side bearings.

4) Remove ring gear bolts and tap ring gear off carrier using a soft drift and hammer. Using an INCH lb. torque wrench, check torque required to rotate drive pinion. If no preload reading is obtained, check looseness of pinion assembly. Looseness indicates pinion bearings should be replaced.

5) Install holder (J-8614-11 or equivalent) on flange with notches toward flange. Remove pinion nut and washer and remove flange. Install pinion nut half way on pinion. Install differential cover using 2 bolts. Tap end of pinion using soft drift and large hammer to remove pinion.

NOTE — *Care MUST be used not to damage pinion bearings when removing pinion from differential housing.*

6) Remove differential cover and remove pinion assembly. Remove pinion oil seal and front bearing from housing. Inspect bearings and bearing cups and replace as required. Discard oil seal, pinion nut and collapsible spacer.

CLEANING & INSPECTION

Clean all parts in cleaning solvent. Inspect all bearings, bearing cups, races and rollers for scoring, chipping or excessive wear. Inspect axle shaft and side gear splines for excessive wear. Inspect ring gear and pinion for scoring, cracking or chipping. Inspect differential case, pinion side gears, thrust washers and pinion shaft for cracks, scoring, galling or excessive wear.

REASSEMBLY & ADJUSTMENT

Case Assembly — Install ring gear squarely (use guide pins if necessary) onto case and tighten ring gear bolts evenly and alternately. Install side gears, differential pinions and thrust washers into case. Install differential pinion shaft and lock screw and tighten lock screw finger tight.

Drive Pinion Depth & Bearing Preload — 1) Drive pinion rear bearing shim thickness must be determined whenever a new axle housing, ring and pinion set, or pinion bearings are installed. Shim pack thickness is determined by using suitable gauging tool set (J-21777).

2) If removed, install pinion bearing cups into housing; then place lubricated pinion bearings into cups. Position gauge plate (J-21777-29 for 8½"; J-21777-36 for 8⅞"; or J-21777-85 for 9½" ring gear) and rear pinion bearing pilot on

GENERAL MOTORS 8½", 8⅞", 9½" RING GEAR (Cont.)

preload stud. Then install through rear pinion bearing, front pinion bearing, and front pinion bearing disc (J-21777-42). Install hex nut until snug, then rotate bearings to insure proper seating. Hold preload stud stationary with a wrench on flats, then tighten hex nut until 20 INCH lbs. are required to rotate bearings. *See Fig. 4.*

3) Mount side bearing gauging discs (J-21777-45) on ends of arbor, then place arbor into carrier making sure discs are properly seated. Install side bearing caps and bolts, then tighten bolts to avoid movement. Position dial indicator on mounting post of arbor, with contact button resting on top surface of plunger. Preload dial indicator ½ revolution, then tighten in this position.

4) Place plunger onto gauging area of gauge plate. Rock plunger rod slowly back and forth across gauging area until dial indicator reads greatest deflection, then set indicator to zero. Repeat rocking action several times to verify setting. Once zero reading is obtained, swing plunger until it is removed from gauging area. Dial indicator will now read required pinion shim thickness for a "nominal pinion". Record this reading.

5) Check drive pinion for painted or stamped markings on pinion stem, or a stamped code number on small end of pinion gear. If marking is found to be plus or minus number (for example, +2 or −5) add or subtract that many thousandths from indicator reading. This will then be thickness of rear pinion bearing shim pack.

NOTE — *If no markings are found on pinion, use dial indicator reading as shim thickness.*

6) Remove bearing caps and gauging tool from housing. Place selected shim pack on pinion gear, then install lubricated pinion bearing onto pinion shaft using suitable press.

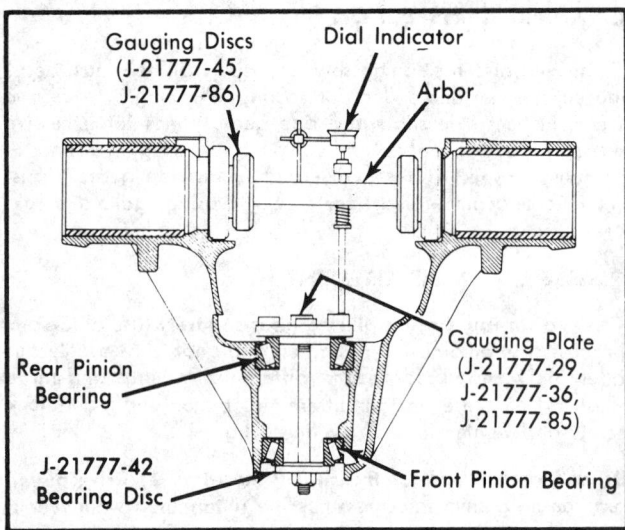

Fig. 4 Sectional View Showing Use of Pinion Depth Tool Set (J-21777)

7) Install a new collapsible spacer over pinion gear shaft, then position pinion assembly in housing. While holding pinion forward, carefully drive front pinion bearing onto pinion gear shaft until a few threads are exposed. Install seal, pinion flange, washer and nut, and tighten until all end play is removed. Rotate pinion several times to seat bearings, then check preload using an INCH lb. torque wrench. Continue tightening nut and checking preload until specified preload is obtained.

CAUTION — *Do not back off nut to lessen preload. If preload is exceeded, a new collapsible spacer must be installed and nut retightened until proper preload is obtained.*

Side Bearing Preload — 1) Lubricate bearings with suitable lubricant. Place differential assembly into position in housing. Hold in place by hand.

2) Install suitable bearing strap (J-22779-6) on left bearing. Tighten bolts evenly to a snug fit. Install right bearing cap. Tighten bolts to a snug fit.

3) Position ring gear tight against pinion so that backlash is .000-.001". Insert a suitable gauging tool (J-22779) between left bearing cup and carrier housing.

4) While moving tool up and down, tighten adjusting nut until a slight drag is felt. Tighten lock bolt on side of tool.

5) Install adjustment spacer (.170") and shim between right bearing and carrier. Insert a feeler gauge thick enough to create a slight drag between shim and carrier.

6) To determine correct side bearing shim thickness, measure thickness of adjusted gauging tool. Record measurement. Add together dimensions of shim, spacer and feeler gauge. Record measurement.

7) Subtract .010" from ring gear (left) side measurement and add .010" to opposite (right) side measurement. This allows for correct backlash adjustment.

8) To obtain correct preload, add .004" to both measurements. The total is the correct shim pack thickness for both sides.

Example:

Ring Gear Side (Left) Shim Pack
  +.265" (Gauging Tool Measurement)
  −.010" (Backlash Adjustment)
  +.004" (Bearing Preload)
  =.259" (Ring Gear Side Shim Pack)
Opposite Ring Gear Side (Right) Shim Pack
  +.250" (Combined Measurement Total)
  +.010" (Backlash Adjustment)
  +.004" (Bearing Preload)
  =.264" (Opposite Ring Gear Side Shim Pack)

9) Install ring gear side shim first, then wedge opposite side shim between bearing cup and spacer. Install shim so that chamfered side is against spacer.

NOTE — *If shim is not chamfered enough and it scrapes spacer when it is installed, file or grind chamfer before installation.*

10) It may be necessary to partially remove differential when right side shim is being installed. Tap shim into place with a soft faced hammer. Tighten bearing cap bolts to 60 ft. lbs.

GENERAL MOTORS 8½", 8⅞", 9½" RING GEAR (Cont.)

Backlash & Final Assembly — 1) Check backlash at four locations around ring gear, using a dial indicator mounted to axle housing. Variation should not exceed .001". If backlash is not wihtin specifications, adjust side bearing shims as necessary.

CAUTION — *Total shim pack thickness must not be changed. If a shim is removed from one side, the same thickness shim must be added to the other side.*

2) After adjustment is completed, make a tooth contact pattern test and make any necessary corrections. Install axle shafts, wheel and housing covers.

TIGHTENING SPECIFICATIONS

Application	Ft. Lbs.
Ring Gear-to-Differential Case	
8½" & 8⅞" Ring Gear	105
9½" Ring Gear	60
Side Bearing Cap	
8½" & 8⅞"	60
9½" Ring Gear	70
Pinion Shaft Lock Bolt	25
Housing Cover	20

AXLE ASSEMBLY SPECIFICATIONS

Application	Specification
Ring Gear Backlash	.005-.008"
Side Bearing Preload	.008"
Pinion Bearing Preload	
Used Bearings	10-15 INCH Lbs.
New Bearings	20-25 INCH Lbs.

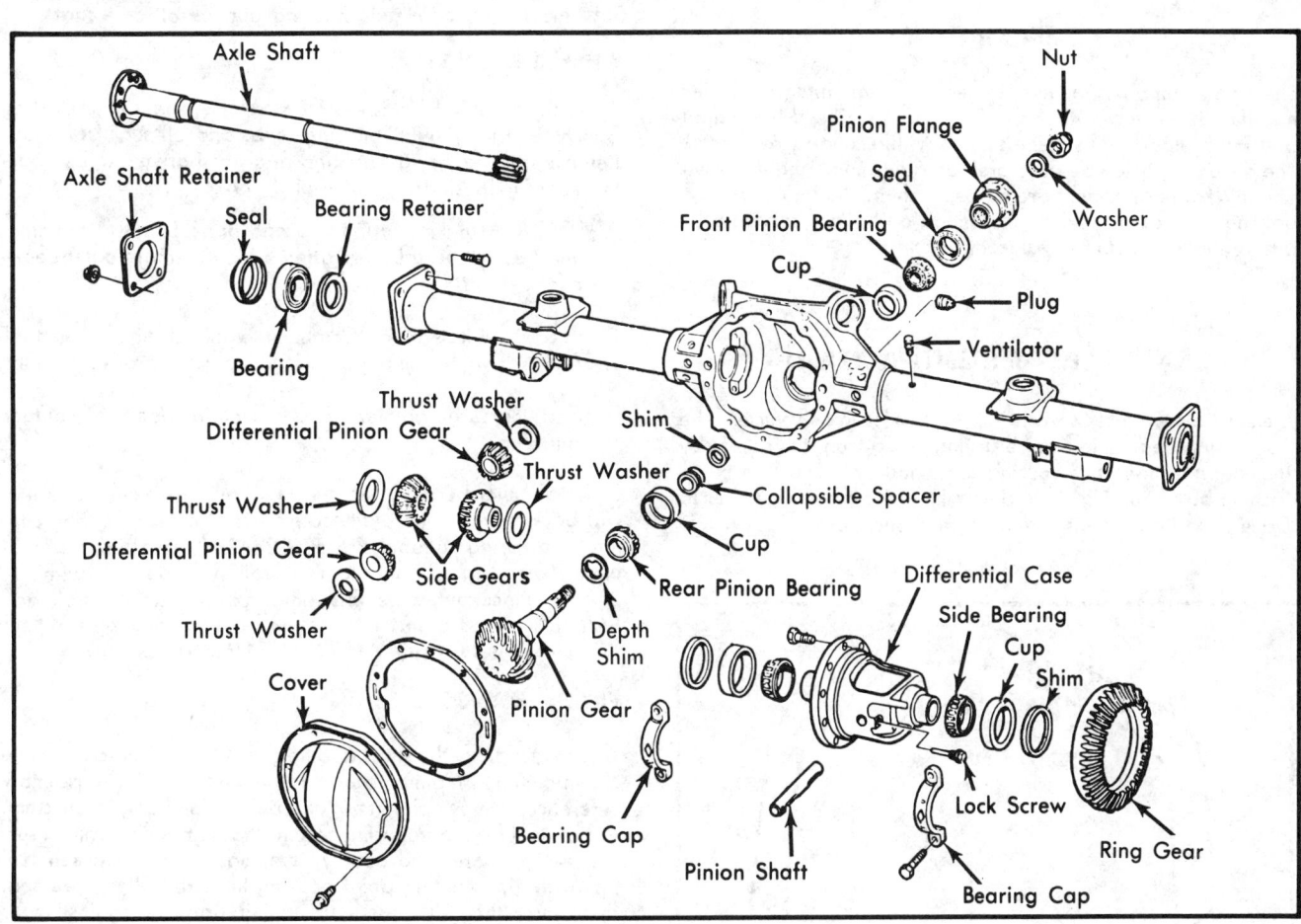

***Fig. 5** Exploded View of General Motors 8½", 8⅞" and 9½" Ring Gear Axle Assembly*

Drive Axles

GENERAL MOTORS 10½" RING GEAR

Chevrolet & GMC
 C20/30 Models
 G30 Models
 K20/30 Models
 P20/30 Models

NOTE — *SERIES IDENTIFICATION* — *The vehicle series numbers used in this article have been abbreviated for common reference to both Chevrolet and GMC models. Chevrolet models use numerical designations as listed; GMC models are identified as follows: 10 = 1500; 20 = 2500; 30 = 3500.*

NOTE — *DRIVE AXLE USAGE* — *The General Motors 10½" ring gear drive axle is used on C20/30 and K20/30 models (except those equipped with dual rear wheels), on all G30 models, and on P30 models (except those equipped with 4.11:1 or 5.43:1 axle ratios). Some C20/30 and K20/30 models may use Spicer (Dana) axles, however.*

DESCRIPTION

The axle assembly is the hypoid gear type with integral carrier housing. It is used with full floating axles. The drive pinion bearing preload adjustment is made with a collapsible spacer. The differential side bearing preload adjustment and the drive pinion depth adjustment are made by shims. A removeable 14 bolt housing cover permits inspection and minor servicing of differential without removal from vehicle.

AXLE RATIO & IDENTIFICATION

General Motors uses several types of axles in its vehicles. The 10½" ring gear axle can be distinguished from the others by the configuration of its housing cover and by the number of attaching bolts. *See Fig. 1.* To determine drive axle ratio, refer to *Drive Axle Ratio Identification* in this Section.

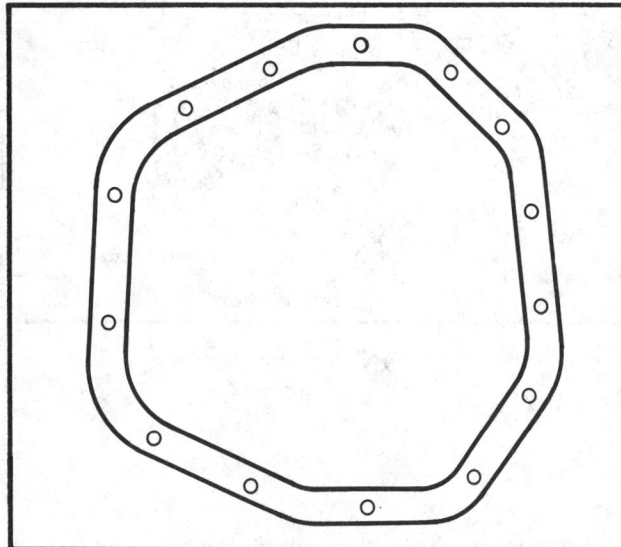

Fig. 1   10½" Ring Gear Housing Cover Gasket for Identification Purposes

REMOVAL & INSTALLATION

AXLE SHAFTS

Remove axle shaft attaching bolts from wheel hub and hit flange on axle shaft with a soft faced hammer to loosen shaft. Grip rib on end of flange with pliers and twist axle shaft to begin removal. When shaft is loose, remove it from housing. To install, reverse removal procedure, using new gaskets.

WHEEL HUB & SEAL

Remove axle shaft, then remove lock nut retainer, lock nut, adjusting nut retainer, adjusting nut and thrust washer from axle housing. Pull hub and drum assembly straight off axle housing. Pry old oil seal from wheel hub, using care not to damage bore surface. Thoroughly clean seal contact area, then pack cavity between seal lips with high melting point wheel bearing lubricant. Position seal in hub bore, then carefully press seal into hub using suitable tool (J-24428) until seal is flush with edge of hub. Install hub onto axle housing and install axle shaft.

WHEEL BEARINGS

1) With wheel hub removed from vehicle, use a long drift or punch to drive INNER bearing, cup, and oil seal from hub. Remove outer bearing retaining ring, then drive OUTER bearing out of hub using suitable tool (J-24426).

CAUTION — *Inner bearing cup and outer bearing retaining ring must be removed before attempting to remove outer bearing cup.*

2) Place OUTER bearing assembly into hub. Using suitable tool (J-8608), drive bearing past retaining ring groove in hub.

NOTE — *Be sure chamfer of tool (J-8608) does not contact bearing cup.*

3) Install outer bearing retaining ring, and drive outer bearing cup back against ring until seated. Place INNER bearing cup into hub. Using suitable driver (J-24427), drive cup into hub until seated against shoulder. Install new oil seal with (J-24428). Place hub assembly onto axle housing. Install adjusting nut, and adjust rear wheel bearing. See *Rear Wheel Bearing Adjustment* in WHEEL ALIGNMENT Section.

PINION FLANGE & SEAL

Disconnect propeller shaft and tie out of way, then scribe a line down pinion nut, pinion stem and pinion flange for reassembly reference. Remove pinion nut and pull pinion flange from stem. Pry oil seal from bore, using care not to damage machined surfaces. Clean area thoroughly, then pack cavity between seal lips with high melting point bearing lubricant. Place new seal into bore, then drive seal in until it bottoms against inner shoulder. Install pinion flange, pinion nut and propeller shaft.

AXLE ASSEMBLY

Raise vehicle and support weight at frame side rails. Remove rear wheels, then disconnect propeller shaft and tie out of way. Remove wheel hub, disconnect parking brake cable at lever and at flange plate, then disconnect hydraulic brake hose at connector on axle housing. Disconnect shock absorbers at axle brackets, then raise axle assembly slightly to relieve tension on springs. Remove spring "U" bolts and lower axle assembly to floor. To install, reverse removal procedure.

Drive Axles

GENERAL MOTORS 10½" RING GEAR (Cont.)

OVERHAUL

DISASSEMBLY

1) Drain lubricant, then remove housing cover and axle shafts. Note and record ring gear backlash and pinion bearing preload for reassembly reference. Remove adjusting nut lock retainers from bearing caps, mark bearing caps for reassembly reference, then remove bearing caps. Loosen side bearing adjusting nuts and remove differential case assembly from axle housing.

2) Remove pinion bearing retainer bolts, then remove pinion and bearing retainer assembly. Note and record number and thickness of shims removed. Remove pinion flange and press pinion gear out of bearing retainer, then press rear pinion bearing from gear. Drive front and rear pinion bearing cups and pinion oil seal from bearing retainer. Drive pinion straddle bearing from axle housing.

3) Mark differential case halves for reassembly reference, then remove ring gear bolts and ring gear and split case halves. Remove side gears, differential spider, differential pinion gears and thrust washers.

REASSEMBLY & ADJUSTMENT

Case Assembly — 1) Lubricate differential pinion gears, side gears and thrust washers with hypoid gear oil, then place pinion gears and thrust washers on differential spider. Install side gears and spider assembly into left half of differential case, then assemble two halves of case, making sure alignment marks on both halves are together.

2) Install two guide pins in ring gear, directly opposite each other. Start guide pins through holes in case flange and tap ring gear lightly with soft face hammer until ring gear attaching bolts can be started. Tighten bolts evenly until ring gear is flush with case flange. Remove guide pins and tighten all ring gear bolts alternately and evenly.

Pinion Depth & Bearing Preload — 1) With pinion bearing retainer mounted in vise, install pinion gear and bearing assembly into retainer, then place pinion flange on gear stem. Install new pinion nut and tighten nut in small increments until specified pinion bearing preload is obtained.

2) If original ring and pinion gears are to be reinstalled, use new pinion shims of same number and thickness as those removed. If new gears are to be installed, determine correct shims as follows: Compare pinion depth code number of new pinion gear with that of original pinion gear. From these two codes, determine correction factor by referring to following chart. Combine correction factor with thickness of original shim pack to obtain necessary thickness of new shim pack. Place new shim pack onto carrier housing and install pinion bearing retainer assembly. Tighten retainer bolts in a crosswise sequence.

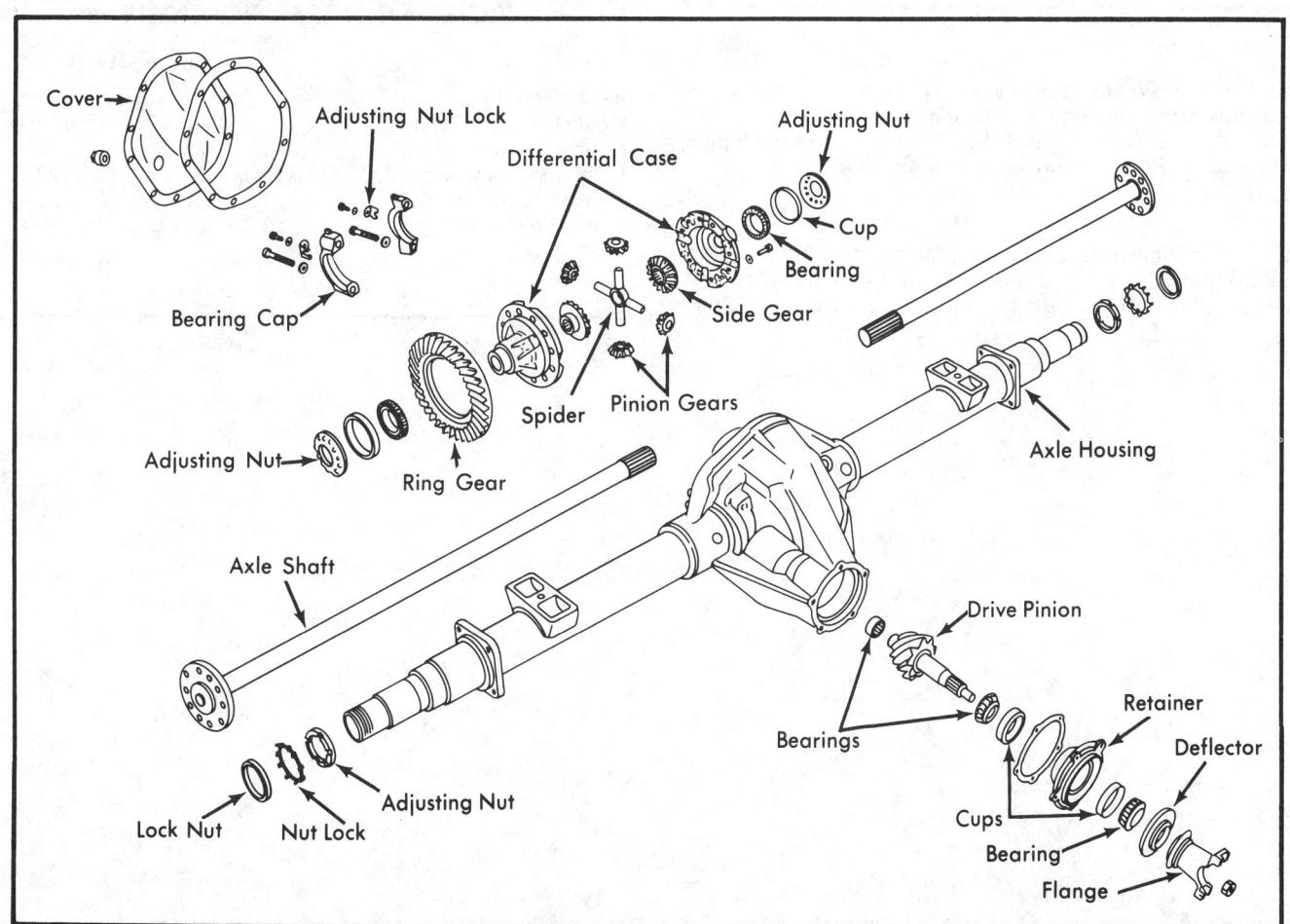

Fig. 2   Exploded View of General Motors 10½" Ring Gear Axle Assembly

GENERAL MOTORS 10½″ RING GEAR (Cont.)

Pinion Depth Codes		
Original Code	Service Code	Correction (In.)
+2	+2	0
+2	+1	−.001
+2	0	−.002
+2	−1	−.003
+2	−2	−.004
+1	+2	+.001
+1	+1	0
+1	0	−.001
+1	−1	−.002
+1	−2	−.003
0	+2	+.002
0	+1	+.001
0	0	0
0	−1	−.001
0	−2	−.002
−1	+2	+.003
−1	+1	+.002
−1	0	+.001
−1	−1	0
−1	−2	−.001
−2	+2	+.004
−2	+1	+.003
−2	0	+.002
−2	−1	+.001
−2	−2	0

Backlash & Final Assembly — 1) Place lubricated bearing cups onto differential side bearings and place differential assembly into carrier. Install bearing caps in their original positions and tighten cap bolts until just snug.

2) Loosen right side bearing adjusting nut and tighten left side adjusting nut until zero backlash is obtained. Back off left adjusting nut two slots to a locking position, then tighten right adjusting nut until case is in firm contact with left adjusting nut. Loosen right adjusting nut until it is free of bearing, then retighten nut until it just contacts bearing. Tighten right adjusting nut additional two slots (used bearings) or three slots (new bearings) to properly preload differential side bearings.

3) Using a dial indicator, measure ring gear backlash in at least four locations around ring gear. Adjust to specifications by moving adjusting nuts in or out as necessary.

CAUTION — *If one adjusting nut is loosened the other nut must be tightened an EQUAL AMOUNT to maintain side bearing preload.*

4) With backlash adjustment complete, install adjusting nut lock fingers into slots in nuts and attach fingers to bearing caps. Tighten bearing cap bolts and perform gear tooth contact pattern check. Install axle housing cover.

AXLE ASSEMBLY SPECIFICATIONS

Ring Gear Backlash
  Preferred .... .005-.008″
  Acceptable .... .003-.012″
Pinion Bearing Preload
  New Bearings .... 25-35 in. lbs.
  Used Bearings .... 5-15 in. lbs.

TIGHTENING SPECIFICATIONS

Application	Torque (Ft. Lbs.)
Ring Gear	120
Side Bearing Cap	135
Drive Pinion Nut	①
Differential Bearing Adjusting Lock	20
Pinion Bearing Retainer	65
Housing Cover	30

① — Torque as necessary to obtain correct preload, tighten to approximately 350 ft. lbs.

GENERAL MOTORS 12¼" RING GEAR

Chevrolet and GMC
P30 Models

NOTE — *DRIVE AXLE USAGE — The General Motors 12¼" ring gear drive axle is used on Chevrolet P30 and GMC P3500 models when equipped with 4.11:1 or 5.43:1 axle ratio.*

DESCRIPTION

The axle has a banjo-type housing with a removeable carrier. The drive pinion is straddle mounted on removeable carrier. There is no adjustment for drive pinion depth or bearing preload. The preload on the differential side bearings is set by adjusting nuts on which the bearing cups rest. The differential has a 2-piece case and 4 differential pinion gears.

AXLE RATIO & IDENTIFICATION

The 12¼" ring gear drive axle assembly is the only one used by General Motors vehicles that has a removeable carrier. To determine axle ratio, refer to Drive Axle Ratio Identification in this Section

REMOVAL & INSTALLATION

AXLE SHAFTS

Remove axle shaft hub cap and install slide hammer into hole on axle shaft flange. Pull shaft straight out of housing. To install, reverse removal procedure, using a new gasket on hub cap, and making sure axle flange splines index into wheel hub splines.

WHEEL HUB & SEAL

Remove axle shaft, then remove lock nut retainer, lock nut, adjusting nut and thrust washer from axle housing. Pull hub and drum assembly straight off axle housing, using care not to drop bearing inner race and roller assembly. Pry old seal from wheel hub, using care not to damage bore surface. Thoroughly clean seal contact area, then pack cavity between seal lips with high melting point wheel bearing lubricant. Position seal in hub bore, then carefully press seal into hub using suitable tool (J-22354) until seal is flush with edge of hub. Install hub onto axle housing and install axle shaft.

WHEEL BEARINGS

1) With wheel hub removed from vehicle, place suitable length of ½" bar stock behind INNER bearing cup and index in notches in hub. Using press tool against bar stock, press out cup.

2) Using suitable tool (J-22380), remove OUTER bearing retaining ring. Drive against axle shaft spacer, using splined flange end cut from an old axle shaft to remove OUTER bearing cup.

3) Place axle shaft spacer in hub, then insert outer bearing, with larger O.D. toward outside of hub. Position outer bearing cup in hub and press in until squarely seated. Install bearing retainer, then press outer cup into contact with retainer ring.

4) Using suitable tool (J-8093), press inner bearing cup into hub bore until seated against shoulder. Install new hub oil seal. Place hub assembly onto axle housing and install adjusting nut. Adjust rear wheel bearing. *See Rear Wheel Bearing Adjustment in WHEEL ALIGNMENT Section.*

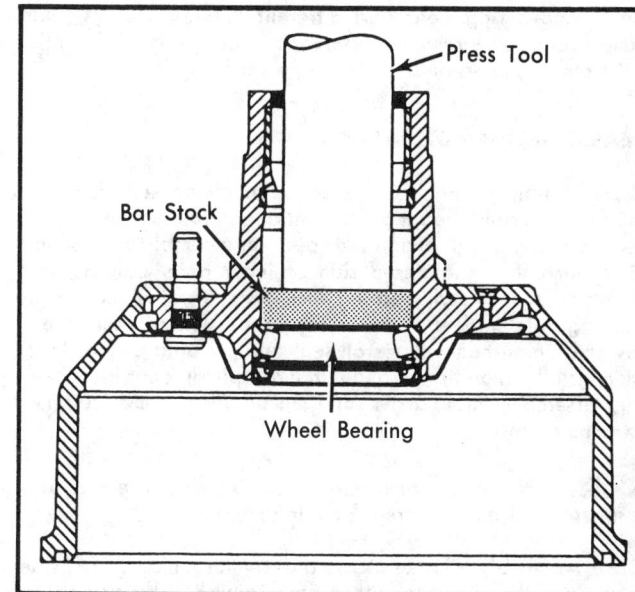

Fig. 1 Sectional View Showing Inner Bearing Cup Removal

PINION FLANGE & SEAL

Disconnect propeller shaft and tie out of way, then scribe a line down pinion nut, pinion stem and pinion flange for reassembly reference. Remove pinion nut and pull pinion flange from stem, then remove oil seal retainer bolts and remove retainer from carrier. Pry old seal from bore, using care not to damage machined surfaces. Clean area thoroughly, then pack cavity between seal lips with high melting point bearing lubricant. Place seal into bore, then drive seal in until it bottoms against shoulder in retainer. Install retainer to carrier; then install pinion flange, pinion nut and propeller shaft.

DIFFERENTIAL CARRIER

Drain lubricant, then remove axle shafts and axle housing cover. Remove trunnion bearing "U" bolts and split universal joint. Tie propeller shaft out of way and remove carrier-to-housing attaching bolts. Support carrier on suitable lift and remove from axle housing. To install, reverse removal procedure.

OVERHAUL

DISASSEMBLY

1) With carrier assembly mounted in suitable holding device, loosen thrust pad lock nut and remove thrust pad. Remove differential adjusting nut locks and bearing cap bolts. Mark bearing caps and carrier for reassembly reference, then remove adjusting nuts and bearing caps. Remove differential and ring gear assembly from carrier.

CAUTION — *Do not attempt to pry cap from carrier, as this may damage machined face of cap.*

Drive Axles

GENERAL MOTORS 12¼" RING GEAR (Cont.)

2) Remove pinion seal retainer bolts, then remove pinion gear and bearing assembly from carrier. Remove pinion nut, pinion flange and pinion seal retainer from pinion gear, then press bearings from gear.

3) Mark differential case halves for reassembly reference, then remove ring gear and differential side bearings. Split case halves and remove differential side gears, differential spider and pinion gears, and thrust washers.

REASSEMBLY & ADJUSTMENT

Drive Pinion — Pack cavity between pinion seal lips with high melting point bearing lubricant and install seal into pinion seal retainer. Install pinion rear bearing assembly onto pinion shaft such that chamfered side of inner race seats against shoulder, then install bearing lock ring. Install pinion front bearing onto shaft such that extended portion of inner race is toward pinion head. Place oil seal retainer onto pinion shaft, then install pinion flange and nut. Place pinion gear and bearing assembly into carrier and install pinion seal retainer attaching bolts.

NOTE — *Pinion depth and pinion bearing preload adjustments are not required for this axle.*

Case Assembly—1) Lubricate differential pinion gears, side gears and thrust washers, then place pinion gears and thrust washers on differential spider. Install side gears and spider assembly into left half of differential case, then assemble two halves of case, making sure alignment marks on both halves are together.

2) Install two guide pins in ring gear, directly opposite each other. Start guide pins through holes in case flange and tap ring gear lightly with soft face hammer until ring gear attaching bolts can be started. Tighten bolts evenly until ring gear is flush with case flange. Remove two guide pins and tighten all ring gear bolts alternately and evenly.

Backlash & Final Assembly—1) Install differential case assembly, bearing adjusting nuts and side bearing caps into carrier. With bearing caps loosened to permit turning of adjusting nuts, adjust bearings to remove all backlash from ring gear and pinion.

2) Loosen left adjusting nut one or two notches to a locking position, then tighten right adjusting nut to force differential against left adjusting nut. Back off right adjusting nut slightly, then retighten snugly against bearing. Tighten right nut additional one or two notches to a locking position.
NOTE — *This adjustment provides for proper preload of differential side bearings.*

3) Mount dial indicator to carrier and check backlash at four locations around ring gear. Adjust backlash to specifications and tighten bearing cap bolts. Install bearing adjusting nut locks and check tooth contact pattern. Install ring gear thrust pad and tighten until pad just touches back face of ring gear while rotating gear. Back off thrust pad screw 1/12 turn and tighten lock nut.

CAUTION — *If one adjusting nut is loosened the other nut must be tightened an EQUAL AMOUNT to maintain side bearing preload.*

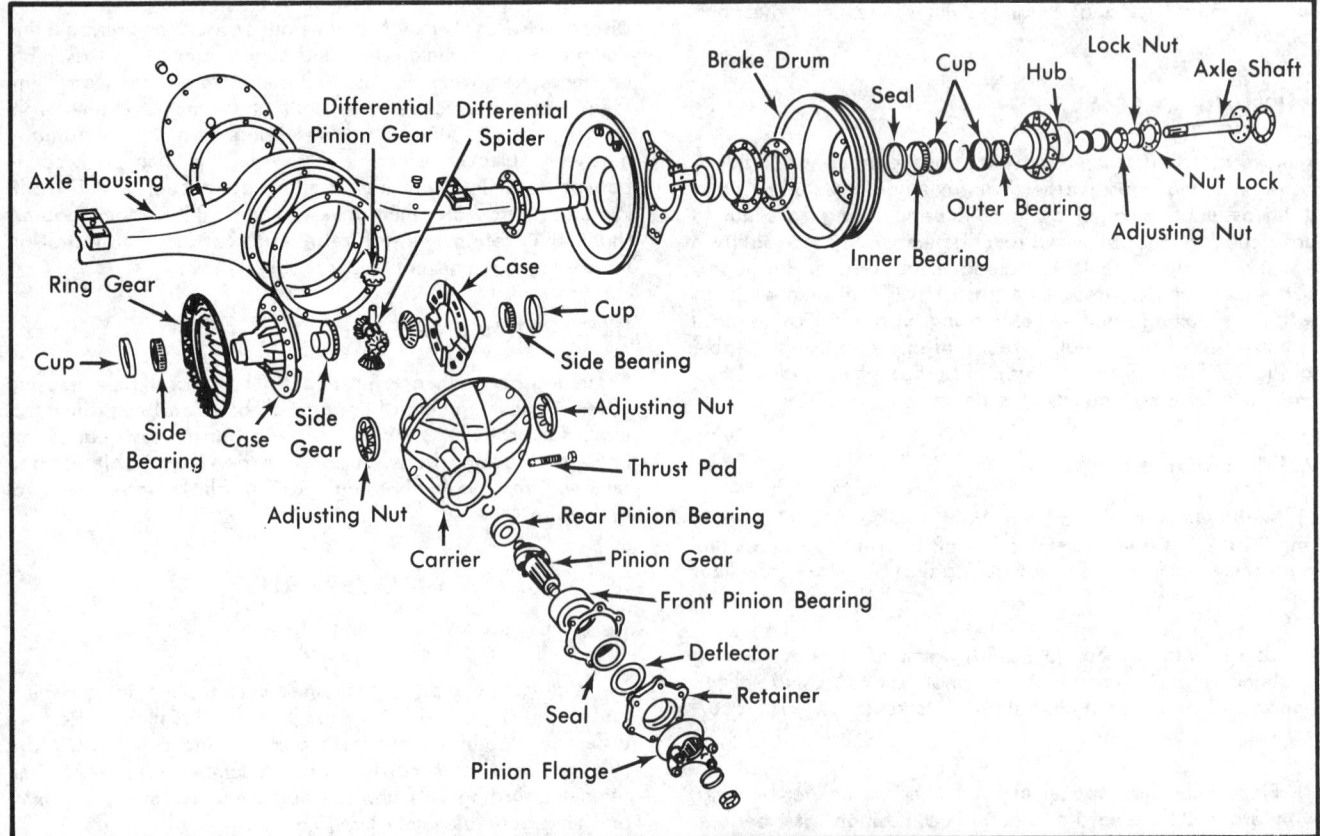

Fig. 2   Exploded View of General Motors 12¼" Ring Gear Drive Axle Assembly

GENERAL MOTORS 12¼" RING GEAR (Cont.)

Lock Nut

Adjusting Screw

Fig. 3   Ring Gear Thrust Pad Adjustment

AXLE ASSEMBLY SPECIFICATIONS

Ring Gear Backlash
  Preferred .... .005-.008"
  Acceptable .... .003-.012"
Thrust Pad Clearance .... .005-.007"

TIGHTENING SPECIFICATIONS

Application	Torque (Ft. Lbs.)
Ring Gear	105
Side Bearing Cap	205
Drive Pinion Nut	220
Differential Carrier	85
Differential Bearing Adjusting Lock	15
Pinion Seal Retainer	165
Thrust Pad Lock Nut	135

Drive Axles

JEEP 8 ⅞" RING GEAR

Cherokee
CJ Models
J10 Models
Scrambler
Wagoneer

DESCRIPTION

The Jeep 8-⅞" ring gear axle assembly is a hypoid gear type with integral carrier housing. Unit is used as rear drive axle on all CJ, Scrambler, some Cherokee, J10 trucks and Wagoneer models. Unit is a semi-floating axle type with tapered axle shafts on CJ and Scrambler models, and flanged axle shaft on Cherokee, J10 trucks and Wagoneer models. Pinion bearing preload is adjusted by varying shim thickness. A removable housing cover allows access to differential for inspection or minor servicing without removing axle assembly.

AXLE RATIO & IDENTIFICATION

The Jeep unit has a 10 bolt cover. Some jeep models use a Spicer (Dana) axle. Refer to *Spicer (Dana) Semi-Floating* or *Full-Floating* articles in this section, for correct identification. All models with Trac-Lok differential have a tag secured to cover by one bolt. Tag indicates that only Jeep Trac-Loc differential lubricant be used. To determine drive axle ratio, refer to *Drive Axle Ratio Identification in this section.*

REMOVAL & INSTALLATION

AXLE HUB

Removal (CJ & Scrambler Models) — Remove dust cap, nut and washer. Raise vehicle and remove tire and wheel. Remove brake drum retaining screws and remove drum. Using a suitable puller (J-25109-01), remove hub. Inspect hub for loose or damaged wheel studs. Check keyway and tapered center bore for wear or cracks, and replace hub if necessary.

CAUTION — *Do not use a knockout or slide hammer-type puller to remove hub. This type of puller may damage axle assembly.*

Installation (Original Hub) — Align axle key and hub keyway. Slide hub onto axle shaft as far as possible. Install nut and washer, drum, retaining screws, and wheel and tire. Lower vehicle and tighten nut to 250 ft. lbs. Tighten nut to align cotter key hole, DO NOT back nut off.

NOTE — *Installation procedures for a new hub and an old hub will differ. If axle shaft is replaced, hub must also be replaced, but a new hub can be installed on an old axle shaft.*

Installation (New Hub) — 1) Align axle key and hub keyway. Slide hub onto axle shaft as far as possible. Install two lubricated thrust washers and axle shaft nut. Install drum, retaining screws, and wheel and tire. Lower vehicle. See Fig. 1.

2) Tighten axle shaft nut until distance from outer hub face to end of axle is 1⁵⁄₁₆". Pressing hub on to this dimension is necessary to form hub serrations correctly. Remove axle shaft nut and one washer. Install nut and tighten to 250 ft. lbs. Tighten nut to align cotter key hole. DO NOT back off nut.

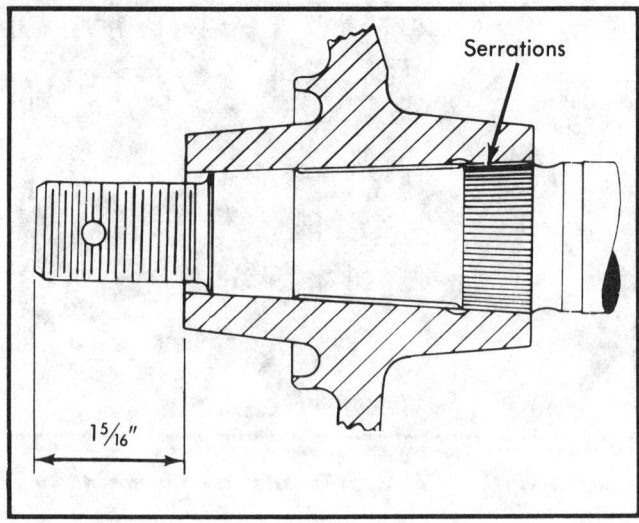

Fig. 1   View Showing Hub Installation Measurement

AXLE SHAFTS & BEARINGS

Removal (CJ & Scrambler Models) — 1) Remove axle hub as previously outlined. Disconnect parking brake cable at equalizer and brake line at wheel cylinder. Remove backing plte, oil seal and shims from axle shaft.

2) Using a suitable puller (J-2498) remove axle shaft. Remove and discard inner seal. Bearing cone is press fit on axle shaft and must be removed using an arbor press and suitable mandrels.

Installation (CJ & Scrambler Models) — 1) Press new axle bearing onto shaft with small diameter of cone towards outer end of shaft. Coat inner axle shaft seal with a light coat of oil. Coat outer surface of metal retainer with non-hardening sealer. Install inner seal in axle housing using a suitable installer (J-21788).

NOTE — *Tapered axle shaft bearings have no provision for lubrication and should be packed with a good wheel bearing lubricant before installation.*

2) Place axle shaft in housing and align splined end with differential gears. Install outer bearing cup. Coat backing plate with sealer at mounting area. Install original shims, oil seal assembly, and backing plate. Tighten backing plate bolts to 35 ft. lbs. Oil seal and retainer are located on outside of backing plate. If left axle was removed, end play must be adjusted.

3) To adjust end play, remove left axle hub if not previously removed. Strike ends of both axles with a lead hammer to seat bearings. Attach a suitable tool (J-2092) and a dial indicator to left axle. Move axles back and forth to measure end play. End play should be .004"-.008" with .006" recommended. Add shims to increase end play and remove shims to decrease end play. Install hub and drum as previously outlined. Adjust brakes and bleed brake hydraulic system.

JEEP 8 ⅞ " RING GEAR (Cont.)

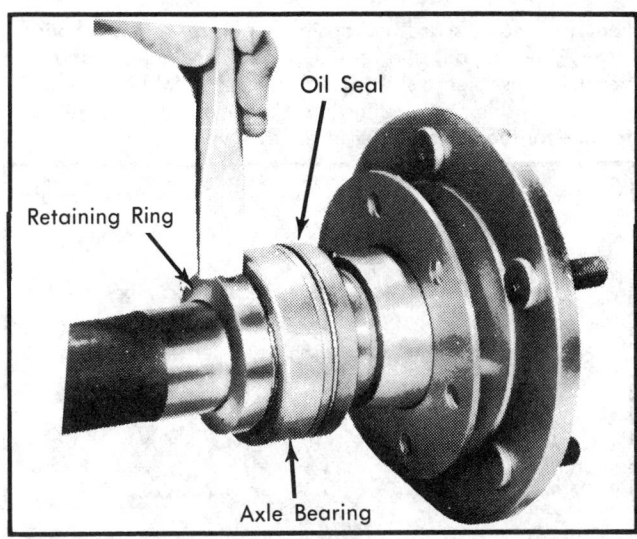

Fig. 2   Removing Bearing Retaining Ring (Cherokee, J-10 & Wagoneer)

Removal (All Others) — 1) Raise and support vehicle and remove rear wheels. Remove brake drum. Remove nuts and lock washers attaching support plate and retainer to axle tube flange.

2) Install suitable slide hammer and adapter tool (J-2619-01 & J-21579) on axle flange and remove axle shaft. Remove and discard oil seal from axle housing and wipe seal bore in housing clean.

3) Mount axle shaft in vise. Drill a ¼ " hole in retaining ring approximately ¾ way through ring thickness, making sure not to let drill contact axle shaft. See Fig. 2.

4) Position chisel over drilled hole in retaining ring and cut or split ring removing it from axle shaft. Cut through oil seal using hacksaw and remove seal and retainer plate, making sure not to damage seal contact surface.

5) Remove axle shaft bearing using arbor press and suitable mandrels.

CAUTION — *DO NOT use a torch to remove axle shaft retaining ring or bearing.*

Installation (All Others) — 1) Install retainer plate on axle shaft. Pack wheel bearing lubricant in oil seal cavity and between oil seal lips and install seal on axle shaft with outer face of seal facing axle flange.

2) Pack new axle bearing with wheel bearing lubricant. Install bearing on axle shaft making sure bearing cup rib ring is facing axle flange.

3) Install bearing retainer ring. Press axle shaft bearing and retaining ring on axle shaft simultaneously, making sure both are seated properly against axle shaft shoulder.

4) Install new oil seal in axle housing using a suitable installer (J-21788), and install axle shaft through support plate. Coat outside diameter of bearing cup with wheel bearing lubricant before installing in bearing bore.

5) Tap flanged end of axle shaft lightly using rawhide (or equivalent) mallet to position axle shaft bearing in bearing bore of housing. Install axle shaft retainer and brake support plate to axle tube flange.

6) Install attaching lockwashers and nuts and tighten to 35 ft. lbs. Install brake drums and rear wheels. Lower vehicle.

PINION FLANGE & SEAL

Removal — Raise and support vehicle and remove both rear wheels and tires, and brake drums. Disconnect propeller shaft from flange. Mark propeller shaft position with flange. Connect an INCH Lb. torque wrench to flange nut. Rotate several times and measure torque required to turn pinion. Record reading for assembly. Hold flange and remove nut. Mark position of flange on drive pinion. Discard pinion nut. Using a suitable puller, remove flange. If surface is damaged or grooved, replace flange. Pry out old seal and discard.

Installation — 1) Coat seal lip with axle lubricant before installing. Install seal using a suitable installer tool (J-22661). Align drive pinion shaft and flange marks and install flange on drive pinion.

2) Tighten replacement nut only enough to remove end play. Check torque required to turn drive pinion. Refer to reading recorded during flange removal.

3) Tighten nut enough to exceed recorded reading by 5 INCH lbs. Repeat these steps until desired torque is obtained. Install propeller shaft aligning marks. Install brake drums, wheels and tires.

CAUTION — *DO NOT loosen and retighten nut. DO NOT overtighten nut, if correct torque is exceeded, a new collapsible spacer MUST be installed and drive pinion preload MUST be reset.*

AXLE ASSEMBLY

Removal — Raise and support vehicle forward of rear springs. Remove wheels and tires. Mark propeller shaft position with flange and disconnect propeller shaft. Disconnect shock absorbers and brake line at "T" fitting. Plug open ends of lines to prevent dirt entering system. Disconnect parking brake cable at equalizer. Support axle housing with a floor jack. Remove "U" bolts at spring. If vehicle has springs mounted below axles, disconnect shackle bolts and lower spring from axle. Slide axle housing out from under vehicle.

Installation — To install axle assembly, reverse removal procedure. Bleed brake hydraulic system and check axle lubricant level.

OVERHAUL

DISASSEMBLY

NOTE — *It is not necessary to remove complete axle assembly from vehicle for overhaul.*

Drive Axles

JEEP 8 ⅞ " RING GEAR (Cont.)

1) Remove axle shaft dust caps and retaining nuts. Raise and support vehicle. Remove axle housing cover and drain lubricant. Remove axle hubs as previously outlined. Mark differential side bearing caps with a center punch for reassembly. Loosen bearing cap bolts until they are retained by just a few threads, then pull bearing cap back on bolts. This will prevent differential from falling out. Pry differential loose in housing. Now remove bearing caps and differential. Secure bearing shims to their respective bearing caps and cups. See *Fig. 3.*

2) Use a suitable puller (J-2497-01) to remove side bearings from differential. Make sure puller pulls against bearing cone and not bearing cage or rollers. Remove ring gear retaining bolts and tap ring gear off differential using a brass hammer. Drive out pinion shaft lock pin using a ³⁄₁₆" drift punch. Drive out pinion shaft using a punch. With shaft removed, withdraw thrust block. Roll pinion gears around on side gears until they can be removed. Remove side gears and thrust washers. See *Fig. 4.*

3) With propeller shaft removed, hold flange with a suitable tool and remove flange retaining nut. Remove flange using a suitable puller. Install housing cover with two bolts. Remove pinion seal. Strike end of drive pinion with a soft mallet. This will unseat front bearing cone from gear. Remove bearing cone.

Remove and discard collapsible spacer. Remove housing cover, drive pinion, and rear bearing. Remove front and rear bearing cups using a slide hammer and a suitable adapter. Pinion depth shims are behind rear bearing cone. Secure shims to cone for reassembly reference.

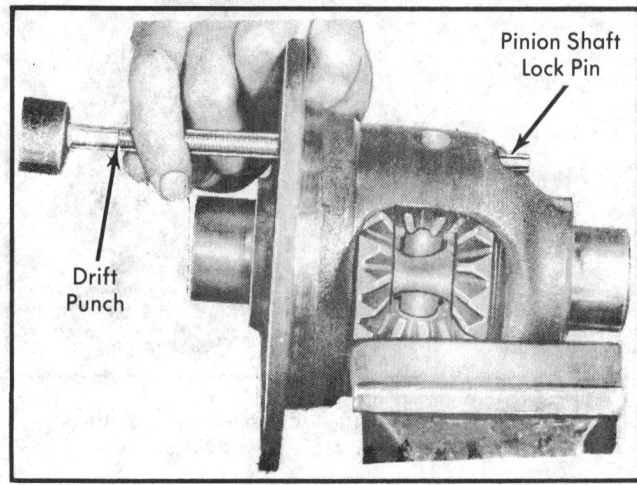

Fig. 4   Removal of Pinion Shaft Lock Pin

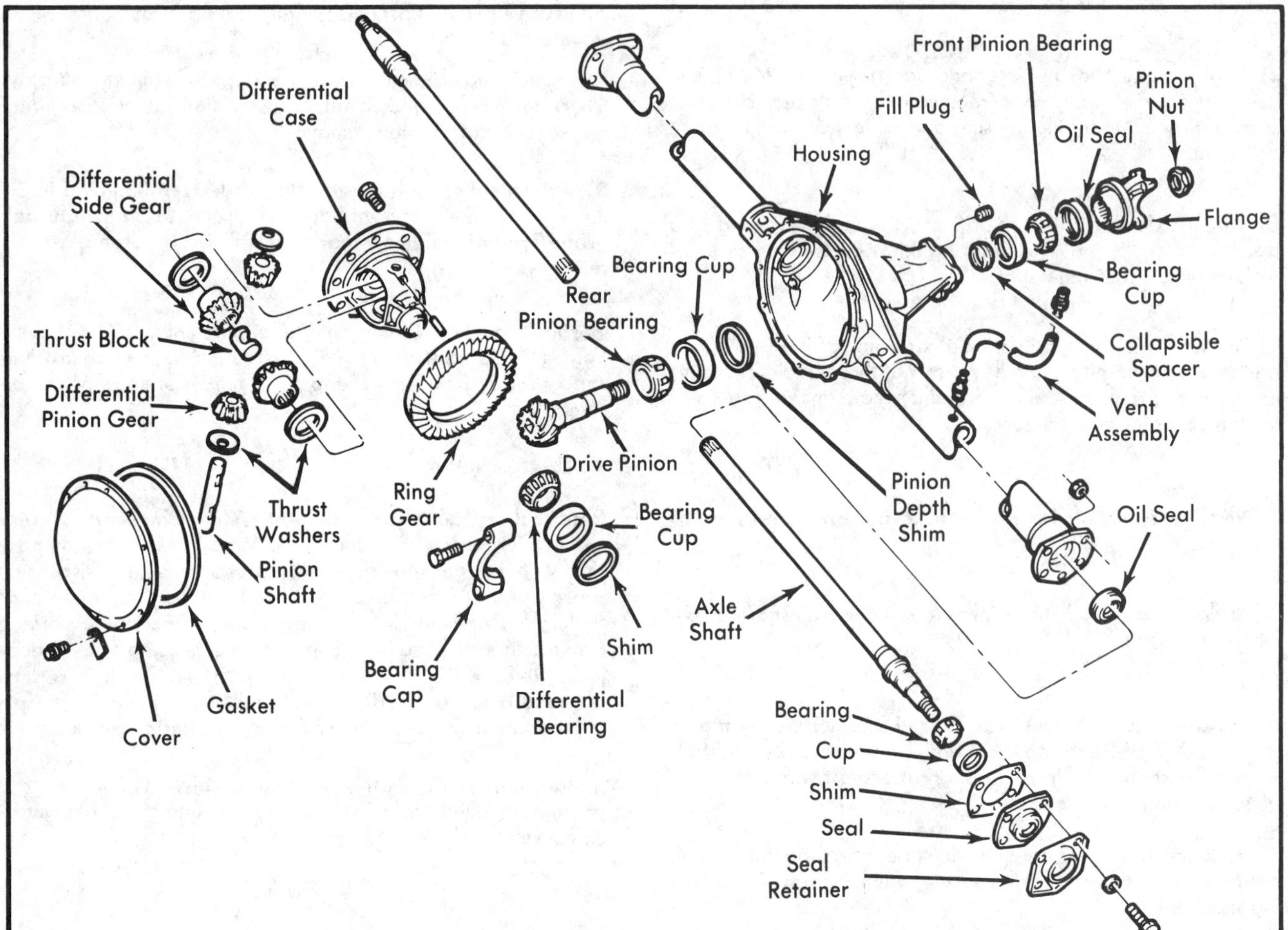

Fig. 3   Exploded View of Drive Axle Assembly (CJ & Scrambler Models)

JEEP 8 ⅞ " RING GEAR (Cont.)

CLEANING & INSPECTION

Clean all components in a suitable solvent. Allow bearings to air dry. Inspect all machined surfaces for smoothness or raised edges. Inspect all bearings and cups for wear or pitting and replace as necessary. Inspect all gear teeth for wear or chipping and replace as necessary. Inspect all splined components for wear or damage and replace as necessary.

REASSEMBLY & ADJUSTMENT

Drive Pinion (Installation & Depth Adjustment) — 1) Pinion gear depth is distance from end face of pinion to the axle shaft centerline. This dimension is controlled by shims installed between pinion gear bearing and axle housing. See Fig. 5.

2) There are 2 numbers painted on pinion gear and one number painted on ring gear. The first number on pinion gear and number on ring gear identify both as a matched set.

NOTE — *Ring and pinion gears should not be used if numbers do not match, or if replacement gear sets are marked ±.009 or more.*

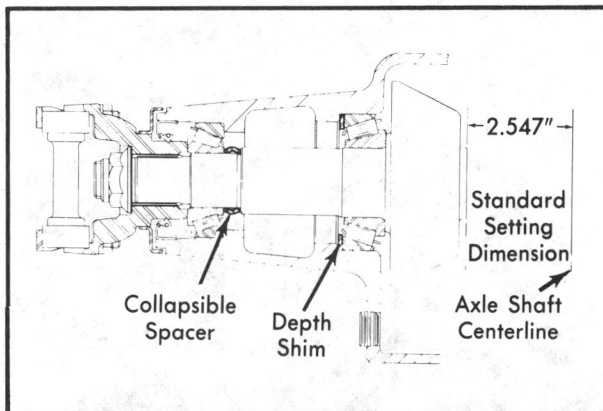

Fig. 5 Sectional View Showing Pinion Depth, Shim Location and Collapsible Spacer Location

3) Second number on pinion gear represents pinion depth variance. This indicates (in thousandths of an inch) the amount that ring and pinion gear varied from standard setting to obtain the correct gear tooth contact pattern.

EXAMPLE: Standard pinion depth is 2.547". If pinion gear is marked 2, the set varied from the standard setting by .002". This means that .002" less shim will be required than a gear set marked 0.

NOTE — *Some factory installed sets may have .010" or .020" machined off the pinion gear end face. Identifying numbers will appear different. For example, if gear is machined .010", the identifying number will appear as +16. This indicates that .010" was removed from end face and that pinion depth variance is .006". A gear machined .020" would be identified in the same manner only a 2 will be used rather than a 1.*

4) To determine a starter shim thickness to measure pinion depth and determine the correct shim thickness, measure thickness of shim removed during disassembly. Note pinion depth variance on old and new pinion gears.

5) Using Pinion Depth Variance Chart, determine amount to be added or subtracted from original shim thickness to determine starter shim thickness.

EXAMPLE: If the old pinion is marked −3 and the new pinion is marked +2, the chart indicates −.005". This means that .005" would be reduced from original shim thickness to determine starter shim.

NOTE — *DO NOT use starter shim thickness as final shim thickness.*

6) Install rear bearing on pinion gear. Make sure large diameter of bearing cage faces gear end of pinion. Make sure bearing is fully pressed against rear face of gear.

7) Make sure pinion gear bearing bores are clean in housing. Install starter shim in rear bearing cup bore. If shim is chamfered, make sure chamfered side faces bottom of bore.

8) Install front and rear bearing cups using suitable mandrels and drivers. Install pinion gear in position in housing.

9) Install front bearing, rear universal joint yoke and original pinion nut. Tighten pinion nut only enough to remove all end play.

NOTE — *DO NOT install new pinion nut or collapsible spacer at this time. These will be installed when pinion bearing preload is adjusted.*

10) Note pinion depth variance marked on pinion gear. Add or subtract this from standard pinion depth. This is correct pinion depth. Record this figure.

11) Assemble pinion depth measuring gauge arbor tool (J-5223-4) and centering discs (J-5223-23). Install gauge assembly, with discs fully seated, in differential bearing cup bores. Install bearing caps and tighten bolts securely.

12) Position gauge block (J-5223-20) on end face of pinion. Make sure anvil end of gauge block is seated on gear and gauge block plunger is under arbor tool.

13) Attach gauge block clamp (J-5223-14 and bolt J-5223-24) to housing cover bolt. Tighten clamp bolt down against gauge block to prevent block from moving. See Fig. 6.

14) Loosen gauge block thumb screw and allow gauge block plunger to contact arbor tool. Now tighten thumb screw securing plunger in position. Remove clamp and then remove gauge block.

15) Using a 2 to 3 inch micrometer, measure distance from end of anvil on gauge block to end of plunger. This represents measured pinion depth. Record this measurement.

JEEP 8⅞" RING GEAR (Cont.)

16) Remove bearing caps, then remove arbor and disc assembly. Remove pinion gear, bearing cup and depth shim from axle.

17) Measure thickness of starter shim. Add this to measurement obtained in step **15)**. From this total, subtract desired pinion depth measurement obtained in step **10)**. The result is the shim thickness required to obtain correct pinion depth.

EXAMPLE:
Standard Pinion Depth		2.547"
Pinion Depth Variance		+.007"
Desired Pinion Depth		=2.554"
Measured Pinion Depth		2.550"
Starter Shim Thickness		+.098"
Total Measured Pinion Depth		=2.648"
Total Measured Pinion Depth		2.648"
Desired Pinion Depth		−2.554"
Correct Shim Thickness		=.094"

Drive Pinion Bearing Preload — 1) Install correct pinion gear depth shim(s) in housing bore. Install pinion gear and rear bearing.

2) Install new collapsible spacer and front bearing in housing. Install pinion oil seal using tool (J-22661). Install universal joint yoke and a new retaining nut. Tighten nut finger tight.

3) Now hold yoke with a suitable tool and tighten nut. Rotate pinion while tightening to make sure bearings seat evenly.

4) Using an INCH lb. torque wrench, measure torque required to turn pinion. If pinion bearing preload is not to specification, continue tightening yoke retaining nut until correct preload is obtained.

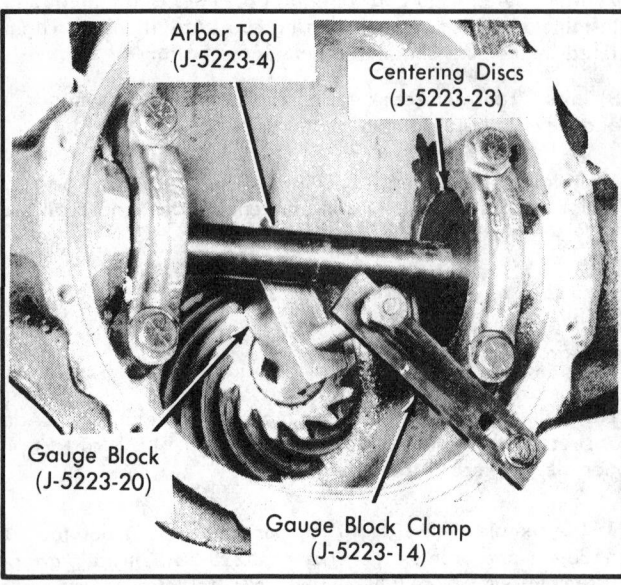

Fig. 6   Measuring Pinion Depth

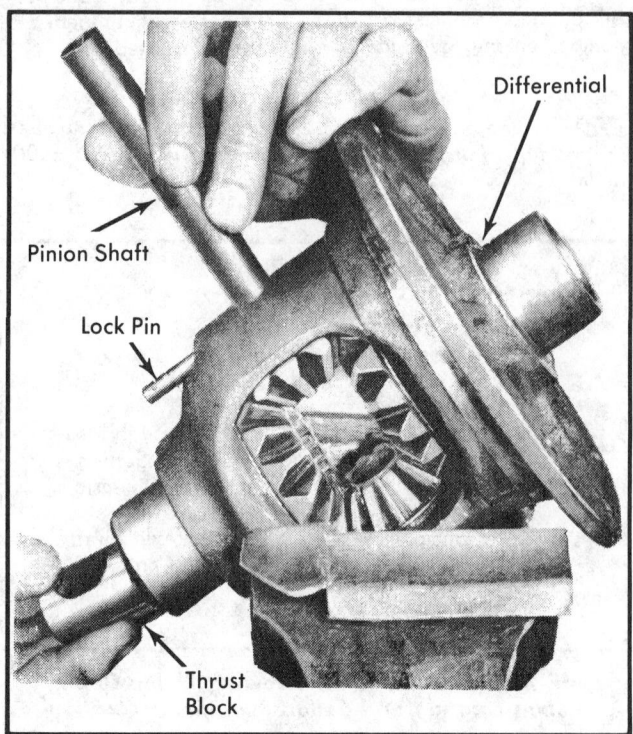

Fig. 7   Installing Pinion Shaft and Thrust Block

PINION DEPTH VARIANCE CHART (INCH)

Old Pinion Marking	New Pinion Marking								
	−4	−3	−2	−1	0	+1	+2	+3	+4
+4	+0.008	+0.007	+0.006	+0.005	+0.004	+0.003	+0.002	+0.001	0
+3	+0.007	+0.006	+0.005	+0.004	+0.003	+0.002	+0.001	0	−0.001
+2	+0.006	+0.005	+0.004	+0.003	+0.002	+0.001	0	−0.001	−0.002
+1	+0.005	+0.004	+0.003	+0.002	+0.001	0	−0.001	−0.002	−0.003
0	+0.004	+0.003	+0.002	+0.001	0	−0.001	−0.002	−0.003	−0.004
−1	+0.003	+0.002	+0.001	0	−0.001	−0.002	−0.003	−0.004	−0.005
−2	+0.002	+0.001	0	−0.001	−0.002	−0.003	−0.004	−0.005	−0.006
−3	+0.001	0	−0.001	−0.002	−0.003	−0.004	−0.005	−0.006	−0.007
−4	0	−0.001	−0.002	−0.003	−0.004	−0.005	−0.006	−0.007	−0.008

JEEP 8⅞" RING GEAR (Cont.)

CAUTION — *DO NOT exceed specified torque. If torque is exceeded, a new collapsible spacer MUST be installed and preload MUST be reset. DO NOT loosen nut to reduce torque.*

Assembling Differential Carrier — 1) Using suitable tools, install differential bearings onto case. Install thrust washers on differential gears (oil pocket side toward gear), then install gears into bores in differential case. Install thrust washers behind differential pinion gears, then mesh gears with differential gears so holes are opposite and in line with each other. Roll gears around until differential pinion gear holes are aligned with shaft holes in case. See Fig. 7.

2) Install thrust block through a differential gear, aligning hole in block with pinion shaft holes. Install pinion shaft, with lock pin hole in shaft aligned with lock pin hole in case. Measure any existing clearance between differential gears and case, using two feeler gauges on opposite sides of one gear. Clearance should be zero.

Adjusting Differential Bearings — 1) Place bearing cup over each differential bearing, then install differential case assembly in axle housing. As a starting point, install an .080" shim on each side. Install bearing caps and tighten bolts finger tight. Mount a dial indicator to housing so that plunger contacts ring gear mounting flange on differential. Using two screwdrivers, pry between shims and housing. Pry assembly to one side, zero indicator, then pry assembly to opposite side and read indicator.

NOTE — *DO NOT read or zero indicator while prying.*

2) The amount read on indicator is amount of shim to be added to arrive at a no preload and no end play condition. Shims are available in thicknesses ranging from .080 to .110" in .002" increments. With all side play eliminated, check ring gear mounting flange for runout. Runout should not exceed .002". Remove differential case from housing and retain shims used to eliminate side play.

Ring Gear Installation — Place ring gear on differential housing case and install retaining bolts. Two bolts installed in opposite holes may be used to pull ring gear into place. Tighten bolts to specification.

Backlash Adjustment — Install differential assembly in housing using shims selected to remove side play. Tighten bearing cap screws to 87 ft. lbs. Attach a dial indicator to housing so that indicator plunger contacts drive side of a tooth on ring gear and is at a right angle to it. Rock ring gear and note movement on dial indicator. Backlash should be .005-.009", with .008" desired. To increase backlash, install a thinner shim on ring gear side. To decrease backlash, reverse procedure, however do not change total thickness of shims.

Differential Bearing Preload — 1) Differential bearings are preloaded by increasing each shim thickness by .004". Install differential bearing shims in axle housing bearing bores. Assemble bearing cups on bearings (cups should completely cover rollers), then position differential so that bearings just start in axle housing bearing bores. Keep assembly square in housing and push in as far as possible. Using a soft hammer, tap outer edge of bearing cups until seated in housing.

CAUTION — *DO NOT distort shims by hammering them into housing.*

2) Install bearing caps, aligning marks made at disassembly, then install and tighten bolts. Preloading differential bearings may change backlash setting, therefore recheck backlash and correct as necessary. After all adjustments have been made, make a gear tooth pattern check to insure correct assembly. Install propeller shaft, axle shafts, bearings, seals, brake backing plate, hubs and drums, reversing disassembly procedures. Fill rear axle with suitable lubricant.

AXLE ASSEMBLY SPECIFICATIONS

Axle Shaft End Play	.004-.008"
Pinion Bearing Preload	17-25 INCH Lbs.
Differential Bearing Preload (Shims)	.008"
Backlash	.005-.009"
Pinion Gear Depth (Std. Setting)	2.547"

TIGHTENING SPECIFICATIONS

Application	Ft. Lbs.
Differential Bearing Cap Bolts	87
Ring Gear Bolts	105
Backing Plate Bolts	32
Rear Wheel Hub-to-Axle Nut	250 (Min.)
"U" Joint Bolt Clamp	13

SPICER (DANA) SEMI-FLOATING AXLES

Chrysler Corp.
Ford
General Motors
Jeep

NOTE — *FRONT AXLE USAGE* — *The Spicer (Dana) models 30 & 50 are used as front drive axles. The models 44 & 60 are used as both front and rear drive axles, with semi-floating axles. The model 60 is also available with full-floating axles. See Spicer (Dana) Full-Floating Axles in this section.*

NOTE — *For removal and installation instructions, see appropriate articles on Locking Hubs and 4-Wheel Drive Steering Knuckles in this section.*

DESCRIPTION

The axle assembly is the hypoid gear type with integral carrier housing and an over-hung mounted drive pinion. The drive pinion depth, pinion bearing preload and side bearing preload are all set or adjusted by shims. Other than the components required for front wheel drive units, service and overhaul procedures for all axle models are the same except for drive pinion depth and some torque specifications.

All Spicer (Dana) drive axles have a removable rear cover plate. The cover plate has a unique shape, that allows positive identification of Spicer (Dana) drive axles on any vehicle. See *Fig. 1*. The axle model is often cast into the differential housing, or it can be determined by measuring the diameter off the ring gear. See the following chart. To determine the drive axle ratio, refer to Drive Axle Ratio Identification in this section.

AXLE RATIO & IDENTIFICATION

Model I.D. By Ring Gear Diameter

Model I.D.	Ring Gear Diameter
Model 30	7.25"
Model 44	8.50"
Model 50	9.25"
Model 60	9.75"

REMOVAL & INSTALLATION

NOTE — *For front axle shaft and bearing removal, see Spicer (Dana) Full-Floating Axles or 4-Wheel Drive Steering Knuckles in this section.*

AXLE SHAFTS & BEARINGS

NOTE — *Spicer (Dana) semi-floating axles do not require an end play adjustment.*

Removal — **1)** Raise vehicle and support with safety stands. Remove wheel, brake drum retaining clips, and brake drum.

NOTE — *If it is necessary to back off brake shoes to remove drum, be sure that automatic adjuster lever is held away from starwheel before rotating starwheel.*

2) Remove bearing retainer bolts and pull axle shaft out of housing. If axle seems stuck, install wheel to flange and use wheel for leverage.

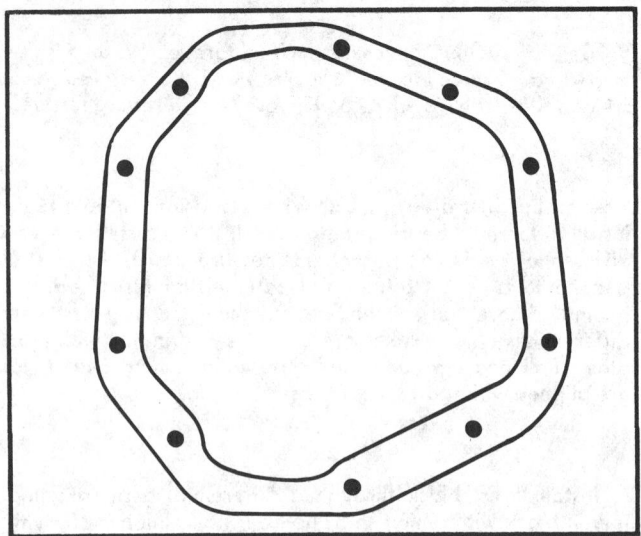

Fig. 1   Spicer (Dana) Housing Cover Gasket for Identification Purposes

CAUTION — *Do not strike axle shaft to free it.*

3) Using a suitable puller, remove bearing cup and oil seal from bore of axle housing. To remove bearing from axle, cut through bearing retaining ring with a cold chisel without nicking axle shaft. With retainer removed, press bearing off shaft. Remove outer oil seal and retainer plate from axle shaft.

CAUTION — *Do not use heat from any source to remove retaining ring.*

NOTE — *If old bearing is to be reused and is still installed on axle shaft, it can be lubricated as follows: Push bearing retainer and seal towards flange end of shaft, being careful that seal does not come off machined part of shaft. Fill cavity between seal and bearing with grease. Wrap masking tape around seal and bearing to retain grease. With masking tape in place, pull seal up towards bearing, forcing grease into bearing. If grease does not appear at small end of rollers, repeat procedures.*

CAUTION — *Be sure that no grease is on flange side of seal.*

Be Sure Lubricant Squeezes Out Here

Lift Seal & Tape Together

Fig. 2   Lubricating Bearing Installed on Axle Shaft

SPICER (DANA) SEMI-FLOATING AXLES (Cont.)

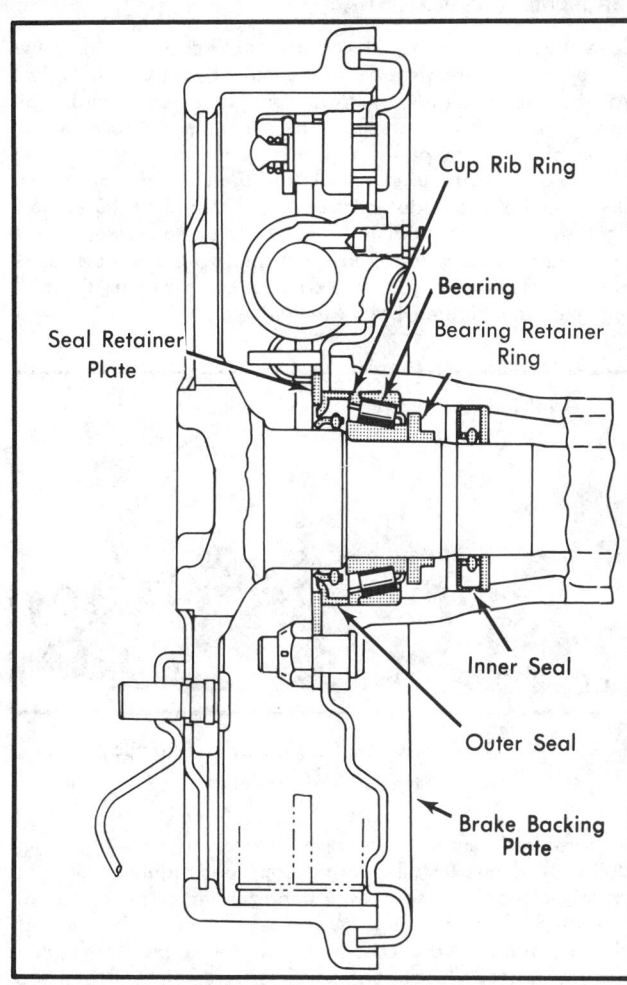

Fig. 3   Sectional View of Flanged Shaft End With Non-Adjustable Bearing

Labels in figure: Cup Rib Ring, Bearing, Bearing Retainer Ring, Seal Retainer Plate, Inner Seal, Outer Seal, Brake Backing Plate

Removal — 1) Raise vehicle and support with safety stands. Remove wheel and tire assembly, and brake caliper.

2) Remove brake backing plate and bearing retaining plate nuts through access hole in axle shaft flange.

3) Bolt a suitable adapter (J-21579) to lug bolts on axle shaft flange. Attach a slide hammer to adapter and remove axle shaft from housing.

4) Pry out axle shaft oil seal from axle housing.

5) Mount axle shaft in a vise. Drill a ¼" hole in bearing retainer ring. Drill hole to a depth ¾ of ring thickness. Do not allow drill to contact axle shaft.

6) Place a chisel over drilled hole in ring. Using chisel, cut a deep groove in ring. This will enlarge ring and allow it to be removed from axle shaft.

NOTE — *Do not heat retaining ring. Heat will transfer to bearing journal and weaken it.*

7) Position a suitable support plate (J-23674) under bearing. Place bearing and support plate in a hydraulic press and remove bearing from axle shaft.

8) Cut through oil seal using a hacksaw. Remove seal and retainer plate. Inspect seal surface on axle shaft for damage. Repair any scratches with crocus cloth.

Installation — 1) Position retainer plate on axle shaft. Pack a suitable wheel bearing grease between oil seal lips.

2) Install oil seal on axle shaft. Make sure outer face of seal faces axle flange.

3) Position bearing on axle shaft. Make sure cup rib ring is facing axle flange. Install a new bearing retainer ring on axle shaft.

4) Using support plate used during bearing removal, press bearing and retainer ring on axle shaft at same time. Make sure bearing and ring are seated against axle shaft shoulder.

5) Install a new oil seal in axle housing tube. Slide axle shaft assembly into position in tube. Care must be taken not to damage seal lip.

6) Apply wheel bearing grease around outside of bearing before sliding into place. Tap flange with a rubber mallet to drive axle into place.

7) Install brake backing plate and retainer plate nuts and lockwashers. Install brake drum. Install wheel and tire and lower vehicle.

PINION YOKE & SEAL

NOTE — *Pinion seal can be serviced with axle assembly installed in vehicle.*

Removal — 1) Disconnect drive shaft and scribe a line down pinion shaft, yoke and nut. Remove nut using tool (J-8614-01) and yoke using tool (J-8614).

CAUTION — *Do not hammer yoke off. Damage to pinion gear, ring gear and bearing could result.*

2) Pry seal from bore using care not to damage machined surfaces.

Installation — Lubricate cavity between seal lips with a high melting point lubricant. Install seal into bore making sure that it bottoms against shoulder. Place flange on shaft and draw it down with pinion nut. Tighten pinion nut to specifications.

CAUTION — *Failure to tighten pinion nut to full specifications will result in flange or pinion shaft failure. Install drive shaft.*

AXLE ASSEMBLY

Removal — Raise vehicle on hoist and support axle assembly to take weight off springs. Disconnect drive shaft at pinion flange and tie out of way. Remove hub and drum assembly. Disconnect vent tube (if equipped), and disconnect parking brake cable(s) and service brake hydraulic lines. Disconnect shock absorbers at axle brackets. Disconnect springs and remove axle.

Installation — Reverse removal procedure. Do not fully tighten shock absorbers nut until assembly is completed. Bleed hydraulic lines and adjust parking brake before moving vehicle.

SPICER (DANA) SEMI-FLOATING AXLES (Cont.)

OVERHAUL

DISASSEMBLY

NOTE — *Axle housing does not need to be removed to overhaul assembly. However, it is suggested that the entire axle unit be removed from the vehicle and held tight in a stand or rack.*

1) Remove housing cover, and mark differential bearing caps for alignment reference. Loosen bearing cap bolts and install axle housing spreader tool (D-113) with holding clamps. Mount dial indicator on axle housing to measure amount of spread.

CAUTION — *Do not spread housing more than .020". Permanent damage to housing could result.*

2) Remove dial indicator after housing has been spread. Remove bearing cap bolts. Carefully pry differential assembly out of housing. Remove spreader tool immediately so that housing does not take set. Mount differential in vise and using brass drift and hammer, remove ring gear. Remove pinion mate lockpin with small punch. Remove pinion mate shaft and thrust block. Rotate pinion gears until gears are aligned with case opening. Remove gears and thrust washers.

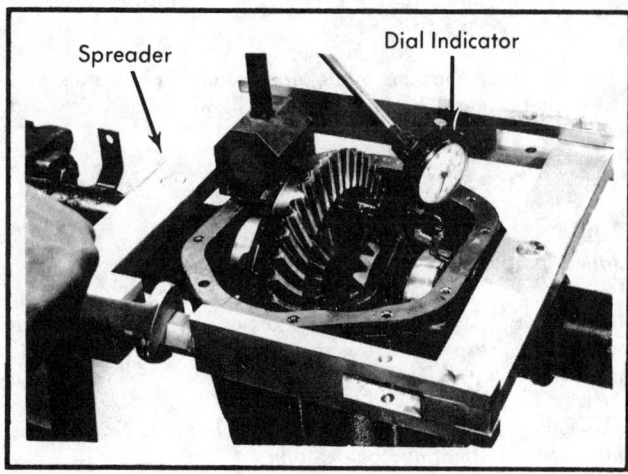

Fig. 4   Correct Procedure to Spread Carrier Housing

3) Remove pinion nut. With suitable puller, remove pinion yoke. Using soft-faced hammer, drive pinion shaft out of housing.

NOTE — *Pinion bearing adjusting shims may remain on pinion shaft, stick to bearing, or fall loose. Collect them and save for reassembly.*

4) From pinion shaft bore, remove oil seal and bearing cone. A baffle or oil slinger may also be present; record the order in which they were removed so that they may be installed correctly. Discard seal. Remove inner bearing cone and press pinion bearing off shaft.

5) Using a suitable puller, remove side bearings from differential case. Often during removal of side bearings, shims between bearings and differential case are mutilated. If so, shims must be individually measured and their thicknesses recorded, so that new shim packs can be secured.

REASSEMBLY & ADJUSTMENT

Case Assembly — 1) Place differential case in holding fixture or vise. Lubricate side and pinion gears and all thrust washers and install in case. Rotate side gears until holes in pinion gears and washers line up with holes in case. Install spacer block (if equipped) and differential pinion shaft. If old thrust washers are used, check for preload of side gears. Clearance between side gears and case should be .000-.006"; if not, shims can be installed (at least one on each side) or new thrust washers used. Install lock pin and peen over hole to retain pin. Inspect ring gear and case for burrs and nicks. Install ring gear and tighten bolts evenly.

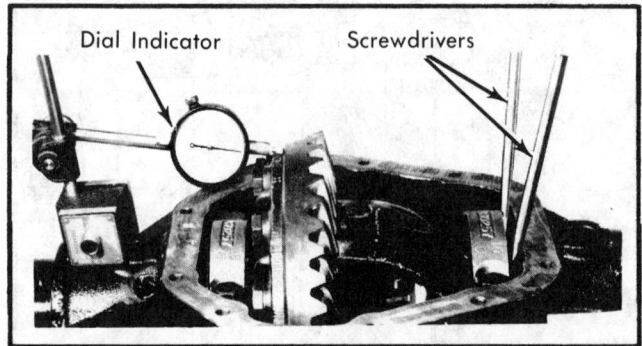

Fig. 5   Measuring Differential End Play With a Dial Indicator

2) Install differential side bearings. Assemble case in housing WITHOUT shims. Install bearing caps and tighten bolts just enough to seat bearing cups. Mount dial indicator to read at back of differential flange. Measure and record amount of side play of differential case by moving back and forth with a screwdriver (see illustration). The measurement will be used later to determine proper shim pack dimension. Remove case from housing.

Pinion Depth & Bearing Preload — 1) Pinion is adjusted by shims placed between inner bearing cup and housing, and by shims placed between pinion shaft shoulder and outer bearing. Shims behind inner bearing cup adjust position of pinion in relation to ring gear. Shims behind outer bearing adjust pinion inner and outer bearing preload.

2) If old pinion and ring gear assembly are used, proceed as follows: Install original shims and inner bearing cup. Install outer bearing cup. Press bearing cone onto pinion shaft and install shaft into housing. Install outer bearing cone, companion flange, and nut. Do not install outer shims or seal at this time. Tighten nut to obtain bearing preload of 10-30 ft. lbs. Use a suitable gauge to measure distance from ring gear center to machined button on end of pinion gear. Add or subtract shims from under inner bearing cup to obtain nominal dimension listed in specifications.

3) If new pinion and ring gear assembly are to be installed, proceed as follows: Determine pinion depth adjustment figure (see illustration) of old and new pinions and find shim adjustment figure from chart. Adjust original shim pack accordingly and proceed as in step **2).**

NOTE — *The previous procedures also apply to pinion adjustment on the FRONT AXLE, which includes the oil slinger between the inner bearing cup and carrier.*

SPICER (DANA) SEMI-FLOATING AXLES (Cont.)

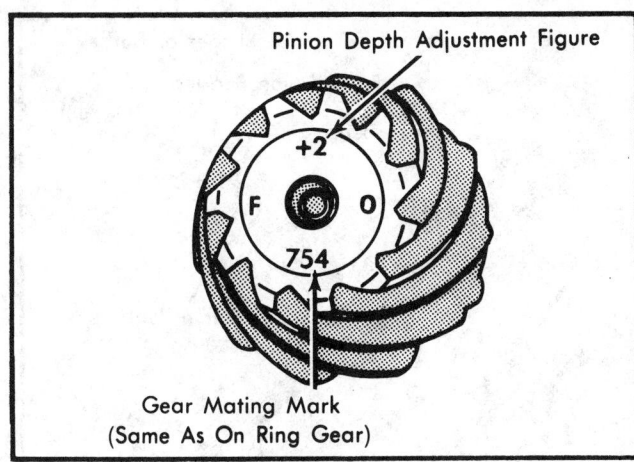

Fig. 6   Pinion Gear Markings Showing
Depth Adjustment Figure

4) Remove pinion gear, rear bearing cup, and starter shim. Install pinion depth shim of correct thickness in housing bearing cup core and reinstall rear bearing cup. Install pinion bearing preload shims. Install pinion gear, front bearing, oil slinger (if equipped), yoke, washer, and old pinion nut. Tighten nut to specified torque, while rotating pinion shaft. Position housing so that pinion shaft is in vertical position, pointing up. With INCH lb. torque wrench, rotate shaft through several revolutions to measure rotating torque.

NOTE — *Ignore torque needed to start shaft rotating.*

5) Check measurement against pinion bearing preload in specifications. To decrease preload, add shims; to increase preload, subtract shims. After adjustment is made, install oil seal and recheck pinion depth.

6) All FRONT AXLES have axle shaft oil seals, which are pressed into the tube ends of the carrier. There are two dif-ferent designs. Check seals in axle housing bores. If condition is questionable, replace, using suitable installer tool.

NOTE — *When installing front axle shaft be sure that these seals are not dislodged.*

Side Bearing Preload — **1)** With pinion installed in housing and depth and preload adjustments properly made, install differential case into housing and set dial indicator so that it reads at back of ring gear. Leave bearing cap bolts loose enough to allow movement of case. Insert screwdriver between bearing cap and housing at opposite end from ring gear. Jam case toward ring gear side and, with force still applied to case, set dial indicator to zero. Jam case the other way (making sure that ring and pinion gears mesh) and record reading. Repeat several times until readings are the same. This reading is amount of shims that will go between case and bearing on ring gear side. Remove indicator and differential case from the carrier. Remove master bearing from differential case. Install these shims.

2) From the figure originally recorded under Case Assembly, subtract amount of shims just installed on case. Add .015" for bearing preload and install new shim pack on end of case opposite ring gear.

Example: +.070" (Original Recorded Sideplay)
         −.032" (Sideplay With Pinion Installed)
         =.038" (Amount Left From Original Sideplay)
         +.015" (Additional Amount For Bearing Preload)
         =.053" (Amount Installed Opposite of Ring Gear)

3) Install spreader to housing, spread housing and install differential case.

NOTE — *Do not spread housing more than .020". Permanent damage to housing could result.*

4) Install differential assembly. Remove spreader and install bearing caps. Make sure that caps are in original position, then tighten caps evenly.

PINION DEPTH SHIM ADJUSTMENT CHART (INCHES)

Old Pinion	New Pinion								
	−4	−3	−2	−1	0	+1	+2	+3	+4
+4	+0.008	+0.007	+0.006	+0.005	+0.004	+0.003	+0.002	+0.001	0
+3	+0.007	+0.006	+0.005	+0.004	+0.003	+0.002	+0.001	0	−0.001
+2	+0.006	+0.005	+0.004	+0.003	+0.002	+0.001	0	−0.001	−0.002
+1	+0.005	+0.004	+0.003	+0.002	+0.001	0	−0.001	−0.002	−0.003
0	+0.004	+0.003	+0.002	+0.001	0	−0.001	−0.002	−0.003	−0.004
−1	+0.003	+0.002	+0.001	0	−0.001	−0.002	−0.003	−0.004	−0.005
−2	+0.002	+0.001	0	−0.001	−0.002	−0.003	−0.004	−0.005	−0.006
−3	+0.001	0	−0.001	−0.002	−0.003	−0.004	−0.005	−0.006	−0.007
−4	0	−0.001	−0.002	−0.003	−0.004	−0.005	−0.006	−0.007	−0.008

SPICER (DANA) SEMI-FLOATING AXLES (Cont.)

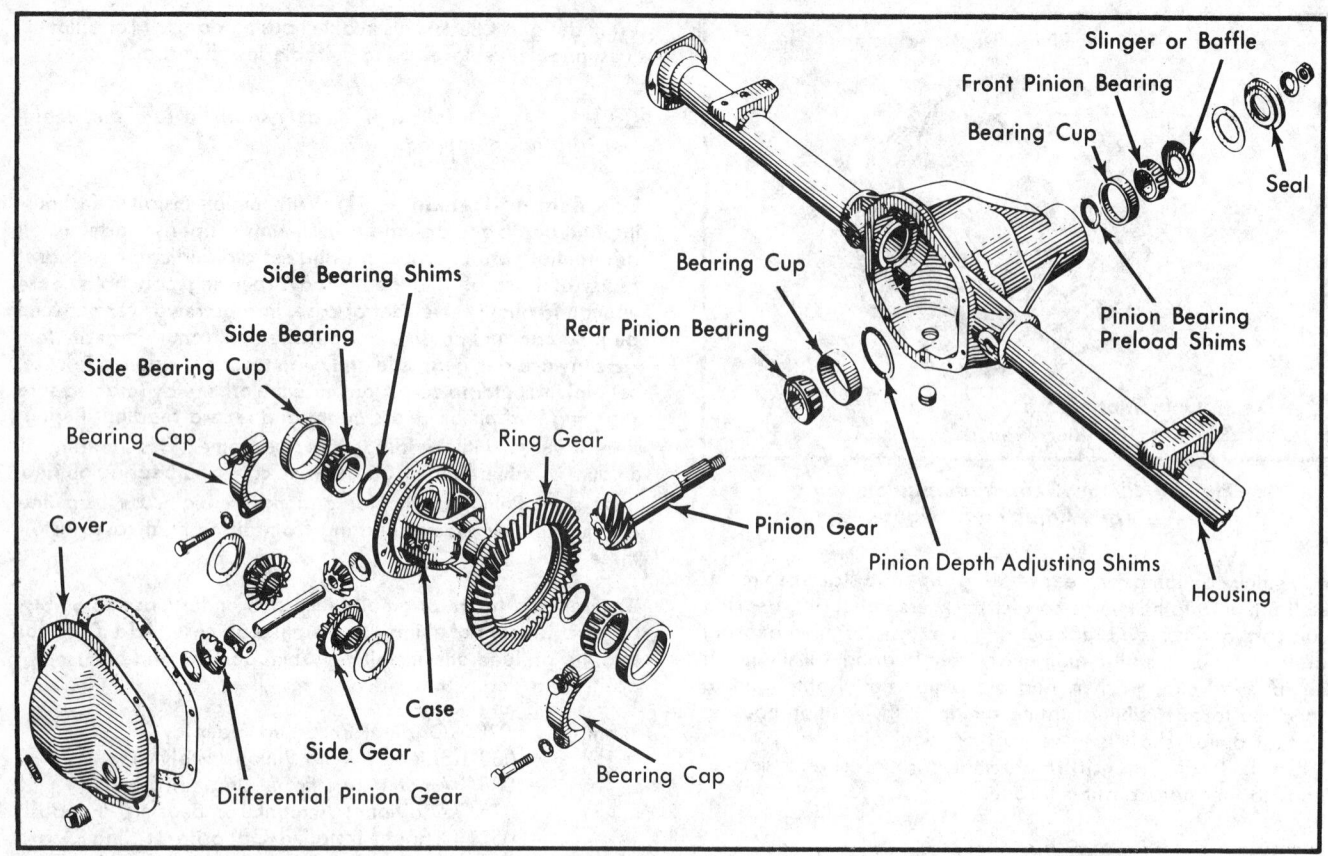

Fig. 7   Exploded View of Spicer (Dana) Model 44 Semi-Floating Axle Assembly

Backlash & Final Assembly — Mount dial indicator to housing and measure ring gear to pinion gear backlash in three places around ring gear (see specifications). Variation between readings should not exceed .002". Adjust to specifications by moving shims from one side of differential case to other, or by changing depth of pinion gear. Check tooth contact pattern (see Tooth Contact Pattern in this section). Install cover and tighten bolts to specifications.

AXLE ASSEMBLY SPECIFICATIONS

Application	Specification
Axle Shaft End Play	Non-Adjustable
Ring Gear Backlash	.005-.010"
Side Bearing Preload	.015"
Pinion Bearing Preload	
New Bearings	20-40 INCH Lbs.
Used Bearings	10-20 INCH Lbs.
Pinion Gear Depth (Nominal Dimension)	
Model 44 (8.500" Ring Gear)	2.625"
Model 30 (7.125" Ring Gear)	2.250"

TIGHTENING SPECIFICATIONS

Application	Ft. Lbs.
Pinion Shaft Flange Nut	210
Differential Side Bearing Cap Bolt	50
Ring Gear-to-Differential Case Bolt	55
Axle Shaft Retainer Bolt	30
Differential Housing Cover Bolt	20

SPICER (DANA) FULL-FLOATING FRONT & REAR AXLES

Chrysler Corp.
Ford
General Motors
Jeep

NOTE — *FRONT AXLE USAGE — With the exception of some C20/30 and K20/30 General Motors models, all front drive axles are Spicer (Dana) Full-Floating front drive axles. All models may use other rear drive axles. See appropriate articles in this section.*

NOTE — *For removal and installation instructions on Locking Hubs and 4-Wheel Drive Steering Knuckles, see appropriate articles in this section.*

DESCRIPTION

Spicer (Dana) axles come in different models for application in vehicles with a wide range of GVW ratings. Service and overhaul procedures for all full-floating axle models are the same, except for drive pinion depth and some torque specifications. The axle assembly has an integral differential carrier and an over-hung mounted drive pinion. The drive pinion depth, pinion bearing preload, and differential side bearing preload are all set by shims. Other than unique components required for front wheel drive units, FRONT and REAR AXLES are identical.

AXLE RATIO & IDENTIFICATION

All Spicer (Dana) axles have an integral carrier with a removable rear cover plate. The cover plate has a unique shape, that allows positive identification of Spicer (Dana) axles on any model vehicle. The axle model is often cast into the differential housing, or it can be determined by measuring the diameter of the ring gear. See following chart. To determine the drive axle ratio, *refer to Drive Axle Ratio Identification in this section.*

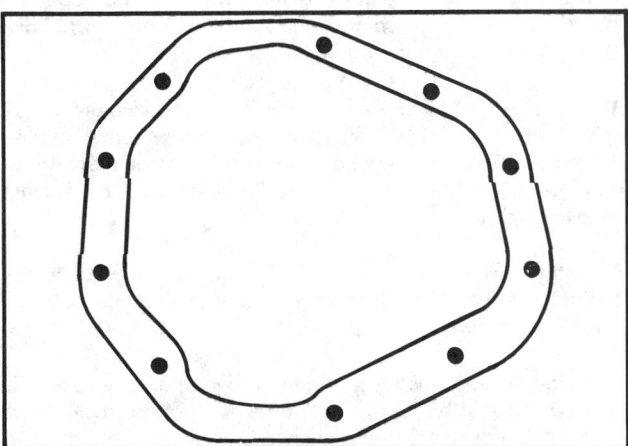

Fig. 1   Spicer (Dana) Housing Cover Gasket for Identification Purposes

Model Identification By Ring Gear Size	
Ring Gear Diameter	**Model Number**
7.125"	30-XX
8.500"	44-XX
9.750"	60-XX
10.500"	70-XX

REMOVAL & INSTALLATION

FRONT AXLE SHAFTS & BEARINGS

Removal (Chrysler Corp. Model 44FBJ Axle) — **1)** Raise vehicle and support with safety stands. Remove wheel and brake caliper assembly. Remove hub cap and snap ring. Remove drive gear and pressure spring. Remove wheel bearing lock nut, lock ring and bearing adjustment nut. Remove hub and assembly. Spring retainer and outer wheel bearing will slide out when hub is removed. Remove hub grease seal, inner wheel bearing cone, inner wheel bearing cup, and outer wheel bearing cup.

2) Remove 6 torque prevailing nuts from brake disc shield. Remove retainer from steering knuckle. If necessary remove brake caliper adapter from steering knuckle. Position a pry bar behind inner axle shaft yoke. Push bearing out of knuckle. Remove "O" ring from steering knuckle (if equipped). Carefully slide out axle shaft assembly. Remove axle seal and stone shield from shaft.

NOTE — *Torque prevailing nuts should be discarded and replaced with new ones during assembly.*

Installation — **1)** Apply RTV sealer to the seal surface of axle shaft housing. Install lip seal on the axle shaft stone shield, with the lip toward the axle spline.

2) Carefully insert axle shaft into the housing so as not to damage the differential seal at the side gears. Install spindle and brake splash shield. Install 6 new nuts and tighten to specifications. Install the rotor, outer bearing nut, washer and locknut onto spindle. Install brake adapter.

3) Install inboard brake shoe on adapter. Slowly slide caliper over disc and into adapter. Install anti-rattle springs and retaining clips and torque to specifications. Install wheel and tire and hub dust cover. Test operation.

Removal (Chrysler Corp. Model 60 Axle) — **1)** Block brake pedal up. Raise vehicle and place on safety stands. Remove wheel and tire. Remove brake caliper. Do not let caliper hang from brake line.

2) Remove cap from center of hub. Remove snap ring. Remove flange nuts and lock washers. Remove drive flange and discard gasket. Straighten tang on lock ring. Remove outer lock nut, lock ring, inner lock nut and outer bearing. Carefully slide hub and rotor off spline.

3) Remove oil seal and inner bearing from hub. Remove bearing cups with a brass drift punch. Remove inner brake pad from adapter. Remove rotor splash shield, brake adapter and spindle to knuckle nuts. Remove spindle from steering knuckle. Slide out inner and outer axle shaft with bronze spacer, seal and oil slinger.

Installation — **1)** Slide axle shaft into position. Place bronze spacer on axle shaft with chamfer side facing toward "U" joint. Install spindle, brake adapter and brake splash shield. Tighten nut to 50-70 ft. lbs.

2) Drive in bearing cups using a suitable installer. Lubricate bearings with suitable lubricant (MOPAR Lubricant Part No. 2525035). Install inner bearing in grease coated hub. Install new seal. Care must be taken not to damage seals.

SPICER (DANA) FULL-FLOATING FRONT & REAR AXLES (Cont.)

3) Install hub and rotor assembly on spindle. Install outer wheel bearing and inner lock nut, tightening to 50 ft. lbs., back off then retighten to 35 ft. lbs. Install outer lock nut and tighten to 65 ft. lbs. Install new gasket on hub, install drive flange lock washers and nuts. Install snap ring and cap in hub, install brake caliper, wheel and tire then lower vehicle.

Removal (Ford) — 1) Raise vehicle and support with safety stands. If equipped with locking hubs, *see removal and installation instructions on Locking Hubs and 4-Wheel Drive Steering Knuckles in appropriate articles in this section.* Remove wheel and brake caliper assembly. Remove hub dust cover and snap ring. Remove drive gear and pressure spring. Remove the wheel bearing lock nut, lock ring, and adjusting nut, using front wheel bearing spanner (T59T-1197-B for F150/250 and Bronco or T78T-1197-A for F350).

2) Remove the hub and disc assembly. Remove the spindle retaining nuts, then carefully remove the spindle from the knuckle studs and axle shaft. It may be necessary to tap the spindle with a rawhide or plastic hammer to break the spindle loose. Remove spindle, splash shield and axle shaft assembly. Remove the stub shaft and slip yoke assembly by removing 3 bolts attaching retainer plate to carrier housing.

3) Place the axle shaft in a vise and drill a ¼" hole in the bearing retainer ring to a depth ¾ the thickness of the ring. With a chisel placed across the hole, strike sharply with a hammer to remove the retaining ring. Replace bearing retaining ring upon assembly. Press the bearing from the axle shaft with the special axle bearing removing tools (T80T-4000-M and T80T-4000-L). Remove the seal and retainer plate from the stub shaft. Discard seal and replace with new seal upon assembly.

Installation — 1) Inspect the retainer plate and stub shaft for nicks or burrs. Replace if necessary. Install retainer plate and new seal on shaft. Coat oil seal with grease. Place the bearing on the shaft. Use axle bearing replacer (T80T-4000-N), and pinion bearing cone remover (T71P-4621-B) to press bearing onto shaft. A .0015" feeler gauge should not fit between the bearing seat and bearing.

2) Install the stub shaft in the carrier and install 3 retainer bolts. Tighten to 40 ft. lbs. Install right-hand axle shaft assembly into slip yoke. Note the blind spline on the axle shaft assembly. Install splash shield and spindle using new nuts. Tighten to 55 ft. lbs. Install hub and disc assembly. Install caliper and wheel assembly.

Removal (General Motors) — 1) Raise vehicle and support on safety stands. Remove wheel and tire. Remove brake caliper. If equipped with locking hubs, *see removal and installation instructions on Locking Hubs and 4-Wheel Drive Steering Knuckles in appropriate articles in this section.* Remove hub lock mechanism.

2) Remove snap ring. Pry out driving hub and spring. Remove wheel bearing lock nut, lock ring and adjusting nut. Outer wheel bearing and retainer will come off with hub. Remove inner bearing, cone and seal from hub using a brass drift punch. Remove inner and outer bearing cups (if necessary) using a brass punch. Remove spindle. Carefully pull axle shaft assembly through hole in steering knuckle.

Installation — 1) Install axle shaft assembly in housing. Care must be taken not to damage seal. Install thrust washer with chamfered end toward slinger on axle. Install spindle. Tighten bolts to 25 ft. lbs. (K10, K1500, K20 and K2500) and to 60 ft. lbs. (K30 and K3500).

2) Install inner and outer bearing cones in hub using suitable drivers. Lubricate cones and bearings with suitable wheel bearing lubricant. Install inner bearing in cone and install new seal. Install outer bearing and retainer in hub.

3) Position hub and rotor assembly on spindle. Install inner adjusting nut, tightening to 50 ft. lbs., back off then retighten to 35 ft. lbs. Install outer lock nut and tighten to 65 ft. lbs. Complete reassembly by reversing removal procedure.

Removal (Jeep "CJ" & Scrambler Models) — 1) Raise vehicle and position on safety stands. Remove wheel and tire. Remove disc brake caliper. Remove drive flange cap from center off hub.

2) Remove drive flange snap ring. Remove bolts securing drive flange to rotor hub. Remove drive flange using a suitable puller (J-25133 or equivalent).

3) Straighten washer lip and remove outer lock nut. Remove washer, inner lock nut and bearing washer. Remove outer bearing and disc brake rotor.

4) Remove disc brake caliper adapter and splash shield. Remove spindle nuts and remove spindle. Carefully pull out axle shaft and "U" joint assembly. Drive inner bearing and seal from hub.

Installation — 1) Make sure all components are clean. Make sure drive flange bolt and bolt hole threads are clean. Install inner bearing and seal in hub.

2) Install axle shaft assembly taking care not to damage seal in axle housing. Install spindle and spindle bearing. Install disc brake caliper adapter and splash shield.

3) Lubricate and install outer bearing in hub assembly. Install hub assembly on spindle. Install washer and adjusting nut and tighten to 50 ft. lbs., then back off ⅙ turn. Install lock washer and lock nut, tightening lock nut to 50 ft. lbs. Bend lockwasher lip over lock nut.

4) Install drive flange and gasket. Coat drive flange bolts with a suitable Adhesive-Sealant (Locktite 242 or equivalent). Install drive flange bolts.

5) Install drive flange snap ring in groove at outer end of axle shaft. Install disc brake caliper. Install hub grease cover. Install wheel and tire and lower vehicle.

REAR AXLE SHAFTS & BEARINGS

Removal — 1) Remove flange nuts from hub studs. Using heavy hammer, rap sharply on center of axle flange to loosen tapered dowels *See Fig. 2.* Remove dowels. Rap center of flange again to cause flange and axle assembly to spring away from hub. Remove axle without using prying devices which might damage axle flange and hub mating surfaces. To service bearings, remove locking devices and bearing ad-

SPICER (DANA) FULL-FLOATING FRONT & REAR AXLES (Cont.)

justing nut. Pull wheel straight off axle housing using care to avoid dropping bearing cones. Remove and discard seal(s). Remove bearing cones from hub or axle housing.

NOTE — *Close inspection of hub and axle type is necessary to determine which procedure applies.*

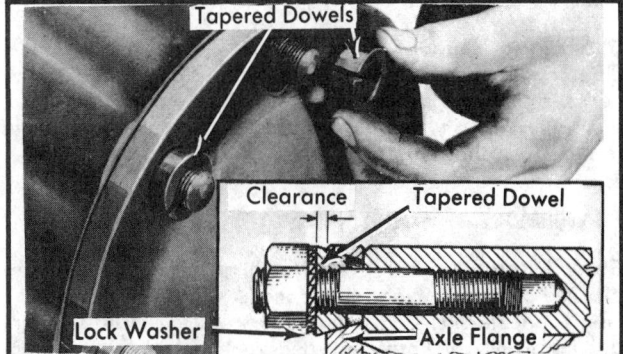

Fig. 2   Detail View of Tapered Dowels

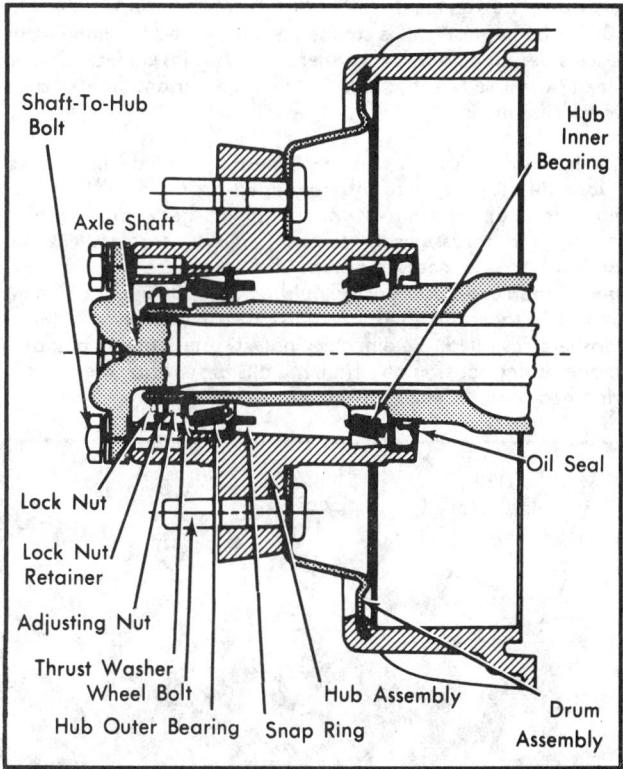

Fig. 3   Sectional View of Axle Shaft and Bearings With Snap Ring Bearing Retainer

2) Two methods are used to position outer bearing cup in hub: Seating cup against a machined shoulder, and seating cup against a removable snap ring set into a machined groove. To remove machined shoulder type, drive each bearing cup out of hub using a long drift or suitable tool. To remove snap ring type, remove inner cup with long drift. Remove snap ring with pliers. Using a suitable tool, drive outer bearing and cup out of hub.

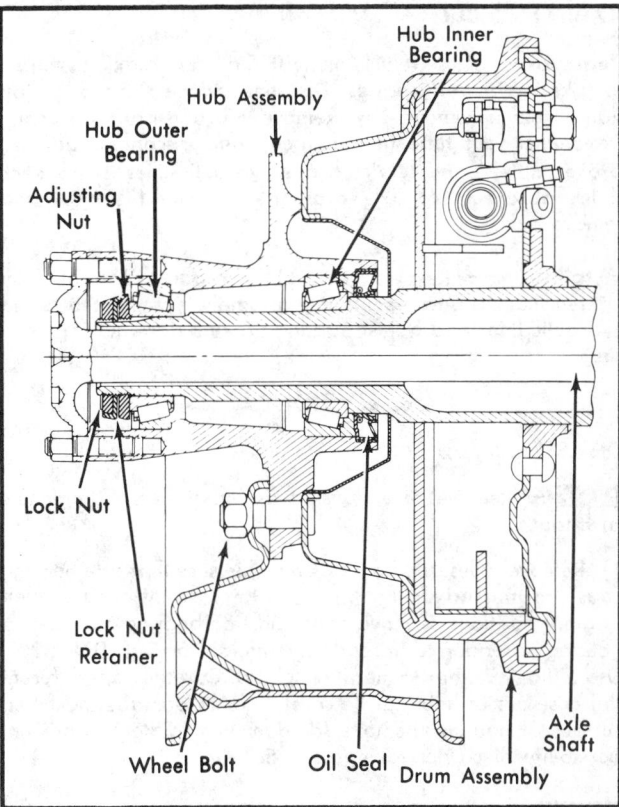

Fig. 4   Sectional View of Axle Shaft and Bearings With Machined Shoulder Bearing Retainer

Installation — To install machined shoulder type, drive or press inner and outer bearing cups into place using a suitable tool. Make sure that cups are firmly seated against shoulders in hub. To install snap ring type, insert outer bearing cone into hub. Insert bearing cup into hub and drive beyond snap ring groove. Install snap ring. Drive cone and cup assembly back against snap ring making sure that it is fully seated. Install inner bearing cup and cone. Install seals. Adjust wheel bearing. *See Rear Wheel Bearing Adjustment in WHEEL ALIGNMENT Section.*

PINION FLANGE & SEAL

NOTE — *Front and rear differentials are the same, except for an oil slinger on the front differential pinion shaft. Pinion seal can be serviced with axle assembly installed in vehicle.*

Removal — Disconnect drive shaft, and scribe a line down pinion shaft, flange and nut. Remove nut, and using suitable tool, remove flange. Pry seal from bore using care not to damage machined surfaces.

CAUTION — *Do not hammer flange off. Damage to pinion gear and bearing could result.*

Installation — Lubricate cavity between seal lips with a high melting point lubricant. Install seal into bore making sure that it bottoms against shoulder. Place flange on shaft and draw it down with pinion nut. Tighten pinion nut to specifications.

CAUTION — *Failure to tighten pinion nut to full specifications will result in flange or pinion shaft failure. Install drive shaft.*

SPICER (DANA) FULL-FLOATING FRONT & REAR AXLES (Cont.)

AXLE ASSEMBLY

Removal — Raise vehicle on hoist and support axle assembly to take weight off springs. Disconnect drive shaft at pinion flange and tie out of way. Remove hub and drum assembly. Disconnect vent tube (if equipped), and disconnect parking brake cable(s) and service brake hydraulic lines. Disconnect shock absorbers at axle brackets. Disconnect springs and remove axle.

Installation — Reverse removal procedure. Do not fully tighten shock absorbers nut until assembly is completed. Bleed hydraulic lines and adjust parking brake before moving vehicle.

OVERHAUL

DISASSEMBLY

NOTE — *Remove axle housing assembly before beginning overhaul.*

1) Remove axles and housing cover. Be sure that side bearing caps are marked so that they can later be installed in their original positions. Remove bolts and side bearing caps. Use a housing spreader to spread differential housing .015-.020". Use a dial indicator to measure spread. Carefully pry differential case out of housing. Be careful not to damage machined surface of housing. Remove spreader immediately to prevent possibility of carrier taking set. See Fig. 5.

CAUTION — *Do not spread housing more than .020". Permanent damage to housing could result.*

2) If differential case is one piece, proceed as follows: Remove bolts holding ring gear to differential case, then tap ring gear off with soft-faced hammer. With a small punch, drive out lock pin. Remove differential shaft and thrust block. Remove differential pinion gears and thrust washers.

3) If differential case is two piece, proceed as follows: Remove bolts holding ring gear to differential case, then tap ring gear off with soft-faced hammer. Mark differentail case halves to aid reassembly. Remove bolts and separate case halves. Remove pinion gear spider, pinion gears, side gears, and all thrust washers.

Fig. 5   Correct Procedure for Spreading Housing

4) Remove pinion nut. With suitable puller, remove pinion flange. Using a soft-faced hammer, drive pinion shaft out of housing. Remove oil seal and bearing cone. If baffle or an oil slinger are also present, record the order in which they were removed so they may be installed correctly. Discard seal. Remove inner bearing cone and press pinion bearing off pinion shaft.

NOTE — *Pinion bearing adjusting shims may remain on pinion shaft, stick to bearing, or fall loose. Collect and save them for reassembly.*

5) Using a suitable puller, remove side bearings from differential case. Often during removal of side bearings, shims between bearings and differential case are mutilated. If so, shims must be individually measured and their thicknesses recorded, so that new shim packs can be secured.

REASSEMBLY & ADJUSTMENT

Case Assembly — **1)** If differential case is one piece, proceed as follows: Place differential case in holding fixture or vise. Lubricate side and pinion gears and all thrust washers and install in case. Rotate side gears until holes in pinion gears and washers line up with holes in case. Install spacer block (if equipped) and differential pinion shaft. If old thrust washers are used, check for preload of side gears by measuring clearance between side gears and case. Clearance should be .000-.006"; if not, shims can be installed (in equal amounts on each side), or new thrust washers installed. Install lock pin and peen over hole to retain pin. Install ring gear and tighten bolts to specifications.

2) If differential case is two piece, proceed as follows: Lubricate all parts with differential lubricant. Install differential side gears and thrust washers, pinion gear spider, pinion gears, and thrust washers in differential case. Check for preload of side gears by measuring clearance between side gears and case. Clearance should be .000-.006"; if not, shims can be installed (in equal amounts on each side), or new thrust washers installed. Rejoin case halves using aligning marks made during reassembly. Tighten bolts to specifications. Install ring gear and tighten bolts to specifications.

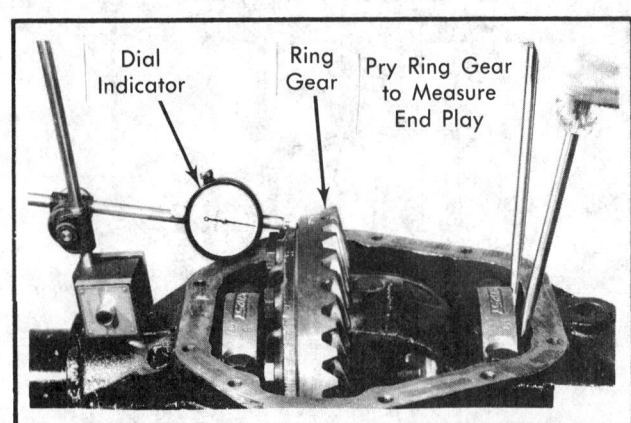

Fig. 6   Using Dial Indicator to Measure Differential End Play

3) Install differential side bearings. Assemble case in housing WITHOUT shims. Install bearing caps and tighten bolts just enough to seat bearing cups. Mount dial indicator to read at back of differential flange. Measure and record amount of

SPICER (DANA) FULL-FLOATING FRONT & REAR AXLES (Cont.)

side play of differential case by moving back and forth with a screwdriver. *See Fig. 6.* The measurement will be used later to determine proper shim pack dimension. Remove case from housing.

Pinion Depth & Bearing Preload — 1) Pinion is adjusted by shims placed between inner bearing cup and housing, and by shims placed between pinion shaft shoulder and outer bearing. Shims behind inner bearing cup adjust position of pinion in relation to ring gear. Shims behind outer bearing adjust pinion inner and outer bearing preload.

2) If old pinion and ring gear assembly are used, proceed as follows: Install original shims and inner bearing cup. Install outer bearing cup. Press bearing cone onto pinion shaft and install shaft into housing. Install outer bearing cone, companion flange, and nut. Do not install outer shims or seal at this time. Tighten nut to obtain bearing preload of 10-30 ft. lbs. Use a suitable gauge to measure distance from ring gear center to machined button on end of pinion gear. Add or subtract shims from under inner bearing cup to obtain nominal dimension listed in specifications.

3) If new pinion and ring gear assembly are to be installed, proceed as follows: Determine pinion depth adjustment figure (*See Fig. 7*) of old and new pinions and find shim adjustment figure from chart. Adjust original shim pack accordingly and proceed as in step **2**).

4) Remove pinion flange and nut, and remove front pinion bearing cone. Install original preload shim pack. Lubricate and install bearing cone. Install pinion flange and nut, and tighten to specifications while rotating pinion shaft. Place housing in position so that pinion shaft is vertical pointing up. Using an INCH lb. torque wrench, rotate shaft through several revolutions to measure rotating torque. Check measurements against pinion bearing preload in specifications. To decrease preload, add shims; to increase preload, subtract shims. After adjustment is made, install oil seal and recheck pinion depth.

NOTE — *Ignore torque needed to start shaft rotating.*

Fig. 7 Pinion and Ring Gear Markings Showing Pinion Depth Adjustment Figure

5) Front axles only: Check seals in axle housing bores. If condition is questionable, replace using suitable installer tool. See Fig. 8.

NOTE — *When installing front axle shaft, be sure that seals are not dislodged.*

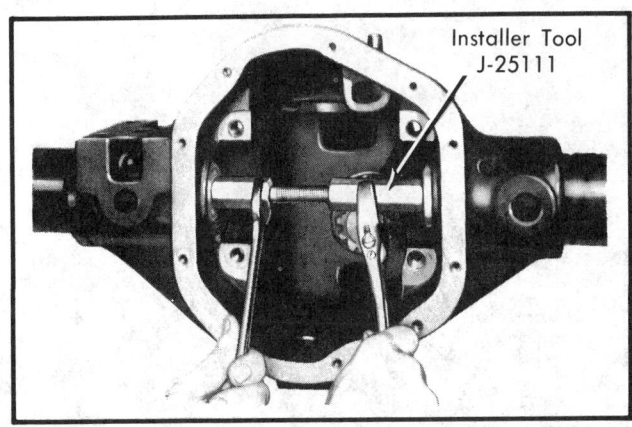

Fig. 8 Correct Procedure for Installing Inner Oil Seals

	PINION DEPTH SHIM ADJUSTMENT CHART (INCHES)								
Old Pinion	New Pinion								
	−4	−3	−2	−1	0	+1	+2	+3	+4
+4	+0.008	+0.007	+0.006	+0.005	+0.004	+0.003	+0.002	+0.001	0
+3	+0.007	+0.006	+0.005	+0.004	+0.003	+0.002	+0.001	0	−0.001
+2	+0.006	+0.005	+0.004	+0.003	+0.002	+0.001	0	−0.001	−0.002
+1	+0.005	+0.004	+0.003	+0.002	+0.001	0	−0.001	−0.002	−0.003
0	+0.004	+0.003	+0.002	+0.001	0	−0.001	−0.002	−0.003	−0.004
−1	+0.003	+0.002	+0.001	0	−0.001	−0.002	−0.003	−0.004	−0.005
−2	+0.002	+0.001	0	−0.001	−0.002	−0.003	−0.004	−0.005	−0.006
−3	+0.001	0	−0.001	−0.002	−0.003	−0.004	−0.005	−0.006	−0.007
−4	0	−0.001	−0.002	−0.003	−0.004	−0.005	−0.006	−0.007	−0.008

Drive Axles

SPICER (DANA) FULL-FLOATING FRONT & REAR AXLES (Cont.)

Side Bearing Preload — 1) With pinion installed in housing and depth and preload adjustments properly made, install differential case into housing and set dial indicator so that it reads at back of ring gear. Leave bearing cap bolts loose enough to allow movement of case. Insert screwdriver between bearing cap and housing at opposite end from ring gear. Jam case toward ring gear side and, with force still applied to case, set dial indicator to zero. Jam case the other way (making sure that ring and pinion gears mesh) and record reading. Repeat several times until readings are the same. This reading is amount of shims that will go between case and bearing on ring gear side. Install these shims.

2) From the figure originally recorded under Case Assembly, subtract amount of shims just installed on case. Add .015" for bearing preload and install new shim pack on end of case opposite ring gear.

Example: +.070" (Original Recorded Sideplay)
—.032" (Sideplay With Pinion Installed)
=.038" (Amount Left From Original Sideplay)

+.015" (Additional Amount For Bearing Preload)
=.053" (Amount Installed Opposite of Ring Gear)

3) Install spreader to housing, spread housing and install differential case. Remove spreader and install bearing caps. Make sure caps are in original position; then tighten caps evenly.

NOTE — *Do not spread housing more than .020". Permanent damage could result.*

Backlash & Final Assembly — Mount dial indicator to housing and measure ring gear to pinion gear backlash in three places around ring gear (see specifications). Variation between readings should not exceed .002". Adjust to specifications by moving shims from one side of differential case to other, or by changing depth of pinion gear. Check tooth contact pattern (see Tooth Contact Pattern in this section). Install cover and tighten bolts to specifications.

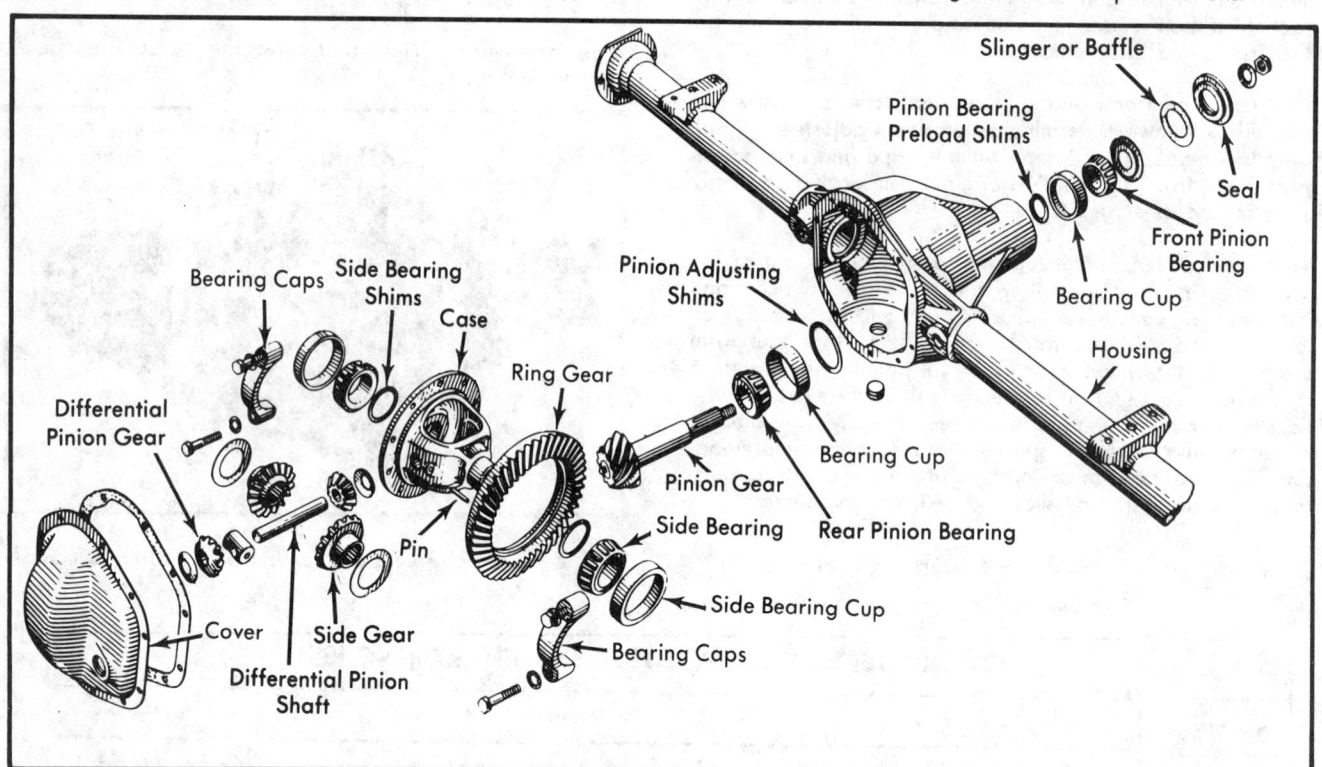

Fig. 9 Exploded View of Spicer (Dana) Full-Floating Axle Assembly (One-Piece Differential Shown)

AXLE ASSEMBLY SPECIFICATIONS

Application	Specification
Ring Gear Backlash	.005-.009"
Side Bearing Preload	.015"
Pinion Bearing Preload	
New Bearings	20-40 INCH Lbs.
Used Bearings	10-20 INCH Lbs.
Pinion Gear Depth (Nominal Dimension)	
Model 30	2.250"
Model 44	2.625"
Model 60	3.125"
Model 70	3.500"

TIGHTENING SPECIFICATIONS

Applications	Ft. Lbs. Models 30 & 44	Ft. Lbs. Models 60 & 70
Pinion Shaft Flange Nut	210	260
Side Bearing Cap		
All (Exc. Model 30)	80	80
Model 30	45	
Ring Gear-to-Case	55	110
Axle Flange-to-Hub		
All (Exc. Model 70)	35	55
Model 70		85
Cover-to-Housing	20	35

Drive Axles

SPICER (DANA) IFS FRONT DRIVE AXLE

Ford

NOTE — *FRONT AXLE USAGE* — *The Spicer (Dana) models 44-IFS, 44-IFS-HD & 50-IFS are used as front axles only. The 44-IFS is used on vehicles with front coil springs. The 44-IFS-HD and 50-IFS axles are used on vehicles with leaf springs.*

NOTE — *For removal and installation instructions, see appropriate articles on Locking Hubs and 4-Wheel Drive Steering Knuckles in this Section.*

DESCRIPTION

The Independent Front Suspension (IFS) front axle is of the integral carrier-housing, hypoid-gear type, with the centerline of the drive pinion mounted above the centerline of the ring gear. The drive pinion bearing preload, and side bearing preload are all set or adjusted by shims. Other than the components required for front wheel drive units, drive pinion depth and some torque specifications, service and overhaul procedures for all axle models are the same.

AXLE RATIO & IDENTIFICATION

All Spicer (Dana) drive axles have an integral carrier with a removable rear cover plate. The cover plate has a unique shape that allows positive identification of Spicer (Dana) drive axles on any vehicle. *See Fig. 1.* A metal tag, stamped with the gear ratio and part number is secured to the housing by one of the carrier bolts. If the axle is equipped with limited slip differential, the axle I.D. tag will have the letters LS following the part numbers. The axle model can be determined by measuring the diameter of the ring gear. See the following chart. To determined the drive axle ratio, *refer to Drive Axle Ratio Identification in this Section.*

Model Identification By Ring Gear Diameter	
Application	**Model**
8.50" Ring Gear	Model 44
9.25" Ring Gear	Model 50

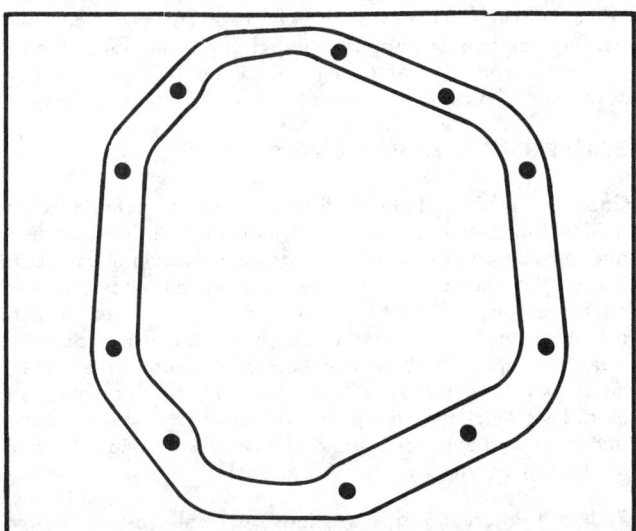

Fig. 1   Spicer (Dana) Housing Cover Gasket for Identification Purposes

REMOVAL & INSTALLATION

AXLE SHAFTS & BEARINGS

Removal — 1) Raise vehicle and support with safety stands. If equipped with locking hubs, *see removal and installation instructions on Locking Hubs and 4-Wheel Drive Steering Knuckles in appropriate articles in this Section.* Remove wheel and brake caliper assembly. Remove hub dust cover and snap ring. Remove drive gear and pressure spring. Remove wheel bearing lock nut, lock ring, and adjusting nut, using front wheel bearing spanner (T59T-1197-B for F150/250 and Bronco, or T78T-1197-A for F350).

2) Remove hub and disc assembly. Remove spindle retaining nuts. Then carefully remove spindle from knuckle studs and axle shaft. It may be necessary to tap spindle with a rawhide or plastic hammer to break it loose. Remove spindle, splash shield, and axle shaft assembly. Remove stub shaft and slip yoke assembly by removing 3 bolts attaching retainer plate to carrier housing.

3) Place axle shaft in a vise, and drill a ¼" hole in housing retainer ring to a depth ¾ the rings thickness. With a chisel placed across hole, strike sharply with a hammer to remove retaining ring. Replace bearing retaining ring upon assembly. Press bearing from axle shaft, using special axle bearing removal tools (T80T-4000-M and T80T-4000-L). Remove seal and retainer plate form stub shaft. Discard seal and replace with new seal upon assembly.

CAUTION — *Do not strike axle shaft to free it. And do not use heat from any source to remove retaining ring.*

NOTE — *If old bearing is to be reused and is still installed on axle shaft, lubricate it as follows: Push bearing retainer and seal toward flange end to shaft, being careful that seal does not come off machined part of shaft. Fill cavity between seal and bearing with grease. Wrap masking tape around seal and bearing to retain grease. With masking tape in place, pull seal up toward bearing, forcing grease into bearing. If grease does not appear at small end of rollers, repeat procedure.*

Installation — 1) Inspect retainer plate and stub shaft for nicks or burrs. Replace if necessary. Install retainer plate and new seal on shaft. Coat oil seal with grease. Place bearing on

Be Sure Lubricant Squeezes Out Here

Lift Seal & Tape Together

Fig. 2   Lubricating Bearing Installed on Axle Shaft

SPICER (DANA) IFS FRONT DRIVE AXLE (Cont.)

shaft. Use axle bearing replacer (T80T-4000-N) and pinion bearing cone remove (T71P-4621-B) to press bearing onto shaft. A .0015" feeler gauge should not fit between bearing seat and bearing.

2) Install stub shaft in carrier, and install 3 retainer bolts. Tighten to 40 ft. lbs. Install right-hand axle shaft assembly into slip yoke. Note blind spline on axle shaft assembly. Install splash shield and spindle, using new nuts. Tighten to 55 ft. lbs. Install hub and disc assembly. Install caliper and wheel assembly.

PINION YOKE & SEAL

NOTE — *Pinion seal can be serviced with axle assembly installed in vehicle.*

Removal — 1) Disconnect drive shaft, and scribe a line down pinion shaft, yoke and nut. Remove nut and yoke using suitable tools.

CAUTION — *Do not hammer yoke off. Damage to pinion gear, ring gear and bearing could result.*

2) Pry seal from bore, using care not to damage machined surfaces.

Installation — Lubricate cavity between seal lips with high melting point lubricant. Install seal into bore, making sure it bottoms against shoulder. Place flange on shaft and draw it down with pinion nut. Tighten pinion nut to specifications. Install drive shaft.

CAUTION — *Failure to tighten pinion nut to full specifications will result in flange or pinion shaft failure.*

AXLE ASSEMBLY

Removal & Installation — Raise vehicle on hoist, supporting axle assembly to take weight off springs. Disconnect drive shaft at pinion flange and tie out of way. Remove hub and disc assemblies. Disconnect vent tube (if equipped), and disconnect shock absorber at axle brackets. Disconnect springs and remove axle. Reverse procedures to complete installation.

OVERHAUL

DISASSEMBLY

NOTE — *Axle housing does not need to be removed to overhaul assembly. However, it is suggested that the entire axle unit be removed from the vehicle and held tight in a stand or rack.*

1) Remove housing cover, and mark differential bearing caps for alignment reference. Loosen bearing cap bolts and install axle housing spreader tool (D-113) with holding clamps. Mount dial indicator on axle housing to measure amount of spread.

CAUTION — *Do not spread housing more than .020". Permanent damage to housing could result.*

2) Remove dial indicator after housing has been spread. Remove bearing cap bolts. Note the matched numbers or letters stamped on the cap and carrier. These letters must be matched upon assembly. Carefully pry differential assembly

out of housing. Remove spreader tool immediately so that housing does not take set. Mount differential in vise and using brass drift and hammer, remove ring gear. Remove pinion mate lockpin with small punch. Remove pinion mate shaft and thrust block. Rotate pinion gears until gears are aligned with case opening. Remove gears and thrust washers.

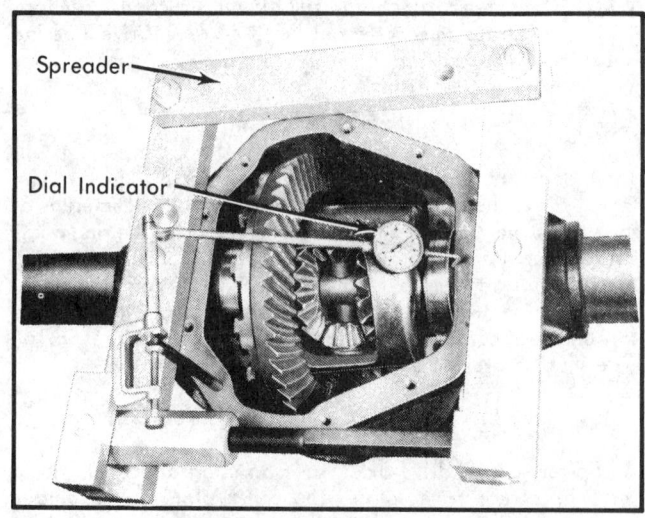

Fig. 3   Spreading Carrier Housing

3) Remove pinion nut. With suitable puller, remove pinion yoke. Using soft-faced hammer, drive pinion shaft out of housing.

NOTE — *Pinion bearing adjusting shims may remain on pinion shaft, stick to bearing, or fall loose. Collect them and save for reassembly.*

4) From pinion shaft bore, remove oil seal and bearing cone. A baffle or oil slinger may also be present. Record the order in which they were removed so that they may be installed correctly. Discard seal. Remove inner bearing cone, and press pinion bearing off shaft.

5) Using a suitable puller, remove side bearings from differential case. During removal of side bearings, shims between bearings and case may be mutilated. If so, shims must be individually measured and their thicknesses recorded, so that new shim packs can be secured.

REASSEMBLY & ADJUSTMENT

Case Assembly — 1) Place differential case in holding fixture or vise. Lubricate side and pinion gears and all thrust washers and install in case. Rotate side gears until holes in pinion gears and washers line up with holes in case. Install spacer block (if equipped) and differential pinion shaft. If old thrust washers are used, check for preload of side gears. Clearance between side gears and case should be .000-.006". If not, shims can be installed (at least one on each side) or new thrust washers used. Install lock pin, and peen over hole to retain pin. Inspect ring gear and case for burrs and nicks. Install ring gear and tighten bolt evenly.

2) Install differential side bearings. Assemble case in housing WITHOUT shims. Install bearings caps, and tighten bolts just enough to seat bearing cups. Mount dial indicator to read at back of differential flange. Measure and record amount of

SPICER (DANA) IFS FRONT DRIVE AXLE (Cont.)

side play of differential case by moving back and forth with a screwdriver. The measurement will be used later to determined proper shim pack dimension. Remove case from housing.

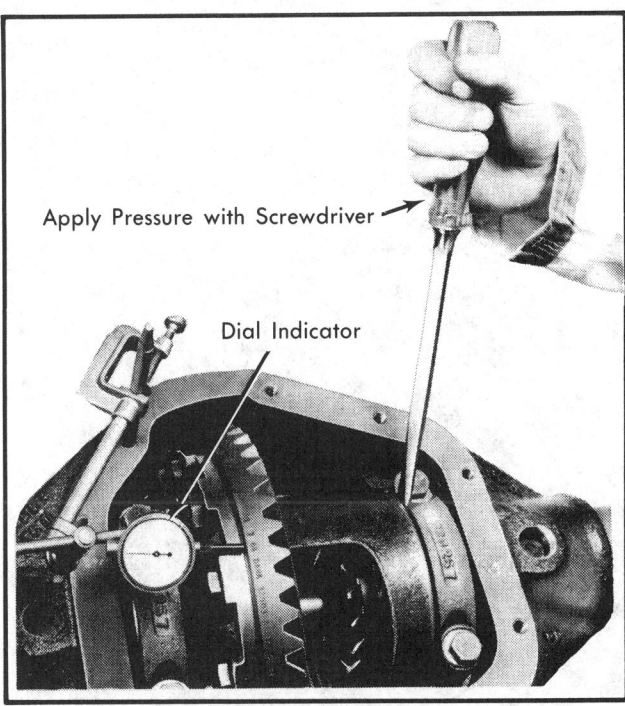

Fig. 4   Measuring Differential End Play With a Dial Indicator

Pinion Depth & Bearing Preload — 1) Pinion is adjusted by shims placed between inner bearing cup and housing, and by shims placed between pinion shaft shoulder and outer bearing. Shims behind inner bearing cup adjust position of pinion in relation to ring gear. Shims behind outer bearing adjust pinion inner and outer bearing preload.

2) If old pinion and ring gear assembly are used, proceed as follows: Install original shims and inner bearing cup. Install outer bearing cup. Press bearing cone onto pinion shaft and install shaft into housing. Install outer bearing cone, companion flange, and nut. Do not install outer shims or seal at this time. Tighten nut to obtain bearing preload of 10-30 ft. lbs. Use a suitable gauge to measure distance from ring gear center to machined button on end of pinion gear. Add or subtract shims from under inner bearing cup to obtain nominal dimension listed in specifications.

3) If new pinion and ring gear assembly are to be installed, proceed as follows: Determine pinion depth adjustment figure of old and new pinions and find shim adjustment figure from chart. Adjust original shim pack accordingly and proceed as in step 2.

NOTE — *An oil slinger (between the inner bearing cone and pinion) and a baffle (between the inner bearing cup and carrier) have been added to the front axle assemblies.*

4) Remove pinion gear, rear bearing cup, and starter shim. Install pinion depth shim of correct thickness in housing bearing cup bore. Reinstall rear bearing cup. Install pinion bearing, oil slinger, yoke, washer, and old pinion nut. Tighten nut to specified torque, while rotating pinion shaft. Position housing

so that pinion shaft is in vertical position, pointing up. With INCH lb. torque wrench, rotate shaft through several revolutions to measure rotating torque.

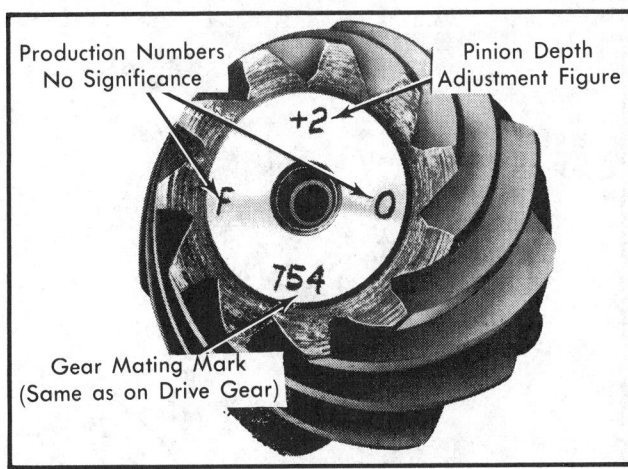

Fig. 5   Pinion Gear Markings Showing Depth Adjustment Figure

NOTE — *Ignore torque needed to start shaft rotating.*

5) Check measurement against pinion bearing preload in specifications. To decrease preload, add shims; to increase preload, subtract shims. After adjustment is made, install oil seal and recheck pinion depth.

6) Check seals in front axle housing bores. If condition is questionable, replace using suitable installer tool.

NOTE — *When installing front axle shafts be sure that these seals are not dislodged.*

Side Bearing Preload — 1) With pinion installed in housing and depth and preload adjustments properly made, install differential case into housing. Set dial indicator so that it reads at back of ring gear. Leave bearing cap bolts loose enough to allow movement of case.

2) Insert screwdriver between bearing cap and housing at opposite end from ring gear. Jam case toward ring gear side and, with force still applied to case, set dial indicator to zero. Jam case the other way making sure that ring gear and pinion gears mesh, and record reading, repeat several times until readings are the same.

3) This reading is the amount of shims that will go between case and bearing on ring gear side. Remove indicator and differential case from the carrier. Remove master bearing from differential case. Install these shims.

4) From the figure originally recorded under Case Assembly, subtract amount of shims just installed on case. Add .015" for bearing preload and install new shim pack on end of case opposite ring gear.

Example: +.070" (Original Recorded Sideplay)
         −.032" (Sideplay With Pinion Installed)
         =.038" (Amount Left From Original Sideplay)
         +.015" (Additional Amount For Bearing Preload)
         =.053" (Amount Installed Opposite of Ring Gear)

5) Install spreader to housing, spread housing and install differential case.

Drive Axles

SPICER (DANA) IFS FRONT DRIVE AXLE (Cont.)

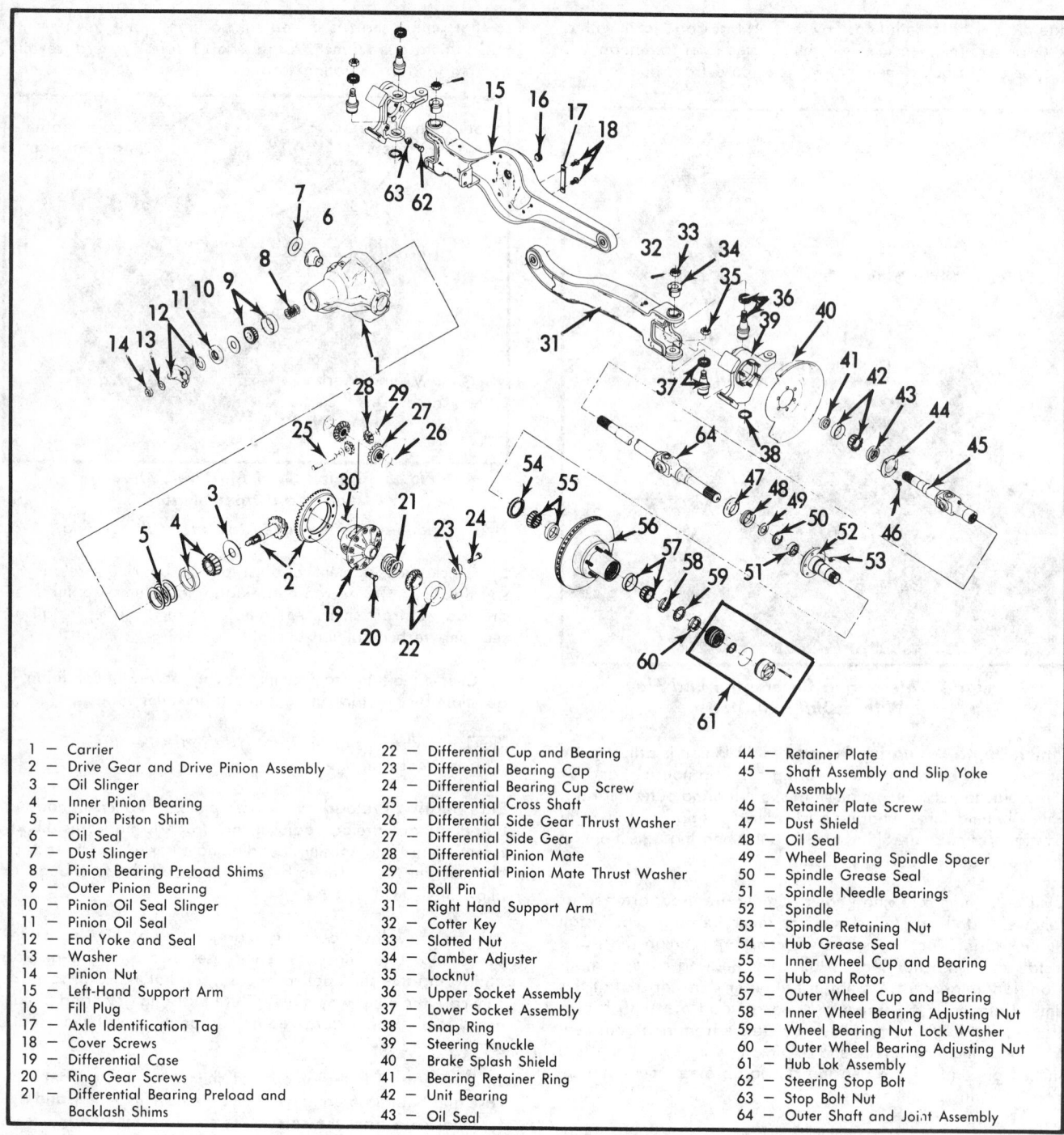

1 — Carrier	22 — Differential Cup and Bearing	44 — Retainer Plate
2 — Drive Gear and Drive Pinion Assembly	23 — Differential Bearing Cap	45 — Shaft Assembly and Slip Yoke
3 — Oil Slinger	24 — Differential Bearing Cup Screw	Assembly
4 — Inner Pinion Bearing	25 — Differential Cross Shaft	46 — Retainer Plate Screw
5 — Pinion Piston Shim	26 — Differential Side Gear Thrust Washer	47 — Dust Shield
6 — Oil Seal	27 — Differential Side Gear	48 — Oil Seal
7 — Dust Slinger	28 — Differential Pinion Mate	49 — Wheel Bearing Spindle Spacer
8 — Pinion Bearing Preload Shims	29 — Differential Pinion Mate Thrust Washer	50 — Spindle Grease Seal
9 — Outer Pinion Bearing	30 — Roll Pin	51 — Spindle Needle Bearings
10 — Pinion Oil Seal Slinger	31 — Right Hand Support Arm	52 — Spindle
11 — Pinion Oil Seal	32 — Cotter Key	53 — Spindle Retaining Nut
12 — End Yoke and Seal	33 — Slotted Nut	54 — Hub Grease Seal
13 — Washer	34 — Camber Adjuster	55 — Inner Wheel Cup and Bearing
14 — Pinion Nut	35 — Locknut	56 — Hub and Rotor
15 — Left-Hand Support Arm	36 — Upper Socket Assembly	57 — Outer Wheel Cup and Bearing
16 — Fill Plug	37 — Lower Socket Assembly	58 — Inner Wheel Bearing Adjusting Nut
17 — Axle Identification Tag	38 — Snap Ring	59 — Wheel Bearing Nut Lock Washer
18 — Cover Screws	39 — Steering Knuckle	60 — Outer Wheel Bearing Adjusting Nut
19 — Differential Case	40 — Brake Splash Shield	61 — Hub Lok Assembly
20 — Ring Gear Screws	41 — Bearing Retainer Ring	62 — Steering Stop Bolt
21 — Differential Bearing Preload and	42 — Unit Bearing	63 — Stop Bolt Nut
Backlash Shims	43 — Oil Seal	64 — Outer Shaft and Joint Assembly

Fig. 6 Exploded View of Spicer (Dana) Model 44-IFS Front Drive Axle

NOTE — *Do not spread housing more than .020". Permanent damage to housing could result.*

6) Remove spreader and install bearing caps. Make sure that caps are in original position. Then tighten caps evenly.

Backlash & Final Assembly — Mount dial indicator to housing, and measure ring gear to pinion gear backlash in 3 places around ring gear. Variation between readings should not exceed .002". Adjust to specifications by moving shims from one side of differential case to the other, or by changing depth of pinion gear. Check tooth contact pattern. See *Tooth Pattern in this Secton.* Install cover and tighten bolts to specifications.

SPICER (DANA) IFS FRONT DRIVE AXLE (Cont.)

TIGHTENING SPECIFICATIONS

Application	Ft. Lbs.
Pinion Shaft Flange Nut	210
Differential Side Bearing Cap Bolt	50
Ring Gear-to-Differential Case Bolt	55
Axle Shaft Retainer Bolt	30
Differential Housing Cover Bolt	20

AXLE ASSEMBLY SPECIFICATIONS

Application	Specifications
Axle Shaft End Play	Non-Adjustable
Ring Gear Backlash	.005-.010″
Side Bearing Preload	
New Bearings	20-40 INCH Lbs.
Used Bearings	10-20 INCH Lbs.
Pinion Gear Depth (Normal Dimension)	
Model 44 (8.50″ Ring Gear)	2.625″
Model 50 (9.25″ Ring Gear)	2.810″

PINION DEPTH SHIM ADJUSTMENT CHART (INCHES)

Old Pinion Marking	New Pinion Marking								
	.4	.3	.2	.1	0	+1	+2	+3	+4
+4	+0.008	+0.007	+0.006	+0.005	+0.004	+0.003	+0.002	+0.001	0
+3	+0.007	+0.006	+0.005	+0.004	+0.003	+0.002	+0.001	+0	−0.001
+2	+0.006	+0.005	+0.004	+0.003	+0.002	+0.001	0	−0.001	−0.002
+1	+0.005	+0.004	+0.003	+0.002	+0.001	0	−0.001	−0.002	−0.003
0	+0.004	+0.003	+0.002	+0.001	0	−0.001	−0.002	−0.003	−0.004
−1	+0.003	+0.002	+0.001	0	−0.001	−0.002	−0.003	−0.004	−0.005
−2	+0.002	+0.001	0	−0.001	−0.002	−0.003	−0.004	−0.005	−0.006
−3	+0.001	0	−0.001	−0.002	−0.003	−0.004	−0.005	−0.006	−0.007
−4	0	−0.001	−0.002	−0.003	−0.004	−0.005	−0.006	−0.007	−0.008

CHRYSLER CORP. SURE-GRIP DIFFERENTIAL

**Dodge & Plymouth with
9¼" Ring Gear**

DESCRIPTION

The cone clutch Sure-Grip is a limited slip type differential, similar in operation to the conventional type differential except for the helix grooved clutch cones that clutch the side gears to the differential case. These grooves assure maximum lubrication of the clutch surface during operation. The clutch cones and side gears are spring preloaded by 2 thrust plates and 4 coil springs to provide an internal resistance to differential action within the case itself. During torque application to axle, the initial spring preloading of the clutch cones is added to by the gear separating forces between side gears and differential pinions which progressively increases the internal resistance (friction) in the differential. This differential is not a positive or locking type unit and will release before excessive driving force can be applied to one wheel.

AXLE RATIO & IDENTIFICATION

Sure-Grip differential is optional on Chrysler axles with 9¼" ring gear. See Chrysler Corp. 8⅜" & 9¼" Ring Gear in this Section.

LUBRICATION

Use only Mopar Hypoid Gear Lubricant (Part No. 3744994) or equivalent.

TESTING ON VEHICLE

1) With rear wheels raised off ground, engine off, automatic transmission in "P" or manual transmission in low and transfer case in "N" (if equipped); grip tread of tire and attempt to rotate wheel.

2) If rotation is extremely difficult or impossible, differential is performing correctly. If either wheel turns relatively easily or continuously, differential is not performing correctly and should be replaced.

REMOVAL & INSTALLATION

Same procedure is used to remove and install Sure-Grip differential as standard differential. See Chrysler Corp. 8⅜" & 9¼" Ring Gear in this Section.

CAUTION — *During removal and installation of axle shafts, DO NOT rotate one axle shaft unless both are in position. Rotation of one axle shaft without the other in place may result in misalignment of two spline segments with which axle shaft splines engage, and will necessitate difficult realignment procedures when shaft is reinstalled.*

OVERHAUL

Sure-Grip differential is serviced as an assembly only.

CAUTION — *Under no circumstances should Sure-Grip differential be disassembled, reassembled, and installed in vehicle.*

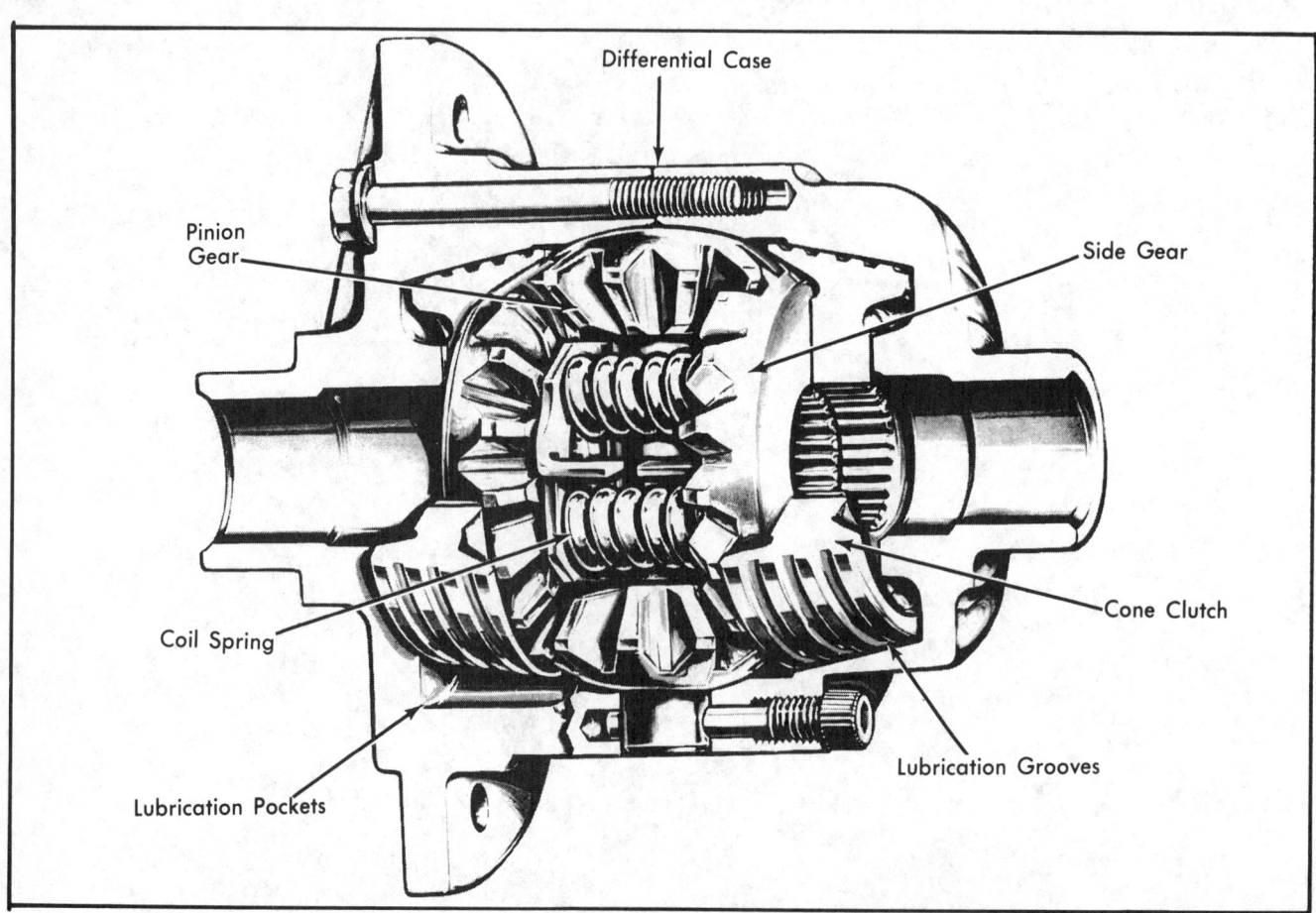

Fig. 1   Cutaway View of Chrysler Corp. Sure-Grip Differential Assembly

Positive Traction Differentials

EATON (ONE PIECE CASE) LOCKING DIFFERENTIAL

Chevrolet & GMC
C, K & G10

DESCRIPTION

The Eaton one piece case locking differential is a 2 pinion type with a clutch disc pack behind each side gear. Unit also utilizes a speed sensitive device which automatically locks both rear wheels if either wheel should spin excessively during slow vehicle operation.

AXLE RATIO & IDENTIFICATION

See *General Motors 8½", 8⅞", & 9½" Ring Gear* article and *Drive Axle Ratio Identification* in this Section.

LUBRICATION

Check lubricant level every 7500 miles or 6 months. Drain and refill every 15,000 miles. Use standard differential lubricant, DO NOT use Positraction lubricant.

TESTING ON VEHICLE

1) Raise vehicle so that both rear wheels can be rotated freely by hand. With one wheel held stationary, rotate other wheel approximately ½ turn every second. Wheel should rotate freely. If both wheels turn, or try to turn, differential is defective.

2) Raise vehicle as high as possible. Leave one technician in vehicle. Start engine and allow to idle at 600-800 RPM. If equipped with automatic transmission, place transmission in drive and apply brakes. If equipped with manual transmission, depress clutch and place transmission in first gear.

3) Pull on one parking brake cable from under vehicle to lock one rear wheel. With engine idling, slowly release brakes on automatic transmission models and slowly release clutch on manual transmission models. Locked rear wheel should remain stationary and free wheel should rotate slowly.

4) As free wheel speed increases, the differential should lock, causing both wheels to rotate or stop.

NOTE — *If equipped with manual transmission, engine may stall.*

5) It may be necessary to accelerate to 10 MPH to lock differential. If speed increases beyond 20 MPH without locking differential, unit is defective. Lock opposite wheel and repeat test.

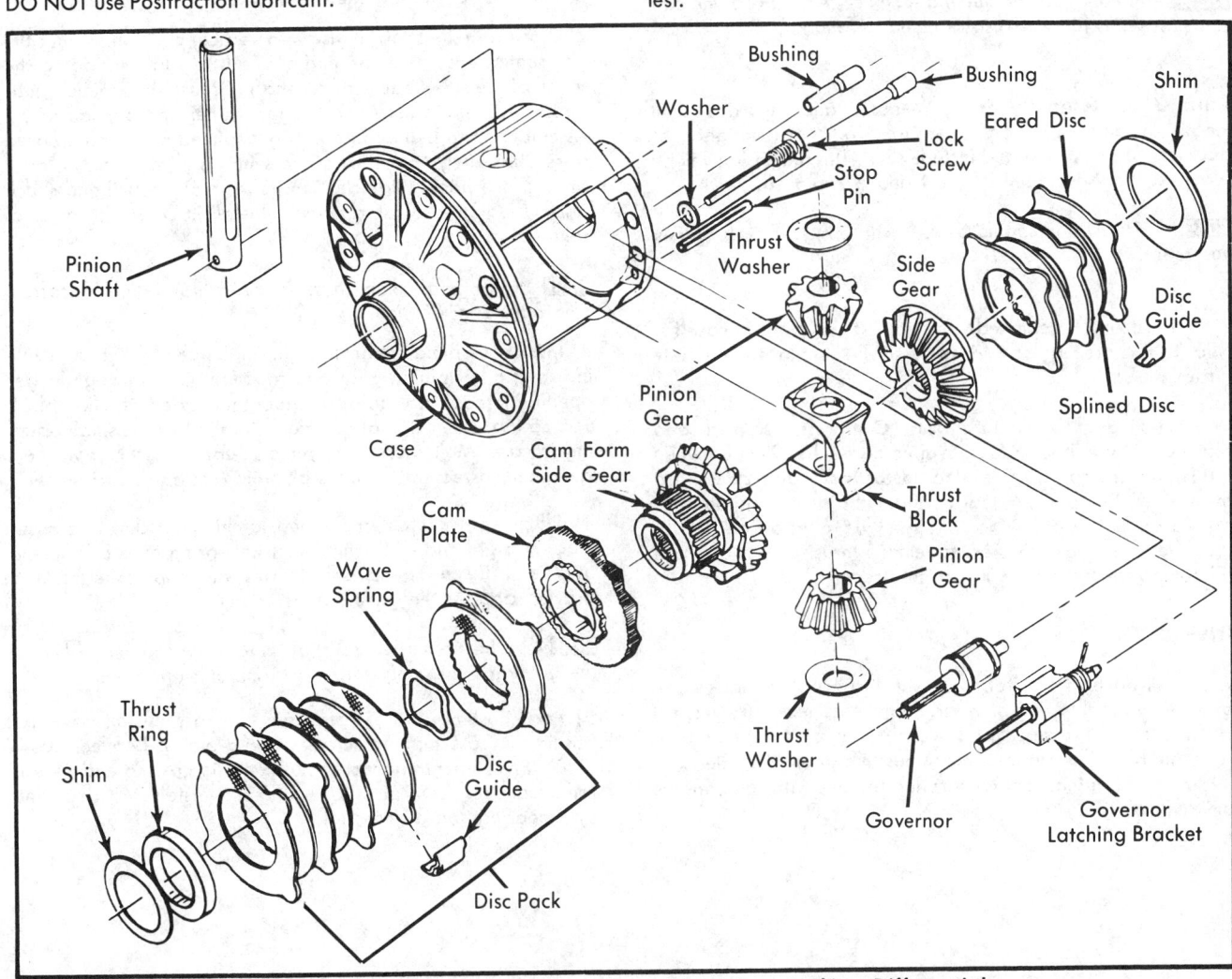

Fig. 1   Exploded View of Eaton One Piece Case Locking Differential

EATON (ONE PIECE CASE) LOCKING DIFFERENTIAL (Cont.)

REMOVAL & INSTALLATION

Same procedure is used to remove and install locking differential as conventional differential. See *General Motors 8½", 8⅞", and 9½" Ring Gear* in this Section.

OVERHAUL

DISASSEMBLY

Differential — 1) With differential removed from housing, remove ring gear and side bearings. Note or mark position of latching bracket and governor assembly for reassembly. Using puller tool (J-26252 or equivalent), remove bushings retaining latching bracket and governor. Remove latching bracket spring while pulling out governor assembly bushing.

2) Remove stop pin by driving through case with drift punch. Remove pinion shaft lock screw and remove pinion shaft. Roll pinion gears out of case. Remove reaction block and pinion thrust washers. Remove cam gears, disc packs and disc pack guide clips on both sides.

NOTE — *If cam gear or clutch discs must be replaced, the cam gear assembly must be disassembled as follows:*

Cam Gear Assembly — 1) Measure and record overall length of gear assembly. Measure from face of gear to backside of thrust ring and include shim. This dimension will be required for reassembly if thrust ring is replaced.

NOTE — *Thrust ring should be replaced only if it is absolutely necessary.*

2) If thrust ring is replaced, check thrust ring bore in case for wear. If bore is scored excessively, replace complete differential.

3) Position gear with hub end up. Compress disc pack and place a suitable bearing removal mandrel (J-22912) between thrust ring and top disc. Beveled side of tool should be toward thrust ring. Position cam gear and tool in a press with tool supported on both sides. Place a 1½-1¾" plug on gear hub. Press against plug with press to remove thrust ring. Make sure all components are kept in correct order.

INSPECTION

Clean all parts in a suitable solvent. Inspect all bearings and gear teeth for chipping or wear. Replace as necessary. Inspect clutch plates and discs for signs of wear or overheating. If reaction block or flange shims must be replaced, measure thickness of original components and replace with components of identical size.

REASSEMBLY

Cam Gear Assembly — 1) Place cam gear on bench with hub end up. Place cam plate on gear so that cam form on plate is against cam form on gear. Position on cam plate two eared discs, one splined disc and one wave spring, alternately in that order. Position on gear hub 2 splined discs and 3 eared discs alternately, starting and ending with an eared disc.

2) Place cam gear in a press with hub end up. Install thrust ring on gear hub with press. Make sure thrust ring is square with hub. Press thrust ring on until it is flush with shoulder. When installing ring, press down on discs to make sure splined disc does not wedge between thrust ring and gear shoulder. When unit is assembled, check for correct disc sequence. Make sure that the first splined disc (large spline) is correctly located on cam plate.

Differential — 1) Install disc pack guide clips on disc ears of cam gear disc pack. Use grease to retain clips on ears. Install cam gear assembly, with original shim in flange end of case. If a new thrust ring has been installed on cam gear, it may be necessary to reshim. Measure overall length of cam gear assembly, including shim. Compare this measurement with one previously recorded. If measurement variation is more than .003" either way, install a new shim that will obtain a reading within .003" of original measurement.

2) Place an axle shaft in vise in a vertical position. Mount the differential case over the end of the axle shaft engaging the spline of the side gear with the shaft. Grease the 2 pinion gear thrust washers and locate them in their proper positions. Assemble on to bell end gear hub 2 splined discs and 3 eared discs alternately. Begin and end with an eared disc. Install 4 small clutch pack guide clips on the ears of the bell end clutch pack using grease for retention. Install in case with original shims.

NOTE — *Original shim must be used to maintain correct clearance specification.*

3) Install one pinion gear through small opening in case, while inserting other pinion gear and reaction block through larger opening in case. Rotate both pinion gears and reaction block 90° so that open side of reaction block is toward small opening in case. Make sure both pinion gears and thrust washers remain in correct position. Install pinion shaft and lock screw.

4) Place governor assembly and latching bracket into case. Place straight end of latching bracket spring over and to the outside of the engagement shaft. This will preload the latching bracket against the governor assembly.

NOTE — *The latching bracket bushing has a tapered hole and the governor assembly bushing has a straight hole.*

5) Press bushing and ¼" stop pin into case. Install governor bushing in case making sure shaft end play is between .004-.020". Press latching bracket bushing into case so end play is removed. Press stop pin flush with case, install ring gear and side bearings on differential.

EATON (TWO PIECE CASE) LOCKING DIFFERENTIAL

Chevrolet & GMC
C20/30
G, K & P30

DESCRIPTION

The Eaton two-piece locking differential is a three pinion type with clutch disc pack behind both side gears. Unit also utilizes a speed-sensitive device which automatically locks both rear wheels if either wheel should spin excessively during slow vehicle operation.

AXLE RATIO & IDENTIFICATION

See General Motors 10½" and 12¼" Ring Gear articles and Drive Axle Ratio Identification in this Section.

LUBRICATION

Check lubricant level every 7500 miles or 6 months. Drain and refill every 15,000 miles. Use standard differential lubricant, DO NOT use Positraction lubricant.

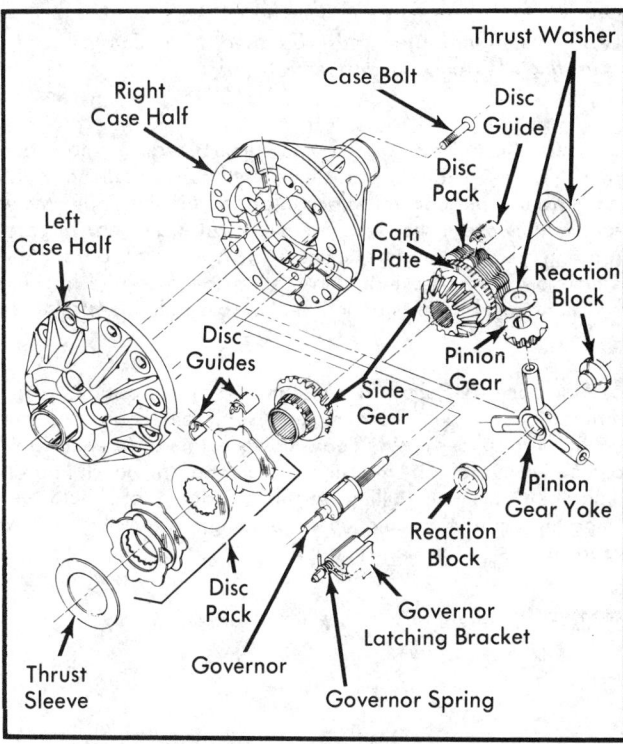

Fig. 1   Exploded View of Eaton Two Piece Case Locking Differential

TESTING ON VEHICLE

1) Raise vehicle so that both rear wheels can be rotated freely by hand. With one wheel held stationary, rotate other wheel approximately ½ turn every second. Wheel should rotate freely. If both wheels turn, or try to turn, differential is defective.

2) Raise vehicle as high as possible. Leave one technician in vehicle. Start engine and allow to idle at 600-800 RPM. If equipped with automatic transmission, place transmission in drive and apply brakes. If equipped with manual transmission, depress clutch and place transmission in first gear.

3) Pull on one parking brake cable from under vehicle to lock one rear wheel. With engine idling, slowly release brakes on automatic transmission models and slowly release clutch on manual transmission models. Locked rear wheel should remain stationary and free wheel should rotate slowly.

4) As free wheel speed increases, the differential should lock, causing both wheels to rotate or stop.

NOTE — *If equipped with manual transmission, engine may stall.*

5) It may be necessary to accelerate to 10 MPH to lock differential. If speed increases beyond 20 MPH without locking differential, unit is defective. Lock opposite wheel and repeat test.

REMOVAL & INSTALLATION

Same procedure is used to remove and install locking differential as conventional differential. See General Motors 10½" and 12¼" Ring Gear articles in this Section.

OVERHAUL

DISASSEMBLY

Differential — 1) With differential removed from housing, remove ring gear and side bearings. Remove 3 screws from front face of ring gear flange. Place differential on right side case half. Using a screwdriver, gently pry case halves apart at yoke hole locations.

2) Remove left side case half. Hold thumb against inside of gear hub when separating case halves. This will prevent side gear from falling out. If governor and latching bracket are only components being replaced, proceed to step **4)** in Reassembly procedures. To further disassemble, pry under pinion gear yoke to remove from case half.

NOTE — *If cam gear or clutch discs must be replaced, the cam gear assembly must be disassembled as follows:*

Cam Gear Assembly — 1) Measure and record overall length of gear assembly. Measure from face of gear to back side of thrust ring and include shim. This dimension will be required for reassembly if thrust ring is replaced.

NOTE — *Thrust ring should be replaced only if it is absolutely necessary.*

2) If thrust ring is replaced, check thrust ring bore in case for wear. If bore is scored excessively, replace complete differential.

3) Position gear with hub end up. Compress disc pack and place suitable bearing removal tool (J-22912) between thrust

EATON (TWO PIECE CASE) LOCKING DIFFERENTIAL (Cont.)

ring and top disc. Beveled side of tool should be toward thrust ring. Position cam gear and tool in press with tool supported on both sides. Place a 1½- 1¾" plug on gear hub. Press against plug with press to remove thrust ring. Make sure all components are in correct order.

INSPECTION

Clean all components in a suitable solvent. Inspect all bearings and gear teeth for chipping or wear. Replace as necessary. Inspect clutch plates and discs for signs of wear or overheating. If reaction blocks or flanges must be replaced, measure thickness of original components and replace with components of comparable size.

REASSEMBLY

NOTE — *If cam gear assembly was disassembled, reassemble as follows:*

Cam Gear Assembly — 1) Place gear on bench with hub end up. Place cam plate on gear so that cam form on plate is against cam form on gear. Install 2 eared discs on cam plate, 1 splined disc and 1 wave spring alternately in that order. Install on gear hub 4 eared discs and 3 splined discs alternately, starting and ending with an eared disc.

2) Place cam gear in a press with hub end up. Install thrust ring on gear hub with press. Make sure thrust ring is square with hub. Press thrust ring on until it is flush with shoulder. When installing ring, press down on discs to make sure splined disc does not wedge between thrust ring and gear shoulder. When unit is assembled, check for correct disc sequence. Make sure that the first splined disc (large spline) is correctly located on cam plate.

Differential — 1) Install disc pack guide clips on disc ears of cam gear disc pack. Use grease to retain clips in ears. Install cam gear assembly and original shim in right case half. If a new thrust ring was installed on cam gear, it may be necessary to reshim. Measure overall length of cam gear assembly, including shim. Compare this measurement with one previously recorded. If measurement variation is more than .003" either way, install a new shim that will obtain a reading within .003" of original measurement.

2) Position right reaction block on gear face with buttonside of block facing up. Replace reaction block only if it is absolutely necessary. If a new block is being installed, measure face-to-face thickness of old block and obtain a new block of same thickness. Install pinion gears and thrust washers on pinion yoke. Place yoke in correct position in housing. Make sure center of yoke is correctly positioned over reaction block button. Tap on yoke lightly to correctly seat it in position.

3) Position left reaction block on yoke with flange end up. Replace block only if it is absolutely necessary. If a new block is being installed, measure face-to-face thickness of old block and obtain a new block of same thickness.

NOTE — *The right and left reaction blocks are not necessarily the same thickness. If the blocks are broke or it is impossible to measure thickness, complete differential must be replaced.*

4) Install governor and latching bracket assemblies in correct position. Place straight end of latching bracket spring over and to the outside of governor shaft. This will preload the latching bracket against the governor assembly. Install the original three eared discs and two splined discs on left side gear alternately, starting and ending with an eared disc.

NOTE — *Original discs must be used to maintain correct operating clearance in differential.*

5) Install the six disc pack guide clips. Use grease to retain clips in place. Install original shim in left case half. Remove disc pack from side gear and place in position in case half. Make sure guides are in correct position. Install side gear in case, rotating gear to engage splines with splines on discs. Hold thumb on right case half. Make sure governor and latching bracket assembly holes are aligned in case halves. Install three screws.

6) Place one axle shaft in a vise in a vertical position. Install differential on axle shaft, making sure splines on axle are engaged in splines in side gear. Slowly rotate differential. This can be easily done by inserting a short shaft or punch in a pinion yoke hole and pulling on shaft. Differential should turn smoothly without locking up or binding. Differential is now ready to be installed in housing.

NOTE — *Differential will lock up if turned rapidly.*

FORD TRACTION-LOK

Bronco
E100/150
F100/150 (2WD)

DESCRIPTION

Traction-Lok positive traction differential employs multiple disc clutch to control differential action. Side gear mounting shims, friction discs, composite plate, clutch hub and guides are housed in differential cover. Located in differential case, between side gears, is one-piece preload plate and block assembly and four calibrated preload springs which apply an initial force to clutch pack. Additional clutch capacity is derived from side gear thrust loads. Traction-Lok differential can have either two or four differential pinion gears.

AXLE RATIO & IDENTIFICATION

To determine the drive axle ratio, *refer to Drive Axle Ratio Identification in this Section.*

LUBRICATION

Check level of lubricant every 5,000 miles or 5 months. Manufacturer recommends no specific drain and refill interval. Use only Ford Hypoid Gear Lubricant (ESW-M2C6119-A) or equivalent.

TESTING ON VEHICLE

Raise one wheel, leaving opposite wheel firmly on ground. Install suitable adapter and torque wrench to wheel mounting studs. With transmission in neutral, note torque required to keep wheel rotating through several revolutions. Torque should be at least 40 ft. lbs. Disregard initial starting torque.

REMOVAL & INSTALLATION

Removal — 1) Position safety stands under rear frame members and support housing with either a floor jack or hoist. Disengage brake line from the clips retaining it to the housing. Disconnect the vent tube from housing.

2) Remove brake backing plate assemblies from the housing, and support them with wire. Do not disconnect the brake line. Disconnect each rear shock absorber from mounting bracket stud on housing bracket. Lower axle slightly to reduce spring tension. At each rear spring, remove U-bolt nuts, U-bolts, and spring seat caps.

Installation — Reverse removal procedure to complete installation.

OVERHAUL

DISASSEMBLY

1) Press differential bearings from journals on case. Remove ring gear attaching bolts and tap gear from case using a soft-faced hammer. Place differential assembly in a suitable press to load case halves so preload of springs is overcome (approximately 1000 lbs.). If press is not available, two $7/16"$ bolts and nuts can be used in ring gear mounting holes (one on each side) to compress case halves and overcome preload tension.

2) With case under pressure, loosen two-case-to-cover retaining screws until one or two threads of each remain engaged. Release pressure, tap on cover to spring it loose, then remove two screws. With cover facing down, lift off case, remove preload spring plate and four preload springs.

3) From cover, remove side gear, four clutch plate ear guides, clutch hub, friction plates, steel clutch discs and shims. Using a drift, drive out pinion shaft lock pins from case. Drive long pinion shaft from case, working from end opposite lock pin hole. Remove two short pinion shafts, working from center outward. Lift out thrust block, then remove pinion gears, thrust washers, side gear and side gear thrust washer.

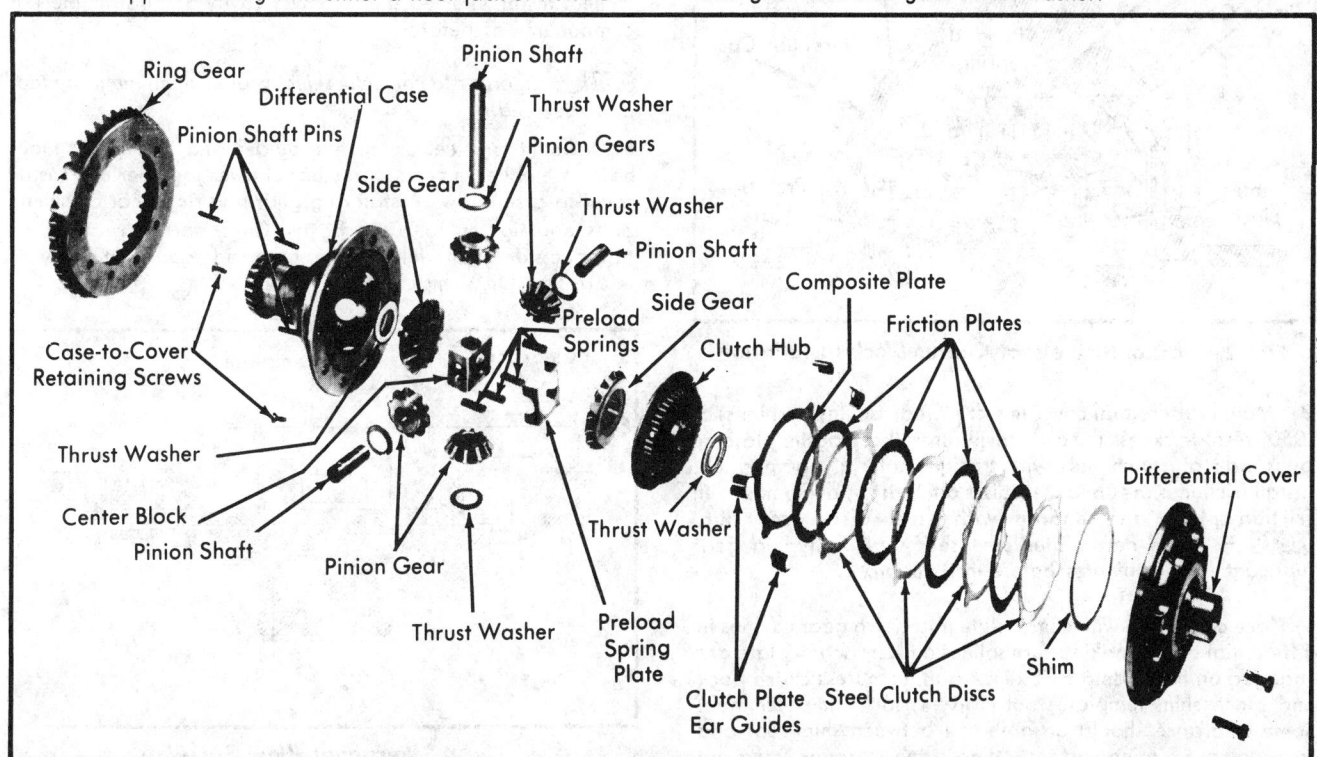

Fig. 1 Exploded View of Typical Ford Traction-Lok Differential Assembly

FORD TRACTION-LOK (Cont.)

INSPECTION

Inspect clutch plates for unevenness or wear. Dog-eared plates must be free of burrs, nicks or scratches. Inspect internally splined clutch plates for condition of bond, bonding material and wear. Replace bonded plates if thickness less than .085″, or if badly worn. Inspect all thrust surfaces and hubs for wear.

REASSEMBLY

1) Lubricate all parts with hypoid gear lubricant prior to assembly. Mount differential case in soft-jawed vise and place a side gear thrust washer and a side gear into counterbore in case. Install pinion thrust washers and place pinion gears on side gear, aligning holes in washers and gears with holes in case. Install center block so holes in block are aligned with holes in pinion gears and case.

2) Using a brass drift, drive pinion shafts into position from outside of case, making sure lock pin holes in shafts are aligned with corresponding holes in case. Install shaft lock pins, making sure pinion and side gears move freely. Place four preload springs in holes provided in center block. Position preload plate over springs, making sure springs are properly seated. Preload plate straddles center block over its narrower, or machined, width.

NOTE — *Center block has 2 machined sides and 2 rough sides. Long shaft is driven through rough side and short shaft is driven through machined side.*

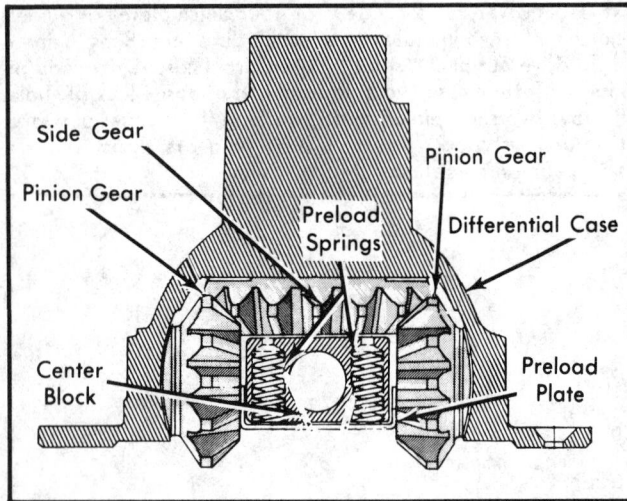

Fig. 2 Sectional View of Center Block Installation

3) Mount differential cover in soft-jawed vise. Insert shim(s) of .050″ total thickness in cover cavity. Install composite plate on back side of clutch hub with friction material against hub. Install friction plates and steel discs alternately, beginning with friction plate and ending with steel disc, onto hub. **NOTE** — *When new plates are used, soak in hypoid gear lubricant for 30 minutes before installation.*

4) Place clutch hub with clutch plate into clutch gear cavities in differential cover, making sure splines on last friction plate are engaged on hub. Using a ⅜ x 2½″ bolt, compress clutch pack and place shim template tool (T68P-4946-A) in clutch hub. Some clearance should be observed between shim tool and cover-to-case mating surface. Using a feeler gauge, measure clearance.

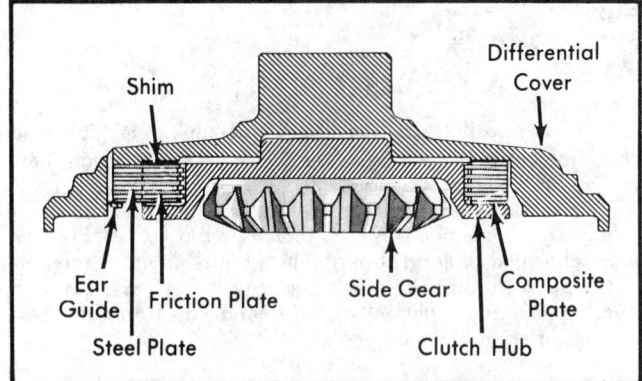

Fig. 3 Sectional View of Clutch Pack Installation

Shim Pack Thickness		
Gauge Reading	**Correction**	**Total Shims**
.001-.002″	None	.050″
.003-.007″	.005″	.045″
.008-.012″	.010″	.040″
.013-.017″	.015″	.035″
.018-.022″	.020″	.030″
.023-.027″	.025″	.025″
.028-.032″	.030″	.020″
.033-.037″	.035″	.015″
.038-.042″	.040″	.010″
.043-.047″	.045″	.005″
.048-.050″	.050″	None

5) Refer to shim pack thickness chart to determine correct amount of shims to subtract from .050″ shim pack originally installed. Install selected shim in cover cavity and install internal components as before.

NOTE — *In order to correctly select proper shim, template tool must be used.*

6) Install four steel clutch ear guides and side gear. Place both assemblies in press, force both halves together and install cover-to-case screws. Install ring gear and ring gear attaching bolts and tighten to 70-85 ft. lbs. Check torque required to turn one side gear while holding other side gear stationary as in "Testing On Vehicle".

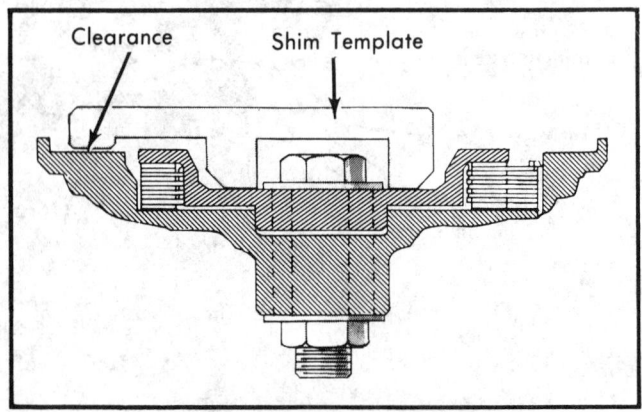

Fig. 4 Sectional View Showing Correct Usage of Shim Template Tool

Positive Traction Differentials

SPICER (DANA) POWER-LOK

Ford
General Motors

DESCRIPTION

The Power-Lok differential uses clutch packs which are preloaded by Belleville spring plates to provide limited slip action. The torque in the axle causes the pinion shafts to move up ramps on the differential case to increase preload on clutch packs. This varies the amount of torque directed to each wheel and causes the wheel with the greatest traction to receive the greatest torque. Power-Lok is used on Spicer (Dana) axles that have a 2-piece differential case and 4 differential pinion gears.

AXLE RATIO & IDENTIFICATION

To determine axle ratio, refer to *Drive Axle Ratio Identification in this Section.*

LUBRICATION

NOTE — *To insure proper operation of unit and to prevent differential chatter, manufacturers recommend that only the special lubricants listed be used.*

Ford — Hypoid Gear Lubricant Part No. ESW-M2C105-A and friction modifier that meets Ford Specification EST-M2C118-A.

General Motors — General Motors Positraction Lubricant.

TESTING ON VEHICLE

With engine off and transmission in Neutral, raise one wheel off ground and block both front and rear of opposite wheel. Install suitable tool across two wheel studs and attach torque wrench to center of tool. Observe torque required to continuously turn wheel smoothly through several revolutions. Repeat test for opposite side. If differential is operating properly, torque should be 40-200 ft. lbs.

NOTE — *Disregard breakaway torque.*

REMOVAL & INSTALLATION

See *Spicer (Dana) Semi-Floating or Full-Floating Axles in this Section.*

OVERHAUL

DISASSEMBLY

CAUTION — *During disassembly, note and record relationship of all parts, especially clutch discs and plates, to each other. Mark case halves, pinion mate shafts and their corresponding ramps and differential spiders for reassembly reference.*

NOTE — *For front axle shaft and bearing removal, see articles on Spicer (Dana) Full-Floating Axles or 4-Wheel Drive Steering Knuckles in this Section.*

1) With axle assembly removed from vehicle, pull axle shafts out far enough to allow clearance for differential removal. Using a housing spreader, spread the carrier. Do not spread carrier over .020". Remove bearing caps, and note letters stamped on caps and carrier. Remove differential. Mark bearing cups to indicate from which side of case they were removed.

2) Scribe marks on both halves of differential case. Place case in vise. Remove case bolts and disassemble case. Keep the stack of plates and discs exactly as they were removed.

INSPECTION

Inspect plates, discs, clutch rings, side gears, pinion mate gears, pinion mate shafts and spacer block for damage or wear. Any part showing extreme wear or scoring should be replaced.

NOTE — *The pinion mate shafts are unlike the shaft of a conventional differential and therefore are not locked to the differential case.*

REASSEMBLY

NOTE — *During assembly, keep all parts clean, and lubricate with limited slip gear lubricant just prior to installation.*

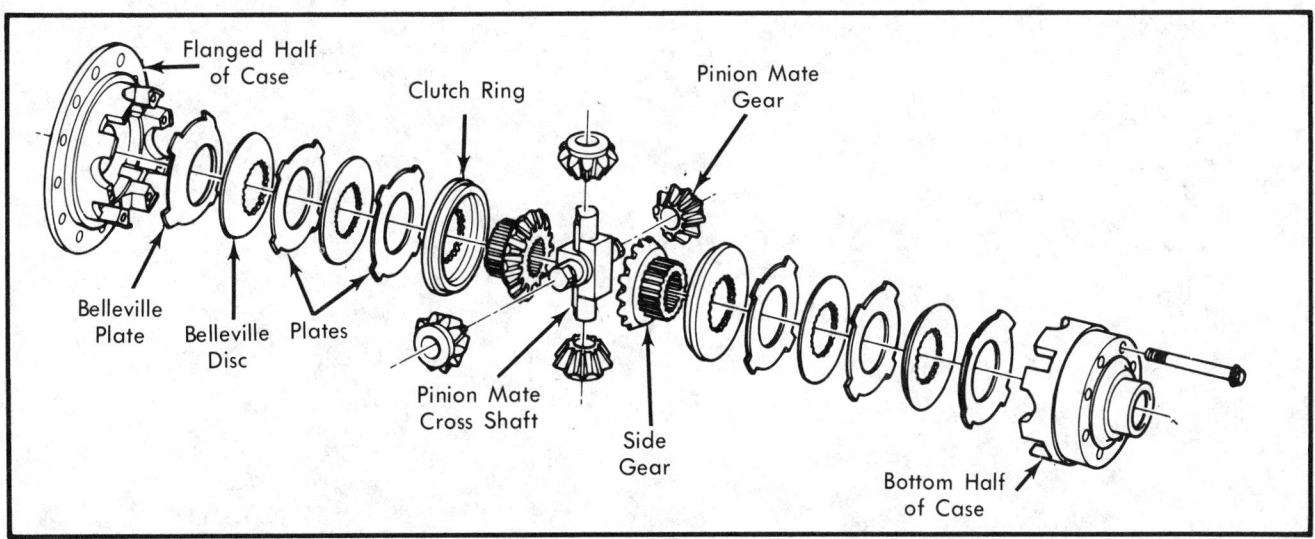

Fig. 1 Exploded View of Spicer (Dana) Power-Lok Differential Assembly

SPICER (DANA) POWER-LOK (Cont.)

NOTE — *All front axles have 3 friction surfaces and rear axles have 5.*

1) Replace plates and disc in exactly the same order as they were removed. Apply proper lubricant on each part. With the plates and disc now assembled to the clutch ring, line up the ears of the plates so they will enter easily into the ring gear case half. Install the side gear, plates and disc on other clutch ring exactly as removed. Apply proper lubricant on each part. Line up ears of plate for case assembly.

2) Assemble bottom half of case making sure scribe marks are lined up. Assemble case bolts finger tight only. Put axle in vise, splined end pointing up and set differential on end of axle. Insert second axle making sure that the splines of side gear and clutch ring are lined up. Also make sure shafts are entered the full depth. Leave shafts in this position and tighten case bolts evenly to 30-40 ft. lbs. Remove shafts.

3) Spread carrier housing to .020" to receive differential assembly. Assemble bearing cups to their correct sides and install differential into housing. Install bearing caps exactly as removed and torque to 70-90 ft. lbs. After axle assembly is completed, refill axle housing with limited slip lubricant.

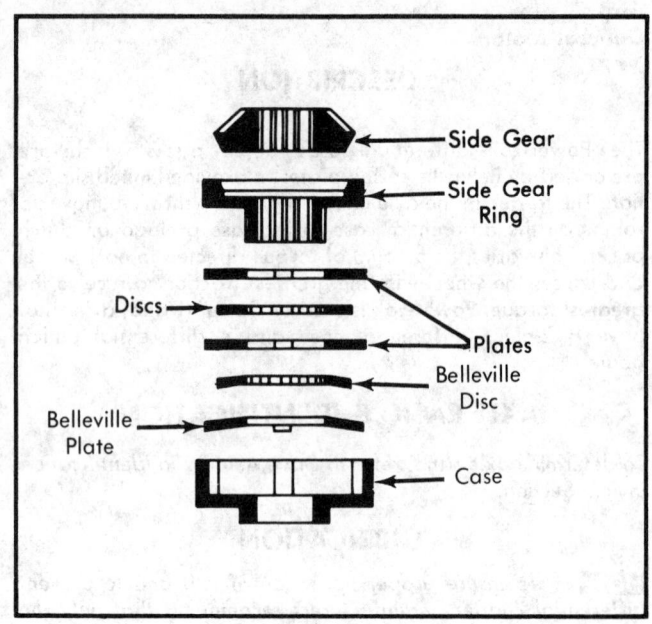

Fig. 2 *Disc and Plate Arrangement for One Side of Power-Lok Differential (Model 70)*

SPICER (DANA) TRAC-LOK

Jeep

DESCRIPTION

The Trac-Lok differential uses clutch packs which are preloaded by Belleville spring plates to provide limited slip action. Multiple disc clutches permit differential action when required for turning corners and transmit equal torque to both wheels when driving straight ahead. When one wheel tries to spin because of reduced traction, the clutch packs automatically provide more torque to the wheel with the greater traction. Trac-Lok is used on Spicer (Dana) axles with a one-piece differential case and 2 differential pinion gears.

AXLE RATIO & IDENTIFICATION

To determine axle ratio, refer to *Drive Axle Ratio Identification* in this Section.

TESTING ON VEHICLE

With engine off and transmission in neutral, raise one wheel off ground and block both front and rear of opposite wheel. Install suitable tool across 2 wheel studs and attach torque wrench to center of tool. Observe torque required to continuously turn wheel smoothly through several revolutions. Repeat test for opposite side. If differential is operating properly, torque should be 40-200 ft. lbs.

NOTE — *Disregard breakaway torque.*

REMOVAL & INSTALLATION

See *Spicer (Dana) Semi-Floating* or *Full-Floating Axles* in this Section.

OVERHAUL

DISASSEMBLY

CAUTION — *During disassembly, note and record relationship of all parts to each other (especially clutch discs and plates). Mark case halves, pinion mate shafts and their corresponding ramps and differential spiders for reassembly reference.*

NOTE — *For front axle shaft and bearing removal, see articles on Spicer (Dana) Full-Floating Axles or 4-Wheel Drive Steering Knuckles, in this Section.*

1) With axle assembly removed from vehicle and axles pulled out from housing, remove cover plate screws and cover. Remove differential bearing caps. Note letters stamped on the bearing caps for reassembly in proper location. Mount spreader to housing. Locate a dial indicator with a magnetic base and extensions. Spread housing to .020", but do not spread wider.

2) Remove differential using two pry bars. Mark differential bearing cups for installation reference later. Place the axle in a vise, with the splined end pointing up 3" above the vise. Assem-

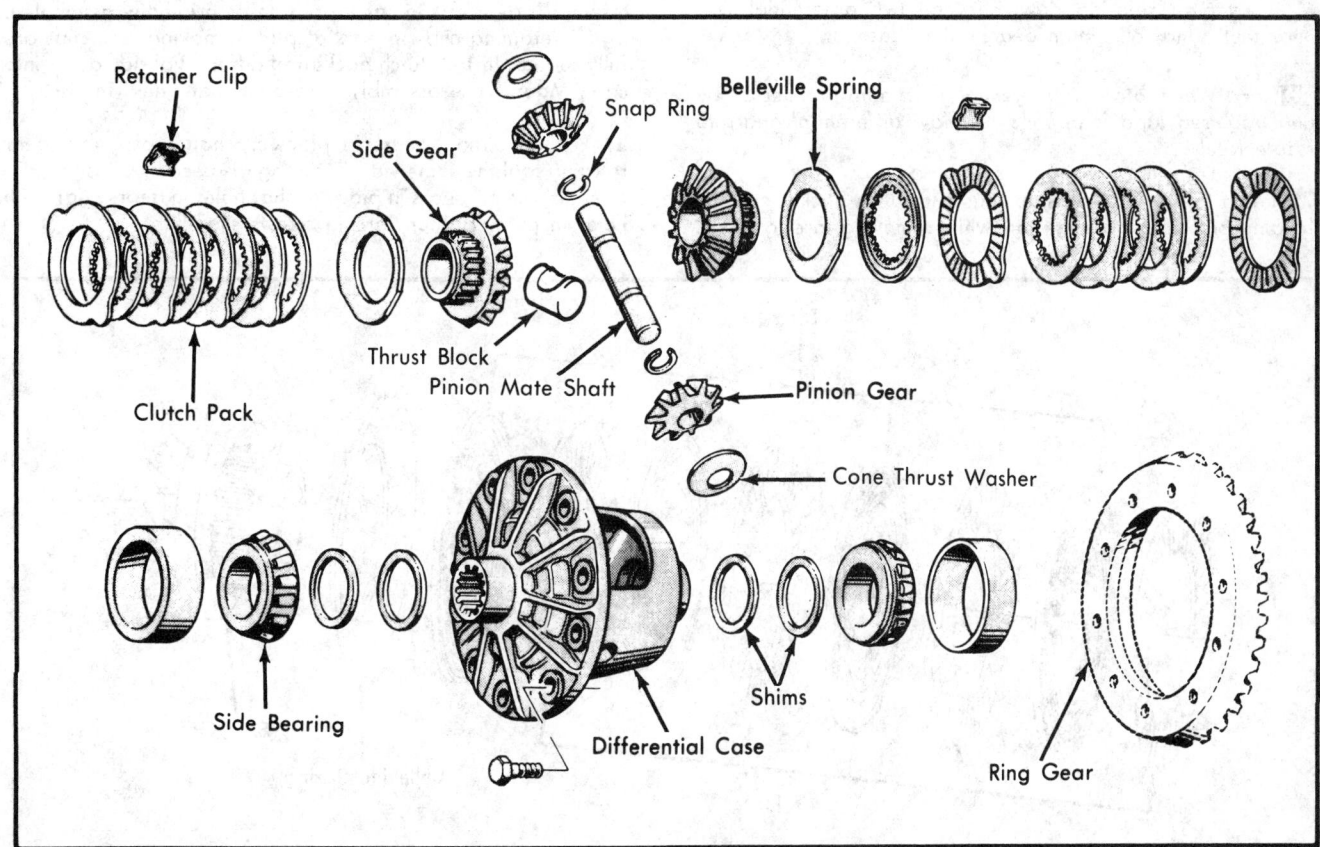

Fig. 1 Exploded View of Spicer (Dana) Trac-Lok Differential Assembly

Labels: Retainer Clip, Side Gear, Snap Ring, Belleville Spring, Clutch Pack, Thrust Block, Pinion Mate Shaft, Pinion Gear, Cone Thrust Washer, Side Bearing, Differential Case, Shims, Ring Gear

SPICER (DANA) TRAC-LOK (Cont.)

ble the differential to the axle shaft with the ring gear screws facing up. Remove ring and disassemble the internal parts of the case. Drive out the lock pin using a long drift.

3) With differential on axle shaft, remove the cross pin and spacer block (if so equipped). Use a hammer and drift.

CAUTION — *Place shop towels over vise jaws to protect gear teeth from becoming nicked after it is free from case.*

NOTE — *On the model 60 Trac-Lok, pinion mate shaft is retained by a single lock pin which should be driven from case at this time, using a ³⁄₁₆" drift.*

NOTE — *Gear Rotating Tool J-23781 is required to perform the following steps. The tool consists of three parts: gear rotating tool, forcing screw and step plate.*

4) Install step plate in lower differential side gear. Position pawl end of gear rotating tool on step plate. Lubricate forcing screw and center hole in step plate before using. Insert forcing screw through top of case and thread into gear rotating tool.

5) Thread forcing screw so that it becomes centered in step plate. Tighten screw until differential side gears move away from pinion gears. This relieves load between gears allowing pinions some freedom of movement. Use shim stock of .030" thickness to remove spherical washers. Loosen forcing screw and retighten until a very slight movement of pinions is detected.

6) Insert gear rotating pawl between two differential side gear teeth and roll pinion gears out of case.

NOTE — *When rotating differential gear, adjust forcing screw until required load is applied to allow differential gears to rotate freely.*

7) Retain top differential side gear and clutch pack in case by holding bottom of rotating tool while removing forcing screw.

Remove rotating tool, step plate, top differential gear and clutch pack from case.

8) Remove case from axle shaft. Invert case and remove remaining side gear and clutch pack. Remove retainer clips from both clutch packs and separate clutch plates and discs.

NOTE — *During disassembly, keep parts in same order as they were removed, so they can be installed in their original positions.*

INSPECTION

Clean and dry all parts. Inspect plates, discs and clips for excessive wear or scoring. Inspect gears for extreme wear, cracks or chips. Inspect case for scoring, wear or metal pickup on machined surfaces.

NOTE — *If any one member of either clutch pack should be replaced, complete clutch pack for both sides should be replaced. If any one gear requires replacement, all differential gears and thrust washers should be replaced.*

REASSEMBLY

NOTE — *Lubricate all parts with positive traction lubricant prior to assembly.*

1) Reassemble Belleville spring plate, disc and plates to differential side gears in same position as originally assembled. Install retaining clips to ears of plates, making sure clips are fully seated. Install clutch packs and differential side gears into case. Mount case assembly onto axle shaft, held in vise.

2) While holding gears in place by hand, assemble gear rotating tool the same way as during disassembly. Position differential pinion gears in place so that holes in gears align with holes in case. Tighten forcing screws slightly.

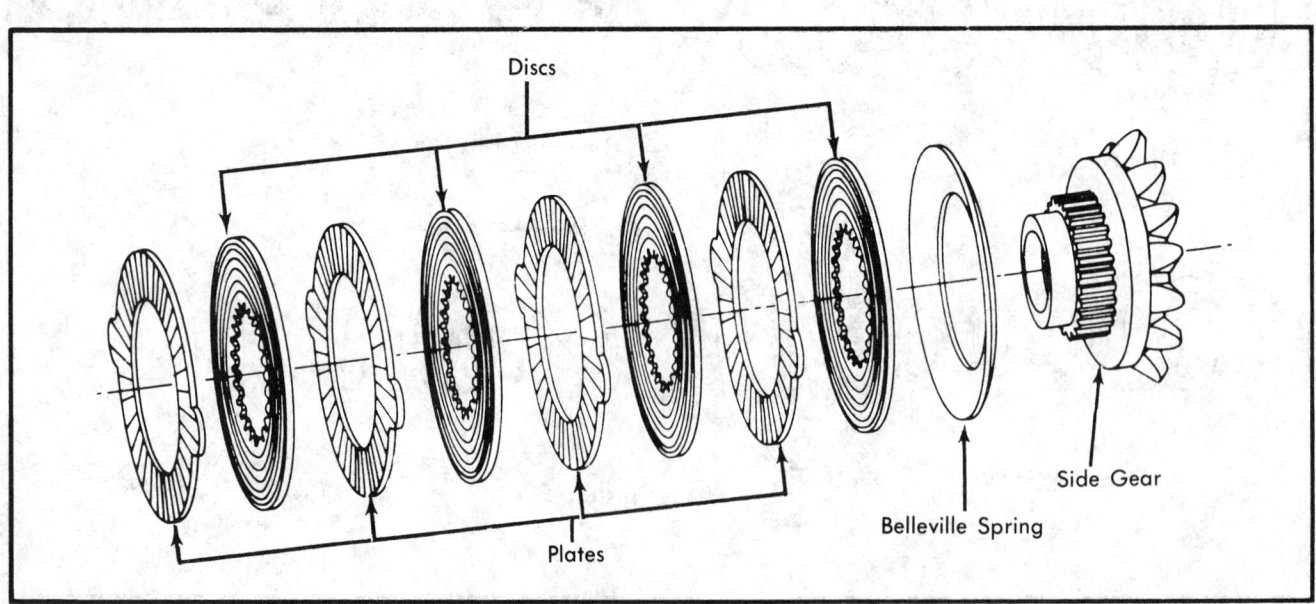

Discs

Plates

Belleville Spring

Side Gear

Fig. 2   View Showing Typical Clutch Pack Arrangement (Not All Combinations Shown)

Positive Traction Differentials

SPICER (DANA) TRAC-LOK (Cont.)

NOTE — *On models with single lock pin through case, make sure hole in shaft is aligned with hole in case.*

3) Install pinion gear thrust washers using small screwdriver to guide washers into position. Remove forcing screw, rotating tool and step plate. Position thrust block between side gears and install differential pinion mate shaft. Be sure snap ring grooves of shaft are exposed enough to install snap rings.

NOTE — *On Model 60 Trac-Lok, align shaft, shaft retaining pin bore, and case pin bore. Tap shaft into position and install retaining pin. If case is mounted in a vise with machined side of ring gear flange facing upward, use a 5/16" diameter punch to install retaining pin.*

4) Seat the pin until the punch bottoms in the case bore. If the case is mounted in a vise, with the machined side of the ring gear flange downward, wrap a length of tape around a 3/16" diameter punch approximately 1¾" from the end of the punch. Install the retaining pin until the edge of the tape is flush with the pin bore.

5) Remove case from axle shaft. Install ring gear on case, using all new ring gear bolts. Do not reuse original bolts. Align ring gear and case bolt holes. Install ring gear bolts finger tight only. Remount case on axle shaft, and tighten bolts evenly to specified torque. Install Trac-Loc differential assembly in axle housing. To complete differential and axle assembly, follow service procedures previously outlined for conventional axles.

STEERING KNUCKLES

Chrysler Corp.
Ford
General Motors
Jeep

DESCRIPTION

Open type steering knuckles are used on all models. Open type knuckles provide a sharper turning angle which will decrease the vehicle turning radius. All of the vehicle weight is carried by the axle housing and steering knuckle; the axle shafts are free floating. The steering knuckles can be attached to axle housing by either ball joints or roller bearings and pivot pins, depending on vehicle model. Other than the unique components required for front-wheel drive, all steering knuckles used on light duty truck application are mechanically identical.

OVERHAUL

BALL JOINT TYPE

Disassembly — 1) Raise vehicle and support on safety stands. Remove wheel and tire assembly. Remove brake caliper. If equipped with locking hubs, see removal and installation instructions on Locking Hubs in this Section. Remove hub lock mechanism.

2) Remove snap ring. Pry out driving hub and spring. Remove wheel bearing lock nut. Outer wheel bearing and retainer will come off with hub. Remove inner bearing, cone and seal from hub using a brass drift punch. Remove inner and outer bearing cups (if necessary) using a brass punch. Remove spindle. Carefully pull axle shaft assembly through hole in steering knuckle.

3) Using suitable tools, press ball sockets from knuckle. Remove threaded sleeve from yoke. Clean all components with suitable solvent and blow dry with compressed air. Inspect all parts for burrs, chips, wear, flat spots or cracks. Replace all damaged parts and parts showing excessive wear.

Reassembly — 1) Place new lower ball socket into position on knuckle. Lower socket has shorter shaft and no cotter pin hole. Using a suitable adapter, press into place in bore. Check bore to socket clearance; it must be less than .0015". Install snap ring, if equipped. Install upper socket into knuckle. Check clearance as with lower socket. Install threaded sleeve into axle end yoke.

2) Adjust threaded sleeve so that approximately two threads are exposed above top of yoke. Assemble knuckle to yoke. Install NEW nut on bottom ball joint and tighten to specifications. Tighten threaded sleeve to specifications (this loads ball joints correctly). Install ball joint upper nut and tighten to specifications. To complete reassembly, reverse disassembly procedure.

NOTE — *When aligning upper ball joint nut to install cotter pin, always tighten nut to align. Never loosen nut to align holes.*

KING PIN TYPE

Disassembly — 1) Raise vehicle and support on safety stands. Remove wheel and tire assembly. Remove brake caliper. If equipped with locking hubs, see removal and installation instructions on Locking Hubs in this Section. Remove hub lock mechanism.

2) Remove snap ring. Pry out driving hub and spring. Remove wheel bearing lock nut. Outer wheel bearing and retainer will come off with hub. Remove inner bearing, cone and seal from hub using a brass drift punch. Remove inner and outer bearing cups (if necessary) using a brass punch. Remove spindle. Carefully pull axle shaft assembly through hole in steering knuckle.

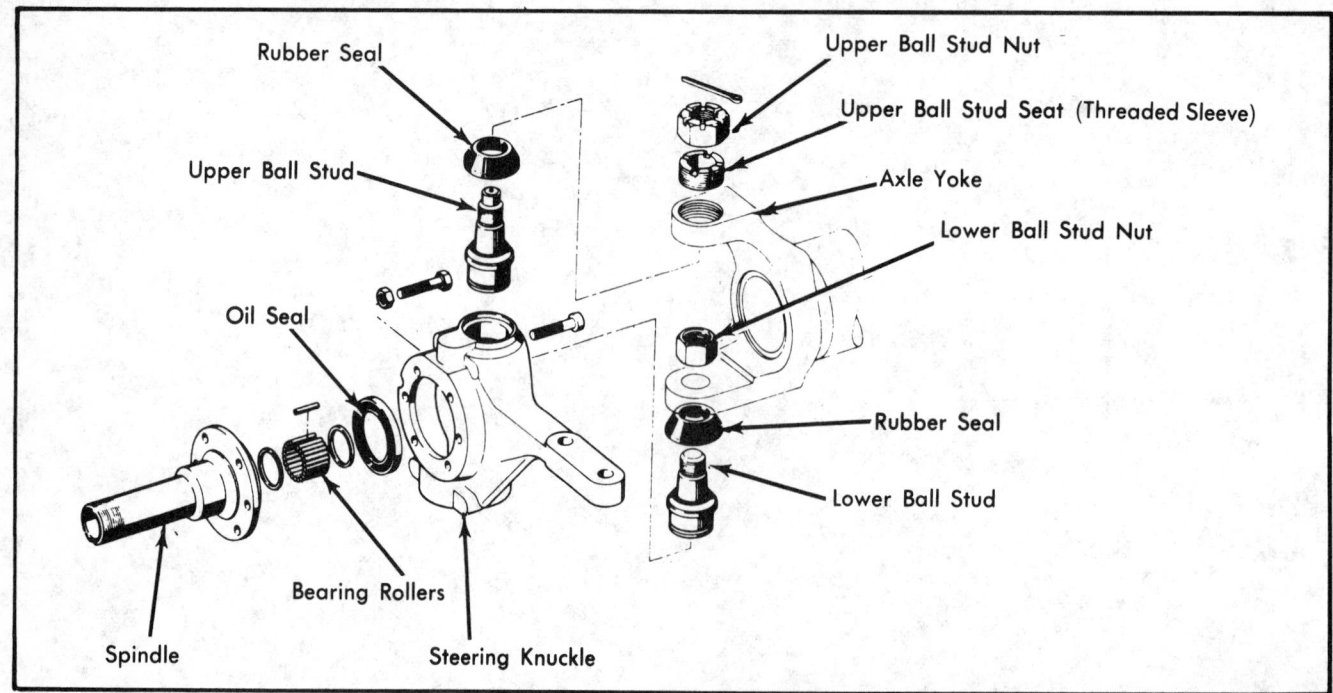

Fig. 1 Exploded View of Ball Joint Type Steering Knuckle Assembly

STEERING KNUCKLES (Cont.)

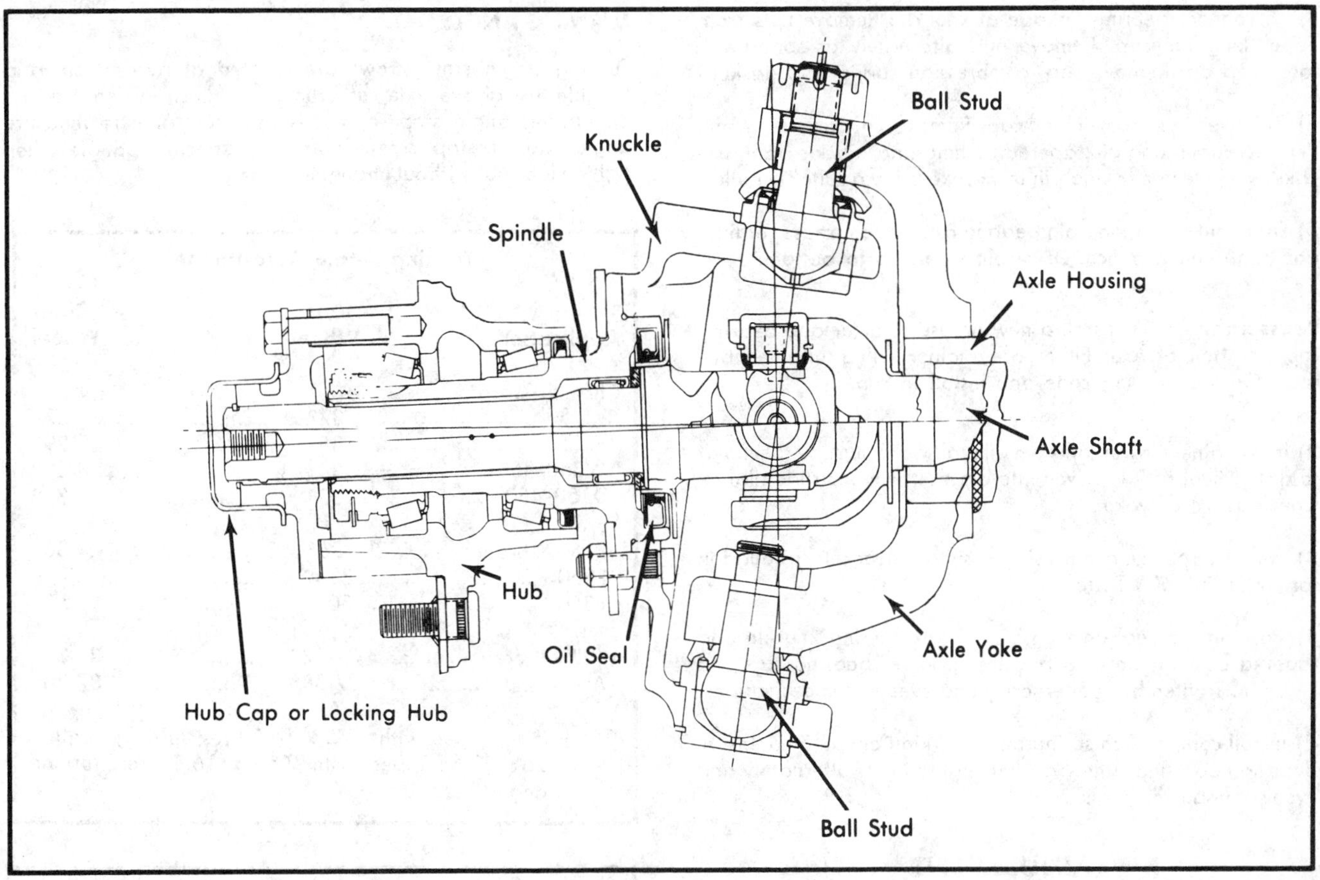

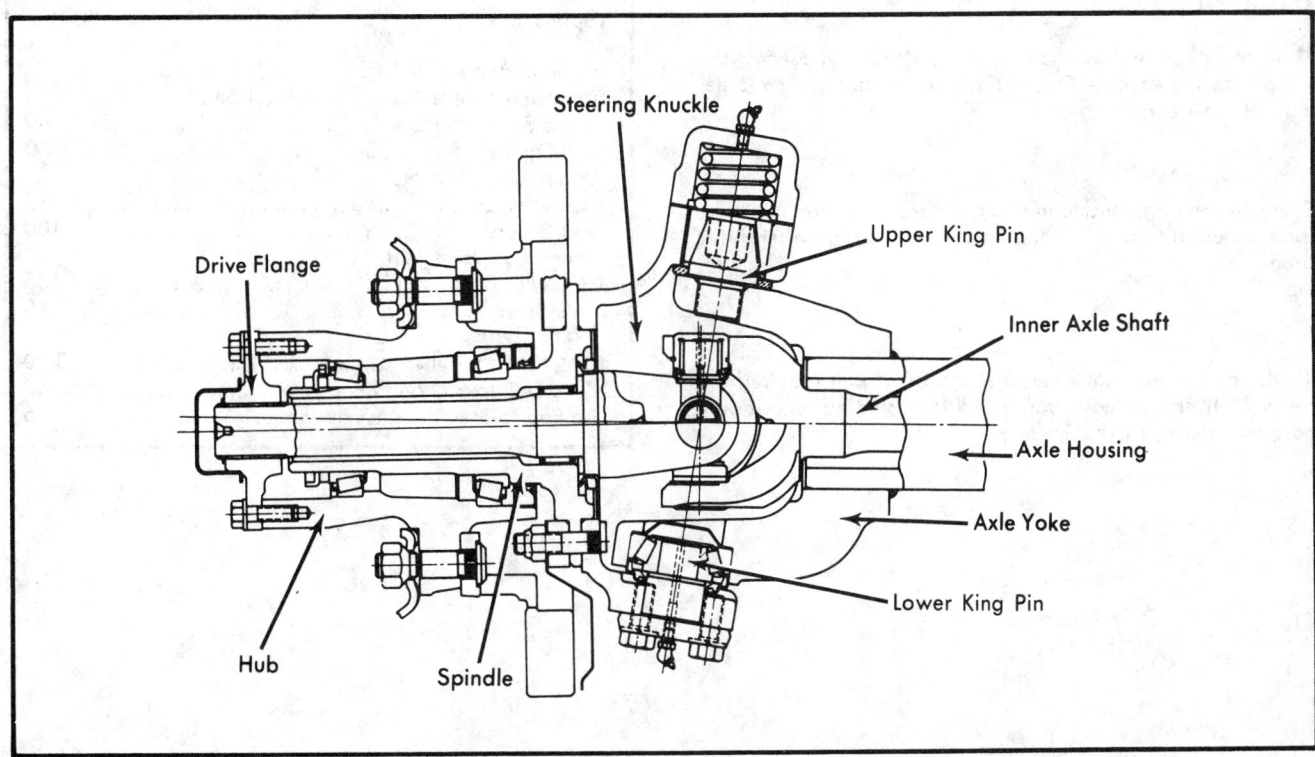

Fig. 2 *Sectional View of Ball Joint Type Steering Knuckle Assembly*

Fig. 3 *Sectional View of King Pin Type Steering Knuckle Assembly*

STEERING KNUCKLES (Cont.)

3) Disconnect steering linkage at knuckle. Remove nuts from upper king pin cap. Remove nuts alternately as spring will force cap up. Remove cap, compression spring and gasket.

4) Remove nuts from lower cap. Remove cap and king pin. Remove upper king pin tapered bushing and knuckle from axle yoke. Remove upper king pin from yoke using a suitable puller.

5) Drive out lower king pin bearing cup, cone, grease retainer and seal with a punch. Drive out from top to bottom.

Reassembly — 1) Install a new grease retainer and bearing cup in bottom of yoke. Fill grease retainer with a suitable lubricant. Grease bearing cone and install in cup.

2) Install a new lower king pin oil seal. Care must be taken not to distort seal as it is driven into place. It will protrude slightly from surface of yoke.

3) Install upper king pin using a suitable socket. Installation torque is 500-600 ft. lbs.

4) Position felt seal on king pin. Install steering knuckle and tapered bushing on king pin. Install lower bearing cap and king pin. Tighten bolts alternately and evenly to specifications.

5) Install compression spring on upper king pin bushing. Install bearing cap using a new gasket. Tighten nuts alternately and evenly to specifications.

ADJUSTMENT

BALL JOINTS

1) Raise vehicle and position on safety stands. Disconnect tie-rod at steering knuckle. Connect a spring tension gauge to tie-rod hole in steering knuckle.

2) Place steering knuckle in straight ahead position. Measure force required to pull steering knuckle to the right after initial breakaway.

3) The pull should not exceed 25 ft. lbs. If pull required exceeds 25 ft. lbs., remove upper ball joint stud nut and loosen adjusting sleeve as required.

TURNING ANGLE

Turning angle stop screws are located at rear of steering knuckle just above axle centerline. To adjust, loosen lock nut on turning angle stop screw. Using a turntable to measure angle, adjust stop screw to obtain specified angle, then tighten lock nut without changing setting.

Turning Angle Adjustment		
Application	**Left Wheel**	**Right Wheel**
Chrysler Corp.		
W150	37°	27°
W250	35°	①29°
W350/450	34°	29°
D150/450	33°	33°
Ford		
F150 & Bronco	36°	36°
F250	33.4°	33.4°
F350	30.3°	30.3°
Jeep		
"CJ" & Scrambler	31-32°	31-32°
All Others	37-38°	37-38°

① — If equipped with 8.75 x 16.5 tires, turning angle is 26°. If equipped with 9.50 x 16.5 tires, turning angle is 24°.

TIGHTENING SPECIFICATIONS	
Application	**Ft. Lbs.**
Ball Joint Type	
Threaded Sleeve (Upper Ball Stud Seat)	
Ford & Chrysler Corp.	40
All Others	50
Upper Ball Joint Nut	
Chrysler Corp.	135
All Others	100
Lower Ball Joint Nut	
Chrysler Corp.	135
All Others	80
King Pin Type	
King Pin Cap Bolts	70-90
Drag Link-to-Steering Knuckle	60
Tie Rod-to-Steering Knuckle	45

Locking Hubs

AUTOMATIC TYPE

Chevrolet
Chrysler Corp.
Ford
GMC

DESCRIPTION

The automatic locking hub automatically engages to lock (and disengages to unlock) the front axle shaft to the front hub. Shifting the transfer case into 4-wheel drive immediately engages the automatic locking hubs. The hubs remain engaged, even during coasting or down-hill operation. The automatic locking hubs disengage when transfer case is shifted into 2-wheel drive and vehicle is slowly moved rearward several feet.

REMOVAL & INSTALLATION

Removal (Chevrolet, GMC & Chrysler Corp.) — 1) Remove 5 cap screws, cover and bearing race spring assembly. Remove sealing ring, seal bridge retainer, and bearing components.

2) Squeeze the tangs of the wire retaining ring together with needle nose pliers and pull the remaining components of the automatic hub from the wheel. *See Fig. 1.*

Removal (Ford) — 1) Remove cap screws and hub cap assembly from wheel hub. Remove cap screw from end of axle shaft.

2) With a knife blade or with a small sharp awl with the tip bent into a hook, remove lock ring seated in the groove of the wheel hub.

3) Remove body assembly from wheel hub. If body assembly does not slide out easily, use an appropriate puller.

4) Unscrew all 4 set screws in spindle lock nut, until heads are flush with edge of lock nut. Remove outer spindle lock nut.

Installation (Chevrolet & Chrysler) — 1) Make sure that the drag sleeve retainer washer is in position between the wheel bearing adjusting nut and the lock nut. Torque wheel bearing adjusting nut to specifications. Make sure that the spacer and retaining ring are in position on the axle shaft.

2) Install the automatic locking hub into the wheel hub, and align the drag sleeve slots with the tabs on the drag sleeve retainer washer. Align the outer clutch housing splines with the splines of the wheel hub.

3) Loosen the cover screws 3 or 4 turns and push in on the cover to allow the retaining ring to expand into the rotor hub groove.

4) Tighten cover screws to 40-50 INCH lbs.

Installation (Ford) — 1) Install slotted lock washer to make sure pin on inner bearing adjusting nut enters one of the slots. Tighten outer spindle lock nut to 15-20 ft. lbs. Tighten down all 4 set screws. Two of the set screws should thread in until they bottom on inner bearing adjusting nut. Firmly push in body assembly until friction shoes are on top of spindle outer lock nut. Install lock ring in groove in wheel hub.

2) Install cap screw into axle shaft. Tighten to 35-50 ft. lbs. Place cap on spindle, and install cap screws. Tighten to 35-50 INCH lbs. Turn dial firmly from stop to stop, causing dialing mechanism to engage body spline. If properly installed, spinning the wheel will cause axle shaft to rotate with the hub when in the "LOCK" position.

NOTE — *Locking hubs should be replaced as a complete unit.*

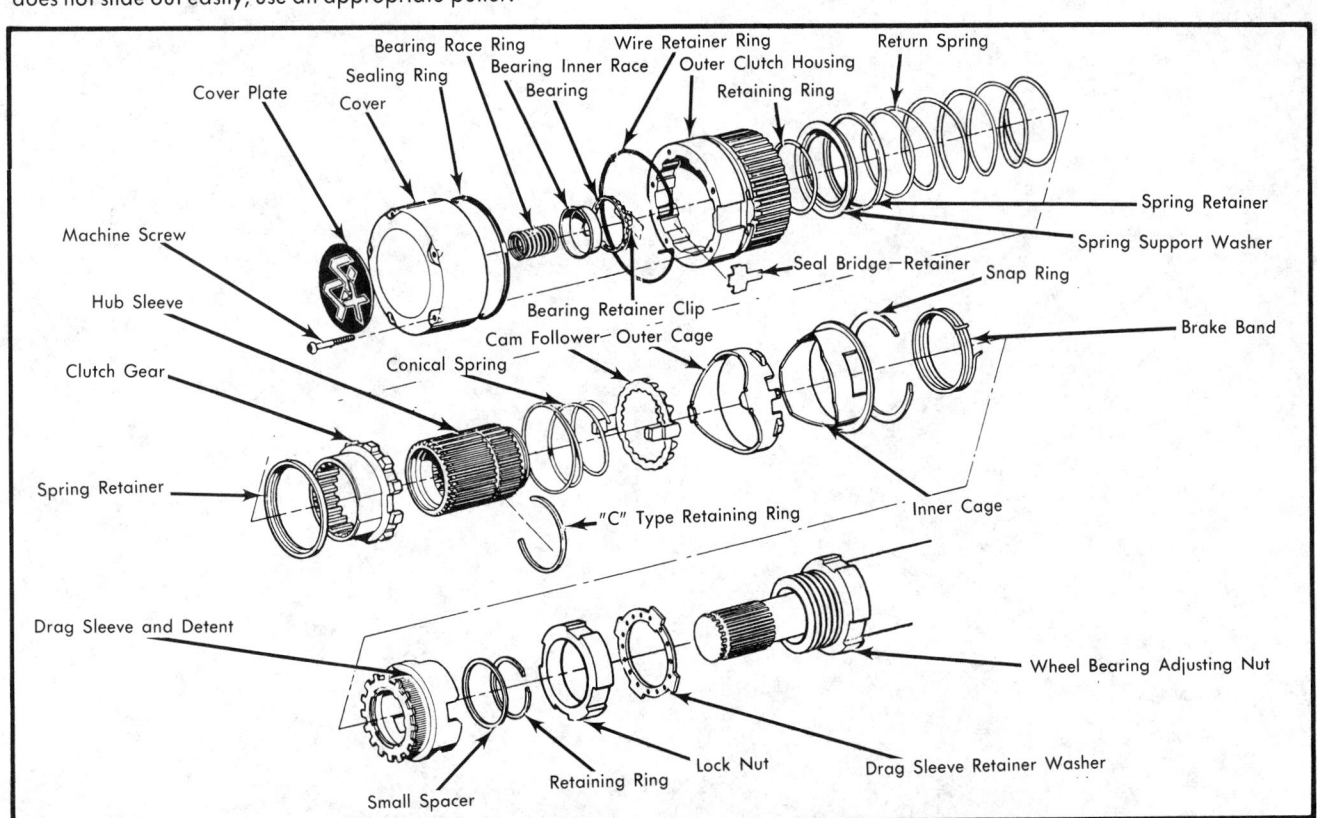

Fig. 1   Automatic Locking Hubs (Chevrolet, GMC & Chrysler Corp.)

Locking Hubs

AUTOMATIC TYPE (Cont.)

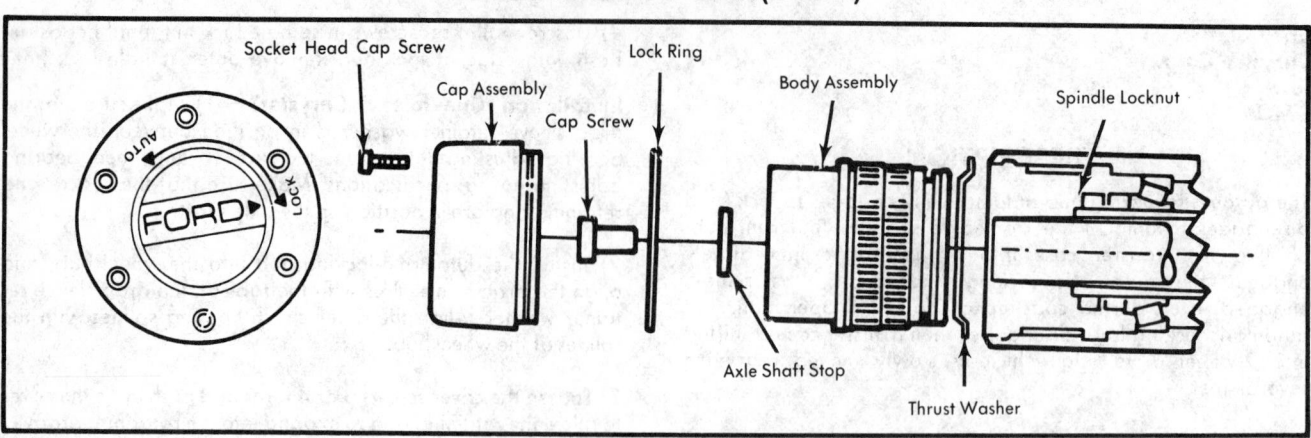

Fig. 2   Automatic Locking Hub (Ford)

Locking Hubs

WARN SELECTIVE MANUAL TYPE

Jeep

DESCRIPTION

Locking hubs provide a means of engagement of front wheels on vehicles with front driving axle. When hub is engaged, full power is transmitted to both front wheels. When hubs are disengaged, front wheels are free to turn but axle shafts and differential will remain idle. Engagement is accomplished through action of gears within hub. With hub in engaged position, clutch body and hub body of hub assembly act as one piece to connect axle shaft to wheel hub. All Warn Selective Manual Hubs function similarly, regardless of differing external appearance.

IDENTIFICATION

All Warn Hubs employ BRASS control knobs to engage and disengage locking mechanism. Model number of hub is stamped into recesses of control knob. Model numbers for Warn Selective Manual Hubs are as follows:

Warn Selective Manual Type Hubs	
Application	**Model No.**
Jeep	
"CJ" & Scrambler M243	
All Other Models M247	

NOTE — *Warn Hubs are not furnished as original equipment by other manufacturers.*

REMOVAL & INSTALLATION

NOTE — *Model M243 and M247 front drive hubs are serviced as either a complete assembly or subassembly, such as the hub body or clutch assembly only. Do not attempt to disassemble*

these units. If the entire hub or a subassembly has malfunctioned, replace the hub assembly or the problem subassembly as a unit only.

Removal (Models M243 & M247) — 1) Remove bolts and tabbed lock washers (if equipped), attaching hub body to axle hub. Retain bolts and washers.

2) Remove retaining ring from axle shaft. Remove hub clutch and bearing assembly. Clean hub components in solvent. Dry them using compressed air, clean shop towels, or air dry. Be sure old lubricant, dirt, water or other foreign materials are flushed out.

CAUTION — *Do not turn the hub control dial until hub has been installed. The hub clutch nut and cup can be damaged serverly if dial is rotated while hub is off vehicle.*

Installation — 1) Lubricate hub components with all purpose chassis lubricant. Apply light coat of lubricant only. Do not pack hub with lubricant. On model M243, install hub clutch, bearing assembly, and retaining ring on axle shaft. Position new gasket on hub body, and install hub body and gasket. On model M247, install hub clutch assembly and small retaining ring on axle shaft. Install large retaining ring in axle hub. Install new O-ring if hub body is being replaced.

2) Align bolt holes in axle and hub body, and install bolts and tabbed lock washers (if equipped). Tighten bolts to 30 ft. lbs. on model M243 and 30 INCH lbs. on model M247. Raise vehicle front end. Turn hub control dials to position "2" and rotate wheels. Wheels should rotate freely. If wheels drag, check hub installation. Also, be sure control dials are fully engaged in 4x4 position.

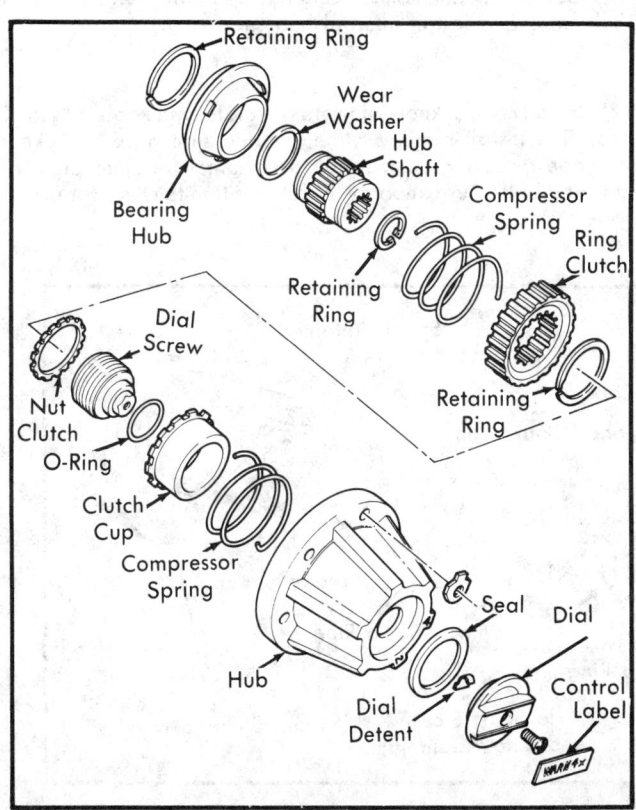

Fig. 1 Exploded View of Warn Hub Model M243

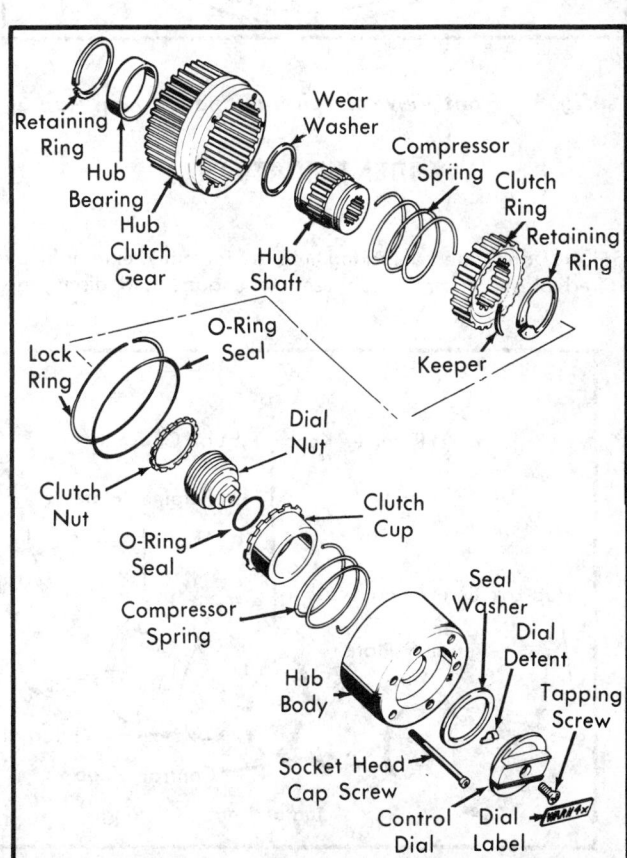

Fig. 2 Exploded View of Warn Hub Model M247

Locking Hubs

SPICER (DANA) INTERNAL LOCKING HUB

DESCRIPTION

Locking hubs provide a means of engagement of front wheels on vehicles with front driving axle. When hubs are engaged, full power is transmitted to both front wheels. When hubs are disengaged, front wheels are free to turn but axle shafts and differential will remain idle. Engagement is accomplished through action of gears within hub. With hub in engaged position, inner clutch ring and axle shaft sleeve act as one piece to connect axle shaft to wheel hub.

Fig. 1   Front View of Spicer (Dana) Locking Hub

IDENTIFICATION

Spicer (Dana) internal locking hubs are identified externally by a red plastic control knob used to engage and disengage

hub. They are identified internally by use of actuating cam to engage and disengage hub.

REMOVAL & INSTALLATION

REMOVAL

With control knob set in "LOCK" position, remove retainer plate attaching bolts. Remove outer retainer plate assembly and separate knob from retainer. Remove internal hub snap ring and slide retainer ring and cam from hub. Relieve pressure on sleeve and ring assembly and remove axle shaft snap ring. Remove sleeve and ring assembly, inner clutch, pressure spring and spring retainer plate.

INSTALLATION

1) Wash all parts in suitable solvent and dry with compressed air. Inspect all parts for wear, cracks or broken teeth. Replace parts as necessary, using new gaskets and seals during reassembly.

2) Lubricate all parts with Moly X-L Hi-Speed Grease. Position spring retainer plate into hub bore, flange side facing bearing, and seat retainer against bearing cup. Install pressure spring in hub with large coils against retainer plate.

NOTE — *Spring is an interference fit. When spring is seated it should extend past spindle nut approximately ⅞".*

3) Place inner clutch ring into axle shaft sleeve and clutch ring assembly and install as a unit onto axle shaft. Force unit in against pressure spring and install axle shaft snap ring. Position actuating cam, cams facing outward, and retainer ring in hub bore and install internal hub snap ring.

4) Install control knob into retainer plate with knob in "LOCK" position. Install retainer plate, making sure grooves in knob engage actuating cam. Install and tighten retainer plate attaching bolts. Turn knob to "FREE" position to check for proper operation.

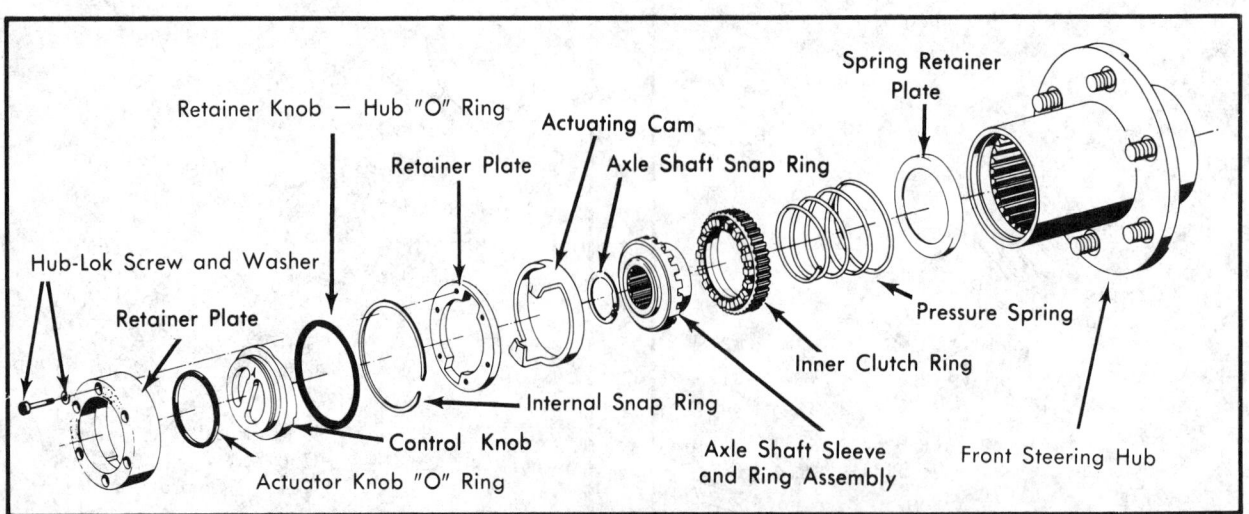

Fig. 2   Exploded View of Spicer (Dana) Internal Locking Hub

Locking Hubs

SPICER (DANA) EXTERNAL LOCKING HUB

DESCRIPTION

Locking hubs provide a means of engagement of front wheels on vehicles with front drive axles. When locking hubs are engaged, full power is transmitted to both front wheels. When hubs are disengaged, front wheels are free to turn but axle shafts and differential will remain idle. Engagement is accomplished through action of gears within hub. With hub in engaged position, the inner clutch gear locks with outer clutch and engages axle shaft with wheel hub.

IDENTIFICATION

Spicer (Dana) external locking hubs are identified externally by a red plastic control knob used to engage and disengage hub. They are identified internally by use of an actuating cam to engage and disengage hub.

REMOVAL & INSTALLATION

REMOVAL

1) Remove hub screws and washers, noting how washers are installed on screws. Loosen gear hub housing and slide away from hub and drum assembly. Remove inner metal gasket and discard. Remove gear hub housing. Remove outer gasket and discard.

2) Wipe clean all exposed components. Apply pressure on clutch gear and remove snap ring. Remove clutch gear and pressure spring from assembly while knob is in "LOCK" position.

3) Turn knob to "FREE" position. Using a drift punch, drive cam lock pin out of assembly. Remove actuating cam from knob. Remove knob from knob retainer.

4) Using a suitable size cap screw, pull out on axle shaft and remove snap ring. Remove bushing and inner clutch assembly. If wear is shown on either the inner or outer clutch gear, replace both as a set.

INSTALLATION

1) Before assembling hub, check splines on axle shaft. Make sure threaded screw holes in wheel hub are clean. Apply Moly XL hi-speed grease to thrust face of bushing and to splines of inner clutch gear.

2) Install inner clutch gear on bushing. Install bushing and inner clutch gear on axle shaft. Make sure splines on inner clutch gear are aligned with splines on axle. Install a new snap ring. Make sure snap ring is fully seated.

3) Apply Parker "O" Ring Lubricant to "O" ring area of control knob. Install "O" ring. Place actuating knob into knob retainer with arrow pointing to "FREE" position. Install knob retainer snap ring. It may be necessary to use a small screwdriver to position snap ring in groove.

4) Place actuating cam on knob, making sure ears of cam are aligned with retainer slots. Install cam lock pin through cam groove and holes in actuator knob. Make sure ends of pin are flush with outside diameter of cam.

5) Turn actuator knob to "LOCK" position. Apply a small amount of Moly XL hi-speed lubricant to cam grooves. Install spring and outer clutch gear. Press down on clutch gear to compress spring. With spring compressed, install snap ring.

6) Turn actuator knob to "FREE" position. Install six dished washers to the six retainer screws. Install two screws and washers into knob retainer to align hub components. Apply a small amount of lubricant to outer splines of outer clutch gear. Remove excess lubricant from retainer gasket surface.

7) Install a new outer retainer gasket. Assemble housing by aligning splines of housing with outer clutch gear splines. Install a new inner metal gasket on hub housing. Install hub assembly to axle using retainer screws as pilots to align gasket holes and wheel hub holes.

8) Tighten retainer screws to secure hub in place. Turn actuator knob to "LOCK" position. Install the four remaining screws. Tighten screws evenly to 30-35 ft. lbs. It my be hard to engage and disengage hub until it has been used several times.

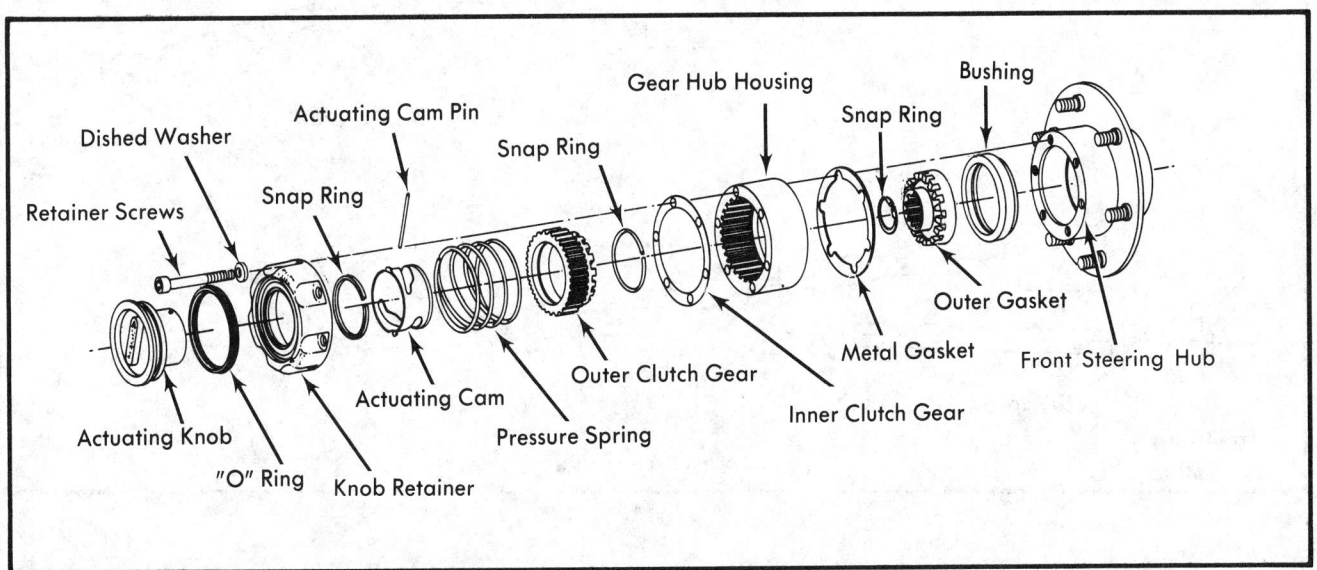

Fig. 1 Exploded View of Spicer (Dana) External Locking Hub

PROPELLER SHAFT ALIGNMENT

All Models
DESCRIPTION

Propeller shafts are balanced, one piece, tubular shafts with universal joints at each end. Number in vehicle varies: one shaft, two shafts with center bearing, and three shafts in four-wheel drive applications. Location of slip joints varies with model and manufacturer. See *Fig. 1.*

INSPECTION

Vibration can come from many sources. Before overhauling driveline, other sources of possible vibration should be checked first.

Tires and Wheels — Check tire inflation and wheel balance. Check for foreign objects in tread, damaged tread, mismatched tread patterns or incorrect tire size.

Center Bearing — Tighten drive shaft center bearing mounting bolts. If bearing insulator is deteriorated or oil soaked, it should be replaced.

Engine and Transmission Mountings — Tighten mounting bolts. If mountings are deteriorated, they should be replaced.

Propeller Shaft — Check propeller shaft for damage or dents that could affect balance. Check for undercoating adhering to shafts. If present, shafts should be thoroughly cleaned.

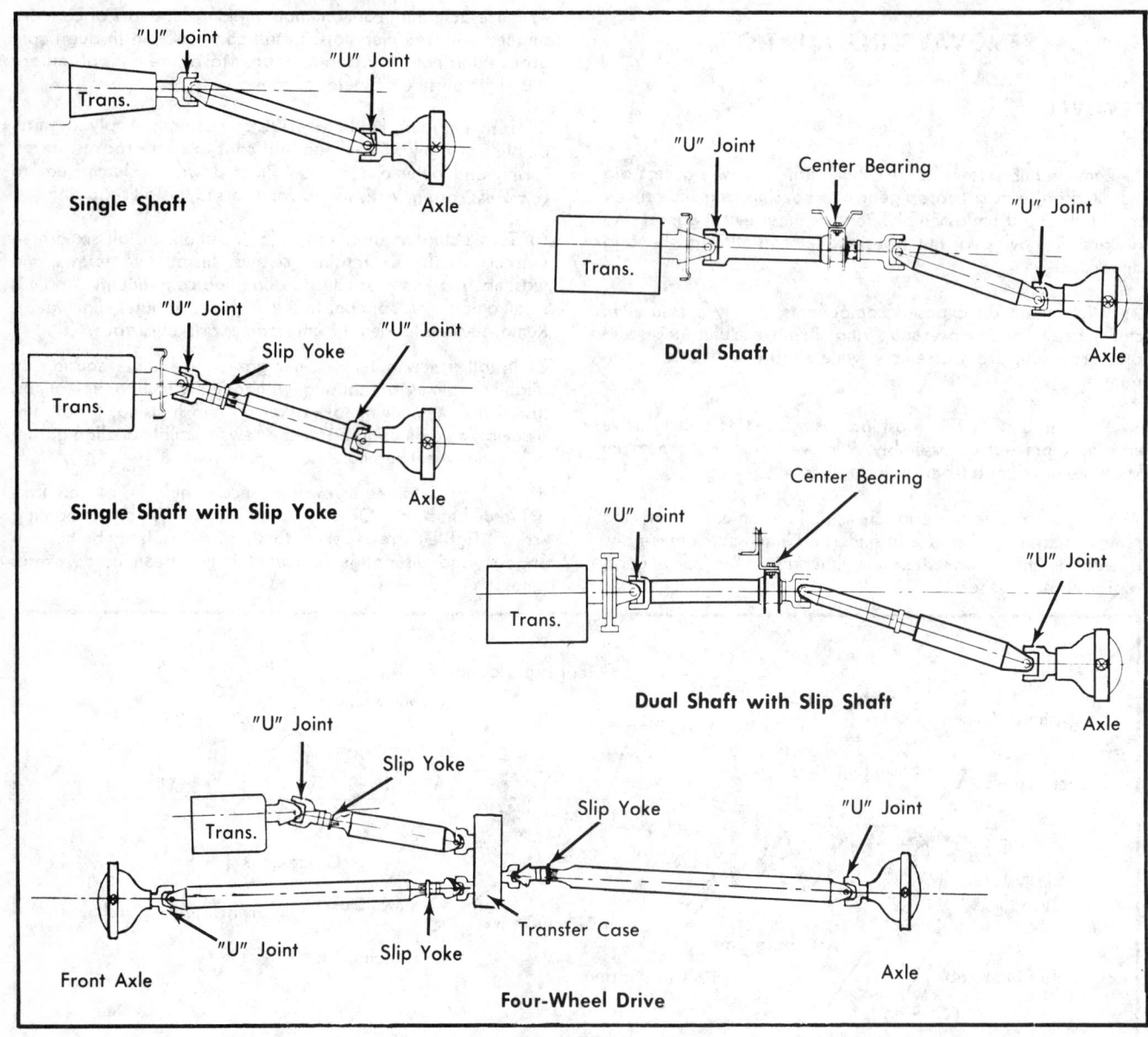

Fig. 1   Five Typical Propeller Shaft Combinations

Propeller Shafts

PROPELLER SHAFT ALIGNMENT (Cont.)

Universal Joints – Check for foreign material stuck in joints. Check for loose bolts and worn bearings.

ADJUSTMENTS

Propeller Shaft Phasing (Chevrolet & GMC) – All models with 32 splines use an alignment key on spline and can mate in correct position only. On "C" and "P" models with two piece shafts, proper phasing is accomplished with a alignment key on spline and can mate in correct position only. On "G" and "K" models with two piece shafts, rotate transmission yoke until trunnion is in vertical position. Install front prop shaft with "U" joint trunnion in horizontal position. Install bearing support to crossmember. Align rear prop shaft with "U" joint trunnion to horizontal position and install shaft.

Propeller Shaft Phasing (All Others) – Check that flanges on either end of drive shaft are in same plane. Often there are arrows on slip joint and drive shaft to aid in alignment. If flanges are not in same plane, disassemble universal joint and align.

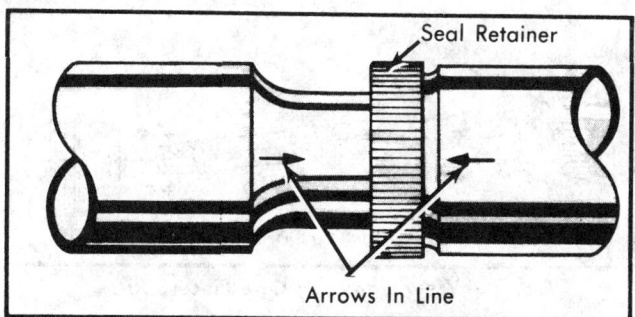

Fig. 2 View Showing Typical Slide Joint Alignment Arrows

Propeller Shaft Balance – **1)** Often propeller shaft imbalance can be cured by disconnecting shaft and rotating it 180° in relation to other components. Test by raising rear wheels off ground and turning shaft with engine.

CAUTION – *Do not run engine with transmission engaged for prolonged periods as overheating of engine or transmission may occur.*

2) On most models, balancing may be done by marking shaft in four positions, 90° apart. Place marks approximately 6" forward of weld at rear end of shaft and number marks 1 through 4.

3) Place a screw type hose clamp in No. 1 position and rotate shaft with engine. If there is little or no change, move clamp to No. 2 position and repeat test. Continue procedure until vibration is at lowest level. If no difference is noted with clamp moved to all four positions, vibrations may not be propeller shaft imbalance.

4) If vibration is lessened but not completely gone, place two clamps at that point and run test again. The combined weight of clamps in one position may worsen vibration. If so, rotate clamps ½" apart, above and below best postion, and repeat test. Continue to rotate clamps as necessary until vibration is at lowest point.

5) When point is reached where vibration has been eliminated, bend end of clamp so it will not loosen. If vibration level is still unacceptable, repeat procedure at front end of propeller shaft.

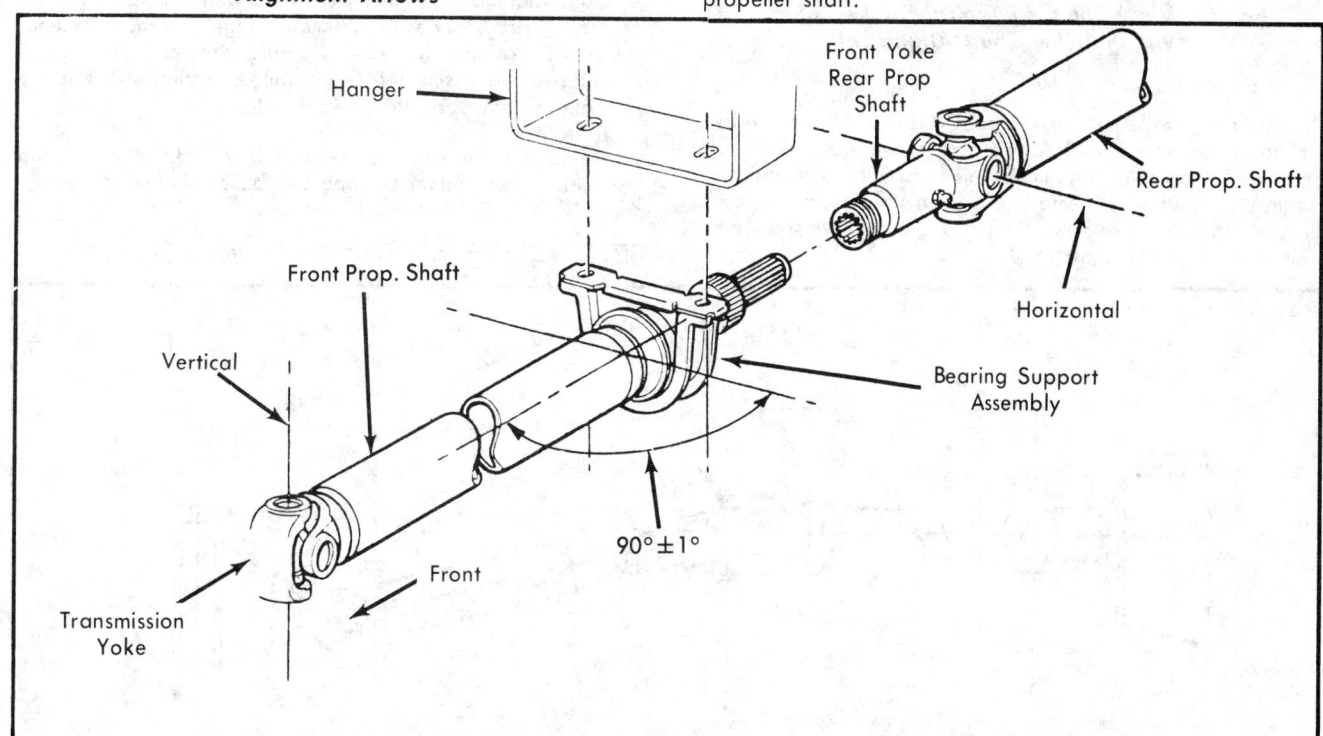

Fig. 3 Propeller Shaft Phase Alignment Chevrolet and GMC Models ("G" & "K" Two Piece Shaft)

PROPELLER SHAFT ALIGNMENT (Cont.)

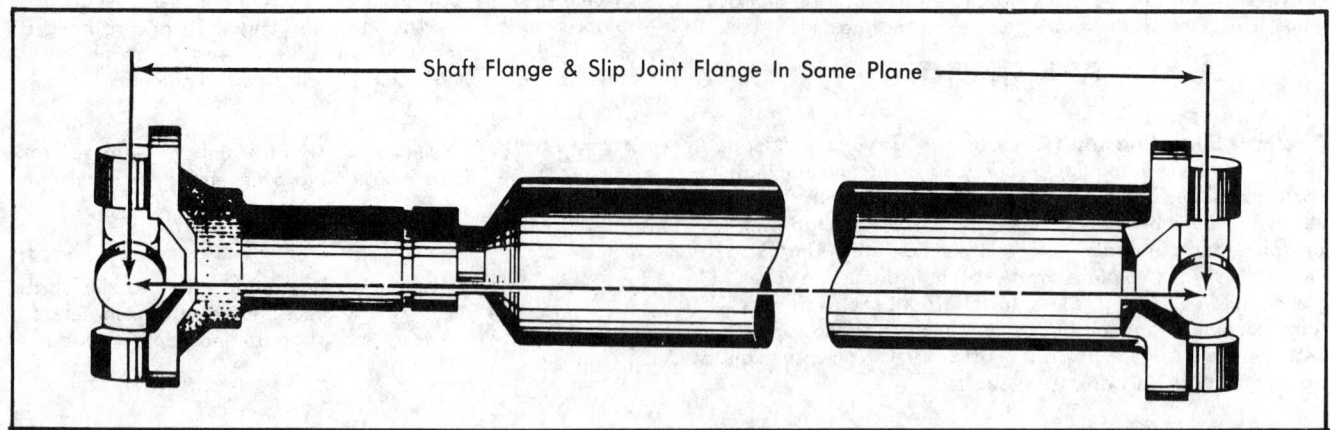

Fig. 4   View Showing Propeller Shaft Phase Alignment

Flange Alignment & Runout — 1) All flanges must be perpendicular in both vertical and horizontal planes to engine crankshaft. The only exception is "broken back" type driveline which has flanges that are not perpendicular in vertical plane. See *Fig. 5.*

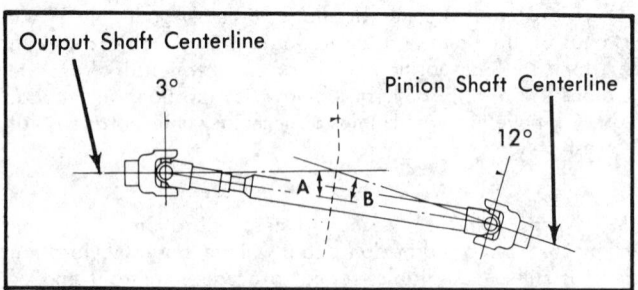

Fig. 5   View Showing Typical "Broken Back" Type Propeller Shaft Alignment

2) With nonparallel or "broken back" type installation, working angles of universal joints of a given drive shaft are equal. See *Fig. 7.* Angle A = Angle B. This is calculated as follows: Angle of output shaft centerline is subtracted from angle of drive shaft. Difference should equal angle of drive shaft subtracted from pinion shaft angle.

3) Parallel type joints maintain a constant velocity between output shaft and pinion shaft. Vibration is minimized and component life maximized when universal joints are parallel.

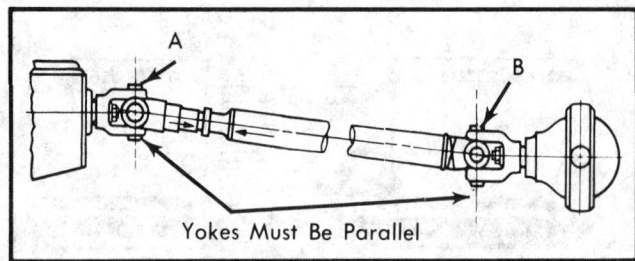

Fig. 7   View Showing One-Piece Shaft Flange Alignment

4) Using dial indicator, measure runout of transmission flange, center bearing flange, and pinion flange. If runout exceeds .003-.005", replace flange. If dial indicator cannot be used, push a rod with a slip fit through flange bearing bore and see if it aligns with opposite bore. If not, replace flange.

5) Rotate transmission flange until it is vertical, measuring from side. Check center bearing and pinion flanges; they cannot be more than 1° off vertical.

NOTE — *See Propeller Shaft Phasing in this Section.*

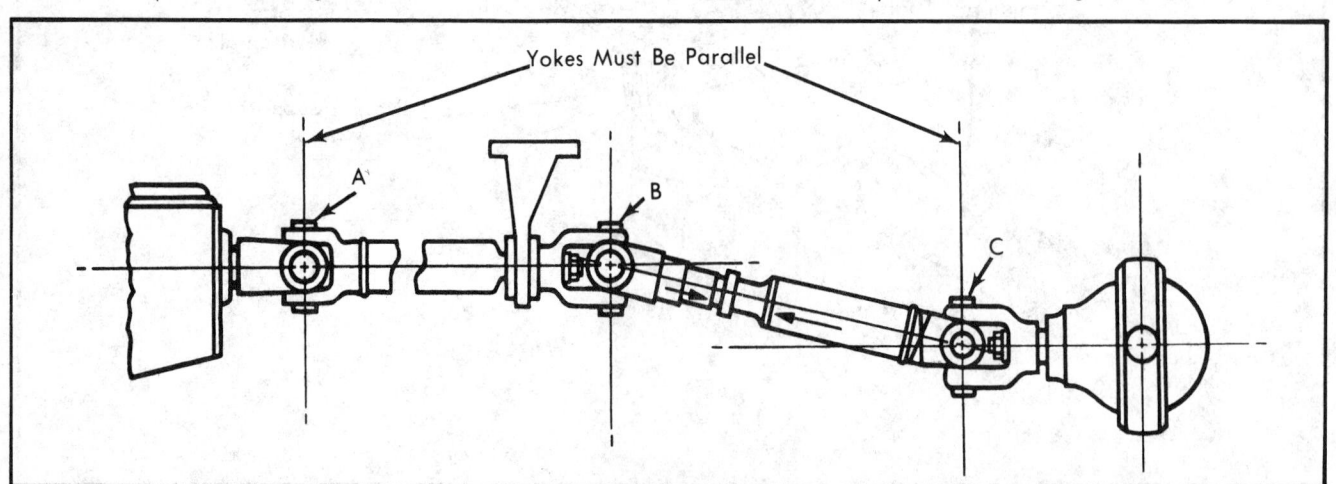

Fig. 6   View Showing Two-Piece Shaft Flange Alignment

PROPELLER SHAFT ALIGNMENT (Cont.)

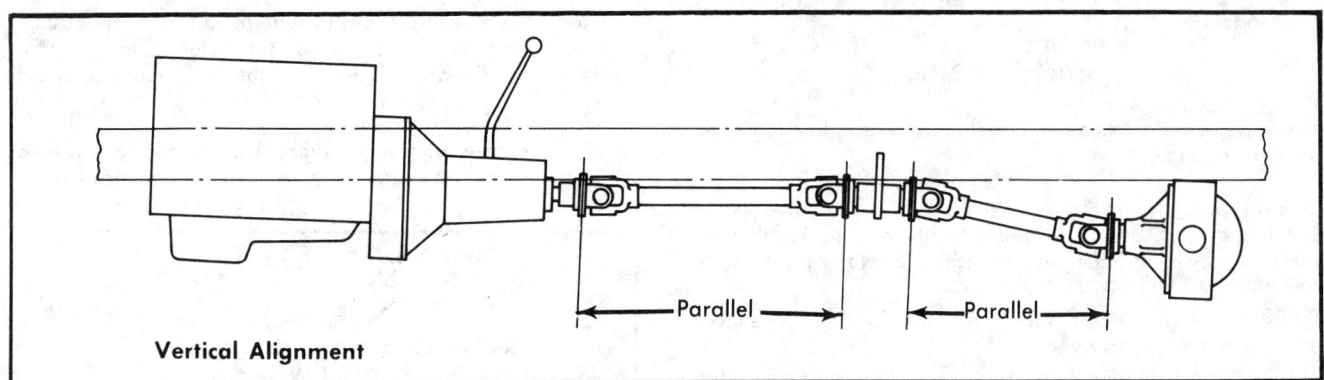

Vertical Alignment

Fig. 8 *View Showing Propeller Shaft Vertical Alignment*

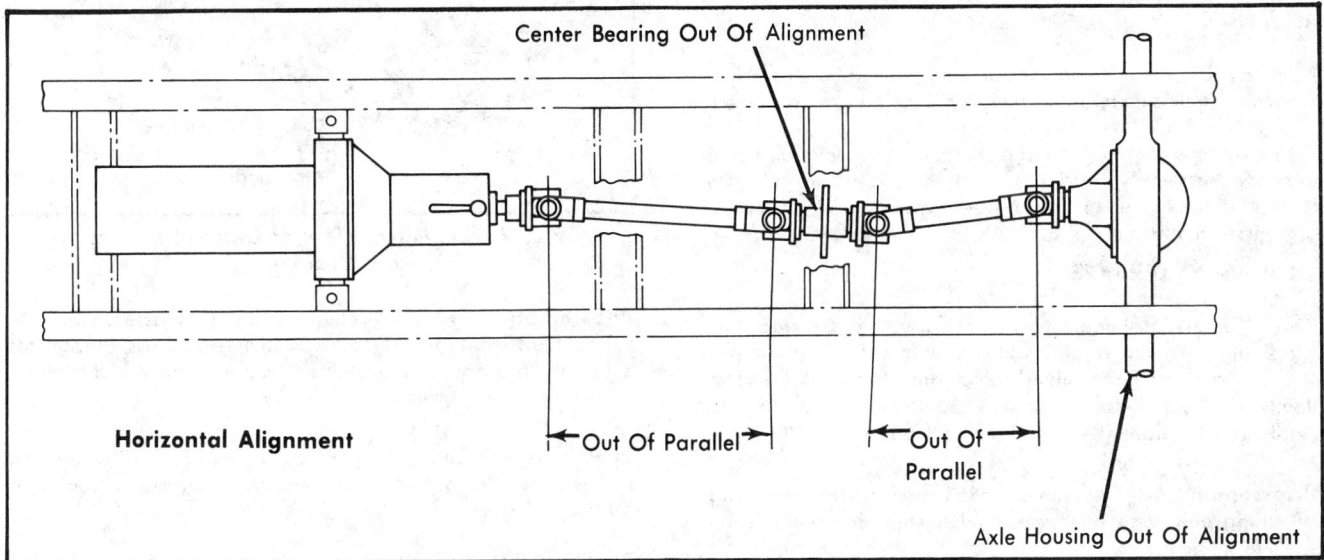

Horizontal Alignment

Fig. 9 *View Showing Propeller Shaft Horizontal Alignment*

6) Rotate transmission flange until it is vertical, measuring from side. Then measure angle from end and record. Check all other flanges for same angle. They must be within ½ ° of each other. Adjust as required.

7) If difficulty is encountered when making above adjustments, horizontal alignment should be checked. As shown in illustration, even though vertical alignment is correct, horizontal alignment can be badly out of adjustment especially after major component replacement or serious accident.

8) To make horizontal alignment checks, set up straightedges as shown in *Fig. 10*. With transmission flange horizontal, clamp a straightedge to it, so that straightedge is horizontal. Do the same with pinion flange. Using a straightedge that is 12" longer than rear wheel track, clamp it to frame side rails using large framing squares to align.

9) Measure distance "X". If two dimensions are not within ⅟₁₆" of each other, transmission flange is misaligned horizontally. Measure distance "W". If two dimensions are not within ⅟₁₆" of each other, pinion flange is misaligned horizontally. Measure

distance "Y", from edge of straightedge to center of axle shaft. If two dimensions are not within ⅛" of each other, axle housing is misaligned.

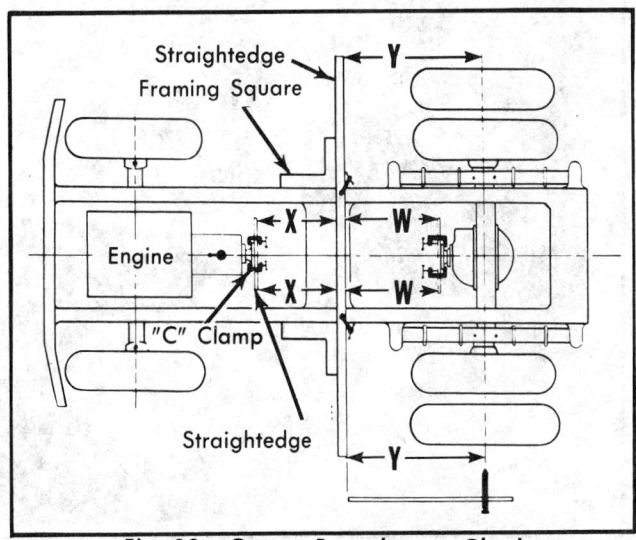

Fig. 10 *Correct Procedure to Check Horizontal Alignment*

Propeller Shafts

UNIVERSAL JOINTS

All Models

MAINTENANCE

If slip yoke has a tendency to stick in extension housing seal, service as follows:

Remove propeller shaft from vehicle and clean yoke with suitable solvent. Lubricate inside diameter of seal with synthetic oil seal lubricant and outside diameter of seal with transmission fluid.

NOTE — *This procedure should also be followed whenever shaft is removed from vehicle.*

OVERHAUL

ALL MODELS

NOTE — *Universal joints should not be disassembled or lubricated unless external leaking or damage has occurred.*

Before disassembly, scribe alignment marks on yoke and shaft to allow reassembly in original position. If joints are rusted or corroded, apply penetrating oil before pressing out bearing cups or trunnion pin.

CROSS & ROLLER TYPE

Two different retaining methods are used for bearing cups, snap ring or nylon retainers. Joints with snap rings may be taken apart and reassembled using same cross and bearings. Joints with nylon retainers are disassembled by braking nylon retainers (therefore, they must be replaced after service).

Disassembly — **1)** Disconnect yoke attaching bolts or flange attaching bolts and remove propeller shaft from vehicle.

NOTE — *Do not use pry bar to hold propeller shaft while loosening bolts as damage to bearing seals may result.*

2) Remove retaining strap (if equipped), remove bushing retainers from yoke, and press out rollers and bushings. Remove last roller and bushing assembly by pressing on end of cross.

3) Remove cross assembly from yoke. Do not remove seal retainers from cross. Cross and retainers are serviced as an assembly.

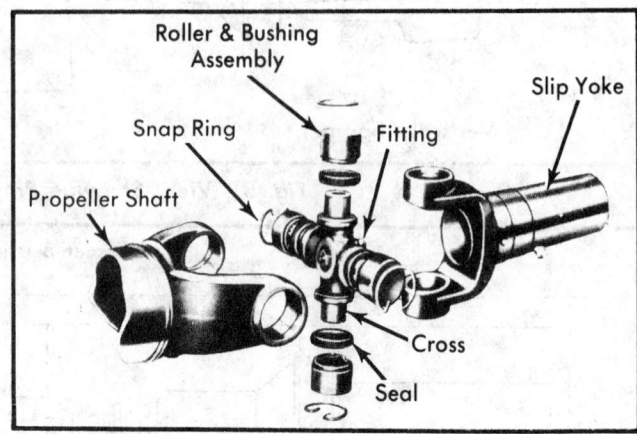

Fig. 2   Exploded View of General Motors Universal Joint

Reassembly — **1)** Coat roller and bearing assemblies with suitable lubricant and fill reservoirs in ends of cross. Place cross assembly in propeller shaft yoke and place roller and bushing assemblies into position.

2) Press both bushing assemblies into yoke until retainers can be installed. Being careful to keep cross aligned in center of bushings.

3) Install retainers, then repeat procedure for remaining bushings. Install strap (if equipped). Install propeller shaft in vehicle, aligning scribe marks.

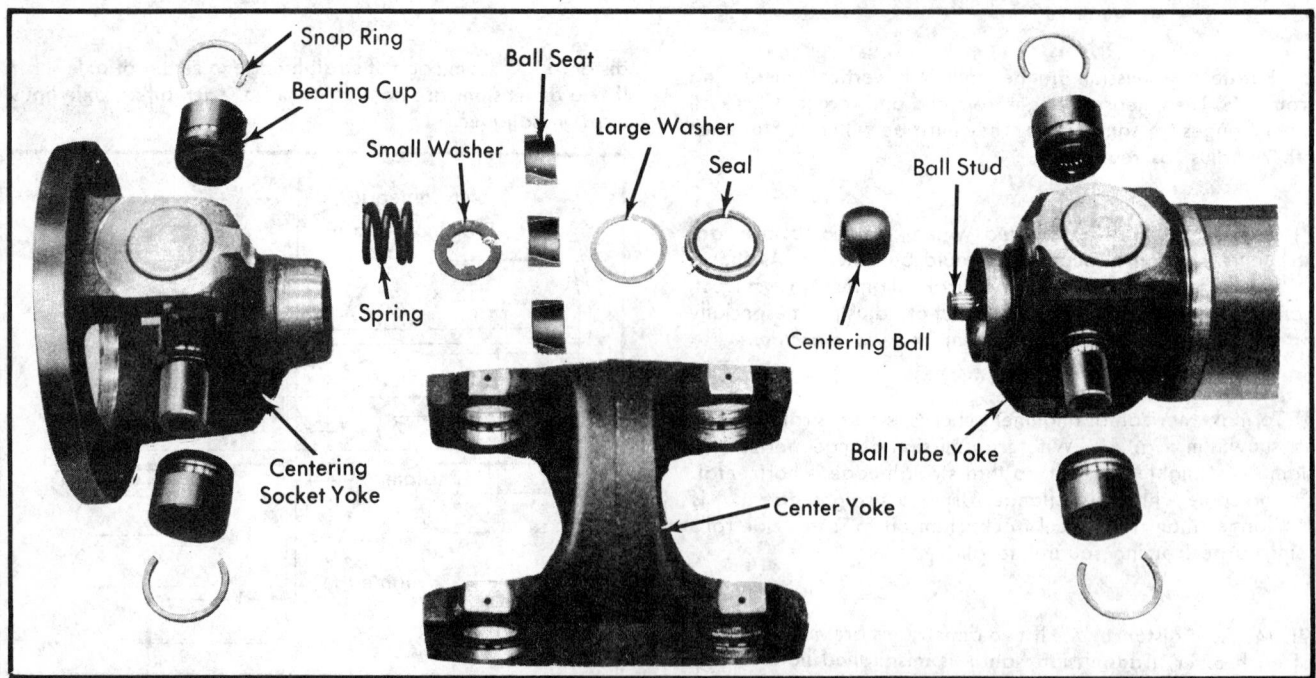

Fig. 1   Exploded View of General Motors and Jeep Constant Velocity Type Universal Joint

UNIVERSAL JOINTS (Cont.)

CONSTANT VELOCITY TYPE

NOTE — *To prevent damage to constant velocity joint, center ball when removing propeller shaft assembly. When handling shaft after removal, support shafts on both sides of constant velocity joint if shaft is being moved horizontally. Do not allow one end to hang free or one shaft to bend at a sharp angle. After removal, shaft may be carried vertically without damage.*

Disassembly; General Motors & Jeep — 1) Disconnect yoke attaching bolts and flange attaching bolts and remove propeller shaft from vehicle. Mark joint so that center yoke, end yoke and crosses will be installed in original positions.

2) Pry out all snap rings and press bearing out enough to allow bearing end to be clamped in a vise. Tap on yoke until it is free of bearing.

3) Repeat procedure for remaining bearings. Remove remaining parts from center yoke assembly.

Reassembly; General Motors & Jeep — 1) Pack all bearings with proper grease and assemble center yoke components in reverse order of disassembly.

2) Using arbor press or vise, press two opposing bearings into position at same time until all bearings are installed. Take caution that crosses and yokes remain aligned during this process.

3) Check for free movement of joint. If bind exists, seat bearings with a sharp rap on yokes with brass hammer.

NOTE — *Never hammer on bearings.*

4) Install propeller shaft in vehicle, making sure marks made during disassembly are aligned.

Disassembly; Ford — 1) With propeller shaft removed from vehicle, position assembly in a vise. Mark position of crosses, center yoke and center socket in relationship with stud yoke welded to propeller shaft tube.

NOTE — *Crosses will have to be installed on bosses in original positions to obtain correct clearance.*

2) Remove snap rings in front of center yoke. Using a "C" clamp type tool (CJ91B or equivalent), tighten screw in tool until bearing protrudes 3/8".

3) Remove propeller shaft from vise. Tighten protruding part of bearing in vise, then rap against center yoke with hammer until bearing is free of yoke. Remove all bearings from cross in this manner.

4) Remove cross from center yoke. Remove centering socket from stud and remove rubber seal from centering ball stud.

5) Remove snap rings from center and drive shaft yokes. Install "C" clamp tool and tighten screws until bearing is pressing outward and center yoke contacts slinger ring.

NOTE — *Do not press beyond this point or slinger will be damaged.*

6) Clamp exposed end of bearing in vise and hammer on center yoke until bearing is free. Press against cross with "C" clamp tool to remove remaining bearing.

7) Remove center yoke from cross and remove cross from propeller shaft using same procedure.

Reassembly; Ford — 1) Clean all components in a suitable cleaning solvent. Place cross in propeller shaft yoke. Make sure cross bosses are installed in original position.

NOTE — *If a repair kit is being installed, bosses will be lubrication plugs.*

2) Press in bearings and install snap rings. Fill sock and relief ball with proper grease. Position center yoke over cross. Press in bearings and install snap rings.

3) Install a new seal on centering ball stud. Place centering socket over stud. Place front cross in yoke. Make sure cross bosses (or lubrication plugs) are installed in original position.

4) Place cross loosely on center stop. Press first set of bearings into center yoke, then install second set. Install snap rings. Apply pressure to center yoke socket and install remaining bearing cup. If replacement kit is used, remove plugs and lubricate "U" joints. Reinstall plugs.

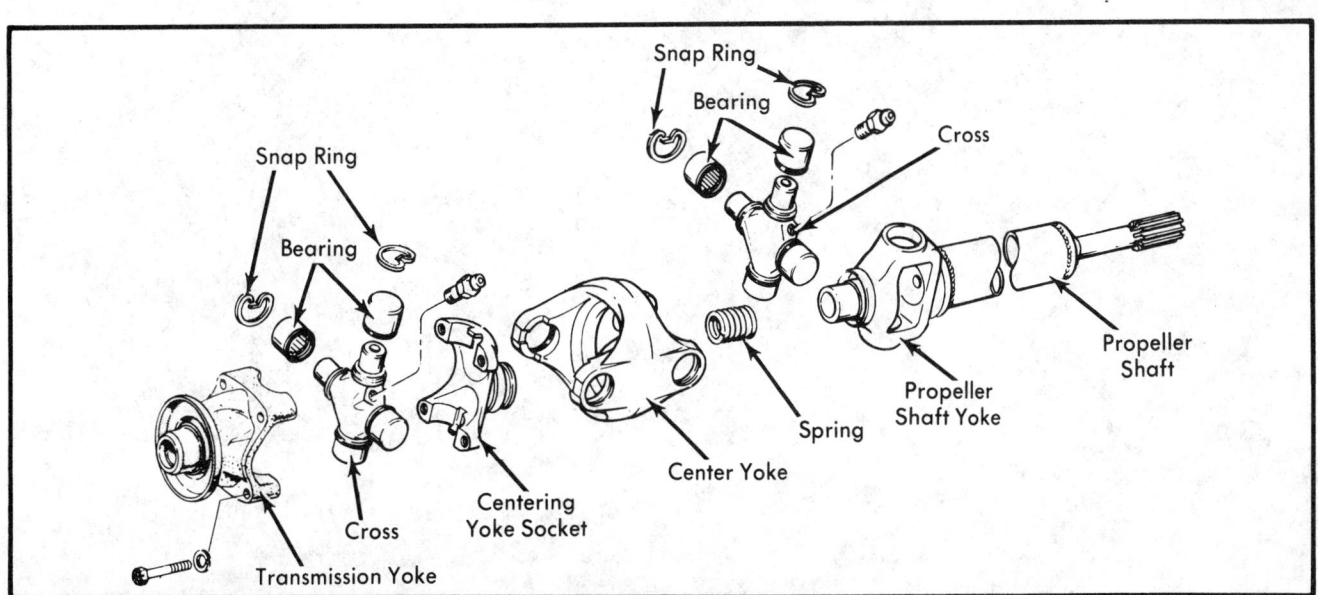

Fig. 3   Exploded View of Ford Constant Velocity Type Universal Joint

Section 10
BRAKES

Contents

NOTE — ALSO SEE GENERAL INDEX.

IMPORTANT

*Because of the great number of model names used by vehicle manufacturers, accurate identification of models is important.
See Model Identification at the front of this publication.*

CHRYSLER CORP.

Application	Type	Make & Design	Master Cylinder	Power Booster
150 Series (All)				
Front	Disc.	Chrysler — Sliding Caliper	Chrysler	Bendix — Single Diaphragm
Rear	Drum	Chrysler — Single Anchor	Dual Piston	
B & PB250				
Front	Disc.	Chrysler — Sliding Caliper	Chrysler	Bendix — Dual Diaphragm
Rear	Drum	Chrysler — Single Anchor	Dual Piston	
D250/450				
Front	Disc.	Chrysler — Sliding Caliper	Chrysler	Bendix — Dual Diaphragm②
Rear	Drum	Bendix — Single Anchor	Dual Piston	
W250①				
Front	Disc.	Chrysler — Sliding Caliper	Chrysler	Bendix — Dual Diaphragm②
Rear	Drum	Bendix — Single Anchor	Dual Piston	
W250/450②				
Front	Disc.	Bendix — Sliding Caliper	Bendix	Bendix — Dual Diaphragm②
Rear	Drum	Bendix — Single Anchor	Dual Piston	
B & PB350, CB & MB350/450				
Front	Disc.	Chrysler — Sliding Caliper	Chrysler	Bendix — Dual Diaphragm③
Rear	Drum	Bendix — Single Anchor	Dual Piston	

① — With Dana/Spicer model 44 front axle.
② — Bendix Hydro-Boost optional on some models.

③ — Bendix Hydro-Boost used on 163″ wheel base models. Single Diaphragm unit used with 3600 lb. front axle.

FORD

Application	Type	Make & Design	Master Cylinder	Power Booster
F100/250① **E100/250①** **Bronco**				
Front	Disc.	Bendix — Sliding Caliper	Ford	Bendix — Single Diaphragm
Rear	Drum	Bendix — Single Anchor	Dual Piston	
F250/350 **E250/350②**				
Front	Disc.	Dayton — Sliding Caliper	Ford	Bendix — Single Diaphragm③
Rear	Drum	Bendix — Single Anchor	Dual Piston	

① — Vehicles under 6900 lbs. GVW.
② — Vehicles above 6900 lbs. GVW.
③ — F350 and E350 models use a Dual Diaphragm.

GENERAL MOTORS

Application ①	Type	Make & Design	Master Cylinder	Power Booster
C10 (Diesel)			Delco — Dual Piston	Bendix-Hydroboost
Front	Disc.	Delco — Floating Caliper		
Rear	Drum	Delco — Single Anchor		
C10 (Gas), K & G10, G20			Delco — Dual Piston	Bendix or Delco Single Diaphragm③
Front	Disc.	Delco — Floating Caliper		Bendix or Delco Dual Diaphragm③
Rear	Drum	Delco — Single Anchor		
C & K20			Delco — Dual Piston	Bendix or Delco Dual Diaphragm
Front	Disc.	Delco — Floating Caliper		
Rear	Drum	Delco — Single Anchor		
C30			Delco — Dual Piston	Bendix or Delco Dual Diaphragm
Front	Disc.	Bendix — Floating Caliper②		Bendix Hydroboost③
Rear	Drum	Delco — Single Anchor		
K30			Delco — Dual Piston	Bendix-Hydroboost③
Front	Disc.	Bendix — Sliding Caliper		
Rear	Drum	Delco — Single Anchor		
P30 Motor Home Chassis			Delco — Dual Piston	Bendix-Hydroboost
Front	Disc.	Bendix — Sliding Caliper		
Rear	Drum⑤	Delco — Single Anchor		
P30 Forward Control			Delco — Dual Piston	Bendix or Delco Dual Piston
Front	Disc.	Bendix — Floating Caliper②		Bendix-Hydroboost③
Rear	Drum⑤	Delco — Single Anchor		
G30			Delco — Dual Piston	Bendix or Delco Dual Diaphragm
Front	Disc.	Delco — Floating Caliper②		
Rear	Drum	Delco — Single Anchor	Bendix-Mini④	Bendix-Hydroboost

① — The vehicle series numbers used in this chart have been abbreviated for common reference to both Chevrolet and GMC models.
② — Models equipped with Bendix Hydroboost are equipped with Bendix Sliding Caliper Disc Brakes
③ — Standard on some models, optional on others.
④ — Used on models with Hydroboost.
⑤ — Bendix sliding caliper discs used on models with 11,000 lb. rear axle.

JEEP

Application	Type	Make & Design	Master Cylinder	Power Booster
"CJ" Models & Scrambler			Delco Dual Piston	Delco — Single Diaphragm
Front	Disc.	Bendix — Floating Caliper		
Rear	Drum	Bendix — Single Anchor①		
Cherokee, Wagoneer & J10 Truck			Delco Dual Piston	Delco — Single Diaphragm
Front	Disc.	Delco — Floating Caliper		
Rear	Drum	Delco — Single Anchor②		
J20 Truck			Delco Dual Piston	Delco — Tandem Diaphragm
Front	Disc.	Delco — Floating Caliper		
Rear	Drum	Delco — Single Anchor②		

① — Cable type adjuster.
② — Lever type adjuster.

Trouble Shooting

BRAKE SYSTEM TROUBLE SHOOTING

NOTE — *This is a general trouble shooting guide. Not all steps will apply to all brake systems.*

CONDITION & POSSIBLE CAUSE

Pull When Brake Applied

- Incorrect tire pressure.
- Front end out of alignment.
- Unmatched tires.
- Restricted brake lines or hoses.
- Malfunctioning caliper.
- Bent shoe or oily linings.
- Loosen suspension parts.
- Loose calipers.

Brake Rough, Chatters or Pulsates

- Excessive lateral runnout.
- Parallelism not to specification.
- Wheel bearings not adjusted.
- Drums out-of-round.
- Disc pad reversed.
- Caliper not sliding.

Excessive Pedal Effort

- Malfunctioning power unit.
- Linings or pads contaminated.
- Linings or pads glazed.
- Worn pads or linings.
- Siezed pistons.
- Worn or scored rotors or drums.
- Incorrect pads or linings.
- Partial system failure.

Low Pedal Effect

- Air in hydraulic sytem.
- Fluid leaks in master clinder.
- Bleed screw loose.

Excessive Pedal Travel

- Partial brake system failure.
- Insufficent or incorrect fluid.
- Rear brakes not adjusted.
- Air in system.
- Bent shoe and lining.
- Excessively worn pads or linings.
- Plugged master cylinder cap.
- Excessive rotor runnout.

Brakes Grab or Uneven Application

- All conditions under "Brake Pulls".
- Malfunction of combination valve.
- Binding brake pedal.
- Linings contaminated.
- Siezed piston(s).
- Incorrect tire pressure.
- Brake line plugged.
- Caliper alignment incorrect.
- Unmatched pads or linings.

CONDITION & POSSIBLE CAUSE

Brake Dragging or Slow Return

- Master cylinder pistons not returning correctly.
- Restricted brake lines or hoses.
- Incorrect parking brake adjustment.
- Parking brake cable frozen.
- Incorrect or misaligned pedal push rod.
- Power booster output rod too long.
- Incorrect installation of pads.

Pedal Travel Decreasing

- Compensating port plugged.
- Swollen master cylinder cup.
- Master cylinder piston not returning.
- Weak shoe retracting springs.
- Wheel cylinder pistons sticking.

Spongy Pedal

- Air in system.
- Swollen brake hoses.
- Incorrect brake fluid.
- Filler cap vent hole plugged.

Pedal Yields Under Slight Pressure

- Deteriorated check valve.
- External fluid leaks.
- Internal leak in master cylinder.

Squeal or Squeak Without Brake Application

- Front linings worn out.
- Dust or oil on drums or rotors.

Shock When Pedal Applied

- Brake drum cracked or distorted.
- Uneven brake drum wear.
- Broken return spring.

Rattling in Front Brakes

- Pad anti-rattle spring clip broken or missing.
- Excessive clearance between pads and caliper.

Brake React Slowly

- Check valve malfunction.
- Vacuum hose blocked or broken.
- Air cleaner restricted.

Leaks in Caliper Piston Cylinder

- Damaged or worn caliper piston seal.
- Deep Scores or corrosion in cylinder bore.

HYDRO-BOOST TROUBLE SHOOTING

NOTE — *This is a general trouble shooting guide. Not all steps will apply to all systems.*

CONDITION & POSSIBLE CAUSE	CONDITION & POSSIBLE CAUSE
No Boost — Hard Pedal • Loose or broken power steering pump belt. • No fluid in power steering reservoir. • Leaks in power steering, booster or accumulator hoses. • Leaks at tube fittings, power steering booster or accumulator connections. • External leakage at accumulator. • Faulty booster piston seal; leakage at flange vent. • Faulty booster input rod seal; leakage at input rod end. • Faulty booster cover seal; leakage between housing and cover. • Faulty booster spool plug seal. • Internal leakage in booster. • Contamination in power steering fluid. • Incorrect routing of hydraulic lines. **Power Steering Pump Noisy on Brake Application** • Insufficient fluid in reservoir. **Brake Pedal Pulls Down on Engine Start** • Restriction in gear or booster return lines.	**Accumulator Leakdown — System Does Not Hold Charge** • External leakage at accumulator. • Internal leakage at accumulator. • Internal leakage at booster accumulator valve. **Brake Grab on Application** • Broken spool return spring. • Faulty spool action due to contamination. **Booster Chatter — Pedal Vibrates** • Power steering pump belt slipping. • Low fluid level in pump reservoir. • Air in system. **Slow Brake Pedal Return** • Excessive seal friction in booster. • Faulty spool action. • Broken piston return spring. • Restriction in return line from booster to pump reservoir. • Broken spool return spring. • Excessive pedal pivot friction.

Brake Servicing

HYDRAULIC BRAKE BLEEDING

DESCRIPTION

Hydraulic system bleeding is necessary any time air has been introduced into system. Bleed brakes at all four wheels if master cylinder lines have been disconnected or master cylinder has been run dry. Bleeding may be done either by using pressure bleeding equipment or by manually pumping brake pedal while using bleeder tubes.

NOTE — *Hydro-boost bleeding is a different procedure than hydraulic brake bleeding. See Hydro-boost bleeding in Hydro-boost article in this Section.*

HYDRAULIC CONTROL VALVES

On disc brake equipped vehicles, metering section of hydraulic control valve must be deactivated before bleeding to permit fluid to flow to front brakes. This is especially important when pressure bleeding. Use suitable tool when applicable (C-4121, Chrysler Corp.; J-23709, General Motors and Jeep with "D" type valve; J-26869, for Jeep with "W" type combination valve). If tool is not available, hold valve open by hand.

CAUTION — *Do not use "C" clamp or other non-yielding device to hold valve in open position.*

PRESSURE TANK BLEEDING

Clean master cylinder cap and surrounding area, then remove cap. With pressure tank at least 1/3 full, connect to master cylinder using suitable adapters. Attach bleeder hose to first bleeder valve to be serviced. *See Bleeding Sequence.* Place other end of hose in clean glass jar partially filled with clean brake fluid so end of hose is submerged in fluid. Open release valve on pressure bleeder. Follow equipment manufacturers pressure instructions unless noted below. Unscrew bleeder valve ¾-1 turn noting fluid flow. When fluid flowing from cylinder to jar is free of bubbles, close bleeder valve securely. Bleed remaining cylinders in correct sequence and in the same manner. Remove tool from control valve.

Pressure Bleeder Settings	
Application	**Psi**
Chrysler Corp.	35
Ford	10-30
General Motors	20-25
Jeep	.....

MANUAL BLEEDING

CAUTION — *During bleeding on disc brakes, air may tend to cling to caliper walls; therefore, lightly tapping caliper will assist in removal of this air.*

Fill master cylinder, then install bleeder hose to first bleeder valve to be serviced. *See Bleeding Sequence.* Place other end of hose in clean glass jar partially filled with clean brake fluid so end of hose is submerged in fluid. Open bleeder valve ¾-1 turn. Depress brake pedal slowly through its full travel. Close bleeder valve, then release pedal. Repeat procedure until flow of fluid shows no signs of air bubbles.

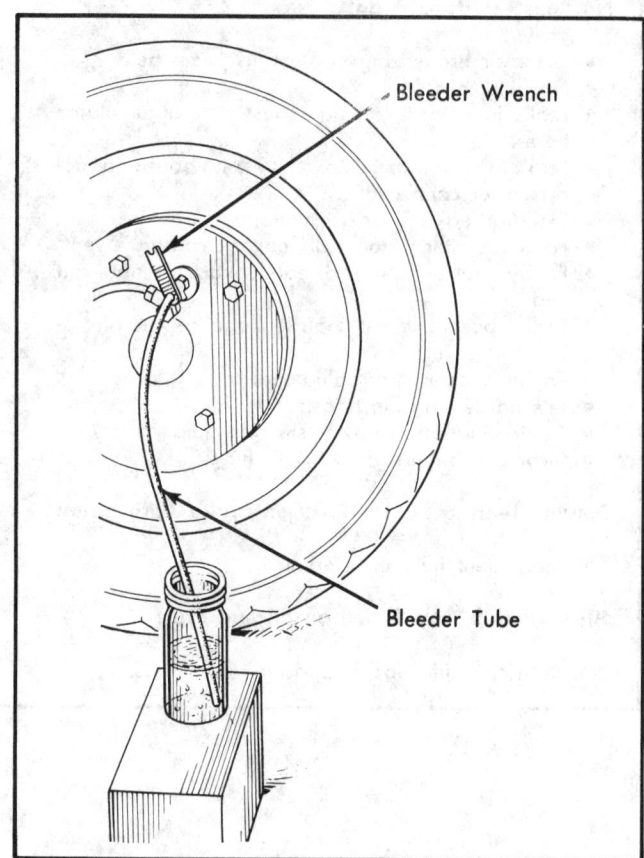

Fig. 1   Wheel Cylinder Bleeding Procedure

BLEEDING SEQUENCE

Before bleeding system, exhaust all vacuum from power unit by depressing brake pedal several times. Bleed master cylinder if equipped with bleeder screws, then bleed slave cylinder on vehicles equipped with remote mount power assist units. Bleed wheel cylinders and calipers in following sequence:

Bleeding Sequence	
Application	**Sequence**
Chrysler Corp.	RR, LR, RF, LF
Ford	RR, LR, RF, LF
General Motors	RR, LR, RF, LF
Jeep	RR, LR, RF, LF, Master Cyl. Lines

HYDRAULIC SYSTEM CONTROL VALVES

DESCRIPTION

All vehicles have some type of hydraulic system control valve or warning switch within the brake hydraulic system. Unit is usually mounted on frame or firewall adjacent to master cylinder. The front and rear brake lines are routed through this valve to their respective caliper or wheel cylinder. Vehicles with drum brakes only use a pressure differential brake warning switch only. Vehicles equipped with disc brakes use a combination pressure differential warning switch with a proportioning valve, or a metering valve, or both.

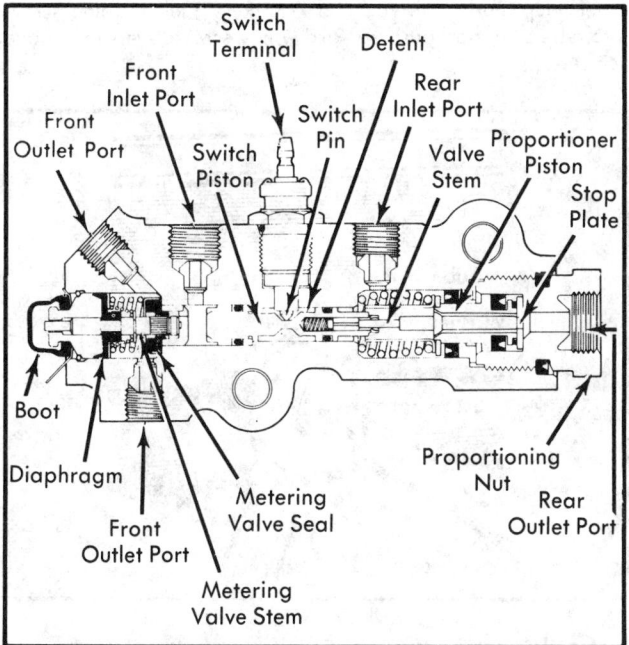

Fig. 1 Sectional View of Typical Hydraulic Control Valve

OPERATION

PRESSURE DIFFERENTIAL BRAKE WARNING SWITCH

This switch is used to warn vehicle operator that one of the hydraulic systems has failed. When hydraulic pressure is equal in both front and rear systems, switch piston remains centered and does not contact terminal in switch. If pressure fails in system, hydraulic pressure moves piston toward failed side. Shoulder of piston then contacts switch terminal to provide ground for brake warning light.

PROPORTIONING VALVE

Valve operates by restricting, at a given ratio, hydraulic pressure to rear brakes when system hydraulic pressure reaches a certain point. This improves front-to-rear brake balance at high speed braking, when a percentage of rear

weight is transferred to front wheels. Valve reduces rear brake pressure, and delays rear wheel skid. On light brake application, valve allows full hydraulic pressure to rear brakes.

METERING VALVE

This valve holds off pressure to front disc brakes to allow rear drum brake shoes to overcome return spring pressure and make contact with rear drums. This prevents locking front brakes on slippery or icy surfaces under light braking conditions. Valve has no effect on front brake pressure during hard braking conditions.

TESTING

BRAKE WARNING LIGHT SYSTEM

Electrical Circuit – Disconnect wire from switch terminal and ground wire to chassis. Turn ignition switch "ON". Warning light should come on. If lamp does not light, bulb or wiring circuit is defective. Replace bulb or wiring as necessary. If lamp lights, turn off ignition and reconnect wire.

Warning Light Switch – Attach a bleeder hose to bleeder screw at either rear brake. Immerse other end of hose in container with brake fluid. Turn ignition "ON". Open bleeder screw while pressure is being applied to brake pedal. Warning lamp should light. Close bleeder screw before pressure is released from pedal. Reapply pedal pressure (moderate to heavy). Light should go out. Repeat test on front brake system. System should function in same manner. Turn ignition "OFF". If lamp does not light during test on either system, but electrical system checked good, the warning light switch portion of valve is defective.

SERVICING

All hydraulic system switches and valves are non-adjustable and non-serviceable. If any part of valve is found to be defective, entire unit must be replaced.

RESETTING SWITCH

All Models – After failed side of system has been repaired, applying brake pedal with moderate force will hydraulically recenter piston and turn off brake warning light.

REMOVAL & INSTALLATION

ALL MODELS

Removal – Disconnect brake warning light connection at switch. Disconnect all brake hydraulic lines at valve. Cover open ends of line to prevent dirt from entering system. Remove valve mounting bolts. Remove valve from vehicle.

Installation – To install control valve, reverse removal procedure. Bleed brake system. See *Hydraulic Brake Bleeding in this Section.* Recenter brake warning light piston as previously outlined.

Master Cylinders

BENDIX/DELCO-MORAINE DUAL PISTON MASTER CYLINDER

Chevrolet
Dodge
GMC
Jeep
Plymouth

NOTE — *Some models may use other units; see Brake Systems Index.*

DESCRIPTION

Bendix and Delco-Moraine tandem dual piston master cylinders are single casting type with front and rear pistons and a separate reservoir and outlet for each piston. Rear piston is operated by push rod connected to brake pedal. Front piston is operated by rear piston. In a combination disc and drum system, reservoir which feeds disc brakes is larger to compensate for larger displacement of disc caliper cylinder.

Master cylinders for General Motors and some Jeep vehicles incorporate a quick take-up feature, that delivers a large volume of fluid at low pressure upon initial application of brakes. This fluid quickly displaces the retracted caliper, placing brake linings in contact with brake rotors and drums.

ADJUSTMENT

BRAKE PEDAL

NOTE — *Adjustment for vehicles equipped with power boosters is accomplished at power booster. See Power Brake Units in this Section.*

All Models — Vehicles without power assisted brakes incorporate a non-adjustable push rod. Brake pedal push rod length is preset by manufacturer.

REMOVAL & INSTALLATION

MASTER CYLINDER

Removal — Disconnect front and rear hydraulic brake lines at master cylinder, and cover ends to prevent entry of foreign matter. On vehicles without power assist units, disconnect brake pedal push rod at brake pedal. Remove master cylinder attaching bolts, and remove cylinder assembly from vehicle.

Installation — Position master cylinder on vehicle and install cylinder attaching bolts. Connect front and rear hydraulic brake lines to cylinder. Connect brake pedal push rod, if removed. Fill reservoir with clean brake fluid, and bleed hydraulic system. *See Hydraulic Brake Bleeding in this Section.*

OVERHAUL

MASTER CYLINDER

Disassembly — 1) Clean outside of cylinder thoroughly and remove cover. Drain fluid, and turning cylinder over, pump piston to remove any remaining fluid. On Jeep Cherokee, Wagoneer and truck models, remove reservoir with a pry bar. Remove reservoir grommets, retaining ring and quick-take-up valve.

2) On manual brake models, remove boot from cylinder to uncover push rod retainer. Pry up retainer tab to release retainer.

On all models, push piston down into cylinder bore. Remove secondary piston stop bolt from front fluid reservoir (if equipped). Remove snap ring from groove in cylinder bore.

3) Remove both piston assemblies. Remove any internal parts remaining in bore. On Jeep "CJ" and Scrambler models, remove push rod from primary piston. Remove and discard all rubber parts from piston assemblies. On General Motors and Jeep "CJ" and Scrambler models, enlarge holes in tube seats using a $^{13}/_{16}$" drill.

4) Place a large flat washer over outlets and thread a $\frac{1}{4}$" x 20 x $\frac{3}{4}$" screw into seat. Remove seat, screw and washer. On all other Jeep models, thread a 6 x 32 x $\frac{5}{8}$" self tapping screw into tube seat, and push upward with 2 screwdrivers to remove seat.

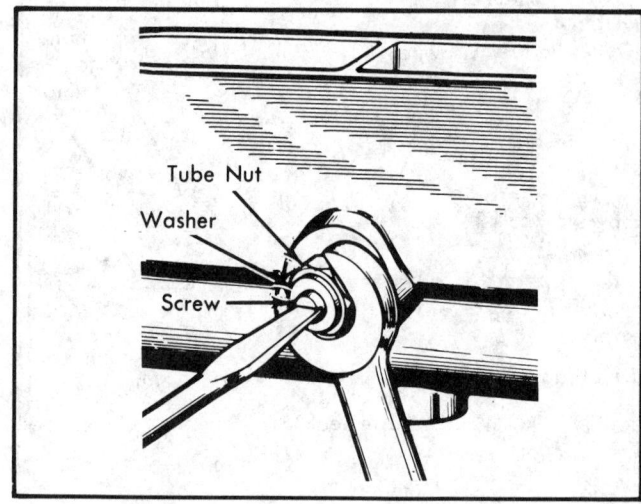

Fig. 1   Removing Tube Seat from Master Cylinder

Inspection — Inspect cylinder bore for scoring or corrosion. Staining which has not pitted or roughened surface of cylinder can be removed with crocus cloth. If cylinder bore is scored, pitted or corroded, it should be replaced.

Reassembly — 1) Install replacement tube seats by threading a spare brake line tube nut into hole and turning nut in until tube seat bottoms. Do not cock tube seat in hole. Remove nut and check for burrs which may have been loosened by nut.

2) Install piston cups on secondary piston, with cup lips facing away from each other. Install seal protector, piston seal, spring retainer and return spring on secondary piston. Install seal so lip faces interior of master cylinder when installed.

3) Lubricate cylinder bore with clean brake fluid and install secondary piston assembly. Lubricate primary piston seals and install primary piston assembly in bore. Hold primary piston down in bore and install snap ring in groove in bore.

4) Install secondary piston stop bolt (if equipped). Install master cylinder reservoir, grommets and quick-take-up valve (if removed). Install master cylinder cover and new diaphragm. On vehicles with manual brakes, assemble brake pedal push rod through retainer (if used), and push retainer over end of master cylinder. Install rubber boot over push rod.

Master Cylinders

BENDIX/DELCO-MORAINE DUAL PISTON MASTER CYLINDER(Cont.)

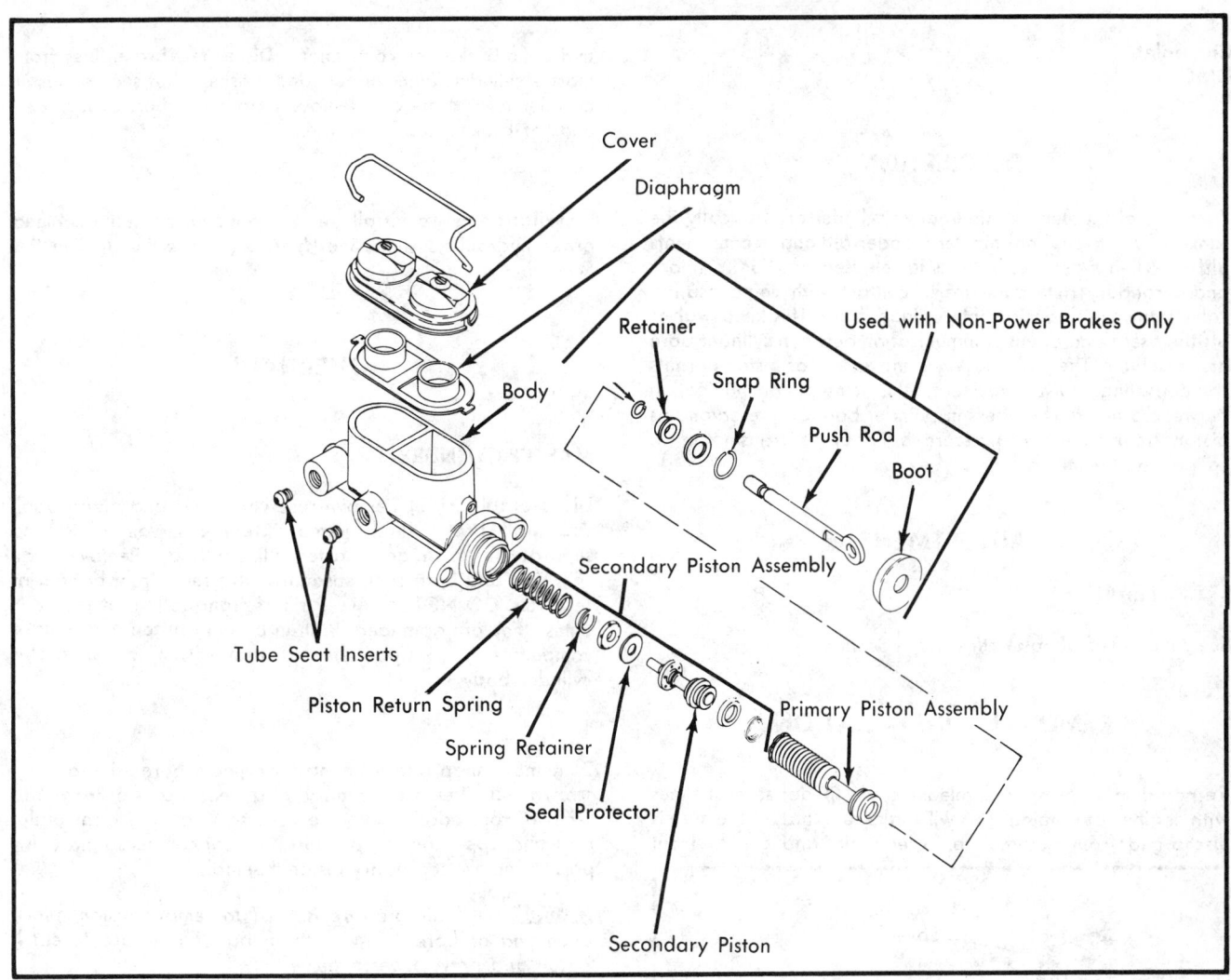

**Fig. 2 Exploded View of Typical Delco-Moraine Master Cylinder
(Bendix Similar)**

Master Cylinders

BENDIX MINI-MASTER CYLINDER

Chevrolet
GMC

DESCRIPTION

Functions of the Bendix Mini-Master cylinder are basically the same as a conventional master cylinder although components differ. When master cylinder is in released position, primary and secondary actuators are in contact with compensating valve stems which project into cylinder bore. This keeps valves off their seat and opens communication between cylinder bore and reservoir. The initial forward movement of piston permits compensating valves to seat, this closes communication between pressure chambers in cylinder bore and reservoir. As piston travels further, pressure build up is transmitted to calipers and wheel cylinders.

ADJUSTMENT

BRAKE PEDAL

See Bendix Hydroboost article in this Section.

REMOVAL & INSTALLATION

Removal — Depress and release brake pedal several times with engine not running. This will make sure that all pressure is discharged from accumulator. Clean dirt and grease from

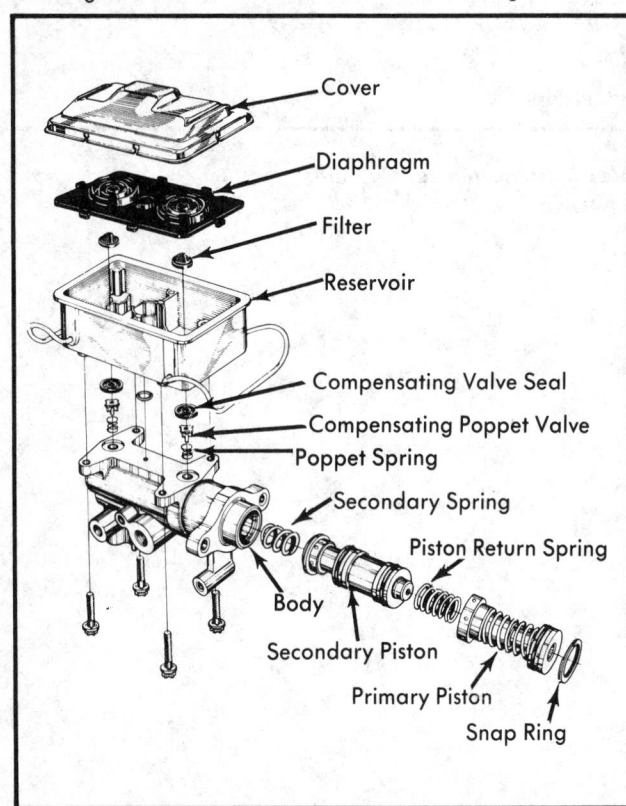

Fig. 1   Exploded View of
Bendix Mini-Master Cylinder

Cover
Diaphragm
Filter
Reservoir
Compensating Valve Seal
Compensating Poppet Valve
Poppet Spring
Secondary Spring
Piston Return Spring
Body
Secondary Piston
Primary Piston
Snap Ring

hydraulic brake line connections. Disconnect brake lines from master cylinder. Remove nuts and washers that secure master cylinder to Hydroboost. Remove master cylinder. Cover open ends of brake lines.

Installation — To install, reverse removal procedure. Bleed brake hydraulic system. *See Hydraulic Brake Bleeding in this Section.*

OVERHAUL

MASTER CYLINDER

Disassembly — 1) Remove reservoir cover and diaphragm. Drain all brake fluid. Remove four reservoir bolts and separate reservoir and master cylinder body. Remove small "O" ring and both compensating valve seals from bottom of reservoir. DO NOT remove 2 filters from bottom of reservoir unless they are damaged. Push in primary piston and remove compensating valve poppets and springs from ports in master cylinder body.

2) Remove snap ring from master cylinder bore using a small screwdriver. Release primary and secondary pistons and remove from bore. It may be necessary to plug front outlet port and apply low air pressure to front compensating valve port to remove secondary piston assembly.

CAUTION — *If air pressure is used to remove piston, place open end of bore 1" away from padded surface to catch piston and prevent personal injury.*

Cleaning & Inspection — Clean all reusable components in clean brake fluid. Make sure filters in bottom of reservoir are clean. If filters do not clean thoroughly, they must be replaced. After cleaning, inspect all components for wear or damage and replace as necessary.

Reassembly — 1) Lubricate primary and secondary pistons, and cylinder bore with clean brake fluid. Position secondary spring (short spring) in open end of secondary piston actuator. Position return spring (long spring) on projection at rear of secondary piston. Place secondary piston, actuator end first in master cylinder bore and press assembly into bottom of bore. Insert primary piston, actuator end first into bore.

2) Using a smooth round end tool with snap ring placed over it, depress piston in bore. Install snap ring in groove. Place compensating valve seals and small "O" ring seal in recesses in bottom of reservoir. Make sure seals are fully seated. Depress pistons and place compensating valve springs and poppets in valve ports. With piston still depressed, place reservoir in position. Install bolts and tighten to 12 to 15 ft. lbs.

CHRYSLER CORP. DUAL PISTON MASTER CYLINDERS – CAST IRON

Dodge
Plymouth

NOTE — *Some models use other units. See Bendix/Delco-Moraine Dual Piston Master Cylinder and Chrysler Corp. Dual Piston Master Cylinder (Aluminum) articles in this section.*

DESCRIPTION

This tandem dual piston master cylinder is the venting type with reservoirs in a single casting and one outlet for each reservoir. Rear piston is operated by push rod connected to brake pedal. Front piston is operated by rear piston.

REMOVAL & INSTALLATION

MASTER CYLINDER

Removal — Disconnect front and rear hydraulic brake lines at master cylinder. Remove bolt attaching push rod to pedal linkage. Remove master cylinder attaching bolts and lift master cylinder from vehicle.

Installation — Position master cylinder on vehicle and install cylinder attaching bolts. Tighten to 200 INCH lbs. Connect front and rear hydraulic brake lines, and connect push rod to brake pedal linkage. Fill reservoir with clean brake fluid and bleed entire brake system. *See Hydraulic Brake Bleeding in this Section.*

OVERHAUL

MASTER CYLINDER

Disassembly — **1)** Clean outside of cylinder and remove cover to drain brake fluid. Use screw extractor to remove tube seats. Remove snap ring from open end of cylinder and slide washer out.

2) Carefully remove primary piston assembly, then slide secondary piston from cylinder. Clean all parts in suitable solvent and blow dry with compressed air.

Inspection — Inspect cylinder bore for scoring or pitting. Light scratches or minor corrosion can usually be removed by using crocus cloth. Deep scratches or scoring may be honed, provided bore diameter is not increased more than .002". If this limit is exceeded, master cylinder must be replaced. Check pistons for scoring, scratches and corrosion. Pistons must be replaced if any of these conditions exist. Replace all rubber parts when overhauling master cylinder.

Reassembly — **1)** Dip all components in brake fluid before reassembly. Carefully slide secondary piston assembly into cylinder bore. Slide primary piston into bore, hold washer in position and install snap ring. Install tube seats.

2) Clamp master cylinder in a vise, being careful not to damage housing, and bleed cylinder as follows: Attach suitable bleeding tubes (C-4029) to outlet ports of cylinder, with ends of tubes in master cylinder reservoirs. Fill reservoirs with clean brake fluid and depress push rod slowly. Allow pistons to return to normal position under spring pressure. Repeat procedure until all air bubbles are expelled. Remove bleeding tubes, and install cylinder cover and diaphragm. Remove cylinder from vise.

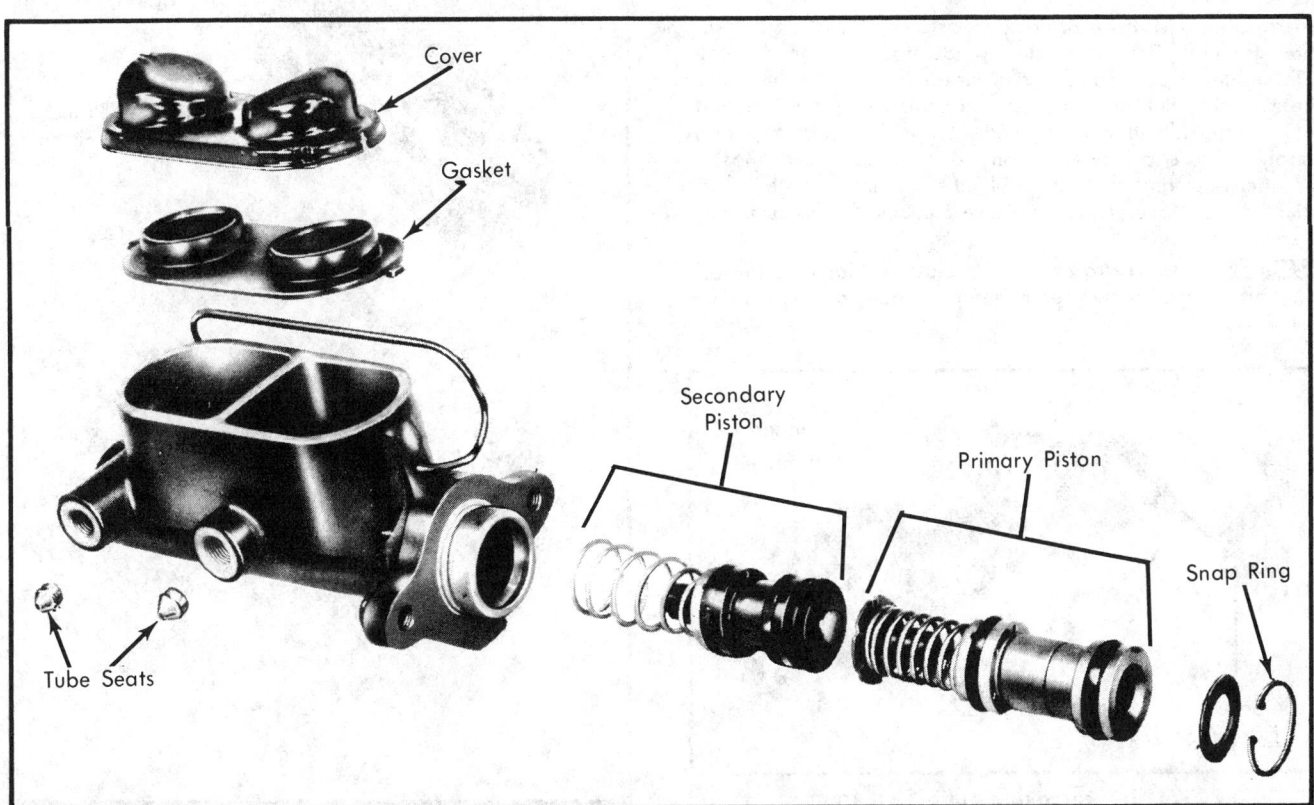

Fig. 1   Exploded View of Cast Iron Master Cylinder

Master Cylinders

CHRYSLER CORP. DUAL PISTON MASTER CYLINDERS – ALUMINUM

Dodge
Plymouth

DESCRIPTION

The new Chrysler tandem dual piston master cylinder is the venting type with nylon reservoir. The front and rear pistons have separate reservoirs and outlets, but may be filled from one cap because reservoirs are connected at the top. Air entrapment is controlled by cup expanders in rear brake wheel cylinders. No residual pressure valves are installed on this master cylinder.

REMOVAL & INSTALLATION

MASTER CYLINDER

Removal (Power Brakes) – Disconnect primary and secondary brake lines from master cylinder and plug outlets. Remove nuts that attach cylinder to power brake unit. Slide master cylinder straight out and away from brake unit.

Installation (Power Brakes) – Position master cylinder over studs of power brake unit, aligning power cylinder brake push rod with cylinder piston. Install and tighten nuts. Connect both brake lines and bleed system. See Hydraulic Brake Bleeding in this Section.

Removal (Manual Brakes) – Disconnect primary and secondary brake lines from master cylinder and plug outlets. Disconnect stop light switch mounting bracket under instrument panel. Grasp brake pedal and pull back to disengage push rod from master cylinder. This will destroy push rod retention grommet. Remove nuts attaching master cylinder to cowl panel. Slide master cylinder straight out and away from cowl.

Installation (Manual Brakes) – Install new push rod retention grommet. Position master cylinder to cowl panel, install and tighten nuts. Connect brake lines and tighten. From under instrument panel, moisten push rod grommet with water and align push rod with master cylinder piston. Using brake pedal, apply pressure to fully seat push rod into piston. Install master cylinder boot and connect stop light switch mounting bracket. Bleed system. See Hydraulic Brake Bleeding in this section.

CAUTION – Use extra care not to cross threads when installing brake lines to master cylinder. Torque to specifications only.

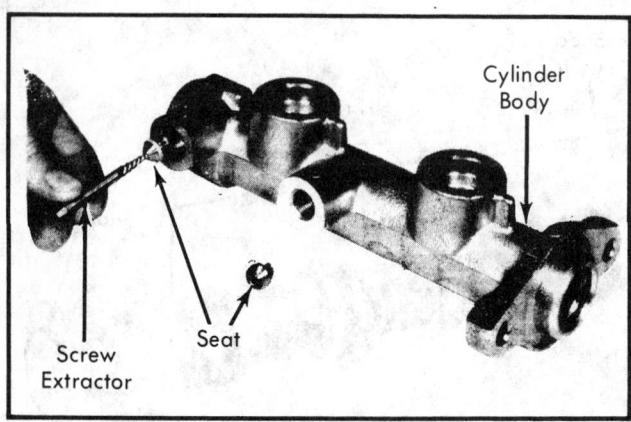

Fig. 1 Removing Tube Seat from Master Cylinder

OVERHAUL

MASTER CYLINDER

Disassembly – 1) Clean outside of reservoir and cylinder body. Remove reservoir caps and empty brake fluid. Position cylinder body in vise and rock reservoir from side to side to remove from cylinder. Remove grommets and use needle nose pliers to remove secondary piston retainer pin from inside master cylinder body. Remove snap ring and slide primary piston out of bore.

2) Tap open end of cylinder on bench to remove secondary piston. If piston sticks, use air pressure to force piston from cylinder. New cups must be installed if air pressure is used.

NOTE – If primary cup on primary piston is damaged or worn, a new primary piston must be installed.

3) If brass tube seats are damaged or worn, use screw extractor to remove seats.

Inspection – 1) Wash master cylinder bore with brake fluid. Inspect bore for pitting, scratches or scoring.

NOTE – Do not hone aluminum master cylinder. If bore is found unservicable, cylinder must be replaced.

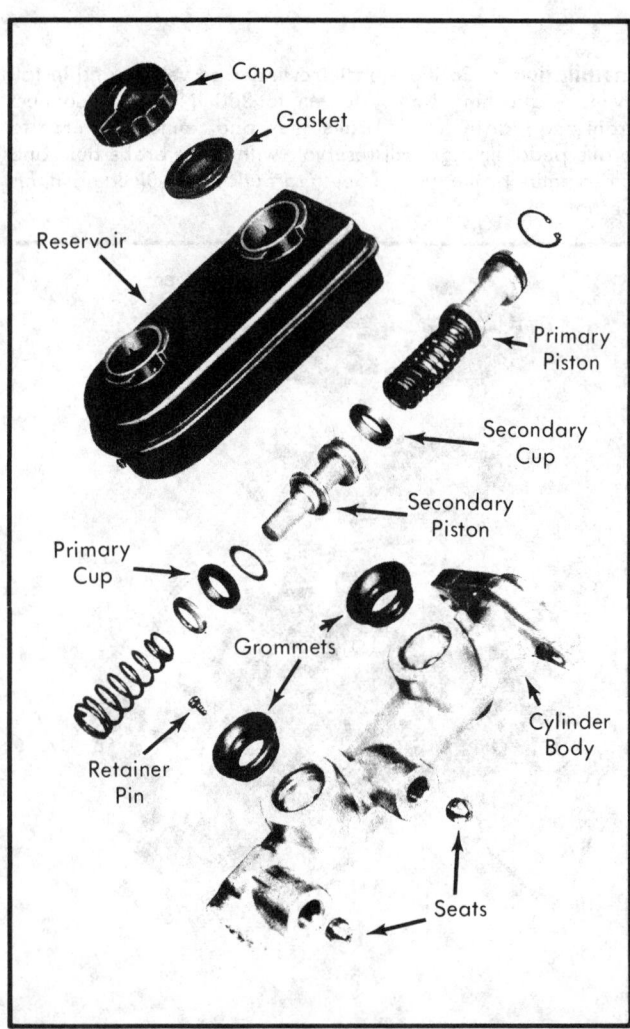

Fig. 2 Exploded View of Aluminum Master Cylinder

CHRYSLER CORP. DUAL PISTON MASTER CYLINDERS — ALUMINUM (Cont.)

2) Inspect piston for corrosion and scoring and replace as necessary. During overhaul, all rubber parts must be replaced.

NOTE — *Internal parts of aluminum master cylinder are not interchangeable with cast iron master cylinder components.*

Reassembly — 1) Dip master cylinder and all components in clean brake fluid. Assembling seals dry could ruin seals.

2) Install check flow washer on secondary piston and carefully work primary cup on end with lip facing away from piston. Slide cup retainer over front end of piston followed by spring.

3) Carefully work secondary piston secondary cup into cylinder bore, with lip away from piston. Install secondary piston into bore. Be careful that lip of cups enters bore evenly in order not to damage sealing of cups.

4) Carefully work secondary cup over rear end of primary piston with larger lip of cup toward piston. Center spring retainer of primary piston on secondary piston. Push piston assemblies into bore up to primary piston cup.

5) Carefully work cup into bore, then push piston into secondary seal. Work lip of primary cup into bore, then push in on piston until seated. Depress piston with brass or wood rod and install snap ring.

TIGHTENING SPECIFICATIONS

Application	Ft. Lbs.
Master Cylinder Attaching Nuts	17
Pedal Link Bolt	30

Application	INCH lbs.
Brake Line Tube Nuts	150

6) Position secondary piston retainer pin in cylinder housing and tap or press in until firmly seated. Install tube seats. Install housing-to-reservoir grommets and using rocking motion, install reservoir on master cylinder body.

NOTE — *Reservoir is keyed to prevent installation in wrong direction.*

7) Bleed cylinder as follows: Clamp master cylinder in vise and attach suitable bleeding tubes (C-4029). Attach residual valves on outlet of each bleeder tube. Fill reservoir with fluid. Using brass or wood rod, depress push rod slowly and allow pistons to return under spring pressure. Repeat until all air is expelled. Remove tubes, plug outlets and install caps.

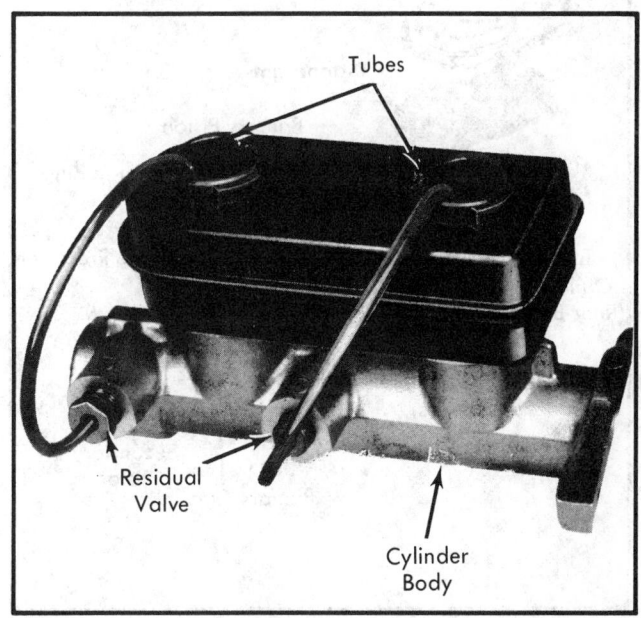

Tubes

Residual Valve

Cylinder Body

Fig. 3   Master Cylinder Bleeding Procedure

FORD DUAL PISTON MASTER CYLINDER

All Models

DESCRIPTION

Ford tandem dual piston master cylinder is a single casting with front and rear piston and a separate reservoir and outlet for each piston. Rear piston is operated by a push rod connected to brake pedal. Front, or floating, piston is operated by rear piston. In a combination drum and disc system, reservoir which feeds disc brakes is larger, to correspond with large size of disc brake caliper cylinders. Master cylinder outlet which feeds drum brake has a residual valve under tube seat. Disc brake outlet has no valve, since disc brakes must not have any residual pressure.

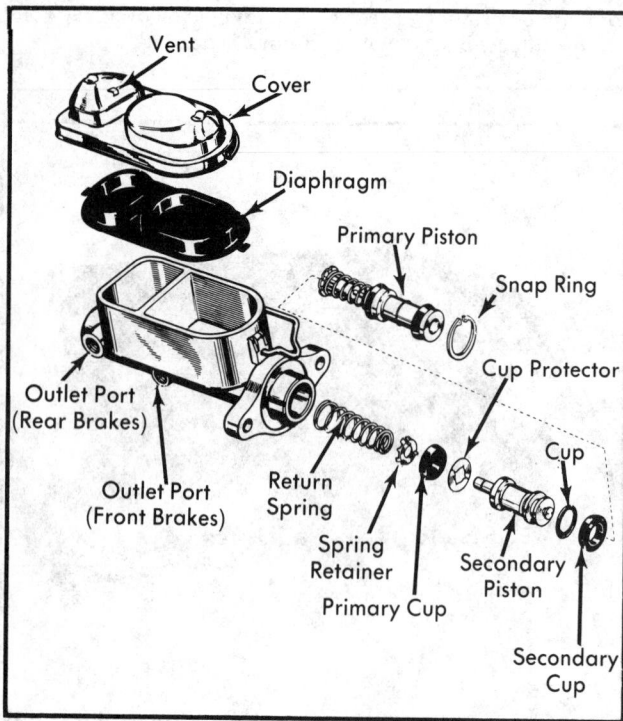

Fig. 1 Exploded View of Master Cylinder Assembly

ADJUSTMENT

BRAKE PEDAL

On dual piston master cylinder or brake mounted vacuum booster equipped vehicles, brake systems are designed to permit full stroke of master cylinder, therefore no brake pedal clearance adjustment is required.

NOTE — *Pedal free-travel will not be correct if power brake booster push rod clearance is not correct. See appropriate Power Brake Unit article in this Section.*

REMOVAL & INSTALLATION

MASTER CYLINDER

Removal (All Power Brake Models) — Depress brake pedal to expel vacuum from brake booster. Disconnect all hydraulic lines at master cylinder. Remove nuts retaining master cylinder to brake booster and remove master cylinder.

Removal (Manual Brake Models) — Disconnect wires from stoplight switch. Remove retaining nut, shoulder bolt, spacers and bushing securing master cylinder push rod to brake pedal. Remove stoplight switch from brake pedal. Disconnect fluid lines. Remove master cylinder to dash panel screws and remove master cylinder. Remove master cylinder push rod boot.

Installation (All Models) — To install, reverse removal procedure, centralize pressure differential valve and bleed system. *See Hydraulic Brake Bleeding in this Section.*

NOTE — *On vehicles equipped with power booster, adjust push rod length prior to installation of master cylinder. (See appropriate article in this section).*

OVERHAUL

MASTER CYLINDER

Disassembly — 1) With master cylinder removed from vehicle, clean outside of cylinder, remove filler cap and diaphragm, and drain any remaining fluid in cylinder. Remove dust boot (if equipped), then remove snap ring retaining piston assemblies.

2) Remove push rod (if equipped), and primary piston assembly from cylinder bore. Apply air pressure to forward outlet port of cylinder and carefully blow secondary piston assembly out of bore. DO NOT place fingers in front of piston. Remove return spring, spring retainer, cup protector and cups from secondary piston.

Inspection — Clean all parts with denatured alcohol, and blow dry with compressed air. Inspect all parts for chipping, excessive wear, or damage. Check all recesses, openings, and internal passages to be sure they are clean and open. Inspect master cylinder bore for signs of corrosion, pitting, etching, or scoring. If any of these conditions exist, manufacturer recommends replacement of master cylinder assembly.

Reassembly — 1) Lubricate all components including cylinder bore with clean brake fluid prior to assembly. Install 2 secondary cups, back-to-back, on secondary piston. Assemble cup protector, primary cup, spring retainer and secondary piston return spring on opposite end of piston. Insert secondary piston assembly into bore in cylinder.

2) On vehicles equipped with standard brakes, position boot, snap ring and push rod retainer on push rod, and seat assembly in primary piston. Install primary piston assembly into cylinder bore. On vehicles equipped with power brakes, position stop plate and snap ring on primary piston, and install primary piston and snap ring to cylinder bore.

3) Before installing master cylinder to vehicle, bleed the unit as follows: Support assembly in a vise and fill both reservoirs with fluid. Install plugs in brake outlet ports. Loosen plug in rear outlet port and depress primary piston slowly to force air out of cylinder. Tighten plug while piston is depressed to prevent air from entering cylinder.

4) Repeat procedure until no air is evident. Procede to the front outlet port when rear is bled, ensuring that rear plug is tight. Piston travel will be greatly restricted when all air is expelled. Remove plugs, install cover and diaphragm.

Power Brake Units

BENDIX SINGLE DIAPHRAGM

Chevrolet
Ford
GMC

DESCRIPTION

Vacuum suspended, self-contained, vacuum-hydraulic unit which utilizes engine manifold vacuum and atmospheric pressure to provide its power. Vacuum power unit contains power piston assembly, which houses control valve, reaction mechanism, and return spring. Control valve consists of air valve, floating control valve assembly, and push rod. Reaction mechanism consists of reaction plate and levers. A vacuum check valve is mounted in front housing for connection to vacuum source.

REMOVAL & INSTALLATION

NOTE — *Power brake unit can be removed without removing master cylinder or disconnecting hydraulic lines.*

Removal — Disconnect vacuum line from check valve or power unit. Remove nuts securing master cylinder to power unit. Pull master cylinder forward away from unit. Disconnect brake pedal from push rod. Remove power unit-to-firewall bolts and remove unit.

Installation — To install power unit, reverse removal procedure.

OVERHAUL

NOTE — *Only Chevrolet and GMC recommend overhaul of power brake unit.*

Disassembly — 1) Scribe mark on housings for reassembly. Remove front housing seal and piston rod. Attach assembly to suitable holding fixture (J-22805). Align tool so that check valve in front housing is not damaged. Loosen lock nut and remove push rod clevis and locknut (if equipped). Remove dust boot retainer, dust boot and silencer from diaphragm plate extension.

2) Partially straighten four deepest tabs on rear housing. Place suitable wrench (J-9504) over studs on rear housing and attach with nuts and washers. Press down on wrench and rotate rear housing clockwise to separate. Remove wrench.

CAUTION — *Housings are under spring pressure.*

3) Remove air filter from diaphragm plate extension. Remove diaphragm from groove in diaphragm plate. Handle diaphragm carefully. Hold diaphragm plate so that push rod is in horizontal position. Depress rod slightly and rotate piston until air valve lock falls from diaphragm plate hub. Remove reaction disc from diaphragm plate bore (use push rod, or suitable tool), to push disc from seat.

CAUTION — *Do not chip diaphragm plate.*

4) Remove rear shell bearing seal with punch or screwdriver. Remove vacuum check valve and grommet.

CAUTION — *Remove rear seal only if a new one is available. Do not reuse old seal.*

Cleaning & Inspection — Use only clean brake fluid to clean all metal, plastic, and rubber parts. Blow out all passages, orifices, and valve holes with clean, dry air, and air dry all parts. Slight rust on inside of housing can be polished with crocus cloth or fine emery cloth. There should be no cut, nicks, or distortion of any rubber part.

Reassembly — 1) Install vacuum check valve grommet (beveled edge on inside), dip check valve in clean, denatured alcohol and install. Install suitable holding fixture (J-22805) on front housing. Install new rear housing seal in center hole, using suitable tool (J-22677) to seat seal in recess (tool bottoms against housing when seal is in place).

2) Assemble diaphragm plate assembly as follows: Lubricate outer diameter of diaphragm plate and extension, bearing surfaces of air valve, and outer edge of valve poppet. Install valve and rod into diaphragm plate extension. Depress push rod slightly and install air lock valve (lock must index and retain air valve). Install rolling diaphragm in diaphragm plate hub groove. Lubricate reaction disc with silicone lubricant and install disc (use master cylinder push rod to seat disc in diaphragm plate bore).

NOTE — *If disc is not seated, push rod height will be gauged incorrectly during adjustment.*

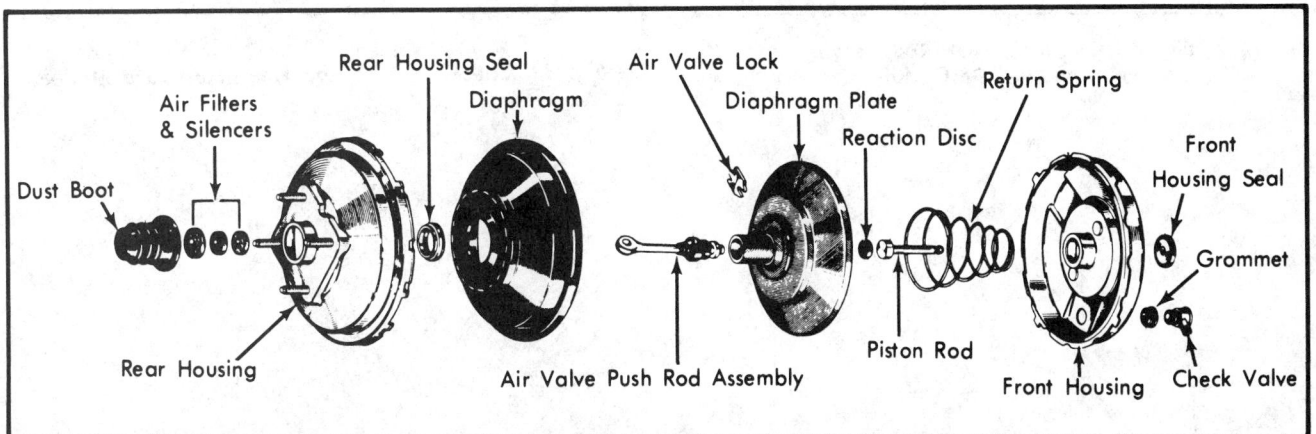

Fig. 1   Exploded View of Bendix Single Diaphragm Assembly

BENDIX SINGLE DIAPHRAGM (Cont.)

3) Lubricate inside of bearing seal and diaphragm bead contact surface of rear shell. Install diaphragm plate assembly in rear housing. Place air filter element over push rod and into diaphragm plate extension. Install filter retainer.

4) With holding fixture in place, position suitable wrench (J-9504) over studs on rear housing and position front and rear housings together. Press down on wrench and rotate rear housing counterclockwise to lock housings. Align scribe marks. Rebend tabs on rear housings. If tabs are cracked or broken, housing must be replaced. Remove wrench.

5) Install air silencers over push rod end. Install push rod boot and boot retainer. On clevis type push rods, install lock nut and push rod clevis. Lightly lubricate piston rod (except rounded end). Guide rod into center bore until fully seated against reaction disc. Press front housing seal into housing until seal is bottomed in recess of housing.

ADJUSTMENT

PUSH ROD

Chevrolet & GMC — 1) Place power unit in a vise with front housing up. Remove front seal to ensure all vacuum is released from unit. Place master cylinder rod, flat end first, in piston rod retainer. Press down on rod with 40 to 50 pounds of pressure to make sure rod is seated.

2) Place a suitable measuring gauge (J22647) over piston rod in such a position that it can be moved from left to right without contacting studs. The center section of gauge has two levels. The piston rod should always contact the lower level and never contact the highest level.

3) If the push rod does not contact gauge correctly, an adjustable push rod must be obtained. Adjust self locking screw on rod to obtain correct clearance with gauge. Apply silicone lubricant on the inside diameter of front housing seal and place seal in position in housing depression.

Ford — Check distance from outer end of push rod to front face of unit. Use a gauge manufactured to specifications shown in *Fig. 3*. Turn push rod screw in or out until length is .980-.995".

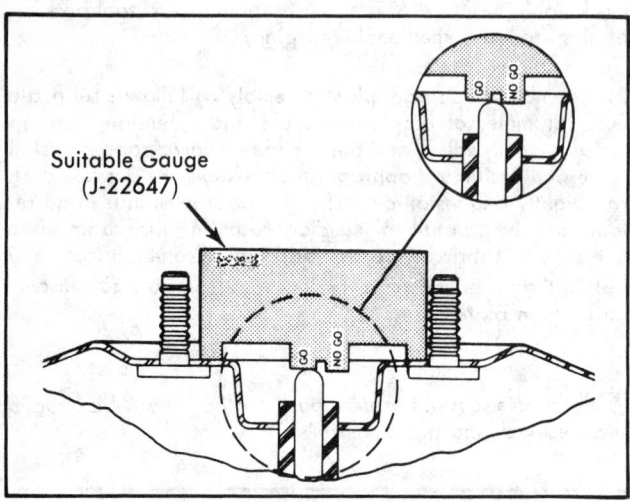

Fig. 2   Checking Push Rod Height
Chevrolet and GMC Models

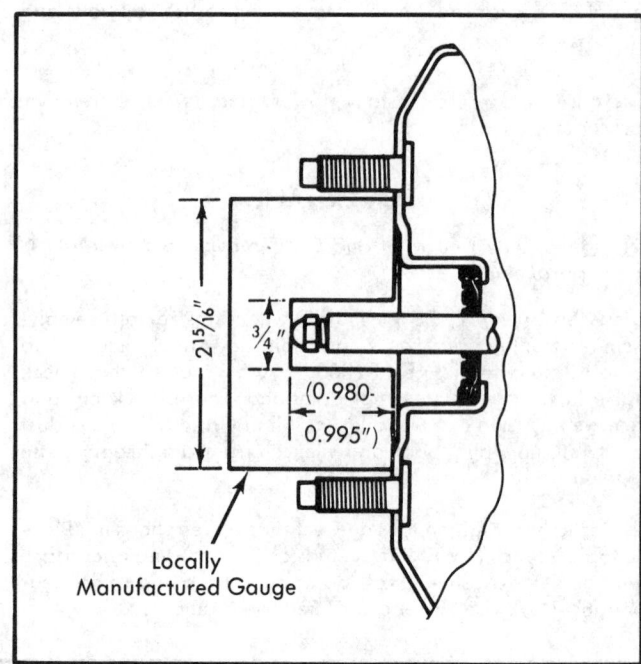

Fig. 3   Checking Push Rod Height on Ford Models

BENDIX TANDEM DIAPHRAGM

Chevrolet
Dodge
Ford
GMC
Plymouth

DESCRIPTION

Vacuum suspended power cylinder used with hydraulic brake system utilizes engine manifold vacuum and atmospheric pressure to provide power assisted brake application. Unit consists of three basic assemblies: vacuum power chamber comprised of front and rear shell, center plate, tandem front and rear diaphragms (with plate assembly), hydraulic push rod and vacuum diaphragm, and diaphragm return spring; mechanically actuated control valve integral with diaphragms; and a master cylinder.

REMOVAL & INSTALLATION

NOTE — *Power brake unit can be removed without disconnecting hydraulic lines at master cylinder.*

Removal — Disconnect vacuum line from check valve or power unit. Remove nuts securing master cylinder to power unit. Pull master cylinder forward away from unit. On Dodge and Plymouth models, remove linkage bellcrank pivot bolt (if equipped). On all models, remove power brake unit from vehicle.

Installation — To install, reverse removal procedure noting the following: Before attaching master cylinder, check push rod for correct length.

OVERHAUL

NOTE — *Only Chevrolet and GMC recommend overhaul of power brake unit.*

Disassembly — **1)** Scribe a mark across front and rear housings for reassembly. Remove master cylinder push rod. Remove both seals from rod.

2) Remove vacuum check valve and grommet. Remove dust boot and silencer from operating valve rod.

3) Using an awl, remove dust guard retainer, dust guard and silencers from rear plate. Reinstall steel retainer on hub.

4) Squirt denatured alcohol down valve operating rod. This will lubricate rubber grommet in valve plunger.

5) Position 2 small blocks of wood on either side of air valve rod and install end of air valve rod in a vise. Leave just enough room to position 2 open end wrenches between vise and retainer on hub of rear plate.

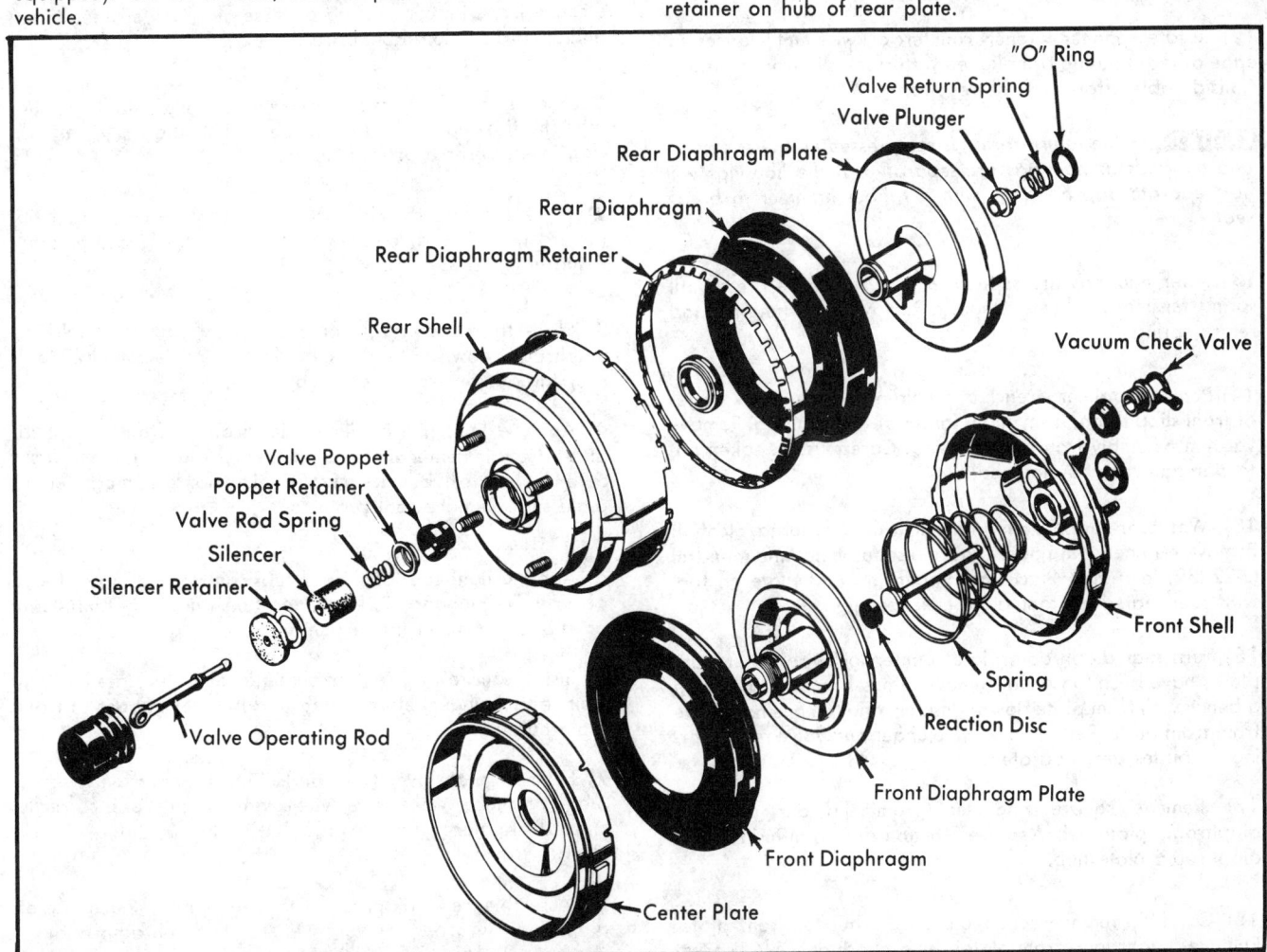

Fig. 1   Exploded View of Bendix Tandem Diaphragm Unit

BENDIX TANDEM DIAPHRAGM (Cont.)

6) Using wrench closest to vise as a pry, force air valve off ball end of rod. Care must be taken not to damage plastic hub or allow vacuum cylinder to fall out.

7) Of the 12 lances at the rear of the housing 4 are deeper than the rest. These must be straightened so that they will clear cutouts in front housing.

NOTE — *If the metal breaks while being straightened, the housing must be replaced.*

8) Remove push rod and vacuum seal from front housing. Attach a suitable holding fixture (J-22805) to front housing studs. Make sure nuts and washers are tight.

9) Place unit and holding fixture in arbor press with rear unit up. Place a 1½" wrench on holding fixture and allow wrench to contact rear of arbor press to prevent unit from turning. See Fig. 2.

10) Using a suitable spanner wrench (J-9504) over studs on rear unit. Bolt wrench to studs. Place a piece of pipe (2" I.D., 3" long) over plastic diaphragm plate hub.

11) Place a piece of flat stock over pipe. Using arbor press, press down on pipe enough to relieve tension of diaphragm rubber lip and spring.

12) Rotate spanner wrench counterclockwise until lances in edge of rear housing are aligned with cutouts in front housing. Considerable effort may be required.

CAUTION — *The return spring is compressed in power section and expands as housings are separated. If the housings will not separate, tap housings with a rubber hammer to break seal.*

13) After housings are separated, slowly release press until spring tension has been released. Remove front housing and return spring.

14) Remove spanner wrench and holding fixture. Work edges of front diaphragm from under lances of rear housing. Remove vacuum assembly from rear housing. Care must be taken not to damage rear housing seal.

15) Wet rear diaphragm retainer with denatured alcohol. Remove retainer with fingers. Place a suitable holding mandrel (J-22839) in a vise. Place the diaphragm and plate on tool with tool seated in front plate hex opening.

16) Turn rear diaphragm plate counterclockwise. After both plates have been loosened, remove plates from tool. Place on a bench with front plate down. Unscrew and remove rear plate from front plate. Retain air valve plunger and valve return spring as plates are separated.

17) Remove square ring seal from shoulder of front diaphragm plate hub. Remove reaction disc from inside front diaphragm plate hub.

18) Carefully remove center plate from hub of front plate. Remove diaphragms from plate. Use a punch or a 1¼" socket to drive seal from rear housings.

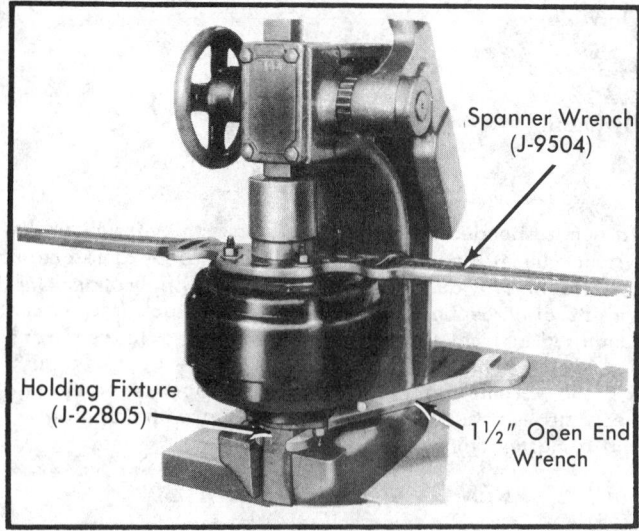

Fig. 2   Using Arbor Press and Suitable Tools to Separate Unit

Cleaning & Inspection — Clean all metal and rubber parts in alcohol. Remove rusted or corroded spots from metal areas with crocus or emery cloth. Dry all components with compressed air. Just before reassembly, rewash all metal components in alcohol. Dry with compressed air. Use all parts included in kit and discard all old rubber parts.

Reassembly — **1)** Press new bearing and seal into rear housing. The flat rubber surface of the seal should be 5/16" below flat, inside surface of rear housing.

2) Place reaction disc in hub of front plate with small tip toward hole. Use a rounded rod to seat disc. Place holding mandrel (J-22839) in a vise.

3) Place front diaphragm on front plate with long fold of diaphragm down. Place a suitable seal protector (J-22733) over threads on front plate hub.

4) Apply a light film of silicone lubricant to front plate hub and to seal in center plate. Guide center plate, seal end first, onto front plate hub. Care must be taken not to damage center plate seal. Remove seal protector.

5) Apply a light coat of silicone lubricant to bearing surfaces of air valve plunger. Care must be taken not to get lubricant on rubber grommet inside plunger.

6) Install square ring seal on shoulder of front plate hub. Install valve plunger return spring and plunger in base of front plate hub.

7) Set rear plate over front plate hub. By hand only, screw plate on hub. Make sure valve and spring are correctly aligned. Tighten plates to 150 INCH lbs. by hand. Check plunger travel.

8) Assemble rear diaphragm to rear plate. Place lip of diaphragm in rear plate groove. Install diaphragm retainer over rear diaphragm and lip of center plate. Press retainer until it seats on shoulder of center plate.

BENDIX TANDEM DIAPHRAGM (Cont.)

9) Apply talcum powder to rear housing inside wall. Apply silicone lubricant to scalloped cutouts of front housing and seal in rear housing.

10) Install diaphragm and plate assembly into rear housing. Carefully guide rear plate hub through seal in rear housing.

11) Bosses on center plate must be aligned between lances in rear housing for reassembly. Work outer rim of front diaphragm into rear housing using a screwdriver. Make sure it is under lances in housing.

12) Attach holding fixture (J-22805) to front housing studs. Position front housing and holding fixture in an arbor press.

13) Place spanner wrench (J-9504) over studs on rear housing. Bolt wrench to studs. Place piece of pipe used during disassembly over plastic diaphragm plate hub. Place a piece of flat stock over pipe.

14) Install return spring so that small end of spring is against housing. Place rear housing over front housing and align scribe marks. Rotate spanner wrench clockwise until housings lock together.

15) Bend tabs in 4 deep lances back to original position. Remove spanner wrench and holding fixture.

16) Wet poppet valve with denatured alcohol. Install in rear plate hub, small end first. Wet poppet retainer with denatured alcohol and assemble with shoulder inside poppet.

17) Install retainer, filters and silencer over ridge on rod. Install return spring over ball end of operating valve rod. Wet grommet in valve plunger with denatured alcohol. Guide air valve rod into valve plunger.

18) Tap end of operating valve rod with plastic hammer to lock ball in grommet. Press filters and silencer into hub and install retainer on hub.

19) Install silencer in dust boot. Wet boot opening with denatured alcohol. Install over operating rod and rear housing flange. Install new check valve and grommet.

20) Apply silicone lubricant to piston end of push rod. Insert in front plate cavity. Twist rod to eliminate air bubbles at reaction disc. Assemble seal over push rod and press into recess in front housing.

ADJUSTMENTS

PUSH ROD ADJUSTMENT

Chevrolet & GMC — 1) Place power unit in a vise with front housing up. Remove front seal to ensure all vacuum is released from unit. Place master cylinder rod, flat end first, in piston rod retainer. Press down on rod with 40 to 50 pounds of pressure to make sure rod is seated.

2) Place a suitable measuring gauge (J-22647) over piston rod and in such a position that it can be moved from left to right without contacting studs. The center section of gauge has two levels. The piston rod should always contact the lower level and never contact the highest level.

3) If the push rod does not contact gauge correctly, an adjustable push rod must be obtained. Adjust self locking screw on rod to obtain correct clearance with gauge. Apply silicone lubricant on the inside diameter of front housing seal and place seal in position in housing depression.

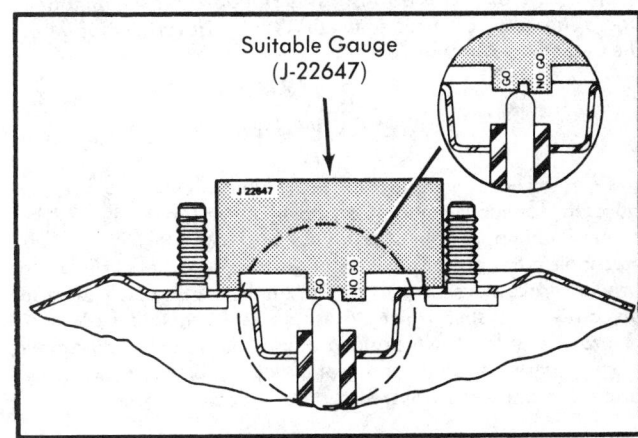

Fig. 3   Checking Push Rod Height
Chevrolet and GMC

Dodge & Plymouth — Push rod length is preset at factory and is non-adjustable.

Ford — Check distance from outer end of booster assembly push rod to front face of booster. Use a gauge manufactured to specifications. See Fig. 4. Turn push rod screw in or out until specified length is obtained.

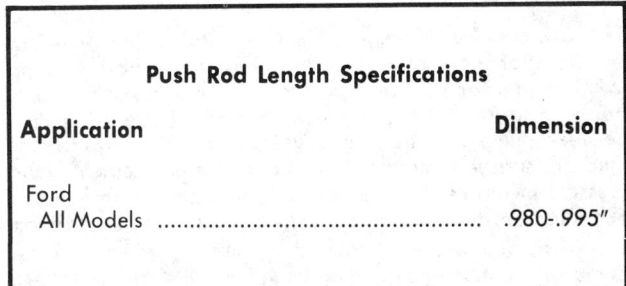

Push Rod Length Specifications	
Application	**Dimension**
Ford All Models	.980-.995"

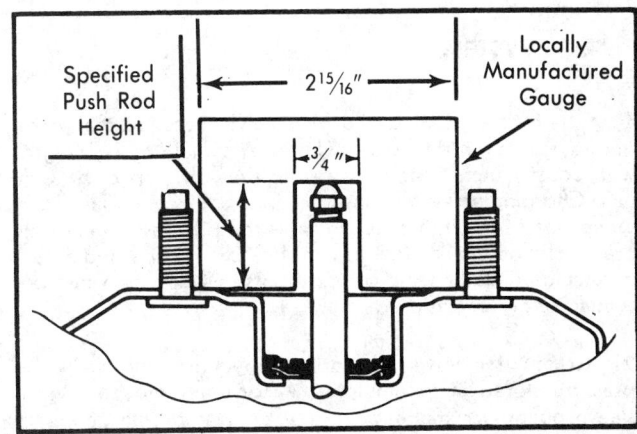

Fig. 4   Checking Push Rod Length on Ford Models

BENDIX HYDRO-BOOST

Chevrolet
Dodge
GMC
Plymouth

NOTE — *The Bendix Hydro-boost is standard on some models and optional on others. See the BRAKE APPLICATION tables at the beginning of this section.*

DESCRIPTION

System utilizes power steering pump fluid pressure to operate booster. Assembly contains an open center spool valve which controls pump pressure magnitude during braking, a lever mechanism to control position of valve, and a boost piston to provide force necessary to operate master cylinder. Unit also has a reserve system which stores sufficient fluid under pressure to provide at least two braking applications in case fluid flow from power steering pump is not available. Brakes can also be applied manually if reserve system is depleted.

OPERATION

RELEASED POSITION (NO BRAKING)

In this position, spool valve return spring holds spool valve open. In open position, spool valve provides unrestricted fluid flow between power steering pump and power steering gear. Fluid pressure is blocked from entering boost pressure chamber by lands on spool valve. As fluid pressure increases with steering demand, it has no effect on boost pressure chamber. Boost pressure chamber is vented through spool valve, to pump return port, and back to power steering pump.

BRAKING POSITION

As brake pedal is depressed, it moves pedal rod and initiates movement of spool valve. This closes fluid return port to pump from boost chamber, and admits fluid into boost chamber from pressure port. Additional valve movement restricts flow between pump and steering gear, causing pump to increase fluid pressure to maintain flow rate to steering gear. As fluid pressure increases in boost chamber, it forces piston forward actuating master cylinder piston, resulting in brake application. If fluid pressure is required for steering while braking, pump pressure will rise and spool valve will shift in an open direction allowing more fluid to flow to steering gear.

RESERVE SYSTEM

1) System consists of a charging valve, accumulator valve, and a spring loaded accumulator. Accumulator is integral with booster unit. System is open to pressure port of booster unit. Charging valve has an orfice and ball check. Fluid from pump passes through orfice in valve, and if pressure exceeds pressure in accumulator, it unseats ball check valve and enters accumulator. Ball check valve prevents reverse flow when accumulator pressure is greater.

2) Accumulator valve is a poppet type valve held closed by pressure stored in accumulator. An actuator on spool valve sleeve opens accumulator valve when a stop with no pump pressure is made that requires use of reserve pressure. Fluid pressure can also enter accumulator from boost chamber through accumulator valve, when boost chamber pressure ex-

ceeds accumulator pressure. A pressure relief valve vents accumulator to pump return port when pressure in accumulator exceeds approximately 1600 psi.

ADJUSTMENT

BRAKE PEDAL

Chevrolet & GMC — 1) Make adjustment in linkage until pedal travel is as specified. Pedal travel is distance pedal moves toward floor from a fully released position. Pump pedal a minimum of 3 times with engine off before making measurement.

2) Specified pedal travel is 3½" on all models except four-wheel disc brake models. Pedal travel is 6" on all four-wheel disc brake models.

NOTE — *Pedal adjustment procedure for Chrysler Corp. vehicles was not available from manufacturer.*

TESTING

NOTE — *Hydro-boost cannot cause noisy brakes, fading brake pedal, or pulling brakes. If one of these conditions exists, other components of brake system are at fault.*

PRELIMINARY CHECKS

Make the following checks, and repair if necessary, before performing any test on the Hydro-Boost system:

- Fluid levels in master cylinder & power steering pump.
- Power steering pump drive belt.
- Power steering hoses for leaks or kinks.
- Air in brake fluid or power steering fluid.
- Engine idle speed.
- Steering pump pressure.

NOTE — *If problem cannot be found in preliminary steps or tests, check areas of brake system that might cause condition. See Trouble Shooting in this section for Hydraulic Brake System Trouble Shooting and Hydro-boost Trouble Shooting.*

HYDRO-BOOST FUNCTIONAL TEST

1) Make all preliminary checks.

2) Place transmission in neutral and stop engine.

3) Apply brake several times to deplete accumulator reserve. Hold brake depressed with medium pressure (40 lbs.).

4) Start engine. Brake pedal should fall slightly then push back against foot.

5) If no action is felt, booster system is not operating properly.

ACCUMULATOR LEAKDOWN TEST

1) Start engine, and charge accumulator by either applying brake with 100 lbs. pedal force or turning steering wheel lock to lock.

BENDIX HYDRO-BOOST (Cont.)

2) Turn off engine and wait one hour. There should be one power assisted brake application with engine off.

3) If reserve system will not retain a charge for one hour, but functions normally immediately following charging, or if accumulator can be heard charging and discharging but will not hold a charge, accumulator valves are at fault and power piston/accumulator must be replaced.

NOTE — *If Hydro-boost is not functioning, ensure power steering system is operating before replacing Hydro-boost unit.*

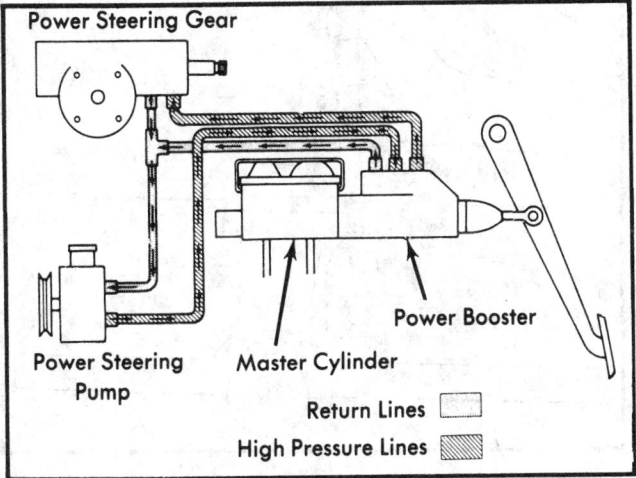

Fig. 1   Hydro-boost Fluid Flow Chart

REMOVAL & INSTALLATION

CHEVROLET & GMC

Removal — 1) Depress and release brake pedal several times to be sure that all pressure is discharged from accumulator prior to disconnecting hoses from booster. Raise Motor Home Chassis on hoist; all others, leave on ground. Clean all dirt from booster at hydraulic line connections and master cylinder. Remove nuts that secure master cylinder to booster and support bracket. Support master cylinder, and cover exposed end with clean cloth.

NOTE — *In most cases, it is not necessary to disconnect master cylinder hydraulic lines to remove booster unit.*

2) On all models except Motor Home Chassis, remove booster pedal push rod cotter pin and disconnect push rod from brake pedal ("C" and "K" models) or booster bracket pivot lever ("G" and "P" models). Remove booster support bracket ("C" and "K" models) or support braces ("G" and "P" models). Remove booster bracket-to-firewall or support bracket nuts and remove booster assembly.

3) On Motor Home Chassis, remove cotter pin, nut and bolt that secure operating lever to vertical brake rod. Remove the six nuts and bolts that secure booster linkage bracket to front and rear support brackets, and remove booster from vehicle by sliding booster off rear support studs. Remove cotter pin, nut, and bolt that secures operating lever to pedal rod. Remove brake pedal rod lever nut and bolt and then remove lever, sleeve and bushings.

Installation — To install, reverse removal procedure noting the following: Lubricate pedal rod and linkage pivot bolts, pins, sleeves and bushings with suitable lubricant (Delco Brake Lube). Bleed booster/power steering hydraulic system. Check brake pedal and stoplamp switch adjustment.

NOTE — *Bleeding Hydro-boost system is a separate procedure from bleeding the hydraulic systems. See Bleeding Hydro-boost Systems in this article.*

DODGE & PLYMOUTH

Removal — Depress brake pedal several times to be sure all pressure is released from accumulator. Remove nuts holding master cylinder to booster. Lay master cylinder aside without kinking lines. Disconnect and plug lines from booster fluid ports. Disconnect brake pedal return spring. Remove bolt from push rod to pedal. Remove mounting nuts and booster from vehicle.

Installation — To install, reverse removal procedure. Tighten all nuts and hose connections. Bleed booster/power steering system. Check brake pedal and stop lamp switch adjustment.

NOTE — *Bleeding Hydro-boost system is a separate procedure from bleeding the hydraulic systems. See Bleeding Hydro-boost Systems in this article.*

BLEEDING

HYDRO-BOOST SYSTEM

NOTE — *If power steering fluid has foamed due to low fluid level, it will be necessary to park vehicle for approximately one hour (reservoir cap loose) so that foam can dissipate.*

Chevrolet & GMC — 1) Fill reservoir with suitable power steering fluid and leave undisturbed for at least 2 minutes. Start engine and run momentarily. Add fluid if necessary. Repeat until fluid level remains constant after running engine. Raise vehicle so front end is off ground. Turn steering wheel right and left, lightly contacting stops. Add fluid if necessary.

2) Start engine and depress brake pedal several times while turning steering wheel from stop to stop. Turn engine off and depress brake pedal several times to deplete accumulator pressure. Add fluid if necessary.

3) If fluid is foamy, or has air in it, let vehicle stand several minutes, then repeat steps 1) and 2). The presence of air in the system will cause fluid level to rise with engine off. Continue to bleed system untill all air is expelled.

Dodge & Plymouth — 1) Check power steering pump reservoir and fill with power steering fluid (MOPAR Power Steering Fluid). Allow fluid to remain undisturbed for 2 minutes. Leave reservoir cap off during operation.

2) Start engine and run for ten seconds. Check fluid level and add fluid if necessary. Repeat procedure until fluid level remains constant. Raise front of vehicle and allow tires to clear floor. Start engine and run at 1500 RPM. Apply and release

BENDIX HYDRO-BOOST (Cont.)

brakes several times, at the same time turn wheels back and forth, lock to lock. Turn off engine and check fluid level. Add fluid if necessary.

3) Lower vehicle. Start engine and run at 1500 RPM. Apply and release brake pedal several times, at the same time turn front wheels back and forth, lock to lock. Turn off engine and check fluid level. Add fluid if necessary. If fluid level is low, repeat bleeding procedure. Place cover on reservoir.

BLEEDING BRAKE CYLINDERS

See Hydraulic Brake Bleeding in this Section.

OVERHAUL

Disassembly —   1) Secure unit in vise (bracket end up) and use chisel to cut bracket nut that secures linkage bracket to power section. Cut nut at slot in threaded section to prevent damage to threads. Remove linkage bracket from unit.

2) Remove pedal rod boot (if equipped) and place rod retainer shearing tool (see tool chart for number) over rod. Place a punch through pedal rod from lower side of tool and push punch on through to rest on higher side of tool. Lift up on punch to shear pedal rod retainer. Remove pedal rod.

3) Remove remnants of rubber grommet from groove near end of pedal rod and from groove inside input rod end. With small

screwdriver, pry plastic guide out of output push rod retainer. Disengage tabs of spring retainer from ledge inside opening near master cylinder mounting flange of booster. Remove retainer, piston return spring and output rod from opening.

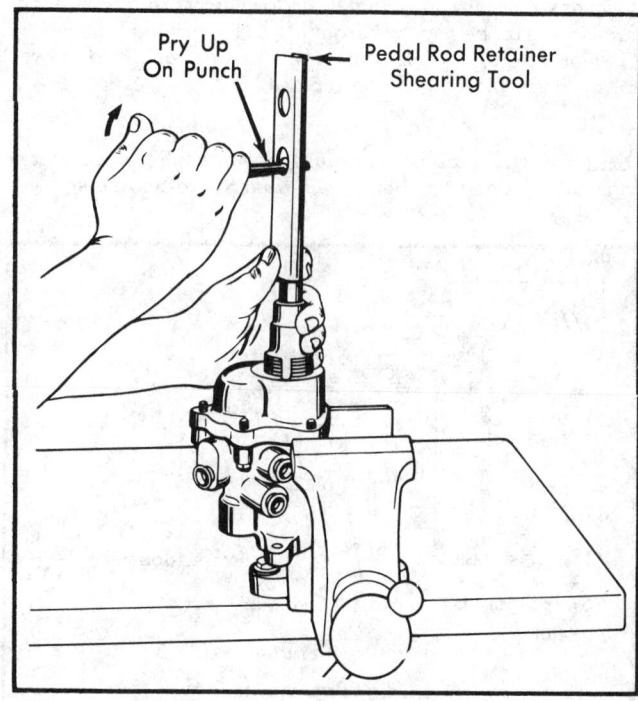

Fig. 2   Procedure for Removing Booster Pedal Rod

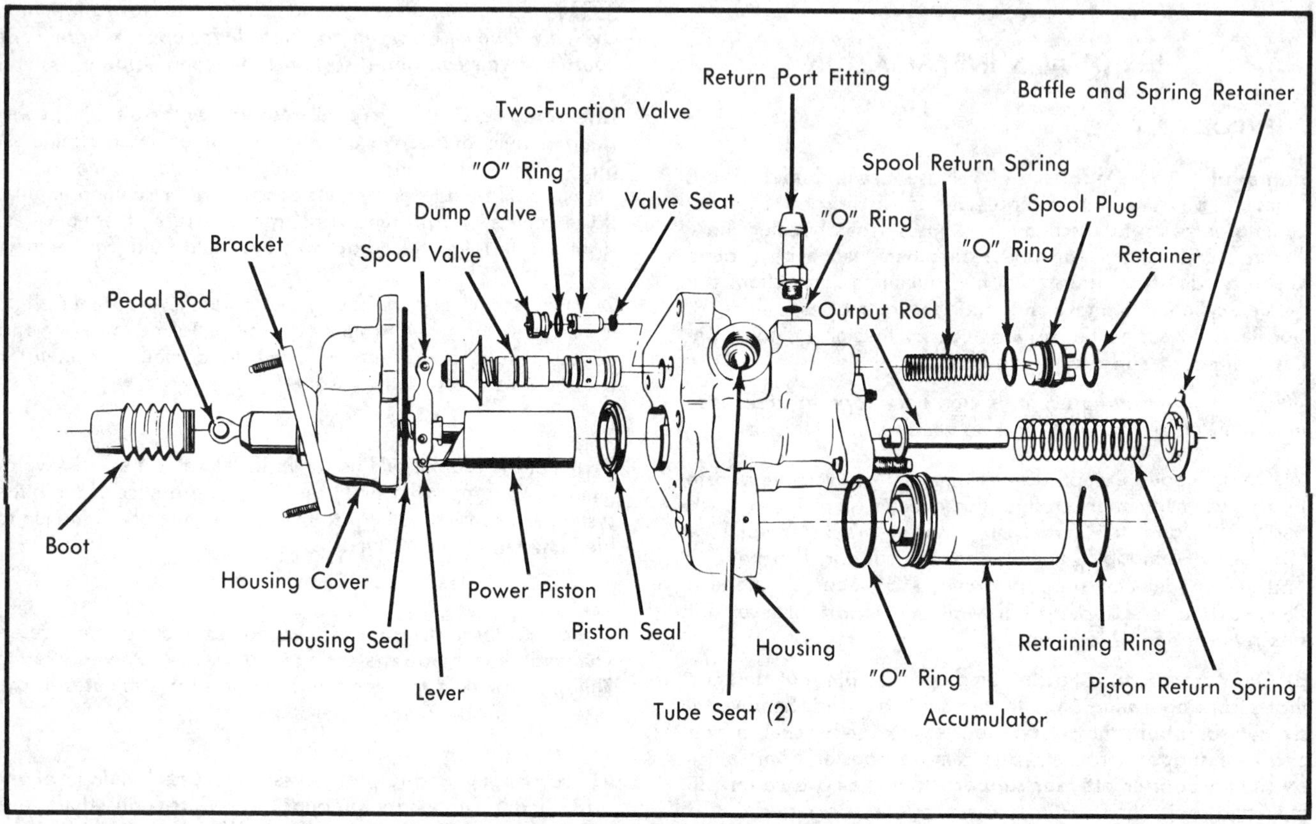

**Fig. 3   Exploded View of Bendix Hydro-boost Assembly Components
(Unit with External Accumulator Shown)**

BENDIX HYDRO-BOOST (Cont.)

4) Place booster cover in a soft-jawed vise and remove 5 screws securing booster housing to cover. Remove booster assembly from vise and while holding over a pan, separate cover from housing. Remove large seal ring from groove in cover and discard.

5) Remove input rod and piston assembly, spool assembly and spool spring from booster housing. If spool valve is defective, the complete assembly must be replaced. Inspect power piston, if deep scratches are evident, input rod and piston must be replaced.

6) Remove input rod seals and piston seal from piston bore. Place retaining cap tool (see tool chart for number) over master cylinder stud and install nut as shown in *Fig. 4*. Using a large "C" clamp, depress accumulator. Insert a punch into hole in housing and remove retaining ring with screwdriver.

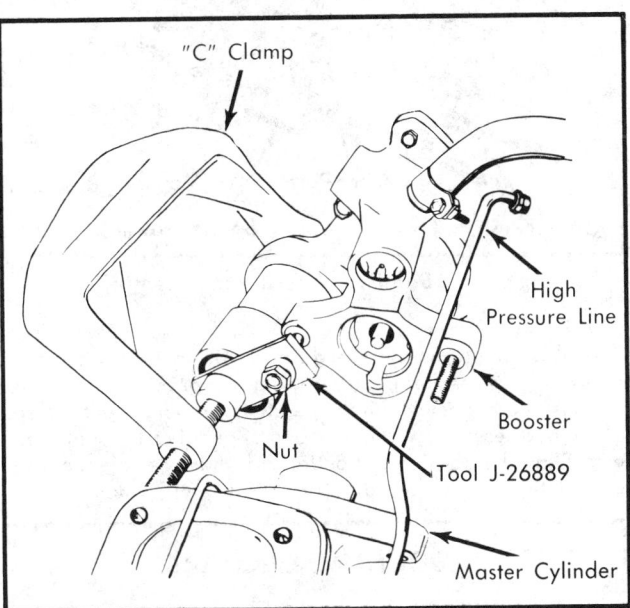

Fig. 4 Compressing Accumulator

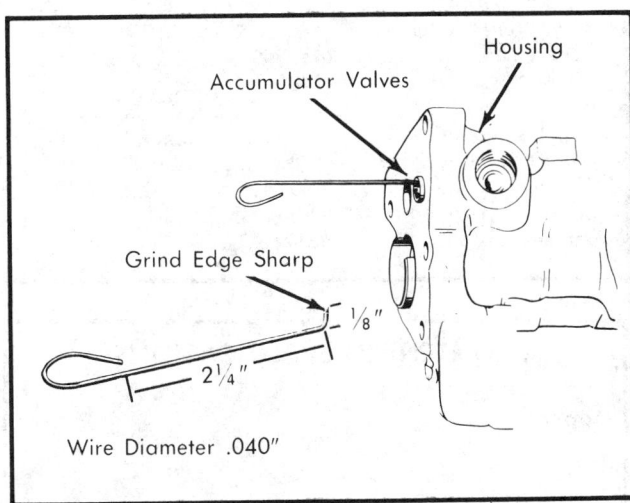

Fig. 5 Removing Accumulator Valves

7) Slowly back off clamp until tension on accumulator is released, then remove accumulator and "O" ring. If accumulator valve is faulty, remove valve using a small diameter wire tool. *See Fig. 5.* Remove the dump valve by catching the tool under the pin guide near the center of the valve, then remove the 2-function valve and seat.

8) Remove return hose "O" ring fitting if it is leaking. Remove spool valve plug, retaining ring and "O" ring. Remove tube seats using a No. 4 Easy Out.

Cleaning & Inspection — 1) Clean all metal parts in a suitable solvent. Inspect valve spool and valve spool bore in booster housing for corrosion, nicks, scoring or other damage. Discoloration of spool or bore, particularly in grooves, is not harmful.

2) If valve spool or spool bore has nicks or scoring that can be felt with a fingernail, particularly on the lands, the entire booster should be replaced as an assembly.

3) Inspect input rod, piston assembly, and piston bore for corrosion, nicks, scoring or other damage. Replace damaged parts.

Reassembly — 1) Be sure that all parts are absolutely clean. Lubricate all seals and metal friction points with power steering fluid.

2) On Chevrolet and GMC models, install tube seat as shown in *Fig. 6*. On Dodge and Plymouth models, position tube seats in booster ports and screw a spare tube nut into each port to seat tube seat. Remove spare nuts and ensure that ports are free from burrs or shavings.

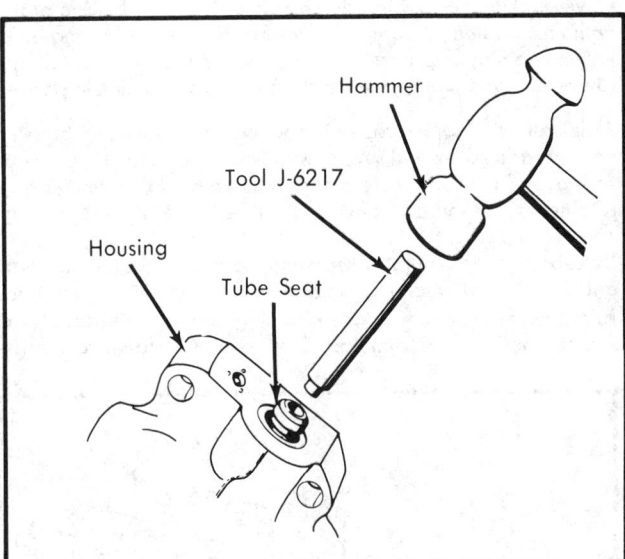

Fig. 6 Installing General Motors Tube Seats

3) On all models, install "O" ring, spool valve plug and retaining ring. Coat piston seal and bore with clean power steering fluid and place seal in bore. Lip of seal must face away from master cylinder mounting flanges. Lubricate input rod end, new input rod seals, and seal installer tool (see tool chart for number) with clean power steering fluid.

Power Brake Units

BENDIX HYDRO-BOOST (Cont.)

4) Slide seals on tool with lip of cups toward open end of tool. *See Fig. 7.* Slide tool over input rod end and down to second groove. Then slide forward seal off tool and into groove. Assemble other seal in first groove. Make sure both seals are seated.

NOTE — *Chevrolet and GMC diesel models use only 1 seal on input rod.*

5) Lubricate piston and piston installation tool (see tool chart for tool number) with clean power steering fluid. Hold the large end of the tool against the piston and slide the tool and piston into the piston bore and through the piston seal. Remove tool. Install return hose "O" ring fitting. If accumulator valve was removed, install new seat in valve bore by installing 2-function valve, which forces seat to bottom in bore.

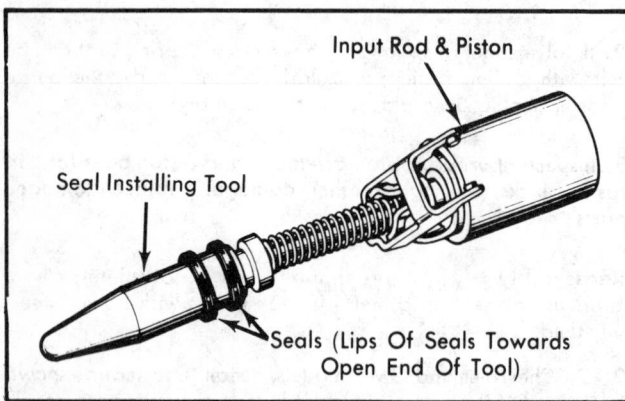

Fig. 7   Installing Input Rod Seals

6) If removed, insert new dump valve over the 2-function valve, making certain the dump valve plunger is held in place until installation is complete. Insert spool valve spring and valve assembly into bore. Extend power piston lever to accept sleeve on spool valve, then slide lever pins into slot in sleeve.

7) Install new seal in groove in housing cover, then join booster housing and cover and secure with 5 screws. Install output rod, spring and new spring retainer. Install new baffle and spring retainer by pushing in on it with a ⅞" socket.

8) Lubricate accumulator seal with clean power steering fluid and install seal and accumulator in housing. Place retaining ring over accumulator. Place retaining cap tool (see tool chart for number) over accumulator. Using a "C" clamp, compress

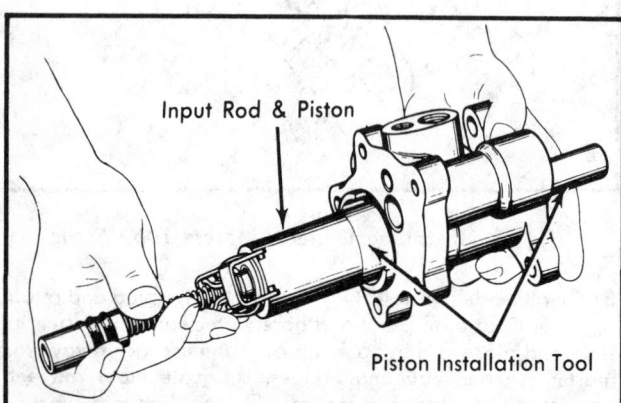

Fig. 8   Installing Input Rod Assembly into Booster

accumulator straight in. Snap retaining ring into the housing groove, and remove "C" clamp and tool.

9) Position mounting on booster. Tab on inside diameter of large hole in bracket should fit into slot in threaded portion of booster hub. Install new bracket nut with staking groove outward on the threaded hub of booster. Using deep socket tool (see tool chart for tool number) and a torque wrench, tighten nut to 110 ft. lbs.

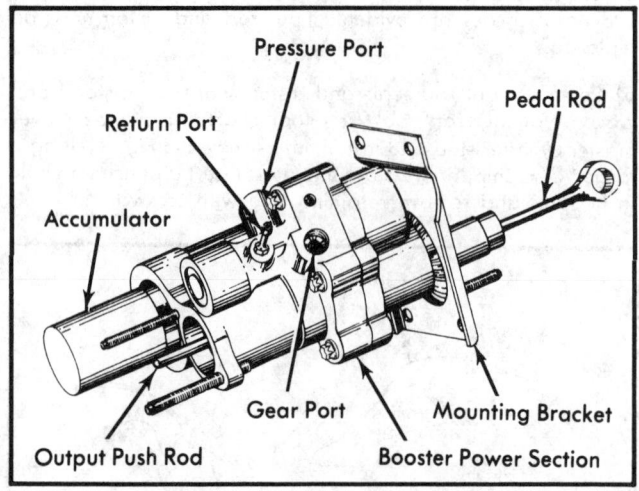

Fig. 9   Bendix Hydro-Boost Assembly

10) Using a hammer and punch, stake the nut in place. Assembly boot (if used) on pedal rod. Assemble new grommet in groove near end of pedal rod. Moisten grommet with water and insert grommet end of the pedal rod into the input rod end of the booster housing. Push on end of pedal rod to seat grommet. Slide the boot on the pedal rod and assemble the large end of the boot onto the hub of the power section.

TOOL NUMBER CHART

Application	GM Number	Chry. Number
Retainer Shearer	J-24569	.... C-4396
Retaining Cap Tool	J-26889	
Input Rod Seal Tool		.... C-4394
Rear Drum Models		
Gasoline	J-24553	
Diesel	J-28485	
Rear Disc Models	J-28497	
Piston Installation Tool		.... C-4393
Diesel Models	J-25083	
All Others	J-24551	
Special Deep Socket ...	J-24554	.... C-4395
Tube Seat Installer	J-6217	

TIGHTENING SPECIFICATIONS

Application	Ft. Lbs.
Booster Housing	20
Mounting Bracket Nut	110
Booster Brackets	25

DELCO-MORAINE SINGLE DIAPHRAGM

Chevrolet
GMC
Jeep

DESCRIPTION

A combined vacuum-hydraulic unit which uses a combination of intake manifold vacuum and atmospheric pressure to provide power assist. Reserve vacuum supply and vacuum check valve allow several brake applications, with vacuum assist, after engine has stopped. Unit is composed of two main sections: vacuum power cylinder and dual master cylinder. Vacuum power cylinder contains power piston assembly, which houses control valve, reaction mechanism, and power piston return spring.

REMOVAL & INSTALLATION

POWER BRAKE UNIT

Disconnect push rod from brake pedal. Disconnect vacuum hose from vacuum check valve. Remove nuts holding master cylinder to power unit and move master cylinder aside. DO NOT disconnect hydraulic lines. Remove nuts holding power unit to dash panel. On Jeep "CJ" and Scrambler models, remove nuts holding bellcrank to dash panel. On all models, remove power unit from vehicle, noting that On Jeep "CJ" and Scrambler models, power unit and bellcrank are removed as an assembly. To install, reverse removal procedure.

OVERHAUL

POWER BRAKE UNIT

NOTE — *Jeep Corp. does not recommend overhaul of this unit. It is serviced as an assembly.*

Disassembly — 1) Scribe marks on housings for reassembly reference and remove boot, front housing seal, vacuum check valve and grommet.

2) Attach power unit front housing to holding fixture base (J-22805-1) and clamp base in vise with power section up.

3) Place a spanner wrench (J-9504) on studs of rear housing. Press down and turn counterclockwise to unlock housings.

NOTE — *Do not put pressure on plastic power piston extension.*

4) Remove power piston bearing, return spring and power piston group. Remove piston rod and reaction retainer.

CAUTION — *Use care not to damage power piston assembly when removing reaction disc. Reaction disc must be replaced.*

5) Use awl, ice pick or similar tool to remove reaction disc. Remove reaction piston.

6) Grasp assembly at outside edge of diaphragm support and diaphragm. Hold pushrod down against a hard surface. Use a slight force or impact to dislodge diaphragm retainer.

NOTE — *Do not disassemble power pushrod assembly.*

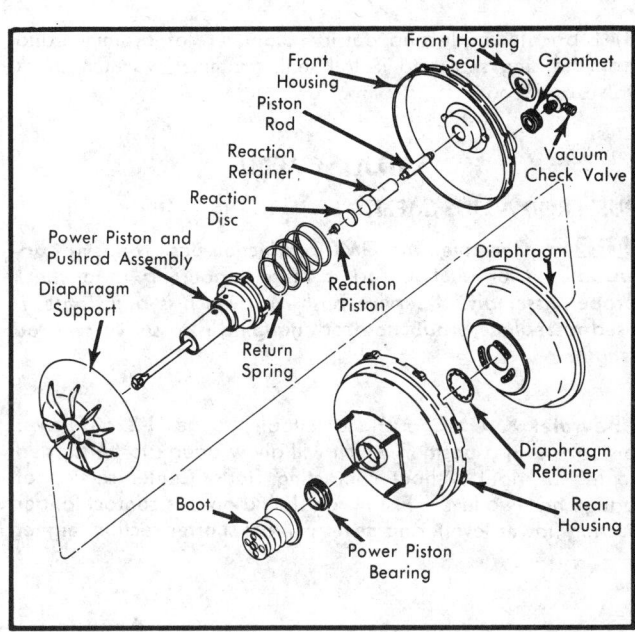

Fig. 1 Exploded View of Typical Delco-Moraine Single Diaphragm Power Brake Unit

Cleaning & Inspection — Clean all metal, plastic, and rubber parts in denatured alcohol. Blow out all passages, orifices, and valve holes with clean, dry air. Air dry all parts. Slight rust on inside of housings can be polished with crocus or emery cloth. There should be no nicks, cuts, or abnormalities of any rubber part. If in doubt about its condition, replace the part.

Reassembly — 1) Lubricate inside diameter of diaphragm lip with silicon lubricant and fit in diaphragm support.

2) Install diaphragm and support over power piston and pushrod assembly, support side first. Install new diaphragm retainer and seat using seating tool (J-28458) and a plastic hammer.

3) Install reaction piston, new reaction disc, reaction retainer and piston rod.

4) Attach holding fixture to front housing and place in vise. Install power piston return spring with white end to front housing.

5) Insert power piston assembly pushrod end through rear housing and place on front housing and return spring.

6) Align scribe marks with spanner on studs of rear housing. Press down and turn clockwise to lock 2 housings.

DELCO-MORAINE SINGLE DIAPHRAGM (Cont.)

NOTE — *Assembly can be aided by connecting a vacuum source to booster.*

7) Stake 2 housing tabs into sockets with screwdriver. Stake at 2 tabs 180° apart.

8) Lubricate inside and outside diameters of grommet and front housing seal and install seal, grommet, vacuum check valve and boot.

ADJUSTMENT

PUSH ROD ADJUSTMENT

NOTE — *Chevrolet and GMC production push rod is not adjustable. If production rod is reused, gauging is to check proper assembly. If service push rod, which is adjustable, is used to replace production rod, gauging is to set correct rod length.*

Chevrolet & GMC — Place suitable gauge (J-22647) over piston rod in a position which will allow gauge to be slipped to left or right without contacting studs. Center section of gauge has two levels. Piston rod should always contact longer section (lower level), and never contact shorter section (higher level). Any variation beyond these two limits would require replacement of production piston rod or adjustment of service piston rod.

Jeep — Piston rod of replacement units is preset at factory and require no field adjustment.

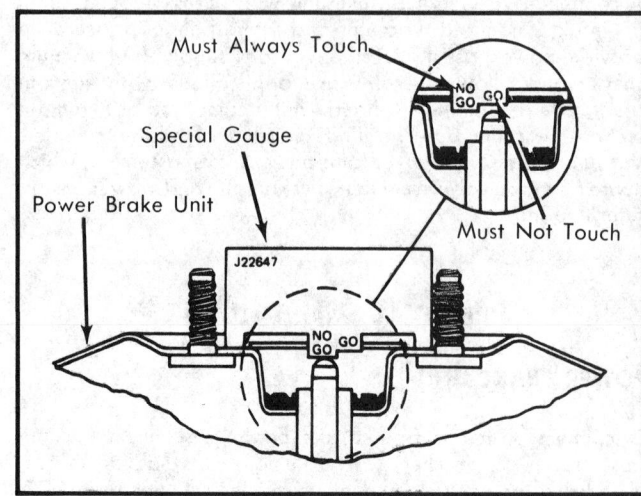

Fig. 2   Checking Piston Rod Height Nonadjustable Production Rod Shown

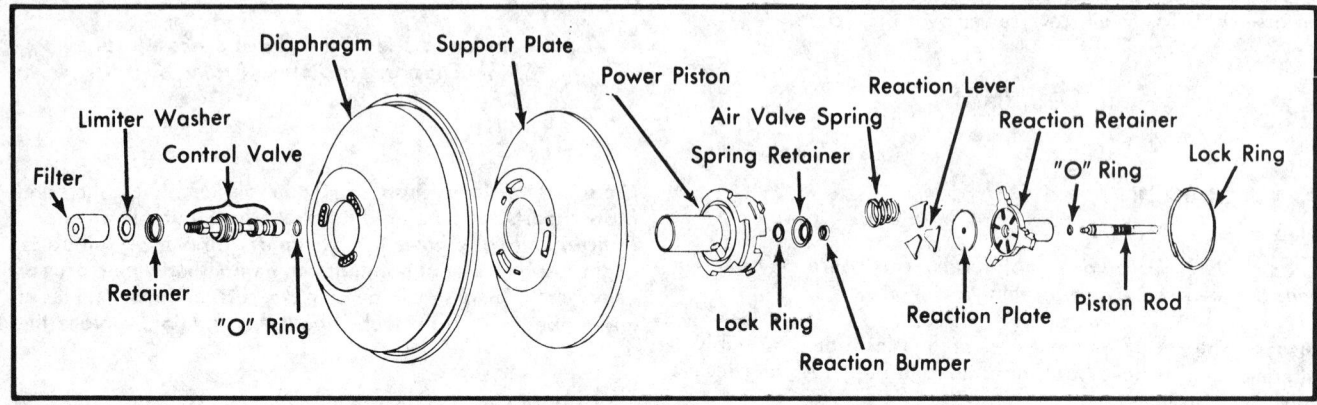

Fig. 3   Exploded View of Power Piston Assembly

Power Brake Units

DELCO-MORAINE TANDEM DIAPHRAGM

Chevrolet
GMC
Jeep

DESCRIPTION

Unit is mounted on firewall and connected directly to brake pedal. A combination of vacuum and atmospheric pressure is used to provide power assist. Power cylinder houses power piston assembly, which contains primary and secondary diaphragms, pistons, floating control valve, reaction piston and disc.

REMOVAL & INSTALLATION

POWER BRAKE UNIT

Removal — Without disconnecting hydraulic lines, remove master cylinder from power unit and position to one side. Disconnect vacuum hose from vacuum check valve. Disconnect power brake push rod from brake pedal. Remove nuts mounting power unit to firewall and remove power unit.

CAUTION — *Do not bend or kink hydraulic lines, and do not force push rod to the side when disconnecting.*

Installation — To install, reverse removal procedures. On Jeep vehicles, use a new bolt to secure push rod to brake pedal.

OVERHAUL

POWER BRAKE UNIT

Disassembly — 1) Remove pushrod boot, silencer, front housing seal, grommet and vacuum check valve.

2) Scribe a mark on front and rear housing for reassembly reference. Attach front housing to suitable holding fixture (J-22805-01).

3) Place spanner wrench (J-9504) over rear housing studs, press down, and turn counterclockwise to unlock housings. Carefully separate housings.

4) Remove power piston group, power piston return spring, and power piston bearing. Remove piston rod, reaction retainer and power head silencer.

5) Grasp assembly at outside edge of divider and diaphragms. Hold with pushrod down against a hard surface. Use a slight force or impact to dislodge diaphragm retainer.

6) Remove primary diaphragm, primary support plate, secondary power piston bearing, housing divider, secondary support plate and diaphragm and power piston assembly.

Cleaning & Inspection — Clean all plastic, metal and rubber parts in denatured alcohol. Blow out all passages, orifices and valve holes. Air dry all parts. Slight rust on housing may be cleaned with crocus or emery cloth. Do not reinstall any rubber parts with cuts, nicks or distortion. If in doubt, replace the part.

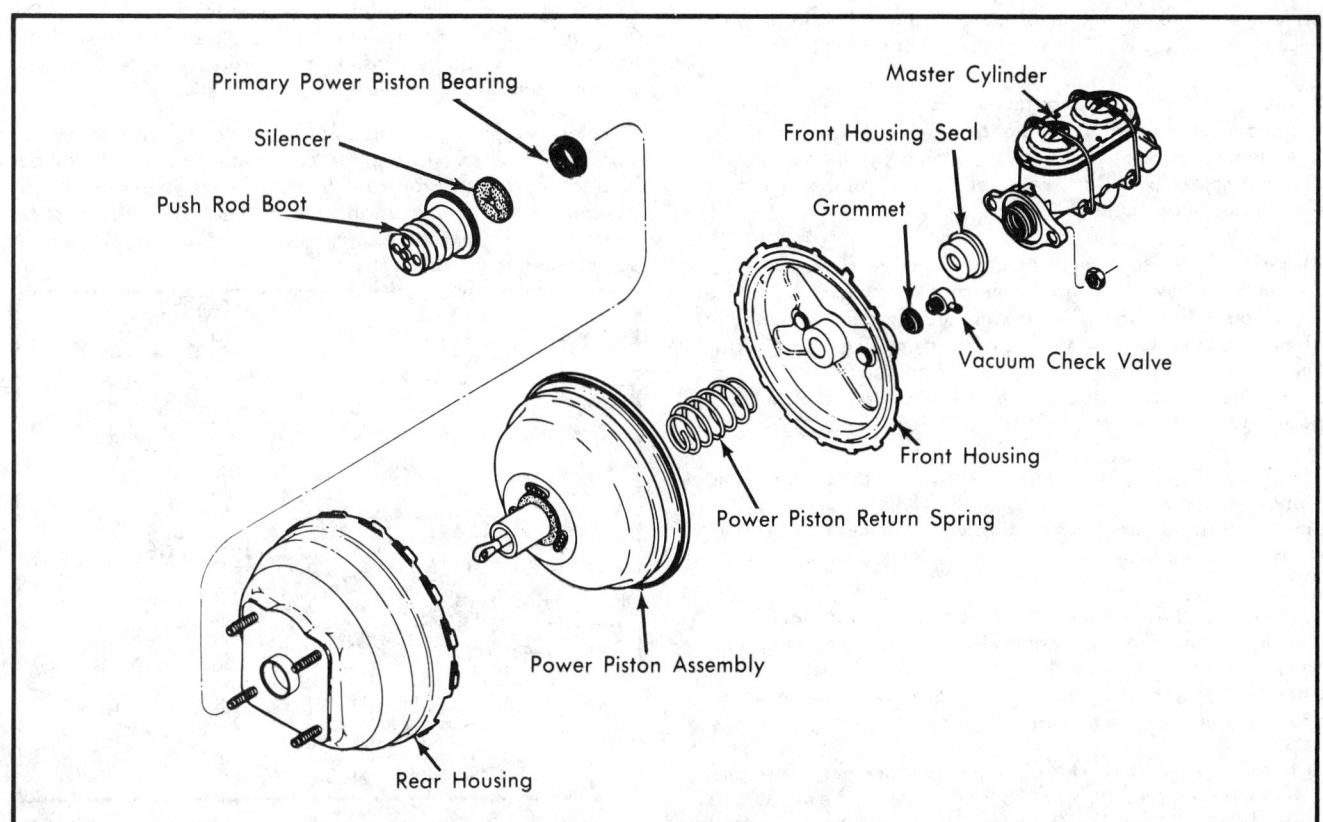

Fig. 1   Exploded View of Delco-Moraine Tandem Power Cylinder

Power Brake Units

DELCO-MORAINE TANDEM DIAPHRAGM (Cont.)

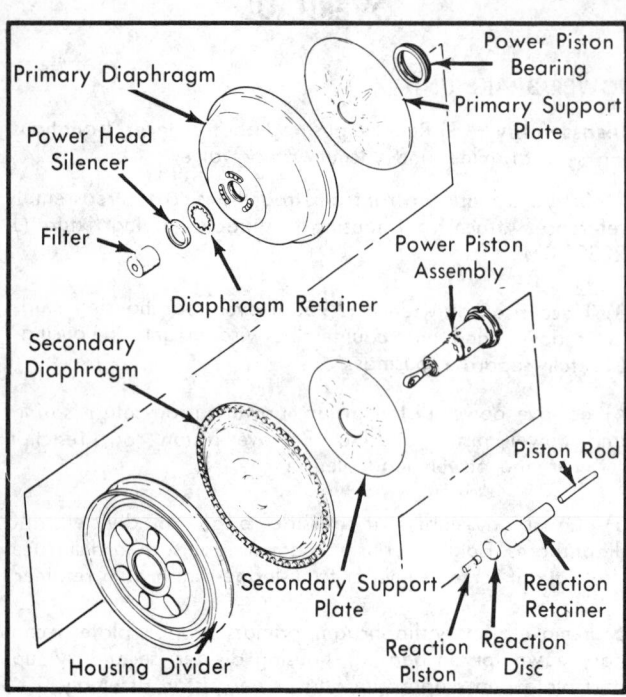

Fig. 2   Exploded View of Delco-Moraine Tandem Power Piston Assembly

NOTE — *Prior to installation of rubber, plastic, and metal friction parts, lubricate with suitable silicone lube (5459912).*

Reassembly — 1) Place power piston on bench with push rod end up. Install assembly cone J-28458 over push rod end of piston. Lubricate inside diameter of secondary diaphragm with silicon lubricant and fit in secondary support plate.

2) Install secondary diaphragm and support plate over power piston and push down until it bottoms. *See Fig. 3.* Lubricate inside diameter of secondary power piston bearing and install in housing divider with flat surface of bearing on the same side as 6 raised lugs on divider.

3) Hold divider so that formed over flange faces up. Press divider down over assembly cone and onto power piston to rest against secondary diaphragm. Lubricate inside diameter of primary diaphragm and install in primary support plate. Remove assembly cone from power piston, place primary support plate and diaphragm assembly over power piston and push down until it bottoms.

4) Place diaphragm retainer over power piston and onto diaphragm. Install assembly cone J-28458 over power piston onto diaphragm retainer and strike with hammer until retainer is locked on neck of power piston. Remove assembly cone.

5) Install reaction retainer, piston rod and power head silencer. Place primary power piston bearing in rear housing center hole. Lubricate with silicon lubricant on inner diameter. Attach front housing to holding fixture and place fixture in vise. Install power piston assembly to rear housing.

6) Install power piston return spring over reaction retainer and lower rear housing onto front housing. Align scribe marks and press down on spanner (J-9504), turning clockwise to lock housings. Stake 2 housing tabs into sockets at 2 locations 180° apart.

7) Lubricate inside and outside diameters of grommet and front housing seal. Install seal, grommet, vacuum check valve, silencer and push rod boot.

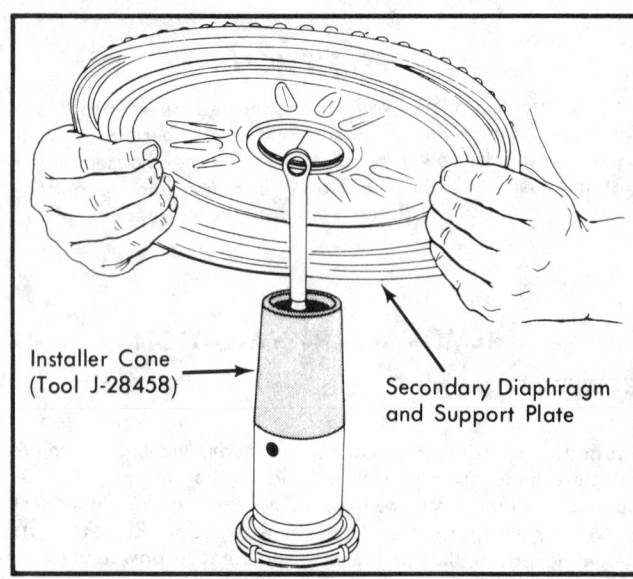

Fig. 3   Installing Secondary Diaphragm and Support Plate

PISTON ROD ADJUSTMENT

NOTE — *This adjustment applies to Chevrolet and GMC only. Jeep push rod is not adjustable.*

1) Place power unit in padded vise with front housing up. Do not clamp tight. Insert master cylinder piston rod, flat end first, into piston rod retainer. Ensure rod is properly seated. Remove front housing seal to assure no vacuum is in unit.

2) Place suitable gauge (J-22647) over piston rod, in a position which will allow gauge to be moved right or left without contacting studs. Piston rod should contact longer section of gauge. Rod is non-adjustable, and if out of limits, must be replaced with adjustable service rod. With service rod, adjust self-locking screw to meet gauging specifications.

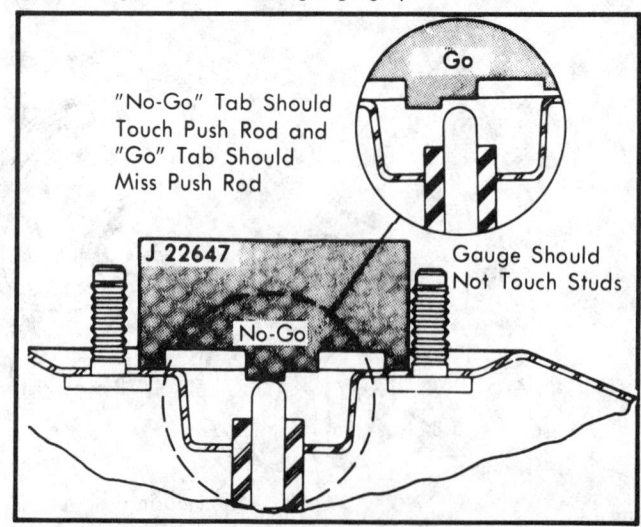

Fig. 4   Gauging Push Rod with Special Gauge (Chevrolet & GMC Models Only)

CHRYSLER CORP. SLIDING CALIPER DISCS

**Dodge
Plymouth**

DESCRIPTION

Chrysler vehicles are quipped with single piston, sliding caliper disc brakes. Brake assembly consists of hub and disc assembly, caliper, disc pads, splash shield and adapter. Cooling fins are cast integrally between machined braking surfaces. When the brake pedal is depressed, hydraulic pressure is applied against brake caliper piston. This force is transmitted to inboard brake pad and inner surface of rotor. As force increases against inboard side, caliper slides inward on machined rotor plate ramps, providing vise-like clamping action on rotor.

ADJUSTMENT & SERVICING

DISC PAD ADJUSTMENT

Pad wear is automatically compensated for by piston moving outward in cylinder bore; therefore, no disc pad adjustment in service is required.

NOTE — *Inspect condition of disc pads whenever wheels are removed. If any pad shows signs of excessive wear, replace complete disc pad set.*

BLEEDING SYSTEM

See Hydraulic Brake Bleeding in this Section.

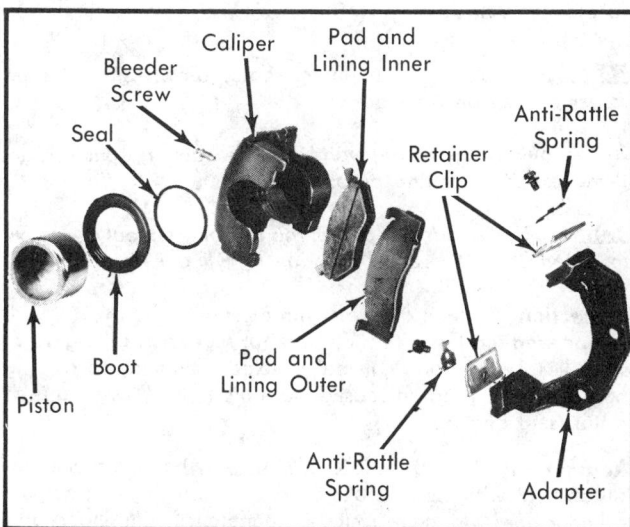

Fig. 1   Exploded View of Chrysler Single Piston Disc Brake Caliper

REMOVAL & INSTALLATION

DISC BRAKE PADS

Removal (W350/450 & W250 Extra) — Siphon fluid from master cylinder until cylinder is $1/3$ full. Raise and support vehicle, and remove wheel. Using a "C" clamp, bottom caliper piston in cylinder bore. Remove clamp. Remove key retaining screws and drive out caliper support key with a brass punch.

Remove caliper support spring and remove caliper from adapter. DO NOT let caliper hang from brake line. Pry outer disc pad from caliper and remove inner disc pad and anti-rattle spring from adapter. If pads are not to be replaced, mark them for reassembly reference.

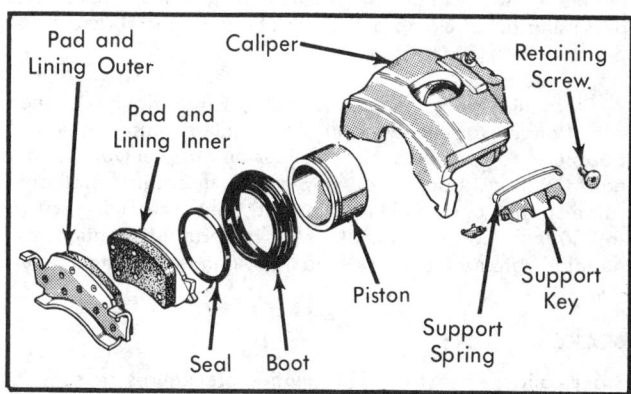

Fig. 2   Exploded View of Bendix Single Piston Disc Brake Caliper

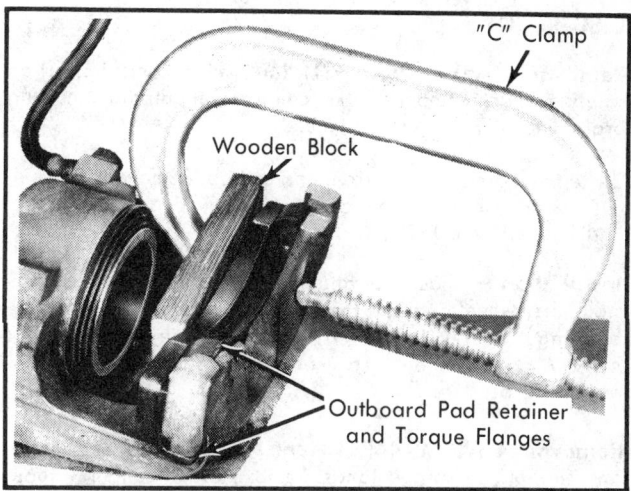

Fig. 3   Installation of Outboard Pad and Liner

Installation — Install anti-rattle spring and inner disc pad in adapter, making sure clips remain in position. Place outer disc pad in position in caliper. If disc pad cannot be installed by hand, press into place using a block of wood and a "C" clamp. Position brake caliper on adapter, making sure hose is not twisted. Position spring over caliper key and install between adapter and lower caliper machined surface. Tap into place using a brass punch and hammer. Install retaining screw, making sure boss on screw fits fully into cut-out on key. Install wheel and tire and refill reservoir in master cylinder to within $1/4$" of top of reservoir. Pump brake pedal several times and recheck fluid level.

Removal (All Remaining Models) — Raise and support vehicle. Remove wheel and tire. Remove caliper retainer and anti-rattle spring assemblies. Carefully lift caliper assembly out and away from rotor. Pry between outer disc pad and fingers of housing to remove outer pad. Support caliper to prevent damage to brake line and remove inner disc pad.

CHRYSLER CORP. SLIDING CALIPER DISCS (Cont.)

Installation — 1) Slowly push piston back into caliper. Care must be taken to ensure reservoir does not overflow while pushing in on piston. Slide outer disc pad into caliper. There should be no free play between disc pad flange and caliper flange. If free play exists, bend disc pad flange until interference fit with caliper is obtained. If necessary, install disc pad using a "C" clamp and block of wood placed across disc pad.

2) Place inner lining on adapter with disc pad flanges aligned with flange ways in adapter. Slide caliper into position in adapter and over disc. Align caliper on adapter, taking care not to pull dust boot away from groove in piston. Install anti-rattle springs and retaining clips and tighten retaining screws to 200 INCH lbs. Pump brake pedal several times until a firm pedal is obtained. Recheck fluid level in master cylinder reservoir.

BRAKE CALIPER

Brake caliper removal and installation procedures are same as for disc brake pads, except it will be necessary to disconnect hydraulic brake hose at caliper.

DISC ROTOR

Removal (2-WD Models) — 1) Raise vehicle and support on safety stands. Remove brake caliper without disconnecting brake line as previously outlined.

2) Remove grease cover from end of hub. Remove cotter pin, nut lock, nut, thrust washer and outer wheel bearing. Pull rotor and hub off wheel spindle.

Installation — Slide rotor and hub into position on spindle. Install outer wheel bearing, thrust washer and nut. Adjust wheel bearing. *See Wheel Bearing Adjustment in WHEEL ALIGNMENT Section.* To complete installation, reverse removal procedure.

Removal (4-WD W/44FBJ Front Axle) — 1) Raise vehicle and support on safety stands. Remove brake caliper without disconnecting brake line as previously outlined.

2) Using tool C-4170, remove wheel bearing adjusting lock nut. Remove locking ring and wheel bearing adjusting nut.

3) Remove rotor assembly; outer wheel bearing and retainer spring plate will slide out as rotor is removed.

NOTE — *Special tools and procedures are required to remove and install inner wheel bearings. See Front Axle Shafts and Bearings in the Dana/Spicer Full-Floating Axle Article in the Drive Axle Section. The following installation procedure is after inner bearings have been installed in rotor hub.*

Installation — 1) Mount rotor on spindle. Position inner wheel bearing in place and install inner lock nut using tool C-4170, and tighten to 50 ft. lbs. to seat bearings. Loosen inner lock nut and retighten to 30-40 ft. lbs. while rotating hub. Back off inner lock nut 135 to 150°.

2) Position locking washer by turning nut so that the pin pressed into the lock nut will enter the nearest hole in locking washer. Install and tighten outer lock nut to 50 ft. lbs. Replace caliper assembly.

Removal (4-WD W/Model 60 Front Axle) — 1) Raise vehicle and support on safety stands. Remove brake caliper without disconnecting brake line as previously outlined.

2) Remove grease cover from end of hub. Remove snap ring from drive axle. Remove flange bolts and flange from hub.

3) Straighten lock tabs on outer wheel bearing lock ring. Using a suitable socket (DD-1241-JD) remove outer lock nut, lock ring, inner nut and outer wheel bearing. Remove rotor and hub assembly.

Installation — Install rotor and hub in position on spindle. Install outer bearing and inner lock nut and adjust wheel bearings. *See Wheel Bearing Adjustment in WHEEL ALIGNMENT Section.* Reverse removal procedure for remaining components.

OVERHAUL

BRAKE CALIPER

Disassembly — 1) Raise vehicle off floor and remove wheel. Remove retainer and anti-rattle spring assemblies. Carefully slide caliper out and away from rotor and support assembly on axle and steering linkage.

2) On vehicles equipped with single piston caliper, carefully depress brake pedal to hydraulically push piston out of bore in caliper. Pedal will fall away when piston has passed bore opening. Prop pedal in any position below first inch of travel to prevent fluid loss.

CAUTION — *Under no conditions should air pressure be used to remove piston from bore.*

3) Disconnect brake hose and remove caliper from vehicle. Remove dust boot and piston seal.

NOTE — *Use wooden or plastic rod to work seal out of groove in piston bore to prevent damage to cylinder.*

Inspection — Clean all parts with alcohol and blow dry with compressed air. Inspect piston bore for scoring or pitting. Light scratches or corrosion can be removed by honing, providing bore diameter is not increased more than .002". Discard used piston seal and boot.

Reassembly (W350/450 & W250 Extra) — Lubricate new piston seal with clean brake fluid and install into groove in cylinder bore, working around circumference with fingers until fully seated. Ensure seal is not twisted. Lubricate new piston boot with brake fluid, and install into caliper by working into outer groove. Plug inlet and bleeder screw hole, lubricate piston and with fingers spreading boot, press piston into boot until boot is forced into groove around piston. Remove plug, and carefully push piston down until bottomed.

Reassembly (All Other Models) — Lubricate new piston seal with brake fluid and install to groove in bore, working around circumference with fingers until fully seated. Ensure seal is not twisted. Coat new boot with brake fluid (leaving a generous amount inside boot) and install to piston. Install piston into bore, pushing past piston seal until bottomed in bore. Position dust boot in counterbore, and using boot installing tools (C-4890 and C-4171), drive boot into counterbore.

CHRYSLER CORP. SLIDING CALIPER DISCS (Cont.)

DISC ROTOR

Mount dial indicator on steering arm with contact tip of indicator against braking surface, approximately 1″ from edge of rotor. Temporarily adjust wheel bearings to zero end play. Measure lateral runout on both sides of rotor. Using micrometer, measure thickness at 12 equally spaced locations around rotor, approximately 1″ from edge. If rotor is scored, warped, or not within specifications, refinish or replace.

CAUTION — If rotor is to be refaced, do not remove more than .015″ of material from each side of rotor.

TIGHTENING SPECIFICATIONS

Application	Ft. Lbs.
Caliper Adapter Bolts	
All with ½″ Bolts	95-125
All with ⅝″ Bolts	140-180

DISC BRAKE SPECIFICATIONS

Application	Dimension
Rotor Thickness	
B, D & P150/250, MB250, AD, AW, PD & PW150,	
(B, CB, MB & PB350 w/3600 lb. Fr. Axle)	1.25″
All Other Models	1.19″
Thickness Variation	
B, D, PB150/250, MB250, AD, AW, & PD150	
B, CB, MB & PB350	.0005″
All Other Models	.001″
Lateral Runout	
B, D, & PB150/250, MB250, AD, AW, PD & PW150	
B, CB, MB & PB350	.004″
All Other Models	.005″

Brake Systems

FORD SLIDING CALIPER DISCS

All Models (Front)

DESCRIPTION

All Ford models equipped with front disc brakes use the sliding caliper type. All 100, 150 and 250 Series (up to 6900 GVW) use a single piston type. All 250 Series (over 6900 GVW) and 350 Series use a dual piston type. On all models, caliper is secured to anchor plate by a retaining key and spring. Ventilated rotor is cast with wheel hub. As brake pedal is depressed, fluid from master cylinder passes through the metering valve and into caliper cylinder.

ADJUSTMENT & SERVICING

DISC PAD ADJUSTMENT

Pad wear is automatically compensated for by piston sliding outward in cylinder bore; therefore, no disc pad adjustment in service is required.

BLEEDING SYSTEM

See Hydraulic Brake Bleeding in this Section.

REMOVAL & INSTALLATION

DISC BRAKE PADS

NOTE — *Always replace both disc brake pads on an axle together. Never service one wheel only.*

Removal (Single Piston Type) — 1) To prevent master cylinder overflow when caliper is depressed, remove a small amount of brake fluid from master cylinder. Raise vehicle and remove front wheel. Place a large "C" clamp on caliper, and tighten clamp to bottom piston in cylinder bore. Remove clamp.

2) Remove key retaining screw, then, using a brass rod and light hammer, drive out caliper support spring. Remove caliper from spindle by pushing it downward against spindle and rotating upper end upward and out of spindle.

CAUTION — *Lay caliper on tie rod or support with wire. Do not allow caliper to hang from brake line.*

3) Remove outer disc pad from caliper. It may be necessary to tap pad to loosen pad flange from caliper. Remove inner disc pad from spindle assembly, then remove pad anti-rattle clip from spindle.

Installation — 1) Install new anti-rattle clip in spindle. Place lower end of inner pad into spindle against anti-rattle clip and slide upper end of pad into position. Be sure clip is still in position.

2) With caliper piston fully bottomed in cylinder bore, position outer pad on caliper and press shoe tabs into place. If shoe cannot be pressed into place by hand, use a large "C" clamp. To complete installation, reverse removal procedure.

Removal (Dual Piston Type) — 1) To prevent master cylinder overflow when caliper is depressed, remove a small amount of brake fluid from master cylinder. Raise vehicle and remove front wheel. Remove key retaining screw.

2) Using a brass rod, and light hammer, drive out key and spring. Remove caliper by rotating key and spring end out away from rotor. Slide opposite end of caliper clear of slide in the support and off the rotor. Do not allow caliper to hang from brake line. Remove caliper disc pad anti-rattle spring. Remove inner and outer disc pad.

Installation — 1) Make sure caliper pistons are fully bottomed in caliper. Install disc pads and anti-rattle spring. Place caliper rail into the slide on support and rotate caliper onto rotor.

2) Place key and spring into position and start inserting between caliper and support. Use a screwdriver if necessary to hold caliper up against support.

NOTE — *Spring is between key and caliper and spring tangs overlap ends of key.*

3) Drive key and spring into position aligning correct notch with existing hole in support. Install key retaining screw and tighten to 12-20 ft. lbs. Check brake fluid level in master cylinder and fill as necessary.

BRAKE CALIPER

Removal & Installation — Caliper removal and installation procedures are same as for disc pad replacement, except it will be necessary to disconnect brake hose. After caliper installation, bleed brake system

DISC ROTOR

Removal (2-WD Models) — Raise vehicle and install safety stands. Remove wheel, tire and caliper assembly. Remove dust cap, cotter pin, nut, washer and outer bearing. Carefully remove hub and rotor assembly from spindle.

Installation — To install hub and rotor assembly, reverse removal procedures and adjust front wheel bearings. *See Wheel Bearing Adjustment in WHEEL ALIGNMENT Section.*

Removal (4-WD Models) — Raise and support vehicle on safety stands. Remove wheel and tire. Remove locking hub assembly as outlined in *Locking Hub article in DRIVE AXLE Section.* Remove wheel bearing lock nut, and adjusting nut using a suitable spanner (T59T-1197 for F100/250 and Bronco, T78T-1197-A for F350). Remove hub and disc assembly.

Installation — To install, reverse removal procedures, ensuring that both hub dials are in the same position. Adjust wheel bearings. *See Wheel Bearing Adjustment in Wheel Alignment Section.*

OVERHAUL

BRAKE CALIPER

Disassembly (Single & Dual Piston) — 1) Remove caliper as previously outlined. Remove plug from inlet port (if equipped) and drain fluid from cylinders. Place a block of wood between caliper and cylinders. Apply low air pressure to brake hose inlet. Air pressure will force out piston(s).

FORD SLIDING CALIPER DISCS (Cont.)

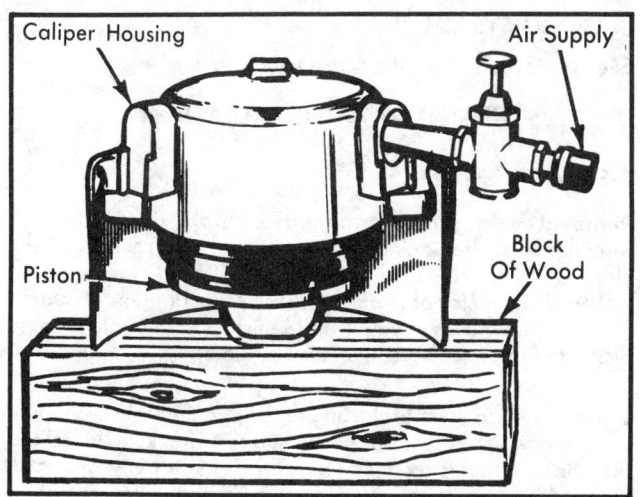

Fig. 1   Using Compressed Air to Remove Caliper Piston

2) If a piston is jammed or cocked and will not easily come out, tap end of piston sharply with a brass hammer to straighten. Do not pry piston from bore. Reapply low air pressure to remove cocked piston. Remove seal and boot from grooves. Discard seals and boots.

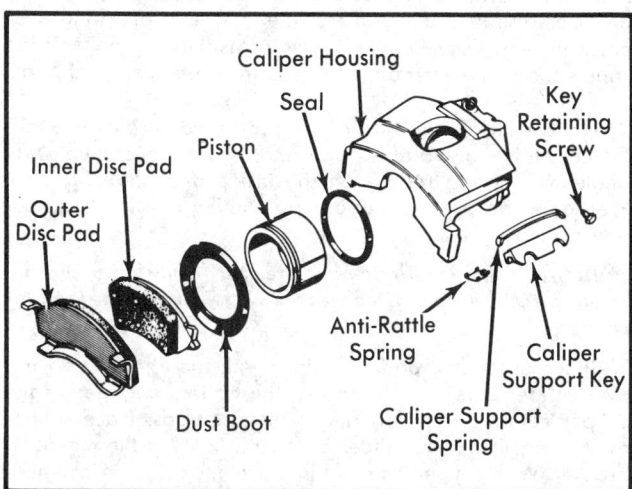

Fig. 2   Exploded View of Single Piston Caliper

Cleaning & Inspection — Clean rust and corrosion from caliper machined surfaces with a wire brush, being careful not to get wire brush in clyinder bores. Clean all components with denatured alcohol and dry with compressed air. Inspect cylinder bore, seal grooves and boot grooves for wear or damage. Replace anti-rattle clip, caliper support spring and key.

Reassembly (Single Piston) — **1)** Lubricate piston seal with clean brake fluid and install in cylinder bore groove. Lubricate cylinder with clean brake fluid. Coat piston and outside beads of dust boot with clean brake fluid. Push piston through boot until boot is around bottom (closed end) of piston.

2) Position piston and boot directly over cylinder bore. Work bead of dust boot into groove near top of cylinder bore. With bead seated in groove, press straight down on piston until it

bottoms in cylinder bore. Care must be taken not to cock or jam piston in cylinder. If necessary use a "C" clamp and a block of wood to bottom piston in cylinder.

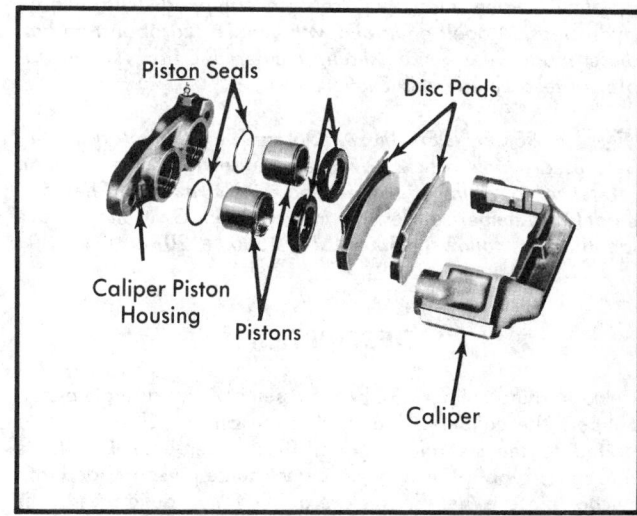

Fig. 3   Exploded View of Dual Piston Caliper

Reassembly (Dual Piston) — **1)** Lubricate new piston seals with clean brake fluid and install seals in grooves in cylinders. Lubricate cylinders with clean brake fluid. Lubricate retaining lips of boots with clean brake fluid and install in grooves in cylinders.

2) Coat pistons with clean brake fluid. Insert into cylinders by hand until they are beyond piston seals. Positon a wood block over one piston and press into cylinder, taking care not to cock piston. Install other piston in same manner.

DISC ROTOR SERVICING

Maximum of .020" material may be taken equally off each braking surface. Fininshed braking surfaces of rotor must be parallel within .0007" for integral hub and disc and .001" or separate hub and disc.

BRAKE SPECIFICATIONS

Application	Dimension
Disc Pad Wear Limit....................	.030" Above Rivet Head
Caliper Piston Diameter	
Single & Dual Piston Type	①2.875"
Resurface Rotor Thickness (Minimum)	
F100 4600 GVW w/Power Brakes	.81"
All Other Single Piston Type	1.120"
Dual Piston Type	1.180"
Rotor Run-Out (Maximum)	
Integral Hub Type	.003"
Separate Hub Type	.010"
Rotor Thickness Variation (Maximum)	
F100 4600 GVW w/Power Brakes	.0005"
F100/350 & Bronco	
w/Integral Hub & Rotor	.005"
All Other Integral Hub & Rotor	.0007"
All Separate Hub & Rotor	.001"

① — F100 4600 GVW w/Power Brakes 2.597".

Brake Systems

GENERAL MOTORS FLOATING CALIPER DISCS

Chevrolet
GMC

NOTE — *Delco floating caliper disc brakes are used on all gasoline engine models, except if equipped with Bendix Hydroboost. Models equipped with Bendix Hydroboost and all diesel models use Bendix sliding caliper disc brakes. See appropriate article in this Section.*

NOTE — *SERIES IDENTIFICATION — The vehicle series numbers used in this article have been abbreviated for common reference to both Chevrolet and GMC models. Chevrolet models use numerical designations as listed. GMC models are identified as follows: 1500 = 10; 2500 = 20; 3500 = 30.*

DESCRIPTION

Delco floating caliper disc brake assembly uses a single piston caliper. The caliper is mounted to an anchor plate which is bolted to the steering knuckle. The caliper assembly floats through 4 rubber bushings on 2 steel guide pins threaded into anchor plate. When brakes are applied, hydraulic pressure is passed to caliper piston. This force is transmitted to inner brake pad against inner rotor braking surface. Pressure then moves caliper inward on guide pins, thus forcing outer disc pad against outer rotor braking surface. When brakes are released, pressure is removed from cylinder and rotor runout moves piston back into caliper cylinder to maintain sufficient rotor-to-pad clearance.

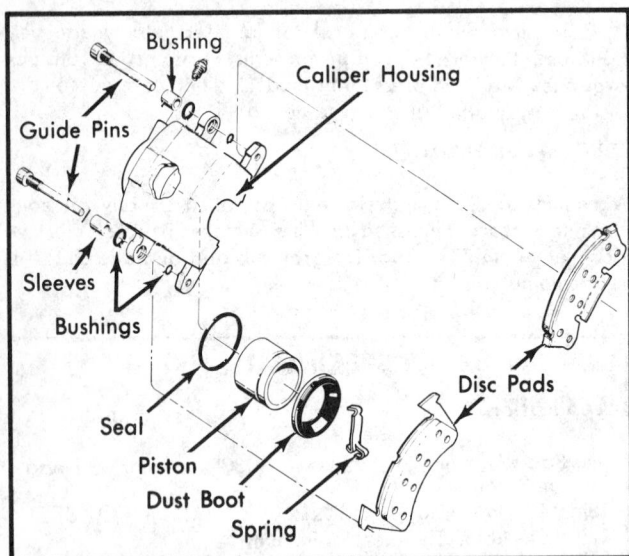

Fig. 1   Exploded View of Floating Caliper Assembly

ADJUSTMENT & SERVICING

DISC PAD ADJUSTMENT

Pad wear is automatically compensated for by piston moving outward in cylinder bore; therefore, no disc pad adjustment in service is required.

NOTE — *Inspect condition of disc pads whenever wheels are removed. If any disc pad is worn to within $\frac{1}{32}$" of rivet heads, replace complete disc pad set.*

BLEEDING SYSTEM

See Hydraulic Brake Bleeding in this Section.

REMOVAL & INSTALLATION

DISC BRAKE PADS

Removal — 1) Remove two-thirds of brake fluid from front reservoir in master cylinder. Raise vehicle and remove wheel. Place a 7" "C" clamp on caliper so that solid side of clamp rests against metal part of outer disc pad. Tighten "C" clamp until caliper moves away from vehicle far enough to push piston to bottom of bore. Remove "C" clamp.

2) Do not disconnect brake line to caliper. Remove two mounting bolts which secure caliper to support bracket. Lift caliper off rotor and remove inner disc pad. Pry out outer disc pad. Place caliper on front suspension arm so that caliper weight is not hanging on brake hose. Remove shoe support spring from cavity in piston. Remove sleeves from inner ear in caliper. Remove rubber bushings from grooves in each of four caliper ears.

Installation — 1) Install new rubber bushings in four caliper ears. Use a suitable installation tool (J-22835) to install sleeves in bushings. Position sleeves so that end toward disc pad is flush with machined surface of ear. Install shoe support spring on inner disc pad. Place the single tang end of spring over notch in center edge of pad. Now press the two tangs at the spring end of the inner disc pad over the bottom edge of pad.

2) Place inner disc pad with spring attached in caliper so that the ear end of disc pad is down and the bottom end up at an angle with spring resting on the inside diameter of piston. Press down on both ends of disc pad until pad is in a flat position resting on piston.

CAUTION — *The inner disc pads are specifically left and right, when correctly installed, the wear sensor will be toward rear of caliper.*

3) Place outer disc pad in caliper with the ears at pad top over caliper ears and the tab at the bottom engaged in the caliper cut-out. Note left and right disc pads. Place caliper over rotor, lining up caliper ears with holes in the mounting bracket. With caliper installed in place, make sure brake hose is not twisted.

4) Start bolts through sleeves in inner caliper ears and through mounting bracket. Make sure that the bolts pass under the retaining ears in the inner disc pad. Push bolts through the holes in the outer disc pads and caliper ears. Thread bolts into mounting bracket. Tighten bolts to 35 ft. lbs.

5) Fill master cylinder with new brake fluid. Pump brake pedal several times to seat disc pads against rotor. Clinch upper ears of outer disc pad using a pair of channel lock pliers with one jaw on top of upper ear and other jaw on bottom of disc pad in notch. After clinching, ears should be flat against caliper housing with no radial clearance. If clearance exists, repeat procedure.

BRAKE CALIPER

Removal & Installation — Brake caliper removal and installation procedures are same as for disc brake pads, except it will be necessary to disconnect brake hose.

GENERAL MOTORS FLOATING CALIPER DISCS (Cont.)

DISC ROTOR

Removal (2-WD Models) — 1) Raise vehicle and position on safety stands. Remove brake caliper without disconnecting brake line as previously outlined.

2) Remove grease cover from end of hub. Remove cotter pin, nut, washer and outer bearing. Remove rotor and hub assembly.

Installation — Install rotor and hub assembly on spindle. Install outer bearing, washer and nut. Adjust wheel bearing. *See Wheel Bearing Adjustment in WHEEL ALIGNMENT Section.*

Removal & Installation (4-WD Models) — Raise and support vehicle on saftey stands. Remove wheel and tire. Remove locking hub as outlined in *Locking Hub article in DRIVE AXLE Section.* Remove wheel bearing lock nut, lock ring and adjuster nut. Remove rotor and hub assembly. To install, reverse removal procedures and adjust wheel bearing. *See Wheel Bearing Adjustment in WHEEL ALIGNMENT Section.*

OVERHAUL

BRAKE CALIPER

Disassembly — Clean exterior of caliper with denatured alcohol and place on clean work surface. Remove brake hose, discarding copper gasket. Drain brake fluid from caliper. Use clean shop towels to pad interior of caliper and use compressed air introduced at caliper inlet to remove piston. Use just enough pressure to ease piston out of bore. Use screwdriver to pry boot out of caliper housing. Remove piston seal from its groove in caliper bore, using a piece of wood or plastic. Do not use metal tool of any type to remove piston seal. Remove bleeder valve from housing.

Inspection — 1) Boot, seal, rubber bushings and sleeves are to be replaced each time caliper is overhauled. Clean all other parts in denatured alcohol. Dry parts with dry, filtered compressed air.

NOTE — *Using lubricated shop air will leave a film of mineral oil on metal parts. This may damage rubber parts upon contact during reassembly.*

2) Check guide pins for corrosion, breaks in plating or other damage. Do not attempt to clean pins; replace them. Check outside diameter of piston for scoring, nicks, corrosion, and worn or damaged plating. If surface defects exist, piston must be replaced.

3) Piston bore should be checked for similar defects. Bore is not plated, therefore, it may be polished with crocus cloth. Thoroughly clean after polishing. Replace caliper housing if bore corrosion cannot easily be cleaned out.

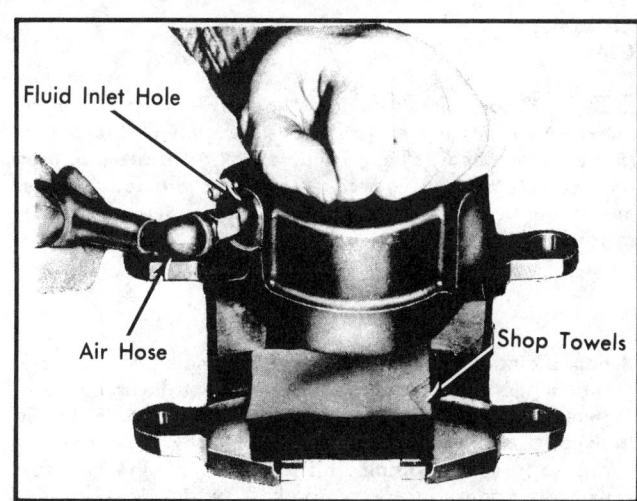

Fig. 2 Using Compressed Air to Remove Caliper Piston

Reassembly — Lubricate bore in caliper housing and new piston seal with clean brake fluid. Position seal in caliper bore groove. Lubricate piston with clean brake fluid and assemble new boot into groove in piston with fold facing open end of piston. Insert piston into caliper bore using care not to unseat seal. Force piston to bottom of bore. Position outer diameter of boot in caliper counterbore and drive in until fully seated. Check boot installation to ensure retaining ring (molded into boot) is not bent, and that boot is installed completely below caliper face. Install brake hose, using new copper gasket.

DISC ROTOR

Lateral Runout — Adjust wheel bearings until all endplay is eliminated. Attach dial indicator with contact tip of indicator approximately one inch from rotor edge. Set indicator to zero and turn rotor through one complete revolution, noting indicator reading.

Parallelism — Check thickness of rotor at four or more points around circumference of rotor. Make all measurements at same distance from edge of rotor. If thickness variation is excessive, refinish or replace rotor as necessary.

TIGHTENING SPECIFICATIONS

Application	Ft. Lbs.
Brake Hose-to-Caliper	32
Caliper Mounting Bolts	35

Application	INCH Lbs.
Hydraulic Line-to-Brake Hose	150
Support Plate-to-Knuckle Bolts	140

DISC BRAKE SPECIFICATIONS

Application	Disc Diameter	Lateral Runout	Parallelism	Original Thickness	Minimum Refinish Thickness	Discard Thickness
All 10 Series & G20	11.86"	.004"	.0005"	1.280"	1.230"	1.215"
All Remaining Models	12.5"①	.004"	.0005"	1.280"②	1.230"③	1.215"③

① — 14.25" rotor on some P30 models.
② — 12.50" x 1.53" rotor on some 30 series models.
③ — For models with 1.53" original thickness rotors, refinish thickness 1.48", discard at 1.465" thickness.

GENERAL MOTORS SLIDING CALIPER DISCS

Chevrolet
GMC

NOTE — *Bendix sliding caliper disc brakes are used on all diesel engine models and all models equipped with Bendix Hydro-boost. Bendix sliding caliper disc brakes are also used on models equipped with four-wheel disc brakes. All other models use Delco floating caliper disc brakes. See appropriate article in this section.*

DESCRIPTION

Bendix sliding caliper disc brakes use a single piston caliper. Front calipers are attached to a mount integral with the steering knuckle. Rear calipers are mounted to an adapter bolted to the drive axle. When brakes are applied, hydraulic pressure is passed to caliper piston. This force is transmitted to inner brake pad against inner rotor braking surface. Pressure then moves caliper inward, thus forcing outer disc pads against outer braking surface. When brakes are released, pressure is removed from caliper cylinder and rotor runout moves piston back into caliper cylinder to maintain sufficient rotor-to-pad clearance.

ADJUSTMENT & SERVICING

DISC PAD ADJUSTMENT

Pad wear is automatically compensated for by piston moving outward in cylinder bore; therefore, no disc pad adjustment in service is required. Inspect condition of disc pads whenever wheels are removed. If any pad is worn to within 1/32" of rivet heads, replace complete pad set.

PARKING BRAKE

See Parking Brake Adjustment in General Motors Single Anchor Brake System in this Section.

BLEEDING SYSTEM

See Hydraulic Brake Bleeding in this Section.

REMOVAL & INSTALLATION

DISC BRAKE PADS

Removal — **1)** To prevent master cylinder overflow when caliper is depressed, remove two-thirds of the brake fluid from master cylinder. Raise vehicle and remove wheel. Place a large "C" clamp on caliper and tighten clamp to bottom piston in cylinder bore. Remove clamp.

2) Remove key retaining screw, then using a brass rod and a light hammer, drive out caliper support key and caliper support spring. Remove caliper by pushing down against mount and rotating upward and away from mount.

CAUTION — *Support caliper with wire. DO NOT let caliper hang with weight on brake hose.*

3) Remove inner disc pad and shoe clip from caliper. Remove outer disc pad from caliper. It may be necessary to tap pad to loosen it in caliper housing.

Installation — **1)** Lubricate caliper and mount sliding surfaces with silicone lubricant. Install new anti-rattle clip in mount. Place lower end of inner pad into mount and against anti-rattle clip, then slide upper end of pad into position. Be sure clip is still in correct position.

2) With caliper piston fully bottomed in cylinder bore, position outer pad on caliper and press tabs into place. If pad cannot be properly positioned by hand, use a large "C" clamp, taking care not to mar lining.

3) With disc pads installed, lift caliper and rest bottom edge of outer pad on outer edge of rotor and ensure there is no clearance between bottom tab of outer pad and caliper abutment. Outer pad should be tight in caliper housing.

4) Position caliper on mounting surface. Place spring over support key and tap into place until key retaining screw can be installed. Tighten screw and replace fluid in master cylinder. Reinstall wheel and lower vehicle.

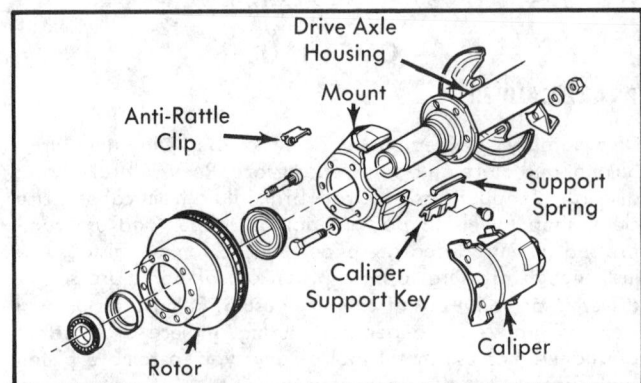

Fig. 1   Rear Sliding Caliper Disc Brake Components

BRAKE CALIPER

Removal & Installation — Caliper removal and installation procedures are the same as those for disc pad replacement, except it will be necessary to disconnect brake hose. Use new copper washers when reconnecting brake hose.

DISC ROTOR

Removal (2-WD Models) — **1)** Raise vehicle and position on safety stands. Remove brake caliper without disconnecting brake line as previously outlined.

2) Remove grease cover from end of hub. Remove cotter pin, nut, washer and outer bearing. Remove rotor and hub assembly.

Installation — Install rotor and hub assembly on spindle. Install outer bearing, washer and nut. Adjust wheel bearing. See *Wheel Bearing Adjustment in WHEEL ALIGNMENT Section.*

Removal & Installation (4-WD Models) — Raise and support vehicle on saftey stands. Remove wheel and tire. Remove locking hub as outlined in *Locking Hub article in DRIVE AXLE Section.* Remove wheel bearing lock nut, lock ring and adjuster nut. Remove rotor and hub assembly. To install, reverse removal procedures and adjust wheel bearing. See *Wheel Bearing Adjustment in WHEEL ALIGNMENT Section.*

GENERAL MOTORS SLIDING CALIPER DISCS (Cont.)

Removal (Optional Rear Wheel Disc Brakes) – 1) Raise vehicle and position on safety stands. Remove brake caliper without disconnecting brake line as previously outlined.

2) Remove axle shaft flange bolts and remove drive axle. Bend lock tab on bearing lock nut and remove lock nut. Remove lock tab assembly. Remove inner bearing adjusting nut and washer. Remove rotor and hub assembly.

Installation – 1) Install rotor and hub assembly into position on axle housing. Install outer bearing and washer. Make sure tang on washer is aligned with groove in axle housing.

2) Install inner bearing nut and adjust wheel bearings. See *Wheel Bearing Adjustment* in *WHEEL ALIGNMENT* Section.

3) Install drive axle shaft using a new flange gasket. Tighten bolts to 115 Ft. Lbs. Install brake caliper as previously outlined.

OVERHAUL

BRAKE CALIPER

Disassembly – 1) With caliper assembly clean, to prevent contamination, remove plug from caliper inlet port and drain fluid from caliper housing. Place caliper assembly on bench with piston side up and place several shop towels between piston and outer legs of caliper housing.

2) Slowly and carefully apply air pressure to caliper inlet port until piston comes out of caliper housing. If piston is seized, free by tapping lightly on and around end of piston with soft-faced hammer.

CAUTION – *Use low air pressure to remove piston. DO NOT place fingers in front of piston when removing, as personal injury may result.*

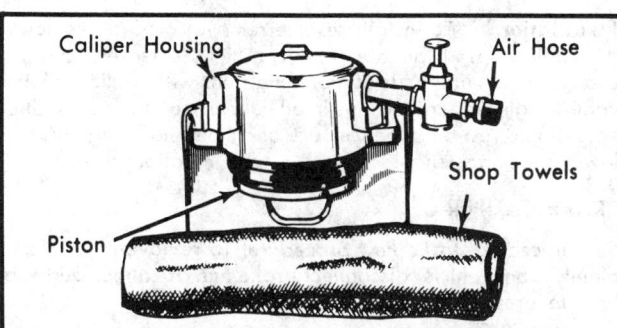

Fig. 2 Using Compressed Air to Remove Caliper Piston

3) Remove boot from piston and seal from cylinder bore. Clean caliper housing and piston with denatured alcohol. Check cylinder bore, seal groove, and boot groove for damage and excessive wear. Replace piston if pitted.

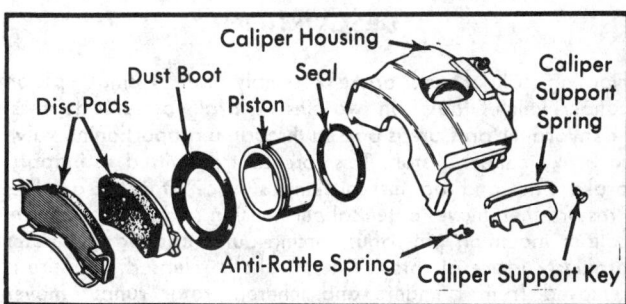

Fig. 3 Exploded View of Sliding Caliper Assembly

Reassembly – To assemble caliper, soak all parts in suitable brake fluid and reverse disassembly procedure. Use large C-clamp to seat piston in cylinder bore.

DISC ROTOR

Lateral Runout – Adjust wheel bearings until all endplay is eliminated. Attach dial indicator with contact tip of indicator on braking surface approximately one inch from rotor edge. Set indicator to zero and turn rotor through one complete revolution, noting indicator reading.

Parallelism – Check thickness of rotor at four or more points around circumference of rotor. Make all measurements at same distance from edge of rotor. If thickness variation is excessive, refinish or replace rotor as necessary.

TIGHTENING SPECIFICATIONS

Application	Ft. Lbs.
Brake Line-to-Caliper	32
Support Key Retaining Screw	18
Caliper Mounting Bolts	35

Application	INCH Lbs.
Hydraulic Line-to-Brake Hose	150
Bleeder Valve Screws	60

DISC BRAKE ROTOR SPECIFICATIONS

Application	Disc Diameter	Lateral Runout	Parallelism	Original Thickness	Minimum Refinish Thickness	Discard Thickness
Diesel Engine Models	11.86"	.004"	.0005"	1.280"	1.230"	1.215"
All Others						
Front (Drum Rear)	12.50"	.004"	.0005"	1.530"	1.480"	1.465"
Front (Disc Rear)	14.25"	.004"	.0005"	1.530"	1.480"	1.465"
Rear①	13.75"	.004"	.0005"	1.530"	1.480"	1.465"

① – Optional on "P" models and Motor Home Chassis with 11,000 lb. axle.

JEEP FLOATING CALIPER DISCS

Cherokee
"J" Models
Wagoneer

DESCRIPTION

Floating caliper disc brake assembly uses a single piston caliper which "floats" on two pins. As brake pedal is depressed, hydraulic pressure is passed through a proportioning valve to brake caliper piston. This force is transmitted to inboard brake pad and against braking surface of rotor or disc. Pressure then moves outer caliper housing and pad inward on caliper mounting pins, thus forcing outer pad against outer braking surface of rotor. When brake is released, pressure is removed from cylinders and inherent rotor runout moves pistons back into cylinders to maintain sufficient rotor-to-pad clearance.

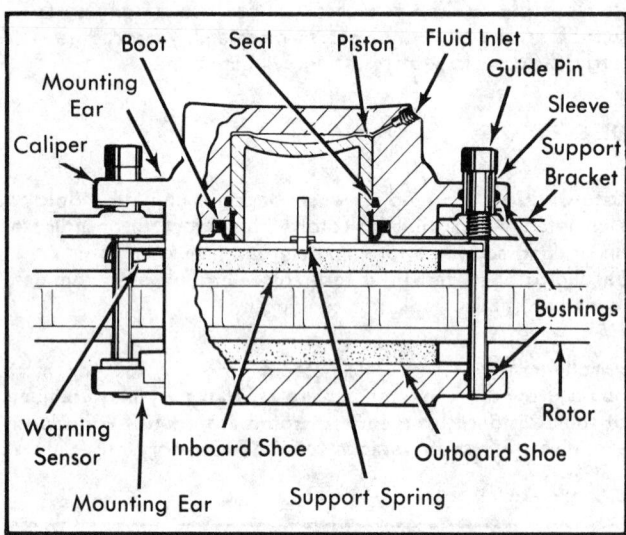

Fig. 1 Cutaway View of Jeep Floating Caliper

ADJUSTMENT & SERVICING

DISC PAD ADJUSTMENT

Automatic adjustment is provided by outward relocation of piston as lining wears.

BLEEDING SYSTEM

See Hydraulic Brake Bleeding in this Section.

REMOVAL & INSTALLATION

BRAKE PADS

Removal — 1) Drain 2/3 of brake fluid from front reservoir using bleeder screw at front outlet port. Raise and support vehicle and remove front wheels. Place "C" clamp on caliper. Solid end of clamp should contact back of caliper, and screw end should contact metal part of outboard shoes. Tighten clamp until caliper moves far enough to force piston to bottom of bore. This will back shoes off rotor surface, easing lining removal and installation.

Fig. 2 Using a "C" Clamp to Bottom Caliper Piston

2) Remove both Allen head mounting bolts and lift caliper off rotor. Rest caliper on front spring or other suitable support. Do not allow brake hose to support weight of caliper. Remove both shoe and lining assemblies (pads). Remove support spring from inboard shoe and note spring position for correct installation later. Remove sleeves from inboard ears of caliper. Remove rubber bushings from all holes in caliper ears.

Installation — To install, reverse removal procedures noting the following: Lubricate new bushings, sleeves, bushing grooves and small ends of mounting bolts with a silicone lubricant. Install rubber bushings in all caliper mounting ears. Shoe ears should rest on upper surface of caliper mounting ears and lower shoe tabs should fit into cutout in caliper.

BRAKE CALIPER

See preceding Brake Pad procedure. To remove caliper completely from vehicle, disconnect brake line at caliper and tape hole to prevent contamination.

DISC ROTOR

Removal — Raise vehicle and support with safety stands. Remove wheel and caliper. On models without front hubs, remove rotor hub cap, drive gear snap ring, drive gear, pressure spring and spring cup. On models with front hubs, remove screws attaching hub body to hub clutch and remove body from clutch. Remove large and small retaining rings. Remove hub clutch from axle shaft. On all models, straighten lip of outer locknut retaining washer. Remove wheel bearing locknuts and washers. Remove rotor and wheel bearings.

Installation — 1) Lubricate bearings with EP-type water proof wheel bearing lubricant. Install bearing and new seal in rotor hub. Install rotor and inner lock nut and retaining washer.

NOTE — *Bearing adjuster inner lock nut has locating peg on one side. When installed, peg must face away from bearing.*

JEEP FLOATING CALIPER DISCS (Cont.)

2) Install wheel but do not tighten nuts. While rotating wheel, tighten inner locknut to 50 ft. lbs., and then back off ⅙ turn. Install outer locknut and retaining washer. Tighten outer locknut to 50 ft. lbs.

NOTE — *Be sure locating peg is engaged in one of the retaining washer holes before installing outer lock nut.*

3) On models without front hubs, install pressure spring cup, pressure spring, drive gear and snap ring. Coat rim of chrome hub cap with Permatex No. 3 (or equivalent) and install cap in rotor hub.

CAUTION — *Spring cup must be installed so recessed side of cup faces outboard bearing and flat side of cup faces pressure spring.*

4) On models with front hubs, install hub clutch on axle. Install large and small hub retaining rings. Install hub body on clutch and tighten to 30 INCH Lbs.

5) On all models, remove drive wheel and install caliper. Reinstall wheel and wheel cover if equipped.

OVERHAUL

Disassembly — **1)** Remove caliper from vehicle and remove pads. If pads are to be reused, mark location in caliper. Clean caliper exterior with clean brake fluid. Drain residual fluid from caliper and place it on a clean working surface. Remove piston from caliper by applying compressed air to fluid port.

CAUTION — *Use just enough pressure to ease piston out of bore. Protect piston from damage with folded cloths, do not try to catch piston with fingers, serious injury could result.*

2) Pry dust boot out of bore with screwdriver. Do not scratch bore. Using a small plastic or wooden stick, pry piston seal from bore. Remove bleeder screw, sleeves and rubber bushings. Clean all parts in clean brake fluid. Blow parts dry with dry, filtered compressed air.

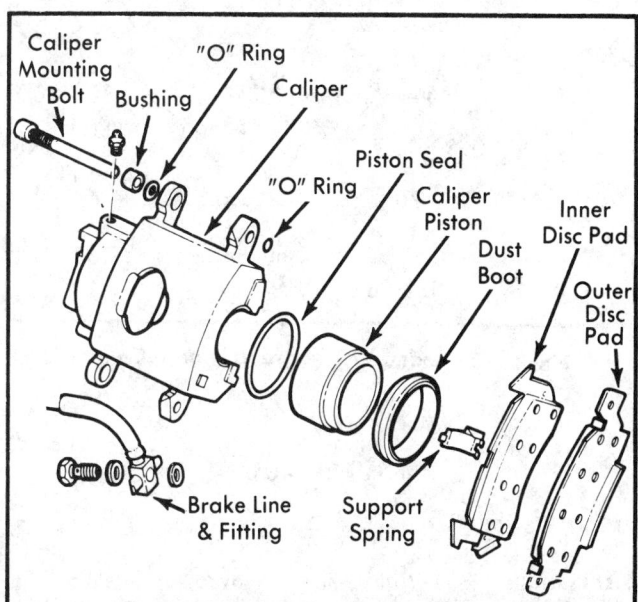

Fig. 3   Exploded View of Floating Disc Brake Caliper Assembly

NOTE — *Do not clean bolts with abrasives, as protective plating may be removed.*

3) Examine parts for rust, corrosion, pitting, scratches, or cracks. Do not attempt to refinish piston in any way. Removal of nickel-chrome plating will lead to pitting, rusting, and eventual cocking in bore. Minor stains on piston bore can be polished with crocus cloth only. Do not use emery cloth or any other abrasive. Wash bore thoroughly with brake fluid after using crocus cloth.

Reassembly — **1)** Lubricate bore and new seal with brake fluid and install seal in groove using fingers. Lubricate piston with brake fluid and install new dust boot on piston. Slide metal retainer portion of dust boot over open end of piston and push retainer towards end of piston until lip on fold seats in piston groove.

2) Push retainer portion of boot forward until boot is flush with rim at open end of piston and snaps into place. Insert piston in bore being careful not to unseat piston seal. Push piston to bottom of bore using hammer handle (approximately 50 lbs. of force are necessary). Position dust boot retainer in counterbore at top of piston.

3) Seat dust boot retainer with suitable tool (J-22904). Metal retainer portion of boot must be evenly seated in counterbore and fit below face of caliper. Install bleeder screw. Connect brake line to caliper using new copper gaskets. Install pads as outlined in *Pad Removal and Installation in this story.* Install caliper over rotor, bleed brakes and install wheel. Test system before moving vehicle.

ROTOR

Runout — Measure rotor lateral runout by mounting a dial indicator on support stand or steering spindle. Position indicator stylus so it contacts center of rotor lining. Zero indicator and turn rotor 360°. Note indicator reading. Runout must not exceed specifications. Refinish if necessary.

Parallelism — Measure rotor parallelism with a micrometer. Measure thickness at 4 or more equally spaced points around rotor circumference and 1″ inward from outside edge of rotor. Variation must not exceed specification. Refinish if necessary.

NOTE — *Replace rotor if machining will cause it to fall below minimum thickness specification.*

BRAKE SPECIFICATIONS

Application	Dimension
Rotor Diameter	
J20	12.5″
All Others	12.0″
Rotor Thickness (Minimum)	1.215″
Parallelism	.001″
Rotor Lateral Runout	.005″

TIGHTENING SPECIFICATIONS

Application	Torque
Bleeder Screw	40-140 INCH Lbs.
Brake Line-to-Caliper	160 INCH Lbs.
Caliper Mounting Bolts	30-40 ft.lbs.

Brake Systems

JEEP SLIDING CALIPER DISCS

"CJ" Models
Scrambler

DESCRIPTION

Sliding caliper disc brake assemblies are single piston type. Calipers are mounted to an anchor mount connected to front drive axle. As brake is depressed, hydraulic pressure is passed to brake caliper piston. This force is transmitted to inboard disc pad and against inner braking surface. As force increases against inner side, caliper slides inward, providing vise-like clamping action on rotor.

ADJUSTMENT & SERVICING

DISC PAD ADJUSTMENT

Pad wear is automatically compensated for by piston moving outward in cylinder bore; therefore, no disc pad adjustment in service is necessary.

BLEEDING SYSTEM

See Hydraulic Brake Bleeding in this Section

REMOVAL & INSTALLATION

DISC BRAKE PADS

Removal — 1) To prevent master cylinder overflow when caliper piston is depressed, remove two-thirds of the brake fluid from master cylinder reservoir. Raise vehicle and remove wheel.

2) Using a screwdriver or "C" clamp, press caliper piston to bottom of bore. Remove support key retaining screw. Drive out support key with a punch and hammer. Lift caliper assembly off anchor mount. Do not let caliper hang from brake line.

3) Remove inner disc pad from anchor mount. Remove anti-rattle spring from inner disc pad. Note position of spring for installation. Remove outer disc pad from caliper.

Installation — 1) Install anti-rattle spring on rear flange of inner disc pad. Make sure looped section of spring faces away from rotor. Install inner disc pad in anchor mount. Make sure anti-rattle spring stays in place.

2) Install outer disc pad in caliper. Place caliper in position over rotor and onto anchor mount. Care must be taken not to tear or dislodge dust boot when installing caliper.

3) Align caliper with anchor mount and install support key and support spring between abutment surfaces at trailing end of caliper and anchor mount. Drive support key into place with a punch and hammer.

4) Install support key screw and tighten to 15 ft. lbs. Fill master cylinder with new brake fluid. Press on brake pedal several times to seat disc brake pads. Install wheel and lower vehicle.

BRAKE CALIPER

Removal & Installation — Caliper removal and installation procedures are same for disc pad replacement, except it will be necessary to disconnect brake hose.

DISC ROTOR

Removal — 1) Raise vehicle and support on safety stands. Remove caliper as previously outlined. Remove bolts attaching hub body to hub clutch and remove hub body. Remove axle shaft retaining ring and remove hub clutch and bearing assembly.

2) Straighten lip of outer lock nut retaining washer. Remove outer lock nut, retaining washer, inner lock nut and inner retainer washer. Remove rotor and wheel bearings.

Installation — 1) Lubricate bearings with EP-type water proof wheel bearing lubricant. Install bearings in rotor, using new oil seal. Install rotor, tabbed inner washer and lock nut. Install wheel but do not tighten wheel nuts. Rotate wheel and tighten inner lock nut to 50 ft. lbs. to seat bearings.

2) Back off inner locknut 1/6 turn. Install outer tabbed washer and lock nut. Tighten lock nut to a minimum of 50 ft. lbs. and bend lip of tabbed washer over locknut. Install hub clutch and bearing assembly on axle shaft. Install retaining ring on axle shaft. Install hub body, gasket and bearing assembly. Align bolt holes in hub body and rotor hub and install bolts and lock washers. Install caliper and wheels.

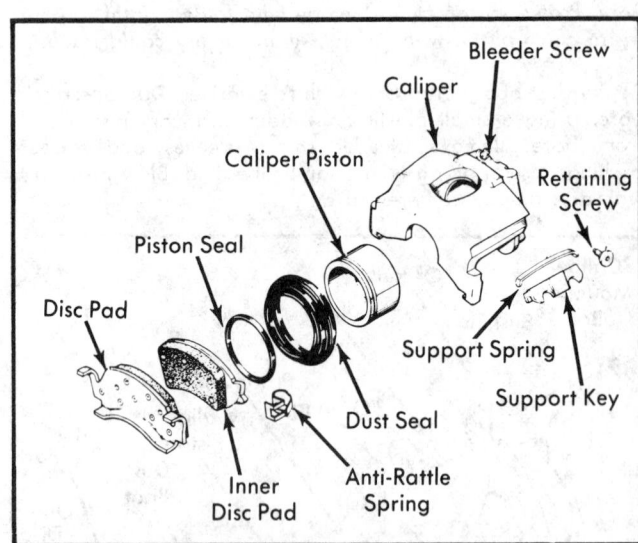

Fig. 1   Exploded View of Jeep Sliding Caliper

OVERHAUL

BRAKE CALIPER

Disassembly — 1) With caliper removed, drain fluid from caliper. Place caliper assembly on bench, piston side up. Place several shop towels between piston and outer legs of caliper housing.

JEEP SLIDING CALIPER DISCS (Cont.)

2) Slowly and carefully apply air pressure to caliper inlet port until piston comes out of caliper housing. Use low air pressure to remove piston, as high pressure may cause piston to pop out with considerable force.

3) Remove dust seal from piston. Remove piston seal from piston bore using a plastic or wooden tool to pry seal out.

CAUTION — *Do not place fingers in front of piston when removing as severe personal injury could result.*

4) Remove bleeder screw and plastic cap. Clean caliper housing and piston with denatured alcohol. Check cylinder bore, seal groove and boot groove for damage and excessive wear. Replace piston if pitted.

Reassembly — **1)** Lubricate piston seal with clean brake fluid and install seal in piston bore groove. Work seal into groove with finger. Install bleeder screw and plastic cap.

2) Place dust seal on piston bore. Do not lubricate seal. Reaching through top of seal, work large lip of seal into seal groove at top of piston bore. Make sure seal is completely seated in groove.

3) Lubricate caliper piston and small lip of dust seal with brake fluid and position piston over seal lip. Hold piston in place on dust seal. Apply reduced air pressure (air pressure should not exceed 15 psi) into caliper inlet port.

4) As air pressure expands dust seal, carefully work caliper piston into dust seal until small lip of seal seats in caliper piston groove. With seal seated in groove, release air pressure and push piston to bottom of bore using a hammer handle.

5) Install caliper as previously outlined. Install brake hose on caliper using a new washer. Tighten brake line bolt to 160 INCH lbs., or if equipped with brake line fitting, tighten fitting to 25 ft. lbs. Fill master cylinder and bleed system. Check brake application and refill master cylinder if necessary.

DISC ROTOR

Lateral Runout — Adjust wheel bearings until all endplay is eliminated. Attach dial indicator with contact tip of indicator on braking surface approximately one inch from rotor edge. Set indicator to zero and turn rotor through one revolution noting indicator reading. If runout exceeds specifications, replace or refinish rotor.

Parallelism — Check thickness of rotor at four or more points around circumferance of rotor. Make all measurements at same distance from edge of rotor. If thickness variation exceeds specifications, replace or refinish rotor.

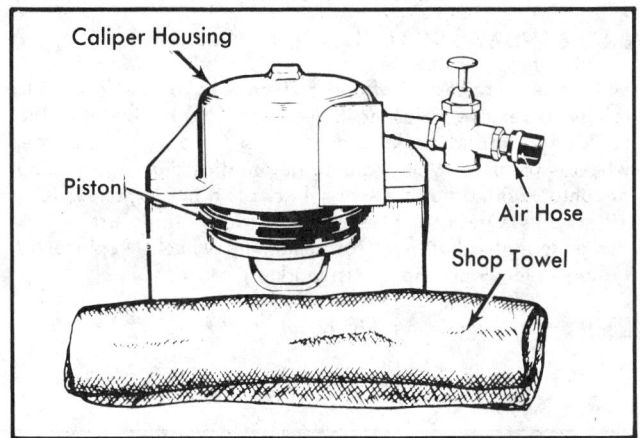

Fig. 2   Using Compressed Air to Remove Caliper Piston

TIGHTENING SPECIFICATIONS

Application	Torque
Brake Hose-to-Caliper	160 INCH Lbs.
Support Key Retaining Screw	15 ft. lbs.

DISC BRAKE ROTOR SPECIFICATIONS

Application	Disc Diameter	Lateral Runout	Parallelism	Original Thickness	Minimum Refinish Thickness	Discard Thickness
"CJ" & Scrambler Models	11.7"	.005"	.001"	.....	.815"	.814"

Brake Systems

CHRYSLER CORP. SINGLE ANCHOR

Dodge
Plymouth

DESCRIPTION

Chrysler Corp. vehicles use both their own and a Bendix type single anchor brake assembly. All 10" brakes are Chrysler type and all 12" and 13" brakes are Bendix type. Both types of brake assemblies consist of a support plate, two brake shoes, return springs, wheel cylinder and a cable type adjuster assembly. The automatic adjuster assembly consists of a cable (with hook and anchor fitting), cable guide, adjuster lever, adjusting screw, pivot, socket and spring.

ADJUSTMENT & SERVICING

BRAKE SHOE ADJUSTMENT

With wheels raised off floor and parking brake lever fully released, remove adjusting hole cover. Using a suitable tool (C-3784), expand brake shoes until slight drag is felt when wheel is rotated. While holding automatic adjusting lever out of contact with adjusting screw, back off adjusting screw 10 or 12 notches. Check for free wheel rotation with no brake shoe drag. Repeat adjustment for remaining wheels. Replace adjusting hole cover and adjust parking brake.

NOTE — *Adjustment must be equal at all wheels.*

BLEEDING SYSTEM

See *Hydraulic Brake Bleeding* in this Section.

PARKING BRAKE ADJUSTMENT

All Models (Exc. "B", "CB", "MB" & "PB") — With service brakes fully adjusted and parking brake fully released, tighten cable adjusting nut until a slight drag is felt while rotating rear wheels. Loosen cable adjusting nut until both rear wheels can be rotated freely, then back off adjusting nut an additional 2 turns. Apply and release parking brake several times, checking for free rotation at rear wheels.

"B", "CB", "MB", & "PB" Models — Raise vehicle high enough to gain access to equalizer and cable adjuster. Make sure parking brake cable adjuster is fully released. Loosen adjuster so there is slack in both cables. Make sure rear brakes are correctly adjusted. Tighten cable adjusting nut at the adjuster until a slight drag is felt while rotating the wheel. Loosen the adjusting nut until both wheels can be rotated freely. Apply and release parking brake, checking for free wheel rotation.

REMOVAL & INSTALLATION

BRAKE SHOES

Removal — Chrysler Brake Assembly (10") — With drum removed, remove brake shoe return springs, noting that secondary spring overlaps primary spring. Slide automatic adjuster

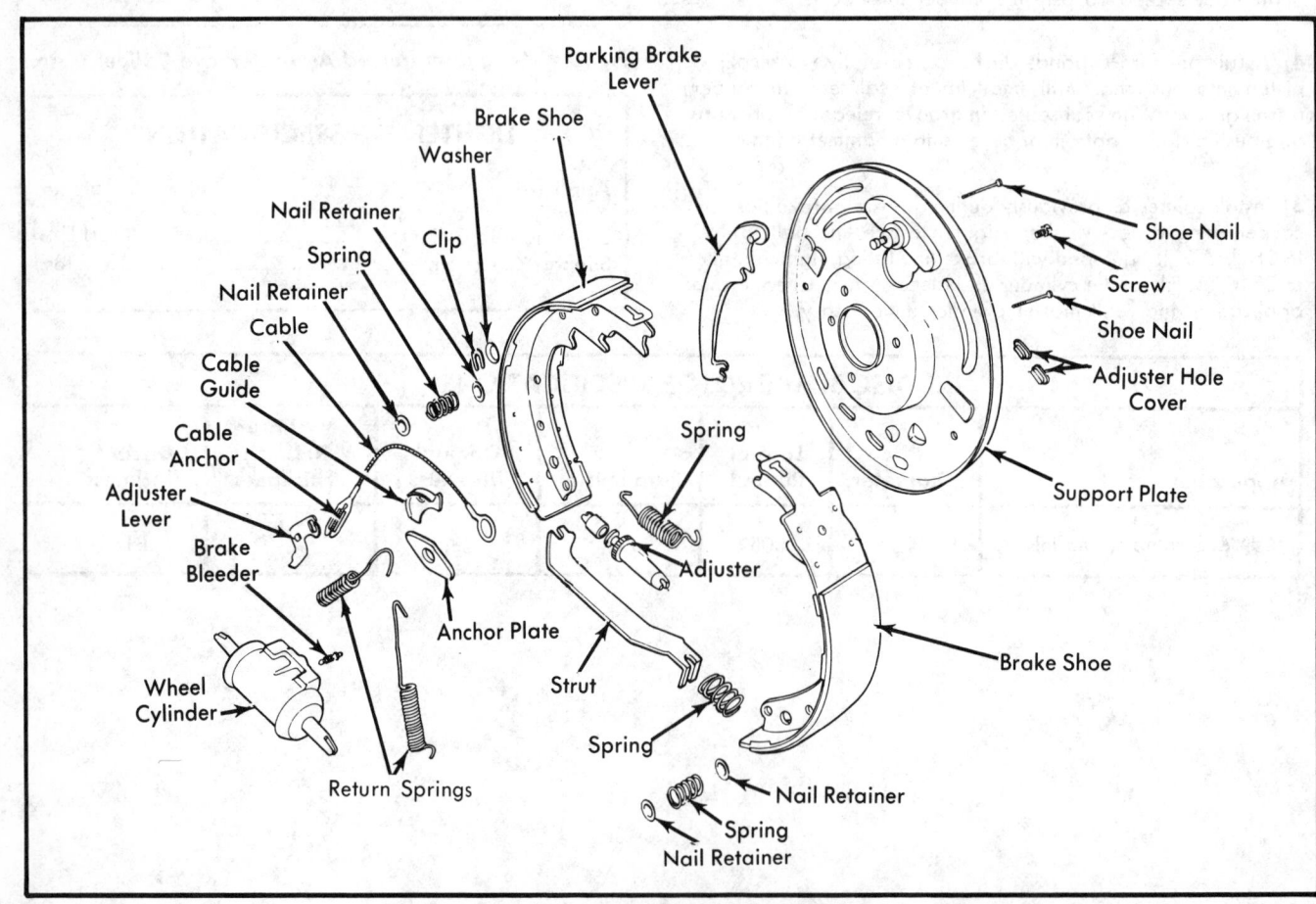

Fig. 1   Exploded View of Chrysler Type Brake Assembly

CHRYSLER CORP. SINGLE ANCHOR (Cont.)

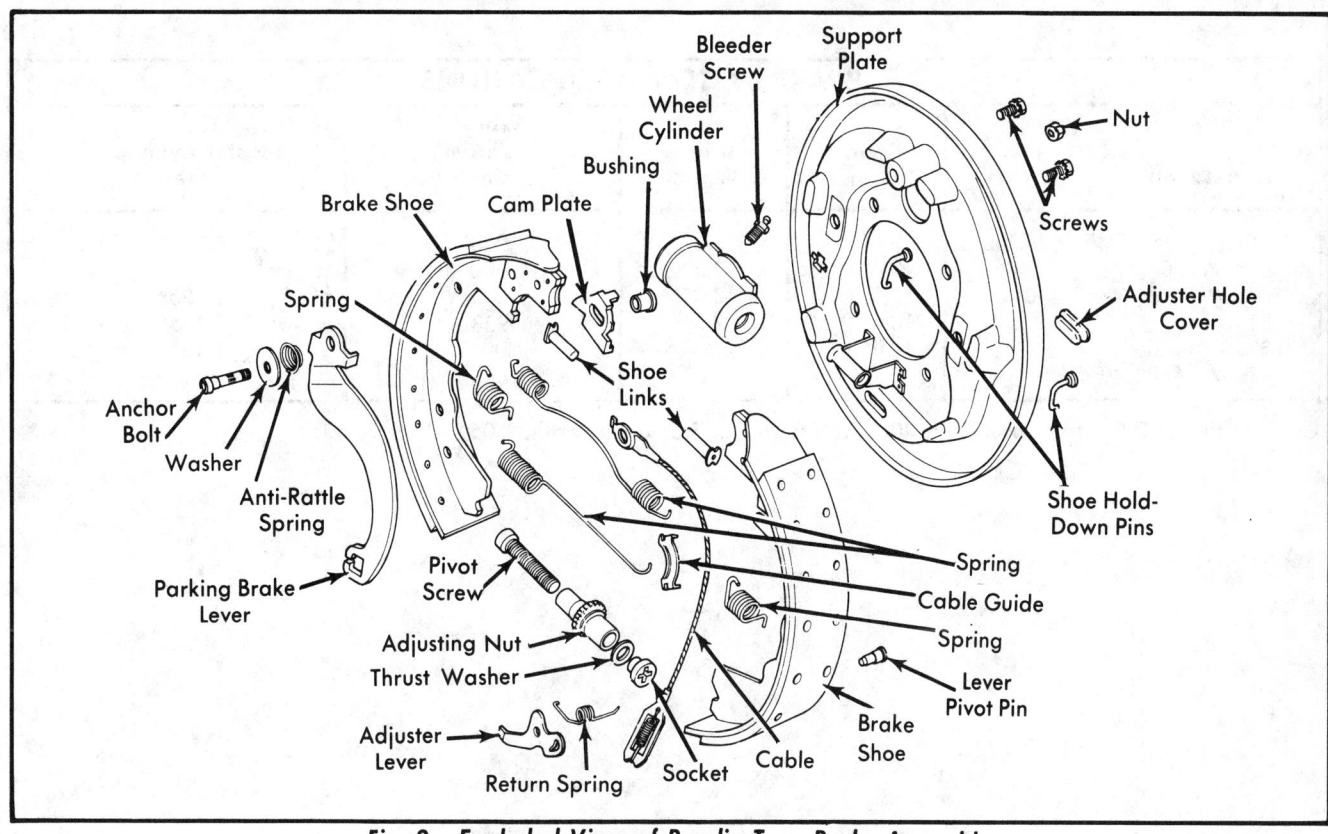

Fig. 2   Exploded View of Bendix Type Brake Assembly

cable eye off anchor and then disconnect cable from adjusting lever. Remove cable, overload spring, cable guide and anchor plate. Disconnect adjuster lever from spring and remove lever. Remove automatic adjuster spring from brake shoes. Remove brake shoe retainers, springs and nails. Spread shoes apart and remove parking brake strut and spring. Disconnect parking brake cable from lever and remove brake shoes.

Installation — To install brake shoes and components, reverse removal procedure.

Removal — Bendix Brake Assembly (12" & 13") — With drum removed, disconnect adjusting lever return spring from lever and remove lever and spring from pivot pin. Disconnect lever from cable. Remove upper spring connecting both shoes. Disconnect and remove shoe hold-down springs. Disconnect parking brake cable from parking brake lever. Remove spring connecting both shoes. Remove both shoes with star wheel adjuster.

Installation — To install brake shoes and components, reverse removal procedure.

WHEEL CYLINDERS

Removal & Installation — 1) Remove wheel, drum and brake shoes. Remove cylinder connecting links and disconnect hydraulic brake line from cylinder.

CAUTION — *On vehicles equipped with vacuum boosters, be sure engine is off and there is no vacuum in system before disconnecting hydraulic lines.*

2) Remove brake cylinder retaining bolts and remove cylinder from backing plate. To install, reverse removal procedure.

OVERHAUL

WHEEL CYLINDERS

Disassembly — With wheel cylinder removed from vehicle, remove rubber boots from ends of cylinders. Remove piston return spring, cylinder cups and pistons from cylinder. Remove bleeder screw and inspect cylinder bore for damage.

Reassembly — If bore of cylinder is pitted or scratched, hone or replace as necessary. Soak all parts in suitable brake fluid or assembly lubricant and reverse disassembly procedure. Clamp brake cylinder pistons against ends of cylinder.

TIGHTENING SPECIFICATIONS

Application	Ft. Lbs.
Brake Hose-to-Wheel Cylinder	
"B", "CB", "MB", & "PB"	7-12
"AD", "AW", "D", "PD", "PW", & "W"	25
Wheel Cylinder Mounting Bolt	11-19
Hydraulic Brake Tube Nuts	
⅜" & ⁷⁄₁₆"	7-12.5
½" & ⁹⁄₁₆"	10-14.5

Brake Systems

CHRYSLER CORP. SINGLE ANCHOR (Cont.)

BRAKE SYSTEM SPECIFICATIONS

Application	Drum Diam.	Drum Width	Wheel Cylinder Diameter	Master Cylinder Diameter
AD, AW, PD, PW, D, W150	10.0"	2.5"	.938"	1.125"
D & W250	12.0"	2.5"	1.00"	1.125"
D250/450 & W350/450	12.0"	3.0"	.....	1.125"
B150/250	10.0"	2.5"	.938"	1.125"
B350	12.0"	2.5"①	1.00"①	1.125"
CB, MB & PB Models	.....	.....	.....	.....

① — With 3,600 lb. front axle. With 4000 lb. front axle, 3.0" drum width, 1.06" wheel cylinder.

FORD SINGLE ANCHOR

All Models (Rear)

DESCRIPTION

The single anchor duo servo brake assembly consists of a support plate, 2 brake shoes, return springs, automatic adjuster components and a wheel cylinder. The automatic adjuster consists of a cable (with hook and anchor fitting), a cable guide, adjusting lever, adjusting screw, pivot nut, socket and spring. The adjuster uses movement of the secondary shoe during reverse brake application to turn brake adjusting screw and maintain proper lining-to-drum clearance.

ADJUSTMENT & SERVICING

BRAKE SHOE ADJUSTMENT

All Models — 1) Adjustment is made with brake drums at room temperature and parking brakes correctly adjusted. Using a suitable measuring gauge (Rotunda 11-0001 for Bronco, 100 and 150 Series; 11-0002 for 250 and 350 Series), measure inside diameter of drum. See *Fig. 1.* Reverse tool and apply to brake shoes on a line parallel to vehicle and through center of axle. Hold automatic adjuster lever away from adjusting screw and turn screw until outside diameter of shoes contacts gauge. See *Fig. 2.*

2) Apply a small amount of lubricant at shoe-to-backing plate contact points. Install brake drum and wheel. Complete adjustment by applying brakes several times while driving vehicle in reverse. Check brake operation by making several stops while driving forward.

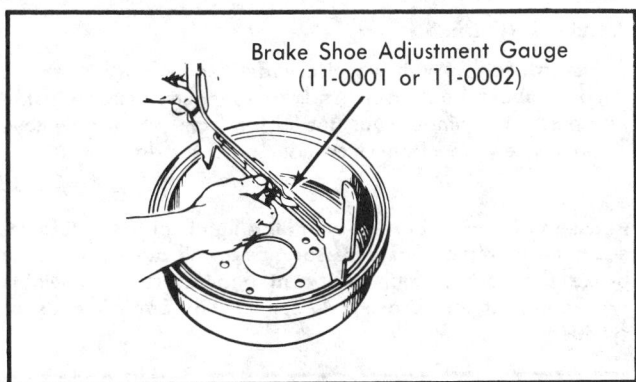

Fig. 1 Measuring Brake Drum Diameter

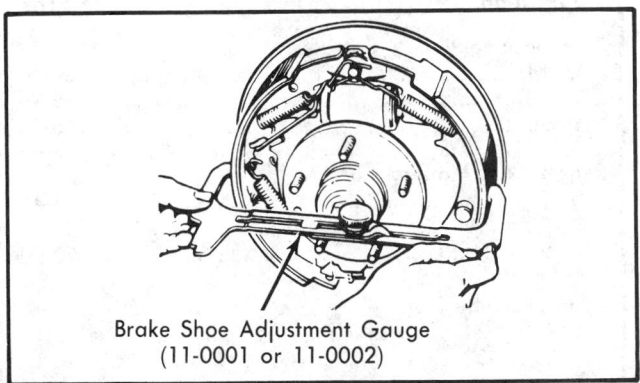

Fig. 2 Measuring Brake Shoe Diameter

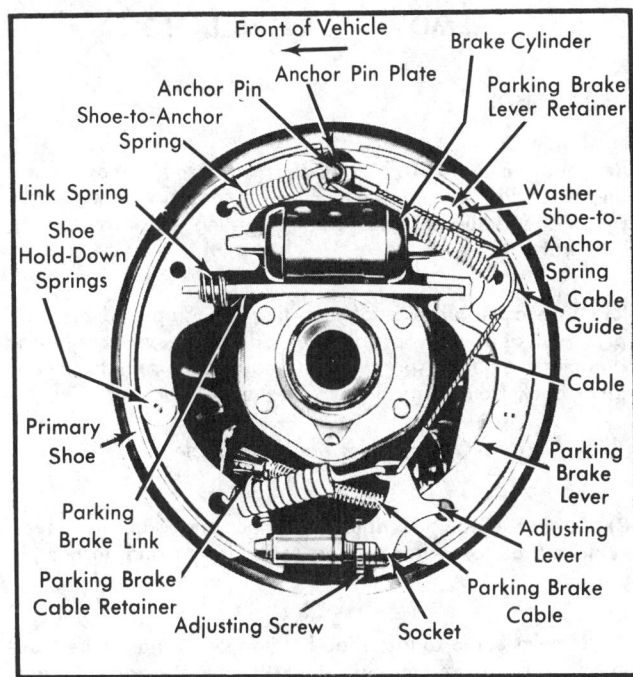

**Fig. 3 Ford Rear Brake Assembly
(E & F100/150 & Bronco Models)**

PARKING BRAKE ADJUSTMENT

NOTE — *If front brake cable tension limiting device is replaced, follow initial adjustment procedure outlined below prior to adjusting cable. If tensioner is not replaced, follow regular parking brake adjustment procedure.*

Initial Adjustment (with new Tension Limiter) — Depress the parking brake pedal. Grip the tension limiter bracket to prevent it from spinning and tighten equalizer nut $2\frac{1}{2}$″ up the rod. Check to make sure the cinch strap has slipped so that less than $1\frac{3}{8}$″ remain exposed.

Regular Cable Adjustment (E100/350) — 1) Release parking brake pedal. Grip automatic adjuster to prevent it from spinning and tighten equalizer nut 6 full turns past its original position.

2) Depress pedal and check tension. Release pedal and check rear wheel drag. If drag is noted on E250/350 models, remove drums and check for clearance between parking brake lever and cam plate. Clearance should be .015″ with brakes fully released. If not to specification, readjust cable.

Regular Cable Adjustment (F100/350 & Bronco) — 1) Depress parking brake pedal 2 notches. Attach suitable tension gauge (Rotunda 210018) behind equalizer assembly. Turn equalizer adjusting nut until tension gauge reads 250 ft. lbs.

2) Back off equalizer nut until tension gauge reads 50 ft. lbs. Retighten adjusting nut until tension gauge reads between 60-100 ft. lbs. Check parking brake operation.

BLEEDING SYSTEM

See *Hydraulic Brake Bleeding* in this Section.

FORD SINGLE ANCHOR (Cont.)

REMOVAL & INSTALLATION

BRAKE SHOES

Removal (E & F100/150 & Bronco) — **1)** Remove wheel and drum. Place a suitable clamp over ends of wheel cylinder. Disengage adjusting lever from adjusting screw by pulling backwards on lever.

2) Move outboard side of adjusting screw up and back off pivot nut as far as possible. Pull adjusting lever, cable and automatic adjuster spring down and toward rear to unhook pivot hook from large hole in secondary shoe.

NOTE — *DO NOT pry pivot hook from hole.*

3) Remove automatic adjuster spring and adjusting lever. Remove shoe to anchor springs, cable anchor and anchor pin plate.

4) Remove cable guide, shoe hold-down springs, shoes, adjusting screw, pivot nut and socket. Remove the parking brake spring and link.

NOTE — *Note color and position of springs as removed for reassembly reference.*

5) Disconnect parking brake cable from lever. Remove secondary shoe and disassemble parking brake lever from shoe by removing retaining clip and spring washer.

Installation — To install, reverse removal procedure, making sure of the following: Adjusting cable is in groove of cable guide, cable does not bind on anchor pin, and adjusting screw is mounted on correct side. If adjuster screw is mounted on wrong side, adjuster will operate incorrectly.

Removal (E & F250/350) — **1)** Remove wheel and brake drum. Remove parking brake assembly retaining nut from backing plate and remove parking brake assembly. Remove adjusting cable assembly from anchor pin, cable guide and adjusting lever.

2) Remove brake shoe return springs, hold down springs and brake shoes. Remove and disassemble adjusting screw assembly.

Installation — Apply a light coat of high temperature grease to contact points of brake assembly and reverse removal procedure.

WHEEL CYLINDER

Removal & Installation — Remove wheel, drum and brake shoes. Remove cylinder connecting links and disconnect hydraulic brake line from cylinder. Remove brake cylinder retaining bolts and remove cylinder from backing plate. To install, reverse removal procedure. Adjust brakes and bleed hydraulic system.

OVERHAUL

WHEEL CYLINDERS

Disassembly — With wheel cylinder removed from vehicle, remove rubber boots from ends of cylinders. Remove piston return spring, cylinder cups and piston from cylinder. Remove bleeder screw and inspect cylinder bore for damage.

Reassembly — If bore of cylinder is lightly pitted or scratched, hone or replace as necessary. Soak all parts in suitable brake fluid or assembly lubricant and reverse disassembly procedure. Clamp brake cylinder pistons against ends of cylinder.

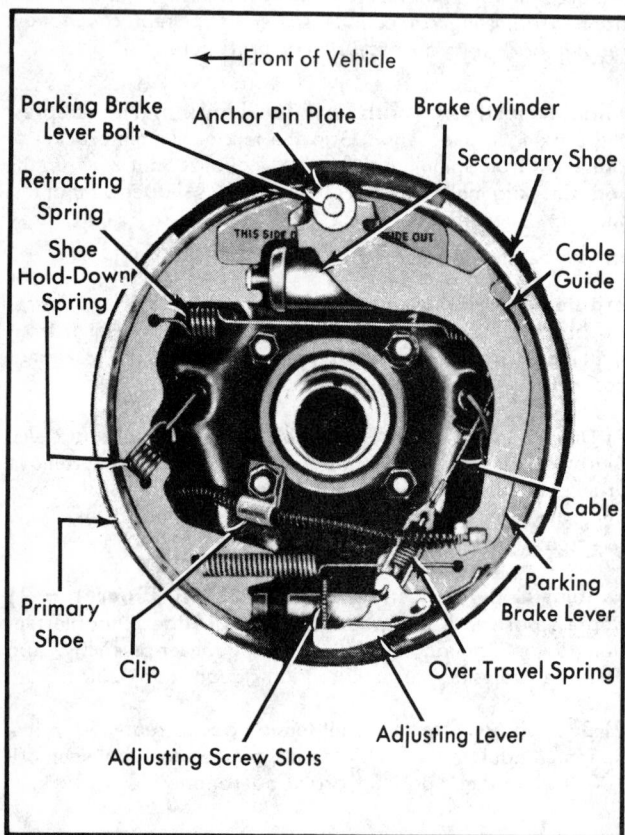

**Fig. 4 Ford Rear Brake Assembly
(E & F250/350 Models)**

TIGHTENING SPECIFICATIONS

Application	Ft. Lbs.
Front Backing Plate-to-Spindle	
7/16"-14	30-50
1/2"-13	55-70
1/2"-20	55-75
1 3/8"-24	30-40
Rear Backing Plate-to-Axle	
7/16"-14	35-45
1/2"-13	75-105
1/2"-20	50-70
Hydraulic Tube Nuts	
3/8" & 7/16"-24	10-15
1/2" & 9/16"-18	10-17

FORD SINGLE ANCHOR (Cont.)

DRUM BRAKE SPECIFICATIONS				
Application	Drum Diam.	Drum Width	Wheel Cylinder Piston Diametr	Master Cylinder Piston Diameter
E100/150 & Bronco	11$\frac{1}{32}$"	2$\frac{1}{4}$"	$\frac{15}{16}$"	1"
E250	12"	2$\frac{1}{2}$"	$\frac{15}{16}$"	1$\frac{1}{16}$"
E350	12"	3"	1$\frac{1}{16}$"①	1$\frac{1}{16}$"
F100②	10"	2$\frac{1}{2}$"	$\frac{15}{16}$"	1"
F100/150	11$\frac{1}{32}$"	2$\frac{1}{4}$"	$\frac{15}{16}$"	1"
F250	12"	2$\frac{1}{2}$"	$\frac{15}{16}$"	1$\frac{1}{16}$"
F250 H.D. & F350	12"	3"	1$\frac{1}{16}$"	$\frac{1}{16}$"

① − School bus wheel cylinder 1".
② − Available with power brakes and 4650/4750 GVW only.

GENERAL MOTORS SINGLE ANCHOR

Chevrolet (Rear Only)
GMC (Rear Only)

NOTE — *For identification purposes, the vehicle series numbers used in this article have been abbreviated for common reference to both Chevrolet and GMC. Chevrolet models use numbers as listed. GMC models are identified as follows: 1500 = 10; 2500 = 20; 3500 = 30.*

DESCRIPTION

Delco single anchor, duo-servo type brake assemblies are used on the rear of all models. The assemblies consist of a support plate, 2 brake shoes, return springs, automatic adjuster components and a duo-servo wheel cylinder. Automatic adjusters consist of a connecting link, override lever, override spring, return spring, actuating lever and an adjusting screw. Normal adjustment is accomplished through movement of actuating lever and secondary shoe during application of brakes when vehicle is operated in reverse.

ADJUSTMENT & SERVICING

BRAKE SHOE ADJUSTMENT

Knock out lanced area in brake drum with a punch. If drum is installed, it must be removed and all metal removed from brake area. Turn adjusting screw, through hole, until brake shoes expand and brake drums can just be turned by hand. The drag should be equal at all wheels. Back off adjusting screw 30 notches at each wheel. If drum still drags, back off an additional one or two notches. Install hole cover in drum.

PARKING BRAKE ADJUSTMENT

Rear Wheel Type (Foot Pedal Actuated) — With service brakes correctly adjusted, raise vehicle until both rear wheels are off ground. Loosen equalizer adjusting nut. Apply parking brake four notches from fully released position. Tighten adjusting nut until a slight drag is felt when wheels are rotated forward. Tighten lock nut. Release parking brake and wheels should rotate forward freely. Lower vehicle.

Rear Wheel Type (Orscheln Lever Actuated) — With service brakes in proper adjustment, turn adjusting knob on lever counterclockwise to stop. Apply parking brake and raise vehicle until both rear wheels are off ground. Loosen intermediate cable equalizer lock nut and adjust front nut until slight drag is felt when rear wheels are rotated forward. Tighten lock nut. Readjust lever adjusting knob to obtain definite snap-over-center feel. Release parking brake and check that no drag is present when wheels are rotated.

Transmission Mounted (Internal Shoe Type) — 1) With at least one rear wheel raised off ground, block wheels and release parking brake. Remove cotter pin and clevis pin connecting pull rod and relay lever. Rotate drum to bring one access hole into line with adjuster screw at bottom of brake shoes (manual transmission) or top of shoes (automatic transmission).

NOTE — *It may be necessary to knock out plug in drum for access hole.*

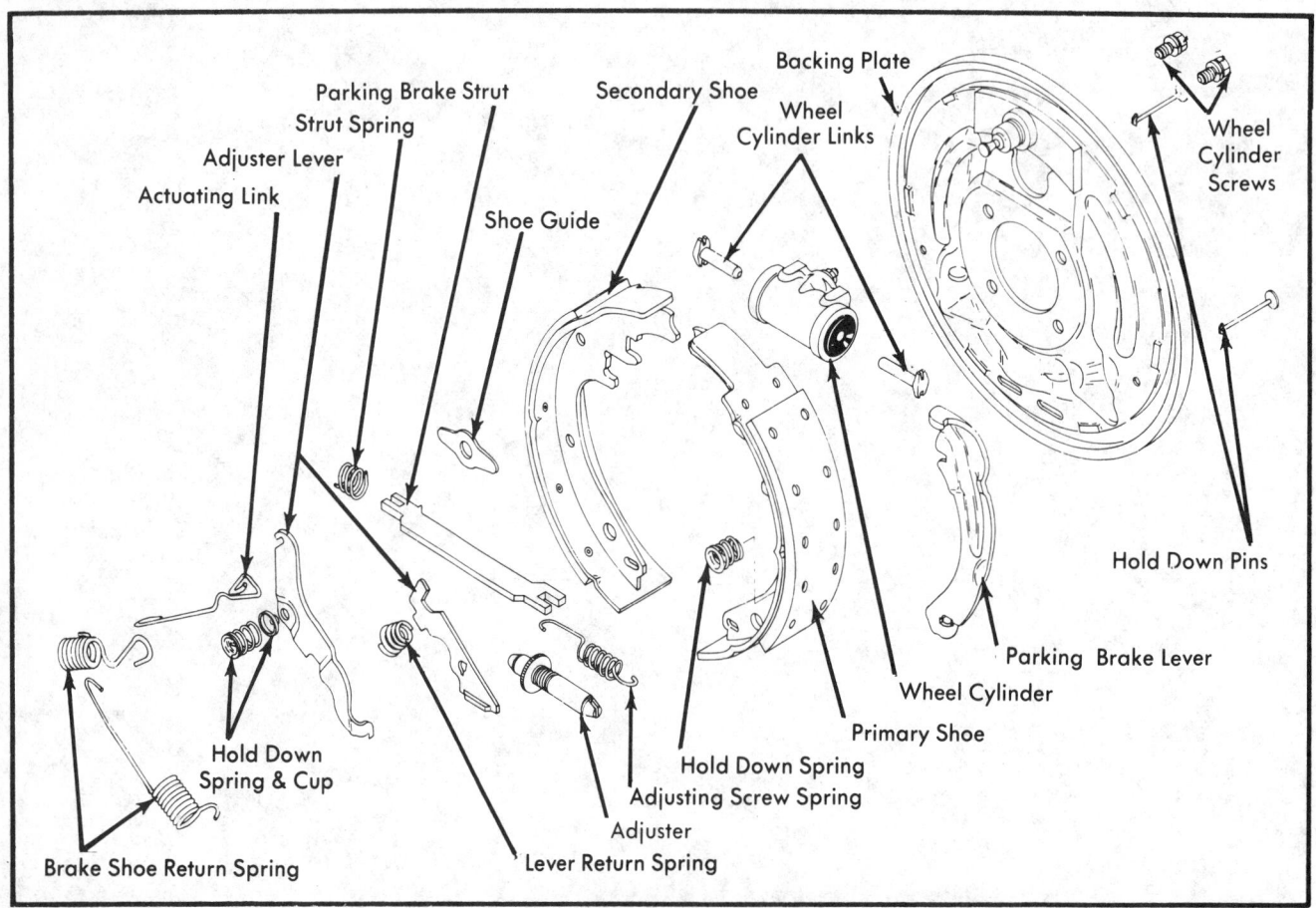

Fig. 1   Exploded View of Single Anchor Brake Assembly

GENERAL MOTORS SINGLE ANCHOR (Cont.)

2) Rotate adjusting screws with a screwdriver to expand shoes until tight against drum. Drum should not be able to be rotated by hand. Back off adjuster screw 10 notches. Place parking brake lever in full released position. Pull on brake cable enough to take up slack in brake linkage. Adjust pull rod clevis to line up with hole in relay lever. Insert clevis pin and roller pin. Tighten clevis lock nut. Install a new plug in access hole in drum and lower vehicle.

BLEEDING SYSTEM

See Hydraulic Brake Bleeding in this Section.

REMOVAL & INSTALLATION

BRAKE SHOES

Removal — 1) Raise vehicle and remove wheel and brake drum. It may be necessary to back off brake shoe adjustment before removing drum. Unlock primary and secondary shoe springs. Remove shoe hold down springs.

NOTE — *On some vehicles, it may be necessary to remove axle shafts to remove hub and drum.*

2) Lift up on actuator, unhook actuating link from anchor pin and remove link. Spread shoes enough to clear wheel cylinder links. Remove parking brake strut and spring. Disconnect cable from lever. Remove brake shoes.

Installation — 1) Lubricate fulcrum end of parking brake lever with suitable brake lubricant. Attach lever to secondary shoe. Make sure lever moves free. Connect brake shoes together with adjuster spring. Place adjuster screw in position. Make sure spring does not contact starwheel portion of adjusting screw. Right hand thread adjusting screw should be on left side.

2) Make sure starwheel lines up with hole in backing plate. Apply a thin coating of brake lubricant to contact surface on backing plate. Position brake shoes on backing plate. Primary shoe (short lining) is to front. Connect cable to parking brake lever. Install strut between shoes.

3) Install actuator, return spring and actuator link. Install shoe hold down springs. Install both primary and secondary shoe springs. Measure inside diameter of brake drum using a suitable measuring gauge (J-21177). Expand brake shoes to dimension obtained on outside caliper portion of tool.

4) Install brake drum and wheel. Bleed system if any portion of the hydraulic system was opened. Check fluid level in master cylinder and add as necessary.

WHEEL CYLINDER

Removal & Installation — Remove wheel, drum and brake shoes. Remove cylinder connecting links and disconnect hydraulic brake line from cylinder. Remove brake cylinder retaining bolts and remove cylinder from support plate. To install, reverse removal procedure.

OVERHAUL

WHEEL CYLINDER

Disassembly — Remove rubber boots from ends of cylinder. Remove piston return spring, cylinder cups, and pistons from cylinder. Remove bleeder screw and inspect bore for damage.

Reassembly — If bore of cylinder is lightly pitted or scratched, hone or replace as necessary. Soak rubber cylinder cups in suitable brake fluid or assembly lubricant and reverse disassembly procedure.

NOTE — *It is not necessary to clamp cylinder ends, as lips of wheel cylinder boots will retain pistons.*

TIGHTENING SPECIFICATIONS

Application	Ft. Lbs.
Brake Hose Attaching Nut	12.5
Rear Brake Anchor Pin	140
Application	**INCH Lbs.**
Bleeder Valves	60
Brake Line Nut	150
Wheel Cylinder Attaching Bolts	50
Brake Line Clips	150

BRAKE DRUM SPECIFICATIONS

Application	Drum Diam.	Drum Width	Wheel Cylinder Piston Diameter	Master Cylinder Piston Diameter
C10 & G10				
to 4900 GVW	11.0"	2.0"	1.0"	1.0"
to 5600 GVW	11.0"	2.0"	1.0"	1.12"
C10 Pickup				
5200-6100 GVW	11.15"	2.75"	1.0"	1.12"
CG & K10				
C, G, K & P20				
to 6800 GVW	11.15"	2.75"	.937"①	1.12"
C, K & P20				
G & P30				
6800-8600 GVW	13.0"	2.5"	1.06"	1.25"
C, G, K & P30	13.0"	3.5"	1.19"	1.34"
P30				
over 10,000 GVW②	.....	.....	.....	.....

① — 1" on some 20 series over 6400 GVW.
② — Rear disc brakes standard. See appropriate article in this section.

Brake Systems

JEEP SINGLE ANCHOR — CABLE ADJUSTER

"CJ" Models
Scrambler

DESCRIPTION

Automatic adjuster brakes are 2 shoe, self-centering type with brake shoe anchor at upper end of shoes above wheel cylinder. Single cylinder is double acting. Automatic adjuster device is cable operated.

ADJUSTMENT & SERVICING

BRAKE SHOE ADJUSTMENT

Brake shoes adjust automatically as brakes are applied when vehicle is operated in reverse. Brake shoes can be manually adjusted by rotating adjuster screw using a suitable tool. Remove access slot cover. Using a small blade screwdriver, push in on adjustment lever to separate from adjustment screw. Turn adjustment screw until brake drum is locked tight, then back screw off until wheel rotates freely. It may also be necessary to back brake shoes off a few notches to remove drum.

PARKING BRAKE ADJUSTMENT

Rear Wheel Integral — Adjustment is not necessary in normal service; automatic service brake adjustments also adjust parking brake. In case of brake overhaul or to compensate for stretched cables, adjust as follows: Check first for binds, kinks, or any frayed condition of cables. Check to see brake shoes are in proper adjustment before proceeding. Release parking brake. Loosen lock nuts at equalizer under vehicle. Tighten cables until wheels, when rotated by hand, have a slight drag from shoes. Loosen cables until wheels rotate freely and no drag is felt. Tighten lock nut and check operation of parking brake.

BLEEDING SYSTEM

See Hydraulic Brake Bleeding in this Section.

REMOVAL & INSTALLATION

BRAKE SHOES

Removal — 1) Raise and support vehicle and remove wheels and drums. Grasp adjusting lever with pliers and remove tang from hole in secondary shoe. Place clamping device over wheel cylinder to retain pistons during further disassembly.

2) Remove secondary return spring, adjuster cable, primary return spring, cable guide, adjuster lever and adjuster springs. Remove hold-down springs and brake shoes. Disengage parking brake cable from parking brake lever.

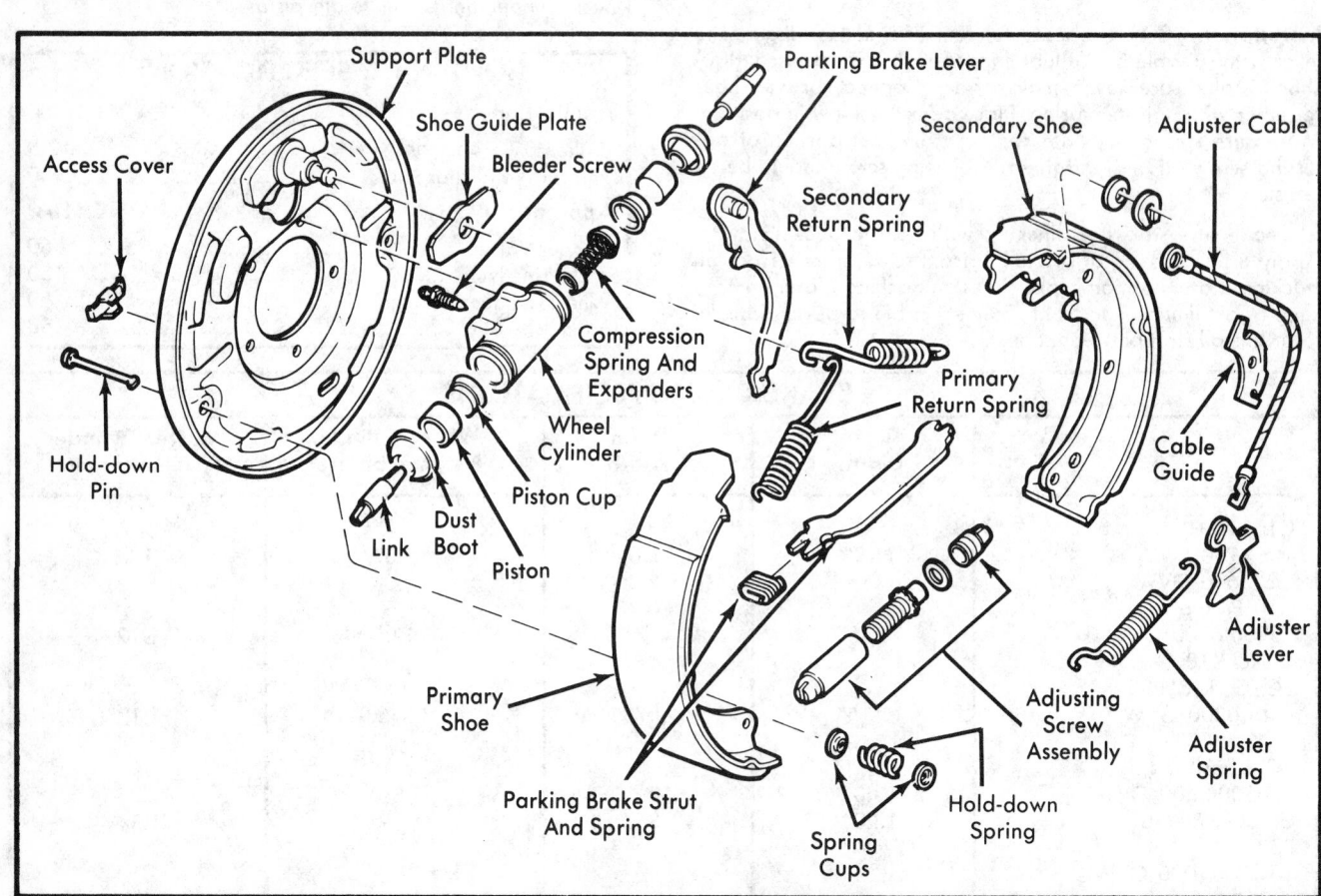

Fig. 1   Exploded View of Jeep Brake Assembly

JEEP SINGLE ANCHOR – CABLE ADJUSTER (Cont.)

Installation – 1) Lubricate support plate ledges, anchor pin, self-adjusting cable guide, adjuster screw threads, and pivot with molydisulphide grease or chassis lubricant. Lubricate parking brake cable lever and install on secondary brake. Install washer and replacement lever retaining "U" clip. Crimp ends of clip to retain it on pivot.

2) Position brake shoe on brake support plate and install hold-down springs. Install parking brake cable in lever, and install parking brake strut and positioning spring. Place adjuster cable eyelet on anchor pin and install primary return spring. Install cable guide to secondary brake shoe and install secondary return spring.

3) Install adjuster screw and spring on brake shoes and insert small hooked end of spring into large hole in primary brake shoe. Install large hooked end of spring in adjuster lever. Position adjuster cable in cable guide groove. Insert hooked end of cable in adjuster lever.

4) Grasp adjuster lever with pliers and hook adjuster lever tang in large hole in bottom of secondary shoe. Initially adjust brakes using clearance gauge (J-21177) or manual adjustment procedure outlined in this story. *See Brake Shoe Adjustment.*

5) Install brake drums, and if brake lines were disconnected, bleed system. Install wheels, lower vehicle, and driving forward and backward make 10-15 brake applications to adjust and balance brake system. Road test vehicle.

WHEEL CYLINDER

Removal – Remove wheels, brake drums, and brake shoes. Disconnect brake line at each wheel cylinder. DO NOT bend line away from cylinder, as when cylinder is moved away from support plate, line will separate easily. Remove cylinder-to-support plate bolts and remove cylinder.

Installation – To install, reverse removal procedure noting the following: Start brake line fitting into cylinder before installing cylinder to support plate.

OVERHAUL

WHEEL CYLINDER

NOTE – *Vehicle manufacturer recommends that cylinders NOT be honed.*

Disassembly – 1) Remove brake shoe links and dust boots. Push pistons, piston cups and expander spring out of bore. Discard piston cups. Clean all cylinder parts with clean brake fluid or brake solvent. Inspect cylinder bore and piston for pitting, wear or other damage and replace if necessary.

2) Light discoloration may be removed by polishing with crocus cloth only. Polish by rotating cylinder around crocus cloth supported on fingers. DO NOT polish in a lengthwise direction.

Reassembly – Lubricate cylinder bore and internal components with brake fluid. Do not lubricate dust boots. Position replacement piston cups on spring expanders and install assembled parts into cylinder bore. Ensure expanders are seated in piston cups and that cups are installed with lips facing one another. Install pistons with flat sides facing interior of bore. Install dust boots and brake shoe links.

TIGHTENING SPECIFICATIONS

Application	INCH Lbs.
Bleeder Screw ¼"-28	40-50
Bleeder Screw ⅜"-24	40-140
Brake Line	120-200

Application	Ft. Lbs.
Support Plate	30-35
Brake Cylinder-to-Support Plate	18

BRAKE SPECIFICATIONS

Application	Specification
Drum Radial Runout	.005"
Maximum Oversize	10.060"

BRAKE SYSTEM SPECIFICATIONS

Application	Drum Diam.	Drum Width	Wheel Cylinder Piston Diameter	Master Cylinder Piston Diameter
"CJ" & Scrambler Models	10"	1¾"	⅞"	1"

JEEP SINGLE ANCHOR — LEVER ADJUSTER

Cherokee
"J" Models
Wagoneer

DESCRIPTION

Single anchor brake assembly consists of a support plate, 2 brake shoes, brake shoe return springs, adjuster lever and single wheel cylinder.

ADJUSTMENT & SERVICING

BRAKE SHOE ADJUSTMENT

Brake shoes adjust automatically when brakes are applied while vehicle is traveling in reverse. Manual adjustment is required if shoes have been removed and reinstalled. See *Brake*

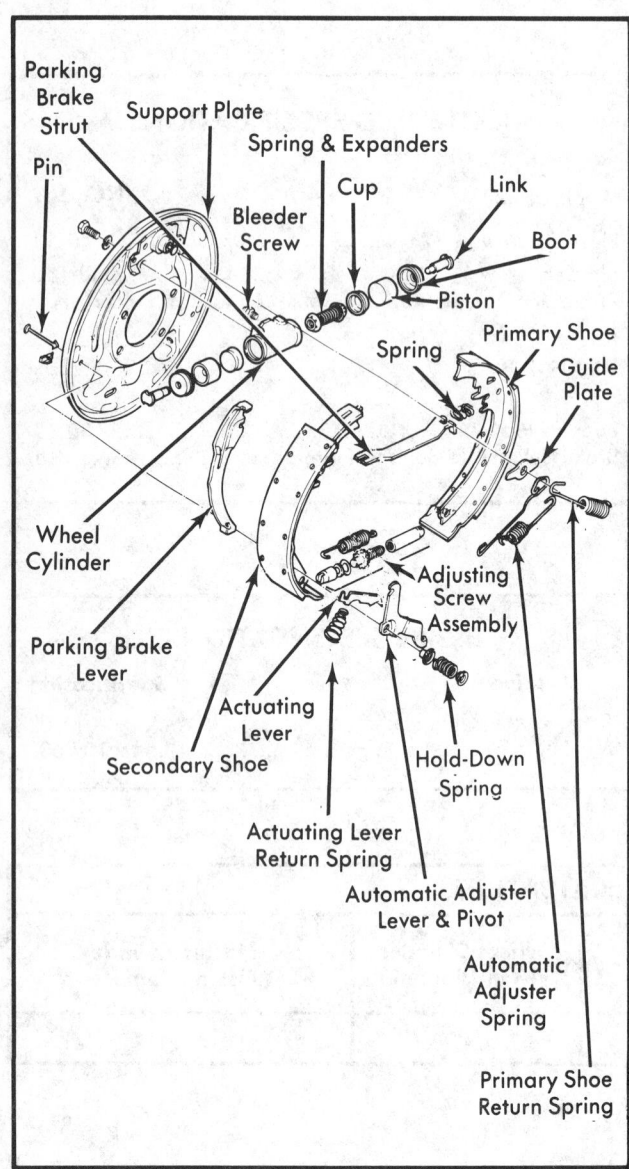

Parking Brake Strut
Support Plate
Pin
Spring & Expanders
Cup
Link
Bleeder Screw
Boot
Piston
Spring
Primary Shoe
Guide Plate
Wheel Cylinder
Parking Brake Lever
Adjusting Screw Assembly
Actuating Lever
Secondary Shoe
Hold-Down Spring
Actuating Lever Return Spring
Automatic Adjuster Lever & Pivot
Automatic Adjuster Spring
Primary Shoe Return Spring

Fig. 1   Exploded View of Jeep Drum Brake Assembly

Shoe Installation in this Article. During overhaul it is sometimes necessary to back off shoes to remove brake drums. This is done by turning star wheel adjuster which is accessible through a hole in brake backing plate. A thin blade screwdriver or similiar tool must be used to disengage automatic adjuster lever while making manual adjustment.

PARKING BRAKE ADJUSTMENT

NOTE — *Brakes Shoes must be adjusted before parking brakes.*

Adjustment is not necessary in normal service; automatic adjusters also adjust parking brake. In case of brake overhaul or to compensate for stretched cables, adjust as follows: Check first for binds, kinks or any frayed condition of cables. Replace as necessary. Release parking brake. Loosen lock nuts at equalizer under vehicle. Tighten cables until wheels, when rotated by hand, have a slight drag from shoes. Loosen cables until wheels rotate freely and no drag is felt. Tighten lock nut and check operation of parking brake.

BLEEDING SYSTEM
See Hydraulic Brake Bleeding in this Section.

REMOVAL & INSTALLATION

BRAKE SHOES

Removal — 1) Raise and support vehicle on safety stands. Remove necessary wheels. On models with full floating rear axle, remove 2 screws that locate drums on hubs. On all models, remove primary return spring, automatic adjuster actuator spring and secondary shoe return spring. Remove hold-down springs and brake shoe assemblies. Disengage parking brake cable from parking brake lever. (Parking brake strut is removed with brake shoe assembly.)

2) Place wheel cylinder clamps over wheel cylinders to retain pistons. Inspect lining wear. Replace riveted linings if worn to within $1/32''$ of rivet heads. Replace bonded linings if worn to total thickness of $1/16''$. Inspect lining wear pattern and replace lining if wear is uneven, checking drum for distortion and run-out.

3) Inspect lining for cracks, charred surface, broken rivets or contamination. Replace linings if conditions described are exhibited. Inspect all springs, parking brake lever, automatic adjuster lever and pivot, and actuating lever. Replace any weak springs, bent levers, or any parts that are worn or broken.

Installation — 1) Apply a thin film of molydisulphide grease or chassis lubricant to support plate ledges, anchor pin, adjuster screw threads and pivot, adjuster lever-to-secondary brakeshoe contact surface, parking brake lever pivot and portion of lever that contacts secondary brakeshoe. Attach parking brake cable to parking brake lever on secondary shoe. Pinch "U" clip to retain lever on shoe.

2) Install secondary brakeshoe, automatic adjuster lever and lever pivot as an assembly and install brakeshoe hold-down

JEEP SINGLE ANCHOR — LEVER ADJUSTER (Cont.)

spring. Install actuating lever and adjusting lever. Large end of tapered spring should rest on brakeshoe. Install primary shoe and hold-down spring.

3) Install guide plate on anchor pin, install parking brake strut and spring on brake shoes. Install adjusting screw and spring. Short hooked end of spring goes on primary brake shoe, and long hooked end goes on secondary brake shoe. Install adjuster spring. Install secondary brake shoe return spring on brake shoe and adjuster spring. Install primary return spring.

4) Perform initial brake adjustment by measuring clearance with gauge (J-21107-01). Set clearance specified by gauge and install drum. If gauge is not available, install drum and adjust star wheel adjuster until drum just drags, then back off adjuster until drum turns freely. Test brake operation before moving vehicle. Make final adjustment by making 10 to 15 forward and reverse stops.

NOTE — *Disengage automatic adjuster with thin bladed screwdriver while making manual adjustment.*

WHEEL CYLINDER

Removal & Installation — Disconnect brake line but do not bend it away from cylinder. When cylinder is moved away from backing plate, line will separate easily. Remove cylinder mounting bolts and remove cylinder. To install, reverse removal procedure.

OVERHAUL

WHEEL CYLINDER

NOTE — *Vehicle manufacturer recommends that wheel cylinders NOT be honed.*

Disassembly — 1) Remove brake shoe links and dust boots. Push pistons, piston cups and expander spring out of bore. Discard piston cups. Clean all cylinder parts with clean brake fluid or brake solvent. Inspect cylinder bore and piston for pitting, wear or other damage and replace if necessary.

2) Light discoloration may be removed by polishing with crocus cloth only. Polish by rotating cylinder around crocus cloth supported by fingers. DO NOT polish in a lengthwise direction.

Reassembly — Lubricate cylinder bore and internal components with brake fluid. Do not lubricate dust boots. Position replacement piston cups on spring expanders and install assembled parts into cylinder bore. Ensure expanders are seated in piston cups and that cups are installed with lips facing each other. Install pistons with flat sides facing interior of bore. Install dust boots and brake shoe links.

TIGHTENING SPECIFICATIONS

Application	INCH Lbs.
Bleeder Screw	
¼"-28	40-50
⅜"-24	40-140
Brake Line	120-200

Application	Ft. Lbs.
Brake Support Plate	
J20	45-55
All Others	35-55

BRAKE SPECIFICATIONS

Application	Specification
Drum Radial Runout	.005"
Maximum Oversize	
11" Drum	11.060"
12" Drum	12.060"

BRAKE SYSTEM SPECIFICATIONS

Application	Drum Diam.	Drum Width	Wheel Cylinder Diameter	Master Cylinder Piston Diameter
Cherokee	11"	2"	$^{15}/_{16}$"	1⅛"
Wagoneer	11"	2"	$^{15}/_{16}$"	1⅛"
J10	11"	2"	$^{15}/_{16}$"	1⅛"
J20	12"	2½"	1⅛"	1⅛"

Contents

Section 11

WHEEL ALIGNMENT

NOTE — ALSO SEE GENERAL INDEX.

IMPORTANT

Because of the great number of model names used by vehicle manufacturers, accurate identification of models is important. See Model Identification at the front of this publication.

Wheel Alignment

WHEEL ALIGNMENT TROUBLE SHOOTING

CONDITION & POSSIBLE CAUSE	CONDITION & POSSIBLE CAUSE
Tire Wear • Tire pressure too low. • Wheel alignment out of tolerance. • Excessively worn wheel bearings. • Improper or no tire rotation. **Grating Tire Noise** • Improper tire pressure. • Wheel alignment out of tolerance. • Damaged or defective spindle or suspension components. **Uneven Tire Wear** • Uneven tire pressure. • Tire pressure too low (shoulders on tire worn).	**Uneven Tire Wear (Cont.)** • Tire pressure to high (center of tread worn). • Bent rotor or wheel. • Improper camber and/or toe setting (one side of tread worn). • Excessive toe-out and/or neg. camber (inside of tread worn). • Excessive toe-in and/or pos. camber (outside of tread worn). • Excessive wheel bearing play. • Brake operation on only one side. **Road Noise** • Abnormal tire wear. • Tire out of balance. • Tire pressure too low.

WHEEL ALIGNMENT SPECIFICATIONS

CHRYSLER CORP.					
Application	**Axle Gap (Inches)**	**Caster (Degrees)**	**Camber (Degrees)**	**Toe-In (Inches)**	**Steering Axis Inclin. (Degrees)**
All "B", "CB", "MB" & "PB"	.....	+1¼ to +3¼	0 to +1	⅛	.....
W150/250	.....	3	1½	⅛	8½
W350/450	.....	3	½	⅛	8½
D150/450	....	+½ ①	+¼	⅛	.....

① — With vehicle loaded.

JEEP					
Application	**Axle Gap (Inches)**	**Caster (Degrees)**	**Camber (Degrees)**	**Toe-In (Inches)**	**Steering Axis Inclin. (Degrees)**
"CJ" & Scrambler	.....	+6 to +7	0 to +½	³⁄₆₄ to ³⁄₃₂	8½
Cherokee, Wagoneer & Truck	.....	+4 to +5	0 to +½	³⁄₆₄ to ³⁄₃₂	8½

WHEEL ALIGNMENT SPECIFICATIONS (Cont.)

FORD MOTOR CO.

Application	Axle Gap (Inches)①	Caster (Degrees)	Camber (Degrees)	Toe-In (Inches)	Steering Axis Inclin. (Degrees)
E100 & 150②	3¼ to 3½	6¼ to 8	−1¾ to −¼	1/32	.....
	3½ to 3¾	5¾ to 7¼	−1½ to +¼	1/32	.....
	3¾ to 4	5 to 6¾	−1 to +¾	1/32	.....
	4 to 4¼	4½ to 5¾	−½ to +1¼	1/32	.....
	4¼ to 4½	4 to 5¼	0 to +1¾	1/32	.....
	4½ to 4¾	3¼ to 4½	+½ to +2¼	1/32	.....
	4¾ to 5	2½ to 4	+1 to +2¾	1/32	.....
	5 to 5¼	2 to 3¼	+1½ to +3¼	1/32	.....
	5¼ to 5½	1½ to 2¾	+2 to +3¾	1/32	.....
E250 & 350③	3¼ to 3½	9 to 10½	−1¾ to −¼	1/32	.....
	3½ to 3¾	8½ to 9¾	−1½ to +¼	1/32	.....
	3¾ to 4	7⅞ to 9	−1 to +¾	1/32	.....
	4 to 4¼	7⅛ to 8½	−½ to +1¼	1/32	.....
	4¼ to 4½	6½ to 7¾	0 to +1¾	1/32	.....
	4½ to 4¾	5¾ to 7	+½ to +2¼	1/32	.....
	4¾ to 5	5¼ to 6½	+1 to +2¾	1/32	.....
	5 to 5¼	4⅝ to 6	+1½ to +3¼	1/32	.....
	5¼ to 5½	4 to 5½	+2 to +3¾	1/32	.....
F100 & 150④ (4x2)	2¼ to 2¾	6 to 10	−3 to −½	1/32	8
	2¾ to 3¼	5 to 9	−2 to +½	1/32	8
	3¼ to 3½	4 to 8	−1¼ to +1¼	1/32	8
	3½ to 4	3 to 7	−¼ to +2¼	1/32	8
	4 to 4¼	2 to 6	+½ to +3	1/32	8
	4¼ to 4¾	1 to 5	+1½ to +4	1/32	8
F250 & 350④ (4x2)	2 to 2¼	5¾ to 9	−2½ to 0	1/32	8
	2¼ to 2¾	4¾ to 8	−1½ to +1	1/32	8
	2¾ to 3¼	3¾ to 7	−¾ to +1¾	1/32	8
	3¼ to 3½	2¾ to 6	+¼ to +2¾	1/32	8
	3½ to 4	1¾ to 5	+1 to +3½	1/32	8
	4 to 4¼	¾ to 4	+2 to +4½	1/32	8
F150 & Bronco④ (4x4)	2¾ to 3¼	6 to 9	−2½ to −¼	1/32	13
	3¼ to 3½	5 to 8	−1¾ to +½	1/32	13
	3½ to 4	4 to 7	−¾ to +1½	1/32	13
	4 to 4¼	3 to 6	0 to +2¼	1/32	13
	4¼ to 4¾	2 to 5	+1 to +3¼	1/32	13
	4¾ to 5	1 to 4	+1¾ to +4	1/32	13
F250 & 350④ (4X4)	4¾ to 5	3 to 5	−2¾ to −¼	1/32	13
	5 to 5½	3⅛ to 5⅛	−1¾ to +¾	1/32	13
	5½ to 6	3⅛ to 5⅛	−¾ to +1¾	1/32	13
	6 to 6¼	3¼ to 5¼	+¼ to +2¾	1/32	13
	6¼ to 6¾	3⅜ to 5⅜	+1¼ to + 4	1/32	13
	6¾ to 7	3½ to 5½	+2½ to + 5	1/32	13

① — Clearance is between top of axle and frame.
② — Toe-in range is 1/32" out to 7/32" in.
③ — Toe-in range is 3/32" out to 5/32" in.
④ — Toe-in range is 1/32" out to 7/32" in.

Wheel Alignment

WHEEL ALIGNMENT SPECIFICATIONS (Cont.)

GENERAL MOTORS					
Application	Axle Gap (Inches)①	Caster (Degrees)	Camber (Degrees)	Toe-In (Inches)	Steering Axis Inclin. (Degrees)
C10	2½	2.4±1.0	0.2±0.7	3/16	.....
	2¾	2.1±1.0	0.2±0.7	3/16	.....
	3	1.8±1.0	0.2±0.7	3/16	.....
	3¼	1.5±1.0	0.2±0.7	3/16	.....
	3½	1.2±1.0	0.2±0.7	3/16	.....
	3¾	1.0±1.0	0.2±0.7	3/16	.....
	4	0.7±1.0	0.2±0.7	3/16	.....
	4¼	0.5±1.0	0.2±0.7	3/16	.....
	4½	0.2±1.0	0.2±0.7	3/16	.....
	4¾	0.1±1.0	0.2±0.7	3/16	.....
	5	0.3±1.0	0.2±0.7	3/16	.....
C20 & 30	2½	1.5±1.0	0.2±0.7	3/16	.....
	2¾	1.2±1.0	0.2±0.7	3/16	.....
	3	0.9±1.0	0.2±0.7	3/16	.....
	3¼	0.6±1.0	0.2±0.7	3/16	.....
	3½	0.3±1.0	0.2±0.7	3/16	.....
	3¾	0.1±1.0	0.2±0.7	3/16	.....
	4	0±1.0	0.2±0.7	3/16	.....
	4¼	−0.1±1.0	0.2±0.7	3/16	.....
	4½	−0.7±1.0	0.2±0.7	3/16	.....
	4¾	−1.0±1.0	0.2±0.7	3/16	.....
	5	−1.2±1.0	0.2±0.7	3/16	.....
K10, 20 & 30	2½ to 5	8③	1.0②③	0	.....
G10 & 20	1½	3.5±1.0	0.5±0.7	3/16	.....
	1¾	3.3±1.0	0.5±0.7	3/16	.....
	2	3.1±1.0	0.5±0.7	3/16	.....
	2¼	2.9±1.0	0.5±0.7	3/16	.....
	2½	2.7±1.0	0.5±0.7	3/16	.....
	2¾	2.6±1.0	0.5±0.7	3/16	.....
	3	2.4±1.0	0.5±0.7	3/16	.....
	3¼	2.2±1.0	0.5±0.7	3/16	.....
	3½	2.1±1.0	0.5±0.7	3/16	.....
	3¾	1.9±1.0	0.5±0.7	3/16	.....
	4	1.8±1.0	0.5±0.7	3/16	.....
	4¼	1.6±1.0	0.5±0.7	3/16	.....
G30	1½	2.8±1.0	0.2±0.7	3/16	.....
	1¾	2.5±1.0	0.2±0.7	3/16	.....
	2	2.2±1.0	0.2±0.7	3/16	.....
	2¼	1.9±1.0	0.2±0.7	3/16	.....
	2½	1.6±1.0	0.2±0.7	3/16	.....
	2¾	1.3±1.0	0.2±0.7	3/16	.....
	3	1.0±1.0	0.2±0.7	3/16	.....
	3¼	0.7±1.0	0.2±0.7	3/16	.....
	3½	0.5±1.0	0.2±0.7	3/16	.....
	3¾	0.2±1.0	0.2±0.7	3/16	.....
	4	0±1.0	0.2±0.7	3/16	.....
	4¼	−0.2±1.0	0.2±0.7	3/16	.....

NOTE — *The vehicle series and model application in this table has been abbreviated for common reference to both Chevrolet and GMC. Chevrolet models use numerical designations as listed; GMC models use numerical designations as follows; 1500 = 10; 2500 = 20; 3500 = 30.*

① — Clearance is between jounce bumper and frame.
② — On K30 models, Camber is 0.5.
③ — No adjustment provision .
④ — Add .3° Caster on vehicles with Hydroboost Brake System.
⑤ — Subtract .4° Caster on vehicles with Dual Rear Wheels.

WHEEL ALIGNMENT SPECIFICATIONS (Cont.)

	GENERAL MOTORS (Cont.)				
Application	Axle Gap (Inches) ①	Caster (Degrees)	Camber (Degrees)	Toe-In (Inches)	Steering Axis Inclin. (Degrees)
P10	2½	2.3±1.0	0.2±0.7	3/16	.....
	2¾	2.0±1.0	0.2±0.7	3/16	.....
	3	1.7±1.0	0.2±0.7	3/16	.....
	3¼	1.5±1.0	0.2±0.7	3/16	.....
	3½	1.2±1.0	0.2±0.7	3/16	.....
	3¾	0.9±1.0	0.2±0.7	3/16	.....
	4	0.6±1.0	0.2±0.7	3/16	.....
	4¼	0.4±1.0	0.2±0.7	3/16	.....
	4½	0.1±1.0	0.2±0.7	3/16	.....
	4¾	−0.1±1.0	0.2±0.7	3/16	.....
	5	−0.3±1.0	0.2±0.7	3/16	.....
P20 & 30	2	2.9±1.0④⑤	0.2±0.7	3/16	.....
	2¼	2.6±1.0④⑤	0.2±0.7	3/16	.....
	2½	2.3±1.0④⑤	0.2±0.7	3/16	.....
	2¾	2.0±1.0④⑤	0.2±0.7	3/16	.....
	3	1.7±1.0④⑤	0.2±0.7	3/16	.....
	3¼	1.4±1.0④⑤	0.2±0.7	3/16	.....
	3½	1.2±1.0④⑤	0.2±0.7	3/16	.....
	3¾	0.9±1.0④⑤	0.2±0.7	3/16	.....
	4	0.6±1.0④⑤	0.2±0.7	3/16	.....
	4¼	0.4±1.0④⑤	0.2±0.7	3/16	.....
	4½	0.2±1.0④⑤	0.2±0.7	3/16	.....
	4¾	0.1±1.0④⑤	0.2±0.7	3/16	.....

NOTE − *The vehicle series and model application in this table has been abbreviated for common reference to both Chevrolet and GMC. Chevrolet models use numerical designations as listed; GMC models use numerical designations as follows; 1500 = 10; 2500 = 20; 3500 = 30.*

① − Clearance is between jounce bumper and frame.
② − On K30 models, Camber is 0.5.
③ − No adjustment provision .
④ − Add .3° Caster on vehicles with Hydroboost Brake System.
⑤ − Subtract .4° Caster on vehicles with Dual Rear Wheels.

Wheel Alignment

WHEEL ALIGNMENT PROCEDURES

PRE-ALIGNMENT CHECKS

NOTE – *Before making wheel alignment adjustments, perform the following checks.*

1) Tires should be equal in size and runout must not be excessive. Tires and wheels should be in balance, and inflated to manufacturer's specifications.

2) Wheel bearings must be properly adjusted.

3) Steering linkage and suspension must not have excessive looseness. Check for wear in tie rod ends and ball joints.

4) Steering gear box must not have excessive play. Check and adjust to manufacturer's specifications.

5) Vehicle must be at curb height with full fuel load, no passengers, spare tire in place but no extra load in vehicle.

6) Vehicle must be on level floor with suspension settled. Bounce front and rear of vehicle several times and allow it to settle to normal riding height.

7) If steering wheel is not centered with front wheels in straight ahead position, correct by shortening one tie rod adjusting sleeve and lengthening opposite sleeve equal amounts.

8) Ensure wheel lug nuts are tightened to manufacturer's specifications.

WHEEL LUG NUTS TIGHTENING SPECIFICATIONS

Application	Ft. Lbs.
Chevrolet & GMC	
C, P & G10 & G20	75-100
All K Models	70-90
C, P, & G30	
W/Single Rear Wheels	90-120
C, P & G30	
W/Dual Rear Wheels	110-140
W/Dual Rear Wheels & ⅝" Studs	130-180
Dodge & Plymouth	
All W & D Models	
W/Cone Type Nut	
½"-20	105
⅝"-18	200
W/Flanged Type Nut	325
All B, CB, MB & PB Models	
W/Cone Type Nut	
½"-20	85-125
⅝"-18	175-225
W/Flanged Type Nut	300-325
Ford Motor Co.	
All Models	
½"-20	90
9/16"-18 W/Single Rear Wheels	145
9/16"-18 W/Dual Rear Wheels	220
Jeep	
All Models (Exc. J20 Truck)	75
J20 Truck	130

CAMBER

Camber is the tilting of the wheel, outward at either top or bottom, as viewed from the front of vehicle. When wheels tilt outward at the top from the centerline of vehicle, camber is said to be positive. When wheels tilt inward at the top, camber is said to be negative. Amount of tilt is measured in degrees from vertical.

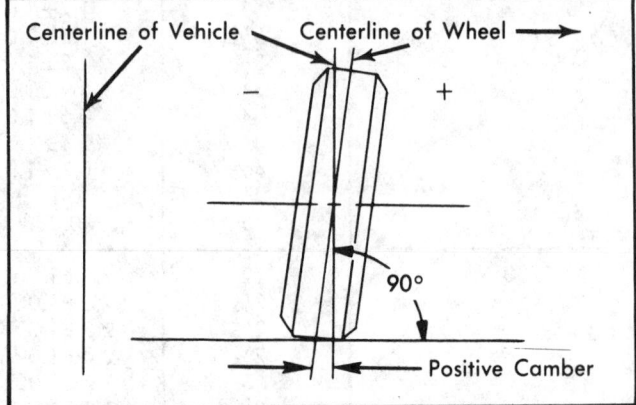

Fig. 1   Camber Angle

CASTER

Caster is the tilting of front steering axis, either forward or backward from vertical, as viewed from side of vehicle. When axis is tilted backward from vertical, caster is said to be positive, creating a trailing action on front wheels. When axis is tilted forward, caster is negative, causing a leading action on front wheels.

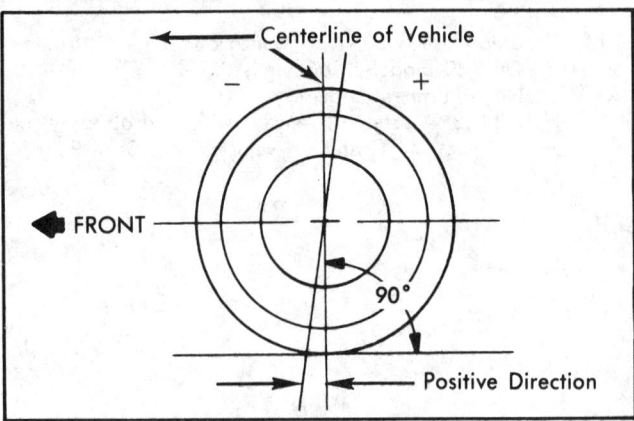

Fig. 2   Caster Angle

TOE-IN ADJUSTMENT

Measure toe-in with front wheels in straight ahead position and steering wheel centered. Adjust toe-in by loosening clamps and turning adjusting sleeve or adjustable end on right and left tie rods equally and in opposite directions to maintain steering wheel in centered position. When tightening clamps, make sure that clamp bolts are positioned so there will be no interference with other parts throughout entire travel of steering linkage.

CAUTION – *Face of tie rod end must be parallel with machined surface of steering rod end to prevent cocking and binding of the ball end in service.*

WHEEL ALIGNMENT PROCEDURES (Cont.)

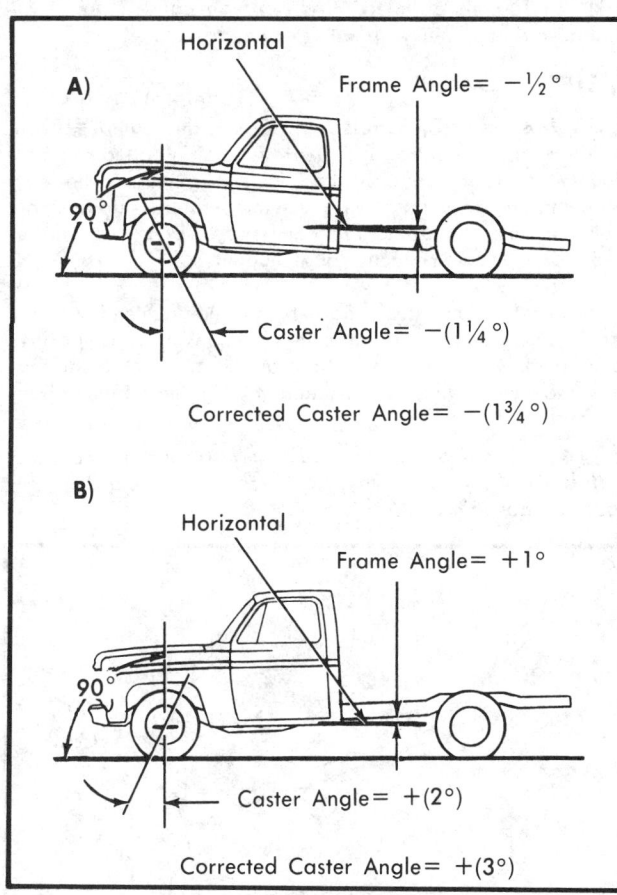

Fig. 3   Determining Corrected Caster Angle

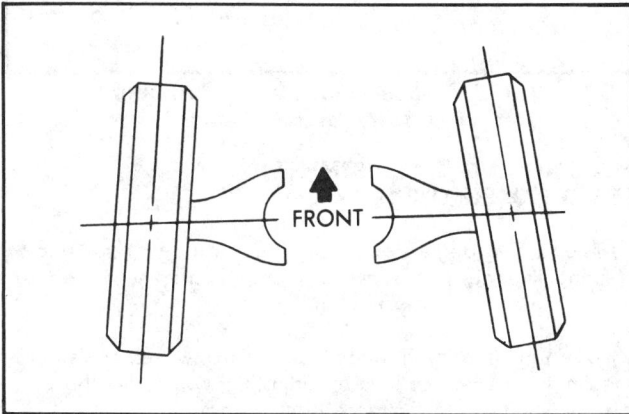

Fig. 4   Wheel Toe-In

TOE-OUT ON TURNS

1) Toe-out check is a check for bent or damaged parts, and not a service adjustment. With caster, camber, and toe-in properly adjusted, check toe-out with weight of vehicle on wheels (use full-floating turn table under each wheel), repeating test with each wheel positioned for right and left turns.

2) Incorrect toe-out generally indicates a bent steering arm. Replace arm and recheck all wheel alignment adjustments.

CAUTION — *Do not attempt to correct by straightening parts.*

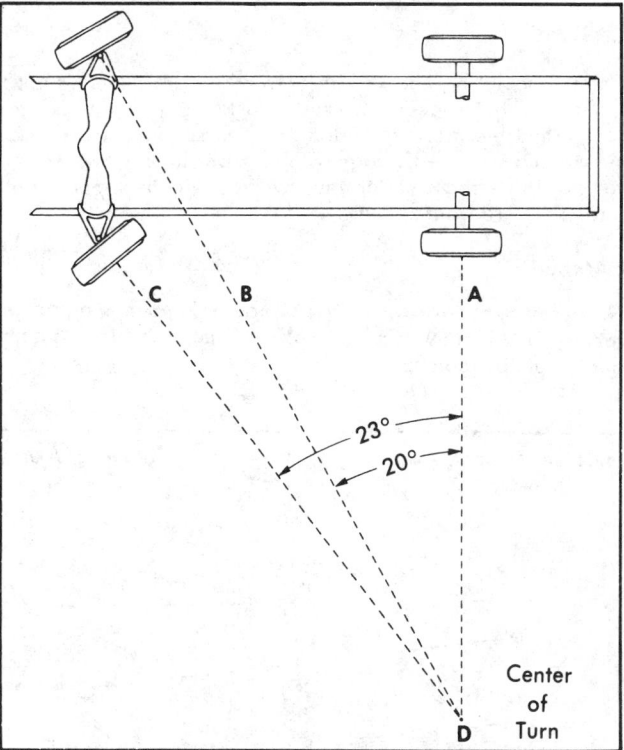

Fig. 5   Wheel Toe-Out on Turns

STEERING AXIS INCLINATION

1) This is a check for bent or damaged parts, and not a service adjustment. Vehicle must be level (crosswise and lengthwise) and camber should be properly adjusted. If camber cannot be brought within limits and steering axis inclination is correct, steering knuckle is bent.

2) If camber and steering axis inclination are both incorrect by approximately the same amount, upper and lower control arms are bent. Replace parts, and recheck all wheel alignment adjustments.

CAUTION — *Do not attempt to correct by straightening parts.*

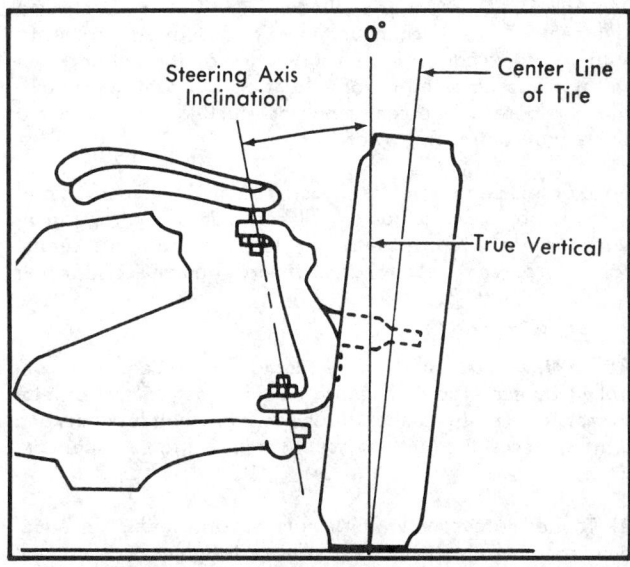

Fig. 6   Steering Axis Inclination

Wheel Alignment

CHRYSLER CORP.

ALL MODELS W/LEAF SPRINGS

CASTER

Caster should be checked after camber and steering axis inclination have been checked. Caster adjustment is accomplished by inserting wedge between spring and axle. To increase caster, insert wedge with thick portion toward rear of vehicle. To decrease caster, insert wedge with thick portion of wedge toward front of vehicle.

CAMBER

No adjustment is provided for camber. Camber is preset at factory, and if not within limits, axle or steering knuckle is bent and should be replaced.

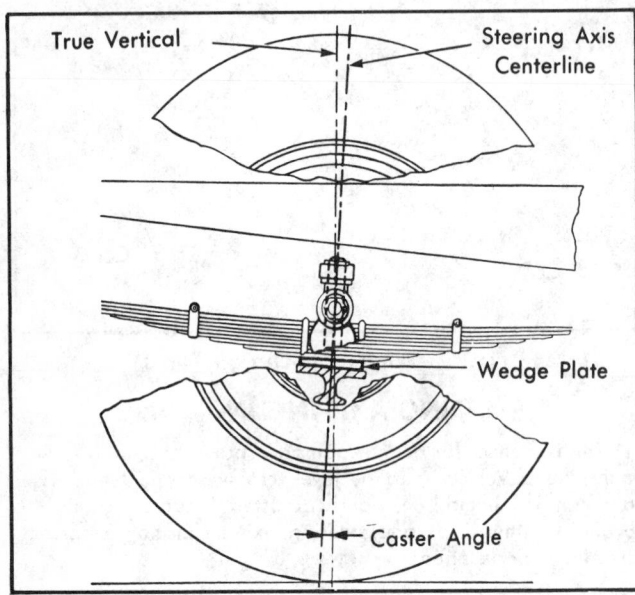

Fig. 1   Caster Angle Adjustment

ALL MODELS W/COIL SPRINGS

CASTER

AD, AW, D, PD, PW and W Models — 1) Caster is controlled by eccentric bolts which mount upper control arm-to-frame. To obtain positive caster, loosen forward eccentric bolt lock nut and turn eccentric bolt to force front part of control arm outward, or loosen rear eccentric bolt lock nut and turn eccentric to pull rear of control arm inward.

2) To obtain negative caster, loosen eccentric bolt lock nut and turn forward eccentric bolt to pull front part of control arm inward, or loosen rear eccentric bolt lock nut and turn eccentric bolt to force rear of control arm outward. Tighten eccentric bolt lock nuts to 70 ft. lbs.

CAMBER

AD, AW, D, PD, PW, and W Models — 1) Camber is controlled by eccentric bolts which mount upper control arm-to-frame. To increase camber, loosen eccentric bolt lock nuts and turn both eccentric bolts an equal amount to force upper control arm outward.

2) To decrease camber, turn both eccentric bolts an equal amount to pull upper control arm inward. Tighten eccentric bolt lock nuts to 70 Lbs.

NOTE — *Turning both eccentric bolts an equal amount will change only camber without affecting caster.*

CASTER & CAMBER

B, CB, MB, and PB Models — 1) Caster and camber is controlled by upper control arm pivot bar. Bar is bolted to frame mounted bracket through slotted holes. Alignment is made by loosening one bolt at a time and prying pivot bar into position. Make alignment adjustment for camber by moving both ends of pivot bar in or out in exactly equal amounts.

2) Adjustment for caster is made by moving each end of bar in exactly equal amounts in opposite directions. Increase positive caster by moving front of pivot bar away from engine and rear of bar toward engine an equal amount. Tighten retaining bolts to 195 ft. lbs.

NOTE — *Do not attempt to make adjustments by loosening both bolts at the same time. Caster should be held as nearly equal as possible on both wheels.*

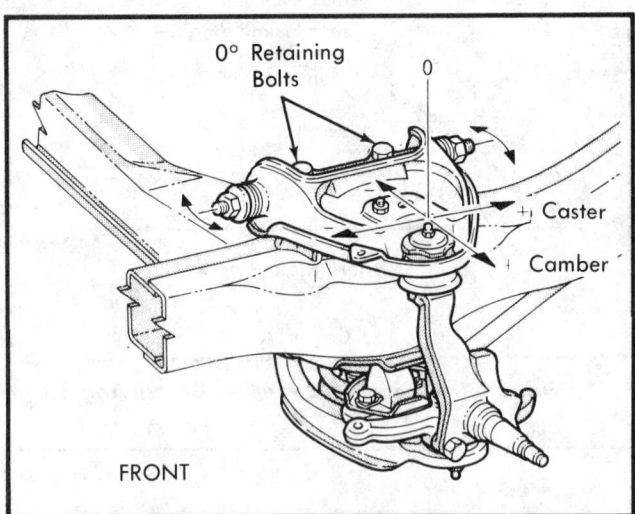

**Fig. 2   Wheel Alignment Adjustments
(B, CB, MB and PB Models)**

TURNING ANGLE ADJUSTMENT (4-WD MODELS ONLY)

1) The turning angle stop screws are located on back side of steering knuckle, just above axle shaft centerline. To adjust, loosen stop screw lock nut.

2) Using full-floating turn table under each wheel, adjust turning angle to specifications by adjusting stop screw IN to increase and OUT to decrease turning angle.

Turning Angle Adjustment (4-WD Models Only)		
Application	Left Wheel	Right Wheel
W150	37°	27°
W250	35°	①29°
W350/450	34°	29°
D150/450	33°	33°

① — If equipped with 8.75 x 16.5" tires, turning angle is 26°. If equipped with 9.50 x 16.5" tires, turning angle is 24°.

FORD

ALL MODELS

RIDING HEIGHT

NOTE — *Before making wheel alignment adjustments, make sure front riding heights are within ⅛" of each other.*

1) With vehicle on level surface, fuel tank full and no other load, bounce both front and rear until suspension settles. On E100-350 models, place 2 height blocks 3½" high between top of axle and flange on lower part of jounce bracket on each axle.

2) Measure clearance at inside area of jounce bracket (toward wheel) between top of axle and spring seat lower surface on frame. On F100-350 and Bronco models, place 2 height blocks 5" high between top of axle and outside lip of jounce bumper on each axle.

3) Measure clearance at inside of spring seat lower surface (toward center of vehicle) between top of axle and spring seat lower surface. If clearance is not correct, height must be corrected by installing proper springs or use of shims.

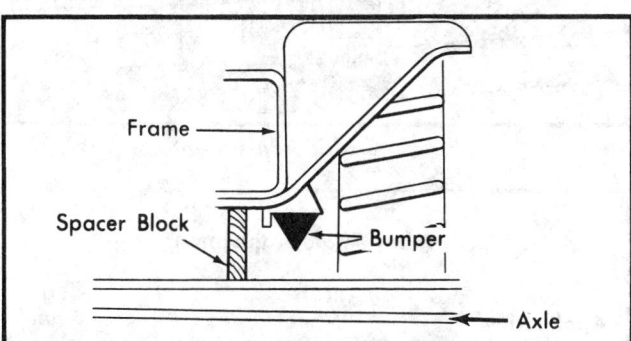

Fig. 1   Setting Riding Height

CASTER

All Models — Caster is built-in at factory and no adjustment is provided. If not within limits, replace parts as required.

CAMBER

All 2-WD Models — Camber is built-in at factory and no adjustment is provided. If not within limits, replace parts as required.

All 4-WD Models — Camber adjustment is provided by a series of interchangeable mounting sleeves for upper ball joint stud. Sleeves are available in 4 ranges of ½° increments from 1½° negative to 1½° positive.

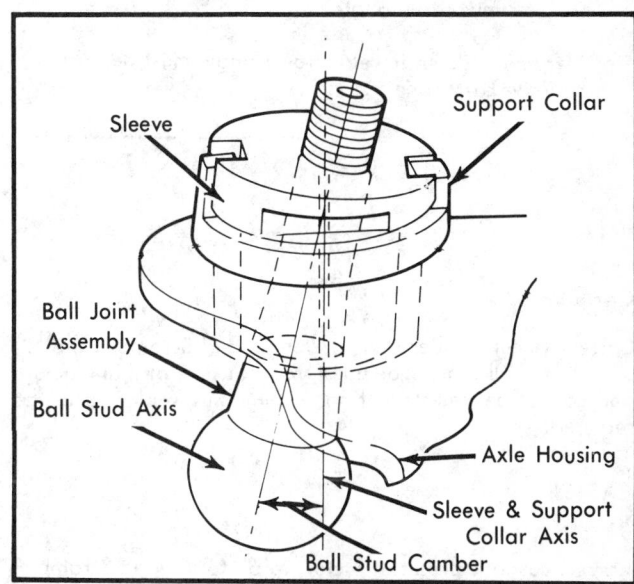

Fig. 2   Camber Adjustment

TURNING ANGLE ADJUSTMENT (4-WD MODELS ONLY)

1) The turning angle stop screws are located on back side of steering knuckle, just above axle shaft centerline. To adjust, loosen stop screw lock nut.

2) Using full-floating turn table under each wheel, adjust turning angle to specifications by adjusting stop screw IN to increase and OUT to decrease turning angle.

Turning Angle Adjustment (4-WD Models Only)		
Application	Left Wheel	Right Wheel
F150 & Bronco	36°	36°
F250	33.4°	33.4°
F350	30.3°	30.3°

GENERAL MOTORS

ALL MODELS

NOTE — *Difference in shim packs must not exceed .300". Front shim pack must be .100" minimum.*

CAMBER

NOTE — *On 4-wheel drive models, camber is built-in at factory and no adjustment is provided. If not within limits, replace parts as required.*

All Models — **1)** Camber is changed by adding or subtracting shims from upper control arm shaft. To increase camber, add equal amounts of shims to both upper control arm attaching bolts.

2) To decrease camber, subtract equal amounts of shims from both control arm attaching bolts.

NOTE — *By adding or subtracting equal amounts of shims, camber may be corrected without affecting caster.*

CASTER

NOTE — *On 4-wheel drive models, caster is built-in at factory and no adjustment is provided. If not within limits, replace parts as required.*

All Models — **1)** Measure frame angle, in relation to level, directly behind cab. Using suitable alignment equipment,

GENERAL MOTORS (Cont.)

determine existing caster. Combine frame angle with caster angle to determine corrected caster angle as follows:

- If frame is down in rear, frame angle must be subtracted from positive caster angle.

- If frame is down in rear, frame angle must be added to negative caster angle.

2) Measure distance from top of jounce bumper bracket on lower control arm to bottom of frame crossmember. Determine correct caster angle for measured clearance and adjust.

3) To increase caster, add shims between forward upper control arm attaching bolt and frame, or subtract shims from rear attaching bolt. To decrease caster, subtract shims from forward bolt, or add shims to rear bolt.

JEEP

ALL MODELS

CAMBER

Correct wheel camber of 1½° for CJ and Scrambler models and 0° for all other models is preset at time of manufacture and cannot be adjusted. If not within limits, replace parts as required.

CASTER

Correct caster is preset at factory to 6° for CJ and Scrambler models, and 4° for all other models. Adjustment is made by inserting shim between spring and axle. To increase caster, insert thick portion toward rear of vehicle. To decrease caster, insert thick portion toward front of vehicle.

TURNING ANGLE ADJUSTMENT

1) The turning angle stop screws are located on back side of steering knuckle, just above axle centerline. To adjust, loosen lock nut on stop screw.

2) Using full-floating turn table under each wheel, adjust stop screw IN to increase turning angle and OUT to decrease turning angle. Tighten lock nut.

Fig. 1   Caster Adjustment

Turning Angle Adjustment		
Application	Left Wheel	Right Wheel
CJ & Scrambler	31-32°	31-32°
All Others	37-38°	37-38°

BALL JOINT CHECKING

FACTORY RECOMMENDED METHOD

CHRYSLER CORP.

Lower Ball Joint — Ball joints are preloaded (zero axial end play). If any axial end play (up and down movement) in excess of .020" is observed, ball joint requires replacement.

FORD MOTOR CO.

F100/350 With Stamped I-Beam Front Axle — 1) Raise vehicle and place safety stand under axle as shown in *Fig. 2*.

2) To check lower ball joints, grasp lower edge of tire and move wheel in and out observing lower spindle arm and lower part of axle jaw.

3) If movement between lower part of axle jaw and lower spindle arm is in excess of 1/32", lower ball joint must be replaced.

4) To check upper ball joints, grasp upper edge of tire and move wheel in and out.

5) If movement between upper spindle arm and upper part of axle jaw is in excess of 1/32", upper ball joint must be replaced.

All Other Models — *Manufacturer gives no method for checking ball joints. See Alternate Method.*

GENERAL MOTORS

"K" Models — Raise vehicle on hoist and place jack stands just inside front springs. Disconnect connecting rod and tie rod to allow independent movement of each steering knuckle. Apply fish scale to tie rod mounting hole of steering knuckle arm. With knuckle assembly in straight ahead position, determine right angle pull required to keep knuckle assembly turning after initial breakaway. Effort must not exceed 25 lbs. in either direction.

All Other Models Upper Ball Joint — The upper ball stud is spring loaded in its socket. This minimizes looseness at this point and compensates for normal wear. If the ball stud has any noticeable lateral shake, or if it can be twisted in its socket with finger pressure, it must be replaced.

All Other Models Lower Ball Joint — Lower ball joints are a loose fit when not connected to the steering knuckle. Wear may be checked without disassembling the ball stud as follows: Raise vehicle and support weight of control arms at wheel hub and drum. Accurately measure the distance between the tip of the ball stud and the tip of the grease fitting below ball joint. Move support so that control arm is supported and wheel and hub are free. Again measure distance between ball stud and grease fitting. If difference between two measurements exceeds 3/32", replace ball joint assembly.

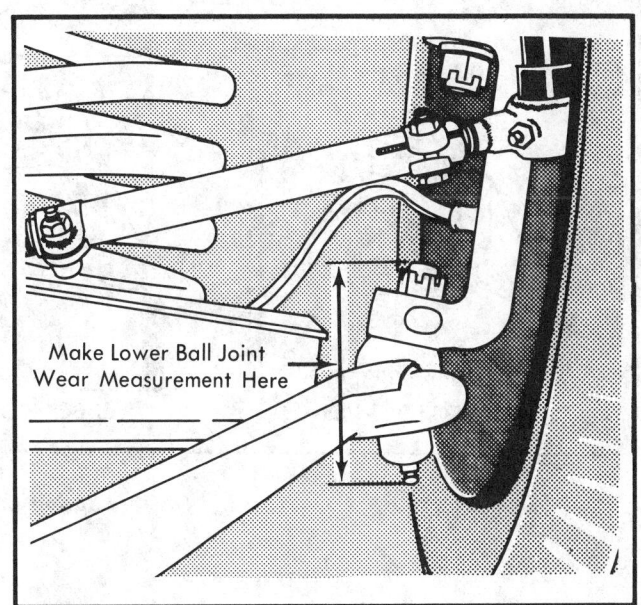

Make Lower Ball Joint Wear Measurement Here

Fig. 1   Checking General Motors Lower Ball Joint

JEEP

All Models — Manufacturer gives no method for checking ball joints. *See Alternate Method.*

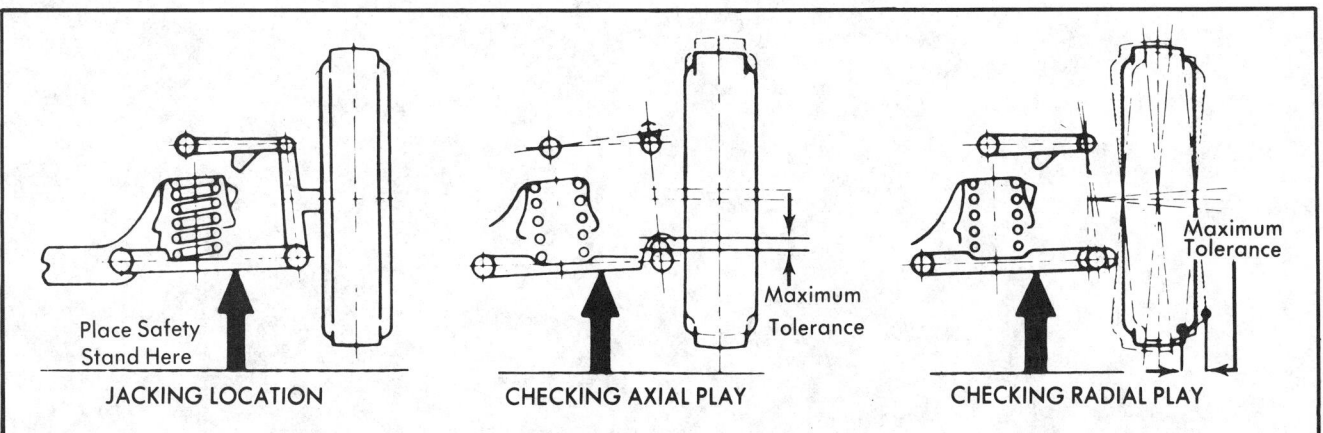

Place Safety Stand Here

JACKING LOCATION

Maximum Tolerance

CHECKING AXIAL PLAY

Maximum Tolerance

CHECKING RADIAL PLAY

Fig. 2   Spring On Lower Control Arm

Ball Joints

BALL JOINT CHECKING (Cont.)

ALTERNATE METHOD

NOTE — *There are two general types of suspensions; one type with spring or torsion bar attached to upper control arm, and other type with spring or torsion bar attached to lower control arm. Check axial play by moving wheel up and down. Check radial play by rocking wheel at top and bottom.*

SPRING ON LOWER CONTROL ARM

Upper Ball Joint — Replace ball joint if there is any perceptible looseness at joint.

Lower Ball Joint — If radial play, measured at bottom of tire on side wall, exceeds .250″, replace ball joint assembly.

SPRING ON UPPER CONTROL ARM

Upper Ball Joint — If radial play, measured at top of tire on side wall, exceeds .250″, replace ball joint assembly.

Lower Ball Joint — Replace ball joint if there is any perceptible looseness at joint.

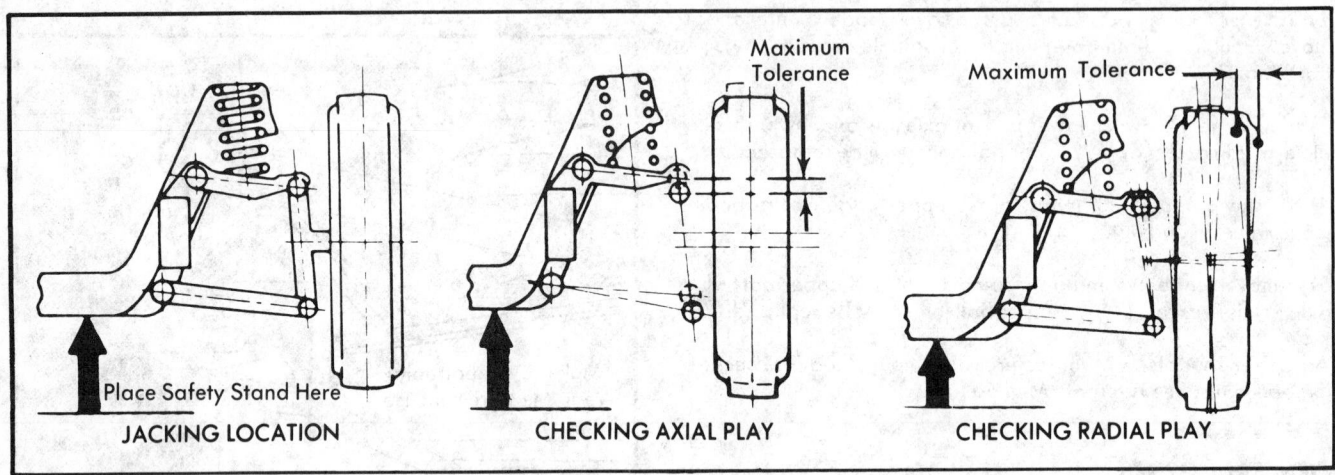

Fig. 3   Spring On Upper Control Arm

FRONT WHEEL BEARING

ADJUSTMENT

NOTE — *For removal and installation of front wheel bearings, see the Spicer (Dana) Full-Floating Axle article in DRIVE AXLE Section.*

NOTE — *Correct wheel bearing adjustment is very important on vehicles with disc brakes, as too much end play in bearings will cause disc wobble and brake damage.*

NOTE — *On all vehicles with disc brakes, caliper assembly must be removed before disc and hub, in order to work on wheel bearings. Caliper-to-disc clearance is very critical on these vehicles. It is not necessary to disconnect brake hoses in order to remove caliper assembly. Wire caliper out of the way (do not hang on brake hose).*

NOTE — *To seat bearings properly, hub must be turning while tightening adjusting nut. If cotter pin holes do not line up, back off nut only enough to insert cotter pin.*

CHRYSLER CORP.

"B", "CB", "MB" & "PB" Models — Tighten wheel bearing adjusting nut to 360 to 480 INCH lbs. while rotating rotor. Back off adjusting nut to release all preload then retighten finger tight. Install nut lock and cotter pin. Install grease cap.

"D" Models — Tighten wheel bearing adjusting nut to 90 ft. lbs. while rotating rotor. Back off adjusting nut to release all preload then retighten finger tight. Install nut lock and cotter pin. Install grease cap.

W150/250, "AW & "PW" Models — Not a bearing adjustment. When installing hub assembly, tighten nut to 100 ft. lbs. Tighten nut to next slot if necessary, to install cotter pin.

W250 (With Extra Equip.), W350/450 — Tighten inner lock nut to 50 ft. lbs. Back nut off and retorque to 30-40 ft. lbs. while turning rotor. Now back off 135-150°. Assemble outer lock nut and lock ring. Tighten lock nut to 65 ft. lbs. Bend tang over inner and outer lock nuts. Correct final end play is .001-.010".

FORD MOTOR CO.

Bronco and F150/350 Models 4-WD — Tighten adjusting nut to 50 ft. lbs. while rotating rotor. Back nut off 90°. Install locking nut and tighten to 50-80 ft. lbs. Final end play should be .001-.010" (.001-.008" for F250 4-WD with Spicer (Dana) 44-9F Axle).

Bronco, "E", and "F" Models 2-WD — Tighten nut to 22-25 ft. lbs. while rotating rotor. Now back off adjusting nut 1/8 turn. Install retainer and cotter pin without backing off nut any more.

GENERAL MOTORS

K10, K1500, K20 & K2500 — Tighten inner adjusting nut to 50 ft. lbs. while rotating rotor. Now back off nut and retighten to 35 ft. lbs. while rotating rotor. Again back off nut 3/8 turn. Install inner nut lock by aligning nearest hole in lock with adjusting nut pin. Install outer lock nut and tighten to 80 ft. lbs.

K30 & K3500 — Tighten inner adjusting nut to 50 ft. lbs. while rotating rotor. Now back off nut and retighten to 35 ft. lbs. while rotating rotor. Again back off nut 3/8 turn. Install lock washer and outer lock nut. Tighten lock nut to 65 ft. lbs. Bend ear of lock washer over outer nut at a minimum of 60°.

"C", "G" & "P" Models — Tighten adjusting nut to 12 ft. lbs. Back off adjusting nut and retighten finger tight. Loosen nut to line up for cotter pin installation but to not loosen more than 1/2 of a flat. Install cotter pin and check that final end play is .001-.005".

JEEP

"CJ" and "Scrambler" Models — Install inner lock washer and adjusting nut. Tighten nut to 50 ft. lbs. while rotating rotor. Now back off nut 1/3 turn. Install outer lock washer and nut. Tighten nut to 50 ft. lbs. Bend lock washer lip over nut.

All Other Models — Install inner adjusting nut. Tighten adjusting nut to 50 ft. lbs. while rotating rotor. Back off nut 1/3 turn. Install inner nut lock washer by aligning nearest hole in lock washer with adjusting nut pin. Install outer lock nut, and tighten to 50 ft. lbs.

NOTE — *Make sure pin on nut faces away from bearing.*

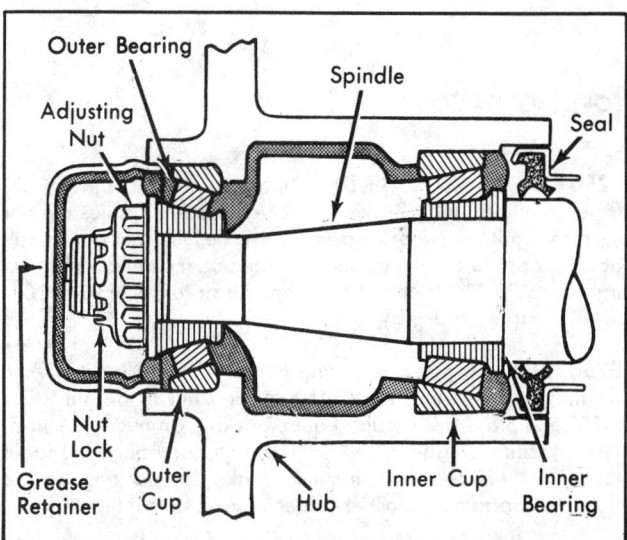

Fig. 1   Typical Front Wheel Bearing Assembly

REAR WHEEL BEARING

ADJUSTMENT

CHRYSLER CORP.

All Models (Double Nut Type) — Tighten inner adjusting nut while rotating brake drum until slight drag is felt. Back off adjusting nut $1/6$ turn to permit free rotation with zero to slight amount of end play. Install nut lock and lock nut. Tighten lock nut to 35-65 ft. lbs. (30-35 ft. lbs. on "M" models). Bend one lock tab over adjusting nut and other tab over lock nut.

NOTE — *Make sure adjusting nut does not turn while tightening lock nut.*

All Models (Wedge Type) — Raise vehicle and install jack stands. Remove axle shaft and nut lock. Loosen adjusting nut, then retighten adjusting nut to 120-140 ft. lbs. while rotating wheel. Back off nut $1/3$ turn to obtain .001-.008" end play. Tap nut lock into spindle keyway. Install new gasket and axle shaft.

GENERAL MOTORS

9¾" & 10½" Ring Gear Models — Tighten bearing adjusting nut to 50 ft. lbs. while rotating brake drum. Back off nut slightly and retighten to 35 ft. lbs. while rotating brake drum. Now back off nut $1/4$ turn. Install nut retainer so that tang will engage nearest slot on adjusting nut. Install outer lock nut and tighten to 65 ft. lbs. There should be .001-.010" bearing end play.

12¼" Ring Gear Models — Tighten bearing adjusting nut to 90 ft. lbs. while rotating brake drum. Back off nut $1/8$ turn. Install nut retainer so that retainer tang will engage nearest slot on adjusting nut. Install outer lock nut and tighten to 250 ft. lbs. There should be no bearing end play. Bearing should be slightly preloaded.

FORD MOTOR CO.

F250/350 (2-WD & 4-WD) — Tighten adjusting nut to 50-80 ft. lbs. while rotating brake drum. Now back off adjusting nut $3/8$ turn. Coat a new lock washer with axle lubricant and install against adjusting nut with smooth side out. Install lock nut and tighten to 90-110 ft. lbs. Wheel should rotate freely with .001-.010" bearing end play.

E250/350 — Tighten adjusting nut to 120-140 ft. lbs. while rotating brake drum. Back off adjusting nut to obtain .001-.010" end play. This should require backing off nut $1/8$-$1/4$ turn. Install locking wedge in key slot. Seat wedge using a suitable tool (T57T-1170-A) and hammer. Make sure locking wedge does not bottom against shoulder of adjusting nut.

NOTE — *The locking wedge and adjusting nut can be reused, providing that the locking wedge cuts a new groove into nylon retainer ring. If it is not possible to obtain the correct end play and install the wedge in uncut nylon, replace locking wedge and adjusting nut.*

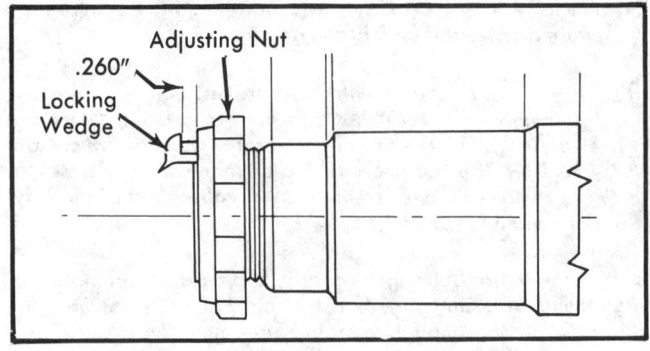

**Fig. 1   Installing Locking Wedge
Chrysler Corp. and Ford E250/350 Models**

JEEP

Truck Models With Spicer (Dana) 60 Axle — Tighten adjusting nut to 50 ft. lbs. while rotating brake drum. Back off adjusting nut $1/6$ turn. Brake drum should rotate freely without any lateral movement. Install lock washer and lock nut. Tighten lock nut to 50 ft. lbs. Bend lock washer lip over lock nut.

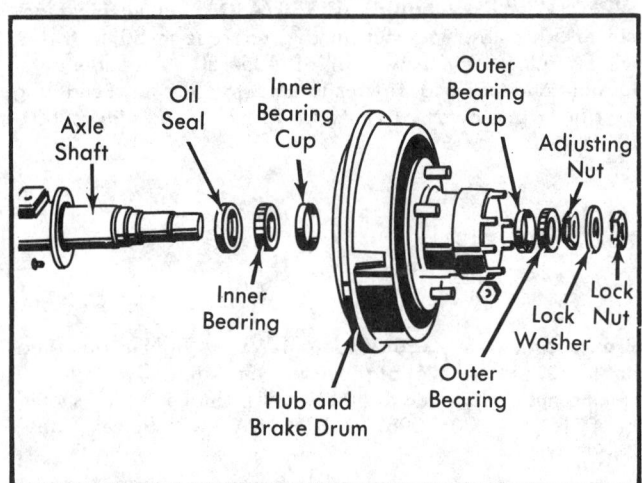

**Fig. 2   Typical Full-Floating
Rear Wheel Bearing**

Section 12

SUSPENSION

Contents

NOTE — ALSO SEE GENERAL INDEX.

IMPORTANT

*Because of the great number of model names used by vehicle manufacturers, accurate identification of models is important.
See Model Identification at the front of this publication.*

SUSPENSION TROUBLE SHOOTING

CONDITION & POSSIBLE CAUSE	CONDITION & POSSIBLE CAUSE

Front End Noise

- Loose wheel lug nuts. Loose or worn wheel bearings, shock absorbers or shock mountings, strut bushings, struts or lower control arm.
- Loose steering gear-to-frame mounting bolts.
- Steering knuckle arm contacting lower control arm wheel stop.
- Worn upper control arm bushings, or lower control arm shaft bushings.
- Insufficient lubrication on ball joints.

Front Wheel Shake, Shimmy or Vibration

- Loose or worn wheel bearings, tie rod ends, strut bushings, upper control arm ball joints, shock absorbers or linkage pivots.
- Tires or wheels out of balance.
- Incorrect front wheel alignment.
- Propeller shaft unbalanced.

Car Pulls to One Side

- Mismatched or uneven tires.
- Broken or sagging springs.
- Loose or worn strut bushings.
- Incorrect front wheel alignment or rear axle alignment.
- Front brakes dragging.

Abnormal Tire Wear

- Unbalanced or non-rotation of tires.
- Sagging or broken springs.
- Front end alignment.
- Faulty shock absorbers.
- Overloaded car.

Scuffed Tires

- Toe-in incorrect.
- Excessive speed on turns.
- Suspension arm bent or twisted.

Springs Bottom Or Sag

- Automobile overloaded.
- Leaking or worn out shocks.
- Loose or broken shackles.
- Bent, broken or improper springs.
- Improper riding height.

Ride Too Soft, Too Hard or Excessive Vertical Motion of Wheels

- Faulty or improper operation of shocks.
- Incorrect springs.

Leaning or Swaying on Corners

- Loose stabilizer bar or missing link.
- Faulty shocks or shock mountings.
- Broken or sagging springs.

Spring Noises

- Loose "U" bolts.
- Loose or worn eye bushings.
- Worn or missing interliners.

Broken Springs

- Loose "U" bolts, or inoperative shock absorbers.

Noisy Shock Absorbers

- Loose bolts or studs.
- Undercoating on shock absorber reservoir.
- Excessively worn bushing.
- Air trapped in system.

Shock Absorber Leaking Fluid

- Worn seals, or crimp in reservoir tube.

Toe Not Adjusted to Specifications

- Lower control arm bent.
- Frame bent.

Camber Not Adjusted to Specifications

- Control arm bent.
- Frame bent.
- Hub and bearing assembly not properly seated on mounting surface.

CHRYSLER CORP. COIL SPRING TYPE

Dodge
Plymouth

DESCRIPTION

Independent front suspension consists of upper and lower control arms, steering knuckles, coil springs, and hydraulic shock absorbers. Upper control arms are mounted to frame side rails, while lower control arms are mounted to crossmember. Steering knuckles are mounted between upper and lower control arms by conventional ball joints. Coil springs are mounted between seat in frame and lower control arm. Double-acting shock absorbers mount inside coil springs, and are fastened to lower control arms and frame.

ADJUSTMENT

WHEEL ALIGNMENT SPECIFICATIONS & PROCEDURES

See Wheel Alignment Specifications & Procedures in WHEEL ALIGNMENT Section.

WHEEL BEARING ADJUSTMENT

See Wheel Bearing Adjustment in WHEEL ALIGNMENT Section.

BALL JOINT CHECKING

See Ball Joint Checking in WHEEL ALIGNMENT Section.

REMOVAL & INSTALLATION

SHOCK ABSORBER

Removal – Raise and support vehicle. Turn wheels to allow best access to upper shock absorber mount. Remove upper mounting nut and retainer. Remove lower mounting bolts, and remove shock absorber from vehicle.

Installation – To install, fully extend shock absorber, and reverse removal procedure.

COIL SPRING

Removal – 1) Block brake pedal in up position. Raise vehicle and position safety stands under frame. Remove wheel and tire. Remove brake caliper retainer and anti-rattle spring. Remove caliper from disc by sliding out and away from disc. Hang caliper out of the way, but do not hang from brake line. Remove inboard brake shoe.

2) On Pick-up models, remove grease cap, cotter key, lock nut, adjusting washer and outer bearing. Carefully slide rotor from steering knuckle. Do not drag seal or inner bearing over steering knuckle threads. Remove splash shield.

3) Remove shock absorber and strut. Disconnect sway bar (if equipped). Install suitable spring compressor (DD-1278), tighten finger tight, then back off ½ turn.

4) Remove cotter keys and ball joint nuts. Install suitable ball joint breaker tool (C-3564-A). Turn threaded portion of tool to

lock against lower stud. Spread tool enough to place lower stud under pressure, then strike steering knuckle with hammer to loosen stud.

5) Remove tool. Slowly loosen spring compressor until all tension is relieved from coil spring. Remove compressor and coil spring.

Installation – To install, reverse removal procedure, and tighten all nuts and bolts.

LOWER CONTROL ARM

Removal – Raise and support vehicle, and remove wheel. Remove coil spring as previously described. Remove lower control arm pivot bolt, and remove lower control arm from vehicle.

Installation – To install, reverse removal procedure. Do not tighten lower control arm pivot bolt until vehicle weight is supported by front suspension. Check wheel alignment.

UPPER CONTROL ARM

Removal – 1) Raise and support vehicle and remove wheel and tire. On Van models, block brake pedal in up position and remove brake caliper retainer and anti-rattle spring. Remove caliper from disc and hang out of the way. Do not hang from brake line. Remove inboard brake shoe.

2) On all models, remove shock absorber and install suitable spring compressor (DD-1278). Tighten finger tight and then back-off ½ turn. Remove cotter keys and ball joint nuts. Position suitable ball joint breaker tool (C-3564-A), with threaded portion of tool locking against upper stud.

3) Spread tool to place stud under pressure, then strike stud with hammer to loosen. Remove tool. Remove retaining bolts and control arm.

Installation – To install, reverse removal procedure. Do not tighten control arm pivot bolts until vehicle weight is supported by front suspension. Check wheel alignment.

LOWER BALL JOINT

Removal – With lower control arm removed, remove ball joint seal. Press out ball joint using a suitable tool (C-4212).

NOTE – *On some models it may be possible to remove ball joint with control arm still in vehicle, but disconnected from steering knuckle and with coil spring removed.*

Installation – Using same tool as used for removal, press ball joint into control arm. Install seal using a suitable tool (C-4034). Install control arm as previously outlined.

UPPER BALL JOINT

Removal – Raise and support vehicle under outer end of lower control arm. Remove wheel and tire. Remove ball joint nuts. Using ball joint breaker tool (C-3564-A), free upper ball joint. Using tool C-3561 unscrew ball joint from control arm.

CHRYSLER CORP. COIL SPRING TYPE (Cont.)

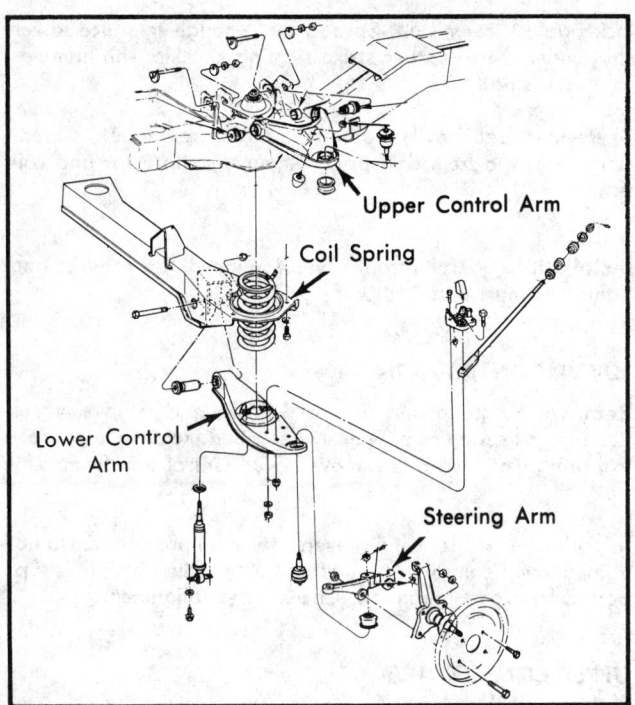

Fig. 1 Exploded View of Front Suspension Assembly

Upper Control Arm

Coil Spring

Lower Control Arm

Steering Arm

Installation — To install, reverse removal procedure, and tighten all nuts and bolts.

STEERING KNUCKLE

Removal — Block brake pedal in up position. Raise vehicle and remove wheel and tire assembly. Remove caliper retainer and anti-rattle spring assemblies. Remove caliper and hang out of way. Do not let caliper hang by hydraulic line. Remove rotor and bearings. Place jack under outer end of lower control arm. Disconnect tie rod at steering knuckle. *See Steering Linkage in STEERING Section.* Separate ball joint studs from steering knuckle as previously described. Remove steering knuckle from vehicle.

Installation — To install, reverse removal procedure, and tighten all nuts and bolts.

TIGHTENING SPECIFICATIONS

Application	Ft. Lbs.
Upper Ball Joint Nut	
D350	50
All Other Models	100
Upper Joint-to-Control Arm	125
Lower Ball Joint Nut	
1¹⁄₁₆″ Nut	135
¾″ Nut	175
Front Strut Bolt	
D150/450	175
All Other Models	135
Rear Strut Nut	
D150/450	85
All Other Models	52
Upper Shock Absorber Mount	①25
Lower Shock Absorber Mount	
All Exc. 4WD	17
All 4WD	55
Upper Control Arm (Eccentric) Bolt	70
Lower Control Arm-to-Crossmember	
"B", "CB", "MB", "PB"	175
All Other Models	210

① — On W150/250 with 44FBJ Axle and W250/350 with 60 Axle, torque is 55 ft. lbs.

FORD 2-WD COIL SPRING TYPE

"F" Models
"E" Models

DESCRIPTION

Front suspension consists of two "I-Beam" reverse Elliot type axles, mounted to a frame pivot bracket at one end, and to the steering knuckle and a radius arm at the other end. Steering knuckle is mounted to the axle by solid, constant diameter kingpin. Either Delrin or bronze bushings are pressed into steering knuckles to provide bearing surfaces for kingpin. Radius arm runs rearward from axle and is attached to a bracket, mounted to frame side rail, at the rear. Coil spring is seated on top of radius arm at bottom of spring, and in a bracket mounted to frame at the top. Hydraulic, double-action shock absorber is mounted between frame and radius arm to dampen road shock.

ADJUSTMENT

WHEEL ALIGNMENT SPECIFICATIONS & PROCEDURES

See Wheel Alignment Specifications & Procedures in WHEEL ALIGNMENT Section.

WHEEL BEARING ADJUSTMENT

See Wheel Bearing Adjustment in WHEEL ALIGNMENT Section.

REMOVAL & INSTALLATION

STEERING KNUCKLE

Removal (Forged & Stamped Front I-Beam Axle) – 1) Raise vehicle and support under front axle. Remove wheel and tire assembly. Remove brake caliper from mount and wire it up out of the way. Remove brake rotor, inner bearing cone and seal and brake dust shield. Disconnect steering linkage from spindle using tool 3290-C.

2) On forged I-beam remove nut and lock washer from locking bolt and remove locking bolt. Remove upper and lower pin plugs, then drive spindle out the top of the axle and remove spindle and bearing. Knock out the spindle pin seal.

3) On stamped I-beam remove the cotter pin from the upper ball joint stud. Remove the nut from the upper and lower ball

joint stud. Strike the bottom of the spindle to pop the ball joints loose from the spindle. Remove the spindle.

NOTE – *Do not use a pickle fork to separate the ball joint from the spindle as it will damage the seal and the ball joint socket.*

Installation (Forged Front I-Beam) – Before installing steering knuckle, pack thrust bearing with chassis lubricant, and position bearing with open end (lip side) down against steering knuckle. Install kingpin in axle and steering knuckle, making sure notch in kingpin is aligned with lock pin hole in steering knuckle. Install king pin so that end with letter "T" stamped on it is up. Install a new lock pin and tighten nut. Install upper and lower spindle plugs. To complete installation, reverse removal procedure.

Installation (Stamped Front I-Beam) – Before assembly, make sure the upper and lower ball joints seals are in place. Place the spindle over the ball joints. Install the nut on the lower ball joint stud and tighten to specification. Install the nut on upper ball joint stud. Tighten to specifications, and continue to tighten the nut until it lines up with hole in stud. Install cotter pin. To complete installation, reverse removal procedure.

KINGPIN BUSHINGS

NOTE – *Delrin bushings do not require special tools for removal or installation, and should not be reamed.*

Removal – Remove steering knuckle from vehicle as previously outlined. Drive bushing out of bore in steering knuckle, using a tool slightly smaller in diameter than bore in steering knuckle. Clean bores in steering knuckle, and make sure lubrication grooves in knuckle are not plugged.

Installation – Position bushing in steering knuckle bore, making sure lubrication hole in bushing is aligned with lubrication fitting in steering knuckle, and open end of oil groove is toward axle. Using a driver which pilots in bushing, drive bushing into place in knuckle (Delrin bushings can be forced into place by hand). Ream bronze bushings until inside diameter of bushing is .001-.003" larger than outside diameter of kingpin. Clean all metal shavings from bushing after reaming. Lubricate bushing and kingpin, and install steering knuckle on vehicle as previously described. Install shims between top of axle and steering knuckle, to obtain .003-.010" axle-to-knuckle clearance.

BALL JOINTS

Removal – Remove steering knuckle from vehicle as previously outlined. Support the upper jaw when pressing out the upper ball joint. Press out lower ball joint.

Installation – Seat the upper ball joint squarely in the hole by hand. Using ball joint installation tool, press the ball joint in until firmly seated. Use the same procedure for pressing the lower ball joint. Axle jaw must be supported before pressing in the ball joint. To complete installation, reverse removal procedure.

COIL SPRING

Removal – Raise front of vehicle, place safety stands under frame and a floor jack under axle. Disconnect lower shock absorber mount. Remove bolts securing upper spring retainer

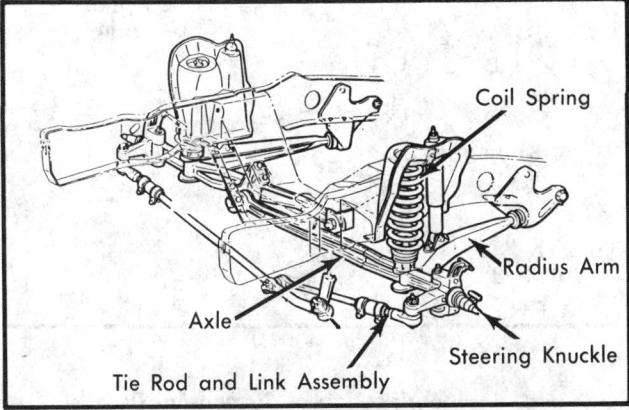

Fig. 1   F100/350 Front Suspension Assembly

Coil Spring

Radius Arm

Steering Knuckle

Axle

Tie Rod and Link Assembly

FORD 2-WD COIL SPRING TYPE (Cont.)

and remove retainer. Remove nut securing lower spring retainer to spring seat and axle. Lower jack under axle and remove spring.

Installation – Place spring in position and raise front axle with jack. Place lower spring retainer over stud and lower seat, and tighten attaching nut. Place upper retainer over the spring and upper seat and tighten bolts. Connect lower shock absorber mount. Remove jack, and safety stands, and lower vehicle.

FRONT AXLE

Removal – Raise vehicle and position safety stands under frame. Remove steering knuckle and front spring as previously outlined. Remove stabilizer bar if equipped. Remove lower spring seat from radius arm. Remove bolt connecting radius arm and bracket to front axle. Remove axle pivot bolt and remove axle.

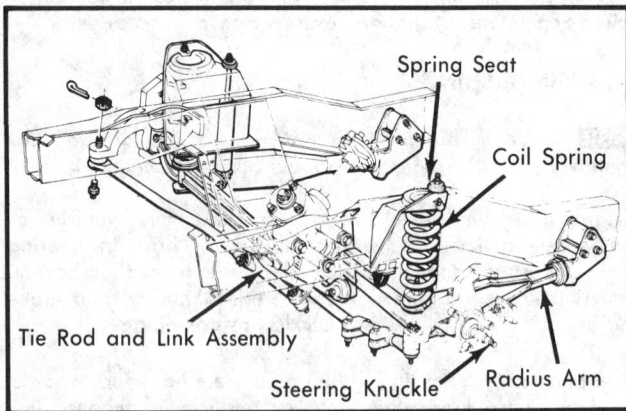

Fig. 2 E100/350 Front Suspension Assembly

Installation – Position axle and install pivot bolt and nut finger tight. Connect radius arm and front bracket, and install and tighten bolt. Install lower spring seat, making sure it aligns over radius arm bolt. Install coil spring as previously outlined. Tighten axle pivot bolt. Install steering knuckle as previously outlined, and stabilizer bar if equipped.

RADIUS ARM

Removal – Raise vehicle and position safety stands under frame and a floor jack under axle. Disconnect lower shock absorber mount. Remove front spring as previously outlined. Remove lower spring seat and remove bolt securing radius arm to axle. Remove nut, rear washer and insulator from rear radius arm mount. Disconnect tie rod and remove radius arm.

Installation – To install radius arm, reverse removal procedure.

STABILIZER BAR

Removal – **1)** Disconnect left and right ends of front stabilizer bar from the link assembly attached to the "I" beam bracket.

2) Disconnect the retainer bolts and remove the stabilizer bar. Disconnect the stabilizer link assembly by loosening left and right locknuts from I-beam brackets.

Installation – **1)** Loosely assemble the entire assembly with both links outboard of the stabilizer bar. Pull stabilizer bar rearward and install bar ends to the links and install link bolts with threads pointing outward.

2) Install link-to-stabilizer bar washers and tighten retaining nuts. Tighten stabilizer bar-to-frame mounting nuts while pushing bar forward to swing the links away from the axle mounting brackets.

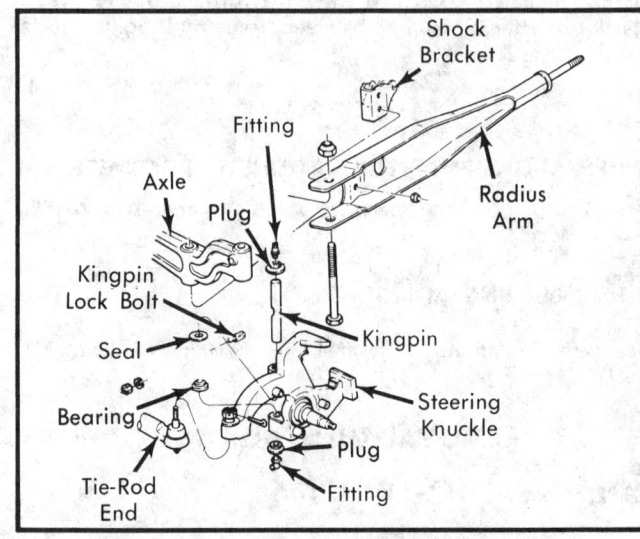

Fig. 3 Identification of Suspension Details "E" Models (Exc. E250 and E350 Steering Knuckle)

3) Ensure that stabilizer bar insulators are properly seated and that bar is centered in vehicle.

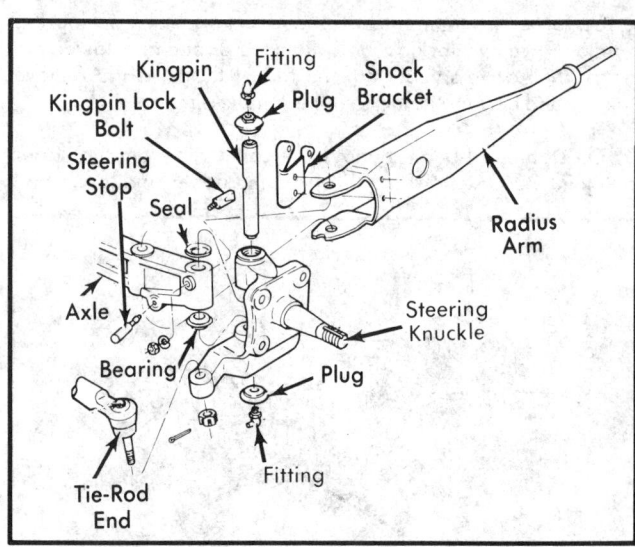

Fig. 4 Identification of Suspension Details E250 and E350 Steering Knuckle

FORD 2-WD COIL SPRING TYPE (Cont.)

SHOCK ABSORBER

1) Insert a wrench from the rear side of the spring upper seat to hold shock upper retaining nut. Loosen the stud by turning the hex on the exposed lower part of the stud.

2) Disconnect the lower end of the shock absorber from the lower bracket bolt and nut. Remove shock absorbers, washers and rubber insulators.

3) To install, reverse removal procedures, making sure to install NEW rubber insulators.

TIGHTENING SPECIFICATIONS

Application	Ft. Lbs.
Upper Shock Absorber Mount	15-25
Shock Absorber Bracket-to-Radius Arm	27-37
Upper Spring Retainer-to-Spring Seat	13-18
Lower Spring Retainer-to-Spring Seat	30-70
Radius Arm-to-Front Axle	240-320
Radius Arm-to-Bracket	80-120
Front Axle Pivot Bolt	120-150
Kingpin Lock Bolt	38-62
Kingpin Plug	35-50
Radius Arm-to-Axle	
Upper Stud	240-260
Lower Bolt	320-340
Radius Arm Bracket-to-Axle Screws	20-26
Stabilizer Bar-to-Frame	27-37
Stabilizer Bar Retaining Nuts	48-65
Upper Ball Joint	85-110
Lower Ball Joint	140-180

Front Suspension

FORD 4-WD COIL SPRING TYPE

Bronco
F150

DESCRIPTION

Front suspension consists of a driving axle, two coil springs, two radius arms, a side strut bar and two hydraulic shock absorbers (some models may be equipped with optional dual quad shock absorbers). Radius arms attach to frame side rails and are clamped around axle housing. If vehicle is equipped with optional quad shock absorbers, the front clamp portion of the radius arm is also the lower shock mount.

Coil springs are mounted to radius arms directly over axle housing and to brackets attached to frame side rails. Standard equipment shock absorbers attach to frame side rails and radius arms behind coil spring. Optional dual quad shock absorbers mount in front of spring in same manner. The side strut bar, used to eliminate axle side movement, is attached to left frame rail and at right side of axle housing.

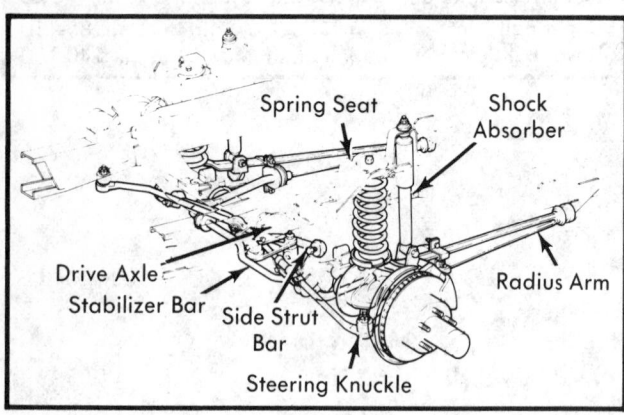

Fig. 1   Identification of Front Suspension Components Bronco & F150

ADJUSTMENT

WHEEL ALIGNMENT SPECIFICATIONS & PROCEDURES

See Wheel Alignment Specifications & Procedures in WHEEL ALIGNMENT Section.

WHEEL BEARING ADJUSTMENT

See Wheel Bearing Adjustment in WHEEL ALIGNMENT Section.

REMOVAL & INSTALLATION

COIL SPRING

Removal (Bronco & F150) — Raise vehicle. Remove shock absorber-to-lower bracket bolt and nut. Remove lower spring retainer nuts. Remove upper spring attaching screw and upper retainer. Place safety stands under frame rails and lower axle enough to relieve tension on spring. Remove spring and lower retainer from vehicle.

Installation — To install, reverse removal procedure. Tighten nuts and bolts to specifications.

RADIUS ARM

Removal (Bronco & F150) — Raise vehicle and place safety stands under frame side rails. Remove shock absorber attaching bolts and remove shock absorber from radius arm. Remove lower spring attaching bolt. Remove radius arm rear insulator. Lower axle and allow axle to move forward. Remove bolt and stud attaching radius arm to axle. Move axle forward and remove radius arm from axle. Pull radius arm from frame brackets.

Installation — Position washer and insulator on rear of radius arm and place radius arm into the frame bracket, loosely installing attaching nut. Position radius arm to axle. Install new bolts and stud and attach radius arm to axle. Position lower spring seat, insulator and retainer to spring and axle and attach. Tighten rear radius rod attaching nut. Install shock absorber and tighten nuts.

STEERING KNUCKLE

Removal & Installation — *See Steering Knuckles in DRIVE AXLE Section for removal and installation.*

DUAL QUAD SHOCK ABSORBERS

Removal — Remove self-locking nut, steel washer and rubber bushings from upper end of shock absorbers. Remove self-locking nut from lower end of shocks. Remove shock absorbers.

Installation — Replace rubber bushings when replacing shock absorbers. Place shock absorbers on mounting brackets with large diameter on top. Install bushings, steel washers and self-locking nuts and tighten.

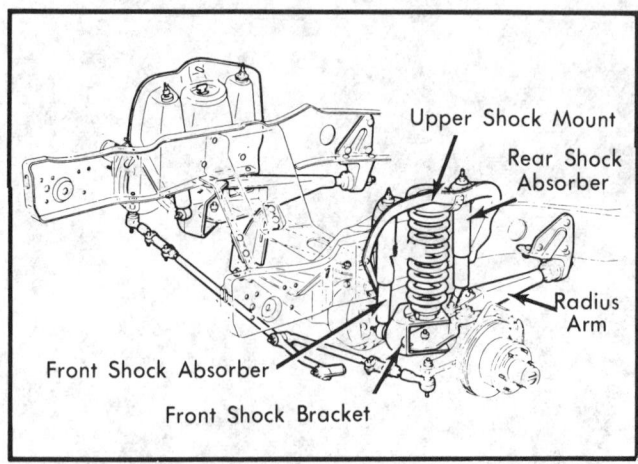

Fig. 2   Dual Quad Shock Absorber Components

STABILIZER BAR

Removal — 1) Remove nuts, bolts and washers connecting stabilizer bar to links. Remove nuts and bolts of stabilizer bar retainer. Remove stabilizer bar insulator assembly.

2) Remove coil spring and lower spring seat. Remove stabilizer bar mounting bracket attaching stud and bracket. Remove stabilizer bar.

FORD 4-WD COIL SPRING TYPE (Cont.)

Installation – 1) Locate the brackets so that the locating tang is positioned in the radius arm notch (or quad shock bracket notch if vehicle has quad shocks).

2) Reposition the spring lower seat and reinstall the spring and retainer. To reinstall the stabilizer bar insulator assembly, assemble all nuts, bolts and washers to the bar, brackets, retainers and links loosely.

3) With the bar positioned correctly, torque retainer nuts, with retainer around the insulator. Then torque all remaining nuts at the link assemblies.

TIGHTENING SPECIFICATIONS

Application	Ft. Lbs.
Upper Spring Retainer	13-18
Lower Spring Retainer	30-70
Radius Arm-to-Bracket	80-120
Shock Absorber Mounting Bolt	
Lower	40-60
Upper	15-25
Radius Arm-to-Axle	
Upper Stud	240-260
Lower Bolt	320-340
Radius Arm Bracket-to-Axle Screws	20-26
Stabilizer Bar-to-Frame	48-65
Stabilizer Bar Retaining Nuts	27-37

Front Suspension

GENERAL MOTORS COIL SPRING TYPE

Chevrolet (2-WD Models)
GMC (2-WD Models)

DESCRIPTION

Independent front suspension consists of upper and lower control arms with steering knuckle mounted between by means of ball joints. Upper and lower control arms are mounted to crossmember by means of pivot shafts, through either rubber or threaded steel bushings. Coil springs are mounted between lower control arm and a formed seat in suspension crossmember. Hydraulic shock absorbers are mounted between lower control arm and frame at rear of suspension. A stabilizer bar is transversely mounted to frame side rails and is connected at ends to lower control arms by link units.

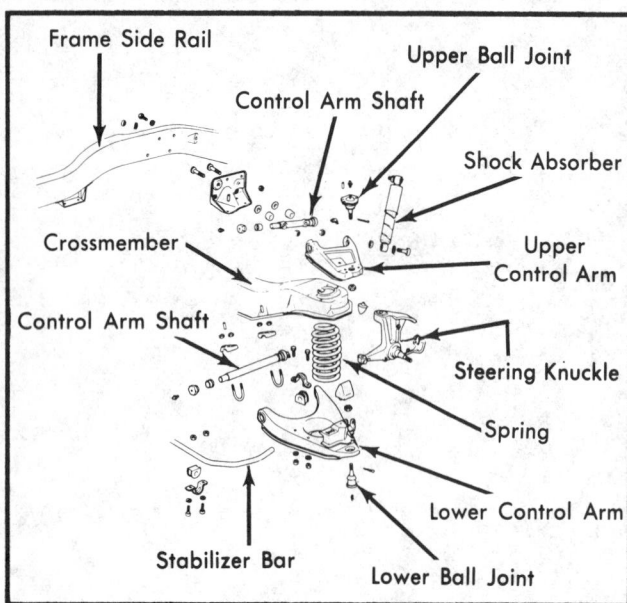

Fig. 1 Exploded View of Front Suspension Assembly

ADJUSTMENT

WHEEL ALIGNMENT SPECIFICATIONS & PROCEDURES

See Wheel Alignment Specifications & Procedures in WHEEL ALIGNMENT Section.

WHEEL BEARING ADJUSTMENT

See Wheel Bearing Adjustment in WHEEL ALIGNMENT Section.

BALL JOINT CHECKING

See Ball Joint Checking in WHEEL ALIGNMENT Section.

REMOVAL & INSTALLATION

SHOCK ABSORBERS

Removal — Remove nuts and eye bolts securing upper and lower ends of shock absorber, and remove shock absorber from vehicle.

Installation — Position shock absorber over mounting bolts or into mounting brackets and install eye bolts. Tighten all bolts and nuts.

STABILIZER BAR

Removal — Raise vehicle, and remove nuts and bolts attaching stabilizer bar brackets to frame. Remove link bolts and bushings at lower control arm and remove stabilizer bar from vehicle.

Installation — Position stabilizer bar on frame and loosely install frame bushings and brackets. Install link units at lower control arms, and tighten all nuts and bolts. Lower vehicle.

COIL SPRINGS

Removal — Raise vehicle and support under frame so that control arms hang free. Disconnect shock absorber and stabilizer bar at lower control arm. Install a suitable support tool (J-23028) onto jack and position tool under lower control arm shaft so that shaft seats in grooves of tool. Install a safety chain through lower control arm and spring. Raise jack to relieve tension on lower control arm shaft and remove control arm shaft bolts. Carefully lower jack until all tension is released from spring, and remove spring from vehicle.

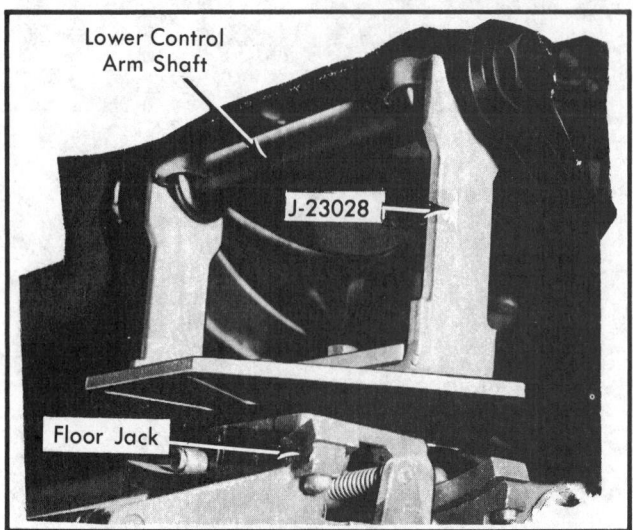

**Fig. 2 Coil Spring Removal
Using a Floor Jack and Special Tool**

Installation — To install coil spring, reverse removal procedure, noting the following; On models with air cylinders in coil springs, check for leaks and damage before installation.

STEERING KNUCKLE

NOTE — It is recommended that front of vehicle be supported with a twin-post hoist so the front coil spring remains compressed, yet the steering knuckle is accessible. If a frame hoist is used, support lower control arm with a jackstand to safely retain spring in its curb height position.

Removal — Raise and support vehicle as described above. Remove wheel, hub, disc rotor and caliper. Remove disc splash shield. Remove upper and lower ball joint cotter pins and LOOSEN nuts. Using suitable tool (J-23742), free steering knuckle from ball studs. Remove ball stud nuts and withdraw steering knuckle.

GENERAL MOTORS COIL SPRING TYPE (Cont.)

Installation – Clean all parts thoroughly, and inspect for damage. To install, reverse removal procedure and tighten all nuts and bolts.

CAUTION – *When installing ball joint nuts, do not loosen nut to install cotter pin. If necessary, tighten one extra notch.*

UPPER BALL JOINT

Removal – Raise vehicle and support front of vehicle on safety stands positioned under lower control arms. Remove cotter pin from upper ball stud and LOOSEN nut 2 turns. Remove brake caliper and suspend it from frame. Do not hang caliper by brake line. Install tool J-23742 between the ball studs. Loosen ball stud and remove tool and stud nut. Drill out rivets and remove ball joint assembly.

Installation – To install, reverse removal procedure. Use nuts and bolts in place of rivets to attach ball joint to control arm.

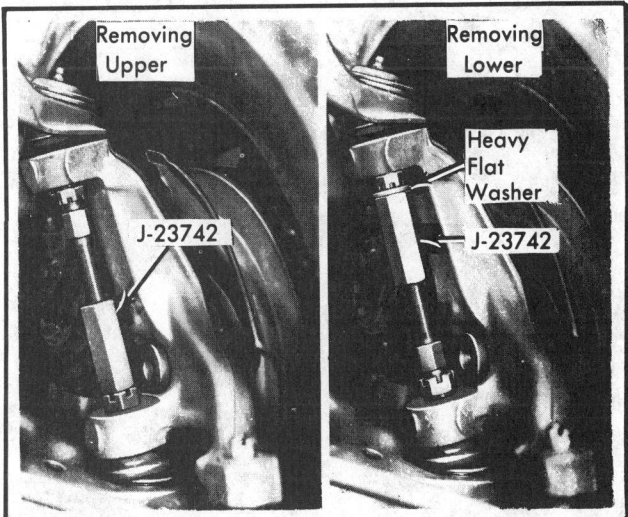

Fig. 3   Removing Upper and Lower Ball Joints

LOWER BALL JOINT

Removal – Raise vehicle and support front of vehicle with safety stands positioned under lower control arms. Remove wheel and tire. Remove lower stud cotter pin and LOOSEN stud nut 2 turns. Remove brake caliper and suspend out of way. Do not suspend by brake line. Install tool J-23742 between the ball studs, and loosen ball stud. Remove tool and ball stud nut. Pull the brake disc and steering knuckle assembly up off the ball stud and support upper control arm with a block of wood. Press lower ball joint out of its seat and remove from vehicle.

Installation – Using tools (J-9519-10 and J-9519-16) install new ball joint into the control arm. Reverse removal procedure, to complete installation.

UPPER CONTROL ARM

Removal – Raise vehicle and support front of vehicle with safety stands positioned under lower control arm. Remove cotter pin from upper ball joint and LOOSEN nut. Remove brake caliper and suspend out of way. Do not suspend by brake line.

Using suitable tool (J-23742), loosen ball joint in steering knuckle. Remove tool and ball joint nut, then raise control arm to clear steering knuckle. Remove nuts and bolts attaching control arm shaft to frame member, and remove control arm from vehicle.

Installation – To install, reverse removal procedure and check wheel alignment. *See WHEEL ALIGNMENT Section*

LOWER CONTROL ARM

Removal – Raise vehicle and place safety stands under frame side rails. Remove coil springs as previously outlined. Support inboard end of control arm after springs are removed. Remove cotter pin from lower stud and LOOSEN stud nut 1 turn. Remove brake caliper and suspend out of way. Do not suspend from brake line. Using suitable tool (J-23742), position large cupped end of tool over upper ball stud nut and pilot threaded end of tool on the lower ball stud. Loosen ball stud, then remove tool and stud nut. Remove nuts attaching control arm to vehicle and remove control arm.

Installation – To install, reverse removal procedure, tighten all nuts and bolts, and check wheel alignment. *See WHEEL ALIGNMENT Section.*

TIGHTENING SPECIFICATIONS

Application	Ft. Lbs.
Lower Control Arm-to-Frame	
G10, 1500, 20, 2500	65
All Others	85
Upper Control Arm-to-Frame	
C & P10, 1500, G10, 1500, 20, 2500	70
All Others	105
Control Arm Rubber Bushings	
C & P10, 1500, G10, 1500, 20, 2500 Only	115
Upper Control Arm Steel Bushings	
C & P20, 2500, 30, 3500, G30, 3500	
New	190
Used	115
Lower Control Arm Steel Bushing	
C & P20, 2500, 30, 3500 , G30, 3500	
New	280
Used	130
G10, 1500, 20, 2500, 30, 3500	
W/Spacer	280
W/O Spacer	130
Upper Ball Joint Nut	
C & P10, 1500, G10, 1500, 20, 2500	50
C & P20, 2500, 30, 3500, G30, 3500	90
Lower Ball Joint Nut	90
Stabilizer Bar	25
Shock Absorber Upper Nut	
C & P Models	140
G Models	75
Shock Absorber Lower Nut	
C & P Models	60
G Models	75

Section 13

STEERING

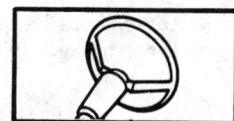

Contents

NOTE — ALSO SEE GENERAL INDEX.

IMPORTANT

Because of the great number of model names used by vehicle manufacturers, accurate identification of models is important. See Model Identification at the front of this publication.

Trouble Shooting

STEERING COLUMN TROUBLE SHOOTING

CONDITION & POSSIBLE CAUSE	CONDITION & POSSIBLE CAUSE

Standard Columns

Noise in Steering Column

- Coupling pulled apart, or bolts not tightened.
- Column not correctly aligned.
- Broken lower joint.
- Horn contact ring not lubricated.
- Lack of grease on bearings or bearing surface.
- Lower or upper shaft bearing worn or broken.
- Shaft lock snap ring not properly seated.
- Plastic spherical joint not lubricated.
- Shroud or housing loose.
- Lock plate retaining ring not seated.
- Loose sight shield.
- Loose cover.
- Coupling bottoming.
- Sheared input shaft plastic joint.
- Improper gear meshload.

High Steering Shaft Effort

- Column assembly misaligned.
- Improperly installed or defective dust shield.
- Damaged upper or lower bearing.
- Flashing on inside diameter of shift tube from plastic joint.
- Tight steering universal joint.

High Shift Effort (Man. & Auto. Trans.)

- Column not aligned correctly.
- Improperly installed or defective dust shield.
- Lack of grease on seals or bearings.
- Improper size screws used for ignition switch, neutral start switch or mounting bracket.
- Burrs on upper or lower end of shift tube.
- Lower bowl bearing assembled wrong.
- Shift tube bent or broken.
- Improper adjustment of shift levers.
- Relay lever loose on shift tube.
- Loose lower shift lever.

Improper Transmission Shifting

- Sheared shift tube joint or lower shaft lever weld joint.
- Improper transmission shift lever adjustment.
- Improper gate plate adjustment.

Excess Play in Mounted Column Assembly

- Instrument panel-to-column bracket mounting bolts loose.
- Broken weld nut on jacket.
- Instrument panel bracket capsule sheared.
- Column bracket-to-jacket bolts loose.

Steering Locks in 2nd Gear (Man. Trans.)

- Shift lever mechanism damaged.
- Defective shift lever gate.
- Loose relay lever on shift tube.

Tilt Columns

NOTE — *Information for standard columns will generally apply to tilt columns. Tilt column information is supplied in addition to and specifically for tilt columns.*

Steering Wheel Loose

- Too much clearance between holes in support or housing and pivot pin diameters.
- Damaged or missing anti-lash spring in centering spheres.
- Upper bearing inner race seal missing, or upper bearing not seated in housing.
- Improperly adjusted tilt and telescopic locking knobs.
- Loose support screws.
- Bearing preload spring missing or broken.
- Housing loose on jacket.

Excess Play in Mounted Column Assembly

- Loose shoes in housing, or loose support screws.
- Loose tilt head pivot pins, or loose shoe lock pin in support.

High Shift Effort

- Wave washer burred.

Housing Scraping on Bowl

- Bowl bent or not concentric with hub.

Steering Wheel Loose in Every Other Tilt Position

- Loose fit between shoe and shoe pivot pin, or shoe not free in slot.

Steering Wheel Will Not Lock in Any Tilt Position

- Shoe siezed on its pivot pin.
- Shoe grooves may have burrs or dirt in them.
- Shoe lock spring weak or broken.

Steering Wheel Fails to Return to Top Position

- Pivot pins are bound up.
- Wheel tilt spring is damaged.
- Turn signal switch wires too tight.

Noise When Tilting Column

- Upper tilt bumpers worn.
- Tilt spring rubbing in housing.

Hard Steering

- Incorrect tire pressure.
- Lack of lubricant in ball joints, steering gear and steering linkage.
- Improper front end alignment.
- Improper steering gear adjustment.

MANUAL STEERING GEAR TROUBLE SHOOTING

CONDITION & POSSIBLE CAUSE	CONDITION & POSSIBLE CAUSE
Rattle or Chucking Noise in Rack and Pinion. • Rack and pinion attachment loose. • Lack of lubricant, or incorrect lubricant in rack and pinion assembly. • Pitman arm loose on shaft, or steering gear mounting bolts loose. • Improper gear adjustment. • Loose or worn steering shaft bearing. **Excessive Play or Looseness** • Front wheel bearing improperly adjusted. • Loose or worn steering linkage, ball joints or steering gear shaft. • Steering arm loose on steering gear shaft. • Incorrect front wheel alignment. • Steering gear housing attachment bolts loose, or steering gear adjustment too loose. • Steering arms loose at knuckles. • Grease, oil or fluid on brake linings. • Rack and pinion mounting loose or out of adjustment. • Tie rod end loose. • Steering wheel loose. • Excessive Pitman shaft-to-ball nut lash. **Hard Steering** • Incorrect tire pressure. • Lack of lubrication in steering linkage. • Steering gear or knuckle ball studs tight. • Front springs sagging. • Steering knuckle bent. • Frozen column bearings. • Worn steering gear or tie rod ends. • Lower coupling flange rubbing against steering shaft. • Bent or broken frame.	**Poor Returnability** • Lack of lubricant in ball joints, steering gear or linkage. • Binding in linkage or ball joints. • Improper front end alignment, steering gear adjustment or tire pressure. • Binding in steering linkage, ball joints, or front axle spindles. • Column misaligned. **Wheel Tramp (Excessive Vertical Motion)** • Improper tire pressure. • Improper balance of wheels, tires or brake rotors. • Worn or faulty shock absorbers. • Loose tie rod ends or steering connections. • Improper wheel alignment. • Loose or worn wheel bearings. **Steering Pulls to One Side** • Improper tire pressure, or mismatch of front tires. • Wheel bearings not adjusted properly. • Bent suspension components, or broken or sagging springs. • Improper wheel alignment. • Brakes dragging. • Steering gear mounting loose or not centered. • Loose wheel lug nuts. **Instability** • Low or uneven tire pressure. • Loose or worn wheel bearings, idler arm bushing or strut bushings. • Incorrect front wheel alignment. • Steering gear not centered. • Broken rear springs or inoperative shock absorbers. • Improper steering cross shaft adjustment. • Bent linkage. • Frozen ball joints or suspension pivots.

POWER STEERING TROUBLE SHOOTING

CONDITION & POSSIBLE CAUSE	CONDITION & POSSIBLE CAUSE
Power Steering Noise Diagnosis **Rattle or Chucking in Steering Gear** • Pressure hoses touching engine parts. • Loose Pitman shaft over center adjustment. • Tie rod ends, or Pitman arm loose. • Rack and pinion attachment loose. • Free play in worm and piston assembly. • Loose sector shaft or thrust bearing adjustment. • Free play in pot coupling, or worn shaft serrations. • Steering gear loose on frame. • Linkage loose. **Growl in Steering Pump** • Excessive back pressure in hoses or steering gear because of restrictions. • Scored pressure plates, thrust plates or rotor. • Extreme wear of cam ring.	**Rattle in Steering Pump** • Vanes not installed properly, or vanes sticking in rotor slots. **Swish Noise in Steering Pump** • Defective flow control valve. **Groan in Steering Pump** • Air in fluid, or poor pressure hose connections. • Low fluid level. **Squawk Noise When Turning** • Damper "O" ring on valve spool cut.

Trouble Shooting

POWER STEERING TROUBLE SHOOTING (Cont.)

CONDITION & POSSIBLE CAUSE	CONDITION & POSSIBLE CAUSE

Power Steering Noise Diagnosis (Cont.)

Moan or Whine in Steering Pump

- Pump shaft bearing scored.
- Air in fluid, or low fluid level.
- Hose or column grounded.
- Valve cover "O" ring missing or damaged.
- Valve cover baffle missing or damaged.
- Interference of components in pumping elements.
- Loose or poor bracket alignment.

Hissing Noise When Parking

- Internal leakage in steering gear. Check valve assembly first.

Chirp Noise in Steering Pump

- Loose or worn power steering pump belt.

Buzzing Noise When Not Steering

- Noisy pump.
- Free play in steering shaft upper bearing or bearing loose on shaft serrations.

Clicking Noise in Pump

- Noise probably caused by pump slippers being too long, broken slipper springs, excessive wear, nicked rotors or damaged cam contour.

Power Steering Handling Diagnosis

Poor Return of Steering Wheel to Center

- Steering wheel rubbing against turn signal housing.
- Lower coupling flange rubbing against steering gear adjuster plug.
- Tight or frozen steering shaft bearings.
- Steering gear adjustment over specifications.
- Sticking or plugged spool valve.
- Improper front end alignment.
- Wheel bearings worn or loose.
- Tie rods or ball joints binding.
- Intermediate shaft joints binding.
- Kinked pressure hoses.
- Loose housing head spanner nut.
- Damaged valve lever.
- Sector shaft or worm thrust bearing adjustment too tight.
- Reaction ring sticking in cylinder or housing head, or seal worn.
- Steering pump internal leakage.
- Steering gear-to-column misalignment.
- Lack of lubrication in steering linkage or ball joints.
- Incorrect tire pressure.
- Steering linkage or ball joints binding.
- Steering shaft poppet valve installed incorrectly.

Momentary Increase in Effort When Turning Left or Right Fast

- High internal pump leakage.
- Power steering pump belt slipping.
- Low fluid level.
- Engine idle speed too low.
- Air in pump fluid system.
- Pump output low.
- Steering gear malfunctioning.

Steering Wheel Surges or Jerks When Turning

- Low fluid level or loose pump belt.
- Insufficient pump pressure.
- Sticky flow control valve.
- Steering linkage hitting engine oil pan at full turn.

Excessive Wheel Kick Back or Free Play

- Air in pump fluid system.
- Worn poppet valve in steering gear.
- Excessive over center lash.
- Loose thrust bearing preload adjustment in steering gear.
- Free play in pot coupling.
- Steering gear flexible coupling loose on shaft, or rubber disc mounting nuts loose.
- Coupling loose on worm shaft serrations.
- Improper sector shaft adjustment.
- Excessive worm piston side play.
- Damaged valve lever.
- Universal joint loose.
- Defective rotary valve.
- Ball studs or wheel bearings loose.
- Steering gear loose on frame.

Lack of Power Assist When Parking

- Sticking flow control valve.
- Insufficient pump pressure output.
- Excessive internal pump leakage.
- Excessive internal gear leakage.
- Lower coupling flange rubbing against steering gear adjuster plug.
- Loose pump belt or low fluid level.
- Engine idle speed too low.
- Steering gear-to-column misalignment.

Lack of Power Assist in Left Turns

- Left turn reaction seal "O" ring worn, damaged or missing.
- Cylinder head "O" ring damaged.

Lack of Power Assist in Right Turns

- Column pot coupling bottomed.
- Right turn reaction seal worn, missing or damaged.
- Excessive internal leakage through piston end plug and/or side plugs.

POWER STEERING TROUBLE SHOOTING (Cont.)

CONDITION & POSSIBLE CAUSE	CONDITION & POSSIBLE CAUSE
Power Steering Handling Diagnosis (Cont.) **Lack of Effort in Turning** • Left or right reaction seal worn or damaged. • Left or right reaction oil passageway not drilled in housing or cylinder head. • Left or right reaction seal ring sticking in housing head. **Car Wanders to One Side** • Front end alignment incorrect. • Unbalanced steering gear valve. • Incorrect tire pressure. • Steering linkage not level. • Ball joints loose. • Oversize or omitted sector cover bushing. • Steering shaft rubbing shift tube. • Insufficient thrust bearing preload.	**Low Pressure Due to Steering Pump** • Flow control valve stuck or inoperative. • Pressure plate not flat against cam ring. • Extreme wear of cam ring. • Scored pressure plate, thrust plate or rotor. • Vanes not installed properly, or vanes sticking in rotor slots. • Cracked or broken thrust or pressure plate. **Low Pressure Due to Steering Gear** • Pressure loss in cylinder due to worn piston ring or scored housing bore. • Leakage at valve rings, or at valve body-to-worm seal connection. **Foaming, Milky Power Steering Fluid, Low Fluid Level or Low Pressure** • Air trapped in fluid, and loss of fluid due to internal pump leakage which creates fluid overflow.

CHRYSLER CORP.

Dodge
Plymouth

REMOVAL & INSTALLATION

HORN BUTTON & STEERING WHEEL

NOTE — *Disconnect battery before removing horn button.*

All Models — If equipped with horn button, pull outward on button until it comes off. If equipped with horn pad, remove 2 retaining screws from behind steering wheel and lift pad off steering wheel. Disconnect horn wire from switch terminal. Remove steering wheel retaining nut. Remove steering wheel using a suitable puller (C-3428B). To install, reverse removal procedure.

CAUTION — *Do not strike steering wheel to remove; severe damage could result.*

DIRECTIONAL SIGNAL INDICATOR SWITCH

NOTE — *On vehicles equipped with speed control, do not completely disconnect turn signal lever but allow to hang loose.*

All Models — Disconnect fusible link under hood at battery. Remove horn switch pad and steering wheel. On tilt column steering systems, remove lock plate and cam assembly. Remove turn signal lever screw and remove lever. Remove switch retainer screws, retainer, wire cover clips and cover. Disconnect switch harness from main harness, lift switch from column, guiding wires and insulator through opening in upper column. Remove switch. To install, reverse removal procedures.

HAZARD FLASHER SWITCH

All Models — Hazard flasher switch is integral with directional signal indicator switch. Combination is removed or installed as a unit. See *Directional Signal Indicator Switch* in this article.

STEERING COLUMN LOCK & IGNITION SWITCH

All Models — 1) Remove steering column from vehicle. See *Steering Columns* in this Section. Clamp column in a soft-jawed vise. Remove horn assembly, steering wheel and turn signal switch. Remove snap ring from upper end of steering shaft.

2) Remove retaining screws and lock lever guide plate which exposes the lock cylinder release hole. Place ignition switch in "LOCK" position and remove key. Insert a small screwdriver or similar tool into lock cylinder release hole and push in to release spring-loaded lock retainer. Pull ignition switch cylinder out of housing bore at same time retainer is depressed. Remove ignition switch assembly.

3) To install, reverse removal procedure noting the following: Ignition key cylinder is installed with cylinder in lock position and key removed. Insert cylinder into lock housing. Place cylinder into place until contact is made with pin on ignition switch cam. Insert key into lock and rotate until slot in cylinder plate lines up with pin. Press key cylinder the remaining way into lock housing, making sure retainer bar snaps into its slot in lock housing.

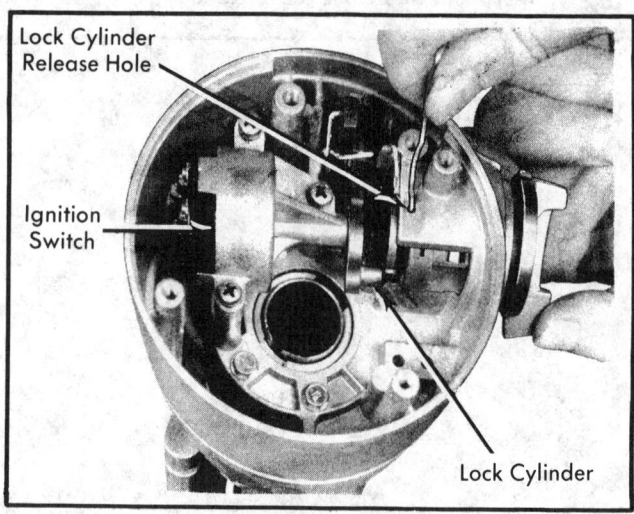

Fig. 1   Depressing Tab for Lock Cylinder Removal

FORD

Bronco
"E" & "F" Models

REMOVAL & INSTALLATION

HORN PAD

All Models — Disconnect battery ground cable. Remove one screw from behind each steering wheel spoke. Remove horn pad switch assembly from steering wheel after disconnecting wire connector. On vehicles with sport wheel option, pry button cover off with screwdriver. On vehicles with speed control, squeeze "J" clip ground wire terminal firmly and remove through hole in steering wheel. To install, reverse procedure.

STEERING WHEEL

All Models — 1) Set wheels in straight ahead position and drive forward a short distance. Mark the relationship of steering wheel with steering column. Remove horn pad assembly as previously outlined.

2) Remove steering wheel retaining nut. Pull off steering wheel using a suitable puller. To install, reverse removal procedure making sure chalk marks made during disassembly are aligned.

FORD (Cont.)

DIRECTIONAL SIGNAL SWITCH & HAZARD FLASHER

All Models — 1) Disconnect battery ground cable. Remove horn pad switch and steering wheel as previously outlined. Remove turn signal switch lever by unscrewing from steering column. Remove column shroud. Disconnect turn signal switch wiring connector by lifting up on tabs and separating.

2) Remove screws securing switch assembly to column. On fixed steering column models, remove switch assembly from vehicle by disconnecting connector plug and guiding switch and connector plug through opening in shaft socket. On fixed column "E" models with automatic transmission, remove shift indicator lamp assembly from shift socket and guide out with switch. To install, reverse removal procedure.

3) On tilt column models, disconnect connector plug from wiring connector by using a wire terminal removal tool. *See Fig. 1*. Record color code and location of each wire as it is removed. Guide switch assembly out of column through shift socket hole. On "E" models with automatic transmission, disconnect lamp wire from turn signal switch harness before removing switch. To install, reverse removal procedure.

IGNITION LOCK CYLINDER

All Models — 1) Disconnect battery ground cable. On non-tilt column models, remove horn pad and steering wheel as

previously outlined. Place automatic transmissions in "Park", or manual transmissions in "Neutral".

2) Turn lock cylinder to "ON" position. Insert a $\frac{1}{8}$" diameter pin or punch in the hole located inside the column near base of lock cylinder housing on standard column models, or in the hole located on the column housing adjacent to the hazard flasher button on tilt column models.

3) On all models, depress retaining pin with punch and pull on lock cylinder to remove it. To install, reverse removal procedures.

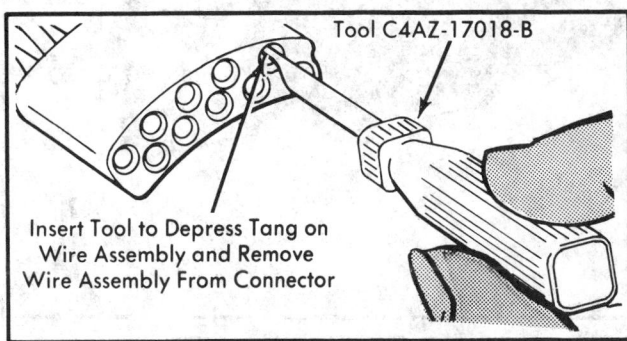

Fig. 1   Removing Wires from Connector Using Wire Terminal Removal Tool

---

GENERAL MOTORS

Chevrolet
GMC

REMOVAL & INSTALLATION

STEERING WHEEL

Removal ("G" & "P" Models) — Disconnect battery. Remove horn button or pad, receiving cup, Belleville spring, and bushing. Mark steering wheel-to-shaft relationship. Remove

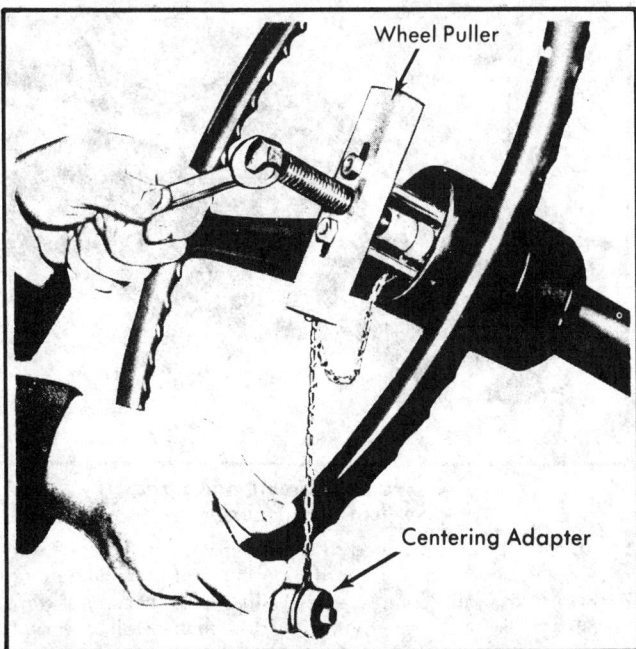

Wheel Puller

Centering Adapter

Fig. 1   Removing Steering Wheel Using Puller

snap ring from steering shaft, then remove nut and washer. Use steering wheel puller (J-2927) to remove steering wheel.

Installation ("G" & "P" Models) — To install steering wheel, reverse removal procedure while noting the following: Directional signal switch must be in neutral position while installing steering wheel to prevent damage to cancelling cam and switch assembly. Install snap ring after steering wheel retaining nut has been tightened.

Removal ("C" & "K" Models) — Disconnect battery. Remove horn button. Remove snap ring from steering shaft, then remove nut and washer. Use steering wheel puller to remove steering wheel.

CAUTION — *Do not hammer on puller while removing wheel.*

Installation ("C" & "K" Models) — To install, reverse removal procedures while noting the following: Directional signal switch must be in neutral position while installing wheel to prevent damage to cancelling cam and switch. Install snap ring after steering wheel retaining nut has been tightened.

DIRECTIONAL SIGNAL SWITCH

"G" & "P" Models — 1) Remove steering wheel, signal switch cancelling cam and spring. Remove column-to-panel trim plate if present. Disconnect signal switch wiring harness at half-moon connector. Pry wiring harness protector out of column retaining slots. Mark location of each wire in half-moon connector, then remove each individual wire from connector using suitable tool (J-22727). Insert tool into connector, then push in until tool bottoms. Remove tool and pull wire from connector. Remove directional signal lever screw and remove lever. Push in on hazard warning knob and unscrew to remove knob.

2) On Tilt Columns only, remove automatic transmission selector dial screws (if equipped) and remove dial and indicator. Remove cap and dial illumination light from housing cover. Un-

GENERAL MOTORS (Cont.)

screw and remove tilt release lever. Use suitable puller tool (J-22708) to remove signal housing cover. On all models, remove 3 signal switch mounting screws. Carefully remove switch assembly from column while guiding wire harness through opening in shift lever housing.

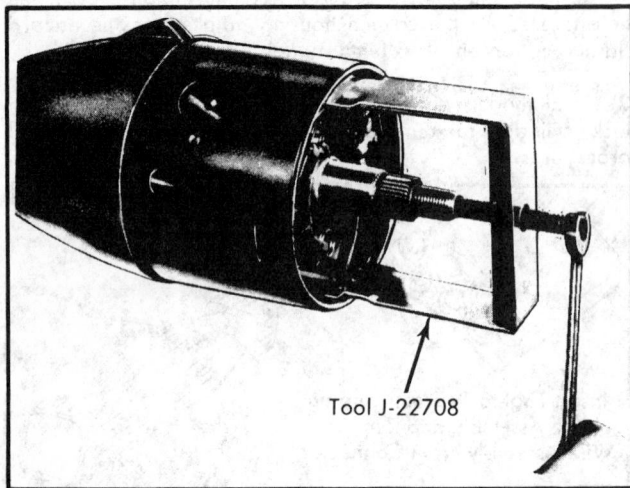

Tool J-22708

Fig. 2   Pulling Directional Signal Housing Cover for Tilt Column Models

3) To install switch, proceed as follows; Wrap ends of signal switch wires with tape and guide them through the opening at lower left side of bearing housing (Tilt Column) and out the lower end of shift lever housing and under dash seal.

CAUTION — *It is extremely important that only specified screws, bolts and nuts be used during reassembly. Use of overlength screws could prevent a portion of column from compressing under impact.*

4) Place directional signal switch in mounting position and install screws. Torque screws to 25 INCH lbs. With Tilt Columns align openings in signal switch cover with proper lever positions and tap cover into place. Install tilt release lever. Install automatic transmission selector dial, pointer, dial illumination light and cap (if equipped).

5) On all models, install signal switch lever and hazard warning knob. Bend wire harness connector tabs out of each wire before installing in half moon connector. Install each wire in its marked position and reconnect signal switch harness. Snap wire harness protector into column retaining slots and install signal canceling cam and spring. Install steering wheel and column-to-instrument panel trim plate (if equipped).

"C" & "K" Models — 1) Remove steering wheel and column-to-instrument panel trim cover. Place screwdriver blade into cover slot and pry up and out to free cover from lock plate. Remove lock plate using suitable compressing tool (J-23653). Screw center post of tool onto steering shaft as far as it will go. Compress lock plate by turning center post nut clockwise. Pry the round wire snap ring out of shaft groove and discard ring. Remove tool and lift lock plate from housing.

CAUTION — *If column is being disassembled on bench, be sure that steering shaft does not slide out of lower end of mast jacket.*

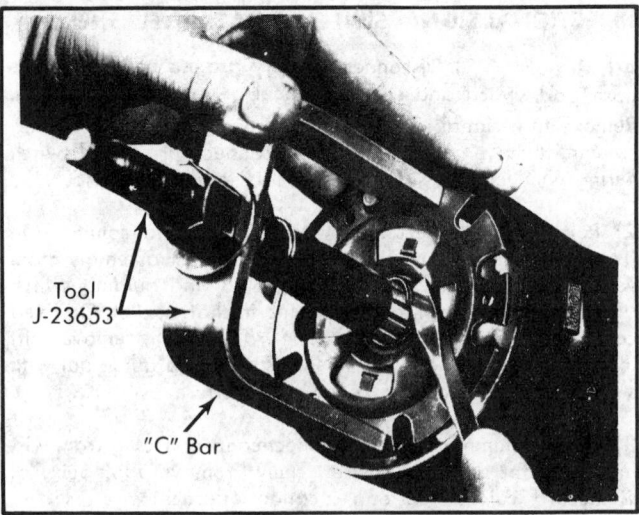

Tool J-23653

"C" Bar

Fig. 3   Depressing Lock Plate for Snap Ring Removal

2) Slide directional signal canceling cam, upper bearing preload spring and thrust washer off shaft end. Remove signal switch lever screw and lever. Push hazard warning knob in and unscrew knob.

3) On standard columns remove 3 switch mounting screws. Pull the switch connector out of bracket on jacket and feed switch connector through column support bracket and pull switch straight up, guiding the wiring harness through column housing and protector. Remove wire protector by pulling downward out of column with pliers on tab.

4) On tilt column, position directional signal and shifter housing in "low" position. Remove harness cover by pulling toward the lower end of the column, being careful not to damage wires. Remove 3 switch mounting screws and pull the switch straight up, guiding wiring harness and cover through column housing.

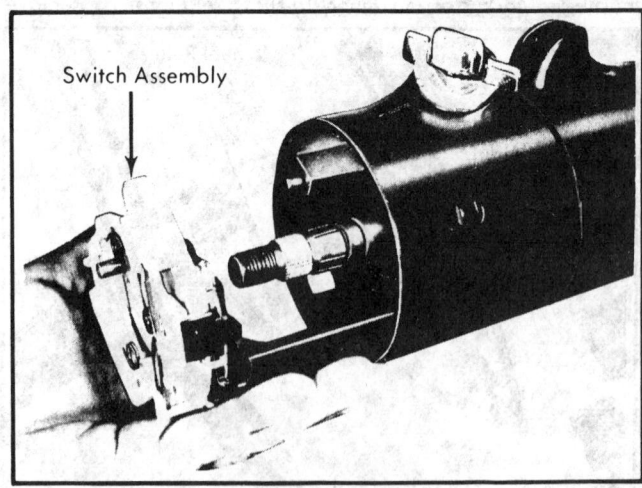

Switch Assembly

Fig. 4   Pulling Directional Signal Switch from Housing

5) To install switch, proceed as follows: Feed wire harness connector and cover down through housing and under mounting bracket. With all columns except Tilt type, check that wire harness is in protector. With Tilt columns, install cover on harness. Install switch mounting screws and clip connector to bracket on column jacket.

GENERAL MOTORS (Cont.)

6) Install trim plate, hazard warning knob and signal lever. Position directional switch in neutral position and pull warning knob out. Slide thrust washer, upper bearing preload spring and canceling cam onto upper end of shaft.

7) Place lock plate over shaft and attach lock plate compressing tool bolt on shaft. Install a new snap ring over tool bolt, place "C" bar of tool over bolt and compress lock plate by turning tool nut. Slide new snap ring down tool bolt and into shaft groove. Install cover on lock plate and snap into place. Install steering wheel and horn button.

NOTE — *Always use a new snap ring during reassembly.*

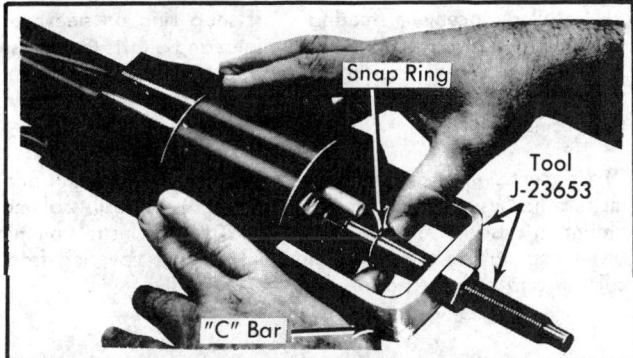

Fig. 5   Installing Lock Plate Snap Ring

HAZARD FLASHER SWITCH

All Models — Hazard flasher switch is integral with directional signal indicator switch. Combination is removed or installed as an assembly. See *Directional Signal Switch in this Section.*

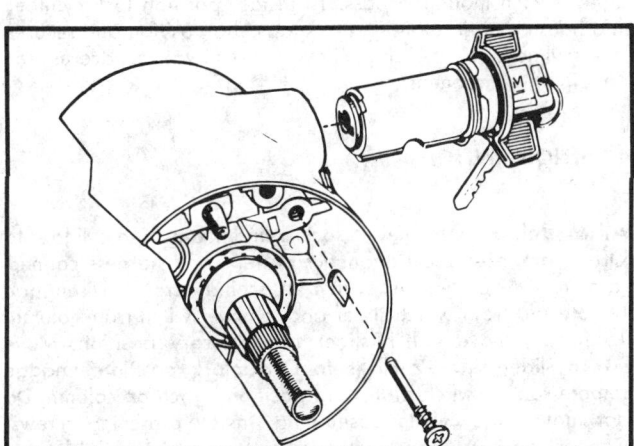

Fig. 6   Lock Cylinder Assembly

STEERING COLUMN LOCK

All Models — **1)** Place key in lock cylinder and rotate to "RUN" position. Remove steering wheel and lift directional signal switch up far enough to slip over end of shaft. It is not necessary to remove it entirely.

2) Remove lock retaining screw and lock cylinder.

CAUTION — *If screw is dropped during removal, disassembly of column may be required.*

IGNITION SWITCH

"C" & "K" Models — **1)** To remove ignition switch, steering column must be lowered, but it is not necessary to remove steering wheel. See *Steering Column Removal in this Section.* If steering is not removed from vehicle, support column before proceding.

2) Place ignition switch in "LOCK" position. If lock cylinder has already been removed, pull up on actuating rod of switch until it stops, then push down one detent. This will position switch in "LOCK" position. Remove two screws, then remove ignition switch.

3) To install, switch and lock cylinder should be in "LOCK" position. With switch in correct position, install activating rod in switch. Install switch on column and tighten mounting screws. Install steering column and check system operation.

NOTE — *Use only specified screws as overlength screws may prevent a portion of column from compressing under impact.*

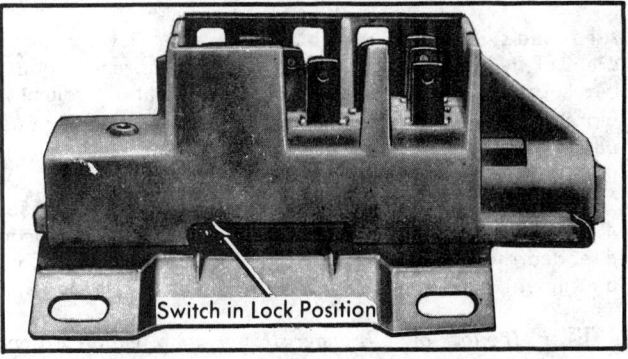

Fig. 7   Ignition Switch Assembly with Switch in Lock Position

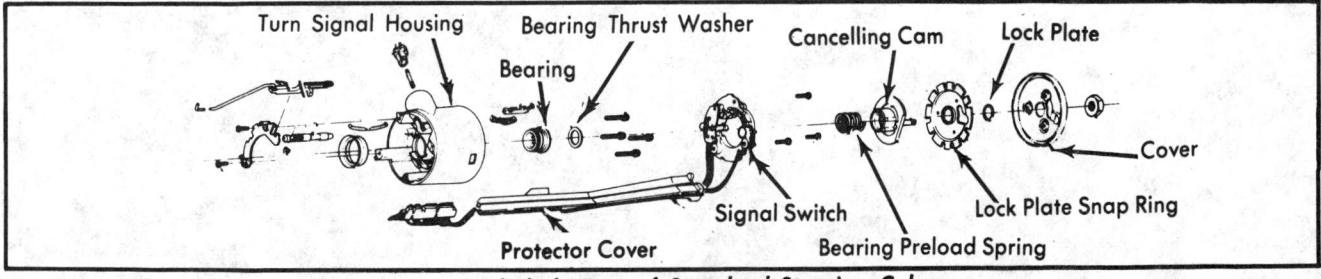

Fig. 8   Exploded View of Standard Steering Column Hub ("C" and "K" Models Shown)

JEEP

All Models

REMOVAL & INSTALLATION

HORN BUTTON & STEERING WHEEL

CAUTION — *Before installing a new steering wheel shaft nut check for Standard American or metric thread. Metric threads have identifying groove in steering wheel splines. Standard American do not have grooves.*

"CJ" & Scrambler Models — Disconnect battery cable, and place front wheels in straight ahead position. Remove horn button by pulling straight up. Remove steering wheel nut and washer. Remove receiver and contact plate. Mark steering wheel and shaft for reassembly reference, and remove steering wheel using puller (J-21232). To install, reverse removal procedures.

Cherokee, Truck & Wagoneer — Disconnect battery cable and place front wheels in straight ahead position. On models with standard steering wheel, remove horn cover attaching screws from underside of wheel and remove cover. On models with sport steering wheel, remove horn button by pulling button upward. On models with standard steering wheel, remove horn wire by disconnecting at steering wheel switch. Unseat retainer that holds horn wire and spring in canceling cam yoke and wire retainer and spring as an assembly. Remove steering wheel nut and washer. On models with sport steering wheel, remove receiver bushing attaching screws and remove bushing, horn botton receiver and contact plate. Index mark steering wheel and shaft and remove steering wheel using puller (J-21232). To install, reverse removal procedure.

DIRECTIONAL SIGNAL SWITCH & HAZARD FLASHER

All Models — **1)** Disconnect battery cable. Cover painted areas of steering column. Remove column-to-instrument panel bezel. Loosen toeplate screws. On vehicles with tilt columns, place column in neutral position. Remove lock plate cover and unseat steering shaft snap ring as follows:

2) If shaft nut is metric threaded, use compressor tool J-23653-4 to compress lock plate and remove snap ring. On American threaded shaft nuts, use tool J-23653 to compress lock plate and unseat snap ring.

NOTE — *The lock plate is under strong spring tension, do not attempt to remove snap ring without using compressor tool.*

3) Remove compressor tool and snap ring. Discard snap ring. Remove lock plate, canceling cam, and upper bearing preload spring. Place turn signal lever in right turn position and remove lever. Press hazard warning knob in and turn counterclockwise to remove.

4) Remove column wiring harness protectors, if equipped. Disconnect wiring harness connectors at base of column. Remove directional switch attaching screws and remove switch from column.

5) To install, install switch in housing and install attaching screws. Tighten to 35 INCH Lbs. Install hazard warning knob and turn signal lever. Install upper bearing preload spring, canceling cam and lock plate on steering shaft.

6) Install replacement steering shaft snap ring on sleeve of compressor tool and install tool on steering shaft. Compress lock plate and seat steering shaft snap ring in shaft groove. Remove tool. Install lock plate cover. Install steering wheel and replacement nut.

7) Connect switch harness connectors at base of column and install harness protectors (if equipped). Install column mounting bracket bolts and tighten to 20 ft. lbs. Install column bezel and tighten toeplate. Remove protective covering from column and connect battery.

STEERING COLUMN LOCK

All Models — Remove horn button, steering wheel and turn signal switch as previously outlined. Position lock cylinder in "LOCK" position on automatic transmission models, or in "ON" position on manual transmission models, then depress key cylinder retaining tab and remove lock cylinder from housing. The retaining tab is accessible through slot adjacent to turn signal switch mounting boss. To install, position lock cylinder into housing until retaining tab snaps into position and secures lock cylinder to housing. Reverse removal prodceres for remaining components.

IGNITION SWITCH

All Models — Insert key in lock cylinder and turn cylinder to Off-Unlock position. Disconnect battery and harness connectors at switch. Remove switch attaching screws. Disengage remote rod from switch slider and remove switch from column. To install, move switch slider to Accessory position. Move switch slider back 2 clicks to Off-Unlock position. Engage remote rod in switch slider and position switch on column. Do not move slider while positioning. Install attaching screws. Connect harness connectors and battery negative cable.

CHRYSLER CORP.

**Dodge
Plymouth**

DESCRIPTION

All models use collapsible type steering columns. All columns have integral ignition switch and locking devices. Tilt wheel features are available in all models. Transmission shift linkage is integral on all models with the exception of floor shift models.

REMOVAL & INSTALLATION

ALL MODELS

Removal – 1) Disconnect battery negative cable. On vehicles equipped with column shift, disconnect link rod(s) by prying rod out of grommet in shift lever. Remove steering shaft lower coupling to worm shaft roll pin. *See Fig. 1.*

NOTE – *Steering shaft may be equipped with either flexible coupling or a "Pot" coupling.*

2) Disconnect wiring connectors at column jacket. Remove steering wheel center pad and horn switch (if equipped). Use tool (C-3428B) to remove steering wheel.

NOTE – *Do not bump or hammer on steering shaft to remove steering wheel.*

3) Remove turn signal lever. Remove floor plate-to-floor pan attaching screws. Remove cluster bezel and panel lower reinforcement to expose steering column bracket. If equipped with automatic transmission, disconnect shift indicator pointer cable from shift housing.

4) Remove nuts attaching steering column bracket to instrument panel support. Carefully remove lower coupling from steering gear worm shaft, then remove column assembly out through passenger compartment.

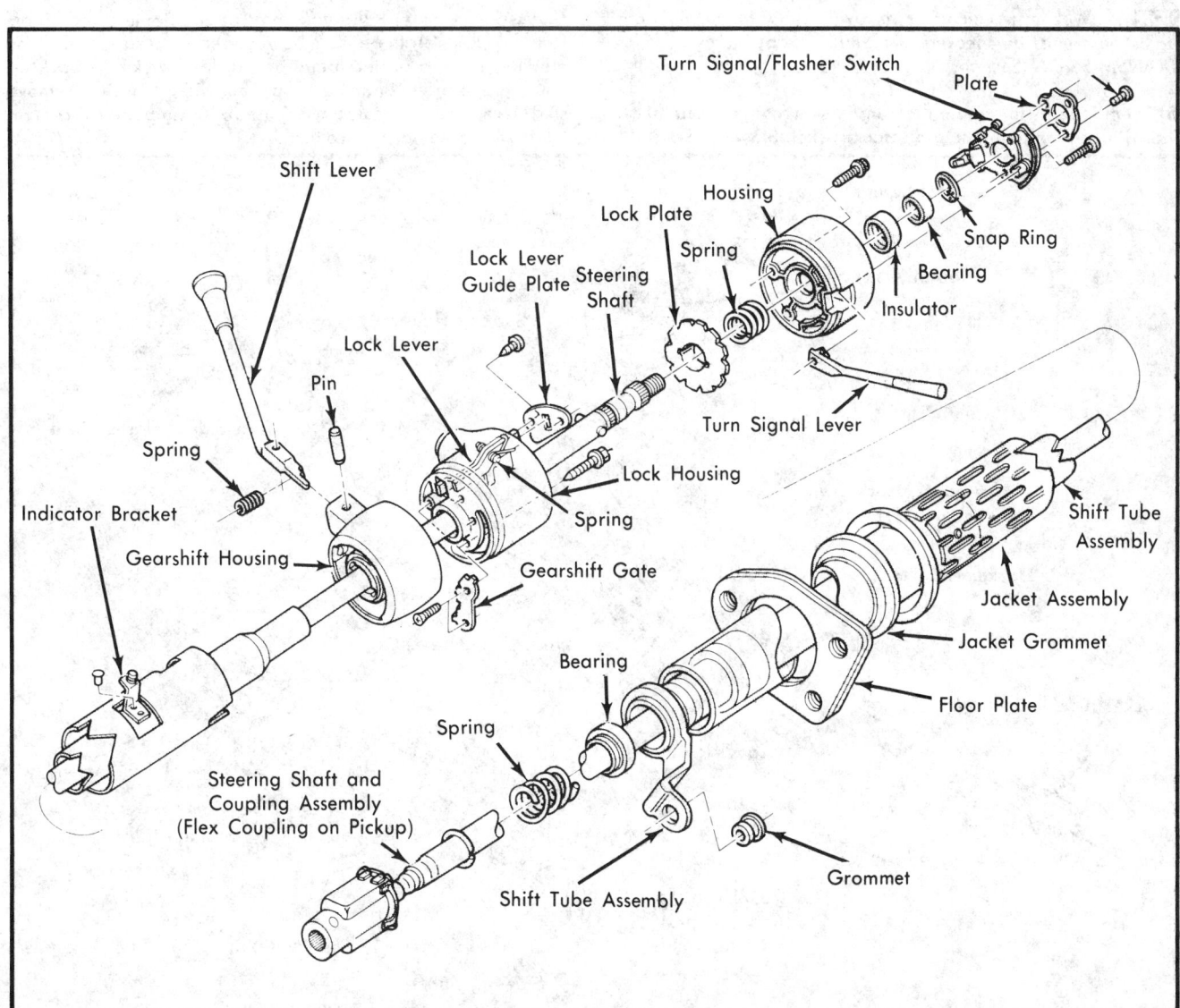

**Fig. 1 Exploded View of Automatic Transmission Steering Column
(Van Models Shown; Pickup Models Similar)**

CHRYSLER CORP. (Cont.)

Installation — 1) Install ground clip on left capsule slot. Plastic capsules should be preassembled in bracket slot. Insert column through floor pan opening. With front wheels straight ahead and splines on wormshaft and coupling aligned, engage coupling and install roll pin.

CAUTION — *Do not apply end load to steering shaft.*

2) Hold column assembly with bracket slots on mounting studs. Loosely install two upper bracket washers and nuts. Be sure both capsules are fully seated in slots in support bracket and tighten nuts to specification.

3) Position floor plate over floor pan opening, centering it around column, then install retaining bolts. Place steering wheel on shaft with splines aligned. Install nut and tighten to specifications.

CAUTION — *Do not drive wheel onto shaft, draw it down with retaining nut.*

4) Install horn switch and connect wiring connector at column jacket. Connect shift links into new grommets.

NOTE — *Whenever column is removed or loosened, linkage adjustment must be checked. See Shift Linkage Adjustment in TRANSMISSION Section.*

5) If equipped with automatic transmission, connect gear shift indicator pointer cable to indicator bracket. Slowly move shift lever from "1" (Low) to "P" (Park) pausing briefly at each position. If necessary, bend indicator bracket to align pointer with each position. Reinstall panel lower reinforcement and cluster bezel. Connect battery and test horn and lights.

FLOOR SHIFT MODELS

The steering column with a floor mounted gear shift is basically the same as previously described. Standard columns and service procedures are identical except as described below.

- Lower steering shaft bearing is mounted in an aluminum support.

- Shift housing has a spring attached between it and column jacket. This keeps housing rotated counterclockwise against rubber bumper. Spring and bumpers are easily removed by hand. See Fig. 2.

OVERHAUL

ALL EXCEPT TILT WHEEL MODELS

Disassembly — 1) Pry out wiring trough retainers and lift off trough. New retainers may be required for reassembly. Use masking tape to protect paint and a deep socket to back up housing and drive retaining roll pin out with a punch to remove shift lever. Secure column in vise by clamping at column bracket. Do not distort column.

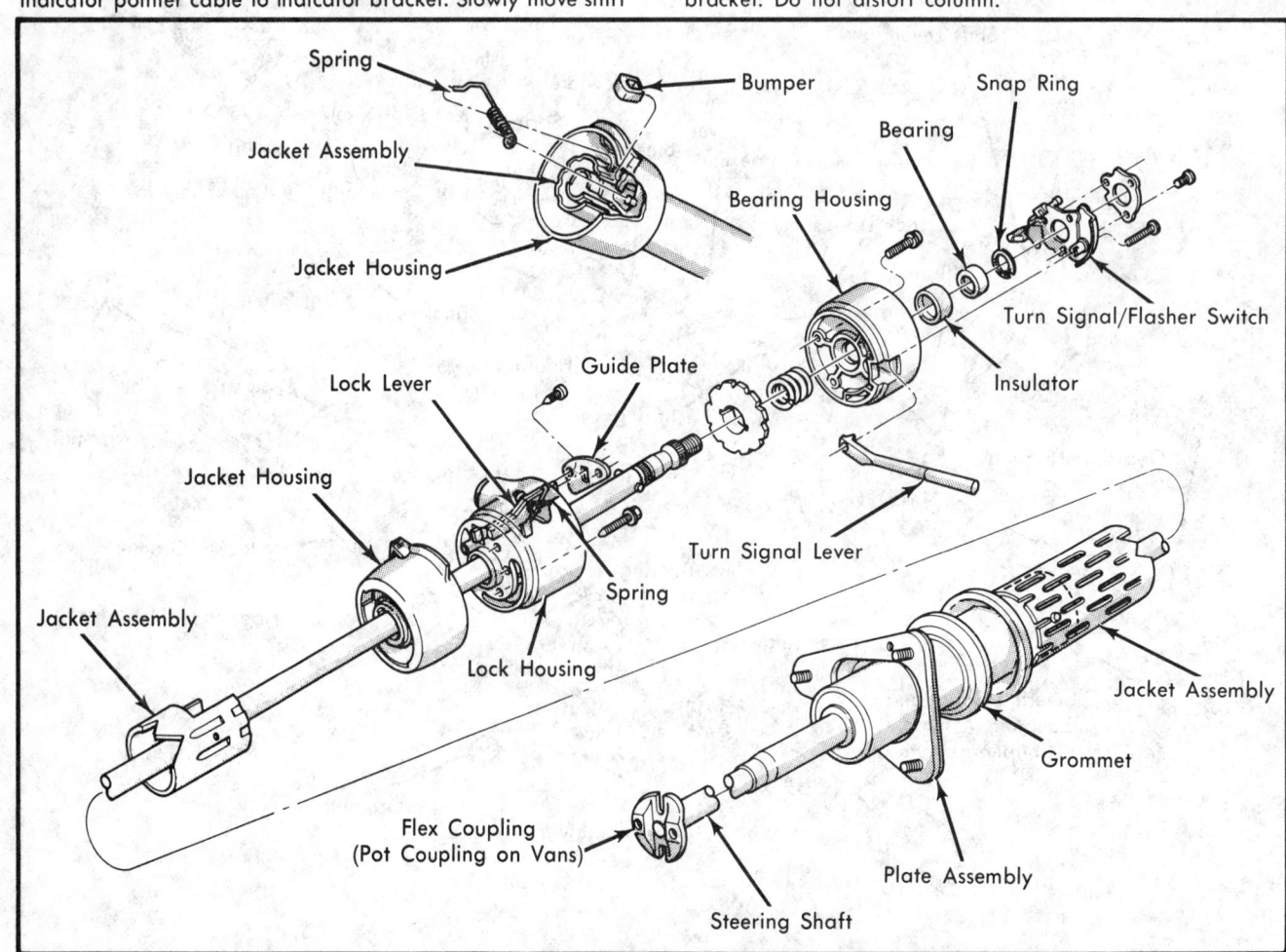

**Fig. 2 Exploded View of Floor Shift Steering Column
(Pickup Models Shown; Van Models Similar)**

CHRYSLER CORP. (Cont.)

2) Remove turn signal switch and upper bearing retaining screws. Remove retainer and lift switch upward out of way. Remove retaining screw and lift ignition key lamp assembly out of way.

3) Remove snap ring from upper end of steering shaft. Remove three screws holding bearing housing-to-lock housing.

NOTE — *These screws must be removed before steering shaft removal.*

4) Remove bearing housing from shaft. Remove coil spring and lock plate from shaft. Remove shaft through lower end of column.

5) Remove two retaining screws and lock lever guide plate. This will expose lock cylinder release hole. Place cylinder in "LOCK" position and remove key.

6) Insert a small diameter screwdriver or similar tool into lock cylinder release hole. Push in to release spring-loaded lock retainer. At same time, pull lock cylinder out of housing bore. Remove three retaining screws and ignition switch assembly. *See Fig. 3.*

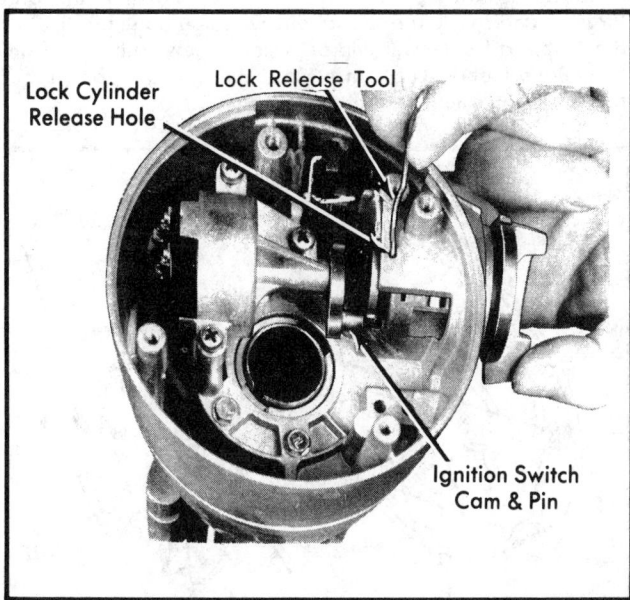

Fig. 3   Removing Lock Cylinder

7) Grasp lock lever and spring assembly and pull straight out of housing. Remove four lock housing-to-column jacket hex head retaining screws and remove housing from jacket.

8) Loosen shift tube set screw in shaft housing. Remove shift tube through lower end of jacket. Remove floor plate and grommet from jacket.

9) To disassemble flexible coupling, remove 4 bolts and 2 cross straps. Remove flexible coupling. Pot coupling is removed by prying cover tangs out of coupling body and lifting seal and cover from body. Drive dowel pin down into coupling and discard. Pull body off shaft and shoe assembly.

Reassembly — 1) During reassembly, coat all friction surfaces with multi-purpose grease NLGI Grade 2, Part Number 2525035 (or equivalent). Clamp column in vise so that both ends of column are accessible. Check column tube-to-mandrel rivets for tightness. If replacement is necessary, use ⅜" diameter by ¾" long (⅜" grip) steel pop rivets.

NOTE — *Never use aluminum rivets.*

2) Install floor plate and grommet on lower end of jacket. On automatic transmission models, position gearshift housing on column jacket. Install dust seal and shift tube support on shift tube. Slide shift tube into jacket. Guide key on upper end of tube into slot in gearshift housing. Position crossover load spring and shift lever in gearshift housing and tap rivet pin into place. Install shift lever gate on lock housing.

3) If equipped, feed gear selector dial lamp wire through hole behind transmission dial on lock housing and route wire through space between housing and jacket. Secure lamp assembly and install gear selector lens assembly. Place shift lever in mid position, seat lock housing on top of jacket and indexing key in housing with slot in jacket. Install housing-to-jacket screws and tighten alternately. Install automatic transmission indicator bracket.

4) Grease and assemble the two lock levers, lock lever spring and pin. Install the assembly into the lock housing. Seat the pin firmly in the bottom of the slots. Make sure the lock lever spring leg is firmly in place in lock casting notch. *See Fig. 4.*

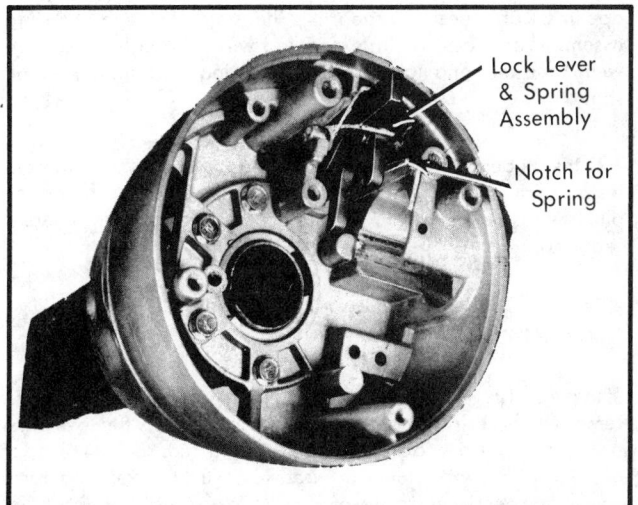

Fig. 4   Lock Lever and Spring Assembly Installed in Housing

5) Install the lock lever guide plate and retaining screws. Position ignition switch to "OFF" position and hand lever in "PARK". Feed wires down through the space between housing and jacket. Position switch in housing and tighten mounting screws.

6) To install ignition lock, turn key to "LOCK" position and remove key. The cylinder will move inward and a spring loaded retainer will snap into place, locking the cylinder into the housing.

CHRYSLER CORP. (Cont.)

7) Fill coupling body $\frac{1}{4}$" full with multi-purpose grease and place cover and seal on shaft. Press shoe pin into steering shaft so it protrudes an equal distance on each side of the shaft. Place spring on side of shaft so it straddles the shoe pin. Place shoes on pin ends with flat side toward spring, engaging tangs.

8) Squeeze shoes together, compressing spring, and push assembly into coupling body. Align master spline mark of coupling body with master spline on upper shaft. Drive in a new dowel pin flush to coupling body outer surface. Position seal and cover on body and crimp cover tangs on body. Move shaft in and out several times to distribute lubricant.

9) Install bearing support (floor shift), bearing and spring on steering shaft and insert steering shaft into column assembly. Install lock plate and new groove pin on steering shaft. Make sure pin is centered. Install steering column shaft lock plate sleeve over shaft lock plate pin and against lock plate. Install bearing lower snap ring on steering shaft. Install coil spring.

10) Install ignition key lamp assembly in housing. Place rubber insulator with grounding staple over column upper bearing and install assembly into bearing housing bore. Use soap solution or rubber lubricant to ease installation. Install turn signal switch in bearing housing, feeding wires through opening in housing. Feed ignition key lamp wires through opening in housing. Install retaining plate over switch and tighten screws.

11) Install turn signal lever or turn signal/speed control lever on turn signal switch. If speed control, feed wires through opening provided in bearing housing. Position housing assembly on steering shaft, feeding wires through space between housing and jacket. Install bearing and snap ring on shaft.

12) Install bearing housing-to-lock housing screws and tighten. Install wiring trough in place over wires, being careful not to pinch wires between trough and jacket. Install new retainers if required.

TILT WHEEL MODELS

Disassembly — 1) Remove steering wheel and column. Remove bracket assembly-to-column jacket bolts. Remove wiring protector from jacket. Attach holding fixture (C-4132) to jacket and mount column in vise. Remove tilt lever and turn signal or speed control lever. Push hazard warning knob in and unscrew to remove. Remove ignition key lamp assembly.

2) Move tilt mechanism to full down tilt. Carefully remove plastic cover from lock plate. Depress lock plate with finger and pry ring out of groove with screwdriver. Remove lock plate, cancelling cam and upper bearing spring.

3) Remove three turn signal switch screws, place shift bowl in low (1) position. Tie up wires and connectors to prevent snagging, remove switch and wiring. To remove lock cylinder, place in "LOCK" position. Insert a thin tool into slot next to switch mounting screw boss (right hand slot) and depress spring latch at bottom of slot to remove lock.

4) Remove housing cover screws and remove housing cover. Reinstall tilt lever and place column in full "UP" position. Remove tilt spring retainer with a phillips screwdriver. Insert screwdriver in opening and press in $\frac{3}{16}$". Turn about $\frac{1}{8}$ turn counterclockwise until ears align with groove in housing and remove spring and guide.

5) Push upper steering shaft in sufficiently to remove steering shaft inner race seat and inner race. Put ignition switch in "ACC" position and remove ignition switch.

6) Place pivot pin remover (C-4016) over pivot pin, thread small portion of screw into pin. Hold screw in position, turn nut clockwise and remove pivot pin from support. Remove opposite pivot pin. Use tilt release lever to disengage lock shoes. Remove bearing housing by pulling upward to extend rack fully. Move housing to left to disengage rack from actuator, remove actuator assembly.

7) Remove roll pin and coupling assembly from lower end of steering shaft. Remove shaft from upper end of column. Disassemble steering shaft by removing center spheres and antilash springs. Remove bolts securing support to lock plate and remove support from end of column jacket. If needed remove attaching screws and shift gate from support.

8) Using screwdriver remove shift tube retaining ring and thrust washer. With a small screwdriver disengage plastic shift tube support from lower end of jacket. Remove shift tube from bowl using tool (C-4120). Insert bushing on end of tool in shift tube and force tube out of bowl. See Fig. 5.

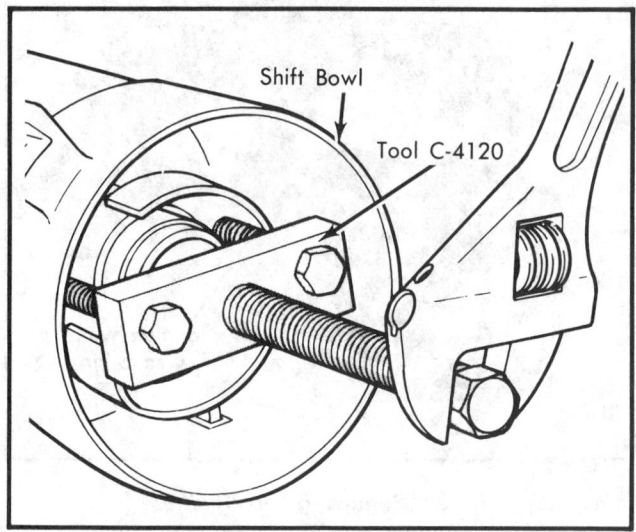

Shift Bowl

Tool C-4120

***Fig. 5   Removing Shift Tube from Bowl
on Tilt Wheel Models***

CAUTION — *Do not hammer or pull on shift tube as plastic joint may be sheared.*

9) Remove shift tube from jacket at lower end. Remove lock plate by sliding out of jacket notches and tapping down toward hub at 12 o'clock position and under jacket opening. Remove wave washer and bowl from jacket. Remove shift lever spring from bowl by winding spring up with pliers and pulling out.

CHRYSLER CORP. (Cont.)

10) Remove tilt lever opening shield and turn signal lever opening shield from housing. Remove lock bolt spring by removing spring retaining screw and moving spring clockwise. Remove snap ring from sector drive shaft. Use a small punch to tap drive shaft from sector. Remove drive shaft, sector and bolt. Remove rack and spring, and also shim if one is used.

11) Using a punch and hammer remove tilt release lever pin. Remove lever and release lever spring. To relieve load on release lever, hold shoes inward and wedge block between top of shoes (over slots) and bearing housing. Remove lock shoe pin with punch and hammer, remove lock shoes and lock shoe springs. *See Fig. 6.*

NOTE — *Do not remove bearings from housing unless they are to be replaced. Never use old bearings.*

Reassembly — 1) Install bearings in housing, if removed. Install lock shoe springs, lock shoes and shoe pin. Use a rod about .180″ diameter to line up shoes. With tilt lever opening on left side, and shoes facing up, the 4 slot shoe is on the left.

Install spring, release lever and pin in bearing housing. Relieve load on release lever as outlined in step **11)** of disassembly procedure. Install drive shaft and tap sector on shaft far enough to install snap ring. Install lock bolt and engage with sector cam surface. Install rack and spring. Block tooth on rack must engage block tooth on sector. Install external tilt release lever, bolt spring and retainer.

2) Install shift lever spring in bowl by winding up with pliers and pushing in. Slide bowl into jacket, install wave washer and lock plate. Work lock plate into notches in jacket and carefully install shift tube in lower end of jacket. Align key in tube with keyway in bowl and use tool (C-4119) to pull tube into bowl. Install thrust washer and retaining ring by pulling bowl up to compress wave washer.

CAUTION — *Do not push hard or tap on end of tube.*

3) Install support by aligning "V" in support with notch in jacket and install retaining screws. Install lower bearing at end of shift tube. Locate about $\frac{3}{16}$″ inside tube (use suitable lubricant to ease installation). Install centering spheres and anti-

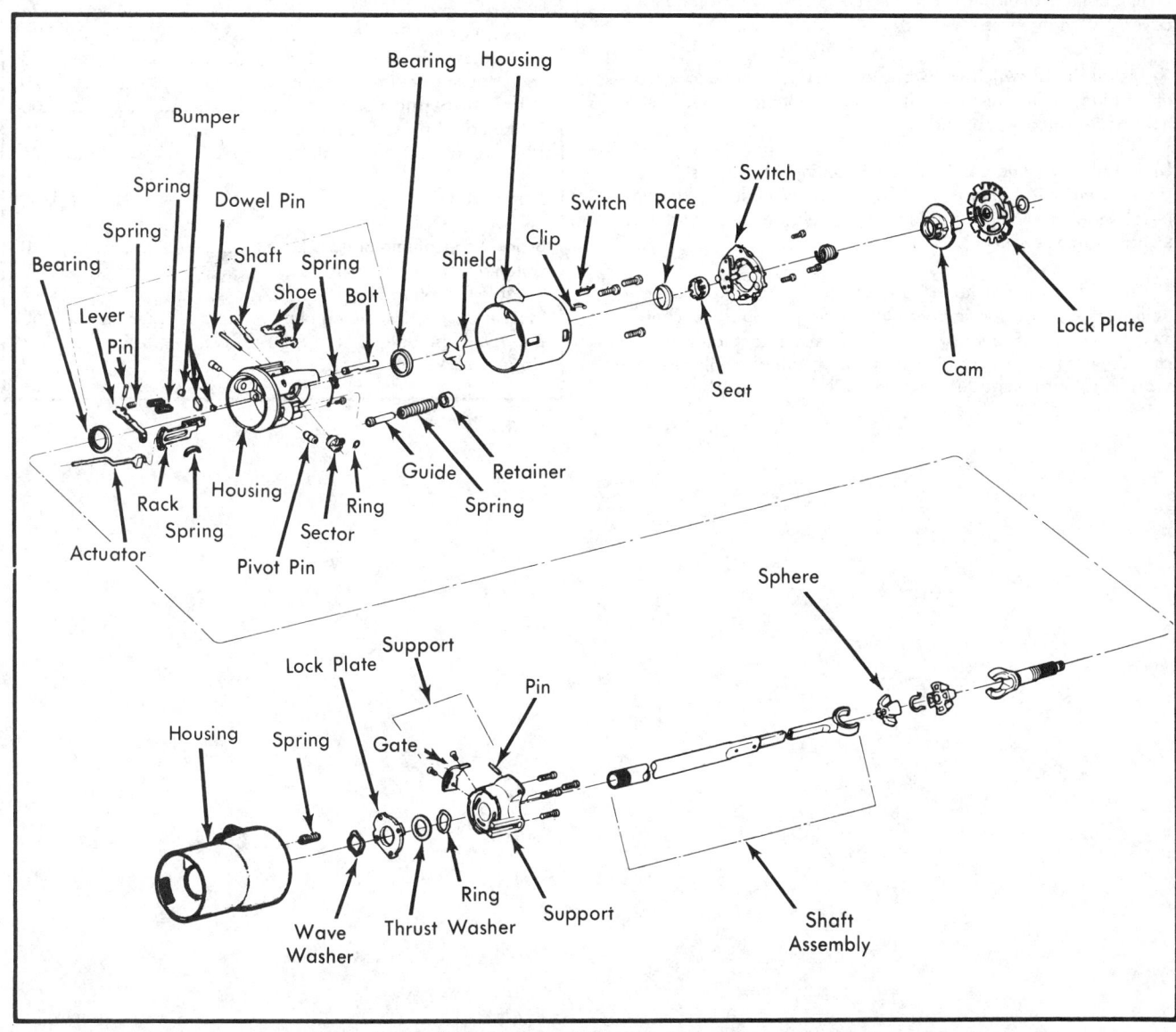

Fig. 6 *Exploded View of Tilt Wheel Column Upper Half*

CHRYSLER CORP. (Cont.)

lash spring in upper steering shaft and lower steering shaft from same side of spheres that spring ends protrude.

4) Check double coupling assembly that master serration of upper shaft will align with master serration of pot coupling. Place housing in full "UP" position, install guide, tilt spring and tilt spring retainer using screwdriver. Turn retainer clockwise to engage. Install steering shaft in shift tube from upper end.

5) Place ignition switch actuator rod through bowl from bottom and insert slot in support. Extend rack downward from bearing housing, assemble housing over steering shaft, and engage rack over end of actuator rod. Install external tilt release lever, and while holding lock shoes in disengaged position, assemble bearing housing over steering shaft until pivot pin holes line up. Install pivot pins.

6) With housing in full "UP" position, install guide, insuring there is grease between guide and peg on support, tilt spring and spring retainer. Using a screwdriver in retainer slot turn retainer clockwise to engage. Install bearing inner race and tilt lever opening shield. Remove tilt release lever, install housing cover and tighten screws.

7) Install signal switch wires and connector. Push hazard warning plunger in, install switch and tighten screws. Install hazard warning knob and pull out.

8) Install cancelling cam spring, cancelling cam and shift lock plate. Using suitable tool (C-4156), depress shift lock plate and install new retaining ring. Install tilt release lever and turn signal switch lever.

9) To install ignition lock, turn key to "LOCK" position and remove key. Insert cylinder into housing enough to contact switch actuator. Press inward to move switch actuator rod up and down to align parts. When aligned, cylinder will move inward and spring loaded retainer will snap into place.

10) When replacing ignition switch, position key cylinder in "ACCESSORY" detent, then place switch in "ACCESSORY" as follows: Spring loaded position at one end is "START". Move slider to extreme other end, this is "ACCESSORY". Fit actuator rod into slider hole and assemble loosely to column.

11) Push switch lightly down column to remove lash in actuator rod and tighten mounting screws. Do not move switch out of detent. Install wire protector over wires on column jacket. Remove column from vise. Remove holding fixture. Position bracket assembly on steering column. Tighten bolts.

12) Align master splines and install coupling assembly on steering shaft. Drive in retaining roll pin. Install column on vehicle, replace steering wheel and road test vehicle.

TIGHTENING SPECIFICATIONS

Application	INCH Lbs.
Bearing Housing-to-Lock Housing Screws	35
Hazard Switch	24
Housing Cover Screws	100
Ignition Switch Screws	35
Lock Housing-to-Jacket	90
Shift Tube Support Screws	60
Tilt Release Spring Retaining Screw	35
Turn Signal Retaining Plate	26

Application	Ft. Lbs.
Bracket-to-Column Bolt	10
Column Clamp Stud Nut	9
Flexible Coupling Bolts	17
Steering Wheel Retaining Nut	60
Support Plate Bolts	17
Upper Bracket Nuts	9

FORD

All Models

DESCRIPTION

All models use steering columns with shift control rod within column tube. Directional signal switch and lever, hazard warning control knob and ignition switch are mounted on columns. Columns are equipped with anti-theft locking device and automatic transmission models have the transmission linkage in the column. Two types of columns are available, a standard column and a tilt column which features 5 positions.

REMOVAL & INSTALLATION

"F" MODELS & BRONCO

Removal — 1) Set parking brake and disconnect negative battery cable. Remove steering wheel. *See Steering Wheels and Column Switches in this Section.* Remove bolt and nut attaching intermediate shaft to steering column. Disconnect shift linkage rods from column.

2) Remove steering floor opening cover plate screws. Remove shroud by loosening screw at bottom, placing shift lever in first gear on manual transmissions, or "1" position on automatic transmissions, and spreading shroud open and pulling it up and away from instrument panel and column.

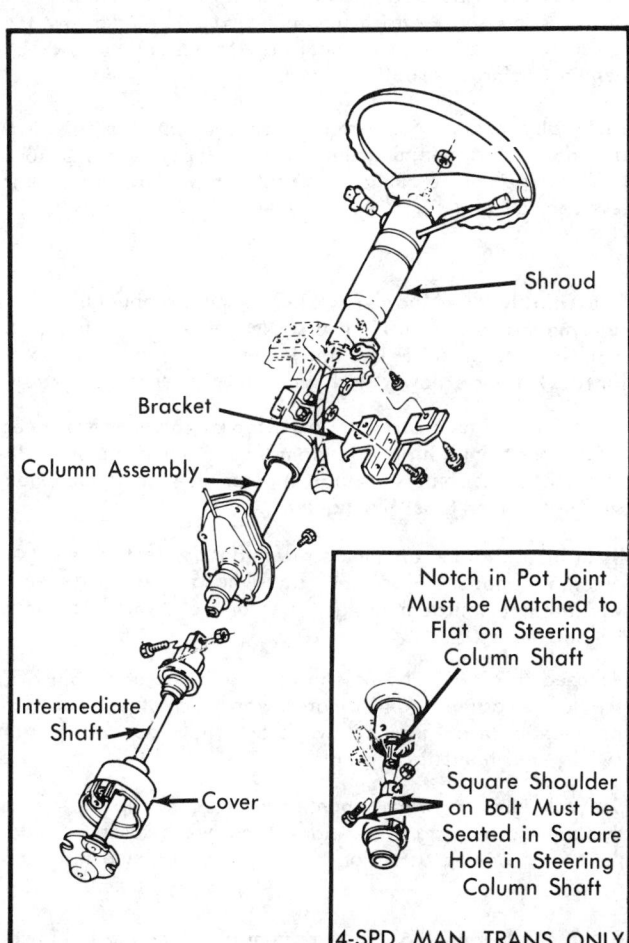

Fig. 1 Steering Column Installation ("F" Models and Bronco)

Shroud

Bracket

Column Assembly

Intermediate Shaft

Cover

Notch in Pot Joint Must be Matched to Flat on Steering Column Shaft

Square Shoulder on Bolt Must be Seated in Square Hole in Steering Column Shaft

4-SPD. MAN. TRANS. ONLY

3) Remove automatic transmission indicator actuation cable. Remove instrument panel column opening cover. Remove column support bracket-to-pedal support bracket bolts. Disconnect turn signal-hazard flasher warning switch and ignition switch wiring harnesses. Remove column from vehicle. Remove support brakcet from column.

Installation — 1) Attach column support bracket, making sure all switch wiring is on outside left of column. Hand start the floor opening cover plate clamp bolt and press plate until clamp butts on column outer tube. Place column in vehicle through opening in floor.

2) Connect turn signal, hazard flasher and ignition switch wiring harnesses. Raise column to pedal support bracket and hand start the bolts. Tighten floor plate cover bolts, support bracket bolts and cover plate clamp bolt. Install and adjust automatic transmission shift indicator cable. Install steering column instrument panel opening cover.

3) Mount shroud by placing manual transmission in first gear, automatic transmission in "1", and spreading shroud around steering column and through opening in instrument panel. Post on interior will index shroud when properly installed. Tighten screw at bottom of shroud. Attach shift linkage rods to column. Fasten intermediate shaft to steering column.

"E" MODELS

Removal — 1) Set parking brake and disconnect negative battery cable. Remove nuts attaching flexible coupling to steering shaft flange. Remove shift linkage rods from column. Remove steering wheel. *See Steering Wheels and Column Switches in this Section.* Remove steering column floor opening cover plate screws.

2) Remove shroud by pulling shroud tabs out of clip at bottom of column. Remove instrument panel column opening cover. Remove bolts attaching column bracket to pedal support bracket. Disconnect turn signal, hazard warning and ignition switch wiring harnesses. Remove steering column.

Installation — 1) Place column in vehicle. Connect turn signal, hazard warning and ignition switch wiring harnesses. Inserting the steering shaft flange through the floor opening so that flange engages the flexible coupling, raise the steering column up to the pedal support bracket and loosely install the support bolts.

2) Loosely install the flexible coupling-to-flange fasteners, and the floor plate fasteners. Install steering wheel. Align steering column and flexible coupling. *See Steering Column Alignment in this Story.* Attach shift linkage rods. Tighten all fasteners. Connect battery.

OVERHAUL

STANDARD COLUMN

Disassembly (All Models) — 1) Remove steering wheel and column. Remove turn signal lever. On 3 speed and automatic transmissions, drive out shift lever pivot pin and remove lever.

2) Remove turn signal-hazard switch retaining screws and partially withdraw switch from upper flange. Remove snap ring

FORD (Cont.)

from upper steering shaft. On "F" and Bronco models, remove lower bearing retainer.

3) Using a light hammer, gently drive the steering shaft out the bottom of the steering column. Clip the ignition switch in the "LOCK" position and remove ignition switch and actuation rod.

4) Remove shift indicator on automatic transmission models. Loosen the upper flange retaining nuts until 1 or 2 threads remain engaged, then pinch the nuts toward each other and pull flange off outer tube.

5) Remove shift tube retaining screw from bottom of shift socket on automatic transmission models. Remove shift socket on 3 speed manual and automatic transmissions, or remove flange extension from outer tube on manual 4 speed transmission.

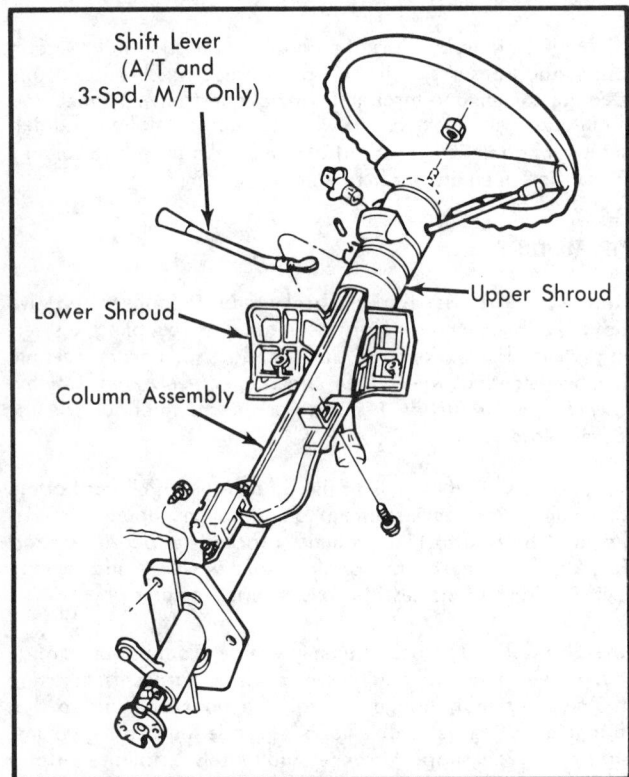

Fig. 2 Steering Column Installation ("E" Models)

6) On "E" models, remove lower bearing retainer on automatic transmission models. Remove shift tube assembly from column bottom on "F" and Bronco models with 3 speed manual or automatic transmission. Remove shift tube assembly from top of column on "E" models with 3 speed manual or automatic transmissions.

7) On "E" models with 3 speed manual transmission withdraw lower shift arms spacer from column outer tube. Remove lamp from flange on automatics and separate turn signal-hazard flasher warning switch from flange.

8) On all models, remove bearing and tire from upper flange by gently tapping opposite side of flange with a light hammer. Disassemble the flange and locking mechanism as described in this story. On "E" models, remove floor opening cover plate from outer tube.

Reassembly ("F" Models & Bronco) — 1) Place bushing in socket retainer in outer tube on 3 speed manual transmissions, and place bushing on upper hub and wave washer on lower hub of shift socket. On automatic transmissions, install shift socket on outer tube. On 4 speed manual transmissions, install flange extension on outer tube.

2) Place wave washer in flange hub on automatics. Install assembled flange onto outer tube by pinching nuts toward each other and pressing flange in place. Retaining bolt "T" head will engage cutouts in outer tube as nuts are tightened.

3) Insert assembled shift tube assembly through lower column opening. Install shift tube retaining screw through bottom of shift socket on automatics. Install steering shaft clip below knurl for upper bearing.

4) Check assembled shaft length. It should be 35.6". Adjust by gently tapping in the appropriate direction. Load shaft up through bottom of column taking care not to collapse steering shaft.

5) Place upper bearing tire onto bearing and press onto knurl on steering shaft until snap ring groove is visible above bearing. Install snap ring. Install turn signal-hazard warning switch.

6) Install lower bearing retainer making sure the centerline of the coupling shaft attachment hole extends $\frac{3}{8}$" below the lower face of the retainer. Minor adjustments can be made by gently tapping the shaft in the appropriate direction.

7) Install ignition switch actuation rod. Mount ignition switch and hand start retaining nuts with the lock cylinder in lock position. Tighten retaining nuts and remove clip. Install shift lever. Install turn signal switch lever.

Reassembly ("E" Models) — 1) On 3 speed manual transmission models, place bushing in socket retainer in outer tube. Place bushing on upper hub and wave washer on lower hub of shift socket. Insert lower shift arms and spacer in outer tube.

2) Insert shift tube assembly from top of column on 3 speed models, or from bottom on automatic transmission models. Install shift socket onto shift tube in outer tube, or flange extension onto outer tube and tighten.

3) Install shift tube retaining screw in bottom of shift socket on automatic models. Place turn signal-hazard warning switch wiring harness through flange. Press lamp and wire into flange on automatics.

4) Feed turn signal harness through shift socket by pinching the flange casting retaining nuts toward each other. Install upper flange. Install ignition switch actuation rod and ignition switch, and hand tighten nuts.

5) With ignition switch mounting nuts loose, clip the switch through the opening in the side of the switch casting. Center the switch on the actuation rod. Tighten retaining nuts and remove clip.

6) Install steering shaft from bottom of column. Install lower bearing retainer. Install upper shaft bearing and tire. Install snap ring on shaft above upper bearing. Install turn signal-hazard warning switch.

FORD (Cont.)

7) Install shift indicator on automatic models. Install shift lever and turn signal lever. Install steering wheel and column in vehicle.

TILT COLUMN

Disassembly — 1) Remove steering wheel. Remove column from vehicle. Remove turn signal lever. Drive out pivot pin and remove shift lever on automatic transmission models. Remove steering shaft lower flange and retaining clamp.

2) Remove lower bearing retainer. On automatic transmission models, remove shift tube retaining screw from bottom of shift socket and withdraw shift tube from bottom of column.

3) Remove lock drive gear. Remove turn signal switch screws, wiring harness to column clips and switch and wiring harness from column.

4) Remove cover casting screws. Lift cover casting up and over the steering shaft and remove casting from column. Unhook upper actuator from lower actuator and remove.

5) Remove and discard screws attaching lower flange to outer tube. Loosen ignition switch retaining screws and remove ignition rod from switch end.

6) Withdraw tilt mechanism, steering shaft and ignition actuation rod from steering column upper end. Remove shift socket from automatic transmission models.

7) Remove screws retaining flange extension on 4 speed manual transmission models, or PRND21 ring on automatics. Remove extension or ring. Remove key release lever mechanism from tilt mechanism on 4 speed manual transmission models.

Reassembly — 1) Attach PRND21 ring to tilt mechanism on automatics, or flange extension to tilt mechanism on manual 4 speed models. Attach key release lever mechanism to tilt mechanism on 4 speed manual transmission models.

2) Install shift socket on automatic models. Install tilt mechanism, feeding the steering shaft down the center of the column and the ignition switch actuation rod through the shift socket/flange extension along the top of the column outer tube.

NOTE — *Care must be taken not to change the length of the steering shaft on "F" and Bronco models because of the telescoping feature.*

3) Install flange retainer assemblies using new hex screws. Install lower bearing retainer. Attach ignition switch loosely to the outer tube.

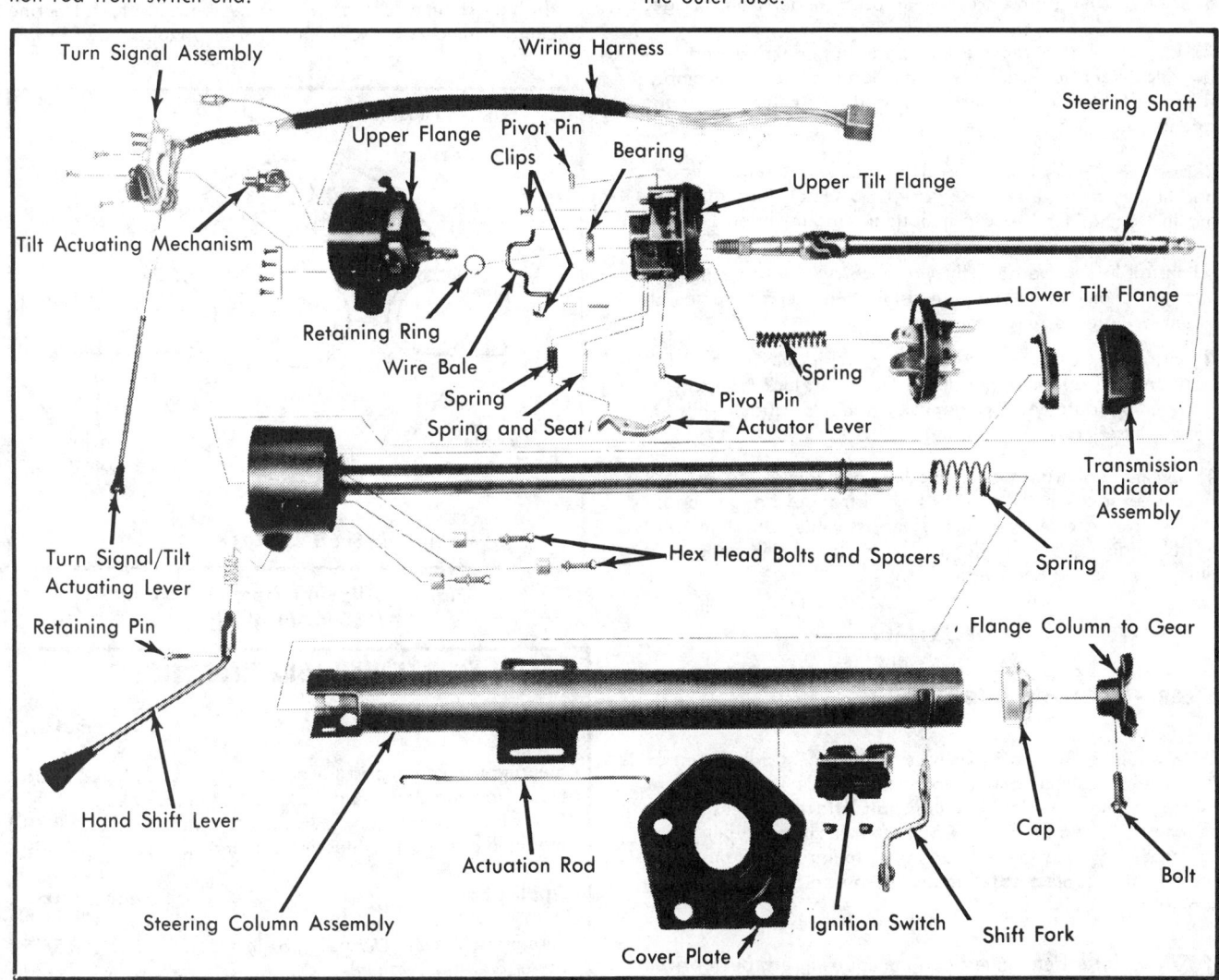

Fig. 3   Exploded View of Tilt Column Assembly

FORD (Cont.)

4) Connect upper and lower actuators. Install cover on column. Install turn signal switch and wiring harness in steering column. Attach wiring harness to steering column clips. Install 2 screws attaching turn signal switch to the flange casting and 1 screw attaching warning buzzer terminal.

5) Install turn signal lever. Install lock drive gear. Install lock cylinder with key in "ON" position. Install the retaining pin flush with cylinder.

6) With ignition switch mounting nuts loose, clip the switch through the opening in the side of the switch casting. Center the switch on the actuation rod. Tighten retaining nuts and remove clip.

7) Install shift lever and pivot pin. Install turn signal lever. Install steering column and steering wheel.

FLANGE & LOCKING MECHANISM

Disassembly (All Non-Tilt Models) — 1) Remove flange retaining bolts. On manual transmission models, remove snap ring and spring from lock release lever assembly. On automatic transmission models, remove shift indicator insert from front of flange. With lock cylinder in "RUN" position, depress retaining pin and remove lock cylinder from flange.

2) On all models, remove lock bearing snap ring and lock bearing. Remove lock drive gear and actuator assembly. Remove lock actuator insert screw and lock actuator through opening in front of flange.

Reassembly — 1) Install lock actuator insert in rear of flange and tighten screw. Insert lock actuator assembly through opening in front of flange until it bottoms against insert.

2) Install lock drive gear through lock cylinder opening such that last gear tooth aligns with last tooth on acutator assembly when actuator is fully rearward.

3) Install lock bearing and snap ring. With cylinder in "RUN" position, and retaining pin depressed, insert lock cylinder into flange. On automatic transmission models, attach shift indicator insert to front of flange.

4) On manual transmission models, position spring on lock release lever assembly through hole in front of flange and install snap ring on lock release lever assembly. On all models, install retaining bolts through holes in flange and hand start nuts 1 to 2 threads on rear side.

ADJUSTMENT

STEERING COLUMN ALIGNMENT

"F" Models & Bronco — There is no alignment adjustment of the steering column and coupling shaft. Alignment is maintained by the slip-joint coupling shaft attaching the steering column to steering gear. Check the flexible coupling for clearance between the slots on the coupling shaft flange and the flexible coupling safety pins. The pin to flange clearance should be .010".

NOTE — *If it is determined that the coupling has been driven in a non-flat position for more than 12,000 miles, coupling should be replaced.*

"E" Models — 1) Remove steering column trim panel. Loosen bolts securing steering column to brake and clutch pedal support. Loosen steering column trim panel. Loosen steering column opening cover plate to dash panel bolts. Loosen lower column clamp.

2) Make sure flexible coupling nuts are tight. With front wheels in straight ahead position, pull up on steering column until the flex coupling is in a flat to a 0.1" concaved position, pointing toward steering wheel.

3) Tighten steering column to support bracket bolts. Tighten steering column opening cover bolts. Insert a .010" shim between right flex coupling safety pin and slot. Now turn steering wheel one revolution clockwise.

4) Check to see if shim is tight. If shim cannot be removed, loosen cover plate clamp and plate attaching bolts. Realign column until shim remains loose enough to be removed when rotating steering wheel.

5) Insert a .010" shim between left flex coupling safety pin and slot. Now turn steering wheel one revolution counterclockwise. Check shim tightness and adjust as described in step 4).

6) Tighten column to support bracket bolts. Tighten steering column opening cover, and install trim panel.

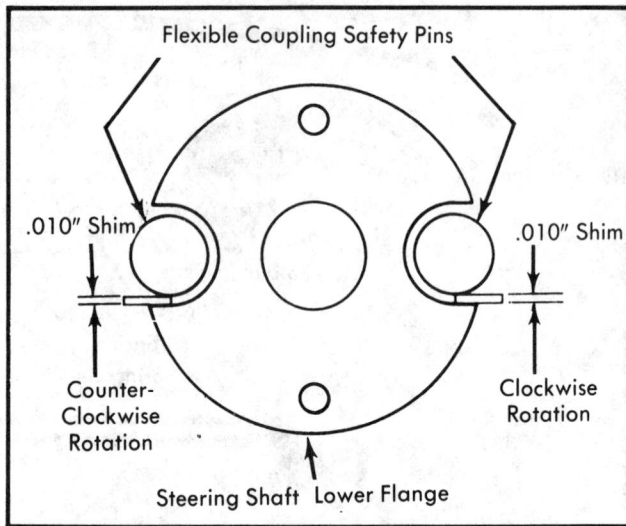

Fig. 4   Aligning Steering Column ("E" Models Only)

TIGHTENING SPECIFICATIONS

Application	Ft. Lbs.
Steering Column Support Bracket	13-38
Floor Opening Cover Plate	5-15
Cover Plate Clamp Bolt	8-18
Intermediate Shaft-to-Steering Column	45-59

Application	INCH-Lbs.
Turn Signal/Hazard Warning Switch	15-25
Lower Bearing Retainer	12-20
Ignition Switch Retaining Nuts	40-65

GENERAL MOTORS

Chevrolet
GMC

DESCRIPTION

All Models — Collapsible steering columns with internal shift linkage and function locking features are used. Tilt steering wheel features are available on all models.

REMOVAL & INSTALLATION

CAUTION — *When working on a collapsible steering column, do not bump or hammer on column components. With the column removed from mounts, it is extremely susceptible to impact damage. A slight impact on the column end may collapse steering shaft or loosen plastic injections which maintain column rigidity. When removing the steering wheel, use a puller but do not hammer on puller to aid removal.*

NOTE — *Correct column installation is important to prevent stress on collapsible components during mounting. Using improper screws, nuts and bolts could prevent assembly from compressing under impact.*

"C" & "K" MODELS

Removal — 1) Loosen front of dash mounting plates. Disconnect battery ground cable. Remove steering wheel. Remove nuts and washers securing flanged end of steering shaft to flexible coupling. Disconnect transmission control linkage from column shift tube levers.

2) Disconnect steering column harness at connector. Disconnect neutral start switch and back-up lamp switch connectors if so equipped. Remove floor pan trim cover screws and remove cover. Remove screws securing two halves of floor pan cover, then remove screws securing halves and seal to floor pan and remove covers. Remove transmission indicator cable if so equipped.

3) Move front seat as far back as possible to provide maximum clearance. Remove two column bracket-to-instrument panel nuts and carefully remove column from vehicle, rotating column so that shift levers will clear hole in floor pan.

Installation — 1) Assemble upper and lower dash covers to seal using seal carrot locks. Attach bracket to steering column. Tighten four retaining bolts to specification.

NOTE — *If rag joint coupling was removed from steering gear shaft, it must be installed before steering column is installed in car.*

2) Position steering column in vehicle. Assemble flange to rag joint. Install lock washers and nuts. Tighten nuts to specification. Loosely install two bracket nuts to dash studs.

3) Install lower clamp (engine side of firewall) and tighten nuts to specification. Install seal, upper and lower covers to cab side of firewall. Tighten two upper bracket nuts to specification.

4) Remove plastic spacers from flexible coupling. Install automatic transmission indicator cable (if equipped with automatic transmission).

5) Install instrument panel trim cover. Connect transmission control linkage. Install steering wheel. Connect battery ground cable.

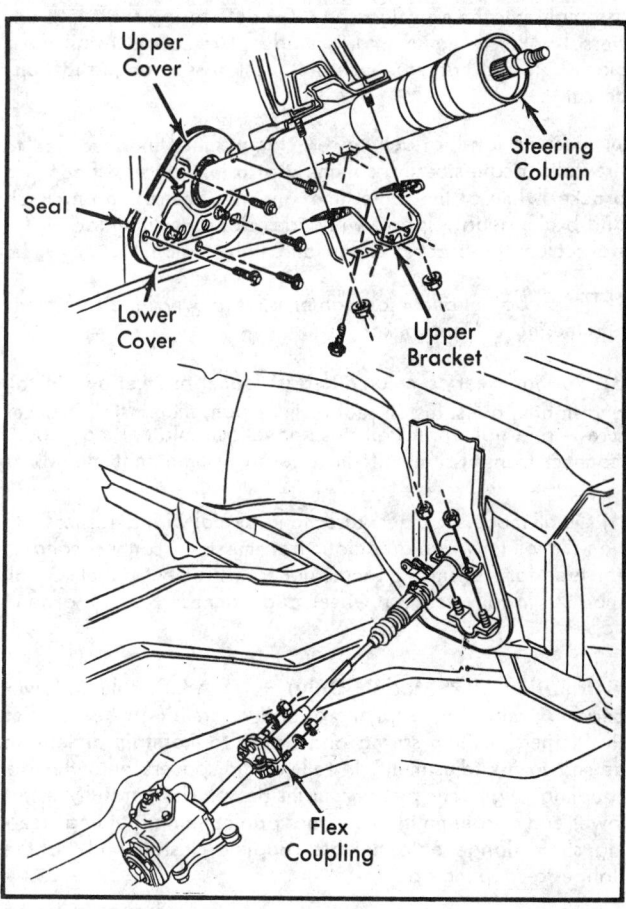

Fig. 1   "C" & "K" Models Steering Column Installation

"G" & "P" MODELS

Removal — 1) Disconnect battery ground cable. On column shift models, disconnect shifter rods at lower end of column. On "G" models, remove steering shaft flange-to-flexible coupling bolts. On "P" models, remove intermediate steering shaft upper universal yoke-to-steering shaft pinch bolt and mark coupling to shaft relationship. On all models, remove column clamp screw(s) on engine side of firewall, if necessary, then slide cover and seal down on column.

2) From inside vehicle, remove screws from floor pan cover and slide cover and seal up column. Remove steering wheel, then reinstall retaining nut and washer to prevent dislocation of steering shaft. Disconnect directional wiring harness. On standard columns with automatic transmission, disconnect conductor tube for transmission indicator at instrument panel.

3) Disconnect single wire at fuse block and unclip it from parking brake bracket on tilt column models with automatic transmission. On all models, remove cap screws from column support bracket at dash panel. Carefully lower, then raise and withdraw column assembly, rotating it so that shift levers clear hole in floor pan.

GENERAL MOTORS (Cont.)

Installation ("P" Models Only) — 1) Applying 50 ft. lbs. force on steering wheel end of steering shaft, adjust lower bearing preload to allow steering shaft end play. Tighten shaft clamp on pot joint bolt. Carefully insert lower end of column assembly into hole in floor pan. Guide steering shaft into universal yoke, lining up marks made at removal. Install yoke pinch bolt and tighten. Pinch bolt must pass through shaft undercut.

2) Position and attach lower clamp mounting bracket to firewall. Locate steering column protrusions against floor pan bracket while at the same time, aligning protrusion on clutch and brake pedal support with index slot on column jacket. Install column-to-bracket clamp and tighten bolt.

NOTE — *Do not allow toe pan bracket to override protrusions on steering column jacket.*

3) Position steering column-to-dash panel bracket and install and tighten bolts. Install seal at floor pan, then install bracket screws and tighten. Install dash panel trim plate, if equipped. Connect transmission shift linkage on column shift models.

4) On all models, connect directional signal wiring harness. On non-tilt columns with automatic transmissions, connect conductor tube for transmission indicator to instrument panel. On all models, install steering wheel and connect battery ground cable.

Installation ("G" Models Only) — 1) Adjust column lower bearing preload by applying a force on steering wheel end of shaft, then position spring and clamp to maintain dimension as shown in Adjustment. Install plastic spacers onto flexible coupling alignment pins. From inside vehicle, carefully insert lower end of column through floor pan opening, guiding steering shaft flange onto flexible coupling. Install and tighten flange-to-coupling bolts

2) Locate index slot in column jacket with protrusion on clutch and brake pedal support. Loosely install column-to-dash bracket and screws. Push column down until steering shaft flange bottoms on plastic spacers on flexible coupling and tighten bracket screws.

3) Remove plastic spacer from alignment pins. Check that the rag joint-to-steering shaft flange clearance is .250-.325". If not within specifications, bracket screws must be loosened and column raised or lowered as required. Retighten screws.

4) Push floor pan seal to floor pan; install and tighten screws. Connect directional signal switch wiring harness. On vehicles with automatic transmissions, connect conductor tube for transmission indicator to instrument panel. On all models, install steering wheel. Connect transmission linkage and battery ground cable.

OVERHAUL

"C" & "K" MODELS
WITHOUT TILT WHEEL

Disassembly — 1) Remove four dash panel bracket-to-column screws and lay bracket in safe place to prevent damage to mounting capsules. Place column in a vise using both weld nuts of set "A" or "B". See Fig. 2.

CAUTION — *Do not place column in vise by clamping onto only one nut or by clamping onto sides of nut not indicated by arrows in Fig. 2.*

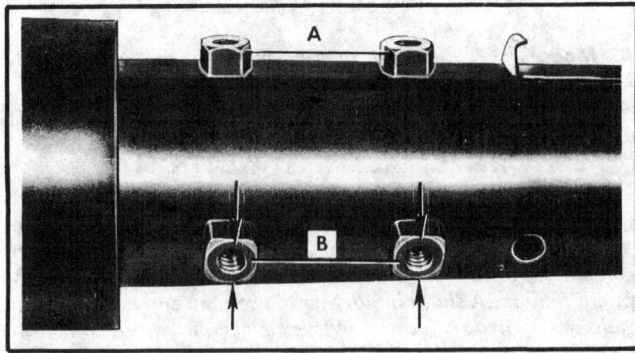

Fig. 2   Correct Installation of Steering Column in Vise

2) Remove directional signal switch, lock cylinder, and ignition switch. Drive out upper shift lever pivot pin and remove shift lever on column shift models. Remove upper bearing thrust washer. Remove four screws attaching directional signal and ignition lock housing to column and remove housing assembly. Remove thrust cap from lower side of housing.

3) Lift ignition switch actuating rod and rack assembly, rack preload spring, and shaft lock bolt and spring assembly out of housing. Remove shift lever detent plate (shift gate). Remove ignition switch actuator sector through lock cylinder hole by pushing firmly on block tooth of sector with a screwdriver or punch. Remove gearshift lever housing and shroud from jacket assembly (transmission control lock tube housing and shroud on floor shift models).

4) Remove shift lever spring from gearshift lever housing (lock tube spring on floor shift models). Pull steering shaft from lower end of jacket assembly. Remove two screws holding back-up switch or neutral start switch to column and remove switch. Remove lower bearing retainer clip. See Fig. 3.

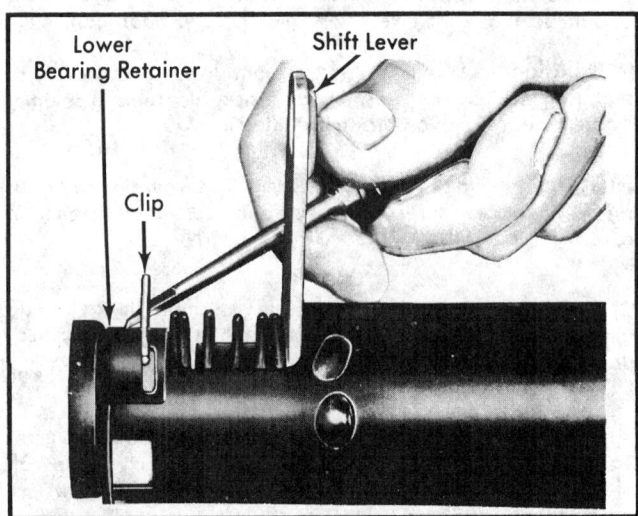

Fig. 3   Removing Lower Bearing Retaining Clip

5) On vehicles with automatic transmission or floorshift, remove lower bearing retainer, bearing adapter assembly, shift tube thrust spring and washer. Lower bearing may be

GENERAL MOTORS (Cont.)

removed from adapter by light pressure on bearing outer race. Slide out shift tube assembly.

6) On vehicles with manual transmission and column shift, remove lower bearing adapter, bearing and 1st-Reverse shift lever. Lower bearing may be removed from adapter by light pressure on bearing outer race. Remove three screws from bearing at lower end and slide out shift tube assembly.

7) On all models with column shift, remove gearshift housing lower bearing from upper end of column.

Reassembly — 1) Apply a thin coat of lithium grease to all friction surfaces. Install sector into directional signal and lock cylinder housing. Install sector in lock cylinder hole over sector shaft with tang end to outside of hole. Press sector over shaft with blunt tool. Install shift lever detent plate onto housing. Insert rack preload spring into housing from bottom side. Long section should be toward handwheel and hook onto edge of housing.

2) Assemble locking bolt onto crossover arm on rack and insert rack and lock bolt assembly into housing from bottom with teeth up (toward handwheel) and toward centerline of column. Align first tooth on sector with last tooth on rack; if aligned properly, block teeth will line up when rack assembly is pushed all the way in.

3) Install thrust cup on bottom hub of housing. Install gearshift housing lower bearing from very end of jacket, while aligning indentations in bearing with projections on jacket.

CAUTION — *If bearing is not properly installed, it will not rest on all the stops provided.*

4) Install shift lever spring into gearshift lever (or lock tube) housing. Install housing and shroud assemblies onto upper end of mast jacket. Rotate housing to be sure it is seated in bearing. With shift lever housing in place, install directional signal and lock cylinder housing onto jacket. Gearshift housing

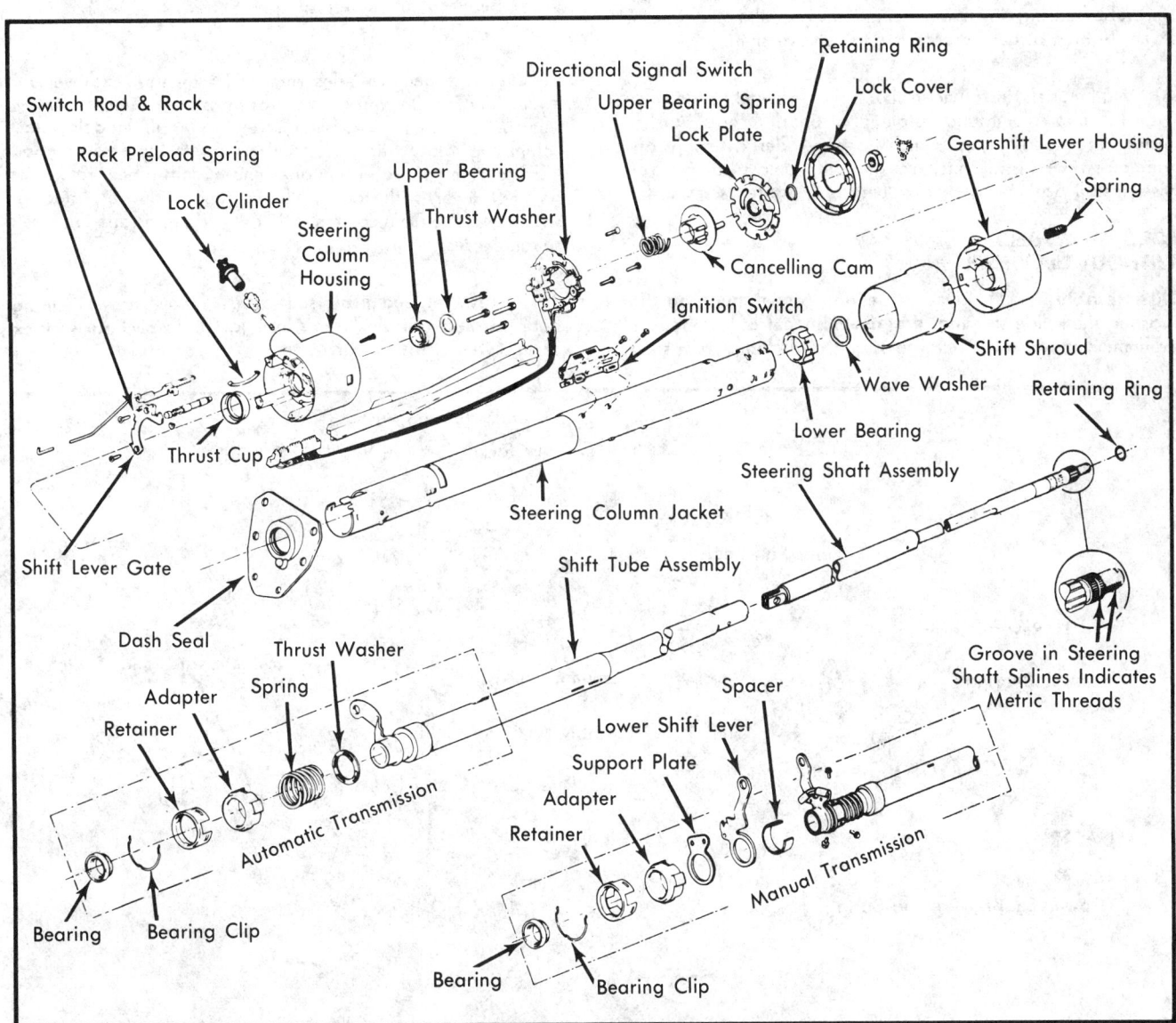

**Fig. 4   Exploded View of Steering Column Assembly
"C" & "K" Models with Column Shift**

GENERAL MOTORS (Cont.)

should be in "PARK" position and rack pulled downward. Be sure directional signal housing is seated on jacket and install and tighten four screws.

5) Press lower bearing into adapter assembly. Insert shift tube assembly into lower end of jacket and rotate until upper shift tube key slides into housing keyway.

6) On vehicles with automatic transmission or floor shift, assemble spring, lower bearing and adapter assembly into bottom of jacket. Holding adapter in place, install lower bearing reinforcement and retainer clip. Be sure clip snaps into jacket and reinforcement slots.

7) On vehicles with manual transmission and column shift, loosely attach three screws in jacket and shift tube bearing. Assemble 1st-Reverse lever and lower bearing and adapter assembly into bottom of jacket. Holding adapter in place, install bearing reinforcement and retaining clip. Be sure clip snaps into jacket and reinforcement slots. Place a .005" shim between 1st-Reverse lever and lever spacer and turn upper shift tube bearing down until definite drag is felt at 1st-Reverse lever. Tighten attaching screws and remove shim.

8) On all models, install neutral or back-up switch. Slide steering shaft into column and install upper bearing thrust washer. Install directional signal switch, lock cylinder assembly and ignition switch. Install shift lever and pin. Remove column from vise. Install dash bracket to column and tighten screws.

"G" & "P" MODELS
WITHOUT TILT WHEEL

Disassembly — 1) Remove steering wheel nut and flat washer, then slide steering shaft assembly out of lower end of column. Remove lower bearing spring and clamp from steering shaft ("G" models) or from steering column ("P" models). Remove back-up lamp switch. Drive out shift lever pin (except floor shift models) and remove shift lever.

2) Remove directional switch cancelling cam and switch lever. Remove column wiring harness cover. Remove directional signal switch screws. Rotate directional signal switch housing counterclockwise and remove housing from column. Remove plastic thrust washer assembly and then remove shift lever housing (or extension housing if floor shift) from column.

NOTE — *Housing and switch cannot be fully removed from column until shift lever housing is removed.*

3) Separate directional signal switch, switch control support assembly, directional signal housing and shift lever housing (or extension housing) assemblies. Press steering shaft upper bearing out of switch contact support. Remove shift lever housing (or extension housing) seat and bushing from upper end of column. Remove bolt and screws from adjusting ring clamp and remove clamp, adjusting ring, and lower bearing. Press lower bearing out of adjusting ring.

4) On three speed columns, remove 1st-Reverse shift lever and lever spacer. On automatic transmission columns, remove selector plate clamping ring screws. On all models, place column upright on floor, supporting it with 2 pieces of wood. Place a block of wood on upper end of shift tube. Press down on shift lever with foot while tapping on wood block to withdraw tube from column jacket. If removal is difficult, use a suitable press.

5) Remove felt seal from shift tube. Remove firewall clamp, floor pan seal and dash seals from jacket. Inspect parts for excessive wear, rust or corrosion.

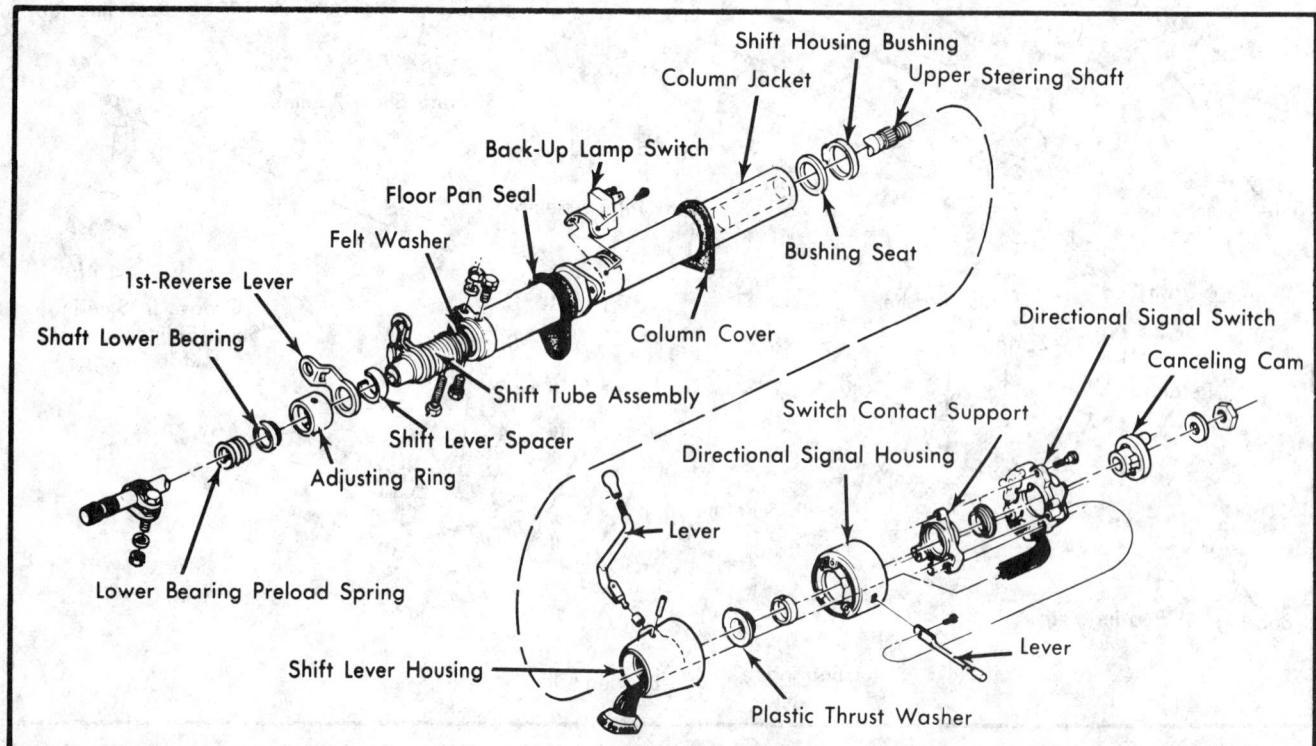

Fig. 5   Exploded View of Steering Column Assembly for "G" & "P" Models

GENERAL MOTORS (Cont.)

Reassembly — 1) When lubrication is called for, use lithium soap grease. Install dash panel seal, floor pan and firewall clamps over end of column. Lubricate all bearing surfaces on shift tube. Place felt seal onto shift tube (next to spring) and place shift tube in jacket.

2) On three speed column shift models, temporarily install spacer, 1st-Reverse shift lever and lower adjusting ring. Place a block of wood on top of adjusting ring and tap until shift tube bottoms. Remove adjusting ring, shift lever, and spacer. On automatic transmission columns, align 3 holes in selector plate with 3 holes in jacket. Shift tube spring retainer must be bottomed against jacket stops. Position clamping ring and install 3 screws.

3) On three speed columns, lubricate and install spacer and 1st-Reverse lever (tang of lever towards top of column). On all columns, install lower bearing in adjusting ring, then install adjusting ring, clamp, and screws. Install shift lever housing (or extension housing) seat and bushing to upper end of housing.

4) Thread directional signal switch wiring harness through switch and shift lever (or extension) housings. Lubricate inner diameter of shift (extension) housing and install onto upper end of column. Install switch housing plastic washer assembly. Press upper bearing into switch contact support.

5) Install directional signal switch housing, contact support, bearing, and switch. Tighten screws. Install column wiring harness cover and back-up lamp switch. Install directional signal and gearshift levers.

6) Loosely install lower bearing preload spring and clamp. Slide steering shaft assembly through column assembly. Install directional signal conceling cam, steering shaft nut and lock washer.

"C" & "K" MODELS
WITH TILT WHEEL

Disassembly — 1) Remove four dash panel bracket-to-column screws and lay bracket in safe place to prevent damage to mounting capsules. Place column in a vise using both weld nuts of set "A" and "B" as shown in *Fig. 2.*

CAUTION — *Do not place column in vise by clamping onto only one nut or by clamping on to sides of nut not indicated by arrows.*

2) Remove directional signal switch, lock cylinder, and ignition switch. Remove tilt release lever, then drive out shift lever pivot pin and remove shift lever and housing. Remove three directional signal housing screws and remove housing.

3) Install tilt release lever and place column in full up position. Remove tilt lever spring retainer by using a phillips screwdriver which just fits into slot opening. Insert screwdriver into slot, press in approximately $\frac{3}{16}$", then rotate $\frac{1}{8}$ turn counterclockwise until retainer ears align with grooves in housing, then remove retainer, spring, and guide. See *Fig. 6.*

4) Remove pot joint-to-steering shaft clamp bolt, then remove intermediate shaft and pot joint assembly. Push upper steering shaft in enough to remove steering shaft upper bearing inner race and seat. Pry off lower bearing retainer clip, then remove bearing reinforcement, bearing, and bearing adapter

assembly from lower end of mast jacket. Remove upper bearing housing pivot pins using special tool (J-21854-1).

Steering Shaft Bearing Lock Nut

Tilt Lever Spring Retainer

Fig. 6   Removing Tilt Lever Spring Retainer

5) With tilt release lever installed, disengage lock shoes. Remove bearing housing by pulling upward to extend rack full down, then move housing to left to disengage ignition switch race from actuator rod. Remove steering shaft assembly from upper end of column. Remove centering spheres and anti-lash spring to disassemble steering shaft.

6) Remove transmission indicator wire, if equipped. Remove steering shaft bearing housing support-to-gearshift housing screws, then remove bearing housing support. Remove ignition switch actuator rod. Use a screwdriver to remove shift tube retaining ring, then remove thrust washer.

7) Install a puller (J-23072) to lock plate, then turn center screw of tool clockwise to force shift tube from housing. Remove shift tube (transmission control lock tube on floor shift models) from lower end of mast jacket, then remove tool from lock plate.

CAUTION — *Guide lower end of shift tube through slotted opening in mast jacket. If tube is allowed to interfere with jacket, damage may result.*

8) Remove housing support lock plate by sliding out of jacket notches, then tipping it down toward housing hub at 12 o'clock position and sliding it under jacket opening. Remove wave washer. Remove shift lever housing from mast jacket (column shift models) or transmission control lock tube housing (floor shift models). Wind up shift lever spring with pliers and pull out. Remove spring plunger on floor shift models.

9) On all columns disassemble bearing housing as follows: Remove tilt lever opening shield, then remove lock bolt spring retaining screw and move spring clockwise to remove it from bolt. Remove sector drive shaft snap ring, then use a small punch to lightly tap drive shaft from sector. Remove drive shaft, sector and lock bolt. Remove rack and rack spring.

10) Use a punch to remove tilt release lever pin. Remove lever and release lever spring. Hold lock shoes inward and wedge a block between top of shoes (over slots) and bearing housing to relieve load on release lever. Remove lock shoe retaining pin using a punch, then remove lock shoes and springs. Remove bearings from housing only if replacement is necessary.

GENERAL MOTORS (Cont.)

Reassembly — 1) Apply a thin coat of lithium grease or equivalent to all friction surfaces. If bearing housing was not disassembled, proceed to step **4)**. To reassemble bearing housing, press bearings into housing (if removed) using a suitable size socket being careful not to damage housing or bearings. Install lock shoe springs, lock shoes, and shoe pin in housing.

NOTE — *Use a .180" diameter rod to line up shoes for pin installation.*

2) Install shoe release lever, spring and pin. If necessary to relieve load on release lever, hold shoes inward and wedge a block between top of shoes (over slots) and bearing housing. Install sector drive shaft into housing and lightly tap sector onto shaft far enough to allow installation of snap ring. Install snap ring.

3) Install lock bolt and engage it with sector cam surface. Install rack and spring while noting that the block tooth on rack should engage block tooth on sector. Install external tilt release lever. Install lock bolt spring and retaining screw and tighten.

4) Wind up shift lever spring with pliers and push into housing. Install plunger on floor shift models. Slide gearshift lever housing onto mast jacket. On all models, install bearing support lock plate wave washer. Install lock plate and work it into notches by tipping plate toward hub a 12 o'clock position and sliding under jacket opening. Slide lock plate into notches in jacket.

5) Install shift tube into lower end of mast jacket, then align keyway of tube with key in shift lever housing. Install wobble plate end of special tool (J-23073) into upper end of shift tube (far enough to reach enlarged portion of tube). Install adapter over end of tool and seat against lock plate. Install nut on end of tool and pull shift tube into housing.

CAUTION — *Do not push or tap on end of shift tube and make sure shift tube lever is aligned with slotted opening at lower end of mast jacket or damage may result.*

6) Pull shift lever housing up far enough to compress wave washer, then install bearing support thrust washer and retaining ring. Install bearing support while ensuring "V" in support is in line with "V" in jacket. Install attaching screws through support and into lock plate, then tighten. Align lower bearing adapter with notches in jacket and push adapter into lower end of mast jacket. Install lower bearing, bearing reinforcement and retaining clip.

NOTE — *Clip must be aligned with slots in reinforcement, jacket and adapter.*

7) Install centering spheres and anti-lash spring into upper shaft. Install lower shaft from same side of spheres that spring ends protrude. Install steering shaft assembly into shift tube from upper end and carefully guide shaft through shift tube and bearing.

8) Install ignition switch actuator rod through shift lever housing and insert into slot in bearing support. Extend rack downward from bearing housing, then assemble bearing housing over steering shaft and engage rack over end of actuator rod. Install tilt release lever, then hold lock shoes in disengaged position and position bearing housing over steering shaft until pivot pin holes line up. Install pivot pins.

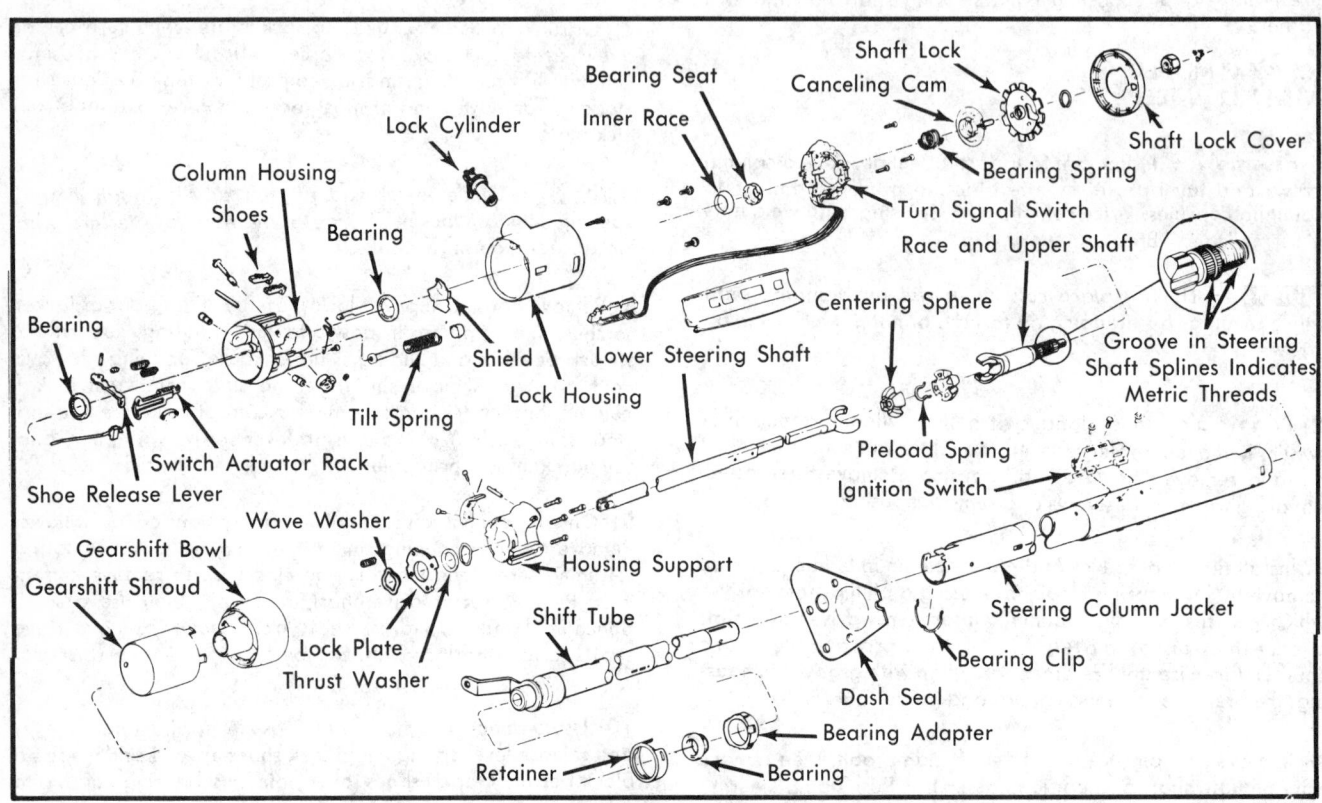

***Fig. 7 Exploded View Of Tilt Wheel Steering Column
"C" & "K" Models with Column Shift***

GENERAL MOTORS (Cont.)

9) Place bearing housing in full up position, then install tilt lever spring guide, spring and spring retainer. Using a phillips screwdriver, push retainer in and turn clockwise to engage in housing. Install upper bearing inner race and race seat, then install tilt lever opening shield. Remove tilt release lever, then install directional signal housing and tighten screws.

10) Install tilt release lever and shift lever, then drive shift lever pin in. Install lock cylinder, directional signal switch, and ignition switch. Install intermediate shaft assembly to upper shaft after aligning groove across upper end of pot joint with flat on steering shaft. Install and tighten clamp while noting that clamp bolt must pass through shaft undercut.

11) Install neutral safety switch or back-up switch. Install dash panel bracket-to-column attaching screws and tighten. The slotted openings in bracket must face upper end of steering column.

"G" & "P" MODELS
WITH TILT WHEEL

Disassembly — 1) Place column in vise using suitable holding fixture (J-22573). Remove directional signal switch. Remove lower steering shaft and pot joint assembly. Remove lower bearing and adapter assembly from column, then press bearing out from adapter. If column shift model, remove shift lever pivot pin and shift lever.

2) Install tilt release lever and place column in full up position. Remove tilt lever spring and retainer using a screwdriver that just fits into slot opening. Insert screwdriver into slot, push in approximately ³⁄₁₆", then rotate clockwise approximately ⅛ turn until retainer ears align with grooves in housing and remove retainer and spring.

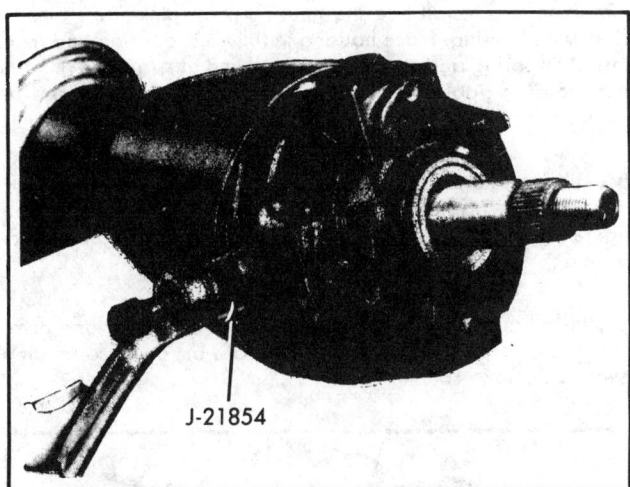

Fig. 8   Removing Bearing Housing Pivot Pins

3) Remove steering shaft bearing lock nut using suitable socket (J-22599). Remove upper bearing race seat and race. Remove two bearing housing pivot pins using suitable tool (J-21854). See *Fig. 8*.

4) Pull up on tilt release lever (to disengage lock shoes) and remove bearing housing. If it is necessary to disassemble bearing housing, proceed as follows: Press upper and lower bearings out of housing. Using suitable puller (J-5822) and slide hammer, pull bearing races from housing. Remove tilt release lever. Drive out shoe release lever pivot pin using a

punch. Remove lever spring and remove wedge. Drive out lock shoe retaining pin with a punch and remove shoes and shoe springs. See *Fig. 9*.

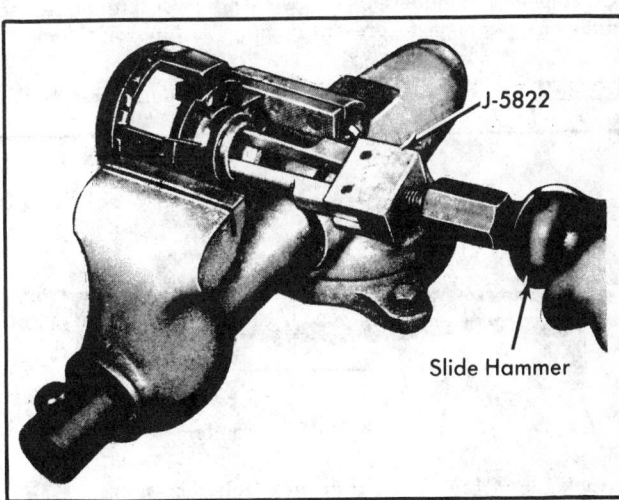

Fig. 9   Using a Puller to Remove Bearing Race

5) Remove steering shaft assembly through upper end of column. If it is necessary to disassemble shaft assembly, proceed as follows: Turn upper shaft 90° to lower shaft and slide upper shaft and centering spheres from lower shaft. Rotate centering spheres 90° and remove centering spheres and preload spring from upper shaft.

6) Remove four bearing housing support screws and remove support. If shift tube index plate (column shift only) must be removed, remove two retaining screws and remove plate. Remove shift tube retaining ring with screwdriver. Remove thrust washer. Remove neutral start switch or back-up lamp switch retaining screws and remove switch. See *Fig. 10*.

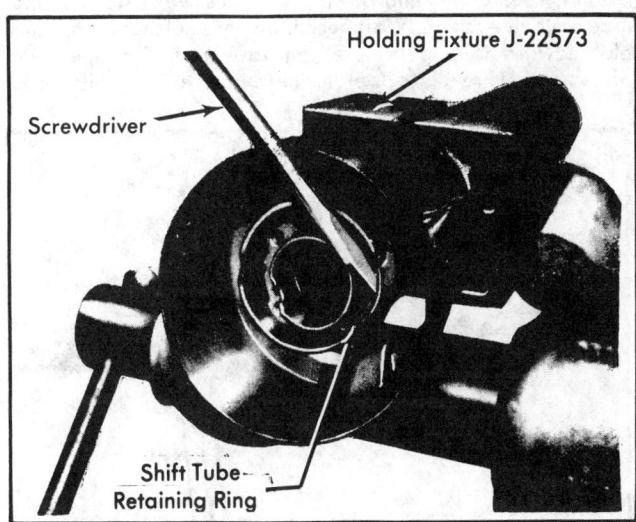

Fig. 10   Removing Shift Tube Retaining Ring

7) Rework a shift tube removing tool (J-22551) by removing ½" from pilot end of tool as shown in *Fig. 11*. Remove shift tube assembly using reworked tool as follows: Insert hooked end of tool into notch in shift tube just below shift lever housing key. Pilot sleeve over threaded end of tool and into upper

GENERAL MOTORS (Cont.)

end of shift tube. Force shift tube out of housing by turning nut onto the tool. If shift tube is not completely free when nut is bottomed on its threads, complete removal by hand. On column shift models, guide lower shift lever through slotted opening in column to prevent damage to tube or column.

CAUTION — *Do not hammer on shift tube during removal.*

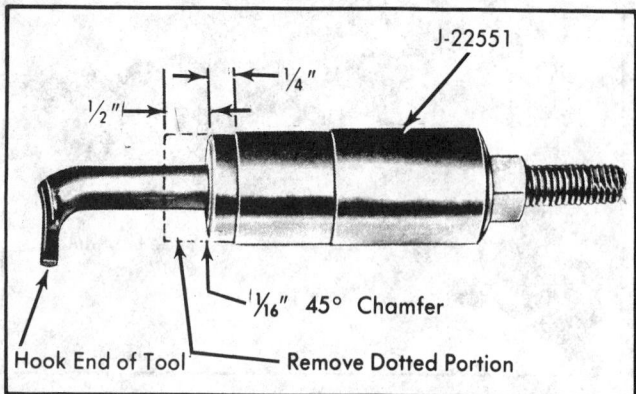

Fig. 11 Reworked Shift Tube Removal Tool

8) On all models, remove lock plate by sliding out of column notches, tipping plate downward toward housing to compress wave washer and then removing wave washer and lock plate. On column shift models, remove shift lever housing and shift lever spring. On all models, remove dash panel seal mounting plate and instrument panel seal from column jacket.

Reassembly — 1) When lubrication is called for, use lithium soap grease. Install dash panel seal, mounting plate and instrument panel seal on column. On column shift models, press a new shift lever spring into shift lever housing. Slide shift lever housing over upper end of column. Place wave washer and lock plate in position. Work lock plate into notches by tipping plate toward housing (compressing wave washer) at open side of column. Lubricate lock plate and upper end of shift tube.

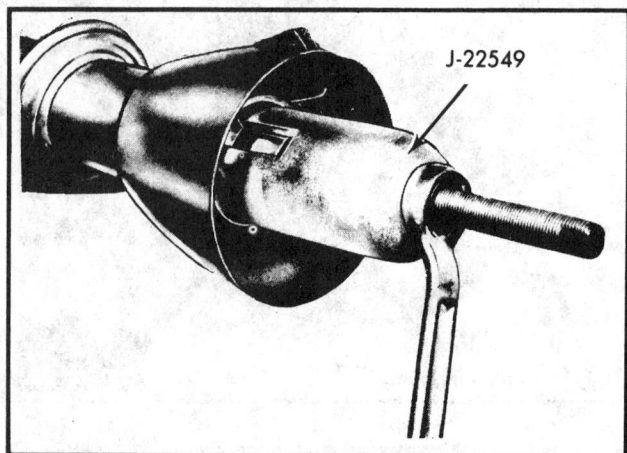

Fig. 12 Installing Shift Pin Tube

2) Carefully install shift tube into lower end of column (make sure foam seal is at lower end of shift tube). Align keyway in tube with key in shift lever housing and complete installation of shift tube using suitable installer tool (J-22549). Shift lever

housing key must bottom in shift tube slot to be fully installed. Remove installer tool from column. Lubricate and push foam seal in flush with column housing. *See Fig. 12.*

CAUTION — *Do not hammer or force tube when installing in column.*

3) Pull up on shift lever housing (to compress wave washer) and install thrust washer and retaining ring. Be sure ring is seated in both slots of shift tube. Lubricate inside diameter of bearing housing support and install support, aligning bolt holes in support with bolt holes in lock plate. Install four support screws and tighten.

4) Assemble steering shaft as follows: Lubricate and assemble centering spheres and preload spring. Install spheres into upper (short) shaft and rotate 90°. Install lower shaft 90° to upper shaft and over centering spheres. Slowly straighten shafts while compressing preload spring.

5) Install shaft assembly into housing from upper end. Install lower bearing and adapter, bearing reinforcement, wire clip, pot joint coupling and lower shaft.

6) Assemble bearing housing as follows: Press new upper and lower bearing races into bearing housing. Lubricate and install bearings into races. Place lock shoe springs in position in housing. Install each shoe in place and compress spring until a suitable size straight punch can be used to hold shoes in position. Once shoes are in place, install retaining pin. Install shoe release lever and drive in pivot pin. Install tilt release lever. Lubricate shoes and release lever.

7) Install bearing housing assembly to support. Hold tilt release lever up until shoes have fully engaged support. Lubricate and install bearing housing pivot pins. Press pins in flush with housing. Place housing in full "UP" position and then install tilt spring and retainer (tapered end of spring first). Push into housing approximately ³⁄₁₆" and rotate counterclockwise ⅛ turn.

8) Lubricate and install upper bearing upper race, race seat and lock nut. Tighten lock nut to remove lash and then further tighten ¹⁄₁₆ to ⅛ turn (column must be in straight-ahead position). Remove tilt release lever.

9) Install directional signal switch. Install shift lever and pivot pin if column shift model. Install neutral-start or back-up lamp switch. Remove column from vise.

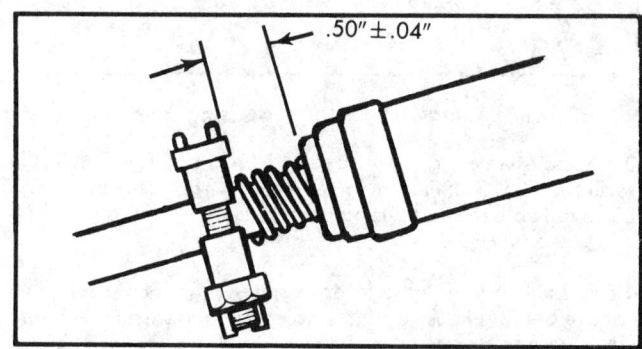

Fig. 13 Steering Column Lower Bearing Adjustment for "G" Models

GENERAL MOTORS (Cont.)

ADJUSTMENTS

LOWER BEARING ADJUSTMENT

"G" & "P" Models — Loosen clamp on steering shaft. Apply 50 lbs. force to steering wheel end of shaft and adjust clamp to obtain clearance of .50±.04" for "G" models and 1.26±.02" for "P" models. See Figs. 13 and 14. Tighten clamp bolts to specifications.

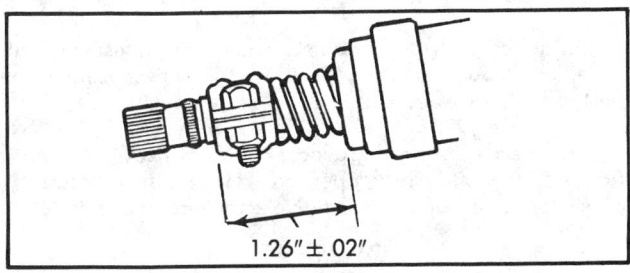

Fig. 14 Steering Column Lower Bearing Adjustment for "P" Models

SHIFTER TUBE ADJUSTMENT ("G" & "P" Models)

Manual Transmissions — Loosen adjusting ring attaching screws and clamp bolt. Rotate adjusting ring to give .005" end play between adjusting ring and lst-Reverse shift lever. Tighten attaching screws and clamp bolt. See Fig. 15.

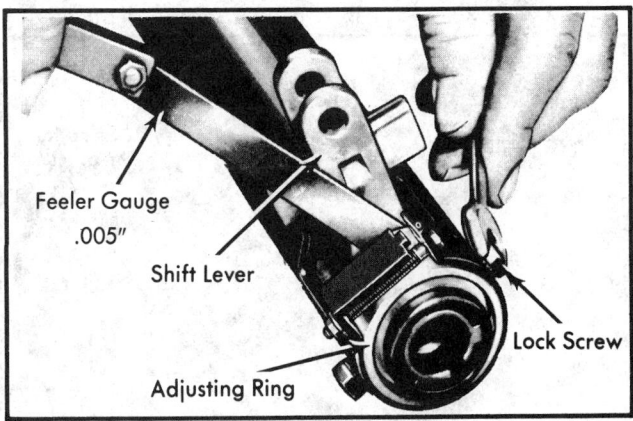

Fig. 15 Shift Tube Adjustment for Manual Transmission "G" & "P" Models

Automatic Transmissions — Place shift tube lever in "N" or "D". Loosen adjusting ring clamp screws and rotate adjusting ring to obtain .33-.36" end play between shift tube lever and adjusting ring. Tighten adjusting ring clamp screws. See Fig. 16.

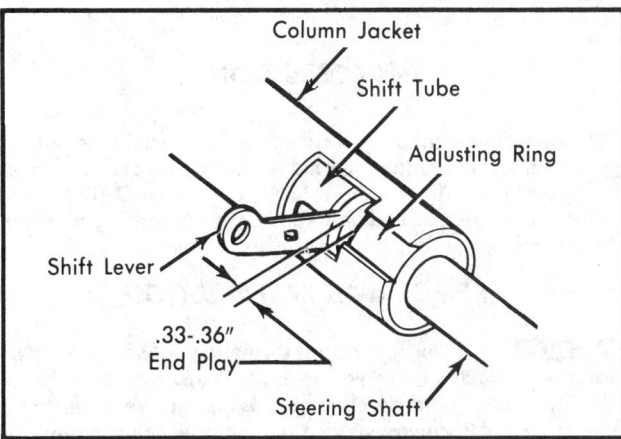

Fig. 16 Shift Tube Adjustment for Automatic Transmission "G" & "P" Models

---

ADJUSTMENT SPECIFICATIONS

Application	Specification
Lower Bearing Adjustment	
"G" Models	.50"±.04"
"P" Models	1.26"±.02"
Shift Tube Adjustment	
Automatic Transmission	.33-.36"
Manual Transmission	.005"

TIGHTENING SPECIFICATIONS

Application	Ft. Lbs.
Flexible Coupling Bolt & Studs	
"P" Models	20
All Others	18
Lower Jacket Bearing Clamp	30
Lower Coupling-to-Worm Shaft Clamp	
"P" Models	75
All Others	30

Application	INCH Lbs.
Column-To-Dash Panel	125
Floor Pan Cover Plate	
"P" Models	24
"G" Models	30
Firewall Bracket Clamp	
"G" Models	150
"P" Models	98
All Others	90
Lower Bearing Adjusting Ring Bolt	70
Ignition Switch Screws	35
Column Lock Plate Cover	20
Turn Signal Housing	45
Lock Bolt Spring Screw (Tilt Wheel)	35
Bearing Housing Support Screw (Tilt Wheel)	60

JEEP

All Models

DESCRIPTION

All models use a collapsible column which is equipped with an anti-theft locking feature. All models are available with an optional Adjust-O-Tilt steering column. The Adjust-O-Tilt steering column is also equipped with the energy-absorbing and anti-theft features.

REMOVAL & INSTALLATION

CAUTION — *When servicing the steering column, use ONLY specified attaching screws and bolts. Screws or bolts longer than specified could damage collapsible feature of the steering column. Attaching nuts and bolts for the column mounting bracket must be tightened to specifications to allow bracket to break away under impact.*

ALL MODELS

Removal — 1) Disconnect battery ground cable. If equipped with automatic transmission, disconnect transmission shift rod at steering column shift lever.

2) On Cherokee and Wagoneer with automatic transmission and power brakes, it will be necessary to shift transmission to "1" detent position to gain access to shift rod retaining clip at shift lever.

3) Remove upper steering shaft to intermediate shaft "U" joint pinch bolt. Do not attempt to separate upper steering shaft and intermediate shaft at this time.

4) On Cherokee and Wagoneer models with air conditioning, remove left duct extension. On all models, remove steering column to instrument panel bezel. On Cherokee, Wagoneer and truck models, bezel screws are located behind lower bezel half.

5) Remove bolts securing steering column mounting bracket to instrument panel. Remove bolts securing mounting bracket to steering column and remove bracket.

CAUTION — *It is recommended that the bracket be stored in a safe place to prevent damage to breakaway capsules.*

6) Remove upper and lower toe-plates. Disconnect wiring harness at ignition switch, removing black connector first.

7) If equipped with Cruise Command, disconnect electrical connector. Separate steering shaft from intermediate "U" joint and remove steering column assembly.

CAUTION — *It is recommended that steering column be handled with care after removal. Blows on end of steering shaft or shift levers, leaning on column assembly, or dropping unit may cause damage to energy absorbing components.*

Installation — 1) Place steering column in vehicle. Connect upper steering shaft to intermediate shaft "U" joint. Install "U" joint pinch bolt and tighten to specification.

2) If equipped with Cruise Command, connect electrical connector. Connect ignition switch connectors, connecting white connector first.

3) Install upper and lower toe plates. Install bolts but do not tighten. Install mounting bracket on steering column. Align column with instrument panel. Install bracket to instrument panel bolts but do not tighten.

4) Pull up on column and tighten bolts to specification. Make sure bolts are tightened while pulling up on column. Tighten toe plate bolts to specification.

5) Install both halves of instrument panel bezel. Install left air conditioning duct extension (if removed). Connect transmission shift rod to shift lever.

6) Connect battery ground cable. Check automatic transmission shift linkage operation and adjust as necessary. Check for correct operation of all electrical components.

OVERHAUL

ALL MODELS
WITHOUT TILT WHEEL

Disassembly (Man. Trans.) — 1) Remove steering column from vehicle as previously outlined. Remove mount bracket from column. Attach a suitable holding fixture (J-23074) to mount bolt holes. Secure column in a vise by clamping on holding fixture.

2) Remove steering wheel. Using two screwdrivers, pry anti-theft cover off lock plate. Compress lock plate using a suitable compressor tool. If steering shaft nut has metric threads, it will have an identifying groove in the steering wheel locating splines. American threaded nuts do not have this groove. For metric threads, use tool J-23653-4. For American threads, use tool J-23653. Remove snap ring from steering shaft.

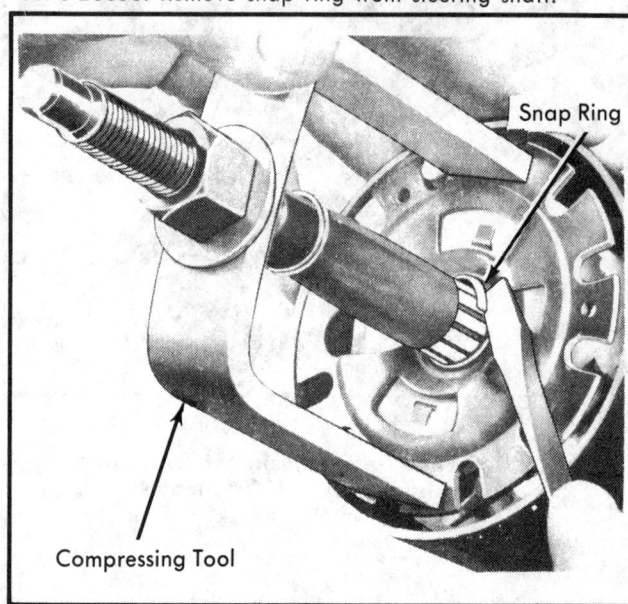

Fig. 1   Removing Lock Plate Snap Ring

3) Remove compressor tool. Remove snap ring and discard. Remove lock plate, directional signal cancelling cam, upper bearing preload spring, and thrust washer from steering shaft.

JEEP (Cont.)

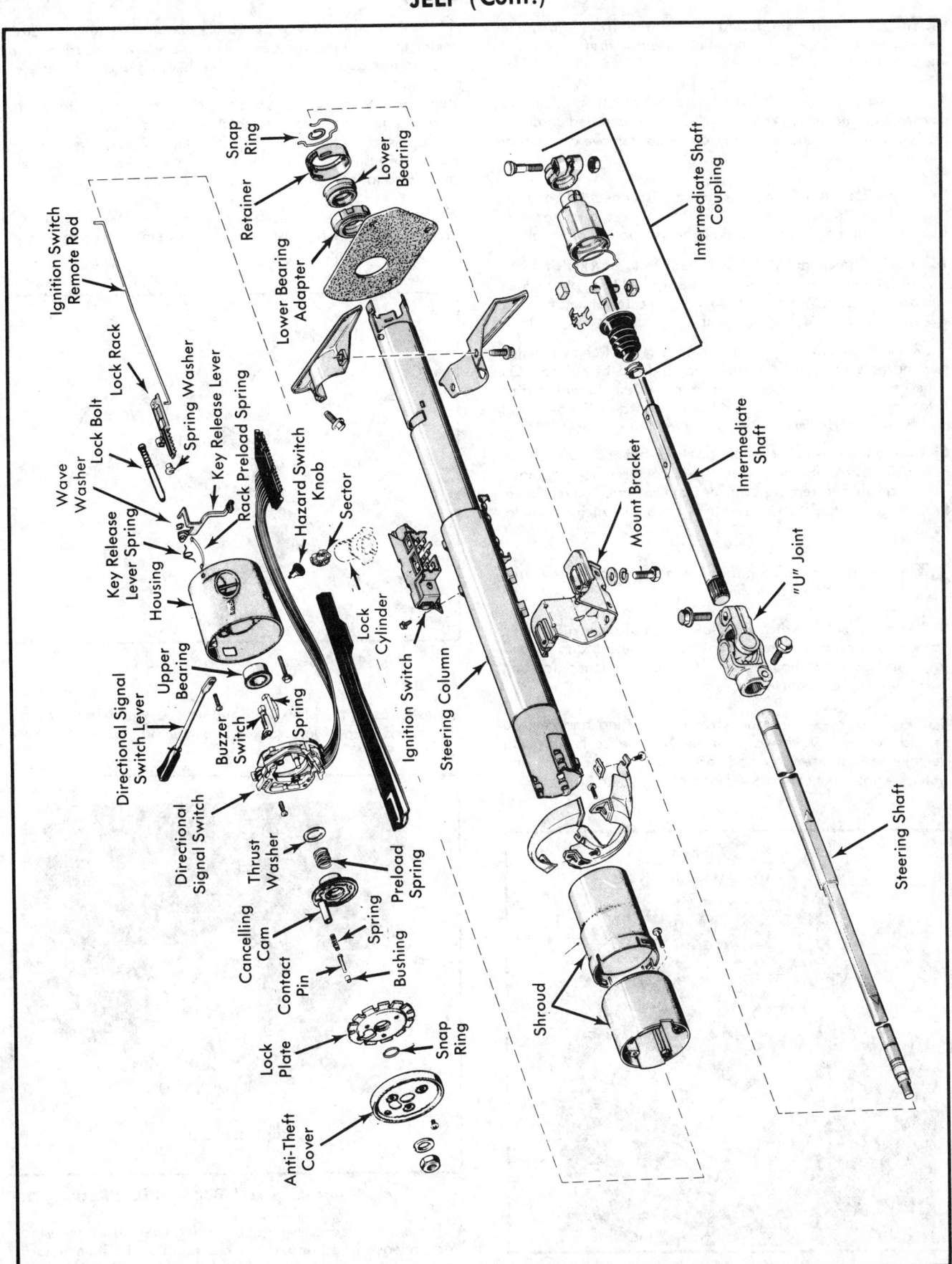

Fig. 2 Exploded View of Steering Column (Manual Transmission Models)

JEEP (Cont.)

CAUTION — *After snap ring is removed from shaft, the steering shaft is free in column. Do not allow shaft to fall out end of column.*

4) Remove steering shaft from lower end of column. Remove hazard warning switch knob by pressing inward and unscrewing. On vehicles without Cruise Command, remove directional signal switch lever.

5) On vehicles with Cruise Command, disconnect two of four wires at switch connector. Fold wires back along harness. Tape wires and a length of string to harness to aid removal.

6) Remove directional switch connector from bracket at lower end of column. Separate switch connector by lifting plastic lock tab on connector. Wrap tape around connector and harness to prevent snagging during removal.

7) Remove directional signal switch screws. Remove switch and harness by pulling straight up and out of column. On vehicles with Cruise Command, remove directional switch lever. Remove Cruise Command switch (in directional signal switch lever) and harness using string taped to harness.

8) Turn ignition switch 2 detent positions beyond "OFF" position. Using a thin bladed screwdriver, compress lock cylinder retaining tab and remove cylinder from column. The retaining tab is reached through slot next to directional switch mounting boss.

NOTE — *If retaining tab is not visible through slot, remove any casting flash that may be in slot.*

9) Remove ignition switch from lower end of column. Remove screws securing directional signal switch housing and shroud to column. Remove housing and shroud. Disconnect ignition switch remote rod from lock rack.

10) Remove screws securing shroud to housing and remove shroud. Remove wave washer from key-release lever pivot. Remove key release lever and spring. Remove lock rack and bolt assembly. Remove rack preload spring. See Fig. 3.

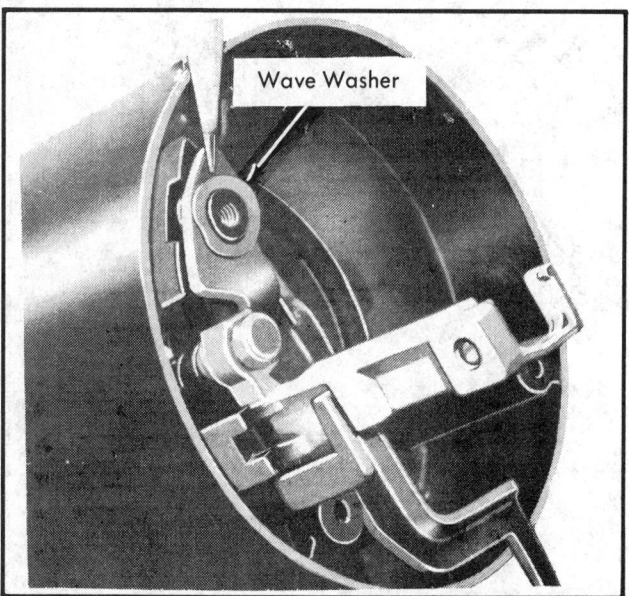

Fig. 3   Wave Washer Removal on Manual Transmission Models

11) Using a punch, push on block tooth of sector and push sector through lock cylinder hole. Remove lower bearing snap ring from retainer. Remove retainer, bearing and adapter.

Reassembly — 1) Coat all friction surfaces with multi-purpose grease before reassembly. Position sector on sector shaft. Insert sector through lock cylinder hole. Use a blunt punch to push sector into place. Make sure sector turns freely after installation.

2) Install rack preload spring. Make sure bowed side of preload spring is against lock rack. Assemble lock rack and lock spring as shown in Fig. 4.

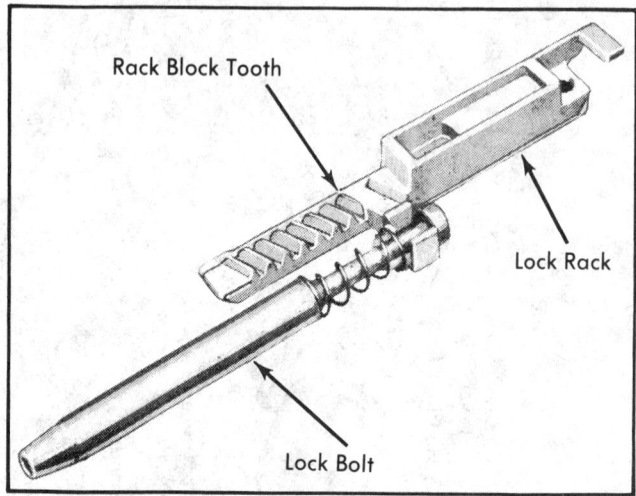

Fig. 4   Assembly Lock Bolt and Lock Rack

3) Install assembled lock bolt and lock rack in housing. Make sure block tooth of lock rack is mated with block tooth of sector. See Fig. 5.

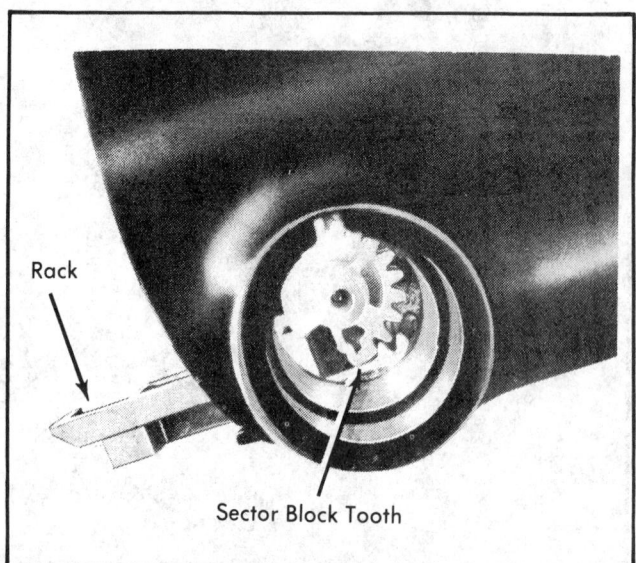

Fig. 5   Installing Lock Bolt and Lock Rack

4) Place key release lever return spring over post in housing. Place release lever finger in lock rack slot. Position hole in lever over threaded hole in housing post. Make sure inner end of spring contacts release lever. See Fig. 6.

JEEP (Cont.)

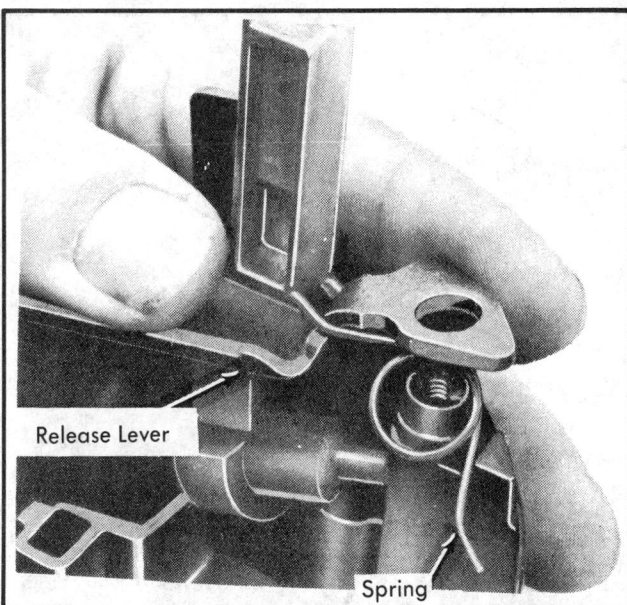

Fig. 6   Installing Release Lever and Spring on Manual Transmission Models

5) Raise lever slightly and place end of lever spring between lever and housing boss. Coat wave washer with multi-purpose grease. Place wave washer on post over release lever.

6) Place shroud on directional signal switch housing. Install and tighten retaining screws. Make sure release lever wave washer is not dislodged when shroud is installed. Install remote rod on lock rack with short end of rod in rack.

7) Place assembled housing and shroud on column. Install and tighten retaining screws. Install lock cylinder to housing. Insert key in lock cylinder. Hold cylinder sleeve and rotate key clockwise until key stops. This will retract actuator.

8) Place lock cylinder in housing bore making sure cylinder tab is aligned with keyway in housing. Push cylinder inward until it bottoms. Rotate key counterclockwise until drive section of cylinder mates with sector. Push cylinder in fully until tab engages in housing groove.

9) Now turn cylinder clockwise to stop, then counterclockwise to stop at "OFF-UNLOCK" position. Place ignition switch on jacket. Move switch to extreme left positon ("ACC"). Now move slider 2 positions to right ("OFF-UNLOCK"). Insert remote rod into switch slider hole. Place switch on column. Install and tighten retaining screws.

10) Install lower bearing, bearing adapter, retainer and snap ring in lower end of column. Insert steering shaft in column through lower end. Bend directional signal switch wires against connector. Feed connector and harness through housing and shroud. Align switch in housing. Install and tighten retaining screws.

11) On vehicles without Cruise Command, install directional signal switch lever. On vehicles with Cruise Command, install lever and switch assembly. Use string taped to harness during disassembly to help feed wires into housing. Remove string and tape. Connect wires to switch terminal and install lever.

12) Install thrust washer, upper bearing preload spring, and cancelling cam on steering shaft. Position cancelling cam as shown. *See Fig. 7.* Place directional signal switch is neutral position and install hazard warning switch knob.

Cancelling Cam

Fig. 7   Directional Signal Switch Cancelling Cam Position

13) Position lock plate on steering shaft. Place new snap ring on sleeve of compressor tool (J-23653 for American threads, J-23653-4 for metric threads). Thread tool sleeve onto end of steering shaft. Compress lock plate with tool and install snap ring in groove in steering shaft. Install anti-theft cover.

14) Remove support tool from steering column. Install mounting bracket and tighten bolts to specification. Connect directional signal switch wire connector to column bracket. Install steering wheel. Install column in vehicle as previously outlined.

Disassembly (Auto. Trans.) — **1)** Remove steering column from vehicle as previously outlined. Remove mount bracket from column. Attach a suitable holding fixture (J-23074) to mount bolt holes. Secure column in a vise by clamping holding fixture.

2) Remove steering wheel. Using two screwdrivers, pry anti-theft cover off lock plate. Compress lock plate using suitable compressor tool (J-23653 for American threaded steering shaft nut, J-23653-4 for metric nut). Remove snap ring from steering shaft.

3) Remove compressor tool. Remove snap ring and discard. Remove lock plate, directional signal cancelling cam, upper bearing preload spring, and thrust washer from steering shaft.

CAUTION — *After snap ring is removed from steering shaft, shaft is free in column. Do not allow shaft to fall out end of column.*

Steering Columns

JEEP (Cont.)

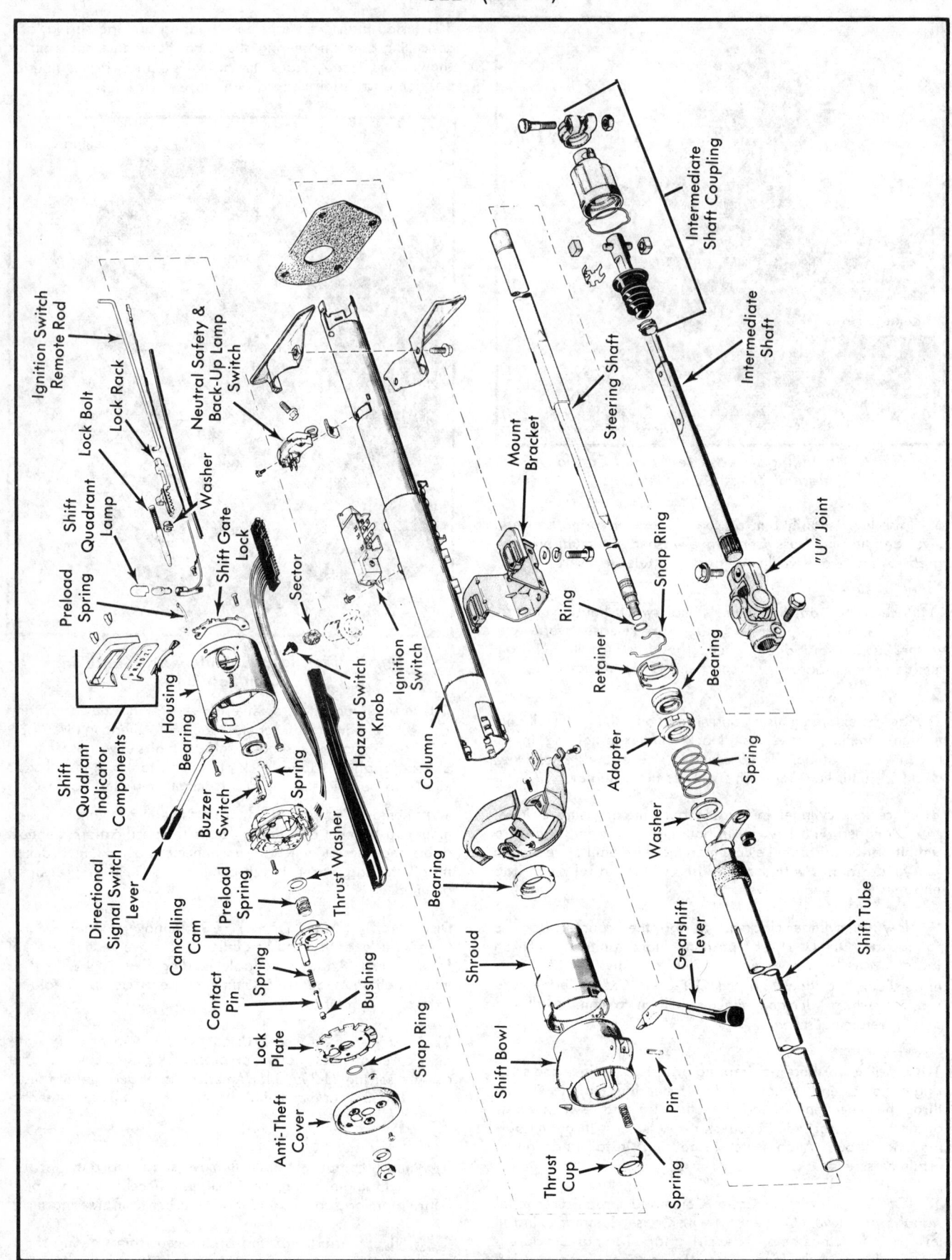

Fig. 8 *Exploded View of Steering Column (Automatic Transmission Models)*

JEEP (Cont.)

4) Remove steering shaft from lower end of column. Remove hazard warning switch knob by pressing inward and unscrewing. On vehicles without Cruise Command, remove directional signal switch lever.

5) On vehicles with Cruise Command, disconnect two of four wires at switch connector. Fold wires back along harness. Tape wires and a length of string to harness to aid removal.

6) Place gearshift lever in "P". Drive out gearshift lever pin using a small drift punch. Remove gearshift lever. Disconnect directional signal switch connector from bracket at lower end of column.

7) Using stiff wire, compress lock tab retaining shift light wire in connector and remove wire from connector. Remove lower bracket and plastic wiring harness connector. Wrap tape around directional switch connector and wiring harness to prevent snagging during removal.

8) Pull switch straight up and out of column to remove. On vehicles with Cruise Command, remove directional signal switch lever. Remove Cruise Command switch (in directional signal switch lever) and harness using string taped to harness.

9) Place lock cylinder in "LOCK" position. Compress cylinder retaining tab and remove lock cylinder. The retaining tab is reached through slot next to directional signal boss in housing.

NOTE – *If retaining tab is not visible through slot, remove any casting flash that may be in slot.*

10) Remove ignition switch from lower end of column. Remove screws securing upper housing to column and remove housing. The ignition switch remote rod and shift quadrant light wire will be removed with upper housing.

11) Remove thrust cup from upper housing. Remove lock bolt and rack. Remove rack and preload spring. Using a blunt punch, remove sector from sector shaft. Note position of sector for reassembly. Remove sector through lock cylinder hole.

12) Remove shift gate lock from upper housing. Inspect shift gate lock detents for wear and replace as necessary. Remove shift quadrant by prying out two clips with a small punch. Remove quadrant light cover and socket assembly.

13) Remove shift bowl from column. Remove lower nylon bowl bearing from upper end of column. Remove lower bearing retainer, retaining ring, preload spring and nylon washer. Remove shift tube and nylon bearing from tube.

Reassembly (Auto. Trans.) – **1)** Apply multi-purpose grease to all friction surfaces. Install shift tube. Install nylon thrust washer in lower end of shift tube, making sure flat side of washer faces upper end of tube.

2) Install preload spring and lower bearing making sure bearing metal face is toward retainer. Install retainer and retainer ring.

3) Install lower nylon bearing in upper end of column. Make sure smaller inside diameter faces toward lower end of tube and bearing notches engage three locator crimps in column.

4) Align shift bowl with shift tube spline and install bowl. Install rack preload spring in upper housing. Place large end

of sector on sector shaft. Place sector into place using a blunt punch.

5) Install shift gate lock and retaining screws. Tighten screws to specification. Install shift quadrant lamp and cover. Install quadrant indicator by pressing retainer clips into place with flat side toward bowl.

6) Assemble lock bolt and lock rack. See *Fig. 4.* Install lock bolt and lock rack in shift bowl. See *Fig. 9.* Make sure block tooth of lock rack engages block tooth of sector. See *Fig. 5.*

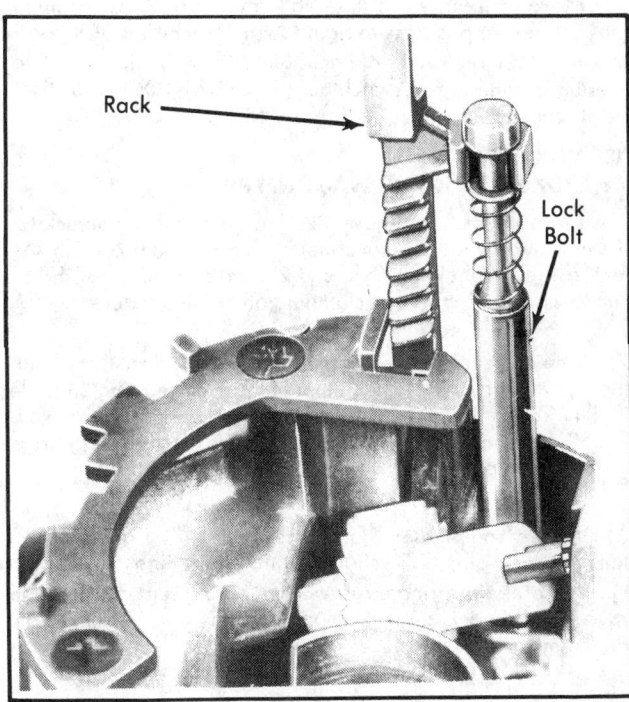

Rack

Lock Bolt

Fig. 9   Installing Lock Rack and Bolt into Shift Bowl

7) Install nylon thrust cup in upper housing, making sure flared end of cup faces outward. Rotate shift bowl as far as possible counterclockwise and install upper housing. Tighten screws to specification.

8) Guide shift quadrant lamp wire and remote lock rod into position between shift bowl and column. Install directional signal switch and harness in column. Remove tape from harness and connector. Place harness in plastic protector. Install and tighten switch retaining screws.

NOTE – *Make sure switch actuating lever pivot is correctly aligned and seated in upper housing boss.*

9) On vehicles without Cruise Command, install directional signal switch lever. On vehicles with Cruise Command, install directional signal switch lever and Cruise Command switch using string taped to harness. Remove string and tape. Connect wires to terminals.

10) Install steering shaft from lower end of column. Install thrust washer, upper bearing preload spring and cancelling cam on steering shaft. Install lock plate, making sure lock plate splines are aligned with steering shaft splines. Make sure cancelling cam shaft protrudes through lock plate opening.

JEEP (Cont.)

11) Install a new steering shaft snap ring on lock plate compressor tool (J-23653 for American threaded steering shaft nut, J-23653-4 for metric threaded nut). Thread tool onto steering shaft. Compress lock plate with tool. Install snap ring in groove in steering shaft. Remove compressor tool.

12) Install anti-theft cover. Install steering wheel. Install gearshift lever. Install lock cylinder in cover. Install ignition switch on column. Place shift bowl in any position but "P". Rotate bowl until lock rack bottoms against lower surface of bowl.

13) Move ignition switch slider to left toward "ACC" position. Move slide two positions to right toward "OFF-UNLOCK" position. Insert remote rod into slider hole. Attach ignition switch to steering column. Move switch out of "OFF-UNLOCK" position. Install column in vehicle as previously outlined.

TILT WHEEL
(CHEROKEE, TRUCK & WAGONEER)

Disassembly — 1) Remove steering column from vehicle as previously outlined. Remove mount bracket from column. Attach a suitable holding fixture (J-23074) to mount bolt holes. Secure column in a vise by clamping on holding fixture.

2) Remove steering wheel. Using two screwdrivers, pry anti-theft cover off lock plate. Compress lock plate using suitable tool (J-23653 for American threaded steering shaft nut, J-23653-4 for metric threaded nut). Remove snap ring from groove in steering shaft. *See Fig. 15.*

3) Remove compressor tool. Remove snap ring and discard. Remove lock plate, directional signal cancelling cam, upper bearing preload spring thrust washer, spring seat and bearing race from steering shaft. Remove gearshift lever retaining pin and remove gearshift lever.

4) On vehicles without Cruise Command, remove directional signal switch lever. On vehicles with Cruise Command, remove wires from Cruise Command switch terminal. Fold two of four wires back and tape along harness. Tape a length of string to harness to aid removal.

5) Remove hazard warning switch knob by pressing in and unscrewing. Disconnect directional signal switch connector at bracket on lower steering column. Remove wiring harness plastic connector from column jacket.

6) Wrap tape around directional signal switch connector to prevent snagging when removing. Remove directional signal switch retaining screws. Pull switch and harness straight up out of column.

7) On vehicles with Cruise Command, remove directional switch lever. Remove Cruise Command switch (in directional signal switch lever) and harness using string taped to harness.

8) Insert ignition key in lock cylinder. Turn key to "LOCK" position. Compress cylinder retaining tab and remove lock cylinder. The retaining tab is reached through slot next to directional signal switch boss in housing.

NOTE — *If retaining tab is not visible through slot, remove any casting flash that may be in slot.*

9) Remove shift quadrant by prying two spring clips out of column. Remove mounting bracket and light socket. Remove tilt release handle. Remove cover retaining screws and remove cover.

10) Remove lock sector tension spring screw. Unhook sector spring from sector shaft. Remove snap ring from sector shaft. Remove sector, shaft and retaining ring. Install tilt release handle. Place column in full upward tilt position.

11) Insert a screwdriver in tilt release spring retainer slot and compress retainer approximately $\frac{3}{16}$". Rotate retainer $\frac{1}{8}$ turn and remove retainer and spring.

CAUTION — *Tilt spring is under strong tension.*

12) Place housing in center position. Using a puller (J-21854-1) remove tilt pivot pins. *See Fig. 10.* Lift tilt release lever to disengage lock shoes and remove housing. Remove both ball bearing assemblies from housing (if necessary).

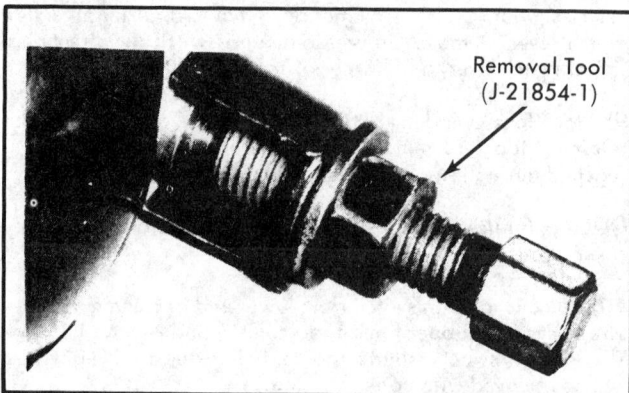

Fig. 10   Removing Tilt Pivot Pins

13) Remove tilt release lever. Using a punch, drive out release lever pin. Compress lock shoe spring to release spring tension on pin. *See Fig. 11.*

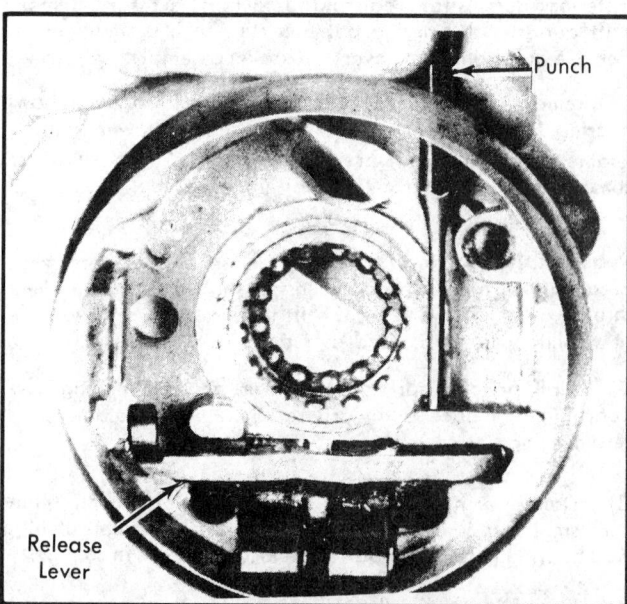

Fig. 11   Removing Release Lever Pin

JEEP (Cont.)

14) Using a punch, drive out lock shoe pin. Compress lock shoe spring to release spring tension on pin. Remove lock shoes and lock shoe springs. Disconnect steering shaft. Remove shaft through upper end of column. *See Fig. 12.*

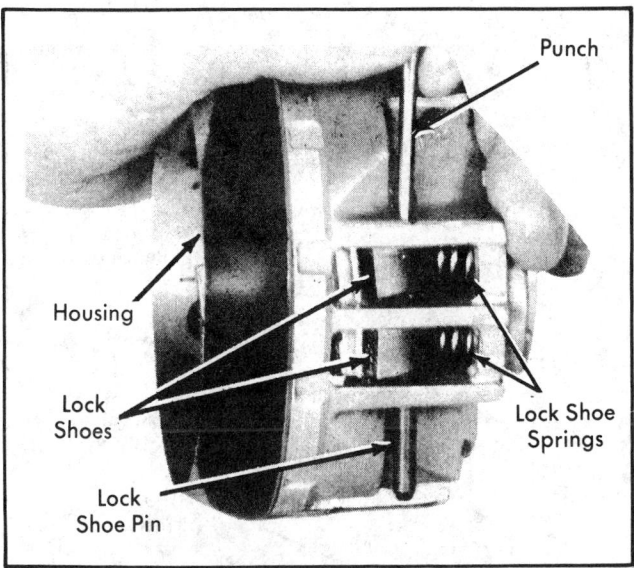

Fig. 12   Removing Lock Shoe Pin

15) Fold shaft at 90° and separate upper and lower halves at flex joint. Remove ignition switch. Remove lock rack and remote rod. Remove lower bearing retainer snap ring, retainer, bearing and adapter.

16) Remove screws securing support to shift bowl. Remove shift gate screws and remove shift gate from support. Remove support and shift tube retaining ring and thrust washer. Using a puller (J-23072), pull shift tube from column.

17) Rotate shift bowl clockwise while sliding retainer plate out of jacket notches. Tip plate down toward shift bowl hub at 12 o'clock position and remove plate, bottom side first.

18) Remove wave washer and shift tube spring. Remove shift bowl from column jacket. Remove lower bearing retainer spring clip. Remove retainer, lower bearing and bearing adapter.

Reassembly — 1) Coat all friction surfaces with multi-purpose grease before reassembly. Mount shift bowl on column. Place shift tube spring, wave washer, and retainer plate in shift bowl.

2) Install shift tube through lower end of column. Make sure tube spline is aligned with shift bowl keyway. Place shift tube installer tools (J-23073-2 and J-23073-4) in shift tube. Make sure spring loaded lower foot of tool is engaged with shift tube inner shoulder and tool guide is seated in shift tube. *See Fig. 13.*

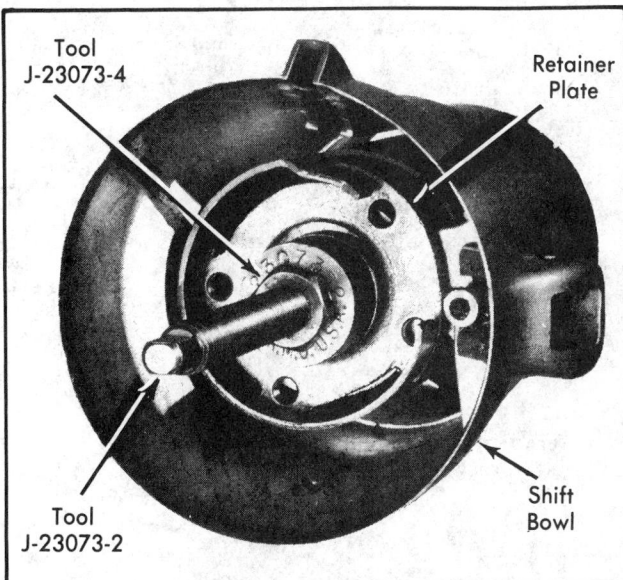

Fig. 13   Positioning Shift Tube Installer Tools

3) Tighten tool spring tension nut until snug. Place installer tools (J-23073-3 and J-23073-4) over puller stud. Tighten tool nut (J-23073-2) and pull tube into place in shift bowl. Remove shift tube installer tools. *See Fig. 14.*

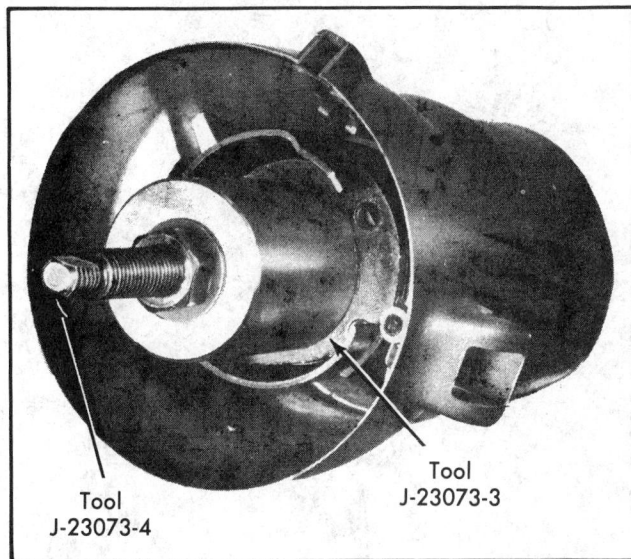

Fig. 14   Pulling Shift Tube into Shift Bowl

4) Install shift tube thrust washer and retainer plate snap ring. Install lower bearing adapter, making sure notched end of adapter faces lower end of column. Install lower bearing in column. Make sure metal face of bearing faces lower end of column. Install lower bearing retainer and retainer spring clip.

5) Install shift gate in support and install shift gate attaching screws. Install support in shift bowl. Make sure "V" notch in support is aligned with notch in column. Install support to shift bowl screws.

JEEP (Cont.)

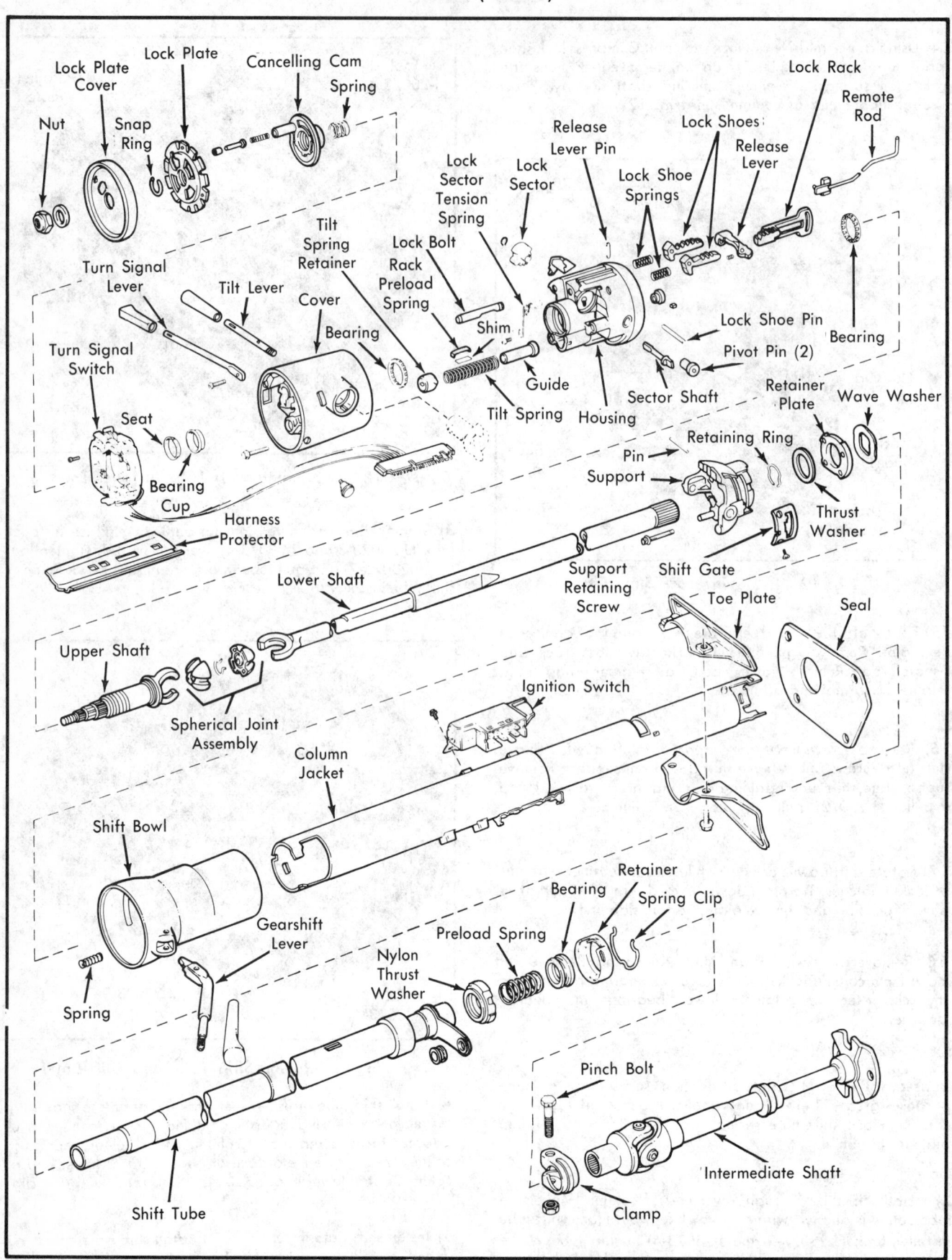

Fig. 15 Exploded View of Tilt Wheel Steering Column (All Except "CJ" & Scrambler Models)

JEEP (Cont.)

6) Assemble upper and lower steering shafts at flexible joint. Install steering shaft through upper end of column. Install ball bearings in housing if removed. Make sure there are 14 balls in each bearing.

7) Install tilt release handle. Insert ignition switch remote rod between shift bowl and column and into guide channel in left side of support. Engage lock rack in remote rod. Guide housing over steering shaft and lock rack, making sure lock shoes align with teeth in support.

8) Align housing and support pivot pin holes and drive in pivot pins using a soft faced mallet. Install lock shoe spring, tilt bumpers and lock pin in housing. Install sector shaft in housing and lock sector in on shaft. Large block tooth of sector must engage large slot in rack.

9) Install sector shaft snap ring. Hook lock sector tension spring on lock bolt. Engage spring with sector and install spring retaining screw. Place housing in full upward tilt position. Install tilt spring and guide in housing.

10) Push tilt spring retainer into housing ³⁄₁₆" and rotate retainer ⅛ turn clockwise to secure retainer tabs in housing lugs. Place housing in center tilt position. Remove tilt release handle. Install cover on housing and install retaining screws.

11) Insert shift quadrant light wire up through housing and between shift bowl and column jacket. Install shift quadrant mounting bracket and connect light socket. Hook base of shift quadrant over tabs on left side of quadrant and place in position.

12) Install quadrant pointer in shift bowl and engage in quadrant. Install quadrant retainer clip with flat side of clip facing downward. Install tilt release handle. Place directional signal switch and harness in column. Guide harness between cover and column.

13) On vehicles without Cruise Command, install directional signal lever. On vehicles with Cruise Command, install directional signal lever and Cruise Command switch assembly. Use string taped to connector during disassembly to install connector.

14) Remove tape and string from connector. Connect four wires to switch terminal. Install and tighten lever screw. Place directional signal switch harness in plastic protector. Align directional signal switch in cover. Install and tighten retaining screws.

NOTE — *Make sure switch actuating lever pivot is correctly aligned and seated in housing pivot boss before installing switch attaching screws.*

15) Install bearing race, bearing race seat, preload spring, and cancelling cam on steering shaft. Align lock plate splines with steering shaft splines. Install lock plate. Make sure cancelling cam shaft protrudes through hole in lock plate.

16) Install new steering shaft snap ring on lock plate compressor tool (J-23653 for American threaded steering shaft nut, J-23653-4 for metric threaded nut). Position tool on steering shaft. Compress lock plate with tool. Install snap ring in groove in steering shaft. Remove tool.

17) Place gearshift lever in shift bowl. Guide gearshift lever over lock sector tension spring and into bowl. Align retaining pin holes with a punch. Drive retaining pin into position using a soft faced hammer.

18) Insert ignition key into lock cylinder. Hold lock cylinder and turn key clockwise to stop. Align cylinder locking lug with keyway in cover and insert cylinder in cover. Push cylinder against lock sector. Rotate cylinder counterclockwise until it engages sector. Push cylinder inward until retainer tab snaps into place.

19) Install steering column as previously outlined. Install steering wheel. Adjust gearshift linkage, and neutral safety and backup lamp switch.

TILT WHEEL
"CJ" & SCRAMBLER MODELS

Disassembly — 1) Remove steering column as previously outlined. Remove mount bracket from column. Attach a suitable holding fixture (J-23074) to mount bolt holes. Secure column in vise by clamping on holding fixture. See Fig. 19.

2) Remove steering wheel. Remove gearshift lever retaining pin and remove lever (if equipped). Remove lock plate cover. Remove tilt and turn signal levers. Remove hazard warning knob by pressing in and turning counterclockwise.

3) Compress lock plate using a suitable compressor tool (J-23653 for American threaded steering shaft nut, J-23653-4 for metric threaded nut). Remove snap ring from groove in steering shaft. Remove tool and discard snap ring.

4) Remove lock plate, cancelling cam and upper bearing preload spring. Disconnect turn signal switch harness at lower end of column. Remove wire harness protector from column. Wrap tape around harness to prevent snagging on removal.

5) Remove turn signal switch attaching screws and remove switch and harness. Pull switch straight up out of column. Insert ignition key in lock cylinder and turn key to "ON" position. Compress lock cylinder retaining tab with small screwdriver and remove cylinder.

Fig. 16 Removing Upper Bearing Race and Seat

JEEP (Cont.)

NOTE — *The retaining tab is accessible through the slot next to turn signal switch mounting boss. If tab is not visible, remove any casting flashing that may be in slot.*

6) Remove cover retaining screws and remove cover. Remove upper bearing race and bearing seat from steering shaft. Reinstall tilt lever and place column in full up position. See Fig. 16.

7) Remove tilt spring, guide and retainer with screwdriver. Press retainer inward and turn counterclockwise until retainer tabs align with housing lugs.

8) Place housing in center position. Remove housing pivot pins using tool J-21854-1. Raise tilt lever to disengage lock shoes and remove housing. Pull housing upward to disengage shoes, and turn housing to one side to separate lock rack from remote rod.

9) Remove tilt lever and shield from housing. Remove lock sector spring retaining screw and spring. Rotate spring clockwise to remove. Remove lock sector retaining ring, lock sector and sector shaft. Tap shaft through sector and out of housing with a hammer and punch. See Fig. 17.

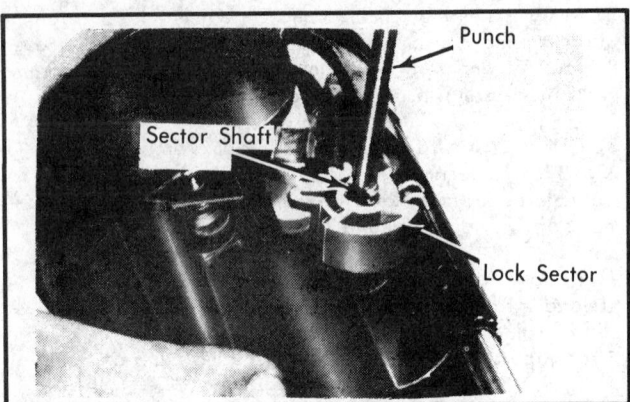

Fig. 17　Removing Lock Sector and Sector Shaft

10) Remove lock bolt, lock rack, rack preload spring, shim and remote rod from housing. Insert wedge between lock shoes and housing to relieve spring tension on tilt and lock shoe pins.

11) Remove tilt lever pin from housing with pin punch. Remove lock shoe pin from housing with pin punch, and remove lock shoes, springs and wedge.

12) Remove upper and lower housing bearings and races, if damaged or worn. If removed, discard and replace with new races and bearings. Disconnect steering shaft at coupling.

13) Remove steering shaft through upper end of column. Remove support attaching bolt and remove support. Remove retainer plate. Tip upper end of plate rearward and turn plate counterclockwise to remove.

14) Remove shroud using twisting-pulling motion. Remove key release lever and lever spring from shroud. Tip lever forward and lift up to remove. See Fig. 18.

15) Disconnect ignition switch wire harness connector and remove switch. Remove snap ring, retainer and bearing assembly from lower end of column.

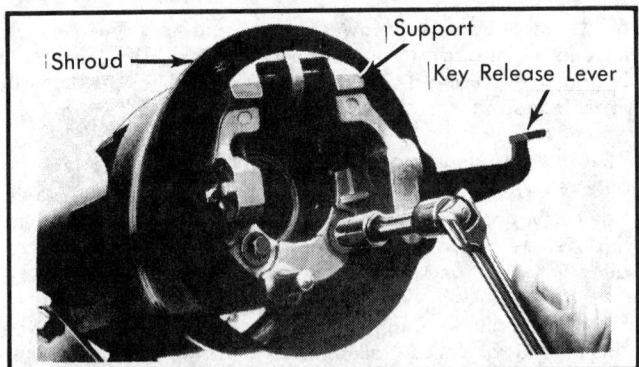

Fig. 18　Removing Support from Housing

Reassembly — 1) Coat all friction surfaces with multipurpose grease before reassembly. Install bearing assembly, bearing retainer and snap ring in lower end of column.

2) Install key release lever spring on lever and install assembled lever and spring in shroud. Align and install shroud on column jacket.

3) Install retainer plate by tipping plate to 12 o'clock position and sliding it under jacket opening. Align column jacket "V" notch with "V" on support and install support in column. Press key release lever down while pressing support into place.

4) Install support attaching screws finger tight then tighten alternately to specifications. Install remote rod in support by guiding rod through upper end of shroud and into rod slot in support.

5) Install steering shaft in column. Install bearings (if removed). Install lock shoes, springs and lock shoe pin in housing. Use .18" diameter rod to align lock shoes and pin.

6) Install release lever, lever spring and lever pin in housing. Insert wedges between housing and lever to relieve spring tension. Install sector shaft in housing. Lightly tap shaft into housing using punch.

7) Install lock sector on shaft. Lightly tap sector onto shaft until shaft snap ring groove is exposed. Install sector snap ring. Install lock bolt in housing and engage bolt in lock sector cam surface.

8) Install lock rack, rack preload spring and shim in housing. Square block tooth of rack must engage square block tooth of sector. Install lock spring and retaining screw.

9) Align and install assembled housing on support. Hold lock shoes in disengaged position to ease housing installation. Align pivot pin in holes in housing and support and install pivot pins. When started in holes, seat pins fully using a hammer and punch. Press housing downward when first installing pins to avoid damage to pin holes.

10) Insert tilt lever in housing and place housing in full upward tilt position. Lubricate tilt guide and spring and install tilt spring on guide. Insert assembled tilt spring and guide in housing and install guide retainer on spring.

11) Install tilt lever shield. Remove tilt lever. Install cover on housing. Install turn signal switch. Guide switch harness and connector through column and into housing. Do not install switch attaching screws at this time.

JEEP (Cont.)

12) Install hazard warning switch knob in turn signal switch and align and install switch attaching screws. Make sure turn signal switch is properly aligned before tightening screws. Pull out on hazard warning knob.

13) Install upper bearing race and seat in housing. Install upper bearing preload spring, cancelling cam and lock plate.

14) Install new steering shaft snap ring on compressor tool (J-23653 for American threaded steering shaft nut, J-23653-4 for metric threaded nut), and install tool on steering shaft. Compress lock plate and seat snap ring. Remove tool.

15) Install tilt and turn signal levers. Install shift lever and retaining pin. Install ignition lock cylinder. Hold cylinder sleeve, turn knob clockwise against stop, align cylinder tab with housing keyway and install cylinder in housing. Turn cylinder knob counterclockwise until cylinder mates with lock sector and push cylinder in until retainer snaps into place.

16) Insert key in cylinder and turn cylinder to "OFF" position. Install ignition switch. Move switch to "ACC" position then back off two clicks to "OFF" position. Remote rod hole should almost be at center.

17) Insert remote rod into hole and install switch on column jacket. Move switch down to eliminate lash and tighten attaching screws. Position switch harness protectors over harness and snap into place.

18) Install lock plate cover. Install steering wheel. Install column in vehicle.

TIGHTENING SPECIFICATIONS

Application	Ft. Lbs.
Column Mounting Bracket Bolt	20
Intermediate Shaft Pinch Bolt	45
Mounting Bracket-to-Instrument Panel Bolts	20
Steering Wheel Nut	30
Toe Plate Bolts	10

Application	INCH Lbs.
Cover Screws	60
Housing Screws	60
Ignition Switch Mounting Screws	35
Lock Sector Tension Spring Screw	35
Shroud Screws (Man. Trans.)	18
Support Screws (Tilt Column)	60
Tilt Lever Screw	35
Turn Signal Lever Screw	①35
Turn Signal Switch Screws	35

① — "CJ" & Scrambler Models 15 INCH lbs.

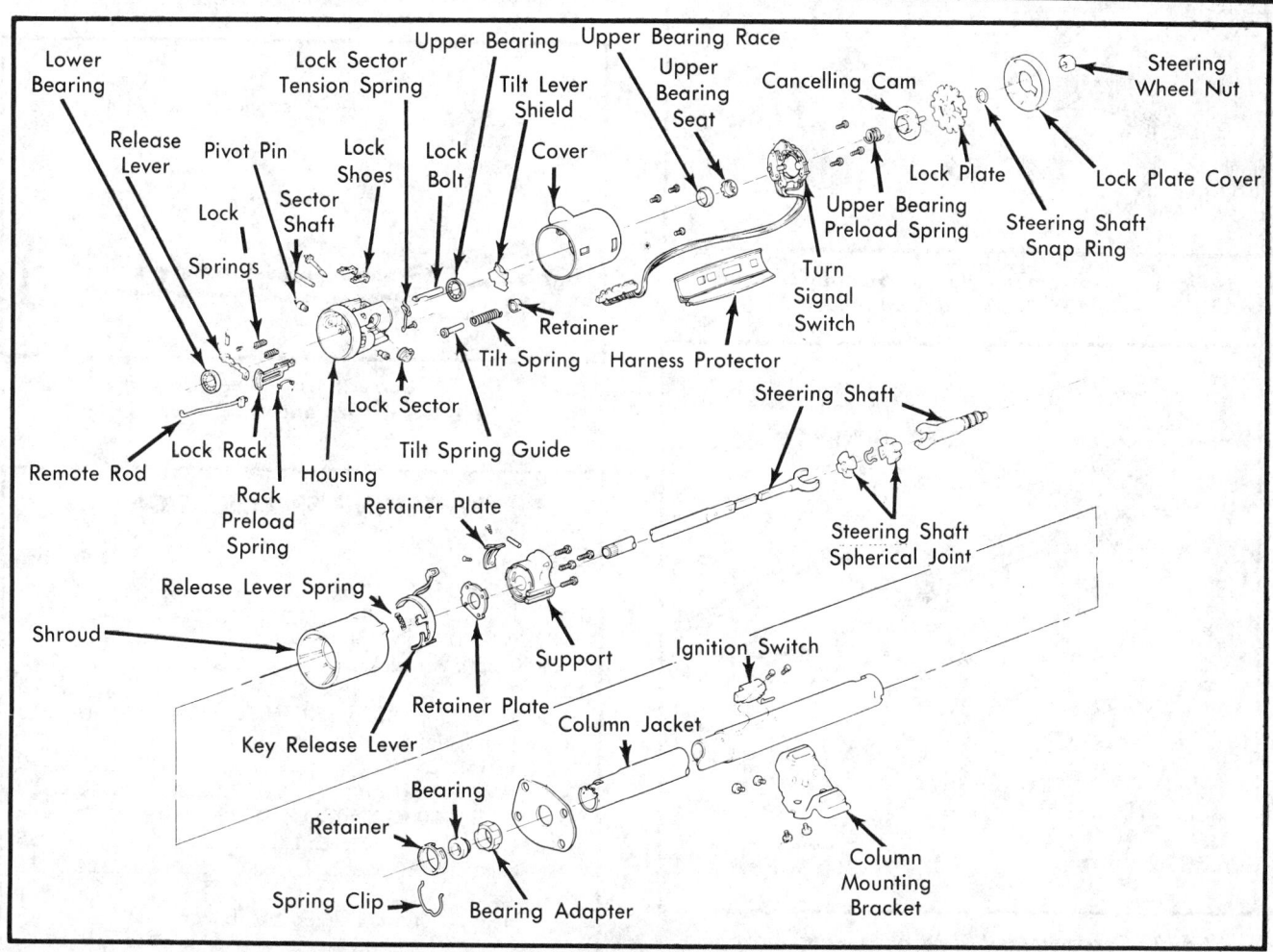

Fig. 19   Exploded View of Tilt Wheel Steering Column ("CJ" & Scrambler Models)

CHRYSLER CORP.

Dodge
Plymouth

"AD", "B", "CB", "MB" & "PB" MODELS (2-WD)

NOTE — *Removal of tie rod ends from steering arm or center link by methods other than using tie rod end puller (C-3894-A) will damage tie rod end seal.*

Tie Rod Replacement — 1) Raise vehicle on hoist and remove cotter key and nut from tie rod end. Install puller (C-3894-A) and remove tie rod end from center link. Loosen sleeve clamping bolt and unscrew tie rod end.

2) Screw new tie rod end onto sleeve. Connect rod end to knuckle arm or center link and torque to specifications. Install cotter key. Lower vehicle and adjust toe-in. Position clamp on sleeve so that bolt is on the bottom on van models, or so that bolt and clamp opening is in line with slot in sleeve on pickup models.

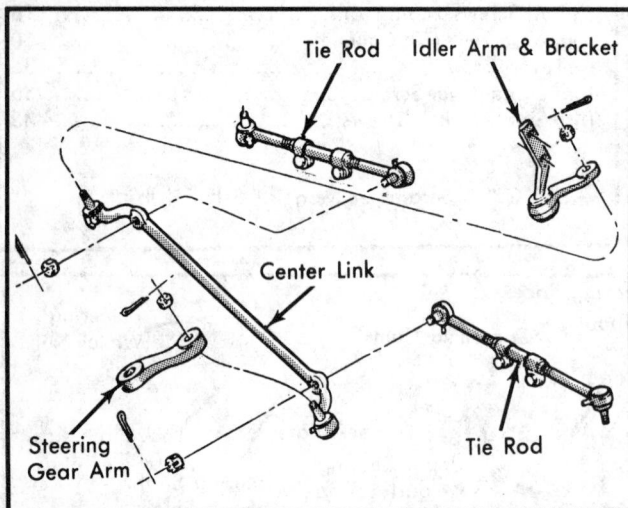

Fig. 1 Disassembled View of Steering Linkage for "D", "AD" and "PD" Models

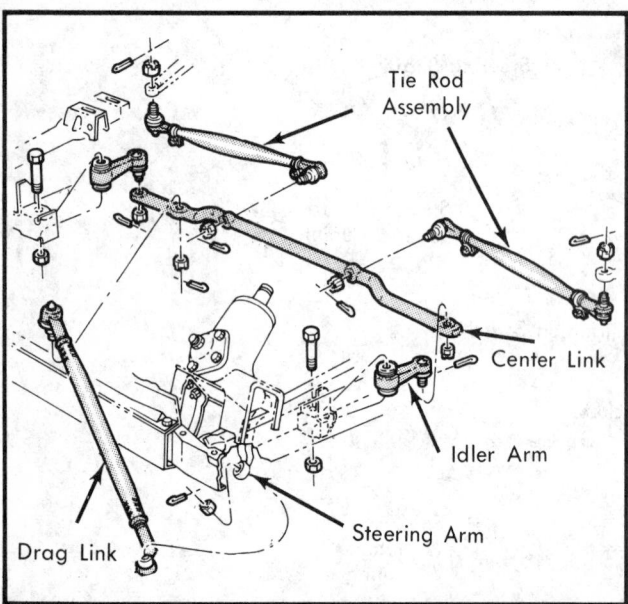

Fig. 2 Disassembled View of Steering Linkage for "B", "CB", "MB" and "PB" Models

Ball Joints — Compression (tension) type lower ball joints are used on all models. Ball joints are of semi-permanent lubricated type except for vehicles used for off-highway use. Lower ball joints should be replaced if axial end play exceeds .020".

"AW", "PW" & "W" MODELS (4-WD)

Ball Joints — Steering linkage ball joint service is the same as on 2-WD models. Servicing ball joints used on steering knubkles requires dismantling of knuckle. *See Steering Knuckles in Suspension Section.* Any end play or looseness in ball joints on 4-WD models requires replacement of ball joints.

Tie Rod Replacement — Raise vehicle. Turn wheels to give best access to tie rod end. Remove cotter key and nut. Loosen clamping bolt nut. Install tool C-3894-A, and remove tie rod end from steering knuckle. Measure and record distance from end of tie rod to outside edge of tie rod end. Unscrew tie rod end. When installing, screw new tie rod end onto tie rod the same distance as recorded when removing old tie rod end. Reverse removal procedures, and position clamping bolt to bottom of tie rod. Adjust toe.

Drag Link — Drag link must be installed to steering knuckle arm with short half ("A") attaching to knuckle arm.

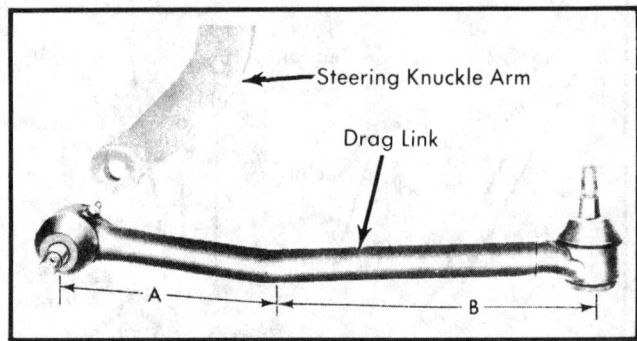

Fig. 3 Correctly Installing Drag Link for "W", "AW" and "PW" Models

TIGHTENING SPECIFICATIONS

Application	Ft. Lbs.
Tie Rod Clamping Bolts	
AD, AW, PD & PW150,	
D150/250, W150/450	13
350/450	25
B & PB150/350, CB350/450, MB150/450	①13
Tie Rod End Nuts	
AD & PD150, D150/450	40
AW & PW150, W150/450	60
B & PB150/350, CB350/450, MB250/450	
9/16" Nut	55
5/8" Nut	75

① — Heavy Duty models 26 Ft. Lb. torque.

FORD

All Models

Tie Rod & Link Replacement — 1) Replace drag link or connecting rods if ball studs are excessively loose, components are bent or threads are stripped. Never try to straighten drag link or connecting rods.

2) Remove cotter pins and nuts from the drag link and tie rod ball studs. Remove drag link ball studs from the right spindle and the pitman arm. Remove the tie rod ball studs from the left spindle and drag link.

3) Turn the drag link and tie rod ends (tie rod ends only on Econoline) into the tie rod end adjustment sleeve to about the same distance the old rods were installed.

4) Equalize the thread engagement of the short and long rod ends in adjustment sleeve for approximate toe-in setting. Position the drag link ball studs into the right spindle and the pitman arm.

5) Position the tie-rod ball studs into the left hand spindle and the drag link. Install all ball stud nuts and tighten. Install new cotter pins and check toe-in. Center adjustment sleeve clamps between locating nibs and tighten.

Pitman Arm Replacement — 1) Replace pitman arm if arm is bent. Remove cotter pin and nut from drag link ball stud. Remove drag link ball stud from pitman arm. Remove pitman arm attaching nut and washer.

2) Remove pitman arm from steering gear sector shaft using tool T64P-3590-F.

3) Install new pitman arm on sector shaft with wheels in straight ahead position. Install pitman arm nut and washer. Install drag link ball stud on pitman arm, and install cotter pin.

TIGHTENING SPECIFICATIONS

Application	Ft. Lbs.
Steering Gear-to-Frame	70
Pitman Arm-to-Steering Gear	170-230
Drag Link Studs	50-75
Rod Clamps	30-42

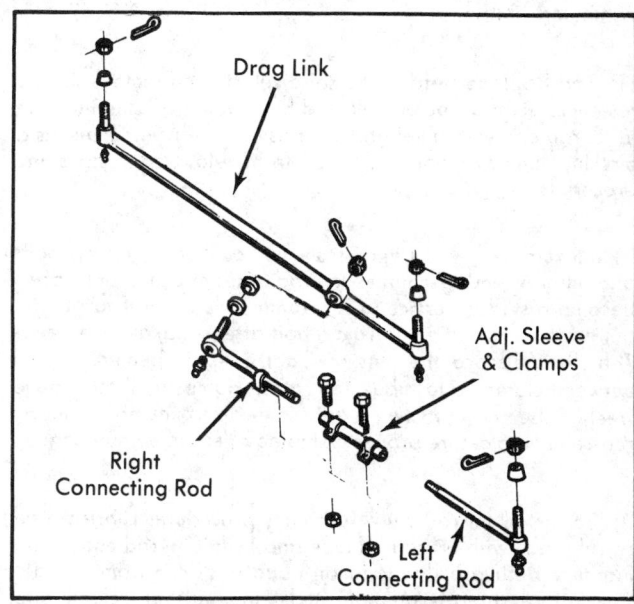

Fig. 1   Disassembled View of Steering Linkage (E100/350, F100/350)

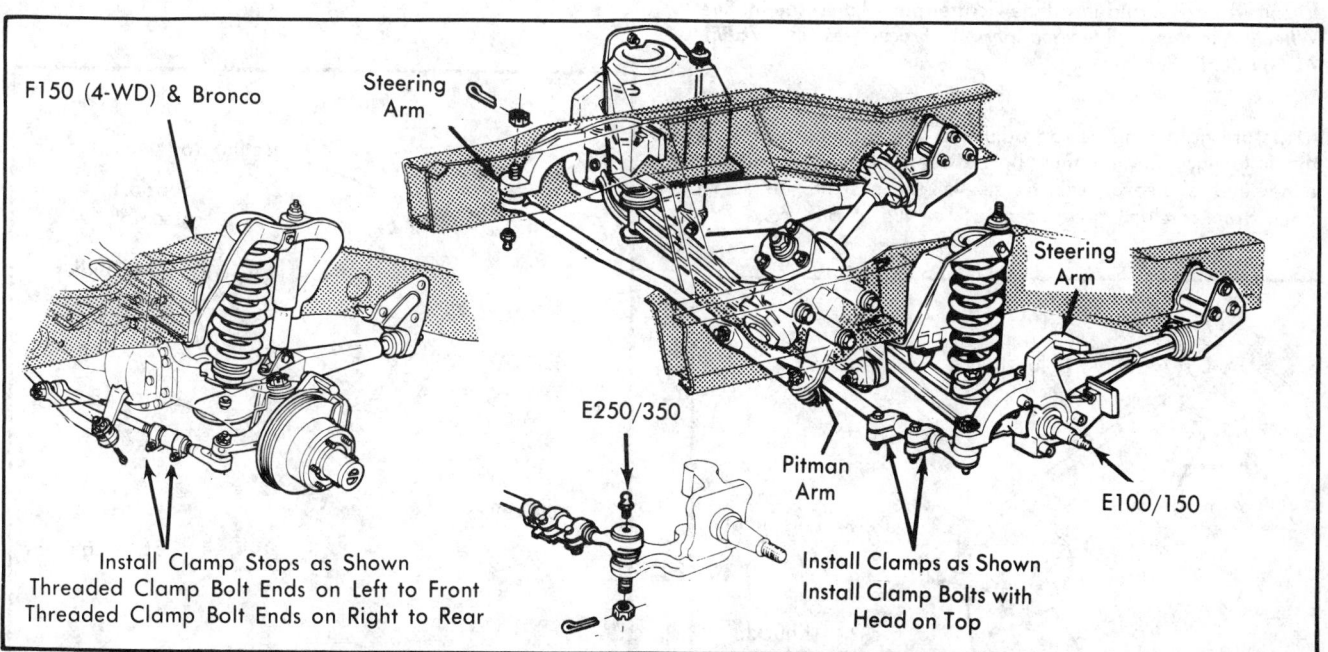

Fig. 2   Steering Linkage & Tie Rod Clamp Positioning "E" Models, F150 4-WD & Bronco Models; "F" Models Similar

GENERAL MOTORS

All Models

Steering System Service Precautions — All steering component fasteners are made of special quality materials. Replacement fasteners must be of same part number or equivalent. Torque all fasteners to specification and install new cotter pins. When installing cotter pins, do not back off castellated nuts to align cotter pin hole, tighten nut to next slot that lines up with hole. Do not hammer on ball studs or damage to threads may result. If threads are not clean and smooth, ball studs may turn in joint when nuts are tightened. Sleeve clamps must always be positioned as specified before tightening bolts.

Tie Rod Replacement — 1) Raise vehicle and remove tie rod fasteners. Remove outer ball stud by tapping on steering arm at tie rod end with a light hammer using a heavy hammer as a backing. Remove inner ball stud from relay rod using same procedure.

2) To remove tie rod ends from tie rod, loosen clamp bolts and unscrew end assemblies. Tie rod adjuster clamp bolts often become rusted in service. It is recommended that if torque required to remove the nut from a bolt after breakaway exceeds 7 ft. lbs., discard the nuts and bolts. Apply penetrating oil between clamps and tube, and rotate clamps until they move freely. Use new fasteners of same part number during reassembly to assure proper clamping at specified nut torque.

3) To install tie rods, use following procedure: Lubricate tie rod threads with EP chassis lube and install tie rod ends making sure both are threaded an equal distance from tie rod. Check that threads on ball studs and nuts are clean and smooth. Check condition of ball stud seals and replace if necessary using suitable tool (J-24434). Install ball studs in steering arms and relay rod. Install ball stud nuts and torque to specifications, and install new cotter pins. Adjust toe-in. See *Wheel Alignment Specifications & Procedures in WHEEL ALIGNMENT Section.*

4) Before tightening tie rod adjusting sleeve clamp bolt, note the following: Clamps must be between locating dimples at either end of sleeve. Adjuster sleeve slot must not be within open area of clamp jaw opening. *See Fig. 6 and 7.*

5) Rotate both inner and outer tie rod housing rearward to limit of ball joint travel before tightening clamps. After tightening clamps, return tie rod assembly to center of travel. Check each tie rod for a rotation of at least 35° using a bubble protractor and a pair of vise grips. Lubricate inner and outer tie rod ends.

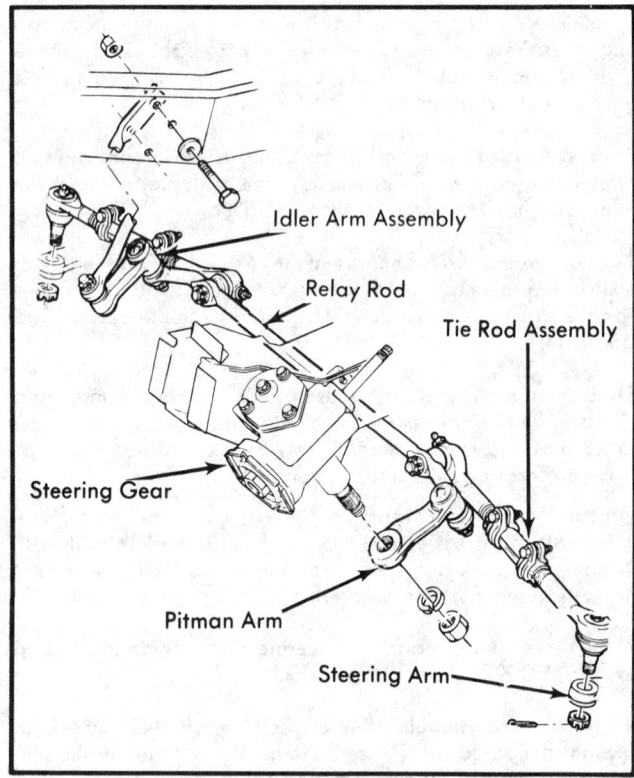

Fig. 2 "G" Model Steering Linkage

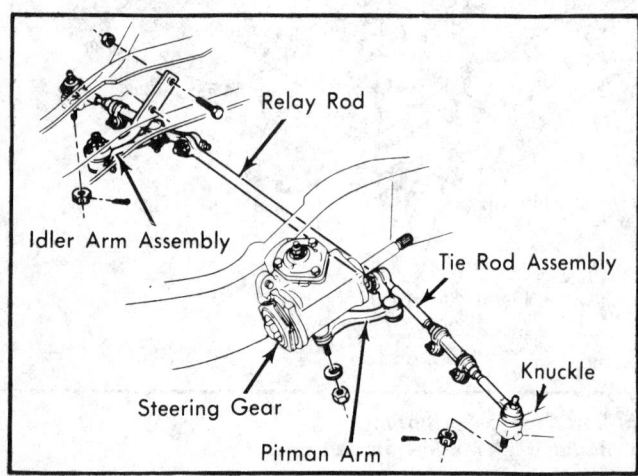

Fig. 1 "C" Model Steering Linkage

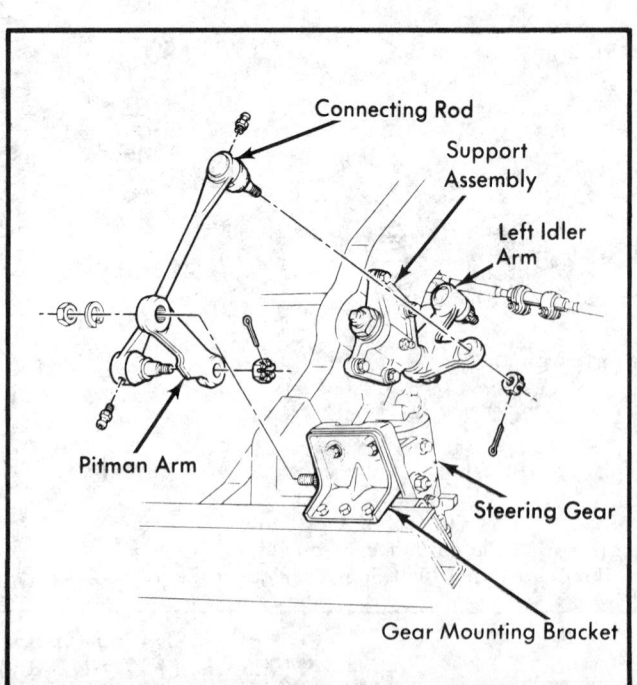

Fig. 3 "P" Model Steering Linkage

GENERAL MOTORS (Cont.)

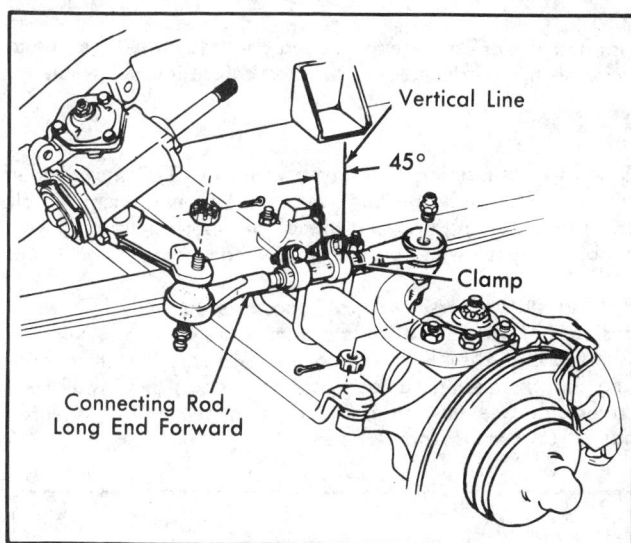

Fig. 4   "K" Model Steering Linkage

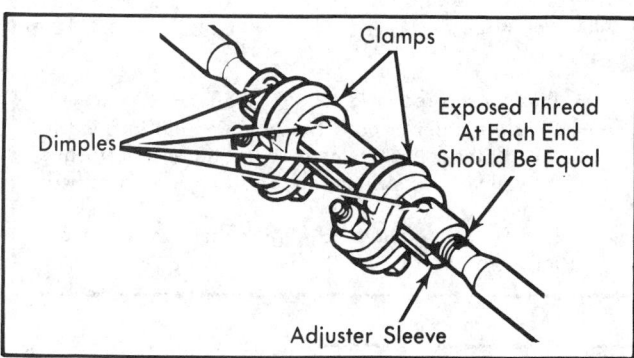

Fig. 5   Position of Tie Rod Clamps

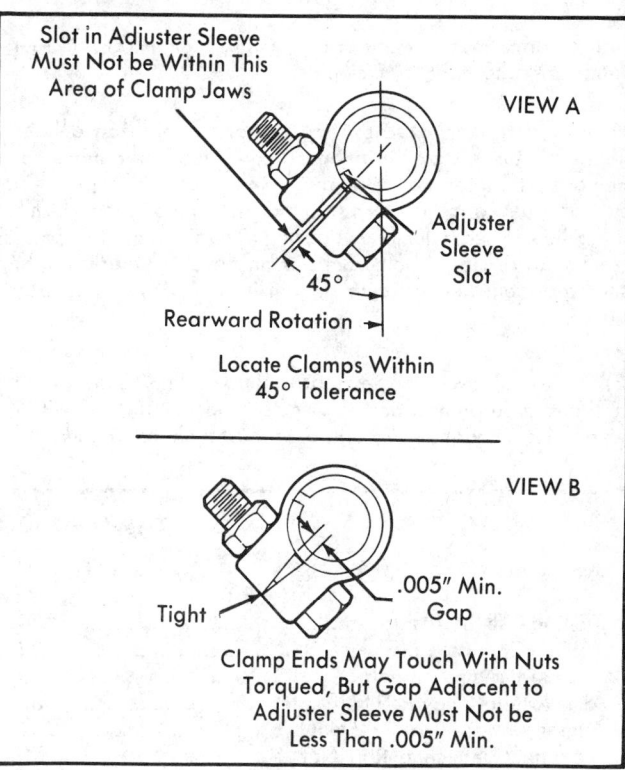

*Fig. 6   Tie Rod Clamp Position
"C", "K" and "P" Models*

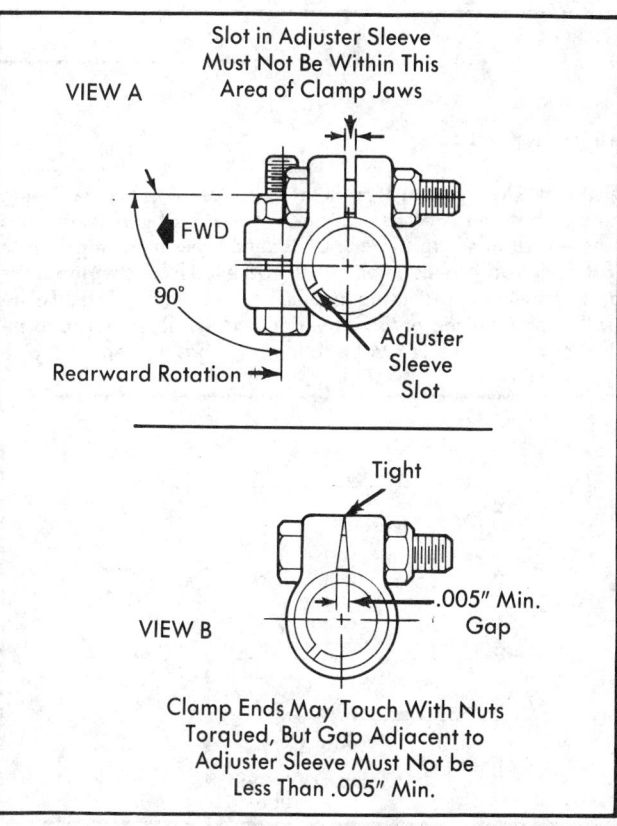

*Fig. 7   Tie Rod Clamp Position
"G" Model*

Relay Rod Replacement — 1) Raise vehicle on hoist. Remove inner ends of tie rods from relay rod. Remove nuts from pitman arm and idler arm ball studs at relay rod. Remove relay rod from pitman and idler arms by tapping on relay rod ball studs bosses with a light hammer while using a heavy hammer as a backing. Remove relay rod.

2) To install, reverse removal procedure and note following: Check ball studs and nuts for clean and smooth threads. Check stud seals and replace if necessary. Torque nuts and install new cotter pins.

Idler Arm Replacement — 1) Place vehicle on hoist. Remove fasteners from ball stud and relay rod. Remove ball stud from relay rod by tapping on relay rod boss with a light hammer, while using a heavy hammer as a backing. Remove idler arm-to-frame bolts and remove idler arm assembly.

NOTE — *Idler arm assembly should always be replaced if it is found that an up and down force of 25 lbs., applied at relay rod end of idler arm, produces a lash of more than ⅛" in straight ahead position.*

2) To install, reverse removal procedure while noting the following: Ensure that threads on studs and nuts are clean and smooth. Check ball stud seals and replace if necessary. Install connecting rod while making sure long end of rod is toward

GENERAL MOTORS (Cont.)

pitman arm. *See illustrations for proper alignment and orientation of connecting rod clamps.*

Pitman Arm Replacement — **1)** Raise vehicle on a hoist. Remove cotter pin from pitman arm ball stud and remove nut. Remove pitman arm or relay rod from ball stud by tapping on side of rod or arm (in which stud mounts) with a hammer while using heavier hammer as a backing. Remove pitman arm nut from shaft or clamp bolt from pitman arm, and mark arm-to-shaft position. Remove pitman arm from shaft using suitable puller.

2) To install, reverse removal procedure and note following: If a clamp type pitman arm is used, spread pitman arm with a wedge just enough to slip arm onto shaft by hand pressure. Do

not hammer or damage to steering gear may result. Be sure to reinstall the hardened steel washer before installing nut.

"K" Models

Steering Connecting Rod Replacement — **1)** Remove cotter pins from ball studs and remove castellated nuts. Remove ball studs from steering arm and pitman arm boss by tapping with a light hammer while using a heavy hammer as a backing.

2) To install, reverse removal procedure and note following: Ensure that threads on studs and nuts are clean and smooth. Check ball stud seals and replace if necessary. Install connecting rod on steering components, torque nuts and install new cotter pins. *See illustration for proper alignment and orientation of connecting rod clamps.*

TIGHTENING SPECIFICATIONS

Application	Ft. Lbs.
Tie Rod Ball Stud Nuts	①50
Tie Rod Clamps	22
Idler Arm Mounting Bolt	30
Idler Arm-to-Relay Rod Nut	②66
Pitman Arm-to-Relay Rod Nut	②66
Steering Connecting Rod Nut	
P10/30 & "P" Motor Home Chassis	③70
K10/20	①50
Steering Connecting Rod Clamps	40
Pitman Arm-to-Pitman Shaft Nut	
K10/20	90

Application	Ft. Lbs.
"P" Motor Home Chassis	125
All Other Models	180

① — Plus torque required to align cotter pin.

② — Seat the taper using a free-spinning nut torqued to 40 ft. lbs., then remove nut and install torque prevailing replacement nut and torque to specification.

③ — Plus torque required to align cotter pin with maximum torque of 100 ft. lbs.

JEEP

All Models

Tie Rod Replacement — Remove cotter pins and retaining nuts at both ends of tie rod and from end of connecting rod where it attaches to tie rod. Disconnect steering damper push rod at tie rod bracket. Remove tie rod ends from steering arms and connecting rod using a puller or expansion fork. To install, attach tie rod ends to steering arms. Tighten nuts and install new cotter pins. Attach connecting rod, tighten nuts, and

install new cotter pin. Attach steering damper. Check and adjust toe-in as necessary.

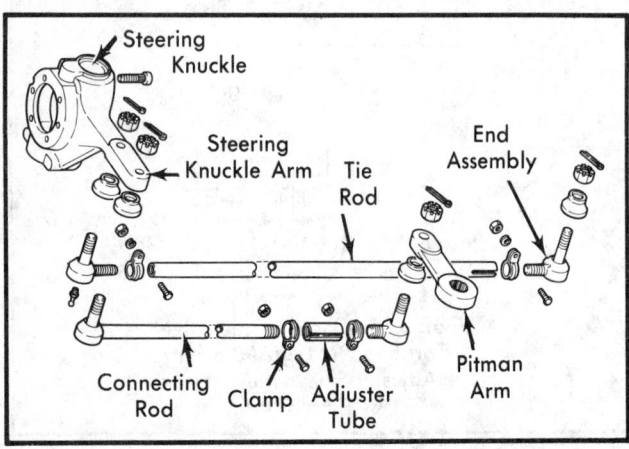

Fig. 1   Disassembled View of Steering Linkage ("CJ" & Scrambler Models)

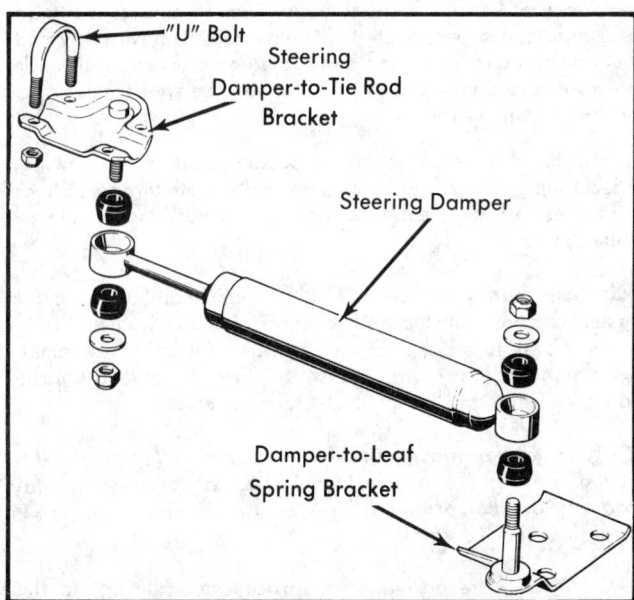

Fig. 2   Positioning of Steering Dampener Bushings All Models Except "CJ" & Scrambler

JEEP (Cont.)

Steering Damper Replacement — With front wheels in straight-ahead position, remove lock nut securing damper to bracket on tie plate, then lift damper off stud. Remove lock nut securing push rod end to tie rod bracket and remove damper assembly. To install, install rubber bushings in damper eyelets, then secure eyelet at push rod end to stud on tie rod bracket with attaching hardware. Install rubber bushings in damper body eyelet. Extend push rod by pulling back on damper body until eyelet can be located on, and secured to, stud on damper bracket. Tighten all lock nuts.

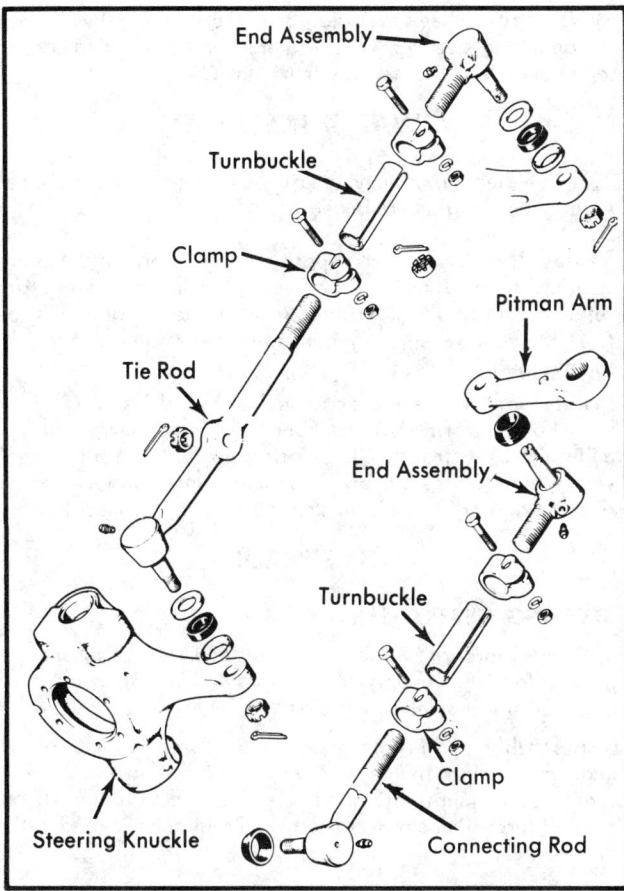

Fig. 3 Disassembled View of Steering Linkage (Cherokee, Wagoneer & Truck Models)

Connecting Rod Replacement — Remove cotter pins and nuts from both ends of connecting rod, then remove rod. When installing be sure wheels are in straight ahead position and steering arm is parallel to centerline of vehicle. Have steering gear steering arm properly indexed, with line marks on steering arm, and gear shaft on center of high point. With steering arm so positioned, install connecting rod.

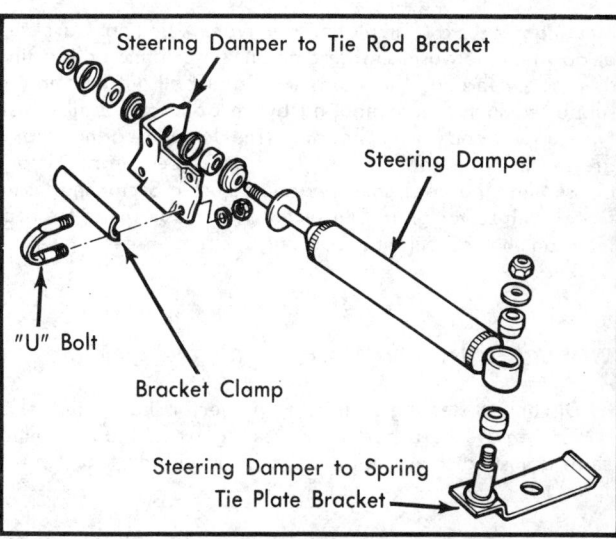

Fig. 4 Steering Damper Assembly "CJ" & Scrambler Models

TIGHTENING SPECIFICATIONS

Application	Ft. Lbs.
Connecting Rod Clamp Bolt	
CJ & Scrambler Models	10-15
All Other Models	25-35
Connecting Rod ⅝"	
(To Castellated Nut Slot)	70 Min.
Connecting Rod ⁹⁄₁₆"	
(To Castellated Nut Slot)	60 Min.
Pitman Arm-to-Shaft	160-210
Tie Rod Clamp Bolt	
CJ & Scrambler Models	10-15
All Other Models	25-35
Tie Rod Stud Nuts	
(To Castellated Nut Slot) CJ & Scrambler	40 Min.
Tie Rod Stud Nuts	
(To Castellated Nut Slot) All Other Models	60 Min.
Steering Damper Lock Nut	
CJ & Scrambler Models	16-28
All Other Models	24-36

Manual Steering Gears

CHRYSLER RECIRCULATING BALL

**Chrysler Corp.
Van Models**

DESCRIPTION

Steering gear is a recirculating ball type. A ball nut travels up or down on the worm shaft, riding on recirculating balls acting as a screw thread. The worm shaft and ball nut assembly is supported in the gear housing by an adjustable ball thrust-type upper and lower bearing. The lower bearing cup is pressed into the gear housing, and the upper bearing cup is pressed into the worm shaft bearing adjuster. Sector shaft is integral with sector gear. The sector gear meshes with the rack teeth on the recirculating ball nut.

ADJUSTMENT

WORM BEARING PRELOAD

1) Disconnect steering gear arm from sector shaft with tool C-4150. Remove horn pad from steering wheel. Loosen sector shaft adjusting screw lock nut and back out adjusting screw 2 turns.

2) Turn steering wheel 2 complete turns from straight ahead position. Place torque wrench tool C-3380A on steering shaft nut. Rotate steering shaft at least 1 turn toward straight ahead position, while testing rotating torque with torque wrench.

3) If reading is not within specifications, adjust as follows: Loosen adjuster lock nut. Use adjuster wrench C-3884 to turn adjuster clockwise to increase preload, or counterclockwise to decrease preload. Hold adjuster from turning and tighten lock nut. Retest worm bearing preload.

BALL NUT RACK & SECTOR MESH

1) With worm bearing preload properly adjusted, turn steering wheel gently from one stop to the other, counting the number of turns. Turn steering back half-way to center position.

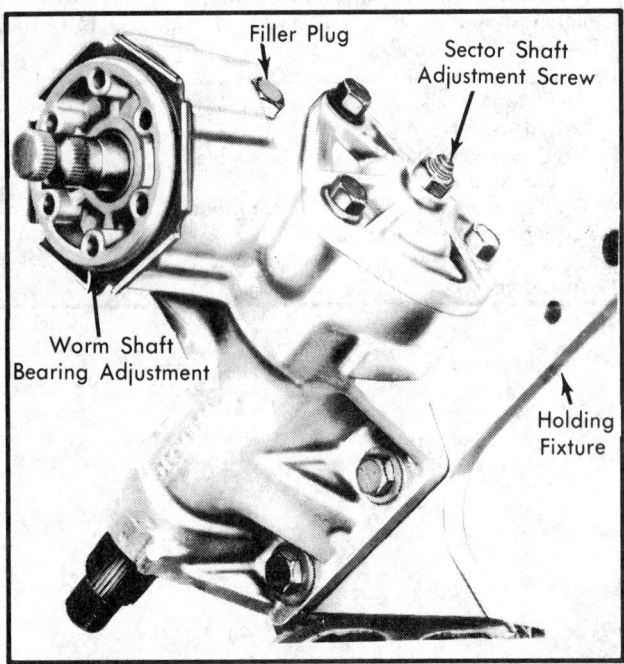

Filler Plug

Sector Shaft
Adjustment Screw

Worm Shaft
Bearing Adjustment

Holding
Fixture

Fig. 1   Steering Gear Adjustment Locations

2) Turn sector shaft adjusting screw clockwise to remove all lash between ball nut rack and sector gear teeth, then tighten adjusting screw lock nut. Turn steering wheel about $\frac{1}{4}$ turn away from center position.

3) With torque wrench tool C-3380 placed on steering wheel nut, measure torque required to rotate steering wheel through high spot at center position. If reading is not to specifications, readjust sector shaft adjusting screw to obtain proper torque reading.

4) Place front wheels in straight ahead position and with steering gear and steering wheel centered, install steering arm on sector shaft and tighten retaining nut.

REMOVAL & INSTALLATION

NOTE – *Steering column must be removed from vehicle before removing steering gear.*

Removal – Disconnect negative battery terminal. Remove steering column. From under vehicle, remove steering arm retaining nut and lock washer. Remove steering arm with tool C-4150. Remove steering gear-to-frame retaining nuts and remove gear.

Installation – Position gear on frame and install retaining nuts. Rotate worm shaft by hand and center sector shaft to mid-point of its travel. Align master serrations on sector shaft with splines in steering arm. Install steering arm lock washer and nut and tighten. Install steering column. Connect battery.

OVERHAUL

STEERING GEAR ASSEMBLY

NOTE – *Thoroughly clean entire outside surface of steering gear before disassembly to avoid contaminating worm shaft and ball nut assembly with dirt.*

Disassembly – 1) With gear removed from vehicle, attach gear to holding fixture C-3323 and place fixture in vise. Loosen sector shaft adjusting screw lock nut and back out screw 2 turns. Remove sector shaft oil seal as described in this article.

2) Position worm shaft in straight ahead position. Remove sector shaft cover bolts and remove sector shaft while sliding arbor tool C-3786 into housing.

3) Remove lock nut from sector shaft adjusting screw and remove screw. Slide adjustment screw and shim out of slot in end of sector shaft. Loosen worm shaft bearing adjuster lock nut with a soft drift punch and remove lock nut. Hold worm shaft from turning while unscrewing adjuster with wrench from tool set C-3884. Slide worm shaft adjuster off shaft.

NOTE – *Handle adjuster carefully to avoid damaging threads. Be sure that ball nut does not run down to either end of worm shaft as ball guide ends can be damaged.*

4) Carefully remove worm and ball nut assembly. Remove sector shaft needle bearing by placing gear housing in an arbor press and inserting tool C-3786 in lower end of housing. Press both bearings through housing.

5) Remove worm shaft oil seal by inserting a blunt punch behind seal and tapping alternately on each side of seal until it

CHRYSLER RECIRCULATING BALL (Cont.)

is driven out of adjuster. Remove worm shaft spacer and upper bearing cup in same manner, being careful not to cock bearing cup.

6) Remove lower bearing cup by positioning locking head jaws of remover tool C-3868 behind bearing cup and expanding remover head. Withdraw bearing cup by turning remover screw nut in a clockwise direction while holding center screw.

Cleaning and Inspection — 1) Wash all parts in clean solvent and dry with compressed air. Test operation of ball nut assembly on worm shaft. If it does not travel smoothly or there is roughness, assembly must be replaced.

2) Inspect sector shaft for wear and check fit of shaft in housing bearings. DO NOT screw worm shaft adjuster into housing without lubrication, or when threads are dirty or damaged. Replace sector shaft and worm shaft oil seals whenever unit is disassembled.

Reassembly — 1) Install sector shaft lower needle bearing by placing bearing on end of tool C-3786 with adapter ring. Press bearing into housing to ½" below end of bore. Install upper needle bearing by placing bearing on tool C-3786 and pressing bearing into housing bore so it is flush with end of bore surface.

2) Install worm shaft bearing cups, position cups and spacer into adjusting nut and press into place with tool C-3865. Install worm shaft oil seal in adjuster with metal retainer UP. Drive seal into place with suitable sleeve so seal is slightly below end of bore in adjuster.

3) Lubricate all moving parts with steering gear lubricant. Lubricate on and around oil seal lips. Clamp holding fixture and housing in vise with bearing adjuster UP. Place a thrust bearing in lower cup in housing.

4) Hold ball nut from turning and insert worm shaft and ball nut assembly into housing with end of worm resting in thrust bearing. Place upper thrust bearing on worm shaft. Lubricate threads on adjuster and threads in housing.

5) Place tape over worm shaft splines and slide adjuster assembly over shaft. Thread adjuster into housing, and with tool C-3884 and splined nut set, tighten adjuster while rotating wormshaft. Loosen adjuster so no bearing preload exists.

6) Adjust worm shaft bearing preload to 1-4.5 INCH lbs. Tighten bearing adjuster lock nut and retest preload. Pack worm shaft cavities in housing with steering gear lubricant. Slide sector shaft adjusting screw and shim into slot in end of shaft.

7) Check end clearance. Screw must be able to turn with .004" maximum end play. Use shims if clearance is not within specifications. Start sector shaft and adjuster screw into bearing in housing cover. Using a screwdriver through hole in cover, turn screw counterclockwise to pull shaft into cover.

8) Install adjusting screw lock nut, but do not tighten. Rotate worm shaft to centralize ball nut. Place new cover gasket on housing cover. Lubricate sector shaft and sector teeth and carefully install shaft and cover assembly into housing.

9) Ensure that some lash exists between sector shaft teeth and ball nut rack. Install and tighten cover bolts. Position sector shaft seal on sector shaft with lip of seal facing gear housing.

10) Place installing adapter SP-3828 from tool C-3880 against seal with short step toward seal. Position nut from tool C-3880 on sector shaft and turn it down against adapter, pressing seal into housing until step on adapter contacts end of housing. Remove tool.

11) Adjust ball nut rack and sector mesh. See "Adjustment" in this article.

SECTOR SHAFT OIL SEAL REPLACEMENT

NOTE — *Sector shaft oil seal can be replaced with steering gear in vehicle or on bench. If replacement is done in vehicle, clean exposed portion of sector shaft before replacing oil seal.*

1) Remove steering gear arm retaining nut and lock washer. Remove arm with tool C-4150.

NOTE — *Tool kit C-3880 must be used to service sector shaft seal. Tool consists of an adapter (SP-3056), half rings (SP-1932), a nut (SP-3610), and installing adapter (SP-3052).*

2) Slide threaded adapter over end of sector shaft and install nut portion of tool on shaft. Maintain pressure on adapter with tool nut while screwing adapter into seal until it grips oil seal firmly.

3) Place two half rings and retainer over both portions of tool. Turn tool nut counterclockwise to withdraw seal from housing.

4) To install, place new seal onto splines of sector shaft with lip of seal facing gear housing. Place installing adapter (SP-3052) against seal and press in until a gap of ¼" exists between adapter and housing.

5) Place nut from tool kit on sector shaft and turn it down against adapter, pressing seal into housing until step on adapter contacts end of housing.

6) Remove tool. Install steering arm, lock washer and retainer nut and tighten.

TIGHTENING SPECIFICATIONS

Application	Ft. Lbs.
Sector Shaft Adj. Screw Lock Nut	35
Steering Arm Retaining Nut	175
Housing Cover Bolts	25
Steering Gear-to-Frame Bolts	100

ADJUSTMENT SPECIFICATIONS

Application	Specification
Ball Nut Rack & Sector Mesh	
Gear in Vehicle	8¼ - 11¼ INCH Lbs.
Gear Removed From Vehicle	7½ - 11½ INCH Lbs.
Worm Bearing Preload	1-4½ INCH Lbs.

Manual Steering Gears

SAGINAW RECIRCULATING BALL

Chrysler Corp.
  (Except Van Models)
Ford
General Motors
Jeep

DESCRIPTION & OPERATION

Steering gear is a recirculating ball type and consists of a ball nut connected to steering worm and in mesh with sector gear. Gears are basically the same for all models and service procedures will apply to all gears unless noted otherwise.

Precision finished helical grooves within ball nut match helical grooves in worm. Ball bearings roll within grooves when steering wheel is turned. There are two complete circuits using tubular ball guides to deflect balls away from their helical path at one end of groove and guide them back to other end.

When steering wheel is turned to right, nut moves upward; when turned to left, nut moves downward. The teeth on sector (forged as part of pitman shaft) and the ball nut are so designed that a tighter fit exists between the two when the front wheels are straight ahead. Proper engagement between sector and ball nut is obtained by an adjusting screw, which moves pitman shaft endwise, permitting desired engagement of tapered teeth of the ball nut and sector gear. Worm bearing adjuster can be turned to provide proper preloading of the upper and lower bearings.

ADJUSTMENT

PRELIMINARY

Worm bearing preload adjustment must be made first; then, make over-center preload adjustment. Do not reverse the order of adjustment. Adjustment of steering gear can be made on or off vehicle in most cases. When making the Worm Bearing Preload adjustment with gear on vehicle, the pitman arm must be disconnected or the steering linkage disconnected from the pitman arm. The torque wrench can be connected directly to the worm shaft (input shaft) or to the steering wheel retaining nut (steering column drag is negligible). When making the Over-Center Preload adjustment, torque wrench is attached to the sector shaft (after removing pitman arm) or the steering wheel nut.

WORM BEARING PRELOAD

Loosen over-center preload adjuster. Tighten worm bearing adjuster until all end play has been removed; then loosen ¼ turn and tighten lock nut. Turn worm shaft carefully to either stop. Do not jam into stop as damage to gear could result. Rotate worm shaft back from stop about ½ turn. Using an INCH lb. torque wrench, measure the torque required to keep worm shaft in motion about one revolution. Adjust rotating torque to specifications, using worm bearing adjuster. Tighten lock nut, and recheck turning torque. Adjust as necessary. Proceed to over-center preload adjustment procedure.

Worm Bearing Preload	
Application	**INCH Lbs.**
All Manufacturers	5-8

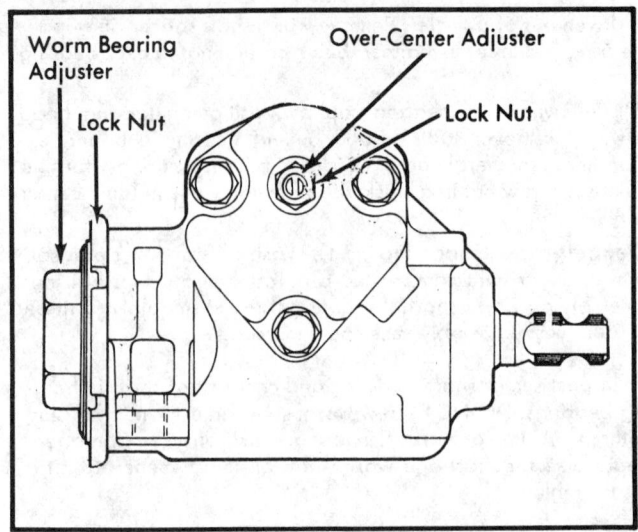

Fig. 1   Adjustment Points for Steering Gear

OVER-CENTER PRELOAD

1) With worm bearing preload adjusted, turn worm shaft slowly from stop to stop while counting total number of turns. Then, turn shaft half-way back to exact center position. Loosen lock nut and turn over-center adjustment screw in until all lash is taken out of shaft. Tighten lock nut.

2) Rotate worm shaft slightly off center (45-90°), then attach an INCH Lbs. torque wrench to worm shaft. Using torque wrench as a lever, rotate worm shaft back through center position and record rotating torque. If rotating torque is not to specifications, repeat procedure. Final rotation of adjustment screw must be clockwise; therefore, if maximum specification was exceeded, screw must be backed out, then rotated in (clockwise) to approximate new setting.

Over-Center Adjustment (INCH Lbs.)		
Application	**Over-Center Preload**	**Preload Maximum Total**
Chrysler Corp.	8	 14
Ford	10	 16
All Other Manufacturers	4-10	 18

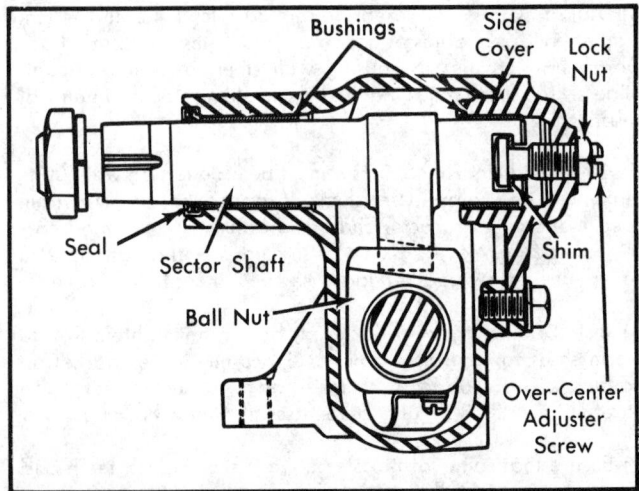

Fig. 2   Cross Section of Steering Gear

SAGINAW RECIRCULATING BALL (Cont.)

REMOVAL & INSTALLATION

NOTE — *All steering component fasteners are made of special quality materials. Replacement fasteners must be of same part number or equivalent. Torque all fasteners and install new cotter pin when used.*

STEERING GEAR

NOTE — *On Chrysler Corp. vehicels, it is recommended that steering column be completely detached from floor and instrument panel before gear removal.*

Chrysler Corp., All Models — 1) Remove 2 bolts from sector shaft coupling. Use tool (C-4150) to disconnect pitman arm from sector shaft. Remove gear-to-frame bolts and remove gear.

2) Position gear on frame and install retaining bolts. Rotate worm shaft by hand and center sector shaft to mid point of its travel. Align serration on sector shaft with splines in pitman arm. Install lock washer and nut, tighten to specifications.

Ford, All Models — 1) Raise vehicle on hoist. Disconnect flex-coupling from steering shaft. Disconnect drag link from pitman arm. Remove pitman arm-to-sector shaft nut, and remove pitman arm. Remove bolts attaching steering gear to frame side rails, and lower steering gear from vehicle. Remove coupling-to-gear attaching bolt, and remove coupling.

2) To install, center worm shaft of steering gear and install gear onto frame side rail. Tighten bolts. Connect pitman arm to sector shaft and drag link to pitman arm. Tighten nuts, and install cotter pins. Attach flex-coupling to steering shaft flange.

General Motors, All Models — 1) Set front wheels in straight-ahead position. Remove flexible coupling-to-steering shaft flange bolts or lower universal joint pinch bolt. Mark position of universal yoke-to-worm shaft. Mark relationship of pitman arm-to-sector shaft. Remove pitman arm using suitable puller (J-6632). Remove steering gear mounting bolts and remove gear assembly.

2) Install flexible coupling on worm shaft aligning flat on coupling with flat on shaft. Push coupling on shaft until shaft hits shoulder and install pinch bolt. Pinch bolt must pass through shaft undercut. Place gear in position, guiding coupling bolt into steering shaft flange.

3) Install gear-to-frame bolts and torque to specification. If flexible coupling alignment pin plastic spacers are used, make sure they are bottomed on pins, then tighten flange bolt nuts and remove plastic spacers. Spacers aid in centering pins and maintain correct coupling-to-flange dimension.

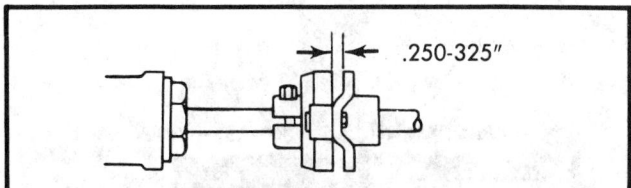

Fig. 3   Adjusting Flexible Coupling for All General Motors Models

4) Check that flexible coupling-to-steering shaft flange dimension is .250-.325". See *Fig. 3*. If flexible coupling alignment pin plastic spacers are not used, center pins in slots in steering shaft flange and tighten flange bolt nuts.

NOTE — *Plastic spacers must be removed before driving vehicle.*

Jeep, All Models — 1) Remove intermediate shaft to worm shaft coupling clamp bolt and disconnect intermediate shaft. Remove pitman arm nut and washer. Pull pitman arm off shaft using a suitable puller (J-6632).

2) On Wagoneer, Cherokee and Truck models, remove steering gear to frame rail bolts and remove steering gear from vehicle. On "CJ" and Scrambler models, raise left side of vehicle slightly to release tension from left front spring. Place safety stand under frame.

3) Remove bolts securing steering gear lower bracket to frame. Remove bolts securing steering gear upper bracket to crossmember. Remove steering gear from vehicle. Remove brackets if necessary. To install, apply Loctite to frame and crossmember bolts, reverse removal procedure.

SECTOR SHAFT SEAL

NOTE — *For models not listed, seal replacement procedure was not available from manufacturer.*

General Motors, All Models — 1) On "K" models, gear must be removed from vehicle to replace seal. On all others, remove pitman arm from sector shaft. Rotate steering wheel (or sector shaft) from stop to stop while counting number of turns. Turn wheel (or sector shaft) back half way, placing gear at center of travel.

2) Remove bolts attaching side cover to housing, and lift sector shaft and side cover assembly from housing. Pry sector shaft seal from housing using a screwdriver being careful not to scratch housing bore. Inspect gear lubricant for contamination, if lubricant is contaminated in any way, gear should be completely overhauled.

3) Lubricate new sector shaft seal with suitable steering gear lubricant (GM 4673M). Position seal in sector shaft bore, and tap it into place using a suitable socket. Remove over-center adjuster lock nut. Remove side cover from sector shaft assembly by turning over-center adjuster screw clockwise. Install sector shaft in gear so center tooth of sector enters center tooth space of ball nut.

4) Fill gear housing with lubricant and install new side cover gasket on gear housing. Install side cover over sector shaft by reaching through cover hole with a screwdriver. Turn over-center adjuster screw counterclockwise until screw bottoms; then back off screw ¼ turn. Install over-center adjuster lock nut, and perform steering gear adjustments.

Jeep, All Models — 1) Mark pitman arm and sector shaft for reassembly reference. Remove pitman arm using puller. Remove seal from sector shaft using a pointed tool or small bladed screwdriver.

2) Inspect condition of gear lubricant. If contaminated, remove and overhaul gear. Wrap pitman arm shaft splines with shim stock to protect replacement seal during installation.

3) Lubricate lip of replacement seal with chassis lubricant, slide seal over shim stock and seat seal in gear housing. Tap seal into place with small plastic hammer. Align index marks, install pitman arm and tighten.

SAGINAW RECIRCULATING BALL (Cont.)

OVERHAUL

DISASSEMBLY

All Models — 1) Place steering gear in a vise, clamping onto one mounting tab or a suitable holding fixture. Worm shaft should be in a horizontal position. Loosen over-center preload adjuster lock nut, and turn adjuster a few turns out. Loosen lock nut on worm shaft adjuster, and turn adjuster out a few turns. Rotate worm shaft from stop to stop, counting number of turns. Then turn shaft back ½ the number of turns to center sector shaft. Place a pan under assembly to catch oil, and remove 3 self-locking bolts holding side cover to housing.

2) Tap on end of sector shaft with a mallet and lift side cover and sector shaft assembly from gear housing. If sector does not clear opening easily, turn worm shaft by hand until sector can be removed. Remove worm shaft adjuster and lock nut assembly with lower worm shaft bearing. Remove worm shaft and ball nut assembly from housing while housing is in a horizontal position to prevent ball nut from running down worm shaft. If ball nut does run down worm shaft with any speed, damage to ball guides will result when nut hits stop. Remove upper bearing from worm guide.

3) Using screwdriver, pry lower bearing retainer from worn adjuster assembly and remove bearing. Remove over-center adjuster lock nut and screw. Slide screw and shim out slot in end of sector shaft. Pry out and discard both sector shaft and worm shaft seals.

CLEANING & INSPECTION

Wash parts with clean solvent and blow dry with air. Inspect bearings and races for signs or wear. Any parts that show signs of wear should be replaced. Inspect sector shaft fit at side cover bushing. If bushing is worn, a new side cover and bushing assembly should be installed. Check ball nut and worm shaft assembly for wear and straightness.

COMPONENT SERVICE

Sector Shaft & Worm Shaft Seals — Pry out seals using a screwdriver. Before installing new seals, check condition of sector shaft bushings and upper worm shaft bearing race. Use a suitable size socket (pressing outer diameter of seal) to replace seal. Avoid installing seal in a cocked position.

Sector Shaft Bushing(s) — Support steering gear in a suitable arbor press and drive sector shaft bushing(s) from housing. Press new bushing(s) into position reversing removal procedure. Replacement bushings are diamond bored to size and need no reaming.

Worm Shaft Bearing Race (In Adjuster) — On gears with horizontal sector shaft, remove worm shaft bearing race using a suitable puller and slide hammer. On vehicles with vertical sector shaft, remove worm shaft bearing race using a hammer and punch. On either type gear, press bearing in place using a suitable tool (J-5755).

Worm Shaft Bearing Race (In Housing) — On vertical sector shaft gears, drive out sheet metal expansion plug using a drift or punch. On all types, drive out housing bearing race with a punch and press new race in with suitable tool (J-5755). On vertical shaft models, install a new expansion plug and press on center of plug to deform it inwards, locking it into place.

Ball Nut & Worm Shaft Assembly — Ball nut disassembly is not necessary unless there is indication of binding or tightness when rotating worm. If disassembly is required, proceed as follows:

1) This first step is going to let loose about 50 ball bearings; be ready to catch them ALL. Remove clamp that retains ball guides and pull guides from ball nut while catching balls in clean pan. Turn nut over and rotate worm until all balls have fallen into pan. Remove worm from ball nut. Wash parts and inspect worm, nut grooves, and ball bearings for indentations. Check ball guides for damage at ends where they deflect or pick up balls from helical path on worm.

Fig. 4   Removing Worm Shaft Bearing Race on Sector Shaft Gear

2) To reassemble ball nut and worm shaft, insert ball nut over worm so that shallow end of ball nut teeth are on left side (looking from steering wheel end of worm shaft). Align grooves in worm and nut by sighting through ball guide holes.

3) There are 2 types of ball guides: those with holes in middle and those with no hole. If ball guides have hole in middle, insert ball guides into holes in ball nut. Divide balls into 2 equal groups and insert each group into a ball guide, while slowly turning worm shaft.

4) If guides have no hole, separate the halves and fill half of each set with balls. Cover filled half with the other half, and plug ends with grease to prevent balls from falling out. Fill each circuit in ball nut with half of remaining balls in one circuit, and half in the other while slowly turning worm shaft. Insert ball guides. On both types, install ball guide retainer.

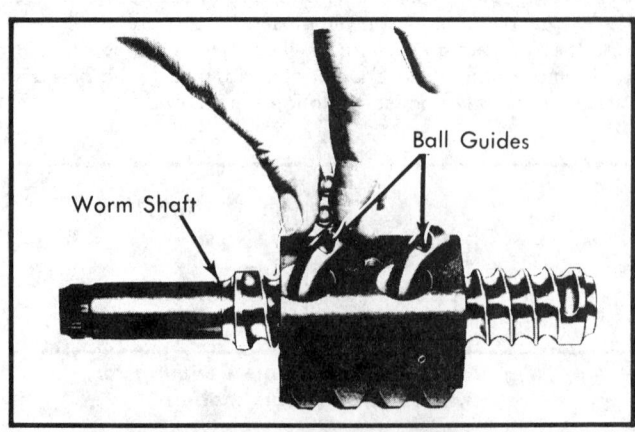

Fig. 5   Filling Ball Circuits Through Holes in Ball Guides

SAGINAW RECIRCULATING BALL (Cont.)

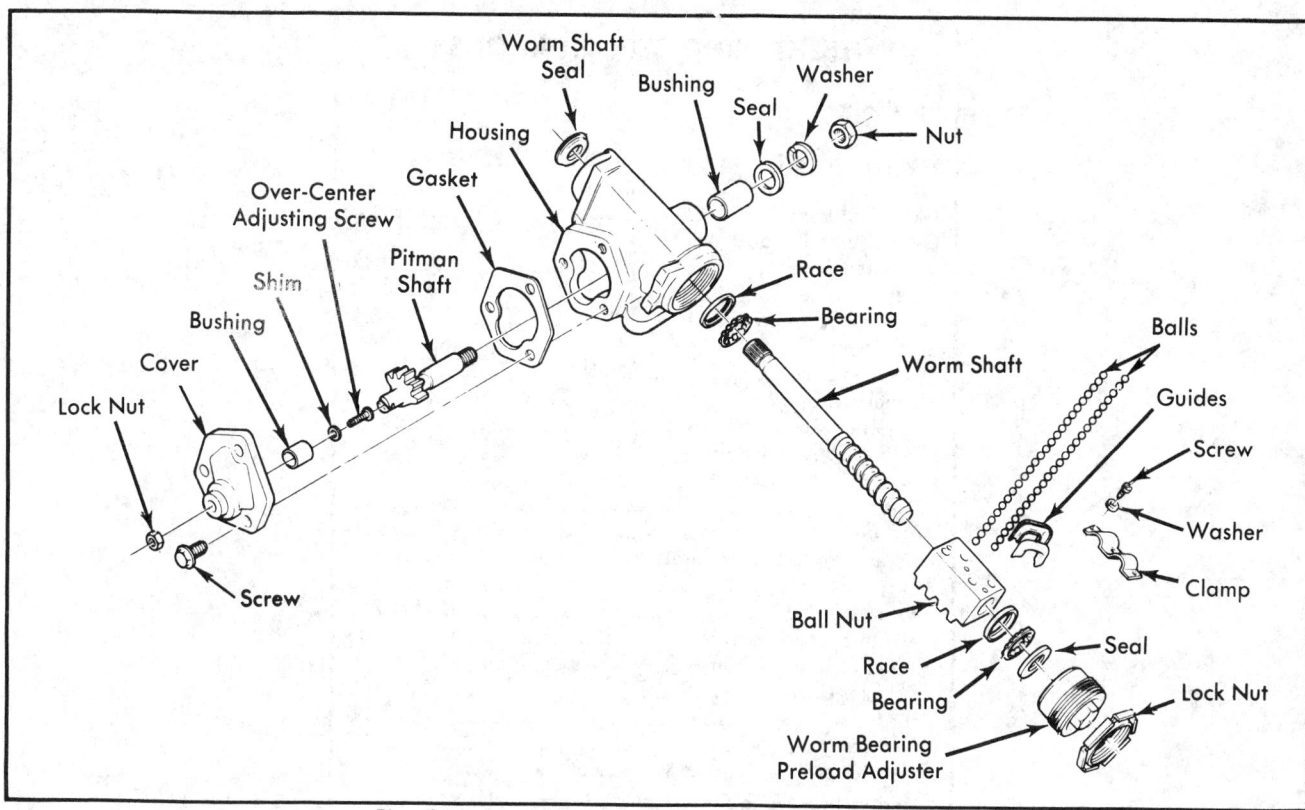

Fig. 6   Exploded View of Recirculating Ball Steering Gear (General Motors Model Shown)

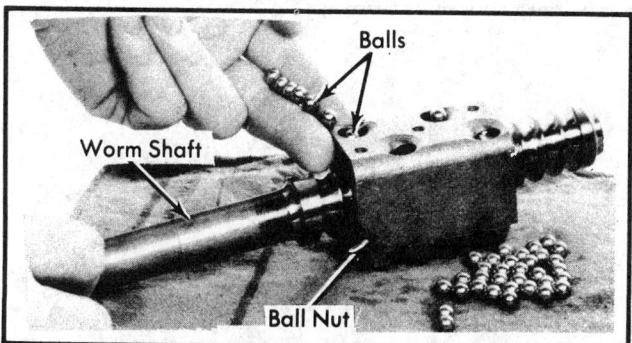

Fig. 7   Filling Ball Circuits Through Holes in Ball Nut

REASSEMBLY

All Models — 1) Place gear housing in a vise with worm shaft bore horizontal and side cover opening facing up. With sector shaft and worm shaft seals, sector shaft bushings, and worm shaft bearing races installed, and ball nut assembly together, proceed as follows: Slip upper ball bearing over worm shaft and insert worm and nut assembly into housing feeding end of shaft through upper ball bearing race and seal. Place ball bearing in adjuster race and press stamped retainer into place with suitable socket. Install adjuster and lock nut into housing carefully guiding worm shaft into bearing until nearly all end play is removed from worm shaft.

2) Position over-center adjuster (with shim) in slotted end of sector shaft. Check end clearance, which should not exceed .002". If clearance is greater than specified, a steering gear over-center adjuster shim kit is available. Lubricate gear as follows: Rotate worm shaft until ball nut is at end of travel, while forcing as much grease as possible into housing without losing it out sector shaft opening. Rotate worm until ball is at other end, and apply more lubricant.

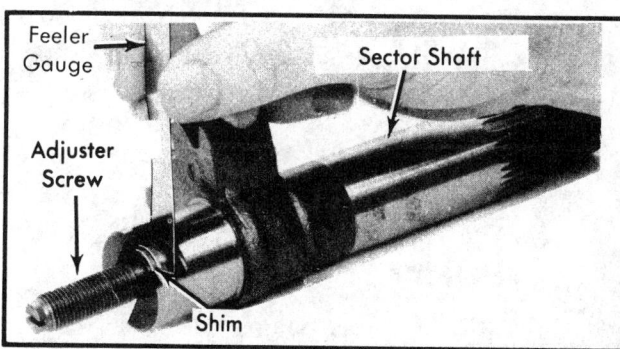

Fig. 8   Checking Over-Center Adjuster Clearance

3) Rotate worm until ball is at center. This will help sector and ball nut engage properly. Insert sector shaft and over-center adjuster screw (without side cover) into housing so center tooth of sector teeth enters center tooth space in ball nut. Apply more lubricant into housing. Install side cover gasket.

4) Install side cover over sector shaft by reaching through cover with a screwdriver. Turn over-center adjuster screw counterclockwise until screw bottoms; then back off screw ½ turn. Loosely install a new lock nut onto adjuster screw. Install and tighten side cover bolts to specifications. Adjust worm bearing preload and over-center preload as previously outlined. See *Adjustments* in this article.

Manual Steering Gears

SAGINAW RECIRCULATING BALL (Cont.)

TIGHTENING SPECIFICATIONS

Application	Ft. Lbs.
Worm Bearing Preload Adj. Lock Nut	
Jeep	90
All Other Manufacturers	85
Over-Center Preload Adj. Lock Nut	
Chrysler Corp.	35
Jeep	23
All Other Manufacturers	25
Side Cover Bolts	
Chrysler Corp.	25
General Motors	45
All Other Manufacturers	30
Flexible Coupling Bolts	
General Motors	20
Jeep	45
All Other Manufacturers	30
Pitman Arm-to-Sector Shaft	
Chrysler Corp.	175
Ford	170210
All Other Manufacturers	185
Steering Gear-to-Frame	
Chrysler Corp.	100
Ford	70
General Motors	80
Jeep (Cherokee, Truck & Wagoneer)	70
Steering Bracket-to-Frame ("CJ" & Scrambler Models)	
Bracket-to-Toe Plate	55
Bracket-to-Gear	70

ALL MODELS

Chrysler Corp.
Ford
General Motors
Jeep

LUBRICATION

SERVICE INTERVALS

Chrysler Corp. – Check fluid every oil change.

Ford – Check with required maintenance checks.

General Motors – Check with every oil change.

Jeep – Check every 5,000 miles or 5 months.

CHECKING FLUID LEVEL

Chrysler Corp. – Check fluid with engine at normal operating temperature. Fluid level should read "FULL" on dipstick.

Ford – With fluid at normal operating temperature, and system properly bled, shut off engine. Fluid level on dipstick should read between "HOT" mark and end of dipstick.

General Motors & Jeep – Check fluid level with engine stopped and fluid hot or cold. Fluid level should be to "FULL HOT" or "FULL COLD" mark on dipstick. On models with remote reservoir, keep fluid level 0.5-1.0" from top of reservoir with wheels fully to the left.

Recommended Fluid

Application	Fluid Type
Chrysler Corp.	Power Steering Fluid (2084329)
Ford	①Power Steering Fluid (C1AZ-19582-A,C,D)
General Motors	Power Steering Fluid (1050017)
Jeep	②Power Steering Fluid

① – Automatic Transmission Fluid.
② – AMC/Jeep Power Steering Fluid or equivalent.

REFILLING & BLEEDING SYSTEM

Chrysler Corp. – Fill pump reservoir with power steering fluid, start engine and check for leaks. Bleed system by turning wheels from stop to stop several times. Shut off engine and check fluid level.

Ford – Fill pump reservoir with fluid and run engine until fluid reaches operating temperature (165-175°F). Turn steering wheel all the way to the left then all the way to the right several times without hitting stops. Check fluid and add if necessary.

General Motors – 1) Fill reservoir to correct level. Let oil settle for two minutes. Start engine and run for two seconds.

Check reservoir and add oil if necessary. Repeat procedure until level in reservoir remains constant after running engine.

2) Raise front of vehicle so that both wheels are off ground. Start engine and increase engine speed to 1500 RPM. Turn wheels right and left, lightly contacting stops. Check fluid and add if necessary. Lower vehicle and turn wheels right and left on ground. Check fluid level and add if necessary.

3) If oil is foamy, allow vehicle to stand still for a few minutes with engine off. Repeat procedure with vehicle raised. Again check fluid level and for air in system. If level is low or there is air in system, repeat complete procedure.

Jeep – 1) Fill reservoir to correct level. Operate engine until fluid reaches normal operating temperature. Stop engine and correct fluid level if necessary. Turn wheels to full left position and add fluid to reservoir to fill to "FULL COLD" mark on dipstick.

2) Start and operate engine at fast idle. Recheck reservoir level and add to "FULL COLD" mark on dipstick. Bleed air from system by turning wheels from side to side without contacting stops. Maintain fluid level just above pump body. Fluid with air in it will have bubbles in it and will have a light tan or tan-orange appearance.

3) Continue to turn wheels until all air is removed from system. When air is removed, return wheels to straight ahead position and operate engine an additional 2-3 minutes and then stop engine. Road test vehicle and recheck fluid level. Level should be at "FULL HOT" position after system has stabilized. Add as necessary but do not overfill.

SERVICE

Belt Tension
Tension (Lbs.) Using Strand Tension Gauge

Application	New Belt	Used Belt
Chrysler Corp.	1	①
Ford		
¼" Belt	80	60
All Other Belts	140	110
General Motors		
5/16" Belt	80 Max.	50 Min.
3/8" Belt	140 Max.	70 Min.
15/32" Belt	165 Max.	90 Min.
Jeep	②125-155	②90-115

① – Belt deflection should be ¼" to 5/16".
② – Calif. models tension 180-200 lbs. new, 140-160 lbs. used.

TESTING

PRESSURE TEST

1) With belt tension correct, disconnect power steering pump pressure hose, keeping hose end raised to prevent fluid loss. Connect pressure hose of suitable gauge to power steering

ALL MODELS (Cont.)

pump fitting and connect second hose from valve side of tester to steering gear inlet. Open valve and run engine until fluid reaches normal operating temperature (170°F). Check fluid level and add if necessary.

NOTE — *For testing Ford vehicles, Power Steering Analyzer D79-33610-A with flow meter is necessary.*

2) If testing Chrysler vehicle, skip intermediate steps and proceed to step **6).** On all other vehicles, note pressure reading with valve open and engine idling. Pressure should be 80-125 psi. On Ford vehicles, note flow. If flow is less than 2 gallons per minute, pump may require repair. At this point, however, continue test. If pressure is above 150 psi on Ford or 200 psi on all other vehicles, check hoses for restrictions and poppet valve (Saginaw gears) for proper assembly.

3) On Ford vehicles, partially close valve to build pressure up to 740 psi for Ford pumps and 620 psi for Saginaw pumps. If flow drops below 1.7 gals./min. for Ford or 1.8 gal./min. for Saginaw pumps, disassemble pump and replace cam pack.

4) On all vehicles, close gate valve completely and re-open 3 times. Record highest reading each time. DO NOT close valve for more than 5 seconds. On Ford vehicles, increase engine speed to 1500 RPM and record flow. On all models, if pressure is less than specification, remove and replace flow control valve. If within specifications on General Motors and Jeep but readings are not within 50 psi of each other, or if above specification on Ford, or if flow varies from step **2)** reading by more than 1 gal./min., remove flow control valve and clean or replace.

5) On all models, with valve open, turn steering wheel all the way from right to left stops and record pressure. DO NOT hold

wheel against stops more than 5 seconds. Pressure should be the same as recorded in step **4).** Note than on Ford vehicles flow should drop 0.5 gal./min. If pump output cannot be matched in either side of gear, gear is leaking internally and must be overhauled. Shut off engine and remove tester, reconnecting hoses.

6) On Chrysler vehicles, idle engine at 600-800 RPM and with valve open, note pressure while turning wheels from side to side to stops. DO NOT hold wheel against stops for more than 5 seconds. A pressure or at least 900 psi should be read. If pressure is low, system is not operating properly. Momentarily close valve and note pressure. If pressure is less than 900 psi, pump is faulty. If pressure is 900 psi but was low at previous reading, steering gear is at fault. Disconnect gauge and reconnect hoses after turning off engine.

Pressure Test Specifications

Application	Idle Pressure	Pump Output Pressure (psi) Relief Pressure
Ford	80-125	①1350-1450
General Motors		
C10/30	80-125	1200-1300
G10/30	80-125	②900-1000
Jeep		
"CJ" & Scrambler	80-125	1100-1200
Cherokee, Wagoneer & Truck	80-125	1400-1500

① — Saginaw pump. For Ford pump, specification is 1400-1500 psi.

② — G30 with hydroboost, pressure is 1350-1450 psi.

Power Steering Gears

CHRYSLER CORP. CONSTANT CONTROL

Dodge
"B", "CB" & "MB" Models
Plymouth
"PB" Models

NOTE – *Some models use other units. See Saginaw Rotary Valve power steering gear in this Section.*

DESCRIPTION

Constant ratio power steering gear consists of a gearbox housing containing a sector shaft with forged sector gear, a rack-piston with gear teeth broached into the side of piston, and a worm shaft. Piston teeth and sector gear are in constant mesh with each other. Worm shaft connects rack-piston to steering shaft through a flexible coupling. Worm shaft is geared to rack-piston through recirculating ball contact. Steering control valve, mounted to top of steering gearbox, directs flow of fluid through the system. Fluid is supplied to the steering gear by an engine driven, constant displacement pump through a high pressure hose. Fluid is returned to pump reservoir from steering gear through a return hose.

LUBRICATION

See *Power Steering General Servicing* in this Section.

TROUBLE SHOOTING & TESTING

See *Power Steering General Servicing* in this Section.

ADJUSTMENT

SECTOR SHAFT PRELOAD

Disconnect steering center link from pitman arm. Start engine and run at idle speed, while turning steering wheel from stop to stop, counting number of turns from one stop to the other. Turn wheel back exactly ½ number of turns to center gear. Loosen sector shaft adjuster screw until backlash is evident in pitman arm. Tighten adjuster until backlash just disappears, then continue tightening ⅜-½ turn from this position. Hold adjuster in position and tighten lock nut.

CONTROL VALVE CENTERING

Start engine, and tap on head or end plug of control valve assembly until unit is not self steering. Turn steering wheel from stop to stop several times to expel all air from system. Check fluid level in pump reservoir. With steering wheel in center position, start and stop engine several times, tapping on valve end plug or valve head, until there is no movement of steering wheel when engine is started or stopped. When steering wheel movement no longer exists, valve is centered. Tighten valve body attaching screws.

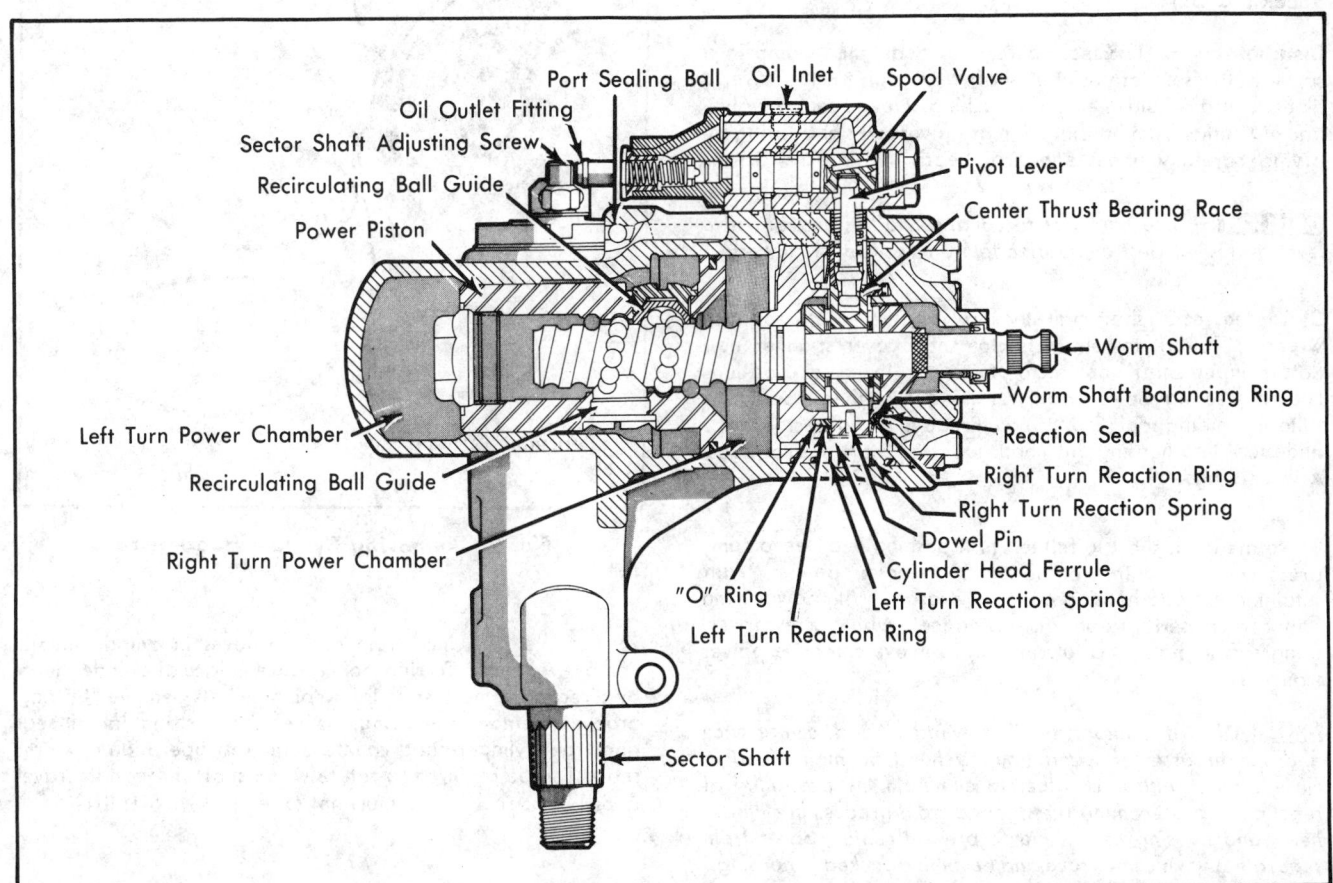

Fig. 1 Cutaway View of Steering Gear Assembly

CHRYSLER CORP. CONSTANT CONTROL (Cont.)

REMOVAL & INSTALLATION

STEERING GEAR

NOTE — *To avoid damage to collapsible steering column, it is recommended that column be completely detached from floor and instrument panel before steering gear is removed. See column removal under STEERING COLUMNS in this Section.*

Removal — Remove battery cable and steering column. Disconnect power steering lines and cap all lines and fittings. Remove pitman arm with tool (C-4150). Remove bolts or nuts from steering gear and remove gear.

Installation — **1)** Position gear on frame and install retaining nuts or bolts. Rotate worm shaft by hand to center sector shaft. Align serrations on sector shaft with splines in pitman arm and install pitman arm.

2) Install and align steering column. Connect power steering lines and fill steering pump with fluid. Start engine and turn wheel from stop to stop to bleed system of air. Stop engine and fill steering pump if necessary. *See procedure given in General Servicing in this section.*

OVERHAUL

STEERING GEAR

Disassembly — **1)** Clean exterior of gear, then clamp in a soft-jawed vise. Rotate input shaft from stop-to-stop several times to drain fluid. Remove attaching screws, control valve, and "O" rings from housing. Remove pivot lever and spring by prying carefully under spherical head with a screwdriver.

CAUTION — *Use care not to collapse slotted end of valve lever as this will destroy bearing tolerances of spherical head.*

2) Loosen sector shaft adjuster lock nut, then use a spanner wrench (C-3988) to remove sector shaft cover spanner nut. Rotate input shaft until sector teeth are in center position. Loosen steering power train retaining nut, then position a suitable holding tool (C-3786) on threaded end of sector shaft. Slide tool into housing until both tool and shaft are engaged with bearings.

3) Rotate input shaft to full left turn position in order to compress power train components. Remove power train retaining nut and housing end tang washer. With power train fully compressed, pry on rack-piston teeth with a screwdriver, using sector shaft as a fulcrum, and remove complete power train assembly.

CAUTION — *It is important that cylinder head, center race and spacer assembly, and housing head be maintained in close contact with each other to eliminate the possibility of reaction rings becoming disengaged from grooves in cylinder head and housing head, and to prevent center spacer from separating from center race and becoming cocked in housing.*

4) Position power train assembly vertically in a soft-jawed vise. Raise housing head until input shaft oil seal just clears end of input shaft. Position suitable arbor tool (C-3929) on top of input shaft and extending into oil seal. Keeping arbor in position, pull up on housing head until arbor is fully positioned in bearing, then remove head and arbor as a unit.

CAUTION — *If input shaft oil seal is to be replaced, perform operation with housing head assembled in steering gear housing.*

5) Remove large "O" ring from groove in housing head. Remove reaction seal by directing compressed air into ferrule chamber. Inspect all grooves for burrs. Make sure passage from ferrule chamber to upper reaction chamber is unobstructed. Remove reaction spring, reaction ring, worn balancing ring, and spacer.

6) While holding worm shaft from turning, turn nut to release staked portions from knurled section of shaft. Wire brush knurled section, and blow out nut and worm shaft to remove metal particles. Remove nut, upper thrust bearing race and upper thrust bearing. Remove center bearing race, lower thrust bearing and lower thrust bearing race. Remove lower reaction ring and spring. Remove cylinder head assembly.

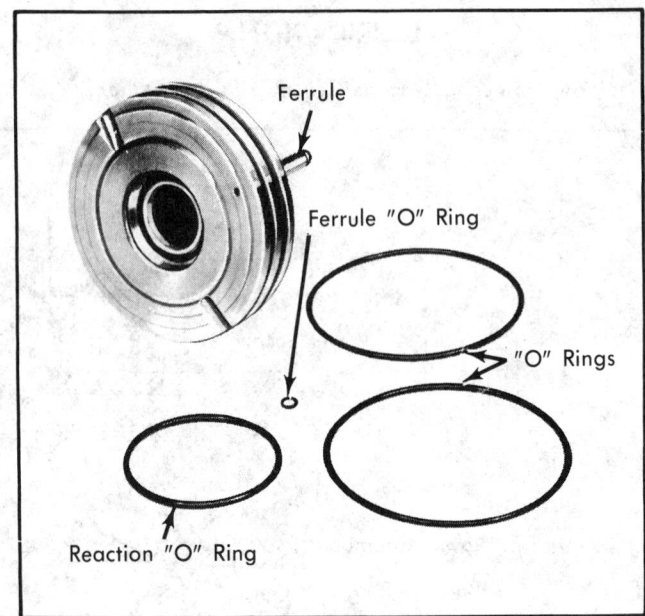

Fig. 2 Removing Cylinder Head Seals

7) Remove "O" rings from outer grooves in cylinder head. Remove reaction "O" ring from groove in face of cylinder head by directing compressed air into oil hole between two "O" ring grooves. Remove snap ring, sleeve, and rectangular oil seal ring from cylinder head counterbore. Test operation of worm shaft. Torque required to rotate worm shaft through its travel in or out of rack piston must not exceed 1½ INCH lbs.

NOTE — *Worm and piston are serviced as an assembly and should not be disassembled.*

CHRYSLER CORP. CONSTANT CONTROL (Cont.)

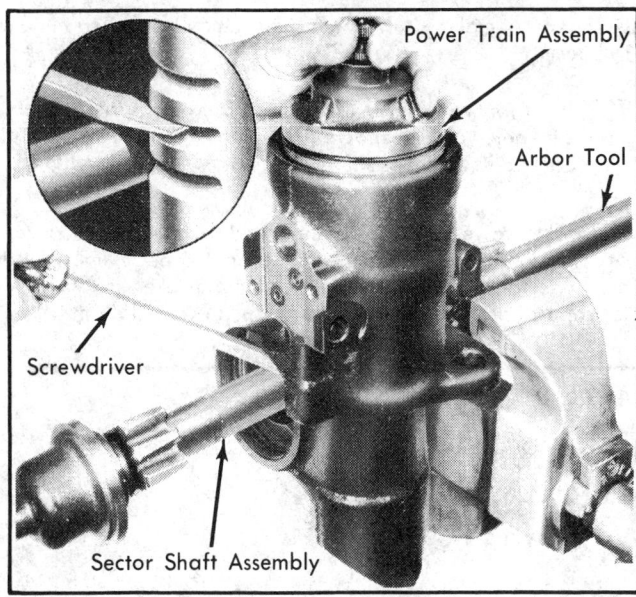

Fig. 3 Removing Power Train

Reassembly — 1) Inspect condition of teflon piston ring for wear and cuts. Replace with new rubber sealing ring and cast iron piston ring if necessary. To install, slide new ring into place in piston groove. Then place piston and ring assembly into suitable holding fixture (C-3676), with lower part of piston and ring resting against land of tool. Press down on piston to seat ring in groove, forcing open ends of ring out for ease of locking ring.

2) Clamp piston assembly in a soft-jawed vise with worm shaft pointing up. Inspect cylinder head ferrule oil passage for obstructions, and inspect lands for burrs. Lubricate large "O" rings and install them in cylinder head grooves. Install worm sleeve seal, sleeve and snap ring, making sure snap ring is fully seated in groove. Install lower reaction "O" ring in cylinder head groove. Slide cylinder head assembly, ferrule end up, onto worm shaft.

CAUTION — *Check worm shaft seal ring, making sure gap is closed, to avoid damaging the ring as the cylinder head moves against the piston flange.*

3) Lubricate power train parts with power steering fluid and install in the following order; lower thrust bearing race, lower thrust bearing, lower reaction spring, lower reaction ring, center bearing race, upper thrust bearing, upper thrust bearing race and thrust bearing adjusting nut. Make sure small hole in reaction spring is over ferrule, lower reaction ring protrudes through reaction spring and adjusting nut is loosely installed.

4) Turn worm shaft ½ turn clockwise. Hold shaft in this position using the splined nut, Tool C-3637, and socket wrench. Tighten adjusting nut to 50 ft. lbs. to prestretch the threads. Hold shaft in position as outlined while performing the following adjustment. Loosen the adjusting nut. Place several rounds of cord around center bearing race. Make a loop in end of cord and attach a suitable distributor breaker arm spring scale to loop. Pull on cord causing bearing race to rotate. Retighten adjusting nut while pulling on cord with spring scale. Adjusting nut is properly tightened when reading on spring scale is 16-24 ozs.

NOTE — *Preferred reading is 20 ozs. with bearing race turning.*

5) Stake upper part of worm shaft bearing adjusting nut into knurled area of shaft. Hold a ¼" flat end punch on centerline of worm shaft end at a slight angle to nut flange. If adjusting nut moves, strike it in the opposite direction to regain proper preload. After retesting for proper preload, stake the nut at three more locations 90° apart around upper part of nut. To test total staking, apply 20 ft. lbs. of torque in each direction. If nut does not move, staking operation is correct.

6) Position spacer assembly over center race, engaging dowel pin of spacer in slot of race, and slot of spacer entered over cylinder head ferrule. This aligns valve pivot lever hole in center bearing race with valve pivot lever hole in center bearing spacer assembly.

NOTE — *The small "O" ring for the ferrule groove should not be installed until after upper reaction spring and spacer have been installed.*

7) Install upper reaction ring on center race, and spacer, with flange down against spacer. Install upper reaction spring over reaction ring, with cylinder head ferrule through hole in reaction spring. Install worm balancing ring (without flange) inside upper reaction ring. Lubricate ferrule "O" ring with Vaseline, and install in groove on cylinder head ferrule. If oil seal was removed from housing head, install new seal using seal installer (C-3650) to drive seal in until tool bottoms on support.

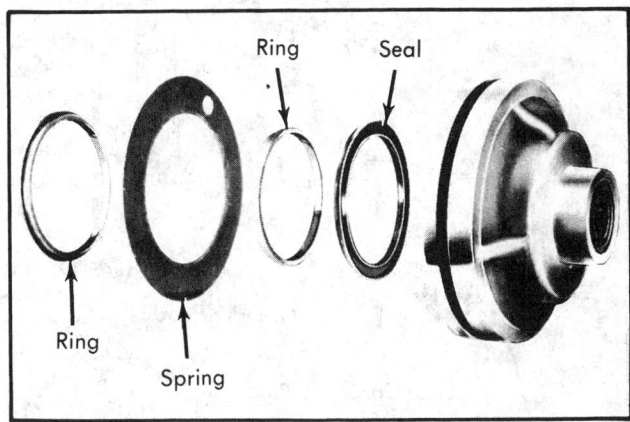

Fig. 4 Installing Reaction Seal and Ring

8) Lubricate and install reaction seal in groove in face of housing head with flat side of seal out. Install "O" ring in groove in housing head. Slide housing head and arbor assembly over worm shaft, engaging cylinder head ferrule and "O" ring and making sure reaction rings enter circular groove in housing head. Power train is now ready for installation in housing.

9) Lubricate power train bore of housing and install power train assembly while noting the following: Keep worm turned fully counterclockwise to keep reaction rings from coming out of their grooves. Piston teeth must be facing to the right, and valve lever hole in center race and spacer must be in the "up" position.

CAUTION — *Make sure cylinder head is bottomed on housing shoulder.*

CHRYSLER CORP. CONSTANT CONTROL (Cont.)

10) Align valve lever hole in center bearing race and center spacer with lever hole in gear housing. Install valve pivot lever, double bearing end first, through hole in housing until engaged in center race and spacer.

CAUTION — *Slots in valve lever must be parallel to worm shaft in order to engage anti-rotation pin in center race.*

11) Lightly tap on end of lever to seat lower pivot pin in center race. Center lever in hole by turning housing head by tapping on a reinforcing rib with a hammer and drift. Install housing head tang washer to index with groove in housing. Install spanner nut, making sure valve lever remains centered in hole in housing.

NOTE — *Turn worm shaft until piston bottoms in both directions, and note valve lever action. Lever must center in hole and snap back to its center position when worm tension is relieved.*

12) Install valve lever spring, small end first. Set power piston at center of travel, install sector shaft and cover assembly, and center sector teeth with piston rack teeth. Make sure "O" ring is properly installed on cover. Install sector cover lock nut.

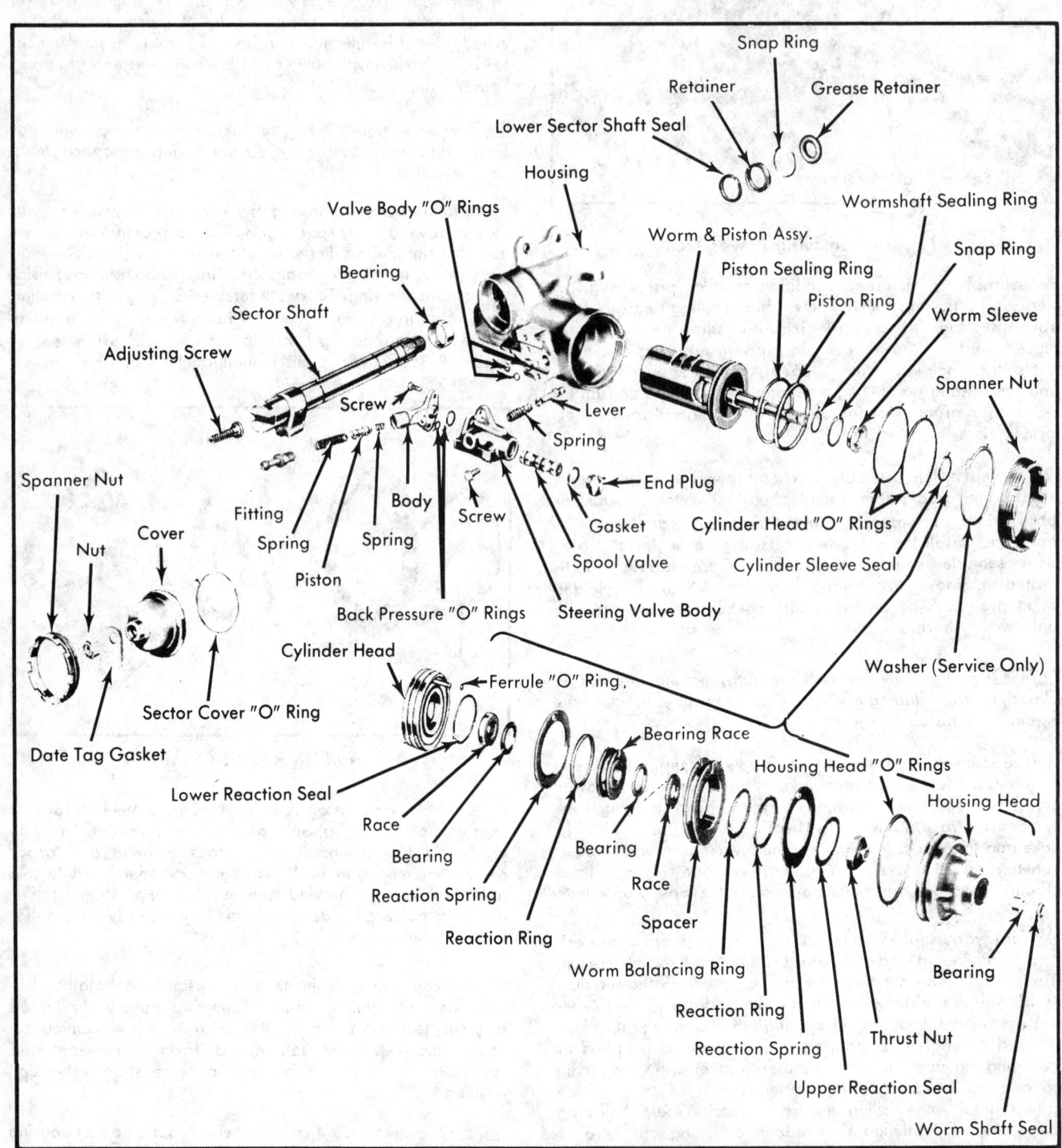

Fig. 5 Exploded View of Steering Gear Components

CHRYSLER CORP. CONSTANT CONTROL (Cont.)

13) Install control valve body on housing, making sure valve pivot lever enters hole in valve spool. Be sure "O" ring seals are in place. Tighten control valve attaching screws. Install new sector shaft seal, followed by seal back-up washer, and snap ring. Install new grease retainer.

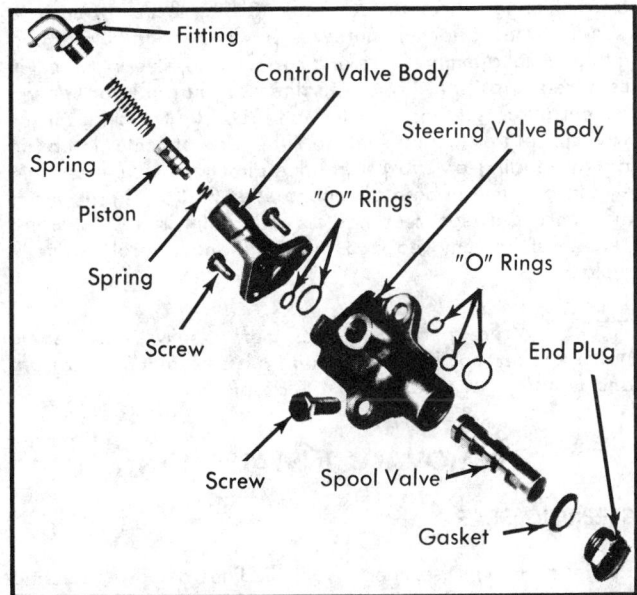

Fig. 6 Disassembled View of Control Valve Assembly

SECTOR SHAFT OIL SEAL

NOTE — *Sector shaft oil seal may be replaced without removing steering gear from vehicle.*

Disassembly — 1) Remove pitman arm attaching nut. Disconnect pitman arm from sector shaft. Slide suitable adapter (SP-3056) over end of sector shaft, and thread tool nut onto sector shaft. Maintain pressure on threaded adapter with tool nut while screwing adapter far enough to engage metal portion of grease retainer.

2) Place two half rings (SP-1932) and tool retainer ring over both portions of tool. Turn tool nut counterclockwise to remove retainer. Remove oil seal snap ring, and seal backup washer. Remove inner seal in same manner, and using same tools as for grease retainer removal.

Reassembly — 1) Place new seal, lip facing down, on flat surface and lubricate inner diameter with power steering fluid. Insert seal protective sleeve in seal, and position seal on sector shaft with lip of seal toward housing. Place tool adapter (SP-3052) with long step against new seal. Install tool nut on sector shaft and tighten nut until shoulder of adapter contacts gear housing.

2) Remove tool nut, adapter, and protector, then install seal backup washer. Install oil seal snap ring with sharp edge out. Fill housing cavity outside retainer and snap ring with a multi-purpose chassis grease. Position oil seal in housing bore.

3) Position adapter tool (SP-3052) with short step of lip against seal. Install tool nut on sector shaft, then tighten until shoulder contacts gear housing. Remove tool, and position steering gear and steering wheel in straight ahead position. Install pitman arm and attaching nut.

TIGHTENING SPECIFICATIONS

Application	Ft. Lbs.
Gear Housing-to-Frame	100
Gear Sector Shaft Adjuster Lock Nut	28
Sector Shaft Cover Spanner Nut	155
Pitman Arm Nut	175
Housing Head Spanner Nut	162
Valve Body End Plug	50
Steering Column Bracket Nuts	9
Steering Wheel Nut	60
Valve Body Attaching Screw	17

Power Steering Gears

FORD TORSION BAR

F100/F350 (2-WD)
F150/350 (4-WD)
Bronco

DESCRIPTION

Torsion bar type power steering unit consists of a worm and one-piece rack-piston, which is meshed to gear teeth on sector shaft. Hydraulic control valve, input shaft, and torsion bar assembly are mounted to end of worm shaft and operated by twisting action of torsion bar. One-piece rack-piston, worm and sector shaft are mounted in one housing, while valve spool is mounted in an attached housing. This allows internal passage of fluid between valve and cylinder, thus eliminating the need for all external lines and hoses, except for pressure and return hoses between pump and gearbox assembly.

LUBRICATION

Check fluid level in pump reservoir every 5000 miles. Steering gear and fluid must be at normal operating temperature. If necessary, add Power Steering Fluid to bring level to proper mark on dipstick.

ADJUSTMENT

OVERCENTER POSITION

Disconnect pitman arm from sector shaft. Disconnect fluid return line at pump reservoir, and cap reservoir return line pipe. Place end of return line in clean container and cycle steering wheel in both directions several times to discharge all fluid from steering gearbox. Remove horn button from steering wheel, and turn steering wheel until positioned 45° from left steering stop. Using an INCH-lb. torque wrench on steering wheel attaching nut, measure force required to turn steering shaft ⅛ turn from 45° position. Turn steering wheel back to center position, and measure force required to move steering shaft back and forth across center position. Loosen lock nut and turn adjusting screw until reading across center position is 14-18 INCH lbs. greater than reading across 45° position. Tighten lock nut while holding adjusting screw in place. Replace pitman arm and reconnect hoses.

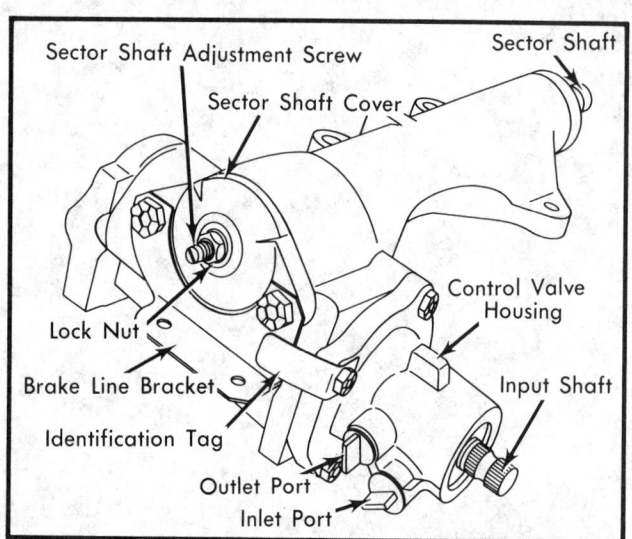

Fig. 1   Ford Torsion Bar Steering Gear Assembly

TESTING

VALVE SPOOL CENTERING

Install a suitable 0-2000 psi pressure gauge and valve assembly between power steering pump and high pressure line. Open gauge valve completely, and remove horn button from steering wheel. Attach an INCH-lb. torque wrench to steering wheel attaching nut. With power steering fluid at normal operating temperature and correct level, steering wheel in centered position, and engine at normal operating temperature, set engine idle to 1000 RPM. Using torque wrench, rotate steering shaft to either side of center to obtain gauge reading of 250 psi in each direction. Torque reading should be same in both directions when 250 psi is reached. If difference between readings exceeds 6 INCH lbs., steering gear must be removed and the shaft and control assembly replaced.

NOTE — *When performing test off vehicle, use same procedure, except take torque and pressure readings at right and left stops instead of either side of center.*

REMOVAL & INSTALLATION

STEERING GEAR

Removal — 1) Disconnect hydraulic lines at power steering gear, and cap lines. Plug ports in steering gear to prevent entry of foreign matter. Remove splash shield from flex coupling. Disconnect flex coupling at steering gear. Raise vehicle and remove pitman arm, attaching nut and washer. Using suitable puller, remove pitman arm from sector shaft, being careful not to damage seals.

2) Support steering gear and remove steering gear attaching bolts. Work the steering gear free of the flex coupling and remove steering gear from vehicle.

Installation — 1) Slide flex coupling into position on steering shaft assembly and turn steering wheel so spokes are in horizontal position. Center steering gear input shaft with indexing flat forward. Install gearbox input shaft into flex coupling and into place on frame. Install and tighten attaching bolts.

2) With wheels in straight ahead position, install pitman arm on sector shaft. Install washer and nut to pitman arm and tighten. Install splash shield. Connect and tighten pressure and return lines to steering gear. Disconnect coil wire. Fill reservoir to proper level. Turn ignition on and turn steering wheel left to right to distribute fluid. Check fluid and add if necessary.

OVERHAUL

NOTE — *If complete gearbox assembly is not to be overhauled, remove unit to be overhauled and proceed to disassembly and reassembly of that unit.*

STEERING GEAR

Disassembly — 1) Drain steering gear completely, and mount gear in a soft-jawed vise. Remove lock nut and washer from adjusting screw. Turn input shaft to either stop, then turn

FORD TORSION BAR (Cont.)

shaft back 2 turns to center gear. Remove sector shaft attaching bolts. Tap lower end of sector shaft with a soft faced hammer to loosen shaft in bore, then lift shaft and cover assembly from housing. Discard cover "O" ring.

2) Turn sector shaft cover counterclockwise to remove it from adjusting screw. Remove valve housing attaching bolts and identification tag. Lift valve housing from steering gear housing while holding piston to prevent it from rotating off worm shaft. Remove valve housing and control valve gasket. Discard gasket.

3) With piston held so that ball guide faces up, remove ball guide clamp screws and ball guide clamp. Over a clean container, place finger over opening in ball guide, turn piston so ball guide faces down and let guide tubes fall into container.

4) Rotate input shaft stop to stop until all balls fall from the piston into the container. Remove valve assembly from piston. Inspect piston bore to make sure all balls have been removed. Install valve body assembly in bench mounted holding fixture (T57L-500-B). Loosen hex head race nut screw from the bearing race nut as shown in *Fig. 2*. Carefully slide input shaft, worn and valve assembly out of valve housing.

piston. Place a minimum of 27 ball bearings in the ball guide while turning worm counterclockwise as viewed from input end of shaft. If all ballls have not been fed into the guide upon reaching the left stop, rotate the input shaft in one direction and then the other while inserting the remaining balls. DO NOT rotate the input shaft more than 3 turns from the left stop or the balls will fall out of the circuit.

3) Secure guides in ball nut with guide clamp. Apply petroleum jelly to Teflon seal on piston and place a new "O" ring on valve housing. Slide piston and valve into gear housing, using care not to damage Teflon seal. Align oil passage in valve housing with passage in gear housing. Place new "O" ring in oil passage hole of gear housing. Install identification tag on housing on upper right valve housing bolt.

4) Loosely install housing attaching bolts, rotate the ball nut so that teeth are in same plane as sector teeth and tighten valve housing bolts. Position sector shaft cover "O" ring in steering gear housing. Turn input shaft as necessary to center piston. Apply petroleum jelly to sector shaft journal, and position sector shaft and cover assembly in gear housing. Install and tighten cover attaching bolts. Adjust steering overcenter position. *See Overcenter Position Adjustment.*

Fig. 2 Removing Worm Bearing Race Nut

CAUTION — *Due to close clearance, cocking of spool may cause it to jam in housing.*

Reassembly — 1) Mount valve housing in a suitable holding fixture with flanged end upward. Apply a light coat of lubricant to Teflon rings on valve sleeve, then carefully install worm and valve in housing. Install race nut in housing and tighten securely. Install Allen head race nut set screw through housing and tighten.

2) Place piston on bench with ball guide holes facing up. Insert worm shaft into piston so that the first groove is in line with the hole nearest the center of the piston. Place the ball guide in the

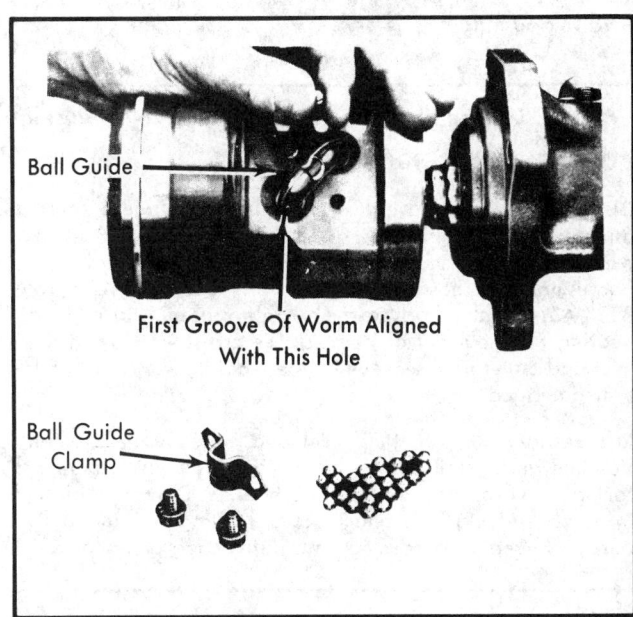

Fig. 3 Installing Piston on Worm Shaft

STEERING GEAR HOUSING

Disassembly & Reassembly — Remove snap ring from lower end of housing. Using a suitable puller, remove dust seal and pressure seal from housing. Lubricate new seals and sector shaft seal bore with Lubriplate. Place dust seal on tool T77L-3576-A so the raised lip of the seal is toward the tool. Place pressure seal on tool so lip is away from tool. Flat back side of pressure seal should be against flat side of dust seal. Insert tool into sector shaft bore and drive in until seals clear snap ring groove. Do not bottom seals against bearing. Install snap ring in housing groove.

Power Steering Gears

FORD TORSION BAR (Cont.)

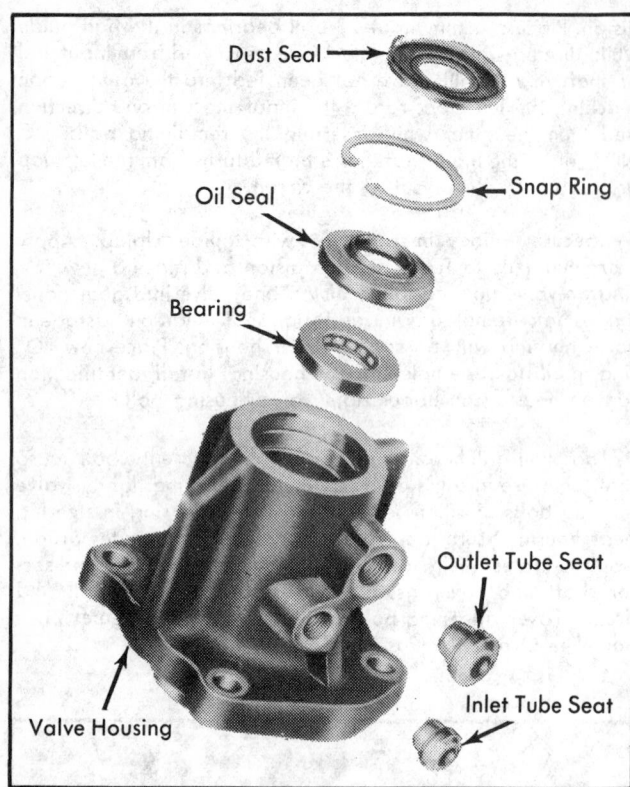

Fig. 4   Disassembled View of Control Valve Housing

CONTROL VALVE HOUSING

Disassembly — Remove dust seal from rear of valve housing using puller (T59C-100-B) and slide hammer (T58L-101-A). Discard seal. Remove snap ring from valve housing. Invert housing and using input shaft bearing/seal tool (T65P-3524-A2 & T65-3524-A3) in valve body assembly opposite oil seal end, tap bearing and seal out of housing. Discard seal. Remove fluid inlet and outlet tube seats with tube seat remover (T74P-3504-L) if damaged.

Reassembly — Coat fluid inlet and outlet tube seats with Vaseline and install bearing with metal side covering rollers facing outward. Press bearing into housing. Dip a new oil seal in power steering fluid and place in housing with metal side out. Drive seal into housing until outer edge does not quite

clear snap ring groove. Place snap ring in housing with dished rubber side out. Drive into place until seal is located behind undercut in input shaft.

WORM & VALVE SLEEVE

Disassembly & Reassembly — Remove rings from sleeve with a small knife. Mount worm end of worm and valve sleeve assembly in a soft-jawed vise and install a suitable mandrel tool (T75L-3517-A1) over the sleeve. Install rings one at a time with the aid of a suitable driver tool (T75L-3517-A2). Rapidly push down on pusher tool to force ring down ramp and into fourth groove of valve sleeve. Repeat three more times, each time adding spacers (Tool T75L-3517-A3) under mandrel tool to line up next groove. After all sleeve rings are installed, install sizing tool (T75L-3517-A4) carefully over valve sleeve rings. Be sure rings are not bent over as tube is slid over them. Remove sizing tool and check condition of rings. They must turn freely.

PISTON & BALL NUT

Disassembly & Reassembly — Remove Teflon ring and "O" ring from piston ball nut assembly. Dip new "O" ring in power steering fluid and install it on piston and ball nut. Install new teflon ring on piston and ball nut, using care not to stretch ring more than necessary.

TIGHTENING SPECIFICATIONS	
Application	**INCH Lbs.**
Ball Return Guide Clamp Screw	42-70
Allen Head Race Nut Setscrew	15-25
Application	**Ft. Lbs.**
Sector Shaft Cover Bolts	55-70
Sector Shaft Adjusting Screw Lock Nut	35-45
Valve Housing-to-Gear Housing Bolts	35-50
Piston End Cap	70-110
Rack Retaining Nut	①

① — Tool used with torque wrench will affect observed reading at torque wrench. To obtain required torque wrench reading, multiply length of torque wrench by desired torque (72 ft. lbs.), and divide this product by sum of torque wrench plus length of tool (5.5").

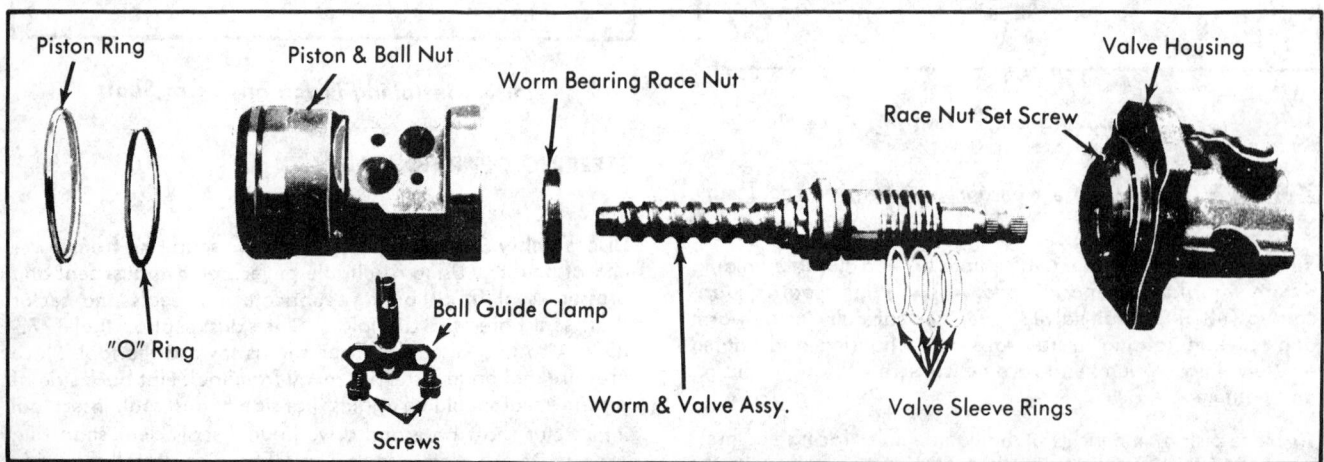

Fig. 5   Disassembled View of Ball Nut & Housing

SAGINAW ROTARY VALVE

Chrysler Corp.
(Exc. "B", "CB", "MB" & "PB" Models)
Ford ("E" Models)
General Motors (All Models)
Jeep (All Models)

DESCRIPTION

Steering gear is a recirculating ball type, available in either a constant or a variable ratio design. Steel balls work as a rolling thread between steering gear worm shaft and rack-piston nut. Worm shaft thrust is taken by a thrust bearing and two races at the lower end, and by a bearing in the adjuster plug at the upper end. This design provides continual spring loaded pressure on worm shaft to prevent loss of thrust bearing preload. The adjuster plug provides initial preload adjustment and the service adjustment when repairing gear. As worm shaft is turned right, the rack-piston is moved upward in gear. As worm shaft is turned left, the rack-piston is moved downward in gear. The rack-piston teeth mesh with the sector, which is forged as part of the sector shaft. Rotating the worm shaft moves the sector shaft, which turns the wheels through mechanical linkage. See Fig. 1.

LUBRICATION, TROUBLE SHOOTING & TESTING

See Power Steering General Servicing in this section.

ADJUSTMENT

THRUST BEARING PRELOAD

1) This procedure is to be performed with steering gear removed from vehicle. Remove adjuster plug lock nut. Turn adjuster plug clockwise with a suitable spanner wrench till plug is seated in housing. Chrysler Corp. and Jeep vehicles will require about 20 ft. lbs. of torque. Ford and General Motors vehicles require about 30 ft. lbs. of torque to seat adjuster plug.

2) Place an index mark on housing opposite one spanner wrench hole in adjuster plug. Measure ½" counterclockwise from mark and again mark housing. Rotate plug counterclockwise until hole in adjuster lines up with second mark. Tighten locknut, making sure adjuster remains in position.

3) Attach an INCH lb. torque wrench to end of input shaft. Turn input shaft to right stop, then back ¼ turn. Using torque wrench, measure rotational torque required to turn shaft. Reading should be taken with beam of torque wrench near vertical while turning it counterclockwise at an even rate. Torque reading should be 4-10 INCH lbs. See Fig. 2.

NOTE — *If reading does not fall within the 4-10 INCH lb. range, the adjuster plug may have turned while lock nut was being tightened. Steering gear may be incorrectly assembled or worm shaft thrust bearings and races may be defective. Repair as required and readjust preload.*

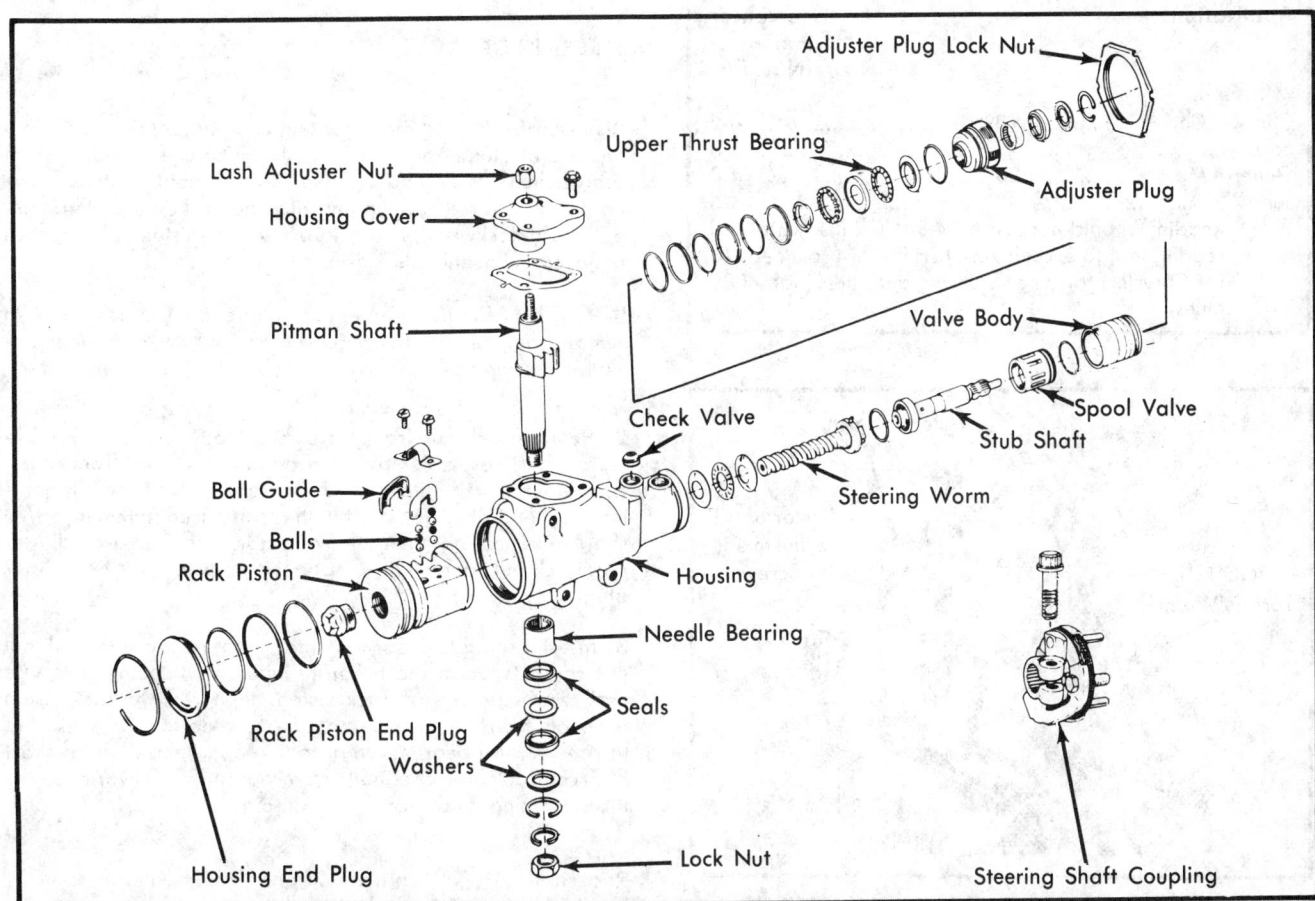

Fig. 1   Exploded View of Saginaw Rotary Valve Power Steering Gear

SAGINAW ROTARY VALVE (Cont.)

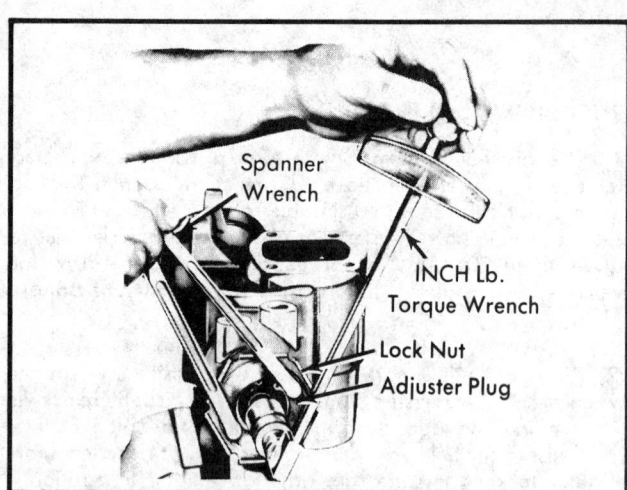

Fig. 2   Measuring Thrust Bearing Preload

OVERCENTER PRELOAD TORQUE

Loosen adjuster screw locknut. Back off adjuster screw until stopped, then turn in 1 full turn. Rotate input shaft from stop to stop counting the number of turns. Turn shaft ½ way back, to center position. Attach an INCH lb. torque wrench to input shaft. Refer to *Overcenter Preload Specifications* and turn shaft from side to side the specified amount of arc on each side of center noting torque reading going overcenter. See *Fig. 3*.

Overcenter Preload Specifications		
Application	**Arc**	**Overcenter Preload① INCH lbs.**
Chrysler Corp.	90°	4-5
Ford	45°	4-6
General Motors	20°	4-8
Jeep	45°	4-5

① — Reading should not exceed 4-8 INCH lbs. with total reading not to exceed 20 INCH lbs. (14 for Jeep, 18 for Chrysler) for a new steering gear (less than 4000 miles).

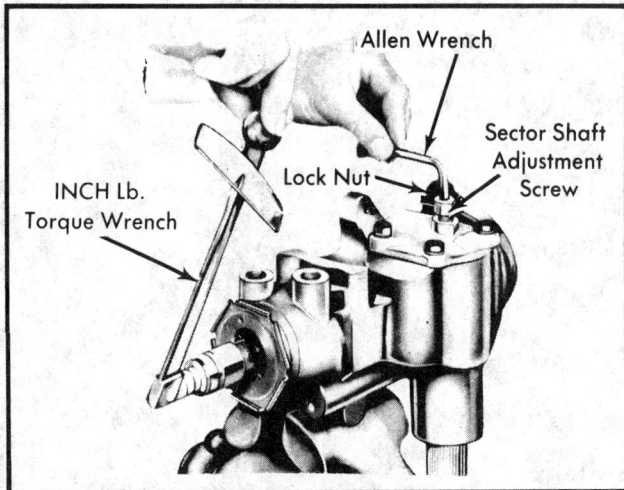

Fig. 3   Measuring Overcenter Preload and Making Adjustment

REMOVAL & INSTALLATION

NOTE — *To avoid damage to collapsible steering column, it is recommended column be completely removed from vehicle before steering gear is removed.*

STEERING GEAR

Removal — Raise and support vehicle, then place a drain pan under steering gear assembly. Center steering gear and tie steering wheel in this position. Disconnect hydraulic hoses from gear and cap ends to prevent fluid loss. Disconnect steering linkage from pitman arm (if necessary) and remove arm from gear. Remove flexible coupling clamp bolt and bolts retaining steering gear to frame, disconnect gear from flexible coupling, and remove gear from vehicle. On Jeep "CJ" and Scrambler models, remove steering gear and mounting bracket as an assembly.

Installation — To install, reverse removal procedures, noting the following. On Ford models, attach flex coupling before placing gear in vehicle.

OVERHAUL

NOTE — *If complete assembly is not to be overhauled, remove subassembly to be serviced, and then proceed with disassembly and reassembly of that unit.*

STEERING GEAR

Disassembly — 1) Rotate housing end plug retainer ring until one end of plug is over hole in housing. Force end of ring from groove in housing and remove. Rotate input shaft counterclockwise to force housing end plug out of housing. Rotate input shaft clockwise ½ turn to draw rack-piston inward, then remove piston and plug from rack-piston.

CAUTION — *Do not rotate shaft more than is necessary to remove plug as ball bearings will fall out of worm and rack piston assembly.*

2) Remove lock nut from sector shaft adjuster, then remove sector shaft cover. Remove and discard "O" ring from cover. Turn input shaft until sector shaft teeth are centered in housing. Tap end of sector shaft with a soft-faced hammer to free shaft from housing, then remove sector shaft. Remove adjuster plug lock nut, and using a spanner wrench, remove adjuster plug.

3) Insert a suitable arbor tool into end of rack-piston until tool just contacts worm shaft. Rotate input shaft counterclockwise until worm is free of rack-piston, then remove rack-piston assembly from housing taking care to keep tool fully inserted to prevent ball bearings from falling out. Remove input shaft and control valve assembly from housing. Lift worm, lower thrust bearing, and races from housing.

Reassembly — 1) Lubricate all parts with clean power steering fluid before reassembly. Install thrust bearing and races on worm. See *Fig. 4*.

SAGINAW ROTARY VALVE (Cont.)

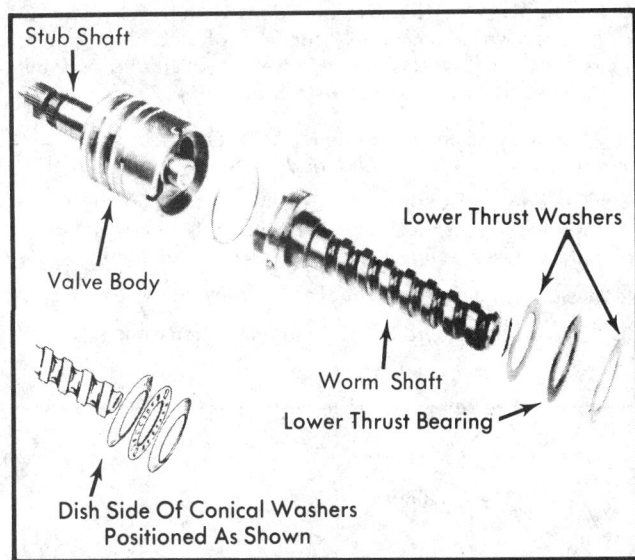

Fig. 4   Reassembly of Valve Body and
Worm Shaft Assembly

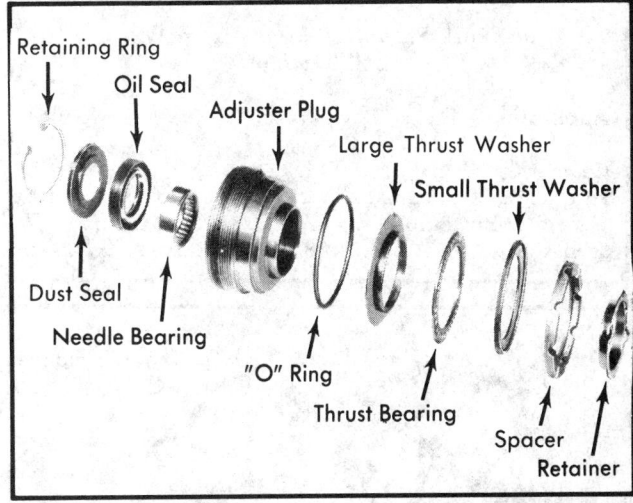

Fig. 5   Disassembled View of Adjuster Plug Assembly

NOTE — *If conical thrust races are used, make sure tapered surfaces are parallel to each other and that cupped sides face toward stub shaft.*

2) Align valve body drive pin on worm with narrow pin slot in valve body, and install "O" ring between valve body and worm head. Install valve body and worm assembly into housing, making sure return hole in gear is fully visible.

3) Position a suitable seal protector over input shaft, install a new adjuster plug "O" ring, then install adjuster plug. Remove seal protector from housing and loosely install adjuster plug lock nut. Adjust thrust bearing preload at this time.

4) Insert arbor tool into rack-piston and place assembly into housing. Force rack-piston into housing until arbor tool contacts worm shaft. Turn input shaft clockwise until middle rack groove in rack-piston is aligned with center of sector shaft roller bearing, then remove arbor tool.

5) Install a new sector shaft cover "O" ring, then thread sector shaft cover onto adjuster screw until bottomed. Back off 1½ turns. Install sector shaft so that center gear tooth meshes with center groove in rack-piston, then install cover attaching bolts.

6) Install adjuster lock nut halfway on, then install piston and plug in rack-piston. Install housing end plug "O" ring, end plug and retainer ring. Adjust overcenter position at this time.

ADJUSTER PLUG

Disassembly — Remove thrust bearing retainer ring with a screwdriver, taking care not to score needle bearing bore. Discard retainer ring. Remove thrust bearing spacer, thrust bearing and bearing races. Remove and discard adjuster plug "O" ring, then remove input shaft seal retainer. Remove and discard dust seal, then pry input shaft seal from adjuster plug. Inspect needle bearing in adjuster plug, and if necessary, remove by pressing out from spacer end. *See Fig. 5.*

Inspection — Inspect thrust bearing for cracks and rollers for pitting, scoring, or cracking. Check thrust races and spacer for damage. Replace parts as necessary.

Reassembly — **1)** Press roller bearing into adjuster plug, identification end facing tool, until bearing bottoms on input shaft seal bore. Install input shaft seal with spring in seal facing adjuster plug.

2) Install dust seal with lip facing upward into adjuster plug, then install retainer ring. Install adjuster plug "O" ring. Assemble thrust bearing, thrust bearing race, and thrust bearing spacer on adjuster plug. Using a brass or wooden dowel, press bearing retainer into needle bearing bore.

RACK-PISTON & WORM

Disassembly — Remove piston ring and back-up "O" ring from rack-piston nut. Remove ball return guide clamp, ball return guide, arbor tool, and all ball bearings from rack-piston.

Inspection — Clean and dry all parts. Inspect worm and rack-piston grooves for scoring. Inspect ball bearings for damage. Check ball guides for pinching of ends. Inspect lower thrust bearing races for cracking, scoring, or pitting.

NOTE — *If either worm or rack-piston are damaged, both must be replaced as a matched set. If any ball bearings are damaged, replace entire set.*

Reassembly — **1)** Install "O" ring and piston ring onto the rack-piston, using care not to twist them. Install worm into rack-piston until worm is against piston shoulder. Install ball bearings into rack-piston while slowly rotating worm counterclockwise.

NOTE — *See following table for number of balls to be installed. BE SURE to install light and dark colored balls alternately, as the black balls are .0005" smaller than the silver balls.*

2) Install correct number of balls in ball guide while alternating colors. Hold balls in place with chassis lubricant and install return ball guide assembly into position. Install clamp and tighten attaching bolts. *See Fig. 6.*

SAGINAW ROTARY VALVE (Cont.)

Rack Piston & Worm Assembly Ball Bearings		
Application	**Rack-Piston**	**Guide**
Chrysler Corp.	19	 5
Ford	16	 6
General Motors	17	 7
Jeep	18	 6

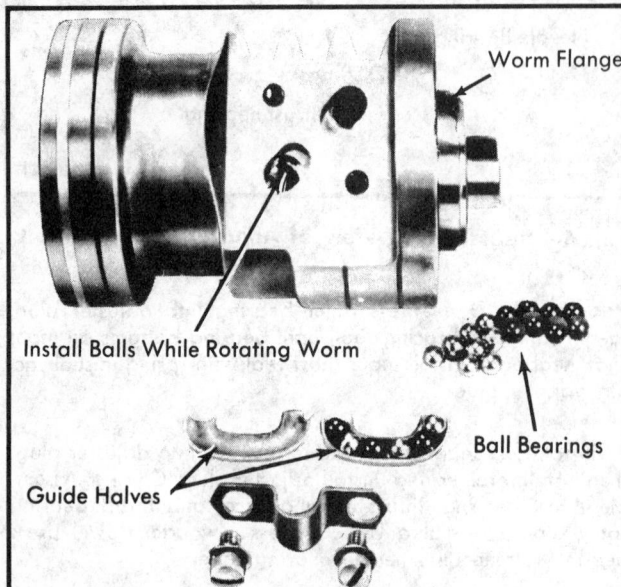

Fig. 6   Installing Ball Bearing into Rack-Piston Assembly

ROTARY VALVE

NOTE — *Complete valve assembly is hydraulically balanced during the manufacturing process. If replacement of any part other than rings or seals is necessary, replace complete valve assembly.*

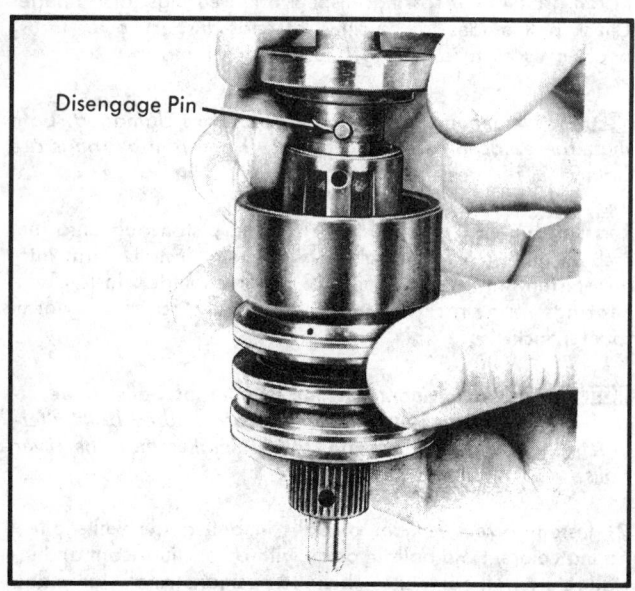

Fig. 7   Pulling Shaft from Valve Assembly

Disassembly — **1)** Remove and discard stub shaft cap "O" ring. Invert valve and lightly tap end of stub shaft against work bench until shaft is free of valve body. Pull stub shaft outward until drive pin hole is visible. *See Fig. 7.*

NOTE — *Do not pull shaft any further than ¼" or spool valve may become cocked in valve body.*

2) Disengage drive pin and carefully remove stub shaft from valve body and spool assembly with a twisting motion. If binding occurs, realign valve and try removal again.

CAUTION — *Do not force spool out of valve body. See Fig. 8.*

3) Remove and discard all "O" ring and Teflon rings.

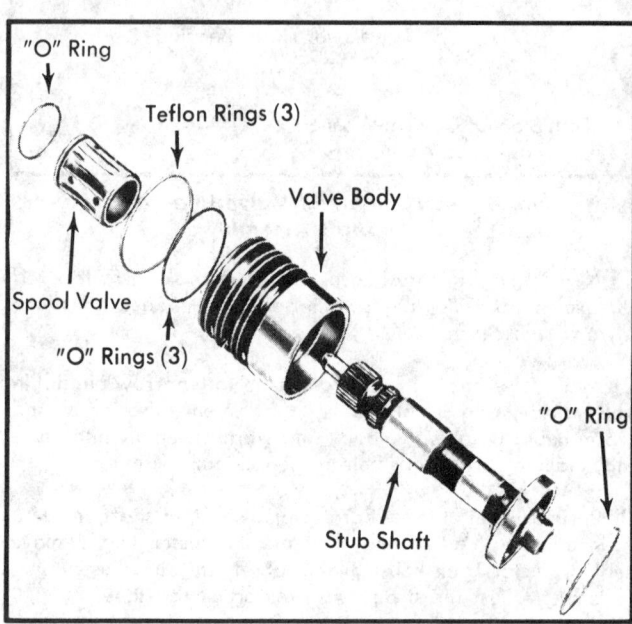

Fig. 8   Disassembled View of Valve Body and Input (Stub) Shaft Assembly

Reassembly — **1)** Lubricate all valve body components with power steering fluid. Install replacement backup "O" rings in seal grooves and install replacement seal rings over backup rings. Take care not to damage seal rings during installation.

NOTE — *Teflon seal rings may appear to be distorted after installation. However, heat of operation will straighten them.*

2) Lubricate replacement spool valve damper "O" ring with petroleum jelly and install on spool valve. Carefully insert spool valve into valve body. Push valve through valve body until locating pin hole is visible at opposite end of valve body and spool valve is flush with notched end of valve.

3) Install stub shaft in spool valve and valve body. Be sure stub shaft locating pin is aligned with spool valve locating hole. Align notch in stub shaft cap with stub shaft locating pin and press stub shaft and spool valve into valve body. Install stub shaft cap "O" ring into valve body. *See Fig. 9.*

CAUTION — *Before installing assembled valve body into gear housing, be sure valve body stub shaft locating pin is fully engaged in stub shaft cap notch. Do not allow stub shaft to disengage from valve body pin.*

SAGINAW ROTARY VALVE (Cont.)

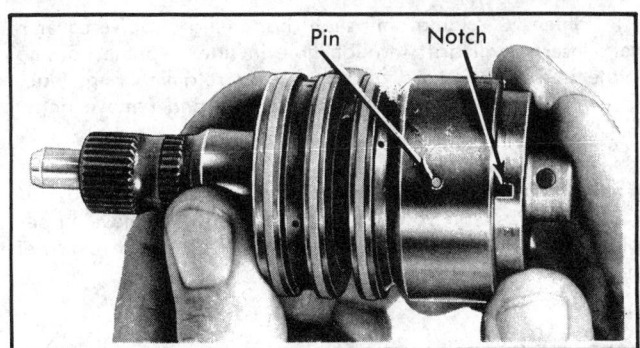

Fig. 9 Aligning Pin and Notch for Input (Stub) Shaft

STEERING GEAR HOUSING

Disassembly — Remove sector shaft seal retaining ring and remove lower spacer washer. Remove lower seal, spacer washer and upper seal from housing. Press sector shaft bearing out of housing from lower end. To remove port seat, tap out seat using a ⅝-18 thread tap, then install a bolt with a flat washer and nut into the seat. Hold bolt from turning and tighten nut to extract seat from housing. Remove check valve and spring from inlet port. See Fig. 10.

Reassembly — Working from upper end, press a new bearing into housing until it is seated .030" below edge of bore. Lubricate new seal with power steering fluid and install single lipped seal, spacer washer, double lipped seal, and second spacer washer. Install sector shaft seal retaining ring.

If port seat was removed, position spring, check valve, and a new seat over opening in housing and drive into place using a brass drift.

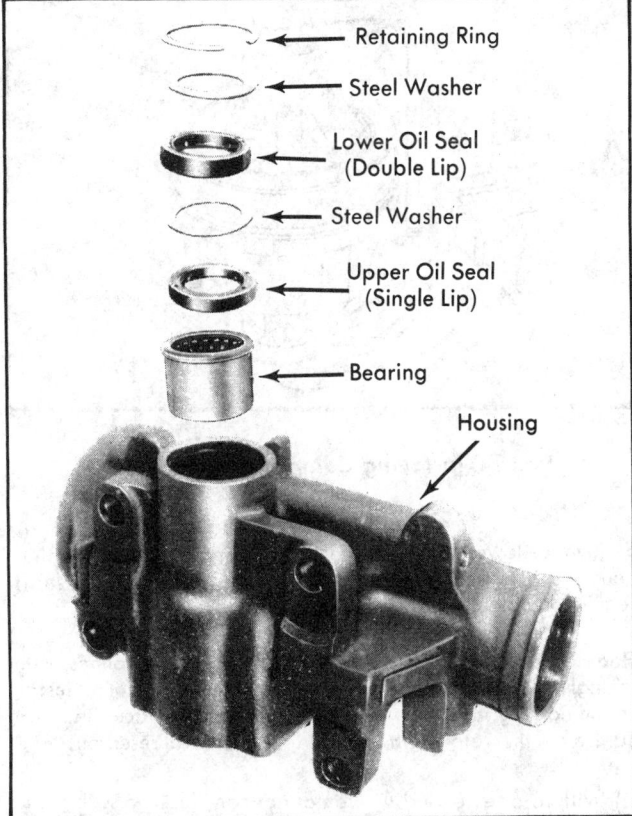

Fig. 10 Gear Housing Seals and Bearing

TIGHTENING SPECIFICATIONS	
Application	**Ft. Lbs.**
Adjuster Plug Lock Nut	
Chrysler Corp.	85
Ford	55-110
General Motors	80
Sector Shaft Adjuster Lock Nut	
Chrysler Corp.	28
Ford	27-37
General Motors	20
Jeep	33
Pitman Arm Attaching Nut	
Chrysler Corp.	175
Ford	170-230
General Motors	180
Jeep	185
Rack Piston End Plug	
Chrysler Corp.	50
Ford	80-140
General Motors & Jeep	75
Gear-to-Frame Attaching Bolts	
Chrysler Corp.	100
Ford	70
General Motors	80
Jeep	
"CJ" & Scrambler Models	55
Cherokee, Wagoneer & Truck Models	70

Power Steering Pumps

FORD C-11

**Bronco
"F" Models**

DESCRIPTION

C-11 power steering pump is a belt driven, slipper type integral pump with a fiber glass nylon reservoir. Reservoir is attached to rear side of pump housing front plate. Pump body is encased within housing and reservoir. Hoses are attached with quick disconnect fittings, located below filler neck at outboard side of reservoir. A pressure sensitive identification tag is attached to reservoir, indicating basic model number.

LUBRICATION, TROUBLE SHOOTING & TESTING

See *Power Steering General Servicing* in this section.

REMOVAL & INSTALLATION

Removal — Disconnect fluid return hose at reservoir and drain fluid. Remove pressure hose from pump. Remove bolts from pump adjustment bracket and loosen pump enough to remove drive belt. Remove pump and adjustment bracket from support bracket. Remove pulley from pump with appropriate pulley puller and remove adjustment bracket attaching bolts. Remove pump.

Installation — Install adjustment bracket on pump and tighten bolts. Install pulley on pump with appropriate pulley installer. Place pump with adjustment bracket and pulley on support bracket. Install and tighten adjustment bracket-to-support bracket bolts. Install and adjust belt on pulley, then tighten adjustment bracket bolts. Install hoses to pump, fill reservoir and start engine, turning wheel from side to side to remove air from system.

OVERHAUL

Disassembly — 1) Remove pulley from pump. Remove outlet fitting, flow control valve, spring and reservoir. Place a "C" clamp in vise. See *Fig. 2*.

2) Install lower support plate tool (T78P-3733-A1) over pump rotor shaft. See *Fig. 1*. Install upper compressor plate tool (T78P-3733-A2) into upper portion of "C" clamp. Holding the upper tool, place the pump assembly into "C" clamp with rotor shaft facing down. See *Fig. 2*.

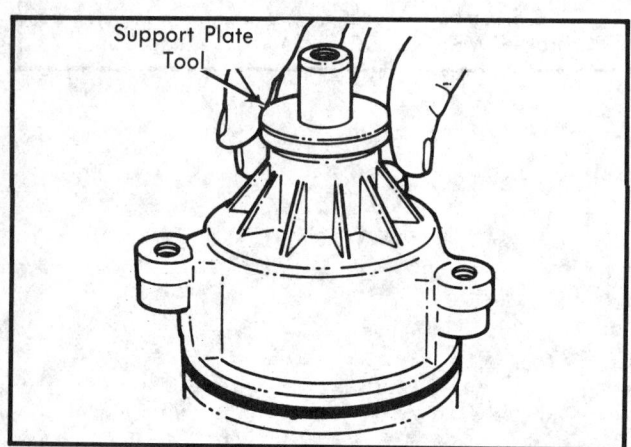

Fig. 1   Installing Lower Support Plate Tool

3) Tighten "C" clamp until slight bottoming of valve cover is felt. Insert small drift through hole in side of pump housing plate and push inward on valve cover retaining ring. Place screwdriver under edge of retaining ring and remove ring.

4) Remove pump from clamp. Remove valve cover and "O" ring seal. Push on rotor shaft and remove. Remove upper plate, rotor and slippers. Remove cam insert and two dowel pins.

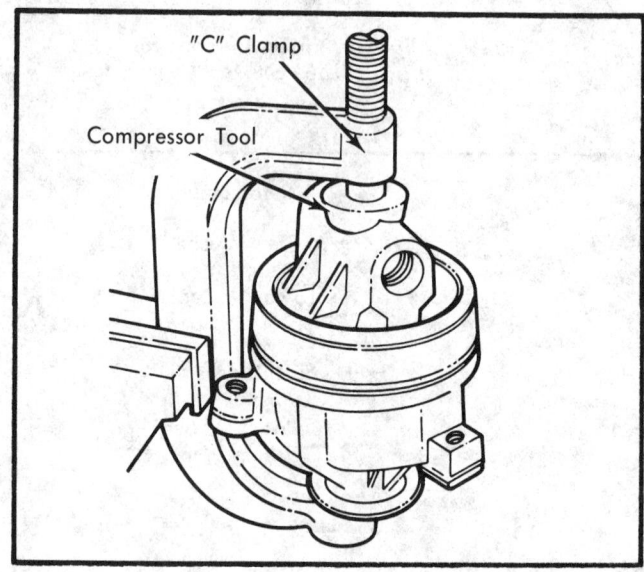

Fig. 2   Installing Compressor Plate Tool

5) Remove lower plate and belleville spring by lightly tapping housing on flat surface, remove "O" ring. Remove rotor shaft seal and seal retainer with a screwdriver.

Reassembly — 1) Place the rotor on rotor shaft splines, with triangle detent in rotor counterbore facing upward. Install retaining ring in groove in end of rotor shaft. Place the insert cam over the rotor with recessed flat toward reservoir.

2) With rotor extended ½ way out of cam, insert a spring into a rotor spring pocket. Work in the rotor cavity directly below recessed flat on the cam. Use one of the slippers to compress the spring and install slipper with groove facing upward.

3) Hold cam stationary and turn rotor either direction one space at a time and install another spring and slipper until all 10 rotor cavities have been filled. Be careful when turning rotor that springs and slippers do not fall out.

4) Install a new rotor shaft seal using seal driver tool (T78P-3733-A3) or equivalent. Using a plastic mallet, drive the seal into the bore until bottomed. Install seal retainer in a similar manner. Place pump housing plate on a flat surface, with pulley side down.

5) Insert 2 dowel pins and Belleville spring into the housing plate. Lubricate the inner and outer "O" ring seals with power steering fluid and install seals on lower pressure plate. Insert

FORD C-11 (Cont.)

pressure plate with seals toward the front of pump into pump housing plate and over dowel pins.

NOTE — *Belleville spring must be installed with dished surface upward.*

6) Place entire assembly into "C" clamp. Use driver tool (T78P-3733-A3) in rotor shaft hole and press lower plate lightly until bottomed in pump plate housing. This will seat "O" ring. Install cam, rotor and slippers, and rotor shaft assembly into pump housing plate over dowel pins.

NOTE — *When installing this assembly, stepped holes must be used for dowel pins, and recessed notch in cam insert must face reservoir and be approximately 180° opposite square pump mounting boss.*

7) Place upper pressure plate over dowel pins. Side of plate with square recessed notch must face toward reservoir and be positioned 180° opposite square pump mounting boss. Place a new "O" ring seal on valve cover and lubricate with power steering fluid.

8) Insert valve cover over dowel pins. Be sure outlet fitting hole in valve cover is directly in line with square mounting boss of pump housing plate. Place the entire assembly in "C" clamp

tool and compress valve cover into pump housing plate, until retaining ring groove is exposed in pump housing plate.

NOTE — *Be sure plastic baffle is securely in place in valve cover. If not, apply petroleum jelly to baffle and install.*

9) Install valve cover retaining ring with ends near access hole in pump housing plate. Remove pump assembly from "C" clamp. Place a new "O" ring seal on pump housing plate. Lubricate seal with power steering fluid. Install power steering reservoir.

10) Install flow control spring and flow control valve in valve cover. Place new "O" ring seals on outlet fitting and lubricate with power steering fluid. Install outlet fitting into valve cover and tighten. Install pulley.

TIGHTENING SPECIFICATIONS

Application	Ft. Lbs.
Pump-to-Adjusting Bracket	30-45
Pressure Hose-to-Rear Fitting	14-29
Return Hose-to-Gear Fitting	17-32
Return Line-to-Frame	11-16
Pump Outlet to Pump Valve Cover	25-34
Adjustment Bracket to Support Bracket	30-45

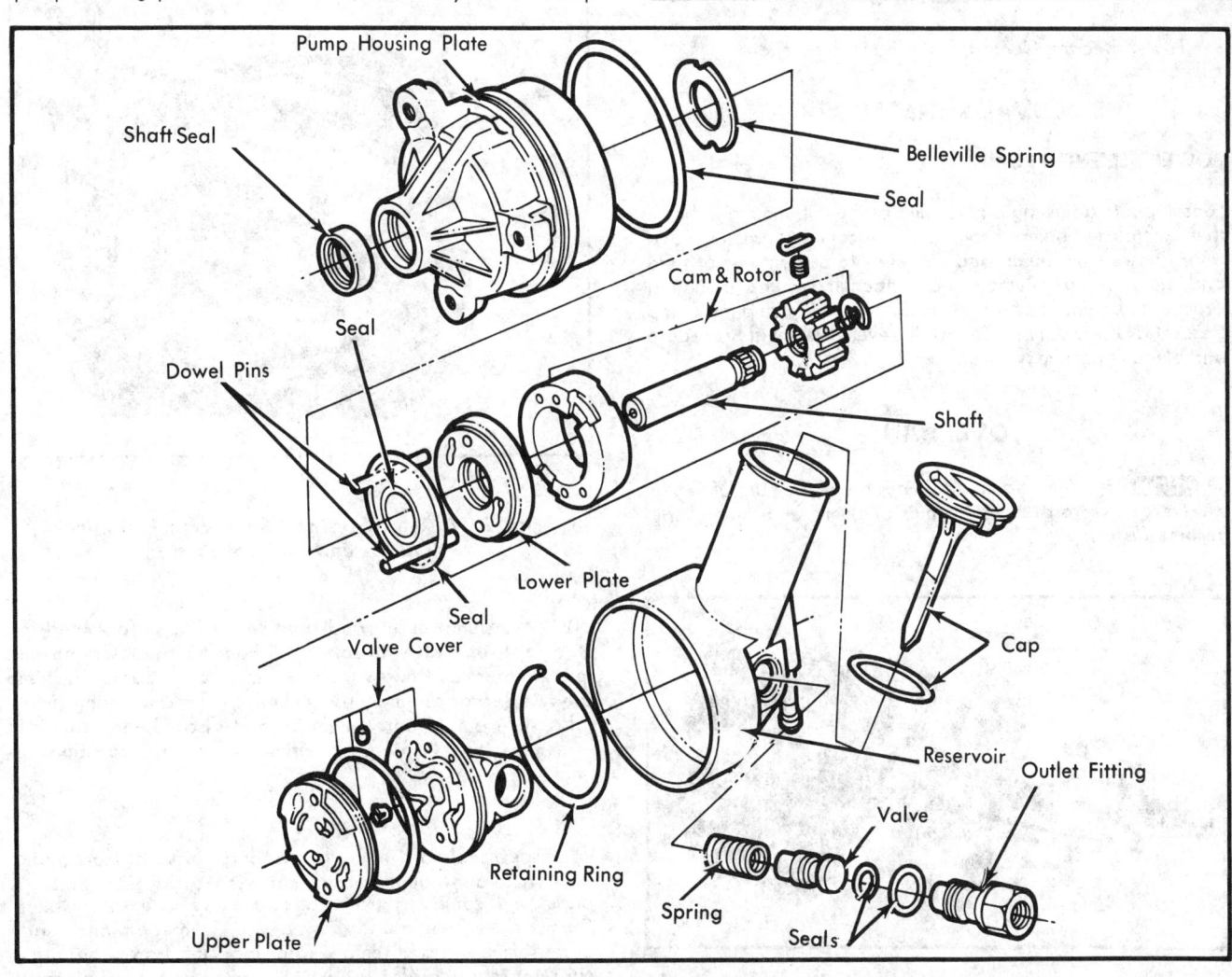

Fig. 3 Disassembled View of C-11 Power Steering Pump

Power Steering Pumps

SAGINAW VANE TYPE

Chrysler Corp.
Ford ("E" Models Only)
General Motors
Jeep

DESCRIPTION

The Saginaw vane type power steering pump can be identified by the "ham can" shape of the fluid reservoir. Internally, rectangular pumping vanes carried by a shaft driven rotor move fluid from intake to pressure cavities of cam ring. As rotor begins to rotate, centrifugal force throws vanes against inside surface of cam ring to pick up residual oil, which is then forced into high pressure area. As more oil is picked up by the vanes, oil is forced into the cavities of the thrust plate and through two cross-over holes in the cam ring and pressure plate (which empty into high pressure area between pressure plate and housing end plate). Filling high pressure area causes oil to flow under vanes in slots of rotor, forcing vanes to follow inside oval surface of cam ring. As vanes rotate to small area of cam ring, oil is forced out from between vanes.

LUBRICATION, TROUBLE SHOOTING & TESTING

See Power Steering General Servicing in this section.

REMOVAL & INSTALLATION

POWER STEERING PUMP

Loosen pump adjusting bolt (or nut) and pump mounting bolts, then withdraw pump drive belt. Disconnect pressure and return hoses from pump and cap ends to prevent loss of fluid and entry of dirt. Remove bolts attaching pump mounting bracket to engine, and withdraw pump, pulley, and mounting bracket as an assembly. To install, reverse removal procedure and bleed hydraulic system.

OVERHAUL

CAUTION — *When clamping pump in vise, be careful not to exert excessive force on front hub of pump as bushing may become distorted.*

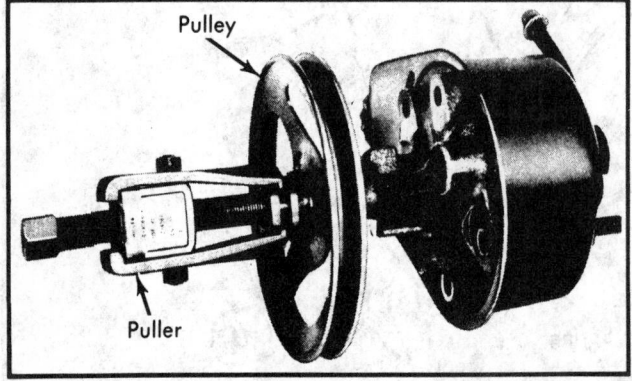

Fig. 1   Using Puller to Remove Pump Pulley

Disassembly — 1) Using a suitable puller, withdraw pulley from shaft. Do not use a hammer to remove pulley. Drain pump reservoir, clean exterior of unit and remove mounting bracket(s). Clamp pump (with shaft pointing downward) in a soft jawed vise, making sure vise grips pump at square boss and shaft housing. Remove pressure line union and "O" ring seal. Remove reservoir retaining studs, then tap against filler tube to loosen reservoir on pump body. Remove reservoir from body, then withdraw and discard "O" ring seals.

2) Using a 1/8" diameter punch, tap end plate retaining ring around until one end of ring is near hole in pump body. Insert punch in hole far enough to disengage ring from groove in pump bore, then use a screwdriver and pry ring out of body. Tap end plate with a soft faced hammer to break it loose; the spring located under the end plate should push plate up. Remove spring. Remove pump from vise.

Fig. 2   Disengaging and Removing Retaining Ring for End Plate of Pump

3) Place pump in inverted position on flat surface, and tap end of drive shaft with soft-faced hammer to loosen pressure plate, rotor, and thrust plate assembly from body. Lift pump body off rotor assembly (flow control valve and spring should also slide out of bore). Remove and discard end plate and pressure plate "O" rings. Pry drive shaft oil seal from body using a screwdriver.

4) Inspect seal bore in housing for burrs, nicks, or score marks that would allow oil to by-pass outer seal surface. Lift pressure plate and cam ring from rotor, then remove rotor vanes. Clamp drive shaft in soft-jawed vise, with rotor and thrust plate facing up, and remove rotor lock ring from shaft, using care not to nick shaft or rotor. Slide rotor and thrust plate off shaft, and remove shaft from vise.

SAGINAW VANE TYPE (Cont.)

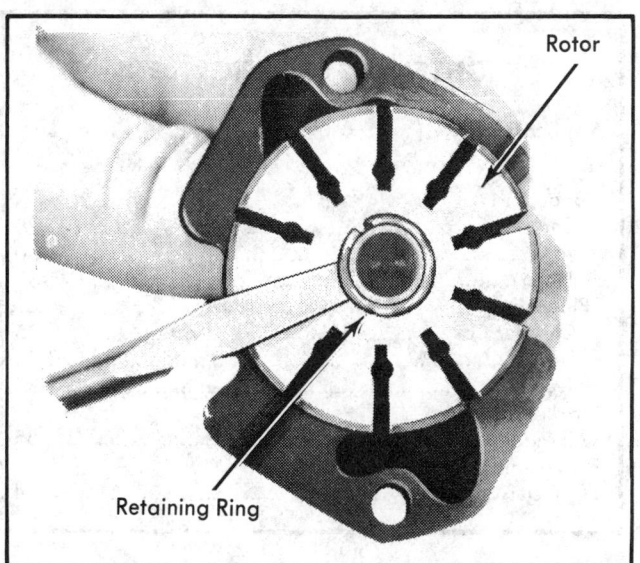

Fig. 3   Removing Pump Rotor Retaining Ring

Cleaning & Inspection — 1) Clean all pump components (except drive shaft seal) in a suitable solvent and blow dry. Inspect flow control valve assembly for wear, scoring, burrs or other damage. Check all machined surfaces of body for scratches or burrs which might allow leaks. Mating surfaces on "O" rings require special attention.

NOTE — *Cam ring is treated with "Lubrite" which leaves a dull gray-black finish on wear surface. Wavy grain appearance inside cam ring is normal.*

2) Inspect pump body drive shaft bushing for excessive wear. If replacement is required, replace pump body and bushing as an assembly. Inspect end cover for nicks and burrs on surface for "O" ring, then polish with a small oil stone if necessary.

3) Inspect rotor ring for roughness or irregularities. Use a small oil stone to correct minor irregularities and replace ring if outside cam surface is badly worn or scored. Check thrust plate and pressure plate for scoring and wear. To remove light scoring, carefully lap using crocus cloth until surface is smooth and flat, then clean thoroughly.

4) Check fit of vanes in rotor to ensure that they slide freely but fit snugly into slots. Use an oil stone to remove burrs or irregularities from vanes. If vanes are excessively loose in slots, the rotor requires replacement. Scoring on rotor may be removed by careful laping using crocus cloth, and then cleaning thoroughly.

Reassembly — 1) Lubricate all "O" rings and seal areas with power steering fluid. On Jeep models, use petroleum jelly to lubricate "O" rings. Place pump body on a flat surface. Drive a new shaft seal in until it bottoms on shoulder in bore. Lubricate seal with power steering fluid, then clamp body in vise with shaft pointing downward. Install end plate and pressure plate "O" rings in groove on body. Install body to reservoir "O" rings and install on pump body.

2) With drive shaft clamped, splined end up, in a soft-jawed vise, install thrust plate on shaft with smooth, ported side up. Slide rotor over splines with counter bore of rotor facing down. Install rotor lock ring making sure it is seated in groove. Install two dowel pins in holes in pump cavity. Carefully insert drive shaft, rotor, and thrust plate assembly in pump cavity, indexing location holes with dowel pins.

NOTE — *Always use new full diameter locking ring.*

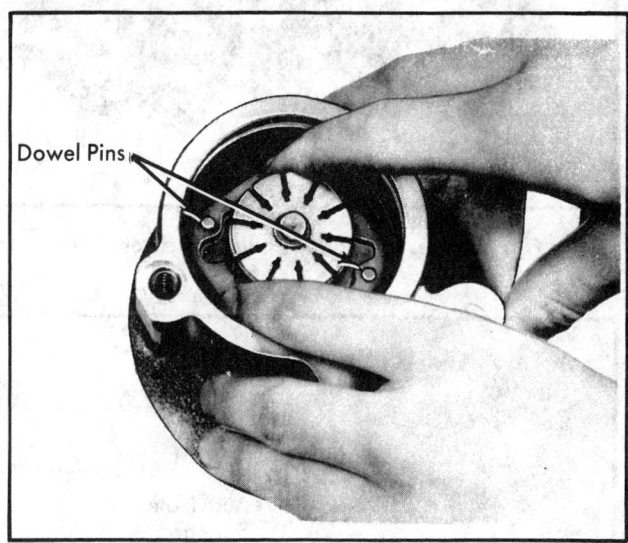

Fig. 4   Installing Drive Shaft Assembly and Aligning Location Holes with Dowel Pins

3) Slide cam ring over rotor and onto dowel pins, with arrow on ring facing up. Install vanes in rotor slots with radius edge facing out towards cam ring inner surface. Position pressure plate on dowel pins. Place a 1¼" socket in groove of pressure plate, and seat entire assembly on "O" ring in pump cavity by pressing down on socket with both thumbs.

4) Place spring in groove in pressure plate and position end cover lip edge up over spring. Press end cover down below retaining ring groove with thumb, and install retaining ring, making sure ring is seated in groove. Care should be taken to prevent cocking end cover in bore or distorting assembly.

5) Using a punch, tap retaining ring ends around in groove until opening is opposite flow control valve bore. This is necessary for maximum retention of retaining ring. Install new reservoir "O" ring, mounting stud "O" rings, and flow control valve "O" ring on pump body, then carefully position reservoir on pump body. Align mounting stud holes until studs can be started in threads.

6) Using a soft-faced hammer, tap reservoir down on pump and install flow control valve spring and valve assembly slotted end up. Install new "O" ring seal on pressure hose fitting, making sure it is installed on the upper groove. Install pressure hose fitting and tighten mounting studs. Tighten hose fitting and rear mounting studs. Remove pump assembly from vise and install mounting bracket and drive pulley.

CAUTION — *Do not hammer pulley on shaft.*

SAGINAW VANE TYPE (Cont.)

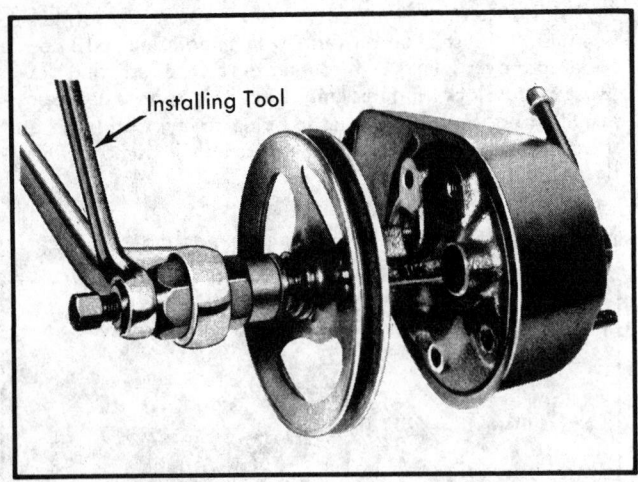

Fig. 5   Pressing Pump Pulley into Position

TIGHTENING SPECIFICATIONS

Application	Ft. Lbs.
Hose Fittings	
Gear End	
Chrysler Corp.	25
Ford	20-30
Jeep	25-35
Pump End	
Chrysler Corp.	35
Ford	20-35
Jeep	25-35
Bracket Bolts	
All Models	35
Flow Control Valve Plug	
Chrysler Corp.	4

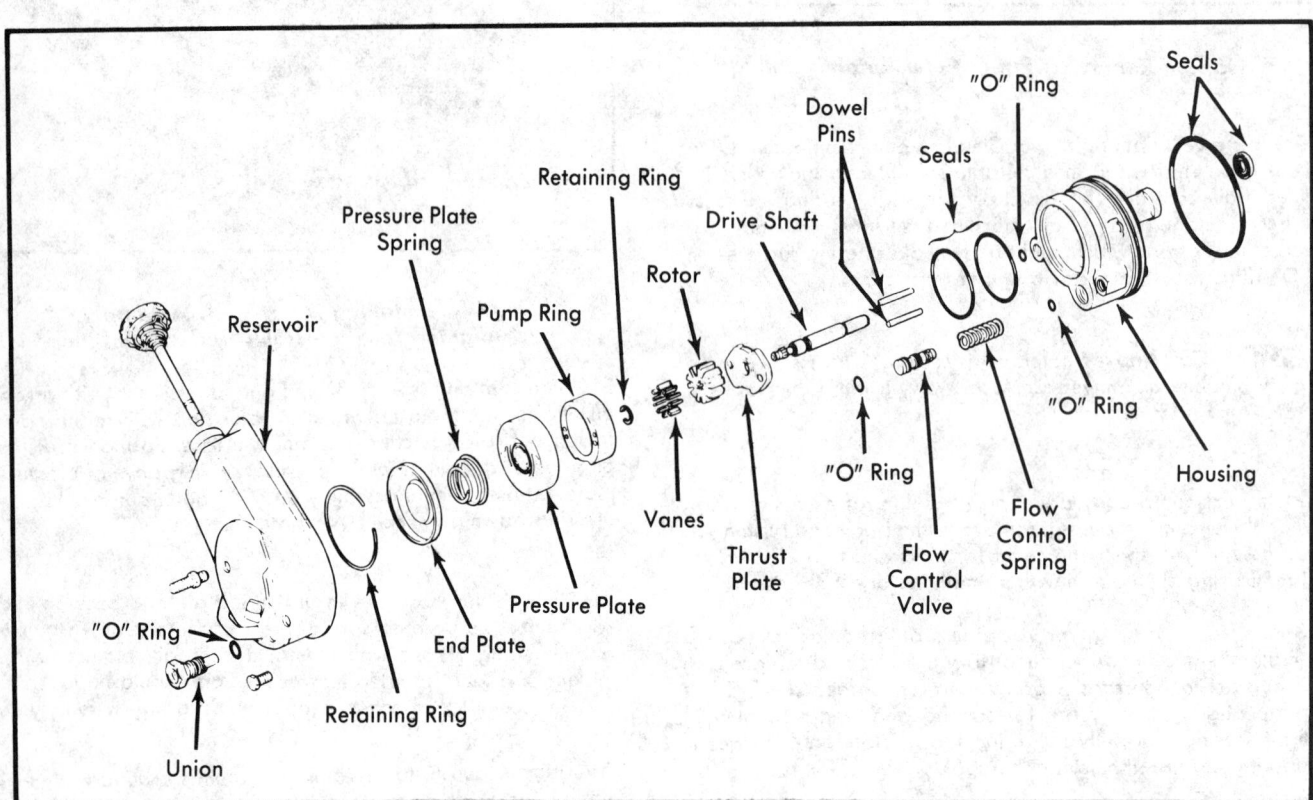

Fig. 6   Exploded View of Power Steering Pump

Contents

Section 14

AUTOMATIC TRANSMISSIONS

NOTE — ALSO SEE GENERAL INDEX.

IMPORTANT

Because of the great number of model names used by vehicle manufacturers, accurate identification of models is important. See Model Identification at the front of this publication.

CHRYSLER CORP. & JEEP TROUBLE SHOOTING

Every diagnosis of automatic transmission problems should begin with a check of the transmission fluid and linkage. Most of the following conditions can be caused by one or more of the following factors:

- *Incorrect fluid level.*
- *Contaminated fluid.*
- *Improperly adjusted linkage.*
- *Damaged or worn linkage.*

CONDITION & POSSIBLE CAUSE	CONDITION & POSSIBLE CAUSE
Harsh Engagement From Neutral to "D" or "R" • Engine idle speed too high. • Valve body malfunction or leakage. • Hydraulic pressures too high. • Worn or faulty rear clutch. • Faulty lock-up clutch. **Delayed Engagement From Neutral to "D" or "R"** • Hydraulic pressures too low. • Valve body malfunction or leakage. • Low-Reverse band or linkage malfunction. • Oil filter clogged. • Faulty oil pump. • Worn or broken input shaft seal rings. • Engine idle speed too low. • Worn or faulty front or rear clutch. • Worn or broken reaction shaft support seal rings. • Worn or faulty front and/or rear clutch. **Runaway Upshifts** • Hydraulic pressures too low. • Valve body malfunction or leakage. • Oil filter clogged. • Worn or broken reaction shaft support seal rings. • Kickdown servo, band or linkage malfunction. • Worn or faulty front clutch. **No Upshifts** • Hydraulic pressures too low. • Valve body malfunction or leakage. • Governor support seal rings worn or broken. • Worn or broken reaction shaft support seal rings. • Governor malfunction. • Kickdown servo, band or linkage malfunction. • Worn or faulty front clutch.	**3-2 Kickdown Runaway** • Hydraulic pressures too low. • Valve body malfunction or leakage. • Kickdown band out of adjustment. • Reaction shaft support seal rings worn or broken. • Kickdown servo, band or linkage malfunction. • Worn or faulty front clutch. **No Kickdown or Normal Downshift** • Valve body malfunction or leakage. • Governor malfunction. • Kickdown servo, band or linkage malfunction. **Erratic Shifts** • Hydraulic pressures too low. • Valve body malfunction or leakage. • Oil filter clogged. • Faulty oil pump. • Worn or broken reaction shaft support seal rings. • Worn or broken governor support seal rings. • Governor malfunction. • Kickdown servo, band or linkage malfunction. • Worn or faulty front clutch. **Slips in Forward Drive Positions** • Hydraulic pressures too low. • Valve body malfunction or leakage. • Oil filter clogged. • Faulty oil pump. • Worn or broken input shaft seal rings. • Overrunning clutch not holding. • Worn or faulty rear clutch. • Overrunning clutch seized or broken.

CHRYSLER CORP. & JEEP TROUBLE SHOOTING (Cont.)

CONDITION & POSSIBLE CAUSE	CONDITION & POSSIBLE CAUSE

Slips in Reverse Only

- Hydraulic pressures too low.
- Low-Reverse band out of adjustment.
- Valve body malfunction or leakage.
- Low-Reverse servo, band or linkage malfunction.
- Faulty oil pump.
- Reaction shaft support seal rings worn or broken.
- Worn or faulty front clutch.

Slips in All Positions

- Hydraulic pressures too low.
- Valve body malfunction or leakage.
- Clogged oil filter.
- Faulty oil pump.
- Input shaft seal rings worn or broken.

No Drive in Any Position

- Hydraulic pressures too low.
- Valve body malfunction or leakage.
- Clogged oil filter.
- Faulty oil pump.
- Planetary gear set broken or seized.

No Drive in Forward Drive Positions

- Hydraulic pressures too low.
- Valve body malfunction or leakage.
- Input shaft seal rings worn or broken.
- Overrunning clutch not holding.
- Worn or faulty rear clutch.
- Planetary gear set worn or broken.
- Overrunning clutch worn, broken or seized.

No Drive in Reverse

- Hydraulic pressures too low.
- Low-Reverse band out of adjustment.
- Valve body malfunction or leakage.
- Low-Reverse servo, band or linkage malfunction.
- Reaction shaft support seal rings worn or broken.
- Worn or faulty front clutch.
- Worn or faulty rear clutch.
- Planetary gear set broken or seized.

Drives in Neutral

- Valve body malfunction or leakage.
- Insufficient clutch plate clearance.
- Worn or faulty rear clutch.
- Rear clutch dragging.

Drags or Locks Up

- Stuck lock-up valve.
- Low-Reverse band out of adjustment.
- Kickdown band too tight.
- Planetary gear set broken or seized.
- Overrunning clutch broken, worn or seized.
- Faulty oil pump.

Hard to Fill, Oil Blows Out Filler Tube

- Clogged oil filter.
- High fluid level.
- Transmission case vent plugged.

Transmission Overheats

- Stuck switch valve.
- Engine idle speed too high.
- Hydraulic pressures too low.
- Faulty oil pump.
- Kickdown band too tight.
- Faulty oil cooler.
- Insufficient clutch plate clearance.

Harsh Upshifts

- Faulty lock-up clutch.
- Incorrect hydraulic pressures.
- Kickdown band out of adjustment.
- Hydraulic pressure too high.

Delayed Upshifts

- Kickdown band out of adjustment.
- Governor support seal rings worn or broken.
- Reaction shaft support seal rings worn or broken.
- Governor malfunction.
- Kickdown servo, band or linkage malfunction.
- Worn or faulty front clutch.

TRANSMISSION NOISY

Grating, Scraping or Growling Noise

- Low-Reverse band out of adjustment.
- Kickdown band out of adjustment.
- Output shaft bearing and/or bushing worn.
- Planetary gear set broken or seized.
- Overrunning clutch broken, worn or seized.

Buzzing Noise

- Faulty oil pump.
- Valve body malfunction or leakage.
- Overrunning clutch inner race damaged.

Automatic Transmissions

FORD TROUBLE SHOOTING

Every diagnosis of automatic transmission problems should begin with a check of the transmission fluid and linkage. Most of the following conditions can be caused by one or more of the following factors:

- *Incorrect fluid level.*
- *Contaminated fluid.*
- *Improperly adjusted linkage.*
- *Worn or damaged linkage.*

CONDITION & POSSIBLE CAUSE	CONDITION & POSSIBLE CAUSE
Slow Initial Engagement • Improper clutch or band application. • Incorrect hydraulic pressures. **Rough Initial Engagement in Either Forward or Reverse** • Engine idle speed too high. • Internal leakage. • Looseness in propeller shaft, "U" joints or engine mounts. • Improper clutch or band application. • Incorrect hydraulic pressures. • Sticking or dirty valve body. • Damaged 2-3 accumulator. **No Drive in Any Gear** • Improper clutch or band application. • Internal leakage. • Valve body loose. • Damaged or worn clutches. • Sticking or dirty valve body. **No Drive Forward (Reverse OK)** • Improper clutch or band application. • Incorrect hydraulic pressures. • Damaged or worn forward clutch. • Damaged or worn governor. • Valve body loose. • Dirty or sticking valve body. • Damaged 2-3 accumulator. **No Drive, Slips or Chatters in Reverse (Forward OK)** • Looseness in propeller shaft, "U" joints or engine mounts. • Reverse band out of adjustment. (C4) • Damaged or worn reverse clutch. (C6) • Incorrect hydraulic pressures. • Damaged or worn reverse clutch or servo. • Valve body loose. • Sticking or dirty valve body.	**No Drive, Slips or Chatters in First Gear in "D" (All Other Gears OK)** • Damaged or worn one-way clutch. **No Drive, Slips or Chatters in Second Gear** • Intermediate band out of adjustment. • Improper clutch or band application. • Incorrect hydraulic pressures. • Damaged or worn servo and/or linkage. • Dirty or sticking valve body. • Polished or glazed band or drum. • Intermediate friction clutch or one way clutch (AOT). **Starts in High in "D", Drag or Lock Up at 1-2 Shift Point or in "2" or "1"** • Damaged or worn governor. • Damaged or worn clutches and/or internal leaks. • Valve body loose. • Dirty or sticking valve body. • Poor mating of valve body-to-case mating surfaces. **Starts Up in 2nd or 3rd** • Improper clutch or band application. • Incorrect hydraulic pressures. • Damaged or worn governor. • Loose valve body. • Dirty or sticking valve body. • Cross leaks between valve body and case mating surface. **Incorrect Shift Points** • Improper vacuum hose routing or leaks (except AOT). • Improper operation of EGR system (except AOT). • Improper speedometer gear installation. • Improper clutch or band application. • Incorrect hydraulic pressures. • Damaged or worn governor. • Dirty or sticking valve body.

FORD TROUBLE SHOOTING (Cont.)

CONDITION & POSSIBLE CAUSE	CONDITION & POSSIBLE CAUSE

No Upshift at Any Speed in "D"

- Vacuum leak to diaphragm assembly.
- Improper clutch or band application.
- Incorrect hydraulic pressures.
- Damaged or worn governor.
- Dirty or sticking valve body.
- Throttle linkage (AOT.)

Shifts 1-3 in "D"

- Intermediate band out of adjustment.
- Damaged intermediate servo and/or internal leakage (except AOT).
- Polished or glazed intermediate band or drum (except AOT).
- Improper clutch or band application.
- Incorrect hydraulic pressures.
- Dirty or sticking valve body.
- Intermediate friction and/or one way clutch (AOT only).

Engine Overspeeds on 2-3 Shift

- Improper clutch or band application.
- Incorrect hydraulic pressures.
- Damaged or worn high clutch.
- Damaged or worn intermediate servo.
- Dirty or sticking valve body.
- Throttle linkage (AOT only).

Mushy 1-2 Shift

- Improper engine performance.
- Intermediate band out of adjustment (except AOT).
- Improper clutch or band application.
- Incorrect hydraulic pressures.
- Worn or damaged high clutch.
- Worn or damaged intermediate servo or band (except AOT).
- Polished or glazed band or drum (except AOT).
- Dirty or sticking valve body.

No Forced Downshift

- Improper clutch or band application.
- Incorrect hydraulic pressures.
- Damaged internal kickdown linkage.
- Dirty or sticking valve body or governor.

Rough 1-2 Shift

- Incorrect engine idle speed or performance.
- Intermediate band out of adjustment (except AOT).
- Improper clutch or band application.
- Incorrect hydraulic pressures.
- Worn or damaged intermediate servo (except AOT).
- Dirty or sticking valve body.

Rough 2-3 Shift

- Incorrect engine performance.
- Improper clutch or band application.
- Incorrect hydraulic pressures.
- Damaged or worn intermediate servo release and high clutch piston check ball (except AOT).
- Dirty or sticking valve body.
- Damaged 2-3 accumulator.

Rough 3-1 Shift at Closed Throttle in "D"

- Incorrect engine idle speed or performance.
- Improper clutch or band application.
- Incorrect hydraulic pressures.
- Improper governor operation.
- Dirty or sticking valve body.

No 3-1 Shift in "D"

- Incorrect engine idle speed or performance.
- Damaged governor.
- Dirty or sticking valve body.

Runaway Engine on 3-2 Downshift

- Intermediate band out of adjustment.
- Improper clutch or band application.
- Incorrect hydraulic pressures.
- Damaged or worn intermediate servo or seals.
- Polished or glazed band or drum.
- Dirty or sticking valve body.

No Engine Braking in Manual First Gear (Except AOT).

- Reverse band out of adjustment. (C4)
- Low-Reverse clutch out of adjustment. (C6)
- Incorrect hydraulic pressures.
- Damaged or worn reverse servo.
- Polished or glazed band or drum.

No Engine Braking in Manual Second Gear

- Intermediate band out of adjustment.
- Improper clutch or band application.
- Incorrect hydraulic pressures.
- Intermediate servo leaking.
- Polished or glazed band or drum.

Automatic Transmissions

FORD TROUBLE SHOOTING (Cont.)

CONDITION & POSSIBLE CAUSE	CONDITION & POSSIBLE CAUSE
TRANSMISSION NOISY **Valve Resonance** • Improper clutch or band application. • Incorrect hydraulic pressures. • Cooler line grounding. • Dirty or sticking valve body. • Internal leakage. • Oil pump cavitation.	**Other Than Valve Resonance** • Faulty torque converter. • Faulty oil pump. • Faulty speedometer driven gear. • Worn or damaged extension housing bushing or seal. • Faulty propeller shaft. • Faulty planetary gear set. • Faulty one-way clutch.

GENERAL MOTORS THM 350 TROUBLE SHOOTING

Every diagnosis of automatic transmissions problems should begin with a check of the transmission fluid level and linkage. Most of the following conditions can be caused by one or more of the following factors:

- *Incorrect fluid level.*
- *Contaminated fluid.*
- *Improperly adjusted linkage.*
- *Worn or damaged linkage.*

CONDITION & POSSIBLE CAUSE	CONDITION & POSSIBLE CAUSE
No Drive in Drive Range • Low hydraulic pressures. • Manual valve disconnect from linkage. • Forward clutch malfunction. • Damaged roller clutch. **1-2 Shift at Full Throttle Only** • Detent valve sticking or out of adjustment. • Vacuum line or fitting leaking. • Valve body gasket damaged. • Detent valve train stuck. • 1-2 shift valve stuck. • Case porosity. **First Speed Only (No 1-2 Shift)** • Governor malfunction. • 1-2 shift valve train stuck closed. • Valve body governor feed channels blocked. • Valve body gaskets damaged. • Case porosity. • Intermediate clutch malfunction.	**Slips in All Ranges** • Vacuum modulator valve sticking. • Oil filter plugged or leaking. • Pressure regulator valve stuck. • Pump-to-case gasket damaged. • Forward clutch slipping due to cross leaks or porosity. **Slipping 1-2 Shift** • Vacuum modulator malfunction. • Modulator valve sticking. • Oil pump pressure regulator valve faulty. • 2-3 accumulator oil ring damaged. • 1-2 accumulator oil ring or bore damaged. • Pump-to-case gasket mispositioned. • Case porosity between channels. • Intermediate clutch porosity. **Rough 1-2 Shift** • Vacuum modulator fittings loose or line plugged. • Modulator valve stuck. • Valve body regulator or boost valve stuck. • Pump-to-case gasket damaged. • Case porosity between channels. • 1-2 accumulator malfunction.

GENERAL MOTORS THM 350 TROUBLE SHOOTING (Cont.)

CONDITION & POSSIBLE CAUSE	CONDITION & POSSIBLE CAUSE
Drives in Neutral • Manual linkage out of adjustment. • Forward clutch not releasing. • Internal linkage: manual valve disconnected or broken. **No Drive, or Slips in Reverse** • Incorrect hydraulic pressures. • Valve body gaskets leaking. • 2-3 valve train stuck in upshift position. • 1-2 valve train stuck in upshift position. • Intermediate servo piston or pin stuck. • Low-Reverse clutch malfunction. • Direct clutch malfunction. • Forward clutch not releasing. **No Engine Braking in "L1"** • Manual low control valve stuck. • Pressure regulator and/or boost valve stuck. • Low-Reverse clutch malfunction. **No Part Throttle Downshift** • Incorrect hydraulic pressures. • Detent valve or linkage worn or damaged. • 2-3 shift valve stuck. **No Detent Downshift** • 2-3 shift valve stuck. • Detent valve or linkage worn or damaged. **Incorrect Shift Points** • Faulty vacuum modulator. • Governor malfunction. • Detent valve or linkage stuck. • 2-3 valve train sticking. • 1-2 shift valve train sticking. • Case porosity. **Will Not Hold in Park** • Manual linkage out of adjustment. • Worn or damaged internal linkage.	**Slipping 2-3 Shift** • Low hydraulic pressures. • Case porosity. • Direct clutch malfunction. **Rough 2-3 Shift** • High hydraulic pressures. • 2-3 accumulator malfunction. **No Engine Braking in "L2"** • Intermediate servo malfunction. • 2-3 accumulator malfunction. • Intermediate band broken or burned. • Pressure regulator and/or boost valve stuck. **Locks Up in Manual Low** **(Usually Hot Only)** • Direct clutch malfunction. • Converter pressure leaking into direct clutch thru stator shaft. **Second Gear Start or** **Slips in Second Gear Only** • Intermediate clutch — Wrong number or clutch plates installed or wrong piston installed. **Locks Up in Reverse** **(Usually Hot Only)** • Wrong forward clutch piston or drum installed. • Direct clutch feeding forward clutch thru stator shaft (check stator shaft index). **Locks in Reverse from** **Park to Reverse Only** • Parking pawl staying in due to a burr on leading edge. **Cold Morning Reverse No** **Drive Until Engine Warms Up** • Pressure regulator bore or sleeve too tight. **Shifts Cold But Not Warm** • Governor nylon gear pin too short. **No Drive But Has Manual Low** • Low-Reverse roller clutch installed backwards.

GENERAL MOTORS THM 400 TROUBLE SHOOTING

Every diagnosis of automatic transmission problems should begin with a check of the transmission fluid and linkage. Most of the following conditions can be caused by one or more of the following factors:

- *Incorrect fluid level.*
- *Contaminated fluid.*
- *Improperly adjusted linkage.*
- *Worn or damaged linkage.*

DIESEL ENGINE NOTE — On Chevrolet and GMC models with a diesel engine, the vacuum source for the vacuum modulator is the Vacuum Regulator Valve. This valve is mounted on the high pressure fuel Pump. When diagnosing shift complaints on these vehicles, it is important to assure that the vacuum pump is providing 22 inches of vacuum to this valve.

CONDITION & POSSIBLE CAUSE	CONDITION & POSSIBLE CAUSE
No Drive in Drive Range • Manual linkage out of adjustment. • Low hydraulic pressures. • Manual valve disconnected from lever. • Forward clutch malfunction. • Damaged roller clutch. **1-2 Shift at Full Throttle Only** • Detent switch sticking. • Detent solenoid loose, gasket leaking or valve stuck open. • Spacer plate gaskets damaged. • Detent valve train sticking. • 3-2 valve sticking. • Case porosity. **First Speed Only** **(No 1-2 Shift)** • Governor valve or shaft damaged. • 1-2 shift valve train stuck closed. • Governor feed channels plugged or leaking. • Spacer plate gaskets damaged. • Intermediate clutch plug leaking or blown out. • Porosity between case channels. • Intermediate clutch malfunction. **Drives in Neutral** • Manual linkage out of adjustment. • Forward clutch not releasing.	**Slips in All Ranges** • Faulty vacuum modulator. • Oil filter plugged or leaking. • Pump regulator or boost valve stuck. • Pump-to-case gasket leaking. • Forward or direct clutch malfunction. **Slipping 1-2 Shift** • Faulty vacuum modulator. • Modulator valve sticking. • Pump pressure regulator valve faulty. • Front accumulator oil seal ring leaking. • 1-2 accumulator valve train sticking. • Valve body or case porosity. • Rear accumulator seal ring or bore damaged. • Pump-to-case gasket leaking. • Intermediate clutch plug leaking. • Intermediate clutch malfunction. **Rough 1-2 Shift** • Vacuum modulator faulty. • Pump regulator or boost valve stuck. • Modulator valve stuck. • Pump-to-case gasket leaking. • 1-2 accumulator valve train sticking. • Valve body bolts loose. • Spacer plate-to-case gasket damaged. • Intermediate clutch ball missing or damaged. • Case porosity. • Faulty rear accumulator. • Extra waved steel plate installed in intermediate clutch.

GENERAL MOTORS THM 400 TROUBLE SHOOTING (Cont.)

CONDITION & POSSIBLE CAUSE	CONDITION & POSSIBLE CAUSE

**First & Second Speeds Only
(No 2-3 Shift)**

- Detent solenoid stuck open.
- Detent switch stuck closed.
- 2-3 shift valve stuck.
- Spacer plate gaskets damaged.
- Direct clutch malfunction.

No Reverse, or Slips in Reverse

- Manual linkage out of adjustment.
- Incorrect hydraulic pressures.
- Spacer plate gaskets damaged.
- Low-Reverse check ball missing from case.
- 2-3 valve train stuck open.
- Rear servo piston seal damaged.
- Rear band apply pin too short.
- Direct clutch malfunction.
- Forward clutch not releasing.

No Engine Braking in "L2"

- Front servo or accumulator oil rings or bore damaged.
- Front servo piston stuck.
- Front band damaged.

No Engine Braking in "L1"

- Low-Reverse check ball missing.
- Rear servo oil seal ring, bore or piston damaged.
- Rear band apply pin too short or improperly installed.
- Rear band damaged.

No Part Throttle Downshift

- Vacuum modulator faulty.
- Modulator valve sticking.
- Pressure regulator valve faulty.
- 3-2 valve stuck, spring missing or broken.

No Detent Downshift

- 3-2 valve stuck, spring missing or broken.
- Detent switch faulty.
- Detent solenoid faulty.
- Detent valve train sticking.

Incorrect Shift Points

- Incorrect hydraulic pressures.
- Governor malfunction.
- Detent solenoid loose or stuck open.
- 3-2 valve train stuck.
- 1-2 shift valve train stuck.
- 1-2 regulator valve stuck.
- Spacer plate-to-case gasket leaking.
- Case porosity.
- Intermediate clutch plug leaking or missing.

Slipping 2-3 Shift

- Faulty vacuum modulator.
- Modulator valve stuck.
- Pump pressure regulator or boost valve stuck.
- Pump-to-case gasket leaking.
- Accumulator piston pin leaking at swedge end.
- Case porosity.
- Direct clutch malfunction.

Rough 2-3 Shift

- Faulty vacuum modulator.
- Modulator valve stuck.
- Pump pressure regulator or boost valve stuck.
- Front accumulator spring damaged or missing.
- Front accumulator piston stuck.
- Extra waved steel plate installed in direct clutch.

Will Not Hold in Park

- Manual linkage out of adjustment.
- Internal parking linkage damaged.
- Parking pawl broken or worn.

TRANSMISSION NOISE

Pump Noise

- Cavitation due to plugged or leaking filter, "O" ring damage, porosity in intake circuit or water in oil.
- Oil pump gears worn, installed backwards, or crescent interference.

**Gear Noise
(1st, 2nd and/or Reverse)**

- Transmission grounded to body.
- Planetary gear set worn or damaged.
- Worn thrust bearings or races.

**Clutch Noise
(During Application)**

- Neutral or Park to Drive — Worn forward clutch plates.
- 1-2 Shift — Intermediate clutch plates worn.
- 2-3 Shift, Neutral or Park to Reverse — Direct clutch plates worn.

Converter Noise

- Damaged needle bearings in converter.

Automatic Transmissions

GENERAL MOTORS CONVERTER CLUTCH TROUBLE SHOOTING

Every diagnosis of automatic transmission or torque converter clutch problems should begin with a check of the transmission fluid and linkage. Road test vehicle to verify complaint. Most of the following conditions can be caused by one or more of the following factors: (1) Incorrect fluid level, (2) Contaminated fluid, (3) Improperly adjusted linkage, or (4) Worn or damaged linkage.

CONDITION & POSSIBLE CAUSE	CONDITION & POSSIBLE CAUSE
Converter Clutch Does Not Apply Or Applies Erratically Or at Wrong Speed During Road Test • Disconnect electrical connector at transmission case. Test female connector for 12 volts (2000 RPM in Neutral). If 12 volts shown, problem is internal; if less than 12 volts, problem is external. **Converter Clutch Applies At a Very Low or High 3rd Speed Gear** • Governor switch malfunction. • Governor switch shorted to ground. • High hydraulic line pressure. • Converter clutch valve sticking or binding. • Solenoid inoperative or shorted to case.	**Converter Clutch Applied in All Ranges. Engine Stalls When Transmission Is Put in Gear** • Converter clutch valve stuck in "Apply" position. **Converter Clutch Applies Erratically With a Shudder, Jerking, Jumping Or Rocking Sensation** • Vacuum hose leak. • Vacuum switch malfunction. • Release oil exhaust orifice at pump blocked or restricted. • Turbine shaft "O" ring damaged. • Converter malfunction. • Clutch pressure plate warped. • "O" ring damaged at solenoid. • Solenoid bolts loose. • Governor pressure switch malfunction.

AUTOMATIC TRANSMISSIONS

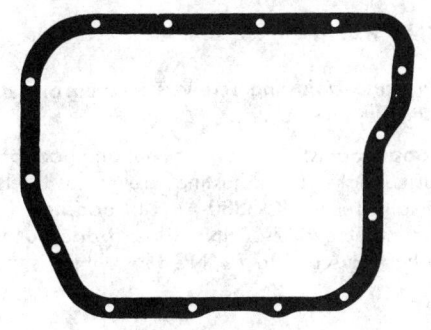

Fig. 1   Chrysler Corp. A727 & A999

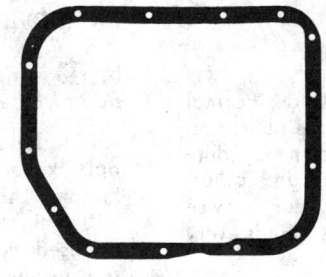

Fig. 2   Chrysler Corp. A904T

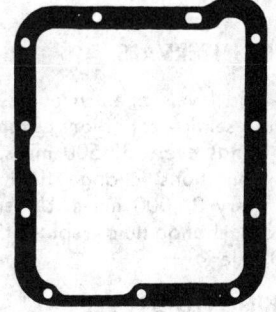

Fig. 3   Ford Motor Co. C-4

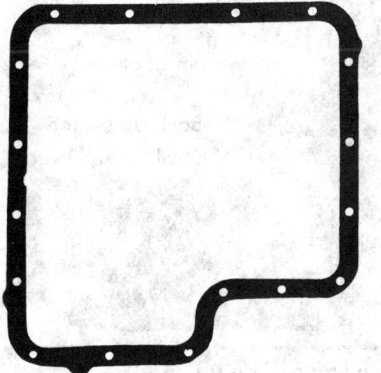

Fig. 4   Ford Motor Co. C-6

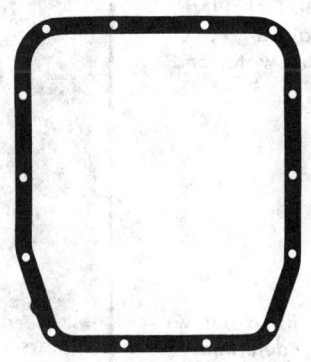

Fig. 5   Ford Motor Co. AOT

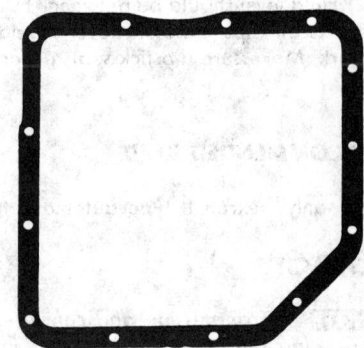

*Fig. 6   General Motors
Turbo Hydra-Matic 350*

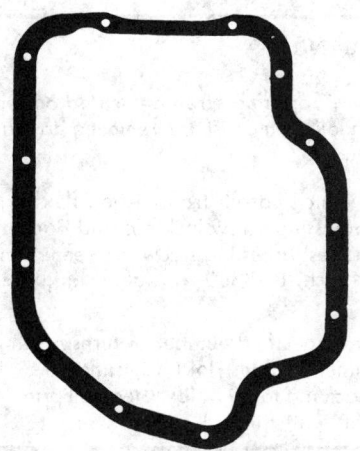

*Fig. 7   General Motors
Turbo Hydra-Matic 400*

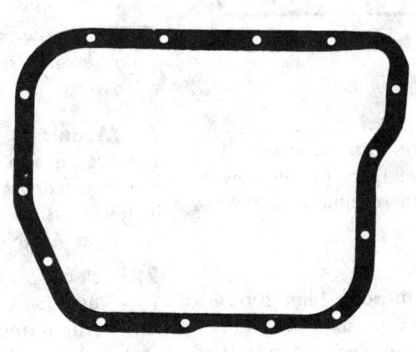

Fig. 8   Jeep 727 & 999

Fig. 9   Jeep 904

CHRYSLER CORP.

LUBRICATION

SERVICE INTERVALS

Check fluid levels at each engine oil change. Under normal light duty service conditions, change fluid, replace filter, and adjust bands every 37,500 miles. Under normal heavy duty service conditions, change fluid, replace filter, and adjust bands every 24,000 miles. Under severe heavy duty service conditions, change fluid, replace filter, and adjust bands every 12,000 miles.

CHECKING FLUID LEVEL

All Models – 1) With vehicle parked on level surface, parking brake applied, engine at curb idle speed and normal operating temperature, move selector lever through all gear ranges, ending in Neutral.

2) Fluid level should be between "FULL" and "ADD ONE PINT" marks on dipstick. Fluid level should never be above "FULL" mark. Make sure dipstick seats properly to seal out water and dirt.

RECOMMENDED FLUID

Use only Dexron II type automatic transmission fluid.

CAPACITY

NOTE – *Transmission and converter capacities listed below are approximate, and correct fluid level should be determined by mark on dipstick, rather than by amount added.*

Transmission Refill Capacities	
Application	**Capacity (Pts.)**
A-727	
Including Converter	
Lock-Up	16.7
Non Lock-Up	17.1
Without Converter	7.7
A-904T/A-999	17.1

DRAINING & REFILLING

All Models – 1) Loosen oil pan bolts, tap pan to break it loose allowing fluid to drain, then remove pan. Install new filter on bottom of valve body and tighten retaining screws. Clean oil pan and install with new gasket.

2) Pour four quarts of transmission fluid through filler tube, start engine, and allow to run at idle for two minutes. Then with engine at curb idle and parking brake applied, move shift selector lever through all ranges, ending in neutral. Add sufficient fluid to bring fluid level to "ADD ONE PINT" mark on dipstick.

CAUTION – *Do not overfill. Reseat dipstick fully to seal out water and dirt. Recheck fluid level when transmission reaches normal operating temperature.*

ADJUSTMENT

KICKDOWN (FRONT) BAND

NOTE – *Kickdown band adjusting screw is located on left side of case near throttle lever shaft.*

All Models – 1) Loosen adjusting screw lock nut and back off approximately 5 turns. Make sure adjusting screw turns freely in case. Using special wrench, (C-3380-A) with adapter (C-3705), tighten adjusting screw 47-50 INCH lbs. If adaptor is not used, tighten adjusting screw to 72 INCH lbs. which is the true torque.

2) Back off adjusting screw specified number of turns given in Kickdown Band Adjustment Table. Hold adjusting screw in this position and tighten lock nut to 35 ft. lbs.

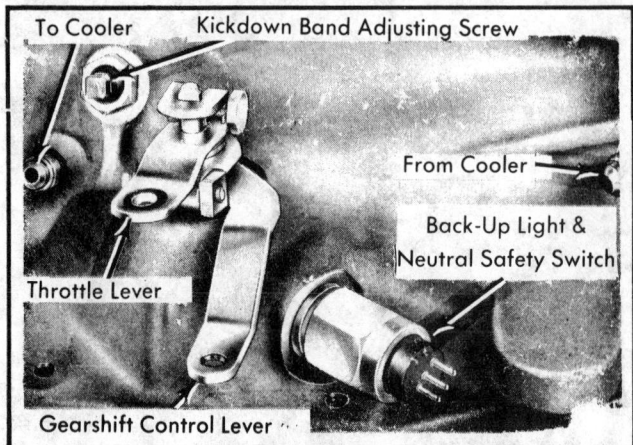

Fig. 1   Adjusting Kickdown Band

Kickdown Band Adjustment Table	
Application	**Back Off Screw**
All Models	2½ Turns

LOW-REVERSE (REAR) BAND

NOTE – *Low-reverse band adjusting screw is located on rear servo lever. Transmission oil pan must be removed to gain access to adjusting screw.*

All Models – 1) Raise vehicle, drain transmission fluid and remove oil pan. Loosen adjusting screw lock nut and back off nut approximately 5 turns. Test adjusting screw for free turning in lever. Using special wrench, (C-3380-A), tighten adjusting screw to 72 INCH lbs.

2) Back off adjusting screw specified number of turns given in Low-Reverse Band Adjustment Table. Hold adjusting screw in this position and tighten lock nut to 30 ft. lbs. Clean oil pan, install new gasket and refill with fluid.

Low-Reverse Band Adjustment Table	
Application	**Back Off Screw**
Models A-904T and A-999	4 Turns
Model A-727	2 Turns

CHRYSLER CORP. (Cont.)

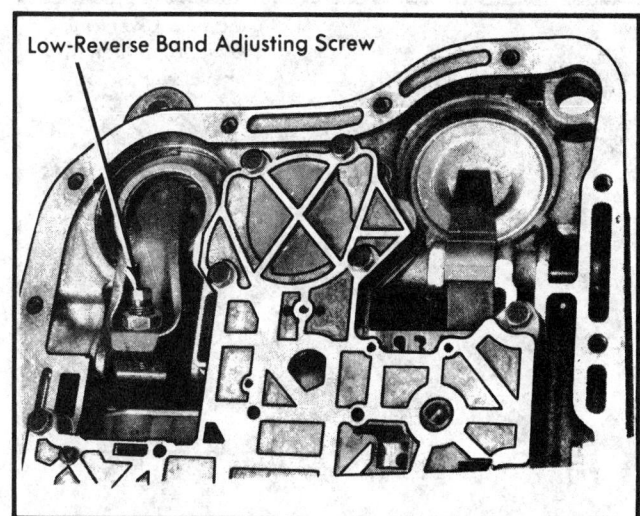

Fig. 2   Adjusting Low-Reverse Band

TRANSMISSION THROTTLE ROD

All Models — 1) With engine at normal operating temperature and carburetor off fast idle cam, adjust idle speed to specifications. Turn off engine and disconnect choke at carburetor or block choke valve in full open position. Open throttle slightly to release fast idle cam and return throttle to curb idle position.

2) Raise vehicle on hoist to make adjustments at transmission throttle lever. Loosen swivel lock screw. Be sure swivel is free to slide along flat end of throttle rod so that preload spring action is not restricted. If necessary, disassemble and clean parts to assure free action.

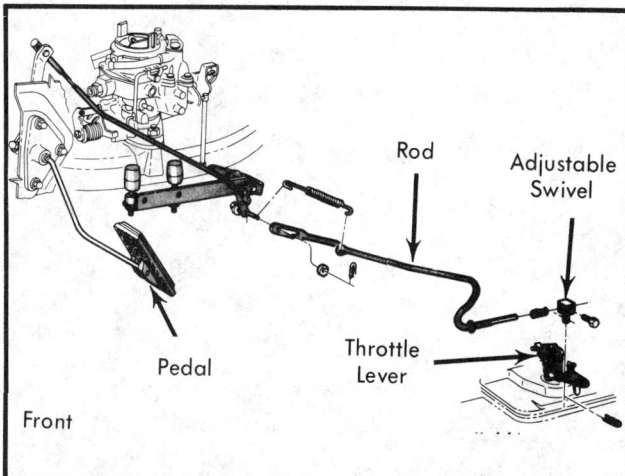

**Fig. 3   Throttle Rod Adjustment Diagram
(3.7L 6-Cyl. Engine)**

3) Hold transmission lever firmly against internal stop and tighten swivel lock screw to 100 INCH lbs. Adjustment is complete and linkage backlash is automatically removed by preload spring.

4) Lower vehicle, reconnect choke and test linkage. Move throttle rod rearward slowly releasing it to confirm it will return fully forward.

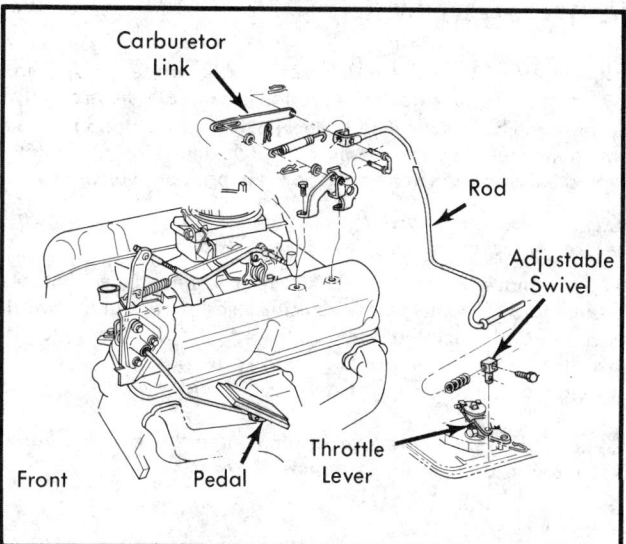

**Fig. 4   Throttle Rod Adjustment Diagram
(5.2L and 5.9L V8 Engines)**

SHIFT LINKAGE

Column Shift Type — Loosen adjustable swivel lock bolt. Place gearshift selector lever in park position and move shift control lever on transmission all the way to the rear to park detent. Set adjustable rod to proper length so no load exists on linkage in either direction, then tighten lock bolt. Check adjustment as follows: Shift effort should be free, detents crisp, and all gate stops positive. Detent position should be close enough to gate stops in neutral and drive so that shift selector lever will not remain out of detent position when placed against gate and released.

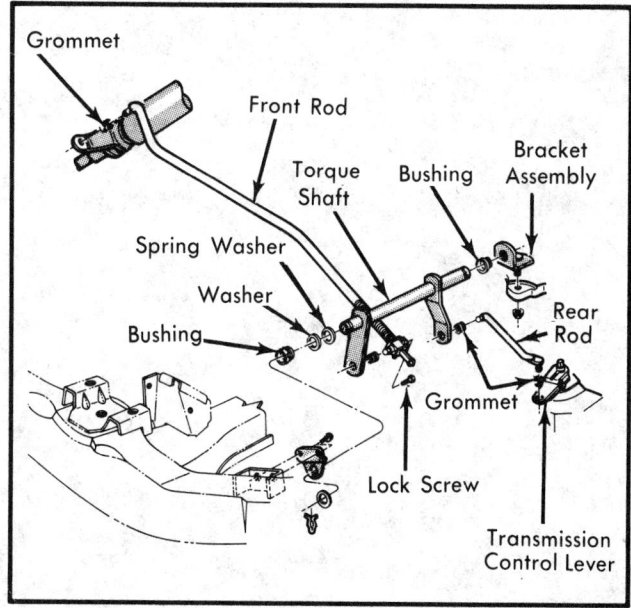

Fig. 5   Column Shift Linkage Adjustment Diagram

CHRYSLER CORP. (Cont.)

NEUTRAL SAFETY SWITCH

All Models — 1) With transmission linkage properly adjusted, switch should allow starter operation in park and neutral only. To test switch, remove wire connector from switch and test for continuity between center pin of switch and case. Continuity should exist only when transmission is in park or neutral.

NOTE — *Be sure gearshift linkage is in proper adjustment before replacing a switch which tests bad.*

2) To replace, remove switch from case and allow fluid to drain into a container. Move selector lever to park and neutral positions and check that switch operating fingers are centered in switch opening. Replace switch with a new seal, retest switch for continuity, and adjust transmission fluid level.

NOTE — *To center switch operation fingers, see Valve Body Assembly in appropriate transmission article.*

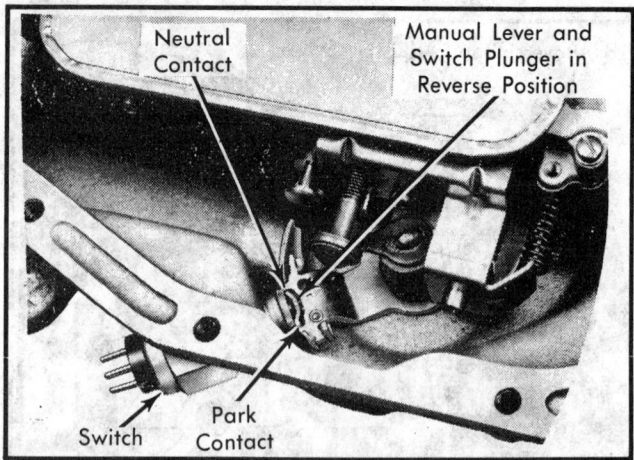

Fig. 6   Back-Up Light and Neutral Safety Switch

FORD

LUBRICATION

SERVICE INTERVALS

All Models — Check fluid level periodically or if leakage is detected. Service intervals for adjusting bands or draining and refilling transmission (severe service or fleet vehicles only) will vary depending upon maintenance schedule code letter.

NOTE — *Vehicles used in normal service do not require scheduled draining and refilling.*

The maintenance schedule code letter is located on the Emission Control Information decal (located on or near engine) or on the Maintenance Schedule Label (located on the rear face of driver's door opening). See the following charts to determine service intervals for maintenance code letters.

NOTE — *If vehicle is used for off-highway operation, check fluid level every 1,000 miles. If vehicle is operated in water, check fluid level daily and drain and refill if necessary.*

Band Adjustment		
Application	**Maintenance Code**	**Service Interval (Miles)**
100 Series W/300"	A or B	10,000 then 20,000 intervals
All Others	A or B	7,500, 22,500 then 22,500 intervals
	E	5,000 then 15,000 intervals
	J or L	6,000 18,000 then 18,000 intervals

Drain & Refill (Severe Service or Fleet Only)		
Application	**Maintenance Code**	**Service Interval (Miles)**
100 Series W/300"	A or B	Every 20,000
All Others	A or B	Every 22,500
	E	20,000 then 15,000 intervals
	J or L	Every 18,000

CHECKING FLUID LEVEL

Transmission At Operating Temperature — With engine at curb idle RPM and parking brake applied, move transmission selector lever through all ranges, ending in "P". Fluid level should check between "ADD" and "FULL" marks on dipstick. If necessary, add fluid through filler tube to raise fluid level to correct position. **CAUTION** — *Do not overfill. Reseat dipstick fully to seal out water and dirt.*

RECOMMENDED FLUID

Use only fluid which has been certified by the supplier as meeting Ford Motor Co. Specifications ESP-M2C138-CJ, Dexron II, Series D or equivalent.

CAPACITY

NOTE — *Transmission and converter assembly capacities listed below are approximate, and correct fluid level should be determined by mark on dipstick rather than amount added.*

Transmission Refill Capacities	
Application	**Capacities (Qts.)**
C-4 Transmission	10.0
C-6 Transmission	
2-WD Models	11.75
4-WD Models	13.5
AOT Transmission	12.0

DRAINING & REFILLING

All Models — 1) On C-4 models, disconnect fluid filler tube from oil pan to drain fluid, then remove pan. On C-6 and AOT models, loosen oil pan bolts and tap pan to break seal loose. Allow fluid to drain, then remove oil pan bolts and oil pan. On all models, clean pan, replace filter, then reinstall. On C-4 model, install filler tube.

2) On all models, add 3 quarts of specified transmission fluid through filler tube. Check fluid level as described. When filling a dry transmission and converter, refer to Transmission Refill Capacity Chart.

3) Recheck fluid level when transmission is at normal operating temperature. Do not overfill.

ADJUSTMENT

INTERMEDIATE (FRONT) BAND

C-4 — Clean all dirt from band adjusting screw area, then remove and discard band adjusting screw lock nut. Install a new lock nut on adjusting screw, then tighten screw to 10 ft. lbs. Back off adjusting screw exactly 1¾ turns, hold screw in this position, and tighten lock nut.

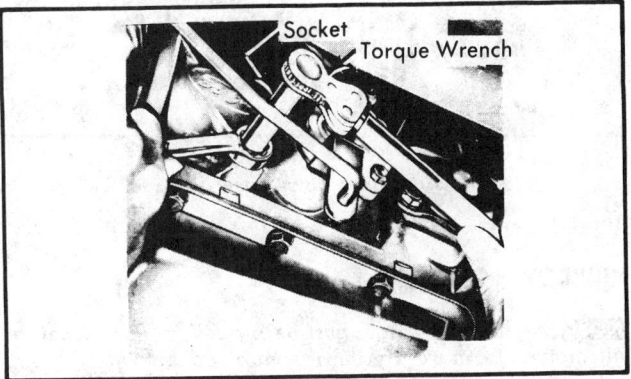

Fig. 1   Adjusting Intermediate Band (C-4)

C-6 — Clean all dirt from band adjusting screw area, then remove and discard band adjusting screw lock nut. Install a

Automatic Transmission Servicing

FORD (Cont.)

new lock nut on adjusting screw, then tighten screw to 10 ft. lbs. Back off adjusting screw exactly 1½ turns, hold screw in this position, and tighten lock nut.

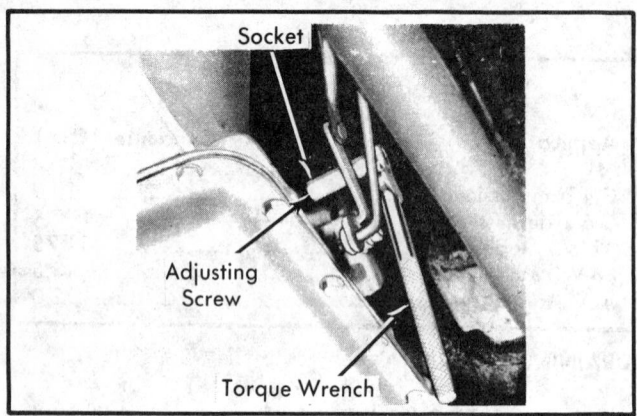

Fig. 2   Adjusting Intermediate Band (C-6)

LOW-REVERSE (REAR) BAND

C-4 — Clean all dirt from band adjusting screw area, then remove and discard band adjusting screw lock nut. Install a new lock nut on adjusting screw, then tighten adjusting screw to 10 ft. lbs. Back off adjusting screw exactly 3 full turns, hold screw in this position, and tighten lock nut.

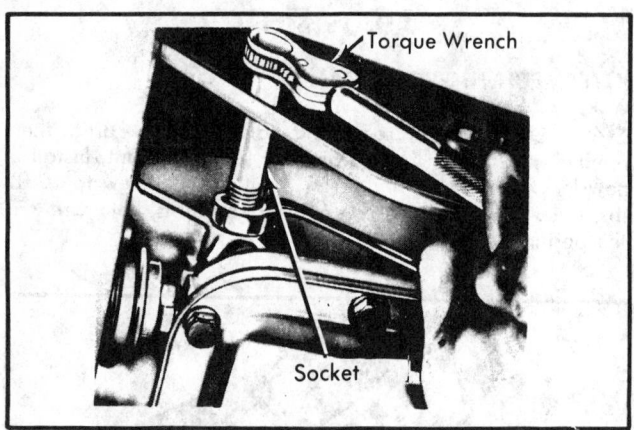

Fig. 3   Adjusting Low-Reverse Band C-4

KICKDOWN CONTROL

NOTE — *Throttle linkage must be properly adjusted before attempting to make kickdown control adjustment.*

All Models (Exc. AOT) — Check for full throttle 1 and full linkage travel at full throttle. When carburetor is at full throttle and throttle linkage is at full throttle stop, there should be a

slight amount of movement left in downshift linkage. Make sure downshift lever return spring is connected and downshift lever returns to closed position.

Automatic Overdrive Transmission (AOT) — 1) Remove air cleaner. Block choke open and release fast idle cam. Connect tachometer and start engine. Check engine idle speed and record reading. Turn engine off.

2) Turn linkage lever adjusting screw to obtain a .005" clearance between end of screw and throttle lever. Start engine and check idle speed again.

3) Compare reading with reading obtained in step **1)**. If idle speed changed by more than 50 RPM, carburetor linkage lever adjustment screw must be reset as described in AOT Idle Speed Adjustment Chart.

NOTE — *If adjustment of linkage lever screw is not possible, then adjustment of the TV control rod at transmission is required.*

AOT Idle Speed Adjustment Chart	
Idle Speed Change	Linkage Lever Adjustment (Turns) ①
Higher	
0-50 RPM	②
50-100 RPM	1½ CC
100-150 RPM	2½ CC
Lower	
0-50 RPM	②
50-100	2½ C
100-150	2½ C
① — CC- Counterclockwise; C- Clockwise.	
② — No change required.	

AOT Throttle Valve (TV) Control Rod — 1) Set engine curb idle speed to specification. Release fast idle cam so that throttle lever is against idle stop.

2) Set shift lever to neutral and apply parking brake. Set linkage lever adjustment screw at it's approximate mid-range.

CAUTION — *Next steps involve working close to exhaust system.*

3) Raise vehicle on hoist. Loosen nut on sliding stud of TV control assembly. Push lower end of control rod to be sure linkage lever at carburetor is against throttle lever. Release force on rod.

4) Push TV control lever on transmission up against internal stop with firm force (approximately 5 Lbs.) and tighten nut on stud.

SHIFT LINKAGE

All Models — 1) Stop engine and apply parking brake. Place selector lever on steering column in "D". Hold against stop by attaching an 8 pound weight to selector lever.

Automatic Transmission Servicing

FORD (Cont.)

2) Loosen nut on slotted shift rod at transmission. Shift manual transmission lever to "D" by moving lever rearward, then forward 2 detents.

3) Tighten nut at slotted lever to 12-18 ft. lbs. Remove weight from selector lever. Operate lever through all positions making sure transmission is in full detent in all positions.

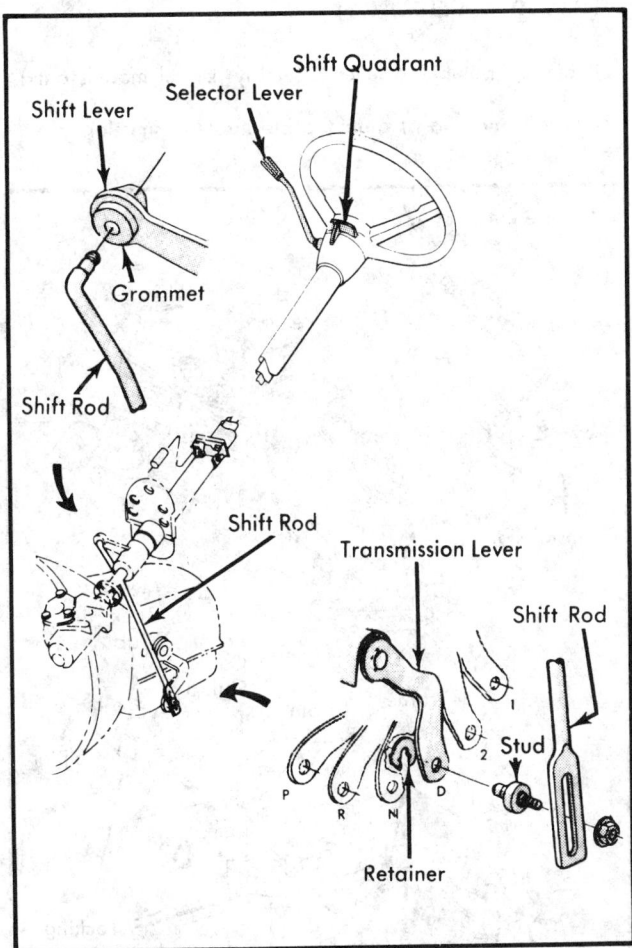

Fig. 4   Adjusting Shift Linkage on 2-WD "F" Models

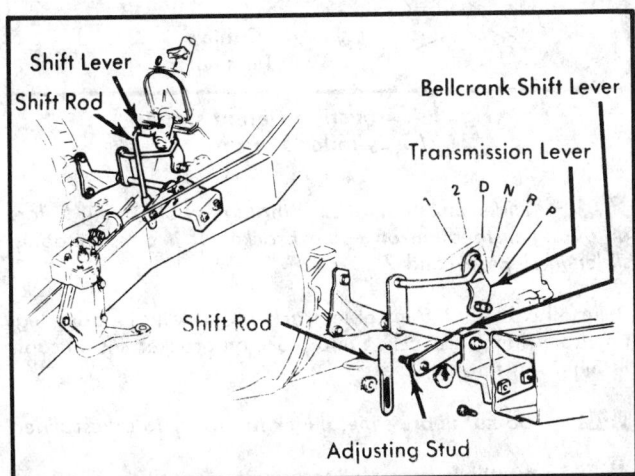

Fig. 5   Adjusting Shift Linkage on 4-WD "F" Models

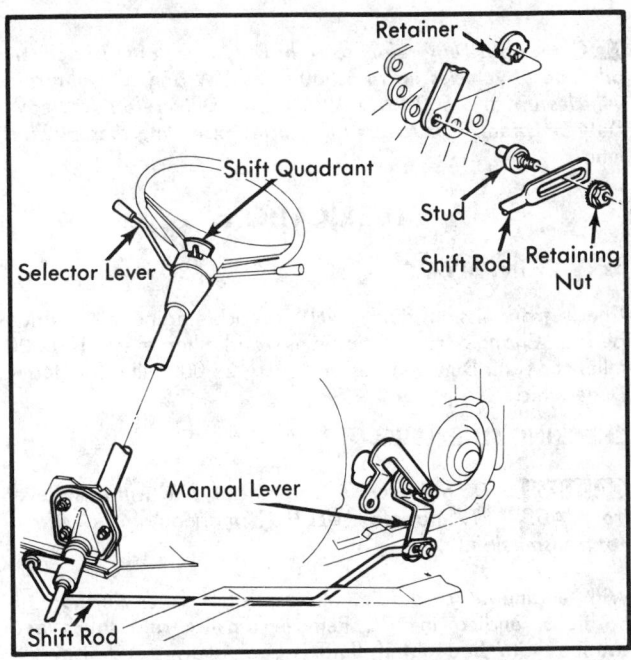

Fig. 6   Adjusting Shift Linkage on "E" Models

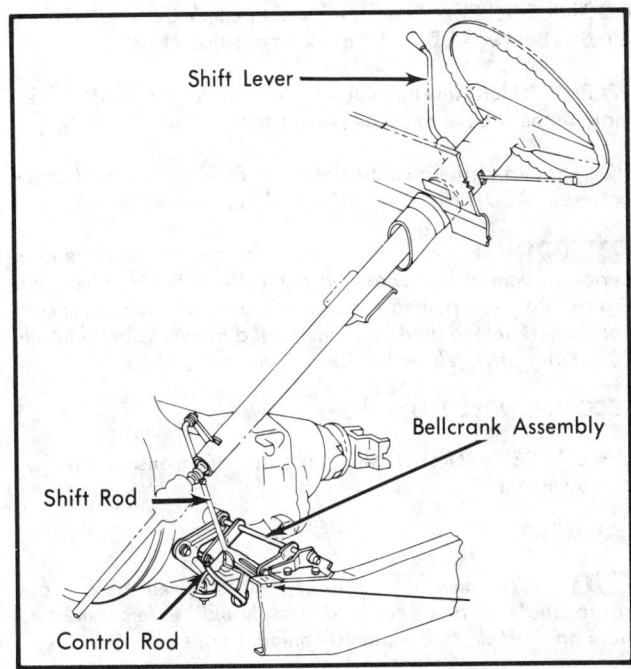

Fig. 7   Adjusting Shift Linkage on AOT Models

NEUTRAL START SWITCH

All Models — 1) Loosen both neutral safety switch bolts at transmission. Rotate manual selector lever against neutral stop.

2) Slide switch until a .091" (no. 43 drill) fits into gauge holes. Tighten switch bolts and remove gauge pin.

3) Check switch operation. Vehicle should start in "N" or "P" only.

GENERAL MOTORS

NOTE — *Light Duty refers to Light Duty Emissions. This covers all Federal vehicles up to 6,000 lbs. GVW and all California vehicles up to 8,500 lbs. GVW. Heavy Duty refers to Heavy Duty Emissions. This covers all vehicles exceeding these weight limits.*

LUBRICATION

SERVICE INTERVALS

Check transmission fluid level at each engine oil change period. Change transmission fluid and filter every 100,000 miles for Light Duty vehicles and every 24,000 miles for Heavy Duty vehicles.

CHECKING FLUID LEVEL

CAUTION — *Do not overfill. One pint of fluid will raise level from "ADD 1 PT." mark to "FULL HOT" mark on dipstick with a hot transmission.*

With engine at curb idle, move selector lever through all positions, ending in "P". Remove dipstick and touch end cautiously to find out if fluid is cool, warm, or hot. Wipe dipstick clean, reinstall, then remove again and inspect level (according to temperature) as follows:

COOL (65-85°F) — Fluid level should check between the two dimples below "ADD 1 PT." mark on dipstick.

WARM — Fluid level should check close to the "ADD 1 PT." mark (either above or below) on dipstick.

HOT (cannot be held comfortably) — Fluid level should check between "ADD 1 PT." and "FULL HOT" marks on dipstick.

CAUTION — *If vehicle has been operated for an extended period of time at high speed, in city traffic in hot weather, or if vehicle has been pulling a trailer, an accurate fluid level cannot be determined until fluid has cooled down (approximately 30 minutes after vehicle has been parked).*

RECOMMENDED FLUID

Use only DEXRON or DEXRON-II automatic transmission fluid or equivalent.

CAPACITY

NOTE — *Transmission refill capacities given below are approximate, and correct fluid level should be determined by mark on dipstick, rather than by amount added.*

Transmission Refill Capacities	
Application	**Capacity (Pts.)**
THM 350 & 350C	6.0
THM 400	7.0

DRAINING & REFILLING

With engine at normal operating, loosen transmission oil pan bolts. Tap side of pan to break loose from transmission and allow fluid to drain. Remove oil pan and filter. Install a a new

filter and gasket. Install oil pan and new gasket. Add sufficient fluid to bring fluid level to proper mark on dipstick.

CAUTION — *Do not overfill transmission.*

ADJUSTMENT

DETENT (DOWNSHIFT) CABLE (THM 350 MODELS ONLY)

1) Remove pump rod lever assembly (Diesel models only).

2) Install one end of detent cable into transmission.

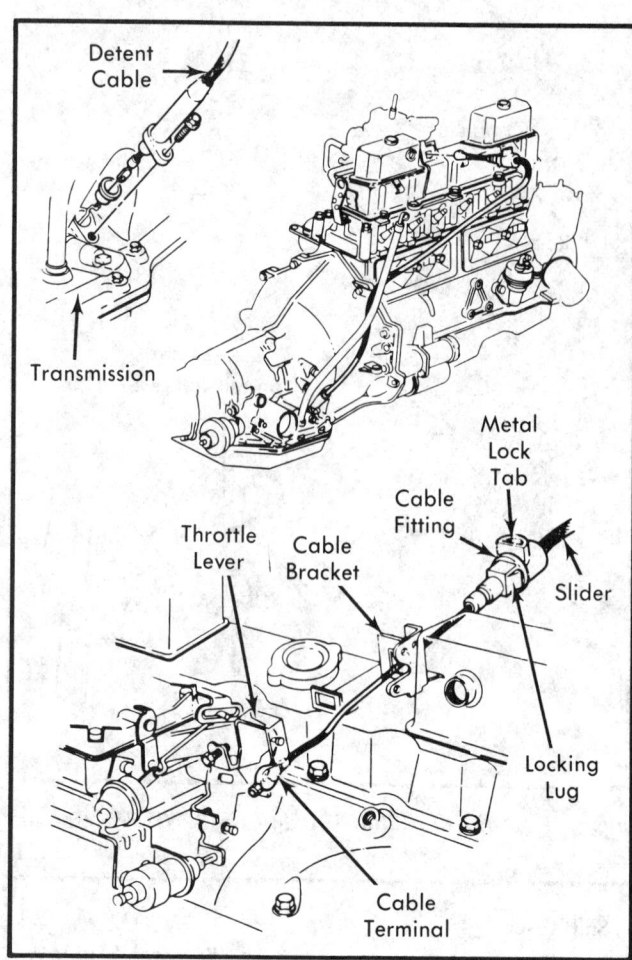

Fig. 1 Adjusting Detent Cable (6-Cylinder Shown)

NOTE — *Slider must not ratchet through cable fitting before or during installation on cable bracket. If it does, re-adjust slider in steps 6) and 7).*

3) Install cable fitting in cable bracket. Check that locking lugs on cable fitting are locked into place on bracket. Install cable terminal on throttle lever.

NOTE — *Do not depress metal lock tab to try to adjust slider.*

4) Open throttle lever to "full throttle stop" position. Slider will automatically adjust to correct setting on cable. Release throttle lever.

GENERAL MOTORS (Cont.)

5) Reconnect pump to lever assembly (Diesel models only).

6) If slider was moved and needs to be re-adjusted, depress and hold metal lock tab. Move slider through cable fitting in direction away from throttle lever until slider stops against cable fitting.

7) Release metal lock tab and repeat step **4)**.

DETENT (DOWNSHIFT) SWITCH (THM 400 ONLY)

With engine off, push detent switch plunger as far forward as possible. This presets switch for adjustment. Depress accelerator pedal to wide open position; switch will then self-adjust. Operation of detent switch circuit can be checked by connecting a test lamp across switch terminals.

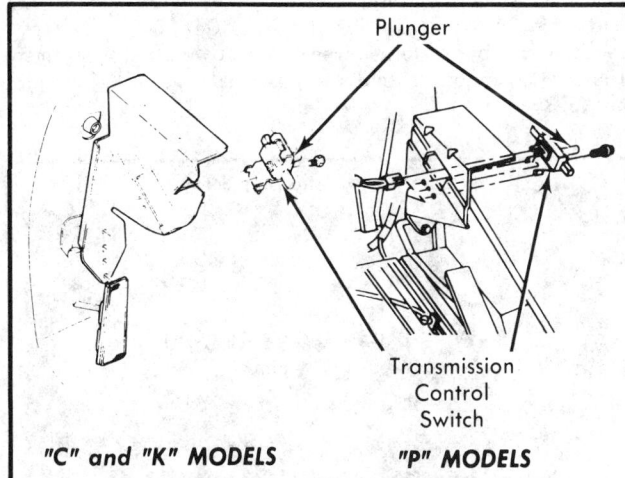

Fig. 2   Detent Switch Installation (THM 400 Only)

SHIFT LINKAGE

"C", "K" & "P" Models — Make sure shift tube and lever are free in steering column. To adjust linkage, remove screw and spring washer from swivel. Move transmission lever counterclockwise to stop, then clockwise three detents. This is neutral position. Place selector lever in neutral using mechanical stops. **NOTE** — *Do not use indicator pointer as reference for positioning selector lever.* Assemble screw, spring washer and swivel. Tighten screw to 20 ft. lbs.

"G" Models — 1) Make sure shift tube and lever assembly are free in steering column. Disconnect shift lever rod from swivel at lower column lever. Move transmission lever counterclockwise to stop, then clockwise three detents. This is neutral position. Place selector lever in neutral using mechanical stops.

NOTE — *Do not use indicator pointer as reference for positioning selector lever.*

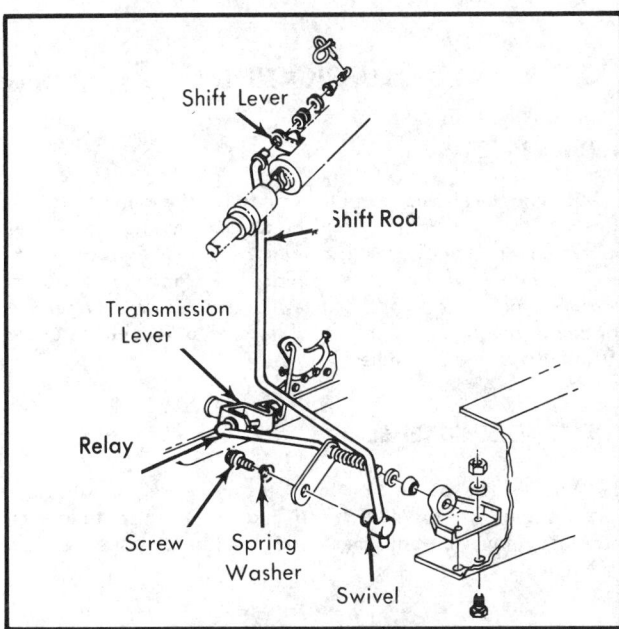

Fig. 3   Adjusting Shift Linkage ("C", "K" and "P" Models)

2) Slide swivel and clamp onto shift lever rod. Install grommets, washers and nut but do not tighten nut. Hold lower column lever against neutral stop on park side. Tighten swivel nut to 18 ft. lbs.

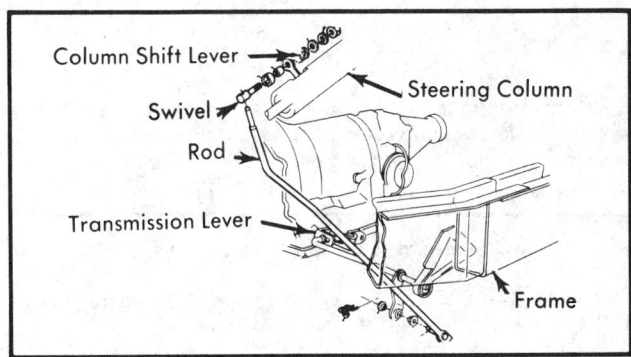

Fig. 4   Adjusting Shift Linkage ("G" Models)

NEUTRAL SAFETY SWITCH

All Models With Column Mounted Switch — Place gearshift selector lever in neutral position and loosen switch attaching screws. Rotate switch on column until a .096" diameter gauge pin can be inserted into switch gauge hole to a depth of 3/8". Tighten switch attaching screws and remove gauge pin. Check for engine starting in neutral or park only.

All Models With Transmission Mounted Switch — Raise and support vehicle and loosen switch mounting bolts. Align hole in switch lever with hole in switch assembly. Insert a .093-.097" diameter gauge pin through switch holes to hold switch in neutral position. With selector lever on transmission in neutral detent, tighten switch mounting bolts and remove gauge pin. Lower vehicle and check operation of switch.

All Models

LUBRICATION

SERVICE INTERVALS

Check fluid level and condition of fluid at each engine oil change. Draining, refilling and band adjustments are not required under normal driving conditions. Under light duty service conditions; change fluid, replace filter and adjust bands every 25 months or 25,000 miles. Under heavy duty service conditions; change fluid, replace filter and adjust bands every 10 months or 10,000 miles.

CHECKING FLUID LEVEL

1) With vehicle parked on level surface, parking brake applied, engine at curb idle speed and normal operating temperature, move selector lever through all gear ranges, ending in Neutral.

2) Fluid level should be between "FULL" and "ADD ONE PINT" marks on dipstick. Fluid level should never be above "FULL" mark. Make sure dipstick seats properly to seal out water and dirt.

RECOMMENDED FLUID

Use only Dexron or Dexron II type automatic transmission fluid.

CAPACITY

NOTE — *Transmission and converter capacities listed below are approximate and correct fluid level should be determined by mark on dipstick rather than by amount added.*

Transmission Refill Capacities	
Application	Capacity (Pts.)
Model 727 & 999	
Including Converter	17.0
Without Converter	8.5
Model 904	
Including Converter	14.2
Without Converter	8.5

DRAINING & REFILLING

1) Loosen oil pan bolts, tap pan to break it loose allowing fluid to drain, then remove pan. Install new filter on bottom of valve body and tighten retaining screws. Clean oil pan and install with new gasket.

2) Pour 8 pints of transmission fluid through filler tube, start engine and allow to run at curb idle for 2 minutes. With engine at curb idle and parking brake applied, move shift selector lever through all ranges, ending in Neutral. Add sufficient fluid to bring fluid level to "ADD ONE PINT" mark on dipstick.

NOTE — *DO NOT overfill. Reseat dipstick fully to seal out water and dirt. Recheck fluid level when transmission reaches normal operating temperature.*

ADJUSTMENT

KICKDOWN (FRONT) BAND

NOTE — *Kickdown band adjusting screw is located on left side of case near throttle lever shaft.*

1) Loosen adjusting screw lock nut and back off approximately 5 turns. After making sure adjusting screw turns freely in case, tighten screw to 36 INCH lbs. if torque wrench, adapter tool and ⁵⁄₁₆" square socket are used.

2) If not, tighten adjusting screw to 72 INCH lbs. (models 727 and 999) or 41 INCH lbs. (model 904). Back off screw specified number of turns given in Kickdown Band Adjustment Table. Hold adjusting screw in this position and tighten lock nut to 35 ft. lbs.

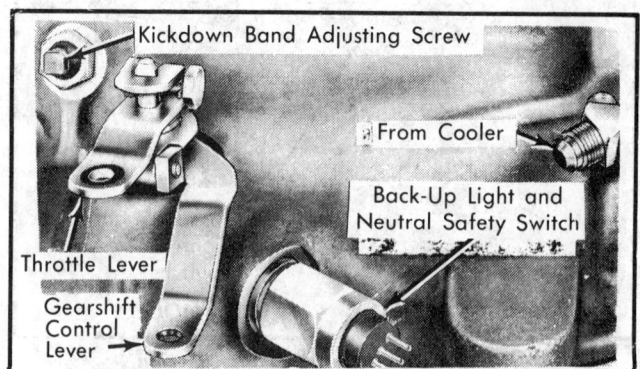

Fig. 1   Adjusting Kickdown Band

Kickdown Band Adjustment Table	
Application	Back Off Screw
Model 727 & 904	2 ½ Turns
Model 999	2 Turns

LOW REVERSE (REAR) BAND

NOTE — *Low-reverse band adjusting screw is located on rear servo lever. Transmission oil pan must be removed to gain access to adjusting screw.*

1) Raise vehicle, drain transmission fluid and remove oil pan. Loosen band adjusting screw lock nut and back off approximately 5 turns. Tighten screw to 41 INCH lbs.

2) Back off screw the specified number of turns given in the Low-Reverse Band Adjustment Table. Hold adjusting screw in this position and tighten lock nut to specifications. Install oil pan and refill transmission with fluid.

JEEP (Cont.)

Low-Reverse Band Adjustment Table	
Application	**Back Off Screw**
Model 727	2 Turns
Model 904	7 Turns
Model 999	4 Turns

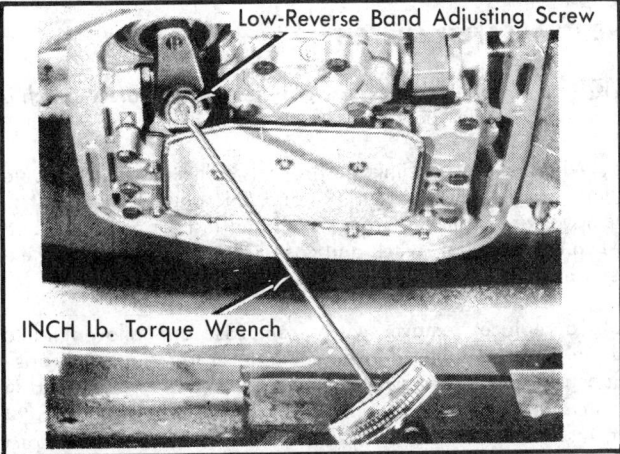

Fig. 2   Adjusting Low-Reverse Band

TRANSMISSION THROTTLE CABLE

4 Cyl. Models — 1) Remove air cleaner and spark plug wire separator from throttle cable bracket. Move separator and wires aside.

2) Use a spare spring to hold throttle valve control lever rearward against stop. Block choke open and release fast idle cam. On vehicles without air conditioning, turn ignition switch to "ON" position to energize throttle stop solenoid.

3) Release T-shaped cable adjuster clamp by lifting upward with small screwdriver. This unlocks throttle control cable. Move cable and cable housing forward until there is no load on throttle cable bellcrank.

NOTE — *Bellcrank is part of carburetor throttle linkage.*

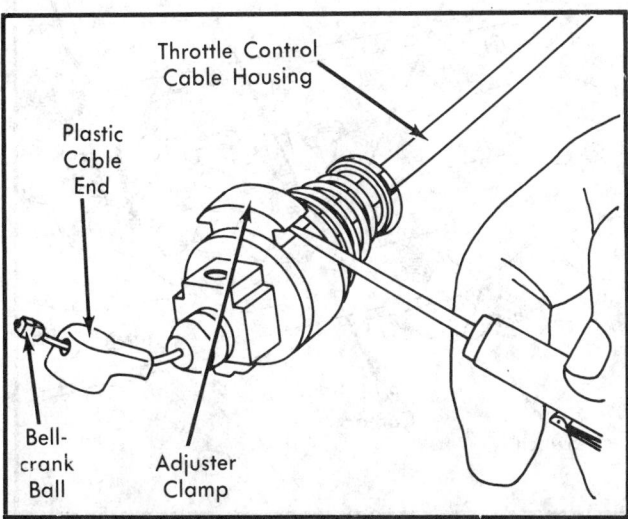

Fig. 3   Throttle Cable Adjustment (4 Cyl. Models)

4) To adjust cable, move cable and cable housing rearward until lash is eliminated between plastic cable end and bellcrank ball. To lock cable, press in T-shaped cable adjuster clamp until it snaps into place.

5) Turn ignition switch to "OFF" position. Install spark plug wire separator and air cleaner. Remove spring holding throttle valve control lever.

TRANSMISSION THROTTLE ROD

6 Cyl. Models — 1) Disconnect throttle control rod spring and use spring to hold transmission throttle valve control lever forward against stop. Block choke open and release fast idle cam.

NOTE — *On carburetors equipped with throttle operated solenoid valve, energize solenoid and open throttle half-way to allow solenoid to lock, then return throttle to idle position.*

2) Loosen retaining bolt on throttle control adjusting link. DO NOT remove spring clip or nylon washer. Pull on end of link to eliminate lash and tighten link retaining bolt. Reconnect throttle control rod spring.

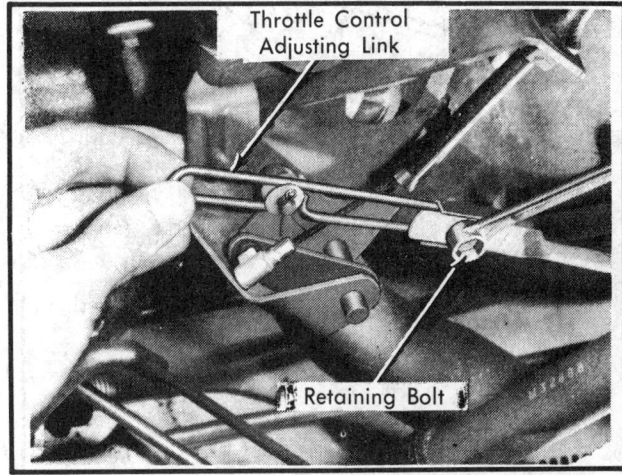

Fig. 4   Throttle Rod Adjustment (6 Cyl. Models)

V8 Models — 1) Disconnect throttle control rod spring and use spring to hold transmission throttle valve control lever forward against stop. Block choke open and release fast idle cam.

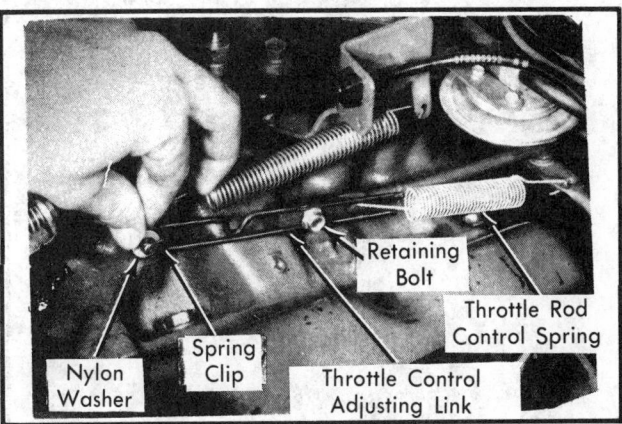

Fig. 5   Throttle Rod Adjustment (V8 Models)

JEEP (Cont.)

NOTE – *On carburetors equipped with throttle operated solenoid valve, energize solenoid and open throttle half-way to allow solenoid to lock, then return throttle to idle position.*

2) Loosen retaining bolt on throttle control adjusting link. Remove spring clip and slide nylon washer to rear of link. Push on end of link to eliminate lash and tighten link retaining bolt. Install nylon washer and spring clip, reconnect throttle control rod spring.

SHIFT LINKAGE

1) Loosen shift rod trunnion jam nuts at transmission lever. Remove lock pin retaining shift rod to bellcrank and disengage trunnion and shift rod at bellcrank. Place selector lever in "P" position and lock steering column. Position transmission shift lever in "Park" detent.

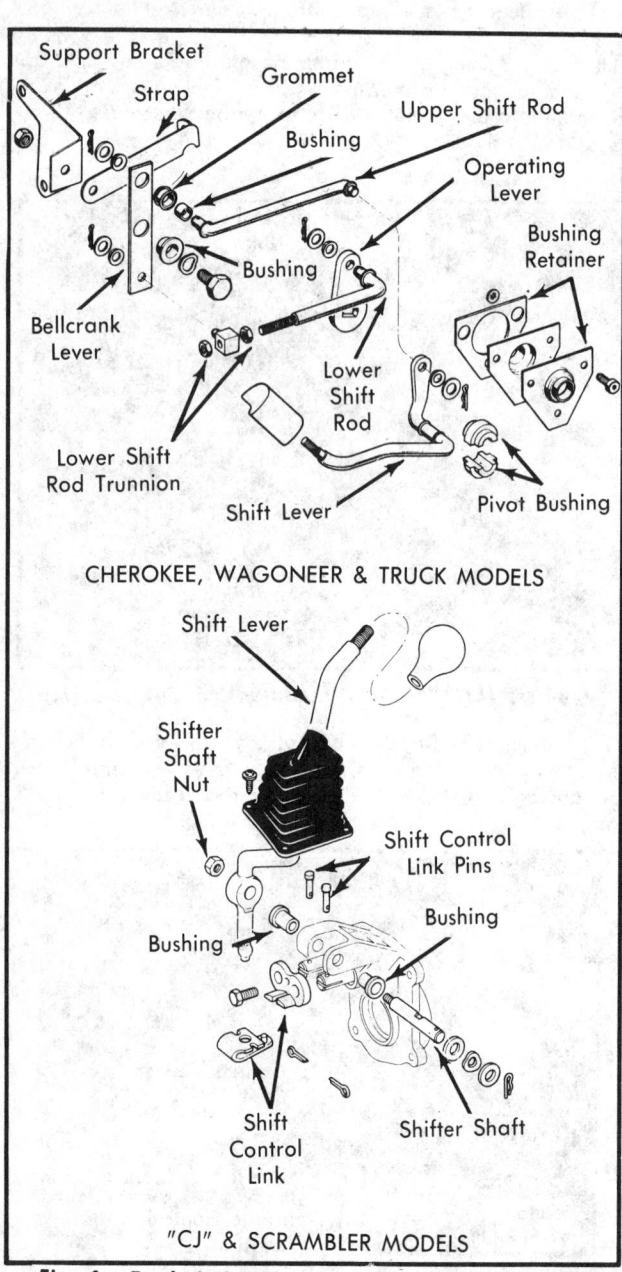

CHEROKEE, WAGONEER & TRUCK MODELS

"CJ" & SCRAMBLER MODELS

Fig. 6 Exploded View of Shift Linkage Assemblies

2) Adjust shift rod trunnion to obtain free pin fit in bellcrank arm and tighten jam nuts. Make sure gearshift linkage lash is eliminated by pulling downward on shift rod and pushing upward on outer bellcrank when tightening jam nuts.

3) Check steering column lock for ease of operation. Move selector lever to "N" position and check for suitable neutral safety switch operation.

NEUTRAL SAFETY SWITCH

NOTE – *Combined back-up light and neutral safety switch is located on lower portion of steering column.*

1) With transmission linkage properly adjusted, switch should allow starter operation in "P" and "N" only. To test switch, remove wire connector from switch and test for continuity between center pin of switch and case. Continuity should only exist when transmission is in "P" or "N".

2) To replace, remove switch from case and allow fluid to drain into a container. Move selector lever to "P" and "N" positions and check that switch operating fingers are centered in switch opening. Install switch and new seal and tighten to 24 ft. lbs. Retest for continuity and refill transmission to correct fluid level.

NOTE – *To center switch operating fingers, see Valve Body Assembly in appropriate transmission article.*

3) Place shift selector lever on column in "P" position and lock ignition switch. Move switch actuating lever until aligned with the letter "P" stamped on back of switch. Insert a 3/32" drill in hole located below the letter "N" stamped on back of switch.

4) Move switch actuating lever until it stops against drill, then install switch on steering column and remove drill. Check operation of switch, engine should start in "N" and "P" positions only and back-up lights should light in "R" position only.

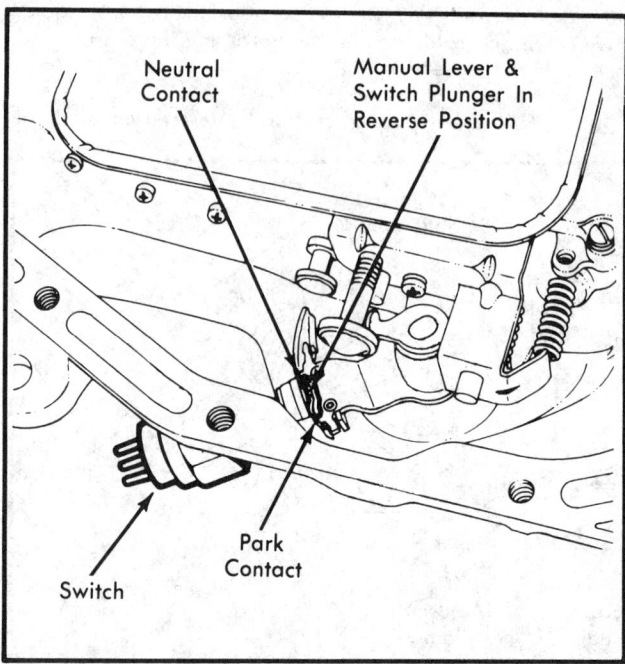

Fig. 7 Back-Up Light and Neutral Safety Switch

CHRYSLER CORP. REMOVAL & INSTALLATION

ALL MODELS

NOTE — *Transmission and converter must be removed and installed as an assembly to prevent damage to converter drive plate, front pump bushing, and oil seal. DO NOT allow weight of transmission to rest on plate during removal or installation.*

Removal — 1) If equipped, remove transfer case. Disconnect negative battery cable. Disconnect and lower exhaust system (if necessary) for transmission removal clearance. Remove engine-to-transmission struts (if equipped). Disconnect cooler lines at transmission. Remove starter, cooler line bracket and converter access cover.

2) Loosen oil pan bolts, tap pan to break it loose and allow fluid to drain. Rotate engine clockwise using suitable socket on vibration damper bolt to position converter-to-drive plate bolts for removal and remove them. Mark propeller shaft for reassembly reference and remove from vehicle.

NOTE — *Crankshaft flange bolt circle, inner and outer circle of holes in drive plate and tapped holes in converter all have 1 hole offset so parts will be installed in original position.*

3) Disconnect wiring connector from back-up light/neutral safety switch. Disconnect gearshift rod and torque shaft assembly from transmission. Disconnect transmission throttle rod from lever and remove oil filler tube. Disconnect speedometer cable.

4) Install a suitable engine support fixture to support rear of engine. Raise transmission with a service jack to relieve load on supports, remove bolts securing crossmember to transmis-sion and frame, then remove crossmember. Remove all converter housing-to-engine attaching bolts.

5) Carefully work transmission and converter assembly rearward off engine block dowels, disengaging converter hub from end of crankshaft. Attach a small "C" clamp to edge of converter housing to hold converter in place while transmission is being removed. Lower transmission and remove from vehicle.

Installation — 1) Reverse removal procedure and note the following: Before installing converter, rotate front pump rotors using a suitable alignment tool (C-3881) until two small holes in tool handle are vertical. Slide torque converter over input and reaction shafts, making sure converter hub slots are vertical and fully engage pump inner rotor lugs. Test for full engagement by placing a straightedge across face of transmission case. Surface of converter front cover lug should be at least ½" to rear of straightedge when converter is fully engaged. Attach a small "C" clamp to edge of converter housing to hold converter in place while installing transmission.

2) Inspect converter drive plate for distortion or cracks and replace if necessary.

NOTE — *When drive plate replacement has been necessary, make sure both transmission dowel pins are in engine block and are protruding far enough to hold transmission in alignment.*

3) Coat converter hub hole in crankshaft with multi-purpose grease. When installing transmission, make sure marks on converter and drive plate (made during removal) are aligned. To complete installation, adjust shift and throttle linkages and fill transmission with fluid.

FORD REMOVAL & INSTALLATION

C-4 ("F" MODELS)

Removal — 1) Remove fluid filler tube from oil pan and allow fluid to drain. Remove converter drain plug access cover, remove converter-to-flywheel attaching nuts and converter drain plug, allow fluid to drain, then reinstall and tighten drain plug. Remove propeller shaft.

2) Disconnect oil cooler lines from transmission. Disconnect manual and downshift linkage rods from transmission control levers. Remove speedometer gear from extension housing. Disconnect starter cable from starter and remove starter. Remove vacuum line(s) from transmission vacuum unit and dis-connect line(s) from retaining clip. Disconnect electrical lead(s) from transmission.

3) Position transmission jack under transmission and secure with safety chain. Remove transmission support crossmember attaching bolts, then raise transmission and remove crossmember. Remove converter housing-to-engine attaching bolts. Move transmission away from engine. Lower transmis-sion and remove it from under vehicle.

Installation — To install, reverse removal procedure and tighten all bolts. Adjust manual and downshift linkage, then fill transmission to proper level with specified fluid.

NOTE — *Converter must rest squarely against flywheel to pre-vent converter pilot from binding in engine crankshaft.*

C-6 ("E" MODELS)

Removal — 1) Working inside vehicle, remove engine compartment cover and disconnect electrical leads at plug connector. Remove flex hose from air cleaner heat tube (V8 models only), then remove the upper converter housing-to-engine attaching bolts. Raise vehicle, drain transmission pan, then remove converter drain plug access cover. Remove converter-to-flywheel attaching nuts and converter drain plug, allow fluid to drain, then reinstall and tighten converter drain plug.

2) Disconnect drive shaft and remove filler tube. Disconnect starter cable and remove starter. Position an engine support bar to side rail and oil pan flanges. Disconnect oil cooler lines and vacuum lines from transmission. Remove speedometer driven gear from extension housing and manual and downshift linkage rods from transmission control levers. Position a transmission jack under transmission and secure with a safety chain.

3) Remove bolt and nut securing rear mount to crossmember and bolts retaining crossmember to side rails, remove two sup-port inserts, raise transmission with jack and remove crossmember. Remove bolt retaining filler tube to cylinder block, then remove filler tube and dipstick from transmission. Remove remaining converter housing-to-engine attaching bolts, lower jack, and remove assembly from vehicle.

FORD REMOVAL & INSTALLATION (Cont.)

Installation — To install, reverse removal procedure and tighten all bolts and nuts. Adjust manual and downshift linkage, then fill transmission to proper level with specified fluid.

NOTE — *Converter must rest squarely against flywheel to prevent converter pilot from binding in engine crankshaft.*

C-6 (BRONCO & "F" MODELS)

Removal — **1)** Remove two upper converter housing-to-engine attaching bolts and bolt securing fluid filler tube to cylinder head. Raise vehicle and drain fluid from transmission and converter. Disconnect propeller shaft and position it out of the way.

2) Disconnect speedometer cable from bearing retainer and disconnect throttle and manual linkage rods from levers at transmission. Disconnect oil cooler lines from transmission. Remove vacuum line(s) from transmission vacuum unit and remove line(s) from retaining clip. Disconnect starter cable from starter and remove starter.

3) Remove two engine rear support crossmember-to-frame attaching bolts. Remove the two engine rear support-to-extension housing attaching bolts and six bolts securing number two crossmember to frame side rails. Raise transmission with a transmission jack and remove both crossmembers.

4) Secure transmission to the jack with safety chain. Remove remaining converter housing-to-engine attaching bolts. Move transmission away from engine, lower the jack and remove converter and transmission assembly from under vehicle.

Installation — To install, reverse removal procedure and tighten all bolts. Adjust throttle and manual linkage and fill transmission to proper level with specified fluid.

NOTE — *Converter must rest squarely against flywheel to prevent converter pilot from binding in engine crankshaft.*

AUTOMATIC OVERDRIVE TRANSMISSION ("F" MODELS)

Removal — **1)** Raise vehicle, drain transmission pan, then remove converter drain plug access cover. Remove nuts attaching converter to flywheel. Remove converter drain plug, allow fluid to drain, then reinstall and tighten converter drain plug. Remove propeller shaft and install seal installation tool in extension housing to prevent fluid leakage.

2) Disconnect starter cable and remove starter. Disconnect neutral start switch wires at connector. Remove bolts securing rear mount to crossmember and bolts retaining crossmember to frame side rails. Remove bolts securing engine rear support to extension housing.

3) Disconnect TV linkage rod and manual rod from transmission. Remove bolts securing bellcrank bracket to converter housing. Raise transmission with jack and remove crossmember. Lower transmission and remove oil cooler lines. Disconnect speedometer cable from extension housing. Remove bolt securing filler tube to engine and remove filler tube.

4) Secure transmission to jack with safety chain. Remove bolts securing converter housing to engine. Move transmission away from engine, lower jack and remove converter and transmission assembly from under vehicle.

Installation — To install, reverse removal procedure and tighten all bolts. Adjust throttle and manual linkage and fill transmission to proper level with specified fluid.

NOTE — *Converter must rest squarely against flywheel to prevent converter pilot from binding in engine crankshaft.*

GENERAL MOTORS REMOVAL & INSTALLATION

ALL EXCEPT "K" MODELS

Removal — **1)** Disconnect battery ground cable. Disconnect detent downshift cable at carburetor. Release parking brake. Raise vehicle on a hoist and disconnect propeller shaft. Disconnect all cables, electrical leads, vacuum lines and linkage rods from transmission. Disconnect oil cooler lines (if equipped) from transmission.

2) Support transmission with suitable transmission jack. Disconnect rear mount from frame crossmember. Remove bolts securing crossmember and remove crossmember. Remove converter under-pan, scribe flywheel-converter relationship for installation, then remove flywheel-to-converter attaching bolts.

3) Lower transmission until jack is barely supporting it. Remove transmission-to-engine mounting bolts and remove oil filler tube at transmission.

NOTE — *On some models it may be necessary to disconnect catalytic converter before transmission can be lowered.*

4) Raise transmission to its normal position, support engine with jack and slide transmission rearward from engine and lower it away from vehicle. Use suitable converter holding tool (J-5384) when lowering transmission or keep rear of transmission lower than front to prevent converter from falling.

Installation — To install, reverse removal procedure and note the following. Before installing flex plate-to-converter bolts, make certain that the weld nuts on converter are flush with the flex plate and the converter rotates freely by hand in this position. Then, hand start all three bolts and tighten finger tight before tightening to specifications.

"K" MODELS

Removal — **1)** Disconnect battery cable and remove transmission dipstick. Disconnect detent downshift cable at carburetor and remove transfer case shift lever knob and boot. Raise vehicle. Remove flywheel cover and remove flywheel-to-converter attaching bolts.

2) Disconnect transmission shift linkage and speedometer cable. Remove engine crossunder pipe-to-manifold bolts. Disconnect vacuum modulator line, line to filler tube clip and detent downshift cable-to-filler tube strap. Disconnect detent cable at transmission and oil cooler lines. Remove transfer case adapter-to-crossmember bolts. Where applicable, disconnect engine-to-transmission support strut rod at transmission. Remove crossmember bolts and remove crossmember.

NOTE – *It may be necessary to raise engine to remove crossmember.*

3) Remove exhaust system hanger bolts. Disconnect rear propeller shaft at transfer case. Disconnect parking brake cable. Disconnect exhaust system and tie aside. Disconnect front propeller shaft at front axle.

4) Support transmission and transfer case with jack and secure with safety chain. Remove transfer case-to-frame bracket bolts. Remove transmission-to-engine bolts and remove transmission and transfer case as a unit.

Installation – To install, reverse removal procedure and tighten all bolts. Adjust shift linkage and fill transmission to proper level with specified fluid.

JEEP REMOVAL & INSTALLATION

REMOVAL

1) Remove transmission dipstick. Raise vehicle on a hoist. Mark front and rear universal joints and yokes for reassembly. On Cherokee, Wagoneer and Truck models, remove parking brake cable lock nut and adjuster nut. Remove clip connecting parking brake cable to crossmember and pull cable out of crossmember.

2) On Cherokee and Wagoneer models with low range reduction unit, remove reduction unit shift lever from shaft. On CJ and Truck models with low range reduction unit, disconnect shift rod at reduction unit shift lever. Disconnect speedometer cable.

3) Mark or tag Emergency Drive control vacuum lines for reassembly. Disconnect Emergency Drive indicator lamp wire. Remove vacuum line bracket bolt at rear of transfer case. Disconnect detent solenoid wire at transmission connector.

4) Remove starter. Remove converter housing cover. Mark relationship of torque converter and drive plate for reassembly. Remove torque converter to drive plate bolts. Remove rear transmission mount to crossmember nuts.

5) Support transmission using a suitable transmission jack. Secure transmission to jack using a safety chain. Remove rear crossmember. On all models (except CJ with 6 cyl.), disconnect exhaust pipe at exhaust manifold. Disconnect exhaust pipe at muffler and remove exhaust pipe.

NOTE – *If equipped with a catalytic converter, disconnect exhaust pipe at converter flange and remove pipe.*

6) Remove spring clip and washer from transmission shift rod trunion. Disengage trunion at bell crank and remove washer from trunion. Remove spring clip securing bell crank to transmission shift lever. Remove bell crank and bracket assembly.

7) Disconnect front propeller shaft at transfer case. Wire shaft to frame out of way. Disconnect cooler lines at transmission. Disconnect vacuum hose at modulator. Place a suitable support under engine. Remove transmission filler tube. Remove converter housing to engine bolts.

8) Move transmission rearward far enough to clear crankshaft. Hold converter in position and lower transmission until it clears engine.

INSTALLATION

Reverse removal procedure and note the following: Do not tighten exhaust pipe attaching bolts until crossmember has been installed and transmission jack has been removed. Make sure all index marks made at removal are in alignment. Fill transmission and transfer case with fluid.

Automatic Transmissions

CHRYSLER CORP. LOADFLITE A727, A904T & A999
& JEEP MODEL 727, 904 & 999

Loadflite A727, A904T & A999
  Dodge
  Plymouth
Jeep 727, 904 & 999
  All Models

TRANSMISSION IDENTIFICATION

A transmission identification number is stamped on transmission oil pan flange, on left side of transmission near throttle lever shaft. Identification number is broken-down as follows:

Chrysler Corp. — First two letters of code is manufacturing plant code; second group of digits (7 numbers) is the transmission part number; third group of numbers is the build date code; last group of numbers is the build sequence number.

Jeep — First group of 7 digits is the transmission part number; second group of numbers is the build date code; final group of numbers is the transmission serial number.

DESCRIPTION

Transmission combines a torque converter and a fully automatic three speed gear system. Converter housing and transmission case are an integral aluminum casting. Transmission consists of two multiple disc clutches, an overrunning clutch, two servos and bands, and two planetary gear sets. Hydraulic system consists of an oil pump and a single valve body which contains all of the valves except governor valve.

In addition, most models are equipped with a lock-up torque converter to improve fuel economy. The lock-up clutch is activated only in direct drive and above a minimum preset vehicle speed. When 2-3 upshift occurs above minimum lock-up speed, lock-up shift will occur immediately after 2-3 upshift. This is possible because the fluid drive with standard automatic transmissions is eliminated and direct drive occurs with the lock-up, thus slippage of fluid drive is reduced.

LUBRICATION & ADJUSTMENT

See Automatic Transmission Servicing in this section.

TESTING

ROAD TEST

1) Before road testing, be certain that fluid level and condition, and control linkage adjustments have been checked and corrected if necessary. During test, transmission should upshift and downshift automatically at approximately the speeds shown in Shift Speed Charts. All shift speeds may vary somewhat due to production tolerances, rear axle ratio, or tire size. The important factor is the quality of the shifts. All shifts should be smooth, responsive, and with no slipping or engine speed flare-up.

2) Slipping or flare-up in any gear usually indicates clutch, band, or overrunning clutch problems. The slipping clutch or band in a particular gear can usually be identified by noting transmission operation in other selector positions, and comparing which internal units are applied in those positions. See Clutch and Band Application Chart.

3) Although this process of elimination can be used (1) to detect any unit which slips and (2) to confirm proper operation of good units, the actual cause of the malfunction usually cannot be determined.

4) Practically any condition can be caused by leaking hydraulic circuits or sticking valves. Therefore, unless an obvious condition exists, transmission should never be disassembled until hydraulic pressure tests have been made.

NOTE — Shift speed specifications for Jeep models were not available from manufacturer.

CLUTCH AND BAND APPLICATION CHART
(ELEMENTS IN USE)

Selector Lever Position	Front Clutch	Rear Clutch	Over-running Clutch	Front (Kickdown) Band	Rear (Low-Reverse) Band
D — DRIVE					
First		X	X		
Second		X		X	
Direct	X	X			
2 — SECOND					
First		X	X		
Second		X		X	
1 — LOW (First)		X			X
R — REVERSE	X				X
NEUTRAL OR PARK — All clutches and bands released and/or ineffective.					

CHRYSLER CORP. LOADFLITE A727, A904T & A999 & JEEP MODEL 727, 904 & 999 (Cont.)

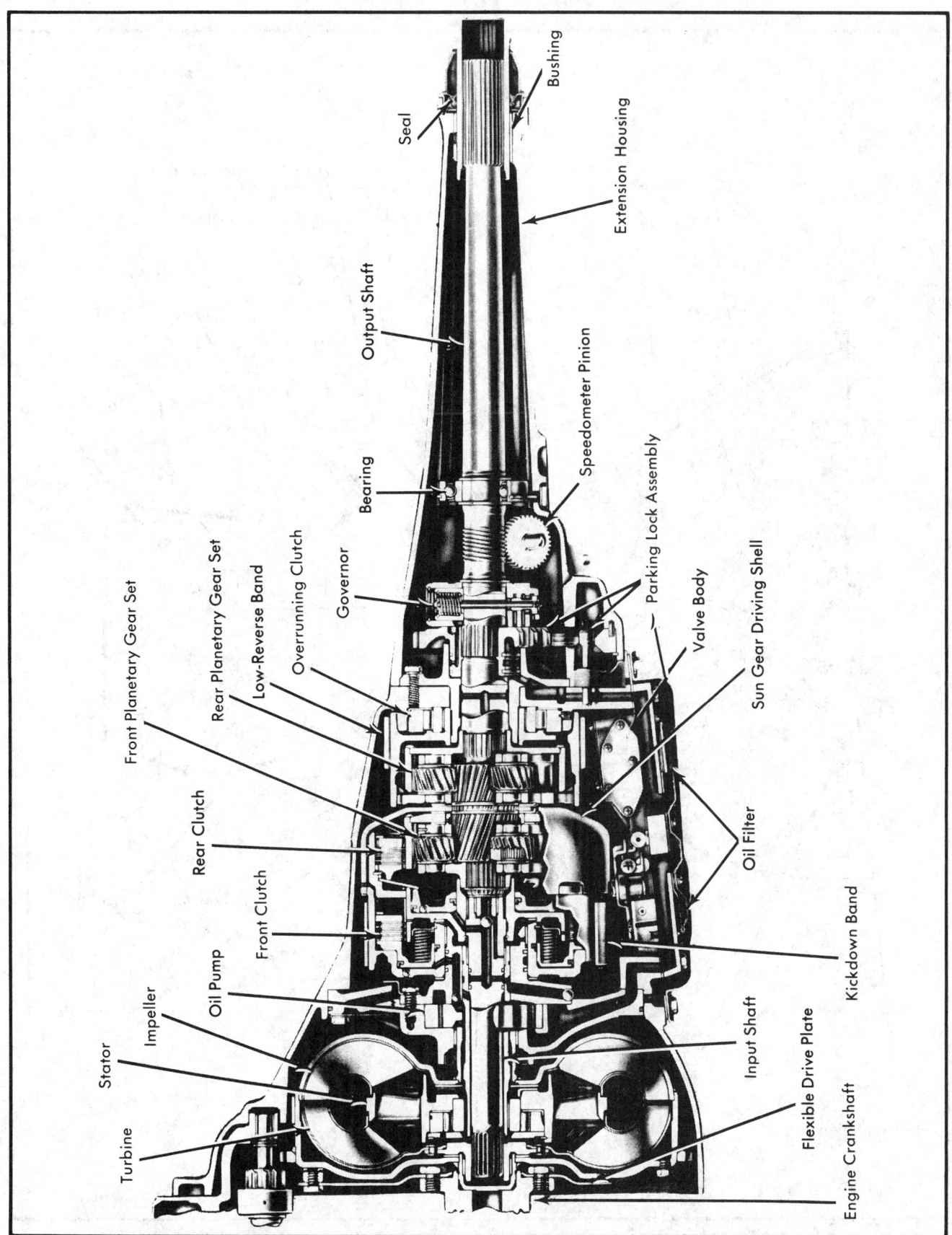

Fig. 1 Cross-Sectional View of Chrysler Corp. Loadflite Automatic Transmission Assembly

CHRYSLER CORP. LOADFLITE A727, A904T & A999
& JEEP MODEL 727, 904 & 999 (Cont.)

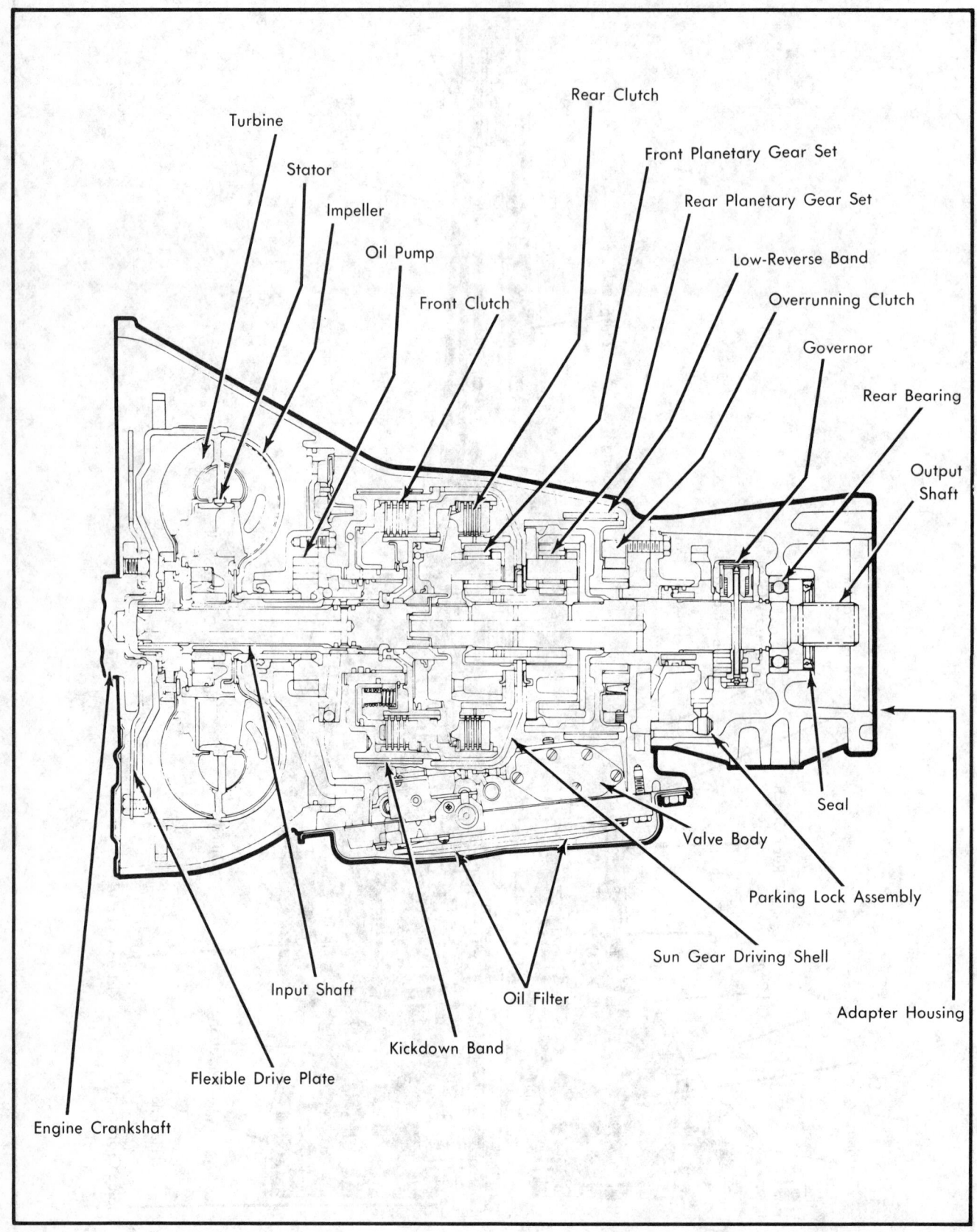

Fig. 2   Cross-Sectional View of Jeep Model 727 Automatic Transmission Assembly

CHRYSLER CORP. LOADFLITE A727, A904T & A999 & JEEP MODEL 727, 904 & 999 (Cont.)

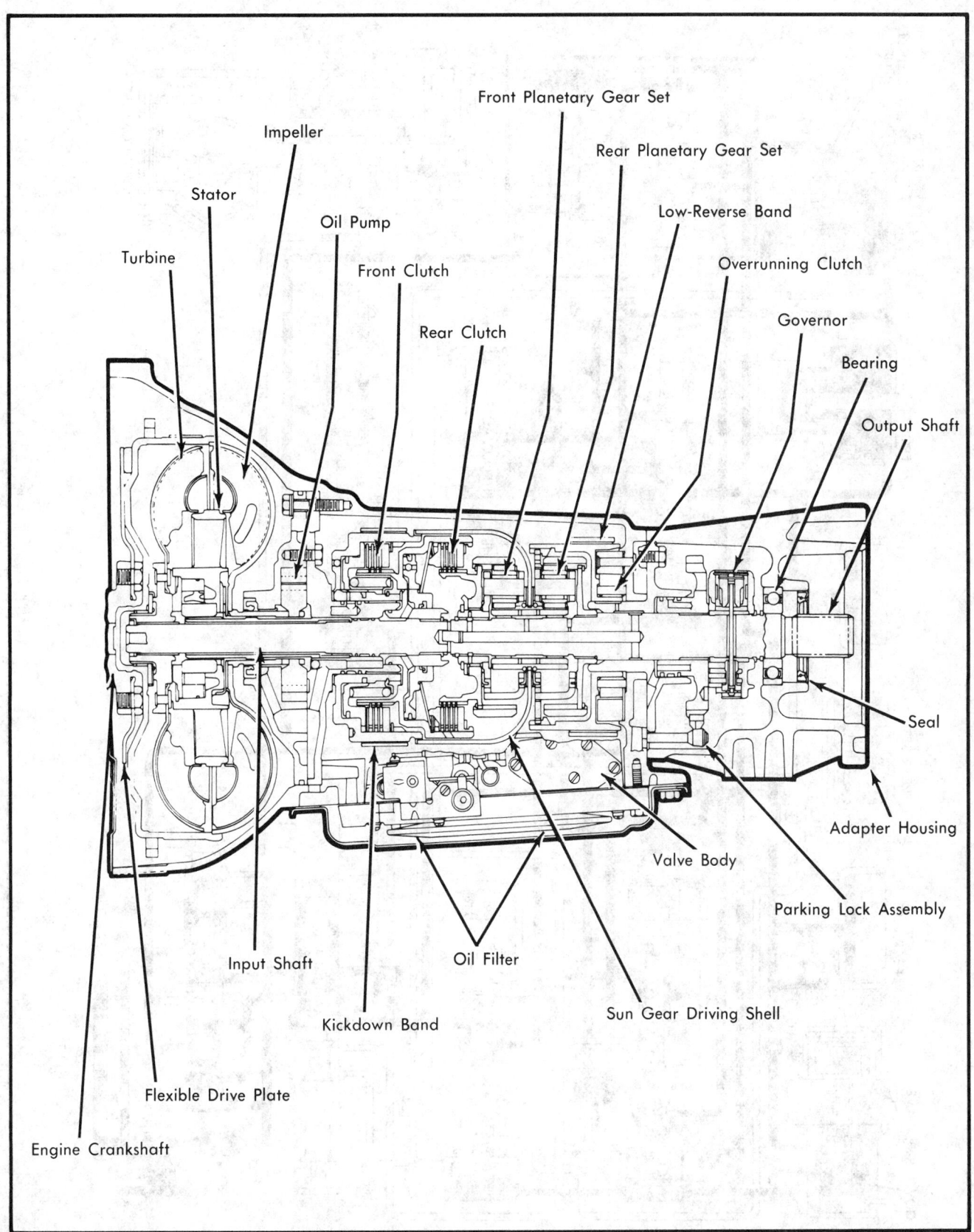

Fig. 3 Cross-Sectional View of Jeep Model 904 & 999 Automatic Transmission Assembly

Automatic Transmissions

CHRYSLER CORP. LOADFLITE A727, A904T & A999 & JEEP MODEL 727, 904 & 999 (Cont.)

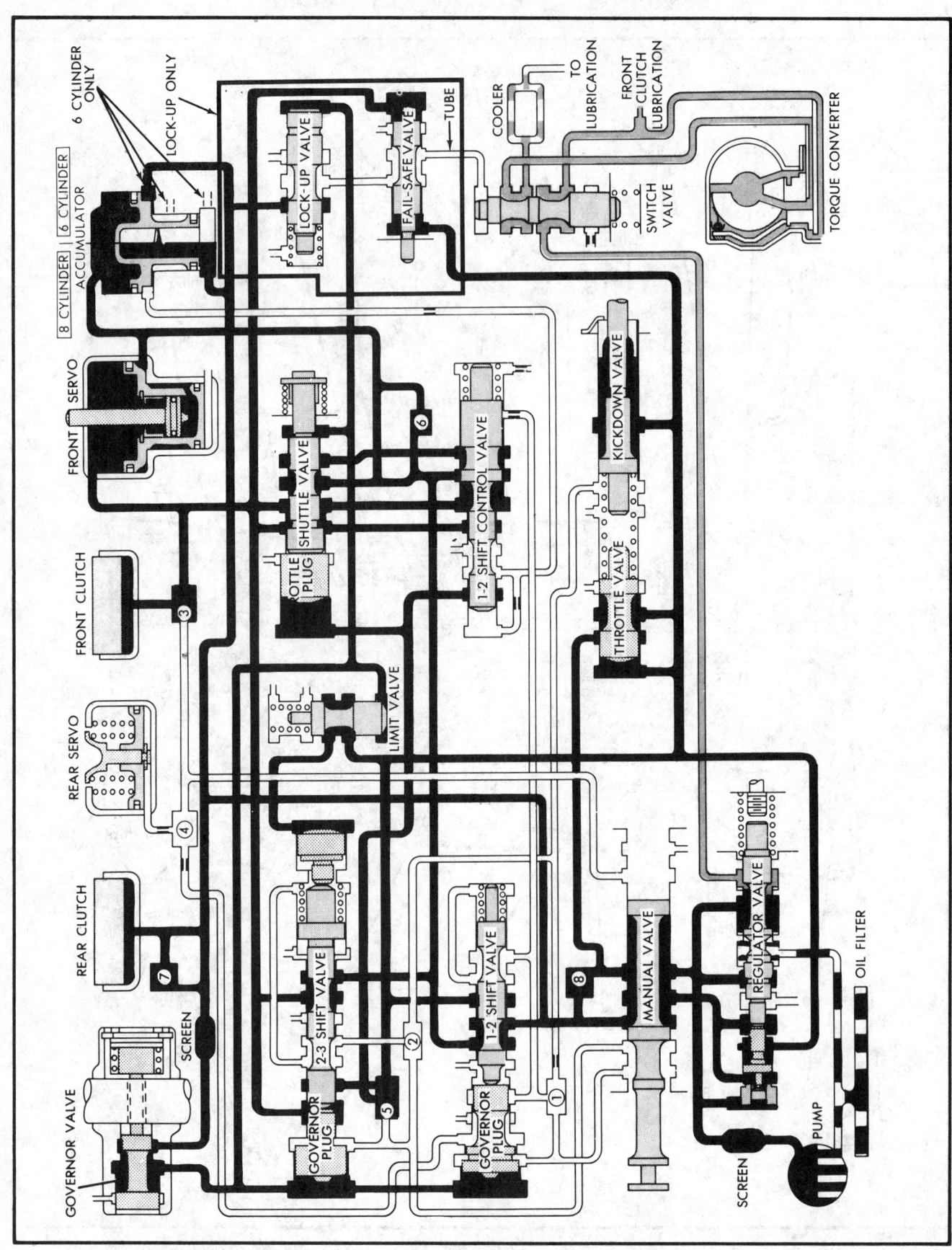

Fig. 4 *Chrysler Corp. Loadflite & Jeep Model 727, 904 & 999 Hydraulic Circuits Diagram*

CHRYSLER CORP. LOADFLITE A727, A904T & A999 & JEEP MODEL 727, 904 & 999 (Cont.)

AUTOMATIC SHIFT SPEEDS & GOVERNOR PRESSURES

NOTE — *Shift speeds shown are approximate. Changes in tire size and/or axle ratio will cause shift points to occur at corresponding higher or lower vehicle speeds.*

CHRYSLER CORP — ALL MODELS

Engine	3.7L (225")		5.2L (318") & 5.9L (360")			
Model	150	250	150	150	250	300/450
Axle Ratio	3.21	3.54	2.71	2.94	4.10	4.56
Tire Size	P195/75R15	8.00x16.5-D	P195/75R15	P195/75R15	8.00x16.5-D	8.00x16.5-E
Throttle Closed						
1-2 Upshift	8-11	8-11	9-12	9-11	7-9	6-8
2-3 Upshift	11-14	11-14	13-17	12-15	9-12	8-11
3-1 Downshift	8-11	8-11	9-12	9-11	7-9	6-8
Throttle Wide Open						
1-2 Upshift	30-40	30-40	36-48	33-44	26-35	23-31
2-3 Upshift	55-60	55-60	65-77	60-71	47-56	42-50
Kickdown Range						
3-2 Downshift	51-61	51-61	60-72	55-67	44-53	39-47
3-1 Downshift	24-33	24-33	29-39	26-36	21-29	19-26
Governor Pressure①						
15 psi	16-18	16-18	19-21	17-19	14-15	12-14
50 psi	39-45	39-45	46-53	43-49	34-39	30-35
75 psi	59-62	59-62	67-74	62-68	48-54	43-48

① — Governor pressure should be from zero to 1.5 psi at stand-still or downshift may not occur.

HYDRAULIC PRESSURE TESTS

Before making pressure tests, be certain that fluid level, condition and control linkage adjustments have been checked and corrected if necessary. Bring transmission to normal operating temperature. Connect tachometer to engine, raise vehicle on hoist to allow rear wheels to turn and position tachometer so it can be read under vehicle. Disconnect throttle rod and shift rod from transmission levers so they can be controlled from under vehicle.

Pressure Test (Selector in "1") — Attach 0-100 psi gauges to line and rear servo ports. Operate engine at 1000 RPM for test. Move selector lever on transmission all the way forward ("1" position). Read pressures on both gauges as throttle lever on transmission is moved from full forward position to full rearward position. Line pressure should read 54-60 psi with throttle lever forward, and should gradually increase as lever is moved rearward to 90-96 psi. Rear servo pressure should read the same as line pressure within 3 psi. This tests pump output, pressure regulation, and condition of rear clutch and rear servo hydraulic circuits.

Pressure Test (Selector in "2") — Install a "T" fitting at rear cooler line fitting. Attach 0-100 psi gauges to "T" connection and line pressure port. Operate engine at 1000 RPM for test. Move selector lever on transmission one detent rearward from

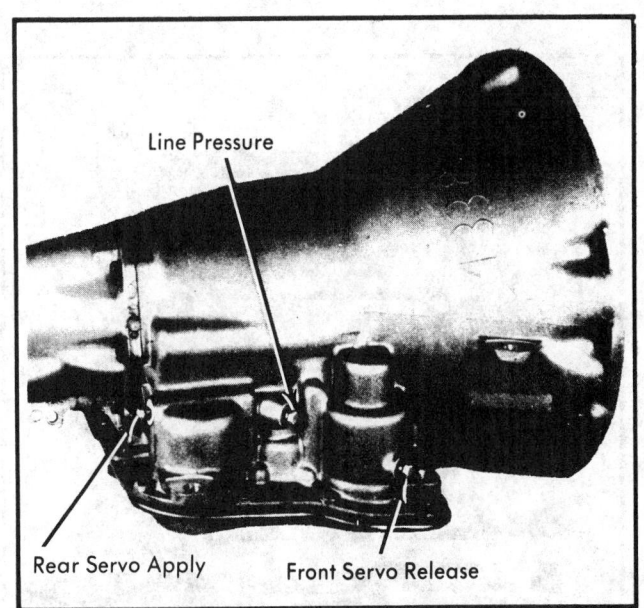

Fig. 5 *Right Side of Transmission Case Showing Pressure Test Ports*

CHRYSLER CORP. LOADFLITE A727, A904T & A999
& JEEP MODEL 727, 904 & 999 (Cont.)

full forward position (into "2" position). Read pressures on both gauges as throttle lever on transmission is moved from full forward position to full rearward position. Line pressure should read 54-60 psi with throttle lever forward, and should gradually increase as lever is moved rearward to 90-96 psi. Lubrication pressure should be 5-15 psi with lever forward, and 10-30 psi with lever rearward. This tests pump output, pressure regulation, and condition of rear clutch and lubrication hydraulic circuits.

Pressure Test (Selector in "D") — Attach 0-100 psi gauges to line and front servo release ports. Operate engine at 1000 RPM for test. Move selector lever on transmission two detents rearward from full forward position (to "D" position). Read pressures on both gauges as throttle lever on transmission is moved from full forward position to full rearward position. Line pressure should read 54-60 psi with throttle lever forward, and should gradually increase as lever is moved rearward. Front servo release is pressurized only in direct drive and should be the same as line pressure (within 3 psi), up to downshift point. This tests pump output, pressure regulation, and condition of front and rear clutch hydraulic circuits.

NOTE — *Use 0-300 psi gauge for reverse pressure test.*

Pressure Test (Selector in Reverse) — Attach gauge to rear servo apply port. Operate engine at 1600 RPM for test. Move selector lever on transmission 4 detents rearward from full forward position (to "R" position). Rear servo pressure should read 145-175 psi with throttle lever forward and should gradually increase as lever is moved rearward to 230-280 psi. This tests pump output, pressure regulation and condition of front clutch and rear servo hydraulic circuits. Move selector lever on transmission to "D" position and check that rear servo pressure drops to zero. This tests for leakage into rear servo due to case porosity, which can cause reverse band to burn out.

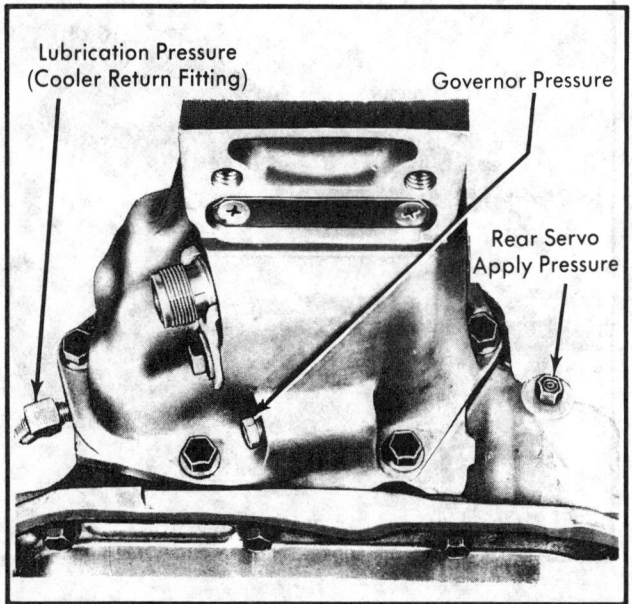

Fig. 6   Rear View of Transmission Case Showing Pressure Test Ports

Pressure Test Indications — If proper line pressure, minimum to maximum, is found in any one test, the pump and pressure regulator are working properly. Low pressure in "D", "1" and "2", but correct pressure in "R", indicates rear clutch circuit leakage. Low pressure in "D" and "R", but correct pressure in "1", indicates front clutch circuit leakage. Low pressure in "R" and "1", but correct pressure in "2", indicates rear servo circuit leakage. Low line pressure in all positions indicates a defective pump, clogged filter, or stuck pressure regulator valve.

Governor Pressure — 1) Connect a 0-100 psi gauge to governor pressure port. Operate transmission in 3rd gear and read pressures. Compare with those shown in Automatic Shift Speeds and Governor Pressure Charts.

NOTE — *Perform governor pressure test only if transmission shifts at wrong vehicle speeds when throttle rod is correctly adjusted.*

2) If governor pressures are incorrect at the given vehicle speeds, governor valve and/or weights are sticking. Governor pressure should return to 0-1½ psi when vehicle is stopped.

NOTE — *High pressure at standstill (above 2 psi) will prevent transmission from downshifting.*

Throttle Pressure — No gauge port is provided for testing throttle pressure. Incorrect throttle pressure should only be suspected if part throttle upshift speeds are either delayed or occur too early in relation to vehicle speeds. Engine runaway on either upshifts or downshifts can also be an indicator of incorrect (low) throttle pressure setting.

NOTE — *DO NOT make throttle pressure adjustment until transmission throttle rod adjustment has been checked and/or made.*

HYDRAULIC PRESSURE ADJUSTMENTS

Throttle Pressure — 1) Throttle pressures cannot be tested accurately; therefore, adjustment should be measured if a malfunction is evident.

2) Remove valve body assembly from transmission. *See Valve Body Assembly in Service (In Vehicle).* Loosen throttle lever stop screw lock nut and back off screw approximately five turns.

3) Insert gauge pin of special tool C-3763 (Chrysler Corp.) or J-24031 (Jeep) between throttle lever cam and kickdown valve. Push in on tool and compress kickdown valve against spring, so valve is completely bottomed inside valve body.

4) As force is being exerted to compress spring, turn throttle lever stop screw with Allen wrench until head of screw touches throttle lever tang with throttle lever cam touching tool and the throttle valve bottomed.

CAUTION — *Be sure adjustment is made with spring fully compressed and valve bottomed in valve body.*

CHRYSLER CORP. LOADFLITE A727, A904T & A999 & JEEP MODEL 727, 904 & 999 (Cont.)

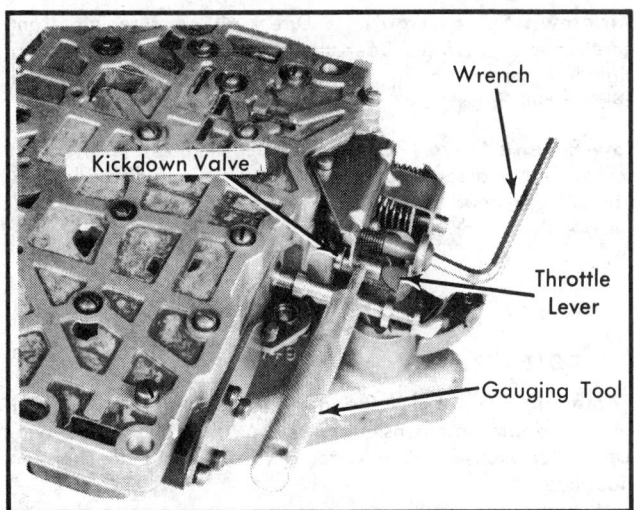

Fig. 7 Adjusting Throttle Pressure Using Special Gauging Tool

Line Pressure — **1)** An incorrect throttle pressure setting will cause incorrect line pressure readings even though line pressure adjustment is correct. Always inspect and correct throttle pressure adjustment before adjusting line pressure.

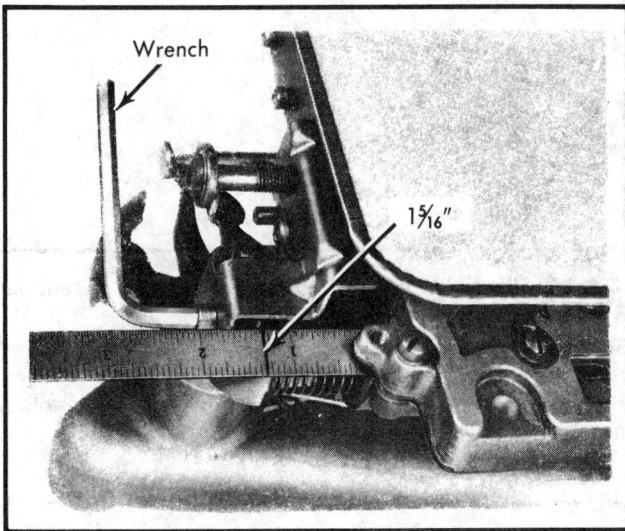

Fig. 8 Measuring Line Pressure Adjustment

2) Turn Allen screw in end of pressure regulator spring bracket so measurement between valve body and inner edge of adjusting nut is 1⁵⁄₁₆". Due to manufacturing tolerances, adjustment can be varied to obtain specified line pressure.

3) One complete turn of adjusting screw changes closed throttle line pressure approximately 1⅔ psi. Turning adjusting screw counterclockwise increases pressure; clockwise decreases pressure.

STALL TEST

CAUTION — *DO NOT allow anyone to stand in front of vehicle during this test.*

1) Check transmission fluid level and correct as necessary. Bring engine to normal operating temperature. Connect tachometer to engine. Block front wheels, fully apply parking brake and service brakes while making test. Test consists of determining engine speed at full throttle in "D" position.

2) Open throttle, but do not hold throttle open any longer than is necessary to obtain maximum engine speed reading and never longer than 5 seconds at a time. If more than one stall speed check is required, operate engine at approximately 1000 RPM in "N" for 20 seconds to cool transmission fluid between checks.

NOTE — *If engine speed exceeds maximum RPM, immediately release throttle as transmission clutch slippage is indicated.*

Stall Speed Specifications	
Application	**Stall RPM**
Chrysler Corp.①	
3.7L 6-Cylinder	1800-2100
5.2L V8	1700-2000
5.9L V8②	1775-2075
Jeep	
2.5L 4-Cyl. (904)③	2050-2350
4.2L 6-Cyl. (999)③	1850-2150
4.2L 6-Cyl. (727)④	1950-2250
5.0L V8 (999)③	1850-2150
6.0L V8 (727)	1700-2000

① — Converter Diameter, 10¾".
② — With 4-Bbl. Carb., 1700-2000.
③ — "CJ" and Scrambler models.
④ — Except "CJ" and Scrambler models.

Stall Speed Below Specification — Low stall speeds (with a properly tuned engine) indicate torque converter stator clutch problems. A road test will be necessary to identify the exact problem. If stall speeds are 250-350 RPM below specifications, and vehicle operates properly at highway speeds but has poor through-gear acceleration, stator overrunning clutch is slipping. If stall speed and acceleration are normal, but abnormally high throttle opening is required to maintain highway speeds, stator clutch has seized (non lock-up converters only). Both of these defects require replacement of torque converter.

Stall Speed Above Specification — If stall speed exceeds maximum limits shown by more than 200 RPM, transmission clutch slippage is indicated. Make hydraulic pressure and air pressure checks to determine cause of slippage.

Noise — A whining or siren-like noise due to fluid flow is normal during stall test with some converters; however, loud metallic noises from loose parts or interference within the assembly indicate a defective converter. To be sure noise originates in converter, raise vehicle on a hoist and operate at light throttle in "D" and "N" while listening under transmission bell housing.

CHRYSLER CORP. LOADFLITE A727, A904T & A999
& JEEP MODEL 727, 904 & 999 (Cont.)

AIR PRESSURE TESTS

NOTE — *When air pressure test is being made on entire transmission, Chrysler recommends that no more than 10 psi be used.*

A "No Drive" condition can exist even with correct fluid pressure because of inoperative clutches and/or bands. The cause can be located by applying compressed air to appropriate case passages after valve body has been removed. If clutches and servos operate correctly, a no upshift and/or erratic shift condition indicates a malfunction in valve body.

NOTE — *Compressed air must be free of any dirt or moisture. Use 30-100 psi pressure for tests.*

Front Clutch — Direct air pressure into front clutch apply passage. Operation of clutch is indicated by a dull thud which may be heard or felt. Hold air pressure on for a few seconds and check system for excessive air leaks.

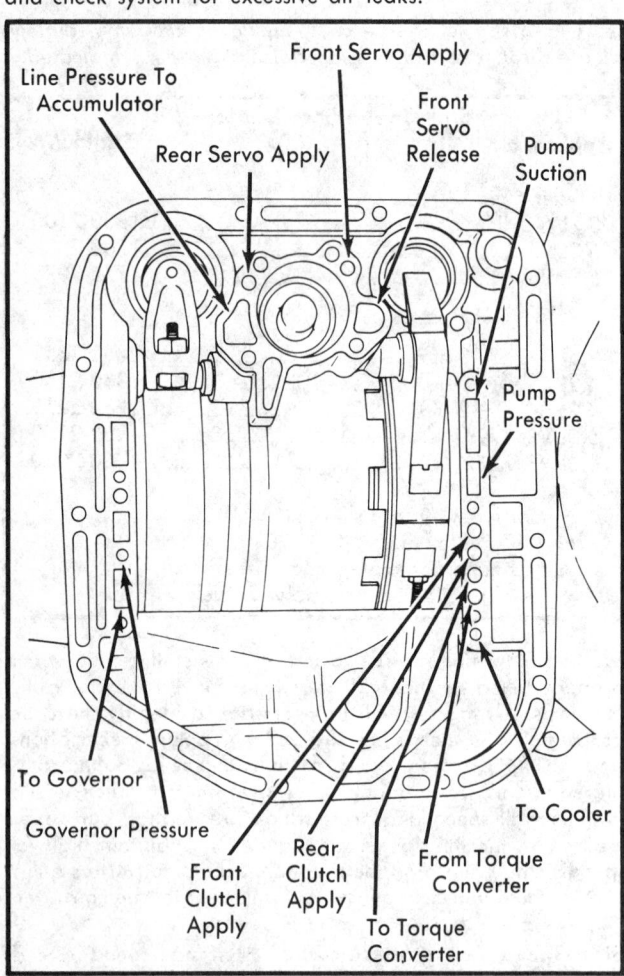

Fig. 9   Bottom View of Transmission Case Showing Air Pressure Test Points

Rear Clutch — Direct air pressure into rear clutch apply passage. Operation of clutch is indicated by a dull thud which may be heard or felt. If a dull thud cannot be heard or felt in clutches, place finger tips on clutch housing and again apply air pressure. Movement of piston can be felt as air is applied. Also check for excessive air leaks.

Kickdown Servo (Front) — Direct air pressure into front servo apply passage. Operation of servo is indicated by a tightening of front band. Spring tension on servo piston should release the band.

Low-Reverse Servo (Rear) — Direct air pressure into rear servo apply passage. Operation of servo is indicated by a tightening of rear band. Spring tension of servo piston should release the band.

SERVICE (IN VEHICLE)

SPEEDOMETER PINION

Removal — Remove bolt and retainer securing speedometer pinion adapter in extension housing. With cable housing connected, carefully work adapter and pinion out of extension housing.

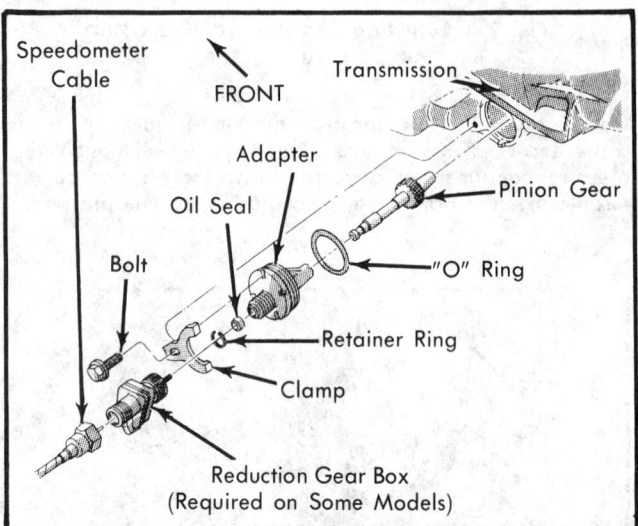

Fig. 10   Exploded View of Speedometer Drive Assembly

Seal Replacement — If transmission fluid is found inside cable housing, replace seal in adapter. Start seal and retainer ring in adapter, then push into adapter using special installation tool C-4004 (Chrysler Corp.) until tool bottoms.

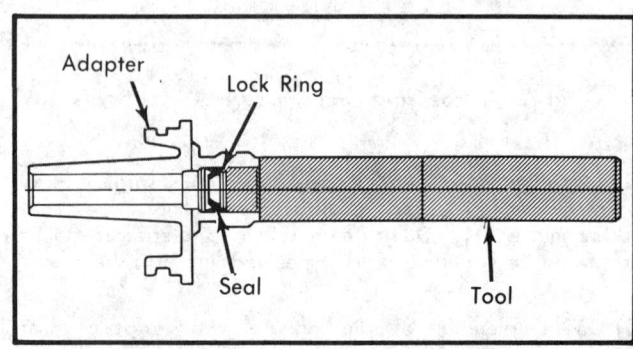

Fig. 11   Installing Speedometer Pinion Seal Using Special Tool

CHRYSLER CORP. LOADFLITE A727, A904T & A999 & JEEP MODEL 727, 904 & 999 (Cont.)

Installation — 1) Note number of gear teeth and install speedometer pinion gear into adapter. Rotate pinion gear and adapter assembly so that number on adapter, corresponding with number of teeth on gear, is in the 6 o'clock position.

NOTE — *To avoid misalignment and possible damage to speedometer pinion gear, make sure adapter flange and its mating surface are clean before installation.*

2) Install pinion gear and adapter assembly. Install retainer and bolt, with tangs in adapter positioning slots. Tap adapter firmly into extension housing and tighten retainer bolt to specifications.

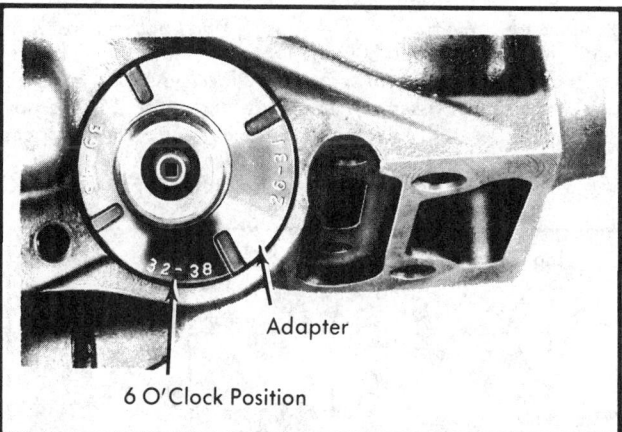

Fig. 12 Correct Installation of Speedometer Pinion and Adapter

NEUTRAL SAFETY SWITCH

See *Automatic Transmission Servicing* in this section.

OUTPUT SHAFT OIL SEAL

Removal — Mark propeller shaft and rear axle flange for reassembly and remove propeller shaft being careful not to nick or scratch splined yoke. Using suitable puller, remove seal from extension housing.

Installation — Position new seal in opening of extension housing, and using a suitable driver, drive seal into extension housing. Install propeller shaft.

EXTENSION HOUSING, BEARING & BUSHING

Removal — 1) Disconnect propeller shaft at rear axle, and slide shaft assembly out of extension housing. Remove speedometer pinion and adapter assembly. Drain approximately two quarts of fluid from transmission. Remove extension housing to crossmember and support bolts, raise transmission slightly, and remove crossmember and support.

NOTE — *When removing or installing extension housing, gearshift lever must be in "1" (Low) position, placing parking lock control rod rearward so it can be disengaged or engaged with parking lock sprag.*

2) Remove extension housing-to-transmission bolts. Remove 2 screws holding plate and gasket to bottom of extension housing mounting pad. With snap ring pliers, spread snap ring on output shaft bearing as far as possible and tap extension housing off output shaft bearing. Pull housing rearward to disengage parking lock control rod knob from sprag and remove housing.

Bushing Replacement — Using a suitable driver, remove bushing from extension housing. Align hole in new bushing with oil slot in extension housing, drive or press bushing into housing, and install new oil seal.

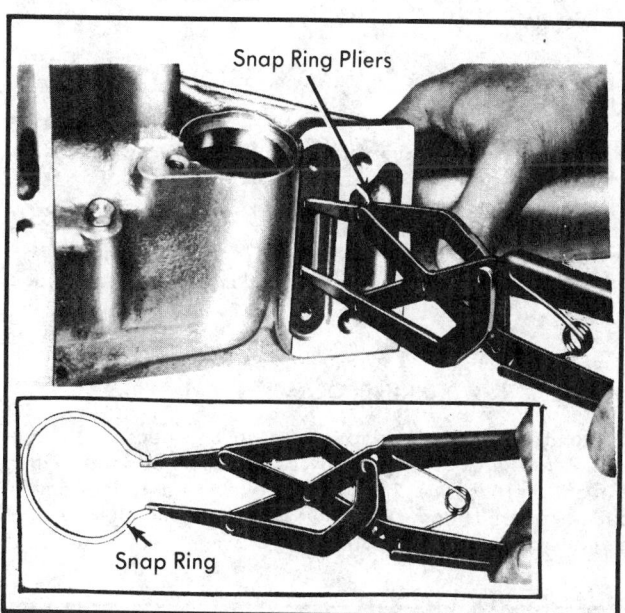

Fig. 13 Spreading Large Snap Ring for Removal of Extension Housing

Bearing Replacement — Remove output shaft bearing rear snap ring and remove bearing from output shaft. To install, replace snap ring in front groove on output shaft (if removed). Install a new bearing on output shaft with ring groove on outer race toward front. Install rear snap ring.

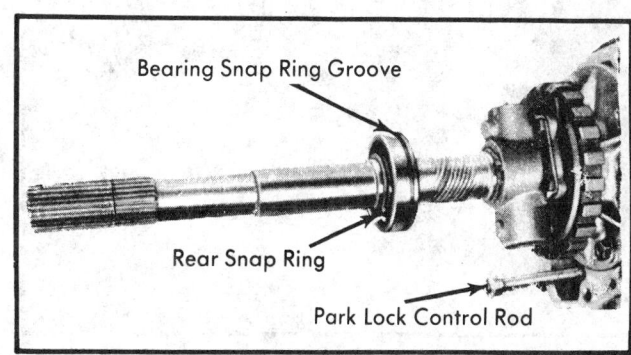

Fig. 14 View of Output Shaft Showing Rear Bearing Installation

Installation — 1) Install a new gasket on transmission case. Position output shaft bearing retaining snap ring in extension

CHRYSLER CORP. LOADFLITE A727, A904T & A999 & JEEP MODEL 727, 904 & 999 (Cont.)

housing. Slide extension housing on output shaft, guiding the parking lock control rod knob past parking sprag. While spreading large snap ring in housing, carefully tap housing into place, and release snap ring.

CAUTION — *Make sure snap ring is fully seated in bearing outer race ring groove.*

2) Install and tighten extension housing-to-transmission case bolts. Install gasket, plate, and screws on bottom of extension housing mounting pad. Install center crossmember and rear mount assembly, lower transmission, and install and tighten extension housing-to-support bolts. Install speedometer pinion and adapter. Install propeller shaft and refill transmission to correct fluid level.

ADAPTER HOUSING BEARING & SEAL (JEEP MODELS)

Removal — Remove seal from adapter housing using screwdriver or punch. Remove snap rings and remove bearing from adapter housing.

Installation — Install new bearing in housing and install snap rings. Install new seal in housing, seating seal flush with edge of seal bore.

GOVERNOR & PARKING GEAR

Removal — 1) With adapter housing or extension housing and output shaft bearing removed, pry snap ring from weight end of governor valve shaft and slide valve and shaft assembly out of governor body. Remove large snap ring from weight end of governor body and lift out governor weight assembly.

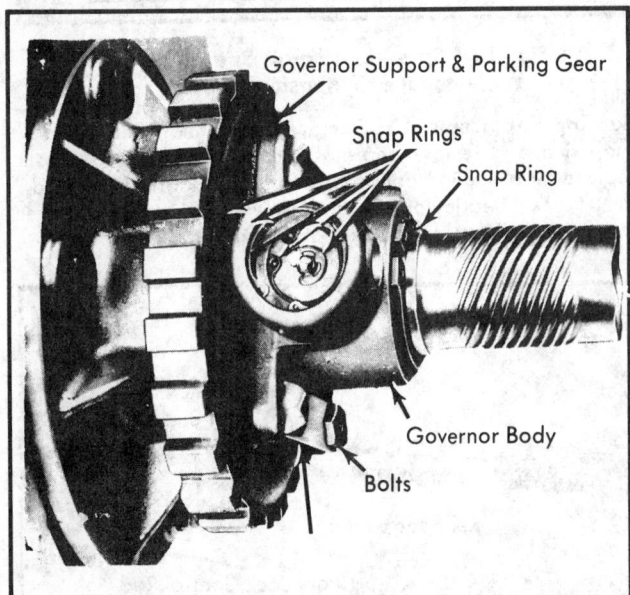

Fig. 15 *View of Parking Gear Assembly Showing Governor and Weight Snap Rings.*

2) Remove snap ring from inside governor weight and remove inner weight and spring. Remove snap ring from behind governor body and slide body and support assembly off output

shaft. Remove bolts and separate governor body from support and parking gear.

Inspection — Inspect all parts for wear or damage, and the spring for distortion. Weights and valves should fall freely in bores when clean and dry. Remove any roughness with crocus cloth.

Installation — 1) Assemble governor body to support and tighten bolts finger tight, making sure oil passage in governor body aligns with passage in support. Position support and governor assembly on output shaft, aligning so valve shaft hole in body mates with hole in output shaft. Slide assembly into place, install snap ring behind governor body, tighten body-to-support bolts, and bend lock tabs over bolt heads.

2) Assemble governor weights and spring, and secure with snap ring inside large governor weight. Place assembly in governor body and install snap ring. Place governor valve on valve shaft, insert assembly into body and through governor weights, and install valve shaft retaining snap ring. Inspect valve and weight assembly for free movement and install output shaft bearing and extension housing or adapter housing.

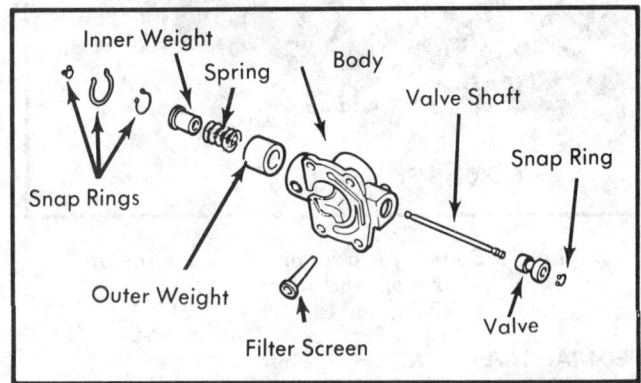

Fig. 16 *Exploded View of Governor Assembly*

PARKING LOCK

Removal — With extension or adapter housing removed, slide shaft out of housing to remove parking sprag and spring. Remove snap ring and slide reaction plug and pin assembly out of housing.

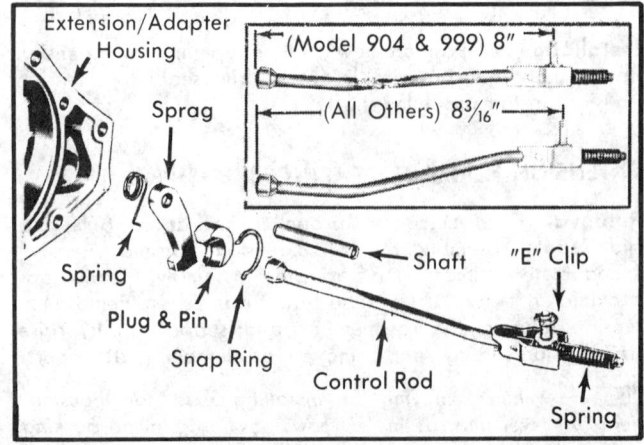

Fig. 17 *Parking Lock Component Installation*

CHRYSLER CORP. LOADFLITE A727, A904T & A999 & JEEP MODEL 727, 904 & 999 (Cont.)

Installation — Install reaction plug and spring assembly in housing and secure with snap ring. Position sprag and spring in housing and insert shaft, making sure square lug on sprag is toward parking gear and spring is positioned so it moves sprag away from gear. Install extension or adapter housing.

VALVE BODY ASSEMBLY & ACCUMULATOR PISTON

Removal — 1) Loosen oil pan bolts, tap pan to break it loose allowing fluid to drain, and remove oil pan. Loosen clamp bolts and remove transmission levers. Remove "E" clip securing parking lock rod to valve body manual lever. Remove neutral safety switch. While holding valve body in position, remove valve body-to-transmission case bolts.

2) While lowering valve body down out of transmission case, disconnect parking lock rod from lever. To remove parking lock rod, pull it forward out of case. If necessary, rotate propeller shaft to align parking gear and sprag to permit knob on end of control rod to pass sprag. Remove accumulator piston and spring from case. Inspect all parts for wear or damage, replace parts as necessary.

Manual Lever Shaft Seal Replacement — If shaft seal requires replacement, drive seal out of case with a punch. Drive a new seal into case using a $^{15}/_{16}$" socket and a hammer.

NOTE — *Seal may be replaced without removing valve body from case by using a small screwdriver to pry seal out of case. Take care not to damage shaft or seal bore in case.*

Installation — 1) Insert parking lock rod through opening in rear of case with knob positioned against plug and sprag. Move front end of rod toward center of transmission while exerting rearward pressure to force it past sprag. If necessary, rotate propeller shaft. Install accumulator piston in transmission case, and accumulator spring on valve body. Place valve body manual lever in LOW position, lift valve body into its approximate position, connect parking lock rod to manual lever, and secure with "E" clip. Position valve body in case and install retaining bolts finger tight.

2) With neutral safety switch installed, place manual valve in neutral position. Shift valve body as necessary to center the neutral finger over neutral switch plunger, snug attaching bolts down evenly, and tighten. Install gearshift lever and tighten clamp bolt, making sure no binding exists when lever is moved through all detent positions. If binding exists, loosen attaching bolts and realign. Make sure throttle shaft seal is in place, install flat washer and lever, and tighten clamp bolt. Connect throttle and gearshift linkage and adjust as required. Install oil pan and refill transmission to correct fluid level.

TRANSMISSION REMOVAL & INSTALLATION

See Transmission Removal & Installation in Automatic Transmission Servicing.

TORQUE CONVERTER

Torque converter is a welded assembly and is not serviceable. If diagnosis indicates a malfunction or if converter becomes contaminated with foreign material, replacement is necessary. DO NOT attempt to repair or flush torque converter.

CAUTION — *Never attempt to interchange lock-up and conventional torque converters. The transmission input shaft and valve body required for lock-up operation are markedly different.*

NOTE — *If starter ring gear on lock-up converter requires replacement, complete converter MUST be replaced.*

TRANSMISSION DISASSEMBLY

INPUT SHAFT END PLAY

Measuring end play before disassembly will usually indicate when a change in thrust washer (located between reaction shaft support and front clutch retainer) is required to properly adjust end play during reassembly (except when major parts are replaced). Attach a dial indicator to transmission bell housing with plunger seated against end of input shaft. Move input shaft in and out to obtain reading. End play should be .034-.084" on model 727 and .022-.091" on all other models. Record reading for reassembly reference.

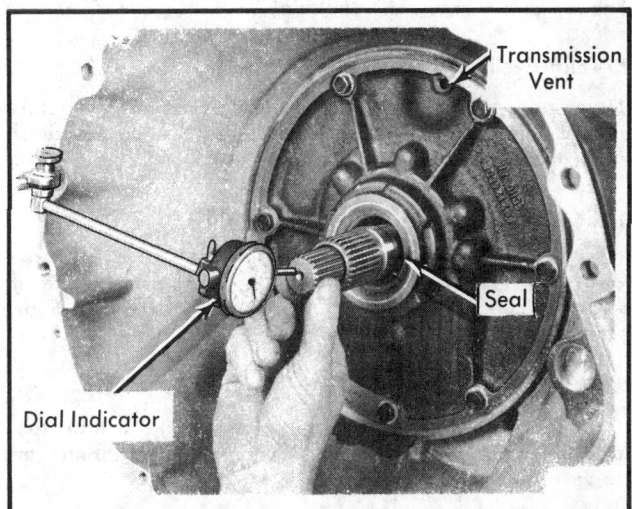

Fig. 18 Measuring Input Shaft End Play

VALVE BODY & ACCUMULATOR PISTON

See Service (In Vehicle).

EXTENSION/ADAPTER HOUSING

See Service (In Vehicle).

GOVERNOR

See Service (In Vehicle).

OIL PUMP & REACTION SHAFT SUPPORT

Tighten front band adjusting screw until band is tight on front clutch retainer, preventing retainer from coming out with pump and damaging clutches. Remove oil pump housing retaining bolts and install two slide hammers in threaded holes in pump housing flange. Operating both hammers evenly, withdraw pump and reaction shaft support assembly from case.

FRONT BAND & FRONT CLUTCH

Loosen front band adjuster, remove band strut, and slide band out of case. Slide front clutch out of case.

CHRYSLER CORP. LOADFLITE A727, A904T & A999
& JEEP MODEL 727, 904 & 999 (Cont.)

INPUT SHAFT & REAR CLUTCH

Grasp input shaft, and slide input shaft and rear clutch assembly out of case.

CAUTION — *Do not lose thrust washer located between rear end of input shaft and forward end of output shaft.*

PLANETARY GEAR ASSEMBLIES, SUN GEAR & DRIVING SHELL

While supporting output shaft and driving shell, carefully slide assembly forward and out through case.

CAUTION — *Do not damage ground surfaces on output shaft during removal.*

REAR BAND & LOW-REVERSE DRUM

Remove low-reverse drum, loosen rear band adjusting screw and thread a ¼" bolt into actuating lever pivot pin and remove pin from case using suitable pliers. Remove lever, linkage and rear band from case.

OVERRUNNING CLUTCH

Note position of overrunning clutch rollers and springs before disassembly to aid in reassembly. Carefully slide out clutch hub, and remove rollers and springs.

KICKDOWN SERVO (FRONT)

Compress kickdown servo using a suitable tool and remove snap ring. Remove rod guide, springs, and piston rod from case, taking care not to damage piston rod or guide. Withdraw piston from transmission case.

LOW-REVERSE SERVO (REAR)

Compress low-reverse servo piston spring using a suitable tool, and remove snap ring. Remove spring retainer, spring, and servo piston and plug assembly from case.

COMPONENT DISASSEMBLY & REASSEMBLY

VALVE BODY DISASSEMBLY

NOTE — *Tag all valves and springs for reassembly reference as they are removed.*

Filter, Transfer Plate & Pressure Regulators — 1) Place valve body assembly on suitable repair stand, remove filter retaining screws and filter. Remove top and bottom screws from spring retainer/adjustment screw bracket. Holding spring retainer firmly against spring pressure, remove last screw from side of valve body and remove spring retainer with line and throttle pressure adjusting screws (do not disturb settings). Remove line pressure and switch valve regulator springs.

2) Slide switch valve and line pressure valve from bores. Remove screws from lock-up module (stiffener plate on non lock-up valve body) and carefully remove tube and lock-up module (or stiffener plate). Disassemble lock-up module tagging springs for reassembly.

3) Remove transfer plate retaining screws and lift off transfer plate and separator plate assembly. Remove screws from stiffener and separator plate and separate parts for cleaning. Remove rear clutch ball check and line pressure regulator screen from separator plate. Remove 7 balls from valve body.

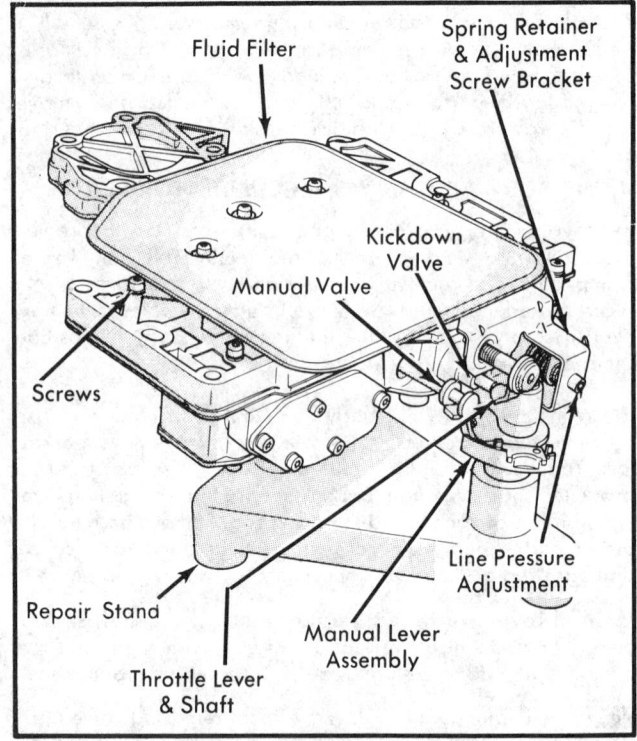

Fig. 19 *View of Valve Body Showing Components and Control Assembly*

NOTE — *Rear clutch ball check valve is used on model 727 only.*

Lock-Up Module — Remove end cover, slide out lock-up spring and valve. Remove fail-safe valve and spring and tag springs for reassembly.

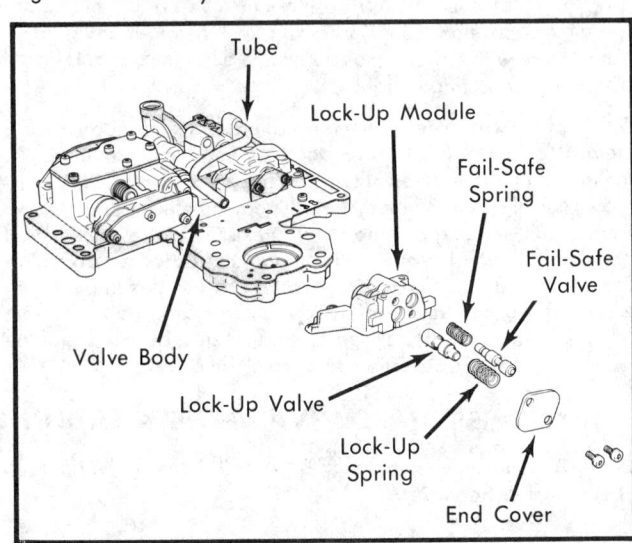

Fig. 20 *Exploded View of Lock-Up Module*

Shuttle Valve & Governor Plugs — Turn valve body over and remove shuttle valve cover plate. Remove governor plug end plate and slide out shuttle valve throttle plug and spring, 1-2 shift valve governor plug, and 2-3 shift valve governor plug. Remove shuttle valve "E" clip and slide shuttle valve from bore. Also remove secondary spring and guides retained by

CHRYSLER CORP. LOADFLITE A727, A904T & A999 & JEEP MODEL 727, 904 & 999 (Cont.)

"E" clip. Remove "E" clip and park control rod from manual lever.

Pressure Regulators & Manual Control — Remove "E" clip and washer from throttle lever shaft. Remove any burrs from shaft, then while holding manual lever detent ball and spring in bore, slide manual lever off throttle shaft. Remove detent ball and spring. Slide manual lever from bore, and remove kickdown detent, kickdown valve, throttle valve spring and throttle valve.

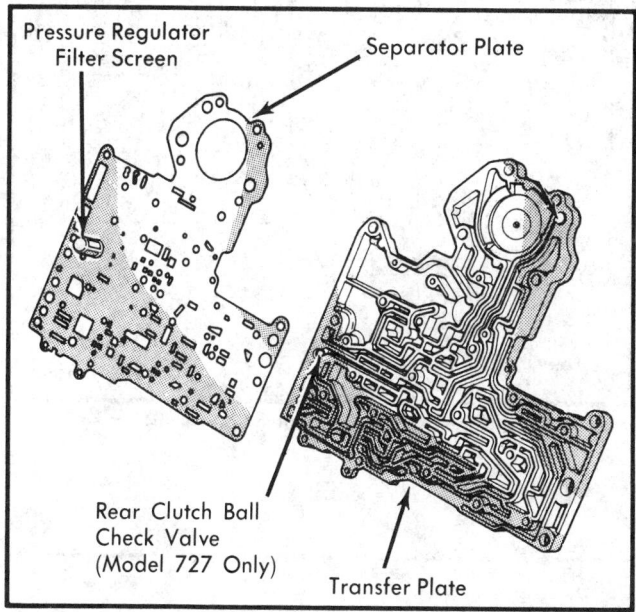

Fig. 21   View of Transfer and Separator Plate

Shift Valves & Regulator Valve Pressure Sensing Plugs — Remove line pressure regulator valve end plate and slide out regulator valve sleeve, line pressure plug, throttle pressure plug and spring. On model 904 & 999, remove downshift valve housing end plate. On model 727, remove downshift valve housing assembly. Remove plug from housing, slide retainer from housing and remove limit valve and spring. Remove 3 springs and shift valves from valve body.

VALVE BODY INSPECTION

- Wash all parts in solvent and dry with compressed air. Inspect all parts for nicks, burrs, scratches or distortion. Small nicks and burrs can be removed with crocus cloth, making sure not to round off any machined surfaces.
- Make sure all passages are clean and free of obstructions and all metering holes in steel plate and valve body are open. Insert a $\frac{1}{32}$" diameter drill through orifice into 1-2 shift control bore to make sure it is open. Inspect all springs for distortion and/or collapsed coils.
- Inspect manual and throttle valve operating levers and shafts for being bent, worn or loose. If lever is loose on shaft, it may be **silver soldered only**, or lever and shaft assembly should be replaced.
- DO NOT attempt to straighten bent levers. When bores, valves and plugs are clean and dry, valves and plugs should fall freely into bores.

VALVE BODY REASSEMBLY

Shift Valves & Regulator Valve Pressure Sensing Plugs — Slide shift valves and springs into proper valve body bores. On model 904 & 999, install downshift valve housing end plate. On model 727, insert limit and spring into downshift housing, and slide spring retainer into groove in housing. Install throttle

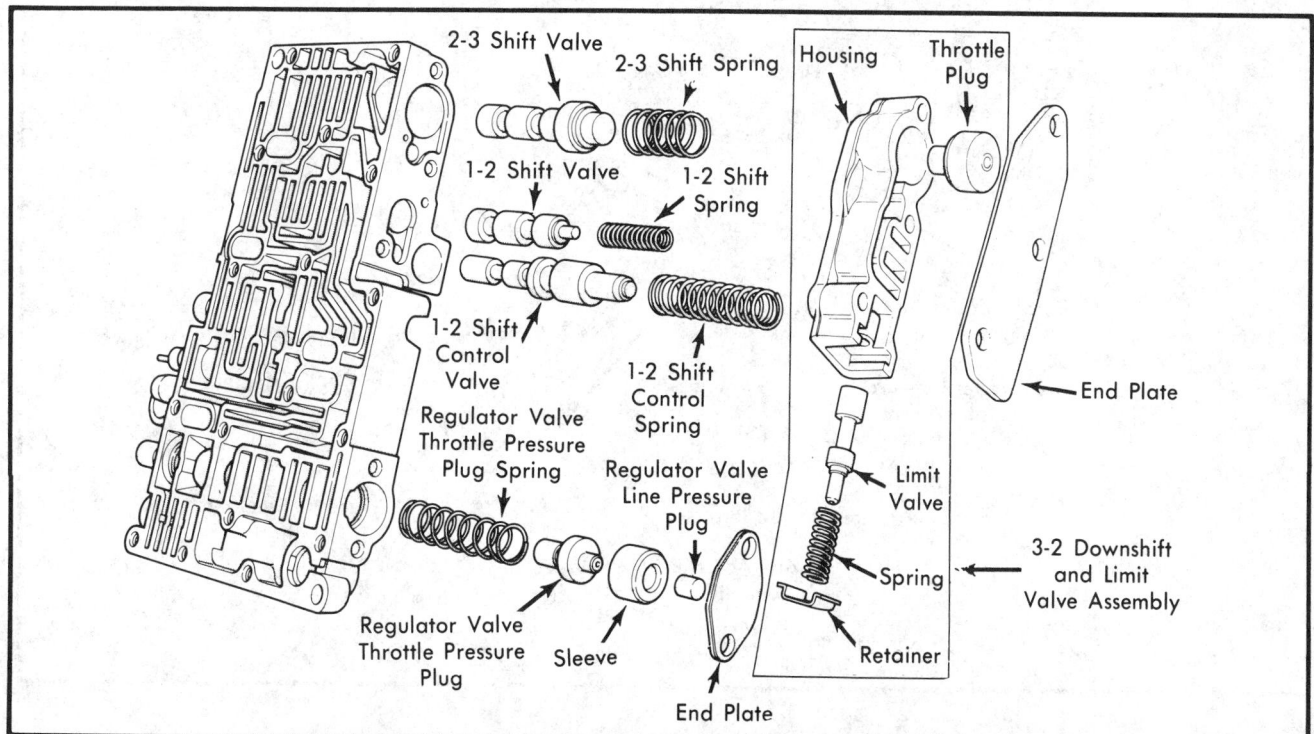

Fig. 22   Exploded View of Shift Valves and Pressure Regulator Valve Plugs

CHRYSLER CORP. LOADFLITE A727, A904T & A999 & JEEP MODEL 727, 904 & 999 (Cont.)

plug in housing bore, then position assembly against shift valve springs. Install end plate and tighten retaining screws. Install throttle pressure spring, plug, sleeve and regulator valve plug. Then install end plate and tighten retaining screws.

Manual Control — Install throttle valve, throttle valve spring, kickdown valve and kickdown detent into bore. Slide manual valve into its bore. Install throttle lever and shaft on valve body. Insert detent ball and spring into bore, depress ball and spring into bore, and slide manual lever over throttle shaft so it engages manual valve and detent ball. Install seal, retaining washer and "E" clip on throttle shaft. Insert switch valve and spring into valve body. Insert line pressure regulator valve and spring into valve body. Install pressure adjusting screw and bracket assembly on the springs and fasten with one screw for now. Use screw which goes into side of valve body. This screw is to be tightened first, after starting the top and bottom screws in a later step.

Shuttle Valve & Governor Plugs — Place 1-2 and 2-3 shift valve governor plugs in bores. Install shuttle valve into bore, then install spring guides, secondary spring, and "E" clip on opposite end of valve. Install primary shuttle valve spring and throttle plug into bore, install governor plug end plate, and install and tighten retaining screws. Install shuttle valve cover plate and tighten retaining screws.

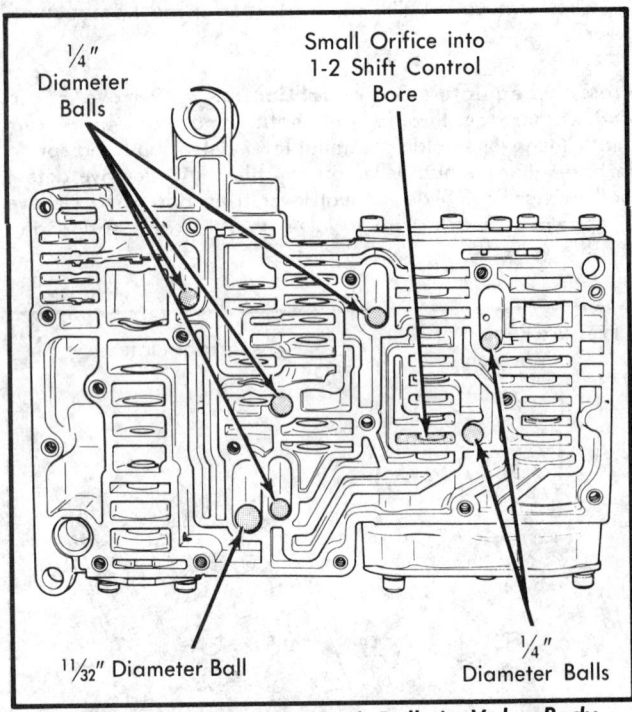

Fig. 23 Location of Check Balls in Valve Body

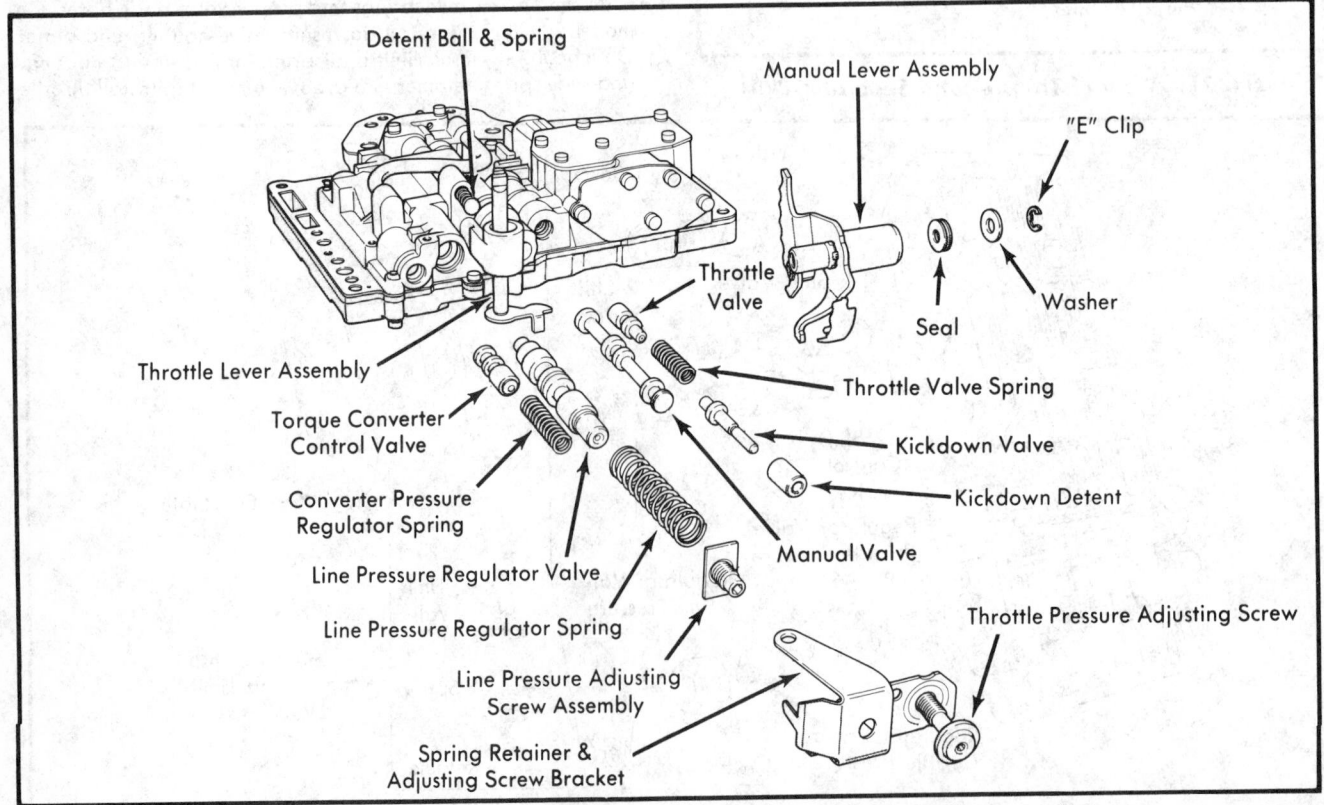

Fig. 24 Exploded View of Pressure Regulators and Manual Controls

CHRYSLER CORP. LOADFLITE A727, A904T & A999 & JEEP MODEL 727, 904 & 999 (Cont.)

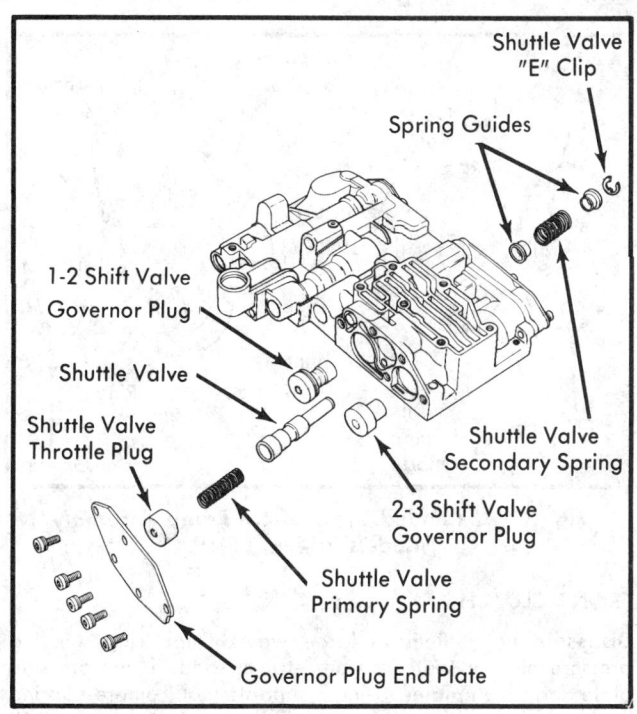

Fig. 25 Exploded View of Shuttle Valve and Governor Plugs

Labels: Shuttle Valve "E" Clip; Spring Guides; 1-2 Shift Valve Governor Plug; Shuttle Valve; Shuttle Valve Throttle Plug; Shuttle Valve Secondary Spring; 2-3 Shift Valve Governor Plug; Shuttle Valve Primary Spring; Governor Plug End Plate

Filter, Transfer Plate & Pressure Regulator — **1)** Install 7 check balls into valve body. See Fig. 23. Install rear clutch ball check valve in transfer plate and regulator valve screen in separator plate. Install 3 screws in separator plate.

2) Place transfer plate assembly on valve body. Install 17 short screws into assembly (3 long screws are for oil filter) finger tight, aligning holes for filter screen at same time. Starting at center and working outward, tighten screws to specifications.

NOTE — *Use screw which goes into side of valve body to fasten adjusting screw bracket. Tighten this screw first after starting top and bottom screws.*

3) Slide switch valve, line pressure valves and springs into respective bores. Install pressure adjusting screw and bracket assembly on the springs and fasten with 1 screw at this time.

4) Install oil filter and tighten screws to specifications. Install lock-up valve and spring, then install fail-safe spring and valve into lock-up module. Install lock-up module to transfer and separator plate assembly with 3 screws (install stiffener plate on non lock-up valve body) and tighten to specifications.

5) After valve body has been reassembled, check throttle and line pressure adjustments. Make adjustments as required unless pressures were correct before disassembly, then do not disturb settings. Install parking lock rod and "E" clip retainer to manual lever.

ACCUMULATOR PISTON & SPRING

Inspection — Inspect seal rings for wear or damage, and ensure they turn freely in grooves. Do not remove seal rings unless replacement is required. Inspect piston for nicks, burrs,

scores, or wear. Check piston bore in case for scores or other damage. Check piston spring for distortion. Replace parts as required.

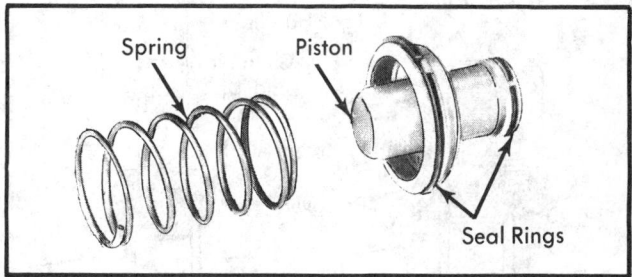

Fig. 26 Accumulator Piston and Spring

Labels: Spring; Piston; Seal Rings

EXTENSION HOUSING BEARING, BUSHING, & OIL SEAL

See Service (In Vehicle).

PARKING SPRAG & LEVER

See Service (In Vehicle).

GOVERNOR

See Service (In Vehicle).

OIL PUMP & REACTION SHAFT SUPPORT

Disassembly — Remove bolts from rear side of reaction shaft support and lift support off pump. Remove rubber seal ring from pump body flange. Drive out oil seal with a blunt punch.

Inspection — Inspect interlocking seal rings on support for wear or broken locks; make sure rings turn freely in grooves. Do not remove rings unless replacement is required. Inspect pump body and support bushings for wear or scores. Check machined surfaces of pump body and support for nicks or burrs, and oil pump rotors for scoring or pitting. With rotors cleaned and installed in pump body, place a straightedge across face of rotors and pump body. Using a feeler gauge, measure clearance between straightedge and rotor faces. Clearance should be .001-.0025". Measure rotor tip clearance between inner and outer rotor teeth. Clearance should be .005-.010" for model 727 and .0045-.0095" for all other models. Clearance between outer rotor and oil pump body bore should be .004-.008" for model 727 and .0035-.0075" for all other models.

NOTE — *Make sure on model 904 & 999 that front clutch retainer-to-reaction shaft thrust washer is .061-.063" thick. Replace if necessary.*

Pump Bushing Replacement — Place pump housing (rotor cavity down) on a clean smooth surface. Using a suitable tool, drive bushing straight down and out of bore, being careful not to cock tool in bore. With hub end of pump housing down, drive new bushing into place in pump cavity using a suitable installing tool. Stake bushing in place using a blunt punch or other suitable tool. Using a narrow bladed knife, remove high points or burrs around staked area. Do not use a file or any tool that would remove more metal than necessary.

CHRYSLER CORP. LOADFLITE A727, A904T & A999
& JEEP MODEL 727, 904 & 999 (Cont.)

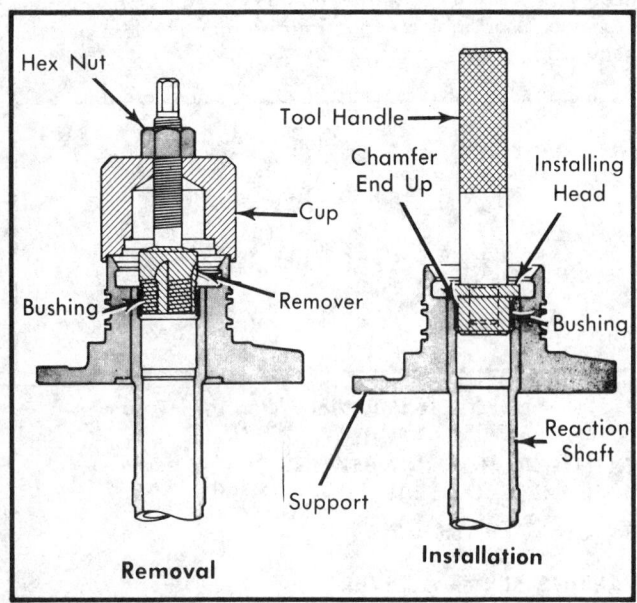

Fig. 27   Replacing Reaction Shaft Bushing

Reaction Shaft Bushing Replacement — Thread a suitable bushing remover tool into bushing, and remove bushing from reaction shaft. Support reaction shaft upright on a clean smooth surface. Using suitable tool, drive new bushing (chamfer end up) into place in reaction shaft. Stake bushing in 2 places to hold.

Reassembly — Install pump rotors and "O" ring in pump housing. Install reaction shaft support, retaining bolts and tighten to specifications. Place new seal in opening of pump housing with lip of seal facing inward and press into place using suitable driver.

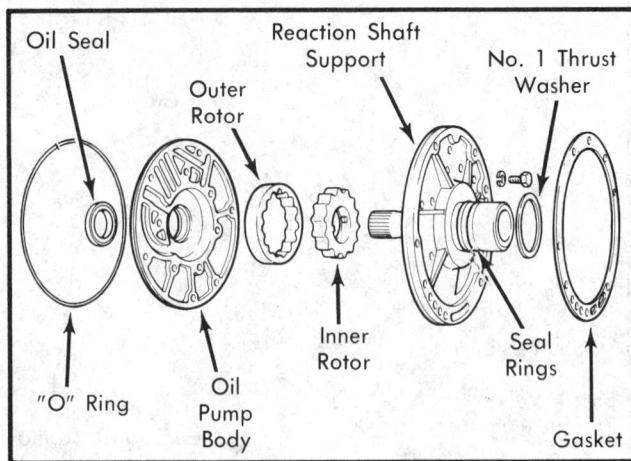

**Fig. 29   Exploded View of Oil Pump Assembly
(Models 904 & 999)**

FRONT CLUTCH

Disassembly — Remove large waved snap ring securing pressure plate in clutch piston retainer, and lift out pressure plate and clutch plates. Using a suitable tool, compress spring retainer and spring(s), remove snap ring and release tool until retainer is free of hub. Remove tool, retainer and spring(s), noting location and number of springs (model 727 only) for reassembly. Remove clutch piston and remove seals from piston and hub.

Inspection — Inspect plates and disc for flatness; they must not be warped or cone-shaped. Inspect facing material on all driving discs, replace if damaged. Inspect discs and plates for wear on splines or lugs, and check clutch retainer for damaged lug grooves or band contacting surface. Make sure ball check in clutch retainer moves freely. Check neoprene seals for wear,

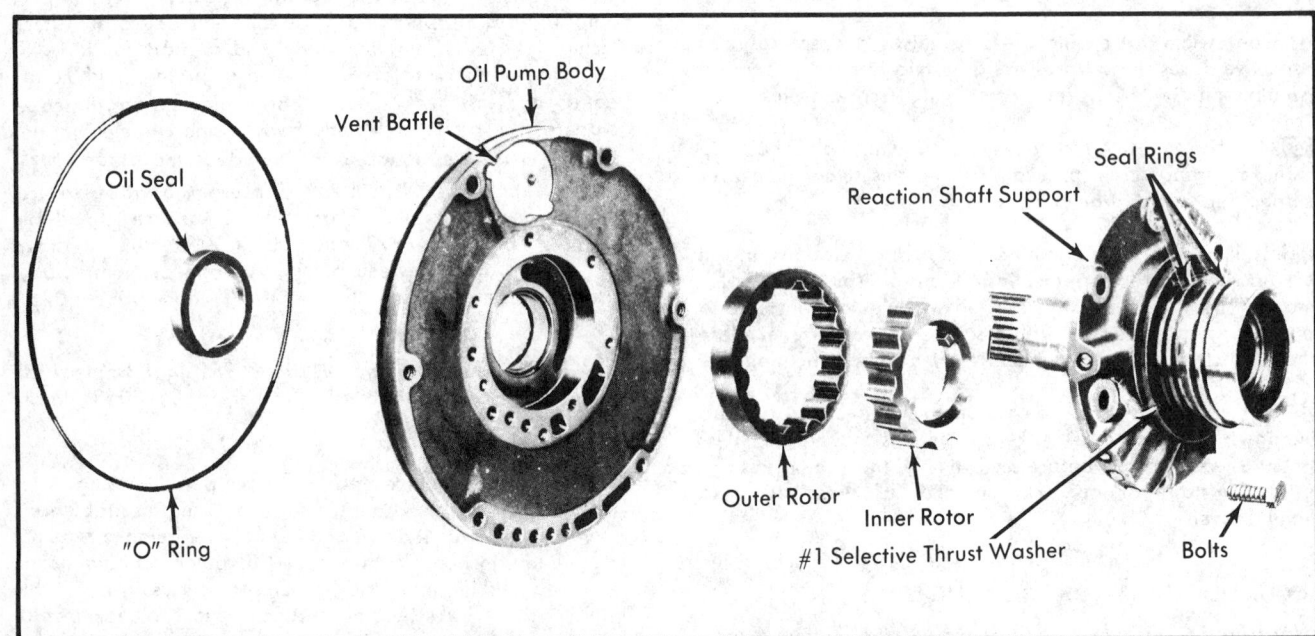

Fig. 28   Exploded View of Oil Pump and Reaction Shaft Support (Model 727)

CHRYSLER CORP. LOADFLITE A727, A904T & A999 & JEEP MODEL 727, 904 & 999 (Cont.)

hardness or deterioration. Inspect piston spring(s), retainer and snap ring for distortion.

Front Clutch Retainer Bushing Replacement — Lay clutch retainer (open end down) on a clean smooth surface. Using a suitable tool, drive bushing straight down and out of bore, taking care not to cock tool in bore. To install, lay clutch retainer (open end up) on a clean smooth surface, and using a suitable tool, drive bushing into place in clutch retainer bore.

Reassembly — 1) Lubricate and install inner seal on hub of clutch retainer. Make sure lip of seal faces down and is properly seated in groove. Install outer seal on clutch piston, with lip of seal toward bottom of clutch retainer. Lubricate seals to ease installation, then install and carefully seat piston in bottom of retainer. Install return spring(s) on piston hub according to correct number used. Position spring retainer and snap ring over hub, compress using suitable tool, and install snap ring in hub groove. Remove compressor tool.

2) Lubricate all clutch plates, then install one steel plate followed by one faced disc until all clutch plates are installed. *See Front Clutch Plate Chart.*

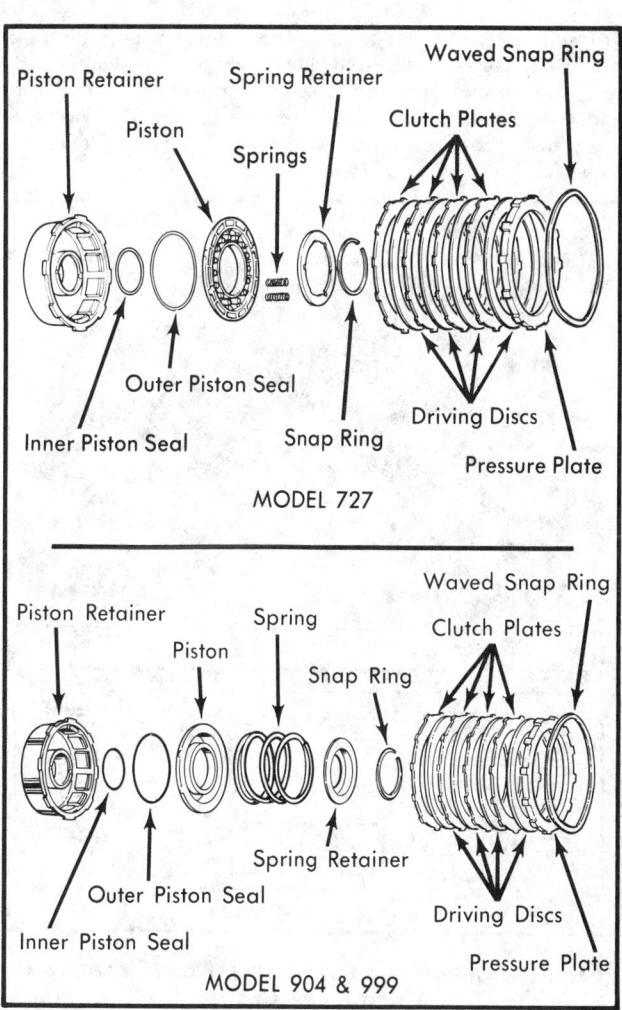

MODEL 727

MODEL 904 & 999

Fig. 31   Exploded View of Front Clutch Assembly

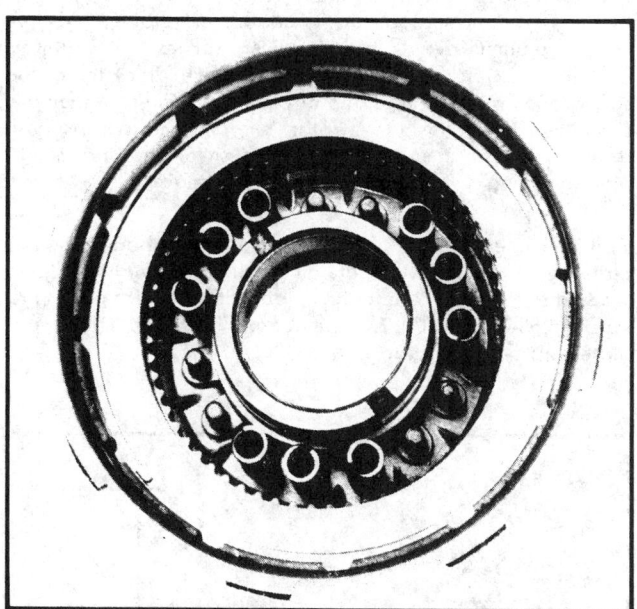

Fig. 30   Spring Installation for Front Clutch (V8 Engines, Model 727)

Front Clutch Plate Chart

Application	Steel Plates	Composition Plates
Chrysler Corp.		
Model A999	5	5
All Other Models	4	4
Jeep		
Model 727	4	4
Model 904	3	3
Model 999	5	5

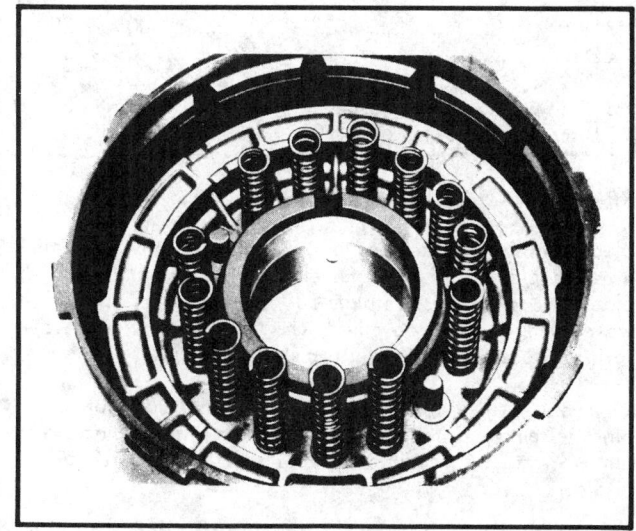

Fig. 32   Spring Installation for Front Clutch (6-Cyl. Engine, Model 727)

CHRYSLER CORP. LOADFLITE A727, A904T & A999 & JEEP MODEL 727, 904 & 999 (Cont.)

3) Install pressure plate and snap ring, making sure snap ring is properly seated. With front clutch completely assembled, insert feeler gauge between pressure plate and waved snap ring. Measure maximum clearance where snap ring is waved away from pressure plate. See Front Clutch Plate Clearance Table for specified clearance.

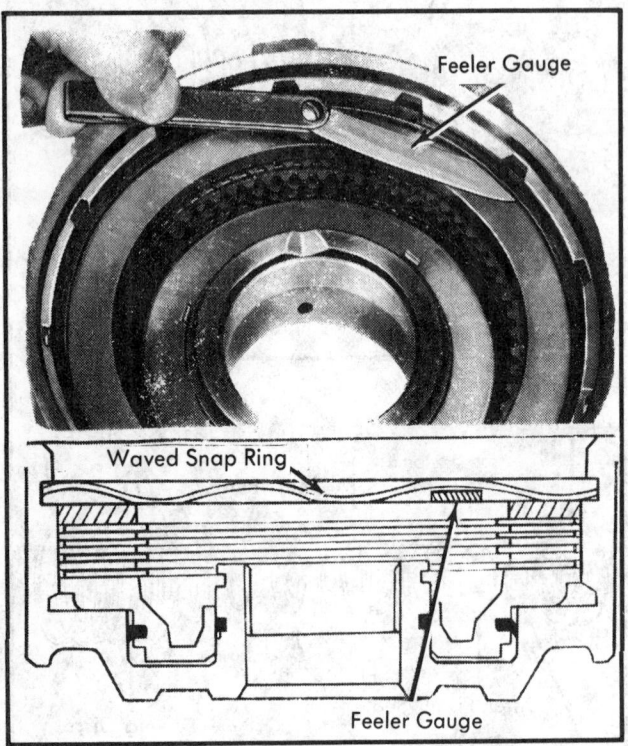

Fig. 33 *Measuring Front Clutch Plate Clearance Using Feeler Gauge*

Front Clutch Plate Clearance Table		
Application	**Model**	**Specification**
3 Disc.	727	.070-.129"
4 Disc.	727	.082-.151"
3 Disc.	904/999	.074-.125"
4 Disc.	904/999	.067-.134"
5 Disc.	904/999	.075-.152"

REAR CLUTCH

Disassembly — 1) Remove large selective snap ring securing pressure plate in clutch retainer. Lift pressure plate, clutch plates and inner pressure plate out of retainer. Pry one end of wave spring out of groove in clutch retainer and remove wave spring, spacer ring and clutch piston spring.

2) Invert clutch piston retainer assembly and bump on wood block to remove piston. Remove seals from piston. If necessary, remove snap ring and press input shaft from clutch piston retainer.

Inspection — Inspect plates and discs for flatness; they must not be warped or cone-shaped. Inspect facing material on all driving discs; replace if damaged. Inspect discs and plates for

wear on splines or lugs, and check lug grooves in clutch retainer for damage. Make sure ball check in piston moves freely. Check seal ring surfaces in clutch retainer for nicks and scratches. Check neoprene seals for wear, hardness, or deterioration. Inspect interlocking seal rings on input shaft for wear or broken locks; make sure rings turn freely in grooves. Do not remove rings unless replacement is required. Check bushing in input shaft for wear or scores. Measure rear clutch-to-front clutch thrust washer for wear; thickness should be .061-.063", replace as necessary.

Input Shaft Bushing Replacement (Model 727) — Clamp input shaft in soft-jawed vise, taking care not to clamp seal ring lands or journals. Thread suitable bushing remover into bushing and withdraw bushing from shaft. Thoroughly clean input shaft to remove any metal chips made by tool. Using suitable installer tool, drive new bushing into place.

Reassembly — 1) If removed, press input shaft into clutch piston retainer and install snap ring. Lubricate and install inner and outer seal rings on clutch piston. Make sure lips of seals face toward head of clutch retainer and are properly seated in grooves. Place piston assembly in retainer, and using a twisting motion, seat piston in bottom of retainer. Position clutch retainer over piston retainer splines and support assembly so clutch retainer remains in place. Place the piston spring and spacer ring on top of piston, making sure they are positioned in retainer recess. Start one end of wave spring in retainer groove, then progressively push or tap spring into place, making sure it is fully seated in groove.

2) Install inner pressure plate in retainer with raised portion of plate against spring. Lubricate all clutch plates, and install one faced disc followed by one steel plate until all clutch plates are installed. See Rear Clutch Plate Chart. Install outer pressure plate and selective snap ring.

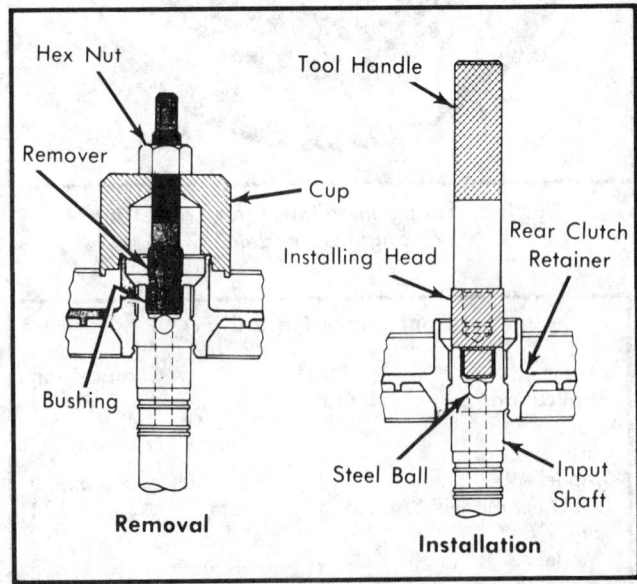

Fig. 34 *Replacing Input Shaft Bushing*

CHRYSLER CORP. LOADFLITE A727, A904T & A999 & JEEP MODEL 727, 904 & 999 (Cont.)

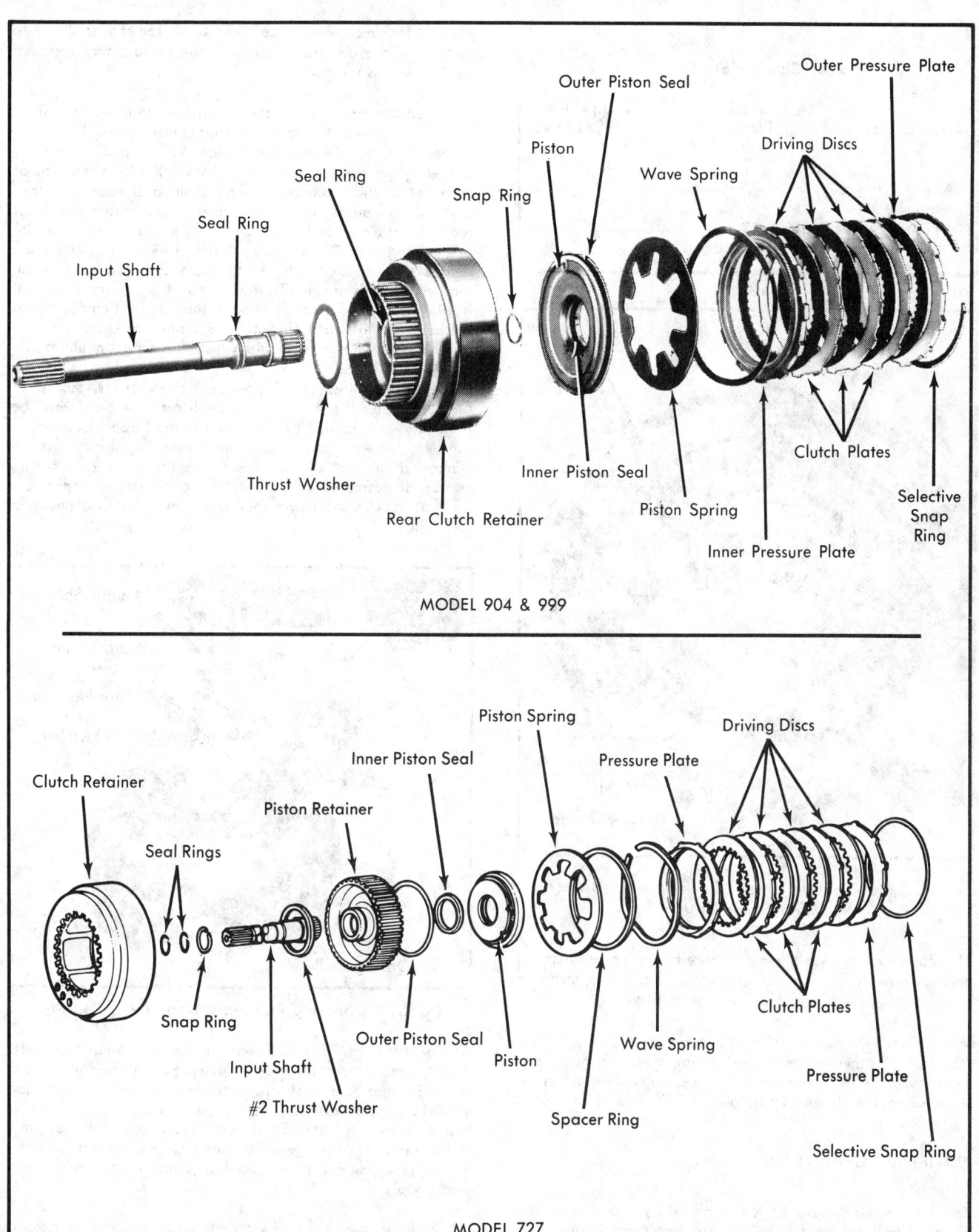

MODEL 904 & 999

MODEL 727

Fig. 35 *Exploded View of Rear Clutch Assembly*

CHRYSLER CORP. LOADFLITE A727, A904T & A999 & JEEP MODEL 727, 904 & 999 (Cont.)

Rear Clutch Plate Chart		
Application	**Steel Plates**	**Composition Plates**
Chrysler Corp.		
All Models	3	 4
Jeep		
All Models	3	 4

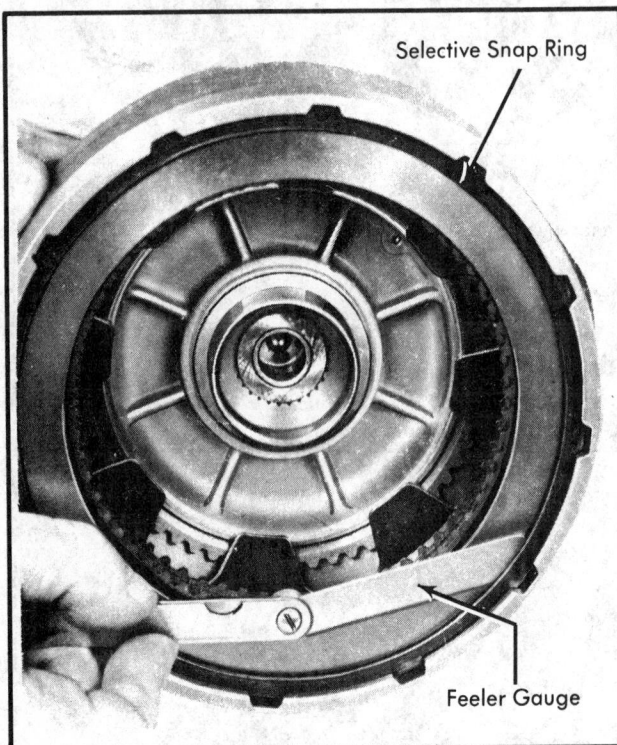

Fig. 36 Measuring Rear Clutch Plate Clearance Using Feeler Gauge

3) Measure rear clutch plate clearance by having an assistant press downward firmly on outer pressure plate, then inserting a feeler gauge between plate and snap ring.

4) Clearance should be .025-.045" for model 727 and .032-.055" for all other models. If not, install snap ring of proper thickness to obtain specified clearance. Selective snap rings are available in thickness of .060", .074", .088" and .106".

PLANETARY GEAR TRAIN

End Play — Measure end play of planetary gear assemblies, sun gear and driving shell before removing from output shaft. With assembly in an upright position, push rear annulus gear support downward on output shaft. Insert a feeler gauge between rear annulus gear support hub and shoulder on output

shaft. Clearance should be .009-.044" for model 727 and .001-.047" for all other models. If not, replace thrust washer and/or necessary parts.

Disassembly — Remove thrust washer and selective snap ring from forward end of output shaft, then slide front planetary assembly off shaft. Slide front annulus gear off planetary gear set, and remove thrust washer from rear side of gear set. Slide sun gear, driving shell, and rear planetary assembly off output shaft. Lift sun gear and driving shell off rear planetary assembly, and remove thrust washer from inside driving shell. Remove snap ring and steel washer from sun gear (rear side of driving shell) and slide gear out of shell, removing front snap ring from sun gear if necessary. Note that front end of sun gear is longer than rear. Remove thrust washer from forward side of rear planetary assembly, and remove planetary gear set and thrust plate from annulus gear.

Inspection — Inspect all parts for nicks, burrs, scores, or other damage. Light scratches, small nicks or burrs may be removed with crocus cloth or a fine stone. Inspect bushings in sun gear for wear or scores; replace assembly if bushings are damaged. Inspect all thrust washers for wear and scores; replace if damaged or worn below specifications. Make sure oil passages in shaft are open and clean. Replace distorted lock rings.

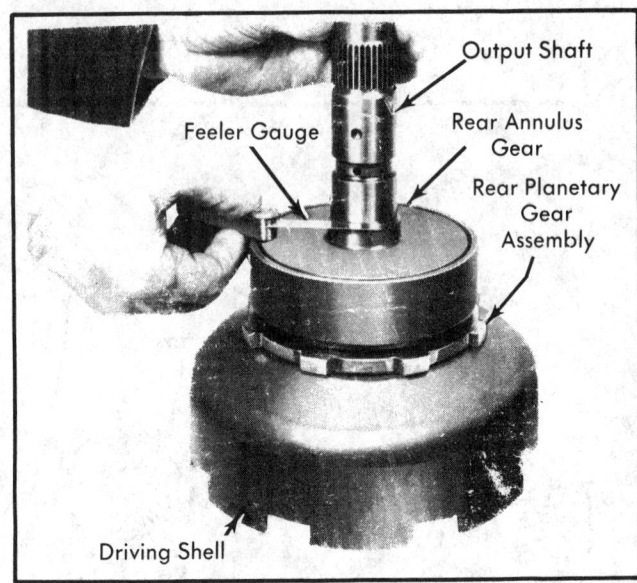

Fig. 37 Checking Planetary Gear Train End Play

Reassembly — 1) Install rear annulus gear on output shaft. Lightly grease thrust plate and place it on shaft and in annulus gear, making sure teeth are over shaft splines. Position rear planetary gear assembly in rear annulus gear, and install thrust washer on front side of gear assembly. Install snap ring in front groove of sun gear (long end of gear). Insert sun gear through front side of driving shell, and install rear steel washer and snap ring.

2) Slide driving shell and sun gear assembly on output shaft, engaging sun gear teeth with rear planetary pinion teeth. Place thrust washer inside front of driving shell. Place thrust washer on rear hub of planetary gear set and slide assembly

CHRYSLER CORP. LOADFLITE A727, A904T & A999 & JEEP MODEL 727, 904 & 999 (Cont.)

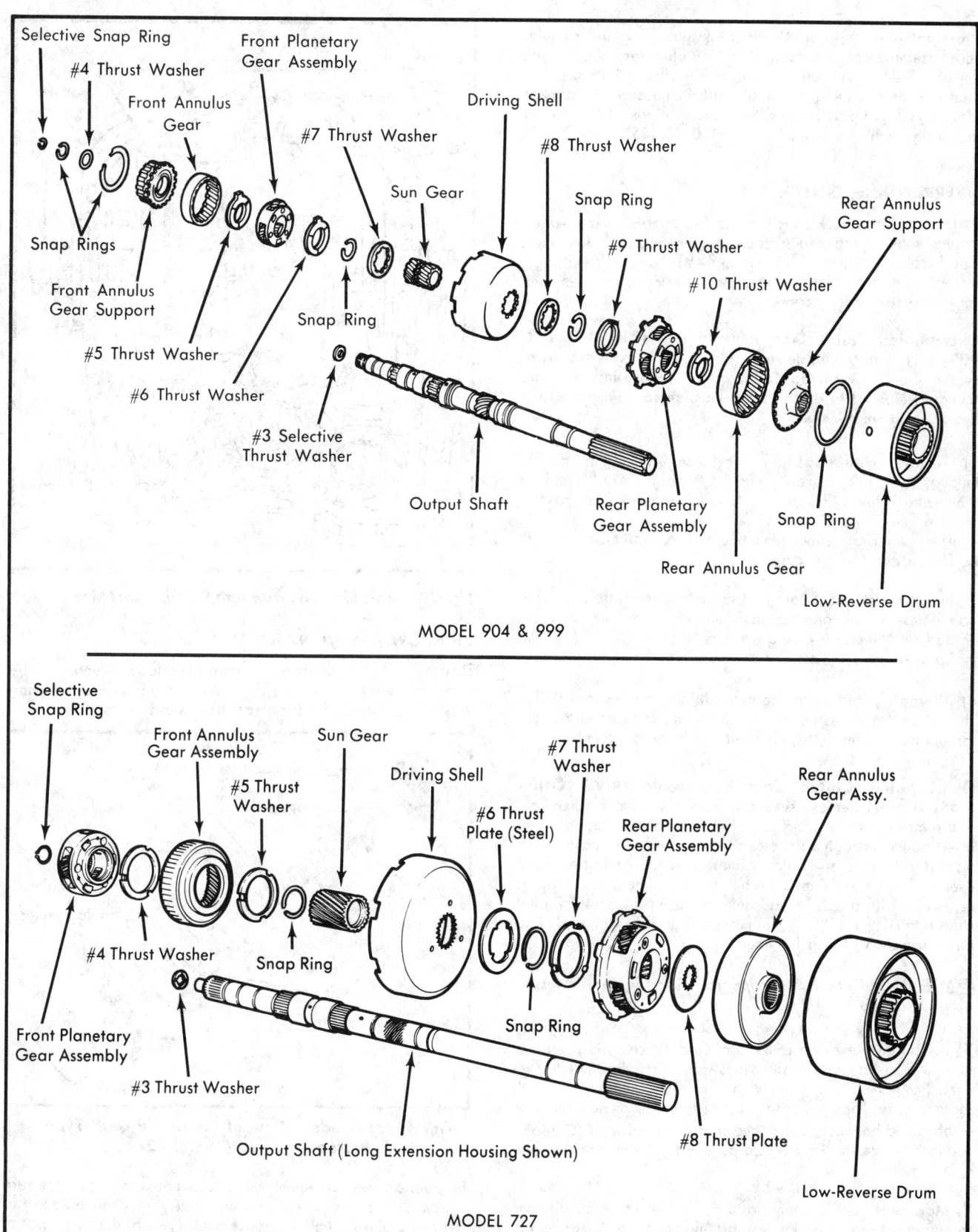

MODEL 904 & 999

MODEL 727

Fig. 38 *Exploded View of Planetary Gear Train and Output Shaft*

CHRYSLER CORP. LOADFLITE A727, A904T & A999 & JEEP MODEL 727, 904 & 999 (Cont.)

into front annulus gear. Work front planetary and annulus gear assembly on output shaft, meshing planetary pinions with sun gear teeth. With all components installed, place selective snap ring on front end of output shaft. Remeasure end play of assembly; if end play is not within specifications, install proper snap ring, available in thicknesses of .048", .055", and .062".

OVERRUNNING CLUTCH

Inspection — Check clutch rollers for smooth round edges. Inspect roller contacting surfaces in cam and race for wear. Check roller springs for distortion, wear, or other damage. Inspect cam set screw for tightness; if loose, tighten and restake case around screw.

Overrunning Clutch Cam Replacement (Model 904 & 999) — **1)** Using suitable center punch, mark rivets exactly in center of each rivet head. Drill out rivet head using $\frac{3}{8}$" drill, being careful not to drill into transmission case. Remove rivet heads using small chisel.

2) Remove rivets and cam from case using blunt punch. Enlarge rivet holes in case using $\frac{17}{64}$" diameter drill. Remove any metal chips, burrs and/or foreign material from case.

NOTE — *Alternate punch from one hole to another so cam will be driven evenly from case.*

3) Install replacement cam and spring retainer into case with bolt holes in cam and retainer aligned with holes in case. Thread retaining screws and washers into cam and install cam in case using soft-faced hammer.

4) Alternately and evenly tighten retaining screws to 8 ft. lbs. Thread 2 pilot studs into case, position support over studs, then tap support firmly into place using soft-faced hammer.

Overrunning Clutch Cam Replacement (All Other Models) — **1)** Remove set screw from case below clutch cam and remove bolts securing output shaft support to rear of case. Insert punch through bolt holes and drive cam from case. Alternate punch from one hole to another so cam will be driven evenly from case. If support requires replacement, tap support rearward with a soft-faced hammer. To install, screw 2 pilot studs into case, position support over studs, then tap firmly into place using soft-faced hammer.

CAUTION — *Output shaft support must be in case to install overrunning clutch cam.*

2) Clean all burrs and chips from case. Place spring retainer on cam, making sure retainer lugs snap firmly into notches on cam. Position cam in case, with cam serrations aligned with those in case. Tap cam evenly into case as far as possible with a soft-faced hammer. Using special tool and adapter (C-3863-A and SP-1524 for Chrysler Corp.), tighten nut on tool to seat cam in case.

3) Make sure cam is firmly bottomed in case, then install cam retaining set screw. Stake case around set screw to prevent it from coming loose. Remove tool and pilot studs, install bolts, and tighten evenly. Stake case around cam in 12 places with a blunt chisel.

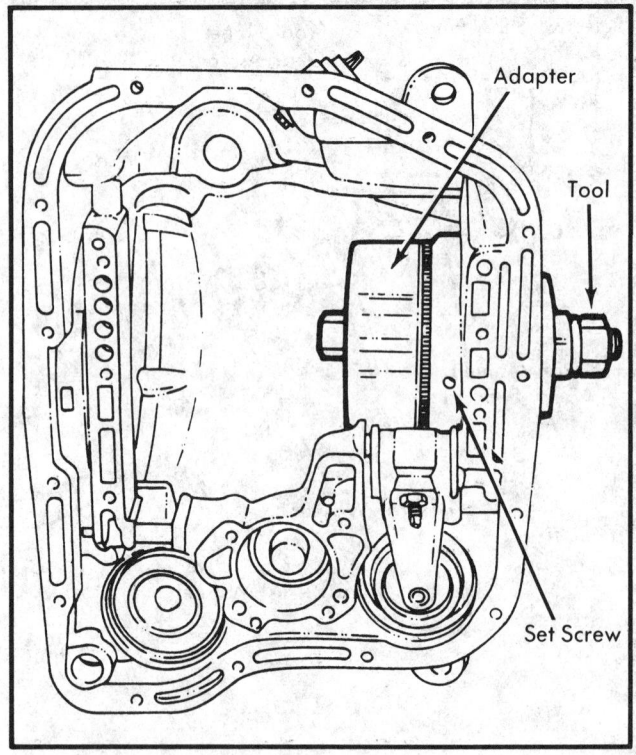

Fig. 39   Installing Overrunning Clutch Cam (Model 727)

KICKDOWN SERVO & BAND

Disassembly — Disassemble controlled load servo piston by removing small snap ring from servo piston, then removing washer, spring, and piston rod from servo piston.

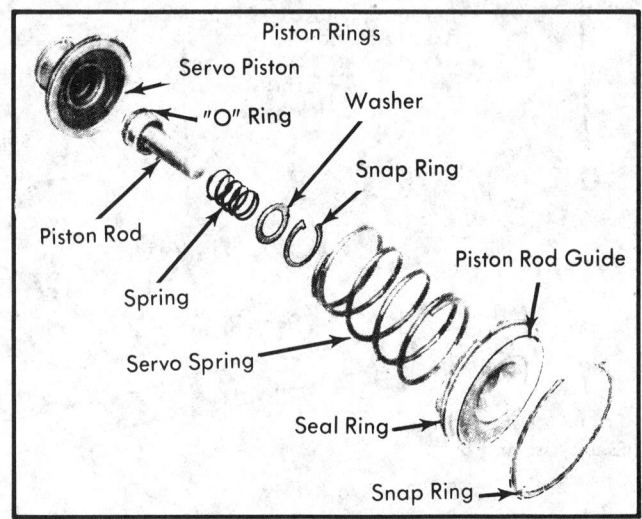

Fig. 40   Exploded View of Controlled Load Type Kickdown Servo (Model 727)

Inspection — Inspect all parts for wear or damage. Be sure piston and guide seal rings turn freely in grooves. Do not remove seal rings unless replacement is required. Inspect piston bore in case for scores or other damage. Inspect fit of guide on piston rod, and piston spring for distortion. If equipped with controlled load servo piston, inspect bore in piston and "O"

CHRYSLER CORP. LOADFLITE A727, A904T & A999
& JEEP MODEL 727, 904 & 999 (Cont.)

ring on piston rod. Inspect band lining for wear or damage; if lining is worn so grooves are not visible at ends or any portion of band, replace band.

Reassembly — Assemble controlled load servo piston as follows: Grease "O" ring and install on piston rod, install piston rod into servo piston, then install spring, flat washer and snap ring.

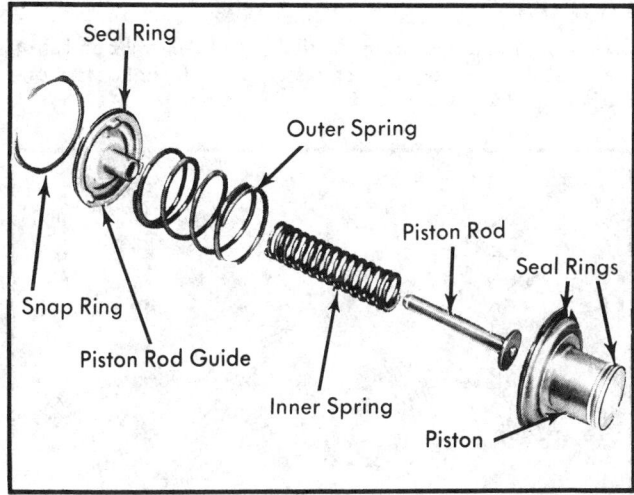

Fig. 41   Exploded View of Non-Controlled Type Kickdown Servo (Model 904 & 999)

LOW-REVERSE SERVO & BAND

Disassembly — Remove snap ring from piston and remove piston plug and spring.

Inspection — Inspect seal for wear, deterioration, and hardness. Inspect piston and plug for cracks, burrs, scores, and wear; piston plug must operate freely in piston. Inspect piston bore for scores or damage. Check springs for distortion. Inspect band lining for wear and bond of lining to band. If lining is worn so grooves are not visible at ends or any portion of band, replace band.

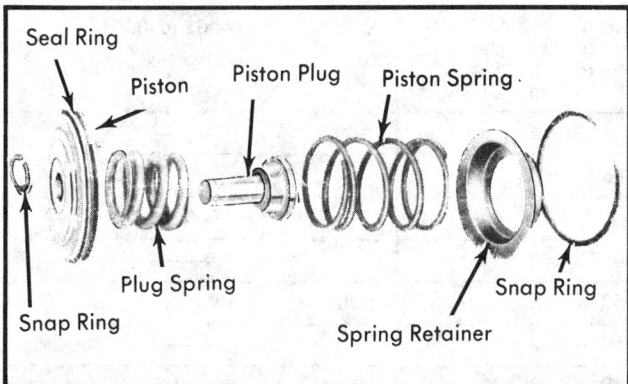

Fig. 42   Exploded View of Low-Reverse Servo

Reassembly — Lubricate and insert piston plug and spring in piston, then secure with snap ring.

TRANSMISSION REASSEMBLY

NOTE — Use only Dexron type Automatic Transmission Fluid to lubricate transmission parts during reassembly.

OVERRUNNING CLUTCH

With transmission case in upright position, insert clutch hub inside cam, then install overrunning clutch rollers and springs exactly as shown in Fig. 43..

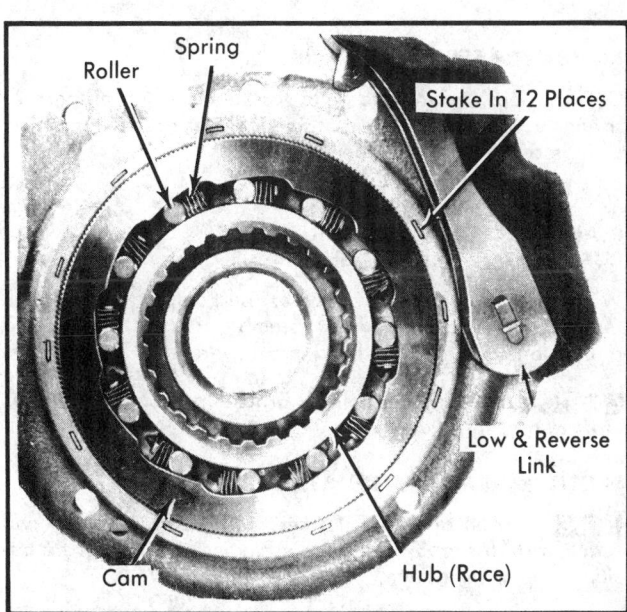

Fig. 43   Installed View of Overrunning Clutch

LOW-REVERSE SERVO & BAND

Carefully work servo piston in case with a twisting motion, then place spring, retainer, and snap ring over piston. Using a

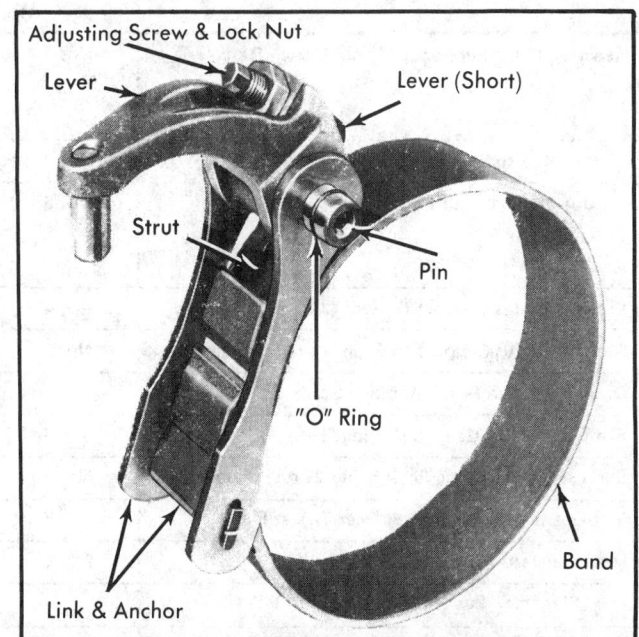

Fig. 44   View of Low-Reverse Band and Linkage

CHRYSLER CORP. LOADFLITE A727, A904T & A999 & JEEP MODEL 727, 904 & 999 (Cont.)

suitable tool, compress low-reverse servo piston and install snap ring. On model 904 & 999, install replacement "O" ring on reaction pin, and insert pin into case until flush with gasket surface. Position band in case so both lugs rest against reaction pin. Install low-reverse drum into rear band, install operating lever and pivot pin. On all other models, position rear band in case, install short strut, then connect long link and anchor to band. Screw in band adjuster enough to hold strut in place. Then, install low-reverse drum.

KICKDOWN SERVO

Carefully push servo piston into case bore. Install piston rod, springs and guide. Using a suitable tool, compress servo piston springs and install snap ring.

PLANETARY GEAR ASSEMBLIES, SUN GEAR & DRIVING SHELL

While supporting assembly in case, insert output shaft through rear support. Carefully work assembly rearward, engaging rear planetary carrier lugs into low-reverse drum slots.

CAUTION — *Do not damage ground surfaces on output shaft during installation.*

FRONT & REAR CLUTCH ASSEMBLIES

NOTE — *Front and rear clutches, front band, oil pump and reaction shaft support are more easily installed with transmission in upright position.*

Apply a coat of grease on input shaft-to-output shaft thrust washer, then install washer on front end of output shaft. Align

front clutch plate inner splines, then place assembly in position on rear clutch, making sure front clutch plate splines are fully engaged on rear clutch splines. Align rear clutch plate inner splines, grasp input shaft, then lower assemblies into case. Carefully work clutch assemblies in a circular motion to engage rear clutch splines over splines of front annulus gear. Make sure front clutch drive lugs are fully engaged in slots of driving shell.

FRONT BAND

Slide front band over front clutch assembly. Install band strut, then screw in band adjuster just enough to hold strut and anchor in place.

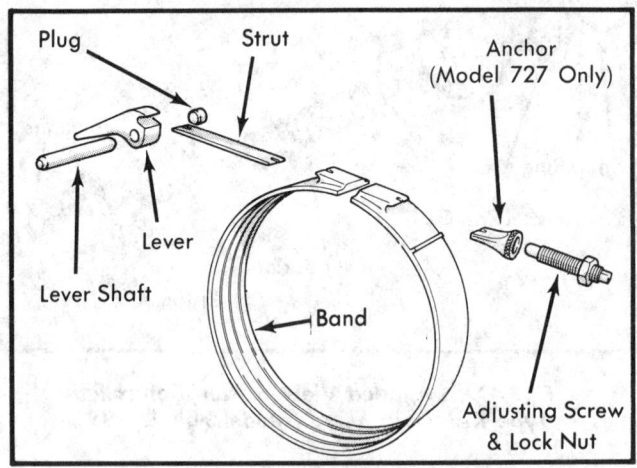

Fig. 45   View of Kickdown Band and Linkage

Thrust Washers	Thrust Washer No. and Transmission Model			
	Model 904 & 999		Model 727	
Reaction Shaft Support to Front Clutch Retainer	No. 1	.061 to .063	No. 1	Selective .061 to .063 — Natural .084 to .086 — Red .102 to .104 — Yellow
Rear Clutch to Front Clutch Retainer	No. 2	.061 to .063	No. 2	.061 to .063 — Natural
Output Shaft to Input Shaft	No. 3	Selective .052 to .054 — Tin .068 to .070 — Red .083 to .085 — Green	No. 3	.062 to .064
Front Annulus Support to Rear Clutch Retainer	No. 4	.121 to .125		———
Front Annulus Support to Front Planetary Gear	No. 5	.048 to .050	No. 4	.059 to .062
Driving Shell to Front Annulus Gear		———	No. 5	.060 to .062
Front Planetary Gear to Driving Shell	No. 6	.048 to .050		———
Sun Gear and Driving Shell Front Thrust Plate	No. 7	.050 to .052	No. 6	.034 to .036
Sun Gear and Driving Shell Rear Thrust Plate	No. 8	.050 to .052		———
Rear Planetary Gear to Driving Shell	No. 9	.048 to .050	No. 7	.059 to .062
Rear Planetary Gear to Rear Annulus Gear		———	No. 8	.034 to .036
Rear Planetary Gear to Rear Annulus Support	No. 10	.048 to .050		

CHRYSLER CORP. LOADFLITE A727, A904T & A999
& JEEP MODEL 727, 904 & 999 (Cont.)

OIL PUMP & REACTION SHAFT SUPPORT

NOTE — *If difficulty was encountered in removing pump assembly due to an exceptionally tight fit, it may be necessary to expand case in pump area with a heat lamp prior to installation.*

1) If input shaft end play was not within specifications, replace thrust washer on reaction shaft support hub with one of proper thickness. Refer to Thrust Washer Chart for sizes available.

2) Screw two pilot studs into pump opening in case, then install a new gasket over studs. Place a new rubber seal ring in groove on outer flange of pump housing, making sure seal is not twisted. Coat seal ring with grease, then install pump assembly into case, tapping lightly with a soft mallet if necessary. Remove pilot studs, install bolts, and snug down evenly. Rotate input and output shafts to see that no binding exists, and tighten pump attaching bolts. Check shafts again for free rotation, and adjust both bands.

GOVERNOR

See Service (In Vehicle).

EXTENSION/ADAPTER HOUSING

See Service (In Vehicle).

VALVE BODY ASSEMBLY & ACCUMULATOR PISTON

See Service (In Vehicle).

TORQUE CONVERTER

See Transmission Removal & Installation in Automatic Transmission Servicing.

TIGHTENING SPECIFICATIONS	
Application	**Ft. Lbs.**
Converter Drive Plate-to-Crankshaft Bolt	105
Extension Housing-to-Transmission Case	
Chrysler Corp.	32
Adapter Housing-to-Transmission Case (Jeep)	24
Extension Housing-to-Insulator	50
Kickdown Band Adjusting Screw Lock Nut	35
Neutral Safety Switch	24
Output Shaft Flange Nut	175
Reverse Band Adjusting Screw Lock Nut	35
Transmission-to-Engine Bolts	
Chrysler Corp. & Jeep	30
Converter Drive Plate-to-Torque Converter	22
Governor Body-to-Support Bolts	8
Kickdown Lever Shaft Plug	13
Cooler Line Fitting	15
Cooler Line Nut	25
Oil Pan Bolts	13
Pump Hsg.-to-Transmission Case	15
Output Shaft Support Bolt	13
Overrunning Clutch Cam Set Screw	3
Overrunning Clutch Cam Retaining Screws	8
Pressure Test Take-Off Plug	9
Reaction Shaft Support-to-Oil Pump	13
Valve Body Screws	3
Valve Body-to-Transmission Case	8

FORD AUTOMATIC OVERDRIVE TRANSMISSION

F100/250

TRANSMISSION IDENTIFICATION

The Automatic Overdrive Transmission (A.O.T.) is identified by the code letter **"T"**. The identification code letter is found on the lower line of Vehicle Certification Label under "TRANS". This label is attached to the left (driver's) side door lock post.

DESCRIPTION

The Automatic Overdrive Transmission (A.O.T.) is a four speed, fully automatic transmission which combines automatic shifting with two fuel saving features: an overdrive gear ratio and mechanical lock-out split torque path in 3rd gear. In this range, 40% of the torque is transmitted hydraulically through the torque converter as in conventional automatic transmissions while the remaining 60% of engine torque is transmitted mechanically.

The torque converter operation is similar to other automatics, but has an added damper assembly and an input shaft which is used in third (direct drive) and overdrive gears.

Overdrive is accomplished by band application which locks the reverse sun gear while driving the planet carrier. In this ratio, engine torque flows through the damper assembly and in doing so, by-passes the torque converter. Power flow from the engine into the transmission is then direct.

Transmission consists basically of the torque converter assembly, four multi-disc clutches, two bands, two one-way roller clutches and a hydraulic control system. The hydraulic system differs from that on other Ford automatic transmissions in that the vacuum diaphragm that is normally used for the

"engine load" input has been eliminated. In place of this vacuum device, mechanical linkage is employed from the carburetor to the transmission. As a result, throttle (TV) fluid pressure is controlled mechanically rather than by vacuum.

LUBRICATION & ADJUSTMENT

See *Automatic Transmission Servicing.*

TESTING

ROAD TEST

1) Check minimum throttle upshifts in "O/D". Transmission should start in first gear, shift to second then shift to third and finally shift to fourth gear at approximately the speeds shown in "Shift Speed Table".

NOTE — *Choke must be "OFF" when checking minimum throttle upshifts. If not, shift points will be affected.*

2) Check partial throttle upshifts in "O/D". Transmission should start in first gear, shift to second, then shift to third and finally shift to fourth gear. *See Shift Speed Table.*

3) With transmission in fourth gear (overdrive), depress accelerator pedal to the floor. Transmission should downshift to third or to second gear, depending on vehicle speed. *See Shift Speed Table.*

4) Since closed throttle downshifts are extremely difficult to detect, it will be necessary to attach pressure gauges to forward and direct clutch pressure taps in order to detect 4-3 and 3-2 coast downshifts.

5) With gauges attached, a 4-3 coast (closed throttle) downshift is signified by the application of the forward clutch

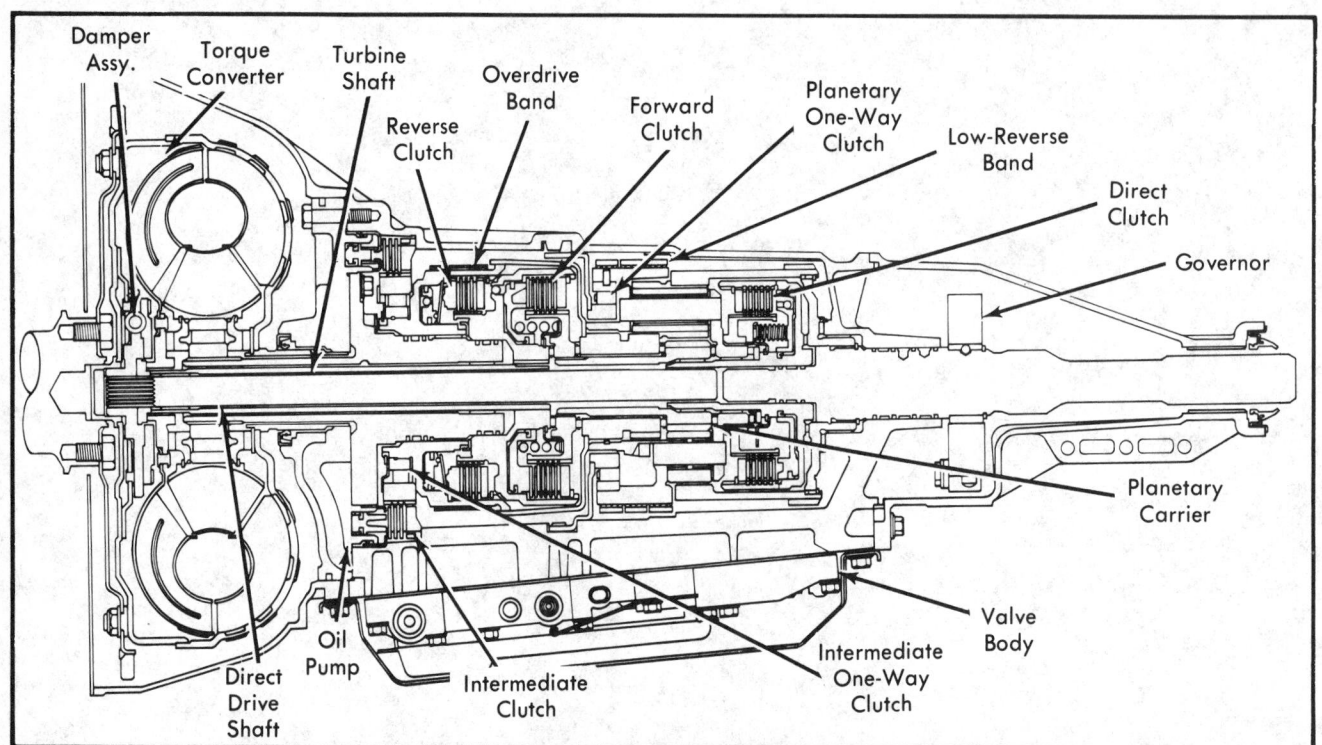

Fig. 1 Cross-Sectional View of Automatic Overdrive Transmission

FORD AUTOMATIC OVERDRIVE TRANSMISSION (Cont.)

and 3-2 coast downshift is signified by the release of the direct clutch. See *Shift Speed Table*.

NOTE — *A 2-1 downshift should not be felt.*

6) With transmission selector lever in "1" (manual low), transmission should operate only in first gear.

7) When selector lever is moved from either overdrive or direct drive ranges to "1" position, transmission should downshift into second gear if vehicle speed is above 25 MPH and into first gear if speed is less than 25 MPH.

NOTE — *The Automatic Overdrive Transmission will not shift into fourth gear (overdrive) at wide open throttle. Also, this transmission will not make a 4-1 downshift.*

SHIFT SPEED SPECIFICATIONS (MPH)

NOTE — *Figures given below are approximate. All shift speeds may vary somewhat due to production tolerances, rear axle ratio, or emission control equipment.*

F100/150 With Federal 5.0L Engine

Throttle	Range	Shift	OPS-R.P.M.	1	2	3	4	5	6
Closed (Minimum)	(D).3	1-2	0260-0500	7-13	7-13	7-14	7-14	6-12	6-12
	(D).3	2-3	0600-0780	15-20	16-20	16-21	17-22	14-18	15-19
	(D)	3-4	1310-1670	53-43	34-44	36-46	37-47	31-39	32-41
	(D)	4-3	1160-1520	30-39	30-40	32-41	33-43	27-36	28-37
	(D).3	3-2	0520-0700	13-18	14-18	14-19	15-20	12-16	13-17
	(D).3	2-1	0100-0450	3-11	3-12	3-12	3-13	2-11	2-11
	1	3-1,2-1	0730-1150	18-29	19-30	20-31	21-33	17-27	18-28
Part Throttle T.V. Pressure 60 PSI	(D).3	1-2	0590-0930	15-24	15-24	16-25	17-26	14-22	14-23
	(D).3	2-3	1110-1550	28-40	29-41	30-42	31-44	26-36	27-38
	(D)	3-4	1900-2320	48-59	50-61	52-63	54-66	45-55	46-57
	(D)	4-3	1570-1910	40-49	41-50	43-52	44-54	37-45	38-46
	(D).3	3-2	0680-1030	17-26	18-27	19-28	19-29	16-24	17-25
	(D).3	2-1	0100-0450	3-11	3-12	3-12	3-13	2-11	2-11
Wide Open Throttle (WOT)	(D).3	1-2	1200-1730	31-44	31-45	33-47	34-49	28-41	29-42
	(D).3	2-3	2330-2680	59-68	61-70	63-73	66-76	55-63	57-65
	(D).3	3-2	1770-2150	45-55	46-56	48-59	50-61	42-51	43-52
	(D).3	2-1	0590-0750	15-19	15-20	16-20	17-21	14-18	14-18

Axle Ratio	Tire Size	Use Col. No.
3.00:1	P195/75R	1
	P205/75R	2
	P215/75R	2
	P235/75R	3
	H78 x 15	3
	L78 x 15	4

Axle Ratio	Tire Size	Use Col. No.
3.25:1	P195/75R	5
	P205/75R	6
	P215/75R	6
	P235/75R	1
	H78 x 15	1
	L78 x 15	2

F100/150 With California 5.0L Engine

Throttle	Range	Shift	OPS-R.P.M.	1	2	3	4	5	6
Closed (Minimum)	(D).3	1-2	0260-0500	07-13	7-13	7-14	7-14	6-12	6-12
	(D).3	2-3	0600-0780	15-20	16-20	16-21	17-22	14-18	15-19
	(D)	3-4	1280-1640	33-42	34-43	35-45	36-46	30-39	31-40
	(D)	4-3	1120-1490	28-39	29-39	30-40	32-42	26-35	27-36
	(D).3	3-2	0520-0700	13-18	14-18	14-19	15-20	12-16	13-17
	(D).3	2-1	0100-0450	3-11	3-12	3-12	3-13	2-11	2-11
	1	3-1,2-1	0730-1150	18-29	19-30	20-31	21-33	17-27	18-28
Part Throttle T.V. Pressure 60 PSI	(D).3	1-2	0590-0930	15-24	15-24	16-25	17-26	14-22	14-23
	(D).3	2-3	1110-1550	28-40	29-41	30-42	31-44	26-36	27-38
	(D)	3-4	1720-2150	44-55	45-56	46-59	49-61	40-51	42-52
	(D)	4-3	1450-1810	37-46	38-47	40-49	41-51	34-43	35-44
	(D).3	3-2	0680-1030	17-26	18-27	19-28	19-29	16-24	17-25
	(D).3	2-1	0100-0450	3-11	3-12	3-12	3-13	2-11	2-11
Wide Open Throttle (WOT)	(D).3	1-2	1200-1730	31-44	31-45	33-47	34-49	28-41	29-42
	(D).3	2-3	2330-2680	59-68	61-70	63-73	66-76	55-63	57-65
	(D).3	3-2	1770-2150	45-55	46-56	48-59	50-61	42-51	43-52
	(D).3	2-1	0590-0750	15-19	15-20	16-20	17-21	14-18	14-18

Axle Ratio	Tire Size	Use Col. No.
3.00:1	P195/75R	1
	P205/75R	2
	P215/75R	2
	P235/75R	3
	H78 x 15	3
	L78 x 15	4

Axle Ratio	Tire Size	Use Col. No.
3.25:1	P195/75R	5
	P205/75R	6
	P215/75R	6
	P235/75R	7
	H78 x 15	7
	L78 x 15	8

FORD AUTOMATIC OVERDRIVE TRANSMISSION (Cont.)

SHIFT SPEED SPECIFICATIONS (MPH) (Cont.)

F250 With Federal 5.0L Engine

Throttle	Range	Shift	OPS-R.P.M	1	2	3	4	5	6
Closed (Minimum)	D,3	1-2	0260-0500	7-13	6-12	6-12	6-12	6-11	6-11
	D,3	2-3	0600-0780	16-20	15-19	14-19	14-18	14-18	13-17
	D	3-4	1310-1670	34-43	32-41	32-40	31-39	30-38	29-37
	D	4-3	1160-1520	30-40	29-38	38-37	27-35	27-35	26-34
	D,3	3-2	0520-0700	14-18	13-17	13-17	12-16	12-16	11-15
	D,3	2-1	0100-0450	3-12	2-11	2-11	2-10	2-10	2-10
	1	3-1,2-1	0730-1150	20-30	19-28	18-28	17-27	17-26	16-26
Part Throttle T.V. Pressure 60 PSI	D3	1-2	0590-0930	15-24	15-23	14-22	14-22	14-21	13-20
	D,3	2-3	1110-1550	29-40	27-38	27-37	26-36	25-35	25-34
	D	3-4	1900-2320	49-60	47-57	46-56	46-54	44-53	42-51
	D	4-3	1570-1910	41-49	39-47	38-46	37-46	36-44	35-42
	D,3	3-2	0680-1030	18-27	17-25	16-25	16-24	16-24	15-23
	D,3	2-1	0100-0450	3-12	2-11	2-11	2-11	2-10	2-10
Wide Open Throttle (WOT)	D3	1-2	1200-1730	31-45	30-43	29-42	28-40	27-40	27-38
	D,3	2-3	2330-2680	61-70	58-66	56-63	54-62	53-61	51-59
	D,3	3-2	1770-2150	46-56	44-53	43-52	41-50	40-49	39-48
	D,3	2-1	0590-0750	15-20	15-19	14-18	14-17	14-17	13-17

Axle Ratio	Tire Size	Use Col. No.
3.54	7.50 × 16	1
	9.50 × 16.5	2
	8.75 × 16.5	3
	8.00 × 16.5	4

Axle Ratio	Tire Size	Use Col. No.
3.73	7.50 × 16	2
	9.50 × 16.5	4
	8.75 × 16.5	5
	8.00 × 16.5	6

F250 With California 5.0L Engine

Throttle	Range	Shift	OPS-R.P.M.	1	2	3	4	5	6
Closed (Minimum)	D ,3	1-2	0260-0500	7-13	6-12	6-12	6-12	6-11	6-11
	D ,3	2-3	0600-0780	6-20	15-19	14-19	14-18	14-18	13-17
	D	3-4	1280-1640	33-43	32-41	31-40	30-38	29-38	28-36
	D	4-3	1490-1120	39-29	37-28	36-27	35-26	34-26	33-25
	D,3	3-2	0520-0700	14-18	13-17	13-17	12-16	12-16	11-15
	D,3	2-1	0100-0450	3-12	2-11	2-11	2-10	2-10	2-10
	1	3-1,2-1	0730-1150	20-30	19-28	18-28	17-27	17-26	16-26
Part Throttle T.V. Pressure 60 PSI	D,3	1-2	0590-0930	15-24	15-23	14-22	14-22	14-21	13-20
	D,3	2-3	1110-1550	29-40	27-38	27-37	26-36	25-35	25-34
	D	3-4	1720-2150	45-56	43-53	42-52	40-50	39-49	38-48
	D	4-3	1450-1810	38-47	36-45	35-44	34-42	33-41	32-39
	D,3	3-2	0680-1030	18-27	17-25	16-25	16-24	16-24	15-23
	D,3	2-1	0100-0450	3-12	2-11	2-11	2-11	2-10	2-10
Wide Open Throttle (WOT)	D,3	1-2	1200-1730	31-45	30-43	29-42	28-40	27-40	27-38
	D,3	2-3	2330-2680	61-70	58-66	56-63	54-62	53-61	51-59
	D,3	3-2	1770-2150	46-56	44-53	43-52	41-50	40-49	39-48
	D,3	2-1	0590-0750	15-20	15-19	14-18	14-17	14-17	13-17

Axle Ratio	Tire Size	Use Col. No.
3.54	7.50 × 16	1
	9.50 × 16.5	2
	8.75 × 16.5	3
	8.00 × 16.5	4

Axle Ratio	Tire Size	Use Col. No.
3.73	7.50 × 16	2
	9.50 × 16.5	4
	8.75 × 16.5	5
	8.00 × 16.5	6

CONTROL PRESSURE TEST

NOTE — When testing line pressure on the Automatic Overdrive Transmission, two readings must be taken; one at idle position (zero T.V.) and the other at wide open, full throttle (full T.V.).

Line Pressure — 1) With engine at normal operating temperature, connect a 0-300 psi pressure gauge to line pressure port tap on left side of transmission case just above control levers.

2) With throttle off fast idle cam, check line pressure in all ranges with engine at idle. Pressures should be approximately as shown in *Control Pressure Specifications Table*.

NOTE — T.V. linkage must be properly adjusted when performing line pressure test.

3) Next, apply parking and service brakes. Check line pressure in all ranges with throttle in wide open position. Pressures should be approximately as shown in *Control Pressure Specifications Table*.

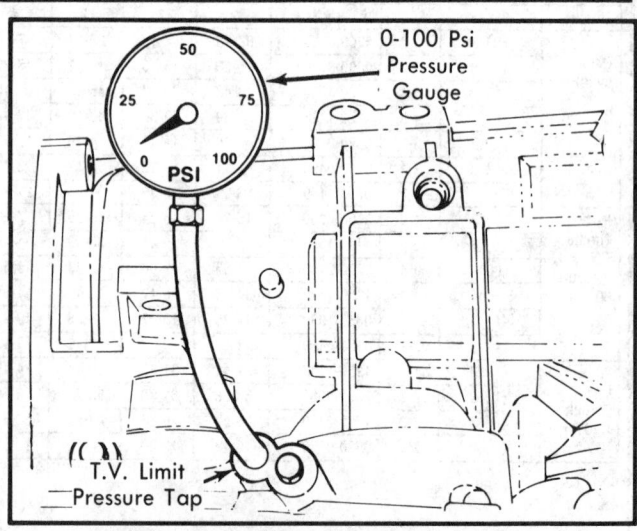

Fig. 2   Right Side of Transmission Case Showing T.V. Limit Pressure Tap

FORD AUTOMATIC OVERDRIVE TRANSMISSION (Cont.)

CLUTCH AND BAND APPLICATION CHART
(ELEMENTS IN USE)

Selector Lever Position	Intermed. Clutch	Intermed. One-Way Clutch	Overdrive Band	Reverse Clutch	Forward Clutch	Planetary One-Way Clutch	Low-Reverse Band	Direct Clutch
O/D — OVERDRIVE								
First Gear					X	X		
Second Gear	X	X			X			
Third Gear	X				X			X
Fourth Gear	X		X					X
3 — OVERDRIVE LOCKOUT								
First Gear					X	X		
Second Gear	X	X			X			
Third Gear	X				X			X
1 — LOW								
First Gear					X	X	X	
Second Gear	X	X	X		X			
R — REVERSE				X			X	
P — PARK							X	
NEUTRAL — All clutches and bands released and/or ineffective.								

CAUTION — *Pressure test at wide open throttle position should be taken at Full Stall conditions. Also, this test must be made as quickly as possible to prevent overheating transmission. Run engine at a fast idle in Neutral for cooling between tests.*

Throttle Valve Pressure — 1) Connect a 0-100 psi pressure gauge to T.V. pressure tap at right side of the transmission case (see Fig. 2). Gauge hose must be long enough so that gauge can be read from under the hood.

2) Make sure throttle lever is at idle stop position (fast idle cam off). Set parking brake firmly, then start engine and let idle in Neutral.

3) Using a 1/16" drill bit, placed between linkage lever adjustment screw and throttle lever, T.V. limit pressure should be 5 psi or lower. If pressure is above 5 psi, throttle linkage is too long. Back off linkage lever adjusting screw 1/2 turn at a time until pressure drops below 5 psi.

Control Pressure Specifications (Psi) (With Governor Pressure At Zero)

Throttle Position	Line Pressure	T.V. Limit Pressure
At Idle		
In "R"	75-90	0
All Other Ranges	55-65	0
At W.O.T.		
In "R"	250-290	79-91
All Other Ranges	180-215	79-91

4) Remove 1/16" drill bit and replace it with a 5/16" drill bit. Now, with engine idling in Neutral, T.V. limit pressure must be

at least 22 psi. If not, turn adjusting screw inward 1/2 turn at a time until pressure is within specifications.

NOTE — *If pressure cannot be adjusted to specifications, it may be necessary to adjust control rod length at transmission. See Automatic Transmission Servicing article.*

CONTROL PRESSURE TEST RESULTS

Low In "P" — Check for faulty valve body or low-reverse servo.

Low In "R" — Check for faulty reverse clutch or low-reverse servo.

Low in "N" — Check for faulty valve body.

Low in "O/D" — Check for faulty forward clutch, overdrive servo or valve body.

Low in "3" — Check for faulty forward clutch and/or intermediate servo.

Low in "1" — Check for faulty forward clutch or reverse clutch or servo.

Low at Idle in All Ranges — Check for low fluid level, restricted intake screen or filter, loose valve body bolts, pump leakage, case leakage, faulty valve body, excessively low engine idle, fluid too hot.

High at Idle in All Ranges — Check T.V. linkage adjustment and condition and for faulty valve body.

Pressure Okay at Idle but Low at W.O.T. — Check for internal leakage, pump leakage, restricted intake screen or filter, damaged or out of adjustment T.V. linkage. Also check for sticking T.V. or T.V. limit valve in valve body.

FORD AUTOMATIC OVERDRIVE TRANSMISSION (Cont.)

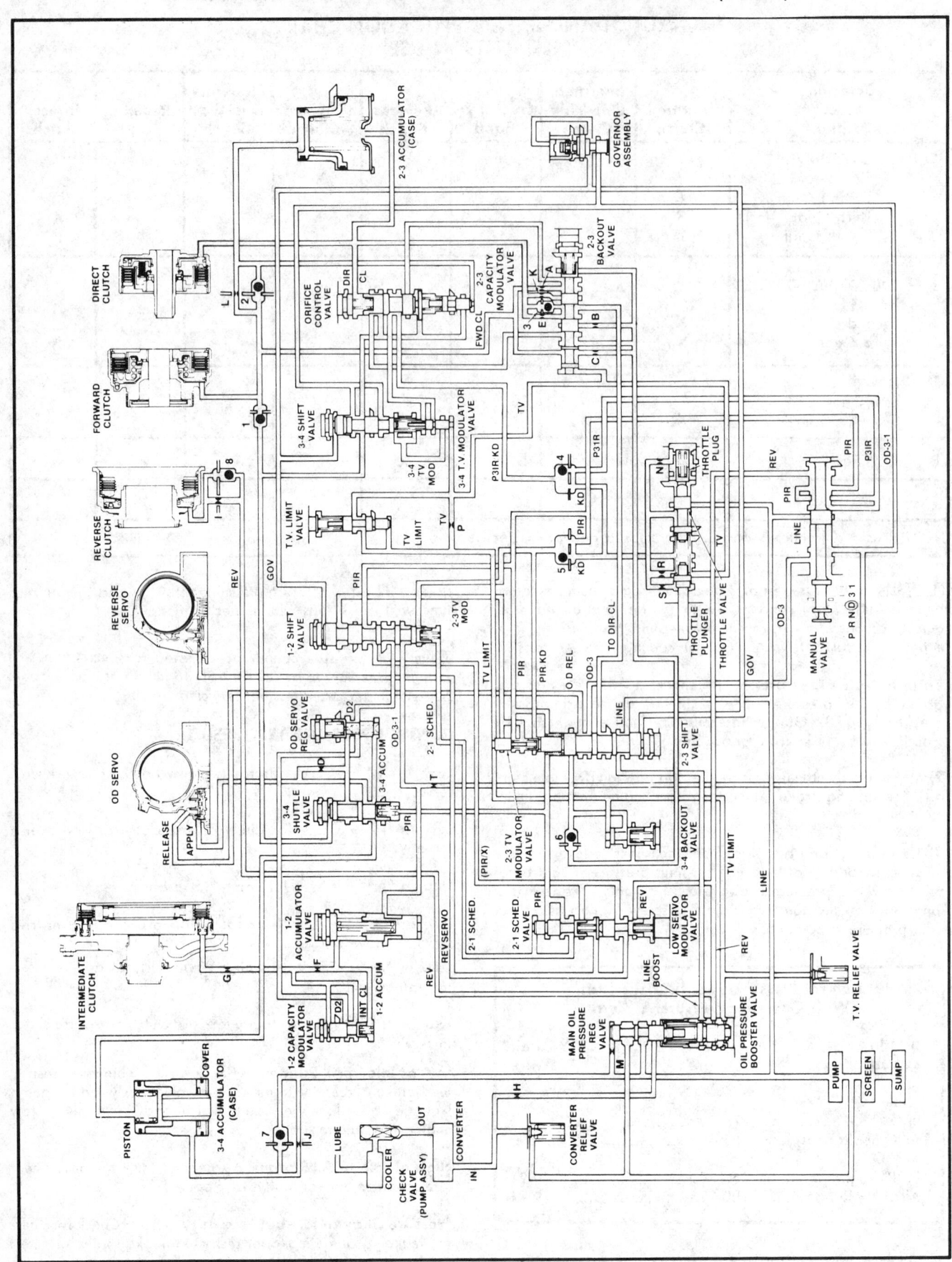

Fig. 3 *Automatic Overdrive Transmission Hydraulic Circuits Diagram*

FORD AUTOMATIC OVERDRIVE TRANSMISSION (Cont.)

GOVERNOR CHECK

Accelerate vehicle to 25 MPH and back off throttle completely. If governor is operating properly, transmission will shift to third gear.

STALL TEST

Testing Precautions — When performing stall test, do not hold throttle open longer than five seconds. Allow a cooling period of 15 seconds with transmission in neutral and engine speed at 1000 RPM between each test. If engine speed exceeds maximum limits shown, release accelerator immediately as this is an indication of clutch or band slippage.

Testing Procedure — With engine at normal operating temperature, tachometer installed, and parking and service brakes applied, stall test transmission in each driving range at full throttle, and note maximum RPM obtained. Engine speed should be within limits shown in following table.

Stall Speed Specifications	
Application	**Stall RPM**
5.0L	1891-2182

STALL TEST RESULTS

Stall Speed Too High — In "O/D", "3", "1" and "R"; general transmission problems are indicated and a control pressure test should be made to locate faulty unit(s). In "O/D" and "3" only; planetary one-way clutch slippage is indicated. In "O/D" "3" and "1"; forward clutch slippage is indicated. In "R" only; reverse clutch and/or low-reverse band slippage is indicated.

Stall Speed Too Low — Converter stator one-way clutch or engine performance is faulty.

AIR PRESSURE TESTS

A "No Drive" condition can exist even with correct transmission fluid pressure, because of inoperative clutches or bands. Erratic shifts could be caused by a stuck governor valve. The inoperative units can be located through a series of checks by substituting air pressure for the fluid pressure to determine location of malfunction. To make air pressure checks, loosen oil pan bolts and allow transmission fluid to drain, then remove oil pan and control valve body assembly. Apply air pressure at points noted in *Fig. 4* and check unit operation as follows:

NOTE — *Air pressure should be regulated to about 25 psi. Compressed air used for test should be filtered and dry to avoid contaminating transmission fluid.*

Forward Clutch — Apply air pressure to transmission case forward clutch passage. A dull thud can be heard when clutch piston is applied, or movement can be felt by placing finger tips on input shell.

Governor — Apply air pressure to line pressure-to-governor passage and listen for sharp clicking or whistling noise, indicating governor valve movement.

Reverse Clutch — Apply air pressure to reverse clutch passage. A dull thud can be heard when clutch piston is applied, or movement can be felt by placing finger tips on clutch drum.

Low-Reverse Servo — Apply air pressure to low-reverse servo apply passage. Low-reverse band should tighten around drum if servo is operating properly. When air is removed, servo piston should be felt to move back against servo cover.

Direct Clutch — Apply air pressure to direct clutch passage. A dull thud can be heard if clutch is operating properly.

Overdrive Servo — First pressurize servo apply passage. Hold pressure and pressurize servo release passage. Piston should be heard to apply band and also heard as it releases against cover when air pressure is removed. A hissing noise indicates a leak.

Intermediate Clutch — Apply air pressure to intermediate clutch apply passage. A dull thud should be heard if clutch is operating properly.

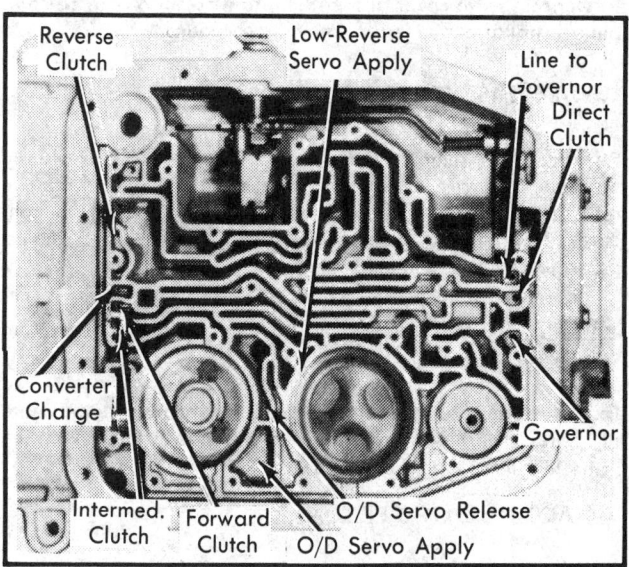

Fig. 4   Bottom View of Transmission Case Showing Hydraulic Passages

SERVICE (IN VEHICLE)

VALVE BODY ASSEMBLY

Removal — 1) Raise vehicle on a hoist. Loosen oil pan attaching bolts and allow transmission fluid to drain. Remove oil pan and gasket.

2) Remove filter-to-valve body attaching bolts and remove filter, grommet and gasket. Remove detent spring attaching bolt and spring. Remove attaching bolts and remove valve body from transmission.

Installation — 1) Using suitable guide pins, position valve body (with new gasket) in case, making sure that inner manual lever and inner T.V. lever are engaged. Install and tighten valve body attaching bolts.

FORD AUTOMATIC OVERDRIVE TRANSMISSION (Cont.)

2) Install and tighten detent spring and attaching bolts. Remove guide pins and install remaining two valve body attaching bolts. Load throttle lever torsion spring against separator plate. To complete installation, reverse removal procedure using new gaskets on filter and oil pan.

OVERDRIVE SERVO ASSEMBLY

Removal — Remove valve body as previously described. Depress overdrive servo piston cover and remove retaining snap ring. Apply air pressure to servo piston release passage to remove piston, cover and spring. Separate piston from cover and remove rubber seals from piston and cover.

Installation — **1)** Install new seals on piston and cover. Lubricate piston seals with automatic transmission fluid or petroleum jelly, then install piston into cover.

2) Lubricate cover seals and overdrive servo pocket in transmission case. Assemble spring to piston, then install assembly into case pocket.

3) Depress servo cover and install retaining snap ring. To complete installation, reverse removal procedure.

LOW-REVERSE SERVO ASSEMBLY

Removal — Remove valve body assembly as previously described. Depress low-reverse servo piston cover and remove retaining snap ring and cover. Remove piston and spring from case by applying compressed air to low-reverse servo release passage in case.

CAUTION — *Low-reverse servo piston may spring free from case when cover is removed.*

Installation — To install, reverse removal procedure and note the following: Make sure that servo piston is installed with the same length rod as was removed.

3-4 ACCUMULATOR PISTON

Removal — Remove valve body assembly as previously described. Depress 3-4 accumulator cover and remove retaining snap ring, then slowly release pressure on cover and remove cover, piston and if equipped, return spring. Remove seals from piston and cover.

NOTE — *If necessary, 3-4 accumulator piston can be removed by applying compressed air to hydraulic apply passage.*

Installation — To install, reverse removal procedures and note the following: Lubricate rubber seals and accumulator pocket in case prior to accumulator installation. Make sure that accumulator cover is seated snug against retaining snap ring.

2-3 ACCUMULATOR PISTON

Removal — Remove valve body assembly as previously described. Depress 2-3 accumulator piston cover and remove retaining snap ring, cover and spring. Remove accumulator piston, then remove seals from piston.

Installation — To install, reverse removal procedure and note the following: Lubricate piston seals and piston pocket in case prior to installation.

EXTENSION HOUSING BUSHING & REAR OIL SEAL

Removal — Raise vehicle on a hoist and disconnect propeller shaft from transmission. Remove oil seal using suitable puller (T74P-77248-A or equivalent). Remove bushing using suitable puller (T77L-7697-A or equivalent), using care not to damage output shaft splines.

Installation — Install new bushing into extension housing using suitable driver (T80L-77034-A or equivalent). Install new seal into housing using suitable driver (761L-7657-A or equivalent). Coat inside diameter of rubber portion of seal with a suitable lubricant. Install propeller shaft.

EXTENSION HOUSING

Removal — **1)** Raise vehicle on a hoist and disconnect parking brake cable from equalizer, if so equipped. Remove propeller shaft and disconnect speedometer cable from extension housing.

2) Remove engine rear support-to-extension housing attaching bolts.

3) Raise transmission just enough to remove weight from rear support. Remove rear support-to-crossmember attaching bolt and remove rear support.

4) Lower transmission and remove extension housing attaching bolts. Slide housing off output shaft and allow fluid to drain. Remove and discard extension housing-to-case gasket.

Installation — Clean mating surface on transmission and extension housing. Position new gasket on transmission. Slide extension housing into place, then install and tighten attaching bolts. To complete installation, reverse removal procedure.

GOVERNOR ASSEMBLY

Removal — Remove extension housing as previously described. Remove governor-to-output shaft retaining snap ring, then using a soft-faced hammer, tap governor assembly off output shaft. Remove governor drive ball. Remove governor-to-counterweight attaching screws and lift governor from counterweight.

Installation — **1)** Lubricate governor parts with clean transmission fluid and make sure valve moves freely in bore. Position governor body on counterweight with cover facing toward front of vehicle. Install and tighten two attaching screws.

2) Position governor drive ball into pocket on output shaft. Align keyway in counterweight with drive ball, then drive assembly onto output shaft with soft-faced hammer. Install governor-to-output shaft retaining snap ring. To complete installation, reverse removal procedure.

FORD AUTOMATIC OVERDRIVE TRANSMISSION (Cont.)

INTERNAL & EXTERNAL SHIFT LINKAGE

Removal — 1) Raise vehicle on a hoist. Apply penetrating oil to outer throttle lever attaching nut to prevent breaking inner throttle lever.

2) Loosen oil pan attaching bolts and allow fluid to drain, then remove oil pan. Disconnect shift rod and throttle valve linkage at transmission.

3) Disconnect inner throttle lever spring, then remove detent spring. Hold outer throttle lever stationary and remove throttle lever attaching nut and lock washer. Using a small screwdriver, remove outer throttle lever seal.

4) Grasp manual lever roll pin with vise grip pliers and remove pin. Hold manual lever firmly in position and remove manual lever attaching nut using a box wrench. Remove outer manual lever from case.

5) Remove inner throttle lever and spring. Remove inner manual lever and park pawl actuating rod. Disconnect park pawl actuating rod from inner manual lever. Remove manual lever oil seal using a screwdriver.

Installation — 1) Install new manual lever oil seal into case using a suitable driver. Partially install outer manual lever into case. Assemble inner manual lever and park pawl actuating rod together.

2) Assemble throttle lever spring and manual lever attaching nut onto inner throttle lever shaft. Assemble actuating rod and inner manual lever onto inner throttle lever shaft.

3) Slide inner throttle lever through I.D. bore of outer manual lever shaft and position park pawl actuating rod into rod guide cup in rear of case.

4) Push outer manual lever all the way into case and start attaching nut on outer manual lever shaft. Reposition outer manual lever (up or down). Assemble inner manual lever to outer manual lever by aligning the flats, then tighten attaching nut.

5) Install new throttle lever seal using a $\frac{3}{8}$″ socket to seat the seal. Install seal .030-.060″ below surface. Install outer throttle lever (aligning flats) and make sure inner and outer throttle levers are in the proper approximate position. Install and tighten throttle lever attaching nut and lock washer.

6) Connect manual lever spring to notch in valve body separator plate. Drive in a new manual lever roll pin. Install detent spring and attaching bolt. Connect transmission manual lever to manual shift linkage making sure that manual lever is in same position as adjustment is necessary.

7) Connect transmission throttle linkage to throttle lever. Install oil pan using a new gasket. Lower vehicle and fill transmission to correct fluid level. Adjust linkage as necessary. See *Automatic Transmission Servicing article for linkage adjustment.*

TRANSMISSION REMOVAL & INSTALLATION

REMOVAL

1) Raise and support vehicle. Loosen oil pan attaching bolts and allow fluid to drain. Remove torque converter drain plug access cover from lower end of converter housing. Remove converter-to-flywheel attaching nuts, then place a wrench on crankshaft pulley attaching bolt and rotate converter until drain plug is accessible. Remove drain plug and drain fluid from converter, then reinstall and tighten drain plug.

2) Remove propeller shaft, then install a seal installation tool into extension housing to prevent fluid leakage. Remove starter motor and disconnect neutral safety switch wires at transmission.

3) Remove rear mount-to-crossmember attaching bolts and crossmember-to-frame attaching bolts. Remove engine rear support-to-extension housing attaching bolts. Disconnect throttle valve and manual linkage from transmission levers. Remove bellcrank-to-converter housing attaching bolts.

4) Raise transmission using a transmission jack, then remove rear mount from crossmember and crossmember from side supports. Lower transmission to gain access to oil cooler lines, then disconnect lines from fittings on transmission. Disconnect speedometer cable from extension housing.

5) Remove bolt attaching transmission fluid filler tube to cylinder block, then lift filler tube and dipstick from transmission.

6) Secure transmission to jack with a safety chain. Remove converter housing-to-engine attaching bolts. Carefully move transmission assembly away from engine and at the same time, lower jack to clear underside of vehicle. Remove converter and mount transmission in a holding fixture.

INSTALLATION

Reverse removal procedure and note the following:

- Position converter on transmission, making sure converter drive flats are fully engaged in pump gear by rotating the converter.
- Lube converter pilot.
- Install new "O" ring on lower end of filler tube.
- Adjust shift and throttle linkage as necessary.
- Fill transmission with transmission fluid.

TORQUE CONVERTER

NOTE — *The torque converter is a sealed unit and cannot be disassembled for service. Replace if found defective. Make the following tests to be certain converter is defective before replacing unit.*

FLUSHING CONVERTER

Whenever transmission has been disassembled to replace worn or damaged parts, or because valve body sticks due to foreign material, converter and oil cooler **must** be cleaned using a mechanically agitated cleaner (Rotunda 14-0028 or equivalent).

CAUTION — *Under no circumstances should an attempt be made to clean converters or oil coolers by hand agitation with solvent.*

TURBINE & STATOR END PLAY CHECK

1) Insert torque converter end play test tool (T77L-7902-D) into converter pump drive hub until it bottoms. Expand sleeve of

FORD AUTOMATIC OVERDRIVE TRANSMISSION (Cont.)

tool in turbine spline by tightening threaded inner post of tool until tool is securely locked into spline.

2) Attach a dial indicator to test tool as shown in *Fig. 5*. Position indicator button on converter pump drive hub, then zero dial indicator. Lift tool upward as far as possible and note indicator reading.

3) Reading is total end play of turbine and stator. If end play exceeds .023" (new or rebuilt converter) or .050" (used converter), replace converter assembly.

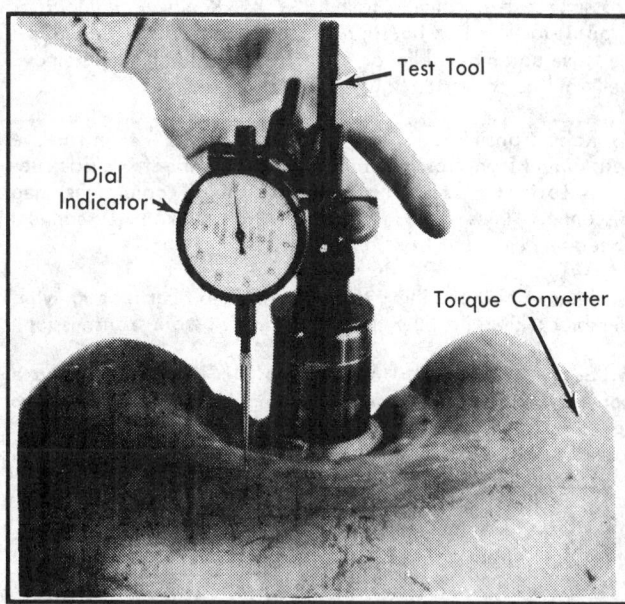

Fig. 5   Measuring Turbine and Stator End Play

STATOR ONE-WAY CLUTCH CHECK

1) Insert one-way clutch holding tool into one of the grooves in stator thrust washer. Insert clutch torquing tool (T77L-7902-B) in converter pump drive hub so as to engage one-way clutch inner race.

2) Attach torque wrench to torquing tool. With clutch holding tool held stationary, turn torque wrench counterclockwise. Converter one-way clutch should lock-up and hold at 10 ft. lbs. force. Repeat lock-up test in at least 5 different locations around converter. If clutch fails to lock-up and hold, replace converter assembly.

NOTE — *One-way clutch should rotate freely in a clockwise direction only.*

STATOR INTERFERENCE CHECK

Stator to Impeller Interference — **1)** Position oil pump assembly on bench with spline end of stator shaft pointing up. Mount torque converter on pump so splines of one-way clutch inner race engage splines of stator support, and converter hub engages pump drive gear.

2) While holding pump stationary, rotate converter counterclockwise. Converter should rotate freely without interference or scraping within assembly. Should this condition exist, replace converter assembly.

Stator to Turbine Interference — **1)** Place converter on bench with front side down. Install oil pump assembly to engage mating splines of stator support and stator, and pump drive gear lugs. Install input shaft, engaging splines with turbine hub.

2) While holding pump stationary, rotate turbine with input shaft. Turbine should rotate freely in both directions without interference or noise. If interference or noise exists, stator front thrust washer may be worn. In such cases, replace converter assembly.

TRANSMISSION DISASSEMBLY

1) Mount transmission in a suitable holding fixture. Remove torque converter. Remove attaching bolts and lift off oil pan and gasket. Remove oil filter, grommet and gasket.

2) Remove detent spring and roller assembly. Remove valve body attaching bolts and lift off valve body and gasket. Push down on 3-4 accumulator cover and remove retaining snap ring, then remove cover, piston and spring.

NOTE — *If necessary, accumulator cover and piston can also be removed by applying compressed air to accumulator hydraulic apply passage. Also, some models do not use a spring on the 3-4 accumulator piston.*

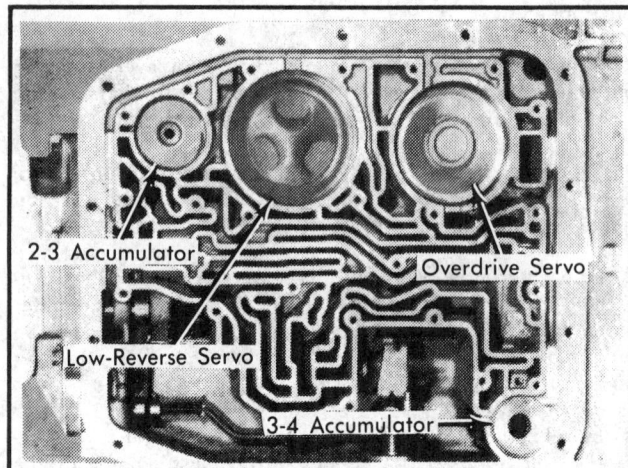

Fig. 6   Bottom View of Transmission Case Showing Accumulators and Servos

3) Following the 3-4 accumulator removal procedure, remove 2-3 accumulator assembly, low-reverse servo assembly and overdrive servo assembly.

4) Remove direct drive shaft by pulling it straight out from case. Remove pump body attaching bolts, then remove pump from case using two slide hammers installed in opposite pump attaching bolt holes. Remove pump-to-case gasket.

5) Grasp turbine shaft and pull intermediate clutch pack, intermediate one-way clutch, reverse clutch and forward clutch from transmission case as an assembly. Disconnect overdrive band from anchor pin and remove band from case.

6) Remove forward clutch hub and No. 3 needle bearing as an assembly. Remove forward sun gear, No. 5 needle bearing, reverse sun gear and drive shell and No. 4 needle bearing from case as an assembly.

FORD AUTOMATIC OVERDRIVE TRANSMISSION (Cont.)

7) Note position of center support snap ring tangs for installation reference, then remove snap ring. Using a screwdriver, pry anti-clunk spring from between center support and case. Remove center support and planetary carrier from case as an assembly.

NOTE — *Prior to removal, note installation position of anti-clunk spring to ensure it is reinstalled in the same position.*

8) Remove reverse band from case. If direct clutch hub did not come out with planetary carrier, remove it from direct clutch.

9) Remove attaching bolts and slide extension housing from transmission, then remove and discard housing-to-case gasket. Remove retaining snap ring and slide governor assembly off output shaft. Remove governor drive ball from output shaft.

NOTE — *If transmission is positioned with output shaft pointing up, do not allow shaft assembly to fall through case when governor is removed.*

10) Remove output shaft, ring gear and direct clutch as an assembly, through front of case. Remove output shaft No. 9 needle bearing from rear of case.

COMPONENT DISASSEMBLY & REASSEMBLY

NOTE — *Handle all parts carefully to avoid damage. Lubricate all parts with clean transmission fluid before reassembly (petroleum jelly may be used on gaskets and thrust washers for easier assembly). Use all new gaskets and seals, and tighten all bolts and screws evenly.*

GOVERNOR ASSEMBLY

Disassembly — Remove attaching screws and separate counterweight from governor body. Remove cover screws and cover. Remove plug, sleeve and valve from governor body.

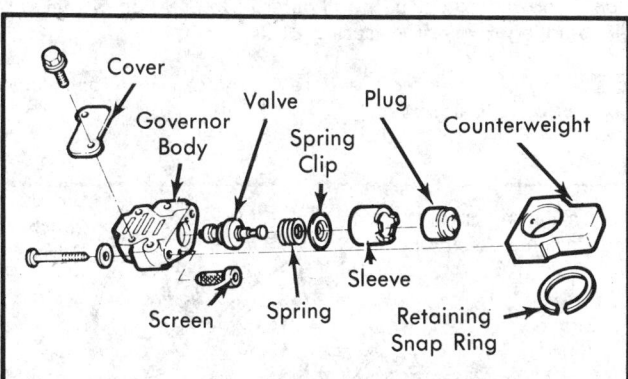

Fig. 7 Exploded View of Governor Assembly

Reassembly — **1)** If removed, install clip and spring on valve, then install valve into governor body. Install sleeve in body with points outward.

2) Install plug in sleeve with knurled face inward. Install cover. Install screen in body with steel band forward and tip of screen facing outward.

3) Position governor body on counterweight and install attaching screws. When correctly assembled, the finished face of governor body should be flush with face of counterweight.

INTERMEDIATE ONE-WAY CLUTCH

Disassembly — Remove clutch retaining ring, then lift off clutch retaining plate. Remove clutch outer race by lifting on race while turning counterclockwise. Carefully lift one-way clutch from inner race.

NOTE — *If a roller is damaged or lost, entire one-way clutch assembly must be replaced.*

Reassembly — Reverse disassembly and make sure outer race is installed over roller clutch with chamfer side facing reverse clutch drum.

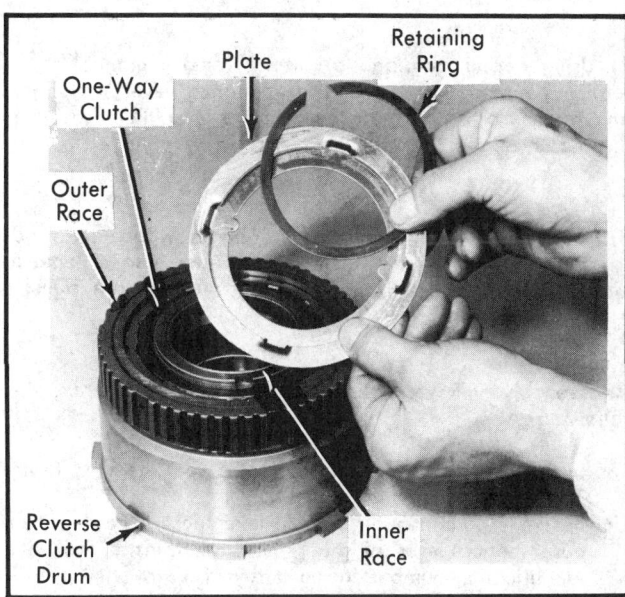

Fig. 8 Intermediate One-Way Clutch Assembly

OUTPUT SHAFT ASSEMBLY

Disassembly — Remove retaining ring and separate output shaft and hub assembly from ring gear. Remove direct clutch from ring gear and No. 8 needle bearing from rear of direct clutch. Remove four output shaft seal rings and hub-to-shaft retaining ring. Separate hub from output shaft. Remove the two direct clutch seal rings from end of output shaft.

Reassembly — To reassemble, reverse disassembly procedure.

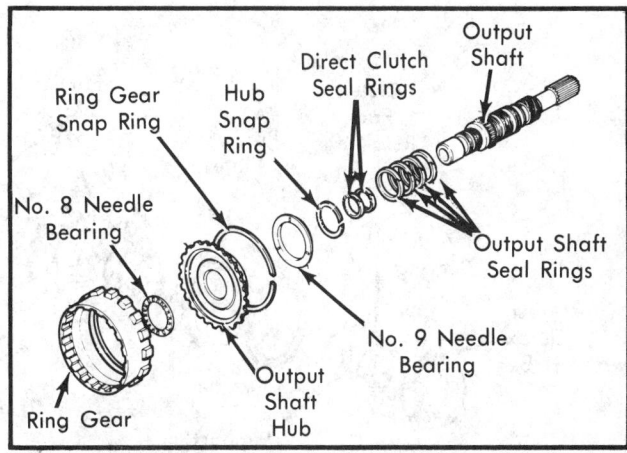

Fig. 9 Exploded View of Output Shaft Assembly

FORD AUTOMATIC OVERDRIVE TRANSMISSION (Cont.)

MANUAL & THROTTLE LINKAGE

Disassembly — 1) Hold outer throttle lever stationary and remove attaching nut, lock washer and throttle lever. Using a small screwdriver, remove oil seal from outer manual lever counterbore.

NOTE — *Failure to hold outer throttle lever stationary when removing attaching nut will allow inner throttle lever to rotate against valve body surface, which could result in damage to surface.*

2) Using a pair of diagonal cutters, remove manual shaft retaining pin from case. Hold inner manual lever stationary and remove attaching nut, then remove lever. Remove inner throttle lever and torsion spring.

3) Remove inner manual lever and parking pawl actuating rod as an assembly. Separate rod from lever if necessary. Remove manual lever shaft seal from case using a suitable seal puller.

Reassembly — Reverse disassembly procedure and note the following:

- Install new manual lever seal using seal installer T74P-77498-A or equivalent tool.
- Before installing outer throttle lever, install new seal in outer manual lever using a 13 mm socket. Install seal with identification number facing outward.

DIRECT CLUTCH ASSEMBLY

Disassembly — 1) Remove No. 7 direct clutch hub inner needle bearing and bearing support. Using a screwdriver, remove clutch pack selective retaining snap ring, then lift out clutch pack.

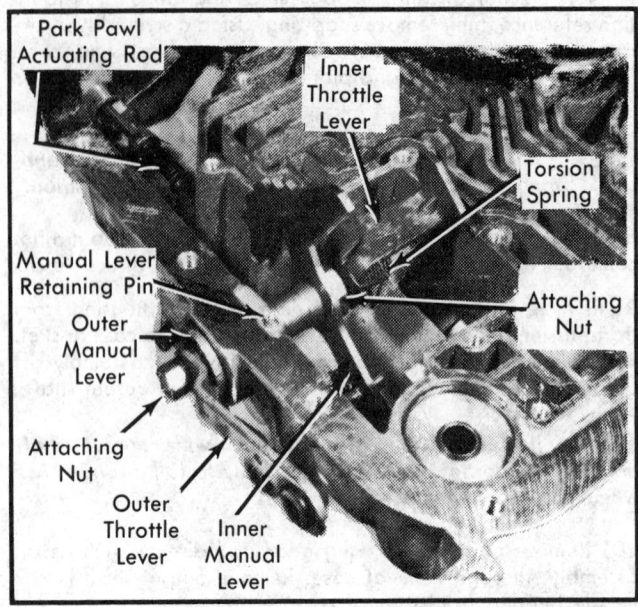

Fig. 10   Bottom View of Transmission Case Showing Manual and Throttle Linkage

2) Using a suitable compressor tool, compress piston return springs and remove retaining snap ring. Remove tool and lift spring retainer assembly and piston from clutch drum. Note position and direction of lip seals, then remove them from drum and piston.

NOTE — *If necessary, piston can be removed from drum by applying compressed air to lubrication hole in clutch drum.*

Reassembly — 1) Using a suitable seal protector (T80L-77234-A), install inner seal on clutch drum hub with sealing lip facing down into drum. Install outer piston seal on piston with lip pointing away from spring posts.

NOTE — *Lubricate seals and seal protector with petroleum jelly prior to installation.*

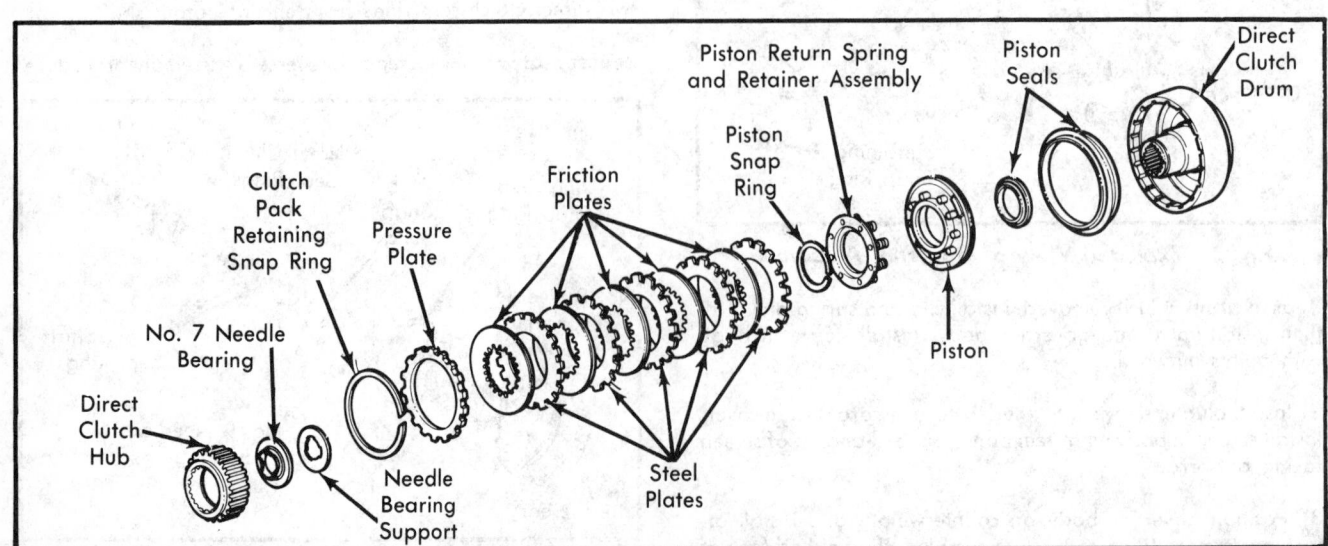

Fig. 11   Exploded View of Direct Clutch Assembly

FORD AUTOMATIC OVERDRIVE TRANSMISSION (Cont.)

2) Coat piston seals, clutch drum sealing area and piston inner seal area with petroleum jelly. Install piston into clutch drum using a suitable seal protector (T80L-77254-A) to prevent damaging seals.

3) Position piston spring and retainer assembly in clutch drum, then compress assembly and install retaining snap ring. Install clutch pack into drum, then install pressure plate on top of clutch pack. Install clutch pack selective retaining ring.

Direct Clutch Plate Usage Chart		
Application	**Steel Plates**	**Friction Plates**
All Models	5	5

4) Using a feeler gauge, measure clearance between clutch pack retaining ring and pressure plate, with pressure plate held downward. Clearance should be .050-.067". If clearance is not within limits, selective snap rings are available in the following thicknesses: .050-.054", .064-.068", .078-.082" and .092-.096". Install correct size snap ring and recheck clearance.

5) Check clutch for proper operation using compressed air (30 psi) as shown in *Fig. 12*. Clutch should be heard and felt to apply smoothly and without leakage.

FORWARD CLUTCH

Disassembly — 1) If not already removed, lift clutch hub and No. 3 needle bearing from forward clutch assembly. Using a screwdriver, pry clutch pack retaining snap ring from drum. Remove clutch pack.

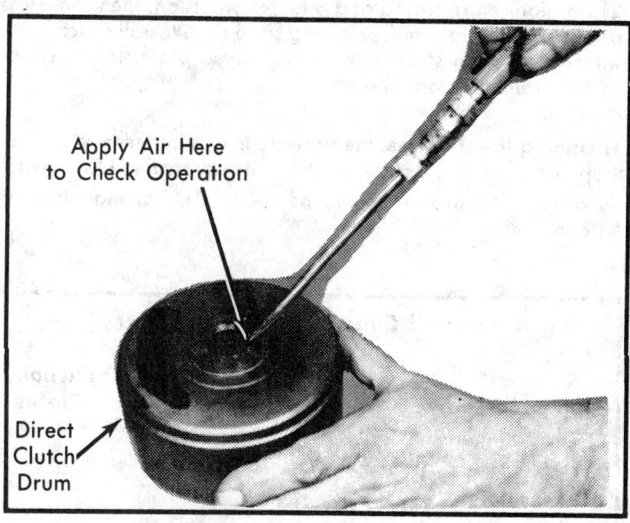

Fig. 12 Using Compressed Air to Check Direct Clutch Operation

2) Using a suitable compressor tool, compress piston return spring and remove retaining snap ring, then lift out retainer and return spring.

3) Remove clutch piston from drum and make sure that two ball checks in forward clutch cylinder are free. Note position of inner and outer piston seals, then remove them.

Reassembly — 1) Lubricate and install inner and outer seals on piston with seal lips facing into clutch drum. Lubricate piston seals and drum sealing area with petroleum jelly, then install piston into drum using a seal protector (T80L-77140-A) to prevent damaging seals.

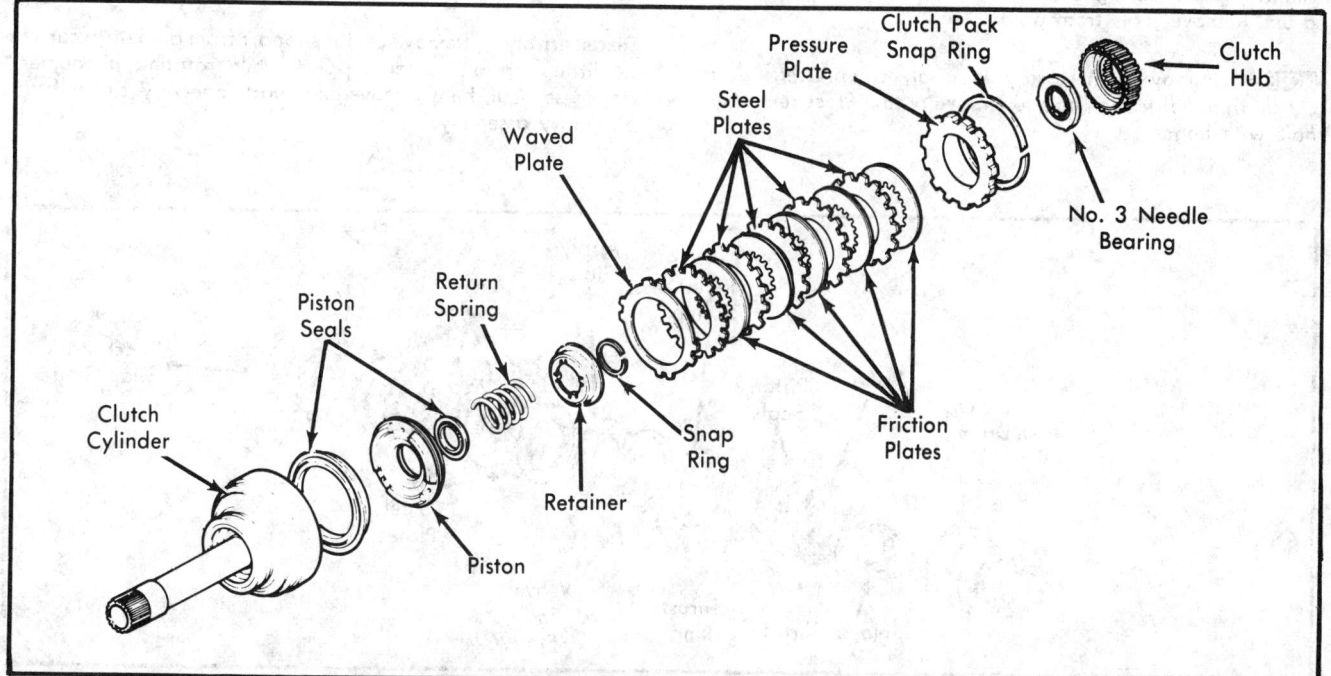

Fig. 13 Exploded View of Forward Clutch Assembly

FORD AUTOMATIC OVERDRIVE TRANSMISSION (Cont.)

2) Position return spring and retainer on piston, then compress return spring and install retaining snap ring. Install clutch pack into clutch drum starting with the waved plate. Install clutch pack retaining snap ring.

3) Using a feeler gauge, measure clearance between retaining snap ring and pressure plate, with pressure plate held downward. Clearance should be .040-.071" for models with 5.0L engine.

Forward Clutch Plate Usage Chart

Application	Steel Plates	Friction Plates
5.0L	4①	4

① — Plus 1 waved plate installed next to piston.

---

4) If forward clutch clearance is not within limits, selective snap rings are available in the following thicknesses: .060-.064", .074-.078", .088-.092" and .102-.106". Install correct size snap ring and recheck clearance.

5) With reassembly completed, use compressed air and check forward clutch operation. Clutch should be heard and felt to apply smoothly and without leakage.

REVERSE CLUTCH

Disassembly — 1) Remove No. 2 thrust washer. Using a screwdriver, pry clutch pack retaining snap ring from clutch drum, then lift out clutch pack.

2) Compress return spring and remove waved snap ring, then remove return spring and thrust ring. Remove piston from drum. Remove seals from piston.

NOTE — *It may be necessary to apply compressed air to clutch drum lubrication hole to remove piston. Block remaining hole with finger.*

Reassembly — 1) Pior to reassembly, make sure that ball check in piston is free. Install new seal on clutch piston, then coat seals and sealing surface in clutch drum with petroleum jelly. Install piston into clutch drum using inner and outer seal protectors (T80L-77403-B and A) to prevent damaging seals.

NOTE — *Seals used on reverse clutch piston are square cut, therefore direction of installation is not important.*

2) Install thrust ring and return spring, then compress return spring and install waved snap ring. Install apply plate into clutch drum with dished side facing piston, then install clutch pack and retaining snap ring.

Reverse Clutch Plate Usage Chart

Application	Steel Plates	Friction Plates
5.0L	2	3

---

3) Using a feeler gauge measure clearance between clutch pack snap ring and pressure plate while pushing down on pressure plate. Clearance should be .030-.056" on models with 5.0L engine.

4) If reverse clutch clearance is not within limits, selective snap rings are available in the following thicknesses: .060-.064", .074-.078", .088-.092" and .102-.106". Install correct size snap ring and recheck clearance.

5) With reverse clutch reassembly completed, check clutch operation using compressed air. Clutch should be heard and felt to apply smoothly and without leakage.

CENTER SUPPORT & PLANETARY ONE-WAY CLUTCH

Disassembly — Remove center support from planetary carrier by lifting up on center support while rotating it counter-clockwise. Carefully remove planetary one-way clutch from planetary assembly.

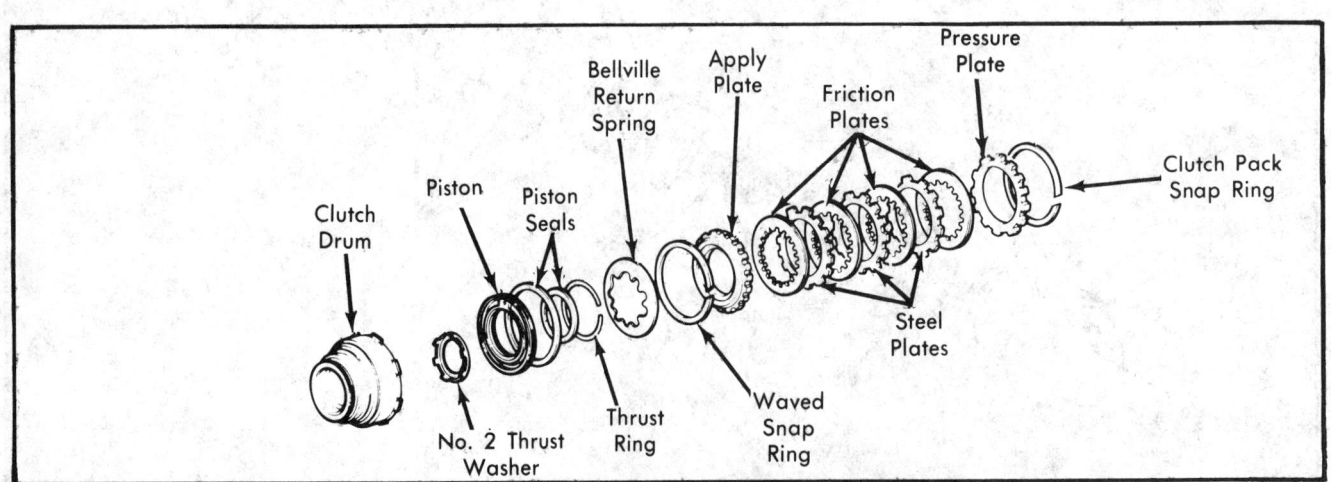

Fig. 14 Exploded View of Reverse Clutch Assembly

FORD AUTOMATIC OVERDRIVE TRANSMISSION (Cont.)

NOTE — *If a roller from planetary one-way clutch is lost or damaged, entire one-way clutch assembly must be replaced.*

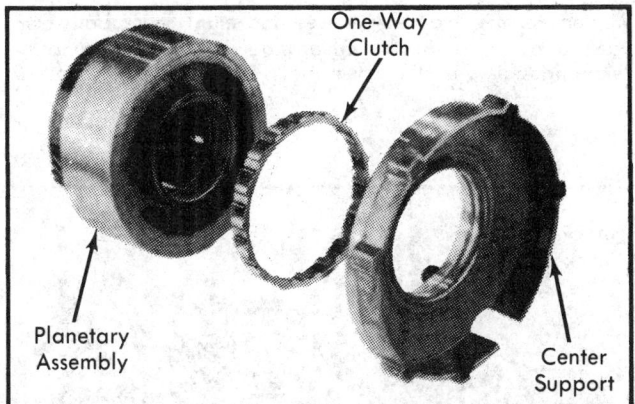

Fig. 15   Center Support and Planetary Assembly

Reassembly — If necessary, assemble one-way clutch as shown in *Fig. 16.* Install one-way clutch in planetary carrier. Install center support into one-way clutch by rotating center support clockwise while pushing down.

NOTE — *Lubricating clutch races and clutch assembly with petroleum jelly may aid in reassembly.*

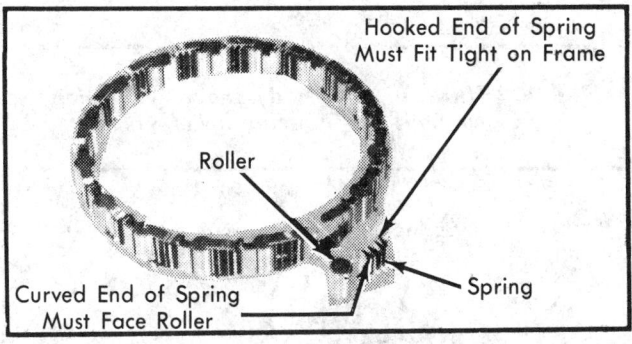

Fig. 16   Assembling Planetary One-Way Clutch

SUN GEAR & DRIVING SHELL

Disassembly — Remove No. 4 needle bearing from driving shell. Remove forward sun gear and No. 5 needle bearing from shell, then remove needle bearing from forward sun gear.

Reassembly — *Sun gear and driving shell will be reassembled as part of Transmission Reassembly.*

Fig. 17   Exploded View of Sun Gear and Driving Shell

OIL PUMP & IMTERMEDIATE CLUTCH PISTON

Disassembly — 1) Lift No. 1 thrust washer from stator support. Remove four seal rings from stator support. Remove pump body-to-case seal and discard.

NOTE — *Reverse clutch seal rings on stator support are larger than forward clutch seal rings.*

2) Remove spring retainer assembly by carefully dislodging the tabs, then lift intermediate clutch piston from pump assembly. Remove attaching bolts and separate stator support from pump body. Remove drive and driven gears from pump body.

Reassembly — 1) Install drive and driven gears into pump body with chamfers on both gears facing into pump body. Stamped triangle on driven gear must face down into pump gear pocket.

2) Position stator support on pump body, then install and tighten attaching bolts. Install pump-to-case seal around outer diameter of pump body.

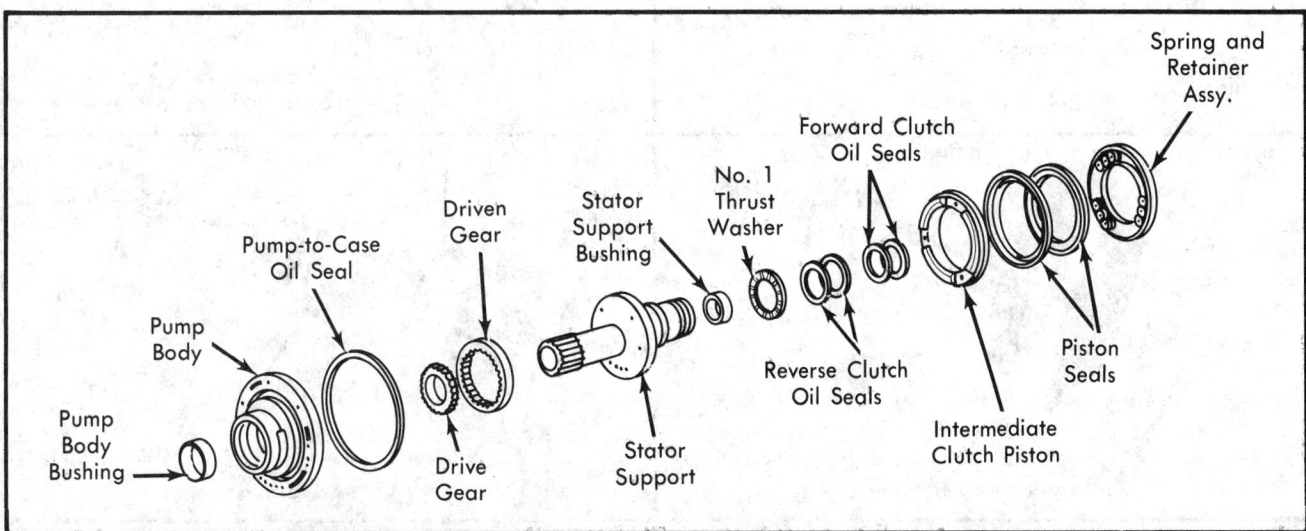

Fig. 18   Exploded View of Oil Pump and Intermediate Clutch Piston

FORD AUTOMATIC OVERDRIVE TRANSMISSION (Cont.)

3) Install new seals on intermediate clutch piston. Seal lips point away from spring posts. Coat piston seal and pump body sealing area with petroleum jelly, then install piston in pump body making sure piston bleed hole is located at 12 o'clock position (toward top of transmission case).

4) Snap spring retainer assembly into place on pump body using even pressure. Install seal rings on stator support.

ACCUMULATORS & SERVOS

3-4 Accumulator — Install new seals on accumulator piston and piston cover. Make sure diagonal cuts on piston seal are aligned properly.

NOTE — Some transmissions use a 3-4 accumulator assembly without a spring. Also, piston and spring construction may differ from that shown in Fig. 19.

2-3 Accumulator — Install new seals on accumulator piston. Make sure diagonal cuts on seals are properly aligned.

Low-Reverse Servo — Inspect sealing edge on both servo cover and piston. Replace cover or piston if necessary.

Overdrive Servo — Separate piston from servo cover. Install new seals on piston and cover. Assemble piston to cover.

VALVE BODY ASSEMBLY

NOTE — Refer to valve body illustrations. As valve trains are removed from each valve body bore, place individual parts in correct order and in relative position to valve body to simplify reassembly. Tag all springs as they are removed for reassembly reference.

Disassembly — **1)** Remove and discard valve body gasket. Remove attaching bolts and remove separator plate, reinforcement plates and separator plate gasket. Discard gasket.

2) Remove the two relief valves and eight check balls from valve body. Note location of orange check ball, it is not interchangeable with the seven black check balls. See Fig. 20.

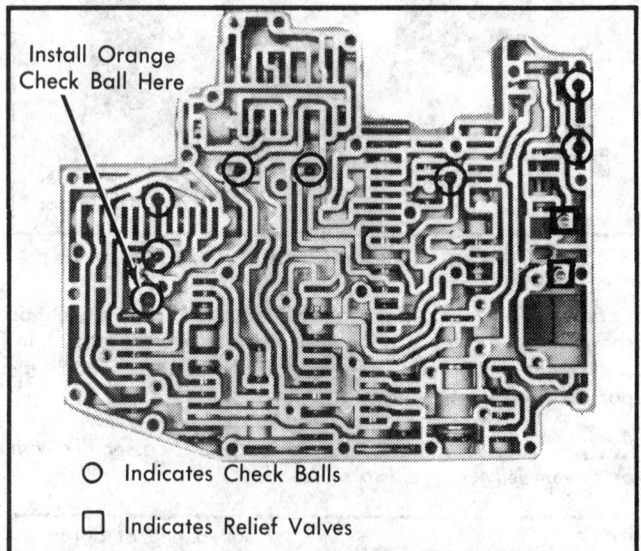

Fig. 20 View of Valve Body Showing Location of Check Balls and Pressure Relief Valves

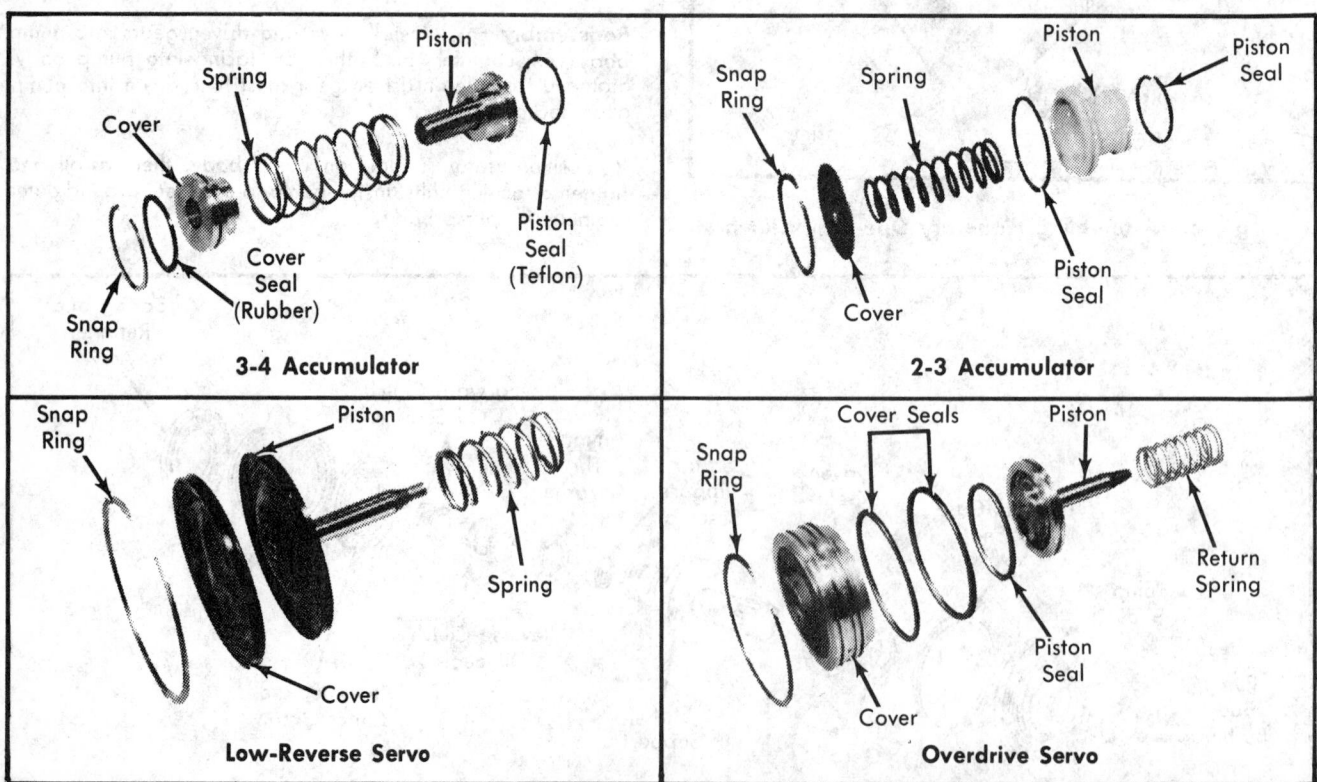

Fig. 19 Exploded View of Accumulator and Servo Assemblies

FORD AUTOMATIC OVERDRIVE TRANSMISSION (Cont.)

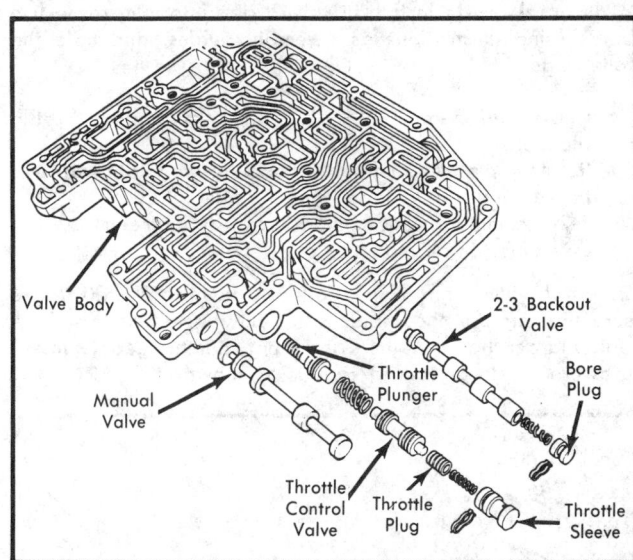

Fig. 21 Exploded View of Manual Valve, Throttle Control Valve Train and 2-3 Backout Valve Train

3) Refer to *Fig. 21* and perform the following:

- Remove manual valve.
- Remove retaining clip and slide throttle control valve train from valve body.
- Remove retaining clip and remove 2-3 backout valve train.

4) Refer to *Fig. 22* and perform the following:

- Remove retaining clip and retaining plate and remove 2-3 capacity modulator valve and orifice control valve trains.
- Remove retaining clip and remove 3-4 T.V. modulator valve and 3-4 shift valve trains.
- Remove retaining plate and remove T.V. limit valve train.
- Remove retaining clip and remove 1-2 shift valve train.
- Remove retaining plate and remove overdrive servo regulator valve train.
- Remove retaining clip and remove 3-4 shuttle valve train.
- Remove retaining clip and remove 1-2 accumulator valve train.
- Remove retaining clip and remove 1-2 capacity modulator valve train.

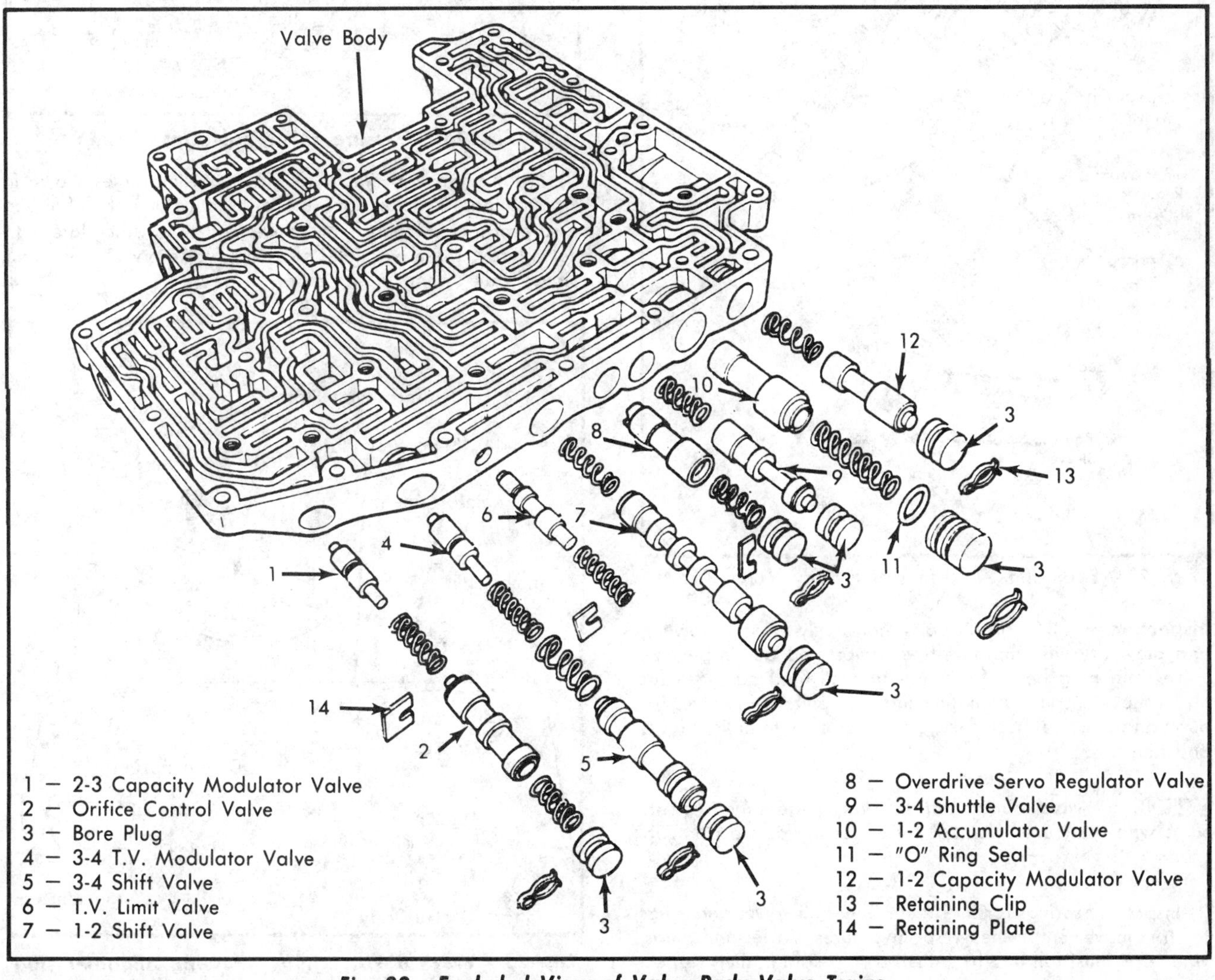

1 — 2-3 Capacity Modulator Valve
2 — Orifice Control Valve
3 — Bore Plug
4 — 3-4 T.V. Modulator Valve
5 — 3-4 Shift Valve
6 — T.V. Limit Valve
7 — 1-2 Shift Valve

8 — Overdrive Servo Regulator Valve
9 — 3-4 Shuttle Valve
10 — 1-2 Accumulator Valve
11 — "O" Ring Seal
12 — 1-2 Capacity Modulator Valve
13 — Retaining Clip
14 — Retaining Plate

Fig. 22 Exploded View of Valve Body Valve Trains

FORD AUTOMATIC OVERDRIVE TRANSMISSION (Cont.)

5) Refer to *Fig. 23* and perform the following:

- Remove retaining clip and remove boost valve and main pressure regulator valve trains.
- Remove two retaining plates and remove 2-1 scheduling valve and low servo modulator valve trains.
- Remove retaining plate and remove 3-4 backout valve train.
- Remove retaining clip and remove 2-3 shift valve and 2-3 T.V. modulator valve trains.

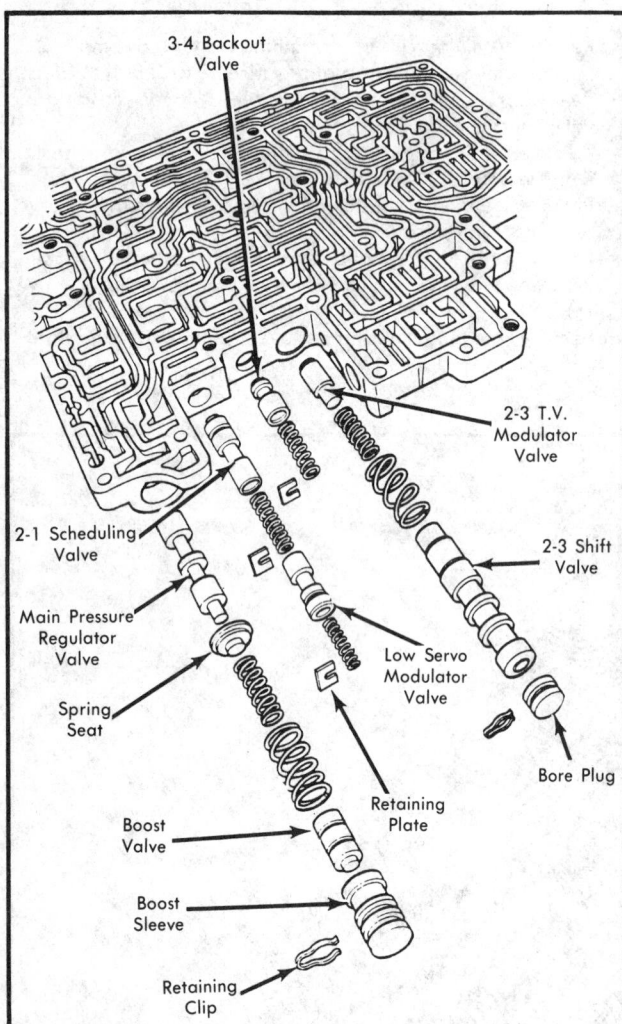

Fig. 23   *Exploded View of Valve Body Valve Trains*

Inspection — 1) Clean all parts thoroughly in clean solvent, and blow dry with moisture-free compressed air. Inspect all valves and plug bores for scores and all fluid passages for obstructions. Inspect all mating surfaces, plugs and valves for burrs and scores. If necessary, use crocus cloth to polish valves and plugs.

CAUTION — *Avoid rounding off the sharp edges of valves and plugs with the crocus cloth. These edges perform a cleaning action.*

2) Inspect all springs for distortion. Check all valves and plugs for free movement in their respective bores. Valves and plugs, when dry, must fall free from their own weight in their respective bores.

Reassembly — 1) Install all valve trains into their respective bores using illustrations as assembly guides, and note the following:

- Chamfered stem of throttle control valve faces throttle plunger.
- Retainer plate used for 2-3 capacity modulator valve is thicker and longer than other retainer plates.
- 1-2 accumulator valve and valve body diameters are not the same for all models.

2) Install valve body check balls as shown in *Fig. 20*. Make sure that orange check ball is correctly installed. This check ball is larger than the others and is not interchangeable. Install pressure relief valves and springs as shown in *Fig. 24*.

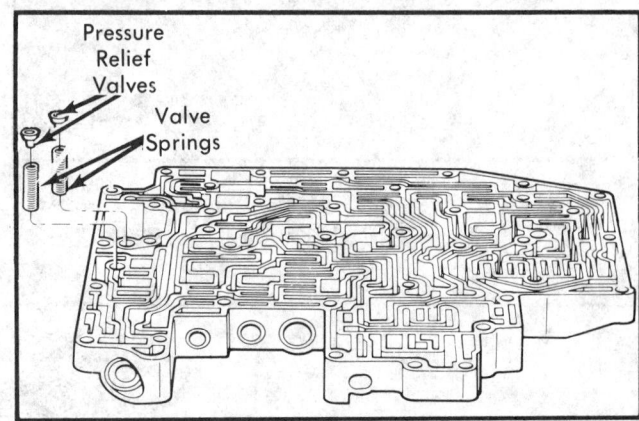

Fig. 24   *Pressure Relief Valve Installation*

3) Install alignment pins (T80L-77100-A) into holes shown in *Fig. 25*. These two holes are smaller than the other bolt holes to assure proper alignment of gasket and separator plate with valve body. These two holes also align valve body gasket and valve body assembly with case.

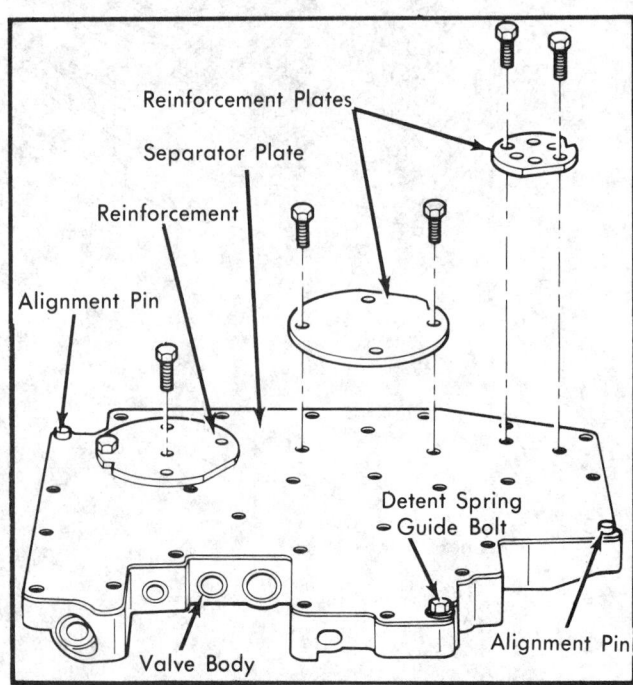

Fig. 25   *View of Valve Body Showing Alignment Pin and Reinforcement Plate Installation*

FORD AUTOMATIC OVERDRIVE TRANSMISSION (Cont.)

4) Using a new separator plate gasket, slide plate and gasket over alignment pins. Position three reinforcment plates and loosely install attaching bolts. Loosely install detent spring guide bolt.

NOTE — *Detent spring guide bolt is the same length as short valve body-to-case attaching bolts.*

5) Starting at center (large) reinforcement plate and working outward, tighten attaching bolts. Remove alignment pins.

TRANSMISSION REASSEMBLY

NOTE — *Handle all parts carefully to avoid damaging bearings and mating surfaces. Lubricate all parts with clean transmission fluid (use petroleum jelly on gaskets, thrust washers and needle bearings to retain in place). Use all new gaskets and seals, and tighten bolts evenly.*

1) Install No. 9 output shaft needle bearing in transmission case. Install bearing support, No. 7 needle bearing and direct clutch hub in direct clutch assembly. Assemble output shaft hub to output shaft and install retaining snap ring. Place No. 8 needle bearing on rear of direct clutch drum, then slide output shaft into direct clutch drum. Attach output shaft hub to ring gear with retaining ring. Install output shaft, ring gear and direct clutch assembly into transmission case.

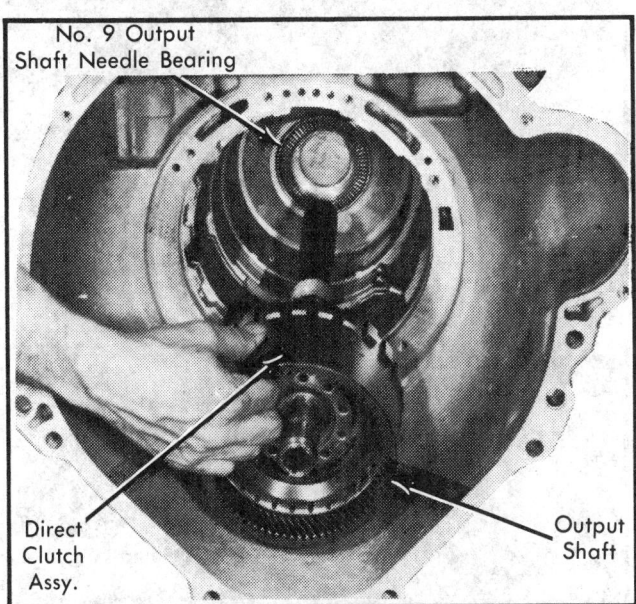

Fig. 26   Direct Clutch Assembly Installation

2) Position governor drive ball in pocket on output shaft. Slide governor assembly onto output shaft with cover and attaching screws facing toward front of case, then install governor retaining snap ring.

3) Install low-reverse band into transmission case and make sure band is seated on anchor pins. When properly installed, center of band actuating rod seat can be seen through servo piston bore.

4) Install center support and planetary assembly into case. If necessary, rotate output shaft to align planet carrier splines with direct clutch hub splines. Install center support anti-clunk spring using a hammer handle or wooden dowel. Install center support retaining ring.

NOTE — *Center support and planet carrier can not be installed unless notch cut in center support is aligned with overdrive band anchor pin.*

5) To determine correct length of low-reverse servo pin to install, proceed as follows:

- Install servo piston and return spring. Do not install cover or retaining ring.
- Install servo selector tool (T80L-77030-A) into servo bore and tighten band apply bolt on tool to 120 INCH lbs.
- Attach a dial indicator as shown in *Fig. 27* and position indicator stem on flat portion of servo piston. Zero dial indicator.
- Thread bolt out of selector tool until piston stops against bottom of tool.
- Read amount of piston travel on dial indicator.
- If travel is .108″ to .241″, correct servo pin is installed. If travel is not within specifications, selective pistons are available in lengths of: 2.936″ (identified by 1 groove), 2.989″ (2 grooves) and 3.043″ (3 grooves). Length is measured from base of piston to end of rod.
- Select proper servo pin to bring servo travel within specifications, then remove selector tool and dial indicator.

6) Install selected low-reverse servo piston. Install servo cover and cover retaining snap ring.

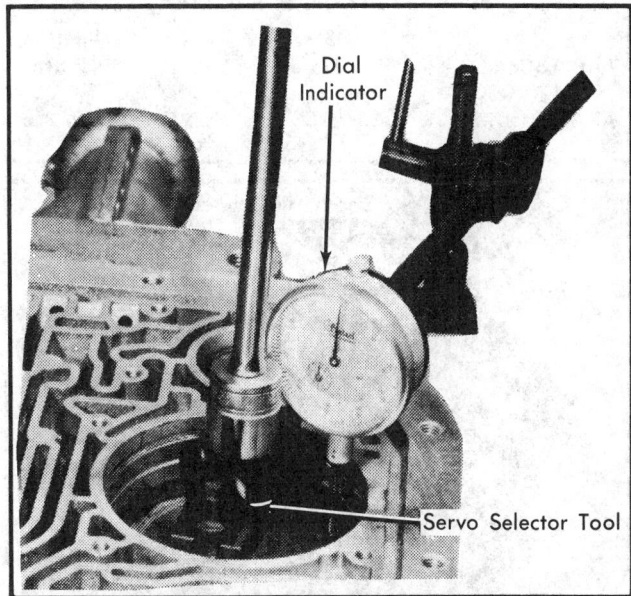

Fig. 27   Low-Reverse Servo Pin Selection

7) Make sure No. 2 thrust washer is in position in reverse clutch, then assemble reverse clutch on forward clutch. Install No. 3 needle bearing and forward clutch hub in forward clutch. Position No. 4 needle bearing on forward clutch hub, then install drive shell over clutch assemblies. Install No. 5 needle bearing and forward sun gear on drive shell, then install complete assembly into case, rotating output to aid in engaging sun gear with planetary gears.

8) Install overdrive band into case and around drive shell assembly and make sure band anchor is properly positioned on anchor pin. Use a screwdriver to hold overdrive band in position, then install overdrive servo.

FORD AUTOMATIC OVERDRIVE TRANSMISSION (Cont.)

NOTE — *With overdrive servo installed, inspect band and apply pin for proper position and engagement. If band anchor and apply pin are not properly engaged, remove servo and reposition band as necessary.*

9) Install intermediate clutch pack components into case in the following order: Pressure plate, clutch pack (starting with a friction plate and alternating steel and friction plates) and selective steel plate. Measure intermediate clutch clearance as follows:

10) Intermediate clutch clearance is measured using a depth micrometer and end play checking tool (T80L-77003-A) as shown in *Fig. 28.* Set end play tool across pump case mounting surface. Locate micrometer end play bar and read depth, then check depth again 180 degrees opposite. Depth at intermediate clutch selective steel plate should be 1.634-1.646". Average of the two measurements should be within this range.

NOTE — *A downward pressure must be applied to clutch pack while measuring intermediate clutch clearance.*

11) If intermediate clutch clearance is not within tolerance, the following size selective steel plates are available: .067-.071", .077-.081", .087-.091" and .097-.101". Install correct size plate and recheck clearance.

Intermediate Clutch Plate Usage

Application	Steel Plates	Friction Plates
All Models	3	3

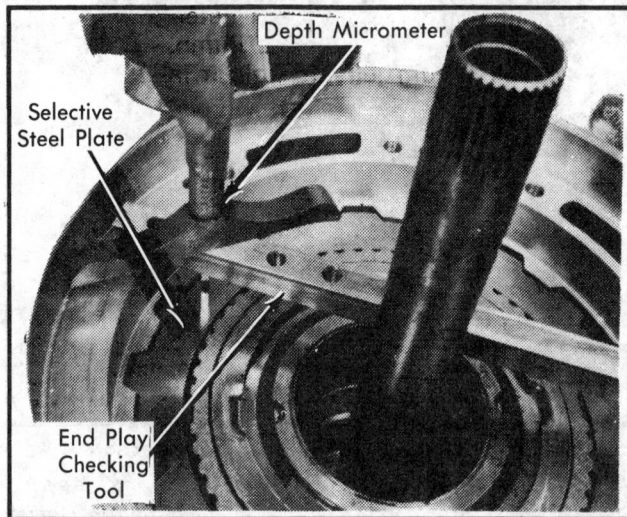

Fig. 28   Measuring Intermediate Clutch Clearance

12) Next, check transmission end play by locating depth micrometer on end play checking tool bar (T80L-77003-A) so that depth is measured at reverse clutch drum thrust face. Check end play 180 degress opposite to determine average depth. Thrust washer controlling transmission end play is located on stator support which is attached to back of pump housing.

13) Transmission end play can be adjusted using one of the selective thrust washers available for service. After measuring depth, select required thrust washer from the following table.

Transmission End Play Thrust Washer Selection Chart

Measured Depth	Washer Thickness	Color Code
1.483-1.500"	.050-.054"	Green
1.501-1.517"	.068-.072"	Yellow
1.518-1.534"	.085-.089"	Natural
1.535-1.551"	.102-.106"	Red
1.552-1.568"	.119-.123"	Blue

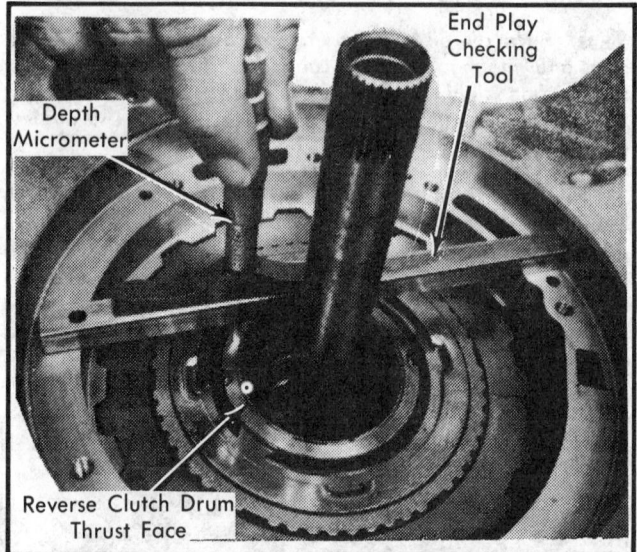

Fig. 29   Measuring Transmission End Play

14) Install selected transmission end play thrust washer on stator support, using petroleum jelly to hold it in place. Install pump alignment dowel, made by cutting the head from a M8-1.25 bolt, into pump mounting bolt hole shown in *Fig. 30.*

Fig. 30   Pump Alignment Dowel Installation

15) Install new pump gasket into case, then install pump assembly into case using two slide hammers to lower it into position. Remove alignment dowel and install the seven pump attaching bolts. Alternately tighten bolts a few turns at a time to draw pump into case.

16) Assemble 3-4 accumulator. Install piston (and spring, if so equipped) into case. Lubricate rubber seal on accumulator cover and top of bore to help cover installation, then install cover and retaining ring. Install 2-3 accumulator assembly.

FORD AUTOMATIC OVERDRIVE TRANSMISSION (Cont.)

NOTE — *After installation, 3-4 accumulator cover must be seated firmly against retaining ring. Use air pressure if necessary to seat cover against ring.*

17) Install 2 valve body alignment pins (T80L-77100-A) into positions shown in *Fig. 31*. Install valve body gasket and valve body assembly over pins, making sure manual and throttle levers are properly positioned before installing valve body attaching bolts.

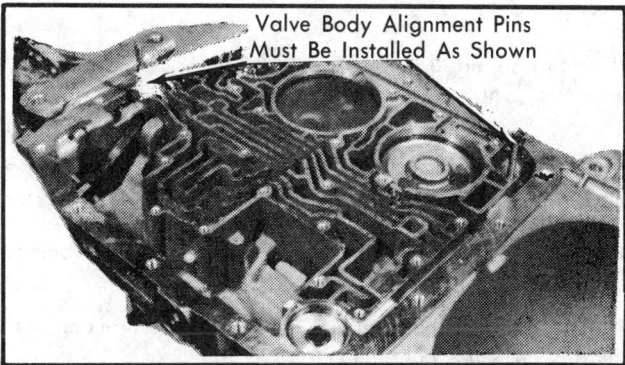

Valve Body Alignment Pins Must Be Installed As Shown

Fig. 31   View of Transmission Showing Valve Body Alignment Pin Installation

18) Loosely install 21 valve body attaching bolts. Starting at center and working outward, tighten bolts. Remove alignment pins and install bolts. Install detent spring and roller assembly and tighten bolts.

NOTE — *Two different length valve body attaching bolts are used. Shorter bolts are used at the four front, one center and three rear locations.*

19) Position torsion spring against separator plate "V" notch. This spring pushes the throttle lever in direction of wide open throttle.

20) Install filter grommet, new filter gasket and filter on valve body. Install filter attaching bolts and tighten. Position new pan gasket on case and install oil pan. Using a new gasket, install extension housing on case.

21) Slide direct drive shaft into turbine input shaft. Install torque converter, making sure it is fully seated in pump.

TIGHTENING SPECIFICATIONS

Application	Ft. Lbs.
Stator Support-to-Pump	16-25
Pump-to-Case	16-20
Oil Pan-to-Case	12-16
Extension-to-Case	16-20
Inner Manual Lever-to-Shaft	30-40
Outer Throttle Lever-to-Shaft	12-16
Cooler Line-to-Case	10-14
Converter Plug-to-Converter	8-28
Neutral Safety Switch-to-Case	8-11
Pressure Plug-to-Case	6-12
Transmission-to-Engine	40-50

Application	INCH Lbs.
Reinforcing Plate-to-Valve Body	80-100
Separator Plate-to-Valve Body	80-100
Valve Body-to-Case	80-100
Filter-to-Valve Body	80-100
Governor Body-to-Counterweight	80-120
Cover-to-Governor Body	34-50

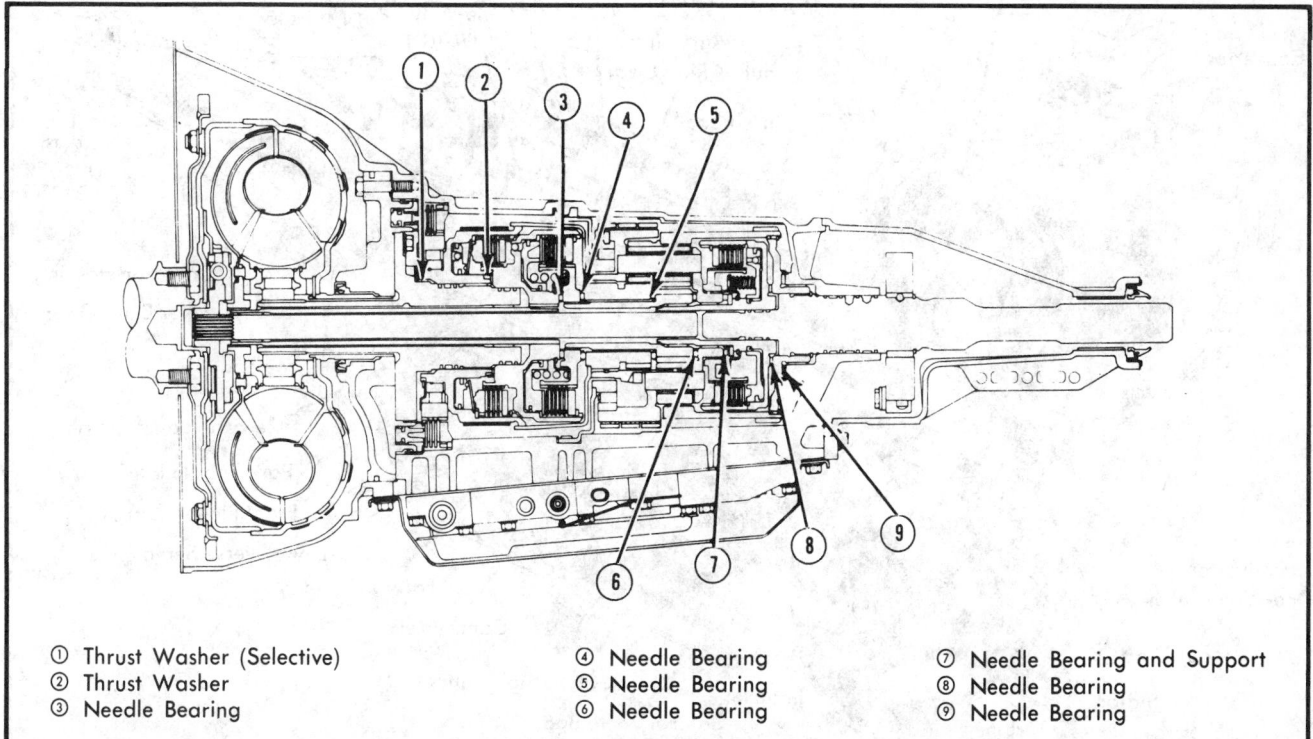

① Thrust Washer (Selective)
② Thrust Washer
③ Needle Bearing
④ Needle Bearing
⑤ Needle Bearing
⑥ Needle Bearing
⑦ Needle Bearing and Support
⑧ Needle Bearing
⑨ Needle Bearing

Fig. 32   Thrust Bearing and Thrust Washer Locations

FORD C-4

F100/150

TRANSMISSION IDENTIFICATION

An identification tag is located under lower front intermediate servo cover bolt. The first line on tag shows transmission model prefix and suffix, and the build date code. A number appearing after the model code suffix indicates internal parts in transmission have been changed after initial production start-up. For example, a PEA-CE1 model transmission that has been changed internally would read PEA-CE2. The lower line of identification tag shows transmission assembly part number.

DESCRIPTION

The C-4 is a 3 speed transmission capable of providing automatic upshifts and downshifts through 3 forward gear ratios and also capable of providing manual selection of 1st and 2nd gears. Transmission consists of a torque converter, planetary gear train with 2 bands, 2 multiple disc clutches, a one-way clutch and hydraulic control system.

LUBRICATION & ADJUSTMENT

See *Automatic Transmission Servicing* in this section.

TESTING

ROAD TEST

1) Check minimum throttle upshifts in "D". Transmission should start in first gear, shift to second, and then shift to third as speed increases. See *Shift Speed table.*

2) With transmission in third gear, depress accelerator pedal through detent (to floor). Transmission should shift from third to second, or third to first, depending on vehicle speed. See *Shift Speed table.*

3) Check closed throttle downshift from third to first by coasting down from about 30 MPH in third gear. Shift should occur as shown in table.

4) With transmission in "2", transmission should operate only in second gear.

5) With transmission in third gear and road speed above 30 MPH, transmission should shift to second gear when selector lever is moved from "D" to "2" or "1". When same manual shift is made below 25 MPH, transmission will shift from second or third to first.

NOTE — *This test will determine if governor pressure and shift control valves are operating properly.*

6) Slipping or engine speed flare-up in any gear usually indicates clutch or band problems. In most cases, the clutch or band that is slipping can be determined by noting transmission operation in all selector positions and comparing which internal units are applied in those positions. See *Clutch And Band Application Chart.*

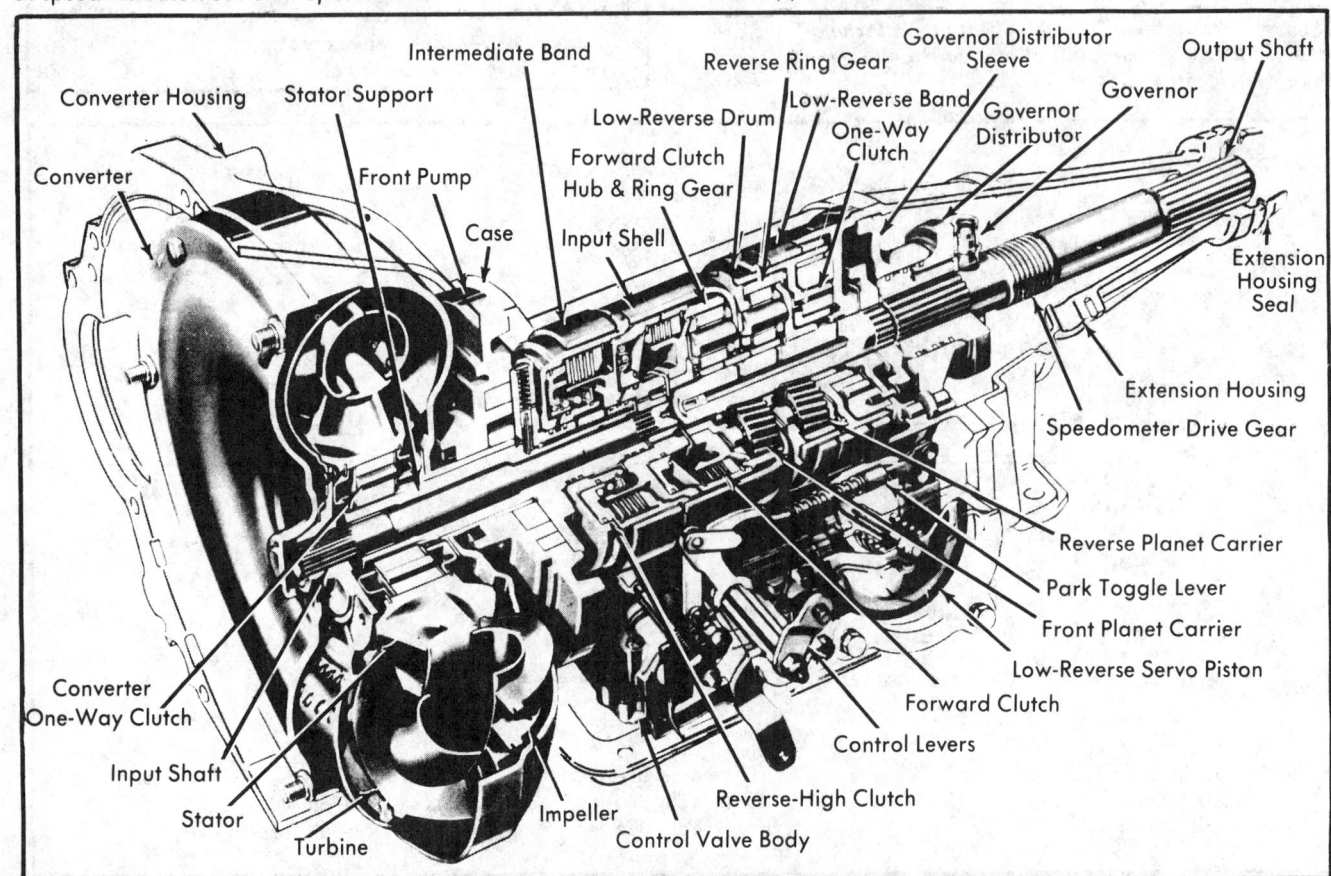

Fig. 1 Cutaway View of Ford C-4 Automatic Transmission Assembly

FORD C-4 (Cont.)

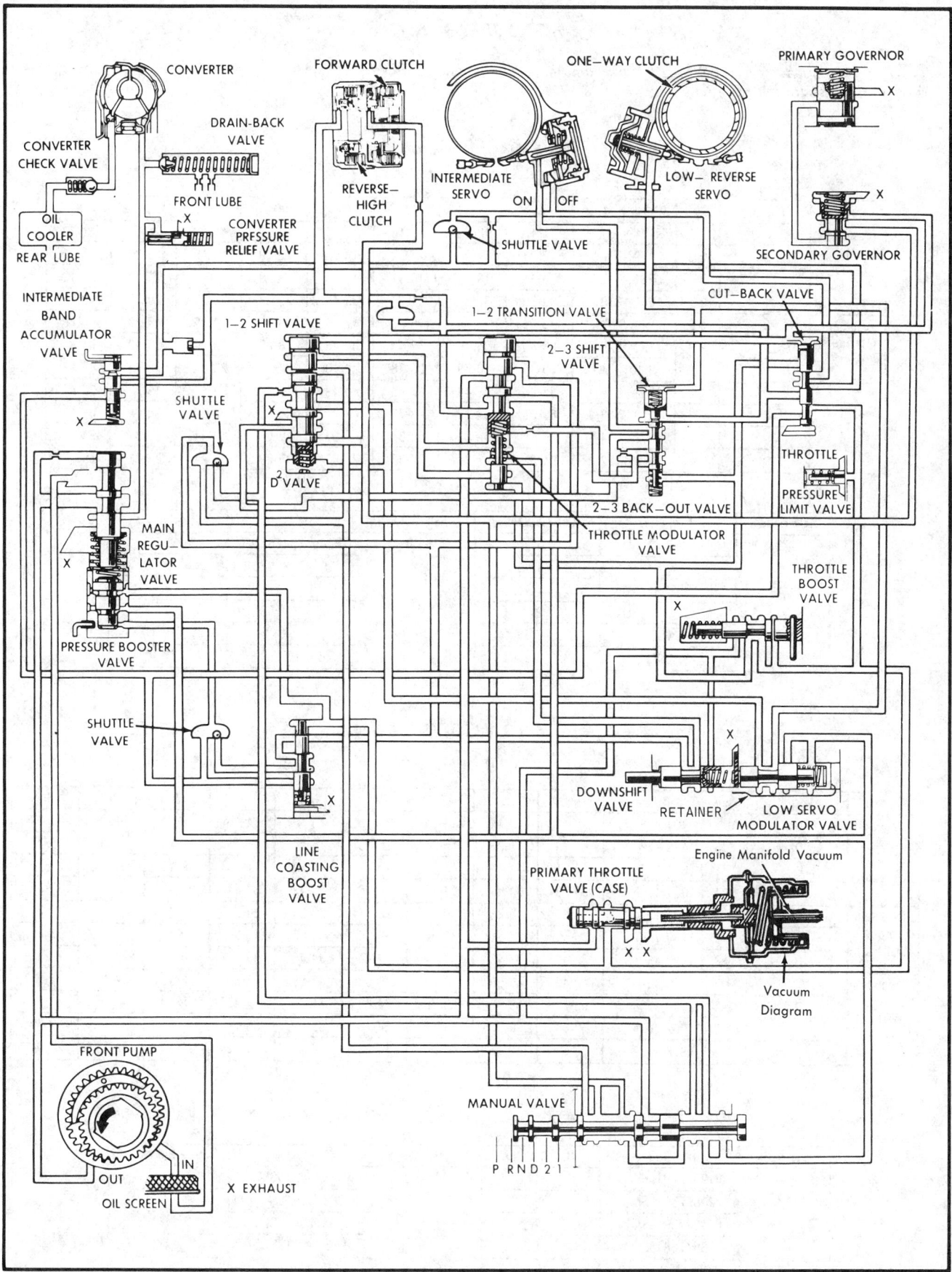

Fig. 2   C-4 Automatic Transmission Hydraulic Circuits Diagram

FORD C-4 (Cont.)

SHIFT SPEEDS (MPH)

NOTE — Shift speeds given below are approximate. All shift speeds may vary somewhat due to production tolerances, axle ratio and emission control equipment.

6-CYLINDER MODELS

Throttle	Range	Shift	OPS-R.P.M.	1	2	3	4	5	6	7	8
Closed (Above 17'' Vacuum)	D	1-2	401-436	11-12	12-13	12-13	13-14	10-11	11-12	11-12	11-12
	D	2-3	449-739	13-21	14-22	14-22	14-23	12-19	12-19	12-20	13-21
	D	3-1	331-366	9-10	10-11	10-11	10-12	9-10	9-10	9-10	9-10
	1	2-1	1061-1268	30-35	32-39	31-37	33-40	27-32	28-33	29-35	30-36
To Detent (Torque Demand)	D	1-2	546-998	15-28	17-30	16-29	17-31	14-26	14-26	15-27	16-28
	D	2-3	1092-1526	30-43	33-46	32-45	34-48	28-39	29-40	30-42	31-43
	D	3-2	908-1291	25-36	28-39	27-38	28-40	23-33	24-34	25-35	26-37
Through Detent (WOT)	D	1-2	1262-1575	35-44	38-48	37-46	40-49	32-40	33-41	58-43	36-45
	D	2-3	2140-2368	60-66	65-72	63-70	67-74	55-60	56-62	58-65	61-67
	D	3-2	1902-2074	53-58	58-63	56-61	60-65	49-53	50-54	52-57	54-59
	D	3-1 2-1	898-1122	25-31	27-34	27-33	28-35	23-29	23-29	25-31	26-32

Axle Ratio	Tire Size	Use Col. No.	Axle Ratio	Tire Size	Use Col. No.
2.75	P195/75R15SL	1	3.00	P195/75R15SL	5
	P205/75R15SL	1		P205/75R15SL	6
	P215/75R15SL	1		P215/75R15SL	6
	P235/75R15SL	2		P235/75R15SL	7
	H78 × 15B	3		L78 × 15C	8
	L78 × 15B	4		H78 × 15B	7

V8 MODELS

Throttle	Range	Shift	OPS-R.P.M.	1	2	3	4	5	6	7	8	9
Closed (Above 17'' Vacuum)	D	1-2	401-436	13-14	13-14	13-14	14-15	13-14	14-15	10-11	11-12	11-12
	D	2-3	449-739	14-23	14-23	15-24	15-25	15-24	16-25	12-19	12-20	13-21
	D	3-1	331-366	10-11	11-12	11-12	11-12	11-12	11-13	9-10	9-10	9-10
	1	2-1	1061-1268	33-39	34-40	34-41	36-43	35-42	37-44	27-32	29-35	30-36
To Detent (Torque Demand)	D	1-2	592-1036	18-32	19-33	19-34	20-35	20-34	20-36	15-27	16-28	17-29
	D	2-3	1169-1607	36-50	37-51	38-52	39-54	39-53	40-55	30-41	32-44	33-46
	D	3-2	1023-1357	32-42	32-43	33-44	34-46	34-45	35-47	26-35	28-37	29-39
Through Detent (WOT)	D	1-2	1350-1575	42-49	43-50	44-51	45-53	45-52	46-54	35-40	37-43	38-45
	D	2-3	2140-2368	66-74	68-75	69-76	72-80	71-78	74-81	55-60	58-65	61-67
	D	3-2	1902-2074	59-64	60-66	61-67	64-70	63-69	65-71	49-53	52-57	54-59
	D	3-1 2-1	898-1122	28-35	29-36	29-36	30-38	30-37	31-39	23-29	25-31	26-32

Axle Ratio	Tire Size	Use Col. No.	Axle Ratio	Tire Size	Use Col. No.
2.47	P195/75R155SL	1	3.00	P195/75R15SL	7
	P205/75R15SL	2		P205/75R15SL	7
	P215/75R15SL	3		P235/75R15SL	8
	P235/75R15SL	4		P215/75R15SL	7
	H78 × 15B	5		H78 × 15B	8
	L78 × 15C	6		L78 × 15C	9

FORD C-4 (Cont.)

CONTROL PRESSURE TEST

Engine Vacuum Method — 1) Attach a tachometer to engine and install a vacuum gauge (using a "T") into manifold vacuum line at vacuum diaphragm unit *(Fig. 3)*. Attach a 0-400 psi pressure gauge to control pressure take-off point on transmission *(Fig. 4)*.

2) Apply both parking and service brakes. With engine at curb idle speed and normal operating temperature, read and record control pressure in all selector positions at specified manifold vacuum. Compare control pressures obtained in tests with pressures given in Control Pressure Table.

CAUTION — *Release throttle immediately if slippage is indicated. Also shift transmission to Neutral and run engine at 1000 RPM to cool transmission fluid between tests.*

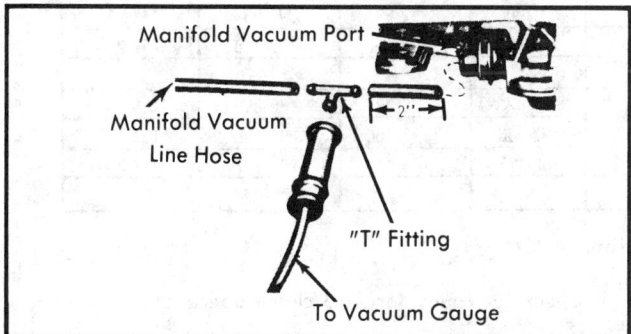

Fig. 3   Connecting Vacuum Gauge for Control Pressure Testing

Vacuum Pump Method — 1) Attach tachometer to engine, and a 0-400 psi pressure gauge to control pressure take-off point at transmission. Disconnect and temporarily plug manifold vacuum line at vacuum diaphragm unit. Connect a suitable remote vacuum source, such as the vacuum pump provided in a distributor tester. Apply both parking and service brakes. Start engine and vacuum pump. Set vacuum at 15 inches, read and record control pressure in all shift selector positions.

2) Increase engine speed to 1000 RPM, and reduce vacuum to 10 inches. Read and record control pressure in "D", "2" and "1". With engine still at 1000 RPM, reduce vacuum to 1 inch. Read and record control pressure in "D", "2", "1" and "R". Compare control pressures obtained in tests with pressures given in Control Pressure Table.

NOTE — *Governor can be checked at same time as Control Pressure Test is performed.*

3) Place selector lever in "2", no load on engine and apply 10" of vacuum. Increase speed slowly while watching speedometer, check speed at which control pressure cutback occurs. It should occur between 10-20 MPH.

4) Decrease vacuum to 0.2" and repeat test. Control pressure cutback should occur between 30-50 MPH. If cutback does not occur within specifications, check shift speeds to make sure that it is the governor and not a stuck cutback valve.

CAUTION — *DO NOT exceed 60 MPH speedometer speed during test. If control pressures are not within specifications, proceed to Control Pressure Test Results to determine problem.*

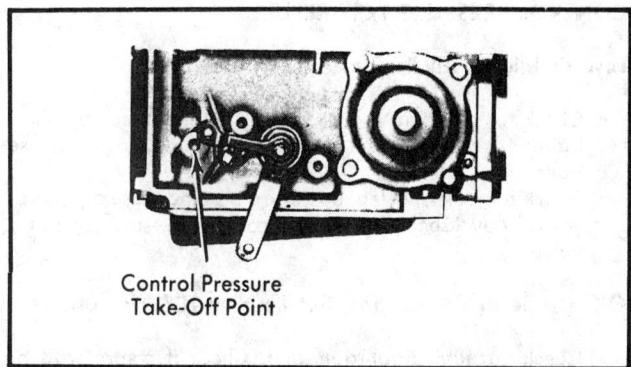

Fig. 4   View of Transmission Case Showing Control Pressure Test Point

CLUTCH AND BAND APPLICATION CHART
(ELEMENTS IN USE)

Selector Lever Position	Intermediate Band	Low-Reverse Band	Forward Clutch	High Clutch	One-Way Clutch
D — DRIVE 　　First Gear 　　Second Gear 　　Third Gear	 X 		 X X X	 X	 X
2 — INTERMEDIATE 　　Second Gear	X		X		
1 — LOW (First)		X	X		
R — REVERSE		X		X	
NEUTRAL OR PARK — All clutches and bands released and/or ineffective.					

Automatic Transmissions

FORD C-4 (Cont.)

CONTROL PRESSURE SPECIFICATIONS

Transmission Models	Range	Idle 15'' & Above	14''	13''	12''	11''	10''	WOT Stall Thru Detent
PEA-CP.CE	D	58-61	58-61	58-69	64-76	71-84	79-91	144-155
PEE-FL.GA	2.1	85-98	91-98	91-98	91-99	91-99	92-99	144-155
PEM-U.AH.AJ.AK	R	151-164	152-164	152-165	152-165	153-165	153-166	243-259
	P.N	58-61	58-62	58-69	—	—	—	—
PEM-C,D,E,AC,	D	58-60	58-66	60-73	67-80	75-87	82-94	149-159
AD.AE.AF.AG	2.1	92-102	94-102	94-102	94-102	95-102	95-103	149-159
	R	157-170	157-170	158-171	158-171	158-171	159-171	248-265
	P.N	58-60	58-66	61-73	—	—	—	—
PEB-N,P,Z,U	D	58-60	58-60	58-64	61-71	69-78	76-85	143-150
PEN-A.B	2.1	79-94	87-95	88-95	88-95	88-95	88-95	143-150
	R	146-158	146-158	146-159	147-159	147-159	147-160	240-251
	P.N	58-60	58-60	58-64	—	—	—	—
PEM-S.W	D	58-64	60-70	67-77	74-83	80-90	87-90	148-155
	2.1	91-98	91-98	91-99	91-99	92-99	92-99	148-155
	R	152-164	152-165	152-165	153-165	153-166	153-166	247-258
	P.N	58-64	60-70	67-77	—	—	—	—
PEJ-AC.AD	D	57-61	57-61	64-75	71-82	79-89	86-89	153-161
	2.1	96-105	97-105	97-105	97-106	97-106	97-106	153-161
	R	161-176	162-176	162-176	162-177	163-177	163-177	257-270
	P.N	57-61	57-61	64-75	—	—	—	—

CONTROL PRESSURE TEST RESULTS

Low at Idle in All Ranges

- Check for low fluid level, restricted intake screen or filter, loose oil tubes, loose valve body or regulator-to-case bolts.
- Check for excessive leakage in front pump, case or control valve body. Check for sticking control pressure regulator valve.

OK at Idle in All Ranges, But Low at 10" Vacuum

- Check vacuum diaphragm unit. Check if control rod or throttle valve is stuck.

High at Idle in All Ranges

- Check vacuum diaphragm unit, manifold vacuum line, throttle rod or control rod.
- Check for sticking regulator boost valve(s).

OK at Idle in All Ranges, OK at 10" Vacuum, But Low at 1" Vacuum

- Check for excessive leakage, low pump capacity or restricted oil pan screen.

Low in "P"

- Check valve body pressure regulator.

Low in "R"

- Check reverse-high clutch and/or low-reverse band or servo.

Low in "N"

- Check valve body for tightness and correct operation.

Low in "D"

- Check for faulty forward clutch operation.

Low in "2"

- Check forward clutch and/or intermediate servo for correct operation.

Low in "1"

- Check forward clutch and/or low-reverse band or servo for correct operation.

VACUUM DIAPHRAGM UNIT

Vacuum Supply Check — 1) Disconnect vacuum line at vacuum unit and connect to vacuum gauge. With engine idling, gauge must show a steady acceptable vacuum. If reading is low, check for vacuum leak and/or poor engine vacuum.

2) If reading is acceptable, rapidly accelerate engine momentarily, vacuum must drop rapidly at acceleration and return immediately upon deceleration. If vacuum reading does not change or changes slowly, vacuum line is plugged, restricted or connected to reservoir supply. Repair as required.

Vacuum Diaphragm Unit Check — 1) Remove unit from transmission. Use suitable tester equipped with vacuum pump. Start pump and set regulator knob so vacuum gauge reads 18" with end of hose blocked off. Connect vacuum hose to port on unit. If gauge still reads 18", unit is not leaking. If vacuum does not hold at 18", unit is leaking and must be replaced.

2) When hose is removed from unit, hold finger over end of control rod. Internal spring of unit should push control rod outward. Also, check for presence of transmission fluid in vacuum side of diaphragm or in vacuum hose. If fluid is present, unit is leaking and must be replaced.

FORD C-4 (Cont.)

STALL SPEED TEST

CAUTION — *DO NOT hold throttle open longer than 5 seconds at a time during testing. If engine speed exceeds maximum limit of stall speed, release throttle immediately as clutches or bands are slipping.*

Testing Procedure — With engine at curb idle speed and normal operating temperature, tachometer installed, parking and service brakes fully applied, stall test transmission in each driving range at full throttle and note maximum RPM obtained. Engine speed should be within limits shown in Stall Speed table.

NOTE — *Allow a cooling period of 15 seconds with transmission in Neutral and engine speed at 1000 RPM between each test.*

Stall Speeds	
Application	Stall RPM
6-Cyl. Models	1572-1824
V8 Models	1422-1685

STALL TEST RESULTS

Stall Speed Too High — In "D", "2", "1", and "R"; general transmission problems are indicated and control pressure check should be made to locate faulty unit(s). In "D", "2", and "1"; indicates forward clutch slippage. In "D" only; planetary gear train one-way clutch slippage is indicated. In "R" only; reverse-high clutch or low-reverse band slippage is indicated.

Stall Speed Too Low — Torque converter stator one-way clutch faulty. **NOTE** — *Make sure engine performance is satisfactory before condemning converter assembly. Converter cannot be overhauled and must be replaced if defective.*

AIR PRESSURE CHECKS

A "No Drive" condition can exist, even with correct transmission fluid pressure, because of inoperative clutches or bands. Erratic shifts could be caused by a stuck governor valve. The inoperative units can be located through a series of checks by substituting air pressure for the fluid pressure to determine location of malfunction. To make air pressure checks, loosen oil pan bolts and allow transmission to drain, then remove oil pan and control valve body. Apply air at points shown in *Fig. 5* and check unit operation as follows:

Forward Clutch — Apply air pressure to transmission case forward clutch passage. A dull thud can be heard when clutch piston is applied, or movement of the piston can be felt by placing finger tips on input shell.

Governor — Apply air pressure to control pressure-to-governor passage and listen for sharp clicking or whistling noise indicating governor valve movement.

Reverse-High Clutch — Apply air pressure to reverse-high clutch passage. A dull thud can be heard when clutch piston is applied, or movement of piston can be felt by placing finger tips on clutch drum.

Intermediate Servo — Hold air nozzle in intermediate servo apply passage. Operation of servo is indicated by tightening of intermediate band around drum. While continuing to apply air pressure at servo apply passage, apply air pressure at intermediate servo release passage. Intermediate servo should then release band against the apply pressure.

Low-Reverse Servo — Apply air pressure to low-reverse servo apply passage. Low-Reverse band should tighten around drum if servo is operating properly.

SERVICE (IN VEHICLE)

VALVE BODY ASSEMBLY

Removal — 1) Raise vehicle. Disconnect fluid filler tube from pan, and allow fluid to drain from pan into container. Remove all pan bolts and remove pan and gasket.

NOTE — *If fluid is to be used again, it should be filtered through a 100-mesh screen.*

2) Shift transmission manual lever to "P" position. Remove 2 bolts that hold detent spring to valve body and case. Remove remaining valve body bolts, hold manual valve in valve body to prevent damage to valve and remove valve body from transmission.

Installation — 1) Clean all gasket material from oil pan mounting face on case. Remove and discard nylon shipping plug from oil pan filler tube hole. Shift manual lever of transmission to "Park" detent and install valve body into case.

NOTE — *Nylon plug is used to retain fluid in transmission during shipment and should be discarded when oil pan is removed.*

2) Position inner downshift lever between downshift lever stop and downshift valve. Make sure both lands on end of manual valve engage actuating pin on manual detent lever. Install valve body-to-case bolts finger tight.

3) Position detent spring to lower valve body and install spring-to-case bolt finger tight. Hold detent spring roller in center of manual detent lever and install and tighten spring-to-lower valve body bolt.

4) Tighten all valve body-to-case bolts to specifications. Install oil filter screen and oil pan with new gasket. Connect filler tube to pan and tighten fitting to specifications. Lower vehicle and refill transmission to correct fluid level.

Automatic Transmissions

FORD C-4 (Cont.)

INTERMEDIATE SERVO

Removal — Remove forward oil cooler line and servo cover-to-case attaching bolts. Remove vacuum tube and line at transmission. Remove servo cover, gasket, piston, and piston return spring, then remove piston from cover. Remove piston seals and cover gasket.

Installation — 1) Install new seals on piston, lubricate seals with transmission fluid, and install servo piston in cover. Install piston return spring into case, place a new seal and gasket on cover, and install piston and cover into case. Use two 5/16-18x1¼ " bolts 180° apart to position cover against case.

2) Install two servo cover retaining bolts in open holes, remove aligning bolts, and install two remaining cover bolts, making sure identification tag is located under lower front bolt. Tighten cover bolts evenly. Install vacuum and oil cooler lines and adjust intermediate band. **NOTE** — *If band cannot be adjusted properly, band struts are not in position. Remove pan and valve body, install struts, then reinstall valve body and oil pan. Adjust band, check and adjust transmission fluid level.*

LOW-REVERSE SERVO

Removal — Loosen reverse band adjusting screw lock nut and tighten band adjusting screw to 10 ft. lbs. **NOTE** — *This will prevent band strut from falling down when servo is removed.* Remove servo cover-to-case attaching bolts, vent tube retaining clip, servo cover and seal from case, then withdraw piston.

NOTE — *The servo piston seal is bonded to piston. If seal is worn or damaged, complete piston must be replaced.*

Installation — 1) Install piston into case. Place a new seal on cover and position cover against case. Use two 5/16-18 x 1¼ " bolts 180° apart to align servo cover on case. Install vent tube retaining clip.

2) Install two servo cover bolts into open holes, remove aligning bolts, install two remaining servo cover bolts, and tighten all bolts evenly. Adjust low-reverse band. **NOTE** — *If band cannot be adjusted properly, band struts are not in position. Remove pan and valve body, install struts, reinstall valve body and oil pan. Adjust band, check and adjust transmission fluid level.*

EXTENSION HOUSING SEAL & BUSHING

Removal — Disconnect propeller shaft from transmission. Remove rear seal using a tapered chisel. Make sure metal chips do not enter extension housing. Remove bushing using special bushing removal tool T77L-7697-A (or equivalent).

CAUTION — *Care must be taken when removing bushing to avoid damaging spline seal.*

Installation — Install new bushing using a suitable driver (T52L-700-HAB). Using replacer tool (T61L-7657-A), install seal, making sure it fits squarely into housing as it is driven into place. Lubricate inside diameter of oil seal. Coat front universal joint splines with lubricant and install propeller shaft.

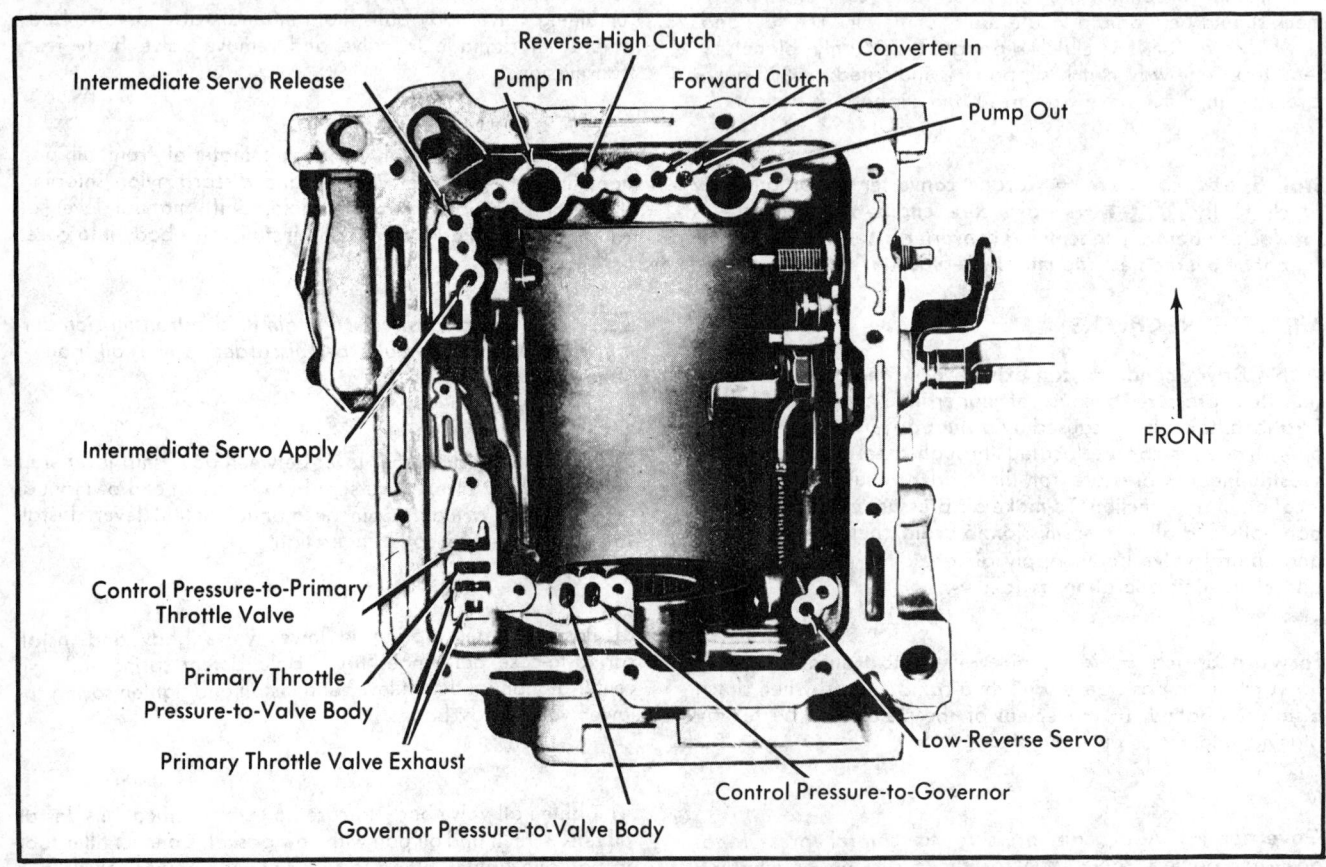

Fig. 5 *Bottom View of Transmission Case Showing Oil Passages*

FORD C-4 (Cont.)

EXTENSION HOUSING

Removal — 1) Remove propeller shaft. Disconnect speedometer cable from extension housing. Remove crossmember-to-extension housing bolts.

2) Lower transmission as required with a transmission jack to provide clearance for removal of housing. Remove extension housing-to-case bolts, pull back extension housing allowing fluid to drain, and remove extension housing.

Installation — Install new gasket on case, install extension housing and attaching bolts, tightening to specifications. Raise transmission and install mount-to-crossmember bolts or nuts. Remove jack, install speedometer cable and propeller shaft. Refill transmission to correct fluid level.

GOVERNOR

Removal — Remove extension housing as previously outlined. Remove governor housing-to-governor distributor attaching bolts, and remove governor housing assembly from distributor.

Installation — Reverse removal procedure and note the following: DO NOT overtighten governor housing attaching bolts.

TRANSMISSION REMOVAL & INSTALLATION

See Transmission Removal & Installation in Automatic Transmission Servicing.

TORQUE CONVERTER

LEAKAGE CHECK

See procedure given in Ford C-6 article.

FLUSHING CONVERTER

See procedure given in Ford C-6 article.

TURBINE & STATOR END PLAY CHECK

See procedure given in Ford C-6 article.

NOTE — Turbine and stator end play on C-4 converters should be .023" (maximum) for new or rebuilt converters, or .050" (maximum) for used converters.

STATOR ONE-WAY CLUTCH CHECK

See procedure given in Ford C-6 article.

STATOR-TO-IMPELLER INTERFERENCE CHECK

See procedure given in Ford C-6 article.

TRANSMISSION DISASSEMBLY

CAUTION — All C-4 transmissions are equipped with high temperature resistance seals. This includes those seals used on the manual and kickdown levers, the "O" rings and oil pan gasket. Under no condition should older design seals be used on 1978 and later transmissions, except the regular service replacement oil pan gasket, which is of special leak prevention design.

1) Remove torque converter from transmission assembly. Remove vacuum unit, gasket and control rod. From vacuum unit hole in case, remove primary throttle valve. Remove two extension housing bolts, and place transmission assembly in a suitable holding fixture. Remove oil pan and gasket, then remove valve body attaching bolts and valve body from case.

2) Loosen intermediate band adjusting screw and remove intermediate band struts from case. Loosen low-reverse band adjusting screw and remove low-reverse band struts.

NOTE — To keep output shaft in alignment during the following transmission end play check, install extension housing oil seal replacer tool or a front universal joint in extension housing.

3) Check transmission end play at this time as follows: Remove one converter housing-to-case attaching bolt and install a dial indicator assembly so indicator contact bears against end of input shaft. With input shaft properly engaged with spline of forward clutch hub, move input shaft and gear train toward rear of transmission. At this time, zero dial indicator. Using a screwdriver inserted behind input shell, move shell and front part of gear train forward, and note dial indicator reading. End play should be .008-.042". If end play is not within specifications, selective thrust washers 1 and 2 must be replaced as required. Remove dial indicator assembly and input shaft.

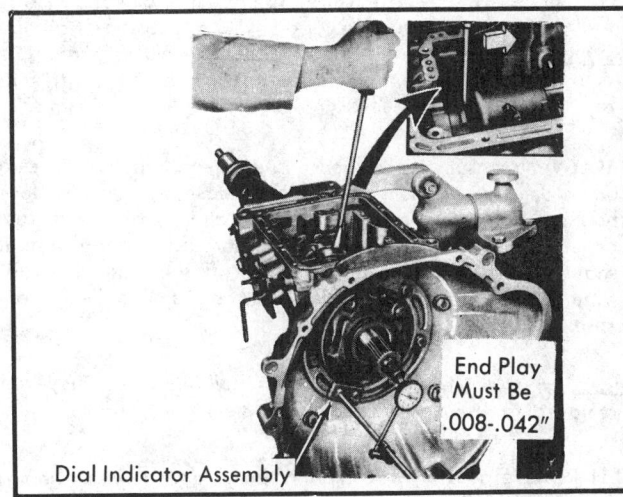

End Play Must Be .008-.042"

Dial Indicator Assembly

Fig. 6 Using a Dial Indicator to Check Transmission End Play

4) Rotate transmission so converter housing faces upward. Remove converter housing and pump-to-case attaching bolts. Remove converter housing from case. Remove front pump by inserting a screwdriver behind input shell and prying shell forward until front pump seal is above edge of case. Remove pump and gasket, making sure thrust washer No. 1 is also removed

NOTE — Ten thrust washers, located between the subassemblies, must be removed and re-installed during transmission overhaul. To properly located and identify thrust washers, position of thrust washers are shown in illustrations. Washers are numbered 1 through 10, with No. 1 thrust washer located at front pump, and No. 10 located at parking pawl ring gear.

FORD C-4 (Cont.)

5) Remove intermediate and low-reverse band adjusting screws from case. Rotate intermediate band to align with clearance holes in case, and remove band. Using a screwdriver between input shell and rear planet carrier, lift input shell upward and remove forward part of gear train assembly.

6) Place forward part of gear train in suitable holding fixture. Remove reverse-high clutch and drum from forward clutch. If No. 2 thrust washer was not removed with front pump, remove from forward clutch cylinder. Remove selective spacer (if used). Remove forward clutch from clutch hub and ring gear. If No. 3 thrust washer was not removed with forward clutch, remove from forward clutch hub.

7) Remove forward clutch hub and ring gear from front planet carrier. Remove No. 4 thrust washer and front planet carrier from input shell. From inside case, remove No. 6 thrust washer from top of reverse planet carrier. Remove reverse planet carrier and No. 7 thrust washer from reverse ring gear and hub.

8) Move output shaft forward and remove reverse ring gear hub-to-output shaft snap ring. Remove reverse ring gear and hub from output shaft. Remove No. 8 thrust washer from low-reverse drum. Remove the low-reverse band from case. Remove the low-reverse drum from one-way clutch inner race. Rotate one-way clutch inner race clockwise and remove from outer race.

9) Remove 12 one-way clutch rollers, springs, and spring retainer from outer race. **NOTE** — *Do not lose or damage springs or rollers. Outer race of one-way clutch cannot be removed from case until extension housing, output shaft, and governor distributor sleeve are removed.*

10) With transmission on bench and extension housing facing upward, remove extension housing-to-case bolts and remove housing. Pull outward on output shaft and remove shaft from governor distributor. Remove governor distributor-to-output shaft snap ring and slide assembly off shaft. Remove distributor sleeve-to-case attaching bolts and remove sleeve from case.

NOTE — *DO NOT bend or distort oil tubes as they are removed from case with distributor sleeve.*

11) Remove parking pawl spring, pawl, and pawl retaining pin from case. Remove parking pawl gear and thrust washer No. 10 from case. Remove one-way clutch outer race-to-case attaching bolts, and as bolts are removed, hold outer race (located inside case) in position. Remove outer race and thrust washer No. 9 from case.

COMPONENT DISASSEMBLY & REASSEMBLY

NOTE — *Handle all parts carefully to avoid damaging bearing or mating surfaces. Lubricate all internal parts with clean automatic transmission fluid only (gaskets and thrust washers may be held in place with vaseline).*

VALVE BODY ASSEMBLY

Disassembly — **1)** Remove oil screen attaching screws, and remove oil screen and gasket from valve body, taking care not to lose throttle pressure limit valve and spring when separating screen from body. Remove attaching screws and separate

lower valve body, gasket and separator plate from upper valve body.

CAUTION — *Take care not to lose upper body shuttle and check valve when separating upper and lower valve bodies.*

2) Remove manual valve retaining ring and slide manual valve out of valve body. **NOTE** — *Retaining ring is used to retain manual valve in its bore during shipment, and should be removed and discarded before sliding manual valve out of valve body.*

3) Pry low servo modulator valve retainer from body and remove retainer plug, spring, and valve. Working in low servo modulator bore, pry downshift valve retainer from body and remove spring and downshift valve. Depress throttle booster plug, remove retaining pin, and remove plug, valve and spring. Remove cover plate, and withdraw cut-back valve, transition valve spring, transition valve, 2-3 back-out valve, and spring from body.

4) Remove shift valve cover plate, and withdraw 2-3 shift valve, spring, throttle modulator valve, 1-2 shift valve, D2 valve, and spring from body. Remove retaining pin, then withdraw intermediate accumulator retainer, valve, and spring. Press main oil pressure booster valve inward and remove retaining pin. Remove main oil pressure booster valve, sleeve, springs, retainer, and main oil pressure regulator valve. Remove retainer, and withdraw spring and line coasting boost valve.

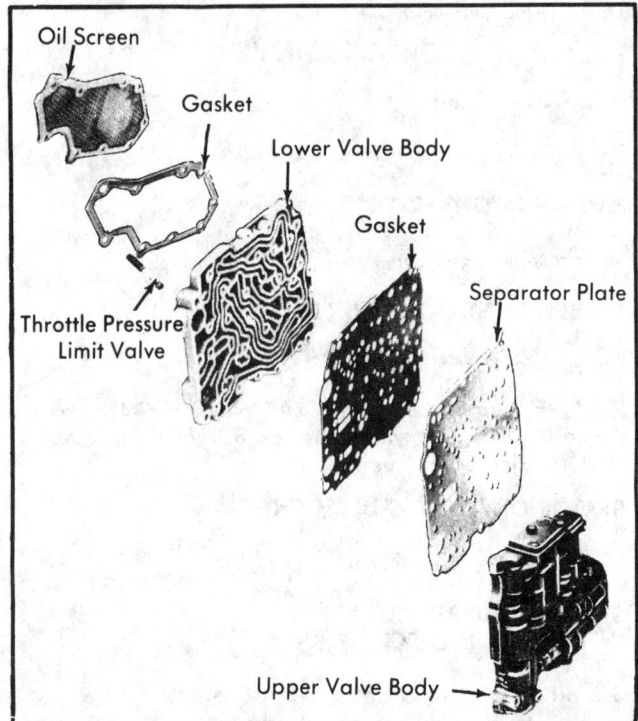

Fig. 7　Disassembled View of Valve Body Components

Reassembly — **1)** Place shuttle valves in upper and lower bodies (see illustration). Position gasket and separator plate on lower body and install but do not tighten attaching bolts. Place lower body and plate assembly on upper body and install attaching screws finger tight. Install oil screen screws

FORD C-4 (Cont.)

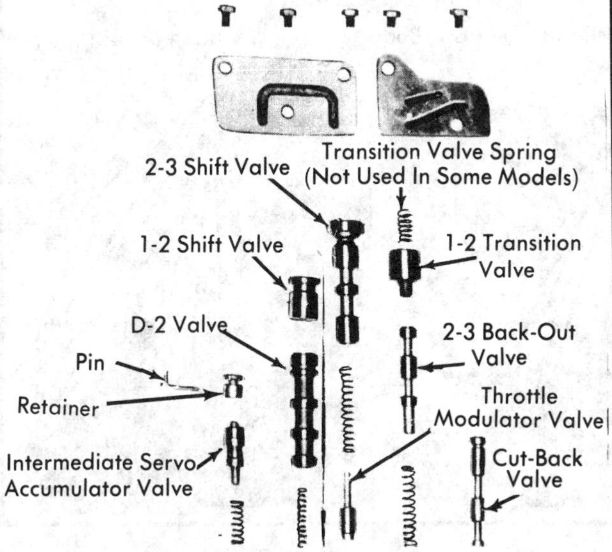

2-3 Shift Valve

Transition Valve Spring (Not Used In Some Models)

1-2 Shift Valve

1-2 Transition Valve

D-2 Valve

2-3 Back-Out Valve

Pin

Retainer

Throttle Modulator Valve

Intermediate Servo Accumulator Valve

Cut-Back Valve

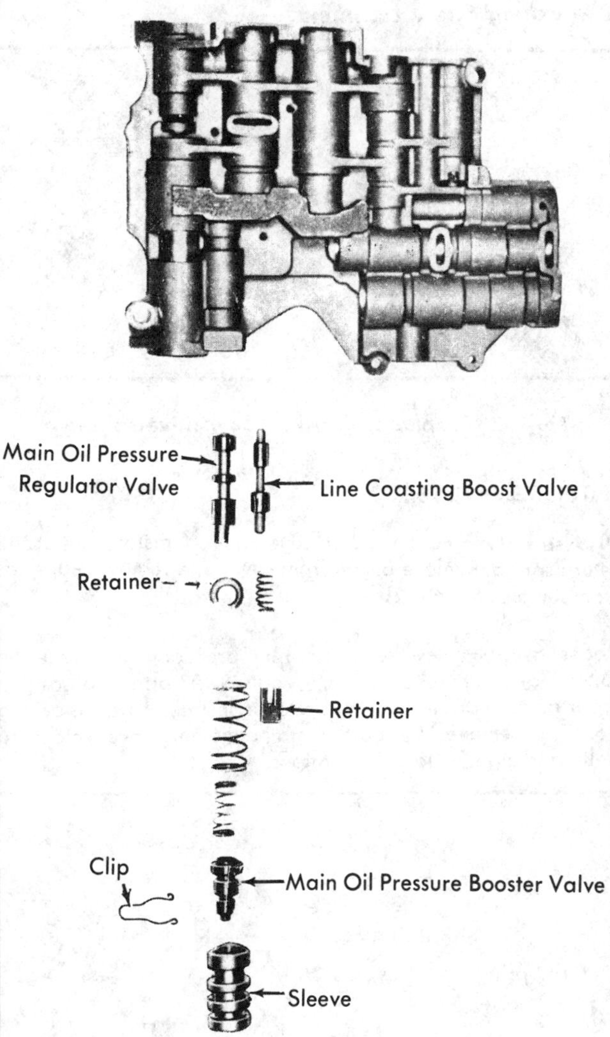

Main Oil Pressure Regulator Valve

Line Coasting Boost Valve

Retainer

Retainer

Clip

Main Oil Pressure Booster Valve

Sleeve

Fig. 8   Exploded View of Upper Valve Body Assembly

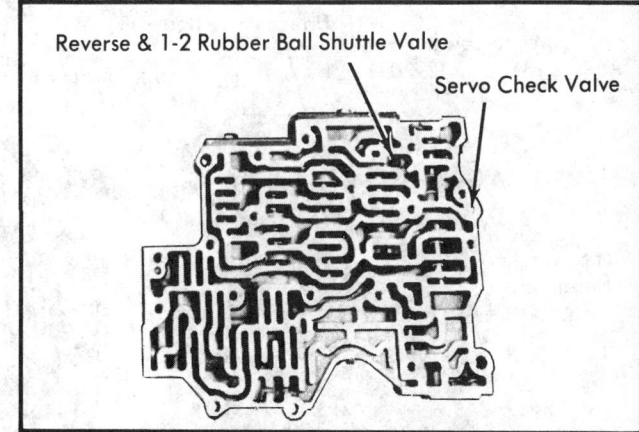

Reverse & 1-2 Rubber Ball Shuttle Valve

Servo Check Valve

Fig. 9   View of Upper Valve Body

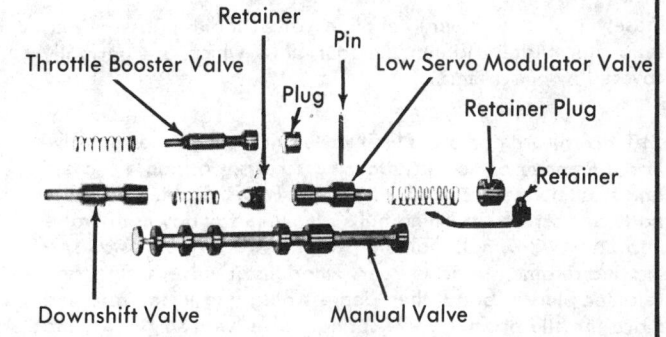

Retainer

Throttle Booster Valve

Pin

Plug

Low Servo Modulator Valve

Retainer Plug

Retainer

Downshift Valve

Manual Valve

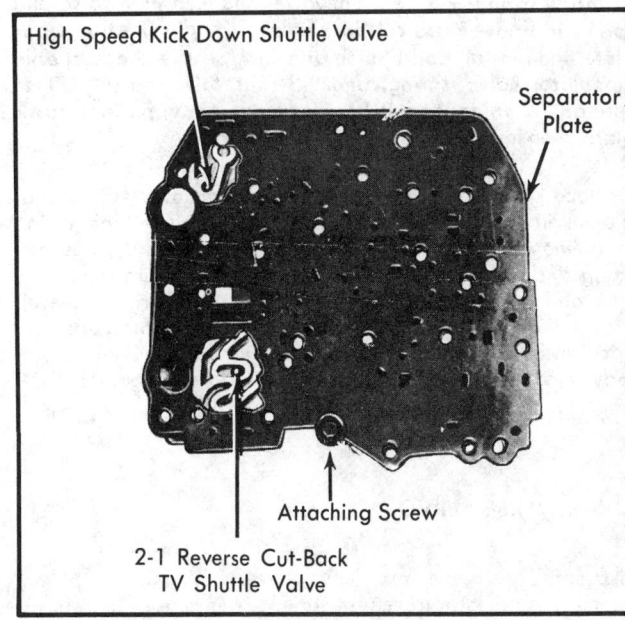

High Speed Kick Down Shuttle Valve

Separator Plate

Attaching Screw

2-1 Reverse Cut-Back TV Shuttle Valve

Fig. 10   View of Lower Valve Body

FORD C-4 (Cont.)

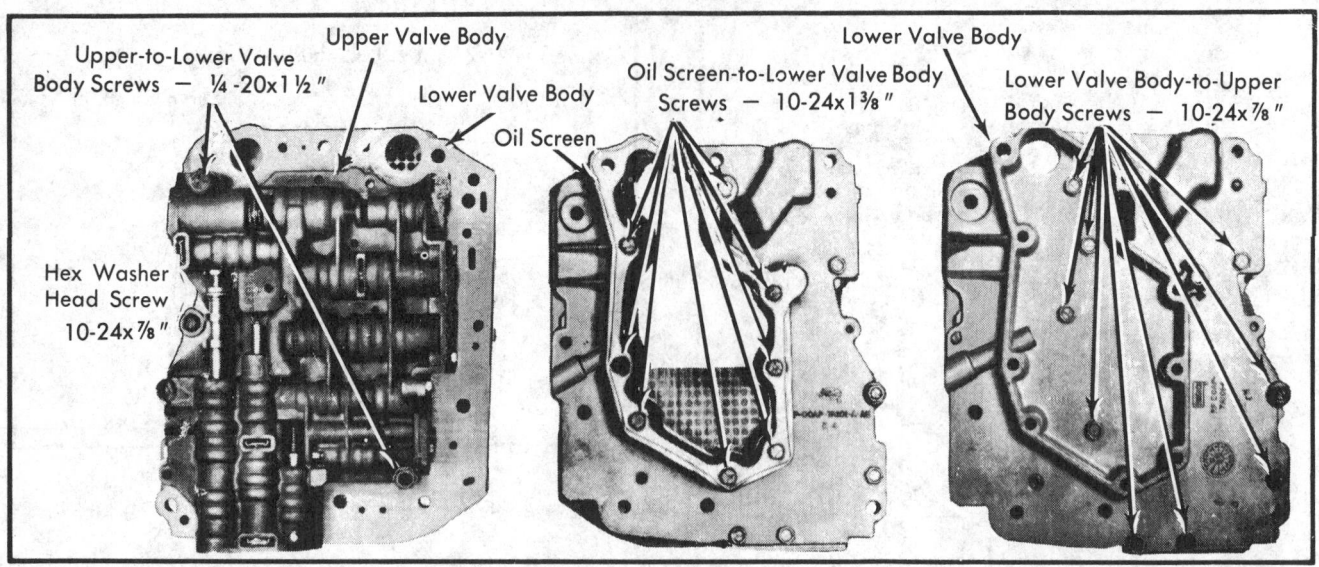

Fig. 11 Views of Valve Body Showing Attaching Screw Locations

loosely (without screen) to align valve bodies, gasket, and separator plate. Tighten the four bolts which are normally covered by oil screen.

2) Place throttle pressure limit valve and spring in lower valve body. Remove oil screen attaching screws, position oil screen and gasket, then reinstall attaching screws. Tighten all valve body and screen attaching bolts evenly. Install downshift valve into body with small diameter facing inward, then install spring and retainer. Insert low servo modulator valve, spring, and retainer plug in body, then depress plug and install retainer. Place throttle booster valve spring, valve (with small end into spring), and plug into body. Depress plug and install retaining pin making sure the 3 grooves are at top of pin as it is installed.

3) Install spring, 2-3 back-out valve, and transition valve and spring in body. Place cut-back valve in body, position cover plate, then install and tighten attaching screws. Place throttle modulator valve, spring, and 2-3 shift valve in body. Place spring, D-2 valve, and 1-2 shift valve in body, position cover plate, then install and tighten attaching screws.

4) Place spring, intermediate servo accumulator valve, and retainer in body, depress retainer, and install retaining pin. Insert line coasting boost valve and spring in body, depress spring and install retainer. Install main oil pressure regulator valve and spring retainer into body. Insert two springs, sleeve, and main oil pressure booster valve, then hold booster valve in place and install retaining pin. Slide manual valve into valve body, making sure end with two lands closest together is inserted first.

LOW-REVERSE SERVO

Disassembly — Remove servo cover, cover seal, piston assembly and piston return spring from case. If seal is damaged, entire piston assembly must be replaced.

Reassembly — Reverse disassembly procedure.

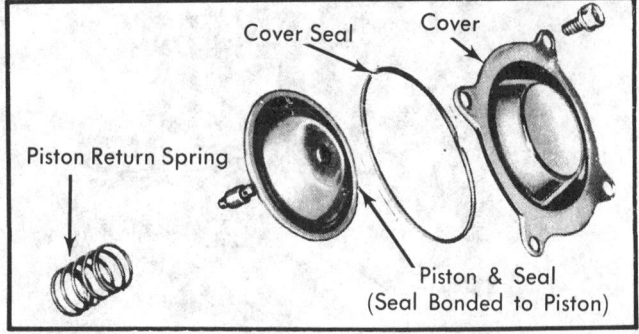

Fig. 12 Exploded View of Low-Reverse Servo

INTERMEDIATE SERVO

Disassembly — Remove servo cover, gasket, piston, and piston return spring. Remove piston from cover and remove seal rings from servo piston and cover.

Reassembly — Reverse disassembly procedure and note the following: Use two $5/16$-18 x $1\frac{1}{4}$" bolts 180° apart, to position cover on case against spring pressure. Install 2 cover attaching bolts and remove $1\frac{1}{4}$" bolts. Install remaining cover attaching bolts and tighten to specifications.

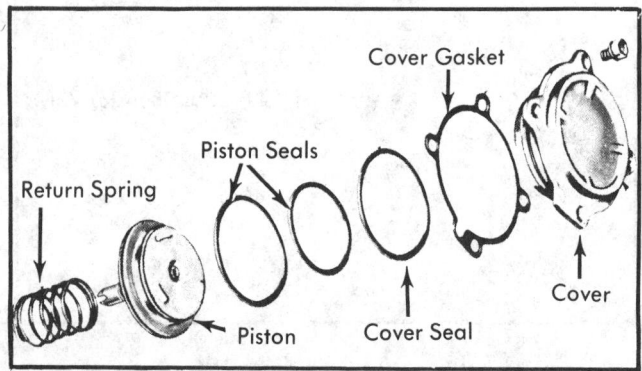

Fig. 13 Exploded View of Intermediate Servo

FORD C-4 (Cont.)

DOWNSHIFT & MANUAL LINKAGE

Disassembly — 1) Apply penetrating oil to outer lever attaching nut to prevent breaking inner lever shaft. Remove downshift outer lever nut and remove downshift outer and inner levers.

2) On vehicles equipped with case mounted neutral safety switch, place screwdriver behind switch and pry switch gently off lever. From inside case, remove upper retaining ring from manual lever link and remove upper end of lever link from case retaining pin.

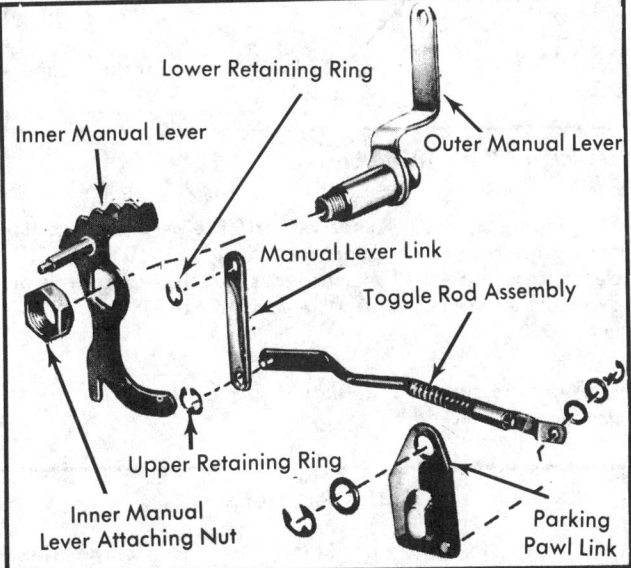

Fig. 14 Exploded View of Transmission Case Internal Linkage

3) From rear of case, remove lower retaining ring and flat washer from parking pawl link and remove link from case retaining pin. Remove parking pawl link, toggle rod and manual lever link as an assembly. Remove rear parking pawl link upper retaining ring, flat washer and link from toggle rod.

4) Remove manual lever link lower retaining ring, flat washer and link from toggle rod. Remove inner manual lever attaching nut and lever, then remove outer manual lever from case. Using suitable tools, replace manual lever seal.

Reassembly — Reverse disassembly procedure and note the following: Position inner manual lever behind manual lever link with cam on lever contacting lower link pin.

FRONT PUMP

Disassembly — Remove four seal rings from stator support. Remove five bolts attaching stator support to front pump housing and remove support. Remove drive and driven gears from pump housing.

Stator Support Bushing Replacement — If front and rear stator support bushings are worn or damaged, remove using a cape chisel. Cut along bushing seam until chisel breaks through bushing wall, pry ends of bushing up and remove. Using a suitable tool (T66L-7003-B9), press new bushing into place.

NOTE — *Oil hole in rear bushing must be aligned with lubrication hole in stator support.*

Pump Housing Bushing Replacement — If bushing is worn or damaged, press out using a suitable remover tool. Install bushing into pump housing using a suitable driver. **NOTE** — *Slot and groove in bushing must be installed toward rear of pump body and 60° below pump horizontal center line. See illustration.*

Reassembly — Reverse disassembly procedure and note the following: When installing gears, chamfered side of gears with identification marks must be positioned downward against face of pump housing. When installing seal rings on stator support, assemble two large rings first in grooves toward front of support. To remove and install front pump seal, mount pump in transmission case, remove seal using a suitable puller, and install using a suitable seal driver.

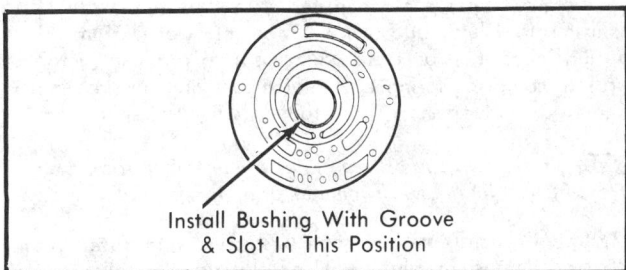

Fig. 15 View of Pump Housing Showing Correct Bushing Installation

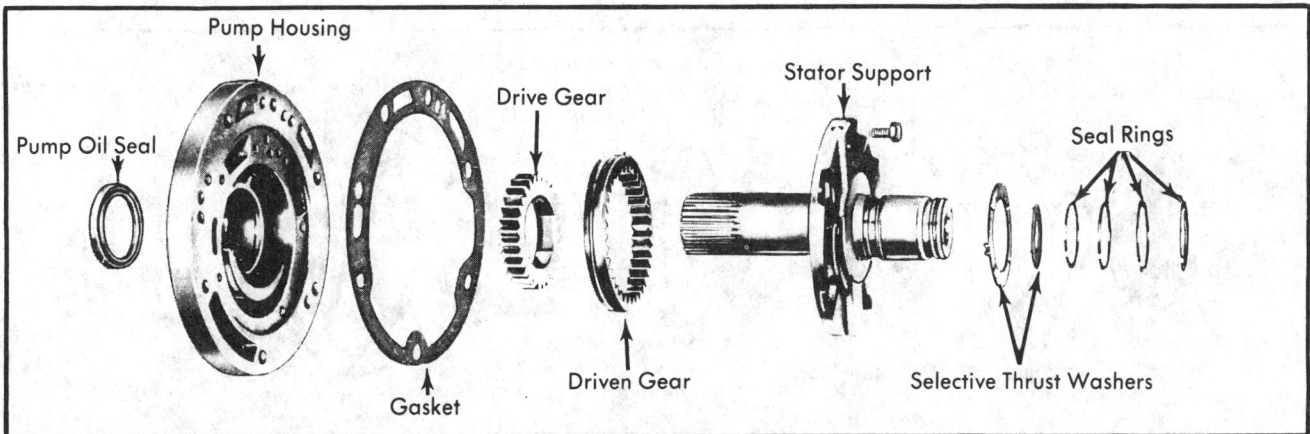

Fig. 16 Exploded View of Oil Pump Assembly

Automatic Transmissions

FORD C-4 (Cont.)

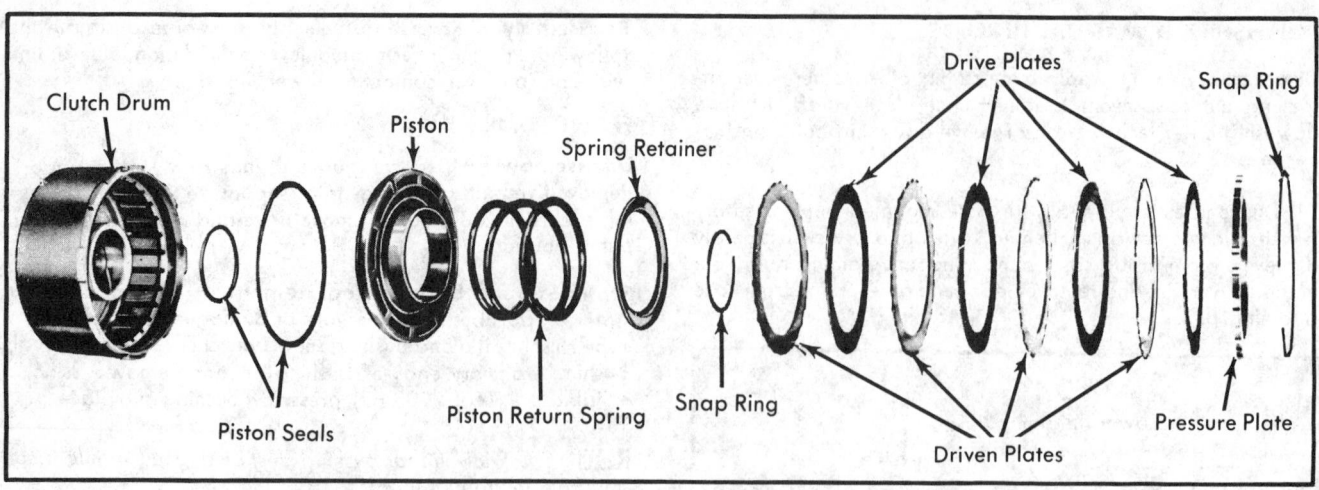

Fig. 17   Exploded View of Reverse-High Clutch Assembly

REVERSE-HIGH CLUTCH

Disassembly — Remove pressure plate retaining snap ring, and remove pressure plate, drive and driven clutch plates. Install clutch hub in an arbor press, compress spring retainer and piston return springs, and remove snap ring. **NOTE** — *When releasing arbor press, guide spring retainer to clear snap ring groove of drum. Remove spring retainer and spring. Remove piston by applying air pressure to piston apply hole in clutch hub. Remove piston outer seal from piston, and piston inner seal from clutch cylinder hub.*

Reassembly — **1)** Install a new inner seal on clutch drum, and a new outer seal on piston. Lubricate seals with clean transmission fluid, and install piston into clutch drum. Place spring in position on piston, place spring retainer on top of spring, compress spring and retainer, making sure retainer is centered to clear snap ring groove and install snap ring.

NOTE — *If new composition plates are installed, soak them in transmission fluid for 15 minutes prior to installation.*

2) Install clutch plates alternately, starting with a steel plate, then a composition plate, until all plates are installed. Make sure last plate installed is pressure plate. Install pressure plate retaining snap ring, making sure it is fully seated in groove.

NOTE — *Last plate installed MUST be the pressure plate.*

3) Using feeler gauge, measure clearance between snap ring and pressure plate. Clearance should be .050-.071". If clearance is not within specifications, selective snap rings are available in thicknesses of .050-.054", .064-.068", .078-.082" and .092-.096".

NOTE — *Pressure plate should be held downward as clearance is checked.*

Clutch Plate Chart		
Application	**Steel Plates**	**Composition Plates**
Reverse-High Clutch	4	4
Forward Clutch	4	5

NOTE — *If new composition plates are installed, soak them in transmission fluid for 15 minutes prior to installation. Install same number of plates that were removed.*

FORWARD CLUTCH

Disassembly — Remove pressure plate retaining snap ring, and remove pressure plate, composition drive plates, and steel

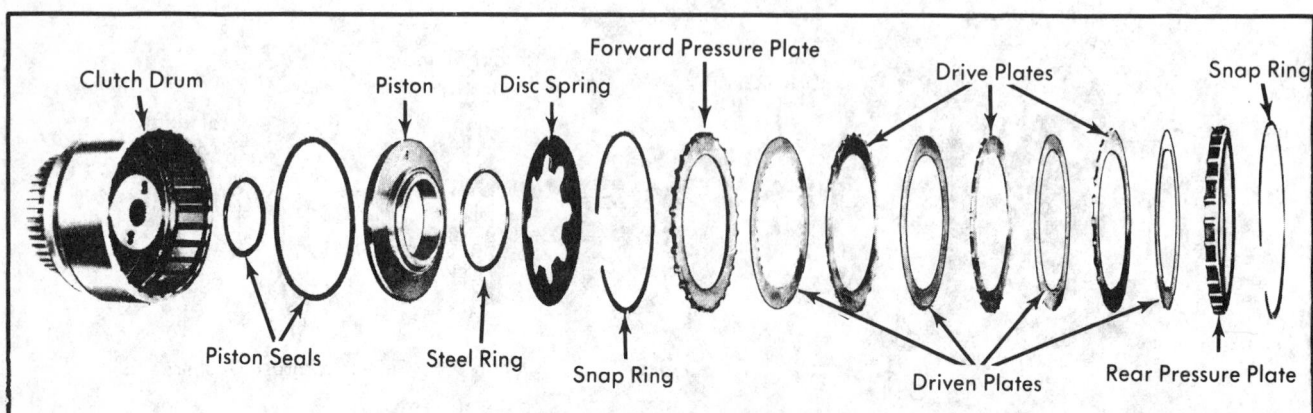

Fig. 18   Exploded View of Forward Clutch Assembly

FORD C-4 (Cont.)

driven plates. Remove disc spring retaining snap ring and disc spring. Apply air pressure to clutch piston pressure hole in drum and remove piston. Remove piston outer seal, and inner seal from clutch hub.

Reassembly — 1) Install new seals on clutch piston and drum. Lubricate seals with clean transmission fluid, install piston into drum, and install disc spring and retaining snap ring. Install lower pressure plate with flat side up and radius side downward. Install one composition plate followed by one steel plate untill all plates are installed.

2) Last plate installed will be top pressure plate. With pressure plate installed, install retaining snap ring, making sure it is fully seated in ring groove of clutch hub. Using a feeler gauge, check clearance between snap ring and pressure plate, pressing downward on plate while checking. Clearance should be .025-.050" on all models.

3) If clearance is not within specifications, selective snap rings are available in thicknesses of .050-.054", .064-.068", .078-.082", and .092-.096". Install correct size snap ring and recheck clearance.

FORWARD CLUTCH HUB & RING GEAR

Disassembly & Reassembly — Remove forward clutch hub retaining snap ring, and withdraw hub from ring gear. When reassembling, make sure hub is bottomed in groove of ring gear, and snap ring is fully seated in groove of ring gear.

Clutch Hub Bushing Replacement — Press old bushing out using an arbor press and a suitable bushing adapter (T66L-7003-B10). Install new bushing with arbor press and suitable bushing driver (T66L-7003-B5).

INPUT SHELL & SUN GEAR

Disassembly — Remove external snap ring and thrust washer No. 5 from sun gear. From inside input shell, remove sun gear. Remove internal snap ring from sun gear.

Sun Gear Bushing Replacement — Remove old bushings by using a sutiable bushing driver and pressing both bushings through and out of gear. Install new bushings separately using a suitable bushing installer (T66L-7003-B2) to press bushings into each end of gear.

Reassembly — Install internal snap ring on sun gear, place sun gear in input shell, position thrust washer No. 5 against input shell, and install external snap ring on sun gear.

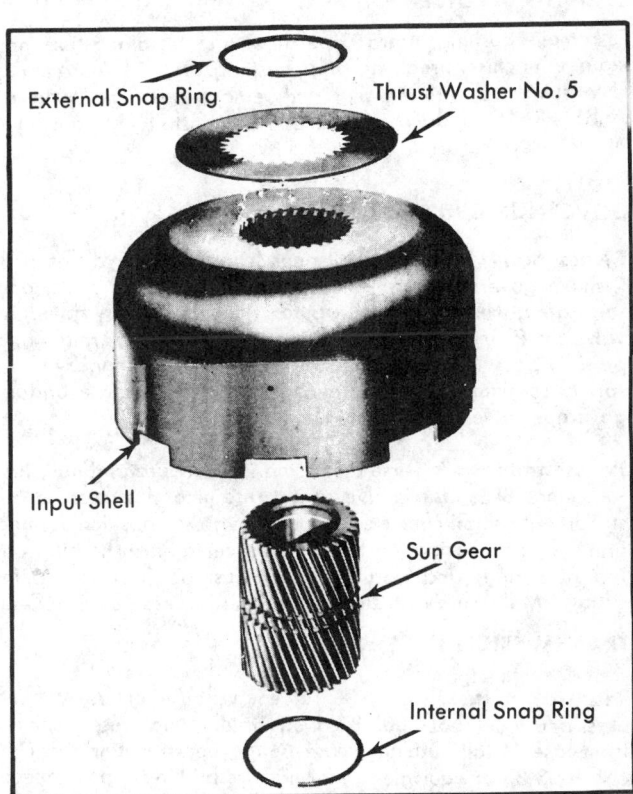

Fig. 19 Exploded View of Input Shell & Sun Gear Assembly

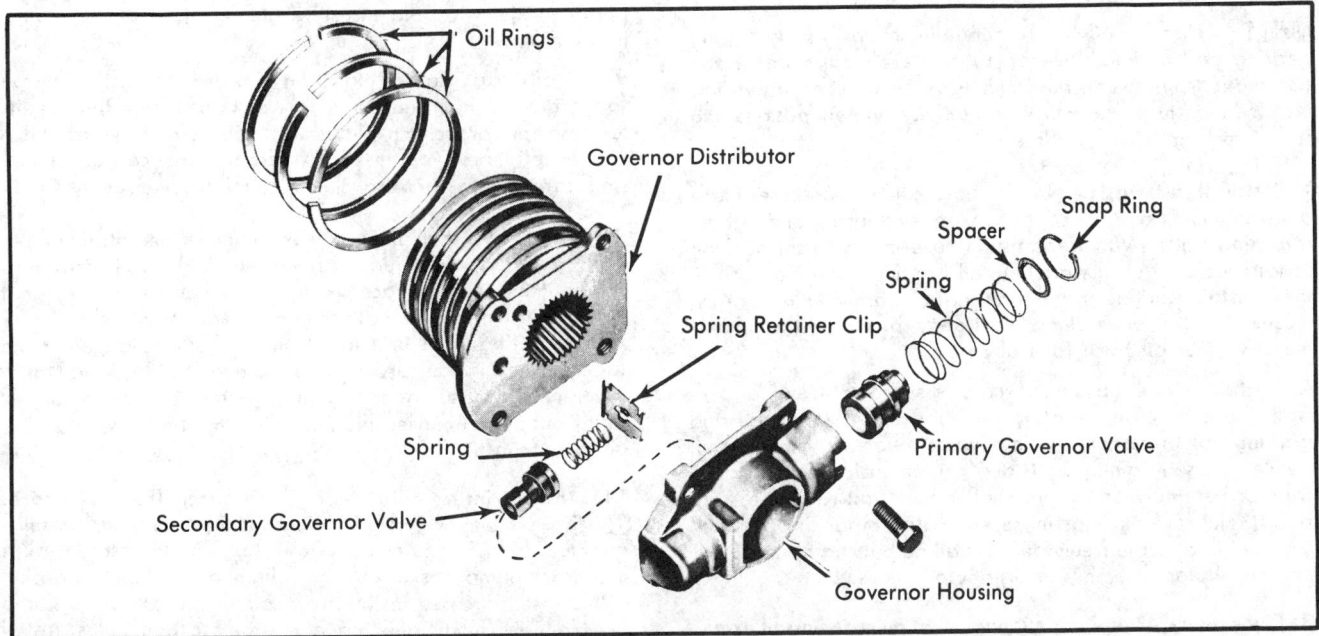

Fig. 20 Exploded View of Governor Assembly

FORD C-4 (Cont.)

REVERSE RING GEAR & HUB

Disassembly & Reassembly — Remove hub retaining snap ring from reverse ring gear, and remove hub from ring gear. When reassembling, make sure hub is fully seated in groove of ring gear, and snap ring is fully seated in groove of ring gear.

LOW-REVERSE BRAKE DRUM BUSHING REPLACEMENT

To remove bushing, use a cape chisel and cut along bushing seam, until chisel breaks through bushing wall. Pry loose ends of bushing up with an awl and remove bushing. Using a sutiable bushing driver (T66L-7003-B6), install new bushing into low-reverse drum.

GOVERNOR & DISTRIBUTOR

Disassembly — Remove oil rings from governor distributor. Remove governor housing-to-distributor attaching bolts, and separate governor from distributor. Remove primary governor valve retaining ring and withdraw washer, spring, and primary governor valve from housing. Remove secondary valve spring retaining clip, and withdraw spring and secondary governor valve from housing.

Reassembly — Reverse disassembly procedure and note the following: Secondary valve spring retaining clip must be installed with small concave area downward to position spring. Primary valve spring washer must be centered in housing on top of spring, and retaining ring must be fully seated in groove. Make sure distributor oil rings turn freely in grooves.

TRANSMISSION CASE BUSHING

Removal & Installation — To remove bushing, use arbor press and tool (T66L-7003-B7 or equivalent) and press bushing from case. Install bushing in case using arbor press and tool (T-66L-7003-B3 or equivalent) making sure bushing is positioned squarely in bore and seated flush with face of case.

TRANSMISSION REASSEMBLY

NOTE — *Handle all parts carefully to avoid damaging bearing and mating surfaces. Lubricate all parts with clean automatic transmission fluid only (gaskets and thrust washers may be held in place with vaseline). Use all new gaskets and seals, and tighten all bolts evenly.*

1) Install thrust washer No. 9 inside transmission case. Place one-way clutch outer race inside case, and install and tighten attaching bolts. With transmission case in a vertical position (back face of case upward), install parking pawl pin in case, then install parking pawl and return spring. Place thrust washer No. 10 on parking pawl gear, and install gear and thrust washer on back face of case.

2) Install two oil tubes in governor distributor sleeve, and install sleeve on case, inserting two tubes in holes in case and parking pawl retaining pin in alignment hole of sleeve. Install sleeve-to-case retaining bolts and tighten. Install governor distributor assembly on output shaft and install retaining snap ring. Make sure oil rings in governor distributor are correctly installed and rotate freely, then install output shaft and governor distributor assembly in distributor sleeve.

3) Place a new extension housing gasket on case, install extension housing, and secure with attaching bolts. Place transmis-

sion in a holding fixture. Rotate transmission to place front pump mounting face upward. Make sure that thrust washer No. 9 is still located at bottom of case.

4) Install one-way clutch spring assembly into outer race, then place inner race inside spring retainer. Make sure face with the step is installed toward rear of case, mating with thrust washer. Install race, and install one-way clutch rollers by slightly compressing each spring and positioning rollers between spring and retainer. When assembled, rotate inner race clockwise to center rollers and spring. Install low-reverse drum, with splines of drum engaging splines of one-way clutch inner race.

NOTE — *Check operation of one-way clutch by rotating low-reverse drum. Clutch should rotate clockwise only.*

5) Install No. 8 thrust washer on low-reverse drum. Install low-reverse band in case, with end of band for small strut toward low-reverse servo. Install reverse ring gear and hub on output shaft. Move output shaft forward and install reverse ring gear hub-to-output shaft retaining ring.

6) Place thrust washers No. 6 and No. 7 on reverse planet carrier. Install planet carrier in reverse ring gear, engaging tabs of carrier with slots in low-reverse drum. On the bench, install forward clutch into reverse-high clutch, rotating units to mesh. Using the end play check reading obtained during disassembly, determine which No. 2 steel backed thrust washer is required as follows:

7) Position stator support vertically on a bench and install correct No. 2 thrust washer (or washer and spacer) to bring end play within limits of .008-.042". Install reverse-high clutch and forward clutch on stator support. Invert complete assembly making sure intermediate brake drum bushing is seated on forward clutch mating surface.

8) Select the thickest plastic washer (No. 1) that can be inserted between stator and intermediate brake drum thrust surfaces and still maintain a slight clearance. DO NOT select a washer that must be forced into position. Remove intermediate brake drum and forward clutch from stator support. Install selected thrust washers No. 1 and No. 2 on stator support, using enough petroleum jelly to hold thrust washer in place during pump installation.

9) Install thrust washer No. 3 on forward clutch, then install forward clutch hub and ring in forward clutch by rotating units to mesh forward clutch plates with splines of forward clutch hub. Install thrust washer No. 4 on front planet carrier, and install carrier into forward clutch hub and ring gear. Check

10) Install input shell and sun gear on gear train, rotating input shell to engage drive lugs of reverse-high clutch. If drive lugs will not engage, outer race (inside forward planet carrier) is not centered to engage end of sun gear (inside input shell). Center thrust bearing race and install input shell. Hold gear train together and install forward part of gear train assembly into case. Input shell sun gear must mesh with reverse pinion gears, and front planet carrier internal splines must mesh with splines on output shaft.

11) Install intermediate band through front of case. **NOTE** — *If a new band is being installed, soak in transmission fluid for 15 minutes prior to installation in case. Install a new front pump gasket on case, aligning bolt holes in gasket with those in case. Install front pump stator support into reverse-high clutch, aligning pump-to-case bolt holes. Install bolts and tighten.*

FORD C-4 (Cont.)

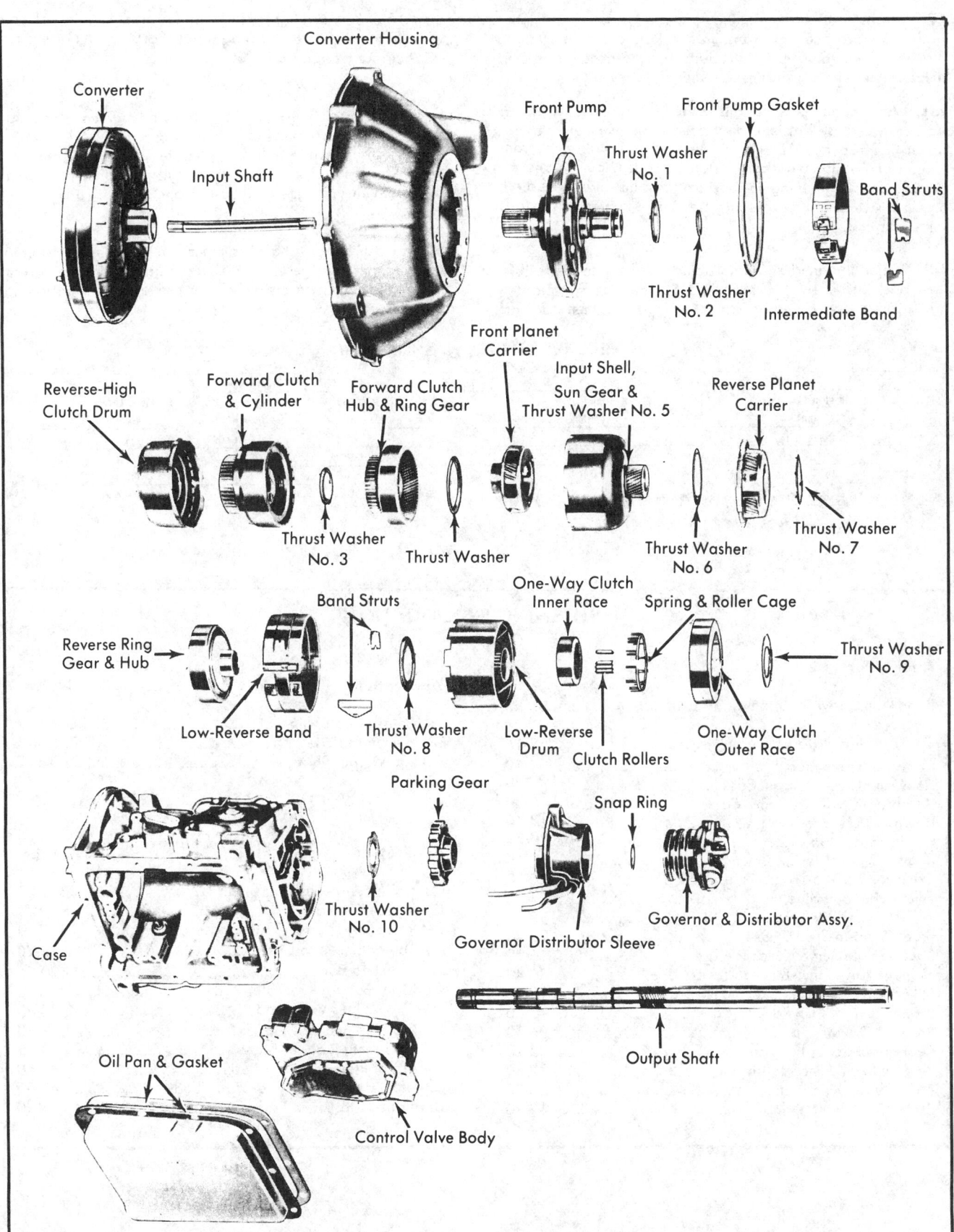

Fig. 21 *Exploded View of Transmission Case and Drive Train Assembly*

FORD C-4 (Cont.)

12) Install input shaft, making sure short splined end is installed toward rear of transmission. Rotate transmission to place it in horizontal position. Using same procedure used at disassembly, check transmission end play.

13) If not within specifications, either wrong selective thrust washers were used or one of the ten thrust washers was installed improperly. Correct as necessary. Install one front pump-to-case attaching bolt. Install converter housing and attaching bolts, tightening to specifications. Install intermediate and low-reverse band adjusting screws in case and install struts for each band.

14) Tighten intermediate band adjusting screw to 10 ft. lbs., then back off screw 1¾ turns and tighten lock nut. Tighten low-reverse band adjusting screw to 10 ft. lbs., then back off

screw 3 full turns and tighten lock nut. Install a "U" joint yoke on output shaft. Rotate input and output shafts in both directions and check for free operation of gear train.

15) Install control valve body, install and tighten attaching screws to specifications. Install oil pan with new gasket. Remove transmission from holding fixture and install 2 remaining extension housing-to-case bolts. Install primary throttle valve, vacuum unit, gasket (if used) and control rod.

16) Make sure input shaft is properly installed in front pump stator support and gear train (short splined end toward rear of transmission), then install torque converter in front pump and converter housing.

SELECTIVE THRUST WASHER CHART

Thrust Washer No. 1		Thrust Washer No. 2	
Nylon Thrust Washer W/Tangs	Color Of Washer	No. Stamped On Washer	Metal Thrust Washer
0.053-0.0575	Red	2	0.056-0.058
0.070-0.0745	Green	3	0.073-0.075
0.087-0.0915	Natural (White)	Spacer	0.032-0.036 ①

① This is a selective spacer. The spacer must be installed next to the stator support to obtain correct end play.

TIGHTENING SPECIFICATIONS

Application	Ft. Lbs.
Band Adj. Screw	35-45
Converter-to-Flywheel	20-30
Converter Cover-to-Converter Hsg.	12-16
Converter Drain Plug	15-26
Converter Hsg.-to-Trans. Case	28-40
Diaphragm Assy.-to-Trans. Case	15-23
Downshift Lever-to-Shaft	12-16
End Plates-to-Body	20-35
Engine Support-to-Crossmember	40-60
Extension Hsg.-to-Trans. Case	28-40
Filler Tube-to-Engine	23-33
Filler Tube-to-Pan	32-42
Front Pump-to-Trans. Case	28-40
Intermediate Servo Cover-to-Case	16-22
Manual Valve Inner Lever-to-Shaft	30-40
Oil Pan-to-Case	12-16
Overrunning Clutch Race-to-Case	13-20
Pressure Gauge Tap	6-12
Rear Servo Cover-to-Case	12-20
Reverse Servo Piston-to-Rod	12-20
Starter Attaching Bolts	20-30
Stator Support-to-Pump	12-20

Application	Ft. Lbs.
Transmission-to-Engine	40-50
TRS Switch-to-Case	4-8
Yoke-to-Output Shaft	60-120

Application	INCH Lbs.
Control Assy.-to-Case	80-120
Cooler Line Fittings	80-120
Detent Spring-to-Lower Valve Body	80-120
Distributor Sleeve-to-Case	12-20
End Plates-to-Body	20-35
Governor Body-to-Collector Body	80-120
Lower-to-Upper Valve Body	40-55
Oil Tube Connector	80-120
Reinforcement Plate-to-Body	40-55
Separator Plate-to-Lower Body	40-60
Screen and Lower Body-to-Upper Body	40-55
Upper Body-to-Lower Body	80-120

FORD C-6

All Models

TRANSMISSION IDENTIFICATION

An identification tag is located under lower front intermediate servo cover bolt. The first line on tag shows transmission model prefix and suffix, and the build date code. A number appearing after the suffix indicates internal parts in transmission have been changed after initial production start-up. For example, a PJD-L12 model transmission that has been changed internally would read PJD-L13. The lower line of identification tag shows transmission assembly part number and serial number.

DESCRIPTION

Transmission is a 3-speed unit capable of providing automatic upshifts and downshifts through 3 forward gear ratios and also providing manual selection of 1st and 2nd gears. Transmission consists basically of a torque converter, compound planetary gear train controlled by a single band, 3 multiple disc clutches, a one-way clutch and hydraulic control system.

CAUTION — *All C-6 transmissions are equipped with high temperature resistant seals. This includes those seals used on the manual and kickdown levers, the "O" rings and oil pan gasket. Under no condition should older design seals be used*

on 1978 and later transmission, except the regular service replacement oil pan gasket, which is of special leak prevention design.

LUBRICATION & ADJUSTMENT

See Automatic Transmission Servicing in this section.

TESTING

ROAD TEST

1) Check minimum throttle upshifts in "D". Transmission should start in first gear, shift to second, and then shift to third as speed increases. *See Shift Table.*

2) With transmission in third gear, depress accelerator through detent (to floor). Transmission should shift from third to second, or third to first, depending on vehicle speed. *See Shift Table.*

3) Check closed throttle downshift from third to first by coasting down from about 30 MPH in third gear. Shift should occur as shown in table.

4) With transmission selector lever in "2" position, transmission should operate only in second gear.

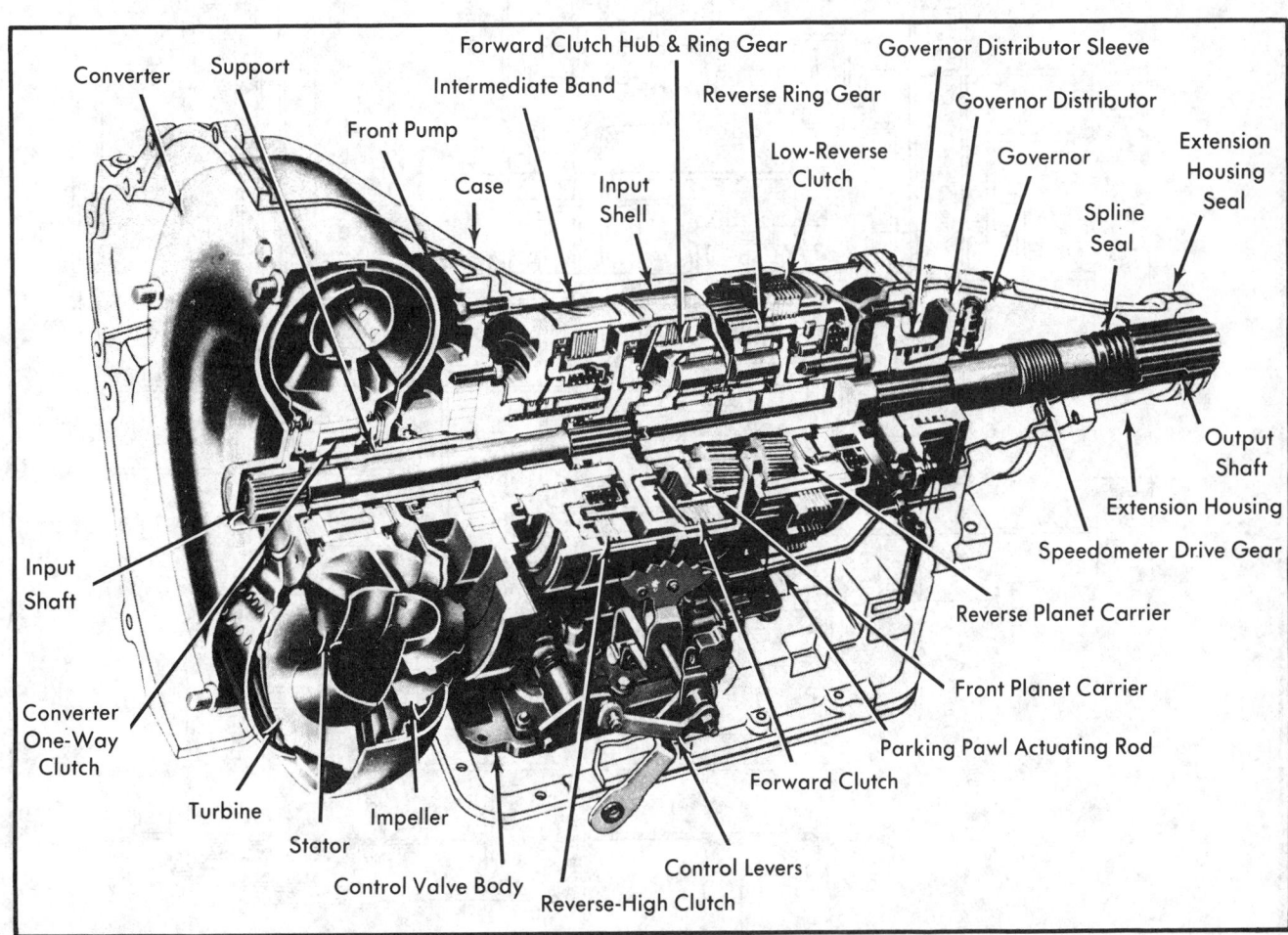

Fig. 1   Cutaway View of Ford C-6 Automatic Transmission Assembly

FORD C-6 (Cont.)

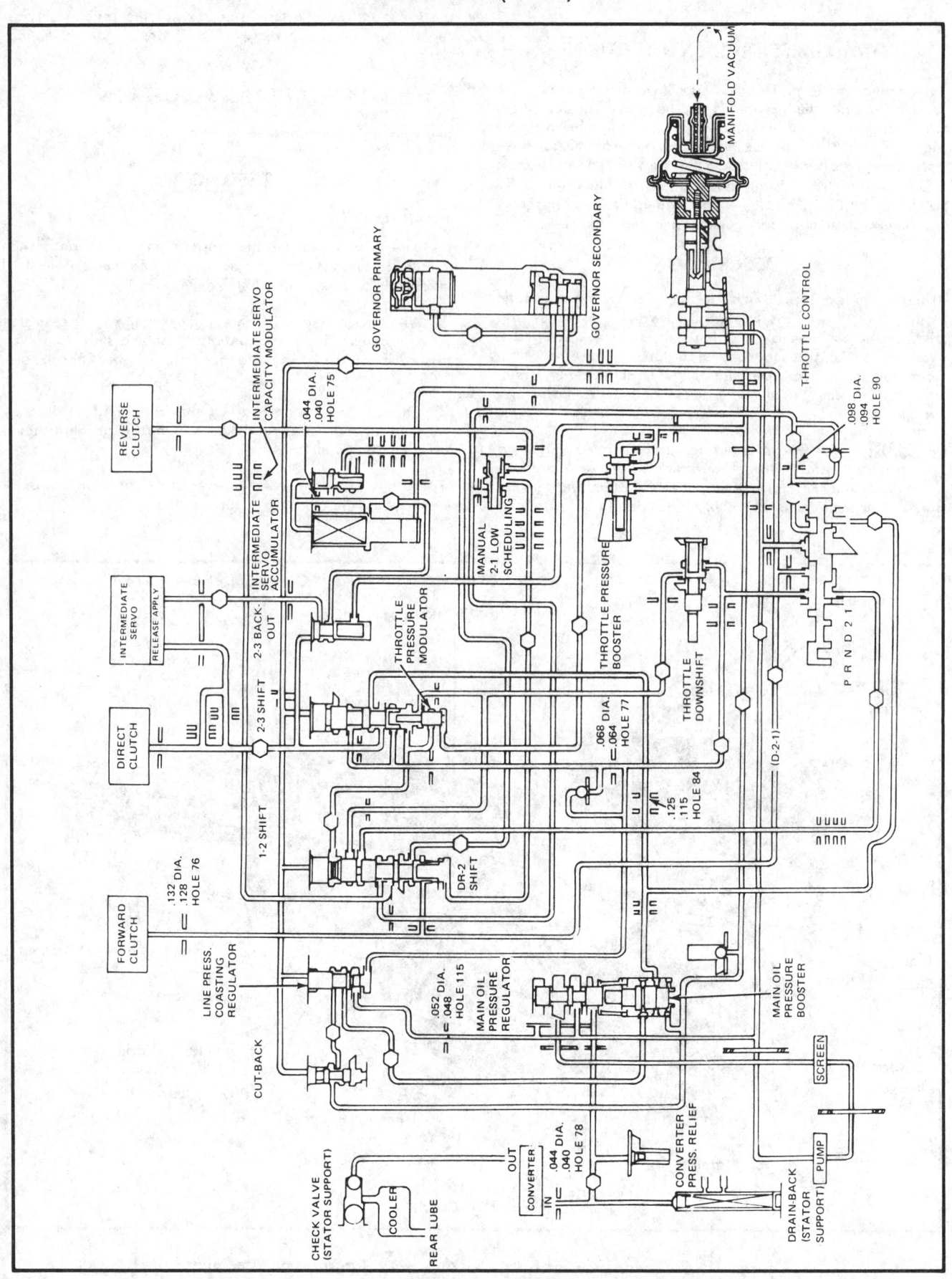

Fig. 2   C-6 Automatic Transmission Hydraulic Circuits Diagram

FORD C-6 (Cont.)

5) With transmission in third gear and road speed above 30 MPH, transmission should shift to second gear when selector lever is moved from "D" into "2" or "1". When manual shift is made below 30 MPH, transmission should shift from second or third to first.

NOTE — *This check will determine if governor pressure and shift control valves are operating properly.*

6) Slipping or engine speed flare-up in any gear usually indicates clutch or band problems. In most cases, the clutch or band that is slipping can be determined by noting transmission operation in all selector positions and comparing which internal units are applied in those positions. *See Clutch and Band Application Chart.*

SHIFT SPEEDS (MPH)

NOTE — *Figures given below are approximate. All shift speeds may vary somewhat due to production tolerances, rear axle ratio, or emission control equipment.*

MODELS PJA-AE, AJ, CJ, DL, DT, DU, DW & Z
MODELS PGD-DJ, DK & DL

Throttle	Range	Shift	OPS-R.P.M	1	2	3	4	5	6	7
Closed (Above 17" Vacuum)	D	1-2	270-560	8-16	8-17	8-16	7-15	7-14	7-14	6-14
	D	2-3	375-870	11-26	11-26	11-25	10-23	10-22	9-21	9-21
	D	3-1	270-330	8-10	8-10	8-9	7-9	7-8	7-8	6-8
	1	2-1	890-1260	26-37	27-38	25-36	23-33	23-32	21-31	20-29
To Detent (Torque Demand)	D	1-2	760-1390	22-41	23-42	22-40	20-37	19-36	19-34	18-32
	D	2-3	1320-2080	39-61	40-63	38-59	35-55	34-53	32-51	31-48
	D	3-2	820-1600	24-47	25-48	23-46	22-42	21-41	20-39	19-37
Through Detent (WOT)	D	1-2	1250-1590	37-47	38-48	36-45	33-42	32-41	30-39	29-38
	D	2-3	2190-2570	64-76	66-78	63-73	58-68	56-66	53-63	51-60
	D	3-2	1990-2340	59-69	60-71	57-67	52-62	51-60	49-57	46-54
	D	3-1 2-1	840-1200	25-35	25-36	24-34	22-32	22-31	20-29	20-28

Axle Ratio	Tire Size	Use Col. No.	Axle Ratio	Tire Size	Use Col. No.
2.47/2.75	P195/75R15SL	1	3.33	750 × 16D	3
	P205/75R15SL	1		750 × 16E	3
	P215/75R15SL	1		800 × 16.5D	4
	P235/75R15XL	2		875 × 16.5E	4
	H78 × 15B	2		875R × 16.5E	4
	L78 × C	2		950 × 16.5E	4
3.00, 3.07	P195/75R15SL	5	3.73	750 × 16D	6
	P205/75R15SL	5		750 × 16E	6
	P215/75R15SL	4		800 × 16.5D	7
	P235/75R16XL	3		800 × 16.5E	7
	H78 × 15B	3		875 × 16.5E	7
	L78 × 15C	3		875R × 16.5E	7
3.25	P215/75R15SL	2		950 × 16.5E	7
	P235/75R15SL	2			
	P235/75R15XL	2			

Throttle	Range	Shift	OPS-R.P.M	1	2	3	4	5
Closed (Above 17" Vacum)	D	1-2	270-560	6-13	6-12	5-11	5-11	5-10
	D	2-3	375-870	9-20	8-18	8-17	7-17	7-16
	D	3-1	270-330	6-8	6-7	5-7	5-6	5-6
	1	2-1	890-1260	20-29	18-26	18-25	17-24	16-23
To Detent (Torque Demand)	D	1-2	760-1390	17-32	16-29	15-28	15-27	14-25
	D	2-3	1320-2080	30-47	28-43	26-42	25-40	24-38
	D	3-2	820-1600	19-36	17-33	16-32	16-31	15-29
Through Detent (WOT)	D	1-2	1250-1590	28-36	26-33	25-32	24-31	23-29
	D	2-3	2190-2570	49-58	46-54	44-51	42-49	40-47
	D	3-2	1990-2340	45-53	41-49	40-47	38-45	36-43
	D	3-1 2-1	840-1200	19-27	18-25	17-24	16-23	15-22

Axle Ratio	Tire Size	Use Col. No.
4.10	7.50 × 16D	1
	7.50 × 16E	1
	8.00 × 16.5D	2
	8.00 × 16.5E	2
	8.75 × 16.5E	2
	8.75R × 16.5E	2
	9.50 × 16.5E	2
4.56	7.50 × 16D	3
	7.50 × 16E	3
	8.00 × 16.5D	4
	8.00 × 16.5E	4
	8.75 × 16.5E	5
	8.75 × 16.5E	5
	9.50 × 16.5E	5

MODELS PJA-DP & DS

Throttle	Range	Shift	OPS-R.P.M	1	2	3	4
Closed (Above 17" Vacuum)	D	1-2	270-640	8-17	8-18	8-18	8-19
	D	2-3	375-930	11-24	11-26	11-26	12-27
	D	3-1	270-330	8-9	8-10	8-10	8-10
	1	2-1	890-1260	25-35	26-36	27-38	28-39
To Detent (Torque Demand)	D	1-2	770-1520	18-42	19-43	19-45	20-46
	D	2-3	1330-2330	30-60	31-63	32-65	33-67
	D	3-2	730-1640	24-44	25-45	25-46	26-48
Through Detent (WOT)	D	1-2	1250-1630	37-48	38-49	39-51	40-52
	D	2-3	2200-2630	63-75	64-77	66-79	68-82
	D	3-2	1980-2380	60-72	62-74	64-76	66-78
	D	3-1 2-1	830-1230	76-37	27-38	28-39	28-40

Axle Ratio	Tire Size
3.00	P205-75R15SL
	P215-75R15SL
	P225-75R15XL
	P235-75R15SL
	P235-75R15XL
	L78 × 15B
	L78 × 15C
3.25	P225-75R15SL
	P235-75R15SL
	P235-75R15XL
	L78 × 15B
	L78 × 15C

MODELS PGD-W & Z

Throttle	Range	Shift	OPS-R.P.M	1	2	3
Closed (Above 17" Vacuum)	D	1-2	270-690	6-15	6-16	6-17
	D	2-3	375-890	8-19	9-20	9-21
	D	3-1	270-330	6-7	6-8	6-8
	1	2-1	880-1210	19-26	20-28	21-29
To Detent (Torque Demand)	D	1-2	1110-1570	24-34	25-36	26-37
	D	2-3	1830-2430	40-53	42-55	44-58
	D	3-2	1100-1640	24-36	25-37	26-39
Through Detent (WOT)	D	1-2	1320-1600	28-35	30-37	31-38
	D	2-3	2230-2560	48-55	51-58	53-61
	D	3-2	1940-2260	42-49	44-51	46-54
	D	3-1 2-1	870-1170	19-25	20-27	21-28

Axle Ratio	Tire Size	Use Col. No.
3.73/4.10	800/16.5D	1
	800/16.5E	2
	950/16.5E	3
	875/16.5D	2
	875/16.5E	2

FORD C-6 (Cont.)

SHIFT SPEEDS (MPH) (Cont.)

MODELS PGD-A, AC, AL, AW, BC, DB, DN, DP & Z

Throttle	Range	Shift	OPS-R.P.M.	1	2	3	4	5	6	7
Closed (Above 17" Vacuum)	D	1-2	270-420	8-15	8-15	7-13	7-13	7-13	7-12	6-12
	D	2-3	375-830	11-24	11-25	11-24	10-22	10-21	9-20	9-19
	D	3-1	270-330	8-10	8-10	8-9	7-9	7-8	7-8	6-8
	1	2-1	890-1200	26-36	27-38	25-35	23-33	23-32	21-30	20-29
To Detent (Torque Demand)	D	1-2	620-1310	19-40	20-41	19-39	17-36	17-35	16-33	15-31
	D	2-3	1030-1910	30-56	31-58	29-55	27-50	26-49	25-47	24-44
	D	3-2	900-1460	26-43	27-44	26-42	24-38	23-37	22-36	21-34
Through Detent (WOT)	D	1-2	1270-1590	38-47	39-49	37-46	34-43	33-42	31-40	30-38
	D	2-3	2190-2560	64-75	66-78	62-73	57-67	56-66	53-62	51-60
	D	3-2	2120-2470	62-73	64-75	61-71	56-65	54-63	52-60	49-57
	D	3-1 2-1	900-1200	25-35	28-38	26-36	24-33	24-32	22-30	21-29

Throttle	Range	Shift	OPS-R.P.M.	1	2	3	4	5
Closed (Above 17" Vacuum)	D	1-2	270-420	6-13	6-11	5-10	5-10	5-9
	D	2-3	375-830	9-19	8-17	8-17	7-16	7-15
	D	3-1	270-330	6-8	6-7	5-7	5-6	5-6
	1	2-1	890-1200	20-28	18-26	18-25	17-24	16-23
To Detent (Torque Demand)	D	1-2	620-1310	15-31	14-28	13-27	13-26	12-25
	D	2-3	1030-1910	23-43	21-40	20-38	20-37	19-35
	D	3-2	900-1460	20-33	19-30	18-29	17-28	16-27
Through Detent (WOT)	D	1-2	1270-1590	29-37	27-34	26-32	24-31	23-29
	D	2-3	2190-2560	50-58	45-51	44-51	42-49	40-47
	D	3-2	2120-2470	48-56	44-50	44-50	40-48	39-45
	D	3-1 2-1	900-1200	21-28	19-26	18-25	18-24	17-23

Axle Ratio	Tire Size	Use Col. No.	Axle Ratio	Tire Size	Use Col. No.
2.47/2.75	P195/75R15SL	1	3.33	7.50 x 16D	3
	P205/75R15SL	1		7.50 x 16E	3
	P215/75R15SL	1		8.00 x 16.5D	4
	P235/75R15SL	2		8.00 x 16.5E	4
	H78 x 15B	2		8.75 x 16.5E	4
	L78 x 15C	2		8.75R x 16.5E	4
				9.50 x 16.5E	4
3.00	P195/75R15SL	5	3.54	7.50 x 16D	5
	P205/75R15SL	5		7.50 x 16E	5
	P215/75R15SL	4		8.00 x 16.5D	6
	P235/75R15XL	3		8.00 x 16.5E	6
	H78 x 15B	3		8.75 x 16.5E	6
	L78 x 15C	3		8.75 x 16.5E	6
				9.50 x 16.5E	6
3.25	P215/75R15SL	2	3.73	7.50 x 16D	6
	P225/75R15SL	2		7.50 x 16E	6
	P235/75R15XL	2		8.00 x 16.5D	7
				8.00 x 16.5E	7
				8.75 x 16.5E	7
				8.75 x 16.5E	7
				9.50 x 16.5E	7

Axle Ratio	Tire Size	Use Col. No.
4.10	7.50 x 16D	1
	7.50 x 16E	1
	8.00 x 16.5D	2
	8.00 x 16.5E	2
	8.75 x 16.5E	2
	8.75R x 16.5E	2
	9.50 x 16.5E	2
4.56	7.50 x 16D	3
	7.50 x 16E	3
	8.00 x 16.5D	5
	8.00 x 16.5E	5
	8.75 x 16.5E	4
	8.75R x 16.5E	4
	9.50 x 16.5E	4

MODELS PGD-CL & CM

Throttle	Range	Shift	OPS-R.P.M.	1	2	3	4
Closed (Above 17" Vacuum)	D	1-2	270-520	8-16	8-17	8-17	8-18
	D	2-3	375-870	11-24	11-26	11-26	12-27
	D	3-1	270-330	8-9	8-10	8-10	8-10
	1	2-1	860-1200	25-35	26-36	27-38	28-39
To Detent (Torque Demand)	D	1-2	640-1440	18-42	19-43	19-45	20-46
	D	2-3	1070-2130	30-60	31-63	32-65	33-67
	D	3-2	840-1530	24-44	25-45	25-46	26-48
Through Detent (WOT)	D	1-2	1280-1640	37-48	38-49	39-51	40-52
	D	2-3	2190-2620	63-75	64-77	66-79	68-82
	D	3-2	2100-2510	60-72	62-74	64-76	66-78
	D	3-1 2-1	890-1250	26-37	27-38	28-39	28-40

Axle Ratio	Tire Size	Use Col. No.
2.47/2.75	P205-75R 15SL	1
	P215-75R 15SL	1
	P225-75R 15SL	2
	P235-75R 15SL	3
	P235-75R 15XL	3
	H78 x 15B	4
	L78 x 15C	4
3.25	P205-75R 15SL	2
	P215-75R 15SL	2
	P225-75R 15SL	2
	P235-75R 15SL	3
	P235-75R 15XL	3
	H78 x 15B	4
	L78 x 15C	4

MODELS PJA-AG, AH, AL, DM & DN

Throttle	Range	Shift	OPS-R.P.M.	1	2	3	4	5	6	7
Closed (Above 17" Vacuum)	D	1-2	270-700	8-21	7-18	7-18	7-17	6-16	6-15	6-15
	D	2-3	375-980	11-29	10-26	10-25	9-24	9-23	9-23	8-21
	D	3-1	270-330	8-10	7-9	7-8	7-8	6-8	6-8	6-7
	1	2-1	890-1260	26-37	23-33	23-32	21-30	20-29	20-29	18-26
To Detent (Torque Demand)	D	1-2	840-1500	25-44	22-39	22-38	20-37	20-35	19-34	18-31
	D	2-3	1430-2040	42-67	38-60	37-59	35-56	33-53	33-52	30-48
	D	3-2	1010-1620	30-48	27-43	26-42	25-40	24-39	24-39	21-34
Through Detent (WOT)	D	1-2	1300-1630	38-48	33-43	33-42	31-40	30-37	29-37	27-34
	D	2-3	2250-2620	66-77	59-69	58-67	55-64	52-61	51-59	47-55
	D	3-2	2030-2360	59-70	53-62	52-61	50-58	45-55	46-54	42-49
	D	3-1 2-1	870-1220	26-36	23-32	22-31	21-30	20-28	20-28	18-25

Axle Ratio	Tire Size	Use Col. No.	Axle Ratio	Tire Size	Use Col. No.
3.00/3.33	750 x 16D	1	3.73	750 x 16D	4
	750 x 16E	1		750 x 16E	4
	800 x 16.5D	2		800 x 16.5D	5
	800 x 16.5E	2		800 x 16.5E	5
	875 x 16.5E	2		875 x 16.5E	5
	875 x 16.5E	2		875R x 16.5E	5
	950 x 16.5E	2		950 x 16.5E	5
3.54	750 x 16D	3	4.10/4.56	750 x 16D	6
	750 x 16E	3		750 x 16E	6
	800 x 16.5D	4		800 x 16.5D	7
	800 x 16.5E	4		800 x 16.5E	7
	875 x 16.5E	4		875 x 16.5E	7
	875 x 16.5E	4		875R x 16.5E	7
	950 x 16.5E	4		950 x 16.5E	7

MODELS PGD-BE, BF, BN, BS, CZ & DC

Throttle	Range	Shift	OPS-R.P.M.	1	2	3	4	5	6	7
Closed (Above 17" Vacuum)	D	1-2	270-460	8-16	8-16	8-15	7-14	7-14	7-13	6-12
	D	2-3	375-920	11-28	11-27	11-26	10-24	10-24	9-22	8-21
	D	3-1	270-330	8-10	8-10	8-9	7-9	7-8	7-8	6-8
	1	2-1	930-1330	29-41	28-40	27-39	25-36	25-35	23-33	22-32
To Detent (Torque Demand)	D	1-2	680-1450	22-45	21-44	20-43	19-39	18-38	17-36	17-35
	D	2-3	1120-2100	33-63	33-62	32-60	29-55	29-54	27-51	26-49
	D	3-2	980-1610	29-49	29-47	28-46	26-42	25-41	24-39	23-37
Through Detent (WOT)	D	1-2	1390-1760	43-54	41-53	35-51	37-47	36-46	34-44	33-42
	D	2-3	2390-2820	72-85	70-83	68-81	63-74	61-72	58-69	56-66
	D	3-2	2310-2720	70-82	68-80	66-78	61-72	59-70	56-66	54-63
	D	3-1 2-1	1000-1380	30-42	29-41	28-39	26-36	26-35	24-34	23-32

Axle Ratio	Tire Size	Use Col. No.	Axle Ratio	Tire Size	Use Col. No.
2.75	P195-75R15SL	2	3.54/3.33	7.50 x 16D	5
	P205-75R15SL	2		7.50 x 16E	5
	P215-75R15SL	2		8.00 x 16.5D	6
	P235-75R15XL	1		8.00 x 16.5E	6
	P235-75R15SL	1		8.75 x 16.5E	6
	H78 x 15B	1		8.75R x 16.5E	6
	L78 x 15C	1		9.50 x 16.5E	7
3.00	P195-75R15SL	5	3.00/3.25	7.50 x 16D	3
	P205-75R15SL	5		7.50 x 16E	3
	P215-75R15SL	4		8.00 x 16.5D	4
	P235-75R15SL	3		8.00 x 16.5E	4
	P235-75R15XL	3		8.75 x 16.5E	4
	H78 x 15B	3		9.50 x 16.5E	4
	L78 x 15B	3				

FORD C-6 (Cont.)

CLUTCH AND BAND APPLICATION CHART
(ELEMENTS IN USE)

Selector Lever Position	Intermediate Band	Reverse Clutch	Forward Clutch	High Clutch	One-Way Clutch
D — DRIVE First Gear Second Gear Third Gear	 X 		 X X X	 X	 X
2 — INTERMEDIATE Second Gear	X		X		
1 — LOW (First)		X	X		
R — REVERSE		X		X	
NEUTRAL OR PARK — Band and all clutches released and/or ineffective.					

CONTROL PRESSURE TEST

Engine Vacuum Method — 1) Attach a tachometer to engine and install a vacuum gauge (using a "T") into manifold vacuum line at vacuum diaphragm unit. Attach a 0-400 psi gauge to control pressure take-off point at transmission.

2) Apply both parking and service brakes. With engine at curb idle speed and normal operating temperature, read and record control pressure in all selector positions at specified manifold vacuum. Compare control pressures obtained in tests with pressures given in Control Pressure Table.

CAUTION — *Release throttle immediately if slippage is indicated. Also shift transmission to Neutral and run engine at 1000 RPM to cool transmission fluid between tests.*

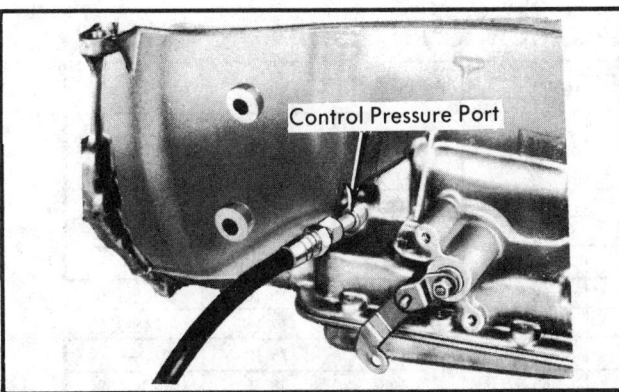

Fig. 3   View of Transmission Case Showing Location of Control Pressure Test Point

Vacuum Pump Method — 1) Attach tachometer to engine and a 0-400 psi gauge to pressure take-off point at transmission. Disconnect and plug manifold vacuum line at diaphragm unit. Connect suitable vacuum source (vacuum pump in distributor tester). Apply both parking and service brakes, start engine and vacuum pump, setting vacuum to 15". Read and record control pressure in all shift selector positions.

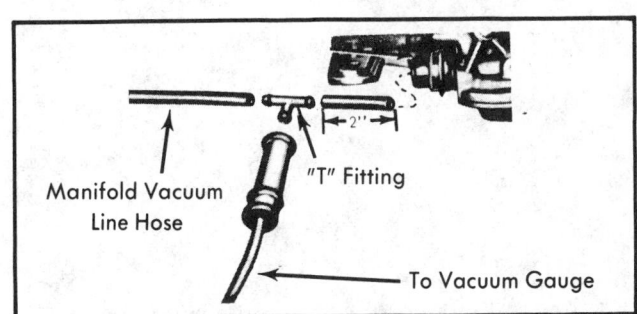

Fig. 4   Connecting Vacuum Gauge for Pressure Test (Engine Vacuum Method)

2) Increase engine to 1000 RPM, and reduce vacuum to 10 inches. Read and record control pressure in "D", "2" and "1". With engine still at 1000 RPM, reduce vacuum to 1 inch. Read and record control pressure in "D", "2", "1" and "R". Compare control pressures obtained in tests with pressures given in Control Pressure Table.

NOTE — *Governor can be checked at same time as Control Pressure Test is performed.*

Automatic Transmissions

FORD C-6 (Cont.)

3) Place selector lever in "2", no load on engine and apply 10" of vacuum. Increase speed slowly while watching speedometer, check speed at which control pressure cutback occurs. It should occur between 10-20 MPH.

4) Decrease vacuum to 0.2" and repeat test. Control pressure cutback should occur between 30-50 MPH. If cutback does not occur within specifications, check shift speeds to make sure that it is the governor and not a stuck cutback valve.

CAUTION — *DO NOT exceed 60 MPH speedometer speed during test. If control pressures are not within specifications, proceed to Control Pressure Test Results to determine problem.*

CONTROL PRESSURE TEST RESULTS

Low at Idle in All Ranges

- Check for low fluid level, restricted intake screen or filter, loose oil tubes, loose valve body or regulator-to-case bolts.

- Check for excessive leakage in front pump, case or control valve body. Check for sticking control pressure regulator valve.

OK at Idle in All Ranges, But Low at 10" Vacuum

- Check vacuum diaphragm unit. Check if control rod or throttle valve is stuck.

High at Idle in All Ranges

- Check vacuum diaphragm unit, manifold vacuum line, throttle rod or control rod.
- Check for sticking regulator boost valve(s).

OK at Idle in All Ranges, OK at 10" Vacuum, But Low at 1" Vacuum

- Check for excessive leakage, low pump capacity or restricted oil pan screen.

Low in "P"

- Check valve body pressure regulator.

Low in "R"

- Check high clutch and/or reverse clutch.

Low in "N"

- Check valve body for tightness and correct operation.

Low in "D"

- Check for faulty forward clutch operation.

Low in "2"

- Check forward clutch and/or intermediate servo.

Low in "1"

- Check forward clutch and/or reverse clutch.

CONTROL PRESSURE SPECIFICATIONS

Transmission Models	Range	(Idle) 15" & Above	14"	13"	12"	11"	10"	WOT Stall Thru Detent
		MANIFOLD VACUUM						
All models with 4.9L, 5.0L, and 5.8L engines	D,2,1	67-91	73-96	80-102	86-108	92-113	99-119	155-180
	R	94-142	115-152	126-159	135-168	144-177	155-186	245-275
	P,N	67-91	73-96	80-102	86-108	92-113	99-119	—
All models with 6.6L engines	D,2,1	42-63	42-71	49-78	58-86	66-93	75-101	155-180
	R	66-99	66-110	77-121	90-135	104-146	117-157	245-275
	P,N	42-63	42-71	49-78	58-86	66-93	75-101	—
All models with high altitude compensating diaphragm	D,2,1	42-61	42-68	48-75	55-82	62-89	68-95	134-159
	R	66-95	66-106	75-117	86-128	97-139	106-148	209-249
	P,N	42-61	42-68	48-75	55-82	62-89	68-95	—

FORD C-6 (Cont.)

VACUUM DIAPHRAGM UNIT

Vacuum Supply Check — 1) Disconnect vacuum line at vacuum unit and connect vacuum gauge. With engine idling, gauge must show a steady acceptable vacuum. If reading is low, check for vacuum leak and/or poor engine vacuum.

2) If reading is acceptable, rapidly accelerate engine momentarily, vacuum must drop rapidly at acceleration and return immediately upon deceleration. If vacuum reading does not change or changes slowly, vacuum line is plugged, restricted or connected to reservoir supply. Repair as required.

Vacuum Diaphragm Unit Check — 1) Remove unit from transmission. Use suitable tester equipped with vacuum pump. Start pump and set regulator knob so vacuum gauge reads 18" with end of hose blocked off. Connect vacuum hose to port on unit. If gauge still reads 18", unit is not leaking. If vacuum does not hold at 18", unit is leaking and must be replaced.

2) When hose is removed from unit, hold finger over end of control rod. Internal spring of unit should push control rod outward. Also, check for presence of transmission fluid in vacuum side of diaphragm or in vacuum hose. If fluid is present, unit is leaking and must be replaced.

Stall Speeds	
Application	**Stall RPM**
4.9L (300") 6-Cyl.	
F100/250	1550-1830
F350 Federal	1525-1776
E100/250 Federal	1560-1850
E350 Federal	1530-1780
E & F350 Calif	1450-1710
5.0L (302") V8	
F100/250 Federal	1550-1860
Bronco ①	1550-1850
E100/250 Federal	1560-1850
E100 Calif.	1525-1790
E150 Calif.	1562-1838
5.8L (351M & W) V8	
F150/250	1550-1836
F350	1480-1760
Bronco	1524-1811
E100/150 Federal	1580-1850
E & F250 Federal	1550-1830
E350	1450-1710
6.6L (400") V8	
E350	1640-1940
7.5L (460") V8	
E350	1620-1960
① — Bronco with 3.50 axle, 1524-1811 RPM.	

STALL SPEED TEST

CAUTION — *DO NOT hold throttle open longer than 5 seconds at a time during testing. If engine speed exceeds maximum limit of stall speed, release throttle immediately as clutches or bands are slipping.*

Testing Procedure — With engine at curb idle and normal operating temperature, tachometer installed, parking and service brakes fully applied, stall test transmission in each driving range at full throttle and note maximum RPM obtained. Engine speed should be within limits shown in Stall Speeds Table.

NOTE — *Allow a cooling period of 15 seconds with transmission in Neutral and engine speed at 1000 RPM between each test.*

STALL TEST RESULTS

Stall Speed Too High — In "D", "2", "1", & "R"; general transmission problems are indicated and a control pressure test should be made to locate faulty unit(s). In "D" only; planetary one-way clutch slippage is indicated. In "D", "2", & "1"; forward clutch slippage is indicated. In "R" only; high and/or reverse clutch slippage is indicated.

Stall Speed Too Low — Converter stator one-way clutch faulty. **CAUTION** — *Make sure engine performance is satisfactory before condemning converter assembly. Converter cannot be overhauled and must be replaced if defective.*

AIR PRESSURE CHECKS

A "No Drive" condition can exist, even with correct transmission fluid pressure, because of inoperative clutches or bands. Erratic shifts could be caused by a stuck governor valve. The inoperative units can be located through a series of checks by substituting air pressure for the fluid pressure to determine location of malfunction. To make air pressure checks, loosen oil pan bolts and allow transmission to drain, then remove oil pan and control valve body. Apply air at points noted (see illustration) and check unit operations as follows:

Forward Clutch — Apply air pressure to transmission case forward clutch passage. A dull thud can be heard when clutch piston is applied, or movement of piston can be felt by placing a finger on input shell.

Governor — Apply air pressure to control pressure-to-governor passage and listen for sharp clicking or whistling noise, indicating governor valve movement.

Reverse-High Clutch — Apply air pressure to reverse-high clutch passage, dull thud should be heard when clutch piston is applied. If not, place finger tips on clutch drum, movement should be felt.

FORD C-6 (Cont.)

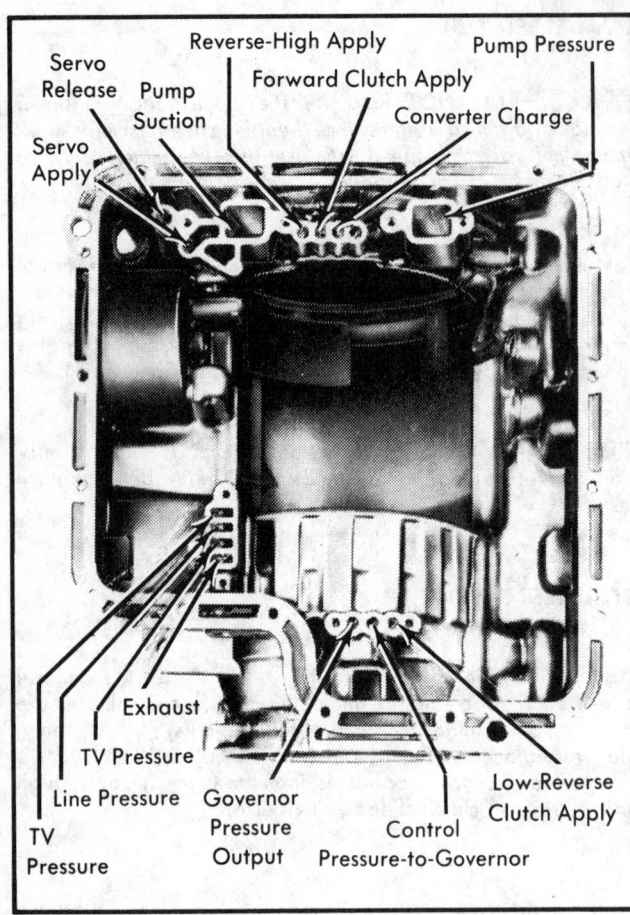

Fig. 5   Bottom View of Transmission Case Showing Fluid Passages for Air Pressure Checks

Intermediate Servo — Hold air nozzle in intermediate servo apply passage. Operation of servo will be indicated by tightening of intermediate band around drum. With air still applied at the apply passage, use second air nozzle to apply air at the servo release passage. Band should now release (combination of air pressure and spring on release side of piston should overcome apply pressure).

Low-Reverse Clutch — Apply air pressure to the reverse clutch apply passage. A dull thud should be heard if clutch is operating properly.

SERVICE (IN VEHICLE)
VALVE BODY

Removal — Loosen oil pan attaching bolts, tap pan to break it loose allowing fluid to drain, then remove oil pan and gasket. Remove and discard nylon shipping plug from filler tube hole. **NOTE** — *This plug is used to retain fluid in transmission during shipment and should be discarded when oil pan is removed.* Remove valve body attaching bolts and lower valve body from transmission case.

Installation — Position valve body to case, making sure selector and downshift levers are engaged. Install and tighten attaching bolts evenly. Install oil pan with new gasket, and tighten attaching bolts evenly.

INTERMEDIATE SERVO

Removal — Remove engine rear support-to-crossmember bolt, crossmember-to-frame attaching bolts, and remove crossmember. Disconnect muffler inlet pipe from exhaust manifolds and allow pipe to hang. Place a drain pan under servo, remove cover attaching bolts, and remove cover, piston, spring, and gasket.

NOTE — *As piston is being removed, screw in band adjusting screw. This keeps tension on band, keeping struts properly engaged in band end notches as piston is removed.*

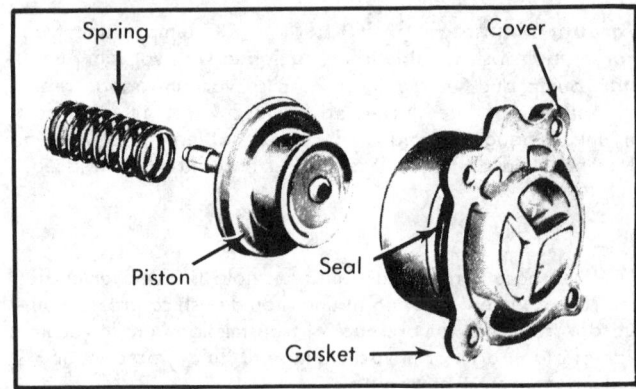

Fig. 6   Disassembled View of Intermediate Servo

Seal Replacement — Apply air pressure to port in servo cover and remove piston and rod. Remove seal from cover. **NOTE** — *Replace complete piston and rod assembly if piston or piston sealing lips are damaged.* Dip new seal in transmission fluid and install on cover. Coat two new gaskets with petroleum jelly and install on cover. Dip piston in transmission fluid and install in cover.

Installation — Reverse removal procedure and note the following: Make sure to back off band adjusting screw as servo cover bolts are being tightened. Make sure service identification tag is located under servo cover bolt. Adjust intermediate band and refill transmission to correct fluid level.

EXTENSION HOUSING SEAL & BUSHING

Removal — Disconnect propeller shaft at transmission. Using a tapered chisel, carefully remove rear seal. Using a bushing remover tool, withdraw bushing from extension housing. **NOTE** — *Use tool carefully so that spline seal is not damaged.*

Installation — Install bushing into extension housing using a suitable bushing driver. Before installing a new seal, inspect sealing surface of propeller shaft yoke for wear or damage. If scores are found, replace yoke. Using a suitable seal driver, install seal in extension housing, making sure it is fully seated in bore. Coat inside of seal and yoke spline with wheel bearing grease, and install propeller shaft.

FORD C-6 (Cont.)

EXTENSION HOUSING & GOVERNOR

Removal — 1) Remove propeller shaft. Remove transfer case (if equipped), and speedometer cable. Remove engine rear support-to-extension housing bolts, then raise transmission with jack to take weight off support and remove support from crossmember.

2) Place drain pan under rear of transmission and remove extension housing-to-case bolts and slide housing off output shaft. Remove governor housing-to-flange bolts and separate governor from flange.

Installation — Reverse removal procedure, tighten all nuts and bolts to specifications. Make sure all mating surfaces are kept clean and refill transmission to correct fluid level.

REMOVAL & INSTALLATION

See *Transmission Removal & Installation in Automatic Transmission Servicing.*

TORQUE CONVERTER

NOTE — *Converter is a sealed unit and cannot be disassembled for service. Replace if found defective. Make the following tests to be certain converter is defective before replacing unit.*

FLUSHING CONVERTER

Whenever transmission has been disassembled to replace worn or damaged parts or because valve body sticks due to foreign material, converter and oil cooler **must** be cleaned using a mechanically agitated cleaner (Rotunda 140028 or equivalent). Under no conditions should converter or oil cooler be cleaned by hand agitation using solvent.

LEAK TEST

NOTE — *If torque converter welds indicate leakage, assemble suitable Torque Converter Leak Detector (Rotunda 720004 or equivalent) to converter and follow detector kit instructions.*

TURBINE & STATOR END PLAY CHECK

1) Insert suitable test tool (T77L-7902-D) into converter pump drive hub until it bottoms. Expand sleeve in turbine spline by tightening threaded inner post of test tool until tool is securely locked into spline.

2) Attach a dial indicator to tool with button on indicator on converter pump drive hub, then zero dial face. Lift tool upward as far as it will go and note indicator reading.

3) Reading is total end play of turbine and stator. If end play exceeds .021″ (new or rebuilt converter) or .040″ (used converter), replace torque converter assembly.

STATOR ONE-WAY CLUTCH CHECK

1) Insert one-way clutch holding tool into one of the grooves in the stator thrust washer. Insert clutch torquing tool (T77L-7902-B) in converter pump drive hub so as to engage one-way clutch inner race.

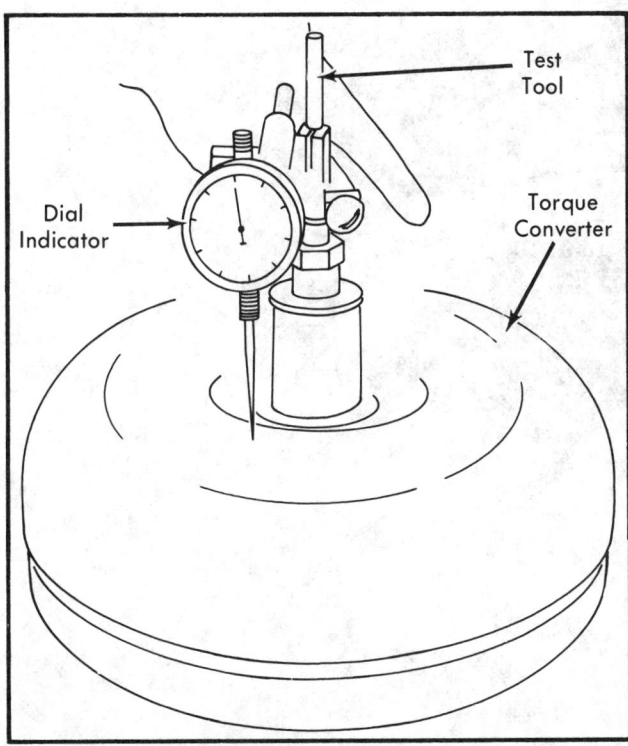

Fig. 7 Checking Torque Converter Turbine & Stator End Play

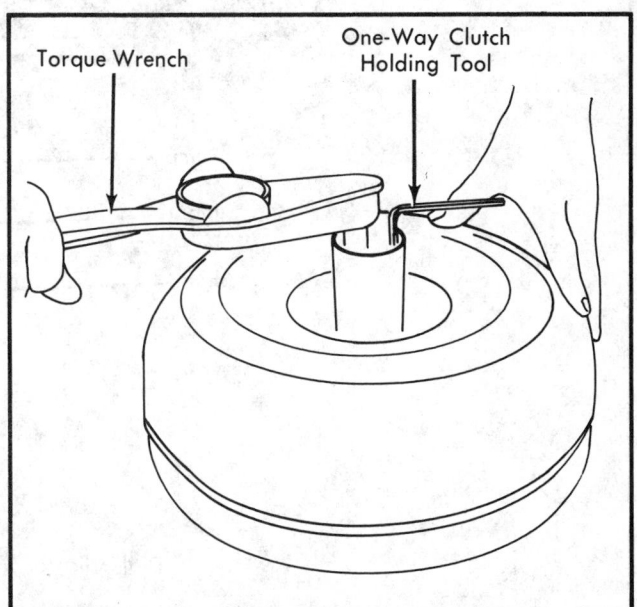

Fig. 8 Stator One-Way Clutch Check

FORD C-6 (Cont.)

2) Attach a torque wrench to torquing tool. With clutch holding tool held stationary, turn torque wrench counter-clockwise. The converter one-way clutch should lock-up and hold a 10 ft. lb. force.

NOTE — *One-way clutch should rotate freely in a clockwise direction.*

3) Repeat lock-up test in at least five different locations around torque converter. If clutch fails to lock-up and hold, replace torque converter.

STATOR INTERFERENCE CHECK

Stator To Impeller Interference Check — Position front pump assembly on bench with spline end of stator shaft pointing up. Mount converter on pump so splines of one-way clutch inner race engage splines of stator support, and converter hub engages pump drive gear. While holding pump stationary, rotate converter counterclockwise. Converter should rotate freely without interference or scraping within assembly. Should this condition exist, replace converter unit.

Stator To Turbine Interference Check — Place converter on bench front side down. Install front pump assembly to engage mating splines of stator support and stator, and pump drive gear lugs. Install input shaft, engaging the splines with turbine hub. While holding pump stationary, rotate turbine with input shaft. Turbine should rotate freely in both directions without interference or noise. If interference or noise exists, stator front thrust washer may be worn. In such cases, replace converter unit.

TRANSMISSION DISASSEMBLY

1) With transmission in a suitable holding fixture, remove oil pan and gasket. Remove attaching bolts and lift valve body assembly from transmission case. Attach a dial indicator to front pump with indicator contact against input shaft. Install oil seal replacer tool (T61L-7657-B) in extension housing to center output shaft. Check transmission end play as follows: Pry gear train to rear of case, then press input shaft inward until bottomed. Zero dial indicator. Pry gear train forward, read and record end play for reassembly reference. Remove checking tools from transmission.

2) Remove vacuum diaphragm, rod, and primary throttle valve from case, and slide input shaft from front pump. Remove front pump attaching bolts, pry gear train forward and remove pump. Loosen band adjusting screw and remove two band struts. Rotate band 90° counterclockwise to align band ends with slot in case, then remove band from reverse-high clutch drum. Remove forward part of gear train from transmission as an assembly.

3) Remove servo cover attaching bolts, servo cover, piston, spring and gasket from case. Remove large snap ring securing reverse planet carrier in low-reverse clutch hub, then lift carrier from drum. Remove snap ring securing reverse ring gear and hub on output shaft and slide assembly from shaft. Rotate low-reverse hub in clockwise direction and remove from case. Remove reverse clutch snap ring and withdraw clutch discs, plates and pressure plate from case.

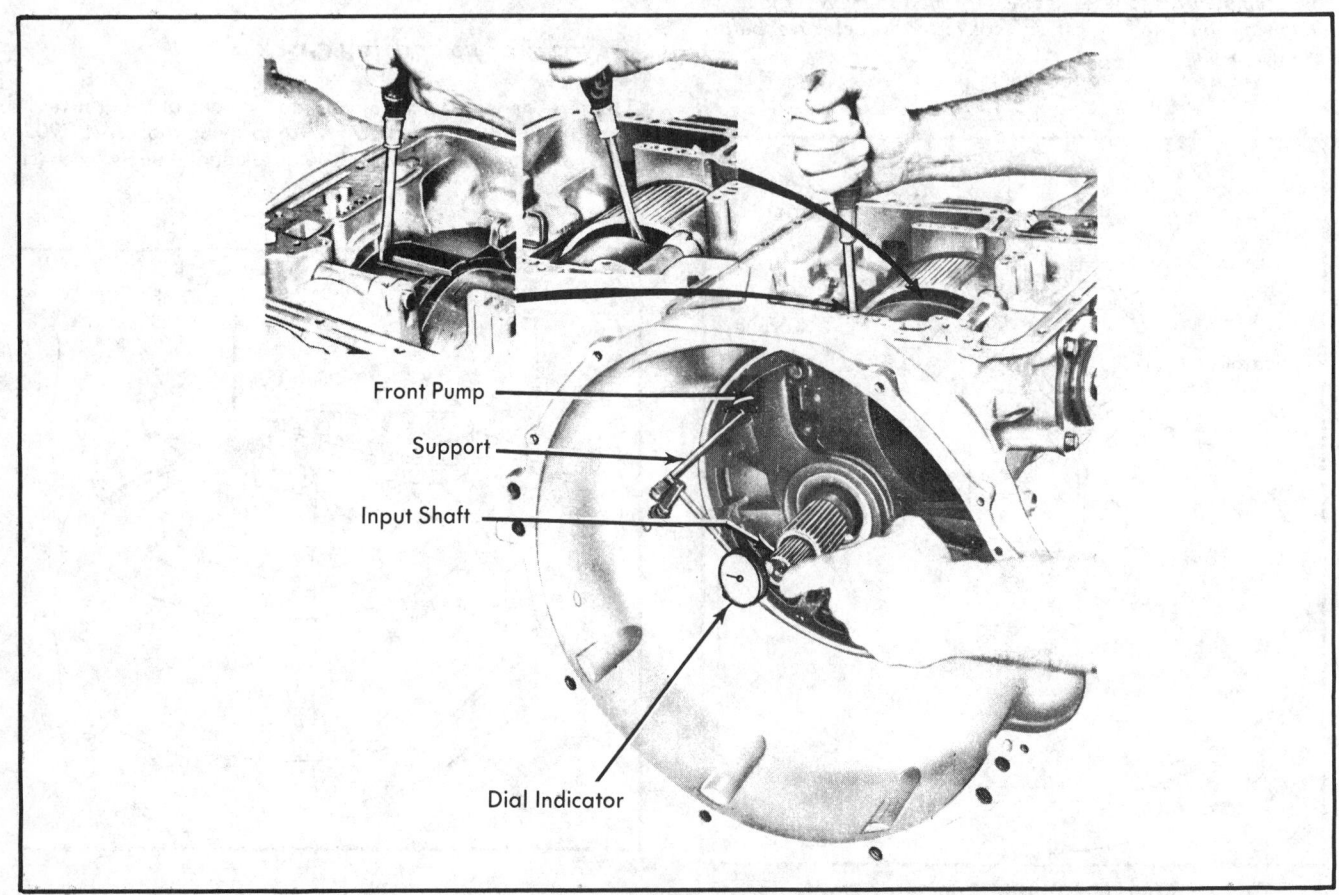

Front Pump

Support

Input Shaft

Dial Indicator

Fig. 9 Checking Transmission End Play

FORD C-6 (Cont.)

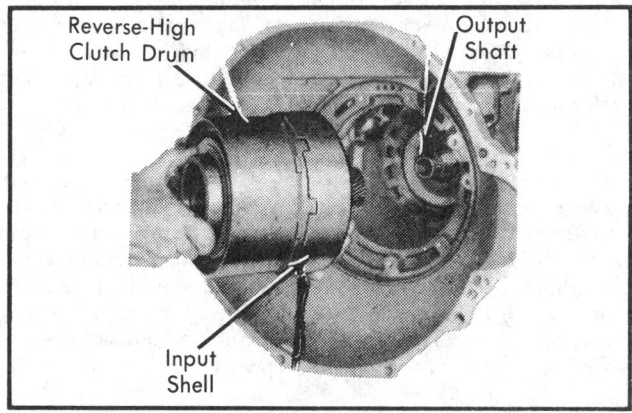

Reverse-High Clutch Drum

Output Shaft

Input Shell

Fig. 10 Removing Forward Part of Gear Train

4) Remove extension housing attaching bolts and vent tube from case. Remove extension housing and gasket. Slide output shaft assembly from case. Remove distributor sleeve attaching bolts, and remove sleeve, parking pawl gear, and thrust washer.

NOTE — *If thrust washer is staked in place, use a sharp chisel and cut off metal from behind thrust washer. Remove any metal particles from case.*

5) Compress reverse clutch piston release spring, remove snap ring and lift out springs and retainer assembly. Remove one-way clutch inner race attaching bolts from rear of case and remove inner race. Remove reverse clutch piston by applying air pressure to low-reverse apply passage in case.

NOTE — *See Fig. 5 for location of low-reverse apply passage.*

COMPONENT DISASSEMBLY & REASSEMBLY

DOWNSHIFT & MANUAL LINKAGE

Disassembly — Remove nut and lock washer securing outer downshift lever to transmission, and remove lever. Slide downshift lever out from inside case, and remove seal from recess in manual lever shaft. On "E" models, remove neutral safety switch bolts and remove switch. Remove "C" ring securing parking pawl actuating rod to manual lever, then remove rod from case. Remove nut securing inner manual lever to shaft. Remove inner lever from shaft, and slide outer lever and shaft from case. Remove seal from case using a suitable puller and slide hammer.

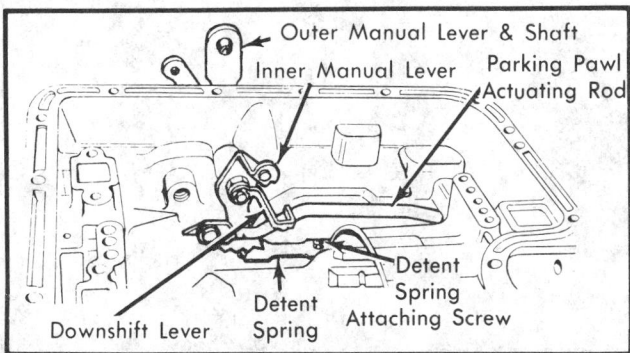

Outer Manual Lever & Shaft

Inner Manual Lever

Parking Pawl Actuating Rod

Downshift Lever

Detent Spring

Detent Spring Attaching Screw

Fig. 11 Installed View of Downshift and Manual Linkage Components

Reassembly — 1) Dip new seal in transmission fluid and install into case using suitable installing tools. Slide outer manual lever and shaft into case. Position inner lever on shaft making sure leaf spring roller is positioned in inner manual lever detent. Install attaching nut and tighten. Install parking pawl actuating rod and secure to inner manual lever with a "C" ring.

2) On "E" models, slide neutral safety switch on outer shaft lever. Install bolt. With manual lever in neutral, rotate switch and install gauge pin (No. 43 drill) into gauge pin hole. Tighten switch retaining bolt. Install a new downshift lever seal in outer lever shaft recess. Slide downshift lever and shaft into position. Place outer downshift lever on shaft. Install and tighten lock washer and nut.

PARKING PAWL LINKAGE

Disassembly — Remove bolts securing parking pawl guide plate to case, and remove plate. Remove spring, parking pawl and shaft from case. Working from pan mounting surface, drill a 1/8" hole through center of cupped plug, and pull plug from case with a wire hook. Unhook end of spring from park plate slot to relieve tension. Thread a 1/4-20 or 8-32 x 1 1/4" screw into park plate shaft. Pull shaft from case with screw. Remove spring and park plate.

Reassembly — Position spring and park plate in case and install shaft. Place end of spring into slot of park plate. Install a new cupped plug to retain shaft. Install parking pawl shaft in case. Slip parking pawl and spring into place on shaft. Position guide plate on case, making sure actuating rod is seated in slot of plate. Secure plate with two bolts and lock washers.

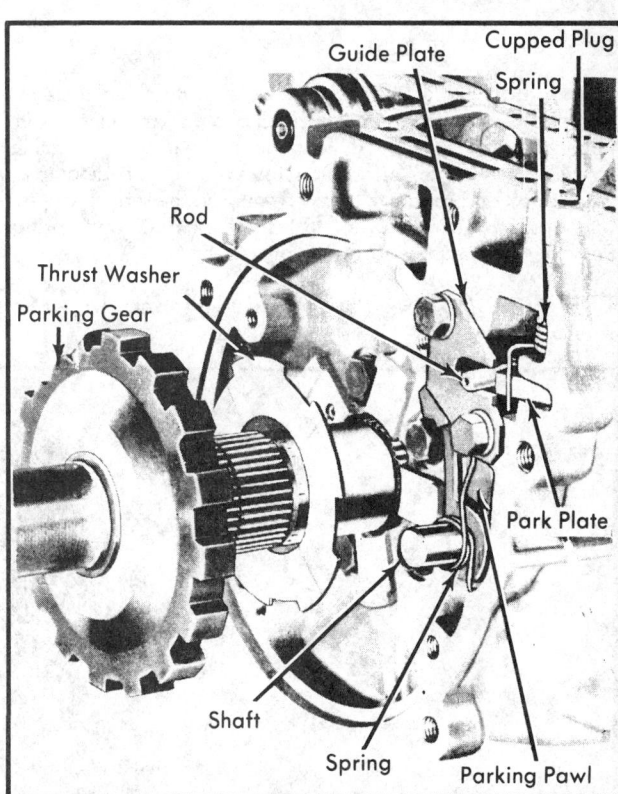

Guide Plate

Cupped Plug

Spring

Rod

Thrust Washer

Parking Gear

Park Plate

Shaft

Spring

Parking Pawl

Fig. 12 Installed View of Parking Pawl Linkage Assembly

FORD C-6 (Cont.)

SERVO APPLY LEVER

Disassembly – Working from inside case, carefully drive on servo apply lever shaft to remove the cup plug; shaft can be withdrawn by hand.

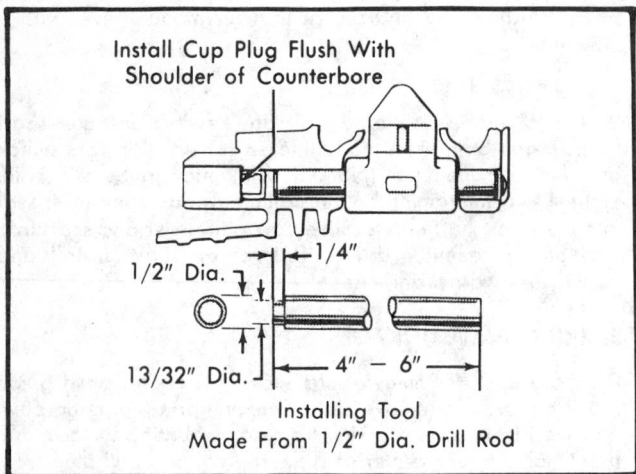

Install Cup Plug Flush With Shoulder of Counterbore

1/4"

1/2" Dia.

13/32" Dia.

4" – 6"

Installing Tool
Made From 1/2" Dia. Drill Rod

Fig. 13   Installing Servo Apply Lever Cup Plug

Reassembly – Hold servo apply lever in position and install shaft. Using fabricated tool shown in *Fig. 13,* drive cup plug into position in case being sure plug is flush with shoulder of counterbore.

NOTE – *Cup plug may be coated with Loctite (or equivalent) to prevent leakage.*

CONTROL VALVE BODY

Disassembly – 1) Remove the 9 screws attaching screen-to-lower valve body and remove screen and gasket. Remove the 5 upper-to-lower valve body and hold down plate attaching screws. Remove the 7 attaching screws from underside of lower valve body and separate bodies, removing the separator plate and gasket. Make sure not to lose check balls and springs. Remove and clean separator plate screen.

NOTE – *DO NOT clean screen gasket in solvent; wipe clean with a lint-free cloth.*

2) Remove manual valve plunger retaining pin from upper valve body, then remove plunger. Slide manual valve out of valve body. Cover downshift valve port with a finger, remove downshift valve retainer, then remove spring and downshift valve.

3) Apply hand pressure on pressure boost valve sleeve and remove retaining clip from underside of valve body. Slowly release hand pressure and remove sleeve and pressure boost valve. Remove 2 springs, retainer and main regulator valve from bore. Apply hand pressure on throttle boost valve plate and remove 2 attaching screws. Release hand pressure and remove plate, throttle boost valve, spring and manual low 2-1 scheduling valve and spring from bore.

4) Apply hand pressure on remaining valve body plate and remove 8 attaching screws. Hold valve body so plate faces upward, release hand pressure on plate and remove. Remove spring and intermediate servo modulator valve from body and remove intermediate servo accumulator valve and springs.

NOTE – *When removing valves from body, keep all ports covered with fingers except bore where valve is being removed.*

5) Remove 2-3 back-out valve, spring and 3-2 shift timing valve plug (if not peened on end). Remove 2-3 shift valve, spring and throttle modulator valve. Remove 1-2 shift valve, DR-2 shift valve and spring. Remove coasting regulator valve and cutback valve from body.

NOTE – *DO NOT attempt to remove 3-2 shift timing plug if end is peened over. Condition will not affect transmission operation.*

Reassembly – Reverse disassembly procedure and note the following: Coat check balls with vaseline to hold in place during reassembly. When installing screen in separator plate, make sure tabs are flush with separator plate surface. Tighten all bolts and screws evenly.

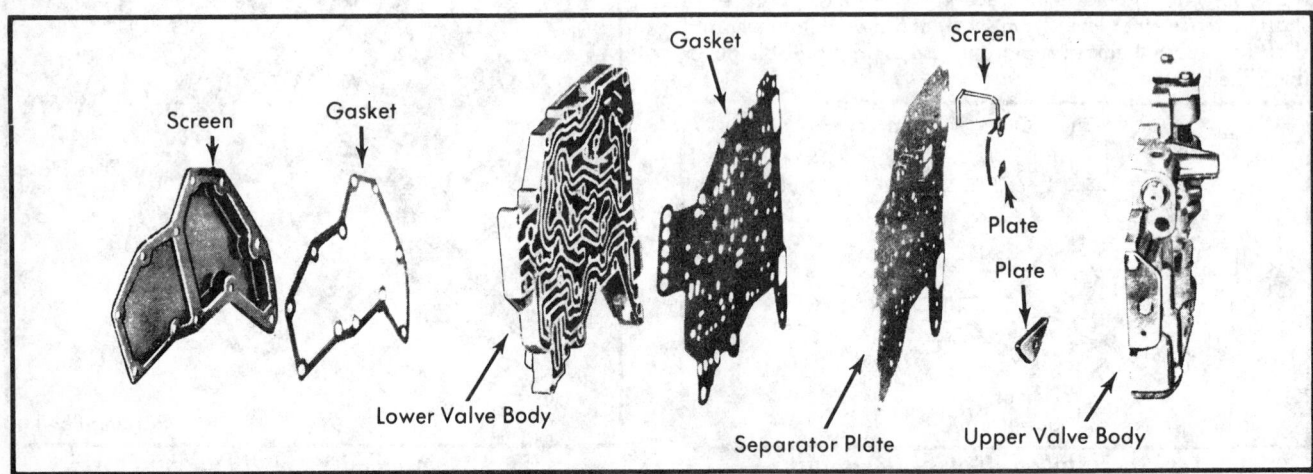

Screen

Gasket

Gasket

Screen

Plate

Plate

Lower Valve Body

Separator Plate

Upper Valve Body

Fig. 14   Exploded View of Control Valve Assembly

FORD C-6 (Cont.)

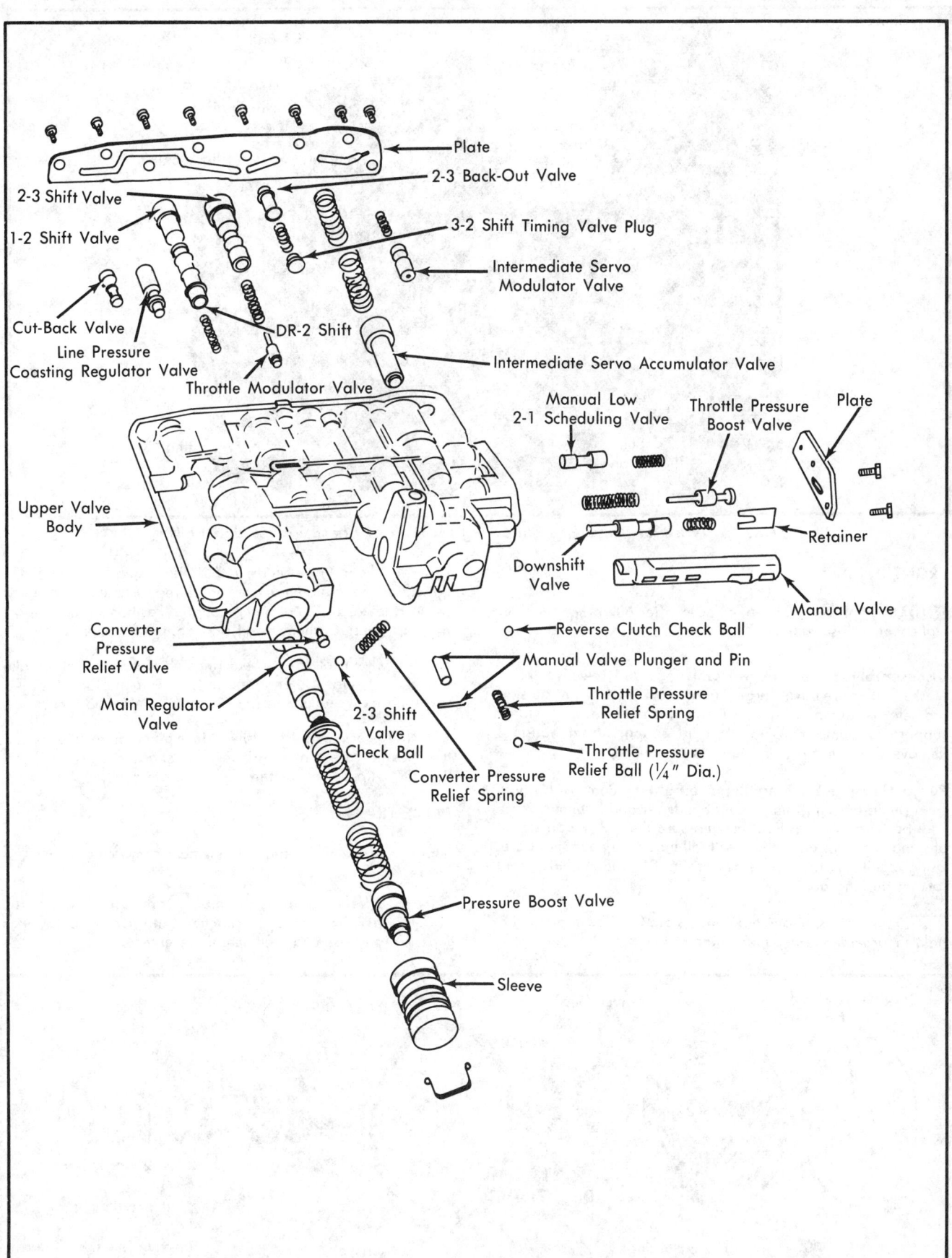

Plate
2-3 Back-Out Valve
2-3 Shift Valve
1-2 Shift Valve
3-2 Shift Timing Valve Plug
Intermediate Servo Modulator Valve
Cut-Back Valve
Line Pressure Coasting Regulator Valve
DR-2 Shift
Throttle Modulator Valve
Intermediate Servo Accumulator Valve
Manual Low 2-1 Scheduling Valve
Throttle Pressure Boost Valve
Plate
Upper Valve Body
Retainer
Downshift Valve
Manual Valve
Converter Pressure Relief Valve
Reverse Clutch Check Ball
Manual Valve Plunger and Pin
Main Regulator Valve
2-3 Shift Valve Check Ball
Throttle Pressure Relief Spring
Converter Pressure Relief Spring
Throttle Pressure Relief Ball (¼" Dia.)
Pressure Boost Valve
Sleeve

Fig. 15 *Exploded View of Upper Valve Body Assembly*

FORD C-6 (Cont.)

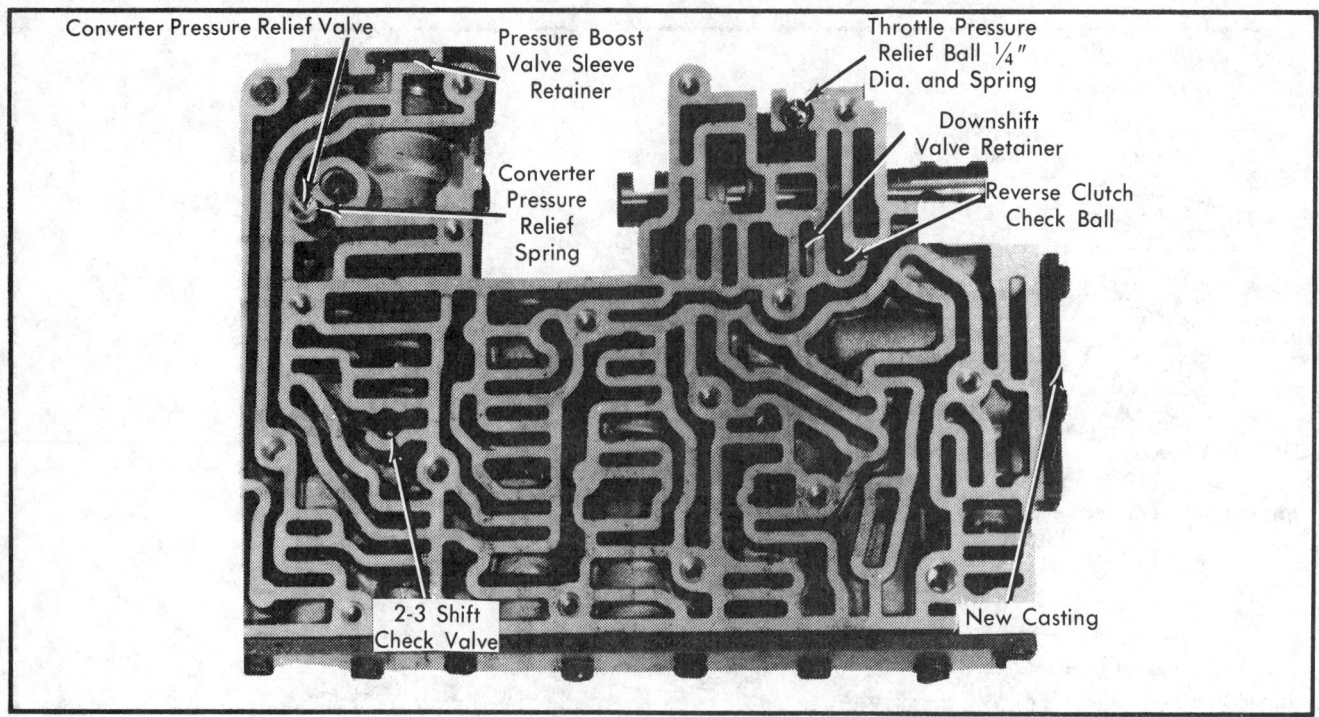

Fig. 16　View of Valve Body Showing Location of Check Valves and Balls

FRONT PUMP

NOTE — *Front seal can be replaced after pump has been installed on transmission.*

Disassembly — Remove two seal rings and selective thrust washer, then remove large square cut seal from outside diameter of pump housing. Remove five bolts securing stator support to pump housing, then lift support from housing. Remove drive and driven gears from housing.

Pump Housing Bushing Replacement — Remove bushing from pump housing using a suitable driver and hammer. Place new bushing into position, making sure the half moon slot in bushing is on top and in line with oil lube hole near seal bore. Using a suitable tool, press bushing in .060-.080″ below front face of bushing bore.

NOTE — *After assembly, half moon slot MUST be in past lube hole to provide proper lubrication.*

Reassembly — 1) Install drive and driven gear in pump housing with identification mark or chamfered surface of each gear installed toward front of pump housing. Position stator support in pump housing, then install and tighten attaching bolts.

2) Carefully install 2 new seal rings on stator support. Make sure ends of rings are engaged to lock them in place. Install a new square cut seal on outside diameter of pump housing.

3) Install selective thrust washer. Place pump on torque converter, making sure that the drive gear engages converter hub. Rotate pump to ensure that gears rotate freely.

DRIVE TRAIN

Separate drive train into subassembly components. See *Fig. 18.*

NOTE — *Different clutch assemblies are used in various models, when disassembling clutches, note number and location of plates used for reassembly reference.*

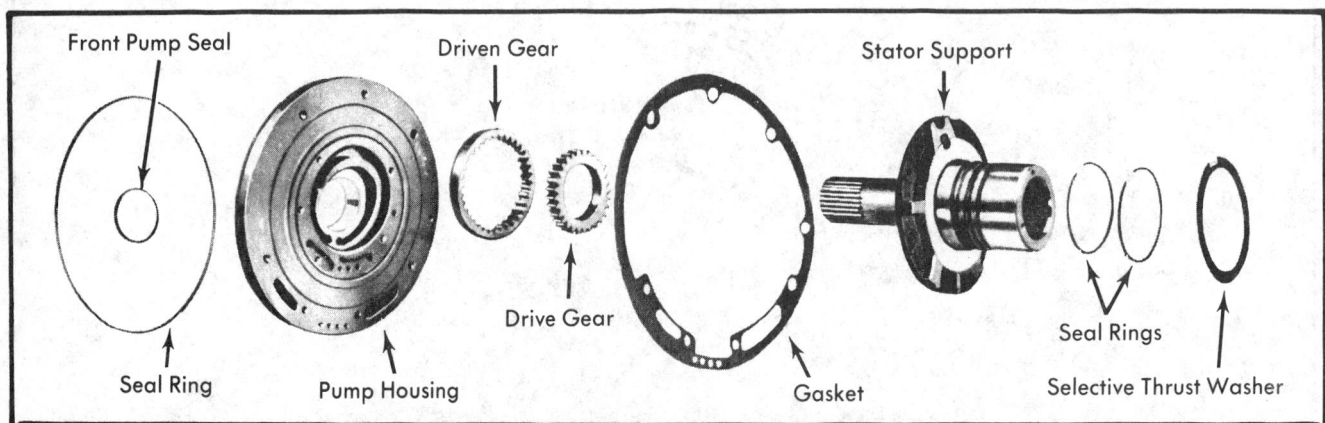

Fig. 17　Exploded View of Front Pump Assembly

FORD C-6 (Cont.)

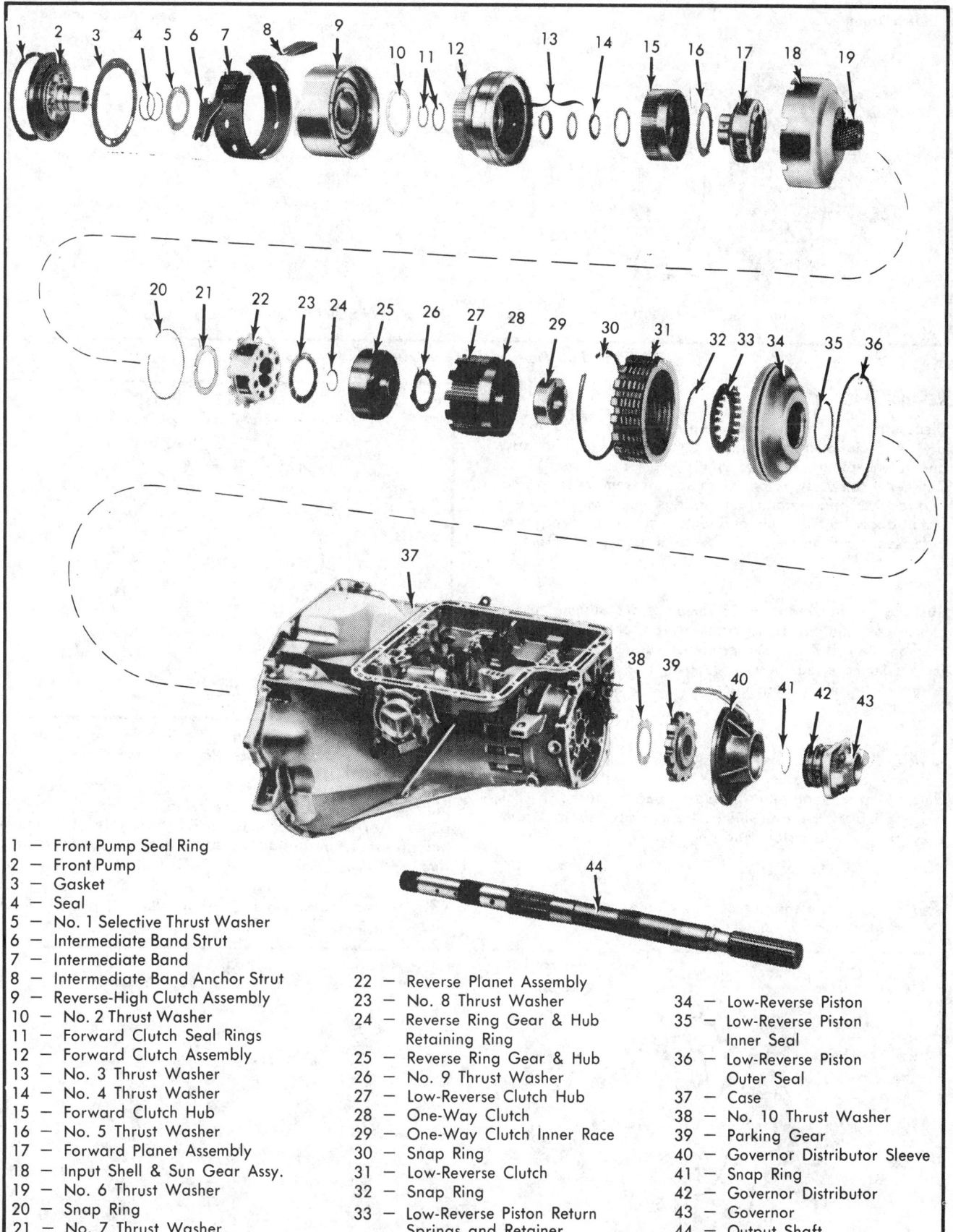

1 — Front Pump Seal Ring
2 — Front Pump
3 — Gasket
4 — Seal
5 — No. 1 Selective Thrust Washer
6 — Intermediate Band Strut
7 — Intermediate Band
8 — Intermediate Band Anchor Strut
9 — Reverse-High Clutch Assembly
10 — No. 2 Thrust Washer
11 — Forward Clutch Seal Rings
12 — Forward Clutch Assembly
13 — No. 3 Thrust Washer
14 — No. 4 Thrust Washer
15 — Forward Clutch Hub
16 — No. 5 Thrust Washer
17 — Forward Planet Assembly
18 — Input Shell & Sun Gear Assy.
19 — No. 6 Thrust Washer
20 — Snap Ring
21 — No. 7 Thrust Washer

22 — Reverse Planet Assembly
23 — No. 8 Thrust Washer
24 — Reverse Ring Gear & Hub
       Retaining Ring
25 — Reverse Ring Gear & Hub
26 — No. 9 Thrust Washer
27 — Low-Reverse Clutch Hub
28 — One-Way Clutch
29 — One-Way Clutch Inner Race
30 — Snap Ring
31 — Low-Reverse Clutch
32 — Snap Ring
33 — Low-Reverse Piston Return
       Springs and Retainer

34 — Low-Reverse Piston
35 — Low-Reverse Piston
       Inner Seal
36 — Low-Reverse Piston
       Outer Seal
37 — Case
38 — No. 10 Thrust Washer
39 — Parking Gear
40 — Governor Distributor Sleeve
41 — Snap Ring
42 — Governor Distributor
43 — Governor
44 — Output Shaft

Fig. 18 Exploded View of Transmission Case and Drive Train Assembly

FORD C-6 (Cont.)

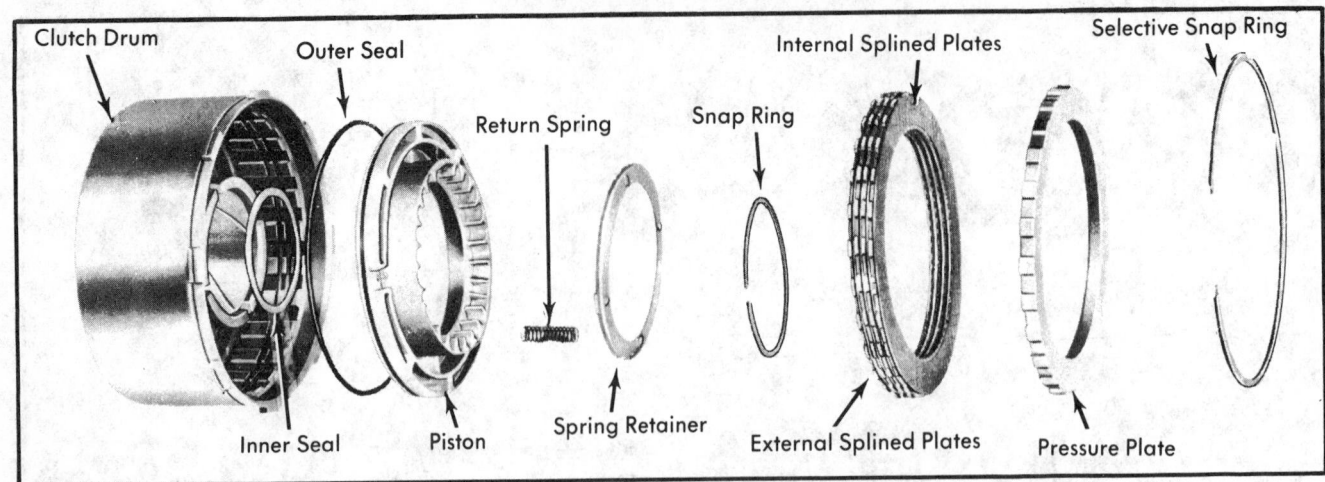

Fig. 19   Exploded View of Reverse-High Clutch Assembly

REVERSE-HIGH CLUTCH

Disassembly — Remove pressure plate retaining snap ring by prying up with a screwdriver, and remove pressure plate, drive and driven plates. Using a suitable compressor tool (T65L-77515-A), compress piston return springs, remove snap ring, and remove spring retainer and springs. Apply air pressure to piston apply hole in drum and remove piston. Remove piston outer seal from piston, and inner seal from clutch drum.

Bushing Replacement — To remove front bushing, use a cape chisel and cut along bushing seam until chisel breaks through bushing wall, then pry loose ends of bushing up to remove. Remove rear bushing using a press ram and bushing adapters. Install bushings using suitable bushing drivers.

Reassembly — 1) Dip new seals in transmission fluid and install one seal on piston and one in drum. Install piston into clutch drum. Position return springs in pockets as shown, then place spring retainer over springs. Using compressor tool, compress springs and install snap ring. See Fig. 20.

NOTE — *Before releasing tool, make sure snap ring is seated INSIDE four snap ring guides on spring retainer.*

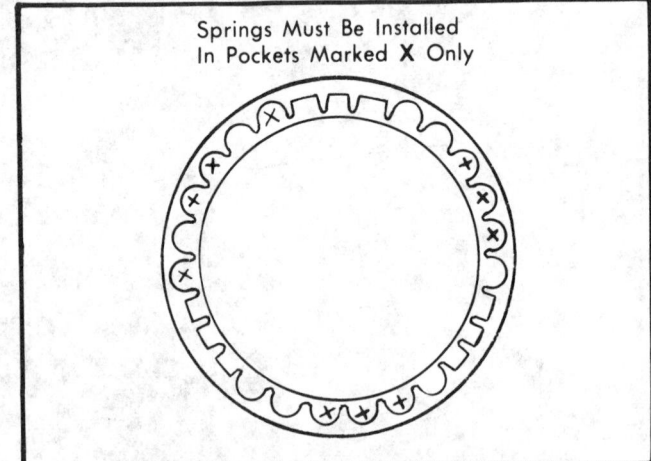

Fig. 20   View Showing Correct Positioning of Reverse-High Clutch Piston Return Springs

2) Install clutch plates alternately starting with a steel drive plate. If new clutch plates are being installed, composition plates must be soaked in transmission fluid for 15 minutes before installation. Install pressure plate and retaining snap ring.

NOTE — *See Clutch Plate Chart for the number of clutch plates required.*

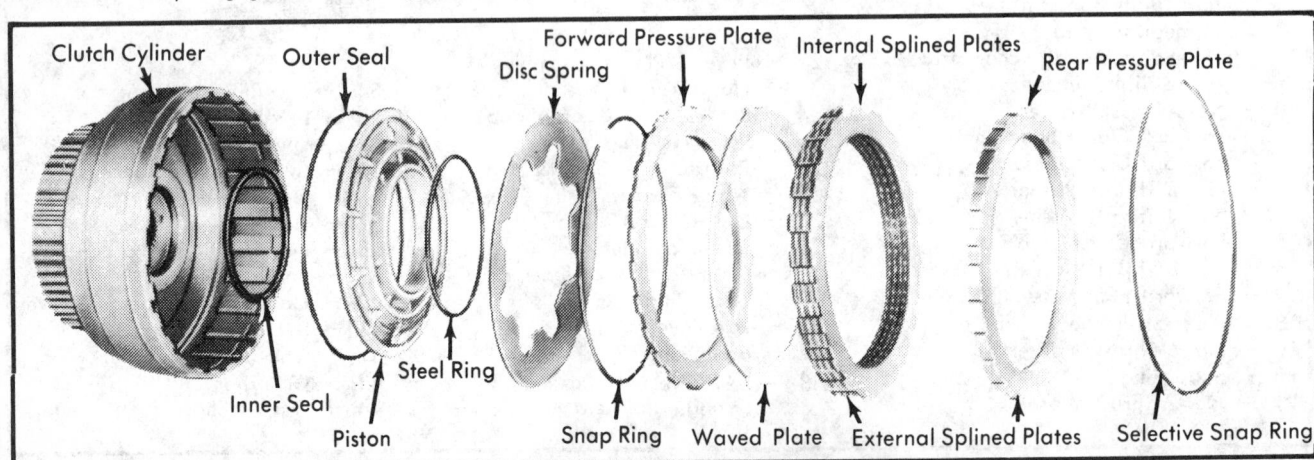

Fig. 21   Exploded View of Forward Clutch Assembly

FORD C-6 (Cont.)

3) Using a feeler gauge, check clearance between pressure plate and snap ring. **NOTE** – *Hold pressure plate downward while measuring.* Clearance should be .022-.036". If clearance is not within specifications, selective snap rings are available in the following thicknesses: .056-.060", .065-.069", .074-.078", .083-.087", .092-.096", .110-.114" and .128-.132". Install correct thickness snap ring and recheck clearance.

Clutch Plate Chart

Application	Flat Steel Plates	Composition Plates
Reverse-High Clutch	3	3
Forward Clutch	①4	4
Low-Reverse Clutch		
Original Case	②5	5
Replacement Case	5	5

① – Plus one WAVED plate installed next to inner pressure plate.
② – Plus one WAVED plate installed next to piston.

FORWARD CLUTCH

Disassembly – Remove clutch pressure plate retaining snap ring, and remove rear pressure plate, drive and driven plates, and forward pressure plate from clutch drum. Remove snap ring securing disc spring in drum and remove disc spring. Apply air pressure to clutch apply passage in drum and remove piston. Remove seals from piston and drum.

Reassembly – 1) Dip two new seals in transmission fluid, and install smaller seal on clutch hub and other seal on piston. Install clutch piston in cylinder. Make sure steel pressure ring is in groove on piston. Place disc spring in clutch drum with dished face downward, then secure in place with retaining snap ring.

NOTE – *If new composition plates are being installed, soak them in transmission fluid for 15 minutes prior to installation.*

2) Install forward pressure plate with flat side up and beveled side downward. Dip the clutch plates in transmission fluid. Install clutch plates starting with the waved plate, then a steel plate and a composition plate. Install remaining plates in this sequence.

NOTE – *See Clutch Plate Chart for the number of clutch plates required.*

3) Using a feeler gauge, check clearance between snap ring and pressure plate. **NOTE** – *Hold pressure plate downward while measuring.* Clearance should be .021"-.046". If clearance is not within specifications, selective snap rings are available in following thicknesses: .056-.060", .065-.069", .074-.078", .083-.087", .092-.096", .110-.114" and .128-.132". Install correct snap ring and recheck clearance.

INPUT SHELL & SUN GEAR

Disassembly – Remove rear (external) snap ring from sun gear and remove thrust washer from sun gear and input shell. Working inside input shell, remove sun gear, then remove internal (forward) snap ring from gear.

Reassembly – Install forward snap ring on short end of sun gear. Working inside input shell, slide sun gear and snap ring into place, making sure longer end of gear is at rear. Place thrust washer on rear end of input shell and sun gear, then install rear snap ring.

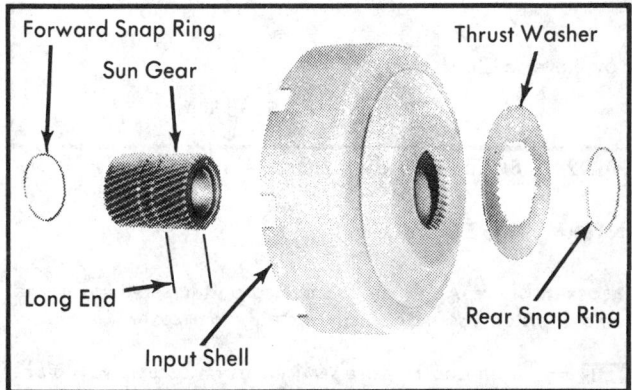

Fig. 22   Exploded View of Input Shell & Sun Gear

OUTPUT SHAFT HUB & RING GEAR

Disassembly & Reassembly – If necessary to remove these parts, remove hub retaining snap ring and lift hub from ring gear. When installing, secure hub with retaining snap ring, making sure snap ring is fully engaged in groove.

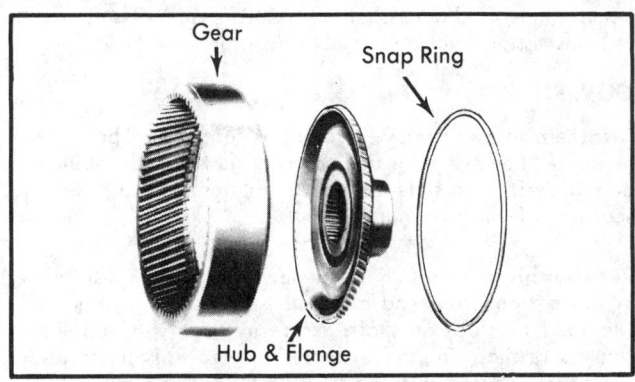

Fig. 23   Output Shaft Hub and Ring Gear

ONE-WAY CLUTCH

Disassembly – Remove snap ring and bushing from rear of low-reverse clutch hub. Remove rollers from spring assembly, then lift spring assembly from hub. Remove remaining snap ring from hub.

Reassembly – Install snap ring in forward groove of low-reverse clutch hub. Place hub on bench with forward end down. Install spring assembly on top of snap ring, then install a roller into each of the spring assembly compartments. Install bushing on top of spring assembly, then install remaining snap ring at rear of clutch hub to secure assembly.

FORD C-6 (Cont.)

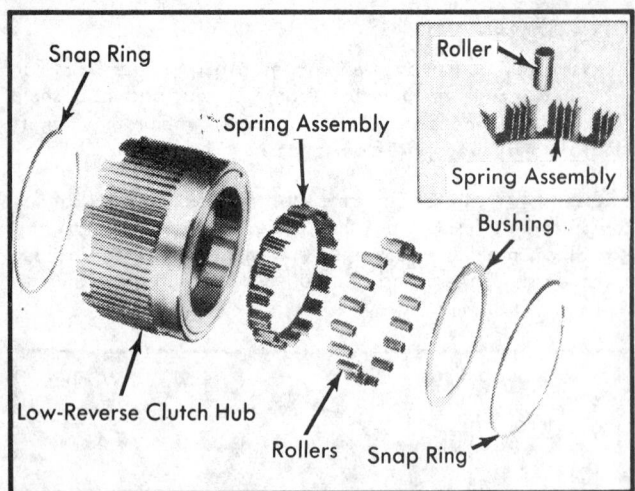

Fig. 24   Exploded View of One-Way Clutch Assembly

INTERMEDIATE SERVO

Disassembly — Apply air pressure to port in servo cover and remove piston assembly. Remove seal from cover.

NOTE — *Piston and rod are serviced as an assembly, replace if piston or sealing lips are damaged.*

Reassembly — Dip new seal in transmission fluid and install on cover. Dip piston assembly in transmission fluid and install in cover.

LOW-REVERSE CLUTCH PISTON

NOTE — *Clutch is assembled as part of transmission reassembly; replace seals as follows:*

Remove inner and outer seals from clutch piston. Dip new seals in transmission fluid and install on piston.

GOVERNOR

Disassembly — Remove governor attaching bolts and governor. Remove snap ring securing governor distributor to output shaft, then slide distributor off front of shaft. Remove seal rings from governor distributor.

Reassembly — Carefully install new seal rings on distributor. Working from front end of output shaft, slide governor distributor into place on shaft. Secure in place with snap ring. Make sure snap ring is fully seated in groove. Position governor on distributor, install and tighten attaching screws.

TRANSMISSION REASSEMBLY

1) With transmission in a holding fixture, tap low-reverse clutch piston into case with a rubber hammer. Hold one-way clutch inner race in position, then install and tighten attaching bolts. Install low-reverse clutch return spring and retainer assembly in clutch piston. Position snap ring on one-way clutch inner race, then compress return spring and retainer and seat snap ring in groove.

2) Place transmission case on bench with front end facing downward. Position parking gear thrust washer and gear on case. It is not necessary to restake thrust washer. Position oil distributor and tubes on rear of case. Install and tighten attaching bolts. Install output shaft and governor as an assembly. Place a new gasket on rear of case, install extension housing and attaching bolts and tighten to specifications. Install vent tube.

3) Coat 2 new servo cover gaskets with petroleum jelly and position them on servo cover. Place servo spring on piston rod and install in case. Install attaching bolts, making sure identification tag is under one of the cover bolts and tighten to specifications. Align low-reverse clutch hub and one-way clutch with inner race at rear of case.

4) Rotate low-reverse clutch hub clockwise while applying pressure to seat it on inner race. Install low-reverse clutch plates, starting with the waved plate next to piston and follow with a steel, then a composition plate until all plates are installed. Retain plates with petroleum jelly. Install pressure plate and snap ring.

5) Test operation of low-reverse clutch assembly by applying air pressure to clutch pressure apply hole in case. Install reverse planet ring gear thrust washer, ring gear and hub assembly. Install snap ring in groove of output shaft. Install front and rear thrust washers onto reverse planet assembly using petroleum jelly to retain.

6) Install assembly into ring gear and install snap ring. Place reverse-high clutch on bench with front end facing downward. Install thrust washer on rear end of assembly and retain with petroleum jelly. Install splined end of forward clutch into open end of reverse-high clutch with splines engaging direct clutch plates.

7) Install thrust washer on front end of forward planet ring gear and hub and retain with petroleum jelly. Install ring gear into forward clutch and install thrust washer on front end of forward planet assembly and retain with petroleum jelly. Install assembly into ring gear, then install input shell and sun assembly.

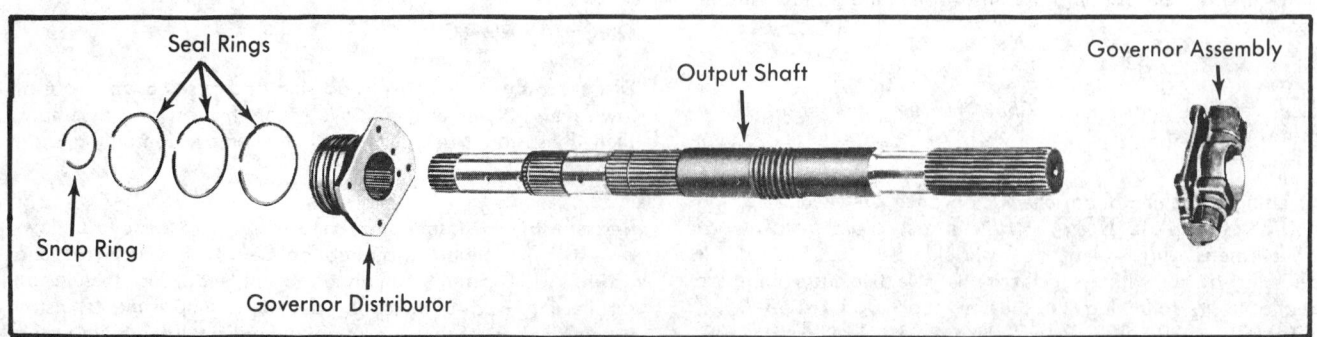

Fig. 25   Exploded View of Output Shaft and Governor Assembly

FORD C-6 (Cont.)

8) Install reverse-high clutch, forward clutch, forward planet assembly, input shell and sun gear as an assembly into case. Install intermediate band around direct clutch drum. Install band struts and tighten band adjusting screw enough to retain band. Place selective bronze thrust washer on rear shoulder of stator support and retain with petroleum jelly.

9) If end play was not within specifications when disassembled, replace washer at this time with one of correct thickness. Using $\frac{5}{16}$ x 3″ bolts, make 2 alignment studs by cutting the heads off and grinding a taper on the cut end. Install the studs opposite each other in case mounting holes. Slide a new gasket onto the studs. Position pump on case, being careful not to damage the seal on pump housing, and remove studs. Install 6 of the mounting bolts and tighten. Tighten intermediate band adjusting screw to 10 ft. lbs.

10) Back off screw exactly $1\frac{1}{2}$ turns. Hold adjusting screw in this position and tighten lock nut to specifications. Install input shaft with long splined end inserted into forward clutch assembly. Check end play again to insure correct assembly. Install control valve body into case, making sure levers engage valves properly.

11) Install primary throttle valve, rod and vacuum diaphragm in case. Install oil pan with new gasket, install attaching bolts and tighten to specifications. Install torque converter.

Selective Thrust Washers

Color Code	Thickness
Blue	.056-.060″
Natural (White)	.073-.077″
Red	.088-.092″

TIGHTENING SPECIFICATIONS

Application	Ft. Lbs.
Converter-to-Flywheel	20-30
Front Pump-to-Case	16-30
Overrunning Clutch Race-to-Case	18-25
Oil Pan-to-Case	12-16
Stator Support-to-Pump	12-16
Converter Cover-to-Housing	12-16
Guide Plate-to-Case	12-16
Intermediate Servo Cover-to-Case	14-20
Diaphragm Assembly-to-Case	12-16
Distributor Sleeve-to-Case	12-16
Extension Housing-to-Case	25-35
Pressure Gauge Tap	9-15
Band Adjusting Screw Lock Nut	35-45
Cooler Tube Connector Lock	20-35
Converter Drain Plug	14-28
Manual Valve Inner Lever-to-Shaft	30-40
Downshift Lever-to-Shaft	12-16
Filler Tube-to-Engine	20-25
Transmission-to-Engine	40-50
Rear Engine Support-to-Frame	40-60
Rear Engine Support-to-Trans.	55-65
TRS Switch Port Plug	6-12
Line Pressure Plug	6-12
Throttle Pressure Plug	6-12
Ext. Hsg.-to-Bearing Ret. Stud	35-50
Bearing Ret.-to-Ext. Housing	35-45

Application	INCH Lbs.
End Plates-to-Valve Body	20-45
Inner Downshift Lever Stop	20-45
Reinforcement Plate-to-Valve Body	20-45
Screen & Lower-to-Upper Valve Body	40-55
Valve Body-to-Case	95-125
Governor Body-to-Collector Body	80-120
Oil Tube Connector	60-120
Detent Spring-to-Case	80-120
Shift Valve Plate-to-Upper Body	20-45
Upper-to-Lower Valve Body	40-55
Right Side Plate-to-Lower Body	20-45
Neutral Switch-to-Case	55-75
Yoke-to-Output Shaft (4-WD)	100-150

GENERAL MOTORS TORQUE CONVERTER CLUTCH (TCC) SYSTEM

All Models With
Turbo Hydra-Matic 350C

DESCRIPTION

The torque converter clutch assembly consists of a 3 element torque converter with the addition of a converter clutch. The converter clutch is an internal mechanism with a friction material attached to the front plate and is splined to the turbine assembly. When operated, it applies against the converter cover providing a mechanical direct drive coupling of the engine to transmission planetary gears. By applying converter clutch, slippage is eliminated, resulting in improved fuel economy and reduced fluid operating temperatures. When converter clutch is released, converter operates in conventional manner.

The converter clutch apply and release is controlled by a series of controls and by drive range selection. On 4-WD vehicles, when transfer case shifter is shifted from 2H to 4L or 4H, circuit to TCC system is opened. In this position (4L or 4H) converter clutch will not apply. When transfer case is shifted back to 2H, TCC system should operate in normal manner. If vehicle does not shift out of 4L or 4H, converter clutch will not apply. Converter clutch is applied in direct drive and above a minimum preset vehicle speed. Clutch apply and release is controlled by the position of the converter clutch apply valve located in an auxiliary valve body in transmission. Apply valve is controlled by a solenoid. The converter clutch is applied when all of the following conditions exist: Transmission is in direct drive range, 3rd gear; Vehicle speed is between 24-30 MPH; Engine coolant temperature is above 130°F; Engine vacuum is above 2.5 in. Hg and brake pedal is released, then governor pressure switch closes, completing the ground circuit and energizes the solenoid.

To further aid the apply and release of the converter clutch during various driving conditions, several controls have been incorporated in the vacuum/electrical system. These controls are external to the transmission and perform the following functions:

Brake Release Switch — Used on all models, switch releases the converter clutch when brakes are applied.

Low Vacuum Switch — Used on all models, switch releases the converter clutch when engine vacuum drops to a pre-set level during moderate acceleration, part-throttle or detent downshifts and during zero throttle coast-down.

High Vacuum Switch — Used on diesel models only, switch releases the converter clutch during zero throttle coast-down.

Thermal Vacuum Valve — Used on gasoline models only, valve prevents the converter clutch from applying at coolant temperatures below 130°F.

TROUBLE SHOOTING

See General Motors Torque Converter Clutch Trouble Shooting Table in AUTOMATIC TRANSMISSION TROUBLE SHOOTING.

TESTING

INTERNAL CONTROLS CHECK

1) Disconnect transmission case connector. Using a 12 volt test light, connect positive lead to female connector and ground negative lead to male connector.

2) Start engine and run at 2000 RPM in "P". If test light comes "ON", governor switch or internal wiring is shorted to ground. Remove oil pan and gasket. Check wiring and/or replace governor pressure switch.

3) If test light remains "OFF", raise rear wheels and run vehicle in "D" range until 3rd gear upshift is obtained, keeping engine at 2000 RPM.

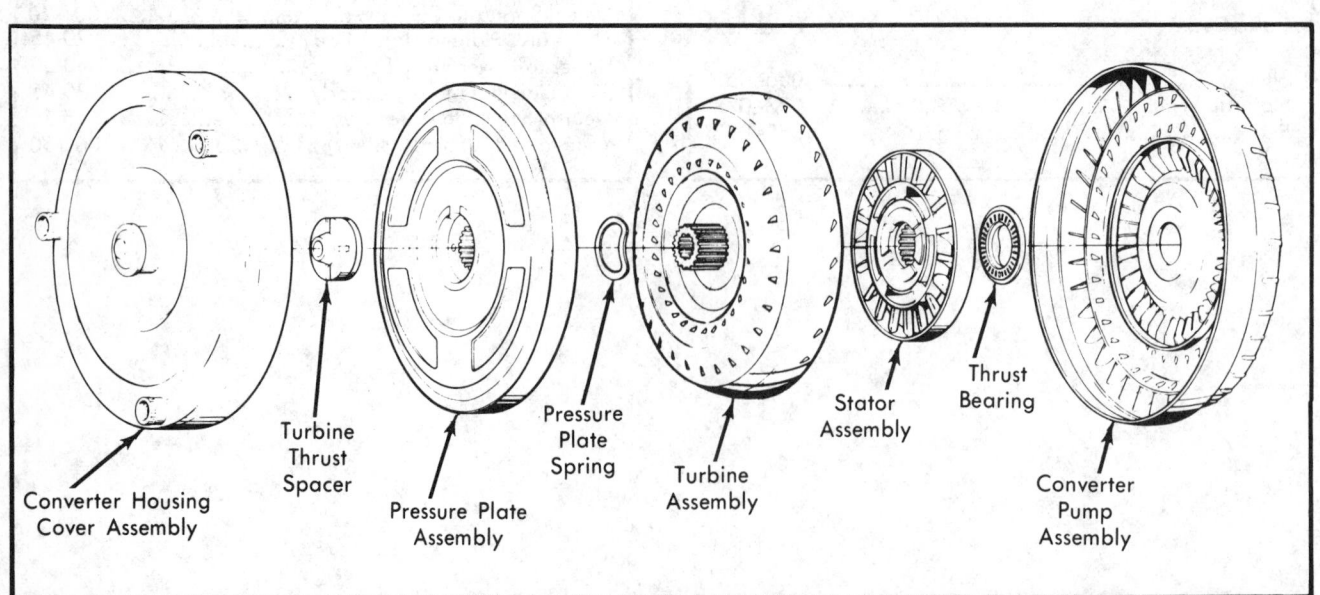

Fig. 1 Exploded View of General Motors Torque Converter Clutch Assembly

GENERAL MOTORS TORQUE CONVERTER CLUTCH (TCC) SYSTEM (Cont.)

4) If test light now comes "ON", verify proper operation of Internal Hydraulic/Mechanical Controls. *See Internal Hydraulic/Mechanical Controls Test.*

5) If test light remains "OFF", there is a solenoid electrical malfunction or governor switch malfunction. Remove oil pan and gasket. Using an external 12 volt source, connect positive lead to case connector terminal. Remove lead wire from governor pressure switch and connect to ground lead of external 12 volt source.

- If solenoid clicks, solenoid is okay electrically, replace governor pressure switch.
- If solenoid does not click, check wiring to solenoid, replace solenoid and recheck.

CAUTION — *Solenoid diode will be damaged if internal voltage source is connected in reverse.*

INTERNAL HYDRAULIC/MECHANICAL CONTROLS CHECK

NOTE — *The following is to test governor for internal hydraulic/mechanical operation.*

1) Obtain a known good governor for testing. Cut two pieces of $5/32"$ vacuum hose into $3/8"$ lengths. Insert one hose under each governor weight as shown in *Fig. 2*.

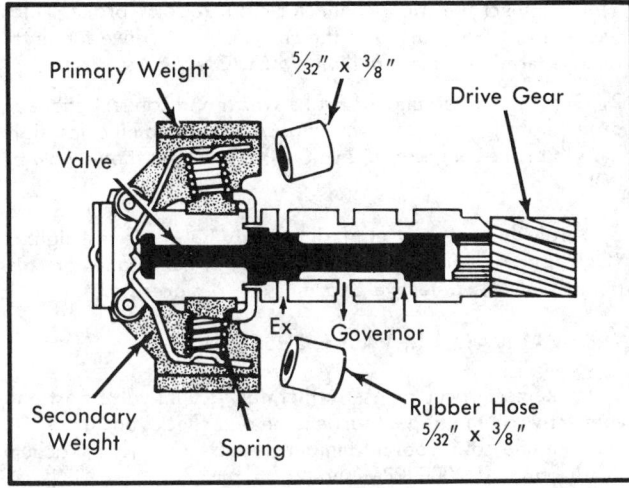

Fig. 2   *Positioning Hoses Under Governor Weights*

2) Remove engine vacuum switch electrical connector. Using a jumper wire, connect both female terminals of electrical connector together. To check for proper hook-ups, turn ignition switch "ON", raise vehicle and check for 12 volts at transmission case female connector. If connections are correct, 12 volts will be present at case connector.

3) Replace governor with test governor. Lower vehicle leaving rear wheels several inches off ground. Apply parking brake (wheels must not turn). Start engine in "P" and run at idle. Depress brake pedal (this will break current flow to solenoid).

4) Place selector lever in "D" range, 3rd gear (transmission will automatically shift into 3rd gear because test governor is causing high governor pressure). Release brake pedal, engine should stall immediately.

5) If engine stalls, converter clutch internal controls are working properly. If engine does not stall, proceed as follows:

- Check for missing or damaged "O" ring at end of turbine shaft.
- Check solenoid for missing plunger.
- Check for loose solenoid bolts.
- Check for defective solenoid ball seat or ball.
- Check converter clutch apply valve for sticking, binding or damage.
- Check direct clutch oil passages in pump for restrictions or being interconnected.
- Check for defective converter.

6) After test, remove test governor and replace it with original governor. If original governor was used for test, remove pieces of hose that were inserted between weights and make sure that weight springs are in correct position before reinstalling in transmission.

EXTERNAL CONTROLS CHECK

1) Turn ignition switch "ON". Check vacuum switch connector for 12 volts and proper operation *(see Vacuum Switch Check).* If no voltage is present at vacuum switch, check the following:

- Converter clutch fuse in fuse block.
- Brake release switch *(see Brake Release Switch Check).*
- Vacuum switch wiring.

2) If 12 volts are present at vacuum switch and switch is okay, reconnect electrical connector to vacuum switch. Using a hand-held vacuum pump, apply 2.5-7.0 inches of vacuum to switch.

3) With ignition switch "ON", again check for 12 volts at female end of connector. If no or low voltage is present, check and/or repair wire between vacuum switch and transmission.

4) If 12 volts are present at transmission, check Thermal Vacuum valve for proper operation. If okay, system is operating properly.

VACUUM SWITCH CHECK
(GASOLINE MODELS ONLY)

1) Disconnect electrical connector and hose from vacuum switch. Ground 1 terminal of vacuum switch electrical connector and connect a test light lead to the other terminal. Connect the remaining lead of test light to a 12 volt battery.

2) Attach a hand vacuum pump (with gauge) to vacuum port of switch. Turn ignition switch "ON" and actuate vacuum pump. Test light should be "OFF" and remain "OFF" until vacuum gauge reads between 2.5-7 in. Hg. At this point, test light should come "ON".

3) Decrease vacuum slowly, light should remain "ON" until vacuum gauge reads between 1.5-2.5 in. Hg. If vacuum switch does not operate as specified, switch is defective and should be replaced.

NOTE — *The high vacuum limit (point at which test light goes "OFF") and low vacuum limit (point at which test light comes back "ON") must have at least 4 in. Hg difference.*

GENERAL MOTORS TORQUE CONVERTER CLUTCH (TCC) SYSTEM (Cont.)

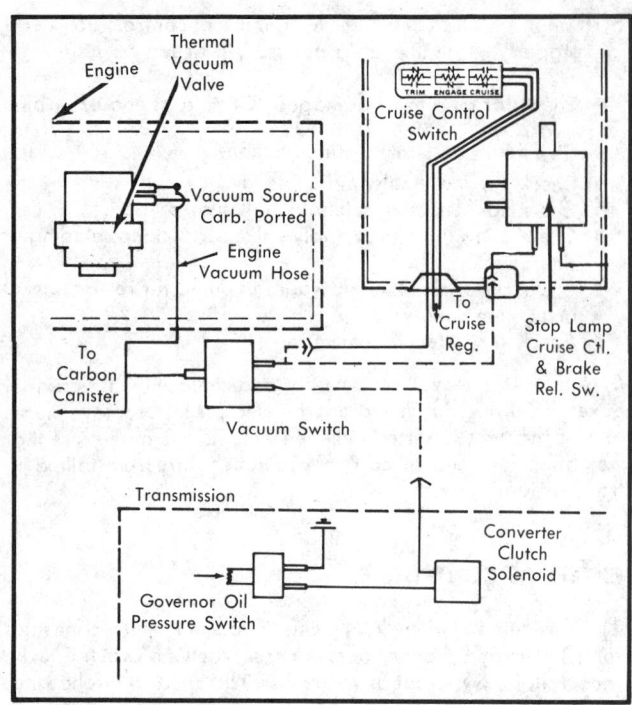

Fig. 3   Torque Converter Clutch System Diagram (Gasoline Models Only)

3) Decrease vacuum slowly, light should remain "OFF" until 12.5 inches of vacuum is obtained. Test light should now come "ON". If high vacuum switch does not turn test light "ON" and "OFF" at specified vacuum level, switch is defective.

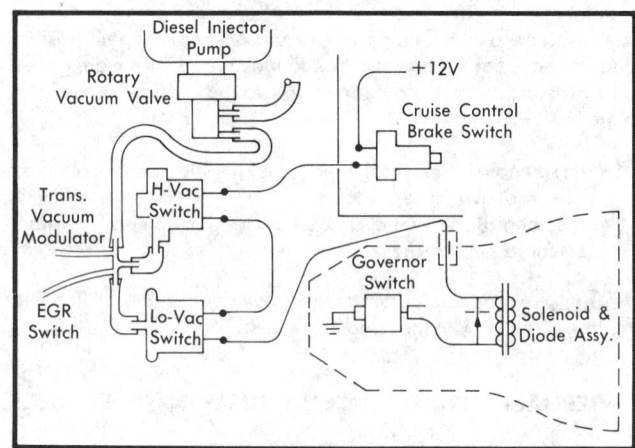

Fig. 4   Torque Converter Clutch System Diagram (Diesel Models Only)

LOW VACUUM SWITCH CHECK (DIESEL MODELS ONLY)

1) Disconnect vacuum hose and electrical connector from low vacuum switch. Attach one lead of test light to either terminal of switch and ground remaining terminal. Attach remaining test light lead to 12 volt ("Hot") side of vacuum switch connector.

2) Attach a hand-held vacuum pump to vacuum port of switch. Turn ignition switch "ON" and apply vacuum to switch. Test light should remain off until about 5.5 inches of vacuum is obtained. Test light should now come "ON".

3) Decrease vacuum slowly, light should remain "ON" until approximately 4.0 inches of vacuum is obtained. Test light should now go "OFF". If vacuum switch does not turn test light "ON" and "OFF" at specified vacuum levels, switch is defective.

HIGH VACUUM SWITCH CHECK (DIESEL MODELS ONLY)

NOTE — *High vacuum switch is used on diesel models only and is located near the low vacuum switch. Switch is identified by vacuum port located on side rather than on end of switch.*

1) Disconnect vacuum hose and electrical connector from high vacuum switch. Connect one lead of test light to either terminal of switch and ground remaining terminal. Attach remaining test light lead to 12 volt ("Hot") side of battery.

2) Attach hand-held vacuum pump to switch vacuum port. Turn ignition switch "ON" and apply vacuum to switch. Test light should remain "ON" until 12.5 inches of vacuum is obtained. Test light should now go "OFF".

BRAKE RELEASE SWITCH CHECK

1) Disconnect electrical connector from rear of brake switch under dash. These are also the cruise control/converter clutch release terminals. Turn ignition switch "ON".

2) Ground one terminal of brake switch and connect one lead of test light to remaining terminal. Attach remaining test light lead to brake connector (12 volt) wire. Test light should now be "ON".

3) Apply brakes, test light should go "OFF". If test light is "OFF" before applying brakes or "ON" when brakes are applied, switch is defective and must be replaced.

THERMAL VACUUM VALVE CHECK

1) Disconnect vacuum hose at thermal vacuum valve port and connect vacuum gauge. Start engine and check vacuum in "P". With engine cold, coolant temperature below 130°F, vacuum at idle and at 2000 RPM should be zero.

2) With engine at normal operating temperature, vacuum at idle should be zero while vacuum at 2000 RPM should be 10 inches Hg minimum.

SOLENOID DIODE CHECKS

CAUTION — *Solenoids may be checked using ONLY a METER READING or SCALE TYPE ohmmeter, set on the x1 scale. Electronic or digital type meters CANNOT be used because a false defective indication can be obtained. DO NOT bench test solenoid by touching leads to an automotive battery.*

Solenoid Diode Testing Procedure — **1)** Set ohmmeter on the x1 scale, touch leads together and zero needle. Attach positive solenoid lead (Red) to positive meter lead and

GENERAL MOTORS TORQUE CONVERTER CLUTCH (TCC) SYSTEM (Cont.)

negative solenoid lead (Black) to negative meter lead. Check ohmmeter reading as follows:

- A reading of 20-40 ohms (depending on solenoid temperature) indicates diode or coil is not shorted.
- A reading of zero ohms indicates diode or coil is shorted.
- An open circuit reading indicates an open coil.

2) Reverse ohmmeter and solenoid lead attachment and check ohmmeter reading again as follows:

- A lower reading than in step **1)** (usually 2-15 ohms), indicates solenoid is okay.
- Same reading as in step **1)** indicates diode is open.

ADJUSTMENT

HIGH VACUUM SWITCH (DIESEL MODELS ONLY)

NOTE — *The high vacuum switch MUST be adjusted whenever the throttle rod, vacuum regulator valve or high idle speed adjustment is changed.*

1) Disconnect high vacuum switch electrical connector. Using a self-powered test light, connect one lead to either terminal of high vacuum switch and connect probe of test light to other switch terminal.

2) Start engine and run at high idle speed, energize fast idle solenoid by disconnecting Pink and Green wire connector from coolant switch located on left rear of intake manifold. Remove seal cap on back of high vacuum switch.

3) High vacuum switch contacts must be closed (test light "ON") before making adjustment. If contacts are open (test light "OFF"), turn switch adjustment screw clockwise until contacts close.

4) Adjust vacuum switch by slowly turning adjustment screw counterclockwise until switch contacts just open (test light "OFF"). Do not turn past this point.

5) Reinstall seal cap on back of switch, reconnect vacuum switch electrical connector and coolant temperature switch connector.

NOTE — *If air cleaner is removed when making high vacuum switch adjustment, EGR solenoid port to EGR valve MUST be plugged to prevent vacuum leak at EGR solenoid.*

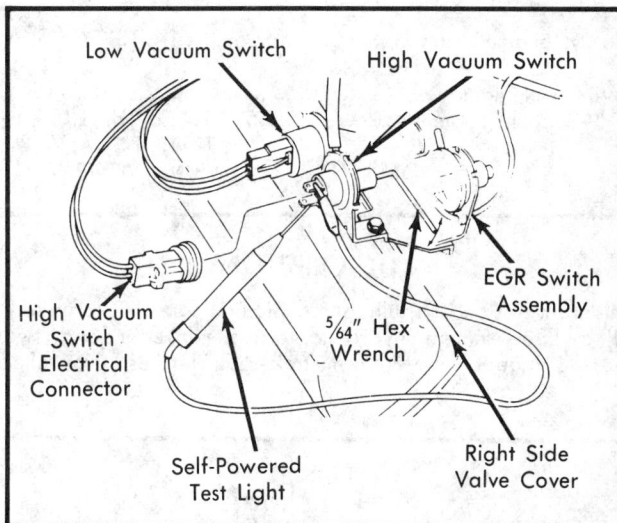

***Fig. 5 High Vacuum Switch Adjustment
(Diesel Models Only)***

Automatic Transmissions

GENERAL MOTORS TURBO HYDRA-MATIC 350 & 350C

Chevrolet
GMC

TRANSMISSION IDENTIFICATION

General Motors THM350 and 350C transmissions have 3 sets of stamped numbers. The unit number is located on right rear vertical surface of transmission oil pan. The VIN number is located on a pad on right front of transmission case. The model number is located on governor cover. Model numbers are decoded as follows:

Transmission Model Code Numbers	
Application	**Model Code**
6 Cyl. Engines	TA, TS, TX, VC, VJ, VL, VN
V8 Diesel Engines	TC
V8 Gasoline Engines	TD, TE, TH, TL, TN, TP, T3, T4, VA, VD, VE, VH, VK, VP, VS, V4, V6

DESCRIPTION

This transmission is a fully automatic unit consisting primarily of a three-element hydraulic torque converter and two planetary gear sets. Four multiple-disc clutches, two roller clutches, and an intermediate overrun band provide friction elements required to obtain desired function of two planetary gear sets. Torque converter couples engine to planetary gears through oil, and hydraulically provides additional torque multiplication when required. The two planetary gear sets give three forward ratios and one reverse.

Changing of gear ratios is fully automatic. A vacuum modulator automatically senses any change in torque input to transmission. The modulator transmits this signal to pressure regulator, which controls line pressure, so all torque requirements are met. The detent valve is activiated by a cable connected to accelerator lever assembly. When throttle is half open, valve is actuated causing throttle downshift at speeds below 50 MPH. When throttle is fully open, detent valve is actuated causing transmission to downshift from 3-1 at speeds below 40 MPH and 3-2 at speeds below 75 MPH.

LUBRICATION & ADJUSTMENT

See *Automatic Transmission Servicing* in this section.

TESTING

ROAD TEST

NOTE — *Some control pressure checks can be performed during road test.*

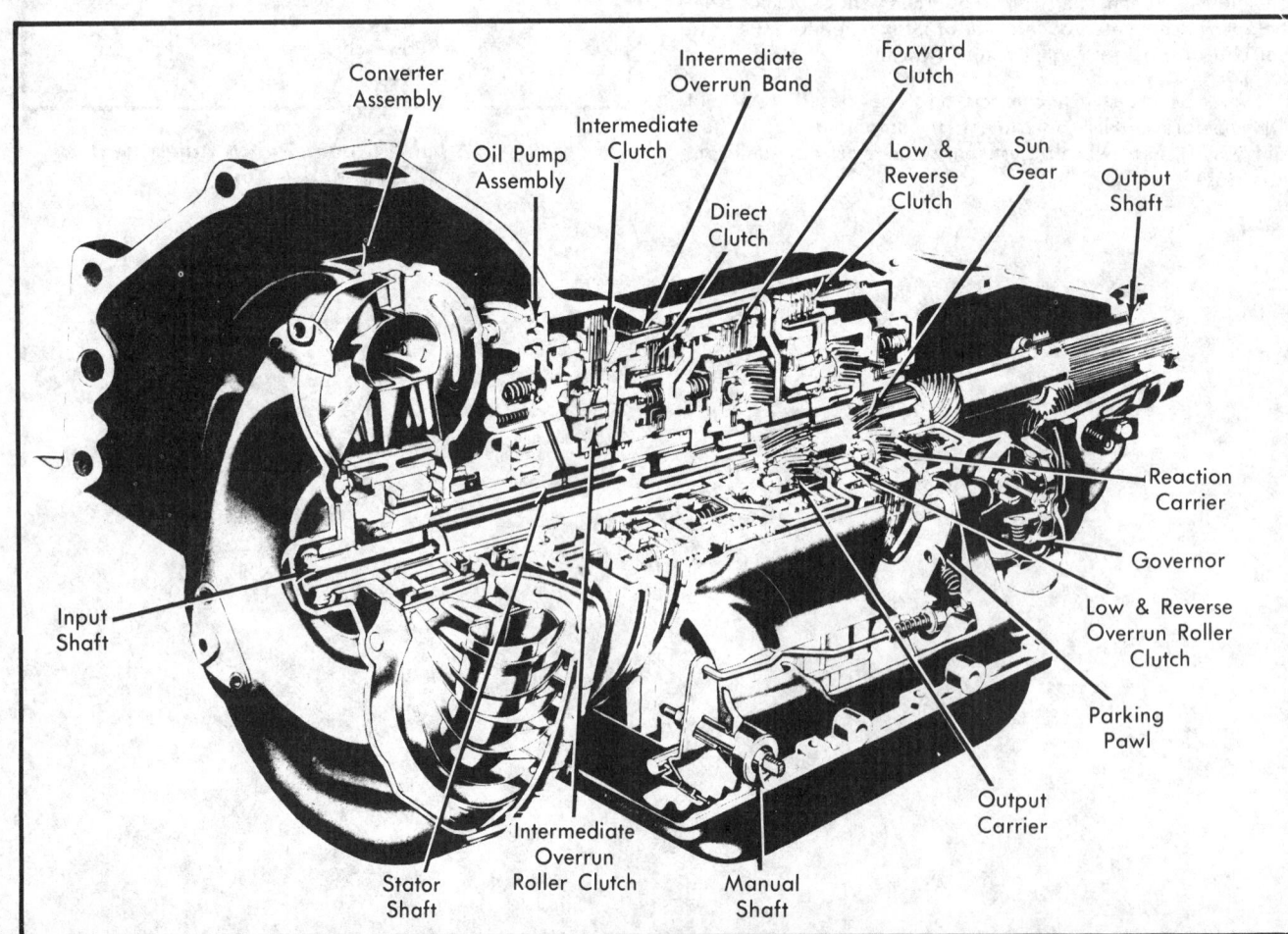

Fig. 1 Cutaway View of General Motors Turbo Hydra-Matic 350 Automatic Transmission Assembly

GENERAL MOTORS TURBO HYDRA-MATIC 350 & 350C (Cont.)

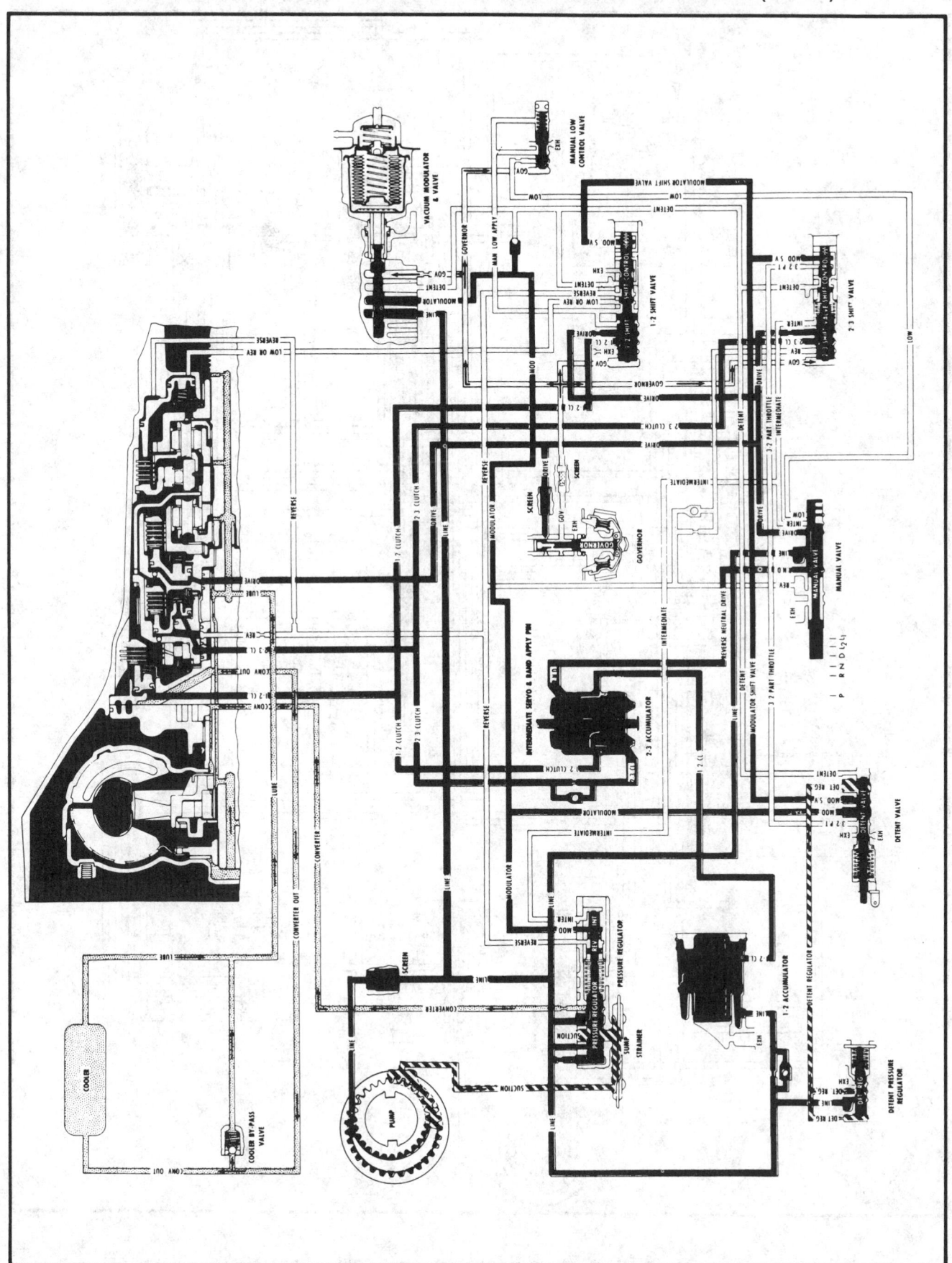

Fig. 2   Turbo Hydra-Matic 350 Hydraulic Circuits Diagram

Automatic Transmissions

GENERAL MOTORS TURBO HYDRA-MATIC 350 & 350C (Cont.)

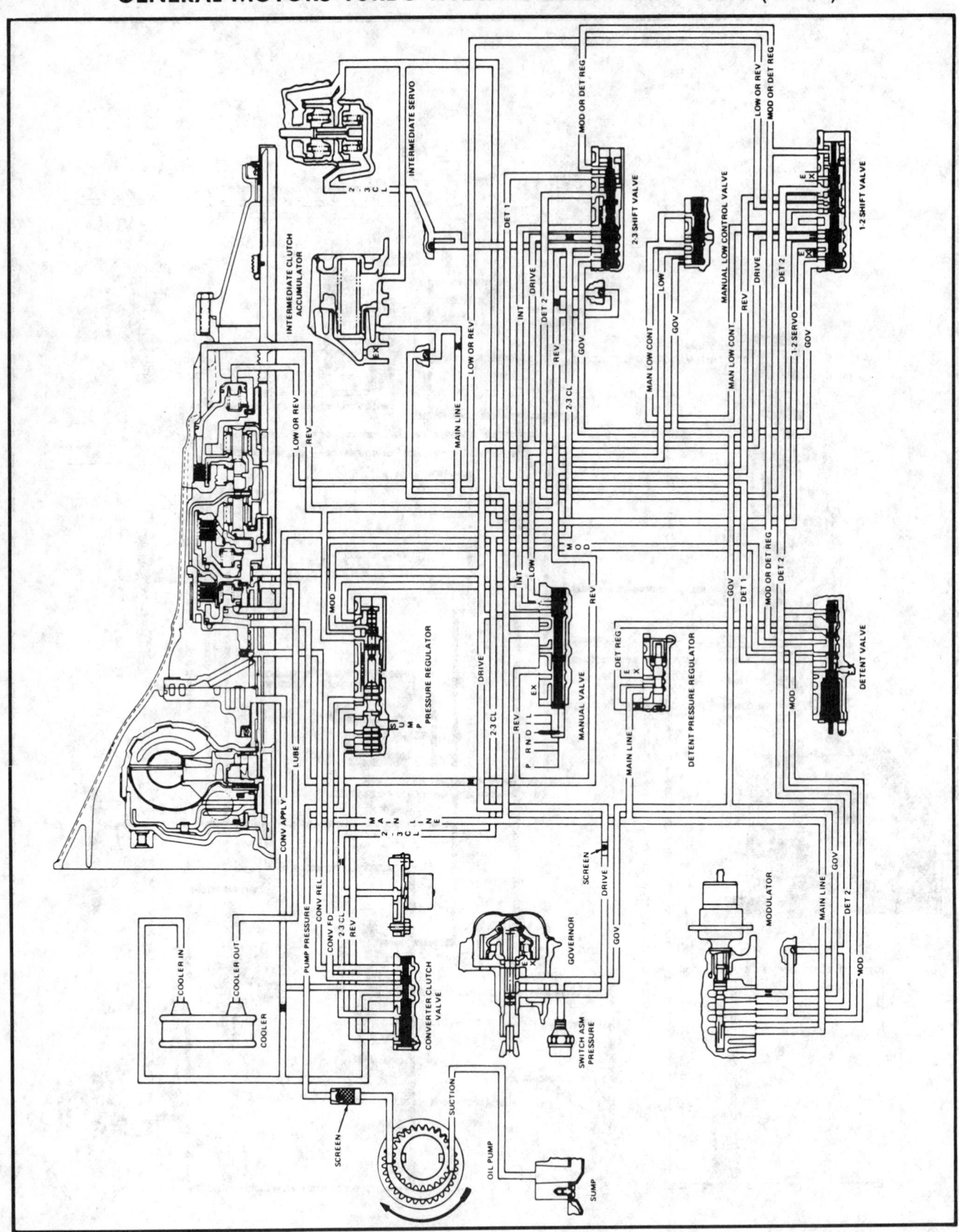

Fig. 3 *Turbo Hydra-Matic 350C Hydraulic Circuits Diagram*
(Torque Converter Clutch Applied)

GENERAL MOTORS TURBO HYDRA-MATIC 350 & 350C (Cont.)

Drive Range — With selector lever in drive range, accelerate vehicle from zero MPH. A 1-2 and 2-3 shift should occur at all throttle openings (shift points will vary with throttle openings). As vehicle speed decreases to zero MPH, 3-2 and 2-1 shifts should occur.

"2" — Forward Range (L-2) — Place selector lever in "2" and accelerate vehicle from zero MPH. A 1-2 shift should occur at all throttle openings (2-3 shift cannot be obtained in this range). The 1-2 shift point will vary with throttle opening. As vehicle speed decreases to zero MPH, a 2-1 shift should occur.

Low Range (L-1) — Place selector in low and accelerate vehicle from zero MPH. No upshift should occur in this range.

2nd Gear (L-2) — Overrun Braking — Connect a 0-300 psi pressure gauge at line pressure take-off point. With selector lever in drive range and vehicle speed at approximately 35 MPH with foot off accelerator, move selector lever to "2" position. Transmission should downshift to 2nd gear. An increase in engine RPM and an engine braking effect should be noticed. Line pressure should change from approximately 100 psi to approximately 125 psi.

1st Gear (L-1) — Overrun Braking — Connect a 0-300 psi pressure gauge at line pressure take-off point. With selector lever in "2" position and vehicle speed approximately 30-50 MPH at closed throttle, move selector lever to low range. Transmission should downshift to 1st gear between 30-45 MPH. An increase in engine RPM and an engine braking effect should be noticed. Line pressure should be approximately 150 psi.

Reverse Range — With selector lever in "R" position, check for suitable reverse operation.

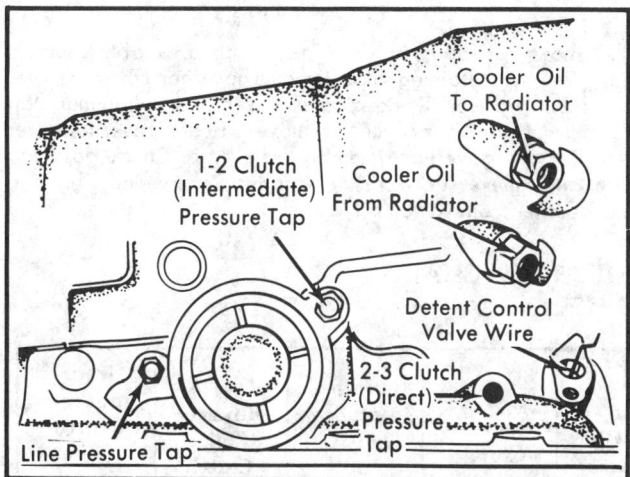

Fig. 4   View of Right Side of Transmission Case Showing Pressure Tap Locations

CONTROL PRESSURE CHECK

NOTE — *Line pressure tap is located just rearward of 1-2 accumulator (on right side of transmission case).*

Connect a tachometer to engine and a 0-300 psi pressure gauge at line pressure take-off point. With transmission fluid at correct level and operating temperature, pressure can be checked by road testing or by running engine with vehicle on stands as follows:

Stationary Check (Modulator Disconnected) — With vehicle stationary (parking brake on), engine speed set to 1200 RPM, vacuum modulator tube disconnected, and gauge installed, transmission control pressure should check approximately as shown in table.

Stationary Check (Modulator Connected) — With vehicle stationary (parking brake on), set engine speed to maintain 12 in Hg absolute manifold vacuum. Connect vacuum modulator tube. Control pressure should check approximately as shown in table.

Control Pressures (Vacuum Modulator Disconnected)	
Shift Lever Position	①**PSI**
Drive, Neutral & Park	167
L-1 or L-2	166
Reverse	254

① — Pressures are given at sea level. As altitude increases, pressure decreases.

Control Pressures (Vacuum Modulator Connected)	
Shift Lever Position	①**PSI**
Drive, Neutral & Park	85
L-1 or L-2	105
Reverse	129

① — Pressures are given at sea level. As altitude increases, pressures will also increase, while engine vacuum will decrease.

CONTROL PRESSURE TEST RESULTS

Line Pressure Too High

- Vacuum leak, vacuum line disconnected, leak in line from engine to modulator, improper engine vacuum or leak in vacuum operated accessories (hoses, vacuum advance).
- Modulator valve stuck, water in modulator, modulator damaged or not operating properly.
- Detent valve or cable stuck in detent position.
- Valve body pressure regulator and/or boost valve stuck, boost valve sleeve broken or defective, incorrect pressure regulator valve spring. 2-3 shift control valve and sleeve installed in pressure regulator bore.
- Pressure regulator exhaust hole not drilled and/or blocked.

Line Pressure Too Low

- Low transmission oil level, defective vacuum modulator assembly, strainer assembly blocked and/or restricted, gasket omitted or damaged.
- Oil pump gear clearance excessive, gears damaged or incorrectly installed, pump-to-case gasket mispositioned, defective pump body and/or cover, bottom seal ring on pump cover hub omitted or damaged, priming valve in pump omitted.

GENERAL MOTORS TURBO HYDRA-MATIC 350 & 350C (Cont.)

- Valve body pressure regulator and/or boost valve stuck, pressure regulator spring too weak, number 1 check ball omitted, loose valve body bolts, spacer plate support omitted or reverse/modulator booster valve stuck.

Line Pressure Low in Drive, But Normal in Neutral or Reverse

- Leak in forward clutch. Check pump oil seal rings or forward clutch seals.

Line Pressure Low in Reverse, Normal in All Other Ranges

- Leak in direct clutch. Check direct clutch outer seal. Check 1-2 and 2-3 accumulator pistons and rings for damage or missing components.
- Intermediate servo piston seal ring broken or omitted. Case assembly check ball missing from cored passage in case face.

No Line Pressure

- Cast flashing blocking suction cavity in case. Priming valve in pump omitted. Front pump drive gear lugs sheared off. Vacuum modulator valve omitted. Pump-to-case gasket incorrectly installed.

VACUUM MODULATOR CHECK

See procedures given in General Motors Turbo Hydra-Matic 400 article in this Section.

SERVICE (IN VEHICLE)

The following units may be removed from transmission without removing transmission from vehicle: Oil pan and gasket, oil filter, valve body, pressure regulator valve, governor, modulator and valve, manual linkage, parking pawl, oil filler pipe and "O" ring, detent cable, front accumulator piston, speedometer driven gear, rear servo and accumulator assembly, and case extension housing and seal. See procedures given in Transmission Disassembly and Transmission Reassembly.

TORQUE CONVERTER

NOTE — For servicing the torque converter clutch converter, see GM Torque Converter Clutch System article in this section. Standard torque converter is a sealed unit and cannot be disassembled for service.

LEAKAGE CHECK

See procedures given in General Motors Turbo Hydra-Matic 400 article in this Section.

END CLEARANCE CHECK

See procedures given in General Motors Turbo Hydra-Matic 400 article in this Section.

TRANSMISSION DISASSEMBLY

CONVERTER & MODULATOR ASSEMBLY

With transmission in a suitable holding fixture, remove torque converter assembly. On Torque Converter Clutch (TCC) converters, it may be necessary to pry converter off of input shaft due to input shaft "O" ring seal. Remove vacuum modulator retaining bolt and retainer. Remove vacuum modulator assembly, "O" ring seal and modulator valve from case.

EXTENSION HOUSING, SPEEDOMETER DRIVEN GEAR, GOVERNOR, OIL PAN & SCREEN

1) Remove extension housing retaining bolts and remove extension housing. Remove square cut "O" ring seal from extension housing. Remove seal from housing using a screwdriver. If extension housing bushing is to be removed, collapse bushing with a screwdriver to remove.

2) Remove speedometer drive gear with a suitable removal tool. Remove retaining clip. Remove governor cover retainer with a screwdriver. Using a screwdriver and a hammer, tap along lip of governor cover to remove. Discard governor cover seal. Remove governor assembly from case. Check governor bore and sleeve for wear or scoring. Remove oil pan and remove filter from valve body.

CLUTCH AND BAND APPLICATION CHART
(ELEMENTS IN USE)

Selector Lever Position	Inter-mediate Clutch	Direct Clutch	Forward Clutch	Low & Reverse Clutch	Inter-mediate Overrun Band	Low & Reverse Roller Clutch	Inter-mediate Overrun Roller Clutch
D — DRIVE							
First Gear			X			X	
Second Gear	X		X				X
Third Gear	X	X	X				
2 — INTERMEDIATE							
Second Gear	X		X		X		X
1 — LOW (First)			X	X		X	
R — REVERSE		X		X			
NEUTRAL OR PARK — Band and all clutches released and/or ineffective.							

GENERAL MOTORS TURBO HYDRA-MATIC 350 & 350C (Cont.)

VALVE BODY & LINKAGE

1) Remove detent spring and roller assembly from valve body. Remove manual control valve link from range selector inner lever. Remove detent control valve link from detent actuating lever. Remove governor pressure switch.

Fig. 5   Removing Governor Assembly From Case

2) Disconnect lead wire from TCC pressure switch (if equipped). Remove auxiliary valve body and solenoid bolts or transfer support plate bolts. Disconnect wire from solenoid (if equipped). Remove auxiliary valve body and solenoid or transfer support plate. Remove lead wire from electrical connector and solenoid wire clip.

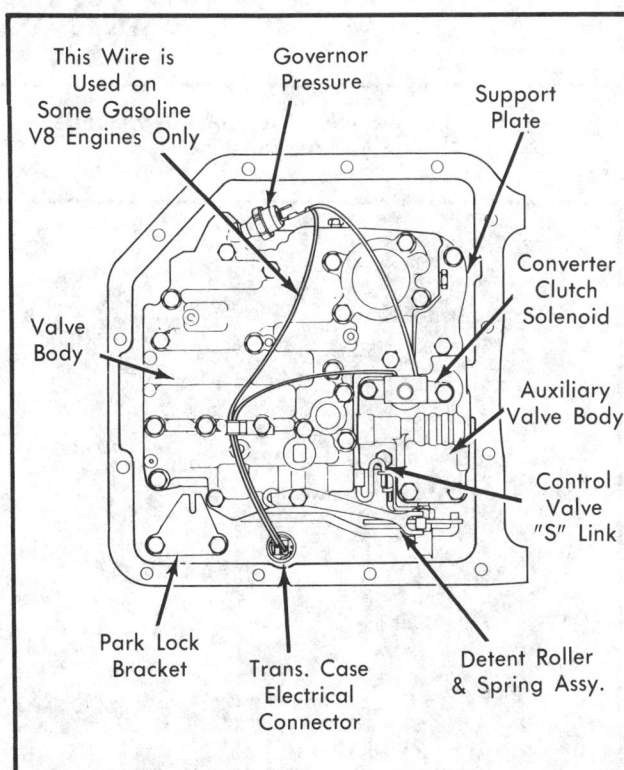

Fig. 6   Bottom View of Transmission Showing Locations of Components for Valve Body Removal

3) Compress fingers on electrical connector sleeve and remove. Remove "O" ring seal from solenoid assembly and inspect solenoid assembly ball check valve for nicks. Remove upper gasket, auxiliary valve body or valve body transfer plate. Remove auxiliary valve body or transfer spacer plate-to-case gasket.

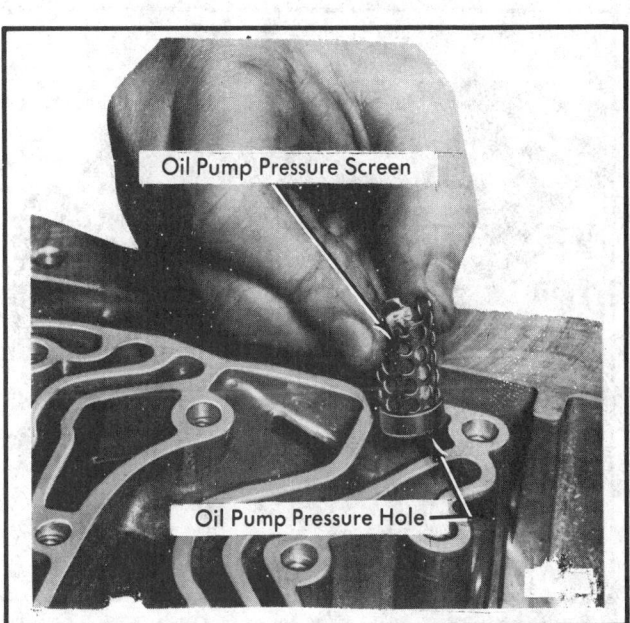

Fig. 7   View of Transmission Case Showing Location of Oil Pump Pressure Screen

4) Remove 4 check balls (5 on TCC transmissions) from passages in case face. Remove oil pump pressure screen from oil pump pressure hole in case. Remove governor feed screen(s) from governor feed hole in case. Remove manual shaft-to-case retainer with a screwdriver.

Fig. 8   View of Transmission Case Showing Location of Governor Feed Screen

GENERAL MOTORS TURBO HYDRA-MATIC 350 & 350C (Cont.)

5) Loosen nut securing range selector inner lever to manual shaft and remove nut and inner lever from manual shaft. Remove inner lever with parking pawl actuating rod from case. Disconnect inner lever from parking pawl actuating rod. Remove manual shaft-to-case lip seal.

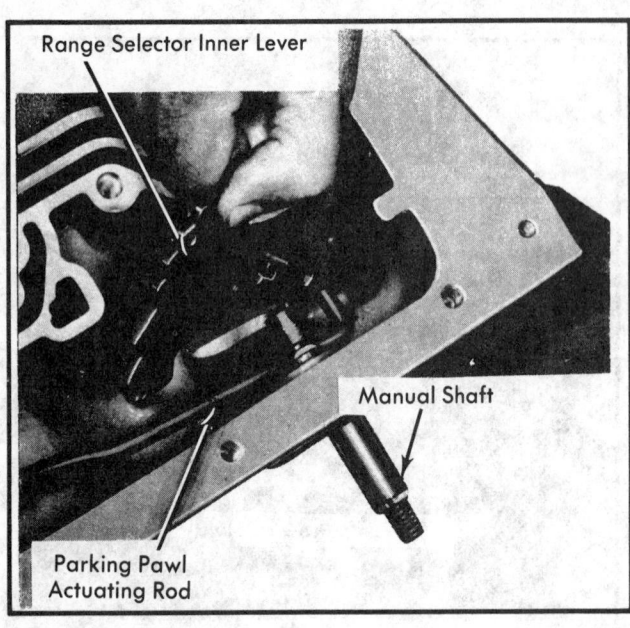

Fig. 9   Removing Manual Linkage From Case

6) Remove parking lock and lock bracket. Remove parking pawl spring, retaining plug, parking pawl shaft and parking pawl. Remove intermediate servo piston and sealing ring. Remove washer, spring seat and apply pin.

Fig. 10   Installed View of Parking Pawl Assembly

OIL PUMP & INTERNAL COMPONENTS

1) Remove oil pump-to-case attaching bolts with washer type seals, then discard seals. Install 2 slide hammers into threaded holes in pump body. Remove pump from case and discard gasket. Remove intermediate clutch cushion spring. Remove intermediate clutch composition and steel plates. Remove intermediate clutch pressure plate and overrun brake band. Pull outward on input shaft and remove the direct and forward clutch assemblies from case.

2) Remove input ring gear front thrust washer. Remove input ring gear snap ring from output shaft and remove input ring gear. Remove input ring gear thrust washer and output carrier assembly. Remove sun gear drive shell assembly and low and reverse roller clutch support-to-case retaining ring. Remove low and reverse clutch support, and race assembly. Remove low and reverse clutch composition and steel plates.

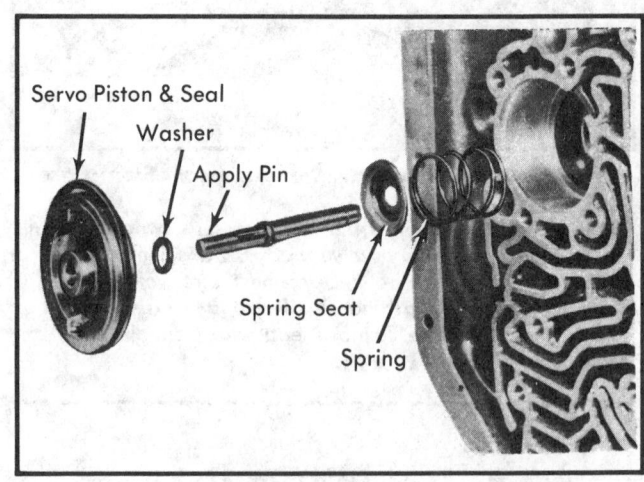

Fig. 11   Disassembled View of Intermediate Servo Assembly

Fig. 12   Removing Intermediate Clutch Plates

GENERAL MOTORS TURBO HYDRA-MATIC 350 & 350C (Cont.)

3) Remove reaction carrier assembly from output ring gear and shaft assembly. Remove output ring gear and shaft assembly from case. Remove reaction carrier-to-output ring gear thrust washer. Remove output ring gear-to-case needle bearing. Compress low and reverse clutch piston spring retainer and remove retaining ring and spring retainer. Remove piston springs from piston.

4) Apply air pressure to hole shown in *Fig. 13* to remove low and reverse clutch piston assembly. Remove low and reverse clutch piston outer seal, center seal, and inner seal. Compress intermediate clutch accumulator with compression tool (J-23069) and remove retaining ring. Remove piston cover and "O" ring seal from case. Remove spring and piston assembly. If piston seals are damaged, replace piston (piston and seals are a single assembly).

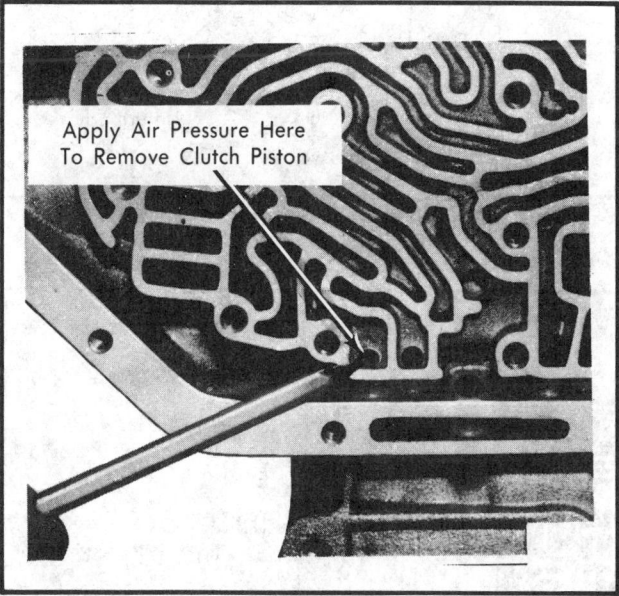

Apply Air Pressure Here To Remove Clutch Piston

Fig. 13   Removing Low and Reverse Clutch Piston

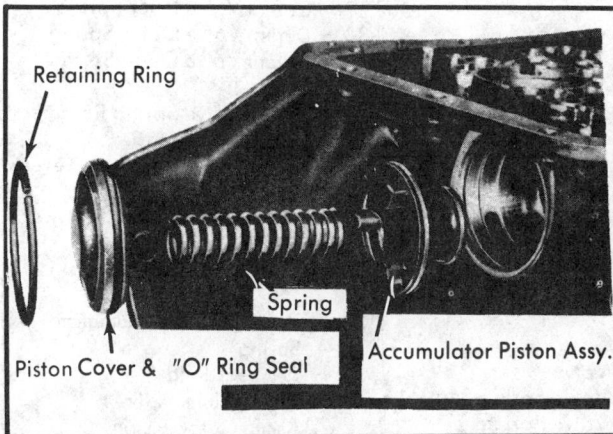

Retaining Ring

Spring

Piston Cover & "O" Ring Seal

Accumulator Piston Assy.

Fig. 14   Disassembled View of Intermediate Clutch Accumulator Assembly

COMPONENT DISASSEMBLY & REASSEMBLY

VALVE BODY

NOTE — *As valve trains are removed from each valve body bore, place individual parts in correct order and in relative position to valve body to simplify reassembly.*

CAUTION — *Valves and springs are not interchangeable, all parts must be installed in correct order and in proper valve body bore. See Fig. 16.*

Disassembly — 1) Position valve body assembly with cored face up and direct clutch accumulator piston pocket positioned at upper left. Remove manual valve from lower left bore.

2) From lower right bore, remove retaining pin and pressure regulator valve train.

3) From next bore up, remove retaining pin and 2-3 shift valve train.

4) From next bore up, remove retaining pin and 1-2 shift valve train.

5) From next bore up, remove retaining pin, plug, manual low control valve spring, and manual low control valve.

6) From next bore up, remove retaining pin, spring, seat, and detent regulator valve.

7) Compress direct clutch accumulator piston with compression tool (J-22269) and remove "E" ring. Remove piston, metal oil seal ring, and spring.

CAUTION — *Do not overcompress piston as damage may occur.*

8) From next bore down from direct clutch accumulator, remove detent actuating lever bracket bolt, bracket, actuating lever and retaining pin, stop, spring retainer, seat, outer spring, inner spring, washer and detent valve.

Cleaning & Inspection — Clean all components in solvent and blow dry with compressed air. Check all valves for scoring or damage and for freedom of movement in their respective bores. Check valve body for cracks or damage, scored bores, interconnected oil passages and flatness of mounting surface. Check all springs for distortion or cracked coils.

Reassembly — Reverse disassembly procedure and note the following: Align piston and oil seal ring when installing direct clutch accumulator piston spring and piston into valve body. Compress spring and piston using same tool as used during disassembly and secure with retaining ring.

AUXILIARY VALVE BODY (TCC MODELS)

Disassembly — Position valve body assembly core face up. From bore, remove retaining pin, seat, spring and converter clutch apply valve.

Cleaning & Inspection — Clean all components in solvent and blow dry with compressed air. Inspect apply valve for scoring, cracks and free movement in bore. Inspect valve body for cracks, scored bores, interconnected oil passages and for flatness of mounting face.

Reassembly — Install apply valve, spring, seat and retaining pin in proper bore. See *Fig. 15*.

GENERAL MOTORS TURBO HYDRA-MATIC 350 & 350C (Cont.)

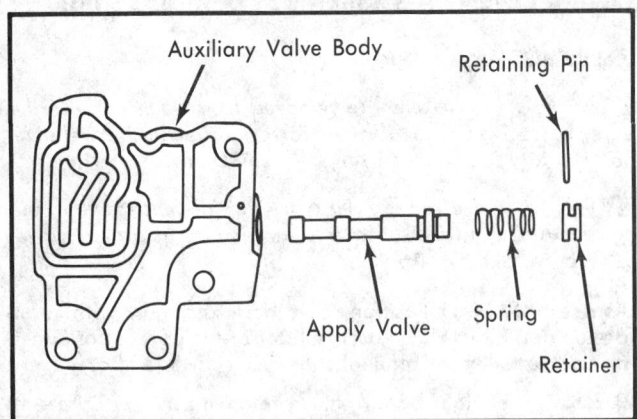

Fig. 15 Exploded View of Auxiliary Valve Body

OIL PUMP

Disassembly — 1) Mark pump body and front cover for proper alignment upon reassembly. Remove cover-to-body attaching bolts, then remove intermediate spring retainer, clutch return springs and clutch piston assembly. Remove clutch piston inner and outer seals. Remove 2 forward clutch-to-pump teflon type oil seal rings and 3 direct clutch drum-to-oil pump hub hook type oil rings.

2) Remove pump cover-to-direct clutch drum needle thrust bearing and shim. Remove pump cover and stator shaft assembly from pump body. Remove pump drive and driven gear. Remove and discard pump-to-case outer "O" ring seal.

3) Fill cooler by-pass passage with grease, using a punch (J-23134) force by-pass valve seat, check ball and spring from pump body. Remove pump body-to-converter hub seal only if seal is damaged.

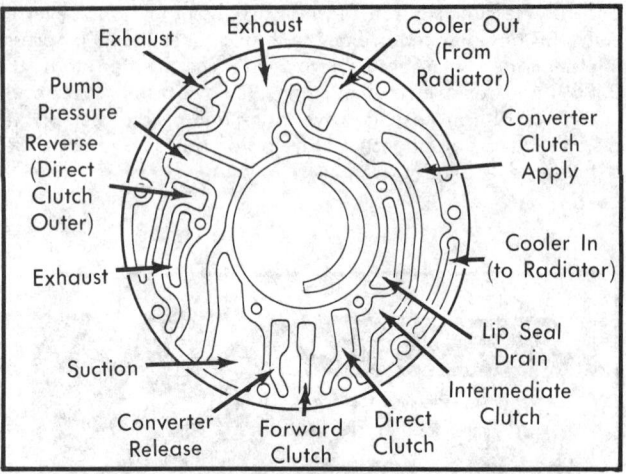

Fig. 17 View of Oil Pump Body Showing Oil Passages

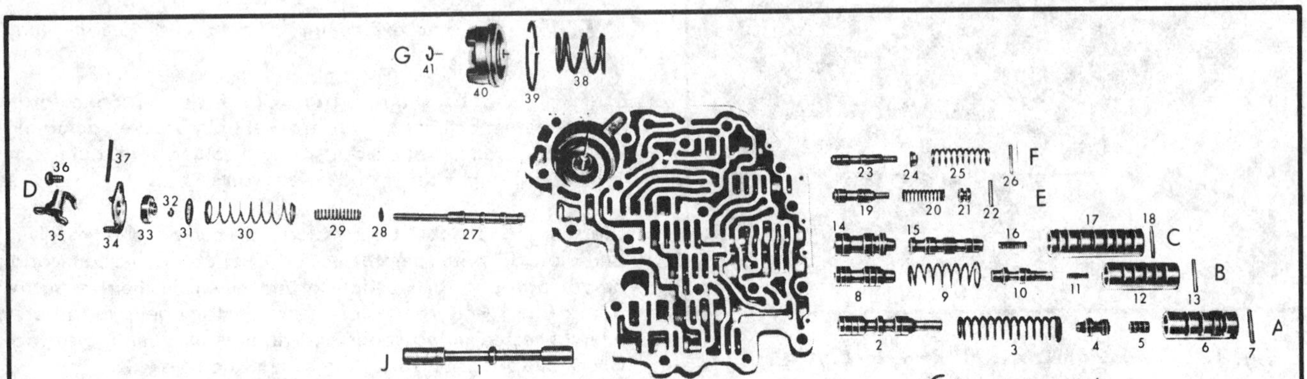

J - 1 — Manual Valve

A {
2 — Pressure Regulator Valve
3 — Pressure Regulator Valve Spring
4 — Reverse & Modulator Boost Valve
5 — Intermediate Boost Valve
6 — Boost Valve Sleeve
7 — Retaining Pin
}

B {
8 — 2-3 Shift Valve
9 — 2-3 Shift Valve Spring
10 — 2-3 Shift Control Valve
11 — 2-3 Shift Control Valve Spring
12 — 2-3 Shift Control Valve Sleeve
13 — Retaining Pin
}

C {
14 — 1-2 Shift Valve
15 — 1-2 Shift Control Valve
16 — 1-2 Shift Control Valve Spring
17 — 1-2 Shift Control Valve Sleeve
18 — Retaining Pin
}

E {
19 — Manual Low Control Valve
20 — Manual Low Control Valve Spring
21 — Plug
22 — Retaining Pin
}

F {
23 — Detent Regulator Valve
24 — Detent Regulator Valve Spring Seat
25 — Detent Regulator Valve Spring
26 — Retaining Pin
}

27 — Detent Valve
28 — Washer
29 — Detent Valve Inner Spring
30 — Detent Valve Outer Spring
31 — Detent Valve Outer Spring Seat

D {
32 — Detent Valve Spring Retainer
33 — Detent Valve Stop
34 — Detent Valve Acutating Lever Bracket
35 — Detent Valve Actuating Lever
36 — Retaining Bolt
37 — Retaining Pin
}

G {
38 — Direct Clutch Accumulator Spring
39 — Oil Seal Ring
40 — Direct Clutch 2-3 Accumulator Piston
41 — Retainer Ring
}

Fig. 16 Exploded View of Valve Body Assembly

GENERAL MOTORS TURBO HYDRA-MATIC 350 & 350C (Cont.)

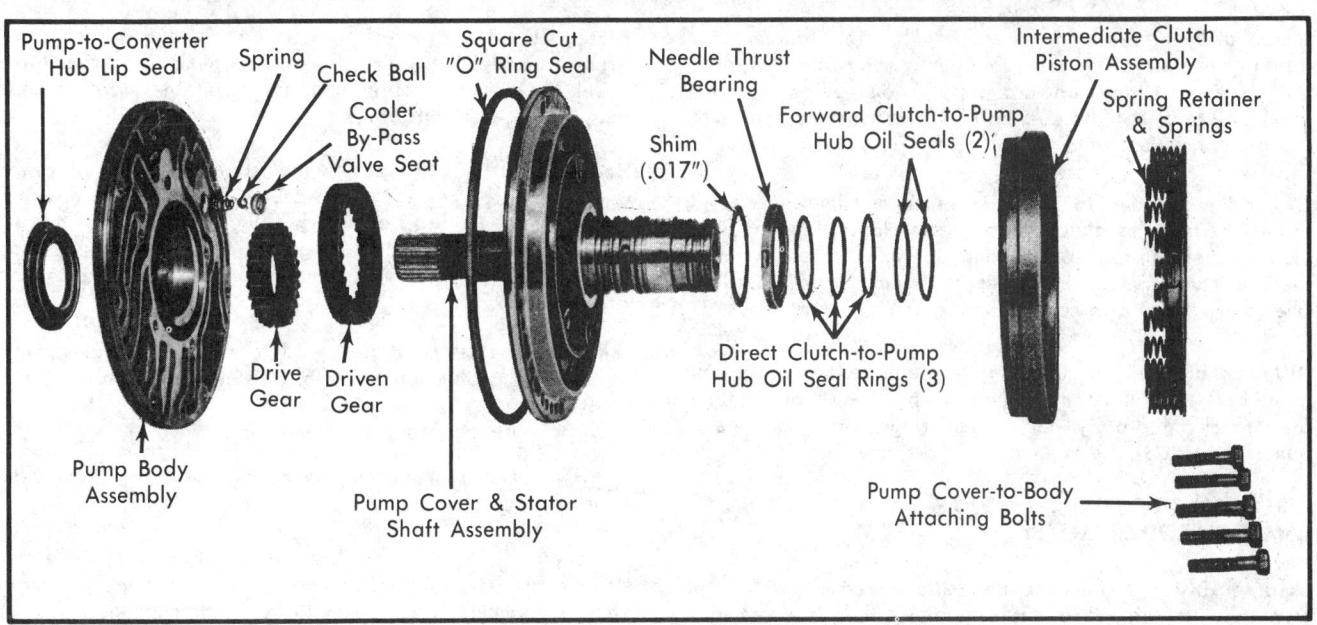

Fig. 18   Exploded View of Oil Pump Assembly

Cleaning & Inspection — 1) Clean all components in solvent and blow dry with compressed air. **CAUTION** — *Do not dry components with shop towels.* Check pump drive and driven gears, gear pocket, and crescent for nicks, scoring, or other damage. Check pump body and cover faces for nicks or scoring. Check clutch hub outside diameter for nicks or burrs that may damage clutch drum bushing.

2) Measure clearance between pump body bushing and converter pump hub. Clearance should not exceed .005". If pump bushing is damaged, oil pump body should be replaced. Check converter housing hub outside diameter for nicks or burrs that may damage pump seal or bushing. With components clean and dry, install pump gears in pump body and check clearance between body face and gear face. Clearance should be .0005-.0015".

Stator Shaft Front Bushing Replacement — With stator shaft properly supported, remove bushing using an outside threaded bushing remover tool (J-21465-15) and slide hammer. Drive in new bushing using a bushing installer (J-21424-7) until bushing is .250" below face.

Stator Shaft Rear Bushing Replacement — With stator shaft properly supported, remove inner and outer bushings using an outside threaded bushing remover tool (J-21465-4) and slide hammer. Drive in a new inner bushing, using bushing installer (J-23062-2) and hammer, until edge of bushing is 1 11/32" below top surface of oil pump delivery sleeve. Drive in outer bushing until edge of bushing is .010" below top surface of oil pump delivery sleeve.

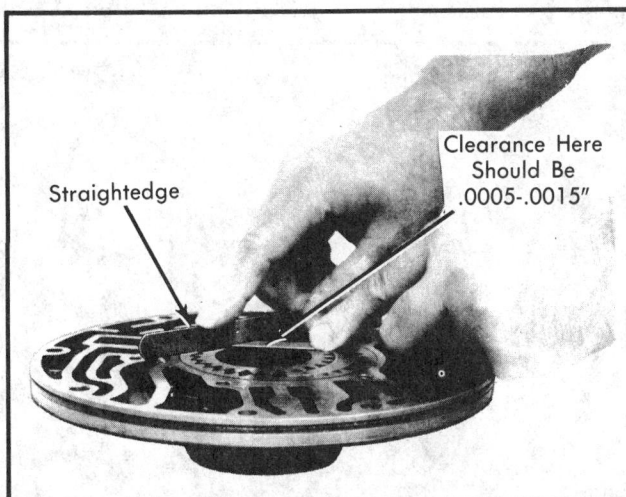

Fig. 19   Measuring Gear Face-to-Pump Face Clearance

Oil Pump Body Bushing Replacement — Support oil pump body on wooden blocks and drive out old bushing. Press new bushing until edge of bushing is .010" below front pump oil seal side of oil pump body.

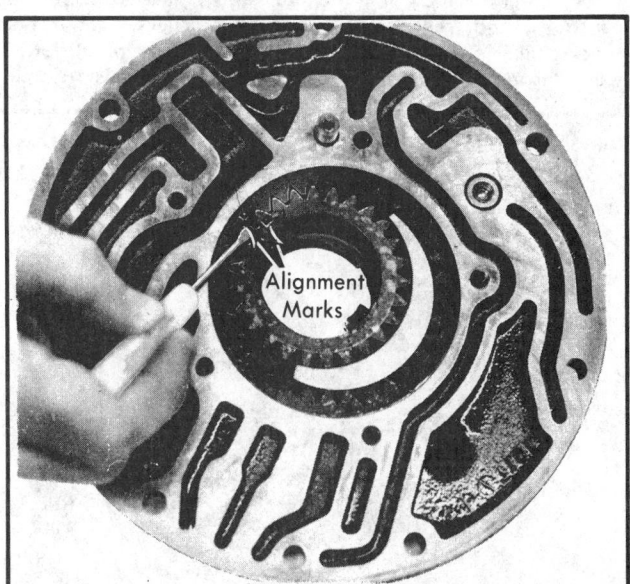

Fig. 20   Installed View of Oil Pump Gears Showing Alignment Marks

Reassembly — 1) If pump body oil seal was removed, place pump on wood blocks, coat outside diameter of new seal with

GENERAL MOTORS TURBO HYDRA-MATIC 350 & 350C (Cont.)

a non-hardening sealer, then install seal fully into counterbore. Install drive and driven gears into pump body with identification marks and tangs upward. Install cooler by-pass spring, check ball and seat into pump body. Press seat into bore until top of seat is flush with face of pump body.

2) Install pump cover to pump body, then install new inner and outer intermediate clutch piston seals. Install intermediate clutch piston. Install springs and spring retainer to intermediate clutch piston. Place clutch aligning strap (J-21368) over pump body and cover, then tighten attaching bolts.

3) Install large square cut "O" ring to outside diameter of oil pump body. Install direct clutch-to-pump hub oil seals (3) then forward clutch-to-pump hub oil seal rings. Make sure the 3 pump cover hub lube holes are not restricted.

DIRECT CLUTCH & INTERMEDIATE OVERRUN ROLLER CLUTCH

Disassembly — 1) Remove intermediate overrun clutch drum front retaining ring and retainer, then withdraw outer race and clutch assembly. **NOTE** — *Inner race is a press fit; do not remove unless replacement is necessary.* Remove direct clutch drum-to-forward clutch housing needle roller bearing.

2) Remove direct clutch pressure plate retaining ring, then withdraw pressure plate, composition and steel clutch plates. Using compressor tools (J-2590-3 and J-2590-5), compress direct clutch piston return spring seat and remove retaining ring. Release compressor tools and remove spring seat and 17 coil return springs. Remove piston, then remove inner and outer seals from piston. Remove piston center seal from clutch drum.

Inspection — Check composition plates and steel plates for signs of burning, scoring, or wear. Inspect springs for collapsed coils or cracking. Check piston for signs of cracking or wear. Check clutch housing for wear, scoring, open oil passages, and freedom of movement of check ball. Inspect roller clutch inner and outer race for scratches or abnormal wear. Inspect roller cage for wear and springs for distortion.

Direct Clutch Bushing Replacement — With direct clutch drum properly supported, drive out bushing using a suitable chisel. Drive in new bushing, using a suitable mandrel, until mandrel contacts clutch drum.

Reassembly — 1) Install new inner and outer seals on piston and new piston center seal in drum with lip facing upward. Install direct clutch piston into housing using a feeler gauge. Install return springs and spring seat. Compress springs using same tool as used during disassembly and install retaining ring.

2) Lubricate steel plates and composition plates with automatic transmission fluid. Install steel plate first and then alternate composition and steel plates until all are installed. Install pressure plate and retaining ring.

NOTE — *Direct clutch plates will be marked with a single light blue stripe.*

3) Install roller clutch assembly, with the 4 holes toward front of transmission. Install clutch overrun outer race, making sure race free-wheels in a counterclockwise direction only. Install overrun clutch retainer and retaining ring.

CAUTION — *If roller clutch rollers fall out during installation, roller must be removed and reinstalled. Roller must be installed from inside to outside to avoid damage to springs.*

Direct Clutch Plate Usage Chart		
Application	Steel Plates	Composition Plates
6 Cyl. and Diesel V8 Models	4	4
V8 Gasoline Models	5	5

FORWARD CLUTCH

Disassembly — Remove forward clutch retaining ring and pressure plate. Remove composition plates, steel plates and

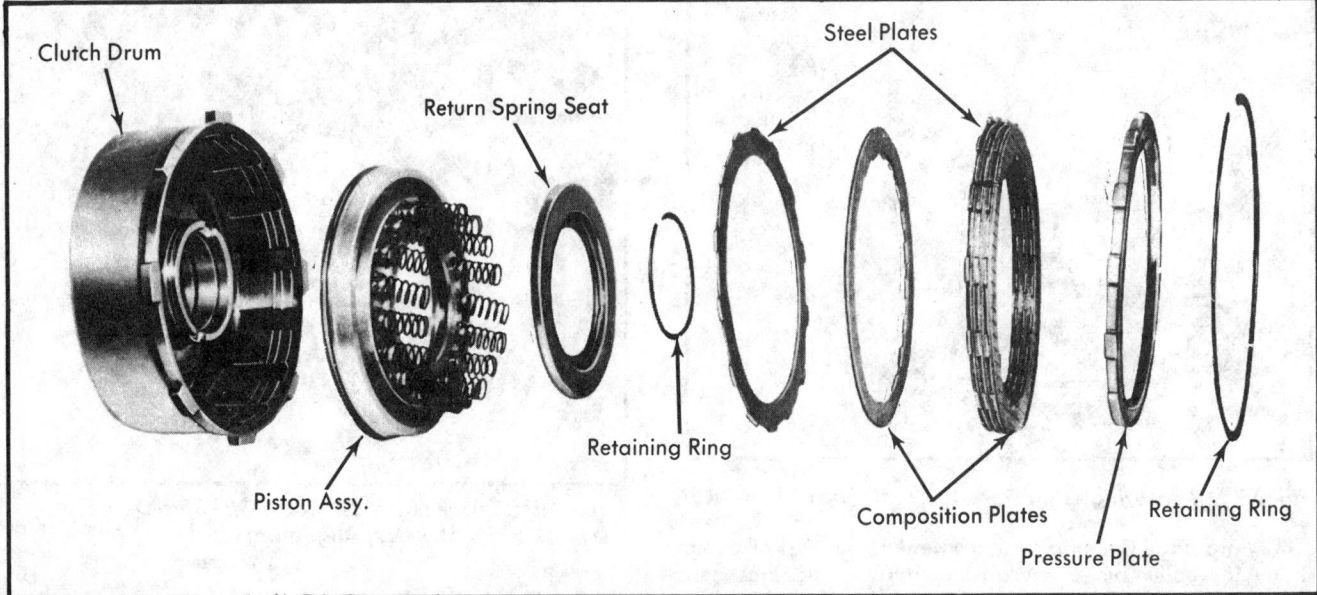

Fig. 21 Exploded View of Direct Clutch Assembly

GENERAL MOTORS TURBO HYDRA-MATIC 350 & 350C (Cont.)

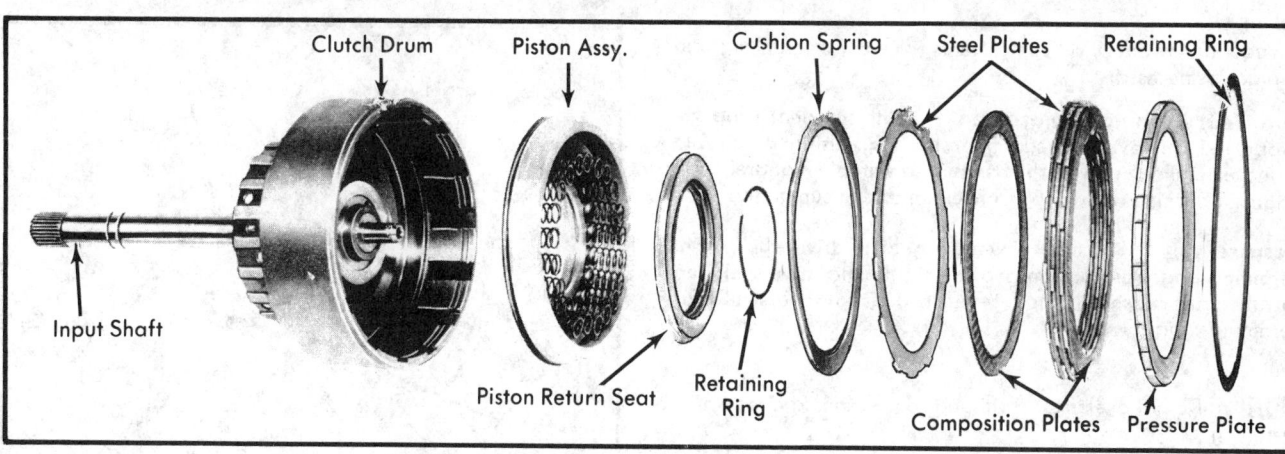

Fig. 22 Exploded View of Forward Clutch Assembly

cushion spring. Using a press and adapters (J-2590-5 and J-2590-4), compress forward clutch piston return spring seat and return springs. Remove forward clutch piston assembly and inner and outer seals from piston.

Inspection — Check composition plates and steel plates for signs of burning, scoring, or wear. Inspect springs for collapsed coils or cracking. Check piston for signs of cracking or wear. Check clutch housing for wear, scoring, open oil passages, and freedom of movement of exhaust check ball. Inspect input shaft for open lubrication passages at each end, damaged splines, worn bushing journals, cracks, or distortion.

Reassembly — 1) Install inner and outer seals on piston. Install forward clutch piston into housing using a .008" feeler gauge as a guide. Compress springs using same tools used during disassembly and install retainer ring.

2) Lubricate clutch plates with transmission fluid. Install cushion spring into drum, follow with 1 steel plate, then alternate composition and steel plates until all plates are installed. Install forward clutch selective fit pressure plate.

NOTE — *Forward clutch plates will be marked with 2 light blue stripes.*

3) Using a feeler gauge, measure clearance between pressure plate and composition plate. Clearance should be .011-.082". If clearance is not to specification, select a thicker or thinner pressure plate to obtain specifications. *See Forward Clutch Pressure Plate Chart.*

Forward Clutch Pressure Plate Chart

Plate I.D. Marks	Thickness In.
None	.245-.255
1	.275-.285
2	.306-.316

Forward Clutch Plate Usage Chart

Application	Steel Plates	Composition Plates
6 Cyl. and Diesel V8 Models	4	4
V8 Gasoline Models	5	5

SUN GEAR & SUN GEAR DRIVE SHELL

Disassembly — Remove sun gear-to-drive shell rear retaining ring. Remove rear steel thrust washer and separate sun gear assembly from drive shell. Remove sun gear-to-drive shell front retaining ring and discard retaining ring.

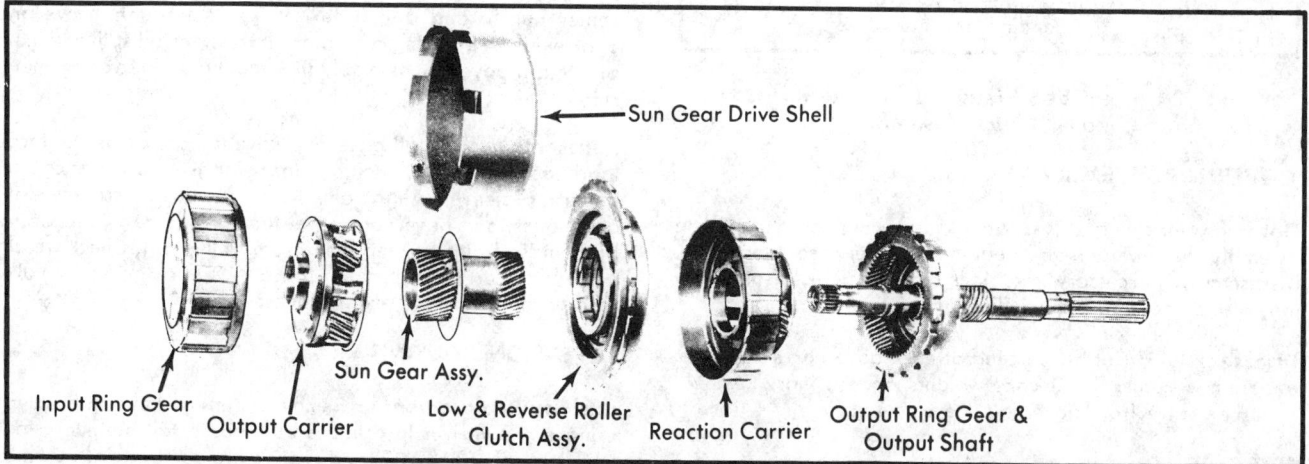

Fig. 23 Exploded View of Planetary Gear Train

GENERAL MOTORS TURBO HYDRA-MATIC 350 & 350C (Cont.)

Inspection — Check all components for wear or cracking and replace as necessary.

Sun Gear Bushing Replacement — With sun gear properly supported, remove two sun gear bushings using a suitable mandrel. Drive in new bushings, using a suitable mandrel, until edges of bushings are .010" from either end of sun gear.

Resassembly — Install new sun gear-to-drive shell front retaining ring. Position sun gear assembly into drive shell and install thrust washer. Install new sun gear-to-drive shell rear retaining ring.

NOTE — *Do not overstress front and rear retaining rings while installing.*

LOW & REVERSE ROLLER CLUTCH ASSEMBLY

Disassembly — Remove low and reverse clutch-to-sun gear thrust washer. Remove overrun clutch inner race and roller clutch retaining ring. Remove roller clutch assembly.

Inspection — Check inner and outer races for scratches or abnormal wear. Check rollers for wear and springs for distortion.

Reassembly — Position low and reverse roller clutch assembly on inner race with oil holes toward rear of transmission. Install overrun clutch outer race and install retaining ring. Install thrust washer.

NOTE — *Low and reverse clutch inner race should free-wheel in a clockwise direction only.*

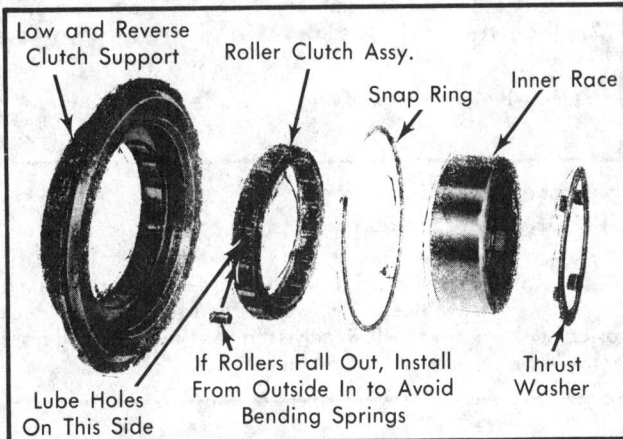

Fig. 24   Exploded View of Low and Reverse Roller Clutch Assembly

GOVERNOR ASSEMBLY

Governor, including driven gear, is serviced as a complete assembly; however, driven gear may be serviced separately. Disassembly is necessary to replace a driven gear. Disassembly may also be necessary due to improper operation.

Disassembly — Cut off one end of each governor weight pin and remove pins, thrust cap, weights and springs. Remove governor valve from governor sleeve.

NOTE — *Governor weights are interchangeable from side to side and need not be identified.*

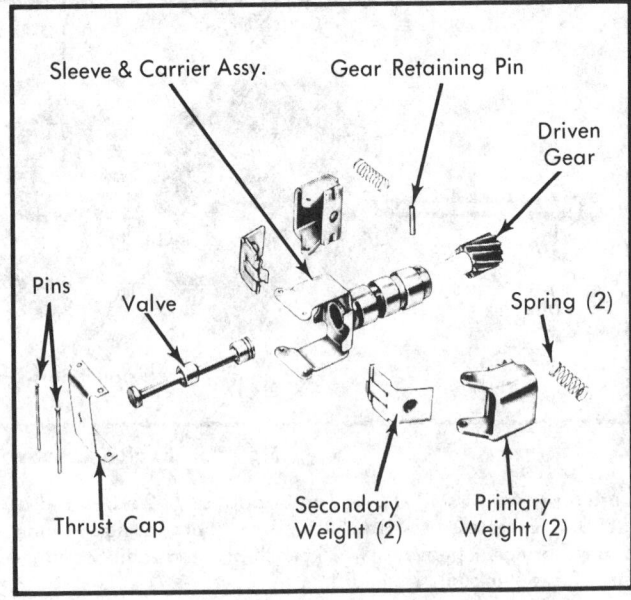

Fig. 25   Exploded View of Governor Assembly

Inspection — Wash all parts, air dry, and blow out all passages. Inspect governor sleeve for nicks, burrs, scoring, or galling. Check governor sleeve for free operation in bore of case. Inspect valve for nicks, burrs, scoring, or galling, and for free operation in bore of governor sleeve. Inspect driven gear for nicks, burrs, damage, or looseness on governor sleeve. Inspect springs for distortion or damage. Check weights for free operation in their retainers. Check valve opening at entry and exhaust (.020" minumum).

Driven Gear Replacement — 1) Drive split retaining pin out of gear. Support governor on 3/16" plates installed in exhaust slots of governor sleeve, place in an arbor press and, with a long punch, press gear out of sleeve. Wash all parts to remove metal chips.

2) Support governor on 3/16" plates installed in exhaust slots of sleeve, position new gear in sleeve and, with a suitabble socket, press gear into sleeve unitl nearly seated. Remove any chips that may have shaved off gear hub, then press gear in until it bottoms on shoulder.

3) Locate a new pin hole position 90° from existing hole, center punch, and drill a new 1/8" hole through sleeve and gear, while supporting governor in press. Install split retaining pin. Wash governor assembly thoroughly to remove any metal chips.

Reassembly — Install governor valve in bore of sleeve (large land end first). Install weights and springs, and thrust cap on governor sleeve. Align pin holes in thrust cap, weight assemblies, and governor sleeve; then, install new pins. Crimp both ends of pins to keep them from falling out. Check weight assemblies for free operation on pins. Check governor valve for free movement in governor sleeve.

EXTENSION HOUSING

Bushing Replacement — Remove extension housing bushing using a screwdriver to collapse bushing. Install bushing using installer tool (J-21424-9) and a drive handle. Edge of bushing should be installed .010" below edge of rear seal counterbore.

GENERAL MOTORS TURBO HYDRA-MATIC 350 & 350C (Cont.)

OUTPUT SHAFT

Bushing Replacement — With output shaft properly supported, remove bushing using a suitable tool and a slide hammer. Using a suitable driver, install bushing on shaft until tool bottoms against shaft.

CASE

Bushing Replacement — With case properly supported, drive bushing out of case using a drive handle and tool (J-23062-3). Using same tools, drive new bushing into case until bushing is .020″ below chamfered edge of case.

REACTION CARRIER

Bushing Replacement — With reaction carrier properly supported, drive out bushing using a suitable mandrel. Drive in new bushing using a suitable mandrel until edge of bushing is flush to .010″ from inside face.

TRANSMISSION REASSEMBLY

INTERNAL COMPONENTS

1) Install low and reverse clutch piston assembly with notch in piston adjacent to parking pawl. Install coil springs and spring seat. Compress coil springs and seat using compressor tool (J-21420-1) and install retaining ring. Install output ring gear thrust bearing in case. Install output ring gear on output shaft. Install reaction carrier to output ring gear thrust washer into output gear support and install output shaft assembly in case.

2) Position reaction carrier into output ring gear. Lubricate low and reverse composition and steel plates with automatic transmission fluid. Starting with a steel plate, alternate steel and composition plates until all are installed. Install low and reverse clutch support retainer spring.

NOTE — *Notch in steel plates is toward bottom of case.*

3) Install low and reverse clutch support assembly, with notch aligned with clutch support retainer spring. Install low and reverse roller clutch inner race-to-sun gear shell thrust washer. Install low and reverse clutch support snap ring with retainer spring between gap. Install rear thrust washer and sun gear drive shell.

CAUTION — *Make sure splines on inner race of roller clutch align with splines on reaction carrier.*

4) Install output carrier assembly. Install input ring gear rear thrust washer and input ring gear. Install new input ring gear-to-output shaft snap ring, taking care not to overstress snap ring. Install input gear front thrust washer, direct clutch assembly and special thrust washer on forward clutch assembly, then install assemblies into case.

NOTE — *Make sure forward clutch composition plates are placed over input ring gear and tangs on direct clutch housing are installed into slots on sun gear drive shell.*

5) Install intermediate band and intermediate clutch pressure plate. Lubricate clutch plates with transmission fluid, then install 1 composition plate followed by 1 steel plate until all plates are installed. Install intermediate clutch cushion spring.

NOTE — *Notch in steel clutch plates is installed toward selector lever inner bracket.*

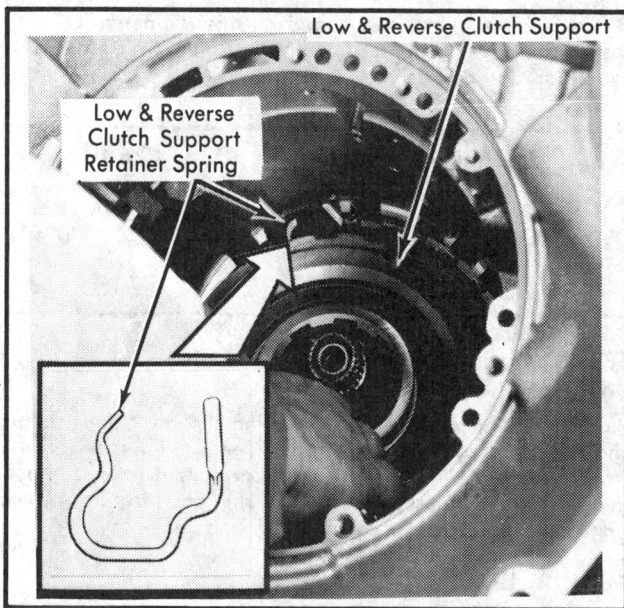

Fig. 26 Installing Low and Reverse Clutch Support Retainer Spring

Low and Reverse Clutch Plate Usage Chart		
Application	Steel Plates	Composition Plates
6 Cyl. and Diesel V8 Models	4	4
V8 Gasoline Models	5	5

6) Lubricate .017″ shim and needle bearing, then install on pump cover hub (face down). Install new gasket, lubricate pump case bore, then install guide pins into case. Install pump to case and remove guide pins. Install pump-to-case bolts.

NOTE — *If input shaft cannot be rotated as pump is being pulled into place with bolts, direct and forward clutch housings are improperly aligned.*

7) Mount a dial indicator so that indicator plunger is contacting end of input shaft. Push up on output shaft and zero indicator. Now push down on shaft and note dial indicator reading. Indicator should read .010-.044″. If not to specifications, remove pump assembly and install correct number of .017″ shims to obtain correct reading.

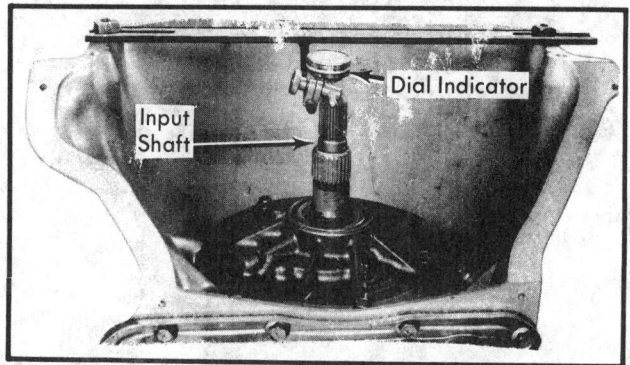

Fig. 27 Measuring Transmission Input Shaft End Play

GENERAL MOTORS TURBO HYDRA-MATIC 350 & 350C (Cont.)

8) Install new pump gasket and outside diameter "O" ring. Install pump using guide pins. Install bolts with new washer type seals and tighten bolts.

Intermediate Clutch Plate Usage Chart		
Application	Steel Plates	Composition Plates
All	3	3

SPEEDOMETER GEARS & EXTENSION HOUSING

Place speedometer drive gear retaining clip into hole in output shaft. Heat a new speedometer drive gear, align speedometer drive gear with retaining clip and carefully drive into place. Install extension housing-to-case "O" ring and position housing on transmission. Install retaining bolts and tighten.

MANUAL LINKAGE

1) If manual shaft-to-case seal was removed, install a new seal using a $\frac{7}{8}$" diameter rod. Install parking pawl in case with tooth toward inside case. Insert parking pawl shaft into case and into parking pawl. Install retainer plug, using a $\frac{3}{8}$" diameter rod to drive plug into place. Edge of plug should be flush to case within .010". Stake plug in position in 3 places.

2) Install disengaging spring with square end hooked on pawl. Install park lock bracket and tighten bolts securely. Position range selector inner lever on parking pawl actuator rod, install manual shaft through case, and connect shaft to inner lever. Install manual shaft retaining nut and tighten. Position spacer clip between case and lever on manual shaft.

VALVE BODY & OIL PAN

1) Install intermediate servo piston, apply pin, spring and spring seat. Install intermediate servo piston and metal oil seal ring. Install 4 check balls (5 on THM 350C torque converter clutch transmission) in correct locations in transmission case pockets. See Fig. 28. Install oil pump pressure screen and governor feed screen.

2) Install valve body transfer plate, auxiliary valve body and gasket. Install valve body-to-transfer plate gasket. Install valve body, connecting manual control valve link to range selector inner lever, install valve body bolts and tighten in random sequence to specifications.

3) Install spacer support plate and bolts, then tighten. On TCC transmissions, install auxiliary valve body. Install valve body. Connect manual control valve link to range selector inner lever. Install manual shaft retaining clip. Tighten valve body bolts, leaving bolt loose for detent roller and spring assembly. Install detent roller and spring assembly to valve body.

4) Install detent control valve wire to detent valve actuating lever, then attach lever to valve body. On TCC transmissions, install solenoid and connect wires. Install governor switch. Align lube holes in strainer with holes in valve body and install strainer and gasket. Install oil pan with new gasket.

NOTE — *If new oil pan is being installed, transfer unit number on right side of old pan to new pan. If new governor cover is being installed, transfer numbers from old cover to new cover.*

GOVERNOR & VACUUM MODULATOR

Install governor assembly, cover and seal, and retainer wire. Install vacuum modulator valve and retainer clip, with tangs on retainer clip pointing toward modulator. Install and tighten retainer bolt.

INTERMEDIATE CLUTCH ACCUMULATOR

Install intermediate clutch accumulator piston assembly in side of transmission case. Install spring and new "O" ring seal in groove in case. Install cover and compress cover using a suitable tool (J-23069) and install retaining ring.

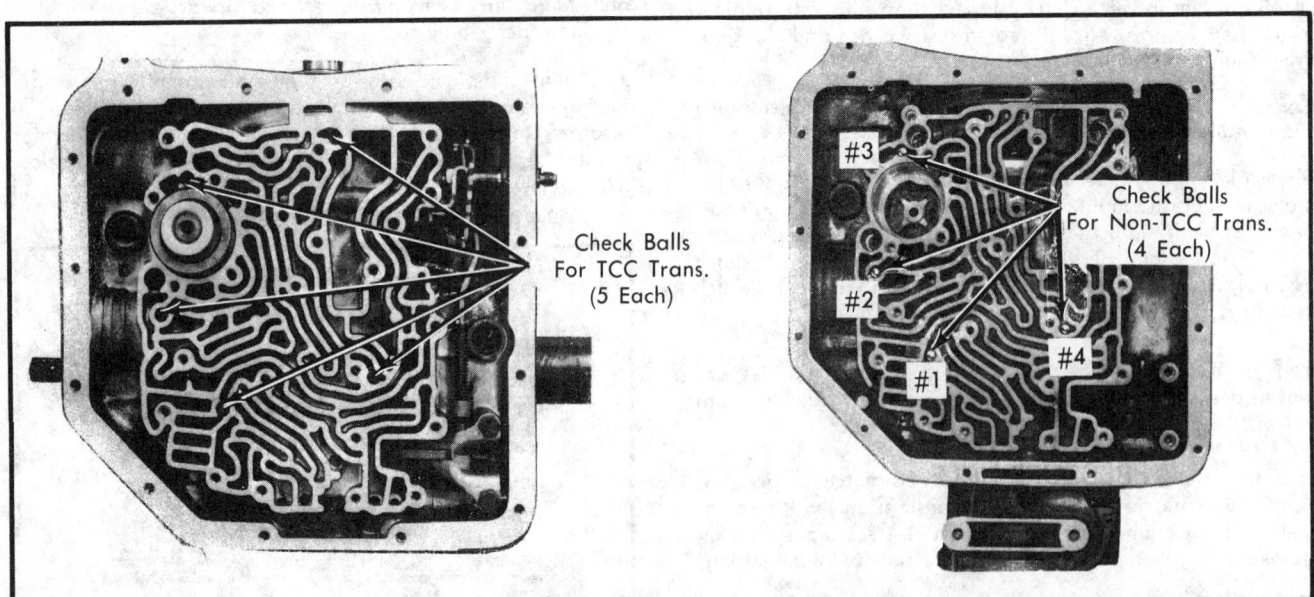

Check Balls For TCC Trans. (5 Each)

#3 #2 #1 #4
Check Balls For Non-TCC Trans. (4 Each)

Fig. 28 Correct Location of Check Balls in Transmission Case Pockets

GENERAL MOTORS TURBO HYDRA-MATIC 350 & 350C (Cont.)

Compressor Tool

Fig. 29 Installing Intermediate Clutch Accumulator

TIGHTENING SPECIFICATIONS

Application	Ft. Lbs.
Oil Pump Cover-to-Pump Body	17
Oil Pump-to-Case	18
Parking Lock Bracket	29
Extension Housing-to-Case	25
Inner Selector Lever-to-Shaft	25
Converter-to-Flywheel	35
Transmission Case-to-Engine	35
Intermediate Band Adjust Nut	15

Application	INCH Lbs.
Valve Body & Support Plate	130
Oil Suction Screen	40
Oil Pan-to-Case	130
Modulator Retainer-to-Case	130
Detent Valve Actuating Bracket	52
Under Pan-to-Transmission Case	110

GENERAL MOTORS TURBO HYDRA-MATIC 400

Chevrolet
GMC

TRANSMISSION IDENTIFICATION

Transmission may be identified by a serial number located on an identification plate (light blue in color) attached to right side of transmission case.

DESCRIPTION

Transmission is a fully automatic unit consisting of a 3 element hydraulic torque converter and a compound planetary gear set. Three multiple disc clutches, 1 gear unit, 1 roller clutch and 2 bands provide friction elements required to obtain desired function of the compound planetary gear set, producing 3 forward gears and reverse. A hydraulic system, pressurized by a gear type pump provides working pressure required to operate friction elements and automatic controls.

LUBRICATION & ADJUSTMENT

See Automatic Transmission Servicing in this section.

TESTING

ROAD TEST

NOTE — Prior to road testing be certain that fluid level and manual linkage adjustment is checked and corrected if necessary.

1) Place selector lever in Drive range and accelerate vehicle from a standstill. A 1-2 and 2-3 shift should occur at all throttle openings (shift points will vary with throttle openings). As vehicle speed decreases to 0 MPH, a 3-2 and 2-1 downshift should occur.

2) Place selector lever in "2" (Intermediate) range and accelerate from a standstill. A 1-2 upshift should occur at all throttle openings (shift point will vary with throttle openings) and no 2-3 shift should occur. As vehicle speed decreases to 0 MPH, a 2-1 downshift should occur.

3) Place selector lever in "1" (Low) range and accelerate vehicle from a standstill. No upshifts should occur regardless of throttle opening.

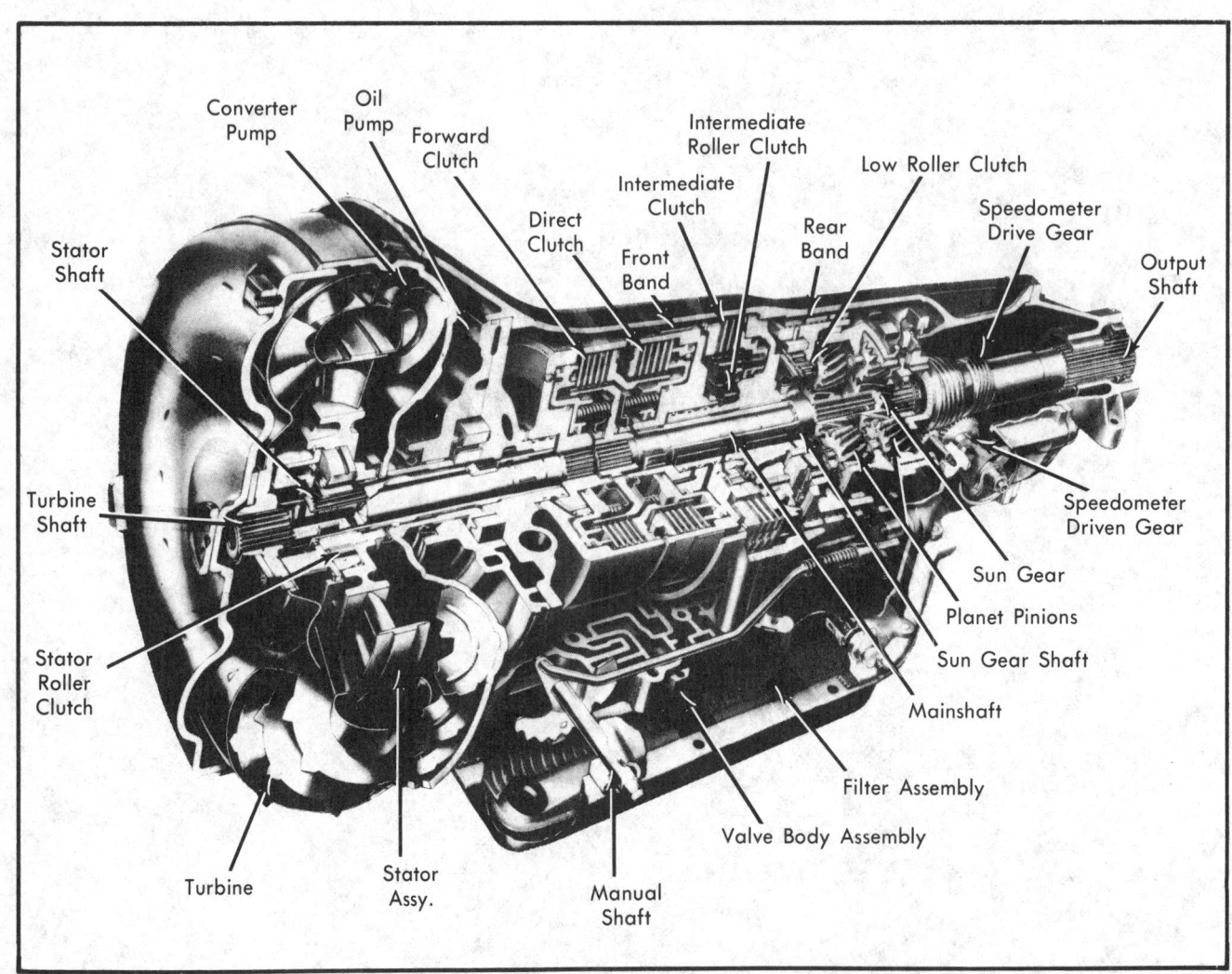

Fig. 1 Cutaway View of Turbo Hydra-Matic 400 Automatic Transmission Assembly

GENERAL MOTORS TURBO HYDRA-MATIC 400 (Cont.)

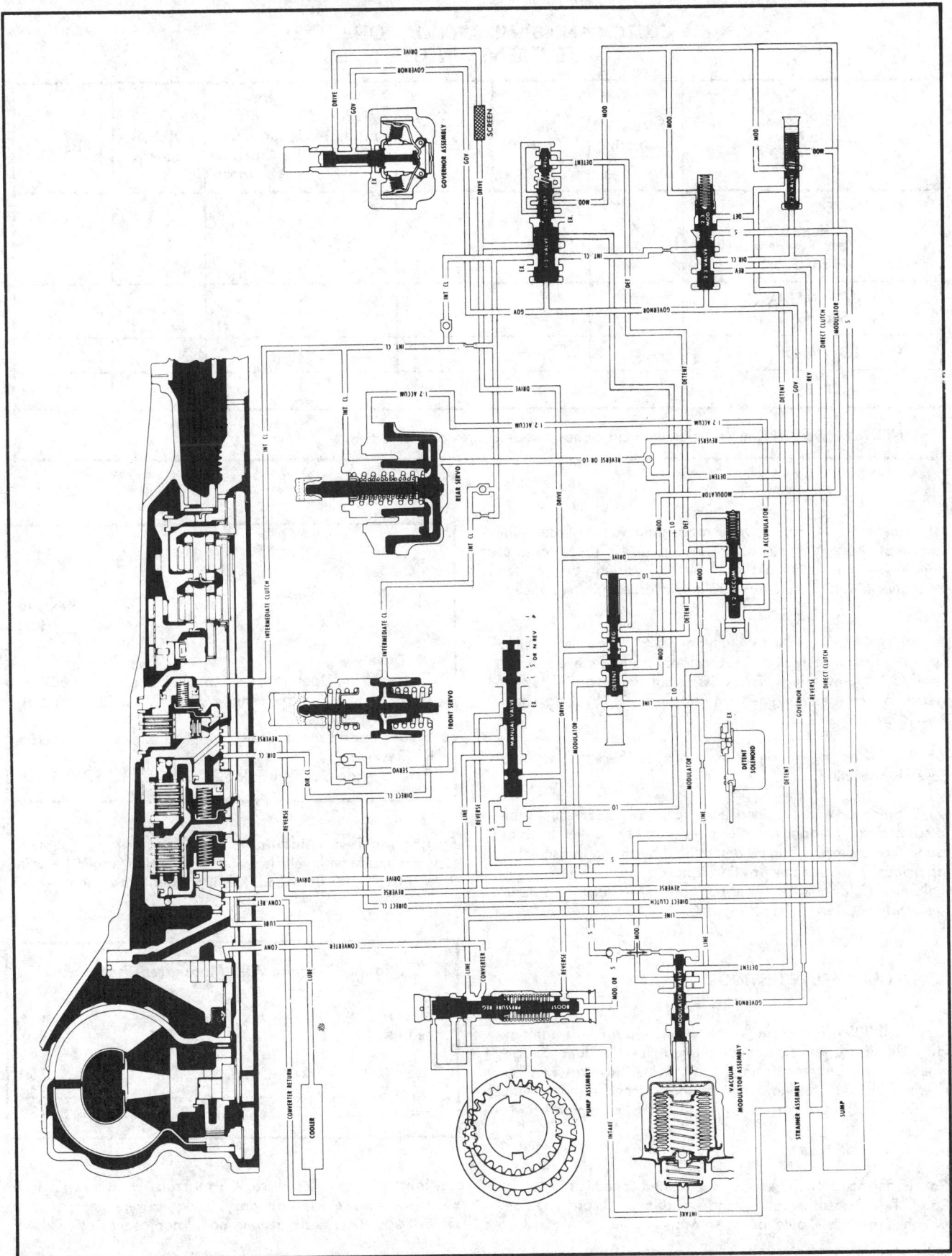

Fig. 2 *Turbo Hydra-Matic 400 Hydraulic Circuits Diagram*

Automatic Transmissions

GENERAL MOTORS TURBO HYDRA-MATIC 400 (Cont.)

CLUTCH AND BAND APPLICATION CHART
(ELEMENTS IN USE)

Selector Lever Position	Forward Clutch	Direct Clutch	Front Band	Intermediate Clutch	Intermediate Roller Clutch Or Sprag	Low Roller Clutch	Rear Band
D - DRIVE							
First Gear	X					X	
Second Gear	X			X	X		
Third Gear	X	X		X			
2 — INTERMEDIATE							
Second Gear	X		X	X	X		
1 — LOW (First)	X					X	X
R — REVERSE		X					X
NEUTRAL OR PARK — All clutches and bands released and/or ineffective.							

4) With selector lever in Drive range and vehicle speed approximately 35 MPH, move selector lever to "2" (Intermediate) range. Transmission should downshift to 2nd gear; an increase in engine RPM and an engine braking effect should be noticed.

5) With selector lever in "2" (Intermediate) range and vehicle speed approximately 30 MPH (constant throttle), move selector lever to "1" (Low) range. Transmission should downshift to first gear; an increase in engine RPM and an engine braking effect should be noticed.

6) With selector lever in Reverse range, check for suitable reverse operation.

7) Slipping or engine speed flare-up in any gear usually indicates clutch or band problems. In most cases, the clutch or band that is slipping can be determined by noting transmission operation in all selector positions and comparing which internal units are applied in those positions. *See Clutch and Band Application Chart.*

CONTROL PRESSURE TESTING

Install a 0-300 psi pressure gauge to pressure take-off point at left side of transmission (near manual lever). Place gauge where it can be seen from driver's seat. Pressures can be checked by road testing or by stationary checks; made with transmission fluid at correct level and operating temperature.

Road Testing — Drive vehicle at indicated speed (as noted in Road Test Pressures table) and read control pressure on gauge. Pressures should be as shown in table.

NOTE — *Vacuum modulator must be CONNECTED during road testing.*

Road Test Pressures

Selector Position	Pressure (Psi)
"D" (Drive)	
Zero to Wide Open Throttle	60-150
Coast at 30 MPH (3rd Gear)	(Min.) 60
"L2" (Intermediate)	
Steady Road Load at 25 MPH	145-155
"R" (Reverse)	
Zero to Wide Open Throttle	95-260

Stationary Test (Modulator Disconnected) — Following tests are made with vehicle stationary, brakes applied, engine RPM set to 1200 RPM and vacuum modulator disconnected.

Stationary Pressure With Modulator Disconnected

Selector Position	Pressure (Psi)
Drive, Neutral, Park	150
"L1" or "L2"	150
Reverse	233

Stationary Test (Modulator Connected) — Following tests are made with vehicle stationary, brakes applied, engine RPM set to 1000 RPM and vacuum modulator connected.

NOTE — *Pressures are not significantly affected by altitude or barometric pressure when vacuum modulator line is connected.*

GENERAL MOTORS TURBO HYDRA-MATIC 400 (Cont.)

Stationary Pressures With Modulator Connected	
Selector Position	Pressure (Psi)
Drive, Neutral, Park	60
"L1" or "L2"	150
Reverse	107

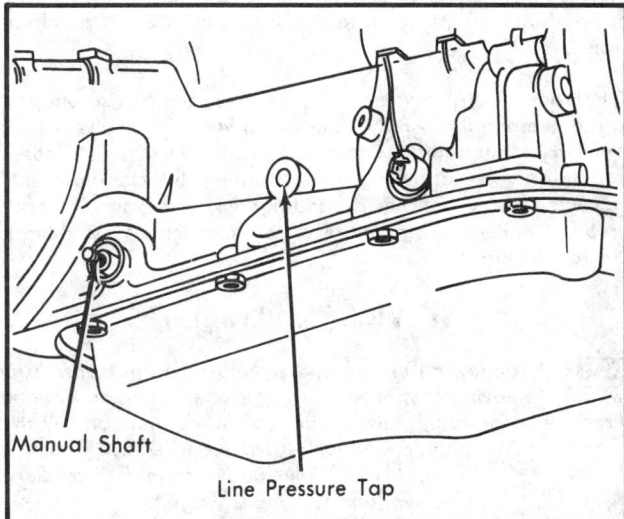

Manual Shaft

Line Pressure Tap

Fig. 3   Location of Control Pressure Test Point

CONTROL PRESSURE TEST RESULTS

Line Pressure Too High

- Vacuum leak, vacuum line disconnected, leak in line from engine to modulator, leak in vacuum operated accessories or improper engine vacuum.
- Vacuum modulator defective, valve stuck, water in modulator or modulator damaged. Detent switch actuated (plunger stuck) or shorted. Detent wiring shorted, solenoid loose or stuck open. Detent feed orifice in spacer plate blocked or restricted. Detent solenoid loose. Detent valve bore plug damaged. Detent regulator valve pin short.
- Pressure regulator and/or boost valve stuck. Incorrect pressure regulator valve spring. Too many pressure regulator valve spacers. Pressure boost valve installed backwards or defective. Pressure boost bushing broken or defective. Oil pump casting bad.

Line Pressure Too Low

- Fluid level low, vacuum modulator assembly defective. Oil filter blocked or restricted, "O" ring seal on intake pipe and/or grommet omitted or damaged. Split or leaking intake pipe. Incorrect oil filter installed.
- Oil pump damaged, worn or drive gear installed backwards. Pressure regulator and/or boost valve stuck. Pressure regulator valve spring too weak or not enough spacers in regulator. Gear clearance excessive. Pump-to-case gasket mispositioned. Defective or mismatched pump body-to-pump case.

Line Pressure Low in Drive, But Normal in Neutral or Reverse

- Leak in forward clutch. Check pump oil seal rings or forward clutch seals.

Line Pressure Low in Reverse, Normal in All Other Ranges

- Leak in direct clutch. Check center support oil seal rings. Check direct clutch outer seal. Check rear servo and front accumulator pistons and/or rings for damage or missing components. Case assembly is porous in intake bore area.
- Intermediate clutch cup plug is leaking or blown out. Low-reverse check ball incorrectly installed or missing (this will cause no reverse and no overrun braking in "1" range.)

GOVERNOR TEST

1) With vehicle on hoist (wheels off ground), disconnect vacuum line to modulator. Connect a pressure gauge to transmission and a tachometer to engine.

2) Start engine, keep foot off brake, move selector lever to Drive range and check line pressure at 1000 RPM. Slowly increase engine speed to 3000 RPM and check for a pressure drop of at least 7 psi for all models.

3) If no pressure drop occurs, inspect governor for stuck valve or weight, or a restricted orifice in valve. Check governor feed system for plugged or restricted screen(s), restrictions in governor pipe, and proper fit of governor pipes in case holes.

4) If specified pressure drop occurs, and transmission is malfunctioning, disassemble, clean and inspect control valve assembly.

VACUUM MODULATOR CHECK

NOTE — *On models equipped with diesel engine, the vacuum source for the vacuum modulator is the Vacuum Regulator Valve. This valve is mounted on injection pump. When diagnosing shift complaints, it is important that the vacuum pump is providing 22 inches of vacuum to this valve.*

Vacuum Diaphragm Leak Check — Insert a pipe cleaner into vacuum connector pipe as far as possible and check for presence of transmission oil. If oil is found, replace modulator.

NOTE — *Gasoline or water vapor may settle in vacuum side of modulator. If this is found without presence of oil, modulator should not be changed.*

Atmospheric Leak Check — Apply a liberal coating of soap bubble solution to vacuum connector pipe seam, crimped upper to lower housing seam, and threaded screw seal (if equipped). Using a short piece of rubber tubing, apply air pressure to vacuum pipe by blowing into tube, then observe for leak bubbles. If bubbles appear, replace modulator.

CAUTION — *Do not use any other method other than human lung power for applying air pressure. Pressures over 6 psi will damage modulator.*

GENERAL MOTORS TURBO HYDRA-MATIC 400 (Cont.)

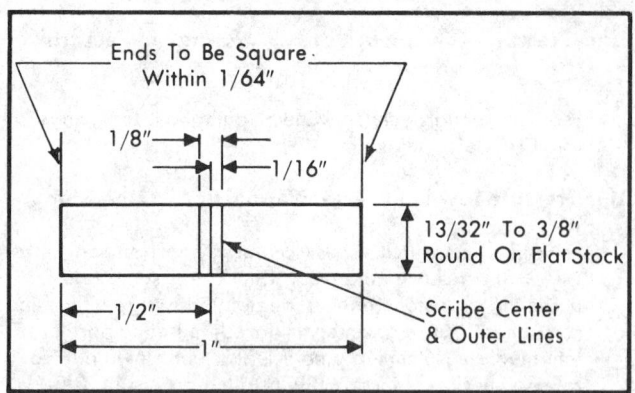

Fig. 4   Dimensions for Bellows Comparison Gauge

Bellows Comparison Check — 1) Using suitable comparison gauge, compare the load of modulator in question with a known good modulator (same part number).

2) Install good modulator on either end of gauge, then install modulator in question on opposite end. Holding modulators in a horizontal position, bring them together under pressure until either modulator sleeve just touches the line in center of gauge.

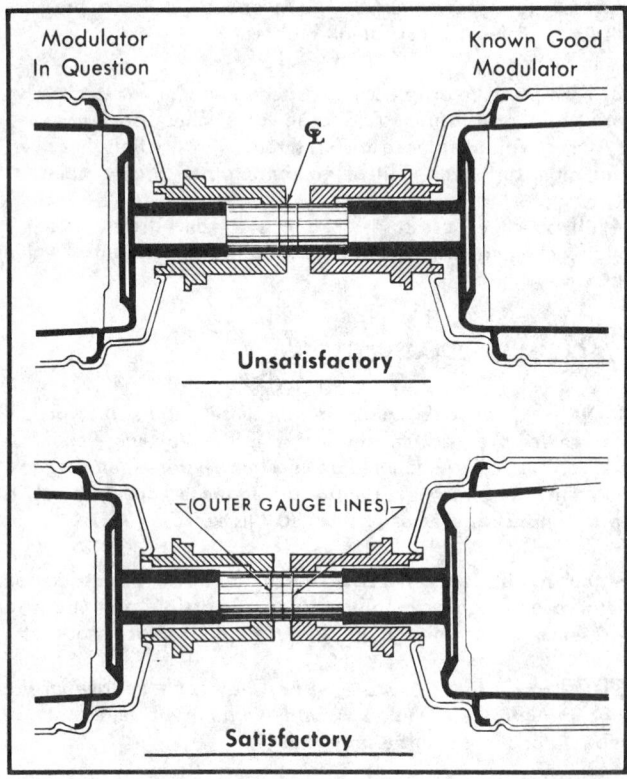

Fig. 5   Vacuum Modulator Bellows Comparison Check

3) Gap between opposite modulator sleeve end and gauge center line should be ¹⁄₁₆" or less. If distance is greater, modulator should be replaced.

Sleeve Alignment Check — Roll main body of modulator on a flat surface and observe the sleeve for concentricity to the cam. If sleeve is concentric and plunger is free, modulator is acceptable.

VACUUM REGULATOR VALVE (DIESEL MODELS ONLY)

1) Check vacuum pump for output of at least 22 inches Hg. Repair or replace as required. Disconnect throttle rod from throttle lever. Install carburetor angle gauge tool (J-26701 & J-26701-15) to injection pump throttle lever.

2) Rotate throttle lever to W.O.T. position and set angle gauge to 0°. Center bubble in level and set angle gauge to 50°. Rotate throttle lever until bubble in gauge is centered. Connect a hand vacuum pump to inboard vacuum port on regulator valve.

3) Connect suitable vacuum gauge to outboard vacuum port on regulator valve. Apply 22 inches of vacuum to valve. Check vacuum gauge reading for 7-8 inches vacuum. If not, loosen regulator valve attaching bolts, rotate valve clockwise until vacuum reads 7-8 inches Hg and tighten valve attaching bolts to 5 ft. lbs. Remove gauges, reconnect vacuum hoses and throttle rod to throttle lever.

SERVICE (IN VEHICLE)

NOTE — *Following units may be removed from transmission without removing transmission from vehicle: Extension Housing, Pressure Regulator Valve, Vacuum Modulator and Valve, Governor Assembly, Speedometer Drive and Driven Gears, Intake Pipe, Oil Pan and Filter, Valve Body Assembly, Rear Servo Assembly, Manual Lever and Parking Linkage.*

REMOVAL & INSTALLATION

See Transmission Removal & Installation in Automatic Transmission Servicing.

TORQUE CONVERTER

LEAKAGE CHECK

Install pressure test plug tool (J-21369 or suitable equivalent) into converter hub and tighten tool to expand it. Install safety strap to prevent tool from blowing out when air pressure is applied. Apply 80 psi air pressure to air valve in tool. Submerge converter in water and check for leaks.

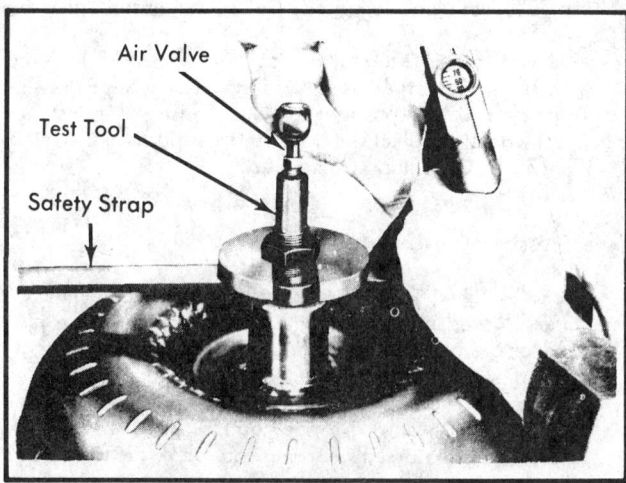

Fig. 6   Assembling Pressure Test Plug to Converter for Torque Converter Leakage Check

GENERAL MOTORS TURBO HYDRA-MATIC 400 (Cont.)

END CLEARANCE CHECK

Install end clearance checking tool (J-21371-8 or suitable equivalent) into converter hub until collet end of tool bottoms. Tighten tool cap nut to 5 ft. lbs. to expand collet. Install support collar (J-21371-3 or suitable equivalent) on converter hub and tighten hex nut to 3 ft. lbs. Install a dial indicator on support collar so that indicator contact bears against test tool cap nut. Set dial indicator at zero. Loosen hex nut while holding cap nut stationary. With hex nut loosened and support collar held firmly against converter hub, reading obtained on dial indicator will be converter end clearance. End clearance should be less than .050". If end clearance is greater, replace converter.

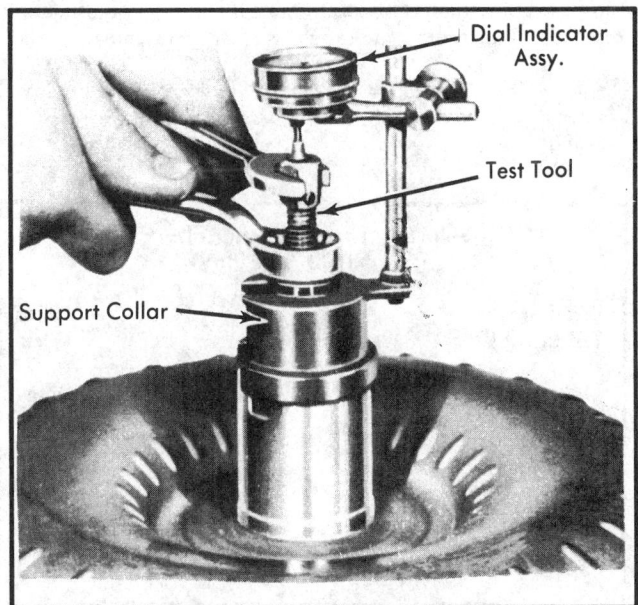

Fig. 7 Assembling Checking Tools to Torque Converter for Converter End Clearance Check

TRANSMISSION DISASSEMBLY

VACUUM MODULATOR & VALVE

Remove modulator attaching screw and retainer, then remove modulator and "O" ring from case. Discard "O" ring, remove modulator valve from transmission case.

GOVERNOR

Remove attaching screws, cover and gasket, then remove governor assembly by pulling straight out of case.

SPEEDOMETER DRIVEN GEAR

Remove speedometer cable, attaching screw and retainer, then apply slight pressure to remove sleeve and driven gear.

INTAKE PIPE, FILTER & OIL PAN

Remove oil pan. Remove filter and intake pipe assembly, discard filter. Remove "O" ring seal from intake pipe and discard seal.

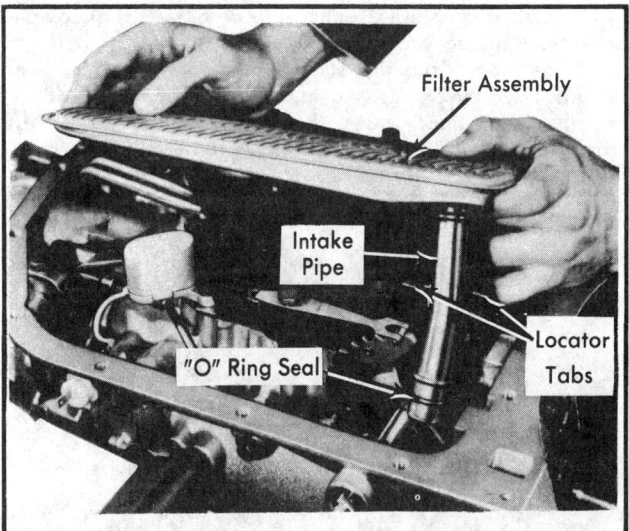

Fig. 8 Removing Filter Assembly and "O" Ring

CONTROL VALVE BODY ASSEMBLY

1) Remove control valve body attaching screws and detent roller and spring assembly (do not remove solenoid attaching screws).

CAUTION — *If transmission is installed in vehicle, front servo parts may drop out as control valve assembly is removed.*

2) Using care not to drop manual valve, remove control valve assembly and governor pipes from case. Remove governor screen assembly from governor feed pipe hole in case or from end of governor feed pipe. Clean screen in solvent and air dry.

3) Remove governor pipes from control valve assembly. Disconnect solenoid lead wire from connector terminal. Remove control valve-to-spacer gasket.

REAR SERVO

Remove servo cover and discard gasket. Remove servo assembly from transmission case. Remove servo accumulator spring. Make a Band Apply Pin Selection Check at this point to select correct pin for reassembly.

NOTE — *This is equivalent to a band adjustment.*

Band Apply Selection Check — 1) Make check at this time to determine possible cause of malfunction. Position band apply pin selector gauge and gauge pin (parts of gauge set J-21370) on transmission case over rear servo bore, and secure with servo cover attaching screws. See Fig. 9.

NOTE — *Make sure gauge pin does not bind in case.*

2) Using torque wrench, apply 25 ft. lbs. of torque to lever on selector gauge. Selection of proper band apply pin is determined by the relation of the flat(s) on gauge pin to the flat machined area around the hole in selector gauge. For models CD and CL pin selection, see Pin Selection Table. For all other models, proceed to step 3).

GENERAL MOTORS TURBO HYDRA-MATIC 400 (Cont.)

3) On all models except CD and CL, if both steps of gauge pin are below gauge surface, long pin (identified by 3 rings) should be used. If gauging surface is between steps, medium pin (identified by 2 rings) should be used. If both steps of pin are above gauging surface, short pin (identified by 1 ring) should be used. Record pin selection for reassembly reference.

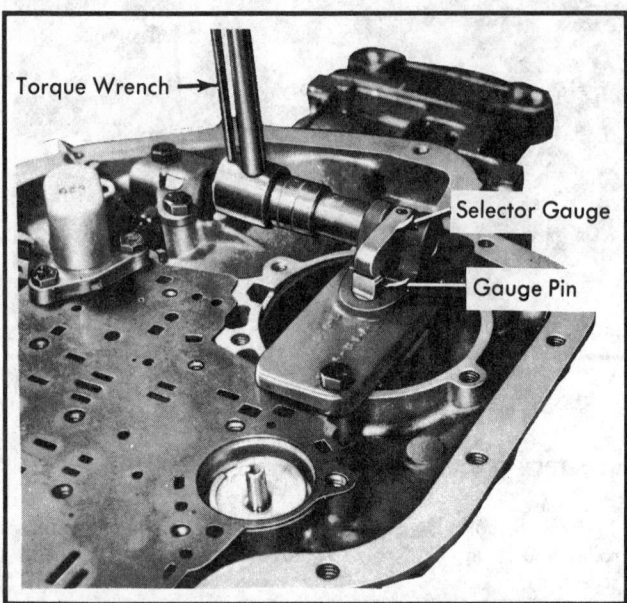

Fig. 9   Installation of Rear Band Apply Pin Checking Tools

Model CD & CL Pin Selection Table

GAGING STEPS LOCATED ON THREE SIDES OF TOOL J-21370-9		PART NO.	PIN IDENTIFICATION
C	LONGEST PIN	THIS STEP: USE PIN NO. 8627195	
		THIS STEP: SIDES B TO C USE PIN NO. 8627194	
B		THIS STEP: USE PIN NO. 8624141	
		THIS STEP: SIDES A TO B USE PIN NO. 8627193	
A		THIS STEP: USE PIN NO. 8624140	
	LOWER STEP SHORTEST PIN	LOWER STEP: USE PIN NO. 8627192	

Note: The Identification Rings are .030" and .100" wide.

DETENT SOLENOID, CONTROL VALVE SPACER & FRONT SERVO

Remove attaching screws and lift off detent solenoid assembly and gasket. Compress connector tangs, withdraw case sleeve connector and "O" ring seal, then discard seal. Remove control valve spacer plate and gasket. Remove 6 check balls; then lift out front servo piston, washer, pin, retainer and springs.

CAUTION — *If transmission is in vehicle, hold plate in a level position so that check balls will not fall out.*

EXTENSION HOUSING

If necessary to replace, pry rear oil seal out of extension housing. Remove extension housing-to-case attaching bolts, then remove extension housing and gasket from case.

NOTE — *Transmission front unit end play should be checked before proceeding with Transmission Disassembly.*

FRONT UNIT END PLAY CHECK

NOTE — *End play should be checked before further disassembly of transmission.*

1) Remove 1 oil pump attaching bolt at either the 10 o'clock or 5 o'clock position and install a 3/8" by 16" rod in bolt hole. Mount dial indicator on rod and index indicator on flat surface on end of turbine shaft.

2) Push turbine shaft rearward and output shaft forward, set indicator to zero, then pull turbine shaft forward and read end play. End play should be .003-.024". If end play adjustment is required, select correct thickness washer from chart.

NOTE — *The selective washer controlling front unit end play is the washer located between pump cover and forward clutch housing.*

Selective Thrust Washer Chart (Front Unit End Play)

Washer Thickness ①	I.D. Number	Color Code
.060-.064"	0	Yellow
.071-.075"	1	Blue
.082-.086"	2	Red
.093-.097"	3	Brown
.104-.108"	4	Green
.115-.119"	5	Black
.126-.130"	6	Purple

① — An oil soaked washer may tend to discolor, so it will be necessary to measure washer for its actual thickness.

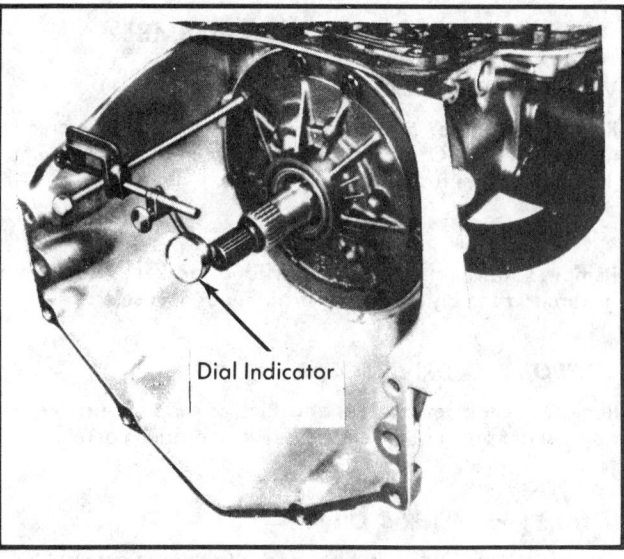

Fig. 10   Using a Dial Indicator to Measure Front Unit End Play

GENERAL MOTORS TURBO HYDRA-MATIC 400 (Cont.)

OIL PUMP

If necessary to replace pump front seal, pry seal out before removing pump. Remove pump attaching screws. Install threaded bolts and slide hammers into two opposite pump mounting bolt holes, and drive pump assembly out of transmission case. Remove and discard pump-to-case seal ring and gasket.

CAUTION — *Drive outward in unison on both slide hammers to prevent cocking pump assembly in transmission case.*

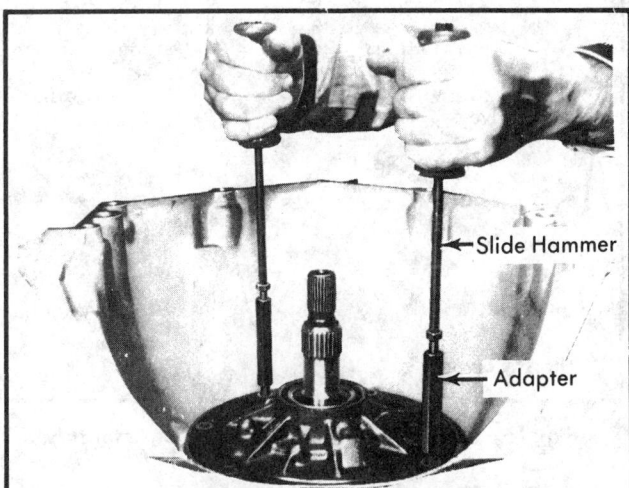

Fig. 11 *Using Slide Hammers to Remove Oil Pump Assembly*

TURBINE SHAFT & FORWARD CLUTCH ASSEMBLY, SUN GEAR SHAFT & FRONT BAND

Remove forward clutch and turbine shaft assembly from transmission, then remove forward clutch hub to direct clutch housing thrust washer. Remove direct clutch and intermediate roller assembly, then remove sun gear shaft. Remove front band assembly.

NOTE — *Make a rear unit end play check before proceeding with transmission disassembly.*

REAR UNIT END PLAY CHECK

1) Install threaded rod into one of the bolt holes in transmission extension housing. Install dial indicator on rod and index indicator on flat surface on end of output shaft and zero dial indicator.

2) Move output shaft in and out and read end play. End play should be .007-.019″. If end play adjustment is required, select correct thickness washer from chart.

Selective Thrust Washer Chart (Rear Unit End Play)	
Washer Thickness	**Identification Notches and/or Numeral**
.074-.078″	None............1
.082-.086″	1 Tab Side......2
.090-.094″	2 Tabs Side......3
.098-.102″	1 Tab O.D.......4
.106-.110″	2 Tabs O.D.......5
.114-.118″	3 Tabs O.D.......6

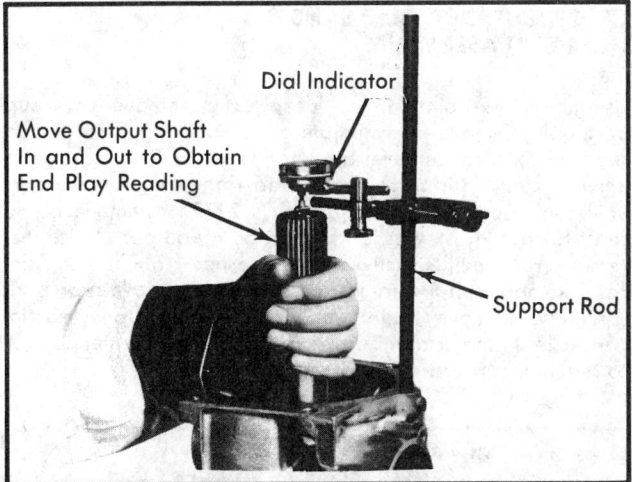

Fig. 12 *Measuring Rear Unit End Play*

MANUAL LINKAGE

NOTE — *Model CD transmission does not have a parking lock mechanism.*

1) If necessary, remove manual linkage as follows:

2) Loosen jam nut holding detent lever to manual shaft. Remove manual shaft retaining pin from case. Remove manual shaft and jam nut from case using care not to lose jam nut as it becomes free from shaft.

3) Remove parking actuator rod and detent lever assembly. Remove attaching screws and parking bracket. Remove parking pawl return spring.

NOTE — *The following step is to be completed only if one or more of the parts require replacement.*

4) Remove parking pawl shaft retainer. Insert a screwdriver between parking pawl shaft and case and pry outward to remove shaft cup plug. Remove parking pawl shaft and parking pawl.

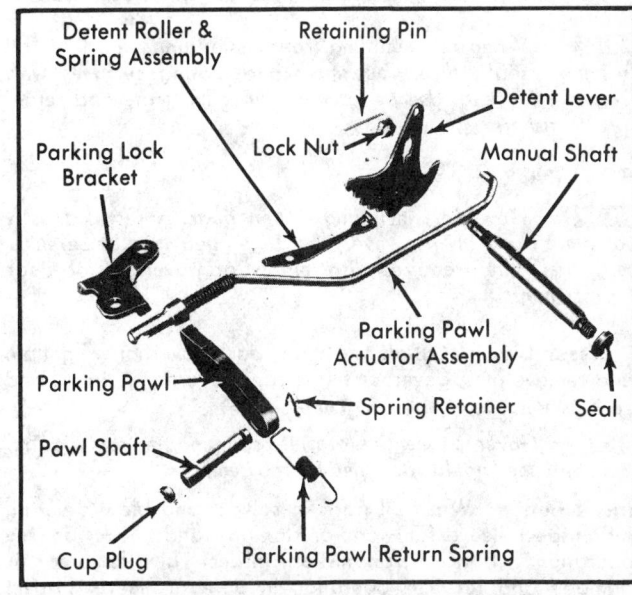

Fig. 13 *Exploded View of Manual Linkage*

GENERAL MOTORS TURBO HYDRA-MATIC 400 (Cont.)

CENTER SUPPORT, REAR BAND & GEAR UNIT ASSEMBLIES

Using a ⅜" 12-point thin wall deep socket, remove center support bolt. Remove intermediate clutch backing plate-to-case snap ring, then remove backing plate and clutch plates. Remove center support-to-case snap ring, then remove gear unit, using suitable removing tool (J-21795). Remove output shaft-to-case thrust washer from rear of output shaft, then remove rear unit selective thrust washer from transmission case. Remove support-to-case spacer, then remove rear band assembly. Remove center support assembly from reaction carrier by lifting straight upward, then remove center support to reaction carrier thrust washer.

Fig. 14 Removing Center Support-to-Case Bolt

COMPONENT DISASSEMBLY & REASSEMBLY

NOTE — *When reassembling transmission units, lubricate all bushings, seals, thrust bearings, and mating surfaces with transmission fluid. Use petroleum jelly to lubricate and retain thrust washers.*

GOVERNOR

NOTE — *Governor, including driven gear, is serviced as a complete assembly. However, the driven gear can be serviced separately and requires disassembly of governor for gear replacement.*

Disassembly — Cut off one end of each governor weight pin and remove pins, governor thrust cap, governor weights, and springs. Remove valve from governor sleeve.

NOTE — *Governor weights are interchangeable from side to side and need not be identified for reassembly.*

Inspection — Wash all parts in solvent and blow dry with air. Inspect sleeve for wear or damage and check for free operation in bore of transmission. Inspect valve for wear or damage and for free operation in bore of sleeve. Inspect driven gear for wear or damage and for looseness on sleeve.

Inspect springs for distortion and weights for free operation in retainers. Check valve opening at entry and exhaust (.020" minimum).

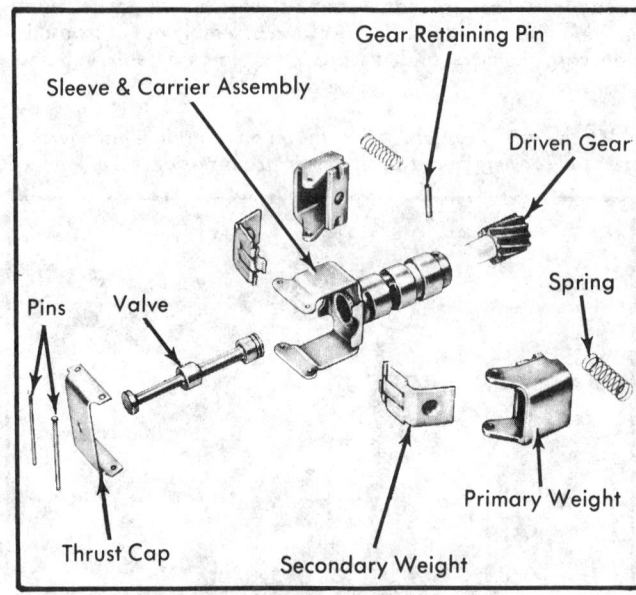

Fig. 15 Exploded View of Governor Assembly

Driven Gear Replacement — With governor disassembled, drive out gear retaining split pin, then support governor assembly on ⁷⁄₆₄" plates installed in exhaust slots of sleeve on an arbor press and press gear out of sleeve. To install gear, support governor in same manner as for gear removal and press gear on until it is almost seated. Carefully remove any chips that may have been shaved off gear and press gear in until it bottoms on shoulder. Drill new ⅛" hole 90° from existing hole, then install retaining pin and completely wash unit.

Reassembly — Install valve in bore of sleeve, inserting large end first. Then install weights, springs, and thrust cap on sleeve. Align pin holes in thrust cap, weight assemblies and sleeve. Install pins, then crimp both ends of pins. Check weight assemblies for free movement.

CONTROL VALVE BODY ASSEMBLY

NOTE — *As valve trains are removed from each valve body bore, place individual parts in correct order and in relative position to valve body to simplify reassembly.*

CAUTION — *Valves and springs are NOT interchangeable. All parts MUST be installed in correct order and in proper valve body bore.*

Disassembly — 1) Place valve body on bench with cored face up and accumulator pocket at bottom. Remove manual valve from upper bore. Compress accumulator piston and remove retaining "E" ring. Remove accumulator piston and spring. See Fig. 16.

2) On right side, next to manual valve, remove 1-2 valve train retaining pin. On CG, CJ and CP model transmissions, remove 1-2 modulator bushing, 1-2 valve spring, 1-2 modulator valve and 1-2 shift valve.

GENERAL MOTORS TURBO HYDRA-MATIC 400 (Cont.)

3) On all other model transmissions, remove 1-2 modulator bushing, 1-2 regulator valve, 1-2 regulator spring, 1-2 detent valve and 1-2 shift valve. Remove retaining pin from next bore down. From bore, remove 2-3 shift valve spring, 2-3 modulator valve bushing, 2-3 modulator valve, 3-2 intermediate spring and 2-3 shift valve.

NOTE — *Model CZ transmission does not use a 2-3 shift valve spring.*

4) Remove retaining pin from next bore down. From bore, remove bore plug, spring, spacer and 3-2 valve. Remove retaining pin from top bore at other end of valve body. From bore, remove bore plug, detent valve, detent regulator valve, spring and spacer.

5) On CK, CP and CZ models, from next bore down, remove grooved retaining pin, bore plug, 1-2 accumulator valve and spring. On CB, CD, CJ and CL models, from next bore down, remove grooved retaining pin, bore plug and 1-2 accumulator valve.

6) On CF, CG, CH, CM, CT and CW models, from next bore down, remove grooved retaining pin, bore plug, 1-2 accumulator secondary spring and 1-2 accumulator valve.

Inspection — 1) Inspect all valves for scoring, cracks and free movement in respective bores. Inspect accumulator piston and oil seal ring for damage.

NOTE — *Do not remove teflon oil seal ring from front accumulator piston unless oil seal ring requires replacement. For service, the oil seal ring is cast iron.*

2) Inspect bushings for cracks, scratches or distortion. Inspect body for cracks or scored bores. Check all springs for distortion or collapsed coils.

Reassembly — Reverse disassembly procedures using *Fig. 16* for reassembly reference.

NOTE — *Manual valve is installed with detent pin groove to the right.*

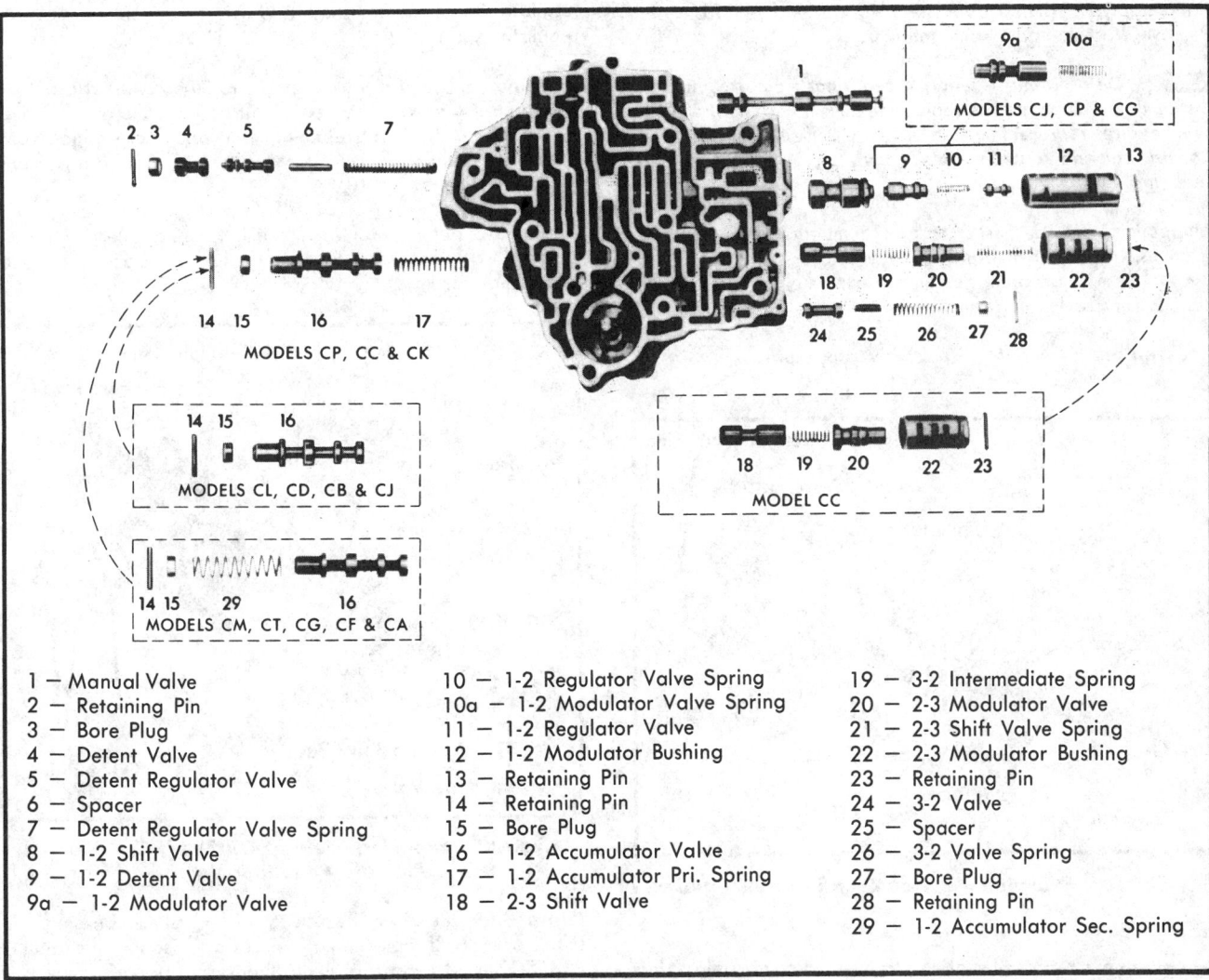

1 — Manual Valve	10 — 1-2 Regulator Valve Spring	19 — 3-2 Intermediate Spring
2 — Retaining Pin	10a — 1-2 Modulator Valve Spring	20 — 2-3 Modulator Valve
3 — Bore Plug	11 — 1-2 Regulator Valve	21 — 2-3 Shift Valve Spring
4 — Detent Valve	12 — 1-2 Modulator Bushing	22 — 2-3 Modulator Bushing
5 — Detent Regulator Valve	13 — Retaining Pin	23 — Retaining Pin
6 — Spacer	14 — Retaining Pin	24 — 3-2 Valve
7 — Detent Regulator Valve Spring	15 — Bore Plug	25 — Spacer
8 — 1-2 Shift Valve	16 — 1-2 Accumulator Valve	26 — 3-2 Valve Spring
9 — 1-2 Detent Valve	17 — 1-2 Accumulator Pri. Spring	27 — Bore Plug
9a — 1-2 Modulator Valve	18 — 2-3 Shift Valve	28 — Retaining Pin
		29 — 1-2 Accumulator Sec. Spring

Fig. 16   Exploded View of Valve Body Assembly

Automatic Transmissions

GENERAL MOTORS TURBO HYDRA-MATIC 400 (Cont.)

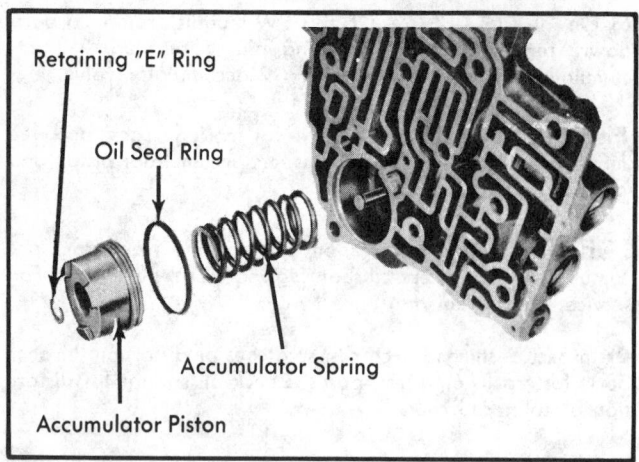

Fig. 17   Disassembled View of Front Accumulator

REAR SERVO

Disassembly — Remove rear accumulator piston from rear servo piston. Remove "E" clip retaining rear servo piston to band apply pin. Remove rear servo piston and seal from pin. Remove washer, spring and retainer.

NOTE — *Do not remove teflon oil seal rings from accumulator piston unless they require replacement. If inner (small) teflon seal requires replacement, use aluminum oil seal ring. If outer (large) seal ring requires replacement, use only the teflon oil seal ring.*

Inspection — Inspect freeness of accumulator rings in piston grooves. Inspect fit of band apply pin in servo piston. Check pin for scores or damage. Inspect accumulator and servo pistons for cracks or porosity.

Reassembly — Reverse disassembly procedure.

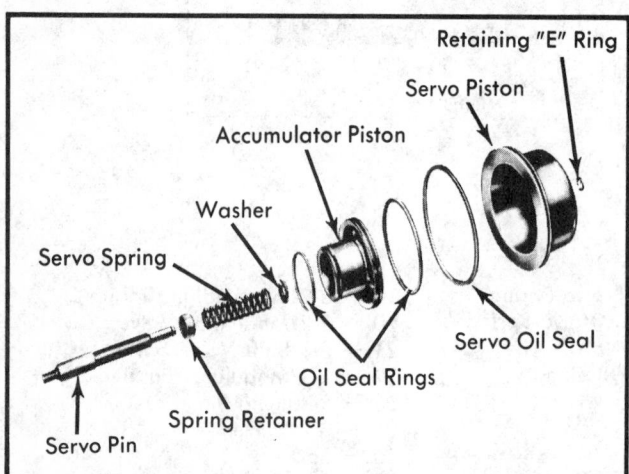

Fig. 18   Exploded View of Rear Servo Assembly

FRONT SERVO

Do not remove teflon oil seal ring from servo piston unless ring requires replacement. For service, the oil seal ring will be aluminum.

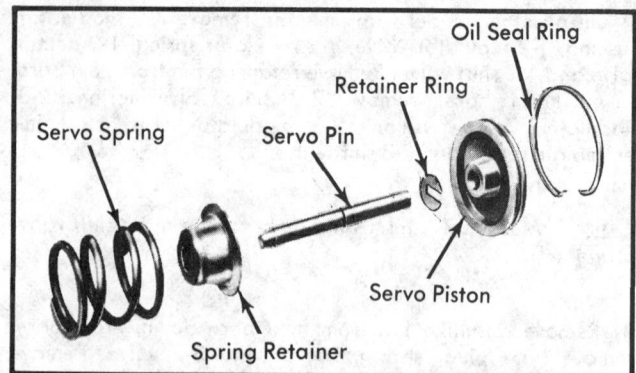

Fig. 19   Exploded View of Front Servo Assembly

Inspection — Inspect servo pin, piston and oil seal ring for damage. Check fit of servo pin in piston and case bore.

OIL PUMP

Disassembly — **1)** Place pump assembly in suitable holding fixture and compress regulator boost valve bushing against pressure regulator spring and remove snap ring. Remove regulator boost valve bushing and valve, then remove pressure regulator spring.

2) Remove regulator valve, spring retainer and spacer(s) (if equipped). Remove pump cover attaching bolts and remove pump cover. Remove retaining pin and bore plug from pressure regulator bore. Remove hook-type oil rings from pump cover.

3) Remove pump-to-forward clutch housing selective thrust washer. Mark drive and driven gears for reassembly reference and remove from pump body.

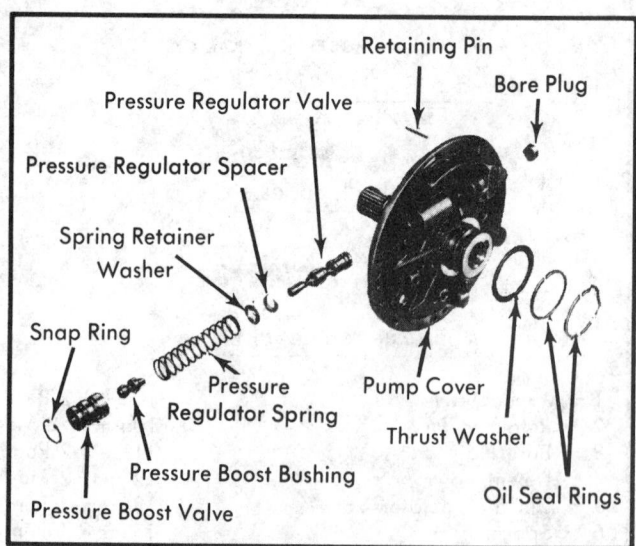

Fig. 20   Exploded View of Oil Pump Cover and Pressure Regulator Valve

Pump Body Bushing Replacement — Check bushing for scores or nicks. If replacement is necessary, use suitable tool (J-21465-17) and remove bushing. From front side of pump, use same tool and install new bushing until it is flush to .010" below gear pocket face.

GENERAL MOTORS TURBO HYDRA-MATIC 400 (Cont.)

Stator Shaft Bushing Replacement — 1) With stator shaft and pump cover properly supported, use suitable tool (J-21465-15) with slide hammer and adapter and remove front bushing. Using suitable tool (J-21465-3), drive replacement bushing into place until tool bottoms.

2) Perform step 1) again, and this time removing rear bushing. Using suitable tool (J-21465-2), drive replacement bushing into place until tool bottoms.

Inspection — Inspect all parts for nicks, scoring, galling, wear or damage. Install pump gears in pump and check pump body face-to-gear face clearance using feeler gauge. Clearance should be .0008-.0035″. Check overall flatness of pump body face. Inspect oil ring grooves for damage and/or wear. Make sure all passages are clean and open. Check pressure regulator and boost valves for free fit in bores. Install pump cover oil rings into counterbore of forward clutch housing and check for proper fit.

CAUTION — *Several different types of pump bodies and covers are in service. The current production pressure regulator valve (solid type) does not contain oil holes or an orifice cup plug, as previous models did. This new type valve must ONLY be used in the pump cover with the squared-off pressure regulator boss.*

Reassembly — Reverse disassembly procedure and note the following:

1) When installing front unit selective thrust washer, make sure it is the proper thickness as determined at disassembly. To align pump body and cover, install attaching bolts, leaving one turn loose.

2) Place pump assembly, less rubber seal ring, upside down into pump bore in transmission case. Tighten pump cover attaching bolts to specifications. Remove pump assembly from case and install pump-to-case "O" ring.

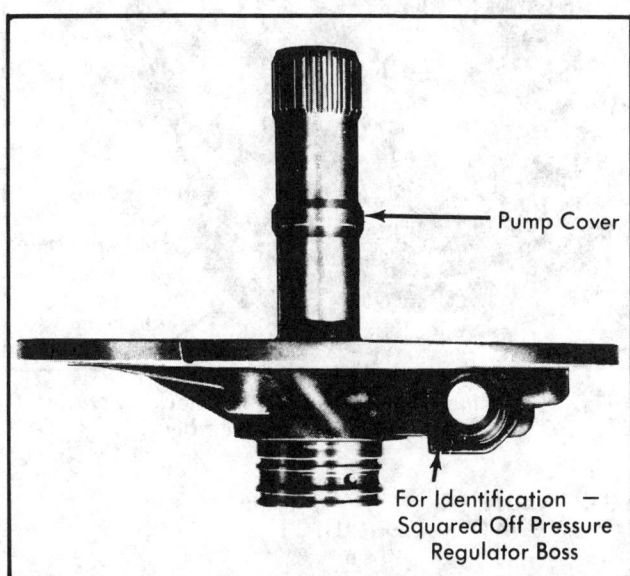

Fig. 21 Pump Cover Used With Pressure Regulator Valve Without Oil Holes or Orifice Cup Plug

Pump Cover

For Identification — Squared Off Pressure Regulator Boss

FORWARD CLUTCH

Disassembly — 1) Remove snap ring which retains forward clutch housing to direct clutch hub. Remove clutch hub from housing. Remove forward clutch hub and thrust washer from each side of hub. Remove steel and composition clutch plates.

NOTE — *Models CL and CD do not use a waved steel plate.*

2) Position forward clutch and turbine shaft in arbor press, and press turbine shaft out of clutch housing. Using a suitable compressor tool, compress forward clutch piston and remove snap ring.

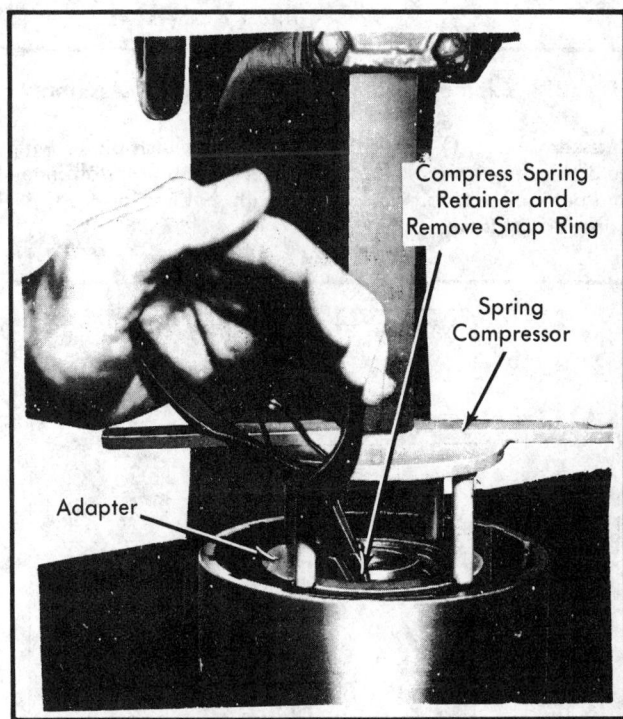

Compress Spring Retainer and Remove Snap Ring

Spring Compressor

Adapter

Fig. 22 Compressing Forward Clutch Piston for Removal of Snap Ring

3) Lift out spring retainer and 16 clutch release springs, keeping springs separated from direct clutch release springs. Remove forward clutch piston. Remove seals from piston and forward clutch housing.

CAUTION — *Production built transmissions use a direct clutch piston without a check ball. The forward and direct clutch pistons are similar in appearance. Be sure the forward clutch piston is identified during disassembly so it will be installed correctly. Also, the production built forward clutch piston will be aluminum or stamped steel.*

Inspection — Inspect clutch plates for burning, scoring, wear or damage. Check release springs for distortion and/or collapsed coils. Inspect all parts for wear, scoring, damage and open oil passages. Check operation of check ball in forward clutch housing.

GENERAL MOTORS TURBO HYDRA-MATIC 400 (Cont.)

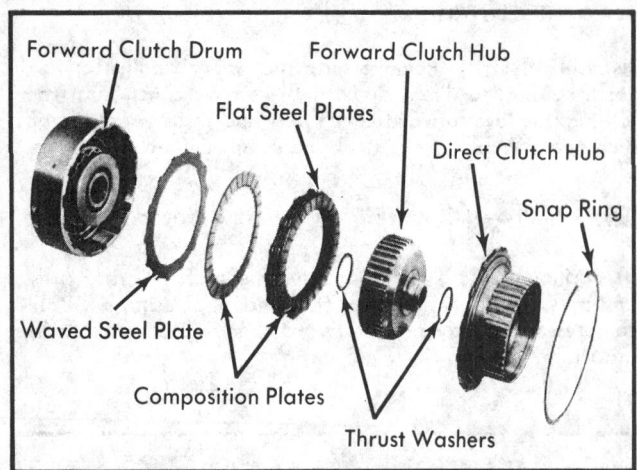

Fig. 23 Exploded View of Forward Clutch Assembly

Reassembly — 1) Lubricate all seals and clutch plates with automatic transmission fluid before reassembly. Install inner and outer oil seals on clutch piston with seal lips facing away from spring pockets.

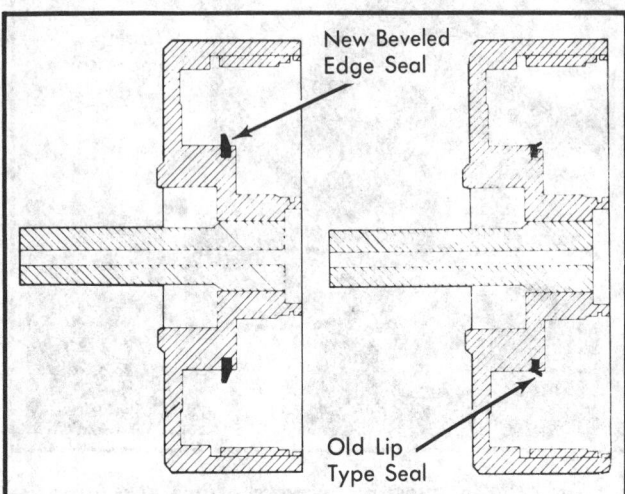

Fig. 24 Forward Clutch Housing Center Seal Application

2) Install center oil seal in clutch housing with beveled edge of seal facing upward and toward open end of housing.

NOTE — *A new type forward clutch housing center seal is being used. It has a beveled edge and is interchangeable with the old type seal. However, the old type seal CANNOT be used in the later model transmissions. Make sure correct seal is installed.*

3) Using suitable seal protectors, install piston into clutch housing using a twisting motion. Install 16 clutch release springs in piston pockets and place retainer over springs. Compress spring retainer and install snap ring.

4) Press short-spline end of turbine shaft into forward clutch housing using an arbor press. Place thrust washers on forward clutch hub. Be sure bronze washer (if used) is installed on side

of hub facing housing. Use petroleum jelly to hold washers in place. Install hub and washers into forward clutch housing.

5) Install clutch plates into clutch housing starting with the waved steel plate, then alternately install composition plates and flat steel plates until all clutch plates are installed. See *Forward Clutch Plate Chart.*

CAUTION — *Do not confuse the flat steel clutch plate (plate with "V" notch) with the waved steel clutch plate (plate with "U" notch). Also, radially grooved composition clutch plates are installed at the factory only. All service composition plates have a smooth surface.*

Forward Clutch Plate Chart

Application	Flat Steel	Composition
All Models	4①	5

① — All models except CL and CD use 1 additional WAVED steel plate installed first. Models CL and CD use 1 additional FLAT steel plate.

6) Install direct clutch hub in clutch housing and install retaining snap ring. Install forward clutch assembly on delivery sleeve of oil pump and apply compressed air to check clutch operation. See *Fig. 25.*

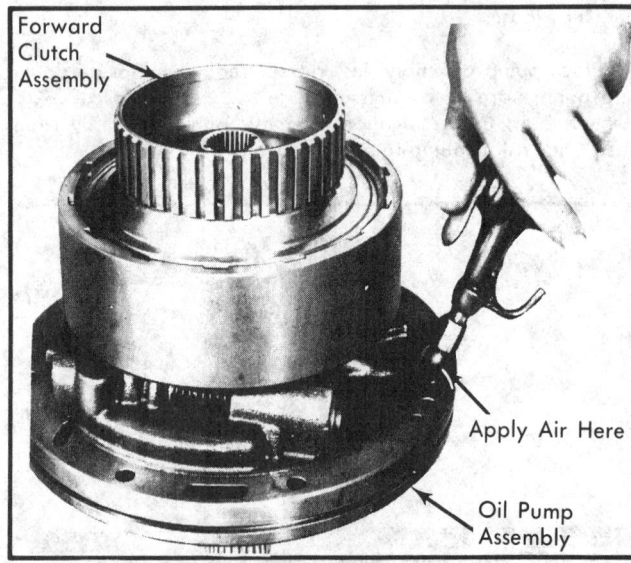

Fig. 25 Using Compressed Air to Check Operation of Forward Clutch Assembly

DIRECT CLUTCH & INTERMEDIATE ROLLER CLUTCH

Disassembly — 1) Remove intermediate roller assembly retainer snap ring and remove spring retainer. Remove roller outer race and roller assembly. Turn unit over and remove backing plate-to-direct clutch housing snap ring.

GENERAL MOTORS TURBO HYDRA-MATIC 400 (Cont.)

2) Remove direct clutch backing plate, composition plates and steel clutch plates. Using suitable compressor tool (J-4670 & J-21664), compress spring retainer and remove snap ring.

3) Remove spring retainer, 14 release springs and direct clutch piston. Remove inner and outer seals from piston and remove center piston seal from direct clutch housing.

Inspection — Inspect roller assembly for popped or loose rollers. Inspect inner cam and outer race for scratches and/or wear. Inspect clutch housing for cracks, wear, open oil passages, wear on clutch plate drive lugs and check clutch plates for wear and/or burning. Inspect backing plate for nicks and/or damage. Inspect clutch piston for cracks. Check release springs for collapsed coils and/or distortion and if one or more springs require replacement, replace all springs with 16 service replacement release springs. Inspect clutch housing for free operation of check ball(s).

NOTE — *Models CB, CD and CL have service replacement pistons containing 2 check balls. In ALL cases, either the direct clutch housing and/or direct clutch piston MUST contain a check ball.*

Reassembly — **1)** Install new inner and outer seals on clutch piston, with seal lips facing away from spring pockets. Install a new center seal on clutch hub with seal lip facing upward. Place suitable seal protectors (J-21362 and J-21409) over hub and clutch housing, then install clutch piston with a rotating motion.

2) If production clutch release springs are being used, install 14 springs into spring pockets of piston, leaving two opposite pockets with no springs. If service replacement springs are being used, install all 16 springs into spring pockets. Place spring retainer on top of springs and snap ring on top of retainer. Using tool used at disassembly, compress springs and install snap ring.

3) Lubricate clutch plates with transmission fluid, then install into clutch housing starting with a waved steel plate (if used), and alternating composition and flat steel plates until all plates are installed. *See Direct Clutch Plate Chart.* Install direct clutch backing plate and retaining snap ring.

NOTE — *Do not confuse the flat steel clutch plate (plate with "V" notch) with the waved steel clutch plate (plate with "U" notch).*

NOTE — *Models CB, CD and CL are equipped with a sprag assembly in place of the intermediate roller clutch.*

Direct Clutch Plate Chart		
Application	**Flat Steel Plates**	**Composition Plates**
Chevrolet & GMC		
Models CB, CD, CL	6	6
Model CW	5	5
Model CZ	3①	4
All Others	4	5
① — Plus one WAVED steel plate installed first.		

4) Install rollers in cage by compressing energizing spring and inserting rollers from outer side of cage. Install clutch roller and outer race on housing using clockwise rotary motion.

NOTE — *When installed, outer race should not rotate counterclockwise.*

5) Install retainer over intermediate clutch roller components and install snap ring. Install direct clutch assembly on center support assembly and apply compressed air to check direct clutch operation. *See Fig. 27.*

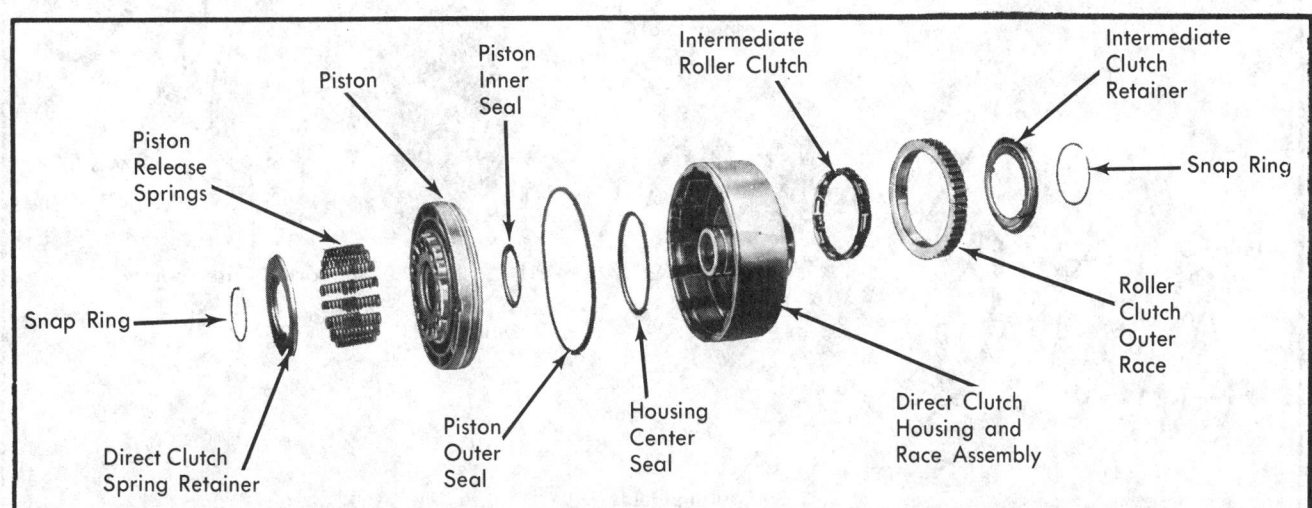

Fig. 26 Exploded View of Direct Clutch and Intermediate Roller Clutch Components

GENERAL MOTORS TURBO HYDRA-MATIC 400 (Cont.)

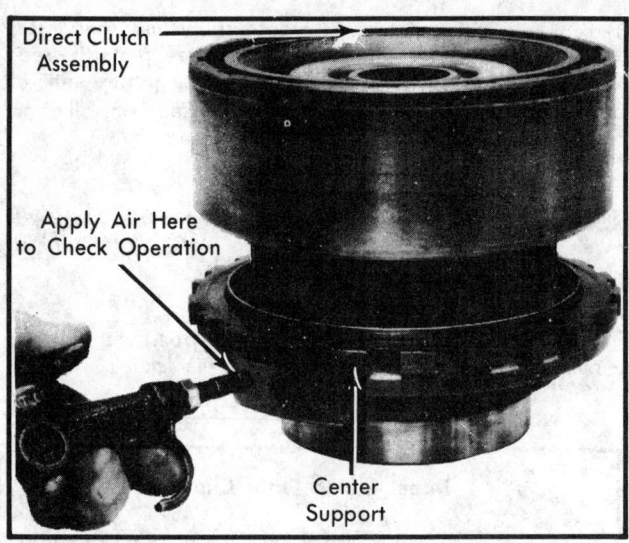

Direct Clutch Assembly

Apply Air Here to Check Operation

Center Support

Fig. 27   Checking Operation of Direct Clutch Assembly

GEAR UNIT

Disassembly — 1) Remove center support assembly and center support-to-reaction carrier thrust washer. Remove center support-to-sun gear races and thrust bearing (1 race may have come out with center support).

2) Remove reaction carrier and roller clutch assembly, then lift roller clutch assembly out of carrier. Remove front internal gear ring from output carrier assembly. Remove sun gear. Remove reaction carrier-to-output carrier thrust washer.

3) Remove "O" ring from output shaft (if equipped). Remove output shaft-to-output carrier snap ring and remove shaft.

Remove output shaft-to-rear internal gear thrust bearing and 2 races. Remove rear internal gear and mainshaft.

4) Remove rear internal gear-to-sun gear thrust bearing and 2 races. If necessary, remove rear internal gear-to-mainshaft snap ring and remove mainshaft.

CENTER SUPPORT & INTERMEDIATE CLUTCH

Disassembly — Remove oil seal rings from center support. Compress spring retainer, remove snap ring, then remove spring retainer and clutch release springs. Remove intermediate clutch spring guide and piston, then remove inner and outer piston seals from piston.

CAUTION — *Do not remove the three screws attaching roller clutch inner race to center support.*

Bushing Replacement — If replacement is required, use a suitable bushing driver (J-21465-6 and J-8092) to remove old bushing, then use same tool to install new bushing. From front side of center support, align elongated slot in bushing with drilled hole in oil delivery sleeve closest to the piston, then drive bushing squarely into bore until bushing is flush to .010" below top of oil delivery sleeve.

Inspection — Inspect all parts for wear, scoring or damage. Inspect release springs for collapsed coils and/or distortion. Check oil ring grooves for damage, rings should fit freely in grooves. Make sure all passages are open. Inspect roller clutch inner race for scratches or indentations. Make sure lubrication hole is open.

NOTE — *Also be sure the constant bleed plug orifice is open. This orifice is approximately .020" in diameter.*

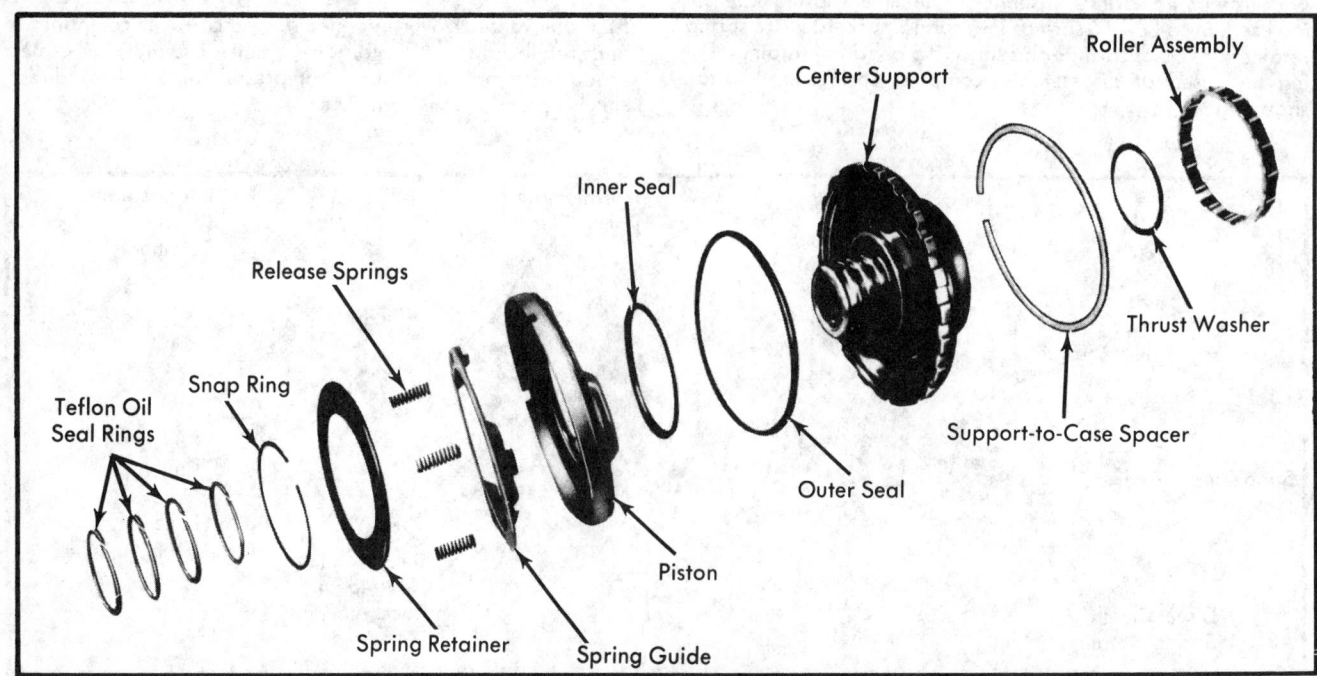

Roller Assembly

Center Support

Inner Seal

Thrust Washer

Release Springs

Support-to-Case Spacer

Snap Ring

Outer Seal

Teflon Oil Seal Rings

Piston

Spring Retainer

Spring Guide

Fig. 28   Exploded View of Center Support Assembly

GENERAL MOTORS TURBO HYDRA-MATIC 400 (Cont.)

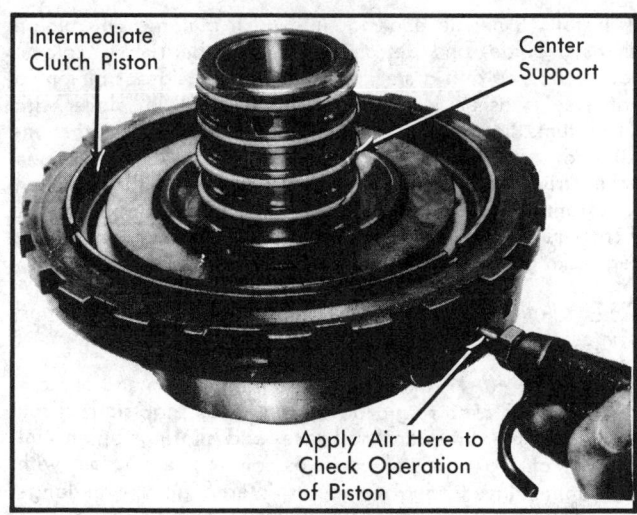

Fig. 29 Checking Operation of Intermediate Clutch Piston

Labels: Intermediate Clutch Piston — Center Support — Apply Air Here to Check Operation of Piston

Reassembly — 1) Lubricate and install new inner and outer seals on piston with lip of seals facing away from spring pocket. Using a suitable seal protector, install piston, indexing spring pockets of piston into cored areas of center support.

2) Install intermediate clutch spring guide. Install 3 release springs into holes of spring guide. Space springs equally during assembly.

3) Place spring retainer and snap ring over springs. Compress springs and install snap ring. Install 4 oil seal rings on center support. Air check operation of intermediate clutch piston . See Fig. 29.

NOTE — When installing teflon oil seal rings on center support, be sure split ends are assembled in the same relation as cut.

GEAR UNIT

Inspection — If reaction carrier is equipped with a spacer ring in an undercut at bottom of roller cam ramps, inspect ring for wear or damage. Inspect reaction carrier bushing for damage; if bushing is damaged, carrier must be replaced. Check pinions for damage, rough bearings, or tilt. Check pinion end play; end play should be .009-.024". Inspect band surface on reaction carrier for burning or scoring. Check all other parts for wear, scoring, or other damage. Make sure all lubrication holes are open.

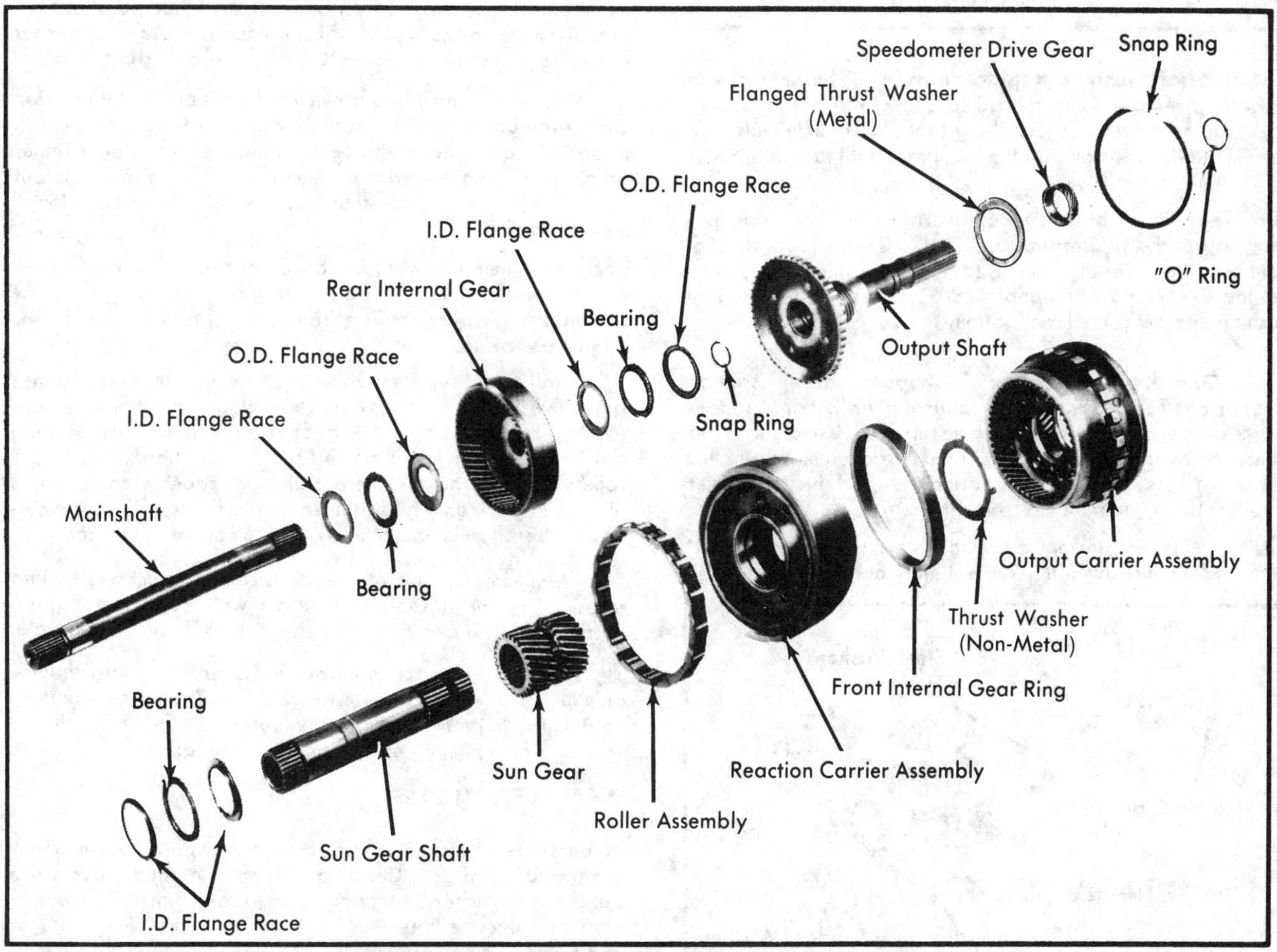

Labels: Speedometer Drive Gear — Snap Ring — Flanged Thrust Washer (Metal) — O.D. Flange Race — I.D. Flange Race — Rear Internal Gear — Bearing — "O" Ring — Output Shaft — Snap Ring — O.D. Flange Race — Bearing — I.D. Flange Race — Mainshaft — Bearing — Output Carrier Assembly — Thrust Washer (Non-Metal) — Front Internal Gear Ring — Reaction Carrier Assembly — Roller Assembly — Sun Gear — Sun Gear Shaft — Bearing — I.D. Flange Race

Fig. 30 Exploded View of Planetary Gear Assembly

GENERAL MOTORS TURBO HYDRA-MATIC 400 (Cont.)

NOTE — *If mainshaft is replaced, make sure that the orifice cup plug in replacement mainshaft is removed before installation.*

NOTE — *Models CA, CF and CG do not have a speedometer drive gear.*

Speedometer Drive Gear Replacement — 1) If nylon gear is used, depress retaining clip and slide gear off output shaft. To install, place retaining clip (square end toward flange of shaft) into hole in output shaft.

2) Align slot in gear with retaining clip and install gear. If steel gear is used, use suitable puller and remove drive gear from output shaft. To install, support output shaft on its front face.

3) Using suitable driver, drive gear onto shaft until distance between rear face of drive gear and end of output shaft is as specified in Speedometer Drive Gear Installation table.

NOTE — *Nylon gear is installed at factory only, all replacement gears are steel.*

Speedometer Drive Gear Installation	
Application	**Distance**
All Models	$5^{21}/_{32}$"

Output Shaft Bushing Replacement — If bushing is worn or galled, remove using thread tool (J-21465-16) in bushing and slide hammer (J-2619). Using tool (J-21465-1) with drive handle (J-8092), install bushing into place until tool bottoms.

Sun Gear Shaft Bushing Replacement — With sun gear shaft properly supported, use tool J-21465-15 with slide hammer J-2619 (or equivalent) to remove bushing. To replace, use tool J-21465-5 with handle J-8092 (or equivalent) to drive bushing into place until tool bottoms.

Pinion Gear Replacement — 1) Support carrier assembly on its front face. Using a ½" diameter drill, remove stake marks from end of pinion pin(s) to be replaced. Using a tapered punch, drive or press pinion pins out of carrier. Remove pinions, thrust washers, and needle bearings. Inspect pinion pocket faces for burrs and remove if present.

NOTE — *This will prevent cracking carrier when pressing out pinions. Do not allow drill to remove any stock from carrier.*

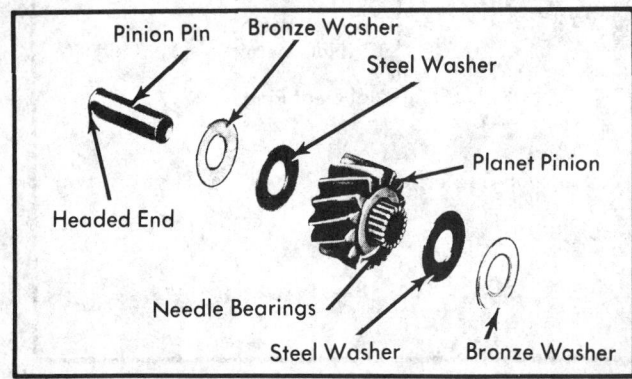

Fig. 31 Exploded View of Planet Pinion Assembly

2) Install 18 needle bearings into each pinion, using pinion pin as a guide, and petrolatum to hold bearings in place. Place a bronze and a steel washer on each side of pinion so that steel washer is against pinion. Hold in place with petrolatum. Place pinion assembly in place in carrier, then install pilot shaft through rear face of assembly, to hold parts in place. Drive a new pinion pin into place while rotating pinion from front, making sure that headed end is flush or below face of carrier. Using a punch as an anvil, place carrier over punch, then stake pinion pin in three places.

NOTE — *Both ends of pinion pins must lie below face of carrier or interference may occur.*

Reassembly — 1) Install rear internal gear on end of main shaft (end with snap ring groove) and install snap ring. Install sun gear-to-internal gear thrust races and bearings against inner face of rear internal gear, as follows, and retain with petrolatum: Place large race against internal gear, with flange facing forward or up, place thrust bearings against race, then place small race against bearing, with inner flange facing into bearing or down.

2) Install output carrier over mainshaft so pinions mesh with rear internal gear. With mainshaft in downward position, install rear internal gear-to-output shaft thrust races and bearings as follows, and retain with petrolatum: Place small diameter race against internal gear, with center flange facing up, place bearing on race, then place second race on bearing, with outer flange cupped over bearing. Install output shaft into output carrier assembly. Install output shaft-to-output carrier snap ring. Install output shaft "O" ring (if required).

3) With output shaft in a downward position, install reaction carrier-to-output carrier thrust washer with tabs facing down in pockets, and retain with petrolatum. Install sun gear (inner splines with chamfer down). Install gear ring over output carrier. Install sun gear shaft with long splined-end down. Install reaction carrier.

NOTE — *When a new output carrier and/or reaction carrier is being installed, and if front internal gear ring prevents assembly of carriers, replace front internal gear ring with the service gear ring.*

4) Install center support-to-sun gear thrust races and bearings as follows, and retain with petrolatum: Install large race (center flange up) over sun gear shaft, install thrust bearing against race, then install second race (center flange up). Install rollers that may have come out of roller cage by compressing energizing spring with forefinger and inserting roller from outer side. Install roller clutch into reaction carrier outer race.

5) Install center support to reaction carrier thrust washer into recess in center support and retain with petrolatum. Install center support into reaction carrier and roller clutch assembly.

NOTE — *With the reaction carrier held, center support should only turn counterclockwise. Install tool (J-21795) on gear unit to hold units in place. Then install output shaft-to-case thrust washer tabs in pockets and retain with petrolatum.*

TRANSMISSION CASE

Inspection — Inspect case for cracks, porosity, or interconnected passages. Check governor and modulator valve bores for scratches or scoring. Check band anchor pin retention, and intermediate clutch driven plate lugs for damage. Inspect snap ring grooves for damage. See that cup plug is properly staked and sealed.

GENERAL MOTORS TURBO HYDRA-MATIC 400 (Cont.)

NOTE — *If transmission case requires replacement, be sure to remove center support-to-case spacer from the existing case and install it in the replacement case. In addition, if a replacement case is required, be sure to remove the nameplate from existing case and transfer it to replacement case.*

Bushing Replacement — With case properly supported, use suitable tool (J-21465-8) and remove bushing. To install, use same tool as for removal with adaptor ring (J-21465-9) and extension (J-21465-13). With lube passage facing front of transmission case, drive replacement bushing into case until it is .040-.055" above selective thrust washer face. Stake bushing with suitable staking tool (J-21465-10), with stake marks in the lubrication grooves.

EXTENSION HOUSING

Inspection — Inspect housing for cracks or porosity, check seal ring groove for damage, make certain rear seal drain back port is not obstructed.

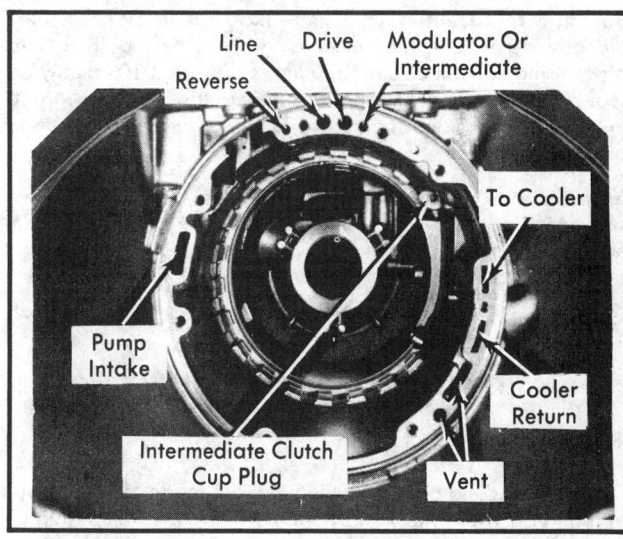

Fig. 32 Front View of Transmission Case Showing Oil Passages

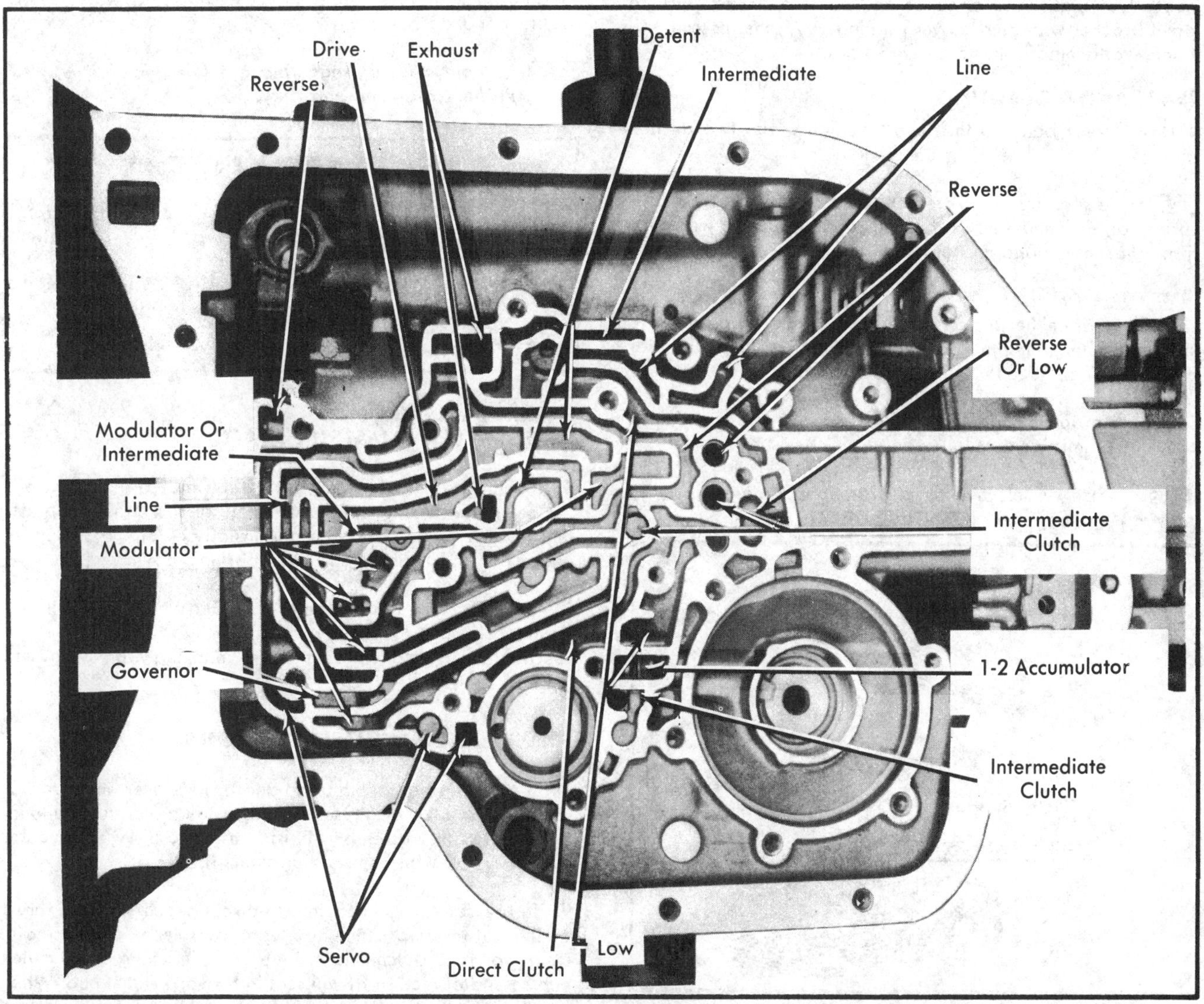

Fig. 33 Bottom View of Transmission Case Showing Oil Passages

GENERAL MOTORS TURBO HYDRA-MATIC 400 (Cont.)

Bushing Replacement — Using suitable tool, drive or press old bushing from extension housing. Press new bushing into place using same tool until bushing is flush to .010" below oil seal counterbore. Stake bushing in place with tool (J-21465-10 or equivalent). Stake marks are to be in bushing lubrication grooves.

Bearing Replacement (Model "CL" Only) — Remove rear seal and snap ring. Using an arbor press or brass rod positioned against bearing outer race, drive or press bearings and bearing spacer from housing.

CAUTION — *Do not bear against inner race or balls. To install, reverse removal procedure.*

TRANSMISSION REASSEMBLY

PARKING PAWL

1) Install parking pawl with tooth toward inside of case. Install parking pawl shaft and shaft retainer. Install new cup plug using a ⅜" diameter rod and drive plug into case until shaft bottoms on case rib.

2) Install parking pawl return spring, with squared end hooked on pawl and opposite end on case. Install parking pawl bracket with guides over parking pawl, then install and tighten attaching bolts to specifications.

REAR BAND & GEAR UNIT

1) Install rear band so that two lugs index with two anchor pins.

NOTE — *Be sure band is seated on lugs. Install support-to-case spacer against shoulder at bottom of case splines, with ring gap adjacent to band anchor pin.*

CAUTION — *Do not confuse this spacer (.040" thick and both sides flat) with either the center support-to-case snap ring (one side is beveled), or the intermediate clutch backing plate-to-case snap ring (.093" thick and both sides flat.)*

2) Install proper rear selective thrust washer into slots inside rear of transmission case.

NOTE — *Size of selective thrust washer was determined by previous end play check during disassembly.*

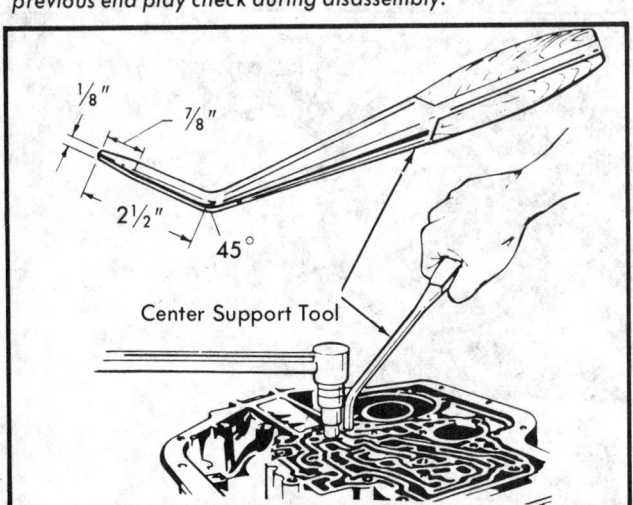

Fig. 34 Installing Center Support Bolt Using Special Locating Tool

With transmission in a vertical position, and with holding tool (J-21795) in end of mainshaft, install complete gear unit assembly into case. Install center support-to-case snap ring, with beveled side up and gap adjacent to band anchor pin. Make sure flat side of snap ring is against center support.

3) Install case-to-center support bolt by placing suitable locating tool into case direct clutch passage. Handle of tool should point to right (as viewed from front of transmission) and parallel to bell housing mounting face. Apply pressure downward on tool handle, which will tend to rotate center support counterclockwise (as viewed from front of transmission). While holding center support firmly counterclockwise against case splines, tighten case-to-center support bolt to specifications.

CAUTION — *Use care not to raise burrs on case valve body mounting face when using locating tool.*

4) Lubricate intermediate clutch plates with transmission fluid and install, starting with a waved steel plate (if used), and alternating composition and steel plates until all clutch plates are installed. Install intermediate clutch backing plate with ridge up. Install backing plate-to-case snap ring, with gap opposite band anchor pin.

NOTE — *Both sides of snap ring are flat and ring is .093" thick. Recheck rear unit end play.*

Intermediate Clutch Plate Chart		
Application	Flat Steel Plates	Composition Plates
Models CB, CD & CL	3	3
All Others	2①	3
① — Plus one WAVED steel plate installed first.		

PARKING LINKAGE, DETENT LEVER & MANUAL SHAFT

1) If removed, install a new shaft seal into case using a ¾" diameter rod to seat seal. Install actuator rod into manual detent lever from side opposite pin. Install actuator rod plunger under parking bracket and over parking pawl.

2) Install manual shaft through case and detent lever. Install detent retaining lock nut on manual shaft and tighten to specifications. Install retaining pin, indexing with groove in manual shaft.

FRONT BAND & CLUTCH ASSEMBLIES

1) Install front band with band anchor hole over band anchor pin and apply lug facing servo hole. Install direct clutch and intermediate roller assembly. Twist housing to allow roller outer race to index with composition clutch plates.

2) Install forward clutch hub-to-direct clutch housing thrust washer on forward clutch hub, using petroleum jelly to retain. Install forward clutch and turbine shaft, indexing direct clutch hub so end of mainshaft will seat in forward clutch hub. When forward clutch is seated, it will be 1¼" from pump mounting face in case.

GENERAL MOTORS TURBO HYDRA-MATIC 400 (Cont.)

OIL PUMP

1) Install and align new gasket on pump and retain with petroleum jelly. Lubricate turbine shaft journals with transmission fluid. Lubricate hook-type oil rings on pump delivery sleeve with petroleum jelly.

2) Install pump assembly into case and install all but 1 pump attaching bolt and seal and tighten to specifications. Install a ⅜"x16" threaded rod into bolt hole in pump and mount dial indicator on rod.

NOTE — *If turbine shaft cannot be rotated as pump is being installed, forward or direct clutch housing is not installed properly. Correct before tightening pump attaching bolts.*

3) Index dial indicator with flat surface on end of turbine shaft. Push turbine shaft rearward and push output shaft forward. Zero dial indicator, pull turbine shaft forward and read end play. End play should be .003-.024".

4) If not, install correct selective thrust washer between pump and forward clutch housing. Install remaining front pump attaching bolt and seal and tighten to specifications. Apply a non-hardening sealer to outside of new front oil seal and install into pump using suitable driver.

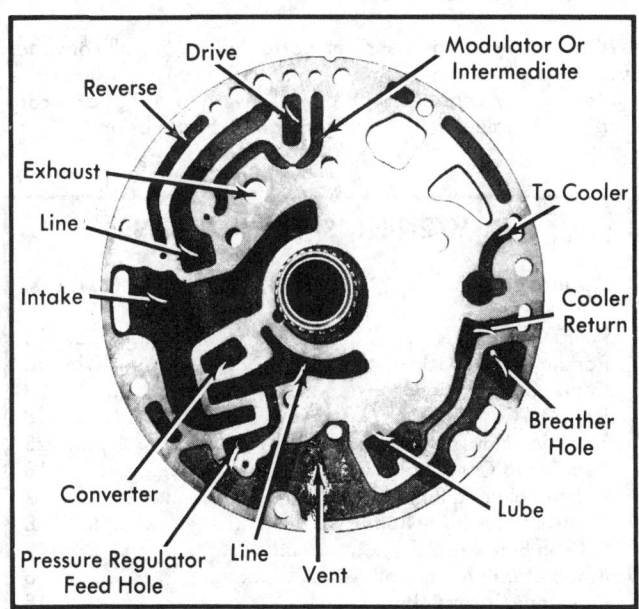

Fig. 35   View of Oil Pump Cover Showing Oil Passages

EXTENSION HOUSING

1) Install a new gasket on extension housing, retaining with petroleum jelly. If applicable, check "O" ring on output shaft for any nicks or flatting and replace if necessary. Install housing on case and tighten attaching bolts.

2) Install new extension housing oil seal, apply a non-hardening sealer to outside of seal and use suitable driver to seat oil seal in housing.

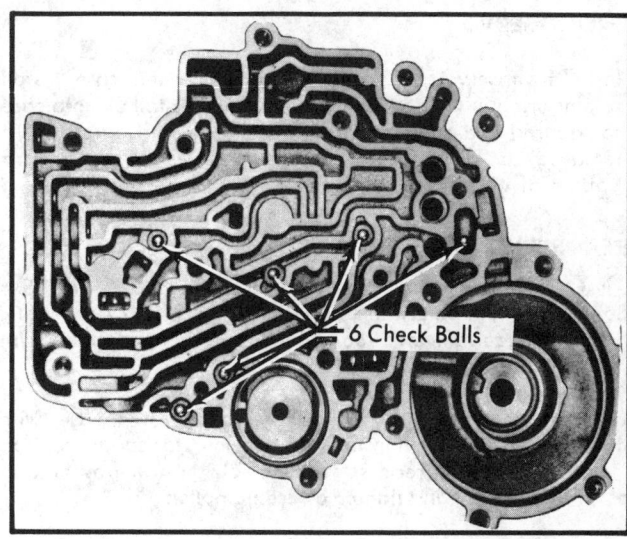

Fig. 36   Bottom View of Transmission Case Showing Location of Check Balls

CONTROL VALVE SPACER & DETENT SOLENOID

1) Install 6 check balls into seats in transmission case. *See Fig. 36.* Install control valve spacer plate-to-case gasket (gasket with extension for detent solenoid and a "C" near front servo location). Install control valve spacer plate and control valve-to-spacer gasket (gasket with a "VB" near front servo).

2) Install detent solenoid and gasket (with connector facing outer edge of case), but do not tighten bolts at this time. Install "0" ring seal on electrical connector. Lubricate and install electrical connector with lock tabs facing into case. Position locator tab in notch on side of case. Connect detent wire and lead wire to electrical connector.

NOTE — *If operation is being performed with transmission in vehicle, install check balls into ball seat pockets in spacer plate. See Fig. 37.*

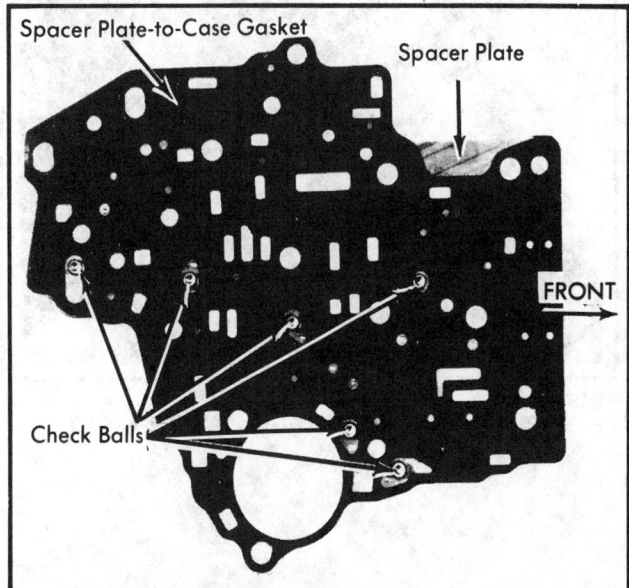

Fig. 37   Location of Check Balls in Spacer Plate With Transmission in Vehicle

GENERAL MOTORS TURBO HYDRA-MATIC 400 (Cont.)

FRONT SERVO

Install front servo spring and spring retainer into case. Install retainer ring in front servo pin groove and install pin into case so tapered end contacts band. Install seal ring on piston (if removed). Install piston on pin with flat side of piston toward bottom of oil pan.

REAR SERVO

NOTE — *Before installing servo, check band apply pin. See Band Apply Pin Selection Check in Transmission Disassembly. Also, make certain that rear band apply lug is aligned with servo pin bore in transmission case.*

Lubricate inner and outer rear servo bores in case with transmission fluid, then install rear accumulator spring in servo inner bore. Install rear servo assembly, install gasket and cover, then install and tighten attaching bolts.

CONTROL VALVE BODY ASSEMBLY

Install governor pipes into control valve assembly (pipes are interchangeable). Install governor screen assembly (open end first) into governor feed pipe hole in case (hole nearest center of transmission). Using two control valve attaching screws with heads cut off as guide pins, install valve assembly and governor pipes on transmission. Ensure gasket and spacer do not become misaligned, that manual valve is indexed properly with pin on detent lever, and that governor pipes are properly seated in case holes. Start control valve assembly attaching bolts, making sure lead wire assembly clip is installed. Remove guide pins, install detent roller and spring assembly, install remaining attaching bolts and tighten all bolts to specified torque.

GOVERNOR

Install governor assembly into case, then install cover with new gasket and install and tighten attaching bolts to specifications.

SPEEDOMETER DRIVEN GEAR

Install speedometer driven gear assembly into case. Install gear retainer with tangs in sleeve positioning bosses and install and tighten retainer attaching screw.

INTAKE PIPE, FILTER & OIL PAN

Install case-to-intake pipe "O" ring on intake pipe and assemble into filter assembly. Install filter and intake pipe. Install filter retainer bolt and tighten to specifications. Install new oil pan gasket on pan and install pan, tightening bolts to specifications.

VACUUM MODULATOR & VALVE

Install modulator valve into case with stem end out. Install "O" ring seal on modulator and install modulator into case. Install modulator retainer and attaching bolt and tighten to specifications.

CONVERTER ASSEMBLY

With transmission on bench or portable jack, install converter assembly into pump assembly making sure converter hub drive slots are fully engaged with pump drive gear tangs and converter is installed fully towards rear of transmission.

Detent Roller & Spring Assembly

Fig. 38   Installing Detent Roller and Spring

TIGHTENING SPECIFICATIONS

Application	Ft. Lbs.
Pump Cover Bolts	18
Parking Pawl Bracket Bolts	18
Center Support Bolts	23
Pump-to-Case Bolts	18
Extension Housing-to-Case Bolts	23
Rear Servo Cover Bolts	18
Detent Solenoid Bolts	7
Control Valve Body Bolts	8
Oil Pan Bolts	12
Modulator Retainer Bolt	18
Governor Cover Bolts	18
Manual Lever-to-Manual Shaft Nut	8
Manual Lever-to-Detent Lever	18
Transmission-to-Engine Bolts	35
Converter-to-Drive Plate Bolts	35
Line Pressure Take-Off Plug	13
Filter Retainer Bolt	10

Contents

Section 15

MANUAL TRANSMISSIONS

NOTE — ALSO SEE GENERAL INDEX.

IMPORTANT

*Because of the great number of model names used by vehicle manufacturers, accurate identification of models is important.
See Model Identification at the front of this publication.*

Manual Transmission Servicing

MANUAL TRANSMISSION TROUBLE SHOOTING

CONDITION & POSSIBLE CAUSE	CONDITION & POSSIBLE CAUSE
Improper Shift Lever Operation • Shift rods out of adjustment. • Steering column shift tube out of alignment. **Transmission Gears Shift Hard** • Clutch pedal free-travel out of adjustment. • Clutch does not release completely. • Low lubricant level. • Incorrect lubricant type. • Shift lever binding or worn. • Worn or damaged internal shift mechanism. • Sliding gears or synchronizer rings binding. • Housing and/or shafts out of alignment. **Transmission Jumps Out of Gear** • Shift linkage damaged or out of adjustment. • Engine, transmission or shift lever bolts loose. • Clutch housing misaligned with crankshaft. • Pilot bushing or bearing worn. • Damaged internal components. • Synchronizer clutch teeth worn. **Noisy In Forward Gears** • Low lubricant level or improper type. • Vehicle body or chassis components grounding on transmission. • Transmission or clutch housing bolts loose. • Power take-off components misaligned. • Clutch housing misaligned with crankshaft. • Worn bearings or gears. • Linkage rattle. • Damaged or worn anti-lash plate.	**Gears Clash When Shifting From Forward Gear to Another** • Engine idle speed too high. • Clutch pedal free-travel out of adjustment. • Shift linkage damaged or out of adjustment. • Pilot bushing or bearing damaged. • Gears or synchronizer assemblies damaged. **Transmission is Locked in One Gear and Cannot Be Shifted Out of That Gear** • Shift linkage damaged or out of adjustment. • Damaged or worn internal components in transmission. • Neutral sensing switch damaged or malfunctioning. • Shift fork loose on shift rail. **Transmission Will Not Shift Into One Gear — Will Shift Into All Others** • Shift linkage out of adjustment. • Shift linkage components worn or damaged. • Damaged or worn internal components in transmission. **Transmission Leaks** • Incorrect type lubricant. • Components other than transmission leaking. • Damaged or worn internal components. • Transmission overfilled. • Rear bearing retainer oil seal worn.

CHRYSLER CORP.

LUBRICATION

SERVICE INTERVALS

Check fluid level at each engine oil change. On vehicles used in normal service, transmission should be drained and refilled every 36,000 miles. For vehicles used in heavy duty service, drain and refill transmission every 18,000 miles.

CHECKING FLUID LEVEL

Check lubricant level at filler plug hole on side of transmission. Lubricant should be level with bottom of filler plug hole. Add lubricant as necessary to bring to correct level.

RECOMMENDED FLUID

New Process 435 4-Speed — Using multi-purpose gear lubricant, if the minimum anticipated atmospheric temperature will be:

- Above 90°F, use SAE 140.
- As low as −10°F, use SAE 90.
- Below −10°F, use SAE 80.

Using engine oil, if the minimum anticipated atmospheric temperature will be:

- Above 32°F, use SAE 50.
- Below 32°F, use SAE 30.

New Process A833 Overdrive 4-Speed — Use Dexron Automatic Transmission Fluid. If objectionable gear rattle is apparent during idle or acceleration, multi-purpose gear lubricant SAE 90 or SAE 80W-90 may be used.

CAPACITY

NOTE — *Transmission assembly capacities are approximate and correct fluid level should be determined by level in transmission rather than by amount added.*

Transmission Refill Capacities	
Application	Capacity (Pts.)
4-Speed	
A833	7.5
435	7.0

ADJUSTMENT

SHIFT LINKAGE

New Process A833 — Install floor shift lever aligning tool to hold levers in neutral crossover position. See *Fig. 1*. Remove all rods from transmission shift levers and place levers in neutral detent positions. Rotate shift rods until they will exactly enter transmission levers. Replace washers and clips, starting with 1st-2nd lever. Remove aligning tool and test shifting action.

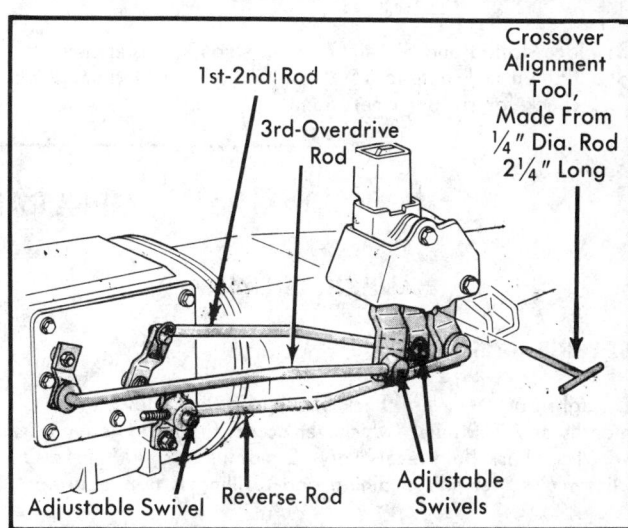

Fig. 1 A833 Gearshift Linkage Adjustment

FORD

LUBRICATION

SERVICE INTERVALS

All Models — Check fluid level whenever malfunction is suspected, leakage is observed, or after operation in water. Periodic draining and refilling is not required.

CHECKING FLUID LEVEL

Check lubricant level at transmission filler plug hole. Lubricant should be level with filler plug hole. Add as necessary.

RECOMMENDED FLUID

Use only Ford Standard Transmission Lubricant, (Ford Part Number D8DZ-19C547-A), meeting Ford Specification ESP-M2C83-C.

CAPACITY

NOTE — *Capacities given below are approximate, and correct fluid level should be determined by level at filler plug hole, rather than by amount added.*

Transmission Refill Capacities	
Application	Capacity (Pts.)
Ford 3-Speed	3.5
New Process 435	7.0
Warner T-18	7.0
4-Speed Overdrive	4.5
Single Rail 4-Speed Overdrive	4.5
4-Speed Overdrive	4.5

ADJUSTMENT

SHIFT LINKAGE

3-Speed — 1) Position shift selector lever in neutral position. Insert a 3/16″ gauge pin through steering column shift levers and plastic spacer.

FORD (Cont.)

2) Loosen shift rod lock nuts, and place both transmission shift levers in neutral position. Tighten lock nuts and remove gauge pin. Check shift linkage operation for smoothness.

4-Speed Overdrive — 1) Disconnect three shift rods and insert a .25" diameter pin in alignment hole in shifter assembly. Put levers in neutral position.

2) Align forward lever (3rd-4th) and rear lever (1st-2nd) in neutral position. Turn middle lever (Reverse) counterclockwise to neutral position. Rotate transmission output shaft to be sure of neutral position.

3) Place slotted end of shift rods on studs in shifter assembly and tighten lock nuts to 15-20 ft. lbs. Remove alignment pin and check for proper operation.

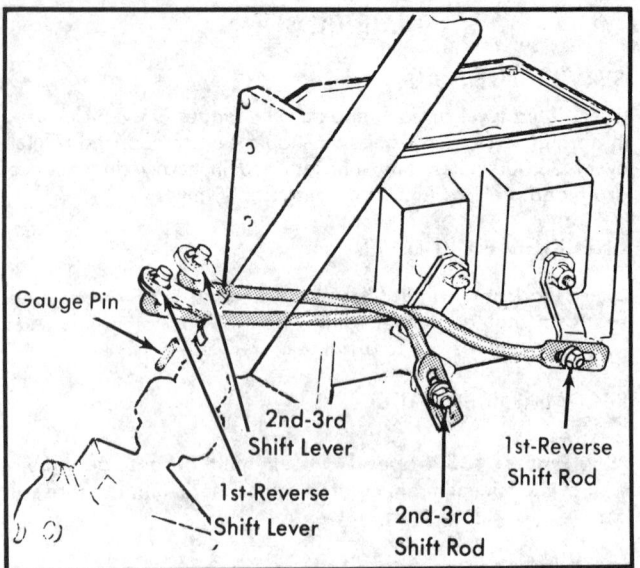

**Fig. 1   Shift Linkage Adjustment
(3-Speed Models)**

GENERAL MOTORS

LUBRICATION

SERVICE INTERVALS

On light duty vehicles, check transmission fluid level every 12 months or 7,500 miles (whichever occurs first). On heavy duty vehicles, check fluid level every 12 months or 6,000 miles. On all vehicles, periodic draining and refilling is not required.

CHECKING FLUID LEVEL

Check lubricant level at transmison filler plug hole. Lubricant should be level with filler plug hole. Add as necessary.

RECOMMENDED FLUID

Use only SAE 80W-90 (GL-5) multi-purpose gear lubricant. In temperatures below 32°F, use only SAE 80W.

CAPACITY

NOTE — *Capacities given below are approximate, and correct fluid level should be determined by level at filler plug hole, rather than by amount added.*

Transmission Refill Capacities	
Application	Capacity (Pts.)
3-Speed (Saginaw)	3.0
3-Speed (Tremac)	3.0
4-Speed (Muncie)	8.0
4-Speed (New Process)	7.5

ADJUSTMENT

SHIFT LINKAGE

NOTE — *Following procedure applies to 3-speed transmissions only. Four-speed transmission requires no external adjustment.*

Loosen bolts or nuts securing swivels to transmission shift rods, then move both shift levers on transmission to neutral position. Align both steering column shift levers in neutral position and place a 3/16" diameter gauge pin in holes in levers to hold in position. Tighten swivel clamp bolts or nuts, making sure all levers remain in neutral positions. Move shift selector lever through all ranges and check linkage operation.

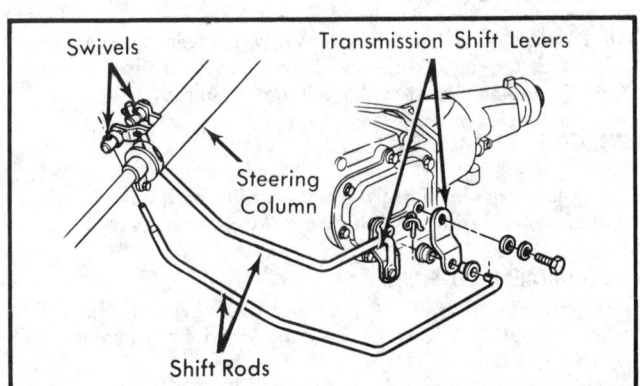

Fig. 1   Shift Linkage Assembly (Typical)

JEEP

LUBRICATION

SERVICE INTERVALS

Under normal driving conditions, check fluid level every 5,000 miles. Under severe driving conditions, check fluid level every 3,000 miles. Transmission lubricant should be changed every 30,000 miles.

CHECKING FLUID LEVEL

Check lubricant level at transmission filler plug hole. Lubricant should be level with filler plug hole. Add as necessary.

RECOMMENDED FLUID

Use only SAE 85W-90 Gear Lubricant.

CAPACITY

NOTE — *Capacities given below are approximate, and correct fluid level should be determined by level at filler plug hole, rather than by amount added.*

Transmission Refill Capacities	
Application	**Capacity (Pts.)**
4-Speed	
SR-4	3.0
T-18	6.5
T-176	3.5

Manual Transmission Servicing

CHRYSLER CORP. MANUAL TRANSMISSION REMOVAL

ALL MODELS

1) Disconnect negative battery cable. Remove retaining screws from floor pan and slide boot up and off shift lever. On models equipped with New Process 435 transmission, remove shift lever retainer by pressing down, rotating retainer clockwise and releasing.

2) On models equipped with New Process A-833 transmission, remove shift lever by inserting a .010" feeler gauge between floor shift assembly and shift lever, and disengaging internal spring clip. Remove bolts and washers securing shift lever to mounting plate on extension housing and remove. See *Fig. 1*.

3) On all models, drain fluid from transmission. On 4-WD models, remove transfer case. See *Transfer Case Removal in TRANSFER CASE Section.* On all vehicles, remove propeller shaft from transmission. On all models, disconnect speedometer cable and back-up light switch.

4) Install engine support fixture (C-3487-A). On models equipped with New Process 435 transmission, place adapters (DD-1279) firmly over frame rails. On all models, make sure support ends of engine fixture tool are up against underside of oil pan flange. Raise engine slightly with fixture.

5) On models with A-833 transmission, disconnect extension housing from removable center crossmember. On all models, support transmission with a suitable jack and remove

crossmember. Remove transmission-to-clutch housing bolts. Slide transmission rearward until drive pinion clears clutch disc, and lower and remove transmission.

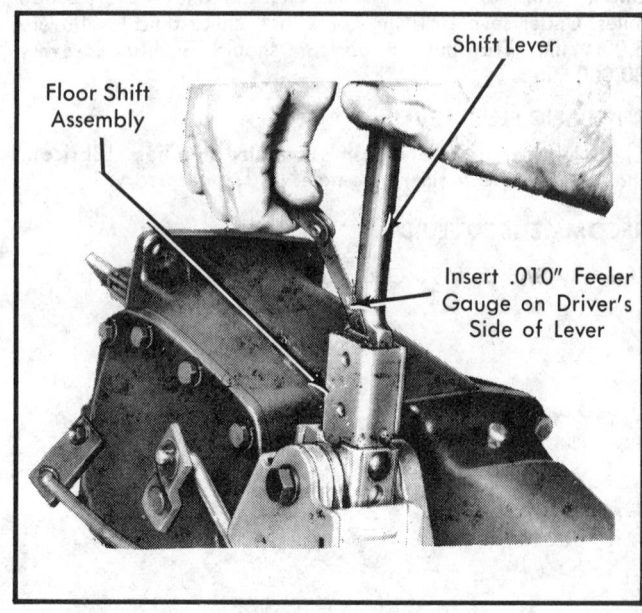

Fig. 1   Removing Shift Lever From A-833 Transmission

FORD MANUAL TRANSMISSION REMOVAL

"E" MODELS EXC. 4-SPEED OVERDRIVE

1) Raise and support vehicle under frame and drain lubricant from transmission. Disconnect driveshaft from flange at transmission. Disconnect speedometer cable and shift control linkage at transmission. Place jack under transmission and secure transmission to jack.

2) Raise transmission slightly and remove four bolts retaining transmission extension housing to insulator and retainer assembly. Remove transmission-to-flywheel housing bolts. Position engine support bar to frame and lower transmission from vehicle.

"E" MODELS WITH 4-SPEED OVERDRIVE

1) Raise and support vehicle. Disconnect drive shaft. Remove speedometer cable and shift rods from housing. Remove bolts connecting shift control to extension housing and nut connecting shift control to transmission case.

NOTE — *A number "6" or "8" referring to 6 cyl. or 8 cyl. is stamped on extension housing by shift control plate. Shift control plate bolts must be placed in proper holes for plate alignment, depending on engine application.*

2) Support engine, remove crossmember to extension housing. Place jack under transmission and remove bolts to flywheel housing. Remove transmission.

CAUTION — *Do not depress clutch pedal when transmission is removed.*

"F" MODELS WITH 3-SPEED TRANSMISSION

1) Raise vehicle and support on safety stands. Support engine with suitable jack. Drain fluid from transmission. Place jack under transmission. Disconnect shift linkage at transmission. Disconnect speedometer cable and back-up switch wires.

2) Disconnect drive shaft. Raise transmission and remove rear support, insulator and retainer. Remove transmission-to-clutch housing attaching bolts. Move transmission rearward until input shaft clears clutch housing and lower transmission.

"F" MODELS & BRONCO WITH NP 435 TRANSMISSION

1) Remove rubber boot from shift lever. Remove floor pan transmission cover or weather pad on F100/350 models. It may be necessary to remove seat assembly. Remove gearshift lever using tool (J-3108) or equivalent. Remove seat and spring. Remove gearshift and disconnect backup light. Raise vehicle and position safety stands. Disconnect speedometer cable and rear driveshaft and wire out of way.

2) Drain transfer case and remove front driveshaft from case and wire out of way. Remove cotter pin holding shift link and remove link. Remove bolts holding support bracket to transfer case. Position transmission jack under transfer case. Remove bolts holding transfer case to transmission and remove transfer case. Place transmission jack under transmission and remove rear support. Remove attaching bolts and remove transmission.

FORD MANUAL TRANSMISSION REMOVAL (Cont.)

"F" MODELS & BRONCO WITH T-18 TRANSMISSION

"F" Models (2-WD) — Disconnect back-up light switch. Remove rubber boot, floor mat, floor pan cover, gearshift lever and weather pad. Raise vehicle and place suitable jack under transmission. Disconnect propeller shaft and clutch linkage. Remove rear support and transmission attaching bolts. Move transmission rearward until input shaft clears clutch housing. Lower transmission.

"F" Models & Bronco (4-WD) — **1)** From inside vehicle, remove shift knobs, shift lever boot assembly, back-up light switch and floor mat. Place shift lever in reverse position and remove floor pan cover. Remove insulator, dust cover, and transmission and transfer case shift levers.

2) Raise vehicle on hoist and drain fluid from transmission. Disconnect front and rear driveshafts from transfer case and place out of the way. Remove retainer ring holding shift link, and remove shift link from transfer case.

3) Remove speedometer cable. Place suitable jack under transfer case, remove bolts and lower transfer case from vehi-cle. Remove bolts holding rear support bracket to transmission. Place suitable jack under transmission and remove rear support bracket and brace. Remove bolts holding transmission to bell housing and remove transmission from vehicle.

"F" MODELS & BRONCO WITH SINGLE RAIL 4-SPEED OVERDRIVE

1) Raise vehicle and support with safety stands. Drain fluid from transmission. Disconnect driveshaft from rear U-joint flange and slide driveshaft off transmission output shaft. Disconnect speedometer cable. Remove screws holding shift lever to turret and remove shift lever.

2) Support engine with suitable jack and remove extension housing-to-rear support bolts. Raise engine high enough to remove weight from crossmember. Remove bolts securing crossmember to frame side supports and remove crossmember. Support transmission with suitable jack and remove transmission-to-flywheel housing bolts. Move transmission rearward until input shaft clears flywheel housing. Remove transmission.

GENERAL MOTORS MANUAL TRANSMISSION REMOVAL

ALL MODELS WITH 3- OR 4-SPEED (EXC. "K" MODELS)

1) Raise and support vehicle under frame, and drain fluid from transmission. Disconnect speedometer cable at transmission. Remove shift controls at transmission. On vehicles equipped with 4-speeds (117 mm), use suitable tool (J-8109) to remove shift lever from top of transmisson. Plug hole with a clean cloth. Remove parking brake lever and controls and back-up switch wire.

2) Disconnect propeller shaft at transmission, and position suitable support under transmission assembly. Remove frame crossmember under transmission, and remove flywheel under-pan. Remove transmission-to-clutch housing attaching bolts, slide transmission rearward until input shaft is clear of clutch hub, then remove assembly from vehicle.

CAUTION — *Support clutch release bearing and support assembly when removing transmission main drive gear from flywheel housing. This will prevent bearing from falling out.*

"K" MODELS WITH 3-SPEED

1) Raise and support vehicle under frame and drain fluid from both transmission and transfer case. Disconnect speedometer cable and propeller shaft at transmission. Remove shift controls from transmission and transfer case. Remove bolts attaching strut to transfer case and engine rear face, and remove strut.

2) Support transfer case with suitable jack and remove transfer case-to-adapter bolts and remove transfer case. Disconnect shift control rods from shift levers at transmission. Support rear of engine and remove adapter mount bolts. Remove 2 top transmission-to-clutch housing cap screws and insert guide pins (J-1126) in holes.

3) Remove 2 lower transmission-to-clutch housing cap screws. Slide transmission and adapter assembly straight back on guide pins until clutch gear is free of splines in clutch disc. Remove transmission and adapter as an assembly.

"K" MODELS WITH 4-SPEED

1) Remove transfer case shift lever boot retainer, and remove floormat (or carpeting) from vehicle. Remove transmission shift lever boot and retainer, and using suitable tool (J-8109), remove transmission shift lever. Remove console, and center floor outlet from heater duct (if equipped). Remove transmission floor cover, and remove transfer case shift lever assembly.

2) Raise and support vehicle under frame, and drain fluid from both transmission and transfer case. Disconnect speedometer cable. Disconnect propeller shaft at both transmission and transfer case. Position suitable supports under both transfer case and transmission and remove frame crossmember.

3) On V8 models, remove exhaust crossover pipe. Remove upper transmission-to-clutch housing bolts, and install suitable guide pins (J-1126) into holes. Remove lower transmission-to-clutch housing bolts and remove transmission and transfer case from vehicle.

JEEP MANUAL TRANSMISSION REMOVAL

ALL MODELS

1) Remove shift lever boot from base of lever. On models with SR-4 transmission, remove shift lever and lever housing from transmission. On models with T-18A transmission, unthread shift lever cap and remove cap, gasket, spring seat, spring and shift lever as an assembly, then remove shift lever locating pins from housing.

2) On models with T-176 transmission, press and turn shift lever retainer to release lever, then remove lever, boot, spring and seat as an assembly. On all models, raise vehicle and support with safety stands. Remove rear propeller shaft from transfer case.

3) On Cherokee and truck models, disconnect front parking brake cable at equalizer. Remove rear cable clip from crossmember. On all models, place a suitable jack under clutch housing to support engine. Remove rear crossmember from frame.

4) Disconnect speedometer cable, back-up light switch wire and four-wheel drive indicator switch wire. Disconnect transfer case vent hose. Remove front propeller shaft.

5) On "CJ" and Scrambler models, remove transfer case shift lever by removing shift shaft retaining nut. Remove cotter pins retaining shift control link pins in shift rods and remove pins. Remove shifter shaft and disengage shift lever from shift control links.

6) On Cherokee and truck models, remove cotter pin and washers connecting link to shift lever and disconnect link. On all models, support transmission and transfer case with suitable jack. Remove bolts securing transmission to clutch housing and remove transmission and transfer case. Remove transfer case from transmission.

FORD 3.03

E100/350
F100/250

TRANSMISSION IDENTIFICATION

A service identification tag is located on right front side of transmission case. First line on tag shows transmission model and service identification codes. Second line of tag shows a build date code and serial number.

DESCRIPTION

Transmission is a 3-speed, fully synchronized unit. All forward gears are constant mesh helical type. Forward speed changes are accomplished through use of blocker-type synchronizer sleeves. Reverse gears are spur type and are not synchronized. Transmission uses a system of detents and interlocks within the case, which maintains gear position and prevents selection of more than one speed at a time.

LUBRICATION

See Lubrication in MANUAL TRANSMISSION SERVICING Section.

TROUBLE SHOOTING

See Manual Transmission Trouble Shooting in MANUAL TRANSMISSION SERVICING Section.

REMOVAL & INSTALLATION

See Manual Transmission Removal in MANUAL TRANSMISSION SERVICING Section.

TRANSMISSION DISASSEMBLY

1) With transmission in a suitable holding fixture, drain transmission lubricant, then remove top cover and gasket. Remove the long spring and detent plug using a magnet. Remove extension housing-to-case bolts and withdraw extension housing and gasket. Remove front bearing retainer-to-case bolts and withdraw front bearing retainer and gasket.

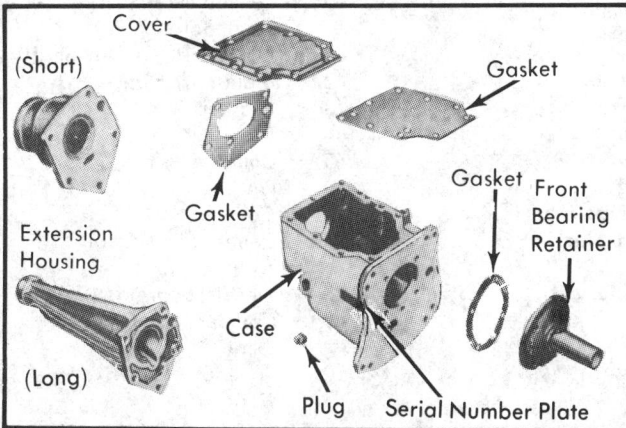

Fig. 1   Exploded View of Transmission Case Assembly

2) Remove filler plug from right side of case and, working through opening, drive roll pin out of case and countershaft using a ¼" punch. Hold countershaft gear with a suitable hook and drive countershaft to rear of case using a suitable dummy countershaft (T63P-7111-B). Remove countershaft from rear of case and allow countershaft (cluster) gear and thrust washers to rest at bottom of case.

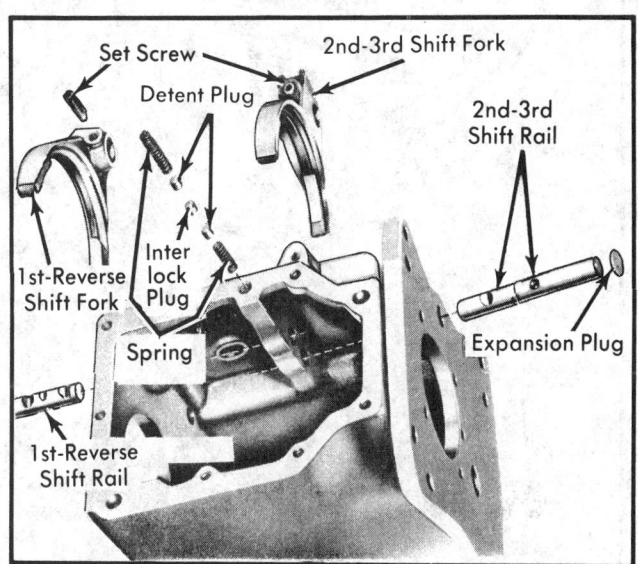

Fig. 2   Shift Rails and Shift Forks Installation

3) Remove speedometer drive gear snap ring and slide gear off shaft. Remove gear lock ball from shaft. Remove bearing snap ring from shaft. Using a suitable puller (T75L-7025-B, C, E, G and J) remove bearing from shaft. Place shift levers in center (neutral) position.

4) Remove set screw that secures 1st-Reverse shift fork to shift rail and slide shift rail out towards rear. Slide 1st-Reverse synchronizer as far forward as possible and rotate shift fork upward and remove. Move 2nd-3rd shift fork to second speed position and remove set screw from fork. Rotate shift rail 90° and lift interlock plug from case with a magnet.

5) Tap on inner end of 2nd-3rd shift rail to remove expansion plug from front of case. Remove shift rail. Remove 2nd-3rd speed shift rail detent plug and spring from detent bore. Pull input gear and shaft from case. Rotate 2nd-3rd shift fork upward and lift from case.

6) Carefully lift output shaft assembly out through top of case. Lift reverse idler gear and two thrust washers from case. Lift out countershaft gear, thrust washer and dummy shaft from case. Remove snap ring from front of output shaft and slide synchronizer and second gear off shaft.

7) Remove snap ring and tabbed thrust washer from output shaft, then withdraw first gear and blocking ring. Remove next snap ring and using an arbor press, withdraw synchronizer hub assembly from shaft.

CAUTION — DO NOT attempt to remove hub by hammering or prying as damage may result.

FORD 3.03 (Cont.)

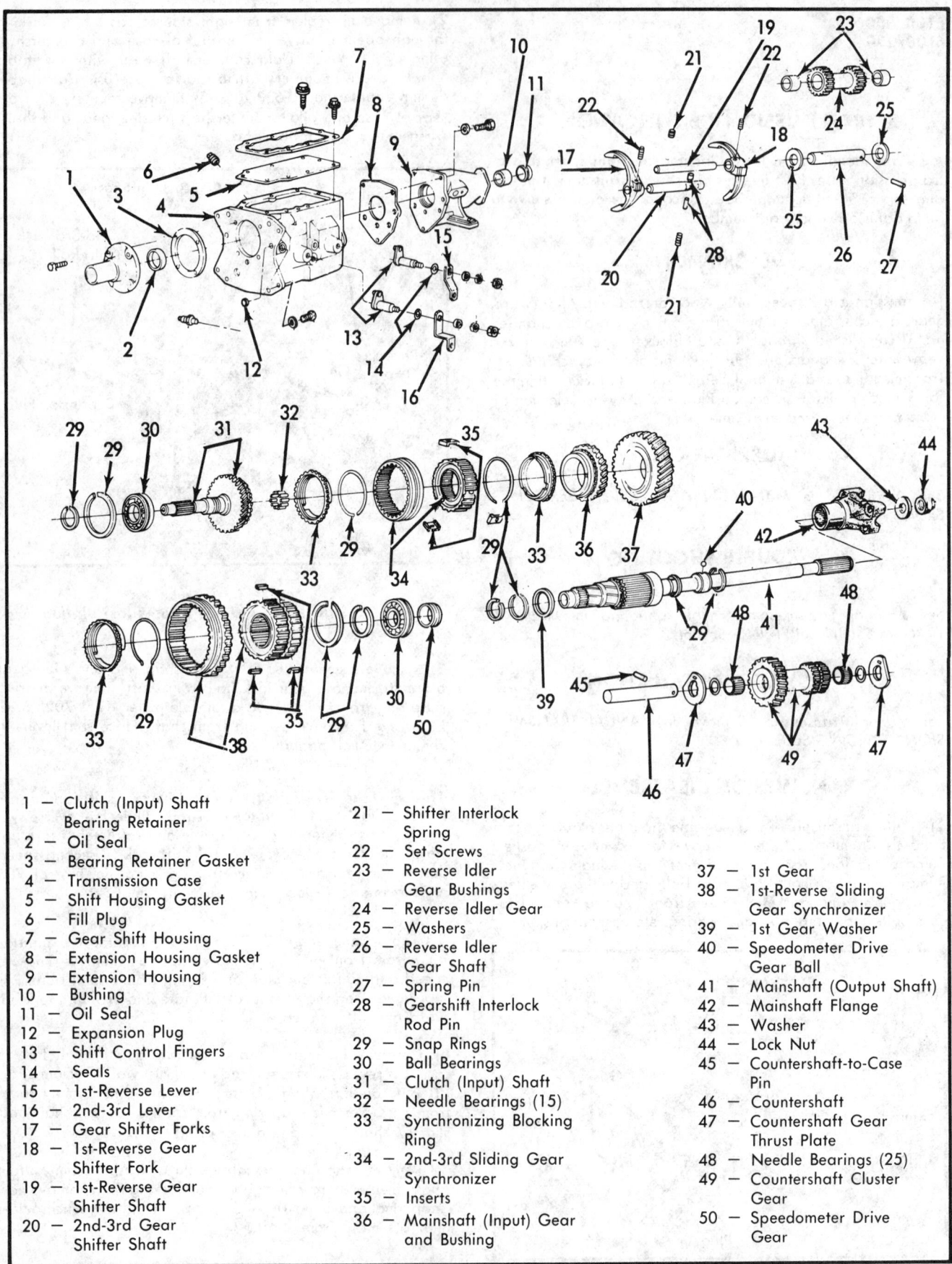

1 — Clutch (Input) Shaft Bearing Retainer
2 — Oil Seal
3 — Bearing Retainer Gasket
4 — Transmission Case
5 — Shift Housing Gasket
6 — Fill Plug
7 — Gear Shift Housing
8 — Extension Housing Gasket
9 — Extension Housing
10 — Bushing
11 — Oil Seal
12 — Expansion Plug
13 — Shift Control Fingers
14 — Seals
15 — 1st-Reverse Lever
16 — 2nd-3rd Lever
17 — Gear Shifter Forks
18 — 1st-Reverse Gear Shifter Fork
19 — 1st-Reverse Gear Shifter Shaft
20 — 2nd-3rd Gear Shifter Shaft

21 — Shifter Interlock Spring
22 — Set Screws
23 — Reverse Idler Gear Bushings
24 — Reverse Idler Gear
25 — Washers
26 — Reverse Idler Gear Shaft
27 — Spring Pin
28 — Gearshift Interlock Rod Pin
29 — Snap Rings
30 — Ball Bearings
31 — Clutch (Input) Shaft
32 — Needle Bearings (15)
33 — Synchronizing Blocking Ring
34 — 2nd-3rd Sliding Gear Synchronizer
35 — Inserts
36 — Mainshaft (Input) Gear and Bushing

37 — 1st Gear
38 — 1st-Reverse Sliding Gear Synchronizer
39 — 1st Gear Washer
40 — Speedometer Drive Gear Ball
41 — Mainshaft (Output Shaft)
42 — Mainshaft Flange
43 — Washer
44 — Lock Nut
45 — Countershaft-to-Case Pin
46 — Countershaft
47 — Countershaft Gear Thrust Plate
48 — Needle Bearings (25)
49 — Countershaft Cluster Gear
50 — Speedometer Drive Gear

Fig. 3 Disassembled View of Ford 3.03 3-Speed Manual Transmission

FORD 3.03 (Cont.)

COMPONENT DISASSEMBLY & REASSEMBLY

SHIFT LEVERS & SEALS

Disassembly — Remove nut, flat washer and lock washer securing each shift lever to lever and shaft in case. Lift off shift lever and slide each lever and shaft out of case. Discard "O" ring from each shaft.

Reassembly — Lubricate new seals with transmission fluid and install on shafts. Install lever and shafts in case, position shift lever on each shaft, and secure with a flat washer, lock washer and nut.

INPUT SHAFT BEARING

Disassembly — Remove snap ring securing input shaft bearing and press out shaft using suitable support tool (T57L-4220-A4).

Reassembly — Press input shaft bearing onto input shaft using suitable press attachment (T53T-4621-B). Install snap ring on shaft.

SYNCHRONIZERS

Disassembly — Punch or etch alignment marks on synchronizer hub before disassembly. Push synchronizer hub from sleeve. Separate inserts and springs from hubs. Use care not to interchange parts between the 2 synchronizers.

Reassembly — 1) Install spring in hub of 1st-Reverse synchronizer. Make sure that spring covers all insert grooves. Start hub on sleeve, making sure that alignment marks are properly indexed. Position three inserts in hub, making sure that small end is on inside of hub. Slide sleeve and reverse gear onto hub.

2) Install one spring into groove of 2nd-3rd synchronizer hub, making sure that all three insert slots are fully covered. With alignment marks properly indexed, start hub into sleeve. Place 3 inserts into slot and install remaining spring. Do not stagger springs. Place synchronizer blocking ring on each end of synchronizer sleeve.

COUNTERSHAFT GEAR BEARINGS

Disassembly — Remove dummy shaft, 50 needle bearings and two bearing retainer washers from countershaft gear.

Reassembly — 1) Coat bore in each end of countershaft gear with grease. Hold dummy shaft in the gear and install 25 needle bearings and a retainer washer in each end of the gear. Position countershaft gear, dummy shaft and needle bearings in case.

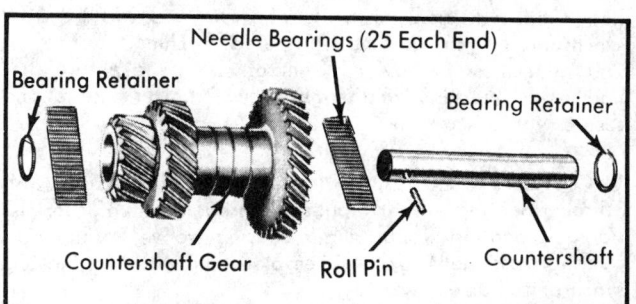

Fig. 5   Countershaft and Gear Assembly

2) Place case in a vertical position. Align gear bore and thrust washers with bores in case and install countershaft. Place case in a horizontal position and check countershaft gear end play with a feeler gauge. End play should be .004-.018". If not to specifications, replace thrust washers. Install dummy shaft and allow countershaft gear to lay in bottom of case until output and input shafts have been installed.

TRANSMISSION REASSEMBLY

1) Coat reverse idler gear thrust surfaces in case with lubricant and position two thrust washers in place. Position reverse idler gear and shaft in place. Align gear bore and thrust washers with case bores and install reverse idler shaft. Measure reverse idler gear end play with a feeler gauge. End play should be .004-.018". If end play is not to specifications, replace thrust washers.

2) Lubricate output shaft splines and machined surfaces. Install 1st-Reverse synchronizer hub on shaft with teeth end of gear facing toward rear of shaft. Press on shaft using an arbor

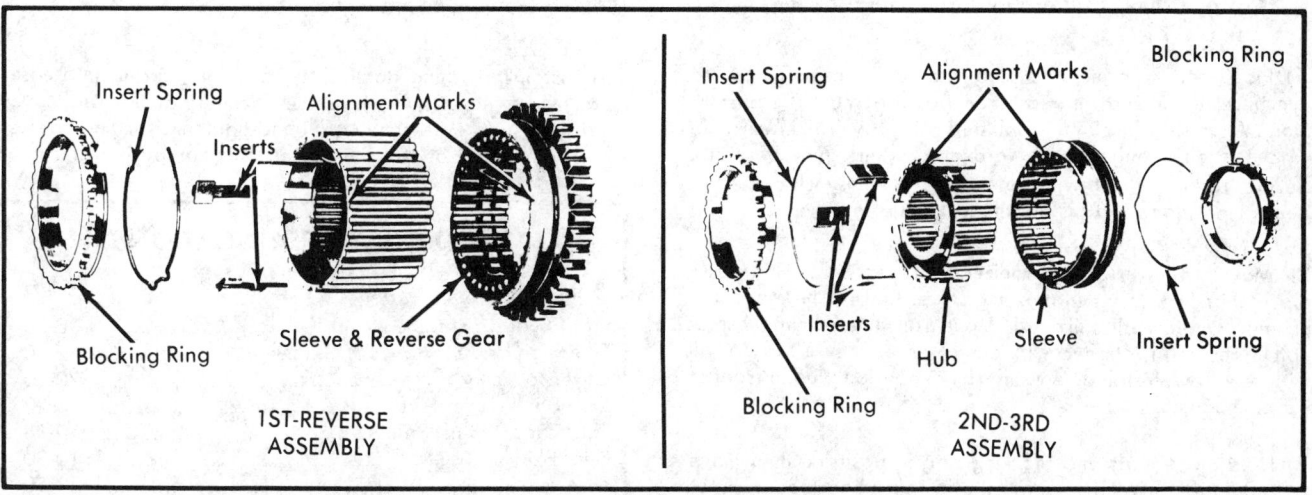

Fig. 4   Exploded View of Synchronizer Assemblies

FORD 3.03 (Cont.)

press, do not attempt to hammer or pry. Secure synchronizer with snap ring (if fitted).

3) Place blocking ring on tapered machined surface of 1st gear and slide 1st gear onto output shaft with blocking ring toward rear of shaft. Rotate gear as necessary to engage three notches in blocking ring with synchronizer inserts. Secure 1st gear with thrust washer and snap ring.

4) Slide blocking ring onto tapered machined surface of 2nd gear. Slide 2nd gear, with blocking ring and 2nd-3rd gear synchronizer onto mainshaft. Tapered machined surface of 2nd gear must be toward front of shaft. Make sure that notches in blocking ring engage synchronizer inserts and secure with a snap ring.

5) Coat bore of input shaft with thin film of grease and install 15 roller bearings. Install input shaft through front of transmission case and install snap ring in bearing groove. Position output shaft assembly in case, then place shift fork on 2nd-3rd synchronizer assembly.

NOTE — *Use only a thin film of grease; a thick application will block lubricating holes.*

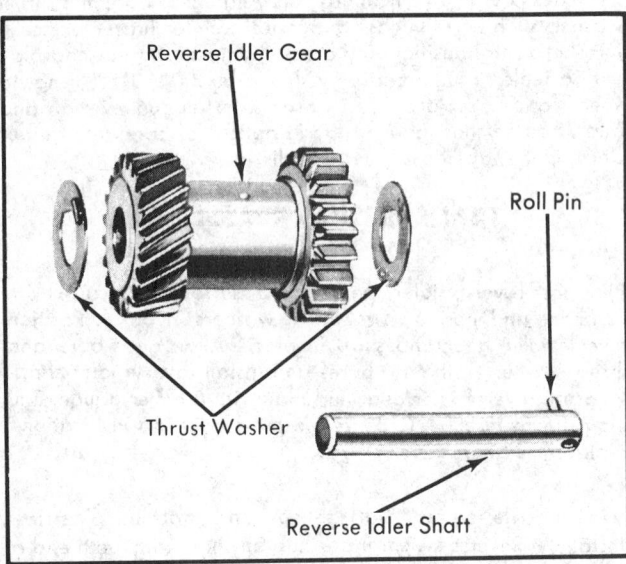

Fig. 6 **Reverse Idler Gear and Shaft Assembly**

6) Place detent spring and plug into case, position 2nd-3rd synchronizer in 2nd gear position (toward rear of transmission). Align shift fork and install shift rail. Move rail inward until detent plug engages forward notch (2nd gear position). Secure fork to shaft with set screw, move synchronizer to neutral position, and install interlock plug in case.

7) Move 1st-Reverse synchronizer to 1st speed position and place shift fork in synchronizer groove. Rotate shift fork into position and install shift rail. Move rail inward until center notch (neutral) is aligned with detent bore. Secure fork to rail with set screw. Install a new shift rail expansion plug in front of transmission.

8) Hold input shaft and blocking ring in position, then move output shaft forward to seat pilot in roller bearings of input gear. Tap input gear bearing into place in case while holding

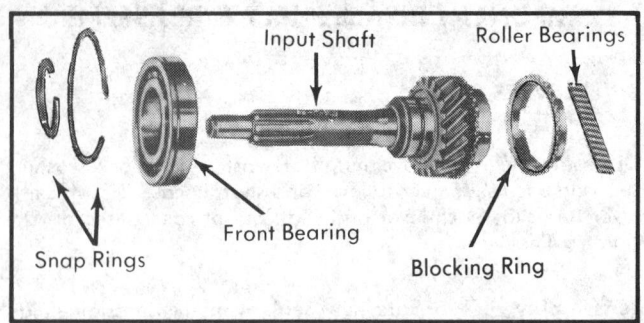

Fig. 7 **Input Shaft and Gear Assembly**

output shaft to prevent roller bearings from dropping. Install front bearing retainer with new gasket, making sure oil return slot of retainer is positioned toward bottom of case. Install and tighten retainer-to-case attaching screws.

9) Install large snap ring on rear bearing and place bearing on output shaft with snap ring toward rear of shaft. Using a suitable bearing installer (T75L-7075-B, E, K & P) press bearing into place. Secure bearing to shaft with snap ring. Hold speedometer drive gear lock ball in detent and slide speedometer drive gear into place. Secure gear with snap ring.

10) Place transmission in vertical position. Working with a screwdriver through bottom drain hole, align bore of countershaft gear with bore of case. Working from rear of case, push dummy shaft out of countershaft gear with countershaft. Ensure that roll pin hole is aligned with hole in case before completely inserting countershaft. Drive shaft into place and install roll pin.

11) Place output shaft bearing retainer into front of extension housing. Coat new extension housing gasket with sealer and install. Install lock washers on 5 attaching screws and dip threads in sealer.

12) Bolt housing to case and tighten to specifications. Place transmission in gear and pour lubricant (ESP-M2C83-C or equivalent) over entire gear train while rotating either input or output shaft.

NOTE — *Refill capacity is 3.5 pts.*

13) Install remaining detent plug and long spring into case. Coat new cover gasket with sealer, Position gasket and cover on transmission case, then install and tighten attaching screws. Check operation of transmission in all gear positions.

TIGHTENING SPECIFICATIONS

Application	Ft. Lbs.
Front Bearing Retainer-to-Case	30-36
Extension Housing-to-Case	42-50
Cover-to-Case	20-25
Outer Shift Lever Nut	18-23
Shift Fork-to-Shift Rail	10-18
Filler Plug	10-20
Transmission-to-Clutch Housing	42-50

GENERAL MOTORS 76 MM

Chevrolet
GMC

DESCRIPTION

The 76 mm 3-speed transmission is identified by the measured distance (76 mm) between centerlines of mainshaft and countergear and by number of forward gears. It is a fully synchronized transmission which provides synchromesh engagement in all forward gears. All gears are helical cut with the forward gears being in constant mesh.

LUBRICATION

See *Lubrication* in MANUAL TRANSMISSION SERVICING Section.

TROUBLE SHOOTING

See *Manual Transmission Trouble Shooting* in MANUAL TRANSMISSION SERVICING Section.

REMOVAL & INSTALLATION

See *Manual Transmission Removal* in MANUAL TRANSMISSION SERVICING Section.

TRANSMISSION DISASSEMBLY

1) Remove side cover assembly, gasket and shift forks. Remove input shaft bearing retainer and gasket. Remove input shaft bearing to shaft snap ring. Remove input shaft bearing by pulling outward on shaft until a screwdriver or other suitable tool can be inserted between bearing snap ring and case to complete removal.

2) Remove speedometer driven gear from extension housing and remove extension housing-to-case bolts. Remove "E" clip from reverse idler shaft. Remove input shaft, mainshaft and extension assembly through rear of case. Remove drive gear, input shaft needle bearings and synchronizer ring from mainshaft.

3) Expand snap ring in extension housing which retains mainshaft rear bearing and remove extension housing. Using a dummy countershaft, drive countershaft and its Woodruff key out rear of case. Dummy shaft will hold roller bearings in position in gear.

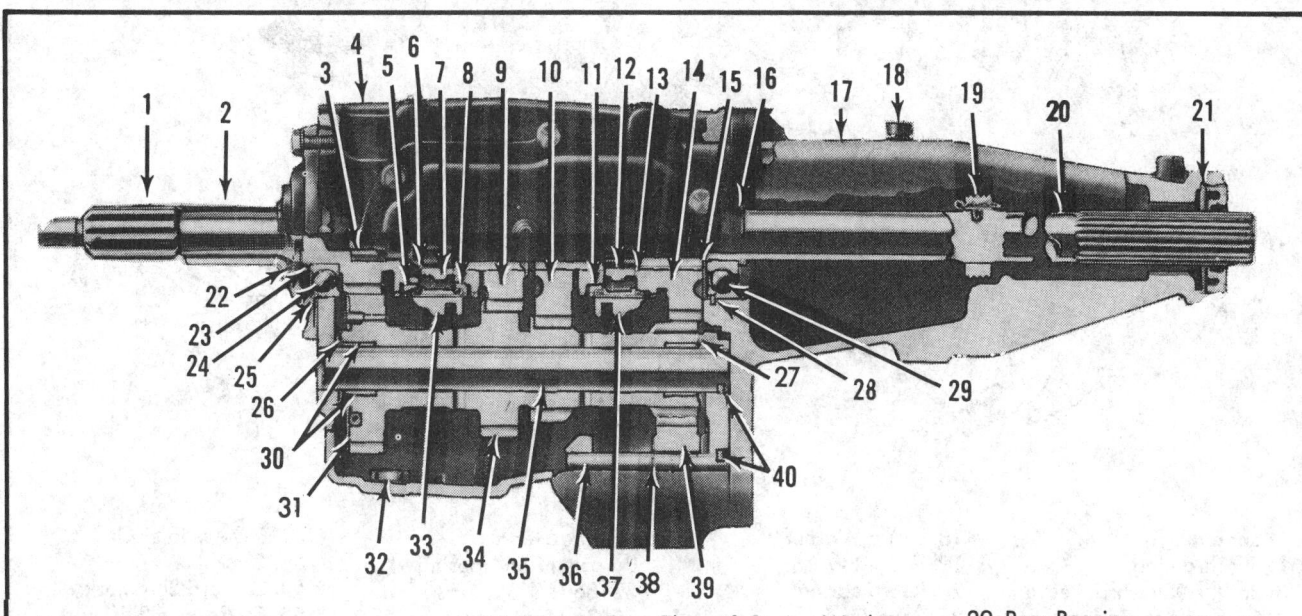

1. Input Shaft	15. Reverse Gear Thrust & Spring Washers	29. Rear Bearing
2. Bearing Retainer	16. Bearing-to-Mainshaft Snap Ring	30. Countergear Roll Bearings
3. Pilot Bearings	17. Extension Housing	31. Anti-Lash Plate Assy.
4. Case	18. Vent	32. Magnet
5. 3rd Gear Blocker Ring	19. Speedo Drive Gear & Clip	33. 2nd-3rd Synchro Sleeve
6. 2nd-3rd Synchro Snap Ring	20. Mainshaft	34. Countergear
7. 2nd-3rd Synchro Hub	21. Rear Oil Seal	35. Countershaft
8. 2nd Gear Blocker Ring	22. Retainer Oil Seal	36. Reverse Idler Shaft
9. 2nd Gear	23. Bearing-to-Gear Snap Ring	37. 1st Gear Synchro Sleeve
10. 1st Gear	24. Input Shaft Bearing	38. "E" Ring
11. 1st Gear Blocker Ring	25. Bearing-to-Case Snap Ring	39. Reverse Idler Gear
12. 1st Gear Synchro Hub	26. Front Thrust Washer	40. Woodruff Key
13. 1st Gear Synchro Snap Ring	27. Rear Thrust Washer	
14. Reverse Gear	28. Extension Housing Snap Ring	

Fig. 1 Cutaway View of General Motors 76 MM Transmission

3-Speed Manual Transmissions

GENERAL MOTORS 76 MM (Cont.)

4) Remove countergear, bearings and thrust washers. Using a long drift (or other suitable tool), drive the reverse idler shaft and Woodruff key out rear of case. Lift out reverse idler gear.

CLEANING & INSPECTION

Wash all components in cleaning solvent and dry with air. Inspect transmission case for cracks, damaged bearing bores, or damaged threads. Remove all small nicks and burrs from front and rear face of case. Check ball bearings for roughness by slowly turning race by hand. Inspect bearing rollers, shafts and washers for wear or damage. Inspect bushing in reverse gear and reverse idler gear for wear or damage. If worn or damaged, replace gear. Their bushings are not serviced separately. Check all other components for wear, chipped or broken teeth, and damage. Replace parts as necessary.

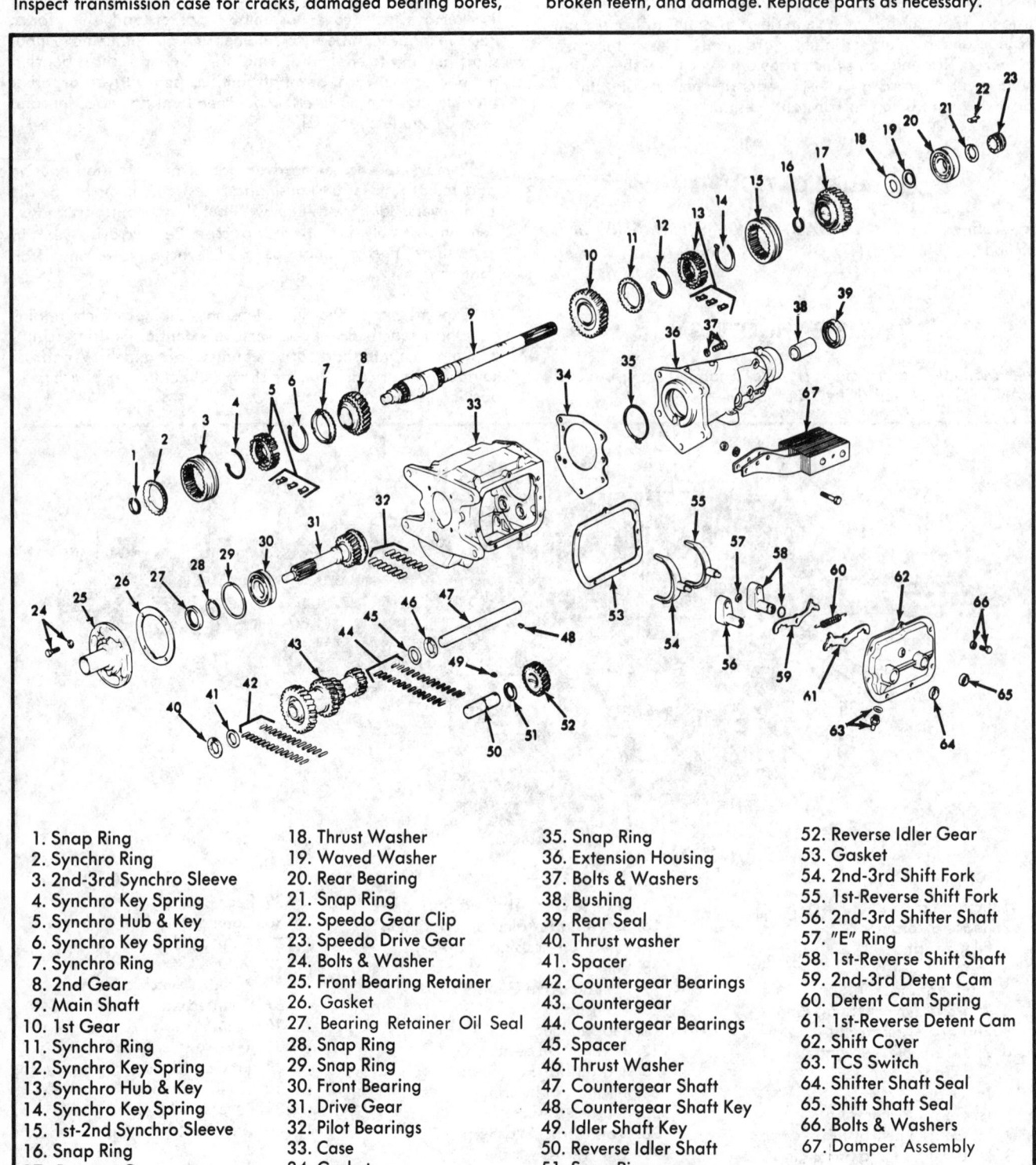

1. Snap Ring
2. Synchro Ring
3. 2nd-3rd Synchro Sleeve
4. Synchro Key Spring
5. Synchro Hub & Key
6. Synchro Key Spring
7. Synchro Ring
8. 2nd Gear
9. Main Shaft
10. 1st Gear
11. Synchro Ring
12. Synchro Key Spring
13. Synchro Hub & Key
14. Synchro Key Spring
15. 1st-2nd Synchro Sleeve
16. Snap Ring
17. Reverse Gear
18. Thrust Washer
19. Waved Washer
20. Rear Bearing
21. Snap Ring
22. Speedo Gear Clip
23. Speedo Drive Gear
24. Bolts & Washer
25. Front Bearing Retainer
26. Gasket
27. Bearing Retainer Oil Seal
28. Snap Ring
29. Snap Ring
30. Front Bearing
31. Drive Gear
32. Pilot Bearings
33. Case
34. Gasket
35. Snap Ring
36. Extension Housing
37. Bolts & Washers
38. Bushing
39. Rear Seal
40. Thrust washer
41. Spacer
42. Countergear Bearings
43. Countergear
44. Countergear Bearings
45. Spacer
46. Thrust Washer
47. Countergear Shaft
48. Countergear Shaft Key
49. Idler Shaft Key
50. Reverse Idler Shaft
51. Snap Ring
52. Reverse Idler Gear
53. Gasket
54. 2nd-3rd Shift Fork
55. 1st-Reverse Shift Fork
56. 2nd-3rd Shifter Shaft
57. "E" Ring
58. 1st-Reverse Shift Shaft
59. 2nd-3rd Detent Cam
60. Detent Cam Spring
61. 1st-Reverse Detent Cam
62. Shift Cover
63. TCS Switch
64. Shifter Shaft Seal
65. Shift Shaft Seal
66. Bolts & Washers
67. Damper Assembly

Fig. 2 Exploded View of General Motors 76 MM Transmission

GENERAL MOTORS 76 MM (Cont.)

COMPONENT DISASSEMBLY & REASSEMBLY

MAINSHAFT

Disassembly — 1) Remove 2nd-3rd gear sliding clutch snap ring from mainshaft. Remove clutch assembly, 2nd gear blocker ring and 2nd gear from front of mainshaft. See *Fig. 2.*

2) Depress speedometer gear retaining clip and remove speedometer gear from mainshaft. Remove rear bearing snap ring from groove in mainshaft. Support reverse gear with press plates, press on rear of mainshaft to remove reverse gear, thrust washer, spring washer, rear bearing and snap ring.

3) Remove the 1st-reverse sliding clutch hub snap ring from mainshaft and remove clutch assembly. Remove 1st gear blocker ring and 1st gear from rear of mainshaft.

Reassembly — 1) On front end of mainshaft, install 2nd gear with clutching teeth upward (rear face of gear will butt against flange on mainshaft). Install blocker ring with teeth down over synchronizing surface of 2nd gear. All three blocker rings are the same.

2) Install the 2nd-3rd gear synchronizer assembly, with fork slot downward, on mainshaft. Press into place until it bottoms out. Both synchronizer assemblies used in transmission are the same. See *Fig. 3.*

NOTE — *If sleeve is removed from 2nd-3rd gear hub, the notches on hub O.D. face toward front of mainshaft. Also make sure that notches on blocker ring align with synchronizer.*

3) Install synchronizer hub snap ring. Both synchronizer snap rings are identical. Install 1st gear on rear end of mainshaft, with clutching teeth up. Front face of gear will butt against flange on mainshaft. Install blocker ring with teeth downward over 1st gear.

4) Install 1st-reverse synchronizer assembly with fork slot downward on mainshaft splines.

NOTE — *Make sure blocker ring notches align with synchronizer keys.*

5) Install synchronizer snap ring. Install reverse gear with teeth downward. Install reverse gear thrust washer (steel) and spring washer. Install rear bearing with snap ring slot down on mainshaft. Install bearing snap ring. Install speedometer drive gear and retaining clip.

SYNCHRONIZER CLUTCH ASSEMBLIES

NOTE — *Clutch hubs and sliding sleeves are a selected assembly and should be kept together as originally assembled, but the keys and two springs may be replaced if worn or broken. See Fig. 3.*

Disassembly — Mark hub and sleeve so they can be matched upon reassembly. Push hub from sliding sleeve, then remove keys and springs.

Reassembly — Place three keys and two springs in position (one on each side of hub), so all three keys are engaged by both springs. The tanged end each synchronizer spring should be installed into different key cavities on either side. Slide sleeve onto hub, aligning marks made before assembly.

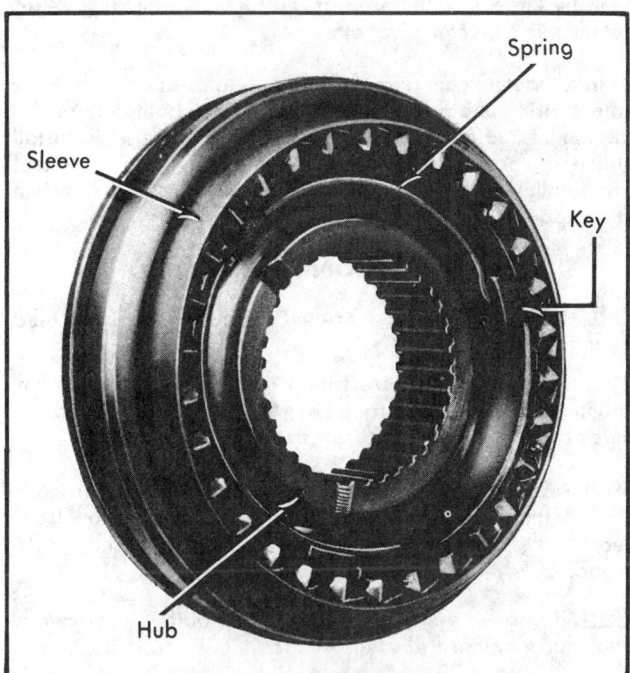

Fig. 3   Synchronizer Assembly

NOTE — *A groove around outside of synchronizer hub identifies the end that must be opposite fork slot in sleeve when assembled. This groove indicates end of hub with a greater recess depth.*

EXTENSION HOUSING OIL SEAL OR BUSHING

If bushing in rear of extension housing requires replacement, remove seal and use a suitable tool to drive bushing into extension housing. Using same tool, drive new bushing into housing from rear. Coat I.D. of bushing and new seal with transmission lubricant. Coat O.D. of seal with sealing compound and use a suitable tool to drive seal into housing.

INPUT SHAFT RETAINER OIL SEAL

If seal in retainer requires replacement, pry old seal out, then use a suitable tool to drive new seal into retainer until seal seats in bore.

NOTE — *When installed, seal lip must face rear of transmission.*

TRANSMISSION CASE COVER

Disassembly — Remove TCS switch (if equipped) from cover. Remove both shift forks from shifter shaft assemblies. Remove both shifter shaft assemblies from cover. Remove detent cam spring, pivot retainer "C" ring, and both detent cams. Inspect and replace damaged parts. Inspect shifter shaft seals and replace as necessary.

Reassembly — 1) With detent spring tang projecting up over the 2nd-3rd shifter shaft cover opening, install the 1st-reverse detent cam pivot pin. With detent spring tang projecting up

3-Speed Manual Transmissions

GENERAL MOTORS 76 MM (Cont.)

over the 1st-reverse shifter shaft cover hole, install the 2nd-3rd detent cam onto cam pivot pin.

2) Install detent cam retaining "C" ring to pivot pin, and hook detent spring into detent cam notches. Install both shifter shaft assemblies into cover taking care not to damage seals. Install both shift forks to shifter shaft assemblies. Lift up on detent cam to allow forks to fully seat into position. Install TCS switch (if equipped).

TRANSMISSION REASSEMBLY

NOTE — *Apply a suitable sealant to all through bolts used during reassembly.*

1) Coat countershaft bore with heavy grease. Insert dummy countershaft into countergear and install needle roller bearings (27) and thrust washer in each end of gear.

2) Place outer gear assembly through rear opening in case along with a tanged thrust washer (with tang away from gear), at each end and install counter gear shaft and Woodruff key from rear of case.

NOTE — *Make sure countershaft picks up both thrust washers and that tangs are aligned in case.*

3) Install reverse idler gear and shaft with Woodruff key from rear of case. Do not install idler shaft "E" clip at this time. Expand snap ring in extension housing and install extension housing over rear of mainshaft and onto rear bearing. Seat snap ring in groove.

4) Coat input shaft cavity with a heavy grease. Install mainshaft pilot bearings (14) into cavity. Install 3rd gear blocking ring on input shaft with teeth facing input gear. Guide input shaft, bearing and 3rd gear blocking ring assembly over front of mainshaft assembly. *See Fig. 4.*

NOTE — *Make sure blocker ring notches align with keys in 2nd-3rd synchronizer assembly.*

5) Install extension housing-to-case gasket. From rear of case, install input shaft, mainshaft and extension housing as an assembly. Install extension housing-to-case bolts.

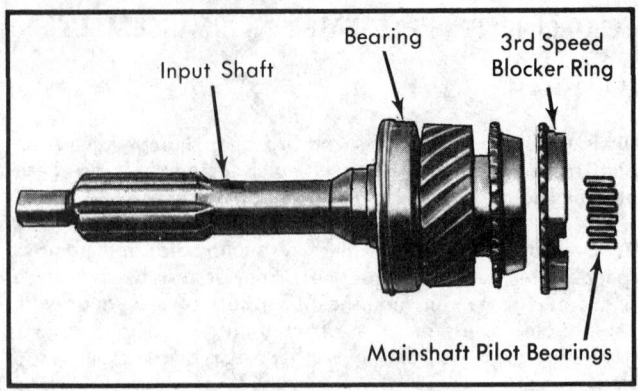

Fig. 4   Input Shaft Assembly

6) Install snap ring on front bearing and place bearing over input shaft. Slide bearing into bore in case. Install snap ring on input shaft. Install input shaft bearing retainer and new gasket to case.

NOTE — *The bearing retainer oil hole should be at bottom.*

7) Install reverse idler gear "E" clip on shaft. Shift synchronizer sleeves to neutral position and install cover, gasket and fork assembly to case. Make sure forks align with synchronizer sleeve grooves. Install speedometer driven gear in extension housing. Rotate input shaft and shift transmission to check operation.

TIGHTENING SPECIFICATIONS

Application	Ft. Lbs.
Input Shaft Retainer-to-Case Bolts	15
Side Cover-to-Case Bolts	15
Ext. Hsg.-to-Case Bolts	45
Filler Plug	13
Shift Lever-to-Shifter Shaft Bolts	25

GENERAL MOTORS 77 MM

Chevrolet
GMC

DESCRIPTION

The 77mm 3-speed transmission is described by number of forward gears and measured distance (77mm) between centerlines of mainshaft and countergear. It is a fully synchronized unit which provides synchromesh engagement in all forward gears. The forward gears are helical cut and are in constant mesh. Reverse gears are spur cut and are not in constant mesh.

LUBRICATION

See Lubrication in MANUAL TRANSMISSION SERVICING Section.

TROUBLE SHOOTING

See Manual Transmission Trouble Shooting in MANUAL TRANSMISSION SERVICING Section.

REMOVAL & INSTALLATION

See Manual Transmission Removal in MANUAL TRANSMISSION SERVICING Section.

TRANSMISSION DISASSEMBLY

1) Remove lower extension housing bolt and drain transmission. See Fig. 1. Remove top cover and gasket. Withdraw long detent spring. See Fig. 2. Using a small magnet, remove detent plug from case. Remove mounting bolts and carefully slide extension housing from mainshaft.

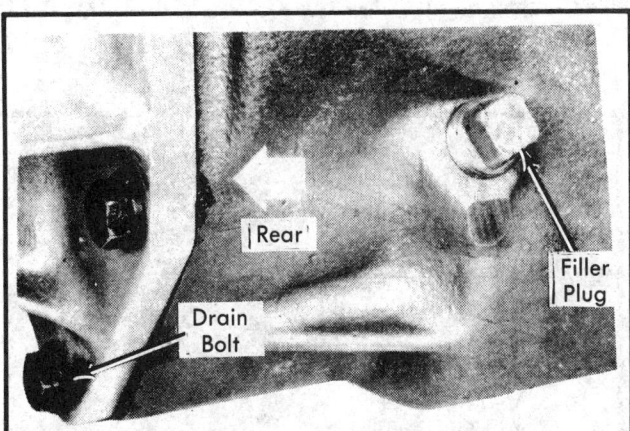

Fig. 1   Transmission Drain and Filler Plug Location

2) Press down on speedometer gear retainer and slide speedometer drive gear and retainer from output shaft. With filler plug removed, use ³⁄₁₆" pin punch through plug opening to drive out countergear roll pin. Using dummy countershaft (J-25232), lightly tap countershaft out rear of case until countershaft can be withdrawn and countergear allowed to rest at bottom of case. See Fig. 3.

NOTE — Countergear roll pin will fall into case where it may be retrieved after gears and shafts have been removed.

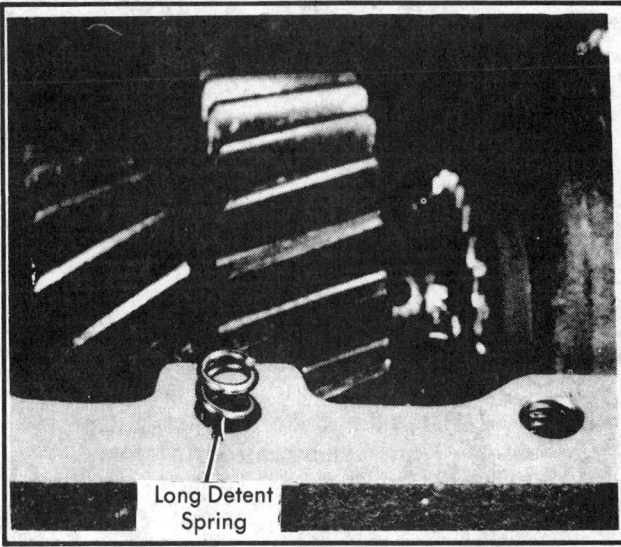

Fig. 2   Upper Long Detent Spring Location

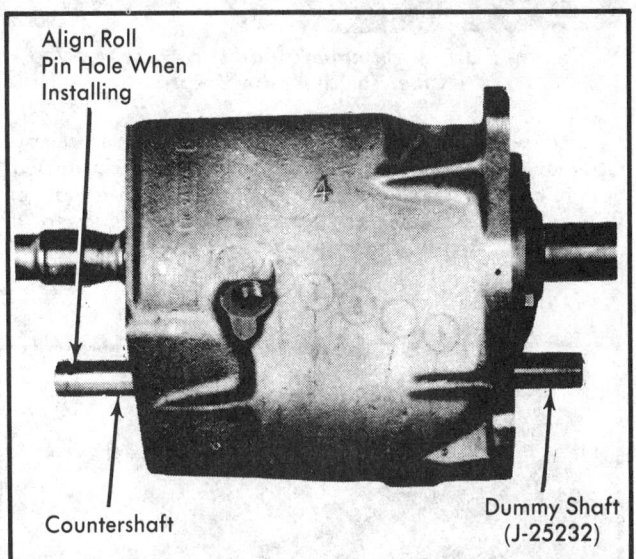

Fig. 3   Removal and Installation of Countershaft Using Special Dummy Shaft

3) Punch alignment marks in front bearing retainer and case for correct assembly location. See Fig. 4. Remove bearing retainer and gasket. Remove large snap ring from front bearing and smaller snap ring from pinion gear shaft. Using a bearing puller (J-6654-01 & J-8433-1), remove front bearing from case.

4) Remove large snap ring from rear bearing and small snap ring from mainshaft. Using bearing puller (J-8157-01), remove rear bearing from mainshaft. Remove setscrew from 1st-Reverse shifter fork and slide shift rail out rear of case. Shift 1st-Reverse sleeve and gear all the way forward and rotate shifter fork upward and out of case. Remove 1st-Reverse detent plug from case.

NOTE — Mainshaft can be blocked using screwdriver between reverse gear assembly and case when removing rear bearing.

GENERAL MOTORS 77 MM (Cont.)

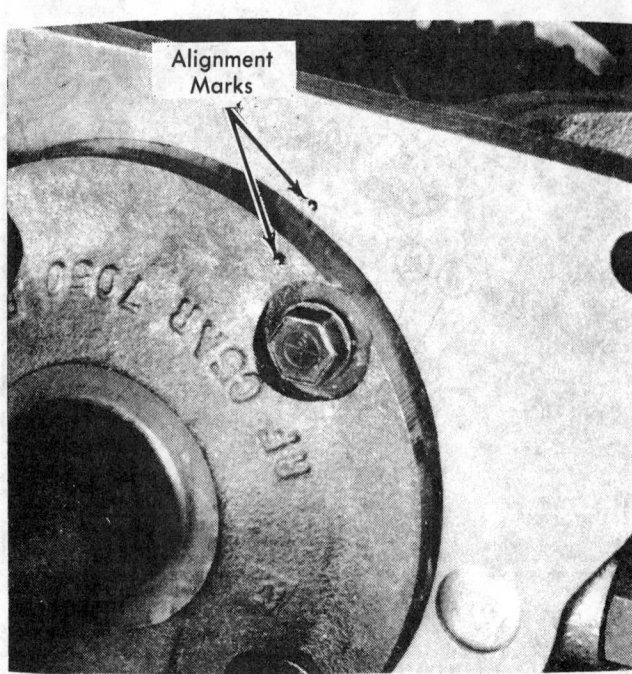

Fig. 4   Placing Alignment Marks in Front Bearing Retainer for Assembly Location

5) Shift second-third shift fork rearward and then remove setscrew. Using a pair of pliers, rotate shift rail 90° to clear bottom detent plug and remove detent plug with a magnet. With a long thin 1/4" punch inserted in access hole in rear of case, drive shift rail and expansion plug out front of case. Rotate second-third shift fork upward and out of case. Remove detent plug and short spring from case. See *Fig. 5.*

Fig. 5   Second-Third Shift Fork Removal

6) Separate clutch gear from output shaft and remove shaft assembly. Tilt spline end of shaft downward and lift gear end upward and out of case. First and reverse sleeve and gear must pass through notch at right end of case. Remove clutch gear and shift fork shafts. With dummy shaft in place, remove countergear, thrust washers and roll pin. See *Fig. 6.*

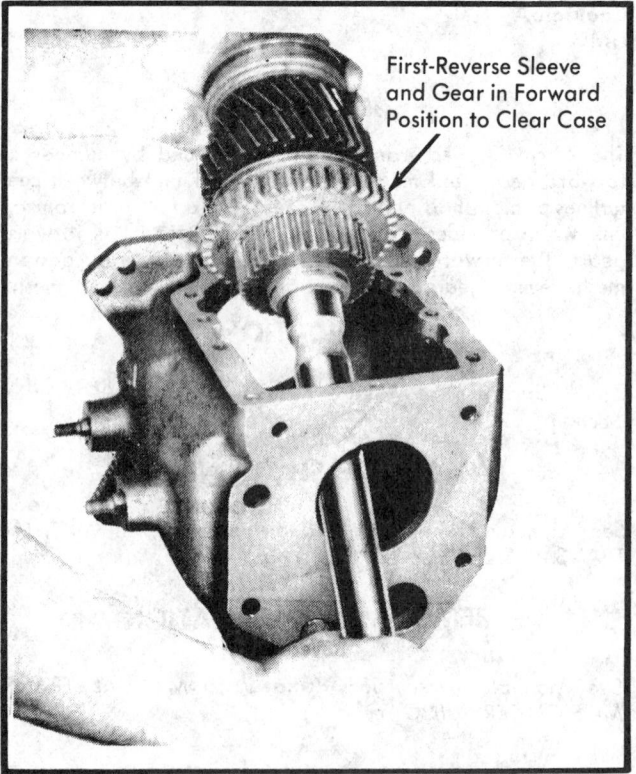

Fig. 6   Removing Mainshaft from Transmission Case

7) Tap reverse idler gear shaft out rear of case until roll pin clears counterbore in case. Remove idler shaft and reverse idler gear. Remove any needle rollers which may have fallen into transmission case. See *Fig. 7.*

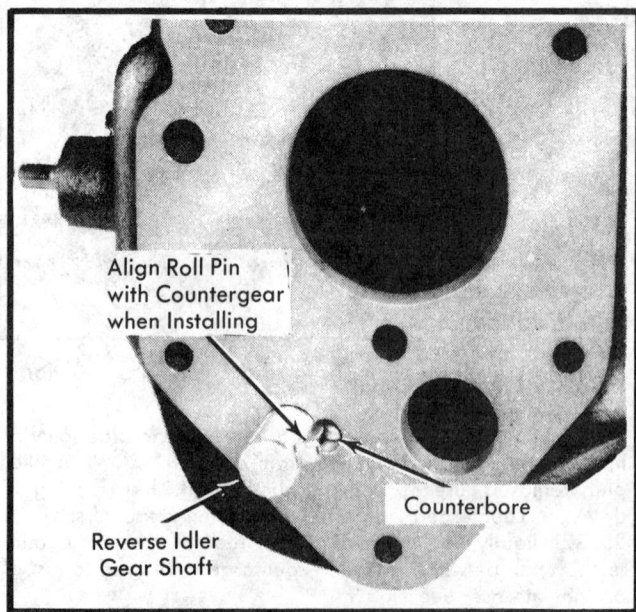

Fig. 7   Removal and Installation of Reverse Idler Shaft

GENERAL MOTORS 77 MM (Cont.)

CLEANING & INSPECTION

Wash all parts in cleaning solvent and dry with air. Inspect transmission case for cracks, damaged bearing bores, or damaged threads. Remove all small nicks or burrs from front or rear face of case. Check ball bearings for roughness by slowly turning race by hand. Inspect needle rollers, shafts and washers for wear or damage. Inspect bushings in reverse gear and reverse idler gear. If worn or damaged, replace gear. Check all other parts for wear, chipped or broken teeth and damage. Replace parts as necessary.

COMPONENT DISASSEMBLY & REASSEMBLY

MAINSHAFT

Disassembly — 1) Mark sleeve and hub on both synchronizer assemblies for reassembly. Remove snap ring from front end of mainshaft. Slide 2nd-3rd synchronizer assembly and 2nd gear from mainshaft. *See Fig. 9.*

2) Remove snap ring and tabbed thrust washer from mainshaft. Slide first gear and blocking ring from mainshaft. Remove first-reverse hub retaining snap ring. Observe position of spring and keys before removal, also, mark hub and sleeve for correct assembly. Remove sleeve and gear, spring, and three keys from hub. Using an arbor press, remove hub from mainshaft. *See Fig. 8.*

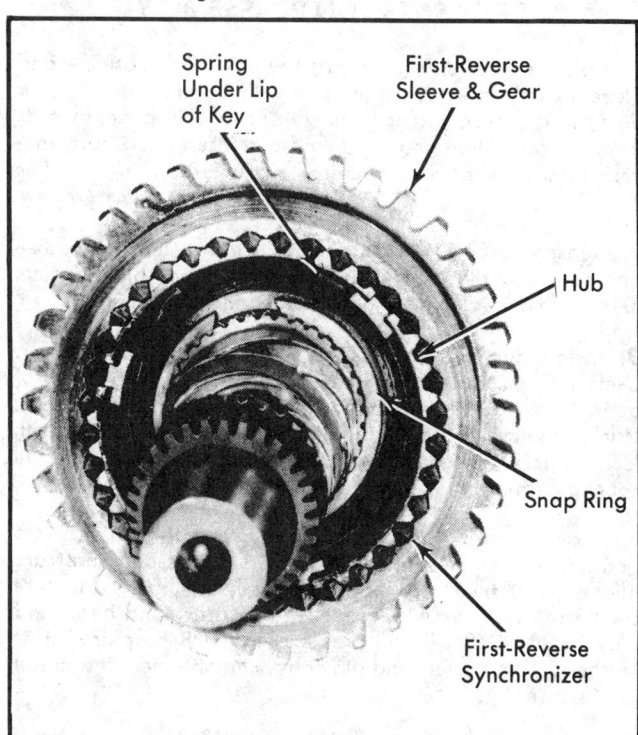

Fig. 8   First-Reverse Synchronizer Assembly

Reassembly — 1) Install first-reverse synchronizer hub on output shaft splines by hand with slotted end of hub facing front of shaft. Use arbor press to complete hub installation and install snap ring in rear groove. Align marks made during disassembly, slide first-reverse sleeve and gear halfway on to hub with gear end of sleeve facing rear of shaft.

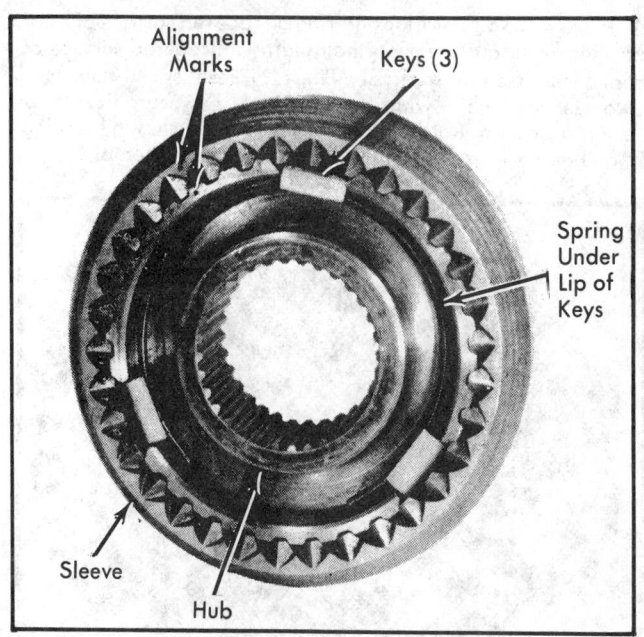

Fig. 9   Second-Third Synchronizer Assembly

2) Install spring in first-reverse hub, making sure spring is bottomed in hub and covers all three key slots. Position three synchronizer keys in hub, with small ends in hub slots and large ends inside hub. Push keys fully into hub so that they seat on spring. Then slide first-reverse sleeve and gear over keys until keys engage in synchronizer sleeve. *See Fig. 8.*

3) Place first gear blocking ring on tapered surface of gear. Install first gear on mainshaft and rotate gear until notches in blocking ring engages keys in first-reverse hub. Place tabbed thrust washer with sharp edge facing out and then install snap ring in mainshaft groove. *See Fig. 10.*

Fig. 10   Installing Tabbed Thrust Washer

GENERAL MOTORS 77 MM (Cont.)

4) Place second gear blocking ring on tapered surface of gear and install second gear on mainshaft with tapered surface of gear facing front of shaft. See Fig. 11. Install second-third synchronizer assembly with flat portion of synchronizer hub facing rearward. Rotate second gear until notches in blocking ring engages keys in second-third synchronizer assembly.

Fig. 11   Installing Second Gear on Mainshaft

5) Install snap ring on mainshaft and measure end play between snap ring and second-third synchronizer hub with a feeler gauge. End play should be .004-.014". If end play exceeds .014", replace thrust washers and all snap rings on mainshaft. See Fig. 12.

Fig. 12   Measuring Mainshaft End Play

SYNCHRONIZER ASSEMBLIES

1) Mark hub and sleeve so they may be matched upon reassembly. Push hub from sliding sleeve, and remove keys and springs.

2) Install one spring into second-third hub. Align second-third sleeve-to-hub marks and start sleeve onto hub. Place the three keys into hub slots and on top of spring. Push sleeve fully onto hub to engage keys in sleeve. See Figs. 8 & 9.

3) Install remaining spring in exact position as 1st spring. Ends of both springs must cover same slots in hub and not be staggered.

NOTE — *Keys have a small lip on each end. When correctly installed, lip will fit over spring.*

EXTENSION HOUSING OIL SEAL OR BUSHING

If bushing in rear housing of extension requires replacement, remove seal and use tool (J-5778) to drive bushing into extension housing. Using same tool, drive new bushing into housing from rear. Coat I.D. of bushing and new seal with transmission lubricant. Coat O.D. of seal with sealing compound and use tool (J-5154) to drive seal into housing.

CLUTCH BEARING OIL SEAL

If lip seal in retainer requires replacement, pry out old seal, then use installer tool (J-25233) to drive new seal into retainer until seal seats in bore.

NOTE — *When installed, lip of seal must face rear of transmission.*

TRANSMISSION REASSEMBLY

1) Coat reverse idler gear thrust washer with Vaseline and place washer in transmission case with locating tabs in case slots. Install reverse idler gear with helical cut gear towards front of case. Align gear and case and insert idler shaft from rear of case with roll pin matching counterbore in case. See Fig. 7.

2) Measure reverse idler gear end play between thrust washer and gear. End play should be .004-.018". If end play exceeds .018", remove idler gear and replace thrust washer.

3) Install dummy shaft (J-25232) in bore of countergear. Using heavy grease, install needle rollers (25) in each end of gear. Install a needle bearing retainer on each end of gear. Using Vaseline, place countergear thrust washer in case with locating tab engaging slot in case. From rear of case, install countershaft far enough to retain thrust washer in case.

4) Align gear and case and insert countershaft part way into gear. Rotate shaft until roll pin holes in case and shaft are aligned and then tap shaft completely into case. Measure countershaft end play between thrust washer and gear. End play is .004-.018". If end play exceeds .018", replace thrust washers. After correct end play has been obtained, install roll pin in case.

5) Install short detent spring and detent plug into case. See Fig. 13. Install shifter fork shafts in case with pivot lugs facing up. Using Vaseline, install needle bearings (15) in pinion gear bore. Place blocking ring on pinion gear and position gear through top of case and in front of case bore. Place first-reverse sleeve and gear in neutral and lower mainshaft into transmission case. Insert forward end of mainshaft into pinion gear roller bearings.

NOTE — *DO NOT use heavy grease to retain roller bearings, as grease could plug lubricant holes in shaft.*

GENERAL MOTORS 77 MM (Cont.)

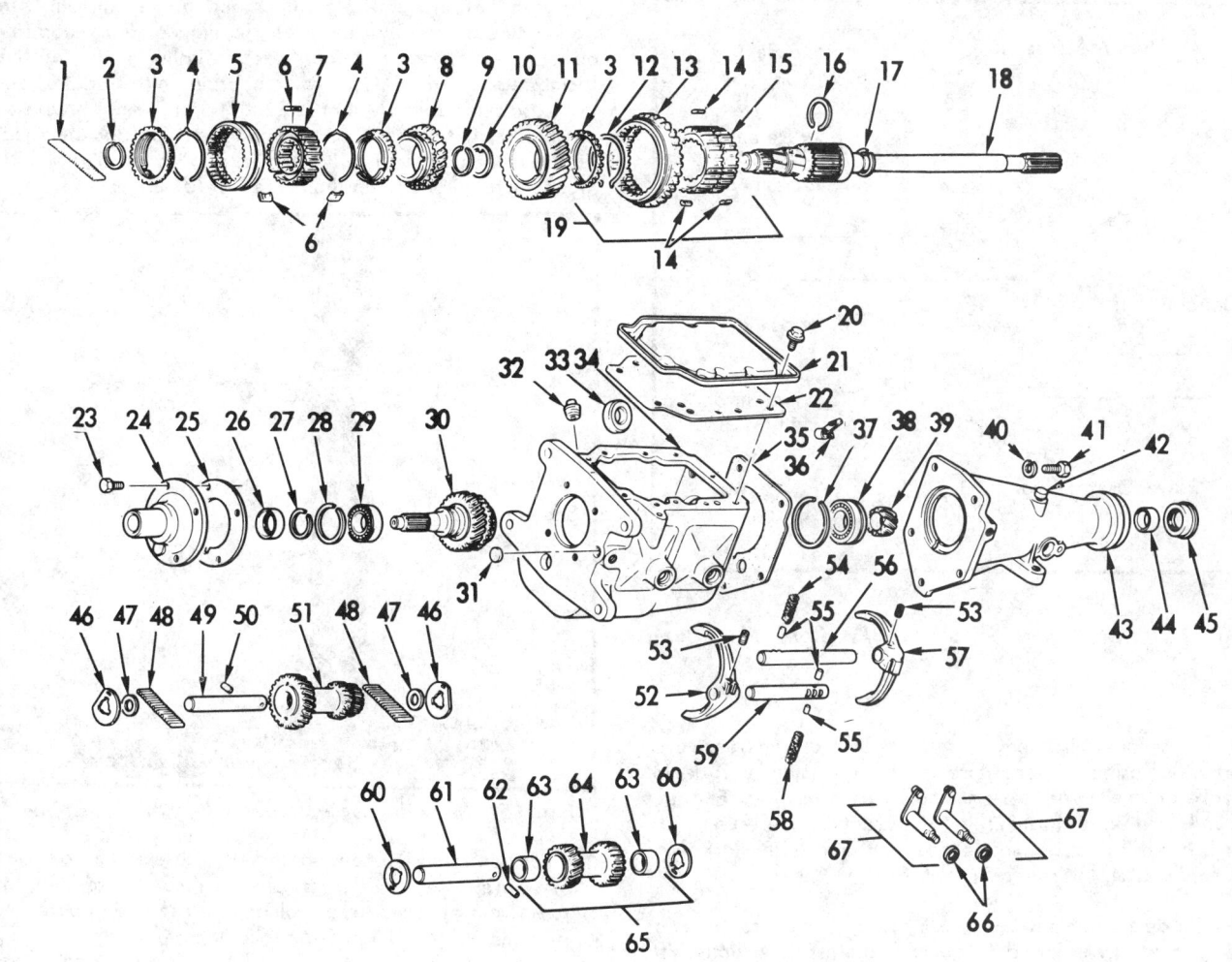

1. Needle Rollers
2. Snap Ring
3. Synchro Blocker Ring
4. 2nd & 3rd Synchro Spring
5. 2nd & 3rd Synchro Sleeve
6. 2nd & 3rd Synchro Keys
7. 2nd & 3rd Synchro Hub
8. Second Gear
9. Snap Ring
10. 1st Gear Tabbed Washer
11. 1st Gear
12. Reverse Synchro Spring
13. 1st & Reverse Synchro Sleeve
14. Reverse Synchro Keys
15. 1st & Reverse Synchro Hub
16. Snap Ring
17. Snap Ring
18. Mainshaft
19. Reverse Synchro Assy.
20. Cover Bolts
21. Top Cover
22. Gasket
23. Bearing Retainer Bolts

24. Bearing Retainer
25. Gasket
26. Seal
27. Snap Ring
28. Snap Ring
29. Front Bearing
30. Pinion Gear & Shaft
31. Expansion Plug
32. Filler Plug
33. Case Magnet
34. Transmission Case
35. Gasket
36. Speedometer Gear Retainer
37. Snap Ring
38. Rear Bearing
39. Speedometer Drive Gear
40. Washer
41. Extension Housing Bolt
42. Ventilator Assy.
43. Extension Housing
44. Bushing
45. Oil Seal
46. Thrust Washer

47. Spacer
48. Needle Bearing
49. Countershaft
50. Roll Pin
51. Countergear
52. 2nd & 3rd Shift Fork
53. Locking Screw
54. Upper Detent Spring
55. Detent Plugs
56. 1st & Reverse Shift Rail
57. 1st & Reverse Shift Fork
58. Lower Detent Spring
59. 2nd & 3rd Shift Rail
60. Thrust Washer
61. Reverse Idler Gear Shaft
62. Roll Pin
63. Bushing
64. Reverse Idler Gear
65. Reverse Idler Gear Assy.
66. "O" Rings
67. Shift Shaft & Lever Assy.

Fig. 13 *Exploded View of General Motors 77 MM 3-Speed Transmission*

GENERAL MOTORS 77 MM (Cont.)

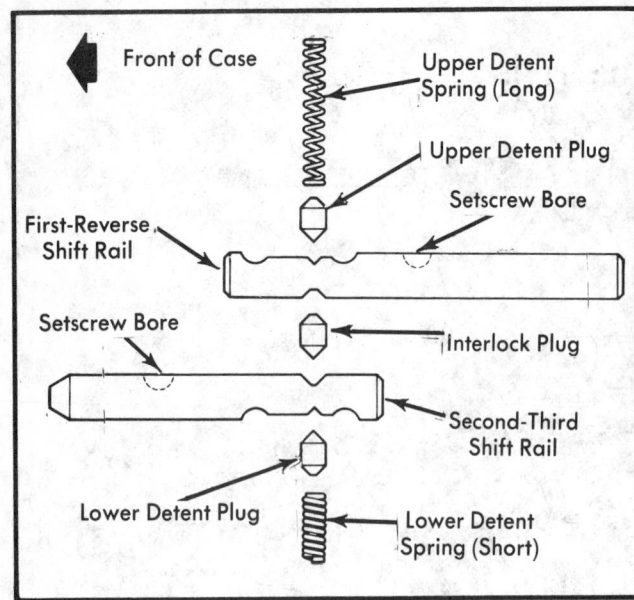

Fig. 14   Installation Sequence of Detent Plugs and Springs

6) Place second-third sleeve in second gear position (rearward position). Position second-third shifter fork (smaller fork) in groove of sleeve with setscrew hole facing upward. Engage second-third shifter fork in shifter fork shaft and insert second-third shift rail through front of case and into shifter fork with tapered end of shift rail facing forward.

7) With detent notches in shift rail facing downward, insert a Phillips screwdriver into detent bore and press down until shift rail can be pushed into rear bore of case. Move rail until detent plug engages forward notch (second gear position) in shift rail. Install shift fork setscrew and place fork in neutral (centered) position.

8) With second-third synchronizer in neutral position, install interlock plug in detent bore. Top of plug will be slightly below surface of first-reverse shift rail bore. Move first-reverse synchronizer forward to first gear position. Place first-reverse shift fork in groove of sleeve with setscrew hole facing upward. Engage fork in shifter fork shaft and insert shift rail through rear of case and shift fork.

9) With shift rail detent notches facing upward, move rail inward until setscrew can be installed in shift fork. Place first-reverse sleeve and gear into neutral (centered) position. Install large snap ring on front bearing and drive bearing onto pinion gear shaft and into case using a suitable tool (J-24433). Install small snap ring on pinion gear shaft.

10) Install front bearing retainer and gasket, making sure gasket cutout and oil drain holes are aligned. Place snap ring on rear bearing and position it over mainshaft with snap ring facing rear of transmission. Drive bearing onto mainshaft and into case using suitable tool (J-22609). Install small snap ring on mainshaft to retain bearing. Engage speedometer gear retainer on mainshaft with loop facing forward and slide speedometer gear into position. See *Fig. 15.*

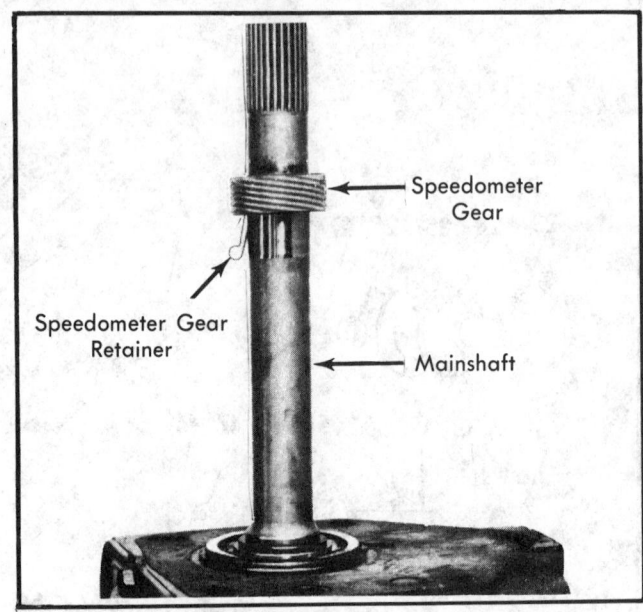

Fig. 15   Installing Speedometer Retainer and Gear

11) Position extension housing gasket on case and install housing to case. Install expansion plug in second-third shift rail bore in front of case. Be sure plug is fully seated in bore and approximately 1/16" below front face of case. Install upper detent plug in detent bore, then install long detent spring on top of plug. See *Fig. 14.* Install fill plug, top cover and gasket.

TIGHTENING SPECIFICATIONS

Application	Ft. Lbs.
Front Bearing Retainer	35
Top Cover	30
Extension Housing	45
Shift Lever	25
Filler Plug	15
Transmission-to-Clutch Housing	75
Crossmember-to-Frame	25
Crossmember-to-Mount	40
2-3 Crossover Shaft Bracket	18
1-Reverse Swivel Bolt	20
Mount-to-Transmission	50

FORD 4-SPEED – RUG – OVERDRIVE

E100/350

TRANSMISSION IDENTIFICATION

Transmission may be identified by a tag located on the right side of case at the front. The first line on tag will show transmission model prefix and suffix, service identification code (when required), and build date code. Lower line on tag shows transmission serial number. Additionally, a serial number is stamped on top side of flange on the transmission case for further identification.

DESCRIPTION

The 4-speed overdrive transmission is fully synchronized with all gears except the reverse sliding gear being in constant mesh. All forward speed changes are accomplished with synchronizer sleeves. All forward speed gears are helical type. Reverse sliding gear and the external teeth of the first and second speed synchronizer sleeve are spur type. With overdrive design, third speed is obtained by shifting gears into direct drive, and overdrive range is obtained by placing gears in what would normally be third speed position.

LUBRICATION

See Lubrication in MANUAL TRANSMISSION SERVICING Section.

TROUBLE SHOOTING

See Manual Transmission Trouble Shooting in MANUAL TRANSMISSION SERVICING Section.

REMOVAL & INSTALLATION

See Manual Transmission Removal in MANUAL TRANSMISSION SERVICING Section.

TRANSMISSION DISASSEMBLY

1) Mount transmission in a holding fixture. Drain lubricant by removing the lower extension housing attaching bolt. Remove cover and gasket from case. Remove long spring which retains detent plug in case and remove detent plug using a small magnet. Remove extension housing bolts, washers and gasket, then remove extension housing from case.

2) Remove input shaft bearing retainer bolts and slide retainer off input shaft. Support countershaft gear with a wire hook. Push countershaft out rear of case. Lower countershaft gear to bottom of case and remove hook. Remove set screw from 1st-2nd speed shift fork. Slide 1st-2nd speed shift rail out rear of case. Using a magnet, remove interlock detent from between 1st-2nd and 3rd-Overdrive shift rails. See Fig. 1.

3) Shift transmission into overdrive position. Remove set screw from 3rd-Overdrive shift fork. Remove the side detent bolt, plug and spring. Rotate 3rd-Overdrive shift rail 90° clockwise, then tap it out through front of case. Remove interlock plug from top of case with a magnet. See Fig. 2.

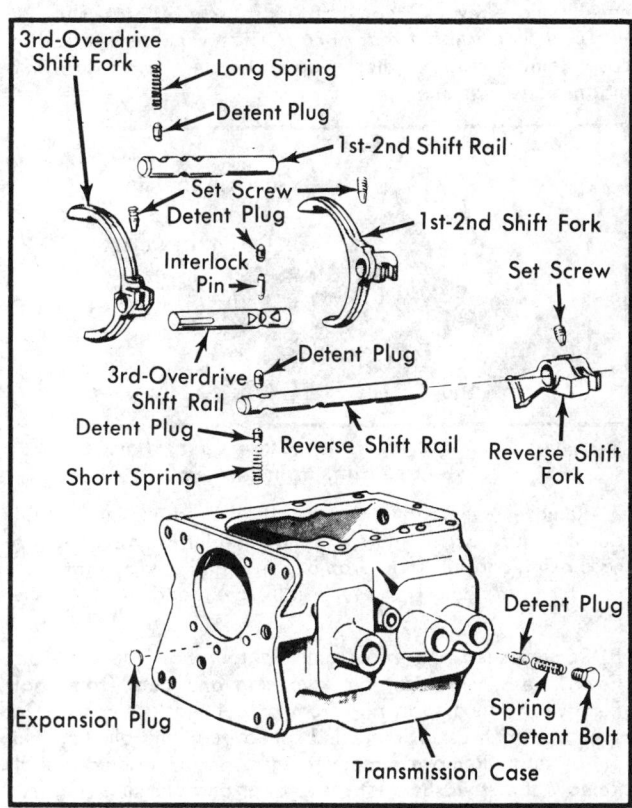

Fig. 1 Exploded View of Shift Rails & Forks

4) Remove snap ring securing speedometer drive gear on output shaft. Slide gear off shaft and remove speedometer gear drive ball. Remove snap ring securing output shaft bearing to shaft. Remove snap ring from outside diameter of bearing. Using suitable bearing puller, pull output shaft bearing from shaft.

5) Remove snap ring securing input shaft bearing to shaft. Remove snap ring from outside diameter of bearing. Use suitable bearing puller to remove bearing from input shaft and transmission case. Remove input shaft and blocking ring from front of case. Move output shaft to right side of case, then rotate shift forks up and out of case.

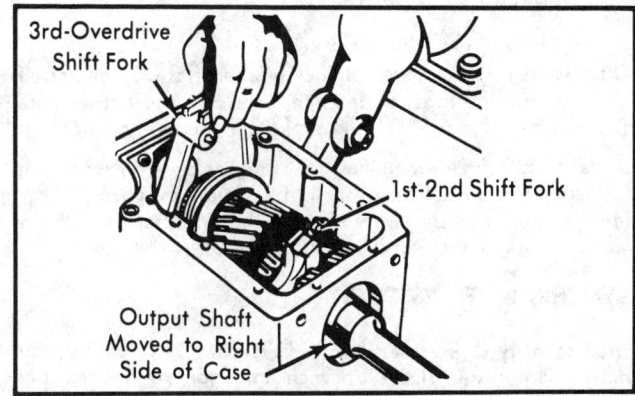

Fig. 2 Removing Shift Forks from Case

6) Support thrust washer and 1st speed gear to prevent them from sliding off shaft, then lift output shaft assembly from

FORD 4-SPEED – RUG – OVERDRIVE (Cont.)

case. Remove reverse gear shift fork set screw. Rotate shift rail 90° and slide rail out rear of case. Lift reverse shift fork from case. Remove reverse detent plug and spring from case with a magnet. See *Fig. 3*.

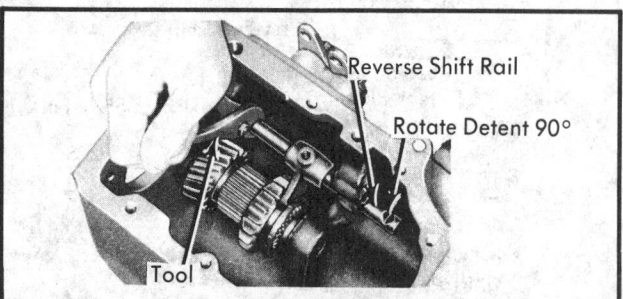

Fig. 3   View of Transmission Case Showing Reverse Shift Rail Removal

7) Remove reverse idler gear shaft from case using suitable dummy shaft. Lift countershaft gear and thrust washers out of case being careful not to drop bearings and dummy shaft from countershaft gear. Lift reverse idler gear and thrust washer from case.

8) Remove snap ring from front of output shaft, then slide 3rd-Overdrive synchronizer blocking ring and gear from shaft. Remove the next snap ring from output shaft, then slide 2nd speed gear thrust washer, 2nd speed gear and blocking ring off of shaft. Remove remaining snap ring from output shaft. Remove thrust washer, 1st speed gear and blocking ring from rear of shaft.

CLEANING & INSPECTION

- Wash all parts in a suitable cleaning solvent and air dry. Inspect ball and roller bearings for wear or damage.

- Inspect transmission case for cracks, wear, damaged bearing bores or damaged threads. Remove all small nicks or burrs from front of case.

- Check all other parts for wear, chipped or broken teeth and/or damage. Replace parts as necessary.

COMPONENT DISASSEMBLY & REASSEMBLY

SHIFT LEVERS AND SEALS

Disassembly — Remove nut, lock washer, flat washer and lift shift levers off shafts. Slide each lever and shaft from case. Remove and discard "O" ring seal from each lever and shaft.

Reassembly — Lubricate new "O" ring seals with transmission lubricant and install them on shafts. Install levers and shafts into case. Position shift lever on each shaft and secure with flat washer, lock washer and nut.

SYNCHRONIZER ASSEMBLY

Disassembly & Reassembly — 1) Punch or scribe alignment marks on hub and sleeve of synchronizer before disassembly. Push hub from each synchronizer sleeve. Separate inserts and insert springs from hubs.

CAUTION — *DO NOT mix parts of the 1st-2nd speed synchronizer with the 3rd-Overdrive speed synchronizer.*

2) To reassemble synchronizers, proceed as follows: Install hub in sleeve, making sure alignment marks are properly indexed. Place the three inserts into place on hub. Install insert springs making sure that the irregular surface (hump) is seated in one of the inserts. DO NOT stagger springs. See *Fig. 4*.

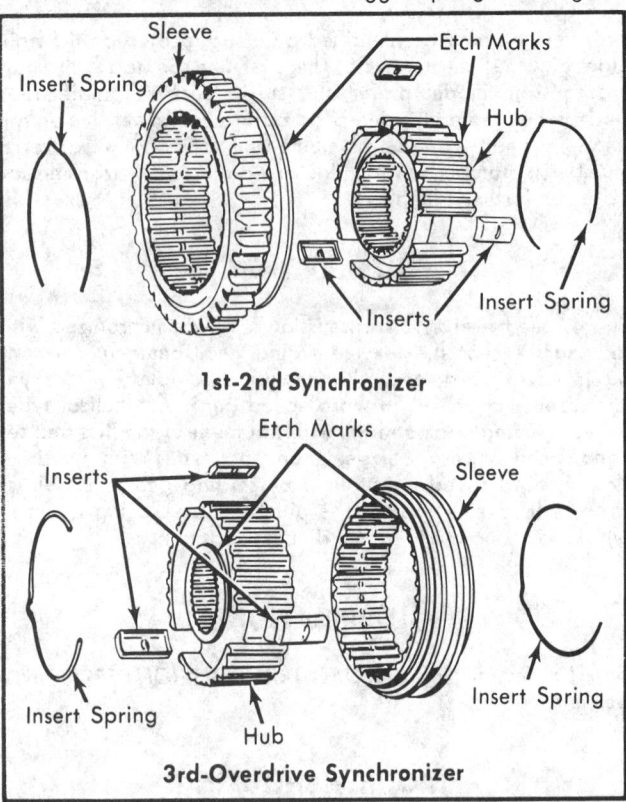

Fig. 4   Exploded View of Synchronizer Assemblies

COUNTERSHAFT GEAR BEARINGS

Disassembly — Remove dummy shaft, 2 bearing retainer washers and the 21 roller bearings from each end of countershaft gear. See *Fig. 5*.

Reassembly — Coat bore in each end of gear and install 21 roller bearings and a retainer washer in each end of gear.

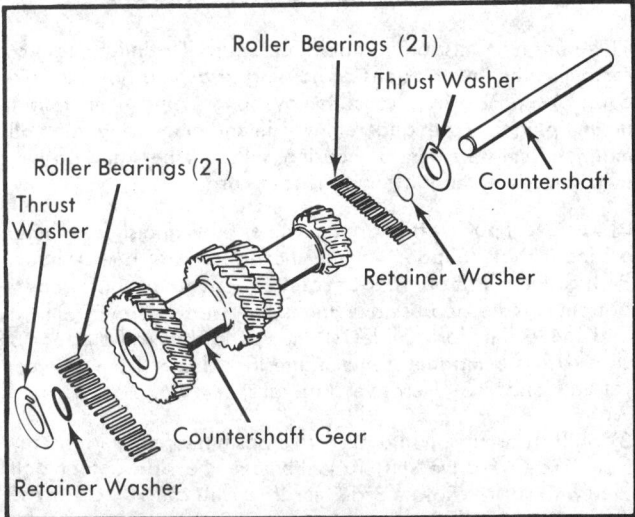

Fig. 5   Exploded View of Countershaft Gear

FORD 4-SPEED – RUG – OVERDRIVE (Cont.)

REVERSE IDLER GEAR BEARINGS

Disassembly – Slide reverse idler sliding gear off reverse idler gear. Remove dummy shaft, 2 bearing retainer washers and 44 roller bearings from reverse idler gear. See *Fig. 6.*

Reassembly – **1)** Coat bore in each end of idler gear with grease. Hold dummy shaft in gear and install 22 roller bearings and a retainer washer in each end of gear.

2) Install sliding gear on reverse idler gear making sure that shift fork groove is toward the front.

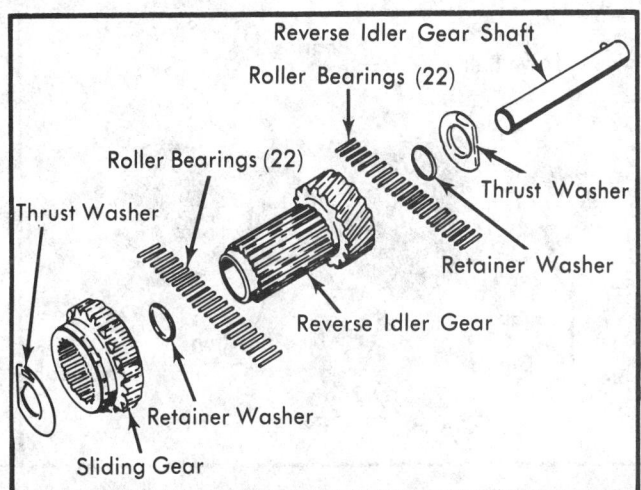

Fig. 6 Exploded View of Reverse Idler Gear Assembly

INPUT SHAFT SEAL

Removal & Installation – Using suitable seal puller, remove seal from input shaft bearing retainer. To install, coat sealing surface with lubricant and drive seal into place.

TRANSMISSION REASSEMBLY

1) Coat countershaft gear thrust surfaces in case with a thin film of lubricant and position a thrust washer at each end of case. Position countershaft gear, dummy shaft, and roller bearings in case. Place case in vertical position. Align gear bore and thrust washers with bores in case and install countershaft. Place case horizontal and check countershaft gear end play with a feeler gauge. End play should be .004-.018"; if not within specifications, replace thrust washers.

2) With end play correctly set, install dummy shaft in countershaft gear and allow the gear to remain at bottom of case. Coat reverse idler gear thrust surfaces with lubricant and position the two thrust washers in place. Position reverse idler gear, sliding gear, dummy shaft, and the roller bearings in place making sure that the shift fork groove in sliding gear is toward front of case. Align gear bore and thrust washers with case bores and install reverse idler shaft. Measure reverse idler gear end play with a feeler gauge. End play should be .004-.018"; if not within specifications, replace thrust washers.

3) Position reverse gear shift rail detent spring and plug in case. Hold reverse shift fork in place on reverse idler sliding gear, then install shift rail from rear of case. Secure fork to rail with set screw. Install 1st-2nd speed synchronizer into front of output shaft, making sure shift fork groove is toward rear of

shaft. Install synchronizer hub with teeth end of gear facing toward rear of shaft.

4) Position blocking ring on 2nd speed gear. Slide gear onto front of shaft, making sure inserts in synchronizer engage notches in blocker ring. Install 2nd speed gear thrust washer and snap ring. Slide overdrive gear onto shaft with synchronizer coned surface toward the front. Place blocking ring on overdrive gear.

5) Slide 3rd-Overdrive synchronizer onto shaft ensuring that inserts engage notches in blocking ring and that the thrust surface is toward overdrive gear. Install snap ring on front of output shaft. Position blocking ring on 1st speed gear. Slide 1st gear onto rear of output shaft ensuring that notches of blocking ring engage synchronizer inserts. Install heavy thrust washer on rear of output shaft.

6) Support thrust washer and 1st speed gear to prevent them from sliding off, then carefully lower output shaft assembly into case. Position 1st-2nd shift fork and 3rd-Overdrive shift forks in place on their respective gears and rotate them into place. Install spring and detent plug into detent bore. Place reverse shift rail into neutral position. See *Fig. 7.*

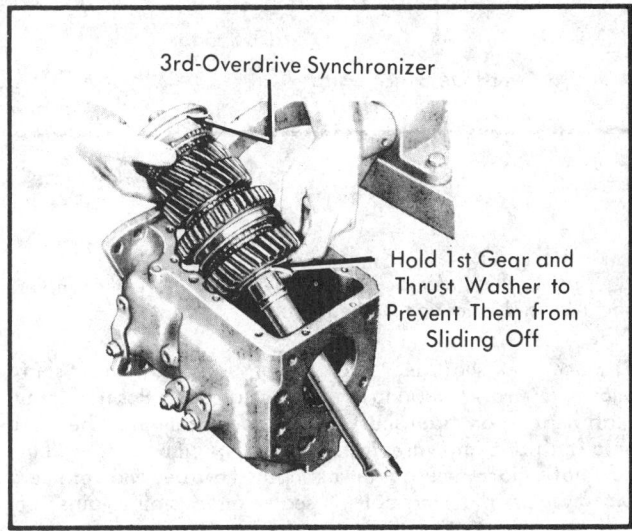

Fig. 7 Installing Output Shaft Assembly

7) Coat 3rd-Overdrive shift rail interlock pin (tapered ends) with grease and position it in shift rail. Align 3rd-Overdrive shift fork with shift rail bores and slide rail into place ensuring that the three detents are facing toward outside of case. Place front synchronizer into overdrive position and install set screw in 3rd-Overdrive shift fork. Move synchronizer to neutral position. Install 3rd-Overdrive detent plug, spring and bolt in left side of case. Place detent plug (tapered ends) in detent bore in case.

NOTE – *A missing or improperly installed interlock pin could allow the transmission to be shifted into first and reverse gear at the same time.*

8) Align 1st-2nd shift fork with case bores and slide shift rail into place, securing shift fork with set screw. Coat input gear bore with thin film of grease, then install 15 roller bearings into bore. Place front blocking ring in 3rd-Overdrive synchronizer. Place dummy bearing (T77L-7025-B) on output shaft to support and align shaft assembly in case. See *Fig. 8.*

FORD 4-SPEED – RUG – OVERDRIVE (Cont.)

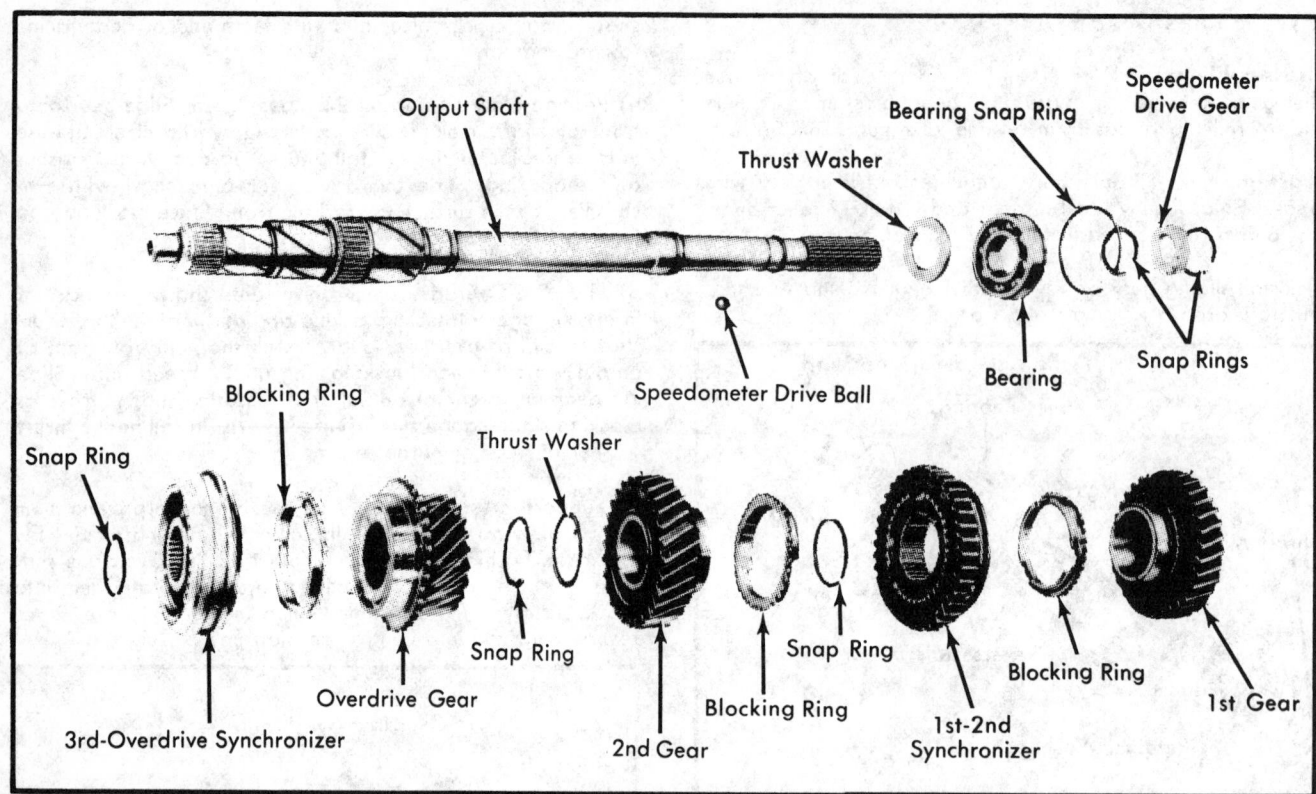

Fig. 8   Exploded View of Output Shaft Assembly

NOTE — *A thick film of grease could plug lubrication holes and restrict lubrication of bearings.*

9) Place input shaft gear into case, ensuring that output shaft pilot enters roller bearings in input gear bore. Position input shaft bearing on input shaft. Slowly and evenly press bearing onto shaft and into case. Install snap rings on bearing and input shaft. Place new gasket on input shaft bearing retainer. Dip retainer attaching bolts in sealer and install retainer on case. *See Fig. 9.*

10) Remove dummy bearing from output shaft. Press output shaft bearing onto output shaft and into case. Install snap rings on output shaft and output shaft bearing.

NOTE — *Make sure that output shaft bearing is aligned with case bore and that countershaft is not interfering with output shaft assembly.*

11) Position transmission in a vertical position. Align countershaft gear bore and thrust washers with bore in case. Install countershaft into case. Pour lubricant over entire gear train while rotating input shaft.

NOTE — *Use sealer on all attaching bolts as transmission is assembled.*

12) Place each shift fork in all positions to ensure proper operation. Install remaining detent plug in case. Install long spring (retained by case) to secure detent plug. Install cover with new gasket. Coat 3rd-Overdrive shift rail plug bore with sealant and install new expansion plug.

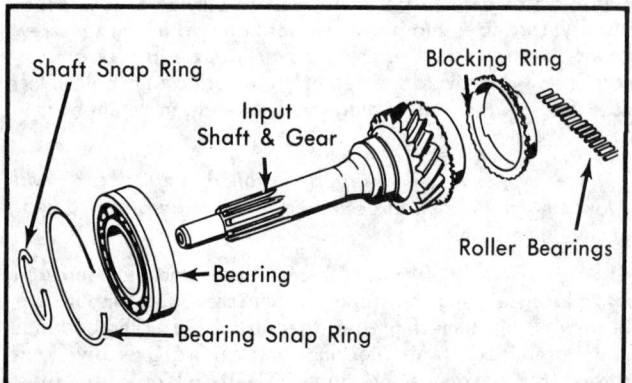

Fig. 9   Exploded View of Input Shaft Assembly

TIGHTENING SPECIFICATIONS

Application	Ft. Lbs.
Input Shaft Bearing Retainer	19-25
Extension Housing Bolts	42-50
Access Cover-to-Case Screw	20-25
Gear Shift Lever Attaching Nuts	18-23
Filler Plug	10-20
Detent Bolt-to-Case	10-15

FORD 4-SPEED S.R.O.D.

Bronco
F100/250
F150 4-WD

TRANSMISSION IDENTIFICATION

Transmission may be identified by a tag located on the right side of case at the front. The first line on tag will show transmission model prefix and suffix, service identification code (when required), and build date code. Lower line on tag shows transmission assembly number and serial number. Additionally, a serial number is stamped on top side of flange on the transmission case for further identification.

DESCRIPTION

The 4-speed overdrive transmission is fully synchronized with all gears except the reverse sliding gear being in constant mesh. All forward speed changes are accomplished with synchronizer sleeves. All forward speed gears are helical type. Reverse sliding gear and the external teeth of the first and second speed synchronizer sleeve are spur type. With overdrive design, third speed is obtained by shifting gears into direct drive, and overdrive range is obtained by placing gears in what would normally be third speed position.

LUBRICATION

See Lubrication in MANUAL TRANSMISSION SERVICING Section.

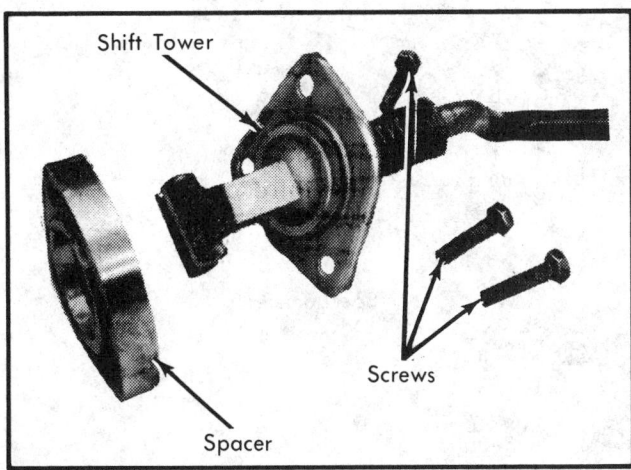

Fig. 1   View of Shift Tower Removed from Turret

TROUBLE SHOOTING

See Manual Transmission Trouble Shooting in MANUAL TRANSMISSION SERVICING Section.

REMOVAL & INSTALLATION

See Manual Transmission Removal in MANUAL TRANSMISSION SERVICING Section.

TRANSMISSION DISASSEMBLY

1) Mount transmission in a holding fixture. Drain lubricant by removing the lower extension housing attaching bolt. Remove cover and gasket from case. Remove long spring which retains

detent plug in case and remove detent plug using a magnet. Remove attaching bolts and washers, then remove extension housing and gasket from case. See Fig. 2.

2) Remove backup lamp switch, snap ring and dust cover from rear of extension housing turret assembly. Remove shifter shaft. Remove extension housing bolts and washers, then remove extension housing and gasket from case. See Figs. 3, 4, and 5.

3) Remove snap ring, speedometer drive gear and ball from mainshaft. Remove rear bearing snap ring and rear bearing from mainshaft. Working from front of case, push countershaft out rear of case using dummy shaft. Let countershaft gear lie at bottom of case.

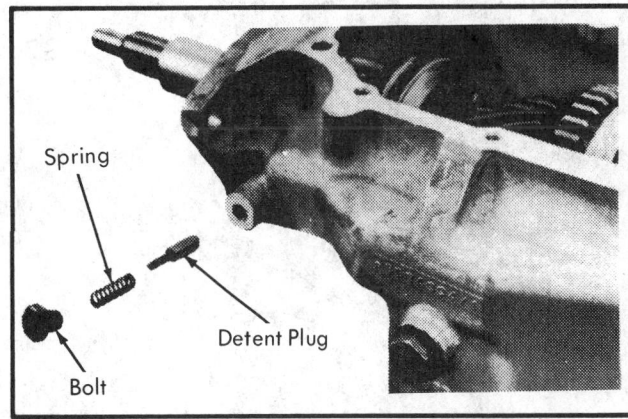

Fig. 2   View of Detent Spring and Plug

4) Remove snap ring securing output shaft bearing to shaft and remove bearing from output shaft (slip fit).

5) Use a dummy shaft and from front of case, push countershaft out rear of case. Lower countershaft to bottom of case. Remove input shaft bearing retainer and gasket. Discard gasket.

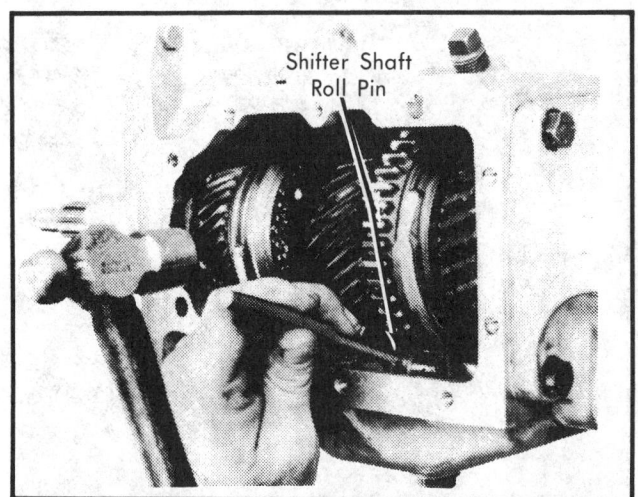

Fig. 3   View Showing Shifter Shaft Roll Pin Removal

6) Remove snap ring securing input shaft bearing to shaft, then remove bearing (slip fit). Remove input shaft and blocking

FORD 4-SPEED S.R.O.D. (Cont.)

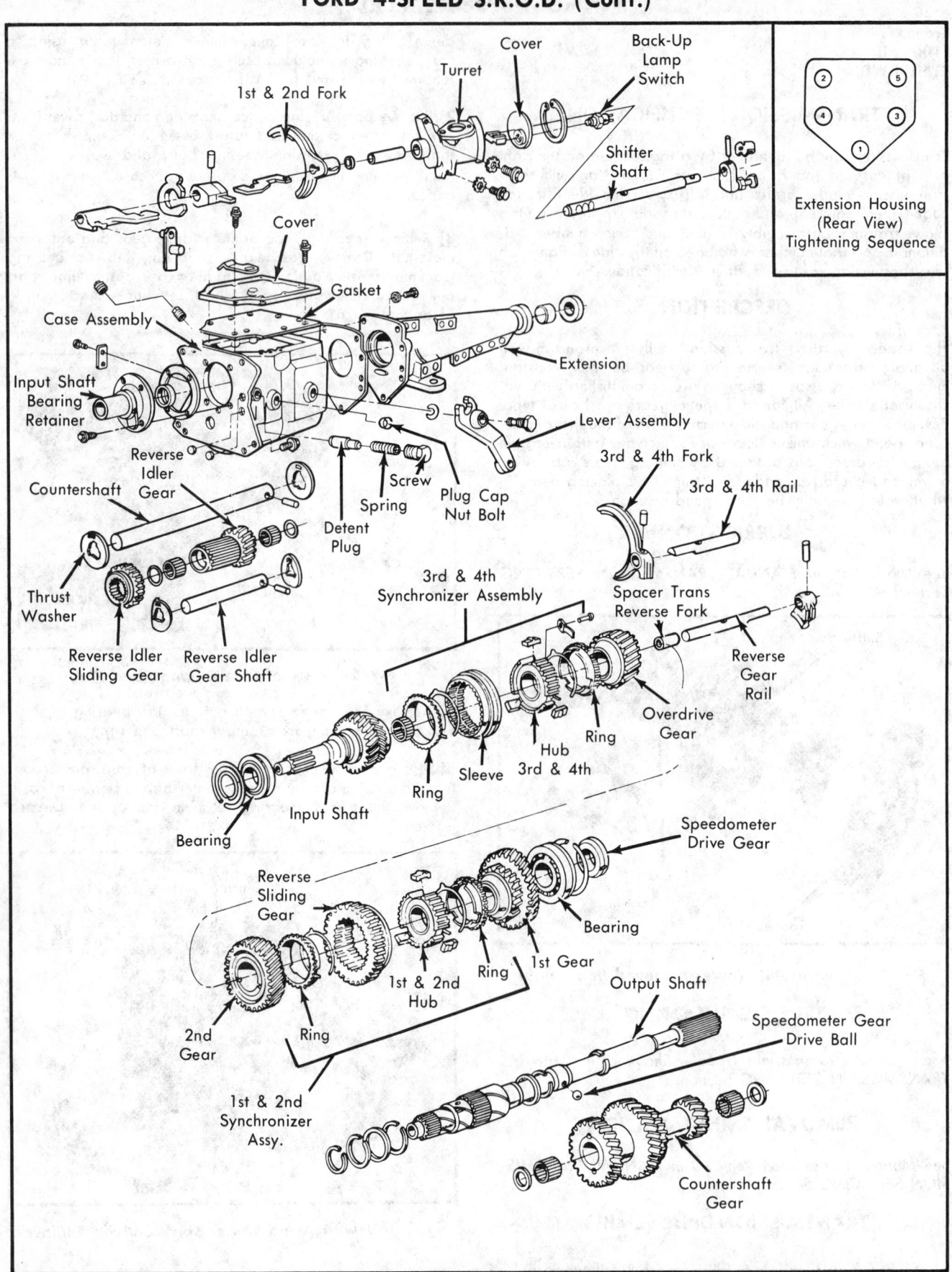

Fig. 4   Exploded View of Ford (Rug) 4-Speed Single Rail Overdrive (S.R.O.D.) Transmission Assembly

FORD 4-SPEED S.R.O.D. (Cont.)

ring from case including roller bearings. Remove overdrive shift pawl and gear selector interlock plate.

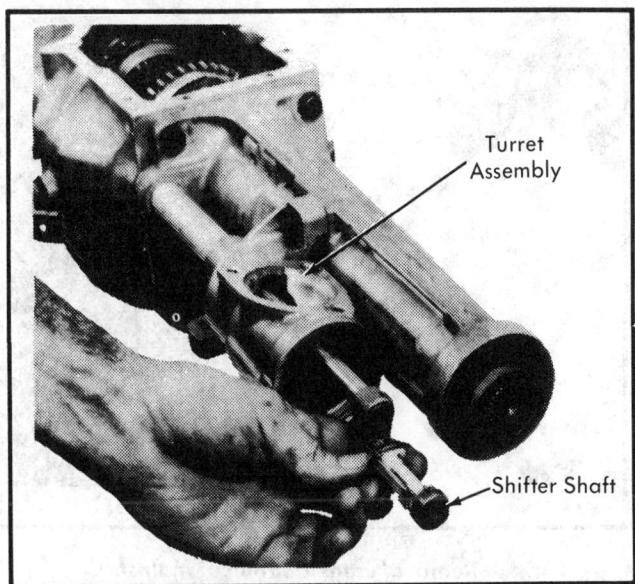

Fig. 5   Shifter Shaft Removal and Installation

7) Remove 1st-2nd gearshift selector arm plate. Remove roll pin from 3rd-overdrive shift fork. Remove 3rd-overdrive shift rail. Remove 1st-2nd and 3rd-overdrive speed shift forks.

8) Remove countershaft gear and thrust washers from case.

CAUTION — *Do not drop bearings or dummy shaft from countershaft.*

9) Remove snap ring from front of output shaft. Slide 3rd-overdrive synchronizer blocking ring and gear from shaft. Remove the next snap ring and thrust washer, then remove 1st speed gear and blocking ring from rear of shaft (slip fit).

10) Remove roll pin from reverse fork, slide reverse shifter rail through rear of case and remove reverse gearshift fork. Drive reverse gear shaft out rear of case, then remove reverse idler gear, thrust washers and roller bearings.

11) Remove retaining clip, reverse gearshift relay lever and reverse gear selector fork pivot pin.

12) Remove overdrive shift control link assembly; shift shaft seal from rear of case and shift shaft rail hole expansion plug from front of case.

TRANSMISSION REASSEMBLY

1) Reverse disassembly procedure and apply lubricants prior to completion of assembly as follows: Transmission mainshaft bearing roller, extension housing bushing, reverse idler bearing rollers and countershaft gear bearing rollers are to be lubricated with long life multi-purpose type grease.

NOTE — *Use suitable sealer on all external bolts. Tighten extension housing bolts in sequence shown in Fig. 4.*

2) Lubricate low gear, 2nd gear and overdrive journal on output shaft with gear oil prior to assembly, and use about ½ pint of approved lubricant to saturate all other components.

3) Lubricate transmission shifter shaft and gear shift damper bushing with multi-purpose grease prior to assembling to transmission. Fill transmission with 4.5 pints of standard transmission lubricant prior to functional operation.

4) Seal both ends of gear shift shaft sleeve and turret cover assembly with B5A-19554-A or equivalent sealer to prevent road contamination. Welch plug at front of intermediate and high rail must be seated firmly and not protrude above front of case or more than .06″(1.5 mm) below front face of case.

GEAR END PLAY

1) Gear end play for 1st, 2nd, and overdrive gears must meet the following specifications: 1st gear, .005-.024″; 2nd gear, .003-.021″; and overdrive gear, .009-.023″.

NOTE — *To obtain actual gear end play in an assembled transmission, subtract output shaft end play from measured gear end play.*

2) Countershaft end play should be .004 to .018″. Rebuild with new components if dimensions exceed the specifications.

TIGHTENING SPECIFICATIONS	
Application	**Ft. Lbs.**
Input Shaft Bearing Retainer	11-25
Extension Housing Bolts	42-50
Access Cover-to-Case Screw	20-25
Filler Plug	10-25
Detent Bolt-to-Case	10-15
Back Up Lamp Switch	8-12
Turret Assembly	8-12

GENERAL MOTORS 117 MM CH 465

Chevrolet
GMC

DESCRIPTION

The 117 mm CH 465 4-speed transmission is described by number of forward gears and measured by distance (117 mm) between centerlines of mainshaft and countergear. It's a heavy duty unit with all helical gears except reverse. First gear is a constant mesh type that engages with the second gear synchronizer sleeve. Second, third and fourth speed gears are synchronized.

LUBRICATION

See Lubrication in MANUAL TRANSMISSION SERVICING Section.

TROUBLE SHOOTING

See Manual Transmission Trouble Shooting in MANUAL TRANSMISSION SERVICING Section.

SERVICE (IN VEHICLE)

REAR BEARING RETAINER OIL SEAL

1) Drain oil from transmission and disconnect propeller shaft. Remove parking brake from rear of transmission. Disconnect speedometer cable and remove speedometer driven gear from mainshaft rear bearing cap. Using flange or yolk holding tool, remove output "U" joint or companion flange nut from mainshaft. Remove mainshaft rear bearing cap and gasket. Discard gasket. Remove oil seal from rear bearing cap, and discard seal.

2) Coat outer diameter of new oil seal with a suitable sealing cement. Install seal in bearing cup using seal driver tool (J-22834). Press seal in flush with outside of bearing cap. To reassemble components, reverse removal procedure and fill transmission with suitable lubricant.

REMOVAL & INSTALLATION

See Manual Transmission Removal in MANUAL TRANSMISSION SERVICING Section.

TRANSMISSION DISASSEMBLY

COVER & SHIFT FORK MECHANISM

Mount transmission in suitable holding fixture and remove cover screws. Move reverse shifter fork so reverse idler gear is partially engaged before removing cover. Forks must be set so rear edge of slot in reverse fork is in line with front edge of slot in forward forks as viewed through tower opening. If necessary, insert two bolts in cover flange threaded holes and turn evenly to raise cover dowel pins from case.

OUTPUT "U" JOINT FLANGE (OUTPUT YOKE) & REAR BEARING RETAINER

Set transmission in 2 gears at once to lock mainshaft, and remove "U" joint flange nut. Remove "U" joint front flange and brake drum (if equipped). On models equipped with a transfer case, use suitable tool (J-23070) to remove mainshaft rear bearing lock nut. See Fig. 1. Remove parking brake and brake flange plate (if equipped). Remove rear bearing retainer and slide speedometer drive gear off mainshaft.

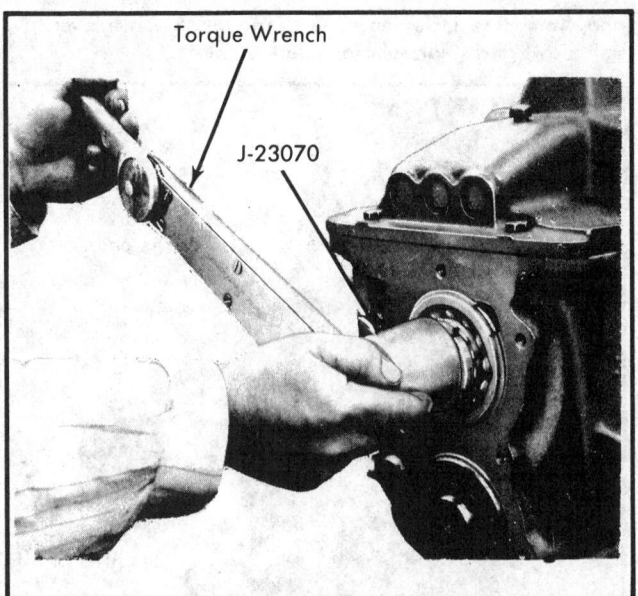

Fig. 1   Removal or Installation of Mainshaft Rear Bearing Lock Nut (4-WD)

COUNTERGEAR

Remove drive pinion bearing retainer and countergear front bearing cap. Pry countergear front bearing out by inserting tool (J-28509) into groove at cast slots in case. Remove countergear rear bearing snap ring from shaft. Using suitable puller tools (J-22832 & J-8433-1), remove countergear rear bearing. This will allow countergear to rest on bottom for mainshaft removal. See Fig. 2.

NOTE — Make sure puller engages full circumference of groove in bearing to prevent tool damage.

Fig. 2   Removal of Rear Countergear Bearing

GENERAL MOTORS 117 MM CH 465 (Cont.)

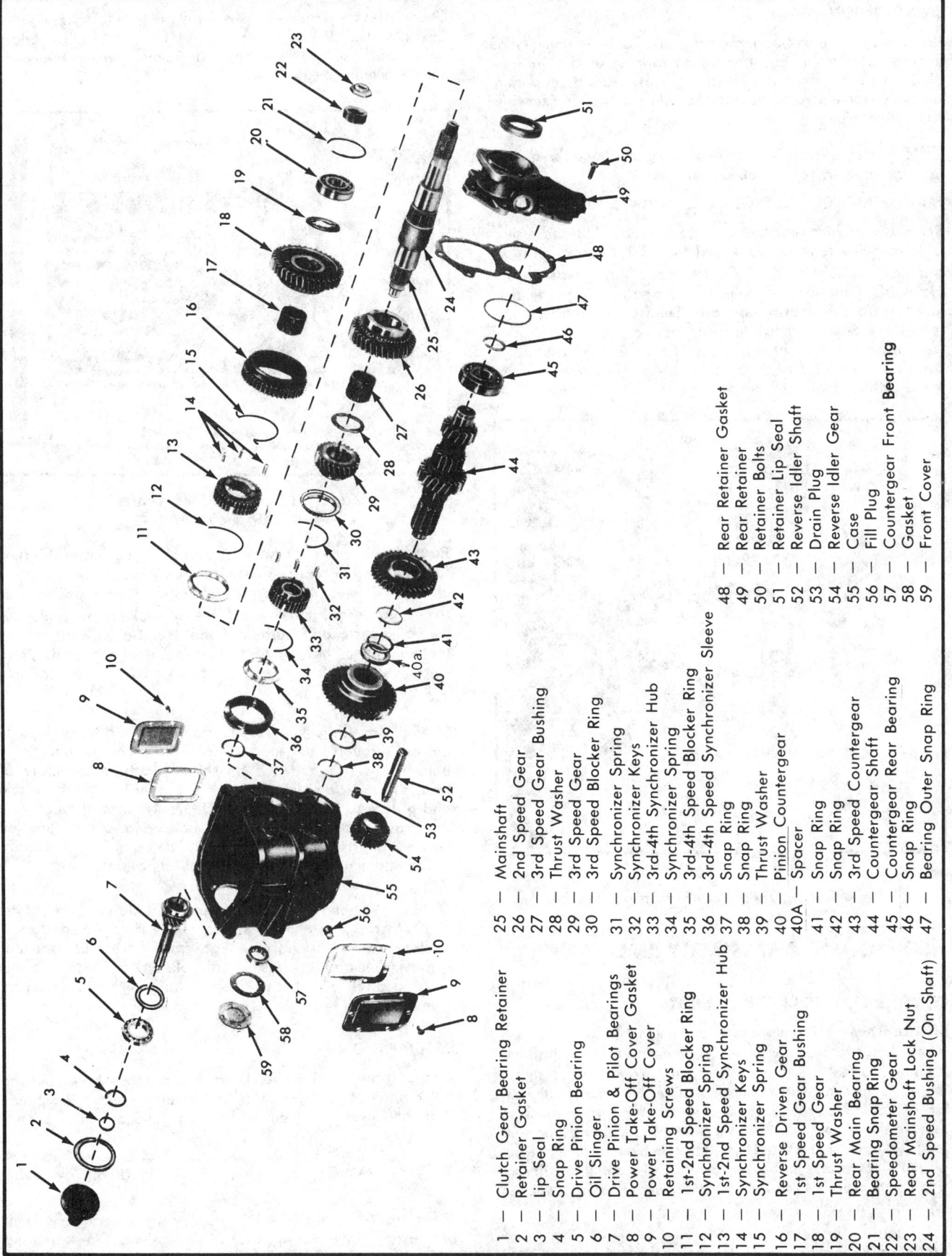

1 — Clutch Gear Bearing Retainer
2 — Retainer Gasket
3 — Lip Seal
4 — Snap Ring
5 — Drive Pinion Bearing
6 — Oil Slinger
7 — Drive Pinion & Pilot Bearings
8 — Power Take-Off Cover Gasket
9 — Power Take-Off Cover
10 — Retaining Screws
11 — 1st-2nd Speed Blocker Ring
12 — Synchronizer Spring
13 — 1st-2nd Speed Synchronizer Hub
14 — Synchronizer Keys
15 — Synchronizer Spring
16 — Reverse Driven Gear
17 — 1st Speed Gear Bushing
18 — 1st Speed Gear
19 — Thrust Washer
20 — Rear Main Bearing
21 — Bearing Snap Ring
22 — Speedometer Gear
23 — Rear Mainshaft Lock Nut
24 — 2nd Speed Bushing (On Shaft)

25 — Mainshaft
26 — 2nd Speed Gear
27 — 3rd Speed Gear Bushing
28 — Thrust Washer
29 — 3rd Speed Gear
30 — 3rd Speed Blocker Ring
31 — Synchronizer Spring
32 — Synchronizer Keys
33 — 3rd-4th Synchronizer Hub
34 — Synchronizer Spring
35 — 3rd-4th Speed Blocker Ring
36 — 3rd-4th Speed Synchronizer Sleeve
37 — Snap Ring
38 — Snap Ring
39 — Thrust Washer
40 — Pinion Countergear
40A — Spacer
41 — Snap Ring
42 — Snap Ring
43 — 3rd Speed Countergear
44 — Countergear Shaft
45 — Countergear Rear Bearing
46 — Snap Ring
47 — Bearing Outer Snap Ring

48 — Rear Retainer Gasket
49 — Rear Retainer
50 — Retainer Bolts
51 — Retainer Lip Seal
52 — Reverse Idler Shaft
53 — Drain Plug
54 — Reverse Idler Gear
55 — Case
56 — Fill Plug
57 — Countergear Front Bearing
58 — Gasket
59 — Front Cover

Fig. 3   Exploded View of General Motors 117 MM CH 465 Transmission

GENERAL MOTORS 117 MM CH 465 (Cont.)

DRIVE PINION

Remove drive pinion bearing outer race to case retaining ring. Remove drive pinion and bearing by tapping on bottom side of drive pinion shaft and prying out at bearing snap ring groove at same time. Remove 4th speed gear synchronizer ring when drive pinion is removed.

NOTE — *Cutout section of drive pinion gear should be down, to clear countergear for pinion removal.*

MAINSHAFT, COUNTERGEAR & REVERSE IDLER GEAR

Remove mainshaft rear bearing retainer snap ring and, using suitable puller tools (J-22832 and J-8433-1), remove bearing from case. See Fig. 4. Slide 1st speed thrust washer off mainshaft. Raise rear of mainshaft and move rearward, then lift shaft front up and out of case. Remove synchronizer cone from shaft. Slide reverse idler gear rearward and move countergear back until front end is free of case. Remove assembly. Drive reverse idler gear shaft out of case from front to rear, using a drift. Remove reverse idler gear.

Fig. 4   Removal of Rear Mainshaft Bearing

COMPONENT DISASSEMBLY & REASSEMBLY

COVER & SHIFT FORK MECHANISM

Disassembly — Drive out pins retaining 1st-2nd and 3rd-4th speed shifter forks to shifter shafts, and also remove shaft expansion plugs. Note that pin retaining 3rd-4th speed shifter must be removed before removing shifter head pin. With shifter shafts in neutral position, drive shafts out of cover to remove shifter forks. Ensure that detent balls, springs, and interlock pins are not lost as shifter shafts are removed. Drive out pin holding reverse shifter head and drive out shaft. Ensure that detent balls are not lost as they are under spring tension in rear rail boss holes.

Cleaning & Inspection — Wash all parts in clean solvent and inspect forks and gates for wear at pads and lever slots.

Check forks for alignment. Check roll pin fit in forks and gates. Check neutral notches of shift shafts for wear from interlock balls. Shafts which are indented at points adjacent to neutral notches should be replaced.

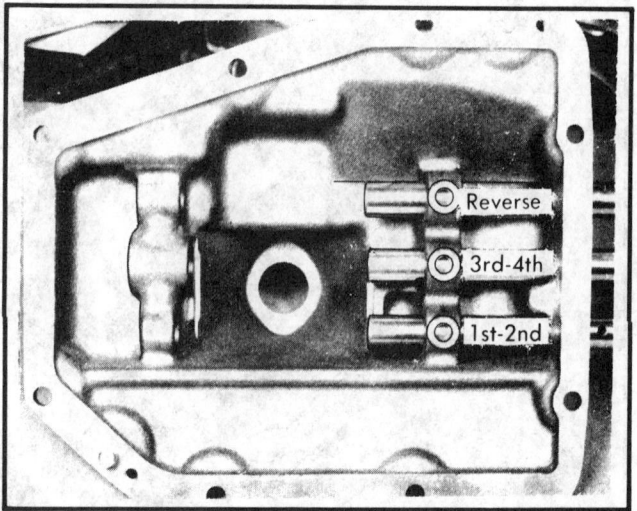

Fig. 5   Location of Shift Shafts in Shift Housing

Reassembly — 1) Reassemble cover installing shifter shafts in following order: reverse shaft, 3rd-4th shaft and 1st-2nd shaft. Place fork detent ball springs and balls in hole positions in cover. Start shafts into cover, depressing yoke detent balls with a small punch, and push shaft on over balls. Starting with reverse shifter shaft, hold fork in position and push shaft through yoke. Install cotter pin in fork and shaft, then position fork in neutral position.

2) Hold 3rd-4th fork in position and push shaft through yoke, but not through front support bore. Place two interlock balls between reverse and 3rd-4th shifter shafts in crossbore of front support boss. Install interlock pin in 3rd-4th shaft hole and grease to hold in place. Push 3rd-4th shaft through fork and cover bore, keeping both balls and pin in position between shafts until retaining holes line up in fork and shaft. Install retaining pin and move to neutral position.

3) Place two interlock balls between 1st-2nd shaft and 3rd-4th shaft in crossbore of front support boss. Hold 1st-2nd fork in position and push shaft through cover bore and fork until retainer hole and fork line up with hole in shaft. Install retainer pin and move to neutral position. Install new shaft hole expansion plugs.

DRIVE PINION

Disassembly — Remove 17 mainshaft pilot bearings and roller retainer. Remove snap ring holding bearing on pinion shaft and press shaft out of bearing using an arbor press.

NOTE — *DO NOT remove snap ring on inside of drive gear.*

Cleaning & Inspection — Wash parts in cleaning solvent and inspect roller bearings for pits or galling. Check bearing surface in shaft recess for galling. Inspect gear teeth for wear and pinion pilot for wear. Check pinion bearing for roughness.

GENERAL MOTORS 117 MM CH 465 (Cont.)

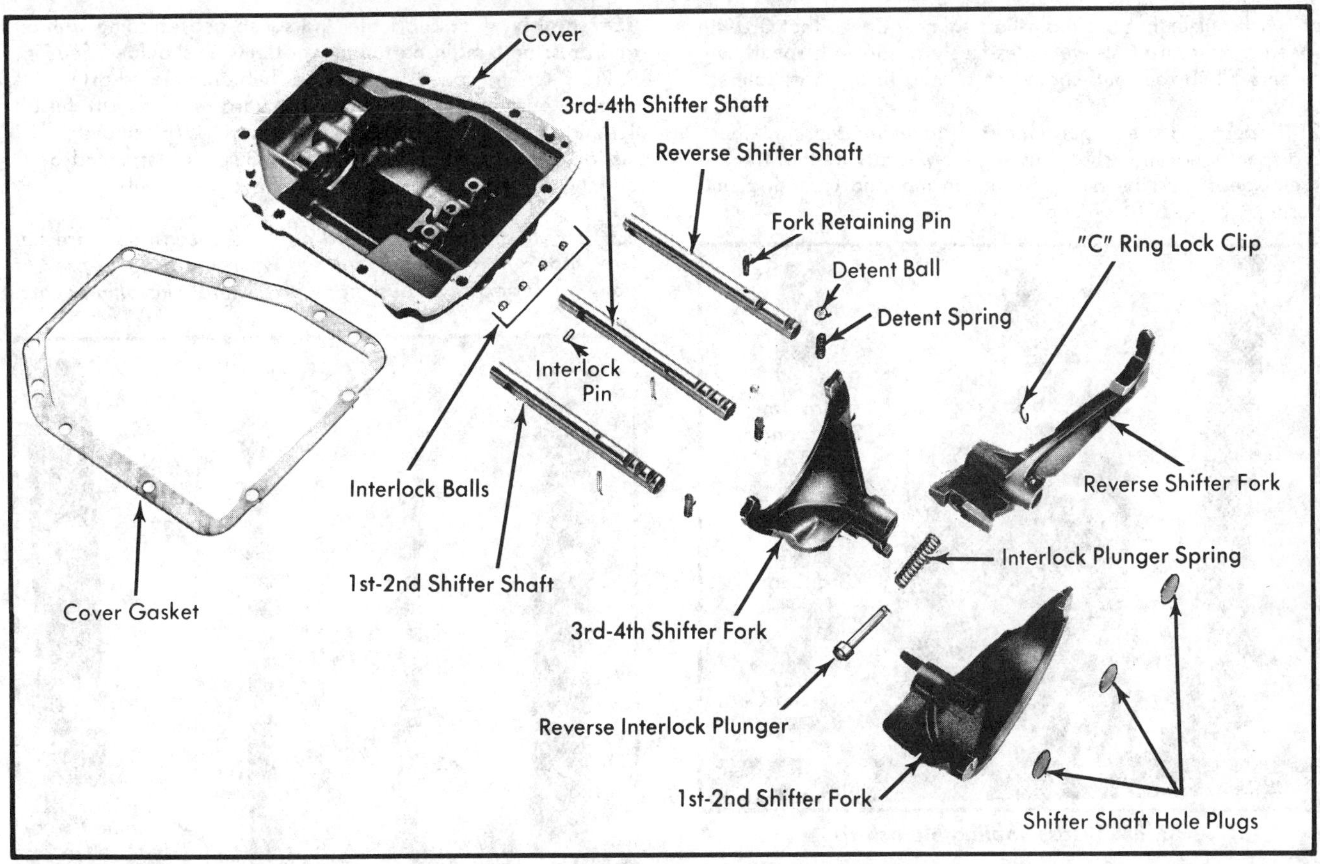

Cover

3rd-4th Shifter Shaft

Reverse Shifter Shaft

Fork Retaining Pin

Detent Ball

Detent Spring

"C" Ring Lock Clip

Interlock Pin

Interlock Balls

Reverse Shifter Fork

Interlock Plunger Spring

1st-2nd Shifter Shaft

Cover Gasket

3rd-4th Shifter Fork

Reverse Interlock Plunger

1st-2nd Shifter Fork

Shifter Shaft Hole Plugs

Fig. 6   Exploded View of Cover and Shift Assembly

Reassembly — Press bearing and new oil slinger onto drive pinion. Slinger should be located flush with bearing shoulder on drive pinion. Install snap ring on pinion to secure bearing, then install retainer ring in groove on outside diameter of bearing. Ensure bearing turns freely after installed on shaft. Install snap ring in mainshaft pilot bearing bore (if previously removed). Apply grease to bearing surface and install roller bearings (17) and bearing retainer.

NOTE — *Roller bearing retainer holds bearings in position and is pushed forward into recess by mainshaft pilot during final assembly.*

DRIVE PINION OIL SEAL

Remove retainer, and oil seal assembly. Pry oil seal from retainer and replace with a new seal. Install new seal with suitable installer tool (J-22833). Insert seal in retainer so lip of seal is toward flange of installer tool. Install retainer with a new gasket and tighten bolts.

MAINSHAFT

Disassembly — Remove first speed gear and thrust washer. Remove snap ring in front of 3rd-4th synchronizer assembly. Withdraw reverse driven gear. Press behind second speed gear to remove 3rd-4th synchronizer, third speed gear, and second speed gear with third gear bushing and thrust washer. Remove second speed synchronizer ring. Support second speed synchronizer hub on front face and press mainshaft through removing first gear bushing and second speed synchronizer hub. Split second gear bushing with a chisel and remove bushing from shaft.

NOTE — *Use care not to damage mainshaft.*

Cleaning & Inspection — 1) Wash all parts in clean solvent and inspect mainshaft for scoring or wear at thrust surfaces and splines. Check synchronizer hub and sleeve for excessive wear. Sleeve should slide freely on synchronizer hub. Check fit

Oil Slinger

J-22872

J-358-1

Fig. 7   Installing Drive Gear Bearing

GENERAL MOTORS 117 MM CH 465 (Cont.)

of synchronizer hub on mainshaft splines. Check that 3rd-4th speed synchronizer sleeve slides freely on 3rd-4th speed synchronizer hub, but hub should be a snug fit on shaft splines.

2) Inspect 3rd speed gear thrust surfaces for scoring. Check 3rd speed gear mainshaft bushing for wear. Note that the 3rd speed gear must be a running fit on mainshaft bushing and bushing, a press fit on shaft.

Fig. 8　Disassembling Mainshaft

3) Check 2nd speed gear and thrust washer for scoring or excessive wear. Check synchronizer springs for looseness or breakage. Inspect 2nd speed gear synchronizer blocker ring and bronze synchronizer cone on 2nd speed gear for excessive wear or damage. Also inspect 3rd speed gear synchronizer cone for wear.

4) The 1st-Reverse sliding gear must have a sliding fit on synchronizer hub and must not have excessive radial movement or rotational play. If gear is not free on hub, check for burrs on front end of half-tooth internal splines. Remove burrs by honing as necessary. Check all gears for excessive tooth wear or damage.

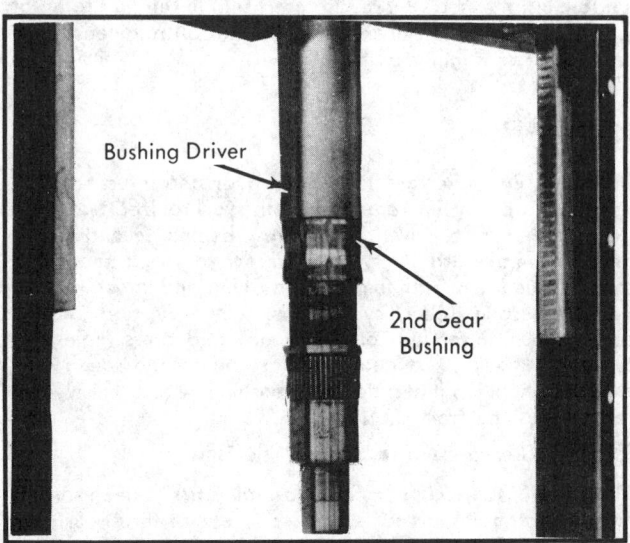

Fig. 9　Installing 2nd Gear Bushing

Reassembly — 1) Lubricate 2nd speed gear bushing with oil and press onto mainshaft until it bottoms on shoulder. *See Fig. 9.* Press 1st-2nd speed synchronizer hub onto mainshaft until it bottoms on shoulder with annulus toward rear of shaft. Install 1st-2nd speed synchronizer keys and springs (if removed). Using an arbor press, and tool J-22873, press 1st speed gear bushing on mainshaft until it bottoms against hub.

NOTE — *Bushings for 1st, 2nd and 3rd speed gears are sintered iron and care must be used when installing to prevent damage. Lubricate all bushings with oil before installing gears.*

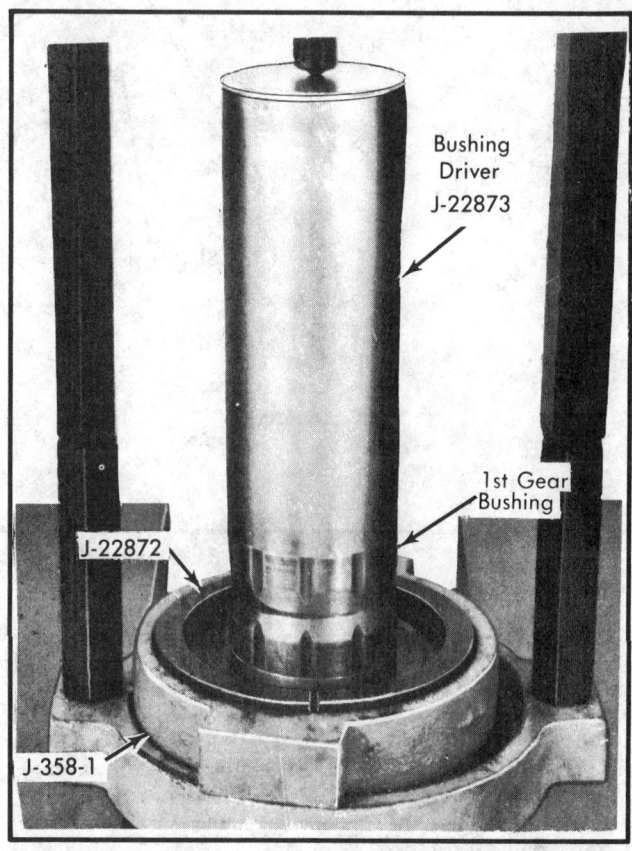

Fig. 10　Installing 1st Gear Bushing

2) Install synchronizer blocker ring and 2nd speed gear on mainshaft and against synchronizer hub. Index synchronizer key slots with keys in hub. Install 3rd speed gear thrust washer on mainshaft with tang in slot on shaft and against 2nd speed gear bushing. Press 3rd speed gear bushing on mainshaft using arbor and suitable tool (J-22875), until it bottoms on thrust washer. See Fig. 11.

3) Install 3rd speed gear and 3rd speed synchronizer blocker ring on mainshaft, against 3rd speed gear thrust washer. Index synchronizer ring key slots with keys. Using an arbor press and tool J-22873, press 3rd-4th speed synchronizer hub assembly onto mainshaft and against 3rd speed gear with thrust face toward 3rd speed gear.

4) Retain synchronizer assembly with snap ring. Install reverse driven gear with fork groove toward rear. Install 1st speed gear on mainshaft and against 1st-2nd speed synchronizer hub. Install 1st speed gear thrust washer.

GENERAL MOTORS 117 MM CH 465 (Cont.)

Fig. 11   Installing 3rd Gear Bushing

COUNTERGEAR & SHAFT

Disassembly — Remove front countergear shaft snap ring and thrust washer. Discard snap ring. Install suitable press plates (J-22832) on countershaft with open side to spacer. See Fig. 13. Support assembly in an arbor press and press countershaft out of clutch countergear assembly. Countergear is a slip fit and pressing may not be required. Remove clutch countergear rear retaining ring and discard. Remove and discard 3rd speed countergear retaining ring. Position assembly on an arbor press and press shaft from 3rd speed countergear.

Cleaning & Inspection — Wash countergear components in clean solvent and inspect gear teeth for wear and damage.

Reassembly — 1) Position 3rd speed countergear on shaft with machined surface toward front of shaft. Press gear on shaft with arbor press with a minimum force of 1500 lbs. If gear can be installed with less than 1500 lbs., replace gear.

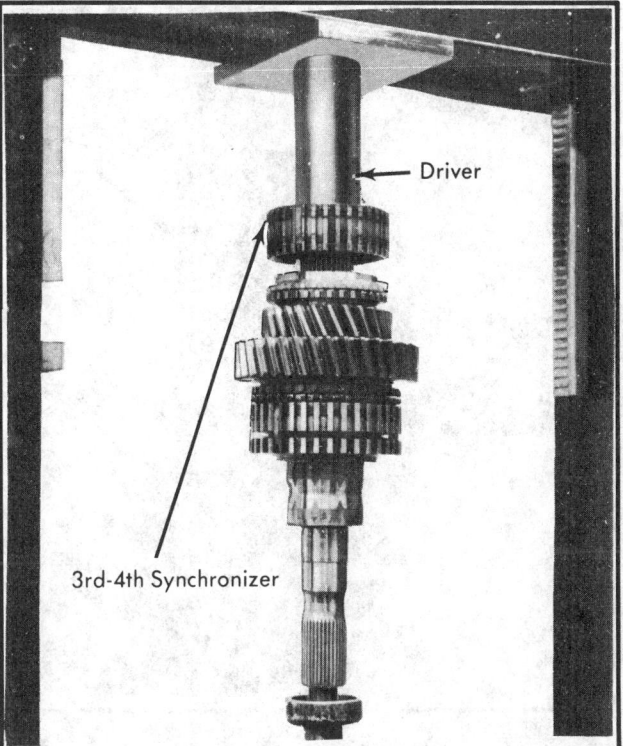

Fig. 12   Installing 3rd-4th Synchronizer

2) Install new countergear rear snap ring using suitable sleeve tools (J-22830 & J-22873) and snap ring pliers as follows: Install inner sleeve over shaft and place snap ring over tool.

3) Push outer tool down on snap ring until it engages groove on shaft. Using snap ring pliers, carefully expand ring until it just slides onto splines, then push ring down until it engages groove on shaft. DO NOT over-stress snap ring.

4) Position clutch countergear and spacer on shaft using a suitable driver (J-22873). Install countergear thrust washer and retaining ring. Position clutch countergear and spacer on shaft using a suitable driver. (J-22873). Install countergear thrust washer and retaining ring.

CAUTION — *Do not overstress snap ring.*

Fig. 13   Removal of Countergear

GENERAL MOTORS 117 MM CH 465 (Cont.)

Fig. 14   Installing Countergear Snap Ring

Fig. 15   Installing Countergear

TRANSMISSION REASSEMBLY

MAINSHAFT, COUNTERGEAR & REVERSE IDLER GEAR

1) Place countergear in bottom of case. Install reverse idler gear in case with gear teeth toward front. Install idler gear shaft from rear to front with slot in shaft end facing down. Shaft slot face must be at least flush with case.

2) Install mainshaft assembly in case with rear of shaft extending out rear bearing hole in case. Position suitable tool (J-22874-5) in pinion gear case front opening and engage front part of mainshaft in tool. See Fig. 16. Lay case on front end. If not previously installed, install 1st speed gear thrust washer. Install mainshaft bearing snap ring and position bearing on shaft. Using suitable driver, drive bearing into case. See Fig. 16. Rotate case, remove tools and install synchronizer cone on pilot end of mainshaft. Slide synchronizer cone rearward to clutch hub.

NOTE — *The 3 cutout sections of 4th speed synchronizer cone must align with 3 clutch keys in clutch assembly.*

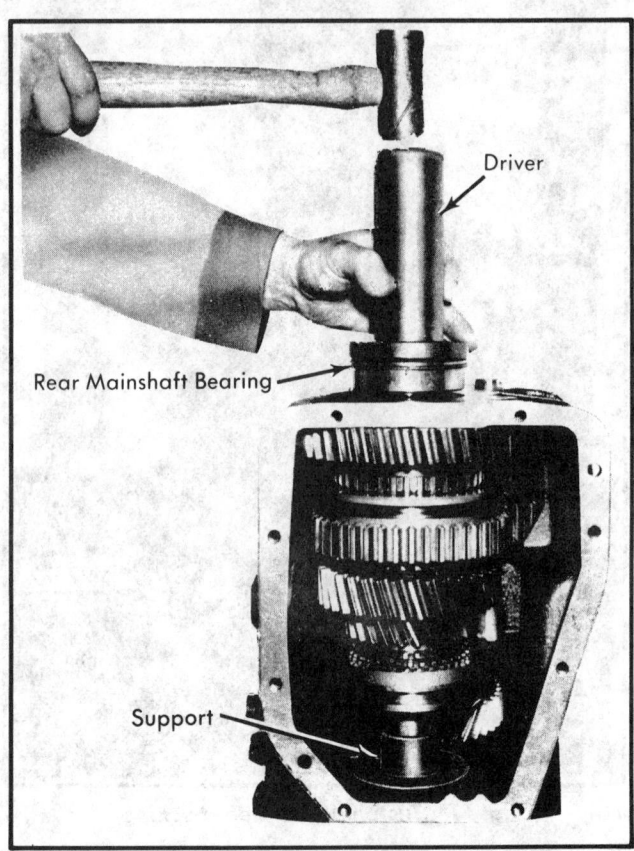

Fig. 16   Installing Rear Mainshaft Bearing

DRIVE PINION

Install drive pinion bearing outer snap ring. Position cutout portion of pinion gear teeth for mainshaft clearance when installing drive pinion. Raise mainshaft to engage drive pinion and 4th speed synchronizer, and tap bearing outer race with a plastic head hammer to install pinion. Install drive pinion bearing retainer using new gasket and tighten bolts to 15-18 ft. lbs.

COUNTERSHAFT

1) Install suitable tool (J-22874-5) in countergear front bearing opening in case to support countergear. See Fig. 17.

2) Lay transmission case on front end and install outer snap ring on countergear rear bearing. Then position bearing on

GENERAL MOTORS 117 MM CH 465 (Cont.)

countergear and using suitable tool (J-22874-1), drive bearing into place.

3) Install snap ring on countershaft at rear bearing and remove tool. Tap countergear front bearing assembly into case and install front bearing retainer with new gasket. Tighten retainer screws to 20-30 INCH lbs.

Fig. 17   Countergear Front Support Tool

OUTPUT YOKE & REAR BEARING RETAINER

1) Slide speedometer drive gear over mainshaft to bearing. Install rear bearing retainer with new gasket and ensure that snap ring ends are in lube slot and cutout in bearing retainer.

2) Install bolts and tighten to 15-18 ft. lbs. Install brake backing plate assembly (if equipped). On models with transfer case, install rear bearing lock nut and washer using suitable tool (J-23070), tighten nut to 120 ft. lbs. and bend washer tangs to fit slots in nut.

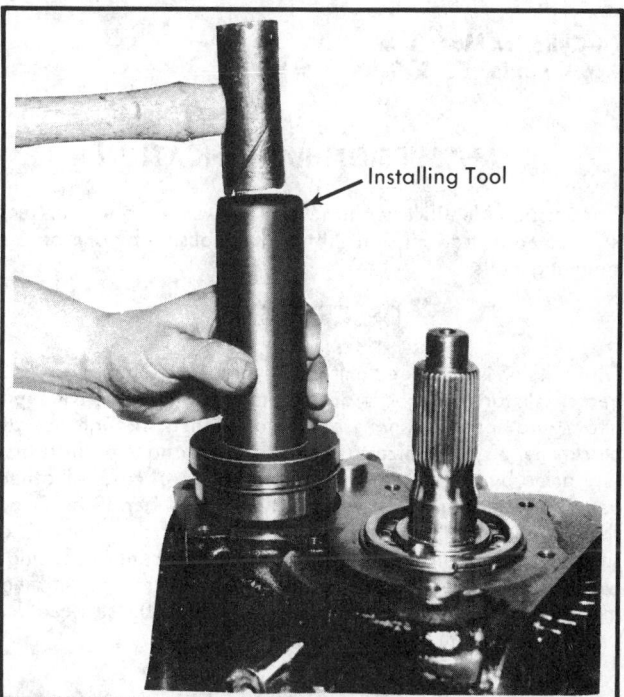

Fig. 18   Installing Rear Countergear Bearing

3) Install parking brake drum and/or universal joint flange. Apply light coat of oil to seal surface. Lock transmission in 2 gears at once and install flange lock nut and tighten to 90-120 ft. lbs.

COVER & SHIFT FORK MECHANISM

Move transmission gears to neutral except reverse idler gear which should be engaged about ⅜". Install cover with new gasket. Shifting forks must slide into their proper positions on clutch sleeves and reverse idler gear. Forks must be positioned as in removal. Install cover bolts and tighten to specification.

TIGHTENING SPECIFICATIONS	
Application	**Ft. Lbs.**
Cover-to-Case Bolts	20
Clutch Gear Bearing-to-Case Bolts	25
Extension and Retainer-to-Case Bolts	
Upper	20
Lower	30
Drain & Filler Plug	30
Shift Lever-to-Shifter Shaft Nut	20
Mount-to-Transmission Bolts	32

JEEP SR-4

Jeep
4-Cylinder Models &
6-Cylinder CJ & Scrambler

TRANSMISSION IDENTIFICATION

Transmission identification tag which shows Jeep part number, is attached to transmission shift control housing by one of the mounting bolts.

DESCRIPTION

Transmission is a 4-speed unit, fully synchronized in all forward gears. All forward gears are constant mesh helical cut type gears and speed changes are accomplished through use of blocker type synchronizer assemblies. Input and mainshaft are supported by ball bearings in front and rear of case. All other gears are supported by needle type roller bearings. Gear shifting is controlled through a top-mounted shift lever. The shifting mechanism is located within the shift control housing, which also serves as the transmission cover. The shifting mechanism requires no adjustment and can be serviced independently of the transmission.

LUBRICATION

See *Lubrication in MANUAL TRANSMISSION SERVICING Section.*

TROUBLE SHOOTING

See *Manual Transmission Trouble Shooting in MANUAL TRANSMISSION SERVICING Section.*

REMOVAL & INSTALLATION

See *Manual Transmission Removal in MANUAL TRANSMISSION SERVICING Section.*

TRANSMISSION DISASSEMBLY

CAUTION — *Except for gearshift lever attaching bolts and fill plug, all threaded holes and bolts used in transmission are metric size. DO NOT attempt to substitute a different thread-type bolt, if original ones are lost or damaged. See Fig. 1 for location of cover dowel-type alignment bolts.*

1) With transfer case removed, mount transmission and adapter housing in suitable holding fixture. Drain lubricant by removing lower adapter housing mounting bolt. Remove flanged nut holding offset lever to shift rail and remove offset lever. Remove adapter housing, transmission cover (shift control housing) and gasket from transmission.

2) Remove reverse lever pivot bolt "C" clip, pivot volt, and remove reverse lever and lever fork as an assembly. Mark front bearing cap for reassembly reference and remove cap and gasket. Remove locating and retaining snap rings from front and rear bearings. Using suitable puller, remove front bearing, clutch shaft, and rear bearing from output shaft.

3) Remove output shaft and gear train as an assembly, ensuring that 1st-2nd or 3rd-4th synchro sleeves do not separate from hubs during removal. Push reverse idler gear shaft out rear of case and remove gear. Using dummy shaft inserted

through front of case, push countershaft from case. Remove countershaft gear and dummy shaft as an assembly and take out any washers or bearings that fell into case during disassembly.

NOTE — *Countershaft gear front washer is plastic and rear washer is metal.*

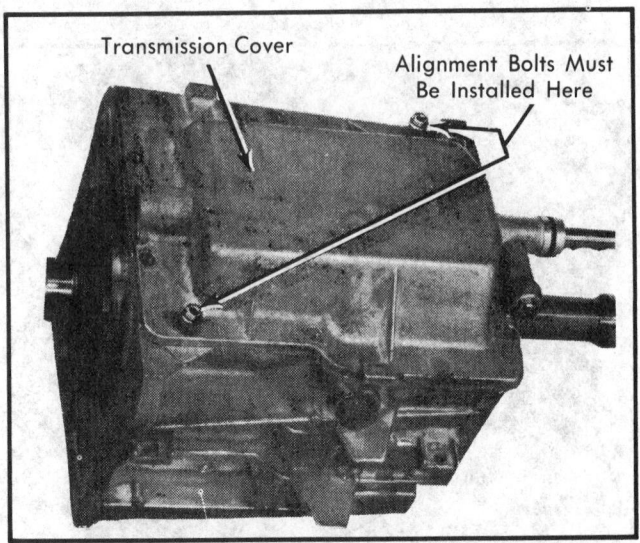

Fig. 1   Location of Transmission Cover Alignment Bolts

COMPONENT DISASSEMBLY & REASSEMBLY

OUTPUT SHAFT

Disassembly — 1) Scribe alignment marks on 3rd-4th synchronizer hub and sleeve for reassembly reference. Remove output shaft snap ring and remove 3rd-4th synchronizer assembly. Disassemble 3rd-4th synchronizer assembly. Remove blocking rings, insert springs, and inserts, then separate sleeve from hub. Slide 3rd gear off output shaft.

2) Remove 2nd gear retaining snap ring, tabbed thrust washer and 2nd gear and blocking ring. Remove 1st gear thrust washer and 1st gear roll pin from rear of output shaft. Remove 1st gear and blocking ring. Scribe alignment marks on 1st-2nd sleeve and output shaft hub for reassembly reference. Remove insert spring and inserts from 1st-2nd sleeve and remove sleeve from shaft hub.

NOTE — *DO NOT attempt to remove 1st-2nd-Reverse hub from output shaft. Hub and shaft are assembled and machined as a matched unit during manufacture.*

Reassembly — 1) Coat output shaft and gear bores with transmission lubricant. Align and install 1st-2nd synchronizer sleeve on output shaft using reference marks made at disassembly. Install three 1st-2nd synchronizer inserts and two insert springs in 1st-2nd synchronizer sleeve. Engage tang end of each insert spring in same synchronizer insert but position open ends of springs so they face away from one another.

2) Place blocking ring on 1st gear and install gear on output shaft, ensuring that synchronizer inserts engage notches in 1st gear blocking ring. Install 1st gear roll pin in output shaft.

JEEP SR-4 (Cont.)

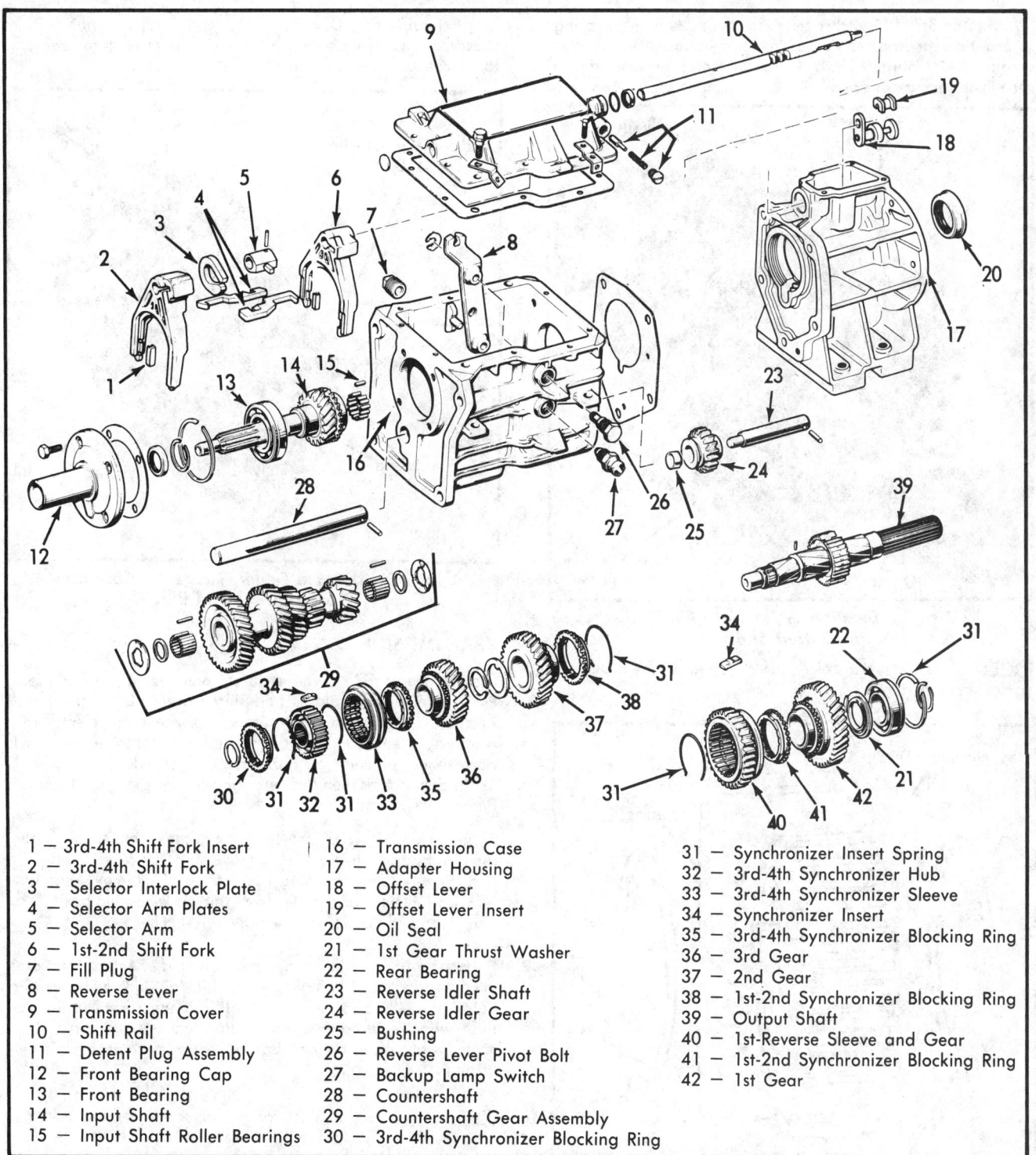

1 — 3rd-4th Shift Fork Insert	16 — Transmission Case	31 — Synchronizer Insert Spring
2 — 3rd-4th Shift Fork	17 — Adapter Housing	32 — 3rd-4th Synchronizer Hub
3 — Selector Interlock Plate	18 — Offset Lever	33 — 3rd-4th Synchronizer Sleeve
4 — Selector Arm Plates	19 — Offset Lever Insert	34 — Synchronizer Insert
5 — Selector Arm	20 — Oil Seal	35 — 3rd-4th Synchronizer Blocking Ring
6 — 1st-2nd Shift Fork	21 — 1st Gear Thrust Washer	36 — 3rd Gear
7 — Fill Plug	22 — Rear Bearing	37 — 2nd Gear
8 — Reverse Lever	23 — Reverse Idler Shaft	38 — 1st-2nd Synchronizer Blocking Ring
9 — Transmission Cover	24 — Reverse Idler Gear	39 — Output Shaft
10 — Shift Rail	25 — Bushing	40 — 1st-Reverse Sleeve and Gear
11 — Detent Plug Assembly	26 — Reverse Lever Pivot Bolt	41 — 1st-2nd Synchronizer Blocking Ring
12 — Front Bearing Cap	27 — Backup Lamp Switch	42 — 1st Gear
13 — Front Bearing	28 — Countershaft	
14 — Input Shaft	29 — Countershaft Gear Assembly	
15 — Input Shaft Roller Bearings	30 — 3rd-4th Synchronizer Blocking Ring	

Fig. 2   Exploded View of Model SR-4 4-Speed Transmission Assembly

Place blocking ring on 2nd gear and install gear on output shaft. Install 2nd gear thrust washer and snap ring on output shaft.

NOTE — *Sharp edge of thrust washer faces outward and tab should be engaged in output shaft notch.*

3) Measure 2nd gear end play by inserting a feeler gauge between 2nd gear and thrust washer. End play should be .004-.014". If end play is not within specifications, replace thrust

washer and snap ring. Also, inspect synchronizer hub for excessive wear on thrust surfaces.

NOTE — *If any output shaft gear is replaced, countershaft gear must also be replaced to maintain proper gear mesh and avoid noisy operation.*

4) Place blocking ring on 3rd gear and install gear on output shaft. Align and install 3rd-4th synchronizer sleeve on 3rd-4th synchronizer hub using reference marks made at disassembly.

JEEP SR-4 (Cont.)

Install three 3rd-4th synchronizer inserts and two insert springs in 3rd-4th synchronizer sleeve. Install assembled 3rd-4th synchronizer on output shaft with machined groove in synchronizer facing forward and install output shaft snap ring.

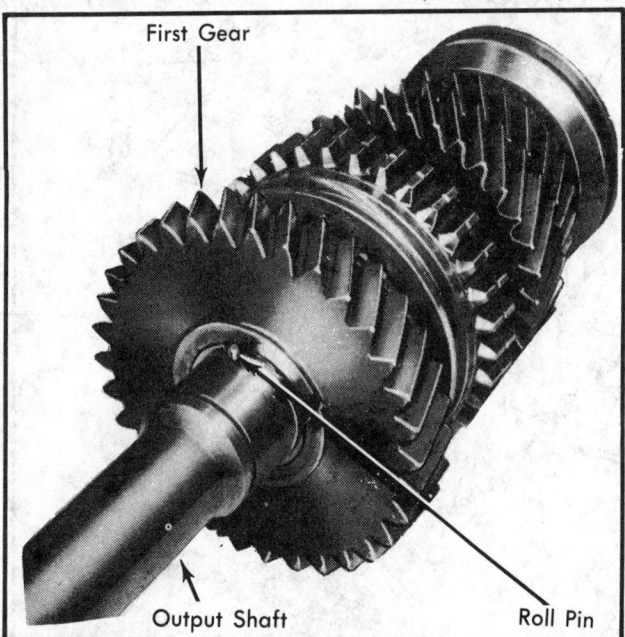

Fig. 3   Location of 1st Gear Roll Pin in Output Shaft

NOTE — *Ensure synchronizer inserts engage notches in 3rd gear blocking ring.*

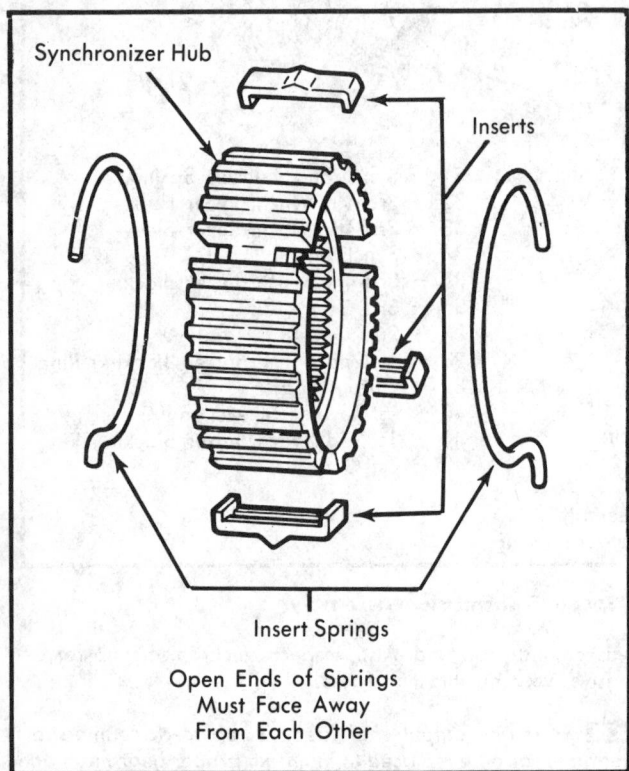

Fig. 4   Synchronizer Insert Spring Positioning

5) Measure output shaft end play using a feeler gauge inserted between snap ring and 3rd-4th synchronizer hub. End play should be .004-.014". If end play is not within specifications, replace snap ring and inspect synchronizer hub for excessive wear on thrust faces.

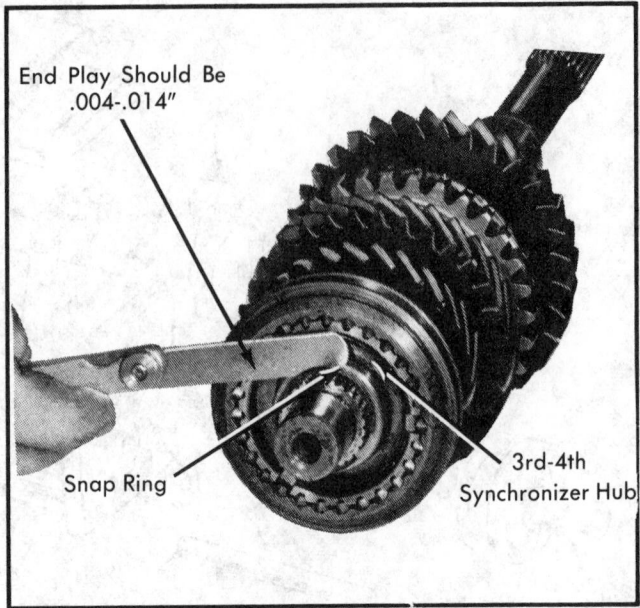

Fig. 5   Using a Feeler Gauge to Measure Output Shaft End Play

TRANSMISSION COVER

Disassembly — 1) Remove detent plug, spring and plunger. Place selector arm plates and shift rail in neutral (centered) position. Rotate shift rail counterclockwise until selector arm disengages selector arm plates and selector arm roll pin is accessible. Pull shift rail rearward until selector arm contacts 1st-2nd shift fork. Remove selector arm roll pin using a punch. Remove shift rail.

2) Remove shift forks, selector arm plates, selector arm and roll pin, and interlock plate. Remove shift rail oil seal and "O" ring. Remove shift rail plug using a punch. Remove nylon inserts and selector arm plates from shift forks, noting position of inserts and plates for reassembly reference.

Reassembly — 1) Install nylon inserts and selector arm plates in shift forks. Install rail plug. Coat shift rail and rail bores with petroleum jelly and insert shift rail into cover until rail end is flush with inside edge of cover. Position 1st-2nd shift fork in cover with offset facing rear of cover and push shift rail through fork.

NOTE — *The 1st-2nd shift fork is the larger of the 2 forks.*

2) Position selector arm and "C" shaped interlock plate in cover and insert rail through arm. Note that widest part of interlock plate must face away from cover and selector arm roll pin hole must face downward and toward rear of cover. Place 3rd-4th shift fork in cover with offset facing rear of cover. 3rd-4th shift fork selector arm plate must be positioned under 1st-2nd shift fork selector arm plate.

3) Insert shift rail through 3rd-4th shift fork and into front bore in cover. Rotate shift rail until plate at forward end of rail faces away from, but is parallel to, cover. Align roll pin holes in selector arm and shift rail and install roll pin. Install

JEEP SR-4 (Cont.)

detent plunger, spring and plug. Install "O" ring in groove of shift rail oil seal. Install shift rail oil seal.

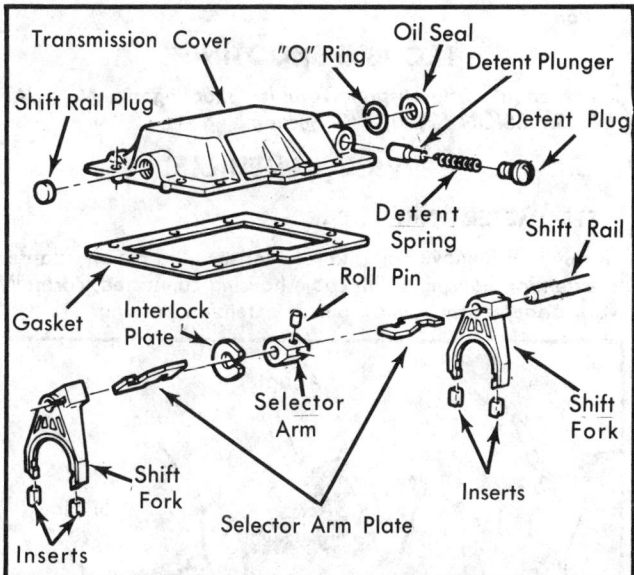

Fig. 6 Exploded View of Transmission Cover Assembly

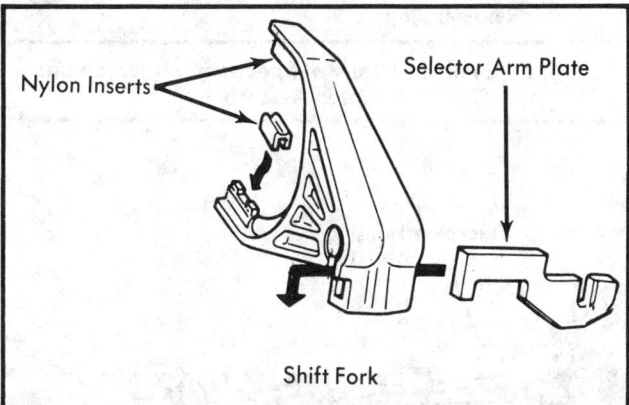

Fig. 7 Assembling Shift Forks and Selector Arm Plates

TRANSMISSION REASSEMBLY

1) Coat countershaft gear thrust washers with petroleum jelly and position in case, ensuring that plastic washer is at front and metal washer at rear. Insert dummy shaft into countershaft gear and install 50 needle bearings in bores at front and rear of gear, then install needle bearing retainers. Use petroleum jelly on needle bearings during installation.

2) Place assembled countershaft gear in case and install countershaft from rear of case. Use care not to displace thrust washers during installation of countershaft and gear. Position reverse idler gear in case with shift lever groove facing front of case. Install reverse idler shaft from rear of case.

3) Using care not to disturb position of synchronizer assemblies, install output shaft and gear train in case. Synchro inserts must engage notch in blocking ring. Coat pilot roller bearing bore of input shaft with petroleum jelly and install 15 roller bearings. Install input shaft in case and engage with 3rd-4th synchro sleeve and blocking ring.

4) Start front bearing onto input shaft and position output shaft 1st gear against rear of case. Align bearing with bearing bore in case and drive bearing completely onto input shaft and into case. Note that rear bearing race has an identification notch while front bearing does not. Install front bearing retaining and locating snap rings.

5) Install front bearing cap oil seal in cap. Install front bearing cap and gasket. Ensure groove in cap is aligned with cutout in gasket and oil hole in case. Install 1st gear thrust washer on output shaft. Ensure side of washer with oil grooves faces 1st gear. Install rear bearing. Install retaining and locating snap rings on rear bearing.

6) Position reverse lever in case. Apply non-hardening sealer to threads of reverse lever pivot bolt and partially install bolt in case. Mount reverse lever on pivot bolt, install spring clip and tighten pivot bolt to specified torque. Ensure that reverse lever fork is engaged in reverse idler gear.

7) Rotate input (clutch) and output shaft gears. If blocking rings tend to stick on gear cones, release rings by gently prying them off cones using a screwdriver. Check blocking ring-to-gear clutch tooth face clearance.

8) Remove oil seal from adapter housing using punch or screwdriver. Install new seal, with metal face of seal flush with or slightly below edge of seal bore.

9) Place reverse lever in Neutral position. Position transmission cover gasket and cover assembly on transmission case. Install cover bolts, tightening them evenly and alternately.

NOTE — The two cover dowel bolts must be installed in proper location to maintain cover alignment. See Fig. 1.

10) Position adapter housing gasket on case and carefully install adapter housing. Install lubricant in case and install transfer case on transmission.

Transmission End Play Specifications	
Application	**End Play**
Countershaft Gear End Play	.004-.018"
Second Gear End Play	.004-.014"
Output Shaft End Play	.004-.014"
Blocking Ring-to-Cone Seat Clearance (Min.)	.001"

TIGHTENING SPECIFICATIONS

Application	Ft. Lbs.
Back-Up Lamp Switch	8-12
Adapter Housing Bolts	18-27
Detent Plug (In Cover)	8-12
Fill Plug	15-25
Front Bearing Cap Bolts	11-15
Gear Shift Lever Bolts	14-22
Offset Lever Nut	8-12
Reverse Lever Pivot Bolt	15-25
Transmission Cover Bolts	7-12
Transmission-to-Clutch Hsg. Bolts	45-65
Universal Joint Clamp Bolt	12-18

NEW PROCESS A833 OVERDRIVE

Chrysler Corp.
General Motors

TRANSMISSION IDENTIFICATION

Transmission may be identified by a number stamped on a machined pad on right side of case. First two letters of code identify manufacturing plant, next three numbers designate transmission type (833), next four numbers indicate manufacturing date, and last four numbers are the production sequence number. A derivative of the Vehicle Identification Number is also stamped on all Chrysler production installed transmissions.

DESCRIPTION

Transmission is a four speed unit providing clash-free shifting in all forward gears due to the use of two synchronizer assemblies. The drive pinion (input shaft) is supported by a ball bearing in the front of transmission case and an oilite bushing pressed in rear of crankshaft. The front end of the mainshaft is supported by roller bearings in the end of the drive pinion and by a ball bearing in the front of the extension housing. The rear end of the mainshaft is supported by the sliding yoke of the propeller shaft, which is supported by a bushing in extension housing. The countershaft gear is supported by a double row of needle-type roller bearings at each end, and gear thrust is taken up by means of thrust washers located between ends of gear and case. The reverse idler gear is supported in case by a bronze bushing which is pressed into gear.

LUBRICATION

See Lubrication in MANUAL TRANSMISSION SERVICING Section

TROUBLE SHOOTING

See Manual Transmission Trouble Shooting in MANUAL TRANSMISSION SERVICING Section.

SERVICE (IN VEHICLE)

SPEEDOMETER PINION GEAR

Removal — Remove bolt and retainer securing pinion adapter to extension housing. With cable housing connected, carefully work adapter and pinion out of extension housing.

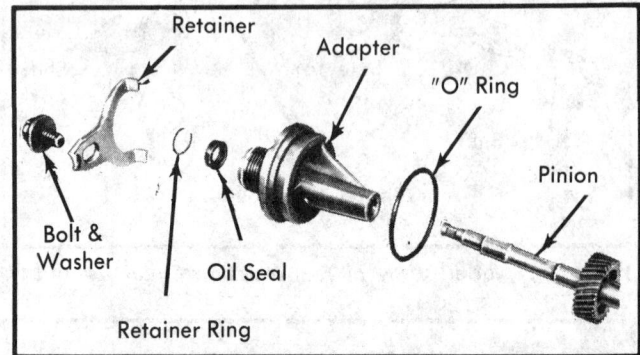

Fig. 1   Exploded View of Speedometer Pinion and Adapter Assembly

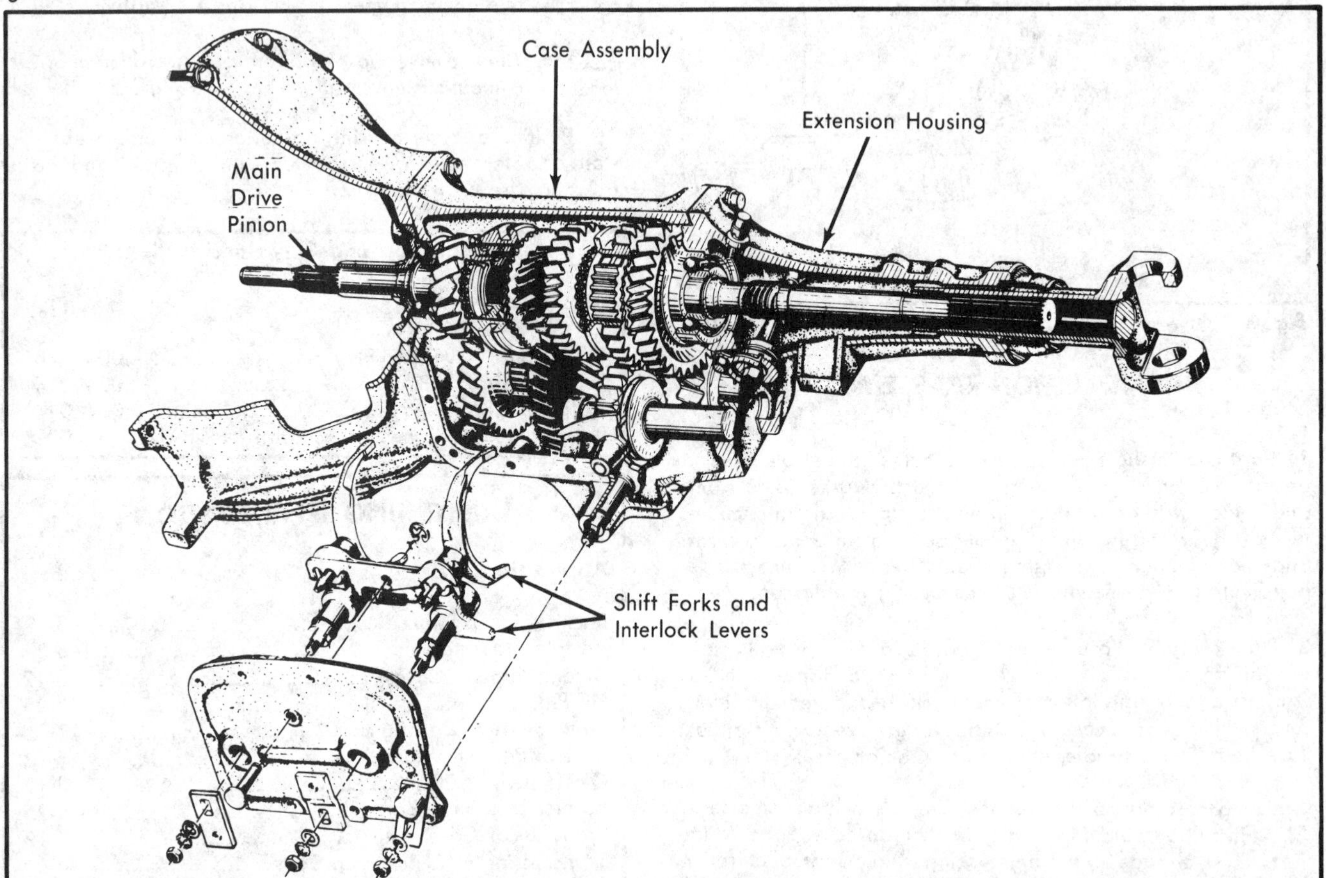

Fig. 2   Cutaway View of Overdrive Transmission

NEW PROCESS A833 OVERDRIVE (Cont.)

Seal Replacement — If transmission fluid is found in cable housing, replace seal in adapter. Start new seal and retainer ring in adapter, then push them into adapter with Tool C-4004 (or equivalent) until tool bottoms.

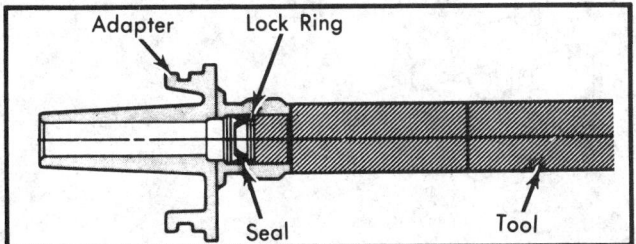

Fig. 3   Installing Speedometer Pinion Seal

CAUTION — *Before installation, make sure adapter flange and its mating area on extension housing are clean and lubricated. Dirt or sand will cause mis-alignment, resulting in pinion gear damage.*

Installation — **1)** Note number of gear teeth and install speedometer pinion gear into adapter. Rotate pinion gear and adapter assembly so that number of teeth on adapter, corresponding to number of teeth on gear, is in the 6 o'clock position as assembly is installed.

2) Install retainer and bolt, with retainer tangs in adapter positioning slots. Tap adapter firmly into extension housing and tighten retaining bolt to specifications.

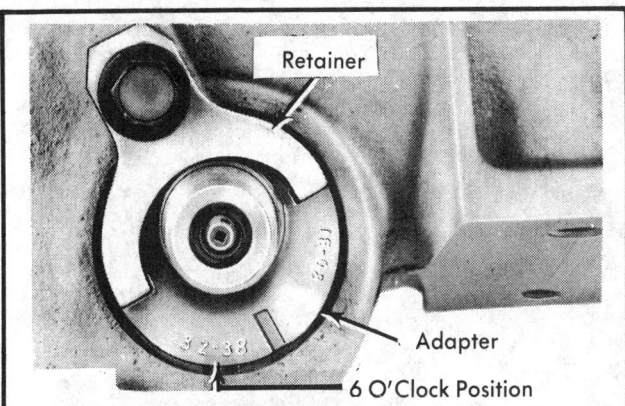

Fig. 4   Installed View of Speedometer Pinion and Adapter

EXTENSION HOUSING YOKE SEAL

Removal — Mark rear universal joint for reassembly, then disconnect and remove propeller shaft. Remove oil seal from housing using tool (C-3985 or equivalent).

CAUTION — *DO NOT nick or scratch ground surface on sliding spline yoke during removal and installation of shaft assembly.*

Installation — Position new seal in opening of extension housing and drive into housing with tool (C-3972 or equivalent). Install propeller shaft, aligning marks made at removal.

REMOVAL & INSTALLATION

See *Manual Transmission Removal* in MANUAL TRANS-MISSION SERVICING Section.

TRANSMISSION DISASSEMBLY

GEARSHIFT HOUSING & MECHANISM

1) Remove reverse shifter lever from shaft, then remove bolts attaching gearshift housing to transmission case. Place all levers in neutral position, then pull housing out and away from case. Work forks out of sleeves and case.

NOTE — *Shift forks may remain in engagement with synchronizer sleeves.*

2) If oil leakage is visible around lever shafts or if interlock levers are cracked, proceed as follows: Remove shift levers and shafts, making sure shafts are free of burrs before removing.

3) Remove "O" ring retainers and "O" rings from housing. Remove "E" ring from interlock lever pivot pin and remove interlock levers and spring from housing. Remove reverse detent spring and ball from bore in side of case.

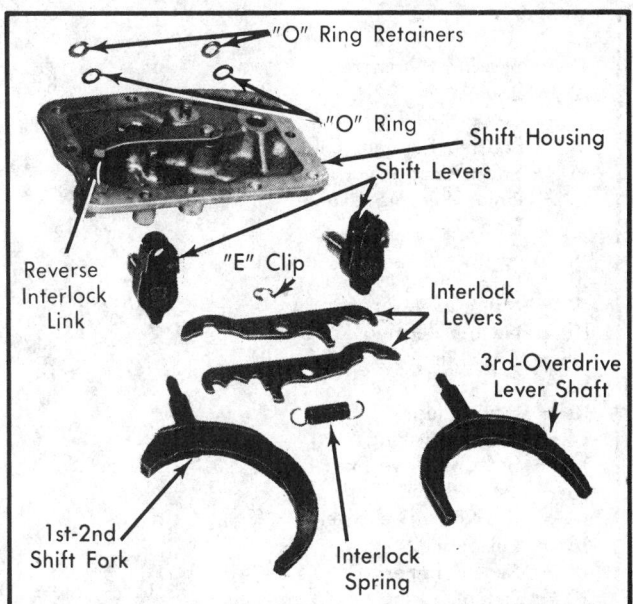

Fig. 5   Exploded View of Gearshift Housing and Mechanism

EXTENSION HOUSING, MAINSHAFT & DRIVE PINION

1) Remove speedometer pinion and adapter from extension housing. Remove bolts attaching extension housing to transmission case. Rotate extension housing on output shaft to expose rear of countershaft. Install 1 extension housing bolt to hold extension housing in inverted position.

2) With centerpunch or drill, make hole in countershaft expansion plug at front of case. Working through this hole, drive countershaft forward and remove Woodruff key. Now push countershaft forward until expansion plug is driven out of case.

NEW PROCESS A833 OVERDRIVE (Cont.)

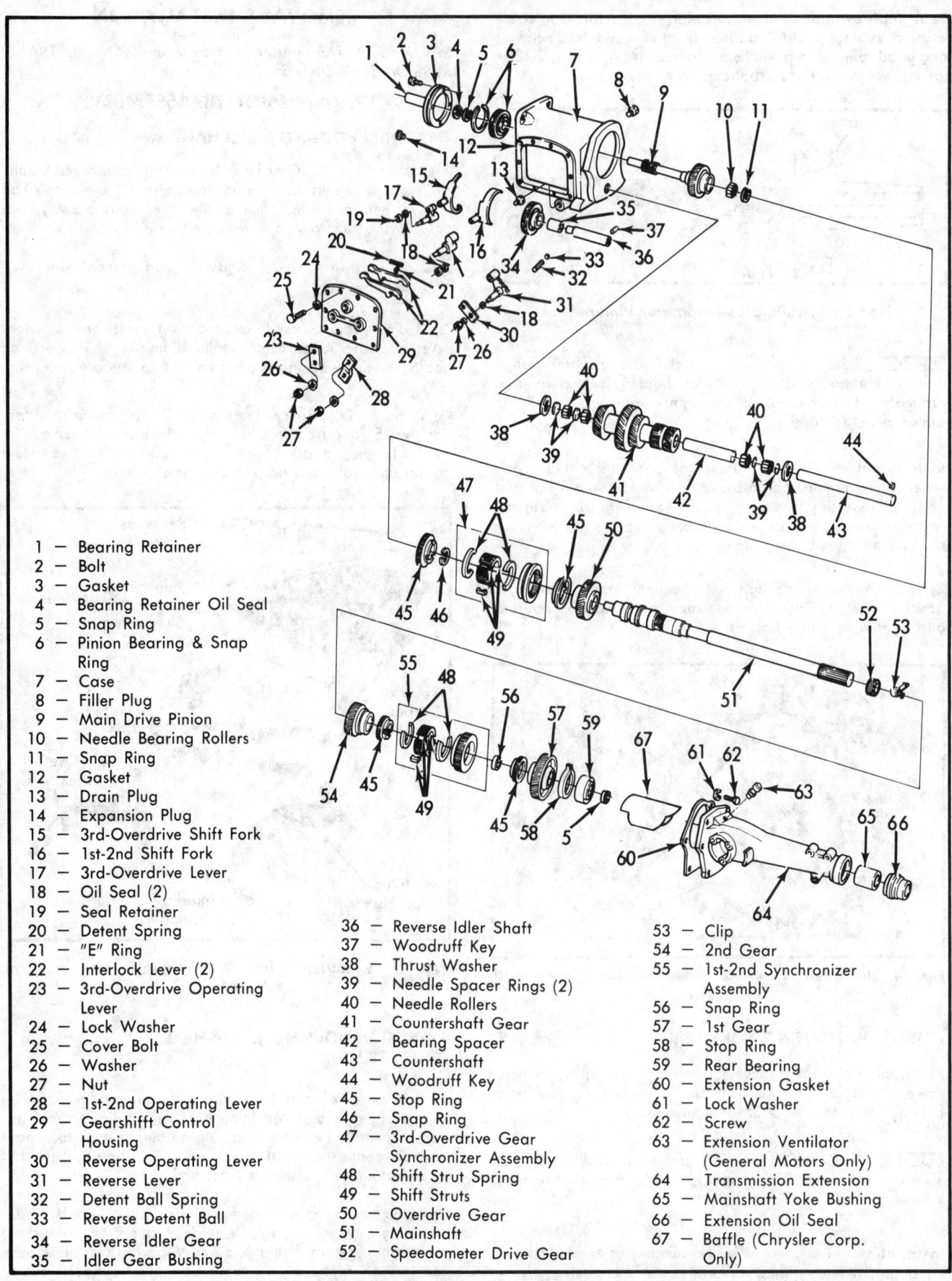

1 — Bearing Retainer
2 — Bolt
3 — Gasket
4 — Bearing Retainer Oil Seal
5 — Snap Ring
6 — Pinion Bearing & Snap Ring
7 — Case
8 — Filler Plug
9 — Main Drive Pinion
10 — Needle Bearing Rollers
11 — Snap Ring
12 — Gasket
13 — Drain Plug
14 — Expansion Plug
15 — 3rd-Overdrive Shift Fork
16 — 1st-2nd Shift Fork
17 — 3rd-Overdrive Lever
18 — Oil Seal (2)
19 — Seal Retainer
20 — Detent Spring
21 — "E" Ring
22 — Interlock Lever (2)
23 — 3rd-Overdrive Operating Lever
24 — Lock Washer
25 — Cover Bolt
26 — Washer
27 — Nut
28 — 1st-2nd Operating Lever
29 — Gearshift Control Housing
30 — Reverse Operating Lever
31 — Reverse Lever
32 — Detent Ball Spring
33 — Reverse Detent Ball
34 — Reverse Idler Gear
35 — Idler Gear Bushing

36 — Reverse Idler Shaft
37 — Woodruff Key
38 — Thrust Washer
39 — Needle Spacer Rings (2)
40 — Needle Rollers
41 — Countershaft Gear
42 — Bearing Spacer
43 — Countershaft
44 — Woodruff Key
45 — Stop Ring
46 — Snap Ring
47 — 3rd-Overdrive Gear Synchronizer Assembly
48 — Shift Strut Spring
49 — Shift Struts
50 — Overdrive Gear
51 — Mainshaft
52 — Speedometer Drive Gear

53 — Clip
54 — 2nd Gear
55 — 1st-2nd Synchronizer Assembly
56 — Snap Ring
57 — 1st Gear
58 — Stop Ring
59 — Rear Bearing
60 — Extension Gasket
61 — Lock Washer
62 — Screw
63 — Extension Ventilator (General Motors Only)
64 — Transmission Extension
65 — Mainshaft Yoke Bushing
66 — Extension Oil Seal
67 — Baffle (Chrysler Corp. Only)

Fig. 6 Exploded View of Overdrive Transmission

NEW PROCESS A833 OVERDRIVE (Cont.)

3) Using arbor tool (C-3938 or equivalent), push countershaft out rear of case. Lower countershaft gear to bottom of case. Rotate extension housing back to normal position. Remove drive pinion bearing retainer and gasket from transmission, remove seal from retainer.

4) Using a brass drift, tap pinion and bearing assembly out through front of case. Slide 3rd-Overdrive synchronizer sleeve slightly forward, slide reverse idler gear to the center of its shaft, and tap housing and mainshaft from case.

5) Remove snap ring retaining 3rd-Overdrive synchronizer on mainshaft. Then slide assembly off mainshaft, followed by overdrive gear and stop ring. Compressing the snap ring holding mainshaft ball bearing in extension housing, pull mainshaft and bearing out of housing.

6) Remove snap ring retaining mainshaft bearing on shaft, place steel plates on front side of 1st gear and press or drive mainshaft through bearing. Remove bearing, retainer ring, 1st gear and stop ring from shaft.

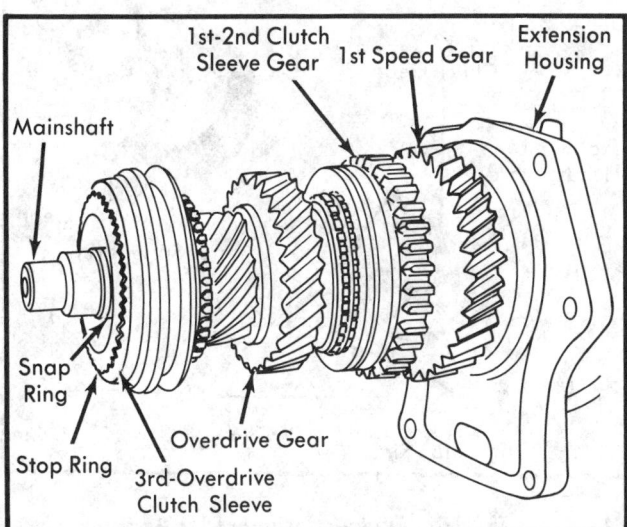

Fig. 7 Assembled View of Mainshaft Assembly

7) Remove snap ring retaining 1st-2nd synchronizer assembly on mainshaft, slide synchronizer assembly off mainshaft followed by 2nd gear.

NOTE — *DO NOT disassemble synchronizer assembly unless replacement of parts is required.*

DRIVE PINION & COUNTERSHAFT GEAR

Remove pinion bearing inner snap ring and remove ball bearing from drive pinion. Remove snap ring and 16 bearing rollers from cavity in drive pinion. Remove countershaft gear from bottom of case and withdraw arbor, 76 needle roller bearings, thrust washers and spacers from center of countershaft gear.

REVERSE GEAR, LEVER & FORK

1) Remove reverse idler gear shaft using tool (C-3638 or equivalent and a $7/16''$ socket). Place tool in case with socket

against end of shaft and tool against case. Press shaft out of case. Remove Woodruff key from shaft.

2) Remove back-up light switch and gasket. If oil leakage is visible around reverse gearshift lever shaft, remove burrs from shaft, push shaft inward and remove from case. Remove "O" ring and "O" ring retainer from case bore.

Fig. 8 Reverse Idler Gear and Shaft

CLEANING & INSPECTION

After cleaning all parts with solvent and drying with compressed air, inspect all bearings, rollers, races and spacers for roughness, galling, flat spots or brinelling. Check gears for chipping, burrs, nicks, cracks or excessive wear. Inspect synchronizers for chipping or excessive wear. Replace parts as required.

TRANSMISSION REASSEMBLY

REVERSE GEAR, LEVER & FORK

1) Coat new oil seal "O" ring and "O" ring retainer with Multipurpose grease. Install reverse shift lever in case bore, followed by "O" ring and "O" ring retainer. Place reverse idler gear shaft in end of case.

2) Press in shaft far enough to position reverse idler gear on shaft with fork slot toward rear and engage slot with reverse shift fork. Press shaft further into case and install Woodruff key. Press shaft flush with end of case and install back-up light switch and gasket, tighten to specifications.

COUNTERSHAFT GEAR & DRIVE PINION

1) Coat inner bore of countershaft gear with heavy grease and install roller bearing spacer so it is centered. Insert same arbor tool used at disassembly and center it in gear. Coat needle bearings with heavy grease, then at each end of gear, install 19 rollers followed by a spacer ring and 19 more roller bearings and one spacer ring. Coat thrust washers with heavy grease and install them over arbor with tang side toward case

NEW PROCESS A833 OVERDRIVE (Cont.)

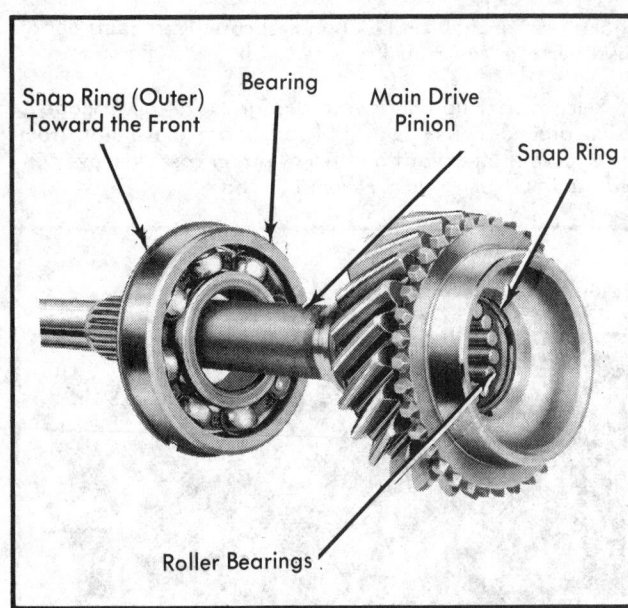

Fig. 9   Assembled View of Drive Pinion

boss. Install countershaft gear in bottom of case, making sure thrust washers stay in position.

2) Press main drive bearing on pinion shaft (outer snap ring groove toward front), and seat bearing fully against shoulder on gear. Install a new inner snap ring (selective fit) on shaft to retain bearing and give minimum end play. Be sure snap ring is fully seated. Place pinion shaft in a soft jawed vise and install 16 bearing rollers in cavity of shaft, coat rollers with grease and install retaining snap ring. Using seal installing tool (C-3789 or equivalent), install new oil seal in retainer bore.

EXTENSION HOUSING BUSHING REPLACEMENT

Remove extension housing yoke seal. Drive bushing out of housing with Tool C-3974 (or equivalent). Slide a new bushing on installing end of tool. Align hole in bushing with oil slot in housing, then drive bushing into place. Drive a new oil seal into housing with Tool C-3972 or equivalent.

MAINSHAFT

CAUTION — *Synchronizers are serviced as an assembly. Except for stop rings, synchronizer parts should not be interchanged. If synchronizers were disassembled for inspection, and parts are in good condition, reassemble as outlined below.*

1) Sub assemble synchronizer parts as follows: Place a stop ring flat on bench followed by clutch gear and sleeve. Drop struts in their slots and snap in a strut spring, placing tang inside one strut. Turn assembly over on stop ring and install second strut spring tang in a different strut.

2) Slide 2nd speed gear over mainshaft (sychronizer cone toward rear) and down against shoulder on shaft. Slide 1st-2nd synchronizer assembly (including stop ring with lugs indexed in hub slots), over mainshaft, down against 2nd gear cone and secure with a new snap ring. Slide next stop ring over shaft and index lugs into clutch hub slots. Slide 1st speed gear (synchronizer cone toward clutch sleeve just installed) over mainshaft into position against clutch sleeve gear. Install

mainshaft bearing retaining ring, followed by mainshaft rear bearing. Using an arbor and a suitable tool, drive or press bearing down into position. Install a new snap ring on shaft to secure bearing.

NOTE — *The snap ring is a select fit for minimum end play.*

3) Install partially assembled mainshaft into extension housing far enough to engage bearing retaining ring in slot in extension housing. Compress ring with pliers so that mainshaft ball bearing can move in to bottom against its thrust shoulder in extension housing. Release ring and seat it all around its groove in housing.

4) Slide overdrive gear over mainshaft (synchronizer cone toward front), and follow with stop ring. Install 3rd-Overdrive synchronizer assembly on mainshaft (shift fork slot toward rear), making sure to index stop ring with shift struts. Install retaining ring. Grease and install front stop ring on synchronizer, indexing ring lugs with shift struts.

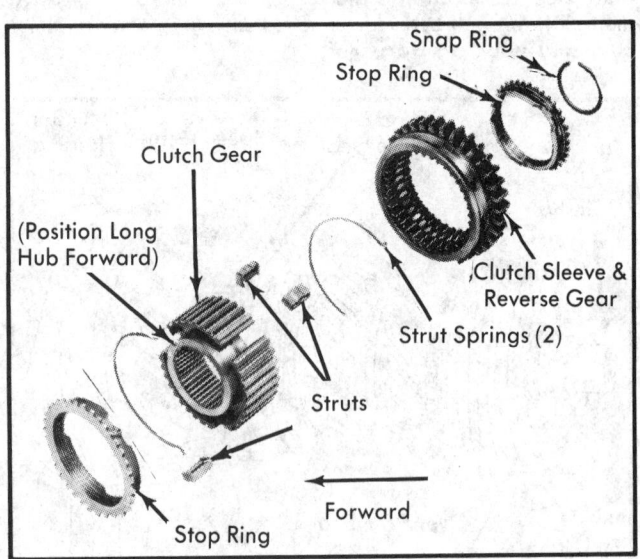

Fig. 10   Exploded View of 1st-2nd Synchronizer Assembly

5) Coat a new extension housing-to-case gasket with grease and install on extension housing. To provide assembly clearance, slide reverse idler gear to center of its shaft and move 3rd-Overdrive synchronizer sleeve as far forward as possible (do not lose struts). Slowly insert mainshaft assembly into case, tilting it as required to clear idler and cluster gears. Place 3rd-Overdrive synchronizer in neutral position.

6) Rotate extension housing on output shaft to expose rear of countershaft. Install 1 extension housing bolt to hold extension housing in inverted position. Install snap ring in drive pinion bearing groove and install drive pinion into case indexing it with mainshaft.

NOTE — *Snap ring should bottom on case. If not, internal parts are not in correct position.*

7) Turn transmission upside down while holding countershaft gear assembly to prevent damaging it. Lower countershaft gear assembly into position, with teeth meshed with drive pi-

NEW PROCESS A833 OVERDRIVE (Cont.)

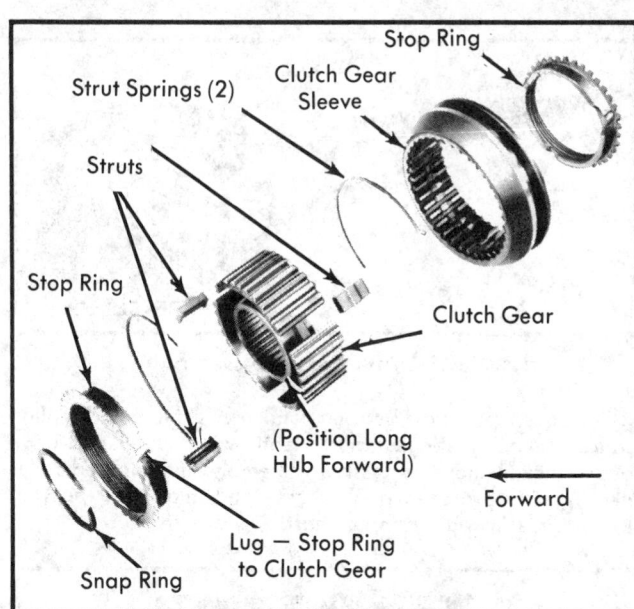

Fig. 11 *Exploded View of 3rd-Overdrive Synchronizer Assembly*

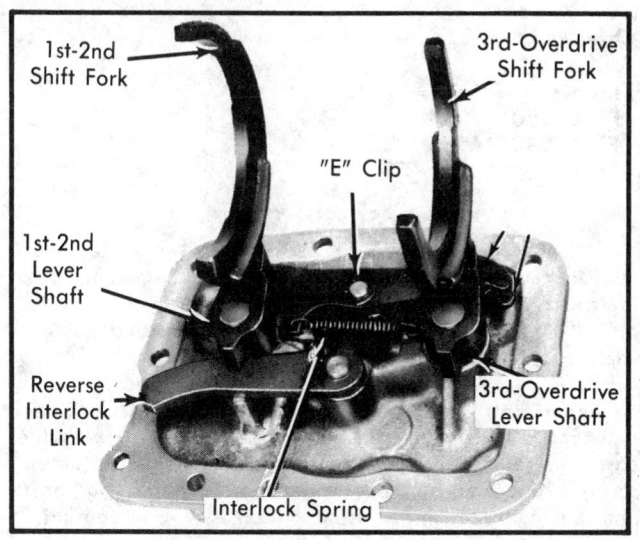

Fig. 12 *Assembled View of Gearshift Mechanism*

nion gear. Make sure thrust washers remain in position and tangs are aligned with slots in case.

8) Install countershaft into bore from rear of case and push forward until installed approximately half-way. Install Woodruff key, then push shaft forward until end is flush with rear of case and arbor tool is removed.

9) Rotate extension housing into place, install and tighten attaching bolts to specifications. Install new seal in drive pinion bearing retainer, place new gasket on retainer and position on case. Coat bolt threads with sealer and install, tightening to specifications. Install new expansion plug in countershaft bore at front of case.

GEARSHIFT HOUSING & MECHANISM

1) Install interlock levers on pivot pin and fasten with "E" ring. Use pliers to install spring on interlock lever hangers. Coat new oil seal "O" rings and "O" ring retainers with Multi-purpose grease.

2) Install each shift lever shaft into its proper bore, followed by an "O" ring and "O" ring retainer. Install operating levers and retaining nuts and tighten to specifications.

3) Rotate each shaft fork bore to Neutral (straight up), and install 3rd-Overdrive shift fork in its bore and under both interlock levers. Position both synchronizer sleeves in Neutral. Place 1st-2nd shift fork in groove of 1st-2nd synchronizer sleeve.

4) Slide reverse idler gear to Neutral. Lay transmission on its right-hand side, coat gearshift housing gasket with grease and position on case. Install reverse detent ball and spring into its bore in side of case.

5) As shift housing is lowered into place, guide 3rd-Overdrive shift fork into 3rd-Overdrive synchronizer groove. Position shaft of synchronizer 1st-2nd shift fork into bore of 1st-2nd

shift lever. Hold reverse interock link against 1st-2nd shift lever to provide clearance as shift cover is lowered into position.

6) Using screwdriver, raise interlock lever against spring tension to allow 1st-2nd shift fork shaft to slip under levers. Install housing bolts finger tight, shift transmission through all gears to insure proper operation.

7) The reverse shift lever and 1st-2nd shift lever have cam surfaces which mate in reverse position to lock 1st-2nd shift lever, fork and synchronizer in Neutral. Grease reverse shaft and install operating lever and retaining nut and tighten to specifications.

NOTE — *Eight of the shift housing bolts are shoulder bolts, 1 has a longer shoulder and acts as a dowel at center of rear flange. Two bolts installed at lower rear of cover are standard.*

8) Install speedometer drive pinion gear and adapter making sure correct range number (corresponding to number of teeth on pinion gear) is in 6 o'clock position.

Transmission Specifications

Application	Specifications
Countershaft-to-Case Bore Dia.	.005-.0065"
Countershaft Gear End Play	.015-.029"
Clutch Housing Face Squareness	.006" Max.
Clutch Housing Bore Run-Out	.008" Max.

TIGHTENING SPECIFICATIONS

Application	Ft Lbs.
Back-Up Light Switch	15
Input Bearing Retainer Bolts	30
Extension Hsg.-to-Case Bolts	50
Gearshift Mount-to-Plate Bolts	24
Gearshift Mount-to-Ext. Hsg. Bolts	12
Shift Lever Nuts	18
Transmission-to-Clutch Hsg. Bolts	50
Drain Plug	15
Speedometer Pinion Adapter Bolt	8

NEW PROCESS 435

Chrysler Corp.
Ford
  Bronco
  F150/350
  F150/250 4-WD

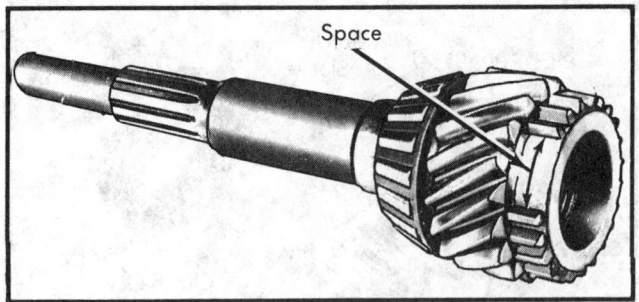

Fig. 1 Input Shaft Assembly

DESCRIPTION

New Process 4-Speed transmission uses a direct-mounted shift lever and cover. 1st and Reverse gears are spur type. 2nd, 3rd, and 4th gears are helical, constant mesh type and are synchronized for easier shifting.

The input shaft is supported at front by tapered roller bearings. End play is controlled by gasket thickness between the case and bearing retainer. The front of the mainshaft (output shaft) is supported by a pilot roller bearing in the input shaft. The rear of the mainshaft is supported by a ball bearing.

Countershaft gear is a solid, 1-piece unit, supported by caged roller bearings at each end. A roller-type thrust bearing and race are provided at rear of countershaft gear, with a thrust washer at front of gear.

Reverse idler gear uses roller bearings in Ford models and bronze bushings in Chrysler Corp. models. 3rd-4th speed synchronizer is mounted at front of mainshaft, 2nd speed synchronizer and 1st speed sliding gear at rear of mainshaft.

LUBRICATION

See *Lubrication* in MANUAL TRANSMISSION SERVICING Section.

TROUBLE SHOOTING

See *Manual Transmission Trouble Shooting* in MANUAL TRANSMISSION SERVICING Section.

REMOVAL & INSTALLATION

See *Manual Transmission Removal* in MANUAL TRANSMISSION SERVICING Section.

TRANSMISSION DISASSEMBLY

SHIFT CONTROL COVER

Mount transmission assembly in holding fixture and remove drain and filler plugs if not previously removed. Place gearshift lever in neutral position, remove shift control cover screws and remove cover by lifting while rotating slightly counterclockwise to provide clearance for shift forks. Remove and discard gasket. See *Fig. 7.*

INPUT SHAFT & MAINSHAFT

1) Lock transmission in 2 gears. Remove mainshaft flange nut and mainshaft flange (if equipped). Remove extension housing and slide speedometer drive gear off mainshaft. Measure and record synchronizer outer stop ring and 3rd speed gear end play for reference during reassembly. See *Fig. 4.*

2) Remove input shaft bearing retainer. Rotate gear to align space in input shaft gear clutch teeth with countershaft drive gear teeth. Remove input shaft assembly and tapered roller bearing. Remove snap ring, washer and pilot roller bearing from recess in rear of input shaft. See *Fig. 1.*

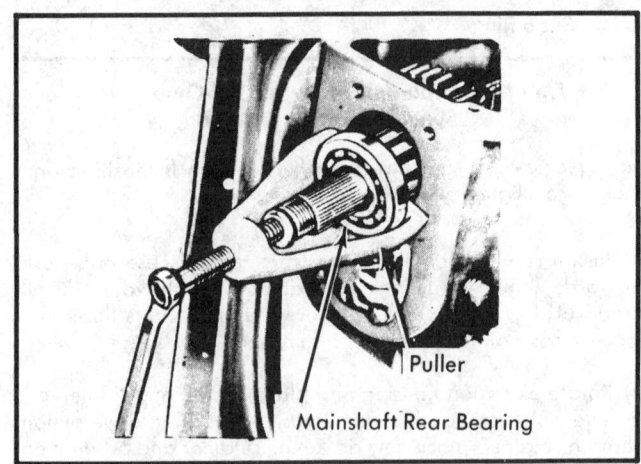

Fig. 2 Removing Rear Mainshaft Bearing

3) Place brass drift in front center of mainshaft and drive mainshaft to rear. Remove rear bearing with suitable puller. Move mainshaft to rear and tilt front of mainshaft up. Remove roller type thrust bearing. Remove synchronizer and stop rings separately. Remove mainshaft assembly. See *Figs. 2 and 3.*

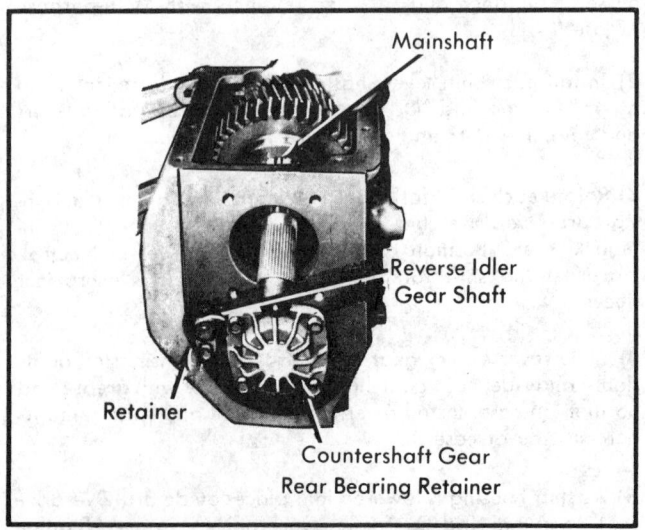

Fig. 3 Removal of Mainshaft from Case

NEW PROCESS 435 (Cont.)

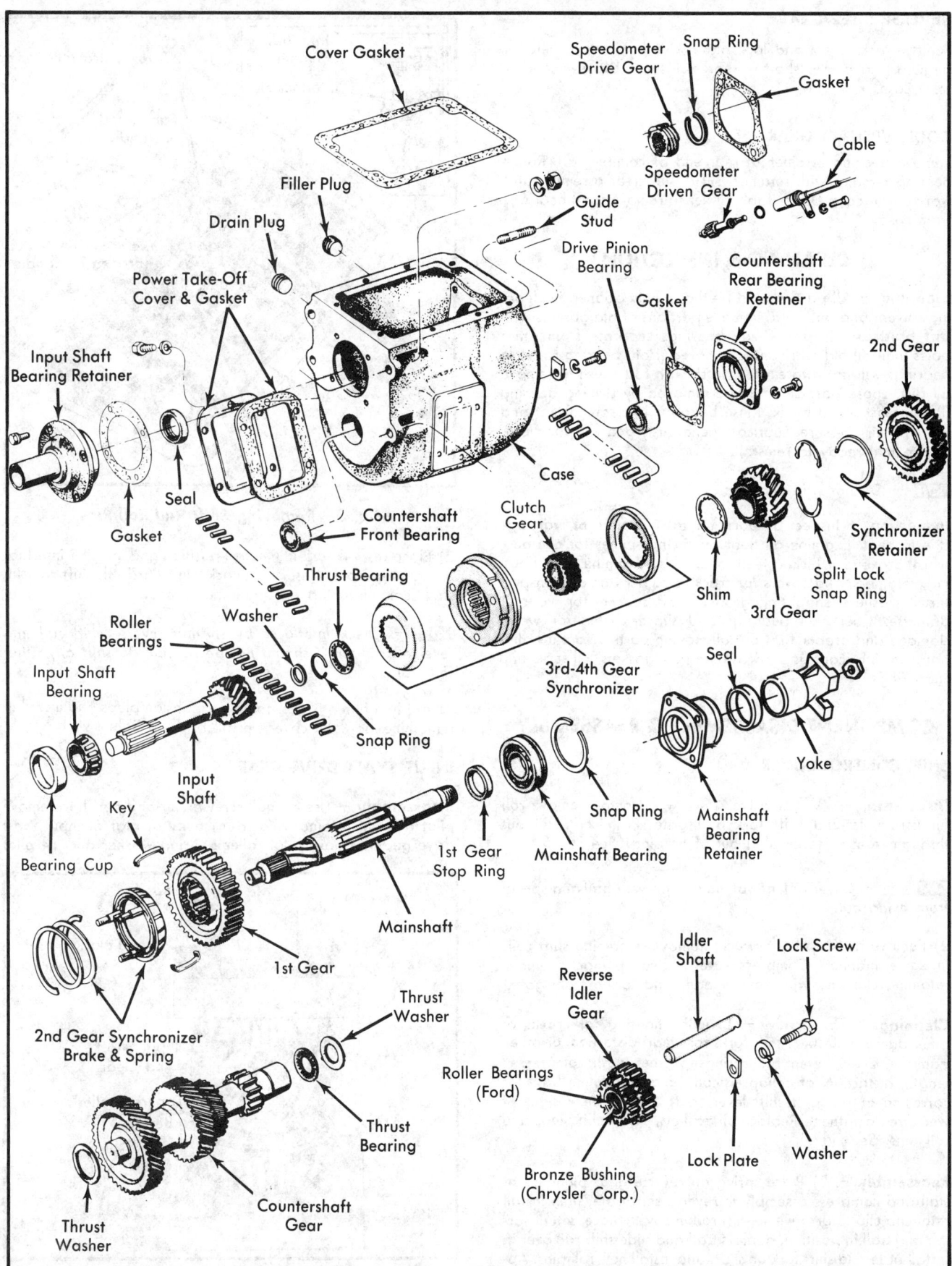

Fig. 4 Exploded View of New Process 435 4-Speed Transmission

NEW PROCESS 435 (Cont.)

REVERSE IDLER GEAR

Remove lock screw and lock plate. Use brass drift, held at angle, to drive idler shaft to rear. Pull shaft. Lift reverse idler from case.

COUNTERSHAFT GEAR

Remove bearing retainer at rear end of countershaft. Roller bearing remains with retainer. Tilt cluster gear assembly and work out of case. Use suitable driver to remove front bearings from case.

CLEANING & INSPECTION

Cleaning — All parts should be thoroughly cleaned in cleaning solvent and air dried. Remove portions of old gaskets with stiff brush or scraper. Clean bearings separate from other parts until all old lubricant is removed. Hold bearing races so bearings will not rotate, then brush with soft brush to remove all dirt. Loose particles may be removed by striking bearing flat against wood block. Rinse bearings in clean solvent and dry with air pressure. Lubricate generously and wrap in clean paper until ready to reinstall.

NOTE — *Do not spin bearings.*

Inspection — Inspect all parts for discoloration or warpage due to heat. Examine all gear teeth and splines for chipped, worn, broken, or nicked teeth or splines. Examine case, housing, retainers, and covers for cracks or other damage. Inspect thrust washers, snap ring grooves and spacers for wear or damage. Check all bearings and synchronizers for wear, damage and proper fit. Coat all moving parts before installation with lubricant and always use new gaskets, oil seals and snap rings.

COMPONENT DISASSEMBLY & REASSEMBLY

SHIFT CONTROL COVER

Disassembly — **1)** Using No. 2 screw extractor, remove roll pins from 1st-2nd shift fork and gate. Push shift rail out through front to force plug out of housing. *See Fig. 5.*

CAUTION — *Cover detent ball hole to prevent ball and spring from flying out.*

2) Remove back-up light switch. Remove remaining shift rails in same manner. Compress reverse gear plunger, remove retaining clip and withdraw plunger and spring from gate.

Cleaning & Inspection — Examine housing for cracks or other damage. Inspect shift forks for wear, distortion, or other damage. Check detent ball springs for free length, compressed length, distortion, or collapsed coils. Examine detent balls for corrosion or wear. If shift lever shaft detents show signs of wear, replace them. Replace all gaskets, expansion plugs and roll pins. *See Fig. 7.*

Reassembly — **1)** Place spring on reverse gear plunger, install and compress assembly in reverse shift gate, then install retaining clip. Start reverse shift rail in cover, place detent spring and ball in position, depress ball and slide shift rail over it. Install gate and shift fork on shaft and install new roll pins. Apply a film of sealer to plug seat at front of cover. Install a new plug in reverse shift rail bore.

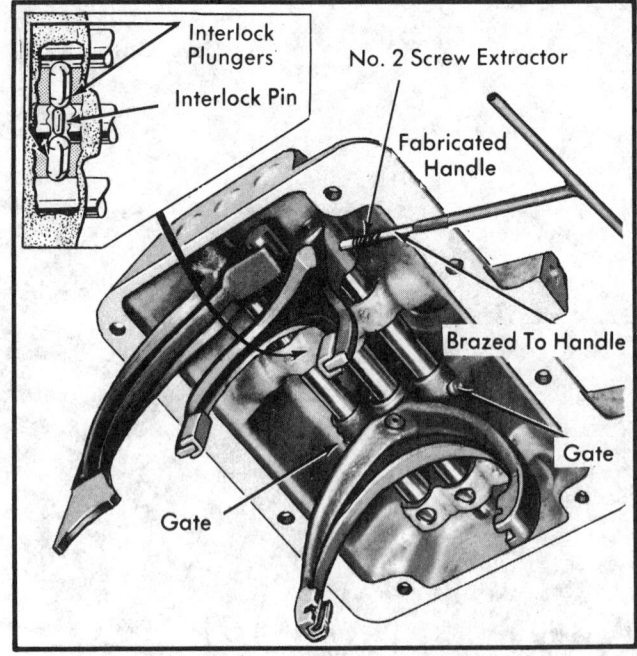

Fig. 5　Removing Shift Rail Roll Pins

2) Place reverse fork in Neutral position and install 2 interlock plungers in bores. Insert interlock pin in 3rd-4th shift rail. Install remaining shift rails in same manner.

NOTE — *Check interlocks by shifting reverse shift rail into reverse position. It should not be possible to shift any other shift rails.*

3) Apply a film of sealer to new expansion plugs and install in remaining bores in cover. Install back-up light switch.

INPUT SHAFT DRIVE GEAR

Disassembly — Use a small screwdriver and punch to remove pilot bearing retainer ring from cavity at rear of input shaft drive gear. Remove pilot roller bearing washer and 14 pilot

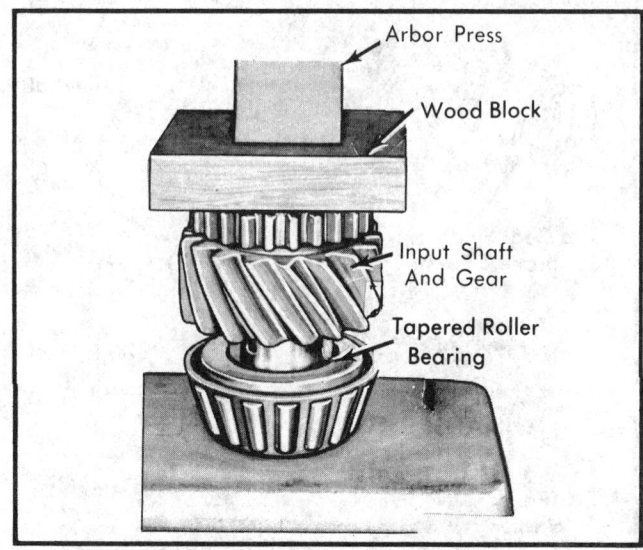

Fig. 6　Installing Tapered Roller Bearing on Input Shaft

NEW PROCESS 435 (Cont.)

bearing rollers from gear. Using a bearing puller, remove tapered roller bearing.

Reassembly – Press tapered bearing cone and roller assembly onto input shaft. Lubricate 14 pilot bearing rollers with light grease and insert them into cavity at rear of input shaft (inside gear). Position roller bearing washer over pilot bearing rollers, and install retaining ring in groove of gear. *See Fig. 6.*

MAINSHAFT

Disassembly – Remove clutch gear snap ring, then withdraw clutch gear, synchronizer outer stop ring-to-third gear shim(s), and third speed gear. Remove special split lock ring with two screwdrivers, and withdraw second speed gear and synchronizer assembly. Remove 1st-Reverse sliding gear from shaft.

Reassembly – **1)** Place mainshaft assembly in a soft jawed vise with rear end upward. Install 1st-Reverse gear making

sure 2 spline springs are in place inside gear as it is installed on shaft.

2) Move mainshaft in vise so that forward end is upward. Install synchronizer spring and brake on 2nd gear, secure brakes with snap ring making sure snap ring tangs are away from gear.

3) Slide 2nd gear assembly onto mainshaft making sure synchronizer brake is toward rear. Secure gear to shaft with split lock snap rings, then install 3rd gear.

NOTE – *Synchronizer clutching gear must be installed with BOTH oil slots facing 3rd gear. Oil slots must NOT face thrust bearing. See Fig. 8.*

4) Install correct shim(s) between 3rd gear and 3rd-4th synchronizer stop ring. Refer to end play measurement obtained during disassembly to bring end play within specifications.

NOTE – *Exact determination of end play will be made after mainshaft and main drive gear are installed in case.*

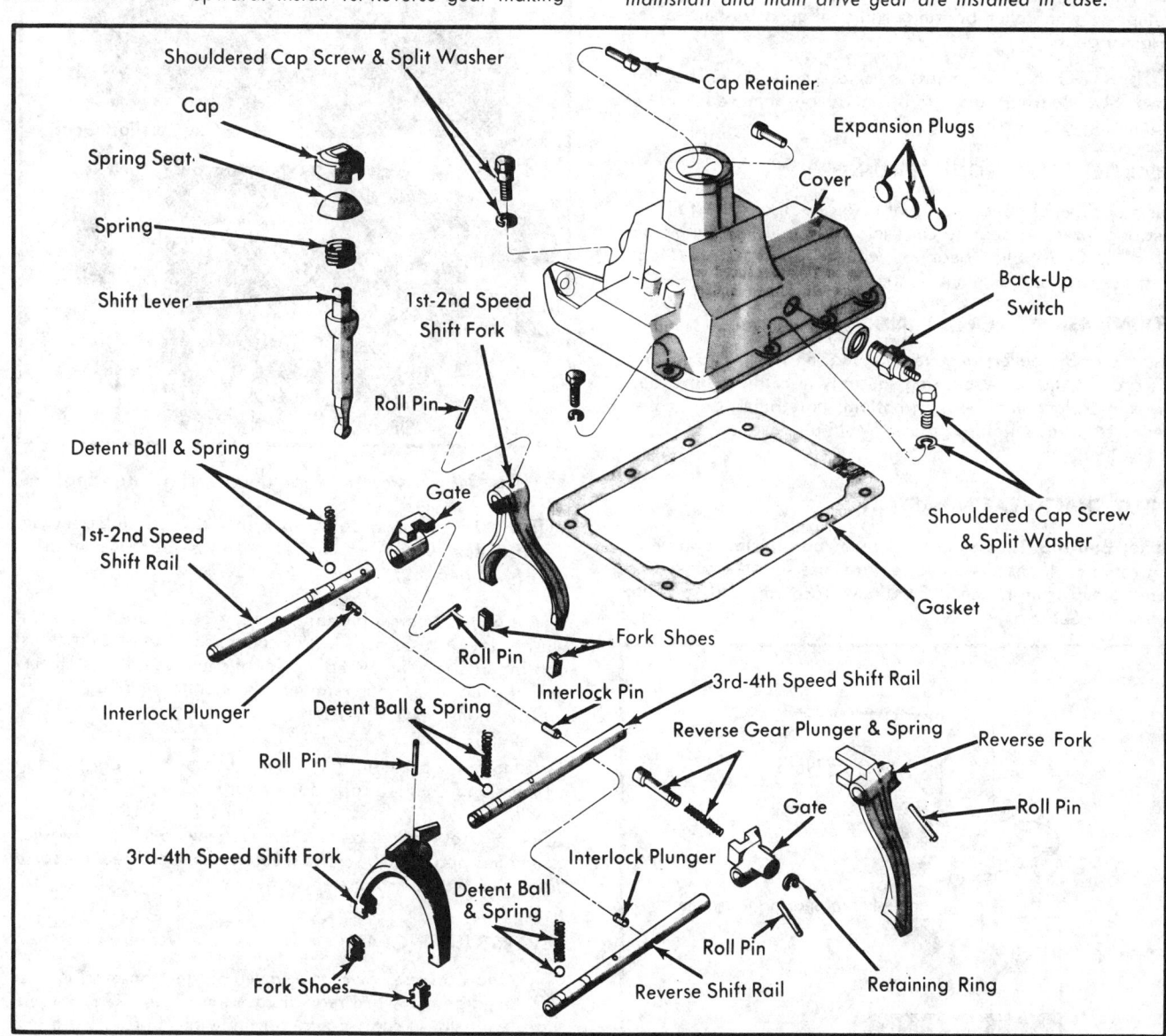

Fig. 7 *Exploded View of Shift Control Cover Assembly*

NEW PROCESS 435 (Cont.)

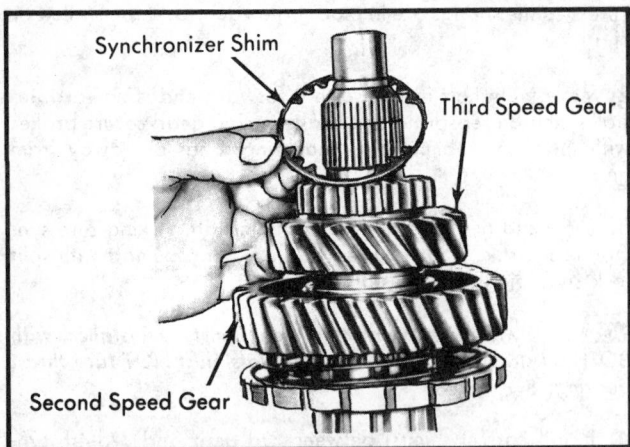

Fig. 8   Installing Synchronizer Shims

REVERSE IDLER GEAR

Gear is serviced by replacement only. Replacement gear is equipped with roller bearings rather than a bushing as on original gear.

NOTE – DO NOT attempt to disassemble roller bearing assembly. Bearing lock ring cannot be removed without damaging gear or bearing.

COUNTERSHAFT FRONT BEARING

Press or drive old bearing out of case and discard. Install new bearing, pressing bearing cage into case until flush with front of case. Coat roller bearings with suitable grease (Multi-purpose grade 2 or equivalent).

COUNTERSHAFT REAR BEARING

Using suitable puller, remove rear bearing from retainer and discard. Position new bearing squarely in retainer bore and press into place until bearing bottoms in retainer. Coat roller bearings with suitable grease (Multi-purpose grade 2 or equivalent).

INPUT SHAFT BEARING RETAINER

Roller Bearing Race – Bearing race cup is installed in bearing retainer. If necessary to replace, use suitable puller and remove cup from retainer. Press new race cup squarely into retainer. See Fig. 9.

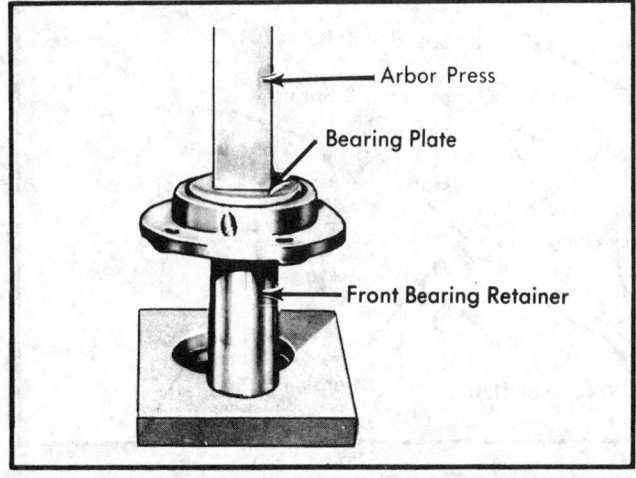

Fig. 9   Installing Front Bearing Race

Oil Seal Replacement – Pry old oil seal out of retainer, and press new seal into place using a suitable sleeve.

NOTE – Lip of oil seal should point toward gasket surface of retainer.

TRANSMISSION REASSEMBLY

COUNTERSHAFT GEAR

1) Position transmission case on work bench with front of case down. Coat front thrust washer with grease and position it in case over countershaft front bearing.

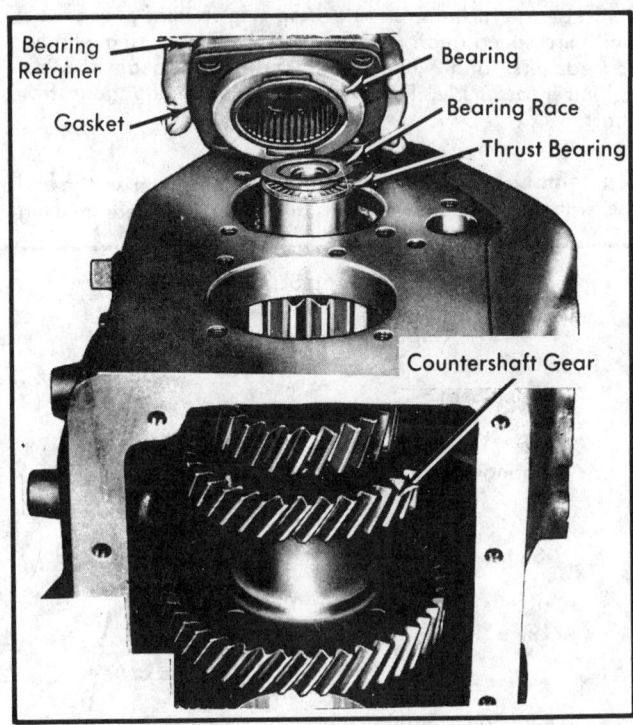

Fig. 10   Installing Rear Countershaft Bearing

NOTE – Tangs on thrust washer fit into cast slots in case. Thrust washer bore is off-center, make sure bore is concentric with front bearing.

2) Position countershaft gear in case, making sure front thrust washer is not disturbed. Install countershaft gear rear thrust bearing and race on pilot diameter of countershaft. Install new gasket, rear bearing retainer and bolts and tighten to specifications. See Fig. 10.

3) Using new gasket, install gasket, countershaft rear bearing retainer and countershaft rear bearing.

NOTE – Use sealing cement on 4 screw and lock washer assemblies and tighten screws securely. Check by feel for some slight end play of countershaft gear.

REVERSE IDLER GEAR

1) Position reverse idler gear assembly in transmission case with large gear toward rear of case. Insert reverse idler gear shaft, with slot in shaft down, partially into bore of case and idler gear. Coat outer end of idler gear shaft with sealing cement.

NEW PROCESS 435 (Cont.)

2) Coat lock screw with sealer. Drive idler gear shaft into idler gear and transmission case. Position lock plate in groove of idler shaft and install lock screw and tighten to specifications.

MAINSHAFT

1) Lower rear end of mainshaft into case and maneuver through rear bearing opening. Make sure synchronizer and shims remain in position on mainshaft. Install roller thrust bearing. See Fig. 11.

2) Place a block of wood between front end of mainshaft and front of case. Install 1st gear stop ring and rear bearing onto mainshaft, drive into case until bearing snap ring is flush with case.

INPUT SHAFT DRIVE GEAR

1) With area of input shaft drive clutch gear with missing teeth down, to permit for passage over countershaft gear, guide input shaft and gear assembly into transmission case and over front end of mainshaft.

NOTE — Be sure 3rd-4th speed synchronizer stop ring engages teeth of drive gear.

2) Position input shaft bearing retainer (without gasket) against transmission case. While holding bearing retainer concentric with input shaft, measure clearance between retainer and face of case with a feeler gauge. See Fig. 12.

3) Remove bearing retainer, then reinstall with gasket shim pack .010-.015" thicker than measured clearance between retainer and case. Using a dial indicator to measure input shaft and gear end play, bring end play within specifications. See Fig. 13.

NOTE — End play of input shaft and gear is necessary to allow for normal heat expansion of parts during operation.

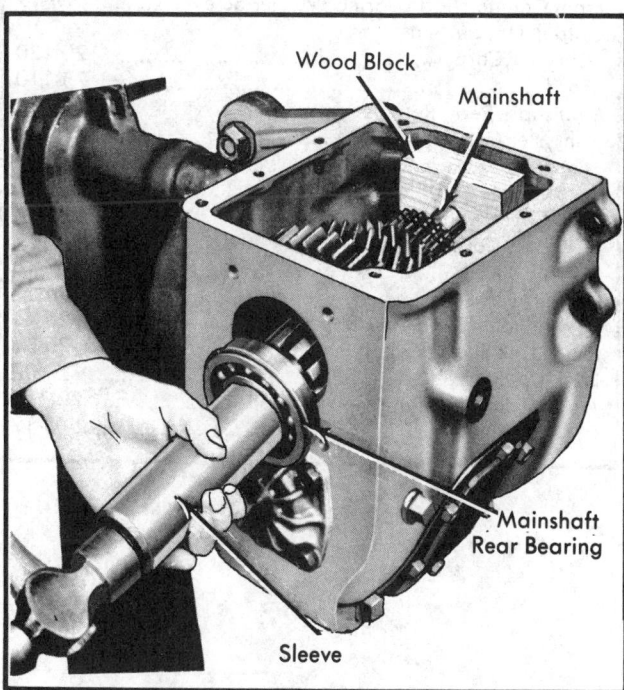

Fig. 11   Installing Rear Mainshaft Bearing

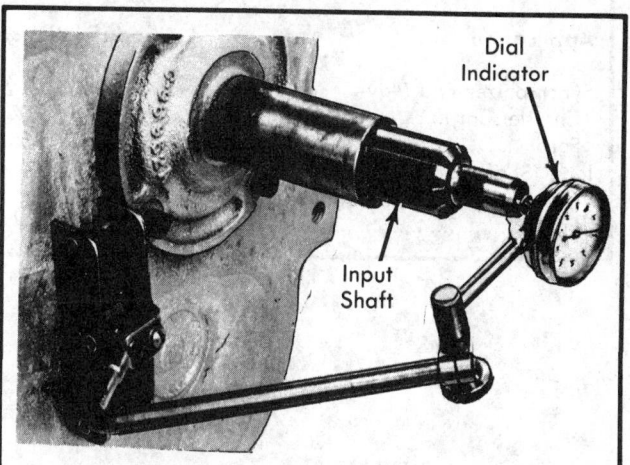

Fig. 13   Measuring Input Shaft Drive Gear End Play

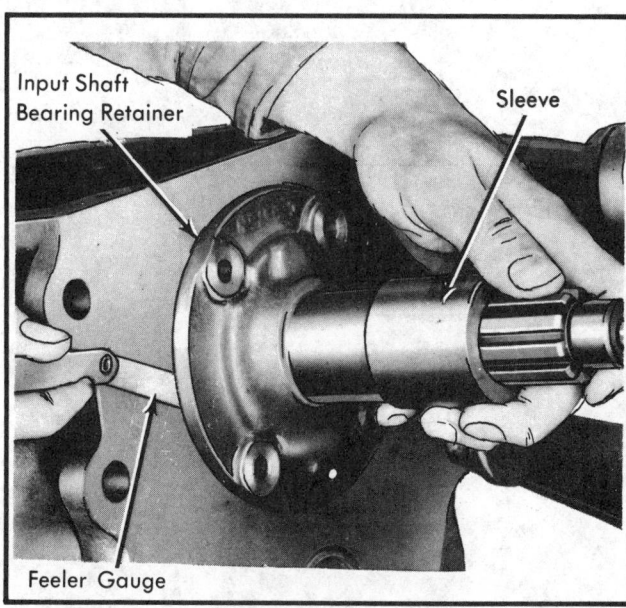

Fig. 12   Measuring Bearing Retainer Clearance

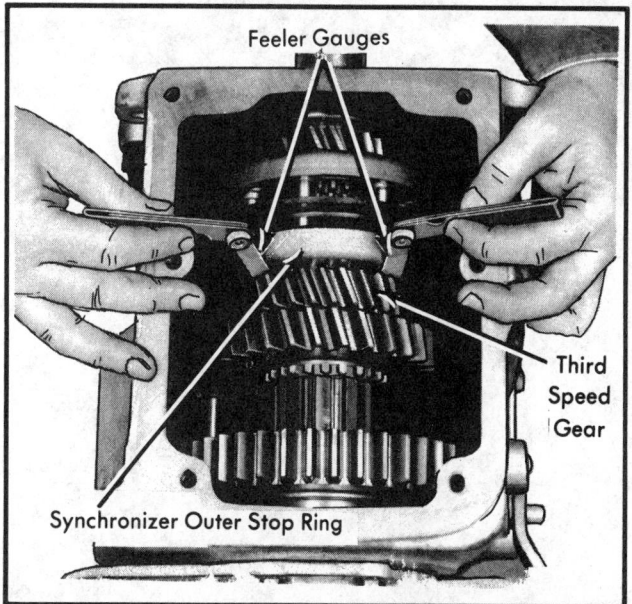

Fig. 14   Measuring Synchronizer End Play

NEW PROCESS 435 (Cont.)

4) Check synchronizer end play after all mainshaft components are in position and properly tightened. Two equal size feeler gauges are used to measure synchronizer end play. Keep gauges as close as possible to both sides of mainshaft. Disassemble mainshaft and add or subtract shims to bring end play within specifications. *See Fig. 14.*

SHIFT CONTROL COVER

1) Make sure all internal parts of transmission are well lubricated before installing shift control cover. Coat gasket surface on top of transmission case with gasket cement and position new gasket on top of case.

2) Place all gears in transmission in neutral position. Position all shift rails in shift control cover in neutral position. Lower cover with new gasket into place, carefully engaging shift forks and lugs into proper gears. Attach cover to case with 8 screws and washers and tighten to specifications.

NOTE — *Second screw from front on each side is shouldered and has a split washer for installation alignment. Install and check gears for free rotation. Install remaining screws.*

Transmission Specifications

Application	Specifications
Synchronizer End Play	
Chrysler Corp.	.050-.070"
Ford	.070-.095"
Input Shaft and Gear End Play	
Chrysler Corp.	.007-.017"
Ford	.007-.014"

TIGHTENING SPECIFICATIONS

Application	Ft. Lbs.
Shift Cover Screw	20-40
Input Shaft Bearing Retainer Screw	25-35
Front Countershaft Retainer Bolt	18-22
Front Countershaft Bearing Washer Screw	15-19
Output Flange Nut	
Chrysler Corp.	120-130
Ford	75-110
Mainshaft Rear Retainer Bolt	
Chrysler Corp.	18-22
Ford	35-45
Rear Countershaft Retainer Bolt	20-40
PTO Cover Bolt	
Chrysler Corp.	8-12
Ford	12-18
Drain & Filler Plugs	25-35
Reverse Idler Shaft Lock Bolt	20-40
Brake Link Shoulder Bolt	25-35
Back-Up Light Switch	20-30
Transmission-to-Clutch Housing Bolt	70-110
Case Breather	8-12

WARNER T-18 & T-18A

Ford
  Bronco
  F100/350
  F150/350 4-WD
Jeep
  J-20 Truck Only

TRANSMISSION IDENTIFICATION

An identification tag is attached to one of the shift control housing-to-case attaching bolts. Tag shows vehicle manufacturer part number and vendor part tag.

DESCRIPTION

Transmission is a 4-speed unit, synchronized in 2nd, 3rd, and 4th gears only. First and reverse gears are spur type, while 2nd, 3rd, and 4th gears are constant mesh helical type. The clutch (input) shaft is supported at the front with a ball bearing. The mainshaft (output shaft) is supported at the front by a pilot bearing in the input shaft and at the rear by a ball bearing. All other gears are supported by needle-type roller bearings.

LUBRICATION

See *Lubrication* in MANUAL TRANSMISSION SERVICING Section.

TROUBLE SHOOTING

See *Manual Transmission Trouble Shooting* in MANUAL TRANSMISSION SERVICING Section.

REMOVAL & INSTALLATION

See *Manual Transmission Removal* in MANUAL TRANSMISSION SERVICING Section.

TRANSMISSION DISASSEMBLY

1) Mount transmission in a suitable holding fixture and drain lubricant. Position shift lever in reverse (Jeep) or 2nd gear (Ford) and remove shift control housing. On 2-WD models, lock in 2 gears, then remove "U" joint flange nut, flange, oil seal, speedometer driven gear and bearing assembly. Remove mainshaft (output shaft) bearing retainer or extension housing, speedometer drive gear snap ring, retainer and gear with spacer.

2) On 4-WD models, remove adapter housing. On all models, remove mainshaft (output shaft) bearing retainer, rear bearing spacer, and bearing. Using suitable puller, remove input shaft bearing and take off oil baffle or retaining washer.

3) Remove mainshaft (output shaft) assembly from case, using care not to lose 22 needle bearings from input shaft. Remove input shaft assembly from case by pushing rearward and removing from inside case. Remove lock plate retaining bolt from countershaft and reverse gear idler shaft. Remove lock plate.

NOTE — *Input shaft may be removed through front bearing bore on Jeep 6-cylinder models.*

4) Use brass drift to drive countershaft toward rear of case until front end of shaft is approximately even with inside of case. Insert dummy shaft (arbor tool) 1.115" in diameter by 9.85" long in countershaft bore. Drive countershaft out rear of case, keeping tool in contact with shaft at all times. Remove assembly carefully along with bearings and washers. Remove reverse idler gear shaft and remove gear assembly from case.

NOTE — *On Ford applications, it may be necessary to remove reverse idler shaft and gear prior to removal of countershaft assembly.*

COMPONENT DISASSEMBLY & REASSEMBLY

MAINSHAFT

Disassembly — **1)** Scribe alignment marks on mainshaft splines and synchronizer hub assemblies for reassembly. Remove pilot bearing spacer from front of mainshaft (if equipped). Remove 3rd-4th synchronizer snap ring from mainshaft.

2) Remove 3rd-4th synchronizer assembly and 3rd gear from mainshaft. Check end play of 2nd speed gear, it should be .005-.024". Remove 1st-2nd gear snap ring from mainshaft. Slide 1st-2nd gear synchronizer assembly from mainshaft.

NOTE — *All end play is controlled by selective thickness snap rings.*

3) Move 2nd gear rearward to gain clearance and remove snap ring. Slide 2nd gear off mainshaft. Punch alignment marks on synchronizer clutch hubs and sleeves for reassembly.

4) Remove insert springs and shift plates from 3rd-4th gear synchronizer assembly. Separate sleeve and hub. Mark position of insert spring and plates for reassembly.

5) Place 1st-2nd gear synchronizer assembly on bench with shift fork groove up. Wrap a shop towel around sleeve (to avoid loosing shift plate lock balls) and separate sleeve and hub. Remove shop towel and remove lock balls, springs, and shift plates.

Reassembly — **1)** Use 3rd-4th gear clutch hub as an assembly tool for reassembling 1st-2nd gear synchronizing assembly. Place 3rd-4th gear synchro hub on work bench. Position 1st-2nd clutch sleeve over hub with shift groove down.

NOTE — *Coat all parts with petroleum jelly prior to reassembly.*

2) Align punch marks made during disassembly and position 1st-2nd synchronizing hub in sleeve with lock ball holes facing up. Insert shift plates in hub slots.

3) Install spring through shifting plate. Compress spring and lock ball while pressing on shift plate until ball is held in position by synchronizer sleeve.

4) Repeat procedure until all shifting plates, springs and lock balls are installed. Press down on hub and pull up on sleeve to complete assembly.

5) Align punch marks on 3rd-4th gear synchronizing clutch hub and trynchronizer sleeve made during disassembly. Insert 3 shifting plates in hub slots. Install retaining ring so that one end of each ring is retained in the same shifting plate.

WARNER T-18 & T-18A (Cont.)

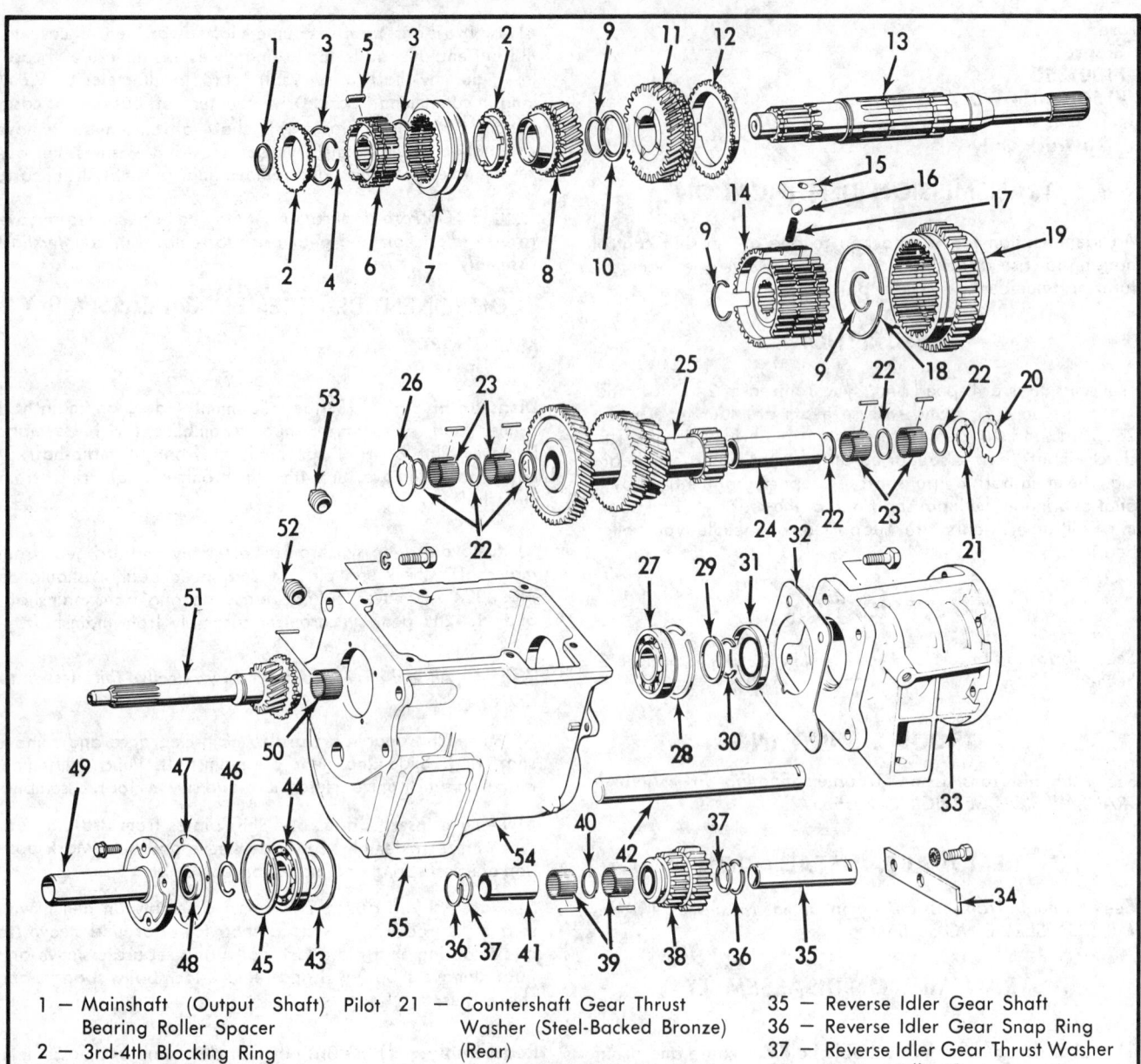

1 — Mainshaft (Output Shaft) Pilot Bearing Roller Spacer
2 — 3rd-4th Blocking Ring
3 — 3rd-4th Retaining Ring
4 — 3rd-4th Synchronizer Snap Ring
5 — 3rd-4th Shifting Plate (3)
6 — 3rd-4th Clutch Hub
7 — 3rd-4th Clutch Sleeve
8 — 3rd Gear
9 — Mainshaft Snap Ring
10 — 2nd Gear Thrust Washer
11 — 2nd Gear
12 — 2nd Gear Blocking Ring
13 — Mainshaft (Output Shaft)
14 — 1st-2nd Clutch Hub
15 — 1st-2nd Shifting Plate (3)
16 — Poppet Ball
17 — Poppet Spring
18 — 1st-2nd Insert Ring
19 — 1st-2nd Clutch Sleeve
20 — Countershaft Gear Thrust Washer (Steel) (Rear)

21 — Countershaft Gear Thrust Washer (Steel-Backed Bronze) (Rear)
22 — Countershaft Gear Bearing Washer
23 — Countershaft Gear Bearing Rollers (88)
24 — Countershaft Gear Bearing Spacer
25 — Countershaft Gear
26 — Countershaft Gear Thrust Washer (Front)
27 — Rear Bearing
28 — Rear Bearing Locating Snap Ring
29 — Rear Bearing Spacer Ring
30 — Rear Bearing Snap Ring
31 — Adapter Plate Seal
32 — Adapter Plate To Transmission Gasket
33 — Transmission Adapter
34 — Countershaft-Reverse Idler Shaft Lockplate

35 — Reverse Idler Gear Shaft
36 — Reverse Idler Gear Snap Ring
37 — Reverse Idler Gear Thrust Washer
38 — Reverse Idler Gear
39 — Reverse Idler Gear Bearing Rollers (74)
40 — Reverse Idler Gear Bearing Washer
41 — Reverse Idler Shaft Sleeve
42 — Countershaft
43 — Front Bearing Retainer Washer
44 — Front Bearing
45 — Front Bearing Locating Snap Ring
46 — Front Bearing Lock Ring
47 — Front Bearing Cap Gasket
48 — Front Bearing Cup Seal
49 — Front Bearing Cap
50 — Mainshaft Pilot Bearing Rollers
51 — Clutch Shaft
52 — Drain Plug
53 — Filler Plug
54 — Transmission Case
55 — P.T.O. (Side) Cover and Gasket

**Fig. 1 Exploded View of Warner Model T-18A 4-Speed Transmission
(Jeep Model Shown, Ford Model Similar)**

WARNER T-18 & T-18A (Cont.)

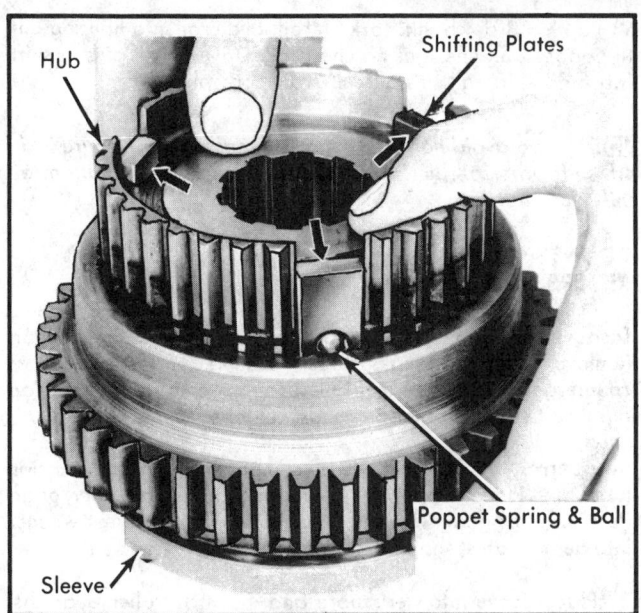

Fig. 2   Assembling 1st-2nd Gear Synchronizer

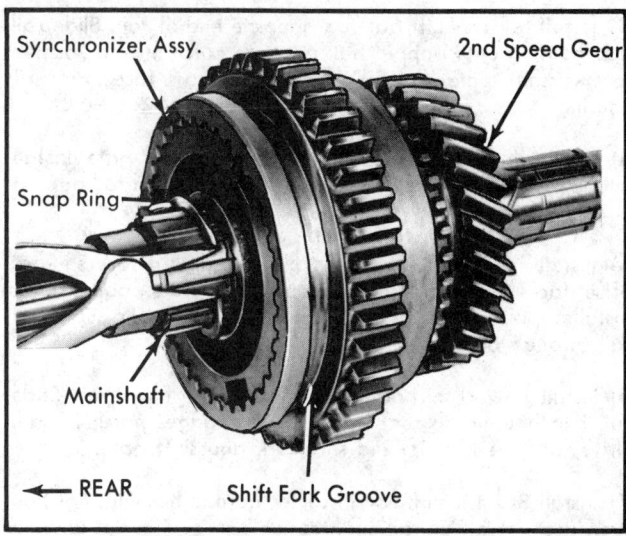

Fig. 4   Installing 1st-2nd Gear Synchronizer Snap Ring

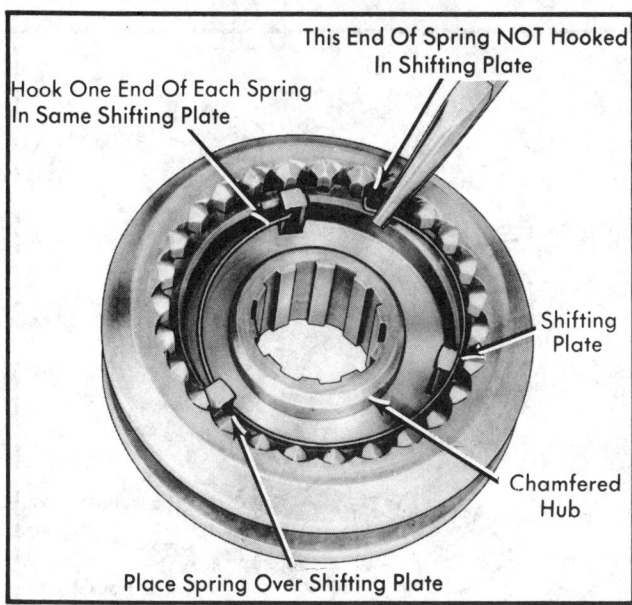

Fig. 3   Assembling 3rd-4th Gear Synchronizer

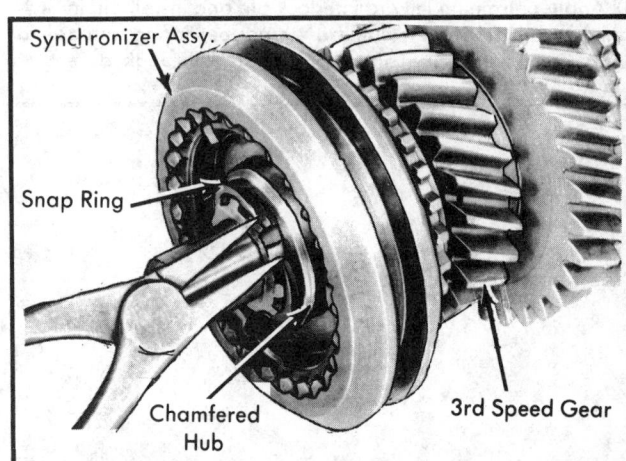

Fig. 5   Installing 3rd-4th Gear Synchronizer Snap Ring

6) Slide 2nd gear and thrust washer on front of mainshaft, making sure step bore of thrust washer is toward front. Install snap ring, positioning step bore of thrust washer over snap ring.

7) From rear of mainshaft, install 2nd gear rear snap ring, blocking ring, 1st-2nd gear synchronizer assembly and snap ring. Make sure 1st-2nd gear synchronizer shift fork groove faces rear of mainshaft.

8) Install 3rd gear, blocking ring, 3rd-4th synchronizer assembly, snap ring, and main drive gear roller bearing thrust washer. Make sure 3rd-4th gear synchronizer chamfered side of hub is facing front of mainshaft.

GEAR SHIFT CONTROL HOUSING

Disassembly — 1) Unscrew shift lever cap. Remove cap, gasket (if equipped), spring seat, spring and shift lever as an assembly. Remove shift lever locating pins from housing.

2) Place housing in a vise with shift forks facing up. Remove back-up light switch and TCS switch (if equipped). Using a hammer and a punch, remove shift rail bore plugs.

3) Move shift rails to neutral position. Drive out roll pins that secure shift gates to shift rails.

4) Place tape over poppet ball holes to prevent losing balls or springs during disassembly. Drive shift rails out of housing using a hammer and a punch.

5) Remove interlock pin from 3rd-4th shift rail. Remove shift forks and shift gates. Note location of forks and gates for reassembly.

6) Remove poppet balls and springs from housing. Remove interlock plungers from housing. Remove retaining clip from reverse shift gate. Remove spring and plunger from gate.

Reassembly — 1) Replace breather in housing if damaged or restricted. Install spring and plunger in reverse shift gate. Compress spring by hand and install retaining clip.

2) Install reverse shift rail into housing. Position reverse shift fork on rail. Slide rail up to shift rail poppet bore. Install poppet spring and ball in bore. Compress spring and slide rail through bore.

WARNER T-18 & T-18A (Cont.)

3) Install reverse shift gate on opposite end of rail. Slide rail into housing until poppet ball engages notch in rail. Position reverse shift gate so that plunger pin boss faces rear of housing.

4) Drive roll pins into reverse shift fork and shift gate. Install interlock plungers in pockets between housing shift rail poppet bores.

5) Install 1st-2nd shift rail. Install 1st-2nd shift fork so fork offset faces rear of housing. Slide shift rail up to poppet bore. Install poppet spring and ball. Compress spring and slide shift rail through bore.

6) Install 1st-2nd shift gate on opposite end of shift rail. Slide rail into housing so that poppet ball engages notch in rail. Drive roll pins into 1st-2nd shift fork and shift gate.

7) Install 3rd-4th shift rail in center bore in housing. Position 3rd-4th shift gate on rail and position gate so that flat tang on gate faces front of housing.

8) Apply petroleum jelly to interlock pin and install pin in 3rd-4th shift rail pin bore. Install 3rd-4th poppet spring and ball in bore. Compress spring and slide shift rail through bore.

9) Position 3rd-4th shift fork on rail. Slide rail into housing until poppet ball engages notch in rail. Drive in roll pins in shift fork and shift rail. Install shift rail bore plugs.

NOTE — *To avoid hard shifting after reassembly, be sure 3rd-4th shift gate roll pin is installed so it is flush with bottom of shift gate notch.*

COUNTERGEAR & REVERSE IDLER GEAR

Disassembly — Remove arbor tool from countergear. Remove roller bearings, thrust washers and spacer from countergear. Remove snap rings from reverse idler gear. Tap out thrust washer, roller bearings, center spacer, and sleeve.

Reassembly — 1) Lubricate all components with transmission lubricant. Place snap ring in one end of reverse idler gear. Position idler gear with snap ring down. Insert thrust washer into gear against snap ring.

2) Place sleeve into gear bore and insert 37 roller bearings. Install spacer and 37 more roller bearings. Install second thrust washer and snap ring.

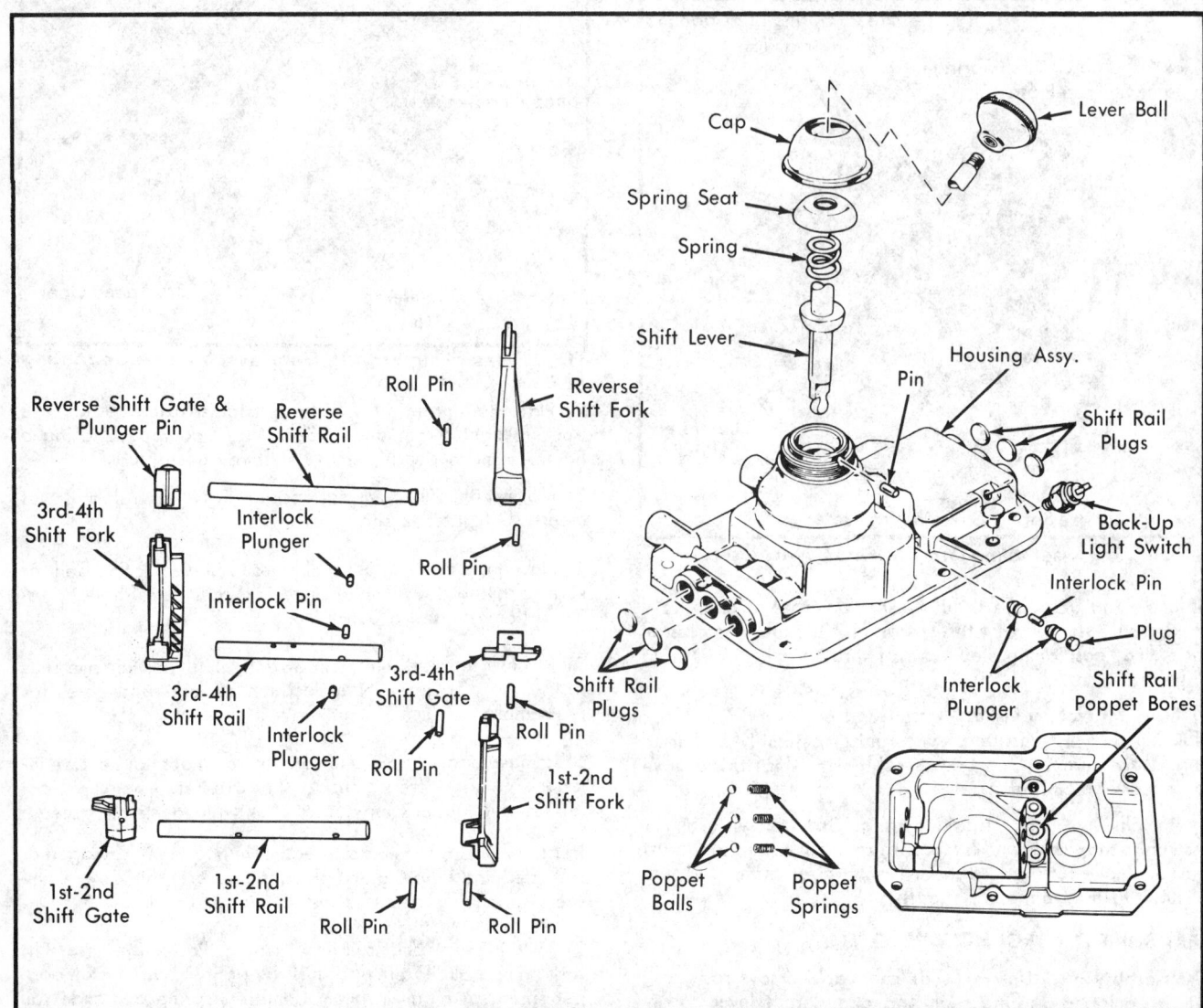

Fig. 6 Exploded View of Gear Shift Control Housing

WARNER T-18 & T-18A (Cont.)

3) Install sleeve and arbor into countergear. Place one spacer ring over arbor against spacer sleeve. Insert 22 roller bearings and slide on second spacer ring. Insert 22 more roller bearings and third spacer ring. Repeat same operation at opposite end of countergear. Leave arbor installed in gear.

TRANSMISSION REASSEMBLY

1) Lubricate all components with transmission lubricant before assembly. Place both countergear thrust washers in case. Place countergear into position (with arbor still installed). Care must be taken not to move thrust washers or roller bearings out of position.

2) Carefully drive countergear shaft into place while driving arbor shaft out rear of transmission case. Make sure slot in countergear shaft is positioned so that it can be engaged by retaining plate.

3) Check countergear end play. It may be necessary to remove countergear and install thicker or thinner snap rings to obtain correct countergear end play.

4) Place reverse idler gear in position in case (larger gear end must face rear of case). Install reverse idler shaft from rear of case. Make sure shaft is positioned so that slot can be engaged by retaining plate. Install countershaft and reverse idler gear shaft retaining plate.

5) Install the 22 pilot roller bearings in inner end of input shaft. Use grease to hold bearings in place. Place input shaft in case. Place 4th gear synchronizer blocking ring on input shaft. Install mainshaft in transmission case, taking care not to move pilot bearings out of position.

6) Install input shaft oil baffle. Temporarily install front bearing cap or suitable tool (T75L-7025-Q) on transmission input shaft to hold shaft in place while installing mainshaft bearing. Install snap ring on mainshaft bearing and drive bearing into case until snap ring is seated.

7) Remove bearing cap or holding tool. Install input shaft bearing washer, with dished side of washer facing mainshaft. Install bearing on shaft and into bearing bore in case. Drive bearing into place against input shaft gear and washer.

CAUTION – *Avoid wedging blocking ring on its mating tapered surface during front bearing installation.*

8) Install thickest of 4 available snap rings in input shaft groove. Pull input shaft bearing out of case just far enough to install bearing locating snap ring. Install bearing retainer with new gasket and tighten bolts to specification.

9) On 4-WD models, install rear oil seal in transfer case adapter. Lip of seal must face toward transfer case. *See Fig. 7.* Install adapter plate with new gasket. Use nonhardening sealer on bolts. Install adapter housing and tighten to specifications.

10) On 2-WD models, install speedometer drive gear and spacer (if equipped) over mainshaft lock ball. Install snap ring. Install rear bearing retainer or extension housing with new gasket. Tighten bolts to specification.

11) On all models, lock transmission in 2 gears. On 2-WD models, install "U" joint flange, and tighten nut to specification. On 4-WD models, install transfer case drive gear spacer, drive gear, flat washer and lock nut. Tighten nut to specification.

NOTE – *Use nonhardening sealer on all case and cover bolts.*

12) Move synchronizer sleeves to Neutral position. Install power take-off (side) cover and gasket (if removed). Install new shift housing gasket on transmission. Place shift housing into position, making sure that shift forks engage grooves in synchronizing hubs. Install bolts and tighten to specificaton. Fill transmission to proper level with specified lubricant and shift through all gears to check operation.

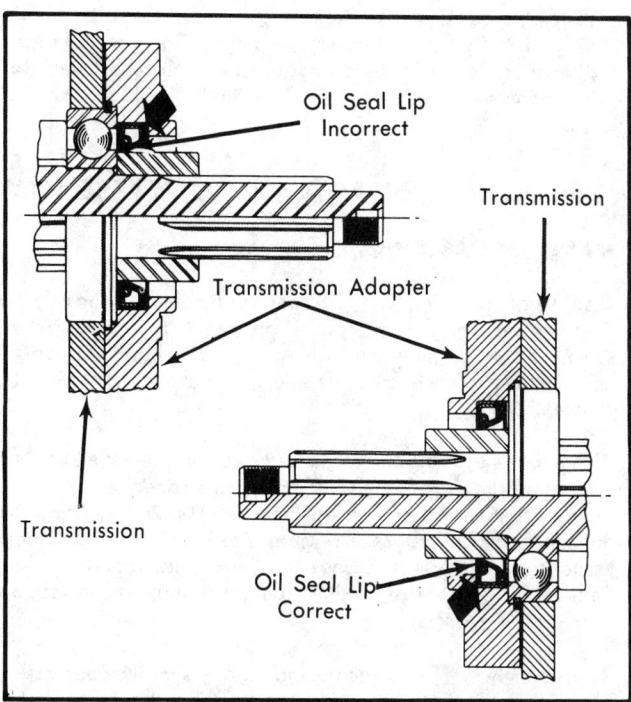

Fig. 7 Transmission Case Oil Seal Position

TIGHTENING SPECIFICATIONS

Application	Ft. Lbs.
Input Shaft Bearing Retainer	10-15
Shift Housing-to-Case	12
"U" Joint Flange Nut (Ford)	75-110
Transfer Case Gear Nut (Jeep)	150
Transfer Case Adapter-to-Case (Jeep)	30
Extension Housing (Ford)	15
P.T.O. Cover Bolts (Ford)	25-35
All Others	12
Mainshaft Rear Retainer Bolts	
3/8"	25-35
1/2"	40-50
Countershaft Rear Retainer	25-35

WARNER T-176

Jeep
6-Cylinder and
V8 Models Except
J-20 Trucks

TRANSMISSION IDENTIFICATION

Transmission identification tag which shows Jeep part number, is attached to transmission shift control housing by one of the mounting bolts.

DESCRIPTION

Transmission is a 4-speed unit, fully synchronized in all forward gears. All forward gears are constant mesh helical cut type gears and speed changes are accomplished through use of blocker type synchronizer assemblies. Input and mainshaft are supported by ball bearings in front and rear of case. All other gears are supported by needle type roller bearings. Gear shift is controlled through top mounted, cane type shifter assembly.

LUBRICATION

See Lubrication in MANUAL TRANSMISSION SERVICING Section.

TROUBLE SHOOTING

See Manual Transmission Trouble Shooting in MANUAL TRANSMISSION SERVICING Section.

REMOVAL & INSTALLATION

See Manual Transmission Removal in MANUAL TRANSMISSION SERVICING Section.

TRANSMISSION DISASSEMBLY

NOTE — Two shift control housing bolts are dowel type. Mark location of these bolts on housing for reassembly.

1) Remove bolts attaching transfer case to transmission, remove transfer case. Remove shift control housing assembly (if not removed during transmission removal). Using suitable arbor tool (J-29342), remove countershaft by tapping out rear of case and let countergear lie at bottom of case.

2) Remove locating ring and retaining snap ring from rear bearing. Remove rear bearing using suitable puller (J-25152). Punch alignment marks in front bearing retainer and case for reassembly. Remove front bearing retainer and gasket. Remove and discard front bearing retainer oil seal.

3) Remove locating ring and retaining snap ring from front bearing. Remove input shaft and front bearing using suitable puller and adapter (J-25152 & J-29344). Remove 3rd-4th blocking ring from clutch (input) shaft or synchronizer hub. Remove mainshaft pilot bearing rollers from clutch (input) shaft.

4) Position 3rd-4th synchronizer sleeve rearward to 3rd gear position and lift front end of shaft upward and remove mainshaft assembly from case. Remove countershaft gear, arbor tool, thrust washers and any needle bearing rollers that may have fallen into case.

5) Working through front of case, tap reverse idler shaft out rear of case until roll pin clears case, then remove shaft. Remove reverse idler gear and thrust washers from case. Remove needle bearings and bearing retainers from gear assembly. Remove sliding gear from idler gear noting position for reassembly.

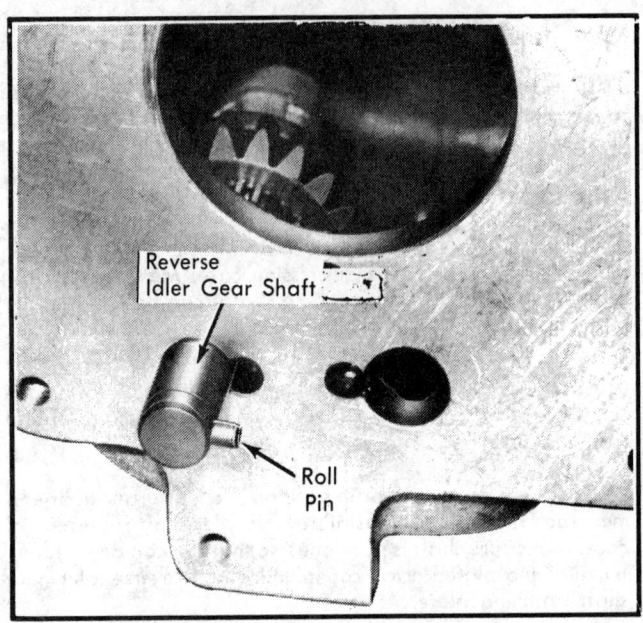

Fig. 1   Removing Reverse Idler Gear Shaft

CLEANING & INSPECTION

Wash all parts in cleaning solvent and dry with compressed air (except bearings). Let bearings air dry in clean shop cloth. Inspect transmission case for cracks, damaged bearing bores, or damaged threads. Remove all small nicks or burrs from front or rear of case. Check ball bearings for roughness by slowly turning race by hand. Inspect needle bearing rollers, shafts and washers for wear or damage. Check all other parts for wear, damage, chipped or broken teeth. Replace parts as necessary.

COMPONENT DISASSEMBLY & REASSEMBLY

MAINSHAFT ASSEMBLY

Disassembly — **1)** Mark sleeves and hubs for reassembly. Remove snap ring from front of mainshaft and slide 3rd-4th synchronizer assembly and 3rd gear from shaft. On 3rd-4th synchronizer, slide hub out of sleeve, remove insert springs for reassembly.

2) Remove snap ring retaining 2nd gear and remove 2nd gear and blocking ring from shaft. Remove tabbed washer from mainshaft. Remove snap ring retaining 1st-2nd synchronizer hub and remove hub, reverse gear and sleeve as an assembly. Remove insert springs, 3 inserts, sleeve and gear from hub. Remove 1st gear thrust washer from shaft and remove 1st gear and blocking ring.

Reassembly — **1)** Lubricate mainshaft, synchronizer assemblies and gear bores with transmission lubricant. Align reassembly marks and assemble 1st-2nd synchronizer hub,

WARNER T-176 (Cont.)

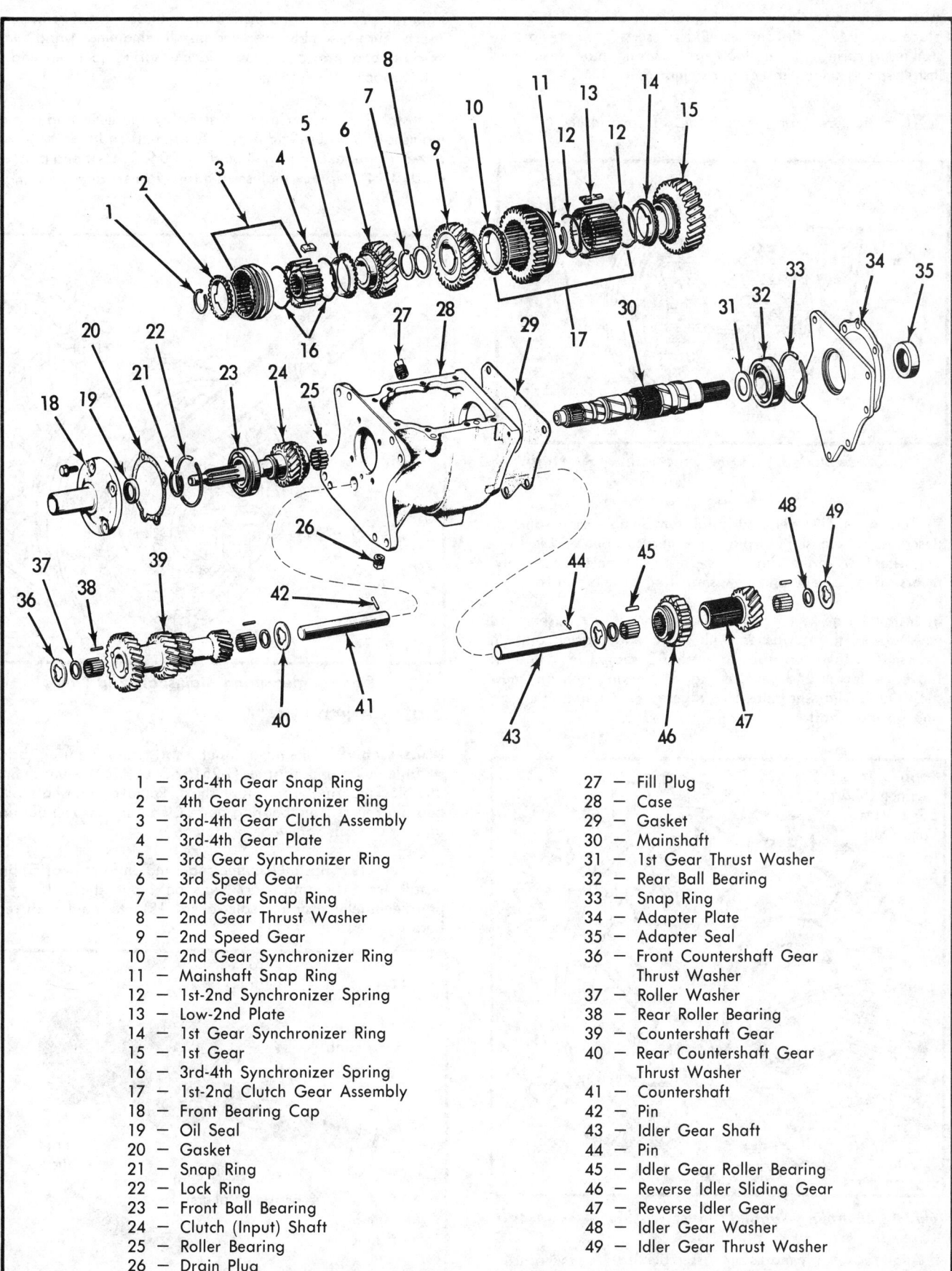

1 — 3rd-4th Gear Snap Ring	27 — Fill Plug
2 — 4th Gear Synchronizer Ring	28 — Case
3 — 3rd-4th Gear Clutch Assembly	29 — Gasket
4 — 3rd-4th Gear Plate	30 — Mainshaft
5 — 3rd Gear Synchronizer Ring	31 — 1st Gear Thrust Washer
6 — 3rd Speed Gear	32 — Rear Ball Bearing
7 — 2nd Gear Snap Ring	33 — Snap Ring
8 — 2nd Gear Thrust Washer	34 — Adapter Plate
9 — 2nd Speed Gear	35 — Adapter Seal
10 — 2nd Gear Synchronizer Ring	36 — Front Countershaft Gear Thrust Washer
11 — Mainshaft Snap Ring	37 — Roller Washer
12 — 1st-2nd Synchronizer Spring	38 — Rear Roller Bearing
13 — Low-2nd Plate	39 — Countershaft Gear
14 — 1st Gear Synchronizer Ring	40 — Rear Countershaft Gear Thrust Washer
15 — 1st Gear	41 — Countershaft
16 — 3rd-4th Synchronizer Spring	42 — Pin
17 — 1st-2nd Clutch Gear Assembly	43 — Idler Gear Shaft
18 — Front Bearing Cap	44 — Pin
19 — Oil Seal	45 — Idler Gear Roller Bearing
20 — Gasket	46 — Reverse Idler Sliding Gear
21 — Snap Ring	47 — Reverse Idler Gear
22 — Lock Ring	48 — Idler Gear Washer
23 — Front Ball Bearing	49 — Idler Gear Thrust Washer
24 — Clutch (Input) Shaft	
25 — Roller Bearing	
26 — Drain Plug	

Fig. 2 Disassembled View of Warner T-176 4-Speed Manual Transmission

WARNER T-176 (Cont.)

reverse gear and sleeve. Install gear and sleeve on hub and place assembly on flat surface. Place inserts into hub slots, install insert spring, placing loop end of spring in one insert and install spring under lips of remaining inserts.

NOTE — *Be sure spring is under lip of each insert.*

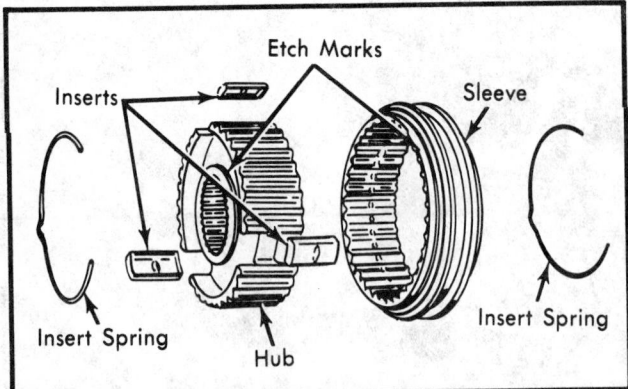

Fig. 3   Exploded View of Synchronizer Assembly

2) Turn assembly over and install remaining spring same as described previously, but placing spring so open end is 180° opposite first spring. Install 1st-2nd synchronizer assembly, reverse gear, sleeve and new snap ring on mainshaft.

3) Install 1st gear, 1st gear blocking ring, thrust washer and new tabbed thrust washer (with sharp edge facing out) on mainshaft. Make sure tabbed washer is seated in mainshaft tab bore. Install 2nd gear, 2nd gear blocking ring and new snap ring on mainshaft. Install 3rd gear and 3rd gear blocking ring on mainshaft.

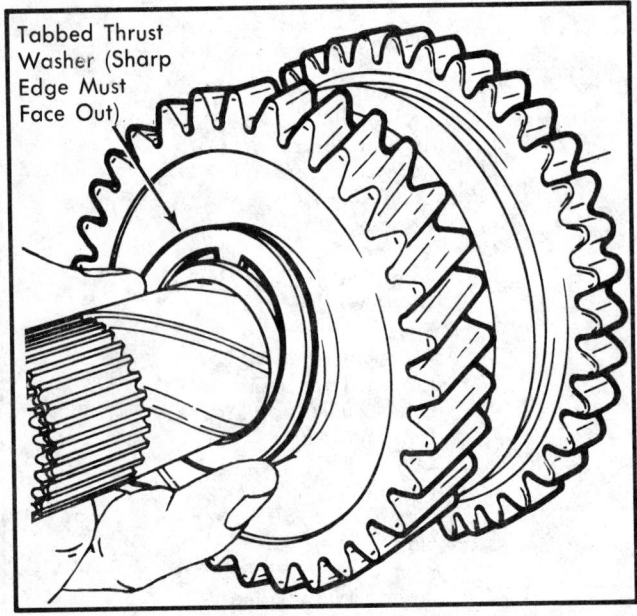

Fig. 4   Installing Tabbed Thrust Washer in Mainshaft

4) Align reassembly marks and assemble 3rd-4th synchronizer hub and sleeve. Place assembly on flat surface and place inserts into hub slots, install insert spring, placing loop end of

spring in one insert and install spring under lips of remaining inserts. Turn assembly over and install remaining spring same as described previously, but placing spring so open end is 180° opposite first spring.

5) Install 3rd-4th synchronizer assembly and new snap ring on mainshaft. Measure end play between hub and snap ring with a feeler gauge. End play should be .004-.014". If end play exceeds .014", replace mainshaft thrust washers and snap rings.

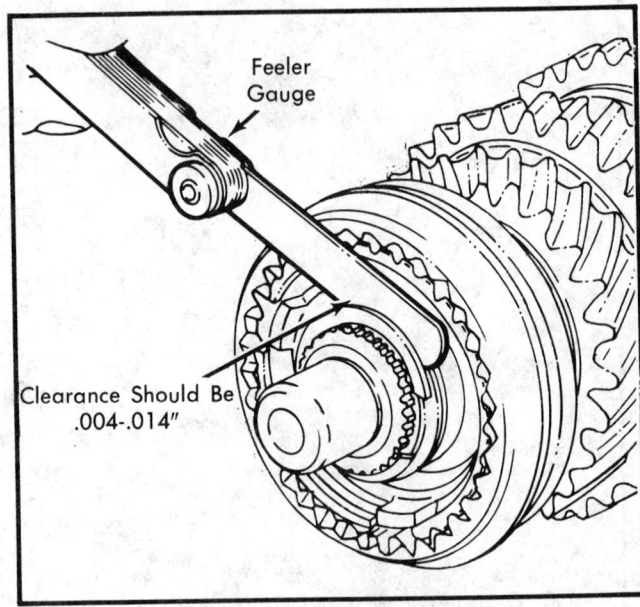

Fig. 5   Measuring Mainshaft End Play

CLUTCH (INPUT) SHAFT

Disassembly — Remove input shaft front bearing using suitable puller and adapter (J-25152 & J-29344). Remove 3rd-4th blocking ring from input shaft. Remove mainshaft pilot bearing rollers from bearing bore. Clean and inspect bearing and input shaft for wear or damage.

Reassembly — Install locating snap ring on front bearing and install front bearing part way on input shaft. Using a petroleum jelly, install needle rollers (15) into input shaft rear bearing bore.

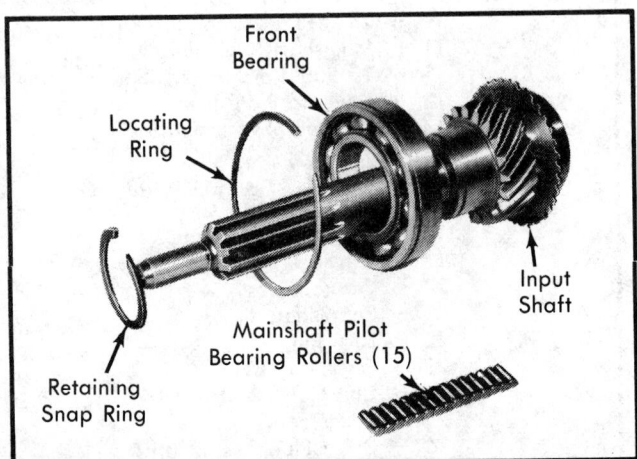

Fig. 6   Clutch (Input) Shaft & Bearing Assembly

WARNER T-176 (Cont.)

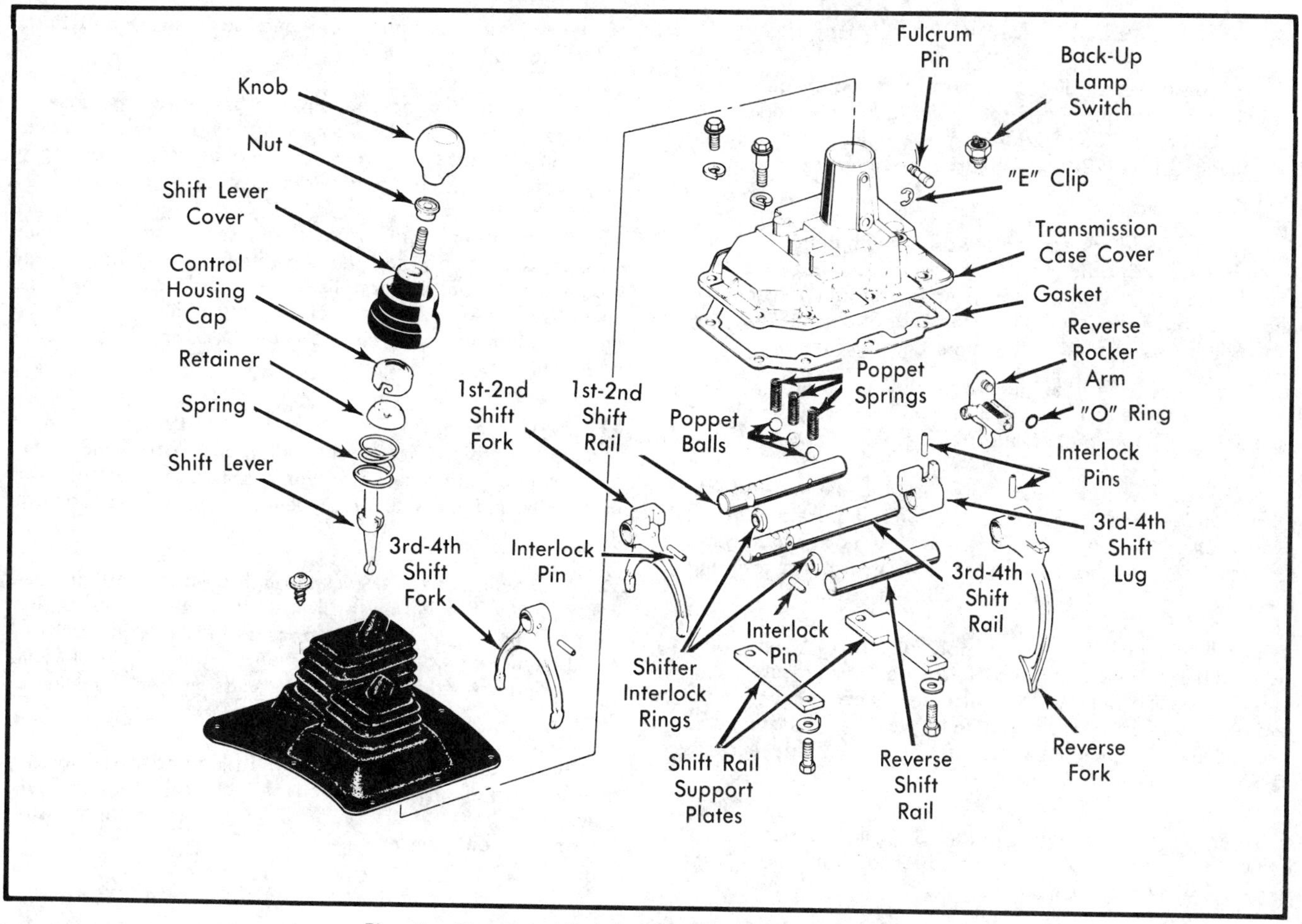

Knob
Nut
Shift Lever Cover
Control Housing Cap
Retainer
Spring
Shift Lever
3rd-4th Shift Fork
1st-2nd Shift Fork
1st-2nd Shift Rail
Interlock Pin
Poppet Balls
Fulcrum Pin
Back-Up Lamp Switch
"E" Clip
Transmission Case Cover
Gasket
Reverse Rocker Arm
"O" Ring
Interlock Pins
Poppet Springs
3rd-4th Shift Lug
3rd-4th Shift Rail
Reverse Fork
Reverse Shift Rail
Interlock Pin
Shift Rail Support Plates
Shifter Interlock Rings

Fig. 7 Disassembled View of Shift Control Housing

SHIFT CONTROL HOUSING

Disassembly — 1) Remove shift lever cover, control housing cap, retainer, shift lever and spring. Position transmission case cover in vise so shift forks are facing upward. Use wooden blocks to protect cover.

2) Place shift rails in Neutral position and carefully remove shift forks and rails, noting position of components for reassembly. Remove poppet balls and springs, remove roll pins attaching shift forks to shift rails and remove shift forks.

CAUTION — *DO NOT lose poppet balls when shift rails are removed.*

Reassembly — 1) With transmission case cover in vise, lubricate shift rails and rail grooves with petroleum jelly. Install poppet springs and balls (one on each spring). Position reverse gear shift rail and fork on reverse rocker arm in cover.

NOTE — *Be sure notch on shift rail is positioned over reverse poppet ball and that reverse rocker arm is engaged in reverse fork slot.*

2) Install 3rd-4th shift rail and shift fork in cover. Be sure interlock pin is in position in shift rail. Install 1st-2nd shift rail and shift fork. Be sure rail notch is over poppet ball. Install shifter interlock rings in cover and between poppet balls.

3) Press downward evenly on rails to compress poppet balls and springs. Position shift rail retaining plates on housing and secure with bolts and tabbed washers.

4) Tighten bolts to 12-15 ft. lbs. and check tabbed washer position before bending over tabs. Check shift rail operation. Install shift lever, spring, spring retainer, and control housing cap.

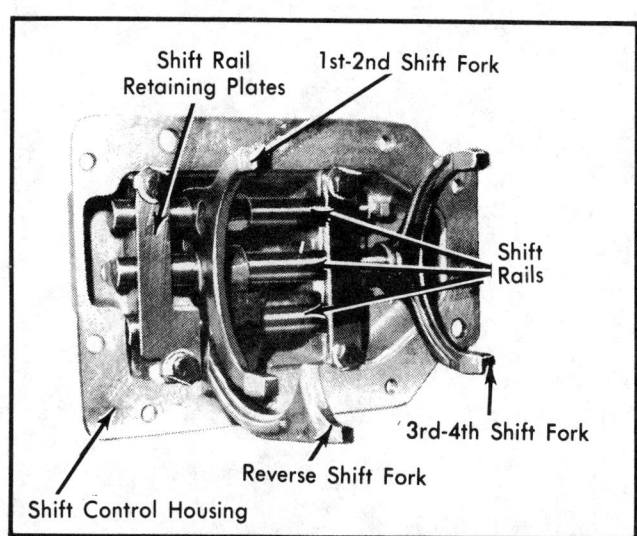

Shift Rail Retaining Plates
1st-2nd Shift Fork
Shift Rails
3rd-4th Shift Fork
Reverse Shift Fork
Shift Control Housing

Fig. 8 Assembled View of Shift Control Housing

WARNER T-176 (Cont.)

TRANSMISSION REASSEMBLY

1) Lubricate reverse idler gear bore and sliding gear with transmission lubricant and install sliding gear on reverse idler gear. Install arbor tool (J-29343) in reverse idler gear and install needle rollers (22) and 1 bearing retainer at each end of gear.

2) Coat reverse idler gear thrust washers with petroleum jelly, place in case with flats of washers facing mainshaft and tabs engaging slots in case. Install reverse idler gear assembly, align gear bore and install shaft from rear of case making sure shaft roll pin is aligned with counterbore in case.

3) Measure reverse idler gear end play by inserting feeler gauge between thrust washer and gear. End play should be .004-.018". If end play exceeds .018", replace thrust washers.

4) Coat countershaft gear bore and needle rollers with petroleum jelly. Insert arbor tool (J-29342) in bore and install needle rollers (21) and 1 bearing retainer at each end of gear. Coat countershaft gear thrust washers with petroleum jelly and place in case with tabs engaging slots in case.

5) Install countershaft gear assembly, align gear bore and install shaft from rear, part way into case, making sure arbor tool enters shaft bore at front of case. Measure countergear end play by inserting feeler gauge between thrust washer and gear. End play should be .004-.018". If end play exceeds .018", replace thrust washers.

6) After correct end play is obtained, push arbor tool back into countergear, remove shaft at rear of case and allow countergear to lie at bottom of case.

NOTE — *Countergear must remain at bottom of case to provide clearance for installation of mainshaft assembly.*

7) Install mainshaft assembly in case, making sure synchronizers are in Neutral position. Coat 3rd-4th blocking ring with transmission lubricant and install on input shaft. Support mainshaft assembly and install input shaft through front bearing bore in case.

8) Align and seat mainshaft pilot hub in input shaft bore and tap front bearing and input shaft into case using rawhide (or equivalent) mallet. Install front bearing retainer and bolts, tightening bolts finger tight.

9) Position rear bearing on mainshaft and install into case using suitable tool (J-29345). Remove tool and complete installation using rawhide (or equivalent) mallet. When bearing is fully seated, install bearing retaining snap ring.

10) Remove front bearing retainer and seat front bearing fully on input shaft and install bearing retaining snap ring. Apply sealer to front bearing retainer gasket and position on case. Install front bearing retainer oil seal in retainer and position on case aligning notch with oil drain back hole. Install bolts and tighten to specifications.

11) Install locating ring on rear bearing and reseat bearing if necessary. Position case on end with input shaft facing down. Align countershaft gear bores with thrust washers, install shaft from rear and tap into place being careful not to damage thrust washers.

12) Shift synchronizer sleeves through all gear positions and make sure no binding exists. If input shaft and mainshaft appear to bind in Neutral position, check blocking rings for any possibly sticking on tapered portion of gears. Free blocking rings using screwdriver. Place transmission back in Neutral position.

13) Install new shift control housing gasket and install housing assembly. Install and tighten bolts to specification making sure dowel type bolts (2) are placed in their correct holes. Install transmission on transfer case.

TIGHTENING SPECIFICATIONS

Application	Ft. Lbs.
Backup Light Switch	15
Drain & Filler Plugs	15
Front Bearing Retainer Bolts	13
Shift Control Housing	13

Section 16
TRANSFER CASES

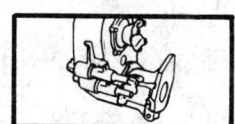

Contents

NOTE — ALSO SEE GENERAL INDEX.

IMPORTANT

Because of the great number of model names used by vehicle manufacturers, accurate identification of models is important.
See Model Identification at the front of this publication.

Trouble Shooting

TRANSFER CASE TROUBLE SHOOTING

CONDITION & POSSIBLE CAUSE	CONDITION & POSSIBLE CAUSE
Hard Shifting or Will Not Shift • Shift linkage loose or improperly adjusted. • Lack of lubricant in shift linkage. • Shift linkage jammed with road dirt. • Shifter shafts or shift rail binding in case. • Shift fork bent. • Shifting detent ball scored. • Control lever bracket or stabilizer loose. • Stabilizer bracket-to-shift lever bolt too tight. • Low lubricant level or incorrect type. • Internal components binding, worn or damaged. • Vehicle speed too high. • Vehicle operated for extended period in 4-WD on dry pavement.	**Slips Out of Either "LOC" Position** • Shift linkage out of adjustment. • Detent springs weak, broken or missing. • Detent ball worn or missing. • Detent plug loose. • Shift rail detent notches worn. • Shift forks worn or bent. • Thrust washers worn or broken. • Gears or sliding clutch gears damaged or worn.
Excessive Noise • Low lubricant level or incorrect type. • Incorrect tire pressure. • Wrong type wheels and/or tires. • Bearing, chain, or gears worn or damaged. • Propeller shafts or "U" joints misaligned. • "U" joint yoke bolts loose. • Adapter bolts loose.	**Backlash** • Improper adjustment of stabilizer and/or control rods. • Companion yoke loose. • Transfer case loose on mounting bolts. • Adapter bolts loose. • Worn or damaged internal components.
Front-Wheel Drive Disengages • Improper linkage adjustment. • De-clutch lever rod improperly adjusted. • Shift linkage loose or binding. • Range fork cracked. • Inserts worn or binding on shift rail. • Gears or sliding clutch gears worn or damaged. • Annulus gear and/or lock plate worn or damaged. • Shift rail poppet ball or spring missing or worn. • Excessive end play in front output shaft. • Worn detent notches in shift rail. • Shift fork worn or bent.	**Lubricant Leakage** • Case overfilled. • Vent clogged. • Output shaft or yoke seals worn. • Incorrect type lubricant. • Seal contact surfaces on companion shaft loose. • Cracked case. • Loose or damaged bearings. • Seals installed incorrectly. **Overheating** • Lubricant level too high or low. • Bearings too tight.

BORG-WARNER 1345

Ford

DESCRIPTION

Transfer case is a 2-piece part time unit, using planetary gearing, a chain drive, and an aluminum case. The unit is lubricated by a positive displacement oil pump that channels oil flow through drilled holes in rear output shaft. Pump turns with the rear output shaft and allows towing of the vehicle for extended distances without disconnecting rear propeller shaft.

LUBRICATION

SERVICE INTERVALS

Check fluid level whenever malfunction is suspected or fluid leakage or contamination is observed. Also check after operation in water.

FLUID TYPE

Use fluid labeled Dextron II Automatic Transmission Fluid.

CAPACITY

Capacity is 6.5 pints.

ADJUSTMENTS

Adjust shift linkage so that all positions may be selected without interference or binding. Inspect all swivels, rods and mountings for wear or damage, and replace as necessary.

REMOVAL & INSTALLATION

TRANSFER CASE

Removal – 1) Raise and support vehicle. Drain fluid from case. Disconnect 4-WD indicator switch wire connector at transfer case. Remove skid plate from frame (if equipped). Disconnect front propeller shaft from front output yoke.

2) Disconnect rear propeller shaft from rear output shaft yoke. Disconnect speedometer driven gear from transfer case rear bearing retainer. Remove retaining clips and shift rod from transfer case control lever and transfer case shift lever. Disconnect vent hose from transfer case.

3) Remove heat shield from engine mount bracket and transfer case, taking care not to get burned on catalytic converter. Support transfer case with a transmission jack. Remove bolts retaining transfer case to transmission adapter.

4) Slide transfer case rearward off of transmission output shaft and lower transfer case from vehicle. Remove gasket between transfer case and adapter.

Installation – 1) Install heat shield on transfer case (if equipped). Place a new gasket between transfer case and adapter. Raise transfer case with a transmission jack so transmission output shaft aligns with splined transfer case input shaft.

2) Slide transfer case forward onto transmission output shaft and onto the aluminum pin. Install bolts retaining transfer case to adapter and tighten. Remove transmission jack from transfer case. Connect rear propeller shaft to rear output shaft yoke and tighten nuts.

3) Place shift rod on transfer case shift lever and transfer case control rod and attach with retaining rings. Connect speedometer driven gear. Connect 4-WD indicator switch wire connector at transfer case. Connect front propeller shaft to front output yoke and tighten nut.

4) Attach heat shield to engine monting bracket and mounting lug on transfer case (if equipped). Install skid plate to frame and tighten. Install drain plug. Remove filler plug and fill transfer case with appropriate amount of fluid. Lower vehicle.

DISASSEMBLY

TRANSFER CASE

1) Remove transfer case from vehicle and drain fluid. Remove both output shaft yoke nuts and remove output yokes from transfer case. Remove 4-WD indicator switch. Separate cover from case by removing attaching bolts. Pry case and cover apart by inserting a screwdriver in pry bosses.

2) Remove magnetic chip collector from bottom case half. Slide shift collar hub off rear output shaft. Compress shift fork spring and remove upper and lower spring retainers from shaft. See *Fig. 1.*

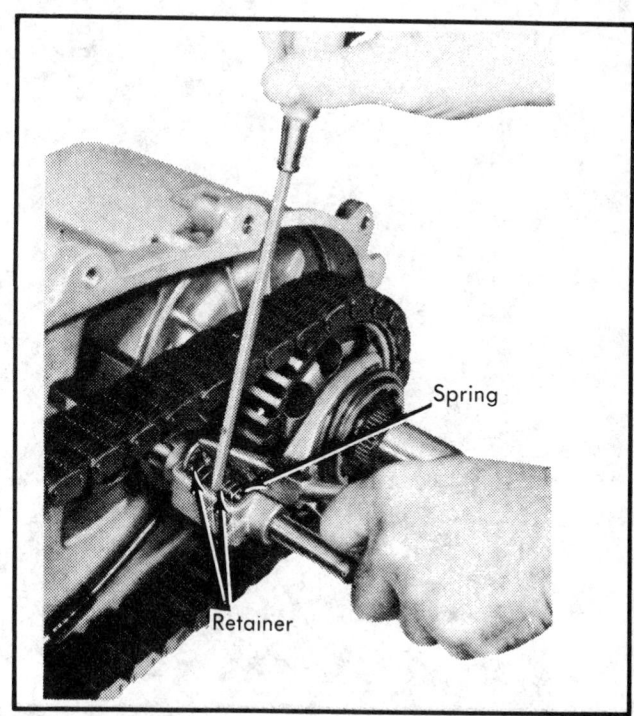

Fig. 1 Removing Spring Retainers

3) Remove 4-WD lockup fork and lockup shift collar from case as an assembly. Take care not to lose nylon wear pads on fork. Remove snap ring and thrust washer from front output shaft. Grip chain and sprockets, and lift straight up to remove drive sprocket, driven sprocket, and chain from ouput shafts.

4) Remove thrust washer from rear output shaft. Remove front output shaft from case. Remove oil pump attaching bolts and remove oil pump, rear cover, pickup tube, pump body and

Transfer Cases

BORG-WARNER 1345 (Cont.)

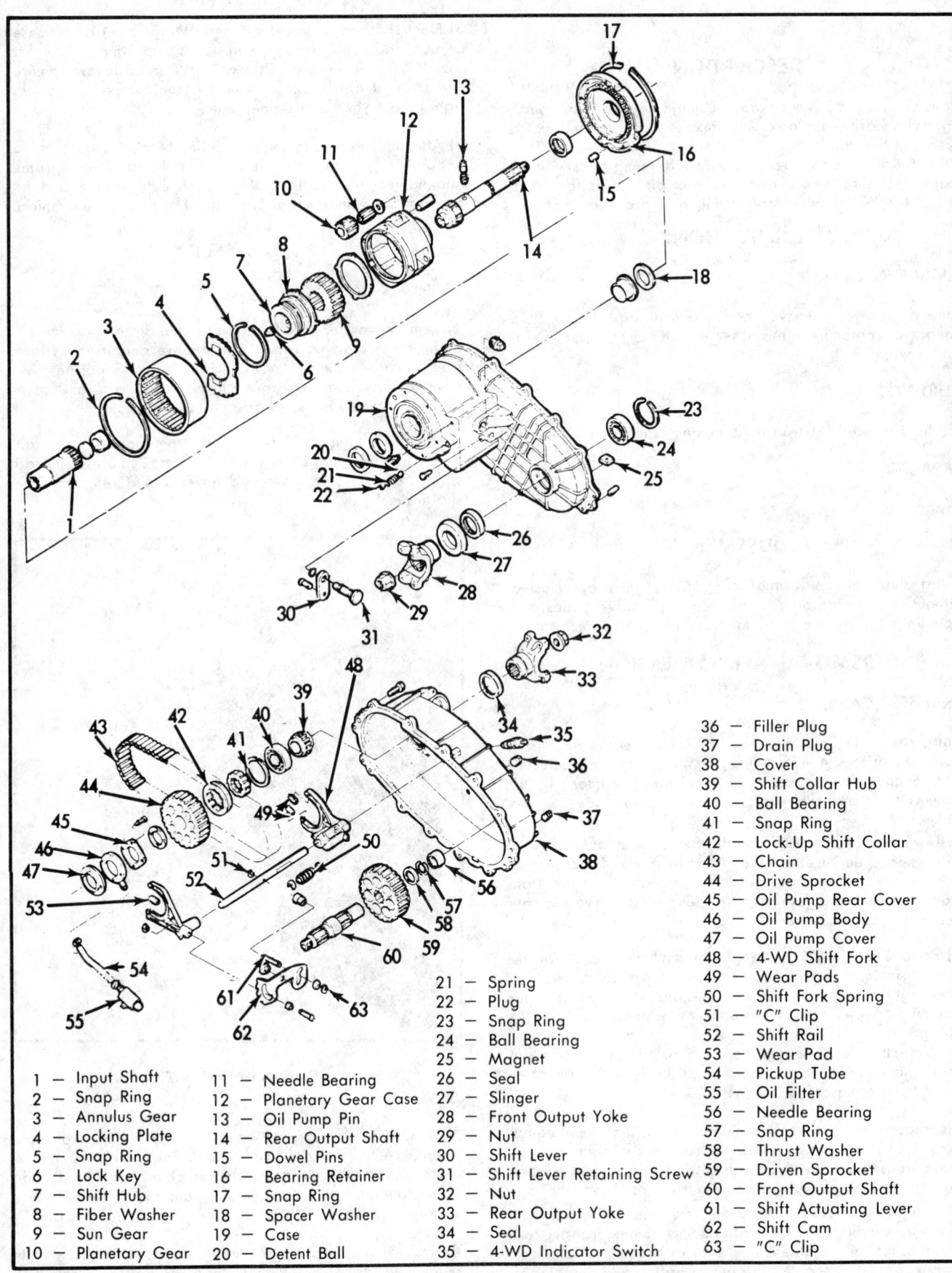

36 — Filler Plug
37 — Drain Plug
38 — Cover
39 — Shift Collar Hub
40 — Ball Bearing
41 — Snap Ring
42 — Lock-Up Shift Collar
43 — Chain
44 — Drive Sprocket
45 — Oil Pump Rear Cover
46 — Oil Pump Body
47 — Oil Pump Cover
48 — 4-WD Shift Fork
49 — Wear Pads
50 — Shift Fork Spring
51 — "C" Clip
52 — Shift Rail
53 — Wear Pad
54 — Pickup Tube
55 — Oil Filter
56 — Needle Bearing
57 — Snap Ring
58 — Thrust Washer
59 — Driven Sprocket
60 — Front Output Shaft
61 — Shift Actuating Lever
62 — Shift Cam
63 — "C" Clip

1 — Input Shaft
2 — Snap Ring
3 — Annulus Gear
4 — Locking Plate
5 — Snap Ring
6 — Lock Key
7 — Shift Hub
8 — Fiber Washer
9 — Sun Gear
10 — Planetary Gear

11 — Needle Bearing
12 — Planetary Gear Case
13 — Oil Pump Pin
14 — Rear Output Shaft
15 — Dowel Pins
16 — Bearing Retainer
17 — Snap Ring
18 — Spacer Washer
19 — Case
20 — Detent Ball

21 — Spring
22 — Plug
23 — Snap Ring
24 — Ball Bearing
25 — Magnet
26 — Seal
27 — Slinger
28 — Front Output Yoke
29 — Nut
30 — Shift Lever
31 — Shift Lever Retaining Screw
32 — Nut
33 — Rear Output Yoke
34 — Seal
35 — 4-WD Indicator Switch

Fig. 2   Exploded View of Borg-Warner Transfer Case

BORG-WARNER 1345 (Cont.)

filter, 2 pump pins, pump spring and oil pump front cover from rear output shaft. Disconnect oil pickup tube from the front of pump body.

5) Remove bearing retainer snap ring from inside case and lift out rear output shaft while tapping on bearing retainer with a plastic hammer. Lift rear output shaft and bearing retainer from case, noting that 2 dowel pins will fall into case.

6) Remove rear output shaft from bearing retainer. If necessary, press needle bearing assembly out from bearing retainer. Remove "C" clip holding shift cam to shift actuating lever inside the case. Remove shift lever retaining screw and remove lever from case. See *Fig. 3.*

Fig. 3   Removing Shift Cam "C" Clip

NOTE — *Shift cam will disengage from shift lever shaft and may release detent ball and spring when removing lever.*

7) Remove planetary gear set, shift rail, shift cam, input shaft and shift forks from case as an assembly. Take care not to loose 2 nylon wear pads on shift fork. See *Fig. 4.* Remove spacer washer from bottom of case, and using a drift, drive plug out from detent spring bore.

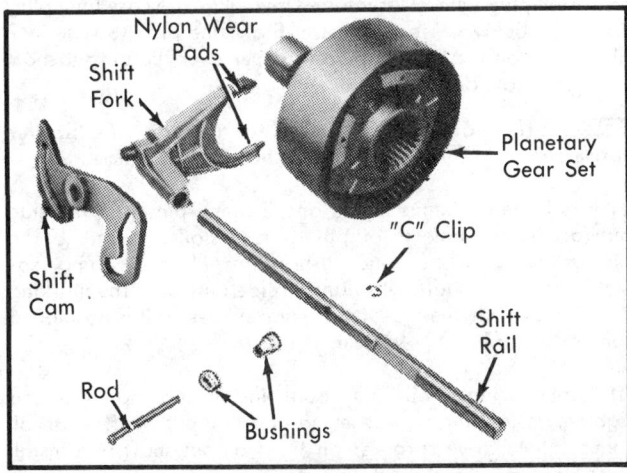

Fig. 4   Shifter Mechanism

PLANETARY GEAR SET

1) Slide input shaft rearward out of planetary gear set. Remove snap ring from annulus gear. Remove shift hub and planetary gear case from annulus gear. Unlock locking plate from hub. See *Fig. 5.*

2) Remove shift hub snap ring. Remove "T" shaped lock key. Lift shift hub from the assembly. Remove outer fiber washer, sun gear and inner fiber washer, rotating inner washer slightly to allow positioning tabs to clear planetary gears.

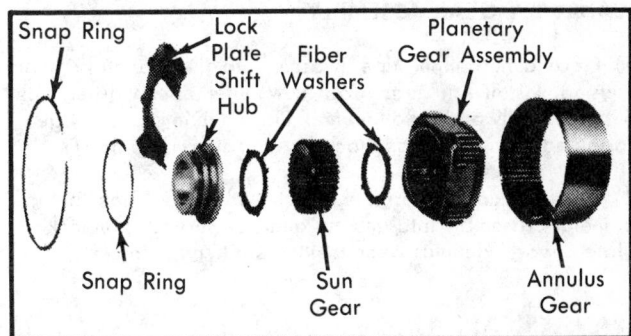

Fig. 5   Planetary Gear Set

COVER

1) Remove snap ring retaining rear output shaft ball bearing assembly in cover. Turn cover over and remove rear output shaft seal with seal remover and slide hammer (1175-AC and T50T-100-A). Remove speedometer drive gear.

2) Press out rear output shaft ball bearing from cover. Remove speedometer gear adapter. Using appropriate slide hammer and puller, (T50T-100-A and D80L-100T from D80-100-A) remove front output shaft inner needle bearing.

CASE

Remove snap ring retaining front output shaft ball bearing assembly in case. Remove output shaft seal and 2 input shaft seals. Press front output shaft bearing and input shaft bushing from case.

CLEANING & INSPECTION

1) Clean all parts in cleaning solvent. Be sure to remove all traces of gaskets from surfaces where used. Dry parts with compressed air, being careful not to spin bearings. Check all gear teeth and splines for burrs, nicks, or excessive damage. Inspect all snap rings and thrust washers for excessive wear, distortion or damage.

2) Inspect 2 case halves for cracks, porosity, damaged mating surfaces, stripped bolt threads or distortion. Inspect condition of all bearings and retainers. Inspect condition of chain and oil pump.

REASSEMBLY

CASE

Press new input shaft bushing in case. Ensure that lug is in downward position. Install new output shaft ball bearing and

BORG-WARNER 1345 (Cont.)

snap ring. Press input shaft seals into case. Press front output shaft seal into case.

COVER

Press a new needle bearing into cover. Press a new ball bearing into cover and install snap ring. Turn cover over and install speedometer drive gear. Install new output shaft seal. Install speedometer gear adapter.

PLANETARY GEAR ASSEMBLY

1) Place a new inner fiber washer into the planetary gear housing. Install sun gear. Coat new outer fiber washer with petroleum jelly and install on hub. Place hub in planetary gear cage and install "T" shape lock key and snap ring. See Fig. 5.

2) Install locking plate on shift hub with dished side toward planetary assembly into annulus gear. Be sure tabs on locking plate engage annulus gear teeth. Install snap ring.

TRANSFER CASE

1) Lubricate all parts with Dextron II Automatic Transmission Fluid. Assemble the planetary gear set, shift rail, shift cam, and shift fork together as an assembly. Ensure that the boss on the shift cam is installed toward the case. Install spacer washer on input shaft.

2) Place rear output shaft in planetary gear set, making sure shift cam engages shift fork actuating pin. Lay case on its side. Insert rear output shaft and planetary gear set into case. Ensure spacer washer remains on input shaft.

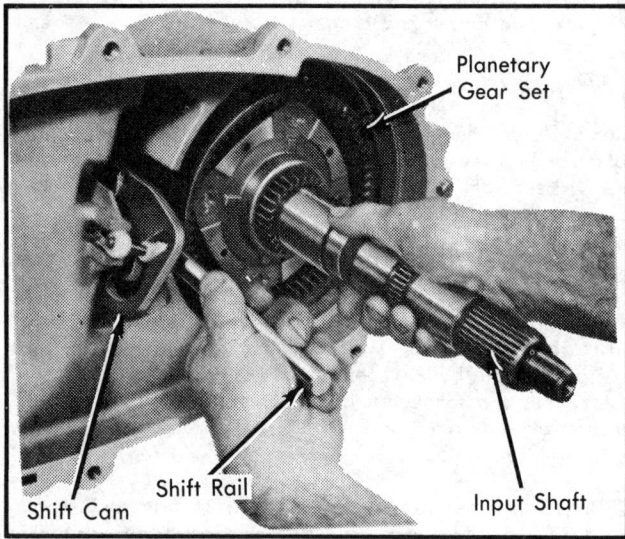

**Fig. 6   Installing Planetary Gear Set
& Shifter Mechanism**

3) Install shift rail into hole in case. Install outer roller bushing into guide in case. Remove rear output shaft and position shift fork in neutral. Place shift control lever shaft through cam and install clip ring.

4) Ensure shift control lever is pointed downward and is parallel to front face of the case. Check shift fork and planetary gear engagement. Unit should operate freely without binding. Press new needle bearing into bearing retainer (if removed).

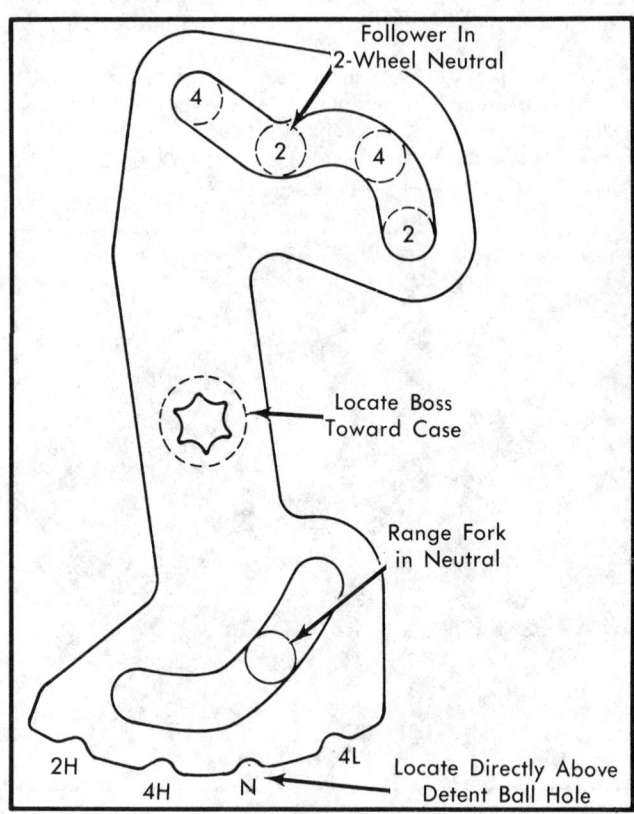

Fig. 7   Shift Cam Engagement

5) Insert output shaft through bearing retainer from the bottom side and facing outward. Insert rear output shaft pilot into the input shaft rear bushing. Align dowel holes and lower bearing into position. Install dowel pins. Install bearing retainer snap ring.

6) Insert detent ball and spring in detent bore in case half. Coat seal plug with RTV sealant. Drive plug into case until plug lip is 1/32" below surface of case. Stake the plug to case in 2 places. Install the oil pump front cover over the output shaft with flanged side down.

NOTE — The marking "TOP" must face the top of the transfer case as it is positioned for installation in the vehicle.

7) Install the oil pump spring and 2 pump pins with flat side outward in the hole in output shaft. Install oil pump body, pickup tube and filter, and push in pins. Place oil pump rear cover on output shaft with flanged side outward. The marking "TOP" must face the top of the transfer case as it is positioned for installation in the vehicle.

8) Apply Loctite to oil pump bolts, install to pump cover and tighten. Install thrust washer to rear output shaft near oil pump. Place drive sprocket on front output shaft and install snap ring and thrust washer. Install chain on drive and driven sprockets.

BORG-WARNER 1345 (Cont.)

9) Lower chain and sprockets into piston in the case. The driven sprocket should be installed over front output shaft and the drive sprocket should be installed to rear output shaft. Engage 4-WD shift fork on shift collar. Slide shift fork over shift shaft and shift collar over rear output shaft.

10) Ensure nylon wear pads are installed on shift fork tips and necked down portion of shift collar is facing rearward. Push 4-WD shift spring down and install upper spring retainer. Push spring upward and install lower spring retainer. Install shift collar hub on rear output shaft.

11) Apply RTV sealant to the case mounting surface. Lower the cover over rear output shaft. Align shift rail to blind hole in cover. Ensure the front output shaft is seated in support bearing. Install attaching bolts and tighten. Install 4-WD indicator switch.

12) Press oil slinger on front yoke. Install front and rear output shaft yokes. Apply Loctite to threads of output shafts and faces of yoke nuts and tighten. Refill transfer case, install in vehicle, and test for correct operation.

TIGHTENING SPECIFICATIONS

Application	Ft. Lbs.
Case Half Attaching Bolts	40-45
4-WD Indicator Switch	8-12
Output Yolks-to-Transfer Case	100-130
Drain Plug	6-14
Fill Plug	15-25
Transfer Case-to-Transmission Adapter	25-43
Heat Shield-to-Transfer Case	
Upper Bolt	40-45
Lower Bolt	11-16
Skid Plate-to-Frame	11-16
Front Propeller Shaft-to-Front	
Output Yoke	8-15
Rear Propeller Shaft-to-Rear	
Output Yoke	20-28

Transfer Cases

NEW PROCESS MODEL 205

Chevrolet
Chrysler Corp.
GMC

DESCRIPTION

A four-position transfer case providing two gear ratios in four-wheel drive (high and low), a two-wheel drive high, and a neutral position. Sliding clutch gears are used in controlling the various selections of gear combinations. The transfer case contains constant-mesh helical cut gears with shafts mounted in ball and roller bearings.

LUBRICATION

SERVICE INTERVALS

Chrysler Corp. — Check fluid level and fill as necessary every 12 months or 7,500 miles. Drain and refill transfer case every 36,000 miles.

General Motors — Check fluid level and fill as necessary every 4 months or 6,000 miles.

FLUID TYPE

Chrysler Corp. — Using multi-purpose gear oil, if minimum anticipated temperature is:

- Above 90°F, use SAE 140.
- Below 90°F but above −10°F, use SAE 90.
- Below −10°F, use SAE 80.

Using engine oil, if air temperature is:

- Above 32°F, use SAE 50.
- Below 32°F, use SAE 30.

General Motors — Use fluid of the type labeled Dextron II Automatic Transmission Fluid.

CAPACITY

Chrysler Corp. — Capacity is 4.5 pints.

General Motors — Capacity is 5.2 pints.

ADJUSTMENTS

SHIFT LINKAGE

Adjust shift linkage so that all positions may be selected without interference or binding. Inspect all swivels, rods and mountings for wear and/or damage and replace as necessary.

REMOVAL & INSTALLATION

TRANSFER CASE

Removal — **1)** Raise vehicle and drain transfer case. Disconnect speedometer cable. Remove skid plate, crossmember and strut rods (if equipped). Disconnect and secure out of way front and rear propeller shafts from flanges at transfer case.

2) Disconnect shift selector levers at transfer case (at shift rail link on some models). Secure transfer case to transmission jack and remove mount bolts. Move transfer case to rear until input shaft clears adapter and remove from vehicle.

Installation — To install, reverse removal procedure. Ensure that all attaching bolts are tight and fill transfer case with recommended lubricant.

DISASSEMBLY

REAR OUTPUT SHAFT & YOKE ASSEMBLY

1) Loosen rear output shaft yoke nut. Remove rear output shaft housing bolts and remove housing and retainer from case. Remove retaining nut and yoke from shaft. Then remove shaft assembly from housing. Remove snap ring and discard.

2) Remove thrust washer and washer pin. Remove tanged bronze washer. Remove gear and gear needle bearings (32 per row). Remove spacer and 2nd row of needle bearings. Remove tanged bronze thrust washer from shaft.

3) Remove pilot rollers from shaft (15 rollers). Remove pilot roller retainer ring and washer and discard retainer ring. Remove oil seal, retainer, ball bearing, speedometer gear and spacer. Discard all gaskets. Press out bearing and remove oil seal.

FRONT OUTPUT SHAFT ASSEMBLY

1) Remove lock nut, washer and yoke. Remove front bearing retainer attaching bolts and retainer. Remove front output shaft rear bearing retainer attaching bolts.

2) Using a soft-faced hammer, tap on output shaft and remove shaft, gear assembly, and rear bearing retainer from case. See *Fig. 1*. Remove the sliding clutch from output high gear, and remove washer and bearing remaining in case.

3) Remove snap ring and gear retaining ring from the shaft. Discard retaining ring. Remove thrust washer and pin from shaft. Remove gear, needle bearings (32 per row) and spacer.

Fig. 1   Removing Front Output Shaft Assembly from Transfer Case Using a Soft-Faced Hammer

NEW PROCESS MODEL 205 (Cont.)

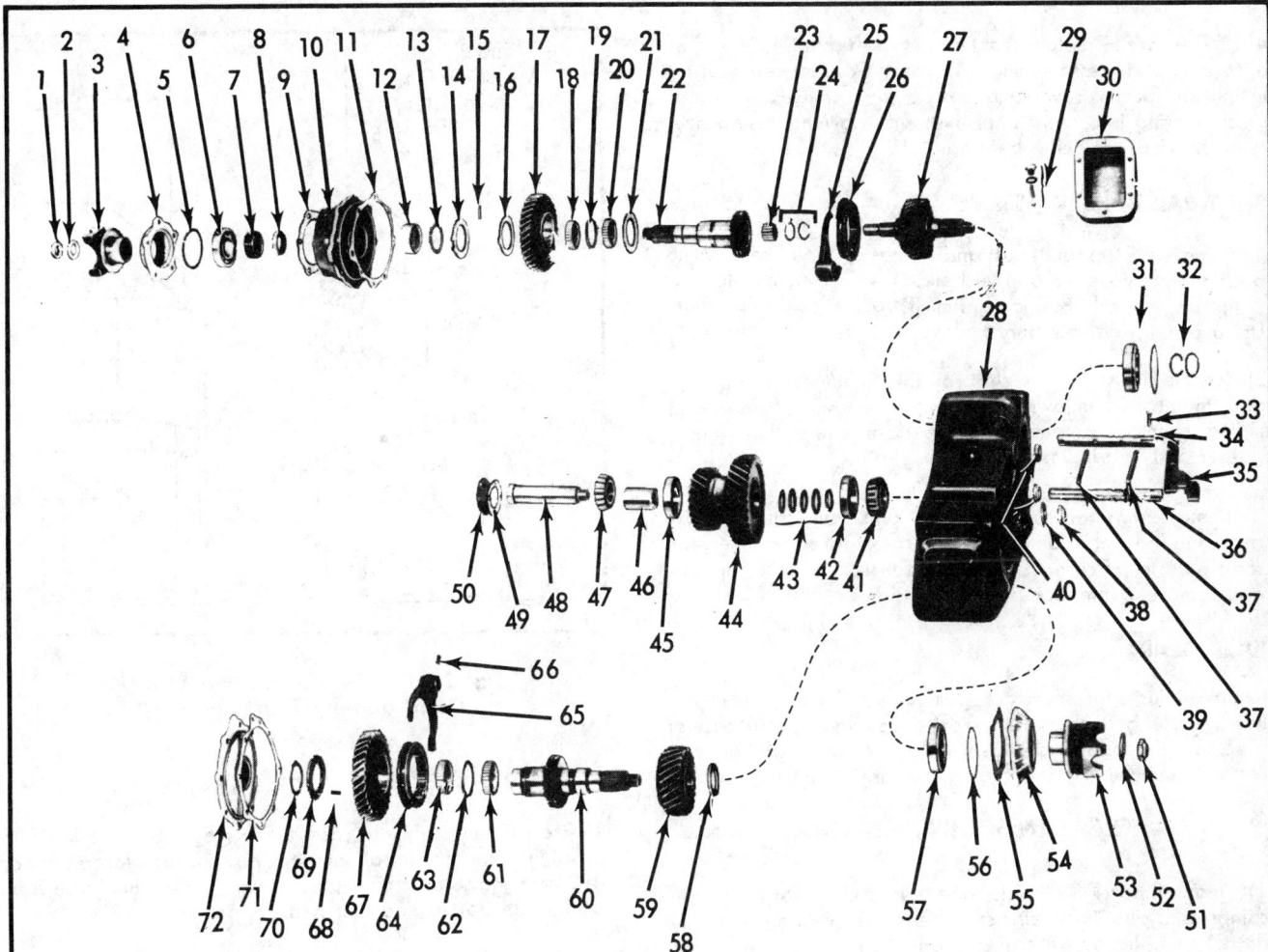

1 — Rear Output Shaft Lock Nut	26 — Sliding Clutch	51 — Front Output Shaft Lock Nut
2 — Washer	27 — Input Shaft	52 — Washer
3 — Rear Output Shaft Yoke	28 — Transfer Case	53 — Yoke
4 — Bearing Retainer & Seal	29 — Poppet Plug, Spring & Ball	54 — Bearing Retainer & Seat
5 — Snap Ring	30 — P.T.O. Gasket & Cover	55 — Gasket
6 — Bearing	31 — Input Shaft Bearing & Snap Ring	56 — Snap Ring
7 — Speedometer Gear	32 — Snap Ring & Rubber "O" Ring	57 — Front Bearing
8 — Spacer	(General Motors Only)	58 — Thrust Washer
9 — Gasket	33 — Shift Link Clevis Pin	59 — Front Wheel High Gear
10 — Rear Output Shaft Housing	34 — Range Shift Rail	60 — Front Output Shaft
11 — Gasket	35 — Shift Rail Connector Link	61 — Needle Bearing
12 — Bearing	36 — Front Wheel Drive Shift Rail	62 — Spacer
13 — Snap Ring	37 — Interlock Pins	63 — Needle Bearing
14 — Thrust Washer	38 — Rear Idler Lock Nut	64 — Sliding Clutch Gear
15 — Thrust Washer Lock Pin	39 — Washer	65 — Shift Fork
16 — Thrust Washer (Tanged)	40 — Shift Rail Seals	66 — Roll Pin
17 — Low Speed Gear	41 — Idler Shaft Bearing	67 — Front Output Low Gear
18 — Needle Bearings	42 — Bearing Cup	68 — Thrust Washer Lock Pin
19 — Spacer	43 — Shims	69 — Thrust Washer
20 — Needle Bearings	44 — Idler Gear	70 — Snap Ring
21 — Tanged Thrust Washer	45 — Bearing Cup	71 — Rear Cover Gasket
22 — Rear Output Shaft	46 — Spacer	72 — Rear Cover & Bearing
23 — Pilot Rollers	47 — Idler Shaft Bearing	
24 — Washer & Retainer	48 — Idler Shaft	
(General Motors Only)	49 — Cover Gasket	
25 — Shift Fork	50 — Rear Cover	

Fig. 2 **Exploded View of New Process Model**
205 Transfer Case

NEW PROCESS MODEL 205 (Cont.)

4) If necessary to replace front output shaft rear bearing, support cover and press bearing from cover. Position new bearing to outside face of cover and using a pipe or piece of wood, press bearing into cover until flush with opening. Use a new retainer when replacing bearing.

SHIFT RAIL & FORK ASSEMBLIES

1) Remove the 2 poppet nuts and springs on top of case. Using a magnet, remove the poppet balls. Drive cup plugs into case using a ¼″ punch. Position both shift rails in neutral position. Using a long, narrow punch, drive shift fork pins into case.

2) Remove clevis pins and shift rail link. Remove shift rails, upper range rail, then lower (4-WD) rail. Remove shift forks and sliding clutch from case. Remove front output high gear, washer and bearing from case.

3) Remove shift rail cup plugs and pins from case. Remove snap ring in front of bearing. Using a soft-faced hammer, tap shaft out rear of case. Tap bearing out front of case. Tip case and remove 2 interlock pins from inside.

IDLER GEAR

Remove idler gear shaft nut. Remove idler shaft rear cover. Remove idler gear shaft using a soft-faced hammer. Tilt case at a 45° angle, and roll idler gear to front output shaft hole and remove. Remove bearing cups as required from idler gear.

CLEANING & INSPECTION

1) Clean all parts in suitable solvent, and blow parts dry with compressed air. Direct air across bearings, ensuring that they do not spin. Remove all traces of gaskets from surfaces where used.

2) Examine all individual roller bearing surfaces for wear or evidence of chipping or cracks. Replace bearings as necessary. Bearings are nonadjustable, and if worn or damaged, they must be replaced.

3) Inspect teeth of all gears for excessive wear or damage. Replace any gear where these conditions exist.

4) Carefully examine spline shaft for scoring or evidence of twisting. Sliding clutch gears must move freely on splines. Parts should be replaced if spline clearance is excessive or if shaft is scored or twisted.

REASSEMBLY

IDLER GEAR

1) Using a press, install 2 bearing cups in idler gear. Assemble 2 bearing cones, spacer, shims and idler gear on dummy shaft with bore up. Check end play. Limits are .001-.002″. See *Fig. 3.* Install idler gear assembly with dummy shaft into case. Install through front output bore, large end first.

2) Install idler shaft from large bore side, and drive through using soft-faced hammer. Install washer and new lock nut. Check for end play and free rotation. Tighten lock nut to 150 ft. lbs. Install idler shaft cover and gasket, and tighten bolts.

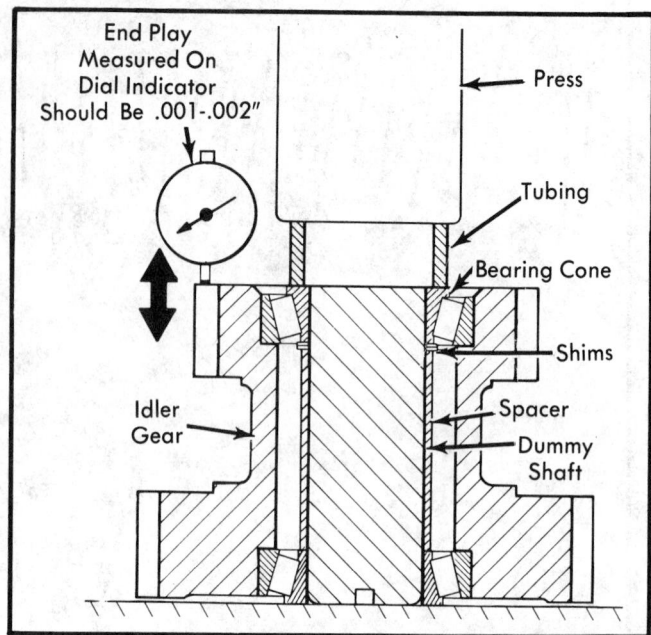

Fig. 3   Checking Idler Gear End Play Using Dummy Shaft and Press

SHIFT RAIL & FORK ASSEMBLIES

1) Press 2 rail seals into case. Seals should be installed with metal lip outward. Install interlock pins through large bore or PTO opening. Start front output drive shift rail into case from back, with slotted end first and poppet notches up.

2) Install shift fork (with long end inward) into rail. Push rail through to neutral position. Install input shaft bearing and shaft into case. Start range rail into case from front, with poppet notches up.

3) Install sliding clutch onto fork, placing over input shaft in case. Position to receive range rail, and push rail through to neutral position. Install new lock pins through holes at top of case and drive into forks. Tip case on PTO opening when installing range rail lock pin.

FRONT OUTPUT SHAFT & GEAR ASSEMBLY

1) Install 2 rows of 32 needle bearings, separated by spacer, in front low output gear. Retain with a sufficient amount of grease. Place front output shaft in a soft-jawed vise, with spline end down. Install front low gear over shaft with clutch gear facing down.

2) Install thrust washer pin, thrust washer and new snap ring. Position snap ring so opening is opposite the pin. Position front wheel high gear and washer in case. Install sliding clutch in fork. Then put shift fork and rail in front wheel drive position with clutch teeth in mesh with teeth of front wheel high gear.

3) Line up washer, high gear, and sliding clutch with bearing bore. Insert front output shaft and low gear assembly through the high gear assembly. Install new seal in bearing retainer, using special tool (J-22836). Install front output bearing and retainer in case.

NEW PROCESS MODEL 205 (Cont.)

4) Clean and grease rollers in front output bearing rear retainer. Install onto case using 1 gasket. Dip bolts into sealant. Install bolts and tighten. Install front output yoke, washer and lock nut. Tighten to specification.

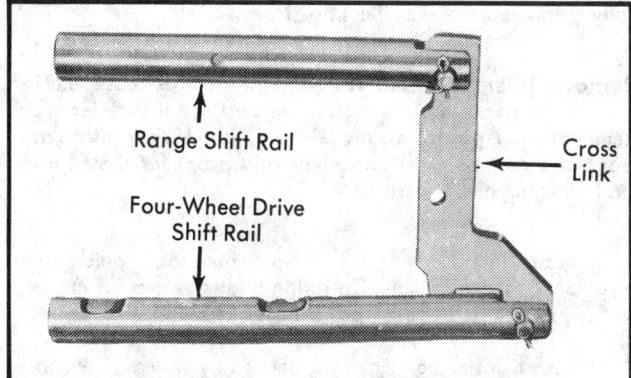

Fig. 4   Shift Rail Components and Position

REAR OUTPUT SHAFT ASSEMBLY

1) Install 2 rows of 32 needle bearngs, separated by spacer, into output low gear. Use grease to retain bearings. Install thrust washer onto rear output shaft, with tang down in clutch gear groove. Install output low gear onto shaft with clutch teeth facing down.

2) Install thrust washer over gear, with tab pointing up and away from gear. Install washer pin and also large thrust washer over shaft and pin. Rotate washer until tab fits into slot, approximately 90° away from pin. Install snap ring and check end play. End play should be within .002-.027".

3) Grease pilot bore or rear output shaft, and install 15 pilot rollers. Install thrust washer and speedometer gear. Install bearing. Install rear bearing retainer seal and bearing retainer onto housing, using 1 or 2 gaskets, depending on clearance. Tighten bolts, install yoke, washer, and lock nut on output shaft.

4) Position range rail in "High" and install output shaft and retainer assembly on transfer case. Tighten bolts. Install PTO cover and gasket. Install and seal cup plugs and rail pin holes (if necessary). Install drain and filler plugs. Install shift rail cross link, clevis pins and lock pins.

TIGHTENING SPECIFICATIONS	
Application	**Ft. Lbs.**
Yoke Lock Nuts	150
Idler Shaft Lock Nut	150
Input & Output Bearing	
Retainer Bolts	35
Transfer Case-to-Adapter Bolts	30
Idler Shaft Cover Bolts	20
Drain & Fill Plugs	30
PTO Cover Bolts	15

Transfer Cases

NEW PROCESS MODEL 208

Chevrolet
Chrysler Corp.
Ford
GMC
Jeep

DESCRIPTION

The Model 208 is a part-time, 4-wheel drive unit having an integral 4-wheel low range. This model is a 4-position unit, providing 2 gear ratios in 4-wheel drive (high and low), a 2-wheel drive high and neutral. A chain drive is used with front and rear output shafts mounted in ball and roller bearings, 2 drive sprockets and a plantary gear assembly, consisting of a 4-pinion carrier and annulus gear housed in a 2-piece aluminum case.

LUBRICATION

SERVICE INTERVALS

Check fluid level, and fill as necessary every 4 months or 6000 miles. Drain and refill transfer case every 36,000 miles.

FLUID TYPE

Jeep — Use a quality grade 10W-30 motor oil.

Except Jeep — Use automatic transmission fluid labeled Dexron II.

CAPACITY

Chrysler Corp. & Jeep — Capacity is 6 pints.
Ford — Capacity is 7 pints.
General Motors — Capacity is 8 pints.

ADJUSTMENTS

Adjust shift linkage so that all positions may be selected without interference or binding. Inspect all swivels, rods and mountings for wear or damage, and replace as necessary.

REMOVAL & INSTALLATION

TRANSFER CASE

Removal (Chrysler Corp. & Jeep) — 1) Raise vehicle and drain transfer case. Disconnect speedometer cable and indicator switch wires. Disconnect shift lever link from operating lever.

2) Place transmission jack under transfer case, and remove crossmember. Mark transfer case front and rear output shaft yokes and propeller shafts for installation alignment reference. Disconnect front and rear propeller shafts at yokes, and secure to frame with wire.

3) If necessary, disconnect parking brake cable guide from pivot on right frame rail, and remove bolts attaching exhaust pipe support bracket-to-transfer case. Remove transfer case-to-transmission bolts. Move assembly rearward until free of output shaft, and remove from vehicle.

Removal (Ford) — 1) Raise vehicle and drain transfer case. Disconnect indicator switch wire, speedometer driven gear and operating lever assembly from transfer case. Remove skid plate from frame, if so equipped. Remove heat shield from transfer case.

2) Place transmission jack under transfer case. Disconnect front and rear propeller shafts at yokes, and secure to frame with wire. Remove transfer case-to-transmission adapter bolts. Lower and remove transfer case from vehicle.

Removal (General Motors) — 1) Place transfer case selector lever in "4H" position. Raise vehicle and drain transfer case. Remove cotter pin from shift lever swivel. Mark transfer case front and rear output shaft yokes and propeller shaft for installation alignment reference.

2) If necessary, disconnect parking brake cable guide from pivot on right frame rail. On automatic transmission models, remove engine strut rod from transfer case.

3) Place transmission jack under transfer case. Remove transfer case-to-transmission adapter bolts. Move assembly rearward until free of output shaft, and remove from vehicle.

Installation (All Models) — Install new transmission-to-transfer case gasket and align transfer case to transmission. Rotate transfer case output shaft until transmission output shaft engages transfer case input shaft. Move transfer case until case seats flush against transmission. Install transfer case attaching bolts, and complete installation by reversing removal procedure.

DISASSEMBLY

TRANSFER CASE

1) Remove fill and drain plugs. Remove front and rear yokes. Discard yoke seal washers and nuts. Place transfer case on end and position front case on wood blocks.

NOTE — *It may be necessary to notch blocks to clear mounting studs in front case.*

2) Remove lock mode switch and washer. Remove detent bolt, spring and ball. Mark rear retainer and case for reassembly. Remove rear retainer attaching bolts, retainer and pump housing as an assembly. See *Fig. 2*. Tap retainer from case using plastic mallet. DO NOT pry retainer.

3) Remove pump housing from retainer, remove and discard pump seal. Remove speedometer drive gear from mainshaft. Remove oil pump from mainshaft. Mark position of pump for reassembly (side facing case interior is recessed). Remove rear case-to-front case attaching bolts and remove rear case.

NOTE — *To remove rear case, insert screwdrivers into slots in case ends and gently pry apart. DO NOT pry case halves apart at any point on mating surface.*

4) Remove front output shaft rear thrust bearing assembly, marking position of bearing and races for reassembly. Remove driven sprocket retaining snap ring. Remove drive sprocket retaining snap ring, thrust washer and spacer washer (if equipped).

NEW PROCESS MODEL 208 (Cont.)

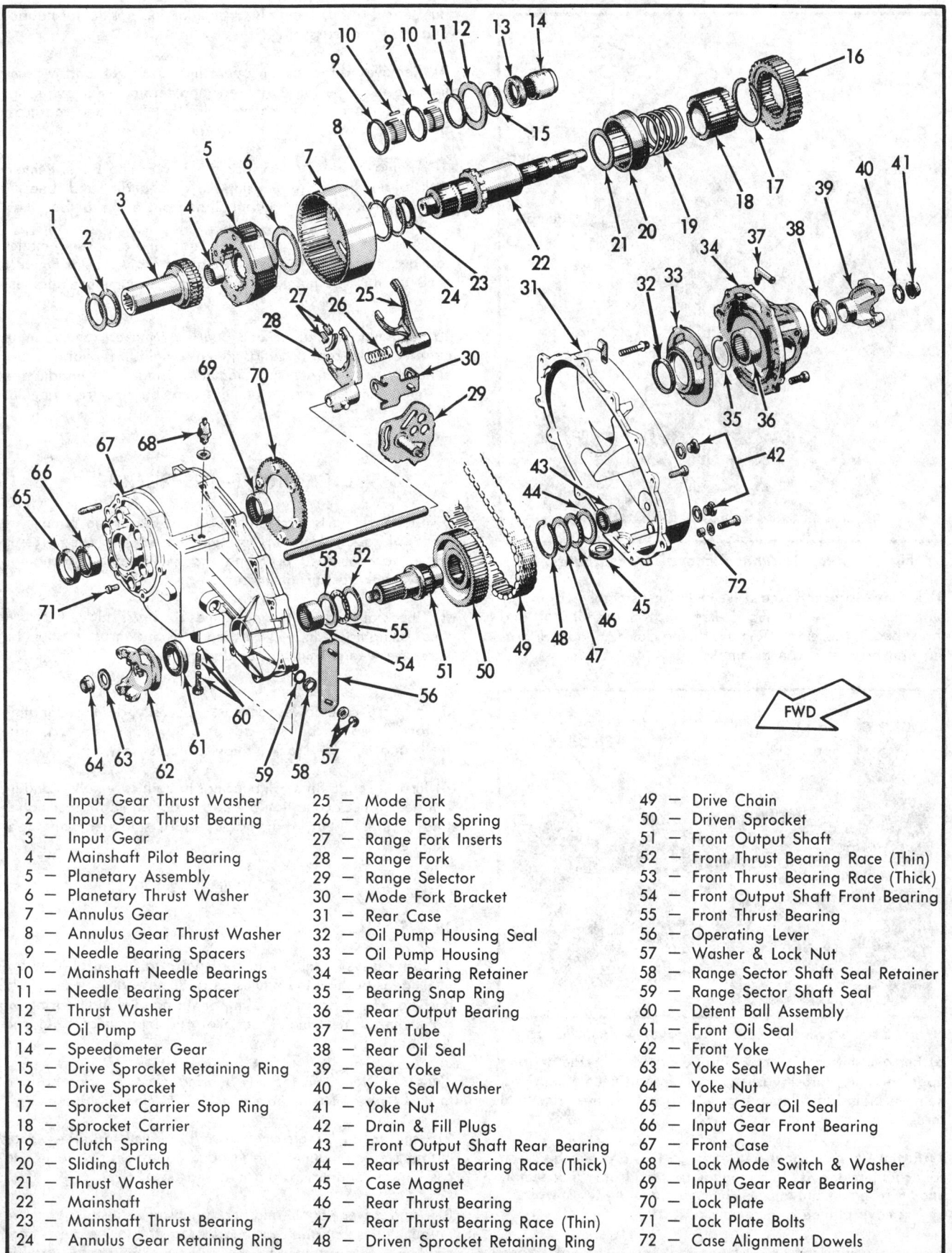

1 — Input Gear Thrust Washer	25 — Mode Fork	49 — Drive Chain
2 — Input Gear Thrust Bearing	26 — Mode Fork Spring	50 — Driven Sprocket
3 — Input Gear	27 — Range Fork Inserts	51 — Front Output Shaft
4 — Mainshaft Pilot Bearing	28 — Range Fork	52 — Front Thrust Bearing Race (Thin)
5 — Planetary Assembly	29 — Range Selector	53 — Front Thrust Bearing Race (Thick)
6 — Planetary Thrust Washer	30 — Mode Fork Bracket	54 — Front Output Shaft Front Bearing
7 — Annulus Gear	31 — Rear Case	55 — Front Thrust Bearing
8 — Annulus Gear Thrust Washer	32 — Oil Pump Housing Seal	56 — Operating Lever
9 — Needle Bearing Spacers	33 — Oil Pump Housing	57 — Washer & Lock Nut
10 — Mainshaft Needle Bearings	34 — Rear Bearing Retainer	58 — Range Sector Shaft Seal Retainer
11 — Needle Bearing Spacer	35 — Bearing Snap Ring	59 — Range Sector Shaft Seal
12 — Thrust Washer	36 — Rear Output Bearing	60 — Detent Ball Assembly
13 — Oil Pump	37 — Vent Tube	61 — Front Oil Seal
14 — Speedometer Gear	38 — Rear Oil Seal	62 — Front Yoke
15 — Drive Sprocket Retaining Ring	39 — Rear Yoke	63 — Yoke Seal Washer
16 — Drive Sprocket	40 — Yoke Seal Washer	64 — Yoke Nut
17 — Sprocket Carrier Stop Ring	41 — Yoke Nut	65 — Input Gear Oil Seal
18 — Sprocket Carrier	42 — Drain & Fill Plugs	66 — Input Gear Front Bearing
19 — Clutch Spring	43 — Front Output Shaft Rear Bearing	67 — Front Case
20 — Sliding Clutch	44 — Rear Thrust Bearing Race (Thick)	68 — Lock Mode Switch & Washer
21 — Thrust Washer	45 — Case Magnet	69 — Input Gear Rear Bearing
22 — Mainshaft	46 — Rear Thrust Bearing	70 — Lock Plate
23 — Mainshaft Thrust Bearing	47 — Rear Thrust Bearing Race (Thin)	71 — Lock Plate Bolts
24 — Annulus Gear Retaining Ring	48 — Driven Sprocket Retaining Ring	72 — Case Alignment Dowels

Fig. 1   Exploded View of New Process Model 208 Transfer Case

Transfer Cases

NEW PROCESS MODEL 208 (Cont.)

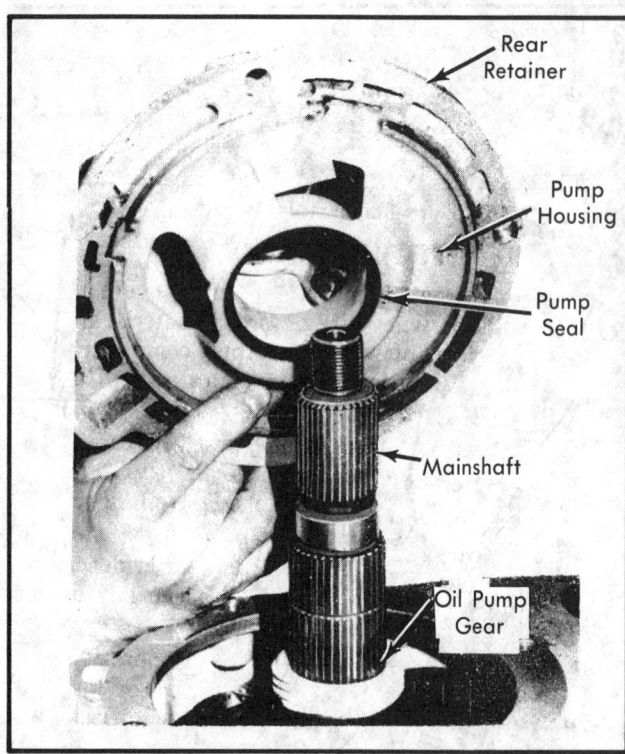

Fig. 2   Rear Retainer Removal & Installation

5) Remove sprockets and drive chain as assembly. Lift evenly on both to remove. See *Fig. 3*. Remove front output shaft and thrust bearing assembly. Remove sliding clutch, mode fork, spring and bracket as an assembly.

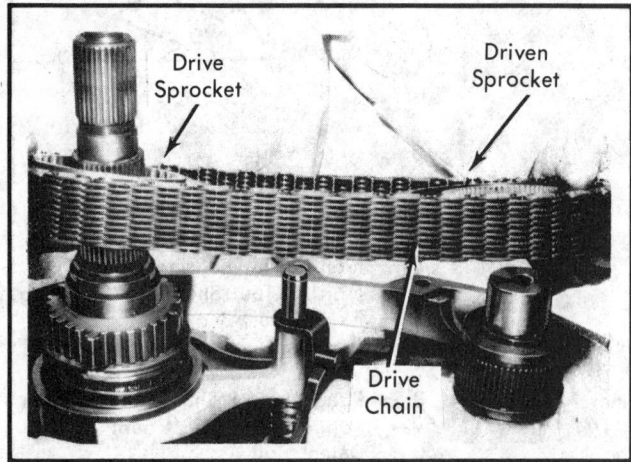

Fig. 3   Sprocket & Chain Removal & Installation

6) Remove shift rail. Remove sprocket carrier, needle bearing upper retainer, thrust washer and mainshaft needle bearings. Remove mainshaft. Remove annulus gear retaining ring and thrust washer.

7) Remove annulus gear and range fork as an assembly. Turn fork counterclockwise to disengage fork lug from range sector, and lift assembly out of case. Remove planetary thrust washer, and remove planetary assembly.

8) Remove mainshaft thrust bearing from input gear, and remove gear by lifting straight up and out of case. Remove input gear thrust bearing and race, marking position of bearing and race for reassembly.

9) Remove range sector operating lever nut and washer. Remove lever, sector shaft, seal and retainer. Remove range sector. Remove output shaft seals from front and rear case bores.

10) Remove and discard lock plate attaching bolts. Remove lock plate from case. Using driver handle and bearing remover, remove front output shaft front and rear bearings.

11) Remove rear output bearing snap ring and, using mallet, tap bearing out of retainer. Using screwdriver or drift punch (and taking care not to nick or damage aluminum retainer), remove rear seal.

12) Using driver handle and bearing remover, remove input gear front and rear bearings. Remove mainshaft pilot bearing, either by hand or with slide hammer. Using driver handle and bushing remover, remove annulus gear bushing from annulus gear.

CLEANING & INSPECTION

1) Clean all parts in cleaning solvent. Be sure to remove all traces of gaskets from surfaces where used. Apply compressed air to each oil feed port and channel in each case half to remove any obstruction or residue.

2) Check all gear teeth and splines for burrs, nicks, excessive wear or damage. Inspect all snap rings and thrust washers for excessive wear, distortion or damage.

3) Inspect 2 case halves for cracks, porosity, damaged mating surfaces, stripped bolt threads or distortion. Check lock plate teeth and hub for cracks, chips or excessive wear.

4) Inspect condition of all bearings in both case halves and input gear. Check condition of bearing bores in both case halves and in input gear, rear output shaft, side gear and rear retainer.

REASSEMBLY

TRANSFER CASE

1) Using driver handle and bushing installer, install new annulus gear bushing in annulus gear. Remove any pieces of old bushing from installation. Using driver handle and bearing installer, install new mainshaft pilot and input gear front and rear bearings.

NOTE — *After replacing any bearing, check bearing position to make sure oil feed hole is not obstructed or blocked.*

2) Using driver handle and bearing installer, install new rear output bearing making sure shielded side of bearing faces into case. Install snap ring and new rear seal.

3) Using driver handle and bearing installer, install new front output shaft front and rear bearings. Install lock plate in front case half. Apply sealer to new attaching bolts and install in case.

NEW PROCESS MODEL 208 (Cont.)

4) Install input gear race and thrust bearing in front case. Install input gear. Install mainshaft thrust bearing in input gear. Install range sector shaft seal and retainer. Install range sector. Install operating lever, washer and lock nut on range sector shaft.

5) Install planetary assembly over input gear making sure planetary is fully seated and meshed with gear. Install washer on planetary hub. Install inserts in range fork (if removed).

6) Engage range fork in annulus gear and install gear over planetary assembly. Install annulus gear thrust washer and snap ring. Align shift rail bores in case and range fork and install shift rail.

NOTE — *Make sure range fork lug is fully inserted in range sector slot and that shift rail bore in case is completely dry and does not contain any oil.*

7) Install mainshaft making sure thrust bearing is properly seated in input gear. Coat sprocket carrier bore with petroleum jelly, and position bearing retainer at center of carrier bore.

8) Coat mainshaft needle bearings with petroleum jelly and install needle bearings (60) in each end of sprocket carrier bore. Install bearing retainer in each end, and position thrust washer on bottom of carrier.

9) Align assembled carrier and needle bearings and install on mainshaft. Assemble mode fork, spring, bracket and engaging fork in sliding clutch and install on shift rail and mainshaft.

10) Install clutch spring and stop ring in upper groove of sprocket carrier. Install front output shaft thrust bearing assembly in front case. Correct sequence is: thick race, thrust bearing, thin race. Install front output shaft.

11) Position sprockets in chain, align sprockets with shafts, and install assembly making sure drive sprocket recessed side is facing into case. Install spacer and thrust washer on drive sprocket. *See Fig. 3.* Install snap ring.

12) Install driven sprocket retaining ring. Install front output shaft rear thrust bearing assembly on front output shaft. Correct sequence is: thin race, thrust bearing, thick race.

13) Install oil pump on mainshaft making sure recessed side of pump faces into case. Install speedometer drive gear. Install magnet in front case (if removed).

14) Apply sealer to mating surface of case halves. Install rear case on front case, making sure front output shaft rear thrust bearing assembly is seated in rear case. Align bolt holes and dowels. Install attaching bolts.

NOTE — *Install flat washers on 2 bolts installed at opposite ends of case.*

15) Install seal in pump housing. Coat pump housing tabs with petroleum jelly and install housing in rear retainer. Apply sealer to mating surface of rear retainer, align and install retainer and bolts. *See Fig. 1.*

16) Coat rear oil seal with petroleum jelly. Install indicator switch and washer. Apply small amount of sealer to detent retainer bolt and install detent ball, spring and bolt.

17) Install yoke with collar on front output shaft. Install rear yoke. Install yoke seal washers and nuts. Refill with specified lubricant and install fill plug.

TIGHTENING SPECIFICATIONS

Application	Ft. Lbs.
Detent Retainer Bolt	20-25
Drain & Fill Plugs	15-20
Indicator Switch	15-20
Lock Plate Bolts	25-35
Operating Lever Lock Nut	15-20
Rear Case-to-Front Case Bolts	20-25
Rear Retainer Bolts	20-25
Yoke Nuts	90-130

SPICER (DANA) MODEL 300

Jeep

DESCRIPTION

The Model 300 is a 4-position, dual range, part-time 4-wheel drive unit with integral low range. It provides 4-wheel undifferentiated high and low ranges, a neutral position and 2-wheel high range. Manual locking front hubs are standard.

LUBRICATION

SERVICE INTERVALS

Jeep — Check fluid level and refill as required every 5 months or 5,000 miles in normal service, 3 months or 3,000 miles in severe service. Change fluid every 30 months or 30,000 miles.

FLUID TYPE

Use gear lubricant of SAE quality 85W-90 API grade GL-5.

CAPACITY

Refill capacity is 4.0 pints.

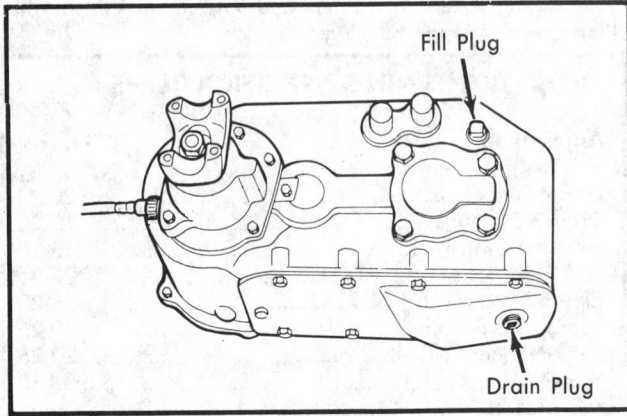

Fig. 1   Drain and Refill Plug Locations

REMOVAL & INSTALLATION

TRANSFER CASE

Removal — 1) Remove shift lever knob, trim ring and boot from transfer case shift lever(s). Remove floor covering (if equipped) and remove transmission access cover. Raise vehicle and drain transfer case. Support transmission and remove rear crossmember.

2) Mark front and rear yokes and driveshafts for reassembly, disconnect driveshaft flanges at transfer case. Disconnect speedometer cable at transfer case. Disconnect parking brake cable at equalizer.

3) Disconnect exhaust pipe support bracket at transfer case (if equipped). Remove transfer case-to-transmission attaching bolts and remove case and gasket.

Installation — 1) Install transmission-to-transfer case gasket on transmission. Shift transfer case to "4L" position. Rotate

transfer case output shaft until transmission output shaft engages transfer case input shaft. Move case forward until case seats against transmission.

NOTE — *DO NOT install transfer case attaching bolts until case is completely seated against transmission.*

2) Install attaching bolts and tighten to specifications. Install drain plug and refill case to specifications. Connect speedometer driven gear to case. Connect shift levers and control links to shift rods. Align reassembly marks and install driveshafts to flanges at transfer case.

3) Install rear crossmember and remove transmission support. Install parking brake cable at equalizer and connect exhaust pipe support bracket at transfer case (if equipped). Lower vehicle and install transmission access cover and floor covering (if equipped). Install shift lever boot, trim ring, lever(s) and shift knob.

DISASSEMBLY

TRANSFER CASE

1) Remove shift lever assembly. Using a putty knife to break the seal, remove bottom cover. Using yoke remover (J-8614-01), remove front and rear yokes and discard lock nuts.

2) Remove screws attaching input shaft support to case. Using a putty knife to break the seal, remove support, rear output shaft gear and input shaft as assembly.

3) Remove rear output shaft clutch sleeve from case. Remove and discard snap ring retaining rear output shaft gear on input shaft. Remove gear. Remove and discard input shaft bearing snap ring. Using a plastic mallet to tap end, remove input shaft and bearing from support. *See Fig. 3.*

4) Using arbor press, remove bearing and shims from input shaft. Remove and discard seal from input shaft support. Remove intermediate shaft lockplate bolt and lockplate. Using a brass punch and plastic mallet, tap intermediate shaft out of case.

5) Remove and discard intermediate shaft seal. Making note of location of tabs on thrust washers for reassembly, remove thrust washers and intermediate gear assembly. Remove 48 needle bearings and 3 bearing spacers from intermediate gear.

6) Remove rear bearing cap bolts. Using a putty knife to break the seal and a plastic mallet to tap output shaft, remove rear bearing cap. Remove end play shims and speedometer drive gear from rear output shaft. Remove and discard rear output shaft seal. Remove bearings and races from rear bearing cap.

7) Remove front and rear output shaft shift forks from shift rods. *See Fig. 2.* Using a punch inserted in pin holes in rods, rotate rods to remove them from case, taking care not to lose poppet balls and springs. Remove shift forks from case.

8) Remove bolts attaching front bearing cap-to-case. Using a putty knife to break the seal, remove front cap. Remove front output shaft from front cap. Remove and discard shift rod oil seals from front cap. Using bearing remover (J-29168), remove bearing race from front cap.

SPICER (DANA) MODEL 300 (Cont.)

9) Remove cover plate and shims from case (keep shims together for reassembly). Move front output shaft toward front of case and remove rear bearing race from case. Remove rear output shaft front bearing.

10) Position case on wood blocks to allow for rear output shaft removal clearance. Seat clutch gear on case interior surface. Using rawhide mallet, tap shaft out of bearing.

NOTE — *If necessary, use an arbor press and press tool to press rear output shaft from bearing.*

11) Remove thrust washer, clutch gear and output shaft from case. Using arbor press and press tool, remove front output shaft rear bearing. Remove case from arbor press and remove front output shaft, clutch gear and sleeve and shaft rear bearing from case.

12) Using arbor press and press tool (J-22912-01), remove front output shaft front bearing. Remove gear from front output shaft. Support rear output shaft in a vise and, using bearing remover (J-29369-1), remove input shaft rear needle bearing from shaft. Use 3/8" drive, 7/16" socket and extension to tap shift rod thimbles out of case.

Fig. 2   Removing Shift Fork

CLEANING & INSPECTION

1) Clean all parts in suitable cleaning solvent and dry with compressed air. Be sure to remove all traces of gaskets from surfaces where used.

CAUTION — *DO NOT dry any bearings with compressed air. Use clean shop towels only.*

2) Inspect all individual bearing surfaces for wear, chipping or cracking. Inspect teeth of all gears for excessive wear or damage. Replace as necessary.

3) Replace any shaft that has damaged splines, threads or bearing surfaces. Check shift rods and rod bores in case for wear or damage. Replace as necessary.

REASSEMBLY

TRANSFER CASE

1) Apply Loctite 220 sealant or equivalent to shift rod thimbles and install. Install gear on front output shaft making sure gear clutch teeth face shaft gear teeth. Using arbor press and press tool, install front bearing on front output shaft. Make sure bearing is seated against gear.

2) Install front output shaft in case and install clutch sleeve and gear on shaft. Using arbor press and press tool, install front output shaft rear bearing. Using bearing installer (J-29179), install input shaft rear needle bearing in rear output shaft.

3) Position rear output shaft clutch gear in case and insert rear output shaft into gear. Using arbor press and press tool, install thrust washer and front bearing on rear output shaft and shims and bearing on input shaft.

4) Using seal installer (J-29184), install new oil seal in input shaft support. Install input shaft, bearing and snap ring in support. Install rear output shaft gear and snap ring on input gear.

5) Using feeler gauge, measure clearance between input gear and gear retaining snap ring. If clearance exceeds .003", disassemble input shaft and add shims between input shaft and shaft bearing until tolerance is attained. Install clutch sleeve on rear output shaft.

6) Apply Loctite 515 sealant or equivalent to mating surface of input shaft support. Using 2 support bolts to align support on case, tap support into position with a plastic mallet and install support, shaft and gear assembly into case.

7) Using press tool (J-9276-3), install rear bearing cap front bearing race. Using press tool (J-29182), install rear bearing cap rear bearing race. Position rear output shaft rear bearing in rear bearing cap and, using seal installer (J-25160), install seal. Install speedometer gear and shims on rear output shaft.

8) Apply Loctite 515 sealant or equivalent to mating surface of rear bearing cap. Using 2 cap bolts to align bolt holes, tap rear bearing cap into position with a plastic mallet and install cap on case. Install rear output shaft yoke. Use spanner wrench (J-8614-01) to hold yoke while tightening nut.

9) Clamp dial indicator (J-8001) onto bearing cap and position indicator stylus so it contacts end of shaft. See *Fig. 4*. Pry rear output shaft back and forth to check end play. End play should be .001-.005". If end play is not correct, remove or add shims between speedometer drive gear and output shaft rear bearing.

10) Install front output shaft rear bearing race, front output shaft end, shims and cover plate. Apply Loctite 220 sealant or equivalent to cover plate bolt threads and install bolts. Using driver (J8092) and press tool (J-29181), install front output shaft front bearing race.

11) Using seal installer (J-25160), install front output shaft yoke oil seal. Using punch (J-25167), install shift rod oil seals. Apply Loctite 515 sealant or equivalent to mating surface of front bearing cap. Using 2 bolts to align cap-to-case bolt holes, tap front bearing cap into position and install on case.

12) Tap end of front output shaft with plastic mallet to seat rear bearing cup against cover plate. Mount dial indicator on front bearing cap and position indicator stylus against end of output shaft. Pry front output shaft back and forth to check end play. End play should be .001-.005". If end play is not

Transfer Cases

SPICER (DANA) MODEL 300 (Cont.)

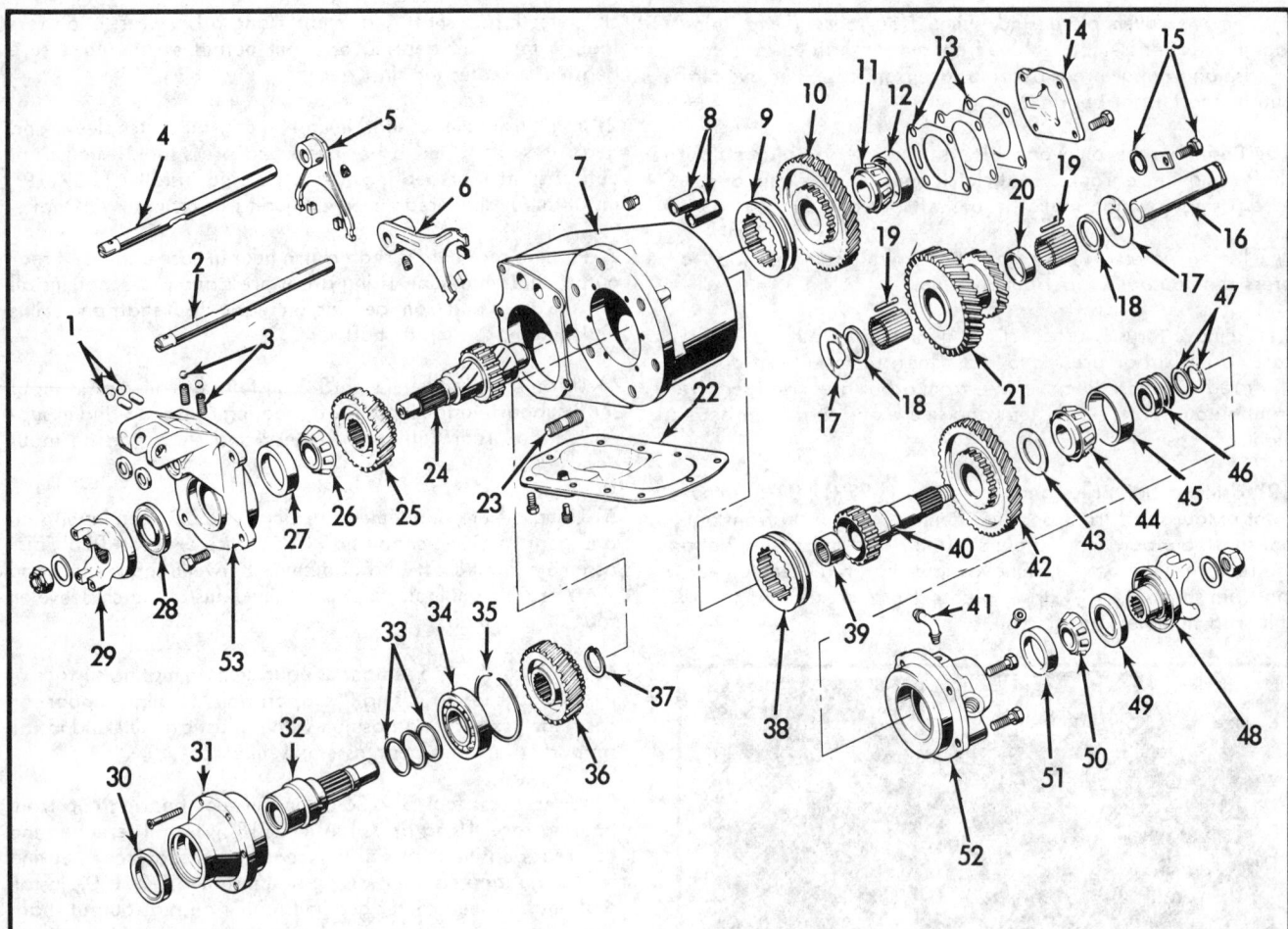

1. Interlock Plugs & Interlocks
2. Rear Output Shaft Shift Rod
3. Poppet Balls & Springs
4. Front Output Shaft Shift Rod
5. Frt. Output Shaft Shift Fork
6. Rear Output Shaft Shift Fork
7. Transfer Case
8. Thimble Covers
9. Frt. Output Shaft Clutch Sleeve
10. Frt. Output Shaft Clutch Gear
11. Frt. Output Shaft Rear Bearing
12. Bearing Race
13. Frt. Output Shaft End Play Shims
14. Cover Plate
15. Lock Plate, Bolt & Washer
16. Intermediate Gear Shaft
17. Thrust Washer
18. Bearing Spacer (Thin)

19. Intermed. Gear Shaft Needle Bearings
20. Bearing Spacer (Thick)
21. Intermediate Gear
22. Bottom Cover
23. Case-to-Trans. Stud
24. Front Output Shaft
25. Frt. Output Shaft Gear
26. Frt. Output Shaft Frt. Bearing
27. Bearing Race
28. Oil Seal
29. Front Yoke
30. Seal
31. Input Shaft Support
32. Input Shaft
33. Shims
34. Input Shaft Bearing
35. Bearing Snap Ring
36. Rear Output Shaft Gear

37. Snap Ring
38. Rear Output Shaft Clutch Sleeve
39. Input Shaft Rear Bearing
40. Rear Output Shaft
41. Vent
42. Rear Output Shaft Clutch Gear
43. Thrust Washer
44. Rear Output Shaft Frt. Bearing
45. Bearing Race
46. Speedometer Drive Gear
47. End Play Shims
48. Rear Yoke
49. Rear Output Shaft Oil Seal
50. Rear Output Shaft Rear Bearing
51. Bearing Race
52. Rear Bearing Cap
53. Front Bearing Cap

Fig. 3 Exploded View of New Process Model 300 Transfer Case

correct, remove or add shims between cover plate and case. Reseat rear bearing cup before rechecking end play.

13) Install front output shaft yoke. Use spanner wrench (J-8614-01) to hold yoke while tightening nut. Insert front and rear output shaft shift forks into case. Compress and install poppet ball and spring in front bearing cap. Install front out-put shaft shift rod part way in case through shift fork and align set screw hole on fork and rod.

14) Compress and install remaining poppet ball and spring in front bearing cap. Install rear output shaft shift rail part way in case through shift fork and align set screw hole on fork and rod. Install and tighten set screws.

SPICER (DANA) MODEL 300 (Cont.)

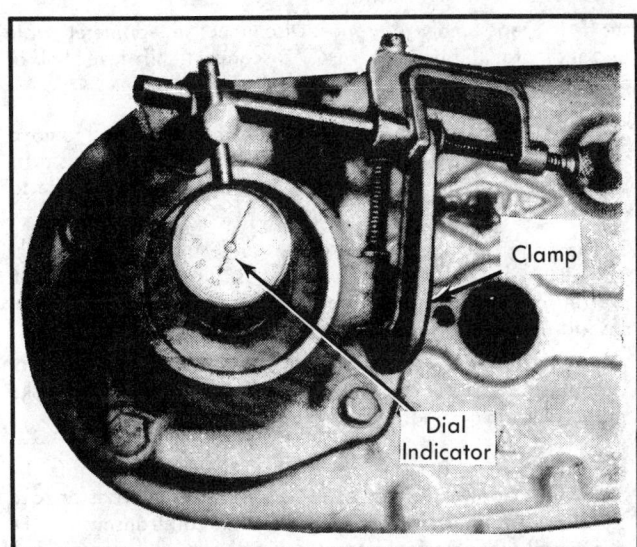

Fig. 4   Checking Rear Output Shaft End Play

15) Insert holding tool (J-25142) in intermediate gear and install needle bearings and spacers in gear. Install intermediate

gear thrust washers in case making sure washer tags align with grooves in case. Install new seal on intermediate shaft.

16) Position intermediate gear in case. Install intermediate shaft in case bore. Using plastic mallet, tap intermediate shaft into gear until shaft forces holding tool (J-25142) out of case and shaft is in place.

17) Install intermediate shaft lockplate and bolt. Apply Loctite 515 sealant or equivalent to mating surface of bottom cover. Use new gasket and install bottom cover.

TIGHTENING SPECIFICATIONS

Application	Ft. Lbs.
Bottom Cover Bolts	15
Cover Plate Bolts	35
Front/Rear Bearing Cap Bolts	35
Front/Rear Yoke Lock Nuts	120
Input Shaft Support Screws	10
Lock Plate Bolts	23
Shift Fork Set Screws	14

QUADRA-TRAC MODEL 219

Jeep

DESCRIPTION

The Model 219 transfer case is a full time 4-wheel drive unit. It provides 4-wheel high and low ranges, a neutral position and a 4-wheel high Lock position when vehicle is immobile due to excessive wheel spin. The model 219 provides full time, fully differentiated 4-wheel drive in 4H range only. In 4H, fully differentiated operation is accomplished through a torque biasing viscous (fluid) coupling and an open type differential (same principal as an open type rear axle) connected to the coupling. The 4L and Lock ranges provide undifferentiated drive modes. The model 219 is a chain drive unit consisting of 2 drive sprockets and an interconnecting drive chain.

NOTE — *Front drive hubs are not available and not recommended for vehicles equipped with the model 219 transfer case.*

The differential assembly consists of the side gear, rear output shaft, viscous coupling and differential pinion gear assembly. The viscous coupling functions as a torque biasing slip limiting unit. It consists of an enclosed housing containing 2 sets of fixed clutch plates and a special silicone fluid. The differential pinion gears are located in the open center section of the coupling.

LUBRICATION

SERVICE INTERVALS

Check fluid level and fill as required every 5 months or 5,000 miles. Drain and refill transfer case lubricant every 30 months or 30,000 miles. *See Fig. 1.*

FLUID TYPE

Use only SAE 10W-30 engine oil with an SE rating.

NOTE — *Do not use any type of anti-friction additives in transfer case.*

CAPACITY

Capacity is 4 pints.

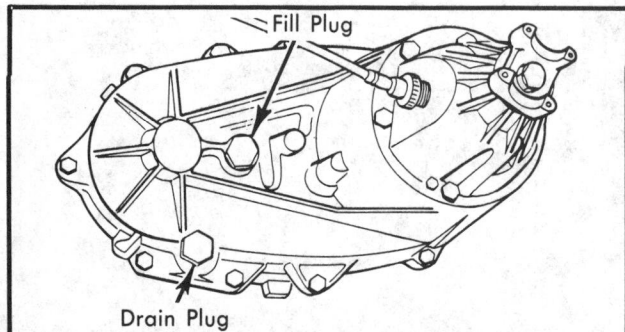

Fig. 1   Drain and Fill Plug Locations

REMOVAL & INSTALLATION

Removal — **1)** Raise vehicle and drain lubricant from transfer case. Mark front and rear output shaft yokes and propeller

shafts for reassembly reference. Disconnect speedometer cable and indicator light switch wires. Disconnect shift lever link at operating lever.

2) Place suitable support stand under transmission and remove rear crossmember. Disconnect front and rear propeller shafts at transfer case yokes and secure to frame rails with wire to keep out of way.

3) Disconnect parking brake cable guide from pivot on right frame rail (if required). Remove exhaust pipe support bracket-to-transfer case attaching bolts (if equipped). Remove transfer case-to-transmission bolts.

4) Move transfer case rearward to disengage transmission output shaft and remove transfer case. Remove all gasket material from rear of transmission adapter housing.

Installation — Reverse removal procedure and note the following: Apply suitable sealer to both sides of transfer case-to-transmission gasket and position gasket on transmission. Do not install any transfer case attaching bolts until transfer case is completely seated against transmission.

DISASSEMBLY

NOTE — *Transfer case is disassembled into subassemblies, then subassembly disassembly procedures are given.*

TRANSFER CASE

1) Remove front and rear output shaft yokes, discard yoke seal washers and nuts. Mark rear retainer and case for reassembly reference. Remove retainer attaching bolts and remove retainer. *See Fig. 3.*

NOTE — *DO NOT pry retainer off rear case. Use plastic mallet to loosen retainer if necessary.*

Case Notch

Screwdriver

Fig. 2   Removing Rear Case Assembly

2) Remove differential shim(s) and speedometer drive gear from rear output shaft. Tag shim(s) for reassembly reference. Remove rear output bearing snap ring and remove bearing from retainer using plastic mallet.

3) Using screwdriver, pry rear output shaft seal from rear retainer. Position front case assembly on wood blocks. Remove rear case-to-front case attaching bolts and using screwdrivers inserted in notches at case ends, pry rear case off front case. *See Fig. 2.*

QUADRA-TRAC MODEL 219 (Cont.)

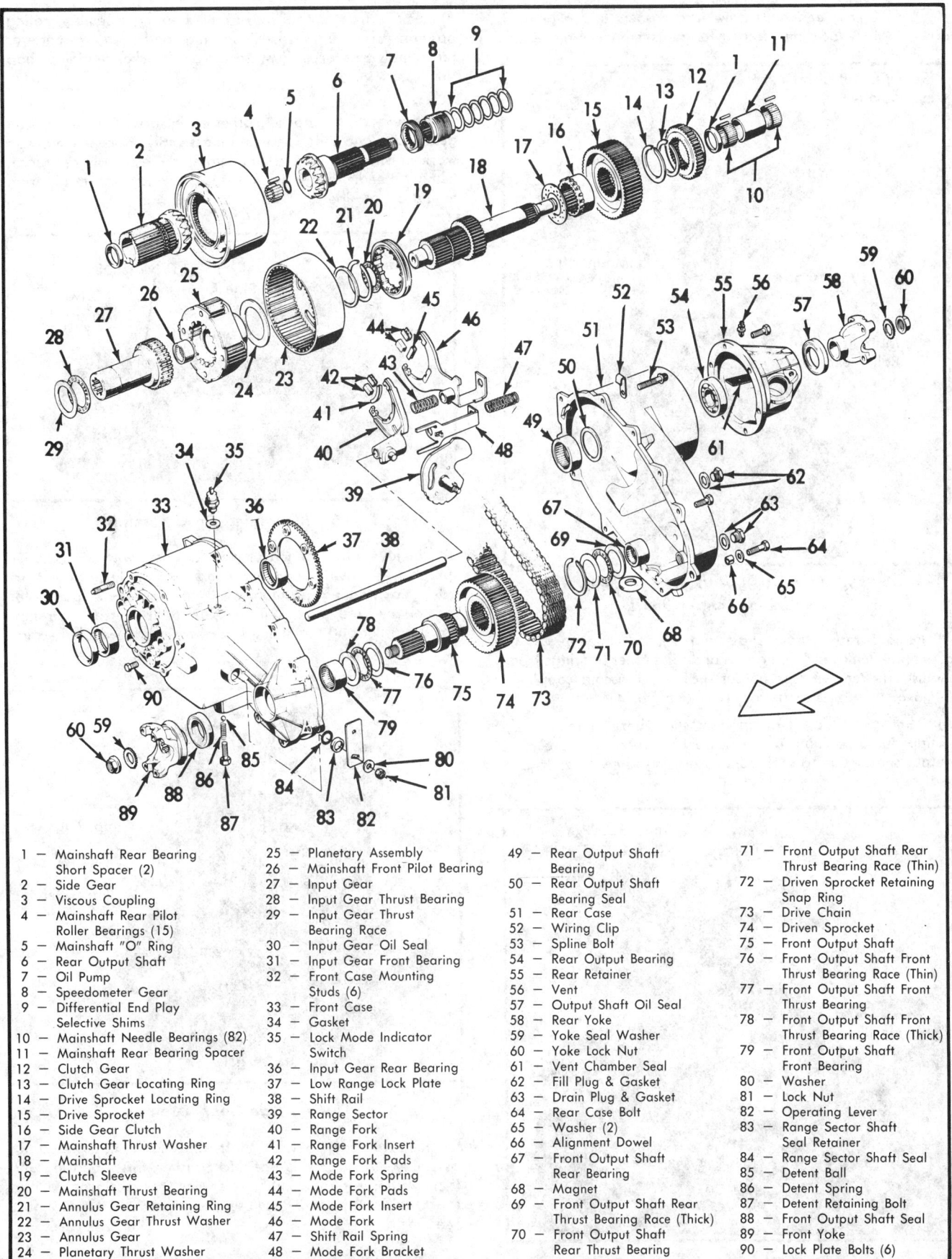

1 — Mainshaft Rear Bearing Short Spacer (2)	25 — Planetary Assembly	49 — Rear Output Shaft Bearing	71 — Front Output Shaft Rear Thrust Bearing Race (Thin)
2 — Side Gear	26 — Mainshaft Front Pilot Bearing	50 — Rear Output Shaft Bearing Seal	72 — Driven Sprocket Retaining Snap Ring
3 — Viscous Coupling	27 — Input Gear	51 — Rear Case	73 — Drive Chain
4 — Mainshaft Rear Pilot Roller Bearings (15)	28 — Input Gear Thrust Bearing	52 — Wiring Clip	74 — Driven Sprocket
5 — Mainshaft "O" Ring	29 — Input Gear Thrust Bearing Race	53 — Spline Bolt	75 — Front Output Shaft
6 — Rear Output Shaft	30 — Input Gear Oil Seal	54 — Rear Output Bearing	76 — Front Output Shaft Front Thrust Bearing Race (Thin)
7 — Oil Pump	31 — Input Gear Front Bearing	55 — Rear Retainer	77 — Front Output Shaft Front Thrust Bearing
8 — Speedometer Gear	32 — Front Case Mounting Studs (6)	56 — Vent	78 — Front Output Shaft Front Thrust Bearing Race (Thick)
9 — Differential End Play Selective Shims	33 — Front Case	57 — Output Shaft Oil Seal	79 — Front Output Shaft Front Bearing
10 — Mainshaft Needle Bearings (82)	34 — Gasket	58 — Rear Yoke	80 — Washer
11 — Mainshaft Rear Bearing Spacer	35 — Lock Mode Indicator Switch	59 — Yoke Seal Washer	81 — Lock Nut
12 — Clutch Gear	36 — Input Gear Rear Bearing	60 — Yoke Lock Nut	82 — Operating Lever
13 — Clutch Gear Locating Ring	37 — Low Range Lock Plate	61 — Vent Chamber Seal	83 — Range Sector Shaft Seal Retainer
14 — Drive Sprocket Locating Ring	38 — Shift Rail	62 — Fill Plug & Gasket	84 — Range Sector Shaft Seal
15 — Drive Sprocket	39 — Range Sector	63 — Drain Plug & Gasket	85 — Detent Ball
16 — Side Gear Clutch	40 — Range Fork	64 — Rear Case Bolt	86 — Detent Spring
17 — Mainshaft Thrust Washer	41 — Range Fork Insert	65 — Washer (2)	87 — Detent Retaining Bolt
18 — Mainshaft	42 — Range Fork Pads	66 — Alignment Dowel	88 — Front Output Shaft Seal
19 — Clutch Sleeve	43 — Mode Fork Spring	67 — Front Output Shaft Rear Bearing	89 — Front Yoke
20 — Mainshaft Thrust Bearing	44 — Mode Fork Pads	68 — Magnet	90 — Lock Plate Bolts (6)
21 — Annulus Gear Retaining Ring	45 — Mode Fork Insert	69 — Front Output Shaft Rear Thrust Bearing Race (Thick)	
22 — Annulus Gear Thrust Washer	46 — Mode Fork	70 — Front Output Shaft Rear Thrust Bearing	
23 — Annulus Gear	47 — Shift Rail Spring		
24 — Planetary Thrust Washer	48 — Mode Fork Bracket		

Fig. 3 Exploded View of Quadra-Trac Model 219 Transfer Case

QUADRA-TRAC MODEL 219 (Cont.)

NOTE — *2 case end bolts have flat washers and alignment dowels. Mark location of each for reassembly reference.*

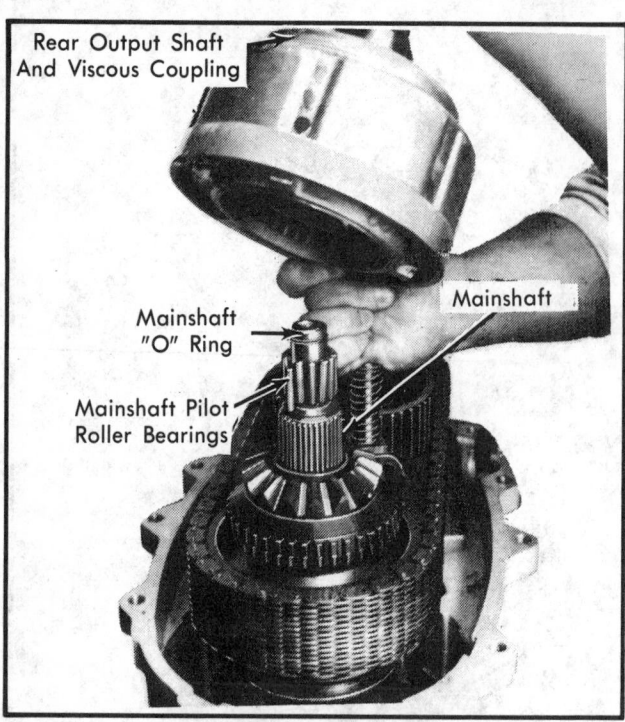

**Fig. 4   Removing Viscous Coupling
and Rear Output Shaft**

4) Remove rear output shaft and viscous coupling as an assembly. Remove "O" ring seal and pilot roller bearings from mainshaft. Remove rear output shaft from viscous coupling. Remove shift rail spring from rail. *See Fig. 4.*

5) Remove plastic oil pump from shaft bore in rear case, noting pump position for reassembly reference. Remove rear output shaft bearing seal from case using screwdriver to pry seal out.

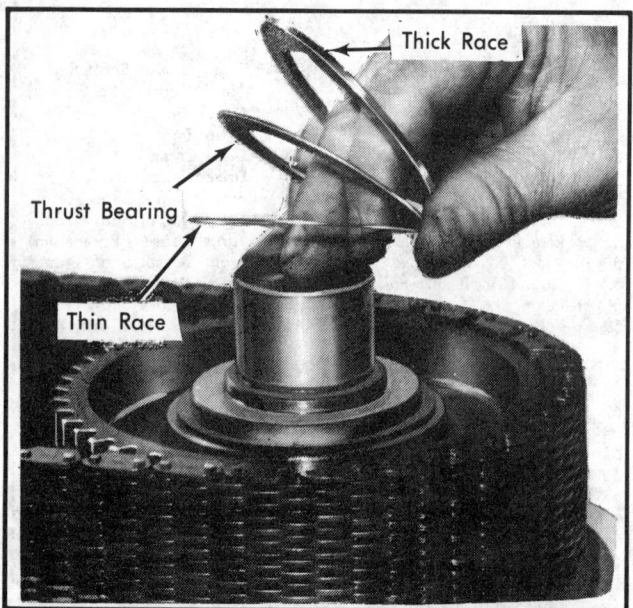

**Fig. 5   Removing Front Output Shaft
Rear Thrust Bearing Assembly**

6) Remove front output shaft thrust bearing assembly, noting position of thick washer, bearing and thin washer for reassembly reference. Remove driven sprocket retaining snap ring. *See Fig. 5.*

7) Remove drive sprocket, drive chain, driven sprocket, side gear clutch and clutch gear as an assembly. Place assembly on work bench and mark components for reassembly reference. Remove needle bearings (82) and bearing spacers (3) from mainshaft or side gear bore. *See Fig. 6.*

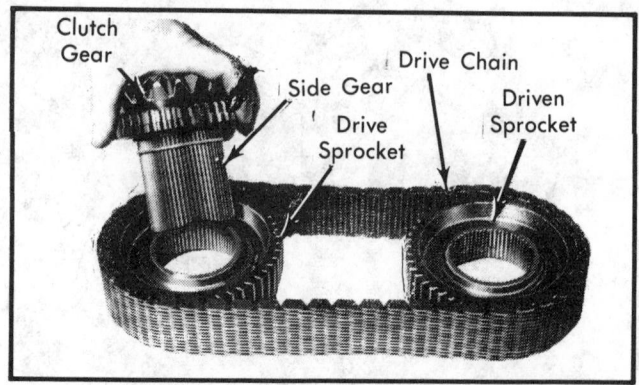

Fig. 6   Identifying Drive Assembly

8) Remove side gear/clutch gear assembly from drive sprocket. Remove 2 snap rings and remove clutch gear from side gear, noting position of snap rings and gears for reassembly reference. Remove side gear clutch, mainshaft thrust washer and remaining (short) mainshaft needle bearing spacer. *See Fig. 7.*

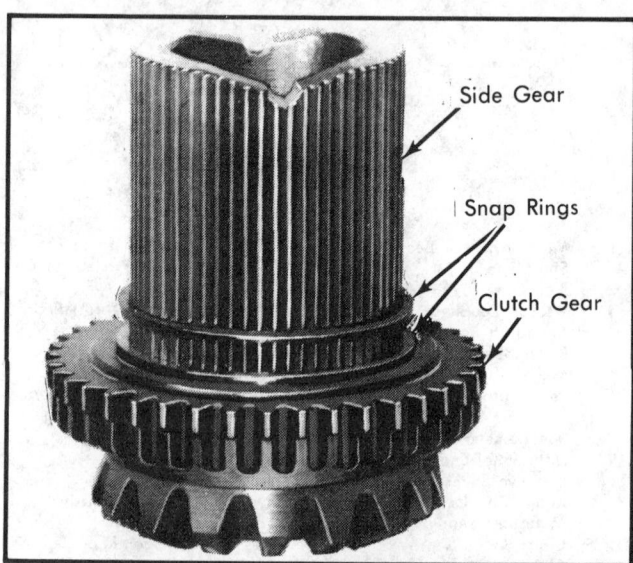

Fig. 7   Side Gear Assembly

9) Remove front output shaft and shaft thrust bearing assembly, noting position of thick washer, thrust bearing and thin washer for reassembly reference. Remove front output shaft seal from front of case using screwdriver to pry seal out. *See Fig. 8.*

10) Remove clutch sleeve, mode fork and spring as assembly, noting position of components for reassembly reference.

QUADRA-TRAC MODEL 219 (Cont.)

Remove mainshaft thrust washer and remove mainshaft. Move range operating lever downward to last detent position. Disengage range fork lug from range sector slot.

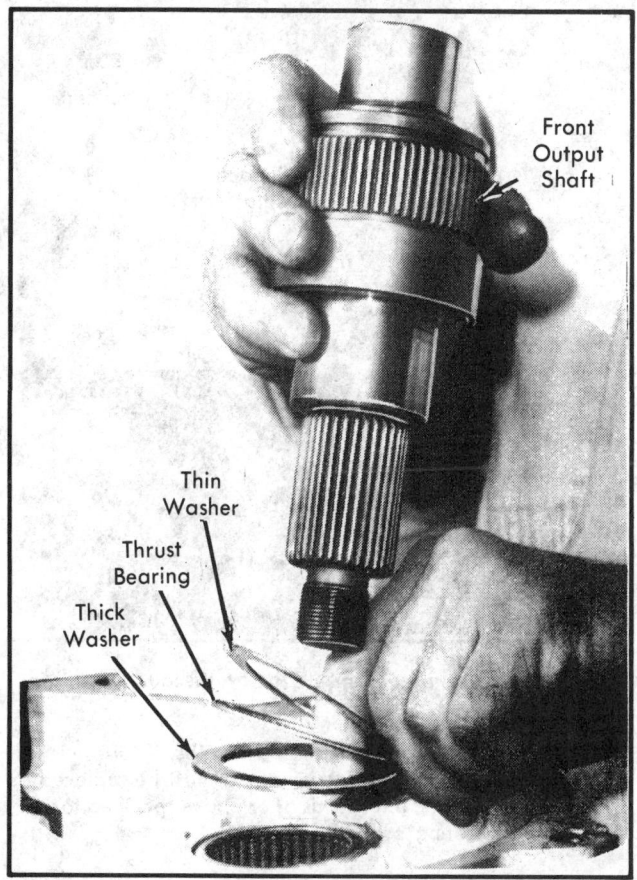

Fig. 8   Removing Front Output Shaft Assembly

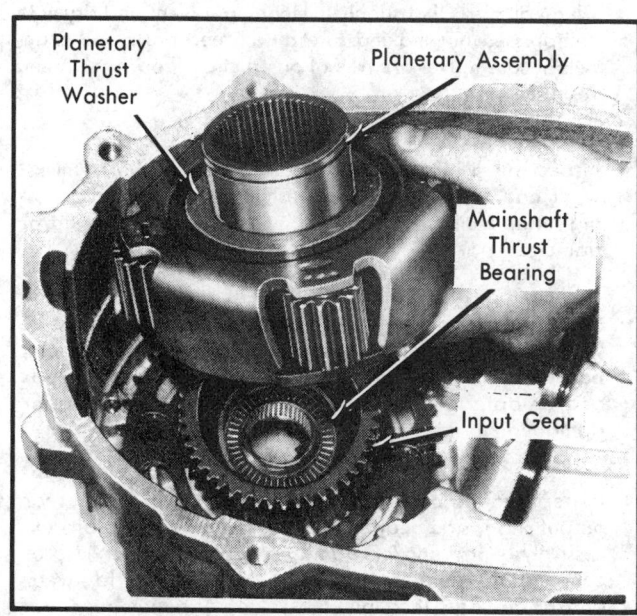

Fig. 9   Removing Planetary Assembly

11) Remove annulus gear retaining snap ring and thrust washer. Remove annulus gear and range fork as an assembly. Remove planetary thrust washer from planetary hub assembly and remove planetary assembly from case. *See Fig. 9.*

12) Remove mainshaft thrust bearing from input gear. Remove input gear, input gear thrust bearing and race. Remove range sector detent ball and spring retaining bolt and remove detent ball and spring.

13) Remove range sector and operating lever attaching nut and lock washer and remove lever. Remove range sector. Remove range sector shaft "O" ring and retainer. Remove input gear oil seal from front case using screwdriver to pry seal out. *See Fig. 10.*

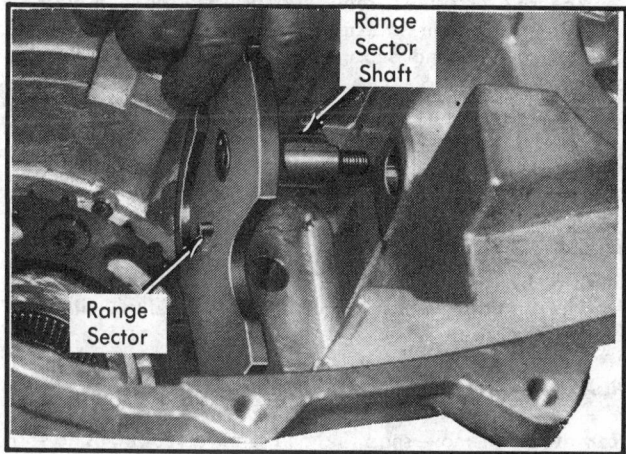

Fig. 10   Removing Range Sector Assembly

LOCKPLATE

Removal — Remove and discard lockplate attaching bolts. Remove lockplate from case and inspect for cracked, broken, chipped or excessively worn teeth and/or hub.

Installation — Coat case and lockplate surfaces around bolt holes with Loctite 515 or equivalent sealer. Position lockplate in case, align bolt holes and install and tighten new attaching lockplate bolts to specifications.

REAR OUTPUT SHAFT BEARING

Removal — Remove bearing using tool (J-8092 & J-29165 or equivalent).

Installation — Install new bearing using tool (J-8092 & J-29166 or equivalent), making sure the bearing oil feed hole is not covered.

FRONT OUTPUT SHAFT FRONT BEARING

Removal — Remove bearing using tool (J-8092 & J-29168 or equivalent).

Installation — Install new bearing using tool (J-8092 & J-29167 or equivalent), making sure the bearing oil feed hole is not covered.

QUADRA-TRAC MODEL 219 (Cont.)

FRONT OUTPUT SHAFT REAR BEARING

Removal — Remove bearing using tool (J-26941 & J-2619-01 or equivalent).

Installation — Install new bearing using tool (J-8092 & J-29163 or equivalent), making sure the bearing oil feed hole is not covered and bearing is seated flush with edge of bore in case.

INPUT GEAR FRONT & REAR BEARINGS

Removal — Remove bearings using tool (J-8092 & J-29170 or equivalent).

Installation — Install new bearings one at a time, installing rear bearing first, then front bearing, using tool (J-8092 & J-29169 or equivalent), making sure the bearing oil feed holes are not covered and bearings are seated flush with bore in case.

MAINSHAFT FRONT PILOT BEARING

Removal — If bearing cannot be removed by hand, remove bearing using tool (J-2619-01 & J-29369-1 or equivalent).

Installation — If necessary, install new bearing using tool (J-8092 & J-29174 or equivalent), making sure the bearing oil feed hole is not covered and bearing is seated flush with edge of bearing bore.

REAR OUTPUT BEARING & SEAL

Removal — Remove snap ring and remove bearing using soft-faced mallet (rawhide or equivalent) and brass punch.

Installation — Install new bearing using tool (J-8092 & J-7818 or equivalent), making sure the shielded side of bearing faces interior of transfer case. Install snap ring. Install new seal using tool (J-29162 or equivalent).

ANNULUS GEAR BUSHING

Removal & Installation — Remove bushing using tool (J-8092 & J-29185 or equivalent). Install using same tool, making sure to remove any chips from annulus gear after removal or installation.

TORQUE BIAS CHECK FOR VISCOUS COUPLING

1) Install clutch gear on side gear and install assembly in viscous coupling. Mount viscous coupling assembly in vise, placing wood blocks between vise jaws and side gear, clamping assembly firmly. *See Fig. 11.*

NOTE — *Wood blocks MUST be placed between vise jaws and side gear to prevent damaging side gear.*

2) Make sure clutch gear is fully engaged in viscous coupling. If necessary, loosen vise and reposition wood blocks to support gear in coupling. Install rear output shaft in viscous coupling.

3) Install yoke and nut on rear output shaft. Rotate rear output shaft using suitable torque wrench and measure torque required to rotate shaft in coupling.

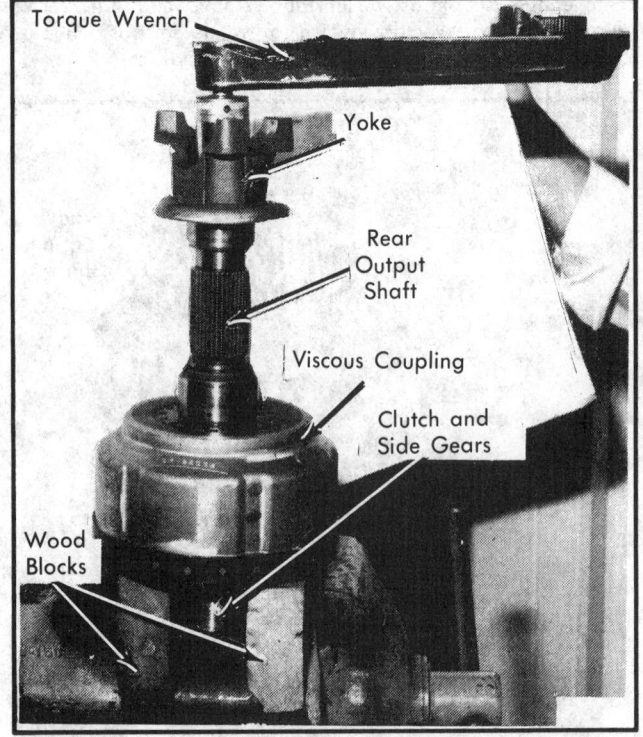

Fig. 11 Checking Torque Bias of Viscous Coupling

4) Torque should be a minimum of 25 ft. lbs. If torque is less than specified, coupling is defective and must be replaced as unit is not serviceable. If torque is at or above specified torque, coupling is operating properly.

CLEANING & INSPECTION

- Clean all parts thoroughly in cleaning solvent and dry with compressed air, making sure all oil feed ports and channels in case halves are free of obstructions and/or cleaning residue.

- Inspect all gear teeth and gear splines for burrs, nicks, wear and/or damage. Remove minor burrs and nicks using suitable oilstone. Replace any excessively worn and/or damaged parts.

- Inspect all snap rings and thrust washers for excessive wear and/or damage. Inspect case halves for cracks, porosity, damaged mating surfaces, stripped bolt threads and/or distortion. Replace any excessively worn and/or damaged parts.

- Inspect bearing bores in both case halves, input gear, rear output shaft, side gear and rear retainer. Replace any excessively worn and/or damaged parts. Inspect viscous coupling for fluid leakage and pinion gears for wear and/or damage. If coupling is leaking or pinion gears are worn or damaged in any way, replace viscous coupling as an assembly.

QUADRA-TRAC MODEL 219 (Cont.)

REASSEMBLY

TRANSFER CASE

1) Install new input gear and rear output shaft bearing oil seals, seating flush with edge of seal bore or in seal groove in case. Coat seal lips with petroleum jelly. Install input gear thrust bearing race in case counterbore.

2) Install input gear thrust bearing on input gear and install assembly into case. Install mainshaft thrust bearing in bearing recess in input gear. Install planetary assembly on input gear, making sure planetary pinion teeth mesh fully with input gear.

3) Install planetary thrust washer on planetary hub. Install new sector shaft "O" ring and retainer in shaft bore in case. Install range sector in front case. Install operating lever, washer and lock nut, tightening lock nut to specifications.

4) Install detent spring, ball and retaining bolt in front case detent bore, tightening bolt to specifications. Move range sector to last detent position. Assemble annulus gear and range fork, installing assembly on and over planetary assembly, making sure annulus gear is fully meshed with planetary pinions.

5) Insert range fork lug in range sector detent slot. Install annulus thrust washer and retaining ring on annulus gear hub. Install mainshaft, making sure shaft is fully seated in input gear, aligning mainshaft thrust washer in input gear if necessary.

6) Install mainshaft thrust washer on mainshaft. Install short mainshaft needle bearing spacer on shaft. Coat mainshaft with petroleum jelly and install 41 needle bearings on shaft. Make sure bearings seat on short spacer. See Fig. 12.

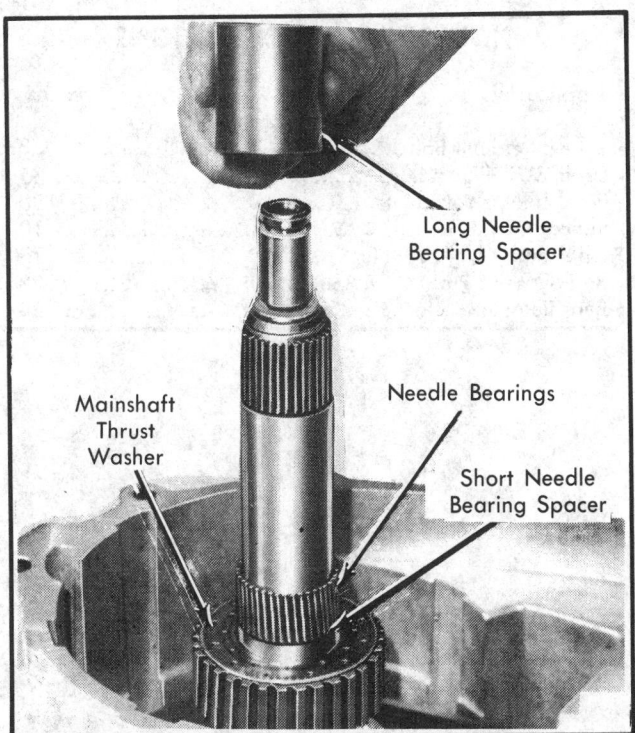

Fig. 12 Installing Mainshaft Needle Bearings

7) Install long mainshaft needle bearing spacer on shaft. Lower spacer onto already installed needle bearings, being careful not to disturb needle bearings. Align shift rail bore in case with bore in range fork and install shift rail.

NOTE — *Remove all traces of oil from case shift rail bore before installing shift rail. Oil in case bore may prevent shift rail from completely seating, preventing rear case installation.*

8) Assemble mode fork, mode fork spring and bracket. Install clutch sleeve in mode fork, making sure sleeve is installed so I.D. numbers on sleeve face upward after sleeve is installed. See Fig. 13.

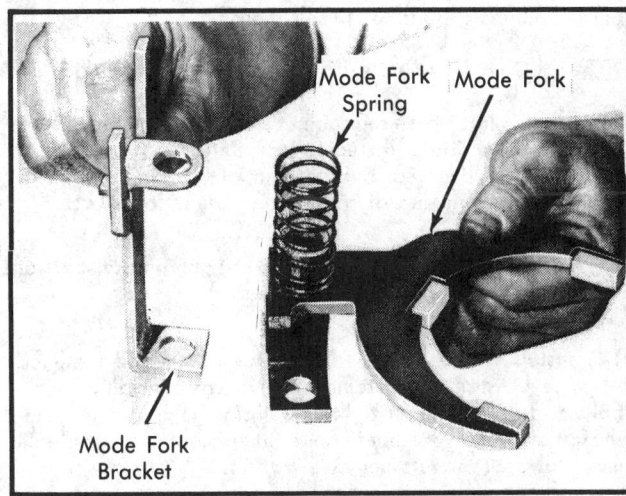

Fig. 13 Exploded View of Mode Fork Spring and Bracket

9) Align clutch sleeve and mode fork assembly with shift rail and install assembly on shift rail and mainshaft, making sure clutch sleeve is meshed with mainshaft gear. Install remaining 41 needle bearings on mainshaft. Install side gear clutch on mainshaft with clutch gear teeth facing downward, making sure gear teeth mesh with clutch sleeve.

10) Install remaining short mainshaft needle bearing spacer, being careful not to disturb already installed needle bearings. Install front output shaft front thrust bearing assembly in front case, installing thick washer first, then thrust bearing and thin washer.

11) Install front output shaft in front case. Install clutch gear on side gear (tapered side of clutch gear teeth must face side gear teeth). Install clutch gear and drive sprocket locating snap rings on side gear, making sure snap rings face each other.

12) Position drive and driven sprockets in drive chain and install assembled side and clutch gears in drive sprocket. Install drive assembly, making sure to keep assembly level while lowering at same time onto both shafts. Make sure not to disturb mainshaft needle bearings during installation of drive assembly.

13) Install driven sprocket retaining snap ring. Install front output shaft rear thrust bearing assembly on front output shaft, installing thin washer first, then thrust bearing and thick washer. Install shift rail spring on shift rail. Install new "O" ring on mainshaft pilot bearing hub.

QUADRA-TRAC MODEL 219 (Cont.)

14) Coat mainshaft pilot bearing hub with petroleum jelly. Install mainshaft pilot roller bearings on shaft. Install rear output shaft in viscous coupling, making sure shaft is fully seated. Install viscous coupling assembly and rear output shaft on mainshaft.

15) Align clutch gear teeth with viscous coupling teeth and seat coupling fully onto clutch gear. When correctly installed, clutch gear teeth will not be visible or extend out of coupling. Install magnet in front case (if removed).

16) Apply Loctite 515 or equivalent sealer to mating surface of front case and to all case attaching bolts. Install rear case on front case aligning case dowels and install case attaching bolts, tightening bolts to specifications.

NOTE — *2 case end dowel bolts require flat washers.*

17) Install oil pump on rear output shaft and seat it in case. Install pump so side with recess faces interior of case. Install speedometer drive gear and differential shim on output shaft, making sure long end of speedometer gear faces case.

NOTE — *Speedometer gear fits correctly on output shaft one way only, long end faces case.*

18) Install vent chamber seal in rear retainer (if removed). Align and install rear retainer on rear case. Install attaching bolts and tighten finger tight only. Install yoke on rear output shaft, tightening yoke nut finger tight only. Mount suitable dial indicator on rear retainer. See Fig. 14.

19) Position dial indicator stem on top of yoke nut. Install yoke on front output shaft and rotate front shaft 10 complete revolutions. Zero dial indicator and rotate front output shaft again, noting end play. End play should be between .002-.010".

20) If end play was incorrect, remove rear retainer and add or subtract differential shims and check end play again until correct. Remove both output shaft yokes and install new front and rear yoke seals.

21) Remove rear retainer attaching bolts and remove rear retainer. Apply Loctite 515 or equivalent sealer to mating surface of retainer and to attaching bolts. Install rear retainer and attaching bolts, tightening to specifications.

22) Install new yoke seal washers on output shafts. Install yokes and nuts and tighten to specifications. Install drain plug.

Refill transfer case with lubricant to correct fluid level and install fill plug, tightening drain and fill plugs to specifications.

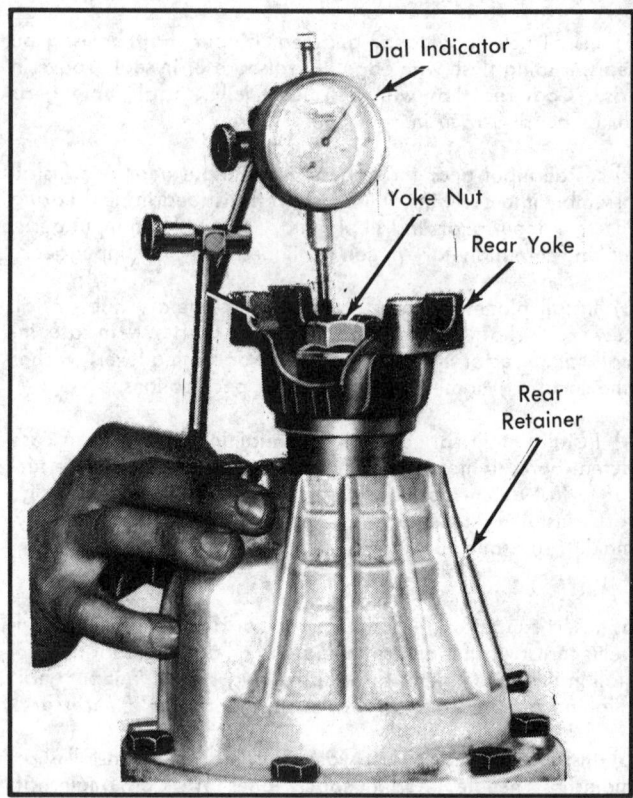

Fig. 14 Checking Differential End Play

TIGHTENING SPECIFICATIONS

Application	Ft. Lbs.
Detent Retainer Bolt	23
Drain & Fill Plugs	35
Front & Rear Yoke Nuts	120
Indicator Switch	18
Operating Lever Lock Nut	18
Rear Case-to-Front Case Bolts	23
Rear Retainer Bolts	23

English-Metric Conversion Chart

FRACTIONS TO INCHES & METRIC EQUIVALENTS

Fractions	Inches	MM	Fractions	Inches	MM
1/64	.016	.397	33/64	.516	13.097
1/32	.031	.794	17/32	.531	13.494
3/64	.047	1.191	35/64	.547	13.891
1/16	.063	1.588	9/16	.563	14.288
5/64	.078	1.984	37/64	.578	14.684
3/32	.094	2.381	19/32	.594	15.081
7/64	.109	2.778	39/64	.609	15.478
1/8	.125	3.175	5/8	.625	15.875
9/64	.141	3.572	41/64	.641	16.272
5/32	.156	3.969	21/32	.656	16.669
11/64	.172	4.366	43/64	.672	17.066
3/16	.188	4.763	11/16	.687	17.463
13/64	.203	5.159	45/64	.703	17.859
7/32	.219	5.556	23/32	.719	18.256
15/64	.234	5.953	47/64	.734	18.653
1/4	.250	6.350	3/4	.750	19.050
17/64	.266	6.747	49/64	.766	19.447
9/32	.281	7.144	25/32	.781	19.844
19/64	.297	7.541	51/64	.797	20.241
5/16	.313	7.938	13/16	.813	20.638
21/64	.328	8.334	53/64	.828	21.034
11/32	.344	8.731	27/32	.844	21.431
23/64	.359	9.128	55/64	.859	21.828
3/8	.375	9.525	7/8	.875	22.225
25/64	.391	9.922	57/64	.891	22.622
13/32	.406	10.319	29/32	.906	23.019
27/64	.422	10.716	59/64	.922	23.416
7/16	.438	11.113	15/16	.938	23.813
29/64	.453	11.509	61/64	.953	24.209
15/32	.469	11.906	31/32	.969	24.606
31/64	.484	12.303	63/64	.984	25.003
1/2	.500	12.700			

CONVERSION FACTORS

Unit	To	Unit	Multiply By
LENGTH			
Millimeters		Inches	.03937
Inches		Millimeters	25.4
Meters		Feet	3.28084
Feet		Meters	.3048
Kilometers		Miles	.62137
Miles		Kilometers	1.60935
AREA			
Square Centimeters		Square Inches	.155
Square Inches		Square Centimeters	6.45159
VOLUME			
Cubic Centimeters		Cubic Inches	.06103
Cubic Inches		Cubic Centimeters	16.38703
Liters		Cubic Inches	61.025
Cubic Inches		Liters	.01639
Liters		Quarts	1.05672
Quarts		Liters	.94633
Liters		Pints	2.11344
Pints		Liters	.47317
Liters		Ounces	33.81497
Ounces		Liters	.02957

Unit	To	Unit	Multiply By
WEIGHT			
Grams		Ounces	.03527
Ounces		Grams	28.34953
Kilograms		Pounds	2.20462
Pounds		Kilograms	.45359
WORK			
Centimeter Kilograms		Inch Pounds	.8676
Inch Pounds		Centimeter Kilograms	1.15262
Meter Kilograms		Foot Pounds	7.23301
Foot Pounds		Meter Kilograms	.13826
PRESSURE			
Kilograms/ Sq. Centimeter		Pounds/Sq.Inch	14.22334
Pounds/Sq.Inch		Kilograms/Sq.Centimeter	.07031
Bar		Pounds/Sq.Inch	14.504
Pounds/Sq.Inch		Bar	.06895
Atmosphere		Pounds/Sq.Inch	14.696
Pounds/Sq.Inch		Atmosphere	.06805
TEMPERATURE			
Centigrade Degrees		Fahrenheit Degrees	$(C° \times 9/5) + 32$
Fahrenheit Degrees		Centigrade Degrees	$(F° - 32) \times 5/9$

English-Metric Conversion Chart

MILLIMETERS TO INCHES

Conversion Factor — Multiply known millimeter figure by .03937

MM	Inches	MM	Inches	MM	Inches	MM	Inches	MM	Inches
1	.039	21	.827	41	1.614	61	2.402	81	3.189
2	.079	22	.866	42	1.654	62	2.441	82	3.228
3	.118	23	.906	43	1.693	63	2.480	83	3.268
4	.157	24	.945	44	1.732	64	2.520	84	3.307
5	.197	25	.984	45	1.772	65	2.559	85	3.346
6	.236	26	1.024	46	1.811	66	2.598	86	3.386
7	.276	27	1.063	47	1.850	67	2.638	87	3.425
8	.315	28	1.102	48	1.890	68	2.677	88	3.465
9	.354	29	1.142	49	1.929	69	2.717	89	3.504
10	.394	30	1.181	50	1.969	70	2.756	90	3.543
11	.433	31	1.220	51	2.008	71	2.795	91	3.583
12	.472	32	1.260	52	2.047	72	2.835	92	3.622
13	.512	33	1.299	53	2.087	73	2.874	93	3.661
14	.551	34	1.339	54	2.126	74	2.913	94	3.701
15	.591	35	1.378	55	2.165	75	2.953	95	3.740
16	.630	36	1.417	56	2.205	76	2.992	96	3.780
17	.669	37	1.457	57	2.244	77	3.031	97	3.819
18	.709	38	1.496	58	2.283	78	3.071	98	3.858
19	.748	39	1.535	59	2.323	79	3.110	99	3.898
20	.787	40	1.575	60	2.362	80	3.150	100	3.937

INCHES TO MILLIMETERS

Conversion Factor — Multiply known inch figure by 25.40

Inches	MM	Inches	MM	Inches	MM	Inches	MM	Inches	MM
.001	.025	.040	1.016	.340	8.636	.640	16.256	.940	23.876
.002	.051	.050	1.270	.350	8.890	.650	16.510	.950	24.130
.003	.076	.060	1.524	.360	9.144	.660	16.764	.960	24.384
.004	.102	.070	1.778	.370	9.398	.670	17.018	.970	24.638
.005	.127	.080	2.032	.380	9.652	.680	17.272	.980	24.892
.006	.152	.090	2.286	.390	9.906	.690	17.526	.990	25.146
.007	.178	.100	2.540	.400	10.160	.700	17.780	1.000	25.400
.008	.203	.110	2.794	.410	10.414	.710	18.034	2.000	50.800
.009	.229	.120	3.048	.420	10.668	.720	18.288	3.000	76.200
.010	.254	.130	3.302	.430	10.922	.730	18.542	4.000	101.600
.011	.279	.140	3.556	.440	11.176	.740	18.796	5.000	127.000
.012	.305	.150	3.810	.450	11.430	.750	19.050		
.013	.330	.160	4.064	.460	11.684	.760	19.304		
.014	.356	.170	4.318	.470	11.938	.770	19.558		
.015	.381	.180	4.572	.480	12.192	.780	19.812		
.016	.406	.190	4.826	.490	12.446	.790	20.066		
.017	.432	.200	5.080	.500	12.700	.800	20.320		
.018	.457	.210	5.334	.510	12.954	.810	20.574		
.019	.483	.220	5.558	.520	13.208	.820	20.828		
.020	.508	.230	5.842	.530	13.462	.830	21.082		
.021	.533	.240	6.096	.540	13.716	.840	21.336		
.022	.559	.250	6.350	.550	13.970	.850	21.590		
.023	.584	.260	6.604	.560	14.224	.860	21.844		
.024	.610	.270	6.858	.570	14.478	.870	22.098		
.025	.635	.280	7.112	.580	14.732	.880	22.352		
.026	.652	.290	7.366	.590	14.986	.890	22.606		
.027	.686	.300	7.620	.600	15.240	.900	22.860		
.028	.711	.310	7.874	.610	15.494	.910	23.114		
.029	.737	.320	8.128	.620	15.748	.920	23.368		
.030	.762	.330	8.382	.630	16.002	.930	23.622		

Torque & Drill Conversion Chart

TORQUE CONVERSIONS
FOOT POUNDS TO METER KILOGRAMS

Ft. Lbs.	Mkg	Ft. Lbs.	Mkg	Ft. Lbs.	Mkg	Ft. Lbs.	Mkg
1	.14	26	3.60	51	7.05	76	10.51
2	.28	27	3.73	52	7.19	77	10.65
3	.41	28	3.87	53	7.33	78	10.78
4	.55	29	4.01	54	7.47	79	10.92
5	.69	30	4.15	55	7.60	80	11.06
6	.83	31	4.29	56	7.74	81	11.20
7	.97	32	4.42	57	7.88	82	11.34
8	1.11	33	4.56	58	8.02	83	11.48
9	1.24	34	4.70	59	8.16	84	11.61
10	1.38	35	4.84	60	8.30	85	11.75
11	1.52	36	4.98	61	8.43	86	11.89
12	1.66	37	5.12	62	8.57	87	12.03
13	1.80	38	5.25	63	8.71	88	12.17
14	1.94	39	5.39	64	8.85	89	12.31
15	2.07	40	5.53	65	8.99	90	12.44
16	2.21	41	5.67	66	9.13	91	12.58
17	2.35	42	5.81	67	9.26	92	12.72
18	2.49	43	5.95	68	9.40	93	12.86
19	2.63	44	6.08	69	9.54	94	13.00
20	2.77	45	6.22	70	9.68	95	13.13
21	2.90	46	6.36	71	9.82	96	13.27
22	3.04	47	6.50	72	9.95	97	13.41
23	3.18	48	6.64	73	10.09	98	13.55
24	3.32	49	6.77	74	10.23	99	13.69
25	3.46	50	6.91	75	10.37	100	13.83

DRILL SIZE & IDENTIFICATION

Drill Diam.	Drill Size	Drill Diam.	Drill Size	Drill Diam.	Drill Size	Drill Diam.	Drill Size
.413"	Z	.2280"	1	.1440"	27	.0550"	54
.404"	Y	.2210"	2	.1405"	28	.0520"	55
.397"	X	.2130"	3	.1360"	29	.0465"	56
.386"	W	.2090"	4	.1285"	30	.0430"	57
.377"	V	.2055"	5	.1200"	31	.0420"	58
.368"	U	.2040"	6	.1160"	32	.0410"	59
.358"	T	.2010"	7	.1130"	33	.0400"	60
.348"	S	.1990"	8	.1110"	34	.0390"	61
.339"	R	.1960"	9	.1100"	35	.0380"	62
.332"	Q	.1935"	10	.1065"	36	.0370"	63
.323"	P	.1910"	11	.1040"	37	.0360"	64
.316"	O	.1890"	12	.1015"	38	.0350"	65
.302"	N	.1850"	13	.0995"	39	.0330"	66
.295"	M	.1820"	14	.0980"	40	.0320"	67
.290"	L	.1800"	15	.0960"	41	.0310"	68
.281"	K	.1770"	16	.0935"	42	.0292"	69
.277"	J	.1730"	17	.0890"	43	.0280"	70
.272"	I	.1695"	18	.0860"	44	.0260"	71
.266"	H	.1660"	19	.0820"	45	.0250"	72
.261"	G	.1610"	20	.0810"	46	.0240"	73
.257"	F	.1590"	21	.0785"	47	.0225"	74
.250"	E	.1570"	22	.0760"	48	.0210"	75
.246"	D	.1540"	23	.0730"	49	.0200"	76
.242"	C	.1520"	24	.0700"	50	.0180"	77
.238"	B	.1495"	25	.0670"	51	.0160"	78
.234"	A	.1470"	26	.0635"	52	.0145"	79
				.0595"	53	.0135"	80

BONUS

MEDIUM & HEAVY DUTY TRUCK ENGINE SPECIFICATIONS SECTION

ENGINE	IGNITION TIMING		DISTRIBUTOR		SPARK PLUGS		CARBURETOR	No.
	Man. Trans.	Auto. Trans.	Cam Angle	Point Gap	Type	Gap	Make & Type	
CHRYSLER CORP								
360"-3 V8	4°B②	4°B②	①	①	CH RF-10	.035"	Holley 2245	1
446" V8	5°B	5°B	①	①	CH RBN-13Y	.035"	Holley 4150G	2
FORD								
370" V8								
2-Bbl	6°B	6°B	①	①	MC ASF-32	.044"	Holley 2300EG	3
4-Bbl	6°B②	6°B②	①	①	MC ASF-32	.044"	Holley 4180EG	4
429" V8	6°B	6°B	①	①	MC ASF-32	.044"	Holley 4180EG	5
477" & 534" V8	10°B	10°B	①	①	MC BYSF-31-4	.040"	Holley 4150EG	6
GENERAL MOTORS								
292" 6 Cyl	8°B	8°B	①	①	AC R44T	.035"	Roch 1ME	7
350" V8	4°B	4°B	①	①	AC R44T	.045"	Roch 2G	8
366" V8	8°B	8°B	①	①	AC R43T	.045"	Holley 4150EG	9
427" & 454" V8	8°B	8°B	①	①	AC R42T	.045"	Holley 4150EG	10
IHC								
345" V8	TDC	TDC	①	①	CH RJ6	.030"	Holley 2300EG	11
392" V8	TDC	TDC	①	①	CH RJ6	.030"	Holley 2300EG	12
404" V8								
2-Bbl	9°B	9°B	①	①	CH RBN-13Y	.030"	Holley 2300EG	13
4-Bbl	9°B	9°B	①	①	CH RBN-13Y	.030"	Holley 4150G	14
446" V8	5°B	5°B	①	①	CH RBN-13Y	.030"	Holley 4150G	15
537" V8	7°B	7°B	①	①	CH RBN-11Y	.030"	Holley 4150G	16

IGNITION TIMING: B — BTDC; **A** — ATDC.

SPARK PLUGS: AL — Autolite; **CH** — Champion; **MC** — Motorcraft.

CARBURETORS: Roch — Rochester.

No.	HOT IDLE		FAST IDLE			Remarks
	Man. Trans.	Auto. Trans.	Man. Trans.		Auto. Trans.	
			RPM	Cam Step	RPM	
1	700③	700③	1600	High	1600	①Electronic Ignition.
2	650	650	2400	.....	2400	②On models with carb TQ9261S, set at 10°.
						③On models with carb TQ9261S, set to 750 RPM.
3	600	600	2200	High	2200	①Electronic Ignition.
4	600	600	2500	High	2500	②Calif models, 2°.
5	600	600	2700	High	2700	
6	600	600	2500	High	2500	
7	700	700	2400	High	2400	①Electronic Ignition.
8	700	700	②	②	②	②See Tune-Up Decal.
9	700	700	2200	High	2200	
10	700	700	2200	High	2200	
11	650	650	2000	.....	2000	①Electronic Ignition.
12	650	650	2000	.....	2000	
13	550	650	1800	.....	1800	
14	550	650	2400	.....	2400	
15	650	650	2400	.....	2400	
16	525	625	2000	.....	2000	

CHRYSLER CORP.

GENERAL SPECIFICATIONS

Engine	Net HP At RPM	Torque (Ft. Lbs. at RPM)	Compr. Ratio	Bore	Stroke	Displ. Cu. Ins.
318"-3	160@4000	180@3600	8.5:1	3.910"	3.310"	318.31"
360"-3	180@3600	260@2000	8.40:1	4.000"	3.580"	360.10"
413"-3	220@3200	325@2000	7.54:1	4.180"	3.750"	413.40"

VALVES

Engine & Valve	Head Diam.	Face Angle	Seat Angle	Seat Width	Stem Diameter	Stem Clearance	Valve Lift
318"-3							
Int.	1.806-1.816"	45°	45°	.080-.105"	.3720-.3730"	.017" Max.	.373"
Exh.	1.512-1.522"	45°	45°	.090-.100"	.3710-.3720"	.017" Max.	.400"
360"-3							
Int.	1.875-1.885"	45°	45°	.065-.085"	.3720-.3730"	.017" Max.	.410"
Exh.	1.595-1.605"	43°	43°	.040-.060"	.3710-.3720"	.017" Max.	.400"
413"							
Int.	1.875-1.885"	45°	45°	.063-.094"	.3720-.3730"	.0010-.0020"	.360"
Exh.	1.495-1.505"	45°	45°	.094-.109"	.4330-.4340"	.0030-.0050"	.360"

VALVE SPRINGS

Engine	Free Length	PRESSURE (LBS.)	
		Valve Closed	Valve Open
318"-3			
Int.	2.000"	78-88@1.687"	170-184@1.313"
Exh.	1.813"	78-88@1.687"	170-184@1.313"
360-3"			
Int.	2.000"	78-88@1.687"	170-184@1.313"
Exh.	2.000"	78-88@1.687"	170-184@1.313"
413"			
Int.	2.313"	75-85@1.859"	173-187@1.469"
Exh.	2.125"	80-90@1.750"	168-182@1.328"

CAMSHAFT

Engine	Journal Diam.	Clearance	Lobe Lift
318"-3 & 360"-3	.....	005" Max.	.....
No. 1	1.9980-1.9990"		
No. 2	1.9820-1.9830"		
No. 3	1.9670-1.9680"		
No. 4	1.9510-1.9520"		
No. 5	1.5605-1.5615"		
413"	.....	.001-.003"	.....
No. 1	2.0000"		
No. 2	1.9840"		
No. 3	1.9690"		
No. 4	1.9530"		
No. 5	1.7500"		

CRANKSHAFT MAIN & CONNECTING ROD BEARINGS

	MAIN BEARINGS				CONNECTING ROD BEARINGS		
Engine	Journal Diam.	Clearance	Thrust Bearing	Crankshaft End Play	Journal Diam.	Clearance	Side Play
318"-3	2.4995-2.5005"	.0005-.0015"	No. 3	.002-.007"	2.1235-2.1245"	.0010-.0020"	.006-.014"
360"-3	2.8095-2.8105"	.0005-.0015"	No. 3	.002-.007"	2.1240-2.1250"	.0005-.0025"	.006-.014"
413"	2.7495-2.7505"	.0015-.0025"	No. 3	.002-.009"	2.3740-2.3750"	.0010-.0020"	.009-.017"

CHRYSLER CORP. (Cont.)

PISTONS, PINS, RINGS

| Engine | PISTONS | PINS | | RINGS | | |
	Clearance	Piston Fit	Rod Fit	Rings	End Gap	Side Clearance
318"-3	.0005-.0015"	.00045-.00075"	.0007-.0014"	1&2	.010-.020"	.0015-.0030"
				3	.015-.055"	.0005-.0050"
360"-3	.0005-.0015"	.00025-.00075"	.0007-.0017"	1&2	.010-.020"	.0015-.0030"
				3	.015-.055"	.0005-.0050"
413"	.0003-.0013"	.00045-.00075"	.0007-.0014"	1&2	.013-.023"	.0010-.0025"
				3	.013-.025"	.0010-.0025"

OIL PUMP SPECIFICATIONS

318" & 360"

Pump Cover Wear	.0015" Max.
Clearance Over Rotors	.004" Max.
Outer Rotor Diameter	2.469" Min.
Inner & Outer Rotor Thickness	.649" Min.
Outer Rotor-to-Pump Body	.014" Max.
Relief Valve Spring	16.2-17.2 lbs. @ 1.344"

413"

Pump Cover Wear	.0015" Max.
Outer Rotor Thickness	.943" Min.
Inner Rotor Thickness	.942" Min.
Outer Rotor Diameter	2.469" Min.
Outer Rotor-to-Pump Body	.014" Max.
Clearance Over Rotors	.004" Max.
Tip Clearance Between Rotors	.010" Max.
Relief Valve Spring	22.3-23.3 lbs. @ 1.549"

TIGHTENING SPECIFICATIONS

318" & 360"

Application	Ft. Lbs.
Cylinder Head Bolts①	95
Main Bearing Cap Bolts	85
Connecting Rod Cap Nuts	45
Vibration Damper-to-Crankshaft Bolt	100
Flywheel Bolts	55

① — See cylinder head tightening sequence.

413"

Application	Ft. Lbs.
Cylinder Head Bolts①	70
Main Bearing Cap Bolts	85
Connecting Rod Cap Nuts	45
Vibration Damper-to-Crankshaft Bolt	135
Flywheel Bolts	5

① — See cylinder head tightening sequence.

CYLINDER HEAD TIGHTENING SEQUENCE

318" & 360"   413"

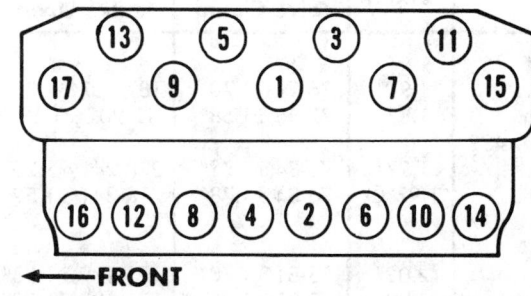

← FRONT

FORD MOTOR CO.

GENERAL SPECIFICATIONS

Engine	Net HP At RPM	Torque (Ft. Lbs. at RPM)	Compr. Ratio	Bore	Stroke	Displ. Cu. Ins.
300″	119@3200	243@1200	8.9:1	4.00″	3.98″	300″
370″ 2V	174@3600	274@2200	8.4:1	4.05″	3.59″	370″
370″ 4V	196@3600	293@2600	8.0:1	4.05″	3.59″	370″
429″	223@4000	343@2700	8.0:1	4.36″	3.59″	429″
475″	.....	.....	.....	4.50″	3.75″	475″
477″	210@3200	393@2300	7.2:1	4.50″	3.75″	477″
534″	227@3200	431@2100	7.3:1	4.50″	4.20″	534″

PISTONS, PINS, RINGS

Engine	PISTONS Clearance	PINS Piston Fit	PINS Rod Fit	RINGS Rings	RINGS End Gap	RINGS Side Clearance
300″	.0014-.0022″	.0002-.0004″	Press Fit	1	.010-.020″	.0019-.0036″
				2	.010-.020″	.0020-.0040″
				3	.010-.035″	①
370″	.0018-.0039″	.0003-.0006″	Press Fit	1	.010-.022″	.0019-.0039″
				2	.010-.023″	.0020-.0040″
				3	②	.0015-.0030″③
429″	.0019-.0037″	.0003-.0006″	Press Fit	1	.013-.025″	.0019-.0036″
				2	.010-.020″	.0020-.0040″
				3	.013-.028″	.0020-.0035″
475″, 477″, 534″	.0028-.0034″	.0003-.0005″	.0002-.0004″	1	.018-.028″	.0029-.0046″
				2	.015-.025″	.0029-.0046″
				3	.013-.028″	.0014″-.0031″

① — Ring should be snug fit in groove with no visible side play.
② — Steel rail type ring, gap not measured.
③ — On 370″ 2V, ring should be snug fit in groove with no visible side play.

CRANKSHAFT MAIN & CONNECTING ROD BEARINGS

Engine	MAIN BEARINGS Journal Diam.	MAIN BEARINGS Clearance	MAIN BEARINGS Thrust Bearing	MAIN BEARINGS Crankshaft End Play	CONNECTING ROD BEARINGS Journal Diam.	CONNECTING ROD BEARINGS Clearance	CONNECTING ROD BEARINGS Side Play
300″	2.3982-2.3990″	.0008-.0015″	No. 3	.004-.008″	2.1228-2.1236″	.0008-.0015″	.006-.013″
370″, 429″	2.9994-3.0002″	.0008-.0026″	No. 3	.004-.008″	2.4992-2.5000″	.0008-.0028″	.010-.020″
475″, 477″, 534″	3.1246-3.1254″	.0019-.0028″	No. 3	.004-.008″	2.7092-2.7100″	.0019-.0037″	.006-.014″

VALVE SPRINGS

Engine	Free Length	PRESSURE (LBS.) Valve Closed	PRESSURE (LBS.) Valve Open
300″			
Int.	1.99″	76-84@1.70″	187-207@1.30″
Exh.	1.87″	77-85@1.58″	12-202@1.18″
370″, 429″			
Int.	1.97″	76-84@1.72″	218-241@1.26″
Exh.	1.97″①	76-84@1.78″	218-241@1.52″
475″, 477″, 534″			
Int.	2.02″	73-81@1.70″	171-189@1.28″
Exh.	2.02″	73-81@1.70″	171-189@1.28″

① — 370″ 2V is 2.03″

CAMSHAFT

Engine	Journal Diam.	Clearance	Lobe Lift
300″	2.017-2.018″	.001-.003″	.249″
370″, 429″	2.1238-2.1348″	.001-.003″	.2526″①
475, 477″			
No. 1	2.474-2.475″	.001-.003″	.2777″
No. 2, 3, 4, 5	2.370-2.371″		
534″			
No. 1	2.474-2.475″	.001-.002″	.2777″
No. 2, 3, 4, 5	2.370-2.371″		

① — Exhaust lobe lift is .265″

FORD MOTOR CO. (Cont.)

VALVES

Engine & Valve	Head Diam.	Face Angle	Seat Angle	Seat Width	Stem Diameter	Stem Clearance	Valve Lift
300″							
Int.	1.772-1.790″	44°	45°	.060-.080″	.3416-.3423″	.0010-.0027″	403″
Exh.	1.551-1.569″	44°	45°	.070-.090″	.3416-.3423″	.0010-.0027″	.403″
370″ 2V							
Int.	1.779-1.789″	44°	45°	.060-.080″	.3711-.3718″	.0010-.0027″	.4377″
Exh.	1.557-1.567″	44°	45°	.070-.090″	.3701-.3708″	.0020-.0037″	.4809″
370″ 4V							
Int.	1.779-1.789″	44°	45°	.060-.080″	.3717-.3718″	.0010-.0027″	.4377″
Exh.	1.557-1.567″	44°	45°	.090-.100″	.3703-.3712″	.0016-.0035″	.4809″
429″							
Int.	2.059-2.069″	44°	45°	.060-.080″	.3711-.3718″	.0010-.0027″	.4377″
Exh.	1.667-1.677″	44°	45°	.093-.108″	.3703-.3712″	.0016-.0035″	.4809″
475″, 477″							
Int.	2.015-2.025″	44°	45°	.090-.105″	.4349-.4358″	.0010-.0026″	.4388″
Exh.	1.630-1.640″	44°	45°	.100-.115″	.4335-.4344″	.0024-.0040″	.4388″
534″							
Int.	2.015-2.025	44°	45°	.090-.105″	.4358-.4359″	.0010-.0026″	.4388″
Exh.	1.630-1.640″	44°	45°	.100-.115″	.4335-.4344″	.0024-.0040″	.4388″

OIL PUMP SPECIFICATIONS

300″

Relief Valve Spring Tension	20.6-22.6lbs@2.49″
Shaft-to-Housing Clearance	.0015-.0029″
Relief Valve Clearance	.0015-.0029″
Rotor Assembly End Clearance	.004″ Max.
Outer Race-to-Housing Clearance	.001-.013″

370 & 429″

Relief Valve Spring Tension	11.1-11.8lbs@1.56″
Shaft-to-Housing Clearance	.0015-.0030″
Relief Valve Clearance	.0015-.0030″
Rotor Assembly End Clearance	.004″ Max.
Outer Race-to-Housing Clearance	.001-.013″

475″, 477″ & 534″

Relief Valve Spring Tension	10.7-11.9lbs. @1.07″
Shaft-to-Housing Clearance	.0015-.0030″
Relief Valve Clearance	.0015-.0030″
Rotor Assembly End Clearance	.004″ Max.
Outer Race-to-Housing Clearance	.006-.011″

TIGHTENING SPECIFICATIONS
300″

Application	Ft. Lbs.
Cylinder Head Bolts①	
Step One	55
Step Two	65
Step Three	70-85
Manifold-to-Cylinder Head	22-32
Intake manifold-to-Exhaust Manifold	28-33
Main Bearing Cap Bolts	60-70
Connecting Rod Cap Nuts	40-45
Vibration Damper	130-150
Flywheel Bolts	75-85

370″ & 429″

Application	Ft. Lbs.
Cylinder Head Bolts①	
Step One	70-80
Step Two	100-110
Step Three	130-140
Manifold-to-Cylinder Head — Intake	22-32
Manifold-to-Cylinder Head — Exhaust	28-33
Main Bearing Cap Bolts	95-105
Connecting Rod Cap Nuts	45-50
Vibration Damper-to-Crankshaft	150-175
Flywheel Bolts	75-85

475″, 477″ & 534″

Application	Ft. Lbs.
Cylinder Head Bolts①	
Step One	140
Step Two	160
Step Three	180
Manifold-to-Cylinder Head — Intake	25-32
Manifold-to-Cylinder Head — Exhaust	22-32
Main Bearing Cap Bolts	150-165
Connecting Rod Cap Nuts	60-65
Damper-to-Crankshaft	130-175
Flywheel-to-Crankshaft	75-85

① — See cylinder head tightening sequence.

FORD MOTOR CO. (Cont.)

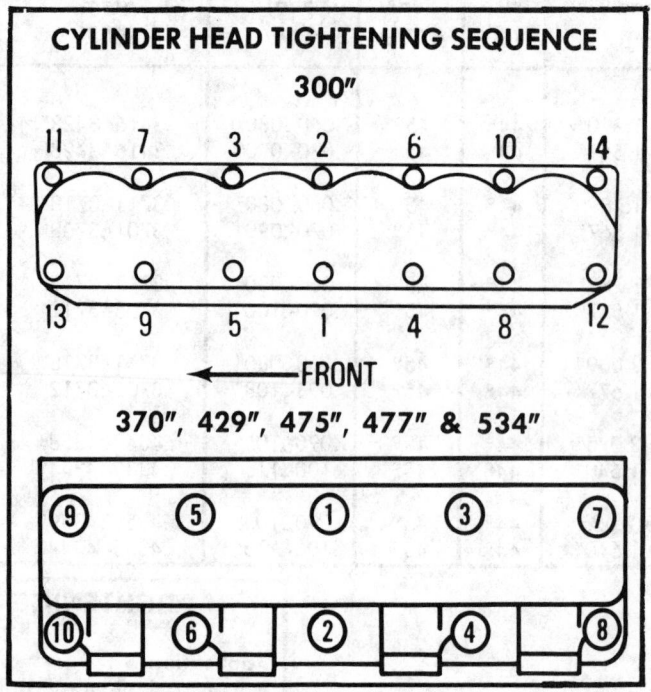

GENERAL MOTORS

GENERAL SPECIFICATIONS

Engine	Net HP At RPM	Torque (Ft. Lbs. at RPM)	Compr. Ratio	Bore	Stroke	Displ. Cu. Ins.
292"	125@3600	225@1600	7.8:1	3.875"	4.12"	292"
350"	161@3600	275@2400	8.0:1	4.000"	3.48"	350"
366"	190@4000	305@2400	7.6:1	3.937"	3.76"	366"
427"	210@3800	340@2400	7.5:1	4.250"	3.76"	427"
454"	210@3800	340@2800	7.9:1	4.250"	4.00"	454"

VALVES

Engine & Valve	Head Diam.	Face Angle	Seat Angle	Seat Width	Stem Diameter	Stem Clearance	Valve Lift
292"							
Int.	1.72"	45°	46°	.031-.063"	.3410-.3417"	.0010-.0027"	.....
Exh.	1.50"	5°	46°	.063-.094"	.3410-.3417"	.0015-.0032"	.....
350"							
Int.	1.94"	45°	46°	.031-.063"	.3410-.3417"	.0010-.0027"	.....
Exh.	1.50"	45°	46°	.0630.094"	.3410-.3417"	.0010-.0027"	.....
366"							
Int.	.....	45°	46°	.031-.063"	.....	.0010-.0027"	.....
Exh.	.....	45°	46°	.363-.094"	.....	.0012-.0029"	.....
427"							
Int.	.....	45°	46°	.031-.063"	.....	.0010-.0027"	.....
Exh.	.....	45°	46°	.063-.094"	......	0014-.0029"	.....
454"							
Int.	.....	45°	46°	.031-.063"	.3715-.3722"	.0010-.0027"	.....
Exh.	.....	45°	46°	.063-.094"	.3713-.3720"	.0014-.0027"	.....

VALVE SPRINGS

Engine	Free Length	PRESSURE (LBS.) Valve Clossed	PRESSURE (LBS.) Valve Open
292"	1.90"	85-93@1.69"	174-184@1.30"
350	2.03"	76-84@1.69"	194-206@1.25"
366"	2.05"	84-96@1.80"	210-230@1.40"
427"	2.05"	84-96@1.80"	210-230@1.40"
454"	2.05"	84-96@1.80"	210-230@1.40"

CAMSHAFT

Engine	Journal Diam.	Clearance	Lobe Lift
292"	1.8682-1.8692"	.....	.2315"
350"	1.8682-1.8692"	.....	.2600"
366"	1.9487-1.9497"	.....	.2343"
427"	1.9487-1.9497"	.....	.2343"
454"	1.9482-1.9492"	.....	.2588"

PISTONS, PINS, RINGS

Engine	PISTONS Clearance	PINS Piston Fit	PINS Rod Fit	Rings	End Gap	Side Clearance
292"	.0026-.0036"	.00015-.00025"	.0008-.0016"	1	.010-.020"	.0020-.0040"
				2	.010-.020"	.0020-.0040"
				3	.015-.055"	.0050-.0055"
350"	.0016-.0026"	.00016-.00026"	.0008-.0016"	1	.010-.020"	.0012-.0032"
				2	.013-.025"	.0012-.0032"
				3	.015-.055"	.0020-.0070"
366"	.0030-.0040"	.00025-.00035"	.0008-.0021"	1	.010-.020"	.0018-.0032"
				2	.010-.020"	.0018-.0032"
				3	.010-.030"	.0025-.0035"
427"	.0039-.0049"	.00025-.00035"	.0008-.0021"	1	.010-.020"	.0018-.0032"
				2	.010-.020"	.0018-.0032"
				3	.010-.030"	.0005-.0065"
454"	.0034-.0044"	.00025-.00035"	.0013-.0021"	1	.010-.020"	.0018-.0032"
				2	.010-.020"	.0018-.0032"
				3	.010-.030"	.0020-.0035"

GENERAL MOTORS (Cont.)

CRANKSHAFT MAIN & CONNECTING ROD BEARINGS

Engine	MAIN BEARINGS		Thrust Bearing	Crankshaft End Play	CONNECTING ROD BEARINGS		
	Journal Diam.	Clearance			Journal Diam.	Clearance	Side Play
292"	2.2983-2.2993"	.0008-.0034"	No. 7	.002-.006"	2.0990-2.1000"	.0007-.0027"	.006-.017"
350"							
No. 1	2.4484-2.4493"	.0008-.0020"	No. 5	.002-.006"	2.1990-2.2000"	.0013-.0035"	.008-.014"
No. 2, 3, 4	2.4481-2.4493"	.0011-.0023"					
No. 5	2.4479-2.4488"	.0017-.0033"					
366"							
No. 1, 2, 3, 4	2.7481-2.7490"	.0013-.0025"	No. 5	.006-.010"	2.1990-2.2000"	.0013-.0035"	.013-.023"
No. 5	2.7473-2.7483"	.0029-.0045"					
427"							
No. 1, 2, 3, 4	2.7481-2.7490"	.0013-.0025"	No. 5	.006-.010"	2.1990-2.2000"	.0014-.0030"	.013.023"
No. 5	2.7473-2.7483"	.0029-.0045"					
454"							
No. 1	2.7485-2.7495"	.0013-.0025"	No. 5	.006-.010"	2.1990-2.2000"	.0014-.0030"	.013-.023"
No. 2, 3, 4	2.7481-2.7490"	.0013-.0025"					
No. 5	2.7478-2.7488"	.0024-.0040"					

TIGHTENING SPECIFICATIONS

292"

Application	Ft. Lbs
Cylinder Head Bolts①	95
Intake Manifold-to-Head	35
Exhaust Manifold Bolts	30
Main Bearing Cap Bolts	65
Connecting Rod Cap Nuts	40
Flywheel Bolts	110
Harmonic Balancer Bolt	60

① — See cylinder head tightening sequence.

350"

Application	Ft. Lbs.
Cylinder Head Bolts①	65
Intake Manifold	30
Exhaust Manifold	②20
Main Bearing Cap Bolts	70
Connecting Rod Cap Nuts	45
Flywheel Bolts	60

① — See cylinder head tightening sequence.
② — Tighten two center bolts to 30 ft. lbs.

366", 427" & 454"

Application	Ft. Lbs.
Cylinder Head Bolts①	80
Intake Manifold	30
Exhaust Manifold	20
Main Bearing Cap Bolts	110
Connecting Rod Cap Nuts	50
Flywheel Bolts	65
Torsional Damper	85

① — See cylinder head tightening sequence.

CYLINDER HEAD TIGHTENING SEQUENCE

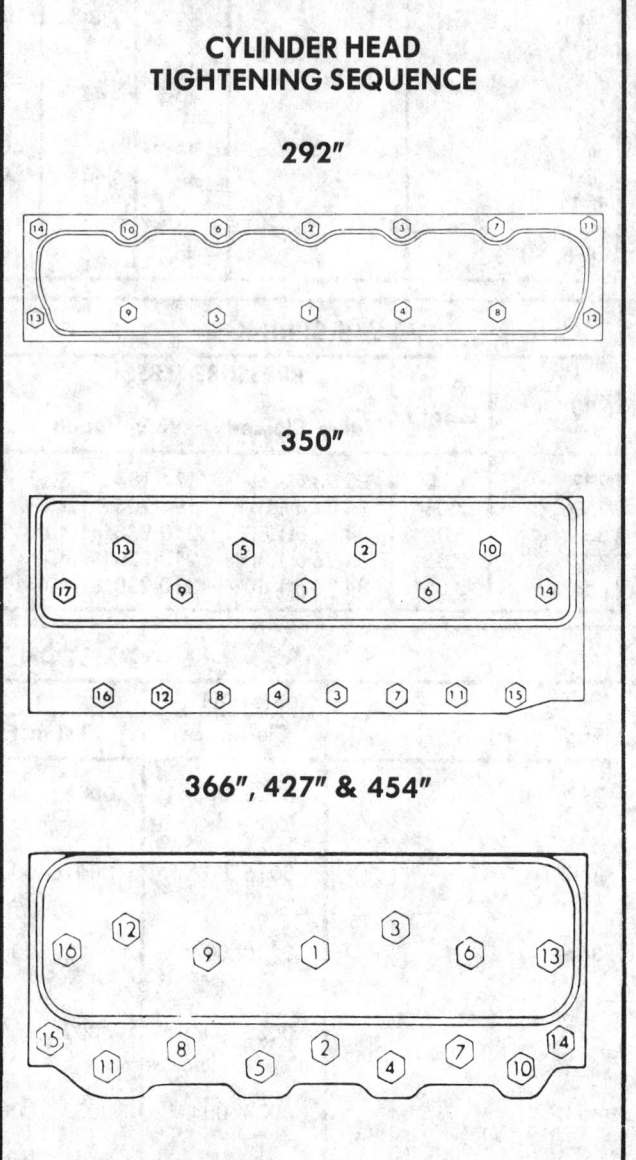

292"

350"

366", 427" & 454"

INTERNATIONAL HARVESTER

GENERAL SPECIFICATIONS

Engine	Net HP At RPM	Torque (Ft. Lbs. at RPM)	Compr. Ratio	Bore	Stroke	Displ. Cu. Ins.
345" ①	282@2200	154@3600	8.28:1	3.880"	3.66"	345.00"
392"	302@2800	185@3600	8.00:1	4.120"	3.66"	390.90"
404" 2V ②	326@2200	189@3600	8.00:1	4.125"	3.74"	399.80"
404" 4V	336@2600	206@3600	8.00:1	4.125"	3.74"	399.80"
446" ③	385@2600	227@3600	8.00:1	4.125"	4.18"	446.89"
478"	384@2200	209@3400	7.60:1	4.500"	3.75"	477.20"
537" 2V	410@1800	203@3200	7.50:1	4.625"	4.00"	537.60"
537" 4V	236@3200	429@2200	7.50:1	4.625"	4.00"	537.20"
549"	227@3200	446@2000	7.60:1	4.500"	4.31"	548.70"

① — Calif. models 115 HP, 281 ft. lbs. torque.
② — Calif. models 183 HP, 323 ft. lbs. torque.
③ — Calif. models 221 HP, 380 ft. lbs. torque.

VALVES

Engine & Valve	Head Diam.	Face Angle	Seat Angle	Seat Width	Stem Diameter	Stem Clearance	Valve Lift
345"							
Int.	.....	45°	45°	.063-.094"	.3720-.3730"	.0010-.0035"	.440"
Int.	.....	45°	45°	.078-.109"	.3715-.3725"	.0015-.0040"	.395"
392"							
Int.	.....	30°	30°	.063-.094"	.3720-.3730"	.0010-.0035"	.440"
Exh.	.....	45°	45°	.078-.109"	.4140-.4150"	.0015-.0040"	.395"
404"							
Int.	.....	45°	45°	.060-.090"	.37215-.37285"	.00115-.00285"	.435"
Exh.	.....	45°	45°	.085-.105"	.37165-.37265"	.00165-.00235"	.435"
446"							
Int.	.....	45°	45°	.060-.090"	.37215-.37285"	.00115-.00285"	.435"
Exh.	.....	45°	45°	.085-.105"	.37165-.37235"	.00165-.00235"	.435"
478"							
Int.	.....	15°	15°	.063-.094"	.4340-.4350"	.0015-.0040"	.....
Exh.	.....	45°	45°	.094-.125"	.4330-.4340"	.0025-.0050"	.....
537"							
Int.	.....	15°	15°	.060-.090"	.4341-.4349"	.0016-.0034"	.465"
Exh.	.....	45°	45°	.090-.120"	.4338-.4345"	.0020-.0037"	.465"
549"							
Int.	.....	15°	15°	.063-.094"	.4340-.4350"	.0015-.0040"	.....
Exh.	.....	45°	45°	.094-.125"	.4330-.4340"	.0025-.0050"	.....

CRANKSHAFT MAIN & CONNECTING ROD BEARINGS

Engine	MAIN BEARINGS				CONNECTING ROD BEARINGS		
	Journal Diam.	Clearance	Thrust Bearing	Crankshaft End Play	Journal Diam.	Clearance	Side Play
345"	2.7484-2.7494"	.0010-.0040"	No.3	.0044-.0094"	2.3730-2.3740"	.0011-.0036"	.008-.016"
392"	2.7484-2.7494"	.0010-.0040"	No.3	.0044-.0094"	2.3730-2.3740"	.0011-.0036"	.008-.016"
404"	3.1228-3.1236"	.0010-.0036"	No.3	.0025-.0085"	2.4980-2.4990"	.0011-.0036"	.008-.020"
446"	3.1228-3.1236"	.0010-.0036"	No.3	.0025-.0085"	2.4980-2.4990"	.0011-.0036"	.008-.020"
478"	3.1230-3.1240"	.0014-.0044"	No.3	.0040-.0090"	2.6230-2.6240"	.0017-.0042"	.010-.018"
537"	3.1235-3.1245"	.0015-.0035"	No.3	.0060-.0120"	2.6230-2.6240"	.0011-.0036"	.008-.018"
549"	3.1230-3.1240"	.0014-.0044"	No.3	.0040-.0090"	2.6230-2.6240"	.0017-.0042"	.010-.018"

INTERNATIONAL HARVESTER (Cont.)

PISTONS, PINS, RINGS

| Engine | PISTONS | PINS | | RINGS | | |
	Clearance	Piston Fit	Rod Fit	Rings	End Gap	Side Clearance
345″	.0035″	.0005-.0009″	.0006-.0012″	1&2 3	.010-.020″ .015-.055″	.0015-.0030″ .0000-.0084″
392″	.0035″	.0005-.0009″	.0006-.0012″	1&2 3	.013-.023″ .013-.028″	.0015-.0030″ .0020-.0035″
404″	.0012-.0017″	.0002-.0006″	.0004-.0008″	1&2 3	.013-.023″ .013-.023″	.0020-.0040 .0020-.0040″
446″	.0012-.0017″	.0002-.0006″	.0004-.0008″	1&2 3	.013-.023″ .013-.023″	.0020-.0040″ .0020-.0040″
478″	.0020″	.0001-.0004″	.0008-.0011″	1&2 3	.013-.025″ .013-.028″	.0035-.0050″ .0010-.0030″
537″	.0012-.0022″	.0001-.0004″	.0008-.0011″	1 2 3	.012-.022″ .014-.024″ .012-.022″	.0020-.0040″ .0020-.0040″ .0020-.0040″
549″	.0020″	.0001-.0004″	.0008-.0011″	1,2&3 4	.013-.025″ .013-.028″	.0035-.0050″ .0010-.0030″

VALVE SPRINGS

| Engine | Free Length | PRESSURE (LBS.) | |
		Valve Closed	Valve Open
345″	2.065″	.....	188.1@1.429″
392″	2.065″	.....	188.1@1.429″
404″	2.065″	.....	188.1@1.429″
446″	2.065″	.....	188.1@1.429″
478″			
Inner	2.281″	.....	79-87@1.538″
Outer	2.563″	.....	112-121@1.663″
537″	2.075″	.....	200@1.397″
549″			
Inner	2.281″	.....	79-87@1.538″
Outer	2.563″	.....	112-121@1.663″

CAMSHAFT

Engine	Journal Diam.	Clearance	Lobe Lift
345″ & 392″	.....	.0015-.0035″	.....
No. 1	2.0990-2.1000″		
No. 2	2.0890-2.0900″		
No. 3.	2.0790-2.0800″		
No. 4	2.0690-2.0700″		
No. 5	2.0590-2.0600″		
404″	2.0990-2.1000″	.0010-.0035″	.....
446″	2.0990-2.1000″	.0010-.0035″	.....
478″ & 549″	.....	.0010-.0030″	.....
No. 1	2.3470-2.3480″		
No. 2	2.3160-2.3170″		
No. 3	2.2900-2.2910″		
No. 4	2.2470-2.2480″		

OIL PUMP SPECIFICATIONS

345″ & 392″

Gear End Play	.0015-.0060″
Gear Side Clearance	.0007-.0027″
Shaft Clearance	.0010-.0025″
Gear Backlash	.0107″
Pressure Regulator Spring	1.812″ @13.33lbs.

404″ & 446″

Body Gear End Clearance	.0015-.0065″
Body-to-Gear Clearance	.0014-.0054″
Pump Shaft Diameter	.4885-.4890″
Shaft Clearance in Body	.0010-.0025″
Body Gear Backlash	.0107″ Max.
Idler Shaft Diameter	.4845-.4855″
Idler Gear Clearance on Shaft	.0015-.0040″

INTERNATIONAL HARVESTER (Cont.)

OIL PUMP SPECIFICATIONS (Cont.)

537"

Body-to-Gear End Clearance .... .0030-.0045"
Body-to-Gear Clearance .... .0007-.0027"
Gear Backlash .... .0005-.0065"

478" & 549"

Body Gear End Clearance .... .0015-.0090"
Pump Body-to-Gear Clearance .... .0046-.0086"
Pump Shaft Diameter .... .4905-.4910"
Pump Shaft Clearance in Bore .... .0015-.0030"
Body Gear Backlash .... .0030-.0150"

TIGHTENING SPECIFICATIONS

345" & 392"

Application	Ft. Lbs.
Cylinder Head Bolts①	90-100
Main Bearing Cap Bolts	75-85
Connecting Rod Cap Nuts .... ②	45-55
Crankshaft Pulley Bolt	100-110
Flywheel Bolts	45-55

① — See cylinder head tightening sequence.
② — Tighten V-392 engine to 40-45 ft. lbs.

404" & 446"

Application	Ft. Lbs.
Cylinder Head Bolts① ....②	90-100
Main Bearing Cap Bolts	90-110
Connecting Rod Cap Nuts	38-44
Crankshaft Vibration Damper	80-100
Flywheel Bolts	45-60

① — See cylinder head tightening sequence.
② — On engines below serial number 38949, tighten to 80-90 ft. lbs.

478" & 549"

Application	Ft. Lbs.
Cylinder Head Bolts①	80-90
Main Bearing Cap Bolts	100-110
Connecting Rod Cap Nuts	60-70
Flywheel-to-Crankshaft	90-100

① — See cylinder head tightening sequence.

537"

Application	Ft. Lbs.
Cylinder Head Bolts①	80-90
Main Bearing Cap Bolts	125-130
Connecting Rod Cap Nuts	65-70
Crankshaft Pulley	260-290
Flywheel-to-Crankshaft	110-120
Idler Pulley	70-85

① — See cylinder head tightening sequence

CYLINDER HEAD TIGHTENING SEQUENCE

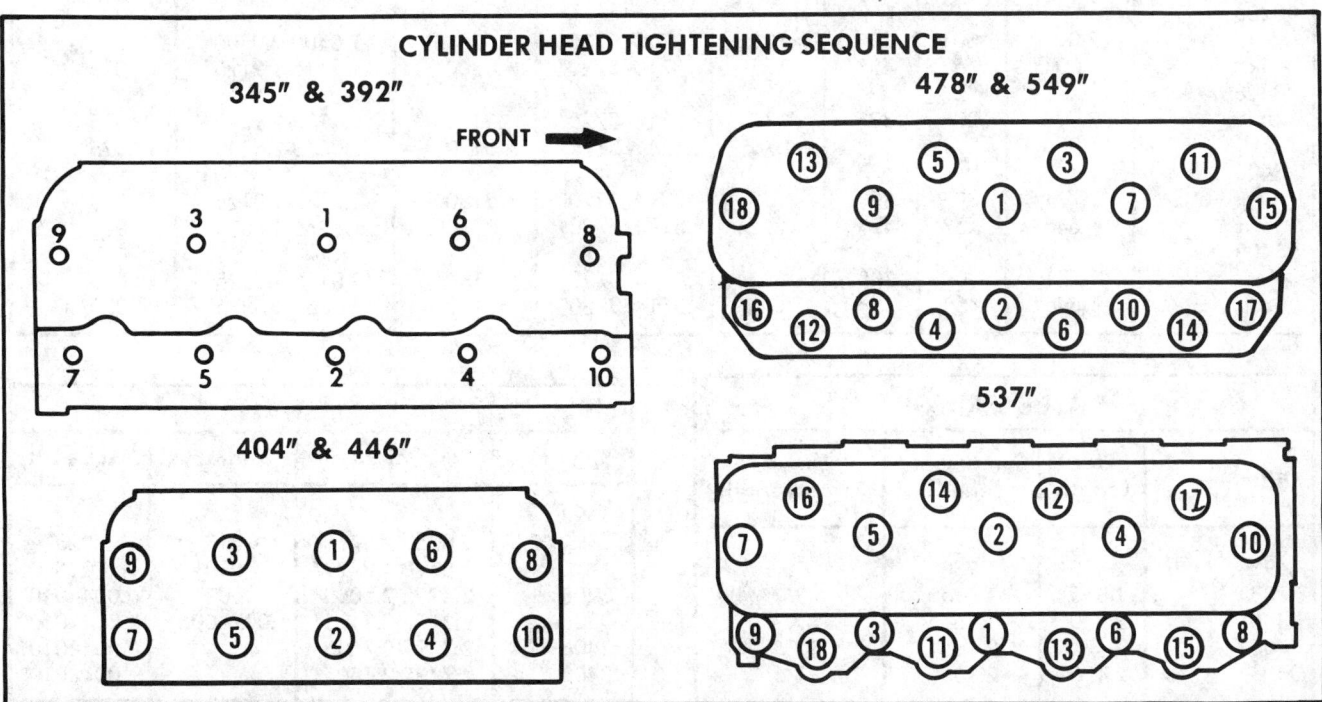

CATERPILLAR

GENERAL SPECIFICATIONS

Engine	Cycle	Displ. Cu. Ins.	Compr. Ratio	Bore	Stroke	Firing Order	Inj. Timing ①
1693	4	893″	16.0:1	5.40″	6.50″	1,5,3,6,2,4	11.0°
3208	4	636″	16.4:1	4.50″	5.00″	1,2,7,3,4,5,6,8	16.0°
3306	4	638″	17.5:1	4.75″	6.00″	1,5,3,6,2,4	13.5°
3406	4	893″	14.5:1	5.40″	6.50″	1,5,3,6,2,4	10.0°
3408	4	1099″	16.5:1	5.40″	6.00″	1,8,4,3,6,5,7,2	①11.00°

① — Unless noted otherwise, all Injection Timing is BTDC.
② — Direct Injection Turbocharged Model is 28°BTDC.

NORMAL OPERATING SPECIFICATIONS

Engine	Idle RPM	Max. RPM	Oil Temp.	Oil Press.	Coolant Temp.	Compression Pressure (PSI) @ RPM (Sea Level)
1693	550	2100	210°	45-65	210°	.....
3208	650	3070	210°	55-85	210°	.....
3306	600	2400	210°	45-60	210°	.....
3406	600	2300	210°	45-70	210°	.....
3408	700	2340	210°	55-69	210°	.....

VALVES & SEATS

Engine	Head Diameter	Face Angle	Seat Angle	Seat Width	Stem Diameter	Stem Clearance	Valve Seat Insert O.D.	Valve Clearance
1693								
Int.	1.771″	44¼°	45°	.060″	.3715-.3725″	.0007″	1.8115-1.8125″	.018″
Exh.	1.646″	44¼°	45°	.060″	.3715-.3725″	.0007″	1.6865-1.6875″	.030″
3208								
Int.	2.094″	30°	30°	.120″	.3720-.3730″	.0200″	2.0400-2.0500″	.015″
Exh.	1.804″	45°	45°	.105″	.3710-.3720″	.0200″	1.9115-1.9125″	.025″
3306								
Int.	2.094″	29°	30°	.076″	.3714-.3720″	.0170″	2.1280-2.1290″	.015″
Exh.	1.896″	29°	30°	.076″	.3714-.3720″	.0170″	2.0030-2.0040″	.025″
3406								
Int.	1.771″	30°	30°	.....	.3714-.3720″	.0180″	1.8115-1.8125″	.015″
Exh.	1.646″	45°	45°	.....	.3714-.3720″	.0180″	1.6865-1.6875″	.030″
3408								
Int.	1.771″	30°	30°	.....	.3714-.3720″	.0180″	1.8115-1.8125″	.015″
Exh.	1.646″	45°	45°	.....	.3714-.3720″	.0180″	1.6865-1.6875″	.030″

VALVE SPRINGS

Engine	Free Length	Compressed Length	Lbs. @ Comp. Length
1693	2.310″	1.950″	35
3208	1.855″	1.715″	35
3306	2.050″	1.766″	57.7
3406	2.470″	2.165″	77.5
3408	2.470″	2.165″	77.5

CAMSHAFT

Engine	Journal Diam.	Clearance	Lobe Lift
1693			
No.1,2,3	2.8750-2.8760″	.010″	.025″
No.4	1.8710-1.8720″	.010″	.025″
3208	2.4995-2.5000″	.007″	.004-.010″
3306	2.3105-2.3115″	.002-.006″	.004-.010″
3406	2.7495-2.7505″	.....	.004-.010″
3408	2.7495-2.7505″	.....	.004-.010″

CATERPILLAR (Cont.)

ROCKER ARMS & VALVE BRIDGES

Engine	Rocker Shaft O.D.	Rocker Arm I.D.	Rocker Arm Clearance	Bridge Guide O.D.	Bridge I.D.	Bridge Height Above Head
1693	.....	.....	.....	.....	.....	.....
3208	.8580-.8588"	.8595-.8611"	.005"	.....	.....	.....
3306	.7240-.7250"	.7258-.7268"	.008"	.....	.....	.....
3406	.9740-.9750"	.9760-.9770"	.010"	.4333-.4335"	.4338.4362"	2.080-2.120"
3408	.9740-.9750"	.9760-.9770"	.010"	.4333-.4335"	.4338-4362"	2.080-2.120"

PISTONS, PINS, RINGS

Engine	PISTONS Clearance	PINS Piston Fit	PINS Rod Fit	RINGS Rings	RINGS End Gap	RINGS Side Clearance
1693	.....	.003-.011"	.0009-.0019"	1	.021-.036"	.0057-.0071"
				2	.035-.050"	.0030-.0048"
				3	.015-.030"	.0015-.0030"
3208	.....	.003"	.003"	1	.015-.030"	.0030-.0055"
				2	.010-.025"	.0015-.0035"
3306	.....	.003-.013"	.003"	1	.0175-.0325"	.0028-.0046"
				2	.0175-.0325"	.0023-.0041"
				3	.0130-.0280"	.0015-.0035"
3406	.....	.003-.013"	.003"	1	.021-.036"	①
				2	.035-.050"	①
				3	.015-.030"	.010-.030"
3408	.....	.003-.011"	.003"	1	.021-.036"	①
				2	.035-.050"	①
				3	.015-.030"	.010-.030"

① — Ring should be a snug fit in groove, with no visible side play.

CRANKSHAFT & MAIN BEARINGS

Engine	Journal Diameter	Bearing Clearance	Crankshaft End Play	Thrust Location	Thrust Washer Thickness	Number of Main Bearings
1693	4.4995-4.5005"	.0035-.0066"	.0060-.0180"	.....	.....	7
3208	3.4990-3.5000"	.0060"	.0030-.0090"	.....	.....	5
3306	3.4984-3.5000"	.0030-.0065"	.0025-.0145"	Front	.1835-.1865"	7
3406	4.7495-4.7508"	.0037-.0068"	.0060-.0200"	Center	.....	7
3408	4.7492-4.7508"	.0036-.0073"	.0060-.0200"	Center	.....	5

CYLINDER LINER & BORE

Engine	Type	Liner Bore	Liner Protrusion
1693	Wet	5.400-5.402"	.002-.007"
3208	.....	①4.500-4.510"	.....
3306	Wet	4.750-4.752"	.001"
3406	Wet	5.400-5.402"	.002-.008"
3408	Wet	5.400-5.402"	.002-.008"

① — Liners not used on Model 3208

CONNECTING RODS & BEARINGS

Engine	Journal Diameter	Bearing Clearance	Sideplay
1693	3.5395-3.5405"	.003-.006"	.....
3208	2.7496-2.7504"	.007"	.....
3306	2.9984-2.3000"	.0030-.0066"	.....
3406	3.8195-3.8205"	.003-.006"	.....
3408	3.8192-3.8208"	.0028-.0066"	.....

CATERPILLAR (Cont.)

OIL PUMP SPECIFICATIONS

1693

Type	Gear
Shaft Diameter	1.2275-1.2281"
Bore in Bushings	1.2300-1.2310"
Clearance Between Gear and Cover	.001-.004"
Relief Valve Spring	
Compressed Length	4.02"@34 lbs.
Free Length	4.38"

3208

Type	Rotary
Clearance Pump Gear Rotor Tip	.002-.006"
Relief Valve Spring	
Compressed Length	2.579"@37.3 lbs.
Free Length	3.500"

3306

Type	Gear
Bore in Idler Gear Bearing	1.1236-1.1284"
Idler Shaft Diameter	1.1250-1.1260"
Clearance Bearing-to-Shaft	.0006-.0064"
Drive Shafts Diameter	.8745-.8749"
Drive Shaft Bearings I.D.	.8760-.8766"
Clearance Drive Shafts-to-Bearings	.0011-.0022"
Clearance all Gears and Housing	.0032-.0068"

3406

Type	Gear
Drive Shaft Diameter	.8745-.8749"
Drive Shaft Bearing Bore	.8760-.8766"
Idler Shaft Bearing Bore	.8760-.8766"
Gear Length	3.1245-3.1255"
Gear Bore Depth	3.1292-3.1308"
Pressure Relief Valve Spring	
Length Compressed @110 lbs.	4.640"
Free Length	6.020"

3408

Type	Gear
Drive Shaft Diameter	.8745-.8749"
Drive Shaft Bearing Bore	.8760-.8766"
Idler Shaft Diameter	.8745-.8749"
Idler Shaft Bearing Bore	.8760-.8766"
Gear Length	3.1240-3.1260"
Gear Bore Depth	3.1292-3.1308"
Pressure Relief Valve Spring	
Length Compressed @110lbs.	4.640"
Free Length	6.020"

TIGHTENING SPECIFICATIONS

1693

Application	Ft. Lbs.
Cylinder Head Bolts①	
Step One	200
Step Two	330
Step Three	330
Main Bearing Cap Bolts②	75
Connecting Rod Cap Bolts③	50
Vibration Damper-to-Crankshaft	138-159
Flywheel Bolts④	375

① — See cylinder head tightening sequence.
② — Mark each bolt and cap, tighten bolt 120°.
③ — Mark each bolt and nut, tighten nut 180°.
④ — Engine with brakesaver, without brakesaver 265 Ft.Lbs.

3208

Application	Ft. Lbs.
Cylinder Head Bolts①	
Step One — Bolts 1-18	60
Step Two — Bolts 1-18	95
Step Three — Bolts 1-18	95
Bolts 19-22	32
Main Bearing Caps②	30
Connecting Rod Caps③	30
Pulley and Damper	460
Flywheel Bolts	55
Fuel Injection Pump	70

① — See cylinder head tightening sequence.
② — Mark each bolt and cap, tighten bolts 120°.
③ — Mark each bolt and nut, tighten nuts 60°.

3306

Application	Ft. Lbs.
Cylinder Head Bolts①	
Step One — All Numbered Bolts	115
Step Two — All Numbered Bolts	175
Step Three — All Numbered Bolts	175
Step Four — All Bolts in Letter Sequence	22
Step Five — All Bolts in Letter Sequence	32
Step Six — All Bolts in Letter Sequence	32
Main Bearing Caps②	30
Connecting Rod Caps③	30
Crankshaft Hub and Damper	230

① — See cylinder head tightening sequence.
② — Mark each bolt and cap, tighten bolts 90°.
③ — Mark each bolt and nut, tighten nuts 90°.

CATERPILLAR (Cont.)

TIGHTENING SPECIFICATIONS (Cont.)

3406

Application	Ft. Lbs.
Cylinder Head Bolts①	
Step One — Bolts 1-20	200
Step Two — Bolts 1-20	330
Step Three — Bolts 1-20	330
Step Four — Install Rocker Arm Groups	
Step Five — Bolts 21-26	200
Step Six — Bolts 21-26	330
Step Seven — Bolts 21-26	330
Step Eight — Tighten Remaining 12 Bolts	32
Main Bearing Caps②	190
Connecting Rod Caps③	60
Flywheel-to-Crankshaft Bolts	210

① — See cylinder head tightening sequence.
② — Mark each bolt and cap, tighten bolts 120°.
③ — Mark each bolt and nut, tighten nuts 120°.

3408

Application	Ft. Lbs.
Cylinder Head Bolts①	
Step One — Bolts 1-14	200
Step Two — Bolts 1-14	330
Step Three — Bolts 1-14	330
Step Four — Install Rocker Arms	
Step Five — Bolts 15-18	200
Step Six — Bolts 15-18	330
Step Seven — Bolts 15-18	330
Step Eight — Nine Small Bolts	32
Main Bearing Caps②	190
Connecting Rod Caps③	60
Flywheel Bolts	200
Vibration Damper	100

① — See cylinder head tightening sequence.
② — Mark each bolt and cap, tighten bolts 120°.
③ — Mark each bolt and nut, tighten nuts 120°.

CYLINDER HEAD TIGHTENING SEQUENCE

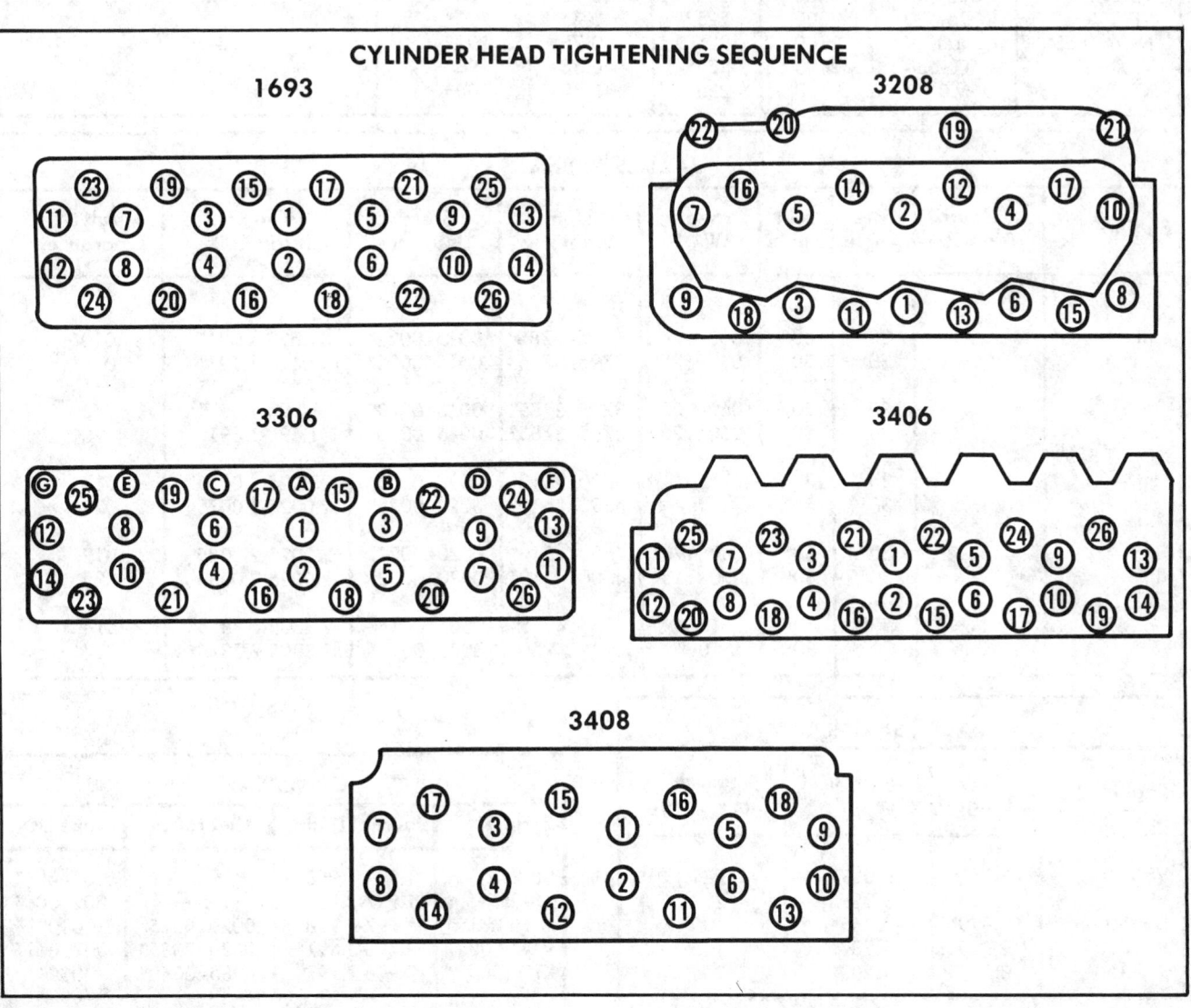

CUMMINS

GENERAL SPECIFICATIONS

Engine	Cycle	Displ. Cu. Ins.	Compr. Ratio	Bore	Stroke	Firing Order ②	Inj. Timing ①
V8-210	4	504″	17.0:1	4.625″	3.750″	1,5,4,8,6,3,7,2	③24.5°
V8-555	4	555″	17.0:1	4.625″	4.125″	1,5,4,8,6,3,7,2	④22.5°
NH/NT 855	4	855″	15.8:1	5.4995″	6.000″	R-1,5,3,6,2,4 L-1,4,2,6,3,5	20.0°
V/VT 903	4	903″	15.5:1	5.4995″	4.750″	1,5,4,8,6,3,7,2	21.0°
KT 1150	4	1150″	14.5:1	6.250″	6.250″	1,5,3,6,2,4	⑤.2032″

① — Unless noted otherwise, all Injection Timing is BTDC.
② — R- Right-hand rotation. L- Left-hand rotation.
③ — "H" Model is 15.5°BTDC.
④ — "H" Model is 14.5°BTDC.
⑤ — Piston travel with 0.1080″ push rod travel. Use of special tools required.

NORMAL OPERATING SPECIFICATIONS

Engine	Idle RPM	Max. RPM	Oil Temp.	Oil Press.	Coolant Temp.	Compression Pressure (PSI) @ RPM (Sea Level)
V8-210	525-600	3300	240°	40-58	190°	.....
V8-555	525-620	3300	225°	40-75	200°	.....
NH/NT855	600	2100	225°	40-75	200°	.....
V/VT903	600-650	2600	225°	40-65	190°	.....
KT1105	600	2100	225°	45-70	200°	.....

VALVES & SEATS

Engine	Head Diameter	Face Angle	Seat Angle	Seat Width	Stem Diameter	Stem Clearance	Valve Seat Insert O.D.	Valve Clearance
V8-210								
Int.	.....	30°	30°	.060-.125″	.3795-.3785″	.0015-.0022″	1.690-1.691″	.010″
Exh.	.....	30°	30°	.060-.125″	.3795-.3785″	.0015-.0022″	1.690-1.691″	.020″
V8-555								
Int.	.....	30°	30°	.060-.125″	.3795-.3785″	.0015-.0020″	1.690-1.691″	.010″
Exh.	.....	30°	30°	.060-.125″	.3795-.3785″	.0015-.0020″	1.690-1.691″	.020″
NH/NT 855								
Int.	.....	30°	30°	.125″	.4500-.4510″	.0022-.0025″	2.0025-2.0035″	.014″
Exh.	.....	30°	30°	.125″	.4500-.4510″	.0022-.0025″	2.0025-2.0035″	.029″
V/VT 903								
Int.	.....	30°	30°	.060-.125″	.4500-.4510″	.0020-.0022″	2.0025-2.0035″	.012″
Exh.	.....	30°	30°	.060-.125″	.4500-.4510″	.0020-.0022″	2.0025-2.0035″	.025″
KT 1150								
Int.	.....	30°	30°	.100″	.4945-.4955″	.0005-.0016″	2.3805-2.3815″	.014″
Exh.	.....	30°	30°	.100″	.4945-.4955″	.0005-.0016″	2.3805-2.3815″	.027″

VALVE SPRINGS

Engine	Free Length	Compressed Length	Lbs. @ Comp. Length
V8-210	1.953″	1.329″	221
V8-555	1.953″	1.329″	221
NH/NT 855	2.890″	1.765″	108
V/VT 903	2.350″	1.287″	136
KT 1150	3.349″	1.908″	266

CAMSHAFT

Engine	Journal Diam.	Clearance	Lobe Lift
V8-210	1.997-1.998″	.....	.002-.006″
V8-555	1.997-1.998″	.....	.002-.006″
NH/NT 855	1.997-1.998″	.0020-.0025″	.010″
V/VT 903	2.496-2.497″	.0030-.0035″	.007-.011″
KT 1150	2.996-2.997″	.0035-.0040″	.009″

CUMMINS (Cont.)

ROCKER ARMS & VALVE BRIDGES

Engine	Rocker Shaft O.D.	Rocker Arm I.D.	Rocker Arm Clearance	Bridge Guide O.D.	Bridge I.D.	Bridge Height Above Head
V8-210	1.1230-1.1240"	1.1245-1.1280"	.0015-.0040"	.3750-.3755"	.376-.378"	2.040-2.060"
V8-555	1.1230-1.1240"	1.1245-1.1280"	.0015-.0040"	.3750-.3755"	.376-.378"	2.040-2.060"
NH/NT 855	1.1230-1.1240"	1.1245-1.1275"	.0015-.0035"	.4330-.4335"	.440-.442"	1.860-1.880"
V/VT 903	1.1855-1.1865"	1.1875-1.1905"	.0020-.0040"	.4330-.4335"	.434-.436"	1.860-1.880"
KT 1150	1.3720-1.3725"	1.3755-1.3765"	.0015-.0040"	.4330-.4335"	.434-.436"	2.350-2.370"

PISTONS, PINS, RINGS

Engine	PISTONS		PINS		RINGS		
	Clearance	Piston Fit	Rod Fit	Rings	End Gap	Side Clearance	
V8-210	.0085-.0110"	.0003"	Press Fit	1	.013"	.005"	
				2	.025"	.005"	
				3	.010"	.005"	
V8-555	.0085-.0110"	.0003"	Press Fit	1	.013"	.005"	
				2	.025"	.005"	
				3	.010"	.005"	
NH/NT 855	.0125-.0130"	.0002"	Press Fit	1	.023"	.005"	
				2	.019"	.005"	
				3	.019"	.005"	
				4	.010"	.005"	
V/VT 903	.0095-.0120"	.0003"	Press Fit	1	.017"	.005"	
				2	.013"	.005"	
				3	.010"	.005"	
KT 1150	.0112-.0115"	.0003"	Press Fit	1	.025"	.005"	
				2	.025"	.005"	
				3	.012"	.005"	

CRANKSHAFT & MAIN BEARINGS

Engine	Journal Diameter	Bearing Clearance	Crankshaft End Play	Thrust Location	Thrust Washer Thickness	Number of Main Bearings
V8-210	3.4990-3.5000"	.0015-.0045"	.004-.014"	No.5	.1490-.1510"	5
V8-555	3.4990-3.5000"	.0015-.0045"	.004-.014"	No.5	.1490-.1510"	5
NH/NT 855	4.4985-4.5000"	.0015-.0050"	.007-.022"	No.7	.2450-.2470"	7
V/VT 903	3.7490-3.7500"	.0020-.0090"	.005-.015"	Front	.1505-.1735"	5
KT 1150	5.4985-5.5000"	.0026-.0065"	.004-.016"	No.6	.1505-1735"	7

CYLINDER LINER & BORE

Engine	Type	Liner Bore	Liner Protrusion
V8-210	Wet	4.6245-4.6260"	.006-.009"
V8-555	Wet	4.6245-4.6260"	.006-.009"
NH/NT 855	Wet	5.4995-5.5010"	.003-.006"
V/VT 903	Wet	5.4995-5.5010"	.003-.006"
KT 1150	Wet	6.2495-6.2550"	.003-.006"

CONNECTING RODS & BEARINGS

Engine	Journal Diameter	Bearing Clearance	Sideplay
V8-210	2.4990-2.5000"	.0015-.0045"	.008-.018"
V8-555	2.7490-2.7500"	.0015-.0045"	.008-.018"
NH/NT 855	3.1235-3.1250"	.0015-.0045"	.....
V/VT 903	3.1240-3.1250"	.0050"	.005-.020"
KT 1150	3.9985-4.0000"	.0050"	.....

CUMMINS (Cont.)

OIL PUMP SPECIFICATIONS

V8-210 & V8-555

Type	Gear
Idler Gear Bushing I.D.	.6195-.6205″
Pump Drive Shaft Bushing I.D.	.6165-.6175″
Drive Shaft Diameter	.6150-.6155″
Idler Shaft Diameter	.6180-.6185″
Driven-to-Idler Gear Backlash	.016-.020″

NH/NT 855

Type	Gear
Bushings I.D.	.8400-.8405″
Idler and Drive Shaft Diameter	.8375-.8380″
Driven Shaft Protrusion	.580-.610″
Drive Shaft Protrusion	.050-.070″
Drive Shaft End Play	.004-.010″
Pressure Relief Valve Open	130PSI

V903 & VT903

Type	Gear
Shaft Bores	.8770-.8775″
Drive Shaft Diameter	.8740″min
Idler Shaft Diameter	.8750″min
Pump Gears	2.397″min
Gear Housing Diameter	2.415″max
Gear Housing Depth	1.252″max
Clearance Driven Gear From Shaft End	.5450-.5750″
Clearance Scavenger Drive Gear-to-Body	.0020-.0040″
Clearance Drive Gear From Shaft End	1.232-1.290″
Clearance Main Drive Gear From Shaft End	.0000-.0200″

KT1150

Type	Gear
Bushing I.D.	.8765-.8775″
Idler Shaft Diameter	.8745-.8750″
Drive Shaft Diameter	.8745-.8750″
Clearance Drive Gear-to-Body	.1300-.1500″
Shaft Protrusion From Mounting Surface	1.030-1.050″
Drive Shaft End Clearance	.0025-.0065″

TIGHTENING SPECIFICATIONS

V8-210

NOTE — *Use minimum two steps to torque all nuts and bolts.*

Application	Ft. Lbs.
Cylinder Head Bolts①	110-115
Main Bearing Cap Bolts	175-185
Connecting Rod Cap Nuts	55
Flywheel Bolts	100-105
Pulley-to-Crankshaft	90-100

① — See cylinder head tightening sequence.

TIGHTENING SPECIFICATIONS (Cont.)

V8-555

NOTE — *Use minimum two steps to torque all nuts and bolts.*

Application	Ft. Lbs.
Cylinder Head Bolts①	135-140
Main Bearing Cap Bolts	165-175
Connecting Rod Cap Nuts	85-90
Flywheel Bolts	135-140
Vibration Damper-to-Crankshaft	135-140

① — See cylinder head tightening sequence.

NH/NT 855

NOTE — *Use minimum two steps to torque all nuts and bolts.*

Application	Ft. Lbs.
Cylinder Head Bolts①	280-300
Main Bearing Cap Bolts	300-310
Connecting Rod Cap Nuts	140-150
Flywheel Bolts	200-220
Vibration Damper and Pulley-to-Crankshaft	180-200

① — See cylinder head tightening sequence.

V903 & VT903

NOTE — *Use minimum two steps to torque all nuts and bolts.*

Application	Ft. Lbs.
Cylinder Head Bolts①	280-300
Main Bearing Cap Bolts	340-350
Connecting Rod Cap Nuts	95-100
Flywheel Bolts	200-210
Vibration Damper and Pulley-to-Crankshaft	200-205

① — See cylinder head tightening sequence.

KT1150

NOTE — *Use minimum two steps to torque all nuts and bolts.*

Application	Ft. Lbs.
Cylinder Head Bolts①	
Cadium Plated	250-260
Lubrited	350-370
Main Bearing Cap Bolts	440-450
Connecting Rod Cap Nuts	210-220
Flywheel Bolts	200-220
Vibration Damper and Pulley-to-Crankshaft	320-340

① — See cylinder head tightening sequence.

CUMMINS (Cont.)

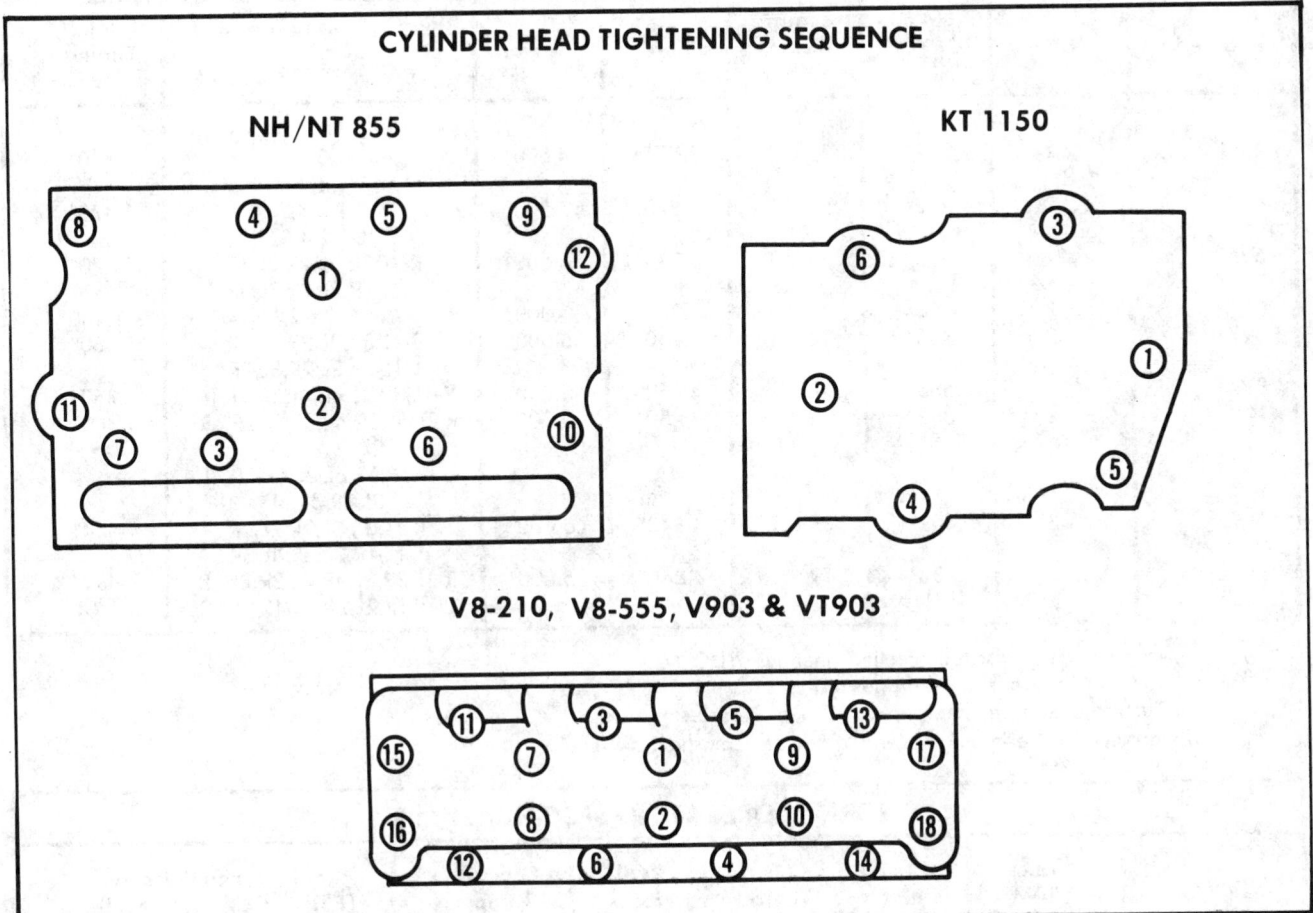

CYLINDER HEAD TIGHTENING SEQUENCE

NH/NT 855

KT 1150

V8-210, V8-555, V903 & VT903

DETROIT DIESEL

GENERAL SPECIFICATIONS

Engine	Cycle	Displ. Cu. Ins.	Compr. Ratio ③	Bore	Stroke	Firing Order ②	Inj. Timing ①
4-53	2	212"	17.0:1	3.875"	4.500"	R-1,3,4,2 L-1,2,4,3	1.470"
4-53N	2	212"	21.0:1	3.875"	4.500"	R-1,3,4,2 L-1,2,4,3	1.470"
6V53	2	318"	21.0:1	3.875"	4.500"	R-1L,3R,3L,2R,2L,1R L-1L,1R,2L,2R,3L,3R	1.470"
6-71N	2	426"	18.7:1	4.250"	5.000"	1,5,3,6,2,4	④1.460"
6V71	2	426"	18.7:1	4.250"	5.000"	R-1L,3R,3L,2R,2L,1R L-1L,1R,2L,2R,3L,3R	1.460"
8V71	2	568"	18.7:1	4.250"	5.000"	R-1L,3R,3L,4R,4L,2R,2L,1R	1.460"
12V71	2	852"	18.7:1	4.250"	5.000"	R-1L,5L,3R,4R,3L,4L,2R,6R, 2L,6L,1R,5R L-1L,5R,1R,6L,2L,6R,2R,4L, 3L,4R,3R,5L	1.460"
6V92	2	552"	19.0:1	4.840"	5.000"	R-1L,3R,3L,2R,2L,1R L-1L,1R,2L,2R,3L,3R	1.484"
8V92	2	736"	19.0:1	4.840"	5.000"	R-1L,3R,3L,4R,4L,2R,2L,1R L-1L,1R,2L,2R,4L,4R,3L,3R	1.484"

① — Unless noted otherwise, all Injection Timing is BTDC.
② — R-Right-hand rotation. L-Left-hand rotation.
③ — All Turbocharged engines have a 17.0:1 compression ratio.
④ — Timing on all 71 series engines with advanced camshaft is 1.484".

NORMAL OPERATING SPECIFICATIONS

Engine	Idle RPM	Max. RPM	Oil Temp.	Oil Press.	Coolant Temp.	Compression Pressure (PSI) @ RPM (Sea Level)
4-53	600	2800	240°	40-60	185°	540-590@600
4-53N	600	2800	240°	40-60	185°	540-590@600
6V53	600	2800	240°	40-60	185°	430-480@600
6-71N	600	2100	225°	40-60	185°	515-565@600
V71	600	2300	235°	50-70	185°	425-475@600
8V71	600	2300	235°	50-70	185°	425-475@600
12V71	600	2300	235°	50-70	185°	425-475@600
6V92	600	2100	235°	50-70	185°	430-480@600
8V92	600	2100	235°	50-70	185°	430-480@600

ROCKER ARMS & VALVE BRIDGES

Engine	Rocker Shaft O.D.	Rocker Arm I.D.	Rocker Arm Clearance	Bridge Guide O.D.	Bridge I.D.	Bridge Height Above Head
4-53	.8735-.8740"	.8750-.8760"	.0010-.0025"	.....	.....	.....
4-53N	.8735-.8740"	.8750-.8760"	.0010-.0025"	.....	.....	.....
6V53	.8735-.8740"	.8750-.8760"	.0010-.0025"	.....	.....	.....
6-71N	.8735-.8740"	.8750-.8760"	.0010-.0025"	.....	.....	2.040"
6V71	.8735-.8740"	.8750-.8760"	.0010-.0025"	.....	.....	2.040"
8V71	.8735-.8740"	.8750-.8760"	.0015-.0025"	.....	.....	2.040"
12V71	.8735-.8740"	.8750-.8760"	.0010-.0025"	.....	.....	2.040"
6V92	.8735-.8740"	.8750-.8760"	.0010-.0025"	.....	.....	2.040"
8V92	.8735-.8740"	.8750-.8760"	.0010-.0025"	.....	.....	2.040"

DETROIT DIESEL (Cont.)

VALVES & SEATS

Engine ①	Head Diameter	Face Angle	Seat Angle	Seat Width	Stem Diameter	Stem Clearance	Valve Seat Insert O.D.	Valve Clearance
4-53	0.910"	30°	30°	.0468-.0781"	.2480-.2488"	.0017-.0035"	1.1615"	.025"
4-53N	0.910"	30°	30°	.0468-.0781"	.2480-.2488"	.0017-.0035"	1.1615"	.025"
6V53	0.910"	30°	30°	.0468-.0781"	.2480-.2488"	.0017-.0035"	1.1615"	.025"
6-71N								
2V	1.180"	30°	30°	.0625-.0937"	.3417-.3425"	.0002-.0038"	1.6260-1.6270"	.013"
4V	1.180"	30°	30°	.0468-.0937"	.3100-.3105"	.0002-.0035"	1.2600-1.2610"	.013"
6V71								
2V	0.980"	30°	30°	.0630-.0940"	.3417-.3425"	.0020-.0038"	1.6260-1.6270"	.011"
4V	0.980"	30°	30°	.0470-.0940"	.3100-.3105"	.0020-.0035"	1.2600-1.2610"	.015"
8V71								
2V	0.980"	30°	30°	.0630-.0940"	.3417-.3425"	.0020-.0038"	1.6260-1.6270"	.011"
4V	0.980"	30°	30°	.0470-.0940"	.3100-.3105"	.0020-.0035"	1.2600-1.2610"	.015"
12V71								
2V	0.980"	30°	30°	.0630-.0940"	.3417-.3425"	.0020-.0038"	1.6260-1.6270"	.011"
4V	0.980"	30°	30°	.0470-.0490"	.3100-.3105"	.0020-.0035"	1.2600-1.2610"	.015"
6V92	1.300"	30°	31°	.078"	.3100-.3108"	.0017-.0035"	1.4420"	.015"
8V92	1.300"	30°	31°	.078"	.3100-.3108"	.0017-.0035"	1.4420"	.015"

① — Detroit Diesel engines do not use intake valves, specifications given are for exhaust valves only.

VALVE SPRINGS

Engine	Free Length	Compressed Length	Lbs. @ Comp. Length
4-53	.....	1.930"	25
4-53N	.....	1.930"	25
6V53	.....	1.930"	25
6-71N			
2V	.....	2.200"	25
4V	.....	1.800"	25
6V71			
2V	.....	2.200"	25
4V	.....	1.800"	25
8V71			
2V	.....	2.200"	25
4V	.....	1.800"	25
12V71			
2V	.....	2.200"	25
4V	.....	1.800"	25
6V92	.....	1.800"	25
8V92	.....	1.800"	25

CAMSHAFT

Engine	Journal Diam.	Clearance	Lobe Lift
4-53	2.1820-2.1825"	.0045-.0060"	.005-.015"
4-53N	2.1820-2.1825"	.0045-.0060"	.005-.015"
6V53	2.1820-2.1825"	.0045-.0060"	.005-.015"
6-71N			
No.1-5	1.4970-1.4975"	.0025-.0040"	.004-.012"
No.2-3-4	1.4980-1.4985"	.0025-.0050"	
6V71			
No.1-5	1.4970-1.4975"	.0025-.0040"	.004-.012"
No.2-3-4	1.4980-1.4985"	.0025-.0050"	
8V71			
No.1-5	1.4960-1.4965"	.0035-.0050"	.004-.012"
No.2-3-4	1.4980-1.4985"	.0025-.0050"	
12V71			
No.1-5	1.4970-1.4975"	.0025-.0040"	.004-.012"
No.2-3-4	1.4980-1.4985"	.0025-.0050"	
6V92			
No.1-5	1.4970-1.4975"	.0025-.0040"	.004-.012"
No.2-3-4	1.4980-1.4985"	.0025-.0050"	
8V92			
No.1-5	1.4960-1.4965"	.0035-.0050"	.004-.012"
No.2-3-4	1.4980-1.4985"	.0025-.0050"	

DETROIT DIESEL (Cont.)

	PISTONS	PINS		RINGS		
Engine	Clearance	Piston Fit	Rod Fit	Rings	End Gap	Side Clearance
4-53	.0031-.0068″	.0025-.0034″	.0010-.0019″	Chrome		
				1	.020-.046″	.0030-.0060″
				2	.020-.046″	.0070-.0100″
				3	.020-.046″	.0050-.0080″
				4	.020-.046″	.0050-.0080″
				5	.010-.025″	.0015-.0055″
				6	.010-.025″	.0015-.0055″
				Iron		
				1	.020-.036″	.0030-.0060″
				2	.020-.036″	.0070-.0100″
				3	.020-.036″	.0050-.0080″
				4	.020-.036″	.0050-.0080″
				5	.010-.025″	.0015-.0055″
				6	.010-.025″	.0015-.0055″
4-53N	.0031-.0068″	.0025-.0034″	.0010-.0019″	Chrome		
				1	.020-.046″	.0030-.0060″
				2	.020-.046″	.0070-.0100″
				3	.020-.046″	.0050-.0080″
				4	.020-.046″	.0050-.0080″
				5	.010-.025″	.0015-.0055″
				6	.010-.025″	.0015-.0055″
				Iron		
				1	.020-.036″	.0030-.0060″
				2	.020-.036″	.0070-.0100″
				3	.020-.036″	.0050-.0080″
				4	.020-.036″	.0050-.0080″
				5	.010-.025″	.0015-.0055″
				6	.010-.025″	.0015-.0055″
6V53	.0031-.0068″	.0025-.0034″	.0010-.0019″	Chrome		
				1	.020-.046″	.0030-.0060″
				2	.020-.046″	.0070-.0100″
				3	.020-.046″	.0050-.0080″
				4	.020-.046″	.0050-.0080″
				5	.010-.025″	.0015-.0055″
				6	.010-.025″	.0015-.0055″
				Iron		
				1	.020-.036″	.0030-.0060″
				2	.020-.036″	.0070-.0100″
				3	.020-.036″	.0050-.0080″
				4	.020-.036″	.0050-.0080″
				5	.010-.025″	.0015-.0055″
				6	.010-.025″	.0015-.0055″
6-71N Trunk Type	.0040-.0078″	.0025-.0034″	.0015-.0024″	1	.023-.038″	.0040-.0060″
				2	.018-.043″	.0100-.0130″
				3	.018-.043″	.0040-.0070″
				4	.018-.043″	.0040-.0070″
				5	.008-.023″	.0015-.0055″
				6	.008-.023″	.0015-.0055″
Crosshead Type	.0045-.0083″	①.0870-.0880″	.....	1	.023-.038″	.0010-.0050″
				2	.018-.043″	.0100-.0130″
				3	.018-.043″	.0040-.0070″
				4	.002-.021″	.0005-.0030″
				②5	.008-.023″	.0010-.0035″
				②6	.008-.023″	.0015-.0055″

① — Thickness of slipper bushing at center on all Crosshead type pistons.
② — Ring end gap for rings 5 and 6 on turbocharged engines is .005-.014″.

DETROIT DIESEL (Cont.)

Engine	PISTONS Clearance	PINS		RINGS		
		Piston Fit	Rod Fit	Rings	End Gap	Side Clearance
6V71 Trunk Type	① .0040-.0078″	.0025-.0034″	.0015-.0024″	1	.023-.038″	.0040-.0070″
				2	.018-.043″	.0095-.0130″
				3	.018-.043″	.0075-.0110″
				4	.018-.043″	.0055-.0090″
				5	.008-.023″	.0015-.0055″
				6	.008-.023″	.0015-.0055″
6V71N Trunk Type	① .0040-.0078″	.0025-.0034″	.0015-.0024″	1	.023-.038″	.0040-.0070″
				2	.018-.043″	.0100-.0130″
				3	.018-.043″	.0040-.0070″
				4	.018-.043″	.0040-.0070″
				5	.008-.023″	.0015-.0055″
				6	.008-.023″	.0015-.0055″
6V71N&T Crosshead Type	.0045-.0083″	① .0870-.0880″	.....	1	.023-.038″	.0010-.0050″
				2	.018-.043″	.0100-.0130″
				3	.018-.043″	.0040-.0070″
				4	.002-.021″	.0005-.0030″
				5	.008-.023″	.0010-.0035″
				6	.008-.023″	.0015-.0055″
8V71 Trunk Type	① .0040-.0078″	.0025-.0034″	.0015-.0024″	1	.023-.038″	.0040-.0070″
				2	.018-.043″	.0095-.0130″
				3	.018-.043″	.0075-.0110″
				4	.018-.043″	.0055-.0090″
				5	.008-.023″	.0015-.0055″
				6	.008-.023″	.0015-.0055″
8V71N Trunk Type	① .0040-.0078″	.0025-.0034″	.0015-.0024″	1	.023-.038″	.0040-.0070″
				2	.018-.043″	.0100-.0130″
				3	.018-.043″	.0040-.0070″
				4	.018-.043″	.0040-.0070″
				5	.008-.023″	.0015-.0055″
				6	.008-.023″	.0015-.0055″
8V71N&T Crosshead Type	.0045-.0083″	① .0870-.0880″	.....	1	.023-.038″	.0010-.0050″
				2	.018-.043″	.0100-.0130″
				3	.018-.043″	.0040-.0070″
				4	.002-.021″	.0005-.0030″
				5	.008-.023″	.0010-.0035″
				6	.008-.023″	.0015-.0055″
12V71 Trunk Type	② .0040-.0078″	.0025-.0034″	.0015-.0024″	1	.023-.038″	.0040-.0070″
				2	.018-.043″	.0095-.0130″
				3	.018-.043″	.0075-.0110″
				4	.018-.043″	.0055-.0090″
				5	.008-.023″	.0015-.0055″
				6	.008-.023″	.0015-.0055″
12V71N Trunk Type	② .0040-.0078″	.0025-.0034″	.0015-.0024″	1	.023-.038″	.0040-.0070″
				2	.018-.043″	.0100-.0130″
				3	.018-.043″	.0040-.0130″
				4	.018-.043″	.0040-.0130″
				5	.008-.023″	.0015-.0055″
				6	.008-.023″	.0015-.0055″

① — Thickness of slipper bushing at center on all Crosshead type pistons.

② — With 70 mm injectors, clearance is .0045-.0083″.

DETROIT DIESEL (Cont.)

PISTONS, PINS, RINGS

Engine	PISTONS Clearance	PINS Piston Fit	PINS Rod Fit	RINGS Rings	RINGS End Gap	RINGS Side Clearance
12V71N&T Crosshead Type	.0045-.0083"	① .0870-.0880"	.....	1 2 3 4 5 6	.023-.038" .018-.043" .018-.043" .002-.021" .008-.023" .008-.023"	.0010-.0050" .0100-.0130" .0040-.0070" .0005-.0030" .0010-.0035" .0015-.0055"
6V92	.0120"	① .0870-.0880"	.....	1 2 3 4 5 6	.025-.040" .025-.040" .025-.040" .002-.017" .010-.020" .010-.020"	.0010-.0050" .0100-.0130" .0040-.0070" .0005-.0030" .0010-.0040" .0015-.0055"
8V92	.0120"	① .0870-.0880"	.....	1 2 3 4 5 6	.025-.040" .025-.040" .025-.040" .002-.017" .010-.020" .010-.020"	.0010-.0050" .0100-.0130" .0040-.0070" .0005-.0030" .0010-.0040" .0015-.0055"

① — Thickness of slipper bushing at center on all Crosshead type pistons.

CRANKSHAFT & MAIN BEARINGS

Engine	Journal Diameter	Bearing Clearance	Crankshaft End Play	Thrust Location	Thrust Washer Thickness	Number of Main Bearings
4-53	2.9990-3.0000"	.0010-.0040"	.004-.011"	No.5	.119-.122"	5
4-53N	2.9990-3.0000"	.0010-.0040"	.004-.011"	No.5	.119-.122"	5
6V53	3.4990-3.5000"	.0010-.0040"	.004-.011"	No.4	.119-.122"	4
6-71N	3.4990-3.5000"	.0014-.0044"	.004-.014"	No.7	.119-.122"	7
6V71	4.4990-4.5000"	.0016-.0050"	.004-.014"	No.4	.119-.122"	4
8V71	4.4990-4.5000"	.0016-.0050"	.004-.014"	No.5	.119-.122"	5
12V71	4.4990-4.5000"	.0016-.0050"	.004-.014"	No.7	.119-.122"	7
6V92	4.4990-4.5000"	.0016-.0050"	.004-.011"	No.4	.119-.122"	4
8V92	4.4990-4.5000"	.0016-.0050"	.004-.011"	No.5	.119-.122"	5

CONNECTING RODS & BEARINGS

Engine	Journal Diameter	Bearing Clearance	Sideplay
4-53	2.4990-2.5000"	.0015-.0045"	.006-.012"
4-53N	2.4990-2.5000"	.0015-.0045"	.006-.012"
6V53	2.7490-2.7500"	.0011-.0041"	.008-.016"
6-71N	2.7514-2.7534"	.0014-.0044"	.006-.012"
6V71	2.9990-3.0000"	.0014-.0044"	.008-.016"
8V71	2.9990-3.0000"	.0014-.0044"	.008-.016"
12V71	2.9990-3.0000"	.0014-.0044"	.008-.016"
6V92	2.9990-3.0000"	.0010-.0040"	.004-.011"
8V92	2.9990-3.0000"	.0010-.0040"	.004-.011"

CYLINDER LINER & BORE

Engine	Type	Liner Bore	Liner Protrusion ①
4-53	Wet	3.8752-3.8767"	.0465-.0500"
4-53N	Wet	3.8752-3.8767"	.0465-.0500"
6V53	Wet	3.8752-3.8767"	.0465-.0500"
6-71N	Wet	4.2495-4.2511"	.0450-.0500"
6V71	Wet	4.2495-4.2511"	.0450-.0500"
8V71	Wet	4.2495-4.2511"	.0450-.0500"
12V71	Wet	4.2495-4.2511"	.0450-.0500"
6V92	Wet	4.8395-4.8411"	.0418-.0482"
8V92	Wet	4.8395-4.8411"	.0418-.0482"

① — All measurements are DEPTH BELOW block surface.

DETROIT DIESEL (Cont.)

OIL PUMP SPECIFICATIONS

4-53, 4-53N & 6V53

Type	Rotary
Clearance Between Inner and Outer Rotors at Each Lobe	.0040-.0110"
Depth Between Face and Rotors	.0010-.0035"
Pressure Relief Valve Opening	52psi

6-71N

Type	Gear
Shaft Bore	.6213-.6225"
Shaft Diameter	.6230"
Clearance Body Bushing	.0008-.0025"
Clearance Cover Bushing	.0010-.0027"
Distance Gear From Shaft End	6.4690"
Clearance Driven Gear-to-Housing	.0050"
Pressure Relief Regulator Opening	50psi
Pressure Relief Valve Opening	105psi

6V71 & 8V71

Type	Gear
Clearance Drive Shaft-to-Bushing	.0010-.0025"
Shaft Shoulder Below Front Cover	.0000-.0200"
Pressure Relief Valve Opening	100psi

12V71

Type	Gear
Shaft Bore	.8787-.8799"
Shaft Diameter	.8781"
Clearance Shaft-to-Bushing	.0015-.0032"
Gear Backlash	.0060-.0120"
Pressure Regulator Valve Opening	50psi
Pressure Relief Valve Opening	120psi

6V92 & 8V92

Type	Gear
Clearance Drive Shaft-to-Bushing	.0010-.0025"
Shaft Shoulder Below Front Cover	.0000-.0200"
Pressure Relief Valve Opening	100psi

TIGHTENING SPECIFICATIONS

Application	Ft. Lbs.
Cylinder Head Bolts①	170-180
Main Bearing Bolts	120-130
Flywheel Bolts	110-120
Crankshaft End Bolt	200-220
Camshaft and Balance Shaft Nut	300-325
Connecting Rod Nuts	40-45

① — See cylinder head tightening sequence.

TIGHTENING SPECIFICATIONS (Cont.)

6-71N

NOTE — Aluminum engine only.

Application	Ft. Lbs.
Cylinder Head Nuts①	140-160
Main Bearing Nuts	120-140
Flywheel Bolts	150-160
Crankshaft End Bolt	290-310
Camshaft and Balance Shaft Nut	300-325
Connecting Rod Nuts	60-70

① — See cylinder head tightening sequence.

6-71N

NOTE — Cast iron engine only.

Application	Ft. Lbs.
Cylinder Head Bolts①	175-185
Main Bearing Bolts	180-190
Main Bearing Nuts	155-185
Flywheel Bolts	180-190
Crankshaft End Bolt	290-310
Connecting Rod Nut	60-70
Crosshead Piston Pin to Connecting Rod Bolt	55-60

① — See cylinder head tightening sequence.

6V71, 8V71 & 12V71

Application	Ft. Lbs.
Cylinder Head Bolts①	175-185
Main Bearing Bolts	180-190
Flywheel Bolts	180-190
Crankshaft End Bolt	290-310
Camshaft and Balance Shaft Nut	300-325
Connecting Rod Nuts	60-70
Crosshead Piston Pin to Connecting Rod Bolt	55-60

① — See cylinder head tightening sequence.

6V92 & 8V92

Application	Ft. Lbs.
Cylinder Head Bolts①	230-240
Main Bearing Bolts	230-240
Flywheel Bolts	180-190
Crankshaft End Bolt	290-310
Camshaft Nut	300-325
Connecting Rod Nut	60-70
Crosshead Piston Pin to Connecting Rod Bolt	55-60

① — See cylinder head tightening sequence.

DETROIT DIESEL (Cont.)

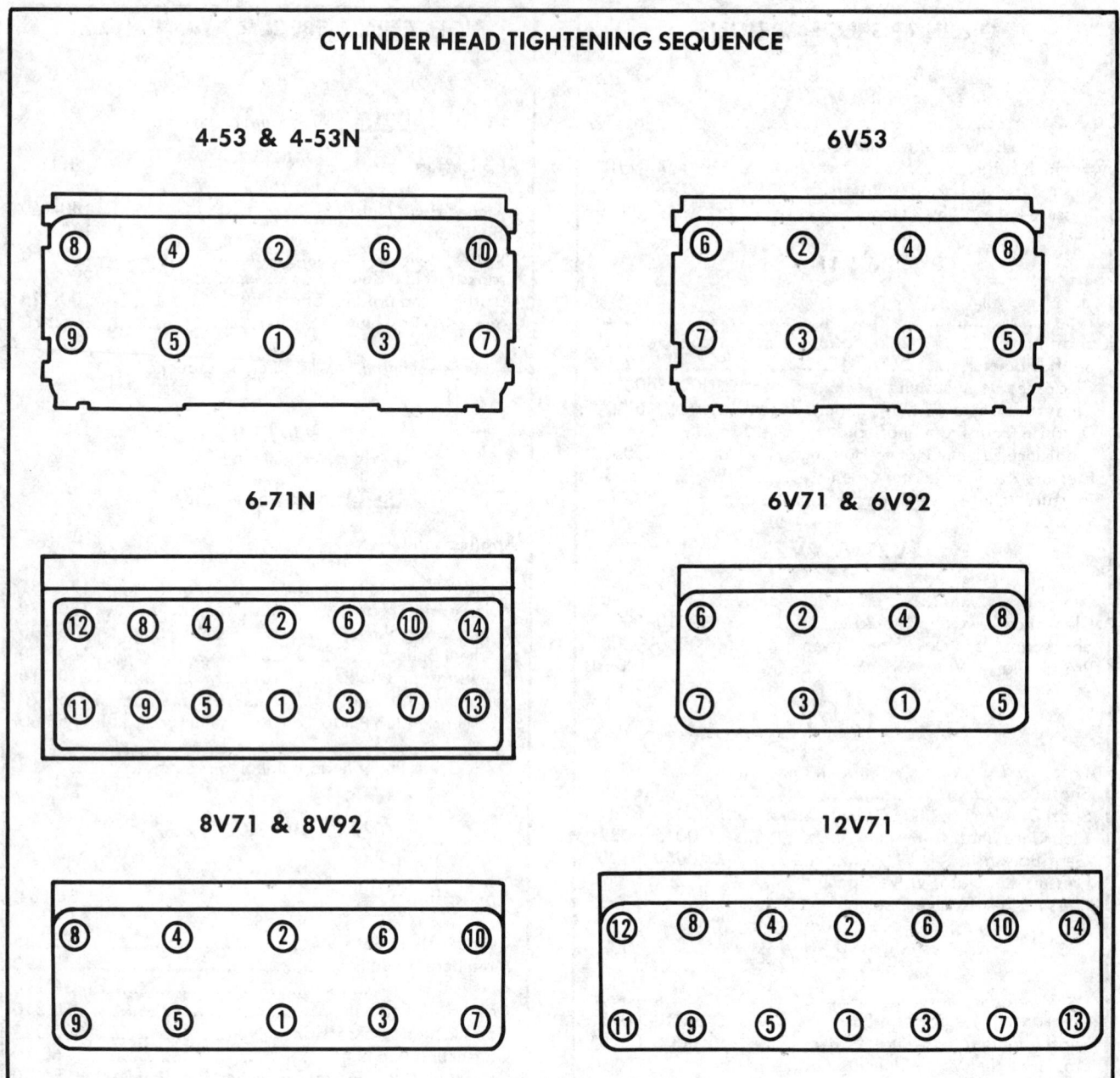

CYLINDER HEAD TIGHTENING SEQUENCE

4-53 & 4-53N

6V53

6-71N

6V71 & 6V92

8V71 & 8V92

12V71

INTERNATIONAL HARVESTER CORP.

GENERAL SPECIFICATIONS

Engine	Cycle	Displ. Cu. Ins.	Compr. Ratio	Bore	Stroke	Firing Order	Inj. Timing ①
D-150	4	461″	17.0:1	4.125″	4.313″	1,8,7,3,6,5,4,2	.207″
D-170	4	549″	17.0:1	4.500″	4.313″	1,8,7,3,6,5,4,2	.207″
D-190	4	549″	17.0:1	4.500″	4.313″	1,8,7,3,6,5,4,2	.207″
DT-466	4	466″	15.1:1	4.300″	5.350″	1,5,3,6,2,4	②13.0°
V-800	4	798″	16.0:1	5.313″	4.500″	1,8,7,3,6,5,4,2	22.0°

① — Unless noted otherwise, all Injection Timing is BTDC.
② — Timing for Model DTI-466, Intercooled is 15.0° static.

NORMAL OPERATING SPECIFICATIONS

Engine	Idle RPM	Max. RPM	Oil Temp.	Oil Press.	Coolant Temp.	Compression Pressure (PSI) @ RPM (Sea Level)
D-150	550-600	3000	220°	45-60	190°	375-425@ ①
D-170	550-600	3000	220°	45-60	190°	375-425@ ①
D-190	550-600	3000	220°	45-60	190°	375-425@ ①
DT-466	675	2920	230°	40-65	202°	.....
DTI-466	675	2935	230°	40-60	202°	.....
V-800	625-675	2860	220°	45-65	190°	400-470@234

① — Cranking Speed.

VALVES & SEATS

Engine	Head Diameter	Face Angle	Seat Angle	Seat Width	Stem Diameter	Stem Clearance	Valve Seat Insert O.D.	Valve Clearance
D-150								
Int.	1.1810″	45°	45°	.080-.090″	.3725-.3730″	.0080-.0230″	.....	.014″
Exh.	1.030″	45°	45°	.080-.090″	.3720-.3725″	.0080-.0230″	.....	.016″
D-170								
Int.	1.990″	45°	45°	.080-.090″	.3725-.3730″	.0080-.0230″	.....	.014″
Exh.	1.740″	45°	45°	.080-.090″	.3720-.3725″	.0080-.0230″	.....	.016″
D-190								
Int.	1.990″	45°	45°	.080-.090″	.3725-.3730″	.0080-.0230″	.....	.014″
Exh.	1.740″	45°	45°	.080-.090″	.3720-.3725″	.0080-.0230″	.....	.016″
DT-466								
Int.	1.965-1.975″	30°	30°	.075-.085″	.3718-.3725″	.0015-.0032″	1.996-1.997″	①.019-.021″
Exh.	1.595-1.605″	45°	45°	.075-.085″	.3718-.3725″	.0015-.0032″	1.624-1.625″	①.024-.026″
V-800								
Int.	1.500″	30°	30°	.080″	.3718-.3725″	.0015-.0032″	.....	.013″
Exh.	1.260″	30°	30°	.080″	.3718-.3725″	.0015-.0032″	.....	.025″

① — Clearance is with engine cold.

INTERNATIONAL HARVESTER CORP. (Cont.)

VALVE SPRINGS

Engine	Free Length	Compressed Length	Lbs. @ Comp. Length
D-150	2.075″	1.397″	200
D-170	2.075″	1.397″	200
D-190	2.075″	1.397″	200
DT-466	2.340″	1.552″	156-165
V-800	1.835″	1.571″	58-62

CAMSHAFT

Engine	Journal Diam.	Clearance	Lobe Lift
D-150, D-170 & D-190			
No.1	2.346-2.347″	.0015-.0035″	.0035-.0115″
No.2	2.315-2.316″	.0015-.0035″	.0035-.0115″
No.3	2.289-2.290″	.0015-.0035″	.0035-.0115″
No.4	2.246-2.247″	.0015-.0035″	.0035-.0115″
DT-466	2.2814-2.2825″	.0020-.0066″	.0050-.0130″
V-800	2.346-2.347″	.0020-.0065″	.0050-.0130″

ROCKER ARMS & VALVE BRIDGES

Engine	Rocker Shaft O.D.	Rocker Arm I.D.	Rocker Arm Clearance	Bridge Guide O.D.	Bridge I.D.	Bridge Height Above Head
D-150	.....	.....	.0011-.0045″	.....	.....	1.219″
D-170	.....	.....	.0011-.0045″	.....	.....	1.219″
D-190	.....	.....	.0011-.0045″	.....	.....	1.219″
DT-466	.8491-.8501″	.851-.853″	.0009-.0039″	.....	.....	.....
V-800	.9990-1.0010″	.....	.....	.....	.....	0.910″

PISTONS, PINS, RINGS

Engine	PISTONS Clearance	PINS Piston Fit	PINS Rod Fit	RINGS Rings	RINGS End Gap	RINGS Side Clearance
D-150	.0055-.0065″	.0009-.0015″	Press Fit	1	.013-.023″	.0035-.0050″
				2	.013-.023″	.0035-.0050″
				3	.013-.028″	.0015-.0030″
D-170	.0060-.0070″	.0009-.0015″	Press Fit	1	.013-.023″	.0035-.0050″
				2	.013-.023″	.0035-.0050″
				3	.013-.028″	.0015-.0030″
D-190	.0060-.0070″	.0009-.0015″	Press Fit	1	013-.023″	.0035-.0050″
				2	.013-.023″	.0035-.0050″
				3	.013-.028″	.0015-.0030″
DT-466	.0045-.0065″	.0005-.0010″	.0006-.0010″	1	.016-.026″	.0000-.0280″
				2	.020-.030″	.0045-.0215″
				3	.010-.020″	.002-.004″
V-800	.0060-.0090″	.0005-.0011″	Press Fit	1	.018-.028″	.0020-.0040″
				2	.020-.030″	.0000-.0150″
				3	.008-.018″	.0015-.0035″

CRANKSHAFT & MAIN BEARINGS

Engine	Journal Diameter	Bearing Clearance	Crankshaft End Play	Thrust Location	Thrust Washer Thickness	Number of Main Bearings
D-150	3.123-3.1240″	.0018-.0048″	.004-.010″	No.3	.....	5
D-170	3.123-3.1240″	.0018-.0048″	.004-.010″	No.3	.....	5
D-190	3.123-3.1240″	.0018-.0048″	.004-.010″	No.3	.....	5
DT-466	3.3742-3.3755″	.0018-.0051″	.006-.012″	No.7	.....	7
V-800	3.7477-3.7490″	.0026-.0059″	.003-.011″	No.5	.....	5

INTERNATIONAL HARVESTER CORP. (Cont.)

CYLINDER LINER & BORE

Engine	Type	Liner Bore	Liner Protrusion
D-150	①	.....	.....
D-170	①	.....	.....
D-190	①	.....	.....
DT-466	Wet	4.300-4.301″	.002-.005″
V-800	Wet	5.3125-5.3135″	.003-.006″

① — Liners are not used.

CONNECTING RODS & BEARINGS

Engine	Journal Diameter	Bearing Clearance	Sideplay
D-150	2.753-2.754″	.0018-.0048″	.....
D-170	2.753-2.754″	.0018-.0048″	.....
D-190	2.753-2.754″	.0018-.0048″	.....
DT-466	2.9977-2.9990″	.0018-.0051″	.007-.015″
V-800	2.9972-2.9982″	.0026-.0059″	.....

OIL PUMP SPECIFICATIONS

D-150, D-170 & D-190

Type	Gear
Shaft Diameter	.4905-.4912″
Clearance in Bore	.0013-.0030″
Clearance Gear-to-Housing	.0014-.0054″
Gear Backlash	.0005-.0065″

DT-466

Type	Gerotor
End clearance, outer rotor-to-housing	.0015-.0040″
End clearance, inner rotor-to-housing	.0018-.0044″
Radial clearance, outer rotor and housing	.0055-.0085″

V-800

Type	Gear
Drive Shaft Diameter	.7385-.7390″
Idler Shaft Diameter	.5901-.5904″
Running Clearance	.0020-.0035″
Clearance Gear-to-Housing	.0040-.0055″
Pumping Gears Backlash	.0080-.0120″
Idler and Crankshaft Gears Backlash	.0040-.0140″
Drive Shaft End Play	.003-.006″

TIGHTENING SPECIFICATIONS

D-150, D-170 & D-190

NOTE — *Use minimum two steps to torque all nuts and bolts.*

Application	Ft. Lbs.
Cylinder Head Bolts①	110
Main Bearing Cap Bolts	130
Connecting Rod Cap Bolts	55
Crankshaft Pulley Nut	150
Flywheel Bolts	110

① — See cylinder head tightening sequence.

DT-466

Application	Ft. Lbs.
Cylinder Head Bolts①	165
Main Bearing Cap Bolts	115
Connecting Rod Cap Bolts	130
Crankshaft Pulley Bolts	125
Flywheel Bolts	125

① — See cylinder head tightening sequence and tighten in minimum of two steps.

V-800

NOTE — *Use minimum two steps to torque all nuts and bolts.*

Application	Ft. Lbs.
Cylinder Head Bolts①	220
Main Bearing Cap Bolts	390
Connecting Rod Cap Nuts	130
Vibration Damper-to-Crankshaft Nut	350
Flywheel Bolts	235

① — See cylinder head tightening sequence.

INTERNATIONAL HARVESTER CORP. (Cont.)

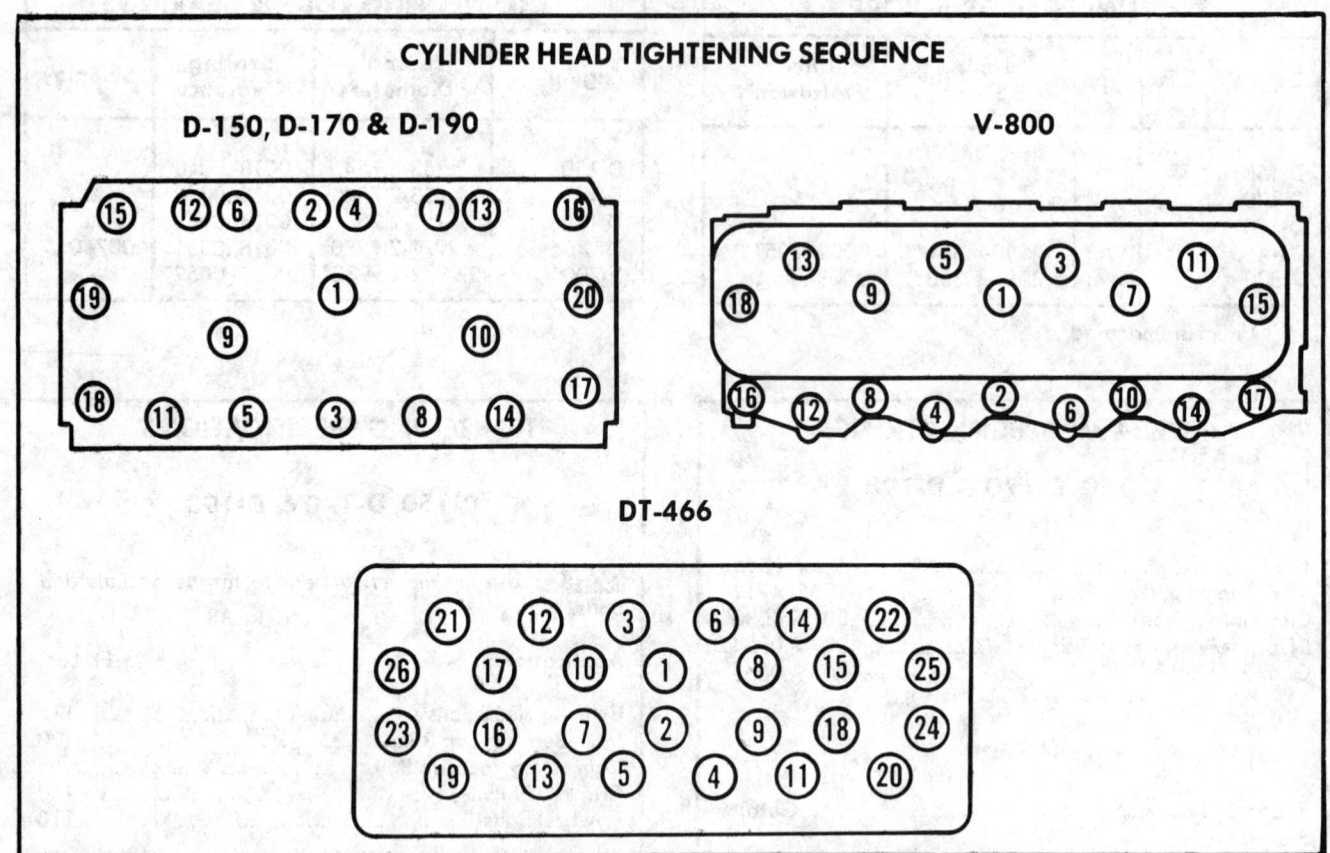

CYLINDER HEAD TIGHTENING SEQUENCE

D-150, D-170 & D-190   V-800

DT-466

MACK

GENERAL SPECIFICATIONS

Engine	Cycle	Displ. Cu. Ins.	Compr. Ratio	Bore	Stroke	Firing Order	Inj. Timing ①
END475	4	475"	16.5:1	4.530"	4.920"	1,5,3,6,2,4	24.0°
ENDT475	4	475"	15.5:1	4.530"	4.920"	1,5,3,6,2,4	25.0°
ENDT673	4	672"	16.11:1	4.875"	6.000"	1,5,3,6,2,4	29.0°
ENDT673C	4	672"	14.99:1	4.875"	6.000"	1,5,3,6,2,4	28.0°
ENDT673E	4	672"	16.11:1	4.875"	6.000"	1,5,3,6,2,4	30.0°
ENDT/B675	4	672"	14.99:1	4.875"	6.000"	1,5,3,6,2,4	29.0°
ENDT/B676	4	672"	14.99:1	4.875"	6.000"	1,5,3,6,2,4	22.0°
END707	4	707"	15.21:1	5.000"	6.000"	1,5,3,6,2,4	30.0°
ENDT/B865	4	866"	15.7:1	5.250"	5.000"	1,5,4,8,6,3,7,2	25.0°
ENDT/B866	4	866"	15.7:1	5.250"	5.000"	1,5,4,8,6,3,7,2	25.0°

① — Unless otherwise noted, all Injection Timing is BTDC.

NORMAL OPERATING SPECIFICATIONS

Engine	Idle RPM	Max. RPM	Oil Temp.	Oil Press.	Coolant Temp.	Compression Pressure (PSI) @ RPM (Sea Level)
END475	450	2600	.....	75	①170°	490-540@1000
ENDT475	500	2600	.....	75	①170°	430-470@1000
ENDT673	500-575	2280	.....	45-75	①170°	575@1000
ENDT673C	525-575	2280	.....	40-75	①170°	460@1000
ENDT673E	500-575	2280	.....	40-75	①170°	530@1000
ENDT/B675	500-575	2270	.....	40-75	①170°	460-1000
ENDT/B676	525-575	2310	.....	40-94	①170°	460@1000
END707	525-575	2285	.....	45-75	①170°	530@1000
ENDT/B865	600-650	2650	.....	40-95	①170°	②530@1000
ENDT/B866	600-650	2500	.....	40-95	①170°	③540@1000

① — Thermostat open temperature.
② — Prior to engine serial no. T865-7WO-030, 485@1000.
③ — Prior to engine serial no. T866-7WO-515, 485@1000

ROCKER ARMS & VALVE BRIDGES

Engine	Rocker Shaft O.D.	Rocker Arm I.D.	Rocker Arm Clearance	Bridge Guide O.D.	Bridge I.D.	Bridge Height Above Head
END475	.8654-.8656"	.8661-.8669"	.0005-.0015"	.....	.....	.....
ENDT475	.8654-.8656"	.8661-.8669"	.0005-.0015"	.....	.....	.....
ENDT673	1.1286-1.1291"	1.1296-1.1301"	.0005-.0015"	.....	.....	.....
ENDT673C	1.1286-1.1291"	1.1296-1.1301"	.0005-.0015"	.....	.....	.....
ENDT673E	1.1286-1.1291"	1.1296-1.1301"	.0005-.0015"	.....	.....	.....
ENDT/B675	1.1286-1.1291"	1.1296-1.1301"	.0005-.0015"	.....	.....	.....
ENDT/B676	1.1286-1.1291"	1.1296-1.1301"	.0005-.0015"	.....	.....	.....
END707	1.1286-1.1291"	1.1296-1.1301"	.0005-.0015"	.....	.....	.....
ENDT/B865	1.1286-1.1291"	1.1296-1.1301"	.0005-.0015"	.....	.....	.....
ENDT/B866	1.1286-1.1291"	1.1296-1.1301"	.0005-.0015"	.....	.....	.....

MACK (Cont.)

VALVES & SEATS								
Engine	Head Diameter	Face Angle	Seat Angle	Seat Width	Stem Diameter	Stem Clearance	Valve Seat Insert O.D.	Valve Clearance
END475 Int.	2.170"	30°	29½°	.047-.059"	.....	.0060"	.....	.012"Hot 014"Cold
Exh.	1.854"	30°	29½°	.047-.059"	.....	.0060"	.....	.016"Hot .018"Cold
ENDT475 Int.	2.170"	30°	29½°	.047-.059"	.....	.0060"	.....	.012"Hot .014"Cold
Exh.	1.854"	30°	29½°	.047-.059"	.....	.0060"	.....	.026"Hot .028"Cold
ENDT673 Int.	2.050"	30°	30°	.063-.094"	.4965-.4975"	.0030-.0050"	2.4405-2.4415"	.014"Hot .016"Cold
Exh.	1.690"	30°	30°	.063-.094"	.4955-.4965"	.0030-.0050"	2.0855-2.0865"	.022"Hot .024"Cold
ENDT673C Int.	2.050"	30°	30°	.063-.094"	.4965-.4975"	.0030-.0050"	2.4405-2.4415"	.014"Hot ①.016"Cold
Exh.	1.690"	30°	30°	.063-.094"	.4955-.4965"	.0030-.0050"	2.0855-2.0865"	.022"Hot .024"Cold
ENDT673E Int.	2.050"	30°	30°	.063-.094"	.4965-.4975"	.0030-.0050"	2.4405-2.4415"	.014"Hot ①.016"Cold
Exh.	1.690"	30°	30°	.063-.094"	.4955-.4965"	.0030-.0050"	2.0855-2.0865"	.022"Hot .024"Cold
ENDT/B675 Int.	2.050"	30°	30°	.063-.094"	.4965-.4975"	.0030-.0050"	2.4405-2.4415"	.014"Hot ①.016"Cold
Exh.	1.690"	30°	30°	.063-.094"	.4955-.4965"	.0030-.0050"	2.0855-2.0865"	.022"Hot .024"Cold
ENDT/B676 Int.	2.050"	30°	30°	.063-.094"	.4965-.4975"	.0020-.0040"	2.4405-2.4415"	.014"Hot ①.016"Cold
Exh.	1.690"	30°	30°	.063-.094"	.4955-.4965"	.0030-.0050"	2.0855-2.0865"	.022"Hot .024"Cold
END707 Int.	2.050"	30°	30°	.063-.094"	.4965-.4975"	.0020-.0040"	2.4405-2.4415"	.014"Hot ①.016"Cold
Exh.	1.690"	30°	30°	.063-.094"	.4955-.4965"	.0020-.0040"	2.0855-2.0865"	.022"Hot .024"Cold
ENDT/B865 Int.	2.050"	30°	30°	.063-.094"	.4965-.4975"	.0020-.0040"	2.4370-2.4380"	.015"Hot ①.016"Cold
Exh.	1.690"	30°	30°	.063-.094"	.4955-.4965"	.0030-.0050"	2.1760-2.1770"	.024"Hot .026"Cold
ENDT/B866 Int.	2.050"	30°	30°	.063-.094"	.4965-.4975"	.0020-.0040"	2.4370-2.4380"	.015"Hot ①.016"Cold
Exh.	1.690"	30°	30°	.063-.094"	.4955-.4965"	.0030-.0050"	2.1760-2.1770"	.024"Hot .026"Cold

① — Set valve clearance COLD STATIC ONLY on all B&C model engines which are equipped with Dynatard Engine Brake.

MACK (Cont.)

CAMSHAFT

Engine	Journal Diam.	Clearance	Lobe Lift
END475			
No.1	2.6825"	.0020-.0030"	.004-.010"
No.2	2.6800"	.0015-.0030"	.004-.010"
No.3	2.6750"	.0015-.0030"	.004-.010"
No.4	2.3600"	.0015-.0030"	.004-.010"
ENDT475			
No.1	2.6825"	.0020-.0030"	.004-.010"
No.2	2.6800"	.0015-.0030"	.004-.010"
No.3	2.6750"	.0015-.0030"	.004-.010"
No.4	2.3600"	.0015-.0030"	.004-.010"
ENDT673			
No.1-6	2.4390-2.4400"	.0015-.0045"	.008-.014"
No.7	2.2510-2.2520"	.0015-.0045"	.008-.014"
ENDT673C			
No.1-6	2.4390-2.4400"	.0015-.0045"	.008-.014"
No.7	2.2510-2.2520"	.0015-.0045"	.008-.014"
ENDT673E			
No.1-6	2.4390-2.4400"	.0015-.0045"	.008-.014"
No.7	2.2510-2.2520"	.0015-.0045"	.008-.014"
ENDT/B675			
No.1-6	2.4390-2.4400"	.0015-.0045"	.008-.014"
No.7	2.2510-2.2520"	.0015-.0045"	.008-.014"
ENDT/B676			
No.1-6	2.4390-2.4400"	.0010-.0050"	.008-.014"
No.7	2.2510-2.2520"	.0015-.0030"	.008-.014"
END707			
No.1-6	2.4390-2.4400"	.0020-.0040"	.008-.014"
No.7	2.2510-2.2520"	.0015-.0030"	.008-.014"
ENDT/B865	2.4390-2.4400"	.0010-.0050"	.008-.014"
ENDT/B866	2.4390-2.4400"	.0010-.0050"	.008-.014"

VALVE SPRINGS

Engine	Free Length	Compressed Length	Lbs. @ Comp. Length
END475			
Inner	2.313"	1.250"	45
Outer	2.594"	1.406"	106
ENDT475			
Inner	2.313"	1.250"	45
Outer	2.594"	1.406"	106
ENDT673			
Inner	3.031"	2.031"	77.2
Outer	3.406"	2.156"	99
ENDT673C			
Inner	3.031"	2.031"	77.2
Outer	3.406"	2.156"	99
ENDT673E			
Inner	3.031"	2.031"	77.2
Outer	3.406"	2.156"	99
ENDT/B675			
Inner	3.031"	2.031"	77.2
Outer	3.406"	2.156"	99
ENDT/B676			
Inner	3.031"	2.031"	77.2
Outer	3.406"	2.156"	99
END707			
Inner	3.031"	2.156"	77.2
Outer	3.406"	2.156"	99
ENDT/B865	3.125"	2.563"	90
ENDT/B866	3.125"	2.563"	90

CYLINDER LINER & BORE

Engine	Type	Liner Bore	Liner Protrusion
END475	Dry	4.5270"	.0027-.0040"
ENDT475	Dry	4.5270"	.0027-.0040"
ENDT673	Dry	4.8670-4.8770"	.0035-.0075"
ENDT673C	Dry	4.8670-4.8770"	.0035-.0075"
ENDT673E	Dry	4.8670-4.8770"	.0035-.0075"
ENDT/B675	Dry	4.8670-4.8770"	.0035-.0075"
ENDT/B676	Dry	4.8760-4.8770"	.0035-.0075"
END707	Dry	5.0010-5.0020"	.0035-.0075"
ENDT/B865	Wet	5.2415-5.2425"	.0005-.0045"
ENDT/B866	Wet	5.2415-5.2425"	.0005-.0045"

CONNECTING RODS & BEARINGS

Engine	Journal Diameter	Bearing Clearance	Sideplay
END475	2.9510"	.0020-.0040"	.008-.010"
ENDT475	2.9510"	.0020-.0040"	.008-.010"
ENDT673	2.9970-2.9980"	.0011-.0036"	.006-.012"
ENDT673C	2.9970-2.9980"	.0011-.0036"	.006-.012"
ENDT673E	2.9970-2.9980"	.0011-.0036"	.006-.012"
ENDT/B675	2.9970-2.9980"	.0011-.0036"	.006-.012"
ENDT/B676	2.9970-2.9980"	.0011-.0039"	.007-.012"
END707	2.9970-2.9980"	.0011-.0031"	.007-.012"
ENDT/B865	3.7470-3.7480"	.0016-.0046"	.007-.0015"
ENDT/B866	3.7470-3.7480"	.0016-.0046"	.007-.015"

MACK (Cont.)

CRANKSHAFT & MAIN BEARINGS

Engine	Journal Diameter	Bearing Clearance	Crankshaft End Play	Thrust Location	Thrust Washer Thickness	Number of Main Bearings
END475	3.3465"	.0020-.0045"	.002-.010"	No.7	.....	7
ENDT475	3.3465"	.0020-.0045"	.002-.010"	No.7	.....	7
ENDT673①	3.9980-3.9990"	.0020-.0050"	.004-.010"	No.4	.090-.103"	7
ENDT/B675	3.9980-3.9990"	.0020-.0050"	.004-.010"	No.4	.090-.103"	7
ENDT/B676	3.9980-3.9990"	.0020-.0050"	.004-.010"	No.4	.090-.103"	7
END707	3.9980-3.9990"	.0020-.0050"	.004-.010"	No.4	.090-.103"	7
ENDT/B865	3.9980-3.9990"	.0026-.0056"	.004-.010"	No.3	.....	5
ENDT/B866	3.9980-3.9990"	.0026-.0056"	.004-.010"	No.3	.....	5

① — ENDT673 E&C Models have same specifications.

PISTONS, PINS, RINGS

Engine	PISTONS Clearance	PINS Piston Fit	Rod Fit	Rings	RINGS End Gap	Side Clearance
END475	.0060"	.0015-.0050"	.0005-.0015"	1	.020-.028"	①
				2	.012-.024"	.0025"
				3	.012-.024"	.0020"
				4	.012-.024"	.0016"
				5	.012-.024"	.0016"
ENDT475	.0060"	.0015-.0050"	.0005-.0015"	1	.020-.028"	①
				2	.012-.024"	.0025"
				3	.012-.024"	.0020"
				4	.012-.024"	.0016"
				5	.012-.024"	.0016"
ENDT673	.0075-.0085"	.0003"	.0011-.0016"	1	.013-.025"	①
				2	.013-.025"	①
				3	.013-.025"	.0020-.0060"
				4	.013-.025"	.0010-.0045"
ENDT673C	.0075-.0085"	.0003"	.0011-.0016"	1	.013-.025"	①
				2	.013-.025"	①
				3	.013-.025"	.0020-.0060"
				4	.013-.025"	.0010-.0045"
ENDT673E	.0075-.0085"	.0003"	.0011-.0016"	1	.013-.025"	①
				2	.013-.025"	①
				3	.013-.025"	.0020-.0060"
				4	.013-.025"	.0010-.0045"
ENDT/B675	.0075-.0085"	.0003"	.0011-.0016"	1	.013-.025"	①
				2	.013-.025"	①
				3	.013-.025"	.0020-.0060"
				4	.013-.025"	.0010-.0045"
ENDT/B676	.0015-.0060"	.0011-.0039"	.0011-.0016"	1	.013-.025"	.0057"
				2	.013-.025"	.0052"
				3	.013-.025"	.0015-.0035"
END707	.0090-.0100"	.0001-.0002"	.0008-.0012"	1	.013-.025"	①
				2	.013-.025"	①
				3	.013-.025"	①
				4	.013-.025"	.0010-.0045"
ENDT/B865	.0080"	.0004-.0007"	.0008-.0055"	1	.020-.030"	.0060"
				2	.020-.030"	.0060"
				3	.016-.026"	.0060"
				4	.018-.028"	.0040-.0050"

① — Ring should be snug in groove with no visible side play.

MACK (Cont.)

OIL PUMP SPECIFICATIONS

END475, ENDT475

Type .... Rotor	
Clearance Bushing-to-Inner Rotor Shaft ..... .0015-.0025"	
Drive Gear-to-Idler Gear Backlash .... .0020-.0040"	
Idler Gear-to-Crankshaft Gear Backlash .... .0020-.0040"	
Type .... Gear	
Clearance Pump Gear-to-Housing .... .0020-.0040"	

ENDT673, ENDT673C, ENDT673E
ENDT/B675

Type .... Gear	
Clearance Gear-to-Side, Cavity .... .0035-.0060"	
Clearance Gear-to-Cover .... .0025-.0050"	
Pump Gear Backlash .... .0235-.0295"	
Pump Gear-to-Pump Driven Gear Backlash .0072-.0138"	
Pump Spring	
Compressed Length @40 lbs. .... 3.078"	
Free Length .... 3.875"	
Pressure Relief Valve Opening 65-100psi	

ENDT/B676

Type .... Gear	
Clearance Gear-to-Side, Cavity .... .0035-.0060"	
Clearance Gear-to-Cover .... .0025-.0050"	
Pump Gear Backlash .... .0235-.0295"	
Pump Gear-to-Pump Driven Gear Backlash .0072-.0138"	
Pump Spring	
Compressed Length @40 lbs. .... 3.078"	
Free Length .... 3.469"	
Pressure Relief Valve Opening 65-100psi	

END707

Type .... Gear	
Clearance Gear-to-Housing Side .... .0025-.0045"	
Clearance Gear-to-Housing End .... .0015-.0020"	
Gear Backlash .... .0270"max	
Pump Spring	
Compressed Length @40 lbs. .... 3.078"	
Free Length .... 3.469"	

ENDT/B865, ENDT/B866

Type .... Gear	
Drive Gear-to-Idler Gear Backlash .... .0050-.0070"	
Clearance Gear-to-Housing Cover .... .0025-.0050"	
Clearance Gear-to-Side, Cavity .... .0035-.0060"	
Pump Gear Backlash .... .0250-.0290"	
Idler Gear-to-Crankshaft Gear Backlash .... .0032-.0058"	
Idler Gear Bushing Bore .... 1.0015-1.0025"	
Idler Gear End Clearance .... .0015-.0040"	
Pump Spring	
Compressed Length @72.75 lbs. .... 3.085"	
Free Length .... 4.275"	
Relief Valve Spring	
Compressed Length @29.7 lbs. .... 3.875"	
Free Length .... 4.875"	

TIGHTENING SPECIFICATIONS

NOTE — *Use minimum two steps to torque all nuts and bolts.*

END475, ENDT475

Application	Ft. Lbs.
Cylinder Head Nuts①	140
Main Bearing Cap Nuts	150
Connecting Rod Bearing Cap Bolts	80
Vibration Damper-to-Crankshaft	542
Camshaft Gear Retaining Nut	220
Flywheel Bolts	149

① — See cylinder head tightening sequence.

ENDT673, ENDT673C, ENDT673E
ENDT/B675

Application	Ft. Lbs.
Cylinder Head Nuts①	175
Main Bearing Cap Bolts	
11/16" Bolt	200
5/8" Bolt	150
Connecting Rod Bearing Cap Bolts	150
Vibration Damper-to-Crankshaft	300
Flywheel Bolts	150-175

① — See cylinder head tightening sequence.

ENDT/B676

Application	Ft. Lbs.
Cylinder Head Nuts①	175
Main Bearing Cap Bolts	
11/16" Bolt	200
5/8" Bolt	150
Connecting Rod Bearing Cap Bolts	150
Vibration Damper-to-Crankshaft	300
Flywheel Bolts	150

① — See cylinder head tightening sequence.

END707

Application	Ft. Lbs.
Cylinder Head Nuts①	175
Main Bearing Cap Bolts	200
Connecting Rod Bearing Cap Bolts	150
Vibration Damper-to-Crankshaft	275
Flywheel Bolts	150-175

① — See cylinder head tightening sequence.

ENDT/B865, ENDT/B866

Application	Ft. Lbs.
Cylinder Head Bolts①	225
Main Bearing Cap Bolts	350
Connecting Rod Bearing Cap Bolts	150
Vibration Damper-to-Crankshaft	300
Flywheel Bolts	150

① — See cylinder tightening sequence.

MACK (Cont.)

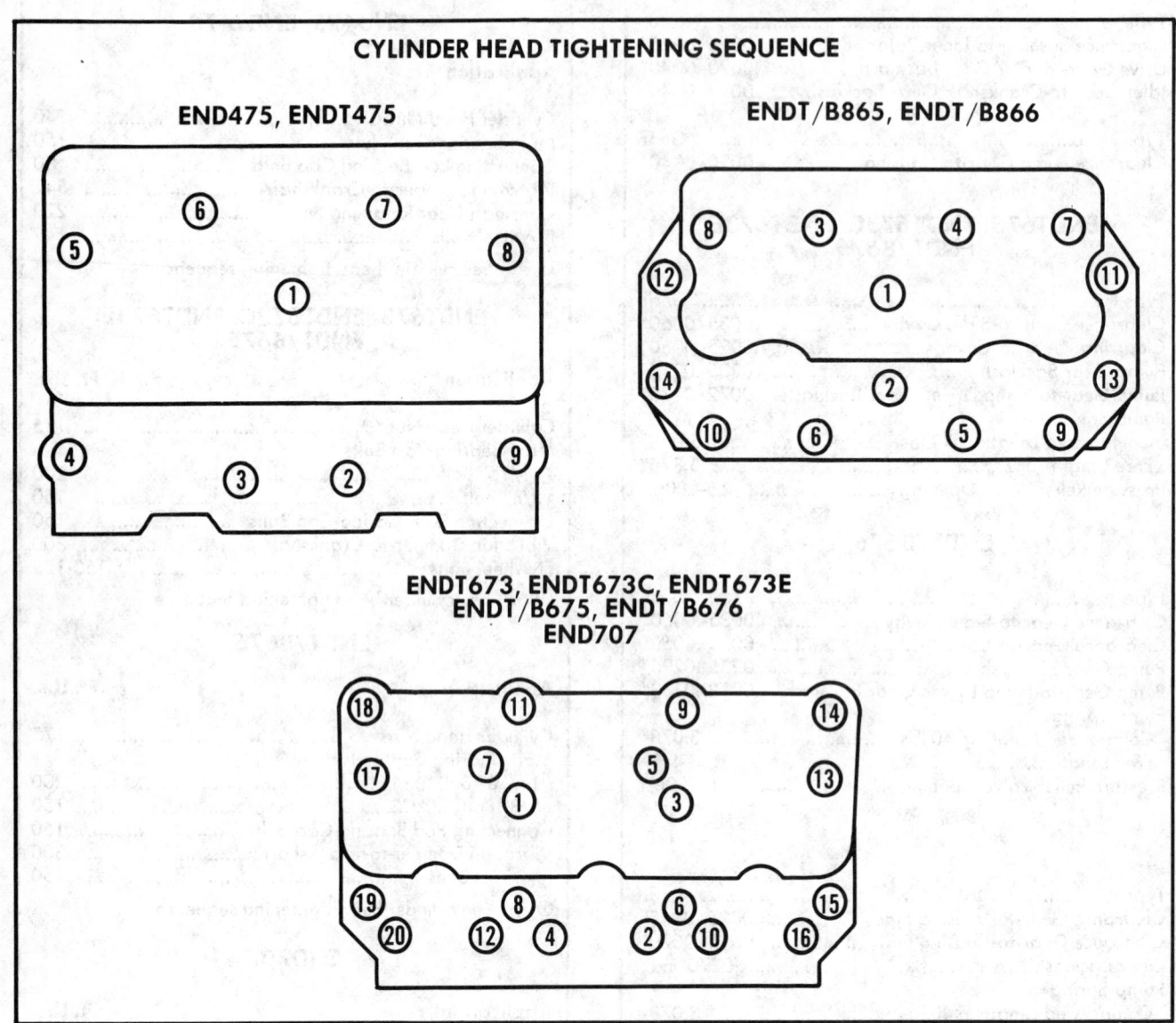

CYLINDER HEAD TIGHTENING SEQUENCE

END475, ENDT475

ENDT/B865, ENDT/B866

ENDT673, ENDT673C, ENDT673E
ENDT/B675, ENDT/B676
END707

PERKINS

GENERAL SPECIFICATIONS

Engine	Cycle	Displ. Cu. Ins.	Compr. Ratio	Bore	Stroke	Firing Order	Inj. Timing ①
6-354	4	354"	16.0:1	3.875"	5.00"	1,5,3,6,2,4	24.0°

① — Unless noted otherwise, all Injection Timing is BTDC.

NORMAL OPERATING SPECIFICATIONS

Engine	Idle RPM	Max. RPM	Oil Temp.	Oil Press.	Coolant Temp.	Compression Pressure (PSI) @ RPM (Sea Level)
6-354	500-550	3100	.....	25-50	.....	430@375

VALVES & SEATS

Engine	Head Diameter	Face Angle	Seat Angle	Seat Width	Stem Diameter	Stem Clearance	Valve Seat Insert O.D.	Valve Clearance
6-354 Int.	.....	45°	45°	.094"	.3725-.3735"	.0015-.0035"	.....	.010"
Exh.	.....	45°	45°	.109"	.3720-.3730"	.0020-.0040"	.....	.010"

VALVE SPRINGS

Engine	Free Length	Compressed Length	Lbs. @ Comp. Length
6-354 Inner	.....	1.5625"	13.4-17.4
Outer	.....	1.7800"	38-42

CAMSHAFT

Engine	Journal Diam.	Clearance	Lobe Lift
6-354		①.0025-.0055"	.3005-.3035"
No.1	1.9965-1.9975"		
No.2	1.9865-1.9875"		
No.3	1.9765-1.9775"		
No.4	1.9665-1.9675"		

① — No. 1 journal only is .0025-.0045".

ROCKER ARMS & VALVE BRIDGES

Engine	Rocker Shaft O.D.	Rocker Arm I.D.	Rocker Arm Clearance	Bridge Guide O.D.	Bridge I.D.	Bridge Height Above Head
6-354	.7485-.7495"	.7505-.7520"	.0010-.0035"	.....	.....	.....

PERKINS (Cont.)

CRANKSHAFT & MAIN BEARINGS

Engine	Journal Diameter	Bearing Clearance	Crankshaft End Play	Thrust Location	Thrust Washer Thickness	Number of Main Bearings
6-354	2.9985-2.9990"	.0025-.0045"	.002-.014"	4	.089-.091"	7

PISTONS, PINS, RINGS

Engine	PISTONS Clearance	PINS Piston Fit	Rod Fit	RINGS Rings	End Gap	Side Clearance
6-354	.0059-.0074"	Push Fit	.00075-.00170"	1	.015-.019"	.0019-.0039"
				2	.011-.016"	.0019-.0039"
				3	.011-.016"	.0019-.0039"
				4	.011-.016"	.0025-.0045"
				5	.011-.016"	.0025-.0045"

CYLINDER LINER & BORE

Engine	Type	Liner Bore	Liner Protrusion
6-354	Dry	3.8770-3.8785"	①.030-.035"

① Engine No. 8123411 is flush to .010" below face of block.

CONNECTING RODS & BEARINGS

Engine	Journal Diameter	Bearing Clearance	Sideplay
6-354	2.4990-2.4995"	.0015-.0030"	.0095-.0130"

OIL PUMP SPECIFICATIONS

Type	Rotor
Outer Rotor Diameter	2.2530-2.2540"
Rotor Shaft Bore Diameter	.6875-.6885"
Rotor Shaft Diameter	.6855-.6860"
Shaft Clearance	.0015-.0030"
Rotor Depth	2.1250-2.1260"
Clearance Between Inner and Outer Rotors	.0040"
Rotor End Clearance	.0025"

TIGHTENING SPECIFICATIONS

Application	Ft. Lbs.
Cylinder Head Nuts①	
7/16"	55-60
1/2"	75-80
Main Bearing Cap Bolts	145-150
Connecting Rod Cap Nuts	65-70
Flywheel-to-Crankshaft Bolts	75
Crankshaft End Bolt	250

① — See cylinder head tightening sequence.

CYLINDER HEAD TIGHTENING SEQUENCE

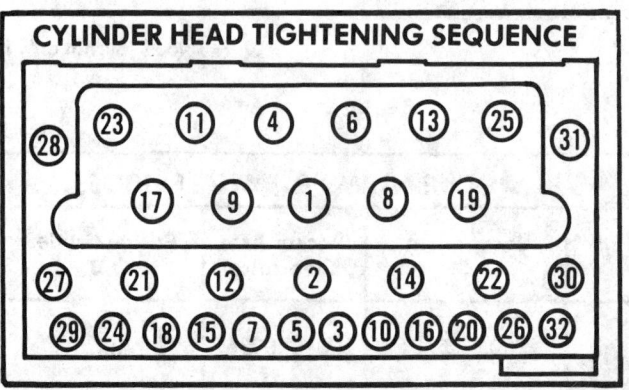

Notes

Notes

Notes

Notes

NOTE — The Latest Changes and Corrections represent a collection of last minute 1981 information which arrived too late to be included into the regular data pages. In addition, we have included information on prior year models which we have received since the publication of last year's edition.

FOR 1981 & EARLIER MODELS

TUNE-UP & FUEL SYSTEMS — SECTIONS 1 & 2

CHRYSLER CORP.

▶ 1981 CHRYSLER CORP. LIGHT DUTY TRUCKS WITH 318" ENGINE, 2-BBL. CARBURETOR, AUTOMATIC TRANSMISSION AND FEDERAL ASPIRATOR EMISSION SYSTEM: REDUCED ENGINE SURGE AND IMPROVED FUEL ECONOMY — If a light surge during highway cruising exists, drive the vehicle with the EGR valve vacuum hose disconnected and plugged. If the surge is eliminated, proceed to repair procedure.

1) Remove original EGR valve from intake manifold.

2) Using the original valve part number, select the proper replacement valve from the list below.

3) Install the correct replacement EGR valve, using a new gasket.

4) Check operation of new EGR valve.

Chrysler Corp. EGR Valve Part List

Original EGR Valve Part No.	Replacement EGR Valve Part No.
4104985/4105085	4240166
4104077/4105077	4240167
4104033/4105033	4186338
4104086/4105086	3879729

▶ 1979-80 CHRYSLER CORP. TRUCKS, VANS AND MOTOR HOMES WITH 36 AND 45 GALLON PLASTIC FUEL TANKS: REPEATED FUEL PUMP FAILURES — Fuel pump failures on these models may be due to poor retention of the in-tank filter sock to the fuel pick-up tube in the fuel tank. A filter sock that has slipped off the pick-up tube could allow plastic machining chips to be sucked into the fuel pump, jamming the check valves open and causing a loss of pumping action.

It is recommended that in cases of repeated fuel pump failure, the sending unit be pulled and the filter sock be clamped to the pick-up tube using a Keystone No. 120 clamp or equivalent. Also, back flush the chassis fuel line between the fuel pump and the tank using mineral spirits, to remove any plastic chips trapped in the fuel tube.

▶ 1981 CHRYSLER CORP. PICK-UP MODELS: FUEL TANK SENDING UNIT — Fuel tank sending units on these models are filled with grease or wax to prevent mud packing in this area. This prevents corrosion of the wiring connections and sending unit. If the sending unit is removed for any reason, the grease or wax must be removed to prevent it from entering the fuel tank. If additional cleaning of this area is required, mineral spirits, kerosene or alcohol should be used.

When a sending unit is reinstalled into the fuel tank, carefully fill the cavity formed by the retainer and sending unit with a suitable grease or wax. Special care must be taken to prevent plugging any of the three fuel tubes with grease or wax.

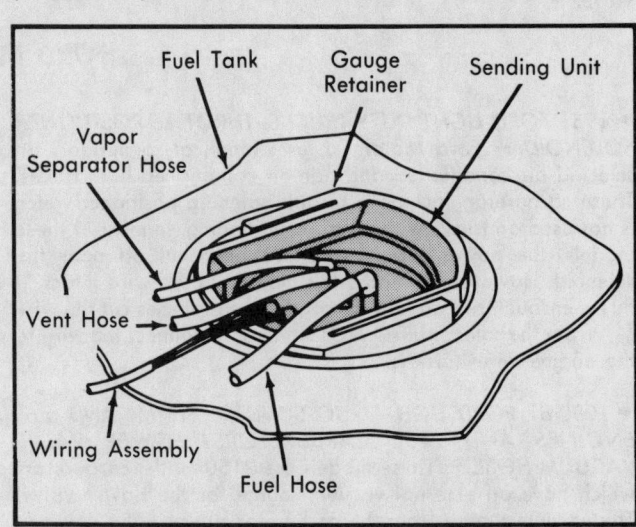

Chrysler Corp. Fuel Tank Sending Unit

▶ 1980 CHRYSLER CORP. TRUCKS WITH 318" ENGINE, 2-BBL. CARBURETOR, AIR PUMP, AUTOMATIC TRANSMISSION, FEDERAL EMISSIONS AND 3:21, 3:55 OR 3.54 REAR AXLE RATIO: WARM ENGINE SURGING — On these models, the engine may surge during a steady cruise down the road after full warm-up. This can be corrected by installing a field fix package (part no. 4240159), as follows:

1) Replace the existing EGR valve with a new one supplied in the package.

2) Replace the main metering jets in the carburetor with ones supplied in the package.

3) Install a new carburetor identification tag under the bowl cover screw closest to the vacuum kick diaphragm on front of carburetor.

4) For vehicles not equipped with an OSAC valve, but with a 25 gallon fuel tank, install an OSAC valve as described in steps 5) through 7). For vehicles not equipped with an OSAC valve, but with a fuel tank bigger than 25 gallons, install the OSAC valve as described in steps 8) through 10).

5) Remove the cover plate and bolts on the passenger side of the air cleaner. Using the same bolts, install the new OSAC valve.

6) Disconnect the vacuum hose on the carburetor that goes to the distributor and connect it to the top nipple on the OSAC

FOR 1981 & EARLIER MODELS

TUNE-UP & FUEL SYSTEMS — SECTION 1 & 2 (Cont.)

CHRYSLER CORP. (Cont.)

valve. Connect one end of the vacuum hose, which comes in the package, to the carburetor nipple previously exposed. Connect the other end to the bottom nipple on the OSAC valve.

7) Install the strap supplied in the package around the hoses at the OSAC valve.

8) Remove the cover plate and bolts on the passenger side of the air cleaner. Using the same bolts, install the new OSAC valve.

9) Locate the vacuum hose between the distributor and the "T" connector. Disconnect this hose from the "T" connector and connect it to the top nipple on the OSAC valve. Connect one end of the vacuum hose supplied in the package to the "T" connector and the other end to the bottom nipple on the OSAC valve.

10) Install the strap supplied in the package around the hoses at the OSAC valve.

FORD MOTOR CO.

5 ▶ *1981 FORD LIGHT DUTY TRUCKS: THROTTLE POSITIONER SOLENOID* — Ford Motor Co. uses identical carburetors on selected air conditioned and non-air conditioned light trucks. These carburetors include a throttle solenoid positioner which is not used on trucks without air conditioning. In most of these models, the power supply wire has been cut off near the solenoid. However, some models may have this wire intact. If this is encountered on non-air conditioned vehicles cut the wire ¼" from the solenoid. DO NOT attempt to connect the wire to the engine wire harness.

6 ▶ *1980-81 FORD LIGHT TRUCKS WITH 5.8L "M" AND 6.6L ENGINES AND 2150 CARBURETORS: POWER VALVE VACUUM HOSE* — These models use 2150 model carburetors which have an external vacuum source for the power valve. The vacuum tubing from the carburetor power valve cover to the intake manifold is made of a special fuel resistant rubber. Standard vacuum hose which is not fuel resistant must not be used for these applications. Only fuel resistant hose should be used.

7 ▶ *FORD LIGHT TRUCKS WITH CALIFORNIA EMISSIONS, 4.9L ENGINE, 8,500 LBS. OR LESS GVW AND CALIBRATION NUMBERS 1-51S, 1-51T, 1-52S AND 1-52T: LEAN SURGE, ROUGH IDLE AND POWER REDUCTION* — If any of these models experience any of the conditions listed above and it cannot be corrected using normal diagnostic procedures, replace the pulse feedback solenoid assembly on the Carter YFA carburetor.

NOTE — *A possible clicking noise may be apparent after installation of the new pulse feedback solenoid. In addition, engines built after Feb. 7, 1981, may also exhibit a similar clicking noise. This noise is normal and should not be mistaken for an abnormal engine component noise.*

8 ▶ *1981 FORD LIGHT TRUCKS UNDER 8,500 LBS. GVW WITH 4.9L ENGINES: SPARK KNOCK DURING ACCELERATION* — Spark knock which occurs during sudden acceleration on these models can be serviced with the following procedure.

1) Check initial timing and distributor mechanical and vacuum advance. Adjust as necessary to proper specifications.

2) If the initial timing was changed, reset the curb and fast idle speeds to proper specifications.

3) Assemble the vacuum harness which is shown in the illustration.

4) Disconnect the hose at the distributor diaphragm and connect the hose to the "D" end of the tee. Connect the hose from the "C" end to the diaphragm.

5) Disconnect the hose from the manifold vacuum fitting at the intake manifold, which connects to the air cleaner, and connect the hose to the "A" end of the assembly. Connect the hose from the "B" end to the manifold vacuum fitting.

6) Make sure the black side of the check valve is positioned toward the "C"-"D" end of the assembly.

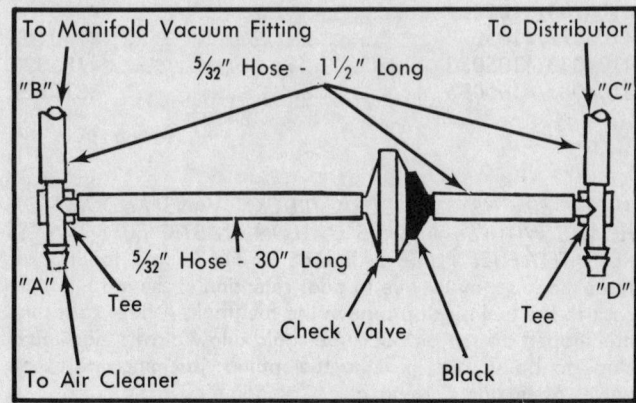

Vacuum Harness Assembly To Correct Spark Knock

9 ▶ *1979-81 FORD E250/350 AND F350 TRUCKS WITH 5.8L "M" ENGINES AND CALIBRATION NUMBERS 9-71J-R10 AND 9-72J-R11: UNSATISFACTORY PERFORMANCE AND/OR POOR FUEL ECONOMY* — The following procedure should be used to correct these conditions on subject vehicles.

1) Remove existing distributor (part no. D7TE-12127-AHA) and replace it with distributor EOPZ-12127-AM.

2) Set ignition timing to 6° BTDC.

3) Recheck all vacuum hose connections to ensure there are no leaks.

4) Install an Authorized Modifications decal.

FOR 1981 & EARLIER MODELS

EMISSION CONTROL — SECTION 3

CHRYSLER CORP.

1 ▶ *1976-81 CHRYSLER CORP. TRUCKS WITH UNDERFLOOR CATALYTIC CONVERTERS: CATALYTIC CONVERTER PIPE REPAIR* — If the catalytic converter inlet or outlet pipes become rusted out, they can be repaired using a catalytic converter pipe repair package as follows:

1) Remove the broken pipes and catalytic converter from the vehicle.

2) Using a hacksaw, cut off the pipes from the converter can. Cut as close to the welds as possible.

3) Check the converter to ensure that it is not damaged or inoperable. If it is, replace the converter assembly.

4) Grind the ends of the converter can to provide a clean welding surface.

5) Install replacement pipes into the converter can and reinstall on the vehicle. Check system alignment and tack weld pipes to converter.

CAUTION — *Attach a ground clamp to exhaust system to prevent damage to vehicle electrical system.*

6) Remove converter assembly from vehicle and complete welding pipes to converter joints using an arc welder or MIG welder.

7) Reinstall converter on vehicle and check for alignment and leaks.

ACCESSORIES & EQUIPMENT — SECTION 6

CHRYSLER CORP.

1 ▶ *1981 CHRYSLER CORP. "D" AND "W" 150 THROUGH 400 MODEL TRUCKS: HEATER CORE NOISE* — Some early production vehicles may exhibit an objectionable "singing" or "humming" noise caused by a high coolant flow through the heater core. This condition is most noticeable just before the transmission shift point during rapid acceleration. This condition can be diagnosed as follows:

A/C Equipped Models — When the noise is noticeable, switch the A/C heater control to "OFF" or "MAX A/C." If noise disappears, proceed to repair procedure.

Non-A/C Equipped Models — When the noise is noticeable, use a pair of pinch-off pliers and pinch close the heater supply hose. If noise disappears, proceed to repair procedure.

Repair Procedure

1) Using pinch-off pliers, pinch off the inlet hose to the heater core and pinch off the outlet hose to the heater core approximately 8" from the core outlet.

2) Disconnect the heater outlet hose from heater core. Insert a restrictor (part no. 118749) $\frac{1}{8}$" connector into the heater outlet hose.

3) Connect the heater outlet hose and remove all pinch-off pliers.

4) Start engine and check for leaks.

FORD MOTOR CO.

2 ▶ *1981 FORD "F" SERIES AND BRONCO MODEL TRUCKS: HEADLAMP SWITCH* — All 1981 "F" Series and Bronco model trucks use new headlamp switches which are not interchangeable with 1980 type switches. The 1980 type switches contain 2 circuit breakers, the main circuit breaker protecting the headlights, and the auxiliary circuit breaker protecting all other external lamps as well as the instrument panel lights.

Switches for 1981 have the auxiliary circuit breaker deleted, leaving only the main circuit breaker. Circuits previously controlled by the auxiliary circuit breaker are now protected by a fuse mounted in the fuse panel. Use of a 1980 headlamp switch in 1981 models will override the circuit protection.

GENERAL MOTORS

3 ▶ *CHEVROLET AND GMC LIGHT DUTY TRUCKS: AUXILIARY FUEL TANK SWITCHING* — The operation of the fuel tank switching mechanism for models with auxiliary fuel tanks has changed for 1981. The auxiliary fuel tank control is located on the instrument panel just to the left of the ashtray. The switch controls both fuel tank switching and fuel gauge indication in a single operation. It operates as follows:

Depress the rocker switch at the top for the right hand tank, and at the bottom for the left hand tank. When depressing the switch, a detent will be felt. Continue pressing beyond the detent and hold momentarily to fully activate the tank switching unit. Release the switch and it will return to the detent position.

Latest Changes & Corrections

ENGINES — SECTION 7

GENERAL MOTORS

▶ *CHEVROLET AND GMC TRUCK WITH DIESEL ENGINE: COMPRESSION TESTER MODIFICATION* — When performing a compression test on diesel engines using compression tester J-26999, an interference may exist between the nozzle hold-down clamp and a rib on the compression tester quick disconnect coupling. To correct, file a flat on one side of the interfering rib. This will provide clearance and allow the quick disconnect coupling to fully engage the compression test head adapter.

▶ *1974-1980 GENERAL MOTORS TRUCKS WITH 305", 350" AND 400" V8 ENGINES: INCORRECT CRANKSHAFT CONNECTING ROD JOURNAL SPECIFICATION* — An incorrect specification may appear in some Mitchell publications. The correct specification for crankshaft connecting rod journal is 2.0988-2.0998".

▶ *1981 CHEVROLET AND GMC LIGHT TRUCKS WITH DIESEL ENGINE: IDENTIFICATION OF FUEL INJECTION PUMPS* — The following information should be used for identification of diesel fuel injection pumps on 1980-81 trucks. Inspection for the correct injection pump should be made after the pump has been removed from the vehicle and prior to replacement.

Diesel Injection Pump Identification

Usage	Part No.	Tag No.	Color Code
1980	22510915	0915	Green/White
1981			
Except Calif.	22510362	0362	
California	22510363	0363	

JEEP

▶ *1981 JEEP 6-CYLINDER ENGINES WITH ENGINE BLOCK HEATER: "O" RING SEAL NOT CONTACTING BLOCK* — Vehicles with block heaters, built prior to engine code 011C01, may have coolant leaks at the "O" ring seal where the block contacts the block heater. This is caused by variations in engine block thickness, allowing the block heater to be too deep in the engine. Correction requires checking block thickness and installing a spacer if necessary, as follows:

1) Drain coolant from engine. Disconnect electrical wiring from block heater. Remove block heater from engine block.

CAUTION — *Do not drain coolant from engine with cooling system hot and under pressure. This could cause serious injury.*

2) Measure thickness of engine block wall at horizontal center of machined boss. If wall thickness is less than .36", it will be necessary to install a spacer on block heater.

NOTE — *Block thickness varies from top to bottom. Be sure to measure at horizontal center of machined boss surface.*

3) Check block heater "O" ring for damage. Install block heater and spacer assembly (part number 8133736), in engine block. Tighten "T" bolt type heater fastener to 20 INCH lbs. Tighten compression nut type heater fastener to 10 ft. lbs.

4) Connect electrical wiring to heater. Fill system with coolant.

▶ *ALL 1980-81 JEEP VEHICLES: CARBON KNOCK* — All engines used in 1980-81 Jeep vehicles may develop a knock caused by carbon build-up on the pistons and combustion chambers. The knock is more likely to occur on high mileage engines but may appear on low mileage engines depending upon the type of driving involved. Carbon knock is not sensitive to engine loading and is most noticeable when the engine is not under load. The knock may be loudest when engine is cold and may continue after engine warms up. Correction requires removing carbon build-up using Jeep Carburetor and Combustion Area Cleaner (part no. 8993813) as follows:

1) Remove air cleaner top. Operate engine until it is at normal operating temperature.

2) Operate engine at fast idle speed and spray the cleaner directly into the carburetor venturi until the container is empty.

3) Stop engine and allow cleaner to penetrate for 5 minutes.

4) Start engine and open and close throttle rapidly for 2 minutes. Replace air cleaner top.

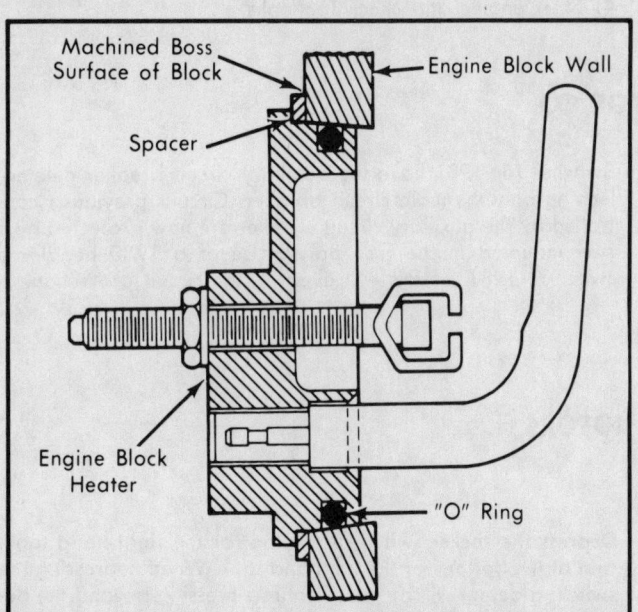

Jeep Engine Block Heater Installation

FOR 1981 & EARLIER MODELS

ENGINES — SECTION 7 (Cont.)

JEEP (Cont.)

▶ *1981 CALIFORNIA JEEP VEHICLES WITH 6-CYLINDER ENGINES, POWER STEERING, AIR CONDITIONING AND 55 OR 63 AMP ALTERNATORS: SERPENTINE DRIVE BELT TENSION* — Some of these vehicles may be equipped with a serpentine drive belt that cannot be adjusted to the proper tension. Correction requires replacing the drive belt and adjusting the new belt to the proper tension as follows:

1) Loosen the alternator pivot and adjusting bolts.

2) Loosen the power steering pump adjusting bolts.

3) Place the power steering pump in the full down position.

4) Place the alternator adjusting bracket in the full up position and finger tighten the alternator pivot and adjusting bolts.

5) Remove the backside idler and shield. Remove the original serpentine drive belt.

6) Install replacement serpentine drive belt (part no. 3241096). Be sure belt is seated in all pulleys.

7) Install backside idler and shield.

8) Position power steering pump so that clearance of 1.2" exists between upper corner of steering pump and flat area on underside of air pump. Tighten adjusting bolts to 30 ft. lbs.

9) Adjust serpentine belt tension by adjusting alternator position. Use ½" square drive hole in alternator mounting bracket to move alternator and adjust belt to correct tension. Tighten alternator pivot and adjusting bolts to 28 ft. lbs.

CLUTCHES — SECTION 8

FORD MOTOR CO.

▶ *1975-81 FORD E100/150 MODELS WITH MANUAL TRANSMISSION: EXCESSIVE CLUTCH PEDAL EFFORT* — The following procedure should be used to correct high clutch pedal effort and/or hard transmission shifting on subject models.

1) Remove the clutch linkage rods from clutch pedal lever and idler bellcrank lever assembly. Remove clutch control rod from idler bellcrank lever assembly and equalizer bar assembly. Inspect both rods for worn or damaged ends and/or worn or missing bushings. Inspect clutch release lever pivot for damaged or worn bushings by removing boot and looking into flywheel housing.

2) Remove clutch idler bellcrank lever assembly from clutch idler bellcrank lever pivot bracket assembly. Save spring washer and retaining ring.

3) Remove idler bellcrank lever pivot bracket assembly from left hand frame side rail.

4) Assemble a new clutch idler bellcrank lever assembly (part no. 7B585) to a new idler bellcrank pivot bracket (part no. 7B587).

5) Attach the idler bellcrank lever assembly and pivot assembly to the left hand frame side rail. Tighten nuts to 35-50 ft. lbs.

6) Install new bushings (part no. 388115) to clutch pedal rod and attach rod to clutch pedal lever and idler bellcrank lever assembly. Lubricate bushings with suitable lubricant.

7) Install new bushings on clutch content rod and attach rod to idler bellcrank lever assembly and to equalizer bar assembly. Lubricate with suitable lubricant.

8) Adjust clutch pedal freeplay to obtain ½" to 1" in order to obtain a minimum of 1" of clutch pedal reserve.

DRIVE AXLES — SECTION 9

CHRYSLER CORP.

▶ *1981 CHRYSLER CORP. TRUCKS WITH 4WD AND AUTOMATIC LOCKING HUBS: HUBS WILL NOT ENGAGE OR DISENGAGE* — If the locking hubs will not engage or disengage, use the following procedures to diagnose and repair the problem.

Diagnosis

NOTE — *Shifts between 2H and 4H must be made while the vehicle is stopped. The hubs will automatically lock when the vehicle is put into motion.*

1) To engage the front drive components, stop the vehicle and shift the transfer case to 4H. Drive the vehicle about 5 feet, taking care not to reverse motion.

2) Raise the vehicle on a hoist and check if the hubs are locked. If the hubs fail to lock, the problem could be caused by an incorrect drag sleeve retainer washer being installed behind the wheel bearing lock nut on the axle shaft.

3) To disengage the front drive components, stop the vehicle and shift the transfer case to 2H. Then shift the transmission to reverse and move the vehicle back about 5 feet.

FOR 1981 & EARLIER MODELS

DRIVE AXLES — SECTION 9 (Cont.)

CHRYSLER CORP. (Cont.)

4) Raise the vehicle on a hoist and see if the hubs are unlocked. If the hubs fail to unlock, perform the following procedure.

Repair Procedure

1) Remove the automatic locking hub.

2) Inspect the locking washer located behind the wheel bearing lock nut.

3) There are 4 tabs on the locking washer that should be visible. If the tabs are not visible, the wrong locking washer is installed and it should be replaced with a new washer (part no. 4219120).

4) Remove the wheel bearing locking nut with socket tool C-4170A.

5) Remove the incorrect locking washer and install the new washer. Reinstall the locking nut. Reinstall the locking hub and test operation.

FORD MOTOR CO.

▶ *1981 FORD 4WD PICKUP AND BRONCO MODELS: FRONT DRIVE AXLE LUBRICANT LEAKAGE* — A lubricant leakage occurring between the differential carrier and the left hand axle arm (carrier cover) may occur on some vehicles due to an interaction of the gear lube and the anti-corrosion coating on the axle arm. This can be serviced as follows:

1) Remove lock hubs, brake rotors, spindles, left and right axle shafts and front drive shaft so that the carrier can be removed from the left hand axle.

2) Loosen the bolts retaining carrier-to-axle arm and drain the lubricant. Remove the differential retaining bolts and remove the carrier.

3) Completely remove all RTV sealant and corrosion resistant coating from the axle arm on the surface where it mounts to the carrier and from carrier mounting surface.

4) Apply a ½" by ½" bead of RTV sealant on the mating surface of the carrier. Gaskets are not to be used.

5) Mount the axle arm to the carrier using 2 guide pins, being careful not to smear the RTV sealant. Install and tighten retaining bolts to 30-40 ft. lbs.

NOTE — *Use new bolts with encapsulated adhesive, or wire brush the old bolts and apply thread locking compound to them.*

6) Allow 1 hour curing time before installing lubricant and operating vehicle.

7) Assemble the wheel end components and drive shaft. Fill carrier assembly with suitable lubricant.

NOTE — *Add 2 ounces of friction modifier to Dana front limited-slip axles.*

▶ *1976-81 FORD E250/350 AND F250/350 WITH DANA MODEL 60-2, 60-3, 70 STD AND 70 HD LIMITED SLIP REAR AXLES: REAR AXLE CHATTER* — A chattering noise (not accompanied by perceptable shake or vibration) noted on vehicles when exiting from a highway, after sustained roadspeeds or when on curving type exit ramps, is a normal and temporary vehicle condition and will not result in damage to the rear axle limited slip differential components. This chatter condition is the result of a temporary contact between the differential clutch plates, caused by the axle lubricant being thrown off of the plates by centrifugal action during straight-ahead vehicle operation since no internal axle differential action is required. During vehicle operation at lower road speeds and during normal turning maneuvers, the lubricant will again be distributed on the plates and will result in a normal, quiet limited slip rear axle operation. If the chattering noise is accompanied by a shake, vibration or ratcheting feel, the differential should be serviced.

STEERING — SECTION 13

GENERAL MOTORS

▶ *1980 GMC TRUCKS WITH MODEL 605 POWER STEERING GEAR: DISASSEMBLY NOTES* — Whenever a power steering gear requires adjustment, the gear should be drained of fluid. This is done by placing the assembly over a container with the fluid ports pointing down toward the container. Cycle the rack-piston-nut from stop to stop several times to drain fluid. When a gear has been disassembled, the side cover must be firmly seated against its retaining ring before any adjustment is attemped. To seat side cover, tap on the end of the pitman shaft with a soft hammer.

FOR 1981 & EARLIER MODELS
AUTOMATIC TRANSMISSIONS – SECTION 14

CHRYSLER CORP.

▶ *ALL 1980 CHRYSLER CORP. TRUCKS AND VANS WITH A-727 AUTOMATIC TRANSMISSION: OVERRUNNING CLUTCH FAILURE* — Overrunning clutch failure may be the result of poor retention of the output shaft bearing by the bearing snap ring under a high load condition. This results in rearward movement of the output shaft which may cause the overrunning clutch to bear against the case and carry the full gear train thrust load. This in turn causes excessive wear of the race into the case and overrunning clutch failure.

The output shaft bearing shown in the illustration may have an improperly machined snap ring groove in the outside diameter of the bearing outer race, which allows the snap ring to spread and release during heavy throttle operation.

All known overrunning clutch failures have resulted from bearings date coded with this symbol. ■ If the transmission output shaft bearing has the date code shown, the bearing, snap ring and case must be replaced. Output shaft bearing is part no. 2466224, and output shaft bearing snap ring is part no. 2400320.

Repair of the transmission requires complete disassembly, cleaning to remove all metallic contamination; and replacement of all seals and gaskets, overrunning clutch assembly and those components damaged by overrunning clutch debris.

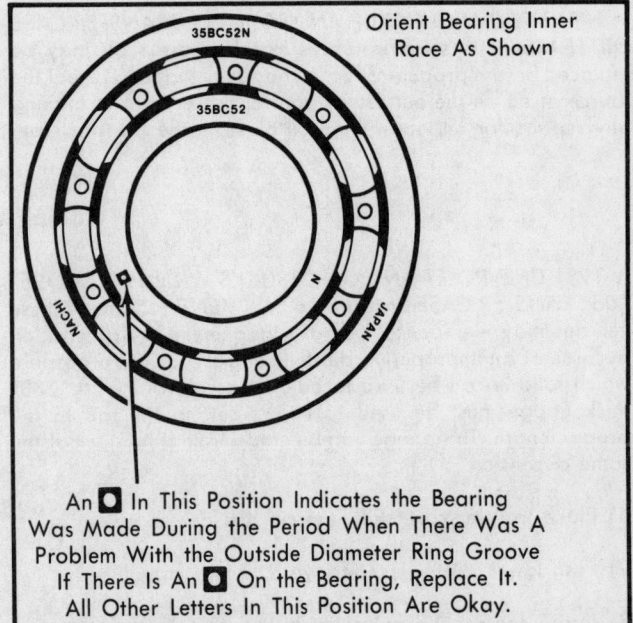

Orient Bearing Inner Race As Shown

An ■ In This Position Indicates the Bearing Was Made During the Period When There Was A Problem With the Outside Diameter Ring Groove If There Is An ■ On the Bearing, Replace It. All Other Letters In This Position Are Okay.

Chrysler Corp. A-727 Transmission Output Shaft Bearing

MANUAL TRANSMISSIONS – SECTION 15

JEEP

▶ *1981 CJ AND SCRAMBLER MODELS WITH SR4 4-SPEED TRANSMISSION: TRANSMISSION VENT LUBRICANT LEAK* — On some of these models built prior to March, 1981, a small amount of transmission lubricant may occasionally escape from the transmission vent located in the transmission adapter. This condition occurs primarily during cold weather warm-up and may be caused by the normal increase in working pressure within the transmission. If inspection indicates that a small amount of fluid is leaking, it can be corrected by drilling an auxiliary vent hole in the transmission top cover as follows:

1) Remove transmission and transfer case shift lever knobs. Remove floor carpeting, if equipped.

2) Remove screws attaching transmission access cover to floor pan and remove access cover and shift lever boots as an assembly.

3) Clean transmission top cover surface thoroughly.

4) Locate, mark and counterpunch position of additional vent hole in transmission top cover. *See illustration.* Scribe a vertical mark in line with trailing edge of letter "R" on casting and be sure horizontal mark is scribed 5/8" upward from top edge of casting letters as shown in illustration.

NOTE — *It is important that vent hole be located as accurately as possible. Use an accurate steel rule and a sharp scriber to locate and mark hole position.*

5) Apply a generous coating of grease to 1/16" diameter drill bit and carefully drill vent hole in transmission top cover. Clean chips from cover after drilling.

CAUTION — *There is only a small clearance between the shift fork retainer and the cover. Do not allow the drill bit to contact the retainer when the bit penetrates the cover.*

6) Install transmission access cover and shift lever boots. Install floor carpeting, if equipped.

7) Install shift lever knobs. Check and adjust transmission lubricant level if required.

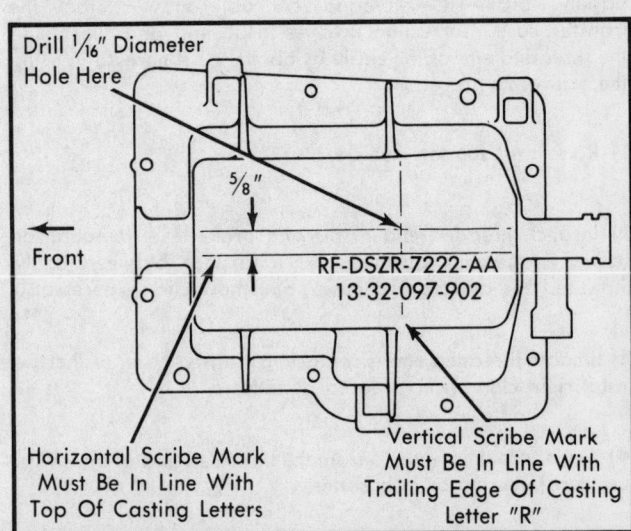

Drill 1/16" Diameter Hole Here

5/8"

Front

RF-DSZR-7222-AA
13-32-097-902

Horizontal Scribe Mark Must Be In Line With Top Of Casting Letters

Vertical Scribe Mark Must Be In Line With Trailing Edge Of Casting Letter "R"

Locating Auxiliary Vent Hole in SR4 Transmission

FOR 1981 & EARLIER MODELS
TRANSFER CASES — SECTION 16
FORD MOTOR CO.

▶ *1981 FORD 4WD PICKUP AND BRONCO: TRANSFER CASE OIL LEAKS* — In some instances transfer case seals may be replaced before proper inspection has been made to reveal the source of oil on the outside of transfer cases. Prior to making any repairs for oil leaks, wipe all oil from the transfer case.

Identify the source of leaks. They may be from overfilling at the supplier plant. Also, front and rear output shaft seals are packed with grease for easier assembly and, after running the unit, the grease melts and can be improperly identified as transmission fluid seal leakage. This condition is normal and does not require servicing.

GENERAL MOTORS

▶ *1981 CHEVROLET AND GMC TRUCKS WITH 4WD: MODEL 208 TRANSFER CASE SHIFTER ADJUSTMENT* — Some of these vehicles may experience lock disengagement in 4HI position because of an improperly adjusted control rod. The procedure which follows can be used to adjust the control rod. A .200" thick gauge must be used to ensure setting the rod to the proper length. This gauge can be made from shim stock of the same dimension.

1) Place transfer case shift lever in 4HI detent.

2) Push lower shifter lever forward to 4HI stop.

3) Install control rod swivel in shift lever hole.

4) Hang the .200" thick gauge over the control rod, behind the swivel.

5) Run the rear rod nut against the fabricated gauge with the shifter against the 4HI stop.

6) Remove the fabricated gauge and push the swivel rearward against the rod nut.

7) Run the front rod nut against the swivel and tighten the nut.

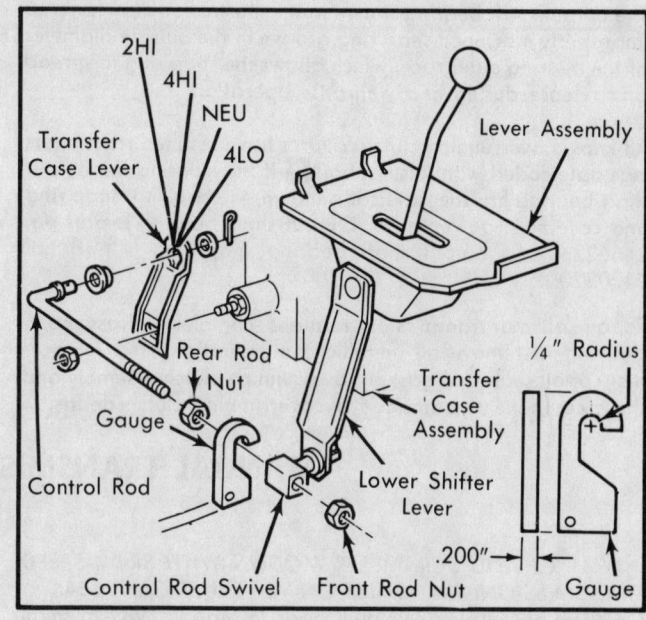

Model 208 Transfer Case Linkage Adjustment

JEEP

▶ *1981 JEEP CHEROKEE, WAGONEER AND TRUCK MODELS WITH 6-CYLINDER ENGINE AND AUTOMATIC TRANSMISSION* — On some of these models the threaded end of the parking brake lever-to-equalizer cable may contact the transfer case. Correction involves inspecting and shortening the threaded end of the cable by about ½" if necessary, using the following procedure.

1) Raise and support vehicle.

2) Inspect threaded end of parking brake lever-to-equalizer cable. If there is at least ½" clearance between cable threaded end and transfer case, no further action is necessary.

3) If cable threaded end is contacting transfer case, or there is insufficient clearance, proceed as follows:

4) Cut approximately ½" from the threaded end of the cable, using a hacksaw or bolt cutter.

5) Remove supports and lower vehicle.

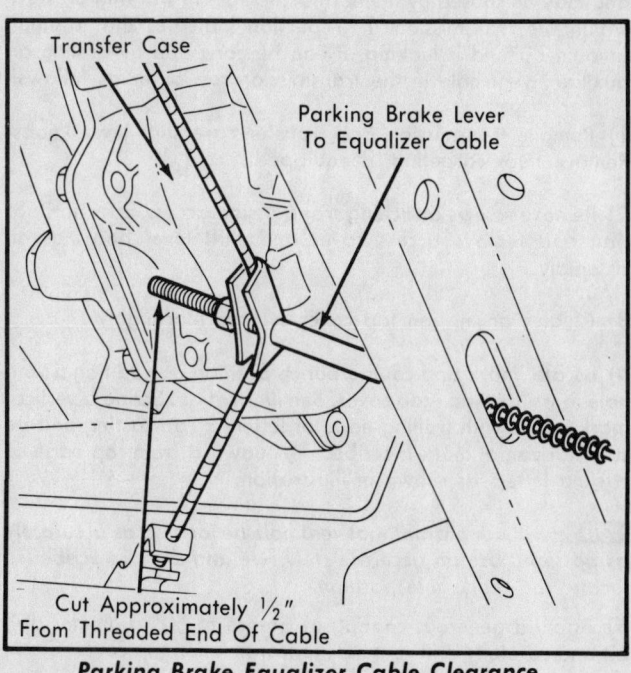

Parking Brake Equalizer Cable Clearance

"WE LISTEN"

We will greatly appreciate receiving your comments or corrections so that we may continue to publish the world's best automotive manuals. **Mail this card today. We'd like to hear from you!**

☐ Domestic ☐ Imported ☐ Trucks
☐ A/C Service ☐ Tune-Up ☐ Mechanical ☐ Transmissions ☐ Emission Control

Section No._____ Page No._____ Vehicle Model, year _____

Comments: _____

_____

_____

Company Name _____ Phone ___(___)_____

Address _____ Zip _____

"WE LISTEN"

We will greatly appreciate receiving your comments or corrections so that we may continue to publish the world's best automotive manuals. **Mail this card today. We'd like to hear from you!**

☐ Domestic ☐ Imported ☐ Trucks
☐ A/C Service ☐ Tune-Up ☐ Mechanical ☐ Transmissions ☐ Emission Control

Section No._____ Page No._____ Vehicle Model, year _____

Comments: _____

_____

_____

Company Name _____ Phone ___(___)_____

Address _____ Zip _____

"WE LISTEN"

We will greatly appreciate receiving your comments or corrections so that we may continue to publish the world's best automotive manuals. **Mail this card today. We'd like to hear from you!**

☐ Domestic ☐ Imported ☐ Trucks
☐ A/C Service ☐ Tune-Up ☐ Mechanical ☐ Transmissions ☐ Emission Control

Section No._____ Page No._____ Vehicle Model, year _____

Comments: _____

_____

_____

Company Name _____ Phone ___(___)_____

Address _____ Zip _____

BUSINESS REPLY CARD

FIRST CLASS   PERMIT NO. 3701   SAN DIEGO, CA

POSTAGE WILL BE PAID BY ADDRESSEE

MITCHELL MANUALS, INC.

P.O. BOX 26260
San Diego, California 92126

NO POSTAGE
NECESSARY
IF MAILED
IN THE
UNITED STATES

BUSINESS REPLY CARD

FIRST CLASS   PERMIT NO. 3701   SAN DIEGO, CA

POSTAGE WILL BE PAID BY ADDRESSEE

MITCHELL MANUALS, INC.

P.O. BOX 26260
San Diego, California 92126

NO POSTAGE
NECESSARY
IF MAILED
IN THE
UNITED STATES

BUSINESS REPLY CARD

FIRST CLASS   PERMIT NO. 3701   SAN DIEGO, CA

POSTAGE WILL BE PAID BY ADDRESSEE

MITCHELL MANUALS, INC.

P.O. BOX 26260
San Diego, California 92126

NO POSTAGE
NECESSARY
IF MAILED
IN THE
UNITED STATES

NO POSTAGE
NECESSARY
IF MAILED
IN THE
UNITED STATES

Turn Page ➚

AIR CONDITIONING & HEATING SERVICE MANUAL

The manual that's used and respected by the people who KNOW the air conditioning industry. Now you can service any air conditioning or heating system—profitably! You get everything you need to make system servicing quick and easy: in-depth trouble shooting and diagnosis...servicing, repair and overhaul data...thousands of illustrations...hundreds of spec tables and charts...factory bulletins...labor estimating section...and more! Total coverage for all factory-installed systems produced in this country since 1972! Big two-volume set!
Price: only $60.00

AIR CONDITIONING OLDER MODELS

Covers vehicles from 1966-1971. **Price: only $25.00**

AIR CONDITIONING BASIC TRAINING MANUAL

Now you can have the most complete basic training manual available for air conditioning systems! This book covers all the important aspects of air conditioning service: Theory, components, operation, diagnosis, servicing, and compressor repair. A handy trouble-shooting wall chart is also included! **Price: only $6.95**

DOMESTIC EMISSION CONTROL SERVICE MANUAL

Tough new pollution laws mean big profits for you in emission control servicing! Cash in on it with Mitchell! You get the most complete and current data available... anywhere! Description, operation, trouble-shooting, maintenance, repair and overhaul info for all domestic car emission systems produced since 1966! PLUS—you get a complete fuel system section, engine I.D., all system wiring and vacuum diagrams. Also included: handy system application charts that give you instant access to the data you need! **Price: only $50.00**

IMPORTED EMISSION CONTROL SERVICE MANUAL

Imported cars need pollution control servicing too... and that means more profit opportunities for your shop! Cash in on it with this fantastic coverage — over 30 foreign manufacturers are covered in complete detail since 1968. Description, operation, trouble-shooting, maintenance, repair, and overhaul — you get it all with Mitchell, PLUS...you get a complete carburetion and fuel injection section, emission system wiring and vacuum diagrams, and more! Over 3,800 pages—it's the most in-depth, money making repair tool you'll find. Start enjoying big emission control servicing profits today! **Price: only $50.00**